Pocket Oxford–Hachette French Dictionary

Fourth edition

French ⟶ English
English ⟶ French

Chief Editor
Marie-Hélène Corréard

XFORD
VERSITY PRESS

OXFORD

UNIVERSITY PRESS

Great Clarendon Street, Oxford OX2 6DP

Oxford University Press is a department of the University of Oxford.
It furthers the University's objective of excellence in research, scholarship,
and education by publishing worldwide in

Oxford New York

Auckland Cape Town Dar es Salaam Hong Kong Karachi
Kuala Lumpur Madrid Melbourne Mexico City Nairobi
New Delhi Shanghai Taipei Toronto

With offices in

Argentina Austria Brazil Chile Czech Republic France Greece
Guatemala Hungary Italy Japan Poland Portugal Singapore
South Korea Switzerland Thailand Turkey Ukraine Vietnam

Oxford is a registered trade mark of Oxford University Press
in the UK and in certain other countries

Published in the United States
by Oxford University Press Inc., New York

British Library Cataloguing in Publication Data

Data available

Library of Congress Cataloging in Publication Data

Data available

Typeset by Datagrafix, Inc
Printed in Great Britain by Clays Ltd, St Ives plc

ISBN 978-0-19-957615-9

10 9 8 7 6 5 4 3 2 1

Preface

This new edition of the *Pocket Oxford-Hachette French Dictionary* has been extensively updated to reflect recent additions to both the French and English languages. It provides comprehensive coverage of core vocabulary across a broad spectrum of contemporary written and spoken language, incorporating many idiomatic phrases and expressions. New words and senses have been drawn from an exciting initiative, the Oxford Languages Tracker, which enables us to track the latest developments in French and other modern languages. Additionally, for the first time in a dictionary of this size, 2000 of the most frequently used words in French and English have been marked.

Essential information on grammar, style, and pronunciation is provided in a convenient and accessible format, making the dictionary an ideal reference tool and study aid. The user is guided in selecting appropriate translations by clear examples of usage and construction and by information on the register of language, where required.

All grammatical terms used are explained in a glossary at the back of the dictionary, and French verbs are cross-referenced to a set of verb tables.

This new edition also includes an expanded and updated A–Z of French life and culture, providing information on contemporary French society, a calendar of traditions, festivals and holidays in France, a practical guide to writing letters and emails in French, a guide to text messaging, and a new section on navigating online services in French. A series of sample letters illustrates the differences between French and English usage, highlighting important features of style and format in a variety of situations.

Designed to meet the needs of a wide range of users, from the student at intermediate level and above to the enthusiastic traveller or business professional, the *Pocket Oxford-Hachette Dictionary* is an invaluable practical resource for learners of contemporary, idiomatic French in the twenty-first century.

The Editors

Editors and contributors

First edition

Chief Editor
Marie-Hélène Corréard

Editors
Frances Illingworth
Natalie Pomier

Associate Editor
Mary O'Neill

Second edition

Chief Editors
Marianne Chalmers
Martine Pierquin

Third edition

Chief Editors
Joanna Brough
Isabelle Stables

A–Z of French Life and Culture
Calendar of French traditions, festivals, and holidays
Penelope Isaac
Ella Associates
Valerie Grundy

Summary of French Grammar
Glynnis Chantrell

Fourth edition

Joanna Rubery
Isabelle Stables
Bénédicte Adriaens

Note on proprietary status

This dictionary includes some words which have, or are asserted to have, proprietary status as trademarks or otherwise. Their inclusion does not imply that they have acquired for legal purposes a non-proprietary or general significance, nor any other judgement concerning their legal status.

In cases where the editorial staff have some evidence that a word has proprietary status this is indicated in the entry for that word by the symbol ®, but no judgement concerning the legal status of such words is made or implied thereby.

Contents

The structure of French-English entries

headword •——————— **délice** /delis/ *nm* delight

délicieusement /delisjøzmɑ̃/ *adv* **(a)** deliciously

délicieux, -ieuse /delisjø, øz/ *adj* **(a)** delicious •————— feminine form of the headword

demandeur¹, -euse /dəmɑ̃dœʀ, øz/ *nm,f* applicant.

■ ~ **d'asile** asylum-seeker; ~ **d'emploi** job-seeker •——— compounds in block at end of entry

words marked •——— **ᵍ épaule** /epol/ *nf* shoulder
with this symbol are
among the most
frequent 2000 words
in French

IDIOMS **changer son fusil d'~** to change one's •——— idioms in block at tactics; **avoir la tête sur les ~s** to have one's end of entry head screwed on (colloq)

épicier, -ière /episje, ɛʀ/ *nm,f* grocer •——————— pronunciation in IPA

grammatical •——— **francophone** /fʀɑ̃kɔfɔn/ **1** *adj* French-
categories speaking; ‹*literature*› in the French language
2 *nmf* French speaker

part of speech •——— **free-lance** /fʀilɑ̃s/ *nmf* freelance, freelancer;
plus gender

juguler /ʒygyle/ [1] *vtr* to stamp out ‹*epidemic,* •——— number of verb group referring to the French verb

sense categories •——— **liquider** /likide/ [1] *vtr* **(a)** to settle ‹*accounts*›; tables at the end of to liquidate ‹*company, business*›; the dictionary **(b)** to clear ‹*goods, stock*›

lot /lo/ *nm* **(a)** (of inheritance) share; (of land) plot •——— sense indicators **(b)** (in lottery) prize; **gagner le gros ~** to hit the jackpot

field labels for •——— **luth** /lyt/ *nm* **(a)** (Mus) lute
specialist terms **(b)** (Zool) leatherback

magner: se magner /maɲe/ [1] *v refl* •——— style labels (+ *v être*) (slang) to get a move on (colloq)

pomponner: se pomponner /pɔ̃pɔne/ [1]
grammatical •——— *v refl* (+ *v être*) to get dolled up
information

précédent, ~e /pʀesedɑ̃, ɑ̃t/ **1** *adj* •——— translations
previous
2 *nm,f* **le ~, la ~e** the previous one

profaner /pʀɔfane/ [1] *vtr* to desecrate
typical collocates •——— ‹*temple*›; to defile ‹*memory*›; to debase
– words used with ‹*institution*›
the headword,
shown to help select **RN** /ɛʀɛn/ *nf* (*abbr* = **route nationale**) ≈ A •——— approximate
the right translation road (GB), highway (US) translation
examples, with •——— **souci** /susi/ *nm* **(a)** **se faire du ~** to worry
a swung dash **(b)** problem; **j'ai d'autres ~s (en tête)** I've got
representing the other things to worry about
headword
transfusé, ~e /tʀɑ̃sfyze/ **1** *pp* ▶ •——— cross-reference
TRANSFUSER

· ·

The structure of English-French entries

· ·

headword •——— **battery** n pile f; (in car) batterie f

battery charger n chargeur m de
batteries • ——— separate entries for compounds
battery farming n élevage m en batterie

words marked • ——— ✧ **beat** ① n (a) (of drum, heart) battement m …
with this symbol ■ **beat back** repousser ⟨group, flames⟩ • ——— phrasal verbs
are among the ■ **beat down** ⟨rain⟩ tomber à verse (**on**
most frequent sur)
2000 words in
English **cat** n (domestic) chat m; (female) chatte f; the
big ∼s les grands félins mpl
IDIOMS **to let the** ∼ **out of the bag** vendre la • ——— idioms in block at
mèche; **to rain** ∼**s and dogs** pleuvoir des end of entry
cordes

grammatical • ——— **clutter** ① n désordre m
categories ② vtr (also ∼ **up**) encombrer
and parts of
speech **edge** ① n (a) (outer limit) bord m; (of wood,
clearing) lisière f; **the film had us on the** ∼ **of** • ——— sense categories
our seats le film nous a tenus en haleine
(b) (of blade) tranchant m

sense indicators • ——— **especially** adv (a) (above all) surtout, en
particulier; **him** ∼ lui en particulier; ∼ **as**
it's so hot d'autant plus qu'il fait si chaud
(b) (on purpose) exprès, spécialement

fishy adj (a) ⟨smell, taste⟩ de poisson
(b) (colloq) (suspect) louche (colloq) • ——— style labels

field labels for • ——— **message window** n (Comput) fenêtre f de
specialist terms message
mushroom n (a) (Bot, Culin) champignon

non-smoking adj non fumeur inv • ——— grammatical
information
translations • ——— **nuisance** n (gen) embêtement m; (Law)
nuisance f; **what a** ∼! que c'est agaçant!

official ① n fonctionnaire mf; (of party,
union) officiel/-ielle m/f; (at town hall) • ——— feminine ending in
employé/-e m/f translation

typical collocates • ——— **plump** adj ⟨person, arm, leg⟩ potelé/-e;
– words used with ⟨cheek, face⟩ rond/-e, plein/-e
the headword, shown **plunge** ① vtr plonger (**into** dans)
to help select the ② vi ⟨road, cliff, waterfall⟩ plonger; ⟨bird,
right translation plane⟩ piquer

secondary school n ≈ école f • ——— approximate
secondaire translation
equivalent
examples, with • ——— **shut** ① adj fermé/-e; **her eyes were** ∼ elle
a swung dash avait les yeux fermés; **to slam the door** ∼
representing the claquer la porte (pour bien la fermer); **to**
headword **keep one's mouth** ∼ (colloq) se taire

these ▶ THIS • ——— cross-reference

The pronunciation of French

Vowels

a	as in	patte	/pat/
ɑ		pâte	/pɑt/
ɑ̃		clan	/klɑ̃/
e		dé	/de/
ɛ		belle	/bɛl/
ɛ̃		lin	/lɛ̃/
ə		demain	/dəmɛ̃/
i		gris	/gʀi/
o		gros	/gʀo/
ɔ		corps	/kɔʀ/
ɔ̃		long	/lɔ̃/
œ		leur	/lœʀ/
œ̃		brun	/bʀœ̃/
ø		deux	/dø/
u		fou	/fu/
y		pur	/pyʀ/

Semi-vowels

j	as in	fille	/fij/
ɥ		huit	/ɥit/
w		oui	/wi/

Consonants

b	as in	bal	/bal/
d		dent	/dɑ̃/
f		foire	/fwaʀ/
g		gomme	/gɔm/
k		clé	/kle/
l		lien	/ljɛ̃/
m		mer	/mɛʀ/
n		nage	/naʒ/
ɲ		gnon	/ɲɔ̃/
ŋ		dancing	/dɑ̃siŋ/
p		porte	/pɔʀt/
ʀ		rire	/ʀiʀ/
s		sang	/sɑ̃/
ʃ		chien	/ʃjɛ̃/
t		train	/tʀɛ̃/
v		voile	/vwal/
z		zèbre	/zɛbʀ/
ʒ		jeune	/ʒœn/

The symbols used in this dictionary for the pronunciation of French are those of the IPA (International Phonetic Alphabet). Certain differences in pronunciation are shown in the phonetic transcription, although many speakers do not observe them—e.g. the long 'a' /ɑ/ in *pâte* and the short 'a' /a/ in *patte*, or the difference between the nasal vowels 'un' /œ̃/ as in *brun* and 'in' /ɛ̃/ as in *brin*.

Transcription

Each entry is followed by its phonetic transcription between slashes, with a few exceptions.

Morphological variations

The phonetic transcription of the plural and feminine forms of certain nouns and adjectives does not repeat the root, but shows only the change in ending. Therefore, in certain cases, the presentation of the entry does not correspond to that of the phonetic transcripton e.g. *électricien, -ienne* /elɛktʀisjɛ̃, ɛn/.

Phrases

Full phonetic transcription is given for adverbial or prepositional phrases which are shown in alphabetical order within the main headword e.g. *emblée, d'emblée* /dɑ̃ble/, *plain-pied, de plain-pied* /d(ə)plɛ̃pje/.

Consonants

Aspiration of 'h'

Where it is impossible to make a liaison this is indicated by /'/ immediately after the slash e.g. *haine* /'ɛn/.

Assimilation

A voiced consonant can become unvoiced when it is followed by an unvoiced consonant within a word e.g. *absorber* /apsɔʀbe/.

Vowels

Open 'e' and closed 'e'

A clear distinction is made at the end of a word between a closed 'e' and an open 'e' e.g. *pré* /pʀe/ and *près* /pʀɛ/, *complet* /kɔ̃plɛ/ and *combler* /kɔ̃ble/.

Within a word the following rules apply:
- 'e' is always open in a syllable followed by a syllable containing a mute 'e' e.g. *règle* /ʀɛgl/, *réglementaire* /ʀɛgləmɑ̃tɛʀ/

- in careful speech 'e' is pronounced as a closed 'e' when it is followed by a syllable containing a closed vowel (y, i, e) e.g. *pressé* /pʀese/
- 'e' is pronounced as an open 'e' when it is followed by a syllable containing an open vowel e.g. *pressant* /pʀɛsɑ̃/.

Mute 'e'

The pronunciation of mute 'e' varies considerably depending on the level of language used and on the region from which the speaker originates. As a general rule it is only pronounced at the end of a word in the South of France or in poetry and it is, therefore, not shown. In an isolated word the mute 'e' preceded by a single consonant is dropped e.g. *parfaitement* /paʀfɛtmɑ̃/, but *probablement* /pʀɔbabləmɑ̃/. In many cases the pronunciation of the mute 'e' depends on the surrounding context. Thus one would say *une reconnaissance de dette* /ynʀəkɔnɛsɑ̃sdədɛt/, but, *ma reconnaissance est éternelle* /maʀkɔnɛsɑ̃sɛtetɛʀnɛl/. The mute 'e' is shown in brackets in order to account for this phenomenon.

Stress

There is no real stress as such in French. In normal unemphasized speech a slight stress falls on the final syllable of a word or group of words, providing that it does not contain a mute 'e'. This is not shown in the phonetic transcription of individual entries.

Abbreviations

abbr	abbreviation	Naut	nautical
adj	adjective	phr	phrase
adv	adverb	pl	plural
Anat	anatomy	Pol	politics
Archit	architecture	pop	populaire (very informal)
Aut	automobile	pp	past participle
aux	auxiliary	pp adj	past participle adjective
Bot	botany	pr n	proper noun
colloq	colloquial	pref	prefix
Comput	computing	prep	preposition
conj	conjunction	pres p adj	present participle adjective
Culin	culinary	pron	pronoun
dem pron	demonstrative pronoun	qch	quelque chose (something)
det	determiner	qn	quelqu'un (somebody)
Econ	economy	quantif	quantifier
excl	exclamation	®	registered trademark
fam	familiar	rel pron	relative pronoun
f	feminine	sb	somebody
Fr	French	Sch	school
GB	British English	sg	singular
gen	generally	sth	something
Hist	history, historical	subj	subjunctive
indic	indicative	Tech	technology
inv	invariable	Univ	university
liter	literary	US	American English
m	masculine	v	verb
Med	medicine	v aux	auxiliary verb
Mil	military	vi	intransitive verb
Mus	music	v impers	impersonal verb
n	noun	v inf	very informal
nf	feminine noun	v refl	reflexive verb
nm	masculine noun	vtr	transitive verb
nmf	masculine and feminine noun	Zool	zoology
nm,f	masculine and feminine noun		

Aa

a¹, A /a, ɑ/ **1** *nm inv* a, A; **démontrer qch à qn par A plus B** to demonstrate sth conclusively to sb

2 A *nf* (*abbr* = **autoroute**) motorway (GB), freeway (US)

a² /a/ ▶ AVOIR¹

ɔˢ **à** /a/ *prep*

■ **Note** You will find translations for expressions such as *machine à écrire, aller à la pêche* etc, at the entries MACHINE, PÊCHE etc.

— For the uses of *à* with the verbs *aller, être, avoir, penser* etc, see the entries for these verbs.

(a) to; **aller ~ Paris** to go to Paris; **se rendre au travail** to go to work

(b) at; in; **~ la maison** at home; **être ~ Paris** to be in Paris; **au printemps** in (the) spring; **~ midi** at midday; **~ quatre kilomètres d'ici** four kilometres (GB) from here; **~ 100 kilomètres-heure** at 100 kilometres (GB) per *or* an hour; **un timbre ~ 0,46 euros** a 0.46 euro stamp; (de) **huit ~ dix heures par jour** between eight and ten hours a day

(c) with; **le garçon aux cheveux bruns** the boy with the dark hair

(d) **~ qui est cette montre?** whose is this watch?; **elle est ~ elle** it's hers; **je suis ~ vous tout de suite** I'll be with you in a minute; **c'est ~ qui de jouer?** whose turn is it?

(e) **il est ~ plaindre** he's to be pitied

(f) **~ nous tous on devrait y arriver** between all of us we should be able to manage; **~ trois on est serrés** with three people it's a squash

(g) **~ ce qu'il paraît** apparently; **~ ta santé, ~ la tienne!** cheers!; **~ tes souhaits!** bless you!

abaisser /abese/ [1] **1** *vtr* to pull down ‹*lever*›; to lower ‹*safety curtain, window*›

2 s'abaisser *v refl* (+ *v être*) (a) ‹*stage curtain*› to fall

(b) **s'~ à faire** to stoop to doing

abandon /abɑ̃dɔ̃/ *nm* (a) **être à l'~** ‹*house*› to be abandoned; ‹*garden*› to be neglected

(b) (of project, method) abandonment; (of right) relinquishment

(c) (from race, competition) withdrawal

abandonné, ~e /abɑ̃dɔne/ **1** *pp*

▶ ABANDONNER

2 *pp adj* (a) ‹*spouse, friend, cause*› deserted; ‹*vehicle, house, nation*› abandoned

(b) ‹*path, factory*› disused

ɔˢ **abandonner** /abɑ̃dɔne/ [1] *vtr* (a) (gen) to give up; (in school) to drop ‹*subject*›

(b) (from game, tournament) to withdraw; to retire

(c) to leave ‹*person, place*›; to abandon ‹*car, object*›

(d) to abandon ‹*child, animal*›; to desert ‹*home, post, cause*›

(e) ‹*courage, chance*› to fail ‹*person*›

abat-jour /abaʒuʀ/ *nm inv* lampshade

abats /aba/ *nm pl* offal; (of poultry) giblets

abattement /abatmɑ̃/ *nm*

(a) despondency

(b) **~ fiscal** tax allowance (GB) *or* deduction (US)

abattoir /abatwaʀ/ *nm* abattoir, slaughterhouse

ɔˢ **abattre** /abatʀ/ [61] **1** *vtr* (a) to shoot [sb] down ‹*person*›; to shoot ‹*animal*›; to slaughter ‹*cattle, sheep*›

(b) to pull down ‹*building*›; to knock down ‹*wall*›; ‹*person*› to fell ‹*tree*›; ‹*storm*› to bring down ‹*tree*›

(c) to show ‹*card, hand*›

(d) to demoralize

(e) **~ de la besogne** to get through a lot of work

2 s'abattre *v refl* (+ *v être*) **s'~ sur** ‹*storm*› to break over; ‹*rain*› to beat down on; ‹*bird of prey*› to swoop down on

abbaye /abei/ *nf* abbey

abbé /abe/ *nm* (a) priest

(b) abbot

abc /abese/ *nm* ABC, rudiments

abcès /apsɛ/ *nm inv* abscess; **crever l'~** to resolve a crisis

abdication /abdikasjɔ̃/ *nf* abdication

abdiquer /abdike/ [1] *vi* ‹*sovereign*› to abdicate

abdomen /abdɔmɛn/ *nm* abdomen, stomach

abdominal, ~e, mpl -aux /abdɔminal, o/ **1** *adj* abdominal

2 abdominaux *nm pl* abdominal muscles

abeille /abɛj/ *nf* bee

aberrant, ~e /abeʀɑ̃, ɑ̃t/ *adj* (a) absurd

(b) aberrant

aberration /abeʀasjɔ̃/ *nf* aberration

abêtir /abetiʀ/ [3] **s'abêtir** *v refl* (+ *v être*) to become stupid

abêtissant, ~e /abetisɑ̃, ɑ̃t/ *adj* mindless

abîme /abim/ *nm* (a) abyss

(b) (figurative) gulf

abîmer /abime/ [1] **1** *vtr* to damage

2 s'abîmer *v refl* (+ *v être*) ‹*object*› to get damaged; ‹*fruit*› to spoil

abject, ~e /abʒɛkt/ *adj* despicable, abject

ablation /ablasjɔ̃/ *nf* excision, removal

abnégation /abnegasjɔ̃/ *nf* self-sacrifice

a

aboiement /abwamɑ̃/ *nm* barking

abolir /abɔliʀ/ [3] *vtr* to abolish

abominable /abɔminabl/ *adj* abominable

abomination /abɔminasjɔ̃/ *nf*
abomination

abondamment /abɔ̃damɑ̃/ *adv* ‹drink›
a lot; ‹illustrate› amply; **rincer** ~ rinse
thoroughly

abondance /abɔ̃dɑ̃s/ *nf* (a) (of information)
wealth; (of resources) abundance
(b) affluence

abondant, ~e /abɔ̃dɑ̃, ɑ̃t/ *adj* ‹food›
plentiful; ‹illustrations› numerous;
‹vegetation› lush

abonder /abɔ̃de/ [1] *vi* to be plentiful; to
abound
IDIOM ~ **dans le sens de qn** to agree wholeheartedly with sb

abonné, ~e /abɔne/ ① *pp* ▶ ABONNER
② *nm,f* (a) subscriber
(b) season ticket holder

abonnement /abɔnmɑ̃/ *nm*
(a) subscription
(b) (**carte d'**)~ season ticket

abonner /abɔne/ [1] ① *vtr* ~ **qn à qch** (to
magazine) to take out a subscription
for sb; (for theatre) to buy sb a season ticket
for sth
② **s'abonner** *v refl* (+ *v être*) to subscribe
(à to); to buy a season ticket (à for)

♂ **abord** /abɔʀ/ ① *nm* (a) **elle est d'un** ~
difficile she is rather unapproachable
(b) **être d'un** ~ **aisé** ‹subject, book› to be
accessible
(c) **au premier** ~ at first sight
② **d'abord** *phr* first; **tout d'**~ first of all
③ **abords** *nm pl* surrounding area, area
around

abordable /abɔʀdabl/ *adj* ‹product, price›
affordable; ‹text› accessible

abordage /abɔʀdaʒ/ *nm* (by pirates)
boarding

♂ **aborder** /abɔʀde/ [1] ① *vtr* (a) to tackle
‹problem›
(b) to approach ‹person›
(c) to reach ‹place, shore›
② *vi* ‹traveller, ship› to land

aboutir /abutiʀ/ [3] ① **aboutir à** *v+prep*
to lead to
② *vi* ‹negotiations, project› to succeed

aboutissants /abutisɑ̃/ *nm pl* **les tenants
et les** ~ **de qch** the ins and outs of sth

aboutissement /abutismɑ̃/ *nm*
(a) culmination
(b) (successful) outcome

aboyer /abwaje/ [23] *vi* ‹dog› to bark (**après**
at)

abracadabrant, ~e /abʀakadabʀɑ̃,
ɑ̃t/ *adj* bizarre

♂ indicates a very frequent word

abrasif, -**ive** /abʀazif, iv/ *adj* abrasive

abrégé /abʀeʒe/ *nm* (book) concise guide

abréger /abʀeʒe/ [15] *vtr* (a) to shorten
‹word, expression›
(b) to cut short ‹visit, career›

abreuver: **s'abreuver** /abʀøve/ [1] *v refl*
(+ *v être*) ‹animal› to drink

abreuvoir /abʀøvwaʀ/ *nm* drinking
trough

abréviation /abʀevjasjɔ̃/ *nf* abbreviation

abri /abʀi/ *nm* (a) shelter; **à l'**~ **de** sheltered
from; (figurative) safe from
(b) shed

abricot /abʀiko/ *nm* apricot

abricotier /abʀikɔtje/ *nm* apricot tree

abriter /abʀite/ [1] ① *vtr* (a) ‹building› to
shelter ‹people, animals›
(b) ‹country, region› to provide a habitat for
‹animals, plant life›
② **s'abriter** *v refl* (+ *v être*) to take shelter

abrogation /abʀɔgasjɔ̃/ *nf* repeal

abroger /abʀɔʒe/ [13] *vtr* to repeal

abrupt, ~e /abʀypt/ *adj* (a) ‹hill, road›
steep; ‹cliff› sheer
(b) ‹person, tone› abrupt

abruti, ~e /abʀyti/ *nm,f* (offensive) moron
(colloq)

abrutir /abʀytiʀ/ [3] ① *vtr* ‹noise› to
deafen; ‹alcohol, medication, fatigue› to have
a numbing effect on; ‹blow› to stun
② **s'abrutir** *v refl* (+ *v être*) (a) to become
dull-witted
(b) **s'**~ **de travail** to wear oneself out with
work

abrutissant, ~e /abʀytisɑ̃, ɑ̃t/ *adj*
‹music, noise› deafening; ‹job› mind-numbing

♂ **absence** /apsɑ̃s/ *nf* (a) absence
(b) lack; **l'**~ **de pluie** the lack of rain

absent, ~e /apsɑ̃, ɑ̃t/ ① *adj* (a) **être** ~ to
be away; (for brief spell) to be out
(b) ‹pupil, employee› absent
(c) (missing) absent (**de** from)
(d) absent-minded
② *nm,f* absentee

absentéisme /apsɑ̃teism/ *nm*
absenteeism

absenter: **s'absenter** /apsɑ̃te/ [1] *v refl*
(+ *v être*) to go away; to go out

♂ **absolu**, ~e /apsɔly/ *adj* absolute; ‹rule›
hard and fast

♂ **absolument** /apsɔlymɑ̃/ *adv* absolutely

absolution /apsɔlysjɔ̃/ *nf* absolution

absolutisme /apsɔlytism/ *nm* absolutism

absorbant, ~e /apsɔʀbɑ̃, ɑ̃t/ *adj*
(a) ‹substance› absorbent
(b) ‹job, work› absorbing

absorber /apsɔʀbe/ [1] *vtr* (a) ‹material,
plant› to absorb
(b) to take ‹food, medicine›
(c) to occupy ‹mind›

absorption /apsɔʀpsjɔ̃/ *nf* **(a)** (of liquid)
absorption
(b) (of food, medicine) taking
abstenir: s'abstenir /apstəniʀ/ [36] *v refl*
(+ *v être*) **(a)** (from voting) to abstain
(b) s'~ **de faire** to refrain from doing
abstention /apstɑ̃sjɔ̃/ *nf* abstention
abstinence /apstinɑ̃s/ *nf* abstinence
abstraction /apstʀaksjɔ̃/ *nf* abstraction;
faire ~ **de** to set aside
abstrait, ~e /apstʀɛ, ɛt/ [1] *adj* abstract
[2] *nm* (gen) abstract; (art) abstract art
absurde /apsyʀd/ *adj, nm* absurd
absurdité /apsyʀdite/ *nf* absurdity
abus /aby/ *nm inv* abuse
abuser /abyze/ [1] [1] *vtr* to fool
[2] **abuser de** *v+prep* **(a)** ~ **de l'alcool** to
drink to excess
(b) ~ **de** to exploit ‹situation, credibility›
(c) ~ **de qn** to sexually abuse sb
[3] *vi* to go too far; **je ne voudrais pas** ~ I
don't want to impose
[4] **s'abuser** *v refl* (+ *v être*) **si je ne
m'abuse** if I'm not mistaken
abusif, -ive /abyzif, iv/ *adj* **(a)** excessive
(b) unfair
(c) improper
(d) over-possessive
acabit /akabi/ *nm* **du même** ~ of that sort
acacia /akasja/ *nm* **(a)** (European) **(faux)** ~
locust tree
(b) (tropical) acacia
académicien, -ienne /akademisjɛ̃,
ɛn/ *nm,f* academician
académie /akademi/ *nf* (Sch) ≈ local
education authority (GB), school district (US)
académique /akademik/ *adj* **(a)** (gen)
academic; of the Académie française
(b) (Sch, Univ) ≈ of the local education
authority (GB) *or* school district (US)
(c) (in art) academic
acajou /akaʒu/ *nm* mahogany
acariâtre /akaʀjɑtʀ/ *adj* cantankerous
accablant, ~e /akablɑ̃, ɑ̃t/ *adj* **(a)** ‹heat,
silence› oppressive
(b) ‹evidence, testimony› damning
accabler /akable/ [1] *vtr* **(a)** ‹bad news› to
devastate; **être accablé par** to be overcome
by ‹heat, grief›
(b) ‹testimony, person› to condemn
accalmie /akalmi/ *nf* **(a)** lull
(b) slack period
accaparant, ~e /akapaʀɑ̃, ɑ̃t/ *adj* very
demanding
accaparer /akapaʀe/ [1] *vtr* to corner
‹market›; to monopolize ‹person, power›
accédant, ~e /aksedɑ̃, ɑ̃t/ *nm,f* ~ **à la
propriété** home-buyer
accéder /aksede/ [14] *v+prep* **(a)** ~ **à** to
reach ‹place›
(b) ~ **à** to achieve ‹fame, glory›; to obtain

‹job›; to rise to ‹high office›
accélérateur /akseleʀatœʀ/ *nm*
accelerator
accélération /akseleʀasjɔ̃/ *nf*
acceleration
accélérer /akseleʀe/ [14] [1] *vtr* to speed
up ‹rhythm, process›; ~ **le pas** to quicken
one's step
[2] *vi* ‹driver› to accelerate
[3] **s'accélérer** *v refl* (+ *v être*) ‹pulse,
movement› to become faster; ‹phenomenon›
to accelerate
accent /aksɑ̃/ *nm* **(a)** (of person, region)
accent
(b) (on a letter) accent
(c) (on a syllable) ~ **tonique** stress; **mettre
l'~ sur qch** to emphasize sth, to put the
emphasis on sth
(d) ~ **de sincérité** hint of sincerity
accentuer /aksɑ̃tɥe/ [1] [1] *vtr* **(a)** (gen) to
emphasize, to accentuate
(b) to heighten ‹tension›; to increase
‹tendency›
(c) (in pronouncing) to stress ‹syllable›
[2] **s'accentuer** *v refl* (+ *v être*) to become
more marked
acceptable /aksɛptabl/ *adj* **(a)** acceptable
(b) passable; satisfactory
acceptation /aksɛptasjɔ̃/ *nf* acceptance
⚔ **accepter** /aksɛpte/ [1] *vtr* to accept; to
agree to
acception /aksɛpsjɔ̃/ *nf* sense; **dans toute
l'~ du terme** *or* **mot** in every sense of the
word
⚔ **accès** /aksɛ/ *nm inv* **(a)** access; **d'un** ~
facile ‹place› easy to get to; **'~ aux quais'**
'to the trains'; **'~ interdit'** 'no entry'; **l'~ à**
access to ‹profession, course›; admission to
‹club, school›
(b) ~ **de colère** fit of anger; ~ **de fièvre** bout
of fever; **par** ~ by fits and starts
(c) (Comput) access
accessible /aksesibl/ *adj* **(a)** ‹place, book,
information› accessible
(b) ~ **à** ‹job› open to
(c) ‹price, fare› affordable
accession /aksesjɔ̃/ *nf* ~ **à** accession to
‹throne, power›; attainment of ‹independence›
accessoire /akseswaʀ/ [1] *adj* incidental
[2] *nm* **(a)** accessory; attachment; ~**s de
toilette** toilet requisites
(b) (in the theatre) ~**s** props
accessoirement /akseswaʀmɑ̃/ *adv*
(a) incidentally, as it happens
(b) if desired
accessoiriste /akseswaʀist/ *nmf* props
man/woman
⚔ **accident** /aksidɑ̃/ *nm* **(a)** accident
(b) hitch; mishap; ~ **de parcours** (fam) hitch
▪ ~ **domestique** accident in the home
accidenté, ~e /aksidɑ̃te/ [1] *adj*
(a) ‹person› injured; ‹car› involved in an ⋯⋗

accident
(b) ‹*road, ground*› uneven
2 *nm,f* accident victim
accidentel, -elle /aksidɑ̃tɛl/ *adj* accidental
accidentellement /aksidɑ̃tɛlmɑ̃/ *adv*
(a) in an accident
(b) by accident, accidentally
acclamation /aklamasjɔ̃/ *nf* cheering
acclamer /aklame/ [1] *vtr* to cheer, to acclaim
acclimater /aklimate/ [1] 1 *vtr* to acclimatize
2 **s'acclimater** *v refl* (+ *v être*) to become acclimatized; to adapt
accointances /akwɛ̃tɑ̃s/ *nf pl* contacts
accolade /akɔlad/ *nf* embrace
accommoder /akɔmɔde/ [1] 1 *vtr* to prepare
2 *vi* ‹*eyes*› to focus
3 **s'accommoder** *v refl* (+ *v être*) **s'~ de qch** to make the best of sth; to put up with sth
accompagnateur, -trice /akɔ̃paɲatœʀ, tʀis/ *nm,f* **(a)** (Mus) accompanist
(b) (with children) accompanying adult; (with tourists) courier
accompagnement /akɔ̃paɲmɑ̃/ *nm* accompaniment
ꝑ **accompagner** /akɔ̃paɲe/ [1] *vtr*
(a) ‹*person*› to accompany, to go with, to come with
(b) to accompany ‹*phenomenon, event*›
(c) (Mus) to accompany
(d) ‹*wine*› to be served with
ꝑ **accomplir** /akɔ̃pliʀ/ [3] 1 *vtr* to accomplish ‹*task*›; to fulfil (GB) ‹*obligation*›
2 **s'accomplir** *v refl* (+ *v être*) to be fulfilled
accomplissement /akɔ̃plismɑ̃/ *nm* (of mission) accomplishment, fulfilment (GB); (of ambition, aim) realization, achievement
ꝑ **accord** /akɔʀ/ *nm* **(a)** agreement; (tacit) understanding; **d'~** all right, OK (colloq); **je suis d'~** I agree (**avec** with); **se mettre** *or* **tomber d'~** to come to an agreement
(b) harmony
(c) (in grammar) **~ en genre/en nombre** gender/number agreement
(d) (Mus) chord
accordéon /akɔʀdeɔ̃/ *nm* accordion
ꝑ **accorder** /akɔʀde/ [1] 1 *vtr* **(a)** **~ qch à qn** to grant sb sth ‹*favour, loan, interview, permission, right*›; to give sb sth ‹*grant, reduction, chance*›; **il n'a pas entièrement tort, et je te l'accorde** he's not entirely wrong, I'll give you that
(b) to attach ‹*importance, value*› (**à** to); to pay ‹*attention*›
(c) (Mus) to tune ‹*instrument*›

ꝑ indicates a very frequent word

(d) to make [sth] agree ‹*word, adjective*›
2 **s'accorder** *v refl* (+ *v être*) **(a)** to give oneself ‹*rest, time off*›
(b) to agree (**sur** about, on)
(c) ‹*colours, clothes*› to go (together) well
(d) ‹*adjective, verb*› to agree (**avec** with)
accordeur /akɔʀdœʀ/ *nm* tuner
accostage /akɔstaʒ/ *nm* docking
accoster /akɔste/ [1] 1 *vtr* to accost ‹*person*›
2 *vi* ‹*ship*› to dock
accotement /akɔtmɑ̃/ *nm* verge
accouchement /akuʃmɑ̃/ *nm* delivery
accoucher /akuʃe/ [1] *vi* to give birth (**de** to)
accoucheur /akuʃœʀ/ *nm* obstetrician
accouder: s'accouder /akude/ [1] *v refl* (+ *v être*) to lean on one's elbows
accoudoir /akudwaʀ/ *nm* arm-rest
accouplement /akupləmɑ̃/ *nm* mating
accourir /akuʀiʀ/ [26] *vi* to run up
accoutrement /akutʀəmɑ̃/ *nm* get-up (colloq)
accoutrer: s'accoutrer /akutʀe/ [1] *v refl* (+ *v être*) to get oneself up (**de** in)
accoutumance /akutymɑ̃s/ *nf* addiction
accoutumer /akutyme/ [1] 1 *vtr* to accustom (**à** to)
2 **s'accoutumer** *v refl* (+ *v être*) to grow accustomed (**à** to)
accrédité, ~e /akʀedite/ *adj* authorized; accredited
accréditer /akʀedite/ [1] *vtr* **(a)** to give credence to ‹*rumour*›
(b) to accredit ‹*ambassador*›
accro /akʀo/ *adj* (fam) hooked (colloq) (**à** on)
accroc /akʀo/ *nm* tear (**à** in)
accrochage /akʀoʃaʒ/ *nm* (between people) clash; (between vehicles) collision
accrocher /akʀoʃe/ [1] 1 *vtr* **(a)** to hang (**à** from)
(b) to hook [sth] on (**à** to)
(c) to catch ‹*stocking, sweater*› (**à** on)
(d) to catch ‹*eye, attention*›
2 **s'accrocher** *v refl* (+ *v être*) **(a)** (to ledge) to hang on; (to post) to cling (**à** to)
(b) ‹*person*› **s'~ à qn** to cling to sb
(c) **l'hameçon s'est accroché à ma veste** the hook got caught in my jacket
(d) (fam) **s'~ pour faire** to try hard to do
IDIOM avoir le cœur *or* **l'estomac bien accroché** to have a strong stomach
accrocheur, -euse /akʀoʃœʀ, øz/ *adj* ‹*song, tune*› catchy; ‹*picture, title*› eye-catching
accroissement /akʀwasmɑ̃/ *nm* growth
accroître /akʀwɑtʀ/ [72] *vtr*, **s'accroître** *v refl* (+ *v être*) to increase
accroupir: s'accroupir /akʀupiʀ/ [3] *v refl* (+ *v être*) to squat (down); to crouch (down)

accru, ~**e** /akry/ ▸ ACCROÎTRE

⚹ **accueil** /akœj/ *nm* (a) welcome
(b) reception desk

accueillant, ~**e** /akœjã, ãt/ *adj*
(a) hospitable, welcoming
(b) homely (GB), homey (US)

⚹ **accueillir** /akœjiʀ/ [27] *vtr* (a) to welcome
(b) to receive, to greet
(c) ‹*room, hotel*› to accommodate
(d) ‹*hospital, organization*› to cater for

accumulation /akymylasjɔ̃/ *nf*
(a) accumulation
(b) storage

accumuler /akymyle/ [1] **1** *vtr* (a) to
store (up) ‹*things*›; to accumulate ‹*capital*›; to
make a succession of ‹*mistakes*›
(b) to store (up) ‹*energy*›
2 **s'accumuler** *v refl* (+ *v être*) ‹*snow,
rubbish*› to pile up; ‹*stocks, debts*› to accrue

accusateur, **-trice** /akyzatœʀ,
tʀis/ **1** *adj* ‹*silence, finger*› accusing;
‹*presence, speech*› accusatory
2 *nm,f* accuser; ~ **public** public prosecutor

accusation /akyzasjɔ̃/ *nf* (a) accusation;
(Law) charge
(b) **l'**~ the prosecution

accusé, ~**e** /akyze/ **1** *pp* ▸ ACCUSER
2 *pp adj* ‹*wrinkles*› deep; ‹*relief*› marked
3 *nm,f* defendant; **les** ~**s** the accused
■ ~ **de réception** acknowledgement (of
receipt)

⚹ **accuser** /akyze/ [1] **1** *vtr* (a) to accuse
‹*person*›; to blame ‹*fate*›; ‹*evidence*› to point
to ‹*person*›; ‹*judge*› to charge ‹*defendant*› (de
with)
(b) to show, to register ‹*fall, deficit*›
2 **s'accuser** *v refl* (+ *v être*) (a) ‹*person*›
to take the blame
(b) to become more marked
IDIOM ~ **le coup** to be visibly shaken

acerbe /asɛʀb/ *adj* acerbic

acéré, ~**e** /aseʀe/ *adj* sharp

acharné, ~**e** /aʃaʀne/ *adj* ‹*supporter*›
passionate; ‹*work*› unremitting; ‹*struggle*›
fierce

acharnement /aʃaʀnəmã/ *nm* furious
energy

acharner: s'acharner /aʃaʀne/ [1] *v refl*
(+ *v être*) (a) to persevere; **s'**~ **contre** to fight
against ‹*project*›
(b) **s'**~ **sur** ‹*person, animal*› to keep going at
‹*victim, prey*›; (figurative) to hound ‹*person*›; **la
malchance s'acharne contre lui** he is dogged
by bad luck

achat /aʃa/ *nm* purchase

acheminement /aʃ(ə)minmã/ *nm*
transportation

acheminer /aʃ(ə)mine/ [1] **1** *vtr* to
transport
2 **s'acheminer** *v refl* (+ *v être*) **s'**~
vers to make one's way toward(s); to move
toward(s)

⚹ **acheter** /aʃte/ [18] **1** *vtr* to buy; ~ **qch à
qn** to buy sth from sb; to buy sth for sb
2 **s'acheter** *v refl* (+ *v être*) (a) **s'**~ **qch**
to buy oneself sth
(b) **cela s'achète où?** where can you get it?

acheteur, **-euse** /aʃtœʀ, øz/ *nm,f* buyer

⚹ **achever** /aʃve/ [16] **1** *vtr* (a) to finish
‹*work*›; to conclude ‹*discussions*›; to complete
‹*project, inquiry*›; to end ‹*life*›
(b) to destroy ‹*animal*›; to finish off ‹*person*›
2 **s'achever** *v refl* (+ *v être*) to end

achoppement /aʃɔpmã/ *nm* **pierre d'**~
stumbling block

acide /asid/ *adj*, *nm* acid

acidité /asidite/ *nf* acidity, tartness,
sharpness

acidulé, ~**e** /asidyle/ *adj* slightly acid;
tangy

acier /asje/ **1** *adj inv* steel(y)
2 *nm* steel; **d'**~ ‹*girder, column*› steel;
‹*nerves*› of steel

aciérie /asjeʀi/ *nf* steelworks

acné /akne/ *nf* acne; ~ **juvénile** teenage
acne

acolyte /akɔlit/ *nmf* henchman, acolyte

acompte /akɔ̃t/ *nm* (a) deposit
(b) part payment

acoquiner: s'acoquiner /akɔkine/ [1] *v
refl* (+ *v être*) **s'**~ **avec qn** to get thick (colloq)
with sb

à-côté, *pl* ~**s** /akote/ *nm* (a) perk
(b) extra expense
(c) extra profit

à-coup, *pl* ~**s** /aku/ *nm* jolt; **par** ~**s** by fits
and starts

acoustique /akustik/ **1** *adj* acoustic
2 *nf* acoustics

acquéreur /akeʀœʀ/ *nm* buyer, purchaser

⚹ **acquérir** /akeʀiʀ/ [35] *vtr* (a) to acquire; (by
buying) to purchase
(b) to acquire ‹*reputation*›

acquiescement /akjɛsmã/ *nm* **donner
son** ~ **à** to acquiesce to

acquiescer /akjese/ [12] *vi* to acquiesce

acquis, ~**e** /aki, iz/ **1** *pp* ▸ ACQUÉRIR
2 *pp adj* (a) ‹*skills*› acquired
(b) ‹*principle, right*› accepted, established;
les avantages ~ the gains made; **tenir qch
pour** ~ to take sth for granted
3 *nm inv* (a) acquired knowledge
(b) ~ **sociaux** social benefits
IDIOM **bien mal** ~ **ne profite jamais** (Proverb)
ill-gotten gains never prosper

acquisition /akizisjɔ̃/ *nf* (a) purchase
(b) acquisition

acquit /aki/ *nm* **je le ferai par** ~ **de
conscience** I'll do it to put my mind at rest

acquittement /akitmã/ *nm* (Law)
acquittal

acquitter /akite/ [1] **1** *vtr* (Law) to acquit
2 **s'acquitter** *v refl* (+ *v être*) **s'**~ **de son** ⋯⋗

a

devoir to do one's duty; **s'~ d'une dette** to pay off a debt

acre /akʀ/ *nf* acre

âcre /ɑkʀ/ *adj* ‹taste› sharp; ‹smell› acrid

acrobate /akʀɔbat/ *nmf* acrobat

acrobatie /akʀɔbasi/ *nf* acrobatics

acronyme /akʀɔnim/ *nm* acronym

acrylique /akʀilik/ *adj, nm* acrylic

ᕁ **acte** /akt/ *nm* **(a)** act; **~ manqué** Freudian slip; **être libre de ses ~s** to do as one wishes; **faire ~ de candidature** to put oneself forward as a candidate
(b) (Law) deed; **~ de naissance** birth certificate
(c) (in play) act

ᕁ **acteur, -trice** /aktœʀ, tʀis/ *nm,f* **(a)** actor/ actress
(b) protagonist

ᕁ **actif, -ive** /aktif, iv/ ① *adj* (gen) active; ‹market› buoyant; **la vie active** working life
② *nm* **(a) l'~** the assets
(b) à l'~ de qn in sb's favour (GB)

ᕁ **action** /aksjɔ̃/ *nf* **(a)** action, act; **une bonne ~** a good deed
(b) l'~ action; **moyens d'~** courses of action; **en ~** in operation
(c) effect; **l'~ de qn sur** sb's influence on
(d) ~ en justice legal action
(e) (in finance) share

actionnaire /aksjɔnɛʀ/ *nmf* shareholder

actionner /aksjɔne/ [1] *vtr* to activate

activement /aktivmɑ̃/ *adv* actively

activer /aktive/ [1] ① *vtr* **(a)** to speed up ‹work›; to stimulate ‹digestion›
(b) ‹wind› to stir up ‹flames›
(c) to stoke ‹fire›
② **s'activer** *v refl* (+ *v être*) (fam) to hurry up

activiste /aktivist/ *adj, nmf* activist

ᕁ **activité** /aktivite/ *nf* **(a)** activity; **~ professionnelle** occupation
(b) être en pleine ~ ‹street› to be bustling with activity; ‹person› to be very busy; **volcan en ~** active volcano

actrice ▸ ACTEUR

actualisation /aktɥalizasjɔ̃/ *nf* (process) updating; (result) update

actualiser /aktɥalize/ [1] *vtr* to update

actualité /aktɥalite/ ① *nf* **(a)** current affairs; **l'~ culturelle** cultural events
(b) d'~ topical; **toujours d'~** still relevant today
② **actualités** *nf pl* **(a)** news
(b) newsreel

ᕁ **actuel, -elle** /aktɥɛl/ *adj* **(a)** present, current
(b) ‹film, discussion› topical

ᕁ **actuellement** /aktɥɛlmɑ̃/ *adv* **(a)** at the moment

(b) currently

actus /akty/ *nfpl* (TV, Radio, fam) news

acuité /akɥite/ *nf* **(a)** acuity
(b) shrillness
(c) (of pain) intensity

acupuncteur, -trice /akypɔ̃ktœʀ, tʀis/ *nm,f* acupuncturist

acupuncture /akypɔ̃ktyʀ/ *nf* acupuncture

adage /adaʒ/ *nm* saying, adage

adaptable /adaptabl/ *adj* **(a)** (flexible) adaptable (**à** to)
(b) ‹height, pressure› adjustable; **~ à toutes les circonstances** *or* **tous les besoins** all-purpose

adaptateur, -trice /adaptatœʀ, tʀis/ ① *nm,f* (for cinema, theatre) adapter
② *nm* (Tech) adapter

adaptation /adaptasjɔ̃/ *nf* adaptation

adapté, ~e /adapte/ *adj* **(a)** suitable
(b) ~ à ‹solution› suited to
(c) (for TV, stage) adapted

ᕁ **adapter** /adapte/ [1] ① *vtr* **(a)** to fit (**à** to)
(b) to adapt ‹equipment›
(c) to adapt ‹novel›
② **s'adapter** *v refl* (+ *v être*) **(a)** ‹tool, part› to fit
(b) to adapt, to adjust (**à** to)

addition /adisjɔ̃/ *nf* **(a)** addition
(b) bill (GB), check (US)

additionner /adisjɔne/ [1] *vtr* to add up

adduction /adyksjɔ̃/ *nf* adduction; **~ d'eau** water conveyance

adepte /adɛpt/ *nmf* **(a)** (of theory) supporter; (of person) disciple
(b) enthusiast

adéquat, ~e /adekwa, at/ *adj*
(a) appropriate, suitable
(b) adequate

adéquation /adekwasjɔ̃/ *nf*
(a) (correspondence) appropriateness (**à, avec** to)
(b) (of model) adequacy (**à** to)

adhérence /adeʀɑ̃s/ *nf* (of tyre, sole) grip

adhérent, ~e /adeʀɑ̃, ɑ̃t/ *nm,f* member

adhérer /adeʀe/ [14] *v+prep* **~ à** ‹glue› to stick to; ‹tyre› to grip
(b) ~ à to join

adhésif, -ive /adezif, iv/ *adj* adhesive

adhésion /adezjɔ̃/ *nf* **(a)** membership
(b) support

adieu, *pl* **~x** /adjø/ *nm* goodbye, farewell

adipeux, -euse /adipø, øz/ *adj* fatty

adjectif /adʒɛktif/ *nm* adjective

adjoint, ~e /adʒwɛ̃, ɛ̃t/ *nm,f* assistant; deputy; **~ au maire** deputy mayor

adjudant /adʒydɑ̃/ *nm* ≈ warrant officer

adjudication /adʒydikasjɔ̃/ *nf* auction; **~ judiciaire** sale by order of the court

---

ᕁ indicates a very frequent word

adjuger /adʒyʒe/ [13] *vtr* to auction; **une fois, deux fois, adjugé!** going, going, gone!

adjuvant /adʒyvɑ̃/ *nm* additive

ADM /adeɛm/ *fpl* (*abbr* = **armes de destruction massive**) WMD

⚥ **admettre** /admɛtʀ/ [60] *vtr* (a) to accept, to admit ‹fact›
(b) to admit ‹person, student›; **être admis à un examen** to pass an exam
(c) ~ **que** to suppose (that)

administrateur, -trice /administʀatœʀ, tʀis/ *nm,f* (a) administrator
(b) director
(c) trustee

administratif, -ive /administʀatif, iv/ *adj* (a) ‹staff, building› administrative
(b) ‹report› official

⚥ **administration** /administʀasjɔ̃/ *nf*
(a) administration
(b) civil service
(c) **être placé sous** ~ **judiciaire** to go into receivership
(d) management
(e) (of drugs, sacrament) administration, giving

administrer /administʀe/ [1] *vtr* (a) to administer ‹funds›; to run ‹company›
(b) to administer, to give ‹drug, sacrament›

admirable /admiʀabl/ *adj* admirable

admirablement /admiʀabləmɑ̃/ *adv* ‹do› admirably; ‹done› superbly

admirateur, -trice /admiʀatœʀ, tʀis/ *nm,f* admirer

admiration /admiʀasjɔ̃/ *nf* admiration

admirer /admiʀe/ [1] *vtr* to admire

admis, ~**e** /admi, iz/ 1 *pp* ▶ ADMETTRE
2 *pp adj* accepted; ‹candidate› successful

admissible /admisibl/ *adj* (a) acceptable
(b) eligible

admission /admisjɔ̃/ *nf* admission; **service des** ~**s** reception

ado /ado/ *nmf* (fam) teenager

adolescence /adɔlesɑ̃s/ *nf* adolescence

adolescent, ~**e** /adɔlesɑ̃, ɑ̃t/ 1 *adj* teenage
2 *nm,f* teenager, adolescent

adonner: s'adonner /adɔne/ [1] *v refl* (+ *v être*) **s'**~ **à** to devote all one's time to; **il s'adonne à la boisson** he drinks too much

⚥ **adopter** /adɔpte/ [1] *vtr* to adopt ‹child, method›; to pass ‹law›

adoptif, -ive /adɔptif, iv/ *adj* (a) ‹child, country› adopted
(b) ‹parent› adoptive

adoption /adɔpsjɔ̃/ *nf* (a) adoption
(b) passing

adorable /adɔʀabl/ *adj* adorable

adorateur, -trice /adɔʀatœʀ, tʀis/ *nm,f* worshipper (GB)

adoration /adɔʀasjɔ̃/ *nf* worship, adoration

⚥ **adorer** /adɔʀe/ [1] *vtr* to adore, to worship

adosser: s'adosser /adose/ [1] *v refl* (+ *v être*) **s'**~ **à** to lean back on

adoucir /adusiʀ/ [3] 1 *vtr* to soften ‹skin, water›; to moderate ‹tone of voice›; to soothe ‹throat›; to ease ‹suffering›
2 **s'adoucir** *v refl* (+ *v être*) ‹temperature› to become milder; ‹slope› to become more gentle

adoucissant, ~**e** /adusisɑ̃, ɑ̃t/ 1 *adj* soothing
2 *nm* softener

adrénaline /adʀenalin/ *nf* adrenalin

⚥ **adresse** /adʀɛs/ *nf* (a) address; **se tromper d'**~ to get the wrong address; (figurative) to pick the wrong person; **remarque lancée à l'**~ **de qn** remark directed at sb
(b) dexterity
(c) skill
■ ~ **email** email address

⚥ **adresser** /adʀese/ [1] 1 *vtr* (a) to direct ‹criticism› (à at); to make ‹request, declaration, appeal›; to deliver ‹ultimatum›; to present ‹petition›; to aim ‹blow›; ~ **la parole à qn** to speak to sb
(b) to send ‹letter›
(c) to refer [sb] (à to)
2 **s'adresser** *v refl* (+ *v être*) (a) **s'**~ **à qn** to speak to sb
(b) **s'**~ **à** to contact ‹embassy›; **s'**~ **au guichet 8** to go to window 8
(c) **s'**~ **à** ‹measure› to be aimed at

adroit, ~**e** /adʀwa, at/ *adj* skilful (GB)

ADSL /adeɛsɛl/ *fpl* (*abbr* = **asymmetrical digital subscriber line**) ADSL

⚥ **adulte** /adylt/ *adj, nmf* adult

adultère /adyltɛʀ/ 1 *adj* adulterous
2 *nm* adultery

advenir /advəniʀ/ [36] *v impers* (a) to happen; **advienne que pourra** come what may
(b) ~ **de** to become of

adverbe /advɛʀb/ *nm* adverb

⚥ **adversaire** /advɛʀsɛʀ/ *nmf* (gen) opponent; (Mil) adversary

adverse /advɛʀs/ *adj* (a) opposing
(b) opposite

adversité /advɛʀsite/ *nf* adversity

aérer /aeʀe/ [14] 1 *vtr* (a) to air
(b) to space out
2 **s'aérer** *v refl* (+ *v être*) to get some fresh air

aérien, -ienne /aeʀjɛ̃, ɛn/ *adj* ‹transport› air; ‹photography› aerial; **métro** ~ elevated section of the underground (GB), elevated railroad (US)

aéro-club, *pl* ~**s** /aeʀoklœb/ *nm* flying club

aérodrome /aeʀodʀom/ *nm* aerodrome (GB), (small) airfield

a

aérodynamique /aeʀodinamik/ *adj*
aerodynamic

aérogare /aeʀogaʀ/ *nf* air terminal

aéroglisseur /aeʀoglisœʀ/ *nm* hovercraft

aéronautique /aeʀonotik/ *nf* aeronautics

aérophagie /aeʀofaʒi/ *nf* aerophagia

aéroport /aeʀopɔʀ/ *nm* airport

aéroporté, ~e /aeʀopɔʀte/ *adj* ‹troops›
airborne; ‹equipment› transported by air

aérosol /aeʀosɔl/ *nm* (a) aerosol
(b) spray

aérospatiale /aeʀospasjal/ *nf* aerospace
industry

affabulation /afabylasjɔ̃/ *nf* fabrication

affaiblir /afɛbliʀ/ [3] ⚊1⚊ *vtr* to weaken
⚊2⚊ **s'affaiblir** *v refl* (+ *v être*) to get weaker

affaiblissement /afɛblismɑ̃/ *nm*
(a) weakening
(b) weakened state

ˢ **affaire** /afɛʀ/ ⚊1⚊ *nf* (a) affair; (political)
crisis, affair; (moral) scandal; (legal) case
(b) affair, matter; **une ~ délicate** a delicate
matter; **c'est l'~ de quelques jours** it'll only
take a few days; **j'en fais mon ~** I'll deal with
it; **c'est une autre ~** that's another matter;
c'est une ~ d'argent there's money involved;
et voilà toute l'~ and that's that; **c'est toute
une ~, ce n'est pas une petite ~** it's quite
a business
(c) (skill, trade) **il connaît bien son ~** he
knows his job; **la mécanique, c'est leur ~**
mechanics is their thing
(d) deal; **faire ~ avec** to do a deal with; **avoir
~ à** to be dealing with
(e) bargain; **la belle ~!** (fam) big deal (colloq);
ça fera l'~ that'll do
(f) business, concern
(g) (difficulty) **être tiré d'~** to be out of danger
⚊2⚊ **affaires** *nf pl* (a) business
(b) (personal) business affairs; **occupe-toi de
tes ~s!** mind your own business!
(c) things, belongings
■ **~s courantes** daily business

affairer: s'affairer /afeʀe/ [1] *v refl* (+ *v
être*) to bustle about (**à faire** doing)

affairisme /afeʀism/ *nm* wheeling and
dealing (colloq)

affaisser: s'affaisser /afese/ [1] *v refl* (+
v être) (a) to subside
(b) ‹shoulders, roof› to sag
(c) ‹person› to collapse

affaler: s'affaler /afale/ [1] *v refl* (+ *v être*)
(a) to collapse
(b) (fam) to fall

affamé, ~e /afame/ ⚊1⚊ *pp* ▶ AFFAMER
⚊2⚊ *pp adj* (a) starving
(b) **~ de** hungry for

affamer /afame/ [1] *vtr* to starve

affectation /afɛktasjɔ̃/ *nf* (a) allocation
(à to)

ˢ indicates a very frequent word

(b) appointment (**à** to); posting (**à** to)
(c) affectation

affecter /afɛkte/ [1] *vtr* (a) to feign, to
affect ‹interest›; to affect ‹behaviour›; **~ de
faire/d'être** to pretend to do/to be
(b) to allocate ‹funds› (**à** to)
(c) to appoint (**à** to); to post (**à, en** to)
(d) to affect ‹market, person›

affectif, -ive /afɛktif, iv/ *adj* (a) emotional
(b) affective

affection /afɛksjɔ̃/ *nf* (a) affection; **prendre
qn en ~** to become fond of sb
(b) (Med) disease

affectionner /afɛksjone/ [1] *vtr* to be
fond of

affectivité /afɛktivite/ *nf* feelings

affectueusement /afɛktɥøzmɑ̃/ *adv*
affectionately, fondly

affectueux, -euse /afɛktɥø, øz/ *adj*
affectionate

affermir /afɛʀmiʀ/ [3] ⚊1⚊ *vtr* to strengthen
‹will›; to consolidate ‹power›; to firm up
‹muscles›
⚊2⚊ **s'affermir** *v refl* (+ *v être*) ‹power› to
be consolidated; ‹voice› to become stronger;
‹muscles› to firm up; ‹ground› to become
firmer

affermissement /afɛʀmismɑ̃/ *nm* (of
power, recovery) consolidation; (of will, muscles,
voice) strengthening; (economic) improvement
(**de** in)

affichage /afiʃaʒ/ *nm* (a) billsticking;
campagne d'~ poster campaign
(b) (Comput) display
■ **~ à cristaux liquides** liquid crystal display,
LCD

affiche /afiʃ/ *nf* poster; (official) notice; **à l'~
‹film› now showing; ‹play› on; **quitter l'~** to
come off
■ **~ de théâtre** playbill

affiché, ~e /afiʃe/ ⚊1⚊ *pp* ▶ AFFICHER
⚊2⚊ *pp adj* (a) ‹ad, picture› (put) up;
‹information› posted (up)
(b) ‹result› published
(c) ‹optimism, opinion› declared
(d) (Comput) ‹data› displayed

afficher /afiʃe/ [1] ⚊1⚊ *vtr* (a) to put up
‹poster, notice›
(b) to display ‹prices, result›; **~ complet**
‹film, play› to be sold out; ‹hotel› to be fully
booked
(c) ‹market› to show ‹rise›
(d) to declare ‹ambitions›; to display ‹scorn›;
to flaunt ‹opinions, liaison›
⚊2⚊ **s'afficher** *v refl* (+ *v être*) (a) to flaunt
oneself
(b) ‹smile› to appear (**sur** on)

afficheur /afiʃœʀ/ *nm* (a) poster (GB) *or*
billboard (US) sticker
(b) (Comput) visual display unit, VDU

affichiste /afiʃist/ *nmf* poster artist

affilé, ~e¹ /afile/ *adj* ‹blade› sharpened

affilée²: d'affilée /dafile/ *phr* in a row

affiler /afile/ [1] *vtr* to sharpen

affilier: s'affilier /afilje/ [2] *v refl* (+ *v être*) to become affiliated

affiner /afine/ [1] ⃞1 *vtr* (a) to hone ‹*style*› (b) to slim down ‹*waistline*›
⃞2 **s'affiner** *v refl* (+ *v être*) (a) ‹*style, taste*› to become (more) refined
(b) ‹*waistline*› to slim down

affinité /afinite/ *nf* affinity

affirmatif, -ive¹ /afiʀmatif, iv/ *adj* affirmative; **faire un signe de tête** ∼ to nod agreement

affirmation /afiʀmasjɔ̃/ *nf* assertion; **l'**∼ **de soi** assertiveness

affirmative² /afiʀmativ/ ⃞1 *adj f*
▶ AFFIRMATIF
⃞2 *nf* affirmative

♂ **affirmer** /afiʀme/ [1] ⃞1 *vtr* (a) to maintain; ∼ **faire** to claim to do
(b) to assert ‹*talent, authority*›
(c) to declare, to affirm ‹*will*›
⃞2 **s'affirmer** *v refl* (+ *v être*) ‹*tendency*› to become apparent; ‹*personality*› to assert itself

affleurer /aflœʀe/ [1] *vi* ‹*reef*› to show on the surface; ‹*rock*› to come through the soil

affligeant, ∼e /afliʒɑ̃, ɑ̃t/ *adj* pathetic

affliger /afliʒe/ [13] *vtr* (a) to afflict (**de** with)
(b) to distress

affluence /aflɥɑ̃s/ *nf* crowd(s)

affluent /aflɥɑ̃/ *nm* tributary

affluer /aflɥe/ [1] *vi* ‹*people*› to flock (**à, vers** to); ‹*letters*› to pour in

affolant, ∼e /afɔlɑ̃, ɑ̃t/ *adj* (fam) frightening

affolement /afɔlmɑ̃/ *nm* panic

affoler /afɔle/ [1] ⃞1 *vtr* to throw [sb] into a panic
⃞2 **s'affoler** *v refl* (+ *v être*) to panic

affranchi, ∼e /afʀɑ̃ʃi/ *nm,f* emancipated slave

affranchir /afʀɑ̃ʃiʀ/ [3] ⃞1 *vtr* (a) to stamp ‹*letter*›
(b) to free ‹*slave, country*›
⃞2 **s'affranchir** *v refl* (+ *v être*) to free oneself

affranchissement /afʀɑ̃ʃismɑ̃/ *nm* (a) stamping; (cost) postage
(b) liberation; freeing

affres /afʀ/ *nf pl* (of pain) agony; (of hunger) pangs; (of jealousy) throes; **les** ∼ **de la mort** death throes

affréter /afʀete/ [14] *vtr* to charter

affréteur /afʀetœʀ/ *nm* charter company

affreusement /afʀøzmɑ̃/ *adv* (fam) terribly

affreux, -euse /afʀø, øz/ *adj* (a) hideous
(b) awful, dreadful

affront /afʀɔ̃/ *nm* affront

affrontement /afʀɔ̃tmɑ̃/ *nm* confrontation

affronter /afʀɔ̃te/ [1] *vtr* to face ‹*situation*›; to brave ‹*weather*›

affubler /afyble/ [1] *vtr* ∼ **qn de** to deck sb out in ‹*clothes*›; to saddle sb with ‹*nickname*›

affût /afy/ *nm* **se tenir** *or* **être à l'**∼ to lie in wait; (figurative) to be on the lookout (**de** for)

affûter /afyte/ [1] *vtr* (a) to sharpen
(b) to grind

♂ **afin** /afɛ̃/ ⃞1 **afin de** *phr* ∼ **de faire** in order to do
⃞2 **afin que** *phr* so that

AFP /aɛfpe/ *nf* (*abbr* = **Agence France-Presse**) AFP (*French news agency*)

♂ **africain, ∼e** /afʀikɛ̃, ɛn/ *adj* African

Afrique /afʀik/ *pr nf* Africa

AG /aʒe/ *nf: abbr* ▶ ASSEMBLÉE

agaçant, ∼e /agasɑ̃, ɑ̃t/ *adj* annoying

agacement /agasmɑ̃/ *nm* irritation

agacer /agase/ [12] *vtr* to annoy, to irritate

agapes /agap/ *nf pl* feast, banquet

agate /agat/ *nf* (a) agate
(b) marble

♂ **âge** /aʒ/ *nm* (a) age; **faire son** ∼ to look one's age; **un homme d'un certain** ∼ a middle-aged man
(b) old age; **avec l'**∼ as one gets older; **prendre de l'**∼ to grow old
(c) age, era
■ **l'**∼ **bête** *or* **ingrat** the awkward *or* difficult age; **l'**∼ **mûr** maturity

âgé, ∼e /aʒe/ *adj* old

agence /aʒɑ̃s/ *nf* (a) agency
(b) (of bank) branch
■ ∼ **immobilière** estate agents (GB), real-estate agency (US); **Agence nationale pour l'emploi, ANPE** *French national employment agency*; ∼ **de placement** employment agency

agencer /aʒɑ̃se/ [12] *vtr* to lay out ‹*room*›

agenda /aʒɛ̃da/ *nm* diary

agenouiller: s'agenouiller /aʒnuje/ [1] *v refl* (+ *v être*) to kneel (down)

♂ **agent** /aʒɑ̃/ *nm* (a) officer, official
(b) agent
(c) employee
■ ∼ **de change** stockbroker; ∼ **de la circula-tion** traffic policeman; ∼ **commercial** sales representative; ∼ **de police** policeman

agglomération /aglɔmeʀasjɔ̃/ *nf* town; village; **l'**∼ **lyonnaise** Lyons and its suburbs

aggloméré /aglɔmeʀe/ *nm* chipboard

agglomérer /aglɔmeʀe/ [14] ⃞1 *vtr* to agglomerate
⃞2 **s'agglomérer** *v refl* (+ *v être*) ‹*people*› to gather together; ‹*houses*› to be grouped together

agglutiner: s'agglutiner /aglytine/ [1] *v refl* (+ *v être*) ‹*onlookers*› to crowd together (**à** at); ‹*insects*› to cluster together

aggravation /agʀavasjɔ̃/ nf (of situation) worsening; (in debt) increase

aggraver /agʀave/ [1] **1** vtr to aggravate, to make [sth] worse
2 **s'aggraver** v refl (+ v être) to get worse

agile /aʒil/ adj agile, nimble

agilité /aʒilite/ nf agility

agios /aʒjo/ nm pl bank charges

✔ **agir** /aʒiʀ/ [3] **1** vi (a) to act
(b) to behave; ∼ **en lâche** to act like a coward
(c) ⟨medicine⟩ to take effect, to work
2 **s'agir de** v impers (+ v être) **de quoi s'agit-il?** what is it about?; **il s'agit de votre mari** it's about your husband; **mais il ne s'agit pas de ça!** but that's not the point!; **il s'agit de faire vite** we must act quickly

âgisme /ɑʒism/ nm ageism

agissements /aʒismɑ̃/ nm pl activities

agitateur, -trice /aʒitatœʀ, tʀis/ nm,f agitator

agitation /aʒitasjɔ̃/ nf (a) restlessness
(b) bustle (**de** in); activity
(c) unrest

agité, ∼e /aʒite/ adj (a) ⟨sea⟩ rough, choppy; ⟨sleep⟩ troubled; ⟨period⟩ turbulent; ⟨night⟩ restless
(b) ⟨street⟩ bustling; ⟨life⟩ hectic

✔ **agiter** /aʒite/ [1] **1** vtr to wave ⟨hand⟩; to shake ⟨can⟩; to shake up ⟨liquid⟩
2 **s'agiter** v refl (+ v être) (a) to fidget; (in bed) to toss and turn
(b) to sway (in the wind)
(c) to bustle about
(d) to become restless

agneau, pl ∼x /aɲo/ nm (a) lamb
(b) lambskin

agonie /agɔni/ nf death throes

agonir /agɔniʀ/ [3] vtr ∼ **qn d'injures** to hurl insults at sb; **en rentrant, il s'est fait ∼** when he got home he was told off soundly

agoniser /agɔnize/ [1] vi to be dying

agrafe /agʀaf/ nf (a) (for paper) staple
(b) (on waistband, bra) hook
(c) (Med) skin clip

agrafer /agʀafe/ [1] vtr (a) to staple [sth] (together)
(b) to fasten

agrafeuse /agʀaføz/ nf stapler

agraire /agʀɛʀ/ adj agrarian; **réforme ∼** land reform

agrandir /agʀɑ̃diʀ/ [3] **1** vtr (a) to enlarge ⟨town, photo⟩; to extend ⟨house⟩
(b) to expand ⟨organization⟩
2 **s'agrandir** v refl (+ v être) ⟨hole⟩ to get bigger; ⟨town, family⟩ to expand; ⟨eyes⟩ to widen

agrandissement /agʀɑ̃dismɑ̃/ nm enlargement

✔ indicates a very frequent word

✔ **agréable** /agʀeabl/ adj nice, pleasant; ∼ **à vivre** ⟨person⟩ pleasant to be with

agréer /agʀee/ [11] vtr (a) to agree to ⟨request⟩; **veuillez ∼ mes salutations distinguées** yours faithfully; yours sincerely
(b) to register ⟨taxi, doctor⟩; **agent agréé** authorized dealer

agrégat /agʀega/ nm aggregate; (figurative) jumble

agrégation /agʀegasjɔ̃/ nf: high-level competitive examination for the recruitment of teachers

agrément /agʀemɑ̃/ nm (a) charm; **plein d'∼** very pleasant; full of charm; **sans ∼** dull; unattractive; cheerless; **voyage d'∼** pleasure trip
(b) (by official body) approval

agrémenter /agʀemɑ̃te/ [1] vtr to liven up ⟨story⟩; to brighten up ⟨garden⟩

agrès /agʀɛ/ nm pl (Sport) apparatus

agresser /agʀese/ [1] vtr (a) to attack
(b) to mug
(c) to be aggressive with

agresseur /agʀesœʀ/ nm (a) attacker
(b) (in war) aggressor

agressif, -ive /agʀesif, iv/ adj
(a) aggressive
(b) violent; ear-splitting; harsh

agression /agʀesjɔ̃/ nf (a) attack
(b) mugging
(c) act of aggression

agressivité /agʀesivite/ nf aggressiveness, aggression

agricole /agʀikɔl/ adj **produit ∼** farm produce; **coopérative ∼** farming cooperative

agriculteur, -trice /agʀikyltœʀ, tʀis/ nm,f farmer

agriculture /agʀikyltyʀ/ nf farming

agripper /agʀipe/ [1] **1** vtr to grab
2 **s'agripper** v refl (+ v être) to cling (**à** to)

agro-alimentaire, pl ∼s /agʀoalimɑ̃tɛʀ/ adj food-processing

agrocarburant /agʀokaʀbyʀɑ̃/ nm biofuel

agrochimie /agʀoʃimi/ nf agro-chemistry

agronomie /agʀɔnɔmi/ nf agronomy

agrume /agʀym/ nm citrus fruit

aguerrir /ageʀiʀ/ [3] **1** vtr to harden ⟨person⟩
2 **s'aguerrir** v refl (+ v être) to become hardened

aguets: aux aguets /ozagɛ/ phr **être aux ∼** to be on one's guard

agulcher /agiʃe/ [1] vtr to lead [sb] on

aguicheur, -euse /agiʃœʀ, øz/ adj alluring

✔ **ah** /ɑ/ excl oh!; ∼ **oui?**, ∼ **bon?** really?

ahuri, ∼e /ayʀi/ adj (a) dazed
(b) stunned

ahurissant, **∼e** /ayʀisɑ̃, ɑ̃t/ *adj* ‹*news, strength*› incredible; ‹*figure*› staggering

ai /ε/ ▶ AVOIR¹

aide¹ /εd/ **1** *nmf* assistant
2 **aide-** (*combining form*) **∼-soignant** nursing auxiliary (GB), nurse's aide (US)
■ **∼ à domicile** carer, home help; **∼ familiale** mother's help

✒ **aide²** /εd/ *nf* (a) (from individual, group) help, assistance; (from state) assistance; **apporter son ∼ à qn** to help sb
(b) (financial) aid; **∼ au développement** foreign aid; **∼ judiciaire** legal aid
■ **∼ en ligne** online help

aide-éducateur, -trice /εdedykatœʀ, tʀis/ *nmf* classroom assistant

Aïd el-Fitr /aidεlfitʀ/ *nm* Eid ul-Fitr

Aïd el-Kebir /aidεlkebiʀ/ *nm* Eid al-Adha

✒ **aider** /ede/ [1] **1** *vtr* (a) to help (à faire to do)
(b) to aid, to give aid to
2 **aider à** *v+prep* to help toward(s) ‹*understanding, funding*›
3 **s'aider** *v refl* (+ v être) (a) **s'∼ de** to use ‹*dictionary, tool*›
(b) to help each other

aie /ε/ ▶ AVOIR¹

aïe /aj/ *excl* (in pain) ouch!; (in concern) **∼** (**∼ ∼**), **que se passe-t-il?** oh dear, what's going on?; (in anticipation) **∼ ∼ ∼!**... oh no!...

aient /ε/ ▶ AVOIR¹

aies /ε/ ▶ AVOIR¹

aïeul, **∼e** /ajœl/ *nm,f* grandfather/ grandmother

aïeux /ajø/ *nm pl* ancestors

aigle /εgl/ *nm, nf* eagle

aiglefin /εgləfε̃/ *nm* haddock

aigre /εgʀ/ *adj* ‹*smell, taste*› sour

aigre-doux, -douce, *pl* **algres-doux, aigres-douces** /εgʀədu, dus/ *adj* (Culin) ‹*fruit, taste*› bitter-sweet; ‹*sauce*› sweet and sour

aigrette /εgʀεt/ *nf* (Zool) (bird) egret; (plumes) crest

aigreur /εgʀœʀ/ *nf* (a) sourness; sharpness
(b) **∼s d'estomac** heartburn
(c) (figurative) bitterness

aigrir /egʀiʀ/ [3] *vtr* to embitter

aigu, aiguë /egy/ **1** *adj* (a) ‹*sound, voice*› high-pitched
(b) ‹*pain, symptom*› acute
(c) ‹*sense*› keen
2 *nm* (Mus) treble; high notes

aigue-marine, *pl* **aigues-marines** /εgmaʀin/ *nf* aquamarine

aiguillage /eguija3/ *nm* (for trains) points (GB), switch (US); **une erreur d'∼** a signalling (GB) error

aiguille /eguij/ *nf* (a) needle; **∼ à coudre** sewing needle
(b) (of watch, chronometer) hand; (of gauge)

needle; (of weighing scales) pointer; **dans le sens des ∼s d'une montre** clockwise

aiguiller /eguije/ [1] *vtr* (a) to direct ‹*person*›; to send ‹*mail*›
(b) (towards career) to guide ‹*person*›

aiguilleur /eguijœʀ/ *nm* **∼ du ciel** air traffic controller

aiguillonner /eguijɔne/ [1] *vtr* (a) to spur ‹*person*›; to stimulate ‹*ambition*›; **la faim m'aiguillonnant...** driven by hunger...
(b) to goad ‹*ox*›

aiguiser /egize/ [1] *vtr* (a) to sharpen ‹*knife*›
(b) to whet ‹*appetite*›; to arouse ‹*curiosity*›

aiguiseur /egizœʀ/ *nm* knife grinder

ail, *pl* **∼s** or **aulx** /aj, o/ *nm* garlic

✒ **aile** /εl/ *nf* (gen) wing; (of windmill) sail; (of car) wing (GB), fender (US); (of army) flank
IDIOMS **battre de l'∼** to be in a bad way; **se sentir pousser des ∼s** to feel exhila-rated; **prendre un coup dans l'∼** to suffer a setback; **voler de ses propres ∼s** to stand on one's own two feet

aileron /εlʀɔ̃/ *nm* (of bird) wing tip; (of shark) fin; (of plane) aileron; (of ship) fin

ailier /elje/ *nm* (in football) winger; (in rugby) wing three-quarter

✒ **ailleurs** /ajœʀ/ **1** *adv* elsewhere
2 **d'ailleurs** *phr* besides, moreover
3 **par ailleurs** *phr* **ils se sont par ∼ engagés à faire** they have also undertaken to do
IDIOM **être ∼** to be miles away

aimable /εmabl/ *adj* (a) ‹*word*› kind
(b) ‹*remark*› polite

aimablement /εmabləmɑ̃/ *adv* politely; kindly

aimant, **∼e** /εmɑ̃, ɑ̃t/ **1** *pp* ▶ AIMER
2 *pp adj* affectionate
3 *nm* magnet

aimé, **∼e** /eme/ ▶ AIMER

✒ **aimer** /eme/ [1] **1** *vtr* (a) to love ‹*person*›; **∼ qn à la folie** to adore sb
(b) to like, to be fond of ‹*person, activity, thing*›; **∼ faire** to like doing; **il aime autant le vin que la bière** he likes wine as much as he likes beer; **j'aime autant te dire que** I may as well tell you that; **∼ mieux** to prefer; **il n'a rien de cassé? j'aime mieux ça!** (in relief) nothing's broken? thank goodness!; **j'aime mieux ça!** (threateningly) that's more like it!
2 **s'aimer** *v refl* (+ v être) (a) to love each other
(b) to like each other

aine /εn/ *nf* groin

aîné, **∼e** /ene/ **1** *adj* elder; eldest
2 *nm,f* (a) elder son/daughter, elder child
(b) eldest son/daughter, eldest child
(c) elder brother/sister
(d) elder; oldest

✒ **ainsi** /ε̃si/ **1** *adv* (a) thus; **le mélange ∼ obtenu** the mixture obtained in this ⋯⋗

a

way; **Charlotte, c'est ~ qu'on m'appelait**
Charlotte, that's what they used to call me;
s'il en est ~ if that's the way it is; **le jury se**
compose ~ the panel is made up as follows;
~ soit-il amen
(b) thus, so
② **ainsi que** *phr* **(a)** as well as
(b) as; **~ que nous en avions convenu** as we
had agreed

⚜ **air** /ɛʀ/ *nm* **(a)** air; **le bon ~** clean air;
concert en plein ~ open-air concert;
activités de plein ~ outdoor activities; **aller**
prendre l'~ to go and get some fresh air; **on**
manque d'~ ici it's stuffy in here; **être dans**
l'~ ⟨*reform, idea*⟩ to be in the air; **regarder**
en l'~ to look up; **avoir le nez en l'~** to
daydream; **en l'~** ⟨*threat, words*⟩ empty;
⟨*plan, idea*⟩ vague; **tout mettre en l'~** (fam)
to make a dreadful mess; **de l'~!** (fam) get
lost (colloq)
(b) il y a de l'~ (in room) there's a draught
(GB) *or* draft (US); (outside) there's a breeze;
il n'y a pas d'~ there's no wind; **un courant**
d'~ a draught (GB) *or* draft (US)
(c) manner; expression; **avoir un drôle d'~**
to look odd; **d'un ~ fâché** angrily; **il y a un ~**
de famille entre vous deux you two share a
family likeness; **cela m'en a tout l'~** it seems
like it to me; **j'aurais l'~ de quoi?** I'd look
a right idiot!; **cela a l'~ d'être une usine** it
looks like a factory; **il a l'~ de vouloir faire**
beau it looks as if it's going to be fine
(d) tune; **un ~ d'opéra** an aria
IDIOMS il ne manque pas d'~! (fam) he's got
a nerve!; **se donner de grands ~s** to put
on airs; **j'ai besoin de changer d'~** I need a
change of scene

aire /ɛʀ/ *nf* **(a)** (surface) area
(b) eyrie
■ **~ d'atterrissage** (for plane) landing strip; (for
helicopter) landing pad; **~ de jeu** playground;
~ de services motorway (GB) *or* freeway (US)
service station; **~ de stationnement** parking
area

airelle /ɛʀɛl/ *nf* **(a)** bilberry
(b) cranberry

aisance /ɛzɑ̃s/ *nf* **(a)** ease
(b) affluence, comfort

aise /ɛz/ ① **aises** *nf pl* **aimer ses ~s** to
like one's creature comforts; **il prenait ses**
~s sur le canapé he was stretched out on
the sofa
② **à l'aise** *phr* **être à l'~** *or* **à son ~**
(physically) to be comfortable; (financially) to be
comfortably off; (psychologically) to be at ease;
mal à l'~ ill at ease; **à votre ~!** as you wish
or like!

aisé, ~e /eze/ *adj* **(a)** easy
(b) wealthy

aisément /ezemɑ̃/ *adv* easily

aisselle /ɛsɛl/ *nf* armpit

⚜ indicates a very frequent word

ait /ɛ/ ▶ AVOIR¹

Aix-la-Chapelle /ɛkslaʃapɛl/ *pr n* Aachen

ajonc /aʒɔ̃/ *nm* gorse bush

ajouré, ~e /aʒuʀe/ *adj* ⟨*tablecloth*⟩
openwork; ⟨*edge, border*⟩ hemstitched

ajournement /aʒuʀnəmɑ̃/ *nm* (of decision)
postponement; (of trial) adjournment

ajourner /aʒuʀne/ [1] *vtr* to postpone
⟨*decision, plan*⟩; to adjourn ⟨*debate, trial*⟩

ajout /aʒu/ *nm* addition
■ **~ de mémoire** memory upgrade

⚜ **ajouter** /aʒute/ [1] ① *vtr* to add (à to)
② **s'ajouter** *v refl* (+ *v être*) **s'~ à** to be
added to

ajustement /aʒystəmɑ̃/ *nm* **(a)** (Tech) fit
(b) adjustment; **~ des prix** price adjustment

ajuster /aʒyste/ [1] *vtr* **(a)** to adjust ⟨*strap,*
price, timetable⟩; to alter ⟨*garment*⟩ (à to); to
calibrate ⟨*weighing scales*⟩; **~ qch à** *or* **sur**
qch to make sth fit sth; **corsage ajusté** close-
fitting bodice
(b) to arrange ⟨*hair*⟩; to straighten ⟨*hat, tie*⟩
(c) ~ son tir to adjust one's aim

ajusteur /aʒystœʀ/ *nm* fitter

alaise ▶ ALÈSE

alambic /alɑ̃bik/ *nm* still

alambiqué, ~e /alɑ̃bike/ *adj* ⟨*expression,*
style⟩ convoluted; ⟨*explanation*⟩ tortuous

alangui, ~e /alɑ̃gi/ *adj* **(a)** languid
(b) listless

alarmant, ~e /alaʀmɑ̃, ɑ̃t/ *adj* alarming

alarme /alaʀm/ *nf* alarm

alarmer /alaʀme/ [1] ① *vtr* to alarm
② **s'alarmer** *v refl* (+ *v être*) to become
alarmed (**de qch** about sth)

albanais, ~e /albanɛ, ɛz/ ① *adj* Albanian
② *nm* (language) Albanian

Albanie /albani/ *pr nf* Albania

albâtre /albɑtʀ/ *nm* alabaster

albatros /albatʀos/ *nm inv* albatross

albinos /albinos/ *adj inv, nmf inv* albino

album /albɔm/ *nm* **(a)** illustrated book; **~**
de bandes dessinées comic strip book
(b) album
■ **~ à colorier** colouring (GB) book

albumine /albymin/ *nf* albumin

alchimie /alʃimi/ *nf* alchemy

alcool /alkɔl/ *nm* **(a)** alcohol; **~ de poire**
pear brandy; **teneur en ~** alcohol content
(b) drink; **l'~ au volant** drink-driving
(c) un ~ a spirit
■ **~ à brûler** methylated spirits; **~ à 90°**
≈ surgical spirit (GB), rubbing alcohol (US)

alcoolémie /alkɔlemi/ *nf* presence of
alcohol in the blood

alcoolique /alkɔlik/ *adj, nmf* alcoholic

alcoolisé, ~e /alkɔlize/ *adj* alcoholic

alcoolisme /alkɔlism/ *nm* alcoholism

alcootest /alkɔtɛst/ *nm* **(a)** Breathalyzer®
(b) breath test

alcôve /alkov/ *nf* alcove

aléas /alea/ *nm pl* vagaries; (financial) hazards

aléatoire /aleatwaʀ/ *adj* (a) ‹*events*› unpredictable; ‹*profession*› insecure (b) ‹*number*› random

alentours /alɑ̃tuʀ/ *nm pl* surrounding area

alerte /alɛʀt/ ⚀ *adj* alert; lively ⚁ *nf* alert; **donner l'~** to raise the alarm; **~ générale** full alert ■ **~ à la bombe** bomb scare

alerter /alɛʀte/ [1] *vtr* to alert (**sur** to)

alèse /alɛz/ *nf* undersheet, mattress protector

alexandrin /alɛksɑ̃dʀɛ̃/ *adj m, nm* alexandrine

algèbre /alʒɛbʀ/ *nf* algebra

Algérie /alʒeʀi/ *pr nf* Algeria

algérien, -ienne /alʒeʀjɛ̃, ɛn/ *adj* Algerian

algue /alg/ *nf* (a) **des ~s** algae (b) seaweed

alias ⚀ *nm* (Comput) alias ⚁ *adv* alias

alibi /alibi/ *nm* (a) (Law) alibi (b) excuse

aliénation /aljenasjɔ̃/ *nf* alienation

aliéné, ~e /aljene/ *nm, f* insane person

alignement /alin(ə)mɑ̃/ *nm* (a) row, line (b) alignment (c) **~ de qch sur qch** ‹*currency, salaries*› bringing into line of sth with sth

aligner /aline/ [1] ⚀ *vtr* (a) to line [sth] up (b) **~ qch sur qch** to bring sth into line with sth (c) to give a list of ‹*figures*› (d) to line up ‹*players*› ⚁ **s'aligner** *v refl* (+ *v être*) (a) ‹*houses, trees*› to be in a line (b) ‹*people*› to line up (c) **s'~ sur** to align oneself with ‹*country, party, ideas*›

aliment /alimɑ̃/ *nm* (gen) food; (for farm animals) feed; (for plants) nutrient

alimentaire /alimɑ̃tɛʀ/ *adj* ‹*needs, habits*› dietary; ‹*industry, shortage*› food; **régime ~** diet

alimentation /alimɑ̃tasjɔ̃/ *nf* (a) diet (b) feeding (c) food; **magasin d'~** food shop (d) food industry (e) supply, feeding; **l'~ en eau** the water supply

alimenter /alimɑ̃te/ [1] ⚀ *vtr* (a) to feed ‹*person, animal*› (b) to feed, to supply ‹*engine, boiler*› (c) to fuel ‹*conversation, hostility*› ⚁ **s'alimenter** *v refl* (+ *v être*) (a) ‹*person*› to eat; ‹*animal*› to feed (b) (with water, gas) **s'~ en** to be supplied with

alinéa /alinea/ *nm* (a) indentation (b) indented line (c) paragraph

alité, ~e /alite/ *adj* **être ~** to be confined to bed

alla /ala/ ▶ ALLER¹

allai /alɛ/ ▶ ALLER¹

allaient /alɛ/ ▶ ALLER¹

allais /alɛ/ ▶ ALLER¹

allait /alɛ/ ▶ ALLER¹

allaitement /alɛtmɑ̃/ *nm* (a) breast-feeding (b) suckling

allaiter /alete/ [1] *vtr* (a) to breast-feed (b) to suckle

allâmes /alɑm/ ▶ ALLER¹

allant, ~e /alɑ̃, ɑ̃t/ ⚀ *pp* ▶ ALLER¹ ⚁ *adj* active, lively ⚂ *nm* drive, lively; **avoir de l'~, être plein d'~** to have plenty of drive, to be full of bounce; **perdre son ~** to run out of steam

allâtes /alɑt/ ▶ ALLER¹

allé, ~e /ale/ ▶ ALLER¹

allécher /aleʃe/ [14] *vtr* to tempt (**avec** with)

allée /ale/ ⚀ *nf* (a) (in garden, wood) path; (leading to house) drive; (in town) avenue (b) aisle ⚁ **allées** *nf pl* **~ et venues** comings and goings

allégé, ~e /aleʒe/ ⚀ *pp* ▶ ALLÉGER ⚁ *pp adj* low-fat; ‹*chocolate*› diet

allégeance /aleʒɑ̃s/ *nf* allegiance

allégement /aleʒmɑ̃/ *nm* (of charges) reduction; (of restrictions, controls) relaxing; **~ fiscal** tax relief

alléger /aleʒe/ [15] ⚀ *vtr* (a) to lighten ‹*load, weight*› (b) to reduce ‹*debt*› (**de** by); to cut ‹*taxes*›; to relax ‹*control, restrictions*› ⚁ **s'alléger** *v refl* (+ *v être*) (a) ‹*load*› to get lighter (b) ‹*debt, taxation*› to be reduced; ‹*embargo*› to be relaxed

allégorie /alegɔʀi/ *nf* allegory

allègre /alɛgʀ/ *adj* ‹*style*› light; ‹*tone*› light-hearted; ‹*step, mood*› buoyant

allégrement /alegʀəmɑ̃/ *adv* joyfully; (ironic) blithely

allégresse /alegʀɛs/ *nf* joy

allegro /alegʀo/ *adv* allegro

alléguer /alege/ [14] *vtr* (a) to invoke (b) to allege

Allemagne /almaɲ/ *pr nf* Germany

✓ **allemand, ~e** /almɑ̃, ɑ̃d/ ⚀ *adj* German ⚁ *nm* (language) German

✓ **aller¹** /ale/ [9] ⚀ *v aux* **je vais apprendre l'italien** I'm going to learn Italian; **j'allais partir quand il est arrivé** I was about to leave when he arrived; **il est allé voir l'exposition** ⋯⟫

a

he went to see the exhibition; **va leur parler**
go and speak to them
⚏ *vi* (+ *v être*) (a) **comment vas-tu, comment
ça va?** how are you?; **ça va (bien)** I'm fine; **∼
beaucoup mieux** to be much better; **bois ça,
ça ira mieux** drink this, you'll feel better; **les
affaires vont bien** business is good; **qu'est-ce
qui ne va pas?** what's the matter?; **ne pas ∼
sans peine** *or* **mal** not to be easy; **ça devrait
∼ de soi** it should be obvious; **ça va pas
non?** (fam), **ça va pas la tête?** (fam) are you
crazy? (colloq)
(b) to go; **où vas-tu?** where are you going?;
∼ nager/au travail to go swimming/to work;
vas-y, demande-leur! go on, ask them!;
allons-y! let's go!; **allons!, allez!** come on!; **∼
et venir** to pace up and down; to run in and
out; **les nouvelles vont vite** news travels fast;
j'y vais (answering phone, door) I'll get it; (when
leaving) (fam) I'm off (colloq); **∼ contre la loi** to
break the law; to be against the law
(c) **ça va, ça ira** (fam), **ça peut aller** (fam) that'll
do; it'll do; **ça va comme ça** it's all right as it
is; **ça ne va pas du tout** that's no good at all;
lundi ça (te) va? would Monday suit you?
(d) **∼ à qn** to fit sb
(e) **∼ à qn** to suit sb; **ta cravate ne va pas
avec ta chemise** your tie doesn't go with
your shirt
(f) **∼ jusqu'à tuer** to go as far as to kill; **la
voiture peut ∼ jusqu'à 200 km/h** the car can
do up to 200 km/h; **la période qui va de 1918
à 1939** the period between 1918 and 1939; **∼
sur ses 17 ans** to be going on 17
(g) **y ∼ de sa petite larme** to shed a little
tear
⚌ **s'en aller** *v refl* (+ *v être*) (a) **s'en aller**
to go, to leave, to be off; to go away
(b) **la tache ne s'en va pas** the stain won't
come out
(c) (formal) to pass away, to die
⚍ *v impers* (a) **il y va de ma réputation** my
reputation is at stake
(b) **il en va de même pour toi** that goes for
you too
aller² /ale/ *nm* (a) **j'ai pris le bus à l'∼** I took
the bus there; I took the bus here; **il n'arrête
pas de faire des ∼s et retours entre chez lui
et son bureau** he's always going to and fro
between the house and the office
(b) **∼ (simple)** single (ticket) (GB), one-way
ticket (**pour** to); **∼ retour** return ticket,
round trip (US)
(c) (Sport) (**match**) **∼** first leg
allèrent /alɛʀ/ ▶ ALLER¹
allergie /alɛʀʒi/ *nf* (Med) allergy
allergique /alɛʀʒik/ *adj* allergic (**à** to)
allergologue /alɛʀɡɔlɔɡ/ *nmf* allergist
aller-retour /alɛʀ(ə)tuʀ/ *nm* return ticket
allez /ale/ ▶ ALLER¹
alliage /aljaʒ/ *nm* (a) alloy

⚡ indicates a very frequent word

(b) (figurative) combination
alliance /aljɑ̃s/ *nf* (a) wedding ring
(b) alliance
allié, ∼e /alje/ ⚏ *pp* ▶ ALLIER
⚌ *pp adj* allied
⚍ *nm,f* (a) ally; **les ∼s** the Allies
(b) relative
allier /alje/ [2] ⚏ *vtr* (a) to combine (**et,
à** with)
(b) (Tech) to alloy ‹*metals*› (**à, avec** with)
⚌ **s'allier** *v refl* (+ *v être*) to form an
alliance
alliez /alje/ ▶ ALLER¹
alligator /aligatɔʀ/ *nm* alligator
allions /aljɔ̃/ ▶ ALLER¹
allô /alo/ *excl* hello!, hallo!
allocation /al(l)ɔkasjɔ̃/ *nf* (a) allocation,
granting
(b) benefit (GB), benefits (US)
■ **∼ chômage** unemployment benefit (GB) *or*
benefits (US); **∼s familiales** family allowance
allocution /al(l)ɔkysjɔ̃/ *nf* address
allongé, ∼e /alɔ̃ʒe/ *adj* (a) **être ∼** ‹*person*›
to be lying down; to be reclining
(b) elongated
allonger /alɔ̃ʒe/ [13] ⚏ *vtr* (a) to lay [sb]
down
(b) to extend ‹*list, holiday*›; **cette coiffure
t'allonge le visage** that hairstyle makes your
face look longer
(c) to water [sth] down ‹*coffee*›
⚌ **s'allonger** *v refl* (+ *v être*) (a) to lie
down
(b) to get longer
allons /alɔ̃/ ▶ ALLER¹
allouer /alwe/ [1] *vtr* to allocate ‹*sum,
allowance, budget*›; to grant ‹*loan*›; to allot
‹*time*›
allumage /alymaʒ/ *nm* (Aut) ignition
allumé, ∼e /alyme/ *adj* (fam) (a) mad
(colloq)
(b) tipsy (colloq)
allume-gaz /alymɡaz/ *nm inv* gas lighter
⚡ **allumer** /alyme/ [1] ⚏ *vtr* (a) to light
‹*candle, gas*›; to start ‹*fire*›
(b) to switch [sth] on, to turn [sth] on; **laisser
ses phares allumés** to leave one's headlights
on
⚌ **s'allumer** *v refl* (+ *v être*) (a) ‹*heating,
radio, lighting*› to come on
(b) **son regard s'alluma** his face lit up
allumette /alymɛt/ *nf* match, matchstick
allumeur, -euse /alymœʀ, øz/ *nm,f* (fam)
tease
allure /alyʀ/ *nf* (a) (of walker) pace; (of vehicle)
speed; **ralentir son ∼** to slow down; **à toute
∼** at top speed; **à cette ∼** at this rate
(b) (of animal) gait
(c) (of person) appearance
(d) style; **avoir de l'∼** to have style

allusif, -ive /alyzif, iv/ *adj* ‹remark›
allusive; ‹person› indirect

allusion /alyzjɔ̃/ *nf* allusion (à to); faire ∼
à to allude to

alluvial, ∼e, *mpl* **-iaux** /alyvjal, o/ *adj*
alluvial

alluvion /alyvjɔ̃/ *nf* alluvium; des ∼s
alluvia

almanach /almana(k)/ *nm* almanac

aloi /alwa/ *nm* un succès de bon ∼ a
well-deserved success; une plaisanterie de
mauvais ∼ a tasteless joke; une gaieté de
bon ∼ a simple cheerfulness

⚭ **alors** /alɔʀ/ **1** *adv* (a) then; il avait ∼
18 ans he was 18 at the time; la mode d'∼
the fashion in those days; jusqu'∼ until then
(b) then; (mais) ∼ cela change tout! but that
changes everything!; et (puis) ∼? so what?
(c) so; il y avait une grève des trains, ∼ j'ai
pris l'autobus there was a train strike, so I
took the bus
(d) ou ∼ or else
(e) (fam) so; ∼ il me dit… so he said to me…
(f) non mais ∼! honestly!
2 alors que *phr* (a) while
(b) when
3 alors même que *phr* even though

alouette /alwɛt/ *nf* lark

alourdir /aluʀdiʀ/ [3] **1** *vtr* (a) to weigh
[sb] down ‹person›; to make [sth] tense
‹atmosphere›
(b) to increase ‹tax, charges›
2 s'alourdir *v refl* (+ *v être*) ‹eyelids› to
begin to droop; ‹air› to grow heavy

alourdissement /aluʀdismɑ̃/ *nm* (of tax,
deduction) increase (de in)

alpestre /alpɛstʀ/ *adj* alpine

alphabet /alfabɛ/ *nm* alphabet

alphabétique /alfabetik/ *adj*
alphabetical

alphabétiser /alfabetize/ [1] *vtr* to teach
[sb] to read and write

alpin, ∼e /alpɛ̃, in/ *adj* alpine

alpinisme /alpinism/ *nm* mountaineering

alpiniste /alpinist/ *nmf* mountaineer,
climber

altération /alteʀasjɔ̃/ *nf* (of faculties)
impairment (de of); (of foodstuff) spoiling (de
of); (in environment) deterioration (de in)

altérer /alteʀe/ [14] *vtr* (a) to affect ‹taste,
health›
(b) to spoil ‹foodstuff›; to fade ‹colour›
(c) to distort ‹text›; to adulterate ‹substance›

alternance /altɛʀnɑ̃s/ *nf* alternation; en
∼ avec alternately with

alternateur /altɛʀnatœʀ/ *nm* alternator

alternatif, -ive¹ /altɛʀnatif, iv/ *adj*
(a) (gen) alternate
(b) ‹current› alternating
(c) ‹culture, theatre› alternative

alternative² /altɛʀnativ/ **1** *adj f*
▶ ALTERNATIF
2 *nf* alternative

alterner /altɛʀne/ [1] **1** *vtr* to alternate
2 *vi* (a) to alternate
(b) ∼ avec qn pour faire to take turns with
sb (at) doing

altesse /altɛs/ *nf* (a) highness
(b) prince/princess

altier, -ière /altje, ɛʀ/ *adj* haughty

altitude /altityd/ *nf* altitude; en ∼ high up
(in the mountains)

alto /alto/ **1** *adj* alto
2 *nm* (a) (instrument) viola
(b) viola player (GB), violin (US)
(c) (voice) alto

altruiste /altʀɥist/ *adj* altruistic

aluminium /alyminjɔm/, **alu** (fam) /aly/
nm aluminium (GB), aluminum (US)

alvéole /alveɔl/ *nf* (a) (in honeycomb) cell
(b) (in rock) cavity

alvéolé, ∼e /alveɔle/ *adj* honeycombed

amabilité /amabilite/ *nf* (a) kindness
(b) courtesy

amadouer /amadwe/ [1] *vtr* to coax, to
cajole

amaigrir /amegʀiʀ/ [3] *vtr* to make [sb]
thinner

amaigrissant, ∼e /amegʀisɑ̃, ɑ̃t/ *adj*
slimming

amalgame /amalgam/ *nm* (a) (gen)
mixture
(b) (in dentistry, chemistry) amalgam

amalgamer /amalgame/ [1] *vtr* (a) to
lump together ‹problems›; to mix ‹feelings,
people›
(b) to blend, to amalgamate ‹ingredients›

amande /amɑ̃d/ *nf* (a) almond
(b) kernel

amanite /amanit/ *nf* amanita; ∼ phalloïde
death cap

amant /amɑ̃/ *nm* lover

amarre /amaʀ/ *nf* rope; les ∼s moorings

amarrer /amaʀe/ [1] *vtr* (a) to moor ‹boat›
(b) to tie (à, sur to)

amas /ama/ *nm inv* pile; heap

amasser /amase/ [1] **1** *vtr* to amass, to
accumulate ‹fortune, books›; to collect ‹proof›
2 s'amasser *v refl* (+ *v être*) ‹snow,
objects› to pile up; ‹proof, evidence› to build
up

amateur /amatœʀ/ **1** *adj inv* amateur
2 *nm* (a) (non-professional) amateur
(b) (of sport, photography) enthusiast; (of wine)
connoisseur
(c) il vend sa voiture, vous êtes ∼? he's
selling his car, are you interested?

amazone /amazon/ *nf* en ∼ sidesaddle

ambassade /ɑ̃basad/ *nf* embassy

a

ambassadeur /ãbasadœʀ/ *nm*
ambassador

ambassadrice /ãbasadʀis/ *nf*
(a) ambassador
(b) ambassador's wife

ambiance /ãbjãs/ *nf* atmosphere

ambiant, ∼**e** /ãbjã, ãt/ *adj* (a) ⟨air⟩
surrounding; **à température** ∼**e** at room
temperature
(b) prevailing

ambigu, ambiguë /ãbigy/ *adj* ⟨remark,
situation⟩ ambiguous; ⟨feeling, attitude⟩
ambivalent

ambiguïté /ãbiguite/ *nf* ambiguity;
enigmatic nature; ambivalence

ambitieux, -ieuse /ãbisjø, øz/ *adj*
ambitious

ambition /ãbisjõ/ *nf* ambition

ambitionner /ãbisjone/ [1] *vtr* to aspire to

ambivalent, ∼**e** /ãbivalã, ãt/ *adj*
ambivalent

ambre /ãbʀ/ *nm* (a) ∼ (jaune) amber
(b) ∼ (gris) ambergris

ambulance /ãbylãs/ *nf* ambulance

ambulancier, -ière /ãbylãsje, ɛʀ/ *nm,f*
ambulance driver

ambulant, ∼**e** /ãbylã, ãt/ *adj* ⟨circus⟩
travelling (GB); **vendeur** ∼ (in station) snack
trolley man; **un cadavre** ∼ (fam) a walking
skeleton (colloq)

⚜ **âme** /ɑm/ *nf* soul; **Dieu ait son** ∼ God rest
his/her soul; **socialiste dans l'**∼ a socialist
to the core; **en mon** ∼ **et conscience** in all
honesty; **pas** ∼ **qui vive** not a (single) soul;
∼ **sœur** soul mate

amélioration /ameljoʀasjõ/ *nf*
improvement

⚜ **améliorer** /ameljoʀe/ [1] *vtr*,
s'améliorer *v refl* (+ *v être*) to improve

amen /amɛn/ *nm inv* amen

aménagé, ∼**e** /amenaʒe/ ⊡ *pp*
▸ AMÉNAGER
⊡ *pp adj* (a) converted
(b) equipped

aménagement /amenaʒmã/ *nm* (a) (of
region, town) development
(b) (of roads) construction; (of parks, green
spaces) creation
(c) (of house, boat) fitting
(d) (of timetable) adjustment; **l'**∼ **du temps de
travail** flexible working hours

aménager /amenaʒe/ [13] *vtr* (a) to
convert; to do up ⟨house, attic⟩
(b) to equip ⟨kitchen⟩; to develop ⟨region⟩
(c) to create ⟨parks, green spaces⟩; to build
⟨road⟩; to lay out ⟨garden⟩
(d) to arrange ⟨timetable⟩; to adjust
⟨regulations⟩

amende /amãd/ *nf* fine

amendement /amãdmã/ *nm* (a) (in law)
amendment (**à** to; **sur** on)
(b) (of soil) enrichment

⚜ **amener** /amne/ [16] *vtr* (a) ∼ **qn quelque
part** to take sb somewhere
(b) (accompany) ∼ **qn (quelque part)** to bring
sb (somewhere)
(c) (controversial) ∼ **qch (à qn)** to bring (sb) sth
(d) to cause ⟨problems, illness⟩; to bring
⟨rain, fame⟩
(e) to bring up ⟨issue, subject⟩; **être bien
amené** ⟨conclusion⟩ to be well-presented
(f) ∼ **qn à qch/faire** to lead sb to sth/to do

amenuiser: s'amenuiser
/amənɥize/ [1] *v refl* (+ *v être*) ⟨supplies⟩ to
dwindle; ⟨risk⟩ to lessen

amer, -ère /amɛʀ/ *adj* bitter

⚜ **américain**, ∼**e** /ameʀikɛ̃, ɛn/ ⊡ *adj*
American; **à l'**∼**e** (gen) in the American
style; (Culin) à l'américaine
⊡ *nm* American English

Amérindien, -ienne /ameʀɛ̃djɛ̃, ɛn/ *nm,f*
Amerindian, American Indian

Amérique /ameʀik/ *pr nf* America

amerrir /ameʀiʀ/ [3] *vi* ⟨hydroplane⟩ to land
(on water); ⟨spacecraft⟩ to splash down

amertume /amɛʀtym/ *nf* bitterness

ameublement /amœbləmã/ *nm*
(a) furniture
(b) furniture trade
(c) (of room, house) furnishing

ameuter /amøte/ [1] *vtr* (a) ⟨person, noise⟩
to bring [sb] out
(b) to stir [sb] up

⚜ **ami**, ∼**e** /ami/ ⊡ *adj* friendly
⊡ *nm,f* friend; **en** ∼ as a friend; **un** ∼ **des
bêtes** an animal lover; ▸ FAUX¹
IDIOM **les bons comptes font les bons** ∼**s**
(Proverb) a debt paid is a friend kept

amiable: à l'amiable
/alamjabl/ ⟨separate⟩ on friendly terms;
⟨separation⟩ amicable; ⟨divorce⟩ by mutual
consent; ▸ CONSTAT

amiante /amjãt/ *nm* asbestos

amical, ∼**e**¹, *pl* **-aux** /amikal, o/ *adj*
friendly

amicale² /amikal/ *nf* association

amicalement /amikalmã/ *adv* (a) ⟨greet,
receive⟩ warmly; ⟨compete⟩ in a friendly way
(b) (at end of letter) (**bien**) ∼ best wishes

amidon /amidõ/ *nm* starch

amincir /amɛ̃siʀ/ [3] *vtr* to make [sb] look
slimmer

amiral, *mpl* **-aux** /amiʀal, o/ *nm* admiral

⚜ **amitié** /amitje/ ⊡ *nf* friendship; **se lier
d'**∼ **avec qn** to strike up a friendship with sb
⊡ **amitiés** *nf pl* (at end of letter) kindest
regards

ammoniac /amɔnjak/ *nm* (gas) ammonia

ammoniaque /amɔnjak/ *nf* ammonia

amnésie /amnezi/ *nf* amnesia

⚜ indicates a very frequent word

amnésique /amnezik/ *adj* amnesic

amnistie /amnisti/ *nf* amnesty

amocher /amɔʃe/ [1] (fam) **1** *vtr* to bash (colloq) [sb/sth] up ‹*person, car*›
2 **s'amocher** *v refl* (+ *v être*) to bash oneself up (colloq); **s'~ le nez** to bash up (colloq) one's nose

amoindrir /amwɛ̃dʀiʀ/ [3] *vtr* to reduce ‹*resistance*›; to weaken ‹*person*›

amonceler /amɔ̃sle/ [19] **1** *vtr* to pile up
2 **s'amonceler** *v refl* (+ *v être*) ‹*clouds, snow*› to build up; ‹*evidence, problems*› to pile up

amoncellement /amɔ̃sɛlmɑ̃/ *nm* pile; mass

amont /amɔ̃/ *nm* (of river) upper reaches; **en ~** upstream (**de** from); **naviguer d'~ en aval** to sail downstream

amoral, ~e, *mpl* **-aux** /amɔʀal, o/ *adj* amoral

amorce /amɔʀs/ *nf* (**a**) (of discussion) initiation
(**b**) bait
(**c**) (of explosive) cap, primer; (of gun) cap

amorcer /amɔʀse/ [12] *vtr* (**a**) to begin
(**b**) to prime

amorphe /amɔʀf/ *adj* apathetic

amortir /amɔʀtiʀ/ [3] *vtr* (**a**) to deaden ‹*noise*›; to absorb ‹*shock, impact*›; to break ‹*fall*›
(**b**) to pay off ‹*debt*›
(**c**) **j'ai amorti mon ordinateur en quelques mois** my computer paid for itself in a few months

amortissement /amɔʀtismɑ̃/ *nm* (**a**) (of noise) deadening; (of shock) absorption; (of fall) cushioning
(**b**) (of debt) paying off
(**c**) (of equipment) depreciation

amortisseur /amɔʀtisœʀ/ *nm* shock absorber

⚘ **amour** /amuʀ/ **1** *nm* love; **pour l'~ de** for the sake of; out of love for; **c'était un ~ de jeunesse** it was a youthful romance
2 **amours** *nm pl or nf pl* (**a**) (Zool) mating
(**b**) love affairs; **à tes ~s!** (to somebody sneezing) bless you!

amouracher: s'amouracher /amuʀaʃe/ [1] *v refl* (+ *v être*) **s'~ de** to become infatuated with

amourette /amuʀɛt/ *nf* passing infatuation

⚘ **amoureux, -euse** /amuʀø, øz/ *adj* in love

amour-propre /amuʀpʀɔpʀ/ *nm* self-esteem; pride

amovible /amɔvibl/ *adj* detachable; removable

ampère /ɑ̃pɛʀ/ *nm* amp, ampère

amphibie /ɑ̃fibi/ *adj* (Zool, Aut) amphibious

amphithéâtre /ɑ̃fiteatʀ/ *nm* (**a**) (natural, ancient) amphitheatre (GB)

(**b**) (at university) lecture hall

amphore /ɑ̃fɔʀ/ *nf* amphora

ample /ɑ̃pl/ *adj* (**a**) ‹*coat, dress*› loose-fitting; ‹*skirt, sleeve*› full; ‹*gesture*› sweeping
(**b**) ‹*quantity*› ample; ‹*harvest*› abundant; ‹*details*› full

amplement /ɑ̃pləmɑ̃/ *adv* fully; **c'est ~ suffisant** that's more than enough!

ampleur /ɑ̃plœʀ/ *nf* (of problem) size; (of project, subject, survey) scope; (of event, disaster, task) scale; (of damage, reaction) extent

amplificateur /ɑ̃plifikatœʀ/ *nm* amplifier

amplification /ɑ̃plifikasjɔ̃/ *nf* (**a**) (in physics) amplification
(**b**) (extension) (of relations) development; (of strike) escalation; (of debate) expansion

amplifier /ɑ̃plifje/ [2] **1** *vtr* to amplify ‹*sound, current*›; to magnify ‹*rumour*›
2 **s'amplifier** *v refl* (+ *v être*) ‹*sound*› to grow louder; ‹*trade*› to increase; ‹*strike*› to intensify

ampoule /ɑ̃pul/ *nf* (**a**) **~ (électrique)** (light) bulb
(**b**) (Med) (drinkable) phial; (injectable) ampoule
(**c**) blister

ampoulé, ~e /ɑ̃pule/ *adj* bombastic

amputation /ɑ̃pytasjɔ̃/ *nf* amputation

amputer /ɑ̃pyte/ [1] *vtr* (**a**) (Med) to amputate ‹*limb*›; to perform an amputation on ‹*person*›
(**b**) to cut [sth] drastically ‹*budget*›

amusant, ~e /amyzɑ̃, ɑ̃t/ *adj*
(**a**) entertaining
(**b**) funny

amuse-gueule /amyzgœl/ *nm inv* cocktail snack (GB), munchies (US)

amusement /amyzmɑ̃/ *nm* entertainment

⚘ **amuser** /amyze/ [1] **1** *vtr* (**a**) to entertain; to amuse
(**b**) to distract
2 **s'amuser** *v refl* (+ *v être*) (**a**) to play; **pour s'~** for fun
(**b**) **bien s'~** to have a good time

amuseur, -euse /amyzœʀ, øz/ *nm,f* entertainer

amygdale /amidal/ *nf* tonsil

⚘ **an** /ɑ̃/ *nm* year; **avoir huit ~s** to be eight (years old); **en l'~ deux mille** in the year two thousand; **l'~ 55 avant J.-C./après J.-C.** 55 BC/AD
IDIOM bon ~, mal ~ year in, year out

anabolisant /anabolizɑ̃/ *nm* anabolic steroid

anachronique /anakʀɔnik/ *adj* anachronistic

anachronisme /anakʀɔnism/ *nm* anachronism

anal, ~e, *mpl* **-aux** /anal, o/ *adj* anal

analogie /analɔʒi/ *nf* analogy

analogue /analɔg/ *adj* similar (**à** to)

analphabète /analfabɛt/ *adj, nmf*
illiterate

analphabétisme /analfabetism/ *nm*
illiteracy

analyse /analiz/ *nf* (a) analysis; **faire l'~
de qch** to analyse (GB) sth
(b) (Med) test
(c) psychoanalysis
■ ~ **coût-efficacité** cost-benefit analysis

♂ **analyser** /analize/ [1] *vtr* (a) (gen) to
analyse (GB)
(b) (Med) to test ‹*blood, urine*›

ananas /anana(s)/ *nm inv* pineapple

anarchie /anaʀʃi/ *nf* anarchy

anarchiste /anaʀʃist/ ① *adj* anarchistic
② *nmf* anarchist

anatomie /anatɔmi/ *nf* anatomy

ancêtre /ɑ̃sɛtʀ/ *nmf* ancestor

anchois /ɑ̃ʃwa/ *nm inv* anchovy

♂ **ancien, -ienne**[1] /ɑ̃sjɛ̃, ɛn/ ① *adj*
(a) ‹*champion, president, capital*› former
(b) ‹*history, language*› ancient
(c) ‹*style, book, building*› old; ‹*car*› vintage;
‹*piece of furniture*› antique
(d) **c'est lui le plus ~** (in job) he's been here
longest
② *nm* (a) (in tribe, congregation) elder; (in
company) senior member; **les ~s** the older
people
(b) old member; former student
(c) **l'~** older property; (furniture) antiques
■ ~ **combattant** veteran

ancienne[2]: **à l'ancienne** /alɑ̃sjɛn/ *phr*
‹*jam, piece of furniture*› traditional-style

anciennement /ɑ̃sjɛnmɑ̃/ *adv* formerly

ancienneté /ɑ̃sjɛnte/ *nf* (a) (of person)
seniority; **trois ans d'~** three years' service
(b) (of tradition, relic) antiquity; (of building) age

ancre /ɑ̃kʀ/ *nf* (Naut) anchor

ancrer /ɑ̃kʀe/ [1] ① *vtr* (a) to anchor ‹*ship*›
(b) to fix ‹*idea*›; to establish ‹*custom*›
② **s'ancrer** *v refl* (+ *v être*) (a) to anchor
(b) ‹*idea*› to become fixed; ‹*custom*› to
become established

Andorre /ɑ̃dɔʀ/ *pr nf* Andorra

andouille /ɑ̃duj/ *nf* (a) (Culin) andouille
(b) (fam) fool

âne /ɑn/ *nm* (a) (Zool) donkey, ass
(b) (fam) dimwit (colloq)
IDIOM **faire l'~ pour avoir du son** to act
dumb to find out more

anéantir /aneɑ̃tiʀ/ [3] *vtr* (a) to ruin ‹*crops,
harvest*›; to lay waste to ‹*town*›; to shatter
‹*hopes*›
(b) ‹*news*› to crush; ‹*strain*› to exhaust

anéantissement /aneɑ̃tismɑ̃/ *nm*
(a) destruction, devastation
(b) (of hope) shattering
(c) (of person) total collapse

♂ indicates a very frequent word

anecdote /anɛkdɔt/ *nf* anecdote

anémie /anemi/ *nf* (a) anaemia
(b) weakness

anémier /anemje/ [2] ① *vtr* (a) (Med) to
make [sb] anaemic ‹*person*›
(b) (figurative) to weaken
② **s'anémier** *v refl* (+ *v être*) (a) (Med) to
become anaemic
(b) (figurative) to grow feeble

anémique /anemik/ *adj* (a) anaemic
(b) weak

anémone /anemɔn/ *nf* anemone

ânerie /anʀi/ *nf* (a) silly remark
(b) silly blunder

ânesse /anɛs/ *nf* she-ass, female donkey

anesthésie /anɛstezi/ *nf* anaesthesia

aneth /anɛt/ *nm* dill

anfractuosité /ɑ̃fʀaktɥozite/ *nf* crevice

♂ **ange** /ɑ̃ʒ/ *nm* angel
IDIOM **être aux ~s** to be in (one's) seventh
heaven

angélique[1] /ɑ̃ʒelik/ *adj* angelic

angélique[2] /ɑ̃ʒelik/ *nf* angelica

angelot /ɑ̃ʒlo/ *nm* cherub

angine /ɑ̃ʒin/ *nf* throat infection

♂ **anglais, ~e**[1] /ɑ̃glɛ, ɛz/ ① *adj* English
② *nm* (language) English

Anglais, ~e /ɑ̃glɛ, ɛz/ *nm,f* Englishman/
Englishwoman

anglaise[2] /ɑ̃glɛz/ ① *adj f* ▶ ANGLAIS 1
② *nf* ringlet

angle /ɑ̃gl/ *nm* (a) angle
(b) corner

Angleterre /ɑ̃glətɛʀ/ *pr nf* England

anglo-américain, ~e, mpl ~s
/ɑ̃gloameʀikɛ̃, ɛn/ ① *adj* (a) Anglo-American
(b) American English
② *nm* (language) American English

anglo-normand, ~e, mpl ~s
/ɑ̃glonɔʀmɑ̃, ɑ̃d/ *adj* Anglo-Norman

Anglo-Normande /ɑ̃glonɔʀmɑ̃d/ *adj f*
les îles ~s the Channel Islands

anglophone /ɑ̃glɔfɔn/ ① *adj* English-
speaking
② *nmf* English speaker; Anglophone

anglo-saxon, -onne, mpl ~s /ɑ̃glosaksɔ̃,
ɔn/ *adj* Anglo-Saxon

angoissant, ~e /ɑ̃gwasɑ̃, ɑ̃t/ *adj*
‹*prospect*› alarming; ‹*film, silence*›
frightening

angoisse /ɑ̃gwas/ *nf* anxiety

angoissé, ~e /ɑ̃gwase/ *adj* anxious

angoisser /ɑ̃gwase/ [1] ① *vtr* to worry
② *vi* (fam) to be anxious, to be nervous

anguille /ɑ̃gij/ *nf* eel

angulaire /ɑ̃gylɛʀ/ *adj* angular

anicroche /anikʀɔʃ/ *nf* hitch; **sans ~(s)**
without a hitch

♂ animal, ~e, *mpl* -aux /animal, o/ ① *adj* animal
② *nm* animal; ~ **familier** pet; ~ **domestique** domestic animal; ~ **nuisible** pest

animalier, -ière /animalje, ɛʀ/ ① *adj* wildlife
② *nm, f* (in a lab) animal keeper
③ *nm* wildlife artist

animateur, -trice /animatœʀ, tʀis/ *nm, f*
(a) (of group of holidaymakers, club) coordinator; (of association) leader; (of festival) organizer
(b) presenter

animation /animasjɔ̃/ *nf* (a) (of group, exhibition, festival) organization; (of sales) coordination
(b) life, liveliness; **ville qui manque d'~** dull town
(c) (of street, market) hustle and bustle; (of people) excitement

animé, ~e /anime/ *adj* (a) animated; lively; busy
(b) ~ **de mauvaises intentions** spurred on by bad intentions

♂ animer /anime/ [1] ① *vtr* (a) to lead ‹discussion, group›; to run ‹course, show›; to present ‹programme›
(b) to liven up ‹town, story, meeting›
② **s'animer** *v refl* (+ *v être*)
(a) ‹conversation› to become lively; ‹meeting› to liven up; ‹face› to light up
(b) ‹statue› to come to life

animosité /animozite/ *nf* animosity
(**envers** toward(s); **entre** between)

anis /ani/ *nm inv* (a) anise
(b) aniseed

ankyloser: **s'ankyloser** /ãkiloze/ [1] *v refl* (+ *v être*) to get stiff

annales /anal/ *nf pl* (a) annals
(b) (of exams) (book of) past papers

anneau, *pl* ~x /ano/ *nm* ring

♂ année /ane/ *nf* year; **l'~ en cours** this year, the current year; **avec les ~s** over the years; **d'~ en ~** year by year; **ces dix dernières ~s** over the last ten years; **souhaiter la bonne ~ à qn** to wish sb a happy new year; (**dans**) **les ~s 80** (in) the eighties; **location à l'~** annual rent
■ ~ **bissextile** leap year; ~ **civile** calendar year; ~ **universitaire** academic year

année-lumière, *pl* **années-lumière** /anelymjɛʀ/ *nf* light-year

annexe¹ /anɛks/ *adj* (a) ‹room› adjoining
(b) ‹questions› additional; ‹file, document› attached

annexe² /anɛks/ *nf* (a) (building) annexe (GB), annex (US)
(b) (document) appendix

annexer /anɛkse/ [1] *vtr* to annex

annihiler /aniile/ [1] *vtr* to destroy ‹efforts, hopes›; to cancel out ‹effect, results›

anniversaire /anivɛʀsɛʀ/ ① *adj* date *or* jour ~ **de** anniversary of
② *nm* (a) birthday
(b) anniversary

annonce /anɔ̃s/ *nf* (a) announcement
(b) advertisement, ad (colloq); **petite ~** classified advertisement
(c) declaration; **faire une ~** (in bridge) to bid
(d) sign

♂ annoncer /anɔ̃se/ [12] ① *vtr* (a) to announce
(b) to forecast ‹rain, event›
(c) ‹event, signal› to herald
② **s'annoncer** *v refl* (+ *v être*) (a) ‹crisis, storm› to be brewing
(b) **la récolte 92 s'annonce excellente** the '92 harvest promises to be very good

annonciateur, -trice /anɔ̃sjatœʀ, tʀis/ *adj* ‹sign, signal› warning

annoter /anɔte/ [1] *vtr* to annotate ‹work›; to write notes on ‹worksheet, homework›

annuaire /anɥɛʀ/ *nm* (a) directory
(b) yearbook

annuel, -elle /anɥɛl/ *adj* (gen) annual, yearly; ‹contract› one-year

annulaire /anylɛʀ/ *nm* ring finger

annulation /anylasjɔ̃/ *nf* (a) (gen) cancellation; (of law) repeal
(b) (Law) (of verdict) quashing; (of elections) cancellation (GB); (of marriage) annulment

annuler /anyle/ [1] ① *vtr* (a) to cancel ‹appointment, trip›; to write off ‹debt›; to discount ‹result of match›
(b) (Law) to declare [sth] void ‹elections›; to quash ‹verdict›
② **s'annuler** *v refl* (+ *v être*) to cancel each other out

anodin, ~e /anodɛ̃, in/ *adj* ‹subject› safe, neutral; ‹question, joke› innocent

anomalie /anɔmali/ *nf* (a) anomaly
(b) fault

anonymat /anɔnima/ *nm* (a) anonymity
(b) confidentiality

anonyme /anɔnim/ *adj* anonymous

anorexie /anɔʀɛksi/ *nf* anorexia

anormal, ~e, *mpl* -aux /anɔʀmal, o/ *adj* abnormal

ANPE /aɛnpeœ/ *nf* (*abbr* = **Agence nationale pour l'emploi**) *French national employment agency*

anse /ãs/ *nf* (of cup, basket) handle

antagoniste /ãtagɔnist/ *adj* ‹groups› opposing; ‹interests› conflicting

antan: d'antan /dãtã/ *phr* ‹wars, festivals› of old; ‹prestige› former; **les métiers d'~** the old trades; **le Lyon d'~** the Lyons of yesteryear

antarctique /ãtaʀktik/ *adj* Antarctic

Antarctique /ãtaʀktik/ *pr nm*
(a) Antarctic; **océan ~** Antarctic Ocean
(b) Antarctica

antécédent, ∼e /ɑ̃tesedɑ̃, ɑ̃t/ **1** *adj* previous
2 *nm* **(a)** past history
(b) medical history
(c) (in grammar, mathematics) antecedent

antenne /ɑ̃tɛn/ *nf* **(a)** (of radio, television) aerial; (of radar, satellite) antenna; **passer à l'**∼ ⟨*programme, person*⟩ to go on the air
(b) (of organization, service) branch
(c) (of insect, shrimp) antenna; **avoir des** ∼**s** (figurative) to have a sixth sense

antérieur, ∼e /ɑ̃teʀjœʀ/ *adj* **(a)** ⟨*situation, work*⟩ previous
(b) ⟨*limb, ligament*⟩ anterior

anthracite /ɑ̃tʀasit/ *adj inv* charcoal grey (GB), charcoal gray (US)

anthropologie /ɑ̃tʀɔpɔlɔʒi/ *nf* anthropology

anthropophage /ɑ̃tʀɔpɔfaʒ/ *nmf* cannibal

antiaérien, -ienne /ɑ̃tiaeʀjɛ̃, ɛn/ *adj* anti-aircraft

antiatomique /ɑ̃tiatɔmik/ *adj* (anti-) radiation; **abri** ∼ nuclear shelter

antibiotique /ɑ̃tibjɔtik/ *adj, nm* antibiotic

antibrouillard /ɑ̃tibʀujaʀ/ *adj inv* **phare** ∼ fog light

antibruit /ɑ̃tibʀɥi/ *adj inv* soundproof

antichambre /ɑ̃tiʃɑ̃bʀ/ *nf* anteroom

antichoc /ɑ̃tiʃɔk/ *adj inv* **(a)** **casque** ∼ crash helmet
(b) ⟨*watch*⟩ shockproof

anticipation /ɑ̃tisipasjɔ̃/ *nf* anticipation; **roman d'**∼ science fiction novel

anticipé, ∼e /ɑ̃tisipe/ *adj* early

anticiper /ɑ̃tisipe/ [1] **1** *vtr* to anticipate ⟨*reaction, change, movement*⟩
2 *vi* **(a)** to get ahead of oneself
(b) to think ahead

anticonformiste /ɑ̃tikɔ̃fɔʀmist/ *adj, nmf* nonconformist

anticorps /ɑ̃tikɔʀ/ *nm inv* antibody

antidater /ɑ̃tidate/ [1] *vtr* to backdate

antidémocratique /ɑ̃tidemɔkʀatik/ *adj* undemocratic

antidérapant, ∼e /ɑ̃tideʀapɑ̃, ɑ̃t/ *adj* ⟨*tyre*⟩ nonskid; ⟨*sole*⟩ nonslip

antidopage /ɑ̃tidɔpaʒ/ *adj* ⟨*measure*⟩ anti-doping; **contrôle** ∼ dope test

antidote /ɑ̃tidɔt/ *nm* antidote

antigang /ɑ̃tigɑ̃g/ *adj inv* **brigade** ∼ crime squad

antigel /ɑ̃tiʒɛl/ *adj inv, nm* antifreeze

anti-inflammatoire, *pl* ∼**s** /ɑ̃tiɛ̃flamatwaʀ/ *adj, nm* anti-inflammatory

antillais, ∼e /ɑ̃tijɛ, ɛz/ *adj* West Indian

Antilles /ɑ̃tij/ *pr nf pl* **les** ∼ the West Indies; **les Petites/Grandes** ∼ the Lesser/ Greater Antilles

antilope /ɑ̃tilɔp/ *nf* antelope

antimite /ɑ̃timit/ *adj, nm* moth-repellent

antimondialisme /ɑ̃timɔ̃djalism/ *nm* anti-globalization

antipathie /ɑ̃tipati/ *nf* antipathy

antipathique /ɑ̃tipatik/ *adj* unpleasant

antipelliculaire /ɑ̃tipɛlikylɛʀ/ *adj* antidandruff

antipoison /ɑ̃tipwazɔ̃/ *adj inv* **centre** ∼ poisons unit

antiquaire /ɑ̃tikɛʀ/ *nmf* antique dealer

antique /ɑ̃tik/ *adj* ancient

antiquité /ɑ̃tikite/ **1** *nf* antique
2 **antiquités** *nf pl* antiquities

Antiquité /ɑ̃tikite/ *nf* antiquity

antireflet /ɑ̃tiʀəflɛ/ *adj inv* nonreflective; (in photography) antiglare

antirouille /ɑ̃tiʀuj/ *adj inv* **(a)** rust-proofing
(b) rust-removing

antisèche /ɑ̃tisɛʃ/ *nf* (fam) (students' slang) crib (colloq)

antisémite /ɑ̃tisemit/ **1** *adj* anti-Semitic
2 *nmf* anti-Semite

antitabac /ɑ̃titaba/ *adj inv* antismoking

antiterroriste /ɑ̃titɛʀɔʀist/ *adj* **lutte** ∼ fight against terrorism

antithèse /ɑ̃titɛz/ *nf* antithesis

antituberculeux, -euse /ɑ̃titybɛʀkylø, øz/ *adj* **vaccin** ∼ tuberculosis vaccine

antivirus /ɑ̃tiviʀys/ *nm* antivirus software

antivol /ɑ̃tivɔl/ *nm* (of bicycle, motorbike) lock; (of car) anti-theft device

anus /anys/ *nm inv* anus

Anvers /ɑ̃vɛʀ/ *pr n* Antwerp

anxiété /ɑ̃ksjete/ *nf* anxiety

anxieux, -ieuse /ɑ̃ksjø, øz/ *adj* ⟨*person*⟩ anxious; ⟨*attitude*⟩ concerned

aorte /aɔʀt/ *nf* aorta

♂ **août** /u(t)/ *nm* August

apaisant, ∼e /apɛzɑ̃, ɑ̃t/ *adj* **(a)** soothing
(b) calming

apaiser /apeze/ [1] **1** *vtr* **(a)** to pacify, to appease
(b) to ease ⟨*conflict*⟩
(c) to calm ⟨*rage*⟩
2 **s'apaiser** *v refl* (+ *v être*) **(a)** to die down
(b) to calm down

apanage /apanaʒ/ *nm* **être l'**∼ **de qch/qn** to be the prerogative of sth/sb

aparté /apaʀte/ *nm* **en** ∼ in private; (in a play) in an aside

apathie /apati/ *nf* **(a)** apathy
(b) stagnation

apatride /apatʀid/ *adj* stateless

♂ indicates a very frequent word

APEC /apɛk/ *nf* (*abbr* = **Agence pour l'emploi des cadres**) *executive employment agency*

✦ **apercevoir** /apɛRsəvwaR/ [5] **1** *vtr* (a) to make out
(b) to catch sight of
2 s'apercevoir *v refl* (+ *v être*) (a) **s'~ que** to realize that; **s'~ de** to notice ‹*mistake*›
(b) to catch sight of each other
(c) to meet briefly

aperçu /apɛRsy/ **1** *pp* ▶ APERCEVOIR
2 *nm* (a) glimpse
(b) outline
(c) insight

apéritif /apeRitif/ *nm* drink

apesanteur /apəzɑ̃tœR/ *nf* weightlessness

à-peu-près /apøpRɛ/ *nm inv* vague approximation

apeuré, ~e /apœRe/ *adj* (scared) frightened; (shy) timid

aphone /afɔn/ *adj* **être ~** to have lost one's voice

aphte /aft/ *nm* mouth ulcer

apiculture /apikyltyR/ *nf* beekeeping

apitoiement /apitwamɑ̃/ *nm* pity (**sur** for)

apitoyer /apitwaje/ [23] **1** *vtr* to move [sb] to pity
2 s'apitoyer *v refl* (+ *v être*) **s'~ sur (le sort de) qn** to feel sorry for sb

aplanir /aplaniR/ [3] *vtr* to level

aplati, ~e /aplati/ **1** *pp* ▶ APLATIR
2 *pp adj* (a) flattened
(b) ‹*nose*› flat

aplatir /aplatiR/ [3] *vtr* (a) to flatten
(b) to smooth out ‹*cushion*›; to smooth down ‹*hair*›
(c) to press ‹*seams*›

aplomb /aplɔ̃/ **1** *nm* (a) confidence; **vous ne manquez pas d'~!** you've got a nerve!
(b) plumb, perpendicularity
2 d'aplomb *phr* (a) **être d'~** to be straight, to be plumb vertical
(b) (*fam*) **ça va te remettre d'~** it will put you back on your feet

apocalypse /apɔkalips/ *nf* apocalypse

apogée /apɔʒe/ *nm* (a) (of moon, satellite) apogee
(b) (of career, empire) peak

apologie /apɔlɔʒi/ *nf* panegyric; apologia; **faire l'~ de** to justify; to praise

a posteriori /apɔsteRjɔRi/ *phr* after the event

apostolat /apɔstɔla/ *nm* (a) apostolate
(b) (figurative) apostolic mission

apostrophe /apɔstRɔf/ *nf* apostrophe

apostropher /apɔstRɔfe/ [1] *vtr* to heckle

apothéose /apɔteoz/ *nf* (a) (of show) high point
(b) (of career, work) culmination

apôtre /apotR/ *nm* apostle

✦ **apparaître** /apaRɛtR/ [73] **1** *vi* (+ *v être*)
(a) ‹*person, problem*› to appear; ‹*sun, moon*› to come out
(b) **laisser** *or* **faire ~** to show
(c) to seem
2 *v impers* **il apparaît que** it appears that

apparat /apaRa/ *nm* grandeur; **d'~** ceremonial

✦ **appareil** /apaRɛj/ *nm* (a) device
(b) appliance
(c) telephone; **qui est à l'~?** who's calling please?
(d) aircraft
(e) system; **l'~ digestif** the digestive system
(f) apparatus; **l'~ du parti** the party apparatus
■ **~ auditif** hearing aid; **~ (dentaire)** brace (GB), braces (US); **~ à sous** slot machine; **~ photo** camera
IDIOM **être dans son plus simple ~** to be in one's birthday suit

appareiller /apaReje/ [1] *vi* to cast off

apparemment /apaRamɑ̃/ *adv*
(a) apparently
(b) seemingly

✦ **apparence** /apaRɑ̃s/ *nf* appearance

apparent, ~e /apaRɑ̃, ɑ̃t/ *adj* (a) visible
(b) ‹*embarrassment*› apparent
(c) seeming, apparent

apparenté, ~e /apaRɑ̃te/ *adj* (a) ‹*person*› related (**à** to)
(b) ‹*company*› allied

apparenter: s'apparenter /apaRɑ̃te/ [1] *v refl* (+ *v être*) **s'~ à** to resemble

apparition /apaRisjɔ̃/ *nf* (a) (of product) appearance; (of problem) emergence
(b) apparition

✦ **appartement** /apaRtəmɑ̃/ *nm* flat (GB), apartment; **~ témoin** show flat (GB), show apartment (US)

appartenance /apaRtənɑ̃s/ *nf* membership (**à** of)

✦ **appartenir** /apaRtəniR/ [36]
1 appartenir à *v+prep* (a) **à ~ to belong to**
(b) **~ à** to be a member of
2 *v impers* **il appartient à qn de faire** it is up to sb to do

appât /apɑ/ *nm* (a) bait
(b) lure

appâter /apate/ [1] *vtr* (a) to bait
(b) to lure

appauvrir /apovRiR/ [3] **1** *vtr* to impoverish
2 s'appauvrir *v refl* (+ *v être*) to become impoverished

✦ **appel** /apɛl/ *nm* (a) call; (urgent) appeal; **~ à** a call for ‹*solidarity*›; appeal for ‹*calm*›; **~ au secours** cry for help; cry for help; **faire ~ à** to appeal to ‹*person*›; to call ‹*fire brigade*›; ‹*task*› to call for ‹*skills*›
(b) roll call; (Sch) registration

···✦

a

(c) (Mil) call up (GB), draft (US)
(d) (Law) appeal; **faire ~ to** appeal
(e) (Sport) take off
■ **~ d'air** draught (GB), draft (US); **~ de phares** flash of headlights (GB) or high beams (US)

appelé, **~e** /aple/ ① *pp* ▶ APPELER
② *pp adj* **~ à qch/à faire** destined for sth/ to do
③ *nm* (Mil) conscript, draftee (US)

◆ **appeler** /aple/ [19] ① *vtr* (a) to call; **~ (qn) à l'aide** to call (to sb) for help
(b) to phone (GB), to call
(c) to call ‹*doctor, taxi*›; to send for ‹*pupil*›; **~ qn sous les drapeaux** (Mil) to call sb up
(d) **~ qn à faire** to call on sb to do; **~ à la grève** to call for strike action
(e) **mon travail m'appelle à beaucoup voyager** my work involves a lot of travel
② **en appeler à** *v+prep* to appeal to
③ **s'appeler** *v refl* (+ *v être*) to be called; **comment t'appelles-tu?** what's your name?; **je m'appelle Vladimir** my name is Vladimir; **voilà ce qui s'appelle une belle voiture!** now, that's what you call a nice car!
IDIOM **~ les choses par leur nom, ~ un chat un chat** to call a spade a spade

appellation /apɛlɑsjɔ̃/ *nf* name, appellation

appendice /apɛ̃dis/ *nm* (Anat) appendix
appendicite /apɛ̃disit/ *nf* appendicitis
appesantir: s'appesantir /apəzɑ̃tiʀ/ [3] *v refl* (+ *v être*) **s'~ sur** to dwell on
appétissant, **~e** /apetisɑ̃, ɑ̃t/ *adj* appetizing
appétit /apeti/ *nm* appetite
applaudir /aplodiʀ/ [3] ① *vtr* to applaud
② *vi* (a) to applaud, to clap
(b) (figurative) to approve; **~ des deux mains** to approve heartily
applaudissement /aplodismɑ̃/ *nm*
(a) applause
(b) acclaim
applicateur /aplikatœʀ/ *nm* applicator
◆ **application** /aplikasjɔ̃/ *nf* (a) care; **il manque d'~** he doesn't apply himself
(b) implementation, enforcement; **mettre en ~** to apply ‹*theory*›; to implement ‹*law*›
(c) (of device, program) **~s** applications
(d) (of ointment) application
(e) (Comput) application program
applique /aplik/ *nf* wall light
appliqué, **~e** /aplike/ *adj* (a) hardworking
(b) ‹*work*› careful
(c) ‹*science*› applied
◆ **appliquer** /aplike/ [1] ① *vtr* (a) to apply ‹*ointment*› (**sur** to); to put ‹*stamp*› (**sur** on)
(b) to implement ‹*policy, law*›
(c) to apply ‹*technique*› (**à** to)
② **s'appliquer** *v refl* (+ *v être*) (a) to take great care (**à faire** to do)

(b) **s'~ à qn/qch** ‹*law, remark*› to apply to sb/sth

appoint /apwɛ̃/ *nm* (a) exact change; **faire l'~** to give the exact change
(b) **d'~** ‹*salary*› supplementary; ‹*heating*› additional
appointements /apwɛ̃tmɑ̃/ *nm pl* salary
apport /apɔʀ/ *nm* (a) provision
(b) contribution
◆ **apporter** /apɔʀte/ [1] *vtr* (a) to bring ‹*improvement, news*›; to bring in ‹*revenue*›; to bring about ‹*change*›; **~ qch à qn** to bring sb sth, to take sb sth
(b) to give ‹*support, explanation*›
apposer /apoze/ [1] *vtr* to affix (**sur** on)
apposition /apozisjɔ̃/ *nf* apposition
appréciable /apʀesjabl/ *adj*
(a) substantial
(b) **c'est ~** it's nice
appréciatif, **-ive** /apʀesjatif, iv/ *adj*
(a) appreciative
(b) appraising
appréciation /apʀesjasjɔ̃/ *nf* (a) (of quantity) estimate
(b) (financial) evaluation
(c) (of quality) assessment; **être laissé à l'~ de qn** to be left to sb's discretion
◆ **apprécier** /apʀesje/ [2] *vtr* (a) to appreciate ‹*art*›; to like ‹*person*›
(b) (financially) to value
(c) to estimate ‹*distance*›
(d) to assess ‹*situation*›
appréhender /apʀeɑ̃de/ [1] *vtr* (a) to arrest
(b) to dread
(c) to comprehend, to understand
appréhension /apʀeɑ̃sjɔ̃/ *nf* apprehension
◆ **apprendre** /apʀɑ̃dʀ/ [52] *vtr* (a) to learn (**à faire** to do)
(b) to learn ‹*truth*›; to hear (about) ‹*news*›
(c) to teach
(d) **~ qch à qn** to tell sb sth
apprenti, **~e** /apʀɑ̃ti/ *nm,f* (a) apprentice, trainee
(b) novice; **~ poète** novice poet
◆ **apprentissage** /apʀɑ̃tisaʒ/ *nm*
(a) training, apprenticeship
(b) learning
apprêté, **~e** /apʀete/ ① *pp* ▶ APPRÊTER
② *pp adj* (a) affected
(b) ‹*hairstyle*› fussy
apprêter: s'apprêter /apʀete/ [1] *v refl* (+ *v être*) **s'~ à faire** to get ready to do
apprivoiser /apʀivwaze/ [1] *vtr* to tame
approbateur, **-trice** /apʀɔbatœʀ, tʀis/ *adj* **sourire ~** smile of approval
approbation /apʀɔbasjɔ̃/ *nf* approval
◆ **approche** /apʀɔʃ/ *nf* approach
◆ **approcher** /apʀɔʃe/ [1] ① *vtr* (a) **~ qch de la fenêtre** to move sth near to the window

---

◆ indicates a very frequent word

(b) to go up to; to come up to
(c) to come into contact with
2 approcher de *v*+*prep* to be (getting) close to
3 *vi* to approach
4 s'approcher *v refl* (+ *v être*) **s'~ de** to go near; to come near

approfondi, ~**e** /apʀɔfɔdi/ **1** *pp*
▸ APPROFONDIR
2 *pp adj* detailed, in-depth

approfondir /apʀɔfɔdiʀ/ [3] *vtr* **(a)** to go into [sth] in depth
(b) ~ **ses connaissances en français** to improve one's knowledge of French
(c) to make [sth] deeper

approprié, ~**e** /apʀɔpʀije/ *adj* appropriate

approprier: s'approprier
/apʀɔpʀije/ [2] *v refl* (+ *v être*) **(a)** to take, to appropriate ‹object, idea›
(b) to seize ‹power›

approuver /apʀuve/ [1] *vtr* **(a)** to approve of; **je t'approuve d'avoir accepté** I think you were right to accept
(b) to approve ‹budget›

approvisionnement
/apʀɔvizjɔnmɑ̃/ *nm* supply **(en** of)

approvisionner /apʀɔvizjɔne/ [1] **1** *vtr*
(a) to supply **(en** with); **mal approvisionné** ‹shop› badly stocked
(b) to pay money into ‹account›
2 s'approvisionner *v refl* (+ *v être*)
(a) **s'~ en** to get one's supplies of **(auprès de** from)
(b) to stock up **(en** on, **with)**

approximatif, -ive /apʀɔksimatif, iv/ *adj* ‹estimate, translation› rough

approximation /apʀɔksimasjɔ̃/ *nf*
(a) rough estimate
(b) approximation

appui /apɥi/ *nm* support; **à l'~ de** in support of ‹theory›; **prendre ~ sur** to lean on

appui-tête, *pl* **appuis-tête** /apɥitɛt/ *nm* headrest

appuyé, ~**e** /apɥije/ **1** *pp* ▸ APPUYER
2 *pp adj* **(a)** ‹look› intent
(b) ‹joke› laboured (GB)

♂ **appuyer** /apɥije/ [22] **1** *vtr* **(a)** to rest **(sur** on); to lean **(sur** on)
(b) to press **(contre** against)
(c) to support, to back (up)
2 *vi* **(a)** ~ **sur** to press ‹switch›; to put one's foot on ‹brake›
(b) ~ **sur** to stress ‹word›
3 s'appuyer *v refl* (+ *v être*) **(a)** to lean **(sur** on: **contre** against)
(b) **s'~ sur** to rely on ‹theory›; to draw on ‹report›

âpre /ɑpʀ/ *adj* **(a)** ‹taste, cold› bitter
(b) ‹voice› harsh
(c) ‹struggle› fierce; ‹argument› bitter

♂ **après** /apʀɛ/ **1** *adv* afterward(s), after; later; **peu/bien ~** shortly/long afterward(s); **une heure ~** one hour later; **peu ~ il y a un lac** a bit further on there's a lake; **et ~?** and then what?; **so what?** (colloq)
2 *prep* after; ~ **mon départ** after I leave; **after I left;** ~ **coup** afterward(s); **il est toujours ~ son fils** (fam) he's always on at his son (colloq)
3 d'après *phr* **(a)** **d'~ moi** in my opinion; **d'~ lui/la météo** according to him/the weather forecast; **d'~ ma montre** by my watch
(b) from; based on; **d'~ un dessin de Gauguin** from a drawing by Gauguin
(c) **l'année d'~** the year after; **la fois d'~** the next time
4 après que *phr* after; ~ **qu'il a parlé** after he had spoken
5 après- *(combining form)* **l'~-guerre** the postwar years

après-demain /apʀɛdmɛ̃/ *adv* the day after tomorrow

après-midi /apʀemidi/ *nm inv or nf inv* afternoon

après-rasage, *pl* ~**s** /apʀɛʀazaʒ/ *adj inv*, *nm* after-shave

après-shampooing /apʀɛʃɑ̃pwɛ̃/ *nm* conditioner

après-ski /apʀeski/ *nm inv* snowboot

après-vente /apʀevɑ̃t/ *adj inv* after-sales

a priori /apʀijɔʀi/ **1** *phr* a priori
2 *phr* ~, **ça ne devrait pas poser de problèmes** on the face of it there shouldn't be any problems

à-propos /apʀɔpo/ *nm inv* **intervenir avec** ~ to make an apposite remark; **agir avec** ~ to do the right thing

apte /apt/ *adj* ~ **à qch/à faire** capable of sth/of doing; fit for sth/to do

aptitude /aptityd/ *nf* aptitude; fitness

aquarelle /akwaʀɛl/ *nf* **(a)** watercolours (GB)
(b) watercolour (GB)

aquarium /akwaʀjɔm/ *nm* aquarium, fish tank

aquatique /akwatik/ *adj* **(a)** aquatic
(b) **sport** ~ water sport

aqueduc /akdyk/ *nm* aqueduct

aquilin /akilɛ̃/ *adj m* aquiline

aquitain, ~**e** /akitɛ̃, ɛn/ *adj* of Aquitaine; **le bassin** ~ the Aquitaine Basin

♂ **arabe** /aʀab/ **1** *adj* **(a)** Arab
(b) Arabic
2 *nm* (language) Arabic

Arabe /aʀab/ *nmf* Arab

arabesque /aʀabɛsk/ *nf* arabesque

Arabie /aʀabi/ *pr nf* Arabia
■ ~ **Saoudite** Saudi Arabia

arabique /aʀabik/ *adj* Arabian

arachide /aʀaʃid/ *nf* groundnut, peanut

araignée /aʀeɲe/ nf spider
■ ~ de mer spider crab
IDIOM avoir une ~ au plafond (fam) to have a screw loose (colloq)
arbalète /aʀbalɛt/ nf crossbow
arbitraire /aʀbitʀɛʀ/ adj arbitrary
arbitrairement /aʀbitʀɛʀmɑ̃/ adv arbitrarily
arbitre /aʀbitʀ/ nm (a) referee, umpire
(b) arbitrator
arbitrer /aʀbitʀe/ [1] **1** vtr (a) to referee, to umpire
(b) to arbitrate in
2 vi to arbitrate (entre between)
arborer /aʀbɔʀe/ [1] vtr (a) to wear ‹smile›; to sport ‹badge›
(b) to bear ‹banner›; to fly ‹flag›
arboriculture /aʀbɔʀikyltyʀ/ nf arboriculture
✦ **arbre** /aʀbʀ/ nm (a) tree
(b) (Tech) shaft
■ ~ généalogique family tree
arbrisseau, pl ~x /aʀbʀiso/ nm small tree
arbuste /aʀbyst/ nm shrub
arc /aʀk/ nm (a) (Sport) bow
(b) arc
(c) arch
arcade /aʀkad/ nf arcade; ~s archways
■ ~ sourcilière arch of the eyebrow
arc-bouter: s'arc-bouter /aʀkbute/ [1] v refl (+ v être) to brace oneself
arceau, pl ~x /aʀso/ nm (a) arch
(b) (in croquet) hoop
(c) (in car) roll bar
arc-en-ciel, pl **arcs-en-ciel** /aʀkɑ̃sjɛl/ nm rainbow
archaïque /aʀkaik/ adj archaic
archange /aʀkɑ̃ʒ/ nm archangel
arche /aʀʃ/ nf arch; ~ de Noé Noah's Ark
archéologie /aʀkeɔlɔʒi/ nf archaeology
archéologique /aʀkeɔlɔʒik/ adj archaeological
archet /aʀʃɛ/ nm (Mus) bow
archétype /aʀketip/ nm archetype
archevêché /aʀʃəveʃe/ nm
(a) archdiocese
(b) archbishop's palace
archevêque /aʀʃəvɛk/ nm archbishop
archi /aʀʃi/ pref (fam) ~connu really well-known
archipel /aʀʃipɛl/ nm archipelago
architecte /aʀʃitɛkt/ nmf architect
architecture /aʀʃitɛktyʀ/ nf
(a) architecture
(b) structure
archives /aʀʃiv/ nf pl archives, records
arctique /aʀktik/ adj arctic

Arctique /aʀktik/ pr nm Arctic
ardemment /aʀdamɑ̃/ adv passionately
ardent, ~e /aʀdɑ̃, ɑ̃t/ adj (a) ‹ember› glowing; ‹sun› blazing
(b) ‹faith› burning; ‹patriot› fervent; ‹speech› impassioned; ‹nature› passionate
ardeur /aʀdœʀ/ nf (of person) ardour (GB); (of beliefs) fervour (GB); (of beginner) enthusiasm
ardoise /aʀdwaz/ nf (a) slate
(b) (fam) account
ardu, ~e /aʀdy/ adj (a) arduous
(b) taxing
arène /aʀɛn/ nf (a) arena
(b) bullring
(c) ~s amphitheatre (GB)
arête /aʀɛt/ nf (a) fishbone
(b) (of roof, mountain) ridge; (of prism) edge; (of nose) bridge
✦ **argent** /aʀʒɑ̃/ nm (a) money
(b) silver
■ ~ liquide cash
IDIOM prendre qch pour ~ comptant to take sth at face value
argenté, ~e /aʀʒɑ̃te/ adj (a) silver-plated
(b) (in colour) silvery
argenterie /aʀʒɑ̃tʀi/ nf silverware, silver
Argentine /aʀʒɑ̃tin/ pr nf Argentina
argile /aʀʒil/ nf clay
argot /aʀgo/ nm slang
arguer /aʀge/ [1] **1** vtr ~ que to claim that
2 **arguer de** v+prep to give [sth] as a reason
✦ **argument** /aʀgymɑ̃/ nm argument
argumentation /aʀgymɑ̃tasjɔ̃/ nf line of argument
argumenter /aʀgymɑ̃te/ [1] vi to argue
argus /aʀgys/ nm inv: used car prices guide
aride /aʀid/ adj arid
aridité /aʀidite/ nf aridity
aristocratie /aʀistɔkʀasi/ nf aristocracy
aristocratique /aʀistɔkʀatik/ adj aristocratic
arithmétique /aʀitmetik/ **1** adj arithmetical
2 nf arithmetic
arlequin /aʀləkɛ̃/ nm harlequin
armateur /aʀmatœʀ/ nm shipowner
armature /aʀmatyʀ/ nf (a) (of tent) frame
(b) (in construction) framework
✦ **arme** /aʀm/ **1** nf (a) weapon; charger une ~ to load a gun; rendre les ~s to surrender; en ~s armed; à ~s égales on equal terms; faire ses premières ~s dans l'enseignement to start out as a teacher
(b) branch of the armed services
2 **armes** nf pl coat of arms
■ ~ blanche weapon with a blade; ~ de destruction massive weapon of mass destruc-

tion; ~ à feu firearm

armé, ~e¹ /aRme/ [1] *pp* ▸ ARMER

[2] *pp adj* **(a)** armed; **vol à main ~e** armed robbery

(b) equipped (**de** with; **contre** against)

✓ **armée²** /aRme/ *nf* army

■ ~ **de l'air** air force; **l'~ de réserve** the reserves; **l'~ de terre** the army

armement /aRməmɑ̃/ *nm* **(a)** armament; arming

(b) arms, weapons

(c) (of rifle) cocking; (of camera) winding on

(d) (of ship) fitting out

✓ **armer** /aRme/ [1] [1] *vtr* **(a)** to arm (**de** with; **contre** against)

(b) to fit out ⟨ship⟩

(c) to wind on ⟨camera⟩; to cock ⟨rifle⟩

[2] **s'armer** *v refl* (+ *v être*) to arm oneself

armistice /aRmistis/ *nm* armistice

armoire /aRmwaR/ *nf* **(a)** cupboard

(b) wardrobe

■ ~ **à glace** wardrobe with a full length mirror; **c'est une ~ à glace** (fam) he/she is built like a tank (colloq); ~ **métallique** metal locker; ~ **à pharmacie** medicine cabinet; ~ **de toilette** bathroom cabinet

armoiries /aRmwari/ *nf pl* arms

armure /aRmyR/ *nf* armour (GB)

armurier /aRmyRje/ *nm* **(a)** gunsmith

(b) armourer (GB)

arobas(e) /aRɔbas, -baz/ *nm* (Comput) at sign

aromates /aRɔmat/ *nm pl* herbs and spices

aromathérapeute /aRɔmateRapøt/ *nmf* aromatherapist

aromatique /aRɔmatik/ *adj* aromatic

aromatiser /aRɔmatize/ [1] *vtr* to flavour (GB)

arôme /aRom/ *nm* **(a)** aroma

(b) flavouring (GB)

arpège /aRpɛʒ/ *nm* arpeggio

arpenter /aRpɑ̃te/ [1] *vtr* **(a)** to stride along

(b) to pace up and down

(c) to survey ⟨piece of land⟩

arqué, ~e /aRke/ *adj* ⟨brows⟩ arched; ⟨nose⟩ hooked; ⟨legs⟩ bandy

arquer /aRke/ [1] [1] *vtr* to bend ⟨bar⟩

[2] **s'arquer** *v refl* (+ *v être*) to become bowed

arrachage /aRaʃaz/ *nm* (of crop) picking; (of tooth, post) pulling out; (of scrub, root) digging out; ~ **des mauvaises herbes** weeding

arraché /aRaʃe/ *nm* snatch; **obtenir à l'~** to snatch ⟨victory⟩; **vol à l'~** bag snatching

arrache-pied: d'arrache-pied /daRaʃpje/ *phr* ⟨work⟩ flat out

✓ **arracher** /aRaʃe/ [1] [1] *vtr* **(a)** to pull up *or* dig up ⟨weeds⟩; to pull out ⟨tooth⟩; to tear

down ⟨poster⟩; to rip out ⟨page⟩; to tear off ⟨mask⟩; to uproot ⟨tree⟩; to blow off ⟨tiles⟩

(b) ~ **à qn** to snatch [sth] from sb ⟨bag, victory⟩; to extract [sth] from sb ⟨promise⟩; to get [sth] from sb ⟨smile⟩

(c) ~ **qn à** to uproot sb from ⟨home⟩; to drag sb away from ⟨work⟩; to rouse sb from ⟨thoughts⟩; to rescue sb from ⟨poverty⟩

[2] **s'arracher** *v refl* (+ *v être*) **(a)** ~ **qch** to fight over sth

(b) **s'~ à** to rouse oneself from ⟨thoughts⟩; to tear oneself away from ⟨work⟩

IDIOMS c'est à s'~ les cheveux! (fam) it's enough to make you tear your hair out!; ~ **les yeux à** *or* **de qn** to scratch sb's eyes out

arracheur /aRaʃœR/ *nm* **mentir comme un ~ de dents** to be a born liar

arraisonner /aRɛzɔne/ [1] *vtr* to board and inspect

arrangeant, ~e /aRɑ̃ʒɑ̃, ɑt/ *adj* obliging

arrangement /aRɑ̃ʒmɑ̃/ *nm* arrangement

arranger /aRɑ̃ʒe/ [13] [1] *vtr* **(a)** to arrange, to organize

(b) to sort out; **pour ne rien ~, pour tout ~** to make matters worse

(c) to arrange ⟨flowers⟩

(d) to tidy ⟨hair⟩; to straighten ⟨skirt⟩

(e) (Mus) to arrange

(f) ⟨events⟩ to suit ⟨person⟩

[2] **s'arranger** *v refl* (+ *v être*) **(a)** to get better, to improve

(b) **s'~ avec qn** to arrange it with sb

(c) to manage

(d) **on s'arrangera après** we'll sort it out later

(e) (fam) **elle ne sait pas s'~** she doesn't know how to make the most of herself

arrangeur, -euse /aRɑ̃ʒœR, øz/ *nm,f* (Mus) arranger

arrestation /aREstasjɔ̃/ *nf* arrest

✓ **arrêt** /aRE/ *nm* **(a)** (gen) stopping; (of conflict) cessation; (of delivery) cancellation; (in production) halt

(b) stop; **sans ~** ⟨travel⟩ nonstop; ⟨interrupt⟩ constantly; **à l'~** ⟨vehicle⟩ stationary; ⟨machine⟩ idle; ⟨electrical appliance⟩ off; **marquer un temps d'~** to pause; **être aux ~s** (Mil) to be under arrest

(c) stop; **un ~ de bus** a bus stop

(d) (Law) ruling

■ ~ **du cœur** heart failure; ~ **sur image** freeze-frame, still; ~ **de jeu** stoppage time; ~ **de mort** death sentence; ~ **de travail** stoppage of work; sick leave; sick note

arrêté, ~e /aRete/ [1] *pp* ▸ ARRÊTER

[2] *pp adj* **(a)** ⟨matter⟩ settled

(b) ⟨ideas⟩ fixed

[3] *nm* order, decree

✓ **arrêter** /aRete/ [1] [1] *vtr* **(a)** to stop (**de faire** doing); **être arrêté pour trois semaines** to be given a sick note for three weeks

(b) to switch off ⟨machine⟩; to halt ⟨process⟩

(c) to give up (**de faire** doing)

···≳

a

(d) to arrest
(e) to decide on ‹plan›
2 *vi* to stop; **arrête!** stop it!
3 s'arrêter *v refl* (+ *v être*) (a) to stop
(b) to give up (**de faire** doing)
(c) to end
(d) **s'~ sur** to dwell on; **s'~ à** to focus on

arrhes /aʀ/ *nf pl* deposit

ơ⁺ **arrière** /aʀjɛʀ/ **1** *adj inv* back; rear
2 *nm* (a) rear; **à l'~** (in car) in the back; (on plane, train, ship) at the rear; **en ~** backward(s); (position) behind; **pencher la tête en ~** to tilt one's head back; **revenir en ~** ‹person› to turn back; (figurative) to take a backward step; (on tape) to rewind
(b) (Sport) fullback

arriéré, ~e /aʀjeʀe/ **1** *adj* (a) outdated
(b) backward
(c) behind the times
(d) retarded
2 *nm* arrears

arrière-cour, *pl* ~**s** /aʀjɛʀkuʀ/ *nf* backyard

arrière-goût, *pl* ~**s** /aʀjɛʀgu/ *nm* aftertaste

arrière-grand-mère, *pl* **arrière-grands-mères** /aʀjɛʀgʀɑ̃mɛʀ/ *nf* great-grandmother

arrière-grand-père, *pl* **arrière-grands-pères** /aʀjɛʀgʀɑ̃pɛʀ/ *nm* great-grandfather

arrière-grands-parents /aʀjɛʀgʀɑ̃paʀɑ̃/ *nm pl* great-grandparents

arrière-pays /aʀjɛʀpei/ *nm inv* hinterland

arrière-pensée, *pl* ~**s** /aʀjɛʀpɑ̃se/ *nf*
(a) ulterior motive
(b) **sans ~** without reservation

arrière-petits-enfants /aʀjɛʀpətizɑ̃fɑ̃/ *nm pl* great-grandchildren

arrière-plan, *pl* ~**s** /aʀjɛʀplɑ̃/ *nm* (of picture) background

arrière-saison, *pl* ~**s** /aʀjɛʀsɛzɔ̃/ *nf* late autumn (GB), late fall (US)

arrière-train, *pl* ~**s** /aʀjɛʀtʀɛ̃/ *nm* hindquarters

arrimer /aʀime/ [1] *vtr* (a) to fasten
(b) (Naut) to stow

arrivage /aʀivaʒ/ *nm* delivery, consignment

arrivant, ~e /aʀivɑ̃, ɑ̃t/ *nm,f* **un nouvel ~** a newcomer

arrivé, ~e¹ /aʀive/ **1** *pp* ▶ ARRIVER
2 *pp adj* (a) **le premier ~** the first person to arrive
(b) **être ~** to have made it (socially)

ơ⁺ **arrivée²** /aʀive/ *nf* (a) arrival; **trains à l'~** arrivals
(b) (in race) finish
(c) (Tech) inlet

ơ⁺ indicates a very frequent word

ơ⁺ **arriver** /aʀive/ [1] (+ *v être*) **1** *vi* (a) (gen) to arrive; (Sport) to finish; **~ à/de Paris** to arrive in/from Paris
(b) to come; **~ en courant** to come running up
(c) **~ à** to reach ‹level, agreement›; to find ‹solution›; **~ (jusqu')à qn** to reach sb
(d) **~ à faire** to manage to do; **je n'y arrive pas** I can't do it; **~ à ses fins** to achieve one's ends
(e) **en ~ à** to come to
(f) to happen
2 *v impers* **qu'est-il arrivé?** what happened? (à to); **il m'arrive d'y aller, il arrive que j'y aille** I sometimes go there

arrivisme /aʀivism/ *nm* ruthless ambition

arrogance /aʀɔgɑ̃s/ *nf* arrogance

arrogant, ~e /aʀɔgɑ̃, ɑ̃t/ *adj* arrogant

arroger: s'arroger /aʀɔʒe/ [13] *v refl* (+ *v être*) to appropriate ‹title›; to assume ‹right, role›

arrondi, ~e /aʀɔ̃di/ **1** *adj* rounded; round
2 *nm* (of face) roundness; (of shoulder) curve

arrondir /aʀɔ̃diʀ/ [3] **1** *vtr* (a) to round off ‹edge›; **coiffure qui arrondit le visage** hairstyle that makes one's face look round
(b) to open wide ‹eyes›
(c) to round off ‹figure› (à to)
2 s'arrondir *v refl* (+ *v être*) (a) ‹object› to become round(ed); ‹eyes› to widen
(b) ‹face› to fill out
(c) ‹fortune› to be growing
IDIOM **~ les angles** to smooth the rough edges

arrondissement /aʀɔ̃dismɑ̃/ *nm* (a) (in city) arrondissement
(b) (region) *administrative division in France*

arrosage /aʀozaʒ/ *nm* watering

arroser /aʀoze/ [1] **1** *vtr* (a) to water, to spray; **on va se faire ~!** (fam) we're going to get soaked!
(b) to baste ‹meat›; to sprinkle ‹cake›
(c) to drink to
(d) **repas arrosé au bourgogne** meal washed down with Burgundy
2 s'arroser *v refl* (+ *v être*) (fam) **ça s'arrose** that calls for a drink

arroseur /aʀozœʀ/ *nm* sprinkler

arrosoir /aʀozwaʀ/ *nm* watering can

arsenal, *pl* **-aux** /aʀsənal, o/ *nm* (a) naval shipyard
(b) arsenal
(c) (fam) gear

ơ⁺ **art** /aʀ/ *nm* (a) art
(b) art, skill; **avoir l'~ de faire** to have a knack of doing
■ **~ dramatique** drama; **~ lyrique** opera; **~ de vivre** art of living; **~s ménagers** home economics; **~s plastiques** plastic arts

Artaban /aʀtabɑ̃/ *n pr* **fier comme ~** proud as a peacock

artère /aʀtɛʀ/ *nf* (a) (Anat) artery
(b) arterial road
(c) main street

artériel, -ielle /aʀteʀjɛl/ *adj* arterial

arthrite /aʀtʀit/ *nf* arthritis

arthrose /aʀtʀoz/ *nf* osteoarthritis

artichaut /aʀtiʃo/ *nm* (globe) artichoke
IDIOM **avoir un cœur d'~** to be fickle (*in love*)

⚜ **article** /aʀtikl/ *nm* (a) (in paper, law) article;
(in contract) clause
(b) (in grammar) article
(c) item; **~s de consommation courante**
basic consumer goods; **faire l'~ à qn** to give
sb the sales pitch
IDIOM **être à l'~ de la mort** to be at death's
door

articulaire /aʀtikylɛʀ/ *adj* articular

articulation /aʀtikylasjɔ̃/ *nf* (a) (Anat)
joint
(b) (of lamp, sunshade) mobile joint
(c) (in phonetics) articulation
(d) (in sentence) link
(e) (of speech, essay) structure

⚜ **articuler** /aʀtikyle/ [1] **1** *vtr* (a) to
articulate; **articule!** speak clearly!
(b) to utter
(c) to structure ⟨*ideas*⟩
2 s'articuler *v refl* (+ *v être*) **s'~ autour**
de to be based on, to hinge on

artifice /aʀtifis/ *nm* (a) trick
(b) device; **les ~s du style** stylistic devices
(c) **sans ~** unpretentious

artificiel, -ielle /aʀtifisjɛl/ *adj*
(a) artificial; man-made
(b) superficial; forced

artificier /aʀtifisje/ *nm* (a) bomb disposal
expert
(b) explosives manufacturer
(c) fireworks manufacturer

artillerie /aʀtijʀi/ *nf* artillery

artisan /aʀtizɑ̃/ *nm* (a) artisan, craftsman
(b) architect, author

artisanal, ~e, *mpl* -aux /aʀtizanal, o/ *adj*
⟨*method*⟩ traditional; **de fabrication ~e**
hand-crafted; home-made

artisanat /aʀtizana/ *nm* (a) craft industry,
cottage industry
(b) artisans
■ **~ d'art** arts and crafts

⚜ **artiste** /aʀtist/ **1** *adj* (a) artistic
(b) **il est un peu ~** he's a bit of a dreamer
2 *nmf* (a) artist; **~ peintre** painter
(b) (on stage) performer; (in music hall) artiste;
~ lyrique opera singer

artistique /aʀtistik/ *adj* artistic

as¹ /a/ ▶ AVOIR¹

as² /ɑs/ *nm inv* ace
IDIOMS **être plein aux ~** (fam) to be loaded (colloq); **passer à l'~** (fam) ⟨*money*⟩ to go down the
drain; ⟨*holidays*⟩ to go by the board; **être fagoté**
comme l'~ de pique (fam) to look a mess

ascendance /asɑ̃dɑ̃s/ *nf* descent,
ancestry

ascendant, ~e /asɑ̃dɑ̃, ɑ̃t/ **1** *adj* ⟨*curve*⟩
rising; ⟨*movement*⟩ upward; ⟨*star*⟩ ascending
2 *nm* (a) influence (**sur** over)
(b) (Law) ascendant

ascenseur /asɑ̃sœʀ/ *nm* lift (GB), elevator
(US)
IDIOM **renvoyer l'~** to return the favour (GB)

ascension /asɑ̃sjɔ̃/ *nf* (a) ascent; **faire l'~**
de to climb
(b) (figurative) rise

ascensionnel, -elle /asɑ̃sjɔnɛl/ *adj*
⟨*movement*⟩ upward; **parachute ~**
parascending

ascète /asɛt/ *nmf* ascetic

ascétisme /asetism/ *nm* asceticism

aseptique /asɛptik/ *adj* aseptic

aseptisé, ~e /asɛptize/ *adj* ⟨*art*⟩ sanitized;
⟨*world*⟩ sterile; ⟨*decor*⟩ impersonal

aseptiser /asɛptize/ [1] *vtr* to disinfect
⟨*wound*⟩; to sterilize ⟨*instrument*⟩

asexué, ~e /asɛksɥe/ *adj* asexual

asiatique /azjatik/ *adj* Asian

Asie /azi/ *pr nf* Asia; **~ Mineure** Asia Minor

asile /azil/ *nm* (a) refuge; **chercher ~ à** to
seek refuge
(b) (political) asylum
(c) **~ de vieillards** old people's home; **~ de**
nuit night shelter

asocial, ~e, *mpl* -iaux /asɔsjal, o/ **1** *adj*
antisocial
2 *nm,f* social misfit

⚜ **aspect** /aspɛ/ *nm* (a) side; **voir qch sous**
son ~ positif to see the good side of sth
(b) aspect; **par bien des ~s** in many respects
(c) appearance

asperge /aspɛʀʒ/ *nf* (a) asparagus
(b) (fam) beanpole (colloq), string bean (US)

asperger /aspɛʀʒe/ [13] *vtr* to spray; to
splash

aspérité /aspeʀite/ *nf* (in terrain) bump

asphalte /asfalt/ *nm* asphalt

asphyxiant, ~e /asfiksjɑ̃, ɑ̃t/ *adj*
asphyxiating

asphyxie /asfiksi/ *nf* asphyxiation

asphyxier /asfiksje/ [2] **1** *vtr* (a) to
asphyxiate ⟨*person*⟩
(b) to paralyse ⟨*network, company*⟩
2 s'asphyxier *v refl* (+ *v être*) (a) to
suffocate to death
(b) to gas oneself
(c) ⟨*network, company*⟩ to become paralysed

aspirateur /aspiʀatœʀ/ *nm* vacuum
cleaner, hoover® (GB)

aspiration /aspiʀasjɔ̃/ *nf* (a) aspiration
(**à** for)
(b) sucking up, drawing up
(c) inhalation

aspirer /aspiʀe/ [1] **1** *vtr* **(a)** to breathe in, to inhale
(b) to suck [sth] up
(c) consonne aspirée aspirated consonant
2 aspirer à *v+prep* to yearn for; to aspire to

aspirine® /aspiʀin/ *nf* aspirin
IDIOM **être blanc comme un cachet d'~** to be lily white

assagir: s'assagir /asaʒiʀ/ [3] *v refl* (+ *v être*) to quieten down (GB), to quiet down (US)

assaillant, ~e /asajɑ̃, ɑ̃t/ *nm,f*
(a) attacker
(b) (Mil) **les ~s** the attacking forces

assaillir /asajiʀ/ [28] *vtr* **(a)** to attack
(b) to plague; **~ qn de questions** to bombard sb with questions

assainir /aseniʀ/ [3] *vtr* **(a)** to clean up
(b) to stabilize ‹*economy*›; to streamline ‹*company*›

assainissement /asenismɑ̃/ *nm*
(a) cleaning up
(b) (of economy) stabilization; (of company) streamlining

assaisonnement /asɛzɔnmɑ̃/ *nm* (Culin) seasoning; (on salad) dressing

assaisonner /asɛzɔne/ [1] *vtr* to season ‹*dish*›; to dress ‹*salad*›

assassin, ~e /asasɛ̃, in/ **1** *adj*
(a) murderous
(b) ‹*campaign*› vicious
2 *nm* **(a)** murderer
(b) assassin

assassinat /asasina/ *nm* **(a)** murder
(b) assassination

assassiner /asasine/ [1] *vtr* **(a)** to murder
(b) to assassinate
(c) (fam) to slate (colloq)

assaut /aso/ *nm* attack, assault; **se lancer** *or* **monter à l'~ de** to launch an attack on; **prendre d'~** to storm; **les ~s du froid** the onslaught of cold weather

assécher /aseʃe/ [14] *vtr* **(a)** to drain
(b) ‹*heat*› to dry up

ASSEDIC /asedik/ *nf* (abbr
= **Association pour l'emploi dans l'industrie et le commerce**)
organization managing unemployment contributions and payments

assemblage /asɑ̃blaʒ/ *nm* **(a)** (of motor) assembly (**de** of)
(b) (of ideas) assemblage; (of objects) collection; (of colours) combination

✓ **assemblée** /asɑ̃ble/ *nf* **(a)** gathering
(b) meeting
(c) assembly
■ **~ générale, AG** general meeting; **l'Assemblée nationale** the French National Assembly

assembler /asɑ̃ble/ [1] **1** *vtr* to assemble, to put together
2 s'assembler *v refl* (+ *v être*) ‹*crowd*› to gather; ‹*ministers*› to assemble
IDIOM **qui se ressemble s'assemble** (Proverb) birds of a feather flock together

asséner /asene/ [14] *vtr* **~ un coup à qn/ qch** to deal sb/sth a blow

assentiment /asɑ̃timɑ̃/ *nm* assent, consent

✓ **asseoir** /aswaʀ/ [41] **1** *vtr* **(a)** to sit [sb] down; (in bed) to sit [sb] up; **faire ~ qn** to make sb sit down; (politely) to offer a seat to sb
(b) to establish ‹*reputation*›
(c) (fam) to stagger, to astound
2 s'asseoir *v refl* (+ *v être*) to sit (down); (in bed) to sit up

assermenté, ~e /asɛʀmɑ̃te/ *adj* sworn, on oath

assertion /asɛʀsjɔ̃/ *nf* assertion

asservir /asɛʀviʀ/ [3] *vtr* **(a)** to enslave ‹*person*›
(b) to subjugate ‹*country*›

asservissement /asɛʀvismɑ̃/ *nm* **(a)** (of country, people) subjugation
(b) subjection
(c) subservience

assesseur /asesœʀ/ *nm* magistrate's assistant

✓ **assez** /ase/ *adv* **(a)** enough; **~ fort** strong enough; **j'en ai ~** I've got enough; I'm fed up (colloq)
(b) quite; **je suis ~ pressé** I'm in rather a hurry; **je suis ~ d'accord** I tend to agree

assidu, ~e /asidy/ *adj* **(a)** diligent
(b) ‹*care*› constant
(c) ‹*presence, visits*› regular
(d) devoted

assiduité /asidɥite/ *nf* **(a)** diligence; **avec ~** ‹*work*› diligently; ‹*train*› assiduously; ‹*read*› regularly
(b) regular attendance
(c) ~s assiduities

assiégeant, ~e /asjeʒɑ̃, ɑ̃t/ *nm,f* besieger

assiéger /asjeʒe/ [15] *vtr* to besiege

✓ **assiette** /asjɛt/ *nf* **(a)** (for food) plate
(b) ~ (fiscale) tax base
■ **~ anglaise** assorted cold meats; **~ en carton** paper plate; **~ creuse** soup plate; **~ à dessert** dessert plate
IDIOM **ne pas être dans son ~** to be out of sorts

assignation /asiɲasjɔ̃/ *nf* **(a)** allocation
(b) (Law) summons

assigner /asiɲe/ [1] *vtr* **(a)** to assign ‹*task*›
(b) to set ‹*objective*›
(c) to ascribe ‹*value, role*› (**à** to)
(d) (Law) **~ à comparaître** to summons; **~ qn à résidence** to put sb under house arrest

assimilation /asimilasjɔ̃/ *nf*
(a) comparison

✓ indicates a very frequent word

(b) assimilation

assimilé, ~e /asimile/ *adj* similar

assimiler /asimile/ [1] **1** *vtr* (a) to assimilate; **être assimilé cadre** to have executive status
(b) ~ **qn/qch à** to liken sb/sth to
2 s'assimiler *v refl* (+ *v être*) (a) **s'~ à** ‹method› to be comparable to; ‹person› to compare oneself to
(b) ‹minority› to become assimilated; ‹substances› to be assimilated

assis, ~e¹ /asi, iz/ **1** *pp* ▶ ASSEOIR
2 *pp adj* (a) seated; **être ~** to be sitting down; (in bed) to be sitting up; **reste ~** don't get up; (as reprimand) sit still
(b) ‹reputation› well-established
(c) (fam) staggered

assise² /asiz/ *nf* basis, foundation

assises /asiz/ *nf pl* (a) meeting
(b) (Law) assizes

assistanat /asistana/ *nm* (a) (Univ) assistantship
(b) (state aid) (pej) charity

assistance /asistɑ̃s/ *nf* (a) assistance; aid
(b) audience
(c) attendance (**à** at)
■ **~ respiratoire** artificial respiration; **l'Assistance publique** ≈ welfare services

assistant, ~e /asistɑ̃, ɑ̃t/ *nm,f* assistant
■ **~ social** social worker

assisté, ~e /asiste/ **1** *pp* ▶ ASSISTER
2 *pp adj* (a) assisted (**de** by)
(b) receiving benefit (GB), on welfare (US)
(c) **~ par ordinateur** computer-aided
(d) **direction ~e** power steering
3 *nm,f*: person receiving benefit (GB) or welfare (US)

⚘ **assister** /asiste/ [1] **1** *vtr* to assist; to aid
2 assister à *v+prep* (a) **~ à** to be at, to attend
(b) **~ à** to witness

associatif, -ive /asɔsjatif, iv/ *adj*
(a) ‹memory› associative
(b) **vie associative** community life

⚘ **association** /asɔsjasjɔ̃/ *nf* (a) association
(b) combination

associé, ~e /asɔsje/ **1** *adj* ‹member› associate; ‹companies› associated
2 *nm,f* associate, partner

⚘ **associer** /asɔsje/ [2] **1** *vtr* (a) **~ qn à** to include sb in ‹success›; to make sb a partner in ‹business›; to give sb a share of ‹profits›
(b) **~ qch à** to combine sth with; to associate sth with
2 s'associer *v refl* (+ *v être*) (a) to go into partnership, to link up; **s'~ pour faire** to join forces to do
(b) **s'~ à** to join ‹movement›; to share in ‹grief›
(c) to combine

assoiffé, ~e /aswafe/ *adj* (a) thirsty
(b) **~ de** thirsting for

assombrir /asɔ̃bʀiʀ/ [3] **1** *vtr* (a) to make [sth] dark, to darken
(b) to spoil; **la tristesse assombrit son visage** his/her face clouded
2 s'assombrir *v refl* (+ *v être*) (a) ‹sky› to darken
(b) ‹face› to become gloomy

assommant, ~e /asɔmɑ̃, ɑ̃t/ *adj* (fam)
(a) (dull) deadly boring (colloq)
(b) (irritating) **tu es ~ avec tes questions** you're a real pain (colloq) with your questions

assommer /asɔme/ [1] *vtr* (a) to knock [sb] senseless
(b) (fam) **~ qn** to get on sb's nerves
(c) (fam) ‹news› to stagger; ‹heat› to overcome

assorti, ~e /asɔʀti/ *adj* (a) matching
(b) assorted

assortiment /asɔʀtimɑ̃/ *nm* (a) set
(b) assortment, selection
(c) (in shop) stock

assortir /asɔʀtiʀ/ [3] **1** *vtr* to match (**à** to; **avec** with)
(b) **~ qch de qch** to add sth to sth
2 s'assortir *v refl* (+ *v être*) (a) **s'~ à** or **avec** to match
(b) **s'~ de** to come with

assoupir /asupiʀ/ [3] **1** *vtr* (a) to make [sb] drowsy
(b) to dull ‹senses, passion›
2 s'assoupir *v refl* (+ *v être*) to doze off

assoupissement /asupismɑ̃/ *nm* drowsiness; (sleep) doze

assouplir /asupliʀ/ [3] **1** *vtr* (a) to soften ‹washing›
(b) to make [sth] more supple ‹body, leather›
(c) to relax ‹rule›
2 s'assouplir *v refl* (+ *v être*) (a) to get softer
(b) to become more supple
(c) ‹person, rule› to become more flexible

assouplissant /asuplisɑ̃/ *nm* fabric softener

assouplissement /asuplismɑ̃/ *nm*
(a) (of leather, woollens) softening; (of washing) conditioning
(b) (Sport) **faire des ~s** or **des exercices d'~** to limber up
(c) (of rules, policy, attitude) relaxing

assouplisseur /asuplisœʀ/ *nm* fabric conditioner

assourdir /asuʀdiʀ/ [3] *vtr* (a) to deafen
(b) to muffle

assouvir /asuviʀ/ [3] *vtr* to satisfy ‹hunger›; to assuage ‹anger›

assouvissement /asuvismɑ̃/ *nm* (a) (of hunger) satisfying; (of anger) assuaging
(b) satisfaction

assujetti, ~e /asyʒeti/ *adj* **~ à** liable for ‹tax›; subject to ‹rule›

assujettir /asyʒetiʀ/ [3] **1** *vtr* (a) to subject (**à** to)
(b) to subjugate, to subdue ⸱⸱⸱▷

(c) to secure
2 **s'assujettir** *v refl* (+ *v être*) ‹person› to submit (**à** to)

assumer /asyme/ [1] 1 *vtr* **(a)** to take ‹responsibility›; to hold ‹post›; to meet ‹costs›
(b) to come to terms with ‹conditions, identity, past›; to accept ‹consequences›
2 **s'assumer** *v refl* (+ *v être*) **(a)** to take responsibility for oneself
(b) to come to terms with oneself

assurable /asyRabl/ *adj* insurable

assurance /asyRɑ̃s/ *nf* **(a)** (self-)confidence, assurance; **avec** ~ confidently
(b) assurance; **donner à qn l'**~ **que** to assure sb that
(c) insurance (policy)
(d) insurance company
(e) insurance (premium)
(f) insurance (sector)
(g) benefit (GB), benefits (US)
■ ~ **au tiers** third-party insurance; ~ **maladie** health insurance; sickness benefit (GB) *or* benefits (US); ~ **tous risques** comprehensive insurance; ~**s sociales** social insurance

assurance-crédit, *pl* **assurances-crédit** /asyRɑ̃skRedi/ *nf* credit insurance

assurance-vie, *pl* **assurances-vie** /asyRɑ̃svi/ *nf* life insurance

assuré, ~**e** /asyRe/ 1 *pp* ▶ ASSURER
2 *pp adj* **(a)** sure, certain (**de faire** of doing); **soyez** ~ **de ma reconnaissance** I am very grateful to you
(b) insured
3 *adj* **(a)** ‹step, air› confident; ‹hand› steady; **mal** ~ ‹step, voice› faltering; ‹gesture› nervous
(b) certain, assured
4 *nm,f* insured party
■ ~ **social** social insurance contributor

assurément /asyRemɑ̃/ *adv* **(a)** definitely
(b) most certainly

♂ **assurer** /asyRe/ [1] 1 *vtr* **(a)** ~ **à qn que** to assure sb that; **ce n'est pas drôle, je t'assure** believe me, it's no joke
(b) ~ **qn de** to assure sb of ‹support›
(c) to insure ‹property, goods›
(d) to carry out ‹maintenance›; to provide ‹service›; ~ **la liaison entre** ‹train, bus, ferry› to operate between; ~ **la gestion de** to manage
(e) to ensure ‹victory›; to secure ‹right, post› (**à qn** for sb); to assure ‹future›; ~ **un revenu à qn** to give sb an income; ~ **ses vieux jours** to provide for one's old age
(f) to secure ‹rope›; to belay ‹climber›
2 **s'assurer** *v refl* (+ *v être*) **(a)** **s'**~ **de qch** to make sure of sth
(b) to secure ‹advantage, help›
(c) to take out insurance
(d) (figurative) **s'**~ **contre** to insure against ‹eventuality, risk›

───────────
♂ indicates a very frequent word

assureur /asyRœR/ *nm* **(a)** insurance agent
(b) insurance company

astérisque /asteRisk/ *nm* asterisk
asthmatique /asmatik/ *adj, nmf* asthmatic
asthme /asm/ *nm* asthma
asticot /astiko/ *nm* maggot
astigmate /astigmat/ *adj* astigmatic
astiquer /astike/ [1] *vtr* to polish
astral, ~**e**, *mpl* **-aux** /astRal, o/ *adj* astral
astre /astR/ *nm* star
astreindre /astRɛ̃dR/ [55] 1 *vtr* ~ **qn à qch** ‹person› to force sth upon sb; ‹rule› to bind sb to sth; ~ **qn à faire** to compel sb to do
2 **s'astreindre** *v refl* (+ *v être*) **s'**~ **à qch** to subject oneself to sth
astringent, ~**e** /astRɛ̃ʒɑ̃, ɑ̃t/ *adj* astringent
astrologie /astRɔlɔʒi/ *nf* astrology
astrologique /astRɔlɔʒik/ *adj* astrological
astrologue /astRɔlɔg/ *nmf* astrologer
astronaute /astRɔnot/ *nmf* astronaut
astronautique /astRɔnotik/ *nf* astronautics
astronomie /astRɔnɔmi/ *nf* astronomy
astronomique /astRɔnɔmik/ *adj* astronomical
astrophysique /astRɔfizik/ *nf* astrophysics
astuce /astys/ *nf* **(a)** cleverness
(b) shrewdness, astuteness
(c) trick
(d) pun; joke
astucieux, **-ieuse** /astysjø, øz/ *adj*
(a) clever
(b) shrewd, sharp
asymétrique /asimetRik/ *adj* asymmetrical
atchoum /atʃum/ *nm* atishoo
atelier /atəlje/ *nm* **(a)** (place) workshop; (artist's) studio
(b) working group
(c) (seminar) workshop
atermoyer /atɛRmwaje/ [23] *vi* to procrastinate
athée /ate/ 1 *adj* atheistic
2 *nmf* atheist
athéisme /ateism/ *nm* atheism
athénien, **-ienne** /atenjɛ̃, ɛn/ *adj* Athenian
athlète /atlɛt/ *nmf* athlete
athlétique /atletik/ *adj* athletic
athlétisme /atletism/ *nm* athletics (GB), track and field events
Atlantique /atlɑ̃tik/ *pr nm* **l'**~ the Atlantic
atlas /atlas/ *nm inv* atlas

atmosphère /atmɔsfɛʀ/ *nf* atmosphere

atoll /atɔl/ *nm* atoll

atome /atom/ *nm* atom
  IDIOM **avoir des ~s crochus avec qn** (fam) to get on well with sb

atomique /atɔmik/ *adj* atomic

atomiseur /atɔmizœʀ/ *nm* spray, atomizer

atone /atɔn/ *adj* **(a)** lifeless, apathetic
  (b) ⟨*syllable*⟩ unstressed

atours /atuʀ/ *nm pl* finery

atout /atu/ *nm* **(a)** trump (card); trumps
  (b) (figurative) asset; trump card; **mettre tous les ~s dans son jeu** to leave nothing to chance

âtre /atʀ/ *nm* hearth

atroce /atʀɔs/ *adj* atrocious, dreadful, terrible

atrocité /atʀɔsite/ *nf* **(a)** atrocity
  (b) monstrosity

atrophie /atʀɔfi/ *nf* atrophy

atrophier: **s'atrophier** /atʀɔfje/ [2] *v refl* (+ *v être*) to atrophy; **bras atrophié** wasted arm

attabler: **s'attabler** /atable/ [1] *v refl* (+ *v être*) to sit down at (the) table

attachant, ~e /ataʃɑ̃, ɑ̃t/ *adj* engaging

attache /ataʃ/ *nf* **(a)** tie; string; rope; strap; **~s familiales** family ties
  (b) **avoir des ~s fines** to have delicate ankles and wrists

attaché, ~e /ataʃe/ *nm,f* attaché
  ■ **~ de presse** press attaché

attachement /ataʃmɑ̃/ *nm* **(a)** (to person) attachment
  (b) (to principle, cause) commitment

⚡ **attacher** /ataʃe/ [1] **1** *vtr* **(a)** to tie ⟨*person, hands, laces*⟩ (**à** to); to tether ⟨*horse, goat*⟩; to chain ⟨*dog*⟩ (**à** to); to lock ⟨*bicycle*⟩ (**à** to); to tie up ⟨*person, parcel*⟩
  (b) to fasten ⟨*belt*⟩
  (c) to attach ⟨*importance*⟩
  (d) **les privilèges attachés à un poste** the privileges attached to a post
  2 **s'attacher** *v refl* (+ *v être*) **(a)** to fasten
  (b) **s'~ à qn/qch** to become attached to sb/sth

attaquable /atakabl/ *adj* **(a)** ⟨*place*⟩ **facilement ~** easy to attack
  (b) ⟨*theory, position*⟩ shaky
  (c) ⟨*will*⟩ contestable

attaquant, ~e /atakɑ̃, ɑ̃t/ *nm,f* attacker

⚡ **attaque** /atak/ **1** *nf* **(a)** attack; (on bank) raid; **passer à l'~** to move into the attack; (figurative) to go on the attack; **~ à main armée** armed raid
  (b) (Med) stroke; **~ cardiaque** heart attack
  2 **d'attaque** *phr* (fam) on (GB) *or* in (US) form; **être d'~ pour faire** to feel up to doing

⚡ **attaquer** /atake/ [1] **1** *vtr* **(a)** to attack; to raid ⟨*bank*⟩
  (b) (Law) to contest ⟨*contract, will*⟩; **~ qn en**

justice to bring a lawsuit against sb
  (c) to tackle ⟨*problem*⟩
  2 *vi* **(a)** (in tennis, golf) to drive
  (b) ⟨*speaker*⟩ to begin (brusquely)
  3 **s'attaquer** *v refl* (+ *v être*) **s'~ à** to attack ⟨*person, policy*⟩; to tackle ⟨*problem*⟩

attardé, ~e /ataʀde/ **1** *adj* retarded
  2 *nm,f* mentally retarded person

attarder: **s'attarder** /ataʀde/ [1] *v refl* (+ *v être*) **(a)** to stay until late; to linger
  (b) **s'~ sur** to dwell on ⟨*point*⟩

⚡ **atteindre** /atɛ̃dʀ/ [55] **1** *vtr* **(a)** to reach ⟨*place, age, level, target*⟩; to achieve ⟨*aim*⟩
  (b) ⟨*projectile, marksman*⟩ to hit ⟨*target*⟩
  (c) ⟨*illness*⟩ to affect
  2 **atteindre à** *v+prep* to reach; to achieve

atteint, ~e¹ /atɛ̃, ɛ̃t/ **1** *pp* ▸ ATTEINDRE
  2 *pp adj* **(a)** affected (**de, par** by); **être ~ de** to be suffering from ⟨*illness*⟩
  (b) hit (**de, par** by)

atteinte² /atɛ̃t/ **1** *nf* **~ à** attack on; **porter ~ à** to undermine ⟨*prestige*⟩; to damage ⟨*reputation*⟩; to endanger ⟨*security*⟩; to infringe ⟨*right*⟩; **~ à la vie privée** breach of privacy
  2 **hors d'atteinte** *phr* **hors d'~** ⟨*person*⟩ beyond reach; ⟨*target*⟩ out of range

attelage /atlaʒ/ *nm* **(a)** (of horse) harness; (of oxen) yoke, (of wagon) coupling, (of trailer) towing attachment
  (b) (animals) team; (of oxen) yoke
  (c) horse-drawn carriage

atteler /atle/ [19] **1** *vtr* to harness ⟨*horse*⟩; to yoke ⟨*oxen*⟩; to couple ⟨*wagon*⟩
  2 **s'atteler** *v refl* (+ *v être*) **s'~ à une tâche** to get down to a job

attelle /atɛl/ *nf* (Med) splint

attenant, ~e /atnɑ̃, ɑ̃t/ *adj* adjacent

⚡ **attendre** /atɑ̃dʀ/ [6] **1** *vtr* **(a)** to wait for ⟨*person, event*⟩; **j'attends de voir pour le croire** I'll believe it when I see it; **se faire ~** to keep people waiting; **la réaction ne se fit pas ~** the reaction was instantaneous; **~ son jour** *or* **heure** to bide one's time; **en attendant mieux** until something better turns up; **on ne t'attendait plus!** we'd given up on you!
  (b) to await, to be in store for ⟨*person*⟩
  (c) to expect; **~ qch de qn/qch** to expect sth from sb/sth; **elle attend un bébé** she's expecting a baby
  2 *vi* to wait; (on phone) to hold; **faire ~ qn** to keep sb waiting; **en attendant** in the meantime; all the same, nonetheless; **tu me perds rien pour ~!** (fam) I'll get you (colloq), just you wait!
  3 **s'attendre** *v refl* (+ *v être*) **s'~ à qch** to expect sth; **s'~ à ce que qn fasse** to expect sb to do

attendrir /atɑ̃dʀiʀ/ [3] **1** *vtr* to touch, to move ⟨*person*⟩; **se laisser ~** to soften   ⸱⸱⸱⟩

a

2 **s'attendrir** *v refl* (+ *v être*) to feel moved

attendrissant, ~**e** /atɑ̃dʀisɑ̃, ɑ̃t/ *adj* touching, moving; ‹*innocence*› endearing

attendrissement /atɑ̃dʀismɑ̃/ *nm* emotion

attendu¹: **attendu que** /atɑ̃dy/ *phr*
(a) given *or* considering that
(b) (Law) whereas

attendu², ~**e** /atɑ̃dy/ *adj* (a) expected
(b) le jour (tant) ~ the long-awaited day

attentat /atɑ̃ta/ *nm* assassination attempt, attack; ~ **à la bombe** bomb attack
■ ~ **à la pudeur** (Law) indecent assault; ~ **suicide** suicide attack

❖ **attente** /atɑ̃t/ *nf* (a) waiting; wait; **mon** ~ **a été vaine** I waited in vain; **dans l'**~ **de vous lire** looking forward to hearing from you; **en** ~ ‹*passenger*› waiting; ‹*file*› pending; ‹*call*› on hold
(b) expectation; **répondre à l'**~ **de qn** to come up to sb's expectations

attenter /atɑ̃te/ [1] *v+prep* ~ **à ses jours** to attempt suicide; ~ **à la vie de qn** to make an attempt on sb's life

attentif, -ive /atɑ̃tif, iv/ *adj* attentive; **sous l'œil** ~ **de leur mère** under the watchful eye of their mother

❖ **attention** /atɑ̃sjɔ̃/ **1** *nf* (a) attention; **faire** ~ **à qch** to mind ‹*cars, step*›; to watch out for ‹*black ice*›; to take care of ‹*clothes, belongings*›; to watch ‹*diet, health*›; to pay attention to ‹*fashion, details*›; **faire** ~ **à qn** to pay attention to sb; to keep an eye on sb; to take notice of sb
(b) kind gesture; **être plein d'**~**s pour qn** to be very attentive to sb
2 *excl* (a) (cry) look out!, watch out!; (written) attention!; (in case of danger) warning!; (on road sign) caution!
(b) ~**, je ne veux pas dire…** don't get me wrong, I don't mean…

attentionné, ~**e** /atɑ̃sjɔne/ *adj* attentive, considerate

attentisme /atɑ̃tism/ *nm* wait-and-see attitude

attentivement /atɑ̃tivmɑ̃/ *adv*
(a) attentively
(b) carefully

atténuantes /atenɥɑ̃t/ *adj f pl* **circonstances** ~ (Law) mitigating circumstances

atténuer /atenɥe/ [1] **1** *vtr* to ease ‹*pain, distress*›; to lessen ‹*impact*›; to smooth over ‹*differences*›; to weaken ‹*effect*›; to soften ‹*blow*›; to reduce ‹*inequalities*›; to dim ‹*light*›; to make [sth] less strong ‹*smell, taste*›
2 **s'atténuer** *v refl* (+ *v être*) ‹*pain*› to ease; ‹*anger, grief*› to subside; ‹*corruption, pessimism*› to lessen; ‹*gaps*› to be reduced;

‹*wrinkles, colour*› to fade; ‹*storm, noise*› to die down

atterrant, ~**e** /atɛʀɑ̃, ɑ̃t/ *adj* (a) appalling
(b) shattering

atterré, ~**e** /atere/ *adj* (a) appalled
(b) shattered

atterrir /ateʀiʀ/ [3] *vi* to land

atterrissage /ateʀisaʒ/ *nm* landing

attestation /atɛstasjɔ̃/ *nf* (a) attestation
(b) certificate

attester /atɛste/ [1] *vtr* (a) to vouch for; to testify to
(b) to prove, to attest to

attirail /atiʀaj/ *nm* gear, equipment

attirance /atiʀɑ̃s/ *nf* attraction

attirant, ~**e** /atiʀɑ̃, ɑ̃t/ *adj* attractive

❖ **attirer** /atiʀe/ [1] **1** *vtr* (a) to attract ‹*person, capital*›; to draw ‹*crowd, attention*›; ~ **qn dans un coin** to take sb into a corner; ~ **qn dans un piège** to lure sb into a trap
(b) ‹*country, profession*› to appeal to
(c) to bring ‹*shame, anger*›; ~ **des ennuis à qn** to cause sb problems
2 **s'attirer** *v refl* (+ *v être*) **s'**~ **le soutien de qn** to win sb's support; **s'**~ **des ennuis** to get into trouble

attiser /atize/ [1] *vtr* (a) to kindle ‹*feeling*›; to fuel ‹*discord*›; to stir up ‹*hatred*›
(b) to fan ‹*fire*›

attitré, ~**e** /atitʀe/ *adj* ‹*chauffeur*› official
(b) ‹*customer*› regular

❖ **attitude** /atityd/ *nf* (a) bearing; posture
(b) attitude

attouchement /atuʃmɑ̃/ *nm*
(a) molesting
(b) fondling
(c) (by healer) laying on of hands

attractif, -ive /atʀaktif, iv/ *adj* attractive

attraction /atʀaksjɔ̃/ *nf* attraction
■ ~ **terrestre** earth's gravity; ~ **universelle** gravitation

attrait /atʀɛ/ *nm* (a) appeal, attraction; lure
(b) **l'**~ **de qn pour qn/qch** sb's liking for sb/ sth

attraper /atʀape/ [1] *vtr* (a) to catch; **se faire** ~ to get caught; **attrapez-le!** stop him!
(b) to catch hold of ‹*rope, hand, leg*›
(c) (fam) to catch ‹*cold, illness*›
(d) (fam) to tell [sb] off

attrayant, ~**e** /atʀɛjɑ̃, ɑ̃t/ *adj*
(a) attractive
(b) pleasant

❖ **attribuer** /atʀibɥe/ [1] **1** *vtr* (a) to allocate ‹*seat, task*›; to grant ‹*right*›; to award ‹*prize*›; to lend ‹*importance*›; ~ **qch à la fatigue** to put sth down to tiredness
(b) ~ **qch à qn** to credit sb with sth ‹*quality*›; to attribute sth to sb ‹*work*›
2 **s'attribuer** *v refl* (+ *v être*) **s'**~ **la meilleure part** to give oneself the largest

---

❖ indicates a very frequent word

share; **s'~ tout le mérite** to take all the credit

attribut /atʀiby/ *nm* **(a)** (quality, symbol) attribute

(b) (in grammar) complement; **adjectif ~** predicative adjective; **nom ~** complement

attribution /atʀibysjɔ̃/ **1** *nf*
(a) allocation
(b) awarding
2 attributions *nf pl* (of individual) remit; (of court) competence

attristant, ~e /atʀistɑ̃, ɑ̃t/ *adj*
(a) distressing, upsetting
(b) depressing; **d'une bêtise ~e** depressingly stupid

attrister /atʀiste/ [1] *vtr* to sadden; **j'ai été attristé d'apprendre** I was sorry to hear

attroupement /atʀupmɑ̃/ *nm* gathering

attrouper: s'attrouper /atʀupe/ [1] *v refl* (+ *v être*) to gather

⚘ **au** /o/ (= **à le**) ▸ à

aubade /obad/ *nf* dawn serenade

aubaine /obɛn/ *nf* **(a)** godsend
(b) bargain

aube /ob/ *nf* **(a)** dawn
(b) alb; cassock

aubépine /obepin/ *nf* hawthorn

auberge /obɛʀʒ/ *nf* inn; **~ de jeunesse** youth hostel
IDIOM **tu n'es pas sorti de l'~!** (fam) you're not out of the woods yet!

aubergine /obɛʀʒin/ *nf* aubergine, eggplant

aubergiste /obɛʀʒist/ *nmf* innkeeper

⚘ **aucun, ~e** /okœ̃, yn/ **1** *adj* no, not any; **en ~ cas** under no circumstances
2 *pron* none; **je n'ai lu ~ de vos livres** I haven't read any of your books; **~ de ses arguments n'est convaincant** none of his arguments are convincing

aucunement /okynmɑ̃/ *adv* in no way

audace /odas/ *nf* **(a)** boldness
(b) daring
(c) audacity, nerve (colloq); impudence

audacieux, -ieuse /odasjø, øz/ *adj*
(a) bold
(b) audacious, daring

au-delà /od(ə)la/ **1** *nm* **l'~** the hereafter
2 *adv* beyond; **jusqu'à 150 euros mais pas ~** up to 150 euros but no more
3 au-delà de *phr* beyond; over

au-dessous /odəsu/ **1** *adv* **(a)** below
(b) under; **les enfants de dix ans et ~** children of ten years and under
2 au-dessous de *phr* below; **être ~ de tout** (fam) to be absolutely useless

au-dessus /odəsy/ **1** *adv* above; **les enfants de 10 ans et ~** children of 10 and over; **la taille ~** the next size up
2 au-dessus de *phr* above; **~ de chez moi** in the apartment above mine; **un pont ~ de la rivière** a bridge over the river; **se**

pencher ~ de la table to lean across the table

au-devant: au-devant de /odəvɑ̃də/ *phr* **aller ~ de qn** to go to meet sb; **aller ~ des ennuis** to let oneself in for trouble

audible /odibl/ *adj* audible

audience /odjɑ̃s/ *nf* **(a)** (Law) hearing; **salle d'~** courtroom
(b) (interview) audience
(c) (public) audience

Audimat® /odimat/ *nm* audience ratings

audiovisuel, -elle /odjovisɥɛl/ **1** *adj*
(a) broadcasting
(b) audiovisual
2 *nm* **(a)** broadcasting
(b) audiovisual equipment
(c) audiovisual methods

audit /odit/ *nm* audit

auditeur, -trice /oditœʀ, tʀis/ *nm,f* listener

auditif, -ive /oditif, iv/ *adj* ‹nerve› auditory; ‹problems› hearing; ‹memory› aural

audition /odisjɔ̃/ *nf* **(a)** (sense) hearing
(b) audition
(c) (Law) hearing, examination

auditionner /odisjone/ [1] *vtr*, *vi* to audition

auditoire /oditwaʀ/ *nm* audience

auge /oʒ/ *nf* (for animal feed) trough

augmentation /ogmɑ̃tasjɔ̃/ *nf* increase; **une ~ (de salaire)** a pay rise (GB) or raise (US)

⚘ **augmenter** /ogmɑ̃te/ [1] **1** *vtr* to raise, to increase; to extend; **~ le loyer de qn** to put sb's rent up
2 *vi* to increase, to go up, to rise

augure /ogyʀ/ *nm* **(a)** omen
(b) augury

augurer /ogyʀe/ [1] *vtr* **que peut-on ~ de cette attitude?** what should we expect from this attitude?

auguste /ogyst/ *adj* august, noble

⚘ **aujourd'hui** /oʒuʀdɥi/ *adv* **(a)** today
(b) nowadays, today; **la France d'~** present-day France

aulne /on/ *nm* alder

aumône /omon/ *nf* hand-out, alms; **demander l'~** to ask for charity

aumônerie /omonʀi/ *nf* chaplaincy

aumônier /omonje/ *nm* chaplain

aune /on/ ▸ AULNE

⚘ **auparavant** /oparavɑ̃/ *adv* before; beforehand; previously; formerly

⚘ **auprès: auprès de** /opʀɛdə/ *phr* **(a)** next to, beside; **il s'est rendu ~ de sa tante** he went to see his aunt
(b) compared with
(c) **s'excuser ~ de qn** to apologize to sb; **renseigne-toi ~ de la mairie** ask for information at the town hall; **représentant ~** ⋯⧽

de l'ONU representative to the UN

⚹ **auquel** ▶ LEQUEL

aura /ɔʀa/ ▶ AVOIR[1]

aurai /ɔʀɛ/ ▶ AVOIR[1]

auras /ɔʀa/ ▶ AVOIR[1]

auréole /ɔʀeɔl/ *nf* (a) (stain) ring
(b) halo

auréolé, ~e /ɔʀeɔle/ *adj* ~ **de** basking in
the glow of

aurez /ɔʀe/ ▶ AVOIR[1]

auriculaire /ɔʀikylɛʀ/ **1** *adj* auricular
2 *nm* little finger, pinkie

aurifère /ɔʀifɛʀ/ *adj* (a) ‹mineral›
auriferous
(b) **valeurs ~s** gold stocks

aurons /ɔʀɔ̃/ ▶ AVOIR[1]

auront /ɔʀɔ̃/ ▶ AVOIR[1]

aurore /ɔʀɔʀ/ *nf* dawn; ~ **boréale** Northern
Lights, aurora borealis

auscultation /ɔskyltasjɔ̃/ *nf* examination

ausculter /ɔskylte/ [1] *vtr* (Med) to
examine

auspices /ospis/ *nm pl* auspices

⚹ **aussi** /osi/ **1** *adv* (a) too, as well, also; **il
sera absent et moi ~** he'll be away and so
will I
(b) ~ **bien que** as well as; ~ **âgé que** as
old as
(c) so; **je ne savais pas qu'il était ~ vieux** I
didn't know he was so old; **dans une ~ belle
maison** in such a nice house
2 *conj* so, consequently

⚹ **aussitôt** /osito/ **1** *adv* (a) immediately,
straight away
(b) ~ **arrivé** as soon as he arrived; ~ **dit ~
fait** no sooner said than done
2 **aussitôt que** *phr* as soon as

austère /ɔstɛʀ, ostɛʀ/ *adj* austere; severe

austérité /osteʀite/ *nf* austerity; severity

austral, ~e, mpl ~s /ɔstʀal/ *adj* southern,
south

Australie /ɔstʀali/ *pr nf* Australia

australien, -ienne /ɔstʀaljɛ̃, ɛn/ *adj*
Australian

⚹ **autant** /otɑ̃/ **1** *adv* **il n'a jamais ~ neigé**
it has never snowed so much; **je t'aime
toujours ~** I still love you as much; **essaie
d'en faire ~** try and do the same; **je les hais
tous ~ qu'ils sont** I hate every single one of
them; **j'aime ~ partir tout de suite** I'd rather
leave straight away; ~ **dire que la réunion
est annulée** in other words the meeting is
cancelled (GB); ~ **parler à un mur** you might
as well be talking to the wall; ~ **que je sache**
as far as I know; ~ **que tu peux** as much as
you can
2 **autant de** *quantif* (a) ~ **de cadeaux**
so many presents; **il y a ~ de femmes que
d'hommes** there are as many women as

(there are) men
(b) ~ **de gentillesse** such kindness; **je n'ai
pas eu ~ de chance que lui** I haven't had as
much luck as he has
3 **d'autant** *phr* **cela va permettre de
réduire d'~ les coûts de production** this will
allow an equivalent reduction in production
costs; **d'~ plus!** all the more reason!; **d'~
moins** even less, all the less; **d'~ que** all the
more so as
4 **pour autant** *phr* for all that; **sans
pour ~ tout modifier** without necessarily
changing everything; **pour ~ que je sache**
as far as I know

autarcie /otaʀsi/ *nf* autarky; **vivre en ~** to
be self-sufficient

autel /otɛl/ *nm* altar

⚹ **auteur** /otœʀ/ *nm* (a) author
(b) creator; (of song) composer; (of crime)
perpetrator
■ ~ **dramatique** playwright

auteur-compositeur, *pl* **auteurs-
compositeurs** /otœʀkɔ̃pozitœʀ/ *nm*
songwriter

authenticité /otɑ̃tisite/ *nf* authenticity

authentifier /otɑ̃tifje/ [2] *vtr* to
authenticate

authentique /otɑ̃tik/ *adj* ‹story› true;
‹painting, document› authentic; ‹feeling›
genuine

autiste /otist/ *nm,f* autistic person

⚹ **auto** /oto/ *nf* car, automobile (US)
■ ~ **tamponneuse** bumper car, dodgem

autobiographie /otobjɔgʀafi/ *nf*
autobiography

autobus /otɔbys/ *nm inv* bus

autocar /otɔkaʀ/ *nm* coach (GB), bus (US)

autochtone /otɔkton/ *adj, nmf* native

autocollant, ~e /otɔkɔlɑ̃, ɑ̃t/ **1** *adj*
self-adhesive
2 *nm* sticker

autocuiseur /otokɥizœʀ/ *nm* pressure
cooker

autodéfense /otodefɑ̃s/ *nf* self-defence
(GB)

autodestructeur, -trice
/otodɛstʀyktœʀ, tʀis/ *adj* self-destructive

autodestruction /otodɛstʀyksjɔ̃/ *nf*
self-destruction

autodétruire: s'autodétruire
/otodetʀɥiʀ/ [69] *v refl* (+ *v être*) ‹person›
to destroy oneself; ‹tape› to self-destruct;
‹missile› to autodestruct

autodidacte /otodidakt/ *nmf* self-
educated person

auto-école, *pl* **~s** /otoekɔl/ *nf* driving
school

autogérer: s'autogérer /otoʒeʀe/ [14]
v refl (+ *v être*) ‹company› to be run on a
cooperative basis

autographe /otɔgʀaf/ *adj, nm* autograph

⚹ indicates a very frequent word

automate /ɔtɔmat/ *nm* robot, automaton

automatique /ɔtɔmatik/ ① *adj*
(a) automatic
(b) inevitable
② *nm* (a) automatic (revolver)
(b) automatic camera

automatiquement /ɔtɔmatikmɑ̃/ *adv*
(a) automatically
(b) (fam) inevitably

automatiser /ɔtɔmatize/ [1] *vtr* to
automate

automatisme /ɔtɔmatism/ *nm*
automatism; automatic functioning;
acquérir des ~s to acquire automatic
reflexes

automne /otɔn/ *nm* autumn (GB), fall (US)

automobile /otɔmɔbil/ ① *adj* (a) car
(b) (Sport) ‹racing› motor; ‹circuit› motor
racing
② *nf* (a) (motor) car, automobile (US)
(b) the motor (GB) or automobile (US)
industry

automobiliste /otɔmɔbilist/ *nmf*
motorist

autonome /otɔnɔm/ *adj* autonomous;
independent; self-sufficient

autonomie /otɔnɔmi/ *nf* (a) autonomy
(b) (of car, plane) range; ~ **de vol** flight range

autonomiste /otɔnɔmist/ *adj, nmf*
separatist

autoportrait /otopɔrtrɛ/ *nm* self-portrait

autopsie /otɔpsi/ *nf* postmortem
(examination)

autoradio /otoradjo/ *nm* car radio

autorisation /otɔrizasjɔ̃/ *nf*
(a) permission; authorization
(b) permit

autorisé, ~**e** /otɔrize/ *adj* authorized;
legal; accredited; permitted

⚹ **autoriser** /otɔrize/ [1] *vtr* (a) to allow, to
authorize
(b) ~ **qn à faire** to entitle sb to do
(c) to make [sth] possible

autoritaire /otɔritɛr/ *adj, nmf*
authoritarian

⚹ **autorité** /otɔrite/ *nf* (a) authority; **faire
qch d'**~ to do sth without consultation; **il n'a
aucune** ~ **sur ses enfants** he has no control
over his children; **faire** ~ ‹person› to be an
authority; ‹work› to be authoritative
(b) (person) authority, expert

autoroute /otɔrut/ *nf* motorway (GB),
freeway (US); ~ **à péage** toll motorway
■ ~ **de l'information** information highway

autoroutier, -ière /otɔrutje, ɛr/ *adj*
motorway (GB), freeway (US)

auto-stop /otostɔp/ *nm* hitchhiking

auto-stoppeur, -euse *mpl* ~**s**
/otostɔpœr, øz/ *nm,f* hitchhiker

⚹ **autour** /otur/ ① *adv* **un parterre de fleurs
avec des pierres** ~ a flower bed with stones

around it; **tout** ~ all around
② **autour de** *phr* (a) around, round (GB);
~ **de la table** around the table
(b) around, about; ~ **de 10 heures** around
10 o'clock
(c) about, on; **un débat** ~ **du thème du
pouvoir** a debate on the theme of power

⚹ **autre** /otr/ ① *det* (a) other; **une** ~ **histoire**
another story; **rien d'**~ nothing else; **l'effet
obtenu est tout** ~ the effect produced is
completely different
(b) (fam) **nous** ~**s professeurs/Français** we
teachers/French
② *pron* (a) **où sont les** ~**s?** where are the
other ones?; **je t'ai pris pour un** ~ I mistook
you for someone else; **ils se respectent les
uns les** ~**s** they respect each other; **chez
lui c'est tout l'un ou tout l'**~ with him it's
all or nothing; **à d'**~**s!** (fam) pull the other
one! (colloq)
(b) **prends-en un** ~ have another one; **si je
peux je t'en apporterai d'**~**s** if I can I'll bring
you some more
③ **autre part** *phr* somewhere else

⚹ **autrefois** /otrəfwa/ *adv* in the past; before,
formerly; in the old days; ~, **quand Paris
s'appelait Lutèce** long ago, when Paris was
called Lutetia; **les légendes d'**~ old legends

⚹ **autrement** /otrəmɑ̃/ *adv* (a) differently,
in a different way; **c'est comme ça, et pas** ~
that's just the way it is; **je n'ai pas pu faire**
~ **que de les inviter** I had no alternative but
to invite them; **on ne peut y accéder** ~ **que
par bateau** you can only get there by boat;
je ne l'ai jamais vue ~ **qu'en jean** I've never
seen her in anything but jeans; ~ **dit** in
other words
(b) otherwise
(c) (fam) ~ **grave** (much) more serious;
il n'était pas ~ **impressionné** he wasn't
particularly impressed

Autriche /otriʃ/ *pr nf* Austria

autrichien, -ienne /otriʃjɛ̃, ɛn/ *adj*
Austrian

autruche /otryʃ/ *nf* ostrich
IDIOM pratiquer la politique de l'~ to bury
one's head in the sand

autrui /otrɥi/ *pron* others, other people

auvent /ovɑ̃/ *nm* (a) canopy
(b) awning

aux /o/ (= **à les**) ▶ À

auxiliaire /oksiljɛr/ ① *adj* (a) ‹verb›
auxiliary
(b) ‹equipment, service› auxiliary; ‹motor›
back-up
(c) **maître** ~ assistant teacher; **infirmier** ~
nursing auxiliary (GB), nurse's aide (US)
② *nmf* assistant, helper
③ *nm* auxiliary (verb)

auxquels, auxquelles ▶ LEQUEL

avachir: s'avachir /avaʃir/ [3] *v refl* (+ *v
être*) (a) ‹chair› to sag ┅┅▷

a

(b) ⟨person⟩ to let oneself go

avaient /avɛ/ ▶ AVOIR¹

avais /avɛ/ ▶ AVOIR¹

avait /avɛ/ ▶ AVOIR¹

aval /aval/ nm (a) (of river) lower reaches; **en ~** downstream
(b) approval

avalanche /avalɑ̃ʃ/ nf avalanche

avaler /avale/ [1] vtr (a) to swallow; '**ne pas ~**' (Med) 'not to be taken internally'
(b) to inhale ⟨smoke, fumes⟩

avaleur /avalœʀ/ nm **~ de sabres** sword swallower

à-valoir /avalwaʀ/ nm inv instalment (GB)

♂ **avance** /avɑ̃s/ ① nf (a) advance
(b) lead; **avoir/prendre de l'~ sur** to be/pull ahead of
(c) **une ~** (sur salaire) an advance (on one's salary)
② **à l'avance** phr in advance
③ **d'avance** phr in advance; **avoir cinq minutes d'~** to be five minutes early
④ **en avance** phr (a) early
(b) **être en ~ sur qn** to be ahead of sb
(c) **il est en ~ pour son âge** he's advanced for his age
⑤ **avances** nf pl advances

avancé, ~e¹ /avɑ̃se/ ① pp ▶ AVANCER
② pp adj ⟨ideas⟩ progressive; **la saison est bien ~e** it's late in the season; **te voilà bien ~!** that's done you a lot of good!

avancée² /avɑ̃se/ nf (of roof, rock) overhang

avancement /avɑ̃smɑ̃/ nm (a) promotion
(b) progress
(c) **~ de l'âge de la retraite** lowering of the retirement age

♂ **avancer** /avɑ̃se/ [12] ① vtr (a) to move [sth] forward ⟨object⟩; to push [sth] forward ⟨plate⟩
(b) to bring forward ⟨trip, meeting⟩
(c) **~ sa montre de cinq minutes** to put one's watch forward (by) five minutes
(d) to get ahead with ⟨work⟩; **cela ne nous avance à rien** that doesn't get us anywhere
(e) **~ de l'argent à qn** ⟨bank⟩ to advance money to sb
(f) to put forward ⟨argument, theory⟩; to propose ⟨figure⟩
② vi (a) ⟨person, vehicle⟩ to move (forward); ⟨army⟩ to advance; **elle avança vers le guichet** she went up to the ticket office
(b) to make progress, to progress; **faire ~ la science** to further science
(c) **ma montre avance de deux minutes** my watch is two minutes fast
(d) ⟨teeth, chin⟩ to stick out; ⟨peninsula⟩ to jut out
③ **s'avancer** v refl (+ v être) (a) **s'~ vers qch** to move toward(s) sth; **s'~ vers qn** to go toward(s) sb; to come up to sb

(b) to get ahead
(c) to jut out, to protrude
(d) **je me suis un peu avancé en lui promettant le dossier pour demain** I shouldn't have committed myself by promising him/her I'd have the file ready for tomorrow

♂ **avant¹** /avɑ̃/ ① adv before; first; **bien ~** long before; **il l'a mentionné ~ dans l'introduction** he mentioned it earlier in the introduction
② prep before; **~ mon retour** before I get back; before I got back; **~ le 1ᵉʳ juillet** by 1 July; **~ peu** shortly; **~ tout, ~ toute chose** above all; first and foremost
③ **d'avant** phr **la séance d'~** the previous performance; **la fois d'~ nous nous étions déjà perdus** we got lost the last time as well
④ **avant de** phr **~ de faire** before doing
⑤ **avant que** phr before
⑥ **en avant** phr forward(s); **en ~ toute!** full steam ahead!; **mettre en ~ le fait que** to point out the fact that; **se mettre en ~** to push oneself forward
⑦ **en avant de** phr ahead of ⟨group⟩

avant² /avɑ̃/ ① adj inv ⟨wheel, seat, paw⟩ front
② nm (a) **l'~** the front; **aller de l'~** to forge ahead
(b) (Sport) forward
③ **avant-** (combining form) **l'~-Thatcher** the pre-Thatcher era

♂ **avantage** /avɑ̃taʒ/ nm (a) advantage; **tirer ~ de qch** to take advantage of sth; **paraître à son ~** to look one's best
(b) benefit; **~ fiscaux** tax benefits

avantager /avɑ̃taʒe/ [13] vtr (a) ⟨person⟩ to favour ⟨GB⟩; ⟨situation⟩ to be to the advantage of
(b) ⟨clothes⟩ to show [sb/sth] off to advantage

avantageusement /avɑ̃taʒøzmɑ̃/ adv favourably (GB)

avantageux, -euse /avɑ̃taʒø, øz/ adj
(a) ⟨conditions, offer⟩ favourable (GB), advantageous; ⟨rate, price⟩ attractive; **tirer un parti ~ de qch** to use sth to one's advantage
(b) ⟨description, outfit⟩ flattering

avant-bras /avɑ̃bʀa/ nm inv forearm

avant-centre, pl **avants-centres** /avɑ̃sɑ̃tʀ/ nm centre (GB) forward; **jouer ~** to play centre (GB) forward

avant-coureur, pl **~s** /avɑ̃kuʀœʀ/ adj **signes ~s** early warning signs

avant-dernier, -ière, pl **~s** /avɑ̃dɛʀnje, ɛʀ/ ① adj penultimate; **l'~ jour** the last day but one
② nm,f the last but one; **l'~ d'une famille de cinq enfants** the second youngest of five children

avant-garde, pl **~s** /avɑ̃gaʀd/ nf
(a) avant-garde
(b) vanguard; **à l'~** in the vanguard

avant-goût, pl **~s** /avɑ̃gu/ nm foretaste

♂ indicates a very frequent word

avant-guerre, *pl* ~**s** /avɑ̃gɛʀ/ *nm or f*
l'~ the prewar period; **l'Espagne d'**~ prewar
Spain

avant-hier /avɑ̃tjɛʀ/ *adv* the day before
yesterday

avant-poste, *pl* ~**s** /avɑ̃pɔst/ *nm* (Mil)
outpost; **être aux** ~**s** to be in the vanguard

avant-première, *pl* ~**s** /avɑ̃pʀəmjɛʀ/ *nf*
preview

avant-propos /avɑ̃pʀɔpo/ *nm inv*
foreword

avant-veille, *pl* ~**s** /avɑ̃vɛj/ *nf* two days
before

avare /avaʀ/ ⟦1⟧ *adj* mean, miserly; ~ **de**
sparing with
⟦2⟧ *nmf* miser

avarice /avaʀis/ *nf* meanness (GB),
miserliness

avarier: **s'avarier** /avaʀje/ ⟦2⟧ *v refl* (+ *v
être*) ⟨*meat, fish*⟩ to go rotten

avatar /avataʀ/ *nm* (**a**) mishap
(**b**) change

◦* **avec** /avɛk/ ⟦1⟧ *adv* (fam) **elle est partie** ~
she went off with it
⟦2⟧ *prep* with; ~ **attention** carefully; **et** ~
cela, que désirez-vous? what else would you
like?; **je fais tout son travail et** ~ **ça il n'est
pas content!** I do all his work and he's still
not happy!; **sa séparation d'**~ **sa femme** his
separation from his wife

avenant, ~**e** /avnɑ̃, ɑ̃t/ ⟦1⟧ *adj* pleasant
⟦2⟧ **à l'avenant** *phr* in keeping

avènement /avɛnmɑ̃/ *nm* (**a**) (of monarch)
accession; (of politician, era) advent; ~ **au trône**
accession to the throne
(**b**) Advent

◦* **avenir** /avniʀ/ *nm* future; **d'**~ ⟨*job*⟩ with a
future; ⟨*technique, science*⟩ of the future

◦* **aventure** /avɑ̃tyʀ/ *nf* (**a**) adventure
(**b**) **il m'est arrivé une drôle d'**~ something
strange happened to me
(**c**) venture
(**d**) (love) affair
IDIOM dire la bonne ~ **à qn** to tell sb's
fortune

aventurer: **s'aventurer** /avɑ̃tyʀe/ ⟦1⟧ *v
refl* (+ *v être*) to venture

aventurier, -ière /avɑ̃tyʀje, ɛʀ/ *nm,f*
adventurer/adventuress

avenue /avny/ *nf* avenue

avérer: **s'avérer** /aveʀe/ ⟦14⟧ *v refl* (+ *v
être*) **s'**~ **utile** to prove useful; **il s'avère que**
it turns out that

averse /avɛʀs/ *nf* shower

aversion /avɛʀsjɔ̃/ *nf* aversion; **avoir qn/
qch en** ~ to loathe sb/sth

averti, ~**e** /avɛʀti/ ⟦1⟧ *pp* ▶ AVERTIR
⟦2⟧ *pp adj* (**a**) ⟨*reader*⟩ informed
(**b**) experienced

avertir /avɛʀtiʀ/ ⟦3⟧ *vtr* (**a**) to inform
(**b**) to warn

avertissement /avɛʀtismɑ̃/ *nm*
(**a**) warning
(**b**) (Sport) caution
(**c**) (in book) foreword

avertisseur /avɛʀtisœʀ/ *nm* (**a**) alarm
(**b**) (of car) horn

aveu, *pl* ~**x** /avø/ *nm* confession; admission

aveuglant, ~**e** /avœglɑ̃, ɑ̃t/ *adj* blinding

aveugle /avœgl/ ⟦1⟧ *adj* (**a**) blind
(**b**) ⟨*faith, love*⟩ blind; ⟨*violence*⟩
indiscriminate
⟦2⟧ *nmf* blind person; **les** ~**s** the blind

aveuglement /avœgləmɑ̃/ *nm* blindness

aveuglément /avœglemɑ̃/ *adv* blindly

aveugler /avœgle/ ⟦1⟧ *vtr* to blind

aveuglette: **à l'aveuglette**
/alavœglɛt/ *phr* (**a**) blindly
(**b**) at random

avez /ave/ ▶ AVOIR¹

aviateur /avjatœʀ/ *nm* airman

aviation /avjasjɔ̃/ *nf* (**a**) aviation
(**b**) aircraft industry
(**c**) l'~ the air force

aviatrice /avjatʀis/ *nf* woman pilot

aviculteur, -trice /avikyltœʀ, tʀis/ *nm,f*
(**a**) (of fowl) poultry farmer
(**b**) (of birds) aviculturist

aviculture /avikyltyʀ/ *nf* (**a**) (of fowl)
poultry farming
(**b**) (of birds) aviculture

avide /avid/ *adj* (**a**) greedy
(**b**) ~ **de** avid for, eager for

avidement /avidmɑ̃/ *adv* ⟨*eat*⟩ greedily;
⟨*read*⟩ avidly; ⟨*look, search*⟩ eagerly

avidité /avidite/ *nf* (**a**) greed
(**b**) eagerness

aviez /avje/ ▶ AVOIR¹

avilir /aviliʀ/ ⟦3⟧ *vtr* to demean

avilissant, ~**e** /avilisɑ̃, ɑ̃t/ *adj* demeaning

avilissement /avilismɑ̃/ *nm* degradation

aviné, ~**e** /avine/ *adj* ⟨*person*⟩ inebriated;
⟨*look, face*⟩ drunken

◦* **avion** /avjɔ̃/ *nm* (**a**) (aero)plane (GB),
airplane (US), aircraft; **aller à Rome en** ~ to
fly to Rome; **'par** ~**'** 'by air mail'
(**b**) flight
■ ~ **de chasse** fighter; ~ **à réaction** jet; ~ **de
tourisme** light passenger aircraft

avions /avjɔ̃/ ▶ AVOIR¹

aviron /aviʀɔ̃/ *nm* (**a**) rowing
(**b**) oar

◦* **avis** /avi/ *nm inv* (**a**) opinion; **je suis de ton**
~ I agree with you; **changer d'**~ to change
one's mind
(**b**) advice; **sauf** ~ **contraire** unless
otherwise informed
(**c**) (of jury, commission) recommendation
(**d**) notice; **lancer un** ~ **de recherche** to issue
a description of a missing person/wanted
person ⋯⟫

a

■ ∼ **au lecteur** foreword; ∼ **de passage** calling card (*left by postman etc*)

avisé, ∼**e** /avize/ *adj* sensible; **être bien/ mal** ∼ to be well-/ill-advised

aviser /avize/ [1] **1** *vtr* to notify

2 *vi* to decide

3 **s'aviser** *v refl* (+ *v être*) **ne t'avise pas de recommencer** don't dare do that again

aviver /avive/ [1] **1** *vtr* (a) to intensify ‹*feeling*›; to stir up ‹*quarrel*›; to make [sth] more acute ‹*pain*›

(b) to liven up ‹*colour*›

(c) to kindle ‹*fire*›

2 **s'aviver** *v refl* (+ *v être*) ‹*desire, anger*› to grow; ‹*pain, grief*› to become more acute

⚜ **avocat** /avɔka/ *nm* (a) lawyer, solicitor (GB), attorney (at law) (US)

(b) barrister (GB), (trial) lawyer (US); ∼ **de l'accusation** counsel for the prosecution

(c) (of idea) advocate; (of cause, person) champion

(d) avocado (pear)

avocate /avɔkat/ *nf* woman lawyer

avoine /avwan/ *nf* oats

⚜ **avoir¹** /avwaʀ/ [8]

──────────

■ **Note** You will find translations for expressions such as *avoir raison, avoir beau, en avoir marre* etc, at the entries RAISON, BEAU, MARRE etc.

──────────

1 *v aux* to have; **j'ai perdu mon briquet** I've lost my lighter; **il aurait aimé te parler** he would have liked to speak to you

2 *vtr* (a) to have (got) ‹*child, book, room, time*›; **elle avait les larmes aux yeux** there were tears in her eyes

(b) to get ‹*object, job*›; to catch ‹*train, plane*›; (on the phone) **j'ai réussi à l'**∼ I managed to get through to him

(c) to wear, to have [sth] on

(d) to feel; ∼ **du chagrin** to feel sad; **qu'est-ce que tu as?** what's wrong with you?

(e) **avoir faim/froid/20 ans** to be hungry/ cold/20 years old

(f) to beat; to have (colloq), to con (colloq); **j'ai été eu** I've been had

3 **avoir à** *v+prep* to have to; **tu n'as pas à le critiquer** you shouldn't criticize him; **j'ai beaucoup à faire** I have a lot to do; **tu n'as qu'à leur écrire** all you have to do is write to them

4 **en avoir pour** *v+prep* (a) **vous en avez pour combien de temps?** how long will it take you?; how long are you going to be?

(b) **j'en ai eu pour 75 euros** it cost me 75 euros

5 **il y a** *v impers* (a) there is/there are; **qu'est-ce qu'il y a?** what's wrong?; **il y a qu'elle m'énerve** she's getting on my nerves, that's what's wrong; **il y a à manger pour quatre** there's enough food for four; **il y en a toujours qui se plaignent** there's always someone who complains; **il n'y en a que pour leur chien** their dog comes first

──────────

⚜ indicates a very frequent word

(b) **il y a longtemps** a long time ago; **il n'y a que cinq ans que j'habite ici** I have only been living here for five years

(c) **combien y a-t-il jusqu'à la gare?** how far is it to the station?; **il y a au moins 15 kilomètres** it's at least 15 kilometres (GB) away

avoir² /avwaʀ/ *nm* (a) credit

(b) credit note

(c) assets, holdings

avoisinant, ∼**e** /avwazinɑ̃, ɑ̃t/ *adj* neighbouring (GB)

avoisiner /avwazine/ [1] *vtr* (a) ‹*costs, sum*› to be close to, to be about

(b) ‹*place*› to be near

avons /avɔ̃/ ▶ AVOIR¹

avortement /avɔʀtəmɑ̃/ *nm* (Med) abortion

avorter /avɔʀte/ [1] *vi* (a) (Med) to have an abortion

(b) ‹*cow, ewe*› to abort, to miscarry

(c) ‹*plan*› to be aborted; ‹*uprising*› to fail

avorton /avɔʀtɔ̃/ *nm* runt

avouable /avwabl/ *adj* worthy; respectable

avoué, ∼**e** /avwe/ **1** *pp* ▶ AVOUER

2 *pp adj* ‹*enemy*› declared; ‹*intention*› avowed

3 *nm* ≈ solicitor (GB), attorney(-at-law) (US)

⚜ **avouer** /avwe/ [1] **1** *vtr* to confess, to admit

2 *vi* to confess; to own up

3 **s'avouer** *v refl* (+ *v être*) **s'**∼ **rassuré** to say one feels reassured; **s'**∼ **vaincu** to admit defeat

⚜ **avril** /avʀil/ *nm* April

axe /aks/ *nm* (a) axis

(b) (Tech) axle

(c) major road

(d) **dans l'**∼ **du bâtiment** in a line with the building; **la cible est dans l'**∼ **du viseur** the target is lined up in the sights

axer /akse/ [1] *vtr* (a) to centre (GB) ‹*screw*›; to line up ‹*part*›

(b) to base, to centre (GB) (**sur** on)

axiome /aksjom/ *nm* axiom

ayant /ɛjɑ̃/ ▶ AVOIR¹

ayant droit, *pl* **ayants droit** /ɛjɑ̃dʀwa/ *nm* (a) legal claimant, beneficiary

(b) assignee

ayez /aje/ ▶ AVOIR¹

ayons /ajɔ̃/ ▶ AVOIR¹

azalée /azale/ *nf* azalea

Azerbaïdjan /azɛʀbajdʒɑ̃/ *pr nm* Azerbaijan

azimut /azimyt/ *nm* (a) (in astronomy) azimuth

(b) (figurative) **une offensive tous** ∼**s** an all-out offensive; **dans tous les** ∼**s** everywhere

azote /azɔt/ *nm* nitrogen

aztèque /astɛk/ *adj* Aztec

azur /azyʀ/ *nm* azure

azyme /azim/ *adj* unleavened

Bb

b, B /be/ *nm inv* b, B; **le b a ba** the rudiments

baba /baba/ *adj inv* (fam) **en être** *or* **rester ∼** to be flabbergasted (colloq)

babillage /babijaʒ/ *nm* babbling

babiller /babije/ [1] *vi* to babble, to chatter

babines /babin/ *nf pl* lips; **retrousser les ∼** ‹dog› to bare its teeth; **se lécher les ∼** to lick one's chops

babiole /babjɔl/ *nf* **(a)** trinket
(b) trifle

bâbord /babɔʀ/ *nm* port (side)

babouche /babuʃ/ *nf* oriental slipper

babouin /babwɛ̃/ *nm* baboon

baby-foot /babifut/ *nm inv* table football (GB), table soccer

bac /bak/ *nm* **(a)** (fam) *abbr*
= BACCALAURÉAT
(b) ferry
(c) tub; **évier à deux ∼s** double sink
■ **∼ à sable** sandpit (GB), sandbox (US)

baccalauréat /bakalɔʀea/ *nm* baccalaureate (*school-leaving certificate taken at 17–18*); **∼ professionnel** vocational baccalaureate (*vocationally-oriented school-leaving certificate*)

bâche /baʃ/ *nf* tarpaulin

bachelier, -ière /baʃəlje, ɛʀ/ *nm,f: holder of the baccalaureate*

bâcher /baʃe/ [1] *vtr* to cover [sth] with tarpaulin ‹vehicle›; **un camion bâché** a covered truck

bachotage /baʃɔtaʒ/ *nm* (Sch, fam) cramming

bâcler /bakle/ [1] *vtr* to dash [sth] off ‹piece of work›; to rush through ‹ceremony›

bactérie /bakteʀi/ *nf* bacterium

badaud, ∼e /bado, od/ *nm,f* **(a)** passerby
(b) onlooker

badigeonner /badiʒɔne/ [1] *vtr* **(a)** to paint
(b) to daub (**de** with)
(c) (Culin) to brush (**de** with)

badin, ∼e /badɛ̃, in/ *adj* ‹tone› bantering

baffe /baf/ *nf* (fam) clout, slap

baffle /bafl/ *nm* **(a)** speaker
(b) baffle

bafouille /bafuj/ *nf* (fam) letter

bafouiller /bafuje/ [1] *vtr, vi* to mumble

bagage /bagaʒ/ *nm* piece of luggage; **faire ses ∼s** to pack
IDIOM **plier ∼** (fam) to pack up and go

bagagiste /bagaʒist/ *nm* baggage handler

bagarre /bagaʀ/ *nf* fight, scuffle

bagarrer: se bagarrer /bagaʀe/ [1] *v refl* (+ *v être*) (fam) to fight

bagarreur, -euse /bagaʀœʀ, øz/ *adj* (fam) aggressive

bagatelle /bagatɛl/ *nf* **(a)** trifle, triviality
(b) **pour la ∼ de** (ironic) for the trifling sum of

bagne /baɲ/ *nm* penal colony

bagou(t) /bagu/ *nm* (fam) **avoir du ∼** to have the gift of the gab

bague /bag/ *nf* **(a)** ring
(b) (around pipe) collar

baguette /bagɛt/ *nf* **(a)** baguette, French stick
(b) stick; **mener qn à la ∼** to rule sb with a rod of iron; **∼ de chef d'orchestre** conductor's baton
(c) drumstick
(d) chopstick
■ **∼ magique** magic wand

bahut /bay/ *nm* **(a)** sideboard
(b) (students' slang) school
(c) (fam) truck

bai, ∼e¹ /bɛ/ *adj* bay

baie² /bɛ/ *nf* **(a)** bay
(b) berry
(c) **∼ (vitrée)** picture window

baignade /bɛɲad/ *nf* swimming

baigner /beɲe/ [1] ① *vtr* **(a)** to give [sb] a bath
(b) to bathe ‹wound›
② *vi* **∼ dans l'huile** to be swimming in grease
③ **se baigner** *v refl* (+ *v être*) to go swimming
IDIOM **ça baigne** (fam) things are going fine

baigneur, -euse /bɛɲœʀ, øz/ *nm,f* swimmer

baignoire /bɛɲwaʀ/ *nf* bathtub; **∼ sabot** hip bath

bail, *pl* **baux** /baj, bo/ *nm* lease; **ça fait un ∼** (fam) it's been ages (**que** since)

bâiller /baje/ [1] *vi* **(a)** to yawn
(b) to gape (open)

bailleur, bailleresse
/bajœʀ, bajʀɛs/ *nm,f* lessor
■ **∼ de fonds** backer, silent partner

bâillon /bajɔ̃/ *nm* gag

bain /bɛ̃/ *nm* **(a)** bath
(b) swim
(c) **grand/petit ∼** deep/shallow pool
■ **∼ de bouche** mouthwash; **∼ de foule** walkabout; **prendre un ∼ de soleil** to sunbathe
IDIOM **se remettre dans le ∼** to get back into the swing of things

b

baïonnette /bajɔnɛt/ *nf* bayonet

baiser /beze/ *nm* kiss

baisse *nf* (a) (gen) fall; **en ~** falling
(b) (Econ) (of power, sales) decline; (of prices)
cut; **la ~ du dollar** the fall in the value of the
dollar; **une ~ des loyers de 2%** a 2% drop
in rents; **être en ~** ‹*rates, stocks, shares*› to
be going down; ‹*results*› to be decreasing;
le marché est à la ~ (Econ) the market is
bearish; **revoir des prévisions à la ~** to
revise estimates downward(s); **spéculations
à la ~** bear speculations (c) (of light) fading

✧ **baisser** /bese/ [1] **1** *vtr* (a) to lower
‹*blind*›; to wind [sth] down ‹*window*›; to turn
down ‹*collar*›; **~ les bras** (figurative) to give
up; **~ le nez** (figurative) to hang one's head
(b) to turn down ‹*volume*›; to dim ‹*light*›; to
cut ‹*prices*›

2 *vi* to go down, to fall, to drop (à to; de by);
(drop in value) (*price, profit, rates, production*) to
fall; ‹*wages, shares*› to go down; ‹*purchasing
power, unemployment*› to decrease;
‹*productivity, market*› to decline; ‹*budget*› to
be cut; ‹*currency*› to slide; ‹*water*› to subside;
‹*sight*› to fail; ‹*hearing*› to deteriorate; **~ d'un
ton** (fam) ‹*person*› to calm down

3 **se baisser** *v refl* (+ *v être*) (a) to bend
down
(b) to duck
(c) to go down

baissier, -ière /besje, ɛR/ **1** *adj* bearish
2 *nm* (on stock exchange) bear

bajoue /baʒu/ *nf* cheek

bal /bal/ *nm* (a) ball, dance
(b) dancehall

balade /balad/ *nf* walk; ride

balader /balade/ [1] (fam) **1** *vtr* (a) to take
[sb] for a walk/drive
(b) to carry [sth] around
2 **se balader** *v refl* (+ *v être*) to go for a
walk/ride/drive

IDIOM envoyer qn ~ (fam) to send sb packing
(colloq)

baladeur /baladœR/ *nm* walkman®,
personal stereo
■ **~ MP3** MP3 player

balafre /balafR/ *nf* (a) scar
(b) slash, gash

balai /balɛ/ *nm* broom; **passer le ~** to
sweep the floor; **du ~!** (fam) go away!

balance /balɑ̃s/ *nf* (a) (weighing) scales;
faire pencher la ~ (figurative) to tip the scales
(b) (Econ) balance; **~ commerciale** balance
of trade; **~ des comptes, ~ des paiements**
balance of payments

Balance /balɑ̃s/ *pr nf* Libra

balancelle /balɑ̃sɛl/ *nf* swing seat

balancement /balɑ̃smɑ̃/ *nm* swaying;
swinging

balancer /balɑ̃se/ [12] **1** *vtr* (a) to sway;
to swing
(b) (fam) to chuck (colloq) (**sur** at); to chuck
out (colloq) ‹*old clothes, junk*›
(c) (fam) to squeal on (colloq)
2 *vi* (a) to sway
(b) to hesitate
3 **se balancer** *v refl* (+ *v
être*) (a) ‹*person*› to sway; ‹*boat*› to rock
(b) (fam) **je m'en balance** I couldn't care less

balancier /balɑ̃sje/ *nm* pendulum

balançoire /balɑ̃swaR/ *nf* swing

balayer /baleje/ [21] *vtr* (a) to sweep (up);
~ le sol ‹*coat*› to brush the ground
(b) to brush [sth] aside ‹*objections*›
(c) ‹*radar*› to scan

balayette /balɛjɛt/ *nf* (short-
handled) brush

balayeur, -euse /balɛjœR, øz/ *nm,f*
roadsweeper

balbutiement /balbysimɑ̃/ *nm* **les ~s du
cinéma** the early days of the cinema

balbutier /balbysje/ [2] *vtr, vi* to mumble

balcon /balkɔ̃/ *nm* (a) balcony
(b) (in theatre, cinema) balcony, circle

Bâle /bɑl/ *pr n* Basel

baleine /balɛn/ *nf* (a) whale
(b) whalebone; stay; rib

balisage /balizaʒ/ *nm* (in port,
channel) beaconing; (on path) marking

balise /baliz/ *nf* (a) beacon
(b) signpost, waymark
(c) (Comput) tag

baliser /balize/ [1] *vtr* (a) to mark [sth] out
with beacons
(b) to signpost, to waymark
(c) (Comput) to tag ‹*text*›

balistique /balistik/ *nf* ballistics

baliverne /balivɛRn/ *nf* nonsense

ballade /balad/ *nf* ballad; ballade

balle /bal/ *nf* (a) ball; **renvoyer la ~ (à
qn)** (figurative) to retort (to sb); **se renvoyer
la ~** to keep up an animated discussion; to
keep passing the buck
(b) (in ball games) shot; **faire des ~s** to knock
the ball around; **~ de jeu** game point
(c) bullet
(d) (fam) franc

ballerine /balRin/ *nf* (a) ballerina
(b) ballet pump

ballet /balɛ/ *nm* ballet

✧ **ballon** /balɔ̃/ *nm* (a) ball
(b) balloon
(c) wine glass
(d) **~ (alcootest)** Breathalyzer®
■ **~ dirigeable** airship (GB), blimp (US);
~ d'eau chaude hot water tank; **~ ovale**
rugby ball; **~ rond** soccer ball

ballonnement /balɔnmɑ̃/ *nm* bloating

ballot /balo/ *nm* (fam) nerd (colloq), fool

✧ indicates a very frequent word

ballottage /balɔtaʒ/ *nm: absence of an absolute majority in the first round of an election*

ballotter /balɔte/ [1] *vtr* **(a)** ‹sea› to toss [sb/sth] around; ‹movement› to jolt
(b) être ballotté entre sa famille et son travail to be torn between one's family and one's job

balluchon ▶ BALUCHON

balnéaire /balneɛR/ *adj* ‹resort› seaside

balte /balt/ *adj* Baltic; les pays ~s the Baltic States

baluchon /balyʃɔ̃/ *nm* bundle

balustrade /balystRad/ *nf* **(a)** parapet
(b) railing
(c) balustrade

bambin, ~e /bɑ̃bɛ̃, in/ *nm,f* kid (colloq), child

bambou /bɑ̃bu/ *nm* bamboo

ban /bɑ̃/ **1** *nm* round of applause
2 **bans** *nm pl* banns
IDIOM mettre qn au ~ de la société to ostracize sb

banal, ~e /banal/ *adj* **(a)** commonplace, ordinary; peu ~ unusual
(b) trivial, trite

banalisation /banalizasjɔ̃/ *nf* la ~ de l'informatique the way in which computing has become part of everyday life

banaliser /banalize/ [1] *vtr* **(a)** to make [sth] commonplace
(b) voiture banalisée unmarked car

banalité /banalite/ *nf* **(a)** ordinariness
(b) triteness
(c) trite remark

banane /banan/ *nf* **(a)** banana
(b) quiff
(c) bumbag (GB), fanny pack (US)

banc /bɑ̃/ *nm* **(a)** bench
(b) (of fish) shoal
■ ~ des accusés dock; ~ d'essai test bench; testing ground; ~ de sable sandbank

bancaire /bɑ̃kɛR/ *adj* **(a)** ‹business› banking
(b) ‹card› bank

bancal, ~e /bɑ̃kal/ *adj* **(a)** ‹chair› rickety
(b) ‹solution› unsatisfactory

♂ **bande** /bɑ̃d/ *nf* **(a)** gang; group; ~ de crétins! you bunch of idiots!; ils font ~ à part they don't join in
(b) (of animals) pack
(c) (of material, paper) strip; band
(d) bandage
(e) broad stripe
(f) (for recording) tape
■ ~ d'arrêt d'urgence, BAU hard shoulder; ~ dessinée, BD (fam) comic strip; comic book; ~ de fréquences waveband; ~ originale (of film) original soundtrack

bande-annonce, *pl* **bandes-annonces** /bɑ̃dɑnɔ̃s/ *nf* trailer

andeau, *pl* ~x /bɑ̃do/ *nm* **(a)** blindfold

(b) eye patch
(c) headband

bandelette /bɑ̃dlɛt/ *nf* bandage

bander /bɑ̃de/ [1] *vtr* **(a)** to bandage
(b) ~ les yeux à qn to blindfold sb

banderole /bɑ̃dRɔl/ *nf* banner

bande-son, *pl* **bandes-son** /bɑ̃dsɔ̃/ *nm* soundtrack

bandit /bɑ̃di/ *nm* **(a)** bandit; ~ de grand chemin highwayman
(b) crook
(c) rascal

banditisme /bɑ̃ditism/ *nm* le (grand) ~ (organized) crime

bandoulière /bɑ̃duljɛR/ *nf* shoulder strap

bang /bɑ̃g/ *nm* sonic boom

banlieue /bɑ̃ljø/ *nf* **(a)** suburbs; de ~ suburban
(b) suburb

banlieusard, ~e /bɑ̃ljøzaR, aRd/ *nm,f* suburbanite

bannière /banjɛR/ *nf* banner; la ~ étoilée the star-spangled banner
IDIOM c'est la croix et la ~ it's hell (pour faire doing)

bannir /baniR/ [3] *vtr* **(a)** to banish (de from)
(b) to ban

bannissement /banismɑ̃/ *nm* banishment (de from)

♂ **banque** /bɑ̃k/ *nf* **(a)** bank
(b) banking
■ ~ de données data bank

banqueroute /bɑ̃kRut/ *nf* bankruptcy

banquet /bɑ̃kɛ/ *nm* **(a)** banquet
(b) feast

banquette /bɑ̃kɛt/ *nf* (in café) wall seat; (in car, train) seat

banquier /bɑ̃kje/ *nm* banker

banquise /bɑ̃kiz/ *nf* ice floe

baptême /batɛm/ *nm* **(a)** baptism, christening
(b) (of ship) christening; (of bell) blessing
■ ~ de l'air first flight

baptiser /batize/ [1] *vtr* **(a)** to baptize, to christen
(b) to call, to name; to nickname
(c) to christen ‹ship›; to bless ‹bell›

bar /baR/ *nm* **(a)** bar
(b) (Zool) sea bass

baragouiner /baRagwine/ [1] *vtr* (fam) to gabble ‹sentence›; to speak [sth] badly ‹language›

baraka /baRaka/ *nf* (fam) luck

baraque /baRak/ *nf* **(a)** shack
(b) (fam) pad (colloq), house

baraqué, ~e /baRake/ *adj* (fam) hefty

baraquement /baRakmɑ̃/ *nm* **(a)** group of huts
(b) hut

⋯⋯❯

b

(c) army camp

baratin /baʀatɛ̃/ *nm* (fam) **(a)** sales pitch **(b)** sweet-talk; smooth talk (GB) (colloq)

baratiner /baʀatine/ [1] *vtr* (fam) **(a)** to give [sb] the spiel (colloq) **(b)** to chat [sb] up (colloq) **(c)** to try to persuade

baratineur, -euse /baʀatinœʀ, øz/ *nm,f* (fam) smooth talker (colloq); (dishonest) liar

barbant, ~e /baʀbɑ̃, ɑ̃t/ *adj* (fam) boring

barbare /baʀbaʀ/ ① *adj* barbaric; barbarian ② *nmf* barbarian

barbarie /baʀbaʀi/ *nf* barbarity, barbarism

❡ **barbe** /baʀb/ ① *nf* beard; **~ naissante** stubble ② *excl* (fam) **la ~!** I've had enough!; **la ~ avec leurs consignes!** to hell with their orders (colloq) ■ **~ à papa** candyfloss (GB), cotton candy (US) IDIOM **à la ~ de qn** under sb's nose

barbelé /baʀbəle/ *nm* barbed wire (GB), barbwire (US)

barbiche /baʀbiʃ/ *nf* **(a)** goatee (beard) **(b)** (on goat) (small) beard

barbier /baʀbje/ *nm* barber

barbiturique /baʀbityʀik/ *nm* barbiturate

barboteuse /baʀbɔtøz/ *nf* romper suit

barbouiller /baʀbuje/ [1] ① *vtr* **(a)** to smear (**de** with) **(b)** to daub (**de** with) **(c)** **~ des toiles** to do daubs; **~ du papier** to write drivel **(d)** **être barbouillé** to feel queasy ② **se barbouiller** *v refl* (+ *v être*) **se ~ le visage de qch** to get one's face all covered in sth

barbu, ~e /baʀby/ *adj* bearded; **il est ~** he has a beard

barde /baʀd/ *nf* thin slice of bacon, bard

bardé, ~e /baʀde/ *adj* covered (**de** in)

barème /baʀɛm/ *nm* scale; **~ des prix** price list **~ d'imposition** tax schedule *or* scale

baril /baʀil/ *nm* barrel, cask; keg; drum

barillet /baʀijɛ/ *nm* cylinder

bariolé, ~e /baʀjɔle/ *adj* multicoloured (GB)

baromètre /baʀɔmɛtʀ/ *nm* barometer

baron /baʀɔ̃/ *nm* baron

baronne /baʀɔn/ *nf* baroness

baroque /baʀɔk/ *adj* **(a)** baroque **(b)** bizarre

baroudeur /baʀudœʀ/ *nm* **(a)** fighter, warrior **(b)** adventurer

barque /baʀk/ *nf* (small) boat

barquette /baʀkɛt/ *nf* punnet (GB), basket (US); tub; container

barrage /baʀaʒ/ *nm* **(a)** dam **(b)** roadblock; barricade; **faire ~ à** to block

barre /baʀ/ *nf* **(a)** bar, rod **(b)** (of chocolate) piece **(c)** tiller, helm **(d)** band, stripe **(e)** stroke; **la ~ du t** the cross on the t **(f)** (of goal) crossbar; (in high jump) bar **(g)** (in ballet practice) barre **(h)** (Law) bar; ≈ witness box (GB), witness stand (US) **(i)** mark; **franchir la ~ des 13%** to go over the 13% mark ■ **~ fixe** horizontal bar; **~ oblique** slash; **~ des tâches** (Comput) taskbar IDIOM **avoir un coup de ~** (fam) to feel drained all of a sudden

barreau, *pl* **~x** /baʀo/ *nm* **(a)** (of cage) bar **(b)** rung **(c)** (Law) **le ~** the Bar

barrer /baʀe/ [1] *vtr* **(a)** to block ‹*way*›; **'route barrée'** 'road closed' **(b)** to cross out

barrette /baʀɛt/ *nf* (hair) slide (GB), barrette (US)

barreur, -euse /baʀœʀ, øz/ *nm,f* (gen) helmsman; (in rowing) cox; **avec ~** coxed; **sans ~** coxless

barricade /baʀikad/ *nf* barricade

barrière /baʀjɛʀ/ *nf* **(a)** fence **(b)** gate **(c)** barrier

barrique /baʀik/ *nf* barrel

barrir /baʀiʀ/ [3] *vi* ‹*elephant*› to trumpet

bar-tabac, *pl* **bars-tabac** /baʀtaba/ *nm* café (*selling stamps and cigarettes*)

baryton /baʀitɔ̃/ *adj, nm* baritone

❡ **bas, basse¹** /bɑ, bɑs/ ① *adj* low; ‹*room*› low-ceilinged; ‹*land*› low-lying; **le ciel est ~** the sky is overcast; **un enfant en ~ âge** a very young child; **être au plus ~** ‹*prices*› to have reached rock bottom; **les cours sont au plus ~** (en Bourse) prices have reached rock bottom ② *adv* **(a)** low; **comment peut-on tomber si ~!** how can one sink so low! **(b)** **voir plus ~** see below **(c)** quietly; **tout ~** ‹*speak*› in a whisper; ‹*sing*› softly **(d)** **être au plus ~** to be extremely weak; to be at one's lowest ③ *nm inv* **(a)** bottom; **le ~ du visage** the lower part of the face; **les pièces du ~** the downstairs rooms **(b)** stocking ④ **en bas** *phr* downstairs; down below; at the bottom ■ **~ de gamme** *adj* low-quality; *nm* lower end of the market; **~ morceaux** (Culin) cheap cuts **basse saison** low season

---

❡ indicates a very frequent word

IDIOMS avoir des hauts et des ∼ to have one's ups and downs; **à ∼ les tyrans!** down with tyranny!

basané, ∼e /bazane/ *adj* swarthy

bas-côté, *pl* ∼**s** /bɑkote/ *nm* **(a)** verge (GB), shoulder (US)
(b) (side) aisle

basculant, ∼e /baskylɑ̃, ɑ̃t/ *adj* **pont ∼** bascule bridge; **camion à benne ∼e** dump truck

bascule /baskyl/ *nf* **fauteuil à ∼** rocking chair

basculer /baskyle/ [1] ① *vtr* to transfer ‹*call*›
② *vi* **(a)** to topple over; **faire ∼** to tip up ‹*skip*›; to tip out ‹*load*›; to knock [sb] off balance ‹*person*›
(b) (figurative) to change radically

✧ **base** /baz/ *nf* **(a)** base; **le riz forme la ∼ de leur alimentation** rice is their staple diet
(b) basis; **reposer sur des ∼s solides** to rest on a firm foundation; **à la ∼ de qch** at the root *or* heart of sth; **salaire de ∼** basic salary; **repartir sur de nouvelles ∼s** to make a fresh start
(c) (in politics) **la ∼** the rank and file
■ **∼ de données** database; **∼ de lancement** launching site

✧ **baser** /baze/ [1] ① *vtr* to base (**sur** on)
② **se baser** *v refl* (+ *v être*) **se ∼ sur qch** to go by sth

bas-fond, *pl* ∼**s** /bɑfɔ̃/ ① *nm* **(a)** shallows
(b) dip
② **bas-fonds** *nm pl* seedy areas

basilic /bazilik/ *nm* basil

basilique /bazilik/ *nf* basilica

basket /baskɛt/ *nm* **(a)** basketball
(b) trainer (GB), sneaker (US)
IDIOM être bien *or* **à l'aise dans ses ∼s** (fam) to be very together (colloq)

basque /bask/ *adj, nm* Basque

basse² /bɑs/ ① *adj* ▶ BAS 1
② *nf* (Mus) bass

basse-cour, *pl* **basses-cours** /bɑskur/ *nf* **(a)** poultry-yard
(b) poultry

bassement /bɑsmɑ̃/ *adv* basely

bassesse /bɑsɛs/ *nf* **(a)** baseness
(b) base act

bassin /basɛ̃/ *nm* **(a)** pond; fountain; pool
(b) (in geography) basin
(c) pelvis
(d) bedpan
■ **∼ houiller** coal field

bassine /basin/ *nf* bowl; basin

bassiste /basist/ *nmf* bass player

bastingage /bastɛ̃gaʒ/ *nm* ship's rail

bas-ventre, *pl* ∼**s** /bavɑ̃tʀ/ *nm* lower abdomen

ât /bɑ/ *nm* pack-saddle
˙IOM c'est là que le ∼ blesse that's where the shoe pinches

✧ **bataille** /bɑtɑj/ ① *nf* **(a)** battle
(b) fight
② **en bataille** *phr* ‹*hair*› dishevelled (GB); ‹*eyebrows*› bushy

batailler /bɑtɑje/ [1] *vi* to fight, to battle

bataillon /bɑtɑjɔ̃/ *nm* battalion; **Dupont?, inconnu au ∼** Dupont?, never heard of him

bâtard, ∼e /bɑtaʀ, aʀd/ ① *adj* **(a)** ‹*dog*› mongrel
(b) ‹*work, style*› hybrid
(c) (offensive) ‹*child*› bastard
② *nm,f* **(a)** mongrel
(b) (offensive) bastard

✧ **bateau,** *pl* ∼**x** /bato/ ① *adj inv* hackneyed
② *nm* **(a)** boat, ship; **∼ à voile/moteur/ vapeur** sailing/motor/steam boat; **faire du ∼** to go boating; to go sailing
(b) dropped kerb (GB) *or* curb (US)
■ **∼ amiral** flagship; **∼ pneumatique** rubber dinghy; **∼ de sauvetage** lifeboat

bateau-école, *pl* **bateaux-écoles** /batoekɔl/ *nm* training ship

bateau-mouche, *pl* **bateaux- mouches** /batomuʃ/ *nm: large river boat for sightseeing*

bateleur, -euse /batlœʀ, øz/ *nm, f* tumbler, juggler

batelier, -ière /batəlje, ɛʀ/ *nm,f* boatman/ boatwoman

bâti, ∼e /bɑti/ ① *pp* ▶ BÂTIR
② *pp adj* **(a)** built; **terrain ∼** developed site
(b) **un homme bien ∼** a well-built man

batifoler /batifɔle/ [1] *vi* **(a)** to romp about
(b) to flirt

✧ **bâtiment** /bɑtimɑ̃/ *nm* **(a)** building
(b) building trade
(c) ship

bâtir /bɑtiʀ/ [3] *vtr* **(a)** to build
(b) to tack ‹*hem*›

bâtisse /bɑtis/ *nf* (dwelling) house; (structure) building

bâtisseur, -euse /bɑtisœʀ, øz/ *nm, f* master-builder; (figurative) builder

bâton /bɑtɔ̃/ *nm* **(a)** stick
(b) vertical stroke
(c) (Hist) (fam) ten thousand francs
■ **∼ de rouge (à lèvres)** lipstick
IDIOMS discuter à ∼s rompus to talk about this and that; **mettre des ∼s dans les roues de qn** to put a spoke in sb's wheel

bâtonnet /bɑtɔnɛ/ *nm* stick
■ **∼ de poisson** fish finger (GB), fish stick (US)

batracien /batʀasjɛ̃/ *nm* batrachian

battage /bataʒ/ *nm* (fam) publicity, hype (colloq)

battant, ∼e /batɑ̃, ɑ̃t/ ① *adj* **le cœur ∼** with a beating heart
② *nm,f* fighter
③ *nm* **porte à deux ∼s** double door

batte /bat/ *nf* (Sport) bat (GB), paddle (US)

battement /batmɑ̃/ *nm* **(a)** beating; beat; fluttering; flutter
(b) break, gap; wait

batterie /batʀi/ *nf* **(a)** percussion section
(b) drum kit
(c) battery
■ ~ **de cuisine** pots and pans

batteur /batœʀ/ *nm* **(a)** percussionist
(b) drummer
(c) whisk

ⷮ **battre** /batʀ/ [61] **1** *vtr* **(a)** (defeat) to beat ‹opponent›; to break ‹record›
(b) (hit) to beat ‹person, animal, carpet›; to thresh ‹corn›
(c) ‹rain, sea› to beat against
(d) to whisk ‹eggs›; to whip ‹cream›
(e) to shuffle ‹cards›
(f) (Mus) ~ **la mesure** to beat time
(g) to scour ‹countryside›
2 battre de *v+prep* ~ **des ailes** to flap its wings; ~ **des cils** to flutter one's eyelashes; ~ **des mains** to clap (one's hands)
3 *vi* **(a)** ‹heart, pulse› to beat
(b) ‹door› to bang
4 se battre *v refl* (+ *v être*) to fight
IDIOMS ~ **en retraite devant qch** to retreat before sth; ~ **son plein** to be in full swing

battu, ~**e** /baty/ **1** *pp* ▶ BATTRE
2 *pp adj* ‹child, wife› battered

BAU /beay/ *nf: abbr* ▶ BANDE

baudet /bodɛ/ *nm* (fam) donkey, ass

baume /bom/ *nm* balm, balsam

baux /bo/ ▶ BAIL

bavard, ~**e** /bavaʀ, aʀd/ **1** *adj*
(a) talkative
(b) indiscreet
(c) long-winded
2 *nm,f* **(a)** chatterbox
(b) blabbermouth (colloq)

bavardage /bavaʀdaʒ/ *nm* **(a)** gossip
(b) idle chatter

bavarder /bavaʀde/ [1] *vi* **(a)** to talk, to chatter
(b) to chat
(c) to gossip (**sur** about)

bavarois, ~**e** /bavaʀwa, az/ **1** *adj* Bavarian
2 *nm* (Culin) Bavarian cream, bavarois

bave /bav/ *nf* dribble; spittle; slaver; slime

baver /bave/ [1] *vi* **(a)** ‹person› to dribble; ‹animal› to slaver
(b) ‹pen› to leak; ‹brush› to drip; ‹ink, paint› to run
IDIOM **il leur en a fait** ~ (fam) he gave them a hard time

bavette /bavɛt/ *nf* **(a)** bib
(b) (Culin) flank

bavoir /bavwaʀ/ *nm* bib

bavure /bavyʀ/ *nf* **(a)** smudge

(b) blunder

bazar /bazaʀ/ *nm* **(a)** general store
(b) (fam) mess
(c) (fam) clutter
(d) bazaar

bazarder /bazaʀde/ [1] *vi* (fam) to throw out

BCBG /besebeʒe/ *adj* (fam) (*abbr* = **bon chic bon genre**) chic and conservative, Sloaney (GB)

BCG /beseʒe/ *nm* (*abbr* = **bacille bilié de Calmette et Guérin**) BCG

BD /bede/ (fam) *abbr* ▶ BANDE

béant, ~**e** /beɑ̃, ɑ̃t/ *adj* gaping

béat, ~**e** /bea, at/ *adj* ‹person› blissfully happy; ‹smile› blissful, beatific

ⷮ **beau**, **bel** *before vowel or mute h*, **belle**[1], *mpl* ~**x** /bo, bɛl/ **1** *adj*
(a) beautiful; handsome; **se faire** ~ to do oneself up; **ce n'est pas** ~ **à voir!** (fam) it's not a pretty sight!
(b) good; fine; nice; lovely; **un** ~ **geste** a noble gesture; **fais de** ~**x rêves!** sweet dreams!; **au** ~ **milieu de** right in the middle of; **c'est bien** ~ **tout ça, mais…** (fam) that's all well and good, but…
(c) ‹sum› tidy; ‹salary› very nice
2 *nm* **qu'est-ce que tu as fait de** ~? done anything interesting?
3 avoir beau *phr* **j'ai** ~ **essayer, je n'y arrive pas** it's no good my trying, I can't do it
4 bel et bien *phr* **(a)** well and truly
(b) definitely
■ ~ **fixe** fine weather; ~**x jours** fine weather; good days
IDIOMS **faire le** ~ ‹dog› to sit up and beg; **c'est du** ~! (fam) (ironic) lovely!

ⷮ **beaucoup** /boku/ **1** *adv* **(a)** a lot; much; **c'est** ~ **dire** that's going a bit far; **c'est déjà** ~ **qu'elle soit venue** it's already quite something that she came; ~ **moins de livres** far fewer books; **c'est** ~ **trop** it's far too much; ~ **trop longtemps** far too long, much too long
(b) ~ **de** a lot of, a great deal of; much; many; **il ne reste plus** ~ **de pain** there isn't much bread left; **avec** ~ **de soin** very carefully; ~ **d'entre eux** many of them
2 de beaucoup *phr* by far
3 pour beaucoup *phr* **être pour** ~ **dans** to have a lot to do with

beauf /bof/ *nm* (fam) **(a)** (*abbr* = **beau-frère**) brother-in-law
(b) (yokel) boor (colloq); boor (colloq)

beau-fils, *pl* **beaux-fils** /bofis/ *nm*
(a) son-in-law
(b) stepson

beau-frère, *pl* **beaux-frères** /bofʀɛʀ/ *nm* brother-in-law

beau-parent, *pl* **beaux-parents** /bopaʀɑ̃/ *nm* **(a)** parent-in-law
(b) step-parent

ⷮ indicates a very frequent word

beau-père, pl **beaux-pères** /bopɛʀ/ nm
(a) father-in-law
(b) stepfather

⚘ **beauté** /bote/ nf beauty; **se faire une ~**
to do oneself up; **finir en ~** to end with a
flourish

beaux-arts /bozaʀ/ nm pl fine arts and
architecture

⚘ **bébé** /bebe/ nm baby

bec /bɛk/ nm (a) beak; **donner des coups
de ~** to peck; **il a toujours la cigarette au ~**
(fam) he's always got a cigarette stuck in his
mouth
(b) (of jug) lip; (of teapot) spout; (of wind
instrument) mouthpiece; **~ verseur**
pourer(-spout)
IDIOMS **clouer le ~ à qn** (fam) to shut sb up
(colloq); **tomber sur un ~** (fam) to come across
a snag

bécane /bekan/ nf (fam) bike, bicycle

bécasse /bekas/ nf woodcock

bec-de-lièvre, pl **becs-de-lièvre**
/bɛkdəljɛvʀ/ nm harelip

bêche /bɛʃ/ nf (a) spade
(b) garden fork

bêcher /beʃe/ [1] vtr to dig (with a spade)

becquée /beke/ nf beakful; **donner la ~ à**
to feed ⟨fledgling⟩

bedaine /bədɛn/ nf (fam) paunch

bédéphile /bedefil/ nmf comic strip fan

bedonnant, **~e** /bədɔnɑ̃, ɑ̃t/ adj
(fam) ⟨person⟩ paunchy

bée /be/ adj f **être bouche ~** to stand open-
mouthed or gaping

beffroi /befʀwa/ nm belfry

bégaiement /begɛmɑ̃/ nm stammer,
stutter

bégayer /begeje/ [21] vtr, vi to stammer

bègue /bɛg/ adj **être ~** to stammer

béguin /begɛ̃/ nm (fam) **avoir le ~ pour qn**
to have a crush on sb

beige /bɛʒ/ adj, nm beige

beignet /bɛɲɛ/ nm (a) fritter
(b) doughnut, donut (US) (colloq)

bel ▸ BEAU 1, 4

bêler /bele/ [1] vi to bleat

belette /bəlɛt/ nf weasel

⚘ **belge** /bɛlʒ/ adj Belgian

Belgique /bɛlʒik/ pr nf Belgium

bélier /belje/ nm (a) ram
(b) battering ram

Bélier /belje/ pr nm Aries

belle² /bɛl/ **1** adj f ▸ BEAU 1
2 nf decider, deciding game
3 **de plus belle** phr with renewed
vigour (GB)
IDIOMS **(se) faire la ~** (fam) to do a bunk
(GB) (colloq), to take a powder (US) (colloq);
en faire voir de ~s à qn (fam) to give sb a
hard time

belle-famille, pl **belles-familles**
/bɛlfamij/ nf in-laws

belle-fille, pl **belles-filles** /bɛlfij/ nf
(a) daughter-in-law
(b) stepdaughter

belle-mère, pl **belles-mères**
/bɛlmɛʀ/ nf (a) mother-in-law
(b) stepmother

belle-sœur, pl **belles-sœurs**
/bɛlsœʀ/ nf sister-in-law

belligérant /beliʒeʀɑ̃/ nm (a) belligerent,
warring party
(b) combatant

belliqueux, **-euse** /belikø, øz/ adj
aggressive

bémol /bemɔl/ nm (Mus) flat; **mi ~** E flat

bénédiction /benediksjɔ̃/ nf blessing

bénéfice /benefis/ nm (a) profit
(b) benefit, beneficial effect
(c) advantage

bénéficiaire /benefisjɛʀ/ nmf beneficiary

⚘ **bénéficier** /benefisje/ [2] v+prep **~ de** to
receive ⟨help⟩; to enjoy ⟨immunity⟩; to get
⟨special treatment⟩

bénéfique /benefik/ adj beneficial

Bénélux /benelyks/ pr nm Benelux

benêt /bənɛ/ nm half-wit

bénévolat /benevɔla/ nm voluntary work

bénévole /benevɔl/ **1** adj voluntary
2 nmf voluntary worker

bénévolement /benevɔlmɑ̃/ adv on a
voluntary basis

bénin, **-igne** /benɛ̃, iɲ/ adj minor; benign

béni-oui-oui /beniwiwi/ nm inv (fam) yes-
man

bénir /beniʀ/ [3] vtr to bless

bénit, **~e** /beni, it/ adj blessed; holy

bénitier /benitje/ nm holy water font

benjamin, **~e** /bɛ̃ʒamɛ̃, in/ nm, f youngest
child

benne /bɛn/ nf (a) skip (GB), dumpster®
(US)
(b) (colliery) wagon
(c) (cable) car

BEPC /beapese, bɛps/ nm (abbr = **Brevet
d'études du premier cycle**) former
examination at the end of the first stage of
secondary education

béquille /bekij/ nf (a) crutch
(b) kickstand

bercail /bɛʀkaj/ nm (fam) home

berceau, pl **~x** /bɛʀso/ nm cradle

bercer /bɛʀse/ [12] **1** vtr to rock ⟨baby⟩
2 **se bercer** v refl (+ v être) **se ~**
d'illusions to delude oneself

berceuse /bɛʀsøz/ nf lullaby

béret /beʀɛ/ nm beret

bergamote /bɛʀgamɔt/ nf bergamot

berge /bɛʀʒ/ nf (of river, canal) bank

b

berger, -ère /bɛʀʒe, ɛʀ/ nm,f shepherd/
shepherdess
■ ~ **allemand** Alsatian (GB), German shepherd
bergerie /bɛʀʒəʀi/ nf sheepfold
berlue /bɛʀly/ nf (fam) **avoir la** ~ to be
seeing things
bermuda /bɛʀmyda/ nm bermudas
Bermudes /bɛʀmyd/ pr nf pl **les** ~**s**
Bermuda
berner /bɛʀne/ [1] vtr to fool, to deceive
besace /bəzas/ nf pouch
besogne /bəzɔɲ/ nf job
✔ **besoin** /bəzwɛ̃/ ⓵ nm need (**de** for; **de
faire** to do); **avoir** ~ **de** to need; **répondre à
un** ~ to meet a need; **au** ~ if need be; **pour
les** ~**s de la cause** for the good of the cause;
être dans le ~ to be in need
⓶ **besoins** nm pl needs; **subvenir aux** ~**s
de qn** to provide for sb
IDIOM **faire ses** ~**s** (fam) ‹person› to relieve
oneself; ‹animal› to do its business
bestial, ~**e,** mpl **-iaux** /bɛstjal, o/ adj
brutish, bestial
bestiaux /bɛstjo/ nm pl **(a)** livestock
(b) cattle
bestiole /bɛstjɔl/ nf (fam) **(a)** creepy-crawly
(colloq), bug
(b) animal
bétail /betaj/ nm livestock; cattle
✔ **bête** /bɛt/ ⓵ adj stupid, silly; **je suis restée
toute** ~ I was dumbfounded
⓶ nf creature; animal
■ ~ **à bon Dieu** ladybird (GB), ladybug (US);
~ **noire** bête noire (GB), pet hate
IDIOMS **il est** ~ **comme ses pieds** (fam) he's
as dumb as can be; **chercher la petite** ~
(fam) to nit-pick (colloq); **reprendre du poil de
la** ~ (fam) to perk up; **travailler comme une** ~
(fam) to work like crazy (colloq)
bêtement /bɛtmɑ̃/ adv stupidly; **il suffit
(tout)** ~ **de faire** you simply need to do
bêtise /betiz/ nf **la** ~ stupidity; **faire une** ~
to do something stupid; **dire des** ~**s** to talk
nonsense; **surtout pas de** ~**s!** be good now!
bêtisier /betizje/ nm collection of howlers
(colloq)
béton /betɔ̃/ nm concrete;
(figurative) watertight
■ ~ **armé** reinforced concrete
bétonnière /betɔnjɛʀ/ nf concrete mixer
betterave /bɛtʀav/ nf beet; ~ **rouge**
beetroot; ~ **sucrière** sugar beet
beugler /bøgle/ [1] vi to moo; to bellow
beur /bœʀ/ nmf (fam) second-generation
North African (*living in France*)
beurette /bœʀɛt/ nf second-generation
North African girl (*living in France*)
✔ **beurre** /bœʀ/ nm butter; ~ **doux** unsalted
butter

■ ~ **d'escargot** garlic and parsley butter; ~ **noir**
black butter; **œil au** ~ **noir** (fam) black eye
IDIOMS **faire son** ~ (fam) to make a packet
(colloq); **compter pour du** ~ (fam) to count for
nothing; **vouloir le** ~ **et l'argent du** ~ (fam) to
want to have one's cake and eat it
beurré, ~**e** /bœʀe/ adj (fam) drunk,
plastered (colloq)
beurrer /bœʀe/ [1] vtr to butter
beurrier /bœʀje/ nm butter dish
beuverie /bœvʀi/ nf drinking session
biais /bjɛ/ ⓵ nm inv **(a)** (of material) bias
(b) way; **par le** ~ **de qn** through sb; **par le** ~
de qch by means of sth
⓶ **de biais, en biais** phr **couper une
étoffe en** ~ to cut material on the cross
biaiser /bjɛze/ [1] vi to hedge
bibelot /biblo/ nm ornament
biberon /bibʀɔ̃/ nm (baby's) bottle (GB),
(nursing) bottle (US)
bible /bibl/ nf bible; **la Bible** the Bible
bibliographie /biblijɔgʀafi/ nf
bibliography
bibliographique /biblijɔgʀafik/ adj
bibliographical
bibliothécaire /biblijɔtekɛʀ/ nmf
librarian
✔ **bibliothèque** /biblijɔtɛk/ nf **(a)** library
(b) bookcase
biblique /biblik/ adj biblical
bic® /bik/ nm biro®
bicarbonate /bikaʀbɔnat/ nm
bicarbonate
bicentenaire /bisɑ̃tnɛʀ/ nm bicentenary,
bicentennial
biceps /bisɛps/ nm inv biceps
biche /biʃ/ nf doe
bichonner /biʃɔne/ [1] vtr (fam) to pamper
bicolore /bikɔlɔʀ/ adj ‹flag› two-coloured
(GB); ‹fabric› two-tone
bicoque /bikɔk/ nf (fam) dump (colloq),
house
bicyclette /bisiklɛt/ nf **(a)** bicycle
(b) cycling
bidasse /bidas/ nm (fam) soldier
bidet /bidɛ/ nm bidet
bidon /bidɔ̃/ ⓵ adj inv (fam) bogus; phoney
(colloq)
⓶ nm **(a)** can; drum; flask
(b) (fam) stomach, paunch
(c) (fam) **c'est du** ~ it is a load of hogwash
(colloq)
bidonner: se bidonner /bidɔne/ [1] v refl
(+ v être) (fam) to laugh, to fall about (colloq)
bidonville /bidɔ̃vil/ nm shanty town
bidule /bidyl/ nm (fam) thingy (GB) (colloq),
thingamajig (colloq)
bielle /bjɛl/ nf connecting rod
✔ **bien** /bjɛ̃/ ⓵ adj inv **(a)** **être** ~ **dans un rô**
to be good in a part; **être** ~ **de sa personne**

✔ indicates a very frequent word

to be good-looking; **ce n'est pas ~ de mentir** it's not nice to lie; **ça fait ~ d'aller à l'opéra** (fam) it's the done thing to go to the opera
(b) well; **ne pas se sentir ~** not to feel well; **t'es pas ~!** (fam) you're out of your mind (colloq)
(c) je suis ~ dans ces bottes these boots are comfortable; **on est ~ au soleil!** isn't it nice in the sun!
(d) (fam) **un quartier ~** a nice district; **des gens ~** respectable people
⟨2⟩ *adv* **(a)** well; ⟨*function*⟩ properly; ⟨*interpret*⟩ correctly; **~ joué!** well done!; **aller ~** ⟨*person*⟩ to be well; ⟨*business*⟩ to go well; **ni ~ ni mal** so-so; **j'ai cru ~ faire** I thought I was doing the right thing; **c'est ~ fait pour elle!** it serves her right!; **tu ferais ~ d'y aller** it would be a good idea for you to go
(b) ⟨*mix*⟩ thoroughly; ⟨*fill*⟩ completely; ⟨*listen*⟩ carefully
(c) ⟨*presented*⟩ well; ⟨*furnished*⟩ tastefully; ⟨*live*⟩ comfortably; **femme ~ faite** shapely woman; **aller ~ ensemble** to go well together; **aller ~ à qn** to suit sb; **~ prendre une remarque** to take a remark in good part
(d) ⟨*nice, sad*⟩ very; ⟨*fear, enjoy*⟩ very much; ⟨*simple, true*⟩ quite; **il y a ~ longtemps** a very long time ago; **merci ~** thank you very much; **~ rire** to have a good laugh; **c'est ~ compris?** is that clear?; **~ au contraire** on the contrary; **~ mieux** much *or* far better; **~ sûr** of course; **~ entendu** *or* **évidemment** naturally; **il y a ~ des années** a good many years ago; **~ des fois** often, many a time
(e) je veux ~ t'aider I don't mind helping you; **j'aimerais ~ essayer** I would love to try
(f) il faut ~ que ça finisse it has just got to come to an end
(g) ça montre ~ que it just goes to show that; **je sais ~ que** I know that; **insiste ~** make sure you insist; **on verra ~** well, we'll see; **il le fait ~ lui, pourquoi pas moi?** if he can do it, why can't I?; **tu peux très ~ le faire toi-même** you can easily do it yourself; **que peut-il ~ faire à Paris?** what on earth can he be doing in Paris?
(h) definitely; **c'est ~ ce qu'il a dit** that's exactly what he said; **tu as ~ pris les clés?** are you sure you've got the keys?; **c'est ~ de lui!** it's just like him!; **c'est ~ le moment!** (ironic) great timing!; **c'est ~ le moment de partir!** (ironic) what a time to leave!
(i) at least; **elle a ~ 40 ans** she's at least 40
⟨3⟩ *nm* **(a)** good; **le ~ et le mal** good and evil; **ça fait du ~ aux enfants** it's good for the children; **vouloir le ~ de qn** to have sb's best interests at heart; **vouloir du ~ à qn** to wish sb well; **dire du ~/le plus grand ~ de qn** to speak well/very highly of sb
(b) possession; **des ~s considérables** substantial assets
⟨4⟩ **bien que** *phr* although
■ **~s de consommation** consumer goods; **~s immobiliers** real estate; **~s mobiliers**

personal property; **~s personnels** private property
bien-être /bjɛnɛtʀ/ *nm* **(a)** well-being
(b) welfare
(c) comforts
bienfaisance /bjɛ̃fəzɑ̃s/ *nf* charity
bienfaisant, ~e /bjɛ̃fəzɑ̃, ɑ̃t/ *adj* beneficial, beneficent
bienfait /bjɛ̃fɛ/ *nm* **(a)** kind deed; **~ du ciel** godsend
(b) beneficial effect
bienfaiteur, -trice /bjɛ̃fɛtœʀ, tʀis/ *nm,f* benefactor/benefactress
bien-fondé /bjɛ̃fɔ̃de/ *nm* (of idea) validity; (of claim) legitimacy
bien-pensant, ~e, mpl ~s /bjɛ̃pɑ̃sɑ̃, ɑ̃t/ *adj* **(a)** right-thinking
(b) self-righteous
bienséance /bjɛ̃seɑ̃s/ *nf* propriety; **les règles de la ~** the rules of polite society
✏ **bientôt** /bjɛ̃to/ *adv* soon; **à ~** see you soon
bienveillant, ~e /bjɛ̃vɛjɑ̃, ɑ̃t/ *adj* benevolent
bienvenu, ~e¹ /bjɛ̃vəny/ *adj* welcome
bienvenue² /bjɛ̃vəny/ *nf* welcome
bière /bjɛʀ/ *nf* **(a)** beer; **~ (à la) pression** draught (GB) *or* draft (US) beer
(b) coffin, casket (US)
■ **~ blonde** lager; **~ brune** ≈ stout; **~ rousse** brown ale
bifteck /biftɛk/ *nm* steak
IDIOM **gagner son ~** (fam) to earn a living
bifurcation /bifyʀkasjɔ̃/ *nf* (in road) fork
bifurquer /bifyʀke/ [1] *vi* **(a)** ⟨*road*⟩ to fork
(b) ⟨*driver*⟩ to turn off
(c) (in career) to change tack
bigame /bigam/ *adj* bigamous
bigamie /bigami/ *nf* bigamy
bigarré, ~e /bigaʀe/ *adj* **(a)** multicoloured (GB)
(b) ⟨*crowd*⟩ colourful (GB)
bigleux, -euse /biglø, øz/ *adj* (pej) (fam) poor-sighted; **complètement ~** as blind as a bat (colloq)
bigorneau, pl ~x /bigɔʀno/ *nm* winkle
bigot, ~e /bigo, ɔt/ *nm,f* religious zealot
bigoudi /bigudi/ *nm* roller, curler
bijou, pl ~x /biʒu/ *nm* **(a)** piece of jewellery (GB) *or* jewelry (US)
(b) jewel; (figurative) gem
bijouterie /biʒutʀi/ *nf* (shop) jeweller's (GB), jewelry store (US)
bilan /bilɑ̃/ *nm* **(a)** balance sheet; **déposer son ~** to file a petition in bankruptcy
(b) outcome
(c) (after disaster) toll
(d) assessment; **~ de santé** check-up
(e) report
bilatéral, ~e, mpl -aux /bilateʀal, o/ *adj* bilateral

bile /bil/ *nf* bile
  IDIOM se faire de la ∼ (fam) to worry
bilingue /bilɛ̃g/ *adj* bilingual
billard /bijaʀ/ *nm* (a) billiards
  (b) billiard table
  ■ ∼ américain pool; ∼ anglais snooker
  IDIOM passer sur le ∼ (fam) to have an
  operation
bille /bij/ *nf* (a) marble
  (b) (billiard) ball
⚬ **billet** /bijɛ/ *nm* (a) bank note, note (GB),
  bill (US)
  (b) ticket
  ■ ∼ doux love letter
billetterie /bijɛtʀi/ *nf* cash dispenser
billion /biljɔ̃/ *nm* billion (GB), trillion (US)
bimensuel /bimɑ̃sɥɛl/ *nm* fortnightly
  magazine (GB), semimonthly (US)
bimoteur /bimɔtœʀ/ *nm* twin-engined plane
binaire /binɛʀ/ *adj* binary
biniou /binju/ *nm* Breton bagpipes
binocles /binɔkl/ *nf pl* (fam) specs (colloq),
  glasses
bio /bjo/ ⨐ *adj inv* (natural) aliments ∼
  health foods; produits ∼ organic produce;
  yaourt ∼ bio yoghurt
  ⨑ *nf* (fam) biography
biocarburant /bjokaʀbyʀɑ̃/ *nm* biofuel
biochimie /bjoʃimi/ *nf* biochemistry
biodégradable /bjodegʀadabl/ *adj*
  biodegradable
biodiversité /bjodivɛʀsite/ *nf* biodiversity
biographie /bjɔgʀafi/ *nf* biography
biologie /bjɔlɔʒi/ *nf* biology
biophysique /bjofizik/ *nf* biophysics
bip /bip/ *nm* beep; ∼ sonore tone
bipède /bipɛd/ *nm* biped
biplace /biplas/ *adj, nm* two-seater
bique /bik/ *nf* (fam) une vieille ∼ an old bag
  (colloq)
biréacteur /biʀeaktœʀ/ *nm* twin-engined
  jet
bis¹ /bis/ *adv* (a) (in address) bis; 33 ∼ rue
  Juliette Lamber 33 bis rue Juliette Lamber
  (b) (at show, concert) encore
bis², ∼e¹ /bi, biz/ *adj* greyish (GB) *or*
  grayish (US) brown
bisannuel, -elle /bizanɥɛl/ *adj* biennial
biscornu, ∼e /biskɔʀny/ *adj* quirky
biscotte /biskɔt/ *nf* continental toast
biscuit /biskɥi/ *nm* biscuit (GB), cookie
  (US)
  ■ ∼ à la cuillère sponge finger (GB), ladyfinger
  (US); ∼ salé cracker
bise² /biz/ ⨐ *adj f* ▶ BIS²
  ⨑ *nf* (a) (fam) kiss; faire la ∼ à qn to kiss sb
  on the cheeks
  (b) North wind

biseau, *pl* ∼**x** /bizo/ *nm* (a) bevel (edge);
  tailler en ∼ to bevel
  (b) (tool) bevel
bison /bizɔ̃/ *nm* (a) bison
  (b) buffalo
bissextile /bisɛkstil/ *adj* année ∼ leap
  year
bistouri /bisturi/ *nm* (Med) bistoury
bistro(t) /bistʀo/ *nm* (fam) bistro, café
bit /bit/ *nm* bit
BIT /beite/ *nm* (*abbr* = **Bureau**
  international du travail) ILO
bitume /bitym/ *nm* (on road) asphalt
bivouac /bivwak/ *nm* bivouac
bizarre /bizaʀ/ *adj* odd, strange
blafard, ∼e /blafaʀ, aʀd/ *adj* pale
blague /blag/ *nf* (fam) (a) joke; ∼ à part
  seriously
  (b) fib (colloq)
  (c) trick; faire une ∼ à qn to play a trick on sb
blaguer /blage/ [1] *vi* (fam) to joke
blagueur, -euse /blagœʀ, øz/ *nm,f*
  (fam) joker
blaireau, *pl* ∼**x** /blɛʀo/ *nm* (a) badger
  (b) shaving brush
blâmer /blɑme/ [1] *vtr* to criticize; to blame
⚬ **blanc, blanche¹** /blɑ̃, blɑ̃ʃ/ ⨐ *adj*
  (gen) white; ⟨page⟩ blank; ∼ cassé off-white
  ⨑ *nm* (a) white; habillé/peint en ∼ dressed
  in/painted white
  (b) household linen
  (c) white meat
  (d) (egg) white
  (e) blank; gap; j'ai eu un ∼ my mind went
  blank
  (f) (fam) correction fluid
  (g) tirer à ∼ to fire blanks
  ⨒ **blancs** *nm pl* (in chess, draughts) white
Blanc, Blanche /blɑ̃, blɑ̃ʃ/ *nm,f* white
  man/woman
blanc-bec, *pl* **blancs-becs** /blɑ̃bɛk/ *nm*
  greenhorn
blanchâtre /blɑ̃ʃɑtʀ/ *adj* whitish
blanche² /blɑ̃ʃ/ ⨐ *adj f* ▶ BLANC 1
  ⨑ *nf* (Mus) minim (GB), half note (US)
blanchiment /blɑ̃ʃimɑ̃/ *nm* (a) (of
  money) laundering
  (b) (of fabric, paper, pulp) bleaching
blanchir /blɑ̃ʃiʀ/ [3] ⨐ *vtr* (a) to whiten
  ⟨shoes⟩
  (b) to clear ⟨name⟩
  (c) to launder ⟨money⟩
  ⨑ *vi* (a) to turn grey (GB) *or* gray (US)
  (b) faire ∼ to blanch ⟨vegetables⟩
  ⨒ **se blanchir** *v refl* (+ *v être*) to clear
  oneself
blanchisserie /blɑ̃ʃisʀi/ *nf* laundry
blanchisseur /blɑ̃ʃisœʀ/ *nm* (shop) laundry
blanchisseuse /blɑ̃ʃisøz/ *nf* laundress
blasé, ∼e /blaze/ *adj* blasé

⚬ indicates a very frequent word

blason /blazɔ̃/ *nm* coat of arms
  IDIOM **redorer son** ∼ to restore one's reputation
blasphème /blasfɛm/ *nm* blasphemy
blasphémer /blasfeme/ [14] *vi* to blaspheme
blatte /blat/ *nf* cockroach
blé /ble/ *nm* wheat; ∼ **noir** buckwheat
bled /blɛd/ *nm* (fam) village
blême /blɛm/ *adj* pale
blessant, ∼**e** /blesɑ̃, ɑ̃t/ *adj* ⟨remark⟩ cutting
blessé, ∼**e** /blese/ *nm,f* injured *or* wounded man/woman; casualty
blesser /blese/ [1] **1** *vtr* **(a)** to injure, to hurt; to wound; **il a été blessé à la tête** he sustained head injuries
  (b) to hurt ⟨person, feelings⟩; to wound ⟨pride⟩
  2 se blesser *v refl* (+ *v être*) to hurt oneself
blessure /blesyʀ/ *nf* injury; wound
blet, **blette** /blɛ, blɛt/ *adj* overripe
♂ **bleu**, ∼**e** /blø/ **1** *adj* **(a)** blue
  (b) ⟨steak⟩ very rare
  2 *nm* **(a)** blue
  (b) bruise
  (c) ∼ **de travail** overalls
  (d) blue cheese
  IDIOM **avoir une peur** ∼**e de qch** to be scared stiff (colloq) of sth
bleuâtre /bløɑtʀ/ *adj* bluish
bleuet /bløɛ/ *nm* (Bot) cornflower
blindé, ∼**e** /blɛ̃de/ *adj* armoured (GB)
blinder /blɛ̃de/ [1] *vtr* to put security fittings on ⟨door⟩; to armour-plate (GB) ⟨car⟩
blizzard /blizaʀ/ *nm* blizzard
bloc **1** *nm* **(a)** block; **faire** ∼ **avec/contre qn** to side with/unite against sb
  (b) notepad; ∼ **de papier à lettres** writing pad
  (c) (Comput) block
  2 à bloc *phr* ⟨screw⟩ tightly; ⟨inflate⟩ fully
  3 en bloc *phr* ⟨deny⟩ outright
  ■ ∼ **opératoire** surgical unit
blocage /blɔkaʒ/ *nm* blocking; ∼ **des salaires** wage freeze
blockhaus /blɔkos/ *nm inv* blockhouse
bloc-notes, *pl* **blocs-notes** /blɔknɔt/ *nm* notepad
blocus /blɔkys/ *nm inv* blockade
♂ **blog**, **blogue** /blɔg/ *nm* blog
blogger /blɔgœʀ/ *nm* blogger
♂ **blond**, ∼**e** /blɔ̃, ɔ̃d/ **1** *adj* **(a)** blonde (GB), blond (US)
  (b) ⟨wheat⟩ golden; ⟨tobacco⟩ light
  2 *nm,f* (female) blonde (GB), blond (US); (male) blond
bloqué, ∼**e** /blɔke/ **1** *pp* ▶ BLOQUER
  2 *pp adj* **(a)** blocked
  (b) ⟨mechanism, door⟩ jammed; **elle/la voiture est** ∼**e** she/the car is stuck

(c) être ∼ ⟨activity⟩ to be at a standstill; ⟨situation⟩ to be deadlocked
bloquer /blɔke/ [1] **1** *vtr* **(a)** to block ⟨road⟩
  (b) to lock ⟨steering wheel⟩; to wedge ⟨door⟩; (accidentally) to jam ⟨mechanism, door⟩
  (c) to stop ⟨vehicle, traveller⟩
  (d) to freeze ⟨prices⟩
  (e) to stop ⟨project⟩
  (f) to lump [sth] together ⟨days⟩
  2 se bloquer *v refl* (+ *v être*) **(a)** ⟨brakes, door⟩ to jam; ⟨wheel⟩ to lock
  (b) to retreat
blottir: se blottir /blɔtiʀ/ [3] *v refl* (+ *v être*) **se** ∼ **contre** to huddle up against; to snuggle up against
blouse /bluz/ *nf* **(a)** overall
  (b) coat; ∼ **blanche** white coat
  (c) blouse
blouson /bluzɔ̃/ *nm* **(a)** blouson; ∼ **d'aviateur** bomber jacket
  (b) ∼ **noir** ≈ rocker
blue-jean, *pl* ∼**s** /bludʒin/ *nm* jeans
bluffer /blœfe/ [1] *vtr*, *vi* (fam) to bluff
BN /beɛn/ *nf* (*abbr* = **Bibliothèque nationale**) *national library in Paris*
boa /bɔa/ *nm* boa
bobard /bɔbaʀ/ *nm* (fam) fib (colloq), tall story
bobine /bɔbin/ *nf* (of film, cable) reel
bobo /bɔbo/ *nm* (fam) (baby talk) **(a)** pain
  (b) scratch
bocage /bɔkaʒ/ *nm* hedged farmland
bocal, *pl* **-aux** /bɔkal, o/ *nm* jar; bowl
bœuf /bœf, *pl* bø/ *nm* **(a)** bullock (GB), steer (US)
  (b) ox
  (c) beef
  IDIOM **faire un effet** ∼ (fam) to make a fantastic (colloq) impression
bof /bɔf/ *excl* (fam) **'tu préfères la mer ou la montagne?'—'**∼**!'** 'which do you prefer, the sea or the mountains?'—'I don't mind'
bogue /bɔg/ *or nf* *nm* (Comput) bug
bohème /bɔɛm/ **1** *adj* bohemian
  2 *nf* **la** ∼ bohemia
bohémien, **-ienne** /bɔemjɛ̃, ɛn/ *nm,f* Romany, gypsy
♂ **boire** /bwaʀ/ [70] **1** *vtr* **(a)** to drink
  (b) ⟨paper⟩ to soak up
  2 se boire *v refl* (+ *v être*) **ce vin se boit frais** this wine should be drunk chilled
  IDIOMS ∼ **comme un trou** (fam) to drink like a fish (colloq); **il y a à** ∼ **et à manger dans leur théorie** there's both good and bad in their theory
♂ **bois** /bwa/ **1** *nm inv* wood; **en** ∼ ⟨chair⟩ wooden; ⟨cheque⟩ dud (colloq); ∼ **mort** firewood
  2 *nm pl* **(a)** antlers
  (b) woodwind section ⋯⟶

b

IDIOMS être de ~ to be insensitive; **il va voir de quel ~ je me chauffe** (fam) I'll show him
boisé, ~**e** /bwaze/ adj wooded
boiserie /bwazʀi/ nf ~**(s)** panelling (GB)
boisson /bwasɔ̃/ nf drink
♂ **boîte** /bwat/ nf (a) (container) box
(b) (for food) tin (GB), can; **petits pois en ~** canned peas
(c) (club) ~ **(de nuit)** nightclub
(d) (fam) (company) firm; office
■ ~ **crânienne** cranium; ~ **à gants** glove compartment; ~ **à** or **aux lettres** post box (GB), mailbox (US); ~ **à** or **aux lettres électronique** (Comput) electronic mailbox; ~ **à musique** musical box (GB), music box (US); ~ **noire** black box; ~ **à outils** toolbox; ~ **postale, BP** PO Box; ~ **de vitesses** gearbox
IDIOM **mettre qn en ~** (fam) to tease sb
boiter /bwate/ [1] vi to limp
boiteux, -euse /bwatø, øz/ 1 adj
(a) lame
(b) ‹chair› wobbly
(c) ‹argument, alliance› shaky
2 nm,f lame person
boîtier /bwatje/ nm (gen) case; (of camera) body
boitiller /bwatije/ [1] vi to limp slightly
bol /bɔl/ nm (a) bowl; ~ **d'air** breath of fresh air
(b) (fam) luck; **coup de ~** stroke of luck
bolée /bɔle/ nf ~ **de cidre** bowl of cider
bolide /bɔlid/ nm high-powered car
bombage /bɔ̃baʒ/ nm (action) graffiti spraying; (result) (sprayed) graffiti
bombardement /bɔ̃baʀdəmɑ̃/ nm (Mil) bombardment; bombing; shelling; ~ **aérien** air raid
bombarder /bɔ̃baʀde/ [1] vtr (a) to bombard; to bomb; to shell
(b) ~ **qn de questions** to bombard sb with questions
(c) (fam) ~ **qn à un poste** to catapult sb into a job
bombardier /bɔ̃baʀdje/ nm (a) bomber
(b) bombardier
bombe /bɔ̃b/ nf (a) bomb; **faire l'effet d'une ~** to come as a bombshell
(b) ~ **(aérosol)** spray
(c) riding hat
IDIOM **partir à toute ~** (fam) to rush off
bombé, ~e /bɔ̃be/ adj (a) ‹forehead› domed; ‹shape› rounded
(b) ‹road› cambered
bomber /bɔ̃be/ [1] 1 vtr ~ **le torse** to thrust out one's chest; (figurative) to swell with pride
2 vi (a) ‹plank› to bulge out
(b) (fam) to belt along (colloq)

 dindicates a very frequent word

♂ **bon, bonne¹** /bɔ̃, bɔn/ 1 adj (a) good; **prends un ~** pull take a warm jumper; **elle est (bien) bonne!** (fam) that's a good one!; (indignantly) I like that!; **voilà une bonne chose de faite!** that's that out of the way!; **nous sommes ~s derniers** we're well and truly last; **il n'est pas ~ à grand-chose** he's pretty useless; **il serait ~ qu'elle le sache** she ought to know; **à quoi ~?** what's the point?
(b) ‹person, words› kind; ‹smile› nice; **avoir ~ cœur** to be good-hearted
(c) ‹time, answer› right; **c'est ~, vous pouvez y aller** it's OK, you can go
(d) ‹ticket› valid; **tu es ~ pour la vaisselle, ce soir!** you're in line for the dishes tonight!
(e) **bonne nuit/chance** good night/luck
2 nm,f **les ~s et les méchants** good people and bad people; (in films) the good guys and the bad guys (colloq)
3 nm (a) coupon; voucher
(b) **il y a du ~ dans cet article** there are some good things in this article
4 adv **ça sent ~!** that smells good!; **il fait ~** the weather's mild; **il fait ~ dans ta chambre** it's nice and warm in your room
5 **pour de bon** phr (a) really; **tu dis ça pour de ~?** are you serious?
(b) for good
■ ~ **de commande** order form; ~ **enfant** good-natured; ~ **de garantie** guarantee slip; ~ **marché** cheap; ~ **mot** witticism; ~ **à rien** good-for-nothing; ~ **sens** common sense; ~ **du Trésor** Treasury bond; ~ **vivant** bon viveur; **bonne action** good deed; **bonne femme** (derogatory) (fam) woman, dame (US) (colloq); wife, old lady (colloq); **bonne pâte** good sort; **bonne sœur** (fam) nun

bonbon /bɔ̃bɔ̃/ nm sweet (GB), candy (US)
bonbonne /bɔ̃bɔn/ nf (a) demijohn; (bigger) carboy
(b) (for gas) cylinder
bond /bɔ̃/ nm (a) leap; **se lever d'un ~** to leap to one's feet
(b) (in time) jump
(c) (in profits, exports) leap; (in prices) jump (de in); **la médecine a fait un ~ en avant avec cette découverte** this discovery was a medical breakthrough
IDIOMS **saisir la balle au ~** to seize the opportunity; **faire faux ~ à qn** to let sb down
bonde /bɔ̃d/ nf (a) (of swimming pool) outlet; (of sink) plughole
(b) (stopper) (in pool) outlet cover; (in sink) plug
bondé, ~e /bɔ̃de/ adj packed (de with)
bondir /bɔ̃diʀ/ [3] vi (a) to leap; ~ **de joie** to jump for joy
(b) ~ **sur qn/qch** to pounce on sb/sth
(c) ‹animal› to leap about
(d) **ça m'a fait ~** I was absolutely furious (about it)
♂ **bonheur** /bɔnœʀ/ nm (a) happiness
(b) pleasure; **faire le ~ de qn** ‹present› to make sb happy; ‹event, exhibition› to delight sb

(c) par ~ fortunately; **au petit ~ (la chance)** at random; **tu ne connais pas ton ~!** you don't realize how lucky you are! IDIOM **alors, tu as trouvé ton ~?** (fam) did you find what you wanted?

bonhomie /bɔnɔmi/ *nf* good-nature

bonhomme, *pl* ~**s, bonshommes** /bɔnɔm, bõzɔm/ ⟦1⟧ *adj* good-natured ⟦2⟧ *nm* (fam) **(a)** fellow, chap (colloq) **(b)** husband, old man (colloq) ∎ ~ **de neige** snowman IDIOM **aller** *or* **suivre son petit ~ de chemin** to go peacefully along

bonification /bɔnifikɑsjõ/ *nf* **(a)** (in sport) bonus points **(b)** (financial) bonus

boniments /bɔnimã/ *nm pl* stories; **raconter des ~ à qn** to give sb some story (colloq) **(à propos de** about); to smooth-talk sb

✍ **bonjour** /bõʒuʀ/ *nm, excl* hello IDIOM **être simple comme ~** (fam) to be very easy

bonne² /bɔn/ ⟦1⟧ *adj f* ▶ BON 1 ⟦2⟧ *nf* **(a)** maid, servant **(b) tu en as de ~s, toi!** you must be joking! ∎ ~ **d'enfants** nanny

bonnement /bɔnmã/ *adv* **tout ~** (quite) simply

bonnet /bɔnɛ/ *nm* **(a)** hat; (for baby) bonnet **(b)** (on bra) cup ∎ ~ **de nuit** nightcap; (figurative) wet blanket (colloq)

bonneterie /bɔnɛtʀi/ *nf* hosiery

bonshommes ▶ BONHOMME

bonsoir /bõswaʀ/ *nm, excl* good evening, good night

bonté /bõte/ *nf* **(a)** kindness **(b)** (of God) goodness

bonus /bɔnys/ *nm inv* no-claims bonus

boom /bum/ *nm* boom; **en plein ~** booming

✍ **bord** /bɔʀ/ *nm* **(a)** (of plate, bed) edge; (of road) side; (of river) bank; **au ~ de** on *or* at the edge of; (figurative) on the verge of; **au ~ de la mer** at the seaside; by the sea; ~ **à ~** edge-to-edge **(b)** (of cup) rim; (of hat) brim **(c)** à ~ ⟨work⟩ on board; **de ~** ⟨instruments, staff⟩ on board; **on fera** (fam) **avec les moyens du ~** we'll make do with what we've got **(d)** side; **être du même ~** to be on the same side

bordeaux /bɔʀdo/ ⟦1⟧ *adj inv* burgundy ⟦2⟧ *nm* Bordeaux; ~ **rouge** claret

border /bɔʀde/ [1] *vtr* **(a)** to line (de with) **(b)** ⟨plants⟩ to border ⟨lake⟩ **(c)** to tuck [sb] in **(d)** to edge ⟨garment⟩ (de with)

bordereau, *pl* ~**x** /bɔʀdəʀo/ *nm* form, slip

bordure /bɔʀdyʀ/ ⟦1⟧ *nf* **(a)** (of sports ground, carpet) border **(b)** (of road, platform) edge

⟦2⟧ **en bordure de** *phr* **(a)** next to ⟨park, canal, track⟩ **(b)** on the edge of ⟨park⟩; on the side of ⟨road⟩ **(c)** just outside ⟨village⟩

boréal, ~**e**, *mpl* -**aux** /bɔʀeal, o/ *adj* boreal

borgne /bɔʀɲ/ *adj* one-eyed

borne /bɔʀn/ ⟦1⟧ *nf* **(a)** ~ **(kilométrique)** kilometre (GB) marker **(b)** bollard (GB), post (US) **(c)** (fam) kilometre (GB) **(d)** (for electricity) terminal ⟦2⟧ **bornes** *nf pl* **leur ambition est sans ~s** their ambition knows no bounds ∎ ~ **téléphonique** emergency telephone; taxi stand telephone

borné, ~**e** /bɔʀne/ *adj* narrow-minded

borner: se borner /bɔʀne/ [1] *v refl* (+ *v être*) **(a) se ~ à faire** to content oneself with doing **(b) se ~ à faire** to be limited to doing

bornette /bɔʀnɛt/ *nf*: docking station for a hired bicycle

bosquet /bɔskɛ/ *nm* grove

bosse /bɔs/ *nf* **(a)** hump **(b)** bump **(c)** dent IDIOMS **avoir la ~ de** (fam) to have a flair for; **rouler sa ~** to knock about

bosseler /bɔsle/ [19] *vtr* to dent; (in metalwork) to emboss

bosser /bɔse/ [1] *vi* (fam) to work

bossu, ~**e** /bɔsy/ *adj* hunchbacked

bot /bo/ *adj m* **pied** ~ club foot

botanique /bɔtanik/ ⟦1⟧ *adj* botanical ⟦2⟧ *nf* botany

botte /bɔt/ *nf* **(a)** boot **(b)** (of flowers) bunch; (of hay) bale ∎ ~**s de caoutchouc** wellington boots

botter /bɔte/ [1] *vtr* **(a) ça le botte!** (fam) he loves it! **(b)** to kick

bottin® /bɔtɛ̃/ *nm* telephone directory

bottine /bɔtin/ *nf* ankle-boot

bouc /buk/ *nm* **(a)** billy goat **(b)** goatee ∎ ~ **émissaire** scapegoat

boucan /bukã/ *nm* (fam) din, racket (colloq)

✍ **bouche** /buʃ/ *nf* mouth; **faire la fine ~ devant qch** to turn one's nose up at sth ∎ ~ **d'aération** air vent; ~ **d'égout** manhole; ~ **d'incendie** fire hydrant; ~ **de métro** tube (GB) *or* subway (US) entrance

bouché, ~**e¹** /buʃe/ ⟦1⟧ *pp* ▶ BOUCHER¹ ⟦2⟧ *pp adj* **(a)** blocked **(b)** ⟨profession⟩ oversubscribed **(c)** (fam) dim (colloq) **(d) cidre ~** bottled cider

bouche-à-bouche /buʃabuʃ/ *nm inv* mouth-to-mouth resuscitation

bouche-à-oreille /buʃaɔʀɛj/ *nm inv* le ~ word of mouth

bouchée² /buʃe/ *nf* mouthful; **pour une ~ de pain** for next to nothing; **mettre les ~s doubles** to double one's efforts

boucher¹ /buʃe/ [1] **1** *vtr* (a) to cork
(b) to block; to clog (up)
(c) to fill ‹crack›
2 **se boucher** *v refl* (+ *v être*) (a) **se ~ le nez** to hold one's nose; **se ~ les oreilles** to put one's fingers in one's ears
(b) to get blocked
IDIOM **en ~ un coin à qn** (fam) to amaze sb

boucher², **-ère** /buʃe, ɛʀ/ *nm,f* butcher

boucherie /buʃʀi/ *nf* (a) butcher's shop
(b) butcher's trade
(c) slaughter

bouchon /buʃɔ̃/ *nm* (a) cork
(b) (screw)cap
(c) (of wax) plug
(d) traffic jam
(e) (in fishing) float

boucle /bukl/ *nf* (a) buckle; **~ d'oreille** earring
(b) curl
(c) loop
(d) (Comput) loop

bouclé, **~e** /bukle/ *adj* curly

boucler /bukle/ [1] *vtr* (a) to fasten ‹belt›
(b) (fam) to lock ‹door›
(c) (fam) to cordon off ‹district›
(d) (fam) to complete ‹investigation›
(e) (fam) to lock [sb] up
IDIOMS **la ~** (fam) to shut up; **~ la boucle** to come full circle

bouclier /buklije/ *nm* shield

bouddhisme /budism/ *nm* Buddhism

bouder /bude/ [1] *vi* to sulk

bouderie /budʀi/ *nf* sulking

boudin /budɛ̃/ *nm* ≈ blood sausage

boudiné, **~e** /budine/ *adj* podgy

boudiner /budine/ [1] *vtr* **être boudiné dans qch** to be squeezed into sth

boue /bu/ *nf* (a) (gen) (figurative) mud
(b) silt

bouée /bwe/ *nf* (a) rubber ring
(b) buoy
■ **~ de sauvetage** *or* **de secours** lifebelt (GB), life preserver (US)

boueux, **-euse** /buø, øz/ *adj* muddy

bouffant, **~e** /bufã, ãt/ *adj* (a) baggy
(b) ‹sleeves› puffed
(c) ‹hairstyle› bouffant

bouffe /buf/ *nf* (fam) (a) eating
(b) food
(c) meal

bouffée /bufe/ *nf* (of tobacco, steam) puff; **une ~ d'air frais** a breath of fresh air
■ **~ de chaleur** hot flush (GB), hot flash (US)

♂ indicates a very frequent word

bouffer /bufe/ (fam) [1] **1** *vtr* to eat
2 *vi* to eat; (greedily) to stuff oneself (colloq)

bouffi, **~e** /bufi/ *adj* puffy

bouffon /bufɔ̃/ *nm* (a) clown
(b) jester; buffoon

bouffonnerie /bufɔnʀi/ *nf*
(a) (actions) antics
(b) (for comic effect) buffoonery
(c) (intrinsic stupidity) ridiculousness
(d) (in theatre) farce

bougeoir /buʒwaʀ/ *nm* (a) candleholder
(b) candlestick

bougeotte /buʒɔt/ *nf* (fam) **avoir la ~** to be restless

♂ **bouger** /buʒe/ [13] **1** *vtr* to move
2 *vi* (a) to move
(b) (fam) ‹sector, company› to be on the move
(c) (fam) **ville qui bouge** lively town
3 **se bouger** *v refl* (+ *v être*) (fam) (a) to get a move on (colloq)
(b) to put some effort in

bougie /buʒi/ *nf* (a) candle
(b) (Tech) spark plug

bougonner /bugɔne/ [1] *vi* to grumble

bouillabaisse /bujabɛs/ *nf* fish soup

bouillant, **~e** /bujã, ãt/ *adj* boiling (hot)

bouille /buj/ *nf* (fam) face

bouilli, **~e** /buji/ ▶ BOUILLIR

bouillie /buji/ *nf* (a) gruel; **en ~** mushy; **mettre qn/qch en ~** to reduce sb/sth to a pulp
(b) baby cereal

bouillir /bujiʀ/ [31] *vi* (a) to boil
(b) to be seething (**de** with)

bouilloire /bujwaʀ/ *nf* kettle

bouillon /bujɔ̃/ *nm* (a) broth
(b) (Culin) stock
(c) **bouillir à gros ~s** to boil fiercely

bouillonnant, **~e** /bujɔnã, ãt/ *adj* ‹water› foaming; ‹person› lively

bouillonner /bujɔne/ [1] *vi* (a) to bubble
(b) **~ d'activité** to be bustling with activity

bouillotte /bujɔt/ *nf* hot-water bottle

♂ **boulanger**, **-ère** /bulãʒe, ɛʀ/ *nm,f* baker

♂ **boulangerie** /bulãʒʀi/ *nf* bakery

boulangerie-pâtisserie, *pl*
boulangeries-pâtisseries
/bulãʒʀipatisʀi/ *nf* bakery (*selling cakes and pastries*)

boule /bul/ *nf* (gen) ball; (in bowling) bowl; **mettre qch en ~** to roll sth up into a ball
■ **~ de neige** snowball; **~ Quiès®** earplug
IDIOMS **il a perdu la ~** (fam) he's gone mad; **mettre qn en ~** (fam) to make sb furious

bouleau, *pl* **~x** /bulo/ *nm* birch

bouledogue /buldɔg/ *nm* bulldog

boulet /bulɛ/ *nm* (a) **~ (de canon)** cannonball
(b) ball and chain
(c) (figurative) millstone

boulette /bulɛt/ *nf* (a) (of bread, paper) pellet

(b) ~ de viande meatball
(c) (fam) blunder
boulevard /bulvaʀ/ *nm* boulevard
■ ~ périphérique ring road (GB), beltway (US)
bouleversant, ~**e** /bulvɛʀsɑ̃, ɑ̃t/ *adj*
deeply moving
bouleversement /bulvɛʀsəmɑ̃/ *nm*
upheaval
bouleverser /bulvɛʀse/ [1] *vtr* **(a)** to move
[sb] deeply
(b) ‹experience› to shatter
(c) to turn [sth] upside down ‹house, files›
(d) to disrupt ‹schedule›
(e) to change [sth] dramatically ‹lifestyle›
boulier /bulje/ *nm* abacus
boulimie /bulimi/ *nf* bulimia
boulon /bulɔ̃/ *nm* bolt
boulot, -otte /bulo, ɔt/ [1] *adj* tubby
[2] *nm* (fam) **(a)** work
(b) job
boulotter /bulɔte/ [1] *vtr, vi* (fam) to eat
boum¹ /bum/ *nm* **(a)** bang
(b) (fam) en plein ~ ‹business› booming; faire
un ~ ‹birth rates› to soar
boum² /bum/ *nf* party
bouquet /bukɛ/ *nm* **(a)** ~ (de fleurs) bunch
of flowers; bouquet
(b) (of firework display) final flourish; c'est le
~! (fam) (figurative) that's the limit! (colloq)
bouquin /bukɛ̃/ *nm* (fam) book
bouquiner /bukine/ [1] *vtr, vi* (fam) to read
bourbier /buʀbje/ *nm* quagmire
bourde /buʀd/ *nf* blunder
bourdon /buʀdɔ̃/ *nm* bumblebee
bourdonnement /buʀdɔnmɑ̃/ *nm*
(of insect) buzzing; (of engine) hum; (of
plane) drone
bourdonner /buʀdɔne/ [1] *vi* to buzz; to
hum
bourg /buʀ/ *nm* market town
bourgeois, ~e /buʀʒwa, az/ [1] *adj*
bourgeois
[2] *nm,f* **(a)** middle-class person
(b) (in Ancien Regime) bourgeois
(c) burgher
bourgeoisie /buʀʒwazi/ *nf* **(a)** middle
classes
(b) bourgeoisie
bourgeon /buʀʒɔ̃/ *nm* bud; en ~s in bud
bourgeonner /buʀʒɔne/ [1] *vi* to bud
bourrage /buʀaʒ/ *nm* ~ de crâne
brainwashing
bourrasque /buʀask/ *nf* (of wind) gust
bourratif, -ive /buʀatif, iv/ *adj* very
filling, stodgy
bourre /buʀ/ *nf* (fam) être à la ~ to be
pushed for time
bourré, ~e /buʀe/ *adj* ‹train, museum›
packed; ‹case, bag› bulging (de with); ~ de
fric (fam) stinking rich (colloq)

bourreau, *pl* ~**x** /buʀo/ *nm* executioner
bourrelet /buʀlɛ/ *nm* roll of fat
bourrer /buʀe/ [1] *vtr* **(a)** to cram [sth] full;
to fill ‹pipe›
(b) (fam) ~ qn de to dose sb up with ‹medicine›
bourricot /buʀiko/ *nm* donkey
bourrique /buʀik/ *nf* **(a)** donkey
(b) (fam) pig-headed person
bourru, ~e /buʀy/ *adj* gruff
bourse /buʀs/ *nf* **(a)** grant (GB),
scholarship (US)
(b) purse
Bourse /buʀs/ *nf* **(a)** stock exchange
(b) shares; une société de ~ a broking
(GB) *or* brokerage (US) firm
boursicoter /buʀsikɔte/ [1] *vi* to dabble in
stocks and shares
boursier, -ière /buʀsje, ɛʀ/ [1] *adj* le
marché ~ share prices
[2] *nm,f* grant holder (GB), scholarship
student (US)
boursouflé, ~e /buʀsufle/ *adj*
(a) blistered
(b) puffy
(c) ‹body› bloated
bousculade /buskylad/ *nf* **(a)** jostling;
(accidental) crush
(b) rush
bousculer /buskyle/ [1] [1] *vtr* **(a)** to
push, to jostle ‹person›
(b) to rush
[2] se bousculer *v refl* (+ *v être*) to fall
over each other (pour faire to do)
bouse /buz/ *nf* une ~ (de vache) a cowpat
bousiller /buzije/ [1] *vtr* (fam) to wreck
‹engine›; to smash up ‹car›
boussole /busɔl/ *nf* compass
bout /bu/ *nm* **(a)** end; tip; (of shoe) toe; au ~
du jardin at the bottom of the garden; aller
jusqu'au ~ to go all the way; aller (jusqu') au
~ de to follow through ‹idea, demand›; elle
est à ~ she can't take any more; ne me
pousse pas à ~ don't push me; être à ~
d'arguments to have run out of arguments;
venir à ~ de to overcome ‹difficulty›; to get
through ‹task, meal›; au ~ du compte in the
end; à ~ portant at point-blank range
(b) (of bread, paper) piece; (of land) bit
■ ~ de chou (fam) sweet little thing (colloq);
~ d'essai screen test
IDIOMS tenir le bon ~ (fam) to be on the right
track; ne pas être au ~ de ses peines not to
be out of the woods yet
boutade /butad/ *nf* witticism
boute-en-train /butɑ̃tʀɛ̃/ *nmf inv* live
wire (figurative)
bouteille /butɛj/ *nf* (gen) bottle; (of
gas) cylinder
IDIOM prendre de la ~ (fam) to be getting
on (a bit)
boutique /butik/ *nf* shop (GB), store (US)

boutiquier, -ière /butikje, ɛʀ/ *nm,f* shopkeeper

bouton /butɔ̃/ *nm* **(a)** (on clothes) button
(b) (knob; button
(c) (Med) spot (GB), pimple (US)
(d) (flower) bud
■ ~ **démarrer** (Comput) start button; ~ **de fièvre** cold sore; ~ **de manchette** cuff link; ~ **d'or** buttercup; ~ **de porte** doorknob; ~ **retour** (Comput) back button

boutonner /butɔne/ [1] *vtr*, **se boutonner** *v refl* (+ *v être*) to button up

boutonneux, -euse /butɔnø, øz/ *adj* spotty (GB), pimply (US)

boutonnière /butɔnjɛʀ/ *nf* buttonhole

bouture /butyʀ/ *nf* cutting

bovin, ~e /bɔvɛ̃, in/ **1** *adj* bovine
2 *nm* bovine; **des ~s** cattle

box, *pl* **boxes** /bɔks/ *nm* **(a)** lock-up garage
(b) (for horse) stall
(c) (in bar) alcove
■ ~ **des accusés** (Law) dock

boxe /bɔks/ *nf* (Sport) boxing; ~ **française** savate

boxer /bɔkse/ [1] *vi* (Sport) to box

boxeur /bɔksœʀ/ *nm* (Sport) boxer

boyau, *pl* ~**x** /bwajo/ *nm* **(a)** gut
(b) catgut
(c) (for sausage) casing
(d) tubeless tyre (GB) *or* tire (US)

boycotter /bɔjkɔte/ [1] *vtr* to boycott

BP *written abbr* ▶ BOÎTE

bracelet /bʀaslɛ/ *nm* **(a)** bracelet; bangle
(b) wristband; ~ **de montre** watchstrap

braconnier /bʀakɔnje/ *nm* poacher

brader /bʀade/ [1] *vtr* **(a)** to sell cheaply
(b) to sell off

braderie /bʀadʀi/ *nf* **(a)** street market
(b) discount store
(c) clearance sale

braguette /bʀaɡɛt/ *nf* flies (GB), fly (US)

braille /bʀaj/ *nm* Braille

brailler /bʀaje/ [1] *vi* (fam) **(a)** to yell
(b) ⟨child, singer⟩ to bawl

braire /bʀɛʀ/ [58] *vi* to bray

braise /bʀɛz/ *nf* live embers

brancard /bʀɑ̃kaʀ/ *nm* stretcher

branchage /bʀɑ̃ʃaʒ/ *nm* branches

⚡ **branche** /bʀɑ̃ʃ/ *nf* **(a)** (of tree) branch
(b) **céleri en ~s** sticks of celery
(c) field, sector
(d) (of family) branch
(e) (of candelabra) branch; (of spectacles) arm; (of star) point

branché, ~e /bʀɑ̃ʃe/ *adj* (fam) trendy (colloq)

branchement /bʀɑ̃ʃmɑ̃/ *nm*
(a) (electrical) connection

⚡ indicates a very frequent word

(b) (for water) branch pipe; (for electricity) lead (GB), cable (US)

brancher /bʀɑ̃ʃe/ [1] *vtr* **(a)** to plug in
(b) to connect (up) ⟨water, electricity⟩
(c) (fam) ~ **qn sur** to get sb onto ⟨topic⟩
(d) (fam) **je vais au cinéma, ça te branche?** I'm going to the cinema, are you interested?

branchie /bʀɑ̃ʃi/ *nf* (of fish) gill

brandir /bʀɑ̃diʀ/ [3] *vtr* to brandish

branlant, ~e /bʀɑ̃lɑ̃, ɑ̃t/ *adj* ⟨chair⟩ rickety; ⟨tooth⟩ loose; ⟨argument⟩ shaky

branle /bʀɑ̃l/ *nm* **mettre qch en ~** to set [sth] in motion ⟨project, convoy⟩

branle-bas /bʀɑ̃lba/ *nm inv* commotion
■ ~ **de combat** (Mil) action stations

branler /bʀɑ̃le/ [1] *vi* ⟨wall⟩ to wobble; ⟨chair⟩ to be rickety; ⟨tooth⟩ to be loose

braquage /bʀakaʒ/ *nm* (fam) robbery

braquer /bʀake/ [1] **1** *vtr* **(a)** to point ⟨gun, camera⟩ (**sur, vers** at); to turn *or* fix ⟨eyes⟩ (**sur, vers** on)
(b) ~ **à gauche/droite** to turn hard left/right
(c) (fam) to point a gun at
(d) (fam) to rob ⟨bank⟩
(e) (fam) ~ **qn contre qn/qch** to turn sb against sb/sth
2 *vi* ⟨driver⟩ to turn the wheel full lock (GB) *or* all the way (US)
3 **se braquer** *v refl* (+ *v être*) to dig one's heels in

⚡ **bras** /bʀa/ *nm inv* **(a)** arm; ~ **dessus ~ dessous** arm in arm; **porter qch à bout de ~** (figurative) to keep sth afloat; **en ~ de chemise** in one's shirtsleeves
(b) manpower, labour (GB)
(c) (of river) branch; ~ **de mer** sound
(d) (of armchair) arm
■ ~ **droit** right hand man; ~ **de fer** arm wrestling; (figurative) trial of strength
IDIOMS **les ~ m'en tombent** I'm absolutely speechless; **avoir le ~ long** to have a lot of influence

brasier /bʀazje/ *nm* inferno

bras-le-corps: **à bras-le-corps** /abʀalkɔʀ/ *phr* ⟨lift⟩ bodily

brassage /bʀasaʒ/ *nm* **(a)** (of beer) brewing
(b) (mixing) (of people) intermingling; (of ideas, cultures) cross-fertilization

brassard /bʀasaʀ/ *nm* armband

brasse /bʀas/ *nf* (Sport) breaststroke

brasser /bʀase/ [1] *vtr* **(a)** to toss around ⟨ideas⟩; to shuffle around ⟨papers⟩; to intermingle ⟨population⟩; **il brasse des millions** he handles big money
(b) to brew ⟨beer⟩

brasserie /bʀasʀi/ *nf* **(a)** brasserie
(b) brewery

brasseur, -euse /bʀasœʀ, øz/ *nm,f* brewer

brassière /bʀasjɛʀ/ *nf* **(a)** baby's top
(b) crop top

brave /bʀav/ *adj* **(a)** nice; **un ∼ homme** a nice man
(b) brave; **un homme ∼** a brave man
braver /bʀave/ [1] *vtr* to defy ‹*person*›; to brave ‹*storm*›
bravo /bʀavo/ *excl* bravo!; well done!
bravoure /bʀavuʀ/ *nf* bravery
break /bʀɛk/ *nm* estate car (GB), station wagon (US)
brebis /bʀəbi/ *nf inv* ewe
brèche /bʀɛʃ/ *nf* **(a)** hole, gap
(b) (Mil) breach
bréchet /bʀeʃɛ/ *nm* wishbone
bredouille /bʀəduj/ *adj* empty-handed
bredouiller /bʀəduje/ [1] *vtr, vi* to mumble
☞ **bref, brève¹** /bʀɛf, bʀɛv/ ① *adj* brief; short
② *adv* **(en) ∼** in short
breloque /bʀəlɔk/ *nf* (on bracelet) charm
Brésil /bʀezil/ *pr nm* Brazil
Bretagne /bʀətaɲ/ *pr nf* Brittany
bretelle /bʀətɛl/ ① *nf* **(a)** (gen) strap
(b) slip road (GB), ramp (US)
② **bretelles** *nf pl* braces
breton, -onne /bʀətɔ̃, ɔn/ ① *adj* Breton
② *nm* (language) Breton
breuvage /bʀœvaʒ/ *nm* beverage
brève² /bʀɛv/ ① *adj f* ▸ BREF 1
② *nf* news flash
brevet /bʀəvɛ/ *nm* **∼ (d'invention)** patent
■ **∼ de pilote** pilot's licence (GB); **∼ de secourisme** first aid certificate; **∼ de technicien supérieur, BTS** advanced vocational diploma
breveter /bʀəvte/ [20] *vtr* **(faire) ∼** to patent
bréviaire /bʀevjɛʀ/ *nm* breviary
bribes /bʀib/ *nf pl* (of conversation) snatches
bric: de bric et de broc /dəbʀikeð(ə) bʀɔk/ *phr* ‹*furnished*› with bits and pieces
bric-à-brac /bʀikabʀak/ *nm inv* bric-à-brac
bricolage /bʀikɔlaʒ/ *nm* DIY (GB), do-it-yourself
bricole /bʀikɔl/ *nf* **acheter une ∼** to buy a little something; **des ∼s** bits and pieces
bricoler /bʀikɔle/ [1] ① *vtr* (fam) **(a)** to tinker with
(b) to throw [sth] together
② *vi* to do DIY (GB), to fix things (US)
bride /bʀid/ *nf* **(a)** bridle
(b) button loop
IDIOMS partir à ∼ abattue to dash off; **avoir la ∼ sur le cou** to have free rein
bridé, ∼e /bʀide/ *adj* **yeux ∼s** slanting eyes
brièvement /bʀijɛvmã/ *adv* briefly
brigade /bʀigad/ *nf* **(a)** (Mil) brigade
(b) (in police) squad
brigadier /bʀigadje/ *nm* **(a)** ≈ corporal

(b) fire chief
brigand /bʀigã/ *nm* brigand, bandit
brillamment /bʀijamã/ *adv* brilliantly
brillant, ∼e /bʀijã, ãt/ ① *adj* **(a)** bright; shiny; glistening
(b) brilliant
② *nm* (cut) diamond, brilliant
☞ **briller** /bʀije/ [1] *vi* **(a)** ‹*sun*› to shine; ‹*flame*› to burn brightly; ‹*gem*› to sparkle; ‹*nose*› to be shiny
(b) **∼ de** ‹*eyes*› to blaze with ‹*anger*›
(c) ‹*person*› to shine; **elle brille par son esprit** she's extremely witty
brimade /bʀimad/ *nf* bullying
brimer /bʀime/ [1] *vtr* **(a)** to bully
(b) **se sentir brimé** to feel picked on
brin /bʀɛ̃/ *nm* **(a)** (of parsley) sprig; (of straw) wisp; (of grass) blade
(b) **un ∼ de** a bit of
brindille /bʀɛ̃dij/ *nf* twig
bringue /bʀɛ̃g/ *nf* (fam) **(a)** drinking party
(b) rave-up (colloq)
(c) (girl) **(grande) ∼** beanpole
brinquebaler /bʀɛ̃kbale/ [1] *vi* ‹*load*› to rattle about; ‹*vehicle*› to jolt along
brio /bʀijo/ *nm* brilliance; (Mus) brio
brioche /bʀijɔʃ/ *nf* **(a)** brioche, (sweet) bun
(b) (fam) paunch
brioché, ∼e /bʀijɔʃe/ *adj* (Culin) brioche
brique /bʀik/ *nf* **(a)** brick
(b) (for milk, juice) carton
briquer /bʀike/ [1] *vtr* to polish [sth] up
briquet /bʀikɛ/ *nm* (cigarette) lighter
brise /bʀiz/ *nf* breeze; **bonne ∼** fresh breeze
brise-glace /bʀizglas/ *nm inv* icebreaker
☞ **briser** /bʀize/ [1] ① *vtr* **(a)** (gen) to break; to break down ‹*resistance*›
(b) to shatter ‹*dream*›
(c) to destroy ‹*organisation*›; to break ‹*person*›; to wreck ‹*career*›
② **se briser** *v refl* (+ *v être*) **(a)** to break
(b) ‹*dream*› to be shattered
(c) ‹*voice*› to break
brise-tout /bʀiztu/ *nm inv* (person) butterfingers
briseur, -euse /bʀizœʀ, øz/ *nm,f* wrecker
■ **∼ de grève** strike breaker
brisure /bʀizyʀ/ *nf* **(a)** crack
(b) fragment
britannique /bʀitanik/ *adj* British
Britannique /bʀitanik/ *nmf* **un/une ∼** a British man/woman; **les ∼s** the British (people)
broc /bʀo/ *nm* ewer
brocante /bʀɔkãt/ *nf* **(a)** bric-à-brac trade
(b) flea market
broche /bʀoʃ/ *nf* **(a)** brooch
(b) (for roasting) spit
(c) (in surgery) pin

brocher /bʀɔʃe/ [1] *vtr* to bind [sth] (with paper) ‹book›; **livre broché** paperback

brochet /bʀɔʃɛ/ *nm* (Zool) pike

brochette /bʀɔʃɛt/ *nf* (a) skewer
(b) kebab

brochure /bʀɔʃyʀ/ *nf* (a) booklet
(b) (travel) brochure

brocoli /bʀɔkɔli/ *nm* broccoli

broder /bʀɔde/ [1] *vtr, vi* to embroider

broderie /bʀɔdʀi/ *nf* embroidery

bromure /bʀɔmyʀ/ *nm* bromide

bronche /bʀɔ̃ʃ/ *nf* **les** ~**s** the bronchial tubes

broncher /bʀɔ̃ʃe/ [1] *vi* **sans** ~ without turning a hair

bronchite /bʀɔ̃ʃit/ *nf* bronchitis

bronzage /bʀɔ̃zaʒ/ *nm* (sun)tan

bronze /bʀɔ̃z/ *nm* bronze

bronzé, ~**e** /bʀɔ̃ze/ *adj* ‹person› (sun-)tanned

bronzer /bʀɔ̃ze/ [1] *vi* to get a tan, to go brown

brossage /bʀɔsaʒ/ *nm* (of hair, teeth) brushing

brosse /bʀɔs/ *nf* brush; **donner un coup de** ~ **à qch** to give sth a brush; **avoir les cheveux (taillés) en** ~ to have a crew cut

brosser /bʀɔse/ [1] **1** *vtr* (a) to brush; to scrub
(b) to give a quick outline of
2 se brosser *v refl* (+ *v être*) to brush oneself down; **se** ~ **les dents** to brush one's teeth

brouette /bʀuɛt/ *nf* wheelbarrow

brouhaha /bʀuaa/ *nm* hubbub

brouillard /bʀujaʀ/ *nm* fog

brouille /bʀuj/ *nf* (a) quarrel
(b) rift

brouiller /bʀuje/ [1] **1** *vtr* (a) to make [sth] cloudy ‹liquid›; to blur ‹text, vision›; ~ **les cartes** to confuse *or* cloud the issue
(b) to jam ‹signal›; to interfere with ‹reception›
2 se brouiller *v refl* (+ *v être*) (a) to fall out (**avec with**)
(b) ‹liquid› to become cloudy; ‹vision› to become blurred; ‹mind› to become confused; **avoir le teint brouillé** to look ill

brouillon, -**onne** /bʀujɔ̃, ɔn/ **1** *adj*
(a) untidy
(b) disorganized
(c) muddled
2 *nm* (a) rough draft
(b) rough paper

broussaille /bʀusaj/ *nf* (a) undergrowth
(b) scrub
(c) bushes

brousse /bʀus/ *nf* bush; **en pleine** ~ (fam) in the sticks (colloq)

brouter /bʀute/ [1] *vtr* to nibble; to graze

⚘ indicates a very frequent word

brouteur, -**euse** /bʀutœʀ, øz/ *nm,f* browser

broyer /bʀwaje/ [23] *vtr* (a) to grind ‹wheat›
(b) to crush
IDIOM ~ **du noir** to brood

broyeur, -**euse** /bʀwajœʀ, øz/ *nm* (machine) crusher, grinder

bru /bʀy/ *nf* daughter-in-law

brugnon /bʀyɲɔ̃/ *nm* nectarine

bruiner /bʀɥine/ [1] *v impers* to drizzle

bruissement /bʀɥismɑ̃/ *nm* (of leaves) rustle; (of brook) babbling

⚘ **bruit** /bʀɥi/ *nm* (a) noise; ~ **étouffé** thud; **un** ~ **de ferraille** a clang
(b) noise, din; ~ **infernal** *or* **d'enfer** awful racket; **sans** ~ silently
(c) **le film a fait beaucoup de** ~ the film attracted a lot of attention
(d) ~ **(de couloir)** rumour (GB)

bruitage /bʀɥitaʒ/ *nm* sound effects

bruiteur /bʀɥitœʀ/ *nm* sound effects engineer

brûlant, ~**e** /bʀylɑ̃, ɑ̃t/ *adj* (a) ‹tea› boiling hot; ‹sand, radiator, person› burning hot; ‹sun› blazing
(b) ‹issue› burning
(c) ‹passion› burning

brûlé, ~**e** /bʀyle/ **1** *nm,f* **un grand** ~ a third degree burns victim; **service des grands** ~**s** burns unit
2 *nm* **ça sent le** ~ there's a smell of burning

brûle-parfum(s) /bʀylpaʀfœ̃/ *nm inv* incense burner

brûle-pourpoint: à brûle-pourpoint /abʀylpuʀpwɛ̃/ *phr* point-blank

⚘ **brûler** /bʀyle/ [1] **1** *vtr* (a) to burn ‹papers›; to set fire to ‹house›
(b) to burn ‹fuel›; to use ‹electricity›
(c) ‹acid› to burn; ‹water› to scald; **j'ai les yeux qui me brûlent** my eyes are stinging
(d) (fam) ~ **un feu (rouge)** to jump (colloq) the lights
2 *vi* (a) ‹wood› to burn; ‹forest, town› to be on fire
(b) ~ **(d'envie) de faire** to be longing to do
3 se brûler *v refl* (+ *v être*) to burn oneself

brûlure /bʀylyʀ/ *nf* (a) burn; ~**s d'estomac** heartburn
(b) burn mark

brume /bʀym/ *nf* mist; fog; haze

brumeux, -**euse** /bʀymø, øz/ *adj* (a) hazy; misty
(b) ‹idea› hazy

brun, ~**e** /bʀœ̃, bʀyn/ **1** *adj* brown, dark; dark-haired
2 *nm,f* dark-haired man/woman
3 *nm* brown

brunir /bʀyniʀ/ [3] *vi* (a) ‹skin› to tan
(b) (Culin) to brown

brushing /bʀœʃiŋ/ *nm* blow-dry
brusque /bʀysk/ *adj* (a) ‹tone, person›
abrupt
(b) ‹movement› sudden; ‹bend› sharp
brusquement /bʀyskəmã/ *adv*
(a) abruptly
(b) suddenly; ‹brake› sharply
brusquer /bʀyske/ [1] *vtr* (a) to be brusque
with
(b) to rush
brut, ~e¹ /bʀyt/ *adj* (a) ‹material› raw; ‹oil›
crude; ‹stone› rough; ‹sugar› unrefined
(b) ‹cider, champagne› dry
(c) ‹salary› gross
brutal, ~e, *mpl* **-aux** /bʀytal, o/ *adj*
(a) ‹blow› violent; ‹pain, death› sudden
(b) ‹tone› brutal; ‹gesture, temper› violent
(c) stark
brutalement /bʀytalmã/ *adv* (a) ‹repress›
brutally; ‹close› violently
(b) ‹die, stop› suddenly
brutaliser /bʀytalize/ [1] *vtr* to ill-treat
brutalité /bʀytalite/ *nf* (a) brutality
(b) suddenness
brute² /bʀyt/ **1** *adj f* ▶ BRUT
2 *nf* brute; comme une ~ ‹hit› savagely
Bruxelles /bʀysɛl/ *pr n* Brussels
bruyant, ~e /bʀɥijã, ãt/ *adj* (a) noisy; loud
(b) resounding
BTS /beteɛs/ *nm; abbr* ▶ BREVET
bu, ~e /by/ ▶ BOIRE
buanderie /bɥãdʀi/ *nf* laundry room
buccal, ~e, *mpl* **-aux** /bykal, o/ *adj* oral
bûche /byʃ/ *nf* (a) log (of wood)
(b) (fam) tumble, fall
(c) (Culin) ~ de Noël yule log
bûcher¹ /byʃe/ [1] *vi* (fam) to slog away
(colloq)
bûcher² /byʃe/ *nm* (a) le ~ the stake
(b) (funeral) pyre
bûcheron /byʃʀɔ̃/ *nm* lumberjack
bûchette /byʃɛt/ *nf* (for fire) stick
bucolique /bykɔlik/ *adj* bucolic, pastoral
budget /bydʒɛ/ *nm* budget
budgétaire /bydʒetɛʀ/ *adj* ‹deficit› budget;
‹year› financial (GB), fiscal (US)
budgétiser /bydʒetize/ [1] *vtr* to include
[sth] in the budget
buée /bɥe/ *nf* (a) condensation
(b) steam
buffet /byfɛ/ *nm* (a) sideboard
(b) dresser
(c) (station) buffet
(d) (Culin) buffet
buffle /byfl/ *nm* buffalo
buis /bɥi/ *nm* (a) box tree
(b) boxwood
buisson /bɥisɔ̃/ *nm* (a) bush
(b) shrub

buissonnière /bɥisɔnjɛʀ/ *adj f* faire
l'école ~ to play truant (GB), to play hooky
(US) (colloq)
bulbe /bylb/ *nm* (Bot) bulb
bulgare /bylgaʀ/ *adj, nm* Bulgarian
Bulgarie /bylgaʀi/ *pr nf* Bulgaria
bulldozer /byldozœʀ/ *nm* bulldozer
bulle /byl/ *nf* (a) bubble
(b) speech bubble
bulletin /byltɛ̃/ *nm* (a) bulletin, report;
~ de santé medical bulletin
(b) certificate; ~ de naissance birth
certificate
(c) form; ~ de salaire payslip; ~ de
participation entry form
(d) bulletin, official publication
(e) ballot *or* voting paper; ~ de vote d'un
(électeur) absent absentee ballot
bulletin-réponse, *pl* **bulletins-
réponse** /byltɛ̃ʀepɔ̃s/ *nm* reply coupon
bulot /bylo/ *nm* whelk
buraliste /byʀalist/ *nmf* (a) (for smokers'
supplies) tobacconist; (for cigarettes and
newspapers) newsagent (GB), newsdealer (US)
(b) (counter staff) clerk
⚡ **bureau,** *pl* **~x** /byʀo/ *nm* (a) desk
(b) study
(c) office
(d) board
(e) (Comput) desktop
▪ ~ d'accueil reception; **Bureau international
du travail, BIT** International Labour Office,
ILO; ~ de poste post office; ~ de tabac
tobacconist's; ~ de vote polling station
bureaucratie /byʀokʀasi/ *nf*
bureaucracy
bureautique /byʀotik/ *nf* office
automation
burin /byʀɛ̃/ *nm* chisel
buriné, ~e /byʀine/ *adj* ‹face› craggy
burlesque /byʀlɛsk/ *adj* ludicrous; farcical
bus /bys/ *nm inv* bus
buse /byz/ *nf* (a) buzzard
(b) (fam) clot (GB) (colloq), clod (colloq)
business /biznɛs/ *nm inv*
(commercial) business; (private) affairs
busqué, ~e /byske/ *adj* ‹nose› hooked
buste /byst/ *nm* (a) (in sculpture) bust
(b) (Anat) chest
(c) bust, breasts
bustier /bystje/ *nm* (a) long-line bra
(b) bustier
⚡ **but** /by(t)/ *nm* (a) goal; aim, purpose; **aller
droit au ~** to go straight to the point
(b) (in football) goal
(c) (in archery) target
IDIOM déclarer de ~ en blanc to declare
point-blank
buté, ~e /byte/ *adj* stubborn, obstinate
buter /byte/ [1] *vi* ~ contre qch to trip over
sth; to bump into sth; ~ sur *or* contre to
come up against ‹obstacle›

butin /bytɛ̃/ nm (from robbery) haul
butiner /bytine/ [1] vi to gather pollen
butte /byt/ nf mound
   IDIOM **être en ~ à** to come up against
   ‹difficulties›; to be the butt of ‹jokes›
buvable /byvabl/ adj (a) ‹medicine› to be
   taken orally

(b) drinkable
buvard /byvaʀ/ nm **(papier)** ~ blotting
   paper
buvette /byvɛt/ nf refreshment area
buveur, -euse /byvœʀ, øz/ nm,f drinker;
   c'est un gros ~ he's a heavy drinker; **un** ~
   de thé/bière a tea/beer drinker

Cc

---

c, C /se/ nm inv c, C; **c cédille** c cedilla
c' ▶ CE 2
CA written abbr ▶ CHIFFRE
◦ **ça** /sa/ pron **(a)** that; this; **c'est pour ~**
   qu'il est parti that's why he left; **sans ~**
   otherwise; **~, c'est bizarre** that's strange; **la**
   rue a ~ de bien qu'elle est calme one good
   thing about the street is that it's quiet
   (b) it; that; **~ fait mal** it hurts; that hurts; **~**
   criait de tous les côtés there was shouting
   everywhere
   IDIOMS **~ alors!** well I never! (colloq); **~, oui!**
   (fam) definitely!; **elle est bête et méchante**
   avec ~ she's stupid and what's more she's
   nasty; **et avec ~?** anything else?; **rien que**
   ~! (ironic) is that all!; **c'est ~!** that's right!; **~**
   y est, ~ recommence! here we go again!; **~**
   y est, j'ai fini! that's it, I've finished!
caban /kabã/ nm sailor's jacket
cabane /kaban/ nf **(a)** hut
   (b) shed
   (c) (pop) prison
cabaret /kabaʀɛ/ nm cabaret
cabas /kaba/ nm shopping bag
cabillaud /kabijo/ nm cod
cabine /kabin/ nf cabin; cab; booth; cubicle
   ■ **~ d'essayage** fitting room; **~ de pilotage**
   cockpit; **~ téléphonique** phone box (GB),
   phone booth
cabinet /kabinɛ/ ⟦1⟧ nm **(a)** (gen) office;
   (of doctor, dentist) surgery (GB), office (US); (of
   judge) chambers
   (b) practice; **~ de médecins** medical
   practice; **ouvrir un ~** to set up in practice
   (c) agency
   (d) (Pol) cabinet; **~ ministériel** minister's
   personal staff
   ⟦2⟧ **cabinets** nm pl toilet
   ■ **~ de toilette** bathroom
cabinet-conseil, pl **cabinets-**
conseil /kabinɛkɔ̃sɛj/ nm firm of
   consultants
câble /kɑbl/ nm **(a)** cable; rope
   (b) cable television

câbler /kɑble/ [1] vtr **(a)** to install cable
   television in ‹house, town›
   (b) to cable ‹message›
cabochard, ~e /kabɔʃaʀ, aʀd/ adj
   (fam) stubborn
caboche /kabɔʃ/ nf (fam) head
cabosser /kabɔse/ [1] vtr to dent
cabot /kabo/ nm (fam) dog, mutt (colloq)
cabotin, ~e /kabɔtɛ̃, in/ adj **être ~** to like
   playing to the gallery
cabrer: se cabrer /kabʀe/ [1] v refl (+ v
   être) **(a)** ‹horse› to rear **(devant** at)
   (b) ‹person› to jib
cabri /kabʀi/ nm (Zool) kid
cabriole /kabʀijɔl/ nf (of clown, child) caper
CAC® /kak/ nm (abbr = **Compagnie**
   des agents de change) **indice ~ 40,**
   ~ 40 Paris Stock Exchange index
caca /kaka/ nm (baby talk) poo (GB) (colloq),
   poop (US) (colloq)
cacahuète /kakawɛt/ nf peanut
cacao /kakao/ nm cocoa
cacatoès /kakatɔes/ nm cockatoo
cachalot /kaʃalo/ nm sperm whale
cache¹ /kaʃ/ nm **se servir d'un ~ pour**
   apprendre une liste de vocabulaire to cover
   up the answers while learning a list of
   vocabulary
cache² /kaʃ/ nf **~ d'armes** arms cache
caché, ~e /kaʃe/ ⟦1⟧ pp ▶ CACHER
   ⟦2⟧ pp adj ‹beauty, sense› hidden; ‹pain,
   desire› secret
cache-cache /kaʃkaʃ/ nm inv hide and
   seek (GB), hide-and-go-seek (US)
cache-col /kaʃkɔl/ nm inv scarf
cachemire /kaʃmiʀ/ nm cashmere
cache-nez /kaʃne/ nm inv scarf, muffler
cache-pot /kaʃpo/ nm inv flowerpot
   holder
◦ **cacher** /kaʃe/ [1] ⟦1⟧ vtr to hide; **~ son jeu**
   (figurative) to keep one's cards close to one's
   chest; **~ qch à qn** to conceal sth from sb
   ⟦2⟧ **se cacher** v refl (+ v être) **(a)** to hide;
   (temporarily) to go into hiding; **il ne s'en cache**

◦ indicates a very frequent word

pas he makes no secret of it
(b) ‹sun› to disappear

cache-sexe /kaʃsɛks/ nm inv G-string

cachet /kaʃɛ/ nm (a) tablet
(b) (for letter) stamp; seal; ~ **de la poste** postmark
(c) (of actor) fee

cacheter /kaʃte/ [20] vtr to seal

cachette /kaʃɛt/ nf hiding place; **en** ~ on the sly

cachot /kaʃo/ nm (a) prison cell
(b) dungeon

cachotterie /kaʃɔtʀi/ nf little secret

cachottier, -ière /kaʃɔtje, ɛʀ/ adj secretive

cachou /kaʃu/ nm cachou

cacophonie /kakɔfɔni/ nf cacophony

cactus /kaktys/ nm inv cactus

c-à-d (written abbr = **c'est-à-dire**) ie

cadastre /kadastʀ/ nm (a) land register
(b) land registry

cadavérique /kadaveʀik/ adj ‹complexion› deathly pale

cadavre /kadavʀ/ nm corpse, body

caddie® /kadi/ nm shopping trolley

cadeau, pl ~**x** /kado/ [1] nm present, gift; **faire un** ~ **à qn** to give sb a present; **il ne fait pas de** ~**x** (examiner, judge) he's very strict
[2] (-)**cadeau** (combining form) gift; **papier(-)** ~ wrapping paper

cadenas /kadna/ nm padlock

cadence /kadɑ̃s/ nf (a) rhythm
(b) (of work) rate

cadet, -ette /kadɛ, ɛt/ [1] adj (a) younger
(b) youngest
[2] nm,f (a) younger son/daughter, younger child
(b) youngest child
(c) younger brother/sister
(d) (Sport) athlete between the ages of 15 and 17
IDIOM c'est le ~ **de mes soucis** it's the least of my worries

cadrage /kadʀaʒ/ nm (a) framing
(b) composition

cadran /kadʀɑ̃/ nm (of watch) face; (of meter) dial; ~ **solaire** sundial

♂ **cadre** /kadʀ/ [1] nm (a) frame
(b) setting; surroundings
(c) **cela sort du** ~ **de mes fonctions** that's not part of my duties
(d) framework
(e) executive; ~ **supérieur** senior executive; **les** ~**s moyens** middle management
(f) **faire partie des** ~**s** to be on the company's books
(g) (of bicycle) frame
(h) (on form) space, box
[2] **dans le cadre de** phr (a) on the occasion of
(b) (of negotiations) within the framework of;

(of campaign, plan) as part of

cadrer /kadʀe/ [1] [1] vtr to centre
(GB) ‹picture›
[2] vi to tally, to fit (**avec** with)

cadreur /kadʀœʀ/ nm cameraman

caduc, caduque /kadyk/ adj (a) obsolete
(b) (Law) null and void
(c) ‹leaf› deciduous

cætera ▶ ET CÆTERA

cafard /kafaʀ/ nm (a) (fam) depression; **avoir le** ~ to be down in the dumps (colloq)
(b) cockroach

cafardeux, -euse /kafaʀdø, øz/ adj glum; gloomy

♂ **café** /kafe/ nm (a) coffee; ~ **en grains** coffee beans; ~ **soluble** instant coffee
(b) café
■ ~ **crème** espresso with milk; ~ **au lait** coffee with milk; **peau** ~ **au lait** coffee-coloured (GB) skin

café-concert, pl **cafés-concerts** /kafekɔ̃sɛʀ/ nm café with live music

caféine /kafein/ nf caffeine

cafétéria /kafeteʀja/ nf cafeteria

cafetière /kaftjɛʀ/ nf coffee pot; coffee maker

cafouillage /kafujaʒ/ nm (fam) bungling (colloq)

cafouiller /kafuje/ [1] vi (fam) ‹person› to get flustered; ‹machine› to be on the blink (colloq); ‹organization› to get in a muddle

cage /kaʒ/ nf (a) cage
(b) (Sport, fam) goal
■ ~ **d'ascenseur** lift (GB) or elevator (US) shaft; ~ **d'escalier** stairwell; ~ **à lapins** rabbit hutch; ~ **thoracique** rib cage

cageot /kaʒo/ nm crate

cagette /kaʒɛt/ nf tray

cagibi /kaʒibi/ nm store cupboard

cagnotte /kaɲɔt/ nf (a) kitty
(b) jackpot

cagoule /kagul/ nf balaclava; hood

cahier /kaje/ nm (a) notebook;
(Sch) exercise book
(b) (in printing) section
■ ~ **de brouillon** rough book; ~ **de textes** homework notebook

cahin-caha /kaɛ̃kaa/ adv (fam) with difficulty

cahot /kao/ nm jolt

cahoter /kaɔte/ [1] vi ‹vehicle› to bounce along

cahoteux, -euse /kaɔtø, -øz/ adj ‹road› rough, bumpy

cahute /kayt/ nf hut, shack

caïd /kaid/ nm (in criminal underworld) boss; **jouer les** ~**s** to act tough

caillasse /kajas/ nf stones

caille /kɑj/ nf (Zool) quail

cailler /kaje/ [1] **1** **se cailler** *v refl* (+ *v être*) **(a)** ⟨*milk*⟩ to curdle
  (b) (fam) ⟨*person*⟩ to be freezing
  2 *v impers* (fam) **ça caille** it's freezing
caillot /kajo/ *nm* clot
caillou, *pl* ~**x** /kaju/ *nm* **(a)** pebble; **gros** ~ stone
  (b) (fam) nut (colloq); **ne plus avoir un poil sur le** ~ to be as bald as a coot (colloq)
caillouteux, -euse /kajutø, øz/ *adj* stony
caïman /kaimã/ *nm* cayman
Caire /kɛʀ/ *pr n* **le** ~ Cairo
caisse /kɛs/ *nf* **(a)** crate
  (b) (of car) shell, body
  (c) (pop) car
  (d) (for money) till; cash register; cash box; **les** ~**s de l'État** the Treasury coffers; **voler la** ~ to steal the takings
  (e) cash desk; (in supermarket) checkout (counter); (in bank) cashier's desk
  (f) fund
  ■ ~ **d'épargne** ≈ savings bank; ~ **noire** slush fund; ~ **à outils** toolbox
caissette /kɛsɛt/ *nf* small box *or* case
caissier, -ière /kesje, ɛʀ/ *nm,f* cashier
cajoler /kaʒɔle/ [1] *vtr* to cuddle ⟨*child*⟩
cajoleur, -euse /kaʒɔlœʀ, øz/ *adj* affectionate
cajou /kaʒu/ *nm* **noix de** ~ cashew nut
cake /kɛk/ *nm* fruit cake
cal /kal/ *nm* callus
calamar /kalamaʀ/ *nm* squid
calamité /kalamite/ *nf* disaster, calamity
calandre /kalãdʀ/ *nf* (Aut) (radiator) grille (GB)
calcaire /kalkɛʀ/ **1** *adj* ⟨*water*⟩ hard; ⟨*soil*⟩ chalky; ⟨*rock*⟩ limestone
  2 *nm* **(a)** limestone
  (b) fur (GB), sediment (US)
calciner /kalsine/ [1] *vtr* **(a)** to char; (in oven) to burn [sth] to a crisp
  (b) (in chemistry) to calcine
calcium /kalsjɔm/ *nm* calcium
calcul /kalkyl/ *nm* **(a)** calculation; **faire le** ~ **de qch** to calculate sth
  (b) arithmetic; ~ **mental** mental arithmetic
  (c) (scheming) calculation; **agir par** ~ to act out of self-interest
  (d) (Med) stone
calculateur, -trice¹ /kalkylatœʀ, tʀis/ *adj* calculating
calculatrice² /kalkylatʀis/ *nf* (pocket) calculator
calculer /kalkyle/ [1] **1** *vtr* **(a)** to calculate, to work out
  (b) to weigh up ⟨*advantages, chances*⟩; **tout bien calculé** all things considered
  (c) ~ **son coup** to plan one's move
  2 *vi* to calculate, to compute

calculette /kalkylɛt/ *nf* pocket calculator
cale /kal/ *nf* **(a)** wedge; (for wheel) chock; (for raising vehicle) block
  (b) (Naut) (ship's) hold
calé, ~e /kale/ *adj* (fam) bright; ~ **en qch** brilliant at sth
calebasse /kalbas/ *nf* calabash, gourd
calèche /kalɛʃ/ *nf* barouche, carriage
caleçon /kalsɔ̃/ *nm* **(a)** boxer shorts; ~ **long** long johns (colloq)
  (b) (for woman) leggings
calédonien, -ienne /kaledɔnjɛ̃, ɛn/ *adj* **(a)** New Caledonian
  (b) Caledonian
calembour /kalãbuʀ/ *nm* pun, play on words
calendrier /kalãdʀije/ *nm* **(a)** calendar
  (b) schedule
  (c) dates
cale-pied, *pl* ~**s** /kalpje/ *nm* toe clip
calepin /kalpɛ̃/ *nm* notebook
caler /kale/ [1] **1** *vtr* **(a)** to wedge ⟨*wheel*⟩; to steady ⟨*piece of furniture*⟩; to support ⟨*row of books*⟩; **bien calé dans mon fauteuil** ensconced in my armchair
  (b) (fam) **ça cale** it fills you up
  2 *vi* ⟨*car*⟩ to stall
  3 **se caler** *v refl* (+ *v être*) to settle (**dans** in)
calfeutrer /kalføtʀe/ [1] **1** *vtr* to stop up ⟨*crack*⟩; to draughtproof ⟨*door*⟩
  2 **se calfeutrer** *v refl* (+ *v être*) to shut oneself away
calibre /kalibʀ/ *nm* **(a)** (of gun) bore, calibre (GB); (of pipe, cable) diameter; **arme de gros** ~ large-bore weapon
  (b) (of eggs, fruit) size, grade
  (c) gauge
calibrer /kalibʀe/ [1] *vtr* **(a)** (Tech) to calibrate
  (b) to grade, to size ⟨*eggs, fruit*⟩
calice /kalis/ *nm* chalice
calife /kalif/ *nm* caliph
califourchon: à califourchon /akalifuʀʃɔ̃/ *phr* astride
câlin, ~e /kalɛ̃, in/ **1** *adj* affectionate
  2 *nm* cuddle
câliner /kaline/ [1] *vtr* to cuddle
calleux, -euse /kalø, øz/ *adj* calloused
calligraphie /kaligʀafi/ *nf* calligraphy
calligraphier /kaligʀafje/ [2] *vtr* to write [sth] in a decorative hand
callosité /kalozite/ *nf* callus
calmant, ~e /kalmã, ãt/ **1** *adj* soothing
  2 *nm* sedative
calmar /kalmaʀ/ *nm* squid
✦ **calme** /kalm/ **1** *adj* **(a)** ⟨*sea, situation*⟩ calm; ⟨*night*⟩ still; ⟨*place, life*⟩ quiet
  (b) ⟨*person*⟩ calm
  2 *nm* **(a)** peace (and quiet)

✦ indicates a very frequent word

(b) calm; (of crowd) calmness; (of night) stillness; **dans le** ~ peacefully **(c)** composure; **conserver son** ~ to keep calm; **du** ~**!** calm down!; quiet!

calmement /kalməmɑ̃/ *adv* calmly

calmer /kalme/ [1] **1** *vtr* **(a)** to calm down ‹person›; to calm ‹stock market›; to defuse ‹situation›; to tone down ‹discussion›; ~ **les esprits** to calm people down
(b) to ease ‹pain›; to take the edge off ‹hunger›; to quench ‹thirst›
2 **se calmer** *v refl* (+ *v être*) **(a)** ‹person, situation› to calm down; ‹agitation, storm› to die down; ‹debate› to quieten (GB) *or* quiet (US) down; ‹ardour› to cool
(b) ‹pain› to ease

calomnie /kalɔmni/ *nf* slander

calomnier /kalɔmnje/ [2] *vtr* to slander

calorie /kalɔri/ *nf* calorie

calorifère /kalɔrifɛr/ *adj* heat-conveying

calorique /kalɔrik/ *adj* calorie; **ration/ valeur** ~ calorie intake/content

calotte /kalɔt/ *nf* **(a)** skull cap
(b) (fam) slap
(c) ~ **glaciaire** icecap

calque /kalk/ *nm* **(a)** tracing
(b) tracing paper
(c) replica

calquer /kalke/ [1] *vtr* **(a)** to copy ‹behaviour›
(b) to trace ‹pattern, design› (**sur** from)

calumet /kalymɛ/ *nm* ~ **de la paix** peace pipe

calvados /kalvados/ *nm* calvados (*apple brandy distilled in Normandy*)

calvaire /kalvɛr/ *nm* **(a)** ordeal
(b) (monument) wayside cross
(c) Calvary

calvitie /kalvisi/ *nf* baldness

camaïeu /kamajø/ *nm* monochrome

⚘ **camarade** /kamarad/ *nmf* **(a)** friend; ~ **d'atelier** workmate
(b) comrade

camaraderie /kamaradri/ *nf* comradeship

Cambodge /kɑ̃bɔdʒ/ *pr nm* Cambodia

cambouis /kɑ̃bwi/ *nm* dirty grease

cambré, ~**e** /kɑ̃bre/ *adj* ‹back› arched; ‹foot, shoe› with a high instep

cambrer /kɑ̃bre/ [1] **1** *vtr* to curve, to arch
2 **se cambrer** *v refl* (+ *v être*) to arch one's back

cambriolage /kɑ̃brijɔlaʒ/ *nm* burglary

cambrioler /kɑ̃brijɔle/ [1] *vtr* to burgle (GB), to burglarize (US)

cambrioleur, -euse /kɑ̃brijɔlœr, øz/ *nm,f* burglar

cambrousse /kɑ̃brus/ *nf* (fam) **la** ~ the sticks (colloq), the country; **en pleine** ~ in the middle of nowhere

cambrure /kɑ̃bryr/ *nf* curve; (of foot) arch
■ ~ **des pieds** instep; ~ **des reins** small of the back

camée /kame/ *nm* cameo

caméléon /kameleɔ̃/ *nm* chameleon

camelote /kamlɔt/ *nf* (fam) junk (colloq)

camembert /kamɑ̃bɛr/ *nm*
(a) (Culin) Camembert
(b) (fam) pie chart

camer: se camer /kame/ [1] *v refl* (+ *v être*) (slang) to be on drugs

caméra /kamera/ *nf* (cine-)camera (GB), movie camera (US)

caméscope® /kameskɔp/ *nm* camcorder

⚘ **camion** /kamjɔ̃/ *nm* truck

camion-citerne, *pl* **camions-citernes** /kamjɔ̃sitɛrn/ *nm* tanker

camionnette /kamjɔnɛt/ *nf* van

camionneur /kamjɔnœr/ *nm* truck driver

camisole /kamizɔl/ *nf* camisole; ~ **de force** straitjacket

camomille /kamɔmij/ *nf* camomile

camouflage /kamuflaʒ/ *nm*
(a) (Mil) camouflage
(b) (figurative) concealing; disguising (**en** as)

camoufler /kamufle/ [1] *vtr* **(a)** (Mil) to camouflage
(b) to cover up ‹crime, mistake, truth›; to conceal ‹intention, feelings›
(c) to hide ‹money›

⚘ **camp** /kɑ̃/ *nm* **(a)** (gen) camp
(b) (Sport, Pol) side
IDIOM ficher (fam) **le** ~ to split (colloq), to leave

campagnard, ~**e** /kɑ̃paɲar, ard/ **1** *adj* country, rustic
2 *nm,f* country person

⚘ **campagne** /kɑ̃paɲ/ *nf* **(a)** country; (open) countryside
(b) campaign; **faire** ~ to campaign

campanule /kɑ̃panyl/ *nf* bellflower

campement /kɑ̃pmɑ̃/ *nm* camp, encampment

camper /kɑ̃pe/ [1] **1** *vtr* to portray ‹character›; to depict ‹landscape, scene›
2 *vi* to camp
3 **se camper** *v refl* (+ *v être*) **se** ~ **devant qn/qch** to stand squarely in front of sb/sth

campeur, -euse /kɑ̃pœr, øz/ *nm,f* camper

camphre /kɑ̃fr/ *nm* camphor

camping /kɑ̃piŋ/ *nm* **(a)** camping; **faire du** ~ **sauvage** to camp rough
(b) campsite (GB), campground (US)

camping-car, *pl* ~**s** /kɑ̃piŋkar/ *nm* camper, camper van (GB)

camping-gaz® /kɑ̃piŋgaz/ *nm inv* (gas) camping stove

campus /kɑ̃pys/ *nm inv* campus

Canada /kanada/ *pr nm* Canada

Canadair® /kanadɛʀ/ *nm* water bomber

♂ **canadien, -ienne¹** /kanadjɛ̃, ɛn/ *adj* Canadian

canadienne² /kanadjɛn/ *nf* (a) sheepskin-lined jacket
(b) ridge tent

canal, *pl* **-aux** /kanal, o/ *nm* (a) canal
(b) channel
(c) (Anat) duct

canalisation /kanalizasjɔ̃/ *nf* (a) pipe
(b) mains

canaliser /kanalize/ [1] *vtr* (a) to canalize ‹river›
(b) (figurative) to channel

canapé /kanape/ *nm* (a) sofa; ∼ convertible sofa bed
(b) (Culin) canapé

canaque /kanak/ *adj* Kanak

canard /kanaʀ/ *nm* (a) duck; ∼ laqué Peking duck
(b) (fam) rag (colloq), newspaper
(c) (Mus) wrong note
IDIOM ça ne casse pas trois pattes à un ∼ (fam) it's nothing to write home about

canarder /kanaʀde/ [1] *vtr* (fam) to snipe at

canari /kanaʀi/ *nm* canary

canasson /kanasɔ̃/ *nm* (pop) nag (colloq), horse

cancan /kɑ̃kɑ̃/ *nm* (a) (fam) gossip
(b) cancan

cancaner /kɑ̃kane/ [1] *vi* (fam) to gossip

cancer /kɑ̃sɛʀ/ *nm* cancer

Cancer /kɑ̃sɛʀ/ *pr nm* Cancer

cancéreux, -euse /kɑ̃seʀø, øz/ *adj* ‹cell› cancerous; ‹person› with cancer

cancérigène /kɑ̃seʀiʒɛn/ *adj* carcinogenic

cancérologie /kɑ̃seʀɔlɔʒi/ *nf* cancer research; service de ∼ cancer ward

cancre /kɑ̃kʀ/ *nm* dunce

cancrelat /kɑ̃kʀəla/ *nm* cockroach

candeur /kɑ̃dœʀ/ *nf* ingenuousness

candi /kɑ̃di/ *adj nm* sucre ∼ sugar candy

♂ **candidat, ∼e** /kɑ̃dida, at/ *nm,f*
(Pol) candidate; (for job) applicant; (in competition) contestant; être ∼ aux élections to stand for election (GB), to run for office (US); être ∼ (à un poste) to apply (for a post); pour la vaisselle, il n'y a pas beaucoup de ∼s! (humorous) when it comes to doing the dishes, there aren't many takers

candidature /kɑ̃didatyʀ/ *nf*
(a) candidature, candidacy; retirer sa ∼ to stand down (GB), to drop out (US)
(b) (for a post) application; faire acte de ∼ to apply

candide /kɑ̃did/ *adj* ingenuous

cane /kan/ *nf* (female) duck

caneton /kantɔ̃/ *nm* duckling

canette /kanɛt/ *nf* (a) ∼ (de bière) (small) bottle of beer
(b) can; ∼ de bière can of beer
(c) (of sewing machine) spool

canevas /kanva/ *nm inv* (a) canvas
(b) tapestry work
(c) (figurative) framework

caniche /kaniʃ/ *nm* poodle

canicule /kanikyl/ *nf* (a) scorching heat
(b) heatwave

canif /kanif/ *nm* penknife

canin, ∼e¹ /kanɛ̃, in/ *adj* canine

canine² /kanin/ *nf* canine (tooth)

caniveau, *pl* ∼**x** /kanivo/ *nm* gutter

cannabis /kanabis/ *nm* cannabis

canne /kan/ *nf* (a) (walking) stick
(b) (Bot) cane
■ ∼ à pêche fishing rod

canneberge /kanbɛʀʒ/ *nf* cranberry

cannelle /kanɛl/ *nf* cinnamon

cannette ▶ CANETTE

cannibale /kanibal/ *adj*, *nmf* cannibal

canoë /kanɔe/ *nm* (a) canoe
(b) canoeing

canoë-kayak /kanɔekajak/ *nm* canoeing

canon /kanɔ̃/ [1] *adj m inv* droit ∼ canon law
[2] *nm* (a) (big) gun; cannon; tirer un coup de ∼ to fire a gun; entendre des coups de ∼ to hear cannon fire
(b) (of firearm) barrel
(c) (Mus) canon; chanter en ∼ to sing in a round
(d) (rule, principle) canon
(e) (in religion) canon

cañon /kanjɔ̃, kanjɔn/ *nm* canyon

canonique /kanɔnik/ *adj* droit ∼ canon law; d'âge ∼ (humorous) of a venerable age

canoniser /kanɔnize/ [1] *vtr* to canonize

canot /kano/ *nm* (small) boat, dinghy; ∼ pneumatique rubber dinghy; ∼ de sauvetage (on ship) lifeboat; (on plane) life raft

canotier /kanɔtje/ *nm* boater

canson® /kɑ̃sɔ̃/ *nm* drawing paper

cantaloup /kɑ̃talu/ *nm* cantaloupe melon

cantate /kɑ̃tat/ *nf* cantata

cantatrice /kɑ̃tatʀis/ *nf* (opera) singer

cantine /kɑ̃tin/ *nf* (a) canteen (GB), cafeteria; manger à la ∼ ‹child› to have school dinners
(b) tin trunk

cantique /kɑ̃tik/ *nm* hymn, canticle

canton /kɑ̃tɔ̃/ *nm* canton

cantonade: à la cantonade /alakɑ̃tɔnad/ *phr* parler à la ∼ to speak to no-one in particular

cantonais, ∼e /kɑ̃tɔnɛ, ɛz/ [1] *adj* Cantonese
[2] *nm* (language) Cantonese

cantonal, ∼e, *mpl* **-aux** /kɑ̃tɔnal, o/ *adj* cantonal

cantonner /kɑ̃tɔne/ [1] *vtr* ~ qn dans un lieu to confine sb to a place; ~ qn dans le rôle de to reduce sb to the role of

cantonnier /kɑ̃tɔnje/ *nm* road-mender

cantonnière /kɑ̃tɔnjɛʀ/ *nf* pelmet

canular /kanylaʀ/ *nm* hoax

canule /kanyl/ *nf* cannula

canyon ▶ CAÑON

caoutchouc /kautʃu/ *nm* **(a)** rubber
(b) rubber plant
(c) rubber band

caoutchouteux, -euse /kautʃutø, øz/ *adj* rubbery

cap /kap/ *nm* **(a)** (in geography) cape
(b) mark; passer le ~ de la cinquantaine to pass the fifty mark
(c) (direction) course; maintenir le ~ to hold one's course; mettre le ~ sur to head for

Cap /kap/ *pr n* le ~ Cape Town

CAP /seape/ *nm*: *abbr* ▶ CERTIFICAT

✦ **capable** /kapabl/ *adj* capable (de faire of doing); ils sont bien ~s de nous mentir I wouldn't put it past them to lie to us

✦ **capacité** /kapasite/ ⒈ *nf* **(a)** ability
(b) capacity
⒉ **capacités** *nf pl* (talent) abilities

cape /kap/ *nf* cape; cloak
IDIOM rire sous ~ to laugh up one's sleeve

capeline /kaplin/ *nf* wide-brimmed hat

CAPES /kapɛs/ *nm* (*abbr* = certificat d'aptitude professionnelle à l'enseignement secondaire*) *secondary school teaching qualification*

capharnaüm /kafaʀnaɔm/ *nm* shambles (colloq)

capillaire /kapilɛʀ/ ⒈ *adj* **(a)** capillary
(b) soins ~s hair care
⒉ *nm* capillary

✦ **capitaine** /kapitɛn/ *nm* **(a)** (Mil) (in army, navy) ≈ captain
(b) (Sport) captain

capitainerie /kapitɛnʀi/ *nf* port authority

✦ **capital, ~e¹**, *mpl* **-aux** /kapital, o/ ⒈ *adj* **(a)** ⟨importance⟩ major; ⟨role, question⟩ key; il est ~ de faire it's essential to do
(b) ⟨letter⟩ capital
(c) peine ~e capital punishment
⒉ *nm* **(a)** capital
(b) le ~ humain/industriel human/industrial resources
⒊ **capitaux** *nm pl* capital, funds

capitale² /kapital/ *nf* **(a)** capital (city)
(b) capital (letter); en ~s d'imprimerie in block capitals

capitalisation /kapitalizasjɔ̃/ *nf* capitalization

capitaliser /kapitalize/ [1] *vtr* to capitalize

capitalisme /kapitalism/ *nm* capitalism

capitaliste /kapitalist/ *adj*, *nmf* capitalist

capitonner /kapitɔne/ [1] *vtr* to pad

capitulation /kapitylasjɔ̃/ *nf* capitulation (devant to); ~ sans conditions unconditional surrender

capituler /kapityle/ [1] *vi* to capitulate

caporal, *pl* **-aux** /kapɔʀal, o/ *nm* (Mil) (in army) ≈ corporal

capot /kapo/ *nm* (Aut) bonnet (GB), hood (US)

capotage /kapɔtaʒ/ *nm* collapse

capote /kapɔt/ *nf* **(a)** great-coat
(b) (of car, pram) hood (GB), top
(c) (fam) ~ (anglaise) condom

capoter /kapɔte/ [1] *vi* **(a)** to collapse
(b) ⟨car⟩ to overturn

câpre /kɑpʀ/ *nf* caper

caprice /kapʀis/ *nm* **(a)** (of person) whim; céder aux ~s de qn to indulge sb's whims; c'est un ~ de la nature (of plant, animal) it's a freak of nature
(b) faire un ~ to throw a tantrum

capricieusement /kapʀisjøzmɑ̃/ *adv* capriciously; whimsically

capricieux, -ieuse /kapʀisjø, øz/ *adj* ⟨person⟩ capricious; ⟨machine⟩ temperamental; ⟨weather⟩ changeable; ⟨destiny⟩ fickle

capricorne /kapʀikɔʀn/ *nm* capricorn beetle

Capricorne /kapʀikɔʀn/ *pr nm* Capricorn

capsule /kapsyl/ *nf* **(a)** (of bottle) cap; top
(b) (Med) capsule
(c) ~ spatiale space capsule

capter /kapte/ [1] *vtr* **(a)** to get ⟨channel, programme⟩; to pick up ⟨signal⟩
(b) to catch ⟨attention⟩
(c) to soak up ⟨light⟩

captif, -ive /kaptif, iv/ *adj*, *nm,f* captive

captivant, ~e /kaptivɑ̃, ɑ̃t/ *adj* enthralling; gripping; riveting; captivating

captiver /kaptive/ [1] *vtr* ⟨beauty⟩ to captivate; ⟨music⟩ to enthrall; ⟨story, person⟩ to fascinate

captivité /kaptivite/ *nf* captivity

capture /kaptyʀ/ *nf* capture

capturer /kaptyʀe/ [1] *vtr* to capture

capuche /kapyʃ/ *nf* hood; à ~ with a hood

capuchon /kapyʃɔ̃/ *nm* **(a)** (of garment) hood
(b) (of pen) cap

capucine /kapysin/ *nf* nasturtium

caquet /kake/ *nm* prattle; rabattre le ~ à qn (fam) to put sb in his/her place

caqueter /kakte/ [20] *vi* ⟨hen⟩ to cackle

✦ **car¹** /kaʀ/ *conj* because, for

car² /kaʀ/ *nm* bus; ~ de police police van; ~ (de ramassage) scolaire school bus

carabine /kaʀabin/ *nf* rifle

carabiné, ~e /kaʀabine/ adj (fam) ⟨fever⟩ raging; ⟨cold⟩ stinking (colloq)

caracoler /kaʀakɔle/ [1] vi (a) to be well ahead
(b) ⟨horse⟩ to prance; ⟨rider⟩ to parade

♂ **caractère** /kaʀaktɛʀ/ nm
(a) (written) character; ~s d'imprimerie block capitals; en petits/gros ~s in small/large print
(b) nature, temperament; avoir mauvais ~ to be bad-tempered
(c) (personality) character; il n'a aucun ~ he's got no backbone
(d) (of house, place) character
(e) characteristic
(f) nature; à ~ commercial of a commercial nature
IDIOM avoir un ~ de cochon (fam), avoir un sale ~ to have a vile temper

caractériel, -ielle /kaʀakteʀjɛl/ adj ⟨problems⟩ emotional; ⟨person⟩ disturbed

caractériser /kaʀakteʀize/ [1] **1** vtr to characterize
2 se caractériser v refl (+ v être) to be characterized

♂ **caractéristique** /kaʀakteʀistik/ **1** adj characteristic
2 nf characteristics

carafe /kaʀaf/ nf carafe

caraïbe /kaʀaib/ adj Caribbean

Caraïbes /kaʀaib/ pr nf pl Caribbean (islands)

carambolage /kaʀɑ̃bɔlaʒ/ nm pile-up

caramboler /kaʀɑ̃bɔle/ [1] vtr to collide with

caramel /kaʀamɛl/ nm (a) caramel
(b) toffee (GB), toffy (US); ~ mou ≈ fudge

carapace /kaʀapas/ nf shell, carapace

carat /kaʀa/ nm carat; or 18 ~s 18-carat gold

caravane /kaʀavan/ nf (a) caravan (GB), trailer (US)
(b) (convoy) caravan

caravelle /kaʀavɛl/ nf (boat) caravel

carbone /kaʀbɔn/ nm (a) carbon
(b) carbon paper
(c) sheet of carbon paper

carbonique /kaʀbɔnik/ adj carbonic; neige ~ dry ice

carbonisé, ~e /kaʀbɔnize/ adj burned-out; charred; burned to a cinder

carboniser /kaʀbɔnize/ [1] vtr (a) to carbonize
(b) to reduce [sth] to ashes

carburant /kaʀbyʀɑ̃/ nm fuel

carburateur /kaʀbyʀatœʀ/ nm carburettor (GB), carburetor (US)

carburer /kaʀbyʀe/ [1] vi (a) il carbure au vin rouge he runs on red wine

(b) to work flat out

carcan /kaʀkɑ̃/ nm (a) (device) iron collar
(b) ~ administratif administrative constraints

carcasse /kaʀkas/ nf carcass

carcéral, ~e, mpl -aux /kaʀseʀal, o/ adj prison

cardan /kaʀdɑ̃/ nm universal joint

cardiaque /kaʀdjak/ adj être ~ to have a heart condition; crise ~ heart attack

cardinal, ~e, mpl -aux /kaʀdinal, o/
1 adj cardinal
2 nm (a) cardinal
(b) cardinal number

cardiologie /kaʀdjɔlɔʒi/ nf cardiology

cardiologue /kaʀdjɔlɔg/ nmf cardiologist

carême /kaʀɛm/ nm le ~ Lent

carence /kaʀɑ̃s/ nf (a) (Med) deficiency
(b) lack
(c) les ~s de la loi the shortcomings of the law

carène /kaʀɛn/ nf hull (below the waterline)

caressant, ~e /kaʀɛsɑ̃, ɑ̃t/ adj affectionate; soft

caresse /kaʀɛs/ nf caress, stroke; faire une ~ or des ~s à to stroke

caresser /kaʀese/ [1] vtr (a) to stroke, to caress; ~ qn du regard to look at sb lovingly
(b) to entertain ⟨hope, idea⟩; to cherish ⟨dream⟩
IDIOM ~ qn dans le sens du poil to stay on the right side of sb

cargaison /kaʀgɛzɔ̃/ nf (a) cargo
(b) (fam) load

cargo /kaʀgo/ nm (Naut) freighter, cargo ship

caricatural, ~e, mpl -aux /kaʀikatyʀal, o/ adj (a) grotesque
(b) caricatural

caricature /kaʀikatyʀ/ nf caricature; c'est une ~ de procès it's a mockery of a trial

caricaturer /kaʀikatyʀe/ [1] vtr to caricature

caricaturiste /kaʀikatyʀist/ nmf caricaturist

carie /kaʀi/ nf la ~ (dentaire) (tooth) decay; avoir une carie to have a hole in one's tooth

carié, ~e /kaʀje/ adj decayed

carier: se carier /kaʀje/ [2] v refl (+ v être) ⟨tooth⟩ to decay

carillon /kaʀijɔ̃/ nm (a) (of church) (set of) bells; (tune) chimes
(b) (chiming) clock; (sound) chimes
(c) (door) chimes

carillonner /kaʀijone/ [1] vi (a) ⟨bells⟩ to ring out, to peal out
(b) (at door) to ring (loudly)

caritatif, -ive /kaʀitatif, iv/ adj charitable; une association caritative a charity

carlingue /kaʀlɛ̃g/ nf (of plane) cabin

carmin /kaʀmɛ̃/ nm, adj inv carmine

carnage /kaʀnaʒ/ nm carnage, massacre

carnassier, -ière /kaʀnasje, ɛʀ/ adj carnivorous

carnaval, pl ~s /kaʀnaval/ nm carnival

carnet /kaʀnɛ/ nm (a) notebook
(b) (of tickets, vouchers, stamps) book
■ ~ de chèques chequebook (GB), checkbook (US); ~ de correspondance (Sch) mark book; ~ de santé health record

carnivore /kaʀnivɔʀ/ ① adj carnivorous
② nm carnivore

carotide /kaʀɔtid/ adj, nf carotid

carotte /kaʀɔt/ nf carrot
IDIOM manier la ~ et le bâton to use stick-and-carrot tactics

caroube /kaʀub/ nf carob

carpe¹ /kaʀp/ nm (Anat) carpus

carpe² /kaʀp/ nf (fish) carp
IDIOM il est resté muet comme une ~ he never said a word

carpette /kaʀpɛt/ nf (a) rug
(b) (fam) doormat (colloq)

⚬ **carré, ~e** /kaʀe/ ① adj (a) ⟨shape⟩ square; il est ~ d'épaules he has broad shoulders
(b) ⟨metre, root⟩ square
② nm (a) square
(b) (of sky, ground) patch; (of chocolate) piece; avoir une coupe au ~ to have one's hair cut in a bob; ~ blanc 'suitable for adults only' sign on French TV
(c) (in mathematics) square
(d) ~ d'agneau rack of lamb

carreau, pl ~x /kaʀo/ nm (a) (floor) tile; (wall) tile
(b) window-pane; faire les ~x to clean the windows
(c) (on paper) square; (on fabric) check
(d) (in cards) diamonds
IDIOMS rester sur le ~ (fam) to be left high and dry (colloq); se tenir à ~ (fam) to watch one's step

carrefour /kaʀfuʀ/ nm (a) junction; crossroads
(b) (figurative) crossroads

carrelage /kaʀlaʒ/ nm (a) tiled floor
(b) tiles

carreler /kaʀle/ [19] vtr to tile

carrelet /kaʀlɛ/ nm plaice

carrément /kaʀemɑ̃/ adv (a) la situation devient ~ inquiétante quite frankly the situation is becoming worrying; il vaut ~ mieux les jeter it would be better just to throw them out
(b) completely; dans un cas pareil, appelle ~ la police in such a case, don't hesitate to call the police
(c) ⟨ask, say⟩ straight out; ⟨express⟩ clearly
(d) allez-y ~! go straight ahead!

⚬ **carrière** /kaʀjɛʀ/ nf (a) career; faire ~ dans to make a career in

(b) quarry; ~ de sable sandpit

carriole /kaʀjɔl/ nf (a) cart
(b) (fam) jalopy (colloq), car

carrossable /kaʀɔsabl/ adj suitable for motor vehicles

carrosse /kaʀɔs/ nm (horse-drawn) coach

carrosserie /kaʀɔsʀi/ nf (a) bodywork
(b) coachbuilding
(c) body repair work

carrossier /kaʀɔsje/ nm coachbuilder

carrousel /kaʀuzɛl/ nm merry-go-round, carousel

carrure /kaʀyʀ/ nf (a) shoulders
(b) calibre (GB)

cartable /kaʀtabl/ nm (a) schoolbag, satchel
(b) briefcase

⚬ **carte** /kaʀt/ nf (a) card; ~ à jouer playing card
(b) pass
(c) map; chart
(d) ~ génétique genetic map
(e) menu; repas à la ~ à la carte meal
■ ~ d'abonnement season ticket; ~ d'adhérent membership card; ~ bleue® credit card; ~ de crédit credit card; ~ grise logbook; ~ d'identité ID card; ~ orange® season ticket (in the Paris region); ~ postale postcard; ~ à puce smart card; ~ de réduction discount card; ~ de retrait (automatique) cashcard; ~ de séjour resident's permit; ~ SIM SIM card; ~ vermeil® senior citizen's railcard; ~ des vins wine list; ~ de visite (social) visiting card; (professional) business card; ~ vitale social insurance smart card; ~ de vœux greetings card

cartel /kaʀtɛl/ nm (a) cartel
(b) coalition

carter /kaʀtɛʀ/ nm (of engine) crankcase; (of gearbox) casing

cartilage /kaʀtilaʒ/ nm (a) (Anat, Zool) cartilage
(b) (Culin) gristle

cartomancie /kaʀtɔmɑ̃si/ nf fortune-telling

cartomancien, -ienne /kaʀtɔmɑ̃sjɛ̃, ɛn/ nm,f fortune-teller

carton /kaʀtɔ̃/ nm (a) cardboard; en ~ ⟨folder⟩ cardboard; ⟨cups⟩ paper
(b) (cardboard) box
(c) card
■ ~ à dessin portfolio
IDIOM faire un ~ (fam) to do great (colloq)

cartonné, ~e /kaʀtɔne/ adj couverture ~e (of book) hard cover

cartonner /kaʀtɔne/ (fam) [1] vi
(a) (Sport) to score
(b) (do well) ⟨film⟩ to be extremely successful

carton-pâte /kaʀtɔ̃pɑt/ nm inv pasteboard

cartouche /kaʀtuʃ/ *nf* **(a)** cartridge; (of gas) refill
(b) ∼ **de cigarettes** carton of cigarettes

♂ **cas** /ka/ 1 *nm inv* case; **auquel** ∼ in which case; **au** ∼ **où il viendrait** in case he comes; **prends ta voiture, au** ∼ **où** take your car, just in case; **en** ∼ **de besoin** if necessary; **en** ∼ **de décès** in the event of death; **le** ∼ **échéant** if need be; **dans le** ∼ **contraire, vous devrez…** should the opposite occur, you will have to…; **dans le meilleur/pire des** ∼ at best/worst; **en aucun** ∼ under no circumstances; **c'est le** ∼ **de le dire!** you can say that again!; **être dans le même** ∼ **que qn** to be in the same position as sb; **n'aggrave pas ton** ∼ don't make things worse for yourself; **un** ∼ **rare** a rare occurrence; **c'est un** ∼ **de renvoi** it's grounds for dismissal
2 **en tout cas**, **en tous les cas** *phr* **(a)** in any case, at any rate
(b) at least
■ ∼ **de conscience** moral dilemma; ∼ **social** socially disadvantaged person
IDIOM il a fait grand ∼ **de son avancement** he made a big thing of his promotion

casanier, -ière /kazanje, ɛʀ/ *adj* ‹person› stay-at-home; ‹existence› unadventurous

casaque /kazak/ *nf* (of jockey) jersey, silk

cascade /kaskad/ *nf* **(a)** waterfall
(b) stunt

cascadeur, -euse /kaskadœʀ, øz/ *nm,f* stuntman/stuntwoman

case /kaz/ *nf* **(a)** hut, cabin
(b) (in board games) square
(c) (on form) box
■ ∼ **départ** (in board game) start; **retour à la** ∼ **départ** (figurative) back to square one
IDIOM il lui manque une ∼ (fam) he's got a screw loose (colloq)

caser /kaze/ (fam) [1] 1 *vtr* **(a)** to put, to stick (colloq)
(b) to marry off
(c) to find a place *or* job for
2 **se caser** *v refl* (+ *v être*) to get married

caserne /kazɛʀn/ *nf* barracks
■ ∼ **de sapeurs-pompiers** fire station

casher /kaʃɛʀ/ *adj inv* kosher

casier /kazje/ *nm* **(a)** (in gym) locker
(b) pigeonhole
(c) ∼ **judiciaire** police record

casino /kazino/ *nm* casino

casque /kask/ *nm* **(a)** helmet; crash helmet; safety helmet
(b) headphones
(c) hairdryer

casqué, ∼e /kaske/ *adj* helmeted

casquette /kaskɛt/ *nf* cap; **porter plusieurs** ∼**s** (figurative) to wear several hats

cassant, ∼e /kasã, ãt/ *adj* **(a)** brittle
(b) curt, abrupt

♂ indicates a very frequent word

casse[1] /kas/ *nm* (pop) break-in, heist (US) (colloq)

casse[2] /kas/ *nf* **(a)** breakage
(b) breaker's yard, scrap yard; **mettre à la** ∼ to scrap

cassé, ∼e /kase/ *adj* ‹voice› hoarse

casse-cou /kasku/ *nmf inv* daredevil

casse-croûte /kaskrut/ *nm inv* snack

casse-noisettes /kasnwazɛt/, **casse-noix** /kasnwa/ *nm inv* nutcrackers

♂ **casser** /kase/ [1] 1 *vtr* to break ‹object, bone›; to crack ‹nut›; ∼ **les prix** to slash prices; ∼ **la figure** (fam) **à qn** to beat sb up (colloq)
2 *vi* **(a)** to break
(b) (fam) ‹couple› to split up
3 **se casser** *v refl* (+ *v être*) **(a)** to break
(b) **se** ∼ **une** *or* **la jambe** to break one's leg; **se** ∼ **la figure** (fam) ‹pedestrian› to fall over (GB) *or* down; ‹venture› to fail; ‹people› to have a scrap (colloq); **il ne s'est pas cassé la tête** (fam) he didn't exactly strain himself
(c) (fam) to go away
IDIOMS ∼ **les pieds** (fam) **à qn** to annoy sb; ∼ **la croûte** to eat; **ça te prendra trois heures, à tout** ∼ (fam) it'll take you three hours at the very most

casserole /kasʀɔl/ *nf* saucepan, pan
IDIOM chanter comme une ∼ (fam) to sing atrociously

casse-tête /kastɛt/ *nm inv* **(a)** headache, problem
(b) puzzle

cassette /kasɛt/ *nf* **(a)** tape, cassette
(b) casket

casseur /kasœʀ/ *nm* **(a)** scrap dealer
(b) rioting demonstrator

cassis /kasis/ *nm inv* **(a)** blackcurrant
(b) (in road) dip

cassonade /kasɔnad/ *nf* soft brown sugar

cassoulet /kasulɛ/ *nm*: meat and bean stew

cassure /kasyʀ/ *nf* **(a)** break
(b) split

castagnettes /kastaɲɛt/ *nf pl* castanets

caste /kast/ *nf* **(a)** caste
(b) (derogatory) (social) class

castor /kastɔʀ/ *nm* beaver

castrer /kastʀe/ [1] *vtr* to castrate

cataclysme /kataklism/ *nm* cataclysm

catacombes /katakɔ̃b/ *nf pl* catacombs

catadioptre /katadjɔptʀ/ *nm* reflector

catalepsie /katalɛpsi/ *nf* catalepsy

catalogue /katalɔg/ *nm* catalogue (GB); **acheter sur** ∼ to buy by mail order

cataloguer /katalɔge/ [1] *vtr* **(a)** to catalogue (GB) ‹objects›
(b) to label ‹people›

catalyse /kataliz/ *nf* catalysis

catalytique /katalitik/ *adj* catalytic

catamaran /katamaRɑ̃/ *nm* catamaran

cataplasme /kataplasm/ *nm* poultice

catapulter /katapylte/ [1] *vtr* to catapult

cataracte /kataRakt/ *nf* cataract

catastrophe /katastʀɔf/ *nf* disaster; **en ∼** in a panic; **atterrissage en ∼** crash landing

catastropher /katastʀɔfe/ [1] *vtr* to devastate

catastrophique /katastʀɔfik/ *adj* disastrous

catch /katʃ/ *nm* wrestling

catcheur, -euse /katʃœR, øz/ *nm,f* wrestler

catéchisme /kateʃism/ *nm* catechism

⚬ **catégorie** /kategɔʀi/ *nf* **(a)** category; **de première/deuxième ∼** top-/low-grade
(b) (of staff) grade
(c) (in sociology) group
(d) (Sport) class

catégorique /kategɔʀik/ *adj* categorical

cathédrale /katedʀal/ *nf* cathedral

cathode /katɔd/ *nf* cathode

catholicisme /katɔlisism/ *nm* (Roman) Catholicism

⚬ **catholique** /katɔlik/ *adj, nmf* Catholic; **ce n'est pas très ∼** (humorous) (fam) it's a bit unorthodox

cauchemar /koʃmaR/ *nm* nightmare

causant, ∼e /kozɑ̃, ɑ̃t/ *adj* (fam) talkative

⚬ **cause** /koz/ *nf* **(a)** cause; **pour la ∼ de la liberté** in the cause of freedom
(b) reason; **pour ∼ de maladie** because of illness; **avoir pour ∼ qch** to be caused by sth; **à ∼ de** because of
(c) case; **être en ∼** ⟨*system, fact*⟩ to be at issue; ⟨*person*⟩ to be involved; **mettre hors de ∼** (gen) to clear; **remettre en ∼** to call [sth] into question ⟨*policy, right*⟩; to cast doubt on ⟨*project, efficiency*⟩; to undermine ⟨*efforts*⟩; **remise en ∼** (of system) reappraisal; **avoir gain de ∼** to win one's case
IDIOM en toute connaissance de ∼ in full knowledge of the facts

⚬ **causer** /koze/ [1] **1** *vtr* **(a)** to cause; **∼ des soucis** to give cause for concern
(b) (fam) to talk about; **∼ travail** to talk shop
2 causer de *v+prep* to talk about
3 *vi* to talk; to chat

causette /kozɛt/ *nf* (fam) chat; **faire la ∼** to have a little chat

caustique /kostik/ *adj* caustic

cautériser /koteRize/ [1] *vtr* to cauterize

caution /kosjɔ̃/ *nf* **(a)** (when renting) deposit; (in finance) guarantee, security; (Law) bail
(b) support

cautionner /kosjone/ [1] *vtr* **(a)** to give one's support to
(b) to stand surety for

cavalcade /kavalkad/ *nf* **(a)** stampede, rush
(b) cavalcade

cavale /kaval/ *nf* (fam) escape; **en ∼** on the run

cavaler /kavale/ [1] *vi* (fam) to rush about

cavalerie /kavalʀi/ *nf* cavalry

cavaleur, -euse /kavalœR, øz/ *adj* (fam) **être ∼** to be a womanizer/man-chaser

cavalier, -ière /kavalje, ɛR/ **1** *adj* cavalier
2 *nm,f* **(a)** (horse) rider; **être bon ∼** to be a good rider
(b) (dancing) partner
3 *nm* **(a)** cavalryman
(b) (in chess) knight
IDIOM faire ∼ seul to go it alone

cave /kav/ *nf* cellar; **avoir une bonne ∼** to have good wines

caveau, pl ∼x /kavo/ *nm* vault

caverne /kavɛRn/ *nf* cavern

caviar /kavjaR/ *nm* caviar

cavité /kavite/ *nf* cavity

CCP /sesepe/ *nm: abbr* ▶ COMPTE

CD /sede/ *nm* (*abbr* = **compact disc**) CD

CD-I /sedei/ *nm inv* (*abbr* = **compact disc interactif**) CD-I

⚬ **ce** /sə/ **1** (**cet** /sɛt/ *before vowel or mute h*, **cette** /sɛt/, *pl* **ces** /se/) *adj* **(a)** this; that; **∼ crayon(-ci)** this pencil; **∼ livre(-là)** that book; **cette nuit** tonight; last night; **un de ces jours** one of these days
(b) (fam) **cet entretien, ça s'est bien passé?** how did the interview go?
(c) **et pour ces dames?** what are the ladies having?
(d) **elle a eu cette chance que la corde a tenu** she was lucky in that the rope held
(e) **cette arrogance!** what arrogance!; **j'ai un de ces rhumes!** I've got an awful cold!
2 (**c'** *before e*) *pron* **qui est-∼?** who's that?; who is it?; **∼ faisant** in so doing; **c'est tout dire** that says it all; **fais ∼ que tu veux** do what you like; **c'est ∼ à quoi il a fait allusion** that's what he was alluding to; **il a fait faillite, ∼ qui n'est pas surprenant** he's gone bankrupt, which is hardly surprising; **il tient à ∼ que vous veniez** he's very keen that you should come; **∼ que c'est grand!** it's so big!

CE /sea/ *nm: abbr* ▶ COURS

CEAM *nf* (*abbr* = **Carte Européenne d'Assurance Maladie**) EHIC

⚬ **ceci** /səsi/ *pron* this; **à ∼ près que** except that; **cet hôtel a ∼ de bien que...** one good thing about this hotel is that...

cécité /sesite/ *nf* blindness

⚬ **céder** /sede/ [14] **1** *vtr* **(a)** to give up ⟨*seat, share*⟩; to yield ⟨*right*⟩; to make over ⟨*property*⟩; **∼ le passage** to give way; **∼ la place** (figurative) to give way
(b) to sell
2 céder à *v+prep* to give in to, to yield to
3 *vi* **(a)** to give in
(b) ⟨*beam*⟩ to give way; ⟨*handle*⟩ to break off; ⟨*door*⟩ to yield

cédille /sedij/ nf cedilla
cèdre /sɛdʀ/ nm cedar
CEE /seəə/ nf: abbr ▶ COMMUNAUTÉ
CEEA /seəəa/ nf (abbr = **Communauté européenne de l'énergie atomique**) EAEC
CEI /seəi/ nf: abbr ▶ COMMUNAUTÉ
ceinture /sɛ̃tyʀ/ nf (a) belt
(b) waistband
(c) girdle
(d) waist; **avoir de l'eau jusqu'à la ~** to be waist-deep in water
(e) (Sport) waist hold; **~ noire** black belt
(f) ring
■ **~ de sauvetage** lifebelt; **~ de sécurité** safety or seat belt
IDIOMS faire **~** (fam) to go without; **se serrer la ~** to tighten one's belt
ceinturer /sɛ̃tyʀe/ [1] vtr to encircle
ceinturon /sɛ̃tyʀɔ̃/ nm belt
⚜ **cela** /səla/ pron

■ Note Cela and ça are equivalent in many cases. See the entry ça for more information.
– Cela is used in formal contexts and in the expressions shown below.

(a) it; that; **quant à ~** as for that; **~ dit** having said that
(b) **~ va sans dire** it or that goes without saying; **voyez-vous ~!** did you ever hear of such a thing!
célébration /selebʀasjɔ̃/ nf celebration
⚜ **célèbre** /selebʀ/ adj famous
célébrer /selebʀe/ [14] vtr (a) to celebrate ‹event, mass›; to perform ‹rite›
(b) to praise ‹person›
célébrité /selebʀite/ nf (a) fame
(b) celebrity
céleri /sɛlʀi/ nm (a) celery
(b) celeriac
céleri-rave, pl **céleris-raves** /sɛlʀiʀav/ nm celeriac
céleste /selɛst/ adj celestial; heavenly; divine
célibat /seliba/ nm (a) single status
(b) celibacy
célibataire /selibatɛʀ/ **1** adj single
2 nmf bachelor/single woman
celle ▶ CELUI
celle-ci ▶ CELUI-CI
celle-là ▶ CELUI-LÀ
celles-ci ▶ CELUI-CI
celles-là ▶ CELUI-LÀ
cellier /selje/ nm cellar
cellophane® /selɔfan/ nf cellophane®
cellulaire /selylɛʀ/ adj cell; cellular
cellule /selyl/ nf (a) cell
(b) unit; **~ familiale** family unit
cellulite /selylit/ nf (a) cellulite
(b) cellulitis

⚜ indicates a very frequent word

celte /sɛlt/ adj, nm Celtic
Celte /sɛlt/ nmf Celt
⚜ **celui** /səlɥi/, **celle** /sɛl/, mpl **ceux** /sø/, fpl **celles** /sɛl/ pron the one; **le train du matin ou ~ du soir?** the morning train or the evening one?; **ceux, celles** those; the ones; **ceux d'entre vous qui veulent partir** those of you who want to leave; **ceux qu'il a vendus** the ones he sold; **faire ~ qui n'entend pas** to pretend not to hear
celui-ci /səlɥisi/, **celle-ci** /sɛlsi/, mpl **ceux-ci** /søsi/, fpl **celles-ci** /sɛlsi/ pron
(a) this one; **ceux-ci, celles-ci** these
(b) **je n'ai qu'une chose à dire et c'est celle-ci** I have only one thing to say and it's this
(c) **elle essaya la fenêtre mais celle-ci était coincée** she tried the window but it was jammed; **il entra, suivi de son père et de son frère; ~ portait un paquet** he came in, followed by his father and his brother; the latter was carrying a parcel
celui-là /səlɥila/, **celle-là** /sɛlla/, mpl **ceux-là** /søla/, fpl **celles-là** /sɛlla/ pron
(a) that one; **ceux-là, celles-là** those (ones)
(b) **si je n'ai qu'un conseil à te donner, c'est ~** if I only have one piece of advice for you, it's this
(c) the former
(d) **il fit une autre proposition, plus réaliste celle-là** he made another proposal, a more realistic one this time
(e) **il exagère, ~!** that guy's pushing it a bit! (colloq)
(f) (fam) **elle est bien bonne, celle-là!** that's a good one!; **je ne m'attendais pas à celle-là** I didn't expect that!; **~ même** the very one
cendre /sɑ̃dʀ/ nf ash
cendré, **~e** /sɑ̃dʀe/ adj blond **~** ash blond
cendrier /sɑ̃dʀije/ nm ashtray
Cène /sɛn/ nf la **~** the Last Supper
censé, **~e** /sɑ̃se/ adj être **~** faire to be supposed to do
censeur /sɑ̃sœʀ/ nm (Sch) school official in charge of discipline
censure /sɑ̃syʀ/ nf (a) censorship
(b) board of censors
(c) censure
censurer /sɑ̃syʀe/ [1] vtr (a) to censor
(b) to ban
⚜ **cent** /sɑ̃/ **1** adj a hundred, one hundred
2 nm (a) hundred
(b) (division of euro) (cent)
3 **pour cent** phr per cent
IDIOMS faire les **~** pas to pace up and down; être aux **~** coups (fam) to be worried sick (colloq); attendre **~** sept ans (fam) to wait for ages
⚜ **centaine** /sɑ̃tɛn/ nf (a) hundred
(b) **une ~** about a hundred
centenaire /sɑ̃tnɛʀ/ **1** adj hundred-year-old, centenarian
2 nmf **c'est une ~** she's a hundred years old
3 nm centenary, centennial

centième /sɑ̃tjɛm/ *adj* hundredth

centilitre /sɑ̃tilitʀ/ *nm* centilitre (GB)

centime /sɑ̃tim/ *nm* (Hist) centime; ∼ [d'euro] cent

centimètre /sɑ̃timɛtʀ/ *nm* **(a)** centimetre (GB)
(b) ne pas avancer d'un ∼ not to move an inch
(c) tape measure

♦ **central**, ∼**e**[1], *mpl* **-aux** /sɑ̃tʀal, o/ [1] *adj* **(a)** central; **court** ∼ (in tennis) centre (GB) court; **ordinateur** ∼ host computer
(b) main
[2] *nm* ∼ **(téléphonique)** (telephone) exchange

centrale[2] /sɑ̃tʀal/ *nf* **(a)** power station
(b) prison

centraliser /sɑ̃tʀalize/ [1] *vtr* to centralize

centralisme /sɑ̃tʀalism/ *nm* centralism

♦ **centre** /sɑ̃tʀ/ *nm* centre (GB); **il se prend pour le ∼ du monde** he thinks the whole world revolves around him
■ ∼ **aéré** children's outdoor activity centre (GB); ∼ **commercial** shopping centre (GB); ∼ **de documentation et d'information, CDI** learning resources centre (GB); ∼ **hospitalier** hospital complex; ∼ **hospitalier universitaire, CHU** ≈ teaching hospital

centrer /sɑ̃tʀe/ [1] *vtr* to centre (GB)

centre-ville, *pl* **centres-villes** /sɑ̃tʀəvil/ *nm* town centre (GB), city centre (GB)

centrifuge /sɑ̃tʀifyʒ/ *adj* centrifugal

centrifugeuse /sɑ̃tʀifyʒøz/ *nf* **(a)** juice extractor
(b) centrifuge

centriste /sɑ̃tʀist/ *adj, nmf* centrist

centuple /sɑ̃typl/ *nm* **dix mille est le ∼ de cent** ten thousand is a hundred times one hundred; **au ∼** a hundred times over

cep /sɛp/ *nm* ∼ **(de vigne)** vine stock

cépage /sepaʒ/ *nm* grape variety; ∼ **cabernet** Cabernet grape

cèpe /sɛp/ *nm* cep

♦ **cependant** /səpɑ̃dɑ̃/ [1] *conj* yet, however
[2] **cependant que** *phr* whereas, while

céramique /seʀamik/ *nf* **(a)** ceramic
(b) ceramics

cerceau, *pl* ∼**x** /sɛʀso/ *nm* hoop

♦ **cercle** /sɛʀkl/ *nm* **(a)** circle; **en ∼** in a circle; **décrire des ∼s** ‹plane, bird› to circle (overhead); **le ∼ de famille** the family circle
(b) circle, society; club
(c) hoop

cercler /sɛʀkle/ [1] *vtr* to hoop ‹barrel›; **les noms cerclés en rouge** the names circled in red

cercueil /sɛʀkœj/ *nm* coffin

céréale /seʀeal/ *nf* cereal, grain

céréalier, -ière /seʀealje, ɛʀ/ *adj* ‹production› cereal; ‹region› cereal-growing

cérébral, ∼**e**, *mpl* **-aux** /seʀebʀal, o/ *adj* **(a)** cerebral
(b) intellectual

cérémonial, *pl* ∼**s** /seʀemɔnjal/ *nm* ceremonial

cérémonie /seʀemɔni/ [1] *nf* ceremony; **tenue** *or* **habit de** ∼ ceremonial dress
[2] **cérémonies** *nf pl* ceremony; **faire des ∼s** to stand on ceremony; **sans ∼s** ‹dinner, invitation› informal; ‹receive› informally

cérémonieux, -ieuse /seʀemɔnjø, øz/ *adj* ceremonious; **d'un air ∼** ceremoniously

cerf /sɛʀ/ *nm* stag

cerfeuil /sɛʀfœj/ *nm* chervil

cerf-volant, *pl* **cerfs-volants** /sɛʀvɔlɑ̃/ *nm* **(a)** kite
(b) stag beetle

cerise /s(ə)ʀiz/ *nf* cherry

cerisier /s(ə)ʀizje/ *nm* cherry (tree)

cerne /sɛʀn/ *nm* ring

cerné, ∼**e** /sɛʀne/ *adj* **avoir les yeux ∼s** to have rings under one's eyes

cerner /sɛʀne/ [1] *vtr* **(a)** to surround
(b) to define ‹problem›; to figure out ‹person›; to determine ‹personality›
(c) to outline ‹drawing›

♦ **certain**, ∼**e** /sɛʀtɛ̃, ɛn/ [1] *adj* **(a)** **être ∼ de** to be certain *or* sure of
(b) ‹fact› certain, sure; ‹date, price, influence› definite; ‹rate› fixed
[2] *det* **elle restera un ∼ temps** she'll stay for some time; **un ∼ nombre d'erreurs** a certain number of mistakes; **d'une ∼e manière** in a way; **il avait déjà un ∼ âge** he was already getting on in years
[3] **certains, certaines** *det pl* some; **à ∼s moments** sometimes, at times
[4] **certains, certaines** *pron pl* some people; **∼s d'entre eux** some of them

♦ **certainement** /sɛʀtɛnmɑ̃/ *adv* **(a)** most probably
(b) certainly; **mais ∼!** certainly!, of course!

♦ **certes** /sɛʀt/ *adv* **ce ne sera ∼ pas facile mais...** admittedly it won't be easy but...

certificat /sɛʀtifika/ *nm* **(a)** certificate
(b) testimonial
■ ∼ **d'aptitude professionnelle, CAP** vocational training qualification; ∼ **de décès** death certificate; ∼ **médical** medical certificate; ∼ **de résidence** proof of residence; ∼ **de scolarité** proof of attendance (at school or university); ∼ **de travail** document from a previous employer giving dates and nature of employment

certifié, ∼**e** /sɛʀtifje/ *adj* **professeur ∼** fully qualified teacher

certifier /sɛʀtifje/ [2] *vtr* **(a)** to certify; **copie certifiée conforme** certified copy
(b) **elle m'a certifié que** she assured me that

certitude /sɛʀtityd/ *nf* (a) certainty; **on sait avec ~ que** we know for certain that (b) **avoir la ~ que** to be certain that

cérumen /seʀymɛn/ *nm* earwax

✓ **cerveau**, *pl* ~**x** /sɛʀvo/ *nm* (a) brain
(b) mind
(c) (person) brain (colloq); **exode** *or* **fuite des ~x** brain drain; **c'est un ~** he/she has an outstanding mind
(d) brains; nerve centre (GB)
IDIOM **avoir le ~ dérangé** to be deranged

cervelas /sɛʀvəla/ *nm* saveloy

cervelet /sɛʀvəlɛ/ *nm* cerebellum

cervelle /sɛʀvɛl/ *nf* (a) brains; ~ **de veau** (Culin) calf's brains
(b) (fam) **il n'a rien dans la ~** he's brainless; ~ **d'oiseau** birdbrain (colloq)

cervical, ~**e**, *mpl* -**aux** /sɛʀvikal, o/ *adj* cervical

ces ▸ CE 1

CES /seəɛs/ *nm: abbr* ▸ COLLÈGE

césar /sezaʀ/ *nm* César (*film award*)

césarienne /sezaʀjɛn/ *nf* caesarian (section)

cessation /sesasjɔ̃/ *nf* suspension

✓ **cesse** /sɛs/ **sans ~** constantly

✓ **cesser** /sese/ [1] **1** *vtr* to stop, to cease; to end; ~ **de faire** to stop doing; to give up doing
2 *vi* ‹activity› to cease; ‹wind› to drop; ‹rain› to stop; **faire ~** to put an end *or* a stop to, to end

cessez-le-feu /seselfø/ *nm inv* ceasefire

cession /sesjɔ̃/ *nf* transfer

c'est-à-dire /setadiʀ/ *phr* (a) that is (to say)
(b) ~ **que** which means (that); **'le travail est trop dur'—'~?'** 'the work is too hard'—'what do you mean?'

cet ▸ CE 1

CET /seate/ *nm: abbr* ▸ COLLÈGE

cette ▸ CE 1

ceux ▸ CELUI

ceux-ci ▸ CELUI-CI

ceux-là ▸ CELUI-LÀ

CFDT /seɛfdete/ *nf* (*abbr* = **Confédération française démocratique du travail**) CFDT (*French trade union*)

CGC /seʒese/ *nf* (*abbr* = **Confédération générale des cadres**) CGC (*French trade union*)

CGT /seʒete/ *nf* (*abbr* = **Confédération générale du travail**) (*French trade union*)

chacal, *pl* ~**s** /ʃakal/ *nm* jackal

✓ **chacun**, ~**e** /ʃakœ̃, yn/ *pron* (a) each (one); **ils ont ~ sa** *or* **leur chambre** they each have their own room
(b) everyone; ~ **pour soi** every man for himself

chagrin, ~**e** /ʃagʀɛ̃, in/ **1** *adj* despondent
2 *nm* grief; **faire du ~ à qn** to cause sb grief; **avoir du ~** to be sad; **avoir un gros ~** to be very upset; ~ **d'amour** unhappy love affair

chagriner /ʃagʀine/ [1] *vtr* (a) to pain, to grieve
(b) to worry

chahut /ʃay/ *nm* racket (colloq)

chahuter /ʃayte/ [1] **1** *vtr* to play up ‹teacher›; to heckle ‹speaker›
2 *vi* to mess around

✓ **chaîne** /ʃɛn/ **1** *nf* (a) chain; **attacher qn avec des ~s** to chain sb up; **des catastrophes en ~** a series of disasters; **réaction en ~** chain reaction
(b) assembly line; **produire (qch) à la ~** to mass-produce (sth)
(c) network; ~ **de solidarité** support network
(d) ~ **(de télévision)** (television) channel
(e) ~ **hi-fi/stéréo** hi-fi/stereo system
2 **chaînes** *nf pl* snow chains
■ ~ **de fabrication** production line

chaînette /ʃɛnɛt/ *nf* chain

chaînon /ʃɛnɔ̃/ *nm* link; ~ **manquant** missing link

✓ **chair** /ʃɛʀ/ **1** *adj inv* flesh-coloured (GB)
2 *nf* flesh; meat; **bien en ~** plump
■ ~ **de poule** gooseflesh, goose pimples; **donner la ~ de poule à qn** ‹cold› to give sb gooseflesh; ‹fear› to make sb's flesh creep

chaire /ʃɛʀ/ *nf* (a) pulpit
(b) (at university) chair
(c) rostrum

✓ **chaise** /ʃɛz/ *nf* chair
■ ~ **haute** high-chair; ~ **longue** deckchair; ~ **roulante** wheelchair
IDIOM **être assis entre deux ~s** to be in an awkward position

châle /ʃɑl/ *nm* shawl

chalet /ʃalɛ/ *nm* chalet

✓ **chaleur** /ʃalœʀ/ **1** *nf* (a) heat; warmth; **coup de ~** heat stroke; ~ **animale** body heat
(b) (of person, welcome, colour) warmth
(c) (Zool) **(être) en ~** (to be) on heat
2 **chaleurs** *nf pl* **les grandes ~s** the hot season

chaleureusement /ʃaløʀøzmɑ̃/ *adv* warmly; wholeheartedly

chaleureux, -**euse** /ʃaløʀø, øz/ *adj* ‹person, greeting› warm; ‹audience› enthusiastic

challenge /ʃalɑ̃ʒ/ *nm*
(a) (Sport) tournament
(b) trophy

challenge(u)r /ʃalɑ̃ʒœʀ/ *nm* challenger

chaloupe /ʃalup/ *nf* (a) rowing boat (GB), rowboat (US)
(b) (motor) launch

✓ indicates a very frequent word

chalumeau, *pl* ∼**x** /ʃalymo/ *nm* blowtorch

chalut /ʃaly/ *nm* trawl

chalutier /ʃalytje/ *nm* **(a)** trawler
(b) trawlerman

chamailler: se chamailler /ʃamaje/ [1]
v refl (+ *v être*) (fam) to squabble

chamarré, ∼**e** /ʃamaʀe/ *adj* **(a)** richly
ornamented
(b) brightly coloured (GB)

chambard /ʃɑ̃baʀ/ *nm* (fam) din, racket
(colloq)

chambardement /ʃɑ̃baʀdəmɑ̃/ *nm*
(fam) **(a)** shake-up (colloq)
(b) mess

chambouler /ʃɑ̃bule/ [1] *vtr* (fam) **(a)** to
upset ⟨*plans, routine*⟩
(b) to turn [sth] upside down ⟨*house*⟩; to mess
[sth] up ⟨*papers*⟩

chambranle /ʃɑ̃bʀɑ̃l/ *nm* frame

✦ **chambre** /ʃɑ̃bʀ/ *nf* **(a)** bedroom; room;
∼ **pour une personne** single room; ∼ **à deux
lits** twin room; **faire** ∼ **à part** to sleep in
separate rooms
(b) musique de ∼ chamber music
(c) (in parliament) house
(d) (in administration) chamber
■ ∼ **à air** inner tube; ∼ **d'amis** guest room;
∼ **de commerce** chamber of commerce; ∼ **à
coucher** bedroom; bedroom suite; **'**∼**s d'hôte'**
'bed and breakfast'; ∼ **noire** camera obscura;
darkroom

chambrée /ʃɑ̃bʀe/ *nf* (Mil) soldiers
occupying barrack room

chambrer /ʃɑ̃bʀe/ [1] *vtr* **(a)** to bring [sth]
to room temperature
(b) (fam) (mock) to tease

chameau, *pl* ∼**x** /ʃamo/ *nm* (Zool) camel

chamelier /ʃaməlje/ *nm* camel driver

chamelle /ʃamɛl/ *nf* she-camel

chamois /ʃamwa/ *nm* (Zool) chamois

✦ **champ** /ʃɑ̃/ **1** *nm* field; (figurative) field,
domain; **en pleins** ∼**s** in open country; **avoir
le** ∼ **libre** to have a free hand
2 **à tout bout de champ** *phr* (fam) all
the time
■ ∼ **de courses** racetrack

champagne /ʃɑ̃paɲ/ *nm* champagne

champagnisé /ʃɑ̃paɲize/ *adj* **vin** ∼
sparkling wine

champenois, ∼**e** /ʃɑ̃pənwa, az/ *adj* **(a)** of
the Champagne region
(b) méthode ∼**e** champagne method

champêtre /ʃɑ̃pɛtʀ/ *adj* ⟨*scene*⟩ rural;
bal ∼ village dance; **déjeuner** ∼ country
picnic

✦ **champignon** /ʃɑ̃piɲɔ̃/ *nm*
(a) (Culin) mushroom; ∼ **vénéneux** toadstool
(b) (Bot, Med) fungus
(c) (fam) throttle, accelerator
■ ∼ **atomique** mushroom cloud; ∼ **de Paris**
button mushroom (GB), champignon (US)

champion, **-ionne** /ʃɑ̃pjɔ̃, ɔn/ *nm,f*
champion; **le** ∼ **en titre** the titleholder

championnat /ʃɑ̃pjɔna/ *nm*
championship

✦ **chance** /ʃɑ̃s/ *nf* **(a)** (good) luck; **coup de**
∼ stroke of luck; **avoir de la** ∼ to be lucky;
avoir la ∼ **de trouver une maison** to be
lucky enough to find a house; **par** ∼ luckily,
fortunately; **tenter** *or* **courir sa** ∼ to try
one's luck
(b) chance (**de** of); **il y a de fortes** ∼**s**
(pour) **que** there's every chance that; **il a ses**
∼**s** he stands a good chance; **mettre toutes
les** ∼**s de son côté** to take no chances; **'il
va pleuvoir?'—'il y a des** ∼**s'** 'is it going to
rain?'—'probably'
(c) chance, opportunity

chancelant, ∼**e** /ʃɑ̃slɑ̃, ɑ̃t/ *adj* **(a)** ⟨*gait*⟩
unsteady; ⟨*object*⟩ rickety, shaky; ⟨*person*⟩
staggering; **d'un pas** ∼ unsteadily
(b) ⟨*courage, faith*⟩ wavering; ⟨*empire*⟩
tottering

chanceler /ʃɑ̃sle/ [19] *vi* **(a)** ⟨*person*⟩ to
stagger; ⟨*object*⟩ to wobble
(b) ⟨*courage*⟩ to waver
(c) ⟨*empire*⟩ to totter; ⟨*health*⟩ to be precarious

chancelier /ʃɑ̃səlje/ *nm* chancellor

chancellerie /ʃɑ̃sɛlʀi/ *nf* Ministry of
Justice

chanceux, **-euse** /ʃɑ̃sø, øz/ *adj* lucky

chandail /ʃɑ̃daj/ *nm* sweater, jumper (GB)

chandelier /ʃɑ̃dəlje/ *nm* candelabra (GB)

chandelle /ʃɑ̃dɛl/ *nf* **(a)** candle; **un dîner
aux** ∼**s** a candlelit dinner
(b) (Sport) shoulder stand
IDIOMS devoir une fière ∼ **à** to be hugely
indebted to; **faire des économies de bouts
de** ∼**s** to make cheeseparing economies

change /ʃɑ̃ʒ/ *nm* **(a)** exchange rate
(b) (foreign) exchange; **perdre au** ∼
(figurative) to lose out

changeant, ∼**e** /ʃɑ̃ʒɑ̃, ɑ̃t/ *adj* changeable

✦ **changement** /ʃɑ̃ʒmɑ̃/ *nm* change; ∼ **en
mieux/pire** change for the better/worse
■ ∼ **climatique** climate change

✦ **changer** /ʃɑ̃ʒe/ [13] **1** *vtr* **(a)** to exchange
⟨*object*⟩; to change ⟨*secretary, job*⟩
(b) to change ⟨*money*⟩; to cash ⟨*traveller's
cheque*⟩
(c) to change ⟨*purchased item*⟩
(d) ∼ **qch de place** to move sth
(e) to change ⟨*situation, appearance*⟩;
cette coiffure te change you look different
with your hair like that; **qu'est-ce que ça
change?** what difference does it make?; **cela
ne change rien au fait que** that doesn't alter
the fact that
(f) ∼ **qn/qch en** to turn sb/sth into
(g) cela nous change de la pluie it makes a
change from the rain; **pour ne pas** ∼ as usual
(h) to change ⟨*baby*⟩
2 **changer de** *v+prep* to change; ∼ **d'avis** ┈┊

c

to change one's mind; ~ **de domicile** to move house; ~ **de trottoir** to cross over to the other side of the road; **nous avons changé de route au retour** we came back by a different route
3 *vi* to change
4 se changer *v refl* (+ *v être*) **(a)** to get changed
(b) se ~ **en** to turn *or* change into
changeur, -euse /ʃɑ̃ʒœʀ, øz/ **1** *nm,f* money changer
2 *nm* change machine
chanoine /ʃanwan/ *nm* canon
⚜ **chanson** /ʃɑ̃sɔ̃/ *nf* **(a)** song; **vedette de la** ~ singing star
(b) c'est toujours la même ~ (fam) it's always the same old story; **je connais la** ~ (fam) I've heard it all before
chansonnier, -ière /ʃɑ̃sɔnje, ɛʀ/ *nm,f* cabaret artist
⚜ **chant** /ʃɑ̃/ *nm* **(a)** singing
(b) (of bird, whale) song; (of cock) crow(ing); (of cricket) chirp(ing); (of cicada) shrilling
(c) song
(d) ode; canto
■ ~ **de Noël** Christmas carol
chantage /ʃɑ̃taʒ/ *nm* blackmail
chantant, ~e /ʃɑ̃tɑ̃, ɑ̃t/ *adj* singsong
⚜ **chanter** /ʃɑ̃te/ [1] **1** *vtr* **(a)** to sing
(b) (fam) **qu'est-ce qu'il nous chante?** what's he talking about?
2 chanter à *v+prep* (fam) **ça te chante d'y aller?** do you fancy (colloq) going?
3 *vi* **(a)** to sing; ~ **juste/faux** to sing in tune/out of tune
(b) ‹*bird*› to sing; ‹*cock*› to crow
(c) faire ~ **qn** to blackmail sb
chanteur, -euse /ʃɑ̃tœʀ, øz/ *nm,f* singer
chantier /ʃɑ̃tje/ *nm* **(a)** building site; **en** ~ ‹*building*› under construction; **notre maison sera en** ~ **tout l'hiver** the work on our house will go on all winter; **mettre en** ~ to undertake ‹*project*›
(b) builder's yard
(c) (fam) mess
chantonner /ʃɑ̃tɔne/ [1] *vtr, vi* to hum
chantre /ʃɑ̃tʀ/ *nm* eulogist (**de** of); ((poet)) bard
chanvre /ʃɑ̃vʀ/ *nm* hemp
chaos /kao/ *nm inv* chaos
chaotique /kaɔtik/ *adj* chaotic
chaparder /ʃapaʀde/ [1] *vtr* (fam) to pinch (colloq)
chape /ʃap/ *nf* ~ **de béton** concrete screed
⚜ **chapeau,** *pl* ~**x** /ʃapo/ **1** *nm* hat
2 *excl* (fam) well done!
■ ~ **haut de forme** top hat; ~ **melon** bowler (hat) (GB), derby (hat) (US); ~ **de roue** (Aut) hubcap; **démarrer sur les** ~**x de roues** (fam) ‹*car, driver*› to shoot off at top speed
IDIOM tirer son ~ **à** to take one's hat off to

⚜ indicates a very frequent word

chapeauter /ʃapote/ [1] *vtr* (fam) to head; **le ministère chapeaute notre équipe** our team works under the ministry
chapelet /ʃaplɛ/ *nm* **(a)** rosary
(b) (of onions, insults, islands) string
chapelier, -ière /ʃapəlje, ɛʀ/ *nm,f* hatter
chapelle /ʃapel/ *nf* **(a)** chapel
(b) clique, coterie
chapelure /ʃaplyʀ/ *nf* breadcrumbs
chaperon /ʃapʀɔ̃/ *nm* chaperon(e)
chapiteau, *pl* ~**x** /ʃapito/ *nm* **(a)** marquee (GB), tent; (of circus) big top
(b) (of pillar) capital
⚜ **chapitre** /ʃapitʀ/ *nm* **(a)** (of book) chapter
(b) subject
IDIOM avoir voix au ~ to have a say in the matter
chapka /ʃapka/ *nf* fur hat
⚜ **chaque** /ʃak/ *det* each, every
char /ʃaʀ/ *nm* **(a)** (Mil) tank
(b) chariot
(c) (in carnival) float
■ ~ **d'assaut** (Mil) tank; ~ **à bœufs** oxcart; ~ **à voile** (Sport) sand yacht; ice yacht
charabia /ʃaʀabja/ *nm* (fam) gobbledygook (colloq)
charade /ʃaʀad/ *nf* riddle
charbon /ʃaʀbɔ̃/ *nm* coal; ~ **de bois** charcoal
IDIOM être sur des ~**s ardents** to be like a cat on a hot tin roof
charcuter /ʃaʀkyte/ [1] *vtr* (fam) to hack [sb] about
charcuterie /ʃaʀkytʀi/ *nf* **(a)** cooked pork meats
(b) pork butcher's
charcutier, -ière /ʃaʀkytje, ɛʀ/ *nm,f* pork butcher
chardon /ʃaʀdɔ̃/ *nm* thistle
charentais, ~e[1] /ʃaʀɑ̃tɛ, ɛz/ *adj* from the Charente region
charentaise[2] /ʃaʀɑ̃tɛz/ *nf* carpet slipper
⚜ **charge** /ʃaʀʒ/ **1** *nf* **(a)** burden, load; (of vehicle) load; (of ship) cargo, freight; **prise en** ~ (in taxi) minimum fare
(b) avoir la ~ **de qn/qch** to be responsible for sb/sth; **avoir trois enfants à** ~ to have three children to support; **prendre en** ~ ‹*guardian*› to take charge of ‹*child*›; ‹*social security system*› to accept financial responsibility for ‹*sick person*›; to take care of ‹*fees*›
(c) ~ **de notaire** ≈ solicitor's office
(d) (legal) charge
(e) (Mil) charge
2 charges *nf pl* **(a)** expenses, costs
(b) (payable by tenant) ~**s** (**locatives**) service charges
■ ~**s patronales** employer's social security contributions
IDIOM revenir à la ~ to try again

chargé, ~e /ʃaʀʒe/ 〔**1**〕 ▸ CHARGER
〔**2**〕 *pp adj* **être ~ de** to be heavy *or* laden (with); **un regard ~ de menaces** a threatening look; **être ~ de famille** to have dependents
〔**3**〕 *adj* ‹person, vehicle› loaded; ‹day› busy; **avoir un casier judiciaire ~** to have had several previous convictions
■ **~ d'affaires** chargé d'affaires; **~ de cours** part-time lecturer; **~ de mission** representative

chargement /ʃaʀʒəmɑ̃/ *nm*
(a) (goods) load; cargo
(b) (action) loading

⚡ **charger** /ʃaʀʒe/ [13] 〔**1**〕 *vtr* **(a)** to load
(b) to charge ‹battery›
(c) **~ qn de faire** to give sb the responsibility of doing; **c'est lui qui est chargé de l'enquête** he is in charge of the investigation
(d) to bring evidence against ‹accused›
(e) ‹police› to charge at ‹crowd›
〔**2**〕 **se charger** *v refl* (+ *v être*) **se ~ de** to take responsibility for; **je m'en charge** I'll see to it

chargeur /ʃaʀʒœʀ/ *nm* **(a)** (Mil) magazine
(b) (of camera) cartridge
(c) (Comput) loader

chariot /ʃaʀjo/ *nm* **(a)** trolley (GB), cart (US)
(b) truck
(c) waggon (GB)
(d) (of typewriter) carriage

charisme /kaʀism/ *nm* charisma

charitable /ʃaʀitabl/ *adj* charitable

charitablement /ʃaʀitabləmɑ̃/ *adv* charitably; kindly

charité /ʃaʀite/ *nf* **(a)** charity
(b) **par (pure) ~** out of the kindness of one's heart

charlatan /ʃaʀlatɑ̃/ *nm* **(a)** quack (colloq)
(b) con man
(c) (politician) fraud

charlot /ʃaʀlo/ *nm* (fam) clown

charlotte /ʃaʀlɔt/ *nf* **(a)** (Culin) charlotte
(b) mobcap

charmant, ~e /ʃaʀmɑ̃, ɑ̃t/ *adj* charming

charme /ʃaʀm/ 〔**1**〕 *nm* **(a)** charm; **faire du ~ à qn** to make eyes at sb; **cela ne manque pas de ~** (lifestyle, novel) it's not without its charms; (proposition) it's not unattractive
(b) spell
〔**2**〕 **charmes** *nm pl* (euphemistic) physical attributes
IDIOM **se porter comme un ~** to be as fit as a fiddle

charmer /ʃaʀme/ [1] *vtr* to charm

charmeur, -euse /ʃaʀmœʀ, øz/ 〔**1**〕 *adj* winning, engaging
〔**2**〕 *nm,f* charmer

charnel, -elle /ʃaʀnɛl/ *adj* carnal

charnier /ʃaʀnje/ *nm* mass grave

charnière /ʃaʀnjɛʀ/ *nf* **(a)** hinge
(b) (figurative) bridge; junction; **rôle(-)~**
pivotal role

charnu, ~e /ʃaʀny/ *adj* ‹lip› fleshy, thick

charogne /ʃaʀɔɲ/ *nf* rotting carcass

charpente /ʃaʀpɑ̃t/ *nf* (of roof) roof structure; (of building) framework; (of person) build

charpentier /ʃaʀpɑ̃tje/ *nm* carpenter

charpie /ʃaʀpi/ *nf* **réduire** *or* **mettre qch en ~** to tear sth to shreds

charretier /ʃaʀtje/ *nm* carter
IDIOM **jurer comme un ~** to swear like a trooper

charrette /ʃaʀɛt/ *nf* cart; **~ à bras** handcart

charrier /ʃaʀje/ [2] 〔**1**〕 *vtr* **(a)** to carry, to haul
(b) ‹river› to carry [sth] along
(c) (fam) to tease [sb] unmercifully
〔**2**〕 *vi* (fam) to go too far

charrue /ʃaʀy/ *nf* plough (GB), plow (US)
IDIOM **mettre la ~ avant les bœufs** to put the cart before the horse

charte /ʃaʀt/ *nf* charter

charter /ʃaʀtɛʀ/ *adj inv* ‹plane› charter

⚡ **chasse** /ʃas/ *nf* **(a)** hunting; shooting; **~ au trésor** treasure hunt; **la ~ est ouverte** it's the open season
(b) **~ gardée** private hunting (ground); (figurative) preserve
(c) **donner la ~ à, prendre en ~** to chase
■ **~ à courre** hunting; **~ d'eau** (toilet) flush; **tirer la ~** to pull the chain
IDIOM **qui va à la ~ perd sa place** (Proverb) leave your place and you lose it

chassé-croisé, *pl* **chassés-croisés** /ʃasekʀwaze/ *nm* continual coming and going

chasse-neige /ʃasnɛʒ/ *nm inv* snowplough (GB), snowplow (US)

⚡ **chasser** /ʃase/ [1] 〔**1**〕 *vtr* **(a)** ‹animal› to hunt ‹prey›
(b) ‹hunter› to shoot (GB), to hunt
(c) ‹person› to chase away ‹animal, intruder›; ‹rain› to drive away ‹tourists›; to fire ‹domestic servant›
(d) to dispel ‹smoke, doubt›
〔**2**〕 *vi* to go hunting

chasseur, -euse /ʃasœʀ, øz/ 〔**1**〕 *nm,f* hunter
〔**2**〕 *nm* **(a)** (Mil) fighter (aircraft); fighter pilot
(b) ((in hotel)) bellboy
■ **~ alpin** *soldier trained for mountainous terrain*; **~ de têtes** head-hunter

châssis /ʃɑsi/ *nm inv* **(a)** (of window) frame
(b) (Aut) chassis

chaste /ʃast/ *adj* (gen) chaste; ‹person› celibate

chasteté /ʃastəte/ *nf* chastity

⚡ **chat¹** /ʃa/ *nm* cat; tomcat
■ **~ de gouttière** ordinary cat; alley cat; **~ perché** off-ground tag   ····⟩

IDIOMS donner sa langue au ~ to give in; **il n'y a pas un** ~ the place is deserted; **avoir un** ~ **dans la gorge** to have a frog in one's throat; **il ne faut pas réveiller le** ~ **qui dort** (Proverb) let sleeping dogs lie; **s'entendre comme chien et** ~ to fight like cat and dog

chat² /tʃat/ *nm* (on mobile) chat

châtaigne /ʃatɛɲ/ *nf* (sweet) chestnut

châtaignier /ʃatɛɲe/ *nm* (sweet) chestnut (tree); **une table de** *or* **en** ~ a chestnut table

châtain /ʃatɛ̃/ *adj m* ‹hair› brown

⚘ **château**, *pl* ~**x** /ʃato/ *nm* (a) castle
(b) palace
(c) mansion
■ ~ **de cartes** house of cards; ~ **d'eau** water tower; ~ **fort** fortified castle
IDIOM mener la vie de ~ to live the life of Riley (GB), to live like a prince

châtelain, ~**e** /ʃatlɛ̃, ɛn/ *nm,f* (a) lord/ lady of the manor
(b) owner of a manor

châtier /ʃatje/ [2] *vtr* to punish

chatière /ʃatjɛʀ/ *nf* catflap

châtiment /ʃatimɑ̃/ *nm* punishment

chatoiement /ʃatwamɑ̃/ *nm* shimmering

chaton /ʃatɔ̃/ *nm* (a) kitten
(b) catkin

chatouille /ʃatuj/ *nf* (fam) tickle

chatouiller /ʃatuje/ [1] *vtr* to tickle
IDIOM ~ **les côtes à qn** (euphemistic) to tan sb's hide

chatouilleux, -euse /ʃatujø, øz/ *adj*
(a) ticklish
(b) touchy (**sur** about)

chatoyant, ~**e** /ʃatwajɑ̃, ɑ̃t/ *adj* shimmering; iridescent

chatoyer /ʃatwaje/ [23] *vi* to shimmer

châtrer /ʃatʀe/ [1] *vtr* to castrate

chatte /ʃat/ *nf* (female) cat

⚘ **chaud**, ~**e** /ʃo, ʃod/ **1** *adj* (a) hot; warm
(b) ‹colour, voice› warm
(c) **ils n'ont pas été très** ~**s pour faire** they were not very keen on doing
(d) ‹region› turbulent; ‹discussion› heated; **un des points** ~**s du globe** one of the flash points of the world
(e) **quartier** ~ (fam) red light district
2 *adv* **il fait** ~ it's warm; it's hot; **ça ne me fait ni** ~ **ni froid** it doesn't matter one way or the other to me
3 *nm* heat; **avoir** ~ to be warm; to be hot; **nous avons eu** ~ (figurative) we had a narrow escape; **se tenir** ~ to keep warm
4 **à chaud** *phr* **à** ~ ‹analyse› on the spot; ‹reaction› immediate
■ ~ **et froid** (Med) chill

chaudement /ʃodmɑ̃/ *adv* (gen) warmly; ‹recommend› heartily

chaudière /ʃodjɛʀ/ *nf* boiler

⚘ indicates a very frequent word

chaudron /ʃodʀɔ̃/ *nm* cauldron

chaudronnerie /ʃodʀɔnʀi/ *nf* boilermaking industry; boilerworks

chaudronnier, -ière /ʃodʀɔnje, ɛʀ/ *nm,f* boilermaker

chauffage /ʃofaʒ/ *nm* (a) heating
(b) heater

chauffagiste /ʃofaʒist/ *nmf* heating engineer

chauffant, ~**e** /ʃofɑ̃, ɑ̃t/ *adj* heating

chauffard /ʃofaʀ/ *nm* (fam) reckless driver

chauffe /ʃof/ *nf* (Tech) fire chamber

chauffe-eau /ʃofo/ *nm inv* water-heater

chauffe-plat /ʃofpla/ *nm inv* dish warmer

chauffer /ʃofe/ [1] **1** *vtr* (a) to heat ‹house›; to heat (up) ‹object, meal›
(b) ‹sun› to warm
2 *vi* (a) ‹food, oven› to heat up; ‹engine› to warm up; to overheat
(b) ‹radiator› to give out heat
(c) (fam) **ça va** ~! there's going to be big trouble!
3 **se chauffer** *v refl* (+ *v être*) (a) **se** ~ **au soleil** to bask in the sun
(b) **se** ~ **au charbon** to have coal-fired heating

chaufferie /ʃofʀi/ *nf* (a) boiler room
(b) (in boat) stokehold

chauffeur /ʃofœʀ/ *nm* (a) driver
(b) chauffeur

chauffeuse /ʃoføz/ *nf* low armless easy chair

chaume /ʃom/ *nm* (a) (in field) stubble
(b) thatch

chaumière /ʃomjɛʀ/ *nf* (a) thatched cottage
(b) **faire jaser dans les** ~**s** to cause tongues to wag

chaussée /ʃose/ *nf* (a) roadway, highway; (in town) street
(b) (road) surface
(c) causeway

chausse-pied, *pl* ~**s** /ʃospje/ *nm* shoehorn

chausser /ʃose/ [1] **1** *vtr* to put [sth] on ‹shoes, spectacles›
2 *vi* **je chausse du 41** I take a (size) 41
3 **se chausser** *v refl* (+ *v être*) (a) to put (one's) shoes on
(b) to buy (one's) shoes

chaussette /ʃosɛt/ *nf* sock
IDIOM laisser tomber qn comme une vieille ~ (fam) to cast sb off like an old rag

chausseur /ʃosœʀ/ *nm* shoe shop manager; shoemaker

chausson /ʃosɔ̃/ *nm* (a) slipper
(b) bootee
(c) ballet shoe
■ ~ **aux pommes** (Culin) apple turnover

⚘ **chaussure** /ʃosyʀ/ *nf* shoe; ~ **montante** ankle boot

IDIOM trouver ∼ à son pied ‹man, woman› to find the right person

chauve /ʃov/ adj bald

chauve-souris, pl **chauves-souris** /ʃovsuʀi/ nf (Zool) bat

chauvin, ∼e /ʃovɛ̃, in/ adj chauvinistic

chaux /ʃo/ nf lime

chavirer /ʃaviʀe/ [1] **1** vtr to overwhelm
2 vi **(a)** ‹boat› to capsize
(b) faire ∼ les cœurs to be a heartbreaker
(c) ‹objects› to tip over

✧ **chef** /ʃɛf/ nm **(a)** leader
(b) superior, boss (colloq)
(c) head; (of sales department) manager; architecte en ∼ chief architect
(d) ∼ cuisinier or de cuisine chef
(e) (fam) ace; se débrouiller comme un ∼ to manage splendidly
(f) de mon/leur (propre) ∼ on my/their own initiative
(g) au premier ∼ primarily, first and foremost
■ ∼ d'accusation (Law) count of indictment; ∼ d'atelier (shop) foreman; ∼ d'équipe foreman; (Sport) team captain; (of seasonal workers) (pejorative) gangmaster; ∼ d'État head of state; ∼ de gare stationmaster

chef-d'œuvre, pl **chefs-d'œuvre** /ʃedœvʀ/ nm masterpiece

chef-lieu, pl **chefs-lieux** /ʃɛfljø/ nm administrative centre

✧ **chemin** /ʃ(ə)mɛ̃/ nm **(a)** country road; lane; ∼ (de terre) dirt track; path
(b) way; sur le ∼ du retour on the way back; reprendre le ∼ du bureau to go back to work; on a fait un bout de ∼ ensemble we walked along together for a while; ∼ faisant, en ∼ on or along the way; l'idée fait son ∼ the idea is gaining ground; prendre le ∼ de la faillite to be heading for bankruptcy; s'arrêter en ∼ to stop off on the way; (figurative) to stop
■ ∼ de fer railway (GB), railroad (US)

cheminée /ʃ(ə)mine/ nf **(a)** chimney; chimney stack
(b) fireplace
(c) mantelpiece
(d) (of ship) funnel

cheminement /ʃ(ə)minmɑ̃/ nm **(a)** slow progression
(b) le ∼ de sa pensée his/her train of thought

cheminer /ʃ(ə)mine/ [1] vi **(a)** to walk (along)
(b) ‹idea› to progress, to develop

cheminot /ʃ(ə)mino/ nm railway worker (GB), railroader (US)

✧ **chemise** /ʃ(ə)miz/ nf **(a)** shirt
(b) folder
■ ∼ de nuit nightgown; (for man) nightshirt
IDIOMS je m'en moque comme de ma première ∼ (fam) I don't give two hoots (GB) (colloq) or a hoot (US) (colloq); **changer**

d'avis comme de ∼ (fam) to change one's mind at the drop of a hat

chemiserie /ʃ(ə)mizʀi/ nf shirt-making trade; shirt factory; shirt shop

chemisier /ʃ(ə)mizje/ nm blouse

chenal, pl **-aux** /ʃənal, o/ nm channel, fairway

chenapan /ʃənapɑ̃/ nm scallywag (colloq), rascal

chêne /ʃɛn/ nm **(a)** oak (tree)
(b) oak

chenet /ʃənɛ/ nm firedog, andiron

chenil /ʃənil/ nm **(a)** (dog) kennel
(b) kennels

chenille /ʃənij/ nf (Aut, Zool) caterpillar

cheptel /ʃɛptɛl/ nm ∼ (vif) livestock

chèque /ʃɛk/ nm cheque (GB), check (US)
■ ∼ en blanc blank cheque (GB) or check (US); ∼ en bois (fam) rubber cheque (GB) (colloq) or check (US); ∼ sans provision bad cheque (GB) or check (US), ∼ de voyage traveller's cheque (GB), traveler's check (US)

chèque-cadeau, pl **chèques-cadeaux** /ʃɛkkado/ nm gift token

chèque-voyage, pl **chèques-voyage** /ʃɛkvwajaʒ/ nm traveller's cheque (GB), traveler's cheque (US)

chéquier /ʃekje/ nm chequebook (GB), checkbook (US)

✧ **cher, chère¹** /ʃɛʀ/ **1** adj **(a)** dear; beloved; un être ∼ a loved one
(b) (as term of address) dear
(c) expensive; pas ∼ cheap
2 nm,f mon ∼/ma chère my dear
3 adv **(a)** a lot (of money); coûter plus/moins ∼ to cost more/less; acheter ∼ to buy at a high price
(b) (figurative) ‹pay, cost› dearly
IDIOM ne pas donner ∼ de la peau de qn (fam) not to rate sb's chances highly

✧ **chercher** /ʃɛʀʃe/ [1] **1** vtr **(a)** to look for ‹person, object, trouble›; to try to find ‹answer, ideas›; to try to remember ‹name›; ∼ fortune to seek one's fortune; ∼ qn du regard to look about for sb
(b) ∼ à faire to try to do
(c) aller ∼ qn/qch to go and get sb/sth; to pick sb/sth up
(d) où est-il allé ∼ cela? what made him think that?
(e) une maison dans ce quartier, ça va ∼ dans les 200 000 euros a house in this area must fetch (GB) or get (US) about 200,000 euros
2 se chercher v refl (+ v être) **(a)** to try to find oneself
(b) se ∼ des excuses to try to find excuses for oneself
(c) (fam) to be out to get each other (colloq)

✧ **chercheur, -euse** /ʃɛʀʃœʀ, øz/ nm,f researcher
■ ∼ d'or gold-digger

chère² /ʃɛʀ/ **1** adj f ▶ CHER
2 nf faire bonne ∼ to eat well

c

chèrement /ʃɛʀmɑ̃/ *adv* ~ acquise gained at great cost

chéri, ~**e** /ʃeʀi/ **1** *pp* ▶ CHÉRIR
2 *pp adj* beloved
3 *nm,f* (a) darling
(b) (fam) boyfriend/girlfriend

chérir /ʃeʀiʀ/ [3] *vtr* to cherish ‹person›; to hold [sth] dear ‹idea›

chérubin /ʃeʀybɛ̃/ *nm* cherub

chétif, -ive /ʃetif, iv/ *adj* ‹child› puny

ƌ **cheval**, *pl* **-aux** /ʃ(ə)val, o/ **1** *nm*
(a) horse; **monter à** ~ to ride a horse; **remède de** ~ strong medicine; **fièvre de** ~ raging fever
(b) (Sport) horse-riding
(c) horsemeat
2 **à cheval sur** *phr* (a) astride
(b) spanning
(c) in between
(d) **être à** ~ **sur qch** to be a stickler for sth
■ ~ **à bascule** rocking horse; ~ **de bataille** hobbyhorse; **chevaux de bois** merry-go-round horses

chevaleresque /ʃ(ə)valʀɛsk/ *adj*
(a) ‹literature› courtly
(b) ‹person› chivalrous

chevalerie /ʃ(ə)valʀi/ *nf* chivalry

chevalet /ʃ(ə)valɛ/ *nm* easel

chevalier /ʃ(ə)valje/ *nm* knight

chevalière /ʃ(ə)valjɛʀ/ *nf* signet ring

cheval-vapeur, *pl* **chevaux-vapeur** /ʃ(ə)valvapœʀ, ʃ(ə)vovapœʀ/ *nm* horsepower

chevauchée /ʃ(ə)voʃe/ *nf* ride

chevaucher /ʃ(ə)voʃe/ [1] **1** *vtr* (a) to sit astride ‹animal, chair›
(b) to overlap
2 **se chevaucher** *v refl* (+ *v être*) to overlap

chevelu, ~**e** /ʃəvly/ *adj* long-haired

chevelure /ʃəvlyʀ/ *nf* hair

chevet /ʃəvɛ/ *nm* bedhead; **être au** ~ **de qn** to be at sb's bedside

ƌ **cheveu**, *pl* ~**x** /ʃəvø/ **1** *nm* hair; **être à un** ~ **de** to be within a hair's breadth of; **ne tenir qu'à un** ~ to hang by a thread
2 **cheveux** *nm pl* hair
IDIOMS **avoir un** ~ **sur la langue** to have a lisp; **venir comme un** ~ **sur la soupe** to come at an awkward moment; **se faire des** ~**x (blancs)** (fam) to worry oneself to death; **couper les** ~**x en quatre** to split hairs; **être tiré par les** ~**x** to be far-fetched

cheville /ʃ(ə)vij/ *nf* (a) (Anat) ankle
(b) Rawlplug®; peg; dowel
IDIOMS **il n'arrive pas à la** ~ **de Paul** he can't hold a candle to Paul; **être en** ~ **avec qn** (fam) to be in cahoots with sb (colloq)

chèvre¹ /ʃɛvʀ/ *nm* goat's cheese

chèvre² /ʃɛvʀ/ *nf* goat; nanny-goat

IDIOM **devenir** ~ (fam) to go nuts (slang)

chevreau, *pl* ~**x** /ʃəvʀo/ *nm* (Zool) kid

chèvrefeuille /ʃɛvʀəfœj/ *nm* honeysuckle

chevreuil /ʃəvʀœj/ *nm* (a) roe (deer); roebuck
(b) (Culin) venison

chevronné, ~**e** /ʃəvʀɔne/ *adj* ‹person› experienced

chevrotant, ~**e** /ʃəvʀɔtɑ̃, ɑ̃t/ *adj* ‹voice› quavering

chevroter /ʃəvʀɔte/ [1] *vtr, vi* to quaver

chevrotine /ʃəvʀɔtin/ *nf* buckshot

ƌ **chez** /ʃe/ *prep* (a) ~ **qn** at sb's place; **rentre** ~ **toi** go home; **de** ~ **qn** ‹telephone› from sb's place; **fais comme** ~ **toi** make yourself at home
(b) (referring to shop, office) **aller** ~ **le boucher** to go to the butcher's; **être convoqué** ~ **le patron** to be called in before the boss
(c) (referring to a region) ~ **nous** where I come from; where I live
(d) among; ~ **l'animal** in animals
(e) **ce que j'aime** ~ **elle, c'est son humour** what I like about her is her sense of humour (GB)
(f) in; ~ **Cocteau** in Cocteau

chic /ʃik/ **1** *adj* (a) smart (GB), chic
(b) (fam) chic, fashionable
(c) (fam) ‹person› nice
2 *nm* chic; **avoir le** ~ **pour faire** to have a knack for doing; **avec** ~ with style

chicane /ʃikan/ *nf* chicane; (on road, ski slope) double bend; **en** ~ on alternate sides

chicaner /ʃikane/ [1] *vi* to squabble

chiche /ʃiʃ/ **1** *adj* (a) mean (GB), stingy
(b) **être** ~ **de faire** (fam) to be quite capable of doing
2 *excl* **'je vais le faire'—'**~**!'** (fam) 'I'll do it'—'I dare you!'

chichement /ʃiʃmɑ̃/ *adv* ‹live› frugally; ‹give› stingily; ‹pay› poorly

chichi /ʃiʃi/ *nm* fuss

chicon /ʃikɔ̃/ *nm* chicory

chicorée /ʃikɔʀe/ *nf* (a) (plant) chicory; (salad vegetable) endive (GB), chicory (US)
(b) (Culin) (powder) chicory; (drink) chicory coffee

ƌ **chien, chienne¹** /ʃjɛ̃, ʃjɛn/ **1** *adj* (fam) **ne pas être** ~ not to be too hard
2 *nm* (a) dog
(b) (of rifle) hammer
3 **de chien** *phr* (fam) ‹job, weather› rotten; **ça me fait un mal de** ~ it hurts like hell (colloq)
■ ~ **d'aveugle** guide dog; ~ **de berger** sheepdog; ~ **de garde** guard dog; (figurative) watchdog; ~ **de race** pedigree dog
IDIOMS **être couché en** ~ **de fusil** to be curled up; **ce n'est pas fait pour les** ~**s** (fam) it's there to be used

---

ƌ indicates a very frequent word

chiendent /ʃjɛ̃dɑ̃/ nm couch grass; **brosse de ~** scrubbing brush

chienlit /ʃjɑ̃li/ nf havoc, chaos

chien-loup, pl **chiens-loups** /ʃjɛ̃lu/ nm Alsatian (GB), German shepherd

chienne² /ʃjɛn/ **1** adj f ▸ CHIEN **2** nf (animal) bitch

chiffon /ʃifɔ̃/ nm (a) rag, (piece of) cloth; **parler ~s** to talk (about) clothes (b) duster

chiffonné, **~e** /ʃifɔne/ adj (a) ‹face› tired-looking (b) (fam) ‹person› troubled, ruffled

chiffonner /ʃifɔne/ [1] **1** vtr (a) to crease, to crumple (b) (fam) to bother ‹person› **2** **se chiffonner** v refl (+ v être) to crease

chiffonnier /ʃifɔnje/ nm **se battre comme des ~s** to fight like cat and dog

chiffrable /ʃifrabl/ adj calculable; **les pertes ne sont pas ~s** it's impossible to put a figure on the losses

 chiffre /ʃifr/ nm (a) figure (b) monogram ■ **~ d'affaires**, CA turnover (GB), sales (US); **~ arabe** Arabic numeral; **~ romain** Roman numeral; **~ de vente** sales (figures)

chiffrer /ʃifre/ [1] **1** vtr (a) to put a figure on ‹cost, loss›; to cost ‹job›; **~ à** to put the cost of [sth] at ‹job› (b) to encode ‹message› **2** vi (fam) to add up; **ça chiffre vite** it soon adds up **3** **se chiffrer** v refl (+ v être) **se ~ à** to amount to, to come to

chignole /ʃiɲɔl/ nf hand drill

chignon /ʃiɲɔ̃/ nm bun; chignon

chiisme /ʃiizm/ nm Shiism

chiite /ʃiit/ adj, nmf Shiite

Chili /ʃili/ pr nm Chile

chimère /ʃimɛr/ nf (a) pipe dream (b) (in mythology) Chimaera

chimérique /ʃimerik/ adj ‹hope› wild; ‹person› fanciful

chimie /ʃimi/ nf chemistry

chimiothérapie /ʃimjoterapi/ nf chemotherapy

chimique /ʃimik/ adj (a) chemical; ‹fibre› man-made (b) ‹food, taste› synthetic

chimiste /ʃimist/ nmf chemist

chimpanzé /ʃɛ̃pɑ̃ze/ nm chimpanzee

Chine /ʃin/ pr nf China

chiné, **~e** /ʃine/ adj chiné

chiner /ʃine/ [1] vi (fam) to bargain-hunt, to antique (US)

 chinois, **~e** /ʃinwa, az/ **1** adj Chinese **2** nm (language) Chinese **IDIOM pour moi c'est du ~** it's double-Dutch (GB) or Greek to me

chiot /ʃjo/ nm puppy, pup

chiper /ʃipe/ [1] vtr (fam) to pinch (colloq)

chipie /ʃipi/ nf (fam) little monkey (colloq)

chipoter /ʃipɔte/ [1] vi (fam) (a) to quibble (sur over) (b) to pick at one's food

chipoteur, **-euse** /ʃipɔtœr, øz/ adj (fam) (a) difficult (b) fussy

chips /ʃips/ nf inv crisp (GB), potato chip (US)

chique /ʃik/ nf plug (of tobacco) **IDIOM couper la ~ à qn** to shut sb up (colloq)

chiqué /ʃike/ nm (fam) (a) **c'est du ~** it's a put-on (b) **faire du ~** to put on or give oneself airs

chiquenaude /ʃiknod/ nf flick

chiquer /ʃike/ [1] vtr **tabac à ~** chewing tobacco

chiromancie /kiromɑ̃si/ nf palmistry

chirurgical, **~e**, mpl, **-aux** /ʃiryrʒikal, o/ adj surgical

chirurgie /ʃiryrʒi/ nf surgery

chirurgien /ʃiryrʒjɛ̃/ nm surgeon

chlore /klɔr/ nm chlorine

chlorer /klɔre/ [1] vtr to chlorinate

chlorhydrique /klɔridrik/ adj hydrochloric

chloroforme /klɔrɔfɔrm/ nm chloroform

chlorophylle /klɔrɔfil/ nf chlorophyll

chlorure /klɔryr/ nm chloride

choc /ʃɔk/ **1** adj inv **'prix ~!'** 'huge reductions' **2** nm (a) impact, shock; collision; **sous le ~** under the impact (b) (noise) crash, smash; thud; clang; chink (c) (confrontation) (gen, Mil) clash; (Sport) encounter; **de ~** ‹journalist› ace (colloq) (d) (emotional, physical) shock

 chocolat /ʃɔkɔla/ nm chocolate; **~ noir** or **à croquer** plain (GB) or dark (US) chocolate

chœur /kœr/ nm (a) choir; (in opera, play) chorus; (figurative) chorus (**de** of); **en ~** ‹say› in unison; ‹laugh› all together (b) (in church) chancel, choir

choir /ʃwar/ [51] vi to fall; **laisser ~ qn** to drop sb

 choisir /ʃwazir/ [3] vtr to choose

 choix /ʃwa/ nm inv (a) choice; **arrêter son ~ sur** to settle or decide on (b) **de ~** ‹item› first-rate; ‹candidate›; **les places de ~** the best seats; **un morceau de ~** (of meat) a prime cut; **de second ~** of inferior quality

choléra /kɔlera/ nm cholera

cholestérol /kɔlɛsterɔl/ nm cholesterol

chômage /ʃomaʒ/ nm unemployment; **mettre qn au ~** to make sb redundant (GB), to lay sb off ■ **~ technique** layoffs

chômé, ∼e /ʃome/ *adj* jour ∼ day off; fête
∼e national holiday

chômer /ʃome/ [1] *vi* (a) to be idle
(b) to be out of work

chômeur, -euse /ʃomœʀ, øz/ *nm,f*
unemployed person

chope /ʃɔp/ *nf* beer mug, tankard

choquant, ∼e /ʃɔkã, ãt/ *adj* shocking

choquer /ʃɔke/ [1] *vtr* (a) to shock ‹person›;
to offend ‹sight, sensibility›
(b) ‹news› to shake ‹person›; ‹accident› to
shake [sb] (up)

chorale /kɔʀal/ *nf* choir

chorégraphie /kɔʀegʀafi/ *nf*
choreography

choriste /kɔʀist/ *nmf* chorister; member
of the choir; member of the chorus

chorus /kɔʀys/ *nm inv* chorus; faire ∼ avec
qn (figurative) to join in with sb

✧ **chose** /ʃoz/ *nf* (a) (object, abstract) thing;
de deux ∼s l'une it's got to be one thing or
the other; une ∼ communément admise a
widely accepted fact; en mettant les ∼s au
mieux at best; mettre les ∼s au point to clear
things up; avant toute ∼ before anything
else; above all else
(b) matter; la ∼ en question the matter in
hand
(c) être un peu porté sur la ∼ (fam) to be
keen on sex

chou, *pl* ∼x /ʃu/ *nm* (a) cabbage
(b) choux bun (GB), pastry shell (US)
(c) dear, darling
■ ∼ de Bruxelles Brussels sprout; ∼ à la
crème cream puff; ∼ rave kohlrabi
IDIOMS bête comme ∼ really easy; faire
∼ blanc (fam) to draw a blank; faire ses
∼x gras de qch (fam) to use sth to one's
advantage; rentrer dans le ∼ de qn (fam) to
beat sb up; to give sb a piece of one's mind

choucas /ʃuka/ *nm* jackdaw

chouchou /ʃuʃu/ *nm* (fam)
(a) (teacher's) pet; (of adoring public) darling
(b) (for hair) scrunchie

chouchouter /ʃuʃute/ [1] *vtr* (fam) to
pamper

choucroute /ʃukʀut/ *nf*
(a) (vegetable) sauerkraut
(b) (hairstyle) beehive

chouette /ʃwɛt/ ① *adj* (fam) great (colloq),
neat (US) (colloq)
② *nf* (a) owl
(b) vieille ∼ old harridan

chou-fleur, *pl* **choux-fleurs**
/ʃuflœʀ/ *nm* cauliflower

chourer /ʃuʀe/ [1] *vtr* (fam) to pinch (colloq);
se faire ∼ qch to have sth pinched

choyer /ʃwaje/ [23] *vtr* to pamper

✧ indicates a very frequent word

✧ **chrétien, -ienne** /kʀetjɛ̃, ɛn/ *adj*, *nm,f*
Christian

chrétienté /kʀetjɛ̃te/ *nf* la ∼ Christendom

Christ /kʀist/ *pr n* le ∼ Christ

christianisme /kʀistjanism/ *nm*
Christianity

chromatique /kʀɔmatik/ *adj* chromatic

chrome /kʀom/ *nm* chromium

chromosome /kʀomozom/ *nm*
chromosome

chronique /kʀɔnik/ ① *adj* chronic
② *nf* (in newspaper) column, page

chroniqueur, -euse /kʀɔnikœʀ, øz/ *nm,f*
columnist, editor

chronologie /kʀɔnɔlɔʒi/ *nf* chronology

chronologique /kʀɔnɔlɔʒik/ *adj*
chronological

chronomètre /kʀɔnɔmɛtʀ/ *nm* stopwatch

chronométrer /kʀɔnɔmetʀe/ [14] *vtr* to
time

chrysalide /kʀizalid/ *nf* chrysalis

ch'ti, *pl* **ch'tis** /ʃti/ (fam) ① *adj* from
Northern France
② *nmf* person from Northern France

chu ▶ CHOIR

CHU /seaʃy/ *nm: abbr* ▶ CENTRE

chuchotement /ʃyʃɔtmã/ *nm*: whisper

chuchoter /ʃyʃɔte/ [1] *vtr*, *vi* to whisper

chuintant, ∼e /ʃɥɛ̃tã, ãt/ *adj* bruit ∼
hissing sound

chuinter /ʃɥɛ̃te/ [1] *vi* ‹steam› to hiss
gently; ‹tyre› to swish

chum /tʃœm/ *nm* (fam) friend; boyfriend

chut /ʃyt/ *excl* shh!, hush!

✧ **chute** /ʃyt/ *nf* (a) (gen) fall; (of
empire) collapse; (of hair) loss; (of pressure) drop
(b) (of film) ending; (of story) punch line
(c) (of cloth) offcut
■ ∼ d'eau waterfall; la ∼ des reins the small
of the back

Chypre /ʃipʀ/ *pr n* Cyprus

✧ **ci** /si/ ① *det* cette page-∼ this page; ces
jours-∼ (past) these last few days; (future) in
the next few days; (present) at the moment
② *pron* this; ∼ et ça this and that

ci-après /siapʀɛ/ *adv* below

cible /sibl/ *nf* target

cibler /sible/ [1] *vtr* to target

ciboulette /sibulɛt/ *nf* (Bot) chive; (Culin)
chives

cicatrice /sikatʀis/ *nf* scar

cicatrisant, ∼e /sikatʀizã, ãt/ *adj*
healing

cicatrisation /sikatʀizasjõ/ *nf* healing

cicatriser /sikatʀize/ [1] *vtr*, **se
cicatriser** *v refl* (+ *v être*) to heal

ci-contre /sikõtʀ/ *adv* opposite

ci-dessous /sidəsu/ *adv* below

ci-dessus /sidəsy/ *adv* above

cidre /sidʀ/ *nm* cider

cidrerie /sidʀəʀi/ *nf* cider-works

ơ **ciel** /sjɛl/, *pl* **cieux** /sjø/ *nm* (a) sky; **carte du ~** star chart; **à ~ ouvert** ‹*pool*› open-air; ‹*sewer*› open
(b) heaven; **c'est le ~ qui t'envoie** you're a godsend

cierge /sjɛʀʒ/ *nm* (church) candle

cieux ▸ CIEL

cigale /sigal/ *nf* cicada

cigare /sigaʀ/ *nm* cigar

cigarette /sigaʀɛt/ *nf* cigarette

ci-gît /siʒi/ *phr* here lies

cigogne /sigɔɲ/ *nf* stork

ci-inclus, **~e** /siɛ̃kly, yz/ *adj, adv* enclosed

ci-joint, **~e** /siʒwɛ̃, ɛ̃t/ *adj, adv* enclosed

cil /sil/ *nm* eyelash

ciller /sije/ [1] *vi* **~ (des yeux)** to blink; **sans ~** without batting an eyelid *or* eyelash

cime /sim/ *nf* ‹*tree*›top

ciment /simɑ̃/ *nm* cement

cimenter /simɑ̃te/ [1] **1** *vtr* to cement
2 se cimenter (+ *v être*) *v refl* ‹*friendship*› to grow stronger

cimenterie /simɑ̃tʀi/ *nf* cement works

cimetière /simtjɛʀ/ *nm* cemetery, graveyard

cinéaste /sineast/ *nmf* film director

ciné-club, *pl* **~s** /sineklœb/ *nm* film club

ơ **cinéma** /sinema/ *nm* (a) **(salle de) ~** cinema (GB), movie theater (US)
(b) cinema; film industry; **faire du ~** to be in films
(c) (figurative) (fam) **arrête ton ~** cut out the play-acting; stop making such a fuss (colloq)
■ **~ d'art et d'essai** cinema showing art films (GB), art house (US)

cinémathèque /sinematɛk/ *nf* film archive

cinématographique /sinematɔgʀafik/ *adj* film (GB), movie (US)

cinéphile /sinefil/ *nmf* cinema enthusiast

cinglant, **~e** /sɛ̃glɑ̃, ɑ̃t/ *adj* (a) ‹*wind*› biting; ‹*rain*› driving
(b) ‹*remark, irony*› scathing

cinglé, **~e** /sɛ̃gle/ *adj* (fam) mad (colloq), crazy (colloq)

cingler /sɛ̃gle/ [1] *vtr* (a) ‹*rain, wind*› to sting ‹*face*›
(b) (with whip) to lash

cinoche /sinɔʃ/ *nm* (fam) cinema (GB), movie theater (US)

ơ **cinq** /sɛ̃k/ *adj inv, pron, nm inv* five

cinquantaine /sɛ̃kɑ̃tɛn/ *nf* **une ~** about fifty

cinquante /sɛ̃kɑ̃t/ *adj inv, pron, nm inv* fifty

cinquantenaire /sɛ̃kɑ̃tnɛʀ/ *nm* fiftieth anniversary

cinquantième /sɛ̃kɑ̃tjɛm/ *adj* fiftieth

cinquième /sɛ̃kjɛm/ **1** *adj* fifth
2 *nf* (a) (Sch) *second year of secondary school, age 12–13*
(b) (Aut) fifth (gear)

cintre /sɛ̃tʀ/ *nm* (a) (clothes) hanger
(b) (in architecture) curve

cintré, **~e** /sɛ̃tʀe/ *adj* ‹*coat*› waisted; ‹*shirt*› tailored

cirage /siʀaʒ/ *nm* (shoe) polish
IDIOM **être dans le ~** (fam) to be half-conscious

circoncire /siʀkɔ̃siʀ/ [64] *vtr* to circumcise

circoncision /siʀkɔ̃sizjɔ̃/ *nf* male circumcision

circonférence /siʀkɔ̃feʀɑ̃s/ *nf* circumference

circonflexe /siʀkɔ̃flɛks/ *adj* **accent ~** circumflex (accent)

circonscription /siʀkɔ̃skʀipsjɔ̃/ *nf* district

circonscrire /siʀkɔ̃skʀiʀ/ [67] *vtr* (a) to contain ‹*fire, epidemic*›; to limit ‹*subject*›
(b) to define

circonspection /siʀkɔ̃spɛksjɔ̃/ *nf* caution

ơ **circonstance** /siʀkɔ̃stɑ̃s/ **1** *nf*
(a) circumstance
(b) situation; **en toute ~** in any event; **pour la ~** for the occasion
2 de circonstance *phr* ‹*poem*› for the occasion; **faire une tête de ~** to assume a suitable expression
■ **~s atténuantes** (Law) extenuating *or* mitigating circumstances

circuit /siʀkɥi/ *nm* (a) (Sport, Tech) circuit
(b) (in tourism) tour
(c) (figurative) **être mis hors ~** ‹*person*› to be put on the sidelines; **vivre en ~ fermé** to live in a closed world

circulaire /siʀkylɛʀ/ *adj, nf* circular

circulation /siʀkylasjɔ̃/ *nf* (a) traffic; **~ alternée** contraflow
(b) circulation; **la libre ~ des personnes** the free movement of people; **disparaître de la ~** to go out of circulation

circulatoire /siʀkylatwaʀ/ *adj* circulatory

circuler /siʀkyle/ [1] *vi* (a) ‹*train, bus*› to run
(b) ‹*person*› to get around; to move about; (by car) to travel
(c) ‹*banknotes, rumour, information*› to circulate; **faire ~** to circulate; to spread ‹*rumour*›
(d) ‹*blood, air*› to circulate

cire /siʀ/ *nf* wax

ciré /siʀe/ *nm* oilskin

cirer /siʀe/ [1] *vtr* to polish ‹*shoes, floor*›

ơ **cirque** /siʀk/ *nm* (a) circus
(b) (figurative) (fam) racket (colloq); **arrête ton ~!** stop your nonsense!

c

cirrhose /siʁoz/ *nf* cirrhosis

cisaille /sizɑj/ *nf* pair of shears; ~s shears

cisailler /sizɑje/ [1] *vtr* **(a)** to shear; to cut
(b) to shear off

ciseau, *pl* ~**x** /sizo/ ⊞ *nm* **(a)** (Tech) chisel
(b) (Sport) scissors jump; scissors hold
⊡ **ciseaux** *nm pl* scissors

ciseler /sizle/ [17] *vtr* to chisel

ciselure /sizlyʁ/ *nf* chasing

citadelle /sitadɛl/ *nf* citadel

citadin, ~**e** /sitadɛ̃, in/ ⊞ *adj* city
⊡ *nm,f* city-dweller

citation /sitasjɔ̃/ *nf* quotation

⚜ **cité** /site/ *nf* **(a)** (gen) city; town
(b) housing estate
■ ~ **universitaire** student halls of residence
(GB), dormitories (US)

⚜ **citer** /site/ [1] *vtr* **(a)** to quote ⟨author,
passage⟩
(b) to name ⟨title, book⟩; to cite ⟨person,
example, fact⟩
(c) (Law) to summon ⟨witness⟩

citerne /sitɛʁn/ *nf* tank

⚜ **citoyen**, **-enne** /sitwajɛ̃, ɛn/ *nm,f* citizen

citoyenneté /sitwajɛnte/ *nf* citizenship

citrique /sitʁik/ *adj* citric

citron /sitʁɔ̃/ *nm* **(a)** lemon
(b) (fam) head, nut (colloq)
■ ~ **givré** lemon sorbet; ~ **vert** lime

citronnade /sitʁɔnad/ *nf* lemon squash
(GB), lemonade (US)

citronnelle /sitʁɔnɛl/ *nf* (Bot) citronella

citronnier /sitʁɔnje/ *nm* lemon tree

citrouille /sitʁuj/ *nf* pumpkin

civet /sivɛ/ *nm* ≈ stew

civière /sivjɛʁ/ *nf* stretcher

⚜ **civil**, ~**e** /sivil/ ⊞ *adj* (gen) civilian;
⟨marriage⟩ civil; ⟨funeral⟩ non religious
⊡ *nm* civilian; **en** ~ in civilian clothes; in
plain clothes; **dans le** ~ in civilian life

⚜ **civilisation** /sivilizasjɔ̃/ *nf* civilization

civiliser /sivilize/ [1] *vtr* to civilize

civilité /sivilite/ *nf* **(a)** (status) title (*Mr,
Mrs, Ms*)
(b) (dated) (politeness) civility

civique /sivik/ *adj* civic

claie /klɛ/ *nf* **(a)** wicker rack
(b) fence, hurdle

⚜ **clair**, ~**e** /klɛʁ/ ⊞ *adj* **(a)** ⟨colour⟩ light;
⟨complexion⟩ fair
(b) ⟨room⟩ bright
(c) ⟨weather, water⟩ clear
(d) ⟨text⟩ clear; **passer le plus** ~ **de son
temps** to spend most of one's time
⊡ *adv* ⟨speak⟩ clearly; **il faisait** ~ it was
already light; **voir** ~ to see well
⊟ *nm* **(a)** light; **mettre ses idées au** ~ to get
one's ideas straight; **tirer une affaire au** ~ to

⚜ indicates a very frequent word

get to the bottom of things
(b) light colours (GB)
■ ~ **de lune** moonlight
IDIOM **c'est** ~ **comme de l'eau de roche** it's
crystal clear

⚜ **clairement** /klɛʁmɑ̃/ *adv* clearly

clairière /klɛʁjɛʁ/ *nf* clearing, glade

clairon /klɛʁɔ̃/ *nm* **(a)** bugle
(b) bugler

claironnant, ~**e** /klɛʁɔnɑ̃, ɑ̃t/ *adj*
strident

claironner /klɛʁɔne/ [1] *vtr* to shout [sth]
from the rooftops

clairsemé, ~**e** /klɛʁsəme/ *adj* ⟨houses⟩
scattered; ⟨hair⟩ thin; ⟨population⟩ sparse

clairvoyance /klɛʁvwajɑ̃s/ *nf*
perceptiveness

clairvoyant, ~**e** /klɛʁvwajɑ̃, ɑ̃t/ *adj*
perceptive

clamer /klame/ [1] *vtr* to proclaim

clameur /klamœʁ/ *nf* roar

clan /klɑ̃/ *nm* clan

clandestin, ~**e** /klɑ̃dɛstɛ̃, in/ *adj*
⟨organization⟩ underground; ⟨immigration⟩
illegal; **passager** ~ stowaway

clandestinement /klɑ̃dɛstinmɑ̃/ *adv*
illegally

clandestinité /klɑ̃dɛstinite/ *nf* secret
or clandestine nature; **dans la** ~ ⟨live⟩ in
hiding; ⟨operate⟩ in secret

clap /klap/ *nm* clapperboard

clapet /klapɛ/ *nm* **(a)** valve
(b) (fam) mouth, trap (colloq)

clapier /klapje/ *nm* rabbit hutch

clapoter /klapɔte/ [1] *vi* to lap

claquage /klakaʒ/ *nm* pulled *or* strained
muscle

claque /klak/ *nf* **(a)** slap
(b) (fam) slap in the face
(c) (in theatre) claque
IDIOM **en avoir sa** ~ (fam) to be fed up

claqué, ~**e** /klake/ *adj* (fam) knackered
(pop), done in (colloq)

claquement /klakmɑ̃/ *nm* (of door) bang;
(of whip) crack; (of tongue) click; (of
flag) flapping

claquemurer: se claquemurer
/klakmyʁe/ [1] *v refl* (+ *v être*) to shut oneself
away (**dans** in)

claquer /klake/ [1] ⊞ *vtr* **(a)** to slam ⟨door⟩
(b) (fam) to exhaust ⟨person⟩
(c) (fam) to blow (colloq) ⟨money⟩
⊡ *vi* ⟨door⟩ to bang; (closing) to slam shut;
⟨flag⟩ to flap; **elle claque des dents** her teeth
are chattering
⊟ **se claquer** *v refl* (+ *v être*) **se** ~ **un
muscle** to pull *or* strain a muscle

claquettes /klakɛt/ *nf pl* tap dancing

clarifier /klaʁifje/ [2] *vtr* to clarify

clarinette /klaʁinɛt/ *nf* clarinet

clarté /klaʁte/ *nf* **(a)** light

(b) (of water) clarity; (of complexion) fairness
(c) (of style) clarity

⚡ **classe** /klas/ *nf* **(a)** (Sch) (group) class, form (GB); (level) year, form (GB), grade (US); **après la ∼** after school
(b) (Sch) classroom
(c) (in society, transport) class; **les ∼s sociales** social classes
(d) avoir de la ∼ to have class
(e) (Mil) **faire ses ∼s** to do one's basic training
■ **∼ d'âge** age group; **∼ verte** *educational schooltrip to the countryside*; **∼s préparatoires (aux grandes écoles)** *preparatory classes for entrance to Grandes Écoles*

classement /klasmã/ *nm*
(a) classification
(b) filing; **faire du ∼ dans ses papiers** to sort one's papers out
(c) grading; **∼ trimestriel** (Sch) termly position (in class)
(d) (Sport) ranking; **en tête du ∼** in first place
(e) (of hotel) rating

classer /klase/ [1] **1** *vtr* **(a)** to classify
(b) to file (away) ‹*documents*›
(c) (Law) to close ‹*case*›
(d) to list ‹*old building*›
(e) to class ‹*country, pupils*›; to rank ‹*song, player*›
(f) (fam) to size [sb] up
2 **se classer** *v refl* (+ *v être*) to rank

classeur /klasœR/ *nm* **(a)** ring binder
(b) file

classicisme /klasisism/ *nm* **(a)** (in art) classicism
(b) (in clothes, tastes) traditionalism

classification /klasifikasjɔ̃/ *nf* classification

classifier /klasifje/ [2] *vtr* to classify

⚡ **classique** /klasik/ **1** *adj* **(a)** classical; **faire des études ∼s** (Sch) to do classics
(b) classic; ‹*method*› classic, standard; ‹*consequence*› usual; **de coupe ∼** of classic cut; **c'est∼!** (fam) it's typical!; **c'est le coup∼!** (fam) it's the same old story!
2 *nm* classic

clause /kloz/ *nf* clause

claustrophobie /klostʀɔfɔbi/ *nf* claustrophobia

clavecin /klavsɛ̃/ *nm* harpsichord

clavicule /klavikyl/ *nf* collarbone

clavier /klavje/ *nm* keyboard; **∼ numérique** numeric keypad

claviste /klavist/ *nmf* **(a)** typesetter
(b) (Comput) keyboarder

⚡ **clé** /kle/ **1** *nf* **(a)** (of lock, tin) key; **sous ∼** under lock and key; **fermer à ∼** to lock; **prix ∼s en main** ‹*car*› on the road price (GB), sticker price (US); **usine ∼s en main** turnkey factory
(b) (solution) key (**de** to)

(c) spanner (GB), wrench
(d) (of flute) key; (of violin) peg; **∼ de fa** bass clef
2 **(-)clé** (*combining form*) **poste/mot(-)∼** key post/word
3 **à la clé** *phr* at stake; **avec, à la ∼, une récompense** with a reward thrown in
■ **∼ anglaise, ∼ à molette** adjustable spanner (GB) *or* wrench (US); **∼ USB** USB key

clef ▸ CLÉ

clément, ∼e /klemã, ãt/ *adj* **(a)** ‹*judge*› lenient
(b) ‹*temperature, winter*› mild

clémentine /klemãtin/ *nf* clementine

cleptomanie /klɛptɔmani/ *nf* kleptomania

clerc /klɛR/ *nm* (Law) clerk

clergé /klɛRʒe/ *nm* clergy

cliché /kliʃe/ *nm* **(a)** snapshot
(b) cliché

⚡ **client, ∼e** /klijã, ãt/ *nm,f* (of shop) customer; (of solicitor) client; (of hotel) guest; (in taxi) fare
IDIOM c'est à la tête du ∼ it depends whether they like the look of you

clientèle /klijãtɛl/ *nf* (of shop) customers; (of solicitor) clients; (of doctor) patients; **se faire une ∼** to build up a clientele

cligner /kliɲe/ [1] *v+prep* **∼ des yeux** to blink; **∼ de l'œil** to wink

clignotant /kliɲɔtã/ *nm* (Aut) indicator (GB), blinker (US)

clignoter /kliɲɔte/ [1] *vi* ‹*light*› to flash; to flash on and off; ‹*star*› to twinkle

climat /klima/ *nm* climate

climatique /klimatik/ *adj* climatic

climatisation /klimatizasjɔ̃/ *nf* air-conditioning

climatiser /klimatize/ [1] *vtr* to air-condition

climatiseur /klimatizœR/ *nm* air-conditioner

clin /klɛ̃/ *nm* **∼ d'œil** wink; (figurative) allusion; **en un ∼ d'œil** in a flash

clinique /klinik/ **1** *adj* clinical
2 *nf* private hospital; **∼ vétérinaire** veterinary clinic

clinquant, ∼e /klɛ̃kã, ãt/ *adj* flashy (colloq)

clip /klip/ *nm* **(a)** pop video
(b) clip-on (earring)

clique /klik/ *nf* clique; **prendre ses ∼s et ses claques** to pack up and go

cliquer /klike/ [1] *vi* (Comput) to click (**sur** on); **∼ à droite/gauche** to right-click/left-click

cliqueter /klikte/ [20] *vi* ‹*keys*› to jingle; ‹*chain, machine*› to rattle

clitoris /klitɔris/ *nm* clitoris

clivage /klivaʒ/ *nm* divide; **∼ d'opinion** division of opinion

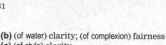

clochard, ∼e /klɔʃaʀ, aʀd/ *nm,f* tramp

cloche /klɔʃ/ *nf* (a) bell
(b) (fam) clod (colloq), idiot
(c) ∼ à fromage cover of cheese dish
IDIOMS entendre plusieurs sons de ∼ to hear several versions; sonner les ∼s à qn to bawl sb out (colloq)

cloche-pied: à cloche-pied /aklɔʃpje/ *phr* sauter à ∼ to hop

clocher¹ /klɔʃe/ [1] *vi* (fam) il y a quelque chose qui cloche there's something wrong

clocher² /klɔʃe/ *nm* steeple; church *or* bell tower; querelle de ∼ local quarrel

clochette /klɔʃɛt/ *nf* (little) bell

cloison /klwazɔ̃/ *nf* (a) partition
(b) screen; ∼ extensible folding room-divider

cloisonner /klwazɔne/ [1] *vtr* (a) to partition ‹room›; to divide up ‹space›
(b) to divide up ‹society›; to compartmentalize ‹administration›

cloître /klwatʀ/ *nm* cloister

cloîtrer /klwatʀe/ [1] **1** *vtr* to shut [sb] away
2 **se cloîtrer** *v refl* (+ *v être*) to shut oneself away

clone /klon/ *nm* clone

clope /klɔp/ *nm or f* (fam) fag (GB) (colloq), ciggy (colloq), cigarette

clopin-clopant /klɔpɛ̃klɔpɑ̃/ *phr* (fam) aller ∼ to hobble along

cloporte /klɔpɔʀt/ *nm* woodlouse

cloque /klɔk/ *nf* blister

clore /klɔʀ/ [79] **1** *vtr* (a) to close ‹debate›
(b) to end, to conclude ‹programme›
(c) to close ‹eyes›
2 **se clore** *v refl* (+ *v être*) to end (par with)

clos, ∼e /klo, oz/ **1** *pp* ▶ CLORE
2 *pp adj* ‹system› closed; ‹area› enclosed; monde ∼ self-contained world

clôture /klotyʀ/ *nf* (a) fence; wire fence; railings
(b) (of debate, session) close; (of subscription) closing; discours de ∼ closing speech

clôturer /klotyʀe/ [1] *vtr* (a) to fence in ‹land›
(b) to close ‹list›; to end ‹debate›

clou /klu/ **1** *nm* (a) nail; stud
(b) (of show) star attraction; (of evening) high point
(c) (Med) boil
2 **clous** *nm pl* (a) pedestrian crossing (GB), crosswalk (US)
(b) (fam) des ∼s! no way!
■ ∼ de girofle (Bot, Culin) clove
IDIOM enfoncer le ∼ to drive the point home

⚲ indicates a very frequent word

clouer /klue/ [1] *vtr* to nail down ‹lid›; to nail together ‹planks›; ∼ au sol (figurative) to pin [sb] down; être cloué au lit to be confined to bed

clown /klun/ *nm* clown

clownerie /klunʀi/ *nf* clowning; arrête tes ∼s stop clowning about

club /klœb/ *nm* (a) club
(b) ∼ de vacances holiday camp

CM /seɛm/ *nm*: *abbr* ▶ COURS

CMU /seɛmy/ *n* (*abbr* = **Couverture Médicale Universelle**) *free health care for people on low incomes*

CNPF /seɛnpeɛf/ *nm* (*abbr* = **Conseil national du patronat français**) *national council of French employers*

CNRS /seɛnɛʀɛs/ *nm* (*abbr* = **Centre national de la recherche scientifique**) *national centre for scientific research*

coaguler /kɔagyle/ [1] *vi*, **se coaguler** *v refl* (+ *v être*) ‹blood› to coagulate

coalition /kɔalisjɔ̃/ *nf* coalition

coasser /kɔase/ [1] *vi* to croak

cobaye /kɔbaj/ *nm* guinea pig

cobra /kɔbʀa/ *nm* cobra

cocaïne /kɔkain/ *nf* cocaine

cocarde /kɔkaʀd/ *nf* (a) rosette; (on uniform) cockade
(b) (on vehicle) official badge

cocasse /kɔkas/ *adj* comical

coccinelle /kɔksinɛl/ *nf* ladybird (GB), ladybug (US)

coccyx /kɔksis/ *nm* coccyx

coche /kɔʃ/ *nm* (stage)coach
IDIOM manquer le ∼ to miss the boat

cocher¹ /kɔʃe/ [1] *vtr* to tick (GB), to check (US)

cocher² /kɔʃe/ *nm* coachman; cabman

cochère /kɔʃɛʀ/ *adj f* porte ∼ carriage entrance

cochon, -onne /kɔʃɔ̃, ɔn/ **1** *adj* (fam) (a) ‹film› dirty; ‹person› dirty-minded
(b) ‹person› messy, dirty
2 *nm,f* (fam) (a) pig (colloq), slob (colloq); de ∼ ‹job› botched; ‹weather› lousy (colloq)
(b) sex maniac
3 *nm* (a) (Zool) pig, hog
(b) (Culin) pork
■ ∼ d'Inde Guinea pig; ∼ de lait sucking pig

cochonnaille /kɔʃɔnaj/ *nf* (fam): *products made from pork such as salami, bacon, pâté and ham*

cochonnerie /kɔʃɔnʀi/ *nf* (fam) (a) junk (colloq); il ne mange que des ∼s he only eats junk food
(b) mess; faire des ∼s to make a mess

cocker /kɔkɛʀ/ *nm* (cocker) spaniel

cocktail /kɔktɛl/ *nm* (a) cocktail

(b) (figurative) mixture
(c) cocktail party

coco /koko/ *nm* coconut

cocon /kɔkɔ̃/ *nm* cocoon

cocorico /kɔkɔRiko/ *nm* cock-a-doodle-do

cocotier /kɔkɔtje/ *nm* coconut palm

cocotte /kɔkɔt/ *nf* **(a)** (fam) (baby talk) hen
(b) (fam) **ma ∼** honey (colloq)
(c) (Culin) casserole (GB), pot

cocotte-minute®, *pl* **cocottes-minute** /kɔkɔtminyt/ *nf* pressure cooker

codage /kɔdaʒ/ *nm* coding, encoding

⚡ **code** /kɔd/ ① *nm* code
　② **codes** *nm pl* (of vehicle) dipped (GB) *or* dimmed (US) (head)lights, low beam
　■ **∼ accès** password; **∼ agence** sort code (GB), routing number (US); **∼ (à) barres** bar code; **∼ confidentiel** personal identification number, PIN; **∼ guichet** ▶ CODE AGENCE; **∼ de la nationalité** regulations as to nationality; **∼ postal** post code (GB), zip code (US); **∼ de la route** (Aut) highway code (GB), rules of the road (US); **passer son ∼** (fam) to take the written part of a driving test

coder /kɔde/ [1] *vtr* to code, to encode

codétenu, **∼e** /kɔdetny/ *nm,f* fellow prisoner

codifier /kɔdifje/ [2] *vtr* to codify *‹laws›*; to standardize *‹language, custom›*

codirecteur, **-trice** /kɔdiRɛktœr, tRis/ *nm,f* joint manager; joint director

coefficient /kɔefisjɑ̃/ *nm* **(a)** ratio
(b) margin
(c) *weighting factor in an exam*; **la chimie est au ∼ 4** chemistry results are multiplied by 4
(d) (in arithmetic, physics) coefficient

coéquipier, **-ière** /koekipje, ɛR/ *nm,f* team mate

⚡ **cœur** /kœR/ ① *nm* **(a)** heart; **il a le ∼ malade** he has a heart condition; **serrer qn sur** *or* **contre son ∼** to hold sb close; **écouter son ∼** to go with one's feelings; **aller droit au ∼ de qn** to touch sb deeply; **avoir un coup de ∼ pour qch** to fall in love with sth; **ça me fait mal au ∼ de voir** it sickens me to see; **problème de ∼** emotional problem; **parler à ∼ ouvert** to speak openly; **avoir bon ∼** to be kind-hearted; **je n'ai plus le ∼ à rien** I don't feel like doing anything any more
(b) (Culin) heart
(c) (figurative) (of fruit, rock) core; (of problem, debate) heart; **au ∼ de** (of region, town) in the middle of; (of building, problem, system) at the heart of; **au ∼ de l'hiver** in the dead of winter
(d) (person) **mon (petit) ∼** sweetheart
(e) courage; **le ∼ m'a manqué** my courage failed me; **redonner du ∼ à qn** to give sb new heart
(f) (Games) (card) heart; (suit) hearts
　② **à cœur** *phr* **avoir à ∼ de faire** to be

intent on doing; **prendre qch à ∼** to take sth seriously
　③ **de bon cœur** *phr* willingly; **rire de bon ∼** to laugh heartily
　④ **par cœur** *phr* by heart; **connaître qn par ∼** to know sb inside out
　IDIOMS **avoir mal au ∼** to feel sick (GB) *or* nauseous (US); **avoir du ∼ au ventre** to be brave; **avoir le ∼ sur la main** to be open-handed; **il ne le porte pas dans son ∼** he's not his favourite (GB) person; **j'irai mais le ∼ n'y est pas** I'll go but my heart isn't in it; **si le ∼ t'en dit** if you feel like it; **avoir qch sur le ∼** to be resentful about sth

coexister /kɔegziste/ [1] *vi* to coexist

coffre /kɔfR/ *nm* **(a)** chest; **∼ à jouets** toy box
(b) (for valuables) safe; (individual) safety deposit box; **la salle des ∼s** the strongroom
(c) (of car) boot (GB), trunk (US)
IDIOM **avoir du ∼** (fam) to have a powerful voice

coffre-fort, *pl* **coffres-forts** /kɔfRǝfɔR/ *nm* safe

coffret /kɔfRɛ/ *nm* **(a)** casket; **∼ à bijoux** jewellery (GB) *or* jewelry (US) box
(b) (of records, cassettes, books) boxed set

cogérer /kɔʒeRe/ [14] *vtr* to co-manage

cogestion /kɔʒɛstjɔ̃/ *nf* joint management

cogiter /kɔʒite/ [1] *vi* to cogitate, to think

cognac /kɔɲak/ *nm* cognac (*brandy from the Cognac area*)

cogner /kɔɲe/ [1] ① *vtr* to knock
　② *vi* **(a) ∼ contre** *‹shutter›* to bang against; *‹branch›* to knock against; *‹projectile›* to hit; **∼ à la porte** to bang on the door
(b) (fam) *‹boxer›* to hit out
(c) *‹heart›* to pound
　③ **se cogner** *v refl* (+ *v être*) to bump into something; **se ∼ le pied contre une pierre** to stub one's toe on a stone

cognitif, **-ive** /kɔgnitif, iv/ *adj* cognitive

cohabitation /koabitasjɔ̃/ *nf* **(a)** living with somebody
(b) *situation where the French President is in political opposition to the government*

cohabiter /koabite/ [1] *vi ‹people›* to live together; *‹things›* to coexist

cohérence /kɔeRɑ̃s/ *nf* **(a)** coherence; consistency
(b) (in physics) cohesion

cohérent, **∼e** /kɔeRɑ̃, ɑ̃t/ *adj* coherent; consistent

cohéritier, **-ière** /koeRitje, ɛR/ *nm,f* joint heir

cohésion /kɔezjɔ̃/ *nf* cohesion

cohorte /koɔRt/ *nf* (fam) crowd, group

cohue /kɔy/ *nf* crowd; **c'est la ∼** it's a crush

coi, **coite** /kwa, kwat/ *adj* **se tenir ∼** to remain quiet

coiffant, ~e /kwafɑ̃, ɑ̃t/ *adj* **gel** ~ styling gel

coiffe /kwaf/ *nf* (gen) headgear; (of nun) wimple

coiffer /kwafe/ [1] **1** *vtr* (a) ~ **qn** to do sb's hair; to comb sb's hair
(b) **coiffé d'une casquette** wearing a cap
2 **se coiffer** *v refl* (+ *v être*) (a) to do *or* comb one's hair
(b) **se** ~ **de qch** to put sth on
IDIOM ~ **qn au poteau** (fam) *or* **sur le fil** (fam) to beat sb by a whisker

coiffeur, **-euse**[1] /kwafœR, øz/ *nm,f* hairdresser

coiffeuse[2] /kwaføz/ *nf* dressing table

coiffure /kwafyR/ *nf* (a) hairstyle
(b) hairdressing
(c) headgear

🗣 **coin** /kwɛ̃/ **1** *nm* (a) corner; **à tous les** ~**s de rue** everywhere; **aux quatre** ~**s de la ville** all over the town; **aller au** ~ (as punishment) to go and stand in the corner; **j'ai dû poser mon sac dans un** ~ I must have put my bag down somewhere; **au** ~ **du feu** by the fire
(b) (of eye, mouth) corner; **un sourire en** ~ a half-smile; **un regard en** ~ a sidelong glance
(c) (of ground) plot; (of lawn) patch; **un** ~ **de paradis** an idyllic spot
(d) (in region) **un** ~ **de France** a part of France; **dans le** ~ around here, in these parts; around there, in those parts; **le café du** ~ the local café; **les gens du** ~ the locals; **connaître les bons** ~**s pour manger** to know all the good places to eat
(e) (for photograph) corner; (for file) reinforcing corner
(f) (Tech) wedge
2 **coin(-)** (*combining form*) ~**-repas**/ **-salon** dining/living area

coincé, ~e /kwɛ̃se/ **1** *pp* ▸ COINCER
2 *pp adj* (a) stuck; trapped; ~ **entre** ‹house› wedged between
(b) (fam) **j'ai le dos** ~, **je suis** ~ my back has gone (colloq)
(c) (figurative) (fam) stuck (colloq)
(d) (fam) ill at ease
(e) (fam) uptight (colloq)

coincer /kwɛ̃se/ [12] **1** *vtr* (a) to wedge ‹object›; to wedge [sth] open/shut ‹door›; ‹snow› to trap ‹person›
(b) to jam ‹drawer, zip›
(c) (fam) to catch ‹person›; **se faire** ~ **par to** get caught by
(d) (fam) to catch [sb] out ‹person›
2 *vi* (a) ‹zip, drawer› to stick
(b) (fam) **ça coince** there's a problem
3 **se coincer** *v refl* (+ *v être*) (a) ‹object› to get stuck *or* jammed
(b) **se** ~ **les doigts** to get one's fingers caught

coïncidence /kɔɛ̃sidɑ̃s/ *nf* coincidence

coïncider /kɔɛ̃side/ [1] *vi* to coincide

coing /kwɛ̃/ *nm* quince

coite ▸ COI

col /kɔl/ *nm* (a) collar
(b) (in mountains) pass
(c) (of bottle) neck
(d) (Anat) neck
■ ~ **blanc** white-collar worker

🗣 **colère** /kɔlɛR/ *nf* (a) anger; **être en** ~ to be angry; **passer sa** ~ **sur qn** to take out *or* vent one's anger on sb; **sous le coup de la** ~ in a fit of anger
(b) **faire** *or* **piquer** (fam) **une** ~ to have a fit; to throw a tantrum

coléreux, **-euse** /kɔleRø, øz/ *adj* ‹person› quick-tempered

colifichet /kɔlifiʃɛ/ *nm* trinket; knick-knack

colimaçon /kɔlimasɔ̃/ *nm* snail; **escalier en** ~ spiral staircase

colin /kɔlɛ̃/ *nm* (fish) hake; coley

colin-maillard /kɔlɛ̃majaR/ *nm* **jouer à** ~ to play blind man's buff

colique /kɔlik/ *nf* (a) diarrhoea
(b) stomach pain; (in babies) colic

colis /kɔli/ *nm* parcel
■ ~ **piégé** parcel bomb; ~ **postal** parcel sent by mail

colite /kɔlit/ *nf* colitis

collaborateur, **-trice** /kɔlabɔRatœR, tRis/ *nm,f* (a) colleague; assistant
(b) employee
(c) (journalist) contributor
(d) (derogatory) collaborator

collaboration /kɔlabɔRasjɔ̃/ *nf*
(a) (to newspaper) contribution; (work on project) collaboration
(b) (in Second World War) collaboration

collaborer /kɔlabɔRe/ [1] *vi* (a) ~ **à** to contribute to ‹newspaper›; to collaborate on ‹project›
(b) (as working partner) to collaborate

collage /kɔlaʒ/ *nm* collage; (in photography) montage

collant, ~e /kɔlɑ̃, ɑ̃t/ **1** *adj*
(a) ‹substance, object› sticky
(b) ‹dress› skintight
2 *nm* tights (GB), panty hose (US)

collation /kɔlasjɔ̃/ *nf* light meal

colle /kɔl/ *nf* (a) glue; (wallpaper) paste
(b) (fam) (hard question) poser (colloq); test
(c) (students' slang) detention

collecte /kɔlɛkt/ *nf* (a) collection; **faire une** ~ to raise funds
(b) (prayer) collect

collecter /kɔlɛkte/ [1] *vtr* to collect

collecteur, **-trice** /kɔlɛktœR, tRis/ *nm,f* collector
■ ~ **de fonds** fundraiser; ~ **d'impôts** tax collector

collectif, -ive /kɔlɛktif, iv/ **1** *adj*
collective; ‹dismissals› mass; ‹heating›
shared; ‹ticket› group
2 *nm* (a) collective
(b) action group

collection /kɔlɛksjɔ̃/ *nf* (a) collection;
~ **de timbres** stamp collection
(b) (of books) series; (by same author) set

collectionner /kɔlɛksjɔne/ [1] *vtr* (a) to
collect
(b) (figurative) ~ **les erreurs** to make one
mistake after another

collectionneur, -euse
/kɔlɛksjɔnœʀ, øz/ *nm,f* collector

collectivement /kɔlɛktivmɑ̃/ *adv*
(gen) collectively; ‹resign› en masse, as a
body

collectivité /kɔlɛktivite/ *nf* (a) group
(b) community
■ ~ **locale** local authority (GB), local
government (US)

collège /kɔlɛʒ/ *nm* (a) secondary school
(GB), junior high school (US) (*up to age 16*)
(b) college, ~ **électoral** (Pol) electoral college
■ ~ **d'enseignement secondaire, CES**
secondary school (GB), junior high school
(US); ~ **d'enseignement technique, CET**
technical secondary school in France

collégial, ~e, mpl -iaux /kɔleʒjal, o/ *adj*
‹church› collegial; ‹system› collegiate

collégien, -ienne /kɔleʒjɛ̃, ɛn/ *nm,f*
schoolboy/schoolgirl

collègue /kɔlɛg/ *nmf* colleague

coller /kɔle/ [1] **1** *vtr* (a) to stick, to glue
‹wood, paper›; to paste up ‹poster›; to hang
‹wallpaper›; to stick [sth] on ‹label›; to stick
down ‹envelope›
(b) ~ **qch contre** or **à qch** to press sth
against sth; **il la colla contre le parapet** he
pushed her up against the parapet
(c) (fam) to stick (colloq); **je leur ai collé
la facture sous le nez** I stuck the bill
(right) under their noses; ~ **une amende/
une gifle à qn** to fine/slap sb
(d) (fam) (in exam) **se faire** ~ to fail
(e) (fam) to give [sb] detention ‹pupil›
2 *vi* (a) to stick
(b) (fam) ~ **avec** to fit *or* be consistent with
3 se coller *v refl* (+ *v être*) (a) **se** ~ **à**
or **contre qn/qch** to press oneself against
sb/sth
(b) (fam) **dès qu'il rentre, il se colle devant
son ordinateur** as soon as he comes in he's
glued (colloq) to his computer

collerette /kɔlʀɛt/ *nf* (a) ruff
(b) ruffle

collet /kɔlɛ/ *nm* **être** ~ **monté** to be prim

collier /kɔlje/ *nm* (a) necklace; ~ **de perles**
string of pearls
(b) (of animal) collar
(c) beard
IDIOM donner un coup de ~ to get one's

head down; to put one's back into it

collimateur /kɔlimatœʀ/ *nm* **avoir qn
dans le** ~ (fam) to have it in for sb (colloq)

colline /kɔlin/ *nf* hill

collision /kɔlizjɔ̃/ *nf* collision

colloque /kɔl(l)ɔk/ *nm* conference,
symposium

collyre /kɔliʀ/ *nm* eyedrops

colmater /kɔlmate/ [1] *vtr* to plug, to seal
off ‹leak›; to seal ‹crack›

colocation /kɔlɔkasjɔ̃/ *nf* (in an
apartment) flat-sharing; (in a house) house-
sharing

colombe /kɔlɔ̃b/ *nf* dove

colombier /kɔlɔ̃bje/ *nm* dovecote

colon /kɔlɔ̃/ *nm* colonist

côlon /kolɔ̃, kɔlɔ̃/ *nm* colon

colonel /kɔlɔnɛl/ *nm* (Mil) (in army) ≈ colonel;
(in air force) ≈ group captain (GB), ≈ colonel
(US)

colonial, ~e, mpl -iaux /kɔlɔnjal, o/ *adj,
nm,f* colonial

colonialisme /kɔlɔnjalism/ *nm*
colonialism

colonie /kɔlɔni/ *nf* (gen) colony; ~ **(de
vacances)** holiday camp (*for children*)

colonnade /kɔlɔnad/ *nf* colonnade

colonne /kɔlɔn/ *nf* column
■ ~ **vertébrale** (Anat) spinal column

colorant, ~e /kɔlɔʀɑ̃, ɑ̃t/ **1** *adj*
colouring (GB)
2 *nm* (a) colouring (GB) agent
(b) dye
(c) (in chemistry) stain
(d) (Culin) colouring (GB)

coloration /kɔlɔʀasjɔ̃/ *nf* (a) colouring
(GB); dyeing; staining; tinting
(b) colour (GB)

coloré, ~e /kɔlɔʀe/ *adj* (a) (gen) coloured (GB)
(b) ‹life, crowd› colourful (GB); ‹style› lively

colorer /kɔlɔʀe/ [1] *vtr* to colour (GB); to
tint; to stain; to dye

colorier /kɔlɔʀje/ [2] *vtr* to colour in (GB),
to color (US)

coloris /kɔlɔʀi/ *nm inv* colour (GB); shade

colossal, ~e, mpl -aux /kɔlɔsal, o/ *adj*
colossal, huge

colosse /kɔlɔs/ *nm* giant

colporter /kɔlpɔʀte/ [1] *vtr* (a) to spread
‹news›
(b) to peddle ‹goods›

coltiner: se coltiner /kɔltine/ [1] *v refl*
(+ *v être*) (fam) (a) to lug (colloq) ‹heavy object›
(b) to get stuck with (colloq) ‹chore, person›

colza /kɔlza/ *nm* rape

coma /kɔma/ *nm* coma

comateux, -euse /kɔmatø, øz/ *adj*
comatose

combat /kɔ̃ba/ *nm* (a) (Mil) fighting; ~**s
aériens** air battles; **mettre hors de** ~ to
disable

(b) (in politics) struggle; **livrer un ~ to**
campaign
(c) (Sport) bout; **hors de ~** out of action
■ **~ de coqs** cock fight

combatif, -ive /kɔ̃batif, iv/ *adj*
(a) assertive
(b) aggressive

combativité /kɔ̃bativite/ *nf* fighting spirit

combattant, ~e /kɔ̃batã, ãt/ *nm,f*
combatant

⚔ **combattre** /kɔ̃batʀ/ [61] *vtr, vi* to fight

⚔ **combien¹** /kɔ̃bjɛ̃/ 1 *adv* **(a) ~ mesure**
le salon? how big is the lounge?; **j'aimerais**
savoir ~ il a payé son costume I'd like
to know how much he paid for that suit;
~ êtes-vous? how many of you are there?
(b) (to what extent) **je ne saurais te dire ~ il me**
manque I can't tell you how much I miss him
2 **combien de** *det* **(a)** how many, how
much
(b) ~ de temps faut-il? how long does it
take?

combien² /kɔ̃bjɛ̃/ *nmf inv* **(a) tu es le/la**
~? (in queue) how many people are before
you?
(b) le ~ sommes-nous? what's the date
today?
(c) (for measurements) **tu chausses du ~?**
what size shoes do you take?
(d) tu le vois tous les ~? how often do you
see him?

combinaison /kɔ̃binɛzɔ̃/ *nf*
(a) combining; combination
(b) (of safe) combination
(c) (full-length) slip
(d) jumpsuit
(e) overalls (GB), coveralls (US)
■ **~ de plongée** wetsuit

combine /kɔ̃bin/ *nf* (fam) trick (colloq);
scheme

combiné /kɔ̃bine/ *nm* handset, receiver

combiner /kɔ̃bine/ [1] *vtr* **(a)** to combine
(b) to work out ‹*plan*›

comble /kɔ̃bl/ 1 *adj* ‹*room*› packed
2 *nm* **(a) le ~ de l'injustice/du mauvais**
goût the height of injustice/of bad taste;
pour ~ de malchance j'ai... I...; c'est un
or le~! (fam) that's the limit!
(b) roof space; **de fond en ~** from top to
bottom; completely
3 **combles** *nm pl* attic

combler /kɔ̃ble/ [1] *vtr* **(a)** to fill (in) ‹*ditch*›
(b) to fill in ‹*gaps*›; to make up ‹*deficit*›
(c) to fulfil (GB) ‹*need, desire*›; **la vie m'a**
comblé I've had a wonderful life; **~ qn** to fill
sb with joy

combustible /kɔ̃bystibl/ 1 *adj*
combustible
2 *nm* fuel; **~ nucléaire** nuclear fuel

combustion /kɔ̃bystjɔ̃/ *nf* combustion

⚔ indicates a very frequent word

comédie /komedi/ *nf* **(a)** comedy
(b) play-acting; **jouer la ~** to put on an act
(c) (fam) scene; **faire une ~** to make a scene
■ **~ musicale** musical

comédien, -ienne /komedjɛ̃, ɛn/ 1 *adj*
il est (un peu) ~ (figurative) he puts it on
2 *nm,f* actor/actress

comestible /komɛstibl/ 1 *adj* edible
2 **comestibles** *nm pl* food

comète /komɛt/ *nf* comet

comique /komik/ 1 *adj* **(a)** comic
(b) funny
2 *nmf* comic actor/actress; comedian
3 *nm* **(a)** clown
(b) comedy

⚔ **comité** /komite/ *nm* **(a)** committee
(b) group

commandant /komãdã/ *nm* (in
army) ≈ major; (in air force) ≈ squadron
leader (GB), ≈ major (US)
■ **~ de bord** captain

commande /komãd/ *nf* **(a)** order
(b) commission; **passer ~ de qch à qn** to
commission sb to do sth
(c) (Tech) control; **levier de ~** control lever;
être aux *or* **tenir les ~s** to be at the controls;
(figurative) to be in control
(d) (Comput) command

commandement /komãdmã/ *nm*
(a) (Mil) command
(b) (in religion) commandment

⚔ **commander** /komãde/ [1] 1 *vtr* **(a)** to
order [sth] **(à qn** from sb)
(b) to commission ‹*book, survey*›
(c) (Mil) to command ‹*army*›; to order ‹*attack*›
(d) ~ qn to order sb about
(e) les circonstances commandent la
prudence the circumstances call for caution
(f) ‹*machine*› to control ‹*mechanism*›
2 **commander à** *v+prep* **(a) ~ à** to be in
command of
(b) ~ à to order, to command
3 *vi* to give the orders, to be in charge
4 **se commander** *v refl* (+ *v être*) **ça ne**
se commande pas it's not something you
can control

commanditer /komãdite/ [1] *vtr* **(a)** to
finance ‹*company*›
(b) to sponsor ‹*project*›
(c) to be behind ‹*crime*›

commando /komãdo/ *nm* commando

⚔ **comme** /kɔm/ 1 *adv* how
2 *conj* **(a)** as; **ici ~ en Italie** here as in Italy;
il est paresseux, ~ sa sœur d'ailleurs he's
lazy, just like his sister; **jolie ~ tout** really
pretty
(b) (in comparisons) **il est grand ~ sa sœur**
he's as tall as his sister; **c'est tout ~** (fam) it
comes to the same thing; **elle me traite ~ un**
enfant she treats me like a child
(c) like; **un manteau ~ le tien** a coat like
yours; **~ ça** like that; **puisque c'est ~ ça** if

that's the way it is
(d) as if, as though; **~ pour faire** as if to do
(e) (fam) **elle a eu ~ un évanouissement** she sort of fainted
(f) **avare ~ il est, il ne te donnera rien** he's so mean, he won't give you anything
(g) as; **travailler ~ jardinier** to work as a gardener
(h) as, since; **~ elle était seule** as or since she was alone
(i) as; **~ il traversait la rue** as he was crossing the road
IDIOMS ~ quoi! which just shows!; **~ ci ~ ça** (fam) so-so (colloq)

commémoration /kɔmemɔrasjɔ̃/ *nf* commemoration

commémorer /kɔmemɔre/ [1] *vtr* to commemorate

commencement /kɔmɑ̃smɑ̃/ *nm* beginning

✧ **commencer** /kɔmɑ̃se/ [12] **1** *vtr* **(a)** to start, to begin
(b) **~ à** or **de faire** to start or begin to do; **ça commence à bien faire!** (fam) it's getting to be a bit much!
2 *vi* to start, to begin; **pour ~** for a start; **vous êtes tous coupables à ~ par toi** you're all guilty starting with you
3 *v impers* **il commence à neiger** it's starting or beginning to snow

✧ **comment** /kɔmɑ̃/ *adv* **(a)** how; **~ faire?** how can it be done?; **~ t'appelles-tu?** what's your name?; **~ ça se fait?** (fam) how come? (colloq)
(b) **~? qu'est-ce que tu dis?** pardon? what did you say?; **Paul ~?** Paul who?
(c) **~ est leur maison/fils?** what's their house/son like?; **~ trouvez-vous ma robe?** what do you think of my dress?
(d) **~ cela?** what do you mean?; **~ donc!** but of course!; **et~ (donc)!** (fam) and how! (colloq); **'c'était bon?'—'et~!'** (fam) 'was it nice?'—'it certainly was!'

✧ **commentaire** /kɔmmɑ̃tɛr/ *nm*
(a) comment
(b) commentary

commentateur, -trice /kɔmmɑ̃tatœr, tris/ *nm,f* commentator

commenter /kɔmmɑ̃te/ [1] *vtr* **(a)** to comment on ‹decision, event›
(b) to give a commentary on ‹film, visit›
(c) to commentate on ‹match›

commérage /kɔmeraʒ/ *nm* gossip

commerçant, ~e /kɔmɛrsɑ̃, ɑ̃t/ **1** *adj* ‹street› shopping; ‹nation› trading
2 *nm,f* shopkeeper, storekeeper (US); retailer

✧ **commerce** /kɔmɛrs/ *nm* **(a)** shop, store (US); **dans le ~** in the shops or stores (US)
(b) business
(c) trade; **faire le ~ de** to trade in; **faire ~ de** to sell; **faire du ~** to be in business

✧ **commercial, ~e,** *mpl* **-iaux** /kɔmɛrsjal, o/ **1** *adj* **(a)** commercial; **carrière ~e** career in sales and marketing
(b) trade
2 *nm,f* sales and marketing person

commercialisation /kɔmɛrsjalizasjɔ̃/ *nf* marketing

commercialiser /kɔmɛrsjalize/ [1] *vtr* to market

commère /kɔmɛr/ *nf* gossip

✧ **commettre** /kɔmɛtr/ [60] *vtr* to make ‹error›; to commit ‹crime›; to carry out ‹attack›

commis /kɔmi/ *nm* **(a)** (in office) clerk
(b) shop assistant (GB), salesclerk (US)

commissaire /kɔmisɛr/ *nm* **(a)** **~ (de police)** ≈ police superintendent
(b) commissioner
(c) (of sports event) steward; (of exhibition) organizer

commissaire-priseur, *pl* **commissaires-priseurs** /kɔmisɛrprizœr/ *nm* auctioneer

commissariat /kɔmisarja/ *nm* **~ (de police)** police station

✧ **commission** /kɔmisjɔ̃/ **1** *nf*
(a) committee
(b) commission; **payé à la ~** paid on a commission basis
(c) errand
(d) **faire la ~ à qn** to give sb the message
2 commissions *nf pl* (fam) shopping

commissionnaire /kɔmisjɔnɛr/ *nm* (Econ) agent, broker

commissure /kɔmisyr/ *nf* corner

commode /kɔmɔd/ **1** *adj*
(a) (gen) convenient; ‹tool› handy
(b) easy
(c) **ne pas être (très) ~** to be strict; to be difficult (to deal with)
2 *nf* chest of drawers

commodité /kɔmɔdite/ *nf* convenience

commotion /kɔmɔsjɔ̃/ *nf* **(a)** **~ (cérébrale)** concussion (*of the brain*)
(b) (figurative) shock

✧ **commun, ~e¹** /kɔmœ̃, yn/ **1** *adj*
(a) common; ‹policy, property› joint; ‹friend› mutual; ‹room, memories, experience› shared; **d'un ~ accord** by mutual agreement; **après dix ans de vie ~e** after living together for ten years
(b) ‹person, tastes› common; ‹face› plain
(c) **elle est d'une beauté peu ~e** she's uncommonly beautiful
2 *nm* ordinary; **le ~ des mortels** ordinary mortals; **hors du ~** exceptional
3 en commun *phr* ‹work, write› jointly, together; **avoir qch en ~** to have sth in common; **nous mettons tout en ~** we share everything

communal, ~e, *mpl* **-aux** /kɔmynal, o/ *adj* ‹budget, resources› local ⋯⋯

council (GB), local government (US); ‹*building*› local council (GB), community (US)

communautaire /kɔmynotɛʀ/ *adj*
(a) (referring to the EC) ‹*budget, law*› Community
(b) **la vie** ~ life in a community

✧ **communauté** /kɔmynote/ *nf*
(a) community
(b) commune; **vivre en** ~ to live in a commune
■ **Communauté économique européenne, CEE** European Economic Community, EEC; **Communauté des États indépendants, CEI** Commonwealth of Independent States, CIS

✧ **commune²** /kɔmyn/ ⓵ *nf* village; town
⓶ **communes** *nf pl* **la Chambre des** ~**s** the (House of) Commons

communément /kɔmynemã/ *adv* generally

communicatif, -ive /kɔmynikatif, iv/ *adj* (a) ‹*person*› talkative
(b) ‹*gaiety*› infectious

✧ **communication** /kɔmynikasjɔ̃/ *nf* (a) ~ **(téléphonique)** (telephone) call; **mettre qn en** ~ **avec qn** to put sb through to sb
(b) report; (at conference) paper
(c) **demander** ~ **d'un dossier à qn** to ask sb for a file
(d) (between people) communication, contact
(e) (media) communications
(f) (by phone, radio) **moyens de** ~ communications

communier /kɔmynje/ [2] *vi* to receive Communion

communion /kɔmynjɔ̃/ *nf* (a) Communion
(b) (figurative) communion
■ ~ **(privée)** first communion

communiqué /kɔmynike/ *nm*
(a) communiqué, press release
(b) statement

✧ **communiquer** /kɔmynike/ [1] ⓵ *vtr*
(a) to announce ‹*date, result*›; to give ‹*address*›
(b) ‹*person*› to pass on ‹*document*›; to convey ‹*idea*›
⓶ *vi* (a) to communicate
(b) ‹*rooms*› to be adjoining
⓷ **se communiquer** *v refl* (+ *v être*)
(a) ‹*people*› to pass [sth] on to each other
(b) ‹*fire, disease*› to spread

communisme /kɔmynism/ *nm* communism

commutateur /kɔmytatœʀ/ *nm* switch
commuter /kɔmyte/ [1] *vtr* to commute
compact, ~e /kɔpakt/ *adj* (a) ‹*fog, crowd*› dense; ‹*earth*› compact
(b) ‹*car*› compact

compagne /kɔ̃paɲ/ *nf*
(a) (female) companion
(b) (female animal) mate

✧ **compagnie** /kɔ̃paɲi/ *nf* (a) company; **en** ~ **de** together with

(b) **salut la** ~! hello everybody!
(c) (commercial) company
(d) theatre company
■ ~ **aérienne** airline; ~ **d'assurance** insurance company; ~ **pétrolière ou** company

✧ **compagnon** /kɔ̃paɲɔ̃/ *nm* (a) companion
(b) partner
(c) mate
(d) journeyman
■ ~ **de route** fellow traveller (GB)

comparable /kɔ̃paʀabl/ *adj* comparable
comparaison /kɔ̃paʀɛzɔ̃/ *nf*
(a) comparison; **c'est sans** ~ **le plus confortable** it's far and away the most comfortable
(b) simile
(c) **adjectif de** ~ comparative adjective

comparaître /kɔ̃paʀɛtʀ/ [73] *vi* (Law) to appear

comparatif, -ive /kɔ̃paʀatif, iv/ *adj* comparative

comparé, ~e /kɔ̃paʀe/ *adj* ‹*literature, law*› comparative

✧ **comparer** /kɔ̃paʀe/ [1] ⓵ *vtr* to compare
⓶ **se comparer** *v refl* (+ *v être*) (a) **se** ~ **à qn/qch** to compare oneself with sb/sth
(b) to be comparable

comparse /kɔ̃paʀs/ *nmf* (a) (in theatre) extra
(b) sidekick (colloq)

compartiment /kɔ̃paʀtimã/ *nm* compartment

compartimenter /kɔ̃paʀtimãte/ [1] *vtr* (a) ~ **un grenier** to divide up a loft with partitions
(b) (figurative) to compartmentalize ‹*administration*›

compas /kɔ̃pa/ *nm* compass
compassion /kɔ̃pasjɔ̃/ *nf* compassion
compatible /kɔ̃patibl/ *adj* compatible
compatir /kɔ̃patiʀ/ [3] *vi* to sympathize
compatissant, ~e /kɔ̃patisã, ãt/ *adj* compassionate

compatriote /kɔ̃patʀiɔt/ *nmf* fellow-countryman/-countrywoman, compatriot

compensation /kɔ̃pãsasjɔ̃/ *nf* compensation

compensé, ~e /kɔ̃pãse/ *adj* (a) **semelle** ~**e** wedge heel
(b) (Med) compensated

compenser /kɔ̃pãse/ [1] *vtr* to compensate for; to make up for; to offset

compère /kɔ̃pɛʀ/ *nm* partner; accomplice

✧ **compétence** /kɔ̃petãs/ *nf* (a) ability; competence, skill
(b) (Law) competence; **relever de la** ~ **de qn** to fall within the competence of sb
(c) domain

compétent, ~e /kɔ̃petã, ãt/ *adj* competent

✧ indicates a very frequent word

compétitif, -ive /kɔ̃petitif, iv/ *adj*
competitive

compétition /kɔ̃petisjɔ̃/ *nf* competition;
en ~ pour competing for; **faire de la ~** to
compete; **sport de ~** competitive sport

complaire: **se complaire** /kɔ̃plɛʀ/ [59]
v refl (+ *v être*) **se ~ à faire** to take pleasure
in doing

complaisance /kɔ̃plɛzɑ̃s/ *nf* (a) kindness
(b) (derogatory) soft attitude; **décrire la
situation sans ~** to give an objective
assessment of the situation
(c) (derogatory) complacency

complaisant, ~e /kɔ̃plɛzɑ̃, ɑ̃t/ *adj*
(a) obliging
(b) (derogatory) indulgent
(c) (derogatory) complacent, self-satisfied

complément /kɔ̃plemɑ̃/ *nm* (a) **~ de
salaire** extra payment
(b) (to funding, programme) supplement
(c) **~ de nom** possessive phrase; **~ d'objet
direct/indirect** direct/indirect object

complémentaire /kɔ̃plemɑ̃tɛʀ/ *adj*
(a) ⟨*training, information*⟩ further; ⟨*activity,
amount*⟩ supplementary
(b) complementary

⚜ **complet, -ète** /kɔ̃plɛ, ɛt/ [1] *adj*
(a) (gen) complete; ⟨*failure*⟩ total; ⟨*inquiry,
range*⟩ full; ⟨*survey*⟩ comprehensive
(b) ⟨*train, hotel*⟩ full; **être (réuni) au
(grand) ~** to be all present
[2] *nm* suit; **~ veston** two-/three-piece suit

⚜ **complètement** /kɔ̃plɛtmɑ̃/ *adv*
completely; ⟨*read*⟩ right through; **~ réveillé**
fully awake

compléter /kɔ̃plete/ [14] [1] *vtr* (a) to
complete ⟨*collection*⟩; to top up ⟨*sum*⟩
(b) ⟨*person*⟩ to complement ⟨*person*⟩
(c) to complete ⟨*sentence*⟩
[2] **se compléter** *v refl* (+ *v
être*) ⟨*elements, people*⟩ to complement each
other

⚜ **complexe** /kɔ̃plɛks/ [1] *adj* complex
[2] *nm* (a) (psychological) complex; **il n'a pas
de ~** he has no inhibitions
(b) (place) complex; **un ~ sportif** a sports
complex

complexer /kɔ̃plekse/ [1] *vtr* (fam) to give
[sb] a complex

complexité /kɔ̃plɛksite/ *nf* complexity

complication /kɔ̃plikasjɔ̃/ *nf*
complication

complice /kɔ̃plis/ [1] *adj* (a) **être ~ de
qch** to be a party to sth
(b) ⟨*air*⟩ of complicity
[2] *nmf* accomplice

complicité /kɔ̃plisite/ *nf* (a) complicity
(b) bond

compliment /kɔ̃plimɑ̃/ [1] *nm*
compliment
[2] **compliments** *nm pl* (gen) compliments;
(tous) mes ~s! congratulations!

complimenter /kɔ̃plimɑ̃te/ [1] *vtr* to
compliment

compliqué, ~e /kɔ̃plike/ *adj* complicated;
⟨*mind*⟩ tortuous

compliquer /kɔ̃plike/ [1] [1] *vtr* to
complicate
[2] **se compliquer** *v refl* (+ *v être*) (a) to
become more complicated
(b) **se ~ la vie** *or* **l'existence** to make life
difficult for oneself

complot /kɔ̃plo/ *nm* plot

comploter /kɔ̃plote/ [1] *vtr, vi* to plot

⚜ **comportement** /kɔ̃pɔʀtəmɑ̃/ *nm*
(a) (gen) behaviour (GB)
(b) (of sportsman, car) performance

⚜ **comporter** /kɔ̃pɔʀte/ [1] [1] *vtr* (a) to
include
(b) to comprise, to consist of
(c) to entail, to involve
[2] **se comporter** *v refl* (+ *v être*) (a) to
behave, to act
(b) ⟨*sportsman, car*⟩ to perform

composant /kɔ̃pozɑ̃/ *nm* (Tech) component

composante /kɔ̃pozɑ̃t/ *nf* element;
component

composé, ~e /kɔ̃poze/ [1] *adj* ⟨*salad*⟩
mixed
[2] *nm* (in chemistry) compound

⚜ **composer** /kɔ̃poze/ [1] [1] *vtr*
(a) ⟨*elements, people*⟩ to make up
(b) ⟨*person*⟩ to put [sth] together
⟨*programme, menu*⟩; to select ⟨*team*⟩; to make
up ⟨*bouquet*⟩
(c) ⟨*artist*⟩ to compose ⟨*piece of music*⟩; to
paint ⟨*picture*⟩
(d) to dial ⟨*number*⟩
[2] **se composer** *v refl* (+ *v être*) **se ~ de**
to be made up of

compositeur, -trice /kɔ̃pozitœʀ, tʀis/
nm,f (a) (Mus) composer
(b) typesetter

composition /kɔ̃pozisjɔ̃/ *nf* (a) (of
government, delegation) make-up; (of
team) line-up; (of product) ingredients; (of
drug) composition
(b) (of government) formation; (of
team) selection; (of list, menu) drawing up; **de
ma ~** of my invention
(c) (of piece of music, picture) composition; (of
letter) writing
(d) (Sch) end-of-term test
(e) typesetting
IDIOM **être de bonne ~** to be good-natured

composter /kɔ̃pɔste/ [1] *vtr* to (date)
stamp; to punch ⟨*ticket*⟩

compote /kɔ̃pɔt/ *nf* (Culin) stewed fruit,
compote

compréhensible /kɔ̃pʀeɑ̃sibl/ *adj*
(a) understandable
(b) comprehensible

compréhensif, -ive /kɔ̃pʀeɑ̃sif, iv/ *adj*
understanding

compréhension /kɔ̃pʀeɑ̃sjɔ̃/ *nf*
understanding; comprehension

✓ **comprendre** /kɔ̃pʀɑ̃dʀ/ [52] **1** *vtr* **(a)** to understand; **c'est à n'y rien ~** it's completely baffling; **mal ~** to misunderstand; **être compris comme une menace** to be interpreted as a threat; **se faire ~** to make oneself understood
(b) to consist of, to comprise
(c) to include
2 se comprendre *v refl* (+ *v être*)
(a) ‹people› to understand each other *or* one another
(b) je me comprends I know what I'm trying to say
(c) ‹attitude› to be understandable

compresse /kɔ̃pʀɛs/ *nf* compress

compresser /kɔ̃pʀese/ [1] *vtr* to compress

compression /kɔ̃pʀesjɔ̃/ *nf*
(a) (Tech) compression
(b) reduction
(c) cut; **~s budgétaires** budget cut

comprimé /kɔ̃pʀime/ *nm* tablet

comprimer /kɔ̃pʀime/ [1] *vtr* **(a)** to constrict; to squeeze ‹tube›
(b) (Med) to compress
(c) (Tech) **air comprimé** compressed air

compris, **~e** /kɔ̃pʀi, iz/ **1** *pp*
▶ COMPRENDRE
2 *pp adj* including; **service ~/non ~** service included/not included
3 tout compris *phr* in total, all in (GB) (colloq)
4 y compris *phr* including

compromettant, **~e** /kɔ̃pʀɔmetɑ̃, ɑ̃t/ *adj* compromising

compromettre /kɔ̃pʀɔmɛtʀ/ [60] **1** *vtr*
(a) to endanger, to jeopardize
(b) to compromise ‹person›; to damage ‹reputation›
2 se compromettre *v refl* (+ *v être*) to compromise oneself

compromis /kɔ̃pʀɔmi/ *nm* compromise

comptabiliser /kɔ̃tabilize/ [1] *vtr* to count

comptabilité /kɔ̃tabilite/ *nf*
(a) accountancy
(b) bookkeeping; **faire sa ~** to do one's accounts
(c) accounts department

comptable /kɔ̃tabl/ **1** *adj* **(a)** ‹year› accounting; ‹department› accounts
(b) ‹noun› countable
2 *nmf* accountant; bookkeeper

comptant /kɔ̃tɑ̃/ *adv* cash

✓ **compte** /kɔ̃t/ **1** *nm* **(a)** count; **faire le ~ de qch** to work out ‹expenditure›; to count (up) ‹objects›; **comment fais-tu ton ~ pour faire…?** (figurative) how do you manage to do…?; **tout ~ fait** all things considered; **en**

✓ indicates a very frequent word

fin de ~ at the end of the day
(b) (of money) amount; (of objects, people) number; **il n'y a pas le ~** that's not the right amount; that's not the right number; **il a son ~** (fam) he's done for (colloq); (drunk) he's had a drop too much; **nous avons eu notre ~ d'ennuis** (figurative) we've had more than our fair share of problems; **à ce ~-là** in that case
(c) prendre qch en ~, tenir ~ de qch to take sth into account
(d) être *or* **travailler à son ~** to be self-employed; **pour le ~ de qn** on behalf of sb; **y trouver son ~** to get something out of it
(e) account; **~ en banque** bank account; **mettre qch sur le ~ de qn** to charge sth to sb's account; (figurative) to put sth down to sb
(f) rendre ~ de qch à qn to give an account of sth to sb; to account for sth to sb; **devoir rendre des ~s à qn** to be answerable to sb; **demander des ~s à qn** to ask for an explanation from sb
(g) se rendre ~ de to realize; to notice
(h) dire qch sur le ~ de qn to say sth about sb
(i) (in boxing) count
2 à bon compte *phr* **s'en tirer à bon ~** to get off lightly
■ **~ chèques** current account (GB), checking account (US); **~ d'épargne** savings account; **~ épargne logement** savings account (for purchasing a property);; **~ chèque postal, CCP** post office account; **~ joint** joint account; **~ à rebours** countdown

compte-gouttes /kɔ̃tgut/ *nm inv* dropper; **au ~** (figurative) sparingly

✓ **compter** /kɔ̃te/ [1] **1** *vtr* **(a)** to count; **on compte deux millions de chômeurs** there is a total of two million unemployed; **il a toujours compté ses sous** he has always watched the pennies; **sans ~** ‹give, spend› freely; **ses jours sont comptés** his/her days are numbered
(b) ~ une bouteille pour trois to allow a bottle between three people
(c) (as fee, price) **~ qch à qn** to charge sb for sth
(d) to count, to include; **sans ~ les soucis** not to mention the worry
(e) to have; **notre club compte des gens célèbres** our club has some well-known people among its members
(f) ~ faire to intend to do
(g) il comptait que je lui prête de l'argent he expected me to lend him some money
2 *vi* **(a)** to count; **~ au nombre de, ~ parmi** to be counted among
(b) to matter; **c'est l'intention qui compte** it's the thought that counts; **ça compte beaucoup pour moi** it means a lot to me
(c) to count; **ça ne compte pas, il a triché** it doesn't count, he cheated
(d) ~ avec to reckon with; to take [sb/sth] into account; **~ sans** not to take [sb/sth] into account

(e) ∼ **sur** to count on ‹person, help›; (for support) to rely on ‹person, resource›; (in anticipation) to reckon on ‹sum, income›
③ **se compter** v refl (+ v être) leurs victoires se comptent par douzaines they have had dozens of victories
④ **à compter de** phr as from
⑤ **sans compter que** phr and what is more; especially as

compte(-)rendu, pl **comptes(-)rendus** /kɔ̃tʁɑ̃dy/ nm (gen) report; (of book) review

compteur /kɔ̃tœʁ/ nm meter; clock
■ ∼ **kilométrique** ≈ milometer; ∼ **de vitesse** speedometer

comptine /kɔ̃tin/ nf nursery rhyme

comptoir /kɔ̃twaʁ/ nm **(a)** (of café) bar
(b) (of shop) counter

comte /kɔ̃t/ nm (title) count; earl

comté /kɔ̃te/ nm county

comtesse /kɔ̃tɛs/ nf countess

con, conne /kɔ̃, kɔn/ nm, f (vulgar) bloody idiot (GB) (slang), stupid jerk (colloq); **idée à la** ∼ lousy idea (colloq)

concasser /kɔ̃kase/ [1] vtr (Culin, Tech) to crush

concave /kɔ̃kav/ adj concave

concéder /kɔ̃sede/ [14] vtr to concede

concentration /kɔ̃sɑ̃tʁasjɔ̃/ nf concentration

concentré, ∼e /kɔ̃sɑ̃tʁe/ ① pp
▶ CONCENTRER
② pp adj **(a)** un air ∼ a look of concentration
(b) concentrated; ‹lait› condensed
③ nm (Culin) ∼ **de tomate** tomato purée (GB) or paste (US)

concentrer /kɔ̃sɑ̃tʁe/ [1] ① vtr to concentrate
② **se concentrer** v refl (+ v être) to concentrate; ‹attention› to be concentrated

✓ **concept** /kɔ̃sɛpt/ nm concept

✓ **conception** /kɔ̃sɛpsjɔ̃/ nf **(a)** conception
(b) design
(c) idea

concernant /kɔ̃sɛʁnɑ̃/ prep
(a) concerning
(b) as regards, with regard to

✓ **concerner** /kɔ̃sɛʁne/ [1] vtr **(a)** to concern
(b) to affect

concert /kɔ̃sɛʁ/ ① nm (Mus) concert
② **de concert** phr ils ont agi de ∼ they worked together

concertation /kɔ̃sɛʁtasjɔ̃/ nf
(a) consultation
(b) cooperation

concerté, ∼e /kɔ̃sɛʁte/ adj concerted

concerter: se concerter /kɔ̃sɛʁte/ [1] v refl (+ v être) to consult each other

concerto /kɔ̃sɛʁto/ nm concerto

concession /kɔ̃sesjɔ̃/ nf
(a) (compromise) concession; **film sans** ∼**s** uncompromising film
(b) (awarding of right) concession (**de** of)
(c) (right, contract) (of mine, site) concession; (Aut) dealership

concessionnaire /kɔ̃sesjɔnɛʁ/ nmf (commercial) agent; (Aut) dealer

✓ **concevoir** /kɔ̃s(ə)vwaʁ/ [5] ① vtr **(a)** to design ‹product, system›
(b) to conceive ‹child›
(c) to understand ‹attitude›
(d) to see ‹phenomenon, activity›
(e) (formal) to conceive ‹hatred›
② **se concevoir** v refl (+ v être) **(a)** to be conceivable
(b) to be understandable

concierge /kɔ̃sjɛʁʒ/ nmf caretaker (GB), superintendent (US)

concile /kɔ̃sil/ nm council

conciliabule /kɔ̃siljabyl/ nm consultation, confab (colloq)

conciliant, ∼e /kɔ̃siljɑ̃, ɑ̃t/ adj conciliatory

conciliation /kɔ̃siljasjɔ̃/ nf conciliation

concilier /kɔ̃silje/ [2] vtr to reconcile

concis, ∼e /kɔ̃si, iz/ adj concise

concision /kɔ̃sizjɔ̃/ nf conciseness

concitoyen, -enne /kɔ̃sitwajɛ̃, ɛn/ nm, f fellow-citizen

conclave /kɔ̃klav/ nm conclave

conclu, ∼e /kɔ̃kly/ ▶ CONCLURE

concluant, ∼e /kɔ̃klyɑ̃, ɑ̃t/ adj conclusive

✓ **conclure** /kɔ̃klyʁ/ [78] vtr **(a)** to conclude (**que** that)
(b) to conclude ‹deal, agreement›; 'marché conclu!' 'it's a deal!'
(c) ‹person› to conclude ‹speech›
(d) to bring [sth] to a close ‹festival›

✓ **conclusion** /kɔ̃klyzjɔ̃/ ① nf
(a) conclusion; **tirer les** ∼**s d'une expérience** to learn from an experience; **ne tire pas de** ∼**s hâtives** don't jump to conclusions
(b) (of deal, treaty) conclusion
(c) (of speech, session) close
② **conclusions** nf pl **(a)** (of analysis, autopsy) results; (of inquiry) findings
(b) (Law) (of expert) opinion; (of jury) verdict; (of plaintiff) pleadings

concocter /kɔ̃kɔkte/ [1] vtr (fam) to concoct ‹dish›; to devise ‹programme›

concombre /kɔ̃kɔ̃bʁ/ nm cucumber

concordance /kɔ̃kɔʁdɑ̃s/ nf concordance; compatibility
■ ∼ **des temps** sequence of tenses

concorder /kɔ̃kɔʁde/ [1] vi ‹results, evidence› to tally; ‹estimates› to agree

concourir /kɔ̃kuʁiʁ/ [26] ① vi to compete
② **concourir à** v+prep ∼ **à qch/à faire** ‹factors› to combine to bring about sth/to do; ‹factor, person› to help bring about sth/do

concours /kɔ̃kuʀ/ *nm inv*
(a) (gen) competition; (agricultural) show; ∼ de beauté beauty contest
(b) competitive examination; ∼ d'entrée entrance examination
(c) help, assistance; support; cooperation
■ ∼ de circonstances combination of circumstances

concret, -ète /kɔ̃kʀɛ, ɛt/ *adj* (a) ⟨*result*⟩ concrete
(b) ⟨*mind, person*⟩ practical

concrètement /kɔ̃kʀɛtmɑ̃/ *adv* (a) in concrete terms
(b) in practical terms

concrétisation /kɔ̃kʀetizasjɔ̃/ *nf* concrete expression; fulfilment (GB); achievement

concrétiser /kɔ̃kʀetize/ [1] **1** *vtr* to make [sth] a reality ⟨*plan, project*⟩
2 **se concrétiser** *v refl* (+ *v être*) ⟨*dream*⟩ to become a reality; ⟨*offer*⟩ to materialize

concubin, ∼e /kɔ̃kybɛ̃, in/ *nm,f* common law husband/wife

concubinage /kɔ̃kybinaʒ/ *nm* cohabitation

concurrence /kɔ̃kyʀɑ̃s/ *nf* competition; prix défiant toute ∼ unbeatable price; jusqu'à ∼ de up to a limit of

concurrencer /kɔ̃kyʀɑ̃se/ [12] *vtr* to compete with

concurrent, ∼e /kɔ̃kyʀɑ̃, ɑ̃t/ **1** *adj* rival
2 *nm,f* (for a job) rival; (Sport) competitor; (in competitive examination) candidate

concurrentiel, -ielle /kɔ̃kyʀɑ̃sjɛl/ *adj* competitive

condamnable /kɔ̃danabl/ *adj* reprehensible

condamnation /kɔ̃danasjɔ̃/ *nf*
(a) (Law) conviction; sentence
(b) condemnation

condamné, ∼e /kɔ̃dane/ **1** *adj*
(a) ⟨*person*⟩ terminally ill
(b) ⟨*door*⟩ sealed up
2 *nm,f* convicted prisoner

♂ **condamner** /kɔ̃dane/ [1] *vtr* (a) (Law) to sentence; ∼ qn à une amende to fine sb; ∼ qn pour vol to convict sb of theft
(b) ⟨*law*⟩ to punish ⟨*thieving, smuggling*⟩
(c) ⟨*person, country*⟩ to condemn ⟨*act, decision*⟩
(d) ∼ qn à faire to compel sb to do
(e) to seal up ⟨*window*⟩; to shut up ⟨*room*⟩
(f) (figurative) to spell death for ⟨*society, industry*⟩
(g) les médecins l'ont condamné the doctors have given up hope of saving him

condensation /kɔ̃dɑ̃sasjɔ̃/ *nf* condensation

condensé /kɔ̃dɑ̃se/ *nm* summary; digest

condenser /kɔ̃dɑ̃se/ [1] *vtr*, **se condenser** *v refl* (+ *v être*) to condense

condescendance /kɔ̃desɑ̃dɑ̃s/ *nf* condescension

condescendant, ∼e /kɔ̃desɑ̃dɑ̃, ɑ̃t/ *adj* condescending

condiment /kɔ̃dimɑ̃/ *nm* (Culin) seasoning; condiment

condisciple /kɔ̃disipl/ *nmf* fellow student

♂ **condition** /kɔ̃disjɔ̃/ **1** *nf* (a) condition; à ∼ d'avoir le temps provided (that) one has the time; sous ∼ ⟨*freed*⟩ conditionally; sans ∼(s) ⟨*acceptance*⟩ unconditional; ⟨*accept*⟩ unconditionally; imposer ses ∼s to impose one's own terms; ∼ préalable precondition
(b) (Law) (of contract, treaty) term
(c) la ∼ ouvrière (the conditions of) working-class life
(d) ∼ (sociale) social status
2 **conditions** *nf pl* (a) conditions; dans ces ∼s in these conditions; in that case
(b) terms

conditionnel, -elle /kɔ̃disjɔnɛl/ **1** *adj* conditional
2 *nm* conditional

conditionnement /kɔ̃disjɔnmɑ̃/ *nm*
(a) conditioning
(b) packaging
■ ∼ sous vide vacuum packing

conditionner /kɔ̃disjɔne/ [1] *vtr* (a) to condition
(b) to package

condoléances /kɔ̃dɔleɑ̃s/ *nf pl* condolences

condom /kɔ̃dɔm/ *nm* condom

condor /kɔ̃dɔʀ/ *nm* condor

conducteur, -trice /kɔ̃dyktœʀ, tʀis/
1 *adj* (a) conductive
(b) ⟨*principle*⟩ guiding
2 *nm,f* (of vehicle) driver
3 *nm* conductor

♂ **conduire** /kɔ̃dɥiʀ/ [69] **1** *vtr* (a) to take ⟨*person*⟩; (in car) to drive
(b) ⟨*leader, studies*⟩ to lead; la route qui conduit à Oxford the road that goes to Oxford; ∼ qn au désespoir to drive sb to despair
(c) to drive ⟨*car, train*⟩; to ride ⟨*motorbike*⟩
(d) to conduct ⟨*research*⟩; to carry out ⟨*project*⟩; to run ⟨*business*⟩
(e) to conduct ⟨*electricity, heat*⟩
2 **se conduire** *v refl* (+ *v être*) to behave

conduit¹, ∼e /kɔ̃dɥi, ɥit/ ▶ CONDUIRE

conduit² /kɔ̃dɥi/ *nm* (a) conduit
(b) (Anat) canal
■ ∼ de fumée flue; ∼ de ventilation ventilation shaft

♂ **conduite** /kɔ̃dɥit/ *nf* (a) behaviour (GB); (of pupil) conduct
(b) (of inquiry) conducting; (of building works) supervision; (of company) management
(c) (of vehicle) driving; (of motorbike) riding

♂ indicates a very frequent word

(d) (Aut) **voiture avec ∼ à gauche** left-hand drive car
(e) (exam) driving test
(f) pipe
cône /kon/ *nm* cone
confection /kɔ̃fɛksjɔ̃/ *nf* **(a)** clothing industry
(b) making
confectionner /kɔ̃fɛksjɔne/ [1] *vtr* (gen) to make; to prepare ‹meal›
confédération /kɔ̃fedeʀasjɔ̃/ *nf* confederation
■ **la Confédération helvétique** Switzerland
confédéré, ∼**e** /kɔ̃fedeʀe/ *adj* confederate
ℱ **conférence** /kɔ̃feʀɑ̃s/ *nf* **(a)** lecture
(b) conference
(c) debate
■ ∼ **au sommet** summit meeting
conférencier, -ière /kɔ̃feʀɑ̃sje, ɛʀ/ *nm,f* speaker; lecturer
conférer /kɔ̃feʀe/ [14] *vtr* to give; to confer
confesser /kɔ̃fese/ [1] ① *vtr* **(a)** to confess ‹sin›
(b) ∼ **qn** to hear sb's confession
② **se confesser** *v refl* (+ *v être*) **(a)** to go to confession
(b) se ∼ à un ami to confide in a friend
confession /kɔ̃fesjɔ̃/ *nf* **(a)** confession
(b) faith
confessionnal, *pl* **-aux** /kɔ̃fesjɔnal, o/ *nm* confessional
confetti /kɔ̃feti/ *nm* confetti
ℱ **confiance** /kɔ̃fjɑ̃s/ *nf* **(a)** trust; **de ∼** ‹person› trustworthy; ‹mission› which requires trust; **avoir ∼ en qn, faire ∼ à qn** to trust sb; **mettre qn en ∼** to win sb's trust
(b) (in ability, self) confidence; ∼ **en soi** (self-) confidence
confiant, ∼**e** /kɔ̃fjɑ̃, ɑ̃t/ *adj* **(a)** confident
(b) (self-)confident
(c) trusting
confidence /kɔ̃fidɑ̃s/ *nf* secret, confidence; **être dans la ∼** to be in on the secret
confident, ∼**e** /kɔ̃fidɑ̃, ɑ̃t/ *nm,f* confidant/ confidante
confidentialité /kɔ̃fidɑ̃sjalite/ *nf* confidentiality
confidentiel, -ielle /kɔ̃fidɑ̃sjɛl/ *adj* confidential
ℱ **confier** /kɔ̃fje/ [2] ① *vtr* **(a)** ∼ **qch à qn** to entrust sb with sth ‹mission›; to entrust sth to sb ‹money, letters›
(b) ∼ **qch à qn** to confide sth to sb ‹intentions›
② **se confier** *v refl* (+ *v être*) to confide
configuration /kɔ̃figyʀasjɔ̃/ *nf* **(a)** shape; **la ∼ des lieux** the layout of the premises
(b) configuration
(c) set-up
configurer /kɔ̃figyʀe/ *vtr* to configure

confiné, ∼**e** /kɔ̃fine/ *adj* **(a)** ‹atmosphere› stuffy; ‹air› stale
(b) ‹space› confined, restricted
confiner /kɔ̃fine/ [1] ① *vtr* to confine
② **confiner à** *v+prep* to border on
③ **se confiner** *v refl* (+ *v être*) to shut oneself away or up
confins /kɔ̃fɛ̃/ *nm pl* boundaries
confirmation /kɔ̃fiʀmasjɔ̃/ *nf* confirmation
ℱ **confirmer** /kɔ̃fiʀme/ [1] ① *vtr* to confirm ‹order, fact›; to uphold ‹decision›; to be evidence of ‹attitude, quality›; to affirm ‹intention›
② **se confirmer** *v refl* (+ *v être*) ‹news› to be confirmed; ‹testimony› to be corroborated
confiserie /kɔ̃fizʀi/ *nf* **(a)** confectioner's (shop)
(b) confectionery
confisquer /kɔ̃fiske/ [1] *vtr* to confiscate, to seize
confit, ∼**e** /kɔ̃fi, it/ ① *adj* ‹fruits› crystallized
② *nm* confit; ∼ **de canard** confit of duck
confiture /kɔ̃fityʀ/ *nf* (Culin) jam, preserve; marmalade
IDIOM donner de la ∼ aux cochons to cast pearls before swine
conflictuel, -elle /kɔ̃fliktɥɛl/ *adj* ‹subject› controversial; ‹relationship› confrontational
ℱ **conflit** /kɔ̃fli/ *nm* conflict
■ ∼ **de générations** generation gap; ∼ **social** industrial strife
confluence /kɔ̃flyɑ̃s/ *nf* confluence; (figurative) convergence
confluent /kɔ̃flyɑ̃/ *nm* confluence
ℱ **confondre** /kɔ̃fɔ̃dʀ/ [53] ① *vtr* **(a)** to mix up, to confuse; **tous secteurs confondus** all sectors taken together
(b) to merge
(c) (formal) to stagger, to amaze
(d) to expose ‹traitor›
② **se confondre** *v refl* (+ *v être*)
(a) ‹shapes, colours› to merge; ‹events, facts› to become confused
(b) ‹interests, hopes› to coincide
(c) (formal) **se ∼ en excuses** to apologize profusely
conforme /kɔ̃fɔʀm/ *adj* **(a)** **être ∼ à** to comply with ‹regulations›
(b) **être ∼ à l'original** to conform to the original
conformément /kɔ̃fɔʀmemɑ̃/ *adv* ∼ **à** in accordance with
conformer: se conformer /kɔ̃fɔʀme/ [1] *v refl* (+ *v être*) to comply with ‹regulations›
conformisme /kɔ̃fɔʀmism/ *nm* conformity
conformiste /kɔ̃fɔʀmist/ *adj, nmf* conformist

conformité /kɔ̃fɔʀmite/ *nf* (a) ∼ à la loi compliance with the law; **en** ∼ **avec** ‹*act*› in accordance with
(b) similarity; **vérifier la** ∼ **de la traduction à l'original** to check that the translation is faithful to the original
(c) (of tastes, points of view) correspondence

confort /kɔ̃fɔʀ/ *nm* comfort; **maison tout** ∼ house with all mod cons (GB) (colloq) *or* modern conveniences

confortable /kɔ̃fɔʀtabl/ *adj* comfortable

confortablement /kɔ̃fɔʀtabləmɑ̃/ *adv* comfortably

conforter /kɔ̃fɔʀte/ [1] *vtr* to consolidate ‹*position*›; to reinforce ‹*situation*›

confrère /kɔ̃fʀɛʀ/ *nm* (at work) colleague; (in association) fellow member

confrérie /kɔ̃fʀeʀi/ *nf* brotherhood

confrontation /kɔ̃fʀɔ̃tasjɔ̃/ *nf* (a) (of ideas, witnesses) confrontation; (of texts) comparison
(b) (between people) debate; clash

confronter /kɔ̃fʀɔ̃te/ [1] *vtr* (a) to confront ‹*witnesses*›
(b) to compare ‹*texts*›

confus, ∼**e** /kɔ̃fy, yz/ *adj* (a) confused
(b) ‹*feeling, fear*› vague
(c) sorry; embarrassed

confusément /kɔ̃fyzemɑ̃/ *adv* ‹*explain*› confusedly; ‹*feel*› vaguely

confusion /kɔ̃fyzjɔ̃/ *nf* (a) confusion
(b) embarrassment
(c) mix-up

congé /kɔ̃ʒe/ *nm* (a) leave; **prendre quatre jours de** ∼ to take four days off; **être en** ∼ **de maladie** to be on sick leave
(b) notice; **donner (son)** ∼ **à qn** to give sb notice
(c) **prendre** ∼ **de qn** to take leave of sb

congédier /kɔ̃ʒedje/ [2] *vtr* to dismiss

congélateur /kɔ̃ʒelatœʀ/ *nm* freezer; (in refrigerator) freezer compartment

congelé, ∼**e** /kɔ̃ʒle/ *adj* frozen; **produits** ∼**s** frozen foods

congeler /kɔ̃ʒle/ [17] **1** *vtr* to freeze
2 se congeler *v refl* (+ *v être*) to freeze

congénital, ∼**e**, *mpl* **-aux** /kɔ̃ʒenital, o/ *adj* congenital

congère /kɔ̃ʒɛʀ/ *nf* snowdrift

congestion /kɔ̃ʒɛstjɔ̃/ *nf* congestion
■ ∼ **cérébrale** stroke

congestionner /kɔ̃ʒɛstjone/ [1] *vtr* (a) **il est tout congestionné** he's all flushed
(b) to congest ‹*street*›

conglomérat /kɔ̃ɡlɔmeʀa/ *nm*
(a) conglomerate
(b) (mixture) conglomeration

congrégation /kɔ̃ɡʀeɡasjɔ̃/ *nf* congregation; (humorous) assembly

congrès /kɔ̃ɡʀɛ/ *nm* conference; **le Congrès** (US) Congress

♂ indicates a very frequent word

congressiste /kɔ̃ɡʀesist/ *nmf* (conference) delegate

conifère /kɔnifɛʀ/ *nm* conifer

conique /kɔnik/ *adj* cone-shaped

conjecture /kɔ̃ʒɛktyʀ/ *nf* conjecture; **vaines** ∼**s** idle speculation

conjecturer /kɔ̃ʒɛktyʀe/ [1] *vtr* to speculate

conjoint, ∼**e** /kɔ̃ʒwɛ̃, ɛ̃t/ **1** *adj* ‹*action*› joint; ‹*questions*› linked
2 *nm,f* spouse; **les** ∼**s** the husband and wife

conjointement /kɔ̃ʒwɛ̃tmɑ̃/ *adv*
(a) jointly
(b) at the same time

conjonction /kɔ̃ʒɔ̃ksjɔ̃/ *nf* conjunction

conjonctivite /kɔ̃ʒɔ̃ktivit/ *nf* conjunctivitis

conjoncture /kɔ̃ʒɔ̃ktyʀ/ *nf* situation; circumstances

conjoncturel, **-elle** /kɔ̃ʒɔ̃ktyʀɛl/ *adj* ‹*situation*› economic

conjugaison /kɔ̃ʒygɛzɔ̃/ *nf* (a) (of verb) conjugation
(b) (figurative) combination

conjugal, ∼**e**, *mpl* **-aux** /kɔ̃ʒygal, o/ *adj* ‹*love*› conjugal; ‹*life*› married

conjugalement /kɔ̃ʒygalmɑ̃/ *adv* ‹*live*› as man and wife

conjuguer /kɔ̃ʒyge/ [1] *vtr* (a) to conjugate ‹*verb*›
(b) to combine ‹*efforts*›

conjuration /kɔ̃ʒyʀasjɔ̃/ *nf* (a) conspiracy
(b) (of evil spirits) conjuration

conjurer /kɔ̃ʒyʀe/ [1] *vtr* (a) to avert ‹*crisis*›; to ward off ‹*danger*›
(b) **je vous en conjure** I beg you

♂ **connaissance** /kɔnesɑ̃s/ *nf*
(a) knowledge; **prendre** ∼ **d'un texte** to acquaint oneself with a text; **en** ∼ **de cause** with full knowledge of the facts
(b) consciousness; **sans** ∼ unconscious
(c) acquaintance; **faire (plus ample)** ∼ **avec qn** to get to know sb (better); **en pays de** ∼ among familiar faces; on familiar ground

connaisseur, **-euse** /kɔnɛsœʀ, øz/ *nm,f* connoisseur, expert

♂ **connaître** /kɔnɛtʀ/ [73] **1** *vtr* (a) to know; **faire** ∼ **à qn** to make [sth] known to sb ‹*decision*›; to introduce sb to ‹*music*›; **je l'ai connu en Chine** I met him in China; **tu connais la nouvelle?** have you heard the news?
(b) to experience ‹*hunger, failure*›; to enjoy ‹*success*›; to have ‹*difficulties*›; ∼ **une forte croissance** to show a rapid growth
2 se connaître *v refl* (+ *v être*) (a) to know oneself
(b) to know each other; **ils se sont connus à Rome** they met in Rome
(c) **s'y** ∼ **en vin** to know all about wine

IDIOMS on connaît la chanson *or* **musique!** we've heard it all before!; ~ **qch comme sa poche** to know sth like the back of one's hand

conne (vulgar) ▶ CON

connecter /kɔnɛkte/ [1] *vtr* to connect

connexion /kɔnɛksjɔ̃/ *nf* connection

connivence /kɔnivɑ̃s/ *nf* connivance; **signe de** ~ sign of complicity

connotation /kɔnɔtasjɔ̃/ *nf* connotation

connu, ~**e** /kɔny/ ▶ CONNAÎTRE

conquérant, ~**e** /kɔ̃keRɑ̃, ɑ̃t/ *nm,f* conqueror

conquérir /kɔ̃keRiR/ [35] *vtr* to conquer; to capture ‹market›; to win over› ‹audience› **IDIOM se croire en pays** *or* **terrain conquis** to lord it over everyone

conquête /kɔ̃kɛt/ *nf* conquest

conquis, ~**e** ▶ CONQUÉRIR

consacré, ~**e** /kɔ̃sakRe/ *adj* **formule** ~**e** time-honoured (GB) expression; **artiste** ~ recognized artist

◦ **consacrer** /kɔ̃sakRe/ [1] **1** *vtr* **(a)** to devote; **pouvez-vous me** ~ **un instant?** can you spare me a moment?
(b) to sanction
(c) to consecrate
2 se consacrer *v refl* (+ *v être*) **se** ~ **à** to devote oneself to

consanguin, ~**e** /kɔ̃sɑ̃gɛ̃, in/ *adj* ‹marriage› between blood relations

consciemment /kɔ̃sjamɑ̃/ *adv* consciously

◦ **conscience** /kɔ̃sjɑ̃s/ *nf* **(a)** conscience; **avoir bonne/mauvaise** ~ to have a clear/a guilty conscience
(b) awareness; **prendre** ~ **de** to become aware of; **prise de** ~ realization; **perdre** ~ to lose consciousness
■ ~ **professionnelle** conscientiousness

consciencieusement /kɔ̃sjɑ̃sjøzmɑ̃/ *adv* **(a)** conscientiously
(b) dutifully

consciencieux, -ieuse /kɔ̃sjɑ̃sjø, øz/ *adj* conscientious

conscient, ~**e** /kɔ̃sjɑ̃, ɑ̃t/ *adj* **(a)** aware
(b) conscious

conscrit /kɔ̃skRi/ *nm* conscript (GB), draftee (US)

consécration /kɔ̃sekRasjɔ̃/ *nf* **(a)** (of author) recognition
(b) consecration

consécutif, -ive /kɔ̃sekytif, iv/ *adj* consecutive; ~ **à** resulting from; following

consécutivement /kɔ̃sekytivmɑ̃/ *adv* consecutively

◦ **conseil** /kɔ̃sɛj/ *nm* **(a)** advice; **quelques** ~**s de prudence** a few words of warning; **il est de bon** ~ he always gives good advice; ~**s d'entretien** cleaning *or* care instructions
(b) council

(c) consultant
■ ~ **d'administration** board of directors; ~ **de classe** (Sch) staff meeting; ~ **de discipline** disciplinary committee; ~ **général** council of a French department

◦ **conseiller¹, -ère** /kɔ̃seje, ɛR/ **1** *nm,f*
(a) adviser (GB)
(b) counsellor (GB)
2 *nm* councillor (GB)
■ ~ **commercial** commercial counsellor (GB); ~ **culturel** cultural counsellor (GB); ~ **en développement personnel** life coach; ~ **d'État** member of the Council of State; ~ **général** councillor (GB) *for a French department*; ~ **municipal** town councillor (GB); ~ **d'orientation** careers adviser

conseiller² /kɔ̃seje/ [1] *vtr* to recommend; to advise; ~ **à qn de faire** to advise sb to do

consensus /kɔ̃sɛ̃sys/ *nm inv* consensus

consentant, ~**e** /kɔ̃sɑ̃tɑ̃, ɑ̃t/ *adj* willing; (Law) consenting

consentement /kɔ̃sɑ̃tmɑ̃/ *nm* consent

consentir /kɔ̃sɑ̃tiR/ [30] **1** *vtr* to grant; to allow
2 consentir à *v+prep* ~ **à qch/à faire** to agree to sth/to do

◦ **conséquence** /kɔ̃sekɑ̃s/ *nf* consequence; **être lourd de** ~**s** to have serious consequences; **sans** ~**(s)** of no consequence; **ne pas tirer à** ~ to be of no consequence; **avoir pour** ~ **le chômage** to result in unemployment; **agir en** ~ to act accordingly; **avoir des qualifications et un salaire en** ~ to have qualifications and a corresponding salary

◦ **conséquent**, ~**e** /kɔ̃sekɑ̃, ɑ̃t/ **1** *adj*
(a) substantial
(b) consistent
2 par conséquent *phr* therefore, as a result

conservateur, -trice /kɔ̃sɛRvatœR, tRis/
1 *adj* **(a)** conservative
(b) produit ~ preservative
2 *nm,f* **(a)** conservative
(b) (museum) curator

conservation /kɔ̃sɛRvasjɔ̃/ *nf* conservation; preservation; **lait longue** ~ long-life milk (GB)

conservatoire /kɔ̃sɛRvatwaR/ *nm* academy; ~ **de musique** conservatoire

conserve /kɔ̃sɛRv/ **1** *nf* **(a) la** ~, **les** ~**s** canned food; **boîte de** ~ can
(b) preserve
2 de conserve *phr* ‹act› in concert

◦ **conserver** /kɔ̃sɛRve/ [1] *vtr* **(a)** to keep; to retain; ~ **l'anonymat** to remain anonymous
(b) (Culin) to preserve; (in vinegar) to pickle
(c) ‹activity› to keep [sb] young

conserverie /kɔ̃sɛRvəRi/ *nf* **(a)** cannery, canning plant
(b) canning industry

considérable /kɔ̃sideʀabl/ *adj*
considerable, significant; **l'enjeu est** ~ the
stakes are high

considération /kɔ̃sideʀasjɔ̃/ *nf*
(a) consideration; **prendre qch en** ~ to
consider sth, to take sth into account; **en** ~
de in view of; **sans** ~ **de** irrespective of
(b) consideration, factor
(c) respect, esteem

⚔ **considérer** /kɔ̃sideʀe/ [14] ① *vtr* **(a)** to
consider, to take into account
(b) to consider, to regard; ~ **qn/qch comme**
(étant) to consider sb/sth to be, to regard sb/
sth as being; **être bien considéré** to be highly
regarded
② **se considérer** *v refl* (+ *v être*) se ~
(comme) **(a)** to consider oneself (to be)
(b) to regard one another (as being)

consignation /kɔ̃siɲasjɔ̃/ *nf* **(a)** deposit
(b) en ~ on consignment

consigne /kɔ̃siɲ/ *nf* **(a)** orders,
instructions; **passer la** ~ **à qn** to pass
the word on to sb; **'**~**s à suivre en cas**
d'incendie' 'fire regulations'
(b) left luggage office (GB), baggage
checkroom (US)
(c) (on bottle) deposit
■ ~ **automatique** left luggage lockers (GB),
baggage lockers (US)

consigné, ~**e** /kɔ̃siɲe/ *adj* ‹*bottle*›
returnable

consigner /kɔ̃siɲe/ [1] *vtr* **(a)** to record, to
write down
(b) to confine ‹*soldier*›; to give [sb] detention
‹*pupil*›

consistance /kɔ̃sistɑ̃s/ *nf*
(a) consistency; **avoir de la/manquer de** ~ to
be quite thick/to be too runny
(b) substance, weight; **sans** ~ ‹*person*›
spineless; ‹*rumour*› groundless

consistant, ~**e** /kɔ̃sistɑ̃, ɑ̃t/ *adj* ‹*meal,
investment*› substantial; ‹*dish*› nourishing

⚔ **consister** /kɔ̃siste/ [1] *vi* **(a)** ~ **en** *or* **dans**
to consist in; ~ **à faire** to consist in doing
(b) ~ **en** to consist of, to be made up of; **en**
quoi consiste cette aide? what form does
this aid take?

consœur /kɔ̃sœʀ/ *nf* **(a)** female colleague
(b) counterpart

consolant, ~**e** /kɔ̃sɔlɑ̃, ɑ̃t/ *adj* comforting

consolation /kɔ̃sɔlasjɔ̃/ *nf* consolation

console /kɔ̃sɔl/ *nf* console; ~ **de jeu vidéo**
games console

consoler /kɔ̃sɔle/ [1] ① *vtr* to console; **si**
ça peut te ~ if it is any comfort to you
② **se consoler** *v refl* (+ *v être*) to find
consolation; **se** ~ **de** to get over

consolidable /kɔ̃sɔlidabl/ *adj* **(a)** ‹*debt*›
fundable
(b) ‹*structure*› reinforceable

⚔ indicates a very frequent word

consolidation /kɔ̃sɔlidasjɔ̃/ *nf* **(a)** (of
wall) strengthening; (of position) consolidation
(b) (of debt) consolidation, funding; (of
turnover, balance sheet) consolidation; (of
currency) strengthening

consolider /kɔ̃sɔlide/ [1] ① *vtr* to
consolidate, to strengthen
② **se consolider** *v refl* (+ *v être*) **(a)** to
grow stronger, to be strengthened
(b) to consolidate

consommable ① *adj* edible; drinkable
② **consommables** *nm pl* (Econ,
Comput) consumables

consommateur, -trice
/kɔ̃sɔmatœʀ, tʀis/ *nm,f* **(a)** consumer
(b) (in bar) customer

consommation /kɔ̃sɔmasjɔ̃/ *nf*
(a) consumption; **faire une grande** ~ **de** to
use a lot of; **de** ~ ‹*goods, society*› consumer
(b) drink
(c) consummation

consommé, ~**e** /kɔ̃sɔme/ *nm* consommé

consommer /kɔ̃sɔme/ [1] *vtr* **(a)** to
consume; to use
(b) to eat ‹*food*›; to drink ‹*tea*›; to take ‹*drugs*›

consonance /kɔ̃sɔnɑ̃s/ *nf* consonance;
mot aux ~**s étrangères** foreign-sounding
word

consonne /kɔ̃sɔn/ *nf* consonant

conspirateur, -trice
/kɔ̃spiʀatœʀ, tʀis/ *nm,f* conspirator

conspiration /kɔ̃spiʀasjɔ̃/ *nf* conspiracy

conspirer /kɔ̃spiʀe/ [1] ① *vi* to conspire,
to plot
② **conspirer à** *v+prep* to conspire to
bring about; ~ **à faire** to conspire to do

constamment /kɔ̃stamɑ̃/ *adv* constantly

constance /kɔ̃stɑ̃s/ *nf* **(a)** consistency;
constancy
(b) steadfastness

constant, ~**e**¹ /kɔ̃stɑ̃, ɑ̃t/ *adj* **(a)** constant;
consistent
(b) continuous; continual

constante² /kɔ̃stɑ̃t/ *nf* constant

constat /kɔ̃sta/ *nm* certified *or* official
report
■ ~ **(à l')amiable** *accident report drawn up by
the parties involved*; ~ **d'échec** admission
of failure

constatation /kɔ̃statasjɔ̃/ *nf* observation

⚔ **constater** /kɔ̃state/ [1] *vtr* **(a)** to notice, to
note; ~ **(par) soi-même** to see for oneself
(b) to ascertain, to establish
(c) to record

constellation /kɔ̃stɛlasjɔ̃/ *nf*
constellation

constellé, ~**e** /kɔ̃stɛlle/ *adj* ~ **de**
spangled with; riddled with; spotted with

consternant, ~**e** /kɔ̃stɛʀnɑ̃, ɑ̃t/ *adj*
(a) distressing
(b) appalling

consternation /kɔ̃stɛʀnasjɔ̃/ nf
consternation

consterner /kɔ̃stɛʀne/ [1] vtr to fill [sb]
with consternation, to dismay

constipation /kɔ̃stipasjɔ̃/ nf constipation

constipé, ~e /kɔ̃stipe/ adj constipated

constiper /kɔ̃stipe/ [1] vtr to make [sb]
constipated

constitué, ~e /kɔ̃stitɥe/ adj (a) personne
bien/mal ~e person of sound/unsound
constitution
(b) constituted

ℱ **constituer** /kɔ̃stitɥe/ [1] **1** vtr (a) to be,
to constitute ‹crime, reason›
(b) to form, to set up ‹team, commission›
(c) to make up ‹whole›
(d) (Law) to settle; ~ qn héritier to appoint
sb as heir
2 **se constituer** v refl (+ v être) (a) to
build up ‹network, reserve›
(b) se ~ en to form ‹party›
(c) se ~ prisonnier to give oneself up

constitutif, -ive /kɔ̃stitytif, iv/ adj
(a) (basic) constituent
(b) (Pol) founding; constitutional

ℱ **constitution** /kɔ̃stitysjɔ̃/ nf (a) (of
company) setting up; (of capital) accumulation;
(of application) preparing
(b) constitution

constructeur, -trice /kɔ̃stʀyktœʀ, tʀis/
nm,f (a) (car) manufacturer
(b) builder

constructif, -ive /kɔ̃stʀyktif, iv/ adj
constructive

ℱ **construction** /kɔ̃stʀyksjɔ̃/ nf
(a) construction; building; en ~ under
construction; de ~ japonaise Japanese built
(b) la ~ the construction industry; ~ navale
shipbuilding

ℱ **construire** /kɔ̃stʀɥiʀ/ [69] **1** vtr to build;
to construct
2 **se construire** v refl (+ v être) (a) ça
s'est beaucoup construit par ici there's been
a lot of building here
(b) se ~ avec le subjonctif to take the
subjunctive

consul /kɔ̃syl/ nm consul

consulat /kɔ̃syla/ nm consulate

consultant, ~e /kɔ̃syltɑ̃, ɑ̃t/ nm,f
consultant

consultation /kɔ̃syltasjɔ̃/ nf
(a) consultation; consulting; ~ électorale
election
(b) surgery hours (GB), office hours (US)

ℱ **consulter** /kɔ̃sylte/ [1] **1** vtr to consult;
~ le peuple to hold a general election
2 vi ‹doctor› to see patients
3 **se consulter** v refl (+ v être) to
consult together; se ~ du regard to
exchange glances

consumer /kɔ̃syme/ [1] **1** vtr ‹fire› to
consume
2 **se consumer** v refl (+ v être) to burn

ℱ **contact** /kɔ̃takt/ nm (a) contact; garder le
~ to keep in touch; entrer en ~ avec to get
in touch with; elle est devenue plus sociable
à ton ~ she's become more sociable through
spending time with you
(b) mettre/couper le ~ to switch on/switch
off the ignition

contacter /kɔ̃takte/ [1] vtr to contact, to
get in touch with

contagieux, -ieuse /kɔ̃taʒjø, øz/ adj
(a) contagious
(b) ‹laughter› infectious

contagion /kɔ̃taʒjɔ̃/ nf contagion

contamination /kɔ̃taminasjɔ̃/ nf
contamination

contaminer /kɔ̃tamine/ [1] vtr to
contaminate; to infect

conte /kɔ̃t/ nm tale, story

contemplatif, -ive /kɔ̃tɑ̃platif, iv/ adj
contemplative

contemplation /kɔ̃tɑ̃plasjɔ̃/ nf
contemplation

contempler /kɔ̃tɑ̃ple/ [1] vtr to survey; to
contemplate; to look at

ℱ **contemporain, ~e** /kɔ̃tɑ̃pɔʀɛ̃, ɛn/ adj,
nm,f contemporary

contenance /kɔ̃t(ə)nɑ̃s/ nf (a) (of
container) capacity
(b) bearing, attitude; perdre ~ to lose one's
composure

contenant /kɔ̃t(ə)nɑ̃/ nm packaging

conteneur /kɔ̃t(ə)nœʀ/ nm container
■ ~ vert (for bottles) bottle bank

ℱ **contenir** /kɔ̃t(ə)niʀ/ [36] **1** vtr (a) to
contain ‹substance, error›
(b) ‹container› to hold; ‹hall› to accommodate
‹spectators›
(c) to contain ‹crowd›
2 **se contenir** v refl (+ v être) to contain
oneself

ℱ **content, ~e** /kɔ̃tɑ̃, ɑ̃t/ **1** adj happy,
pleased, glad; ~ de soi pleased with oneself
2 nm avoir son ~ de to have had one's
fill of

contentement /kɔ̃tɑ̃tmɑ̃/ nm
contentment

ℱ **contenter** /kɔ̃tɑ̃te/ [1] **1** vtr to satisfy
‹customer, curiosity›; facile à ~ easy to please
2 **se contenter** v refl (+ v être) se ~ de
qch to content oneself with sth

contentieux /kɔ̃tɑ̃sjø/ nm (a) bone of
contention
(b) legal department
(c) litigation

ℱ **contenu, ~e** /kɔ̃t(ə)ny/ **1** pp ▸ CONTENIR
2 pp adj restrained; suppressed
3 nm contents; content

conter /kɔ̃te/ [1] vtr to tell, to recount

contestable /kɔ̃tɛstabl/ *adj* questionable

contestataire /kɔ̃tɛstatɛʀ/ **1** *adj* anti-authority

2 *nmf* protester

contestation /kɔ̃tɛstasjɔ̃/ *nf* (a) protest
(b) challenging; être sujet à ∼, prêter à ∼ to be questionable; sans ∼ possible beyond dispute
(c) la ∼ dissent

conteste: **sans conteste** /sɑ̃kɔ̃tɛst/ *phr* unquestionably

contesté: ∼e /kɔ̃tɛste/ *adj* controversial

contester /kɔ̃tɛste/ [1] **1** *vtr* to question; to contest; to dispute; to challenge
2 *vi* (a) to raise objections
(b) to protest

⚘ **contexte** /kɔ̃tɛkst/ *nm* context

contextuel, -elle /kɔ̃tɛkstɥɛl/ *adj* menu ∼ pop-up menu

contigu, -uë /kɔ̃tigy/ *adj* ⟨rooms⟩ adjoining

continent, ∼e /kɔ̃tinɑ̃, ɑ̃t/ **1** *adj* continent
2 *nm* (a) continent
(b) mainland

continental, ∼e, *mpl* **-aux** /kɔ̃tinɑ̃tal, o/ *adj* (a) continental
(b) mainland

contingent /kɔ̃tɛ̃ʒɑ̃/ *nm* (a) contingent; (Mil) conscripts, draft (US)
(b) quota
(c) (Law, figurative) share

continu, ∼e /kɔ̃tiny/ *adj* continuous

continuation /kɔ̃tinɥasjɔ̃/ *nf* continuation

continuel, -elle /kɔ̃tinɥɛl/ *adj* continual

⚘ **continuer** /kɔ̃tinɥe/ [1] **1** *vtr* to continue
2 *vi* to continue, to go on

continuité /kɔ̃tinɥite/ *nf* continuity

contondant, ∼e /kɔ̃tɔ̃dɑ̃, ɑ̃t/ *adj* blunt

contorsion /kɔ̃tɔʀsjɔ̃/ *nf* contortion

contorsionner: se contorsionner /kɔ̃tɔʀsjɔne/ [1] *v refl* (+ *v être*) to tie oneself in knots

contorsionniste /kɔ̃tɔʀsjɔnist/ *nmf* contortionist

contour /kɔ̃tuʀ/ *nm* (a) outline, contour
(b) ∼s (of road, river) twists and turns

contourner /kɔ̃tuʀne/ [1] *vtr* to go round; to by-pass ⟨town⟩; to get round ⟨problem⟩

contraceptif, -ive /kɔ̃tʀasɛptif, iv/
1 *adj* contraceptive
2 *nm* contraceptive

contraception /kɔ̃tʀasɛpsjɔ̃/ *nf* contraception

contractant, ∼e /kɔ̃tʀaktɑ̃, ɑ̃t/ **1** *adj* contracting
2 *nm,f* contracting party

contracter /kɔ̃tʀakte/ [1] **1** *vtr* (a) to tense ⟨muscle⟩

⚘ indicates a very frequent word

(b) to incur ⟨debt⟩; to take out ⟨loan⟩
(c) to contract ⟨disease⟩
2 **se contracter** *v refl* (+ *v être*) ⟨muscle, word⟩ to contract; ⟨face, person⟩ to tense up

contraction /kɔ̃tʀaksjɔ̃/ *nf* (a) tenseness
(b) contraction

contractuel, -elle /kɔ̃tʀaktɥɛl/ **1** *adj* contractual; personnel ∼ contract staff
2 *nm,f* (a) contract employee
(b) traffic warden (GB), meter reader (US)

contradiction /kɔ̃tʀadiksjɔ̃/ *nf* contradiction

contradictoire /kɔ̃tʀadiktwaʀ/ *adj* contradictory; ∼ à in contradiction to

contraignant, ∼e /kɔ̃tʀɛɲɑ̃, ɑ̃t/ *adj* restrictive

contraindre /kɔ̃tʀɛ̃dʀ/ [54] **1** *vtr* (a) ∼ qn à faire to force sb to do
(b) to restrain, to curb
2 **se contraindre** *v refl* (+ *v être*) se ∼ à to force oneself to

contraint, ∼e¹ /kɔ̃tʀɛ̃, ɛ̃t/ *adj* (a) ∼ et forcé (Law) under duress
(b) strained, forced

contrainte² /kɔ̃tʀɛ̃t/ *nf* (a) pressure; coercion
(b) constraint
(c) sans ∼ without restraint, freely

⚘ **contraire** /kɔ̃tʀɛʀ/ **1** *adj* (a) opposite; contrary; ⟨interests⟩ conflicting; être ∼ aux usages to be contrary to custom; dans le cas ∼ (should it be) otherwise
(b) adverse
2 *nm* le ∼ the opposite, the contrary; ne dites pas le ∼ don't deny it; au ∼! on the contrary!

contrairement /kɔ̃tʀɛʀmɑ̃/ *adv* ∼ à ce qu'on pourrait penser contrary to what one might think; ∼ à qn unlike sb

contrariant, ∼e /kɔ̃tʀaʀjɑ̃, ɑ̃t/ *adj*
(a) ⟨person⟩ contrary
(b) ⟨event⟩ annoying

contrarier /kɔ̃tʀaʀje/ [2] *vtr* (a) to upset
(b) to annoy
(c) to frustrate, to thwart

contrariété /kɔ̃tʀaʀjete/ *nf* vexation

contraste /kɔ̃tʀast/ *nm* contrast

contrasté, ∼e /kɔ̃tʀaste/ *adj*
(a) contrasting
(b) ⟨photo⟩ with good contrast
(c) ⟨results⟩ uneven

contraster /kɔ̃tʀaste/ [1] **1** *vtr* to contrast ⟨colours⟩; to give contrast to ⟨photo⟩
2 *vi* to contrast

⚘ **contrat** /kɔ̃tʀa/ *nm* contract
■ ∼ emploi solidarité, CES part-time low-paid work for the long-term unemployed

contravention /kɔ̃tʀavɑ̃sjɔ̃/ *nf*
(a) parking ticket; speeding ticket; fine
(b) minor offence (GB)

◆ **contre¹** /kɔ̃tʀ/ ① *prep* (a) against; **22%
~ 18% hier** 22% as against 18% yesterday;
allongés l'un ~ l'autre lying side by side
(b) versus
(c) (in exchange) for; **échange-la ~ une
bleue** exchange it for a blue one
② **par contre** *phr* on the other hand
contre² /kɔ̃tʀ/ ① *nm* (a) **le pour et le ~**
the pros and cons
(b) (Sport) counter-attack
② *pref* counter
contre-accusation, *pl* ~**s**
/kɔ̃tʀakyzasjɔ̃/ *nf* counter-charge
contre-allée, *pl* ~**s** /kɔ̃tʀale/ *nf* service
road; side path
contre-attaque, *pl* ~**s** /kɔ̃tʀatak/ *nf*
counter-attack
contrebalancer /kɔ̃tʀəbalɑ̃se/ [12] *vtr*
(a) to counterbalance
(b) to offset
contrebande /kɔ̃tʀəbɑ̃d/ *nf* (a) smuggling
(b) smuggled goods, contraband
contrebandier, -ière
/kɔ̃tʀəbɑ̃dje, ɛʀ/ *nm,f* smuggler
contrebas: **en contrebas**
/ɑ̃kɔ̃tʀəbɑ/ *phr* (down) below; **en ~ de** below
contrebasse /kɔ̃tʀəbas/ *nf* double bass
contrecarrer /kɔ̃tʀəkaʀe/ [1] *vtr* to
thwart, to foil; to counteract
contrechamp /kɔ̃tʀəʃɑ̃/ *nm* reverse shot
contrecœur: à contrecœur
/akɔ̃tʀəkœʀ/ *phr* reluctantly
contrecoup /kɔ̃tʀəku/ *nm* effects; after-
effects; **par ~** as a result
contre-courant, *pl* ~**s** /kɔ̃tʀəkuʀɑ̃/ *nm*
counter-current; **nager à ~** to swim against
the current; **aller à ~ de la mode** to go
against the fashion
contredire /kɔ̃tʀədiʀ/ [65] ① *vtr* to
contradict
② **se contredire** *v refl* (+ *v être*) (a) to
contradict oneself
(b) to contradict each other
contrée /kɔ̃tʀe/ *nf* (a) land
(b) region
contre-enquête, *pl* ~**s** /kɔ̃tʀɑ̃kɛt/ *nf*
second enquiry (GB)
contre-espionnage, *pl* ~**s**
/kɔ̃tʀɛspjɔnaʒ/ *nm* counter-intelligence
contre-expertise, *pl* ~**s**
/kɔ̃tʀɛkspɛʀtiz/ *nf* second opinion
contrefaçon /kɔ̃tʀəfasɔ̃/ *nf* (a) forging,
counterfeiting
(b) forgery, counterfeit
contrefacteur /kɔ̃tʀəfaktœʀ/ *nm*
(of notes, credit cards, paintings) forger;
(of coins) counterfeiter; (of software,
invention) pirate
contrefaire /kɔ̃tʀəfɛʀ/ [10] *vtr* (a) to forge,
to counterfeit
(b) to imitate

(c) to disguise
contrefort /kɔ̃tʀəfɔʀ/ *nm* (a) foothills
(b) buttress
(c) (of shoe) back
contre-indiqué, ~**e**, *mpl* ~**s** /kɔ̃tʀɛ̃dike/
adj contra-indicated; inadvisable
contre-interrogatoire, *pl* ~**s**
/kɔ̃tʀɛ̃teʀɔgatwaʀ/ *nm* cross-examination
contre-jour, ~**s** /kɔ̃tʀəʒuʀ/ *nm*
backlighting; **à ~** against *or* into the light
contremaître, -esse /kɔ̃tʀəmɛtʀ,
kɔ̃tʀəmɛtʀɛs/ *nm,f* foreman/forewoman
contrepartie /kɔ̃tʀəpaʀti/ *nf*
(a) equivalent
(b) compensation; **en ~** in compensation; in
return; **mais la ~ est que le salaire est élevé**
but this is offset by the high salary
contre-pied, *pl* ~**s** /kɔ̃tʀəpje/ *nm* **prendre
le ~ de ce que dit qn** to say the opposite of
what sb says
contreplaqué /kɔ̃tʀəplake/ *nm* plywood
contrepoids /kɔ̃tʀəpwa/ *nm*
counterweight
contrer /kɔ̃tʀe/ [1] *vtr* to counter; to block
contresens /kɔ̃tʀəsɑ̃s/ *nm*
(a) misinterpretation
(b) mistranslation
(c) **à ~** in the opposite direction; the wrong
way; against the grain
contretemps /kɔ̃tʀətɑ̃/ *nm inv*
(a) setback, contretemps
(b) **à ~** (Mus) on the off-beat; out of time;
(figurative) at the wrong moment
contre-valeur, *pl* ~**s** /kɔ̃tʀəvalœʀ/ *nf*
exchange value
contrevenir /kɔ̃tʀəvəniʀ/ [36] *v+prep* ~ **à**
to contravene
contribuable /kɔ̃tʀibɥabl/ *nmf* taxpayer
◆ **contribuer** /kɔ̃tʀibɥe/ [1] *v+prep* ~ **à** to
contribute to; to pay one's share of; **cela y a
beaucoup contribué** it was a major factor
contribution /kɔ̃tʀibysjɔ̃/ *nf*
(a) contribution; **mettre qn à ~** to call upon
sb's services
(b) ~**s** taxes; tax office
contrit, ~**e** /kɔ̃tʀi, it/ *adj* contrite,
apologetic
◆ **contrôle** /kɔ̃tʀol/ *nm* (a) control
(b) check; ~ **de police** police check; ~ **des
billets** ticket inspection
(c) (Sch) test; ~ **de géographie** geography
test
(d) check-up
(e) monitoring; **sous ~ médical** under
medical supervision
■ ~ **continu (des connaissances)** continuous
assessment; ~ **fiscal** tax investigation;
~ **technique (des véhicules)** MOT (test)
◆ **contrôler** /kɔ̃tʀole/ [1] ① *vtr* (a) to
control   ⋯⋰

(b) to monitor
(c) to check; to inspect; to test
2 **se contrôler** *v refl* (+ *v être*) to control oneself

contrôleur, -euse /kɔ̃trolœr, øz/ *nm,f* inspector; ~ **aérien** air-traffic controller

contrordre /kɔ̃trɔrdr/ *nm* **(a) ordres et** ~**s** conflicting orders; **j'irai vendredi, sauf** ~ I'll go on Friday, unless I hear to the contrary
(b) counter command

controverse /kɔ̃trɔvɛrs/ *nf* controversy

controversé, ~e /kɔ̃trɔvɛrse/ *adj* controversial

contusion /kɔ̃tyzjɔ̃/ *nf* bruise

convaincant, ~e /kɔ̃vɛ̃kɑ̃, ɑ̃t/ *adj*
(a) convincing
(b) persuasive

✍ **convaincre** /kɔ̃vɛ̃kr/ [57] **1** *vtr* to convince; to persuade
2 **se convaincre** *v refl* (+ *v être*) to convince oneself

convaincu, ~e /kɔ̃vɛ̃ky/ **1** *pp*
▶ CONVAINCRE
2 *pp adj* **(a)** convinced; **d'un ton** ~ with conviction
(b) ‹*supporter*› staunch

convalescence /kɔ̃valesɑ̃s/ *nf* convalescence

convalescent, ~e /kɔ̃valesɑ̃, ɑ̃t/ *adj, nm,f* convalescent

convenable /kɔ̃vnabl/ *adj* **(a)** suitable
(b) reasonable
(c) decent; proper; respectable

convenablement /kɔ̃vnabləmɑ̃/ *adv* properly; reasonably well; decently

convenance /kɔ̃vnɑ̃s/ *nf* **(a) pour** ~ **personnelle** for personal reasons; **à votre** ~ at your convenience
(b) ~**s** (social) conventions

✍ **convenir** /kɔ̃vnir/ [36] **1** *vtr* **(a)** to admit
(b) to agree
2 **convenir à** *v+prep* to suit; to be suitable for
3 **convenir de** *v+prep* **(a)** ~ **de** to admit, to acknowledge
(b) ~ **de** to agree on
4 *v impers* **(a) il convient de faire/que vous fassiez** one/you should do
(b) ce qu'il est convenu d'appeler le réalisme what is commonly called realism; **comme convenu** as agreed

✍ **convention** /kɔ̃vɑ̃sjɔ̃/ *nf* **(a)** agreement
(b) convention; **de** ~ conventional

conventionné, ~e /kɔ̃vɑ̃sjone/ *adj* ‹*doctor, costs*› national health service; ‹*clinic*› registered; **médecin non** ~ private doctor

conventionnel, -elle /kɔ̃vɑ̃sjonɛl/ *adj*
(a) conventional
(b) contractual

✍ indicates a very frequent word

convenu, ~e /kɔ̃v(ə)ny/ **1** *pp*
▶ CONVENIR
2 *pp adj* **(a)** ‹*date, terms*› agreed
(b) ‹*phrase*› conventional; ‹*smile*› polite

convergence /kɔ̃vɛrʒɑ̃s/ *nf* convergence

converger /kɔ̃vɛrʒe/ [13] *vi* to converge

✍ **conversation** /kɔ̃vɛrsasjɔ̃/ *nf* conversation; **avoir de la** ~ to be a good conversationalist; **dans la** ~ **courante** in everyday speech

converser /kɔ̃vɛrse/ [1] *vi* to converse

conversion /kɔ̃vɛrsjɔ̃/ *nf* conversion

converti, ~e /kɔ̃vɛrti/ **1** *pp*
▶ CONVERTIR
2 *nm,f* convert

convertible /kɔ̃vɛrtibl/ *adj*
(a) convertible
(b) canapé ~ sofa-bed

convertir /kɔ̃vɛrtir/ [3] **1** *vtr* to convert
2 **se convertir** *v refl* (+ *v être*) to convert; ‹*company*› to change products

convertisseur /kɔ̃vɛrtisœr/ *nm* converter

convexe /kɔ̃vɛks/ *adj* convex

conviction /kɔ̃viksjɔ̃/ *nf* conviction

convier /kɔ̃vje/ [2] *vtr* to invite ‹*person*›

convive /kɔ̃viv/ *nmf* guest

convivial, ~e, *mpl* **-iaux** /kɔ̃vivjal, o/ *adj*
(a) convivial
(b) user-friendly

convivialité /kɔ̃vivjalite/ *nf*
(a) friendliness; conviviality
(b) user-friendliness

convocation /kɔ̃vɔkasjɔ̃/ *nf* **(a)** (of meeting) convening; (of person) summoning; (Mil) calling up
(b) notice to attend; (Law) summons; ~ **aux examens** notification of examination timetables

convoi /kɔ̃vwa/ *nm* **(a)** convoy; '~ **exceptionnel'** (Aut) 'wide *or* dangerous load'
(b) train

convoiter /kɔ̃vwate/ [1] *vtr* to covet

convoitise /kɔ̃vwatiz/ *nf* **la** ~ covetousness; ~ **de** lust for

convoquer /kɔ̃vɔke/ [1] *vtr* to call, to convene ‹*meeting*›; to send for ‹*pupil*›; to summon ‹*witness*›; to call up ‹*soldier*›; **être convoqué à un examen** to be asked to attend an exam

convoyer /kɔ̃vwaje/ [23] *vtr* to escort

convoyeur, -euse /kɔ̃vwajœr/ *nm,f*
(a) prison escort
(b) courier; ~ **de fonds** security guard

convulsif, -ive /kɔ̃vylsif, iv/ *adj*
(a) convulsive
(b) ‹*laughter*› nervous

convulsion /kɔ̃vylsjɔ̃/ *nf* convulsion

convulsionner /kɔ̃vylsjone/ [1] *vtr* to convulse

coopératif, -ive /kɔɔpeʀatif, iv/ **1** *adj* cooperative

2 coopérative *nf* cooperative

coopération /kɔɔpeʀasjɔ̃/ *nf*
(a) cooperation
(b) cultural/technical aid

coopérer /kɔɔpeʀe/ [14] *vi* to cooperate

coordinateur, -trice /kɔɔʀdinatœʀ, tʀis/
1 *adj* coordinating
2 *nm, f* coordinator

coordination /kɔɔʀdinasjɔ̃/ *nf*
(a) coordination
(b) joint committee

coordonné, ~e /kɔɔʀdɔne/ **1** *pp*
▶ COORDONNER
2 *pp adj* coordinated; coordinating
3 *nm pl* (in fashion) coordinates

coordonnées /kɔɔʀdɔne/ *nf pl* (a) (on graph, map) coordinates
(b) information
(c) address and telephone number

coordonner /kɔɔʀdɔne/ [1] *vtr* to coordinate

copain, copine /kɔpɛ̃, in/ **1** *adj* pally (GB) (colloq), chummy (colloq)
2 *nm, f* (a) friend
(b) boyfriend/girlfriend

copeau, *pl* ~**x** /kɔpo/ *nm* shaving

Copenhague /kɔpɛnag/ *pr n* Copenhagen

copie /kɔpi/ *nf* (a) copying; copy
(b) (Sch) paper

copier /kɔpje/ [2] *vtr* (a) to copy
(b) (Sch) ~ sur qn to copy *or* crib from sb

copier-coller /kɔpjekɔle/ [1] *vtr* (Comput) to copy and paste

copieur, -ieuse /kɔpjœʀ, øz/ **1** *nm, f* (Sch) cheat
2 *nm* photocopier

copieusement /kɔpjøzmɑ̃/ *adv* heartily; lavishly; copiously

copieux, -ieuse /kɔpjø, øz/ *adj* ‹meal› hearty; ‹portion› generous; ‹notes› copious

copilote /kɔpilɔt/ *nmf* co-pilot; co-driver

copine ▶ COPAIN

coprésident, ~e /kɔpʀezidɑ̃, ɑ̃t/ *nm, f* joint president; co-chair

coproduction /kɔpʀɔdyksjɔ̃/ *nf* co-production

copropriété /kɔpʀɔpʀijete/ *nf* joint ownership; co-ownership

coq /kɔk/ *nm* cockerel, rooster; cock; **au chant du** ~ at cockcrow; **le** ~ **du village** (figurative) the local Casanova
■ ~ **de bruyère** grouse
IDIOMS **être comme un** ~ **en pâte** to be in clover; **sauter du** ~ **à l'âne** to hop from one subject to another

coque /kɔk/ *nf* (a) (of boat) hull; (of hydroplane) fuselage; (of car) body
(b) cockle
(c) (of nut) shell

coquelicot /kɔkliko/ *nm* poppy

coqueluche /kɔklyʃ/ *nf* (a) whooping-cough
(b) (fam) idol

coquet, -ette /kɔkɛ, ɛt/ *adj* (a) être ~ to be particular about one's appearance
(b) pretty
(c) (fam) ‹sum› tidy (colloq)

coquetier /kɔktje/ *nm* eggcup

coquetterie /kɔkɛtʀi/ *nf* interest in one's appearance; vanity; **par** ~ out of vanity

coquillage /kɔkijaʒ/ *nm* (a) shellfish
(b) shell

coquille /kɔkij/ *nf* (a) shell
(b) scallop-shaped dish; ~ **de saumon** salmon served in a shell
(c) misprint
(d) (Med) spinal jacket
■ ~ **Saint-Jacques** scallop; scallop shell

coquillette /kɔkijet/ *nf* small macaroni

coquin, ~e /kɔkɛ̃, in/ **1** *adj*
(a) mischievous
(b) naughty, saucy
2 *nm, f* rascal

cor /kɔʀ/ *nm* (a) (Mus) horn
(b) (Med) corn
IDIOM **réclamer** *or* **demander qch à** ~ **et à cri** to clamour (GB) for sth

corail, *pl* **-aux** /kɔʀaj, o/ *adj inv, nm* coral

Coran /kɔʀɑ̃/ *pr nm* **le** ~ the Koran

corbeau, *pl* ~**x** /kɔʀbo/ *nm* (a) crow; **grand** ~ raven
(b) (fam) writer of a poison-pen letter

corbeille /kɔʀbɛj/ *nf* (a) basket
(b) dress circle

corbillard /kɔʀbijaʀ/ *nm* hearse

corde /kɔʀd/ *nf* (a) rope
(b) ~ (**à sauter**) skipping rope
(c) (of racket, instrument) string
■ ~ **à linge** clothes line; ~ **raide** tightrope; ~**s vocales** vocal chords
IDIOMS **mériter la** ~ to deserve to be hanged; **pleuvoir** *or* **tomber des** ~**s** to be raining cats and dogs (colloq); **tirer sur la** ~ to push one's luck; **faire jouer la** ~ **sensible** to tug at the heartstrings; **usé jusqu'à la** ~ threadbare

cordée /kɔʀde/ *nf* roped party (of climbers)

cordelière /kɔʀdəljɛʀ/ *nf* cord

cordial, ~e, *mpl* **-iaux** /kɔʀdjal, o/ *adj* cordial; warm-hearted; warm

cordialement /kɔʀdjalmɑ̃/ *adv* warmly; ~ (**vôtre** *or* **à vous**) yours sincerely

cordialité /kɔʀdjalite/ *nf* warmth; friendliness

cordillère /kɔʀdijɛʀ/ *nf* cordillera

cordon /kɔʀdɔ̃/ *nm* (a) cord; string; lace
(b) flex (GB), cord (US)
(c) cordon

⋯⟐

(d) row
(e) ribbon
■ ~ ombilical umbilical cord
cordonnerie /kɔʀdɔnʀi/ *nf*
(a) shoemaking
(b) shoe repairing
(c) cobbler's
cordonnier /kɔʀdɔnje/ *nm* cobbler
IDIOM les ~s sont toujours les plus mal chaussés it's always the baker's children who have no bread
Corée /kɔʀe/ *pr nf* Korea
coriace /kɔʀjas/ *adj* tough
coriandre /kɔʀjɑ̃dʀ/ *nf* coriander
Corinthe /kɔʀɛ̃t/ *pr n* raisins de ~ currants
corne /kɔʀn/ *nf* (a) horn; antler; à ~s horned; **blesser d'un coup de** ~ to gore
(b) (Mus) horn
(c) (fam) **avoir de la** ~ **aux pieds** to have calluses on one's feet
■ ~ d'abondance horn of plenty, cornucopia; ~ de brume foghorn
cornée /kɔʀne/ *nf* cornea
corneille /kɔʀnɛj/ *nf* crow
cornemuse /kɔʀnəmyz/ *nf* bagpipes
corner /kɔʀne/ [1] *vtr* to turn down the corner of ‹page›; **page cornée** dog-eared page
cornet /kɔʀnɛ/ *nm* (a) (paper) cone
(b) (ice-cream) cone, cornet (GB)
■ ~ à dés dice cup; ~ à pistons cornet
corniche /kɔʀniʃ/ *nf* (a) cornice
(b) moulding (GB), molding (US)
(c) ledge (of rock)
(d) cliff road
cornichon /kɔʀniʃɔ̃/ *nm* gherkin
Cornouailles /kɔʀnuɑj/ *pr nf* Cornwall
corollaire /kɔʀɔlɛʀ/ *nm* corollary
corolle /kɔʀɔl/ *nf* (a) corolla
(b) en ~ ‹skirt› flared
coron /kɔʀɔ̃/ *nm* miners' terraced houses
corporatif, -ive /kɔʀpɔʀatif, iv/ *adj* corporate
corporation /kɔʀpɔʀasjɔ̃/ *nf* corporation
corporel, -elle /kɔʀpɔʀɛl/ *adj* ‹needs› bodily; ‹punishment› corporal
♂ **corps** /kɔʀ/ *nm inv* body; (combat) ~ à ~ hand-to-hand combat; **se donner** ~ **et âme à** to give oneself body and soul to; **faire** ~ **avec** ‹person› to stand solidly behind; ‹building› to be joined to; **prendre** ~ to take shape
■ ~ enseignant teaching profession; ~ et biens (to sink) with all hands; ~ expéditionnaire expeditionary force; ~ gras fatty substance; ~ médical medical profession
IDIOM **tenir au** ~ to be nourishing
corpulence /kɔʀpylɑ̃s/ *nf* stoutness

corpulent, ~e /kɔʀpylɑ̃, ɑ̃t/ *adj* stout, corpulent
correct, ~e /kɔʀɛkt/ *adj* (a) ‹calculation› correct; ‹copy› accurate
(b) ‹outfit› proper; ‹conduct› correct
(c) (fam) ‹result, wine› reasonable, decent
(d) ‹person› polite; fair, correct
correctement /kɔʀɛktəmɑ̃/ *adv*
(a) correctly
(b) properly
(c) decently, reasonably well
correcteur, -trice /kɔʀɛktœʀ, tʀis/
1 *adj* corrective
2 *nm,f* (a) examiner (GB), grader (US)
(b) proofreader
correction /kɔʀɛksjɔ̃/ *nf* (a) correcting; proofreading; marking (GB), grading (US)
(b) correction
(c) thrashing
(d) correctness; good manners
correctionnel, -elle[1] /kɔʀɛksjɔnɛl/ *adj* tribunal ~ magistrate's court
correctionnelle[2] /kɔʀɛksjɔnɛl/ *nf* magistrate's court
corrélation /kɔʀelasjɔ̃/ *nf* correlation; être en ~ avec qn to be related to sth
correspondance /kɔʀɛspɔ̃dɑ̃s/ *nf*
(a) letters; mail; correspondence; **faire sa** ~ to write some letters; **vendu par** ~ available by mail order
(b) correspondence
(c) connection; **trains**/**vols en** ~ connecting trains/flights
correspondant, ~e /kɔʀɛspɔ̃dɑ̃, ɑ̃t/
1 *adj* corresponding
2 *nm,f* correspondent; (Sch) pen pal
♂ **correspondre** /kɔʀɛspɔ̃dʀ/ [6]
1 **correspondre à** *v+prep* to correspond to; to match; to suit ‹tastes›
2 *vi* to correspond, to write
3 **se correspondre** *v refl* (+ *v être*) to correspond
corrida /kɔʀida/ *nf* bullfight
corridor /kɔʀidɔʀ/ *nm* corridor
corrigé /kɔʀiʒe/ *nm* (Sch) correct version
corriger /kɔʀiʒe/ [13] 1 *vtr* (a) to correct; to proofread ‹manuscript›; to mark (GB), to grade (US) ‹exam papers›; to redress ‹situation›
(b) to adjust ‹position›; to modify ‹theory›; ~ **le tir** (Mil) to alter one's aim; (figurative) to adjust one's tactics
(c) to give [sb] a hiding (colloq); to spank ‹child›
2 **se corriger** *v refl* (+ *v être*) (a) to correct oneself
(b) se ~ d'un défaut to cure oneself of a fault
corroborer /kɔʀɔbɔʀe/ [1] *vtr* to corroborate
corroder /kɔʀɔde/ [1] *vtr* to corrode
corrompre /kɔʀɔ̃pʀ/ [53] *vtr* (a) to bribe
(b) to corrupt

♂ indicates a very frequent word

corrompu, ~**e** /kɔʀɔ̃py/ **1** *pp*
▶ CORROMPRE
  2 *pp adj* corrupt
corrosif, **-ive** /kɔʀɔzif, iv/ *adj*
  (a) ‹*substance*› corrosive
  (b) ‹*humour*› caustic
corrosion /kɔʀɔzjɔ̃/ *nf* corrosion
corruption /kɔʀypsjɔ̃/ *nf* **(a)** corruption
  (b) bribery
corsage /kɔʀsaʒ/ *nm* **(a)** blouse
  (b) bodice
corsaire /kɔʀsɛʀ/ *nm* **(a)** corsair
  (b) pedal pushers
corse /kɔʀs/ *adj, nm* Corsican
Corse /kɔʀs/ *pr nf* Corsica
corsé, ~**e** /kɔʀse/ *adj* ‹*coffee*› strong;
‹*sauce, story*› spicy; ‹*problem*› tough; ‹*bill*›
steep
corser /kɔʀse/ [1] **1** *vtr* **(a)** to make [sth]
more difficult; **pour ~ l'affaire** (just) to
complicate matters
  (b) to make [sth] spicier ‹*sauce*›
  2 **se corser** *v refl* (+ *v être*) to get more
complicated
corset /kɔʀsɛ/ *nm* corset
corso /kɔʀso/ *nm* ~ **fleuri** procession of
floral floats
cortège /kɔʀtɛʒ/ *nm* procession
corvée /kɔʀve/ *nf* chore; (Mil) fatigue (duty)
cosmétique /kɔsmetik/ *adj, nm* cosmetic
cosmique /kɔsmik/ *adj* cosmic
cosmonaute /kɔsmɔnot/ *nmf* cosmonaut
cosmopolite /kɔsmɔpɔlit/ *adj*
cosmopolitan
cosse /kɔs/ *nf* (of pea) pod; (of grain) husk
cossu, ~**e** /kɔsy/ *adj* ‹*person*› well-to-do;
‹*interior*› plush; ‹*house*› smart
costaud /kɔsto/ *adj* (fam) strong, sturdy;
hefty (colloq)
costume /kɔstym/ *nm* **(a)** suit
  (b) costume; **répétition en ~** dress rehearsal
costumer: se costumer /kɔstyme/ [1]
v refl (+ *v être*) **se ~** en to dress up as; **soirée**
costumée fancy-dress party
cotation /kɔtasjɔ̃/ *nf* quotation
cote /kɔt/ *nf* **(a)** (of stocks,
commodities) quotation; (stock exchange) list
  (b) (of stamp) quoted value
  (c) (at races) odds
  (d) (of person, film) rating; **avoir la ~**
(fam) **auprès de** to be popular with; to be well
thought of by
  (e) (on plan) dimension
  (f) (on map) spot height
■ ~ **d'alerte** flood level; (figurative) danger level;
~ **de popularité** popularity rating
coté, ~**e** /kɔte/ **1** *pp* ▶ COTER
  2 *pp adj* **être ~** to be well thought of
ꜰ **côte** /kot/ **1** *nf* **(a)** coast
  (b) hill; **dans une ~** on a hill
  (c) rib

  (d) chop; ~ **de bœuf** rib roast
  2 **côte à côte** *phr* side by side
■ **Côte d'Azur** French riviera
ꜰ **côté** /kote/ **1** *nm* **(a)** side; **du ~ droit/**
gauche on the righthand/lefthand side;
chambre ~ rue room overlooking the street;
par certains ~s in some respects; ~ **santé**
healthwise; **de mon ~, je pense que...** for
my part, I think that...; **d'un ~... d'un autre**
~**...** on the one hand... on the other hand...
  (b) way, direction; **de tous ~s** ‹*come*› from
all directions; ‹*run*› all over the place; **du ~**
de Nice ‹*live*› near Nice; **aller du ~ de Dijon**
to head for Dijon
  2 **à côté** *phr* **(a)** nearby; **les gens d'à**
~ the people next door; **à ~ de** next to;
le ballon est passé à ~ (du but) the ball
went wide (of the goal); **répondre à ~** (by
mistake) to miss the point; (on purpose) to
sidestep the question
  (b) by comparison
  (c) on the side; **elle est étudiante et travaille**
à ~ she's a student and works on the side
  3 **de côté** *phr* **(a)** sideways
  (b) aside; **mettre qch de ~** to put sth aside
‹*money, object*›
  4 **aux côtés de** *phr* **aux ~s de qn** ‹*to*
be› at sb's side; ‹*to work*› alongside sb
coteau, *pl* ~**x** /kɔto/ *nm* **(a)** hillside
  (b) hill
  (c) (sloping) vineyard
côtelette /kotlɛt/ *nf* (Culin) chop
coter /kɔte/ [1] *vtr* **(a)** to quote, to list
‹*shares*›; to price ‹*car*›
  (b) to rate ‹*film*›
côtier, **-ière** /kotje, ɛʀ/ *adj* coastal; inshore
cotisation /kɔtizasjɔ̃/ *nf* **(a)** contribution
  (b) subscription
cotiser /kɔtize/ [1] **1** *vi* **(a)** to pay one's
contributions
  (b) to pay one's subscription (à to)
  2 **se cotiser** *v refl* (+ *v être*) to club
together (GB), to go in together
co-titulaire /kotitylɛʀ/ *nmf* joint account-
holder
coton /kɔtɔ̃/ *nm* **(a)** cotton
  (b) thread
  (c) cotton wool (GB), cotton (US)
IDIOMS **filer un mauvais ~** to be in a bad
way; **élever un enfant dans du ~** to give
a child a very sheltered upbringing; **j'ai**
les jambes en ~ (after shock) my legs have
turned to jelly
cotonnade /kɔtɔnad/ *nf* cotton fabric
cotonneux, **-euse** /kɔtɔnø, øz/ *adj* ‹*fog*›
like cotton-wool; ‹*cloud*› fleecy
côtoyer /kotwaje/ [23] **1** *vtr* to walk
alongside ‹*river*›; to move in ‹*milieu*›; to mix
with ‹*people*›; to be in close contact with
‹*death*›
  2 **se côtoyer** *v refl* (+ *v être*) ‹*people*›
to mix

cotte /kɔt/ *nf* overalls
■ ~ **de mailles** coat of mail

⚜ **cou** /ku/ *nm* neck; **être endetté jusqu'au** ~ to be up to one's eyes in debt

couchage /kuʃaʒ/ *nm* bedding; **un studio avec** ~ **pour six** a studio that sleeps six

couchant /kuʃɑ̃/ **1** *adj* **au soleil** ~ at sunset
2 *nm* **(a)** sunset
(b) west

⚜ **couche** /kuʃ/ *nf* **(a)** layer; (of paint) coat
(b) nappy (GB), diaper (US)
(c) class, sector

couché, ~e /kuʃe/ **1** *pp* ▶ COUCHER
2 *pp adj* ‹grass› flattened; ‹writing› sloping

couche-culotte, *pl* **couches-culottes** /kuʃkylɔt/ *nf* disposable nappy (GB) *or* diaper (US)

⚜ **coucher** /kuʃe/ **1** *nm* bedtime
2 *vtr* **(a)** to put [sb] to bed; to lay out ‹wounded person›
(b) to lay [sth] on its side; to lay [sth] down
(c) to flatten ‹grass›
3 *vi* to sleep; ~ **sous les ponts** to sleep rough (GB) *or* outdoors
4 **se coucher** *v refl* (+ *v être*) **(a)** to lie (down)
(b) to go to bed
(c) ‹stem› to bend; ‹boat› to list; **se** ~ **sur** ‹cyclist› to lean forward over ‹handlebars›
(d) ‹sun› to set
■ ~ **de soleil** sunset

couchette /kuʃɛt/ *nf* couchette, berth

couci-couça /kusikusa/ *adv* (fam) so-so (colloq)

coucou /kuku/ **1** *nm* **(a)** cuckoo
(b) cowslip
(c) (fam) (old) crate (colloq), plane
(d) cuckoo clock
2 *excl* (fam) **(a)** cooee!
(b) peekaboo!

coude /kud/ *nm* **(a)** elbow; **travailler** ~ **à** ~ to work shoulder to shoulder
(b) (in river, pipe) bend
IDIOM **se serrer les** ~**s** to stick together

coudé, ~e¹ /kude/ *adj* bent at an angle

coudée² /kude/ *nf* **avoir les** ~**s franches** to have elbow room

cou-de-pied, *pl* **cous-de-pied** /kudpje/ *nm* instep

couder /kude/ [1] *vtr* to bend

coudre /kudʀ/ [76] *vtr* to sew; to sew [sth] on; to stitch [sth] on; to stitch (up)
IDIOM **leur histoire est cousue de fil blanc** you can see right through their story

couenne /kwan/ *nf* (bacon) rind

couette /kwɛt/ *nf* duvet

couffin /kufɛ̃/ *nm* Moses basket (GB), bassinet (US)

⚜ indicates a very frequent word

couiner /kwine/ [1] *vi* to squeak, to squeal

coulant, ~e /kulɑ̃, ɑ̃t/ *adj* ‹camembert› runny; ‹person› easy-going

coulée /kule/ *nf* ‹of lava› flow; (of paint) drip

⚜ **couler** /kule/ [1] **1** *vtr* **(a)** to cast ‹metal, statue›; to pour ‹concrete›
(b) to sink ‹ship›
(c) (fam) to put [sth] out of business; to bring [sb] down
2 *vi* **(a)** ‹blood› to flow; ‹paint, cheese› to run; **faire** ~ **qch** to run ‹bath›
(b) ‹tap, pen› to leak; ‹nose› to run
(c) ‹boat› to sink; ‹company› to go under
3 **se couler** *v refl* (+ *v être*) **se** ~ **dans/ entre** to slip into/between

⚜ **couleur** /kulœʀ/ *nf* **(a)** colour (GB); **de** ~ ‹person› coloured (GB); **sans** ~ colourless (GB); **plein de** ~ colourful (GB)
(b) paint
(c) **les** ~**s** (washing) coloureds (GB); (flag) the colours (GB)
(d) (in cards) suit
(e) **sous** ~ **de faire** while pretending to do
IDIOMS **ne pas voir la** ~ **de qch** (fam) never to get a sniff of sth (colloq); **il m'en a fait voir de toutes les** ~**s** (fam) he put me through the mill

couleuvre /kulœvʀ/ *nf* grass snake
IDIOM **avaler des** ~**s** (fam) to believe anything one is told

coulissant, ~e /kulisɑ̃, ɑ̃t/ *adj* sliding

coulisse /kulis/ *nf* **(a)** **les** ~**s**, **la** ~ the wings; **en** ~ backstage; (figurative) behind the scenes
(b) runner

coulisser /kulise/ [1] *vi* to slide

couloir /kulwaʀ/ *nm* **(a)** corridor (GB), hallway; passage; **bruits de** ~**s** rumours (GB)
(b) lane; ~ **aérien** air (traffic) lane

⚜ **coup** /ku/ *nm* **(a)** knock; blow; ~ **à la porte** knock at the door; **à** ~**s de bâton** with a stick; **donner un** ~ **de qch à qn** to hit sb with sth; **donner un** ~ **de poing à qn** to punch sb; **porter un** ~ **(sévère) à** (figurative) to deal [sb/sth] a (severe) blow; **sa fierté en a pris un** ~ it was a blow to his/her pride; **sous le** ~ **de la colère** in (a fit of) anger; **être sous le** ~ **d'une forte émotion** to be in a highly emotional state
(b) (noise) knock; bang; thump, thud; **au douzième** ~ **de minuit** on the last stroke of midnight; **sur le** ~ **de dix heures** (fam) around ten; ~ **de sifflet** whistle blast
(c) **un (petit)** ~ **de chiffon** a (quick) wipe; **un** ~ **de peinture** a lick of paint
(d) (in tennis, golf, cricket) stroke; shot; (in chess) move; (with dice) throw; (in boxing) punch; **tous les** ~**s sont permis** no holds barred
(e) ~ **de feu/fusil** (gun)shot/(rifle) shot
(f) (fam) job (colloq), racket (colloq); trick (colloq); **monter un** ~ to plan a job (colloq); **il a**

raté son ∼ (fam) he blew it (colloq); **être dans le ∼** to be in on it; to be up to date; **qui a fait le ∼?** who did it?

(g) time; **du premier ∼** first time; **à tous les ∼s** every time; **ce ∼-ci** this time; **du ∼** (fam) as a result; **après ∼** afterward(s); **∼ sur ∼** in succession; **tout d'un ∼**, **tout à ∼** suddenly, all of a sudden; **d'un ∼**, **d'un seul ∼** just like that; **en un seul ∼** in one go (colloq); **sur le ∼** at the time; instantly, on the spot; **pleurer un bon ∼** to have a good cry **(h) à ∼s de subventions** by means of subsidies

(i) (fam) drink

■ ∼ **bas** blow below the belt; ∼**s et blessures** assault and battery; ∼ **dur** blow; ∼ **franc** free kick; ∼ **monté** put-up job; ∼ **de tête** *or* **de boule** (fam) headbutt

■ **Note** For translations of expressions such as *coup d'envoi, coup de fil* etc., look up the entries at ENVOI, FIL etc.

IDIOMS **tenir le ∼** ‹shoes› to last out; ‹repair› to hold; ‹person› to hold on; **être aux cent ∼s** (fam) to be worried sick (colloq); **faire les quatre cents ∼s** (fam) to be a real tearaway; **attraper le ∼ pour faire** (fam) to get the knack of doing

⚜ **coupable** /kupabl/ **1** *adj* guilty; ‹negligence› culpable; ‹indifférence› shameful **2** *nmf* culprit

coupant, **∼e** /kupɑ̃, ɑ̃t/ *adj* sharp

coup-de-poing, *pl* **coups-de-poing** /kudpwɛ̃/ *nm* ∼ **américain** knuckle-duster (GB), brass knuckles (US)

coupe /kup/ *nf* **(a)** cutting; cutting out; cut **(b)** haircut

(c) (Sport) cup; **la ∼ du Monde** the World Cup

(d) (fruit) bowl; (champagne) glass

(e) section; ∼ **transversale** cross section

■ ∼ **en brosse** crew cut

IDIOMS **la ∼ est pleine** enough is enough; **être sous la ∼ de qn** to be under sb's control

coupe-feu /kupfø/ *nm inv* firebreak

coupe-gorge /kupgɔʀʒ/ *nm inv* rough place; rough area

coupe-papier /kuppapje/ *nm inv* paper knife

⚜ **couper** /kupe/ **[1]** **1** *vtr* **(a)** to cut; to cut down; to chop; to cut out; to cut off; ∼ **qch en tranches** to slice sth

(b) ‹road› to cut across; ∼ **la route à qn** to cut in on sb

(c) to cut off ‹road, supplies›; to spoil ‹appetite›; to take the edge off ‹hunger›; to turn off ‹water›; ∼ **le souffle à qn** to take sb's breath away; ∼ **la parole à qn** to interrupt sb **(d)** ∼ **qn de qn/qch** to cut sb off from sb/sth **(e)** to dilute ‹wine›

(f) (in cards) to cut ‹pack›; to trump ‹card›

2 *vi* **attention ça coupe!** be careful, it's sharp; ∼ **à travers champs** to cut across country

3 **se couper** *v refl* (+ *v être*) to cut

oneself

IDIOM **c'est ton tour de faire à manger, tu n'y couperas pas** it's your turn to cook, you won't get out of it

couper-coller /kupekɔle/ **[1]** *vtr* (Comput) to cut and paste

couperet /kupʀɛ/ *nm* cleaver; (of guillotine) blade; **la nouvelle est tombée comme un ∼** the news came as a bolt from the blue

couperose /kupʀoz/ *nf* broken veins

coupe-vent /kupvɑ̃/ *nm inv*
(a) windcheater (GB), windbreaker (US)
(b) windbreak

⚜ **couple** /kupl/ *nm* **(a)** couple; pair
(b) relationship

couplet /kuplɛ/ *nm* **(a)** verse
(b) couplet

coupole /kupɔl/ *nf* cupola, dome

coupon /kupɔ̃/ *nm* **(a)** remnant
(b) ticket voucher
(c) multiuse ticket (*in travel pass*)

coupon-réponse, *pl* **coupons-réponses** /kupɔ̃ʀepɔ̃s/ *nm* reply coupon

coupure /kupyʀ/ *nf* **(a)** cut; ∼ **d'électricité** *or* **de courant** power cut
(b) break
(c) gap
(d) (bank)note (GB), bill (US)

■ ∼ **de journal** *or* **de presse** (newspaper) cutting

⚜ **cour** /kuʀ/ *nf* **(a)** courtyard; (school) playground; (farm) yard
(b) (of sovereign) court; (of celebrity) entourage
(c) courtship
(d) (Law) court

■ ∼ **d'arrivée** arrivals area; ∼ **de départ** departures area; ∼ **martiale** court-martial; ∼ **de récréation** playground

⚜ **courage** /kuʀaʒ/ *nm* **(a)** courage, bravery; **avoir du ∼** to be brave
(b) energy; **je n'ai même pas le ∼ de me doucher** I don't even have the energy to have a shower; **bon ∼!** good luck!; **perdre ∼** to lose heart; **je n'ai pas eu le ∼ de dire non** I didn't have the heart to say no

courageusement /kuʀaʒøzmɑ̃/ *adv* courageously, bravely

courageux, **-euse** /kuʀaʒø, øz/ *adj* courageous, brave

couramment /kuʀamɑ̃/ *adv* **(a)** fluently
(b) ‹used› widely; **cela se fait ∼** it's very common

courant¹ /kuʀɑ̃/ *prep* ∼ **janvier** (some time) in January

⚜ **courant²**, **∼e** /kuʀɑ̃, ɑ̃t/ **1** *adj* **(a)** ‹word, practice, mistake› common
(b) ‹language› everyday; ‹procedure› usual, ordinary; ‹size› standard
(c) ‹month, price› current; **le 15 du mois ∼** the 15th of this month
2 *nm* **(a)** current; **il n'y a plus de ∼** the power has gone off

⋯⟩

c

(b) trend; **un** ~ **politique** a political trend
(c) **dans le** ~ **de** in the course of
3 **au courant** phr **être au** ~ **de** to know about ‹news›; to be up to date on ‹technique›; **mettre qn au** ~ **to** put sb in the picture; **tenir qn au** ~ to keep sb posted
■ ~ **d'air** draught (GB), draft (US)
courbatu, ~**e** /kuʀbaty/ adj stiff
courbature /kuʀbatyʀ/ nf ache; **avoir des** ~**s** to be stiff
courbaturé, ~**e** /kuʀbatyʀe/ adj stiff; aching
courbe /kuʀb/ 1 adj curved
2 nf (a) curve
(b) bend
■ ~ **de température** temperature chart; ~ **d'apprentissage** learning curve
courber /kuʀbe/ [1] vtr to bend; ~ **le dos** (figurative) to bow down
courbette /kuʀbɛt/ nf (low) bow; **faire des** ~**s** (figurative) to bow and scrape
courbure /kuʀbyʀ/ nf curve
coureur, -euse /kuʀœʀ, øz/ nm,f runner; ~ **automobile** racing driver; ~ **de jupons** philanderer
courge /kuʀʒ/ nf gourd; (vegetable) marrow
courgette /kuʀʒɛt/ nf courgette (GB), zucchini (US)
⚜ **courir** /kuʀiʀ/ [26] 1 vtr (a) to compete in ‹trials›
(b) ~ **le monde** to roam the world
(c) ~ **les cocktails** to do the round of the cocktail parties; ~ **les boutiques** to go round the shops (GB) or stores (US)
(d) ~ **un (grand) danger** to be in (great) danger; ~ **un (gros) risque** to run a (big) risk; **faire** ~ **un risque à qn** to put sb at risk
(e) (fam) ~ **les filles** to chase after girls
2 vi (a) to run; to race; ~ **après qn/qch** to run after sb/sth; to chase after sb/sth; **les voleurs courent toujours** the thieves are still at large; ~ **à la catastrophe** to be heading for disaster
(b) ‹rumour› to go around
IDIOMS **tu peux toujours** ~! (fam) you can go whistle for it! (colloq); **laisser** ~ (fam) to let things ride
couronne /kuʀɔn/ nf (a) crown
(b) ~ **de fleurs** garland; wreath
(c) ring-shaped loaf
(d) (in Paris) **la petite/grande** ~ the inner/ outer suburbs
couronnement /kuʀɔnmɑ̃/ nm coronation
couronner /kuʀɔne/ [1] vtr to crown
courre /kuʀ/ vtr **chasse à** ~ hunting
courriel /kuʀjɛl/ nm e-mail
courrier /kuʀje/ nm (a) mail, post (GB); **faire son** ~ to write letters

⚜ indicates a very frequent word

(b) ~ **du cœur** problem page; ~ **électronique** electronic mail; ~ **des lecteurs** letters to the editor
courroie /kuʀwa/ nf (a) strap
(b) (on machine) belt
⚜ **cours** /kuʀ/ nm inv (a) lesson, class; **avoir** ~ to have a class; **faire** ~ to teach
(b) course book, textbook
(c) school; ~ **de théâtre** drama school
(d) price; exchange rate
(e) (of river) course
(f) (of tale, events) course; (of ideas) flow; **la vie reprend son** ~ life returns to normal; **donner libre** ~ **à** to give free rein to ‹imagination›; **au** or **dans le** ~ **de** in the course of, during; **en** ~ ‹month› current; ‹project› under way; ‹work› in progress; **en** ~ **de journée** in the course of the day
■ ~ **d'eau** watercourse; ~ **élémentaire première année**, **CE1** second year of primary school, age 7–8; ~ **moyen première année**, **CM1** fourth year of primary school, age 9–10; ~ **particulier(s)** private tuition (GB), private tutoring (US); ~ **préparatoire**, **CP** first year of primary school, age 6–7
⚜ **course** /kuʀs/ nf (a) running; run; racing; race; **faire la** ~ **avec qn** to race sb; **c'est la course tous les matins pour me préparer** I'm always in a rush in the morning to get ready
(b) (in taxi) journey; **c'est 10 euros la** ~ the fare is 10 euros
(c) **faire une** ~ to run an errand; **faire les** ~**s** to do the shopping
(d) (of star, planet) path; (of clouds) passage
■ ~ **de haies** (in athletics) hurdles; (for horses) steeplechase; ~ **d'obstacles** obstacle race; (figurative) obstacle course; ~ **de vitesse** (in athletics) sprint; (on motorbikes) speedway race
IDIOMS **ne plus être dans la** ~ to be out of touch; **être à bout de** ~ to be worn out
coursier, -ière /kuʀsje, ɛʀ/ nm,f messenger
⚜ **court, -e** /kuʀ, kuʀt/ 1 adj (a) short; **de** ~**e durée** short-lived; short-term; **avoir le souffle** ~ to get out of breath easily
(b) ‹defeat, victory, majority› narrow
2 adv **couper** ~ **à qch** to put paid to sth; **s'arrêter** ~ to stop short
3 nm ~ **de tennis** tennis court
■ ~ **métrage** short (film); ~**e échelle: faire la** ~**e échelle à qn** to give sb a leg up (colloq)
IDIOMS **être à** ~ **de** to be short of ‹money›; **prendre qn de** ~ to catch sb unprepared
court-circuit, pl ~**s** /kuʀsiʀkɥi/ nm shortcircuit
courtier, -ière /kuʀtje, ɛʀ/ nm,f broker
courtiser /kuʀtize/ [1] vtr to woo
courtois, ~**e** /kuʀtwa, az/ adj ‹person, tone› courteous; ‹genre, tradition› courtly
courtoisie /kuʀtwazi/ nf courtesy
couru, ~e /kuʀy/ 1 pp ▶ COURIR
2 pp adj ‹place› popular
IDIOM **c'est** ~ **d'avance** (fam) it's a foregone conclusion

cousin, ∼e /kuzɛ̃, in/ *nm,f* cousin

coussin /kusɛ̃/ *nm* cushion

cousu, ∼e /kuzy/ ▸ COUDRE

✎ **coût** /ku/ *nm* cost; ∼ de la vie cost of living

coûtant /kutɑ̃/ *adj m* prix ∼ cost price

✎ **couteau**, *pl* ∼x /kuto/ *nm* **(a)** knife;
donner un coup de ∼ **à qn** to stab sb
(b) razor shell (GB) *or* clam (US)
(c) knife edge
IDIOMS **être à** ∼**x tirés avec qn** to be at
daggers drawn with sb; **avoir le** ∼ **sous la
gorge** to have a pistol to one's head

✎ **coûter** /kute/ [1] **1** *vtr* to cost
2 *vi* to cost; ∼ **cher** to be expensive; **ça m'a
coûté de m'excuser** it was hard for me to
apologize
3 *v impers* **il t'en coûtera d'avoir fait cela**
you will pay for doing this; **coûte que coûte**,
quoi qu'il en coûte at all costs
IDIOM ∼ **les yeux de la tête** to cost an arm
and a leg (colloq)

coûteux, **-euse** /kutø, øz/ *adj* costly

coutume /kutym/ *nf* custom; **avoir** ∼ **de
faire** to be in the habit of doing
IDIOM **une fois n'est pas** ∼ it does no harm
just this once

coutumier, **-ière** /kutymje, ɛʀ/ *adj*
customary

couture /kutyʀ/ *nf* **(a)** sewing;
dressmaking; **faire de la** ∼ to sew
(b) seam
IDIOMS **sous toutes les** ∼**s** from every
angle; **battre qn à plates** ∼**s** to beat sb
hollow

couturier /kutyʀje/ *nm* dress designer

couturière /kutyʀjɛʀ/ *nf* dressmaker

couvent /kuvɑ̃/ *nm* convent

couver /kuve/ [1] **1** *vtr* **(a)** to sit on ⟨eggs⟩;
la poule couve the hen is brooding
(b) to overprotect; ∼ **qn/qch du regard** to
look fondly at sb/sth; to gaze longingly at
sb/sth
(c) to be coming down with ⟨illness⟩
2 *vi* ⟨rebellion⟩ to brew; ⟨fire, anger⟩ to
smoulder (GB), to smolder (US)

couvercle /kuvɛʀkl/ *nm* **(a)** lid
(b) screwtop

couvert, ∼e /kuvɛʀ, ɛʀt/ **1** *pp*
▸ COUVRIR
2 *pp adj* **(a)** covered (de in, with); **être** ∼
de diplômes to have a lot of qualifications
(b) ⟨pool⟩ indoor; ⟨market⟩ covered
(c) ⟨sky⟩ overcast
3 *nm* **(a)** place setting; **mettre le** ∼ to lay
the table; **un** ∼ **en argent** a silver knife, fork
and spoon
(b) cover charge
4 **à couvert** *phr* **se mettre à** ∼ to take
cover
5 **sous le couvert de** *phr* under the
pretence (GB) of; **sous** ∼ **de la plaisanterie**
under the guise of a joke

couverture /kuvɛʀtyʀ/ *nf* **(a)** blanket;
(small) rug (GB), lap robe (US)
(b) (of book, magazine) cover
(c) (media, mobile phone) coverage
IDIOM **tirer la** ∼ **à soi** to turn a situation to
one's own advantage

couveuse /kuvøz/ *nf* incubator

couvre-feu, *pl* ∼**x** /kuvʀəfø/ *nm* curfew

couvre-lit, *pl* ∼**s** /kuvʀəli/ *nm* bedspread

couvreur /kuvʀœʀ/ *nm* roofer

✎ **couvrir** /kuvʀiʀ/ [32] **1** *vtr* **(a)** to cover
⟨furniture, wall, fire, card⟩; to roof ⟨house⟩;
∼ **qn de qch** (with blows, jewels, compliments) to
shower sb with sth
(b) ⟨sound⟩ to drown out
(c) ⟨transmitter, inspector⟩ to cover ⟨region⟩
(d) to wrap [sb] up; to cover [sb] up
(e) to cover up for ⟨mistake, person⟩
(f) (with gun) to cover ⟨soldier⟩
(g) to cover ⟨distance⟩
(h) ⟨book, journalist⟩ to cover ⟨story, event⟩
(i) ⟨sum⟩ to cover ⟨expenses⟩
2 **se couvrir** *v refl* (+ *v être*) **(a)** to wrap
up; to put on a hat
(b) ⟨sky⟩ to become overcast
(c) **se** ∼ **de** to become covered with
(d) (against accusations) to cover oneself

CP /sepe/ *nm: abbr* ▸ COURS

crabe /kʀab/ *nm* crab

crachat /kʀaʃa/ *nm* spit

crachement /kʀaʃmɑ̃/ *nm* **(a)** spitting
(b) crackling

cracher /kʀaʃe/ [1] **1** *vtr* **(a)** to spit out;
c'est le portrait de sa mère tout craché
(fam) she's the spitting image of her mother
(b) to belch (out) ⟨flames, smoke⟩
2 *vi* to spit; **je ne cracherais pas dessus**
(fam) I wouldn't turn up my nose at it

cracheur /kʀaʃœʀ/ *nm* ∼ **de feu** fire-eater

crachin /kʀaʃɛ̃/ *nm* drizzle

crachoir /kʀaʃwaʀ/ *nm* spittoon

crachoter /kʀaʃote/ [1] *vi* **(a)** to cough and
splutter
(b) to crackle

crack /kʀak/ *nm* **(a)** (genius) ace
(b) (fam) (drug) crack (colloq)

craie /kʀɛ/ *nf* chalk

✎ **craindre** /kʀɛ̃dʀ/ [54] *vtr* **(a)** to fear, to be
afraid of
(b) to be sensitive to ⟨cold⟩; to dislike ⟨sun⟩

craint, ∼**e**[1] /kʀɛ̃, ɛ̃t/ ▸ CRAINDRE

✎ **crainte**[2] /kʀɛ̃t/ *nf* fear; **avoir des** ∼**s au
sujet de qn** to be worried about sb; **n'ayez** ∼,
soyez sans ∼ have no fear

craintif, **-ive** /kʀɛ̃tif, iv/ *adj* timorous,
timid

cramoisi, ∼**e** /kʀamwazi/ *adj* crimson

crampe /kʀɑ̃p/ *nf* cramp

crampon /kʀɑ̃pɔ̃/ *nm* crampon;
chaussures à ∼**s** (for football) boots with studs
(GB) *or* cleats (US); (for running) spiked shoes

cramponner: **se cramponner**
/kʀɑ̃pɔne/ [1] *v refl* (+ *v être*) to hold on tightly

cran /kʀɑ̃/ **1** *nm* **(a)** notch; (in belt) hole; **monter d'un ∼** to move up a notch
(b) nick
(c) (fam) **avoir du ∼** to have guts (colloq)
(d) (in hair) wave
2 **à cran** *phr* **être à ∼** to be on edge
■ **∼ d'arrêt** flick knife (GB), switchblade (US); **∼ de sûreté** safety catch

crâne /kʀɑn/ *nm* **(a)** skull
(b) (fam) head; **ne rien avoir dans le ∼** to have no brains; **bourrer le ∼ à qn** (fam) to brainwash sb

crânement /kʀɑnmɑ̃/ *adv* gallantly; proudly

crânien, -ienne /kʀɑnjɛ̃, ɛn/ *adj* cranial; **boîte crânienne** cranium

crapaud /kʀapo/ *nm* toad

crapule /kʀapyl/ *nf* crook

crapuleux, -euse /kʀapylø, øz/ *adj* villainous

craqueler: **se craqueler** /kʀakle/ [19] *v refl* (+ *v être*) to crack

craquement /kʀakmɑ̃/ *nm* **(a)** creaking sound, creak
(b) cracking sound, crack

craquer /kʀake/ [1] **1** *vtr* **(a)** to split ‹*trousers*›
(b) to strike ‹*match*›
2 *vi* **(a)** ‹*seam*› to split; ‹*branch*› to crack
(b) ‹*floor*› to creak
(c) (fam) ‹*person*› to crack up (colloq)

crasher: **se crasher** /kʀaʃe/ [1] *v refl* (+ *v être*) ‹*computer*› to crash

crasse /kʀas/ *nf* grime, filth

crasseux, -euse /kʀasø, øz/ *adj* filthy, grimy

cratère /kʀatɛʀ/ *nm* crater

cravache /kʀavaʃ/ *nf* whip

cravate /kʀavat/ *nf* tie

crawl /kʀol/ *nm* crawl

⚜ **crayon** /kʀɛjɔ̃/ *nm* pencil; **∼ noir** lead pencil; **∼ optique** light pen

créance /kʀeɑ̃s/ *nf* **(a)** debt (*owed by a debtor*)
(b) letter of credit

créancier, -ière /kʀeɑ̃sje, ɛʀ/ *nm,f* creditor

créateur, -trice /kʀeatœʀ, tʀis/ *nm,f* creator; designer

créatif, -ive /kʀeatif, iv/ *adj* creative

⚜ **création** /kʀeasjɔ̃/ *nf* **(a)** creation; **la ∼ d'une entreprise** the setting up of a company; **la ∼ d'un nouveau produit** the development of a new product; **tous les livres de la ∼** all the books in the world
(b) (work of art) creation; (play) first

production; (commercial) new product

créativité /kʀeativite/ *nf* creativity

⚜ **créature** /kʀeatyʀ/ *nf* creature

crèche /kʀɛʃ/ *nf* **(a)** crèche (GB), day-nursery
(b) (at Christmas) crib (GB), crèche (US)

crédibilité /kʀedibilite/ *nf* credibility

crédible /kʀedibl/ *adj* credible

crédit /kʀedi/ *nm* **(a)** funds; **les ∼s de la recherche** research funding
(b) credit; **accorder un ∼** to grant credit terms; **faire ∼ à qn** to give sb credit; **porter une somme au ∼ d'un compte** to credit sb's account with a sum of money; **mettre** *or* **porter qch au ∼ de qn** (figurative) to give sb credit for sth

créditer /kʀedite/ [1] *vtr* to credit

créditeur, -trice /kʀeditœʀ, tʀis/ *adj* **être ∼** to be in credit

credo /kʀedo/ *nm* creed

crédule /kʀedyl/ *adj* gullible, credulous

⚜ **créer** /kʀee/ [11] **1** *vtr* (gen) to create; to develop ‹*new product*›; to set up ‹*company*›
2 **se créer** *v refl* (+ *v être*) **se ∼ des problèmes** to bring trouble on oneself

crémaillère /kʀemajɛʀ/ *nf* **pendre la ∼** to have a house-warming (party)

crémation /kʀemasjɔ̃/ *nf* cremation

crématoire /kʀematwaʀ/ *nm* crematorium

crème¹ /kʀɛm/ *adj inv* cream

crème² /kʀɛm/ *nf* **(a)** cream
(b) cream dessert
(c) (fam) **la ∼ des linguistes** the very best linguists
■ **∼ Chantilly** whipped cream; **∼ glacée** dairy ice cream; **∼ de marrons** chestnut spread; **∼ renversée** caramel custard

crémerie /kʀɛmʀi/ *nf* cheese shop (GB) *or* store (US)

crémeux, -euse /kʀemø, øz/ *adj* creamy

créneau, *pl* **∼x** /kʀeno/ *nm* **(a)** parallel parking
(b) (Econ) market
(c) gap, niche
(d) crenel; **les ∼x** crenellations
■ **∼ horaire** time slot; **∼ publicitaire** advertising slot

créole /kʀeɔl/ *adj*, *nm* Creole

crêpe¹ /kʀɛp/ *nm* **(a)** crepe
(b) black veil

crêpe² /kʀɛp/ *nf* pancake, crêpe

crêper /kʀepe/ [1] *vtr* to backcomb (GB), to tease ‹*hair*›

crépi /kʀepi/ *nm* rendering

crépitement /kʀepitmɑ̃/ *nm* crackling, crackle; sizzling

crépiter /kʀepite/ [1] *vi* ‹*fire*› to crackle; ‹*oil*› to sizzle; ‹*rain*› to patter

---

⚜ indicates a very frequent word

crépon /kʀepɔ̃/ *nm* crepe paper

crépu, **~e** /kʀepy/ *adj* frizzy

crépuscule /kʀepyskyl/ *nm* twilight, dusk

crescendo /kʀeʃɛndo/ **1** *adv* **aller ~** ‹noise› to intensify
2 *nm* crescendo

cresson /kʀɛsɔ̃, kʀəsɔ̃/ *nm* watercress

crête /kʀɛt/ *nf* **(a)** (of cock) comb; (of bird) crest
(b) (of mountain, wave) crest; (of roof) ridge

crétin, **~e** /kʀetɛ̃, in/ *nm,f* moron (colloq)

creuser /kʀøze/ [1] **1** *vtr* **(a)** to dig a hole in ‹ground›; to drill a hole in ‹tooth›; to dig into ‹rock›
(b) to dig ‹hole, canal, grave›; to sink ‹well›
(c) ‹wrinkles› to furrow ‹face›; **~ les reins** to arch one's back
(d) to deepen, to increase ‹deficit, inequalities›
(e) to go into [sth] in depth ‹question, subject›
2 **se creuser** *v refl* (+ *v être*) ‹cheeks› to become hollow; ‹gap› to widen
IDIOMS **ça creuse** (fam) it really gives you an appetite; **se ~ (la tête** *or* **la cervelle)** (fam) to rack one's brains

creux, **-euse** /kʀø, øz/ **1** *adj* **(a)** ‹trunk, tooth, sound, cheeks› hollow; ‹stomach, speech› empty; ‹analysis› shallow; **un plat ~** a shallow dish; **assiette creuse** soup dish
(b) ‹day, period› slack, off-peak
2 *adv* **sonner ~** to make a hollow sound
3 *nm* **(a)** hollow; **le ~ des reins** the small of the back; **le ~ de l'aisselle** the armpit; **le ~ de la vague** the trough of the wave; **être au ~ de la vague** (figurative) to be at rock bottom
(b) (fam) **avoir un petit ~** to have the munchies (colloq)

crevaison /kʀəvɛzɔ̃/ *nf* puncture

crevasse /kʀəvas/ *nf* **(a)** crevasse
(b) crack, fissure
(c) chapped skin

crève /kʀɛv/ *nf* (fam) chill; **attraper la ~** to catch a chill *or* one's death (of cold)

crever /kʀəve/ [16] **1** *vtr* to puncture, to burst; **~ les yeux de qn** to blind sb; to poke sb's eyes out; **ça crève les yeux** it's blindingly obvious; **ça crève le cœur** it's heartbreaking
2 *vi* **(a)** to burst; to burst open
(b) to die; **~ de faim** to be starving
(c) **~ d'envie** to be eaten up with envy; **~ d'orgueil** to be terribly full of oneself
3 **se crever** *v refl* (+ *v être*) **il s'est crevé un œil** he put one of his eyes out
IDIOM **marche ou crève** sink or swim

crevette /kʀəvɛt/ *nf* **~ grise** shrimp; **~ rose** prawn

✦**cri** /kʀi/ *nm* **(a)** cry; shout; scream; **un ~ aigu** a shriek; **à grands ~s** loudly; **pousser les hauts ~s** to protest loudly
(b) (of bird) call

criant, **~e** /kʀijɑ̃, ɑ̃t/ *adj* clear, striking

criard, **~e** /kʀiaʀ, aʀd/ *adj* ‹voice› shrill; ‹colour› garish

crible /kʀibl/ *nm* (for minerals) screen; (for sand) riddle; **passer au ~** (figurative) to sift through

cribler /kʀible/ [1] *vtr* **(a)** **~ qn/qch de balles** to riddle sb/sth with bullets
(b) **~ qn de reproches** to heap reproaches on sb

cric /kʀik/ *nm* (for car) jack

criée /kʀije/ *nf* **(vente à la) ~** auction

✦**crier** /kʀije/ [2] **1** *vtr* **(a)** to shout
(b) to proclaim; to protest ‹innocence›
2 **crier à** *v+prep* **on a crié au scandale quand...** there was an outcry when...
3 *vi* **(a)** to shout; to cry; to scream
(b) ‹animal› to give a cry; ‹monkey› to chatter; ‹gull› to cry; ‹pig› to squeal

crieur, **-leuse** /kʀijœʀ, øz/ *nm,f* **~ de journaux** news vendor

✦**crime** /kʀim/ *nm* **(a)** crime
(b) murder; **~ crapuleux** murder for money

criminalité /kʀiminalite/ *nf* crime

criminel, **-elle** /kʀiminɛl/ **1** *adj* criminal
2 *nm,f* **(a)** criminal
(b) murderer

crin /kʀɛ̃/ *nm* horsehair; **à tout ~** (figurative) dyed-in-the-wool

crinière /kʀinjɛʀ/ *nf* mane

crique /kʀik/ *nf* cove

criquet /kʀikɛ/ *nm* locust

✦**crise** /kʀiz/ *nf* **(a)** crisis; **~ agricole** crisis in the agricultural industry; **la ~** the economic crisis, the slump
(b) shortage; **~ de l'emploi** job shortage
(c) (Med) attack; **~ d'appendicite** appendicitis; **~ de toux** coughing fit
(d) fit; **~ de colère** fit of rage; **faire une ~** to have a tantrum; to have a fit (colloq)
■ **~ cardiaque** heart attack; **~ de foie** indigestion; **~ de nerfs** hysterics

crisper /kʀispe/ [1] **1** *vtr* **l'angoisse crispait son visage** his/her face was tense with worry
2 **se crisper** *v refl* (+ *v être*) ‹hands› to clench; ‹face, person› to tense (up); ‹smile› to freeze

crisser /kʀise/ [1] *vi* ‹shoes, chalk› to squeak; ‹snow› to crunch; ‹tyres, brakes› to screech

cristal, *pl* **-aux** /kʀistal, o/ *nm* crystal

cristallin, **~e** /kʀistalɛ̃, in/ **1** *adj*
(a) crystalline
(b) crystal clear
2 *nm* (of eye) (crystalline) lens

cristalliser /kʀistalize/ [1] *vtr, vi, v refl* (+ *v être*) to crystallize

critère /kʀitɛʀ/ *nm* **(a)** criterion; **~s de gestion/de confort** standards of

···>

management/comfort; **le ~ déterminant** the crucial factor
(b) specification; **remplir les ~s d'âge et de diplôme** to meet the requirements as far as age and qualifications are concerned

critiquable /kʁitikabl/ *adj* questionable

critique¹ /kʁitik/ ⒈ *adj* critical
⒉ *nmf* critic

❖ **critique²** /kʁitik/ *nf* **(a)** criticism; **faire une ~ à qn** to criticize sb
(b) review; **faire la ~ d'un film** to review a film
(c) la ~ littéraire literary criticism

critiquer /kʁitike/ [1] *vtr* to criticize

croasser /kʁɔase/ [1] *vi* to caw

croc /kʁo/ *nm* fang

croche /kʁɔʃ/ *nf* quaver (GB), eighth note (US); **double ~** semiquaver (GB), sixteenth note (US)

croche-pied, *pl* **~s** /kʁɔʃpje/ *nm* (fam) **faire un ~ à qn** to trip sb up

crochet /kʁɔʃɛ/ *nm* **(a)** hook
(b) picklock
(c) crochet hook; **faire du ~** to crochet
(d) square bracket
(e) faire un ~ to make a detour
(f) (in boxing) hook
(g) fang
IDIOM **vivre aux ~s de qn** (fam) to sponge off sb (colloq)

crocheter /kʁɔʃte/ [18] *vtr* to pick ‹lock›

crochu, **~e** /kʁɔʃy/ *adj* ‹nose› hooked; ‹hands› clawed

crocodile /kʁɔkɔdil/ *nm* crocodile

❖ **croire** /kʁwaʁ/ [71] ⒈ *vtr* **(a)** to believe; **faire ~ à qn** to make sb believe
(b) to think; **je crois savoir que** I happen to know that; **il est malin, faut pas~!** (fam) he's clever, believe me!; **tu ne crois pas si bien dire** you don't know how right you are; **on croirait de la soie** it looks *or* feels like silk
(c) si l'on en croit l'auteur, à en ~ l'auteur if we are to believe the author; **crois-en mon expérience** take my word for it
⒉ **croire à** *v+prep* to believe ‹story›; to believe in ‹ghosts›
⒊ **croire en** *v+prep* to believe in
⒋ **se croire** *v refl* (+ *v être*) **il se croit beau** he thinks he's handsome

croisade /kʁwazad/ *nf* crusade

croisé, **~e¹** /kʁwaze/ ⒈ *pp* ▶ CROISER
⒉ *pp adj* **(a)** ‹legs› crossed; ‹arms› folded
(b) crossbred
(c) ‹agreements› reciprocal

croisée² /kʁwaze/ *nf* **(a)** junction; **à la ~ des chemins** at the crossroads
(b) window

croisement /kʁwazmã/ *nm*
(a) crossroads; crossing, junction
(b) (of threads, straps) crossing

(c) crossbreeding; hybrid, cross(breed)

❖ **croiser** /kʁwaze/ [1] ⒈ *vtr* **(a)** to cross; **~ les bras** to fold one's arms
(b) ~ qn/qch to pass sb/sth (coming the other way)
(c) to meet; **mon regard croisa le sien** our eyes met
(d) to cross(breed)
⒉ **se croiser** *v refl* (+ *v être*) ‹cars› to pass each other; ‹letters› to cross in the post (GB) *or* mail (US); ‹roads› to intersect; ‹lines› to cross

croisière /kʁwazjɛʁ/ *nf* cruise

croissance /kʁwasãs/ *nf* growth

croissant /kʁwasã/ *nm* **(a)** croissant
(b) crescent; **~ de lune** crescent moon

Croissant-Rouge /kʁwasãʁuʒ/ *nm* **le ~** Red Crescent

croître /kʁwatʁ/ [72] *vi* **(a)** to grow; **faire ~** to grow
(b) ‹noise› to get *or* grow louder

croix /kʁwa/ *nf* cross; **bras en ~** arms out on either side of the body
IDIOMS **ton argent, tu peux faire une ~ dessus** (fam) you can kiss your money goodbye; **un jour à marquer d'une ~** a red-letter day

Croix-Rouge /kʁwaʁuʒ/ *nf* **la ~** the Red Cross

croquant, **~e** /kʁɔkã, ãt/ *adj* crunchy

croque-madame /kʁɔkmadam/ *nm inv*: toasted ham and cheese sandwich topped with a fried egg

croque-monsieur /kʁɔkməsjø/ *nm inv*: toasted ham and cheese sandwich

croque-mort, *pl* **~s** /kʁɔkmɔʁ/ *nm* (fam) undertaker

croquer /kʁɔke/ [1] ⒈ *vtr* **(a)** to crunch
(b) to sketch; **belle à ~** as pretty as a picture
⒉ *vi* **(a)** to be crunchy
(b) ~ dans une pomme to bite into an apple

croquette /kʁɔkɛt/ *nf* croquette

croquis /kʁɔki/ *nm* sketch

crosse /kʁɔs/ *nf* **(a)** (of rifle) butt
(b) (of cane) crook
(c) (Sport) stick

crotte /kʁɔt/ *nf* dropping; **c'est de la ~ de chien** it's dog mess

crotter /kʁɔte/ [1] *vtr* to muddy; **bottes crottées** muddy boots

crottin /kʁɔtɛ̃/ *nm* **(a)** dung
(b) (small round) goat's cheese

crouler /kʁule/ [1] *vi* **(a)** to collapse; to crumble
(b) ~ sous to be weighed down by ‹parcels, debts, work›; **~ sous le poids de** ‹table› to groan under the weight of ‹books›

croupe /kʁup/ *nf* (of horse) croup

croupi, **~e** /kʁupi/ *adj* stagnant

croupier /kʁupje/ *nm* croupier

croupir /kʀupiʀ/ [3] *vi* (a) *‹water›* to stagnate
(b) ~ **en prison** to rot in jail
croustillant, ~**e** /kʀustijã, ãt/ *adj*
(a) crispy; crunchy
(b) *‹story, details›* spicy
croustiller /kʀustije/ [1] *vi ‹bread›* to be
crusty; *‹chocolate›* to be crunchy
croûte /kʀut/ *nf* (a) (of bread) crust; (of
cheese) rind; **casser la** ~ (fam) to have a bite
to eat
(b) (Culin) **pâté en** ~ pâté en croute *or* in pastry
(c) (Med) scab
(d) (fam) daub, bad painting
croûton /kʀutɔ̃/ *nm* (a) crust
(b) (Culin) crouton
croyance /kʀwajɑ̃s/ *nf* belief
croyant, ~**e** /kʀwajã, ãt/ *adj* **être** ~ to be
a believer
CRS /seɛʀɛs/ *nm* (*abbr* = **compagnie
républicaine de sécurité**) **un** ~ *a
member of the French riot police*
cru¹, ~**e¹** /kʀy/ ▶ CROIRE
cru², ~**e²** /kʀy/ 1 *adj* (a) raw; uncooked;
‹milk› unpasteurized; **se faire manger tout** ~
(fam) to be eaten alive (colloq)
(b) *‹light, colour›* harsh
(c) *‹language›* crude
2 *nm* vineyard; vintage; vintage year; **du
meilleur** ~ *‹collection›* vintage; **du** ~ *‹wine,
author›* local
crû³, **crue** /kʀy/ ▶ CROÎTRE
cruauté /kʀyote/ *nf* cruelty
cruche /kʀyʃ/ *nf* jug (GB), pitcher (US)
crucial, ~**e**, *mpl* **-iaux** /kʀysjal, o/ *adj*
crucial
crucifier /kʀysifje/ [2] *vtr* to crucify
crucifix /kʀysifi/ *nm* crucifix
crudité /kʀydite/ *nf* ~**s** raw vegetables,
crudités
crue⁴ /kʀy/ 1 *adj f* ▶ CRU² 1
2 *nf* rise in water level; flood; **en** ~ in spate
cruel, **-elle** /kʀyɛl/ *adj* cruel
cruellement /kʀyɛlmɑ̃/ *adv* (a) cruelly
(b) **manquer** ~ **de qch** to be desperately
short of sth
(c) terribly; **la pénurie de carburant se fait** ~
sentir the fuel shortage is being sorely felt
crûment /kʀymɑ̃/ *adv* (a) bluntly
(b) crudely
crustacé /kʀystase/ *nm* shellfish
crypte /kʀipt(ə)/ *nf* crypt
crypté, ~**e** /kʀipte/ *adj* coded; encrypted
cube /kyb/ 1 *adj* cubic
2 *nm* (a) cube
(b) building block
cubique /kybik/ *adj* (a) cubic
(b) cube-shaped
cucul /kyky/ *adj* (fam) corny (colloq); silly
cueillette /kœjɛt/ *nf* (a) (of fruits,
flowers) picking
(b) crop
cueilli, ~**e** /kœji/ ▶ CUEILLIR

cueillir /kœjiʀ/ [27] *vtr* (a) to pick *‹fruit,
flowers›*
(b) (fam) to arrest *‹criminal›*
⚜ **cuiller**, **cuillère** /kɥijɛʀ/ *nf* spoon;
spoonful; ~ **à café** teaspoon; coffee spoon
IDIOMS **il n'y va pas avec le dos de la** ~
(fam) he doesn't do things by halves; **en deux
coups de** ~ **à pot** in two shakes of a lamb's
tail (colloq)
cuillerée /kɥij(ə)ʀe/ *nf* spoonful
cuir /kɥiʀ/ *nm* (a) leather
(b) rawhide; hide
■ ~ **chevelu** scalp
cuirassé /kɥiʀase/ *nm* battleship
cuire /kɥiʀ/ [69] 1 *vtr* (a) to cook; to bake;
to roast; ~ **à la vapeur** to steam; **à** ~ *‹apple›*
cooking
(b) to fire *‹porcelain›*
2 *vi* (a) *‹food›* to cook; to be cooking;
laissez ~ **à petit feu** allow to simmer gently
(b) (fam) **on cuit sur la plage** it's baking
(hot) on the beach
(c) *‹graze›* to sting; **ça me cuit** it stings
cuisant, ~**e** /kɥizã, ãt/ *adj* (a) *‹defeat,
regret›* bitter; *‹remark›* stinging
(b) *‹pain›* burning
⚜ **cuisine** /kɥizin/ *nf* (a) kitchen
(b) galley
(c) kitchen furniture
(d) cooking
(e) (fam) intrigues
cuisiner /kɥizine/ [1] *vtr*, *vi* to cook
cuisinier, **-lère¹** /kɥizinje, ɛʀ/ *nm,f* cook;
chef
cuisinière² /kɥizinjɛʀ/ *nf* cooker
cuissarde /kɥisaʀd/ *nf* wader; thighboot
cuisse /kɥis/ *nf* thigh; **des** ~**s de
grenouille** frogs' legs
cuisson /kɥisɔ̃/ *nf* (a) cooking; baking;
roasting
(b) (of pottery) firing
cuistot /kɥisto/ *nm* (fam) cook
cuit, ~**e¹** /kɥi, kɥit/ ▶ CUIRE
IDIOMS **c'est** ~ (fam) we've had it (colloq); **c'est
du tout** ~ (fam) it's a piece of cake (colloq);
it's in the bag (colloq); **elle attend que ça (lui)
tombe tout** ~ (fam) she expects things to fall
straight into her lap
cuite² /kɥit/ *nf* **tenir une** ~ to be plastered
(colloq)
cuivre /kɥivʀ/ 1 *nm* (a) ~ **(rouge)** copper
(b) ~ **(jaune)** brass
2 **cuivres** *nm pl* (a) copperware
(b) brass
(c) (Mus) **les** ~**s** the brass
cul /ky/ *nm* (a) (pop) bottom, arse
(GB) (vulgar), ass (US) (slang)
(b) (of bottle) bottom; ~ **sec!** (fam) bottoms
up! (colloq)
culasse /kylas/ *nf* (a) cylinder head
(b) breechblock
culbute /kylbyt/ *nf* somersault

culbuter /kylbyte/ [1] *vi* ⟨person⟩ to take a tumble; ⟨vehicle⟩ to overturn

cul-cul (fam) ▶ CUCUL

cul-de-jatte, *pl* **culs-de-jatte** /kydʒat/ *nmf* person who has had both legs amputated

cul-de-sac, *pl* **culs-de-sac** /kydsak/ *nm*
(a) cul-de-sac
(b) dead end

culinaire /kylinɛR/ *adj* culinary

culminant, **~e** /kylminɑ̃, ɑ̃t/ *adj* point
~ (of mountain) highest point *or* peak; (of career) peak; (of crisis) height; (of holiday) high point

culminer /kylmine/ [1] *vi* (a) **~ au-dessus de qch** to tower above sth
(b) ⟨inflation, unemployment⟩ to reach its peak

culot /kylo/ *nm* (fam) cheek (colloq); **y aller au ~** to bluff

culotte /kylɔt/ *nf* (a) pants (GB), panties (US)
(b) **en ~(s) courte(s)** in short trousers (GB) *or* pants (US)

culotté, **~e** /kylɔte/ *adj* (fam) cheeky

culpabilisation /kylpabilizasjɔ̃/ *nf* making guilty; feeling of guilt

culpabiliser /kylpabilize/ [1] **1** *vtr* to make [sb] feel guilty
2 *vi* to feel guilty

culpabilité /kylpabilite/ *nf* guilt

culte /kylt/ *nm* (a) cult
(b) religion

cultivateur, **-trice** /kyltivatœR, tRis/ *nm,f* farmer

cultiver /kyltive/ [1] **1** *vtr* to grow; to cultivate
2 **se cultiver** *v refl* (+ *v être*) to improve one's mind

✍ **culture** /kyltyR/ **1** *nf* (a) cultivation; **la ~ du blé** wheat growing
(b) crop; **~ d'hiver** winter crop
(c) (in biology) culture
(d) (of society) culture; **~ de masse** mass culture
(e) knowledge; **~ classique** classical education
(f) arts; **subventionner la ~** to subsidize the arts
2 **cultures** *nf pl* cultivated land
■ **~ physique** physical exercise

✍ **culturel**, **-elle** /kyltyRɛl/ *adj* cultural

culturisme /kyltyRism/ *nm* body-building

cumin /kymɛ̃/ *nm* cumin

cumul /kymyl/ *nm* (a) **~ de fonctions** holding of several posts concurrently
(b) (Law) **~ des peines** ≈ sentences to be served consecutively

cumuler /kymyle/ [1] *vtr* (a) to hold [sth] concurrently ⟨offices⟩; to draw [sth]

concurrently ⟨salaries⟩
(b) to accumulate ⟨handicaps, degrees⟩
(c) to combine ⟨results⟩; to add up ⟨amounts⟩

cumulus /kymylys/ *nm inv* cumulus

cupide /kypid/ *adj* grasping

cupidité /kypidite/ *nf* avarice, greed, cupidity

cure /kyR/ *nf* **faire une ~** to go for a course of treatment in a spa
■ **~ d'amaigrissement** slimming course (GB), reducing treatment (US); **~ de sommeil** sleep therapy

curé /kyRe/ *nm* (parish) priest

cure-dents /kyRdɑ̃/ *nm inv* toothpick

curer /kyRe/ [1] **1** *vtr* to clean out ⟨pipe, pond⟩
2 **se curer** *v refl* (+ *v être*) **se ~ les ongles** to clean one's nails

curieusement /kyRjøzmɑ̃/ *adv* (a) oddly, strangely
(b) oddly enough

✍ **curieux**, **-ieuse** /kyRjø, øz/ **1** *adj*
(a) inquisitive, curious
(b) strange
(c) esprit **~** person with an enquiring mind; **être ~ d'apprendre** to be keen to learn
2 *nm,f* onlooker

curiosité /kyRjozite/ *nf* curiosity

curriculum vitae /kyRikylɔmvite/ *nm inv* curriculum vitae, résumé (US)

curry /kyRi/ *nm* (a) curry powder
(b) curry

curseur /kyRsœR/ *nm* cursor

cursus /kyRsys/ *nm inv* course

cutané, **~e** /kytane/ *adj* ⟨irritation⟩ skin

cutter /kytœR/ *nm* Stanley knife®

cuve /kyv/ *nf* vat; tank

cuvée /kyve/ *nf* vatful; **la ~ 1959** the 1959 vintage; **~ du patron** house wine

cuvette /kyvɛt/ *nf* (a) bowl; **~ des wc** lavatory bowl *or* pan
(b) (in land) basin

CV /seve/ *nm* (a) (*abbr* = **curriculum vitae**) CV (GB), résumé (US)
(b) (*written abbr* = **cheval-vapeur**) HP

cybercafé /sibɛRkafe/ *nm* cybercafé

cyberjargon /sibɛRʒaRgɔ̃/ *nm* netspeak

cyclable /siklabl/ *adj* **piste ~** cycle track

cycle /sikl/ *nm* (a) cycle; **~ infernal** vicious cycle
(b) series
(c) (Sch) **premier ~** first two years of a university degree course leading to a diploma; **deuxième ~** final two years of a university degree course; **troisième ~** postgraduate (GB) *or* graduate (US) studies
(d) (bi)cycle

cyclique /siklik/ *adj* cyclic

cyclisme /siklism/ *nm* cycling; cycle racing

✍ indicates a very frequent word

cycliste /siklist/ [1] *adj* ‹club› cycling; ‹race› cycle; **coureur** ~ racing cyclist [2] *nmf* cyclist; **short de** ~ cycling shorts

cyclone /siklon/ *nm* (a) cyclone (b) (in weather) depression

cygne /siɲ/ *nm* swan; ~ **mâle** cob; ~ **femelle** pen; **jeune** ~ cygnet

cylindre /silɛ̃dʀ/ *nm* (a) cylinder

(b) roller

cylindrée /silɛ̃dʀe/ *nf* capacity, size; ~ **de 1200 cm³** 1200 cc engine

cymbale /sɛ̃bal/ *nm* cymbal

cynique /sinik/ *adj* cynical

cynisme /sinism/ *nm* cynicism

cyprès /sipʀɛ/ *nm* cypress

cystite /sistit/ *nf* cystitis

d

D d

d, D /de/ *nm inv* d, D

d' ▶ DE

DAB /deabe/ *nm* (*abbr* = **distributeur automatique de billets**) automatic teller machine, ATM

dactylographie /daktilɔgʀafi/ *nf* typing

dada /dada/ *nm* (fam) (a) (baby talk) horsie (colloq) (b) hobby (c) hobbyhorse

dadais /dadɛ/ *nm inv* (fam) clumsy youth; **espèce de grand** ~**!** you great oaf!

daigner /deɲe/ [1] *vtr* to deign (**faire de do**)

daim /dɛ̃/ *nm* (a) (fallow) deer (b) venison (c) buckskin (d) suede

dallage /dalaʒ/ *nm* paving

dalle /dal/ *nf* (a) slab (b) flagstone (c) concrete foundation slab IDIOMS **avoir la** ~ (fam) to be ravenous; **que** ~ (pop) nothing at all, zilch (colloq)

daller /dale/ [1] *vtr* to pave

daltonien, -ienne /daltɔnjɛ̃, ɛn/ *adj* colour (GB) -blind

dam /dɑ(m)/ *nm* **au grand** ~ **de** to the great displeasure of

⚜ **dame** /dam/ [1] *nf* (a) lady (b) (in cards, chess) queen; (in draughts) King [2] **dames** *nf pl* draughts (GB), checkers (US)

damier /damje/ *nm* draughtboard (GB), checkerboard (US)

damnation /danasjɔ̃/ *nf* damnation

damner /dɑne/ [1] [1] *vtr* to damn [2] **se damner** *v refl* (+ *v être*) to damn oneself; **se** ~ **pour qch** (fam) to sell one's soul for sth

dancing /dɑ̃siŋ/ *nm* dance hall

dandiner: se dandiner /dɑ̃dine/ [1] *v refl* (+ *v être*) ‹duck› to waddle

Danemark /danmaʀk/ *pr nm* Denmark

⚜ **danger** /dɑ̃ʒe/ *nm* danger ■ ~ **public** danger to the public; (figurative) menace

dangereusement /dɑ̃ʒʀøzmɑ̃/ *adv* dangerously

⚜ **dangereux, -euse** /dɑ̃ʒʀø, øz/ *adj* dangerous

danois, ~e /danwa, az/ [1] *adj* Danish [2] *nm* (a) (language) Danish (b) (dog) Great Dane

⚜ **dans** /dɑ̃/ *prep* (a) in; **être** ~ **la cuisine** to be in the kitchen; **être** ~ **un avion/bateau** to be on a plane/boat (b) into; **entrer** ~ **une pièce** to go into a room; **monter** ~ **un avion** to get on a plane (c) **boire** ~ **un verre** to drink out of a glass; **prendre qch** ~ **un placard** to take sth out of a cupboard (d) ~ **deux heures** in two hours; **fait** ~ **les deux heures** done within two hours; **je t'appellerai** ~ **la journée** I'll phone you during the day (e) ~ **les 30 euros** about 30 euros

danse /dɑ̃s/ *nf* (a) dance (b) dancing; **faire de la** ~ to take dancing classes ■ ~ **classique** classical ballet

⚜ **danser** /dɑ̃se/ [1] *vtr, vi* to dance IDIOM **ne pas savoir sur quel pied** ~ not to know what to do

danseur, -euse /dɑ̃sœʀ, øz/ *nm,f* dancer; ~ **étoile** principal dancer

dard /daʀ/ *nm* (a) (Zool) sting (b) spear

dare-dare /daʀdaʀ/ *adv* (fam) double quick

darne /daʀn/ *nf* (fish) steak

dartre /daʀtʀ/ *nf* scurf patch

⚜ **date** /dat/ *nf* (a) date; ~ **limite** deadline; ~ **limite de vente** sell-by date (b) time; **depuis cette** ~ from that time; **un ami de longue** ~ a longstanding friend; **le dernier scandale en** ~ the latest scandal

dater /date/ [1] [1] *vtr* to date; **à** ~ **du 31 juillet** as from 31 July ⋯⟶

② *vi* (a) ~ **de** to date from
(b) to be dated

dation /dasjɔ̃/ *nf* ~ **(en paiement)** payment in kind

datte /dat/ *nf* (Bot, Culin) date

dattier /datje/ *nm* date palm

daube /dob/ *nf* **bœuf en** ~ beef casserole

dauphin /dofɛ̃/ *nm* (a) dolphin
(b) heir apparent
(c) dauphin

daurade /dɔʀad/ *nf* (sea) bream

✒ **davantage** /davɑ̃taʒ/ *adv* (a) more
(b) longer; **rester** ~ to stay longer

DCA /desea/ *nf* (*abbr* = **défense contre les aéronefs**) antiaircraft defence (GB)

DDASS /das/ *nf* (*abbr* = **Direction départementale de l'action sanitaire et sociale**) regional social services department

✒ **de, d'** *before vowel or mute h* /də, d/

■ **Note** You will find translations for expressions such as *d'abord, de travers, pomme de terre, chemin de fer* etc, at the entries ABORD, TRAVERS, POMME, CHEMIN etc.

① *prep* (a) from; **venir** ~ **Paris** to come from Paris; **il est** ~ **père italien** his father is Italian
(b) by; **un poème** ~ **Victor Hugo** a poem by Victor Hugo
(c) of; **les chapeaux** ~ **Paul** Paul's hats; **le 20 du mois** the 20th of the month; **deux heures d'attente** a two-hour wait; **deux heures** ~ **libres** two hours free
(d) than; **plus/moins** ~ **dix** more/less than ten
(e) in; **d'un ton monocorde** in a monotone
(f) with; **pousser qch du pied** to push sth aside with one's foot
(g) travailler ~ **nuit** to work at night; **ne rien faire** ~ **la journée** to do nothing all day
(h) **être content** ~ **faire** to be happy to do
② *det* **de, de l', de la, du** some; any; **voulez-vous** ~ **la bière?** would you like some beer?; **je n'ai pas d'argent** I haven't got any money

dé /de/ *nm* (a) dice; **les** ~**s sont jetés** the die is cast
(b) ~ **(à coudre)** thimble

DEA /deəa/ *nm* (*abbr* = **diplôme d'études approfondies**) postgraduate certificate (*prior to doctoral thesis*)

déambulateur /deɑ̃bylatœʀ/ *nm* zimmer® (frame)

déambuler /deɑ̃byle/ [1] *vi* to wander (about)

débâcle /debɑkl/ *nf* (a) (Mil) rout
(b) (figurative) collapse

déballage /debalaʒ/ *nm* (fam) jumble; outpouring

déballer /debale/ [1] *vtr* (a) to unpack
(b) to display

débandade /debɑ̃dad/ *nf* (a) stampede
(b) disarray

✒ indicates a very frequent word

débarbouiller /debaʀbuje/ [1] ① *vtr* to wash
② **se débarbouiller** *v refl* (+ *v être*) to wash one's face

débarcadère /debaʀkadɛʀ/ *nm* landing stage, jetty

débardeur /debaʀdœʀ/ *nm* tank top

débarquement /debaʀkəmɑ̃/ *nm* (a) (of goods) unloading
(b) (of passengers) disembarkation
(c) (Mil) landing

débarquer /debaʀke/ [1] ① *vtr* to unload ‹goods›
② *vi* (a) to disembark
(b) (Mil) to land
(c) (fam) to turn up (colloq) (**chez qn** at sb's place)

débarras /debaʀa/ *nm inv* (a) junk room
(b) **bon**~**!** (fam) good riddance!

débarrasser /debaʀase/ [1] ① *vtr* (a) to clear (out)
(b) ~ **qn de** to free sb from ‹complex›; ~ **qn (de son manteau)** to take sb's coat
② **se débarrasser** *v refl* (+ *v être*) **se** ~ **de**; to get rid of; to dispose of
IDIOM ~ **le plancher** (fam) to clear off (colloq)

✒ **débat** /deba/ *nm* debate

débattre /debatʀ/ [61] ① *vtr* to negotiate
② **débattre de** *or* **sur** *v+prep* (a) ~ **de** *or* **sur** to discuss
(b) ~ **de** *or* **sur** to debate
③ **se débattre** *v refl* (+ *v être*) to struggle

débauche /debof/ *nf* (a) debauchery
(b) profusion

débaucher /debofe/ [1] *vtr* (a) to corrupt
(b) to lay [sb] off
(c) (fam) to tempt [sb] away

débile /debil/ ① *adj* (fam) daft (colloq)
② *nmf* ~ **mental** (Med) retarded person

débilité /debilite/ *nf* (a) debility
(b) (fam) stupidity

débiner /debine/ (fam) [1] ① *vtr* to badmouth (colloq)
② **se débiner** *v refl* (+ *v être*) to clear off (colloq); to make oneself scarce (colloq)

débit /debi/ *nm* (a) debit; **la somme est inscrite au** ~ the sum has been debited
(b) (when speaking) delivery
(c) (of river) rate of flow
(d) (of liquid) flow; (of gas) output
(e) (Comput) **haut** ~ broadband
■ ~ **de boissons** bar

débiter /debite/ [1] *vtr* (a) to debit
(b) to reel [sth] off; ~ **des bêtises** to talk a lot of nonsense
(c) to cut [sth] up

débiteur, -trice /debitœʀ, tʀis/ ① *adj* **compte** ~ debit account; **pays** ~ debtor nation
② *nm,f* debtor

déblayer /debleje/ [21] *vtr* (a) to clear away ‹earth, snow›
(b) to clear ‹place›

débloquer /deblɔke/ [1] **1** *vtr*
(a) to unlock ‹*steering wheel*›; to unjam ‹*mechanism*›
(b) to unfreeze ‹*prices*›; to end the deadlock in ‹*situation*›
(c) to make [sth] available ‹*credit*›
2 *vi* (fam) to be off one's rocker (colloq)

déboires /debwaʀ/ *nm pl*
(a) disappointments
(b) trials, difficulties
(c) setbacks

déboiser /debwaze/ [1] *vtr* to deforest

déboîter /debwate/ [1] **1** *vtr* to disconnect ‹*tubes*›
2 *vi* ‹*car*› to pull out
3 **se déboîter** *v refl* (+ *v être*) se ~ le genou to dislocate one's knee

débonnaire /debɔnɛʀ/ *adj* good-humoured (GB); kindly

débordant, **~e** /debɔʀdã, ãt/ *adj*
(a) ‹*imagination*› overactive
(b) ~ de brimming with ‹*energy*›; bursting with ‹*health*›

débordé, **~e** /debɔʀde/ **1** *pp*
▶ DÉBORDER
2 *pp adj* (a) overwhelmed
(b) overloaded

débordement /debɔʀdəmã/ *nm* (of protest) flood; (of enthusiasm) excess; **parking de ~** overflow car park

déborder /debɔʀde/ [1] **1** *vtr*
(a) ‹*problem, feeling*› to go beyond
(b) **se laisser ~** to let oneself be overwhelmed
(c) (Mil, Sport) to outflank
2 **déborder de** *v+prep* to be brimming over with; to be bursting with
3 *vi* (a) ‹*river*› to overflow
(b) ‹*liquid*› to overflow; to boil over
(c) to jut out

débouché /debuʃe/ *nm* (a) market; **~s à l'exportation** export outlets
(b) job opportunity

déboucher /debuʃe/ [1] **1** *vtr* (a) to unblock
(b) to open; to uncork
2 *vi* **~ sur** ‹*street*› to open onto; ‹*talks*› to lead to
3 **se déboucher** *v refl* (+ *v être*) (a) to come unblocked
(b) ‹*ears*› to pop
(c) **se ~ les oreilles/le nez** to unblock one's ears/nose

débouler /debule/ [1] **1** *vtr* to charge down
2 *vi* (a) to tumble down
(b) (fam) to turn up

déboulonner /debulɔne/ [1] *vtr* to unbolt

débourser /debuʀse/ [1] *vtr* to pay out

déboussoler /debusɔle/ [1] *vtr* (fam) to confuse

✔ **debout** /dəbu/ **1** *adj inv, adv*
(a) standing; ‹*object*› upright; **se mettre ~**

to stand up; **je ne tiens plus ~** I'm falling asleep on my feet
(b) **ton histoire tient ~** (fam) your story seems likely
(c) (out of bed) **être ~** to be up
2 *excl* get up!

déboutonner /debutɔne/ [1] **1** *vtr* to unbutton
2 **se déboutonner** *v refl* (+ *v être*) to come undone

débraillé, **~e** /debʀaje/ *adj* ‹*person*› dishevelled (GB); ‹*clothes, style*› sloppy

débrancher /debʀãʃe/ [1] *vtr* to unplug ‹*appliance*›; to disconnect ‹*alarm system*›

débrayer /debʀeje/ [21] *vi* (Aut) to declutch

débridé, **~e** /debʀide/ *adj* unbridled

débris /debʀi/ *nm inv* (a) fragment; **des ~ de verre** broken glass
(b) piece of wreckage

débrouillard, **~e** /debʀujaʀ, aʀd/ *adj* resourceful

débrouiller /debʀuje/ [1] **1** *vtr* (a) to disentangle ‹*threads*›
(b) to solve ‹*riddle*›
2 **se débrouiller** *v refl* (+ *v être*) (a) to manage
(b) to get by; **il se débrouille bien en espagnol** he speaks good Spanish

débroussailler /debʀusaje/ [1] *vtr* to clear the undergrowth from; (figurative) to do the groundwork on

débusquer /debyske/ [1] *vtr* to flush [sb/sth] out

♂ **début** /deby/ **1** *nm* beginning; start
2 **débuts** *nm pl* (a) debut
(b) early stages

débutant, **~e** /debytã, ãt/ **1** *adj* ‹*driver, skier*› novice; ‹*engineer*› recently qualified
2 *nm,f* beginner

débuter /debyte/ [1] *vi* (a) ‹*day, novel*› to begin, to start; ‹*person*› to start off
(b) to start out (**comme** as)
(c) ‹*performer*› to make one's debut

deçà /dəsa/ **1** *adv* **~, delà** here and there
2 **en deçà** *phr* (a) on this side
(b) below

décacheter /dekaʃte/ [20] *vtr* to unseal

décade /dekad/ *nf* (a) 10-day period
(b) (controversial) decade

décadence /dekadãs/ *nf* decadence; decline

décadent, **~e** /dekadã, ãt/ *adj*
(a) decadent
(b) in decline

décaféiné, **~e** /dekafeine/ *adj* decaffeinated

décalage /dekalaʒ/ *nm* (a) gap
(b) discrepancy
(c) interval, time-lag
(d) shift
■ **~ horaire** time difference

décalcomanie /dekalkɔmani/ *nf*
transfer

décaler /dekale/ [1] ① *vtr* **(a)** to bring
forward ‹*date, departure time*›
(b) to put (GB) *or* move (US) back
(c) to move [sth] forward ‹*object*›
(d) to move [sth] back ‹*object*›
② **se décaler** *v refl* (+ *v être*) **se ~ sur la
droite** to move *or* shift to the right

décalquer /dekalke/ [1] *vtr* **(a)** to trace
(**sur** from)
(b) to transfer (**sur** onto)

décamper /dekɑ̃pe/ [1] *vi* (fam) to run off

décanter /dekɑ̃te/ [1] ① *vtr* to allow [sth]
to settle ‹*liquid*›; to clarify ‹*waste water*›
② **se décanter** *v refl* (+ *v être*) **(a)** ‹*liquid*›
to settle
(b) ‹*situation, ideas*› to become clearer

décapant, **~e** /dekapɑ̃, ɑ̃t/ *adj*
(a) scouring
(b) (fam) ‹*humour*› abrasive, caustic

décaper /dekape/ [1] *vtr* **(a)** to clean
(b) to strip ‹*furniture*›; **~ avec un abrasif**
to scour
(c) (fam) ‹*alcohol, soap*› to be harsh

décapitation /dekapitasjɔ̃/ *nf*
decapitation; beheading

décapiter /dekapite/ [1] *vtr* to behead; to
decapitate

décapotable /dekapɔtabl/ *adj* **une
(voiture) ~** a convertible

décapsuler /dekapsyle/ [1] *vtr* to take
the top off

décapsuleur /dekapsylœʀ/ *nm* bottle-
opener

décathlon /dekatlɔ̃/ *nm* decathlon

décéder /desede/ [14] *vi* (+ *v être*) to die

décelable /deslabl/ *adj* detectable

déceler /desle/ [17] *vtr* **(a)** to detect
(b) to reveal ‹*anomaly, feeling*›
(c) to indicate ‹*presence*›

✔ **décembre** /desɑ̃bʀ/ *nm* December

décemment /desamɑ̃/ *adv* decently

décence /desɑ̃s/ *nf* decency

décennie /deseni/ *nf* decade

décent, **~e** /desɑ̃, ɑ̃t/ *adj* **(a)** decent
(b) proper

décentraliser /desɑ̃tʀalize/ [1] *vtr* to
decentralize

décentrer /desɑ̃tʀe/ [1] *vtr* to move away
from the centre (GB)

déception /desɛpsjɔ̃/ *nf* disappointment

décerner /desɛʀne/ [1] *vtr* to award

décès /desɛ/ *nm inv* death

décevant, **~e** /desəvɑ̃, ɑ̃t/ *adj*
disappointing

décevoir /desəvwaʀ/ [5] *vtr* **(a)** to
disappoint

✔ indicates a very frequent word

(b) to fail to fulfil (GB) ‹*hope*›

déchaîné, **~e** /deʃene/ ① *pp*
▶ DÉCHAÎNER
② *pp adj* stirred up; **~ contre** furious with

déchaîner /deʃene/ [1] ① *vtr* to rouse
‹*feelings*›; to excite ‹*people*›
② **se déchaîner** *v refl* (+ *v être*) **(a)** ‹*sea*›
to rage; ‹*feelings*› to burst out
(b) to go wild

déchanter /deʃɑ̃te/ [1] *vi* to become
disenchanted

décharge /deʃaʀʒ/ *nf* **(a)** (of
firearm) discharge
(b) **~ municipale** (municipal) dump
(c) **~ électrique** electric shock
(d) (Law) acquittal

décharger /deʃaʀʒe/ [13] ① *vtr* **(a)** to
unload ‹*vessel, goods*›
(b) to unload ‹*firearm*›
(c) to fire ‹*gun*›
(d) **~ qn de** to relieve sb of ‹*task*›
(e) to discharge ‹*battery*›
(f) to unburden ‹*conscience*›
② **se décharger** *v refl* (+ *v être*) **(a)** **se ~
de qch** to off-load sth
(b) ‹*battery*› to run down

décharné, **~e** /deʃaʀne/ *adj* ‹*body*›
emaciated; ‹*finger*› bony

déchausser: se déchausser
/deʃose/ [1] *v refl* (+ *v être*) **(a)** to take off
one's shoes
(b) ‹*teeth*› to work loose due to receding
gums

dèche /dɛʃ/ *nf* (fam) **être dans la ~** to be
broke (colloq)

déchéance /deʃeɑ̃s/ *nf* **(a)** decline
(b) degeneration

déchet /deʃɛ/ ① *nm* **(a)** scrap
(b) waste
(c) wreck
② **déchets** *nm pl* waste material,
waste; **~s industriels** industrial waste; **~s
nucléaires** nuclear waste

déchetterie /deʃɛtʀi/ *nf* waste reception
centre (GB)

déchiffrer /deʃifʀe/ [1] *vtr* **(a)** to decipher
(b) (Mus) to sight-read

déchiqueté, **~e** /deʃikte/ ① *pp*
▶ DÉCHIQUETER
② *pp adj* jagged, ragged

déchiqueter /deʃikte/ [20] *vtr* **(a)** to tear
[sth] to shreds
(b) ‹*machine, animal*› to tear to pieces

déchirant, **~e** /deʃiʀɑ̃, ɑ̃t/ *adj* **(a)** heart-
rending
(b) agonizing

déchirer /deʃiʀe/ [1] ① *vtr* **(a)** to tear up
‹*paper, material*›
(b) to tear ‹*garment*›
(c) to split ‹*group*›; **déchiré entre X et Y** torn
between X and Y
② **se déchirer** *v refl* (+ *v être*) **(a)** to tear

(b) se ~ un muscle to tear a muscle
(c) to tear each other apart

déchirure /deʃiRyR/ *nf* (gen, Med) tear

déchoir /deʃwaR/ [51] *vi* to demean oneself; **~ de son rang** to come down in the world

déchu, ~e /deʃy/ 1 *pp* ▶ DÉCHOIR
2 *adj* ‹monarch› deposed; ‹angel› fallen

décibel /desibɛl/ *nm* decibel

décidé, ~e /deside/ 1 *pp* ▶ DÉCIDER
2 *pp adj* determined; resolute

décidément /desidemã/ *adv* really

◆ **décider** /deside/ [1] 1 *vtr* (a) to decide; **c'est décidé** it's settled
(b) to persuade (à faire to do)
2 **décider de** *v+prep* to decide on; to fix
3 **se décider** *v refl* (+ *v être*) (a) to make up one's mind
(b) se ~ pour to decide on

décideur /desidœR/ *nm* decision-maker

décimal, ~e¹, mpl -aux /desimal, o/ *adj* decimal

décimale² /desimal/ *nf* decimal

décimer /desime/ [1] *vtr* to decimate

décisif, -ive /desizif, iv/ *adj* (a) decisive
(b) conclusive

◆ **décision** /desizjɔ̃/ *nf* (a) decision
(b) decisiveness

déclamer /deklame/ [1] *vtr* to declaim

◆ **déclaration** /deklaRasjɔ̃/ *nf* (a) statement; declaration
(b) notification
(c) (Law) statement; **~ de vol/perte** report of theft/loss
■ **~ d'impôts** (income-)tax return

déclaré, ~e /deklaRe/ *adj* ‹enemy› avowed; ‹hatred› professed

◆ **déclarer** /deklaRe/ [1] 1 *vtr* (a) to declare; **il a été déclaré coupable** he was found guilty
(b) to declare ‹goods, revenue›; to report ‹theft›; to register ‹birth›; **non déclaré** undeclared; illegal
2 **se déclarer** *v refl* (+ *v être*) (a) ‹fire, epidemic› to break out; ‹fever› to start
(b) se ~ pour/contre to come out for/against

déclenchement /deklɑ̃ʃmɑ̃/ *nm* (of mechanism) release; (of illness) onset; (of reaction) start

déclencher /deklɑ̃ʃe/ [1] 1 *vtr* (a) to spark (off) ‹protest›; to cause ‹reaction, explosion›; to start ‹avalanche›
(b) to launch ‹offensive›; to start ‹strike, debate›
(c) to set off ‹mechanism›
2 **se déclencher** *v refl* (+ *v être*) (a) to go off; to be activated
(b) to break out; to begin

déclic /deklik/ *nm* (a) trigger
(b) (of camera) click

déclin /deklɛ̃/ *nm* decline

déclinaison /deklinɛzɔ̃/ *nf* declension

décliner /dekline/ [1] 1 *vtr* (a) to decline; to turn [sth] down
(b) ~ son identité to give one's name
(c) to decline
2 *vi* ‹light, talent› to fade; ‹health› to deteriorate; ‹enthusiasm› to wane; ‹sun› to go down
3 **se décliner** *v refl* (+ *v être*) to decline

décocher /dekɔʃe/ [1] *vtr* to shoot ‹arrow›

décoder /dekode/ [1] *vtr* to decode

décodeur /dekodœR/ *nm* decoder

décoiffer /dekwafe/ [1] *vtr* **~ qn** to ruffle sb's hair

décoincer /dekwɛ̃se/ [12] *vtr* to unjam ‹mechanism, door›; to free ‹key›

décollage /dekɔlaʒ/ *nm* take-off

décoller /dekɔle/ [1] 1 *vtr* to peel off ‹sticker›
2 *vi* ‹plane› to take off
3 **se décoller** *v refl* (+ *v être*) to come off

décolleté, ~e /dekɔlte/ 1 *adj* low-cut
2 *nm* low neckline

décolleuse /dekɔløz/ *nf* steam stripper

décolonisation /dekɔlɔnizasjɔ̃/ *nf* decolonization

décolorant, ~e /dekɔlɔRɑ̃, ɑ̃t/ *adj* bleaching

décolorer /dekɔlɔRe/ [1] *vtr* (a) to bleach
(b) to cause to fade

décombres /dekɔ̃bR/ *nm pl* rubble

décommander /dekɔmɑ̃de/ [1] 1 *vtr* to call [sth] off
2 **se décommander** *v refl* (+ *v être*) to cry off (GB), to beg off

décomposer /dekɔ̃poze/ [1] 1 *vtr* (a) to break down ‹argument, water›
(b) to distort ‹features›
2 **se décomposer** *v refl* (+ *v être*) (a) to decompose
(b) to fall apart

décomposition /dekɔ̃pozisjɔ̃/ *nf*
(a) decomposition
(b) disintegration

décompte /dekɔ̃t/ *nm* (a) discount
(b) count; **faire le ~ de** to count [sth] up ‹votes, points›

décompter /dekɔ̃te/ [1] *vtr* (a) to deduct (de from)
(b) to count ‹votes, points›

déconcentrer /dekɔ̃sɑ̃tRe/ [1] *vtr* to distract

déconcertant, ~e /dekɔ̃sɛRtɑ̃, ɑ̃t/ *adj* disconcerting; **d'une facilité ~e** ridiculously easy

déconcerter /dekɔ̃sɛRte/ [1] *vtr* to disconcert

déconfit, ~e /dekɔ̃fi, it/ *adj* crestfallen

déconfiture /dekɔ̃fityR/ *nf* (a) (of person) failure; (of party, team) defeat
(b) (of company) collapse

décongeler /dekɔ̃ʒle/ [17] *vtr, vi* to defrost

décongestionner /dekɔ̃ʒɛstjɔne/ [1]
⓵ *vtr* **(a)** to ease the pressure on
‹*university, services*›; ‹*motorway*› to relieve
congestion in ‹*street, town*›
(b) to clear ‹*nose*›
⓶ **se décongestionner** *v refl* (+ *v
être*) to clear

déconnecter /dekɔnɛkte/ [1] *vtr* **(a)** to
disconnect ‹*appliance*›
(b) to dissociate

déconner /dekɔne/ [1] *vi* (pop) **(a)** to kid
around (colloq); **faut pas** ∼! come off it! (colloq)
(b) to mess around (colloq); to piss around
(GB) (slang)
(c) to play up (colloq)

déconseiller /dekɔ̃seje/ [1] *vtr* to advise
against

déconsidérer /dekɔ̃sidere/ [14] ⓵ *vtr*
to discredit
⓶ **se déconsidérer** *v refl* (+ *v être*) **tu
t'es déconsidéré** it was unworthy of you

décontenancer /dekɔ̃tnɑ̃se/ [12] *vtr* to
disconcert

décontracté, ∼**e** /dekɔ̃tRakte/ ⓵ *pp*
▶ DÉCONTRACTER
⓶ *pp adj* **(a)** relaxed
(b) casual
(c) laid-back (colloq)

décontracter /dekɔ̃tRakte/ [1] *vtr*, **se
décontracter** *v refl* (+ *v être*) to relax

décontraction /dekɔ̃tRaksjɔ̃/ *nf*
(a) relaxation
(b) ease
(c) casual attitude

déconvenue /dekɔ̃vəny/ *nf*
disappointment

décor /dekɔR/ *nm* **(a)** decor
(b) setting; **j'ai besoin de changer de** ∼ I
need a change of scene; **partir dans le** ∼
(fam) to drive off the road
(c) (of film) set; **tourné en** ∼ **naturel** shot on
location

décorateur, -trice /dekɔRatœR, tRis/ *nm,
f* **(a)** interior decorator
(b) set designer

décoratif, -ive /dekɔRatif, iv/ *adj*
(a) ornamental
(b) decorative

décoration /dekɔRasjɔ̃/ *nf* **(a)** decorating
(b) (gen, Mil) decoration
(c) interior design

décorer /dekɔRe/ [1] *vtr* to decorate

décortiquer /dekɔRtike/ [1] *vtr* to shell
‹*nut*›; to peel ‹*prawn*›

décote /dekɔt/ *nf* (Econ) drop

découcher /dekuʃe/ [1] *vi* to spend the
night away from home

découdre /dekudR/ [76] ⓵ *vtr* to undo, to
unpick (GB) ‹*hem, seam*›
⓶ *vi* **en** ∼ to have a fight (**avec** with)

ꝸ indicates a very frequent word

découler /dekule/ [1] *vi* **(a)** to follow (**de**
from)
(b) to result (**de** from)

découpage /dekupaʒ/ *nm* cut-out

découper /dekupe/ [1] *vtr* to cut up ‹*tart*›;
to carve ‹*roast*›; to divide up ‹*land*›

découragé, ∼**e** /dekuRaʒe/ *adj* ‹*person*›
disheartened; ‹*expression*› despondent; ‹*tone*›
dejected

décourageant, ∼**e** /dekuRaʒɑ̃, ɑ̃t/ *adj*
disheartening

découragement /dekuRaʒmɑ̃/ *nm*
discouragement, despondency

décourager /dekuRaʒe/ [13] *vtr* **(a)** to
dishearten
(b) to discourage
(c) to deter

décousu, ∼**e** /dekuzy/ ⓵ *pp* ▶ DÉCOUDRE
⓶ *pp adj* ‹*hem*› which has come undone
⓷ *adj* ‹*story*› rambling; ‹*conversation*›
casual

découvert, ∼**e¹** /dekuvɛR, ɛRt/ ⓵ *pp*
▶ DÉCOUVRIR
⓶ *pp adj* **(a)** bare; **avoir la tête** ∼**e** to be
bare-headed
(b) ‹*truck*› open; ‹*car*› open-topped
⓷ *nm* overdraft; **être à** ∼ to be overdrawn

ꝸ **découverte²** /dekuvɛRt/ *nf* discovery

ꝸ **découvrir** /dekuvRiR/ [32] ⓵ *vtr* **(a)** to
discover; **faire** ∼ **qch à qn** to introduce sb
to sth
(b) to show ‹*arm, back*›
(c) to leave [sth] exposed ‹*border*›
⓶ **se découvrir** *v refl* (+ *v être*) **(a)** to
remove one's hat
(b) **elle s'est découvert un talent** she found
she had a talent

décrasser /dekRase/ [1] *vtr* to get [sb/sth]
clean

décrépit, ∼**e** /dekRepi, it/ *adj* ‹*person*›
decrepit; ‹*building*› dilapidated; ‹*wall*›
crumbling

décrépitude /dekRepityd/ *nf*
degeneration; decay; decrepitude

décret /dekRɛ/ *nm* decree

décréter /dekRete/ [14] *vtr* **(a)** to order
(b) to decree (**que** that)
(c) to declare (**que** that)

ꝸ **décrire** /dekRiR/ [67] *vtr* **(a)** to describe
(b) to follow

décrocher /dekRɔʃe/ [1] ⓵ *vtr* **(a)** to take
down ‹*picture*›
(b) to uncouple ‹*wagon*›
(c) ∼ **son téléphone** to pick up the receiver;
to take the phone off the hook
(d) (fam) to get ‹*contract*›
⓶ *vi* to give up
IDIOM ∼ **le gros lot** to hit the jackpot

décroissant, ∼**e** /dekRwasɑ̃, ɑ̃t/ *adj*
fading; lessening; **par** *or* **en ordre** ∼ in
descending order

décroître /dekʀwɑtʀ/ [72] *vi* ‹level› to fall; ‹moon› to wane; ‹day› to get shorter; ‹light, noise› to fade; ‹inflation› to go down

décrypter /dekʀipte/ [1] *vtr* (a) to decipher ‹signs›
(b) to interpret ‹statement›

déçu, **~e** /desy/ ▸ DÉCEVOIR

déculpabiliser /dekylpabilize/ [1] *vtr* to free [sb] of guilt

décupler /dekyple/ [1] *vtr*, *vi* to increase tenfold

dédaigner /dedeɲe/ [1] *vtr* to despise

dédaigneux, -euse /dedɛɲø, øz/ *adj* disdainful, scornful; **être ~ du danger** to be unmindful of danger

dédain /dedɛ̃/ *nm* contempt, disdain

dédale /dedal/ *nm* (a) (of buildings) maze
(b) (of laws, formalities) labyrinth

⚔ **dedans** /dədɑ̃/ **1** *adv* inside
2 **en dedans** *phr* inside

dédicace /dedikas/ *nf* (a) dedication (**à qn** to sb)
(b) inscription

dédicacer /dedikase/ [12] *vtr* (a) to dedicate ‹book› (**à** to)
(b) to sign ‹book, photo›

dédier /dedje/ [2] *vtr* (a) to dedicate ‹novel› (**à** to)
(b) to devote ‹life› (**à** to)

dédire: **se dédire** /dediʀ/ [65] *v refl* (+ *v être*) to back out

dédommagement /dedɔmaʒmɑ̃/ *nm* compensation

dédommager /dedɔmaʒe/ [13] *vtr* (a) to compensate
(b) **~ qn de qch** to make it up to sb for sth

dédouaner /dedwane/ [1] *vtr* to clear through customs

dédoubler: **se dédoubler** /deduble/ [1] *v refl* (+ *v être*) ‹rail› to split; ‹image› to split in two; ‹cable› to come apart

dédramatiser /dedʀamatize/ [1] *vi* to play things down

déductible /dedyktibl/ *adj* deductible (**de** from); **~ des impôts** tax-deductible

déduction /dedyksjɔ̃/ *nf* deduction

déduire /deduiʀ/ [69] **1** *vtr* (a) to deduce
(b) to infer
(c) to deduct
2 **se déduire** *v refl* (+ *v être*) (a) to be inferred
(b) to be deduced
(c) to be deducted

déesse /dees/ *nf* goddess

défaillance /defajɑ̃s/ *nf* failure

défaillant, ~e /defajɑ̃, ɑ̃t/ *adj* (a) ‹motor, system› faulty
(b) ‹organization› inefficient
(c) ‹health, memory› failing; ‹person› fainting

défaillir /defajiʀ/ [28] *vi* (a) to faint; **se sentir ~** to feel faint

(b) ‹health, memory› to fail; **soutenir qn sans ~** to show unflinching support for sb

défaire /defɛʀ/ [10] **1** *vtr* to undo; to untie
2 **se défaire** *v refl* (+ *v être*) (a) to come undone
(b) **se ~ de** to get rid of; to part with; to rid oneself of
(c) ‹face› to fall; **avoir la mine défaite** to look haggard

défaite /defɛt/ *nf* defeat

⚔ **défaut** /defo/ **1** *nm* (a) fault, failing; **prendre qn en ~** to catch sb out
(b) defect; flaw; **présenter des ~s** to be faulty; **~ de fabrication** manufacturing fault; **~ de prononciation** speech impediment
(c) shortage; **faire ~** ‹money, resources› to be lacking
2 **à défaut de** *phr* **à ~ de (quoi)** failing (which); **à ~ de pouvoir acheter, elle loue** since she can't buy, she has to rent

défaveur /defavœʀ/ *nf* **il s'est trompé de 5 euros en ma ~** he overcharged me by 5 euros

défavorable /defavɔʀabl/ *adj* ‹situation› unfavourable (GB) (**à** to); ‹person› opposed (**à** to)

défavorisé, ~e /defavɔʀize/ *adj*
(a) underprivileged
(b) disadvantaged

défavoriser /defavɔʀize/ [1] *vtr* (a) to discriminate against
(b) to put [sb] at a disadvantage

défection /defɛksjɔ̃/ *nf* (a) defection
(b) non-appearance
(c) (of friends) desertion

défectueux, -euse /defɛktɥø, øz/ *adj* ‹material› faulty, defective; ‹reasoning› flawed

⚔ **défendre** /defɑ̃dʀ/ [6] **1** *vtr* (a) **~ à qn de faire** to forbid sb to do
(b) to defend ‹person, country, interests›
(c) to fight for ‹right›; to stand up for ‹friend, principle›; **~ une cause** to champion a cause
(d) (Law, Sport) to defend
2 **se défendre** *v refl* (+ *v être*) (a) to defend oneself; to stand up for oneself
(b) to be tenable
(c) to protect oneself
(d) (fam) to get by
(e) **on ne peut se ~ de penser que...** one can't help thinking that...

⚔ **défense** /defɑ̃s/ *nf* (a) **'~ de fumer'** 'no smoking'; **~ d'en parler devant lui** don't mention it in front of him
(b) (Med, Mil, Sport) defence (GB)
(c) protection; **sans ~** helpless; unprotected; **la ~ de l'environnement** the protection of the environment; **prendre la ~ de** to stand up for
(d) (Zool) tusk

défenseur /defɑ̃sœʀ/ *nm* defender

d

défensive /defãsiv/ *nf* **sur la ∼** on the defensive

déférence /defeʀãs/ *nf* **marques de ∼** marks of respect

déferler /defɛʀle/ [1] *vi* (a) ‹*wave*› to break (**sur** on)
(b) ‹*violence*› to erupt
(c) **∼ sur** ‹*people*› to pour into ‹*country, town*›

défi /defi/ *nm* (a) challenge; **mettre qn au ∼ de faire** to challenge sb to do
(b) **air de ∼** defiant look

défiance /defjãs/ *nf* distrust, mistrust

défiant, ∼e /defjã, ãt/ *adj* distrustful, wary

déficience /defisjãs/ *nf* deficiency

déficit /defisit/ *nm* (a) deficit
(b) (Med) deficiency

déficitaire /defisitɛʀ/ *adj* showing a deficit; showing a loss; showing a shortfall

défier /defje/ [2] *vtr* (a) to challenge ‹*rival*›
(b) to defy ‹*danger, death*›; **prix défiant toute concurrence** unbeatable price

défigurer /defigyʀe/ [1] *vtr* to disfigure

défilé /defile/ *nm* (a) parade
(b) (protest) march
(c) (of visitors, candidates) stream
(d) gorge
■ **∼ aérien** flypast (GB), flyover (US); **∼ militaire** march-past; **∼ de mode** fashion show

défiler /defile/ [1] **1** *vi* (a) to parade; ‹*protesters*› to march
(b) ‹*people*› to come and go
(c) ‹*images, landscape*› to unfold
(d) (Comput) to scroll
2 se défiler *v refl* (+ *v être*) (fam) to wriggle out of it

✔ définir /definiʀ/ [3] *vtr* to define

définitif, -ive /definitif, iv/ **1** *adj* ‹*accounts, report*› final; ‹*edition*› definitive; ‹*refusal*› flat
2 en définitive *phr* at the end of the day

✔ définition /definisjɔ̃/ *nf* definition

définitivement /definitivmã/ *adv* for good

défiscalisé, ∼e /defiskalize/ *adj* tax-exempt

déflagration /deflagʀasjɔ̃/ *nf* detonation

défoncer /defɔ̃se/ [12] *vtr* to break down ‹*door*›; to smash in ‹*back of a car*›

déformation /defɔʀmasjɔ̃/ *nf*
(a) distortion
(b) deformity
(c) **c'est de la ∼ professionnelle** it's a habit that comes from the job

déformé, ∼e /defɔʀme/ *adj* ‹*face, image, truth*› distorted; ‹*object, mind*› warped; **chaussée ∼e** uneven (road) surface

déformer /defɔʀme/ [1] **1** *vtr* (a) to bend [sth] (out of shape)
(b) to distort
(c) **on a déformé mes propos** my words have been twisted
2 se déformer *v refl* (+ *v être*) to lose its shape

défoulement /defulmã/ *nm* letting off steam

défouler /defule/ [1] **1** *vtr* **ça me défoule** it helps me (to) unwind
2 se défouler *v refl* (+ *v être*) (a) to let off steam
(b) **se ∼ sur qn** to take it out on sb

défraîchi, ∼e /defʀeʃi/ *adj* ‹*garment, curtain*› worn; ‹*material, beauty*› faded

défrayer /defʀeje/ [21] *vtr* (a) **∼ la chronique** to be the talk of the town
(b) **∼ qn** to pay *or* meet sb's expenses

défricher /defʀiʃe/ [1] *vtr* to clear, to reclaim

défriser /defʀize/ [1] *vtr* to straighten

défroisser /defʀwase/ [1] *vtr* to smooth out

défunt, ∼e /defœ̃, œ̃t/ **1** *adj* (a) former
(b) late
2 *nm,f* **le ∼** the deceased

dégagé, ∼e /degaʒe/ *adj* (a) ‹*road, sky*› clear; ‹*forehead*› bare
(b) ‹*look*› casual

dégagement /degaʒmã/ *nm* (a) clearing
(b) (in football) clearance

✔ dégager /degaʒe/ [13] **1** *vtr* (a) to free; **∼ qn d'une responsabilité** to relieve sb of a responsibility; **∼ des crédits** to make funds available
(b) to unblock ‹*nose*›
(c) to clear ‹*way*›; '**dégagez, s'il vous plaît**' 'move along please'; **dégage!** (fam) get lost! (colloq)
(d) to find ‹*idea, sense*›
(e) to emit ‹*odour, gas*›; **∼ de la chaleur** to give off heat
2 se dégager *v refl* (+ *v être*) (a) to free oneself/itself
(b) ‹*weather, sky*› to clear
(c) **se ∼ de** to come out of
(d) to become clear

dégaine /degɛn/ *nf* (fam) odd appearance

dégainer /degene/ [1] *vtr* to draw ‹*gun*›

dégarnir: se dégarnir /degaʀniʀ/ [3] *v refl* (+ *v être*) to be going bald

dégât /dega/ *nm* damage

dégel /deʒɛl/ *nm* thaw

dégeler /deʒle/ [17] **1** *vtr* (a) to improve ‹*relations*›
(b) to unfreeze ‹*credit*›
2 *vi* to thaw (out)
3 se dégeler *v refl* (+ *v être*) (a) ‹*relations, situation*› to thaw
(b) ‹*audience*› to warm up

✔ indicates a very frequent word

dégénérer /deʒeneʀe/ [14] *vi* (a) ⟨*incident*⟩ to get out of hand; ∼ **en** to degenerate into (b) ⟨*plant, species*⟩ to degenerate

dégingandé, ∼**e** /deʒɛ̃gɑ̃de/ *adj* lanky

dégivrer /deʒivʀe/ [1] *vtr* (a) to de-ice ⟨*windscreen*⟩
(b) to defrost ⟨*fridge*⟩

déglingué, ∼**e** /deglɛ̃ge/ *adj* (fam) dilapidated

déglutir /deglytiʀ/ [3] *vtr*, *vi* to swallow

dégonflé, ∼**e** 1 *adj* ⟨*balloon*⟩ deflated; ⟨*tyre*⟩ flat
2 *nm,f* (fam) chicken (colloq), coward

dégonfler /degɔ̃fle/ [1] 1 *vtr* to deflate ⟨*tyre*⟩
2 *vi* ⟨*swelling, bump*⟩ to go down
3 **se dégonfler** *v refl* (+ *v être*) (a) to deflate; to go down
(b) (fam) to chicken out (colloq)

dégot(t)er /degote/ [1] *vtr* (fam) to find

dégouliner /deguline/ [1] *vi* (a) to trickle
(b) to drip (**de** with)

dégoupiller /degupije/ [1] *vtr* ∼ **une grenade** to pull the pin out of a grenade

dégourdi, ∼**e** /deguʀdi/ *adj* smart

dégourdir: se dégourdir /deguʀdiʀ/ [3] *v refl* (+ *v être*) **se** ∼ **les jambes** to stretch one's legs

dégoût /degu/ *nm* disgust

dégoûtant, ∼**e** /degutɑ̃, ɑ̃t/ *adj* (a) filthy
(b) (fam) disgusting; revolting

dégoûté, ∼**e** /degute/ *adj* disgusted; **faire le** ∼ to turn one's nose up

dégoûter /degute/ [1] *vtr* (a) to disgust
(b) to make [sb] feel sick
(c) ∼ **qn de qch/de faire** to put sb off sth/off doing

dégradant, ∼**e** /degʀadɑ̃, ɑ̃t/ *adj* degrading

dégradation /degʀadasjɔ̃/ *nf* (a) damage
(b) deterioration
(c) decline; **la** ∼ **des conditions de vie** the deterioration in the standard of living; **la** ∼ **du pouvoir d'achat** the erosion in purchasing power

dégradé, ∼**e** /degʀade/ 1 *adj* **tons** ∼**s** shaded tones; **coupe** ∼**e** layered cut
2 *nm* (in colours) gradation

dégrader /degʀade/ [1] 1 *vtr* (a) to damage
(b) (Mil) to cashier ⟨*officer*⟩
(c) to degrade ⟨*person*⟩
2 **se dégrader** *v refl* (+ *v être*) to deteriorate

dégrafer /degʀafe/ [1] 1 *vtr* to undo
2 **se dégrafer** *v refl* (+ *v être*) to come undone

dégraisser /degʀese/ [1] *vtr* to trim the fat off

degré /dəgʀe/ *nm* (a) degree; **par** ∼**s** gradually; **à un moindre** ∼ to a lesser extent;

susceptible au plus haut ∼ extremely touchy; **brûlures du premier** ∼ first-degree burns; ∼ **de parenté** degree of kinship
(b) step; **enseignement du second** ∼ secondary education; **c'est à prendre au deuxième** ∼ it is not to be taken literally
(c) **titrer 40° d'alcool** ≈ to be 70% proof
■ ∼ **Celsius** degree Celsius; ∼ **Fahrenheit** degree Fahrenheit

dégressif, **-ive** /degʀesif, iv/ *adj* ⟨*tax*⟩ graduated; **tarifs** ∼**s** tapering charges

dégringolade /degʀɛ̃gɔlad/ *nf* (fam)
(a) (gen) fall
(b) (Econ) collapse

dégringoler /degʀɛ̃gɔle/ (fam) [1] 1 *vtr* to race down ⟨*stairs, hill*⟩
2 *vi* (a) ⟨*person*⟩ to take a tumble; ⟨*books*⟩ to tumble down
(b) to drop sharply

dégriser /degʀize/ [1] *vtr* (a) to sober [sb] up
(b) to bring [sb] to his/her senses

déguerpir /degɛʀpiʀ/ [3] *vi* to leave

déguisé, ∼**e** /degize/ *adj* (a) in fancy dress; in disguise
(b) ⟨*party*⟩ fancy-dress
(c) ⟨*attempt*⟩ concealed; ⟨*compliment*⟩ disguised

déguisement /degizmɑ̃/ *nm* costume

déguiser /degize/ [1] 1 *vtr* (a) to dress [sb] up (**en** as)
(b) to disguise
2 **se déguiser** *v refl* (+ *v être*) (a) to dress up
(b) to disguise oneself

dégustation /degystasjɔ̃/ *nf* tasting

déguster /degyste/ [1] *vtr* to savour (GB) ⟨*drink, victory*⟩; to enjoy ⟨*performance*⟩

déhanchement /deɑ̃ʃmɑ̃/ *nm*
(a) swaying hips
(b) lopsidedness

déhancher: se déhancher /deɑ̃ʃe/ [1] *v refl* (+ *v être*) to wiggle one's hips

✧ **dehors** /dəɔʀ/ 1 *adv* outside; **mettre qn** ∼ to throw sb out; to fire sb; to expel sb
2 *excl* get out!
3 **en dehors de** *phr* (a) outside
(b) apart from

✧ **déjà** /deʒa/ *adv* (a) already
(b) before, already; **je te l'ai** ∼ **dit** I've told you before
(c) (fam) **il s'est excusé, c'est** ∼ **quelque chose** he apologized, that's something at least; **elle est** ∼ **assez riche!** she's rich enough as it is; **c'est combien,** ∼**?** how much was it again?

déjà-vu /deʒavy/ *nm inv* déjà vu; **c'est du** ∼ (fam) we've seen it all before

déjeuner[1] /deʒœne/ [1] *vi* to have lunch

✧ **déjeuner**[2] /deʒœne/ *nm* lunch

déjouer /deʒwe/ [1] *vtr* to frustrate ⟨*precaution, manoeuvre*⟩; to foil ⟨*plan*⟩; to evade ⟨*inspection*⟩

✔ **delà** /dəla/ *adv* **deçà** *or* **de-ci,** ∼ here and
there

délabré, ∼**e** /delabʀe/ *adj* ⟨*house,
equipment*⟩ dilapidated; ⟨*health*⟩ damaged

délabrement /delabʀəmɑ̃/ *nm*
dilapidation

délabrer /delabʀe/ [1] **1** *vtr* to ruin
2 se délabrer *v refl* (+ *v être*) ⟨*house*⟩ to
become run-down; ⟨*business, country*⟩ to go
to rack and ruin; ⟨*health*⟩ to deteriorate

délacer /delase/ [12] *vtr* to undo; to unlace

délai /delɛ/ *nm* **(a) dans un** ∼ **de 24 heures**
within 24 hours; **respecter un** ∼ to meet a
deadline; **dans les meilleurs** ∼**s** as soon as
possible
(b) extension; **demander un** ∼ to ask for
extra time
■ ∼ **de livraison** delivery *or* lead time

délaisser /delese/ [1] *vtr* **(a)** to abandon
⟨*activity*⟩
(b) to neglect ⟨*friends*⟩

délassement /delɑsmɑ̃/ *nm* relaxation

délasser /delɑse/ [1] *vtr, v refl* (+ *v être*) to
relax; **ça délasse** it's relaxing

délateur, -trice /delatœʀ, tʀis/ *nm,f*
informer

délation /delɑsjɔ̃/ *nf* informing

délavé, ∼**e** /delave/ *adj* **(a)** ⟨*colour, sky*⟩
washed-out; ⟨*jeans*⟩ faded
(b) waterlogged

délayer /deleje/ [21] *vtr* to thin ⟨*paint*⟩; to
mix ⟨*flour*⟩

délectation /delɛktasjɔ̃/ *nf* delight

délecter: se délecter /delɛkte/ [1] *v refl*
(+ *v être*) **se** ∼ **à faire/en faisant** to delight
in doing

délégation /delegasjɔ̃/ *nf* delegation

délégué, ∼**e** /delege/ *nm,f* delegate
■ ∼ **syndical** union representative

déléguer /delege/ [14] *vtr* **(a)** to appoint
[sb] as a delegate
(b) to delegate ⟨*responsibility, power*⟩

délestage /delɛstaʒ/ *nm* **parking de** ∼
overflow car park

délester /delɛste/ [1] *vtr* **(a)** to get rid of
the ballast from
(b) to divert traffic away from

délibération /deliberasjɔ̃/ *nf*
deliberation; **mettre qch en** ∼ to debate sth

délibéré, ∼**e** /delibeʀe/ *adj* ⟨*act, violation*⟩
deliberate; ⟨*choice, policy*⟩ conscious

délibérément /deliberemɑ̃/ *adv* ⟨*wound,
provoke*⟩ deliberately; ⟨*accept, choose*⟩
consciously

délibérer /delibeʀe/ [14] **1 délibérer
de** *or* **sur** *v+prep* to discuss
2 *vi* to be in session

délicat, ∼**e** /delika, at/ *adj* **(a)** ⟨*dish*⟩
subtle; ⟨*person*⟩ refined

(b) tactful
(c) thoughtful; **des procédés peu** ∼**s**
unscrupulous means
(d) ⟨*balance, task*⟩ delicate; ⟨*business,
moment*⟩ sensitive; ⟨*mission*⟩ tricky
(e) ⟨*skin*⟩ delicate

délicatement /delikatmɑ̃/ *adv*
(a) delicately
(b) tactfully

délicatesse /delikatɛs/ *nf* **(a)** delicacy; **la**
∼ **de ses traits** his/her fine features
(b) sensitivity
(c) delicacy, trickiness

délice /delis/ *nm* delight

délicieusement /delisjøzmɑ̃/ *adv*
(a) deliciously
(b) delightfully

délicieux, -ieuse /delisjø, øz/ *adj*
(a) delicious
(b) ⟨*feeling, music*⟩ delightful; ⟨*joy*⟩ exquisite

délié, ∼**e** /delje/ *adj* **(a)** ⟨*waist*⟩ slender
(b) ⟨*movement*⟩ loose
(c) ⟨*mind*⟩ nimble

délier /delje/ [2] *vtr* to untie; ∼ **qn de** to
release sb from] ⟨*promise*⟩
IDIOM ∼ **la langue à qn** to loosen sb's tongue

délimiter /delimite/ [1] *vtr* **(a)** to mark the
boundary of
(b) to form the boundary of
(c) to define ⟨*role*⟩; to define the scope of
⟨*subject*⟩

délinquance /delɛ̃kɑ̃s/ *nf* crime; **la** ∼
juvénile juvenile delinquency

délinquant, ∼**e** /delɛ̃kɑ̃, ɑ̃t/ **1** *adj*
delinquent
2 *nm,f* offender

déliquescence /delikesɑ̃s/ *nf* decline

délirant, ∼**e** /deliʀɑ̃, ɑ̃t/ *adj* **(a)** ⟨*welcome*⟩
ecstatic
(b) (fam) ⟨*scenario*⟩ crazy (colloq)

délire /deliʀ/ *nm* **(a)** (Med) delirium
(b) (fam) madness
(c) frenzy; **salle en** ∼ ecstatic audience

délirer /deliʀe/ [1] *vi* **(a)** (Med) to be delirious
(b) (fam) to be mad

délit /deli/ *nm* offence (GB)
■ ∼ **de fuite** hit-and-run offence; ∼ **d'initie**
insider dealing

délivrance /delivʀɑ̃s/ *nf* relief

délivrer /delivʀe/ [1] *vtr* **(a)** to free, to
liberate; ∼ **qn de** to relieve sb of
(b) to issue ⟨*passport*⟩

délocalisation /delɔkalizasjɔ̃/ *nf*
relocation; ∼ **industrielle** *relocation in
search of cheap labour*

délocaliser /delɔkalize/ *vtr* to offshore

déloger /delɔʒe/ [13] *vtr* **(a)** to evict ⟨*tenant*⟩
(b) to flush out ⟨*rebels, game*⟩
(c) to remove ⟨*dust*⟩

déloyal, ∼**e,** *mpl* **-aux** /delwajal, o/ *adj*
⟨*person*⟩ disloyal; ⟨*competition*⟩ unfair

deltaplane /dɛltaplan/ *nm* hang-glider

✔ indicates a very frequent word

déluge /delyʒ/ *nm* downpour; ~ **de** flood of ‹*tears, complaints*›; **le Déluge** the Flood
IDIOM **après moi le** ~ I don't care what happens after I'm gone

déluré, ~e /delyʀe/ *adj* (a) smart, resourceful
(b) forward

démagogie /demaɡɔʒi/ *nf* demagoguery, demagogy; **faire de la** ~ to try to gain popularity

démagogique /demaɡɔʒik/ *adj* demagogic

𝄞 **demain** /dəmɛ̃/ *adv* tomorrow; **l'Europe de** ~ the Europe of the future
IDIOMS ~ **il fera jour** tomorrow is another day; **ce n'est pas** ~ **la veille!** that's not going to happen in a hurry!

démancher: se démancher /demɑ̃ʃe/ [1] *v refl* (+ *v être*) ‹*tool*› to come off its handle

𝄞 **demande** /dəmɑ̃d/ *nf* (a) request, application, claim (**de** for); ~ **de dommages et intérêts** claim for damages; **faire une** ~ **de mutation** to apply for a transfer
(b) (in economics) demand
(c) application form
∎ ~ **d'emploi** job application; **'~s d'emploi'** 'situations wanted'; ~ **en mariage** marriage proposal

demandé, ~e /dəmɑ̃de/ *adj* **très** ~ ‹*destination*› very popular; ‹*product*› in great demand

𝄞 **demander** /dəmɑ̃de/ [1] **1** *vtr* (a) to ask for ‹*advice, money, help*›; to apply for ‹*nationality*›; to claim ‹*damages*›; ~ **le divorce** to sue for divorce; ~ **en mariage** to propose to; **'on demande un plombier'** 'plumber wanted'; **fais ce qu'on te demande!** do as you're told!; **je ne demande pas mieux** there's nothing I would like better
(b) ~ **qch à qn** to ask sb sth; **il m'a demandé de tes nouvelles** he asked after you
(c) to send for ‹*priest*›; to dial ‹*number*›; **le patron vous demande** the boss wants to see you
(d) to call for ‹*reforms*›; to require ‹*effort, qualification*›; to need ‹*attention*›
2 **se demander** *v refl* (+ *v être*) to wonder

demandeur¹, -euse /dəmɑ̃dœʀ, øz/ *nm,f* applicant
∎ ~ **d'asile** asylum-seeker; ~ **d'emploi** job-seeker

demandeur², -eresse /dəmɑ̃dœʀ, d(ə)ʀɛs/ *nm,f* (Law) plaintiff

démangeaison /demɑ̃ʒɛzɔ̃/ *nf* itch

démanger /demɑ̃ʒe/ [13] *vtr* **ça me démange** it itches, it's itching; **l'envie de le gifler me démangeait** I was itching to slap him

démanteler /demɑ̃tle/ [17] *vtr* to dismantle; to break up

démaquillage /demakijaʒ/ *nm* make-up removal

démaquillant, ~e /demakijɑ̃, ɑ̃t/ **1** *adj* ‹*milk*› cleansing
2 *nm* make-up remover

démaquiller: se démaquiller /demakije/ [1] *v refl* (+ *v être*) to remove one's make-up

démarcation /demaʀkasjɔ̃/ *nf* demarcation

démarchage /demaʀʃaʒ/ *nm* door-to-door selling; ~ **électoral** canvassing; ~ **téléphonique** cold calling

𝄞 **démarche** /demaʀʃ/ *nf* (a) walk
(b) step; **faire une** ~ **auprès de qn** to approach sb; **faire des** ~**s pour obtenir qch** to take steps to obtain sth
(c) reasoning; ~ **de la pensée** thought process

démarcher /demaʀʃe/ [1] *vtr* (a) to sell door-to-door
(b) to canvass

démarque /demaʀk/ *nf* (of goods) mark-down (**de** of)

démarquer /demaʀke/ [1] **1** *vtr* to mark down ‹*goods*›
2 **se démarquer** *v refl* (+ *v être*) (a) **se** ~ **de** to distance oneself from
(b) (Sport) to get free of one's marker

démarrage /demaʀaʒ/ *nm* (a) starting up
(b) spurt
∎ ~ **en côte** hill start

démarrer /demaʀe/ [1] **1** *vtr* to start (up)
2 *vi* (a) ‹*vehicle*› to pull away; ‹*engine*› to start; ‹*driver*› to drive off; ‹*business*› to start up; ‹*campaign*› to get under way; ‹*person*› to start off
(b) (Sport) to put on a spurt

démarreur /demaʀœʀ/ *nm* (in car) starter

démasquer /demaske/ [1] *vtr* to unmask ‹*person*›; to uncover ‹*plot*›

démazouter /demazute/ [1] *vtr* to clean the oil from ‹*beach*›

démêlé /demele/ *nm* wrangle; **avoir des** ~**s avec la justice** to get into trouble with the law

démêler /demele/ [1] *vtr* (a) to disentangle; to untangle
(b) to sort out ‹*situation*›

démembrement /demɑ̃bʀəmɑ̃/ *nm*
(a) break-up, dismemberment
(b) (of estate) division

démembrer /demɑ̃bʀe/ [1] *vtr* to divide up, to dismember

déménagement /demenaʒmɑ̃/ *nm*
(a) moving house; move
(b) removal; **entreprise de** ~**s** removals firm (GB), moving company (US)

déménager /demenaʒe/ [13] **1** *vtr* (a) to move ‹*furniture*›; to relocate ‹*offices*›
(b) to clear ‹*room*›

⋯⟩

2 *vi* **(a)** to move (house)
(b) (fam) to push off (colloq)
(c) (fam) to be off one's rocker (colloq)

déménageur /demenaʒœr/ *nm* removal
(GB) *or* moving (US) man

démence /demɑ̃s/ *nf* **(a)** insanity
(b) dementia

démener: se démener /dem(ə)ne/ [16] *v
refl* (+ *v être*) **(a)** to thrash about
(b) to put oneself out, to exert oneself

dément, ~e /demɑ̃, ɑ̃t/ *adj* **(a)** insane, mad
(b) (fam) terrific (colloq)

démenti /demɑ̃ti/ *nm* denial

démentiel, -ielle /demɑ̃sjɛl/ *adj* insane

démentir /demɑ̃tir/ [30] *vtr* **(a)** to deny
(b) ⟨person⟩ to refute ⟨statement⟩; ⟨fact⟩ to give
the lie to ⟨statement⟩; to belie ⟨appearance⟩

démesure /deməzyr/ *nf* **(a)** (of
ambition) excesses
(b) excessive size

démesuré, ~e /deməzyre/ *adj* excessive,
immoderate

démettre /demɛtr/ [60] **1** *vtr* **(a)** to
dislocate ⟨joint⟩
(b) to dismiss ⟨employee⟩
2 se démettre *v refl* (+ *v être*) **se ~
l'épaule** to dislocate one's shoulder

demeurant: au demeurant
/odəmœrɑ̃/ *phr* as it happens, for all that

demeure /dəmœr/ **1** *nf* **(a)** residence
(b) mettre qn en ~ de faire to require sb
to do
2 à demeure *phr* permanently;
permanent
IDIOM il n'y a pas péril en la ~ there's no
rush

demeuré, ~e /dəmœre/ *adj* retarded

✓ **demeurer** /dəmœre/ [1] **1** *vi* **(a)** (+ *v
avoir*) to reside, to live
(b) (+ *v être*) to remain
2 *v impers* **il n'en demeure pas moins que**
nonetheless, the fact remains that

✓ **demi, ~e¹** /d(ə)mi/ **1 et demi, et
demie** *phr* and a half; **il est trois heures et
~e** it's half past three
2 *nm,f* half
3 *nm* **(a)** glass of beer
(b) (Sport) **~ de mêlée/d'ouverture** scrum/
stand-off half
4 à demi *phr* half; **à ~ éveillé** half awake
5 demi- (*combining form*) **(a)** half; **une
~-pomme** half an apple
(b) partial; **une ~-victoire** a partial victory

demi-cercle, *pl* **~s** /d(ə)misɛrkl/ *nm*
semicircle

demie² /d(ə)mi/ **1** *adj* ▶ DEMI 1, 2
2 *nf* **il est déjà la ~** it's already half past

demi-écrémé, ~e, mpl ~s
/d(ə)miekreme/ *adj* semi-skimmed

demi-finale, *pl* **~s** /d(ə)mifinal/ *nf*
semifinal

demi-fond, *pl* **~s** /d(ə)mifɔ̃/ *nm* middle-
distance running

demi-frère, *pl* **~s** /d(ə)mifrɛr/ *nm* half-
brother; stepbrother

demi-gros /d(ə)migro/ *nm inv* wholesale
direct to the public

demi-heure, *pl* **~s** /d(ə)mijœr/ *nf* half
an hour

demi-journée, *pl* **~s** /d(ə)miʒurne/ *nf*
half a day; **à la ~** on a half-day basis

démilitariser /demilitarize/ [1] *vtr* to
demilitarize

demi-litre, *pl* **~s** /d(ə)militr/ *nm* half a
litre (GB)

demi-mesure, *pl* **~s** /d(ə)mim(ə)zyr/ *nf*
half-measure

demi-mot: à demi-mot /ad(ə)mimo/ *phr*
j'ai compris à ~ I didn't need to have it spelt
out

déminer /demine/ [1] *vtr* to clear [sth] of
mines

demi-pension /d(ə)mipɑ̃sjɔ̃/ *nf* half
board

demi-pensionnaire, *pl* **~s**
/d(ə)mipɑ̃sjɔnɛr/ *nmf* (Sch) pupil who has
school lunches

démis, ~e /demi, iz/ **1** *pp* ▶ DÉMETTRE
2 *pp adj* dislocated

demi-sel /d(ə)misɛl/ *adj* ⟨butter⟩ slightly
salted

demi-sœur, *pl* **~s** /d(ə)misœr/ *nf* half-
sister; stepsister

démission /demisjɔ̃/ *nf* **(a)** resignation
(**de** from)
(b) (figurative) failure to take responsibility

démissionner /demisjɔne/ [1] *vi* **(a)** to
resign (**de** from)
(b) to abdicate one's responsibilities

demi-tarif, *pl* **~s** /d(ə)mitarif/ **1** *adj*
half-price
2 *adv* half-price
3 *nm* half-price ticket

demi-tour, *pl* **~s** /d(ə)mitur/ *nm* half-
turn; **faire ~** to turn back

démobiliser /demobilize/ [1] *vtr* **(a)** to
demobilize
(b) to demotivate

démocrate /demɔkrat/ **1** *adj*
democratic
2 *nmf* democrat

✓ **démocratie** /demɔkrasi/ *nf* democracy

démocratique /demɔkratik/ *adj*
democratic

démocratiser: se démocratiser
/demɔkratize/ [1] *v refl* (+ *v être*) **(a)** to
become more democratic
(b) to become more accessible

démodé, ~e /demɔde/ *adj* old-fashioned

✓ indicates a very frequent word

démoder: se **démoder** /demɔde/ [1] *v*
refl (+ *v être*) to go out of fashion

démographie /demɔgʀafi/ *nf*
demography

démographique /demɔgʀafik/ *adj*
demographic

demoiselle /d(ə)mwazɛl/ *nf* (a) young
lady
(b) single woman
■ ∼ d'honneur bridesmaid

démolir /demɔliʀ/ [3] *vtr* to demolish; to
wreck; to destroy

démolition /demɔlisjɔ̃/ *nf* demolition

démon /demɔ̃/ *nm* demon, devil
■ ∼ de midi ≈ middle-age lust

démoniaque /demɔnjak/ *adj* demonic

démonstrateur, -trice
/demɔ̃stʀatœʀ, tʀis/ *nm,f* (for
products) demonstrator

démonstratif, -ive /demɔ̃stʀatif, iv/ *adj*
demonstrative

démonstration /demɔ̃stʀasjɔ̃/ *nf*
(a) display; ∼ de courage display of
courage; ∼s d'amitié a show of friendship
(b) demonstration
(c) (of theory) demonstration, proof

démontable /demɔ̃tabl/ *adj* ‹furniture›
that can be taken apart

démonté, ∼e /demɔ̃te/ *adj* ‹sea› stormy

démonte-pneu, *pl* ∼s /demɔ̃t(ə)pnø/ *nm*
tyre-lever (GB), tire iron (US)

démonter /demɔ̃te/ [1] **1** *vtr* (a) to
dismantle, to take [sth] to pieces ‹machine›;
to remove ‹wheel›
(b) (fam) to fluster; ne pas se laisser ∼ to
remain unruffled
2 se **démonter** *v refl* (+ *v être*)
(a) ‹furniture› to come apart
(b) (fam) ‹person› to become flustered

✔ **démontrer** /demɔ̃tʀe/ [1] *vtr* to
demonstrate, to prove

démoralisant, ∼e /demɔʀalizɑ̃, ɑ̃t/ *adj*
demoralizing

démoraliser /demɔʀalize/ [1] *vtr* to
demoralize

démordre /demɔʀdʀ/ [6] *v+prep* il n'en
démord pas he sticks by it, he's sticking to it

démotiver /demɔtive/ *vtr* demotivate

démouler /demule/ [1] *vtr* to turn [sth]
out of the tin (GB) *or* pan (US) ‹cake›; to
remove [sth] from the mould (GB) *or* mold
(US) ‹statue›

démultiplier /demyltiplije/ [2] *vtr* (a) to
reduce ‹speed›
(b) to increase ‹powers, capacity›

démuni, ∼e /demyni/ *adj* destitute;
penniless; ∼ de devoid of, without ‹talent›

démunir /demyniʀ/ [3] **1** *vtr* to divest
(de of)
2 se **démunir** *v refl* (+ *v être*) se ∼ de
qch to leave oneself without sth

démystifier /demistifje/ [2] *vtr* (a) ∼ qn
to dispel sb's illusions
(b) to demystify

démythifier /demitifje/ [2] *vtr* to
demythologize

dénatalité /denatalite/ *nf* fall in the
birthrate

dénationaliser /denasjɔnalize/ [1] *vtr* to
denationalize

dénaturé, ∼e /denatyʀe/ *adj* (a) ‹alcohol›
denatured
(b) ‹tastes› warped; ‹parents› unnatural

dénaturer /denatyʀe/ [1] *vtr* (a) to
denature
(b) to distort ‹facts›
(c) to spoil ‹taste, sauce›

dénicher /denife/ [1] *vtr* (a) (fam) to dig out
(colloq) ‹object›; to track down ‹person›; to find
‹right address›
(b) to flush out ‹thief, animal›

dénier /denje/ [2] *vtr* to deny

deniers /dənje/ *nm pl* money; ∼s publics
or de l'État public funds

dénigrement /denigʀəmɑ̃/ *nm*
denigration

dénigrer /denigʀe/ [1] *vtr* to denigrate

dénivellation /denivɛlasjɔ̃/ *nf*
(a) difference in level
(b) gradient

dénombrable /denɔ̃bʀabl/ *adj* countable;
non ∼ uncountable

dénombrement /denɔ̃bʀəmɑ̃/ *nm* count

dénombrer /denɔ̃bʀe/ [1] *vtr* to count

dénomination /denɔminasjɔ̃/ *nf* name,
designation

dénommer /denɔme/ [1] *vtr* to name

dénoncer /denɔ̃se/ [12] **1** *vtr* to
denounce
2 se **dénoncer** *v refl* (+ *v être*) to give
oneself up

dénonciation /denɔ̃sjasjɔ̃/ *nf*
denunciation

dénoter /denɔte/ [1] *vtr* denote

dénouement /denumɑ̃/ *nm*
(a) denouement
(b) outcome

dénouer /denwe/ [1] **1** *vtr* (a) to undo
‹knot›
(b) to unravel ‹intrigue›; to resolve ‹crisis›
2 se **dénouer** *v refl* (+ *v être*) (a) ‹laces›
to come undone
(b) ‹crisis› to resolve itself

dénoyauter /denwajote/ [1] *vtr* to stone
(GB), to pit (US)

denrée /dɑ̃ʀe/ *nf* (a) foodstuff; ∼ de base
staple
(b) commodity

dense /dɑ̃s/ *adj* dense; concentrated; heavy

densité /dɑ̃site/ *nf* (a) density
(b) denseness

d

✦ **dent** /dɑ̃/ nf **(a)** tooth; **à pleines** or **belles ~s**
with relish; **ne rien avoir à se mettre sous la
~** to have nothing to eat
(b) (of comb) tooth; (of fork) prong; **en ~s de
scie** ‹blade› serrated; ‹results› which go up
and down
(c) crag
■ **~ de lait** milk tooth
IDIOMS avoir une ~ contre qn to bear
sb a grudge; **avoir les ~s longues** to be
ambitious

dentaire /dɑ̃tɛʀ/ adj dental

denté, ~e /dɑ̃te/ adj **(a)** toothed
(b) dentate

dentelé, ~e /dɑ̃t(ə)le/ adj ‹coast› indented;
‹crest› jagged; ‹stamp› perforated; ‹leaf›
dentate

dentelle /dɑ̃tɛl/ nf lace
IDIOM il ne fait pas dans la ~ he's not one to
bother with niceties

dentelure /dɑ̃tlyʀ/ nf (of stamp)
perforation; (of crest) jagged outline; (of
leaf) serration

dentier /dɑ̃tje/ nm dentures

dentifrice /dɑ̃tifʀis/ nm toothpaste

dentiste /dɑ̃tist/ nmf dentist

dentition /dɑ̃tisjɔ̃/ nf dentition

dénuder /denyde/ [1] **1** vtr to strip
2 se dénuder v refl (+ v être) **(a)** to strip
(off)
(b) to become bare

dénué, ~e /denɥe/ adj **~ de** lacking in; **~
de sens** senseless

dénuement /denɥmɑ̃/ nm destitution;
bareness

déodorant, ~e /deɔdɔʀɑ̃, ɑ̃t/ **1** adj
deodorant
2 nm deodorant

déontologie /deɔ̃tɔlɔʒi/ nf
(professional) ethics

dépannage /depanaʒ/ nm repair

dépanner /depane/ [1] vtr **(a)** to fix ‹car,
machine›
(b) to tow away
(c) (fam) to help [sb] out

dépanneur, -euse¹ /depanœʀ, øz/ nm,f
engineer

dépanneuse² /depanøz/ nf breakdown
truck (GB), tow truck (US)

dépareillé, ~e /depaʀeje/ adj **(a)** odd;
articles ~s oddments
(b) incomplete

déparer /depaʀe/ [1] vtr to spoil, to mar

✦ **départ** /depaʀ/ nm **(a)** departure; **~
des grandes lignes** main line departures;
téléphone avant ton ~ phone before you
leave; **être sur le ~** to be about to leave
(b) resignation; **le ~ en retraite** retirement
(c) (gen, Sport) start; **donner le (signal du) ~**

─────────────────
✦ indicates a very frequent word

aux coureurs to start the race; **prendre un
nouveau ~** (figurative) to make a fresh start;
au ~ at first; at the outset; **de ~** initial;
‹language› source; ‹salary› starting

départager /depaʀtaʒe/ [13] vtr to decide
between ‹competitors›

département /depaʀtəmɑ̃/ nm
department

départemental, ~e, mpl **-aux**
/depaʀtəmɑ̃tal, o/ adj ‹election› local; ‹road›
secondary

dépassé, ~e /depɑse/ adj **(a)** outdated,
outmoded
(b) (fam) overwhelmed

dépassement /depɑsmɑ̃/ nm
(a) overtaking
(b) overrun; **~ d'horaire** overrunning
the schedule; **le ~ de la dose prescrite**
exceeding the stated dose
(c) **~ de soi** surpassing oneself
■ **~ budgétaire** cost overrun; **~ de capacité**
(Comput) overflow

✦ **dépasser** /depɑse/ [1] **1** vtr **(a)** to
overtake (GB), to pass (US) ‹car, pedestrian›;
to go past ‹place›
(b) to exceed ‹figure, dose, limit›; **elle le
dépasse de cinq centimètres** she's five
centimetres (GB) taller than him; **il a
dépassé la cinquantaine** he's over or past
fifty; **~ la mesure** or **les bornes** to go too far
(c) to be ahead of, to outstrip ‹rival›; **ça me
dépasse!** it's beyond me!
2 vi to jut or stick out; ‹underskirt› to show

dépassionner /depɑsjɔne/ [1] vtr to
defuse ‹discussion›

dépatouiller: se dépatouiller
/depatuje/ [1] v refl (+ v être) (fam) to get by

dépaysé, ~e /depeize/ adj **il est
complètement ~** he's like a fish out of water;
il n'est pas ~ ici he feels at home here

dépaysement /depeizmɑ̃/ nm **(a)** change
of scenery
(b) disorientation

dépayser /depeize/ [1] vtr **(a)** to provide
[sb] with a pleasant change of scenery
(b) to disorient

dépecer /dep(ə)se/ [16] vtr to tear apart,
to cut up

dépêche /depɛʃ/ nf dispatch

dépêcher /depeʃe/ [16] **1** vtr to dispatch
(à to)
2 se dépêcher v refl (+ v être) to hurry
up

dépeigné, ~e /depeɲe/ adj dishevelled
(GB)

dépeindre /depɛ̃dʀ/ [55] vtr to depict

dépenaillé, ~e /depənaje/ adj ragged

dépénaliser /depenalize/ [1] vtr to
decriminalize

dépendance /depɑ̃dɑ̃s/ nf
(a) dependence, dependency

(b) outbuilding

(c) dependency, dependent territory

dépendant, **~e** /depɑ̃dɑ̃, ɑ̃t/ *adj* dependent (**de** on); **~s l'un de l'autre** interdependent

⚜ **dépendre** /depɑ̃dʀ/ [6] *v+prep* **(a)** **~ de** to depend on

(b) **~ de** to be dependent on

(c) **~ de** ‹*organization*› to come under the control of; ‹*employee*› to be responsible to

(d) **~ de** ‹*environment*› to be the responsibility of

(e) **~ de** ‹*territory*› to be a dependency of

(f) **~ de** ‹*building, land*› to belong to

dépens /depɑ̃/ *nm pl* **aux ~ de** at the expense of; **vivre aux ~ des autres** to live off other people

dépense /depɑ̃s/ *nf* **(a)** spending, expenditure; **~s publiques** public expenditure

(b) expense; **réduire ses ~s** to cut down on expenses

(c) outlay; **une ~ de 300 euros** an outlay of 300 euros

(d) consumption; **~ d'énergie physique** expenditure of physical energy

dépenser /depɑ̃se/ [1] **1** *vtr* to spend ‹*money, time*›; to use up ‹*energy, fuel*›

2 **se dépenser** *v refl* (*+ v être*) to get (enough) exercise

dépensier, -ière /depɑ̃sje, ɛʀ/ *adj* extravagant

déperdition /depɛʀdisjɔ̃/ *nf* loss

dépérir /depeʀiʀ/ [3] *vi* ‹*person*› to waste away; ‹*plant*› to wilt; ‹*economy*› to be on the decline

dépêtrer: **se dépêtrer** /depɛtʀe/ [1] *v refl* (*+ v être*) **se ~ de** to extricate oneself from

dépeuplement /depœpləmɑ̃/ *nm* depopulation

dépeupler /depœple/ [1] *vtr* to depopulate ‹*region*›; to reduce the wildlife in ‹*forest*›

déphasé, ~e /defɑze/ *adj* **(a)** (fam) out of step

(b) out of phase

dépiauter /depjote/ [1] *vtr* (fam) to skin ‹*animal*›

dépilation /depilasjɔ̃/ *nf* hair removal

dépilatoire /depilatwaʀ/ *adj* depilatory, hair-removing

dépistable /depistabl/ *adj* detectable

dépistage /depistaʒ/ *nm* screening (**de** for); **test de ~ du sida** Aids test

dépister /depiste/ [1] *vtr* **(a)** to track down ‹*criminal, game*›

(b) to detect ‹*illness*›

dépit /depi/ **1** *nm* pique; **par ~** out of pique

2 **en dépit de** *phr* in spite of; **en ~ du bon sens** in a very illogical way

dépité, ~e /depite/ *adj* piqued (**de** at)

déplacé, ~e /deplase/ *adj* inappropriate; **c'est ~** it's out of place; it's uncalled for

déplacement /deplasmɑ̃/ *nm* **(a)** trip; **ça vaut le ~!** it's worth the trip!; **frais de ~** travelling (GB) expenses

(b) moving; shifting; transfer (**vers** to)

(c) displacement

■ **~ de vertèbre** slipped disc

⚜ **déplacer** /deplase/ [12] **1** *vtr* to move ‹*object, person*›; to displace ‹*population*›; to shift ‹*attention*›; to change ‹*issue*›

2 **se déplacer** *v refl* (*+ v être*) **(a)** to move; **se ~ une vertèbre** to slip a disc

(b) to get about; to travel

(c) ‹*doctor*› to go out on call

déplaire /deplɛʀ/ [59] **1** *vi* **le spectacle a déplu** the show was not well received

2 **déplaire à** *v+prep* **cela m'a déplu** I didn't like it; **la situation n'est pas pour me ~** the situation quite suits me

3 *v impers* **ne vous en déplaise** (ironic) whether you like it or not

déplaisant, ~e /deplɛzɑ̃, ɑ̃t/ *adj* unpleasant

déplâtrer /deplɑtʀe/ [1] *vtr* to remove the cast from ‹*limb*›

dépliant /deplijɑ̃/ *nm* **(a)** leaflet

(b) fold-out page

déplier /deplije/ [2] *vtr* to unfold ‹*newspaper*›; to open out ‹*map*›

déploiement /deplwamɑ̃/ *nm* **(a)** display; array

(b) deployment

déplorable /deplɔʀabl/ *adj* **(a)** regrettable

(b) appalling, deplorable

déplorer /deplɔʀe/ [1] *vtr* to deplore

déployer /deplwaje/ [23] *vtr* **(a)** to display ‹*talent, wealth*›; to expend ‹*energy*›

(b) to deploy ‹*troops*›

(c) to spread ‹*wings*›; to unfurl ‹*sail*›

déplumer: **se déplumer** /deplyme/ [1] *v refl* (*+ v être*) ‹*bird*› to lose its feathers

dépoli, ~e /depɔli/ *adj* **verre ~** frosted glass

dépolitiser /depɔlitize/ [1] *vtr* to depoliticize

dépolluer /depɔlɥe/ [1] *vtr* to rid [sth] of pollution, to clean up

dépollution /depɔlysjɔ̃/ *nf* cleanup

dépopulation /depɔpylasjɔ̃/ *nf* depopulation

déportation /depɔʀtasjɔ̃/ *nf* **(a)** internment in a concentration camp

(b) deportation

déporté, ~e /depɔʀte/ *nm,f* **(a)** prisoner interned in a concentration camp

(b) transported convict

déporter /depɔʀte/ [1] **1** *vtr* **(a)** to send [sb] to a concentration camp

(b) to deport

2 **se déporter** *v refl* (*+ v être*) to swerve

déposant, ∼**e** /depozɑ̃, ɑ̃t/ *nm,f*
(a) depositor
(b) deponent

ℐ **déposer** /depoze/ [1] ① *vtr* (a) to dump
‹*rubbish*›; to lay ‹*wreath*›; to drop off, to leave
‹*parcel, passenger*›; to deposit ‹*money*›; ∼ **les
armes** to lay down one's arms
(b) to register ‹*trademark*›; to submit ‹*file,
offer*›; to lodge ‹*complaint*›; ∼ **son bilan** to
file a bankruptcy petition
(c) ‹*river*› to deposit ‹*alluvium*›
② *vi* (Law) to make a statement, to testify
③ **se déposer** *v refl* (+ *v être*) ‹*dust*› to
settle; ‹*deposit*› to collect

dépositaire /depozitɛʀ/ *nmf* (a) agent; ∼
agréé authorized dealer
(b) trustee

déposition /depozisjɔ̃/ *nf* (Law) statement;
deposition; evidence

déposséder /deposede/ [14] *vtr* to
dispossess

dépôt /depo/ *nm* (a) warehouse; depot
(b) outlet; **l'épicerie fait** ∼ **de pain** the
grocer's sells bread
(c) (of trademark) registration; (of
bill) introduction
(d) **date limite de** ∼ **des déclarations d'impôt**
deadline for income tax returns
(e) deposit
(f) police cells
■ ∼ **de bilan** voluntary liquidation; ∼
d'ordures (rubbish) tip *or* dump (GB);
garbage dump (US)

dépotoir /depotwaʀ/ *nm* (a) dump
(b) (fam) shambles (colloq)

dépôt-vente, *pl* **dépôts-ventes**
/depovɑ̃t/ *nm* secondhand shop (GB) *or* store
(*where goods are sold on commission*)

dépouille /depuj/ *nf* (a) skin, hide
(b) body; ∼ **mortelle** mortal remains
(c) ∼**s** spoils

dépouillé, ∼**e** /depuje/ *adj* (a) ‹*style*› spare
(b) ‹*tree*› bare

dépouillement /depujmɑ̃/ *nm* (a) (of
votes) counting, count; (of mail) going through
(b) asceticism
(c) (of style) sobriety

dépouiller /depuje/ [1] *vtr* (a) to skin
‹*animal*›
(b) to lay [sth] bare ‹*region*›
(c) to rob ‹*person*›
(d) to count ‹*votes*›; to go through ‹*mail*›

dépourvu, ∼**e** /depuʀvy/ ① *adj* ∼ **de**
devoid of ‹*interest, charm*›; without ‹*heating*›
② *nm* **prendre qn au** ∼ to take sb by surprise

dépoussiérer /depusjere/ [14] *vtr* to dust;
(figurative) to revamp

dépravation /depʀavasjɔ̃/ *nf* depravity

dépraver /depʀave/ [1] *vtr* to deprave

dépréciation /depʀesjasjɔ̃/ *nf*
depreciation

ℐ indicates a very frequent word

déprécier /depʀesje/ [2] *vtr* (a) to
depreciate
(b) to disparage, to depreciate

déprédateur, **-trice** /depʀedatœʀ, tʀis/
nm,f vandal

déprédations /depʀedasjɔ̃/ *nf pl* damage

dépressif, **-ive** /depʀesif, iv/ *adj, nm,f*
depressive

dépression /depʀesjɔ̃/ *nf* depression;
∼ **nerveuse** nervous breakdown

dépressurisation /depʀesyʀizasjɔ̃/ *nf*
(a) depressurization
(b) loss of pressure

déprimant, ∼**e** /depʀimɑ̃, ɑ̃t/ *adj*
depressing

déprime /depʀim/ *nf* (fam) depression

déprimer /depʀime/ [1] ① *vtr* to depress
② *vi* (fam) to be depressed

déprogrammer /depʀogʀame/ [1] *vtr* to
cancel

ℐ **depuis** /dəpɥi/ ① *adv* since; ∼ **je n'ai
plus de nouvelles** since then I haven't had
any news
② *prep* (a) since; ∼ **quand vis-tu là-bas?**
how long have you been living there?; ∼ **le
début jusqu'à la fin** from start to finish
(b) for; **il pleut** ∼ **trois jours** it's been raining
for three days; ∼ **quand?** how long?; ∼ **peu**
recently; ∼ **toujours** always
(c) from; ∼ **ma fenêtre** from my window
③ **depuis que** *phr* since, ever since; **il
pleut** ∼ **que nous sommes arrivés** it's been
raining ever since we arrived

député /depyte/ *nm* (a) (in politics) deputy;
(in GB) member of Parliament; **être** ∼ **au
Parlement européen** to be a Euro-MP *or*
member of the European Parliament
(b) representative

député-maire, *pl* **députés-maires**
/depytemɛʀ/ *nm* deputy and mayor

déqualifier /dekalifje/ [2] *vtr* to deskill

der /dɛʀ/ *nf* (fam) last; **la** ∼ **des** ∼**s** the war
to end all wars

déraciné, ∼**e** /deʀasine/ *nm,f* uprooted
person

déracinement /deʀasinmɑ̃/ *nm*
(a) uprooting
(b) rootlessness

déraciner /deʀasine/ [1] *vtr* (a) to uproot
(b) to eradicate ‹*prejudice*›

déraillement /deʀajmɑ̃/ *nm* derailment

dérailler /deʀaje/ [1] *vi* (a) to be derailed;
faire ∼ **un train** to derail a train
(b) (fam) to lose one's marbles (colloq); to talk
through one's hat (colloq)

dérailleur /deʀajœʀ/ *nm* derailleur

déraisonnable /deʀɛzɔnabl/ *adj*
unrealistic; senseless; unreasonable

déraisonner /deʀɛzɔne/ [1] *vi* to talk
nonsense

dérangé, ∼**e** /deʀɑ̃ʒe/ *adj* (a) upset
(b) (fam) deranged

dérangeant, ~e /deʀɑ̃ʒɑ̃, ɑ̃t/ *adj*
disturbing

dérangement /deʀɑ̃ʒmɑ̃/ *nm* **(a)** trouble, inconvenience
(b) ~ **intestinal** stomach upset
(c) être en ~ ‹*lift, phone*› to be out of order

déranger /deʀɑ̃ʒe/ [13] ▯ *vtr* to disturb ‹*person*›; to upset ‹*routine, plans*›; to affect ‹*mind*›; **excusez-moi de vous** ~ (I'm) sorry to bother you; **est-ce que la fumée vous dérange?** do you mind if I smoke?
▯ **se déranger** *v refl* (+ *v être*) **(a)** to go out, to come out; **je me suis dérangé pour rien, c'était fermé** I wasted my time going there, it was shut
(b) to get up; to move
(c) to put oneself out

dérapage /deʀapaʒ/ *nm* **(a)** skid
(b) blunder
(c) loss of control

déraper /deʀape/ [1] ▯ *vi* **(a)** ‹*prices, discussion*› to get out of control
(b) ‹*knife*› to slip
(c) to skid
(d) ‹*skier*› to sideslip

dératisation /deʀatizasjɔ̃/ *nf* pest control (*for rats*)

déréglé, ~e /deʀegle/ *adj* ‹*mind*› unbalanced; ‹*life*› irregular; ‹*mechanism*› out, disturbed

dérèglement /deʀɛɡləmɑ̃/ *nm* **(a)** (in machine) fault
(b) disorder

déréglementer /deʀegləmɑ̃te/ [1] *vtr* to deregulate

dérégler /deʀegle/ [14] *vtr* to affect ‹*weather, organ*›; to upset ‹*process, mechanism*›; ~ **la radio** to lose the station on the radio; ~ **le réveil** to set the alarm clock wrong

dérider /deʀide/ [1] ▯ *vtr* to cheer [sb] up
▯ **se dérider** *v refl* (+ *v être*) to start smiling

dérision /deʀizjɔ̃/ *nf* scorn, derision; **tourner qn/qch en** ~ to ridicule sb/sth

dérisoire /deʀizwaʀ/ *adj* pathetic; trivial

dérivatif, **-ive** /deʀivatif, iv/ ▯ *adj* derivative
▯ *nm* **(a)** diversion (à from)
(b) (Med) derivative

dérivation /deʀivasjɔ̃/ *nf* diversion (GB), detour

dérive /deʀiv/ *nf* drift; **à la** ~ adrift

dérivé, ~e /deʀive/ *nm* by-product

dériver /deʀive/ [1] ▯ **dériver de** *v+prep* **(a)** ~ **de** to stem from
(b) ~ **de** to be derived from
▯ *vi* to drift

dermatologie /dɛʀmatɔlɔʒi/ *nf* dermatology

derme /dɛʀm/ *nm* dermis

✦ **dernier**, **-ière**[1] /dɛʀnje, ɛʀ/ ▯ *adj*
(a) last; ‹*floor, shelf*› top; **je les veux jeudi** ~ **délai** I want them by Thursday at the latest
(b) latest; **les dernières nouvelles** the latest news; **ces** ~ **temps** recently
(c) **du** ~ **ridicule** utterly ridiculous; **c'était la dernière chose à faire** it was the worst possible thing to do
▯ *nm,f* last; **arriver le** ~ to arrive last; **c'est bien le** ~ **de mes soucis** that is the least of my worries; **être le** ~ **de la classe** to be bottom of the class; **le petit** ~ the youngest child; **ce** ~ the latter; **le** ~ **des** ~**s** the lowest of the low
▯ **en dernier** *phr* last; **j'irai chez eux en** ~ I'll go to them last
■ ~ **cri** latest fashion; **dernières volontés** last requests

dernière[2] /dɛʀnjɛʀ/ *nf* **(a)** **la** ~ the latest
(b) last performance

dernièrement /dɛʀnjɛʀmɑ̃/ *adv* recently

dernier-né, **dernière-née**, *mpl* **derniers-nés** /dɛʀnjene, dɛʀnjɛʀne/ *nm,f*
(a) youngest (child)
(b) latest model

dérobade /deʀɔbad/ *nf* evasion

dérobé, ~e /deʀɔbe/ ▯ *adj* ‹*door, stairs*› concealed
▯ **à la dérobée** *phr* furtively

dérober /deʀɔbe/ [1] ▯ *vtr* to steal
▯ **se dérober** *v refl* (+ *v être*) **(a)** to be evasive
(b) to shirk responsibility
(c) **se** ~ **à** to shirk ‹*duty*›
(d) ‹*ground, knees*› to give way

dérogation /deʀɔgasjɔ̃/ *nf*
(a) (special) dispensation
(b) infringement (à of)

dérogatoire /deʀɔgatwaʀ/ *adj* special; **clause** ~ derogation clause

déroger /deʀɔʒe/ [13] *v+prep* ~ **à** to infringe ‹*law*›; to depart from ‹*principles*›; to ignore ‹*obligation*›; to break with ‹*tradition*›

dérouiller /deʀuje/ [1] (fam) *vi* to get a hiding (colloq) or beating; to suffer

déroulant /deʀulɑ̃/ *adj* **menu** ~ pop-up menu

déroulement /deʀulmɑ̃/ *nm* **(a)** **le** ~ **des événements** the sequence of events; **veiller au bon** ~ **de** to make sure [sth] goes smoothly; ~ **de carrière** career development
(b) uncoiling, unwinding

✦ **dérouler** /deʀule/ [1] ▯ *vtr* to unroll ‹*carpet*›; to uncoil ‹*rope*›; to unwind ‹*wire, film*›
▯ **se dérouler** *v refl* (+ *v être*) **(a)** to take place
(b) ‹*negotiations*› to proceed; ‹*story*› to unfold

déroutant, ~e /deʀutɑ̃, ɑ̃t/ *adj* puzzling

déroute /deʀut/ *nf* crushing defeat, rout; **mettre en** ~ to rout; **en** ~ in disarray

d

dérouter /deʀute/ [1] *vtr* **(a)** to puzzle
(b) to divert

⟨ **derrière¹** /dɛʀjɛʀ/ **1** *prep* behind; ∼ **les
apparences** beneath the surface; **il faut
toujours être** ∼ **son dos** you have to keep
after him
2 *adv* behind; (of room) at the back; (in
car) in the back

derrière² /dɛʀjɛʀ/ *nm* **(a)** (of house,
object) back; **de** ∼ ⟨*bedroom*⟩ back
(b) (fam) behind (colloq), backside (colloq)

des /de/ **1** *det* ▸ UN 1
2 *det* ▸ DE

⟨ **dès** /dɛ/ **1** *prep* from; ∼ **(l'âge de) huit ans**
from the age of eight; ∼ **maintenant** straight
away; **je vous téléphone** ∼ **mon arrivée** I'll
phone you as soon as I arrive; ∼ **Versailles il
y a des embouteillages** there are traffic jams
from Versailles onwards
2 **dès que** *phr* as soon as
3 **dès lors** *phr* **(a)** from then on, from
that time on, henceforth
(b) therefore, consequently
4 **dès lors que** *phr* **(a)** once, from the
moment that
(b) since

désabonner: **se désabonner**
/dezabɔne/ [1] *v refl* (+ *v être*) (gen) to
cancel one's subscription (à to); (Comput) to
unsubscribe

désabusé, ∼**e** /dezabyze/ *adj*
disillusioned; cynical

désaccord /dezakɔʀ/ *nm* disagreement;
être en ∼ to disagree (**avec** with; **sur** over)

désaccordé, ∼**e** /dezakɔʀde/ *adj* out-
of-tune

désaccoutumer: **se désaccoutumer**
/dezakutyme/ [1] *v refl* **se** ∼ **de qch** to break
one's dependence on sth

désactiver /dezaktive/ *vt* to deactivate

désaffecté, ∼**e** /dezafɛkte/ *adj* disused

désaffection /dezafɛksjɔ̃/ *nf* disaffection
(**pour** with)

désagréable /dezagʀeabl/ *adj*
unpleasant

désagrégation /dezagʀegasjɔ̃/ *nf*
disintegration, break-up, collapse

désagréger: **se désagréger**
/dezagʀeʒe/ [15] *v refl* (+ *v être*) to
disintegrate, to break up

désagrément /dezagʀemɑ̃/ *nm*
inconvenience

désaltérant, ∼**e** /dezalteʀɑ̃, ɑ̃t/ *adj*
thirst-quenching

désaltérer /dezalteʀe/ [14] **1** *vtr* ∼ **qn** to
quench sb's thirst
2 **se désaltérer** *v refl* (+ *v être*) to
quench one's thirst

désamorcer /dezamɔʀse/ [12] *vtr* to
defuse ⟨*explosive, crisis*⟩; to drain ⟨*pump*⟩

⟨ indicates a very frequent word

désappointement /dezapwɛ̃tmɑ̃/ *nm*
disappointment

désappointer /dezapwɛ̃te/ [1] *vtr* to
disappoint

désapprobateur, -trice
/dezapʀɔbatœʀ, tʀis/ *adj* disapproving

désapprobation /dezapʀɔbasjɔ̃/ *nf*
disapproval

désapprouver /dezapʀuve/ [1] *vtr* to
disapprove of

désarçonner /dezaʀsɔne/ [1] *vtr* **(a)** to
throw ⟨*rider*⟩
(b) to take [sb] aback

désargenté, ∼**e** /dezaʀʒɑ̃te/ *adj*
(fam) hard up (colloq), penniless

désarmant, ∼**e** /dezaʀmɑ̃, ɑ̃t/ *adj*
disarming

désarmé, ∼**e** /dezaʀme/ **1** *pp*
▸ DÉSARMER
2 *pp adj* **(a)** disarmed
(b) ⟨*ship*⟩ laid up

désarmement /dezaʀməmɑ̃/ *nm*
(a) disarmament
(b) (of ship) laying up

désarmer /dezaʀme/ [1] **1** *vtr* **(a)** to
disarm
(b) to lay up ⟨*ship*⟩
2 *vi* **(a)** to disarm
(b) ⟨*person*⟩ to give up the fight; ⟨*anger*⟩ to
abate

désarroi /dezaʀwa/ *nm* distress; confusion

désarticulé, ∼**e** /dezaʀtikyle/ *adj* ⟨*chair*⟩
wrecked; ⟨*puppet*⟩ with broken joints

désastre /dezastʀ/ *nm* disaster

désastreux, -euse /dezastʀø, øz/ *adj*
disastrous

désavantage /dezavɑ̃taʒ/ *nm*
(a) disadvantage
(b) drawback, disadvantage

désavantager /dezavɑ̃taʒe/ [13]
vtr to put [sb/sth] at a disadvantage, to
disadvantage

désavantageux, -euse
/dezavɑ̃taʒø, øz/ *adj* unfavourable (GB),
disadvantageous

désaveu /dezavø/ *nm* **(a)** denial
(b) rejection

désavouer /dezavwe/ [1] *vtr* **(a)** to deny
(b) to disown

désaxé, ∼**e** /dezakse/ **1** *pp* ▸ DÉSAXER
2 *pp adj* deranged
3 *nm,f* deranged person

désaxer /dezakse/ [1] *vtr* **(a)** to put [sth]
out of true ⟨*wheel*⟩
(b) to unbalance ⟨*person*⟩

desceller /desele/ [1] **1** *vtr* to work [sth]
free
2 **se desceller** *v refl* (+ *v être*) to work
loose

descendance /desɑ̃dɑ̃s/ *nf* descendants

descendant, ~e /desãdã, ãt/ *nm,f*
descendant

⚹ **descendre** /dɛsãdʀ/ [6] **1** *vtr* (+ *v
avoir*) **(a)** to take [sb/sth] down (**à** to), to
bring [sb/sth] down (**de** from)
(b) to lower ‹*shelf, blind*›; to wind [sth] down
‹*window*›
(c) to go down, to come down ‹*road, steps,
river*›; ~ **la rivière à la nage** to swim down
the river
(d) (fam) to bump off (colloq) ‹*person*›; to shoot
down ‹*plane*›
(e) (fam) to down ‹*bottle*›
2 *vi* (+ *v être*) **(a)** to go down (**à** to), to
come down (**de** from); ‹*night*› to fall; **tu es
descendu à pied?** did you walk down?; **la
route descend en pente douce** the road
slopes down gently
(b) ~ **de** to step off ‹*step*›; to get off ‹*train,
bike, horse*›; to get out of ‹*car*›
(c) ‹*temperature, prices*› to drop, to go down;
‹*tide*› to go out
(d) ~ **dans le Midi** to go down to the South
(of France)
(e) ~ **dans un hôtel** to stay at a hotel
(f) ~ **de** to be descended from

descente /desãt/ *nf* **(a)** descent; **la** ~ **a
pris une heure** it took an hour to come down
(b) **à ma** ~ **du train** when I got off the train
(c) ~ **de police** police raid; **la police a fait
une** ~ **dans l'immeuble** the police raided the
building
(d) (in skiing) downhill (event)
■ ~ **de lit** (bedside) rug

descriptif, -ive /deskʀiptif, iv/ *adj*
descriptive

⚹ **description** /deskʀipsjɔ̃/ *nf* description;
faire une ~ **de qch** to describe sth

désembuer /dezãbɥe/ [1] *vtr* to demist
(GB), to defog (US)

désemparé, ~e /dezãpaʀe/ **1** *pp*
▶ DÉSEMPARER
2 *pp adj* distraught, at a loss

désemparer /dezãpaʀe/ [1] *vtr* to throw
[sb] into confusion

désemplir /dezãpliʀ/ [3] *vi* **ne pas** ~ to be
always full

désenchanté, ~e /dezãʃãte/ *adj*
disillusioned, disenchanted (**de** with)

désenchantement /dezãʃãtmã/ *nm*
disillusionment, disenchantment

désenclaver /dezãklave/ [1] *vtr* to open
up ‹*region*›

désendettement /dezãdɛtmã/ *nm*
reduction of the debt

désenfler /dezãfle/ [1] *vi* to become less
swollen, to go down

désengagement /dezãɡaʒmã/ *nm*
(a) (Econ) disengagement
(b) withdrawal (**de** from)

désengager: se désengager
/dezãɡaʒe/ [13] *v refl* (+ *v être*) to withdraw

(de from)

désensibiliser /desãsibilize/ [1] *vtr* to
desensitize

désenvoûter /dezãvute/ [1] *vtr* to break
the spell on

désépaissir /dezepesiʀ/ [3] *vtr* **(a)** to thin
‹*sauce*›
(b) to thin [sth] out ‹*hair*›

déséquilibre /dezekilibʀ/ *nm*
(a) unsteadiness; **en** ~ ‹*table*› unstable;
‹*person*› off balance
(b) imbalance
(c) derangement

déséquilibré, ~e /dezekilibʀe/ **1** *pp*
▶ DÉSÉQUILIBRER
2 *pp adj* (Med) unbalanced
3 *nm,f* lunatic

déséquilibrer /dezekilibʀe/ [1] *vtr* **(a)** to
make [sb] lose their balance; to make [sth]
unstable
(b) to destabilize ‹*country*›
(c) (Med) to unbalance

⚹ **désert**, ~e /dezɛʀ, ɛʀt/ **1** *adj*
(a) uninhabited; **île** ~e desert island
(b) deserted
2 *nm* desert

déserter /dezɛʀte/ [1] *vtr, vi* to desert

déserteur /dezɛʀtœʀ/ *nm* deserter

désertion /dezɛʀsjɔ̃/ *nf* **(a)** desertion
(b) defection

désertique /dezɛʀtik/ *adj* **(a)** ‹*climate,
region*› desert
(b) barren

désespérant, ~e /dezɛspeʀã, ãt/ *adj*
‹*person, situation*› hopeless

désespéré, ~e /dezɛspeʀe/ **1** *pp*
▶ DÉSESPÉRER
2 *pp adj* ‹*person*› in despair; ‹*situation*›
hopeless; ‹*attempt*› desperate; **cri** ~ cry of
despair

désespérément /dezɛspeʀemã/ *adv*
despairingly; desperately; hopelessly

désespérer /dezɛspeʀe/ [14] **1** *vtr* to
drive [sb] to despair
2 **désespérer de** *v+prep* ~ **de qn** to
despair of sb; **il ne désespère pas de le
sauver** he hasn't given up hope of saving
him
3 *vi* to despair, to lose hope
4 **se désespérer** *v refl* (+ *v être*) to
despair

désespoir /dezɛspwaʀ/ *nm* despair; **mettre**
or **réduire qn au** ~ to drive sb to despair

déshabillé /dezabije/ *nm* negligee

déshabiller /dezabije/ [1] **1** *vtr* to
undress
2 **se déshabiller** *v refl* (+ *v être*) **(a)** to
undress
(b) to take one's coat off

déshabituer /dezabitɥe/ [1] *vtr* ~ **qn du
tabac** to get sb out of the habit of smoking

désherbant /dezɛRbɑ̃/ nm weedkiller

désherber /dezɛRbe/ [1] vtr to weed

déshérité /dezeRite/ ① pp ▶ DÉSHÉRITER
② pp adj underprivileged; disadvantaged; deprived
③ nm,f les ∼s the underprivileged

déshériter /dezeRite/ [1] vtr to disinherit

déshonorant, ∼e /dezɔnɔRɑ̃, ɑ̃t/ adj dishonourable (GB), degrading

déshonorer /dezɔnɔRe/ [1] ① vtr to bring disgrace on ‹family›; to bring [sth] into disrepute ‹profession›
② se déshonorer v refl (+ v être) to disgrace oneself

déshumaniser /dezymanize/ [1] ① vtr to dehumanize
② se déshumaniser v refl (+ v être) to become dehumanized

déshydratation /dezidRatasjɔ̃/ nf
(a) dehydration
(b) drying

déshydrater /dezidRate/ [1] vtr to dehydrate

desiderata /deziderata/ nm pl wishes

désignation /deziɲasjɔ̃/ nf designation

✓ **désigner** /deziɲe/ [1] vtr (a) ‹word› to designate; ‹triangle› to represent
(b) to point out
(c) to choose; être tout désigné pour to be just right for

désillusion /dezil(l)yzjɔ̃/ nf disillusion

désimlocker /desimlɔke/ [1] vtr to unblock ‹mobile phone›

désincarcérer /dezɛ̃kaRseRe/ [14] vtr to free

désincarné, ∼e /dezɛ̃kaRne/ adj disembodied

désinence /dezinɑ̃s/ nf ending

désinfectant, ∼e /dezɛ̃fɛktɑ̃, ɑ̃t/ ① adj disinfecting
② nm disinfectant

désinfecter /dezɛ̃fɛkte/ [1] vtr to disinfect

désintégrer: se désintégrer /dezɛ̃tegRe/ [14] v refl (+ v être) to disintegrate

désintéressé, ∼e /dezɛ̃teRese/ ① pp ▶ DÉSINTÉRESSER
② pp adj ‹person, act› selfless, unselfish; ‹advice› disinterested

désintéressement /dezɛ̃teRɛsmɑ̃/ nm
(a) disinterestedness; agir avec ∼ to act disinterestedly
(b) (Econ) paying off

désintéresser: se désintéresser /dezɛ̃teRese/ [1] v refl (+ v être) se ∼ de to lose interest in

désintérêt /dezɛ̃teRɛ/ nm lack of interest

désintoxiquer /dezɛ̃tɔksike/ [1] vtr to detoxify; se faire ∼ to undergo detoxification

désinvolte /dezɛ̃vɔlt/ adj casual, offhand

désinvolture /dezɛ̃vɔltyR/ nf casual manner

✓ **désir** /deziR/ nm wish, desire; prendre ses ∼s pour des réalités to delude oneself

désirable /dezirabl/ adj desirable

✓ **désirer** /deziRe/ [1] vtr to want; effets non désirés unwanted effects; que désirez-vous? what would you like?; laisser à ∼ to leave something to be desired

désistement /dezistəmɑ̃/ nm withdrawal

désister: se désister /deziste/ [1] v refl (+ v être) to stand down (GB), to withdraw

désobéir /dezɔbeiR/ [3] v+prep to disobey; ∼ à qn to disobey sb

désobéissance /dezɔbeisɑ̃s/ nf disobedience

désobéissant, ∼e /dezɔbeisɑ̃, ɑ̃t/ adj disobedient

désobligeant, ∼e /dezɔbliʒɑ̃, ɑ̃t/ adj discourteous

désobliger /dezɔbliʒe/ [13] vtr to offend

désodorisant /dezɔdɔRizɑ̃/ nm deodorant

désodoriser /dezɔdɔRize/ [1] vtr to freshen

désœuvré, ∼e /dezœvRe/ adj at a loose end (GB) (colloq), at loose ends (US) (colloq)

désœuvrement /dezœvRəmɑ̃/ nm par ∼ for lack of anything better to do

désolation /dezɔlasjɔ̃/ nf (a) grief
(b) desolation

désolé, ∼e /dezɔle/ ① pp ▶ DÉSOLER
② pp adj (a) sorry
(b) desolate

désoler /dezɔle/ [1] ① vtr (a) to upset, to distress
(b) to depress; tu me désoles! I despair of you!
② se désoler v refl (+ v être) to be upset

désopilant, ∼e /dezɔpilɑ̃, ɑ̃t/ adj hilarious

désordonné, ∼e /dezɔRdɔne/ adj ‹person› untidy; ‹meeting› disorderly; ‹movements› uncoordinated; ‹existence› wild

désordre /dezɔRdR/ ① adj inv (fam) faire ∼ to look untidy or messy
② nm (a) untidiness; mess; pièce en ∼ untidy room; il a tout mis en ∼ he made such a mess
(b) chaos; semer le ∼ to cause chaos
(c) dans le ∼ in any order; gagner dans le ∼ (at races) to win with a combination forecast
(d) disorder; ∼s mentaux mental disorders

désorganisation /dezɔRganizasjɔ̃/ nf disruption; disorganization

désorganisé, ∼e /dezɔRganize/ adj disorganized

désorienter /dezɔRjɑ̃te/ [1] vtr (a) to disorientate (GB)
(b) to confuse, to bewilder

✓ indicates a very frequent word

désormais /dezɔRmɛ/ *adv* **(a)** from now on
(b) from then on

désosser /dezose/ [1] *vtr* (Culin) to bone

despote /dɛspɔt/ *nm* despot

despotique /dɛspɔtik/ *adj* despotic

desquelles ▸ LEQUEL

desquels ▸ LEQUEL

DESS /deøɛsɛs/ *nm* (abbr = **diplôme d'études supérieures spécialisées**) *postgraduate degree taken after a Master's*

dessaisir /desɛziR/ [3] **1** *vtr* **(a)** ~ qn de to relieve sb of ⟨responsibility⟩
(b) ~ qn de to divest sb of ⟨property⟩
2 se dessaisir *v refl* (+ *v être*) se ~ de to relinquish

dessaler /desale/ [1] *vtr* **(a)** to desalinate
(b) (Culin) to desalt

dessécher /deseʃe/ [14] **1** *vtr* to dry [sth] out; **arbre desséché** withered tree
2 se dessécher *v refl* (+ *v être*) ⟨hair⟩ to become dry; ⟨tree⟩ to wither; ⟨ground⟩ to dry out

dessein /desɛ̃/ *nm* design, intention; **à ~** deliberately

desserré, **~e** /deseRe/ *adj* loose

desserrement /deseRmã/ *nm*
(a) loosening
(b) (Econ) relaxation; **~ du crédit** relaxation of credit

desserrer /deseRe/ [1] **1** *vtr* **(a)** to loosen; to release; to relax
(b) to relax ⟨grip, credit⟩
2 se desserrer *v refl* (+ *v être*) ⟨screw⟩ to work loose; ⟨knot⟩ to come undone
IDIOM **il n'a pas desserré les dents** he never once opened his mouth

dessert /deseR/ *nm* dessert

desserte /deseRt/ *nf*
(a) (transport) service; **la ~ d'une ville par les transports en commun** public transport services to and from a city
(b) sideboard

desservir /deseRviR/ [30] *vtr* **(a)** ⟨train⟩ to serve ⟨town⟩
(b) to lead to ⟨room, floor⟩
(c) ⟨hospital⟩ to serve

dessin /desɛ̃/ *nm* **(a)** drawing; **tu veux que je te fasse un~?** (fam) do I have to spell it out for you?
(b) design
(c) pattern
(d) outline
■ **~ animé** cartoon

dessinateur, **-trice** /desinatœR, tRis/ *nm,f* **(a)** draughtsman (GB), draftsman (US)
(b) designer
■ **~ de bande dessinée** (strip) cartoonist

dessiner /desine/ [1] **1** *vtr* **(a)** to draw
(b) to design ⟨material, decor⟩; to draw up

⟨plans⟩
2 *vi* to draw
3 se dessiner *v refl* (+ *v être*) **(a)** ⟨future⟩ to take shape
(b) se ~ à l'horizon to appear on the horizon; **il se dessinait nettement dans la lumière** he was clearly outlined in the light

dessoûler /desule/ [1] *vtr* to sober up

dessous¹ /dəsu/ **1** *adv* underneath
2 en dessous *phr* **(a)** underneath; **il habite juste en ~** he lives on the floor below
(b) **la taille en ~** the next size down
3 en dessous de *phr* below; **les enfants en ~ de 13 ans** children under 13

dessous² /dəsu/ **1** *nm inv* (of plate, tongue) underside; (of arm) inside (part); **le ~ du pied** the sole of the foot; **l'étagère de** or **du ~** the shelf below; the bottom shelf
2 *nm pl* **(a)** underwear
(b) inside story

dessous-de-plat /d(ə)sudpla/ *nm inv*
(a) table mat
(b) plate stand
(c) trivet

dessous-de-table /d(ə)sudtabl/ *nm inv* backhanders (colloq (GB), bribes

dessus¹ /dəsy/ *adv* on top; **le prix est marqué ~** the price is on it; **passe ~** go over it; **compte ~** count on it; **'ton rapport est fini?'—'non, je travaille** or **suis ~'** 'is your report finished?'—'no, I'm working on it'

dessus² /dəsy/ *nm inv* (of shoe) upper; (of table, head) top; (of hand) back; **les voisins du ~** the people who live on the floor above
IDIOM **reprendre le ~** to regain the upper hand; (after illness) to get back on one's feet

dessus-de-lit /d(ə)sydli/ *nm inv* bedspread

déstabiliser /destabilize/ [1] *vtr* to unsettle ⟨person⟩; to destabilize ⟨country⟩

destin /destɛ̃/ *nm* **(a)** fate
(b) destiny

destinataire /dɛstinatɛR/ *nmf*
(a) addressee
(b) beneficiary
(c) payee

destination /dɛstinasjɔ̃/ **1** *nf* destination
2 à destination de *phr* ⟨train⟩ bound for

destinée /dɛstine/ *nf* destiny

destiner /dɛstine/ [1] **1** *vtr* **(a)** ~ qch à qn to design sth for sb; **être destiné à faire** to be designed or intended to do; to be destined to do
(b) **la lettre ne leur était pas destinée** the letter wasn't for them
2 se destiner *v refl* (+ *v être*) **elle se destine à une carrière de juriste** she's decided on a legal career

destituer /dɛstitɥe/ [1] *vtr* to discharge ⟨*officer*⟩; to depose ⟨*monarch*⟩

destitution /dɛstitysjɔ̃/ *nf* discharge; deposition

destructeur, -trice /dɛstryktœʀ, tʀis/ *adj* destructive

destruction /dɛstryksjɔ̃/ *nf* destruction

désuet, -ète /dezɥɛ, ɛt/ *adj* ⟨*decor*⟩ old-world; ⟨*style*⟩ old-fashioned; ⟨*word*⟩ obsolete

désunion /dezynjɔ̃/ *nf* (a) division
(b) discord

désunir /dezyniʀ/ [3] *vtr* to divide, to break up

détachant /detaʃɑ̃/ *nm* stain remover

détaché, ~e /detaʃe/ 1 *pp* ▶ DÉTACHER
2 *pp adj* (a) detached, unconcerned
(b) ⟨*teacher, diplomat*⟩ on secondment (GB), transferred

détachement /detaʃmɑ̃/ *nm*
(a) detachment (**de** from)
(b) (Mil) detachment
(c) secondment

détacher /detaʃe/ [1] 1 *vtr* (a) to untie; to unfasten; to undo
(b) to take down ⟨*poster*⟩
(c) ~ **les yeux** *or* **le regard de qch** to take one's eyes off sth
(d) to second (GB), to transfer
(e) to remove the stain(s) from
2 **se détacher** *v refl* (+ *v être*)
(a) ⟨*prisoner, animal*⟩ to break loose; ⟨*boat*⟩ to come untied
(b) to come undone
(c) ⟨*coupon*⟩ to come out; ⟨*wallpaper*⟩ to come away
(d) to grow away from ⟨*person*⟩
(e) ⟨*pattern*⟩ to stand out
(f) **se ~ de** to detach oneself from; to pull away from

⚜ **détail** /detaj/ *nm* (a) detail
(b) breakdown; **analyse de ~** detailed analysis
(c) retail; **acheter (qch) au ~** to buy (sth) retail

détailler /detaje/ [1] *vtr* (a) to detail; to itemize
(b) to scrutinize

détartrer /detaʀtʀe/ [1] *vtr* (a) to descale ⟨*kettle*⟩
(b) to scale ⟨*teeth*⟩

détaxe /detaks/ *nf* (a) tax removal
(b) tax refund
(c) export rebate

détecter /detɛkte/ [1] *vtr* to detect

détecteur /detɛktœʀ/ *nm* detector; ~ **de mines** mine detector

détection /detɛksjɔ̃/ *nf* detection

détective /detɛktiv/ *nm* detective

déteindre /detɛ̃dʀ/ [55] *vi* (a) ⟨*garment*⟩ to fade

(b) ⟨*colour*⟩ to run
(c) (figurative) to rub off

détendre /detɑ̃dʀ/ [6] 1 *vtr* (a) to release ⟨*spring*⟩
(b) to slacken ⟨*rope, spring*⟩
(c) to relax ⟨*muscle*⟩; to calm ⟨*atmosphere, mind*⟩
2 *vi* (a) to be relaxing
(b) to be entertaining
3 **se détendre** *v refl* (+ *v être*) (a) ⟨*rope, spring*⟩ to slacken
(b) ⟨*person, muscle*⟩ to relax

détendu, ~e /detɑ̃dy/ 1 *pp* ▶ DÉTENDRE
2 *pp adj* (a) relaxed
(b) slack

détenir /det(ə)niʀ/ [36] *vtr* (a) to keep ⟨*objects*⟩; to hold ⟨*power, record*⟩; to possess ⟨*arms*⟩; to have ⟨*secret, evidence*⟩
(b) to detain ⟨*suspect*⟩

détente /detɑ̃t/ *nf* (a) relaxation
(b) détente
(c) (on gun) trigger
IDIOM **être lent** *or* **dur à la ~** (fam) to be slow on the uptake

détention /detɑ̃sjɔ̃/ *nf* (a) (of passport, drugs, record) holding; (of arms, secret) possession
(b) detention; ~ **préventive** custody

détenu, ~e /detəny/ *nm,f* prisoner

détergent /detɛʀʒɑ̃/ *nm* detergent

détériorer /deteʀjɔʀe/ [1] 1 *vtr* to damage
2 **se détériorer** *v refl* (+ *v être*) ⟨*situation, weather*⟩ to deteriorate; ⟨*foodstuff*⟩ to go bad

déterminant, ~e /detɛʀminɑ̃, ɑ̃t/ *adj* ⟨*role, factor*⟩ decisive

détermination /detɛʀminasjɔ̃/ *nf* determination

déterminé, ~e /detɛʀmine/ 1 *pp* ▶ DÉTERMINER
2 *pp adj* (a) determined
(b) given

⚜ **déterminer** /detɛʀmine/ [1] *vtr* (a) to determine ⟨*reason, responsibility*⟩
(b) to work out ⟨*policy, terms*⟩
(c) to determine ⟨*attitude, decision*⟩
(d) ~ **qn à faire** to make sb decide to do

déterrer /deteʀe/ [1] *vtr* to dig [sb/sth] up

détestable /detɛstabl/ *adj* ⟨*style, weather*⟩ appalling; ⟨*habits*⟩ revolting; ⟨*person*⟩ hateful

détester /detɛste/ [1] *vtr* (a) to detest, to loathe ⟨*person*⟩
(b) to hate

détonateur /detɔnatœʀ/ *nm* (a) detonator
(b) (figurative) catalyst

détonation /detɔnasjɔ̃/ *nf* detonation

détonner /detɔne/ [1] *vi* to be out of place

détordre /detɔʀdʀ/ [6] *vtr* to straighten ⟨*iron bar*⟩; to unwind ⟨*cable*⟩

détour /detuʀ/ *nm* (a) detour; **ça vaut le ~** it's worth the trip

---

⚜ indicates a very frequent word

(b) roundabout means
(c) circumlocution; **il me l'a dit sans ~s** he told me straight
(d) (in road, river) bend

détourné, ~e /deturne/ **1** *pp*
▶ DÉTOURNER
2 *pp adj* ‹reference› oblique; ‹means› indirect

détournement /deturnəmã/ *nm*
(a) misappropriation
(b) hijacking
(c) (of traffic) diversion
■ **~ de mineur** (Law) corruption of a minor

détourner /deturne/ [1] **1** *vtr* **(a)** to divert ‹attention›
(b) **~ les yeux** *or* **le regard** *or* **la tête** to look away
(c) to divert ‹traffic, river, flight›; **~ la conversation** to change the subject
(d) to hijack ‹plane, ship›; to misappropriate ‹funds›
2 **se détourner** *v refl* (+ *v être*) **(a) se ~ de** to turn away from ‹friend›
(b) to look away

détracteur, -trice /detraktœr, tris/ *nm,f* detractor

détraqué, ~e /detrake/ *nm,f* (fam) deranged person

détraquer /detrake/ [1] **1** *vtr* **(a)** to bust [sth] (colloq); to make [sth] go wrong
(b) (fam) ‹medicine› to upset ‹stomach›; to damage ‹health›
2 **se détraquer** *v refl* (+ *v être*) ‹mechanism› to break down; ‹weather› to break

détremper /detrãpe/ [1] *vtr* to saturate ‹ground›; to soak ‹garment›

détresse /detres/ *nf* distress

détriment: **au détriment de** /odetrimãdə/ *phr* to the detriment of

détritus /detrity(s)/ *nm pl* refuse, rubbish (GB), garbage (US)

détroit /detrwa/ *nm* straits

détromper /detrõpe/ [1] **1** *vtr* to set [sb] straight
2 **se détromper** *v refl* (+ *v être*)
détrompez-vous! don't you believe it!

détrôner /detrone/ [1] *vtr* to dethrone

détruire /detruir/ [69] *vtr* to destroy

dette /det/ *nf* debt; **avoir une ~ envers qn** to be indebted to sb

DEUG /dœg/ *nm* (*abbr* = **diplôme d'études universitaires générales**) *university diploma taken after two years' study*

deuil /dœj/ *nm* **(a)** bereavement
(b) mourning, grief
IDIOM **faire son ~ de qch** (fam) to kiss sth goodbye (colloq)

deux /dø/ **1** *adj inv* **(a)** two; **~ fois** twice; **des ~ côtés de la rue** on either side *or*

both sides of the street; **tous les ~ jours** every other day; **à nous ~** I'm all yours; (to enemy) it's just you and me now
(b) a few, a couple of
(c) second; **le deux mai** the second of May (GB), May second (US)
2 *pron* **elles sont venues toutes les ~** they both came
3 *nm inv* two
IDIOMS **faire ~ poids, ~ mesures** to have double standards; **un tiens vaut mieux que ~ tu l'auras** (Proverb) a bird in the hand is worth two in the bush; **en ~ temps, trois mouvements** very quickly; **je n'ai fait ni une ni ~** I didn't have a second's hesitation

deuxième /døzjɛm/ **1** *adj* second; **dans un ~ temps nous étudierons…** secondly, we will study…
2 *nmf* second
■ **~ classe** second class, standard class (GB)

deuxièmement /døzjɛmmã/ *adv* secondly

deux-points /døpwɛ̃/ *nm inv* colon

deux-roues /døru/ *nm inv* two-wheeled vehicle

dévaler /devale/ [1] *vtr* to hurtle down; to tear down

dévaliser /devalize/ [1] *vtr* **(a)** to rob ‹person, bank, safe›
(b) to clean out (colloq) ‹shop, larder›

dévaloriser /devalɔrize/ [1] **1** *vtr* **(a)** to depreciate
(b) to belittle
2 **se dévaloriser** *v refl* (+ *v être*) **(a)** to lose value; to lose prestige
(b) to put oneself down

dévaluation /devaluasjõ/ *nf* devaluation

dévaluer /devalɥe/ [1] *vtr* to devalue

devancer /dəvãse/ [12] *vtr* **(a)** to be ahead of, to outstrip ‹competitor›
(b) to anticipate ‹demand, desire›; to forestall ‹attack, criticisms›

devant[1] /dəvã/ **1** *prep* **(a)** in front of; **tous les hommes sont égaux ~ la loi** all men are equal in the eyes of the law; **fuir ~ le danger** to run away from danger; **le bus est passé ~ moi sans s'arrêter** the bus went straight past me without stopping
(b) outside; **il attendait ~ la porte** he was waiting outside the door; he was waiting by the door
(c) ahead of; **la voiture ~ nous** the car ahead *or* in front of us; **laisser passer quelqu'un ~ (soi)** to let somebody go first; **avoir toute la vie ~ soi** to have one's whole life ahead of one
2 *adv* **(a)** 'où est la poste?'—'tu es juste ~' 'where's the post office?'—'you're right in front of it'
(b) **pars ~, je te rejoins** go ahead, I'll catch up with you
(c) (of hall, theatre) at the front; (in car) in the front

devant² /dəvɑ̃/ *nm* front
IDIOM prendre les ∼**s** to take the initiative
devanture /dəvɑ̃tyʀ/ *nf* **(a)** (shop)front
(b) shop *or* store (US) window
dévastation /devastasjɔ̃/ *nf* devastation
dévaster /devaste/ [1] *vtr* **(a)** ‹army› to lay
waste to; ‹storm, fire› to destroy
(b) ‹burglar› to wreck
déveine /devɛn/ *nf* (fam) rotten luck (colloq),
bad luck
 ✓ **développement** /devlɔpmɑ̃/ *nm*
(a) development; **pays en voie de** ∼
developing nation *or* country
(b) (in photography) developing
 ✓ **développer** /devlɔpe/ [1] **1** *vtr* to
develop
2 se développer *v refl* (+ *v être*) ‹body,
ability› to develop; ‹plant, company, town›
to grow
 ✓ **devenir¹** /dəvniʀ/ [36] *vi* (+ *v être*) to
become; **et Paul, qu'est-ce qu'il devient?** and
what is Paul up to these days?
devenir² /dəvniʀ/ *nm* future
dévergonder: se dévergonder
/devɛʀgɔ̃de/ [1] *v refl* (+ *v être*) to be going
to the bad
déverser /devɛʀse/ [1] **1** *vtr* to pour
‹liquid›; to drop ‹bombs›; to dump ‹refuse,
sand›; to discharge ‹waste›; to disgorge
‹crowd›; ∼ **du pétrole** to dump oil; to spill oil
2 se déverser *v refl* (+ *v être*) ‹river› to
flow; ‹sewer, crowd› to pour
dévêtir /devetiʀ/ [33] **1** *vtr* to undress
2 se dévêtir *v refl* (+ *v être*) to get
undressed
déviation /devjasjɔ̃/ *nf* **(a)** diversion (GB),
detour (US)
(b) departure, deviation
(c) (of compass) deviation
(d) (of light) deflection
dévider /devide/ [1] *vtr* to unwind ‹cable›
dévier /devje/ [2] **1** *vtr* to deflect ‹ball,
trajectory›; to divert ‹traffic›
2 *vi* **(a)** ‹bullet, ball› to deflect; ‹vehicle› to
veer off course
(b) ∼ **de** to deviate from ‹plan›
(c) ‹tool› to slip
(d) ‹conversation› to drift
devin /dəvɛ̃/ *nm* soothsayer, seer
deviner /dəvine/ [1] *vtr* **(a)** to guess ‹secret›;
to foresee, to tell ‹future›
(b) to sense ‹danger›
(c) to make out, to discern
devinette /dəvinɛt/ *nf* riddle
devis /d(ə)vi/ *nm inv* estimate, quote
dévisager /devizaʒe/ [13] *vtr* to stare at
devise /dəviz/ *nf* **(a)** currency
(b) (foreign) currency
(c) motto

✓ indicates a very frequent word

deviser /dəvize/ [1] *vi* to converse
dévisser /devise/ [1] *vtr* to unscrew
dévoiler /devwale/ [1] *vtr* **(a)** to unveil
(b) to reveal; to uncover
 ✓ **devoir¹** /dəvwaʀ/ [44] **1** *v aux* **(a)** to have
to; **je dois aller au travail** I've got to *or* I must
go to work; **il a dû accepter** he had to accept;
il aurait dû partir he should have left
(b) **il a dû accepter** he must have accepted;
elle doit avoir 13 ans she must be about
13 years old
(c) **cela devait arriver** it was bound to
happen; **un incident qui devait avoir de
graves conséquences** an incident which was
to have serious consequences; **ils doivent
arriver vers 10 heures** they're due to arrive
around 10 o'clock
2 *vtr* to owe; **il me doit des excuses** he
owes me an apology
3 se devoir *v refl* (+ *v être*) **(a)** **je me dois
de le faire** it's my duty to do it
(b) **les époux se doivent fidélité** spouses owe
it to each other to be faithful
(c) **un homme de son rang se doit d'avoir un
chauffeur** a man of his standing has to have
a chauffeur
4 comme il se doit *phr* **(a)** **agir comme
il se doit** to behave in the correct way
(b) **comme il se doit, elle est en retard!** as
you might expect, she's late!
devoir² /dəvwaʀ/ *nm* **(a)** duty; **il est de mon
∼ de** it's my duty to
(b) test; homework
dévolu /devɔly/ *nm* **jeter son ∼ sur** to set
one's heart on ‹object›; to set one's cap at
‹person›
dévorant, ∼e /devɔʀɑ̃, ɑ̃t/ *adj* ‹hunger›
voracious; ‹flames, passion› all-consuming
dévorer /devɔʀe/ [1] *vtr* **(a)** to devour ‹food,
book›; ∼ **qn de baisers** to smother sb with
kisses
(b) ‹obsession› to consume
dévot, ∼e /devo, ɔt/ *adj* devout
dévotion /devɔsjɔ̃/ *nf* **(a)** devoutness
(b) (religious) devotion (à to)
(c) passion (pour for)
dévoué, ∼e /devwe/ *adj* devoted (à to)
dévouement /devumɑ̃/ *nm* devotion
dévouer: se dévouer /devwe/ [1] *v refl*
(+ *v être*) **(a)** to devote *or* dedicate oneself
(b) to put oneself out
dévoyer /devwaje/ [23] **1** *vtr* to deprave
[sb], to lead [sb] astray
2 se dévoyer *v refl* (+ *v être*) to go astray
dextérité /dɛksteʀite/ *nf* dexterity, skill
dézipper /dezipe/ *vt* (Comput) to unzip
diabète /djabɛt/ *nm* diabetes
diabétique /djabetik/ *adj, nmf* diabetic
diable /djɑbl/ **1** *nm* **(a)** devil; **en** ∼
diabolically; fiendishly; **un (petit)** ∼ a little
devil

(b) two-wheeled trolley (GB), hand truck (US)
2 *excl* my God!; **pourquoi** ~ why on earth IDIOMS **habiter au** ~ to live miles from anywhere; **que le** ~ **t'emporte!** to hell with you!; **ce n'est pas le** ~**!** it's not that difficult!; **avoir le** ~ **au corps** to be like someone possessed; **tirer le** ~ **par la queue** to live from hand to mouth

diablement /djablɑmɑ̃/ *adv* terrifically

diabolique /djabɔlik/ *adj* **(a)** diabolic; ‹*invention*› fiendish
(b) ‹*person*› demonic; ‹*scheme, smile*› devilish
(c) ‹*precision*› uncanny

diabolo /djabɔlo/ *nm* ~ **menthe** mint cordial and lemonade (GB) *or* soda (US)

diadème /djadɛm/ *nm* **(a)** tiara
(b) diadem

diagnostic /djagnɔstik/ *nm* (gen, Med) diagnosis

diagnostiquer /djagnɔstike/ [1] *vtr* to diagnose

diagonal, ~**e**[1], *mpl* **-aux** /djagɔnal, o/ *adj* diagonal

diagonale[2] /djagɔnal/ *nf* diagonal; **lire qch en** ~ to skim through sth

diagramme /djagʀam/ *nm* graph

dialecte /djalɛkt/ *nm* dialect

⚬ **dialogue** /djalɔg/ *nm* dialogue (GB)

dialoguer /djalɔge/ [1] *vi* to have talks

dialoguiste /djalɔgist/ *nmf* screenwriter

dialyse /djaliz/ *nf* dialysis

diamant /djamɑ̃/ *nm* diamond

diamantaire /djamɑ̃tɛʀ/ *nm* **(a)** diamond cutter
(b) diamond merchant

diamétralement /djametʀalmɑ̃/ *adv* diametrically

diamètre /djamɛtʀ/ *nm* diameter

diapason /djapazɔ̃/ *nm* **(a)** (note) diapason
(b) tuning fork
IDIOM **se mettre au** ~ to fall in step

diaphragme /djafʀagm/ *nm* diaphragm

diapo /djapo/ *nf* (fam) slide

diaporama /djapɔʀama/ *nm* slide show

diapositive /djapozitiv/ *nf* slide, transparency

diarrhée /djaʀe/ *nf* diarrhoea

dico /diko/ *nm* (fam) dictionary

dictateur /diktatœʀ/ *nm* dictator

dictature /diktatyʀ/ *nf* dictatorship

dictée /dikte/ *nf* dictation

dicter /dikte/ [1] *vtr* **(a)** to dictate
(b) to motivate

diction /diksjɔ̃/ *nf* diction; elocution

dictionnaire /diksjɔnɛʀ/ *nm* dictionary

dicton /diktɔ̃/ *nm* saying

didacticiel /didaktisjɛl/ *nm* educational software program

didactique /didaktik/ *adj* **(a)** ‹*work, tone*› didactic
(b) ‹*term, language*› technical, specialist

dièse /djɛz/ 1 *adj* sharp
2 *nm* **(a)** (Mus) do ~ C sharp
(b) (on phone) **la touche** ~ the hash key (GB), the pound key (US)

diesel /djezɛl/ *nm* diesel

diète /djɛt/ *nf* (Med) light diet

diététicien, -ienne /djetetisjɛ̃, ɛn/ *nm,f* dietitian

diététique /djetetik/ 1 *adj* dietary; **produits** ~**s** health foods; **magasin** ~ health-food shop
2 *nf* dietetics

⚬ **dieu,** *pl* ~**x** /djø/ *nm* **(a)** god
(b) **sur le terrain c'est un** ~ he's brilliant on the sports field
IDIOMS **nager comme un** ~ to be a superb swimmer; **être dans le secret des** ~**x** to be privy to the secrets of those on high

Dieu /djø/ *nm* God
IDIOMS **se prendre pour** ~ **le père** to think one is God Almighty; **chaque jour que** ~ **fait** day in, day out; **il vaut mieux s'adresser à** ~ **qu'à ses saints** (Proverb) always go straight to the top

diffamation /difamasjɔ̃/ *nf* slander; (Law) libel

diffamatoire /difamatwaʀ/ *adj* (in writing) libellous; (verbally) slanderous; **écrit** ~ libel

diffamer /difame/ [1] *vtr* (gen) to slander, to defame; (Law) to libel

différé, ~**e** /difeʀe/ 1 *pp* ▶ DIFFÉRER
2 *pp adj* **(a)** postponed
(b) ‹*payment*› deferred
(c) ‹*programme*› pre-recorded
3 *nm* (of match, event) recording

différemment /difeʀamɑ̃/ *adv* differently

⚬ **différence** /difeʀɑ̃s/ *nf* difference; **à la** ~ **de** unlike; **le droit à la** ~ the right to be different

différenciation /difeʀɑ̃sjasjɔ̃/ *nf* differentiation

différencier /difeʀɑ̃sje/ [2] 1 *vtr* **(a)** to differentiate; **rien ne les différencie** there's no way of telling them apart
(b) to make [sb/sth] different
2 **se différencier** *v refl* (+ *v être*)
(a) ‹*person, organization*› to differentiate oneself
(b) to differ
(c) to become different

différend /difeʀɑ̃/ *nm* disagreement

⚬ **différent,** ~**e** /difeʀɑ̃, ɑ̃t/ *adj* different, various; **pour** ~**es raisons** for various reasons

différentiel, -ielle /difeʀɑ̃sjɛl/ *adj* differential

différer /difeʀe/ [14] 1 *vtr* to postpone ‹*departure, meeting*›; to defer ‹*payment*›
2 *vi* to differ

d

♂ **difficile** /difisil/ *adj* (a) (gen) difficult;
‹*victory*› hard-won; **le plus ~ reste à faire** the
worst is yet to come
(b) ‹*person, personality*› difficult
(c) fussy (**sur** about); **tu n'es pas ~!** you're
easy to please!

difficilement /difisilmã/ *adv* with
difficulty; **~ supportable** hard to bear

♂ **difficulté** /difikylte/ *nf* difficulty

difforme /difɔʀm/ *adj* ‹*body, limb*›
deformed; ‹*object*› strangely shaped; ‹*tree*›
twisted

difformité /difɔʀmite/ *nf* deformity

diffus, ~e /dify, yz/ *adj* ‹*light, heat*› diffuse;
‹*feeling*› vague

diffuser /difyze/ [1] *vtr* (a) to broadcast
(b) to spread; **~ le signalement de qn** to
send out a description of sb
(c) to distribute ‹*article, book*›
(d) to diffuse ‹*light, heat*›

diffusion /difyzjɔ̃/ *nf* (a) broadcasting; **la
~ du film** the showing of the film
(b) dissemination, diffusion
(c) (commercial) distribution
(d) (of newspaper) circulation

digérer /diʒeʀe/ [14] *vtr* (a) to digest
(b) (fam) to swallow ‹*insult*›; to stomach
‹*defeat*›

digeste /diʒɛst/ *adj* easily digestible

digestif, -ive /diʒɛstif, iv/ ① *adj* digestive
② *nm* liqueur (*taken after dinner*); brandy

digestion /diʒɛstjɔ̃/ *nf* digestion

digicode® /diʒikɔd/ *nm* digital
(access) lock

digital, ~e, *mpl* **-aux** /diʒital, o/ *adj*
digital

♂ **digne** /diɲ/ *adj* (a) dignified
(b) worthy; **~ de confiance** *or* **de foi**
trustworthy

dignement /diɲmã/ *adv* (a) with dignity
(b) fittingly

dignité /diɲite/ *nf* (a) dignity; **avoir sa ~** to
have one's pride
(b) (title) dignity

digression /digʀesjɔ̃/ *nf* digression

digue /dig/ *nf* (a) sea wall
(b) dyke (GB), dike (US)
(c) harbour (GB) wall

dilapider /dilapide/ [1] *vtr* to squander

dilatation /dilatasjɔ̃/ *nf* (a) (of
gas) expansion
(b) (Med) dilation

dilater /dilate/ [1] *vtr* (a) to dilate ‹*pupil,
cervix*›; to distend ‹*stomach*›
(b) to expand ‹*gas*›

dilemme /dilɛm/ *nm* dilemma

dilettante /dilɛtãt/ *nmf* amateur

dilettantisme /dilɛtãtism/ *nm*
amateurism; (pejorative) dilettantism

diligence /diliʒãs/ *nf* (a) stagecoach
(b) haste

diligent, ~e /diliʒã, ãt/ *adj* diligent

diluant /dilɥã/ *nm* thinner

diluer /dilɥe/ [1] *vtr* (a) to dilute
(b) to thin [sth] down

diluvien, -ienne /dilyvjɛ̃, ɛn/ *adj* **pluies
diluviennes** torrential rain

♂ **dimanche** /dimãʃ/ *nm* Sunday
IDIOM **ce n'est pas tous les jours ~** not
every day is a holiday

♂ **dimension** /dimãsjɔ̃/ *nf* (a) dimension
(b) size
(c) dimension, aspect
(d) (of problem) dimensions

diminué, ~e /diminɥe/ ① *pp* ▶ DIMINUER
② *pp adj* ‹*person*› weak

diminuer /diminɥe/ [1] ① *vtr* (a) to
reduce; to lower
(b) to dampen ‹*enthusiasm, courage*›
(c) to belittle ‹*person, achievement*›
(d) to weaken ‹*person*›; to sap ‹*strength*›
② *vi* (a) to come *or* go down; to be reduced;
to fall; to decrease; **les jours diminuent** the
days are getting shorter
(b) ‹*activity, violence*› to fall off; ‹*tension*›
to decrease; ‹*noise, flames, rumours*› to die
down; ‹*strength*› to diminish

diminutif /diminytif/ *nm* (a) diminutive
(b) pet name

diminution /diminysjɔ̃/ *nf* decrease;
reduction; (in production, trade) fall-off

dinde /dɛ̃d/ *nf* turkey (hen)

dindon /dɛ̃dɔ̃/ *nm* turkey (cock)
IDIOM **être le ~ de la farce** to be fooled *or*
duped

dindonneau, *pl* **~x** /dɛ̃dɔno/ *nm* turkey

dîner¹ /dine/ [1] *vi* to have dinner
IDIOM **qui dort dîne** (Proverb) when you're
asleep you don't feel hungry

♂ **dîner²** /dine/ *nm* dinner

dînette /dinɛt/ *nf* doll's tea set

dingo /dɛ̃go/ *adj inv* (fam) crazy (colloq)

dingue ① *adj* (a) ‹*person*› crazy (colloq)
(b) ‹*noise, success*› wild; ‹*price, speed*›
ridiculous
② *nmf* (a) nutcase (colloq)
(b) **un ~ de musique** a music freak (colloq)

dinosaure /dinozɔʀ/ *nm* dinosaur

diocèse /djɔsɛz/ *nm* diocese

dioxyde /dijɔksid/ *nm* dioxide

diphtongue /diftɔ̃g/ *nf* diphthong

diplomate /diplɔmat/ ① *adj* diplomatic
② *nmf* diplomat

diplomatie /diplɔmasi/ *nf* diplomacy

diplomatique /diplɔmatik/ *adj*
diplomatic

diplôme /diplom/ *nm* (a) certificate,
diploma; **il n'a aucun ~** he hasn't got any
qualifications
(b) (at university) degree; diploma
(c) (in army, police) staff exam

♂ indicates a very frequent word

diplômé, **~e** /diplome/ [1] *adj* une
infirmière **~e** a qualified nurse
[2] *nm,f* graduate

✧ **dire¹** /diʀ/ [65] [1] *vtr* **(a)** to say *‹words,
prayer›*; to read *‹lesson›*; to tell *‹story, joke›*; **~**
qch entre ses dents to mutter sth
(b) to tell; **c'est ce qu'on m'a dit** so I've been
told; **faire ~ à qn que** to let sb know that…;
je me suis laissé ~ que… I heard that…;
c'est pas pour ~, mais… (fam) I don't want
to make a big deal of it, but… (colloq); **à qui le
dites-vous!** (fam) don't I know it!; **je ne vous
le fais pas~!** (fam) you don't need to tell me!;
dis donc, où tu te crois? (fam) hey! where do
you think you are?
(c) to say **(que** that); **on dit que…** it is said
that…; **si l'on peut ~** if one might say so;
autant ~ que… you might as well say that…;
si j'ose ~ if I may say so; **c'est (tout) ~!**
need I say more?; **cela dit** having said that;
tu peux le·~! (fam) you can say that again!
(colloq); **à vrai ~** actually; **entre nous soit
dit** between you and me; **soit dit en passant**
incidentally; **c'est ~ si j'ai raison** it just goes
to show I'm right; **c'est beaucoup ~** that's
going a bit far; **c'est vite dit** that's easy for
you to say; **ce n'est pas dit** I'm not that sure;
comment ~? how shall I put it?; **pour ainsi
~** so to speak; **autrement dit** in other words;
comme dirait l'autre (fam) as they say; **il n'y
a pas à ~, elle est belle** (fam) you have to
admit, she's beautiful
(d) *‹law›* to state; *‹measuring device›* to show;
vouloir ~ to mean
(e) **~ à qn de faire** to tell sb to do
(f) to think; **on dirait de l'estragon** it looks
or tastes like tarragon; **ça ne me dit rien de
faire** I don't feel like doing; **notre nouveau
jardinier ne me dit rien (qui vaille)** I don't
think much of our new gardener
[2] **se dire** *v refl* (+ *v être*) **(a)** to tell
oneself; **il faut (bien) se ~ que…** one must
realize that…
(b) to exchange *‹insults›*; **se ~ adieu** to say
goodbye to each other
(c) to claim to be
(d) **ça ne se dit pas** you can't say that
[3] **se dire** *v impers* **il ne s'est rien dit
d'intéressant à la réunion** nothing of interest
was said during the meeting

dire² /diʀ/ *nm* **au ~ de, selon les ~s de**
according to

✧ **direct** /diʀɛkt/ [1] *adj* **(a)** *‹contact,
descendant, tax›* direct; *‹superior›* immediate
(b) *‹route, access›* direct; **ce train est ~ pour
Lille** this train is nonstop to Lille
(c) direct, frank
[2] *nm* **(a)** live broadcasting; **en ~ de** live
from
(b) (in boxing) jab; **~ du gauche** left jab
(c) express (train)

✧ **directement** /diʀɛktəmã/ *adv* **(a)** *‹travel,
go›* straight

(b) directly

✧ **directeur**, **-trice** /diʀɛktœʀ, tʀis/ [1] *adj*
principe ~ guiding principle; **idée directrice
d'un ouvrage** central theme of a book
[2] *nm,f* **(a)** headmaster/headmistress (GB),
principal (US); (of private school) principal
(b) (of hotel, cinema) manager/manageress
(c) director; head
■ **~ de banque** bank manager; **~ général**
managing director (GB), chief executive
officer (US); **~ de prison** prison governor
(GB), warden (US); **~ sportif** (team) manager

✧ **direction** /diʀɛksjõ/ *nf* **(a)** direction; **il a
pris la ~ du nord** he headed north; **en ~ de**
toward(s); **indiquer la ~ à qn** to tell sb the
way; **prenez la ~ Nation** take the train going
to 'Nation'
(b) (gen) management; supervision;
(of newspaper) editorship; (of movement)
leadership; **orchestre sous la ~ de**
orchestra conducted by
(c) management; **la ~ et les ouvriers**
management and workers
(d) manager's office; head office
(e) (Aut) steering

directive /diʀɛktiv/ *nf* directive

directrice ▶ DIRECTEUR

dirigeable /diʀiʒabl/ *adj, nm* dirigible

dirigeant, **-e** /diʀiʒã, ãt/ [1] *adj* *‹class›*
ruling
[2] *nm* leader

✧ **diriger** /diʀiʒe/ [13] [1] *vtr* **(a)** to be in
charge of *‹people›*; to run *‹service, party›*; to
manage *‹company›*; to lead *‹investigation›*; to
direct *‹operation›*
(b) to steer; to pilot; **il vous dirigera dans la
ville** he'll guide you around the town
(c) to turn *‹light, jet›* **(sur** on); to point *‹gun,
telescope›* **(sur** at)
(d) to dispatch *‹goods›*; to direct *‹convoy›*
(e) (Mus) to conduct
(f) to direct *‹actors›*; to manage *‹theatre
company›*
[2] **se diriger** *v refl* (+ *v être*) **se ~ vers** to
make for; **avoir du mal à se ~ dans le noir** to
have difficulty finding one's way in the dark

dirigisme /diʀiʒism/ *nm* planned economy

discale /diskal/ *adj f* **hernie ~** slipped disc

discernement /disɛʀnəmã/ *nm*
judgment

discerner /disɛʀne/ [1] *vtr* **(a)** to detect
‹sign, smell, expression›; to make out *‹shape,
noise›*
(b) to make out *‹motives›*; **~ le vrai du faux**
to discriminate between truth and untruth

disciple /disipl/ *nmf* **(a)** follower
(b) disciple

disciplinaire /disiplinɛʀ/ *adj* disciplinary

discipline /disiplin/ *nf* **(a)** discipline
(b) discipline, specialism
(c) (Sch) subject
(d) sport

d

discipliner /disipline/ [1] *vtr* **(a)** to
discipline
(b) to control ⟨*troops*⟩; to discipline
⟨*thoughts, feelings*⟩
(c) to keep [sth] under control ⟨*hair*⟩

disco /disko/ ① *adj inv* disco
② *nm* disco music

discontinu, **~e** /diskɔ̃tiny/ *adj*
⟨*movement*⟩ intermittent; ⟨*line*⟩ broken

discordance /diskɔʀdɑ̃s/ *nf* **(a)** (of
opinions) conflict
(b) (of colours) clash
(c) (of sounds) dissonance

discordant, **~e** /diskɔʀdɑ̃, ɑ̃t/ *adj*
(a) ⟨*sound, instrument*⟩ discordant; ⟨*voice*⟩
strident
(b) ⟨*colours*⟩ clashing
(c) ⟨*opinions*⟩ conflicting

discorde /diskɔʀd/ *nf* discord, dissension

discothèque /diskɔtɛk/ *nf* **(a)** music
library
(b) record collection
(c) discotheque

discourir /diskuʀiʀ/ [26] *vi* ~ de *or* sur
qch to hold forth on sth

ⓡ **discours** /diskuʀ/ *nm inv* **(a)** speech (**sur**
on)
(b) talk; **assez de ~, des actes!** let's have
less talk and more action!
(c) views; **il tient toujours le même ~** his
views haven't changed
(d) (in linguistics) speech; discourse

discrédit /diskʀedi/ *nm* disrepute; **jeter le
~ sur** to discredit

discréditer /diskʀedite/ [1] *vtr* to
discredit

discret, **-ète** /diskʀɛ, ɛt/ *adj* **(a)** ⟨*person*⟩
unassuming; ⟨*colour*⟩ sober; ⟨*charm*⟩ subtle;
⟨*lighting*⟩ subdued; ⟨*smile, perfume*⟩ discreet;
⟨*place*⟩ quiet
(b) discreet (**sur** about)
(c) not inquisitive

discrètement /diskʀɛtmɑ̃/ *adv*
discreetly; soberly; quietly

discrétion /diskʀesjɔ̃/ ① *nf* discretion;
dans la plus grande ~ in the greatest
secrecy
② **à discrétion** *phr* **il y avait à boire à ~**
you could drink as much as you liked
③ **à la discrétion de** *phr* at the
discretion of

discrimination /diskʀiminasjɔ̃/ *nf*
discrimination

discriminatoire /diskʀiminatwaʀ/ *adj*
discriminatory (**à l'encontre de** against)

discriminer /diskʀimine/ [1] *vtr* to
discriminate between ⟨*things, people*⟩

disculper /diskylpe/ [1] ① *vtr* to
exculpate
② **se disculper** *v refl* (+ *v être*) to

vindicate oneself (**auprès de qn** in the eyes
of sb)

ⓡ **discussion** /diskysjɔ̃/ *nf* **(a)** discussion;
relancer la ~ to revive the debate
(b) argument

discutable /diskytabl/ *adj* debatable;
questionable

discuté, **~e** /diskyte/ ① *pp* ▶ DISCUTER
② *pp adj* controversial

ⓡ **discuter** /diskyte/ [1] ① *vtr* **(a)** to discuss,
to debate
(b) to question
② **discuter de** *v+prep* to discuss
③ *vi* **(a)** to talk (**avec qn** to sb)
(b) to argue
④ **se discuter** *v refl* (+ *v être*) **ça se
discute, ça peut se ~** that's debatable

diseur, **-euse** /dizœʀ, øz/ *nm,f* **~ de
bonne aventure** fortune-teller

disgrâce /disgʀɑs/ *nf* disgrace

disgracieux, **-ieuse** /disgʀasjø, øz/ *adj*
ugly; unsightly

disjoindre /diszwɛ̃dʀ/ [56] ① *vtr* **(a)** to
loosen
(b) to separate
② **se disjoindre** *v refl* to come loose

disjoncter /diszɔ̃kte/ [1] *vi* **ça a disjoncté**
the trip switch has gone

disjoncteur /diszɔ̃ktœʀ/ *nm* circuit
breaker

dislocation /dislɔkasjɔ̃/ *nf*
(a) dismemberment
(b) ~ (**articulaire**) dislocation (of a joint)

disloquer /dislɔke/ [1] *vtr* **(a)** to
dismember ⟨*empire, state*⟩
(b) to dislocate ⟨*shoulder, arm*⟩

ⓡ **disparaître** /dispaʀɛtʀ/ [73] *vi* **(a)** to
disappear; to vanish; **disparaissez!** out of
my sight!; **des centaines de personnes
disparaissent chaque année** hundreds of
people go missing every year
(b) ⟨*pain, smell*⟩ to go; ⟨*stain*⟩ to come out;
⟨*fever*⟩ to subside; **faire ~** to get rid of ⟨*pain,
dandruff*⟩; to remove ⟨*stain*⟩
(c) (euphemistic) to die; to die out; to become
extinct; **voir ~** to witness the end of
⟨*civilization*⟩

disparate /dispaʀat/ *adj* ill-assorted;
mixed

disparition /dispaʀisjɔ̃/ *nf*
(a) disappearance; (of species) extinction; **une
espèce en voie de ~** an endangered species
(b) (euphemistic) death

disparu, **~e** /dispaʀy/ ① *pp*
▶ DISPARAÎTRE
② *pp adj* **(a)** missing; **porté ~** (Mil) missing
in action
(b) ⟨*civilization, traditions*⟩ lost; ⟨*species*⟩
extinct
(c) (euphemistic) dead
③ *nm,f* **(a)** missing person
(b) **les ~s** the dead

ⓡ indicates a very frequent word

dispendieux, **-ieuse** /dispɑ̃djø, øz/ *adj* expensive, extravagant

dispense /dispɑ̃s/ *nf* (a) exemption (de from)
(b) certificate of exemption

dispenser /dispɑ̃se/ [1] **1** *vtr* (a) to give ‹*lessons, advice*›
(b) ~ qn de (faire) qch to exempt sb from (doing) sth; to excuse sb from (doing) sth; **je vous dispense de commentaire** I don't need any comment from you
2 se dispenser *v refl* (+ *v être*) **se ~ de (faire) qch** to spare oneself (the trouble of doing) sth

disperser /dispɛʀse/ [1] **1** *vtr* to scatter ‹*objects, family*›; to disperse ‹*crowd, smoke*›; to break up ‹*gathering, collection*›
2 se disperser *v refl* (+ *v être*) to disperse; to scatter; to break up

disponibilité /dispɔnibilite/ **1** *nf* availability
2 disponibilités *nf pl* available funds

✓ **disponible** /dispɔnibl/ *adj* available

dispos, **~e** /dispo, oz/ *adj* **frais et ~** fresh as a daisy

disposé, **~e** /dispoze/ **1** *pp* ▶ DISPOSER
2 *pp adj* (a) arranged; laid out
(b) ~ à faire willing to do
(c) être bien ~ to be in a good mood; être bien ~ à l'égard de *or* envers qn to be well-disposed toward(s) sb

✓ **disposer** /dispoze/ [1] **1** *vtr* (a) to arrange; to position
(b) **les machines dont nous disposons** the machines we have at our disposal
2 se disposer *v refl* (+ *v être*) (a) **se ~ à faire** to be about to do
(b) **se ~ en cercle autour de qn** to form a circle around sb

dispositif /dispozitif/ *nm* (a) device; system
(b) operation; **~ policier** police operation

✓ **disposition** /dispozisjɔ̃/ **1** *nf*
(a) arrangement; layout; position
(b) disposal; **à la ~ du public** for public use
(c) measure, step
2 dispositions *nf pl* aptitude

disproportionné, **~e** /dispʀɔpɔʀsjɔne/ *adj* ‹*effort, demand*› disproportionate; ‹*head*› out of proportion with one's body

dispute /dispyt/ *nf* argument

disputé, **~e** /dispyte/ *adj* (a) ‹*title, match*› keenly contested
(b) ‹*place, person*› sought-after (de by)
(c) ‹*issue, plan*› controversial

disputer /dispyte/ [1] **1** *vtr* (a) to compete in ‹*competition*›; to compete for ‹*cup*›; to play ‹*match*›; to run ‹*race*›
(b) (fam) to tell [sb] off
2 se disputer *v refl* (+ *v être*) (a) to argue (sur about; pour over); **nous nous**

sommes disputés we had an argument
(b) to fight over ‹*inheritance, bone*›
(c) ‹*tournament*› to take place

disquaire /diskɛʀ/ *nmf* record dealer

disqualifier /diskalifje/ [2] **1** *vtr* to disqualify; **se faire ~ (par)** to be disqualified (by)
2 se disqualifier *v refl* (+ *v être*) to discredit oneself (**en faisant** by doing)

✓ **disque** /disk/ *nm* (a) record; **passer un ~** to play a record
(b) (gen, Tech) disc; (Comput) disk
(c) (Sport) discus
■ **~ compact** compact disc; **~ dur** hard disk; **~ souple** flexi-disc; floppy disk; **~ de stationnement** parking disc

disquette /diskɛt/ *nf* diskette, floppy disk

dissection /disɛksjɔ̃/ *nf* dissection

dissemblable /disɑ̃blabl/ *adj* dissimilar, different

dissémination /diseminasjɔ̃/ *nf* spread; dispersal; scattering; dissemination

disséminer /disemine/ [1] **1** *vtr* to spread ‹*germs, ideas*›; to disperse ‹*pollen*›
2 se disséminer *v refl* (+ *v être*) ‹*people*› to scatter; ‹*germs, ideas*› to spread

dissension /disɑ̃sjɔ̃/ *nf* disagreement (**au sein de** within)

disséquer /diseke/ [14] *vtr* to dissect

dissert /disɛʀ/ *nf* essay

dissertation /disɛʀtasjɔ̃/ *nf* essay

disserter /disɛʀte/ [1] *vi* to speak (**sur** on)

dissidence /disidɑ̃s/ *nf* (a) dissent; dissidence; rebellion
(b) **la ~** the dissidents

dissident, **~e** /disidɑ̃, ɑ̃t/ **1** *adj* dissident
2 *nm,f* (a) dissident
(b) dissenter

dissimulation /disimylasjɔ̃/ *nf* concealment

dissimuler /disimyle/ [1] *vtr* to conceal (**qch à qn** sth from sb)

dissipation /disipasjɔ̃/ *nf* (a) (of misunderstanding) clearing up
(b) (of fog, clouds) clearing
(c) (of attention) wandering
(d) restlessness

dissipé, **~e** /disipe/ *adj* ‹*pupil*› badly-behaved; ‹*life*› dissipated

dissiper /disipe/ [1] **1** *vtr* (a) to dispel ‹*doubt*›; to clear up ‹*misunderstanding*›; to disperse ‹*smoke*›
(b) to distract ‹*person*›
2 se dissiper *v refl* (+ *v être*) (a) ‹*doubt*› to vanish; ‹*misunderstanding*› to be cleared up; ‹*mist*› to clear
(b) to behave badly

dissocier /disɔsje/ [2] *vtr* to separate (de from)

dissolu, ∼e /disɔly/ adj ‹life› dissolute;
‹morals› loose
dissolution /disɔlysjɔ̃/ nf dissolution
dissolvant, ∼e /disɔlvɑ̃, ɑ̃t/ **1** adj
solvent
2 nm (a) nail varnish
(b) solvent
dissonance /disɔnɑ̃s/ nf dissonance
dissonant, ∼e /disɔnɑ̃, ɑ̃t/ adj ‹voice›
dissonant; ‹colours› clashing
dissoudre /disudʀ/ [75] **1** vtr (a) to
dissolve ‹assembly›; to disband ‹movement›
(b) to dissolve ‹substance›
2 **se dissoudre** v refl (+ v être)
(a) ‹organization› to disband
(b) ‹substance› to dissolve
dissous, -oute /disu, ut/ ▶ DISSOUDRE
dissuader /disɥade/ [1] vtr to dissuade; to
put [sb] off; to deter
dissuasif, -ive /disɥazif, iv/ adj
(a) dissuasive; deterrent
(b) prohibitive
dissuasion /disɥazjɔ̃/ nf (Mil) deterrence
dissymétrie /disimetʀi/ nf asymmetry
ɗ **distance** /distɑ̃s/ nf (a) distance; **Paris
est à quelle ∼ de Londres?** how far is Paris
from London?; **j'ai couru sur une ∼ de deux
kilomètres** I ran for two kilometres (GB);
être à faible ∼ de not to be far (away) from;
prendre ses ∼s avec to distance oneself
from; **tenir** or **garder ses ∼s** to stand aloof;
tenir la ∼ ‹runner› to stay the course; **à ∼**
from a distance; **commande à ∼** remote
control
(b) gap; **à une semaine de ∼** one week apart
distancer /distɑ̃se/ [12] vtr to outdistance;
to outrun; **se laisser ∼** to get left behind
distancier: se distancier /distɑ̃sje/ [2]
v refl (+ v être) to distance oneself (**de** from)
distant, ∼e /distɑ̃, ɑ̃t/ adj (a) ‹place,
noise› distant; ∼s **de trois kilomètres** three
kilometres (GB) apart
(b) ‹person› distant; ‹attitude› reserved;
‹relations› cool
distendre **1** vtr (a) to distend ‹stomach›;
to stretch ‹skin, cable›
(b) to weaken ‹bond, tie›
2 **se distendre** v refl (+ v être) (a) to
slacken
(b) to cool
distiller /distile/ [1] vtr to distil (GB)
distillerie /distilʀi/ nf (a) distillery
(b) distilling
distinct, ∼e /distɛ̃, ɛ̃kt/ adj (a) distinct
(**de** from)
(b) ‹sound› distinct; ‹voice› clear
(c) ‹firm› separate
distinctif, -ive /distɛ̃ktif, iv/ adj ‹mark›
distinguishing; ‹feature› distinctive

ɗ indicates a very frequent word

distinction /distɛ̃ksjɔ̃/ nf (a) distinction;
sans ∼ without discrimination;
indiscriminately
(b) honour (GB); ∼ **honorifique** award
(c) refinement
distingué, ∼e /distɛ̃ge/ adj distinguished
ɗ **distinguer** /distɛ̃ge/ [1] **1** vtr (a) to
distinguish between; **il est difficile de les ∼**
it's difficult to tell them apart
(b) to distinguish, to make out
(c) to discern
(d) to set [sb] apart; to make [sth] different
(e) to single [sb] out for an honour (GB)
2 **se distinguer** v refl (+ v être) (a) **se
∼ de** to differ from; to set oneself apart from
(b) to distinguish oneself
(c) to be distinguishable
(d) to draw attention to oneself
distordre /distɔʀdʀ/ **1** vtr to contort;
distordu par contorted with
2 **se distordre** v refl to become
contorted
distorsion /distɔʀsjɔ̃/ nf distortion
distraction /distʀaksjɔ̃/ nf (a) leisure,
entertainment; **les ∼s sont rares ici** there's
not much to do around here
(b) recreation
(c) absent-mindedness
distraire /distʀɛʀ/ [58] **1** vtr (a) to
amuse; to entertain
(b) ∼ **qn de qch** to take sb's mind off sth
(c) to distract (**de** from; **par** by)
2 **se distraire** v refl (+ v être) (a) to
amuse oneself; to enjoy oneself
(b) **j'ai besoin de me ∼** I need to take my
mind off things
distrait, ∼e /distʀɛ, ɛt/ adj ‹person›
absent-minded; inattentive; ‹air› distracted;
‹look› vague
distraitement /distʀɛtmɑ̃/ adv absent-
mindedly; **regarder ∼ qch** to look vaguely at
sth; **écouter ∼** to listen with half an ear
distrayant, ∼e /distʀɛjɑ̃, ɑ̃t/ adj
entertaining
distribuer /distʀibɥe/ [1] vtr (a) to
distribute (**à** to); to allocate (**à** to); ∼ **les
cartes** to deal; ∼ **le courrier** to deliver the
mail
(b) to supply ‹water, heat›
distributeur, -trice /distʀibytœʀ, tʀis/
1 nm,f distributor
2 nm (a) dispenser; vending machine;
∼ **de tickets** ticket machine; ∼ **de billets (de
banque)** cash dispenser
(b) retailing group
■ ∼ **automatique de billets, DAB** automatic
teller machine, ATM
distribution /distʀibysjɔ̃/ nf
(a) (sector) retailing
(b) (in commerce) distribution
(c) (of water, electricity) supply
(d) (supplying) distribution, handing out; (of

jobs, duties) allocation
(e) (geographically) distribution, layout
(f) (of actors) casting; cast
■ ~ **d'actions gratuites** allocation of bonus shares; ~ **automatique** automatic dispensing; ~ **du courrier** postal delivery

dithyrambique /ditirãbik/ *adj ‹speech, comments›* ecstatic; *‹praise›* extravagant

diurétique /djyretik/ *adj, nm* diuretic

divagation /divagasjɔ̃/ *nf* ravings; rambling

divaguer /divage/ [1] *vi* **(a)** to rave; **la fièvre le fait ~** he's delirious with fever
(b) to ramble; to talk nonsense
(c) to stray

divan /divã/ *nm* divan; couch

divergence /divɛrʒãs/ *nf* divergence; difference

divergent, ~e /divɛrʒã, ãt/ *adj* divergent

diverger /divɛrʒe/ [13] *vi* to diverge (**de** from); to differ (**de** from)

⚡ **divers, ~e** /divɛr, ɛrs/ *adj* **(a)** various; **les gens les plus ~** all sorts of people
(b) miscellaneous

diversement /divɛrsəmã/ *adv* variously, in different ways

diversification /divɛrsifikasjɔ̃/ *nf* diversification; **une entreprise en voie de ~** a company in the process of diversifying; **une ~ de la clientèle** targeting a wider clientele

diversifier /divɛrsifje/ [2] *vtr* to widen the range of; to diversify

diversion /divɛrsjɔ̃/ *nf* (Mil) diversion

diversité /divɛrsite/ *nf* diversity; variety

divertir /divɛrtir/ [3] **1** *vtr* to entertain; to amuse
2 se divertir *v refl* (+ *v être*) to amuse oneself; **pour se ~** for fun

divertissant, ~e /divɛrtisã, ãt/ *adj* amusing; entertaining; enjoyable

divertissement /divɛrtismã/ *nm* entertainment; recreation

dividende /dividãd/ *nm* dividend

⚡ **divin, ~e** /divɛ̃, in/ *adj* divine

divinité /divinite/ *nf* deity; divinity

diviser /divize/ [1] **1** *vtr* to divide
2 se diviser *v refl* (+ *v être*) **(a)** to become divided (**sur** over)
(b) to be divided
(c) to be divisible
(d) to divide; to fork

divisible /divizibl/ *adj* divisible

⚡ **division** /divizjɔ̃/ *nf* division

divisionnaire /divizjɔnɛr/ *adj* **commissaire ~** Chief Superintendent

⚡ **divorce** /divɔrs/ *nm* divorce (**d'avec** from); **prononcer le ~ entre deux époux** to grant a divorce to a couple

divorcé, ~e /divɔrse/ *nm,f* divorcee

divorcer /divɔrse/ [12] *vi* to get divorced

divulgation /divylgasjɔ̃/ *nf* disclosure

divulguer /divylge/ [1] *vtr* to disclose

⚡ **dix** /dis, *but before consonant* di, *before vowel or mute h* diz/ *adj inv, pron, nm inv* ten
IDIOMS **ne rien savoir faire de ses ~ doigts** to be useless; **un de perdu, ~ de retrouvés** (Proverb) there's plenty more fish in the sea

dix-huit /dizɥit/ *adj inv, pron, nm inv* eighteen

dix-huitième /dizɥitjɛm/ *adj* eighteenth

dixième /dizjɛm/ *adj* tenth

dix-neuf /diznœf/ *adj inv, pron, nm inv* nineteen

dix-neuvième /diznœvjɛm/ *adj* nineteenth

dix-sept /dis(s)ɛt/ *adj inv, pron, nm inv* seventeen

dix-septième /dis(s)ɛtjɛm/ *adj* seventeenth

⚡ **dizaine** /dizɛn/ *nf* **(a)** ten
(b) une ~ about ten; **des ~s de personnes** dozens of people

do /do/ *nm inv* (Mus) (note) C; (in sol-fa) doh

docile /dɔsil/ *adj ‹animal, person›* docile

dock /dɔk/ *nm* **(a)** dock
(b) warehouse

⚡ **docteur** /dɔktœr/ *nm* doctor; **jouer au ~** to play doctors and nurses

doctorat /dɔktɔra/ *nm* PhD, doctorate

doctrinaire /dɔktrinɛr/ *adj ‹attitude›* doctrinaire; *‹tone›* sententious

doctrine /dɔktrin/ *nf* doctrine

⚡ **document** /dɔkymã/ *nm* **(a)** document; **~ sonore** audio material; **avec ~s à l'appui** with documentary evidence
(b) document, paper

documentaire /dɔkymãtɛr/ **1** *adj* documentary; **à titre ~** for your information
2 *nm* documentary (**sur** on, about)

documentaliste /dɔkymãtalist/ *nmf* information officer; (school) librarian

documentation /dɔkymãtasjɔ̃/ *nf*
(a) material (**sur** on)
(b) research
(c) brochures
(d) centre de ~ resource centre (GB)

documenter: se documenter /dɔkymãte/ [1] *v refl* (+ *v être*) **se ~ sur qch** to research sth

dodeliner /dɔdline/ [1] *vi* **il dodelinait de la tête** his head was nodding

dodo /dɔdo/ *nm* (baby talk) **faire ~** to sleep

dodu, -e /dɔdy/ *adj* plump

dogmatique /dɔgmatik/ *adj* dogmatic

dogme /dɔgm/ *nm* dogma

dogue /dɔg/ *nm* mastiff

⚡ **doigt** /dwa/ *nm* finger; **petit ~** little finger (GB), pinkie; **bout des ~s** fingertips; **du bout des ~s** (figurative) reluctantly; **connaître une ville sur le bout des ~s** to know a city like ⋯▶

the back of one's hand; **montrer du ~ to point at**; (figurative) to point the finger at
■ **~ de pied** toe
IDIOMS **se brûler les ~s** to get one's fingers burned; **être à deux ~s de** to be a whisker away from; **filer entre les ~s de qn** ‹*money, thief*› to slip through sb's fingers; **se faire taper sur les ~s** to get one's knuckles rapped; **lever le ~** to put one's hand up

doigté /dwate/ *nm* **(a)** tact
(b) (of pianist) fingering

doléance /dɔleɑ̃s/ *nf* complaint

dollar /dɔlaʀ/ *nm* dollar

DOM /dɔm/ *nm inv* (*abbr* = **département d'outre-mer**) *French overseas* (*administrative*) *department*

◆ **domaine** /dɔmɛn/ *nm* **(a)** estate
(b) field, domain
(c) territory

domanial, ~e, *mpl* **-iaux** /dɔmanjal, o/ *adj* state-owned

dôme /dom/ *nm* dome

domestique /dɔmɛstik/ ① *adj* **(a)** ‹*staff, animal*› domestic
(b) ‹*market*› domestic, home
② *nmf* servant

domestiquer /dɔmɛstike/ [1] *vtr* to domesticate ‹*animal*›

domicile /dɔmisil/ ① *nm* place of residence; (of company) registered address
② **à domicile** *phr* **travail à ~** working at *or* from home; **'livraisons à ~'** 'home deliveries'

domicilié, ~e /dɔmisilje/ *adj* **(a)** **être ~ à Arras** to live in Arras
(b) j'habite à Paris, mais je suis ~e à Rennes I live in Paris, but my official address is in Rennes

dominance /dɔminɑ̃s/ *nf* dominance

dominant, ~e¹ /dɔminɑ̃, ɑ̃t/ *adj*
(a) ‹*colour, gene*› dominant; ‹*wind, tendency*› prevailing; ‹*feature, idea*› main
(b) ‹*class*› ruling

dominante² /dɔminɑ̃t/ *nf* **(a)** dominant feature
(b) (Univ) main subject, major

dominateur, -trice /dɔminatœʀ, tʀis/ *adj* domineering; overbearing; imperious

domination /dɔminasjɔ̃/ *nf* domination; **être sous la ~ de** to be dominated by

◆ **dominer** /dɔmine/ [1] ① *vtr* **(a)** to dominate; to tower above; **de là, on domine toute la vallée** from there you get a view of the whole valley
(b) to dominate ‹*match, sector*›
(c) ‹*theme*› to dominate
(d) to master ‹*subject*›; to overcome ‹*fear*›; **~ la situation** to be in control of the situation
② *vi* **(a)** to rule, to hold sway
(b) to be in the lead

◆ indicates a very frequent word

(c) ‹*impression*› to prevail; ‹*duat*› to stand out
③ **se dominer** *v refl* (+ *v être*) to control oneself

dominical, ~e, *mpl* **-aux** /dɔminikal, o/ *adj* ‹*walk, mass*› Sunday

domino /dɔmino/ *nm* domino

◆ **dommage** /dɔmaʒ/ *nm* **(a) c'est ~** it's a shame *or* pity
(b) damage
(c) (Law) tort
■ **~s corporels** personal injury; **~s et intérêts** damages

dommageable /dɔmaʒabl/ *adj* harmful (**pour to**)

dommages-intérêts /dɔmaʒɛteʀɛ/ *nm pl* damages; **5 000 euros de ~** 5,000 euros in damages

dompter /dɔ̃te/ [1] *vtr* to tame ‹*wild animal*›; to bring [sb] to heel ‹*unruly person*›; to subdue ‹*insurgents*›; to overcome ‹*passion*›

dompteur, -euse /dɔ̃tœʀ, øz/ *nm,f* tamer

DOM-TOM /dɔmtɔm/ *nm pl* (*abbr* = **départements et territoires d'outre-mer**) *French overseas departments and territories*

◆ **don** /dɔ̃/ *nm* **(a)** donation; **faire ~ de** to give (à to); **~ de soi** self-sacrifice
(b) gift; **avoir le ~ de faire** to have a talent for doing
■ **~ du sang** blood donation

donation /dɔnasjɔ̃/ *nf* **(a)** donation
(b) (Law) gift

◆ **donc** /dɔ̃k/ *conj* so, therefore; **j'étais ~ en train de lire, lorsque…** so I was reading, when…; **je disais ~ que…** as I was saying…; **entrez ~!** do come in!; **mais où est-il ~ passé?** where on earth has he gone?

donjon /dɔ̃ʒɔ̃/ *nm* (of castle) keep

donne /dɔn/ *nf* (in cards) deal

donné, ~e¹ /dɔne/ ① *pp* ▶ DONNER
② *pp adj* **(a) il n'est pas ~ à tout le monde de faire** not everyone can do
(b) given; **à un moment ~** at one point; **all of a sudden**
(c) cheap
③ **étant donné (que)** *phr* given (that)

◆ **donnée²** /dɔne/ *nf* **(a)** fact, element
(b) data

◆ **donner** /dɔne/ [1] ① *vtr* **(a)** to give ‹*present, headache, advice, dinner, lesson*›; **~ l'heure à qn** to tell sb the time; **je lui donne 40 ans** I'd say he/she was 40; **~ faim à qn** to make sb feel hungry; **elle donne sa fille à garder à mes parents** she has my parents look after her daughter; **j'ai donné ma voiture à réparer** I've taken my car in to be repaired; **les sondages le donnent en tête** the polls put him in the lead
(b) to show ‹*film*›; to put on ‹*play*›; to give ‹*performance*›
(c) to produce, to yield ‹*fruit, juice*›; to produce ‹*results*›

(d) to show ‹signs›
(e) (fam) to inform on ‹accomplice›
2 *vi* **(a) le poirier va bien ~ cette année** the pear tree will yield a good crop this year
(b) ne plus savoir où ~ de la tête (figurative) not to know which way to turn
(c) ~ sur ‹room, window› to overlook; ‹door› to give onto; **~ au nord** to face north; **la cuisine donne dans le salon** the kitchen leads into the living-room
(d) ~ dans to tend toward(s)
(e) ~ de sa personne to give of oneself
3 se donner *v refl* (+ *v être*) **(a) se ~ à** to devote oneself to
(b) se ~ le temps de faire to give oneself time to do
(c) se ~ pour but de faire to make it one's aim to do
(d) se ~ de grands airs to put on airs
(e) se ~ des coups to exchange blows; **se ~ le mot** to pass the word on
IDIOMS donnant donnant: je fais la cuisine, tu fais la vaisselle fair's fair: I cook, you do the washing-up; **avec lui, c'est donnant donnant** he never does anything for nothing
donneur, -euse /dɔnœʀ, øz/ *nm,f* (Med) donor

♂ **dont** /dɔ̃/ *rel pron* **(a)** whose, of which; **la jeune fille ~ on nous disait qu'elle avait 20 ans** the girl who they said was 20; **Sylvaine est quelqu'un ~ on se souvient** Sylvaine is somebody (that) you remember; **la maladie ~ il souffre** the illness which he's suffering from; **la façon ~ il a été traité** the way in which he has been treated
(b) il y a eu plusieurs victimes ~ mon père there were several victims, one of whom was my father; **des boîtes ~ la plupart sont vides** boxes, most of which are empty
dopage /dɔpaʒ/ *nm* **(a)** (of horses) doping
(b) illegal drug-taking
doper /dɔpe/ [1] *vtr* to dope
dorade /dɔʀad/ *nf* (sea) bream
doré, ~e /dɔʀe/ **1** *pp* ▶ DORER
2 *pp adj* **(a)** ‹paint› gold; ‹frame› gilt; ‹dome› gilded; ‹hair› golden; ‹skin› tanned; ‹bread› golden brown; **~ à l'or fin** gilded
(b) ‹exile› luxurious; **jeunesse ~e** gilded youth
3 *nm* gilt
dorénavant /dɔʀenavɑ̃/ *adv* from now on
dorer /dɔʀe/ [1] **1** *vtr* **(a)** to gild
(b) (Culin) to glaze
2 *vi* (Culin) to brown
3 se dorer *v refl* (+ *v être*) **se ~ au soleil** to sunbathe
dorloter /dɔʀlɔte/ [1] *vtr* to pamper
dormeur, -euse /dɔʀmœʀ, øz/ *nm,f* sleeper; **c'est un gros ~** he sleeps a lot
♂ **dormir** /dɔʀmiʀ/ [30] *vi* **(a)** to sleep; **~ debout** (figurative) to be dead on one's feet; **ça m'empêche de ~** it keeps me awake; **il n'en dort plus** he's losing sleep over it
(b) ‹money› to lie idle

IDIOMS ne ~ que d'un œil to sleep with one eye open; **~ sur ses deux oreilles, ~ tranquille** to rest easy; **~ comme un loir** to sleep like a log; **~ à poings fermés** to be fast asleep
dorsal, ~e, *mpl* **-aux** /dɔʀsal, o/ *adj* ‹pain› back; ‹fin› dorsal
dortoir /dɔʀtwaʀ/ **1** *nm* dormitory
2 (-)dortoir (*combining form*) **ville-~** dormitory town
dorure /dɔʀyʀ/ *nf* gilt
♂ **dos** /do/ *nm inv* **(a)** back; **avoir le ~ rond** *or* **voûté** to stoop; **mal de ~** backache; **voir qn de ~** to see sb from behind; **robe décolletée dans le ~** dress with a low back; **il n'a rien sur le ~** (fam) he's wearing hardly anything; **tourner le ~ à** to have one's back to; to turn one's back to; (figurative) to turn one's back on sb
(b) (of book) spine; (of blade) blunt edge
IDIOMS mettre qch sur le ~ de (fam) to blame sth on; **il a bon ~ le réveil!** (fam) it's easy to blame it on the alarm-clock!
dosage /dozaʒ/ *nm* **(a)** amount; measurement
(b) mix; mixing
(c) proportions
dos-d'âne /dodɑn/ *nm inv* hump
dose /doz/ *nf* **(a)** dose; **forcer la ~** (fam) to go a bit far (colloq)
(b) measure
doser /doze/ [1] *vtr* **(a)** to measure
(b) to use [sth] in a controlled way
dossard /dosaʀ/ *nm* number (*worn by an athlete*)
♂ **dossier** /dosje/ *nm* **(a)** file, dossier; **~ médical** medical records; **~ d'inscription** (Sch) registration form; **sélection sur ~** selection by written application
(b) (Law) file; case
(c) le ~ brûlant de la pollution the controversial problem of pollution
(d) file, folder
(e) (of chair) back
dot /dɔt/ *nf* dowry
dotation /dɔtasjɔ̃/ *nf* allocation; endowment
doter /dɔte/ [1] *vtr* **(a) ~ qn de qch** to allocate sth to sb
(b) ~ qn/qch de to equip sb/sth with
(c) ~ qn/qch de to endow sb/sth with
douane /dwan/ *nf* **(a)** customs
(b) (on goods) duty
douanier, -ière /dwanje, ɛʀ/ **1** *adj* customs
2 *nm* customs officer
♂ **double** /dubl/ **1** *adj* double; **l'avantage est ~** the advantage is twofold; **valise à ~ fond** suitcase with a false bottom; **~ nationalité** dual nationality; **avoir le don de ~ vue** to have second sight; **en ~ exemplaire** in duplicate
2 *adv* double
3 *nm* **(a)** double; **leur piscine fait le ~ de** ⋯⟩

d

la nôtre their swimming-pool is twice as big
as ours
(b) copy; un ~ des clés a spare set of keys
(c) (in tennis) doubles

doublé, ~e /duble/ ① *pp* ▶ DOUBLER
② *pp adj* (a) ‹coat› lined
(b) ‹film› dubbed

doublement /dubləmɑ̃/ ① *adv* in two
ways; il est ~ coupable he's guilty on two
counts
② *nm* (of quantity) doubling

doubler /duble/ [1] ① *vtr* (a) to double
(b) to line (de with)
(c) to dub ‹film›; to stand in for ‹actor›
(d) to overtake (GB), to pass (US); 'défense de
~' 'no overtaking' (GB), 'no passing' (US)
② *vi* to double
③ **se doubler** *v refl* (+ *v être*) se ~ de
qch to be coupled with sth

doublure /dublyʀ/ *nf* (a) lining
(b) (for actor) double

douce ▶ DOUX

douceâtre /dusɑtʀ/ *adj* sickly sweet

✍ **doucement** /dusmɑ̃/ *adv* (a) gently; ~
avec le vin! go easy on the wine!
(b) quietly
(c) slowly

doucereux, -euse /dusʀø, øz/ *adj*
‹person› smooth; ‹words› sugary; ‹smile›
unctuous

douceur /dusœʀ/ ① *nf* (a) softness;
mildness; mellowness; smoothness;
gentleness; ~ de vivre relaxed rhythm of
life; avec ~ gently
(b) sweet (GB), candy (US)
② **en douceur** *phr* (a) smoothly;
atterrissage en ~ smooth landing
(b) shampooing qui lave en ~ mild shampoo

✍ **douche** /duʃ/ *nf* shower; ~ froide cold
shower; (figurative) letdown (colloq)
∎ ~ écossaise alternating hot and cold
shower; (figurative) bucket of cold water

doucher /duʃe/ [1] ① *vtr* (a) to give [sb]
a shower
(b) (fam) to dampen ‹enthusiasm›
② **se doucher** *v refl* (+ *v être*) to take a
shower

doué, ~e /dwe/ *adj* (a) gifted, talented; être
~ pour to have a gift for
(b) ~ de endowed with, gifted with

douille /duj/ *nf* (a) cartridge (case)
(b) (light) socket

douillet, -ette /dujɛ, ɛt/ *adj*
(a) oversensitive to pain
(b) cosy (GB), cozy (US)

✍ **douleur** /dulœʀ/ *nf* (a) pain; médicament
contre la ~ painkiller
(b) grief

douloureuse ▶ DOULOUREUX

─────────────

✍ indicates a very frequent word

douloureusement /duluʀøzmɑ̃/ *adv*
(a) grievously; terribly
(b) painfully

douloureux, -euse /duluʀø, øz/ *adj*
(a) painful
(b) ‹event› distressing; ‹question› painful

✍ **doute** /dut/ ① *nm* doubt; laisser qn dans
le ~ to leave sb in a state of uncertainty;
mettre qch en ~ to call sth into question;
dans le ~, j'ai préféré ne rien dire not being
sure I didn't say anything; il fait peu de
~ que there's little doubt that; nul ~ que
there's no doubt that
② **sans doute** *phr* probably; sans aucun
~ without any doubt

✍ **douter** /dute/ [1] ① *vtr* (a) ~ que to doubt
that *or* whether
(b) ~ de qch to have doubts about sth; elle
l'affirme mais j'en doute she says it's true
but I have my doubts; elle ne doute de rien!
(fam) (ironic) she's so sure of herself!
② *vi* to doubt
③ **se douter** *v refl* (+ *v être*) se ~ de to
suspect; je m'en doutais! I thought so!; je me
doute (bien) qu'il devait être furieux I can
(well) imagine that he was furious; nous
étions loin de nous ~ que we didn't have the
least idea that

douteux, -euse /dutø, øz/ *adj*
(a) uncertain
(b) ambiguous
(c) dubious
(d) ‹deal, character› shady

douve /duv/ *nf* moat

Douvres /duvʀ/ *n pr* Dover

✍ **doux, douce** /du, dus/ *adj* ‹light, voice,
substance› soft; ‹cider› sweet; ‹cheese,
shampoo, weather› mild; ‹person, slope› gentle
IDIOMS filer ~ (fam) to keep a low profile;
se la couler douce (fam) to take it easy; en
douce (fam) on the sly

douzaine /duzɛn/ *nf* (a) dozen; à la ~ by
the dozen
(b) une ~ about twelve, a dozen or so

✍ **douze** /duz/ *adj inv, pron, nm inv* twelve

douzième /duzjɛm/ *adj* twelfth

doyen, -enne /dwajɛ̃, ɛn/ *nm,f* (a) oldest
person
(b) the (most) senior member
(c) dean

Dr (*written abbr* = **docteur**) Dr

draconien, -ienne /dʀakɔnjɛ̃, ɛn/ *adj*
draconian; very strict

dragée /dʀaʒe/ *nf* (a) sugared almond
(b) sugar-coated pill

dragon /dʀagɔ̃/ *nm* (a) dragon
(b) (Mil) dragoon

draguer /dʀage/ [1] *vtr* (a) (fam) to come
on to (colloq)
(b) to dredge, to drag ‹river, canal›

dragueur, -euse /dRagœR, øz/ *nm,f* (fam)
c'est un drôle de ∼ (fam) he's a terrible flirt

drain /dRɛ̃/ *nm* drain

drainage /dRɛnaʒ/ *nm* (a) drainage
(b) (Med) draining (off)

drainer /dRɛne/ [1] *vtr* to drain

dramatique /dRamatik/ *adj* (a) tragic; ce
n'est pas ∼ it's not the end of the world
(b) dramatic; art ∼ drama; auteur ∼
playwright

dramatiquement /dRamatikmɑ̃/ *adv*
tragically

dramatiser /dRamatize/ [1] *vtr* to
dramatize

dramaturge /dRamatyRʒ/ *nmf* playwright

drame /dRam/ *nm* (a) tragedy; tourner au
∼ to take a tragic turn
(b) drama; play; ∼ lyrique opera

drap /dRa/ *nm* (a) sheet
(b) woollen (GB) cloth
■ ∼ de plage beach towel
IDIOM se mettre dans de beaux ∼s to land
oneself in a fine mess

drapeau, *pl* ∼x /dRapo/ *nm* flag; être sous
les ∼x to be doing military service

drap-housse, *pl* **draps-housses**
/dRaus/ *nm* fitted sheet

dressage /dRɛsaʒ/ *nm* (a) training; (of
horse) breaking in
(b) dressage

✧ **dresser** /dRese/ [1] **1** *vtr* (a) to train
‹animal›; to break in ‹horse›; to teach [sb]
how to behave ‹person›
(b) to put up ‹scaffolding›
(c) to prick up ‹ears›
(d) to lay out ‹buffet›
(e) to draw up ‹list›; ∼ un procès-verbal à qn
to give sb a ticket
(f) ∼ qn contre to set sb against
2 se dresser *v refl* (+ *v être*) (a) to stand
up
(b) se ∼ contre to rebel against
(c) ‹statue, obstacle› to stand; to tower up

dresseur, -euse /dRɛsœR, øz/ *nm,f* trainer

dribbler /dRible/ [1] *vi* to dribble

drogue /dRɔg/ *nf* drug; la ∼ drugs; c'est
devenu une ∼ it has become an addiction

drogué, ∼e /dRɔge/ *nm,f* drug-addict

droguer /dRɔge/ [1] **1** *vtr* (a) ‹doctor› to
dope
(b) to dope ‹animal, sportsman›; to drug
‹victim›; to doctor ‹drink›
2 se droguer *v refl* (+ *v être*) (a) to dope
oneself (à, de with)
(b) to take drugs

droguerie /dRɔgRi/ *nf* hardware shop
(GB) *or* store (US)

droguiste /dRɔgist/ *nmf* owner of a
hardware shop

✧ **droit, ∼e¹** /dRwa, at/ **1** *adj* (a) ‹line, road,
nose› straight; ‹writing› upright; se tenir

∼ to stand up straight; to sit up straight;
s'écarter du ∼ chemin to stray from the
straight and narrow
(b) right; du côté ∼ on the right-hand side
(c) ‹person› straight(forward)
(d) ‹skirt› straight
(e) ‹angle› right
2 *adv* straight; continuez tout ∼ carry
straight on; marcher ∼ to toe the line
3 *nm* (a) right; être dans son (bon) ∼ to be
within one's rights; cela leur revient de ∼ it's
theirs by right; avoir ∼ à to be entitled to;
il a eu ∼ à une amende (ironic) he got a fine;
avoir le ∼ de faire to be allowed to do; to
have the right to do; avoir le ∼ de vie ou de
mort sur qn to have power of life and death
over sb; il s'imagine qu'il a tous les ∼s he
thinks he can do whatever he likes; être en
∼ de to be entitled to
(b) le ∼ law; faire son ∼ to study law
(c) fee
(d) (in boxing) right
■ (prisonnier de) ∼ commun nonpolitical
prisoner; ∼ d'entrée entrance fee; ∼ de
passage right of way (GB), easement (US);
un ∼ de regard sur a say in; ∼s d'auteur
royalties; ∼s de douane customs duties;
les ∼s de l'homme human rights; ∼s de
succession inheritance tax

✧ **droite²** /dRwat/ *nf* (a) right; la porte de
∼ the door on the right; à ta ∼ on your
right; demander à ∼ et à gauche to ask
everywhere; to ask everybody
(b) voter à ∼ to vote for the right; de ∼
right-wing
(c) straight line

droitier, -ière /dRwatje, ɛR/ *nm,f* right-
hander

droiture /dRwatyR/ *nf* honesty,
uprightness

✧ **drôle** /dRol/ *adj* (a) funny, odd; faire
(tout) ∼ à qn to give sb a funny feeling; faire
une ∼ de tête to make a bit of a face
(b) funny, amusing
(c) (fam) un ∼ de courage a lot of courage
IDIOMS j'en ai entendu de ∼s I heard some
funny things; en faire voir de ∼s à qn to lead
sb a merry dance

drôlement /dRolmɑ̃/ *adv* (a) (fam) really
(b) oddly

drôlerie /dRolRi/ *nf* avec ∼ amusingly

dromadaire /dRɔmadɛR/ *nm* dromedary

dru, ∼e /dRy/ **1** *adj* ‹hair› thick
2 *adv* (a) ‹grow› thickly
(b) la pluie tombait ∼ it was raining heavily

druide /dRɥid/ *nm* druid

DS /deɛs/ *nf*: Citroen car of the 1950s

DST /deɛste/ *nf* (*abbr* = **Direction de la
surveillance du territoire**) *French
counterintelligence agency*

✧ **du** /dy/ ▶ DE

dû, due, *mpl* **dus** /dy/ **1** *pp* ▶ DEVOIR¹ ···⟩

⟨2⟩ *pp adj* **(a)** owed, owing, due (à to); **en bonne et due forme** in due form
(b) ∼ **à** due to
⟨3⟩ *nm* **réclamer son** ∼ to claim one's due

dualité /dyalite/ *nf* duality

dubitatif, -ive /dybitatif, iv/ *adj* sceptical (GB), skeptical (US)

duc /dyk/ *nm* duke

duchesse /dyʃɛs/ *nf* duchess

duel /dyɛl/ *nm* duel (à with); (figurative) battle

dulcinée /dylsine/ *nf* lady-love

dune /dyn/ *nf* dune

duo /dyo, dyo/ *nm* **(a)** duet; **en** ∼ as a duo
(b) double act (GB), duo (US)
(c) (fam) pair

dupe /dyp/ ⟨1⟩ *adj* **être** ∼ to be taken in *or* fooled
⟨2⟩ *nf* dupe; **un marché de** ∼**s** a fool's bargain

duper /dype/ [1] *vtr* to fool; **facile à** ∼ gullible

duperie /dypʀi/ *nf* trickery

duplex /dyplɛks/ *nm inv* maisonette (GB), duplex apartment (US)

duplicata /dyplikata/ *nm inv* duplicate

ᕍ **duquel** ▸ LEQUEL

ᕍ **dur, ∼e** /dyʀ/ ⟨1⟩ *adj* **(a)** ⟨ground, toothbrush, bread⟩ hard; ⟨meat⟩ tough; ⟨brush, cardboard⟩ stiff; ⟨plastic⟩ rigid
(b) ⟨zip, handle, pedal⟩ stiff; ⟨steering⟩ heavy
(c) ⟨sound, light, colour⟩ harsh
(d) ⟨face, expression⟩ severe
(e) ⟨parents, boss⟩ hard; harsh; ⟨policy⟩ hardline
(f) ⟨living conditions⟩ harsh
(g) ⟨job, sport⟩ hard; tough; ⟨climate, necessity⟩ harsh
(h) ⟨exam⟩ hard, difficult
(i) ⟨water⟩ hard
⟨2⟩ *nm,f* **(a)** tough nut (colloq); **jouer les** ∼**s** to act tough
(b) hardliner
⟨3⟩ *adv* ⟨work, hit⟩ hard
⟨4⟩ *nm* **construction en** ∼ permanent structure
⟨5⟩ **à la dure** *phr* **élevé à la** ∼**e** brought up the hard way
IDIOMS ∼ **d'oreille** hard of hearing; **avoir la tête** ∼**e** to be stubborn; to be dense; **avoir la vie** ∼**e** ⟨habit⟩ to die hard; **mener la vie** ∼**e à qn** to give sb a hard time

durable /dyʀabl/ *adj* ⟨impression⟩ lasting; ⟨interest⟩ enduring; ⟨material⟩ durable

durablement /dyʀabləmã/ *adv* on a permanent basis

ᕍ **durant** /dyʀã/ *prep* **(a)** for; **des heures** ∼ for hours and hours
(b) during

durcir /dyʀsiʀ/ [3] ⟨1⟩ *vtr* **(a)** to harden ⟨ground, features, position⟩
(b) to step up ⟨strike action⟩; ∼ **sa politique**

ᕍ indicates a very frequent word

en matière de to take a harder line on
⟨2⟩ *vi* ⟨clay, artery⟩ to harden; ⟨cement, glue⟩ to set; ⟨bread⟩ to go hard
⟨3⟩ **se durcir** *v refl* (+ *v être*) **(a)** to harden
(b) to become harsher; to intensify

durcissement /dyʀsismã/ *nm*
(a) hardening
(b) intensification

ᕍ **durée** /dyʀe/ *nf* **(a)** (of reign, studies) length; (of contract) term; (of cassette) playing time; **séjour d'une** ∼ **de trois mois** three-month stay; **contrat à** ∼ **déterminée** fixed-term contract; **de courte** ∼ ⟨peace⟩ short-lived; ⟨absence⟩ brief; ⟨loan⟩ short-term
(b) ∼ **(de vie)** life; **pile longue** ∼ long-life battery

durement /dyʀmã/ *adv* **(a)** badly
(b) harshly
(c) ⟨look⟩ severely
(d) ⟨hit⟩ hard

ᕍ **durer** /dyʀe/ [1] *vi* **(a)** to last
(b) to go on; **ça ne peut plus** ∼ it can't go on any longer; **faire** ∼ to prolong ⟨meeting⟩; **faire** ∼ **le plaisir** (ironic) to prolong the agony
(c) ⟨festival⟩ to run

dures /dyʀ/ *nf pl* **en faire voir de** ∼ **à ses parents** to give one's parents a hard time

dureté /dyʀte/ *nf* **(a)** (of material, face) hardness; (of meat) toughness; (of brush) stiffness
(b) (of expression, tone, climate) harshness; (of look) severity; **avec** ∼ ⟨look⟩ severely; ⟨punish⟩ harshly

durillon /dyʀijõ/ *nm* callus

durite /dyʀit/ *nf* radiator hose

DUT /deyte/ *nm* (*abbr* = **diplôme universitaire de technologie**) *two-year diploma from a university institute of technology*

duvet /dyvɛ/ *nm* **(a)** (of bird) down
(b) sleeping bag

duveteux, -euse /dyvtø, øz/ *adj* downy

DVD /devede/ *nm* DVD

dynamique /dinamik/ ⟨1⟩ *adj* dynamic, lively
⟨2⟩ *nf* **(a)** dynamics
(b) process

dynamiser /dinamize/ [1] *vtr* to make [sb/sth] more dynamic; to revitalize

dynamisme /dinamism/ *nm* dynamism; **être plein de** ∼ to be very dynamic

dynamite /dinamit/ *nf* dynamite

dynamiter /dinamite/ [1] *vtr* to dynamite; (figurative) to destroy

dynastie /dinasti/ *nf* dynasty

dysenterie /disãtri/ *nf* dysentery

dysfonctionnement /disfõksjɔnmã/ *nm*
(a) (Med) dysfunction
(b) malfunctioning

dyslexie /dislɛksi/ *nf* dyslexia

Ee

e, **E** /ə/ *nm inv* e, E; **e dans l'o** o and e joined together

ơ **eau**, *pl* ∼**x** /o/ ① *nf* **(a)** water; **l'∼ de source** spring water; **prendre l'∼** ‹shoe› to let in water; **être en ∼** to be dripping with sweat; **mettre à l'∼** to launch ‹ship›; **se jeter à l'∼** to throw oneself into the water; (figurative) to take the plunge; **tomber à l'∼** (figurative) to fall through; **nettoyer le sol à grande ∼** to sluice the floor down
(b) rain
② **eaux** *nf pl* **(a)** water; waters
(b) (Med) waters
■ ∼ **bénite** holy water; ∼ **de chaux** limewater; ∼ **douce** fresh water; ∼ **de Javel** ≈ (chloride) bleach; ∼ **de mer** seawater; ∼ **oxygénée** hydrogen peroxide; ∼ **plate** plain water; still mineral water; ∼ **de rose: à l'∼ de rose** ‹novel› sentimental; ∼**x et forêts** forestry commission; ∼**x usées** waste water
IDIOMS **mettre l'∼ à la bouche de qn** to make sb's mouth water; **ou dans ces ∼x-là** (fam) or thereabouts; **vivre d'amour et d'∼ fraîche** to live on love alone

EAU *written abbr* ▶ ÉMIRATS

eau-de-vie, *pl* **eaux-de-vie** /odvi/ *nf* brandy, eau de vie; à l'∼ in brandy

ébahir /ebaiʀ/ [3] ① *vtr* to dumbfound
② **s'ébahir** *v refl* (+ *v être*) to be dumbfounded

ébattre: s'ébattre /ebatʀ/ [61] *v refl* (+ *v être*) to frolic (about), to frisk about; to splash about

ébauche /eboʃ/ *nf* **(a)** (for sculpture) rough shape; (for picture) preliminary sketch; (of novel) preliminary draft; **être encore à l'état d'∼** to be still at an early stage
(b) **l'∼ d'un sourire** a hint of a smile

ébaucher /eboʃe/ [1] ① *vtr* to sketch out ‹picture, solution›; to draft ‹novel, plan›; to rough-hew ‹statue›; to begin ‹conversation›
② **s'ébaucher** *v refl* (+ *v être*) ‹solution, novel› to begin to take shape; ‹friendship› to begin to develop; ‹talks› to start

ébène /eben/ *nf* ebony

ébéniste /ebenist/ *nmf* cabinetmaker

éberluer /ebɛʀlɥe/ [1] *vtr* to dumbfound

éblouir /ebluiʀ/ [3] *vtr* to dazzle

éblouissement /ebluismɑ̃/ *nm* **(a)** dazzle
(b) dizzy spell

éborgner /ebɔʀɲe/ [1] *vtr* ∼ **qn** to blind sb in one eye; (humorous) to poke sb's eye out

éboueur /ebuœʀ/ *nm* dustman (GB), garbageman (US)

ébouillanter /ebujɑ̃te/ [1] *vtr* **(a)** to scald

(b) to blanch ‹vegetables›

éboulement /ebulmɑ̃/ *nm* (of wall, cliff) collapse; ∼ **(de rochers)** rockfall

éboulis /ebuli/ *nm inv* mass of fallen rocks; heap of fallen earth

ébouriffer /eburife/ [1] *vtr* to tousle; to ruffle

ébranler /ebrɑ̃le/ [1] *vtr* **(a)** to rattle ‹windowpane›; to shake ‹house›; to weaken ‹building›
(b) to shake ‹person, confidence›

ébrécher /ebreʃe/ [14] *vtr* to chip ‹cup›

ébriété /ebrijete/ *nf* intoxication

ébrouer: s'ébrouer /ebrue/ [1] *v refl* (+ *v être*) **(a)** ‹horse› to snort
(b) ‹person, dog› to shake oneself/itself; ‹bird› to flap its wings

ébruiter /ebrɥite/ [1] ① *vtr* to divulge
② **s'ébruiter** *v refl* (+ *v être*) ‹news› to get out

ébullition /ebylisjɔ̃/ *nf* (Culin) boiling
IDIOM **être en ∼** ‹crowd› to be in a fever of excitement; ‹country, brain› to be in a ferment

écaille /ekaj/ *nf* **(a)** (on fish, reptile) scale; (on oyster) shell
(b) tortoiseshell; **lunettes en ∼** horn-rimmed glasses
(c) flake

écailler /ekaje/ [1] ① *vtr* **(a)** (Culin) to scale ‹fish›; to open ‹oyster›
(b) ∼ **qch** to chip [sth] off
② **s'écailler** *v refl* (+ *v être*) to flake away

écarlate /ekaʀlat/ *adj* scarlet

écart /ekaʀ/ ① *nm* **(a)** (between objects) distance, gap; (between dates) interval; (between ideas) gap
(b) (between versions, in prices) difference; ∼ **des salaires** pay differential
(c) **faire un ∼** ‹horse› to shy; ‹car› to swerve
(d) lapse; ∼**s de langage** bad language
② **à l'écart** *phr* **être à l'∼** to be isolated; **se tenir à l'∼** to stand apart; to keep oneself to oneself; not to join in; **mettre qn à l'∼** to push sb aside; to ostracize sb; **entraîner qn à l'∼** to take sb aside
③ **à l'écart de** *phr* away from; **tenir qn à l'∼ de** to keep sb away from ‹place›; to keep sb out of ‹activity, talks›

écarté, ∼**e** /ekaʀte/ ① *pp* ▶ ÉCARTER
② *pp adj* **(a)** ‹fingers› spread; ‹knees, legs› apart; ‹teeth› widely spaced
(b) ‹place› isolated

écarteler /ekaʀtəle/ [17] *vtr* (kill) to quarter [sb]

e

écartement /ekaʀtəmɑ̃/ nm distance, space

◆ **écarter** /ekaʀte/ [1] **1** vtr (a) to move [sth] further apart ‹objects›; to open ‹curtains›; to spread ‹fingers, legs›
(b) to move [sth] aside ‹chair›; to remove ‹obstacle›; to push [sb] aside; to move [sb] on
(c) to dispel ‹suspicion›; to eliminate ‹risk, rival›
(d) to reject ‹idea›; to rule out ‹possibility›
2 **s'écarter** v refl (+ v être) (a) ‹crowd, clouds› to part; ‹shutters› to open
(b) to move away; **s'~ de** to move away from ‹direction, standard›; to stray from ‹path, subject›

ecchymose /ekimoz/ nf bruise

ecclésiastique /eklezjastik/ nm cleric

écervelé, ~e /esɛʀvale/ nm,f featherbrain

échafaud /eʃafo/ nm (a) scaffold
(b) guillotine

échafaudage /eʃafodaʒ/ nm scaffolding

échafauder /eʃafode/ [1] vtr to put [sth] together ‹plan›; to develop ‹theory›

échalas /eʃala/ nm inv (a) cane, stake
(b) (fam) beanpole (colloq)

échalote /eʃalɔt/ nf shallot

échancré, ~e /eʃɑ̃kʀe/ adj (a) ‹dress› low-cut; ‹briefs› high-cut; **trop ~** ‹sleeve› cut too wide
(b) ‹blouse› open-necked
(c) ‹coast› indented

◆ **échange** /eʃɑ̃ʒ/ **1** nm (a) exchange; **elles ont fait l'~ de leurs manteaux** they've swapped coats
(b) trade; **~s commerciaux** trade
(c) (cultural, linguistic) exchange
(d) (Sport) rally
2 **en échange** phr in exchange, in return
3 **en échange de** phr in exchange for, in return for
■ **~ de bons procédés** quid pro quo

◆ **échanger** /eʃɑ̃ʒe/ [13] vtr (a) to exchange; **~ des insultes** to trade insults
(b) (Sport) **~ des balles** to rally

échangeur /eʃɑ̃ʒœʀ/ nm interchange (GB), grade separation (US)

échantillon /eʃɑ̃tijɔ̃/ nm sample

échappatoire /eʃapatwaʀ/ nf way out (à of)

échappement /eʃapmɑ̃/ nm (Aut) **(tuyau d')~** exhaust (pipe)

◆ **échapper** /eʃape/ [1] **1** **échapper à** v+prep (a) **~ à** to get away from; (cleverly) to elude
(b) **~ à** to escape ‹death, failure›; (to manage) to avoid ‹accident›
(c) **~ à** to escape from ‹social background›; **je sens qu'il m'échappe** ‹partner› I feel he is drifting away from me; ‹child› I feel he's

growing away from me
(d) **~ à qn** or **des mains de qn** to slip out of sb's hands
(e) **un soupir m'a échappé** I let out a sigh
(f) **le titre m'échappe** the title escapes me
(g) **~ à** to defy ‹logic›; **~ à la règle** to be an exception to the rule
2 **s'échapper** v refl (+ v être) (a) to run away; to fly away; to escape; to get away
(b) ‹gas, smoke› to escape
(c) to get away; **s'~ pour quelques jours** to get away for a few days
IDIOM **l'~ belle** to have a narrow escape

écharde /eʃaʀd/ nf splinter

écharpe /eʃaʀp/ nf (a) scarf
(b) sash

échasse /eʃɑs/ nf stilt

échauder /eʃode/ [1] vtr to put [sb] off
IDIOM **chat échaudé craint l'eau froide** (Proverb) once bitten, twice shy

échauffement /eʃofmɑ̃/ nm (Sport) warm-up

échauffer /eʃofe/ [1] vtr (a) (Sport) to warm up
(b) to stir ‹imagination›; to stir up ‹person, debate›
(c) to start [sth] fermenting
IDIOM **~ les oreilles de qn** to vex sb

échéance /eʃeɑ̃s/ nf (a) (of debt) due date; (of share, policy) maturity date; (of loan) redemption date; **arriver à ~** ‹payment› to fall due; ‹investment, policy› to mature
(b) expiry date
(c) **à longue/brève ~** ‹forecast› long-/short-term; ‹strengthen, change› in the long/short term
(d) payment; repayment
(e) date; deadline

échéancier /eʃeɑ̃sje/ nm schedule of due dates; schedule of repayments

échéant: le cas échéant /ləkazeʃeɑ̃/ phr if need be, should the case arise

échec /eʃɛk/ **1** nm (a) failure; setback; **faire ~ à qn** to thwart sb
(b) (gen, Mil) defeat
(c) **faire ~ au roi** to put the king in check
2 **échecs** nm pl **les ~s** chess; chess set

échelle /eʃɛl/ nf (a) ladder; **~ coulissante** extending ladder (GB), extension ladder (US); **faire la courte ~ à qn** to give sb a leg up
(b) (of map, model) scale; **plan à l'~** scale plan; **à l'~ mondiale** on a worldwide scale; **~ des salaires** pay scale
(c) (fam) (in stocking) ladder

échelon /eʃlɔ̃/ nm (a) (of ladder) rung
(b) grade; **sauter les ~s** to get accelerated promotion
(c) level

échelonner /eʃlɔne/ [1] **1** vtr (a) to space [sth] out ‹objects›
(b) to spread ‹payments, work›; to stagger

◆ indicates a very frequent word

⟨holidays⟩
(c) to grade ⟨exercises⟩
2 **s'échelonner** v refl (+ v être) **(a)** to be positioned at intervals
(b) ⟨payments⟩ to be spread; ⟨departures⟩ to be staggered

écheveau, pl ∼x /eʃvo/ nm hank, skein

échevelé, ∼e /eʃəvle/ adj **(a)** tousled
(b) ⟨rhythm⟩ frenzied; ⟨romanticism⟩ unbridled

échine /eʃin/ nf **(a)** (Anat) spine
(b) (Culin) ≈ spare rib
IDIOM **courber l'**∼ **devant** to submit to

échiquier /eʃikje/ nm **(a)** chessboard
(b) chequered (GB) or checkered (US) pattern

Échiquier /eʃikje/ pr nm **l'**∼ the Exchequer, the Treasury

écho /eko/ nm **(a)** echo; **faire** ∼ **à qch, se faire l'**∼ **de qch** to echo sth
(b) response; **nous n'avons eu aucun** ∼ **des pourparlers** we have heard nothing about the talks

échographie /ekoɡrafi/ nf (Med) scan

échoir /eʃwaʀ/ [51] vi (+ v être) ⟨rent⟩ to fall due; ⟨draft⟩ to be payable

échoppe /eʃɔp/ nf stall

échouer /eʃwe/ [1] **1** vtr to beach ⟨boat⟩
2 **échouer à** v+prep to fail ⟨exam, test⟩
3 vi **(a)** ⟨person, attempt⟩ to fail
(b) to end up (**dans** in)
4 **s'échouer** v refl (+ v être) ⟨boat⟩ to run aground; ⟨whale⟩ to be beached

échu, ∼e /eʃy/ **1** pp ▸ ÉCHOIR
2 adj expired; **payer à terme** ∼ to pay in arrears

éclabousser /eklabuse/ [1] vtr **(a)** to splash
(b) il a été éclaboussé par ces rumeurs the rumours (GB) have damaged his reputation

éclair /eklɛʀ/ **1** adj inv rencontre ∼ brief meeting; **attaque** ∼ lightning strike; **guerre** ∼ blitzkrieg
2 nm **(a)** flash of lightning; **passer comme un** ∼ to flash past
(b) (of explosion, diamonds) flash; (of eyes) glint
(c) (of lucidity, triumph) moment; **il a eu un** ∼ **de génie** he had a brainwave (GB) or brainstorm (US)
(d) (Culin) éclair

éclairage /eklɛʀaʒ/ nm lighting; light; ∼ **au gaz** gaslight

éclairagiste /eklɛʀaʒist/ nm (in theatre, films) electrician

éclairant, ∼e /eklɛʀɑ̃, ɑ̃t/ adj flare

éclaircie /eklɛʀsi/ nf sunny spell

éclaircir /eklɛʀsiʀ/ [3] **1** vtr **(a)** to lighten ⟨colour⟩; to lighten the colour (GB) of ⟨paint, hair⟩
(b) to shed light on [sth]
2 **s'éclaircir** v refl (+ v être) **(a)** ⟨weather⟩ to clear; **l'horizon s'éclaircit** (figurative) the outlook is getting brighter

(b) ⟨colour⟩ to fade; ⟨hair⟩ to get lighter
(c) ⟨situation, mystery⟩ to become clearer
(d) ⟨crowd, forest⟩ to thin out
(e) s'∼ **les cheveux** to lighten one's hair; **s'**∼ **la voix** or **la gorge** to clear one's throat

éclaircissement /eklɛʀsismɑ̃/ nm **(a)** explanation
(b) clarification

éclairé, ∼e /eklɛʀe/ adj ⟨person, advice⟩ enlightened; ⟨art lover⟩ well-informed

ꝰ **éclairer** /eklɛʀe/ [1] **1** vtr **(a)** to light ⟨street, room⟩; to light up ⟨place, object⟩
(b) to give [sb] some light
(c) ⟨remark⟩ to throw light on ⟨text, situation⟩
(d) to enlighten [sb]
2 vi ⟨lamp, candle⟩ to give out light
3 **s'éclairer** v refl (+ v être) **(a)** ⟨screen, face⟩ to light up
(b) s'∼ **à l'électricité** to have electric lighting

éclaireur /eklɛʀœʀ/ nm **(a)** scout (GB), Boy Scout (US)
(b) (Mil) scout

éclaireuse /eklɛʀøz/ nf guide (GB), Girl Guide (US)

ꝰ **éclat** /ekla/ nm **(a)** splinter; **un** ∼ **d'obus** a piece of shrapnel; **voler en** ∼**s** to shatter
(b) (of light, star) brightness; (of spotlight) glare; (of snow) sparkle
(c) (of colour, material) brilliance; (of hair, plumage) shine; (of metal) lustre (GB)
(d) (of face, smile) radiance; (of eyes) sparkle; ⟨eyes⟩ dull; ⟨beauty⟩ lifeless
(e) splendour (GB); **manquer d'**∼ ⟨ceremony⟩ to lack sparkle
(f) scene, fuss; **faire un** ∼ to make a scene
■ ∼ **de colère** fit of anger; ∼ **de rire** roar of laughter; **des** ∼**s de voix** raised voices
IDIOM **rire aux** ∼**s** to roar with laughter

éclatant, ∼e /eklatɑ̃, ɑ̃t/ adj **(a)** ⟨light⟩ dazzling; ⟨sun⟩ blazing
(b) ⟨colour, plumage⟩ bright; **d'une blancheur** ∼**e** sparkling white
(c) ⟨beauty, smile⟩ radiant; ⟨victory⟩ brilliant
(d) ⟨proof⟩ striking
(e) ⟨laughter⟩ ringing

éclaté, ∼e /eklate/ adj (gen) fragmented; ⟨family⟩ divided

éclatement /eklatmɑ̃/ nm **(a)** bursting
(b) explosion
(c) break-up (**en** into)

ꝰ **éclater** /eklate/ [1] vi **(a)** ⟨tyre, bubble⟩ to burst; ⟨shell, firework⟩ to explode; ⟨bottle⟩ to shatter; **faire** ∼ to burst ⟨bubble⟩; to detonate ⟨bomb⟩
(b) ⟨pipe, boil⟩ to burst
(c) ⟨laughter, firing⟩ to break out; ⟨shot⟩ to ring out
(d) ⟨scandal, news⟩ to break; ⟨truth⟩ to come out
(e) ⟨war⟩ to break out; ⟨storm⟩ to break
(f) laisser ∼ **sa joie** to be wild with joy
(g) ⟨coalition⟩ to break up (**en** into); ⟨party⟩ to split

⋯▸

(h) to lose one's temper; $\sim$ **de rire** to burst out laughing

éclectique /eklɛktik/ *adj* eclectic

éclipse /eklips/ *nf* eclipse

éclipser /eklipse/ [1] **1** *vtr* **(a)** to eclipse
(b) to obscure
(c) to outshine
2 **s'éclipser** *v refl* (+ *v être*) (fam) to slip away

éclopé, $\sim$**e** /eklope/ *adj* injured, lame

éclore /eklɔʀ/ [79] *vi* **(a)** ‹*chick, egg*› to hatch; ‹*flower*› to bloom; **faire** $\sim$ **un œuf** to incubate an egg
(b) ‹*idea*› to dawn; ‹*talent*› to bloom

écluse /eklyz/ *nf* lock

écœurant, $\sim$**e** /ekœʀɑ̃, ɑ̃t/ *adj* **(a)** ‹*food, smell*› sickly
(b) nauseating
(c) (humorous) sickening

écœurement /ekœʀmɑ̃/ *nm* nausea

écœurer /ekœʀe/ [1] *vtr* **(a)** to make [sb] feel sick
(b) (figurative) to sicken

éco-guerrier, -ière /ekɔgeʀje, ɛʀ/ *nm,f* eco-warrior

$\checkmark$ **école** /ekɔl/ *nf* **(a)** school
(b) education system
(c) (grande) $\sim$ higher education institution *with competitive entrance examination*; **une** $\sim$ **de commerce** a business school
(d) training (de in); **être à bonne** $\sim$ to be in good hands
(e) (of art) school; **faire** $\sim$ to gain a following
■ $\sim$ **élémentaire** primary school; $\sim$ **d'infirmières** nursing college; $\sim$ **maternelle** nursery school; $\sim$ **normale** primary teacher training college; $\sim$ **primaire** primary school; **École nationale d'administration, ENA** *Grande École for top civil servants*; **École normale supérieure, ENS** *Grande École from which the educational élite is recruited*

écolier, -ière /ekɔlje, ɛʀ/ *nm,f* schoolboy/schoolgirl

écologie /ekɔlɔʒi/ *nf* ecology

écologique /ekɔlɔʒik/ *adj* ecological; ‹*speech*› on the environment; ‹*interest*› environmental; ‹*product*› environment-friendly

écologiste /ekɔlɔʒist/ **1** *adj*
(a) ‹*candidate*› Green
(b) ‹*measure*› ecological
2 *nmf* **(a)** environmentalist
(b) Green (candidate)
(c) ecologist

écomusée /ekomyze/ *nm* ≈ open air museum

éconduire /ekɔ̃dɥiʀ/ [69] *vtr* to turn [sb] away

économat /ekɔnɔma/ *nm* bursar's office

économe /ekɔnɔm/ **1** *adj* thrifty

$\checkmark$ indicates a very frequent word

2 *nm* (Culin) potato peeler

$\checkmark$ **économie** /ekɔnɔmi/ **1** *nf* **(a)** (of country) economy
(b) (discipline) economics
(c) (amount saved) saving; **faire l'**$\sim$ **de** to save the cost of ‹*trip*›
(d) economy, thrift; **par** $\sim$ in order to save money; **s'exprimer avec une grande** $\sim$ **de paroles** to express oneself succinctly
2 **économies** *nf pl* savings; **faire des** $\sim$**s** to save up; to save money
■ $\sim$ **d'entreprise** managerial economics; $\sim$ **de marché** free market (economy)
IDIOM il n'y a pas de petites $\sim$**s** every little helps

$\checkmark$ **économique** /ekɔnɔmik/ *adj* **(a)** ‹*policy, crisis*› economic
(b) economical

économiser /ekɔnɔmize/ [1] *vtr* **(a)** to save (up) ‹*money*›; $\sim$ **ses forces** to pace oneself
(b) to save ‹*petrol, water, energy*›
(c) to economize

économiste /ekɔnɔmist/ *nmf* economist

écoper /ekɔpe/ [1] *vtr* to bail out

écoproduit /ekɔpʀɔdɥi/ *nm* eco-product

écorce /ekɔʀs/ *nf* (of tree) bark; (of fruit) peel; (of chestnut) skin
■ $\sim$ **terrestre** earth's crust

écorché, $\sim$**e** /ekɔʀʃe/ *adj* $\sim$ **(vif)** hypersensitive

écorcher /ekɔʀʃe/ [1] *vtr* **(a)** to skin ‹*animal*›; to flay ‹*person*›
(b) to graze ‹*face, leg*›
(c) to mispronounce ‹*word*›

écorchure /ekɔʀʃyʀ/ *nf* graze

écossais, $\sim$**e** /ekɔsɛ, ɛz/ **1** *adj* Scottish; ‹*whisky*› Scotch; ‹*language*› Scots; ‹*skirt*› tartan
2 *nm* **(a)** (dialect) Scots
(b) (Scottish) Gaelic
(c) tartan (cloth)

Écossais, $\sim$**e** /ekɔsɛ, ɛz/ *nm,f* Scotsman/Scotswoman, Scot

Écosse /ekɔs/ *pr nf* Scotland

écosser /ekɔse/ [1] *vtr* to shell

écot /eko/ *nm* share

écoulement /ekulmɑ̃/ *nm* **(a)** (of water, traffic) flow; (of time) passing
(b) (Med) discharge
(c) (of banknotes, drugs) circulation

écouler /ekule/ [1] **1** *vtr* **(a)** to sell ‹*product*›; **les stocks sont écoulés** stocks are exhausted
(b) to fence ‹*stolen goods*›; to pass ‹*banknote*›
2 **s'écouler** *v refl* (+ *v être*) **(a)** ‹*time, life*› to pass
(b) ‹*river*› to flow
(c) ‹*oil, water*› to escape
(d) ‹*water*› to drain away
(e) ‹*product*› to move

écourter /ekuʀte/ [1] *vtr* to cut short ‹*stay*›

écoute /ekut/ *nf* (a) être à l'∼ de to be listening to ‹programme›; to be (always) ready to listen to ‹problems›
(b) audience; **heure de grande** ∼ peak listening time; peak viewing time
(c) **un centre d'**∼**(s)** monitoring centre (GB); **je suis sur** ∼**(s)** my phone is being tapped

✦ **écouter** /ekute/ [1] **1** *vtr* (a) to listen to [sb/sth]; ∼ **qn chanter** to listen to sb singing; ∼ **aux portes** to eavesdrop
(b) ∼ **son cœur** to follow one's own inclination
2 **s'écouter** *v refl* (+ *v être*) (a) s'∼ **parler** to like the sound of one's own voice
(b) to cosset oneself
(c) **si je m'écoutais** if it was up to me

écouteur /ekutœʀ/ *nm* (a) (on phone) earpiece
(b) earphones
(c) headphones

écoutille /ekutij/ *nf* (Naut) hatch

écrabouiller /ekʀabuje/ [1] *vtr* (fam) to squash

✦ **écran** /ekʀɑ̃/ *nm* (a) (gen) screen; **crever l'**∼ ‹actor› to have a great screen presence; **une vedette du petit** ∼ a TV star
(b) cinema (GB), movie theater (US)
(c) (on machine) display
(d) **crème** ∼ **total** sun block
■ ∼ **antibruit** soundproofing; ∼ **de contrôle** monitor; ∼ **à cristaux liquide** liquid crystal display, LCD; ∼ **solaire** sunscreen; ∼ **tactile** touch screen; ∼ **de visualisation** VDU screen

écrasant, ∼e /ekʀazɑ̃, ɑ̃t/ *adj* (a) ‹weight› enormous
(b) ‹heat› sweltering; ‹victory› resounding; ‹responsibility› heavy

écraser /ekʀaze/ [1] **1** *vtr* (a) to crush ‹finger, person›; to squash, to crush ‹insect, hat, fruit, box›; ‹driver› to run over ‹person, animal›; **se faire** ∼ to get run over
(b) to flatten ‹vegetation›
(c) (Culin) to mash ‹fruit›
(d) ∼ **sa cigarette** to stub out one's cigarette; ∼ **une larme** to wipe away a tear
(e) to press ‹nose, face› (**contre** against)
(f) to crush ‹rebellion›; to thrash (colloq) ‹opponent›
(g) to outshine
(h) to put [sb] down
(i) ‹fatigue, heat› to overcome
2 **s'écraser** *v refl* (+ *v être*) (a) ‹car, train› to crash; ‹driver, motorcyclist› to have a crash; ‹insect› to splatter (**contre** on)
(b) (fam) to shut up (colloq)
(c) (fam) to keep one's head down

écrémé, ∼e /ekʀeme/ *adj* skimmed

écrémer /ekʀeme/ [14] *vtr* (a) to skim ‹milk›
(b) to cream off the best of ‹candidates›

écrevisse /ekʀəvis/ *nf* crayfish (GB), crawfish (US)

écrier: s'écrier /ekʀije/ [2] *v refl* (+ *v être*) to exclaim

écrin /ekʀɛ̃/ *nm* (for jewellery) case

✦ **écrire** /ekʀiʀ/ [67] **1** *vtr* (a) to write
(b) to spell
2 *vi* to write
3 **s'écrire** *v refl* (+ *v être*) (a) to be written
(b) to be spelled

écrit, ∼e /ekʀi, it/ **1** *pp* ▸ ÉCRIRE
2 *pp adj* written; **c'était** ∼ it was bound to happen
3 *nm* (a) work, piece of writing
(b) document; **par** ∼ in writing
(c) written examination
IDIOM **les paroles s'envolent, les** ∼**s restent** never put anything in writing; (as security) get it in writing

écriteau, *pl* ∼**x** /ekʀito/ *nm* sign

écritoire /ekʀitwaʀ/ *nf* writing case

✦ **écriture** /ekʀityʀ/ **1** *nf* (a) handwriting
(b) (in printing) hand
(c) (text, activity) writing
(d) script; ∼ **phonétique** phonetic script
2 **écritures** *nf pl* accounts; **tenir les** ∼**s** to do the books

Écriture /ekʀityʀ/ *nf* **les (saintes)** ∼**s** the Scriptures; **l'**∼ **sainte** Holy Writ

✦ **écrivain** /ekʀivɛ̃/ *nm* writer

écrou /ekʀu/ *nm* (Tech) nut

écrouer /ekʀue/ [1] *vtr* (Law) to commit [sb] to prison

écroulé, ∼e /ekʀule/ *adj* overwhelmed; ∼ **de rire** (fam) doubled up with laughter

écrouler: s'écrouler /ekʀule/ [1] *v refl* (+ *v être*) to collapse; to fade; to crumble

écru, ∼e /ekʀy/ *adj* ‹canvas› unbleached; ‹wool› undyed; ‹silk› raw
(b) (colour) ecru

écu /eky/ *nm* (a) (Hist) (in EU) ecu
(b) ≈ crown
(c) shield

écueil /ekœj/ *nm* (a) reef
(b) (figurative) pitfall

écuelle /ekɥɛl/ *nf* (a) bowl
(b) bowlful

écume /ekym/ *nf* (a) (on water) foam; (on beer) froth; (on metal) dross
(b) (at mouth) foam, froth

écumer /ekyme/ [1] **1** *vtr* (a) to skim
(b) to scour, to search
2 *vi* ‹sea› to foam; ‹wine› to froth

écumoire /ekymwaʀ/ *nf* skimming ladle

écureuil /ekyʀœj/ *nm* squirrel

écurie /ekyʀi/ *nf* (a) stable
(b) (Sport) stable
(c) (figurative) pigsty

écusson /ekysɔ̃/ *nm* (a) (Mil) flash (GB)
(b) (of school) crest, badge; (of club, movement) badge; (of car) insignia
(c) (in heraldry) coat of arms

e

écuyer, -ère /ekɥije, ɛʀ/ **1** *nm,f*
(a) horseman/horsewoman
(b) riding instructor
(c) bareback rider
2 *nm* (a) squire
(b) equerry

eczéma /ɛgzema/ *nm* eczema

éden /edɛn/ *nm* paradise

Éden /edɛn/ *pr nm* Eden

édenté, ~e /edɑ̃te/ *adj* (a) toothless
(b) gap-toothed
(c) ‹comb› broken

EDF /œdeɛf/ *nf* (abbr = **Électricité de France**) *French electricity board*

édicter /edikte/ [1] *vtr* to enact ‹law›

édifiant, ~e /edifjɑ̃, ɑ̃t/ *adj* (a) edifying
(b) enlightening

édifice /edifis/ *nm* (a) building
(b) structure

édifier /edifje/ [2] *vtr* (a) to build [sth]
(b) to build ‹empire›
(c) to edify
(d) to enlighten

Édimbourg /edɛ̃buʀ/ *pr n* Edinburgh

édit /edi/ *nm* edict

éditer /edite/ [1] *vtr* (a) to publish ‹book, author›; to release ‹record›
(b) (Comput) to edit

éditeur, -trice /editœʀ, tʀis/ **1** *nm,f*
editor
2 *nm* (a) publisher
(b) (Comput) editor

❖ **édition** /edisjɔ̃/ **1** *nf* (a) (of book)
publication; (of record) release
(b) (book, print) edition; (record) release
(c) publishing; **société d'~** publishing firm
(d) editing
(e) (paper) **~ du soir** evening edition
2 **éditions** *nf pl* **les ~s de la Roulotte** la
Roulotte (Publishing Company)

éditorial, ~e, *mpl* -iaux /editɔʀjal, o/
1 *adj* ‹policy, service› editorial
2 *nm* editorial, leader

édredon /edʀədɔ̃/ *nm* eiderdown

éducateur, -trice /edykatœʀ, tʀis/
1 *adj* educational
2 *nm,f* youth worker

éducatif, -ive /edykatif, iv/ *adj*
educational

❖ **éducation** /edykasjɔ̃/ *nf* (a) education;
faire l'~ de qn to educate sb
(b) training
(c) manners
■ **Éducation nationale, EN** Ministry of
Education; (system) state education

édulcorer /edylkɔʀe/ [1] *vtr* (a) to sweeten
(b) to tone down ‹letter, remark›

éduquer /edyke/ [1] *vtr* to educate; to train

effacé, ~e /efase/ *adj* retiring

❖ indicates a very frequent word

effacement /efasmɑ̃/ *nm* (a) deletion
(b) (of cassette) erasure
(c) self-effacement

❖ **effacer** /efase/ [12] **1** *vtr* (a) to rub out; to
delete; to erase
(b) to wipe ‹tape›; to clear ‹file›; to clean
‹blackboard›
(c) ‹rain› to erase ‹tracks›; ‹snow› to cover
(up) ‹tracks›; ‹cream› to remove ‹wrinkles›
(d) to blot out ‹memory›; to remove
‹differences›
(e) to write off ‹debt›
2 **s'effacer** *v refl* (+ *v être*) (a) **ça s'efface**
you can rub it out
(b) ‹inscription, drawing, memory› to fade;
‹impression› to wear off; ‹fear› to disappear
(c) to step aside
(d) to stay in the background

effaceur /efasœʀ/ *nm* correction pen

effarant, ~e /efaʀɑ̃, ɑ̃t/ *adj* astounding

effarer /efaʀe/ [1] *vtr* to alarm

effaroucher /efaʀuʃe/ [1] *vtr* (a) to
frighten [sb/sth] away
(b) to alarm

effectif, -ive /efɛktif, iv/ **1** *adj* real
2 *nm* (of school) number of pupils; (of
university) number of students; (of company)
workforce; (of army) strength

❖ **effectivement** /efɛktivmɑ̃/ *adv*
(a) indeed
(b) actually, really

❖ **effectuer** /efɛktɥe/ [1] *vtr* to do ‹work,
repairs›; to make ‹payment, trip›; to carry
out ‹transaction›; to conduct ‹survey›; to
serve ‹sentence›

efféminé, ~e /efemine/ *adj* effeminate

effervescence /efɛʀvesɑ̃s/ *nf*
(a) effervescence
(b) turmoil

effervescent, ~e /efɛʀvesɑ̃, ɑ̃t/ *adj*
(a) effervescent
(b) (figurative) ‹crowd› seething; ‹personality›
effervescent

❖ **effet** /efɛ/ **1** *nm* (a) effect; **prendre ~**
‹measure, law› to take effect; **sous l'~ de
l'alcool** under the influence of alcohol;
couper tous ses ~s à qn to steal sb's
thunder
(b) impression; **être du plus mauvais ~** to be
in the worst possible taste; **faire un drôle d'~**
to make one feel strange; **un ~ de surprise**
an element of surprise
(c) **à cet ~** for that purpose
2 **en effet** *phr* indeed
3 **effets** *nm pl* things, clothes
■ **~ de serre** greenhouse effect; **~s secondaires** (Med) side effects

❖ **efficace** /efikas/ *adj* effective; efficient

efficacement /efikasmɑ̃/ *adv* efficiently;
effectively

efficacité /efikasite/ *nf* (of action, remedy)
effectiveness; (of person, device) efficiency

effigie /efiʒi/ *nf* (a) effigy; à l'~ de ‹medal, stamp› with the head of
(b) logo

effilé, ~**e** /efile/ *adj* ‹almonds› flaked

effiler /efile/ [1] **1** *vtr* (a) to sharpen
(b) to string ‹green beans›
2 **s'effiler** *v refl* (+ *v être*) to fray

effilocher /efiloʃe/ [1] **1** *vtr* to shred
2 **s'effilocher** *v refl* (+ *v être*) to fray

efflanqué, ~**e** /eflɑ̃ke/ *adj* emaciated

effleurer /eflœʀe/ [1] *vtr* to touch lightly, to brush (against); **l'idée ne m'a même pas effleuré** the idea didn't even cross my mind

effluent /eflyɑ̃/ *nm* effluent

effluve /eflyv/ *nm* (a) unpleasant smell
(b) fragrance

effondrement /efɔ̃dʀəmɑ̃/ *nm*
(a) collapse
(b) subsidence

effondrer: s'effondrer /efɔ̃dʀe/ [1] *v refl* (+ *v être*) (a) ‹roof, person› to collapse; ‹dreams› to crumble; ‹hopes› to fall
(b) être effondré par la nouvelle to be distraught at the news

efforcer: s'efforcer /efɔʀse/ [12] *v refl* (+ *v être*) to try hard (**de faire** to do)

⚜ **effort** /efɔʀ/ *nm* (a) effort; **fais un petit ~ d'imagination!** use a bit of imagination!; **avec mon dos, je ne peux pas faire d'~** with this back of mine, I can't do anything strenuous
(b) (in physics) stress; strain

effraction /efʀaksjɔ̃/ *nf* breaking and entering
■ ~ **informatique** computer hacking

effrayant, ~**e** /efʀejɑ̃, ɑ̃t/ *adj* ‹sight, ugliness› frightening; ‹thinness, paleness› dreadful

effrayer /efʀeje/ [21] *vtr* (a) to frighten; to alarm
(b) ‹difficulty, price› to put [sb] off

effréné, ~**e** /efʀene/ *adj* ‹rhythm, competition› frenzied; ‹ambition› wild

effriter /efʀite/ [1] **1** *vtr* to crumble; to break up
2 **s'effriter** *v refl* (+ *v être*) to crumble (away)

effroi /efʀwa/ *nm* dread, terror

effronté, ~**e** /efʀɔ̃te/ *adj* cheeky; shameless

effroyable /efʀwajabl/ *adj* dreadful

effroyablement /efʀwajabləmɑ̃/ *adv*
(a) horribly
(b) (fam) terribly

effusion /efyzjɔ̃/ *nf* effusion
■ ~ **de sang** bloodshed

⚜ **égal**, ~**e**, *mpl* **-aux** /egal, o/ **1** *adj*
(a) equal (à to); **à prix ~, je préfère celui-là** if the price is the same, I'd rather have that one
(b) ‹ground› level; ‹light› even; ‹colour›

uniform; ‹weather› settled; ‹pulse, breathing› steady; **d'un pas ~** at an even pace
(c) **ça m'est ~** I don't mind (either way); I don't care
2 *nm, f* equal; **traiter d'~ à ~ avec qn** to deal with sb as an equal
IDIOMS rester ~ à soi-même to be one's usual self; **combattre à armes ~es** to be on an equal footing

égalable /egalabl/ *adj* **difficilement ~** unparalleled; incomparably superior

⚜ **également** /egalmɑ̃/ *adv* (a) also, too
(b) equally

égaler /egale/ [1] *vtr* (a) to equal ‹record›; to be as good as ‹person›; to be as high as ‹price›
(b) **trois plus trois égalent six** three plus three equals six *or* is six

égalisation /egalizasjɔ̃/ *nf* (a) levelling (GB) out
(b) **le penalty a permis l'~** the penalty evened (GB) *or* tied (US) the score

égaliser /egalize/ [1] **1** *vtr* (a) to level ‹ground›
(b) to make [sth] the same size ‹planks›
2 *vi* (Sport) to equalize (GB), to tie (US)

égalitaire /egalitɛʀ/ *adj, nmf* egalitarian

⚜ **égalité** /egalite/ *nf* (a) equality
(b) (Sport) **être à ~** to be level (GB), to be tied (US); **~!** deuce!

⚜ **égard** /egaʀ/ **1** *nm* (a) consideration; **sans ~ pour** without regard for
(b) **à l'~ de qn** toward(s) sb; **à cet ~** in this respect
2 **égards** *nm pl* **avec des ~s** with respect; **être plein d'~s envers qn** to be attentive to sb's every need

égaré, ~**e** /egaʀe/ *adj* (a) stray
(b) ‹look› wild

égarement /egaʀmɑ̃/ *nm* (a) distraction, madness
(b) confusion
(c) erratic behaviour (GB)

égarer /egaʀe/ [1] **1** *vtr* (a) to lead [sb] astray
(b) to mislay
2 **s'égarer** *v refl* (+ *v être*) (a) to get lost
(b) (figurative) ‹mind› to wander; ‹person› to ramble

égayer /egeje/ [21] *vtr* to enliven; to lighten; to brighten; to cheer [sb] up

égérie /eʒeʀi/ *nf* muse

égide /eʒid/ *nf* aegis

églantine /eglɑ̃tin/ *nf* wild rose, dog-rose

églefin /egləfɛ̃/ *nm* haddock

⚜ **église** /egliz/ *nf* church

ego /ego/ *nm inv* ego

égocentrique /egosɑ̃tʀik/ *adj, nmf* egocentric

égoïsme /egɔism/ *nm* selfishness

égoïste /egɔist/ *adj* selfish

égorger /egɔʀʒe/ [13] *vtr* ~ **qn** to cut sb's throat

égosiller: **s'égosiller** /egozije/ [1] *v refl* (+ *v être)* **(a)** to shout oneself hoarse
(b) to sing at the top of one's voice
(c) to yell

égout /egu/ *nm* sewer

égoutter /egute/ [1] **1** *vtr* to drain
2 **s'égoutter** *v refl* (+ *v être)* ‹*dishes, rice, vegetables*› to drain; ‹*washing*› to drip dry

égouttoir /egutwaʀ/ *nm* draining rack (GB), (dish) drainer (US)

égratigner /egʀatiɲe/ [1] **1** *vtr* to scratch, to graze
2 **s'égratigner** *v refl* (+ *v être)* to scratch oneself; to graze oneself

égratignure /egʀatiɲyʀ/ *nf* scratch; graze

égrener /egʀəne/ [16] *vtr* **(a)** to shell ‹*peas*›; to remove the seeds from ‹*melon*›
(b) to chime out ‹*notes*›; ~ **son chapelet** to tell one's beads

Égypte /eʒipt/ *pr nf* Egypt

égyptien, -ienne /eʒipsjɛ̃, ɛn/ **1** *adj* Egyptian
2 *nm* (language) Egyptian

éhonté, ~e /eõte/ *adj* ‹*liar, lie*› brazen

Éire /ɛʀ/ *pr n* Éire, Republic of Ireland

éjectable /eʒɛktabl/ *adj* **siège** ~ ejector seat (GB), ejection seat (US)

éjecter /eʒɛkte/ [1] *vtr* **(a)** (in accident) to throw [sb/sth] out
(b) (Tech) to eject

élaboration /elabɔʀasjõ/ *nf* development; working out; drafting; putting together

élaboré, ~e /elabɔʀe/ *adj* sophisticated; elaborate

élaborer /elabɔʀe/ [1] *vtr* to work [sth] out; to draw [sth] up; to put [sth] together

élaguer /elage/ [1] *vtr* to prune

élan /elã/ *nm* **(a)** (Sport) run up; **saut sans** ~ standing jump
(b) momentum
(c) impetus
(d) enthusiasm; ~ **patriotique** patriotic fervour (GB)
(e) impulse; ~ **de tendresse** surge of tenderness
(f) (Zool) elk

élancé, ~e /elãse/ *adj* slender

élancement /elãsmã/ *nm* throbbing pain

élancer: **s'élancer** /elãse/ [12] *v refl* (+ *v être)* **(a)** to dash forward
(b) **s'**~ **vers le ciel** ‹*tree, spire*› to soar up toward(s) the sky

élargi, ~e /elaʀʒi/ *adj* enlarged; expanded

élargir /elaʀʒiʀ/ [3] **1** *vtr* **(a)** to widen ‹*road*›; to let out ‹*garment*›
(b) to stretch ‹*shoes, sweater*›
(c) to extend ‹*contacts, law*›; to broaden

‹*knowledge*›; to increase ‹*majority*›
2 **s'élargir** *v refl* (+ *v être)* ‹*group*› to expand; ‹*gap*› to increase; ‹*road*› to widen; ‹*person*› to fill out; ‹*garment*› to stretch

élastique /elastik/ **1** *adj* **(a)** ‹*waistband*› elasticated (GB), elasticized (US)
(b) ‹*gas, fibre*› elastic
(c) ‹*rule, timetable*› flexible; ‹*budget*› elastic
2 *nm* **(a)** rubber band
(b) (in haberdashery) elastic
(c) (Sport) bungee cord
IDIOM les lâcher avec un ~ (fam) to be tight-fisted

élastomère /elastɔmɛʀ/ *nm* elastomer

électeur, -trice /elɛktœʀ, tʀis/ *nm,f* voter

ơ **élection** /elɛksjõ/ *nf* **(a)** election
(b) choice; **mon pays d'**~ my chosen country

électoral, ~e, mpl -aux /elɛktɔʀal, o/ *adj* electoral; election

électorat /elɛktɔʀa/ *nm* electorate, voters

électricien, -ienne /elɛktʀisjɛ̃, ɛn/ *nm,f* electrician

électricité /elɛktʀisite/ *nf* electricity

électrifier /elɛktʀifje/ [2] *vtr* to electrify ‹*railtracks*›

électrique /elɛktʀik/ *adj* **(a)** electrical
(b) (figurative) ‹*atmosphere*› electric

électriser /elɛktʀize/ [1] *vtr* to electrify

électro(-) /elɛktʀo/ *pref* electro; ~**cardiogramme** electrocardiogram

électrochoc /elɛktʀoʃɔk/ *nm* ~**s** electroshock therapy, EST

électrocuter: **s'électrocuter** /elɛktʀɔkyte/ [1] *v refl* (+ *v être)* to be electrocuted

électrode /elɛktʀɔd/ *nf* electrode

électrogène /elɛktʀoʒɛn/ *adj* **groupe** ~ (electricity) generator

électromécanicien, -ienne /elɛktʀomekanisjɛ̃, ɛn/ *nm,f* electrical engineer

électroménager /elɛktʀomenaʒe/ **1** *adj* **m appareil** ~ household appliance
2 *nm* **(a)** domestic electrical appliances
(b) electrical goods industry

électron /elɛktʀõ/ *nm* electron

électronicien, -ienne /elɛktʀonisjɛ̃, ɛn/ *nm,f* electronics engineer

électronique /elɛktʀonik/ **1** *adj*
(a) ‹*circuit*› electronic
(b) ‹*microscope*› electron
2 *nf* electronics

électrophone /elɛktʀofɔn/ *nm* record player

élégamment /elegamã/ *adv* ‹*dress*› elegantly

élégance /elegãs/ *nf* elegance; **avec** ~ ‹*dress*› elegantly; ‹*lose*› gracefully; ‹*behave*› honourably (GB); ‹*resolve problem*› neatly

---

ơ indicates a very frequent word

élégant, ~**e** /elegɑ̃, ɑ̃t/ *adj* elegant; **ce n'est pas très ~ de ta part** it's not very decent of you

✔ **élément** /elemɑ̃/ ① *nm* **(a)** (in structure, ensemble) element; (in device) component; **~ moteur** driving force
(b) factor, element; **l'~-clé de** the key element in
(c) (of furniture) unit
(d) fact; **disposer de tous les ~s** to have all the facts
(e) (person) **bon ~** good pupil; good player
(f) (chemical) element
② **éléments** *nm pl* elements

élémentaire /elemɑ̃tɛʀ/ *adj* **(a)** ⟨*principle*⟩ basic
(b) elementary

éléphant /elefɑ̃/ *nm* elephant

éléphanteau, *pl* ~**x** /elefɑ̃to/ *nm* (elephant) calf

élevage /elvaʒ/ *nm* **(a)** livestock farming; **faire de l'~ de porcs** to breed pigs; **d'~** ⟨*oysters*⟩ farmed; ⟨*pheasant*⟩ captive-bred
(b) farm; **un ~ de visons** a mink farm
(c) stock (**de** of)

élévateur /elevatœʀ/ *nm* elevator

élévation /elevasjɔ̃/ *nf* **(a)** rise (**de** in)
(b) (to rank) elevation
(c) (in architecture) elevation

élevé, ~**e** /elve/ *adj* **(a)** ⟨*level, price, rank*⟩ high
(b) ⟨*plateau*⟩ high
(c) ⟨*sentiment*⟩ fine, ⟨*principles*⟩ high; ⟨*ideal*⟩ lofty; ⟨*language*⟩ elevated

✔ **élève** /elɛv/ *nmf* (gen) student; (Sch) pupil; **~ officier** trainee officer

✔ **élever** /elve/ [16] ① *vtr* **(a)** to put up, to erect
(b) to raise ⟨*temperature, level*⟩
(c) to lift, to raise ⟨*load*⟩
(d) la poésie élève l'âme poetry is elevating *or* uplifting
(e) to raise ⟨*objection*⟩
(f) to bring [sb] up; **c'est mal élevé** it's bad manners (**de faire** to do)
(g) to rear ⟨*cattle*⟩; to keep ⟨*bees*⟩
② **s'élever** *v refl* (+ *v être*) **(a)** ⟨*rate*⟩ to rise
(b) s'~ à ⟨*expenses*⟩ to come to; ⟨*death toll*⟩ to stand at
(c) to rise (up); **s'~ dans les airs** ⟨*smoke*⟩ to rise up into the air; ⟨*bird*⟩ to soar into the air
(d) ⟨*voice, protests*⟩ to be heard
(e) s'~ contre qch to protest against sth
(f) ⟨*statue*⟩ to stand; **s'~ au-dessus de qch** to rise above sth

éleveur, -**euse** /elvœʀ, øz/ *nm,f* breeder

elfe /ɛlf/ *nm* elf

élider /elide/ [1] *vtr* to elide

éligible /eliʒibl/ *adj* eligible for office

élimé, ~**e** /elime/ *adj* threadbare

élimer /elime/ [1] ① *vtr* to wear [sth] thin
② **s'élimer** *v refl* (+ *v être*) to wear thin

élimination /eliminasjɔ̃/ *nf* **(a)** (gen) elimination, defeat
(b) (of stain) removal; **~ déchets** waste disposal

éliminatoire /eliminatwaʀ/ *adj* ⟨*question, match*⟩ qualifying; ⟨*mark*⟩ eliminatory

éliminer /elimine/ [1] *vtr* to eliminate

élire /eliʀ/ [66] *vtr* to elect; **se faire ~** to be elected; **~ domicile** to take up residence

élision /elizjɔ̃/ *nf* elision

élite /elit/ *nf* **l'~** the elite; **d'~** ⟨*troops*⟩ elite, crack; ⟨*student*⟩ high-flying; ⟨*athlete*⟩ top

élitisme /elitism/ *nm* elitism

élixir /eliksiʀ/ *nm* elixir

✔ **elle** /ɛl/ *pron f* she; it; ~**s** they; **je les vois plus souvent qu'~** I see them more often than she does; I see them more often than (I see) her; **le bol bleu est à ~** the blue bowl is hers

ellébore /elebɔʀ/ *nm* hellebore

elle-même, *pl* **elles-mêmes** /ɛlmɛm/ *pron* herself; itself; **elles-mêmes** themselves; **'Mme Roc?'**—'**~**' 'Mrs Roc?'– 'speaking'

elles ► ELLE

ellipse /elips/ *nf* ellipsis

elliptique /eliptik/ *adj* **(a)** elliptical
(b) elliptic

élocution /elɔkysjɔ̃/ *nf* diction; **défaut d'~** speech impediment

éloge /elɔʒ/ *nm* **(a)** praise; **être tout à l'~ de qn** to do sb great credit
(b) eulogy; **~ funèbre** funeral oration

élogieux, -**ieuse** /elɔʒjø, øz/ *adj* full of praise; laudatory

éloigné, ~**e** /elwaɲe/ *adj* **(a)** distant; **~ de tout** remote; **deux usines ~es de cinq kilomètres** two factories five kilometres (GB) apart
(b) ⟨*memories*⟩ distant; ⟨*event*⟩ remote; **~ dans le temps** distant (in time)
(c) ⟨*cousin*⟩ distant

éloignement /elwaɲmɑ̃/ *nm* **(a)** distance
(b) remoteness

✔ **éloigner** /elwaɲe/ [1] ① *vtr* **(a)** to move [sb/sth] away
(b) ils font tout pour l'~ de moi they are doing everything to drive us apart
② **s'éloigner** *v refl* (+ *v être*) **(a)** to move away; **ne t'éloigne pas trop** don't go too far away
(b) s'~ de to move away from ⟨*party line*⟩; to stray from ⟨*subject*⟩

élongation /elɔ̃gasjɔ̃/ *nf* (Med) pulled muscle

éloquence /elɔkɑ̃s/ *nf* eloquence

éloquent, ~**e** /elɔkɑ̃, ɑ̃t/ *adj* eloquent

élu, ~**e** /ely/ *nm,f* **(a)** elected representative
(b) beloved
(c) (in religion) **les ~s** the Chosen Ones

élucider /elyside/ [1] *vtr* to solve ‹crime, problem›; to clarify ‹circumstances›

élucubrations /elykybʀasjɔ̃/ *nf pl* rantings

éluder /elyde/ [1] *vtr* to evade

Élysée /elize/ *pr nm* **(palais de) l'∼** the official residence of the French President

émacier: s'émacier /emasje/ [2] *v refl* (+ *v être*) to become emaciated

e-mail /emaj/ *nm* e-mail

émail, *pl* **-aux** /emaj, o/ *nm* enamel

émaillé, **∼e** /emaje/ *adj* ‹utensil› enamel; ‹metal› enamelled

émanation /emanasjɔ̃/ *nf* emanation; **∼s de gaz** gas fumes

émancipation /emɑ̃sipasjɔ̃/ *nf* emancipation

émanciper /emɑ̃sipe/ [1] **1** *vtr* to emancipate ‹people›; to liberate ‹country›
2 s'émanciper *v refl* (+ *v être*) to become emancipated; **femme émancipée** liberated woman

émaner /emane/ [1] **1** *vi* **∼ de** to emanate from; to come from
2 *v impers* **il émane d'elle un charme fou** she exudes charm

émaux ▶ ÉMAIL

emballage /ɑ̃balaʒ/ *nm* packaging; wrapping; packing
■ **∼ sous vide** vacuum packing

emballant, **∼e** /ɑ̃balɑ̃, ɑ̃t/ *adj* (fam) exciting

emballer /ɑ̃bale/ [1] **1** *vtr* **(a)** to pack, to wrap
(b) (fam) **être emballé par** to be taken with
2 s'emballer *v refl* (+ *v être*) **(a)** ‹horse› to bolt
(b) (fam) to get carried away
(c) to get all worked up (colloq)
(d) (fam) ‹engine› to race
(e) ‹prices, inflation› to shoot up; ‹currency› to shoot up in value

embarcadère /ɑ̃baʀkadɛʀ/ *nm* pier; wharf

embarcation /ɑ̃baʀkasjɔ̃/ *nf* boat

embardée /ɑ̃baʀde/ *nf* (of car) swerve

embargo /ɑ̃baʀgo/ *nm* embargo

embarquement /ɑ̃baʀkəmɑ̃/ *nm* boarding

embarquer /ɑ̃baʀke/ [1] **1** *vtr* **(a)** to load ‹goods›; to take [sb] on board
(b) (fam) to take ‹object›; ‹police› to pick up ‹criminal›
2 *vi* **(a)** to board
(b) to sail (**pour** for)
3 s'embarquer *v refl* (+ *v être*) **(a)** to board
(b) (fam) **s'∼ dans** to launch into ‹explanation›

embarras /ɑ̃baʀa/ *nm inv*
(a) embarrassment
(b) awkward position; difficult situation
(c) n'avoir que l'∼ du choix to have too much to choose from

embarrassant, **∼e** /ɑ̃baʀasɑ̃, ɑ̃t/ *adj*
(a) awkward; embarrassing
(b) cumbersome

embarrassé, **∼e** /ɑ̃baʀase/ **1** *pp*
▶ EMBARRASSER
2 *pp adj* **(a)** embarrassed; **être bien ∼ pour répondre** to be at a loss for an answer
(b) ‹room› cluttered; **∼ d'une grosse valise** weighed down with a large suitcase

embarrasser /ɑ̃baʀase/ [1] **1** *vtr* **(a)** to embarrass
(b) to clutter [sth] (up); **cette armoire m'embarrasse plutôt qu'autre chose** this wardrobe is more of a nuisance than anything else
2 s'embarrasser *v refl* (+ *v être*) **s'∼ de** to burden oneself with ‹baggage, person›

embauche /ɑ̃boʃ/ *nf* appointment (GB), hiring (US); **salaire d'∼** starting salary

embaucher /ɑ̃boʃe/ [1] *vtr* **(a)** to take on (GB), to hire
(b) (fam) to recruit

embaumer /ɑ̃bome/ [1] **1** *vtr* **(a)** ‹smell› to fill ‹place›; ‹place› to smell of ‹wax›
(b) to embalm
2 *vi* to be fragrant

embaumeur, **-euse** /ɑ̃bomœʀ, øz/ *nm,f* embalmer

embellir /ɑ̃beliʀ/ [3] **1** *vtr* **(a)** to improve [sth]; to make [sb] more attractive
(b) to embellish ‹story, truth›
2 *vi* to become more attractive

embellissement /ɑ̃belismɑ̃/ *nm* (of house) improving; **travaux d'∼** improvements

emberlificoter /ɑ̃bɛʀlifikɔte/ [1] (fam) **1** *vtr* **(a)** to entangle
(b) to take [sb] in (colloq)
2 s'emberlificoter *v refl* (+ *v être*) to get entangled; to get tangled up (**dans** in)

embêtant, **∼e** /ɑ̃betɑ̃, ɑ̃t/ *adj* **(a)** annoying
(b) boring

embêtement /ɑ̃betmɑ̃/ *nm* problem

embêter /ɑ̃bete/ [1] **1** *vtr* **(a)** to bother
(b) to pester; to annoy
(c) to bore
2 s'embêter *v refl* (+ *v être*) **(a)** to be bored
(b) **s'∼ à faire** to go to the bother of doing

emblée: d'emblée /dɑ̃ble/ *phr*
(a) straightaway
(b) at first sight

emblématique /ɑ̃blematik/ *adj* emblematic; symbolic

emblème /ɑ̃blɛm/ *nm* emblem

embobiner /ɑ̃bɔbine/ [1] *vtr* (fam) to hoodwink

ᕫ indicates a very frequent word

emboîter /ābwate/ [1] ① *vtr* to fit [sth] together; ∼ qch dans to fit sth into
② **s'emboîter** *v refl* (+ *v être*) ‹part› to fit (dans into); ‹parts› to fit together
IDIOM ∼ le pas à qn to fall in behind sb

embonpoint /ābɔ̃pwɛ̃/ *nm* stoutness; avoir de l'∼ to be stout

embouché, ∼e /ābuʃe/ *adj* mal ∼ coarse; in a foul mood

embouchure /ābuʃyʀ/ *nf* (of river) mouth; (of instrument) mouthpiece; (of pipe) opening

embourber: **s'embourber** /ābuʀbe/ [1] *v refl* (+ *v être*) (a) to get stuck in the mud
(b) to get bogged down

embourgeoiser: **s'embourgeoiser** /ābuʀʒwaze/ [1] *v refl* (+ *v être*) ‹person› to become middle-class; ‹area› to become gentrified

embout /ābu/ *nm* (of cigar, cane) tip; (of hosepipe) nozzle; (of pipe) mouthpiece

embouteillage /ābutɛjaʒ/ *nm* traffic jam

emboutir /ābutiʀ/ [3] *vtr* (a) to stamp, to press ‹part, metal›
(b) (fam) to crash into ‹vehicle›

embranchement /ābʀɑ̃ʃmɑ̃/ *nm*
(a) junction
(b) side road
(c) (on railways) branch line

embrasé, ∼e /ābʀaze/ *adj* (a) burning
(b) glowing

embrasement /ābʀazmɑ̃/ *nm* (a) blaze
(b) dazzling illumination
(c) unrest

embraser /ābʀaze/ [1] ① *vtr* (a) to set [sth] ablaze
(b) to set [sth] alight ‹country›
② **s'embraser** *v refl* (+ *v être*) (a) to catch fire
(b) ‹country› to erupt into violence
(c) ‹sky› to be set ablaze
(d) to burn with desire

✎ **embrasser** /ābʀase/ [1] ① *vtr* (a) to kiss; je t'embrasse lots of love
(b) to embrace; to hug
(c) to take up ‹career, cause›
② **s'embrasser** *v refl* (+ *v être*) (a) to kiss (each other)
(b) to embrace; to hug
IDIOM ∼ qn comme du bon pain to hug sb warmly

embrasure /ābʀazyʀ/ *nf* ∼ de fenêtre window; ∼ de porte doorway

embrayage /ābʀɛjaʒ/ *nm* (a) clutch
(b) clutch pedal

embrayer /ābʀeje/ [21] *vi* ‹driver› to engage the clutch; (Tech) to engage

embrigader /ābʀigade/ [1] *vtr* (a) to recruit
(b) (Mil) to brigade

embrouillamini /ābʀujamini/ *nm* (fam) muddle

embrouille /ābʀuj/ *nf* (fam) shady goings-on (colloq)

embrouiller /ābʀuje/ [1] ① *vtr* (a) to tangle ‹wires›
(b) to confuse ‹matter, person›
② **s'embrouiller** *v refl* (+ *v être*) (a) to become tangled
(b) ‹ideas, person› to become confused

embroussaillé, ∼e /ābʀusaje/ *adj* ‹path› overgrown; ‹hair› bushy

embrumé, ∼e /ābʀyme/ *adj* (a) misty
(b) ‹mind› befuddled; ‹look› glazed

embruns /ābʀœ̃/ *nm pl* spray

embryon /ābʀijɔ̃/ *nm* embryo

embûche /ābyʃ/ *nf* (a) trap; dresser des ∼s to set traps
(b) hazard; pitfall; semé d'∼s hazardous; (figurative) fraught with pitfalls

embuer /ābɥe/ [1] ① *vtr* to mist up, to fog up
② **s'embuer** *v refl* (+ *v être*) ‹window› to mist up, to fog up; ‹eyes› to mist over

embuscade /ābyskad/ *nf* ambush

embusquer: **s'embusquer** /ābyske/ [1] *v refl* (+ *v être*) to lie in ambush

éméché, ∼e /emeʃe/ *adj* (fam) tipsy

émeraude /emʀod/ *nf* emerald

émergence /emɛʀʒɑ̃s/ *nf* emergence

émerger /emɛʀʒe/ [13] *vi* to emerge

émeri /emʀi/ *nm* emery

émérite /emeʀit/ *adj* (a) outstanding
(b) professeur ∼ emeritus professor

émerveiller /emɛʀveje/ [1] ① *vtr* ∼ qn to fill sb with wonder
② **s'émerveiller** *v refl* (+ *v être*) s'∼ de or devant qch to marvel at sth

émetteur, **-trice** /emetœʀ, tʀis/ ① *adj*
(a) ‹station› broadcasting
(b) ‹bank› issuing
② *nm* (a) transmitter
(b) (of loan, card) issuer

émettre /emɛtʀ/ [60] *vtr* (a) to express ‹opinion, wish›; to put forward ‹hypothesis›
(b) to utter ‹cry›; to produce ‹sound, heat›
(c) to issue ‹document›
(d) to broadcast ‹programme›
(e) to send out ‹signal›
(f) to emit ‹radiation›

émeute /emøt/ *nf* riot

émietter /emjete/ [1] ① *vtr* to crumble [sth]
② **s'émietter** *v refl* (+ *être*) to crumble

émigrant, ∼e /emigʀã, ãt/ *nm, f* emigrant

émigration /emigʀasjɔ̃/ *nf* emigration

émigré, ∼e /emigʀe/ *nm, f* emigrant; émigré

émigrer /emigʀe/ [1] *vi* (a) to emigrate
(b) ‹bird› to migrate

émincer /emɛ̃se/ [12] *vtr* to slice [sth] thinly

éminemment /eminamɑ̃/ *adv* eminently

éminence /eminɑ̃s/ *nf* **(a)** hillock
(b) (Anat) protuberance

Éminence /eminɑ̃s/ *nf* Eminence

éminent, **~e** /eminɑ̃, ɑ̃t/ *adj*
distinguished, eminent

émirat /emiʀa/ *nm* emirate

Émirats /emiʀa/ *pr nm pl* **~ arabes unis**,
EAU United Arab Emirates

émis, **~e** /emi, iz/ ▶ ÉMETTRE

émissaire /emisɛʀ/ *nm* emissary

🞜 **émission** /emisjɔ̃/ *nf* **(a)** programme (GB)
(b) (of document) issue
(c) (of waves, signals) emission

emmagasiner /ɑ̃magazine/ [1] *vtr* **(a)** to
store
(b) to stockpile ‹goods›; to store up
‹knowledge›

emmanchure /ɑ̃mɑ̃ʃyʀ/ *nf* armhole

emmêler /ɑ̃mele/ [1] **1** *vtr* **(a)** to tangle
(b) to confuse ‹matter›
2 s'emmêler *v refl* (+ *v être*) to get
tangled up; **s'~ les pieds dans** to get one's
feet caught in

emménagement /ɑ̃menaʒmɑ̃/ *nm*
moving in

emménager /ɑ̃menaʒe/ [13] *vi* to move in

emmener /ɑ̃mne/ [16] *vtr* **(a)** to take
‹person› (à, jusqu'à to); **veux-tu que je
t'emmène en voiture?** do you want a lift (GB)
or a ride (US)?
(b) (fam) (controversial) to take [sth] with one
‹object›
(c) to take [sb] away

emmerder /ɑ̃mɛʀde/ [1] (pop) **1** *vtr* to
annoy, to hassle (colloq); **~ le monde** to be a
pain in the arse (GB) (colloq) *or* ass (US) (slang)
2 s'emmerder *v refl* (+ *v être*) **(a)** to be
bored stiff (colloq)
(b) s'~ à faire to go to the trouble of doing;
tu t'emmerdes pas! you're doing all right for
yourself!; you've got a nerve!

emmitoufler /ɑ̃mitufle/ [1] **1** *vtr* to
wrap [sb/sth] up warmly
2 s'emmitoufler *v refl* (+ *v être*) to wrap
(oneself) up warmly

émoi /emwa/ *nm* agitation, turmoil

émoluments /emolymɑ̃/ *nm pl*
remuneration

émonder /emɔ̃de/ [1] *vtr* to prune

émotif, **-ive** /emɔtif, iv/ *adj* emotional

🞜 **émotion** /emosjɔ̃/ *nf* emotion

émotivité /emɔtivite/ *nf* **enfant d'une
grande ~** highly emotional child

émousser /emuse/ [1] **1** *vtr* **(a)** to blunt
(b) to dull ‹curiosity, sensitivity›
2 s'émousser *v refl* (+ *v être*) **(a)** to
become blunt
(b) ‹curiosity› to become dulled

🞜 indicates a very frequent word

émoustiller /emustije/ [1] *vtr* **(a)** to
exhilarate
(b) to titillate

émouvant, **~e** /emuvɑ̃, ɑ̃t/ *adj* moving

émouvoir /emuvwaʀ/ [43] **1** *vtr* to move,
to touch; **~ l'opinion** to cause a stir
2 s'émouvoir *v refl* (+ *v être*) **(a)** to be
touched *or* moved
(b) s'~ de to become concerned about; to be
bothered by

empailler /ɑ̃paje/ [1] *vtr* to stuff

empailleur, **-euse** /ɑ̃pajœʀ, øz/ *nm,f*
taxidermist

empaler /ɑ̃pale/ [1] **1** *vtr* to impale
2 s'empaler *v refl* (+ *v être*) to become
impaled

empaqueter /ɑ̃pakte/ [20] *vtr* to package;
to wrap [sth] up

emparer: s'emparer /ɑ̃paʀe/ [1] *v refl*
(+ *v être*) **(a) s'~ de** (gen) to get hold of, to
seize; to take over ‹town›; to seize ‹power›
(b) s'~ de ‹feeling› to take hold of [sb]

empâter: s'empâter /ɑ̃pate/ [1] *v refl*
(+ *v être*) to become puffy; to put on weight

empêchement /ɑ̃pɛʃmɑ̃/ *nm* unforeseen
difficulty; **j'ai un ~** something's cropped up

🞜 **empêcher** /ɑ̃peʃe/ [1] **1** *vtr* to prevent,
to stop; **~ qn de faire** to prevent sb (from)
doing
2 s'empêcher *v refl* (+ *v être*) **je n'ai pas
pu m'~ de rire** I couldn't help laughing
3 *v impers* **(il) n'empêche** all the same; **il
n'empêche que** the fact remains that

empereur /ɑ̃pʀœʀ/ *nm* emperor

empesé, **~e** /ɑ̃pəze/ *adj* ‹collar› starched;
‹person, manner› starchy

empester /ɑ̃pɛste/ [16] **1** *vtr* to stink
[sth] out (GB), to stink up (US)
2 *vi* to stink

empêtrer: s'empêtrer /ɑ̃petʀe/ [1] *v
refl* (+ *v être*) **s'~ dans** to get entangled in
‹briars›; to get tangled up in ‹lies›

emphase /ɑ̃faz/ *nf* **(a)** grandiloquence
(b) emphasis

emphatique /ɑ̃fatik/ *adj*
(a) grandiloquent
(b) emphatic

empiècement /ɑ̃pjɛsmɑ̃/ *nm* (of garment)
yoke

empiéter /ɑ̃pjete/ [14] *vi* to encroach

empiffrer: s'empiffrer /ɑ̃pifʀe/ [1] *v refl*
(+ *v être*) (fam) to stuff oneself

empiler /ɑ̃pile/ [1] **1** *vtr* to pile [sth] (up)
2 s'empiler *v refl* (+ *v être*) to pile up

🞜 **empire** /ɑ̃piʀ/ *nm* empire

Empire /ɑ̃piʀ/ *nm* **l'~** the Empire
■ **l'~ d'Orient** the Byzantine Empire; **l'~
d'Occident** the Western Empire

empirer /ɑ̃piʀe/ [1] *vi* to get worse

empirique /ɑ̃piʀik/ *adj* empirical

empirisme /ɑ̃piʀism/ *nm* empiricism

emplacement /ɑ̃plasmɑ̃/ *nm* **(a)** site
(b) parking space

emplette /ɑ̃plɛt/ *nf* purchase

emplir /ɑ̃pliʀ/ [3] *vtr*, **s'emplir** *v refl* (+ *v être*) to fill (**de** with)

✵ **emploi** /ɑ̃plwa/ *nm* **(a)** job
(b) employment
(c) use; **téléviseur couleur à vendre, cause double ~ colour** (GB) TV for sale, surplus to requirements
(d) usage
■ **~ du temps** timetable
IDIOM avoir la tête de l'~ to look the part

employé, ~e /ɑ̃plwaje/ *nm,f* employee
■ **~ de banque** bank clerk; **~ municipal** local authority employee

✵ **employer** /ɑ̃plwaje/ [23] **1** *vtr* to employ ‹*person*›; to use ‹*word, product*›
2 **s'employer** *v refl* (+ *v être*) **(a)** to be used
(b) **s'~ à faire** to apply oneself to doing

employeur, -euse /ɑ̃plwajœʀ, øz/ *nm,f* employer

empocher /ɑ̃pɔʃe/ [1] *vtr* to pocket

empoigner /ɑ̃pwaɲe/ [1] *vtr* to grab (hold of)

empoisonnant, ~e /ɑ̃pwazɔnɑ̃, ɑ̃t/ *adj* (fam) annoying, irritating

empoisonné, ~e /ɑ̃pwazɔne/ **1** *pp*
▶ EMPOISONNER
2 *pp adj* ‹*foodstuff*› poisoned; ‹*atmosphere*› sour

empoisonnement /ɑ̃pwazɔnmɑ̃/ *nm*
(a) poisoning
(b) (fam) trouble

empoisonner /ɑ̃pwazɔne/ [1] **1** *vtr* to poison; **~ la vie de qn** to make sb's life a misery
2 **s'empoisonner** *v refl* (+ *v être*) to poison oneself; **il s'est empoisonné avec une huître pas fraîche** he got food poisoning from eating a bad oyster

empoisonneur, -euse /ɑ̃pwazɔnœʀ, øz/ *nm,f* **(a)** poisoner
(b) (fam) nuisance

emportement /ɑ̃pɔʀtəmɑ̃/ *nm* fit of anger; **avec ~** angrily

✵ **emporter** /ɑ̃pɔʀte/ [1] **1** *vtr* **(a)** to take ‹*object*›; **pizzas à ~** takeaway pizzas (GB), pizzas to go (US)
(b) ‹*ambulance*› to take [sb] away; ‹*plane*› to carry [sb] away
(c) ‹*wind, river*› to sweep [sb/sth] away; ‹*shell, bullet*› to take ‹*ear, leg*›
(d) **une leucémie l'a emporté** he died of leukaemia
(e) to take ‹*position*›
(f) **l'~** to win; to prevail; **l'~ sur qch** to overcome sth
2 **s'emporter** *v refl* (+ *v être*) to lose one's temper

empoté, ~e /ɑ̃pɔte/ *adj* (fam) clumsy, awkward

empreindre: **s'empreindre** /ɑ̃pʀɛ̃dʀ/ [55] *v refl* (+ *v être*) to become marked (**de** with), to become imbued (**de** with)

empreinte /ɑ̃pʀɛ̃t/ *nf* **(a)** footprint; track
(b) stamp, mark
■ **~ écologique** carbon footprint; **~s digitales** fingerprints

empressement /ɑ̃pʀɛsmɑ̃/ *nm*
(a) eagerness; **avec ~** eagerly
(b) attentiveness

empresser: **s'empresser** /ɑ̃pʀese/ [1] *v refl* (+ *v être*) **s'~ de faire** to hasten to do; **s'~ autour** *or* **auprès de qn** to fuss over sb

emprise /ɑ̃pʀiz/ *nf* hold, influence

emprisonnement /ɑ̃pʀizɔnmɑ̃/ *nm* imprisonment; **peine d'~** prison sentence

emprisonner /ɑ̃pʀizɔne/ [1] *vtr* **(a)** to imprison (**à, dans** in)
(b) to keep [sb] prisoner

emprunt /ɑ̃pʀœ̃/ *nm* **(a)** (money) loan; **faire un ~** to take out a loan
(b) borrowing; **d'~** ‹*car, name*› borrowed
(c) (object, book) loan; **c'est un ~ fait à un musée** it's on loan from a museum
(d) (of idea, word) borrowing

emprunté, ~e /ɑ̃pʀœ̃te/ *adj* awkward

emprunter /ɑ̃pʀœ̃te/ [1] *vtr* **(a)** to borrow
(b) to take ‹*road*›

empuantir /ɑ̃pɥɑ̃tiʀ/ [3] *vtr* to stink out (GB), to stink up (US)

ému, ~e /emy/ **1** *pp* ▶ ÉMOUVOIR
2 *pp adj* moved; touched; nervous; **trop ~ pour parler** too overcome to speak
3 *adj* ‹*words*› full of emotion; ‹*memory*› fond

émulation /emylasjɔ̃/ *nf* competitiveness

émule /emyl/ *nmf* imitator; **être l'~ de qn** to model oneself on sb

émulsifiant /emylsifjɑ̃/ *nm* emulsifier

émulsion /emylsjɔ̃/ *nf* emulsion

✵ **en** /ɑ̃/ **1** *prep* **(a)** in; into; to; **vivre ~ ville** to live in town; **aller ~ Allemagne** to go to Germany; **~ hiver/1991** in winter/1991; **~ semaine** during the week; **voyager ~ train** to travel by train
(b) **il est toujours ~ manteau** he always wears a coat
(c) as; **je vous parle ~ ami** I'm speaking (to you) as a friend
(d) into; **traduire ~ anglais** to translate into English
(e) **c'est ~ or** it's (made of) gold; **le même ~ bleu/plus grand** the same in blue/only bigger; **~ hauteur, le mur fait trois mètres** the wall is three metres (GB) high
(f) (*used with gerund*) **je l'ai croisé ~ sortant** I met him as I was leaving; **prends un café ~ attendant** have a cup of coffee while you're waiting; **l'enfant se réveilla ~ hurlant** ⋯⋗

the child woke up screaming; **ouvrez cette caisse ∼ soulevant le couvercle** open this box by lifting the lid; **tu aurais moins chaud ∼ enlevant ta veste** you'd be cooler if you took your jacket off

2 *pron* **(a)** (indicating means) **il sortit son épée et l'∼ transperça** he took out his sword and ran him/her through

(b) (indicating cause) **ça l'a tellement bouleversé qu'il ∼ est tombé malade** it distressed him so much that he fell ill (GB) *or* became sick (US)

(c) (representing person) **ils aiment leurs enfants et ils ∼ sont aimés** they love their children and they are loved by them

(d) (representing thing) **'veux-tu du vin?'—'oui, j'∼ veux'** 'would you like some wine?'—'yes, I'd like some'; **il n'∼ reste pas beaucoup** there isn't much (of it) left; there aren't many left; **j'∼ suis fier** I'm proud of it

(e) (fam) **tu ∼ as un beau chapeau!** what a nice hat you've got!

ENA /ena/ *nf: abbr* ▶ ÉCOLE

énarque /enaʀk/ *nmf* graduate of the ENA

encadré /ɑ̃kadʀe/ *nm* (in newspaper) box

encadrement /ɑ̃kadʀəmɑ̃/ *nm*
(a) supervision
(b) supervisory staff; managerial staff; (Mil) officers
(c) (of picture) frame

encadrer /ɑ̃kadʀe/ [1] *vtr* **(a)** to supervise ‹staff›; to train ‹soldier›
(b) to flank ‹person›; to frame ‹face, window›; **∼ de rouge** to outline [sth] in red
(c) to frame ‹picture›

encaisser /ɑ̃kese/ [1] *vtr* **(a)** to cash ‹cheque, sum of money›
(b) (fam) to take ‹blow, defeat›; **je ne peux pas ∼ ton frère** I can't stand your brother
IDIOM ∼ le coup (fam) to take it all in one's stride

encart /ɑ̃kaʀ/ *nm* insert; **∼ publicitaire** promotional insert

en-cas /ɑ̃ka/ *nm inv* snack

encastrer /ɑ̃kastʀe/ [1] **1** *vtr* to build in ‹oven, refrigerator›; to fit ‹sink, hotplate›; **baignoire encastrée** sunken bath
2 s'encastrer *v refl* (+ *v être*) to fit (**dans** into)

encaustique /ɑ̃kɔstik/ *nf* wax polish

enceinte /ɑ̃sɛ̃t/ **1** *adj f* ‹woman› pregnant
2 *nf* **(a)** (mur d')∼ surrounding wall
(b) (of prison, palace) compound; (of church) interior

encens /ɑ̃sɑ̃/ *nm inv* incense

encenser /ɑ̃sɑ̃se/ [1] *vtr* to sing the praises of ‹person›; to acclaim ‹work of art›

encercler /ɑ̃sɛʀkle/ [1] *vtr* **(a)** to surround, to encircle

✔ indicates a very frequent word

(b) (with pen) to circle

enchaînement /ɑ̃ʃɛnmɑ̃/ *nm* **(a)** (of events) chain
(b) sequence
(c) (in music, sport) transition

enchaîner /ɑ̃ʃɛne/ [1] **1** *vtr* to chain up ‹person, animal›; **∼ à** to chain to
2 *vi* to go on; **∼ avec une nouvelle chanson** to move on to a new song
3 s'enchaîner *v refl* (+ *être*) ‹shots, sequences in film› to follow on

enchantement /ɑ̃ʃɑ̃tmɑ̃/ *nm* enchantment, spell; **comme par ∼** as if by magic

enchanter /ɑ̃ʃɑ̃te/ [1] *vtr* **(a)** to delight; **ça ne m'enchante guère** it doesn't exactly thrill me; **enchanté (de faire votre connaissance)!** how do you do!
(b) **forêt enchantée** enchanted forest

enchanteur, -eresse /ɑ̃ʃɑ̃tœʀ, tʀɛs/
1 *adj* enchanting
2 *nm, f* **(a)** enchanter/enchantress
(b) (figurative) charmer

enchère /ɑ̃ʃɛʀ/ **1** *nf* bid
2 enchères *nf pl* **vente aux ∼s** auction

enchérir /ɑ̃ʃeʀiʀ/ [3] *vi* to bid; **∼ sur qn** to bid more than sb; **∼ sur une offre** to make a higher bid

enchevêtrement /ɑ̃ʃ(ə)vɛtʀəmɑ̃/ *nm* (of threads) tangle; (of corridors, streets) labyrinth

enchevêtrer /ɑ̃ʃ(ə)vetʀe/ [1] **1** *vtr* **(a)** to tangle [sth] up ‹threads›
(b) **être enchevêtré** ‹sentence, plot› to be muddled; ‹case› to be complicated
2 s'enchevêtrer *v refl* (+ *v être*)
(a) ‹branches, threads› to get tangled
(b) ‹phrases, ideas› to become muddled

enclave /ɑ̃klav/ *nf* enclave

enclencher /ɑ̃klɑ̃ʃe/ [1] **1** *vtr* **(a)** to set [sth] in motion ‹process›
(b) to engage ‹mechanism›
2 s'enclencher *v refl* (+ *v être*)
(a) ‹process› to get under way
(b) ‹mechanism› to engage

enclin, ∼e /ɑ̃klɛ̃, in/ *adj* inclined (**à** to)

enclos /ɑ̃klo/ *nm inv* (gen) enclosure; (for animals) pen

enclume /ɑ̃klym/ *nf* (Tech, Anat) anvil

encoche /ɑ̃kɔʃ/ *nf* notch

encoder /ɑ̃kɔde/ [1] *vtr* to encode

encodeur /ɑ̃kɔdœʀ/ *nm* (Comput) encoder

encolure /ɑ̃kɔlyʀ/ *nf* **(a)** (of garment) neckline
(b) collar size
(c) (of animal) neck

encombrant, ∼e /ɑ̃kɔ̃bʀɑ̃, ɑ̃t/ *adj*
(a) bulky; cumbersome
(b) ‹person, matter› troublesome

encombre, sans encombre /sɑ̃zɑ̃kɔ̃bʀ/ *phr* without a hitch

encombré, ~e /ãkõbʀe/ *adj* ‹road, sky›
congested (**de** with); ‹room› cluttered

encombrement /ãkõbʀəmã/ *nm*
(a) traffic congestion
(b) (of switchboard) jamming
(c) (of room) cluttering
(d) (of furniture) bulk

encombrer /ãkõbʀe/ [1] **1** *vtr* **(a)** ‹object,
people› to clutter up ‹room›; to obstruct
‹road, path›
(b) to jam ‹switchboard›; to clutter up ‹mind›
2 **s'encombrer** *v refl* (+ *v être*) **s'~ de** to
burden oneself with; **s'~ l'esprit** to clutter
up one's mind (**de** with)

encontre: **à l'encontre de**
/alãkõtʀədə/ *phr* **(a)** counter to
(b) against
(c) toward(s)

encorder: **s'encorder** /ãkɔʀde/ [1] *v refl*
(+ *v être*) to rope up

✧ **encore** /ãkɔʀ/ **1** *adv* **(a)** still; **il n'est ~
que midi** it's only midday; **tu en es ~ là?**
haven't you got (GB) *or* gotten (US) beyond
that by now?; **qu'il soit impoli passe ~,
mais...** the fact that he's rude is one thing,
but...
(b) **pas ~** not yet; **il n'est pas ~ rentré** he
hasn't come home yet; he still hasn't come
home; **cela ne s'est ~ jamais vu** it has never
been seen before
(c) again; **~ toi!** you again!; **~! encore!**,
more!; **~ une fois** once more, once again;
qu'est-ce que j'ai ~ fait? what have I done
now?
(d) more, **mange ~ un peu** have some more
to eat; **c'est ~ mieux** it's even better
(e) **~ un gâteau?** another cake?; **pendant ~
trois jours** for another three days; **qu'est-ce
qu'il te faut ~?** what more do you need?
(f) **~ faut-il qu'elle accepte** but she still has
to accept; **si ~ il était généreux!** if he were at
least generous!
(g) only, just; **il y a ~ trois mois** only three
months ago
2 **et encore** *phr* if that; **c'est tout au
plus mangeable, et ~!** it's only just edible,
if that!
3 **encore que** *phr* even though

encourageant, ~e /ãkuʀaʒã, ãt/ *adj*
encouraging

encouragement /ãkuʀaʒmã/ *nm*
encouragement

✧ **encourager** /ãkuʀaʒe/ [13] *vtr* **(a)** to
encourage (**à faire** to do)
(b) to cheer [sb] on

encourir /ãkuʀiʀ/ [26] *vtr* to incur

encrasser /ãkʀase/ [1] *vtr* **(a)** to clog
[sth] (up) ‹filter, artery›; to make [sth] sooty
‹chimney›
(b) to dirty; (Aut) to foul up ‹spark plugs›

encre /ãkʀ/ *nf* ink
■ **~ de Chine** Indian (GB) *or* India (US) ink; **~**

sympathique invisible ink
IDIOMS cela a fait couler beaucoup d'~ a lot
of ink has been spilled over this; **se faire un
sang d'~** to be worried sick

encrier /ãkʀije/ *nm* inkwell; ink pot

encroûter: **s'encroûter** /ãkʀute/ [1] *v
refl* (fam) to get in a rut

encyclopédie /ãsiklɔpedi/ *nf*
encyclopedia

endetté, ~e /ãdete/ *adj* in debt

endettement /ãdɛtmã/ *nm* debt

endetter /ãdete/ [1] **1** *vtr* to put [sb]
into debt
2 **s'endetter** *v refl* (+ *v être*) to get into
debt

endiablé, ~e /ãdjɑble/ *adj* ‹rhythm›
furious

endiguer /ãdige/ [1] *vtr* to confine
‹river›; to contain ‹demonstrators›; to curb
‹speculation›

endimanché, ~e /ãdimãʃe/ *adj* in one's
Sunday best

endive /ãdiv/ *nf* chicory (GB), endive (US)

endoctriner /ãdɔktʀine/ [1] *vtr* to
indoctrinate

endolori, ~e /ãdɔlɔʀi/ *adj* aching

endolorir /ãdɔlɔʀiʀ/ [3] *vtr* to make
[sb/sth] ache

endommager /ãdɔmaʒe/ [13] *vtr* to
damage

endormi, ~e /ãdɔʀmi/ *adj* **(a)** ‹person,
animal› sleeping, asleep
(b) ‹village, mind› sleepy

✧ **endormir** /ãdɔʀmiʀ/ [30] **1** *vtr* **(a)** to send
[sb] to sleep ‹child›; ‹person, substance› to put
[sb] to sleep ‹patient›
(b) (from boredom) ‹person, lecture› to send [sb]
to sleep ‹person›
(c) to dupe ‹person, opinion, enemy›
(d) to allay ‹suspicion›; to numb ‹faculties›
2 **s'endormir** *v refl* (+ *v être*) **(a)** to fall
asleep
(b) to get to sleep
(c) (figurative) to sit back

endossable /ãdosabl/ *adj* ‹cheque›
endorsable

endosser /ãdose/ [1] *vtr* **(a)** to take on
‹role, responsibility›
(b) to endorse ‹cheque›

✧ **endroit** /ãdʀwa/ **1** *nm* **(a)** place; **par ~s**
in places; **à quel ~?** where?
(b) (of fabric) right side; **à l'~** (of object) the
right way up; (of garment) the right way
round (GB) *or* around (US)
2 **à l'endroit de** *phr* toward(s)

enduire /ãdɥiʀ/ [69] **1** *vtr* to coat (**de**
with)
2 **s'enduire** *v refl* (+ *v être*) **s'~ de** to put
[sth] on

enduit /ãdɥi/ *nm* **(a)** coating
(b) filler

endurance /ãdyʀãs/ *nf* (a) (of person) stamina; ~ à resistance to
(b) (of engine) endurance

endurant, ~e /ãdyʀã, ãt/ *adj* ‹person, athlete› tough; ‹engine, vehicle› hard-wearing

endurcir /ãdyʀsiʀ/ [3] **1** *vtr* (a) ‹sport, hard work› to strengthen ‹body, character›
(b) ‹ordeal› to harden ‹person›
2 s'endurcir *v refl* (+ *v être*) (a) to become stronger
(b) to become hardened

endurer /ãdyʀe/ [1] *vtr* (a) to endure; faire ~ qch à qn to put sb through sth
(b) to put up with

énergétique /enɛʀʒetik/ *adj* (a) ‹needs, resources› energy
(b) ‹food› high-calorie

✧ **énergie** /enɛʀʒi/ *nf* energy; faire des économies d'~ to save energy; trouver des ~s douces to find safe energy sources; avec l'~ du désespoir driven on by despair; avec ~ ‹work› energetically; ‹protest› strongly
■ ~ éolienne windpower; ~ nucléaire nuclear power *ou* energy; ~ solaire solar power

énergique /enɛʀʒik/ *adj* (a) ‹person, gesture› energetic; ‹handshake› vigorous; ‹face, expression› resolute
(b) ‹action› tough; ‹protest› strong; ‹refusal› firm; ‹intervention› forceful

énergumène /enɛʀɡymɛn/ *nmf* oddball

énervant, ~e /enɛʀvã, ãt/ *adj* irritating

énervé, ~e /enɛʀve/ *adj* (a) irritated
(b) nervous; ‹child› overexcited

énervement /enɛʀvəmã/ *nm*
(a) irritation
(b) agitation; elle pleura d'~ she was so on edge that she cried

énerver /enɛʀve/ [1] **1** *vtr* (a) to put [sb] on edge
(b) ~ qn to get on sb's nerves, to irritate sb
2 s'énerver *v refl* (+ *v être*) to get worked up

✧ **enfance** /ãfãs/ *nf* childhood; la petite ~ early childhood
IDIOM c'est l'~ de l'art it's child's play

✧ **enfant** /ãfã/ *nmf* child; infant; être ~ unique to be an only child
■ ~ de chœur altar boy; ce n'est pas un ~ de chœur (figurative) he's no angel

enfanter /ãfãte/ [1] *vtr* to give birth to

enfantillage /ãfãtijaʒ/ *nm* childishness

enfantin, ~e /ãfãtɛ̃, in/ *adj* (a) simple, easy
(b) mode ~e children's fashion
(c) childish

✧ **enfer** /ãfɛʀ/ *nm* Hell; (figurative) hell; aller à un train d'~ (fam) to go hell for leather (colloq); soirée d'~ (fam) hell of a party (colloq)

enfermer /ãfɛʀme/ [1] **1** *vtr* (a) to shut [sth] in ‹animal›; to lock [sth] up ‹money,

jewellery›; to lock [sb] up ‹person›; elle est bonne à ~ (fam) she's stark raving mad (colloq)
(b) ~ qn dans un rôle to confine sb to a role; ~ qn dans une situation to trap sb in a situation
2 s'enfermer *v refl* (+ *v être*) (a) (gen) to lock oneself in; (accidentally) to get locked in; (in order to be alone) to shut oneself away; ne reste pas enfermé toute la journée! don't stay cooped up indoors all day!
(b) s'~ dans to retreat into; s'~ dans le mutisme to remain obstinately silent

enfiévré, ~e /ãfjevʀe/ *adj* ‹imagination› fevered; ‹atmosphere› feverish; ‹speech› fiery

enfilade /ãfilad/ *nf* (of traps) succession; (of houses, tables) row

enfiler /ãfile/ [1] **1** *vtr* (a) to slip on
(b) to thread ‹piece of thread, needle›
2 s'enfiler *v refl* (+ *v être*) (a) (fam) to guzzle down
(b) s'~ dans to take ‹street›

✧ **enfin** /ãfɛ̃/ *adv* finally; lastly; ~ et surtout last but not least; ~ seuls! alone at last!; mais ~, cessez de vous disputer! for heaven's sake, stop arguing!; il pleut tous les jours, ~ presque it rains every day, well almost

enflammé, ~e /ãflame/ *adj* (a) burning, on fire
(b) ‹person, declaration› passionate; ‹speech› impassioned
(c) (Med) ‹throat, wound› inflamed
(d) ‹sky› ablaze

enflammer /ãflame/ [1] **1** *vtr* (a) to set fire to [sth]
(b) to inflame ‹public opinion, mind›; to fire ‹imagination›; to fuel ‹anger›
2 s'enflammer *v refl* (+ *v être*)
(a) ‹house, paper› to go up in flames; ‹wood› to catch fire
(b) ‹eyes› to blaze; ‹imagination› to be fired (de with; à la vue de by); ‹country› to explode; s'~ pour qn to become passionate about sb; s'~ pour qch to get carried away by sth

enfler /ãfle/ [1] **1** *vtr* to exaggerate ‹story, event›
2 *vi* (a) ‹part of body› to swell (up); ‹river, sea› to swell
(b) ‹rumour, anger› to spread
3 s'enfler *v refl* (+ *v être*) ‹anger› to mount; ‹voice› to rise; ‹rumour› to grow

enfoncement /ãfõsmã/ *nm* (a) recess; dip
(b) l'~ du pays dans la récession the country's slide into recession

enfoncer /ãfõse/ [12] **1** *vtr* (a) to push in ‹cork, stake›; ~ ses mains dans ses poches to dig one's hands into one's pockets; ~ son doigt dans to stick one's finger into; ~ un clou dans qch to knock a nail into sth
(b) to break down ‹door›; to break through ‹enemy lines›; ~ des portes ouvertes to state

---

✧ indicates a very frequent word

the obvious
(c) ne m'enfonce pas davantage don't rub
it in
2 **s'enfoncer** *v refl* (+ *v être*) **(a) s'~
dans la neige** to sink in the snow; **s'~
dans l'erreur** to make error after error; **les
piquets s'enfoncent facilement** the posts go
in easily; **s'~ une épine dans le doigt** to get
a thorn in one's finger; **s'~ dans la forêt** to
go into the forest
(b) (fam) to make things worse for oneself
enfouir /ɑ̃fwiʀ/ [3] 1 *vtr* **(a)** to bury
(b) ~ **qch dans un sac** to shove sth into a
bag
2 **s'enfouir** *v refl* (+ *v être*) **s'~ sous les
couvertures** to burrow under the blankets
enfourcher /ɑ̃fuʀʃe/ [1] *vtr* to mount
‹horse›; to get on ‹motorbike›
enfourner /ɑ̃fuʀne/ [1] *vtr* **(a)** to put [sth]
in the oven
(b) (fam) to stuff down ‹food›
enfreindre /ɑ̃fʀɛ̃dʀ/ [55] *vtr* to infringe
enfuir: s'enfuir /ɑ̃fɥiʀ/ [9] *v refl* (+ *v être*)
(a) to run away; ‹bird› to fly away
(b) to escape
enfumer /ɑ̃fyme/ [1] *vtr* to fill [sth] with
smoke; **tu nous enfumes avec tes cigares!**
you're smoking us out with your cigars!
engagé, **~e** /ɑ̃ɡaʒe/ *nm,f* enlisted man/
woman
engageant, **~e** /ɑ̃ɡaʒɑ̃, ɑ̃t/ *adj* ‹person,
manner› welcoming; ‹dish, place› inviting
⚓ engagement /ɑ̃ɡaʒmɑ̃/ *nm*
(a) commitment; **prendre l'~ de faire** to
undertake to do
(b) involvement
(c) (Mil) enlistment
⚓ engager /ɑ̃ɡaʒe/ [13] 1 *vtr* **(a)** to hire
‹staff›; to enlist ‹soldier›; to engage ‹artist›
(b) to begin ‹process, reform policy›; **nous
avons engagé la conversation** we struck up
a conversation
(c) to commit, to bind ‹person›
(d) to stake ‹honour›; ~ **sa parole** to give
one's word
(e) ~ **qch dans** to put sth in
(f) to lay out ‹capital›
(g) ~ **qn à faire** to urge sb to do
(h) (Sport) ~ **qn dans une compétition** to
enter sb for a competition
(i) to pawn ‹valuables›
2 **s'engager** *v refl* (+ *v être*) **(a)** to
promise (**à faire** to do); **s'~ vis-à-vis de qn** to
make a commitment to sb
(b) **s'~ dans un projet** to embark on a
project
(c) to get involved
(d) **s'~ sur une route** to go into a road
(e) ‹lawsuit› to begin
(f) **s'~ dans l'armée** to join the army
engelure /ɑ̃ʒlyʀ/ *nf* chilblain
engendrer /ɑ̃ʒɑ̃dʀe/ [1] *vtr* **(a)** to engender

(b) ‹woman› to give birth to; ‹man› to father
engin /ɑ̃ʒɛ̃/ *nm* **(a)** device
(b) vehicle
(c) piece of equipment
englober /ɑ̃ɡlɔbe/ [1] *vtr* to include
engloutir /ɑ̃ɡlutiʀ/ [3] *vtr* **(a)** ‹sea, storm,
fog› to engulf, to swallow up
(b) (fam) to gulp [sth] down
(c) ‹person› to squander ‹money›
engoncé, **~e** /ɑ̃ɡɔ̃se/ *adj* **il était ~ dans
une veste trop étroite** he was squeezed into
a tight jacket
engorger /ɑ̃ɡɔʀʒe/ [13] *vtr* **(a)** to block (up)
‹pipes, drains›
(b) to clog up ‹roads›
engouement /ɑ̃ɡumɑ̃/ *nm* (for thing, activity)
passion; (for person) infatuation
engouer: s'engouer /ɑ̃ɡwe/ [1] *v refl* (+ *v
être*) **s'~ de** to develop a passion for
engouffrer: s'engouffrer /ɑ̃ɡufʀe/ [1]
v refl (+ *v être*) (into a room) to rush; (into a taxi)
to dive
engourdi, **~e** /ɑ̃ɡuʀdi/ *adj* ‹limb, body›
numb (**par, de** with); ‹person› drowsy; ‹town›
sleepy; ‹mind› dull(ed)
engourdir: s'engourdir /ɑ̃ɡuʀdiʀ/
[3] *v refl* (+ *v être*) ‹limb› to go numb; ‹mind›
to grow dull
engourdissement /ɑ̃ɡuʀdismɑ̃/ *nm*
(a) (physical) numbness; (mental) drowsiness
(b) (of body) numbing; (of mind) dulling
engrais /ɑ̃ɡʀɛ/ *nm inv* manure; fertilizer
engraisser /ɑ̃ɡʀese/ [1] 1 *vtr* **(a)** to
fatten ‹cattle›
(b) to fertilize ‹soil›
2 *vi* to get fat
3 **s'engraisser** *v refl* (+ *v être*) (fam) **s'~**
(**sur le dos de qn**) to grow fat (off sb's back)
(colloq)
engranger /ɑ̃ɡʀɑ̃ʒe/ [13] *vtr* to gather in
‹harvest›; (figurative) to store; to store up
engrenage /ɑ̃ɡʀənaʒ/ *nm* **(a)** gears
(b) (figurative) (of violence) spiral
engueuler /ɑ̃ɡœle/ (pop) [1] 1 *vtr* to tell
[sb] off; to give [sb] an earful (colloq)
2 **s'engueuler** *v refl* (+ *v être*) to have
a row
enhardir: s'enhardir /ɑ̃aʀdiʀ/ [3] *v refl*
(+ *v être*) to become bolder
énième /ɛnjɛm/ *adj* umpteenth
énigmatique /enigmatik/ *adj* enigmatic
énigme /enigm/ *nf* **(a)** enigma, mystery
(b) riddle; **parler par ~s** to speak in riddles
enivrant, **~e** /ɑ̃nivʀɑ̃, ɑ̃t/ *adj* intoxicating
enivrement /ɑ̃nivʀəmɑ̃/ *nm* intoxication
enivrer /ɑ̃nivʀe/ [1] 1 *vtr* **(a)** to make [sb]
drunk
(b) ~ **qn** ‹success› to go to sb's head
2 **s'enivrer** *v refl* (+ *v être*) to get drunk
enjambée /ɑ̃ʒɑ̃be/ *nf* stride; **avancer/
s'éloigner à grandes ~s** to stride forward/off

enjamber /ɑ̃ʒɑbe/ [1] *vtr* to step over ‹*obstacle*›

enjeu, *pl* ~**x** /ɑ̃ʒø/ *nm* (Games) stake; **analyser l'~ des élections** to analyse (GB) what is at stake in the elections

enjoindre /ɑ̃ʒwɛ̃dʀ/ [56] *vtr* ~ **à qn de faire** to enjoin sb to do

enjôler /ɑ̃ʒole/ [1] *vtr* to beguile

enjoliver /ɑ̃ʒɔlive/ [1] *vtr* to embellish

enjoliveur /ɑ̃ʒɔlivœʀ/ *nm* hubcap

enjoué, ~**e** /ɑ̃ʒwe/ *adj* ‹*character*› cheerful; ‹*tone*› light-hearted

enlacer /ɑ̃lase/ [12] **1** *vtr* to embrace; ‹*snake*› to wrap itself around ‹*prey*›
2 **s'enlacer** *v refl* (+ *v être*) ‹*people*› to embrace; ‹*body*› to intertwine

enlaidir /ɑ̃lediʀ/ [3] *vtr* to spoil ‹*landscape*›; to make [sb] look ugly ‹*person*›

enlevé, ~**e** /ɑ̃lve/ *adj* lively

enlèvement /ɑ̃lɛvmɑ̃/ *nm* kidnapping (GB), abduction

ꝺ **enlever** /ɑ̃lve/ [16] **1** *vtr* (a) to take [sth] away, to remove ‹*piece of furniture, book*›; to take [sth] down ‹*curtains, pictures*›; to take [sth] off ‹*garment*›; to move, to remove ‹*vehicle*›
(b) to remove ‹*stain, paint*›
(c) to take ‹*person, object*› away; ~ **à qn l'envie de partir** to put sb off going
(d) to kidnap; to carry [sb] off
(e) to carry [sth] off ‹*trophy*›; to capture ‹*market*›
2 **s'enlever** *v refl* (+ *v être*) (a) ‹*varnish*› to come off; ‹*stain*› to come out
(b) ‹*part, section*› to be detachable
(c) (fam) **enlève-toi de là** get off (colloq)

enlisement /ɑ̃lizmɑ̃/ *nm* sinking; (of negotiations) stalemate; (of movement) collapse

enliser /ɑ̃lize/ [1] **1** *vtr* to get [sth] stuck
2 **s'enliser** *v refl* (+ *v être*) (a) ‹*boat, vehicle*› to get stuck
(b) ‹*inquiry, negotiations*› to drag on

enluminure /ɑ̃lyminyʀ/ *nf* illumination

enneigé, ~**e** /ɑ̃neʒe/ *adj* ‹*summit*› snowy; ‹*road*› covered in snow

enneigement /ɑ̃nɛʒmɑ̃/ *nm* **bulletin d'~** snow report

ꝺ **ennemi**, ~**e** /ɛnmi/ **1** *adj* (a) (Mil) enemy
(b) (gen) hostile
2 *nm,f* enemy
3 *nm* (Mil) enemy; **passer à l'~** to go over to the enemy

ennui /ɑ̃nɥi/ *nm* (a) boredom; **tromper l'~** to escape from boredom; **quel ~!** what a bore!
(b) problem; **avoir des ~s** to have problems; **j'ai des ~s avec la police** I'm in trouble with the police; **s'attirer des ~s** to get into trouble

ennuyé, ~**e** /ɑ̃nɥije/ *adj* (a) bored

(b) embarrassed; **j'étais très ~ de laisser les enfants seuls** I felt awful about leaving the children on their own
(c) **j'aurais été très ~ si je n'avais pas eu la clé** I would have been in real trouble if I hadn't had the key

ennuyer /ɑ̃nɥije/ [22] **1** *vtr* (a) to bore
(b) to bother; **si ça ne vous ennuie pas trop** if you don't mind
(c) to annoy
(d) to hassle (colloq)
2 **s'ennuyer** *v refl* (+ *v être*) (a) to be bored; to get bored
(b) **s'~ de** to miss ‹*friend*›

ennuyeux, -**euse** /ɑ̃nɥijø, øz/ *adj*
(a) boring
(b) tedious
(c) annoying
IDIOM **être ~ comme la pluie** to be as dull as ditchwater

énoncé /enɔ̃se/ *nm* (a) (of exam subject) wording (de of); **l'~ d'une théorie** the exposition of a theory
(b) (of fact) statement (de of)

énoncer /enɔ̃se/ [12] *vtr* to pronounce ‹*verdict*›; to set out, to state ‹*facts*›; to expound ‹*theory*›

enorgueillir: **s'enorgueillir** /ɑ̃nɔʀɡœjiʀ/ [3] *v refl* (+ *v être*) to pride oneself (de on)

ꝺ **énorme** /enɔʀm/ *adj* (a) ‹*object, person*› huge, enormous
(b) ‹*success, effort*› tremendous; ‹*mistake*› terrible; ‹*lie*› outrageous

énormément /enɔʀmemɑ̃/ *adv* a tremendous amount; a great deal; ~ **de temps** a tremendous amount of time; **ça m'a ~ plu** I liked it immensely

énormité /enɔʀmite/ *nf* (a) (of figure, size) hugeness; (of lie) enormity
(b) outrageous remark

enquérir: **s'enquérir** /ɑ̃keʀiʀ/ [35] *v refl* (+ *v être*) **s'~ de** to enquire about

ꝺ **enquête** /ɑ̃kɛt/ *nf* (a) (Law) inquiry, investigation; (into a death) inquest; ~ **de police** police investigation
(b) (by journalist) investigation
(c) (by sociologist) survey

enquêter /ɑ̃kete/ [1] *vi* ‹*policeman*› to carry out an investigation; ‹*expert*› to hold an inquiry

enquêteur, -**trice** /ɑ̃ketœʀ, tʀis/ *nm,f*
(a) investigating officer
(b) pollster
(c) interviewer

enquiquinant, ~**e** /ɑ̃kikinɑ̃, ɑ̃t/ *adj* (fam) annoying; boring

enquiquiner /ɑ̃kikine/ [1] **1** *vtr* ~ **qn** to get on sb's nerves; to pester sb
2 **s'enquiquiner** *v refl* (+ *v être*) **s'~ à faire** to go to the trouble of doing

ꝺ indicates a very frequent word

enraciner: **s'enraciner** /ɑ̃Rasine/ [1]
v refl (+ *v être*) **(a)** to take root
(b) (figurative) ‹*person*› to put down roots;
‹*custom, idea*› to take root

enragé, **~e** /ɑ̃Raʒe/ *adj* **(a)** fanatical
(b) enraged
(c) (Med) rabid
IDIOM manger de la vache ~e (fam) to go
through hard times

enrageant, **~e** /ɑ̃Raʒɑ̃, ɑ̃t/ *adj* infuriating

enrager /ɑ̃Raʒe/ [13] *vi* to be furious; **faire
~ qn** to tease sb

enrayer /ɑ̃Reje/ [21] **1** *vtr* **(a)** to check
‹*epidemic, development*›; to curb ‹*inflation*›;
to stop [sth] escalating ‹*crisis*›
(b) to jam ‹*mechanism, gun*›
2 s'enrayer *v refl* (+ *v être*) to get
jammed

enregistrement /ɑ̃RəʒistRəmɑ̃/ *nm*
(a) (of music) recording
(b) (of data) recording; (of order) taking down
(c) (of baggage) check-in

enregistrer /ɑ̃RəʒistRe/ [1] *vtr* **(a)** to
record ‹*cassette, album*›
(b) to note ‹*progress, failure*›; to record ‹*rise,
drop*›
(c) to make a record of ‹*expenses*›; to take
‹*order*›; to record ‹*data*›; to set ‹*record*›
(d) to register ‹*birth, claim*›
(e) to check in ‹*baggage*›
(f) **c'est enregistré, j'enregistre** (fam) I've
made a mental note of it

enregistreur DVD /ɑ̃RəʒistRœR
devede/ *nm* DVD writer

enrhumer: **s'enrhumer** /ɑ̃Ryme/ [1] *v
refl* (+ *v être*) to catch a cold

enrichir /ɑ̃RiʃiR/ [3] **1** *vtr* **(a)** to make [sb]
rich ‹*person*›; to bring wealth to ‹*country*›
(b) to enrich, to enhance ‹*collection, book*›
2 s'enrichir *v refl* (+ *v être*) **(a)** ‹*person*› to
become *or* grow rich
(b) to be enriched

enrichissant, **~e** /ɑ̃Riʃisɑ̃, ɑ̃t/ *adj*
‹*experience*› rewarding; ‹*relationship*›
fulfilling

enrober /ɑ̃Robe/ [1] *vtr* **(a)** to coat
(b) (figurative) to wrap up ‹*news*›

enrôlement /ɑ̃Rolmɑ̃/ *nm* (in the army)
enlistment; (in political party) enrolment (GB)

enrôler: **s'enrôler** /ɑ̃Role/ [1] **1** *vtr* to recruit
2 s'enrôler *v refl* (+ *v être*) to enlist

enrouer: **s'enrouer** /ɑ̃Rwe/ [1] *v refl* (+ *v
être*) ‹*voice*› to go hoarse; ‹*person*› to make
oneself hoarse; **d'une voix enrouée** hoarsely

enrouler /ɑ̃Rule/ [1] **1** *vtr* **(a)** to wind
(b) to wrap
2 s'enrouler *v refl* (+ *v être*) **(a)** ‹*thread,
tape*› to wind
(b) ‹*person, animal*› to curl up

ENS /œɛnɛs/ *nf: abbr* ▶ ÉCOLE

ensabler: **s'ensabler** /ɑ̃sable/ [1] *v refl*
(+ *v être*) ‹*vehicle*› to get stuck in the sand;

‹*boat*› to get stranded (*on a sandbank*)

ensanglanter /ɑ̃sɑ̃glɑ̃te/ [1] *vtr* **(a)** to
cover [sth] with blood
(b) to bring bloodshed to ‹*country*›

⚹ **enseignant**, **~e** /ɑ̃seɲɑ̃, ɑ̃t/ **1** *adj* **corps
~** teaching profession
2 *nm,f* (Sch) teacher; (at university) lecturer

enseigne /ɑ̃sɛɲ/ *nf* **(a)** (shop) sign; **~
lumineuse** neon sign
(b) (Mil, Naut) ensign
IDIOM nous sommes logés à la même ~ we
are in the same boat

⚹ **enseignement** /ɑ̃sɛɲmɑ̃/ *nm*
(a) education; **l'~ supérieur** higher
education
(b) teaching; **méthodes d'~** teaching
methods
(c) lesson
∎ **~ par correspondance** distance learning; **~
professionnel** vocational training; **~ religieux**
religious instruction

⚹ **enseigner** /ɑ̃seɲe/ [1] *vtr* to teach

⚹ **ensemble** /ɑ̃sɑ̃bl/ **1** *adv* **(a)** together
(b) at the same time
2 *nm* **(a)** group; **un ~ de personnes** a
group of people; **une vue d'~** an overall
view; **plan d'~ d'une ville** general plan of
a town; **dans l'~** by and large; **dans l'~ de**
throughout; **dans son** *or* **leur ~** as a whole
(b) (of luggage, measures) set
(c) unity, cohesion; **former un bel ~** to form
a harmonious whole
(d) (of gestures) coordination; (of sounds)
unison; **un mouvement d'~** a coordinated
movement
(e) (in mathematics) set
(f) (Mus) ensemble
(g) (of offices) complex; **~ hôtelier** hotel
complex; **~ industriel** industrial estate (GB)
or park (US)
(h) (set of clothes) outfit; suit

ensevelir /ɑ̃səvəliR/ [3] *vtr* to bury

ensoleillé, **~e** /ɑ̃sɔleje/ *adj* sunny

ensommeillé, **~e** /ɑ̃sɔmeje/ *adj* sleepy

ensorcelé, **~e** /ɑ̃sɔRsəle/ *adj* enchanted

ensorceler /ɑ̃sɔRsəle/ [19] *vtr* **(a)** to cast
or to put a spell on
(b) to bewitch, to enchant

ensorceleur, **-euse** /ɑ̃sɔRsəlœR, øz/ *nm,f*
charmer

⚹ **ensuite** /ɑ̃sɥit/ *adv* **(a)** then; after; next;
très bien, mais ~? fine, but then what?; **il ne
me l'a dit qu'~** he only told me later
(b) secondly

ensuivre: **s'ensuivre** /ɑ̃sɥivR/ [19] *v refl*
(+ *v être*) to follow, to ensue

entacher /ɑ̃taʃe/ [1] *vtr* to mar ‹*relations*›

entaille /ɑ̃taj/ *nf* **(a)** cut; gash
(b) notch

entailler /ɑ̃taje/ [1] **1** *vtr* to cut into;
(deeply) to make a gash in
2 s'entailler *v refl* (+ *v être*) **s'~ le doigt**
to cut one's finger, to gash one's finger

entame /ɑ̃tam/ *nf* **(a)** (Culin) first slice
(b) (in cards) lead
entamer /ɑ̃tame/ [1] *vtr* **(a)** to start ‹day, activity›; to initiate ‹procedure›; to open ‹negotiations›
(b) to undermine ‹credibility›
(c) to eat into ‹savings›
(d) to cut into ‹loaf, roast›; to open ‹bottle, jar›; to start eating ‹dessert›
(e) to cut into ‹skin, wood›
(f) to eat into ‹metal›
entartrer /ɑ̃taʁtʁe/ [1] **1** *vtr* to fur up (GB), to scale up
2 **s'entartrer** *v refl* (+ *v être*) to scale up; ‹teeth› to be covered in tartar
entassement /ɑ̃tasmɑ̃/ *nm* **(a)** piling up; cramming together
(b) pile; heap
entasser /ɑ̃tase/ [1] **1** *vtr* **(a)** to pile ‹books, clothes›
(b) to hoard ‹money, old things›
(c) to pack, to cram ‹people, objects› (**dans** into)
2 **s'entasser** *v refl* (+ *v être*) ‹objects› to pile up; ‹people› to squeeze (**dans** into; **sur** onto)
entendement /ɑ̃tɑ̃dmɑ̃/ *nm* understanding; **cela dépasse l'~** it's beyond belief
♂ **entendre** /ɑ̃tɑ̃dʁ/ [6] **1** *vtr* **(a)** to hear ‹noise, word›; **faire ~ un cri** to give a cry; **je n'en ai jamais entendu parler** I've never heard of it; **on n'entend plus parler de lui** his name is not mentioned any more
(b) ‹judge› to hear ‹witness›; **à t'~, tout va bien** according to you, everything is fine; **elle ne veut rien ~** she won't listen
(c) to understand; **il agit comme il l'entend** he does as he likes; **elle a laissé ~ que** she intimated that; **ils ne l'entendent pas de cette oreille** they don't see it that way
(d) to mean; **qu'entends-tu par là?** what do you mean by that?
(e) **~ faire** to intend doing; **j'entends qu'on fasse ce que je dis** I expect people to do what I say
2 **s'entendre** *v refl* (+ *v être*) **(a)** to get on *or* along
(b) to agree (**sur** on)
(c) ‹noise› to be heard
(d) to hear oneself; ‹two or more people› to hear each other
(e) **phrase qui peut s'~ de plusieurs façons** sentence which can be understood in several ways
entendu, ~e /ɑ̃tɑ̃dy/ **1** *pp* ▶ ENTENDRE
2 *pp adj* **(a)** 'tu viens demain?'—'~!' 'will you come tomorrow?'—'OK!' (colloq)
(b) **d'un air ~** with a knowing look
3 **bien entendu** *phr* of course

♂ indicates a very frequent word

entente /ɑ̃tɑ̃t/ *nf* **(a)** harmony; **vivre en bonne ~ avec qn** to be on good terms with sb
(b) understanding
(c) arrangement
entériner /ɑ̃teʁine/ [1] *vtr* **(a)** to ratify
(b) to confirm
enterré, ~e /ɑ̃teʁe/ *adj* buried; **mort et ~** dead and buried
enterrement /ɑ̃tɛʁmɑ̃/ *nm* **(a)** burial
(b) funeral; **faire une tête d'~** (fam) to look gloomy
enterrer /ɑ̃teʁe/ [1] *vtr* to bury
IDIOM **~ sa vie de garçon** to have a stag party
entêtant, ~e /ɑ̃tetɑ̃, ɑ̃t/ *adj* ‹aroma› heady; ‹music› insistent
en-tête, pl ~s /ɑ̃tɛt/ *nm* heading
entêtement /ɑ̃tɛtmɑ̃/ *nm* stubbornness
entêter: s'entêter /ɑ̃tete/ [1] *v refl* (+ *v être*) **(a)** to be stubborn
(b) to persist
enthousiasme /ɑ̃tuzjasm/ *nm* enthusiasm
enthousiasmer /ɑ̃tuzjasme/ [1] *vtr* to fill [sb] with enthusiasm
enthousiaste /ɑ̃tuzjast/ *adj* enthusiastic
enticher: s'enticher /ɑ̃tiʃe/ [1] *v refl* (+ *v être*) **s'~ de** to become infatuated with
♂ **entier, -ière** /ɑ̃tje, ɛʁ/ **1** *adj* **(a)** whole; **manger un pain ~** to eat a whole loaf; **des heures entières** for hours on end; **lait ~** full-fat milk
(b) ‹success, satisfaction› complete; **avoir l'entière responsabilité de qch** to have full responsibility for sth
(c) ‹object, reputation› intact; **le mystère reste ~** the mystery remains unsolved
(d) **avoir un caractère ~** to be thoroughgoing
2 *nm* (in mathematics) integer
♂ **entièrement** /ɑ̃tjɛʁmɑ̃/ *adv* entirely, completely; **~ équipé** fully equipped
entonner /ɑ̃tɔne/ [1] *vtr* to start singing ‹song›
entonnoir /ɑ̃tɔnwaʁ/ *nm* **(a)** funnel
(b) crater
entorse /ɑ̃tɔʁs/ *nf* **(a)** (Med) sprain
(b) (figurative) infringement (**à** of); **faire une ~ au règlement** to bend the rules
entortiller /ɑ̃tɔʁtije/ [1] **1** *vtr* **(a)** to wind (**autour de qch** round (GB) sth)
(b) to tangle up
2 **s'entortiller** *v refl* (+ *v être*) ‹thread, wool› to get entangled (**dans** in)
entourage /ɑ̃tuʁaʒ/ *nm* **(a)** family circle
(b) circle (of friends); **on dit dans son ~ que** people close to him/her say that
entouré, ~e /ɑ̃tuʁe/ **1** *pp* ▶ ENTOURER
2 *adj* **(a)** ‹person› popular
(b) **nos patients sont très ~s** our patients

are well looked after

entourer /ātuʀe/ [1] **1** *vtr* **(a)** to surround
(b) ~ qch de qch to put sth around sth; ~ qch de mystère to shroud sth in mystery
(c) to rally round (GB) *or* around (US) ‹*sick person*›
2 **s'entourer** *v refl* (+ *v être*) **s'**~ **d'objets** to surround oneself with things; **s'**~ **de précautions** to take every possible precaution

entracte /ātʀakt/ *nm* intermission

entraider: **s'entraider** /ātʀede/ [1] *v refl* (+ *v être*) to help each other *or* one another

entrailles /ātʀaj/ *nf pl* (of animal) innards

entrain /ātʀɛ̃/ *nm* **(a)** (of person) spirit, go (GB) (colloq); **retrouver son** ~ to cheer up
(b) (of party, discussion) liveliness; **sans** ~ half-hearted

entraînant, ~**e** /ātʀɛnã, ãt/ *adj* lively

entraînement /ātʀɛnmã/ *nm*
(a) training, coaching
(b) practice (GB); **avoir de l'**~ to be highly trained; **l'**~ **à la lecture** reading practice (GB)
(c) training session

entraîner /ātʀene/ [1] **1** *vtr* **(a)** to lead to; **une panne a entraîné l'arrêt de la production** a breakdown brought production to a standstill
(b) ‹*river, current*› to carry [sb/sth] away ‹*swimmer, boat*›; **il a entraîné qn/qch dans sa chute** he dragged sb/sth down with him
(c) to take, to lead ‹*person*›; ~ **qn à faire** ‹*person*› to make sb do; ‹*circumstances*› to lead sb to do
(d) (figurative) to carry [sb] away ‹*person, group*›
(e) to train, to coach ‹*athlete, team*› (à for); to train ‹*horse, soldier*› (à for)
(f) ‹*engine, piston*› to drive ‹*machine, wheel, turbine*›
2 **s'entraîner** *v refl* (+ *v être*) **(a)** ‹*player, soldiers*› to train
(b) to prepare oneself

entraîneur /ātʀɛnœʀ/ *nm* (of athlete) coach

entrave /ātʀav/ *nf* hindrance; (on freedom) restriction

entraver /ātʀave/ [1] *vtr* to hinder, to impede

entre /ātʀ/ *prep*

■ **Note** You will find translations for expressions such as *entre parenthèses, entre nous* etc, at the entries PARENTHÈSE, NOUS etc.

(a) between; ~ **midi et deux** at lunchtime; **'doux ou très épicé?'—'**~ **les deux'** 'mild or very spicy?'—'in between'; ~ **son travail et l'informatique, il n'a pas le temps de sortir** what with work and his computer he doesn't have time to go out
(b) among; **organiser une soirée** ~ **amis** to organize a party among friends; **chacune d'**~ **elles** each of them; ~ **hommes** as one man to another; ~ **nous** between you and me; **nous sommes** ~ **nous** there's just the

two of us; we're among friends; **les enfants sont souvent cruels** ~ **eux** children are often cruel to each other

entrebâillement /ātʀəbajmã/ *nm* (in door, shutter, window) gap (**de** in)

entrebâiller /ātʀəbaje/ [1] *vtr* to half-open

entrechoquer /ātʀəʃɔke/ [1] **1** *vtr* to clatter ‹*saucepans*›; to clink ‹*glasses*›
2 **s'entrechoquer** *v refl* (+ *v être*)
(a) ‹*glasses*› to clink
(b) ‹*ideas, interests*› to clash

entrecôte /ātʀəkot/ *nf* **(a)** entrecôte (steak)
(b) rib steak

entrecouper /ātʀəkupe/ [1] **1** *vtr* to punctuate
2 **s'entrecouper** *v refl* (+ *v être*) to intersect

entrecroiser /ātʀəkʀwaze/ [1] *vtr* to intertwine

entre-deux-guerres /ātʀədøgɛʀ/ *nm or f inv* interwar period

entrée /ātʀe/ *nf* **(a)** entrance (**de** to); **se retrouver à l'**~ **du bureau** to meet outside the office
(b) (on motorway) (entry) slip road (GB), on-ramp (US)
(c) (in house) hall; (in hotel) lobby; (door) entry
(d) l'~ **dans la récession** the beginning of the recession; **d'**~ **(de jeu)** from the very start
(e) l'~ **d'un pays dans une organisation** the entry of a country into an organization; '~ **libre'** 'admission free'; '~ **interdite'** 'no entry'
(f) ticket; **deux** ~**s gratuites** two free tickets
(g) (of person) entrance; **réussir son** ~ ‹*actor*› to enter on cue
(h) (Culin) starter
(i) (in bookkeeping) ~**s** receipts
■ ~ **des artistes** stage door; ~ **en matière** introduction

entrée-sortie, *pl* **entrées-sorties** /ātʀesɔʀti/ *nf* (Comput) input-output

entrefaites: **sur ces entrefaites** /syʀsezātʀəfɛt/ *phr* at that moment, just then

entrefilet /ātʀəfilɛ/ *nm* brief article

entrejambes /ātʀəʒãb/ *nm inv* crotch

entrelacer /ātʀəlase/ [12] *vtr*, **s'entrelacer** *v refl* (+ *v être*) to intertwine, to interlace

entremêler: **s'entremêler** /ātʀəmele/ [1] *v refl* (+ *v être*) (gen) to be mixed; ‹*hair, branches*› to get tangled

entremets /ātʀəmɛ/ *nm* dessert

entremetteur, **-euse** /ātʀəmɛtœʀ, øz/ *nm,f* **(a)** matchmaker
(b) go-between

entremise /ātʀəmiz/ *nf* intervention; **il l'a su par mon** ~ he heard of it through me

entreposer /ãtRəpoze/ [1] *vtr* to store
entrepôt /ãtRəpo/ *nm* (a) warehouse
(b) stockroom
entreprenant, **~e** /ãtRəpRənã, ãt/ *adj*
enterprising
⚘ **entreprendre** /ãtRəpRãdR/ [52] *vtr* (a) to
start, to undertake; **~ de faire** to set about
doing; to undertake to do
(b) **~ qn sur un sujet** to engage sb in
conversation about sth
entrepreneur, **-euse** /ãtRəpRənœR,
øz/ *nm,f* (a) builder
(b) contractor
(c) owner-manager (*of a small firm*)
⚘ **entreprise** /ãtRəpRiz/ *nf* (a) firm,
business; **petites et moyennes ~s** small and
medium-sized businesses
(b) business, industry; **la libre ~** free
enterprise
(c) undertaking; venture
■ **~ unipersonnelle à responsabilité limitée,
EURL** company owned by a sole proprietor
⚘ **entrer** /ãtRe/ [1] **1** *vtr* (*+ v avoir*) (a) to
bring [sth] in; to take [sth] in
(b) (in computing) to enter
2 *vi* (*+ v être*) (a) to get in, to enter; to
go in; to come in; **fais-la ~** show her in;
'défense d'~' ('on door) 'no entry'; (on gate) 'no
trespassing'; **je ne fais qu'~ et sortir** I can
only stay a minute
(b) to fit (in); **je n'arrive pas à faire ~ la
pièce dans la fente** I can't get the coin into
the slot
(c) **~ dans** to enter ⟨*period, debate*⟩; to
join ⟨*company, army, party*⟩; **~ à** to enter
⟨*school, charts*⟩; to get into ⟨*university*⟩; **~
en** to enter into ⟨*negotiations*⟩; **~ dans la
vie de qn** to come into sb's life; **~ dans la
légende** ⟨*person*⟩ to become a legend; ⟨*fact*⟩
to become legendary; **cela n'entre pas dans
mes attributions** it's not part of my duties; **~
dans une colère noire** to fly into a blind rage
entresol /ãtRəsɔl/ *nm* mezzanine
entre-temps /ãtRətã/ *adv* meanwhile
⚘ **entretenir** /ãtRətniR/ [36] **1** *vtr* (a) to
look after ⟨*garment, house*⟩; to maintain
⟨*road*⟩; **~ sa forme** to keep in shape
(b) to support ⟨*family*⟩; to keep ⟨*mistress*⟩
(c) to keep [sth] going ⟨*conversation, fire*⟩; to
keep [sth] alive ⟨*friendship*⟩
(d) **~ qn de qch** to speak to sb about sth
2 **s'entretenir** *v refl* (*+ v être*) (a) **s'~ de
qch** to discuss sth
(b) **s'~ facilement** ⟨*house, fabric*⟩ to be easy
to look after
⚘ **entretien** /ãtRətjɛ̃/ *nm* (a) (of house)
upkeep; (of car, road) maintenance; (of plant,
skin) care
(b) cleaning
(c) (gen) discussion; (for a job) interview; (in
newspaper) interview

⚘ indicates a very frequent word

entre-tuer: **s'entre-tuer** /ãtRətɥe/ [1] *v
refl* (*+ v être*) to kill each other
entrevoir /ãtRəvwaR/ [46] *vtr* (a) to catch a
glimpse of; (indistinctly) to make out
(b) to glimpse ⟨*truth, solution*⟩
(c) to foresee ⟨*difficulty*⟩; **laisser ~ qch**
⟨*result, sign*⟩ to point to sth
entrevue /ãtRəvy/ *nf* meeting; (Pol) talks
entrouvrir /ãtRuvRiR/ [32] **1** *vtr* to open
[sth] a little
2 **s'entrouvrir** *v refl* (*+ v être*) (gen) ⟨*door,
country*⟩ to half-open; ⟨*lips*⟩ to part
énumération /enymeRasjɔ̃/ *nf* (a) listing
(b) catalogue (GB)
énumérer /enymeRe/ [14] *vtr* to
enumerate
envahir /ãvaiR/ [3] *vtr* (a) ⟨*troops, crowd*⟩ to
invade; ⟨*animal*⟩ to overrun
(b) to flood ⟨*market*⟩
envahissant, **~e** /ãvaisã, ãt/ *adj*
(a) intrusive
(b) pervasive; invasive
envahisseur /ãvaisœR/ *nm* invader
enveloppe /ãvlɔp/ *nf* (a) (for letter)
envelope; **sous ~** in an envelope
(b) (for parcel) wrapping; (of grains) husk; (of
peas, beans) pod
■ **~ budgétaire** budget
enveloppé, **~e** /ãvlɔpe/ *adj* ⟨*person*⟩
plump
envelopper /ãvlɔpe/ [1] **1** *vtr* (a) ⟨*person*⟩
to wrap [sb/sth] (up); ⟨*sheet*⟩ to cover
(b) ⟨*fog, silence*⟩ to envelop; ⟨*mystery*⟩ to
surround
2 **s'envelopper** *v refl* (*+ v être*) to wrap
oneself (up)
envenimer /ãvnime/ [1] **1** *vtr* to inflame
⟨*debate*⟩; to aggravate ⟨*situation*⟩
2 **s'envenimer** *v refl* (*+ v être*) ⟨*dispute*⟩
to worsen; ⟨*situation*⟩ to turn ugly
envergure /ãveRgyR/ *nf* (a) (of plane)
wingspan
(b) (figurative) (of person) stature; (of project)
scale; **un projet d'~** a substantial project;
sans ~ ⟨*project*⟩ limited; ⟨*person*⟩ of no
account
⚘ **envers**[1] /ãveR/ *prep* toward(s), to
IDIOM ~ et contre tous/tout in spite of
everyone/everything
envers[2] /ãveR/ **1** *nm inv* (of sheet of paper)
back; (of piece of cloth) wrong side; (of garment)
inside; (of coin) reverse
2 **à l'envers** *phr* (a) the wrong way
(b) upside down
(c) inside out
(d) back to front
(e) the wrong way round (GB) *or* around
(US); **mettre ses chaussures à l'~** to put
one's shoes on the wrong feet
(f) **passer un film à l'~** to run a film
backward(s)

✛ **envie** /ɑ̃vi/ *nf* **(a)** (gen) urge (**de faire** to do); (for food) craving; **avoir ~ de qch** to feel like sth; **avoir ~ de dormir** to want to go to bed; **mourir d'~ de faire** to be dying to do (colloq); **donner (l')~ à qn de faire** to make sb want to do
(b) envy; **il te fait ~ ce jouet?** would you like that toy?
(c) birthmark

✛ **envier** /ɑ̃vje/ [2] *vtr* to envy

envieux, -ieuse /ɑ̃vjø, øz/ **1** *adj* envious
2 *nm,f* **faire des ~** to make people jealous

✛ **environ** /ɑ̃viʀɔ̃/ *adv* about

environnant, ~e /ɑ̃viʀɔnɑ̃, ɑ̃t/ *adj* surrounding

✛ **environnement** /ɑ̃viʀɔnmɑ̃/ *nm* environment

environner /ɑ̃viʀɔne/ [1] *vtr* to surround

environs /ɑ̃viʀɔ̃/ *nm pl* **être des ~ to** be from the area; **aux ~ de** (place) in the vicinity of; (time, moment) around; (amount) in the region of

envisageable /ɑ̃vizaʒabl/ *adj* possible

✛ **envisager** /ɑ̃vizaʒe/ [13] *vtr* **(a)** to plan (**de faire** to do)
(b) to envisage ‹hypothesis, situation›; to foresee ‹problem, possibility›; **~ le pire** to imagine the worst
(c) to consider

envoi /ɑ̃vwa/ *nm* **(a)** tous les **~** s de colis sont suspendus parcel post is suspended; **faire un ~ de** to send ‹flowers, books›
(b) demander l'~ (immédiat) de troupes to ask for troops to be dispatched (immediately)
(c) l'~ de la fusée the rocket launch; **donner le coup d'~ de** to kick off ‹match›; to open ‹festival›
■ **~ recommandé** registered post (GB) *or* mail (US); **~ contre remboursement** cash on delivery

envol /ɑ̃vɔl/ *nm* (of bird) flight; (of plane) takeoff

envolée /ɑ̃vɔle/ *nf* **(a)** flight of fancy
(b) (in prices) surge (**de** in); (of political party) rise

envoler: s'envoler /ɑ̃vɔle/ [1] *v refl* (+ *v être*) **(a)** ‹bird› to fly off; ‹plane, passenger› to take off; ‹paper, hat› to be blown away
(b) ‹prices› to soar
(c) to vanish
(d) (fam) to do a runner (colloq)

envoûtement /ɑ̃vutmɑ̃/ *nm*
(a) bewitchment
(b) spell

envoûter /ɑ̃vute/ [1] *vtr* to bewitch

envoyé, ~e /ɑ̃vwaje/ **1** *adj* **ça c'est (bien) ~!** (fam) well said!
2 *nm,f* envoy; **~ spécial** special correspondent

✛ **envoyer** /ɑ̃vwaje/ [24] **1** *vtr* **(a)** to send; **~ qn étudier à Genève** to send sb off to study

in Geneva
(b) to throw ‹pebble›; to fire ‹missile›; **~ qch dans l'œil de qn** to hit sb in the eye with sth; **~ le ballon dans les buts** to put the ball in the net
2 **s'envoyer** *v refl* (+ *v être*) to exchange; **s'~ des baisers** to blow each other kisses
IDIOMS **~ qn promener** (fam) to send sb packing (colloq); **tout ~ promener** (fam) to drop the lot (colloq); **il ne me l'a pas envoyé dire** (fam) and he told me in no uncertain terms

enzyme /ɑ̃zim/ *nm or f* enzyme

éolien, -ienne¹ /eɔljɛ̃, ɛn/ *adj* ‹generator› wind

éolienne² /eɔljɛn/ *nf* **(a)** (aeolian) windmill
(b) wind turbine

épagneul /epaɲœl/ *nm* spaniel

épais, épaisse /epɛ, ɛs/ **1** *adj* **(a)** thick; **il n'est pas bien~ ce petit!** (fam) he's a skinny little fellow!
(b) ‹mind› dull
(c) ‹night› deep
2 *adv* a lot, much

épaisseur /epɛsœʀ/ *nf* **(a)** thickness; **couper qch dans (le sens de) l'~** to cut sth sideways
(b) layer

épaissir /epesiʀ/ [3] **1** *vtr* **(a)** to thicken
(b) to deepen ‹mystery›
2 *vi* **(a)** ‹sauce› to thicken; ‹jelly› to set
(b) to put on weight
3 **s'épaissir** *v refl* (+ *v être*) ‹sauce, waist, mist› to thicken; ‹mystery› to deepen

épancher: s'épancher /epɑ̃ʃe/ [1] *v refl* (+ *v être*) to open one's heart (**auprès de** to)

épanoui, ~e /epanwi/ *adj* ‹flower› in full bloom; ‹smile› beaming; ‹person› well-adjusted

épanouir /epanwiʀ/ [3] **1** *vtr* **(a)** ‹sun› to open (out) ‹flower›; ‹joy› to light up ‹face›
(b) (figurative) to make [sb/sth] blossom
2 **s'épanouir** *v refl* (+ *v être*) ‹flower› to bloom; ‹face› to light up; ‹person› to blossom

épanouissant, ~e /epanwisɑ̃, ɑ̃t/ *adj* fulfilling

épanouissement /epanwismɑ̃/ *nm*
(a) (of flower) blooming
(b) (of person) development; (of talent) flowering

épargnant, ~e /epaʀɲɑ̃, ɑ̃t/ *nm,f* saver

épargne /epaʀɲ/ *nf* savings

épargner /epaʀɲe/ [1] **1** *vtr* **(a)** to save ‹money›
(b) to spare; **~ qch à qn** to spare sb sth
2 *vi* to save
3 **s'épargner** *v refl* (+ *v être*) to save oneself

éparpiller /epaʀpije/ [1] *vtr*, **s'éparpiller** *v refl* (+ *v être*) to scatter

épars, ∼**e** /epaʀ, aʀs/ *adj* scattered

épatant, ∼**e** /epatã, ãt/ *adj* (fam) marvellous (GB)

épate /epat/ *nf* (fam) **faire de l'**∼ to show off

épaté, ∼**e** /epate/ *adj* **(a) nez** ∼ pug nose, flat nose
(b) (fam) amazed (**de** by)

épater /epate/ [1] *vtr* (fam) **(a)** to impress; **ça t'épate, hein?** surprised, aren't you?
(b) to amaze

ⱷ **épaule** /epol/ *nf* shoulder
IDIOMS **changer son fusil d'**∼ to change one's tactics; **avoir la tête sur les** ∼**s** to have one's head screwed on (colloq)

épauler /epole/ [1] ① *vtr* **(a)** to help
(b) to take aim with ‹*rifle*›
② *vi* to take aim

épaulette /epolɛt/ *nf* **(a)** shoulder-pad
(b) (shoulder-)strap
(c) (Mil) epaulette

épave /epav/ *nf* **(a)** wreck
(b) (car) (gen) wreck; (after accident) write-off (colloq); write-off (colloq)
(c) (person) wreck

épée /epe/ *nf* sword; **c'est un coup d'**∼ **dans l'eau** it was a complete waste of effort

épeler /eple/ [19] *vtr* to spell ‹*word*›

éperdu, ∼**e** /epɛʀdy/ *adj* ‹*need, desire*› overwhelming; ‹*glance*› desperate; ‹*love*› boundless

éperdument /epɛʀdymã/ *adv* ‹*in love*› madly; **je me moque** ∼ **de ce qu'il pense** I couldn't care less what he thinks

éperon /eprɔ̃/ *nm* spur

épervier /epɛʀvje/ *nm* (Zool) sparrowhawk

éphémère /efemɛʀ/ *adj* ephemeral; fleeting; short-lived

épi /epi/ *nm* **(a)** (of corn) ear; (of flower) spike; ∼ **de maïs** corn cob
(b) cow's lick (GB), cow-lick (US)

épice /epis/ *nf* spice

épicé, ∼**e** /epise/ *adj* spicy; hot

épicentre /episãtʀ/ *nm* epicentre (GB)

épicer /epise/ [12] *vtr* to spice; to add spice to

ⱷ **épicerie** /episʀi/ *nf* **(a)** grocer's (shop) (GB), grocery (store) (US); ∼ **fine** delicatessen
(b) grocery trade
(c) groceries

épicier, -ière /episje, ɛʀ/ *nm,f* grocer

épidémie /epidemi/ *nf* epidemic

épiderme /epidɛʀm/ *nm* skin

épidermique /epidɛʀmik/ *adj* skin; ‹*sensitivity*› extreme; **réaction** ∼ gut reaction

épier /epje/ [2] *vtr* **(a)** to spy on ‹*person, behaviour*›
(b) to be on the lookout for

ⱷ indicates a very frequent word

épilation /epilasjɔ̃/ *nf* removal of unwanted hair

épilepsie /epilɛpsi/ *nf* **crise d'**∼ epileptic fit

épiler /epile/ [1] *vtr* to remove unwanted hair from; to wax ‹*leg*›; to pluck ‹*eyebrows*›

épilogue /epilɔg/ *nm* epilogue (GB)

épiloguer /epilɔge/ [1] *vi* to go on and on (**sur** about)

épinard /epinaʀ/ *nm* spinach
IDIOM **ça met du beurre dans les** ∼**s** (fam) it brings in a nice bit of extra money

épine /epin/ *nf* thorn; ∼ **dorsale** spine
IDIOM **ôter à qn une** ∼ **du pied** to take a weight off sb's shoulders

épineux, -euse /epinø, øz/ *adj* ‹*stem, character*› prickly; ‹*problem*› tricky; ‹*question*› vexed

épingle /epɛ̃gl/ *nf* pin; ∼ **de** *or* **à nourrice**, ∼ **de sûreté** safety pin
IDIOMS **monter qch en** ∼ to blow sth up out of proportion; **être tiré à quatre** ∼**s** (fam) to be immaculately dressed; **tirer son** ∼ **du jeu** to get out while the going is good

épinière /epinjɛʀ/ *adj f* **moelle** ∼ spinal cord

épique /epik/ *adj* epic; **c'était** ∼ (humorous) (fam) it was quite something (colloq)

épisode /epizɔd/ *nm* episode; **roman à** ∼**s** serialized novel

épisodique /epizɔdik/ *adj* sporadic

épistolaire /epistɔlɛʀ/ *adj* epistolary; **ils ont des relations** ∼**s** they correspond

épitaphe /epitaf/ *nf* epitaph

épithète /epitɛt/ *nf* attributive adjective

éploré, ∼**e** /eplɔʀe/ *adj* **(a)** grief-stricken
(b) tearful

éplucher /eplyʃe/ [1] *vtr* to peel; (figurative) to go through [sth] with a fine-tooth comb

épluchure /eplyʃyʀ/ *nf* ∼**s** peelings

éponge /epɔ̃ʒ/ *nf* **(a)** sponge
(b) terry-towelling (GB)
IDIOM **passer l'**∼ to forget the past

éponger /epɔ̃ʒe/ [13] *vtr* **(a)** to mop (up)
(b) to absorb ‹*deficit*›; to pay off ‹*debts*›

épopée /epɔpe/ *nf* **(a)** epic
(b) saga

ⱷ **époque** /epɔk/ *nf* **(a)** time; **vivre avec son** ∼ to move with the times; **quelle** ∼**!** what's the world coming to!; **à mon** ∼ in my day
(b) (historical) era
(c) **en costume d'**∼ in period costume; **des meubles d'**∼ antique furniture

épouse /epuz/ *nf* wife, spouse

épouser /epuze/ [1] *vtr* **(a)** to marry ‹*person*›
(b) to adopt ‹*cause, idea*›

épousseter /epuste/ [20] *vtr* to dust

époustoufler /epustufle/ [1] *vtr* (fam) to amaze

épouvantable /epuvɑ̃tabl/ adj (a) (gen) dreadful
(b) appalling
épouvantail /epuvɑ̃taj/ nm (a) scarecrow
(b) (fam) (ugly person) fright
(c) spectre (GB)
épouvante /epuvɑ̃t/ nf (a) terror
(b) horror
épouvanter /epuvɑ̃te/ [1] vtr (a) to terrify
(b) to horrify
époux /epu/ 1 nm inv husband
2 nm pl les ∼ the (married) couple
éprendre: s'éprendre /eprɑ̃dʀ/ [52] v refl (+ v être) s'∼ de qn to become enamoured of sb
⚜ **épreuve** /epʀœv/ nf (a) ordeal
(b) test; mettre à rude ∼ to put [sb] to a severe test ‹person›; to be very hard on ‹car, shoes›; to tax ‹patience, nerves›; à toute ∼ unfailing; l'∼ du feu ordeal by fire; à l'∼ du feu/des balles fire-/bullet-proof
(c) (part of an) examination; ∼ écrite written examination
(d) (Sport) ∼ d'athlétisme athletics event
(e) (photograph, print) proof
épris, ∼e /epʀi, iz/ adj in love (de with)
éprouvant, ∼e /epʀuvɑ̃, ɑ̃t/ adj gruelling (GB); trying
⚜ **éprouver** /epʀuve/ [1] vtr (a) to feel ‹regret, love›; to have ‹sensation, difficulty›; ∼ de la jalousie to be jealous
(b) to test
(c) ‹death, event› to distress ‹person›; ‹storm› to hit ‹region›
éprouvette /epʀuvɛt/ nf (a) test tube
(b) sample
EPS /œpeɛs/ nf (abbr = **éducation physique et sportive**) PE
épuisant, ∼e /epɥizɑ̃, ɑ̃t/ adj exhausting
épuisé, ∼e /epɥize/ 1 pp ▸ ÉPUISER
2 pp adj (a) exhausted, worn out
(b) ‹publication, livre› out of print; ‹item› out of stock
épuisement /epɥizmɑ̃/ nm (a) exhaustion
(b) jusqu'à ∼ des stocks while stocks last
épuiser /epɥize/ [1] 1 vtr (a) to exhaust, to wear [sb] out
(b) to exhaust ‹subject, mine›
2 s'épuiser v refl (+ v être) (a) to exhaust oneself
(b) ‹stocks, provisions› to be running out
épuisette /epɥizɛt/ nf (a) landing net
(b) shrimp net
épurateur /epyʀatœʀ/ nm purifier
épuration /epyʀasjɔ̃/ nf (a) (of gas, liquid) purification; (of sewage) treatment
(b) purge
épurer /epyʀe/ [1] vtr (a) to purify ‹water, gas›
(b) to purge ‹party›
(c) to expurgate ‹text›

équateur /ekwatœʀ/ nm equator
équation /ekwɑsjɔ̃/ nf equation
équerre /ekɛʀ/ nf (a) set square; en or d'∼ at right angles
(b) flat angle bracket
équestre /ekɛstʀ/ adj equestrian; centre ∼ riding school
⚜ **équilibre** /ekilibʀ/ nm (a) balance; être en ∼ sur ‹object› to be balanced on; ‹person› to balance on
(b) equilibrium; manquer d'∼ to be unstable; retrouver son ∼ to get back to normal
équilibrer /ekilibʀe/ [1] vtr to balance
équilibriste /ekilibʀist/ nmf acrobat
équinoxe /ekinɔks/ nm equinox
équipage /ekipaʒ/ nm crew
⚜ **équipe** /ekip/ nf team; crew; shift; travailler en ∼ to work as a team; ∼ de tournage film crew; l'∼ de nuit the night shift
équipé, ∼e¹ /ekipe/ 1 pp ▸ ÉQUIPER
2 pp adj bien/mal ∼ well-/ill-equipped; cuisine ∼e fitted kitchen
équipée² /ekipe/ nf escapade
équipement /ekipmɑ̃/ nm (a) equipment; kit
(b) ∼s facilities
équiper /ekipe/ [1] 1 vtr to equip ‹hospital, vehicle›; to provide ‹town›; to fit out ‹person›
2 s'équiper v refl (+ v être) to equip oneself
équipier, -ière /ekipje, ɛʀ/ nm,f (a) team member
(b) crew member
équitable /ekitabl/ adj fair-minded; fair
équitablement /ekitabləmɑ̃/ adv equitably, fairly
équitation /ekitɑsjɔ̃/ nf (horse-)riding
équité /ekite/ nf equity
équivalence /ekivalɑ̃s/ nf (a) equivalence
(b) titre admis en ∼ recognized qualification
équivalent, ∼e /ekivalɑ̃, ɑ̃t/ adj
(a) equivalent
(b) identical
équivaloir /ekivalwaʀ/ [45] v+prep ∼ à to be equivalent to ‹quantity›; to amount to ‹effect›
équivoque /ekivɔk/ 1 adj (a) ambiguous
(b) ‹reputation› dubious; ‹behaviour› questionable
2 nf ambiguity; sans ∼ ‹reply› unequivocal; ‹condemn› unequivocally
érable /eʀabl/ nm maple (tree)
érafler /eʀafle/ [1] 1 vtr to scratch
2 s'érafler v refl (+ v être) to scratch oneself
érailler: s'érailler /eʀaje/ [1] v refl (+ v être) to become hoarse

ère /ɛʀ/ *nf* **(a)** era; **en l'an 10 de notre ~** in the year 10 AD
(b) age; **à l'~ atomique** in the nuclear age

érection /eʀɛksjɔ̃/ *nf* erection

éreinter /eʀɛ̃te/ [1] *vtr* (fam) to exhaust

ergot /ɛʀɡo/ *nm* **(a)** (of cock) spur; (of dog) dewclaw
(b) ergot

ergoter /ɛʀɡɔte/ [1] *vi* to split hairs

ériger /eʀiʒe/ [13] **1** *vtr* to erect ‹statue›
2 s'ériger *v refl* (+ *v être*) **s'~ en** to set oneself up as

ermite /ɛʀmit/ *nm* **(a)** hermit
(b) recluse

éroder /eʀɔde/ [1] *vtr* to erode

érosion /eʀozjɔ̃/ *nf* erosion

érotique /eʀɔtik/ *adj* erotic

érotisme /eʀɔtism/ *nm* eroticism

errance /ɛʀɑ̃s/ *nf* restless wandering

errant, ~e /ɛʀɑ̃, ɑ̃t/ *adj* wandering; rootless; **chien ~** stray dog

errer /ɛʀe/ [1] *vi* ‹person, gaze› to wander; ‹animal› to roam

⚐ **erreur** /ɛʀœʀ/ *nf* **(a)** mistake; **~ de jugement** error of judgment; **induire qn en ~** to mislead sb; **sauf ~ de ma part** if I'm not mistaken
(b) (Law) error

erroné, ~e /ɛʀɔne/ *adj* incorrect, erroneous

ersatz /ɛʀzats/ *nm* ersatz

érudit, ~e /eʀydi, it/ *nm,f* scholar

érudition /eʀydisjɔ̃/ *nf* erudition, scholarship

éruption /eʀypsjɔ̃/ *nf* eruption

es /ɛ/ ▶ ÊTRE¹

ès /ɛs/ *prep* **licence ~ lettres** ≈ arts degree, B. A. (degree)

esbroufe /ɛzbʀuf/ *nf* (fam) **faire de l'~** to swank (colloq), to show off

escabeau, *pl* **~x** /ɛskabo/ *nm* stepladder

escadrille /ɛskadʀij/ *nf* squadron

escadron /ɛskadʀɔ̃/ *nm* (Mil) company; **~ de la mort** death squad

escalade /ɛskalad/ *nf* **(a)** (Sport) climbing; ascent
(b) escalation

escalader /ɛskalade/ [1] *vtr* to scale ‹wall›; to climb ‹mountain›

escale /ɛskal/ *nf* (gen) stopover; (for ship) port of call; **~ technique** (for plane) refuelling (GB) stop; (for ship) overhaul

⚐ **escalier** /ɛskalje/ *nm* **(a)** staircase
(b) stairs
■ **~ mécanique** *or* **roulant** escalator; **~ de service** backstairs

escalope /ɛskalɔp/ *nf* escalope

⚐ indicates a very frequent word

escamotable /ɛskamɔtabl/ *adj* ‹landing gear› retractable; ‹ladder› foldaway

escamoter /ɛskamɔte/ [1] *vtr*
(a) ‹magician› to make [sth] disappear
(b) to evade ‹issue›

escampette /ɛskɑ̃pɛt/ *nf* (fam) **prendre la poudre d'~** to scarper (colloq), to skedaddle (colloq)

escapade /ɛskapad/ *nf* escapade

escargot /ɛskaʀɡo/ *nm* snail

escarpé, ~e /ɛskaʀpe/ *adj* **(a)** steep
(b) craggy

escarpement /ɛskaʀpəmɑ̃/ *nm* steep slope

escarpin /ɛskaʀpɛ̃/ *nm* court shoe (GB), pump (US)

escarre /ɛskaʀ/ *nf* bedsore

escient /ɛsjɑ̃/ *nm* **à bon ~** wittingly; **à mauvais ~** ill-advisedly

esclaffer: s'esclaffer /ɛsklafe/ [1] *v refl* (+ *v être*) to guffaw

esclandre /ɛsklɑ̃dʀ/ *nm* scene

esclavage /ɛsklavaʒ/ *nm* slavery; (figurative) tyranny

⚐ **esclave** /ɛsklav/ *nmf* slave

escompte /ɛskɔ̃t/ *nm* discount

escompter /ɛskɔ̃te/ [1] *vtr* to anticipate; **~ faire** to count on doing, to hope to do

escorte /ɛskɔʀt/ *nf* escort

escorter /ɛskɔʀte/ [1] *vtr* to escort

escrime /ɛskʀim/ *nf* fencing

escrimer: s'escrimer /ɛskʀime/ [1] *v refl* (+ *v être*) (fam) **s' ~ à faire** to knock oneself out trying to do (colloq)

escroc /ɛskʀo/ *nm* swindler, crook

escroquer /ɛskʀɔke/ [1] *vtr* to swindle

escroquerie /ɛskʀɔkʀi/ *nf* **(a)** fraud, swindling; **tentative d'~** attempted fraud
(b) swindle

ésotérique /ezɔteʀik/ *adj* esoteric

⚐ **espace** /ɛspas/ *nm* **(a)** space
(b) **~ de loisirs** leisure complex
(c) gap
(d) **en l'~ de** in the space of; **l'~ d'un instant** for a moment
■ **~ vert** open space; **~ vital** living space

espacer /ɛspase/ [12] **1** *vtr* to space [sth] out
2 s'espacer *v refl* (+ *v être*) to become less frequent

espadon /ɛspadɔ̃/ *nm* swordfish

espadrille /ɛspadʀij/ *nf* espadrille

Espagne /ɛspaɲ/ *pr nf* Spain
IDIOM **bâtir des châteaux en ~** to build castles in the air

⚐ **espagnol, ~e** /ɛspaɲɔl/ **1** *adj* Spanish
2 *nm* (language) Spanish

espalier /ɛspalje/ *nm* **(a)** espalier
(b) fruit-wall

◆ **espèce** /ɛspɛs/ **1** *nf* **(a)** species; **l'~ humaine** mankind
(b) kind
2 espèces *nf pl* **en ~s** in cash

espérance /ɛsperɑ̃s/ *nf* hope; **~ de vie** life expectancy

◆ **espérer** /ɛspere/ [14] **1** *vtr* **(a)** **~ qch** to hope for sth
(b) to expect; **je n'en espérais pas tant** it's more than I expected
2 *vi* to hope

espiègle /ɛspjɛgl/ *adj* mischievous

espion, -ionne /ɛspjɔ̃, ɔn/ *nm,f* spy

espionnage /ɛspjɔnaʒ/ *nm* espionage, spying

espionner /ɛspjɔne/ [1] *vtr* to spy on

esplanade /ɛsplanad/ *nf* esplanade

◆ **espoir** /ɛspwaʀ/ *nm* hope; **reprendre ~** to feel hopeful again; **avec ~** hopefully

◆ **esprit** /ɛspʀi/ *nm* **(a)** mind; **avoir l'~ mal placé** to have a dirty mind (colloq); **avoir un ~ de synthèse** to be good at synthesizing information; **avoir l'~ de contradiction** to be contrary; **dans mon ~ c'était facile** the way I saw it, it was easy; **cela ne t'est jamais venu à l'~?** didn't it ever occur to you?; **avoir l'~ ailleurs** to be miles away; **les choses de l'~** spiritual matters
(b) wit; **faire de l'~** to try to be witty; **~ d'à-propos** ready wit
(c) dans un ~ de vengeance in a spirit of revenge; **ils ont l'~ de famille** they're a very close family
(d) l'un des plus grands ~s de son temps one of the greatest minds of his/her time; **calmer les ~s** to calm people down; **les ~s sont échauffés** feelings are running high
(e) spirit; **croire aux ~s** to believe in ghosts
■ **~ de corps** solidarity; **~ d'équipe** team spirit
IDIOMS **perdre ses ~s** to faint; **les grands ~s se rencontrent** great minds think alike

esquimau, -aude, *mpl* **~x** /ɛskimo, od/ **1** *adj* Eskimo; **chien ~** husky
2 *nm* **(a)** Eskimo
(b) ® chocolate-covered ice lolly (GB), ice-cream bar (US)

esquinter /ɛskɛ̃te/ [1] *vtr* (fam) to damage

esquisse /ɛskis/ *nf* **(a)** sketch
(b) outline

esquisser /ɛskise/ [1] *vtr* to sketch ‹portrait›; to outline ‹programme›

esquiver /ɛskive/ [1] **1** *vtr* to dodge, to duck ‹blow›; to sidestep ‹issue›
2 s'esquiver *v refl* (+ *v être*) to slip away

◆ **essai** /ɛsɛ/ **1** *nm* **(a)** (Tech, Med) trial; test; **être à l'~** to undergo trials; to be tested; **~ sur route** road test
(b) try, attempt; **un coup d'~** a try; **prendre qn à l'~** to give sb a try-out
(c) essay
(d) (in rugby) try

2 essais *nm pl* (Aut, Sport) qualifying round

essaim /esɛ̃/ *nm* swarm

essayage /esɛjaʒ/ *nm* fitting

◆ **essayer** /eseje/ [21] **1** *vtr* **(a)** to try; **~ sa force** to test one's strength
(b) to test ‹weapon, product›; to run trials on ‹car›
(c) to try on ‹clothes›; to try ‹size, colour›; to try out ‹car›
2 *vi* to try; **~ à la poste** to try the post office; **j'essaierai que tout se passe bien** I'll try to make sure everything goes all right
3 s'essayer *v refl* (+ *v être*) **s'~ à** to have a go at, to try one's hand at

essayiste /esejist/ *nmf* essayist

◆ **essence** /esɑ̃s/ *nf* **(a)** petrol (GB), gasoline (US)
(b) essential oil
(c) tree species
■ **~ à briquet** lighter fuel (GB), lighter fluid (US); **~ ordinaire** ≈ 2-star petrol (GB), regular gasoline (US); **~ sans plomb** unleaded (petrol) (GB), unleaded gasoline (US); **~ super** ≈ 4-star petrol (GB), premium gasoline (US)

◆ **essentiel, -ielle** /esɑ̃sjɛl/ **1** *adj* essential
2 *nm* **c'est l'~** that's the main thing; **aller à l'~** to get to the heart of the matter; **l'~ des voix** the bulk of the vote; **pour l'~ mainly; en voyage je n'emporte que l'~** when I travel I only take the bare essentials

essentiellement /esɑ̃sjɛlmɑ̃/ *adv*
(a) mainly
(b) essentially

esseulé, -e /esœle/ *adj* forlorn

essieu, *pl* **~x** /esjø/ *nm* axle

essor /esɔʀ/ *nm* (of technology, area) development; **être en plein ~** to be booming

essorage /esɔʀaʒ/ *nm* wringing; spin-drying

essorer /esɔʀe/ [1] *vtr* **(a)** to wring
(b) to spin-dry ‹washing›; to spin ‹lettuce›

essoufflement /esuflǝmɑ̃/ *nm* breathlessness; (figurative) loss of impetus

essouffler /esufle/ [1] **1** *vtr* to leave [sb] breathless; **être essoufflé** to be out of breath
2 s'essouffler *v refl* (+ *v être*) **(a)** to get breathless
(b) to run out of steam

essuie-glace, *pl* **~s** /esɥiglas/ *nm* windscreen wiper (GB), windshield wiper (US)

essuie-mains /esɥimɛ̃/ *nm inv* hand towel

essuie-tout /esɥitu/ *nm inv* kitchen roll, kitchen paper

essuyer /esɥije/ [22] **1** *vtr* **(a)** to dry ‹glass, hands›; to wipe ‹table›; **~ la vaisselle** to dry up; **~ ses larmes** to wipe away one's tears

⋯⋰

(b) to suffer ‹defeat, losses›; to meet with ‹failure›

2 s'essuyer v refl (+ v être) to dry oneself; **s'~ les mains** to dry one's hands

♂ **est¹** /ε/ ▶ ÊTRE¹

♂ **est²** /εst/ **1** adj inv east; eastern

2 nm **(a)** east; **un vent d'~** an easterly wind

(b) l'Est the East; **de l'Est** eastern

estafette® /εstafεt/ nf van

estampe /εstɑ̃p/ nf **(a)** engraving

(b) print

estamper /εstɑ̃pe/ [1] vtr (fam) to rip [sb] off (colloq)

esthète /εstεt/ nmf aesthete

esthéticienne /εstetisjεn/ nf beautician

esthétique /εstetik/ **1** adj aesthetic; ‹decor› aesthetically pleasing; ‹pose› graceful

2 nf aesthetics

estimable /εstimabl/ adj **(a)** worthy

(b) laudable

(c) difficilement ~ hard to estimate

estimation /εstimasjɔ̃/ nf estimate; valuation

estime /εstim/ nf respect

♂ **estimer** /εstime/ [1] vtr **(a)** to feel; **~ nécessaire de faire** to consider it necessary to do

(b) to think highly of ‹friend, artist›

(c) to value ‹painting›; to assess ‹damage›; **une vitesse estimée à 150 km/h** an estimated speed of 150 kph

(d) to reckon

estival, ~e, mpl **-aux** /εstival, o/ adj

(a) summer

(b) summery

estivant, ~e /εstivɑ̃, ɑ̃t/ nm,f summer visitor

estomac /εstɔma/ nm stomach; **avoir l'~ bien accroché** to have a strong stomach

IDIOM **avoir l'~ dans les talons** (fam) to be famished

estomper /εstɔ̃pe/ [1] **1** vtr to blur ‹shape›; to gloss over ‹details›

2 s'estomper v refl (+ v être) ‹landscape› to become blurred; ‹hatred, memories› to fade

estrade /εstʀad/ nf platform

estragon /εstʀagɔ̃/ nm tarragon

estropié, ~e /εstʀɔpje/ nm,f cripple

estropier /εstʀɔpje/ [2] **1** vtr to maim

2 s'estropier v refl (+ v être) to maim oneself

estuaire /εstɥεʀ/ nm estuary

esturgeon /εstyʀʒɔ̃/ nm sturgeon

♂ **et** /e/ conj and; **~ voilà qu'il sort un couteau de sa poche!** and next thing he whips a knife out of his pocket!; **~ alors?** so what?

étable /etabl/ nf cowshed

établi, ~e /etabli/ **1** pp ▶ ÉTABLIR

2 pp adj **(a)** ‹reputation, use› established

(b) ‹power, regime› ruling; ‹order› established

3 nm workbench

♂ **établir** /etabliʀ/ [3] **1** vtr **(a)** to set up ‹home›

(b) to establish ‹rule, link, reputation, innocence, fact›; to introduce ‹tax, discipline›; to set ‹record, standard›

(c) to draw up ‹list, plan, budget, file›; to make out ‹cheque, bill›; to prepare ‹quote›; to make ‹diagnosis›; to draw ‹parallel›

2 s'établir v refl (+ v être) **(a)** ‹person› to settle (à, en in); **s'~ à son compte** to set up one's own business

(b) ‹links› to develop

♂ **établissement** /etablismɑ̃/ nm

(a) organization; **~ bancaire** banking institution

(b) (of relations, regime) establishment; (of tax, sanctions) introduction

(c) premises

■ **~ commercial** commercial establishment; **~ de crédit** finance company; **~ d'enseignement supérieur** higher education institution; **~ scolaire** school

♂ **étage** /etaʒ/ nm **(a)** floor; **le premier ~** the first floor (GB), the second floor (US); **à l'~** upstairs

(b) (of tower) level; (of aquaduct, cake) tier

étagère /etaʒεʀ/ nf shelf

étaient /etε/ ▶ ÊTRE¹

étain /etɛ̃/ nm **(a)** tin

(b) pewter

étais /etε/ ▶ ÊTRE¹

était /etε/ ▶ ÊTRE¹

étal /etal/ nm **(a)** (market) stall

(b) butcher's block

étalage /etalaʒ/ nm **(a)** window display

(b) display; **faire ~ de ses connaissances** to flaunt one's knowledge

étalagiste /etalaʒist/ nmf window dresser

étalement /etalmɑ̃/ nm (of holidays) staggering; (of payments) spreading

étaler /etale/ [1] **1** vtr **(a)** to spread out ‹sheet›; to roll [sth] out ‹pastry›

(b) to scatter

(c) to spread ‹butter, glue›; to apply ‹paint, ointment›

(d) to spread ‹work, payments›; to stagger ‹departures›

(e) to flaunt ‹wealth, knowledge›; to display ‹merchandise›; **~ qch au grand jour** to bring sth out into the open

2 s'étaler v refl (+ v être) **(a)** ‹butter, paint› to spread

(b) ‹person› to sprawl, to spread out

(c) (fam) **s'~ de tout son long** to fall flat on one's face; **s'~** or **se faire ~ à un examen** to fail an exam

étalon /etalɔ̃/ nm **(a)** stallion

(b) standard

étalon-or /etalɔ̃ʀ/ nm inv gold standard

étamine /etamin/ nf stamen

♂ indicates a very frequent word

étanche /etɑ̃ʃ/ *adj* ~ (à l'eau) waterproof; watertight; ~ (à l'air) airtight

étanchéité /etɑ̃ʃeite/ *nf* waterproofness; watertightness; airtightness

étancher /etɑ̃ʃe/ [1] *vtr* to quench ‹thirst›

étang /etɑ̃/ *nm* pond

étant /etɑ̃/ ▶ DONNÉ 3, ÊTRE[1]

♂ **étape** /etap/ *nf* (a) stop
(b) (in journey) stage; (in race) leg
(c) (figurative) stage, step; **brûler les ~s** to go too far too fast

♂ **état** /eta/ [1] *nm* (a) condition; **mettre qn hors d'~ de nuire** to put sb out of harm's way; **leur ~ de santé est excellent** they're in excellent health; **maintenir qch en ~ de marche** to keep sth in working order; **hors d'~ de marche** ‹car› off the road; ‹machine› out of order; **j'ai laissé les choses en l'~** I left everything as it was
(b) state; **être dans un drôle d'~** (fam) to be in a hell of a state (colloq); **être dans un ~ second** to be in a trance; **ce n'est encore qu'à l'~ de projet** it's still only at the planning stage
(c) statement
[2] **faire ~ de** *phr* (a) to cite ‹document›
(b) to mention ‹conversation›
(c) to state ‹preferences›
(d) to make a point of mentioning ‹success›
■ ~ **d'âme** qualm; feeling; ~ **civil** registry office (GB); civil status; ~ **d'esprit** state of mind; ~ **de fait** fact; ~ **des lieux** inventory and report on state of repair; **~s de service** service record

IDIOM **être/se mettre dans tous ses ~s** (fam) to be in/to get into a state (colloq)

État /eta/ *nm* (a) state, State
(b) state, government

étatique /etatik/ *adj* state (GB), public (US)

état-major, *pl* **états-majors** /etamaʒɔR/ *nm* (a) (Mil) staff
(b) headquarters

États-Unis /etazyni/ *pr nm pl* ~ (d'Amérique) United States (of America)

étau, *pl* ~**x** /eto/ *nm* vice (GB), vise (US); (figurative) **l'~ se resserre** the net is tightening

étayer /eteje/ [21] *vtr* (a) to prop up
(b) (figurative) to support ‹theory›

et cætera, **et cetera**, **etcétéra*** /ɛtsetera/ *loc adv* et cetera

♂ **été[1]** /ete/ ▶ ÊTRE[1]

♂ **été[2]** /ete/ *nm* summer

♂ **éteindre** /etɛ̃dR/ [55] [1] *vtr* (a) to put out ‹fire, cigarette›; to blow out ‹candle›
(b) to switch off ‹light, TV, oven›; to turn off ‹gas›
[2] **s'éteindre** *v refl* (+ *v être*) (a) ‹cigarette, fire, light› to go out; ‹radio› to go off
(b) (euphemistic) to pass away *or* on
(c) ‹desire, passion› to fade

éteint, ~**e** /etɛ̃, ɛ̃t/ [1] *pp* ▶ ÉTEINDRE
[2] *pp adj* (a) ‹gaze› dull

(b) ‹volcano› extinct; ‹star› extinct, dead

étendard /etɑ̃daR/ *nm* standard, flag

♂ **étendre** /etɑ̃dR/ [6] [1] *vtr* (a) to stretch ‹arms, legs›
(b) to spread (out) ‹cloth›; ~ **le linge** to hang out the washing
(c) to extend ‹embargo›
[2] **s'étendre** *v refl* (+ *v être*) (a) ‹land, forest› to stretch
(b) ‹strike, epidemic› to spread; ‹town› to expand, to grow
(c) ‹law, measure› **s'~ à** to apply to
(d) ‹period, work› to stretch, to last
(e) to lie down
(f) **s'~ sur** to dwell on

étendu, ~**e[1]** /etɑ̃dy/ [1] *pp* ▶ ÉTENDRE
[2] *pp adj* ‹city› sprawling; ‹region, plain› vast; ‹vocabulary, knowledge, damage› extensive

étendue[2] /etɑ̃dy/ *nf* (a) expanse
(b) size
(c) scale, extent; range

♂ **éternel, -elle** /etɛRnɛl/ *adj* endless; eternal

éternellement /etɛRnɛlmɑ̃/ *adv*
(a) forever
(b) permanently
(c) perpetually
(d) eternally

éterniser: s'éterniser /etɛRnize/ [1] *v refl* (+ *v être*) to drag on; ‹visitor› to stay for ages (colloq)

éternité /etɛRnite/ *nf* eternity

éternuement /etɛRnymɑ̃/ *nm* sneeze

éternuer /etɛRnɥe/ [1] *vi* to sneeze

êtes /ɛt/ ▶ ÊTRE[1]

éther /etɛR/ *nm* ether

éthique /etik/ [1] *adj* ethical
[2] *nf* (a) ethics
(b) code of ethics

ethnie /ɛtni/ *nf* ethnic group

ethnique /ɛtnik/ *adj* ethnic

ethnologie /ɛtnɔlɔʒi/ *nf* ethnology

éthylique /etilik/ *adj, nmf* alcoholic

éthylisme /etilism/ *nm* alcoholism

étiez /etje/ ▶ ÊTRE[1]

étincelant, ~**e** /etɛ̃slɑ̃, ɑ̃t/ *adj* ‹sun› blazing; ‹star› twinkling; ‹gemstone, glass› sparkling; ‹feathers, colour› brilliant

étinceler /etɛ̃sle/ [19] *vi* to twinkle; to sparkle

étincelle /etɛ̃sɛl/ *nf* spark; **jeter des ~s** to glitter; **faire des ~s** to do brilliantly

étioler: s'étioler /etjɔle/ [1] *v refl* (+ *v être*) to wilt

étions /etjɔ̃/ ▶ ÊTRE[1]

étiquetage /etiktaʒ/ *nm* labelling (GB)
■ ~ **génétique** gene tagging

étiqueter /etikte/ [20] *vtr* to label

étiquette /etikɛt/ *nf* (a) label ┈┈⟩

(b) tag; **porter une** ~ to be labelled (GB);
candidat sans ~ independent candidate
(c) etiquette

étirer /etiʀe/ [1] **1** vtr to stretch
2 **s'étirer** v refl (+ v être) **(a)** ⟨person⟩ to
stretch
(b) ⟨procession, road⟩ to stretch out

étoffe /etɔf/ nf **(a)** fabric
(b) (figurative) substance; **avoir l'**~ **d'un grand
homme** to have the makings of a great man

étoffer /etɔfe/ [1] **1** vtr to expand
2 **s'étoffer** v refl (+ v être) to put on weight

⚜ **étoile** /etwal/ nf star
■ ~ **filante** shooting star; ~ **de mer** starfish; ~
polaire Pole Star
IDIOM coucher or **dormir à la belle** ~ to
sleep out in the open

étoilé, ~**e** /etwale/ adj **(a)** starry
(b) ⟨glass, windscreen⟩ crazed

étole /etɔl/ nf stole

étonnamment /etɔnamɑ̃/ adv
surprisingly

étonnant, ~**e** /etɔnɑ̃, ɑ̃t/ adj
(a) surprising
(b) amazing

étonnement /etɔnmɑ̃/ nm surprise

⚜ **étonner** /etɔne/ [1] **1** vtr to surprise
2 **s'étonner** v refl (+ v être) to be surprised

étouffant, ~**e** /etufɑ̃, ɑ̃t/ adj **(a)** stifling
(b) oppressive

étouffé, ~**e** /etufe/ adj **(a)** ⟨sound, voice⟩
muffled
(b) ⟨sob⟩ choked; ⟨laughter⟩ suppressed

étouffement /etufmɑ̃/ nm asphyxiation

étouffer /etufe/ [1] **1** vtr **(a)** to suppress
⟨protest⟩
(b) to hush up ⟨scandal⟩
(c) to suffocate ⟨person⟩; to choke ⟨plant⟩; **la
générosité ne les étouffe pas** generosity is
not their middle name
(d) to smother ⟨fire⟩
(e) to stifle ⟨yawn⟩; to hold back ⟨sigh⟩
(f) to deaden ⟨noise⟩
2 vi to feel stifled; **on étouffe ici!** (fam) it's
stifling in here!; **mourir étouffé** to die of
suffocation
3 **s'étouffer** v refl (+ v être) to choke

étourderie /etuʀdəʀi/ nf absent-
mindedness

étourdi, ~**e** /etuʀdi/ adj **(a)** absent-minded
(b) unthinking

étourdir /etuʀdiʀ/ [3] **1** vtr **(a)** to stun,
to daze
(b) ~ **qn** ⟨noise⟩ to make sb's head spin
2 **s'étourdir** v refl (+ v être) **s'**~ **de
paroles** to become intoxicated with words

étourdissant, ~**e** /etuʀdisɑ̃, ɑ̃t/ adj
⟨noise⟩ deafening; ⟨speed⟩ dizzying

étourdissement /etuʀdismɑ̃/ nm **avoir
un** ~ to feel dizzy

⚜ indicates a very frequent word

⚜ **étrange** /etʀɑ̃ʒ/ **1** adj strange; **chose** ~
elle n'a pas répondu strangely enough she
didn't answer
2 nm **(a)** strangeness
(b) l'~ the bizarre

étrangement /etʀɑ̃ʒmɑ̃/ adv
(a) curiously; **vous me rappelez** ~ **un ami**
it's strange but you remind me of a friend
(b) surprisingly

⚜ **étranger, -ère** /etʀɑ̃ʒe, ɛʀ/ **1** adj
(a) foreign
(b) ~ **à** ⟨person⟩ not involved in ⟨case⟩;
outside ⟨group⟩; ⟨fact⟩ with no bearing on
⟨problem⟩; **se sentir** ~ to feel like an outsider
(c) unfamiliar
2 nm,f **(a)** foreigner
(b) outsider
(c) stranger
3 nm **à l'**~ abroad

étrangeté /etʀɑ̃ʒte/ nf strangeness

étranglé, ~**e** /etʀɑ̃gle/ adj **(a)** ⟨voice⟩
choked; ⟨sound⟩ muffled
(b) ⟨street⟩ narrow

étranglement /etʀɑ̃gləmɑ̃/ nm
(a) strangulation
(b) (of road, valley) narrow section

étrangler /etʀɑ̃gle/ [1] **1** vtr **(a)** to
strangle
(b) to choke
2 **s'étrangler** v refl (+ v être) **(a)** to
strangle oneself
(b) to choke

étrangleur, -euse /etʀɑ̃glœʀ, øz/ nm,f
strangler

⚜ **être¹** /ɛtʀ/ [7] vi (+ v avoir)

■ **Note** You will find translations for fixed
phrases using être such as être en train de, être
sur le point de, quoi qu'il en soit, étant donné etc,
at the entries TRAIN, POINT, QUOI, DONNÉ etc.

(a) to be; **nous sommes pauvres** we are poor
(b) (as auxiliary verb) **elles sont tombées** they
have fallen; they fell; **elle s'était vengée** she
had taken her revenge
(c) (to go) **je n'ai jamais été en Chine** I've
never been to China
(d) (with ce) **est-ce leur voiture?** is it their car?;
c'est grave? is it serious?; **qui est-ce?** who
is he/she?; who is that?; who is it?; **est-ce
que tu parles russe?** do you speak Russian?;
qu'est-ce que c'est? what is it?; **ce sont mes
enfants** these are my children; they are
my children; **c'est cela** that's right; **c'est à
Pierre/lui de choisir** it's Pierre's/his turn to
choose; it's up to Pierre/to him to choose;
**il aurait pu s'excuser, ne serait-ce qu'en
envoyant un mot** he could have apologized if
only by sending a note
(e) (with il) **il est facile de critiquer** it is easy
to criticize; **il n'est pas jusqu'à l'Antarctique
qui ne soit pollué** even the Antarctic is
polluted; **il n'en est rien** this isn't at all the
case
(f) (with en) **où en étais-je?** where was I?;

je ne sais plus où j'en suis I'm lost; 'où
en es-tu de tes recherches?'—'j'en suis à
mi-chemin' 'how far have you got in your
research?'—'I'm halfway through'; j'en suis
à me demander si... I'm beginning to wonder
whether...; ~ en uniforme to be wearing a
uniform
(g) (with *y*) j'y suis I'm with you, I get it
(colloq); je n'y suis pas I don't get it (colloq);
nous partons, vous y êtes? we're leaving,
are you ready?
(h) (with *à* and *de*) ce livre est à moi/à mon
frère this book is mine/my brother's; à qui
est ce chien? whose dog is this?; je suis
à vous tout de suite I'll be with you right
away; je suis à vous I'm all yours; ~ à ce
qu'on fait to have one's mind on what one
is doing; elle est d'un ridicule! she's so
ridiculous!

être² /ɛtʀ/ *nm* (a) ~ humain human being;
les ~s animés et inanimés animate and
inanimate things; un ~ sans défense a
defenceless (GB) creature
(b) person; un ~ cher a loved one
(c) de tout son ~ with one's whole being;
blessé au plus profond de son ~ hurt to
the core

étreindre /etʀɛ̃dʀ/ [55] *vtr* to embrace, to
hug ‹friend›; to clasp ‹opponent›

étreinte /etʀɛ̃t/ *nf* embrace; grip

étrenner /etʀene/ [1] *vtr* to use [sth] for
the first time

étrennes /etʀɛn/ *nf pl* (a) gift
(b) money

étrier /etʀije/ *nm* stirrup
IDIOM mettre à qn le pied à l'~ (figurative) to
get sb started

étriper /etʀipe/ [1] *vtr* (figurative) (fam) ~ qn
to skin sb alive

étriqué, ~e /etʀike/ *adj* ‹jacket› skimpy;
‹life› restricted

étroit, ~e /etʀwa, at/ [1] *adj* (a) narrow;
avoir l'esprit ~ to be narrow-minded
(b) ‹links› close; en ~e collaboration closely
[2] à l'étroit *phr* nous sommes un peu à
l'~ we're a bit cramped; je me sens un peu
à l'~ dans cette jupe this skirt feels a bit
too tight

étroitement /etʀwatmã/ *adv* closely

étroitesse /etʀwatɛs/ *nf* narrowness

étude /etyd/ [1] *nf* (a) study
(b) survey
(c) (mise à l')~ consideration; à l'~ under
consideration
(d) (of lawyer) office
(e) (Sch) study room (GB), study hall (US)
(f) study period
[2] **études** *nf pl* studies; faire des ~s to be
a student; je n'ai pas fait d'~s (supérieures)
I didn't go to university *or* college
■ ~ de marché market research

étudiant, ~e /etydjɑ̃, ɑ̃t/ *nm,f* student

étudié, ~e /etydje/ *adj* (a) carefully
prepared
(b) studied

étudier /etydje/ [2] [1] *vtr* to study; to
examine ‹file, situation›; to learn ‹lesson›
[2] *vi* (a) to be a student
(b) to be studying

étui /etɥi/ *nm* case; ~ à revolver holster

étuve /etyv/ *nf* (a) steam room; le grenier
est une ~ (figurative) the attic is like an oven
(b) incubator

étymologie /etimɔlɔʒi/ *nf* etymology

eu, ~e /y/ ▸ AVOIR¹

eucalyptus /økaliptys/ *nm inv* eucalyptus

eucharistie /økaʀisti/ *nf* (a) Eucharist
(b) Sacrament

eûmes /ym/ ▸ AVOIR¹

eunuque /ønyk/ *nm* eunuch

euphémisme /øfemism/ *nm* euphemism

euphorie /øfɔʀi/ *nf* euphoria

euphorique /øfɔʀik/ *adj* euphoric

euphorisant, ~e /øfɔʀizɑ̃, ɑ̃t/ [1] *adj*
stimulating; uplifting; euphoriant
[2] *nm* (Med) stimulant

eurasien, -ienne /øʀazjɛ̃, ɛn/ *adj*
Eurasian

Euratom /øʀatɔm/ *nf* (*abbr* = **European
atomic energy commission**)
Euratom

eurent /yʀ/ ▸ AVOIR¹

EURL /œyɛʀɛl/ *nf: abbr* ▸ ENTREPRISE

euro /øʀʊøʀo/ *nm* (currency) euro

eurochèque /øʀoʃɛk/ *nm* Eurocheque

euroconnecteur /øʀokɔnɛktœʀ/ *nm*
scart socket; scart plug

eurocrate /øʀokʀat/ *nmf* eurocrat

eurodéputé, -e /øʀodepyte/ *nm,f* Euro
MP

euromarché /øʀomaʀʃe/ *nm* Euromarket

Europe /øʀɔp/ *pr nf* Europe; l'~
communautaire the European community

européaniser /øʀopeanize/ [1] [1] *vtr*
to europeanize; ~ un débat to broaden a
debate to a European level
[2] **s'européaniser** *v refl* (+ *v être*)
‹country› to become europeanized; ‹economy›
to become adapted to a European framework

européen, -éenne /øʀopeɛ̃, ɛn/ *adj*
European

eurosceptique /øʀosɛptik/ *nmf*
eurosceptic

Eurotunnel /øʀotynɛl/ *nm* Eurotunnel

Eurozone /øʀozon/ *nf* Eurozone

eus /y/ ▸ AVOIR¹

eusse /ys/ ▸ AVOIR¹

eussent /ys/ ▸ AVOIR¹

eusses /ys/ ▸ AVOIR¹

eussiez /ysje/ ▸ AVOIR¹

eussions /ysjɔ̃/ ▸ AVOIR¹

eut /y/ ▶ AVOIR¹

eût /yt/ ▶ AVOIR¹

eûtes /yt/ ▶ AVOIR¹

euthanasie /øtanazi/ *nf* euthanasia

✵ **eux** /ø/ *pron* (a) they; **je sais que ce n'est pas ∼ qui ont fait ça** I know they weren't the ones who did it
(b) them; **les inviter, ∼, quelle idée!** invite THEM, what an idea!; **c'est à ∼** it's theirs

eux-mêmes /ømɛm/ *pron* themselves; **les experts ∼ reconnaissent que…** even the experts admit that…

évacuation /evakɥasjɔ̃/ *nf* (a) evacuation
(b) discharge; **il y a un problème d'∼ de l'eau** the water doesn't drain away

évacuer /evakɥe/ [1] *vtr* (a) to evacuate
(b) to drain off
(c) (figurative) to shrug off ‹*problem*›

évader: s'évader /evade/ [1] *v refl* (+ *v être*) (a) to escape; **faire ∼ qn** to help sb to escape
(b) (figurative) to get away (**de** from)

évaluable /evalɥabl/ *adj* assessable

évaluation /evalɥasjɔ̃/ *nf* (a) (of collection, house) valuation; **faire l'∼ de** to value
(b) (of costs, damages) assessment; estimate, appraisal (US)
(c) (of staff) appraisal

✵ **évaluer** /evalɥe/ [1] *vtr* (a) to estimate ‹*size, length*›; to assess ‹*risks, costs*›
(b) to value ‹*inheritance*›
(c) to assess ‹*employee, student*›

Évangile /evɑ̃ʒil/ *nm* Gospel

évanouir: s'évanouir /evanwiʀ/ [3] *v refl* (+ *v être*) (a) to faint
(b) ‹*feeling*› to fade

évanouissement /evanwismɑ̃/ *nm*
(a) blackout, fainting fit
(b) fading

évaporation /evapɔʀasjɔ̃/ *nf* evaporation

évaporer: s'évaporer /evapɔʀe/ [1] *v refl* (+ *v être*) (a) to evaporate
(b) (fam) to vanish

évaser /evaze/ [1] **1** *vtr* to flare
2 **s'évaser** *v refl* (+ *v être*) ‹*duct*› to open out; ‹*skirt*› to be flared

évasif, -ive /evazif, iv/ *adj* evasive

évasion /evazjɔ̃/ *nf* escape

Ève /ɛv/ *pr nf* Eve; **en tenue d'∼** in her birthday suit
IDIOM **elle ne le connaît ni d'∼ ni d'Adam** she doesn't know him from Adam

évêché /eveʃe/ *nm* (a) diocese
(b) bishop's palace

éveil /evɛj/ *nm* awakening

éveiller /eveje/ [1] **1** *vtr* (a) to arouse ‹*curiosity, suspicions*›; to stimulate ‹*intelligence*›; to awaken ‹*conscience*›; **un enfant éveillé** a bright child

(b) to wake (up) ‹*sleeper*›; **être éveillé** to be awake
2 **s'éveiller** *v refl* (+ *v être*) (a) to wake up
(b) ‹*imagination*› to start to develop

✵ **événement** /evenmɑ̃/ *nm* event

événementiel, -ielle /evenmɑ̃sjɛl/ *adj* factual

éventail /evɑ̃taj/ *nm* (a) fan
(b) range

éventaire /evɑ̃tɛʀ/ *nm* stall

éventer: s'éventer /evɑ̃te/ [1] *v refl* (+ *v être*) ‹*perfume, coffee*› to go off; ‹*wine*› to pass its best; ‹*beer, lemonade*› to go flat

éventrer /evɑ̃tʀe/ [1] *vtr* (a) ‹*person*› to disembowel; ‹*bull*› to gore
(b) to rip open

éventualité /evɑ̃tɥalite/ *nf* (a) eventuality
(b) possibility; **dans l'∼ de** in the event of

éventuel, -elle /evɑ̃tɥɛl/ *adj* possible

éventuellement /evɑ̃tɥɛlmɑ̃/ *adv*
(a) possibly
(b) if necessary

évêque /evɛk/ *nm* bishop (**de** of)

évertuer: s'évertuer /evɛʀtɥe/ [1] *v refl* (+ *v être*) to try one's best (**à faire** to do)

éviction /eviksjɔ̃/ *nf* (a) ousting (**de** from)
(b) (Law) eviction

✵ **évidemment** /evidamɑ̃/ *adv* of course

✵ **évidence** /evidɑ̃s/ **1** *nf* (a) obviousness
(b) obvious fact; **se rendre à l'∼** to face the facts; **de toute ∼, à l'∼** obviously
2 **en évidence** *phr* **laisser qch en ∼** to leave sth in an obvious place; **mettre en ∼** to highlight ‹*feature*›

✵ **évident, ∼e** /evidɑ̃, ɑ̃t/ *adj* obvious; **ce n'est pas ∼** (fam) not necessarily; it's not so easy

évider /evide/ [1] *vtr* to hollow out; to scoop out

évier /evje/ *nm* sink

évincer /evɛ̃se/ [12] *vtr* to oust ‹*rival*›

évitable /evitabl/ *adj* avoidable

✵ **éviter** /evite/ [1] *vtr* (a) to avoid; **∼ à qn de faire** to save sb (from) doing
(b) to dodge ‹*bullet, blow*›

évocation /evɔkasjɔ̃/ *nf* (a) evocation; reminiscence
(b) mention (**de** of)

évolué, ∼e /evɔlɥe/ *adj* (a) civilized
(b) evolved

évoluer /evɔlɥe/ [1] *vi* (a) to evolve, to change
(b) to develop
(c) to glide

évolutif, -ive /evɔlytif, iv/ *adj* progressive

✵ **évolution** /evɔlysjɔ̃/ *nf* (a) evolution
(b) development
(c) progress
(d) progression
(e) change; **en pleine ∼** undergoing rapid change

✵ indicates a very frequent word

évolutionniste /evɔlysjɔnist/ *adj* evolutionary

✔ **évoquer** /evɔke/ [1] *vtr* **(a)** to recall
(b) to mention, to bring up
(c) to bring back ‹*memory*›; to be reminiscent of ‹*childhood*›
(d) to evoke

✔ **ex** /ɛks/ *nm* **(a)** (*written abbr* = **exemple**) eg
(b) (*written abbr* = **exemplaire**) copy

ex- /ɛks/ *pref* ~**champion** former champion

exacerber /ɛgzasɛʀbe/ [1] *vtr* to exacerbate

exact, ~**e** /ɛgza(kt), akt/ *adj* **(a)** correct
(b) accurate
(c) exact
(d) punctual

✔ **exactement** /ɛgzaktəmɑ̃/ *adv* exactly

exactitude /ɛgzaktityd/ *nf* **(a)** correctness
(b) accuracy
(c) exactness
(d) punctuality

ex æquo /ɛgzeko/ *adv* **ils sont premiers ~** they've tied for first place

exagération /ɛgzaʒeʀasjɔ̃/ *nf* exaggeration

exagéré, ~**e** /ɛgzaʒeʀe/ *adj*
(a) exaggerated
(b) excessive; **d'une sensibilité** ~**e** oversensitive

exagérément /ɛgzaʒeʀemɑ̃/ *adv* excessively

exagérer /ɛgzaʒeʀe/ [14] **1** *vtr* to exaggerate
2 *vi* to go too far

exaltant, ~**e** /ɛgzaltɑ̃, ɑ̃t/ *adj* thrilling; inspiring

exaltation /ɛgzaltasjɔ̃/ *nf* **(a)** elation
(b) stimulation
(c) glorification

exalté, ~**e** /ɛgzalte/ **1** *pp* ▶ EXALTER
2 *pp adj* impassioned

exalter /ɛgzalte/ [1] *vtr* **(a)** to glorify
(b) to heighten
(c) to elate, to thrill

✔ **examen** /ɛgzamɛ̃/ *nm* **(a)** (Sch, Univ) examination, exam; **passer un** ~ to take an exam; ~ **de rattrapage** retake, resit (GB)
(b) (Med) examination
(c) examination; consideration; review; **être en cours d'**~ to be under review; to be under consideration
(d) inspection
■ ~ **blanc** mock (exam), practice exam; ~ **de conscience** self-examination; ~ **spécial d'entrée à l'université, ESEU** *university entrance exam for students not having the baccalaureate*

examinateur, -trice /ɛgzaminatœʀ, tʀis/ *nm, f* examiner

✔ **examiner** /ɛgzamine/ [1] *vtr* **(a)** to examine; to review; ~ **qch de près** to have a close look at sth
(b) (Med) to examine ‹*patient, wound*›

exaspération /ɛgzaspeʀasjɔ̃/ *nf*
(a) exasperation
(b) intensification

exaspérer /ɛgzaspeʀe/ [14] *vtr* **(a)** to exasperate, to infuriate
(b) to exacerbate

exaucer /ɛgzose/ [12] *vtr* to grant

excavatrice /ɛkskavatʀis/ *nf* excavator

excédant, ~**e** /ɛksedɑ̃, ɑ̃t/ *adj* exasperating, infuriating

excédent /ɛksedɑ̃/ *nm* surplus; ~ **de bagages** excess baggage

excédentaire /ɛksedɑ̃tɛʀ/ *adj* surplus

excéder /ɛksede/ [14] *vtr* **(a)** to exceed
(b) to infuriate

excellence /ɛksɛlɑ̃s/ *nf* excellence

Excellence /ɛksɛlɑ̃s/ *nf* **Son** ~ His/Her Excellency

✔ **excellent**, ~**e** /ɛksɛlɑ̃, ɑ̃t/ *adj* excellent

exceller /ɛksele/ [1] *vi* to excel

excentré, ~**e** /ɛksɑ̃tʀe/ *adj* **(a)** ‹*area*› outlying
(b) être ~ ‹*axis*› to be off-centre (GB)

excentricité /ɛksɑ̃tʀisite/ *nf* eccentricity

excentrique /ɛksɑ̃tʀik/ *adj, nmf* eccentric

excepté, ~**e** /ɛksɛpte/ **1** *pp* ▶ EXCEPTER
2 *prep* except
3 **excepté que** *phr* except that

excepter /ɛksɛpte/ [1] *vtr* **si l'on excepte** except for, apart from

✔ **exception** /ɛksɛpsjɔ̃/ *nf* exception; **faire** ~ to be an exception; **à l'**~ **de, ~ faite de** except for; **sauf** ~ with the occasional exception; **d'**~ ‹*person*› exceptional; ‹*law*› emergency

exceptionnel, -elle /ɛksɛpsjɔnɛl/ *adj* (gen) exceptional; ‹*price*› bargain; ‹*meeting*› extraordinary

exceptionnellement /ɛksɛpsjɔnɛlmɑ̃/ *adv* exceptionally

excès /ɛksɛ/ *nm inv* excess; **commettre des** ~ to go too far; **des** ~ **de langage** bad language; **tomber dans l'**~ **inverse** to go to the opposite extreme; ~ **de confiance/zèle** overconfidence/overzealousness
■ ~ **de vitesse** speeding

excessif, -ive /ɛksesif, iv/ *adj*
(a) excessive
(b) extreme; **il est** ~ he is a man of extremes

excision /ɛksizjɔ̃/ *nf* **(a)** excision
(b) female circumcision

excitant, ~**e** /ɛksitɑ̃, ɑ̃t/ **1** *adj*
(a) ‹*substance*› stimulating
(b) exciting; thrilling
2 *nm* stimulant

excitation /ɛksitasjɔ̃/ *nf* **(a)** excitement ⋯⟩

(b) arousal
(c) stimulation
excité, ~**e** /ɛksite/ **1** *adj* **(a)** ‹crowd› in a
frenzy; ‹atmosphere› frenzied
(b) ‹person› thrilled, excited
(c) (sexually) aroused
2 *nm,f* **(a)** rowdy
(b) fanatic
(c) neurotic
IDIOM être ~ comme une puce (fam) to be
like a cat on a hot tin roof
exciter /ɛksite/ [1] **1** *vtr* **(a)** to arouse
‹anger›; to kindle ‹desire›
(b) to thrill
(c) to arouse
(d) to tease ‹animal›; to get [sb] excited
‹child›; ‹coffee› to get [sb] hyped up
(e) to stimulate ‹palate›
2 **s'exciter** *v refl* (+ *v être*) to get excited
exclamatif, -ive /ɛksklamatif, iv/ *adj*
exclamatory
exclamation /ɛksklamasjɔ̃/ *nf*
exclamation
exclamer: s'exclamer /ɛksklame/ [1] *v*
refl (+ *v être*) to exclaim
exclu, ~**e** /ɛkskly/ **1** *pp* ▶ EXCLURE
2 *pp adj* excluded; c'est exclu! it's out of
the question!; se sentir ~ to feel left out
exclure /ɛksklyʀ/ [78] *vtr* **(a)** to exclude
‹person›; to rule out ‹possibility›
(b) to expel ‹member›
exclusif, -ive /ɛksklyzif, iv/ *adj* exclusive;
concessionnaire ~ sole agent
exclusion /ɛksklyzjɔ̃/ **1** *nf* **(a)** exclusion;
~ sociale social exclusion
(b) expulsion
(c) suspension
2 à l'exclusion de *phr* with the
exception of
exclusivité /ɛksklyzivite/ *nf* exclusive
rights; en ~ ‹publish› exclusively; ‹product›
exclusive
excommunier /ɛkskɔmynje/ [2] *vtr* to
excommunicate
excrément /ɛkskʀemɑ̃/ *nm* excrement
excrétion /ɛkskʀesjɔ̃/ *nf* excretion
excroissance /ɛkskʀwasɑ̃s/ *nf* **(a)** (Med)
growth, excrescence
(b) (in botany) outgrowth
excursion /ɛkskyʀsjɔ̃/ *nf* excursion, trip
excuse /ɛkskyz/ *nf* **(a)** excuse
(b) apology
excuser /ɛkskyze/ [1] **1** *vtr* to forgive; to
pardon; to excuse; **excusez-moi** I'm sorry;
vous êtes tout excusé it's quite all right
2 **s'excuser** *v refl* (+ *v être*) to apologize
exécrable /ɛgzekʀabl/ *adj* loathsome;
dreadful; detestable
exécrer /ɛgzekʀe/ [14] *vtr* to loathe

exécutant, ~**e** /ɛgzekytɑ̃, ɑ̃t/ *nm,f*
(a) performer
(b) il dit n'avoir été qu'un ~ he claims he
was only obeying orders
✔ **exécuter** /ɛgzekyte/ [1] **1** *vtr* **(a)** to carry
out ‹task, mission›; to do ‹exercise›
(b) to carry out ‹orders, threat›; to fulfil (GB)
‹contract›; to enforce ‹law, ruling›
(c) to execute ‹prisoner›; to kill ‹victim›
(d) (Mus) to perform
2 **s'exécuter** *v refl* (+ *v être*) to comply
exécutif, -ive /ɛgzekytif, ive/ *adj*
executive
exécution /ɛgzekysjɔ̃/ *nf* **(a)** execution,
carrying out; enforcement; fulfilment (GB);
mettre à ~ to carry out ‹threat›; travaux
en cours d'~ work in progress; veiller à
la bonne ~ d'une tâche to see that a job is
done well
(b) execution; ~ capitale capital
punishment
exemplaire /ɛgzɑ̃plɛʀ/ **1** *adj*
(a) exemplary; élève ~ model pupil
(b) (Law) exemplary
2 *nm* **(a)** copy; print
(b) specimen
exemplarité /ɛgzɑ̃plaʀite/ *nf* deterrent
nature (de of)
✔ **exemple** /ɛgzɑ̃pl/ **1** *nm* **(a)** example;
sans ~ unprecedented; être l'~ de la
gentillesse to be a model of kindness;
donner qn en ~ to hold sb up as an example
(b) warning (pour to)
2 par exemple *phr* for example; ça par
~! how amazing!; well, honestly!
exemplifier /ɛgzɑ̃plifje/ [2] *vtr* to
exemplify
exempt, ~**e** /ɛgzɑ̃, ɑ̃t/ *adj* exempt; ~
d'impôt tax-free
exempter /ɛgzɑ̃te/ [1] *vtr* to exempt
✔ **exercer** /ɛgzɛʀse/ [12] **1** *vtr* **(a)** to
exercise ‹right›; to exert ‹authority›
(b) to exercise ‹profession›; to practise (GB)
‹art›
(c) to exercise ‹body›
2 **s'exercer** *v refl* (+ *v être*) **(a)** ‹athlete› to
train; ‹musician› to practise (GB)
(b) ‹influence, force› to be exerted
✔ **exercice** /ɛgzɛʀsis/ *nm* exercise; faire
de l'~ to get some exercise; dans l'~ de
ses fonctions in the course of one's duty;
while at work; en ~ ‹minister, president›
incumbent; entrer en ~ to take up one's
duties
exergue /ɛgzɛʀg/ *nm* **(a)** epigraph
(b) inscription
exhaler /ɛgzale/ [1] *vtr* to exhale
exhausser /ɛgzose/ [1] *vtr* to raise
exhaustif, -ive /ɛgzostif, iv/ *adj*
exhaustive
exhiber /ɛgzibe/ [1] **1** *vtr* to flaunt
‹wealth›; to show ‹animal›; to expose ‹body›

✔ indicates a very frequent word

2 s'exhiber *v refl* (+ *v être*) **(a)** to expose oneself
(b) to flaunt oneself
exhibition /ɛgzibisjɔ̃/ *nf* **(a)** (of animals) show; exhibition
(b) (Sport) demonstration, display
(c) (of wealth) parade; (of emotion) display
exhibitionniste /ɛgzibisjɔnist/ *adj, nmf* exhibitionist
exhortation /ɛgzɔʀtasjɔ̃/ *nf* exhortation; ∼ **au calme** call for calm
exhorter /ɛgzɔʀte/ [1] *vtr* to motivate; ∼ **qn à faire** to urge *or* exhort sb to do
exhumer /ɛgzyme/ [1] *vtr* **(a)** to exhume
(b) to excavate
exigeant, ∼e /ɛgziʒã, ãt/ *adj* demanding
exigence /ɛgziʒãs/ *nf* demand (**de qch** for sth)
exiger /ɛgziʒe/ [13] *vtr* **(a)** to demand ‹*answer, reforms*›
(b) to require
exigibilité /ɛgziʒibilite/ *nf* (of tax, bill) payability; (of debt) repayability
exigible /ɛgziʒibl/ *adj* due
exigu, -uë /ɛgzigy/ *adj* ‹*room*› cramped; ‹*entrance*› narrow; ‹*space*› confined
exil /ɛgzil/ *nm* exile; **en** ∼ in exile
exilé, ∼e /ɛgzile/ *nm,f* exile
exiler /ɛgzile/ [1] **1** *vtr* to exile
2 s'exiler *v refl* (+ *v être*) to go into exile
existence /ɛgzistãs/ *nf* **(a)** existence
(b) (fam) life
existentialisme /ɛgzistɑ̃sjalism/ *nm* existentialism
exister /ɛgziste/ [1] *vi* to exist; **si le paradis existe** if there is a heaven; **la maison existe encore** the house is still standing
exode /ɛgzɔd/ *nm* exodus; ∼ **rural** rural depopulation
exonération /ɛgzɔneʀasjɔ̃/ *nf* exemption
exonérer /ɛgzɔneʀe/ [14] *vtr* to exempt
exorbitant, ∼e /ɛgzɔʀbitã, ãt/ *adj* ‹*price*› exorbitant; ‹*demands*› outrageous
exorbité, ∼e /ɛgzɔʀbite/ *adj* bulging
exorciser /ɛgzɔʀsize/ [1] *vtr* to exorcize
exotique /ɛgzɔtik/ *adj* exotic
exotisme /ɛgzɔtism/ *nm* exoticism
expansif, -ive /ɛkspãsif, iv/ *adj* communicative, outgoing
expansion /ɛkspãsjɔ̃/ *nf* **(a)** growth; **en (pleine)** ∼ (rapidly) growing
(b) expansion
expansivité /ɛkspãsivite/ *nf* expansiveness
expatriation /ɛkspatʀijasjɔ̃/ *nf* expatriation
expatrié, ∼e /ɛkspatʀije/ *adj, nm,f* expatriate
expatrier /ɛkspatʀije/ [2] **1** *vtr* to deport
2 s'expatrier *v refl* (+ *v être*) to emigrate

expectative /ɛkspɛktativ/ *nf* **rester dans l'**∼ to wait and see
expédient /ɛkspedjã/ *nm* expedient; **vivre d'**∼**s** to live by one's wits
expédier /ɛkspedje/ [2] *vtr* **(a)** to send; to post (GB), to mail (US); ∼ **qch à qn** to send sb sth
(b) to get rid of ‹*person*›; to polish off ‹*work, meal*›; ∼ **un procès en une heure** to get a trial over within one hour
expéditeur, -trice /ɛkspeditœʀ, tʀis/ *nm,f* sender
expéditif, -ive /ɛkspeditif, iv/ *adj* ‹*person*› brisk; ‹*method*› cursory; **une justice expéditive** summary justice
expédition /ɛkspedisjɔ̃/ *nf* expedition
expéditionnaire /ɛkspedisjɔnɛʀ/ **1** *adj* expeditionary
2 *nmf* **(a)** forwarding agent
(b) copyist
expérience /ɛkspeʀjãs/ *nf* **(a)** experience; **avoir de l'**∼ to be experienced; **j'en ai fait l'**∼ **à mes dépens** I learned that lesson to my cost
(b) experiment
expérimental, ∼e, mpl -aux /ɛkspeʀimãtal, o/ *adj* experimental
expérimentation /ɛkspeʀimãtasjɔ̃/ *nf* experimentation
■ ∼ **animale** experiments on animals
expérimenté, ∼e /ɛkspeʀimãte/ *adj* experienced
expérimenter /ɛkspeʀimãte/ [1] *vtr* to test
expert /ɛkspɛʀ/ *nm* **(a)** expert (**en on**); **l'avis d'un** ∼ expert advice
(b) adjuster
expert-comptable, pl experts-comptables /ɛkspɛʀkɔ̃tabl/ *nm* ≈ chartered accountant (GB), certified public accountant (US)
expert-conseil, pl experts-conseils /ɛkspɛʀkɔ̃sɛj/ *nm* consultant
expertise /ɛkspɛʀtiz/ *nf* **(a)** valuation (GB), appraisal (US); assessment
(b) expertise
expertiser /ɛkspɛʀtize/ [1] *vtr* to value (GB), to appraise (US) ‹*jewellery*›; to assess ‹*damages*›
expier /ɛkspje/ [2] *vtr* to atone for, to expiate
expiration /ɛkspiʀasjɔ̃/ *nf* **(a)** exhalation
(b) expiry (GB), expiration (US)
expirer /ɛkspiʀe/ [1] **1** *vtr* to exhale
2 *vi* **(a)** ‹*contract*› to expire
(b) to breathe out
explicatif, -ive /ɛksplikatif, iv/ *adj* explanatory
explication /ɛksplikasjɔ̃/ *nf* explanation; **nous avons eu une bonne** ∼ we've talked things through

explicite /ɛksplisit/ *adj* ‹text, film› explicit; ‹answer› definite

explicitement /ɛksplisitmɑ̃/ *adv* ‹mention› explicitly; ‹condemn› unequivocally; ‹ask› specifically

expliciter /ɛksplisite/ [1] *vtr* to clarify

⚘ **expliquer** /ɛksplike/ [1] **1** *vtr* (a) to explain
(b) (Sch) to analyse (GB) ‹text›
2 **s'expliquer** *v refl* (+ *v être*) s'~ qch to understand sth; **tout finira par s'~** everything will become clear

exploit /ɛksplwa/ *nm* exploit, feat

exploitant, **~e** /ɛksplwatɑ̃, ɑ̃t/ *nm,f* ~ agricole farmer

exploitation /ɛksplwatasjɔ̃/ *nf*
(a) exploitation
(b) ~ agricole farm; ~ commerciale business concern
(c) (of land, forest) exploitation; (of airline, shipping line) operation

exploiter /ɛksplwate/ [1] *vtr* (a) to exploit ‹person›
(b) to work ‹mine›; to mine ‹coal›; to exploit ‹forest›; to run ‹firm›; to operate ‹airline›
(c) to make the most of ‹gift, knowledge›

explorateur, **-trice** /ɛksplɔRatœR, tRis/ *nm,f* explorer

exploration /ɛksplɔRasjɔ̃/ *nf* exploration

explorer /ɛksplɔRe/ [1] *vtr* to explore

exploser /ɛksploze/ [1] *vi* to explode; to blow up; **faire ~** to cause [sth] to blow up

explosif, **-ive** /ɛksplozif, iv/ **1** *adj* explosive
2 *nm* explosive; **attentat à l'~** bomb attack

explosion /ɛksplozjɔ̃/ *nf* (a) explosion
(b) outburst
(c) (in market) boom

export /ɛkspɔR/ *nm* export

exportateur, **-trice** /ɛkspɔRtatœR, tRis/ *nm,f* exporter

exportation /ɛkspɔRtasjɔ̃/ *nf* export

exporter /ɛkspɔRte/ [1] *vtr* to export

exposé, **~e** /ɛkspoze/ **1** *pp* ▶ EXPOSER
2 *pp adj* (a) exposed; **maison ~e au sud** south-facing house
(b) on show; on display
3 *nm* (a) ~ de account of; **faire un** *or* **l'~ des faits** to give a statement of the facts
(b) (Sch) talk; **faire un ~** to give a talk

⚘ **exposer** /ɛkspoze/ [1] **1** *vtr* (a) to exhibit ‹art›; to display, to put [sth] on display ‹goods›
(b) to state ‹facts›; to outline ‹idea, plan›; to explain ‹situation›
(c) to risk ‹life, reputation›
(d) to expose ‹skin, body›; **ne reste pas exposé au soleil** stay out of the sun
2 **s'exposer** *v refl* (+ *v être*) (a) to put

oneself at risk; **s'~ à** to lay oneself open to ‹criticism›
(b) **s'~ au soleil** to go out in the sun

exposition /ɛkspozisjɔ̃/ *nf* (a) (of art) exhibition; (of animals, plants) show; (for trade) fair
(b) (in shop) display
(c) (of situation, facts) exposition
(d) (of house) aspect
(e) (to light, radiation) exposure

exprès¹ /ɛkspRɛ/ *adv* (a) deliberately, on purpose; **comme par un fait ~** as ill-luck would have it
(b) specially

exprès², **-esse** /ɛkspRɛs/ **1** *adj* express
2 **exprès** *adj inv* **envoyer qch en** *or* **par ~** to send sth special delivery *or* express

express /ɛkspRɛs/ **1** *adj inv* express
2 *nm inv* (a) express (train)
(b) espresso

expressément /ɛkspRɛsemɑ̃/ *adv* expressly

expressif, **-ive** /ɛkspRɛsif, iv/ *adj* expressive

⚘ **expression** /ɛkspRɛsjɔ̃/ *nf* expression; **réduire qch à sa plus simple ~** (figurative) to reduce sth to a minimum
■ **~ corporelle** self-expression through movement

expressivité /ɛkspRɛsivite/ *nf* expressiveness

exprimable /ɛkspRimabl/ *adj* **difficilement ~** hard to express

⚘ **exprimer** /ɛkspRime/ [1] **1** *vtr* to express
2 **s'exprimer** *v refl* (+ *v être*) (a) to express oneself; **si j'ose m'~ ainsi** if I may put it that way
(b) to be expressed

expropriation /ɛkspRɔpRijasjɔ̃/ *nf* compulsory purchase; expropriation

exproprier /ɛkspRɔpRije/ [2] *vtr* **~ qn** to put a compulsory purchase order on sb's property

expulser /ɛkspylse/ [1] *vtr* (a) to evict
(b) to deport
(c) to expel
(d) (Sport) to send [sb] off

expulsion /ɛkspylsjɔ̃/ *nf* (a) eviction
(b) deportation
(c) expulsion

expurger /ɛkspyRʒe/ [13] *vtr* to purge

exquis, **~e** /ɛkski, iz/ *adj* exquisite; delightful

exsangue /ɛgzɑ̃g/ *adj* bloodless

exsuder /ɛksyde/ [1] **1** *vtr* to exude
2 *vi* to ooze (**de** from)

extase /ɛkstɑz/ *nf* ecstasy

extasier: s'extasier /ɛkstazje/ [2] *v refl* (+ *v être*) to go into ecstasy *or* raptures

extatique /ɛkstatik/ *adj* ecstatic

extensible /ɛkstɑ̃sibl/ *adj* (a) extensible

⚘ indicates a very frequent word

(b) extendable

extensif, -ive /ɛkstɑ̃sif, iv/ *adj*
(a) extensive
(b) extended

extension /ɛkstɑ̃sjɔ̃/ *nf* extension; **prendre de l'~** ‹industry› to expand; ‹strike› to spread

exténuer /ɛkstenɥe/ [1] *vtr* to exhaust

⚹ **extérieur, ~e** /ɛksteʀjœʀ/ **1** *adj*
(a) outside
(b) outer
(c) foreign
(d) outward
2 *nm* (a) outside; **à l'~** outside, outdoors; **d'~** outdoor
(b) exterior, appearance
(c) **en ~** ‹filmed› on location

extérieurement /ɛksteʀjœʀmɑ̃/ *adv*
(a) on the outside
(b) outwardly

extérioriser /ɛksteʀjɔʀize/ [1] *vtr* to show

extermination /ɛkstɛʀminasjɔ̃/ *nf* extermination

exterminer /ɛkstɛʀmine/ [1] *vtr* to exterminate; to wipe out

externalisation /ɛkstɛʀnalizasjɔ̃/ *nf* outsourcing

externaliser /ɛkstɛʀnalize/ *vtr* to outsource

externat /ɛkstɛʀna/ *nm* (a) (Sch) day school
(b) **préparer l'~** to prepare for medical school entrance exams; **faire son ~** to be a non-resident student doctor (in a hospital)

externe /ɛkstɛʀn/ **1** *adj* external; outside; exterior
2 *nmf* (a) (Sch) day pupil
(b) (Med) non-residential medical student (GB), extern (US)

extincteur /ɛkstɛ̃ktœʀ/ *nm* fire extinguisher

extinction /ɛkstɛ̃ksjɔ̃/ *nf* (a) (Med) **avoir une ~ de voix** to have lost one's voice
(b) extinction; **espèce en voie d'~** endangered species
(c) **après l'~ de l'incendie** after the fire was put out; **après l'~ des feux** after lights out

extirper /ɛkstiʀpe/ [1] *vtr* (a) to eradicate
(b) (fam) to drag ‹person› (de out of, from)

extorquer /ɛkstɔʀke/ [1] *vtr* to extort

extorsion /ɛkstɔʀsjɔ̃/ *nf* extortion

extra /ɛkstʀa/ **1** *adj inv* (a) (fam) great (colloq)
(b) ‹product› of superior quality
2 *nm inv* (a) extra; **se payer un petit ~** to have a little treat
(b) **faire des ~** to do a few extra jobs
(c) extra worker

extracommunautaire, *pl* ~s
/ɛkstʀakɔmynotɛʀ/ *adj* non-EEC

extraction /ɛkstʀaksjɔ̃/ *nf* (a) (of oil, gas) extraction; (of coal, diamonds) mining; (of marble, slate) quarrying
(b) (of bullet, tooth) extraction

extrader /ɛkstʀade/ [1] *vtr* to extradite

⚹ **extraire** /ɛkstʀɛʀ/ [58] *vtr* (a) to extract ‹mineral›; to mine ‹gold, coal›; to quarry ‹slate, marble›
(b) to extract; to pull out; to remove

extrait /ɛkstʀɛ/ *nm* (a) (from book, film) extract, excerpt; (from speech) extract
(b) essence, extract; **~ de viande** meat extract
■ **~ (d'acte) de naissance** birth certificate; **~ de casier judiciaire (de qn)** copy of (sb's) criminal record; **~ de compte** abstract of accounts

extra-long, -longue, *mpl* ~s /ɛkstʀalɔ̃, ɔ̃g/ *adj* ‹cigarette› king-size; ‹clothing› extra-long

extralucide /ɛkstʀalysid/ *adj* clairvoyant

⚹ **extraordinaire** /ɛkstʀaɔʀdinɛʀ/ *adj*
(a) extraordinary, amazing, remarkable; **c'est quand même ~!** it's incredible!
(b) ‹expenses, measures› extraordinary

extraordinairement /ɛkstʀaɔʀdinɛʀmɑ̃/ *adv* amazingly, extraordinarily

extrapoler /ɛkstʀapɔle/ [1] *vtr, vi* to extrapolate

extrascolaire /ɛkstʀaskɔlɛʀ/ *adj* extracurricular

extraterrestre /ɛkstʀatɛʀɛstʀ/ *nmf* extraterrestrial, alien

extra-utérin, ~e, *mpl* ~s /ɛkstʀayterɛ̃, in/ *adj* **grossesse ~e** ectopic pregnancy

extravagance /ɛkstʀavagɑ̃s/ *nf*
(a) eccentricity
(b) extravagance

extravagant, ~e /ɛkstʀavagɑ̃, ɑ̃t/ *adj*
(a) eccentric
(b) extravagant
(c) exorbitant

extraverti, ~e /ɛkstʀavɛʀti/ *adj, nm,f* extrovert

⚹ **extrême** /ɛkstʀɛm/ **1** *adj* (a) furthest; **dans l'~ nord/sud du pays** in the extreme North/South of the country
(b) extreme
(c) drastic
2 *nm* extreme; **c'est pousser la logique à l'~** that's taking logic to extremes; **à l'~ inverse** at the other extreme

extrêmement /ɛkstʀɛmmɑ̃/ *adv* extremely

Extrême-Orient /ɛkstʀɛmɔʀjɑ̃/ *pr nm* **l'~** the Far East

extrémiste /ɛkstʀemist/ *adj, nmf* extremist

extrémité /ɛkstʀemite/ *nf* (a) end; (of finger) tip; (of mast) top; (of town, field) edge; **aux deux ~s** at both ends ⋯⋯▶

(b) extreme
exubérance /εgzybeʀɑ̃s/ *nf* exuberance
exubérant, ~e /εgzybeʀɑ̃, ɑ̃t/ *adj*
exuberant

exultation /εgzyltasjɔ̃/ *nf* exultation
exulter /εgzylte/ [1] *vi* to be exultant, to
exult (**de** with), to exult (**de faire** at doing)
exutoire /εgzytwaʀ/ *nm* outlet

Ff

f, F /εf/ *nm inv* **(a)** (letter) f, F
(b) F3 2-bedroom flat (GB) *or* apartment
(c) (Hist) (*written abbr* = **franc**) **50 F** 50 F
fa /fa/ *nm inv* (Mus) (note) F; (in sol-fa) fa
fable /fɑbl/ *nf* **(a)** tale
(b) fable
(c) tall story
fabricant /fabʀikɑ̃/ *nm* manufacturer
fabrication /fabʀikasjɔ̃/ *nf* making;
manufacture; **~ en série** mass production
■ **~ assistée par ordinateur, FAO** computer-
aided manufacturing, CAM
fabrique /fabʀik/ *nf* factory
ℐ **fabriquer** /fabʀike/ [1] *vtr* **(a)** to make; to
manufacture
(b) to invent ‹*alibi*›; **qu'est-ce que tu
fabriques?** (fam) what are you up to?
fabulateur, -trice /fabylatœʀ, tʀis/ *nm,f*
compulsive liar
fabuler /fabyle/ [1] *vi* **(a)** to make things up
(b) to confabulate
fabuleusement /fabyløzmɑ̃/ *adv*
fabulously
fabuleux, -euse /fabylø, øz/ *adj* ‹*beauty*›
fabulous; ‹*sum*› fantastic; ‹*creature*› mythical
fac /fak/ *nf* (fam) **(a)** faculty
(b) university
façade /fasad/ *nf* **(a)** (of building) front; **~
nord** north side
(b) façade
ℐ **face** /fas/ ❶ *nf* **(a)** face
(b) side; **le côté ~ d'une pièce** the heads side
of a coin
(c) faire ~ to face up to things; **se faire
~** to face each other; to be opposite one
another; **faire ~ à** to face ‹*place*›; (figurative)
to face ‹*adversary, challenge*›; to cope with
‹*spending*›; to meet ‹*demand*›
❷ **de face** *phr* ‹*photo*› fullface; ‹*lighting*›
frontal
❸ **en face** *phr* **il habite en ~** he lives
opposite; **voir les choses en ~** to see things
as they are; **l'équipe d'en ~** the opposing
team
❹ **en face de** *phr* **(a)** en **~ de l'église**
opposite the church (GB), across from the
church

(b) compared with
❺ **face à** *phr* **(a)** **mon lit est ~ à la fenêtre**
my bed faces the window
(b) ~ à cette situation in view of this
situation
IDIOM se voiler la ~ not to face facts
face-à-face /fasafas/ *nm inv* **(a)** one-to-one
debate (GB), one-on-one debate (US)
(b) encounter
facétie /fasesi/ *nf* facetious remark;
practical joke
facétieux, -ieuse /fasesjø, øz/ *adj*
mischievous
facette /fasεt/ *nf* facet
fâché, ~e /fɑʃe/ ❶ *pp* ▶ FÂCHER
❷ *pp adj* angry; **être ~ avec qn** to have
fallen out with sb
fâcher: se fâcher /fɑʃe/ [1] *v refl* (+ *v
être*) **(a)** to get angry
(b) to fall out
fâcheux, -euse /fɑʃø, øz/ *adj* ‹*influence*›
detrimental; ‹*delay*› unfortunate; ‹*news*›
distressing
facial, ~e, mpl -iaux /fasjal, o/ *adj* facial
faciès /fasjεs/ *nm inv* **(a)** facies
(b) face
ℐ **facile** /fasil/ ❶ *adj* **(a)** easy; **avoir la larme
~** to be quick to cry
(b) easy-going
❷ *adv* (fam) easily
ℐ **facilement** /fasilmɑ̃/ *adv* **(a)** easily
(b) (fam) **j'ai mis ~ deux heures pour venir** it
took me a good two hours to get here
facilité /fasilite/ ❶ *nf* **(a)** (of work)
easiness; (of use, maintenance) ease
(b) fluency
❷ **facilités** *nf pl* **(a)** **donner toutes ~s
pour faire** to afford every opportunity to do
(b) ~s (de paiement) easy terms
faciliter /fasilite/ [1] *vtr* to make [sth]
easier
ℐ **façon** /fasɔ̃/ ❶ *nf* **(a)** way; **de toute ~, de
toutes les ~s** anyway; **de ~ à faire** in order
to do; in such a way as to do; **de ~ (à ce)
qu'elle fasse** so (that) she does; **elle nous a
joué un tour à sa ~** she played a trick of her
own on us; **~ de parler** so to speak
(b) un peigne ~ ivoire an imitation ivory
comb

ℐ indicates a very frequent word

(c) (of garment) making-up

2 **façons** *nf pl* **en voilà des** ∼**s!** what a way to behave!; **sans** ∼**s** ⟨*meal*⟩ informal; ⟨*person*⟩ unpretentious

façonner /fasɔne/ [1] *vtr* **(a)** to manufacture; to make

(b) to hew ⟨*wood*⟩; to fashion ⟨*clay*⟩

(c) to shape, to mould (GB), to mold (US)

fac-similé, *pl* ∼**s** /faksimile/ *nm* facsimile

⚘ **facteur, -trice** /faktœr, tris/ 1 *nm,f* postman/postwoman

2 *nm* factor

factice /faktis/ *adj* ⟨*smile*⟩ forced; ⟨*jewellery*⟩ imitation; ⟨*flower, beauty*⟩ artificial

faction /faksjɔ̃/ *nf* **(a)** faction

(b) (Mil) guard duty

factrice ▶ FACTEUR 1

factuel, -elle /faktɥɛl/ *adj* factual

facturation /faktyrasjɔ̃/ *nf* **(a)** invoicing

(b) invoicing department

facture /faktyr/ *nf* bill; invoice

facturer /faktyre/ [1] *vtr* to invoice ⟨*goods*⟩

facturette /faktyrɛt/ *nf* credit card slip

facturier, -ière¹ /faktyrje, ɛr/ 1 *nm,f* invoice clerk

2 *nm* invoice book

facturière² /faktyrjɛr/ *nf* invoicing machine

facultatif, -ive /fakyltatif, iv/ *adj* optional

faculté /fakylte/ *nf* **(a)** (mental) faculty; ability

(b) option

(c) (at university) faculty

(d) (Law) right

fade /fad/ *adj* ⟨*person, book*⟩ dull; ⟨*food, taste*⟩ tasteless; ⟨*colour*⟩ drab

fadeur /fadœr/ *nf* blandness; dreariness

fagot /fago/ *nm* bundle of firewood

fagoter /fagɔte/ [1] 1 *vtr* to do [sb] up (colloq)

2 **se fagoter** *v refl* to do oneself up (colloq); **(être) mal fagoté** (to be) badly dressed

⚘ **faible** /fɛbl/ 1 *adj* **(a)** (gen) weak; ⟨*sight*⟩ poor; ⟨*constitution*⟩ frail; **être** ∼ **avec qn** to be too soft on sb

(b) ⟨*proportion, increase*⟩ small; ⟨*income, speed*⟩ low; ⟨*means, impact*⟩ limited; ⟨*chance*⟩ slim

(c) ⟨*noise, glow*⟩ faint; ⟨*lighting*⟩ dim; ⟨*wind, rain*⟩ light

(d) ⟨*result*⟩ poor; ⟨*argument*⟩ feeble

(e) ⟨*pupil, class*⟩ slow; ∼ **d'esprit** feeble-minded

(f) le mot est ∼**!** that's putting it mildly!

2 *nmf* weak-willed person

3 *nm* weakness; **avoir un** ∼ **pour qn** to have a soft spot for sb

faiblement /fɛbləmɑ̃/ *adv* weakly; ⟨*influence, increase*⟩ slightly; ⟨*lit*⟩ dimly

faiblesse /fɛblɛs/ *nf* **(a)** weakness; (of invalid) frailty

(b) inadequacy

(c) (of voice) faintness; (of lighting) dimness

faiblir /fɛblir/ [3] *vi* **(a)** ⟨*person, pulse*⟩ to get weaker; ⟨*sight*⟩ to be failing

(b) ⟨*person, currency*⟩ to weaken

(c) ⟨*athlete*⟩ to flag; ⟨*plot*⟩ to decline; ⟨*interest*⟩ to wane; ⟨*speed*⟩ to slacken

(d) ⟨*storm*⟩ to abate; ⟨*noise*⟩ to grow faint

faïence /fajɑ̃s/ *nf* earthenware

IDIOM **se regarder en chiens de** ∼ to look daggers at each other

faille /faj/ *nf* **(a)** (in geology) fault

(b) flaw; **sans** ∼ unfailing

(c) rift

faillir /fajir/ [28] *vi* **(a) elle a failli le gifler** she almost *or* (very) nearly slapped him

(b) sans ∼ unfailingly

faillite /fajit/ *nf* **(a)** bankruptcy

(b) failure

⚘ **faim** /fɛ̃/ *nf* hunger; **avoir** ∼ to be hungry; **mourir de** ∼ to die of starvation; (figurative) to be starving, **je suis resté sur ma** ∼ I was disappointed

fainéant, ∼**e** /feneɑ̃, ɑ̃t/ *adj* lazy

fainéantise /feneɑ̃tiz/ *nf* laziness

⚘ **faire** /fɛr/ [10]

■ **Note** You will find the translations for expressions such as *faire peur*, *faire semblant* etc, at the entries PEUR, SEMBLANT etc.

1 *vtr* **(a)** to make; ∼ **son lit/une faute** to make one's bed/a mistake; ∼ **des jaloux** to make people jealous, **deux et deux font quatre** two and two is four

(b) to do; ∼ **de la recherche** to do research; **j'ai à** ∼ I have things to do; **que fait-il?** what does he do?; what is he doing?; **que veux-tu que j'y fasse?** what do you want me to do about it?; ∼ **médecine/du violon** to do *or* study medicine/to study *or* play the violin; ∼ **une école de commerce** to go to business school; ∼ **un numéro de téléphone/une lettre** to dial a number/to write a letter; ∼ **du tennis/de la couture** to play tennis/to sew; ∼ **un poulet** to do *or* cook a chicken

(c) to do ⟨*distance, journey*⟩; to go round ⟨*shops*⟩; to do (colloq) ⟨*region, museums*⟩; **j'ai fait tous les tiroirs mais je ne l'ai pas trouvé** I went through all the drawers but I couldn't find it

(d) (fam) to have ⟨*diabetes, complex*⟩

(e) ∼ **le malade** to pretend to be ill

(f) leur départ ne m'a rien fait their departure didn't affect me at all; **ça y fait** (fam) it has an effect; **pour ce que ça fait!** (fam) for all the good it does!

(g) to say; **'bien sûr', fit-elle** 'of course,' she said; **le canard fait 'coin-coin'** ducks go 'quack'

(h) ça m'a fait rire it made me laugh; ∼ **manger un bébé** to feed a baby; **fais voir** show me; **fais-leur prendre un rendez-vous** get them to make an appointment; ∼ **traverser la rue à un vieillard** to help an old man across the road

(i) ∼ **réparer sa voiture** to have *or* get one's ⋯⋗

car repaired

(j) je n'en ai rien à ~ (fam) I couldn't care less; **ça ne fait rien!** it doesn't matter!; **qu'est-ce que ça peut bien te**~? (fam) what is it to you?; **il sait y** ~ he's got the knack; **il ne fait que pleuvoir** it never stops raining; **je ne fais qu'obéir aux ordres** I'm only obeying orders

2 *vi* **(a)** to do, to act; **fais comme tu veux** do as you like

(b) to look; ~ **jeune** to look young

(c) ça fait 15 ans que j'habite ici I've been living here for 15 years; **ça fait 2 mètres de long** it's 2 metres (GB) long

(d) to go (to the toilet); **tu as fait?** have you been?

(e) (fam) ~ **avec** to make do with; to put up with

3 **se faire** *v refl* (+ *v être*) **(a) se** ~ **un café** to make oneself a coffee; **se** ~ **comprendre** to make oneself understood

(b) to get, to become; **il se fait tard** it's getting late

(c) s'en ~ to worry; **il ne s'en fait pas!** he's not the sort of person to worry about things!; (as criticism) he's got a nerve!

(d) se ~ **à** to get used to

(e) ça se fait encore ici it's still done here; **ça ne se fait pas** it's not the done thing

(f) ‹colour, style› to be in (fashion)

(g) c'est ce qui se fait de mieux it's the best there is

(h) comment se fait-il que…? how is it that…?, how come…?

faire-part /fɛʀpaʀ/ *nm inv* announcement

faire-valoir /fɛʀvalwaʀ/ *nm inv* **être le** ~ **de** ‹actor› to be a foil for

fais /fɛ/ ▶ FAIRE

faisaient /fɛzɛ/ ▶ FAIRE

faisais /fɛzɛ/ ▶ FAIRE

faisait /fɛzɛ/ ▶ FAIRE

faisan /fəzɑ̃/ *nm* (cock) pheasant

faisane /fəzan/ *nf* (poule) ~ hen pheasant

faisant /fɛzɑ̃/ ▶ FAIRE

faisceau, *pl* ~**x** /fɛso/ *nm* **(a)** beam; ~ **lumineux** beam of light

(b) bundle

faisiez /fɛzje/ ▶ FAIRE

faisions /fɛzjɔ̃/ ▶ FAIRE

faisons /fɛzɔ̃/ ▶ FAIRE

✒ **fait**, ~**e** /fɛ, fɛt/ **1** *pp* ▶ FAIRE

2 *pp adj* **(a)** done; **c'en est** ~ **de** that's the end of; **c'est bien**~ **(pour toi)!** (fam) it serves you right!

(b) ~ **de** *or* **en** made (up) of; **idée toute** ~**e** ready-made idea; **elle est bien** ~**e** she's got a great figure; **la vie est mal** ~**e** life is unfair

(c) ~ **pour qch/pour faire** meant for sth/to do

(d) ‹programme, device› designed

(e) (fam) done for

✒ indicates a very frequent word

(f) un fromage bien ~ a ripe cheese

3 *nm* **(a)** fact; **le** ~ **est là** *or* **les** ~**s sont là**, **il t'a trompé** the fact (of the matter) is that he cheated you; **les** ~**s et gestes de qn** sb's movements

(b) de ce ~ because of this *or* that; **être le** ~ **de qn** to be due to sb

(c) event

(d) aller droit au ~ to go straight to the point

4 ■ **au fait** /ofɛt/ *phr* by the way

5 ■ **de fait** *phr* **(a)** ‹situation› de facto

(b) ‹exist, result in› effectively

(c) indeed

6 ■ **en fait** *phr* in fact, actually

7 ■ **en fait de** *phr* as regards

■ ~ **divers** (short) news item; ~ **de société** fact of life

IDIOMS **être au** ~ **de** to be informed about; **prendre qn sur le** ~ to catch sb in the act

faîte /fɛt/ *nm* (of mountain) summit; (of house) rooftop; (of tree) top

faites /fɛt/ ▶ FAIRE

falaise /falɛz/ *nf* cliff

fallacieux, **-ieuse** /falasjø, øz/ *adj* ‹argument› fallacious; ‹pretext› false

✒ **falloir** /falwaʀ/ [50] **1** *v impers* **(a) il faut qn/qch** we need sb/sth; sb/sth is needed; **il va** ~ **deux jours/du courage** it will take two days/courage; **il me/te/leur faut qch** I/you/they need sth; **il me faut ce livre!** I've got to have that book!

(b) il faut faire we/you etc have (got) to do; we/you etc must do; we/you etc should do; **il ne faut pas la déranger** she mustn't be disturbed; **il fallait le faire** it had to be done; **faut le faire!** (fam) (admiring) it takes a bit of doing!; (critical) would you believe it?; **comme il faut** ‹behave› properly

(c) il faut que tu fasses you have (got) to do, you must do; you should do

2 **s'en falloir** *v refl* (+ *v être*) **peu s'en faut** very nearly; **elle a perdu, mais il s'en est fallu de peu** she lost, but only just

IDIOMS **il faut ce qu'il faut!** there's no point in skimping!; **en moins de temps qu'il ne faut pour le dire** before you could say Jack Robinson

fallu /faly/ ▶ FALLOIR

falsification /falsifikasjɔ̃/ *nf*

(a) falsification

(b) forging

falsifier /falsifje/ [2] *vtr* **(a)** to falsify, to tamper with ‹document›; to distort ‹facts›

(b) to forge

famé, ~**e** /fame/ *adj* **un quartier mal** ~ a disreputable *or* seedy area

famélique /famelik/ *adj* emaciated, scrawny

✒ **fameux**, **-euse** /famø, øz/ *adj* **(a)** much talked-about

(b) famous

(c) excellent

♂ **familial**, ∼e, *mpl* **-iaux** /familjal, o/ *adj*
(a) ‹*meal, life, firm*› family
(b) **voiture** ∼e estate car (GB), station wagon (US)

familiariser /familjaʀize/ [1] *vtr* to familiarize

familiarité /familjaʀite/ *nf* familiarity

familier, -ière /familje, ɛʀ/ *adj* (a) ‹*face, landscape*› familiar
(b) ‹*word*› informal, colloquial
(c) ‹*attitude*› informal; ‹*person, gesture*› familiar
(d) animal ∼ pet

familièrement /familjɛʀmɑ̃/ *adv*
(a) commonly
(b) informally
(c) with undue familiarity

♂ **famille** /famij/ *nf* family; **c'est de** ∼ it runs in the family

famine /famin/ *nf* famine

fanatique /fanatik/ ⟦1⟧ *adj* ‹*believer*› fanatical; ‹*admiration, love*› ardent
⟦2⟧ *nmf* (a) fanatic
(b) (fam) enthusiast, freak (colloq)

fanatisme /fanatism/ *nm* fanaticism

faner /fane/ [1] ⟦1⟧ *vi* (a) to wither
(b) to make hay
⟦2⟧ **se faner** *v refl* (+ *v être*) (a) ‹*plant*› to wither, to wilt
(b) ‹*beauty, colour*› to fade

fanfare /fɑ̃faʀ/ *nf* brass band; **annoncer qch en** ∼ to trumpet sth

fanfaron, -onne /fɑ̃faʀɔ̃, ɔn/ *nm,f* boaster, swaggerer; **faire le** ∼ to boast

fanfaronner /fɑ̃faʀɔne/ [1] *vi* to boast

fanion /fanjɔ̃/ *nm* pennant

fantaisie /fɑ̃tezi/ *nf* (a) imaginativeness; **manquer de** ∼ ‹*person*› to be staid; ‹*life*› to be dull
(b) whim, fancy
(c) **s'offrir une petite** ∼ to spoil oneself; **un bijou** ∼ a piece of costume jewellery (GB) *or* jewelry (US)

fantaisiste /fɑ̃tezist/ *adj* (a) ‹*person*› unreliable; ‹*figures*› doubtful
(b) ‹*idea*› far-fetched

fantasme /fɑ̃tasm/ *nm* fantasy

fantasque /fɑ̃task/ *adj* ‹*character*› unpredictable; ‹*tale*› fanciful

fantassin /fɑ̃tasɛ̃/ *nm* infantryman, footsoldier

fantastique /fɑ̃tastik/ ⟦1⟧ *adj* fantastic
⟦2⟧ *nm* **le** ∼ fantasy

fantoche /fɑ̃tɔʃ/ *adj* puppet

fantôme /fɑ̃tom/ ⟦1⟧ *nm* ghost
⟦2⟧ **(-)fantôme** (*combining form*) ‹*train, city*› ghost; **image(-)**∼ (on screen) ghost; **société(-)**∼ (Law) dummy company

FAO /ɛfao/ *nf* (Comput) (*abbr* = **fabrication assistée par ordinateur**) CAM

faon /fɑ̃/ *nm* (Zool) fawn

faramineux, -euse /faʀaminø, øz/ *adj* (fam) colossal, staggering; incredible

farandole /faʀɑ̃dɔl/ *nf* (dance) farandole; ≈ conga

farce /faʀs/ *nf* (a) practical joke; **magasin de** ∼**s et attrapes** joke shop (GB), novelty store (US)
(b) joke
(c) (in theatre) farce
(d) stuffing, forcemeat

farceur, -euse /faʀsœʀ, øz/ *nm, f* practical joker

farcir /faʀsiʀ/ [3] *vtr* (Culin) to stuff

fard /faʀ/ *nm* make-up; **sans** ∼ ‹*beauty*› natural; ‹*truth*› simple
■ ∼ **à joues** blusher; ∼ **à paupières** eyeshadow
IDIOM **piquer un** ∼ (fam) to go as red as a beetroot (GB), to turn as red as a beet (US)

fardeau, *pl* ∼**x** /faʀdo/ *nm* burden

farder /faʀde/ [1] ⟦1⟧ *vtr* to disguise ‹*truth*›
⟦2⟧ **se farder** *v refl* (+ *v être*) ‹*actor*› to make up; ‹*woman*› to use make-up

farfelu, ∼e /faʀfəly/ *adj* (fam) ‹*idea*› harebrained (colloq); ‹*person*› scatter-brained (colloq); ‹*show*› bizarre

farfouiller /faʀfuje/ [1] *vi* (fam) to rummage around *or* about (**dans** in)

farine /faʀin/ *nf* (a) flour
(b) baby cereal
■ ∼ **d'avoine** oatmeal
IDIOM **se faire rouler dans la** ∼ (fam) to be had (colloq)

farineux, -euse /faʀinø, øz/ *adj* ‹*food*› starchy; ‹*potato*› floury

farniente /faʀnjɛnte/ *nm* **le** ∼ lazing about, lazing around

farouche /faʀuʃ/ *adj* (a) ‹*child, animal*› timid, shy; ‹*adult*› unsociable
(b) ‹*look, warrior*› fierce
(c) ‹*enemy, hatred*› fierce; ‹*adversary*› fierce; ‹*supporter*› staunch; ‹*will*› iron

farouchement /faʀuʃmɑ̃/ *adv* ‹*opposed, independent*› fiercely; ‹*refuse*› doggedly

fascicule /fasikyl/ *nm* (a) booklet
(b) fascicule

fascinant, ∼e /fasinɑ̃, ɑ̃t/ *adj* ‹*person, film*› fascinating; ‹*charm, music*› spellbinding

fascination /fasinasjɔ̃/ *nf* fascination

fasciner /fasine/ [1] *vtr* ‹*speaker, music*› to hold [sb] spellbound; ‹*sea, person*› to fascinate

fascisant, ∼e /faʃizɑ̃, ɑ̃t/ *adj* fascistic

fascisme /faʃism/ *nm* fascism

fasse /fas/ ▶ FAIRE

fassent /fas/ ▶ FAIRE

fasses /fas/ ▶ FAIRE

fassiez /fasje/ ▶ FAIRE

fassions /fasjɔ̃/ ▶ FAIRE

faste /fast/ [1] *adj* auspicious
[2] *nm* splendour (GB), pomp; **avec** ~ with pomp

fastidieux, -ieuse /fastidjø, øz/ *adj* tedious

fatal, ~**e** /fatal/ *adj* (a) inevitable
(b) fatal, disastrous
(c) ⟨*moment, day*⟩ fateful

fatalement /fatalmɑ̃/ *adv* inevitably

fatalisme /fatalism/ *nm* fatalism

fatalité /fatalite/ *nf* (a) **la** ~ fate
(b) mischance
(c) inevitability

fatidique /fatidik/ *adj* fateful

fatigant, ~**e** /fatigɑ̃, ɑ̃t/ *adj* (a) ⟨*sport, journey*⟩ tiring; ⟨*climate*⟩ wearing
(b) ⟨*work*⟩ arduous
(c) ⟨*person*⟩ tiresome; ⟨*film, conversation*⟩ tedious

fatigue /fatig/ *nf* (a) tiredness; **être mort de** ~, **tomber de** ~ to be dead tired
(b) (Med) fatigue; ~ **visuelle** eyestrain

fatigué, ~**e** /fatige/ [1] *pp* ▶ FATIGUER
[2] *pp adj* ⟨*voice*⟩ strained; ⟨*eyes, smile*⟩ weary

fatiguer /fatige/ [1] [1] *vtr* (a) to make [sb/sth] tired; to strain ⟨*eyes*⟩
(b) to tire [sb] out
(c) to wear [sb] out
(d) to wear out ⟨*engine*⟩
[2] *vi* (a) (fam) to get tired
(b) ⟨*engine, car*⟩ to be labouring (GB)
[3] **se fatiguer** *v refl* (+ *v être*) (a) to get tired
(b) to tire oneself out
(c) **se** ~ **les yeux** to strain one's eyes
(d) **se** ~ **à faire** to bother doing

fatras /fatrɑ/ *nm inv* jumble

faubourg /fobur/ *nm* working class area (*on the outskirts*)

fauché, ~**e** /foʃe/ *adj* (fam) broke (colloq), penniless

faucher /foʃe/ [1] *vtr* (a) to mow; to scythe
(b) ⟨*car, bullet*⟩ to mow [sb] down
(c) (fam) to steal

faucheuse /foʃøz/ *nf* mowing machine

faucille /fosij/ *nf* sickle

faucon /fokɔ̃/ *nm* falcon, hawk (US)

faudra ▶ FALLOIR

faufiler /fofile/ [1] [1] *vtr* to baste
[2] **se faufiler** *v refl* (+ *v être*) (a) **se** ~ **à l'extérieur** to slip out
(b) **se** ~ **dans** ⟨*mistakes*⟩ to creep into ⟨*text*⟩
(c) ⟨*route*⟩ to snake in and out

faune /fon/ *nf* (a) wildlife, fauna; **la** ~ **marine** marine life
(b) (derogatory) set, crowd

faussaire /foser/ *nmf* forger

fausse ▶ FAUX¹ 1

ɑ̍ indicates a very frequent word

faussement /fosmɑ̃/ *adv* (a) falsely, wrongly
(b) deceptively

fausser /fose/ [1] *vtr* to distort ⟨*result, mechanism*⟩; to damage ⟨*lock*⟩; to buckle ⟨*blade*⟩
IDIOM ~ **compagnie à qn** to give sb the slip

faut ▶ FALLOIR

ɑ̍ **faute** /fot/ *nf* (a) mistake, error; **il a fait un (parcours) sans** ~ he's never put a foot wrong
(b) (gen) misdemeanour (GB); (Law) civil wrong; **être en** ~ to be at fault; **prendre qn en** ~ to catch sb out
(c) fault; **c'est (de) ma** ~ it's my fault; **par la** ~ **de qn** because of sb; **rejeter la** ~ **sur qn** to lay the blame on sb
(d) ~ **de temps** through lack of time; ~ **de mieux** for want of anything better; ~ **de quoi** otherwise, failing which; **sans** ~ without fail
(e) (Sport) foul; (in tennis) fault

ɑ̍ **fauteuil** /fotœj/ *nm* (a) chair, armchair
(b) (in theatre) seat

fauteur /fotœr/ *nm* ~ **de troubles** troublemaker; ~ **de guerre** warmonger

fautif, -ive /fotif, iv/ [1] *adj* (a) at fault
(b) ⟨*memory*⟩ faulty; ⟨*reference*⟩ inaccurate
[2] *nm, f* culprit

fauve /fov/ [1] *adj* tawny
[2] *nm* (a) wild animal
(b) big cat
(c) (colour) fawn

fauvette /fovɛt/ *nf* warbler

ɑ̍ **faux¹, fausse** /fo, fos/ [1] *adj* (a) ⟨*result, number, idea*⟩ wrong; ⟨*impression, promise, accusation*⟩ false
(b) ⟨*beard, tooth, eyelashes*⟩ false
(c) ⟨*wood, marble, diamonds*⟩ imitation, fake; ⟨*door, drawer*⟩ false
(d) ⟨*passport, money*⟩ forged
(e) ⟨*policeman, bishop*⟩ bogus; ⟨*candour, humility*⟩ feigned
(f) ⟨*hope*⟩ false; ⟨*fear*⟩ groundless
(g) deceitful
[2] *adv* ⟨*play, sing*⟩ out of tune
[3] *nm inv* (a) **le** ~ falsehood
(b) fake; forgery
■ **fausse couche** (Med) miscarriage; **fausse facture** bogus invoice; **fausse fenêtre** blind window; **fausse joie** ill-founded joy; **faire une fausse joie à qn** to raise sb's hopes in vain; **fausse monnaie** forged *or* counterfeit currency; **fausse monnaie** forged *or* counterfeit currency; **fausse note** jarring note; **fausse piste** wrong track; ~ **ami** *foreign word which looks deceptively like a word in one's own language*; ~ **en écriture(s)** falsification of accounts; ~ **frais** extras, incidental expenses; ~ **jeton** (fam) two-faced person; ~ **nom** assumed name; ~ **pas** slip; mistake; faux pas; ~ **pli** crease; ~ **témoignage** perjury

faux² /fo/ *nf inv* scythe

faux-filet, pl ∼s /fofilɛ/ nm sirloin

faux-monnayeur, pl ∼s /fomɔnɛjœʀ/ nm forger, counterfeiter

faux-semblant, pl ∼s /fosɑ̃blɑ̃/ nm les ∼s pretence (GB)

ᵍ **faveur** /favœʀ/ **1** nf favour (GB); régime or traitement de ∼ preferential treatment; des mesures en ∼ des handicapés measures to help the disabled; intervenir en ∼ de qn to intervene on sb's behalf
2 à la faveur de phr thanks to; à la ∼ de la nuit under cover of darkness

favorable /favɔʀabl/ adj favourable (GB); être ∼ à qch to be in favour (GB) of sth

favori, -ite /favɔʀi, it/ **1** adj, nm,f favourite (GB)
2 favoris nm pl sideburns

ᵍ **favoriser** /favɔʀize/ [1] vtr (a) to favour (GB); les milieux favorisés the privileged classes
(b) to encourage, to promote

favorite ▶ FAVORI 1

favoritisme /favɔʀitism/ nm favouritism (GB)

fax /faks/ nm inv (a) fax
(b) fax machine

fayot¹ /fajo/ nm (fam) bean

fayot², -otte /fajo, ɔt/ nm,f (fam) creep (colloq), crawler (colloq)

FB (Hist) (written abbr = **franc belge**) BFr

fébrile /febʀil/ adj (a) ‹emotion, gesture› feverish; ‹person› nervous
(b) (Med) feverish

fébrilité /febʀilite/ nf (a) agitation; avec ∼ agitatedly
(b) nervousness

fécal, ∼e, mpl **-aux** /fekal, o/ adj faecal

fécond, ∼e /fekɔ̃, ɔ̃d/ adj (a) fertile
(b) fruitful

fécondation /fekɔ̃dasjɔ̃/ nf (of female) impregnation; (of plant) pollination; (of egg) fertilization

féconder /fekɔ̃de/ [1] vtr to impregnate ‹female›; to inseminate ‹animal›; to pollinate ‹plant›; to fertilize ‹egg, ovum›

fécondité /fekɔ̃dite/ nf (a) fertility
(b) (of author) productivity

fécule /fekyl/ nf starch

féculent /fekylɑ̃/ nm starch; starchy food

fédéral, ∼e, mpl **-aux** /federal, o/ adj federal

fédéralisme /federalism/ nm federalism

fédératif, -ive /federatif, iv/ adj federal

fédération /federasjɔ̃/ nf federation

fée /fe/ nf fairy; ∼ du logis perfect housewife
IDIOM avoir des doigts de ∼ to have nimble fingers

féerie /fe(e)ʀi/ nf (a) c'est une vraie ∼ it's magical

(b) extravaganza

féerique /fe(e)ʀik/ adj ‹beauty› enchanting; ‹landscape, moment› enchanted

feignant, ∼e /fɛɲɑ̃, ɑ̃t/ ▶ FAINÉANT

feindre /fɛ̃dʀ/ [55] vtr to feign; ∼ de faire/d'être to pretend to do/to be

feinte /fɛ̃t/ nf (a) feint; faire une ∼ (in football, rugby) to dummy (GB), to fake (US)
(b) (fam) trick, ruse

fêlé, ∼e /fele/ adj (fam) cracked (colloq)

fêler /fele/ [1] vtr, **se fêler** v refl (+ v être) to crack

félicitations /felisitasjɔ̃/ nf pl congratulations

féliciter /felisite/ [1] **1** vtr to congratulate
2 se féliciter v refl (+ v être) se ∼ de qch to be very pleased about sth

félin, ∼e /felɛ̃, in/ **1** adj (a) feline; exposition ∼e cat show
(b) ‹grace› feline; ‹eyes› catlike
2 nm feline; les ∼s felines, the cat family

fêlure /felyʀ/ nf crack

femelle /fəmɛl/ **1** adj female; éléphant ∼ cow elephant; moineau ∼ hen sparrow
2 nf female; (in pair) mate

féminin, ∼e /feminɛ̃, in/ **1** adj ‹sex, occupation› female; ‹magazine, record› women's; ‹team, club› ladies'; ‹appearance› feminine
2 nm feminine; au ∼ in the feminine

féminiser: se féminiser /feminize/ [1] v refl (+ v être) ‹profession› to become more open to women; to become predominantly female

féministe /feminist/ adj, nmf feminist

féminité /feminite/ nf femininity

ᵍ **femme** /fam/ nf (a) woman
(b) wife
■ ∼ d'affaires businesswoman; ∼ de chambre chambermaid; ∼ au foyer housewife; ∼ d'intérieur homemaker; ∼ de service cleaner, cleaning lady; ∼ de tête assertive woman;
▶ BON, JEUNE
IDIOM souvent ∼ varie woman is fickle

fémur /femyʀ/ nm thighbone; se casser le col du ∼ to break one's hip

FEN /fɛn/ nf (abbr = **Fédération de l'éducation nationale**) FEN (French teachers' union)

fendiller: se fendiller /fɑ̃dije/ [1] v refl (+ v être) ‹lips› to chap; ‹earth› to craze over; ‹wood› to crack

fendre /fɑ̃dʀ/ [6] **1** vtr (a) to chop ‹wood›; to slit ‹material›
(b) to crack ‹wall, stone›; to split ‹lip›
(c) ∼ le cœur à qn to break sb's heart
(d) ∼ l'air to slice through the air; ∼ la foule to push one's way through the crowd
2 se fendre v refl (+ v être) (a) to crack
(b) (fam) to cough up (colloq) ‹money›; tu ne ⋯⇢

t'es pas fendu! that didn't break the bank!
IDIOMS **se ~ la pêche** (fam) to split one's
sides (colloq); **avoir la bouche fendue
jusqu'aux oreilles** to be grinning from ear
to ear

✧ **fenêtre** /fənɛtʀ/ *nf* window
■ **~ à guillotine** sash window
IDIOM **jeter l'argent par les ~s** to throw
money away

fenouil /fənuj/ *nm* fennel

fente /fɑ̃t/ *nf* **(a)** slit; (for coin, card) slot; (of
jacket) vent
(b) crack; (in wood) split; (in rock) crevice

féodal, ~e, *mpl* **-aux** /feɔdal, o/ *adj* feudal

✧ **fer** /fɛʀ/ *nm* **(a)** iron; **de ~** ‹*discipline, fist,
will*› iron
(b) (on shoe) steel tip
(c) branding iron
(d) croiser le ~ avec to cross swords with
■ **~ à cheval** horseshoe; **~ forgé** wrought iron;
~ à repasser iron
IDIOMS **croire dur comme ~** to believe
wholeheartedly; **tomber les quatre ~s en
l'air** (fam) to fall flat on one's back

fera /fəʀa/ ▶ FAIRE

ferai /fəʀɛ/ ▶ FAIRE

feraient /fəʀɛ/ ▶ FAIRE

ferais /fəʀɛ/ ▶ FAIRE

ferait /fəʀɛ/ ▶ FAIRE

feras /fəʀa/ ▶ FAIRE

fer-blanc, *pl* **fers-blancs** /fɛʀblɑ̃/ *nm*
tinplate

ferez /fəʀe/ ▶ FAIRE

férié, ~e /feʀje/ *adj* **jour ~** public holiday
(GB), holiday (US)

feriez /fəʀje/ ▶ FAIRE

ferions /fəʀjɔ̃/ ▶ FAIRE

✧ **ferme¹** /fɛʀm/ **1** *adj* **(a)** firm
(b) (Law) **peine de prison ~** custodial
sentence
2 *adv* ‹*argue, campaign*› vigorously;
‹*believe*› firmly; **tenir ~** to stand one's
ground
IDIOM **attendre de pied ~** to be ready and
waiting

✧ **ferme²** /fɛʀm/ *nf* farm, farmhouse; **~
éolienne** wind farm

fermement /fɛʀməmɑ̃/ *adv* firmly

ferment /fɛʀmɑ̃/ *nm* ferment

fermenter /fɛʀmɑ̃te/ [1] *vi* to ferment

✧ **fermer** /fɛʀme/ [1] **1** *vtr* **(a)** to close, to
shut ‹*door, book, eyes*›; to clench ‹*fist*›; to
draw ‹*curtain*›; to turn off ‹*tap, gas, radio*›;
to do up ‹*jacket*›; **~ à clé** to lock (up)
(b) to close ‹*shop, airport, road*›; (definitively)
to close [sth] down
2 *vi* to close (down)
3 se fermer *v refl* (+ *v être*) **(a)** ‹*door*›
to shut; ‹*flower*› to close up; ‹*coat, bracelet*›
to fasten

✧ indicates a very frequent word

(b) ‹*person*› to clam up; ‹*face*› to harden
IDIOM **~ les yeux sur** to turn a blind eye to

fermeté /fɛʀməte/ *nf* firmness

fermette /fɛʀmɛt/ *nf* farmhouse-style
cottage

fermeture /fɛʀmətyʀ/ *nf* **(a)** (of business,
account) closing; (definitive) closure, closing
down
(b) (on handbag) clasp; (on garment) fastening
■ **~ éclair®, ~ à glissière** zip (GB), zipper (US)

fermier, -ière /fɛʀmje, ɛʀ/ **1** *adj* free-
range
2 *nm,f* farmer

fermoir /fɛʀmwaʀ/ *nm* (on necklace, bag)
clasp

féroce /feʀɔs/ *adj* **(a)** fierce; ferocious
(b) ‹*appetite*› voracious

férocité /feʀɔsite/ *nf* **(a)** (of animal)
ferociousness
(b) (of remark) savagery
(c) (of person) fierceness

ferons /fəʀɔ̃/ ▶ FAIRE

feront /fəʀɔ̃/ ▶ FAIRE

ferraille /feʀɑj/ *nf* **(a)** scrap metal
(b) scrapheap
(c) (fam) small change

ferrailleur /feʀɑjœʀ/ *nm* scrap (metal)
dealer

ferronnerie /feʀɔnʀi/ *nf* **(a)** ironworks
(b) wrought iron work
(c) iron work

ferroviaire /feʀɔvjɛʀ/ *adj* ‹*transport,
collision*› rail; ‹*station, tunnel*› railway (GB),
railroad (US)

fertile /fɛʀtil/ *adj* fertile; ‹*year*› productive

fertilisant /fɛʀtilizɑ̃/ *nm* fertilizer

fertilité /fɛʀtilite/ *nf* fertility

fervent, ~e /fɛʀvɑ̃, ɑ̃t/ *adj* ‹*believer*›
fervent; ‹*admirer*› ardent

ferveur /fɛʀvœʀ/ *nf* (of prayer) fervour (GB);
(of love) ardour (GB)

fesse /fɛs/ *nf* buttock
IDIOM **coûter la peau des ~s** (fam) to cost an
arm and a leg (colloq)

fessée /fese/ *nf* smack on the bottom,
spanking

festin /fɛstɛ̃/ *nm* feast

festival /fɛstival/ *nm* festival

festivités /fɛstivite/ *nf pl* festivities

festoyer /fɛstwaje/ [23] *vi* to feast

fêtard, ~e /fɛtaʀ, aʀd/ *nm,f* (fam) reveller

✧ **fête** /fɛt/ *nf* **(a)** public holiday (GB), holiday
(US)
(b) (saint's) name-day; **ça va être ma~!** (fam)
I'm going to cop it! (colloq)
(c) festival
(d) (day of) celebration
(e) party; **faire la ~** to live it up (colloq)
(f) fête, fair, celebrations
■ **~ foraine** funfair; **~ du travail** May Day,

Labour Day (GB)
IDIOM faire sa ∼ à qn (fam) to give sb a working over (colloq)

fêter /fete/ [1] *vtr* to celebrate ‹event›

fétiche /fetiʃ/ **1** *adj* lucky
2 *nm* (a) mascot
(b) fetish

fétide /fetid/ *adj* foul; foul-smelling

feu[1], ∼**e** /fø/ *adj* late; ∼ la reine, la ∼e reine the late queen

◆ **feu**[2], *pl* ∼**x** /fø/ *nm* (a) fire ▶ HUILE
(b) light; sous le ∼ des projecteurs under the glare of the spotlights; (figurative) in the spotlight
(c) traffic light; **j'ai le ∼ vert de mon patron** my boss has given me the go-ahead
(d) (on cooker) ring (GB), burner (US); **faire cuire à petit ∼** cook over a gentle heat
(e) **avez-vous du ∼?** have you got a light?
(f) passion; **dans le ∼ de la discussion** in the heat of the discussion
(g) ∼! (Mil) fire!; **faire ∼** to fire; **coup de ∼** shot
(h) (Mil) action
■ ∼ **d'artifice** fireworks display; firework; ∼ **de cheminée** chimney fire, open fire; ∼ **follet** will-o'-the-wisp; ∼ **de joie** bonfire; ∼ **de signalisation**, ∼ **tricolore** traffic light; ∼**x de croisement** dipped (GB) *or* dimmed (US) headlights; ∼**x de détresse** warning lights; ∼**x de route** headlights
IDIOMS **il n'y a pas le ∼!** (fam) there's no rush!; **ne pas faire long ∼** (fam) not to last long; **il n'y a vu que du ∼** (fam) he fell for it; **mourir à petit ∼** to die a slow death

feuillage /fœjaʒ/ *nm* foliage, leaves

◆ **feuille** /fœj/ *nf* (a) (Bot) leaf
(b) (of paper, metal) sheet
■ ∼ **de chou** (fam) rag (colloq), newspaper; ∼ **d'impôts** tax return; ∼ **de maladie** *a form for reclaiming medical expenses from the social security office*; ∼ **de paie** payslip (GB), pay stub (US)

feuillet /fœjɛ/ *nm* (a) (in book) leaf
(b) page

feuilleté, ∼**e** /fœjte/ *adj* **pâte ∼e** puff pastry

feuilleter /fœjte/ [20] *vtr* to leaf through [sth]

feuilleton /fœjtɔ̃/ *nm* serial; soap (opera)

feutre /føtʀ/ *nm* (a) felt
(b) felt-tip (pen)

feutré, ∼**e** /føtʀe/ *adj* ‹atmosphere› hushed; ‹sound› muffled

fève /fɛv/ *nf* (a) broad bean
(b) lucky charm (*hidden in Twelfth Night cake*)

◆ **février** /fevʀije/ *nm* February

FF (Hist) (*written abbr* = **franc français**) FFr

fiabilité /fjabilite/ *nf* reliability

fiable /fjabl/ *adj* reliable

fiançailles /fjɑ̃saj/ *nf pl* engagement

fiancé, ∼**e** /fjɑ̃se/ *nm,f* fiancé/fiancée

fiancer: se fiancer /fjɑ̃se/ [12] *v refl* (+ *v être*) to get engaged

fibre /fibʀ/ *nf* fibre (GB)

ficeler /fisle/ [19] *vtr* to tie up ‹parcel›

ficelle /fisɛl/ *nf* (a) string
(b) trick; **la ∼ est un peu grosse** it's a bit obvious
(c) thin baguette
IDIOM **tirer sur la ∼** to push one's luck

fiche /fiʃ/ *nf* (a) index card; slip
(b) form; ∼ **d'inscription** enrolment (GB) form
(c) plug; **prise à trois ∼s** three-pin plug
■ ∼ **d'état civil** *record of personal details for administrative purposes*; ∼ **de paie** payslip (GB), pay stub (US)

ficher /fiʃe/ [1] **1** *vtr* (a) to put [sth] on a file; to open a file on [sb]; **être fiché (par la police)** to be on police files
(b) to drive ‹stake, nail›
(c) (fam) **qu'est-ce que tu fiches?** what the heck are you doing? (colloq); **n'en avoir rien à ∼** not to give a damn (colloq)
(d) (fam) ∼ **un coup à qn** (figurative) to be a real blow to sb; ∼ **la paix à qn** to leave sb alone
(e) (fam) ∼ **qch quelque part** to chuck sth somewhere (colloq); ∼ **qn dehors** to kick sb out (colloq)
2 **se ficher** *v refl* (+ *v être*) (a) ‹arrow, knife› to stick
(b) (fam) **se ∼ de qn** to make fun of sb; **se ∼ du monde** to have a hell of a nerve (colloq)
(c) (fam) **se ∼ de ce que qn fait** not to give a damn (about) what sb does (colloq)

◆ **fichier** /fiʃje/ *nm* file; (in library) index

fichu **1** *pp* ▶ FICHER 1C, 1D, 1E, 2
2 *adj* (a) ‹weather, job› rotten (colloq); ‹rain› dreadful; ‹car, TV› damned (colloq)
(b) ‹person, car› done for (colloq); **s'il pleut c'est ∼** if it rains that's the end of that
(c) **être bien ∼** to be well designed; ‹book› to be well laid out; **je suis mal ∼** I feel lousy (colloq)
(d) **être ∼ de faire** to be quite capable of doing

fictif, -ive /fiktif, iv/ *adj* imaginary; false

fiction /fiksjɔ̃/ *nf* (a) fiction
(b) (on TV) drama

◆ **fidèle** /fidɛl/ **1** *adj* (a) ‹person, dog› faithful; **être ∼ au poste** to be always there
(b) loyal
(c) true (à to)
(d) ‹translation› faithful
2 *nmf* (a) loyal supporter
(b) **les ∼s** the faithful

fidèlement /fidɛlmɑ̃/ *adv* (a) faithfully
(b) loyally

fidéliser /fidelize/ [1] *vtr* to secure the loyalty of ‹clients›

fidélité /fidelite/ *nf* (a) fidelity
(b) loyalty
(c) (of translation) accuracy

fiduciaire /fidysjɛʀ/ *adj* fiduciary; **société**
~ **trust** company

fief /fjɛf/ *nm* (a) fief
(b) (figurative) territory; (of party) stronghold

fieffé, **~e** /fjefe/ *adj* ~ **menteur**
incorrigible liar

fier¹, **fière** /fjɛʀ/ *adj* proud; **avoir fière**
allure to cut a fine figure

ɟ **fier²**: **se fier** /fje/ [2] *v refl* (+ *v être*) (a) **se**
~ **à** to trust ‹*person, promise*›
(b) **se** ~ **à** to rely on ‹*person, instrument*›; to
trust to ‹*chance*›

fierté /fjɛʀte/ *nf* pride

fièvre /fjɛvʀ/ *nf* (a) (high) temperature;
avoir de la ~ to have a (high) temperature
(b) frenzy
(c) fervour (GB); ~ **électorale** election fever
■ ~ **de cheval** (fam) raging fever

fiévreusement /fjevʀøzmɑ̃/ *adv*
frantically; feverishly

fiévreux, **-euse** /fjevʀø, øz/ *adj* (a) (Med)
feverish
(b) (agitated) frantic
(c) (passionate) feverish

figer /fiʒe/ [13] **1** *vtr* (a) to congeal ‹*grease*›; to
thicken ‹*sauce*›; to clot ‹*blood*›
2 **se figer** *v refl* (+ *v être*) (a) ‹*smile,*
person› to freeze
(b) ‹*grease*› to congeal; ‹*blood*› to clot

fignoler /fiɲɔle/ [1] **1** *vtr* (a) to put the
finishing touches to
(b) to take great pains over
2 *vi* to fiddle about

figue /fig/ *nf* fig; ~ **de Barbarie** prickly pear

figuier /figje/ *nm* fig tree

figurant, **~e** /figyʀɑ̃, ɑ̃t/ *nm,f* (in films)
extra; (in theatre) bit player

figuratif, **-ive** /figyʀatif, iv/ *adj* figurative,
representational; **artiste non** ~ abstract
artist

figuration /figyʀasjɔ̃/ *nf* **faire de la** ~
(in films) to be an extra; (figurative) to have a
token role

ɟ **figure** /figyʀ/ *nf* (a) face
(b) **faire** ~ **d'amateur** to look like an
amateur; **reprendre** ~ **humaine** to look half-
human again
(c) (in history, politics) figure
(d) (in drawing) figure
IDIOMS **prendre** ~ to take shape; **faire bonne**
~ to keep an air of composure; to make the
right impression; to do well

ɟ **figurer** /figyʀe/ [1] **1** *vtr* to represent
2 *vi* ‹*name, object*› to appear
3 **se figurer** *v refl* (+ *v être*) to imagine

figurine /figyʀin/ *nf* figurine

ɟ indicates a very frequent word

ɟ **fil** /fil/ **1** *nm* (a) thread; ▶ COUDRE
(b) yarn
(c) string; ~ **de fer** wire
(d) wire; (on appliance) flex (GB), cord (US); (on
phone) lead; **coup de** ~ (fam) (phone) call; **au**
bout du ~ (fam) on the phone
(e) (of conversation, text) thread; **perdre le** ~
des événements to lose track of events
(f) (of razor) edge
2 **au fil de** *phr* in the course of; **au** ~ **des**
ans over the years; **aller au** ~ **de l'eau** to go
with the flow
■ ~ **conducteur** (of heat) conductor; (of novel)
thread; (of inquiry) lead; ~ **directeur** guiding
principle
IDIOM **ne tenir qu'à un** ~ to hang by a thread

filament /filamɑ̃/ *nm* filament

filature /filatyʀ/ *nf* (a) textile mill
(b) spinning
(c) **prendre qn en** ~ to tail sb (colloq)

file /fil/ *nf* (a) ~ **(d'attente)** queue (GB), line
(US)
(b) line; ~ **indienne** single file
(c) lane; **se garer en double** ~ to double-
park

filer /file/ [1] **1** *vtr* (a) to spin ‹*wool, cotton*›
(b) to spin ‹*web, cocoon*›
(c) to ladder (GB), to get a run in ‹*tights*›
(d) to tail [sb] (colloq)
(e) (fam) to give [sth] (à qn to sb)
2 *vi* (fam) (a) to go off, to leave
(b) to rush
(c) ‹*time*› to fly by; ‹*prisoner*› to get away; ~
entre les mains to slip through one's fingers

filet /filɛ/ *nm* (a) net; ~ **à provisions** string
bag; **coup de** ~ (police) raid
(b) fillet
(c) (of water) trickle; (of smoke) wisp; ~ **de**
citron dash of lemon juice

filial, **~e¹**, *mpl* **-iaux** /filjal, o/ *adj* filial

filiale² /filjal/ *nf* subsidiary

filiation /filjasjɔ̃/ *nf* filiation

filière /filjɛʀ/ *nf* (a) (Sch) course of study
(b) (Econ) field
(c) **suivre la** ~ **habituelle** to climb up the
usual career ladder
(d) official channels
(e) ~ **(clandestine) de la drogue** drugs ring

filiforme /filifɔʀm/ *adj* spindly; threadlike

filigrane /filigʀan/ *nm* filigree

filin /filɛ̃/ *nm* rope

ɟ **fille** /fij/ *nf* (a) daughter
(b) girl; ~ **mère** unmarried mother

fillette /fijɛt/ *nf* (a) little girl
(b) (fam) half bottle

filleul /fijœl/ *nm* godson, godchild

filleule /fijœl/ *nf* goddaughter, godchild

ɟ **film** /film/ *nm* (a) film (GB), movie (US)
(b) (thin) film
■ ~ **d'animation** cartoon

filmer /filme/ [1] *vtr* to film

filmique /filmik/ *adj* film; cinematic

filon /filɔ̃/ *nm* vein, seam

filou /filu/ *nm* crook; cheat; rascal

✧ **fils** /fis/ *nm inv* son; **Dupont ∼ Dupont** Junior

filtre /filtʀ/ *nm* filter

filtrer /filtʀe/ [1] **1** *vtr* (a) to filter
(b) to screen ‹*visitors, calls*›
2 *vi* ‹*information*› to leak out; ‹*idea, liquid*› to filter through

fîmes /fim/ ▸ FAIRE

fin¹, fine /fɛ̃, fin/ **1** *adj* (a) ‹*rain, sand, brush*› fine; ‹*slice, layer*› thin
(b) ‹*ankle, waist*› slender; ‹*features*› fine; ‹*dish*› delicate
(c) ‹*person*› perceptive; ‹*taste, humour*› subtle; **vraiment c'est ∼!** that's really clever!; **jouer au plus ∼ avec qn** to try to outsmart sb; **avoir l'air ∼** (fam) to look a fool
(d) **avoir l'ouïe ∼e** to have a keen sense of hearing
(e) **au ∼ fond de** in the remotest part of ‹*country*›; **le ∼ mot de l'histoire** the truth of the matter
2 *adv* (a) **être ∼ prêt** to be all set
(b) ‹*write, grind*› finely; ‹*slice*› thinly
3 *nm* **le ∼ du ∼** the ultimate
■ **∼e mouche** sly customer (colloq); **∼es herbes** mixed herbs

✧ **fin²** /fɛ̃/ *nf* (a) end, ending; **à la ∼ des années 70** in the late '70s; **tu vas te taire à la∼!** (fam) for God's sake, be quiet!; **chômeur en ∼ de droits** unemployed person no longer entitled to benefit
(b) end, death
(c) end, aim, purpose
■ **∼ de série** oddment

✧ **final, ∼e¹,** *mpl* **-aux** /final, o/ *adj* final

finale² /final/ *nf* (Sport) final

✧ **finalement** /finalmɑ̃/ *adv* (a) in the end, finally
(b) in fact, actually

finaliser /finalize/ [1] *vtr* to finalize; to complete

finalité /finalite/ *nf* (a) purpose, aim
(b) finality

finance /finɑ̃s/ **1** *nf* (a) **la ∼** finance
(b) financiers
2 finances *nf pl* **les ∼s** finances; **moyennant ∼s** for a consideration

financement /finɑ̃smɑ̃/ *nm* financing

financer /finɑ̃se/ [12] *vtr* to finance

✧ **financier, -ière** /finɑ̃sje, ɛʀ/ **1** *adj* financial
2 *nm* (a) financier
(b) small cake

finaud, -e /fino, od/ *nm,f* (Comput) hacker

finesse /fines/ *nf* (a) (of thread, writing) fineness; (of layer, paper) thinness
(b) (of dish) delicacy; (of face) fineness; (of waist) slenderness

(c) (of remark, person) perceptiveness; (of actor) sensitivity
(d) (of senses) keenness
(e) **les ∼s d'une langue** the subtleties of a language

fini, ∼e /fini/ **1** *pp* ▸ FINIR
2 *pp adj* **être ∼** to be over, to be finished
3 *nm* finish

✧ **finir** /finiʀ/ [3] **1** *vtr* (a) to finish (off), to complete; to end ‹*day*›
(b) to use up ‹*supplies*›
2 *vi* to finish, to end; ‹*contract, lease*› to run out; **le film finit bien** the film has a happy ending; **ça va mal ∼!** it'll end in tears!; **∼ par faire** to end up doing; **ils finiront bien par céder** they're bound to give in in the end; **en ∼ avec qn/qch** to have done with sb/sth; **finissons-en!** let's get it over with!

finissant /finisɑ̃/ ▸ FINIR

finition /finisjɔ̃/ *nf* (a) finishing
(b) finish

finlandais, ∼e /fɛ̃lɑ̃dɛ, ɛz/ *adj* Finnish

Finlandais, ∼e /fɛ̃lɑ̃dɛ, ɛz/ *nm,f* Finn

Finlande /fɛ̃lɑ̃d/ *pr nf* Finland

finnois, ∼e /finwa, az/ **1** *adj* Finnish
2 *nm* (language) Finnish

fioriture /fjɔʀityʀ/ *nf* embellishment

fioul /fjul/ *nm* fuel oil

firent /fiʀ/ ▸ FAIRE

firme /fiʀm/ *nf* firm

fis /fi/ ▸ FAIRE

fisc /fisk/ *nm* tax office

fiscal, ∼e, *mpl* **-aux** /fiskal, o/ *adj* fiscal, tax

fiscaliser /fiskalize/ [1] *vtr* (a) to tax
(b) to fund [sth] by taxation

fiscalité /fiskalite/ *nf* (a) taxation
(b) tax system

fisse /fis/ ▸ FAIRE

fissent /fis/ ▸ FAIRE

fisses /fis/ ▸ FAIRE

fissible /fisibl/ *adj* fissionable, fissile

fissiez /fisje/ ▸ FAIRE

fission /fisjɔ̃/ *nf* fission; **∼ nucléaire** nuclear fission

fissionner /fisjɔne/ [1] *vtr, vi* to split

fissions /fisjɔ̃/ ▸ FAIRE

fissure /fisyʀ/ *nf* (a) crack
(b) (Anat) fissure

fissurer /fisyʀe/ [1] *vtr* to crack, to fissure

fit /fi/ ▸ FAIRE

fîtes /fit/ ▸ FAIRE

fixation /fiksasjɔ̃/ *nf* (a) fixing; fastening
(b) (on ski) binding
(c) fixation

fixe /fiks/ *adj* (a) fixed
(b) permanent

fixé, ∼e /fikse/ **1** *pp* ▸ FIXER
2 *pp adj* (a) **tu es ∼ maintenant!** you've got the picture now! (colloq) ····⟩

(b) nous ne sommes pas encore très ∼s we haven't really decided yet

✔ **fixer** /fikse/ [1] **1** *vtr* **(a)** to fix (à to)
(b) to set ‹*date, price*›; to establish ‹*boundaries*›; **∼ son choix sur** to decide on
(c) to fix ‹*colour, emulsion*›
(d) to focus ‹*attention*›; to stare at ‹*person*›
2 se fixer *v refl* (+ *v être*) **(a)** ‹*part*› to be attached
(b) to set oneself ‹*goal, limit*›

flacon /flakɔ̃/ *nm* **(a)** (small) bottle
(b) decanter
(c) (in laboratory) flask

flagada /flagada/ *adj inv* (fam) weary

flageller /flaʒele/ [1] *vtr* to flog; (as religious punishment) to flagellate

flageoler /flaʒɔle/ [1] *vi* **avoir les jambes qui flageolent** to feel wobbly

flageolet /flaʒɔlɛ/ *nm* flageolet

flagrant, ∼e /flagrɑ̃, ɑ̃t/ *adj* ‹*difference*› obvious; ‹*injustice*› flagrant; ‹*lie*› blatant; **prendre qn en ∼ délit** to catch sb red-handed

flair /flɛʀ/ *nm* **(a)** sense of smell, nose
(b) intuition

flairer /flere/ [1] *vtr* **(a)** to sniff ‹*object*›; **le chien a flairé une piste** the dog has picked up a scent
(b) ‹*animal*› to scent; ‹*person*› to smell
(c) to sense ‹*danger*›

flamand, ∼e /flamɑ̃, ɑ̃d/ **1** *adj* Flemish
2 *nm* (language) Flemish

flamant /flamɑ̃/ *nm* flamingo

flambant /flɑ̃bɑ̃/ *adv* **∼ neuf** brand new

flambeau, *pl* **∼x** /flɑ̃bo/ *nm* torch

flambée /flɑ̃be/ *nf* **(a)** fire; **faire une ∼** to light a fire
(b) (of hatred) flare-up; (of prices) explosion

flamber /flɑ̃be/ [1] **1** *vtr* to flambé ‹*pancake*›
2 *vi* to burn

flamboyant, ∼e /flɑ̃bwajɑ̃, ɑ̃t/ *adj* ‹*fire, light*› blazing; ‹*colour*› flaming

✔ **flamme** /flɑm/ *nf* **(a)** flame; **en ∼s** on fire
(b) love, passion
IDIOMS **descendre en ∼s** to shoot down; **être tout feu tout ∼** to be wildly enthusiastic

flan /flɑ̃/ *nm* (Culin) custard tart (GB) *or* flan (US)
IDIOM **en rester comme deux ronds de ∼** (fam) to be dumbfounded

flanc /flɑ̃/ *nm* (of person, mountain) side; (of animal) flank; **être sur le ∼** (fam) to be exhausted

flancher /flɑ̃ʃe/ [1] *vi* (fam) **(a)** to lose one's nerve
(b) to crack up
(c) ‹*heart, engine*› to give out

flanelle /flanɛl/ *nf* flannel

✔ indicates a very frequent word

flâner /flɑne/ [1] *vi* to stroll; to loaf around (colloq)

flâneur, -euse /flɑnœr, øz/ *nm,f*
(a) stroller
(b) loafer (colloq), idler

flanquer /flɑ̃ke/ [1] **1** *vtr* **(a)** to flank; **il est toujours flanqué de son adjoint** his assistant never leaves his side
(b) (fam) to give ‹*blow, fine*›; **∼ qch par terre** to throw sth to the ground; to drop sth; to knock sth to the ground
2 se flanquer *v refl* (+ *v être*) (fam) **se ∼ dans** to run into

flapi, ∼e /flapi/ *adj* (fam) worn out

flaque /flak/ *nf* **∼ (d'eau)** puddle; **∼ d'huile** pool of oil

flash, *pl* **∼es** /flaʃ/ *nm* **(a)** (on camera) flash
(b) ∼ (d'information) news headlines; **∼ publicitaire** advert (GB), commercial (US)

flasque¹ /flask/ *adj* ‹*skin, flesh*› flabby

flasque² /flask/ *nf* flask

flatter /flate/ [1] **1** *vtr* to flatter
2 se flatter *v refl* (+ *v être*) to pride oneself

flatterie /flatri/ *nf* flattery

flatteur, -euse /flatœr, øz/ *adj*
(a) ‹*portrait*› flattering
(b) ‹*person, remarks*› sycophantic

flatulence /flatylɑ̃s/ *nf* wind, flatulence

fléau, *pl* **∼x** /fleo/ *nm* **(a)** scourge
(b) (figurative) curse, plague
(c) (person) pest

flèche /flɛʃ/ *nf* **(a)** arrow; **partir en ∼** to shoot off; **monter en ∼** ‹*prices*› to soar
(b) barbed remark
(c) spire

flécher /fleʃe/ [14] *vtr* to signpost

fléchette /fleʃɛt/ *nf* **(a)** dart
(b) (game) darts

fléchir /fleʃir/ [3] **1** *vtr* **(a)** to bend
(b) to sway ‹*person, opinion*›; to weaken ‹*will*›
2 *vi* **(a)** ‹*knees*› to bend; ‹*legs*› to give way
(b) ‹*attention*› to flag; ‹*courage*› to waver; ‹*will*› to weaken; ‹*demand*› to fall off

flegmatique /flɛgmatik/ *adj* phlegmatic

flegme /flɛgm/ *nm* phlegm, composure

flemmard, ∼e /flemar, ard/ *nm,f* (fam) lazybones (colloq), lazy devil (colloq)

flemme /flɛm/ *nf* (fam) laziness

flétan /fletɑ̃/ *nm* halibut

flétrir /fletrir/ [3] **1** *vtr* to blacken ‹*reputation*›
2 se flétrir *v refl* (+ *v être*) ‹*plant*› to wither; ‹*flower, beauty*› to fade; ‹*fruit*› to shrivel

✔ **fleur** /flœr/ *nf* **(a)** flower; **être en ∼s** ‹*garden*› to be full of flowers; ‹*plant, shrub*› to be in flower; ‹*tree, lilac*› to be in blossom; **à ∼s** flowery
(b) à ∼ d'eau just above the water
■ **∼ des champs** wild flower; **∼ de lys**

fleur-de-lis
IDIOMS être ~ **bleue** to be romantic; **avoir une sensibilité à** ~ **de peau** to be hypersensitive; **avoir les nerfs à** ~ **de peau** to be a bundle of nerves; **faire une** ~ **à qn** (fam) to do sb a favour (GB)

fleuret /flœRε/ *nm* (sword) foil

fleurette /flœRεt/ *nf* (Culin) **crème** ~ whipping cream

fleuri, ~**e** /flœRi/ **1** *pp* ▶ FLEURIR
2 *pp adj* (a) ‹*garden*› full of flowers; ‹*tree*› in blossom; in bloom
(b) ‹*table*› decorated with flowers
(c) ‹*wallpaper*› flowery

fleurir /flœRiR/ [3] *vi* (a) ‹*rose bush*› to flower; ‹*cherry tree*› to blossom
(b) ‹*new buildings*› to spring up; ‹*posters*› to appear
(c) to thrive, to flourish

fleuriste /flœRist/ *nmf* (a) florist
(b) flower shop

⚜ **fleuve** /flœv/ **1** *nm* river
2 (-)**fleuve** (*combining form*) interminable; ▶ ROMAN-FLEUVE

flexible /flεksibl/ *adj* (a) ‹*blade, tube*› flexible; ‹*body*› supple
(b) ‹*person, timetable*› flexible

flexion /flεksjɔ̃/ *nf* (of object) bending; (of arm, leg) flexing

flic /flik/ *nm* (fam) cop (colloq), policeman

flipper /flipœR/ *nm* (Games) (a) pinball machine
(b) (device in machine) flipper
(c) (game) pinball

flirter /flœRte/ [1] *vi* to flirt

flocon /flɔkɔ̃/ *nm* (of snow) flake; (of dust) speck; (of wool) bit; ~**s d'avoine** oat flakes (GB), oatmeal (US)

flop /flɔp/ *nm* (fam) flop

flopée /flɔpe/ *nf* (fam) **(toute) une** ~ **de gamins** masses of kids (colloq)

floraison /flɔRεzɔ̃/ *nf* flowering

floral, ~**e**, *mpl* -**aux** /flɔRal, o/ *adj* floral

floralies /flɔRali/ *nf pl* flower show

flore /flɔR/ *nf* flora

florilège /flɔRilεʒ/ *nm* anthology

florin /flɔRε̃/ *nm* (Dutch currency) guilder

florissant, ~**e** /flɔRisɑ̃, ɑ̃t/ *adj*
(a) ‹*activity*› thriving
(b) ‹*complexion*› ruddy

flot /flo/ **1** *nm* (a) (of letters, refugees) flood; (of visitors) stream
(b) **les** ~**s** the deep, the sea
2 **à flot** *phr* **couler à** ~**(s)** to flow

flottant, ~**e** /flɔtɑ̃, ɑ̃t/ *adj* ‹*wood, line*› floating; ‹*clothes, hair*› flowing

flotte /flɔt/ *nf* (a) fleet
(b) (fam) rain
(c) (fam) water

flottement /flɔtmɑ̃/ *nm* (a) wavering
(b) (of currency) floating

flotter /flɔte/ [1] **1** *vi* (a) to float; ~ **à la dérive** to drift
(b) ‹*mist*› to drift; ‹*flag*› to fly; ~ **au vent** to flutter in the wind; **elle flotte dans ses vêtements** her clothes are hanging off her
(c) ‹*currency*› to float
2 *v impers* (fam) to rain

flotteur /flɔtœR/ *nm* float

flou, ~**e** /flu/ **1** *adj* (a) ‹*outline*› blurred
(b) (figurative) vague, hazy
2 *nm* (a) fuzziness
(b) (figurative) vagueness
■ ~ **artistique** soft focus; (figurative) artistry

flouer /flue/ [1] *vtr* (fam) to cheat; **se faire** ~ to be had (colloq)

fluctuant, ~**e** /flyktɥɑ̃, ɑ̃t/ *adj* ‹*prices, opinions*› fluctuating; ‹*person*› fickle

fluet, -**ette** /flyε, εt/ *adj* ‹*body, person*› slight; ‹*voice*› thin, reedy

fluide /flɥid/ **1** *adj* (a) ‹*oil, paint*› fluid
(b) ‹*style*› fluent; ‹*traffic*› moving freely
2 *nm* (a) (in physics) fluid
(b) (of clairvoyant) (psychic) powers

fluo /flyo/ *adj inv* (fam) fluorescent

fluor /flyɔR/ *nm* fluorine

fluorescent, ~**e** /flyɔRεsɑ̃, ɑ̃t/ *adj* fluorescent

flûte /flyt/ **1** *nf* (a) (Mus) flute; **petite** ~ piccolo
(b) (champagne) flute
(c) French stick
2 *excl* (fam) damn! (colloq), darn it! (colloq)
■ ~ **à bec** recorder; ~ **de Pan** panpipes

fluvial, ~**e**, *mpl* -**iaux** /flyvjal, o/ *adj* fluvial, river

flux /fly/ *nm inv* (a) (gen, Econ) flow
(b) (in physics) flux
(c) **le** ~ **et le reflux** flood tide and ebb tide; (figurative) the ebb and flow
(d) influx

FMI /εfεmi/ *nm: abbr* ▶ FONDS

foc /fɔk/ *nm* jib

focal, ~**e**, *mpl* -**aux** /fɔkal, o/ *adj* focal

focaliser /fɔkalize/ [1] *vtr* to focus ‹*rays*›; to focalize ‹*electron beam*›

fœtus /fetys/ *nm inv* foetus

⚜ **foi** /fwa/ *nf* (a) faith; **avoir la** ~ to be a believer
(b) **ma** ~ **oui** well yes; **en toute bonne** ~ **je crois que** in all sincerity, I believe that; **il est de mauvaise** ~ he doesn't mean a word of it
(c) **sur la** ~ **de témoins** on the evidence of witnesses; **qui fait** *or* **faisant** ~ ‹*text, signature*› authentic; **sous la** ~ **du serment** under oath
IDIOM sans ~ **ni loi** fearing neither God nor man

foie /fwa/ *nm* liver; **crise de** ~ indigestion

foin /fwε̃/ *nm* hay; **tas de** ~ haystack; **la saison des** ~**s** the haymaking season

foire /fwaR/ *nf* (a) fair; ~ **du livre** book fair ⋯⟩

(b) fun fair
(c) (fam) bedlam; **faire la ~** (fam) to live it up (colloq)

✿ **fois** /fwa/ **1** *nf inv* time; **une ~** once; **deux ~** twice; **quatre ~ trois font douze** four times three is twelve; **l'autre ~** last time; **une (bonne) ~ pour toutes** once and for all; **une ~ sur deux** half the time; **une ~ sur trois** every third time; **deux ~ sur cinq** two times out of five; **toutes les ~ que** every time (that); **deux ~ plus petit** half as big; **c'est dix ~ trop lourd!** it's far too heavy!; **régler en trois ~** to pay in three instalments (GB); **pour la énième ~** for the hundredth time; **(à) la première ~** the first time; **la première ~ que je vous ai parlé** when I first talked to you
2 **à la fois** *phr* **deux à la ~** two at a time; **elle est à la ~ intelligente et travailleuse** she's both clever and hardworking
3 **des fois** *phr* (fam) sometimes; **tu n'as pas vu mon chien, des ~?** you wouldn't have seen my dog, by any chance?
4 **des fois que** *phr* (fam) in case
IDIOM **il était une ~** once upon a time there was

foisonner /fwazɔne/ [1] *vi* to abound

fol ▶ FOU 1

folâtrer /fɔlɑtʀe/ [1] *vi* to romp about; to frisk

folichon, -onne /fɔliʃɔ̃, ɔn/ *adj* (fam) **pas ~** far from brilliant

✿ **folie** /fɔli/ *nf* **(a)** madness; **aimer qn/qch à la ~** to be mad (GB) *or* crazy about sb/sth
(b) act of folly; **elle a fait une ~ en acceptant** she was mad to accept
(c) extravagance
■ **~ des grandeurs** delusions of grandeur

folk /fɔlk/ *nm* folk music

folklo /fɔlklo/ *adj* (fam) eccentric, crazy (colloq)

folklore /fɔlklɔʀ/ *nm* **(a)** folklore
(b) (fam) razzmatazz (colloq)

folklorique /fɔlklɔʀik/ *adj* **(a)** ‹music› folk; ‹costume› traditional
(b) (fam) eccentric

folle ▶ FOU 1, 2

follement /fɔlmɑ̃/ *adv* **s'amuser ~** to have a terrific time

follet /fɔlɛ/ *adj m* **feu ~** will-o'-the-wisp

fomenter /fɔmɑ̃te/ [1] *vtr* to instigate

foncé, ~e /fɔ̃se/ *adj* ‹colour› dark; ‹pink› deep

foncer /fɔ̃se/ [12] **1** *vtr* **(a)** to make [sth] darker *or* deeper ‹colour›
(b) (Culin) to line
2 *vi* **(a)** (fam) ‹person, vehicle› to tear along (colloq); **fonce!** get a move on! (colloq); **~ vers/dans** to rush toward(s)/into; **~ sur qch/vers la sortie** to make a dash for sth/for the exit;

~ sur qn to charge at sb; **~ à New York** to dash over to New York
(b) ‹colour› (gen) to darken; ‹pink, mauve› to deepen; ‹fabric› to go darker

fonceur, -euse /fɔ̃sœʀ, øz/ (fam) **1** *adj* dynamic
2 *nm,f* go-getter (colloq)

foncier, -ière /fɔ̃sje, ɛʀ/ *adj* ‹income› from land; **impôt ~** property tax

foncièrement /fɔ̃sjɛʀmɑ̃/ *adv* fundamentally

✿ **fonction** /fɔ̃ksjɔ̃/ *nf* **(a)** (in administration, company) post; duties; **dans l'exercice de leurs ~s** while carrying out their duties; **occuper la ~ de** to hold the position of; **voiture de ~** company car
(b) **en ~ de** according to
(c) function; **avoir pour ~ de faire** to be designed to do; **faire ~ de** to serve as
(d) profession; **~ enseignante** teaching profession
■ **~ publique** civil service

fonctionnaire /fɔ̃ksjɔnɛʀ/ *nmf* civil servant; (higher ranking) government official

fonctionnalité /fɔ̃ksjɔnalite/ *nf* functionality

fonctionnel, -elle /fɔ̃ksjɔnɛl/ *adj* functional

✿ **fonctionnement** /fɔ̃ksjɔnmɑ̃/ *nm* **(a)** (of institution) functioning
(b) (of machinery) working; **mauvais ~** malfunction; **en ~** in service

✿ **fonctionner** /fɔ̃ksjɔne/ [1] *vi* to work; **~ à l'essence** to run on petrol (GB) *or* gas (US)

✿ **fond** /fɔ̃/ **1** *nm* **(a)** (of vessel, lake, valley) bottom; (of cupboard, wardrobe) back; **~ de la mer** seabed; **~ de l'océan** ocean floor; **toucher le ~** (in water) to touch the bottom; (figurative) to hit rock bottom
(b) (of shop, yard) back; (of corridor, room) far end; **la chambre du ~** the back bedroom; **au ~ des bois** deep in the woods; **de ~ en comble** from top to bottom
(c) **les problèmes de ~** the basic problems; **un débat de ~** an in-depth debate; **au ~** *or* **dans le ~, le problème est simple** basically, the problem is simple
(d) (of text) content
(e) **regarder qn au ~ des yeux** (suspiciously) to give sb a searching look; **elle a un bon ~** she's very good at heart
(f) background; **~ musical** background music
(g) **un ~ de porto** a drop of port
(h) (Naut) **il y a 20 mètres de ~** the water is 20 metres (GB) deep
(i) (Sport) **épreuve de ~** long-distance event
2 **à fond** *phr* **(a) connaître qch à ~** to be an expert in sth; **être à ~ pour** (fam) to support wholeheartedly; **respirer à ~** to breathe deeply; **mettre la radio à ~** to turn the radio right up
(b) (fam) **rouler à ~** to drive at top speed
■ **~ d'artichaut** artichoke bottom; **~ de teint**

---

foundation (GB), make-up base (US)

◆ **fondamental, ~e,** *mpl* **-aux** /fɔ̃damɑ̃tal, o/
adj **(a)** basic, fundamental
(b) essential

fondamentalement /fɔ̃damɑ̃talmɑ̃/ *adv*
(a) fundamentally
(b) radically

fondamentaliste /fɔ̃damɑ̃talist/ *nm*
fundamentalist

fondant, ~e /fɔ̃dɑ̃, ɑ̃t/ *adj* **(a)** ⟨ice⟩ melting
(b) ⟨pear⟩ which melts in the mouth

fondateur, -trice /fɔ̃datœr, tris/ *nm,f*
founder; **groupe ~** founding group

fondation /fɔ̃dasjɔ̃/ **1** *nf* foundation
2 fondations *nf pl* foundations

fondé, ~e /fɔ̃de/ **1** *pp* ▶ FONDER
2 *pp adj* justifiable, well-founded,
legitimate; **non ~, mal ~** ⟨accusation⟩
groundless
■ **~ de pouvoir** (of company) authorized representative; (of bank) senior banking executive

fondement /fɔ̃dmɑ̃/ *nm* foundation; **être
sans** *or* **dénué de ~** to be unfounded

◆ **fonder** /fɔ̃de/ [1] **1** *vtr* **(a)** to found
(b) to base
2 se fonder *v refl* (+ *v être*) **se ~ sur**
⟨theory, method⟩ to be based on; ⟨person⟩ to
go on

fonderie /fɔ̃dri/ *nf* **(a)** foundry
(b) casting

fondre /fɔ̃dr/ [6] **1** *vtr* **(a)** to melt down
⟨metal⟩; to smelt ⟨mineral⟩
(b) to cast ⟨statue⟩
2 *vi* **(a)** ⟨snow, butter⟩ to melt
(b) ⟨sugar⟩ to dissolve
(c) ⟨savings⟩ to melt away
(d) (emotionally) to soften; **~ en larmes** to
dissolve into tears
3 se fondre *v refl* (+ *v être*) **se ~ dans**
⟨person, figure⟩ to blend in with

◆ **fonds** /fɔ̃/ **1** *nm inv* **(a)** (in gallery, museum)
collection
(b) fund
2 *nm pl* funds
■ **~ d'amortissement** sinking fund; **~ bloqués**
frozen assets; **~ de commerce** business; **~ de
placement** investment fund; **~ de prévoyance**
provident fund; **~ propres** equity capital;
~ de roulement working capital; **~ de
solidarité** mutual aid fund; **Fonds monétaire
international, FMI** International Monetary
Fund, IMF

fondu, ~e¹ /fɔ̃dy/ **1** *pp* ▶ FONDRE
2 *pp adj* ⟨butter⟩ melted; ⟨metal⟩ molten

fondue² /fɔ̃dy/ *nf* (Culin) fondue; **~
savoyarde** cheese fondue; **~ bourguignonne**
fondue bourguignonne (*meat dipped in hot
oil*)

font /fɔ̃/ ▶ FAIRE

fontaine /fɔ̃tɛn/ *nf* **(a)** fountain
(b) spring

fonte /fɔ̃t/ *nf* **(a)** cast iron

(b) melting down, smelting
(c) thawing; **~ des neiges** thaw

fonts /fɔ̃/ *nm pl* **~ baptismaux** font

◆ **foot** /fut/ (fam) ▶ FOOTBALL

◆ **football** /futbol/ *nm* football (GB), soccer

footballeur, -euse /futbolœr, øz/ *nm,f*
football *or* soccer player

footing /futiŋ/ *nm* jogging

forage /fɔraʒ/ *nm* drilling

forain, -aine /fɔrɛ̃, ɛn/ **1** *adj* fairground
2 *nm* stallkeeper; **les ~s** fairground
people

forçat /fɔrsa/ *nm* **(a)** convict
(b) galley slave

◆ **force** /fɔrs/ **1** *nf* **(a)** strength; **~s**
strength; **avoir de la ~** to be strong; **c'est
au-dessus de mes ~s** it's too much for me;
de toutes ses ~s with all one's might; **ils
sont de ~ égale aux échecs** they are evenly
matched at chess
(b) force; **de ~** by force; **faire manger de ~**
to force [sb] to eat; **entrer de ~ dans un lieu**
to force one's way into a place
(c) ~ de vente sales force; **~s** (Mil) forces;
d'importantes ~s de police large numbers
of police
2 à force *phr* (fam) **à ~, elle l'a cassé** she
ended up breaking it
3 à force de *phr* **réussir à ~ de travail**
to succeed by dint of hard work; **il est
aphone à ~ de crier** he's been shouting so
much (that) he's lost his voice
■ **~ de dissuasion** (Mil) deterrent force; **~ de
frappe** nuclear weapons; **~s de l'ordre** forces
of law and order

forcé, ~e /fɔrse/ **1** *pp* ▶ FORCER
2 *pp adj* **(a)** (gen) forced
(b) ⟨consequence⟩ inevitable; **c'est~!** (fam)
there's no way around it! (colloq)

forcément /fɔrsemɑ̃/ *adv* inevitably; **pas
~** not necessarily

forcené, ~e /fɔrsəne/ **1** *adj* ⟨rhythm⟩
furious; ⟨activity⟩ frenzied
2 *nm,f* **(a)** maniac
(b) crazed gunman

◆ **forcer** /fɔrse/ [12] **1** *vtr* **(a)** to force
(b) to break through ⟨fence, enclosure⟩; **~
la porte de qn** to force one's way into sb's
house; **~ le passage** to force one's way
through
2 forcer sur *v+prep* to overdo ⟨salt,
colour⟩
3 *vi* **(a)** to overdo it
(b) serrez sans ~ do not tighten too much;
ne force pas! don't force it!
4 se forcer *v refl* (+ *v être*) to force
oneself
IDIOM **~ la main à qn** to force sb's hand

forcing /fɔrsiŋ/ *nm* (fam) **faire du ~** to go
all out

forer /fɔre/ [1] *vtr* to drill

forestier, -ière /fɔʀɛstje, ɛʀ/ adj ‹area›
forested; **chemin** ～ forest path; **exploitation
forestière** (place) forestry plantation

foret /fɔʀɛ/ nm drill

ꞵ **forêt** /fɔʀɛ/ nf forest; ～ **tropicale** rain forest
IDIOM **c'est l'arbre qui cache la** ～ you can't
see the wood for the trees

forfait /fɔʀfɛ/ nm (a) fixed rate; **un** ～ **de
8 euros** a fixed price of 8 euros
(b) package; ～ **avion-auto** fly-drive package
(c) ～ **skieur** ski pass
(d) (of player) withdrawal; **déclarer** ～ to give
up; (Sport) to withdraw

forfaitaire /fɔʀfɛtɛʀ/ adj prix ～ contract
or all-inclusive price; **indemnité** ～ basic
allowance

forge /fɔʀʒ/ nf (a) forge
(b) ironworks

forgé, ～**e** /fɔʀʒe/ [1] pp ▶ FORGER
[2] pp adj ‹object, metal› wrought

forger /fɔʀʒe/ [13] vtr (a) to forge
(b) to form ‹character›

forgeron /fɔʀʒəʀɔ̃/ nm blacksmith
IDIOM **c'est en forgeant qu'on devient** ～
(Proverb) practice makes perfect

formaliser: se formaliser
/fɔʀmalize/ [1] v refl (+ v être) to take offence
(GB)

formalité /fɔʀmalite/ nf formality; **les**
～**s à accomplir pour obtenir un visa** the
necessary procedure to obtain a visa; **par
pure** ～ as a matter of form

format /fɔʀma/ nm format, size

formatage /fɔʀmataʒ/ nm (Comput)
formatting; **faire un** ～ to format

formateur, -trice /fɔʀmatœʀ, tʀis/ adj
formative

ꞵ **formation** /fɔʀmasjɔ̃/ nf (a) education;
training; **avoir une** ～ **littéraire** to have an
arts background; **en** ～ undergoing training
(b) training course
(c) (of government, team) forming
(d) group
■ ～ **continue,** ～ **permanente** adult continuing
education; ～ **professionnelle** professional
training

ꞵ **forme** /fɔʀm/ [1] nf (a) shape; form; **en** ～
de in the shape of; **sous** ～ **de** in the form
of; **sans** ～ shapeless; **pour la** ～ as a matter
of form
(b) (of payment) method
(c) (physical condition) form; **en pleine** ～ in
great shape
[2] **formes** nf pl (a) (of person) figure
(b) (of object, building) lines
(c) **faire qch dans les** ～**s** to do sth in the
correct manner; **y mettre les** ～**s** to be tactful

formé, ～**e** /fɔʀme/ [1] pp ▶ FORMER
[2] pp adj (a) made up; formed
(b) educated; trained

ꞵ indicates a very frequent word

(c) ‹writing, sentence› formed

formel, -elle /fɔʀmɛl/ adj (a) ‹refusal,
denial, person› categorical; ‹order› strict; **être**
～ **sur qch** ‹person› to be definite about sth
(b) **c'est purement** ～ it's just a formality

formellement /fɔʀmɛlmɑ̃/ adv
(a) categorically; strictly
(b) officially; ～ **identifié** clearly identified

ꞵ **former** /fɔʀme/ [1] [1] vtr (a) to form
‹circle, rectangle›
(b) to form, to constitute
(c) to train ‹staff›; to educate ‹person, tastes›;
to develop ‹intelligence›
(d) to form ‹abscess, film›
[2] **se former** v refl (+ v être) (a) to form
(b) to be formed
(c) to train, to be trained
(d) ‹character, style› to develop

formidable /fɔʀmidabl/ adj (a) ‹force›
tremendous
(b) (fam) great, marvellous (GB)
(c) (fam) incredible

formol /fɔʀmɔl/ nm formalin

formulaire /fɔʀmylɛʀ/ nm form

formulation /fɔʀmylasjɔ̃/ nf formulation;
wording; **la** ～ **de cette idée est difficile** it's
not easy to express that idea

ꞵ **formule** /fɔʀmyl/ nf (a) expression; ～
toute faite set phrase
(b) (in travel, tourism) option; ～ **à 75€** (in
restaurant) set menu at 75€
(c) method
(d) concept
(e) (in science) formula
(f) (of car) ～ **un** Formula One
(g) (of magazine) format
■ ～ **magique** magic words

formuler /fɔʀmyle/ [1] vtr (gen) to express;
to put [sth] into words ‹idea›

ꞵ **fort,** ～**e** /fɔʀ, fɔʀt/ [1] adj (a) strong; **armée**
～**e de 10 000 hommes** 10,000-strong army;
～ **d'un chiffre d'affaires en hausse** boasting
an increased turnover
(b) ‹noise› loud; ‹light› bright; ‹heat, activity›
intense; ‹temperature, fever, rate› high;
‹blow, jolt› hard; ‹rain› heavy; ‹spice› hot;
‹majority› large; ‹lack, shortage› great; ‹drop,
increase› sharp; ～**e émigration** high level of
emigration
(c) (at school subject) good
(d) ‹person› stout; ‹hips› broad; ‹bust› large;
‹thighs› big
(e) (fam) **c'est un peu** ～! that's a bit much!
(colloq)
[2] adv (a) extremely, very
(b) ‹doubt› very much; **avoir** ～ **à faire** (fam) to
have a lot to do
(c) ‹hit› hard; ‹squeeze› tight; ‹breathe›
deeply; ‹speak› loudly; **y aller un peu** ～ (fam)
to go a bit too far
(d) **il ne va pas très** ～ he's not very well
[3] nm (a) fort
(b) strong person

4 **au plus fort de** *phr* **au plus ~ de l'été** at the height of summer
■ **~e tête** rebel
IDIOM **c'est plus ~ que moi/qu'elle** I/she just can't help it

fortement /fɔʀtəmɑ̃/ *adv* ‹*criticize*› strongly; ‹*rise*› sharply; ‹*industrialized*› highly; ‹*shaken*› deeply; ‹*damaged*› badly; ‹*displease, dislike*› greatly; ‹*armed*› heavily; **il est ~ question de…** it is highly likely that…

forteresse /fɔʀtəʀɛs/ *nf* stronghold

fortiche /fɔʀtiʃ/ *adj* (fam) smart, clever **(en** at)

fortifiant /fɔʀtifjɑ̃/ *nm* (Med) tonic

fortification /fɔʀtifikasjɔ̃/ *nf* fortification

fortifier /fɔʀtifje/ [2] *vtr* **(a)** to strengthen ‹*nails, hair*›
(b) ‹*meal*› to fortify; ‹*holiday, vitamins*› to do [sb] good
(c) to reinforce ‹*construction*›

fortuit, ~e /fɔʀtɥi, it/ *adj* ‹*meeting*› accidental; ‹*incident, discovery*› fortuitous

✓ **fortune** /fɔʀtyn/ *nf* **(a)** fortune
(b) **de ~** makeshift
IDIOM **faire contre mauvaise ~ bon cœur** to put on a brave face

fortuné, ~e /fɔʀtyne/ *adj* wealthy

fosse /fos/ *nf* **(a)** pit
(b) grave
(c) sandpit
■ **~ commune** communal grave; **~ septique** septic tank

fossé /fose/ *nm* **(a)** (gen) ditch; (of castle) moat
(b) (figurative) gap; rift

fossette /fosɛt/ *nf* dimple

fossile /fosil/ *adj, nm* fossil

fossiliser /fosilize/ [1] *vtr*, **se fossiliser** *v refl* (+ *être*) to fossilize

fossoyeur /foswajœʀ/ *nm* gravedigger

✓ **fou, fol** *before vowel or mute h*, **folle** /fu, fɔl/ **1** *adj* **(a)** (insane) mad; **devenir ~** to go mad; **un tueur ~** a crazed killer
(b) ‹*person, idea*› mad (GB), crazy; ‹*look*› wild; ‹*story*› crazy; **être ~ furieux** (fam) to be raving mad; **être ~ à lier** (fam) to be stark raving mad (colloq); **entre eux c'est l'amour ~** they're madly in love; **~ de qn** crazy about sb
(c) ‹*success*› huge; **un monde ~** a huge crowd; **avoir un mal ~ à faire** to find it incredibly difficult to do
(d) ‹*vehicle, horse*› runaway; ‹*lock of hair*› stray; **avoir le ~ rire** to have a fit of the giggles
2 *nm,f* madman/madwoman; **envoyer qn chez les ~s** (fam) to send sb to the nuthouse (colloq); **courir comme un ~** to run like mad; **c'est un ~ d'art contemporain** he's mad about contemporary art
3 *nm* **(a)** fool, court jester
(b) (in chess) bishop

IDIOMS **faire les ~s** (fam) to fool about; **plus on est de ~s plus on rit** (fam) the more the merrier

foudre /fudʀ/ *nf* lightning; **coup de ~** love at first sight; **avoir le coup de ~ pour** to be really taken with

foudroyant, ~e /fudʀwajɑ̃, ɑ̃t/ *adj* ‹*attack*› lightning; ‹*look*› furious; ‹*death*› sudden

foudroyer /fudʀwaje/ [23] *vtr* **(a)** to strike ‹*tree*›; **mort foudroyé** struck dead by lightning; **~ qn du regard** to look daggers at sb (colloq)
(b) ‹*bad news*› to devastate

fouet /fwɛ/ *nm* **(a)** whip; **dix coups de ~** ten lashes of the whip; **le grand air m'a donné un coup de ~** the fresh air invigorated me; **se heurter de plein ~** to collide head-on
(b) (Culin) whisk; **~ mécanique** hand whisk

fouetter /fwɛte/ [1] *vtr* **(a)** to whip, to flog ‹*person*›; to whip ‹*animal*›
(b) **la pluie leur fouettait le visage** the rain lashed their faces
IDIOMS **il n'y a pas de quoi ~ un chat** (fam) it's no big deal (colloq); **avoir d'autres chats à ~** (fam) to have other fish to fry

foufou, fofolle /fufu, fɔfɔl/ *adj* (fam) scatterbrained

fougère /fuʒɛʀ/ *nf* **(a)** fern
(b) bracken

fougue /fug/ *nf* enthusiasm

fougueusement /fugøzmɑ̃/ *adv* enthusiastically

fougueux, -euse /fugø, øz/ *adj* spirited; enthusiastic

fouille /fuj/ *nf* **(a)** (of place, person, baggage) search
(b) excavation

fouillé, ~e /fuje/ **1** *pp* ▶ FOUILLER
2 *pp adj* ‹*study, portrait, piece of work*› detailed; ‹*style*› elaborate

fouiller /fuje/ [1] **1** *vtr* **(a)** to search; to frisk
(b) to dig ‹*site*›
2 *vi* **~ dans** (gen) to rummage through; to search ‹*memory*›; to delve into ‹*past*›

fouillis /fuji/ *nm inv* mess; jumble

fouine /fwin/ *nf* (Zool) stone marten

fouiner /fwine/ [1] *vi* **(a)** to forage about
(b) **~ dans** to rummage through ‹*objects, papers*›; to poke one's nose into ‹*life, past*›

foulard /fulaʀ/ *nm* scarf, headscarf

✓ **foule** /ful/ *nf* **(a)** crowd; mob; **il y avait ~ à la réunion** there were masses of people at the meeting; **venir en ~ à** to flock to
(b) mass

foulée /fule/ *nf* (of horse, athlete) stride; **courir dans la ~ de qn** (Sport) to tail sb; **dans la ~ il a…** while he was at it, he…

fouler /fule/ [1] **1** *vtr* to tread ‹*grapes*›
2 **se fouler** *v refl* (+ *v être*) **(a)** (Med) **se ~** ⋯⋗

le poignet to sprain one's wrist

(b) (fam) **tu ne t'es pas foulé** you didn't kill yourself (colloq)

foulure /fulyʀ/ *nf* sprain

⚡ **four** /fuʀ/ *nm* **(a)** oven; **cuire au ∼** to roast, to bake

(b) furnace; kiln

■ **∼ crématoire** crematory (furnace); **∼ à micro-ondes** microwave oven

fourbu, ∼e /fuʀby/ *adj* exhausted

fourche /fuʀʃ/ *nf* fork; **faire une ∼** to fork

fourcher /fuʀʃe/ [1] *vi* **ma langue a fourché** it was a slip of the tongue

⚡ **fourchette** /fuʀʃɛt/ *nf* **(a)** fork

(b) (of prices, temperature) range; (of income) bracket; **∼ horaire** period

fourchu, ∼e /fuʀʃy/ *adj* ‹branch› forked; **cheveux ∼s** split ends

fourgon /fuʀɡɔ̃/ *nm* **(a)** van

(b) (of train) goods wagon (GB), freight car (US)

■ **∼ à bestiaux** cattle truck

fourgonnette /fuʀɡɔnɛt/ *nf* (small) van

fourguer /fuʀɡe/ (pop) [1] *vtr* to flog (colloq) (**à** to), to sell [sth] off (**à** to)

fourmi /fuʀmi/ *nf* (Zool) ant; **travail de ∼** laborious task

IDIOM **avoir des ∼s dans les jambes** to have pins and needles in one's legs

fourmilier /fuʀmilje/ *nm* anteater

fourmilière /fuʀmiljɛʀ/ *nf* ant hill

fourmillement /fuʀmijmɑ̃/ *nm* **(a)** **un ∼ de gens** a mass of people

(b) tingling sensation

fourmiller /fuʀmije/ [1] **1** **fourmiller de** *v+prep* to be chock-full of ‹mistakes›; to be swarming with ‹visitors›

2 *vi* to abound

fournaise /fuʀnɛz/ *nf* blaze; **la ville est une ∼ en été** the town is baking hot in summer

fourneau, *pl* **∼x** /fuʀno/ *nm* **(a)** (Tech) furnace

(b) stove

fournée /fuʀne/ *nf* batch

fourni, ∼e /fuʀni/ **1** *pp* ▶ FOURNIR

2 *pp adj* ‹hair› thick; ‹grass› lush

⚡ **fournir** /fuʀniʀ/ [3] **1** *vtr* to supply ‹document, equipment›; to provide ‹energy›; to contribute ‹effort›; to produce ‹proof›

2 **se fournir** *v refl* (+ *v être*) **se ∼ chez** *or* **auprès de** to get [sth] from

fournisseur, -euse /fuʀnisœʀ, øz/

1 *adj* **pays ∼** exporting country

2 *nm* supplier; **∼ de drogue** drug dealer

■ **∼ d'accès** (Comput) service provider

fourniture /fuʀnityʀ/ *nf* **(a)** supply, provision

(b) **∼s scolaires/de bureau** school/office stationery; **∼s de laboratoire** laboratory equipment

fourrage /fuʀaʒ/ *nm* forage; **∼ sec** fodder

fourré, ∼e /fuʀe/ **1** *pp* ▶ FOURRER

2 *pp adj* **(a)** (Culin) filled

(b) fur-lined; lined

(c) (fam) **toujours ∼ au café** always hanging about at the café

3 *nm* thicket

fourrer /fuʀe/ [1] **1** *vtr* **(a)** (fam) to stick (colloq); **∼ qch dans la tête de qn** to put sth into sb's head

(b) (Culin) to fill

(c) to line ‹garment›

2 **se fourrer** *v refl* (+ *v être*) (fam) **(a)** **se ∼ dans un coin** to get into a corner

(b) **se ∼ une idée dans la tête** to get an idea into one's head

fourre-tout /fuʀtu/ *adj inv* **sac ∼** holdall (GB), carryall (US)

fourreur /fuʀœʀ/ *nm* furrier

fourrière /fuʀjɛʀ/ *nf* pound; **mettre une voiture à la ∼** to impound a car

fourrure /fuʀyʀ/ *nf* fur, coat

fourvoyer: se fourvoyer /fuʀvwaje/ [23] *v refl* (+ *v être*) to make a mistake

foutoir /futwaʀ/ *nm* (pop) shambles (colloq); complete chaos

foutre /futʀ/ [6] (pop) **1** *vtr* **(a)** **n'en avoir rien à ∼** not to give a damn (colloq)

(b) **∼ qch quelque part** to stick sth somewhere (colloq)

2 **se foutre** *v refl* (+ *v être*) **(a)** **il ne s'est pas foutu de toi!** he's been very generous!; **se ∼ du monde** to have a bloody (GB) *or* hell of a (US) nerve (slang)

(b) not to give a damn (colloq)

IDIOM **∼ le camp** to bugger off (GB) (colloq), to split (US) (colloq)

foutu, ∼e /futy/ (pop) **1** *pp* ▶ FOUTRE

2 *pp adj* **(a)** *before n* bloody awful (GB) (slang), damned (US)

(b) **être ∼** ‹person, garment› to have had it (colloq)

(c) **être mal ∼** to be unattractive; to feel lousy (colloq)

(d) **être ∼ de faire** to be totally capable of doing

foyer /fwaje/ *nm* **(a)** home; **fonder un ∼** to get married

(b) (family) household

(c) hostel

(d) club

(e) (for fire) hearth

(f) (of resistance) pocket; **un ∼ d'incendie** a fire

(g) (of rebellion) seat; (of epidemic) source

(h) (in optics) focus; **lunettes à double ∼** bifocals

■ **∼ fiscal** household for tax purposes; **∼ de placement** foster home

---

⚡ indicates a very frequent word

fracas /fʀaka/ *nm inv* (of falling object) crash; (of waves) roar; (of town, battle) din

fracassant, **~e** /fʀakasɑ̃, ɑ̃t/ *adj* ‹noise› deafening; ‹news› sensational; ‹success› stunning

fracasser /fʀakase/ [1] **1** *vtr* to smash
2 **se fracasser** *v refl* (+ *v être*) to crash

fraction /fʀaksjɔ̃/ *nf* **(a)** (in mathematics) fraction
(b) (of sum of money) part; (of company) section; **en une ~ de seconde** in a split second

fractionnement /fʀaksjɔnmɑ̃/ *nm* division; fragmentation

fractionner /fʀaksjɔne/ [1] *vtr* to divide up ‹work, group›; to split ‹party›

fracture /fʀaktyʀ/ *nf* fracture; **~ du poignet** fractured wrist

fracturer /fʀaktyʀe/ [1] **1** *vtr* to break down ‹door›; to break ‹window›; to force ‹safe›
2 **se fracturer** *v refl* (+ *v être*) **se ~ la cheville** to break one's ankle

fragile /fʀaʒil/ *adj* **(a)** fragile
(b) ‹person› frail; ‹eye› sensitive; ‹heart› weak

fragiliser /fʀaʒilize/ [1] *vtr* to weaken

fragilité /fʀaʒilite/ *nf* **(a)** fragility
(b) frailty

fragment /fʀagmɑ̃/ *nm* **(a)** (of cup, bone) fragment
(b) (of book, novel) passage

fragmentaire /fʀagmɑ̃tɛʀ/ *adj* patchy; sketchy; sporadic

fragmentation /fʀagmɑ̃tasjɔ̃/ *nf*
(a) division; splitting up
(b) fragmentation

fragmenter /fʀagmɑ̃te/ [1] *vtr* to break up ‹substance›; to divide up ‹work›

fraîche ▸ FRAIS 5, 1

fraîchement /fʀɛʃmɑ̃/ *adv* **(a)** freshly, newly
(b) coldly; **elle a été ~ accueillie** she was given a cool reception

fraîcheur /fʀɛʃœʀ/ *nf* **(a)** coolness; coldness; **la ~ du soir** the cold evening air
(b) freshness

ᓯ **frais, fraîche** /fʀɛ, fʀɛʃ/ **1** *adj* **(a)** cool; cold; **'servir ~'** 'serve chilled'
(b) ‹news, snow› fresh; ‹paint› wet
(c) ‹complexion› fresh
(d) ‹troops› fresh; **de l'argent ~** more money
2 *adv* **il fait ~** it's cool
3 *nm* **prendre le ~** to get some fresh air; **mettre au ~** to put in a cool place; to put to cool
4 *nm pl* **(a)** expenses; **aux ~ de l'entreprise** paid for by the company; **rentrer dans ses ~** to cover one's expenses; **faire les ~ de qch** to bear the brunt of sth
(b) fees
(c) costs
5 **à la fraîche** *phr* in the cool of the

morning; in the cool of the evening
■ **~ d'annulation** cancellation fees; **~ de déplacement** (of employee) travel expenses; (for repairman) call-out charge; **~ divers** miscellaneous costs; **~ d'expédition** (for parcel) postage and packing; **~ de fonctionnement** running costs; **~ de garde** childminding fees; **~ d'inscription** (gen) registration fees; (for school) school fees (GB), tuition fees (US); (at university) tuition fees; **~ de port** postage; **~ professionnels** professional expenses; **~ de scolarité** tuition fees, school fees (GB)

fraise /fʀɛz/ *nf* **(a)** strawberry; **~ des bois** wild strawberry
(b) (tool, instrument) reamer; milling-cutter; (of dentist) drill
IDIOM ramener sa ~ (fam) to stick one's nose in (colloq)

fraiseur, -euse¹ /fʀɛzœʀ, øz/ *nm,f* cutter

fraiscuse² /fʀɛzøz/ *nf* milling machine

fraisier /fʀɛzje/ *nm* **(a)** strawberry plant
(b) strawberry gateau

framboise /fʀɑ̃bwaz/ *nf* **(a)** raspberry
(b) raspberry liqueur

framboisier /fʀɑ̃bwazje/ *nm* raspberry cane; raspberry bush

ᓯ **franc, franche** /fʀɑ̃, fʀɑ̃ʃ/ **1** *adj*
(a) ‹person› frank, straight; ‹reply› straight; ‹laughter, expression› open, honest; **jouer ~ jeu** to play fair
(b) duty-free; **~ de port** postage paid
2 *nm* (currency) franc; **~ lourd** (Hist) new franc

ᓯ **français, ~e** /fʀɑ̃sɛ, ɛz/ **1** *adj* French
2 *nm* (language) French

Français, ~e /fʀɑ̃sɛ, ɛz/ *nm,f* Frenchman/ Frenchwoman

France /fʀɑ̃s/ *pr nf* France

franche ▸ FRANC 1

franchement /fʀɑ̃ʃmɑ̃/ *adv* **(a)** frankly, candidly; **je lui ai demandé ~** I asked him straight out
(b) ‹lean› firmly; ‹enter› boldly
(c) really; **il m'a franchement agacé** he really annoyed me; **~!** (well) really!

ᓯ **franchir** /fʀɑ̃ʃiʀ/ [3] *vtr* to cross ‹line›; to get over ‹fence›; to cover ‹distance›

franchise /fʀɑ̃ʃiz/ *nf* **(a)** frankness, sincerity
(b) exemption
(c) (in insurance) excess (GB), deductible (US)
(d) (to sell goods) franchise
■ **~ de bagages** baggage allowance; **~ fiscale** tax exemption; **~ postale** 'postage paid'; **en ~ postale** post free

franchiser /fʀɑ̃ʃize/ [1] *vtr* to franchise

franchissement /fʀɑ̃ʃismɑ̃/ *nm* crossing; clearing; **~ de la ligne continue** crossing the white line

franciser /fʀɑ̃size/ [1] *vtr* to gallicize

franc-jeu /fʀɑ̃ʒø/ *nm* fair play

franc-maçon, -onne, *pl* **francsmaçons, franc-maçonnes** ⋯⋗

/fʁɑ̃masɔ̃, ɔn/ *nm,f* Freemason

franc-maçonnerie, *pl* ~s
/fʁɑ̃masɔnʁi/ *nf* la ~ Freemasonry

franco /fʁɑ̃ko/ *adv* (a) ~ de port postage
paid, carriage paid
(b) (fam) y aller ~ to go right ahead

francophone /fʁɑ̃kɔfɔn/ **1** *adj* French-
speaking; ‹literature› in the French language
2 *nmf* French speaker

francophonie /fʁɑ̃kɔfɔni/ *nf* French-
speaking world

franc-parler /fʁɑ̃paʁle/ *nm* avoir son ~ to
speak one's mind

frange /fʁɑ̃ʒ/ *nf* (a) (on rug, curtain, garment)
fringe
(b) (hair) fringe (GB), bangs (US)

frangin /fʁɑ̃ʒɛ̃/ *nm* (fam) brother

frangine /fʁɑ̃ʒin/ *nf* (fam) sister

franglais /fʁɑ̃ɡlɛ/ *nm* Franglais

franquette: à la bonne franquette
/alabɔnfʁɑ̃kɛt/ *phr* (fam) recevoir qn à la
bonne ~ to have sb over for an informal
meal

frappé, ~e /fʁape/ **1** *pp* ▸ FRAPPER
2 *pp adj* ‹cocktail› frappé; ‹coffee› iced

⚡ **frapper** /fʁape/ [1] **1** *vtr* (a) (gen) to hit, to
strike; ~ à coups de pied to kick; ~ à coups
de poing to punch; ~ un grand coup (gen) to
hit hard; (on door) to knock
(b) to strike ‹coin›
(c) ‹unemployment, epidemic› to hit ‹region›;
les taxes qui frappent les produits français
duties imposed on French goods
(d) ce qui m'a frappé c'est... what struck
me was...; j'ai été frappé de voir que... I was
amazed to see that...
2 *vi* (a) to hit, to strike; ~ dans ses mains
to clap one's hands
(b) to knock; on a frappé there was a knock
at the door
(c) ‹criminals› to strike

frasque /fʁask/ *nf* escapade

fraternel, -elle /fʁatɛʁnɛl/ *adj* fraternal,
brotherly

fraternellement /fʁatɛʁnɛlmɑ̃/ *adv* in a
brotherly fashion

fraternisation /fʁatɛʁnizasjɔ̃/ *nf*
fraternizing

fraterniser /fʁatɛʁnize/ [1] *vi* to fraternize

fraternité /fʁatɛʁnite/ *nf* fraternity

fraude /fʁod/ *nf* (Law) fraud; ~ fiscale tax
fraud; ~ électorale vote *or* election rigging;
en ~ ‹enter› illegally

frauder /fʁode/ [1] *vi* (on public transport) to
travel without a ticket; (in cinema) to slip in
without paying

fraudeur, -euse /fʁodœʁ, øz/ *nm,f*
swindler; tax evader; cheat

⚡ indicates a very frequent word

frauduleux, -euse /fʁodylø, øz/ *adj*
fraudulent

frayer /fʁɛje/ [21] **1** *vtr* ~ un passage à
qn à travers la foule to clear a path for sb
through the crowd; ~ le chemin *or* la voie à
qch (figurative) to pave the way for sth
2 se frayer *v refl* (+ *v être*) se ~ un
chemin dans *or* à travers to make one's way
through

frayeur /fʁɛjœʁ/ *nf* (a) fear
(b) fright

fredonner /fʁədɔne/ [1] *vtr* to hum

free-lance /fʁilɑ̃s/ *nmf* freelance,
freelancer; travailler en ~ to work freelance
or as a freelancer

freezer /fʁizœʁ/ *nm* icebox

frégate /fʁegat/ *nf* (Naut) frigate

frein /fʁɛ̃/ *nm* brake; donner un coup de ~
to slam on the brakes; mettre un ~ à to curb
IDIOM ronger son ~ to champ at the bit

freinage /fʁɛnaʒ/ *nm* braking

freiner /fʁɛne/ [1] **1** *vtr* (a) to slow down
‹vehicle›
(b) to impede ‹person›
(c) to curb ‹inflation›
2 *vi* (a) to brake; ~ à fond to slam on the
brakes
(b) (in skiing) to slow down

frelaté, ~e /fʁəlate/ *adj* ‹alcohol›
adulterated; ‹taste› unnatural

frêle /fʁɛl/ *adj* frail

frelon /fʁəlɔ̃/ *nm* hornet

frémir /fʁemiʁ/ [3] *vi* (a) ‹leaf› to quiver;
‹water› to ripple
(b) (with emotion) ‹lip› to tremble; ‹person› to
quiver; to shudder
(c) (Culin) to start to come to the boil

frémissant, ~e /fʁemisɑ̃, ɑ̃t/ *adj* faire
cuire dans l'eau ~e simmer gently in water

frémissement /fʁemismɑ̃/ *nm* (a) quiver,
tremor
(b) (of person, hand) quiver, shudder

frêne /fʁɛn/ *nm* ash (tree)

frénésie /fʁenezi/ *nf* frenzy

frénétique /fʁenetik/ *adj* frenzied;
frenetic

frénétiquement /fʁenetikmɑ̃/ *adv* ‹fight›
frantically; ‹dance› frenziedly; ‹applaud›
wildly

fréquemment /fʁekamɑ̃/ *adv* frequently

fréquence /fʁekɑ̃s/ *nf* frequency

fréquent, ~e /fʁekɑ̃, ɑ̃t/ *adj* (a) frequent
(b) common

fréquentable /fʁekɑ̃tabl/ *adj* respectable;
ce ne sont pas des gens ~s they are not the
sort of people one should associate with

fréquentation /fʁekɑ̃tasjɔ̃/ *nf*
(a) company; avoir de bonnes/mauvaises
~s to keep good/bad company
(b) ~ des théâtres theatregoing (GB)

fréquenté, ~e /fʀekɑ̃te/ [1] *pp*
▶ FRÉQUENTER
[2] *pp adj* popular, busy; **lieu bien ~** place
that attracts the right sort of people

fréquenter /fʀekɑ̃te/ [1] [1] *vtr* **(a)** to
associate with ‹person›; to move in ‹milieu›
(b) to attend ‹school›; to go to ‹restaurant›
[2] **se fréquenter** *v refl* (+ *v être*) ‹friends›
to see one another

◆ **frère** /fʀɛʀ/ *nm* brother

fresque /fʀɛsk/ *nf* **(a)** fresco
(b) panorama

fret /fʀɛt/ *nm* freight

frétiller /fʀetije/ [1] *vi* ‹fish› to wriggle; **~**
de la queue ‹dog› to wag its tail

freudien, -ienne /fʀødjɛ̃, ɛn/ *adj, nm,f*
Freudian

friable /fʀijabl/ *adj* ‹rock, biscuit› crumbly

friand, ~e /fʀijɑ̃, ɑ̃d/ [1] *adj* **être ~ de qch**
to be very fond of sth
[2] *nm* (Culin) puff; **~ au fromage** cheese
puff

friandise /fʀijɑ̃diz/ *nf* sweet (GB), candy
(US)

fric /fʀik/ *nm* (fam) dough (colloq), money

friche /fʀiʃ/ *nf* waste land

friction /fʀiksjɔ̃/ *nf* **(a)** (Med) rub
(b) friction

frictionner /fʀiksjɔne/ [1] [1] *vtr* to give
[sb] a rub ‹person›, to rub ‹head, feet›
[2] **se frictionner** *v refl* (+ *v être*) to rub
oneself down

frigidaire® /fʀiʒidɛʀ/ *nm* refrigerator

frigide /fʀiʒid/ *adj* frigid

frigo /fʀigo/ *nm* (fam) fridge (colloq)

frigorifique /fʀigɔʀifik/ *adj* refrigerated

frileux, -euse /fʀilø, øz/ *adj* **(a)** sensitive
to the cold
(b) ‹attitude, policy› cautious

frimas /fʀima/ *nm pl* cold weather

frime /fʀim/ *nf* (fam) **pour la ~** for show;
c'est de la ~ it's all an act

frimer /fʀime/ [1] *vi* (fam) to show off (colloq)

frimousse /fʀimus/ *nf* (fam) little face

fringale /fʀɛ̃gal/ *nf* (fam) **j'ai la ~** I'm
absolutely starving (colloq)

fringuer: se fringuer /fʀɛ̃ge/ [1] *v refl*
(+ *v être*) (fam) to dress

friper /fʀipe/ [1] *vtr* **se friper** *v refl* (+ *v*
être) to crease, to crumple

fripon, -onne /fʀipɔ̃, ɔn/ *nm,f* (fam) rascal

fripouille /fʀipuj/ *nf* (fam) crook (colloq)

frire /fʀiʀ/ [64] *vtr, vi* to fry

frisé, ~e¹ /fʀize/ [1] *pp* ▶ FRISER
[2] *pp adj* ‹hair› curly; ‹person› curly-haired

frisée² /fʀize/ *nf* curly endive

friser /fʀize/ [1] [1] *vtr* **(a)** to curl; **se faire**
~ to have one's hair curled
(b) to border on; **cela frise les 10%** it's
approaching 10%

[2] *vi* to curl; ‹person› to have curly hair

frisson /fʀisɔ̃/ *nm* shiver, shudder; **j'ai des**
~s I keep shivering; **grand ~** great thrill

frissonner /fʀisɔne/ [1] *vi* **(a)** (with cold) to
shiver; (with fear) to shudder
(b) ‹leaves› to tremble
(c) ‹water, milk› to simmer

frit /fʀi/ ▶ FRIRE

frite /fʀit/ *nf* (Culin) chip (GB), French fry
(US)

friterie /fʀitʀi/ *nf* chip shop (GB), French-
fries stall (US)

friteuse /fʀitøz/ *nf* deep fat fryer, chip
pan (GB)

friture /fʀityʀ/ *nf* **(a)** frying
(b) (for frying) fat; oil
(c) fried food
(d) (fish) **petite ~** ≈ whitebait
(e) (on radio) crackling

frivole /fʀivɔl/ *adj* frivolous

◆ **froid, ~e** /fʀwa, fʀwad/ [1] *adj* cold;
(figurative) cold, cool
[2] *adv* **il fait ~** it's cold
[3] *nm* **(a)** cold; **coup de ~** chill; **prendre ~**
to catch a cold
(b) coldness; **ils sont en ~ avec moi**
relations between them and me are strained;
jeter un ~ to cast a chill
[4] **à froid** *phr* **démarrage à ~** cold start
IDIOMS **il fait un ~ de canard** (fam) it is
bitterly cold; **donner ~ dans le dos** to send
a shiver down the spine; **ne pas avoir ~ aux**
yeux to be fearless

froidement /fʀwadmɑ̃/ *adv* **(a)** coolly;
abattre ~ to shoot [sb] down in cold blood
(b) **regarder les choses ~** to look at things
with a cool head

froideur /fʀwadœʀ/ *nf* (gen) coldness; (of
reception) coolness

froissement /fʀwasmɑ̃/ *nm* **(a)** (of paper,
fabric) crumpling; (noise) rustling
(b) (Med) strain

froisser /fʀwase/ [1] [1] *vtr* **(a)** to crease
‹fabric›; to crumple ‹paper›
(b) to offend ‹person›
(c) (Med) to strain
[2] **se froisser** *v refl* (+ *v être*) **(a)** to
crease
(b) to be hurt *or* offended
(c) (Med) to strain

frôlement /fʀolmɑ̃/ *nm* **(a)** brushing
(b) rustling; fluttering

frôler /fʀole/ [1] [1] *vtr* **(a)** ‹person› to brush
(against)
(b) ‹bullet, car› to miss narrowly; **il a frôlé la**
mort he came close to dying
[2] **se frôler** *v refl* (+ *v être*) ‹people› to
brush against each other

◆ **fromage** /fʀɔmaʒ/ *nm* cheese; **~ maigre**
low-fat cheese; **~ de tête** brawn (GB), head
cheese (US)

fromager /fʀɔmaʒe/ *nm* **(a)** cheesemaker ···⊱

(b) cheese seller

fromagerie /fʀɔmaʒʀi/ *nf* cheese shop

froment /fʀɔmɑ̃/ *nm* wheat

froncement /fʀɔ̃smɑ̃/ *nm* avoir un léger ~ de sourcils to frown slightly

froncer /fʀɔ̃se/ [12] *vtr* (a) to gather ‹pleats›
(b) ~ les sourcils to frown

fronde /fʀɔ̃d/ *nf* (a) (weapon) sling
(b) (toy) catapult (GB), slingshot (US)
(c) revolt

frondeur, -euse /fʀɔ̃dœʀ, øz/ *adj* rebellious

⚜ **front** /fʀɔ̃/ ① *nm* (a) forehead
(b) (Mil) front
(c) façade
② **de front** *phr* ils marchaient à quatre de ~ they were walking four abreast; **mener plusieurs tâches de** ~ to have several jobs on the go
IDIOM avoir le ~ **de faire** to have the face *or* effrontery to do

frontal, ~e, *mpl* **-aux** /fʀɔ̃tal, o/ *adj* ‹attack› frontal; ‹collision› head-on

frontalier, -ière /fʀɔ̃talje, ɛʀ/ ① *adj* border; **travailleur** ~ person who works across the border
② *nm,f* person living near the border

⚜ **frontière** /fʀɔ̃tjɛʀ/ *nf* (a) frontier, border; ~ **naturelle** natural boundary
(b) ~s **entre les disciplines** boundaries between disciplines

fronton /fʀɔ̃tɔ̃/ *nm* pediment

frottement /fʀɔtmɑ̃/ *nm* (a) rubbing
(b) friction

frotter /fʀɔte/ [1] ① *vtr* (a) to rub
② *vi* to rub
③ **se frotter** *v refl* (+ *v être*) (a) se ~ les yeux to rub one's eyes
(b) to scrub oneself
(c) se ~ à to take on ‹person›
IDIOM qui s'y frotte s'y pique if you go looking for trouble, you'll find it

frottis /fʀɔti/ *nm inv* (Med) smear

froussard, ~e /fʀusaʀ, aʀd/ *nm,f* (fam) chicken (colloq), coward

frousse /fʀus/ *nf* (fam) fright

fructifier /fʀyktifje/ [2] *vi* ‹capital› to yield a profit; ‹business› to flourish

fructueux, -euse /fʀyktɥø, øz/ *adj*
(a) ‹relationship, meeting› fruitful; ‹attempt, career› successful
(b) (financially) profitable

frugal, ~e, *mpl* **-aux** /fʀygal, o/ *adj* frugal

⚜ **fruit** /fʀɥi/ *nm* fruit
■ ~ **de la passion** passion fruit; ~ **sec** dried fruit; ~s **de mer** seafood

fruité, ~e /fʀɥite/ *adj* ‹alcohol, aroma› fruity

fruitier, -ière /fʀɥitje, ɛʀ/ ① *adj* fruit
② *nm,f* fruiterer (GB), fruit seller (US)

fruste /fʀyst/ *adj* unsophisticated

frustrant, ~e /fʀystʀɑ̃, ɑ̃t/ *adj* frustrating

frustré, ~e /fʀystʀe/ *adj* frustrated

frustrer /fʀystʀe/ [1] *vtr* (a) ~ qn to thwart sb
(b) ~ qn de qch to deprive sb of sth; to cheat sb (out) of sth
(c) to frustrate

fuel /fjul/ *nm* ▶ FIOUL

fugace /fygas/ *adj* fleeting; ‹symptom› elusive

fugitif, -ive /fyʒitif, iv/ ① *adj*
(a) ‹prisoner› escaped
(b) fleeting, elusive
② *nm,f* fugitive

fugue /fyg/ *nf* (a) **faire une** ~ to run away
(b) (Mus) fugue

fugueur, -euse /fygœʀ, øz/ *nm,f* runaway (child)

fui, ~e /fɥi/ ▶ FUIR

⚜ **fuir** /fɥiʀ/ [29] ① *vtr* (a) to flee ‹country, oppression›
(b) to avoid ‹discussion, person›; to steer clear of ‹crowd›; to stay out of ‹sun›
② *vi* (a) ‹person› to flee; ‹animal› to run away; **faire** ~ to scare [sb] off ‹person›
(b) ‹tap, gas, pen› to leak
(c) ~ **devant ses responsabilités** not to face up to one's responsibilities

fuite /fɥit/ *nf* (a) (gen) flight; (of prisoner) escape; **prendre la** ~ to flee; to escape
(b) (of information) leak
(c) (of liquid, gas) leak

fulgurant, ~e /fylgyʀɑ̃, ɑ̃t/ *adj* ‹attack› lightning; ‹progression› dazzling; ‹imagination› brilliant

fulminer /fylmine/ [1] *vi* to fulminate

fumé, ~e¹ /fyme/ ① *pp* ▶ FUMER
② *pp adj* (a) (Culin) smoked
(b) ‹lenses› tinted; ‹glass› smoked

⚜ **fumée²** /fyme/ *nf* (a) smoke; ~s (from factory) fumes; **partir en** ~ (figurative) to go up in smoke
(b) steam

⚜ **fumer** /fyme/ [1] ① *vtr* to smoke
② *vi* (a) ‹person, chimney› to smoke
(b) ‹soup› to steam; ‹acid› to give off fumes
IDIOM ~ **comme un pompier** *or* **sapeur** to smoke like a chimney

fûmes /fym/ ▶ ÊTRE¹

fumet /fymɛ/ *nm* (Culin) (of meat) aroma; (of wine) bouquet

fumeur, -euse¹ /fymœʀ, øz/ *nm,f* smoker; **zone non** ~s non-smoking area

fumeux, -euse² /fymø, øz/ *adj* ‹theory, ideas› woolly (GB), woolly (US)

fumier /fymje/ *nm* manure

fumigène /fymiʒɛn/ *adj* **grenade** ~ smoke grenade

⚜ indicates a very frequent word

fumiste /fymist/ *nm,f* (fam) (a) shirker
(b) phoney (colloq)
fumisterie /fymistəri/ *nf* (a) (fam) joke;
c'est de la ∼ it's a joke
(b) chimney engineering; stove fitting
fumoir /fymwar/ *nm* smoking-room
funambule /fynãbyl/ *nmf* tightrope
walker
funèbre /fynɛbr/ *adj* (a) cérémonie/service
∼ funeral ceremony/service
(b) gloomy
funérailles /fyneraj/ *nf pl* funeral
funéraire /fynerer/ *adj* ‹ceremony›
funeral; ‹monument› funerary
funeste /fynɛst/ *adj* fatal; fateful
funiculaire /fynikylɛr/ *nm* funicular
fur: au fur et à mesure /ofyreaməzyr/
phr as one goes along; le chemin se
rétrécissait au ∼ et à mesure qu'on avançait
the path grew progressively narrower as we
went along
furent /fyr/ ▶ ÊTRE[1]
furet /fyrɛ/ *nm* ferret
fureter /fyrte/ [18] *vi* to rummage
fureur /fyrœr/ *nf* (a) rage, fury
(b) frenzy; avec ∼ frenziedly; ce sport fait
∼ en ce moment that sport is all the rage at
the moment
furibond, ∼e /fyribɔ̃, ɔ̃d/ *adj* furious
furie /fyri/ *nf* rage, fury
furieusement /fyrjøzmã/ *adv*
(a) furiously, violently
(b) (fam) j'ai ∼ envie de dormir I'm dying to
go to sleep
furieux, -ieuse /fyrjø, øz/ *adj* (a) furious,
angry
(b) (fam) ‹desire› terrible
(c) ‹battle› intense
furoncle /fyrɔ̃kl/ *nm* boil
furtif, -ive /fyrtif, iv/ *adj* (a) furtive;
marcher d'un pas ∼ to creep along
(b) fleeting
furtivement /fyrtivmã/ *adv* furtively
fus /fy/ ▶ ÊTRE[1]
fusain /fyzɛ̃/ *nm* charcoal crayon; charcoal
drawing
fuseau, *pl* ∼x /fyzo/ *nm* (a) spindle; en ∼
tapering
(b) ski pants

(c) ∼ horaire time zone
fusée /fyze/ *nf* (a) rocket
(b) (Aut) stub axle
fuselage /fyzlaʒ/ *nm* fuselage
fuselé, ∼e /fyzle/ *adj* tapering, spindle-
shaped
fuser /fyze/ [1] *vi* to ring out; les rires
fusaient laughter came from all sides
fusible /fyzibl/ *nm* fuse
fusil /fyzi/ *nm* (a) gun, shotgun; (Mil) rifle
(b) sharpening steel
(c) gas igniter
fusillade /fyzijad/ *nf* (a) gunfire
(b) shoot-out
fusiller /fyzije/ [1] *vtr* (a) to shoot
(b) (fam) to wreck
IDIOM ∼ qn du regard to look daggers at sb
fusil-mitrailleur, *pl* **fusils-
mitrailleurs** /fyzimitrajœr/ *nm* light
machine gun
fusion /fyzjɔ̃/ *nf* (a) (of metal, ice) melting;
roche en ∼ molten rock
(b) (in biology, physics) fusion
(c) (of companies, parties) merger; (of systems,
cultures) fusion; (of peoples) mixing
fusionner /fyzjone/ [1] *vtr, vi* to merge
fusse /fys/ ▶ ÊTRE[1]
fussent /fys/ ▶ ÊTRE[1]
fusses /fys/ ▶ ÊTRE[1]
fussiez /fysje/ ▶ ÊTRE[1]
fussions /fysjɔ̃/ ▶ ÊTRE[1]
fut /fy/ ▶ ÊTRE[1]
fût[1] /fy/ ▶ ÊTRE[1]
fût[2] /fy/ *nm* cask, barrel; drum
futaie /fytɛ/ *nf* forest of tall trees
futé, ∼e /fyte/ [1] *adj* wily, crafty; ce n'est
pas très ∼ that isn't or wasn't very clever
[2] *nm,f* (petit) ∼ cunning little devil
fûtes /fyt/ ▶ ÊTRE[1]
futile /fytil/ *adj* trivial; superficial
futilité /fytilite/ [1] *nf* superficiality
[2] **futilités** *nf pl* (a) banalities
(b) trifles; trifling activities
(c) trivial details
✓ **futur, ∼e** /fytyr/ [1] *adj* future; mon ∼
mari my husband-to-be
[2] *nm* future
fuyant, ∼e /fɥijã, ãt/ *adj* ‹look› shifty
fuyard, ∼e /fɥijar, ard/ *nm,f* runaway

G g

g, G /ʒe/ *nm inv* **(a)** (letter) g, G
  (b) (*written abbr* = **gramme**) 250 g 250 g
gabarit /gabaʀi/ *nm* **(a)** (of vehicle) size
  (b) (fam) (of person) calibre (GB); (physical)
build
gabonais, ~e /gabɔnɛ, ɛz/ *adj* Gabonese
gâcher /gaʃe/ [1] *vtr* **(a)** to waste ‹*food,
talent*›; to throw away ‹*life*›
  (b) to spoil ‹*party*›
gâchette /gaʃɛt/ *nf* **(a)** (of gun) tumbler
  (b) (controversial) trigger
  (c) (on lock) tumbler
gâchis /gaʃi/ *nm inv* **(a)** waste
  (b) mess
gadget /gadʒɛt/ *nm* gadget
gadin /gadɛ̃/ *nm* (fam) **ramasser** *or* **prendre
un ~** to fall flat on one's face
gadoue /gadu/ *nf* (fam) mud
gaélique /gaelik/ *adj, nm* Gaelic
gaffe /gaf/ *nf* (fam) **(a)** blunder; **faire une ~**
to make a blunder
  (b) faire ~ to watch out
gag /gag/ *nm* **(a)** (in film, show) gag
  (b) joke
gaga /gaga/ *adj inv* (fam) **(a)** gaga (colloq)
  (b) silly
gage /gaʒ/ **1** *nm* **(a)** security; **mettre qch
en ~** to pawn sth; **être le ~ de qch** to be a
guarantee of sth
  (b) (Games) forfeit
  (c) pledge
  2 gages (dated) *nm pl* wages; **tueur à ~s**
hired killer
gager /gaʒe/ [13] *vtr* **~ que** to suppose that,
to wager that
gageure /gaʒyʀ/ *nf* challenge
gagnant, ~e /gaɲɑ̃, ɑ̃t/ **1** *adj* winning
  2 *nm,f* winner; winning horse; winning
ticket
gagne-pain /gaɲpɛ̃/ *nm inv* livelihood
gagne-petit /gaɲpəti/ *nmf inv* low-wage
earner
⚔ **gagner** /gaɲe/ [1] **1** *vtr* **(a)** to win; **~
d'une longueur** to win by a length; **c'est
gagné!** we've done it!; **à tous les coups on
gagne!** every one a winner!
  (b) to earn; **il gagne bien sa vie** he makes a
good living
  (c) to gain ‹*reputation, advantage, time*›; **~
de la vitesse** to gather speed
  (d) to save ‹*time*›; **~ de la place en faisant** to
make more room by doing

(e) to win [sb] over
  (f) to reach ‹*place*›
  (g) ‹*blaze, disease*› to spread to ‹*place*›
  (h) ‹*fear*› to overcome
  (i) to beat [sb]; **~ qn de vitesse** to outstrip sb
  2 *vi* **(a)** to win
  **(b) le film gagne à être vu en version
originale** the film is best seen in the original
version
  (c) to gain
  (d) y ~ to come off better; **y ~ en** to gain in
‹*comfort*›
  (e) ‹*sea*› to encroach
gagneur, -euse /gaɲœʀ, øz/ *nm,f* winner
gai, ~e /gɛ/ *adj* **(a)** ‹*person*› happy; ‹*smile,
expression*› cheerful; ‹*conversation*› light-
hearted
  (b) (ironic) **c'est ~** great!
  (c) merry, tipsy
gaiement /gɛmɑ̃/ *adv* **(a)** cheerfully,
merrily; gaily
  (b) (ironic) happily
gaieté /gete/ *nf* gaiety, cheerfulness
gaillard, ~e /gajaʀ, aʀd/ *nm,f* strapping
lad/girl
gain /gɛ̃/ *nm* **(a)** earnings; **mes ~s au jeu**
my winnings
  (b) (on stock exchange) gain
  (c) saving; **c'est un ~ de temps considérable**
it saves a considerable amount of time
gaine /gɛn/ *nf* **(a)** (for dagger) sheath
  (b) girdle
  (c) (Tech) sheathing; casing
  (d) (Bot) sheath
gainer /gene/ [1] *vtr* to sheathe
gala /gala/ *nm* gala
galamment /galamɑ̃/ *adv* gallantly
galant, ~e /galɑ̃, ɑ̃t/ *adj* **(a)** gallant,
gentlemanly
  (b) romantic
galanterie /galɑ̃tʀi/ *nf* gallantry
galaxie /galaksi/ *nf* galaxy
galbe /galb/ *nm* curve
galbé, ~e /galbe/ *adj* shapely
gale /gal/ *nf* **(a)** scabies
  (b) (on dog, cat) mange; (on sheep) scab
  (c) (Bot) scab
galère /galɛʀ/ *nf* **(a)** galley
  (b) (fam) hell (colloq)
  IDIOM être dans la même ~ to be in the
same boat
galérer /galeʀe/ [14] *vi* (fam) to have a hard
time
galerie /galʀi/ *nf* **(a)** gallery

⚔ indicates a very frequent word

(b) tunnel

■ ~ **marchande** shopping arcade; ~ **de toit** roof rack; **Galerie des Glaces** hall of mirrors
IDIOMS amuser la ~ (fam) to play to the gallery; **pour épater la** ~ (fam) to impress the crowd

galet /galɛ/ *nm* **(a)** pebble
(b) (Tech) roller

galette /galɛt/ *nf* **(a)** round flat biscuit (GB), cookie (US)
(b) pancake
■ ~ **des Rois** Twelfth Night cake

Galles /gal/ *pr nf pl* **le pays de** ~ Wales

gallois, ~**e** /galwɑ, az/ **1** *adj* Welsh
2 *nm* (language) Welsh

Gallois, ~**e** /galwɑ, az/ *nm,f* Welshman/ Welshwoman; **les** ~ the Welsh

gallon /galɔ̃/ *nm* gallon

galoche /galɔʃ/ *nf* clog; **menton en** ~ protruding chin

galon /galɔ̃/ *nm* **(a)** (for trimming) braid
(b) (Mil) stripe; **prendre du** ~ to be promoted

galop /galo/ *nm* **(a)** gallop; **petit** ~ canter; **grand** ~ full gallop; **au** ~! (figurative) hurry up!
(b) (Mus) galop
IDIOM chassez le naturel il revient au ~ (Proverb) what's bred in the bone will come out in the flesh

galopade /galopad/ *nf* **(a)** gallop
(b) (fam) (figurative) stampede

galoper /galɔpe/ **1** *vi* **(a)** to gallop
(b) (fam) ‹child› to charge (around)

galopin /galɔpɛ̃/ *nm* rascal

galvaniser /galvanize/ **1** *vtr* (literal and figurative) to galvanize

gamba /gɑ̃ba, *pl* -as/ *nf* large (Mediterranean) prawn

gambader /gɑ̃bade/ **1** *vi* to gambol

gamelle /gamɛl/ *nf* (of soldier) dixie (GB), mess kit; (of camper) billycan (GB), tin dish; (of worker) lunchbox; (for pet) dish
IDIOM prendre une ~ (fam) to fall flat on one's face (colloq); (figurative) to come a cropper

gamin, ~**e** /gamɛ̃, in/ **1** *adj* ‹air, look› youthful; ‹attitude› childish
2 *nm,f* kid (colloq); ~ **des rues** street urchin

gaminerie /gaminri/ *nf* childish behaviour

gamme /gam/ *nf* **(a)** (Mus) scale
(b) range; **produit (de) bas de** ~ low quality product; **cheap product** ~ **de produits** product range

gammée /game/ *adj f* **croix** ~ swastika

ganglion /gɑ̃glijɔ̃/ *nm* ganglion

gangrène /gɑ̃gʁɛn/ *nf* **(a)** (Med) gangrene
(b) (figurative) canker

gangrener /gɑ̃gʁəne/ [16] **1** *vtr* to corrupt

2 se gangrener *v refl* (+ *v être*) **(a)** (Med) to become gangrenous
(b) (figurative) to become corrupt

gangster /gɑ̃gstɛʁ/ *nm* **(a)** gangster
(b) swindler

gant /gɑ̃/ *nm* glove
■ ~ **de boxe** boxing glove; ~ **de ménage** rubber glove; ~ **de toilette** ≈ (face) flannel (GB), wash cloth (US)
IDIOMS son tailleur lui va comme un ~ her suit fits her like a glove; **mettre** *or* **prendre des** ~**s avec qn** to handle sb with kid gloves

⚘ **garage** /gaʁaʒ/ *nm* **(a)** garage
(b) garage, filling station
■ ~ **à vélos** bicycle shed

garagiste /gaʁaʒist/ *nmf* **(a)** garage owner
(b) car mechanic

garant, ~**e** /gaʁɑ̃, ɑ̃t/ **1** *adj* **être** *or* **se porter** ~ **de qn/qch** to vouch for sb/sth
2 *nm,f* guarantor

garanti, ~**e**[1] /gaʁɑ̃ti/ **1** *pp* ▶ GARANTIR
2 *adj* **(a)** with a guarantee
(b) guaranteed

garantie[2] /gaʁɑ̃ti/ *nf* **(a)** (gen, Law) guarantee
(b) (in finance) security; guarantee
(c) (in insurance) cover; **montant des** ~**s** sum insured

⚘ **garantir** /gaʁɑ̃tiʁ/ [3] *vtr* **(a)** to guarantee; ~ **qch à qn** to guarantee sb sth
(b) to safeguard ‹security›
(c) to guarantee ‹loan, product›

⚘ **garçon** /gaʁsɔ̃/ *nm* **(a)** boy
(b) young man; **un brave** *or* **gentil** ~ a nice chap (GB) *or* guy (US)
(c) bachelor
(d) ~ **(de café)** waiter
■ ~ **d'écurie** stableboy; ~ **d'honneur** best man; ~ **manqué** tomboy

garçonnet /gaʁsɔnɛ/ *nm* little boy

garçonnière /gaʁsɔnjɛʁ/ *nf* bachelor flat (GB) *or* apartment

⚘ **garde**[1] /gaʁd/ *nm* **(a)** guard
(b) (for invalid, patient) carer; (in prison) warder
■ ~ **champêtre** ≈ local policeman (*appointed by the municipality*); ~ **du corps** bodyguard; ~ **forestier** forest warden; **Garde des Sceaux** French Minister of Justice

garde[2] /gaʁd/ *nf* **(a)** nurse
(b) (gen, Mil, Sport) guard; **la vieille** ~ the old guard; **monter la** ~ ‹soldier› to mount guard; **monter la** ~ **auprès de qn** to keep watch over sb; to stand guard over sb; **être de** ~ ‹doctor› to be on call; ‹soldier› to be on guard duty
(c) **mettre qn en** ~ to warn sb; **prendre** ~ to watch out; to be careful
(d) (of sword) hilt
(e) (page de) ~ endpaper
■ ~ **à vue** (Law) ≈ police custody

garde-à-vous /gaʁdavu/ *nm inv* **se mettre au** ~ to stand to attention

garde-chasse, *pl* **gardes-chasses**
/gaʁdəʃas/ *nm* game warden; gamekeeper

garde-côte, *pl* ∼s /gaʁdəkot/ *nm*
coastguard ship

garde-fou, *pl* ∼s /gaʁdəfu/ *nm* **(a)** parapet
(b) safeguard

garde-malade, *pl* **gardes-malades**
/gaʁdmalad/ *nmf* home nurse

garde-manger /gaʁdmãʒe/ *nm inv* meat
safe

⚜ **garder** /gaʁde/ [1] **1** *vtr* **(a)** to keep
‹object›; to keep on ‹hat, sweater›; to keep on
‹employee›
(b) ‹soldier› to guard; ‹person› to look after
2 **se garder** *v refl* (+ *v être*) **(a)** se ∼ de
faire to be careful not to do
(b) ‹foodstuff› to keep

garderie /gaʁdəʁi/ *nf* **(a)** day nursery
(b) after-school child-minding facility

garde-robe, *pl* ∼s /gaʁdəʁɔb/ *nf*
wardrobe

gardien, -ienne[1] /gaʁdjɛ̃, ɛn/ *nm,f* **(a)** (in
premises) security guard; (in apartment block)
caretaker (GB), janitor (US); (in park) keeper;
(in prison) warder; (in museum) attendant
(b) (Sport) keeper
■ ∼ **de but** goalkeeper; ∼ **de nuit** night watchman; ∼ **de la paix** police officer

gardiennage /gaʁdjɛnaʒ/ *nm* (of premises)
security; (of apartment block) caretaking

gardienne[2] /gaʁdjɛn/ *nf* **(a)** ▶ GARDIEN
(b) ∼ **(d'enfant)** childminder (GB), day-care
lady (US)

gardon /gaʁdɔ̃/ *nm* roach
IDIOM **être frais comme un** ∼ to be as fresh
as a daisy

gare /gaʁ/ **1** *nf* (railway) station
2 *excl* ∼ **(à toi)!** (threat) careful!, watch it!
(colloq)
■ ∼ **maritime** harbour (GB) station; ∼ **de péage** toll plaza; ∼ **routière** coach station (GB),
bus station (US)
IDIOM **sans crier** ∼ without any warning

garenne /gaʁɛn/ *nf* (rabbit) warren

garer /gaʁe/ [1] *vtr* to park
2 **se garer** *v refl* (+ *v être*) **(a)** to park
(b) ‹vehicle› to pull over

gargariser: se gargariser
/gaʁgaʁize/ [1] *v refl* (+ *v être*) to gargle

gargarisme /gaʁgaʁism/ *nm* **(a)** gargling
(b) mouthwash

gargouille /gaʁguj/ *nf* **(a)** gargoyle
(b) waterspout

gargouiller /gaʁguje/ [1] *vi* ‹water,
fountain› to gurgle; ‹stomach› to rumble

garnement /gaʁnəmã/ *nm* brat (colloq)

garni, ∼e /gaʁni/ **1** *pp* ▶ GARNIR
2 *adj* **bien** ∼ ‹wallet› full; ‹fridge› well-
stocked; ‹buffet› copious

⚜ indicates a very frequent word

garnir /gaʁniʁ/ [3] *vtr* **(a)** ‹objects› to fill
‹room›; ‹person› to stock ‹shelves›
(b) ‹cushion›
(c) (Culin) to decorate ‹cake›; to garnish
‹meat›

garnison /gaʁnizɔ̃/ *nf* garrison

garniture /gaʁnityʁ/ *nf* **(a)** (Culin) side
dish; (for dessert) decoration; (for meat, fish)
garnish
(b) (on hat, garment) trimming
■ ∼ **de cheminée** mantelpiece ornaments

garrigue /gaʁig/ *nf* garrigue, scrubland (*in
southern France*)

garrot /gaʁo/ *nm* **(a)** (Med) tourniquet
(b) (Zool) withers; **le cheval mesure 1,50 m au**
∼ ≈ the horse is 15 hands

gars /ga/ *nm inv* (fam) **(a)** boy
(b) chap (GB) (colloq), guy (US) (colloq)

Gascogne /gaskɔɲ/ *pr nf* Gascony

Gascon, -onne /gaskɔ̃, ɔn/ *nm,f* Gascon
IDIOM **faire une offre de** ∼ to raise false
hopes

gas-oil /gazwal/ *nm* diesel (GB), fuel oil (US)

gaspillage /gaspijaʒ/ *nm* **(a)** wasting;
waste
(b) squandering

gaspiller /gaspije/ [1] *vtr* **(a)** to waste
‹time, food›
(b) to squander ‹resources, talent›

gastronome /gastʁɔnɔm/ *nmf* gourmet,
gastronome

gastronomie /gastʁɔnɔmi/ *nf*
gastronomy

gastronomique /gastʁɔnɔmik/ *adj*
(Culin) gourmet, gastronomic

⚜ **gâteau**, *pl* ∼**x** /gato/ *nm* cake; gâteau
■ ∼ **apéritif** cocktail biscuit; ∼ **de cire** honeycomb; ∼ **de riz** ≈ rice pudding; ∼ **sec** biscuit
(GB), cookie (US)
IDIOMS **c'est du** ∼! (fam) it's a piece of cake!
(colloq); **c'est pas du** ∼! (fam) it's no picnic!

gâter /gate/ [1] **1** *vtr* to spoil; to ruin
‹teeth›
2 **se gâter** *v refl* (+ *v être*) **(a)** to go bad;
to rot
(b) to take a turn for the worse

gâterie /gatʁi/ *nf* little treat

gâteux, -euse /gatø, øz/ *adj* **(a)** senile
(b) **il est** ∼ **avec sa fille** (fam) he's dotty about
his daughter (colloq)

⚜ **gauche**[1] /goʃ/ *adj* **(a)** left
(b) ‹person, manner› awkward; ‹style› clumsy
IDIOM **se lever du pied** ∼ (fam) to get out of
bed on the wrong side (GB), to get up on the
wrong side of the bed (US)

gauche[2] /goʃ/ *nf* **(a)** left; **à** ∼ ‹drive› on
the left; ‹go, look› to the left; ‹turn› left; **de** ∼
‹page›
(b) Left; **de** ∼ left-wing
IDIOMS **passer l'arme à** ∼ (fam) to kick the
bucket (colloq); **jusqu'à la** ∼ (fam) completely;

mettre de l'argent à ∼ (fam) to put money aside

gauchement /goʃmɑ̃/ *adv* awkwardly

gaucher, -ère /goʃe, ɛʀ/ *adj* left-handed

gaucherie /goʃʀi/ *nf* awkwardness

gauchiste /goʃist/ *adj, nmf* leftist

gaufre /gofʀ/ *nf* (a) waffle
(b) honeycomb

gaufrette /gofʀɛt/ *nf* wafer

gaufrier /gofʀije/ *nm* waffle iron

Gaule /gol/ *pr nf* Gaul

Gaulois, ∼e /golwa, az/ *nm,f* Gaul

gaver /gave/ [1] **1** *vtr* to force-feed ‹geese›
2 se gaver *v refl* (+ *v être*) (a) to stuff oneself; **ça me gave** (fam) I've had enough of it (colloq)
(b) se ∼ de to devour ‹novels›

gay /gɛ/ *adj inv, nm* gay, homosexual

gaz /gaz/ **1** *nm inv* gas
2 *nn pl* (a) (Aut) air-fuel mixture; **rouler à pleins** ∼ (fam) to go at full throttle
(b) (Med) wind
■ ∼ **d'échappement** exhaust fumes; ∼ **de ville** mains gas
IDIOM il y a de l'eau dans le ∼ (fam) there's trouble brewing

gaze /gaz/ *nf* gauze

gazéifier /gazeifje/ [2] *vtr* to carbonate ‹drink›

gazelle /gazɛl/ *nf* gazelle

gazer /gaze/ [1] **1** *vtr* to gas
2 *vi* (fam) **ça gaze** things are fine

gazette /gazɛt/ *nf* newspaper

gazeux, -euse /gazø, øz/ *adj* (a) ‹drink› fizzy
(b) gaseous

gazinière /gazinjɛʀ/ *nf* gas cooker (GB), gas stove

gazoduc /gazɔdyk/ *nm* gas pipeline

gazole /gazɔl/ *nm* diesel (oil) (GB), fuel oil (US)

gazon /gazɔ̃/ *nm* (a) grass, turf
(b) lawn

gazouiller /gazuje/ [1] *vi* to twitter; to babble

GDF /ʒedeɛf/ (*abbr* = **Gaz de France**) French gas board

géant, ∼e /ʒeɑ̃, ɑ̃t/ **1** *adj* (a) huge
(b) giant
2 *nm,f* giant/giantess

geignement /ʒɛɲmɑ̃/ *nm* moan, groan

geindre /ʒɛ̃dʀ/ [55] *vi* (in pain) to moan, to groan; to whimper; (complainingly) to whine

gel /ʒɛl/ *nm* (a) frost; **résistant au** ∼ frost-resistant
(b) ∼ **des prix/salaires** price/wage freeze
(c) **après le** ∼ **du projet** after the project had been put on ice
(d) gel

gélatine /ʒelatin/ *nf* gelatine (GB), gelatin (US)

gelé, ∼e¹ /ʒəle/ **1** *pp* ▶ GELER
2 *adj* (a) ‹water, ground› frozen; ‹toe› frost-bitten; **j'ai les oreilles** ∼**es** my ears are frozen
(b) ‹prices, negotiations› frozen

gelée² /ʒəle/ *nf* (a) (from fruit) jelly; (from meat, fish) gelatinous stock; **œuf en** ∼ egg in aspic
(b) gel
(c) frost
■ ∼ **blanche** hoarfrost

geler /ʒəle/ [17] **1** *vtr* (a) to freeze; to nip ‹plant›
(b) to freeze ‹salaries›; to suspend ‹plan›
2 *vi* ‹water, ground, finger, foot› to freeze; ‹plant› to be frosted
3 *v impers* **il gèle** it's freezing

gélule /ʒelyl/ *nf* capsule

Gémeaux /ʒemo/ *pr nm pl* Gemini

gémir /ʒemiʀ/ [3] *vi* to moan; to whimper

gémissement /ʒemismɑ̃/ *nm* moan

gemme /ʒɛm/ *nf* (a) gem, gemstone
(b) resin

gênant, ∼e /ʒɛnɑ̃, ɑ̃t/ *adj* (a) ‹box› cumbersome; ‹problem› annoying
(b) embarrassing

gencive /ʒɑ̃siv/ *nf* gum

gendarme /ʒɑ̃daʀm/ *nm* (a) (Mil) gendarme, French policeman
(b) dried sausage
■ ∼ **couché** road hump

gendarmerie /ʒɑ̃daʀm(ə)ʀi/ *nf*
(a) ≈ police station
(b) ∼ **(nationale)** gendarmerie

gendre /ʒɑ̃dʀ/ *nm* son-in-law

gène /ʒɛn/ *nm* gene

gêne /ʒɛn/ *nf* (a) embarrassment
(b) discomfort
(c) inconvenience
(d) poverty

gêné, ∼e /ʒene/ **1** *pp* ▶ GÊNER
2 *adj* (a) embarrassed
(b) short of money

généalogie /ʒenealɔʒi/ *nf* genealogy

généalogique /ʒenealɔʒik/ *adj* genealogical; **arbre** ∼ family tree

gêner /ʒene/ [1] **1** *vtr* (a) to disturb, to bother
(b) ‹smoke, noise› to bother
(c) to embarrass
(d) ‹belt› to restrict ‹breathing›
(e) ‹person› to get in the way of ‹progress›
2 se gêner *v refl* (+ *v être*) (a) to get in each other's way
(b) **je vais me** ∼ (fam) see if I don't; **ne vous gênez pas pour moi** don't mind me

général, ∼e¹, mpl -aux /ʒeneʀal, o/
1 *adj* general; **de l'avis** ∼ in most people's opinion; **en** ∼, **de façon** ∼**e** generally, in general; **en règle** ∼**e** as a rule ┈┈➤

2 *nm* general

générale² /ʒeneʀal/ *nf* (a) dress rehearsal
(b) general's wife

⚬ **généralement** /ʒeneʀalmɑ̃/ *adv*
generally

généralisation /ʒeneʀalizasjɔ̃/ *nf*
widespread use; generalization; spread

généralisé, ∼e /ʒeneʀalize/ *adj* ‹conflict›
widespread; ‹process› general; ‹cancer›
generalized

généraliser /ʒeneʀalize/ [1] **1** *vtr* to
bring [sth] into general use
2 *vi* to generalize
3 **se généraliser** *v refl* (+ *v être*)
‹technique› to become standard; ‹tax› to
become widely applicable; ‹strike, illness›
to spread

généraliste /ʒeneʀalist/ *adj* non-
specialized; **(médecin) ∼** GP, general
practitioner

généralité /ʒeneʀalite/ *nf* generality

générateur, -trice /ʒeneʀatœʀ, tʀis/
1 *adj* **être ∼ de** to generate
2 *nm* generator

⚬ **génération** /ʒeneʀasjɔ̃/ *nf* generation

générer /ʒeneʀe/ [14] *vtr* to generate

généreusement /ʒeneʀøzmɑ̃/ *adv*
generously; liberally

généreux, -euse /ʒeneʀø, øz/ *adj*
(a) ‹person, nature› generous; ‹idea, gesture›
noble
(b) ‹portion› generous; **poitrine généreuse**
large bust

générique /ʒeneʀik/ **1** *adj* generic
2 *nm* credits; **le ∼ de fin** closing credits

générosité /ʒeneʀozite/ *nf* generosity

genèse /ʒənɛz/ *nf* (a) (of plan) genesis; (of
state) birth
(b) **la Genèse** Genesis

genêt /ʒənɛ/ *nm* (Bot) broom

généticien, -ienne /ʒenetisjɛ̃, ɛn/ *nm,f*
geneticist

génétique /ʒenetik/ **1** *adj* genetic
2 *nf* genetics

génétiquement /ʒenetikmɑ̃/ *adv*
genetically; **∼ modifié** genetically modified

Genève /ʒənɛv/ *pr n* Geneva

genévrier /ʒənevʀije/ *nm* juniper

génial, ∼e, mpl -iaux /ʒenjal, o/ *adj*
(a) brilliant
(b) (fam) great (colloq)

⚬ **génie** /ʒeni/ *nm* (a) genius; **idée de ∼**
brainwave
(b) spirit; genie
(c) engineering

genièvre /ʒənjɛvʀ/ *nm* Dutch gin

génisse /ʒenis/ *nf* heifer

génital, ∼e, mpl -aux /ʒenital, o/ *adj*
genital

⚬ indicates a very frequent word

génocide /ʒenɔsid/ *nm* genocide

génoise /ʒenwaz/ *nf* ≈ sponge cake

⚬ **genou**, *pl* **∼x** /ʒ(ə)nu/ **1** *nm* knee; **sur les
∼x de qn** on sb's lap
2 **à genoux** *phr* **se mettre à ∼x** to kneel
down; to go down on one's knees
IDIOMS faire du ∼ à qn (fam) to play footsie
with sb (colloq); **mettre qn sur les ∼x** (fam) to
wear sb out

genouillère /ʒənujɛʀ/ *nf* (Sport) knee pad;
(Med) knee support

⚬ **genre** /ʒɑ̃ʀ/ *nm* (a) sort, kind, type; **un peu
dans le ∼ de ta robe** a bit like your dress
(b) **pour se donner un ∼** (in order) to make
oneself look different
(c) (in grammar) gender
(d) genre
(e) (Bot, Zool) genus
■ **le ∼ humain** mankind

⚬ **gens** /ʒɑ̃/ *nm pl* (a) people
(b) servants; retinue
■ **∼ d'église** clergymen; **∼ de lettres** writers;
∼ de maison servants; **∼ du voyage** travelling (GB) people

gentil, -ille /ʒɑ̃ti, ij/ *adj* (a) kind, nice
(b) good; **sois ∼** be a good boy
(c) **c'est bien ∼ tout ça, mais...** that's all
very well, but...

gentilhomme, *pl* **gentilshommes**
/ʒɑ̃tijɔm, ʒɑ̃tizɔm/ *nm* gentleman; **∼
campagnard** country gentleman

gentillesse /ʒɑ̃tijɛs/ *nf* (a) kindness
(b) (ironic) **échanger des ∼s** to exchange
insults

gentiment /ʒɑ̃timɑ̃/ *adv* (a) kindly
(b) quietly

géographie /ʒeɔgʀafi/ *nf* geography

geôlier, -ière /ʒolje, ɛʀ/ *nm,f* jailer

géologie /ʒeɔlɔʒi/ *nf* geology

géomètre /ʒeɔmɛtʀ/ *nm,f* land surveyor

géométrie /ʒeɔmetʀi/ *nf* geometry; **à ∼
variable** ‹doctrine› flexible

géométrique /ʒeɔmetʀik/ *adj* geometric

Géorgie /ʒeɔʀʒi/ *pr nf* (a) (in US) Georgia
(b) (in Europe) Georgia

gérable /ʒeʀabl/ *adj* manageable; **situation
difficilement ∼** a situation which is hard to
handle

gérance /ʒeʀɑ̃s/ *nf* management; **mettre en
∼** to appoint a manager for ‹shop, company›;
to appoint a managing agent for ‹property›

géranium /ʒeʀanjɔm/ *nm* geranium

gérant, ∼e /ʒeʀɑ̃, ɑ̃t/ *nm,f* manager; (of
property) (managing) agent

gerbe /ʒɛʀb/ *nf* (a) bouquet; wreath
(b) (of water) spray
(c) (of wheat) sheaf

gercer /ʒɛʀse/ [12] *vi* to become chapped

gerçure /ʒɛʀsyʀ/ *nf* (in skin, lips) crack

gérer /ʒeʀe/ [14] *vtr* (a) to manage
‹production, time›; to run ‹business›

(b) to handle ‹*situation*›

gériatrie /ʒeʁjatʁi/ *nf* geriatrics

germain, **~e** /ʒɛʁmɛ̃, ɛn/ *adj* **(a)** **(cousin)** ~ first cousin
(b) Germanic

germanique /ʒɛʁmanik/ *adj, nm* Germanic

germanophone /ʒɛʁmanɔfɔn/ *nmf* German speaker

germe /ʒɛʁm/ *nm* (of embryo, seed) germ; (of potato) sprout

germer /ʒɛʁme/ [1] *vi* **(a)** ‹*wheat*› to germinate
(b) ‹*idea, suspicion*› to form

gérondif /ʒeʁɔ̃dif/ *nm* gerund, gerundive

gésier /ʒezje/ *nm* gizzard

gésir /ʒeziʁ/ [37] *vi* (formal) **ci-gît Luc Pichon** here lies Luc Pichon

⚔ **geste** /ʒɛst/ *nm* **(a)** movement; gesture; **joindre le ~ à la parole** to suit the action to the word
(b) gesture, act

gesticuler /ʒɛstikyle/ [1] *vtr* **(a)** to gesticulate
(b) to fidget

⚔ **gestion** /ʒɛstjɔ̃/ *nf* **(a)** management
(b) (of situation) handling
(c) (of classroom) management
■ ~ **administrative** administration; ~ **des déchets** waste management; ~ **des stocks** stock (GB) *or* inventory (US) control; ~ **de portefeuille** portfolio management; ~ **de la production assistée par ordinateur** computer-aided production management

gestionnaire /ʒɛstjɔnɛʁ/ *nmf* administrator
■ ~ **de fichiers** (Comput) file-management system; ~ **de portefeuille** portfolio manager

gestuel, -elle¹ /ʒɛstɥɛl/ *adj* gestural

gestuelle² /ʒɛstɥɛl/ *nf* body language

geyser /ʒezɛʁ/ *nm* geyser

ghetto /ɡeto/ *nm* ghetto

gibecière /ʒibsjɛʁ/ *nf* gamebag

gibier /ʒibje/ *nm* game; **gros ~** big game; (figurative) big-time criminals

giboulée /ʒibule/ *nf* shower

giclée /ʒikle/ *nf* spurt; squirt

gicler /ʒikle/ [1] *vi* to spurt; to squirt

gifle /ʒifl/ *nf* slap in the face

gifler /ʒifle/ [1] *vtr* to slap [sb] across the face

gigantesque /ʒiɡɑ̃tɛsk/ *adj* huge, gigantic

gigaoctet /ʒiɡaɔktɛ/ *nm* gigabyte

GIGN /ʒeiʒeɛn/ *nm* (*abbr* = **Groupe d'intervention de la gendarmerie nationale**) *branch of the police specialized in cases of armed robbery, terrorism etc*

gigogne /ʒiɡɔɲ/ *adj* **tables ~s** nest of tables

gigot /ʒiɡo/ *nm* leg of lamb

gigoter /ʒiɡɔte/ [1] *vi* **(a)** to wriggle
(b) to fidget

gilet /ʒilɛ/ *nm* **(a)** cardigan
(b) waistcoat (GB), vest (US)
■ ~ **pare-balles** bulletproof vest; ~ **de sauvetage** lifejacket

gin /dʒin/ *nm* gin; ~ **tonic** gin and tonic

gingembre /ʒɛ̃ʒɑ̃bʁ/ *nm* ginger

girafe /ʒiʁaf/ *nf* (Zool) giraffe

giratoire /ʒiʁatwaʁ/ *adj* gyratory
■ **sens ~** roundabout (GB), traffic circle (US)

girls band /ɡœlzband/ *nm* girl band

girofle /ʒiʁɔfl/ *nm* **un clou de ~** a clove

girolle /ʒiʁɔl/ *nf* chanterelle

girouette /ʒiʁwɛt/ *nf* windvane

gisement /ʒizmɑ̃/ *nm* (of oil, minerals) deposit

gît ▸ GÉSIR

gitan, **~e** /ʒitɑ̃, an/ *nm,f* gypsy (GB)

gîte /ʒit/ *nm* **(a)** shelter
(b) (of hare) form
■ ~ **rural** self-catering cottage

givrant /ʒivʁɑ̃/ *adj m* **brouillard ~** freezing fog

givre /ʒivʁ/ *nm* frost; ice

givré, **~e** /ʒivʁe/ *adj* **(a)** frosty; frost-covered; frozen
(b) (fam) crazy
(c) (Culin) ‹*glass*› frosted

givrer /ʒivʁe/ [1] *vi*, **se givrer** *v refl* (+ *v être*) to frost over

glaçage /ɡlasaʒ/ *nm* (Culin) (on dessert) icing

⚔ **glace** /ɡlas/ *nf* **(a)** ice; **de ~** ‹*face*› stony
(b) ice cream
(c) mirror
(d) sheet of glass; (of shop window) glass; (of car) window
IDIOM rester de ~ to remain unmoved

glacé, **~e** /ɡlase/ *adj* **(a)** ‹*rain*› ice-cold; ‹*hands*› frozen; **thé ~** iced tea
(b) ‹*cake*› iced
(c) ‹*atmosphere*› frosty; ‹*smile*› chilly
(d) ‹*paper*› glossy

glacer /ɡlase/ [12] **1** *vtr* **(a)** to freeze ‹*body*›; to chill [sb] to the bone
(b) to intimidate; ~ **le sang de qn** to make sb's blood run cold
2 **se glacer** *v refl* (+ *v être*) to freeze

glaciaire /ɡlasjɛʁ/ *adj* glacial

glacial, **~e**, *mpl* **~s** *or* **-iaux** /ɡlasjal, o/ *adj* **(a)** icy
(b) ‹*person, reception*› frosty; ‹*silence*› stony; ‹*look*› icy

glacier /ɡlasje/ *nm* **(a)** glacier
(b) ice-cream maker
(c) ice-cream parlour (GB)

glacière /ɡlasjɛʁ/ *nf* coolbox (GB), ice chest (US)

glaçon /ɡlasɔ̃/ *nm* ice cube

glaire /glɛʀ/ nf (a) mucus
(b) albumen

glaise /glɛz/ nf clay

glaive /glɛv/ nm double-edged sword

gland /glɑ̃/ nm (a) acorn
(b) (Anat) glans
(c) tassel

glande /glɑ̃d/ nf (Anat) gland

glaner /glane/ [1] vtr to glean

glapir /glapiʀ/ [3] vi (a) ‹pup› to yap; ‹fox›
to bark
(b) ‹person› to shriek

glas /glɑ/ nm inv toll, knell

glauque /glok/ adj murky; ‹street› squalid

glissade /glisad/ nf slide; skid

glissant, ~e /glisɑ̃, ɑ̃t/ adj slippery

glissement /glismɑ̃/ nm (a) sliding
(b) (in sense) shift; (among voters) swing; (in
prices) fall

♂ **glisser** /glise/ [1] **1** vtr to slip ‹object›
(**dans** into); to slip in ‹remark, criticism›
2 vi (a) to be slippery
(b) to slip
(c) to slide; to glide
(d) ~ **sur** to have no effect on
3 **se glisser** v refl (+ v être) **se ~ dans** to
slip into, to sneak into, to creep into

glissière /glisjɛʀ/ nf slide; **fermeture à ~**
zip (GB), zipper (US)

global, ~e, mpl **-aux** /glɔbal, o/ adj ‹sum›
total; ‹result, cost› overall; ‹agreement,
solution› global; ‹study› comprehensive

globalement /glɔbalmɑ̃/ adv on the
whole

globalisation /glɔbalizasjɔ̃/ nf
globalization

globe /glɔb/ nm (a) ~ **(terrestre)** earth,
globe; **parcourir le ~** to globe-trot
(b) round glass lampshade; glass case
(c) (in architecture) dome
■ ~ **oculaire** eyeball

globule /glɔbyl/ nm globule; blood cell
■ ~ **blanc** white cell; ~ **rouge** red cell

♂ **gloire** /glwaʀ/ nf (a) glory, fame
(b) credit; **faire qch pour la ~** to do sth (just)
for the sake of it
(c) glory, praise
(d) **tirer ~ de** to pride oneself on
(e) celebrity; star

glorieux, -ieuse /glɔʀjø, øz/ adj glorious

glorifier /glɔʀifje/ [2] **1** vtr to glorify
2 **se glorifier** v refl (+ v être) to glory (**de**
in), to boast (**de** about)

glose /gloz/ nf gloss; note

gloser /gloze/ [1] vi to ramble on (**sur**
about)

glossaire /glɔsɛʀ/ nm glossary

glotte /glɔt/ nf glottis

♂ indicates a very frequent word

gloussement /glusmɑ̃/ nm (of hen)
clucking; (of person) chuckle

glousser /gluse/ [1] vi ‹hen› to cluck;
‹person› to chuckle

glouton, -onne /glutɔ̃, ɔn/ adj ‹person›
gluttonous; ‹appetite› voracious

glu /gly/ nf (a) bird lime
(b) glue

gluant, ~e /glyɑ̃, ɑ̃t/ adj (a) sticky
(b) slimy

glucide /glysid/ nm carbohydrate

glycémie /glisemi/ nf **taux de ~** blood
sugar level

glycérine /gliseʀin/ nf glycerin

gnognotte /ɲɔɲɔt/ nf (fam) **c'est pas de la
~!** it's not your common or garden variety

gnome /gnom/ nm gnome

gnon /ɲɔ̃/ nm (fam) dent; bruise; **prendre un
~** to get hit

go: tout de go /go/ phr ‹say› straight out

goal /gol/ nm (fam) goalkeeper, goalie (colloq)

gobelet /gɔblɛ/ nm cup; tumbler; beaker;
~ **en carton** paper cup

gober /gɔbe/ [1] vtr (a) to suck ‹egg›; to
swallow [sth] whole
(b) (fam) to fall for (colloq) ‹story›

godasse /gɔdas/ nf (fam) shoe

godet /gɔdɛ/ nm (a) goblet
(b) pot

goéland /gɔelɑ̃/ nm gull

goémon /gɔemɔ̃/ nm wrack

gogo: à gogo /gogo/ phr (fam) galore; **vin à
~** wine galore

goguette: en goguette /ɑ̃gɔgɛt/ phr
(fam) **partir en ~** to go on a spree

goinfre /gwɛ̃fʀ/ nmf (fam) greedy pig (colloq)

goinfrer: se goinfrer /gwɛ̃fʀe/ [1] v refl
(+ v être) (fam) to stuff oneself (colloq) (**de**
with)

goitre /gwatʀ/ nm goitre (GB)

golden /gɔldɛn/ nf inv Golden Delicious
(apple)

golf /gɔlf/ nm (a) golf
(b) golf course

golfe /gɔlf/ nm gulf; bay

gomme /gɔm/ **1** nf (a) eraser, rubber (GB)
(b) (substance) gum
2 **à la gomme** phr (fam) ‹idea› pathetic,
useless; ‹machine› useless; ‹plan› hopeless
IDIOM mettre (toute) la ~ (fam) to step on it
(colloq); to give it full throttle (colloq); to turn
it up full blast

gommer /gɔme/ [1] vtr (a) to rub [sth] out
(b) to smooth out ‹wrinkle›; to erase ‹past,
boundaries›; to iron out ‹differences›

gond /gɔ̃/ nm hinge; **sortir de ses ~s** to
come off its hinges; to fly off the handle
(colloq)

gondole /gɔ̃dɔl/ nf (a) gondola
(b) sales shelf

gondoler: se gondoler /gɔ̃dɔle/ [1] *v refl*
(+ *v être*) ‹*paper*› to crinkle; ‹*wood*› to warp

gonflable /gɔ̃flabl/ *adj* inflatable

gonflé, ~e /gɔ̃fle/ **1** *pp* ▶ GONFLER
2 *adj* (a) ‹*tyre, balloon*› inflated; ‹*cheeks*›
puffed out
(b) swollen; bloated; puffy; **yeux ~s de
sommeil** eyes puffy with sleep
(c) (fam) **être ~** to have guts (colloq); (critical) to
have a nerve (colloq)

gonfler /gɔ̃fle/ [1] **1** *vtr* (a) to blow up,
to inflate ‹*balloon, tyre*›; to fill ‹*lungs, sail*›;
to puff out ‹*cheeks*›; **être gonflé à bloc** to be
fully inflated; to be raring to go (colloq)
(b) to flex ‹*muscle*›; to make [sth] bulge
‹*pocket, bag*›; to saturate ‹*sponge*›; to make
[sth] swollen ‹*river*›; to swell ‹*bud*›
(c) **il est gonflé d'orgueil** he's full of his own
importance
(d) to increase ‹*profits*›; to push up ‹*prices*›;
to inflate ‹*statistics*›
2 *vi* (gen) to swell (up); (Culin) to rise

gonfleur /gɔ̃flœʀ/ *nm* (air) pump

gong /gɔ̃g/ *nm* (a) gong
(b) (in boxing) bell

googler /gugle/ *vtr* to Google®

goret /gɔʀɛ/ *nm* (a) piglet
(b) (fam) (child) little pig (colloq)

gorge /gɔʀʒ/ *nf* (a) throat; **avoir mal à la
~** to have a sore throat; **tenir qn à la ~** to
have sb by the throat; (figurative) to have a
stranglehold over sb; **avoir la ~ serrée** *or*
nouée to have a lump in one's throat; to have
one's heart in one's mouth; **à ~ déployée,
à pleine ~ sing** at the top of one's voice;
‹*laugh*› uproariously; **ta remarque m'est
restée en travers de la ~** I found your
comment hard to swallow
(b) bosom, breast
(c) gorge
IDIOM faire des ~s chaudes de qn/qch to
laugh at sb/sth; to scorn sb/sth

gorgé, ~e¹ /gɔʀʒe/ *adj* **~ d'eau** ‹*land*›
waterlogged; ‹*sponge*› saturated with water;
fruit ~ de soleil fruit bursting with sunshine

gorgée² /gɔʀʒe/ *nf* sip; gulp

gorger: se gorger /gɔʀʒe/ [13] *v refl* (+ *v
être*) **se ~ de nourriture** to gorge oneself

gorille /gɔʀij/ *nm* (a) gorilla
(b) (fam) bodyguard

gosier /gozje/ *nm* throat, gullet

gosse /gɔs/ *nmf* (fam) (a) kid (colloq); **sale ~**
brat (colloq)
(b) **il est beau ~** he's a good-looking fellow

gothique /gɔtik/ *adj, nm* Gothic

gouache /gwaʃ/ *nf* gouache, poster paint

gouaille /gwaj/ *nf* cheek, cheekiness

goudron /gudʀɔ̃/ *nm* tar

goudronner /gudʀɔne/ [1] *vtr* to tarmac

gouffre /gufʀ/ *nm* chasm, abyss; **le ~ de
Padirac** the caves of Padirac

goujat /guʒa/ *nm* boor

goujon /guʒɔ̃/ *nm* (Zool) gudgeon

goulée /gule/ *nf* (fam) gulp

goulet /gulɛ/ *nm* (a) narrows
(b) gully
■ **~ d'étranglement** bottleneck

goulot /gulo/ *nm* (of bottle) neck

goulu, ~e /guly/ *adj* greedy

goulûment /gulymɑ̃/ *adv* greedily

goupillon /gupijɔ̃/ *nm* (a) bottle brush
(b) holy water sprinkler

gourd, ~e¹ /guʀ, guʀd/ *adj* numb

gourde² /guʀd/ **1** *adj* (fam) dumb (colloq),
gormless (GB) (colloq)
2 *nf* (a) flask; gourd
(b) (fam) dope (colloq)

gourdin /guʀdɛ̃/ *nm* bludgeon, cudgel

gourmand, ~e /guʀmɑ̃, ɑ̃d/ *adj* fond of
good food; **il est ~ (de sucreries)** he has a
sweet tooth

gourmandise /guʀmɑ̃diz/ **1** *nf*
weakness for sweet things; weakness for
good food
2 **gourmandises** *nf pl* sweets (GB),
candies (US)

gourmet /guʀmɛ/ *nm* gourmet

gourmette /guʀmɛt/ *nf* chain bracelet

gourou /guʀu/ *nm* guru

gousse /gus/ *nf* pod; **~ d'ail** clove of garlic

gousset /gusɛ/ *nm* (a) (pocket) fob
(b) gusset

🔊 **goût** /gu/ *nm* (a) (gen) taste; palate; **donner
du ~ à qch** to give sth flavour (GB)
(b) **de bon ~** in good taste; **s'habiller sans ~**
to have no dress sense; **avoir le mauvais ~
de faire** to be tactless enough to do
(c) liking; **ne pas être du ~ de tout le monde**
not to be to everyone's liking; not to be
everyone's cup of tea; **chacun ses ~s** each
to his own; **être au ~ du jour** to be trendy;
faire qch par ~ to do sth for pleasure
IDIOM tous les ~s sont dans la nature
(Proverb) it takes all sorts to make a world

🔊 **goûter¹** /gute/ [1] **1** *vtr* (a) to taste, to try
(b) to enjoy ‹*peace, solitude*›
2 **goûter à** *v+prep* (a) **~ à** to try ‹*food,
drink*›
(b) **~ à** to have a taste of ‹*freedom, power*›

🔊 **goûter²** /gute/ *nm* (a) snack
(b) children's party

goutte /gut/ **1** *nf* (a) drop (**de** of); **~ de
pluie** raindrop; **à grosses ~s** ‹*rain*› heavily;
‹*perspire*› profusely
(b) (Med) gout
2 **gouttes** *nf pl* (Med) drops
IDIOM se ressembler comme deux ~s d'eau
to be as alike as two peas in a pod

goutte-à-goutte /gutagut/ *nm inv* (Med)
drip

gouttelette /gutlɛt/ nf droplet

goutter /gute/ [1] vi to drip

gouttière /gutjɛʀ/ nf gutter; drainpipe

gouvernail /guvɛʀnaj/ nm (a) rudder
(b) helm

gouvernant, ~e¹ /guvɛʀnɑ̃, ɑ̃t/ ⟦1⟧ adj
ruling
⟦2⟧ **gouvernants** nm pl les **~s** the
government

gouvernante² /guvɛʀnɑ̃t/ nf
housekeeper

gouverne /guvɛʀn/ nf **pour votre ~** for
your information

♂ **gouvernement** /guvɛʀnəmɑ̃/ nm
government

gouvernemental, ~e, mpl **-aux**
/guvɛʀnəmɑ̃tal, o/ adj government;
governmental

gouverner /guvɛʀne/ [1] vtr (a) to govern,
to rule
(b) ⟨money⟩ to rule
(c) to steer ⟨ship⟩

gouverneur /guvɛʀnœʀ/ nm governor

GPS (abbr = **Global Positioning
System**) GPS

grabataire /gʀabatɛʀ/ adj bedridden

grabuge /gʀabyʒ/ nm (fam) **faire du ~** to
raise hell (colloq)

♂ **grâce** /gʀɑs/ ⟦1⟧ nf (a) (of person, gesture)
grace; (of landscape) charm
(b) **de bonne ~** with (a) good grace
(c) favour (GB); **faire à qn la ~ d'accepter** to
do sb the honour (GB) of accepting
(d) mercy; **~ présidentielle** presidential
pardon; **je vous fais ~ des détails** I'll spare
you the details
(e) **~ à Dieu!** thank God!
⟦2⟧ **grâce à** phr thanks to

Grâce /gʀɑs/ nf Grace; **votre ~** your Grace

gracier /gʀasje/ [2] vtr to pardon, to
reprieve

gracieusement /gʀasjøzmɑ̃/ adv (a) free
of charge
(b) gracefully

gracieux, -ieuse /gʀasjø, øz/ adj
(a) graceful
(b) gracious

grade /gʀad/ nm rank; **monter en ~** to be
promoted

gradé, ~e /gʀade/ nm,f noncommissioned
officer

gradin /gʀadɛ̃/ nm (in hall) tier; (in arena)
terrace

gradué, ~e /gʀadɥe/ adj **règle ~e** ruler

graduer /gʀadɥe/ [1] vtr (a) to increase
⟨difficulty⟩
(b) to graduate ⟨instrument⟩

graffiti /gʀafiti/ nm pl graffiti

graillon /gʀajɔ̃/ nm (fam) **ça sent le ~** it
smells of stale fat

grain /gʀɛ̃/ nm (a) grain; **nourri au ~** corn-
fed (GB) or grain-fed
(b) grain; **~ de poivre** peppercorn; **~ de
café** coffee bean; **~ de moutarde** mustard
seed; **~ de raisin** grape
(c) speck
(d) **le ~** the grain; **à gros ~** coarse grained
■ **~ de beauté** beauty spot, mole
IDIOMS **avoir un ~** (fam) to be loony (colloq);
mettre son ~ de sel (fam) to put one's oar
in (colloq)

graine /gʀɛn/ nf seed; birdseed; **monter
en ~** ⟨vegetable⟩ to run to seed; ⟨child⟩ to
shoot up
IDIOM **prends-en de la ~** (fam) let that be an
example to you

graisse /gʀɛs/ nf (a) (gen) fat; (of seal, whale)
blubber
(b) (Tech) grease

graisser /gʀese/ [1] vtr to grease ⟨pan⟩; to
lubricate ⟨mechanism⟩

graisseux, -euse /gʀesø, øz/ adj (gen)
greasy; (Med) fatty

grammaire /gʀamɛʀ/ nf grammar

grammatical, ~e, mpl **-aux**
/gʀamatikal, o/ adj grammatical

gramme /gʀam/ nm gram

♂ **grand, ~e** /gʀɑ̃, gʀɑ̃d/ ⟦1⟧ adj (a) ⟨person,
tree, tower⟩ tall; ⟨arm, stride, journey⟩ long;
⟨margin, angle⟩ wide; ⟨place, object, fire⟩ big
(b) ⟨crowd, family, fortune⟩ large, big; **pas
~ monde** not many people; **il fait ~ jour** it's
broad daylight; **laver à ~e eau** to wash [sth]
in plenty of running water; to wash [sth]
down
(c) ⟨dreamer, collector, friend⟩ great; ⟨cheat,
gambler⟩ big; ⟨drinker, smoker⟩ heavy; **c'est
un ~ timide** he's very shy
(d) ⟨discovery, news, expedition⟩ great; ⟨date⟩
important; ⟨role⟩ major; ⟨problem, decision⟩
big
(e) main
(f) ⟨company, brand⟩ leading; **les ~es
industries** the big industries
(g) ⟨painter, wine⟩ great; ⟨heart, spirit⟩ noble
(h) ⟨brother, sister⟩ elder; ⟨pupil⟩ senior (GB),
older; **assez ~ pour faire** old enough to do
(i) ⟨height, length, value, distance⟩ great;
⟨size, quantity⟩ large; ⟨speed⟩ high
(j) ⟨kindness, friendship, danger, interest⟩
great; ⟨noise⟩ loud; ⟨cold⟩ severe; ⟨heat⟩
intense; ⟨wind⟩ strong, high; ⟨storm⟩ big,
violent; **à ma ~e surprise** much to my
surprise
(k) ⟨family, name⟩ great; **la ~e bourgeoisie**
the upper middle class
(l) ⟨reception, plan⟩ grand
(m) ⟨word⟩ big; ⟨phrase⟩ high-sounding; **faire
de ~s gestes** to wave one's arms about; **et
voilà, tout de suite les ~s mots** there you go,
straight off the deep end

♂ indicates a very frequent word

2 *nm,f* big boy/girl; (Sch) senior (GB) *or* older pupil

3 *adv* wide; **ouvrir tout ~ les bras** to throw one's arms open; **ouvrir ~ ses oreilles** to prick up one's ears; **voir ~** to think big

4 *nm* **les ~s de ce monde** the great and the good; the world's leaders

5 **en grand** *phr* ‹open› wide; **faire les choses en ~** to do things on the grand scale
■ **~s axes** main roads; **~ banditisme** organized crime; **le ~ capital** big money; **~ duc** eagle owl; **~ écart** (Sport) splits; **le ~ écran** the big screen; **le ~ ensemble** high-density housing complex; **le ~ large** the high seas; **~ magasin** department store; **le ~ monde** high society; **le Grand Nord** the Far North; **Grand Pardon** Day of Atonement; **~ prêtre** high priest; **~ prix** grand prix; **le ~ public** the general public; **produit ~ public** consumer product; **la ~e banlieue** the outer suburbs; **la ~e cuisine** haute cuisine; **la Grande Guerre** the First World War; **la ~e muraille de Chine** the Great Wall of China; **~e personne** grown-up, adult; **~e puissance** superpower; **~e roue** big wheel (GB), Ferris wheel (US); **~e surface** supermarket; **~es eaux** fountains; **dès qu'on la gronde, ce sont les ~es eaux** the minute you tell her off, she turns on the waterworks; **~es lignes** main train routes; **~es marées** spring tides; **~es ondes** long wave; **les ~s blessés** the seriously injured; **~s fauves** big cats

grand-angle, *pl* **grands-angles** /grɑ̃tɑ̃gl, grɑ̃zɑ̃gl/ *adj* wide-angle; **un (objectif) ~** a wide-angle lens

grand-chose /grɑ̃ʃoz/ *pron* **pas ~** not much, not a lot; **il n'y a plus ~ à faire** there isn't much left to do

Grande-Bretagne /grɑ̃dbrətaɲ/ *pr nf* Great Britain

grandement /grɑ̃dmɑ̃/ *adv* greatly; a great deal; extremely

grandeur /grɑ̃dœr/ *nf* (a) size; **~ nature** ‹reproduction› full-scale; ‹portrait› life-size
(b) scale
(c) greatness

Grand-Guignol /grɑ̃giɲɔl/ *nm* **c'est du ~** it's farcical

grandiloquence /grɑ̃dilɔkɑ̃s/ *nf* pomposity, grandiloquence

grandiloquent, **~e** /grɑ̃dilɔkɑ̃, ɑ̃t/ *adj* pompous, grandiloquent

grandiose /grɑ̃djoz/ *adj* ‹site, decor› grandiose; ‹party› spectacular; ‹gesture› grand

grandir /grɑ̃dir/ [3] **1** *vtr* (a) to magnify
(b) to make [sb] look taller
(c) to exaggerate
2 *vi* (a) to grow; to grow up
(b) ‹company› to expand; ‹crowd, anxiety› to grow
3 **se grandir** *v refl* (+ *v être*) to make oneself (look) taller

grandissant, **~e** /grɑ̃disɑ̃, ɑ̃t/ *adj* growing

♂ **grand-mère**, *pl* **grands-mères** /grɑ̃mɛr/ *nf* grandmother

grand-oncle, *pl* **grands-oncles** /grɑ̃tɔ̃kl, grɑ̃zɔ̃kl/ *nm* great-uncle

grand-peine **1** *nf* **avoir ~ à faire** to have great difficulty doing
2 **à grand-peine** *phr* **à ~** with great difficulty

grand-père, *pl* **grands-pères** /grɑ̃pɛr/ *nm* grandfather

grand-route, *pl* **~s** /grɑ̃rut/ *nf* main road

grand-rue, *pl* **~s** /grɑ̃ry/ *nf* high street

grands-parents /grɑ̃parɑ̃/ *nm pl* grandparents

grand-tante, *pl* **grand(s)-tantes** /grɑ̃tɑ̃t/ *nf* great-aunt

grand-voile, *pl* **grand(s)-voiles** /grɑ̃vwal/ *nf* mainsail

grange /grɑ̃ʒ/ *nf* barn

granit(e) /granit/ *nm* granite

granité, **~e** /granite/ *adj* grained

granulé /granyle/ *nm* granule

graphie /grafi/ *nf* (a) written form
(b) spelling

graphique /grafik/ **1** *adj* (a) ‹work› graphic
(b) ‹screen› graphic; ‹software› graphics
2 *nm* graph

graphisme /grafism/ *nm* (a) style of drawing
(b) handwriting
(c) graphic design

graphologie /grafɔlɔʒi/ *nf* graphology

grappe /grap/ *nf* (of fruit) bunch; (of flowers) cluster

grappiller /grapije/ [1] *vtr* to pick up ‹fruit›; to glean ‹information›

grappin /grapɛ̃/ *nm* **mettre le ~ sur qn** (fam) to get sb in one's clutches

gras, grasse /grɑ, grɑs/ **1** *adj*
(a) ‹substance› fatty; ‹fish› oily; ‹paper› greasy
(b) coarse, vulgar
(c) (in printing) bold
(d) loose, phlegmy
2 *adv* **manger ~** to eat fatty foods
3 *nm* (a) (from meat) fat
(b) grease
(c) (of arm, calf) **le ~** the fleshy part

grassement /grɑsmɑ̃/ *adv* ‹pay› handsomely; ‹feed› lavishly

grassouillet, **-ette** /grasujɛ, ɛt/ *adj* (fam) chubby, plump

graticiel /gratisjɛl/ *nm* freeware

gratifiant, **~e** /gratifjɑ̃, ɑ̃t/ *adj* gratifying

gratification /gratifikasjɔ̃/ *nf*
(a) gratification
(b) bonus

gratifier /gʀatifje/ [2] *vtr* ~ **qn de qch** to give sb sth; **se sentir gratifié** to feel gratified

gratin /gʀatɛ̃/ *nm* (a) gratin (*breadcrumbs and cheese*)
(b) (fam) **le** ~ the upper crust (colloq)

gratiné, ~**e** /gʀatine/ *adj* (a) (Culin) au gratin
(b) (fam) ‹*person*› weird; ‹*problem*› mind-bending (colloq)

gratiner /gʀatine/ [1] *vtr* (faire) ~ **un plat** to brown a dish

gratis /gʀatis/ ⟦1⟧ *adj inv* free
⟦2⟧ *adv* free (GB), for free

gratitude /gʀatityd/ *nf* gratitude; **avoir de la** ~ **pour qn** to be grateful to sb

gratte-ciel /gʀatsjɛl/ *nm inv* skyscraper

gratte-papier /gʀatpapje/ *nm inv* (fam) pen pusher

gratter /gʀate/ [1] ⟦1⟧ *vtr* (a) to scratch; to scrape (off)
(b) to make [sb] itch; **ça me gratte partout** I'm itching all over
⟦2⟧ *vi* ~ **à la porte** to scratch at the door
⟦3⟧ **se gratter** *v refl* (+ *v être*) to scratch; **se** ~ **la tête** to scratch one's head

grattoir /gʀatwaʀ/ *nm* (a) (tool) scraper
(b) (on matchbox) striking strip

✓ **gratuit**, ~**e** /gʀatɥi, it/ *adj* (a) ‹*place, service*› free
(b) ‹*violence*› gratuitous; ‹*accusation*› spurious; ‹*exercise*› pointless

gratuité /gʀatɥite/ *nf* **la** ~ **de l'enseignement** free education

gratuitement /gʀatɥitmɑ̃/ *adv* (a) free (GB), for free
(b) ‹*work*› for nothing
(c) gratuitously

gravats /gʀava/ *nm pl* rubble

✓ **grave** /gʀav/ *adj* (a) ‹*problem, injury*› serious
(b) ‹*expression*› grave, solemn
(c) ‹*voice*› deep; ‹*note*› low; ‹*sound*› low-pitched
(d) (fam) ‹*person*› hopeless

gravement /gʀavmɑ̃/ *adv* (a) gravely, solemnly
(b) seriously

graver /gʀave/ [1] *vtr* (a) to engrave
(b) to burn ‹*CDs etc.*›

graveur, -euse /gʀavœʀ, øz/ ⟦1⟧ *nm,f* engraver; ~ **sur bois** wood engraver
⟦2⟧ *nm* (for CDs etc.) burner

gravier /gʀavje/ *nm* **du** ~ gravel

gravillon /gʀavijɔ̃/ *nm* grit

gravir /gʀaviʀ/ [3] *vtr* to climb up

gravitation /gʀavitasjɔ̃/ *nf* gravitation; ~ **universelle** Newton's law of gravitation

gravité /gʀavite/ *nf* (a) seriousness
(b) solemnity

(c) (in physics) gravity

graviter /gʀavite/ [1] *vi* to orbit

gravure /gʀavyʀ/ *nf* (a) **la** ~ engraving
(b) engraving
(c) print, reproduction

gré /gʀe/ *nm* (a) **contre le** ~ **de qn** against sb's will; **de** ~ **ou de force** one way or another
(b) (formal) **savoir** ~ **à qn de qch** to be grateful to sb for sth
(c) **j'ai flâné au** ~ **de mon humeur** I strolled where the mood took me

✓ **grec, grecque** /gʀɛk/ ⟦1⟧ *adj* Greek; Grecian
⟦2⟧ *nm* (language) Greek

Grec, Grecque /gʀɛk/ *nm,f* Greek

Grèce /gʀɛs/ *pr nf* Greece; ~ **antique** Ancient Greece

grecque ▶ GREC

greffe /gʀɛf/ *nf* (a) (of organ) transplant; (of skin) graft
(b) (in agriculture) grafting; graft

greffer /gʀefe/ [1] ⟦1⟧ *vtr* (a) to transplant ‹*organ*›; to graft ‹*tissue*›
(b) to graft ‹*tree*›
⟦2⟧ **se greffer** *v refl* (+ *v être*) **se** ~ **sur qch** ‹*problem, event*› to come along on top of sth

greffier, -ière /gʀefje, ɛʀ/ *nm,f* clerk of the court (GB), court clerk (US)

grégaire /gʀegɛʀ/ *adj* gregarious

grège /gʀɛʒ/ *adj, nm* oatmeal

grêle /gʀɛl/ ⟦1⟧ *adj* (a) skinny; spindly
(b) ‹*voice*› reedy; ‹*sound*› thin
⟦2⟧ *nf* hail

grêlé, ~**e** /gʀɛle/ *adj* pockmarked

grêler /gʀɛle/ [1] *v impers* **il grêle** it's hailing

grêlon /gʀɛlɔ̃/ *nm* hailstone

grelot /gʀəlo/ *nm* small bell

grelotter /gʀələte/ [1] *vi* to shiver

grenade /gʀənad/ *nf* (a) grenade
(b) pomegranate

Grenade /gʀənad/ ⟦1⟧ *pr n* Granada
⟦2⟧ *pr nf* **la** ~ Grenada

grenadine /gʀənadin/ *nf* grenadine

grenaille /gʀənaj/ *nf* (a) steel filings
(b) lead shot

grenat /gʀəna/ *adj inv* dark red

grenier /gʀənje/ *nm* attic, loft; ~ **à grain** granary

grenouille /gʀənuj/ *nf* frog

grès /gʀɛ/ *nm inv* (a) sandstone
(b) (piece of) stoneware

grésillement /gʀezijmɑ̃/ *nm* (a) crackling
(b) sizzling

grésiller /gʀezije/ [1] *vi* (a) ‹*radio*› to crackle
(b) ‹*butter, oil*› to sizzle

grève /gʀɛv/ *nf* (a) strike; **mouvement de** ~ industrial action
(b) shore

✓ indicates a very frequent word

■ ~ **de la faim** hunger strike; ~ **sur le tas** sit-down strike; ~ **du zèle** work-to-rule

grever /gʀəve/ [16] *vtr* to put a strain on ‹*budget*›; **l'entreprise est grevée de charges** the company has crippling overheads

gréviste /gʀevist/ *nmf* striker

gribouillage /gʀibujaʒ/ *nm* (fam) scribble

gribouiller /gʀibuje/ [1] *vtr* (fam) to scribble

grief /gʀijɛf/ *nm* grievance

grièvement /gʀijɛvmɑ̃/ *adv* ‹*injured*› seriously; ‹*burned*› badly; ‹*affected*› severely

griffe /gʀif/ *nf* **(a)** claw; **tomber entre les ~s de qn** to fall into sb's clutches
(b) (on garment) label
(c) signature stamp
(d) (in jewellery) claw

griffer /gʀife/ [1] **1** *vtr* to scratch
2 se griffer *v refl* (+ *v être*) to scratch oneself

griffonner /gʀifɔne/ [1] *vtr* **(a)** to scrawl
(b) to sketch

griffure /gʀifyʀ/ *nf* scratch

grignoter /gʀiɲɔte/ [1] **1** *vtr* **(a)** to nibble
(b) to encroach on ‹*territory*›; to conquer ‹*corner of market*›
(c) to fritter away ‹*inheritance*›
2 *vi* **(a)** ‹*rodent*› to gnaw
(b) ‹*person*› to nibble

gri-gri, *pl* **gris-gris** /gʀigʀi/ *nm* lucky charm

gril /gʀil/ *nm* grill (GB), broiler (US)

grillage /gʀijaʒ/ *nm* wire netting; chicken wire; wire mesh

grille /gʀij/ *nf* **(a)** railings; (iron) gate; (of sink, sewer) drain; (of air vent) grille; (in oven, fridge) shelf; (in fireplace, stove) grate
(b) (of crossword) grid
(c) (on TV, radio) schedule, listings
(d) (for assessing results) model
(e) (in administration) scale

grillé, ~**e** /gʀije/ **1** *pp* ▸ GRILLER
2 *pp adj* **(a)** ‹*meat*› grilled; ‹*bread*› toasted; ‹*almonds*› roasted
(b) crispy, well-browned
(c) burned out; **l'ampoule est ~e** the bulb has blown
(d) (fam) ‹*spy*› exposed

grille-pain /gʀijpɛ̃/ *nm inv* toaster

griller /gʀije/ [1] **1** *vtr* **(a)** to grill ‹*meat*›; to toast ‹*bread*›; to roast ‹*almonds*›
(b) (fam) to jump (colloq) ‹*light*›; to ignore ‹*give way sign*›
(c) (fam) to give the game away about [sb]
(d) (fam) ~ **un adversaire** to manage to get ahead of one's opponent
2 *vi* **(a)** to grill; **faire** ~ to grill; to toast; to roast
(b) ‹*bulb*› to blow

grillon /gʀijɔ̃/ *nm* cricket

grimaçant, ~**e** /gʀimasɑ̃, ɑ̃t/ *adj* grimacing

grimace /gʀimas/ *nf* grimace; funny face

grimacer /gʀimase/ [12] *vi* to grimace

grimer: se grimer /gʀime/ [1] *v refl* (+ *v être*) to make oneself up

grimpant, ~**e** /gʀɛ̃pɑ̃, ɑ̃t/ *adj* climbing

grimper /gʀɛ̃pe/ [1] **1** *vtr* to climb ‹*stairs*›
2 *vi* **(a)** ~ **aux arbres** to climb (up) trees; **grimpe sur mon dos** get on my back
(b) (fam) ‹*road*› to be steep
(c) (fam) ‹*prices*› to climb

grimpeur, -euse /gʀɛ̃pœʀ, øz/ *nm,f* rock climber

grinçant, ~**e** /gʀɛ̃sɑ̃, ɑ̃t/ *adj* ‹*tone*› scathing; ‹*joke*› caustic; ‹*laugh*› nasty

grincement /gʀɛ̃smɑ̃/ *nm* creak(ing); squeak(ing); screech(ing)

grincer /gʀɛ̃se/ [12] *vi* ‹*door*› to creak; ‹*violin*› to screech; ‹*chalk*› to squeak; ~ **des dents** to grind one's teeth; (figurative) to gnash one's teeth

gringalet /gʀɛ̃galɛ/ *nm* runt

griotte /gʀijɔt/ *nf* morello cherry

grippe /gʀip/ *nf* flu
■ ~ **aviaire** bird flu, avian flu; ~ **intestinale** gastric flu (GB), intestinal flu (US)
IDIOM prendre qn/qch en ~ (fam) to take a sudden dislike to sb/sth

✓ **gris**, ~**e** /gʀi, iz/ **1** *adj* **(a)** grey (GB), gray (US)
(b) dreary; dull
(c) tipsy
2 *nm inv* grey (GB), gray (US)

grisaille /gʀizaj/ *nf* **(a)** dullness
(b) (of weather) greyness (GB), grayness (US)

grisant, ~**e** /gʀizɑ̃, ɑ̃t/ *adj* ‹*speed*› exhilarating; ‹*success*› intoxicating
(b) ‹*perfume*› heady

grisâtre /gʀizɑtʀ/ *adj* ‹*colour, sky*› greyish (GB), grayish (US); ‹*morning*› dull

griser /gʀize/ [1] *vtr* ‹*speed*› to exhilarate; ‹*success*› to intoxicate; **se laisser** ~ **par le pouvoir** to let power go to one's head

griserie /gʀizʀi/ *nf* exhilaration (**de** of)

grisonnant, ~**e** /gʀizɔnɑ̃, ɑ̃t/ *adj* greying

grisonner /gʀizɔne/ [1] *vi* to go grey

grisou /gʀizu/ *nm* firedamp

grive /gʀiv/ *nf* thrush

grivois, ~**e** /gʀivwa, az/ *adj* bawdy; coarse

grivoiserie /gʀivwazʀi/ *nf* suggestive remark

grizzli, grizzly /gʀizli/ *nm* grizzly bear

grogne /gʀɔɲ/ *nf* (fam) discontent

grognement /gʀɔɲəmɑ̃/ *nm* grunt; growl

grogner /gʀɔɲe/ [1] *vi* **(a)** to groan; (figurative) to grumble
(b) ‹*pig*› to grunt; ‹*dog*› to growl

grognon /gʀɔɲɔ̃/ *adj* grouchy (colloq)

groin /gʀwɛ̃/ *nm* snout

g

grommeler /gʀɔmle/ [19] *vi* to grumble

grondement /gʀɔ̃dmɑ̃/ *nm* (of torrent, machine) roar; (of crowd) angry murmur

gronder /gʀɔ̃de/ [1] **1** *vtr* to tell [sb] off
2 *vi* (a) ⟨thunder⟩ to rumble; ⟨machine, wind⟩ to roar
(b) ⟨rebellion⟩ to be brewing

groom /gʀum/ *nm* bellboy (GB), bellhop (US)

ⱱ **gros**, **grosse** /gʀo, gʀos/ **1** *adj* (a) big, large
(b) thick
(c) fat
(d) ⟨customer, market⟩ big; ⟨damage⟩ considerable
(e) ⟨problem⟩ serious, big; ⟨flaw⟩ big, major
(f) ⟨cold⟩ bad; ⟨sobs⟩ loud; ⟨voice⟩ deep; ⟨rain⟩ heavy; ⟨smoker⟩ heavy
2 *adv* (a) ⟨write⟩ big
(b) ⟨bet, lose⟩ a lot of money; (figurative) a lot
3 *nm inv* (a) le ~ de the majority of ⟨spectators⟩; the bulk of ⟨work⟩; most of ⟨winter⟩
(b) wholesale trade
(c) la pêche au ~ game fishing
4 en ~ *phr* (a) roughly; en ~ je suis d'accord avec toi basically, I agree with you
(b) wholesale
(c) in big letters
■ ~ bonnet (fam) big shot (colloq); ~ lot first prize; ~ mot swearword; ~ œuvre shell (of a building); ~ plan close-up; ~ sel cooking salt; ~ titre headline; grosse caisse bass drum; grosse tête (fam) brain (colloq)
IDIOMS en avoir ~ sur le cœur *or* la patate (fam) to be very upset; c'est un peu ~ comme histoire! that's a bit of a tall story!

groseille /gʀozɛj/ *nf* redcurrant; ~ à maquereau gooseberry

grosse ▸ GROS

grossesse /gʀosɛs/ *nf* pregnancy
■ ~ nerveuse phantom pregnancy (GB), false pregnancy

grosseur /gʀosœʀ/ *nf* (a) size
(b) (of thread) thickness
(c) (Med) lump

grossier, **-ière** /gʀosje, ɛʀ/ *adj* (a) ⟨person, gesture⟩ rude; ⟨language⟩ bad
(b) ⟨laugh⟩ coarse
(c) ⟨imitation⟩ crude
(d) ⟨sketch, idea⟩ rough; ⟨work⟩ crude
(e) ⟨error⟩ glaring

grossièrement /gʀosjɛʀmɑ̃/ *adv*
(a) ⟨calculate⟩ roughly
(b) ⟨build⟩ crudely
(c) ⟨speak⟩ rudely

grossièreté /gʀosjɛʀte/ *nf* (a) rudeness
(b) dirty word
(c) coarseness

ⱱ indicates a very frequent word

grossir /gʀosiʀ/ [3] **1** *vtr* (a) to enlarge ⟨image⟩
(b) to increase ⟨numbers⟩; to boost ⟨profits⟩
(c) to exaggerate ⟨incident⟩
(d) to make [sb] look fat
2 *vi* (a) to put on weight
(b) (gen) to grow; ⟨river⟩ to swell

grossissant, ~e /gʀosisɑ̃, ɑ̃t/ *adj* magnifying

grossiste /gʀosist/ *nmf* wholesaler

grosso modo /gʀosomodo/ *adv* roughly

grotesque /gʀotɛsk/ *adj* ridiculous

grotte /gʀot/ *nf* (a) cave
(b) grotto

grouiller /gʀuje/ [1] **1** *vi* to swarm about; to mill about
2 se grouiller *v refl* (+ *v être*) (fam) to get a move on (colloq)

groupage /gʀupaʒ/ *nm* bulking; envoi en ~ collective shipment

ⱱ **groupe** /gʀup/ *nm* (a) (gen, Econ) group; par ~s de deux in pairs, in twos
(b) (of objects) group; cluster
■ ~ d'autodéfense vigilante group; ~ électrogène (electricity) generator; ~ de pression pressure group; ~ sanguin blood group; ~ scolaire school; ~ des Sept, G7 Group of Seven, G7 countries

groupement /gʀupmɑ̃/ *nm*
(a) association, group
(b) grouping

grouper /gʀupe/ [1] **1** *vtr* to put together
2 se grouper *v refl* (+ *v être*) to gather (autour de around); to form a group; se ~ par trois to form groups of three; restez groupés keep together

groupuscule /gʀupyskyl/ *nm* small group

gruau, *pl* ~x /gʀyo/ *nm* (a) gruel
(b) fine wheat flour

grue /gʀy/ *nf* (Tech, Zool) crane
IDIOM faire le pied de ~ (fam) to hang around

grumeau, *pl* ~x /gʀymo/ *nm* lump

gruyère /gʀyjɛʀ/ *nm* Gruyère, Swiss cheese

Guadeloupe /gwadlup/ *pr nf* la ~ Guadeloupe

gué /ge/ *nm* ford; passer un ruisseau à ~ to ford a stream

guenille /gənij/ *nf* rag; en ~s in rags

guenon /gənɔ̃/ *nf* female monkey

guépard /gepaʀ/ *nm* cheetah

guêpe /gɛp/ *nf* wasp

guêpier /gepje/ *nm* (a) wasps' nest
(b) tight corner; dans quel ~ es-tu allé te fourrer? (fam) what kind of mess have you got (GB) or gotten (US) yourself into?

guêpière /gepjɛʀ/ *nf* basque, bodyshaper with suspenders (GB) *or* garters (US)

guère /gɛʀ/ *adv* hardly; il n'avait ~ le choix he didn't really have a choice

guéridon /geʀidɔ̃/ *nm* pedestal table

guérilla /geʀija/ *nf* (a) guerilla warfare
(b) guerillas

guérir /geʀiʀ/ [3] **1** *vtr* (a) to cure ‹person, disease›
(b) ~ qn de to cure sb of ‹habit›
2 *vi* to recover; to heal; to get better
3 **se guérir** *v refl* (+ *v être*) se ~ de to overcome ‹shyness›

guérison /geʀizɔ̃/ *nf* recovery; healing

guérite /geʀit/ *nf* (a) sentry box
(b) (on toll road) booth

♂ **guerre** /gɛʀ/ *nf* war; warfare; **les pays en** ~ the warring nations
■ ~ **chimique** chemical war; chemical warfare; ~ **éclair** blitzkrieg, lightning war; ~ **mondiale** world war; **Première/Deuxième Guerre mondiale** World War I/II; ~ **nucléaire** nuclear war; nuclear warfare; ~ **de 14** 1914–18 war; ~ **de Sécession** American Civil War; ~ **d'usure** war of attrition; ~ **des prix** price war
IDIOMS **à la** ~ **comme à la** ~ in time of hardship you have to make the best of things; **c'est de bonne** ~ it's only fair; **de** ~ **lasse, elle renonça** realizing that she was fighting a losing battle, she gave up

guerrier, -ière /geʀje, ɛʀ/ *nm,f* warrior

guet /gɛ/ *nm* (a) lookout; **faire le** ~ to be on the lookout
(b) (Mil) watch

guet-apens, *pl* **guets-apens** /gɛtapɑ̃/ *nm* ambush; (figurative) trap

guêtre /gɛtʀ/ *nf* (a) (Sport) leggings
(b) gaiter

guetter /gete/ [1] *vtr* (a) to watch ‹prey, criminal, reaction›; to watch out for ‹sign›; to look out for ‹postman›
(b) to threaten

guetteur, -euse /gɛtœʀ, øz/ *nm,f* lookout

gueule /gœl/ *nf* (a) (pop) face; **il a la** ~ **de l'emploi** he really looks the part
(b) (pop) mouth; **(ferme) ta** ~! shut your face (GB) *or* mouth!
(c) (of animal) mouth
■ ~ **de bois** (fam) hangover
IDIOM **faire la** ~ (pop) to be sulking

gueuler /gœle/ (pop) [1] **1** *vtr* to yell; to bawl out
2 *vi* to yell, to bawl; to kick up a real fuss; ~ **après qn** to have a go at sb (colloq)

gui /gi/ *nm* mistletoe

guichet /giʃɛ/ *nm* window; (in bank) counter; (in museum, station) ticket office; (in theatre, cinema) box office; **la pièce se jouera à** ~s **fermés** the play is sold out
■ ~ **automatique** automatic teller machine

guichetier, -ière /giʃtje, ɛʀ/ *nm,f* ticket clerk

guide /gid/ *nm* guide

guider /gide/ [1] *vtr* (a) (gen) to guide
(b) to show [sb] the way

guidon /gidɔ̃/ *nm* handlebars

guigne /giɲ/ *nf* (fam) bad luck

guignol /giɲɔl/ *nm* (a) puppet show; ≈ Punch and Judy show
(b) (derogatory) clown

guillemets /gijmɛ/ *nm pl* inverted commas (GB), quotation marks

guillotine /gijɔtin/ *nf* guillotine

guimauve /gimov/ *nf* (a) (Bot) (marsh) mallow
(b) (confectionery) marshmallow

guimbarde /gɛ̃baʀd/ *nf* Jew's harp

guindé, ~e /gɛ̃de/ *adj* formal

guingois: de guingois /dəgɛ̃gwa/ *phr* **être de** ~ to be lopsided

guirlande /giʀlɑ̃d/ *nf* garland; tinsel
■ ~ **électrique** set *or* string of fairy lights

guise /giz/ *nf* (a) **'à votre** ~' 'just as you like *or* please'
(b) **en** ~ **de** by way of

♂ **guitare** /gitaʀ/ *nf* guitar

guitariste /gitaʀist/ *nm,f* guitarist

gustatif, -ive /gystatif, iv/ *adj* ‹organ› taste

guttural, ~e, *mpl* **-aux** /gytyʀal, o/ *adj* guttural

Guyana /gɥijana/ *pr nf* Guyana; **République de** ~ Republic of Guyana

Guyane /gɥijan/ *pr nf* ~ **(française)** (French) Guyana; ~ **hollandaise** Dutch Guiana

gym /ʒim/ *nf* (fam, Sch) physical education

gymnase /ʒimnaz/ *nm* gymnasium

gymnaste /ʒimnast/ *nm,f* gymnast

gymnastique /ʒimnastik/ *nf* gymnastics; exercises
■ ~ **corrective** ≈ physiotherapy exercises

gynécologie /ʒinekɔlɔʒi/ *nf* gynaecology

gyrophare /ʒiʀofaʀ/ *nm* flashing light, emergency rotating light

H h

h, H /aʃ/ *nm inv* (a) (letter) h, H; **h muet** mute h

(b) (*written abbr* = **heure**) 9 h 10 9.10

ha /'a/ (*written abbr* = **hectare**) ha

habile /abil/ *adj* clever, skilful (GB)

habilement /abilmɑ̃/ *adv* skilfully (GB); cleverly

habileté /abilte/ *nf* skill; skilfulness (GB)

habiliter /abilite/ [1] *vtr* to authorize

habillé, ~e /abije/ *adj* ‹dress› smart; ‹dinner› formal

habillement /abijmɑ̃/ *nm* clothing

habiller /abije/ [1] **1** *vtr* (a) to dress; to dress [sb] up
(b) to clothe; to provide [sb] with clothing
(c) to make [sb's] clothes
(d) **un rien l'habille** she looks good in anything
2 s'habiller *v refl* (+ *v être*) (a) to get dressed; to dress up; **s'~ long/court** to wear long/short skirts
(b) **s'~ chez** to get one's clothes from

habilleur, -euse /abijœʀ, øz/ *nm,f* dresser

habit /abi/ *nm* (a) **~s** clothes
(b) outfit, costume
(c) (of monk, nun) habit
■ **~ de lumière** matador's costume; **~s du dimanche** Sunday best

habitable /abitabl/ *adj* (a) habitable
(b) **surface ~** living space

habitacle /abitakl/ *nm* (a) (Aviat) cockpit; (of rocket) cabin
(b) (Aut) interior
(c) (Naut) binnacle

ℱ **habitant, ~e** /abitɑ̃, ɑ̃t/ *nm,f* inhabitant; resident; **loger chez l'~** to stay as a paying guest

habitat /abita/ *nm* (a) (Bot, Zool) habitat
(b) housing

habitation /abitasjɔ̃/ *nf* (a) house, dwelling; home
(b) living; **immeuble d'~** block of flats (GB), apartment building (US)
■ **~ à loyer modéré, HLM** ≈ (block of) council flats (GB), low-rent apartment (building) (US)

habité, ~e /abite/ *adj* (a) inhabited
(b) ‹rocket› manned

ℱ **habiter** /abite/ [1] **1** *vtr* to live in
2 *vi* to live

ℱ **habitude** /abityd/ **1** *nf* (a) habit; **par ~** out of habit; **ils ont l'~ de se coucher tôt**

they usually go to bed early; **avoir l'~ de** to be used to
(b) custom
2 d'habitude *phr* usually

habitué, ~e /abitɥe/ *nm,f* regular

habituel, -elle /abitɥɛl/ *adj* usual

habituellement /abitɥɛlmɑ̃/ *adv* usually

habituer /abitɥe/ [1] **1** *vtr* (a) **~ qn à** to get sb used to
(b) to teach
2 s'habituer *v refl* (+ *v être*) **s'~ à** to get used to

hache /'aʃ/ *nf* axe (GB), ax (US)
IDIOM **enterrer la ~ de guerre** to bury the hatchet

haché, ~e /'aʃe/ *adj* (a) ‹meat› minced
(b) ‹speech› disjointed

hache-légumes /'aʃlegym/ *nm inv* vegetable chopper

hacher /'aʃe/ [1] *vtr* to mince; to chop

hachette /'aʃɛt/ *nf* hatchet

hachis /'aʃi/ *nm inv* mince; **~ de persil** chopped parsley
■ **~ Parmentier** ≈ shepherd's pie

hachisch /'aʃiʃ/ *nm* hashish

hachoir /'aʃwaʀ/ *nm* (a) mincer
(b) chopper

hachurer /'aʃyʀe/ [1] *vtr* to hatch

haddock /'adɔk/ *nm* smoked haddock

hagard, ~e /'agaʀ, aʀd/ *adj* ‹person› dazed; ‹eyes› wild

haï, ~e /'ai/ ▶ HAÏR

haie /'ɛ/ *nf* (a) hedge
(b) (Sport) hurdle; fence; **course de ~s** hurdle race; steeple chase
(c) line, row; **faire une ~ d'honneur** to form a guard of honour (GB)

haillon /'ajɔ̃/ *nm* rag; **en ~s** in rags

ℱ **haine** /'ɛn/ *nf* hatred; **s'attirer la ~ de qn** to earn sb's hatred

haineux, -euse /'ɛnø, øz/ *adj* full of hatred

haïr /'aiʀ/ [25] *vtr* to hate

haïssable /'aisabl/ *adj* detestable, hateful

halage /'alaʒ/ *nm* **chemin de ~** towpath

hâle /'ɑl/ *nm* (sun)tan

hâlé, ~e /'ɑle/ *adj* tanned

haleine /alɛn/ *nf* breath; breathing; **hors d'~** out of breath; **un travail de longue ~** a long-drawn-out job

haler /'ale/ [1] *vtr* to tow ‹boat›; to haul in ‹chain›

haleter /'alte/ [18] *vi* (a) to gasp for breath; to pant

ℱ indicates a very frequent word

(b) ‹machine› to puff; ‹chest› to heave

hall /'ɔl/ nm entrance hall (GB), lobby (US); ∼ **(de gare)** concourse

halle /'al/ nf covered market

hallucination /alysinasjɔ̃/ nf hallucination; **avoir des** ∼**s** to hallucinate; to be seeing things

halluciné, ∼**e** /alysine/ adj ‹eyes› wild

hallucinogène /alysinɔʒɛn/ adj hallucinogenic

halo /'alo/ nm halo; **entouré d'un** ∼ **de mystère** shrouded in mystery

halogène /alɔʒɛn/ adj halogen

halte /'alt/ **1** nf **(a)** stop
(b) stopping place
2 excl stop!; (Mil) halt!

halte-garderie, pl **haltes-garderies** /'altəɡaʀdəʀi/ nf ≈ playgroup

haltère /altɛʀ/ nm dumbbell; barbell; **faire des** ∼**s** to do weightlifting

haltérophilie /alteʀɔfili/ nf weightlifting

hamac /'amak/ nm hammock

hameau, pl ∼**x** /'amo/ nm hamlet

hameçon /amsɔ̃/ nm hook; **mordre à l'**∼ to take the bait

hanche /'ɑ̃ʃ/ nf (of person) hip

handicap /'ɑ̃dikap/ nm handicap

handicapé, ∼**e** /'ɑ̃dikape/ **1** adj
(a) disabled
(b) être ∼ to be at a disadvantage
2 nm,f disabled person

handicaper /'ɑ̃dikape/ [1] vtr to handicap

hangar /'ɑ̃ɡaʀ/ nm shed; warehouse; hangar

hanneton /'antɔ̃/ nm cockchafer (GB), June bug (US)

hanter /'ɑ̃te/ [1] vtr to haunt

hantise /'ɑ̃tiz/ nf dread

happer /'ape/ [1] vtr to catch ‹insect›; **happé par** ‹arm› caught up in ‹machine›; ‹person› hit by ‹train›; (figurative) swallowed up by ‹crowd›

haranguer /'aʀɑ̃ɡe/ [1] vtr to harangue

haras /'aʀa/ nm inv stud farm

harassement /'aʀasmɑ̃/ nm exhaustion

harasser /'aʀase/ [1] vtr to exhaust

harcèlement /'aʀsɛlmɑ̃/ nm harassment

harceler /'aʀsəle/ [17] vtr **(a)** to pester
(b) to harass

hardi, ∼**e** /'aʀdi/ adj bold, daring

hardiesse /'aʀdjɛs/ nf **(a)** boldness
(b) brazenness

hareng /'aʀɑ̃/ nm herring

hargne /'aʀɲ/ nf aggression

hargneux, **-euse** /'aʀɲø, øz/ adj aggressive

haricot /'aʀiko/ nm (Bot) bean; ∼ **blanc** haricot bean; ∼ **vert** French bean
IDIOM **c'est la fin des** ∼**s** (fam) we've had it (colloq)

harmonica /aʀmɔnika/ nm mouth organ, harmonica

harmonie /aʀmɔni/ nf harmony

harmonieux, **-ieuse** /aʀmɔnjø, øz/ adj harmonious; ‹movements› graceful

harmoniser /aʀmɔnize/ [1] **1** vtr **(a)** to coordinate ‹colours›
(b) to harmonize; to make [sth] consistent; to bring into line
(c) (Mus) to harmonize
2 s'harmoniser v refl (+ v être) **bien s'**∼ ‹colours› to go together well

harnachement /'aʀnaʃmɑ̃/ nm **(a)** (for horse) harness
(b) (fam) (clothes) get-up (colloq)

harnacher /'aʀnaʃe/ [1] vtr **(a)** to harness ‹horse›
(b) (fam) to rig out (colloq) ‹person›

harnais /'aʀnɛ/ nm inv harness

harpe /'aʀp/ nf harp

harpie /'aʀpi/ nf harpy

harpon /'aʀpɔ̃/ nm harpoon

harponner /'aʀpɔne/ [1] vtr to harpoon

✝ **hasard** /'azaʀ/ nm chance; **par** ∼ by chance; **par un curieux** ∼ by a curious coincidence; **par un heureux** ∼ by a stroke of luck; **ce n'est pas un** ∼ **si...** it's no accident that...; **le** ∼ **a voulu que...** as luck would have it,...; **au** ∼ ‹choose› at random; ‹walk› aimlessly; ‹answer› off the top of one's head; **comme par** ∼, **il a oublié son argent** (ironic) surprise, surprise, he's forgotten his money; **à tout** ∼ just in case, on the off chance; **les** ∼**s de la vie** the fortunes of life
IDIOM **le** ∼ **fait bien les choses** fate is a great provider

hasarder /'azaʀde/ [1] **1** vtr **(a)** to venture ‹advice›
(b) to risk ‹life›
2 se hasarder v refl (+ v être) to venture

hasardeux, **-euse** /'azaʀdø, øz/ adj risky

hâte /'ɑt/ nf **(a)** haste; **à la** ∼ hastily
(b) j'ai ∼ **de partir/qu'elle parte** I can't wait to leave/for her to leave

hâter /'ɑte/ [1] **1** vtr to hasten; ∼ **le pas** to quicken one's step
2 se hâter v refl (+ v être) to hurry, to rush

hâtif, **-ive** /'ɑtif, iv/ adj **(a)** ‹judgment› hasty, hurried
(b) ‹plant› early

hâtivement /'ɑtivmɑ̃/ adv hurriedly, hastily

hausse /'os/ nf increase, rise; **être en** ∼ ‹prices› to be rising; ‹goods› to be going up in price; **en** ∼ **de 10%** up 10%

haussement /'osmɑ̃/ nm ∼ **d'épaules** shrug

hausser /'ose/ [1] **1** vtr to raise; ∼ **les épaules** to shrug one's shoulders
2 se hausser v refl (+ v être) **se** ∼ **sur la** ···>

pointe des pieds to stand on tiptoe

ⓢ **haut**, ~**e¹** /'o, 'ot/ **1** adj (a) high; tall; **l'étagère la plus** ~**e** the top shelf; **à** ~**e voix** ⟨speak⟩ loudly; ⟨read⟩ aloud, out loud; **à** ~ **risque** very risky; **au plus** ~ **point** immensely
(b) ⟨rank, society⟩ high; ⟨person, post⟩ high-ranking; ~**e surveillance** close supervision
(c) (in geography) upper; **la** ~**e Égypte** Upper Egypt
(d) **le** ~ **Moyen Âge** the early Middle Ages
2 adv (a) high; **un personnage** ~ **placé** a high-ranking person; **plus** ~ **sur la page** higher up on the page; '**voir plus** ~' see above; **de** ~ from above
(b) (in time) far back
(c) loud(ly); **dire qch tout** ~ to say sth aloud; **n'avoir jamais un mot plus** ~ **que l'autre** never to raise one's voice
3 nm (a) top; **le** ~ **du corps** the top half of the body; **l'étagère du** ~ the top shelf; **les pièces du** ~ the upstairs rooms; **parler du** ~ **d'un balcon** to speak from a balcony
(b) **faire 50 mètres de** ~ to be 50 metres (GB) high
4 **en haut** phr upstairs; on an upper floor; **en** ~ **de** at the top of
■ ~ **en couleur** ⟨character⟩ colourful (GB); ~ **débit** broadband; ~ **fait** heroic deed; ~ **lieu de** centre (GB) of or for; **en** ~ **lieu** in high places; ~**e mer** open sea; ~**es sphères** high social circles
IDIOMS **voir les choses de** ~ to have a detached view of things; **tomber de** ~ to be dumbfounded; **connaître des** ~**s et des bas** to have one's ups and downs; ~ **les mains!** hands up!; **gagner** ~ **la main** to win hands down; **prendre qch de** ~ to react indignantly

hautain, ~**e** /'otɛ̃, ɛn/ adj haughty

hautbois /'obwɑ/ nm inv (a) oboe
(b) oboist

haut-de-forme, pl **hauts-de-formes** /'odfɔRm/ nm top hat

haute² /'ot/ **1** adj f ▶ HAUT 1
2 nf (fam) **les gens de la** ~ the upper crust

haute(-)fidélité, pl **hautes(-)fidélités** /'otfidelite/ nf hi-fi, high fidelity

ⓢ **hauteur** /'otœR/ **1** nf (a) height; **prendre de la** ~ ⟨plane⟩ to climb; **dans le sens de la** ~ upright; **à** ~ **d'homme** at head height
(b) hill; **gagner les** ~**s** to reach high ground
(c) haughtiness
(d) (of voice) pitch
2 **à la hauteur de** phr (a) **arriver à la** ~ **de** to come up to; to draw level with; **raccourcir une jupe à la** ~ **des genoux** to shorten a dress to the knee
(b) (figurative) **être à la** ~ to measure up; **être à la** ~ **de sa tâche** to be equal to one's job
IDIOM **tomber de toute sa** ~ to fall headlong

haut-fond, pl **hauts-fonds** /'ofɔ̃/ nm shallows

ⓢ indicates a very frequent word

haut(-)fourneau, pl
hauts(-)fourneaux /'ofuRno/ nm blast furnace

haut-le-cœur /'olkœR/ nm inv retching, heaving; **avoir un** ~ to retch

haut-parleur, pl ~**s** /'opaRlœR/ nm loudspeaker

havane /'avan/ **1** adj inv tobacco-brown
2 nm (a) Havana tobacco
(b) Havana cigar

havre /'ɑvR/ nm haven

Haye /'ɛ/ pr n **la** ~ the Hague

heaume /'om/ nm helmet

hebdomadaire /ɛbdomadɛR/ adj, nm weekly

hébergement /ebɛRʒəmɑ̃/ nm
(a) accommodation
(b) housing

héberger /ebɛRʒe/ [13] vtr to put [sb] up; to accommodate; to provide shelter for

hébété, ~**e** /ebete/ adj ⟨look⟩ stupid

hébraïque /ebraik/ adj Hebrew

hébreu, pl ~**x** /ebRø/ **1** adj m Hebrew
2 nm (language) Hebrew
IDIOM **pour moi, c'est de l'**~ it's all Greek to me

HEC /aʃəse/ nf (abbr = **Hautes études commerciales**) major business school

hécatombe /ekatɔ̃b/ nf massacre, slaughter

hectare /ɛktaR/ nm hectare

hecto /ɛkto/ **1** nm (abbr = **hectogramme**) hectogram
2 **hecto(-)** (combining form) hecto

hein /'ɛ̃/ excl (fam) what (colloq),?, sorry?; **ça t'étonne**, ~? that's surprised you, hasn't it?

hélas /'elas/ excl alas; ~ **non!** unfortunately not!

héler /'ele/ [14] vtr to hail

hélice /elis/ nf (a) (screw) propeller
(b) helix

hélicoptère /elikɔptɛR/ nm helicopter

héliporté, ~**e** /elipɔRte/ adj helicopter-borne

hellène /ɛllɛn/ adj Hellenic

helvétique /ɛlvetik/ adj Helvetic, Swiss; **la Confédération** ~ Switzerland

helvétisme /ɛlvetism/ nm Swiss French expression

hématologie /ematɔlɔʒi/ nf haematology

hématome /ematom/ nm bruise

hémicycle /emisikl/ nm semicircular auditorium

hémisphère /emisfɛR/ nm hemisphere

hémoglobine /emoglɔbin/ nf haemoglobin

hémophile /emɔfil/ **1** adj haemophilic
2 nmf haemophiliac

hémorragie /emɔRaʒi/ nf
(a) haemorrhage, bleeding

(b) (of capital) outflow

hémorroïdes /emɔʀɔid/ *nf pl* piles, haemorrhoids

henné /'ene/ *nm* henna

hennir /'eniʀ/ [3] *vi* to neigh, to whinny

hépatique /epatik/ ① *adj* hepatic
② *nmf* person with a liver complaint

hépatite /epatit/ *nf* hepatitis

héraldique /eʀaldik/ *adj* heraldic

herbacé, **~e** /ɛʀbase/ *adj* herbaceous

herbage /ɛʀbaʒ/ *nm* pasture

herbe /ɛʀb/ ① *nf* **(a)** grass; **mauvaise ~** weed
(b) (Culin) herb
② **en herbe** *phr* **(a)** ‹wheat› in the blade
(b) ‹musician› budding
IDIOM **couper l'~ sous le pied de qn** to pull the rug from under sb's feet

herbeux, **-euse** /ɛʀbø, øz/ *adj* grassy

herbier /ɛʀbje/ *nm* herbarium

herbivore /ɛʀbivɔʀ/ ① *adj* herbivorous
② *nm* herbivore

herboriste /ɛʀbɔʀist/ *nmf* herbalist

herboristerie /ɛʀbɔʀistəʀi/ *nf* **(a)** herb trade
(b) herbalist's shop (GB) *or* store (US)

héréditaire /eʀeditɛʀ/ *adj* hereditary; (figurative) ‹enemy› traditional

hérédité /eʀedite/ *nf* **(a)** heredity
(b) (of title) hereditary nature

hérésie /eʀezi/ *nf* **(a)** heresy
(b) (humorous) sacrilege

hérétique /eʀetik/ ① *adj* heretical
② *nmf* heretic

hérissé, **~e** /'eʀise/ *adj* ‹hair› bristling, standing up on end; **~ de** spiked with ‹nails›

hérisser /'eʀise/ [1] ① *vtr* **(a)** ‹bird› to ruffle (up) ‹feathers›
(b) **~ qch de** to spike sth with
(c) (fam) **ça me hérisse** it makes my hackles rise
② **se hérisser** *v refl* (+ *v être*) ‹hair› to stand on end

hérisson /'eʀisɔ̃/ *nm* hedgehog

héritage /eʀitaʒ/ *nm* **(a)** inheritance; **laisser qch en ~** to bequeath sth; **recevoir qch en ~** to inherit sth
(b) heritage

hériter /eʀite/ [1] ① *vtr* to inherit
② **hériter de** *v*+*prep* to inherit
③ *vi* to inherit; to come into an inheritance; **~ de qn** to receive an inheritance from sb

héritier, **-ière** /eʀitje, ɛʀ/ *nm,f* heir/ heiress

hermétique /ɛʀmetik/ *adj* **(a)** hermetic; airtight; watertight
(b) ‹milieu› impenetrable; ‹poetry, author› abstruse; ‹face› inscrutable

hermétiquement /ɛʀmetikmɑ̃/ *adv*
(a) ‹sealed› hermetically

(b) ‹speak› abstrusely

hermine /ɛʀmin/ *nf* **(a)** stoat
(b) ermine

hernie /'ɛʀni/ *nf* **(a)** hernia
(b) (in tyre) bulge

héroïne /eʀɔin/ *nf* **(a)** heroine
(b) heroin

héroïque /eʀɔik/ *adj* heroic; epic

héroïsme /eʀɔism/ *nm* heroism

héron /'eʀɔ̃/ *nm* heron

✧ **héros** /'eʀo/ *nm inv* hero

herse /'ɛʀs/ *nf* **(a)** harrow
(b) portcullis

hertzien, **-ienne** /ɛʀtzjɛ̃, ɛn/ *adj* ‹wave› Hertzian; ‹station› radio-relay

hésitant, **~e** /ezitɑ̃, ɑ̃t/ *adj* **(a)** hesitant
(b) ‹start› shaky

hésitation /ezitasjɔ̃/ *nf* **(a)** indecision, hesitancy
(b) hesitation

✧ **hésiter** /ezite/ [1] *vi* to hesitate; **elle hésite encore** she's still undecided; **il n'y a pas à ~** it's got to be done; **j'hésite sur le chemin à prendre** I'm not sure which path to take; **~ à faire** to be hesitant to do

hétéroclite /eteʀɔklit/ *adj* ‹population, work› heterogeneous, ‹objects› miscellaneous

hétérogène /eteʀɔʒɛn/ *adj* mixed, heterogeneous

hétérosexuel, **-elle** /eteʀɔsɛksɥɛl/ *adj, nm,f* heterosexual

hêtre /'ɛtʀ/ *nm* **(a)** beech (tree)
(b) beechwood

✧ **heure** /œʀ/ *nf* **(a)** hour; **24 ~s sur 24** 24 hours a day; **dans l'~ qui a suivi** within the hour; **d'~ en ~** ‹increase› by the hour; **à trois ~s d'avion de Paris** three hours from Paris by plane; **à trois ~s de marche de Paris** a three-hour walk from Paris; **faire du 60 à l'~** (fam) to do 60 km per hour; **payé à l'~** paid by the hour; **une petite ~** an hour at the most
(b) time; **quelle ~ est-il?** what time is it?; **il est 10 ~s** it's 10 (o'clock); **il est 10 ~s 20** it's 20 past 10; **il est 10 ~s moins 20** it's 20 to 10; **mettre sa montre à l'~** to set one's watch; **l'~ tourne** time is passing; **~s d'ouverture** opening times; **être à l'~** to be on time; **à une ~ avancée (de la nuit)** late at night; **de bonne ~** early; **c'est son ~** it's his/her usual time; **à l'~ où je te parle** as we speak; **de la première ~** from the very beginning; **à la première ~** at first light; **ta dernière ~ est arrivée** your time has come; **à l'~ actuelle, pour l'~** at the present time; **l'~ du déjeuner** lunchtime; **l'~ est grave** the situation is serious; **il est peintre à ses ~s** he paints in his spare time; **à la bonne ~!** well done!
(c) era, age; **vivre à l'~ des satellites** to live in the satellite era

■ **~ d'affluence** peak hour; **~ d'été** summer time (GB), daylight saving(s) time; **~ H** (Mil, ⋯⫶

figurative) zero hour; ∼ **d'hiver** winter time
(GB), standard time; ∼ **de pointe** rush hour;
∼**s supplémentaires** overtime

✠ **heureusement** /œRøzmɑ̃/ *adv*
fortunately

✠ **heureux, -euse** /œRø, øz/ *adj* (a) happy;
∼ **en ménage** happily married; **très ∼ de
faire votre connaissance** (very) pleased to
meet you
(b) ⟨*ending*⟩ happy; ⟨*proportions*⟩ pleasing;
⟨*choice*⟩ fortunate; ⟨*surprise*⟩ pleasant
(c) ⟨*winner*⟩ lucky; **'il a réussi!'—'encore ∼!'**
'he succeeded!'—'just as well!'
IDIOM attendre un ∼ événement to be
expecting a baby

heurt /'œR/ *nm* (a) collision
(b) (figurative) (between people) clash; **sans ∼s**
⟨*do*⟩ smoothly; ⟨*relationship*⟩ smooth

heurter /'œRte/ [1] **1** *vtr* ⟨*object*⟩ to hit;
⟨*person*⟩ to collide with, to bump into
(b) (figurative) to go against ⟨*convention*⟩; to
hurt ⟨*feelings*⟩
2 *vi* ∼ **contre** to strike
3 **se heurter** *v refl* (+ *v être*) to collide;
(figurative) to clash; **se ∼ à** to bump into
⟨*table*⟩; to come up against ⟨*refusal, problem*⟩

hévéa /evea/ *nm* rubber tree

hexagonal, ∼e, *mpl* **-aux** /ɛgzagɔnal, o/
adj (a) hexagonal
(b) (fam) ⟨*policy*⟩ inward-looking

hexagone /ɛgzagon/ *nm* (a) hexagon
(b) (fam) **l'Hexagone** France

hiberner /ibɛRne/ [1] *vi* to hibernate

hibou, *pl* **∼x** /'ibu/ *nm* owl

hic /'ik/ *nm* (fam) snag; **voilà le ∼** there's
the snag

hideux, -euse /'idø, øz/ *adj* hideous

✠ **hier** /jɛR/ *adv* yesterday; **ça ne date pas d'∼**
it's nothing new

hiérarchie /'jeRaRʃi/ *nf* hierarchy

hiérarchique /'jeRaRʃik/ *adj* hierarchical;
mon supérieur ∼ my immediate superior;
par la voie ∼ through the correct channels

hiérarchiser /'jeRaRʃize/ [1] *vtr* to
organize [sth] into a hierarchy ⟨*structure*⟩

hiératique /jeRatik/ *adj* hieratic

hiéroglyphe /'jeRɔglif/ *nm* hieroglyph; **les
∼s** hieroglyphics

hi-fi /'ifi/ *adj inv, nf inv* hi-fi

hilarant, ∼e /ilaRɑ̃, ɑ̃t/ *adj* hilarious; **gaz
∼** laughing gas

hilare /ilaR/ *adj* **être ∼** to be laughing

hilarité /ilaRite/ *nf* mirth, hilarity

hindou, ∼e /ɛ̃du/ *adj, nm,f* Hindu

hindouisme /ɛ̃duism/ *nm* Hinduism

hippique /ipik/ *adj* equestrian; **concours
∼** showjumping event (GB), horse show

hippocampe /ipɔkɑ̃p/ *nm* sea horse

---

hippodrome /ipɔdRom/ *nm* racecourse
(GB), racetrack (US)

hippopotame /ipɔpɔtam/ *nm*
hippopotamus

hirondelle /iRɔ̃dɛl/ *nf* swallow

hirsute /'iRsyt/ *adj* dishevelled (GB),
unkempt

hispanique /ispanik/ *adj, nmf* Hispanic

hispano-américain, ∼e, *mpl* **∼s**
/ispanoameRikɛ̃, ɛn/ *adj* Hispanic-
American, Spanish-American

hispanophone /ispanofɔn/ *nmf* Spanish
speaker

hisse /'is/ *excl* **oh ∼!** heave-ho!

hisser /'ise/ [1] **1** *vtr* to hoist ⟨*flag*⟩
2 **se hisser** *v refl* (+ *v être*) to heave
oneself up

✠ **histoire** /istwaR/ *nf* (a) history; **l'∼ jugera**
posterity will be the judge
(b) story; **tout ça, c'est des∼s!** (fam) that's all
fiction!; **une ∼ à dormir debout** a tall story;
raconter des ∼s to tell fibs
(c) matter, business; ∼ **d'amour** love affair;
∼ **de famille** family matter; **il m'est arrivé
une drôle d'∼** a funny thing happened to me
(d) fuss; trouble; **elle fait toujours des ∼s**
she's always making a fuss; **ça va faire des
∼s** it will cause trouble; **c'est une femme à
∼s** she's a troublemaker; **une vie sans ∼s**
an uneventful life; **ça a été toute une ∼ pour
faire** it was a terrible job doing; **au travail,
et pas d'∼s!** (fam) get on with it, no messing
about! (colloq)
(e) (fam) ∼ **de rire** just for fun

historien, -ienne /istɔRjɛ̃, ɛn/ *nm,f*
historian

✠ **historique** /istɔRik/ **1** *adj* (a) historical
(b) historic
(c) **passé ∼** past historic
2 *nm* (Comput) History (button)

hit-parade, *pl* **∼s** /'itpaRad/ *nm* charts

✠ **hiver** /ivɛR/ *nm* winter

hivernage /ivɛRnaʒ/ *nm* wintering

hivernal, ∼e, *mpl* **-aux** /ivɛRnal, o/ *adj*
(a) winter
(b) wintry

hiverner /ivɛRne/ [1] *vi* ⟨*animals*⟩ to winter

HLM /aʃɛlɛm/ *nm or f: abbr* ▶ HABITATION

hochement /'ɔʃmɑ̃/ *nm* nod; shake of
the head

hocher /'ɔʃe/ [1] *vtr* ∼ **la tête** to nod; to
shake one's head

hochet /'ɔʃɛ/ *nm* rattle

hockey /'ɔkɛ/ *nm* hockey

holà /'ɔla/ *excl* hey (there)!
IDIOM mettre le ∼ à qch to put an end *or* a
stop to sth

holding /'ɔldiŋ/ *nm or f* holding company

hold-up, *pl* ∼ *or* ∼**s** /'ɔldœp/ *nm* hold-up

hollandais, ∼e /'ɔlɑ̃dɛ, ɛz/ **1** *adj* Dutch
2 *nm* (language) Dutch

✠ indicates a very frequent word

Hollandais, **~e** /'ɔlɑ̃ dɛ, ɛz/ *nm,f*
Dutchman/Dutchwoman; **les ~** the Dutch
Hollande /'ɔlɑ̃d/ *pr nf* Holland
holocauste /ɔlɔkost/ *nm* holocaust
homard /'ɔmaʀ/ *nm* lobster
homéopathie /ɔmeɔpati/ *nf* homeopathy
homéopathique /ɔmeɔpatik/ *adj*
homeopathic; **à doses ~s** (figurative) in small
doses
homicide /ɔmisid/ *nm* homicide;
manslaughter; murder
hommage /ɔmaʒ/ *nm* homage, tribute;
présenter ses ~s to pay one's respects
hommasse /ɔmas/ *adj* mannish
♂ **homme** /ɔm/ *nm* man; **l'~** man; mankind;
un ~ à la mer! man overboard!; **comme un
seul ~** as one; **leur ~ de confiance** their
right-hand man; **il n'est pas ~ à se venger**
he's not the type to want revenge
∎ **~ d'affaires** businessman; **~ des cavernes**
caveman; **~ d'esprit** wit; **~ d'État** statesman;
~ à femmes womanizer; **~ au foyer** house-
husband; **~ de main** hired hand; **~ de paille**
front man (GB), straw man (US); **~ de terrain**
man with practical experience; **~ à tout faire**
handyman; **~ de troupe** private; **~s en blanc**
surgeons
IDIOM **un ~ averti en vaut deux** (Proverb) fore-
warned is forearmed
homme-grenouille, *pl* **hommes-
grenouilles** /ɔmgʀənuj/ *nm* frogman
homme-orchestre, *pl* **hommes-
orchestres** /ɔmɔʀkɛstʀ/ *nm* one-man
band
homogène /ɔmɔʒɛn/ *adj* homogeneous
homogénéité /ɔmɔʒeneite/ *nf*
homogeneity
homologue /ɔmɔlɔg/ ⊡ *adj* homologous
⊡ *nmf* counterpart, opposite number
homologuer /ɔmɔlɔge/ [1] *vtr* **(a)** to
approve ‹product›
(b) (Sport) to recognize officially
homonyme /ɔmɔnim/ *nm* **(a)** homonym
(b) namesake
homoparentalité /ɔmɔpaʀɑ̃talite/ *nf*
gay parenting
homosexualité /ɔmɔsɛksɥalite/ *nf*
homosexuality
homosexuel, -elle /ɔmɔsɛksɥɛl/ *adj*,
nm,f homosexual
Hongrie /'ɔ̃gʀi/ *pr nf* Hungary
honnête /ɔnɛt/ *adj* **(a)** honest
(b) decent; respectable
(c) fair, reasonable
honnêtement /ɔnɛtmɑ̃/ *adv* **(a)** ‹say,
manage› honestly; ‹reply› frankly; ‹behave›
properly; ‹judge› fairly
(b) fairly, reasonably; **s'acquitter ~ d'une
tâche** to do a decent job
honnêteté /ɔnɛtte/ *nf* honesty

♂ **honneur** /ɔnœʀ/ *nm* **(a)** honour (GB); **à
toi l'~!** you do the honours (GB)!; **j'ai l'~ de
vous informer que** I beg to inform you that;
j'ai l'~ de solliciter I would respectfully
request; **d'~** ‹stairs› main
(b) credit; **c'est tout à leur ~** it's all credit
to them
(c) mettre qn à l'~ to honour (GB) sb; **être à
l' or en ~** to be in favour (GB); **faire ~ à un
repas** to do justice to a meal; **faire les ~s de
la maison à qn** to show sb around the house;
avoir les ~s de la presse to be mentioned
in the press; **en quel~?** (fam) (ironic) any
particular reason why?
IDIOM **en tout bien tout ~** with no hidden
motive
honnir /'ɔniʀ/ [3] *vtr* **honni soit qui mal y
pense** evil unto him who evil thinks
honorabilité /ɔnɔʀabilite/ *nf* integrity
honorable /ɔnɔʀabl/ *adj* **(a)** honourable
(GB)
(b) ‹score› creditable; ‹salary› decent
honorablement /ɔnɔʀabləmɑ̃/ *adv*
(a) honourably (GB)
(b) decently
honoraire /ɔnɔʀɛʀ/ ⊡ *adj* ‹member›
honorary
⊡ **honoraires** *nm pl* fee, fees
honorer /ɔnɔʀe/ [1] *vtr* **(a)** to honour (GB)
‹god, person, memory›
(b) to honour (GB) ‹promise, debt›
(c) to be a credit to ‹country, profession›
honorifique /ɔnɔʀifik/ *adj* honorary
honoris causa /ɔnɔʀiskoza/ *phr*
être nommé docteur ~ to be awarded an
honorary doctorate
♂ **honte** /'ɔ̃t/ *nf* **(a)** shame; **avoir ~ de** to be
ashamed of; **sans fausse ~** quite openly
(b) disgrace; **faire la ~ de** to be a disgrace to;
quelle ~! what a disgrace!
honteusement /'ɔ̃tøzmɑ̃/ *adv*
(a) shamefully
(b) shamelessly
honteux, -euse /'ɔ̃tø, øz/ *adj*
(a) disgraceful
(b) ashamed
♂ **hôpital**, *pl* **-aux** /ɔpital, o/ *nm* hospital
IDIOM **c'est l'~ qui se moque de la charité**
it's the pot calling the kettle black
hoquet /'ɔkɛ/ *nm* **avoir le ~** to have hiccups
hoqueter /'ɔkte/ [20] *vi* ‹person› to hiccup
horaire /ɔʀɛʀ/ ⊡ *adj* per hour, hourly;
tranche *or* **plage ~** time-slot
⊡ *nm* timetable, schedule; **les ~s libres** *or*
à la carte flexitime
horde /'ɔʀd/ *nf* horde
♂ **horizon** /ɔʀizɔ̃/ *nm* horizon
horizontal, **~e¹**, *mpl* **-aux** /ɔʀizɔ̃tal, o/
adj horizontal
horizontale² /ɔʀizɔ̃tal/ *nf* horizontal
horloge /ɔʀlɔʒ/ *nf* clock

h

horloger, -ère /ɔʀlɔʒe, ɛʀ/ *nm,f* watchmaker

horlogerie /ɔʀlɔʒʀi/ *nf* (a) watchmaking (b) watchmaker's (shop)

hormis /'ɔʀmi/ *prep* (formal) save, except (for)

hormonal, ~e, *mpl* **-aux** /ɔʀmɔnal, o/ *adj* ‹problem› hormonal; ‹treatment› hormone

hormone /ɔʀmon/ *nf* hormone

horodateur /ɔʀɔdatœʀ/ *nm* parking ticket machine

horoscope /ɔʀɔskɔp/ *nm* horoscope

✧ **horreur** /ɔʀœʀ/ *nf* (a) horror; **quelle ~!** how horrible!
(b) **dire des ~s de** *or* **sur qn** to say awful things about sb
(c) loathing; **avoir ~ de qn/de faire** to loathe sb/doing

horrible /ɔʀibl/ *adj* (a) horrible
(b) revolting
(c) hideous

horriblement /ɔʀiblǝmɑ̃/ *adv* ‹damaged› horribly; ‹cold› terribly

horrifier /ɔʀifje/ [2] *vtr* to horrify

horripiler /ɔʀipile/ [1] *vtr* to exasperate

✧ **hors** /'ɔʀ/

> ■ **Note** You will find translations for expressions such as *hors série, hors d'usage* etc, at the entries SÉRIE, USAGE etc.

1 *prep* outside; **longueur ~ tout** overall length
2 hors de *phr* out of, outside; **~ d'ici!** get out of here!
IDIOM être ~ de soi to be beside oneself

hors-bord /'ɔʀbɔʀ/ *nm inv* speedboat

hors-d'œuvre /'ɔʀdœvʀ/ *nm inv* starter, hors d'oeuvre

hors-jeu /'ɔʀʒø/ *nm inv* **(pour) ~** for offside

hors-la-loi /'ɔʀlalwa/ *nm inv* outlaw

hors-piste /'ɔʀpist/ *nm inv* off-piste skiing

hortensia /ɔʀtɑ̃sja/ *nm* hydrangea

horticulteur, -trice /ɔʀtikyltœʀ, tʀis/ *nm,f* horticulturist

hospice /ɔspis/ *nm* home; **~ de vieillards** old people's home

hospitalier, -ière /ɔspitalje, ɛʀ/ *adj*
(a) hospital; **centre ~** hospital
(b) hospitable

hospitalisation /ɔspitalizasjɔ̃/ *nf* hospitalization; **~ à domicile** home (medical) care

hospitaliser /ɔspitalize/ [1] *vtr* to hospitalize

hospitalité /ɔspitalite/ *nf* hospitality

hostie /ɔsti/ *nf* Host

hostile /ɔstil/ *adj* hostile

hostilité /ɔstilite/ *nf* hostility

hôte /ot/ **1** *nm* (a) host
(b) occupant
2 *nmf* guest

✧ **hôtel** /otɛl/ *nm* hotel
■ **~ particulier** town house; **~ de passe** hotel used by prostitutes; **~ des ventes** saleroom; **~ de ville** ≈ town hall

hôtelier, -ière /otəlje, ɛʀ/ **1** *adj* ‹industry› hotel; ‹school› hotel management
2 *nm,f* hotelier

hôtellerie /otɛlʀi/ *nf* hotel business

hôtesse /otɛs/ *nf* (at home, at exhibition) hostess; (in company) receptionist; (in boat) stewardess
■ **~ d'accueil** receptionist; **~ de l'air** air hostess

hotte /'ɔt/ *nf* (a) basket
(b) hood
■ **~ aspirante** extractor hood (GB), ventilator (US); **la ~ du Père Noël** Santa Claus's sack

houblon /'ublɔ̃/ *nm* hop, hops

houille /'uj/ *nf* coal

houiller, -ère /'uje, ɛʀ/ *adj* ‹industry› coal; ‹area› coalmining

houle /'ul/ *nf* swell

houlette /'ulɛt/ *nf* (of shepherd) crook; **sous la ~ de** (figurative) under the leadership of

houleux, -euse /'ulø, øz/ *adj* (a) ‹sea› rough
(b) ‹meeting› stormy

houppe /'up/ *nf* (a) (of hair) tuft; (of threads) tassel
(b) powder puff

houppette /'upɛt/ *nf* powder puff

hourra /'uʀa/ *nm* cheer

houspiller /'uspije/ [1] *vtr* to scold

housse /'us/ *nf* cover, slipcover; dustcover; garment bag

houx /'u/ *nm inv* holly

HT (written abbr = **hors taxes**) exclusive of tax

hublot /'yblo/ *nm* (in plane) window; (in boat) porthole

huche /'yʃ/ *nf* (a) chest
(b) **~ à pain** bread bin

huer /'ɥe/ [1] *vtr* to boo

✧ **huile** /'ɥil/ *nf* (a) oil
(b) oil painting
■ **~ de coude** (humorous) elbow grease; **~ solaire** suntan oil
IDIOMS tout/ça baigne dans l'~ (fam) everything/it is going smoothly; **jeter** *or* **verser de l'~ sur le feu** to add fuel to the fire

huiler /'ɥile/ [1] *vtr* to oil

huileux, -euse /'ɥilø, øz/ *adj* oily

huis /'ɥi/ *nm inv* **à ~ clos** (Law) in camera; (figurative) behind closed doors

huissier /'ɥisje/ *nm* (a) **~ (de justice)** bailiff
(b) porter; usher

✧ **huit** /'ɥit, *but before consonant* 'ɥi/ **1** *adj inv* eight; **mardi en ~** a week on Tuesday
2 *pron* eight
3 *nm inv* (a) eight
(b) a figure of eight

huitaine /ˈɥitɛn/ *nf* (a) about a week; **sous ~** within a week
(b) **une ~** about eight

huitième /ˈɥitjɛm/ **1** *adj* eighth
2 *nf* (Sch) *fourth year of primary school, age 9–10*

huître /ɥitʀ/ *nf* oyster

hululement /ˈylylmɑ̃/ *nm* hooting

hululer /ˈylyle/ [1] *vi* to hoot

⚔ **humain, ~e** /ymɛ̃, ɛn/ **1** *adj* (a) human; **pertes ~es** loss of life
(b) ⟨*regime*⟩ humane; ⟨*person*⟩ human, understanding
2 *nm* human (being)

humainement /ymɛnmɑ̃/ *adv*
(a) humanly
(b) humanely

humaniser /ymanize/ [1] **1** *vtr* to humanize
2 s'humaniser *v refl* (+ *v être*) to become more human

humanitaire /ymanitɛʀ/ *adj* humanitarian

⚔ **humanité** /ymanite/ *nf* humanity

humble /œ̃bl/ *adj* humble

humblement /œ̃blømɑ̃/ *adv* humbly

humecter /ymɛkte/ [1] *vtr* to moisten

humer /ˈyme/ [1] *vtr* to sniff; to smell

humeur /ymœʀ/ *nf* (a) mood; **être de bonne/mauvaise ~** to be in a good/bad mood
(b) temperament; **être d'~ égale** to be even-tempered; **être d'~ inégale** to be moody; **elle est connue pour sa bonne ~** she's known for her good humour
(c) bad temper; **geste d'~** bad-tempered gesture; **avec ~** bad-temperedly

humide /ymid/ *adj* (a) damp
(b) ⟨*climate*⟩ humid; ⟨*season*⟩ rainy; **il fait froid et ~** it's cold and damp; **il fait une chaleur ~** it's muggy

humidifier /ymidifje/ [2] *vtr* to humidify

humidité /ymidite/ *nf* (a) dampness, damp
(b) humidity

humiliant, ~e /ymiljɑ̃, ɑ̃t/ *adj* humiliating

humiliation /ymiljasjɔ̃/ *nf* humiliation

humilier /ymilje/ [2] *vtr* to humiliate

humilité /ymilite/ *nf* (a) humility
(b) (of task) humble nature

humoriste /ymɔʀist/ *nmf* (a) humorist
(b) joker

humoristique /ymɔʀistik/ *adj* humorous; **dessin ~** cartoon

humour /ymuʀ/ *nm* humour (GB); **avoir de l'~** to have a sense of humour (GB); **faire de l'~** to make jokes

huppé, ~e /ˈype/ *adj* (a) (fam) ⟨*person*⟩ upper-crust
(b) ⟨*bird*⟩ crested

hurlement /ˈyʀləmɑ̃/ *nm* (of animal) howl, howling; (of person) yell, howl; (of siren) wail, wailing

hurler /ˈyʀle/ [1] **1** *vtr* to yell
2 *vi* (a) to yell; (with pain, anger) to howl
(b) ⟨*siren*⟩ to wail; ⟨*wind*⟩ to roar; ⟨*radio*⟩ to blare
IDIOMS ~ avec les loups to follow the crowd; **~ à la mort** to bay at the moon

hurluberlu, ~e /ˈyʀlybɛʀly/ *nm,f* oddball (colloq)

hutte /ˈyt/ *nf* hut

hybride /ibʀid/ *adj, nm* hybrid

hydratant, ~e /idʀatɑ̃, ɑ̃t/ *adj* moisturizing

hydratation /idʀatasjɔ̃/ *nf* (a) hydration
(b) moisturizing

hydrate /idʀat/ *nm* **~ de carbone** carbohydrate

hydrater /idʀate/ [1] **1** *vtr* (a) to hydrate
(b) to moisturize ⟨*skin*⟩
2 s'hydrater *v refl* (+ *v être*) **bien s'~** to take plenty of fluids

hydraulique /idʀolik/ *adj* hydraulic

hydravion /idʀavjɔ̃/ *nm* seaplane, hydroplane

hydro /idʀo/ *pref* hydro; **~électrique** hydroelectric

hydrocarbure /idʀɔkaʀbyʀ/ *nm* hydrocarbon

hydrocution /idʀɔkysjɔ̃/ *nf* immersion hypothermia

hydrofuge /idʀɔfyʒ/ *adj* water-repellent

hydrogène /idʀɔʒɛn/ *nm* hydrogen

hydroglisseur /idʀɔglisœʀ/ *nm* hydroplane

hydrophile /idʀɔfil/ *adj* absorbent

hydroxyde /idʀɔksid/ *nm* hydroxide

hyène /ˈjɛn/ *nf* hyena

hygiaphone® /iʒjafɔn/ *nm* grill (*perforated communication panel*)

hygiène /iʒjɛn/ *nf* hygiene; **bonne ~ alimentaire** healthy diet
■ **~ corporelle** personal hygiene

hygiénique /iʒjenik/ *adj* (a) hygienic
(b) ⟨*lifestyle*⟩ healthy

hymen /imɛn/ *nm* (a) hymen
(b) nuptial bond

hymne /imn/ *nm* hymn; **~ national** national anthem

hyperactif, -ive /ipɛʀaktif, iv/ *adj* hyperactive

hyperclassique /ipɛʀklasik/ *adj* ⟨*reaction*⟩ absolutely classic; **roman ~** great classic

hypermarché /ipɛʀmaʀʃe/ *nm* hypermarket (GB), large supermarket

hypermétrope /ipɛʀmetʀɔp/ *adj* longsighted

hypernerveux, -euse /ipɛʀnɛʀvø, øz/ *adj* highly strung

hypersensible /ipɛʀsɑ̃sibl/ *adj* hypersensitive

hypersophistiqué, ~e /ipɛʀsɔfistike/ *adj* very sophisticated

hyperspécialisé, ~e /ipɛʀspesjalize/ *adj* highly specialized

hypertension /ipɛʀtɑ̃sjɔ̃/ *nf* ~ **(artérielle)** high blood pressure

hypertexte /ipɛʀtɛkst/ *nm* hypertext

hypertoile /ipɛʀtwal/ *nf* World Wide Web

hypertrophie /ipɛʀtʀɔfi/ *nf* **(a)** (Med) enlargement
(b) (of town) overdevelopment

hypertrophier: s'hypertrophier /ipɛʀtʀɔfje/ [2] *v refl* (+ *v être*) **(a)** (Med) to hypertrophy
(b) ‹town› to become overdeveloped

hypnose /ipnoz/ *nf* hypnosis

hypnotique /ipnɔtik/ *adj, nm* hypnotic

hypnotiser /ipnɔtize/ [1] *vtr* to hypnotize; (figurative) to mesmerize

hypnotiseur, -euse /ipnɔtizœʀ, øz/ *nm,f* hypnotist

hypocalorique /ipɔkalɔʀik/ *adj* low-calorie

hypocondriaque /ipɔkɔ̃dʀijak/ *adj, nmf* hypochondriac

hypocrisie /ipɔkʀizi/ *nf* hypocrisy

hypocrite /ipɔkʀit/ **1** *adj* hypocritical
2 *nmf* hypocrite

hypodermique /ipɔdɛʀmik/ *adj* hypodermic

hypokhâgne /ipɔkaɲ/ *nf*: first year preparatory class in humanities for entrance to École normale supérieure

hypotension /ipɔtɑ̃sjɔ̃/ *nf* ~ **(artérielle)** low blood pressure

hypothécaire /ipɔtekɛʀ/ *adj* mortgage; **créancier/débiteur** ~ mortgagee/mortgager

hypothèque /ipɔtɛk/ *nf* mortgage

hypothéquer /ipɔteke/ [14] *vtr* to mortgage

ᐟ **hypothèse** /ipɔtɛz/ *nf* hypothesis

hypothétique /ipɔtetik/ *adj* hypothetical

hystérie /isteʀi/ *nf* hysteria

hystérique /isteʀik/ *adj* hysterical

I i

i, I /i/ *nm inv* i, I
IDIOM **mettre les points sur les i** to make things crystal clear

ibérique /ibeʀik/ *adj* Iberian

iceberg /ajsbɛʀg, isbɛʀg/ *nm* iceberg

ᐟ **ici** /isi/ *adv* **(a)** here; **c'est** ~ **que...** this is where...; **par** ~ this way; around here; **les gens d'**~ the locals; **je vois ça d'**~**!** I can just picture it!
(b) **jusqu'**~ until now; until then; **d'**~ **peu** shortly; **d'**~ **deux jours** two days from now; **d'**~ **là** by then; **il l'aime bien, mais d'**~ **à ce qu'il l'épouse...** he likes her, but as for marrying her...

ici-bas /isibɑ/ *adv* here below

icône /ikon/ *nf* icon

id. *written abbr* = IDEM

ᐟ **idéal, ~e, mpl -aux** /ideal, o/ **1** *adj* ideal
2 *nm* ideal; **dans l'**~ ideally

idéalisme /idealism/ *nm* idealism

ᐟ **idée** /ide/ *nf* idea; thought; **avoir de l'**~ to be inventive; **avoir une** ~ **derrière la tête** to have something in mind; **se faire des** ~**s** to imagine things; **avoir les** ~**s larges** to be broad-minded; **changer d'**~ to change one's mind; **avoir de la suite dans les** ~**s** to be single-minded; not to be easily deterred;

avoir **dans l'**~ **de faire** to plan to do; **tu ne m'ôteras pas de l'**~ **que...** I still think that...; **ça ne m'est pas venu à l'**~ it never occurred to me
■ ~ **fixe** obsession; ~ **de génie** brainwave (colloq); ~ **noire** dark thought; ~ **reçue** received idea

idem /idɛm/ *adv* ditto

identification /idɑ̃tifikasjɔ̃/ *nf* identification

ᐟ **identifier** /idɑ̃tifje/ [2] **1** *vtr* to identify
2 **s'identifier** *v refl* (+ *v être*) **(a)** to become identified
(b) to identify

identique /idɑ̃tik/ *adj* **(a)** identical
(b) unchanged

ᐟ **identité** /idɑ̃tite/ *nf* **(a)** identity; **vol d'** ~ identity theft
(b) similarity

idéologie /ideɔlɔʒi/ *nf* ideology

idiomatique /idjɔmatik/ *adj* idiomatic

idiome /idjom/ *nm* idiom

idiot, ~e /idjo, ɔt/ **1** *adj* stupid
2 *nm* idiot; **faire l'**~ to behave like an idiot

idiotie /idjɔsi/ *nf* **(a)** stupid thing
(b) stupidity

idolâtrer /idɔlatʀe/ [1] *vtr* to idolize

idole /idɔl/ *nf* idol

idylle /idil/ *nf* **(a)** love affair

ᐟ indicates a very frequent word

(b) (in literature) idyll
idyllique /idilik/ *adj* idyllic
if /if/ *nm* **(a)** yew (tree)
(b) yew (wood)
IFOP /ifɔp/ *nm* (*abbr* = **Institut français d'opinion publique**) French institute for opinion polls
ignare /iɲaʀ/ *adj* ignorant
ignifuge /iɲify3/ *adj* fireproofing
ignifuger /iɲify3e/ [13] *vtr* to fireproof
ignoble /iɲɔbl/ *adj* **(a)** ‹*person, conduct*› vile
(b) ‹*place*› squalid; ‹*food*› revolting
ignominie /iɲɔmini/ *nf* **(a)** ignominy
(b) dreadful thing
ignorance /iɲɔʀɑ̃s/ *nf* ignorance
ignorant, ∼e /iɲɔʀɑ̃, ɑ̃t/ *adj* ignorant
ignoré, ∼e /iɲɔʀe/ *adj* unknown; ignored
✒ **ignorer** /iɲɔʀe/ [1] *vtr* **(a)** j'ignore comment/si I don't know how/whether; **∼** tout de qch to know nothing of *or* about sth; **∼** l'existence de to be unaware of the existence of
(b) to ignore ‹*person*›
iguane /igwan/ *nm* iguana
✒ **il** /il/ [1] *pron m* he; it; **∼s** they
[2] *pron impers* it; **∼** pleut it's raining
✒ **île** /il/ *nf* island
■ l'**∼** de Beauté Corsica
illégal, ∼e, *mpl* **-aux** /ilegal, o/ *adj* illegal
illégalité /ilegalite/ *nf* illegality; être dans l'**∼** to be in breach of the law
illégitime /ileʒitim/ *adj* ‹*child*› illegitimate
illégitimité /ileʒitimite/ *nf* (of child) illegitimacy; (of love) illicitness
illettré, ∼e /iletʀe/ *adj, nm,f* illiterate
illicite /ilisit/ *adj* illicit; unlawful
illico /iliko/ *adv* (fam) straightaway
illimité, ∼e /ilimite/ *adj* unlimited
illisible /ilizibl/ *adj* **(a)** illegible
(b) unreadable
illogique /ilɔʒik/ *adj* illogical
illumination /ilyminasjɔ̃/ [1] *nf*
(a) floodlighting
(b) flash of inspiration
[2] **illuminations** *nf pl* (in town) illuminations
illuminé, ∼e /ilymine/ [1] *adj*
(a) ‹*monument*› floodlit
(b) ‹*face*› radiant
[2] *nm,f* **(a)** visionary
(b) crank
illuminer /ilymine/ [1] [1] *vtr* **(a)** to illuminate; to floodlight
(b) ‹*smile*› to light up ‹*face*›
[2] **s'illuminer** *v refl* (+ *v être*) to light up
✒ **illusion** /ilyzjɔ̃/ *nf* illusion; se faire des **∼**s to delude oneself; il ne fait pas **∼** he doesn't fool anyone

illusionner: s'illusionner /ilyzjɔne/ *v refl* (+ *v être*) to delude oneself (**sur** qch/qn about sth/sb)
illusionniste /ilyzjɔnist/ *nmf* conjurer
illusoire /ilyzwaʀ/ *adj* illusory
illustrateur, -trice /ilystʀatœʀ, tʀis/ *nm,f* illustrator
illustration /ilystʀasjɔ̃/ *nf* illustration
illustre /ilystʀ/ *adj* illustrious
illustré /ilystʀe/ *nm* comic
illustrer /ilystʀe/ [1] [1] *vtr* to illustrate
[2] **s'illustrer** *v refl* (+ *v être*) to distinguish oneself
îlot /ilo/ *nm* **(a)** islet
(b) **∼s de végétation** isolated patches of vegetation
ils ▸ IL 1
✒ **image** /imaʒ/ *nf* **(a)** picture
(b) (on film) frame
(c) reflection, image
(d) à l'**∼** de ses prédécesseurs... just like his/her predecessors...
(e) image; les **∼**s d'un poème the imagery of a poem
■ **∼** d'Épinal *simplistic print of traditional French life*; (figurative) clichéd image; **∼** de marque brand image; corporate image; (public) image
imagé, ∼e /imaʒe/ *adj* ‹*style*› colourful (GB)
imagerie /imaʒʀi/ *nf* **(a)** imagery
(b) print trade
(c) imaging
imaginable /imaʒinabl/ *adj* conceivable, imaginable
imaginaire /imaʒinɛʀ/ *adj* imaginary
imaginatif, -ive /imaʒinatif, iv/ *adj* imaginative
✒ **imagination** /imaʒinasjɔ̃/ *nf* imagination
✒ **imaginer** /imaʒine/ [1] [1] *vtr* **(a)** to imagine, to picture
(b) to suppose
(c) to devise, to think up
[2] **s'imaginer** *v refl* (+ *v être*) **(a)** to imagine, to picture
(b) to picture oneself; s'**∼** à 60 ans to picture oneself at 60
(c) to think
imbattable /ɛ̃batabl/ *adj* unbeatable
imbécile /ɛ̃besil/ [1] *adj* idiotic
[2] *nmf* fool; faire l'**∼** to play the fool
imberbe /ɛ̃bɛʀb/ *adj* beardless
imbiber /ɛ̃bibe/ [1] [1] *vtr* to soak
[2] **s'imbiber** *v refl* (+ *v être*) s'**∼** de to become soaked with
imbriquer: s'imbriquer /ɛ̃bʀike/ [1] *v refl* (+ *v être*) **(a)** ‹*slates*› to overlap
(b) ‹*issues*› to be interlinked; ‹*parts*› to interlock
imbu, ∼e /ɛ̃by/ *adj* full; **∼** de sa personne full of oneself
imbuvable /ɛ̃byvabl/ *adj* **(a)** undrinkable ⋯⟶

(b) (fam) unbearable

imitateur, -trice /imitatœʀ, tʀis/ *nm,f*
(a) impressionist
(b) (of painting) imitator

imitation /imitasjɔ̃/ *nf* imitation; (of person)
impression

imiter /imite/ [1] *vtr* **(a)** to imitate; to forge
‹*signature*›
(b) to do an impression of [sb]
(c) il part, je vais l'~ he's leaving and I'm
going to do the same

immaculé, ~e /imakyle/ *adj* immaculate

immangeable /ɛ̃mɑ̃ʒabl/ *adj* inedible

immanquablement /ɛ̃mɑ̃kabləmɑ̃/ *adv*
inevitably

immatriculation /imatʀikylasjɔ̃/ *nf*
registration; numéro d'~ registration (GB)
or license (US) number

immatriculer /imatʀikyle/ [1] *vtr* to
register; to register (GB) *or* license (US) ‹*car*›

immédiat, ~e /imedja, at/ **1** *adj*
immediate
2 *nm* dans l'~ for the time being

⚡ **immédiatement** /imedjatmɑ̃/ *adv*
immediately

⚡ **immense** /imɑ̃s/ *adj* (gen) huge; ‹*pain,
regret*› immense; ‹*joy, courage*› great

immensité /imɑ̃site/ *nf* (of place)
immensity; (of knowledge) breadth

immerger /imɛʀʒe/ [13] *vtr* to immerse
‹*object*›; to bury [sth] at sea

immersion /imɛʀsjɔ̃/ *nf* **(a)** (of body, object)
immersion; (of corpse) burial at sea
(b) flooding

immettable /ɛ̃metabl/ *adj* (fam)
unwearable

immeuble /imœbl/ *nm* **(a)** building
(b) real asset

immigrant, ~e /imigʀɑ̃, ɑ̃t/ *adj, nm,f*
immigrant

immigration /imigʀasjɔ̃/ *nf* immigration

immigré, ~e /imigʀe/ *adj, nm,f*
immigrant

immigrer /imigʀe/ [1] *vi* to immigrate

imminent, ~e /iminɑ̃, ɑ̃t/ *adj* imminent

immiscer: s'**immiscer** /imise/ [12] *v refl*
(+ *v être*) to interfere

immobile /imɔbil/ *adj* (gen) motionless;
‹*vehicle*› stationary; ‹*stare*› fixed

immobilier /imɔbilje/ *nm* l'~ property
(GB), real estate (US)

immobiliser /imɔbilize/ [1] **1** *vtr* **(a)** to
bring [sth] to a standstill ‹*vehicle*›; to stop
‹*machine*›
(b) to immobilize ‹*person*›
(c) to tie up ‹*capital*›
2 s'**immobiliser** *v refl* (+ *v être*) to come
to a halt; to stop

⚡ indicates a very frequent word

immobilisme /imɔbilism/ *nm* opposition
to change

immobilité /imɔbilite/ *nf* **(a)** immobility
(b) stillness

immodéré, ~e /imɔdeʀe/ *adj*
(a) excessive
(b) immoderate

immoler /imɔle/ [1] *vtr* to sacrifice (à to)

immonde /imɔ̃d/ *adj* **(a)** filthy
(b) revolting

immondices /imɔ̃dis/ *nf pl* refuse (GB),
trash (US)

immoral, ~e, *mpl* **-aux** /imɔʀal, o/ *adj*
immoral

immortaliser /imɔʀtalize/ [1] *vtr* to
immortalize

immortel, -elle¹ /imɔʀtɛl/ *adj* immortal

immortelle² /imɔʀtɛl/ *nf* everlasting
(flower)

immuable /imɥabl/ *adj* **(a)** immutable
(b) unchanging
(c) perpetual

immuniser /imynize/ [1] *vtr* to immunize

immunitaire /imynitɛʀ/ *adj* (Med)
immune

immunité /imynite/ *nf* immunity

impact /ɛ̃pakt/ *nm* impact; mark

impair, ~e /ɛ̃pɛʀ/ **1** *adj* ‹*number*› odd;
‹*day, year*› odd-numbered
2 *nm* indiscretion, faux pas

imparable /ɛ̃paʀabl/ *adj* **(a)** unstoppable
(b) unanswerable
(c) irrefutable

impardonnable /ɛ̃paʀdɔnabl/ *adj*
unforgivable

imparfait, ~e /ɛ̃paʀfɛ, ɛt/ **1** *adj*
imperfect
2 *nm* l'~ the imperfect (tense)

impartial, ~e, *mpl* **-iaux** /ɛ̃paʀsjal, o/ *adj*
impartial

impartir /ɛ̃paʀtiʀ/ [3] *vtr* to give; dans les
temps impartis within the given time

impasse /ɛ̃pas/ *nf* **(a)** dead end
(b) deadlock

impassible /ɛ̃pasibl/ *adj* impassive

impatience /ɛ̃pasjɑ̃s/ *nf* impatience

impatient, ~e /ɛ̃pasjɑ̃, ɑ̃t/ *adj* impatient

impatienter /ɛ̃pasjɑ̃te/ [1] **1** *vtr* to
irritate
2 s'**impatienter** *v refl* (+ *v être*) to get
impatient

impayable /ɛ̃pɛjabl/ *adj* (fam) priceless

impayé, ~e /ɛ̃pɛje/ *adj* unpaid

impeccable /ɛ̃pɛkabl/ *adj* perfect;
impeccable; spotless

impénétrable /ɛ̃penetʀabl/ *adj*
(a) impenetrable
(b) inscrutable

impénitent, ~e /ɛ̃penitɑ̃, ɑ̃t/ *adj* ‹*drinker*›
inveterate; ‹*bachelor*› confirmed

impensable /ɛ̃pɑ̃sabl/ *adj* unthinkable

imper /ɛ̃pɛʀ/ *nm* (fam) raincoat, mac (GB) (colloq)

impératif, -ive /ɛ̃peʀatif, iv/ **1** *adj* imperative
2 *nm* (a) (of situation) imperative; (for quality) necessity
(b) (in grammar) imperative

impératrice /ɛ̃peʀatʀis/ *nf* empress

imperceptible /ɛ̃pɛʀsɛptibl/ *adj* imperceptible

imperfection /ɛ̃pɛʀfɛksjɔ̃/ *nf* imperfection

impérial, ~e¹, mpl -iaux /ɛ̃peʀjal, o/ *adj* imperial

impériale² /ɛ̃peʀjal/ *nf* autobus à ~ double-decker bus

impérialisme /ɛ̃peʀjalism/ *nm* imperialism

impérieux, -ieuse /ɛ̃peʀjø, øz/ *adj*
(a) imperious
(b) pressing

impérissable /ɛ̃peʀisabl/ *adj* imperishable

imperméable /ɛ̃pɛʀmeabl/ **1** *adj*
(a) ‹material› waterproof; ‹ground› impermeable
(b) impervious
2 *nm* raincoat

impertinence /ɛ̃pɛʀtinɑ̃s/ *nf*
(a) impertinence
(b) impertinent remark

impertinent, ~e /ɛ̃pɛʀtinɑ̃, ɑ̃t/ *adj* impertinent

imperturbable /ɛ̃pɛʀtyʀbabl/ *adj* imperturbable; unruffled

imperturbablement
/ɛ̃pɛʀtyʀbabləmɑ̃/ *adv* ‹continue, listen› unperturbed

impétueux, -euse /ɛ̃petɥø, øz/ *adj* (gen) impetuous; ‹torrent› raging

impie /ɛ̃pi/ *adj* impious

impitoyable /ɛ̃pitwajabl/ *adj* merciless, pitiless; relentless; ruthless

implacable /ɛ̃plakabl/ *adj* implacable; tough; harsh

implacablement /ɛ̃plakabləmɑ̃/ *adv* relentlessly; ruthlessly

implantation /ɛ̃plɑ̃tasjɔ̃/ *nf* establishment; setting up; installation; settlement

implanté, ~e /ɛ̃plɑ̃te/ *adj* (a) ‹factory, party› established; ‹population› settled
(b) ‹roots› established; **dents mal ~es** crooked teeth

implanter /ɛ̃plɑ̃te/ [1] **1** *vtr* (a) to establish ‹factory›; to build ‹supermarket›; to open ‹agency›; to introduce ‹product, fashion›; to instil (GB) ‹ideas›
(b) (Med) to implant
2 s'implanter *v refl* (+ *v être*) ‹company,

‹product› to establish itself; ‹factory› to be built; ‹person› to settle; ‹party› to gain a following

implication /ɛ̃plikasjɔ̃/ *nf* (a) involvement
(b) implication
(c) commitment

implicite /ɛ̃plisit/ *adj* implicit

implicitement /ɛ̃plisitmɑ̃/ *adv* implicitly; (Comput) by default

🎵 **impliquer** /ɛ̃plike/ [1] *vtr* (a) to implicate
(b) to involve ‹staff›
(c) to involve (**de faire** doing)
(d) to mean

implorer /ɛ̃plɔʀe/ [1] *vtr* (a) to beseech, to implore
(b) to beg for

imploser /ɛ̃ploze/ [1] *vi* to implode

impoli, ~e /ɛ̃pɔli/ *adj* rude, impolite

impolitesse /ɛ̃pɔlitɛs/ *nf* rudeness

impondérable /ɛ̃pɔ̃deʀabl/ *nm* imponderable

impopulaire /ɛ̃pɔpylɛʀ/ *adj* unpopular

🎵 **importance** /ɛ̃pɔʀtɑ̃s/ *nf* (a) importance; **quelle ~?** what does it matter?
(b) size; (of damage) extent; **prendre de l'~** to increase in size
(c) **prendre de l'~** ‹person› to become more important

🎵 **important, ~e** /ɛ̃pɔʀtɑ̃, ɑ̃t/ **1** *adj*
(a) important
(b) significant; considerable; sizeable; large; lengthy
(c) **prendre un air ~** to adopt a self-important manner
2 *nm,f* **jouer les ~s** to act important (colloq)

importateur, -trice /ɛ̃pɔʀtatœʀ, tʀis/
1 *adj* importing
2 *nm,f* importer

importation /ɛ̃pɔʀtasjɔ̃/ *nf*
(a) importation
(b) import

🎵 **importer** /ɛ̃pɔʀte/ [1] **1** *vtr* to import
2 *v impers* **peu importe** *or* **qu'importe que…** it doesn't matter *or* what does it matter if…; **n'importe quel enfant** any child; **n'importe qui** anybody, anyone; **n'importe lequel** any; **n'importe où** anywhere; **prends n'importe quoi** take anything; **elle dit n'importe quoi** she talks nonsense

importun, ~e /ɛ̃pɔʀtœ̃, yn/ **1** *adj*
(a) troublesome; tiresome; **visiteur ~** unwelcome visitor
(b) ‹visit› ill-timed; ‹remark› ill-chosen
2 *nm,f* unwelcome visitor; tiresome individual

importuner /ɛ̃pɔʀtyne/ [1] *vtr* (a) to bother
(b) to disturb

imposable /ɛ̃pozabl/ *adj* ‹person› liable to tax; ‹income› taxable

imposant, ~e /ɛ̃pozɑ̃, ɑ̃t/ *adj* imposing

⚷ **imposer** /ɛ̃poze/ [1] **1** *vtr* (a) ‹person› to impose ‹sanctions, deadline›; to lay down ‹rule›; **elle nous a imposé le silence** she made us be quiet
(b) to impose ‹idea, opinion›; to set ‹fashion›
(c) to command ‹respect›
(d) to tax
2 **en imposer** *v+prep* **elle en impose à ses élèves** she inspires respect in her pupils
3 **s'imposer** *v refl* (+ *v être*) (a) ‹choice, solution› to be obvious; to be called for; **une visite au Louvre s'impose** a visit to the Louvre is a must
(b) to impose [sth] on oneself; **s'~ de travailler le soir** to make it a rule to work in the evening
(c) to impose (à qn on sb)
(d) **s'~ comme leader** to establish oneself/ itself as the leader; **s'~ sur un marché** to establish itself in a market
(e) ‹person› to make one's presence felt; ‹will› to impose itself

imposition /ɛ̃pozisjɔ̃/ *nf* taxation

impossibilité /ɛ̃pɔsibilite/ *nf* impossibility; **être dans l'~ de faire** to be unable to do

⚷ **impossible** /ɛ̃pɔsibl/ **1** *adj* impossible
2 *nm* **l'~** the impossible; **faire** *or* **tenter l'~** to do everything one can

imposteur /ɛ̃pɔstœʀ/ *nm* impostor

imposture /ɛ̃pɔstyʀ/ *nf* (a) deception
(b) fraud

impôt /ɛ̃po/ *nm* tax; **après ~** after tax
■ **~ sur le revenu** income tax

impotent, ~e /ɛ̃pɔtɑ̃, ɑ̃t/ **1** *adj* infirm
2 *nm,f* person with impaired mobility

impraticable /ɛ̃pʀatikabl/ *adj* impassable

imprécis, ~e /ɛ̃pʀesi, iz/ *adj* ‹outline, memory› vague; ‹concept› hazy; ‹aim› inaccurate; ‹results› imprecise; ‹person› vague

imprécision /ɛ̃pʀesizjɔ̃/ *nf* imprecision; vagueness; inaccuracy

imprégner /ɛ̃pʀeɲe/ [14] **1** *vtr* to impregnate
2 **s'imprégner** *v refl* (+ *v être*) **s'~ de** to become soaked with ‹water›; to immerse oneself in ‹language›

imprenable /ɛ̃pʀənabl/ *adj* **avec vue ~** with unobstructed view guaranteed

imprésario /ɛ̃pʀesaʀjo/ *nm* agent, impresario

⚷ **impression** /ɛ̃pʀesjɔ̃/ *nf* (a) impression; **faire bonne ~** to make a good impression; **j'ai l'~ d'être surveillé** I feel I am being watched
(b) printing; **faute d'~** misprint
(c) pattern

⚷ indicates a very frequent word

impressionnant, ~e /ɛ̃pʀesjɔnɑ̃, ɑ̃t/ *adj*
(a) impressive
(b) disturbing

impressionner /ɛ̃pʀesjɔne/ [1] *vtr* (a) to impress
(b) ‹image› to disturb
(c) to act on ‹retina›

impressionnisme /ɛ̃pʀesjɔnism/ *nm* Impressionism

impressionniste /ɛ̃pʀesjɔnist/ *nmf* Impressionist

imprévisible /ɛ̃pʀevizibl/ *adj* unpredictable

imprévu, ~e /ɛ̃pʀevy/ **1** *adj*
(a) unforeseen
(b) unexpected
2 *nm* (a) hitch
(b) **l'~** the unexpected; **plein d'~** ‹person, film› quirky; ‹trip› with a few surprises
(c) unforeseen expense

imprimante /ɛ̃pʀimɑ̃t/ *nf* printer
■ **~ à jet d'encre** ink-jet printer; **~ (à) laser** laser printer; **~ à marguerite** daisywheel printer; **~ matricielle** dot matrix printer

imprimé, ~e /ɛ̃pʀime/ **1** *pp* ▶ IMPRIMER
2 *pp adj* printed (de with)
3 *nm* (a) form
(b) printed matter
(c) print; **un ~ à fleurs** a floral print

imprimer /ɛ̃pʀime/ [1] *vtr* (a) to print ‹text›
(b) to put ‹stamp, seal›
(c) to leave an imprint of [sth]

imprimerie /ɛ̃pʀimʀi/ *nf* (a) printing; **atelier d'~** printing shop
(b) printing works
(c) printers, print workers

imprimeur /ɛ̃pʀimœʀ/ *nm* printer

improbable /ɛ̃pʀɔbabl/ *adj* unlikely

improductif, **-ive** /ɛ̃pʀɔdyktif, iv/ *adj* unproductive; **capitaux ~s** idle capital

impromptu, ~e /ɛ̃pʀɔ̃pty/ **1** *adj* impromptu
2 *adv* impromptu

impropre /ɛ̃pʀɔpʀ/ *adj* ‹term, usage› incorrect; **~ à** unfit for ‹human consumption›

improvisation /ɛ̃pʀɔvizasjɔ̃/ *nf* improvisation

improvisé, ~e /ɛ̃pʀɔvize/ *adj* ‹speech› improvised; ‹meal› impromptu; ‹means› makeshift; ‹solution› ad hoc; ‹cook› stand-in

improviser /ɛ̃pʀɔvize/ [1] **1** *vtr* to improvise ‹meal, speech›; to concoct ‹excuse, alibi›
2 *vi* to improvise
3 **s'improviser** *v refl* (+ *v être*) (a) **s'~ cuisinier** to act as a cook
(b) **un camp pour réfugiés ne s'improvise pas** you can't create a refugee camp just like that

improviste: **à l'improviste** /alɛ̃pʀɔvist/ *phr* unexpectedly

imprudemment /ɛ̃pʀydamɑ̃/ adv ‹speak› carelessly; ‹act› unwisely

imprudence /ɛ̃pʀydɑ̃s/ nf (a) carelessness (b) **commettre une ~** to do something foolish

imprudent, ~e /ɛ̃pʀydɑ̃, ɑ̃t/ adj ‹person, words› careless; ‹action› rash

impudence /ɛ̃pydɑ̃s/ nf impudence

impudent, ~e /ɛ̃pydɑ̃, ɑ̃t/ adj impudent

impudeur /ɛ̃pydœʀ/ nf immodesty; shamelessness

impuissance /ɛ̃pɥisɑ̃s/ nf (gen, Med) impotence; **~ à faire** inability to do

impuissant, ~e /ɛ̃pɥisɑ̃, ɑ̃t/ adj (a) powerless, helpless (b) (Med) impotent

impulsif, -ive /ɛ̃pylsif, iv/ adj impulsive

impulsion /ɛ̃pylsjɔ̃/ nf (a) (gen) impulse; (Tech) pulse (b) (figurative) impetus

impunément /ɛ̃pynemɑ̃/ adv with impunity; **on ne joue pas ~ avec sa santé** you don't play fast and loose with your health and get away with it

impuni, ~e /ɛ̃pyni/ adj unpunished

impunité /ɛ̃pynite/ nf impunity

impur, ~e /ɛ̃pyʀ/ adj (a) ‹thoughts› impure (b) ‹air› dirty; ‹blood› tainted (c) ‹ore› impure

impureté /ɛ̃pyʀte/ nf impurity

imputable /ɛ̃pytabl/ adj (a) attributable (à to) (b) chargeable (sur to)

imputer /ɛ̃pyte/ [1] vtr to attribute, to impute

inabordable /inabɔʀdabl/ adj (a) ‹coast› inaccessible (b) ‹prices› prohibitive

inacceptable /inaksɛptabl/ adj unacceptable

inaccessible /inaksesibl/ adj (a) inaccessible (b) ‹person› unapproachable

inaccoutumé /inakutyme/ adj unusual

inachevé, ~e /inaʃve/ adj unfinished

inactif, -ive /inaktif, iv/ [1] adj, idle; ‹person› inactive; ‹population› non-working [2] nm,f non-worker; **les ~s** the non-working population

inactivité /inaktivite/ nf inactivity

inadaptation /inadaptasjɔ̃/ nf (a) (of law, equipment) inappropriateness (à for) (b) (emotional, social) maladjustment (à to)

inadapté, ~e /inadapte/ adj (a) ‹child› maladjusted (b) ‹means› inappropriate; ‹tool› unsuitable; ‹law› ill-adapted

inadéquat, ~e /inadekwa, at/ adj inadequate; unsuitable

inadmissible /inadmisibl/ adj (a) intolerable (b) unacceptable

inadvertance: par inadvertance /paʀinadvɛʀtɑ̃s/ phr inadvertently

inaltérable /inalteʀabl/ adj (a) ‹substance› unalterable, non-corroding; ‹colour› fade-resistant (b) ‹character› constant; ‹principle› immutable; ‹hope› steadfast

inaltéré, ~e /inalteʀe/ adj ‹substance› unaltered; ‹sky, air› pure

inamovible /inamɔvibl/ adj irremovable

inanimé, ~e /inanime/ adj ‹matter› inanimate; ‹person› unconscious; lifeless

inanition /inanisjɔ̃/ nf starvation

inaperçu, ~e /inapɛʀsy/ adj **passer ~** to go unnoticed

inapte /inapt/ adj unfit

inaptitude /inaptityd/ nf unfitness

inarticulé, ~e /inaʀtikyle/ adj inarticulate

inassouvi, ~e /inasuvi/ adj ‹appetite› insatiable; ‹person, desire› unsatisfied

inattaquable /inatakabl/ adj (a) (Mil) unassailable (b) irreproachable (c) irrefutable

inattendu, ~e /inatɑ̃dy/ adj unexpected

inattentif, -ive /inatɑ̃tif, iv/ adj (a) inattentive; distracted (b) heedless

inattention /inatɑ̃sjɔ̃/ nf inattention; **faute d'~** careless mistake

inaudible /inodibl/ adj inaudible

inaugural, ~e, mpl -aux /inogyʀal, o/ adj (a) ‹ceremony› inauguration (b) ‹flight› maiden

inauguration /inogyʀasjɔ̃/ nf (of building) inauguration; (of exhibition) opening

inaugurer /inogyʀe/ [1] vtr (a) to unveil ‹statue, plaque›; to open ‹motorway, school› (b) to open ‹conference› (c) to mark the start of ‹period›

inavouable /inavwabl/ adj shameful

inavoué, ~e /inavwe/ adj ‹crime, vice› unconfessed; ‹aim› undisclosed; ‹fear› hidden

incalculable /ɛ̃kalkylabl/ adj (a) innumerable (b) incalculable

incandescent, ~e /ɛ̃kɑ̃dɛsɑ̃, ɑ̃t/ adj incandescent; white-hot; glowing

✗ **incapable** /ɛ̃kapabl/ adj (a) **~ de faire** incapable of doing; unable to do (b) incompetent

incapacité /ɛ̃kapasite/ nf (a) inability; **être dans l'~ de faire** to be unable to do (b) incompetence (c) disability (d) (Law) incapacity

incarcération /ɛ̃kaʀseʀasjɔ̃/ *nf* imprisonment

incarcérer /ɛ̃kaʀseʀe/ [14] *vtr* to imprison

incarnation /ɛ̃kaʀnasjɔ̃/ *nf* incarnation

incarné, **~e** /ɛ̃kaʀne/ *adj* (a) c'est la bêtise **~e** he/she is stupidity itself
(b) ⟨*nail*⟩ ingrowing

incarner /ɛ̃kaʀne/ [1] **1** *vtr* (a) to embody
(b) to play, to portray
2 **s'incarner** *v refl* (+ *v être*) to become incarnate

incartade /ɛ̃kaʀtad/ *nf* (a) misdemeanour (GB)
(b) (in riding) shy; faire une **~** to shy

incassable /ɛ̃kasabl/ *adj* unbreakable

incendiaire /ɛ̃sɑ̃djɛʀ/ **1** *adj* (a) ⟨*bomb*⟩ incendiary
(b) ⟨*statement*⟩ inflammatory
2 *nmf* arsonist

incendie /ɛ̃sɑ̃di/ *nm* fire; **~** criminel arson

incendier /ɛ̃sɑ̃dje/ [2] *vtr* (a) to burn (down), to torch
(b) (fam) to haul [sb] over the coals

incertain, **~e** /ɛ̃sɛʀtɛ̃, ɛn/ *adj* ⟨*person, date, result*⟩ uncertain; ⟨*effect*⟩ unknown; ⟨*colour*⟩ indeterminate; ⟨*smile*⟩ vague; ⟨*weather*⟩ unsettle; ⟨*step*⟩ hesitant

incertitude /ɛ̃sɛʀtityd/ *nf* uncertainty

incessamment /ɛ̃sesamɑ̃/ *adv* very shortly

incessant, **~e** /ɛ̃sɛsɑ̃, ɑ̃t/ *adj* ⟨*noise, rain*⟩ incessant; ⟨*activity*⟩ unceasing

inceste /ɛ̃sɛst/ *nm* incest

incestueux, **-euse** /ɛ̃sɛstɥø, øz/ *adj* incestuous

inchangé, **~e** /ɛ̃ʃɑ̃ʒe/ *adj* unchanged

incidemment /ɛ̃sidamɑ̃/ *adv* (a) in passing
(b) by chance

incidence /ɛ̃sidɑ̃s/ *nf* (a) impact
(b) incidence

incident, **~e** /ɛ̃sidɑ̃, ɑ̃t/ *nm* incident; **~** de parcours hitch; l'**~** est clos the matter is closed

incinérateur /ɛ̃sineʀatœʀ/ *nm*
(a) incinerator
(b) crematorium (GB), crematory (US)

incinération /ɛ̃sineʀasjɔ̃/ *nf* (a) incineration
(b) cremation

incinérer /ɛ̃sineʀe/ [14] *vtr* (a) to burn; to incinerate
(b) to cremate

inciser /ɛ̃size/ [1] *vtr* to make an incision in

incisif, **-ive¹** /ɛ̃sizif, iv/ *adj* ⟨*criticism*⟩ incisive; ⟨*portrait*⟩ telling; ⟨*look*⟩ piercing

incision /ɛ̃sizjɔ̃/ *nf* incision

incisive² /ɛ̃siziv/ **1** *adj f* ▶ INCISIF
2 *nf* incisor

♂ indicates a very frequent word

incitation /ɛ̃sitasjɔ̃/ *nf* (a) incentive
(b) (Law) incitement

inciter /ɛ̃site/ [1] *vtr* ⟨*person, situation*⟩ to encourage; ⟨*event, decision*⟩ to prompt; **~** qn à la prudence to make sb cautious

inclassable /ɛ̃klasabl/ *adj* unclassifiable

inclinable /ɛ̃klinabl/ *adj* adjustable

inclinaison /ɛ̃klinɛzɔ̃/ *nf* (of hill) incline; (of wall, seat) angle; (of roof) slope; (of boat) list

inclination /ɛ̃klinasjɔ̃/ *nf* inclination

incliné, **~e** /ɛ̃kline/ *adj* (a) ⟨*ground*⟩ sloping; ⟨*roof*⟩ steep
(b) ⟨*wall*⟩ leaning

incliner /ɛ̃kline/ [1] **1** *vtr* to tilt ⟨*sunshade*⟩; to tip up ⟨*bottle*⟩; **~** le buste to lean forward
2 **s'incliner** *v refl* (+ *v être*) (a) to lean forward; (politely) to bow
(b) s'**~** devant qch to bow to sth, to accept sth
(c) to give in (colloq)
(d) s'**~** devant le courage de qn to admire sb's courage

inclure /ɛ̃klyʀ/ [78] *vtr* (a) to include
(b) to enclose

inclus, **~e** /ɛ̃kly, yz/ **1** *pp* ▶ INCLURE
2 *pp adj* (a) jusqu'à jeudi **~** up to and including Thursday (GB), through Thursday (US)
(b) enclosed

inclusion /ɛ̃klyzjɔ̃/ *nf* inclusion

inclusivement /ɛ̃klyzivmɑ̃/ *adv* jusqu'au 4 mai **~** till 4 May inclusive

incognito **1** *adv* incognito
2 *nm* garder l'**~** to remain incognito

incohérence /ɛ̃kɔeʀɑ̃s/ *nf*
(a) incoherence
(b) discrepancy

incohérent, **~e** /ɛ̃kɔeʀɑ̃, ɑ̃t/ *adj* ⟨*talk, behaviour*⟩ incoherent; ⟨*attitude*⟩ illogical

incollable /ɛ̃kɔlabl/ *adj* (a) elle est **~** en latin you can't catch her out in Latin
(b) riz **~** easy-cook rice

incolore /ɛ̃kɔlɔʀ/ *adj* colourless (GB); ⟨*glass*⟩ clear

incomber /ɛ̃kɔ̃be/ [1] *v+prep* **~** à ⟨*task*⟩ to fall to; ⟨*responsibility*⟩ to lie with

incommode /ɛ̃kɔmɔd/ *adj*
(a) inconvenient; awkward
(b) uncomfortable

incommodé, **~e** /ɛ̃kɔmɔde/ **1** *pp* ▶ INCOMMODER
2 *pp adj* unwell, indisposed

incommoder /ɛ̃kɔmɔde/ [1] *vtr* to bother

incomparable /ɛ̃kɔ̃paʀabl/ *adj* incomparable

incompatible /ɛ̃kɔ̃patibl/ *adj* incompatible

incompétence /ɛ̃kɔ̃petɑ̃s/ *nf* (gen) incompetence; (Law) incompetency

incompétent, ∼**e** /ɛ̃kɔ̃petã, ãt/ *adj*
incompetent

incomplet, -ète /ɛ̃kɔ̃plɛ, ɛt/ *adj*
incomplete

incompréhensible /ɛ̃kɔ̃pʀeãsibl/ *adj*
incomprehensible

incompréhension /ɛ̃kɔ̃pʀeãsjɔ̃/ *nf*
(a) incomprehension
(b) lack of understanding

incompressible /ɛ̃kɔ̃pʀɛsibl/ *adj*
(a) incompressible
(b) ⟨costs⟩ fixed

incompris, ∼**e** /ɛ̃kɔ̃pʀi, iz/ *nm,f*
misunderstood person

inconcevable /ɛ̃kɔ̃svabl/ *adj*
inconceivable

inconditionnel, -elle
/ɛ̃kɔ̃disjɔnɛl/ ⟨1⟩ *adj* unconditional
⟨2⟩ *nm,f* devoted admirer; fan

inconfortable /ɛ̃kɔ̃fɔʀtabl/ *adj*
(a) uncomfortable
(b) awkward

incongru, ∼**e** /ɛ̃kɔ̃gʀy/ *adj* ⟨behaviour⟩
unseemly; ⟨remark⟩ incongruous

incongruité /ɛ̃kɔ̃gʀɥite/ *nf* incongruity

✔ **inconnu**, ∼**e** /ɛ̃kɔny/ ⟨1⟩ *adj* unknown;
⟨territories⟩ unexplored
⟨2⟩ *nm,f* (a) unknown (person)
(b) stranger

inconsciemment /ɛ̃kɔ̃sjamã/ *adv*
(a) subconsciously
(b) unintentionally, unconsciously

inconscience /ɛ̃kɔ̃sjãs/ *nf*
(a) recklessness
(b) (Med) unconsciousness

inconscient, ∼**e** /ɛ̃kɔ̃sjã, ãt/ ⟨1⟩ *adj*
(a) unthinking; foolhardy
(b) (Med) unconscious
(c) ⟨act, gesture⟩ unconscious, automatic
⟨2⟩ *nm,f* c'est un ∼ he's irresponsible
⟨3⟩ *nm* l'∼ the unconscious

inconséquent, ∼**e** /ɛ̃kɔ̃sekã, ãt/ *adj*
⟨person, behaviour⟩ inconsistent

inconsidéré, ∼**e** /ɛ̃kɔ̃sideʀe/ *adj*
(a) ⟨remark, act⟩ ill-considered
(b) ⟨consumption⟩ excessive

inconsidérément /ɛ̃kɔ̃sideʀemã/ *adv*
⟨drink⟩ to excess; ⟨spend⟩ wildly

inconsistant, ∼**e** /ɛ̃kɔ̃sistã, ãt/ *adj*
⟨argument, plot⟩ flimsy; ⟨programme⟩ lacking
in substance; ⟨person⟩ characterless

inconstant, ∼**e** /ɛ̃kɔ̃stã, ãt/ *adj* fickle

incontestable /ɛ̃kɔ̃tɛstabl/ *adj*
unquestionable, indisputable

incontesté, ∼**e** /ɛ̃kɔ̃tɛste/ *adj* ⟨victory⟩
undisputed; ⟨fact⟩ uncontested

incontinent, ∼**e** /ɛ̃kɔ̃tinã, ãt/ *adj*
incontinent

incontournable /ɛ̃kɔ̃tuʀnabl/ *adj* ⟨facts⟩
that cannot be ignored

incontrôlable /ɛ̃kɔ̃tʀolabl/ *adj*
(a) unverifiable
(b) uncontrollable

inconvenance /ɛ̃kɔ̃vnãs/ *nf* impropriety

inconvenant, ∼**e** /ɛ̃kɔ̃vnã, ãt/ *adj*
unsuitable; improper, unseemly

inconvénient /ɛ̃kɔ̃venjã/ *nm* drawback,
disadvantage; **si vous n'y voyez pas d'**∼ if
you have no objection

incorporer /ɛ̃kɔʀpɔʀe/ [1] *vtr* (a) (Culin)
to blend
(b) to incorporate

incorrect, ∼**e** /ɛ̃kɔʀɛkt/ *adj* (a) incorrect;
faulty; inaccurate
(b) ⟨behaviour⟩ improper; ⟨term⟩ unsuitable;
⟨person⟩ impolite
(c) unfair

incorrection /ɛ̃kɔʀɛksjɔ̃/ *nf* (of style,
language) incorrectness; (of behaviour)
impropriety

incorrigible /ɛ̃kɔʀiʒibl/ *adj* incorrigible

incrédule /ɛ̃kʀedyl/ *adj* incredulous

incrédulité /ɛ̃kʀedylite/ *nf* incredulity

incriminer /ɛ̃kʀimine/ [1] *vtr* ⟨person⟩ to
accuse; ⟨evidence⟩ to incriminate; **l'article
incriminé** the offending article

incroyable /ɛ̃kʀwajabl/ *adj* incredible,
unbelievable; ∼ **mais vrai** strange but true

incrustation /ɛ̃kʀystasjɔ̃/ *nf* (a) inlaying
(b) inlay
(c) encrustation

incruster /ɛ̃kʀyste/ [1] ⟨1⟩ *vtr* (a) to inlay
(b) **incrusté de diamants** encrusted with
diamonds
⟨2⟩ **s'incruster** *v refl* (+ *v être*) ⟨pebble,
shell⟩ to become embedded

incubation /ɛ̃kybasjɔ̃/ *nf* incubation

incuber /ɛ̃kybe/ [1] *vtr* to incubate, to
hatch

inculpation /ɛ̃kylpasjɔ̃/ *nf* (Law) charge

inculpé, ∼**e** /ɛ̃kylpe/ *nm,f* l'∼ ≈ the
accused

inculper /ɛ̃kylpe/ [1] *vtr* (Law) to charge

inculquer /ɛ̃kylke/ [1] *vtr* to inculcate

inculte /ɛ̃kylt/ *adj* uncultivated

incurable /ɛ̃kyʀabl/ *adj, nmf* incurable

incursion /ɛ̃kyʀsjɔ̃/ *nf* incursion, foray

incurver /ɛ̃kyʀve/ [1] *vtr*, **s'incurver**
v refl (+ *v être*), to curve, to bend

Inde /ɛ̃d/ *pr nf* India

indécence /ɛ̃desãs/ *nf* (gen) indecency; (of
remark) impropriety

indécent, ∼**e** /ɛ̃desã, ãt/ *adj* indecent;
⟨luxury⟩ obscene

indéchiffrable /ɛ̃deʃifʀabl/ *adj*
(a) indecipherable
(b) ⟨mystery⟩ incomprehensible

indécis, ∼**e** /ɛ̃desi, iz/ ⟨1⟩ *adj* (a) **il est
encore** ∼ he hasn't decided yet
(b) indecisive ⋯⋗

2 *nm,f* **(a)** indecisive person
(b) (in opinion poll) 'don't know'; (in election) floating voter
indécision /ɛ̃desizjɔ̃/ *nf* **(a)** indecision, uncertainty
(b) indecisiveness
indécrottable /ɛ̃dekʀɔtabl/ *adj* (fam) hopeless (colloq)
indéfini, ~**e** /ɛ̃defini/ *adj* **(a)** ‹*number*› indeterminate
(b) ‹*sadness*› undefined; ‹*duration*› indefinite
(c) (in grammar) indefinite
indéfiniment /ɛ̃definimã/ *adv* indefinitely
indéfinissable /ɛ̃definisabl/ *adj* undefinable
indélébile /ɛ̃delebil/ *adj* indelible
indélicatesse /ɛ̃delikatɛs/ *nf*
(a) indelicacy, tactlessness
(b) dishonesty
(c) act of dishonesty
indemne /ɛ̃dɛmn/ *adj* unscathed, unharmed
indemnisation /ɛ̃dɛmnizasjɔ̃/ *nf*
(a) indemnification
(b) indemnity, compensation
indemniser /ɛ̃dɛmnize/ [1] *vtr* to indemnify
indemnité /ɛ̃dɛmnite/ *nf* **(a)** (Law) indemnity, compensation
(b) allowance
■ ~ **de chômage** unemployment benefit; ~ **journalière** sick pay; ~ **de licenciement** severance pay
indéniable /ɛ̃denjabl/ *adj* undeniable
indentation /ɛ̃dãtasjɔ̃/ *nf* indentation
indépendamment /ɛ̃depãdamã/ 1 *adv* independently
2 **indépendamment de** *phr*
(a) regardless of
(b) in addition to
indépendance /ɛ̃depãdãs/ *nf* independence
indépendant, ~**e** /ɛ̃depãdã, ãt/ 1 *adj*
(a) independent
(b) ‹*room*› separate; **maison** ~**e** detached house
2 *nm,f* freelance, self-employed person
indépendantiste /ɛ̃depãdãtist/ 1 *adj* ‹*organization*› (pro-)independence
2 *nmf* **(a)** freedom fighter
(b) member of an independence movement
indescriptible /ɛ̃dɛskʀiptibl/ *adj* indescribable
indésirable /ɛ̃deziʀabl/ *adj* ‹*person*› undesirable; **effets** ~**s** (Med) adverse reactions
indéterminé, ~**e** /ɛ̃detɛʀmine/ *adj* ‹*form, quantity*› indeterminate; ‹*reason*›

unspecified
index /ɛ̃dɛks/ *nm inv* **(a)** index; **mettre qn/ qch à l'**~ to blacklist sb/sth
(b) forefinger
indexer /ɛ̃dɛkse/ [1] *vtr* **(a)** to index-link; ~ **qch sur qch** to index sth to sth
(b) to index
indicateur, -trice /ɛ̃dikatœʀ, tʀis/
1 *adj* **panneau** *or* **poteau** ~ signpost
2 *nm* **(a)** informer
(b) indicator
(c) gauge, indicator
indicatif, -ive /ɛ̃dikatif, iv/ 1 *adj* indicative
2 *nm* **(a)** (in grammar) indicative
(b) ~ **(téléphonique)** dialling (GB) code
(c) theme tune
indication /ɛ̃dikasjɔ̃/ *nf* **(a)** indication
(b) information; **sauf** ~ **contraire** unless otherwise indicated
(c) (for use) instruction
(d) indication, clue
indice /ɛ̃dis/ *nm* **(a)** sign, indication
(b) (in inquiry) clue
(c) (Econ) index; ~ **du coût de la vie** cost of living index
(d) l'~ **d'écoute** audience ratings
■ ~ **de masse corporel** body mass index
indicible /ɛ̃disibl/ *adj* inexpressible
✓ **indien, -ienne** /ɛ̃djɛ̃, ɛn/ *adj* **(a)** Indian
(b) (North American) Indian
indifféremment /ɛ̃difeʀamã/ *adv*
(a) equally
(b) servir ~ **de salon ou de bureau** to be used either as a living room or a study
indifférence /ɛ̃difeʀãs/ *nf* indifference
indifférent, ~**e** /ɛ̃difeʀã, ãt/ *adj*
(a) indifferent
(b) irrelevant
indifférer /ɛ̃difeʀe/ [14] *vtr* to leave [sb] indifferent
indigence /ɛ̃diʒãs/ *nf* destitution, extreme poverty
indigène /ɛ̃diʒɛn/ 1 *adj* **(a)** ‹*fauna, flora*› indigenous
(b) ‹*population, custom*› local; native
2 *nmf* local; native
indigeste /ɛ̃diʒɛst/ *adj* indigestible
indigestion /ɛ̃diʒɛstjɔ̃/ *nf* **(a)** indigestion
(b) avoir une ~ **de qch** to be fed up with sth (colloq)
indignation /ɛ̃diɲasjɔ̃/ *nf* indignation
indigne /ɛ̃diɲ/ *adj* **(a)** ‹*conduct*› disgraceful; ‹*mother, son*› bad
(b) ~ **de qn** unworthy of sb
indigné, ~**e** /ɛ̃diɲe/ *adj* indignant
indigner /ɛ̃diɲe/ [1] 1 *vtr* to make [sb] indignant, to outrage [sb]
2 **s'indigner** *v refl* (+ *v être*) to be indignant
indignité /ɛ̃diɲite/ *nf* **(a)** despicableness

(b) despicable act, disgraceful act

indigo /ε̃digo/ *adj inv, nm* indigo

indiqué, **~e** /ε̃dike/ [1] *pp* ▶ INDIQUER
[2] *pp adj* **(a)** ‹*treatment*› recommended
(b) à l'heure **~e** at the specified time; **le
village est très mal ~** the village is very
badly signposted

✍ **indiquer** /ε̃dike/ [1] *vtr* **(a)** ‹*person*› to
point out, to point to; ‹*signpost*› to show the
way to; **pouvez-vous m'~ la banque la plus
proche?** can you tell me where the nearest
bank is?
(b) to indicate **(que** that)
(c) je peux t'**~ un bon médecin** I can give
you the name of a good doctor
(d) to give; **l'heure indiquée sur le
programme est fausse** the time given on the
programme (GB) is wrong
(e) ‹*meter, map*› to show; **le restaurant
n'est pas indiqué** there are no signs to the
restaurant

indirect, **~e** /ε̃dirεkt/ *adj* indirect

indiscipline /ε̃disiplin/ *nf* lack of
discipline

indiscipliné, **~e** /ε̃disipline/ *adj*
undisciplined, unruly

indiscret, **-ète** /ε̃diskrε, εt/ *adj*
(a) ‹*person*› inquisitive; **à l'abri des regards
~s** away from prying eyes
(b) ‹*person, question*› indiscreet; **il est ~** he
can't keep a secret

indiscrétion /ε̃diskresjɔ̃/ *nf*
(a) inquisitiveness; **sans ~, combien
gagnez-vous?** if you don't mind my asking,
how much do you earn?
(b) lack of discretion
(c) indiscreet remark

indiscutable /ε̃diskytabl/ *adj*
indisputable, unquestionable

✍ **indispensable** /ε̃dispɑ̃sabl/ [1] *adj*
essential; **être ~ à qn** to be indispensable
to sb
[2] *nm* l'**~** the essentials

indisposé, **~e** /ε̃dispoze/ *adj* unwell,
indisposed

indisposer /ε̃dispoze/ [1] *vtr* **(a)** to annoy
(b) to upset [sb], to make [sb] feel ill

indisposition /ε̃dispozisjɔ̃/ *nf*
indisposition

indissociable /ε̃disɔsjabl/ *adj*
inseparable

indistinct, **~e** /ε̃distε̃, ε̃kt/ *adj* indistinct

✍ **individu** /ε̃dividy/ *nm* **(a)** individual
(b) human being, person
(c) un sinistre **~** a sinister individual *or*
character; **un ~ armé** an armed man
(d) (in scientific study) subject

individualiser /ε̃dividɥalize/ [1] [1] *vtr*
(a) to tailor [sth] to individual needs
(b) to individualize
[2] **s'individualiser** *v refl* (+ *v être*) to
become more individual

individualiste /ε̃dividɥalist/ *adj*
individualistic

✍ **individuel**, **-elle** /ε̃dividɥεl/ *adj* (gen)
individual; ‹*responsibility*› personal; ‹*room*›
single; **maison individuelle** (detached) house

indivisible /ε̃divizibl/ *adj* indivisible

Indochine /ε̃dɔʃin/ *pr nf* Indochina

indo-européen, **-éenne**, *mpl* **~s**
/ε̃doørɔpeε̃, εn/ *adj* Indo-European

indolence /ε̃dɔlɑ̃s/ *nf* laziness, indolence

indolent, **~e** /ε̃dɔlɑ̃, ɑ̃t/ *adj* lazy, indolent

indolore /ε̃dɔlɔr/ *adj* painless

indomptable /ε̃dɔ̃tabl/ *adj* ‹*person,
courage*› indomitable; ‹*anger, passion,
person*› uncontrollable; ‹*animal*› untamable;
avec une énergie ~ with tireless energy

Indonésie /ε̃dɔnezi/ *pr nf* Indonesia

indu, **~e** /ε̃dy/ *adj* ‹*hour*› ungodly (colloq),
unearthly; ‹*remark, reaction*› inappropriate

indubitable /ε̃dybitabl/ *adj* indubitable

indubitablement /ε̃dybitablǝmɑ̃/ *adv*
undoubtedly

induction /ε̃dyksjɔ̃/ *nf* induction

induire /ε̃dɥir/ [69] *vtr* **(a)** ‹*event, measures*›
to lead to, to bring about
(b) to infer, to conclude
(c) to induce; **~ qn en erreur** to mislead sb
(d) to induce ‹*current*›

indulgence /ε̃dylʒɑ̃s/ *nf* **(a)** (of parent,
audience) indulgence
(b) (of jury) leniency

indulgent, **~e** /ε̃dylʒɑ̃, ɑ̃t/ *adj* **(a)** ‹*parent,
audience*› indulgent
(b) ‹*jury*› lenient

industrialisation /ε̃dystrializasjɔ̃/ *nf*
industrialization

industrialiser /ε̃dystrialize/ [1] [1] *vtr* to
industrialize
[2] **s'industrialiser** *v refl* (+ *v être*) to
become industrialized

✍ **industrie** /ε̃dystri/ *nf* **(a)** industry; **l'~
hôtelière** the hotel trade
(b) industrial concern

✍ **industriel**, **-ielle** /ε̃dystrijεl/ [1] [1] *adj*
industrial; **pain ~** factory-baked bread
[2] *nm, f* industrialist, manufacturer

inébranlable /inebrɑ̃labl/ *adj*
(a) unshakeable, unwavering
(b) immovable

inédit, **~e** /inedi, it/ *adj* ‹*book*› (previously)
unpublished; ‹*situation*› (totally) new

ineffable /inefabl/ *adj* ineffable,
unutterable

inefficace /inefikas/ *adj* **(a)** ineffective
(b) inefficient

inefficacité /inefikasite/ *nf*
(a) ineffectiveness, inefficacy
(b) inefficiency

inégal, **~e**, *mpl* **-aux** /inegal, o/ *adj*
unequal; uneven; irregular; ‹*mood*› ⋯⋗

changeable, erratic

inégalable /inegalabl/ *adj* incomparable

inégalé, **~e** /inegale/ *adj* unequalled (GB), unrivalled (GB)

inégalement /inegalmã/ *adv*
(a) unequally
(b) unevenly

inégalité /inegalite/ *nf* (a) disparity
(b) inequality
(c) (of mood) changeability; (of surface) unevenness

inéluctable /inelyktabl/ *adj, nm* inevitable

inénarrable /inenaʀabl/ *adj* hilarious

inepte /inɛpt/ *adj* ‹person› inept; ‹judgment› inane; ‹remark› idiotic

ineptie /inɛpsi/ *nf* (a) inanity
(b) idiotic remark
(c) (action) stupid thing

inépuisable /inepɥizabl/ *adj* inexhaustible

inerte /inɛʀt/ *adj* (a) inert
(b) apathetic

inertie /inɛʀsi/ *nf* (a) inertia
(b) apathy, inertia

inespéré, **~e** /inɛspere/ *adj* ‹victory› unhoped for; **c'est une occasion ~e de faire** this is a heaven-sent opportunity to do

inestimable /inɛstimabl/ *adj* ‹value› inestimable; ‹help› invaluable

inévitable /inevitabl/ *adj* inevitable; unavoidable

inexact, **~e** /inegza, akt/ *adj* inaccurate

inexactitude /inegzaktityd/ *nf*
(a) inaccuracy
(b) unpunctuality

inexcusable /inɛkskyzabl/ *adj* inexcusable

inexistant, **~e** /inegzistã, ãt/ *adj* ‹means, help› nonexistent

inexpérience /inɛkspeʀjãs/ *nf* inexperience

inexpérimenté, **~e** /inɛkspeʀimãte/ *adj* inexperienced

inexplicable /inɛksplikabl/ *adj* inexplicable

inexpressif, **-ive** /inɛkspʀesif, iv/ *adj* inexpressive

inexprimable /inɛkspʀimabl/ *adj* inexpressible

in extremis /inɛkstʀemis/ *phr* at the last minute

infaillible /ɛ̃fajibl/ *adj* infallible

infaisable /ɛ̃fəzabl/ *adj* unfeasible, impossible

infamant, **~e** /ɛ̃famã, ãt/ *adj* (a) ‹remark› defamatory
(b) ‹act› infamous

ⱷ indicates a very frequent word

infâme /ɛ̃fam/ *adj* (a) ‹food, smell› revolting
(b) ‹person› despicable; ‹crime› odious

infamie /ɛ̃fami/ *nf* (a) infamy
(b) infamous act
(c) slanderous remark

infanterie /ɛ̃fɑ̃tʀi/ *nf* infantry

infantile /ɛ̃fɑ̃til/ *adj* (a) ‹illness› childhood; ‹mortality› infant; ‹psychology› child
(b) ‹person, behaviour› infantile, childish

infantilisme /ɛ̃fɑ̃tilism/ *nm* childishness

infarctus /ɛ̃faʀktys/ *nm inv* heart attack

infatigable /ɛ̃fatigabl/ *adj* tireless

infatué, **~e** /ɛ̃fatɥe/ *adj* **être ~ de sa personne** to be full of oneself

infect, **~e** /ɛ̃fɛkt/ *adj* foul; revolting

infecter /ɛ̃fɛkte/ [1] **1** *vtr* (a) (Med) to infect
(b) (figurative) to poison
2 **s'infecter** *v refl* (+ *v être*) to become infected, to go septic

infectieux, **-ieuse** /ɛ̃fɛksjø, øz/ *adj* infectious

infection /ɛ̃fɛksjɔ̃/ *nf* (a) (Med) infection
(b) (figurative) **c'est une ~!** it stinks to high heaven! (colloq)

ⱷ **inférieur**, **~e** /ɛ̃feʀjœʀ/ **1** *adj* (a) lower; ‹size› smaller; ‹length› shorter; **~ à la moyenne** below average; **être en nombre ~** to be fewer in number
(b) inferior
(c) (in mathematics) **si a est ~ à b** if a is less than b
2 *nm,f* inferior

infériorité /ɛ̃feʀjɔʀite/ *nf* inferiority

infernal, **~e**, *mpl* **-aux** /ɛ̃fɛʀnal, o/ *adj* (a) ‹noise, heat› infernal; **cycle ~** unstoppable chain of events
(b) ‹situation› diabolical; **ce gosse est ~** (fam) that child is a monster

infertile /ɛ̃fɛʀtil/ *adj* barren, infertile

infester /ɛ̃fɛste/ [1] *vtr* to infest, to overrun; **infesté de puces** flea-ridden

infidèle /ɛ̃fidɛl/ **1** *adj* unfaithful; disloyal
2 *nmf* infidel

infidélité /ɛ̃fidelite/ *nf* (a) infidelity; **faire des ~s à** to be unfaithful to
(b) disloyalty

infiltration /ɛ̃filtʀasjɔ̃/ *nf* (a) **~s d'eau** water seepage
(b) (of spies) infiltration
(c) (Med) injection

infiltrer /ɛ̃filtʀe/ [1] **1** *vtr* to infiltrate
2 **s'infiltrer** *v refl* (+ *v être*) (a) ‹liquid› to seep; ‹light, cold› to filter in
(b) ‹person› **s'~ dans** to infiltrate ‹group, place›

infime /ɛ̃fim/ *adj* tiny, minute

ⱷ **infini**, **~e** /ɛ̃fini/ **1** *adj* infinite
2 *nm* **l'~** infinity

infiniment /ɛ̃finimã/ *adv* immensely; **~ plus** infinitely more

infinité /ɛ̃finite/ nf l'~ infinity; **une ~ de** an endless number of

infinitif /ɛ̃finitif/ nm infinitive

infirme /ɛ̃fiʀm/ **1** adj (gen) disabled; (because of age) infirm

   2 nmf disabled person; **les ~s** the disabled

infirmer /ɛ̃fiʀme/ [1] vtr (gen, Law) to invalidate

infirmerie /ɛ̃fiʀməʀi/ nf (gen) infirmary; sick room; sick bay

infirmier /ɛ̃fiʀmje/ nm male nurse

infirmière /ɛ̃fiʀmjɛʀ/ nf nurse

infirmité /ɛ̃fiʀmite/ nf (gen) disability; (through old age) infirmity

inflammable /ɛ̃flamabl/ adj flammable

inflammation /ɛ̃flamasjɔ̃/ nf (Med) inflammation

inflammatoire /ɛ̃flamatwaʀ/ adj (Med) inflammatory

inflation /ɛ̃flɑsjɔ̃/ nf inflation

infléchir /ɛ̃fleʃiʀ/ [3] vtr, **s'infléchir** v refl (+ v être) to soften; to deflect

inflexible /ɛ̃flɛksibl/ adj inflexible

infliger /ɛ̃fliʒe/ [13] vtr to impose ‹fine›

influençable /ɛ̃flyɑ̃sabl/ adj impressionable

✧ **influence** /ɛ̃flyɑ̃s/ nf influence

influencer /ɛ̃flyɑ̃se/ [12] vtr to influence ‹person›; to affect ‹situation›

influent, ~e /ɛ̃flyɑ̃, ɑ̃t/ adj influential

influer /ɛ̃flye/ [1] v+prep **~ sur** to have an influence on

informateur, -trice /ɛ̃fɔʀmatœʀ, tʀis/ nm,f (a) (gen) informant

   (b) (police) informer

informaticien, -ienne /ɛ̃fɔʀmatisjɛ̃, ɛn/ nm,f computer scientist

✧ **information** /ɛ̃fɔʀmasjɔ̃/ nf

   (a) information; **une ~** a piece of information

   (b) (in newspaper, on television) **une ~** a piece of news; **écouter les ~s** to listen to the news; **contrôler l'~** to control the media

   (c) (Comput) data, information

✧ **informatique** /ɛ̃fɔʀmatik/ **1** adj computer

   2 nf computer science, computing

informatisation /ɛ̃fɔʀmatizasjɔ̃/ nf computerization

informatiser /ɛ̃fɔʀmatize/ [1] **1** vtr to computerize

   2 **s'informatiser** v refl (+ v être) to become computerized

informe /ɛ̃fɔʀm/ adj shapeless

✧ **informer** /ɛ̃fɔʀme/ [1] **1** vtr to inform

   2 **s'informer** v refl (+ v être) (a) to keep oneself informed

   (b) **s'~ de qch** to enquire about sth

   (c) **s'~ sur qn** to make enquiries about sb

infortune /ɛ̃fɔʀtyn/ nf misfortune

infortuné, ~e /ɛ̃fɔʀtyne/ **1** adj ill-fated

   2 nm,f unfortunate

infra /ɛ̃fʀa/ adv below; **voir ~** see below

infraction /ɛ̃fʀaksjɔ̃/ nf offence (GB); **être en ~** to be in breach of the law

infranchissable /ɛ̃fʀɑ̃ʃisabl/ adj ‹obstacle› insurmountable; ‹border› impassable

infrarouge /ɛ̃fʀaʀuʒ/ adj, nm infrared; **missile guidé par ~** heat-seeking missile

infrastructure /ɛ̃fʀastʀyktyʀ/ nf

   (a) facilities

   (b) (Econ) infrastructure

infructueux, -euse /ɛ̃fʀyktɥø, øz/ adj fruitless

infuser /ɛ̃fyze/ [1] vi ‹tea› to brew, to infuse

infusion /ɛ̃fyzjɔ̃/ nf (a) herbal tea

   (b) infusion

ingénier: s'ingénier /ɛ̃ʒenje/ [2] v refl (+ v être) to do one's utmost (**à faire** to do)

ingénierie /ɛ̃zeniʀi/ nf engineering

ingénieur /ɛ̃ʒenjœʀ/ nm engineer

ingénieur-conseil, pl **Ingénieurs-conseils** /ɛ̃ʒenjœʀkɔ̃sɛj/ nm consulting engineer

ingénieux, -ieuse /ɛ̃ʒenjø, øz/ adj ingenious

ingéniosité /ɛ̃ʒenjozite/ nf ingenuity

ingénu, ~e /ɛ̃ʒeny/ adj ingenuous

ingénuité /ɛ̃ʒenɥite/ nf ingenuousness; **en toute ~** in all innocence

ingérence /ɛ̃ʒeʀɑ̃s/ nf interference (**dans** in)

ingérer /ɛ̃ʒeʀe/ [14] **1** vtr to ingest

   2 **s'ingérer** v refl (+ v être) to interfere

ingestion /ɛ̃ʒɛstjɔ̃/ nf ingestion

ingrat, ~e /ɛ̃gʀa, at/ adj (a) ungrateful

   (b) ‹face, landscape› unattractive

   (c) ‹task, role› thankless; ‹land, soil› unproductive

ingratitude /ɛ̃gʀatityd/ nf ingratitude

ingrédient /ɛ̃gʀedjɑ̃/ nm ingredient

ingurgiter /ɛ̃gyʀʒite/ [1] vtr to gulp down

inhabitable /inabitabl/ adj uninhabitable

inhabité, ~e /inabite/ adj uninhabited

inhabituel, -elle /inabitɥɛl/ adj unusual

inhalation /inalasjɔ̃/ nf inhalation

inhaler /inale/ [1] vtr to inhale

inhérent, ~e /ineʀɑ̃, ɑ̃t/ adj inherent

inhibition /inibisjɔ̃/ nf inhibition

inhumain, ~e /inymɛ̃, ɛn/ adj inhuman

inhumation /inymasjɔ̃/ nf (a) burial

   (b) funeral

inhumer /inyme/ [1] vtr to bury

inimaginable /inimaʒinabl/ adj

   (a) unimaginable

   (b) unthinkable

inimitable /inimitabl/ adj inimitable

ininflammable /inɛ̃flamabl/ *adj*
nonflammable

inintéressant, ~**e** /inɛ̃teʀesɑ̃, ɑ̃t/ *adj*
uninteresting

ininterrompu, ~**e** /inɛ̃teʀɔ̃py/ *adj*
(a) ‹*process*› uninterrupted; ‹*drop*›
continuous; ‹*traffic*› endless
(b) ‹*procession*› unbroken

initial, ~**e**[1], *mpl* **-iaux** /inisjal, o/ *adj*
initial

initiale[2] /inisjal/ *nf* initial

initiateur, **-trice** /inisjatœʀ, tʀis/ *nm,f*
(a) originator; instigator
(b) instructor

initiation /inisjasjɔ̃/ *nf* (a) introduction
(b) initiation

ℱ **initiative** /inisjativ/ *nf* initiative; **avoir
l'esprit d'**~ to have initiative

initié, ~**e** /inisje/ ① *adj* (Comput) ~ **à
l'informatique** computer literate
② *nm,f* (a) initiate
(b) insider trader
(c) (Comput) ~ **à l'informatique** computer-
literate person

initier /inisje/ [2] ① *vtr* (a) to introduce
(b) to initiate
② **s'initier** *v refl* (+ *v être*) **s'**~ **à qch** to
learn sth

injecter /ɛ̃ʒɛkte/ [2] *vtr* to inject

injection /ɛ̃ʒɛksjɔ̃/ *nf* injection

injonction /ɛ̃ʒɔ̃ksjɔ̃/ *nf* injunction,
command

injure /ɛ̃ʒyʀ/ *nf* insult, abuse

injurier /ɛ̃ʒyʀje/ [1] *vtr* to insult, to swear at

injurieux, **-ieuse** /ɛ̃ʒyʀjø, øz/ *adj* ‹*remark*›
abusive; ‹*attitude*› insulting

injuste /ɛ̃ʒyst/ *adj* unfair

injustement /ɛ̃ʒystəmɑ̃/ *adv* unjustly;
unfairly

injustice /ɛ̃ʒystis/ *nf* injustice; unfairness;
réparer une ~ to right a wrong

injustifié, ~**e** /ɛ̃ʒystifje/ *adj* unjustified

inlassable /ɛ̃lasabl/ *adj* ‹*person*› tireless;
‹*curiosity*› insatiable; ‹*efforts*› unremitting

inlassablement /ɛ̃lasabləmɑ̃/ *adv*
tirelessly

inné, ~**e** /inne/ *adj* innate

innocemment /inɔsamɑ̃/ *adv* innocently;
pas ~ disingenuously

innocence /inɔsɑ̃s/ *nf* innocence

innocent, ~**e** /inɔsɑ̃, ɑ̃t/ *adj* innocent

innocenter /inɔsɑ̃te/ [1] *vtr* to prove [sb]
innocent

innombrable /innɔ̃bʀabl/ *adj*
(a) countless
(b) ‹*crowd*› vast

innommable /innɔmabl/ *adj* unspeakable

ℱ indicates a very frequent word

innovateur, **-trice** /inɔvatœʀ, tʀis/ *nm,f*
innovator

innover /inɔve/ [1] *vi* to innovate

inoculer /inɔkyle/ [1] *vtr* to inoculate

inodore /inɔdɔʀ/ *adj* ‹*substance*› odourless
(GB)

inoffensif, **-ive** /inɔfɑ̃sif, iv/ *adj* harmless

inondation /inɔ̃dasjɔ̃/ *nf* (a) flood
(b) flooding

inonder /inɔ̃de/ [1] *vtr* to flood

inopérant, ~**e** /inɔpeʀɑ̃, ɑ̃t/ *adj*
ineffective

inopiné, ~**e** /inɔpine/ *adj* unexpected

inopportun, ~**e** /inɔpɔʀtœ̃, yn/ *adj*
(a) inappropriate
(b) ill-timed

inoubliable /inublijabl/ *adj* unforgettable

inouï, ~**e** /inwi/ *adj* ‹*event*› unprecedented;
‹*success*› incredible; **c'est** ~ that's unheard
of

inox /inɔks/ *nm* inv stainless steel

inoxydable /inɔksidabl/ *adj* ‹*metal*› non-
oxidizing; **acier** ~ stainless steel

inqualifiable /ɛ̃kalifjabl/ *adj* unspeakable

inquiet, **-iète** /ɛ̃kjɛ, ɛt/ *adj* (a) anxious
(b) worried

inquiétant, ~**e** /ɛ̃kjetɑ̃, ɑ̃t/ *adj*
(a) worrying
(b) frightening

inquiéter /ɛ̃kjete/ [14] ① *vtr* (a) to worry
(b) **les douaniers ne l'ont pas inquiété** the
customs officers didn't bother him
② **s'inquiéter** *v refl* (+ *v être*) (a) to worry
(b) **s'**~ **de qch** to enquire about sth

inquiétude /ɛ̃kjetyd/ *nf* (a) anxiety,
concern
(b) worry; **il n'y a pas d'**~ **à avoir** there's
nothing to worry about

inquisiteur, **-trice** /ɛ̃kizitœʀ, tʀis/
① *adj* inquisitive
② *nm,f* inquisitor

inquisition /ɛ̃kizisjɔ̃/ *nf* inquisition

insaisissable /ɛ̃sezisabl/ *adj* ‹*person*,
character› elusive; ‹*nuance*› imperceptible

insalubre /ɛ̃salybʀ/ *adj* insanitary

insanité /ɛ̃sanite/ *nf* (a) rubbish, nonsense
(b) insanity

insatiable /ɛ̃sasjabl/ *adj* insatiable

insatisfaction /ɛ̃satisfaksjɔ̃/ *nf*
dissatisfaction

insatisfait, ~**e** /ɛ̃satisfɛ, ɛt/ *adj*
dissatisfied (**de** with); unsatisfied

inscription /ɛ̃skʀipsjɔ̃/ *nf* (a) (in school)
enrolment (GB); (at university) registration
(b) **l'**~ **au club coûte 40 euros** the
membership fee for the club is 40 euros; ~
électorale registration as a voter
(c) inscription; graffiti

ℱ **inscrire** /ɛ̃skʀiʀ/ [67] ① *vtr* (a) to enrol
(GB) ‹*pupil*›; to register ‹*student*›

(b) to write down ‹*name, date*›
  2 **s'inscrire** *v refl* (+ *v être*) **(a)** to enrol (GB); **s'~ au chômage** to register as unemployed; **s'~ à un parti** to join a party
(b) s'~ dans le cadre de to be in line with
(c) s'~ en faux contre qch to dispute the validity of sth
inscrit, **~e** /ɛ̃skʀi, it/ **1** *pp* ▶ INSCRIRE
  2 *nm,f* registered student; registered voter
insecte /ɛ̃sɛkt/ *nm* insect
insecticide /ɛ̃sɛktisid/ *nm* insecticide
insécurité /ɛ̃sekyʀite/ *nf* insecurity
INSEE *nm* (*abbr* = **Institut National de la Statistique et des Études Économiques**) French national institute of statistics and economic studies
insémination /ɛ̃seminasjɔ̃/ *nf* insemination; **~ artificielle** artificial insemination
insensé, **~e** /ɛ̃sɑ̃se/ *adj* **(a)** insane
(b) (*fam*) ‹*crowd, traffic jam*› phenomenal
insensibiliser /ɛ̃sɑ̃sibilize/ [1] *vtr* (Med) to anaesthetize
insensibilité /ɛ̃sɑ̃sibilite/ *nf* insensitivity
insensible /ɛ̃sɑ̃sibl/ *adj* **(a)** impervious
(b) insensitive
insensiblement /ɛ̃sɑ̃sibləmɑ̃/ *adv* imperceptibly
inséparable /ɛ̃sepaʀabl/ *adj* inseparable
insérer /ɛ̃seʀe/ [14] **1** *vtr* to insert
  2 **s'insérer** *v refl* (+ *v être*) (gen) to be inserted
insertion /ɛ̃sɛʀsjɔ̃/ *nf* **(a)** insertion
(b) integration
insidieux, **-ieuse** /ɛ̃sidjø, øz/ *adj* insidious
insigne /ɛ̃siɲ/ **1** *adj* ‹*honour, favour*› great
  2 *nm* badge
insignifiant, **~e** /ɛ̃siɲifjɑ̃, ɑ̃t/ *adj* insignificant
insinuation /ɛ̃sinɥasjɔ̃/ *nf* insinuation
insinuer /ɛ̃sinɥe/ [1] **1** *vtr* to insinuate
  2 **s'insinuer** *v refl* (+ *v être*) **s'~ dans** ‹*person*› to worm one's way into; ‹*liquid*› to seep into
insipide /ɛ̃sipid/ *adj* insipid
insistance /ɛ̃sistɑ̃s/ *nf* insistence
insistant, **~e** /ɛ̃sistɑ̃, ɑ̃t/ *adj* insistent
♂ **insister** /ɛ̃siste/ [1] *vi* **(a)** to insist; **'ça ne répond pas'—'insiste'** 'there's no reply!'—'keep trying'
(b) ~ sur to stress ‹*danger, need*›; to put the emphasis on ‹*spelling*›
(c) ~ sur to pay particular attention to ‹*stain*›
insolation /ɛ̃sɔlasjɔ̃/ *nf* sunstroke
insolence /ɛ̃sɔlɑ̃s/ *nf* **(a)** insolence
(b) insolent remark

insolent, **~e** /ɛ̃sɔlɑ̃, ɑ̃t/ *adj* **(a)** ‹*child, tone*› insolent
(b) ‹*rival, winner*› arrogant
insolite /ɛ̃sɔlit/ *adj, nm* unusual
insoluble /ɛ̃sɔlybl/ *adj* insoluble
insolvable /ɛ̃sɔlvabl/ *adj* insolvent
insomniaque /ɛ̃sɔmnjak/ *adj, nmf* insomniac
insomnie /ɛ̃sɔmni/ *nf* insomnia
insondable /ɛ̃sɔ̃dabl/ *adj* unfathomable
insonorisation /ɛ̃sɔnɔʀizasjɔ̃/ *nf* soundproofing
insonoriser /ɛ̃sɔnɔʀize/ [1] *vtr* to soundproof
insouciance /ɛ̃susjɑ̃s/ *nf* carefreeness
insouciant, **~e** /ɛ̃susjɑ̃, ɑ̃t/ *adj* carefree
insoumission /ɛ̃sumisjɔ̃/ *nf*
(a) insubordination
(b) (Mil) draft-dodging
insoupçonné, **~e** /ɛ̃supsɔne/ *adj* unsuspected
insoutenable /ɛ̃sutnabl/ *adj* **(a)** ‹*pain*› unbearable
(b) ‹*opinion*› untenable
inspecter /ɛ̃spɛkte/ [1] *vtr* to inspect
inspecteur, **-trice** /ɛ̃spɛktœʀ, tʀis/ *nm,f* inspector
  ■ **~ de police** ≈ detective constable (GB); **~ du travail** health and safety inspector
inspection /ɛ̃spɛksjɔ̃/ *nf* **(a)** inspection
(b) inspectorate
inspiration /ɛ̃spiʀasjɔ̃/ *nf* inspiration
♂ **inspirer** /ɛ̃spiʀe/ [1] **1** *vtr* **(a)** to inspire ‹*person*›; **être bien/mal inspiré de faire** to be well-/ill-advised to do; **un roman inspiré des vieux contes populaires** a novel based on old folk tales
(b) to appeal to; **ça ne m'inspire pas** that doesn't appeal to me
(c) ~ la méfiance à qn to inspire distrust in sb
  2 *vi* to breathe in, to inhale
  3 **s'inspirer** *v refl* (+ *v être*) **s'~ de** to draw one's inspiration from
instabilité /ɛ̃stabilite/ *nf* (gen) instability
instable /ɛ̃stabl/ *adj* (gen) unstable; ‹*weather*› unsettled
installateur, **-trice** /ɛ̃stalatœʀ, tʀis/ *nm,f* fitter
installation /ɛ̃stalasjɔ̃/ **1** *nf*
(a) installation, putting in
(b) system; **~ électrique** (electric) wiring
(c) move; **depuis mon ~ à Paris** since I moved to Paris
  2 **installations** *nf pl* facilities
installé, **~e** /ɛ̃stale/ **1** *pp* ▶ INSTALLER
  2 *pp adj* ‹*person*› living (à in); ‹*company*› based; **être bien ~ dans un fauteuil** to be ensconced in an armchair; **ils sont bien ~s dans leur nouvelle maison** they're very snug in their new home; **c'est un homme ~** ⋯⋙

(figurative) he's very nicely set up

ௗ **installer** /ɛ̃stale/ [1] **1** *vtr* **(a)** to install, to put in ‹*central heating, sink*›; to put up ‹*shelves*›; to connect ‹*gas*›
(b) to put ‹*guest*› (dans in); ~ qn dans un fauteuil to sit sb in an armchair; ~ qn à un poste to appoint sb to a post
2 **s'installer** *v refl* (+ *v être*)
(a) ‹*recession*› to set in; ‹*illness*› to take hold; le doute commence à s'~ dans leur esprit they're beginning to have doubts
(b) s'~ à son compte to set up one's own business
(c) to settle; partir s'~ à l'étranger to go and live abroad; je viendrai te voir quand tu seras installé I'll come and see you when you're settled in; s'~ au soleil to sit in the sun; s'~ à son bureau to settle down at one's desk; installe-toi, j'arrive! make yourself at home, I'm coming!

instamment /ɛ̃stamɑ̃/ *adv* insistently

instance /ɛ̃stɑ̃s/ *nf* **(a)** authority; les ~s d'un parti politique the leaders of a political party
(b) être en ~ de divorce to be engaged in divorce proceedings

ௗ **instant, ~e** /ɛ̃stɑ̃, ɑ̃t/ *nm* moment, instant; à tout *or* chaque ~ all the time; par ~s at times; pour l'~ for the moment; il devrait arriver d'un ~ à l'autre he should arrive any minute now; à l'~ même où just when

instantané, ~e /ɛ̃stɑ̃tane/ **1** *adj* instantaneous; ‹*drink, soup*› instant
2 *nm* snapshot

instar: à l'instar de /alɛstaʀdə/ *phr* following the example of

instaurer /ɛ̃stoʀe/ [1] *vtr* to establish ‹*regime, dialogue*›; to impose ‹*curfew*›

instigateur, -trice /ɛ̃stigatœʀ, tʀis/ *nm,f*
(a) instigator
(b) originator

instigation /ɛ̃stigasjɔ̃/ *nf* à l'~ de qn at sb's instigation

instiller /ɛ̃stile/ [1] *vtr* to instil (GB)

instinct /ɛ̃stɛ̃/ *nm* instinct; d'~ instinctively

instinctif, -ive /ɛ̃stɛ̃ktif, iv/ *adj* instinctive

instituer /ɛ̃stitɥe/ [1] *vtr* to institute

institut /ɛ̃stity/ *nm* **(a)** institute
(b) ~ de beauté beauty salon *or* parlour (GB)
■ Institut universitaire de formation des maîtres, IUFM *primary teacher training college*; Institut universitaire de technologie, IUT university institute of technology

instituteur, -trice /ɛ̃stitytœʀ, tʀis/ *nm,f* (primary school) teacher

ௗ **institution** /ɛ̃stitysjɔ̃/ *nf* **(a)** institution
(b) private school

institutrice ▶ INSTITUTEUR

instructeur /ɛ̃stʀyktœʀ/ *nm* (gen, Mil) instructor

ௗ indicates a very frequent word

instructif, -ive /ɛ̃stʀyktif, iv/ *adj* (gen) instructive; ‹*experience*› enlightening

ௗ **instruction** /ɛ̃stʀyksjɔ̃/ **1** *nf* **(a)** (gen) education; (Mil) training
(b) (Law) preparation of a case for trial
2 **instructions** *nf pl* instructions
■ ~ civique civics; ~ religieuse religious instruction

instruire /ɛ̃stʀɥiʀ/ [69] **1** *vtr* **(a)** to teach ‹*child*›; to train ‹*soldiers*›
(b) (Law) ~ une affaire to prepare a case for trial
2 **s'instruire** *v refl* (+ *v être*) to learn

instruit, ~e /ɛ̃stʀɥi, it/ *adj* educated

ௗ **instrument** /ɛ̃stʀymɑ̃/ *nm* (gen, Mus) instrument; ~ à cordes/à percussion/à vent string/percussion/wind instrument; jouer d'un ~ to play an instrument; être l'~ de qn to be sb's tool
■ ~s de bord controls

insu: à l'insu de /alɛ̃sydə/ *phr* à l'~ de qn without sb knowing

insubordination /ɛ̃sybɔʀdinasjɔ̃/ *nf* insubordination

insubordonné, ~e /ɛ̃sybɔʀdɔne/ *adj* rebellious; insubordinate

insuffisamment /ɛ̃syfizamɑ̃/ *adv* insufficiently; inadequately

insuffisance /ɛ̃syfizɑ̃s/ *nf*
(a) insufficiency, shortage
(b) poor standard; l'~ de la production the shortfall in production
(c) (Med) insufficiency

insuffisant, ~e /ɛ̃syfizɑ̃, ɑ̃t/ *adj*
(a) insufficient
(b) inadequate

insuffler /ɛ̃syfle/ [1] *vtr* to instil (GB); ~ la vie à qn to breathe life into sb

insulaire /ɛ̃sylɛʀ/ *adj* ‹*population*› island; ‹*mentality*› insular

insultant, ~e /ɛ̃syltɑ̃, ɑ̃t/ *adj* insulting

insulte /ɛ̃sylt/ *nf* insult

insulter /ɛ̃sylte/ [1] *vtr* to insult; to shout abuse at; ‹*attitude*› to be an insult to

insupportable /ɛ̃sypɔʀtabl/ *adj* unbearable

insurgé, ~e /ɛ̃syʀʒe/ *nm,f* insurgent, rebel

insurger: s'insurger /ɛ̃syʀʒe/ [13] *v refl* (+ *v être*) **(a)** to rise up
(b) to protest

insurmontable /ɛ̃syʀmɔ̃tabl/ *adj* insurmountable; insuperable; unconquerable

insurrection /ɛ̃syʀɛksjɔ̃/ *nf* insurrection

intact, ~e /ɛ̃takt/ *adj* intact

intarissable /ɛ̃taʀisabl/ *adj* ‹*imagination*› inexhaustible; ‹*source*› never-ending

intégral, ~e, mpl -aux /ɛ̃tegʀal, o/ *adj*
(a) ‹*payment*› full, in full
(b) ‹*tan*› all-over
(c) ‹*text*› unabridged; **version** ~e uncut

version
intégralement /ētegʀalmã/ *adv* ‹pay›
in full
intégralité /ētegʀalite/ *nf* l'~ de leur
salaire their entire salary
intégrante /ētegʀãt/ *adj f* faire partie ~
de qch to be an integral part of sth
intégration /ētegʀasjõ/ *nf* integration
intègre /ētegʀ/ *adj* ‹person, life› honest
intégré /ētegʀe/ *adj* (a) included, inserted
(b) integrated; ‹journalist› embedded
◆ **intégrer** /ētegʀe/ [14] **1** *vtr* (a) to insert
(b) to integrate ‹population›
(c) (fam) il vient d'~ Harvard he has just got
into Harvard
2 **s'intégrer** *v refl* (+ *v être*)
(a) ‹population› to integrate
(b) ‹building› to fit in
intégrisme /ētegʀism/ *nm*
fundamentalism
intégriste /ētegʀist/ *nmf* (religious)
fundamentalist
intégrité /ētegʀite/ *nf* integrity
intellect /ētelekt/ *nm* intellect
◆ **intellectuel, -elle** /ētelektɥel/ **1** *adj*
‹work› intellectual; ‹effort› mental
2 *nm,f* intellectual
◆ **intelligence** /ēteliʒãs/ *nf* (a) intelligence
(b) agir d'~ avec qn to act in agreement
with sb
intelligent, -e /ēteliʒã, ãt/ *adj*
intelligent; clever
intelligible /ēteliʒibl/ *adj* intelligible
intempéries /ētãpeʀi/ *nf pl* bad weather
intempestif, -ive /ētãpestif, iv/ *adj*
untimely; ‹curiosity, zeal› misplaced
intemporel, -elle /ētãpɔʀel/ *adj* timeless
intenable /ēt(ə)nabl/ *adj* (a) ‹situation›
unbearable
(b) ‹child› difficult
intendance /ētãdãs/ *nf* (Sch)
administration
intendant, -e /ētãdã, ãt/ **1** *nm,f* (Sch)
bursar
2 *nm* (Mil) quartermaster; paymaster
intense /ētãs/ *adj* (gen) intense; ‹red, green›
vivid; ‹traffic› heavy
intensif, -ive /ētãsif, iv/ *adj* intensive
intensification /ētãsifikasjõ/ *nf*
intensification
intensifier /ētãsifje/ [2] *vtr*,
s'intensifier *v refl* (+ *v être*) to intensify
intensité /ētãsite/ *nf* intensity
intensivement /ētãsivmã/ *adv*
intensively
intenter /ētãte/ [1] *vtr* ~ un procès à qn
to sue sb
◆ **intention** /ētãsjõ/ *nf* intention; c'est l'~
qui compte it's the thought that counts; à l'~
de qn ‹remark› aimed at sb

intentionné, ~e /ētãsjone/ *adj* bien/mal
~ well-/ill-intentioned
intentionnel, -elle /ētãsjonel/ *adj*
intentional
interaction /ēteʀaksjõ/ *nf* interaction
interbancaire /ēteʀbãkeʀ/ *adj* interbank
intercalaire /ēteʀkaleʀ/ **1** *adj* feuille *or*
feuillet ~ insert
2 *nm* divider
intercaler /ēteʀkale/ [1] *vtr* to insert
intercéder /ēteʀsede/ [14] *vi* to intercede
intercepter /ēteʀsepte/ [1] *vtr* to intercept
interchangeable /ēteʀʃãʒabl/ *adj*
interchangeable
interclasse /ēteʀklas/ *nm* (Sch) break
interdiction /ēteʀdiksjõ/ *nf* (a) banning;
'~ de dépasser' 'no overtaking' (GB), 'no
passing' (US)
(b) ban; lever une ~ to lift a ban
■ ~ de séjour prohibition on residence
◆ **interdire** /ēteʀdiʀ/ [65] *vtr* to ban; ~ à qn
de faire, ~ que qn fasse to forbid sb to do
interdisciplinaire /ēteʀdisiplineʀ/ *adj*
(Sch) cross-curricular; (Univ) interdisciplinary
interdit, ~e /ēteʀdi, it/ **1** *pp* ▶ INTERDIRE
2 *pp adj* prohibited, forbidden; entrée ~e
no entry *or* admittance; film ~ aux moins de
13 ans film unsuitable for children under 13
3 *adj* dumbfounded
4 *nm* proscription; taboo
◆ **intéressant, ~e** /ēteʀesã, ãt/ **1** *adj*
(a) interesting
(b) ‹prices, conditions› attractive; il est plus
~ de payer au comptant qu'à crédit it's
better to pay in cash rather than by credit
2 *nm,f* faire l'~ *or* son ~ to show off
intéressé, ~e /ēteʀese/ **1** *pp*
▶ INTÉRESSER
2 *pp adj* (a) interested
(b) attentive
(c) les parties ~es those concerned; les
personnes ~es aux bénéfices people with a
share in the profits
(d) ‹person› self-interested; ‹action›
motivated by self-interest; ses conseils
étaient ~s he/she had a selfish motive for
giving that advice
3 *nm,f* person concerned
intéressement /ēteʀesmã/ *nm* share in
the profits
◆ **intéresser** /ēteʀese/ [1] **1** *vtr* (a) to
interest; ça ne m'intéresse pas I'm not
interested
(b) ‹problem, decision› to concern
(c) ~ les salariés aux bénéfices to offer a
profit-sharing scheme to employees
2 **s'intéresser** *v refl* (+ *v être*) s'~ à (gen)
to be interested in; to take an interest in
◆ **intérêt** /ēteʀe/ *nm* (a) interest; recherche
digne d'~ worthwhile research; l'~
supérieur de la nation the higher good of the ⋯⟶

country; je ne vois pas l'∼ de cette réforme I can't see the point of this reform; par ∼ ‹act› out of self-interest; ‹marry› for money
(b) (financial) interest

interface /ɛ̃tɛʀfas/ nf interface

interférence /ɛ̃tɛʀfeʀɑ̃s/ nf interference

interférer /ɛ̃tɛʀfeʀe/ [14] vi to interfere

⚜ **intérieur**, ∼e /ɛ̃teʀjœʀ/ **1** adj
(a) internal, interior; ‹sea› inland; ‹pocket› inside; le côté ∼ the inside
(b) domestic; sur le plan ∼ on the domestic front
(c) ‹regulations› internal
2 nm (of box, newspaper) inside; (of car, house) interior; à l'∼ inside; indoors; à l'∼ des terres inland; d'∼ ‹game› indoor; être fier de son ∼ to be proud of one's home

intérim /ɛ̃teʀim/ nm (a) interim (period); président par ∼ acting president; assurer l'∼ de to stand in for
(b) temporary work; travailler en ∼ to temp (colloq)

intérimaire /ɛ̃teʀimɛʀ/ adj ‹committee› interim; ‹minister› acting; ‹job, staff› temporary

intérioriser /ɛ̃teʀjɔʀize/ [1] vtr to internalize

interjection /ɛ̃tɛʀʒɛksjɔ̃/ nf interjection

interligne /ɛ̃tɛʀliɲ/ nm line space

interlocuteur, -trice /ɛ̃tɛʀlɔkytœʀ, tʀis/ nm,f (a) mon ∼ the person I am/was talking to
(b) (in negotiations) representative
(c) Louis est notre seul ∼ Louis is our only contact

interloquer /ɛ̃tɛʀlɔke/ [1] vtr to take [sb] aback

interlude /ɛ̃tɛʀlyd/ nm interlude

intermède /ɛ̃tɛʀmɛd/ nm interlude

intermédiaire /ɛ̃tɛʀmedjɛʀ/ **1** adj ‹rate, stage› intermediate
2 nmf (in negotiations) go-between; (in industry) middleman
3 phr par l'∼ de through

interminable /ɛ̃tɛʀminabl/ adj
(a) interminable, never-ending
(b) endless

intermittence /ɛ̃tɛʀmitɑ̃s/ nf par ∼ ‹rain› on and off; ‹work› intermittently

intermittent, ∼e /ɛ̃tɛʀmitɑ̃, ɑ̃t/ adj ‹rain, fever› intermittent; ‹noise, efforts› sporadic

internat /ɛ̃tɛʀna/ nm boarding school

⚜ **international**, ∼e, mpl -aux /ɛ̃tɛʀnasjɔnal, o/ adj international

interne /ɛ̃tɛʀn/ **1** adj (gen) internal; ‹training› in-house; ‹ear› inner
2 nmf (a) (Sch) boarder
(b) ∼ (en médecine) houseman (GB), intern (US)

internement /ɛ̃tɛʀnəmɑ̃/ nm (Med) committal (to a psychiatric institution)

interner /ɛ̃tɛʀne/ [1] vtr to commit ‹mental patient›

⚜ **Internet** /ɛ̃tɛʀnɛt/ nm Internet; naviguer sur (l') ∼ to surf the Internet

interpellation /ɛ̃tɛʀpelasjɔ̃/ nf procéder à des ∼s to take people in for questioning

interpeller /ɛ̃tɛʀpəle/ [1] vtr (a) to call out to; to shout at
(b) to question; (in police station) to take [sb] in for questioning

interphone® /ɛ̃tɛʀfɔn/ nm (a) intercom
(b) entry phone

interposer: s'interposer /ɛ̃tɛʀpoze/ [1] v refl (+ v être) to intervene; par personne interposée through an intermediary

interprétariat /ɛ̃tɛʀpʀetaʀja/ nm interpreting

⚜ **interprétation** /ɛ̃tɛʀpʀetasjɔ̃/ nf (a) (gen, Mus) interpretation
(b) (profession) interpreting

interprète /ɛ̃tɛʀpʀɛt/ nmf (a) interpreter
(b) performer
(c) spokesperson

interpréter /ɛ̃tɛʀpʀete/ [14] vtr (a) to play ‹role, sonata›; to sing ‹song›
(b) to interpret

interpréteur /ɛ̃tɛʀpʀetœʀ/ nm (Comput) interpreter

interrogateur, -trice /ɛ̃teʀɔgatœʀ, tʀis/ adj enquiring; d'un air ∼ enquiringly

interrogatif, -ive /ɛ̃teʀɔgatif, iv/ adj interrogative

interrogation /ɛ̃teʀɔgasjɔ̃/ nf (a) (of witness) questioning
(b) (in grammar) question
(c) (Sch) test; ∼ orale oral test

interrogatoire /ɛ̃teʀɔgatwaʀ/ nm (gen) interrogation; (by police) questioning

⚜ **interroger** /ɛ̃teʀɔʒe/ [13] **1** vtr (a) (gen) to question; to ask; (figurative) to examine ‹conscience›; être interrogé comme témoin (Law) to be called as a witness
(b) ∼ son répondeur to check one's calls
(c) (Sch) to test
2 s'interroger v refl (+ v être) s'∼ sur to wonder about

interrompre /ɛ̃teʀɔ̃pʀ/ [53] **1** vtr (a) to interrupt; to break off ‹dialogue›; ‹person› to cease ‹activity›; ∼ son repas pour faire to stop eating to do
(b) to put an end to ‹holiday›; to stop ‹treatment›; to terminate ‹pregnancy›
2 s'interrompre v refl (+ v être)
(a) ‹person, conversation› to break off
(b) ‹rain› to stop

interrupteur /ɛ̃teʀyptœʀ/ nm switch

interruption /ɛ̃teʀypsjɔ̃/ nf (a) break; sans ∼ continuously
(b) ending; l'∼ du dialogue entre the breaking off of the dialogue (GB) between

---

⚜ indicates a very frequent word

intersection /ɛ̃tɛʀsɛksjɔ̃/ *nf* intersection

interstice /ɛ̃tɛʀstis/ *nm* (in floor) crack; (in shutters, blinds) chink

intervalle /ɛ̃tɛʀval/ *nm* **(a)** space; **à ∼s réguliers** at regular intervals **(b)** interval; **dans l'∼** meanwhile, in the meantime

◆ **intervenir** /ɛ̃tɛʀvəniʀ/ [36] *vi* **(a)** ‹*changes*› to take place; ‹*agreement*› to be reached **(b)** ‹*speaker*› to speak **(c)** (in emergency) ‹*police*› to intervene **(d)** ∼ **auprès de qn pour qn** to intercede with sb on sb's behalf

◆ **intervention** /ɛ̃tɛʀvɑ̃sjɔ̃/ *nf* **(a)** intervention **(b)** speech; lecture **(c)** (Med) ∼ **(chirurgicale)** operation

intervertir /ɛ̃tɛʀvɛʀtiʀ/ [3] *vtr* to invert

interviewer /ɛ̃tɛʀvjuve/ [1] *vtr* to interview

intestin /ɛ̃tɛstɛ̃/ *nm* bowel, intestine

intestinal, **∼e**, *mpl* **-aux** /ɛ̃tɛstinal, o/ *adj* intestinal

intime /ɛ̃tim/ 1 *adj* **(a)** ‹*life, diary*› private; ‹*friend, relationship*› intimate; ‹*hygiene*› personal **(b)** ‹*gathering*› intimate; ‹*conversation*› private; ‹*dinner*› quiet **(c)** ‹*room*› cosy (GB), cozy (US) **(d)** ‹*knowledge*› intimate 2 *nmf* close friend

intimement /ɛ̃timmɑ̃/ *adv* intimately; **je suis ∼ convaincu que…** I'm absolutely convinced that…

intimidation /ɛ̃timidasjɔ̃/ *nf* intimidation; **d'∼** ‹*measures, remarks*› intimidatory

intimider /ɛ̃timide/ [1] *vtr* to intimidate

intimité /ɛ̃timite/ *nf* **(a)** intimacy **(b)** privacy; **dans la plus stricte ∼** in the strictest privacy **(c)** private life **(d)** (of house, setting) cosiness

intitulé /ɛ̃tityle/ *nm* title, heading

intituler /ɛ̃tityle/ [1] 1 *vtr* to call 2 **s'intituler** *v refl* (+ *v être*) to be called, to be entitled

intolérable /ɛ̃tɔleʀabl/ *adj* intolerable; deeply shocking

intolérance /ɛ̃tɔleʀɑ̃s/ *nf* intolerance

intolérant, **∼e** /ɛ̃tɔleʀɑ̃, ɑ̃t/ *adj* intolerant

intonation /ɛ̃tɔnasjɔ̃/ *nf* intonation

intoxication /ɛ̃tɔksikasjɔ̃/ *nf* **(a)** (Med) poisoning **(b)** (figurative) disinformation

intoxiquer /ɛ̃tɔksike/ [1] 1 *vtr* to poison 2 **s'intoxiquer** *v refl* (+ *v être*) to poison oneself

intraitable /ɛ̃tʀɛtabl/ *adj* inflexible

intra-muros /ɛ̃tʀamyʀos/ *adj inv* **Paris ∼** Paris itself

intransigeance /ɛ̃tʀɑ̃ziʒɑ̃s/ *nf* intransigence

intransigeant, **∼e** /ɛ̃tʀɑ̃ziʒɑ̃, ɑ̃t/ *adj* ‹*attitude*› uncompromising; ‹*person*› intransigent

intraveineuse /ɛ̃tʀavenøz/ *nf* intravenous injection

intrépide /ɛ̃tʀepid/ *adj* intrepid, bold

intrépidité /ɛ̃tʀepidite/ *nf* boldness

intrigant, **∼e** /ɛ̃tʀigɑ̃, ɑ̃t/ *nm,f* schemer

intrigue /ɛ̃tʀig/ *nf* **(a)** intrigue **(b)** plot; **une ∼ policière** a detective story

intriguer /ɛ̃tʀige/ [1] *vtr* to intrigue

intrinsèque /ɛ̃tʀɛ̃sɛk/ *adj* intrinsic

introduction /ɛ̃tʀɔdyksjɔ̃/ *nf* **(a)** (gen) introduction **(b)** (of key, probe) insertion

◆ **introduire** /ɛ̃tʀɔdɥiʀ/ [69] 1 *vtr* **(a)** to insert ‹*object*› **(b)** to usher [sb] in ‹*visitor*›; (surreptitiously) to smuggle [sb] in **(c)** to introduce ‹*person*› **(d)** to introduce ‹*product, idea*› 2 **s'introduire** *v refl* (+ *v être*) **s'∼ dans** to get into

introduit, **∼e** /ɛ̃tʀɔdɥi, it/ ▶ INTRODUIRE

introspection /ɛ̃tʀɔspɛksjɔ̃/ *nf* introspection

introverti, **∼e** /ɛ̃tʀɔvɛʀti/ *nm,f* introvert

intrus, **∼e** /ɛ̃tʀy, yz/ *nm,f* intruder

intrusion /ɛ̃tʀyzjɔ̃/ *nf* **(a)** (gen) intrusion **(b)** interference

intuitif, **-ive** /ɛ̃tɥitif, iv/ *adj* intuitive

intuition /ɛ̃tɥisjɔ̃/ *nf* intuition

inusable /inyzabl/ *adj* hardwearing

inusité, **∼e** /inyzite/ *adj* uncommon

◆ **inutile** /inytil/ *adj* useless; pointless; needless; **(il est) ∼ de faire** there's no point in doing; **∼ de dire que** needless to say; **sans risques ∼s** without unnecessary risks

inutilement /inytilmɑ̃/ *adv* unnecessarily; needlessly; in vain

inutilisable /inytilizabl/ *adj* unusable

inutilité /inytilite/ *nf* (of expense, action) pointlessness

invalide /ɛ̃valid/ 1 *adj* disabled 2 *nmf* disabled person

invalidité /ɛ̃validite/ *nf* (Med) disability

invariable /ɛ̃vaʀjabl/ *adj* invariable

invasion /ɛ̃vazjɔ̃/ *nf* invasion

invendable /ɛ̃vɑ̃dabl/ *adj* unsaleable

invendu, **∼e** /ɛ̃vɑ̃dy/ *adj* unsold

inventaire /ɛ̃vɑ̃tɛʀ/ *nm* **(a)** stocktaking (GB), inventory (US) **(b)** stocklist (GB), inventory (US) **(c)** (of wardrobe, suitcase) list of contents

◆ **inventer** /ɛ̃vɑ̃te/ [1] 1 *vtr* to invent; to devise; **je n'invente rien** I'm not making it up 2 **s'inventer** *v refl* (+ *v être*) **ça ne s'invente pas** that has to be true

⋯⟶

IDIOM il n'a pas inventé la poudre (fam) he is not very bright

inventeur, -trice /ɛ̃vɑ̃tœʀ, tʀis/ nm,f inventor

inventif, -ive /ɛ̃vɑ̃tif, iv/ adj (a) inventive (b) resourceful

invention /ɛ̃vɑ̃sjɔ̃/ nf (a) invention (b) fabrication; **c'est de l'∼ pure** it's a complete fabrication

inventorier /ɛ̃vɑ̃tɔʀje/ [2] vtr to make out an inventory of

inverse /ɛ̃vɛʀs/ **1** adj (gen) opposite; **dans l'ordre ∼** (referring to list) in reverse order **2** nm (gen) **l'∼** the opposite; **à l'∼** conversely; **à l'∼ de ce qu'il croyait** contrary to what he thought

inversement /ɛ̃vɛʀsəmɑ̃/ adv (gen) conversely

inverser /ɛ̃vɛʀse/ [1] vtr (a) to invert ‹position›; to reverse ‹roles›; **image inversée** mirror image (b) to reverse ‹electric current›

inversion /ɛ̃vɛʀsjɔ̃/ nf inversion; reversal

invertébré, ∼e /ɛ̃vɛʀtebʀe/ adj invertebrate

invertir /ɛ̃vɛʀtiʀ/ [3] vtr to reverse; to switch [sth] round ‹words›

investigation /ɛ̃vɛstigasjɔ̃/ nf investigation; **d'∼** investigative

investir /ɛ̃vɛstiʀ/ [3] **1** vtr (a) to invest ‹capital› (b) to invest ‹person, ambassador› (c) ‹police› to go into; ‹tourists, demonstrators› to take over (d) ‹army› to besiege **2 s'investir** v refl (+ v être) **s'∼ dans** to put a lot of oneself into; to invest emotionally in

investissement /ɛ̃vɛstismɑ̃/ nm (gen) investment; (Mil) investing

investisseur /ɛ̃vɛstisœʀ/ nm investor

investiture /ɛ̃vɛstityʀ/ nf investiture

invétéré, ∼e /ɛ̃vetere/ adj ‹drinker, thief› inveterate; ‹liar› compulsive

invincible /ɛ̃vɛ̃sibl/ adj ‹people› invincible

inviolable /ɛ̃vjɔlabl/ adj (gen) inviolable; ‹door, safe› impregnable

invisible /ɛ̃vizibl/ adj (a) invisible; **la route était ∼ depuis la maison** the road could not be seen from the house (b) ‹danger› unseen

invitation /ɛ̃vitasjɔ̃/ nf invitation

invité, ∼e /ɛ̃vite/ nm,f guest

♂ **inviter** /ɛ̃vite/ [1] vtr to invite; **ceci invite à penser que...** this suggests that...

invivable /ɛ̃vivabl/ adj unbearable

invocation /ɛ̃vɔkasjɔ̃/ nf invocation

involontaire /ɛ̃vɔlɔ̃tɛʀ/ adj ‹reaction› involuntary; ‹mistake› unintentional

♂ indicates a very frequent word

invoquer /ɛ̃vɔke/ [1] vtr to invoke

invraisemblable /ɛ̃vʀɛsɑ̃blabl/ adj (a) ‹story› unlikely; ‹explanation› implausible (b) (fam) fantastic, incredible

invraisemblance /ɛ̃vʀɛsɑ̃blɑ̃s/ nf (a) unlikelihood (b) improbability

invulnérable /ɛ̃vylneʀabl/ adj invulnerable

iode /jɔd/ nm iodine

iota /jɔta/ nm inv iota **IDIOMS ne pas changer d'un ∼** not to change one iota; **ne pas bouger d'un ∼** not to move an inch

ira /iʀa/ ▶ ALLER[1]

irai /iʀɛ/ ▶ ALLER[1]

iraient /iʀɛ/ ▶ ALLER[1]

irais /iʀɛ/ ▶ ALLER[1]

irait /iʀɛ/ ▶ ALLER[1]

iras /iʀa/ ▶ ALLER[1]

irascible /iʀasibl/ adj ‹person› quick-tempered

irez /iʀe/ ▶ ALLER[1]

iriez /iʀje/ ▶ ALLER[1]

irions /iʀjɔ̃/ ▶ ALLER[1]

iris /iʀis/ nm inv (a) (flower) iris (b) (of eye) iris

irisé, ∼e /iʀize/ adj iridescent

irlandais, ∼e /iʀlɑ̃dɛ, ɛz/ **1** adj Irish **2** nm (language) Irish

Irlandais, ∼e /iʀlɑ̃dɛ, ɛz/ nm,f Irishman/Irishwoman

Irlande /iʀlɑ̃d/ pr nf Ireland; **la République d'∼** the Republic of Ireland; **l'∼ du Nord** Northern Ireland

IRM /iɛʀɛm/ nf (abbr = **imagerie par résonance magnétique**) MRI

ironie /iʀɔni/ nf irony; **faire de l'∼** to be ironic

ironique /iʀɔnik/ adj ironic

ironiser /iʀɔnize/ [1] vi to be ironic (**sur** about)

irons /iʀɔ̃/ ▶ ALLER[1]

iront /iʀɔ̃/ ▶ ALLER[1]

irradier /iʀadje/ [2] **1** vtr to irradiate **2** vi to radiate

irrattrapable /iʀatʀapabl/ adj irretrievable

irréalisable /iʀealizabl/ adj ‹dream› impossible; ‹plan› unworkable

irrécupérable /iʀekypeʀabl/ adj (a) irrecoverable (b) damaged beyond repair (c) ‹delinquent› beyond help

irréductible /iʀedyktibl/ nmf diehard

irréel, -elle /iʀeɛl/ adj unreal

irréfléchi, ∼e /iʀefleʃi/ adj ill-considered

irréfutable /iʀefytabl/ adj irrefutable

irrégularité /iʀegylaʀite/ *nf* irregularity
irrégulier, -ière /iʀegylje, ɛʀ/ *adj*
 (a) irregular; uneven
 (b) ‹*procedure*› irregular; **immigré en situation irrégulière** illegal immigrant
 (c) ‹*athlete*› whose performance is uneven
irrégulièrement /iʀegyljɛʀmɑ̃/ *adv*
 (a) illegally
 (b) irregularly; unevenly; erratically
irrémédiable /iʀ(ʀ)emedjabl/ *adj* irreparable
irremplaçable /iʀɑ̃plasabl/ *adj* irreplaceable
irréparable /iʀepaʀabl/ ⟨1⟩ *adj* ‹*car*› beyond repair; ‹*damage, crime*› irreparable
 ⟨2⟩ *nm* **commettre l'~** to go beyond the point of no return
irrépressible /iʀepʀesibl/ *adj* (gen) irrepressible; ‹*tears*› uncontrollable
irréprochable /iʀepʀɔʃabl/ *adj* ‹*life, employee*› beyond reproach; ‹*work*› perfect
irrésistible /iʀezistibl/ *adj* irresistible; ‹*person, joke*› hilarious
irrésolu, ~e /iʀezɔly/ *adj* ‹*person*› indecisive; ‹*problem, mystery*› unsolved
irrespirable /iʀespiʀabl/ *adj* ‹*air*› unbreathable; ‹*atmosphere*› stifling
irresponsable /iʀespɔ̃sabl/ *adj* irresponsible
irrévérencieux, -ieuse /iʀeveʀɑ̃sjø, øz/ *adj* irreverent
irréversible /iʀeveʀsibl/ *adj* irreversible
irrévocable /iʀevɔkabl/ *adj* irrevocable
irrigation /iʀigasjɔ̃/ *nf* (a) (of land) irrigation
 (b) (Med) supply of blood
irriguer /iʀige/ ⟨1⟩ *vtr* to irrigate
irritation /iʀitasjɔ̃/ *nf* (gen, Med) irritation
irriter /iʀite/ ⟨1⟩ ⟨1⟩ *vtr* (a) to irritate, to annoy
 (b) (Med) to irritate
 ⟨2⟩ **s'irriter** *v refl* (+ *v être*) (a) to get angry
 (b) (Med) to become irritated
irruption /iʀypsjɔ̃/ *nf* **faire ~ dans** to burst into ‹*room*›
islam /islam/ *nm* **l'~** Islam
islamique /islamik/ *adj* Islamic
islamisme /islamism/ *nm* Islam
islamiste ⟨1⟩ *adj* Islamist, Islamic
 ⟨2⟩ *nmf* Islamist
Islande /islɑ̃d/ *pr nf* Iceland

isolant, ~e /izɔlɑ̃, ɑ̃t/ *adj* insulating
isolation /izɔlasjɔ̃/ *nf* insulation
isolement /izɔlmɑ̃/ *nm* (a) (of village) remoteness; (of house) isolated location
 (b) (of patient, politician) isolation; (of prisoner) solitary confinement
isoler /izɔle/ ⟨1⟩ ⟨1⟩ *vtr* (a) to isolate ‹*sick person, dissident*›; to put [sb] in solitary confinement ‹*prisoner*›
 (b) to isolate ‹*gene, substance*›
 (c) to soundproof; to insulate
 (d) to insulate ‹*wire*›
 ⟨2⟩ **s'isoler** *v refl* (+ *v être*) to isolate oneself
isoloir /izɔlwaʀ/ *nm* voting *or* polling (GB) booth
isotherme /izotɛʀm/ *adj* refrigerated; **boîte ~** ice box; **sac ~** cool bag
✓ **issu, ~e¹** /isy/ *adj* **être ~ de** to come from; to result from
issue² /isy/ *nf* (a) exit; **'sans ~'** 'no exit'
 (b) solution; **situation sans ~** situation with no solution
 (c) outcome; **à l'~ de** at the end of; **à l'~ de trois jours de pourparlers** at the close of three days of talks
 ∎ **~ de secours** emergency exit
Italie /itali/ *pr nf* Italy
✓ **italien, -ienne** /italjɛ̃, ɛn/ ⟨1⟩ *adj* Italian
 ⟨2⟩ *nm* (language) Italian
italique /italik/ *nm* italics
itinéraire /itineʀɛʀ/ *nm* (a) (gen) route; (detailed) itinerary
 (b) (figurative) career
 ∎ **~ bis** alternative route; **~ de délestage** relief route
itinérance /itineʀɔ̃s/ *adj* (mobile phone) roaming
itinérant, ~e /itineʀɑ̃, ɑ̃t/ *adj* ‹*exhibition*› touring; ‹*life*› peripatetic; ‹*circus*› travelling (GB)
IUFM /iyɛfɛm/ *nm*: *abbr* ▶ INSTITUT
IUT /iyte/ *nm*: *abbr* ▶ INSTITUT
ivoire /ivwaʀ/ *adj inv*, *nm* ivory
ivoirien, -ienne /ivwaʀjɛ̃, ɛn/ *adj* of the Ivory Coast
ivre /ivʀ/ *adj* (a) drunk, intoxicated
 (b) **~ de rage** wild with rage
ivresse /ivʀɛs/ *nf* (a) intoxication
 (b) exhilaration
ivrogne /ivʀɔɲ/ *nmf* drunkard

J j

j, J /ʒi/ *nm inv* j, J; **le jour J** D-day

j' ▶ JE

jabot /ʒabo/ *nm* **(a)** (of bird) crop
(b) (of shirt) jabot

jacasser /ʒakase/ [1] *vi* to chatter

jachère /ʒaʃɛʀ/ *nf* **(terre en)** ~ fallow land

jacinthe /ʒasɛ̃t/ *nf* hyacinth

jackpot /(d)ʒakpɔt/ *nm* **(a)** jackpot
(b) slot machine

jacquet /ʒakɛ/ *nm* backgammon

jacter /ʒakte/ [1] *vi* (pop) to jaw (colloq), to talk

jade /ʒad/ *nm* jade

jadis /ʒadis/ *adv* formerly, in the past

jaguar /ʒagwaʀ/ *nm* jaguar

jaillir /ʒajiʀ/ [3] *vi* ‹liquid› to gush out;
‹tears› to flow; ‹flame› to shoot up; ‹truth› to emerge

jais /ʒɛ/ *nm inv* **(a)** jet
(b) **(noir) de** ~ jet-black

jalon /ʒalɔ̃/ *nm* **(a)** marker
(b) (figurative) **poser les** ~**s de** to prepare the ground for

jalonner /ʒalɔne/ [1] *vtr* **(a)** ‹trees› to line ‹road›; ‹incidents› to punctuate ‹career›
(b) to mark out ‹road›

jalousement /ʒaluzmɑ̃/ *adv* jealously; enviously

jalouser /ʒaluze/ [1] *vtr* to be jealous of

jalousie /ʒaluzi/ *nf* **(a)** jealousy
(b) slatted blind

jaloux, -ouse /ʒalu, uz/ **1** *adj* jealous
2 *nm,f* jealous man/woman

✓ **jamais** /ʒamɛ/ *adv* **(a)** never; **rien n'est** ~ **certain** nothing is ever certain; **sait-on** ~? you never know; ~ **de la vie!** never!
(b) ever; **plus belle que** ~ prettier than ever; **si** ~ if
(c) **à tout** ~ forever
(d) **ne…** ~ **que** only; **il ne fait** ~ **que son devoir** he is only doing his duty

✓ **jambe** /ʒɑ̃b/ *nf* leg; **avoir de bonnes** ~**s** to have strong legs; **courir à toutes** ~**s** to run as fast as one's legs can carry one; **j'ai les** ~**s comme du coton** (fam) I feel weak at the knees; **traîner la** ~ (fam) to trudge along
IDIOMS cela me fait une belle ~ (fam) a fat lot of good that does me (colloq); **il ne tient plus sur ses** ~**s** he can hardly stand up; **prendre ses** ~**s à son cou** to take to one's heels; **tenir la** ~ **à qn** to keep talking to sb; **par-dessus** *or* **par-dessous la** ~ in a slipshod manner

✓ **jambon** /ʒɑ̃bɔ̃/ *nm* ham
■ ~ **blanc** *or* **de Paris** cooked ham; ~ **de pays** cured ham

jambonneau, *pl* ~**x** /ʒɑ̃bɔno/ *nm* knuckle of ham

jante /ʒɑ̃t/ *nf* **(a)** rim
(b) wheel

✓ **janvier** /ʒɑ̃vje/ *nm* January

Japon /ʒapɔ̃/ *pr nm* Japan

japonais, -e /ʒapɔnɛ, ɛz/ **1** *adj* Japanese
2 *nm* (language) Japanese

jappement /ʒapmɑ̃/ *nm* yapping

japper /ʒape/ [1] *vi* to yap

jaquette /ʒakɛt/ *nf* **(a)** morning coat
(b) dust jacket
(c) (on tooth) crown

✓ **jardin** /ʒaʀdɛ̃/ *nm* garden (GB), yard (US);
chaise de ~ garden chair (GB), patio chair (US)
■ ~ **d'acclimatation** ▶ JARDIN ZOOLOGIQUE; ~ **d'agrément** ornamental garden; ~ **d'enfants** kindergarten; ~ **potager** vegetable garden; ~ **public** park; ~ **zoologique** zoo

jardinage /ʒaʀdinaʒ/ *nm* gardening

jardiner /ʒaʀdine/ [1] *vi* to do some gardening

jardinier, -ière¹ /ʒaʀdinje, ɛʀ/ **1** *adj* garden
2 *nm,f* gardener

jardinière² /ʒaʀdinjɛʀ/ *nf* jardinière

jargon /ʒaʀgɔ̃/ *nm* **(a)** jargon; ~ **administratif** officialese
(b) gibberish

jarre /ʒaʀ/ *nf* (earthenware) jar

jarret /ʒaʀɛ/ *nm* **(a)** (of human) ham, hollow of the knee
(b) (of animal) hock
(c) (Culin) ~ **de veau** knuckle of veal

jarretelle /ʒaʀtɛl/ *nf* suspender (GB), garter (US)

jars /ʒaʀ/ *nm inv* gander

jaser /ʒaze/ [1] *vi* to gossip

jasmin /ʒasmɛ̃/ *nm* jasmine

jatte /ʒat/ *nf* bowl, basin

jauge /ʒoʒ/ *nf* gauge; ~ **d'huile** dipstick

jaunâtre /ʒonɑtʀ/ *adj* yellowish

✓ **jaune** /ʒon/ **1** *adj* yellow; ~ **d'or** golden yellow; ~ **paille** straw-coloured (GB); ~ **poussin** bright yellow; **teint** ~ sallow complexion
2 *nm* **(a)** yellow

✓ indicates a very frequent word

(b) ~ **(d'œuf)** (egg) yolk
(c) blackleg (GB), scab
IDIOM rire ~ (fam) to give a forced laugh
jaunir /ʒoniʀ/ [3] **1** *vtr* to turn [sth]
yellow, to make [sth] go yellow
2 *vi* to go yellow
jaunisse /ʒonis/ *nf* jaundice; **il va en faire
une** ~**!** (fam) that'll put his nose out of joint!
java /ʒava/ *nf* **(a)** popular dance
(b) (fam) rave-up (colloq)
Javel /ʒavɛl/ *nf* **(eau de)** ~ ≈ bleach
javelliser /ʒavelize/ [1] *vtr* to chlorinate
javelot /ʒavlo/ *nm* javelin
J.-C. (*written abbr* = **Jésus-Christ**) avant
~ BC; après ~ AD
⚜ **je, j'** *before vowel or mute h* /ʒ(ə)/ *pron* I
jean /dʒin/ *nm* **(a)** (pair of) jeans
(b) denim
jeannette /ʒanɛt/ *nf* ≈ Brownie
je-ne-sais-quoi /ʒɔnsɛkwa/ *nm inv* **avoir
un** ~ to have a certain something
jérémiades /ʒeʀemjad/ *nf pl* moaning
jerrican /ʒeʀikan/ *nm* Jerrycan
jersey /ʒɛʀze/ *nm* **(a)** jersey
(b) stocking stitch
jésuite /ʒezɥit/ *adj, nm* Jesuit
Jésus /ʒezy/ *pr n* Jesus
jet¹ /ʒɛ/ *nm* **(a)** throwing; throw
(b) jet; spurt; burst; **passer au** ~ to hose
down; **premier** ~ (figurative) first sketch; **d'un
seul** ~ ‹write› in one go
■ ~ **d'eau** fountain; hosepipe
jet² /dʒɛt/ *nm* jet (plane)
jetable /ʒətabl/ *adj* disposable
jetée /ʒəte/ *nf* pier; jetty
⚜ **jeter** /ʒəte/ [20] **1** *vtr* **(a)** to throw; to hurl;
to throw away *or* out; ~ **qch à qn** to throw
sth to sb ‹ball›; to throw sth at sb ‹stone›;
~ **qn dehors** to throw sb out; ~ **quelques
idées sur le papier** (figurative) to jot down a
few ideas; **bon à** ~ fit for the bin (GB) *or* the
garbage (US)
(b) to give ‹cry, light›; to cast ‹glance,
shadow›
(c) to create ‹confusion, terror›; ~ **l'émoi
dans la ville** to throw the town into turmoil
2 **se jeter** *v refl* (+ *v être*) **(a)** **se** ~ **du
haut d'un pont** to throw oneself off a bridge;
se ~ **sur** to fall upon ‹opponent›; to pounce
on ‹prey, newspaper›; **se** ~ **au cou de qn** to
fling oneself around sb's neck; **se** ~ **à l'eau**
to jump into the water; (figurative) to take the
plunge; **(aller) se** ~ **contre un arbre** to crash
into a tree
(b) ‹river› to flow
jeton /ʒ(ə)tɔ̃/ *nm* (for machine) token; (in board
games) counter; (at casino) chip
⚜ **jeu,** *pl* ~**x** /ʒø/ *nm* **(a) le** ~ play; **un** ~ a
game; **faire un** ~ to play a game; **par** ~ for
fun; **entrer en** ~ to come into the picture;
se prendre *or* **se piquer au** ~ to get hooked;

mettre en ~ to bring [sth] into play; to
stake; **hors** ~ offside; **ils ont beau** ~ **de me
critiquer** it's easy for them to criticize me
(b) le ~ gambling; **ton avenir est en** ~ your
future is at stake
(c) (in cards) hand; **cacher bien son** ~
(figurative) to keep it quiet
(d) (of cards) deck; ~ **d'échecs** chess set
(e) (of actor) acting; (of musician) playing; (of
sportsman) game
(f) (of keys, spanners) set
■ ~ **d'argent** game played for money; ~ **de
construction** construction set; ~ **électronique**
computer game; ~ **de massacre** ≈ coconut shy (GB); ~ **de mots** pun; ~ **de l'oie**
≈ snakes and ladders (GB); ~ **de société**
board game; party game; ~ **télévisé** (TV)
game show; ~**x Olympiques, JO** Olympic
Games; ~**x Paralympiques** Paralympic
Games
IDIOMS **jouer le** ~ to play the game; **c'est
pas de** *or* **du** ~**!** (fam) that's not fair!; **faire le**
~ **de qn** to play into sb's hands
jeu-concours, *pl* **jeux-concours**
/ʒøkɔ̃kuʀ/ *nm* competition
⚜ **jeudi** /ʒødi/ *nm* Thursday
IDIOM **ça aura lieu la semaine des quatre**
~**s!** (fam) it won't happen, not in a month of
Sundays!
jeun: à jeun /aʒœ̃/ *phr* **(a)** on an empty
stomach
(b) (fam) sober
⚜ **jeune** /ʒœn/ **1** *adj* **(a)** (gen) young;
‹industry› new; ‹face, hairstyle› youthful; **nos**
~**s années** our youth; **le** ~ **âge** youth; **le** ~
marié the groom; **la** ~ **mariée** the bride
(b) younger; **mon** ~ **frère** my younger
brother
2 *nmf* young person; **les** ~**s** young people
3 *adv* **s'habiller** ~ to wear young styles;
faire ~ to look young
■ ~ **femme** young woman; ~ **fille** girl; ~
homme young man; ~ **loup** up-and-coming
executive; ~ **premier** romantic lead
jeûne /ʒøn/ *nm* **(a)** fasting; fast
(b) period of fasting
jeûner /ʒøne/ [1] *vi* to fast
⚜ **jeunesse** /ʒœnɛs/ *nf* **(a)** youth; **une
seconde** ~ a new lease of life; **une erreur de**
~ a youthful indiscretion
(b) young people
IDIOMS **il faut que** ~ **se passe** youth will
have its fling; **les voyages forment la** ~
travel broadens the mind
jf *written abbr* = **JEUNE FEMME** *or* **FILLE;**
▶ **JEUNE**
jh *written abbr* = **JEUNE HOMME;** ▶ **JEUNE**
JO /ʒio/ *nm pl: abbr* ▶ **JEU**
joaillerie /ʒoajʀi/ *nf* **(a)** jeweller's shop
(GB), jewelry store (US)
(b) jewellery (GB), jewelry (US)
joaillier, -ière /ʒoalje, ɛʀ/ *nm,f* jeweller
(GB), jeweler (US)

Joconde /ʒɔkɔ̃d/ *n pr* la ~ the Mona Lisa

joggeur, -euse /dʒɔgœʀ, øz/ *nm,f* jogger

✔ **joie** /ʒwa/ *nf* joy; **au comble de la** ~ overjoyed; **se faire une** ~ **de faire** to look forward to doing; to be delighted to do
IDIOM **s'en donner à cœur** ~ to enjoy oneself to the full; (figurative) to have a field day

joignable /ʒwaɲabl/ *adj* **il n'est pas** ~ **en ce moment** he's not available at the moment

✔ **joindre** /ʒwɛ̃dʀ/ [56] **1** *vtr* (a) to get hold of ‹*person*›
(b) to enclose ‹*cheque*›; to attach ‹*card*›
(c) to link ‹*points*›; to put [sth] together ‹*planks, feet*›; ~ **l'intelligence à la simplicité** to be intelligent without being pretentious
2 se joindre *v refl* (+ *v être*) (a) **se** ~ **à** to join ‹*person, group*›; to join in ‹*conversation*›
(b) ‹*lips*› to meet; ‹*hands*› to join
IDIOM ~ **les deux bouts** (fam) to make ends meet

joint¹, ~e /ʒwɛ̃, ɛ̃t/ ▶ JOINDRE

joint² /ʒwɛ̃/ *nm* (in wood) joint; (on pipes) seal

jointure /ʒwɛ̃tyʀ/ *nf* joint

jojo **1** *adj inv* **il n'est pas** ~ **ton chapeau** your hat isn't very nice; **ce n'est pas** ~ **ce qu'ils lui ont fait** what they did to him/her wasn't very nice
2 *nm* **un affreux** ~ a horrible brat (colloq); a weirdo (colloq)

✔ **joli, ~e** /ʒɔli/ **1** *adj* (gen) nice; ‹*face*› pretty; ‹*sum*› tidy; **faire** ~ to look nice
2 *nm* **c'est du** ~! (ironic) very nice!
■ ~ **cœur** smooth talker; **faire le** ~ **cœur** to play Romeo
IDIOM **être** ~ **à croquer** *or* **comme un cœur** to be as pretty as a picture

joliment /ʒɔlimɑ̃/ *adv* (a) prettily, nicely
(b) (fam) ‹*happy, well*› really; ‹*handle*› nicely

jonc /ʒɔ̃/ *nm* rush

joncher /ʒɔ̃ʃe/ [1] *vtr* ‹*papers, leaves*› to be strewn over ‹*ground*›

jonction /ʒɔ̃ksjɔ̃/ *nf* (a) junction
(b) link-up

jongler /ʒɔ̃gle/ [1] *vi* to juggle

jonque /ʒɔ̃k/ *nf* junk

jonquille /ʒɔ̃kij/ *nf* daffodil

jouable /ʒwabl/ *adj* (a) feasible; **le pari est** ~ the gamble might pay off
(b) ‹*piece of music*› playable; **une pièce qui n'est pas** ~ a play that's impossible to stage

joue /ʒu/ *nf* (a) cheek
(b) (Mil) **en** ~! aim!; **mettre qn en** ~ to take aim at sb

✔ **jouer** /ʒwe/ [1] **1** *vtr* (a) to play ‹*match, music*›
(b) to back ‹*horse*›; to stake ‹*money*›; to risk ‹*reputation, life*›; **c'est joué d'avance** it's a foregone conclusion; **tout n'est pas encore joué** the game isn't over yet; ~ **le tout pour le tout** to go for broke (colloq)

✔ indicates a very frequent word

(c) **qu'est-ce qu'on joue au théâtre/cinéma?** what's on at the theatre/cinema?
(d) ~ **les imbéciles** to play dumb
2 jouer à *v+prep* to play ‹*tennis, game*›; to play with ‹*doll*›; ~ **à qui perd gagne** to play 'loser takes all'; ~ **à la marchande** to play shops
3 jouer de *v+prep* (a) ~ **de** to play ‹*instrument*›
(b) ~ **de** to use ‹*influence*›
4 *vi* (a) to play; **arrête de** ~ **avec ta bague!** stop fiddling with your ring!; **à toi de** ~! your turn!; (figurative) the ball's in your court!; **bien joué!** well played!; (figurative) well done!
(b) to gamble; ~ **avec** to gamble with ‹*life, health*›; ~ **aux courses** to bet on the horses; ~ **sur** to bank on ‹*credulity*›
(c) to act; **il joue bien** he's a good actor
(d) ‹*argument, clause*› to apply; ‹*age*› to matter; **faire** ~ **ses relations** to make use of one's connections
5 se jouer *v refl* (+ *v être*) (a) ‹*future, peace*› to be at stake; ‹*drama*› to be played out
(b) **se** ~ **de** to make light of ‹*obstacle*›

jouet /ʒwɛ/ *nm* (a) toy
(b) plaything

✔ **joueur, -euse** /ʒwœʀ, øz/ **1** *adj*
(a) playful
(b) **être** ~/**joueuse** to be a gambling man/woman
2 *nm,f* (a) player; **être beau/mauvais** ~ to be a good/bad loser
(b) gambler

joufflu, ~e /ʒufly/ *adj* ‹*person*› chubby-cheeked; ‹*face*› chubby

joug /ʒu/ *nm* yoke

✔ **jouir** /ʒwiʀ/ [3] *v+prep* ~ **de** to enjoy; to enjoy the use of ‹*property*›; ‹*place*› to have ‹*view, climate*›

jouissance /ʒwisɑ̃s/ *nf* (a) (Law) use
(b) pleasure

joujou, pl ~x /ʒuʒu/ *nm* (baby talk) toy

✔ **jour** /ʒuʀ/ *nm* (a) day; **quel** ~ **sommes-nous?** what day is it today?; **un** ~ **ou l'autre** some day; ~ **pour** ~ to the day; **à ce** ~ to date; **à** ~ up to date; **mettre à** ~ to bring up to date ‹*work*›; to revise ‹*edition*›; **mise à** ~ updating; **de nos** ~s nowadays; **d'un** ~ **à l'autre** ‹*expected*› any day now; ‹*change*› from one day to the next; **du** ~ **au lendemain** overnight; **d'un** ~ ‹*fashion*› passing; ‹*queen*› for a day; **vivre au** ~ **le** ~ to live one day at a time; **le** ~ **se lève** it's getting light; **au lever du** ~ at daybreak; **le petit** ~ the early morning; **de** ~ ‹*work*› days; ‹*travel*› in the daytime
(b) daylight; light; **en plein** ~ in broad daylight; **se faire** ~ ‹*truth*› to come to light; **éclairer qch d'un** ~ **nouveau** to shed new light on sth; **je t'ai vu sous ton vrai** ~ I saw you in your true colours (GB)
(c) (figurative) **donner le** ~ **à qn** to bring sb

into the world; **voir le** ~ ‹person› to come into the world; ‹work of art› to see the light of day; **mes ~s sont comptés** my days are numbered; **des ~s difficiles** hard times; **les beaux ~s reviennent** spring will soon be here
(d) (in wall) gap; ~s openwork (embroidery)
■ ~ **de l'An** New Year's Day; ~ **férié** bank holiday (GB), legal holiday (US); ~ **de fermeture** closing day; ~ **ouvrable** working day

journal, *pl* **-aux** /ʒuʀnal, o/ *nm*
(a) newspaper
(b) magazine
(c) news (bulletin)
(d) journal
■ ~ **de bord** logbook; ~ **intime** diary; **Journal officiel** *government publication listing new acts, laws etc*

journalier, -ière /ʒuʀnalje, ɛʀ/ *adj* daily

journalisme /ʒuʀnalism/ *nm* journalism

journaliste /ʒuʀnalist/ *nmf* journalist

journalistique /ʒuʀnalistik/ *adj* journalistic

journée /ʒuʀne/ *nf* day; ~ **de repos** day off; **dans la** ~ during the day; **la** ~ **d'hier/de mardi** yesterday/Tuesday; **faire des ~s de huit heures** to work an eight-hour day

joute /ʒut/ *nf* (a) (figurative) jousting, battle; ~ **oratoire** *or* **verbale** sparring match
(b) joust

jouvence /ʒuvɑ̃s/ *nf* **fontaine de** ~ Fountain of Youth

jouxter /ʒukste/ [1] *vtr* to adjoin

jovial, ~**e**, *mpl* ~**s** *or* **-iaux** /ʒɔvjal, o/ *adj* jovial

jovialité /ʒɔvjalite/ *nf* joviality

joyau, *pl* ~**x** /ʒwajo/ *nm* jewel, gem

joyeusement /ʒwajøzmɑ̃/ *adv* merrily, cheerfully

joyeux, -euse /ʒwajø, øz/ *adj* merry, cheerful

jubilation /ʒybilasjɔ̃/ *nf* joy, jubilation

jubilé /ʒybile/ *nm* jubilee

jubiler /ʒybile/ [1] *vi* to be jubilant

jucher /ʒyʃe/ [1] *vtr*, **se jucher** *v refl* (+ *v être*) to perch

judaïsme /ʒydaism/ *nm* Judaism

judas /ʒyda/ *nm inv* peephole

judiciaire /ʒydisjɛʀ/ *adj* judicial

judicieux, -ieuse /ʒydisjø, øz/ *adj* judicious, sensible

judo /ʒydo/ *nm* judo

juge /ʒyʒ/ *nm* judge; **être à la fois** ~ **et partie** to be judge and jury
■ ~ **d'instruction** examining magistrate; ~ **de touche** linesman

jugé: au jugé /oʒyʒe/ *phr* ‹value› by guesswork; ‹shoot› blind

jugement /ʒyʒmɑ̃/ *nm* judgment; **passer en** ~ ‹case› to come to court

jugeote /ʒyʒɔt/ *nf* (fam) common sense

juger /ʒyʒe/ [13] **1** *vtr* (a) to judge ‹person, competition›; **mal** ~ **qn** to misjudge sb
(b) to consider; ~ **utile de faire** to consider it useful to do
(c) (Law) to try ‹case›; to judge ‹case›
2 juger de *v+prep* to assess; **j'en jugerai par moi-même** I'll judge for myself; **à en** ~ **par** judging by

juguler /ʒygyle/ [1] *vtr* to stamp out ‹epidemic, uprising›; to curb ‹inflation›

juif, juive /ʒɥif, ʒɥiv/ **1** *adj* Jewish
2 *nm,f* Jew

juillet /ʒɥijɛ/ *nm* July; **le 14** ~ Bastille Day

juin /ʒɥɛ̃/ *nm* June

juive ▶ JUIF

jumeau, -elle[1], *mpl* ~**x** /ʒymo, ɛl/ *adj*, *nm,f* twin

jumelage /ʒymlaʒ/ *nm* twinning

jumeler /ʒymle/ [19] *vtr* to twin

jumelle[2] /ʒymɛl/ *nf*, **jumelles** *nf pl* binoculars; ~**s de théâtre** opera glasses

jument /ʒymɑ̃/ *nf* mare

jungle /ʒœ̃gl/ *nf* jungle

junte /ʒœ̃t/ *nf* junta

jupe /ʒyp/ *nf* skirt
IDIOM **il est toujours dans les ~s de sa mère** he's tied to his mother's apron strings

jupe-culotte, *pl* **jupes-culottes** /ʒypkylɔt/ *nf* culottes, divided skirt

jupette /ʒypɛt/ *nf* short skirt

jupon /ʒypɔ̃/ *nm* petticoat
IDIOM **courir le** ~ to womanize

juré, ~**e** /ʒyʀe/ **1** *pp* ▶ JURER
2 *pp adj* (a) on oath; sworn-in
(b) ‹enemy› sworn
3 *nm* juror; **les ~s** the members of the jury

jurer /ʒyʀe/ [1] **1** *vtr* to swear; **on leur a fait** ~ **le secret** they were sworn to secrecy; ~ **de tuer qn** to vow to kill sb; **ah mais je te jure!** (fam) honestly! (colloq)
2 jurer de *v+prep* to swear to
3 *vi* (a) to swear
(b) ‹colours› to clash
(c) **ne** ~ **que par** to swear by
4 se jurer *v refl* (+ *v être*) (a) to swear [sth] to one another
(b) to vow
IDIOM **il ne faut** ~ **de rien** (Proverb) never say never

juridiction /ʒyʀidiksjɔ̃/ *nf* (a) jurisdiction
(b) courts

juridique /ʒyʀidik/ *adj* legal; **vide** ~ gap in the law

jurisprudence /ʒyʀispʀydɑ̃s/ *nf* case law

juriste /ʒyʀist/ *nmf* (a) jurist
(b) lawyer

juron /ʒyʀɔ̃/ *nm* swearword

jury /ʒyʀi/ *nm* (a) jury

⋯⟩

(b) panel of judges
(c) board of examiners

jus /ʒy/ *nm inv* **(a)** juice
(b) (from meat) juices; gravy
(c) electricity; **prendre le** ∿ to get a shock

✦ **jusque** (**jusqu'** *before vowel*) /ʒysk/
  1 *prep* **(a)** **aller jusqu'à Paris** to go as far as Paris; to go all the way to Paris; **courir jusqu'au bout du jardin** to run right down to the bottom of the garden (GB) *or* the end of the yard (US); **suivre qn** ∿ **dans sa chambre** to follow sb right into his/her room; **la nouvelle est arrivée jusqu'à nous** the news has reached us; **jusqu'où comptez-vous aller?** how far do you intend to go?
  (b) jusqu'à, jusqu'en until, till; **jusqu'à présent, jusqu'ici** (up) until now
  (c) monter jusqu'à 20° to go up to 20°
  (d) to the point of; **aller jusqu'à faire** to go so far as to do
  (e) even; **des détritus** ∿ **sous la table** rubbish everywhere, even under the table
  2 jusqu'à ce que *phr* until

jusque-là /ʒyskəla/ *adv* **(a)** until then, up to then
  (b) up to here; up to there
  IDIOMS en avoir ∿ **de qn/qch** (fam) to have had it up to here with sb/sth (colloq); **s'en mettre** ∿ (fam) to stuff one's face (colloq)

justaucorps /ʒystokɔʀ/ *nm inv* leotard

✦ **juste** /ʒyst/ **1** *adj* **(a)** ‹*person*› just, fair
  (b) ‹*cause*› just; ‹*anger*› righteous; ‹*word, answer*› right, correct
  (c) ‹*balance, watch*› accurate; ∿ **milieu** happy medium; **à** ∿ **titre** with good reason; **dire des choses** ∿**s** to make some valid points; **apprécier qn à sa** ∿ **valeur** to get a fair picture of sb
  (d) (Mus) ‹*piano, voice*› in tune; ‹*note*› true
  (e) c'est un peu ∿ (in width, time) it's a bit tight; (in quantity) it's barely enough
  2 *adv* **(a)** ‹*sing*› in tune; ‹*guess*› right; **elle a vu** ∿ she was right; **viser** ∿ to aim straight
  (b) just; ∿ **à temps** just in time
  (c) (tout) ∿ only just; **j'arrive** ∿ I've only just arrived; **c'est tout** ∿ **s'il sait lire** he can hardly read
  3 au juste *phr* exactly

4 *nm* righteous man; **les** ∿**s** the righteous

✦ **justement** /ʒystəmɑ̃/ *adv* **(a)** precisely
  (b) just
  (c) correctly
  (d) justifiably

justesse /ʒystɛs/ **1** *nf* **(a)** correctness; **avec** ∿ correctly
  (b) accuracy; **avec** ∿ accurately
  2 de justesse *phr* ‹*succeed*› only just

✦ **justice** /ʒystis/ *nf* **(a)** justice; **rendre la** ∿ to dispense justice; **il faut leur rendre cette** ∿ **qu'ils sont…** one has to acknowledge that they are…; **ce n'est que** ∿ it is only fair; **se faire** ∿ to take the law into one's own hands; to take one's own life
  (b) la ∿ the law; the legal system; the courts; **action en** ∿ legal action

justicier, -ière /ʒystisje, ɛʀ/ *nm, f* righter of wrongs

justificatif, -ive /ʒystifikatif, iv/ *nm* documentary evidence; ∿ **de domicile** proof of domicile; ∿ **de frais** receipt

justification /ʒystifikasjɔ̃/ *nf*
  (a) justification
  (b) explanation; documentary evidence

justifié, ∿**e 1** *pp* ▸ **JUSTIFIER**
  2 *pp adj* justified; **non** ∿ unjustified

✦ **justifier** /ʒystifje/ [2] **1** *vtr* to justify ‹*method, absence*›; to vindicate ‹*guilty party*›; to explain ‹*ignorance*›; **les faits ont justifié nos craintes** events proved our fears to have been justified; **tu essaies toujours de la** ∿ you are always making excuses for her
  2 justifier de *v+prep* to give proof of
  3 se justifier *v refl* (+ *v être*) **(a)** to make excuses; (in court) to clear oneself
  (b) ‹*decision*› to be justified (by)

jute /ʒyt/ *nm* jute; **(toile de)** ∿ hessian

juteux, -euse /ʒytø, øz/ *adj* ‹*fruit*› juicy

juvénile /ʒyvenil/ *adj* youthful; juvenile

juxtaposer /ʒykstapoze/ [1] *vtr* to juxtapose

juxtaposition /ʒykstapozisjɔ̃/ *nf* juxtaposition

✦ indicates a very frequent word

K k

k, **K** /ka/ *nm inv* k, K

kafkaïen, -ïenne /kafkajɛ̃, ɛn/ *adj* Kafkaesque

kakatoès /kakatɔɛs/ *nm inv* cockatoo

kaki /kaki/ ① *adj inv* khaki
② *nm* (a) persimmon
(b) khaki

kaléidoscope /kaleidɔskɔp/ *nm* kaleidoscope

kanak ▶ CANAQUE

kangourou /kãguʀu/ ① *adj inv* **poche** ∼ front pocket; **slip** ∼ pouch-front briefs
② *nm* (a) kangaroo
(b) ®baby carrier

karaté /kaʀate/ *nm* karate

karité /kaʀite/ *nm* shea; **beurre de** ∼ shea butter

kart /kaʀt/ *nm* go-kart

karting /kaʀtiŋ/ *nm* go-karting; **faire du** ∼ to go karting

kasher /kaʃɛʀ/ *adj inv* kosher

kayak /kajak/ *nm* kayak; **faire du** ∼ to go kayaking

képi /kepi/ *nm* kepi

kératine /keʀatin/ *nf* keratin

kermesse /kɛʀmɛs/ *nf* fete

kérosène /keʀɔzɛn/ *nm* kerosene

kF *written abbr* ▶ KILOFRANC

kg (*written abbr* = **kilogramme**) kg

kibboutz, *pl* **-tzim** /kibuts, kibutsim/ *nm* kibbutz

kick /kik/ *nm* kick-start

kidnapper /kidnape/ [1] *vtr* to kidnap; **se faire** ∼ to be kidnapped

kidnappeur, -euse /kidnapœʀ, øz/ *nm,f* kidnapper

kif-kif /kifkif/ *adj inv* (fam) **c'est** ∼ (bourricot) it's all the same

kilo¹ /kilo/ *pref* kilo

kilo² /kilo/ *nm* (*abbr* = **kilogramme**) kilo; **prendre des** ∼**s** to put on weight

kilofranc /kilɔfʀɑ̃/ *nm* (Hist) 1,000 French francs

kilogramme /kilɔgʀam/ *nm* kilogram

kilométrage /kilɔmetʀaʒ/ *nm* ≈ mileage

kilomètre /kilɔmɛtʀ/ *nm* kilometre (GB)

kilomètre-heure, *pl* **kilomètres-heure** /kilɔmɛtʀœʀ/ *nm* kilometre (GB) per hour

kilométrique /kilɔmetʀik/ *adj* ‹distance› in kilometres (GB); ‹price› per kilometre (GB)

kilo-octet /kilɔɔktɛ/ *nm* kilobyte

kilotonne /kilɔtɔn/ *nf* kiloton

kilowattheure /kilɔwatœʀ/ *nm* kilowatt-hour

kimono /kimɔno/ *nm* (a) kimono
(b) judo suit

kinésithérapeute /kineziteʀapøt/ *nmf* physiotherapist (GB), physical therapist (US)

kinésithérapie /kineziteʀapi/ *nf* physiotherapy (GB), physical therapy (US)

kiosque /kjɔsk/ *nm* kiosk
■ ∼ **à musique** bandstand

kiwi /kiwi/ *nm* kiwi

klaxon® /klaksɔn/ *nm* (car) horn

klaxonner /klaksɔne/ [1] *vi* to sound one's horn (GB), to honk the horn

kleptomane /klɛptɔman/ *adj, nmf* kleptomaniac

knock-out /nɔkaut/ ① *adj inv* knocked out
② *nm* knockout

Ko (*written abbr* = **kilo-octet**) KB

KO /kao/ ① *adj inv* (*abbr* = **knocked out**) (a) KO'd (colloq); **mettre qn** ∼ to KO sb (colloq)
(b) (fam) exhausted
② *nm* (*abbr* = **knockout**) KO (colloq)

koala /kɔala/ *nm* koala (bear)

kopeck /kɔpɛk/ *nm* kopeck; **ça ne vaut pas un** ∼ it's not worth a penny

krach /kʀak/ *nm* (on stock exchange) crash

kraft /kʀaft/ *nm* (**papier**) ∼ brown paper

kurde /kyʀd/ *adj, nm* Kurdish

Kurde /kyʀd/ *nmf* Kurd

kW (*written abbr* = **kilowatt**) kW

K-way® /kawe/ *nm* windcheater (GB), windbreaker (US)

kyrielle /kiʀjɛl/ *nf* **une** ∼ **de** a string of

kyste /kist/ *nm* cyst

L l

l, L /ɛl/ *nm inv* **(a)** (letter) l, L
(b) (*written abbr* = **litre**) 20 l 20 l

l' ▶ LE

⚡ **la¹** ▶ LE

la² /la/ *nm* (Mus) (note) A; (in sol-fa) lah; **donner
le ~** to give an A; (figurative) to set the tone

⚡ **là** /la/ *adv* **(a)** there; here; **viens ~** come
here; **~ où je travaille** where I work; **pas par
ici, par ~** not this way, that way; **de ~ au
village** from there to the village
(b) then; **d'ici ~** between now and then; by
then; **et ~, le téléphone a sonné** and then
the phone rang; **en ce temps-~** in those
days; **ce jour-~** that day
(c) s'il en est (arrivé) ~, c'est que… if he's
got to that point, it's because…; **alors ~ tu
exagères!** now you're going too far!; **que
vas-tu chercher ~?** what are you thinking
of?; **il a fallu en passer par ~** there was no
alternative; **qu'entendez-vous par ~?** what
do you mean by that?; **si tu vas par ~** if you
are saying that; **de ~** hence; from that

là-bas /labɑ/ *adv* over there

labeur /labœʀ/ *nm* hard work

labo /labo/ *nm* (fam) lab (colloq)

laboratoire /labɔʀatwaʀ/ *nm* laboratory
■ **~ d'analyses médicales** medical laboratory;
~ de langues language laboratory; **~ pharmaceutique** pharmaceutical company

laborieusement /labɔʀjøzmɑ̃/ *adv*
laboriously

laborieux, -ieuse /labɔʀjø, øz/ *adj*
(a) ⟨*work, process*⟩ arduous; ⟨*style*⟩ laboured
(GB)
(b) les classes laborieuses the working
classes

labour /labuʀ/ *nm* ploughing; **cheval de ~**
plough horse

labourer /labuʀe/ [1] *vtr* to plough (GB), to
plow (US)

labyrinthe /labiʀɛ̃t/ *nm* maze; labyrinth

⚡ **lac** /lak/ *nm* **(a)** lake
(b) reservoir

lacer /lase/ [12] *vtr* to lace up ⟨*shoes, corset*⟩

lacérer /laseʀe/ [14] *vtr* to lacerate; to slash

lacet /lasɛ/ *nm* **(a)** lace; **chaussures à ~s**
lace-up shoes; **nouer ses ~s** to do up one's
laces
(b) (in road) **une route en ~s** a twisting road

lâche /lɑʃ/ **1** *adj* **(a)** ⟨*person, crime*⟩
cowardly
(b) ⟨*belt*⟩ loose

(c) ⟨*regulation*⟩ lax
2 *nmf* coward

lâchement /lɑʃmɑ̃/ *adv* **ils se sont ~
enfuis** they fled like cowards; **il a été ~
assassiné** he was foully murdered

lâcher¹ /lɑʃe/ [1] **1** *vtr* **(a)** to drop ⟨*object*⟩;
to let go of ⟨*rope*⟩; **lâche-moi** let go of me;
(figurative) (fam) give me a break (colloq); **~
prise** to lose one's grip
(b) to reveal ⟨*information*⟩; to let out ⟨*scream*⟩
(c) to let [sb/sth] go ⟨*person, animal*⟩
(d) to drop ⟨*friend, activity*⟩; **la peur ne
la lâche plus depuis** she's been living in
constant terror ever since
2 *vi* ⟨*rope*⟩ to give way; ⟨*brakes*⟩ to fail; **ses
nerfs ont lâché** he/she went to pieces

lâcher² /lɑʃe/ *nm* (of balloons, birds) release

lâcheté /lɑʃte/ *nf* **(a)** cowardice; **par ~** out
of cowardice
(b) cowardly act

laconique /lakɔnik/ *adj* laconic; terse

lacrymal, ~e, mpl -aux /lakʀimal, o/ *adj*
lachrymal

lacrymogène /lakʀimɔʒɛn/ *adj* ⟨*grenade,
bomb*⟩ teargas; **gaz ~** teargas

lacté, ~e /lakte/ *adj* **(a)** ⟨*product*⟩ milk
(b) ⟨*liquid*⟩ milky; **la voie ~e** the Milky Way

lacune /lakyn/ *nf* (in knowledge, law) gap

là-dedans /lad(ə)dɑ̃/ *adv* in here; in there;
et moi ~ qu'est-ce que je fais? (fam) and
where do I come in?

là-dessous /lad(ə)su/ *adv* under here;
under there; **il y a quelque chose de louche
~** (fam) there's something fishy about all
this (colloq)

là-dessus /lad(ə)sy/ *adv* **(a)** on here; on
there
(b) qu'as-tu à dire ~? what have you got to
say about it?
(c) ~ il a raccroché with that he hung up

ladite ▶ LEDIT

lagon /lagɔ̃/ *nm* lagoon

lagune /lagyn/ *nf* lagoon

là-haut /lao/ *adv* **(a)** up here; up there; **tout
~** (all the) way up there
(b) upstairs
(c) in heaven

laïc /laik/ *nm* layman

laïcité /laisite/ *nf* secularism; secularity

laid, ~e /lɛ, lɛd/ *adj* **(a)** ugly
(b) disgusting

laideur /lɛdœʀ/ *nf* ugliness

lainage /lɛnaʒ/ *nm* **(a)** woollen (GB) material
(b) woollen (GB) garment

⚡ indicates a very frequent word

laine /lɛn/ *nf* wool; **de** *or* **en** ~ woollen (GB), wool
■ ~ **peignée** worsted; ~ **de verre** glass wool; ~ **vierge** new wool (GB), virgin wool

laïque /laik/ ⒈ *adj* ‹school› nondenominational (GB), public (US); ‹state, mind› secular
⒉ *nmf* layman/laywoman; **les** ~**s** lay people

laisse /lɛs/ *nf* (for dog) lead (GB), leash (US)

laissé-pour-compte, **laissée-pour-compte**, *mpl* **laissés-pour-compte** /lesepuʀkɔ̃t/ *nm,f* **les laissés-pour-compte** (gen) the forgotten people; **les laissés-pour-compte de la révolution technologique** the casualties of the technological revolution

✦ **laisser** /lese/ [1] ⒈ *vtr* to leave; ~ **la liberté à qn** to let sb go free; **je te laisse** I must go; ~ **le choix à qn** to give sb the choice; **laisse ce jouet à ton frère** let your brother have the toy; **laisse-le, ça lui passera** ignore him, he'll get over it; **cela me laisse sceptique** I'm sceptical (GB) *or* skeptical (US)
⒉ *v aux* ~ **qn/qch faire** to let sb/sth do; **laisse-moi faire** let me do it; leave it to me; **laisse faire!** so what!
⒊ **se laisser** *v refl* (+ *v être*) **se** ~ **bercer par les vagues** to be lulled by the waves; **il se laisse insulter** he puts up with insults; **elle n'est pas du genre à se** ~ **faire** she won't be pushed around; **il ne veut pas se** ~ **faire** he won't let you touch him; **se** = **aller** to let oneself go

laisser-aller /leseale/ *nm inv* (a) scruffiness
(b) sloppiness

laissez-passer /lesepase/ *nm inv* pass

✦ **lait** /lɛ/ *nm* milk
■ ~ **de chaux** whitewash; ~ **concentré non sucré** evaporated milk; ~ **demi-écrémé** semi-skimmed milk (GB), two percent milk (US); ~ **écrémé** skimmed milk (GB), skim *or* nonfat milk (US); ~ **maternel** breastmilk; ~ **de poule** eggnog

laitage /lɛtaʒ/ *nm* dairy product

laitance /lɛtɑ̃s/ *nf* (Culin, Zool) soft roe

laiterie /lɛtʀi/ *nf* (a) dairy
(b) dairy industry

laiteux, -euse /lɛtø, øz/ *adj* ‹liquid, white› milky; ‹complexion› creamy

laitier, -ière /lɛtje, ɛʀ/ ⒈ *adj* ‹industry, product› dairy; ‹production, cow› milk
⒉ *nm,f* milkman/milkwoman

laiton /lɛtɔ̃/ *nm* brass

laitue /lɛty/ *nf* lettuce

laïus /lajys/ *nm inv* (fam) speech

lama /lama/ *nm* (a) (animal) llama
(b) (religious leader) lama

lambda /lɑ̃bda/ *adj inv* (fam) average

lambeau, *pl* ~**x** /lɑ̃bo/ *nm* (of cloth) rag; (of paper, hide) strip; (of flesh) bit

lambris /lɑ̃bʀi/ *nm inv* panelling (GB); marble walls; (on ceiling) mouldings (GB), moldings (US)

lambrisser /lɑ̃bʀise/ [1] *vtr* to panel

lame /lam/ *nf* (a) (of knife, saw) blade
(b) knife
(c) sword; **une fine** ~ an expert swordsman
(d) (of metal, wood) strip; (on blind) slat
■ ~ **de fond** ground swell; (figurative) upheaval; ~ **de rasoir** razor blade

lamé /lame/ *nm* lamé; **en** ~ lamé

lamelle /lamɛl/ *nf* (a) (of wood, metal) small strip
(b) (Culin) sliver; **découper en fines** ~**s** to slice thinly
(c) (Bot) (of mushroom) gill

lamentable /lamɑ̃tabl/ *adj* pathetic, awful

lamentablement /lamɑ̃tabləmɑ̃/ *adv* ‹fail› miserably; ‹cry› piteously

lamentation /lamɑ̃tasjɔ̃/ *nf* wailing

lamenter: se lamenter /lamɑ̃te/ [1] *v refl* (+ *v être*) to moan; **se** ~ **sur son propre sort** to feel sorry for oneself

lampadaire /lɑ̃padɛʀ/ *nm* (a) standard (GB) *or* floor (US) lamp
(b) streetlight

✦ **lampe** /lɑ̃p/ *nf* (a) lamp, light
(b) (light) bulb
■ ~ **à bronzer** sun lamp; ~ **de chevet** bedside light; ~ **électrique** torch (GB), flashlight (US); ~ **de poche** pocket torch (GB), flashlight (US); ~ **témoin** indicator light; ~ **tempête** hurricane lamp

lampée /lɑ̃pe/ *nf* (fam) gulp

lampion /lɑ̃pjɔ̃/ *nm* paper lantern

lance /lɑ̃s/ *nf* (gen) spear; (in jousting) lance
■ ~ **d'incendie** fire hose nozzle

lancée /lɑ̃se/ *nf* **sur ma** ~ while I was at it; **continuer sur sa** ~ to continue to forge ahead

lancement /lɑ̃smɑ̃/ *nm* (a) (of ship, company) launching; (of process) setting up
(b) (of product, book) launch; (of loan) floating; (of actor) promotion
(c) (of missile) launching; launch

lance-pierres /lɑ̃spjɛʀ/ *nm inv* catapult
IDIOM payer qn avec un ~ (fam) to pay sb peanuts (colloq)

✦ **lancer¹** /lɑ̃se/ [12] ⒈ *vtr* (a) to throw ‹ball, pebble, javelin›; ~ **le poids** to put the shot
(b) to launch ‹rocket, ship›; to fire ‹arrow›; to drop ‹bomb›; to start up ‹engine›
(c) to throw out ‹smoke, flames›; to give ‹look›; to put about ‹rumour›; to issue ‹ultimatum›; to send out ‹invitation›
(d) to hurl ‹insult›; to make ‹accusation›; **lança-t-il** he said
⒉ *vi* (fam) to throb; **mon doigt me lance** my finger is throbbing
⒊ **se lancer** *v refl* (+ *v être*) (a) **se** ~ **dans des dépenses** to get involved in expense; **se** ~ **dans les affaires** to go into business
(b) **se** ~ **dans le vide** to jump
(c) to throw [sth] to each other ‹ball›; to exchange ‹insults›

lancer² /lɑ̃se/ nm (a) (Sport) ∼ du disque discus event; ∼ du poids shot put (event)
(b) le ∼, la pêche au ∼ rod and reel fishing

lance-roquettes /lɑ̃sʀɔkɛt/ nm inv rocket launcher

lancinant, ∼e /lɑ̃sinɑ̃, ɑ̃t/ adj ‹pain› shooting; ‹music, rhythm› insistent

landau /lɑ̃do/ nm pram (GB), baby carriage (US)

lande /lɑ̃d/ nf moor

⚜ **langage** /lɑ̃gaʒ/ nm language
■ ∼ administratif official jargon; ∼ des sourds-muets sign language

lange /lɑ̃ʒ/ nm (a) swaddling clothes
(b) nappy (GB), diaper (US)

langer /lɑ̃ʒe/ [13] vtr (a) to wrap [sb] in swaddling clothes ‹baby›
(b) to put a nappy (GB) or diaper (US) on ‹baby›

langoureux, -euse /lɑ̃guʀø, øz/ adj languorous

langouste /lɑ̃gust/ nf spiny lobster

langoustine /lɑ̃gustin/ nf langoustine

⚜ **langue** /lɑ̃g/ nf (a) tongue; tirer la ∼ to stick out one's tongue; (for doctor) to put out one's tongue; (figurative) to be dying of thirst; to struggle financially
(b) language; speech
(c) mauvaise ∼ malicious gossip
(d) ∼ de terre spit of land
■ ∼ de bois political cant; ∼ maternelle mother tongue; ∼ verte slang
IDIOMS avoir la ∼ bien pendue (fam) to be very talkative; avoir qch sur le bout de la ∼ to have sth on the tip of one's tongue

languette /lɑ̃gɛt/ nf (on shoe) tongue; (on satchel, bag) strap; (of ham) long narrow strip

langueur /lɑ̃gœʀ/ nf languor

languir /lɑ̃giʀ/ [3] **1** vi (a) ‹conversation› to languish; ‹economy› to be sluggish
(b) je languis de vous revoir I'm longing to see you; faire ∼ qn to keep sb in suspense
2 se languir v refl (+ v être) to pine

languissant, ∼e /lɑ̃gisɑ̃, ɑ̃t/ adj ‹economy› sluggish; ‹conversation› desultory

lanière /lanjɛʀ/ nf (gen) strap; (of whip) lash

lanterne /lɑ̃tɛʀn/ nf (a) lantern
(b) (Aut) sidelight (GB), parking light (US)
IDIOM éclairer la ∼ de qn to enlighten sb

laper /lape/ [1] vtr to lap (up) ‹soup, milk›

lapider /lapide/ [1] vtr (a) to stone [sb] to death
(b) to throw stones at

lapin /lapɛ̃/ nm (a) rabbit; ∼ de garenne wild rabbit; coup du ∼ rabbit punch; (in accident) whiplash injury; cage or cabane à ∼s rabbit hutch; (figurative) (fam) tower block
(b) rabbit(skin)
IDIOMS poser un ∼ à qn (fam) to stand sb up; se faire tirer comme des ∼s (fam) to be

⚜ indicates a very frequent word

picked off like flies; c'est un chaud ∼ (fam) he's a randy devil

lapine /lapin/ nf doe rabbit

laps /laps/ nm inv ∼ de temps period of time

lapsus /lapsys/ nm inv slip

laquais /lakɛ/ nm inv lackey

laque /lak/ nf (a) hairspray
(b) lacquer; gloss paint (GB), enamel (US)

laqué, ∼e /lake/ adj ‹paint› gloss

laquelle ▸ LEQUEL

laquer /lake/ [1] vtr to lacquer; to paint [sth] in gloss (GB) or enamel (US)

larbin /laʀbɛ̃/ nm (derogatory) (fam) servant

lard /laʀ/ nm ≈ fat streaky bacon

larder /laʀde/ [1] vtr (Culin) to lard; ∼ qn de coups de couteau (figurative) to stab sb repeatedly

lardon /laʀdɔ̃/ nm (Culin) bacon cube

⚜ **large** /laʀʒ/ **1** adj (a) ‹shoulders, hips› broad; ‹avenue, bed› wide; ‹coat› loose-fitting; ‹trousers› loose; ‹skirt› full; ‹jumper› big; ‹smile› broad; ‹curve› long; ∼ de trois mètres three metres (GB) wide
(b) ‹advance, profit› substantial; ‹choice, public› wide; ‹majority› large; au sens ∼ in a broad sense
(c) ‹person› generous
(d) ‹life› comfortable
(e) avoir les idées ∼s, être ∼ d'esprit to be broad-minded
2 adv (a) ‹plan› on a generous scale; ‹calculate, measure› on the generous side
(b) s'habiller ∼ to wear loose-fitting clothes
3 nm (a) faire quatre mètres de ∼ to be four metres (GB) wide
(b) open sea; au ∼ offshore
■ ∼ bande broadband
IDIOM ne pas en mener ∼ (fam) to be worried sick (colloq)

⚜ **largement** /laʀʒəmɑ̃/ adv (a) widely
(b) largely, to a large extent; être ∼ responsable de qch to be largely responsible for sth
(c) arriver ∼ en tête to be a clear winner; ∼ en dessous de la limite well under the limit
(d) tu as ∼ le temps you've got plenty of time
(e) easily; une chaîne en or vaudrait ∼ le double a gold chain would easily be worth twice as much
(f) ‹contribute› generously

largesse /laʀʒɛs/ nf generous gift

largeur /laʀʒœʀ/ nf (a) width, breadth; dans le sens de la ∼ widthwise
(b) ∼ d'esprit broad-mindedness

largué, ∼e /laʀge/ adj (fam) (a) lost, out of one's depth
(b) out of touch

larguer /laʀge/ [1] vtr (a) (Mil) to drop ‹bomb, missile›; to drop ‹parachutist›; to release ‹satellite›

(b) to unfurl ‹sail›; ~ **les amarres** to cast off; (figurative) to set off
(c) (fam) to give up ‹studies›; to chuck (colloq) ‹boyfriend, girlfriend›

⚔ **larme** /laʀm/ *nf* **(a)** tear; **elle a ri aux ~s** she laughed till she cried; **avoir la ~ à l'œil** to be a bit weepy
(b) (fam) drop

larmoyant, ~e /laʀmwajɑ̃, ɑ̃t/ *adj*
(a) ‹eyes› full of tears
(b) ‹voice› whining; ‹speech› maudlin

larmoyer /laʀmwaje/ [23] *vi* **(a)** ‹eyes› to water
(b) ‹person› to whine

larron /laʀɔ̃/ *nm* **(a)** (humorous) scoundrel
(b) thief
IDIOM s'entendre comme ~s en foire to be as thick as thieves

larvaire /laʀvɛʀ/ *adj* ‹state› embryonic

larve /laʀv/ *nf* **(a)** (Zool) larva
(b) (person) wimp (colloq)

larvé, ~e /laʀve/ *adj* latent

laryngite /laʀɛ̃ʒit/ *nf* laryngitis

larynx /laʀɛ̃ks/ *nm inv* larynx

las, lasse /lɑ, lɑs/ *adj* weary

lasagnes /lazaɲ/ *nf pl* lasagna

lascar /laskaʀ/ *nm* (fam) fellow

lascif, -ive /lasif, iv/ *adj* ‹person, look› lascivious; ‹temperament› lustful

laser /lazɛʀ/ *nm* laser

lassant, ~e /lasɑ̃, ɑ̃t/ *adj* **(a)** ‹speech› tedious; ‹reproaches› tiresome
(b) tiring

lasser /lase/ [1] **1** *vtr* **(a)** to bore ‹person, audience›
(b) to weary ‹person, audience›
2 **se lasser** *v refl* (+ *v être*) ‹person› to grow tired; **sans se ~** without tiring; patiently

lassitude /lasityd/ *nf* weariness

lasso /laso/ *nm* lasso; **prendre au ~** to lasso

latence /latɑ̃s/ *nf* latency

latent, ~e /latɑ̃, ɑ̃t/ *adj* ‹danger, illness› latent; ‹anxiety, jealousy› underlying

latéral, ~e, *mpl* **-aux** /lateʀal, o/ *adj* ‹door, exit› side; ‹tunnel, aisle› lateral

latéralement /lateʀalmɑ̃/ *adv* sideways

⚔ **latin, ~e** /latɛ̃, in/ **1** *adj* **(a)** ‹text› Latin
(b) ‹temperament› Latin; ‹culture› Mediterranean
(c) **langues ~es** Romance languages
2 *nm* (language) Latin
IDIOM c'est à y perdre son ~ you can't make head or tail of it

latino-américain, ~e, *mpl* **~s** /latinoameʀikɛ̃, ɛn/ *adj* Latin-American

latitude /latityd/ *nf* latitude
IDIOM avoir toute ~ de faire to be entirely free to do

latte /lat/ *nf* **(a)** lath; (of floor) board
(b) (of bed base) slat

laudatif, -ive /lodatif, iv/ *adj* laudatory

lauréat, ~e /lɔʀea, at/ *nm,f* **(a)** (of competition) winner
(b) (in exam) successful candidate

laurier /lɔʀje/ **1** *nm* **(a)** (Bot) laurel; **~ commun** bay (tree)
(b) (Culin) **feuille de ~** bay leaf
2 **lauriers** *nm pl* laurels; **s'endormir sur ses ~s** to rest on one's laurels

laurier-rose, *pl* **lauriers-roses** /lɔʀjeʀoz/ *nm* oleander

lavable /lavabl/ *adj* washable

lavabo /lavabo/ *nm* washbasin, washbowl

lavage /lavaʒ/ *nm* **(a)** washing; cleaning
(b) (washing machine cycle) wash
■ **~ de cerveau** brainwashing; **faire un ~ d'estomac à qn** to pump sb's stomach (out)

lavande /lavɑ̃d/ *adj inv, nf* lavender

lave /lav/ *nf* lava; **coulée de ~** lava flow

lave-glace, *pl* **~s** /lavglas/ *nm* windscreen (GB) *or* windshield (US) washer

lave-linge /lavlɛ̃ʒ/ *nm inv* washing machine

lavement /lavmɑ̃/ *nm* (Med) enema

⚔ **laver** /lave/ [1] **1** *vtr* **(a)** to wash ‹clothes, child, car›; **~ son linge** to do one's washing; **~ la vaisselle** to do the dishes; **~ qch à grande eau** to wash sth down
(b) to clean ‹wound›
(c) to clear; **~ qn d'une accusation** to clear sb of an accusation
2 **se laver** *v refl* (+ *v être*) **(a)** to wash; **se ~ les mains** to wash one's hands; **se ~ les dents** to brush one's teeth
(b) to be washable
(c) **se ~ d'un affront** to take revenge for an insult
IDIOM je m'en lave les mains I'm washing my hands of it

laverie /lavʀi/ *nf* **~ (automatique)** launderette (GB), laundromat® (US)

lave-vaisselle /lavvɛsɛl/ *nm inv* dishwasher

lavis /lavi/ *nm inv* wash drawing

lavoir /lavwaʀ/ *nm* wash house

laxatif /laksatif/ *nm* laxative

laxisme /laksism/ *nm* laxity

laxiste /laksist/ *adj* lax

layette /lɛjɛt/ *nf* baby clothes, layette

⚔ **le, la¹** (**l'** *before vowel or mute h*), *pl* **les** /lə, la, l, le/ **1** *det* **(a)** the; **la table de la cuisine** the kitchen table; **les Dupont** the Duponts; **elle aime les chevaux** she likes horses; **arriver à** *or* **vers les 11 heures** to arrive at about 11 o'clock
(b) **elle s'est cogné ~ bras** she banged her arm
(c) a, an; **9 euros ~ kilo** 9 euros a kilo
(d) (oh) **la jolie robe!** what a pretty dress!
2 *pron* him; her; it; them; **je ne les comprends pas** I don't understand them ⋯⋗

3 *pron neutre* je ~ savais I knew; I knew it; je ~ croyais aussi, mais... I thought so too, but...; espérons-~! let's hope so!

lé /le/ *nm* (of cloth, wallpaper) width

LEA /ɛləa/ *nf pl* (*abbr = **langues étrangères appliquées***) *university language course with emphasis on business and management*

leadership /lidœʀʃip/ *nm* (a) leading role (b) supremacy

lèche-bottes (fam) /lɛʃbɔt/ **1** *nmf inv* crawler (GB) (colloq), bootlicker (colloq) **2** *nm* crawling (GB) (colloq), bootlicking (colloq)

lécher /leʃe/ [1] **1** *vtr* (a) to lick ‹spoon, plate› (b) ‹flames› to lick; ‹sea› to lap against **2** se lécher *v refl* (+ *v être*) se ~ les doigts to lick one's fingers

lèche-vitrines /lɛʃvitʀin/ *nm inv* window-shopping

⚘ **leçon** /ləsɔ̃/ *nf* lesson; ~ particulière private lesson; cela lui servira de ~ that'll teach him a lesson

⚘ **lecteur, -trice** /lɛktœʀ, tʀis/ **1** *nm,f* (a) reader (b) teaching assistant **2** *nm* (a) (Comput) reader; ~ optique optical scanner *or* reader; ~ de disquettes disk drive; ~ DVD DVD reader (b) player; ~ laser CD player

⚘ **lecture** /lɛktyʀ/ *nf* (a) (of book, newspaper) reading; faire la ~ à qn to read to sb (b) reading, interpretation (c) reading material; tu as pris de la ~? have you brought something to read? (d) (of music, X-ray, disk) reading (e) (of cassette, CD) play; playing

ledit, ladite, *pl* **lesdits, lesdites** /lədi, ladit, ledi, ledit/ *adj* the aforementioned

légal, ~e, *mpl* **-aux** /legal, o/ *adj* legal; lawful

légalement /legalmɑ̃/ *adv* legally; lawfully

légaliser /legalize/ [1] *vtr* to legalize

légalité /legalite/ *nf* (a) legality (b) lawfulness

légataire /legatɛʀ/ *nmf* legatee

légendaire /leʒɑ̃dɛʀ/ *adj* legendary

légende /leʒɑ̃d/ *nf* (a) legend (b) (accompanying picture) caption; (on map) key (c) tall story

⚘ **léger, -ère** /leʒe, ɛʀ/ **1** *adj* (a) light; se sentir plus ~ (figurative) to have a great weight off one's mind (b) (Culin) ‹meat› light (c) ‹person› nimble; ‹step› light (d) ‹laugh› gentle; ‹blow, knock› soft; ‹error, delay› slight; ‹taste, hope› faint; ‹wind, rain› light; ‹cloud› thin; ‹injury› minor

⚘ indicates a very frequent word

(e) ‹tea, drink› weak; ‹perfume, wine› light; ‹tobacco› mild (GB), light (US) (f) ‹action› ill-considered; ‹remark› thoughtless; ‹argument, proof› weak (g) (fam) c'est un peu ~ it's a bit skimpy (h) ‹woman, way of life› loose; ‹husband, mood› fickle (i) (Mil) light **2** *adv* ‹travel› light; cuisiner/manger ~ to cook/to eat light meals **3** à la légère *phr* (gen) without thinking; ‹accuse› rashly; prendre qch à la légère not to take sth seriously

légèrement /leʒɛʀmɑ̃/ *adv* (a) ‹move› gently; ‹perfume› lightly; ‹tremble, injured› slightly (b) (Culin) ‹eat› lightly (c) ‹walk, run› lightly, nimbly (d) ‹act, speak› without thinking

légèreté /leʒɛʀte/ *nf* (a) lightness; nimbleness (b) thoughtlessness; fickleness; la ~ de ses mœurs his/her loose morals

légiférer /leʒifeʀe/ [14] *vi* to legislate

légion /leʒjɔ̃/ *nf* (a) (Mil) legion (b) army ■ la Légion (étrangère) the Foreign Legion

légionellose /leʒjɔneloz/ *nf* Legionnaire's disease

légionnaire /leʒjɔnɛʀ/ *nm* (Roman) legionary; (in Foreign Legion) legionnaire

législateur, -trice /leʒislatœʀ, tʀis/ *nm,f* legislator, law-maker

législatif, -ive /leʒislatif, iv/ *adj* legislative; élections législatives ≈ general election

législation /leʒislasjɔ̃/ *nf* legislation

législature /leʒislatyʀ/ *nf* (a) term of office (b) legislature

légiste /leʒist/ *nm* jurist

légitime /leʒitim/ *adj* (a) ‹child, right› legitimate; ‹union, heir› lawful (b) ‹action› legitimate; ‹anger› justifiable (c) ‹reward› just ■ ~ défense self-defence (GB)

légitimité /leʒitimite/ *nf* (a) legitimacy (b) (of an act) lawfulness

legs /lɛg/ *nm inv* (Law, gen) legacy; (of personal belongings) bequest

léguer /lege/ [14] *vtr* (a) (in one's will) to leave (b) to hand down ‹traditions›; to pass on ‹flaw›

⚘ **légume** /legym/ *nm* vegetable; ~s secs pulses

leitmotiv /lajtmɔtiv/ *nm* leitmotiv

Léman /lemɑ̃/ *n pr* le lac ~ Lake Geneva

⚘ **lendemain** /lɑ̃dmɛ̃/ **1** *nm* (a) le ~, la journée du ~ the following day; dès le ~ the (very) next day; le ~ de l'accident the day after the accident; du jour au ~ overnight

(b) au ∼ de (in the period) after; **au ∼ de la guerre** just after the war
(c) le ∼ tomorrow, the future; **sans ∼** ⟨happiness, success⟩ short-lived
2 **lendemains** nm pl **(a)** outcome; consequences
(b) future; **des ∼s difficiles** difficult days ahead

lénifiant, ∼e /lenifjɑ̃, ɑ̃t/ adj soothing

lent, ∼e¹ /lɑ̃, ɑ̃t/ adj slow; ⟨film, vehicle⟩ slow-moving; ⟨poison⟩ slow-acting

lente² /lɑ̃t/ nf (Zool) nit

ơ **lentement** /lɑ̃t(ə)mɑ̃/ adv slowly

lenteur /lɑ̃tœʀ/ nf slowness; **avec ∼** slowly

lentille /lɑ̃tij/ nf **(a)** (Bot, Culin) lentil
(b) lens; ∼s de contact contact lenses

léopard /leɔpaʀ/ nm **(a)** leopard
(b) leopardskin

lèpre /lɛpʀ/ nf leprosy

lépreux, **-euse** /lepʀø, øz/ nm, f leper

ơ **lequel** /ləkɛl/, **laquelle** /lakɛl/, **lesquels** mpl, **lesquelles**, fpl /lekɛl/; (with à) **auquel, auxquels** mpl, **auxquelles** fpl /okɛl/; (with de) **duquel** /dykɛl/, **desquels** mpl, **desquelles** fpl /dekɛl/
1 **lequel, laquelle, lesquels, lesquelles** adj who; which; Il m'a présenté son cousin, ∼ cousin vit en Grèce he introduced me to his cousin, who lives in Greece; **auquel cas** in which case
2 rel pron who; which; **les gens contre lesquels ils luttaient** the people (who) they were fighting against
3 pron which; **lesquels sont les plus compétents?** which are the most competent?

les ▶ LE

lesbienne /lɛsbjɛn/ nf lesbian

lesdites ▶ LEDIT

lesdits ▶ LEDIT

lèse-majesté /lɛzmaʒɛste/ nf inv lese-majesty

léser /leze/ [14] vtr to wrong ⟨person⟩; to prejudice ⟨interests⟩

lésiner /lezine/ [1] vi **ne pas ∼ sur** to be liberal with ⟨ingredients, money, compliments⟩

lésion /lezjɔ̃/ nf (Med) lesion

lesquels, lesquelles ▶ LEQUEL

lessive /lesiv/ nf **(a)** washing powder; washing liquid
(b) washing

lessiver /lesive/ [1] vtr **(a)** to wash
(b) (fam) **être lessivé** to be washed out (colloq)

lessiveuse /lesivøz/ nf boiler, copper (GB)

lest /lɛst/ nm **(a)** ballast; **jeter** or **lâcher du ∼** to jettison ballast
(b) (on fishing net) weight

leste /lɛst/ adj **(a)** ⟨person, animal⟩ agile, nimble
(b) ⟨joke, remark⟩ risqué

lestement /lɛstəmɑ̃/ adv nimbly

lester /lɛste/ [1] vtr **(a)** to ballast
(b) (fam) to stuff

létal, ∼e, mpl **-aux** /letal, o/ adj lethal

léthargie /letaʀʒi/ nf lethargy

léthargique /letaʀʒik/ adj **(a)** ⟨person⟩ lethargic; ⟨industry⟩ sluggish
(b) (Med) lethargic

ơ **lettre** /lɛtʀ/ **1** nf **(a)** (of alphabet) letter; ∼ majuscule or capitale capital letter; ∼ d'imprimerie block letter; **en toutes ∼s** in full; **c'est écrit en toutes ∼s dans le rapport** it's down in black and white in the report; **les Romains furent des urbanistes avant la ∼** the Romans were city planners before the concept was invented; **à la ∼, au pied de la ∼** to the letter; **il prend tout ce qu'on lui dit à la ∼** he takes everything you say literally
(b) (message) letter; ∼ **de rupture** letter ending a relationship
2 **lettres** nf pl **(a)** (university subject) French; (more general) arts (GB), humanities (US)
(b) letters; **femme de ∼s** woman of letters; **avoir des ∼s** to be well read
■ ∼ **explicative** covering letter; ∼ **de recommandation** letter of recommendation; ∼ **recommandée** registered letter; ∼s **classiques** French and Latin; ∼s **modernes** French language and literature
IDIOM **passer comme une ∼ à la poste** (fam) ⟨reform⟩ to go through smoothly; ⟨excuse⟩ to be accepted without any questions

lettré, ∼e /letʀe/ nm, f man/woman of letters

leu: à la queue leu leu /alakølølø/ phr in single file

leucémie /løsemi/ nf leukaemia

ơ **leur** /lœʀ/ **1** pron them; **il ∼ a écrit** he wrote to them; **il ∼ a fallu faire** they had to do
2 det (pl **leurs**) their; **un de ∼s amis** a friend of theirs; **pendant ∼ absence** while they were away
3 **le leur, la leur, les leurs** pron theirs; **c'est le ∼** it's theirs; **il est des ∼s** he's one of them; **ils m'ont demandé d'être des ∼s** they asked me to come along; **ils vivent loin des ∼s** they live far away from their families

leurre /lœʀ/ nm **(a)** illusion
(b) (in fishing, hunting) lure
(c) (Mil) decoy

leurrer /lœʀe/ [1] **1** vtr to delude
2 **se leurrer** v refl (+ v être) to delude oneself

levain /ləvɛ̃/ nm (fermenting agent) starter; (for bread) leaven (GB), sourdough (US)

levant /ləvɑ̃/ **1** adj m **soleil ∼** rising sun
2 nm east; **au ∼** in the east; **du ∼ au couchant** from east to west

levé, ∼e¹ /ləve/ **1** pp ▶ LEVER¹
2 pp adj **(a)** **voter à main ∼e** to vote by a   ⋯>

l

show of hands

(b) up; **elle est toujours la première ∼e** she's always the first up

levée² /ləve/ *nf* **(a)** (of embargo, sentence, martial law) lifting; (of diplomatic immunity) removal; (of secrecy, taboo) ending; (of session) close

(b) (of mail) collection

(c) (embankment) levee

■ **∼ de boucliers** outcry

✑ **lever¹** /ləve/ [16] **1** *vtr* **(a)** to raise; **∼ la main** *or* **le doigt** (for permission to speak) to put up one's hand; **∼ la main sur qn** to raise a hand to sb; **∼ les bras au ciel** to throw up one's hands; **lève les pieds quand tu marches!** don't drag your feet!; **∼ les yeux** *or* **la tête** to look up

(b) to lift ‹object›; to raise ‹barrier›; **∼ son verre** to raise one's glass

(c) (out of bed) to get [sb] up ‹child, sick person›

(d) to lift ‹embargo, restriction›; to raise ‹siege›; to end ‹taboo, secret›; to remove ‹obstacle›; to close ‹session›

(e) to levy ‹tax›

(f) to flush out ‹game, partridges›

2 *vi* **(a)** (Culin) ‹dough› to rise

(b) ‹seedlings, corn› to come up

3 **se lever** *v refl* (+ *v être*) **(a)** to get up

(b) to stand up; **se ∼ de table** to leave the table

(c) ‹person, people› to rise up

(d) ‹sun› to rise; **le jour se lève** it's getting light

(e) ‹wind› to rise

(f) ‹fog, mist› to clear; ‹weather› to clear up

lever² /ləve/ *nm* **(a)** **être là au ∼ des enfants** to be there when the children get up

(b) **au ∼ du jour** at daybreak

lève-tard /lɛvtaʀ/ *nmf inv* late riser

lève-tôt /lɛvto/ *nmf inv* early riser

levier /ləvje/ *nm* lever; **soulever qch avec un ∼** to lever sth up

■ **∼ de changement de vitesse** (Aut) gear lever (GB), gear stick (US); **∼ de commande** control stick

lévitation /levitasjɔ̃/ *nf* levitation

✑ **lèvre** /lɛvʀ/ *nf* lip; **avoir le sourire aux ∼s** to be smiling; **du bout des ∼s** ‹eat› half-heartedly; ‹reply› grudgingly

IDIOM **être suspendu aux ∼s de qn** to hang on sb's every word

lévrier /levʀije/ *nm* greyhound

levure /ləvyʀ/ *nf* yeast; **∼ chimique** baking powder

lexical, **∼e**, *mpl* **-aux** /lɛksikal, o/ *adj* lexical

lexique /lɛksik/ *nm* **(a)** glossary; (bilingual) vocabulary (book)

(b) lexicon, lexis

lézard /lezaʀ/ *nm* **(a)** lizard

(b) lizardskin

lézarde /lezaʀd/ *nf* crack

lézarder /lezaʀde/ [1] **1** *vtr* to crack

2 *vi* (fam) **∼ au soleil** to bask in the sun

3 **se lézarder** *v refl* (+ *v être*) to crack

liaison /ljɛzɔ̃/ *nf* **(a)** link; **la ∼ Calais–Douvres** the Calais–Dover line

(b) **∼ radio** radio contact; **∼ satellite** satellite link

(c) **assurer la ∼ entre différents services** to liaise between different services

(d) (love) affair

(e) (between words) liaison

liane /ljan/ *nf* creeper, liana

liant, **∼e** /ljɑ̃, ɑ̃t/ *adj* sociable

liasse /ljas/ *nf* (of banknotes) wad; (of letters, papers, documents) bundle

Liban /libɑ̃/ *pr nm* Lebanon

libellé /libɛlle/ *nm* wording

libeller /libɛlle/ [1] *vtr* **(a)** to draw up ‹contract›

(b) to word ‹article›

(c) to make out ‹cheque›

libellule /libɛllyl/ *nf* dragonfly

libéral, **∼e**, *mpl* **-aux** /libeʀal, o/ *adj*

(a) liberal

(b) (in politics) Liberal

(c) free-market

libéralisation /libeʀalizasjɔ̃/ *nf* liberalization; **∼ des mœurs** relaxation of moral standards

libéraliser /libeʀalize/ [1] **1** *vtr* to liberalize

2 **se libéraliser** *v refl* (+ *v être*) ‹country, attitudes› to become more liberal

libéralisme /libeʀalism/ *nm* liberalism

libéralité /libeʀalite/ *nf* liberality

libérateur, **-trice** /libeʀatœʀ, tʀis/ **1** *adj* liberating

2 *nm,f* (de pays, ville, personne) liberator

libération /libeʀasjɔ̃/ *nf* **(a)** (of prisoner, hostage) release

(b) (of country, population) liberation; **∼ des femmes** women's liberation

(c) relief

(d) (of prices) deregulation

Libération /libeʀasjɔ̃/ *nf* (of 1944) **la ∼** the Liberation

libéré, **∼e** /libeʀe/ **1** *pp* ▶ LIBÉRER

2 *pp adj* **(a)** ‹man, woman› liberated

(b) ‹country, area, town› free

(c) ‹post, premises› vacant

✑ **libérer** /libeʀe/ [14] **1** *vtr* **(a)** to liberate ‹country, town›; to free ‹companion, hostage›

(b) to release ‹prisoner›; to free ‹slave, animal›

(c) to allow [sb] to go ‹employee›

(d) to liberate ‹person›; (of post, duties) to relieve ‹minister›; **∼ qn de l'emprise de qn** to get sb away from sb's influence

(e) to release ‹emotion›; to give free rein to

✑ indicates a very frequent word

⟨*imagination*⟩
(f) to relieve ⟨*mind, person*⟩; ∼ **sa conscience** to unburden oneself

(g) to vacate ⟨*apartment, office*⟩; ∼ **la chambre avant midi** (in hotel) to check out before noon

(h) to free ⟨**arm, hand**⟩; to release ⟨*spring, catch*⟩

(i) to liberalize ⟨*economy, trade*⟩; to deregulate ⟨*prices*⟩; ∼ **les loyers** to lift rent controls

(j) to release ⟨*gas, energy*⟩

2 **se libérer** *v refl* (+ *v être*) **(a)** to free oneself/itself; **se** ∼ **d'une dette** to pay a debt

(b) j'essaierai de me ∼ **mercredi** I'll try and be free on Wednesday

libertaire /libɛʀtɛʀ/ *adj, nmf* libertarian

⚜ **liberté** /libɛʀte/ *nf* **(a)** (gen) freedom; **être en** ∼ to be free; **élever des animaux en** ∼ to raise animals in a natural habitat; **espèce vivant en** ∼ species in the wild; **l'assassin est toujours en** ∼ the killer is still at large; **prendre la** ∼ **de faire** to take the liberty of doing; ∼ **de pensée** freedom of thought

(b) (Law) **mettre qn en** ∼ **conditionnelle** to release sb on parole; **mise en** ∼ **surveillée** release on probation

libertin, ∼**e** /libɛʀtɛ̃, in/ *adj, nm,f* libertine

libido /libido/ *nf* libido

⚜ **libraire** /libʀɛʀ/ *nmf* bookseller

librairie /libʀɛʀi/ *nf* **(a)** bookshop (GB), bookstore

(b) bookselling business

librairie-papeterie, *pl* **librairies-papeteries** /libʀɛʀipapetʀi/ *nf* stationer's and bookshop (GB)

⚜ **libre** /libʀ/ *adj* **(a)** ⟨*person, country*⟩ free; ∼ **à elle de partir** it's up to her whether she goes or not; **être** ∼ **de ses actes** to do as one wishes

(b) ⟨*person*⟩ free and easy; ⟨*manner*⟩ free; ⟨*opinion*⟩ candid; ⟨*morality*⟩ easygoing

(c) ⟨*hand, thumb*⟩ free; ⟨*road, way*⟩ clear

(d) ⟨*person, room*⟩ available; ⟨*seat*⟩ free

(e) ⟨*WC*⟩ vacant; **la ligne n'est pas** ∼ (on telephone) the number is engaged (GB) *or* busy (US)

■ ∼ **arbitre** free will; ∼ **circulation** freedom of movement

IDIOM **être** ∼ **comme l'air** to be as free as a bird

libre-échange /libʀeʃɑ̃ʒ/ *nm* free trade

librement /libʀəmɑ̃/ *adv* freely

libre-service, *pl* **libres-services** /libʀəsɛʀvis/ 1 *adj inv* self-service

2 *nm* **(a) le** ∼ self-service

(b) self-service shop (GB) *or* store (US); self-service restaurant

■ ∼ **bancaire** automatic teller

lice /lis/ *nf* **être en** ∼ to have entered the lists

licence /lisɑ̃s/ *nf* **(a)** (bachelor's) degree; ∼ **en droit** law degree

(b) (Law) licence (GB); **produit sous** ∼ licensed product

licencié, ∼**e** /lisɑ̃sje/ 1 *pp* ▶ LICENCIER

2 *pp adj* ⟨*student*⟩ graduate

3 *nm,f* **(a)** graduate (GB), college graduate (US)

(b) ∼ **(économique)** redundant employee (GB), laid-off worker

licenciement /lisɑ̃simɑ̃/ *nm* dismissal; ∼ **(économique)** redundancy (GB), lay-off ∼ **abusif** unfair dismissal; ∼ **collectif** mass redundancy (GB); ∼ **sec** compulsory redundancy (GB) (*without compensation*)

licencier /lisɑ̃sje/ [2] *vtr* **(a)** to make [sb] redundant (GB), to lay [sb] off

(b) to dismiss (GB), to let [sb] go

licencieux, -ieuse /lisɑ̃sjø, øz/ *adj* licentious

lichen /likɛn/ *nm* lichen

licite /lisit/ *adj* lawful

licorne /likɔʀn/ *nf* unicorn

lie /li/ *nf* **(a)** dregs, lees

(b) (figurative) dregs

lie-de-vin /lidvɛ̃/ *adj inv* wine-coloured (GB)

liège /ljɛʒ/ *nm* cork; **bouchon en** ∼ cork

liégeois, ∼**e** /ljeʒwa, az/ *adj* of Liège; **café** ∼ iced coffee topped with whipped cream

⚜ **lien** /ljɛ̃/ *nm* **(a)** strap; string

(b) connection, link (**entre** between)

(c) (gen) link, tie (**avec** with); (emotional) tie, bond; ∼**s économiques** economic links; ∼**s de parenté** family ties

⚜ **lier** /lje/ [1] 1 *vtr* **(a)** to tie [sb/sth] up; **il avait les mains liées** his hands were tied

(b) to bind; **ils sont très liés** they are very close

(c) to link ⟨*ideas, events*⟩

(d) ∼ **amitié avec qn** to strike up a friendship with sb

(e) (Mus) to slur ⟨*notes*⟩

2 **se lier** *v refl* (+ *v être*) to make friends

lierre /ljɛʀ/ *nm* ivy

liesse /ljɛs/ *nf* jubilation; **en** ∼ jubilant

⚜ **lieu** /ljø/ 1 *nm* **(a)** *pl* ∼**x** place; ∼ **de passage** thoroughfare; **en tous** ∼**x** everywhere; **en** ∼ **et place de qn** ⟨*sign, act*⟩ on behalf of sb; **en dernier** ∼ lastly; **avoir** ∼ to take place; **tenir** ∼ **de** to serve as ⟨*bedroom, study*⟩; **il y a** ∼ **de s'inquiéter** there is cause for concern; **s'il y a** ∼ if necessary; **donner** ∼ **à** to cause ⟨*scandal*⟩

(b) *pl* ∼**s** coley

2 **au lieu de** *phr* instead of

3 **lieux** *nm pl* **(a) sur les** ∼**x** at *or* on the scene; on the spot; **repérer les** ∼**x** to have a scout around

(b) premises; **visiter les** ∼**x** to visit the premises

■ ∼ **commun** platitude; ∼ **public** public place

lieue /ljø/ *nf* league; ∼ **marine** league

IDIOM **j'étais à cent** *or* **mille** ∼**s d'imaginer** I ⋯⟶

never for a moment imagined

lieutenant /ljøtnɑ̃/ *nm* (a) (Mil) (in army) ≈ lieutenant (GB), ≈ first lieutenant (US); (in air force) ≈ flying officer (GB), ≈ first lieutenant (US)
(b) (on boat) first officer

lièvre /ljɛvʀ/ *nm* (Zool) hare
IDIOM **courir plusieurs ~s à la fois** to try to do too many things at once

lifting /liftiŋ/ *nm* face-lift

ligament /ligamɑ̃/ *nm* ligament

ligaturer /ligatyʀe/ [1] *vtr* (Med) to tie

lignage /liɲaʒ/ *nm* lineage

⚜ **ligne** /liɲ/ *nf* (a) (gen) line; **lire les ~s de la main de qn** to read sb's palm; **~ droite** straight line; (driving) straight piece of road; **la dernière ~ droite avant l'arrivée** the home straight; **je vous écris ces quelques ~s pour vous dire…** this is just a quick note to tell you…; **à la ~!** new paragraph!
(b) (in public transport) service; route; (of train, underground) line; **~ de chemin de fer** railway line; **~s intérieures** domestic flights
(c) cable; **~ aérienne** overhead cable
(d) (telephone) line
(e) figure; **garder la ~** to stay slim
(f) (of body) contours; (of face) shape; (of hills) outline; **la ~ aérodynamique d'une voiture** the aerodynamic lines of a car
(g) (of clothes, furniture, style) look
(h) outline; **raconter un événement dans ses grandes ~s** to give an outline of events
(i) fishing line; **pêche à la ~** angling
(j) line; row; **les ~s ennemies** (Mil) the enemy lines
(k) (Comput) **en ~** on line
■ **~ de conduite** line of conduct; **se donner comme ~ de conduite de faire** to make it a rule to do; **~ de démarcation** (Mil) demarcation line; **~ de mire** line of sight; **~ de tir** line of fire
IDIOMS **être en première ~** to be in the front line; (figurative) to be in the firing line; **entrer en ~ de compte** to be taken into account

lignée /liɲe/ *nf* (a) descendants; lineage; **de haute ~** of noble descent
(b) tradition

lignite /liɲit/ *nm* brown coal, lignite

ligoter /ligɔte/ [1] *vtr* to truss [sb] up

ligue /lig/ *nf* league

liguer: **se liguer** /lige/ [1] *v refl* (+ *v être*) ⟨*people*⟩ to join forces

lilas /lila/ *adj inv, nm* lilac

lilliputien, -ienne /lilipysjɛ̃, ɛn/ *adj, nm,f* Lilliputian

limace /limas/ *nf* (Zool) slug

limaçon /limasɔ̃/ *nm* snail

limaille /limaj/ *nf* filings

limande /limɑ̃d/ *nf* (Zool) dab

limande-sole, *pl* **limandes-soles** /limɑ̃dsɔl/ *nf* (Zool) lemon sole

lime /lim/ *nf* (a) (Tech) file; **~ à ongles** nail file
(b) (Bot) lime
(c) (Zool) lima

limer /lime/ [1] **1** *vtr* (a) to file ⟨*nails, metal*⟩; to file down ⟨*key*⟩
(b) to file through ⟨*bars of cage*⟩
2 se limer *v refl* (+ *v être*) **se ~ les ongles** to file one's nails

limier /limje/ *nm* (a) bloodhound
(b) (fam) sleuth

limitatif, -ive /limitatif, iv/ *adj* limiting, restrictive

limitation /limitasjɔ̃/ *nf* (of power, liberty) limitation, restriction; (of prices, interest rates) control; **~ de vitesse** (Aut) speed limit

⚜ **limite** /limit/ **1** *nf* (a) border
(b) (of estate, piece of land) boundary; (of sea, forest, village) edge
(c) limit; **connaître ses ~s** to know one's (own) limitations; **vraiment, il dépasse les ~s!** he's really going too far!; **à la ~, je préférerais qu'il refuse** I'd almost prefer it if he refused
(d) **à la ~ de** on the verge of; **activités à la ~ de la légalité** activities bordering on the illegal
(e) **dans une certaine ~** up to a point, to a certain extent; **dans la ~ de, dans les ~s de** within the limits of
2 (-)limite (*combining form*) **date(-)~** deadline; **date(-)~ de vente** sell-by date; **vitesse(-)~** maximum speed
■ **~ d'âge** age limit

⚜ **limiter** /limite/ [1] **1** *vtr* to limit, to restrict ⟨*power, duration, number*⟩; **cela limite nos possibilités** that rather limits our scope
2 se limiter *v refl* (+ *v être*) (a) **se ~ à deux verres de bière par jour** to limit oneself to two glasses of beer a day; **je me limiterai à quelques observations** I'll confine myself to a few observations
(b) **se ~ à** to be limited to; **la vie ne se limite pas au travail** there's more to life than work

limitrophe /limitʀɔf/ *adj* ⟨*country, region*⟩ adjacent; ⟨*city*⟩ border

limoger /limɔʒe/ [13] *vtr* to dismiss

limon /limɔ̃/ *nm* (a) silt
(b) (on horse-drawn carriage) shaft

limonade /limɔnad/ *nf* lemonade (GB), lemon soda (US)

limousine /limuzin/ *nf* (Aut) limousine

limpide /lɛ̃pid/ *adj* (a) clear, limpid
(b) (figurative) ⟨*explanation, style*⟩ clear, lucid

limpidité /lɛ̃pidite/ *nf* clarity

lin /lɛ̃/ *nm* (a) flax
(b) linen

linceul /lɛ̃sœl/ *nm* shroud

linéaire /lineɛʀ/ *adj* linear

⚜ indicates a very frequent word

linge /lɛ̃ʒ/ *nm* (a) linen; ∼ **sale** dirty linen
(b) washing; **corde** *or* **fil à** ∼ clothes line
(c) ∼ **(de corps)** underwear
(d) cloth
■ ∼ **de maison** household linen; ∼ **de toilette** bathroom linen

lingère /lɛ̃ʒɛʀ/ *nf* laundry woman

lingerie /lɛ̃ʒʀi/ *nf* (a) linen room
(b) lingerie

lingot /lɛ̃go/ *nm* ingot

linguiste /lɛ̃ɡɥist/ *nmf* linguist

linguistique /lɛ̃ɡɥistik/ **1** *adj* linguistic
2 *nf* linguistics

linotte /linɔt/ *nf* linnet

linteau, *pl* ∼**x** /lɛ̃to/ *nm* lintel

lion /ljɔ̃/ *nm* lion; ∼ **de mer** sealion
IDIOM **avoir mangé du** ∼ (fam) to be full of beans (GB) (colloq), to be full of pep (US) (colloq)

Lion /ljɔ̃/ *pr nm* Leo

lionceau, *pl* ∼**x** /ljɔ̃so/ *nm* lion cub

lionne /ljɔn/ *nf* lioness

lipide /lipid/ *nm* lipid

liquéfier /likefje/ [2] *vtr*, **se liquéfier** *v refl* (+ *v être*) to liquefy

liquette /likɛt/ *nf* (fam) shirt

liqueur /likœʀ/ *nf* liqueur

liquidation /likidasjɔ̃/ *nf* (a) (Law) (of property) liquidation; (of debts) settlement
(b) clearance; ∼ **totale (du stock)** total clearance

liquide /likid/ **1** *adj* (a) liquid; **miel** ∼ clear honey
(b) **argent** ∼ cash
2 *nm* (a) liquid
(b) cash
■ ∼ **correcteur** correction fluid, white-out (fluid) (US); ∼ **de frein** brake fluid

liquider /likide/ [1] *vtr* (a) to settle ‹*accounts*›; to liquidate ‹*company, business*›
(b) to clear ‹*goods, stock*›
(c) (fam) to liquidate (colloq) ‹*enemy, witness*›
(d) (fam) to demolish ‹*meal*›; to empty ‹*glass*›

liquidité /likidite/ *nf* **des** ∼**s** liquid assets

⚔ **lire¹** /liʀ/ [66] *vtr* to read; ∼ **qch en diagonale** to skim through sth; ∼ **sur les lèvres de qn** to lip-read what sb is saying; ∼ **dans les pensées de qn** to read sb's mind

lire² /liʀ/ *nf* lira

lis /lis/ *nm inv* lily

liseré /lizʀe/ *nm*, **liséré** /lizere/ *nm* (on dress) edging; piping

liseron /lizʀɔ̃/ *nm* bindweed, convolvulus

liseuse /lizøz/ *nf* (a) bed jacket
(b) small reading lamp

lisible /lizibl/ *adj* (a) legible
(b) readable

lisière /lizjɛʀ/ *nf* (a) (of wood, field) edge; (of village) outskirts
(b) (on piece of fabric) selvage

lisse /lis/ *adj* ‹*skin, surface*› smooth; ‹*tyre*› worn

lisser /lise/ [1] *vtr* to smooth ‹*hair, garment*›; to stroke ‹*beard*›

⚔ **liste** /list/ *nf* (gen) list; (at election) list (of candidates) (GB), ticket (US)
■ ∼ **d'attente** waiting list; ∼ **électorale** electoral roll; ∼ **de mariage** wedding list
IDIOM **être sur** ∼ **rouge** to be ex-directory (GB), to have an unlisted number (US)

lister /liste/ [1] *vtr* to list

⚔ **lit** /li/ *nm* (a) bed; ∼ **à une place** *or* **d'une personne** single bed; ∼ **à deux places** *or* **de deux personnes** double bed; **aller** *or* **se mettre au** ∼ to go to bed **garder le** ∼ to stay in bed; **tirer qn du** ∼ to drag sb out of bed; **au** ∼! bedtime!; ∼ **métallique** iron bedstead; **le** ∼ **n'était pas défait** the bed had not been slept in
(b) (Law) marriage
(c) (of river) bed; **la rivière est sortie de son** ∼ the river has overflowed its banks
■ ∼ **de camp** camp bed (GB), cot (US); ∼ **pliant** folding bed; ∼**s superposés** bunk beds

litanie /litani/ *nf* litany

literie /litʀi/ *nf* bedding

lithographie /litɔɡʀafi/ *nf* (a) lithography
(b) lithograph

litière /litjɛʀ/ *nf* (a) (for cattle) litter; (for horses) bedding; (for cats) cat litter
(b) (mode of transport) litter

litige /litiʒ/ *nm* dispute; **point de** ∼ bone of contention; **point at issue**; **les parties en** ∼ the litigants

litigieux, -ieuse /litiʒjø, øz/ *adj* ‹*case, point, argument*› contentious

litre /litʀ/ *nm* (a) (measure) litre (GB)
(b) litre (GB) bottle

⚔ **littéraire** /liteʀɛʀ/ **1** *adj* ‹*work, criticism*› literary; **études** ∼**s** arts studies
2 *nm,f* (a) literary person
(b) arts *or* liberal arts (US) student

littéral, -e, *mpl* **-aux** /liteʀal, o/ *adj* literal

littéralement /liteʀalmã/ *adv* literally; verbatim

⚔ **littérature** /liteʀatyʀ/ *nf* literature

littoral, -e, *mpl* **-aux** /litɔʀal, o/ **1** *adj* coastal
2 *nm* coast

liturgie /lityʀʒi/ *nf* liturgy

livide /livid/ *adj* deathly pale

living /liviŋ/ *nm* living-room

livraison /livʀɛzɔ̃/ *nf* delivery; '∼**s à domicile**' 'we deliver'; **il est venu prendre** ∼ **de la commande** he came to pick up the order

⚔ **livre¹** /livʀ/ *nm* book; **c'est mon** ∼ **de chevet** it's my bedside book; (figurative) it's my bible
■ ∼ **blanc** blue book; ∼ **de bord** logbook; ∼ **d'or** visitors' book; ∼ **de poche®** paperback; ⋯⋮>

~ scolaire schoolbook

livre² /livʀ/ *nf* **(a)** pound; **~ sterling** pound sterling; **~ irlandaise** Irish pound, punt **(b)** (unit of weight) half a kilo; (in UK) pound

livrée /livʀe/ *nf* livery

⚜ **livrer** /livʀe/ [1] **1** *vtr* **(a)** to deliver ‹*goods*›; **~ qn** to deliver sb's order

(b) to hand [sb] over ‹*criminal*›; to betray ‹*accomplice, secret*›

(c) être livré à soi-même to be left to one's own devices

(d) il nous livre un peu de lui-même he reveals something of himself

2 **se livrer** *v refl* (+ *v être*) **(a) se ~ à un trafic de drogue** to engage in drug trafficking

(b) se ~ à ‹*criminal*› to give oneself up to

(c) se ~ à un ami to confide in a friend

livret /livʀɛ/ *nm* **(a)** booklet

(b) libretto

■ **~ de caisse d'épargne** ≈ savings book (GB), bankbook (*for a savings account*) (US); **~ de famille** family record book (*of births, marriages and deaths*)

livreur, -euse /livʀœʀ, øz/ *nm,f* delivery man/woman

lobe /lɔb/ *nm* lobe; **~ de l'oreille** ear lobe

⚜ **local, ~e,** *pl* **-aux** /lɔkal, o/ **1** *adj* ‹*newspaper, authorities*› local; ‹*pain, showers*› localized

2 *nm* **(a)** place; **les scouts ont besoin d'un ~** the scouts need a place to meet

(b) ~ commercial commercial premises; **les locaux du journal** the newspaper offices

localement /lɔkalmɑ̃/ *adv* on a local level; **appliquer la crème ~** apply the cream locally

localisation /lɔkalizasjɔ̃/ *nf* **(a)** location

(b) la ~ d'un incendie localizing a fire

localiser /lɔkalize/ [1] *vtr* **(a)** to locate ‹*person, noise*›

(b) to confine, to localize ‹*fire*›

localité /lɔkalite/ *nf* locality

locataire /lɔkatɛʀ/ *nmf* tenant

locatif, -ive /lɔkatif, iv/ *adj* ‹*agreement*› rental

location /lɔkasjɔ̃/ *nf* **(a)** (by owner) renting out; (by tenant) renting; **agence de ~** rental agency

(b) rented accommodation

(c) rent

(d) (of equipment) hire; **~ de voitures** car hire (GB), car rental; **contrat de ~** rental agreement; **~ de vidéos** video rental

(e) (of theatre seats) reservation, booking (GB)

location-vente, *pl* **locations-ventes** /lɔkasjɔ̃vɑ̃t/ *nf* 100% mortgage scheme

locomotion /lɔkɔmɔsjɔ̃/ *nf* locomotion

locomotive /lɔkɔmɔtiv/ *nf* engine, locomotive; **~ à vapeur** steam engine

---

⚜ indicates a very frequent word

locuteur, -trice /lɔkytœʀ, tʀis/ *nm,f* speaker

locution /lɔkysjɔ̃/ *nf* phrase; idiom

logarithme /lɔgaʀitm/ *nm* logarithm, log

loge /lɔʒ/ *nf* **(a)** (caretaker's dwelling) lodge

(b) (of actor) dressing room; (in theatre) box

(c) (in freemasonry) Lodge

(d) loggia

logé, ~e /lɔʒe/ **1** *pp* ▶ LOGER

2 *pp adj* housed; **être ~, nourri, blanchi** to have bed, board and one's laundry done

logement /lɔʒmɑ̃/ *nm* **(a)** accommodation; **~ individuel** flat (GB), apartment (US)

(b) housing; **la crise du ~** the housing crisis

loger /lɔʒe/ [13] **1** *vtr* **(a)** to house ‹*student*›

(b) to put [sb] up ‹*friend*›; to provide accommodation for ‹*refugees*›

(c) ‹*hotel*› to have accommodation for

(d) to put; **je n'ai pas pu ~ tous mes meubles dans le salon** I couldn't fit all my furniture in the living room

(e) ~ une balle dans la tête de qn to shoot sb in the head

2 *vi* **(a)** to live

(b) to stay; **~ à l'hôtel** to stay at a hotel

3 **se loger** *v refl* (+ *v être*) **(a)** to find accommodation; **se nourrir et se ~** to pay for food and accommodation

(b) se ~ dans qch to get stuck in sth; ‹*dust*› to collect in sth; **la balle est venue se ~ dans le genou** the bullet lodged in his/her knee

logeur, -euse /lɔʒœʀ, øz/ *nm,f* lodger

loggia /lɔdʒja/ *nf* loggia

⚜ **logiciel** /lɔʒisjɛl/ *nm* **(a)** software; **~ de base** system(s) software

(b) program

(c) (Comput) **~ de navigation** browser

⚜ **logique** /lɔʒik/ **1** *adj* **(a)** logical; **il n'est pas ~ avec lui-même** he is not consistent

(b) (fam) reasonable; **ce serait ~ qu'ils soient en colère** one could understand why they would be angry

2 *nf* logic; **manquer de ~** to be illogical; **c'est dans la ~ des choses** it's in the nature of things; **en toute ~** logically

logiquement /lɔʒikmɑ̃/ *adv* logically

logis /lɔʒi/ *nm inv* home, dwelling

logistique /lɔʒistik/ *nf* logistics

logo /lɔgo/ *nm* logo

⚜ **loi** /lwa/ *nf* **(a)** law; **voter une ~** to pass a law

(b) la ~ the law; **enfreindre la ~** to break the law; **tomber sous le coup de la ~** to be or constitute an offence (GB); **faire la ~** (figurative) to lay down the law

(c) rule; law; **la ~ du milieu** the law of the underworld; **c'est la ~ des séries** things always happen in a row

■ **~ d'amnistie** act granting amnesty to some offenders; **~ communautaire** community law; **~ informatique et libertés** data protection act; **~ de la jungle** law of the jungle

⚹ loin /lwɛ̃/ **1** *adv* **(a)** a long way, far (away); **c'est ~** it's a long way; **c'est trop ~** it's too far; **il habite plus ~** he lives further *or* farther away; **du plus ~ qu'il m'aperçut** as soon as he saw me; **voir plus ~** (in text) see below
(b) (in time) **tout cela est bien ~** that was all a long time ago; **aussi ~ que je me souvienne** as far back as I can remember; **l'été n'est plus très ~ maintenant** summer isn't far off now
(c) (figurative) **de là à dire qu'il est incompétent, il n'y a pas ~** that comes close to saying he's incompetent; **il n'est pas bête, ~ s'en faut!** he's not stupid, far from it!; **ça va beaucoup plus ~** it goes much further
2 loin de *phr* **(a)** (in space) far from; **est-ce encore ~ d'ici?** is it much further *or* farther from here?
(b) (in time) far from; **cela ne fait pas ~ de quatre ans que je suis ici** I've been here for almost four years now
(c) (figurative) far from, a long way from; **~ de moi cette idée!** nothing could be further from my mind!; **avec l'imprimante, il faut compter pas ~ de 8 000 euros** if you include the printer, you're talking about 8,000 euros or thereabouts
3 de loin *phr* from a distance; **je ne vois pas très bien de ~** I can't see very well at a distance; **c'est de ~ ton meilleur roman** it's by far your best novel
4 au loin *phr* **au ~** in the distance
5 de loin en loin *phr* **(a)** on pouvait voir des maisons de ~ **en ~** you could see houses scattered here and there
(b) every now and then
IDIOM **~ des yeux, ~ du cœur** (Proverb) out of sight, out of mind

lointain, ~e /lwɛ̃tɛ̃, ɛn/ **1** *adj*
(a) ‹*country, past*› distant
(b) ‹*link*› remote
(c) ‹*person*› distant
2 *nm* background; **dans le ~** ‹*see, hear*› in the distance

loir /lwaʀ/ *nm* (edible) dormouse

loisir /lwaziʀ/ *nm* **(a)** spare time; **(tout) à ~** at (great) leisure
(b) avoir tout ~ de faire to have plenty of time to do
(c) leisure activity

lombaire /lɔ̃bɛʀ/ *nf* lumbar vertebra

londonien, -ienne /lɔ̃dɔnjɛ̃, ɛn/ *adj* (of) London

Londres /lɔ̃dʀ/ *pr n* London

⚹ long, longue /lɔ̃, lɔ̃g/ **1** *adj* long; **plus/ trop ~ de deux mètres** two metres (GB) longer/too long; **être ~ (à faire)** ‹*person*› to be slow (to do); **être en longue maladie** to be on extended sick leave; **il guérira, mais ce sera ~** he will get better, but it's going to take a long time; **être ~ à la détente** (fam) to be slow on the uptake (colloq)

2 *adv* **(a) en dire ~/trop ~/plus ~** to say a lot/too much/more **(sur qn/qch** about sb/ sth)
(b) s'habiller ~ to wear longer skirts
3 *nm* **un câble de six mètres de ~** a cable six metres (GB) long, a six-metre (GB) long cable; **en ~** lengthwise; **en ~ et en large** ‹*tell*› in great detail; **marcher de ~ en large** to pace up and down; **en ~, en large et en travers** (fam) ‹*tell*› at great length; **le ~ du mur** along the wall; up *or* down the wall; **tomber de tout son ~** to fall flat (on one's face)
4 à la longue *phr* in the end, eventually
■ **~ métrage** feature-length film

long-courrier, *pl* **~s** /lɔ̃kuʀje/ *nm*
(a) ocean-going ship
(b) long-haul aircraft

longer /lɔ̃ʒe/ [13] *vtr* **(a)** ‹*person, train*› to go along ‹*coast*›; to follow ‹*river*›
(b) ‹*garden, road*› to run alongside ‹*lake, field*›

longévité /lɔ̃ʒevite/ *nf* longevity

longiligne /lɔ̃ʒiliɲ/ *adj* lanky, rangy

longitude /lɔ̃ʒityd/ *nf* longitude

longitudinal, ~e, *mpl* **-aux** /lɔ̃ʒitydinal, o/ *adj* longitudinal, lengthwise

⚹ longtemps /lɔ̃tɑ̃/ *adv* ‹*wait, sleep*› (for) a long time; **il t'a fallu ~?** did it take you long?; **~ avant/après** long before/after; **je peux le garder plus ~?** can I keep it a bit longer?; **il n'y a pas ~ qu'il travaille ici** he hasn't worked here long; **il y a or ça fait ~ qu'il n'a pas téléphoné** he hasn't phoned for ages (colloq); **il est mort depuis ~** he died a long time ago; **il n'y a pas si ~ c'était encore possible** it was still possible until quite recently

⚹ longue ▸ LONG 1, 4

longuement /lɔ̃gmɑ̃/ *adv* ‹*hesitate, talk*› for a long time; ‹*explain, interview*› at length

⚹ longueur /lɔ̃gœʀ/ **1** *nf* **(a)** (in space, time) length; **la maison est tout en ~** the house is long and narrow; **traîner en ~** ‹*film, book*› to go on forever
(b) (in race, swimming) length; **avoir une ~ d'avance sur qn** (Sport) to be one length ahead of sb; (figurative) to be ahead of sb; **le saut en ~** the long *or* broad (US) jump
(c) length
2 longueurs *nf pl* (in film, book, speech) overlong passages
3 à longueur de *phr* **à ~ de journée** all day long; **à ~ d'année** all year round; **à ~ d'émissions** programme (GB) after programme (GB)
■ **~ d'onde** wavelength

longue-vue, *pl* **longues-vues** /lɔ̃gvy/ *nf* telescope

look /luk/ *nm* (fam) look; image

looping /lupiŋ/ *nm* loop

lopin /lɔpɛ̃/ *nm* **~ (de terre)** patch of land

loquace /lɔkas/ *adj* talkative, loquacious

loque /lɔk/ 1 *nf* ~ (humaine) (human) wreck

2 **loques** *nf pl* rags

loquet /lɔkɛ/ *nm* latch

lorgner /lɔʀɲe/ [1] *vtr* (fam) to give [sb] the eye ‹person› (colloq); to cast longing glances at ‹jewel, cake›; to have one's eye on ‹inheritance, job›

lorgnette /lɔʀɲɛt/ *nf* (a) opera-glasses
(b) spy-glass

lorgnon /lɔʀɲɔ̃/ *nm* (a) lorgnette
(b) pince-nez

◊ **lors**: **lors de** /lɔʀ/ *phr* (a) during
(b) at the time of

◊ **lorsque**, (**lorsqu'** *before vowel or mute h*) /lɔʀsk(ə)/ *conj* when

losange /lɔzɑ̃ʒ/ *nm* (shape) lozenge; **en** ~ diamond-shaped

lot /lo/ *nm* (a) (of inheritance) share; (of land) plot
(b) (in lottery) prize; **gagner le gros** ~ to hit the jackpot
(c) (of objects for sale) batch; (at auction) lot
(d) (of person) **être au-dessus du** ~ to be above the average
(e) fate, lot

loterie /lɔtʀi/ *nf* raffle; (in fair) tombola (GB), raffle (US); (large scale) lottery

loti, ~e /lɔti/ *adj* **bien/mal** ~ well/badly off

lotion /losjɔ̃/ *nf* lotion

lotir /lɔtiʀ/ [3] *vtr* **terrain(s) à** ~ plots for sale

lotissement /lɔtismɑ̃/ *nm* housing estate (GB), subdivision (US)

loto /lɔto/ *nm* lotto; **le** ~ **national** the national lottery

lotte /lɔt/ *nf* monkfish; (freshwater) burbot

lotus /lɔtys/ *nm inv* lotus

louable /luabl/ *adj* commendable, praiseworthy

louage /luaʒ/ *nm* **voiture de** ~ hire car (GB), rental car (US)

louange /luɑ̃ʒ/ *nf* praise

loubard /lubaʀ/ *nm* (fam) hooligan, delinquent youth

louche /luʃ/ 1 *adj* ‹person, past, affair› shady; ‹place› seedy
2 *nf* ladle; ladleful

loucher /luʃe/ [1] *vi* to have a squint

louer /lue/ [1] *vtr* (a) ‹owner, landlord› to let (GB), to rent out ‹house›; to hire out ‹premises›; to rent out ‹equipment›; **'à** ~' 'for rent', 'to let' (GB)
(b) ‹tenant› to rent ‹house›; to hire ‹room›; to rent ‹equipment, film›
(c) to hire ‹staff›
(d) to praise; **Dieu soit loué** thank God

loufoque /lufɔk/ *adj* (fam) crazy (colloq)

◊ indicates a very frequent word

louis /lwi/ *nm inv* ~ **d'or** (gold) louis

loukoum /lukum/ *nm* Turkish delight

loulou /lulu/ *nm* (a) spitz
(b) (fam) hooligan, delinquent youth
(c) (fam) pet (GB) (colloq), honey (US)

◊ **loup** /lu/ *nm* (a) wolf; **le grand méchant** ~ the big bad wolf; **à pas de** ~ stealthily
(b) ~ **(de mer)** (sea) bass
(c) domino; mask
■ (vieux) ~ **de mer** old salt, old tar
IDIOMS **avoir une faim de** ~ to be ravenous; **être connu comme le** ~ **blanc** to be known to everybody; **hurler avec les** ~s to follow the herd *or* crowd; **se jeter dans la gueule du** ~ to stick one's head in the lion's mouth; **les** ~s **ne se mangent pas entre eux** (Proverb) (there is) honour (GB) among thieves; **quand on parle du** ~ (**on en voit la queue**) (Proverb) speak of the devil; **l'homme est un** ~ **pour l'homme** (Proverb) dog eat dog

loupe /lup/ *nf* magnifying glass

louper /lupe/ (fam) [1] 1 *vtr* (a) to miss ‹train, opportunity, visitor›; **il n'en loupe pas une** he's always opening his big mouth
(b) to flunk (colloq) ‹exam›; to screw up (colloq) ‹sauce, piece of work›
2 *vi* **j'avais dit que ça se casserait, ça n'a pas loupé** I said it would break, and sure enough it did; **tu vas tout faire** ~ you'll mess everything up

loup-garou, *pl* **loups-garous** /lugaʀu/ *nm* werewolf

loupiote /lupjɔt/ *nf* (fam) small lamp

◊ **lourd**, ~e /luʀ, luʀd/ 1 *adj* (a) ‹person, object, metal› heavy
(b) ‹stomach, head, steps› heavy; ‹gesture› clumsy
(c) ‹meal, food› heavy; ‹wine› heady; ~ **à digérer** heavy on the stomach
(d) ‹equipment, weapons› heavy
(e) ‹fine, taxation› heavy
(f) ‹defeat, responsibility› heavy; ‹mistake› serious
(g) ‹administration, structure› unwieldy; ‹staff numbers› large
(h) ‹person, animal› ungainly; ‹body, object, architecture› heavy; ‹building› cumbersome, ponderous
(i) ‹joke› flat; ‹style› clumsy
(j) ‹atmosphere, silence› heavy; ‹heat› sultry
(k) **être** ~ **de dangers** to be fraught with danger
2 *adv* (a) **peser** ~ to weigh a lot; (figurative) to carry a lot of weight
(b) (of weather) **il fait** ~ it's close
(c) (fam) **pas** ~ not a lot, not much; **dix personnes, ça ne fait pas** ~ ten people, that's not a lot
IDIOMS **avoir la main** ~e to be heavy-handed; **avoir la main** ~e **avec le sel/le parfum** to overdo the salt/the perfume

lourdement /luʀdəmɑ̃/ *adv* (a) heavily; **se tromper** ~ to be gravely mistaken

(b) marcher ~ to walk clumsily; **insister ~ sur** to keep going on about

lourdeur /luʀdœʀ/ *nf* **(a)** (of organization) complexity
(b) heaviness
(c) (of style) clumsiness; (in a text) clumsy expression
(d) weight
(e) (of person) oafishness; (of joke) poorness; (of architecture) ungainliness
(f) (of weather) closeness

loutre /lutʀ/ *nf* **(a)** otter
(b) otterskin

louve /luv/ *nf* she-wolf

louveteau, *pl* ~**x** /luvto/ *nm* (Zool) wolf cub

louvoyer /luvwaje/ [23] *vi* **(a)** ‹ship› to tack
(b) (figurative) to manoeuvre (GB), to maneuver (US)

lover: se lover /lɔve/ [1] *v refl* (⊢ *v être*) ‹snake› to coil itself up; ‹person› to curl up

loyal, ~**e**, *mpl* **-aux** /lwajal, o/ *adj*
(a) ‹friend› true; ‹servant› loyal, faithful
(b) ‹procedure, conduct› honest; ‹competition, game› fair

loyalisme /lwajalism/ *nm* loyalty

loyaliste /lwajalist/ *adj*, *nmf* loyalist

loyauté /lwajote/ *nf* **(a)** loyalty
(b) honesty

loyer /lwaje/ *nm* rent

lu, ~**e** /ly/ ▸ LIRE¹

lubie /lybi/ *nf* whim

lubricité /lybʀisite/ *nf* lechery; lewdness

lubrifiant /lybʀifjɑ̃/ *nm* lubricant

lubrifier /lybʀifje/ [2] *vtr* to lubricate

lubrique /lybʀik/ *adj* ‹person› lecherous; ‹look, dance› lewd

lucarne /lykaʀn/ *nf* (small) window; (in roof) skylight

lucide /lysid/ *adj* clear-headed; lucid

lucidité /lysidite/ *nf* lucidity; clear-headedness; clarity; **juger en toute ~** to judge without any illusions

luciole /lysjɔl/ *nf* firefly

lucratif, **-ive** /lykʀatif, iv/ *adj* lucrative

ludique /lydik/ *adj* ‹activity› play

ludothèque /lydɔtɛk/ *nf* toy library

luette /lyɛt/ *nf* uvula

lueur /lɥœʀ/ *nf* (faint) light; **les ~s de la ville** the city lights; **à la ~ d'une bougie** by candlelight; **à la ~ des événements d'hier** in the light of yesterday's events; **les dernières ~s du soleil couchant** the dying glow of the sunset

luge /lyʒ/ *nf* **(a)** toboggan (GB), sled (US)
(b) (Sport) luge

lugubre /lygybʀ/ *adj* gloomy; mournful

♂ **lui¹** /lɥi/ **1** *pron m* **(a)** he; **elle lit, ~ regarde la télévision** she's reading, he's watching TV; **~ seul a le droit de parler** he alone has the right to talk
(b) him; **à cause de ~** because of him; **je les vois plus souvent que ~** I see them more often than he does; I see them more often than I see him; **c'est à ~** it's his, it belongs to him; it's his turn; **c'est à ~ de choisir** it's up to him to choose
2 *pron mf* it; **le parti lance un appel, apportez-~ votre soutien** the party is launching an appeal—give it your support; **l'Espagne a signé, le Portugal, ~, n'a pas encore donné son accord** Spain has signed while Portugal hasn't yet agreed
3 *pron f* her; **je ~ ai annoncé la nouvelle** I told her the news

lui² /lɥi/ ▸ LUIRE

lui-même /lɥimɛm/ *pron* **(a)** (referring to person) himself; **'M. Greiner?'—'~'** (on phone) 'Mr Greiner?'—'speaking'
(b) (referring to object, concept) itself

♂ **luire** /lɥiʀ/ [69] *vi* to shine; to glow; **leur regard luisait de colère** their eyes blazed with anger

luisant, ~**e** /lɥizɑ̃, ɑ̃t/ *adj* shining; glistening

lumbago /lœbago/ *nm* back pain

♂ **lumière** /lymjɛʀ/ **1** *nf* **(a)** light; **~ naturelle/électrique** natural/electric light; **la ~ du jour** daylight; **il y a une ~ très particulière dans cette région** there's a very special quality to the light in this region; **les ~s de la ville** the city lights; **à la ~ d'une chandelle** by candlelight; **à la ~ des récents événements** in the light of recent events
(b) (person) **ce n'est pas une ~** he'll never set the world on fire
2 lumières *nf pl* **(a)** (of vehicle) lights
(b) (fam) **j'ai besoin de vos ~s** I need to pick your brains

Lumières /lymjɛʀ/ *nf pl* **le siècle des ~** the Age of Enlightenment

luminaire /lyminɛʀ/ *nm* light (fitting)

lumineux, **-euse** /lyminø, øz/ *adj*
(a) luminous; **panneau ~** electronic display (board); **enseigne lumineuse** neon sign; **rayon ~** ray of light
(b) idée lumineuse brilliant idea
(c) ‹smile, gaze› radiant

luminosité /lyminozite/ *nf* brightness, luminosity

lump /lœmp/ *nm* **œufs de ~** lumpfish roe

lunaire /lynɛʀ/ *adj* lunar

lunatique /lynatik/ *nmf* moody person

lunch /lœʃ/ *nm* buffet (lunch); buffet (supper)

♂ **lundi** /lœdi/ *nm* Monday

⚡ **lune** /lyn/ *nf* moon; **pleine** ~ full moon
■ ~ **de miel** honeymoon; ~ **rousse** ≈ April moon
IDIOMS **être dans la** ~ (fam) to have one's head in the clouds; **avoir l'air de tomber de la** ~ to look blank; **demander la** ~ (fam) to cry for the moon; **promettre la** ~ (fam) to promise the earth; **décrocher la** ~ to do the impossible

luné, ~**e** /lyne/ *adj* (fam) **mal** ~ grumpy

lunette /lynɛt/ ⟦1⟧ *nf* lavatory seat
⟦2⟧ **lunettes** *nf pl* **(a)** glasses
(b) (protective) goggles; ~**s de natation** swimming goggles
■ ~ **arrière** (Aut) rear window; ~**s noires** dark glasses; ~**s de soleil** sunglasses

lunule /lynyl/ *nf* (on nail) half-moon

lurette /lyʀɛt/ *nf* (fam) **il y a** *or* **cela fait belle** ~ **que je ne l'ai pas vue** it's been ages since I last saw her (colloq)

luron /lyʀɔ̃/ *nm* fellow

lustre /lystʀ/ ⟦1⟧ *nm* **(a)** (gen) (decorative) ceiling light; (made of glass) chandelier
(b) sheen
(c) (of place, institution) prestigious image; **donner un nouveau** ~ **à** to give fresh appeal to
⟦2⟧ **lustres** *nm pl* (fam) **depuis des** ~**s** for ages (colloq)

lustré, ~**e** /lystʀe/ *adj* **(a)** glossy; (through wear) shiny
(b) ‹fabric› glazed

lustrer /lystʀe/ [1] *vtr* to polish ‹shoes, mirror›

luth /lyt/ *nm* **(a)** (Mus) lute
(b) (Zool) leatherback

luthier /lytje/ *nm* stringed instrument maker

lutin /lytɛ̃/ *nm* goblin

⚡ **lutte** /lyt/ *nf* **(a)** conflict; struggle; fight; ~ **d'influence** power struggle; **la** ~ **contre le cancer** the fight against cancer
(b) (Sport) wrestling
■ ~ **armée** armed conflict; ~ **de classes** class struggle *or* war; ~ **d'intérêts** clash of interests

⚡ **lutter** /lyte/ [1] *vi* to struggle; to fight; ~ **contre qn** to fight against sb; ~ **contre** to fight ‹crime, unemployment, illness›; to fight

against ‹violence›; to contend with ‹noise, bad weather›; **Louis luttait contre le sommeil** Louis was struggling to stay awake

lutteur, -euse /lytœʀ, øz/ *nm,f* (gen) fighter; (Sport) wrestler

luxation /lyksasjɔ̃/ *nf* dislocation

luxe /lyks/ *nm* luxury; **s'offrir le** ~ **de faire** to afford the luxury of doing; (figurative) to give oneself the satisfaction of doing; **je l'ai nettoyé et ce n'était pas du** ~ (fam) I gave it a much needed clean; **avoir des goûts de** ~ to have expensive tastes

Luxembourg /lyksɑ̃buʀ/ *pr nm* Luxembourg

Luxembourgeois, ~e /lyksɑ̃buʀʒwa, az/ *nm,f* **(a)** native of Luxembourg
(b) inhabitant of Luxembourg

luxer: se luxer /lykse/ [1] *v refl* (+ *v être*) **se** ~ **l'épaule** to dislocate one's shoulder

luxueux, -euse /lyksɥø, øz/ *adj* luxurious

luxure /lyksyʀ/ *nf* lust

luxuriant, ~e /lyksyʀjɑ̃, ɑ̃t/ *adj* luxuriant

luzerne /lyzɛʀn/ *nf* alfalfa, lucerne (GB)

⚡ **lycée** /lise/ *nm* secondary school (*preparing students aged 15–18 for the baccalaureate*)

lycéen, -éenne /liseɛ̃, ɛn/ *nm,f* secondary school student

lymphatique /lɛ̃fatik/ *adj* **(a)** lethargic
(b) lymphatic

lyncher /lɛ̃ʃe/ [1] *vtr* to lynch

lynx /lɛ̃ks/ *nm inv* lynx
IDIOM **avoir un œil** *or* **des yeux de** ~ to have very keen eyesight

lyonnais, ~e[1] /ljɔnɛ, ɛz/ *adj* of Lyons

lyonnaise[2] /ljɔnɛz/ *nf* **(a)** (Culin) **à la** ~ à la lyonnaise
(b) *regional game of boules*

lyophiliser /ljɔfilize/ [1] *vtr* to freeze-dry

lyre /liʀ/ *nf* lyre

lyrique /liʀik/ *adj* **(a)** (Mus) ‹song, composer› operatic; ‹singer, season› opera
(b) ‹poetry, poet› lyric; ‹content, tone› lyrical

lyrisme /liʀism/ *nm* lyricism

lys /lis/ *nm inv* lily

⚡ indicates a very frequent word

M m

m, M /ɛm/ *nm inv* **(a)** (letter) m, M
(b) (*written abbr* = **mètre**) 30 m 30 m

m' ▸ ME

⚘ **M.** (*written abbr* = **Monsieur**) Mr

ma ▸ MON

macabre /makabʀ/ *adj* macabre

macadam /makadam/ *nm* tarmac®

macaque /makak/ *nm* macaque

macaron /makaʀɔ̃/ *nm* **(a)** macaroon
(b) lapel badge; sticker

macédoine /masedwan/ *nf* mixed diced
vegetables

macérer /maseʀe/ [14] *vi* ‹plant, fruit› to
soak, to steep; ‹meat› to marinate

mâche /mɑʃ/ *nf* corn salad, lamb's lettuce

mâcher /mɑʃe/ [1] *vtr* to chew
IDIOMS ~ **la besogne** *or* **le travail à qn** to
break the back of the work for sb; **il ne
mâche pas ses mots** he doesn't mince his
words

machette /maʃɛt/ *nf* machete

machiavélique /makjavelik/ *adj*
Machiavellian

machin /maʃɛ̃/ *nm* (fam) **(a)** thing,
thingummy (colloq), whatsit (colloq)
(b) old fogey

Machin, ~e /maʃɛ̃, in/ *nm,f* (fam) what's-
his-name (colloq)/what's her-name (colloq)

machinal, ~e, mpl -aux /maʃinal, o/ *adj*
‹gesture, reaction› mechanical

machination /maʃinasjɔ̃/ *nf* plot

⚘ **machine** /maʃin/ *nf* **(a)** machine; **taper à
la ~** to type; **coudre à la ~** to machine-sew;
faire deux~s (de linge) (fam) to do two loads
of washing
(b) (Naut) engine; **faire ~ arrière** to go astern;
(figurative) to back-pedal
■ ~ **à calculer** calculating machine; ~ **à coudre** sewing machine; ~ **à écrire** typewriter;
~ **à laver** washing machine; ~ **à laver la
vaisselle** dishwasher; ~ **à sous** slot machine,
one-armed bandit

machinerie /maʃinʀi/ *nf* **(a)** machinery
(b) machine room; (Naut) engine room

machiste /ma(t)ʃist/ *adj, nm* male
chauvinist

mâchoire /mɑʃwaʀ/ *nf* jaw

mâchouiller /mɑʃuje/ [1] *vtr* (fam) to
chew (on)

maçon /masɔ̃/ *nm* bricklayer; builder;
mason

maçonnerie /masɔnʀi/ *nf* building;
bricklaying; masonry work

maculer /makyle/ [1] *vtr* to smudge; ~ **qch
de sang** to spatter sth with blood

⚘ **madame, pl mesdames** /madam,
medam/ *nf* **(a)** (addressing a woman whose
name you do not know) **Madame** (in letter)
Dear Madam; **bonsoir ~!** good evening!;
mesdames et messieurs bonsoir good
evening, ladies and gentlemen
(b) (addressing a woman whose name you know, for
example Bon) Mrs, Ms; (in a letter) **Madame** Dear
Ms Bon; **bonjour, ~** good morning, Mrs Bon
(c) (polite form of address) madam; '~ **a
sonné?'** 'you rang, Madam?'

Madeleine /madlɛn/ *pr n* **pleurer comme
une ~** to cry one's eyes out

mademoiselle, pl mesdemoiselles
/madmwazɛl, medmwazɛl/ *nf* **(a)** (addressing
a woman whose name you do not know)
Mademoiselle (in letter) Dear Madam;
bonjour, ~! good morning!; **mesdames,
mesdemoiselles, messieurs** ladies and
gentlemen
(b) (addressing a woman whose name you
know, for example Bon) Miss, Ms; (in a letter)
Mademoiselle Dear Miss Bon; **bonjour, ~**
good morning, Miss Bon
(c) (polite form of address) madam; '~ **a
sonné?'** 'you rang, Madam?'

madone /madon/ *nf* madonna

madrier /madʀije/ *nm* beam

maestria /maɛstʀija/ *nf* brilliance,
panache

maf(f)ia /mafja/ *nf* mafia; **la Mafia** the
Mafia

maf(f)ieux, -ieuse /mafjø, øz/ *adj* mafia

⚘ **magasin** /magazɛ̃/ *nm* **(a)** shop, store;
grand ~ department store; **faire les ~s** to
go shopping
(b) avoir **en ~** to have in stock

magasinier, -ière /magazinje, ɛʀ/ *nm,f*
(a) stock controller
(b) warehouse keeper

⚘ **magazine** /magazin/ *nm* magazine

mage /maʒ/ *nm* magus; **les rois ~s** the
(Three) Wise Men

maghrébin, ~e /magʀebɛ̃, in/ *adj* North
African, Maghrebi

magicien, -ienne /maʒisjɛ̃, ɛn/ *nm,f*
(a) magician/enchantress
(b) conjuror
(c) (figurative) wizard

magie /maʒi/ *nf* **(a)** magic
(b) conjuring

⚘ **magique** /maʒik/ *adj* **(a)** magic; **formule ~**
magic words   ⋯⟶

(b) (figurative) magical

magistère /maʒistɛʀ/ *nm*: *high-level University degree*

magistral, ~e, *mpl* **-aux** /maʒistʀal, o/ *adj* **(a)** brilliant; **réussir un coup ~** to bring off a masterstroke
(b) magisterial

magistrat /maʒistʀa/ *nm* magistrate

magistrature /maʒistʀatyʀ/ *nf*
(a) magistracy
(b) public office

magma /magma/ *nm* **(a)** magma
(b) (figurative) jumble

magnanime /maɲanim/ *adj* magnanimous

magnat /maɲa/ *nm* magnate, tycoon

magner: se magner /maɲe/ [1] *v refl* (*+ v être*) (pop) to get a move on (colloq)

magnésie /maɲezi/ *nf* magnesia

magnétique /maɲetik/ *adj* magnetic

magnétiser /maɲetize/ [1] *vtr* **(a)** to magnetize
(b) to hypnotize, to mesmerize

magnétiseur, -euse /maɲetizœʀ, øz/ *nm,f* healer

magnétisme /maɲetism/ *nm* magnetism

magnéto(phone) /maɲeto(fɔn)/ *nm* tape recorder

magnétoscope /maɲetɔskɔp/ *nm* VCR, video recorder

magnificence /maɲifisɑ̃s/ *nf* magnificence, splendour (GB)

magnifier /maɲifje/ [1] *vtr* **(a)** to idealize ‹*memory, feeling*›
(b) to glorify ‹*heroism, act*›

✧ **magnifique** /maɲifik/ *adj* gorgeous, magnificent

magot /mago/ *nm* (fam) pile (of money) (colloq)

magouille /maguj/ *nf* (fam) **(a)** wangling (colloq), fiddling (colloq)
(b) trick; **~s politiques** political skulduggery; **~s électorales** election rigging

magret /magʀɛ/ *nm* **~ de canard** duck breast

Mahomet /maɔme/ *pr n* Mohammed

✧ **mai** /mɛ/ *nm* May; **le premier ~** May Day

maigre /mɛgʀ/ **1** *adj* **(a)** ‹*person*› thin
(b) ‹*meat*› lean; ‹*cheese*› low-fat
(c) ‹*day*› without meat; **faire** or **manger ~** to abstain from meat
(d) ‹*talents, savings*› meagre (GB); ‹*applause*› scant
(e) ‹*dawn, hair*› sparse
2 *nmf* thin man/woman; **c'est une fausse ~** she looks thinner than she is

maigrement /mɛgʀəmɑ̃/ *adv* ‹*paid*› poorly

maigreur /mɛgʀœʀ/ *nf* **(a)** thinness

(b) meagreness (GB)

maigrichon, -onne /mɛgʀiʃɔ̃, ɔn/ *adj* skinny

maigrir /mɛgʀiʀ/ [3] *vi* to lose weight

✧ **mail** /maj/ *nm* **(a)** mall
(b) (game) pall-mall
(c) e-mail (message)

mailer /majle/ *vt* to e-mail

mailing /mɛliŋ/ *nm* (controversial) **(a)** direct mail advertising
(b) mail shot
(c) mailing pack

maille /maj/ *nf* **(a)** stitch; **une ~ qui file** (in tights) a ladder (GB), a run (US)
(b) mesh; **passer à travers les ~s** to slip through the net
(c) (in fence) link
IDIOM avoir ~ à partir avec qn to have a brush with sb

maillet /majɛ/ *nm* mallet

maillon /majɔ̃/ *nm* (in chain) link

maillot /majo/ *nm* **(a) ~ (de corps)** vest (GB), undershirt (US)
(b) (of footballer) shirt; (of cyclist) jersey
(c) swimsuit
■ **~ de bain** swimsuit; **le ~ jaune** the leader in the Tour de France

✧ **main** /mɛ̃/ *nf* **(a)** hand; **se donner** or **se tenir la ~** to hold hands; **saluer qn de la ~** to wave at sb; **haut les ~s!** hands up!; **demander la ~ de qn** to ask for sb's hand in marriage; **avoir qch bien en ~(s)** to hold sth firmly; (figurative) to have sth well in hand; **si tu lèves la ~ sur elle** if you lay a finger on her; **à la ~** ‹*sew*› by hand; ‹*adjust*› manually; **fait à ~** handmade; **vol à ~ armée** armed robbery; **donner un coup de ~ à qn** to give sb a hand
(b) **une ~ secourable** a helping hand; **une ~ criminelle** someone with criminal intentions
(c) **avoir qch sous la ~** to have sth to hand; **cela m'est tombé sous la ~** I just happened to come across it; **mettre la ~ sur qch** to get one's hands on sth; **je n'arrive pas à mettre la ~ dessus** I can't lay my hands on it; **je l'ai eu entre les ~s mais…** I did have it but…; **être entre les ~s de qn** ‹*power*› to be in sb's hands; **prendre qn/qch en ~s** to take sb/sth in hand; **à ne pas mettre entre toutes les ~s** ‹*book*› not for general reading; **tomber entre les ~s de qn** to fall into sb's hands; **les ~s vides** empty-handed; **je le lui ai remis en ~s propres** I gave it to him/her in person; **de la ~ à la ~** ‹*sell*› privately; **être payé de la ~ à la ~** to be paid cash (in hand)
(d) **écrit de la ~ du président** written by the president himself; **de ma plus belle ~** in my best handwriting
(e) **avoir le coup de ~** to have the knack; **se faire la ~** to practise (GB)
(f) (in cards) hand; deal
(g) **à ~ droite/gauche** on the right/left
■ **~ courante** handrail

✧ indicates a very frequent word

IDIOMS j'en mettrais ma ~ au feu *or* à couper I'd swear to it; **d'une ~ de fer** with an iron rod; **il n'y est pas allé de ~ morte!** (fam) he didn't pull his punches!; **avoir la ~ leste** to be always ready with a slap; **faire ~ basse sur** to help oneself to ‹*goods*›; to take over ‹*market, country*›; **en venir aux ~s** to come to blows; **avoir la ~ heureuse** to be lucky

mainate /mɛnat/ *nm* mynah bird

main-d'œuvre, *pl* **mains-d'œuvre** /mɛ̃dœvʀ/ *nf* labour (GB)

main-forte /mɛ̃fɔʀt/ *nf inv* **prêter ~ à qn** to come to sb's aid

mainmise /mɛ̃miz/ *nf* seizure

maint, ~e /mɛ̃, mɛ̃t/ *det* many, many a; **à ~es reprises** many times

maintenance /mɛ̃tnɑ̃s/ *nf* maintenance

✧ **maintenant** /mɛ̃t(ə)nɑ̃/ *adv* now; nowadays; **commence dès ~** start straightaway

✧ **maintenir** /mɛ̃t(ə)niʀ/ [36] **1** *vtr* **(a)** to keep; to maintain; to keep up, **~ qch debout** to keep sth upright
(b) to support ‹*wall, ankle*›
(c) to stand by ‹*decision*›; **~ que** to maintain that; **~ sa candidature** ‹*politician*› not to withdraw one's candidacy
2 **se maintenir** *v refl* (+ *v être*) ‹*trend*› to persist; ‹*price*› to remain stable; ‹*weather*› to remain fair; ‹*political system*› to remain in force; ‹*currency*› to hold steady

maintien /mɛ̃tjɛ̃/ *nm* **(a)** maintaining; **assurer le ~ de l'ordre** to maintain order
(b) support
(c) deportment

maire /mɛʀ/ *nm* mayor
■ **~ adjoint** deputy mayor

mairie /meʀi/ *nf* **(a)** town council (GB) *or* hall (US); **être élu à la ~ de** to be elected mayor of
(b) town hall (GB), city hall (US)

✧ **mais** /mɛ/ *conj* but; **incroyable ~ vrai** strange but true; **il est bête, ~ bête!** (fam) he's so incredibly stupid!; **~, vous pleurez!** good heavens, you're crying!; **~ j'y pense** now that I come to think of it

maïs /mais/ *nm inv* **(a)** maize (GB), corn (US)
(b) sweetcorn; **épi de ~** corn on the cob

✧ **maison** /mɛzɔ̃/ **1** *adj inv* ‹*product*› home-made
2 *nf* **(a)** house
(b) home
(c) family, household; **gens de ~** domestic staff
(d) firm; **avoir 15 ans de ~** to have been with the firm for 15 years
■ **~ d'arrêt** prison; **~ bourgeoise** *imposing town house*; **~ de campagne** house in the country; **~ close** brothel; **~ de correction** institution for young offenders; **~ de la culture** ≈ community arts centre (GB); **~ des**

jeunes et de la culture, MJC** ≈ youth club; **~ de maître** manor; **~ mère** headquarters; main branch; **~ de passe** brothel; **~ de retraite** old people's *or* retirement home; **~ de santé** nursing home; **la Maison Blanche** the White House

IDIOM **c'est gros comme une ~** (fam) it sticks out a mile

maisonnée /mɛzɔne/ *nf* household; family

✧ **maître, -esse¹** /mɛtʀ, ɛs/ **1** *adj* **(a)** être **~ de soi** to have self-control; **être ~ chez soi** to be master/mistress in one's own house; **être ~ de son véhicule** to be in control of one's vehicle
(b) main; key; major
2 *nm,f* **(a)** teacher
(b) (of house) master/mistress
(c) (of animal) owner
3 *nm* **(a)** ruler; **être (le) seul ~ à bord** to be in sole command; **être son propre ~** to be one's own master/mistress; **régner en ~ absolu** to reign supreme
(b) master; **être passé ~ dans l'art de qch/de faire** to be a past master of sth/at doing; **en ~** masterfully
(c) **Me** Maître (*form of address given to members of the legal profession*)
■ **~ d'hôtel** maître d'hôtel (GB), maître d' (US); **~ à penser** mentor; **maîtresse femme** strong-minded woman

IDIOM **trouver son ~** to meet one's match

maître-assistant, ~e, *mpl* **maîtres-assistants** /mɛtʀasistɑ̃, ɑ̃t/ *nm,f* ≈ senior lecturer (GB), senior instructor (US)

maître-chanteur, *pl* **maîtres-chanteurs** /mɛtʀəʃɑ̃tœʀ/ *nm* blackmailer

maître-nageur, *pl* **maîtres-nageurs** /mɛtʀənaʒœʀ/ *nm* **(a)** swimming instructor
(b) pool attendant

maîtresse² /mɛtʀɛs/ **1** *adj f* ▶ MAÎTRE 1
2 *nf* **(a)** ▶ MAÎTRE 2
(b) mistress

maîtrise /mɛtʀiz/ *nf* **(a)** mastery
(b) perfect command
(c) **~ (de soi)** self-control
(d) master's degree

maîtriser /mɛtʀize/ [1] **1** *vtr* **(a)** to control ‹*feelings*›; to bring [sth] under control ‹*fire*›; to overcome ‹*opponent*›
(b) to master ‹*language*›
2 **se maîtriser** *v refl* (+ *v être*) to have self-control

maïzena® /maizena/ *nf* cornflour

majesté /maʒɛste/ *nf* majesty

majestueux, -euse /maʒɛstɥø, øz/ *adj* majestic; stately

✧ **majeur, ~e** /maʒœʀ/ **1** *adj* **(a)** être **~** to be over 18 *or* of age
(b) main, major; **en ~e partie** for the most part
(c) (Mus) major
2 *nm* middle finger

majoration /maʒɔʀasjɔ̃/ *nf* increase

majordome /maʒɔʀdɔm/ *nm* butler

majorer /maʒɔʀe/ [1] *vtr* to increase

majoritaire /maʒɔʀitɛʀ/ *adj* majority

majoritairement /maʒɔʀitɛʀmɑ̃/ *adv*
(a) by a majority (vote)
(b) province ∼ catholique predominantly
Catholic province

✧ **majorité** /maʒɔʀite/ *nf* (a) majority; ils
sont en ∼ they are in the majority; ce sont,
en ∼, des enfants they are, for the most
part, children
(b) la ∼ the government, the party in power

majuscule /maʒyskyl/ ① *adj* capital
② *nf* capital (letter)

✧ **mal**, *mpl* **maux** /mal, mo/ ① *adj inv*
(a) wrong; qu'a-t-elle fait de ∼? what has
she done wrong?
(b) bad; ce ne serait pas ∼ de déménager it
wouldn't be a bad idea to move out
(c) (fam) il n'est pas mal ⟨film⟩ it's not bad;
⟨man⟩ he's not bad(-looking)
② *nm* (a) trouble, difficulty; avoir du ∼ à
faire to find it difficult to do; se donner du ∼
to go to a lot of trouble; ne te donne pas ce
∼! don't bother!
(b) pain; faire ∼ to hurt, to be painful; se
faire ∼ to hurt oneself; j'ai ∼ it hurts; avoir
∼ partout to ache all over; elle avait très ∼
she was in pain; avoir ∼ à la tête to have a
headache; avoir ∼ à la gorge to have a sore
throat; j'ai ∼ au genou my knee hurts; j'ai ∼
au cœur I feel sick (GB) *or* nauseous
(c) illness, disease
(d) être en ∼ de to be short of ⟨inspiration⟩;
to be lacking in ⟨affection⟩
(e) harm; faire du ∼ à to harm, to hurt; une
douche ne te ferait pas de ∼ (humorous) a
shower wouldn't do you any harm
(f) le ∼ evil; qu'elle parte, est-ce vraiment
un ∼? is it really a bad thing that she is
leaving?; sans penser à ∼ without meaning
any harm; dire du ∼ de qn/qch to speak ill
of sb/sth
③ *adv* (a) badly; not properly; elle travaille
∼ her work isn't good; je t'entends ∼ I can't
hear you very well
(b) with difficulty; on voit ∼ comment it's
difficult to see how
(c) ⟨diagnosed, addressed⟩ wrongly; j'avais
∼ compris I had misunderstood; ∼ informé
ill-informed
(d) se trouver ∼ to faint; être ∼ (assis *or*
couché *or* installé) not to be comfortable;
être au plus ∼ to be critically ill
④ **pas mal** *phr* (a) ⟨travel, read⟩ quite
a lot
(b) il ne s'en est pas ∼ tiré (in exam) he coped
quite well; (in dangerous situation) he got off
lightly
■ ∼ de l'air airsickness; ∼ de mer seasickness;

✧ indicates a very frequent word

∼ du pays homesickness; ∼ du siècle world-
weariness; ∼ des transports travel sickness

✧ **malade** /malad/ ① *adj* ⟨person⟩ ill, sick;
⟨animal⟩ sick; ⟨organ, plant⟩ diseased; tomber
∼ to fall ill *or* sick, to get sick (US); être ∼ en
voiture/en avion to get carsick/airsick; j'en
suis ∼ (figurative) (fam) it makes me sick; ∼
d'inquiétude worried sick
② *nmf* (a) sick man/woman
(b) patient
■ ∼ imaginaire hypochondriac; ∼ mental
mentally ill person

✧ **maladie** /maladi/ *nf* illness, disease; il va
en faire une∼ (fam) (figurative) he'll have a fit
(colloq)
■ ∼ sexuellement transmissible, MST sexually
transmitted disease, STD; ∼ du sommeil
sleeping sickness

maladif, -ive /maladif, iv/ *adj* ⟨child⟩
sickly; ⟨jealousy⟩ pathological

maladresse /maladʀɛs/ *nf* (a) clumsiness,
awkwardness
(b) tactlessness
(c) blunder

maladroit, ∼e /maladʀwa, wat/ ① *adj*
(a) clumsy
(b) tactless
② *nm,f* (a) clumsy person
(b) tactless person

maladroitement /maladʀwatmɑ̃/ *adv*
(a) clumsily, awkwardly
(b) tactlessly; ineptly

malaise /malɛz/ *nm* (a) dizzy turn; avoir
un ∼ to feel faint
(b) (figurative) uneasiness; unrest
■ ∼ cardiaque mild heart attack

malaxer /malakse/ [1] *vtr* (a) to cream
⟨butter⟩; to knead ⟨dough⟩
(b) to mix ⟨cement⟩

malchance /malʃɑ̃s/ *nf* bad luck,
misfortune; par ∼ as ill luck would have it

malchanceux, -euse /malʃɑ̃sø, øz/ *adj*
unlucky

maldonne /maldɔn/ *nf* misunderstanding

mâle /mɑl/ ① *adj* (a) male; ⟨elephant⟩
bull; ⟨antelope, rabbit⟩ buck; ⟨sparrow⟩ cock;
cygne ∼ cob; canard ∼ drake
(b) manly
② *nm* (a) male
(b) (humorous) he-man (colloq)

malédiction /malediksjɔ̃/ *nf* curse

maléfice /malefis/ *nm* evil spell

maléfique /malefik/ *adj* evil

malencontreusement
/malɑ̃kɔ̃tʀøzmɑ̃/ *adv* inopportunely;
unfortunately

malencontreux, -euse /malɑ̃kɔ̃tʀø,
øz/ *adj* unfortunate

malentendant, ∼e /malɑ̃tɑ̃dɑ̃, ɑ̃t/ *nm,f*
les ∼s the hearing-impaired

malentendu /malãtãdy/ *nm* misunderstanding

malfaçon /malfasɔ̃/ *nf* defect

malfaisant, ~e /malfəzã, ãt/ *adj* evil; harmful

malfaiteur /malfɛtœʀ/ *nm* criminal

malformation /malfɔʀmasjɔ̃/ *nf* malformation

malgache /malgaʃ/ *adj, nm* Malagasy

⚜ **malgré** /malgʀe/ *prep* in spite of, despite; ~ cela, ~ tout nevertheless; ~ moi against my wishes; reluctantly

malhabile /malabil/ *adj* clumsy

⚜ **malheur** /malœʀ/ *nm* (a) le ~ misfortune, adversity; faire le ~ de qn to bring sb nothing but unhappiness
(b) misfortune; accident; un grand ~ a tragedy; un ~ est si vite arrivé! accidents can so easily happen!
(c) misfortune; ceux qui ont le ~ de faire those who are unfortunate enough to do; j'ai eu le ~ de le leur dire I made the mistake of telling them; par ~ as bad luck would have it; si par ~ la guerre éclatait if, God forbid, war should break out; porter ~ to be bad luck
IDIOMS faire un ~ (fam) to be a sensation; to go wild; à quelque chose ~ est bon (Proverb) every cloud has a silver lining

⚜ **malheureusement** /malœʀøzmã/ *adv* unfortunately

⚜ **malheureux, -euse** /malœʀø, øz/ [1] *adj*
(a) ‹person, life› unhappy, miserable; ‹victim, choice, word› unfortunate; ‹candidate› unlucky; c'est ~ que it's a pity or shame that
(b) (fam) ‹sum› paltry, pathetic
[2] *nm,f* (a) poor wretch; le ~! poor man!
(b) poor person; les ~ the poor
IDIOM être ~ comme les pierres to be as miserable as sin

malhonnête /malɔnɛt/ *adj* dishonest

malhonnêteté /malɔnɛtte/ *nf* dishonesty

malice /malis/ *nf* (a) mischief
(b) (dated) malice; être sans ~ to be harmless

malicieux, -ieuse /malisjø, øz/ *adj* mischievous

malin, maligne /malɛ̃, malin/ [1] *adj*
(a) clever; j'ai eu l'air ~! (ironic) I looked like a total fool!
(b) malicious
(c) (Med) malignant
[2] *nm,f* c'est un ~ he's a crafty one
IDIOM à ~, ~ et demi (Proverb) there's always someone who will outwit you

malingre /malɛ̃gʀ/ *adj* ‹person, tree› sickly

malintentionné, ~e /malɛ̃tãsjɔne/ *adj* malicious

malle /mal/ *nf* trunk

malléabilité /maleabilite/ *nf* malleability

mallette /malɛt/ *nf* briefcase

malmener /malmøne/ [16] *vtr* (a) to manhandle
(b) to give [sb] a rough ride

malnutrition /malnytʀisjɔ̃/ *nf* malnutrition

malodorant, ~e /malɔdɔʀã, ãt/ *adj* foul-smelling

malotru, ~e /malɔtʀy/ *nm,f* boor

Malouines /malwin/ *pr nf pl* les (îles) ~ the Falklands

malpoli, ~e /malpɔli/ *adj* rude

malpropre [1] *adj* dirty
[2] *nmf* se faire renvoyer comme un ~ to be chucked out (colloq)

malsain, ~e /malsɛ̃, ɛn/ *adj* unhealthy

Malte /malt/ *pr nf* Malta

malthusianisme /maltyzjanism/ *nm* Malthusianism

maltraiter /maltʀete/ [1] *vtr* to mistreat

malus /malys/ *nm inv* loaded premium

malveillance /malvɛjãs/ *nf* malice

malveillant, ~e /malvɛjã, ãt/ *adj* malicious

malvenu, ~e /malvəny/ *adj* out of place

malversation /malvɛʀsasjɔ̃/ *nf*
(a) malpractice
(b) embezzlement

malvoyant, ~ e /malvwajã, ãt/ *nmf* partially sighted person

⚜ **maman** /mamã/ *nf* mum (GB) (colloq), mom (US) (colloq)

mamelle /mamɛl/ *nf* udder; teat

mamelon /mamlɔ̃/ *nm* (a) nipple
(b) hillock

mamie /mami/ *nf* (fam) granny (colloq), grandma (colloq)

mammifère /mamifɛʀ/ *nm* mammal

mammouth /mamut/ *nm* mammoth

mamy ▸ MAMIE

manager¹, manageur /manaʒœʀ/ *nm* manager

manager² /manaʒe/ [13] *vtr* to manage

manche¹ /mɑ̃ʃ/ *nm* (a) (of tool) handle; (of violin) neck
(b) (fam) clumsy idiot
■ ~ à balai broomhandle; broomstick; joystick

⚜ **manche²** /mɑ̃ʃ/ *nf* (a) sleeve; sans ~s sleeveless
(b) (Sport) round; (in cards) hand; (in bridge) game; (in tennis) set
IDIOMS avoir qn dans la ~ to have sb in one's pocket; c'est une autre paire de ~s (fam) it's a different ball game (colloq)

Manche /mɑ̃ʃ/ *pr nf* la ~ the (English) Channel

manchette /mɑ̃ʃɛt/ *nf* (a) (double) cuff
(b) oversleeve
(c) headline

manchot, -otte /mɑ̃ʃo, ɔt/ **1** *adj* one-armed; one-handed; **il est ~** he's only got one arm; **ne pas être ~** (fam) to be pretty good with one's hands (colloq)
2 *nm* penguin

mandarine /mɑ̃daʀin/ *nf* mandarin orange

mandat /mɑ̃da/ *nm* **(a) ~ (postal)** money order
(b) term of office; **exercer son ~** to be in office
(c) mandate
■ **~ d'arrêt** (arrest) warrant; **~ d'expulsion** expulsion order; eviction order; **~ de perquisition** search warrant

mandataire /mɑ̃datɛʀ/ *nmf*
(a) representative, agent
(b) proxy

mandater /mɑ̃date/ [1] *vtr* to appoint [sb] as one's representative; to give a mandate to

mandat-lettre, *pl* **mandats-lettres** /mɑ̃dalɛtʀ/ *nm* postal order

mandibule /mɑ̃dibyl/ *nf* mandible

mandoline /mɑ̃dɔlin/ *nf* mandolin

manège /manɛʒ/ *nm* **(a)** merry-go-round
(b) riding school
(c) (little) trick, (little) game; **j'ai bien observé ton ~** I know what you are up to

manette /manɛt/ *nf* **(a)** lever; joystick
(b) (figurative) **~s** controls

mangeable /mɑ̃ʒabl/ *adj* edible

mangeoire /mɑ̃ʒwaʀ/ *nf* manger; trough; feeding tray

⚜ **manger¹** /mɑ̃ʒe/ [13] **1** *vtr* **(a)** to eat; **il n'y a rien à ~ dans la maison** there's no food in the house
(b) to use up ‹savings›; to go through ‹inheritance›; to take up ‹time›
(c) ‹rust, acid› to eat away
(d) ~ ses mots to mumble
2 *vi* to eat; **~ au restaurant** to eat out; **~ à sa faim** to eat one's fill; **donner à ~ à qn** to feed sb; to give sb something to eat; **faire à ~** to cook; **inviter qn à ~** to invite sb for a meal; **~ chinois** to have a Chinese meal; **on mange mal ici** the food is not good here
3 **se manger** *v refl* (+ *v être*) **ça se mange?** can you eat it?; **le gaspacho se mange froid** gazpacho is served cold

manger² /mɑ̃ʒe/ *nm* food

mangeur, -euse /mɑ̃ʒœʀ, øz/ *nm,f* **bon/gros ~** good/big eater
■ **mangeuse d'hommes** man-eater

mangouste /mɑ̃ɡust/ *nf* **(a)** mongoose
(b) mangosteen

mangue /mɑ̃ɡ/ *nf* mango

maniable /manjabl/ *adj* ‹object, car› easy to handle; ‹book› manageable in size

maniaque /manjak/ **1** *adj* particular, fussy

2 *nmf* **(a)** fusspot (GB), fussbudget (US)
(b) fanatic; **c'est un ~ de l'ordre** he's obsessive about tidiness
(c) maniac
(d) (Med) manic

maniaquerie /manjakʀi/ *nf* fussiness

manichéen, -éenne /manikeɛ̃, ɛn/ *adj* Manichean; dualistic

manie /mani/ *nf* **(a)** habit; **c'est une vraie ~** it's an absolute obsession
(b) quirk, idiosyncrasy
(c) (Med) mania

maniement /manimɑ̃/ *nm* handling; (of machine) operation; (of language) command
■ **~ d'armes** arms drill

manier /manje/ [2] **1** *vtr* to handle
2 **se manier** *v refl* (+ *v être*) **se ~ aisément** ‹tool› to be easy to handle; ‹car› to handle well
IDIOM ~ la fourchette avec entrain (fam) (humorous) to have a hearty appetite

⚜ **manière** /manjɛʀ/ *nf* **(a)** way; **d'une certaine ~** in a way; **leur ~ de vivre/penser** their way of life/thinking; **de toutes les ~s possibles** in every possible way; **de telle ~ que** in such a way that; **de ~ à faire** so as to do; **de ~ à ce que** so that; **à ma ~** my (own) way; **de quelle ~?** how?; **de toute ~, de toutes ~s** anyway, in any case; **la ~ forte** strong-arm tactics, force
(b) style; **à la ~ de qn/qch** in the style of sb/sth
(c) manners; **faire des ~s** to stand on ceremony

maniéré, ~e /manjeʀe/ *adj* affected

manifestant, ~e /manifɛstɑ̃, ɑ̃t/ *nm,f* demonstrator

⚜ **manifestation** /manifɛstasjɔ̃/ *nf*
(a) demonstration
(b) event; **~s sportives** sporting events
(c) (of phenomenon) appearance
(d) (of feeling) expression, manifestation
■ **~ silencieuse** vigil; **~ de soutien** rally

manifeste /manifɛst/ **1** *adj* obvious, manifest
2 *nm* manifesto

⚜ **manifester** /manifɛste/ [1] **1** *vtr* to show ‹courage›; to express ‹desire, fears›; **~ sa présence** to make one's presence known
2 *vi* to demonstrate; **appeler à ~ le 5 juin** to call a demonstration for 5 June
3 **se manifester** *v refl* (+ *v être*)
(a) ‹symptom› to manifest itself; ‹phenomenon› to appear; ‹worry› to show itself
(b) ‹witness› to come forward; ‹person› to appear; to get in touch

manigance /maniɡɑ̃s/ *nf* little scheme

maniganceer /maniɡɑ̃se/ [12] *vtr* **~ quelque chose** to be up to something; **~ un mauvais coup** to hatch up a scheme

⚜ indicates a very frequent word

manipulateur, -trice /manipylatœr, tʀis/ *nm, f* **(a)** technician
(b) (pejorative) manipulator

manipulation /manipylasjɔ̃/ *nf* **(a)** (of object) handling
(b) manipulation
(c) (Sch) experiment

manipuler /manipyle/ [1] *vtr* **(a)** to handle ⟨object⟩; to use ⟨words⟩
(b) to manipulate ⟨person⟩

manitou /manitu/ *nm* (fam) big noise (colloq); **un grand ~ de la finance** a big noise in the financial world

manivelle /manivɛl/ *nf* handle
IDIOM **donner le premier tour de ~** to start filming

manne /man/ *nf* godsend

mannequin /mankɛ̃/ *nm* **(a)** (fashion) model
(b) dummy

manœuvre¹ /manœvʀ/ *nm* unskilled worker

manœuvre² /manœvʀ/ *nf* manœuvre (GB), maneuver (US); **champ de ~** military training area; **fausse ~** mistake

manœuvrer /manœvʀe/ [1] **1** *vtr* **(a)** to manœuvre (GB), to maneuver (US) ⟨vehicle⟩
(b) to operate ⟨machine⟩
(c) to manipulate ⟨person⟩
2 *vi* to manœuvre (GB), to maneuver (US)

manoir /manwaʀ/ *nm* manor (house)

manomètre /manɔmɛtʀ/ *nm* pressure gauge

manquant, ~e /mākā, āt/ *adj* missing

⚜ **manque** /māk/ **1** *nm* **(a)** **~ de** lack of; shortage of; **~ de chance, il est tombé malade** just his luck, he fell ill
(b) gap; **en ~ d'affection** in need of affection; **être en ~** ⟨drug addict⟩ to be suffering from withdrawal symptoms
2 **à la manque** *phr* (fam) **une idée à la ~** a useless idea

manqué, ~e /māke/ **1** *pp* ▶ MANQUER
2 *pp adj* ⟨attempt⟩ failed; ⟨opportunity⟩ missed

⚜ **manquer** /māke/ [1] **1** *vtr* **(a)** to miss; **un film à ne pas ~** a film not to be missed; **tu l'as manquée de cinq minutes** you missed her/it by five minutes
(b) **~ son coup** (fam) to fail
(c) (fam) **la prochaine fois je ne le manquerai pas** next time I won't let him get away with it
2 **manquer à** *v+prep* **(a)** **~ à qn** to be missed by sb; **ma tante me manque** I miss my aunt
(b) **~ à sa parole** to break one's word
3 **manquer de** *v+prep* **(a)** **~ de** to lack; **on ne manque de rien** we don't want for anything; **elle ne manque pas de charme** she's not without charm; **on manque d'air ici** it's stuffy in here

(b) **je ne manquerai pas de vous le faire savoir** I'll be sure to let you know; **et évidemment, ça n'a pas manqué!** (fam) and sure enough that's what happened!
(c) **il a manqué (de) casser un carreau** he almost broke a windowpane
4 *vi* **(a)** **les vivres vinrent à ~** the supplies ran out; **le courage leur manqua** their courage failed them; **ce n'est pas l'envie qui m'en manque** it's not that I don't want to
(b) ⟨person⟩ to be absent; to be missing
5 *v impers* **il lui manque un doigt** he's got a finger missing; **il nous manque deux joueurs pour former une équipe** we're two players short of a team; **il ne manquerait plus que ça!** (fam) that would be the last straw!
6 **se manquer** *v refl* (+ *v être*) to miss each other

mansarde /māsaʀd/ *nf* attic room

mansardé, ~e /māsaʀde/ *adj* ⟨room⟩ attic

mansuétude /māsɥetyd/ *nf* indulgence

⚜ **manteau,** *pl* **~x** /māto/ *nm* coat
■ **~ de cheminée** mantelpiece
IDIOM **sous le ~** illicitly

manucure /manykyʀ/ **1** *nmf* manicurist
2 *nf* manicure

manuel, -elle /manɥɛl/ **1** *adj* manual
2 *nm* manual; (Sch) textbook
■ **~ de conversation** phrase book

manuellement /manɥɛlmā/ *adv* manually

manufacture /manyfaktyʀ/ *nf* **(a)** factory
(b) manufacture

manufacturer /manyfaktyʀe/ [1] *vtr* to manufacture

manu militari /manymilitaʀi/ *adv* forcibly

manuscrit, ~e /manyskʀi, it/ **1** *adj* handwritten
2 *nm* manuscript

manutention /manytāsjɔ̃/ *nf* handling

manutentionnaire /manytāsjɔnɛʀ/ *nm* warehouseman

mappemonde /mapmɔ̃d/ *nf* **(a)** map of the world (in two hemispheres)
(b) globe

maquereau, *pl* **~x** /makʀo/ *nm* mackerel

maquette /makɛt/ *nf* scale model

maquillage /makijaʒ/ *nm* **(a)** making-up
(b) make-up

maquiller /makije/ [1] **1** *vtr* **(a)** to make [sb] up
(b) to doctor ⟨truth⟩; **~ un crime en accident** to disguise a crime as an accident
2 **se maquiller** *v refl* (+ *v être*) **(a)** to put make-up on
(b) to wear make-up

maquilleur, -euse /makijœʀ, øz/ *nm, f* make-up artist

maquis /maki/ *nm inv* maquis; **prendre le ~** to go underground

m

maquisard, ∼e /makizaʀ, aʀd/ nm,f
member of the Resistance
marabout /maʀabu/ nm **(a)** marabou
(b) marabout
maraîchage /maʀɛʃaʒ/ nm market
gardening (GB), truck farming (US)
maraîcher, -ère /maʀɛʃe, ɛʀ/ **1** adj
produits ∼s market garden produce (GB),
truck (US)
2 nm,f market gardener (GB), truck
farmer (US)
marais /maʀɛ/ nm inv marsh; swamp
■ ∼ salant saltern
marasme /maʀasm/ nm stagnation
marathon /maʀatɔ̃/ nm marathon
marathonien, -ienne /maʀatɔnjɛ̃,
ɛn/ nm,f marathon runner
marâtre /maʀɑtʀ/ nf cruel mother
maraude /maʀod/ nf pilfering; en ∼
⟨person⟩ on the prowl
marauder /maʀode/ [1] vi **(a)** to pilfer
(b) to prowl around
maraudeur, -euse /maʀodœʀ, øz/ nm,f
petty thief
marbre /maʀbʀ/ nm **(a)** marble
(b) marble top
(c) marble statue
IDIOMS rester de ∼ to remain stony-faced;
la nouvelle les laissa de ∼ they were completely unmoved by the news
marbrer /maʀbʀe/ [1] vtr to marble
marbrerie /maʀbʀəʀi/ nf marble industry;
marble masonry
marbrier, -ière¹ /maʀbʀije, ɛʀ/ nm,f
marble mason
marbrière² /maʀbʀijɛʀ/ nf marble quarry
marbrure /maʀbʀyʀ/ nf marbling
marc /maʀ/ nm marc
■ ∼ de café coffee grounds
marcassin /maʀkasɛ̃/ nm young wild
boar
✧ **marchand, -e** /maʀʃɑ̃, ɑ̃d/ **1** adj
⟨quality⟩ marketable; ⟨sector⟩ trade; ⟨value⟩
market
2 nm,f shopkeeper; stallholder; ∼
d'armes/de bestiaux arms/cattle dealer; ∼
de charbon/vins coal/wine merchant
■ ∼ ambulant hawker; ∼ de couleurs ironmonger (GB), hardware merchant; ∼ de glaces ice cream vendor; ∼ en gros wholesaler;
∼ de journaux newsagent; news vendor; ∼
des quatre saisons costermonger (GB), fruit
and vegetable merchant; ∼ de sable sand-
man; ∼ de tapis carpet salesman
marchandage /maʀʃɑ̃daʒ/ nm haggling
marchander /maʀʃɑ̃de/ [1] vtr **(a)** to
haggle over
(b) (figurative) ∼ sa peine not to put oneself
out

marchandise /maʀʃɑ̃diz/ nf goods,
merchandise; tromper qn sur la ∼ to swindle
sb
✧ **marche** /maʀʃ/ nf **(a)** walking; walk;
pace, step; faire de la ∼ to go walking; à
10 minutes de ∼ 10 minutes' walk away
(b) march; fermer la ∼ to bring up the rear;
ouvrir la ∼ to be at the head of the march
(c) (of vehicle) progress; (of events) course; (of
time) march; bus en ∼ moving bus; dans le
sens contraire de la ∼ facing backward(s)
(d) (of mechanism) operation; (of organization)
running; en état de ∼ in working order;
mettre en ∼ to start (up) ⟨machine⟩; to switch
on ⟨TV⟩
(e) step; les ∼s the stairs
■ ∼ arrière reverse; faire ∼ arrière to reverse;
(figurative) to backpedal; ∼ avant forward; ∼ à
suivre procedure
IDIOM prendre le train en ∼ to join halfway
through; to climb onto the bandwagon
✧ **marché** /maʀʃe/ nm **(a)** market; faire son
∼ to do one's shopping at the market
(b) deal; conclure un ∼ avec qn to strike
a deal with sb; ∼ conclu! it's a deal!; bon/
meilleur ∼ cheap/cheaper; par-dessus le ∼
(fam) to top it all
■ ∼ de l'emploi job market; ∼ libre free
market; ∼ noir black market; ∼ aux puces
flea market; ∼ du travail labour (GB) market;
Marché commun Common Market
marchepied /maʀʃəpje/ nm **(a)** step
(b) steps
✧ **marcher** /maʀʃe/ [1] vi **(a)** to walk;
⟨demonstrators⟩ to march
(b) to tread; se laisser ∼ sur les pieds
(figurative) to let oneself be walked over
(c) ⟨mechanism, system⟩ to work; ma radio
marche mal my radio doesn't work properly;
faire ∼ qch to get sth to work; ∼ au gaz to
run on gas; les bus ne marchent pas le soir
the buses don't run in the evenings
(d) (fam) ∼ (bien)/∼ mal ⟨work, relationship⟩
to go well/not to go well; ⟨film, student⟩ to do
well/not to do well; ⟨actor⟩ to go down well/
not to go down well
(e) (fam) c'est trop risqué, je ne marche pas
it's too risky, count me out; ça marche! it's
a deal!
(f) (fam) to fall for it
(g) faire ∼ qn to pull sb's leg; faire ∼ son
monde (fam) to be good at giving orders
IDIOM il ne marche pas, il court! (fam) he's as
gullible as they come
marcheur, -euse /maʀʃœʀ, øz/ nm,f
walker
✧ **mardi** /maʀdi/ nm Tuesday
mare /maʀ/ nf **(a)** pond
(b) ∼ de sang pool of ⟨blood⟩
marécage /maʀekaʒ/ nm marsh, swamp
marécageux, -euse /maʀekaʒø, øz/ adj
⟨ground⟩ marshy, swampy; ⟨plant⟩ marsh

✧ indicates a very frequent word

maréchal, *pl* -**aux** /maʀeʃal, o/ *nm* ≈ field marshal (GB), general of the army (US)

maréchal-ferrant, *pl* **maréchaux-ferrants** /maʀeʃalfɛʀɑ̃, maʀeʃofeʀɑ̃/ *nm* farrier

marée /maʀe/ *nf* tide; **la ~ monte/descend** the tide is coming in/is going out; **à ~ haute/ basse** at high/low tide
■ **~ noire** oil slick
IDIOM **contre vents et ~s** come hell or high water; against all odds

marelle /maʀɛl/ *nf* hopscotch

marémoteur, **-trice** /maʀemɔtœʀ, tʀis/ *adj* tidal; **usine marémotrice** tidal power station

mareyeur, **-euse** /maʀɛjœʀ, øz/ *nm,f* fish wholesaler

margarine /maʀɡaʀin/ *nf* margarine

marge /maʀʒ/ 1 *nf* **(a)** margin;
(b) leeway; **on a 10 minutes de ~** we've got 10 minutes to spare
(c) scope; **tu devrais me laisser plus de ~ de décision** you should allow me more scope for making decisions
(d) profit margin; mark-up
2 **en marge de** *phr* vivre en **~ de la loi** to live outside the law; **se sentir en ~** to feel like an outsider
■ **~ bénéficiaire** profit margin; **~ commerciale** gross profit; **~ d'erreur** margin of error; **~ de sécurité** safety margin

marginal, **~e**, *mpl* -**aux** /maʀʒinal, o/ 1 *adj* **(a)** marginal;
(b) ⟨artist⟩ fringe
(c) on the margins of society
2 *nm,f* dropout; **les marginaux** the fringe elements of society

marginaliser /maʀʒinalize/ [1] *vtr* to marginalize

marguerite /maʀɡəʀit/ *nf* daisy

✎ **mari** /maʀi/ *nm* husband

✎ **mariage** /maʀjaʒ/ *nm* **(a)** marriage; **né d'un premier ~** from a previous marriage; **~ de raison** marriage of convenience; **faire un riche ~** to marry into money
(b) wedding
(c) (figurative) (of colours) marriage; (of companies) merger; (of parties) alliance; (of techniques) fusion
■ **~ blanc** marriage in name only; **~ civil** civil wedding; **~ religieux** church wedding

Marianne /maʀjan/ *pr n* Marianne (*female figure personifying the French Republic*)

marié, **~e** /maʀje/ 1 *pp* ▶ MARIER
2 *pp adj* married
3 *nm,f* **le (jeune) ~** the (bride)groom; **la (jeune) ~e** the bride; **les ~s** the newlyweds

✎ **marier** /maʀje/ [2] 1 *vtr* to marry
2 **se marier** *v refl* (+ *v être*) **(a)** to get married
(b) ⟨colours⟩ to blend

marijuana /maʀiʀwana/ *nf* marijuana

✎ **marin**, **~e¹** /maʀɛ̃, in/ 1 *adj* **(a)** ⟨life⟩ marine; ⟨salt⟩ sea; ⟨drilling⟩ offshore
(b) **pull ~** seaman's jersey; **costume ~** sailor suit
2 *nm* sailor
■ **~ d'eau douce** fair-weather sailor; **~ pêcheur** fisherman
IDIOM **avoir le pied ~** not to get seasick

marine² /maʀin/ 1 *adj inv* navy (blue)
2 *nm* marine

marine³ /maʀin/ *nf* navy; **de ~** nautical

mariner /maʀine/ [1] *vtr*, *vi* to marinate

marinière /maʀinjɛʀ/ *nf* smock

marionnette /maʀjɔnɛt/ *nf* **(a)** puppet
(b) **~s** puppet show
■ **~ à fils** marionette

marionnettiste /maʀjɔnetist/ *nmf* puppeteer

maritalement /maʀitalmɑ̃/ *adv* ⟨live⟩ as man and wife

maritime /maʀitim/ *adj* ⟨climate, commerce⟩ maritime; ⟨area⟩ coastal; ⟨company⟩ shipping

marivaudage /maʀivodaʒ/ *nm* **(a)** gallant banter
(b) refined affectation (*in the style of Marivaux*)

marjolaine /maʀʒɔlɛn/ *nf* marjoram

marmaille /maʀmaj/ (fam) *nf* rabble of kids (colloq)

marmelade /maʀməlad/ *nf* stewed fruit

marmite /maʀmit/ *nf* **(a)** (cooking-)pot
(b) potful
IDIOM **faire bouillir la ~** (fam) to bring home the bacon

marmiton /maʀmitɔ̃/ *nm* chef's assistant

marmonner /maʀmɔne/ [1] *vtr* to mumble, to mutter

marmot /maʀmo/ *nm* (fam) kid (colloq), brat (colloq)

marmotte /maʀmɔt/ *nf* **(a)** marmot
(b) (figurative) sleepyhead (colloq)

maroquinerie /maʀɔkinʀi/ *nf* **(a)** leather shop
(b) leather industry; leather trade; **(articles de) ~** leather goods

marotte /maʀɔt/ *nf* **(a)** pet subject, hobby horse; pet *or* favourite (GB) hobby
(b) puppet

marquant, **~e** /maʀkɑ̃, ɑ̃t/ *adj* ⟨fact⟩ memorable; ⟨memory⟩ lasting

✎ **marque** /maʀk/ *nf* **(a)** brand, make; **de ~** ⟨product⟩ branded; ⟨guest⟩ distinguished; ⟨person⟩ eminent
(b) mark; sign; **~ de doigts** fingermarks; **on voit encore les ~s (de coups)** you can still see the bruises; **~ du pluriel** plural marker; **laisser sa ~** to make one's mark
(c) (Sport) score; **à vos ~s, prêts, partez!** on your marks, get set, go!
■ **~ déposée** registered trademark; **~ de** ⋯⟫

fabrication manufacturer's brand name; ~ de
fabrique trademark

marqué, ~**e** /maʀke/ **1** *pp* ▶ MARQUER
2 *pp adj* **(a)** il a le corps ~ de traces de
coups he's bruised all over; elle est restée
~e par la guerre the war left its mark on
her; visage ~ worn face
(b) ‹*difference*› marked

ᕤ **marquer** /maʀke/ [1] **1** *vtr* **(a)** to mark
‹*goods*›; to brand ‹*cattle*›
(b) to mark, to signal ‹*beginning, end*›
(c) to mark ‹*body, object*›
(d) (figurative) ‹*event, work*› to leave its
mark on ‹*person*›; c'est quelqu'un qui m'a
beaucoup marqué he/she was a strong
influence on me
(e) to write [sth] down ‹*information*›; to
mark ‹*price*›; qu'est-ce qu'il y a de marqué?
what does it say?
(f) to show; ~ la mesure (Mus) to beat time; il
faut ~ le coup let's celebrate
(g) ~ un temps (d'arrêt) to pause
(h) (Sport) to score ‹*goal*›; to mark ‹*opponent*›
2 *vi* **(a)** to leave a mark
(b) (Sport) to score

marqueur /maʀkœʀ/ *nm* marker pen

marquis, ~**e** /maʀki, iz/ *nm,f* marquis/
marchioness

marraine /maʀɛn/ *nf* **(a)** godmother
(b) sponsor
■ ~ de guerre *soldier's wartime female
penfriend*

marrant, ~**e** /maʀɑ̃, ɑ̃t/ *adj* (fam) funny

marre /maʀ/ *adv* (fam) en avoir ~ to be fed
up (colloq)

marrer: se marrer /maʀe/ [1] *v refl* (+ *v
être*) (fam) **(a)** to have a great time
(b) to have a good laugh

marron, -onne /maʀɔ̃, ɔn/ **1** *adj* crooked
2 *adj inv* brown; ~ clair/foncé light/dark
brown
3 *nm* **(a)** chestnut
(b) brown
■ ~ glacé marron glacé; ~s chauds roast
chestnuts

marronnier /maʀɔnje/ *nm* chestnut (tree)

ᕤ **mars** /maʀs/ *nm inv* March
IDIOM arriver comme ~ en carême to come
as sure as night follows day

Marseillaise /maʀsɛjez/ *nf* Marseillaise
(*French national anthem*)

marsouin /maʀswɛ̃/ *nm* porpoise

marteau, *pl* ~**x** /maʀto/ *nm* hammer; (of
judge) gavel; (on door) knocker

marteler /maʀtəle/ [17] *vtr* **(a)** to hammer,
to pound
(b) to rap out ‹*words*›

martial, ~**e**, *mpl* **-iaux** /maʀsjal, o/ *adj*
‹*art, law*› martial; ‹*music, step*› military

martinet /maʀtinɛ/ *nm* **(a)** (Zool) swift

(b) whip

martingale /maʀtɛ̃gal/ *nf* **(a)** (on jacket)
half belt
(b) (for horse) martingale

martre /maʀtʀ/ *nf* **(a)** marten
(b) sable

martyr, ~**e**¹ /maʀtiʀ/ **1** *adj* martyred;
enfant ~ battered child
2 *nm,f* martyr

martyre² /maʀtiʀ/ *nm* **(a)** martyrdom
(b) agony; souffrir le ~ to suffer agony

martyriser /maʀtiʀize/ [1] *vtr* **(a)** to
torment ‹*victim, animal*›; to batter ‹*child*›
(b) to martyr

marxisme /maʀksism/ *nm* Marxism

mas /mɑ/ *nm inv* farmhouse (*in Provence*)

mascarade /maskaʀad/ *nf* **(a)** farce; ~ de
justice travesty of justice
(b) masked ball

mascotte /maskɔt/ *nf* mascot

ᕤ **masculin**, ~**e** /maskylɛ̃, in/ **1** *adj*
‹*population, sex, part*› male; ‹*sport*› man's;
‹*magazine, team*› men's; ‹*face, noun*›
masculine
2 *nm* masculine

masochisme /mazɔʃism/ *nm* masochism

masochiste /mazɔʃist/ *nmf* masochist

masque /mask/ *nm* **(a)** mask
(b) face-pack
(c) expression
■ ~ à gaz gas mask; ~ de plongée diving
mask; ~ de soudeur face shield
IDIOM jeter le ~ to show one's true colours
(GB)

masqué, ~**e** /maske/ *adj* **(a)** ‹*bandit*›
masked
(b) (figurative) concealed

masquer /maske/ [1] **1** *vtr* **(a)** to conceal
‹*defect*›; to mask ‹*problem*›
(b) to block ‹*opening, light*›
2 se masquer *v refl* (+ *v être*) to hide
[sth] from oneself ‹*truth*›

massacrante /masakʀɑ̃t/ *adj f* être
d'humeur ~ to be in a foul mood

massacre /masakʀ/ *nm* massacre,
slaughter

massacrer /masakʀe/ [1] *vtr* **(a)** to
massacre, to slaughter
(b) (figurative) (fam) to slaughter (colloq)
‹*opponent*›; to massacre ‹*piece of music*›; to
botch ‹*job*›; to slate ‹*play, actor*›

massage /masaʒ/ *nm* massage

ᕤ **masse** /mas/ *nf* **(a)** mass; ~ rocheuse
rocky mass; une ~ humaine a mass of
humanity
(b) une ~ de a lot of; des ~s de (fam) masses
of; départs en ~ mass exodus
(c) la ~, les ~s the masses; culture de ~
mass culture
■ ~ d'armes mace; ~ monétaire money supply; ~ salariale (total) wage bill

---

ᕤ indicates a very frequent word

IDIOMS (se laisser) tomber comme une ~ to collapse; **dormir comme une** ~ to sleep like a log (colloq)

massepain /maspɛ̃/ nm marzipan cake

masser /mase/ [1] **1** vtr to massage
  2 se masser v refl (+ v être) **(a)** to mass
  (b) se ~ **les jambes** to massage one's legs

masseur, -euse /masœʀ, øz/ nm,f masseur/masseuse

massicot /masiko/ nm (for paper) guillotine

massif, -ive /masif, iv/ **1** adj **(a)** ⟨features⟩ heavy; ⟨silhouette⟩ massive
  (b) ⟨dose⟩ massive; ⟨redundancies⟩ mass
  (c) ⟨gold, oak⟩ solid
  2 nm **(a)** massif
  (b) (flower) bed

massivement /masivmɑ̃/ adv ⟨demonstrate⟩ in great numbers; ⟨inject⟩ in massive doses; ⟨approve⟩ overwhelmingly

mass media /masmedja/ nm pl mass media

massue /masy/ nf (gen, Sport) club, bludgeon

mastic /mastik/ **1** adj inv putty-coloured (GB)
  2 nm (for windows) putty; (for holes) filler

mastiquer /mastike/ [1] vtr to chew

mastoc /mastɔk/ adj inv (fam) huge

mastodonte /mastɔdɔ̃t/ nm **(a)** mastodon
  (b) (figurative) (person) colossus, hulk (colloq); colossus, hulk (colloq); (animal) monster

masturber /mastyʀbe/ [1] vtr, **se masturber** v refl (+ v être) to masturbate

m'as-tu-vu /matyvy/ nmf inv (fam) show-off

mat¹, ~e /mat/ **1** adj **(a)** ⟨paint⟩ matt (GB), matte (US)
  (b) ⟨complexion⟩ olive
  (c) ⟨sound⟩ dull
  2 nm **(échec et)** ~**!** checkmate!

mat² /mat/ nm (colloq) morning

mât /mɑ/ nm **(a)** mast
  (b) pole; climbing pole; ~ **de drapeau** flagpole

matador /matadɔʀ/ nm matador

match /matʃ/ nm match; (in team sports) match (GB), game (US) draw (GB); ~ **nul** draw (GB), tie (US); **faire** ~ **nul** to draw (GB), to tie (US)
  ■ ~ **de classement** league match

matelas /matla/ nm inv mattress; ~ **pneumatique** air bed

matelassé, ~e /matlase/ adj ⟨material⟩ quilted; ⟨door⟩ padded

matelot /matlo/ nm **(a)** sailor
  (b) ≈ ordinary seaman (GB), ≈ seaman apprentice (US)

mater /mate/ [1] vtr to bring [sb/sth] into line ⟨rebels⟩; to take [sb/sth] in hand ⟨child, horse⟩

matérialiser /mateʀjalize/ [1] **1** vtr
  (a) to realize ⟨dream⟩; to make [sth] happen ⟨plan⟩
  (b) to mark; **'chaussée non matérialisée sur 3 km'** 'no road markings for 3 km'
  2 se matérialiser v refl (+ v être) to materialize

matérialisme /mateʀjalism/ nm materialism

matérialiste /mateʀjalist/ adj materialistic

matériau, pl ~x /mateʀjo/ nm material; ~x **de construction** building materials

matériel, -ielle /mateʀjɛl/ **1** adj ⟨cause, conditions⟩ material; ⟨means⟩ practical
  2 nm **(a)** equipment; ~ **agricole** farm machinery
  (b) material
  ■ ~ **informatique** hardware

matériellement /mateʀjɛlmɑ̃/ adv
  (a) **c'est** ~ **possible** it can be done
  (b) financially

maternel, -elle¹ /matɛʀnɛl/ adj
  (a) ⟨instinct⟩ maternal; ⟨love⟩ motherly
  (b) ⟨aunt⟩ maternal; **du côté** ~ on the mother's side

maternelle² /matɛʀnɛl/ nf nursery school

maternellement /matɛʀnɛlmɑ̃/ adv in a motherly way

materner /matɛʀne/ [1] vtr **(a)** to mother
  (b) to mollycoddle

maternité /matɛʀnite/ nf **(a)** motherhood
  (b) pregnancy; **de** ~ ⟨leave⟩ maternity
  (c) maternity hospital

mathématicien, -ienne /matematisjɛ̃, ɛn/ nm,f mathematician

mathématiquement /matematikmɑ̃/ adv **(a)** mathematically
  (b) logically

mathématiques /matematik/ nf pl mathematics

matheux, -euse /matø, øz/ nm,f (fam) mathematician

maths /mat/ nf pl (fam) maths (GB) (colloq), math (US) (colloq)

matière /matjɛʀ/ nf **(a)** material; **fournir la** ~ **d'un roman** to provide the material for a novel
  (b) matter; **en** ~ **d'emploi** as far as employment is concerned; ~ **à réflexion** food for thought
  (c) (Sch) subject
  ■ ~**s fécales** faeces; ~**s grasses** fat; ~ **grise** grey (GB) or gray (US) matter; ~ **première** raw material

Matignon /matiɲɔ̃/ pr n: offices of the French Prime Minister

matin /matɛ̃/ nm morning; **de bon** ~ early in the morning
  IDIOM **être du** ~ to be a morning person

m

matinal, ~e, *mpl* **-aux** /matinal, o/ *adj*
⟨*walk*⟩ morning; ⟨*hour*⟩ early; **être** ~ to be an
early riser, to be up early

mâtiné, ~e /matine/ *adj* **un anglais** ~ **de**
français a mixture of English and French

matinée /matine/ *nf* **(a)** morning
(b) matinée
IDIOM **faire la grasse** ~ to sleep in

matines /matin/ *nf pl* matins

matraquage /matʁakaʒ/ *nm*
(a) bludgeoning
(b) (figurative) ~ **publicitaire** hype (colloq)

matraque /matʁak/ *nf* club; truncheon
(GB), billy (US); **c'est le coup de** ~ (figurative)
(fam) it costs a fortune

matraquer /matʁake/ [1] *vtr* **(a)** to club
(b) ⟨*media*⟩ to bombard ⟨*public*⟩

matriarcal, ~e, *mpl* **-aux** /matʁijaʁkal,
o/ *adj* matriarchal

matrice /matʁis/ *nf* **(a)** matrix
(b) (Tech) die

matricule /matʁikyl/ *nm* reference
number; (Mil) service number

matrimonial, ~e, *mpl* **-iaux**
/matʁimɔnjal, o/ *adj* marriage, matrimonial

matrone /matʁon/ *nf* matronly woman

maturation /matyʁasjɔ̃/ *nf* ripening;
maturing

maturité /matyʁite/ *nf* maturity

maudire /modiʁ/ [80] *vtr* to curse

maudit, ~e /modi, it/ ⓵ *pp* ▶ MAUDIRE
⓶ *adj* (fam) blasted (colloq)
⓷ *nm,f* damned soul; **les** ~**s** the damned

maugréer /mogʁee/ [11] *vi* to grumble
(**contre** about)

maure /moʁ/ *adj* Moorish

maussade /mosad/ *adj* ⟨*mood*⟩ sullen;
⟨*weather*⟩ dull; ⟨*landscape*⟩ bleak

♂ **mauvais**, ~e /mɔvɛ, ɛz/ ⓵ *adj* **(a)** bad,
poor; ⟨*lawyer, doctor*⟩ incompetent; ⟨*wage*⟩
low; **du** ~ **tabac** cheap tobacco
(b) ⟨*address*⟩ wrong
(c) ⟨*day, moment*⟩ bad; ⟨*method*⟩ wrong
(d) bad; ⟨*surprise*⟩ nasty; ⟨*taste, smell*⟩
unpleasant; **par** ~ **temps** in bad weather; **ça**
a ~ **goût** it tastes horrible
(e) ⟨*cold, wound*⟩ nasty; ⟨*sea*⟩ rough
(f) ⟨*person, smile*⟩ nasty; ⟨*intentions,*
thoughts⟩ evil; **préparer un** ~ **coup** to be up
to mischief
⓶ *adv* **sentir** ~ to smell; **sentir très** ~ to
stink; **il fait** ~ the weather is bad
⓷ *nm* **il n'y a pas que du** ~ **dans le projet**
the project isn't all bad
■ ~ **esprit** scoffing person; scoffing attitude;
~ **garçon** tough guy; ~ **traitements** ill-
treatment; ~**e herbe** weed; ~**es rencontres**
bad company
IDIOM **l'avoir** ~**e** (fam) to be furious

♂ indicates a very frequent word

mauve¹ /mov/ *adj*, *nm* mauve

mauve² /mov/ *nf* mallow

mauviette /movjɛt/ *nf* wimp (colloq)

maux ▶ MAL

maxi- /maksi/ *pref* ~**-jupe** maxi-skirt;
~**-bouteille** one-and-a-half litre (GB) bottle

maxillaire /maksilɛʁ/ *nm* jawbone

maxima ▶ MAXIMUM

maximal, ~e, *mpl* **-aux** /maksimal, o/
adj maximum

maxime /maksim/ *nf* maxim

maximum, *pl* ~**s** *or* **maxima**
/maksimɔm, maksima/ ⓵ *adj* maximum
⓶ *nm* **(a)** maximum; **10 euros au grand** ~
10 euros at the very most; **au** ~ ⟨*work*⟩ to
the maximum; ⟨*reduce*⟩ as much as possible;
obtenir le ~ **d'avantages** to get as many
advantages as possible; **faire le** ~ to do one's
utmost
(b) (Law) maximum sentence

mayonnaise /majɔnɛz/ *nf* mayonnaise

mazagran /mazagʁɑ̃/ *nm*: thick china
goblet for coffee

mazout /mazut/ *nm* (fuel) oil

♂ **me** (**m'** *before vowel or mute h*) /m(ə)/ *pron*
(a) me; **tu ne m'as pas fait mal** you didn't
hurt me
(b) myself; **je** ~ **lave (les mains)** I wash (my
hands)

Me *written abbr* ▶ MAÎTRE 3C

méandre /meɑ̃dʁ/ *nm* meander; **les** ~**s de**
l'administration the maze of officialdom; **les**
~**s de ta pensée** the rambling development
of your ideas

mec /mɛk/ *nm* (fam) guy (colloq); **mon** ~ my
man (colloq)

mécanicien, **-ienne** /mekanisjɛ̃,
ɛn/ ⓵ *adj* mechanical
⓶ *nm,f* mechanic
⓷ *nm* (of train) engine driver (GB),
(locomotive) engineer (US); (of plane) flight
engineer; (of boat) engineer

mécanique /mekanik/ ⓵ *adj*
mechanical; ⟨*toy*⟩ clockwork; ⟨*razor*⟩ hand
⓶ *nf* **(a)** mechanics; **une merveille de** ~ a
marvel of engineering
(b) (fam) machine

mécaniquement /mekanikmɑ̃/ *adv*
mechanically; **fabriqué** ~ machine-made

mécaniser /mekanize/ [1] *vtr*, **se**
mécaniser *v refl* (+ *v être*) to mechanize

mécanisme /mekanism/ *nm* mechanism

mécano /mekano/ *nm* (fam) mechanic

mécénat /mesenɑ/ *nm* patronage

mécène /mesɛn/ *nm* patron of the arts

méchamment /meʃamɑ̃/ *adv*
(a) spitefully, maliciously; viciously; **traiter**
qn ~ to treat sb badly
(b) (fam) ⟨*damage*⟩ badly; ⟨*good*⟩ terribly

méchanceté /meʃɑ̃ste/ nf (a) nastiness;
par pure ~ out of pure spite
(b) maliciousness, viciousness
(c) malicious act; malicious remark

◆ **méchant**, ~**e** /meʃɑ̃, ɑ̃t/ **1** adj
(a) ⟨person⟩ nasty, malicious; ⟨animal⟩
vicious; ⟨flu, business⟩ nasty, bad
(b) (fam) fantastic (colloq), terrific (colloq)
2 nm,f (a) villain, baddie (colloq)
(b) naughty boy/girl

mèche /mɛʃ/ nf (a) (of hair) lock
(b) (in hair) streak
(c) (of candle) wick
(d) (Med) packing
(e) (of explosive) fuse
(f) (drill) bit
IDIOMS **être de** ~ **avec qn** (fam) to be in
cahoots with sb (colloq); **vendre la** ~ to let the
cat out of the bag

méchoui /meʃwi/ nm North African style
barbecue; spit-roast lamb

méconnaissable /mekɔnɛsabl/ adj
unrecognizable

méconnaissance /mekɔnɛsɑ̃s/ nf
(a) ignorance
(b) misreading

méconnaître /mekɔnɛtʀ/ [73] vtr to
misread; to be mistaken about

méconnu, ~**e** /mekɔny/ adj ⟨artist, work⟩
neglected; ⟨value⟩ unrecognized

mécontent, ~**e** /mekɔ̃tɑ̃, ɑ̃t/ adj
dissatisfied; ⟨voter⟩ discontented; **pas** ~
rather pleased

mécontentement /mekɔ̃tɑ̃tmɑ̃/ nm
(a) dissatisfaction
(b) discontent
(c) annoyance

mécontenter /mekɔ̃tɑ̃te/ [1] vtr to annoy;
to anger

Mecque /mɛk/ pr n **la** ~ Mecca

médaille /medaj/ nf (a) medal; ~ **d'or** gold
medal
(b) coin
(c) medallion

médaillon /medajɔ̃/ nm (a) locket
(b) (in art, architecture) medallion

◆ **médecin** /medsɛ̃/ nm doctor; ~ **traitant**
general practitioner, GP (GB)
■ ~ **de garde** duty doctor, doctor on duty; ~
légiste forensic surgeon

médecine /medsin/ nf medicine
■ ~ **scolaire** ≈ school health service; ~ **du**
travail ≈ occupational medicine; ~**s douces**
or **parallèles** alternative medicine

◆ **média** /medja/ **1** nm medium
2 **médias** nm pl **les** ~**s** the media

médiateur, -**trice** /medjatœʀ,
tʀis/ **1** adj mediatory
2 nm mediator; ombudsman

médiathèque /medjatɛk/ nf multimedia
library

médiation /medjasjɔ̃/ nf mediation

médiatique /medjatik/ adj ⟨exploitation⟩
by the media; ⟨success⟩ media

médiatisation /medjatizasjɔ̃/ nf media
coverage

médiatiser /medjatize/ [1] vtr to give [sth]
publicity in the media

◆ **médical**, ~**e**, mpl -**aux** /medikal, o/ adj
medical

médicament /medikamɑ̃/ nm medicine,
drug

médication /medikasjɔ̃/ nf medication

médicinal, ~**e**, mpl -**aux** /medisinal,
o/ adj medicinal

médico-légal, ~**e**, mpl -**aux**
/medikolegal, o/ adj forensic; **certificat** ~
autopsy report

médico-pédagogique, pl ~**s**
/medikopedagɔʒik/ adj **institut** ~ special
school

médiéval, ~**e**, mpl -**aux** /medjeval, o/ adj
medieval

médiocre /medjɔkʀ/ adj mediocre; ⟨pupil,
intelligence⟩ below average; ⟨soil, light,
return, food⟩ poor; ⟨interest, success⟩ limited;
⟨income⟩ meagre (GB)

médiocrement /medjɔkʀəmɑ̃/ adv
rather badly

médiocrité /medjɔkʀite/ nf (a) mediocrity
(b) meagreness (GB)

médire /mediʀ/ [65] v+prep ~ **de** to speak
ill of

médisance /medizɑ̃s/ nf malicious gossip

médisant, ~**e** /medizɑ̃, ɑ̃t/ adj malicious

médit /medi/ ▸ MÉDIRE

méditation /meditasjɔ̃/ nf meditation

méditer /medite/ [1] **1** vtr to mull
over; **longuement médité** ⟨plan⟩ carefully
considered
2 vi to meditate; ~ **sur** to meditate on
⟨existence⟩; to ponder on or over ⟨problem⟩

Méditerranée /mediteʀane/ pr nf **la**
(mer) ~ the Mediterranean (Sea)

méditerranéen, -**éenne** /mediteʀaneɛ̃,
ɛn/ adj Mediterranean

médium /medjɔm/ nm medium

méduse /medyz/ nf jellyfish

méduser /medyze/ [1] vtr to dumbfound

meeting /mitiŋ/ nm meeting

méfait /mefɛ/ **1** nm misdemeanour (GB);
crime
2 **méfaits** nm pl detrimental effect

méfiance /mefjɑ̃s/ nf mistrust, suspicion;
~ **de qn envers qn/qch** sb's wariness of sb/
sth

méfiant, ~**e** /mefjɑ̃, ɑ̃t/ adj suspicious; **elle**
est d'un naturel ~ she's always very wary

méfier: se méfier /mefje/ [2] v refl (+ v
être) (a) **se** ~ **de qn/qch** not to trust sb/sth;
sans se ~ quite trustingly ⸱⸱⸱⟩

m

(b) se ~ de qch to be wary of sth; **méfie-toi!** be careful!; watch it!

méga /mega/ *pref* mega; **~hertz** megahertz

mégalomane /megalɔman/ *adj, nmf* megalomaniac

mégaoctet /megaɔktɛ/ *nm* megabyte

mégarde: par mégarde /paʀmegaʀd/ *phr* inadvertently

mégère /meʒɛʀ/ *nf* shrew

mégot /mego/ *nm* cigarette butt

✦ **meilleur**, **~e¹** /mɛjœʀ/ **1** *adj* **(a)** better (que than)
(b) best; **au ~ prix** ‹*buy*› at the lowest price; ‹*sell*› at the highest price
2 *nm,f* **le ~, la ~e** the best one
3 *adv* better; **il fait ~ qu'hier** the weather is better than it was yesterday
4 *nm* **le ~** the best bit; **pour le ~ et pour le pire** for better or for worse
5 meilleure *nf* **ça c'est la ~!** that's the best one yet!

mél /mel/ *nm* (fam) (message) email; (address) email address

mélancolie /melɑ̃kɔli/ *nf* (gen) melancholy; (Med) melancholia

mélancolique 1 *adj* melancholy
2 *nmf* melancholic

mélancoliquement /melɑ̃kɔlikmɑ̃/ *adv* melancholically, in a melancholy fashion

mélange /melɑ̃ʒ/ *nm* (of teas, tobaccos) blend; (of products, ideas) combination; (of colours) mixture; **c'est un ~ (coton et synthétique)** it's a mix (of cotton and synthetic fibres (GB))

mélanger /melɑ̃ʒe/ [13] **1** *vtr* **(a)** to blend ‹*teas, oils, tobaccos*›; to mix ‹*colours, shades*›
(b) to put together ‹*styles, people, objects*›
(c) to mix up; **~ les cartes** to shuffle (the cards)
2 se mélanger *v refl* (+ *v être*) **(a)** ‹*teas, oils, tobaccos*› to blend; ‹*colours, shades*› to mix, to blend together
(b) ‹*ideas*› to get muddled

mélangeur /melɑ̃ʒœʀ/ *nm* mixer

mélasse /melas/ *nf* black treacle (GB), molasses

mêlée /mele/ *nf* **(a)** mêlée; **~ générale** free-for-all
(b) (Sport) scrum
(c) (figurative) fray

✦ **mêler** /mele/ [1] **1** *vtr* **(a)** to mix ‹*products, colours*›; to blend ‹*ingredients, cultures*›; to combine ‹*influences*›
(b) être mêlé à un scandale to be involved in a scandal
2 se mêler *v refl* (+ *v être*) **(a)** ‹*cultures, religions*› to mix; ‹*smells, voices*› to mingle
(b) se ~ à to mingle with ‹*crowd*›; to mix with ‹*people*›; to join in ‹*conversation*›
(c) se ~ de to meddle in; **mêle-toi de tes affaires** (fam) mind your own business

méli-mélo, *pl* **mélis-mélos** /melimelo/ *nm* jumble, mess

mélo /melo/ *adj* (fam) slushy (colloq), schmaltzy (colloq)

mélodie /melɔdi/ *nf* **(a)** melody, tune
(b) melodiousness

mélodrame /melɔdʀam/ *nm* melodrama

mélomane /melɔman/ *nmf* music lover

melon /məlɔ̃/ *nm* **(a)** melon
(b) bowler (hat) (GB), derby (hat) (US)

membrane /mɑ̃bʀan/ *nf* (Anat) membrane

✦ **membre** /mɑ̃bʀ/ *nm* **(a)** member; **les pays ~s** the member countries
(b) limb; **~ postérieur** hind limb

✦ **même** /mɛm/ **1** *adj* **(a)** same
(b) c'est l'intelligence ~ he's/she's intelligence itself
(c) le jour ~ où the very same day that; **c'est cela ~** that's it exactly
2 *adv* **(a)** even; **je ne m'en souviens ~ plus** I can't even remember now
(b) very; **c'est ici ~ que je l'ai rencontré** I met him at this very place
3 de même *phr* **agir** *or* **faire de ~** to do the same; **il en va de ~ pour** the same is true of
4 de même que *phr* **le prix du café, de ~ que celui du tabac, a augmenté de 10%** the price of coffee, as well as that of tobacco, has risen by 10%
5 même si *phr* even if
6 *pron* **le ~, la ~, les ~s** the same; **ce sac est le ~ que celui de Pierre** this bag is the same as Pierre's

mémé /meme/ *nf* (fam) gran (colloq), granny (colloq)

mémento /memɛ̃to/ *nm* guide

mémo /memo/ *nm* (fam) note

Mémo-Appel /memoapɛl/ *nm* reminder call service

mémoire¹ /memwaʀ/ **1** *nm* **(a)** memo
(b) dissertation
2 mémoires *nm pl* memoirs

✦ **mémoire²** /memwaʀ/ *nf* **(a)** memory; **si j'ai bonne ~** if I remember rightly; **ne pas avoir de ~** to have a bad memory; **de ~ d'homme** in living memory; **en ~ de** to the memory of, in memory of; **pour ~** for the record; for reference
(b) (Comput) memory; storage; **mettre des données en ~** to input data
■ **~ centrale** main storage *or* memory; **~ morte** read-only memory, ROM; **~ vive** random access memory, RAM

Mémophone /memɔfɔn/ *nm* public voicemail service

mémorable /memɔʀabl/ *adj* memorable

mémorial, **~e**, *mpl* **-iaux** /memɔʀjal, o/ *nm* memorial

---

✦ indicates a very frequent word

mémoriser /memɔʀize/ [1] *vtr* to memorize

menaçant, ~e /mənasɑ̃, ɑ̃t/ *adj* menacing

⚔ **menace** /mənas/ *nf* threat; **sous la ~** under duress; **sous la ~ d'une arme** at gunpoint

⚔ **menacer** /mənase/ [12] *vtr* (a) to threaten ‹*person*›
(b) to pose a threat to; **être menacé** ‹*stability, economy*› to be in jeopardy; ‹*life*› to be in danger; ‹*population*› to be at risk

ménage /menaʒ/ *nm* (a) household; **se mettre en ~ avec qn** to set up home with sb; **scènes de ~** domestic rows; **monter son ~** to buy the household goods
(b) housework; **faire le ~** to do the cleaning; **faire des ~s** to do domestic cleaning work
IDIOM **faire bon ~** to be compatible

ménagement /menaʒmɑ̃/ *nm* **avec ~s** gently; **sans ~s** ‹*say*› bluntly; ‹*push*› roughly

ménager¹ /menaʒe/ [13] ① *vtr* (a) to handle [sb] carefully; to deal carefully with [sb]; to be gentle with [sb]; to be careful with [sth]; **~ la susceptibilité de qn** to humour (GB) sb
(b) to be careful with ‹*clothes, savings*›; **il ne ménage pas sa peine** he spares no effort
② **se ménager** *v refl* (+ *v être*) to take it easy

ménager², -ère¹ /menaʒe, ɛʀ/ *adj* ‹*jobs*› domestic; ‹*equipment*› household; **appareils ~s** domestic appliances; **travaux ~s** housework

ménagère² /menaʒɛʀ/ *nf* (a) housewife
(b) canteen of cutlery

ménagerie /menaʒʀi/ *nf* menagerie

mendiant, ~e /mɑ̃djɑ̃, ɑ̃t/ *nm,f* beggar

mendicité /mɑ̃disite/ *nf* begging

mendier /mɑ̃dje/ [2] ① *vtr* to beg for
② *vi* to beg

⚔ **mener** /məne/ [16] ① *vtr* (a) **~ qn quelque part** to take sb somewhere; to drive sb somewhere
(b) to lead ‹*people, country*›; to run ‹*company*›; **il ne se laisse pas ~ par sa grande sœur** he won't be bossed about by his sister (colloq)
(c) **~ au village** ‹*road*› to go *or* lead to the village
(d) **~ à** to lead to; **cette histoire peut te ~ loin** it could be a very nasty business; **~ à bien** to complete [sth] successfully; to bring [sth] to a successful conclusion; to handle [sth] successfully
(e) to carry out ‹*study, reform*›; to run ‹*campaign*›; **~ une enquête** to hold an investigation; **~ sa vie comme on l'entend** to live as one pleases
② *vi* (Sport) to be in the lead
IDIOM **~ la danse** *or* **le jeu** to call the tune

ménestrel /menɛstʀɛl/ *nm* minstrel

meneur, -euse /mənœʀ, øz/ *nm,f* leader

menhir /meniʀ/ *nm* menhir

méninge /menɛ̃ʒ/ ① *nf* (Anat) meninx
② **méninges** *nf pl* (fam) brains (colloq)

méningite /menɛ̃ʒit/ *nf* meningitis

ménisque /menisk/ *nm* meniscus

ménopause /menɔpoz/ *nf* menopause

menotte /mənɔt/ ① *nf* tiny hand
② **menottes** *nf pl* handcuffs

⚔ **mensonge** /mɑ̃sɔ̃ʒ/ *nm* (a) lie
(b) **le ~** lying

mensonger, -ère /mɑ̃sɔ̃ʒe, ɛʀ/ *adj* ‹*accusations*› false; ‹*advertising*› misleading

mensualité /mɑ̃sɥalite/ *nf* monthly instalment (GB)

mensuel, -elle /mɑ̃sɥɛl/ ① *adj* monthly
② *nm* monthly magazine

mensuellement /mɑ̃sɥɛlmɑ̃/ *adv* once a month, monthly

mensurations /mɑ̃syʀasjɔ̃/ *nf pl* measurements

⚔ **mental, ~e,** *mpl* **-aux** /mɑ̃tal, o/ *adj* mental; **handicapé ~** mentally handicapped person

mentalité /mɑ̃talite/ *nf* mentality

menteur, -euse /mɑ̃tœʀ, øz/ ① *adj* ‹*person*› untruthful; ‹*statement*› full of lies
② *nm,f* liar

menthe /mɑ̃t/ *nf* (a) mint; **~ poivrée** peppermint; **~ verte** spearmint
(b) mint tea
(c) **~ (à l'eau)** mint cordial

menthol /mɛ̃tɔl/ *nm* menthol

mentholé, ~e /mɛ̃tɔle/ *adj* mentholated; menthol

mention /mɑ̃sjɔ̃/ *nf* (a) mention; **faire ~ de qch** to mention sth
(b) (Sch) **~ passable** pass with 50 to 60%; **~ très bien** pass with 80% upward(s)
(c) note; **rayer la ~ inutile** *or* **les ~s inutiles** delete as appropriate

⚔ **mentionner** /mɑ̃sjɔne/ [1] *vtr* to mention

mentir /mɑ̃tiʀ/ [30] ① *vi* (a) to lie, to tell lies
(b) ‹*figures*› to be misleading
② **se mentir** *v refl* (+ *v être*) (a) to fool oneself
(b) to lie to one another

menton /mɑ̃tɔ̃/ *nm* chin

menu, ~e /məny/ ① *adj* (a) ‹*person*› slight; ‹*foot, piece*› tiny; ‹*writing*› small
(b) ‹*jobs*› small; ‹*details*› minute
② *adv* ‹*write*› small; ‹*chop*› finely
③ *nm* menu
④ **par le menu** *phr* in (great) detail
■ **~ fretin** small fry; **~e monnaie** small change

menuiserie /mənɥizʀi/ *nf* woodwork

menuisier /mənɥizje/ *nm* joiner (GB), finish carpenter

méprendre: se méprendre /mepʀɑ̃dʀ/ [52] *v refl* (+ *v être*) to be mistaken

mépris /mepʀi/ nm inv contempt; **au ~ de la loi** regardless of the law

méprisable /mepʀizabl/ adj contemptible

méprisant, ~e /mepʀizɑ̃, ɑ̃t/ adj ‹gesture› contemptuous; ‹person› disdainful

méprise /mepʀiz/ nf mistake

mépriser /mepʀize/ [1] vtr to despise ‹person, wealth›; to scorn ‹danger, offer›

◇ **mer** /mɛʀ/ nf **(a)** sea; **une ~ d'huile** a glassy sea; **en pleine ~** out at sea; **la ~ monte** the tide is coming in
(b) seaside
IDIOM **ce n'est pas la ~ à boire** it's not all that difficult

mercantile /mɛʀkɑ̃til/ adj mercenary

mercenaire /mɛʀsənɛʀ/ adj, nmf mercenary

mercerie /mɛʀsəʀi/ nf haberdasher's shop (GB), notions store (US)

◇ **merci¹** /mɛʀsi/ nm, excl thank you

merci² /mɛʀsi/ nf mercy; **on est toujours à la ~ d'un accident** there's always the risk of an accident

◇ **mercredi** /mɛʀkʀədi/ nm Wednesday

mercure /mɛʀkyʀ/ nm mercury

mercurochrome® /mɛʀkyʀokʀom/ nm Mercurochrome®, antiseptic

◇ **merde** /mɛʀd/ nf, excl (vulgar) shit (slang)

◇ **mère** /mɛʀ/ **1** nf **(a)** mother
(b) ~ **supérieure** Mother Superior
2 **(-)mère** (combining form) **cellule/maison ~** parent cell/company
■ ~ **célibataire** single mother; ~ **de famille** mother; housewife; ~ **porteuse** surrogate mother; ~ **poule** mother hen

merguez /mɛʀgez/ nf inv spicy sausage

méridien /meʀidjɛ̃/ nm meridian

méridional, ~e /meʀidjɔnal, o/ **1** adj southern
2 nm,f Southerner

meringue /məʀɛ̃g/ nf meringue

mérite /meʀit/ nm merit; credit; **au ~** according to merit; **vanter les ~s de** to sing the praises of

mériter /meʀite/ [1] **1** vtr to deserve; ~ **réflexion** to be worth considering
2 **se mériter** v refl (+ v être) **ça se mérite** it's something that has to be earned

merlan /mɛʀlɑ̃/ nm whiting

merle /mɛʀl/ nm blackbird

mérou /meʀu/ nm grouper

merveille /mɛʀvɛj/ **1** nf marvel, wonder
2 **à merveille** phr wonderfully

◇ **merveilleux, -euse** /mɛʀvɛjø, øz/ adj marvellous (GB), wonderful

mes ▷ MON

mésaventure /mezavɑ̃tyʀ/ nf misadventure

mesdames ▷ MADAME

mesdemoiselles ▷ MADEMOISELLE

mésentente /mezɑ̃tɑ̃t/ nf dissension; disagreement

mésestimer /mezɛstime/ [1] vtr to underrate; to underestimate

mesquin, ~e /mɛskɛ̃, in/ adj **(a)** petty-minded; petty
(b) ‹person› mean (GB), cheap (US) (colloq)

mesquinerie /mɛskinʀi/ nf **(a)** meanness
(b) stinginess
(c) mean trick; mean remark

◇ **message** /mesaʒ/ nm message; ~ **publicitaire** commercial

messager, -ère /mesaʒe, ɛʀ/ nm,f
(a) messenger
(b) envoy

messagerie /mesaʒʀi/ nf freight forwarding
■ ~ **électronique** electronic mail service, e-mail; ~ **vocale** voice messaging

messe /mɛs/ nf mass; ~**s basses** (fam) whispering

messie /mesi/ nm messiah

messieurs ▷ MONSIEUR

◇ **mesure** /məzyʀ/ nf **(a)** measure; **prendre des ~s** to take measures; to take steps
(b) measurement; **c'est du sur ~** it's made to measure; **tu as un emploi sur ~** the job is tailor-made for you; **c'est une adversaire à ta ~** she is a match for you
(c) **unité de ~** unit of measurement; **instrument de ~** measuring device; **deux ~s de lait pour une ~ d'eau** two parts milk to one of water
(d) moderation; **dépasser la ~** to go too far
(e) (Mus) bar; **battre la ~** to beat time
(f) **être en ~ de rembourser** to be in a position to reimburse; **dans la ~ du possible** as far as possible; **dans la ~ où** insofar as

◇ **mesurer** /məzyʀe/ [1] **1** vtr **(a)** to measure; ~ **le tour de cou de qn** to take sb's neck measurement
(b) to measure ‹productivity, gap›; to assess ‹difficulties, risks, effects›; to consider ‹consequences›; ~ **ses paroles** to weigh one's words
2 vi ~ **20 mètres carrés** to be 20 metres (GB) square; **elle mesure 1,60 m** she's 1.60 m tall
3 **se mesurer** v refl (+ v être) **(a)** **se ~ en mètres** to be measured in metres (GB)
(b) **se ~ à** or **avec qn** to pit one's strength against sb

métal, pl -aux /metal, o/ nm metal; **pièce de** or **en ~** metal coin; ~ **jaune** gold

métallique /metalik/ adj **(a)** metal; **c'est ~** it's made of metal
(b) metallic

métallisé, ~e /metalize/ adj ‹green, blue› metallic

◇ indicates a very frequent word

métallurgie /metalyRʒi/ *nf*
(a) metalworking industry
(b) metallurgy
métallurgique /metalyRʒik/ *adj*
metallurgical
métamorphose /metamɔRfoz/ *nf*
metamorphosis
métamorphoser /metamɔRfoze/ [1]
1 *vtr* to transform [sb/sth] completely
2 se métamorphoser *v refl* (+ *v être*)
se ~ en to metamorphose into
métaphore /metafɔR/ *nf* metaphor
métayage /metejaʒ/ *nm* tenant farming,
sharecropping
métayer, -ère /meteje, ɛR/ *nm,f* tenant
farmer (GB), sharecropper (US)
météo /meteo/ *nf* weather forecast
météore /meteɔR/ *nm* meteor
météorite /meteɔRit/ *nm or nf* meteorite
météorologie /meteɔRɔlɔʒi/ *nf*
meteorology
météorologique /meteɔRɔlɔʒik/ *adj*
meteorological; **conditions ~s** weather
conditions
météorologiste /meteɔRɔlɔʒist/,
météorologue /meteɔRɔlɔg/ *nmf*
meteorologist
métèque /metɛk/ *nm* (offensive) foreigner,
dago (offensive)
méthane /metan/ *nm* methane
méthode /metɔd/ *nf* (a) method
(b) (for languages) course book (GB), textbook
(US)
(c) way; **j'ai ma ~ pour le convaincre** I've got
a way of convincing him
méthodique /metɔdik/ *adj* methodical
méthodiquement /metɔdikmɑ̃/ *adv*
methodically; **procédons ~** let's take things
step by step
méticuleux, -euse /metikylø, øz/ *adj*
meticulous; painstaking
métier /metje/ *nm* (a) job; profession;
trade; craft; **avoir 20 ans de ~** to have
20 years' experience; **c'est le ~ qui rentre!**
you learn by your mistakes!
(b) **~ à tisser** weaving loom
métis, -isse /metis/ *nm,f* person of mixed
race
métissage /metisaʒ/ *nm* (of people)
miscegenation; (of plants, animals) crossing
métrage /metraʒ/ *nm* (a) (of material)
length
(b) **long ~** feature(-length) film
mètre /mɛtR/ *nm* (a) metre (GB); **le 60 ~s**
the 60 metres (GB); **piquer un cent ~s** (fam)
to break into a run
(b) rule (GB), yardstick (US); **~ ruban** or **de
couturière** tape measure
métrique /metrik/ *adj* metric
métro /metro/ *nm* underground (GB),
subway (US)

IDIOM **~, boulot, dodo** (fam) the daily grind
métronome /metrɔnɔm/ *nm* metronome
métropole /metrɔpɔl/ *nf* (a) metropolis
(b) major city
(c) Metropolitan France
métropolitain, ~e /metrɔpɔlitɛ̃, ɛn/ *adj*
(a) ‹network› underground (GB), subway (US)
(b) from Metropolitan France
métropolite /metrɔpɔlit/ *nm*
metropolitan
mets /mɛ/ *nm inv* dish, delicacy
mettable /mɛtabl/ *adj* wearable
metteur /mɛtœR/ *nm* **~ en scène** director
mettre /mɛtR/ [60] **1** *vtr* (a) to put; to
put in ‹heating, shower›; to put up ‹curtains,
shelves›; **je mets les enfants à la crèche**
I send the children to a creche; **mets ton
écharpe** put your scarf on; **~ le linge à
sécher** to put the washing out to dry; **faire ~
le téléphone** to have a telephone put in
(b) to wear
(c) **~ qn en colère** to make sb angry
(d) to put on ‹radio, TV, heating›; **mets
moins fort!** turn it down!; **~ le réveil** to set
the alarm
(e) to put up ‹sign›; **qu'est-ce que je dois ~?**
what shall I put?; **je t'ai mis un mot** I've left
you a note; **~ en musique** to set to music; **~
en anglais** to put into English
(f) **y ~ du sien** to put oneself into it;
combien pouvez-vous ~? how much can
you afford?; **elle a mis une heure** it took her
an hour (**pour faire** to do)
(g) (Sch) **je vous ai mis trois sur vingt** I've
given you three out of twenty
(h) (fam) **mettons qu'il vienne, qu'est-ce que
vous ferez?** supposing he comes, what will
you do?
2 *vi* **~ bas** ‹animal› to give birth; to calve
3 se mettre *v refl* (+ *v être*) (a) **se ~
devant la fenêtre** to stand in front of the
window; **se ~ au lit** to go to bed; **se ~
debout** to stand up; **où est-ce que ça se met?**
where does this go?
(b) to spill [sth] on oneself
(c) **je ne sais pas quoi me ~** I don't know
what to put on
(d) **se ~ à l'anglais** to take up English; **il va
se ~ à pleuvoir** it's going to start raining
(e) **je préfère me ~ bien avec lui** I prefer to
get on the right side of him; **se ~ à l'aise** to
make oneself comfortable
meuble /mœbl/ **1** *adj* ‹soil› loose
2 *nm* **un ~** a piece of furniture
IDIOM **sauver les ~s** to salvage something
meublé /mœble/ *nm* furnished apartment
meubler /mœble/ [1] *vtr* to furnish; **la
plante meuble bien la pièce** the plant makes
the room look more cosy (GB) or cozy (US)
meugler /møgle/ [1] *vi* to moo
meule /møl/ *nf* (a) millstone
(b) grindstone

⋯⟶

(c) ∼ de foin haystack

meunier, -ière /mønje, ɛʀ/ *nm, f* miller

meurtre /mœʀtʀ/ *nm* murder

meurtrier, -ière /mœʀtʀije, ɛʀ/ **1** *adj* ‹fighting, repression› bloody; ‹explosion, accident› fatal; ‹epidemic› deadly; ‹arm› lethal

2 *nm, f* murderer

meurtrir /mœʀtʀiʀ/ [3] *vtr* (a) to hurt
(b) to bruise
(c) to wound ‹self-esteem›

meute /møt/ *nf* pack of hounds

mexicain, ∼e /mɛksikɛ̃, ɛn/ *adj* Mexican

Mexico /mɛksiko/ *pr n* Mexico City

Mexique /mɛksik/ *pr nm* Mexico

mezzanine /medzanin/ *nf* mezzanine

MF /ɛmɛf/ *nf* (*abbr* = **modulation de fréquence**) frequency modulation, FM

mi /mi/ *nm inv* (Mus) (note) E; (in sol-fa) mi, me

mi- /mi/ *pref* à la ∼-mai/saison in mid-May/
-season; ∼-chinois, ∼-français half Chinese,
half French

miam-miam /mjammjam/ *excl* (fam) yum-
yum! (colloq)

miauler /mjole/ [1] *vi* to miaow (GB), to
meow

mi-bas /miba/ *nm inv* knee sock, long sock

miche /miʃ/ *nf* round loaf

mi-chemin: à mi-chemin /amiʃmɛ̃/ *phr*
halfway; (figurative) halfway through

mi-clos, ∼e /miklo, oz/ *adj* half-closed

micmac /mikmak/ *nm* (fam) shady goings-
on (colloq)

mi-côte: à mi-côte /amikot/ *phr* halfway
up; halfway down

mi-course: à mi-course /amikuʀs/ *phr*
halfway through the race; (figurative) halfway
through

micro¹ /mikʀo/ *pref* micro

micro² /mikʀo/ *nm* microphone, mike
(colloq); ∼ caché bug

microbe /mikʀɔb/ *nm* germ, microbe

microclimat /mikʀoklima/ *nm*
microclimate

microcosme /mikʀokɔsm/ *nm*
microcosm

micro-cravate, *pl* **micros-cravates**
/mikʀokʀavat/ *nm* lapel-microphone

micro-édition /mikʀoedisjɔ̃/ *nf* desktop
publishing

microfilm /mikʀofilm/ *nm* microfilm

micro-informatique
/mikʀoɛ̃fɔʀmatik/ *nf* microcomputing

micro-ondes /mikʀoɔ̃d/ *nm inv*
microwave

micro-ordinateur, *pl* ∼s
/mikʀoɔʀdinatœʀ/ *nm* microcomputer

microphone /mikʀofɔn/ *nm* microphone

microprocesseur /mikʀopʀɔsɛsœʀ/ *nm*
microprocessor

microscope /mikʀoskɔp/ *nm* microscope

microscopique /mikʀoskɔpik/ *adj*
microscopic; (figurative) tiny

microsillon /mikʀosijɔ̃/ *nm* **(disque)** ∼
microgroove record

mi-cuisse: à mi-cuisse /amikɥis/ *phr*
above one's knees

♂ **midi** /midi/ *nm* (a) twelve o'clock, midday,
noon; je fais mes courses entre ∼ et deux I
go shopping in my lunch hour
(b) lunchtime
(c) le Midi the South of France

midinette /midinɛt/ *nf* bimbo (colloq)

mi-distance: à mi-distance
/amidistɑ̃s/ *phr* halfway

mie /mi/ *nf* bread without the crusts

miel /mjɛl/ *nm* honey
IDIOM être tout sucre tout ∼ to be as nice as
pie (colloq)

mielleux, -euse /mjɛlø, øz/ *adj* ‹tone›
unctuous, honeyed; ‹person› fawning

♂ **mien, mienne** /mjɛ̃, mjɛn/ **1** *det* ces
idées, je les ai faites miennes I adopted
these ideas
2 le mien, la mienne, les miens,
les miennes *pron* mine

miette /mjɛt/ *nf* crumb; réduire en ∼s to
smash (sth) to bits ‹vase›; to shatter ‹hopes›;
elle n'en perd pas une ∼ (fam) she's taking
it all in

♂ **mieux** /mjø/ **1** *adj inv* better; le ∼, la
∼, les ∼ the best; the nicest; the most
attractive; ce qu'il y a de ∼ the best
2 *adv* (a) better; je ne peux pas te dire ∼
that's all I can tell you; qui dit ∼? any other
offers?; any advance on that bid?; de ∼ en
∼ better and better; on la critiquait à qui ∼
∼ each person criticized her more harshly
than the last
(b) le ∼, la ∼, les ∼ the best; (of two) the
better
3 *nm inv* le ∼ est de refuser the best thing
is to refuse; il y a un/du ∼ there is an/some
improvement; je ne demande pas ∼ que de
rester ici I'm perfectly happy staying here;
fais pour le ∼, fais au ∼ do whatever is best;
tout va pour le ∼ everything's fine; elle est
au ∼ avec sa voisine she is on very good
terms with her neighbour (GB)

mièvre /mjɛvʀ/ *adj* vapid; soppy

mièvrerie /mjɛvʀəʀi/ *nf* vapidity; soppiness

mi-figue /mifig/ *adj inv* ∼ mi-raisin ‹smile›
half-hearted; ‹compliment› ambiguous

mignon, -onne /miɲɔ̃, ɔn/ *adj* (a) cute
(b) sweet, kind

migraine /migʀɛn/ *nf* splitting headache

migration /migʀasjɔ̃/ *nf* migration

migratoire /migʀatwaʀ/ *adj* migratory

migrer /migʀe/ [1] *vi* to migrate

♂ indicates a very frequent word

mi-hauteur: **à mi-hauteur** /amiotœʀ/ *phr* halfway up; halfway down

mi-jambe: **à mi-jambe** /amiʒãb/ *phr* (up) to one's knees

mijaurée /miʒoʀe/ *nf* **ne fais pas ta ~** don't put on such airs

mijoter /miʒɔte/ [1] **1** *vtr* (Culin) to prepare
2 *vi* (Culin) to simmer

mijoteuse® /miʒɔtøz/ *nf* slow cooker

mikado /mikado/ *nm* spillikins

mil /mil/ ▶ MILLE 1

milice /milis/ *nf* militia; **~ de quartier** local vigilante group

Milice /milis/ *nf* **la ~** the Milice (*French wartime paramilitary organization which collaborated with the Germans against the Resistance*)

milicien, -ienne /milisjɛ̃, ɛn/ *nm,f*
(a) militiaman/militiawoman
(b) member of the Milice

✐ **milieu**, *pl* **~x** /miljø/ **1** *nm* (a) middle; **au beau** *or* **en plein ~** right in the middle; **au ~ de la nuit** in the middle of the night
(b) middle ground
(c) environment; **en ~ rural** in the country
(d) background, milieu; **le ~** the underworld
2 **au milieu de** *phr* (a) among; **être au ~ de ses amis** to be with one's friends
(b) surrounded by; **au ~ du désastre** in the midst of disaster

✐ **militaire** /militɛʀ/ **1** *adj* military; army
2 *nm* serviceman

militairement /militɛʀmã/ *adv* (a) by military means; **zone occupée ~** military occupied zone
(b) with military efficiency; along military lines

militant, ~e /militã, ãt/ **1** *adj* militant
2 *nm,f* (of organization) active member, activist; (for cause) campaigner

militantisme /militãtism/ *nm* political activism

militariste /militaʀist/ *adj* militaristic

militer /milite/ [1] *vi* (a) to campaign
(b) to be a political activist

✐ **mille** /mil/ **1** *adj inv* a thousand, one thousand; **deux/trois ~** two/three thousand
2 *nm inv* (a) a thousand, one thousand
(b) bull's eye; **taper dans le ~** to hit the bull's-eye; (figurative) to hit the nail on the head
3 *nm* (a) **~ (marin** *or* **nautique)** (nautical) mile
(b) (air) mile
4 **pour mille** *phr* per thousand
IDIOM **je vous le donne en ~** you'll never guess (in a million years)

millénaire /milenɛʀ/ **1** *adj* (a) **un arbre ~** a one-thousand-year-old tree
(b) ‹*tradition*› age-old
2 *nm* (a) **pendant des ~s** for thousands

of years
(b) millennium, millenary

mille-pattes /milpat/ *nm inv* centipede, millipede

millésime /milezim/ *nm* vintage, year

milli /mili/ *pref* milli; **~mètre** millimetre (GB)

✐ **milliard** /miljaʀ/ *nm* billion

milliardaire /miljaʀdɛʀ/ *nmf* multimillionaire, billionaire

millième /miljɛm/ *adj* thousandth

✐ **millier** /milje/ *nm* (a) thousand
(b) **un ~** about a thousand

✐ **million** /miljɔ̃/ *nm* million

millionième /miljɔnjɛm/ *adj* millionth

millionnaire /miljɔnɛʀ/ **1** *adj* **être ~** ‹*firm*› to be worth millions; ‹*person*› to be a millionaire
2 *nmf* millionaire

mime /mim/ *nm* mime

mimer /mime/ [1] *vtr* (a) to mime
(b) to mimic

mimétisme /mimetism/ *nm* (a) (Zool) mimicry
(b) **par ~** through unconscious imitation

mimique /mimik/ *nf* funny face

minable /minabl/ *adj* (fam) (a) ‹*salary, person*› pathetic
(b) ‹*place*› crummy (colloq); ‹*existence*› miserable
(c) (drunk) sloshed (colloq)

minage /minaʒ/ *nm* mining

minaret /minaʀɛ/ *nm* minaret

minauder /minode/ [1] *vi* (a) to mince about
(b) to simper

mince /mɛ̃s/ *adj* (a) slim, slender; ‹*face, slice*› thin
(b) ‹*consolation*› small; ‹*chance*› slim

minceur /mɛ̃sœʀ/ *nf* slimness; slenderness; thinness

mincir /mɛ̃siʀ/ [3] *vi* to lose weight

✐ **mine** /min/ *nf* (a) expression; **faire ~ d'accepter** to pretend to accept; **elle nous a dit, ~ de rien, que** (fam) she told us, casually, that; **il est doué, ~ de rien** (fam) it may not be obvious, but he's very clever
(b) **avoir bonne ~** ‹*person*› to look well
(c) (in pencil) lead
(d) mine; **~ d'or** gold mine
(e) (Mil) mine
IDIOM **ne pas payer de ~** (fam) not to look anything special (colloq)

miner /mine/ [1] *vtr* (a) to sap ‹*morale, energy*›; to undermine ‹*health*›
(b) (Mil) to mine

minerai /minʀɛ/ *nm* ore; **~ de fer** iron ore

minéral, ~e, *mpl* **-aux** /mineʀal, o/ **1** *adj* ‹*water*› mineral; ‹*chemistry*› inorganic
2 *nm* mineral

minéralogique /mineʀalɔʒik/ *adj* plaque ~ number plate (GB), license plate (US)

minerve /minɛʀv/ *nf* (Med) surgical collar (GB), neck brace (US)

minet /minɛ/ *nm* (a) pussycat
(b) (fam) pretty boy (colloq)

minette /minɛt/ *nf* (a) pussycat
(b) (fam) cool chick (colloq)

mineur, ~e /minœʀ/ **1** *adj* (a) (Law) under 18
(b) ‹détail› minor
(c) (Mus) **en ré ~** in D minor
2 *nm,f* (Law) person under 18
3 *nm* miner; **~ de fond** pit worker

mini- /mini/ *pref* mini

miniature /minjatyʀ/ *adj, nf* miniature

miniaturisation /minjatyʀizasjɔ̃/ *nf* miniaturization

minibus /minibys/ *nm inv* minibus

minicassette® /minikasɛt/ *nf* mini-cassette®

minier, -ière /minje, ɛʀ/ *adj* mining

mini-informatique /miniɛ̃fɔʀmatik/ *nf* minicomputing

mini-jupe, *pl* **~s** /miniʒyp/ *nf* mini-skirt

minimal, ~e, *mpl* **-aux** /minimal, o/ *adj* minimal, minimum

minimalisme /minimalism/ *nm* minimalism

minime /minim/ **1** *adj* negligible
2 *nmf* (Sport) junior (*7 to 13 years old*)

minimiser /minimize/ [1] *vtr* to minimize

minimoto /minimoto/ *nf* Minimoto, pocket bike

minimum, *pl* **~s** *or* **minima** /minimɔm, minima/ **1** *adj* minimum
2 *nm* (a) minimum; **un ~ de bon sens** a certain amount of common sense; **il faut au ~ deux heures pour faire le trajet** the journey takes at least two hours
(b) (Law) minimum sentence
■ **~ vital** subsistence level

mini-ordinateur, *pl* **~s** /miniɔʀdinatœʀ/ *nm* minicomputer

minipilule /minipilyl/ *nf* low-dose combined pill

✧ **ministère** /ministɛʀ/ *nm* ministry; (in UK, US) department

ministériel, -ielle /ministeʀjɛl/ *adj* ministerial, cabinet

✧ **ministre** /ministʀ/ *nm* (a) minister; (in UK) Secretary of State; (in US) Secretary
(b) (of religion) minister

Minitel® /minitɛl/ *nm* Minitel (*terminal linking phone users to a database*)

minitéler /minitele/ [14] *vtr* to contact via Minitel

minitéliste /minitɛlist/ *n* Minitel user

minivague /minivag/ *nf* soft perm

minois /minwɑ/ *nm inv* fresh young face

minoration /minɔʀasjɔ̃/ *nf*
(a) undervaluation; underestimation
(b) reduction; **~ des prix** cut in prices

minorer /minɔʀe/ [1] *vtr* (a) to reduce (**de** by)
(b) to undervalue; to underestimate

minoritaire /minɔʀitɛʀ/ *adj* minority

minorité /minɔʀite/ *nf* (a) minority; **être mis en ~** to be defeated
(b) (age) minority
■ **~ de blocage** blocking minority

minoterie /minɔtʀi/ *nf* (a) flour mill
(b) flour-milling

minou /minu/ *nm* pussycat

minuit /minɥi/ *nm* midnight

minuscule /minyskyl/ **1** *adj* ‹person, thing› tiny; ‹quantity› tiny, minute
2 *nf* small letter; (in printing) lower-case letter

minutage /minytaʒ/ *nm* (precise) timing

✧ **minute** /minyt/ *nf* minute; **la ~ de vérité** the moment of truth

minuter /minyte/ [1] *vtr* (a) to time
(b) to work out the timing of

minuterie /minytʀi/ *nf* (a) time-switch
(b) automatic lighting

minuteur /minytœʀ/ *nm* timer

minutie /minysi/ *nf* meticulousness

minutieusement /minysjøzmɑ̃/ *adv* with meticulous care; in great detail

minutieux, -ieuse /minysjø, øz/ *adj* meticulous; ‹description› detailed

mioche /mjɔʃ/ *nmf* (fam) kid (colloq)

mirabelle /miʀabɛl/ *nf* (a) mirabelle (*small yellow plum*)
(b) plum brandy

miracle /miʀakl/ **1** *adj inv* **un médicament ~** a wonder drug; **une méthode ~** a magic formula
2 *nm* (a) miracle; **faire un ~** to work a miracle; (figurative) to work miracles; **comme par ~** as if by magic
(b) miracle play

miraculeux, -euse /miʀakylø, øz/ *adj* miraculous; ‹product, remedy› which works wonders

mirador /miʀadɔʀ/ *nm* watchtower

mirage /miʀaʒ/ *nm* mirage

mi-raisin /miʀɛzɛ̃/ ▶ MI-FIGUE

miraud, ~e /miʀo, od/ *adj* (fam) shortsighted

mirobolant, ~e /miʀɔbɔlɑ̃, ɑ̃t/ *adj* (fam) fabulous (colloq)

✧ **miroir** /miʀwaʀ/ *nm* mirror

miroitement /miʀwatmɑ̃/ *nm* sparkling; shimmering

miroiter /miʀwate/ [1] *vi* to shimmer; **faire ~ qch à qn** to hold out the prospect of sth to sb

---

✧ indicates a very frequent word

mis, **~e¹** /mi, miz/ ▶ METTRE
misanthrope /mizãtʀɔp/ ☐1 *adj*
misanthropic
  ☐2 *nmf* misanthropist, misanthrope
♂ **mise²** /miz/ *nf* **une ~ de cinq euros** a five-euro bet
  ■ **~ à jour** update; **~ de fonds** investment; **~ en plis** set
  IDIOM **être de ~** ‹*conduct*› to be proper
miser /mize/ [1] ☐1 *vtr* to bet
  ☐2 *vi* (a) **~ sur** to bet on, to place a bet on
  (b) **~ sur qn** to place all one's hopes in sb
misérabilisme /mizeʀabilism/ *nm*
  (a) sordid realism
  (b) tendency to dwell on the dark side
misérable /mizeʀabl/ ☐1 *adj* (a) ‹*person*› destitute, poor; ‹*life*› poor
  (b) ‹*salary*› meagre (GB)
  ☐2 *nmf* (a) pauper
  (b) scoundrel
♂ **misère** /mizɛʀ/ *nf* (a) destitution; **réduire qn à la ~** to reduce sb to poverty
  (b) misery, wretchedness
  (c) trouble, woe; **on a tous nos petites ~s** we all have our troubles
  (d) **être payé une ~** to be paid a pittance
miséreux, -euse /mizeʀø, øz/ *nm,f* destitute person; **les ~** the destitute
miséricorde /mizeʀikɔʀd/ *nf, excl* mercy
misogyne /mizɔʒin/ *adj* misogynous
misogynie /mizɔʒini/ *nf* misogyny
missel /misɛl/ *nm* missal
missile /misil/ *nm* missile
♂ **mission** /misjɔ̃/ *nf* mission
missionnaire /misjɔnɛʀ/ *adj, nmf* missionary
missive /misiv/ *nf* missive
mistral /mistʀal/ *nm* mistral
mitaine /mitɛn/ *nf* fingerless mitten
mite /mit/ *nf* (clothes) moth
mi-temps¹ /mitã/ *nm inv* part-time job
mi-temps² /mitã/ *nf inv* (Sport) half-time
miteux, -euse /mitø, øz/ *adj* seedy; shabby
mitigé, ~e /mitiʒe/ *adj* ‹*reception*› lukewarm; ‹*success*› qualified
mitonner /mitɔne/ [1] *vtr* to cook [sth] lovingly
mitoyen, -enne /mitwajɛ̃, ɛn/ *adj* ‹*hedge*› dividing; **mur ~** party wall
mitraille /mitʀaj/ *nf* hail of bullets
mitrailler /mitʀaje/ [1] *vtr* (a) to machine-gun
  (b) **~ qn de questions** to fire questions at sb
  (c) (fam) to take photo after photo of [sb/sth]
mitraillette /mitʀajɛt/ *nf* submachine gun
mitrailleuse /mitʀajøz/ *nf* machine gun
mi-voix: à mi-voix /amivwa/ *phr* in a low voice

mixage /miksaʒ/ *nm* sound mixing
mixer¹ /mikse/ [1] *vtr* to mix
mixer² /miksɛʀ/ ▶ MIXEUR
mixeur /miksœʀ/ *nm* (a) mixer
  (b) blender
mixité /miksite/ *nf* (gen) mixing of sexes; (Sch) coeducation
mixte /mikst/ *adj* (a) ‹*school*› coeducational; ‹*class*› mixed
  (b) ‹*couple, marriage*› mixed; ‹*economy*› mixed; **société ~** joint venture
mixture /mikstyʀ/ *nf* (a) concoction
  (b) (in pharmacy) mixture
  (c) mishmash (colloq)
MJC /ɛmʒise/ *nf* (abbr = **maison des jeunes et de la culture**) ≈ youth club
MLF /ɛmɛlɛf/ *nm* (abbr = **mouvement de libération des femmes**) ≈ Women's Lib
Mlle (*written abbr* = **Mademoiselle**) Ms, Miss
mm (*written abbr* = **millimètre**) mm
MM. (*written abbr* = **Messieurs**) Messrs
Mme (*written abbr* = **Madame**) Ms, Mrs
mnémotechnique /mnemɔtɛknik/ *adj* mnemonic
Mo (*written abbr* = **mégaoctet**) Mb, MB
mobbing /mɔbiŋ/ *nm* psychological harassment at work
mobile /mɔbil/ ☐1 *adj* (gen) mobile; ‹*leaf*› loose
  ☐2 *nm* (a) motive
  (b) mobile
mobilier, -ière /mɔbilje, ɛʀ/ ☐1 *adj* **biens ~** movable property
  ☐2 *nm* furniture
mobilisation /mɔbilizasjɔ̃/ *nf* mobilization
mobiliser /mɔbilize/ [1] ☐1 *vtr* to mobilize ‹*soldier*›; to call up ‹*civilian*›
  ☐2 **se mobiliser** *v refl* (+ *v être*) to rally
mobilité /mɔbilite/ *nf* mobility
mobylette® /mɔbilɛt/ *nf* moped
mocassin /mɔkasɛ̃/ *nm* moccasin, loafer
moche /mɔʃ/ *adj* (fam) (a) ‹*person*› ugly; ‹*garment*› ghastly
  (b) ‹*incident*› dreadful
  (c) ‹*act*› nasty
modalité /mɔdalite/ ☐1 *nf* modality
  ☐2 **modalités** *nf pl* terms; practical details
mode¹ /mɔd/ *nm* (a) way, mode; **~ de paiement** method of payment
  (b) (in grammar) mood
  ■ **~ d'emploi** instructions for use
♂ **mode²** /mɔd/ *nf* (a) fashion; **lancer une ~** to start a trend; **à la ~** ‹*garment, club*› fashionable; ‹*singer*› popular
  (b) fashion industry
♂ **modèle** /mɔdɛl/ ☐1 *adj* (gen) model; ‹*conduct*› perfect, exemplary

···>

m

2 *nm* **(a)** (gen) model; **prendre ~ sur qn** to do as sb does/did; **~ à suivre** somebody to look up to; **la tente grand ~** the large-size tent; **le ~ au-dessus** the next size up; **~ de signature** specimen signature
(b) pattern; **~ déposé** registered pattern
■ **~ réduit** scale model

modeler /mɔdle/ [17] *vtr* to model ‹clay›; to mould (GB), to mold (US) ‹character›

modélisme /mɔdelism/ *nm* modelling (GB)

modération /mɔdeʀasjɔ̃/ *nf* **(a)** moderation
(b) (in price, tax) reduction

modéré, ~e /mɔdeʀe/ *adj* ‹political party, speed, words› moderate; ‹price› reasonable; ‹temperament› even; ‹enthusiasm› mild

modérément /mɔdeʀemɑ̃/ *adv*
(a) relatively
(b) slightly

modérer /mɔdeʀe/ [14] *vtr* to curb ‹expenses›; to moderate ‹language›; to reduce ‹speed›

◆ **moderne** /mɔdɛʀn/ *adj* modern

moderniser /mɔdɛʀnize/ [1] *vtr* to modernize; to update

modernité /mɔdɛʀnite/ *nf* modernity

modeste /mɔdɛst/ *adj* ‹sum, apartment, person› modest; ‹cost› moderate; ‹background› humble

modestement /mɔdɛstəmɑ̃/ *adv* modestly

modestie /mɔdɛsti/ *nf* modesty

modification /mɔdifikasjɔ̃/ *nf* modification

◆ **modifier** /mɔdifje/ [2] *vtr* to change; to alter, to modify

modique /mɔdik/ *adj* ‹sum, resources› modest

modiste /mɔdist/ *nf* milliner

modulation /mɔdylasjɔ̃/ *nf* modulation
■ **~ de fréquence, MF** frequency modulation, FM

module /mɔdyl/ *nm* (gen, Sch) module

moduler /mɔdyle/ [1] *vtr* **(a)** to modulate
(b) to adjust ‹price›; to adapt ‹policy›

moelle /mwal/ *nf* marrow
■ **~ épinière** spinal cord

moelleux, -euse /mwalø, øz/ *adj*
(a) ‹carpet› thick; ‹bed› soft
(b) ‹wine› mellow

mœurs /mœʀ(s)/ *nf pl* **(a)** customs; habits; lifestyle; **l'évolution des ~** the change in attitudes
(b) morals; **des ~ dissolues** loose morals; **la police des ~, les Mœurs** (fam) the vice squad
(c) (of animals) behaviour
IDIOM **autres temps, autres ~** other days, other ways

mohair /mɔɛʀ/ *nm* mohair

◆ **moi¹** /mwa/ *pron* **(a)** I, me; **c'est ~** it's me

(b) me; **pour ~** for me; **des amis à ~** friends of mine; **c'est à ~** it's mine; it's my turn

moi² /mwa/ *nm* **le ~** the self

moignon /mwaɲɔ̃/ *nm* stump

moi-même /mwamɛm/ *pron* myself

◆ **moindre** /mwɛ̃dʀ/ *adj* **(a)** lesser; **à ~ prix** more cheaply
(b) **le ~** the least; **je n'en ai pas la ~ idée** I haven't got the slightest idea

moine /mwan/ *nm* monk
IDIOM **l'habit ne fait pas le ~** (Proverb) you can't judge a book by its cover

moineau, *pl* **~x** /mwano/ *nm* sparrow

◆ **moins¹** /mwɛ̃/ **1** *prep* **(a)** minus
(b) **il est huit heures ~ dix** it's ten (minutes) to eight; **il était ~ une** (fam) it was a close shave (colloq)
2 *adv* (comparative) less; (superlative) **le ~** the least; **le ~ difficile** the less difficult; the least difficult; **de ~ en ~ less** and less; **~ je sors, ~ j'ai envie de sortir** the less I go out, the less I feel like going out; **il n'en est pas ~ vrai que** it's nonetheless true that; **il ressemble à son frère en ~ gros** he looks like his brother, only thinner; **à tout le ~, pour le ~** to say the least; **il y avait deux fourchettes en ~ dans la boîte** there were two forks missing from the box
3 **moins de** *quantif* **~ de livres** fewer books; **~ de sucre** less sugar; **les ~ de 20 ans** people under 20
4 **à moins de** *phr* unless
5 **à moins que** *phr* unless
6 **au moins** *phr* at least
7 **du moins** *phr* at least

moins² /mwɛ̃/ *nm inv* minus
■ **~ que rien** good-for-nothing, nobody

moiré, ~e /mware/ *adj* moiré; watered

◆ **mois** /mwa/ *nm inv* month

moisi /mwazi/ *nm* mould (GB), mold (US)

moisir /mwaziʀ/ [3] *vi* ‹foodstuff› to go mouldy (GB) *or* moldy (US); ‹object, plant› to become mildewed

moisissure /mwazisyʀ/ *nf* **(a)** mould (GB), mold (US)
(b) mildew

moisson /mwasɔ̃/ *nf* harvest

moissonner /mwasɔne/ [1] *vtr* to harvest

moissonneuse /mwasɔnøz/ *nf* reaper

moite /mwat/ *adj* ‹heat› muggy; ‹skin› sweaty

moiteur /mwatœʀ/ *nf* (of air) mugginess; (of skin) sweatiness

◆ **moitié** /mwatje/ *nf* half; **à ~ vide** half empty

moitié-moitié /mwatjemwatje/ *adv* half-and-half

moka /mɔka/ *nm* **(a)** mocha
(b) mocha cake

molaire /mɔlɛʀ/ *nf* molar

molécule /mɔlekyl/ *nf* molecule

◆ indicates a very frequent word

moleskine /mɔlɛskin/ nf (a) imitation leather
(b) moleskin

molester /mɔlɛste/ [1] vtr to manhandle

molette /mɔlɛt/ nf (of spanner) adjusting knob

mollasson, -onne /mɔlasɔ̃, ɔn/ adj (fam) sluggish

molle ▶ MOU 1

mollement /mɔlmɑ̃/ adv (a) idly
(b) ⟨work⟩ without much enthusiasm; ⟨protest⟩ half-heartedly

mollet /mɔlɛ/ **1** adj m œuf ~ soft-boiled egg
2 nm (Anat) calf

molleton /mɔltɔ̃/ nm (a) flannel; flannelette
(b) (table) felt
(c) (ironing board) cover

molletonner /mɔltɔne/ [1] vtr to line with fleece

mollir /mɔliʀ/ [3] vi (a) ⟨courage⟩ to fail; ⟨resistance⟩ to grow weaker; ⟨person⟩ to soften
(b) ⟨knees⟩ to give way; ⟨arm⟩ to go weak

mollusque /mɔlysk/ nm mollusc (GB), mollusk (US)

molosse /mɔlɔs/ nm huge dog

môme /mom/ nmf (fam) kid (colloq); brat (colloq)

moment /mɔmɑ̃/ nm moment; le ~ venu when the time comes/came; il devrait arriver d'un ~ à l'autre he should arrive any minute now; à un ~ donné at some point; at a given moment; à ce ~-là at that time; just then; in that case; au ~ où at the time (when); au ~ où il quittait son domicile as he was leaving his home; jusqu'au ~ où until; du ~ que as long as, provided; il arrive toujours au bon or mauvais ~! he certainly picks his moment to call!; un ~! just a moment!; ça va prendre un ~ it will take a while; au bout d'un ~ after a while; par ~s at times; les ~s forts du film the film's highlights; dans ses meilleurs ~s, il fait penser à Orson Welles at his best, he reminds one of Orson Welles; à mes ~s perdus in my spare time

momentané, ~e /mɔmɑ̃tane/ adj momentary

momentanément /mɔmɑ̃tanemɑ̃/ adv for a moment, momentarily

momie /mɔmi/ nf mummy

mon, ma, pl **mes** /mɔ̃, ma, mɛ/ det my; j'ai ~ idée I have my own ideas about that

monacal, ~e, mpl **-aux** /mɔnakal, o/ adj monastic

monarchie /mɔnaʀʃi/ nf monarchy

monarchiste /mɔnaʀʃist/ adj, nmf monarchist

monarque /mɔnaʀk/ nm monarch

monastère /mɔnastɛʀ/ nm monastery

monceau, pl ~**x** /mɔ̃so/ nm (of rubbish) pile

mondain, ~e /mɔ̃dɛ̃, ɛn/ **1** adj ⟨life, ball⟩ society; ⟨conversation⟩ polite
2 nm,f socialite

monde /mɔ̃d/ nm (a) world; pas le moins du ~ not in the least; aller or voyager de par le ~ to travel the world; c'est le bout du ~! it's in the back of beyond!; ce n'est pas le bout du ~! it's not such a big deal!; à la face du ~ for all the world to see; en ce bas ~ here below; elle n'est plus de ce ~ she's no longer with us; je n'étais pas encore au ~ I wasn't yet born; le ~ médical the medical world; le ~ animal the animal kingdom; un ~ nous sépare we are worlds apart
(b) people; tout le ~ everybody; tout mon petit ~ my family and friends
(c) society; le beau or grand ~ high society
IDIOMS se faire un ~ de qch to get all worked up about sth; depuis que le ~ est ~ since the beginning of time; c'est un ~! (fam) that's a bit much!

mondial, ~e, mpl **-iaux** /mɔ̃djal, o/ adj world; ⟨success⟩ worldwide; seconde guerre ~e Second World War

mondialement /mɔ̃djalmɑ̃/ adv être ~ connu to be world famous

mondialisation /mɔ̃djalizasjɔ̃/ nf globalization

mondialiser /mɔ̃djalize/ [1] vtr to globalize; to cause [sth] to spread worldwide

mondialisme /mɔ̃djalism/ nm internationalism

mondovision /mɔ̃dɔvizjɔ̃/ nf satellite broadcasting

monétaire /mɔnetɛʀ/ adj ⟨system, stability⟩ monetary; ⟨market⟩ money

monétariste /mɔnetaʀist/ adj, nmf monetarist

monétique /mɔnetik/ nf electronic banking

monétiser /mɔnetize/ [1] vtr to monetize

Mongolie /mɔ̃gɔli/ pr nf Mongolia

mongolien, -ienne /mɔ̃gɔljɛ̃, ɛn/ nm,f Down's syndrome child (controversial)

moniteur, -trice /mɔnitœʀ, tʀis/ **1** nm,f (a) (Aut, Sport) instructor
(b) (in holiday camp) group leader (GB), counselor (US)
2 nm (a) (TV) monitor
(b) (Comput) monitor system

monitorat /mɔnitɔʀa/ nm tutoring; tutorial system

monnaie /mɔnɛ/ nf (a) currency; fausse ~ forged or counterfeit currency
(b) change; faire de la ~ to get some change
(c) coin; battre ~ to mint or strike coins; l'hôtel de la Monnaie, la Monnaie the Mint
(d) (Econ) money
■ ~ d'échange trading currency; bargaining chip; ~ de papier paper money
IDIOMS rendre à qn la ~ de sa pièce to ⋯⟩

m

pay sb back in his/her own coin; **c'est ~ courante** it's commonplace

monnayable /mɔnɛjabl/ *adj* **(a)** (in finance) convertible
(b) ‹*skill, qualification*› marketable

monnayer /mɔnɛje/ [21] *vtr* **(a)** to convert [sth] into cash
(b) to capitalize on ‹*talent, experience*›; **~ qch contre qch** to exchange sth for sth

mono¹ /mono/ *pref* mono; **~chrome** monochrome; **~lingue** monolingual

mono² /mono/ *nf* (in hi-fi) mono

monocellulaire /mɔnosɛlylɛʀ/ *adj* **famille ~** nuclear family

monocle /mɔnɔkl/ *nm* monocle

monocorde /mɔnɔkɔʀd/ *adj* ‹*voice, speech*› monotonous; ‹*instrument*› single-string

monogame /mɔnɔgam/ *adj* monogamous

monogamie /mɔnɔgami/ *nf* monogamy

monoï /mɔnɔj/ *nm inv* coconut oil (*used in cosmetics*)

monologue /mɔnɔlɔg/ *nm* monologue (GB)
■ **~ intérieur** stream of consciousness

mononucléose /mɔnonykleoz/ *nf* mononucleosis; **~ infectieuse** glandular fever

monoparental, **~e**, *mpl* **-aux** /mɔnopaʀɑtal, o/ *adj* **famille ~e** single-parent family

monopole /mɔnɔpɔl/ *nm* monopoly

monopoliser /mɔnɔpɔlize/ [1] *vtr* to monopolize

monoprocesseur /mɔnopʀɔsɛsœʀ/ *nm* single-chip computer

monoski /mɔnɔski/ *nm* **(a)** monoski
(b) monoskiing

monothéiste /mɔnoteist/ *adj* monotheistic

monotone /mɔnɔtɔn/ *adj* monotonous

monotonie /mɔnɔtɔni/ *nf* monotony

monoxyde /mɔnɔksid/ *nm* monoxide

Monseigneur, *pl* **Messeigneurs** /mɔsɛɲœʀ, mesɛɲœʀ/ *nm* Your Highness; Your Eminence; **~ le duc de Parme** His Grace, the duke of Parme

ℱ **monsieur**, *pl* **messieurs** /məsjø, mesjø/ *nm* **(a)** (addressing a man whose name you do not know) **Monsieur** (in a letter) Dear Sir; **bonjour ~!** good morning!
(b) (addressing a man whose name you know, for instance Hallé) **Monsieur** (in a letter) Dear Mr Hallé; **bonjour ~!** good morning, Mr Hallé
(c) (polite form of address) **'Monsieur a sonné?'** 'you rang, sir?'
(d) man; **le double messieurs** the men's doubles; **c'était un (grand) ~!** he was a (true) gentleman!

ℱ indicates a very frequent word

■ **~ Tout le Monde** the man in the street

monstre /mɔstʀ/ **1** *adj* (fam) ‹*task, success, publicity*› huge; ‹*nerve*› colossal
2 *nm* **(a)** monster
(b) freak (of nature)
■ **~ marin** sea monster

monstrueux, **-euse** /mɔstʀyø, øz/ *adj*
(a) ‹*crime, cruelty*› monstrous
(b) hideous; **d'une laideur monstrueuse** hideously ugly
(c) ‹*error*› colossal

monstruosité /mɔstʀyozite/ *nf* **(a)** (of conduct) monstrousness
(b) atrocity
(c) monstrosity; **dire des ~s** to say preposterous things

mont /mɔ/ *nm* mountain
■ **le ~ Blanc** Mont Blanc

montage /mɔtaʒ/ *nm* **(a)** set-up
(b) (of machine) assembly; (of tent) putting up; **chaîne de ~** assembly line
(c) (of film) editing; **salle de ~** cutting room
(d) (of gem) setting
■ **~ photo** photomontage; **~ sonore** sound montage

montagnard, **~e** /mɔtaɲaʀ, aʀd/ **1** *adj* ‹*people, plant*› mountain; ‹*custom*› highland
2 *nm,f* mountain dweller

ℱ **montagne** /mɔtaɲ/ *nf* **(a)** mountain
(b) **la ~** the mountains; **de ~** ‹*road, animal*› mountain; **il neige en haute ~** it's snowing on the upper slopes
■ **~s russes** big dipper, roller coaster
IDIOM se faire une ~ de qch to get really worked up about sth

montagneux, **-euse** /mɔtaɲø, øz/ *adj* mountainous

montant, **~e** /mɔtɑ, ɑt/ **1** *adj* **(a)** ‹*cabin, group*› going up
(b) ‹*road*› uphill
(c) ‹*neck*› high; ‹*socks*› long; **chaussures ~es** ankle boots
2 *nm* **(a)** sum; **le ~ des pertes** the total losses; **d'un ~ de** ‹*deficit, savings*› amounting to; ‹*cheque*› to the amount of; ‹*goods*› for a total of
(b) (of door, window) upright, jamb; transom; (of scaffolding) pole; (of ladder) upright

mont-de-piété, *pl* **monts-de-piété** /mɔdpjete/ *nm* pawnshop, pawnbroker's

monte-charge /mɔtʃaʀʒ/ *nm inv* goods lift (GB) *or* elevator (US)

montée /mɔte/ *nf* **(a)** (up slope) climb; (of mountain) ascent
(b) (of plane) climb
(c) rising; rise; **la ~ des eaux** the rise in the water level; **une brusque ~ d'adrénaline** a rush of adrenaline
(d) (in prices) rise; (in danger) increase
(e) hill; **une légère ~** a slight slope

ℱ **monter** /mɔte/ [1] **1** *vtr* (+ *v avoir*) **(a)** to take [sb/sth] up; to take [sb/sth] upstairs; to

bring [sb/sth] up; to bring [sb/sth] upstairs;
impossible de ∼ **le piano par l'escalier** it's
impossible to get the piano up the stairs
(b) to put [sth] up; to raise ‹shelf›
(c) to go up [sth]; ∼ **la colline à bicyclette** to
cycle up the hill
(d) to turn up ‹volume, gas›
(e) ∼ **les blancs en neige** beat *or* whisk the
eggwhites until stiff
(f) ∼ **qn contre qn** to set sb against sb
(g) to ride ‹horse›
(h) (Zool) to mount
(i) to assemble ‹appliance, unit›; to put up
‹tent, scaffolding›; ∼ **un film** to edit a film
(j) to hatch ‹plot›; to set up ‹company›; to
stage ‹play›; **monté de toutes pièces** ‹story›
fabricated from beginning to end
2 *vi* (+ *v être*) **(a)** to go up; to go upstairs; to
come up; to come upstairs; ‹plane› to climb;
‹bird› to fly up; ‹sun, mist› to rise; **tu es monté**
à pied? did you walk up?; did you come up
on foot?; ∼ **sur** to get onto ‹footpath›; to climb
onto ‹stool›; ∼ **à l'échelle** to climb (up) the
ladder; **faites-les** ∼ send them up
(b) ∼ **dans une voiture/dans un train** to get
in a car/on a train; ∼ **sur** to get on ‹bike,
horse›
(c) ‹road› to go uphill, to climb; ‹ground› to
rise; ∼ **jusqu'à** ‹path, wall› to go up to; ∼ **en**
lacets to wind its way up
(d) ‹garment, water› to come up (**jusqu'à** to)
(e) ‹temperature, price› to rise, to go up; ‹tide›
to come in
(f) ∼ **à** *or* **sur Paris** to go up to Paris
(g) ∼ **(à cheval)** to ride
(h) (Mil) ∼ **à l'assaut** *or* **l'attaque** to mount
an attack
(i) ‹employee› to rise, to move up; ‹artist› to
rise
(j) ‹anger, emotion› to mount; ‹tears› to well
up; **le ton monta** the discussion became
heated
(k) ∼ **à la tête de qn** to go to sb's head
(l) (Aut, Tech) ∼ **à 250 km/h** to go up to
250 km/h
IDIOM se ∼ **la tête** (fam) to get worked up
(colloq)

monteur, -euse /mɔ̃tœʀ, øz/ *nm,f*
(a) fitter
(b) (in film-making) editor
(c) paste-up artist

montgolfière /mɔ̃gɔlfjɛʀ/ *nf* hot-air
balloon

monticule /mɔ̃tikyl/ *nm* **(a)** hillock
(b) mound

montrable /mɔ̃tʀabl/ *adj* ‹person›
presentable; ‹images› suitable for viewing

montre /mɔ̃tʀ/ *nf* watch; **trois heures** ∼ **en**
main three hours exactly

Montréal /mɔ̃ʀeal/ *pr n* Montreal

♂ **montrer** /mɔ̃tʀe/ [1] **1** *vtr* **(a)** to show; ∼
qch à qn to show sb sth
(b) to show ‹feelings, knowledge›

(c) ‹person› to point out ‹track, place, object›;
‹survey, table› to show ‹trend, results›; ∼ **qn**
du doigt to point at sb; to point the finger
at sb
2 **se montrer** *v refl* (+ *v être*) **(a)** to show
oneself to be; to prove (to be); **il faut se** ∼
optimiste we must try to be optimistic
(b) ‹person› to show oneself; ‹sun› to come
out
IDIOMS ∼ **les dents** to bare one's teeth; ∼ **le**
bout de son nez to show one's face; to peep
through

monture /mɔ̃tyʀ/ *nf* **(a)** (for rider) mount
(b) (of glasses) frames; (of ring) setting

monument /mɔnymɑ̃/ *nm* **(a)** monument
(b) (historic) building; **visiter les** ∼**s de**
Paris to see the sights of Paris
(c) **un des** ∼**s de la littérature européenne** a
masterpiece of European literature
■ ∼ **historique** ancient monument; ∼ **aux**
morts war memorial

monumental, ∼e, *mpl* **-aux**
/mɔnymɑ̃tal, o/ *adj* monumental

moquer: se moquer /mɔke/ [1] *v refl* (+ *v*
être) **(a)** **se** ∼ **de** to make fun of
(b) **se** ∼ **de** not to care about
(c) **se** ∼ **du monde** to take people for fools

moquerie /mɔkʀi/ *nf* **(a)** mocking remark
(b) mockery

moquette /mɔkɛt/ *nf* wall-to-wall carpet

moqueur, -euse /mɔkœʀ, øz/ *adj*
mocking

♂ **moral, ∼e**[1], *mpl* **-aux** /mɔʀal, o/ **1** *adj*
(a) moral; **n'avoir aucun sens** ∼ to have no
sense of right and wrong
(b) ‹torture› mental; ‹support› moral
(c) ‹person› moral; ‹conduct› ethical
2 *nm* **(a)** morale; **avoir le** ∼ to be in good
spirits; **avoir le** ∼ **à zéro** (fam) to feel very
down; **remonter le** ∼ **de qn** to raise sb's
spirits
(b) ‹mind›; **au** ∼ **comme au physique**
mentally and physically

♂ **morale**[2] /mɔʀal/ *nf* **(a)** morality; **leur** ∼
their moral code
(b) moral; **faire la** ∼ **à qn** to give sb a lecture
(c) **la** ∼ moral philosophy, ethics

moralement /mɔʀalmɑ̃/ *adv* **(a)** morally,
ethically
(b) psychologically

moralisant, ∼e /mɔʀalizɑ̃, ɑ̃t/ *adj*
moralizing

moralisateur, -trice /mɔʀalizatœʀ,
tʀis/ *adj* moralizing, moralistic

moraliser /mɔʀalize/ [1] *vtr* to clean up;
to reform

moraliste /mɔʀalist/ *nmf* moralist

moralité /mɔʀalite/ *nf* **(a)** morals
(b) (of action) morality
(c) moral; ∼**, ne faites confiance à personne**
the moral is: don't trust anybody

morbide /mɔʀbid/ *adj* morbid

morbidité /mɔʀbidite/ *nf* morbidity

ℱ **morceau**, *pl* ∼**x** /mɔʀso/ *nm* (a) piece, bit;
∼ **de sucre** sugar lump; **manger un** ∼ (fam)
to have a snack
(b) (of meat) cut; **bas** ∼ cheap cut
(c) (Mus) piece; ∼ **de piano** piano piece
(d) (from book) extract
IDIOM **recoller les** ∼**x** to patch things up

morceler /mɔʀsəle/ [19] *vtr* to divide [sth]
up

mordant, ∼**e** /mɔʀdɑ̃, ɑ̃t/ **1** *adj*
(a) caustic, scathing
(b) ⟨*cold*⟩ biting
2 *nm* (a) sarcasm
(b) (fam) (of person, team) zip (colloq)

mordiller /mɔʀdije/ [1] *vtr* to nibble at

mordoré, ∼**e** /mɔʀdɔʀe/ *adj* golden brown

mordre /mɔʀdʀ/ [6] **1** *vtr* to bite
2 mordre à *v+prep* ∼ **à l'appât** *or*
l'hameçon to take the bait
3 *vi* (a) ∼ **dans une pomme** to bite into
an apple
(b) ∼ **sur** to go over ⟨*white line*⟩; to encroach
on ⟨*territory*⟩
(c) (fam) to fall for it (colloq)
4 se mordre *v refl* (+ *v être*) **se** ∼ **la
langue** to bite one's tongue
IDIOM **je m'en suis mordu les doigts** I could
have kicked myself

mordu, ∼**e** /mɔʀdy/ **1** *adj* (fam) (a) **être** ∼
de qch to be mad about sth (colloq)
(b) smitten
2 *nm,f* (fam) fan; **les** ∼**s du ski** skiing fans

morfondre: **se morfondre**
/mɔʀfɔ̃dʀ/ [6] *v refl* (+ *v être*) (a) **se** ∼ **à
attendre** *or* **en attendant** to wait dejectedly
(b) to pine

morgue /mɔʀg/ *nf* (a) morgue; (hospital)
mortuary
(b) arrogance

moribond, ∼**e** /mɔʀibɔ̃, ɔ̃d/ **1** *adj*
⟨*person*⟩ dying; ⟨*civilization*⟩ moribund
2 *nm,f* dying man/woman

morille /mɔʀij/ *nf* morel (mushroom)

morne /mɔʀn/ *adj* (a) gloomy; ⟨*face*⟩ glum
(b) ⟨*landscape, life*⟩ dreary

morose /mɔʀoz/ *adj* morose; gloomy

morosité /mɔʀozite/ *nf* gloom

morphine /mɔʀfin/ *nf* morphine

morphologie /mɔʀfɔlɔʒi/ *nf* morphology

morpion /mɔʀpjɔ̃/ *nm* noughts and crosses
(GB), tick-tack-toe (US)

mors /mɔʀ/ *nm inv* bit; **prendre le** ∼ **aux
dents** to take the bit between its/one's teeth

morse /mɔʀs/ *nm* (a) walrus
(b) (code) ∼ Morse code

morsure /mɔʀsyʀ/ *nf* (a) bite; ∼ **de chien**
dogbite
(b) **la** ∼ **du froid** the biting cold

ℱ **mort¹** /mɔʀ/ *nf* death; **mourir de sa belle** ∼
to die peacefully in old age; **il n'y a pas eu** ∼
d'homme there were no fatalities; **trouver la**
∼ to die; **mise à** ∼ (of condemned) killing; (of
bull) dispatch; **à** ∼ ⟨*fight*⟩ to the death; ⟨*war*⟩
ruthless; ⟨*brake, squeeze*⟩ like mad (colloq)
■ ∼ **cérébrale** brain death
IDIOM **la** ∼ **dans l'âme** with a heavy heart

ℱ **mort²**, ∼**e** /mɔʀ, mɔʀt/ **1** *pp* ▶ MOURIR
2 *pp adj* (a) dead
(b) **je suis** ∼ **de froid** I'm freezing to death; **je
suis** ∼ (fam) I'm dead tired
(c) ⟨*district*⟩ dead; ⟨*season*⟩ slack
(d) ⟨*civilization*⟩ dead; ⟨*city*⟩ lost
3 *nm,f* dead person, dead man/woman
4 *nm* (a) fatality; **il y a eu 12** ∼**s** there
were 12 dead
(b) body; **faire le** ∼ to play dead; to lie low
IDIOM **ne pas y aller de main** ∼**e** (fam) not to
pull any punches

mortalité /mɔʀtalite/ *nf* mortality

mort-aux-rats /mɔʀoʀa/ *nf inv* rat
poison

mortel, **-elle** /mɔʀtɛl/ **1** *adj* (a) ⟨*blow,
illness*⟩ fatal; ⟨*poison*⟩ lethal; ⟨*venom*⟩ deadly
(b) ⟨*cold*⟩ deathly
(c) ⟨*enemy*⟩ mortal
(d) ⟨*person, meeting*⟩ deadly boring
(e) ⟨*being*⟩ mortal
2 *nm,f* mortal

mortellement /mɔʀtɛlmɑ̃/ *adv*
(a) ⟨*injured*⟩ fatally
(b) ⟨*boring*⟩ deadly

mortier /mɔʀtje/ *nm* mortar

mort-né, ∼**e**, *mpl* ∼**s** /mɔʀne/ *adj*
(a) stillborn
(b) ⟨*plan*⟩ abortive

mortuaire /mɔʀtɥeʀ/ *adj* **cérémonie** ∼
funeral ceremony; **veillée** ∼ wake

morue /mɔʀy/ *nf* cod

morve /mɔʀv/ *nf* nasal mucus, snot (slang)

mosaïque /mɔzaik/ *nf* mosaic

Moscou /mɔsku/ *pr n* Moscow

mosquée /mɔske/ *nf* mosque

ℱ **mot** /mo/ *nm* (a) word; **à** ∼**s couverts** in
veiled terms; **au bas** ∼ at least; **il est bête et
le** ∼ **est faible!** he's stupid and that's putting
it mildly!; **dire un** ∼ **à qn** to have a word
with sb; **il ne dit jamais un** ∼ **plus haut que
l'autre** he never raises his voice; **avoir son** ∼
à dire to be entitled to one's say
(b) note; **je t'ai laissé un** ∼ I left you a note
■ ∼ **d'esprit** witticism; ∼ **d'ordre** watchword;
∼ **d'ordre de grève** strike call; ∼ **de passe**
password; ∼**s croisés** crossword; ∼**s doux**
sweet nothings
IDIOMS **ne pas avoir peur des** ∼**s** to call a
spade a spade; **manger ses** ∼**s** to mumble;
se donner le ∼ to pass the word around

motard, ∼**e** /mɔtaʀ, aʀd/ **1** *nm,f* (fam)
biker (colloq)
2 *nm* police motorcyclist

ℱ indicates a very frequent word

mot-clé, *pl* **mots-clés** /mokle/ *nm* key word

♂ **moteur, -trice** /mɔtœʀ, tʀis/ **1** *adj*
(a) ‹*force, principle*› driving; **la voiture a quatre roues motrices** the car has four-wheel drive
(b) (Med) **troubles** ∼**s** motor problems
2 *nm* (a) motor
(b) engine
(c) **être le** ∼ **de qch** to be the driving force behind sth
■ ∼ **éolien** wind turbine

♂ **motif** /mɔtif/ *nm* (a) grounds; **des** ∼**s d'espérer** grounds for hope
(b) reason
(c) motive
(d) pattern; **à** ∼ **floral** with a floral pattern

motion /mɔsjɔ̃/ *nf* motion

motivant, ∼**e** /mɔtivɑ̃, ɑ̃t/ *adj* ‹*salary*› attractive; ‹*work*› rewarding

motivation /mɔtivasjɔ̃/ *nf* (a) motivation
(b) motive; ∼**s profondes** deeper motives

motivé, ∼**e** /mɔtive/ *adj* (a) motivated
(b) ‹*complaint*› justifiable

motiver /mɔtive/ [1] *vtr* (a) to motivate
(b) to lead to ‹*decision, action*›; **motivé par** caused by

moto /mɔto/ *nf* (a) (motor)bike
(b) motorcycling

motocyclette /mɔtosiklɛt/ *nf* motorcycle

motocyclisme /mɔtosiklism/ *nm* motorcycle racing

motocycliste /mɔtosiklist/ **1** *adj* motorcycle
2 *nmf* motorcyclist

motoneige /mɔtonɛʒ/ *nf* snowmobile

motoriser /mɔtɔʀize/ [1] *vtr* to motorize; **être motorisé** (fam) to have transport (GB) *or* transportation (US)

motrice ▶ MOTEUR 1

motte /mɔt/ *nf* ∼ **(de terre)** clod (of earth); ∼ **de gazon** sod, piece of turf; ∼ **(de beurre)** slab of butter

motus /mɔtys/ *excl* (fam) ∼ **(et bouche cousue)!** keep it under your hat!

mou (**mol** *before vowel or mute h*) **molle** /mu, mɔl/ **1** *adj* (a) ‹*substance, cushion*› soft; ‹*blow*› dull
(b) ‹*stomach*› flabby
(c) ‹*person*› listless; ‹*growth*› sluggish
(d) ‹*paint*› soft
(e) ‹*speech*› feeble
2 *nm* (a) wimp (colloq)
(b) (in butchery) lights (GB), lungs (US)
(c) (in rope) slack; **donner du** ∼ **à qn** (fam) to give sb a bit of leeway

mouchard, ∼**e** /muʃaʀ, aʀd/ **1** *nm,f* (fam) (a) grass (GB) (colloq), informer
(b) sneak (colloq)
2 *nm* (a) tachograph
(b) spyhole

moucharder /muʃaʀde/ [1] *vtr* (fam) (a) ∼ **qn** to inform on sb; to squeal (colloq) on sb
(b) to sneak (colloq)

mouche /muʃ/ *nf* (a) fly
(b) patch, beauty spot
(c) bull's eye; **faire** ∼ to hit the bull's eye; (figurative) to be right on target
(d) (Sport) (on foil) button
■ ∼ **verte** greenbottle; ∼ **du vinaigre** fruit fly
IDIOMS **quelle** ∼ **les a piqués?** (fam) what's got (GB) *or* gotten (US) into them?; **prendre la** ∼ to fly off the handle

moucher /muʃe/ [1] **1** *vtr* ∼ **qn** to blow sb's nose; (figurative) (fam) to put sb in their place
2 **se moucher** *v refl* (+ *v être*) to blow one's nose
IDIOM **il ne se mouche pas du pied** *or* **du coude** (fam) he's full of airs and graces

moucheron /muʃʀɔ̃/ *nm* midge

moucheté, ∼**e** /muʃte/ *adj* (a) ‹*material*› flecked; ‹*plumage, fish*› speckled; ‹*coat*› spotted; ‹*horse*› dappled
(b) (Sport) ‹*foil*› buttoned

mouchoir /muʃwaʀ/ *nm* handkerchief; tissue

moudre /mudʀ/ [77] *vtr* to grind

moue /mu/ *nf* pout; **faire la** ∼ to pout; (doubtfully) to pull a face

mouette /mwɛt/ *nf* (sea)gull

moufle /mufl/ *nf* mitten

mouiller /muje/ [1] **1** *vtr* (a) to wet; to get [sth] wet
(b) to drop ‹*anchor*›; to lay ‹*mine*›
2 *vi* to anchor, to drop anchor
3 **se mouiller** *v refl* (+ *v être*) to get wet

mouillette /mujɛt/ *nf* (fam) soldier (colloq), finger of bread (*eaten with a boiled egg*)

moulage /mulaʒ/ *nm* (a) casting; **faire un** ∼ **de qch** to take a cast of sth
(b) (of grain) milling

moulant, ∼**e** /mulɑ̃, ɑ̃t/ *adj* tight-fitting

moule¹ /mul/ *nm* (a) mould (GB), mold (US)
(b) tin, pan (US); ∼ **à gaufre** waffle iron

moule² /mul/ *nf* mussel

mouler /mule/ [1] *vtr* (a) to mould (GB), to mold (US) ‹*substance*›; to cast ‹*bronze*›; to mint ‹*medal*›
(b) to take a cast of
(c) ‹*garment*› to hug

moulin /mulɛ̃/ *nm* mill
■ ∼ **à paroles** (fam) chatterbox; ∼ **à vent** windmill
IDIOMS **apporter de l'eau au** ∼ **de qn** to fuel sb's arguments; **on ne peut être à la fois au four et au** ∼ one can't be in two places at once; **on y entre comme dans un** ∼ (fam) one can just slip in

mouliner /muline/ [1] *vtr* to grind, to mill

moulinet /mulinɛ/ *nm* **faire des** ∼**s avec les bras** to wave one's arms about

moulu, **~e** /muly/ **1** pp ▶ MOUDRE
2 pp adj ‹coffee, pepper› ground
3 adj (fam) ~ **(de fatigue)** worn out

moumoute /mumut/ nf (fam) **(a)** toupee
(b) sheepskin jacket

mourant, **~e** /muRã, ãt/ adj ‹person, animal› dying; ‹light› fading; ‹voice› faint

⚜ **mourir** /muRiR/ [34] vi (+ v être) to die; ~ **de froid** to die of exposure; to die of cold; **je meurs de soif/de froid** I'm dying of thirst/freezing to death; **c'était à ~ (de rire)!** it was hilarious!; ~ **debout** to be active to the end
IDIOMS **partir c'est ~ un peu** to say goodbye is to die a little; **je ne veux pas ~ idiot** (fam) I want to know

mouroir /muRwaR/ nm (derogatory) old people's home, twilight home

mousquetaire /muskətɛR/ nm musketeer

mousqueton /muskətɔ̃/ nm snap clasp

moussant, **~e** /musã, ãt/ adj ‹gel› foaming

mousse¹ /mus/ nm ship's apprentice

mousse² /mus/ nf **(a)** moss
(b) foam; (from soap) lather; (on milk) froth; (on beer) head
(c) ~ **au chocolat** chocolate mousse
(d) foam rubber
■ ~ **carbonique** fire foam; ~ **à raser** shaving foam

mousseline /muslin/ nf **(a)** muslin
(b) chiffon

mousser /muse/ [1] vi to foam; to lather
IDIOM **se faire ~** (fam) to blow one's own trumpet

mousseux, **-euse** /musø, øz/ adj
(a) ‹wine› sparkling; ‹beer› fizzy
(b) ‹lace› frothy

mousson /musɔ̃/ nf monsoon

moustache /mustaʃ/ **1** nf moustache (GB), mustache (US)
2 moustaches nf pl (Zool) whiskers

moustachu, **~e** /mustaʃy/ adj ‹person› with a moustache (GB) or mustache (US)

moustiquaire /mustikɛR/ nf mosquito net

moustique /mustik/ nm mosquito

moutarde /mutaRd/ adj inv, nf mustard
IDIOM **la ~ me monte au nez!** (fam) I'm beginning to see red!

mouton /mutɔ̃/ **1** nm **(a)** sheep
(b) mutton
(c) sheepskin
(d) (derogatory) sheep
2 moutons nm pl **(a)** small fleecy clouds
(b) whitecaps
(c) fluff
■ ~ **à cinq pattes** rare bird
IDIOM **revenons à nos ~s** (fam) let's get back to the point

⚜ indicates a very frequent word

mouture /mutyR/ nf **(a)** (of coffee) grind
(b) **première/nouvelle ~** first/new version

mouvant, **~e** /muvã, ãt/ adj **(a)** ‹ground› unstable
(b) ‹group› shifting
(c) ‹opinion› changing

⚜ **mouvement** /muvmã/ nm **(a)** (gen) movement; **faire un ~** to move; ~ **perpétuel** perpetual motion; **accélérer le ~** to speed up
(b) bustle; **suivre le ~** (figurative) to follow the crowd
(c) impulse, reaction; **un ~ de colère** a surge of anger
(d) **le ~ étudiant** the student protest movement; ~ **de grève** strike, industrial action
(e) **le ~ des idées** the evolution of ideas; **un milieu en ~** a changing environment
(f) (Econ) **le ~ du marché** market fluctuations; ~ **de hausse** upward trend

mouvementé, **~e** /muvmãte/ adj
(a) ‹life, week, trip› eventful, hectic
(b) ‹terrain› rough

mouvoir: se mouvoir /muvwaR/ [43] v refl (+ v être) to move

⚜ **moyen, -enne¹** /mwajɛ̃, ɛn/ **1** adj
(a) medium; medium-sized
(b) ‹income› middle; ‹level› intermediate
(c) average, mean; **le Français ~** the average Frenchman
2 nm **(a)** means, way **(de faire** of doing); **employer les grands ~s** to resort to drastic measures; **(il n'y a) pas ~ de lui faire comprendre qu'il a tort** it's impossible to make him realize he's wrong
(b) (of expression, production) means; (of investigation, payment) method
3 au moyen de phr by means of
4 par le moyen de phr by means of
5 moyens nm pl **(a)** means; **faute de ~s** through lack of money; **avoir de petits ~s** not to be very well off
(b) resources; **donner à qn les ~s de faire** to give sb the means to do
(c) ability; **perdre ses ~s** to go to pieces
■ ~ **de locomotion** or **transport** means of transport (GB) or transportation (US); **Moyen Âge** Middle Ages

moyenâgeux, **-euse** /mwajɛnaʒø, øz/ adj **(a)** medieval
(b) antiquated

moyen-courrier, pl **~s** /mwajɛ̃kuRje/ nm medium-haul airliner

moyennant /mwajenã/ prep ~ **finances** for a fee; ~ **quoi** in view of which; in return for which

moyenne² /mwajɛn/ **1** adj f ▶ MOYEN
2 nf **(a)** average; **la ~ d'âge** the average age; **en ~** on average
(b) half marks (GB), 50%
(c) (Aut) average speed

moyennement /mwajɛnmã/ adv ‹intelligent, wealthy› moderately; ‹like› to a certain extent

Moyen-Orient /mwajɛnɔʀjɑ̃/ *pr nm*
Middle East

moyeu, *pl* ~**x** /mwajø/ *nm* hub

MST /ɛmɛste/ *nf*: *abbr* ▶ MALADIE

mû, mue¹ /my/ ▶ MOUVOIR

mucoviscidose /mykovisidoz/ *nf* cystic
fibrosis

mucus /mykys/ *nm inv* mucus

mue² /my/ *nf* **(a)** (of insect) metamorphosis;
(of reptile) sloughing of the skin; (of bird,
mammal) moulting (GB), molting (US); (of stag)
casting
(b) (of snake, insect) slough, sloughed skin
(c) breaking (GB) *or* changing (US) of voice

muer /mɥe/ [1] **1** *vi* **(a)** ‹insect› to
metamorphose; ‹snake› to slough its skin;
‹bird, mammal› to moult (GB), to molt (US)
(b) sa voix mue, il mue his voice is breaking
(GB) *or* changing (US)
2 se muer *v refl* (+ *v être*) **(a)** to be
transformed
(b) to transform oneself

muet, -ette /mɥe, ɛt/ **1** *adj* **(a)** dumb;
speechless
(b) ‹witness› silent
(c) ‹vowel, consonant› mute
(d) ‹film› silent; ‹role› non-speaking
2 *nm, f* mute

mufle /myfl/ **1** *adj* boorish, loutish
2 *nm* **(a)** (Zool) muffle, muzzle
(b) boor, lout

muflerie /myfləʀi/ *nf* boorishness

mugir /myʒiʀ/ [3] *vi* **(a)** to low; to bellow
(b) ‹wind› to howl; ‹siren› to wail; ‹torrent›
to roar

mugissement /myʒismɑ̃/ *nm* **(a)** (of cow)
lowing; (of bull, ox) bellowing
(b) (of wind) howling; (of waves) roar

muguet /mygɛ/ *nm* lily of the valley

mulâtre /mylɑtʀ/ *adj* mulatto

mule /myl/ *nf* **(a)** female mule
(b) (slipper) mule

mulet /mylɛ/ *nm* (male) mule

mulot /mylo/ *nm* fieldmouse

multi /mylti/ *pref* multi; ~**colore**
multicoloured (GB); ~**media** multimedia;
~**programmation** multiple programming

multicarte /myltikaʀt/ *adj inv*
représentant ~ representative for several
firms

multifonction /myltifɔ̃ksjɔ̃/ *adj inv*
multipurpose; (Comput) multifunction

multipare /myltipaʀ/ *adj* multiparous

⚐ **multiple** /myltipl/ **1** *adj* **(a)** ‹reasons,
occasions› numerous, many; ‹births›
multiple; **à choix** ~ multiple-choice
(b) ‹causes, facets› many, various
(c) (in science) multiple
2 *nm* multiple

multipliable /myltiplijabl/ *adj*
multiplicable

multiplication /myltiplikasjɔ̃/ *nf* **(a)** ~
de increase in the number of
(b) (in mathematics, science) multiplication

multiplicité /myltiplisite/ *nf* multiplicity

multiplier /myltiplije/ [2] **1** *vtr* **(a)** to
multiply
(b) to increase ‹risks, fortune›; to increase
the number of ‹trains, accidents›
2 se multiplier *v refl* (+ *v être*)
(a) ‹branches, villas› to grow in number;
‹incidents› to be on the increase; ‹difficulties›
to increase
(b) ‹animals, germs› to multiply

multipropriété /myltipʀopʀijete/ *nf*
time-sharing

multirisque /myltiʀisk/ *adj* **assurance** ~
comprehensive insurance

multisalle /myltisal/ *adj inv* **cinéma** ~
cinema complex, multiplex

multitude /myltityd/ *nf* **(a) une** ~ **de** a
mass of ‹tourists, objects›; a lot of ‹reasons,
ideas›
(b) multitude, throng

municipal, ~**e**, *mpl* -**aux** /mynisipal,
o/ *adj* ‹council› local, town; city; ‹park, pool›
municipal; **arrêté** ~ bylaw

municipales /mynisipal/ *nf pl* local
elections

municipalité /mynisipalite/ *nf*
(a) municipality
(b) town council; city council

munir /myniʀ/ [3] **1** *vtr* to provide, ~ **un**
bâtiment d'un escalier de secours to put a
fire escape on a building; **muni de** fitted with
2 se munir *v refl* (+ *v être*) **se** ~ **de** to
bring; to take

munitions /mynisjɔ̃/ *nf pl* ammunition

muqueuse /mykøz/ *nf* mucous membrane

⚐ **mur** /myʀ/ **1** *nm* wall; **faire les pieds au** ~
to do a handstand against the wall; (figurative)
to tie oneself up in knots
2 murs *nm pl* (of business) premises; (of
palace, embassy) confines; **être dans ses** ~**s** to
own one's own house
■ ~ **portant** *or* **porteur** load-bearing wall; ~
du son sound barrier; **Mur des lamentations**
Wailing Wall
IDIOMS **faire le** ~ to go over the wall; **mettre**
qn au pied du ~ to call sb's bluff; **être au**
pied du ~ to be up against the wall

mûr, ~**e¹** /myʀ/ *adj* **(a)** ripe
(b) mature; **l'âge** ~ middle age; **après** ~**e**
réflexion after careful consideration
(c) ready; **il est** ~ **pour des aveux** he's ready
to confess
(d) ‹situation› at a decisive stage
IDIOM **en voir des vertes et des pas** ~**es**
(fam) to go through a lot

muraille /myʀaj/ *nf* great wall

m

mural, ∼e, *mpl* **-aux** /myʀal, o/ *adj*
⟨*covering, map*⟩ wall; ⟨*plant*⟩ climbing
mûre² /myʀ/ **1** *adj f* ▶ MÛR
2 *nf* blackberry
mûrement /myʀmã/ *adv* ∼ **réfléchi**
carefully thought through
murer /myʀe/ [1] *vtr* to build a wall around
[sth]; to brick [sth] up; to block [sth] off
muret /myʀɛ/ *nm* low wall
mûrier /myʀje/ *nm* mulberry tree
mûrir /myʀiʀ/ [3] **1** *vtr* **(a)** to ripen ⟨*fruit*⟩
(b) to mature ⟨*person*⟩; to develop ⟨*plan*⟩
2 *vi* **(a)** ⟨*fruit*⟩ to ripen
(b) ⟨*person, talent*⟩ to mature; ⟨*plan, idea*⟩ to
evolve; ⟨*passion*⟩ to develop
(c) ⟨*abscess*⟩ to come to a head
murmure /myʀmyʀ/ *nm* **(a)** murmur
(b) ∼s mutterings
(c) (of wind) whisper
murmurer /myʀmyʀe/ [1] **1** *vtr* **(a)** to
murmur
(b) to say; **on murmure qu'il est riche** he is
rumoured (GB) to be rich
2 *vi* ⟨*person*⟩ to murmur; ⟨*wind*⟩ to whisper
musaraigne /myzaʀɛɲ/ *nf* (Zool) shrew
musc /mysk/ *nm* musk
muscade /myskad/ *nf* nutmeg
muscle /myskl/ *nm* muscle
musclé, ∼e /myskle/ *adj* **(a)** muscular
(b) ⟨*music, speech*⟩ powerful; ⟨*reaction*⟩
strong; ⟨*intervention*⟩ tough
(c) (Econ) competitive
muscler /myskle/ [1] **1** *vtr* **(a)** ∼ **les bras**
to develop the arm muscles
(b) to strengthen
2 se muscler *v refl* (+ *v être*) to develop
one's muscles
musculaire /myskylɛʀ/ *adj* muscle;
muscular
musculation /myskylasjõ/ *nf* (**exercices
de**) ∼ (gen) bodybuilding; (Med) exercises to
strengthen the muscles; **salle de** ∼ weights
room
musculature /myskylatyʀ/ *nf*
musculature
muse /myz/ *nf* **(a)** Muse
(b) (figurative) muse
museau, *pl* ∼**x** /myzo/ *nm* **(a)** muzzle;
snout; nose
(b) (fam) face
musée /myze/ *nm* museum; art gallery
(GB), art museum (US); **une ville** ∼ a city of
great historical and artistic importance
museler /myzle/ [19] *vtr* to muzzle
muselière /myzəljɛʀ/ *nf* muzzle
musette¹ /myzɛt/ *nm* accordion music
musette² /myzɛt/ *nf* **(a)** haversack
(b) lunchbag

✔ indicates a very frequent word

muséum /myzeɔm/ *nm* ∼ (**d'histoire
naturelle**) natural history museum
musical, ∼e, *mpl* **-aux** /myzikal, o/ *adj*
⟨*event*⟩ musical; ⟨*critic*⟩ music; ⟨*choice*⟩ of
music
music-hall, *pl* ∼s /mysikol/ *nm* music hall
musicien, **-ienne** /myzisjɛ̃, ɛn/ **1** *adj*
musical
2 *nm,f* musician
✔ **musique** /myzik/ *nf* music; **travailler en**
∼ to work with music in the background;
mettre en ∼ to set [sth] to music; **faire de la**
∼ to play an instrument; **une** ∼ **de film** a
film score
IDIOMS **connaître la** ∼ (fam) to know the
score (colloq); **je ne peux pas aller plus vite
que la** ∼ (fam) I can't go any faster than
I'm already going; **être réglé comme du
papier à** ∼ (fam) ⟨*person*⟩ to be as regular as
clockwork; ⟨*conference, project*⟩ to go very
smoothly
✔ **musulman**, ∼e /myzylmã, an/ *adj, nm,f*
Muslim
mutabilité /mytabilite/ *nf* mutability
mutant, ∼e /mytã, ãt/ *adj, nm,f* mutant
mutation /mytasjõ/ *nf* **(a)** transfer
(b) transformation; **en pleine** ∼ undergoing
radical transformation
(c) mutation
muter /myte/ [1] *vtr* to transfer ⟨*official*⟩
mutilation /mytilasjõ/ *nf* mutilation
mutilé, ∼e /mytile/ *nm,f* disabled person;
∼ **de guerre** disabled war veteran
mutiler /mytile/ [1] *vtr* to mutilate
mutin, ∼e /mytɛ̃, in/ **1** *adj* mischievous
2 *nm* mutineer; rioter
mutiner: se mutiner /mytine/ [1] *v refl*
(+ *v être*) to mutiny; to riot
mutinerie /mytinʀi/ *nf* mutiny; riot
mutisme /mytism/ *nm* silence
mutuel, **-elle¹** /mytɥɛl/ *adj* mutual
mutuelle² /mytɥɛl/ *nf* mutual insurance
company
mutuellement /mytɥɛlmã/ *adv*
mutually; **s'aider** ∼ to help each other
myopathe /mjɔpat/ *nmf* myopathy patient
myopathie /mjɔpati/ *nf* myopathy
myope /mjɔp/ *adj* short-sighted (GB), near-
sighted (US)
myopie /mjɔpi/ *nf* short-sightedness (GB),
near-sightedness (US)
myosotis /mjɔzɔtis/ *nm inv* forget-me-not
myriade /miʀjad/ *nf* myriad (**de** of)
myrrhe /miʀ/ *nf* myrrh
myrtille /miʀtij/ *nf* bilberry, blueberry
✔ **mystère** /mistɛʀ/ *nm* **(a)** mystery
(b) secrecy
(c) rite
mystérieusement /misteʀjøzmã/ *adv*
mysteriously

mystérieux, -ieuse /misteʀjø, øz/ *adj*
mysterious
mysticisme /mistisism/ *nm* mysticism
mystification /mistifikasjɔ̃/ *nf* **(a)** hoax
(b) myth
mystique /mistik/ **1** *adj* mystical
   2 *nf* **(a)** mysticism
   (b) mystique

(c) blind belief
mythe /mit/ *nm* myth
mythique /mitik/ *adj* mythical
mythologie /mitɔlɔʒi/ *nf* mythology
mythologique /mitɔlɔʒik/ *adj*
mythological
mythomane /mitɔman/ *adj, nmf*
mythomaniac

n, N /ɛn/ **1** *nm inv* **(a)** (letter) n, N
   (b) n° (*written abbr* = **numéro**) no
   2 N *nf* (*abbr* = **nationale**) la N7 the N7
n' ▸ NE
nabot, ∼e /nabo, ɔt/ *nm,f* (offensive) dwarf
nacelle /nasɛl/ *nf* **(a)** (of hot-air balloon)
gondola
   (b) carrycot (GB), carrier (US)
   (c) (of worker) cradle
nacre /nakʀ/ *nf* mother-of-pearl
nacré, ∼e /nakʀe/ *adj* pearly
nage /naʒ/ *nf* **(a)** swimming; **200 mètres
quatre ∼s** 200 metres (GB) medley; **traverser
à la ∼** to swim across
   (b) être en ∼ to be in a sweat
   ■ **∼ indienne** sidestroke; **∼ libre** freestyle
nageoire /naʒwaʀ/ *nf* **(a)** (of fish) fin
   (b) (of seal) flipper
nager /naʒe/ [13] **1** *vtr* to swim
   2 *vi* **(a)** to swim
   (b) (figurative) **∼ dans le bonheur** to bask in
contentment; **elle nage dans sa robe** her
dress is far too big for her
   (c) (fam) to be absolutely lost
   IDIOM **∼ entre deux eaux** to run with the
hare and hunt with the hounds
nageur, -euse /naʒœʀ, øz/ *nm,f* swimmer
naguère /nagɛʀ/ *adv* **(a)** quite recently
   (b) formerly
naïf, naïve /naif, iv/ *adj* naïve
nain, ∼e /nɛ̃, nɛn/ **1** *adj* ‹tree› dwarf; ‹dog›
miniature
   2 *nm,f* dwarf
♂ **naissance** /nɛsɑ̃s/ *nf* **(a)** (gen) birth; (of
rumour) start; **de ∼** ‹Italian, French› by birth;
‹deaf› from birth; **à ma ∼** when I was born
   (b) à la ∼ du cou at the base of the neck
naissant, ∼e /nɛsɑ̃, ɑ̃t/ *adj* new
♂ **naître** /nɛtʀ/ [74] *vi* (+ *v être*) **(a)** to be born;
elle est née le 5 juin she was born on 5 June;
le bébé doit ∼ à la fin du mois the baby is
due at the end of the month; **l'enfant à ∼** the
unborn baby *or* child; **je l'ai vu ∼** (figurative) I
have known him since he was a baby

   (b) (figurative) ‹idea› to be born; ‹company› to
come into existence; ‹love› to spring up; ‹day›
to break; **faire ∼** to give rise to ‹hope›; **voir ∼**
to see the birth of ‹newspaper, century›
naïve ▸ NAÏF
naïvement /naivmɑ̃/ *adv* naively;
artlessly
naïveté /naivte/ *nf* naivety
nanisme /nanism/ *nm* dwarfism
nantir /nɑ̃tiʀ/ [3] *vtr* **∼ qn de** to provide sb
with; to award [sth] to sb
nantis /nɑ̃ti/ *nm pl* **les ∼** the well-off
naphtaline /naftalin/ *nf* mothballs
nappe /nap/ *nf* **(a)** tablecloth
   (b) (of oil, gas) layer; (of water, fire) sheet; (of
fog) blanket
napper /nape/ [1] *vtr* (Culin) to coat; to glaze
napperon /napʀɔ̃/ *nm* mat
narcisse /naʀsis/ *nm* (flower) narcissus
narcissisme /naʀsisism/ *nm* narcissism
narco(-) /naʀko/ *pref* drug; **∼-dollars**/
-trafiquant drug money/trafficker
narcotique /naʀkɔtik/ *adj, nm* narcotic
narguer /naʀge/ [1] *vtr* to taunt ‹person›
narine /naʀin/ *nf* nostril
narquois, ∼e /naʀkwa, az/ *adj* mocking
narrateur, -trice /naʀatœʀ, tʀis/ *nm,f*
narrator
narratif, -ive /naʀatif, iv/ *adj* narrative
narration /naʀasjɔ̃/ *nf* narration
narrer /naʀe/ [1] *vtr* to relate
nasal, ∼e, mpl -aux /nazal, o/ *adj* nasal;
hémorragie ∼e heavy nosebleed
naseau, pl ∼x /nazo/ *nm* nostril
nasillard, ∼e /nazijaʀ, aʀd/ *adj* ‹voice›
nasal; ‹instrument› tinny
nasillement /nazijmɑ̃/ *nm* nasal twang
nasiller /nazije/ [1] *vi* **(a)** to speak with a
nasal voice
   (b) ‹duck› to quack
nasse /nas/ *nf* **(a)** keepnet
   (b) (figurative) net

natal, ~**e**, *mpl* ~**s** /natal/ *adj* native
nataliste /natalist/ *adj* ‹*policy*› pro-birth
natalité /natalite/ *nf* (**taux de**) ~ birthrate
natation /natasjɔ̃/ *nf* swimming
natif, -ive /natif, iv/ *adj* ~ **de** native of
⚐ **nation** /nasjɔ̃/ *nf* nation
  ■ **les Nations unies** the United Nations
⚐ **national**, ~**e**[1], *mpl* **-aux** /nasjɔnal, o/ *adj*
  national
nationale[2] /nasjɔnal/ *nf* ≈ A road (GB),
  highway (US)
nationalisation /nasjɔnalizasjɔ̃/ *nf*
  nationalization
nationaliser /nasjɔnalize/ [1] *vtr* to
  nationalize
nationalisme /nasjɔnalism/ *nm*
  nationalism
nationalité /nasjɔnalite/ *nf* nationality
nativité /nativite/ *nf* nativity
natte /nat/ *nf* (**a**) plait (GB), braid (US)
  (**b**) mat
natter /nate/ [1] *vtr* to plait
naturalisation /natyralizasjɔ̃/ *nf*
  naturalization
naturalisé, ~**e** /natyralize/ *adj* naturalized
naturaliser /natyralize/ [1] *vtr* to
  naturalize ‹*foreigner, species*›; to assimilate
  ‹*word, custom*›
naturalisme /natyralism/ *nm* naturalism
⚐ **nature** /natyr/ [1] *adj inv* (**a**) ‹*yoghurt*›
  plain; ‹*tea*› black
  (**b**) (fam) ‹*person*› natural
  [2] *nf* (**a**) nature; **protection de la** ~
  protection of the environment; **en pleine**
  ~ in the heart of the countryside; **lâcher**
  qn dans la ~ to leave sb in the middle of
  nowhere; (figurative) to let sb loose
  (**b**) **de** ~ **à faire** likely to do; **des offres de**
  toute ~ offers of all kinds
  (**c**) **peindre d'après** ~ to paint from life; **plus**
  vrai que ~ larger than life
  (**d**) **en** ~ ‹*pay*› in kind
  ■ ~ **humaine** human nature; ~ **morte** still life;
  ▸ PETIT
⚐ **naturel, -elle** /natyrɛl/ [1] *adj* natural
  [2] *nm* (**a**) nature, disposition; **être d'un** ~
  craintif to be timid by nature
  (**b**) **il manque de** ~ he's not very natural
  (**c**) **au** ~ ‹*rice*› plain; ‹*tuna*› in brine
⚐ **naturellement** /natyrɛlmã/ *adv* (gen)
  naturally; (obviously) of course
naturisme /natyrism/ *nm* nudism
naturiste /natyrist/ *nmf* naturist (GB),
  nudist
naufrage /nofraʒ/ *nm* shipwreck, sinking;
  faire ~ ‹*ship*› to be wrecked; ‹*sailor*› to be
  shipwrecked; ‹*company*› to collapse
naufragé, ~**e** /nofraʒe/ [1] *adj*
  shipwrecked

  [2] *nm,f* survivor (of a shipwreck); castaway
nauséabond, ~**e** /nozeabɔ̃, ɔ̃d/ *adj*
  sickening, nauseating
nausée /noze/ *nf* nausea
nautique /notik/ *adj* ‹*science*› nautical;
  ‹*sports*› water
nautisme /notism/ *nm* water sports
naval, ~**e**, *mpl* ~**s** /naval/ *adj*
  (**a**) ‹*industry*› shipbuilding
  (**b**) (Mil) naval
navet /navɛ/ *nm* (**a**) turnip
  (**b**) rubbishy film (GB), turkey (US) (colloq)
navette /navɛt/ *nf* shuttle; shuttle service;
  faire la ~ (to work) to commute
  ■ ~ **spatiale** space shuttle
navigable /navigabl/ *adj* navigable
navigant, ~**e** /navigɑ̃, ɑ̃t/ *adj* **personnel**
  ~ (on plane) flight personnel; (Naut) seagoing
  personnel; **mécanicien** ~ flight engineer
navigateur, -trice /navigatœr, tris/ *nm,f*
  (**a**) navigator
  (**b**) sailor
  (**c**) (Comput) browser
navigation /navigasjɔ̃/ *nf* navigation
  ■ ~ **de plaisance** boating; yachting
naviguer /navige/ [1] *vi* (**a**) ‹*ship, sailor*› to
  sail; ‹*pilot, plane*› to fly; **en état de** ~ ‹*ship*›
  seaworthy
  (**b**) to navigate
  (**c**) (Comput) to browse; ~ **sur l'Internet** to
  surf the Internet
⚐ **navire** /navir/ [1] *nm* ship
  [2] **navire-** (*combining form*) ~**-école**
  -usine training/factory ship; ~**s-citernes**
  tankers
  ■ ~ **amiral** flagship; ~ **de guerre** warship
navrant, ~**e** /navrɑ̃, ɑ̃t/ *adj* (**a**) depressing
  (**b**) distressing
navré, ~**e** /navre/ *adj* **je suis vraiment** ~ I
  am terribly sorry; **avoir l'air** ~ to look sad
nazi, ~**e** /nazi/ *adj, nm,f* Nazi
nazisme /nazism/ *nm* Nazism
⚐ **ne** /nə/ (**n'** *before vowel or mute h*) *adv*

  ■ **Note** In cases where *ne* is used with *pas,*
  jamais, guère, rien, plus, aucun, personne etc,
  one should consult the corresponding entry. –
  ne + verb + *que* is treated in the entry below.

  je n'ai que 20 euros I've only got 20 euros; **il**
  n'y a que lui pour être aussi désagréable only
  he can be so unpleasant; **tu n'es qu'un raté**
  you're nothing but a loser (colloq); **je n'ai que**
  faire de tes conseils you can keep your advice
né, ~**e** /ne/ [1] *pp* ▸ NAÎTRE
  [2] *pp adj* **bien** ~ highborn; **Madame**
  Masson ~**e Roux** Mrs Masson née Roux
  [3] **(-)né** (*combining form*) **musicien(-)/**
  écrivain(-)~ born musician/writer
⚐ **néanmoins** /neɑ̃mwɛ̃/ *adv* nevertheless
néant /neɑ̃/ *nm* (**a**) **le** ~ nothingness;
  réduire à ~ to destroy ‹*argument, hopes*›
  (**b**) 'revenus: ~' 'income: nil'

⚐ indicates a very frequent word

nébuleux, -euse /nebylø, øz/ *adj* **(a)** ‹sky›
cloudy
(b) ‹idea› vague, nebulous

◆ **nécessaire** /nesesɛʀ/ **1** *adj* necessary
(à for); **plus qu'il n'est ~** more than is
necessary; **les voix ~s pour renverser le
gouvernement** the votes needed in order to
overthrow the government
2 *nm* **(a) faire le ~** to do what is necessary
(b) essentials; **le strict ~** the bare essentials
■ **~ de couture** sewing kit; **~ à ongles** manicure set; **~ de toilette** toiletries

nécessairement /nesesɛʀmɑ̃/ *adv*
necessarily; **passe-t-on ~ par Oslo?** do you
have to go via Oslo?

◆ **nécessité** /nesesite/ *nf* **(a)** necessity; **~
urgente** urgent need; **~ de qch/de faire/
d'être** need for sth/to do/to be; **de première
~** vital; **par ~** out of necessity; **être dans la
~ de faire** to have no choice but to do
(b) need; **être dans la ~** to be in need
IDIOM ~ fait loi (Proverb) necessity knows
no law

nécessiter /nesesite/ **1** *vtr* to require

nécessiteux, -euse /nesesitø, øz/ *nm,f*
needy person; **les ~** the needy

nec plus ultra /nɛkplyzyltʀa/ *nm inv* **le
~** the last word (**de** in)

nécrologie /nekʀɔlɔʒi/ *nf* deaths column
nécrologique /nekʀɔlɔʒik/ *adj* obituary
nectar /nɛktaʀ/ *nm* nectar

néerlandais, ~e /neɛʀlɑ̃dɛ, ɛz/ **1** *adj*
Dutch
2 *nm* (language) Dutch

Néerlandais, ~e /neɛʀlɑ̃dɛ, ɛz/ *nm,f*
Dutchman/Dutchwoman; **les ~** the Dutch

nef /nɛf/ *nf* nave; **~ latérale** side aisle

néfaste /nefast/ *adj* harmful

◆ **négatif, -ive¹** /negatif, iv/ **1** *adj* negative
2 *nm* negative

négation /negasjɔ̃/ *nf* **(a)** negation
(b) (in grammar) negative

négative² /negativ/ **1** *adj f* ▶ NÉGATIF 1
2 *nf* **répondre par la ~** to reply in the
negative

négativement /negativmɑ̃/ *adv*
negatively

négligé, ~e /negliʒe/ **1** *adj* ‹person›
sloppy; ‹house› neglected; ‹injury› untreated
2 *nm* negligee

négligeable /negliʒabl/ *adj* ‹amount›
negligible; ‹person› insignificant

négligemment /negliʒamɑ̃/ *adv*
(a) nonchalantly
(b) carelessly

négligence /negliʒɑ̃s/ *nf* **(a)** negligence
(b) oversight

négligent, ~e /negliʒɑ̃, ɑ̃t/ *adj* ‹employee›
negligent, careless; ‹glance› casual

négliger /negliʒe/ [13] **1** *vtr* (gen) to
neglect; to leave untreated ‹cold›; to ignore

‹rule›; **une offre qui n'est pas à ~** an offer
that's worth considering; **~ de faire** to fail
to do
2 se négliger *v refl* (+ *v être*) **(a)** not to
take care over one's appearance
(b) not to look after oneself

négoce /negɔs/ *nm* trade (**avec** with)

négociable /negɔsjabl/ *adj* negotiable

négociant, ~e /negɔsjɑ̃, ɑ̃t/ *nm,f*
merchant; wholesaler

négociateur, -trice /negɔsjatœʀ,
tʀis/ *nm,f* negotiator

négociation /negɔsjasjɔ̃/ *nf* negotiation

négocier /negɔsje/ [2] *vtr, vi* to negotiate

nègre /nɛgʀ/ *nm* **(a)** (offensive) Negro
(b) ghostwriter

négresse /negʀɛs/ *nf* (offensive) Negress

négritude /negʀityd/ *nf* black identity,
negritude

négroïde /negʀɔid/ *adj* Negroid

◆ **neige** /nɛʒ/ *nf* snow; **~ fondue** slush; sleet;
aller à la ~ to go skiing; **blancs battus en ~**
stiffly beaten eggwhites
IDIOM être blanc comme ~ to be completely
innocent

neiger /neʒe/ [13] *v impers* to snow

nénuphar /nenyfaʀ/ *nm* waterlily

néo /neo/ *pref* neo

néologisme /neɔlɔʒism/ *nm* neologism

néon /neɔ̃/ *nm* **(a)** neon
(b) neon light

néo-zélandais, ~e /neozelɑ̃dɛ, ɛz/ *adj*
New Zealand

Néo-Zélandais, ~e /neozelɑ̃dɛ, ɛz/ *nm,f*
New Zealander

népotisme /nepɔtism/ *nm* nepotism

nerf /nɛʀ/ **(a)** nerve; **être malade des ~s** to
suffer from nerves
(b) spirit, go (colloq); **redonner du ~ à qn** to
put new heart into sb
IDIOMS jouer avec les ~s de qn to be
deliberately annoying; **ses ~s ont lâché** he/
she went to pieces; **avoir les ~s à fleur de
peau** to have frayed nerves; **avoir les ~s en
pelote** (fam) *or* **en boule** (fam) *or* **à vif** to be
really wound up; **être sur les ~s, avoir ses
~s** (fam) to be on edge; **taper** (fam) *or* **porter
sur les ~s de qn** to get on sb's nerves; **être à
bout de ~s** to be at the end of one's tether *or*
rope (US); **passer ses ~s sur** (fam) **qn/qch** to
take it out on sb/sth; **l'argent est le ~ de la
guerre** money is the sinews of war

nerveusement /nɛʀvøzmɑ̃/ *adv*
(a) ‹wait› nervously
(b) **être épuisé ~** to be suffering from
nervous exhaustion

nerveux, -euse /nɛʀvø, øz/ **1** *adj*
(a) ‹person› tense
(b) ‹engine› responsive; ‹horse› vigorous
(c) (Anat) ‹cell› nerve; ‹system› nervous
2 *nm,f* nervous person

nervosité /nɛʀvozite/ *nf* (a) nervousness
(b) excitability
(c) (of engine) responsiveness

nervure /nɛʀvyʀ/ *nf* (of leaf) nervure

n'est-ce pas /nɛspa/ *adv* c'est joli, ∼?
it's pretty, isn't it?; ∼ qu'il est gentil? isn't
he nice?

ᵈ **net, nette** /nɛt/ **1** *adj* (a) ‹price, weight›
net
(b) ‹change› marked; ‹tendency› distinct
(c) ‹victory, memory› clear; ‹situation›
clearcut; ‹handwriting› neat; ‹break› clean;
en avoir le cœur ∼ to be clear in one's mind
about it
(d) ‹house, hands› clean; (figurative)
‹conscience› clear; faire place nette to clear
everything away
2 *adv* ‹stop› dead; ‹kill› outright; ‹refuse›
flatly; la corde a cassé ∼ the rope snapped

Net /nɛt/ *nm* le ∼ the Net

netiquette /netikɛt/ *nf* netiquette

nettement /nɛtmã/ *adv* (a) ‹increase,
deteriorate› markedly; ‹dominate› clearly;
‹prefer› definitely
(b) ‹see, say› clearly; ‹refuse› flatly;
‹remember› distinctly

netteté /nɛtte/ *nf* (a) (of image, features)
sharpness; (of result, statement) definite nature
(b) (of place) cleanness; (of work) neatness

nettoyage /netwajaʒ/ *nm* (a) clean(up); ∼
de printemps spring-cleaning
(b) cleaning; (of skin) cleansing; ∼ à sec
dry-cleaning
(c) opération de ∼ (fam) (by army, police)
mopping-up operation

nettoyant /nɛtwajã/ *nm* cleaning agent

nettoyer /netwaje/ [23] *vtr* (a) (gen) to
clean; to clean up ‹garden›; to clean out
‹river›; to clean off ‹stain›
(b) (figurative) ‹police› to clean up ‹town›

ᵈ **neuf¹** /nœf/ *adj inv, pron, nm inv* nine

ᵈ **neuf², neuve** /nœf, nœv/ **1** *adj* new; tout
∼ brand new; 'état ∼' 'as new'
2 *nm inv* new; quoi de ∼? what's new?;
habillé de ∼ dressed in new clothes; faire du
∼ avec du vieux to revamp things
IDIOM faire peau neuve to undergo a transformation

neurasthénie /nøʀasteni/ *nf* depression

neurasthénique /nøʀastenik/ *nmf*
depressive

neuro /nøʀo/ *pref* neuro

neurone /nøʀɔn/ *nm* neurone

neutralisation /nøtʀalizasjɔ̃/ *nf*
neutralization

neutraliser /nøtʀalize/ [1] *vtr* to
neutralize

neutralité /nøtʀalite/ *nf* neutrality

neutre /nøtʀ/ *adj* neutral; neuter; ∼ en
carbone carbon neutral

neutron /nøtʀɔ̃/ *nm* neutron

neuvième /nœvjɛm/ **1** *adj* ninth
2 *nf* (Sch) third year of primary school,
age 8–9

neveu, *pl* ∼x /n(ə)vø/ *nm* nephew

névralgie /nevʀalʒi/ *nf* neuralgia

névralgique /nevʀalʒik/ *adj* (a) neuralgic
(b) point ∼ key point

névrose /nevʀoz/ *nf* neurosis

névrosé, ∼e /nevʀoze/ *adj, nm,f* neurotic

New York /njujɔʀk/ *pr n* (a) New York
City
(b) l'État de ∼ New York (State)

ᵈ **nez** /ne/ *nm* nose; ∼ en trompette turned-
up nose; ça sent le parfum à plein ∼ (fam)
there's a strong smell of perfume; je n'ai
pas mis le ∼ dehors (fam) I didn't set foot
outside; mettre le ∼ à la fenêtre (fam) to show
one's face at the window; lever le ∼ to look
up; tu as le ∼ dessus (fam) it's staring you in
the face; avoir du ∼, avoir le ∼ fin (figurative)
to be shrewd
IDIOMS mener qn par le bout du ∼ (fam) to
have sb under one's thumb; avoir qn dans
le ∼ (fam) to have it in for sb; avoir un coup
or verre dans le ∼ (fam) to have had one too
many (colloq); au ∼ (et à la barbe) de qn right
under sb's nose; filer *or* passer sous le ∼ de
qn to slip through sb's fingers; se casser le
∼ (fam) to fail

NF /ɛnɛf/ *adj, nf* (*abbr* = **norme
française**) French manufacturing
standard

ᵈ **ni** /ni/ *conj* nor, or; elle ne veut ∼ ne peut
changer she doesn't want to change, nor can
she; elle ne veut pas le voir ∼ lui parler she
doesn't want to see him or talk to him; ∼…
∼ neither… nor; ∼ l'un ∼ l'autre neither of
them; il ne m'a dit ∼ oui ∼ non he didn't say
yes or no
IDIOMS ∼ vu ∼ connu (fam) on the sly (colloq); c'est ∼ fait ∼ à faire (fam) it's a botched
job (colloq); il n'a fait ∼ une ∼ deux (fam) he
didn't have a second's hesitation

niais, ∼e /njɛ, njɛz/ *adj* stupid

niaiserie /njɛzʀi/ *nf* (a) stupidity
(b) stupid *or* inane remark

nicaraguayen, -enne /nikaʀagwajɛ̃,
ɛn/ *adj* Nicaraguan

niche /niʃ/ *nf* (a) kennel, doghouse (US)
(b) recess; (for statue) niche
(c) (fam) trick

nichée /niʃe/ *nf* (of birds) brood; (of mice)
litter

nicher /niʃe/ [1] **1** *vi* (a) ‹bird› to nest
(b) (fam) ‹person› to live
2 se nicher *v refl* (+ *v être*) (a) ‹bird› to
nest
(b) ‹person, cottage› to nestle

ᵈ indicates a very frequent word

nickel /nikɛl/ **1** *adj* (fam) spotless
2 *nm* nickel

nicotine /nikɔtin/ *nf* nicotine

nid /ni/ *nm* nest
■ ~ **d'aigle** eyrie; ~ **d'ange** snuggle suit; ~ **à poussière** dust trap; ~ **de résistance** pocket of resistance

nid-d'abeilles, *pl* **nids-d'abeilles** /nidabɛj/ *nm* honeycomb weave

nid-de-poule, *pl* **nids-de-poule** /nidpul/ *nm* pothole

nièce /njɛs/ *nf* niece

nième /ɛnjɛm/ ▶ ÉNIÈME

nier /nje/ [2] *vtr* to deny ‹fact, existence›

nigaud, **~e** /nigo, od/ *adj* silly

nigérian, **~e** /niʒeRjɑ̃, an/ *adj* Nigerian

nigérien, **-ienne** /niʒeRjɛ̃, ɛn/ *adj* of Niger

nihiliste /niilist/ *adj*, *nmf* nihilist

nîmois, **~e** /nimwa, az/ *adj* of Nîmes

nipper: **se nipper** /nipe/ [1] *v refl* (+ *v être*) (fam) to get rigged out in one's Sunday best (colloq)

nippes /nip/ *nf pl* (fam) rags (colloq), old clothes

nippon, **-onne** /nipɔ̃, ɔn/ *adj* Japanese

niveau, *pl* **~x** /nivo/ *nm* (gen) level; (of knowledge, education) standard; **au ~ du sol** at ground level; **être de ~** to be level; **arrivé au ~ du bus, il...** when he drew level with the bus he...; **bâtiment sur deux ~x** two-storey (GB) *or* two-story (US) building; **'~ bac + 3'** baccalaureate or equivalent plus 3 years' higher education; **de haut ~** ‹athlete› top; ‹candidate› high-calibre (GB), **au plus haut ~** ‹discussion› top-level
■ ~ **de langue** register; ~ **social** social status; ~ **sonore** sound level; ~ **de vie** standard of living

nivelage /nivlaʒ/ *nm* standardization

niveler /nivle/ [19] *vtr* (a) to level ‹ground›
(b) to bring [sth] to the same level ‹salaries›; ~ **par le bas/haut** to level down/up

nobiliaire /nɔbiljɛR/ *adj* nobiliary

noble /nɔbl/ **1** *adj* (gen) noble; ‹family› aristocratic; ‹person› of noble birth
2 *nmf* nobleman/noblewoman

noblement /nɔbləmɑ̃/ *adv* (a) nobly
(b) handsomely

noblesse /nɔblɛs/ *nf* nobility; **la petite ~** the gentry

noce /nɔs/ *nf* (a) (fam) party; **faire la ~** (figurative) (fam) to live it up (colloq), to party (colloq)
(b) wedding party
(c) **~s** wedding

noceur, **-euse** /nɔsœR, øz/ *nm,f* (fam) party animal (colloq)

nocif, **-ive** /nɔsif, iv/ *adj* noxious, harmful

noctambule /nɔktɑ̃byl/ *nmf* night owl

nocturne¹ /nɔktyRn/ *adj* ‹attack› night; ‹animal› nocturnal; **la vie ~ à Londres** nightlife in London

nocturne² /nɔktyRn/ *nf* (a) (in sport) evening fixture
(b) (of shop) late-night opening

Noël /nɔɛl/ *nm* Christmas; **'Joyeux ~'** 'Merry Christmas'; **de ~** ‹tree, gift› Christmas

nœud /nø/ *nm* (a) (gen) knot; **faire un ~ de cravate** to tie a tie
(b) (of matter) crux; (of play) core
■ ~ **coulant** slipknot; ~ **papillon** bow tie; ~ **de vipères** nest of vipers

noir, **~e¹** /nwaR/ **1** *adj* (a) (gen) black; ‹eyes› dark; ‹person, race› black; **être ~ de coups** to be black and blue; **être ~ de monde** to be swarming with people
(b) ‹street› dark; **il fait ~** it's dark
(c) ‹year› bad, bleak; ‹poverty› dire; ‹idea› gloomy, dark
(d) ‹look› black; ‹plot, design› evil, dark; **se mettre dans une colère ~e** to fly into a towering rage
2 *nm* (a) (colour) black
(b) **avoir du ~ sur le visage** to have a black mark on one's face
(c) darkness
(d) **au ~** ‹sell› on the black market; **travailler au ~** to work without declaring one's earnings, to moonlight (colloq)
(e) (fam) **un (petit) ~** an espresso
IDIOM voir tout en ~ to look on the black side (of things)

Noir, **~e** /nwaR/ *nm,f* black man/woman

noirâtre /nwaRɑtR/ *adj* blackish

noiraud, **~e** /nwaRo, od/ *adj* swarthy

noirceur /nwaRsœR/ *nf* (gen) blackness; (of hair, night, eyes) darkness

noircir /nwaRsiR/ [3] **1** *vtr* (a) ‹coal› to make [sth] dirty; ‹smoke› to blacken
(b) (figurative) ~ **du papier** to scribble away; ~ **la situation** to paint a black picture of the situation
2 *vi* ‹banana› to go black; ‹wall› to get dirty; ‹metal› to tarnish; ‹person› to get brown
3 **se noircir** *v refl* (+ *v être*) ‹sky› to darken; **se ~ le visage** to blacken one's face

noire² /nwaR/ **1** *adj f* ▶ NOIR 1
2 *nf* (Mus) crotchet (GB), quarter note (US)

noise /nwaz/ *nf* **chercher ~** *or* **des ~s à qn** to pick a quarrel with sb

noisetier /nwaztje/ *nm* hazel (tree)

noisette /nwazɛt/ *nf* (a) hazelnut
(b) ~ **de beurre** small knob of butter

noix /nwa/ *nf inv* (a) walnut (GB), English walnut (US)
(b) ~ **de beurre** knob of butter
■ ~ **de cajou** cashew nut; ~ **de coco** coconut; ~ **(de) muscade** nutmeg

nom /nɔ̃/ **1** *nm* (a) name; **petit ~** first name; ~ **et prénom** full name; **donner un** ⋯⟶

∼ à to name; **sans** ∼ unspeakable; **George Sand, de son vrai** ∼ **Aurore Dupin** George Sand, whose real name was Aurore Dupin; **parler en son propre** ∼ to speak for oneself
(b) noun
2 **au nom de** *phr* **(a)** in the name of
(b) on behalf of
■ ∼ **de baptême** Christian name; ∼ **d'emprunt** pseudonym; ∼ **de famille** surname; ∼ **de jeune fille** maiden name
IDIOMS **traiter qn de tous les** ∼**s** (fam) to call sb all the names under the sun; **appeler les choses par leur** ∼ to call a spade a spade

nomade /nɔmad/ *nmf* nomad

◆ **nombre** /nɔ̃bʀ/ *nm* number; **un** ∼ **à deux chiffres** a two-digit number; **un certain** ∼ **de** some; **être en** ∼ **inférieur** ⟨*players*⟩ to be fewer in number; ⟨*group*⟩ to be smaller; **ils étaient au** ∼ **de 30** there were 30 of them; **écrasé sous le** ∼ (of people) overcome by sheer weight of numbers; (of letters) overwhelmed by the sheer volume; **bon** ∼ **de** a good many; ∼ **de fois** many times

◆ **nombreux, -euse** /nɔ̃bʀø, øz/ *adj* ⟨*population, collection*⟩ large; ⟨*people, objects*⟩ numerous, many; **ils étaient peu** ∼ there weren't many of them; **ils ont répondu** ∼ **à l'appel** a great many people responded to the appeal; **les touristes deviennent trop** ∼ the number of tourists is becoming excessive

nombril /nɔ̃bʀil/ *nm* navel; **elle se prend pour le** ∼ **du monde** (fam) she thinks she's God's gift to mankind

nombrilisme /nɔ̃bʀilism/ *nm* (fam) navel-gazing (colloq)

nombriliste *adj* (fam) egocentric

nomenclature /nɔmɑ̃klatyʀ/ *nf* nomenclature; (in dictionary) word list

nominal, ∼e, mpl -aux /nɔminal, o/ *adj* (gen) nominal; ⟨*list*⟩ of names

nominatif, -ive /nɔminatif, iv/ **1** *adj* ⟨*list*⟩ of names; ⟨*invitation*⟩ personal; ⟨*share*⟩ registered
2 *nm* nominative

nomination /nɔminasjɔ̃/ *nf* **(a)** appointment
(b) letter of appointment
(c) (controversial) nomination

nominativement /nɔminativmɑ̃/ *adv* by name

nominer /nɔmine/ [1] *vtr* to nominate

nommément /nɔmemɑ̃/ *adv* specifically, by name

◆ **nommer** /nɔme/ [1] **1** *vtr* **(a)** to appoint; **être nommé à Paris** to be posted to Paris
(b) to name ⟨*person*⟩; to call ⟨*thing*⟩; **pour ne** ∼ **personne** to mention no names
2 **se nommer** *v refl* (+ *v être*) **(a)** to be called
(b) to give one's name

◆ indicates a very frequent word

◆ **non** /nɔ̃/ **1** *adv* **(a)** no; **'tu y vas?'—'**∼**'** 'are you going?'—'no, I'm not'; **ah, ça** ∼**!** definitely not!; **faire** ∼ **de la tête** to shake one's head; **je pense que** ∼ I don't think so; **je te dis que** ∼ no, I tell you; **il paraît que** ∼ apparently not; **tu trouves ça drôle? moi** ∼ do you think that's funny? I don't; ∼ **sans raison** not without reason; ∼ **moins difficile** just as difficult; **qu'il soit d'accord ou** ∼ whether he agrees or not; **tu viens, oui ou** ∼**?** are you coming or not?; **sois un peu plus poli,** ∼ **mais!** (fam) be a bit more polite, for heaven's sake!
(b) non; ∼ **alcoolisé** nonalcoholic; ∼ **négligeable** considerable
2 *nm inv* **(a)** no
(b) 'no' vote
3 **non plus** *phr* **je ne suis pas d'accord** ∼ **plus** I don't agree either; **il n'a pas aimé le film, moi** ∼ **plus** he didn't like the film and neither did I
4 **non(-)** (/nɔn/ *before vowel or mute h*) (*combining form*) ∼**-fumeur** nonsmoker; ∼**-syndiqué** non union member

nonagénaire /nɔnaʒenɛʀ/ *adj* **être** ∼ to be in one's nineties

non-aligné, ∼e, mpl ∼s /nɔnaliɲe/ *nm,f* nonaligned country

nonante /nɔnɑ̃t/ *adj inv, pron* ninety

non-assistance /nɔnasistɑ̃s/ *nf* ∼ **à personne en danger** failure to render assistance

nonchalance /nɔ̃ʃalɑ̃s/ *nf* nonchalance

nonchalant, ∼e /nɔ̃ʃalɑ̃, ɑ̃t/ *adj* nonchalant

non-dit /nɔ̃di/ *nm inv* **le** ∼ what is left unsaid

non-figuratif, -ive, mpl ∼s /nɔ̃figyʀatif, iv/ *adj* abstract

non-fonctionnement / nɔ̃fɔ̃ksjɔnmɑ̃/ *nm* failure to operate

non-initié, ∼e, mpl ∼s /nɔninisje/ *nm,f* layman, lay person

non-inscrit, ∼e, mpl ∼s /nɔnɛ̃skʀi, it/ *nm,f* independent

non-lieu, pl ∼x /nɔ̃ljø/ *nm* (Law) dismissal (of a charge); **il y a eu** ∼ the case was dismissed

nonne /nɔn/ *nf* nun

nonnette /nɔnɛt/ *nf* small iced gingerbread

non-recevoir /nɔ̃ʀəsəvwaʀ/ *nm* **fin de** ∼ flat refusal

non-reconduction, pl ∼s /nɔ̃ʀəkɔ̃dyksjɔ̃/ *nf* (of contract) non-renewal

non-respect /nɔ̃ʀɛspɛ/ *nm* ∼ **de** failure to comply with ⟨*clause*⟩; failure to respect ⟨*person*⟩

non-sens /nɔ̃sɑ̃s/ *nm inv* nonsense

non-spécialiste, pl ∼s /nɔ̃spesjalist/ *nmf* layman, lay person

non-violent, ~**e**, *mpl* ~**s** /nɔ̃vjɔlɑ̃, ɑ̃t/ *nm,f* advocate of nonviolence

non-voyant, ~**e**, *mpl* ~**s** /nɔ̃vwajɑ̃, ɑ̃t/ *nm,f* visually handicapped person

⚜ **nord** /nɔʀ/ **1** *adj inv* north; northern
2 *nm* (a) north; **le vent du** ~ the north wind; **le** ~ **de l'Europe** northern Europe
(b) **le Nord** the North; **la Corée du Nord** North Korea
IDIOM **il ne perd pas le** ~**!** (fam) he's got his head screwed on! (colloq)

nord-africain, ~**e**, *mpl* ~**s** /nɔʀafʀikɛ̃, ɛn/ *adj* North African

nord-américain, ~**e**, *mpl* ~**s** /nɔʀamerikɛ̃, ɛn/ *adj* North American

nord-est /nɔʀ(d)ɛst/ **1** *adj inv* northeast; northeastern
2 *nm* northeast

nordique /nɔʀdik/ *adj* Nordic

nord-ouest /nɔʀ(d)wɛst/ **1** *adj inv* northwest; northwestern
2 *nm* northwest

Nord-Sud /nɔʀsyd/ *adj inv* North-South

⚜ **normal**, ~**e**¹, *mpl* **-aux** /nɔʀmal, o/ *adj* normal; **il est** ~ **que** it is natural that; **il n'est pas** ~ **que** it is not right that

normale² /nɔʀmal/ *nf* (a) average
(b) norm; **retour à la** ~ return to normal

normalement /nɔʀmalmɑ̃/ *adv* normally

normalisation /nɔʀmalizasjɔ̃/ *nf*
(a) normalization
(b) standardization

normaliser /nɔʀmalize/ [1] *vtr* (a) to normalize ‹relations›
(b) to standardize ‹sizes›

normalité /nɔʀmalite/ *nf* normality

normand, ~**e** /nɔʀmɑ̃, ɑ̃d/ **1** *adj*
(a) ‹conquest› Norman
(b) ‹coast› Normandy; ‹team› from Normandy
2 *nm* Norman (French)

Normand, ~**e** /nɔʀmɑ̃, ɑ̃d/ *nm,f* Norman
IDIOM **une réponse de** ~ a noncommittal reply

normatif, **-ive** /nɔʀmatif, iv/ *adj* normative

⚜ **norme** /nɔʀm/ *nf* (gen) norm; (Tech) standard

Norvège /nɔʀvɛʒ/ *pr nf* Norway

norvégien, **-ienne** /nɔʀveʒjɛ̃, ɛn/ **1** *adj* Norwegian
2 *nm* (language) Norwegian

nos ▸ NOTRE

nostalgie /nɔstalʒi/ *nf* nostalgia

nostalgique /nɔstalʒik/ *adj* nostalgic

notable /nɔtabl/ **1** *adj* ‹fact› notable; ‹progress› significant
2 *nm* notable

notaire /nɔtɛʀ/ *nm* notary public

⚜ **notamment** /nɔtamɑ̃/ *adv* (a) notably
(b) in particular

notation /nɔtasjɔ̃/ *nf* (a) notation
(b) (of pupil) marking (GB), grading (US); (of staff) grading

⚜ **note** /nɔt/ *nf* (a) bill (GB), check (US); **faire la** ~ **de qn** to write out sb's bill (GB) *or* check (US)
(b) (Mus) note; **forcer la** ~ to overdo it
(c) mark (GB), grade (US); ~ **éliminatoire** fail mark (GB) *or* grade (US)
(d) (written) note; **prendre qch en** ~ to make a note of sth; **prendre (bonne)** ~ **de qch** (figurative) to take (due) note of sth
■ ~ **de frais** expense account; ~ **d'honoraires** bill; ~ **de service** memorandum

⚜ **noter** /nɔte/ [1] *vtr* (a) to write down ‹idea, address›
(b) to notice ‹change›; **notez (bien) que je n'ai rien à lui reprocher** mind you I haven't got anything particular against him; **il faut quand même** ~ it has to be said
(c) to mark (GB), to grade (US) ‹exercise›; to give a mark (GB) *or* grade (US) to; to grade ‹employee›

notice /nɔtis/ *nf* (a) note
(b) instructions

notifier /nɔtifje/ [2] *vtr* ~ **qch à qn** (gen) to notify sb of sth; (Law) to give sb notice of sth

⚜ **notion** /nɔsjɔ̃/ *nf* (a) notion; **perdre la** ~ **de** to lose all sense of
(b) ~**s** basic knowledge

notoire /nɔtwaʀ/ *adj* ‹fact, position› well-known; ‹swindler, stupidity› notorious

notoirement /nɔtwaʀmɑ̃/ *adv* manifestly; notoriously

notoriété /nɔtɔʀjete/ *nf* (a) fame; (of product) reputation; **il est de** ~ **(publique) que** it's common knowledge that
(b) (person) celebrity

⚜ **notre**, *pl* **nos** /nɔtʀ, no/ *det* our; **à nos âges** at our age; **c'était** ~ **avis à tous** we all felt the same; **nos enfants à nous** (fam) our children

nôtre /notʀ/ **1** *det* **nous avons fait** ~**s ces idées** we've adopted these ideas
2 **le nôtre**, **la nôtre**, **les nôtres** *pron* ours; **soyez des** ~**s!** won't you join us?; **les** ~**s** our own people; (team, group) our side

nouer /nwe/ [1] **1** *vtr* (a) (gen) to tie; to knot ‹tie›; to tie up ‹parcel›; **avoir la gorge nouée** to have a lump in one's throat
(b) to establish ‹relations›; to engage in ‹dialogue›
2 **se nouer** *v refl* (+ *v être*) (a) ‹plot› to take shape
(b) ‹diplomatic relations› to be established; ‹dialogue, friendship› to begin

nougat /nuga/ *nm* nougat

nouilles /nuj/ *nf pl* noodles, pasta

nounou /nunu/ *nf* (fam) nanny (GB), nurse

nounours /nunuʀs/ *nm inv* (fam) teddy bear

n

nourrice /nuʀis/ *nf* (a) childminder (GB), babysitter (US)
(b) wet nurse

⚹ **nourrir** /nuʀiʀ/ [3] **1** *vtr* (a) to feed ‹*person, animal*›; to nourish ‹*skin, leather*›; **bien nourri** well-fed; ~ **au sein/au biberon** to breast-/to bottle-feed; **mon travail ne me nourrit pas** I don't make enough to live on
(b) (figurative) to harbour (GB) ‹*hopes*›; to feed ‹*fire*›; to fuel ‹*passion*›
2 se nourrir *v refl* (+ *v être*) ‹*animal*› to feed; ‹*person*› to eat; **se** ~ **de** to live on ‹*vegetables*›; to feed on ‹*illusions*›

nourrissant, ~e /nuʀisɑ̃, ɑ̃t/ *adj* nourishing

nourrisson /nuʀisɔ̃/ *nm* infant

⚹ **nourriture** /nuʀityʀ/ *nf* (a) food
(b) diet

⚹ **nous** /nu/ *pron* (a) (subject) we; (object) us; ~ **sommes en avance** we're early; **donne-**~ **l'adresse** give us the address; **entre** ~, **il n'est pas très intelligent** between you and me, he isn't very intelligent; **une maison à** ~ a house of our own; **pensons à** ~ let's think of ourselves
(b) (with reflexive verb) ~ ~ **soignons** we look after ourselves; ~ ~ **aimons** we love each other

nous-même, *pl* **nous-mêmes** /numɛm/ *pron* ourselves

⚹ **nouveau** (**nouvel** *before vowel or mute h*), **nouvelle¹**, *mpl* ~**x** /nuvo, nuvɛl/ **1** *adj* (gen) new; ‹*attempt, attack*› fresh; **tout** ~ brand-new; **se faire faire un** ~ **costume** to have a new suit made; to have another suit made; **une nouvelle fois** once again; **les** ~**x élus** the newly-elected members; **les** ~**x mariés** the newlyweds
2 *nm, f* (in school) new boy/girl; (in company) new employee; (in army) new recruit
3 *nm* **téléphone-moi s'il y a du** ~ give me a call if there is anything new to report; **j'ai du** ~ **pour toi** I've got some news for you
4 à nouveau, de nouveau *phr* (once) again

nouveau-né, ~e, *mpl* ~**s** /nuvone/ *nm,f* newborn baby

nouveauté /nuvote/ *nf* (a) novelty; **ce n'est pas une** ~! that's nothing new!
(b) (gen) new thing; (book) new publication; (record) new release; (car, machine) new model

nouvel ▶ NOUVEAU 1

nouvelle² /nuvɛl/ **1** *adj f* ▶ NOUVEAU 1
2 *nf* (a) ▶ NOUVEAU 2
(b) news; **une** ~ a piece of news; **tu connais la** ~? have you heard the news?; **recevoir des** ~**s de qn** to hear from sb; (through somebody else) to hear news of sb; **il m'a demandé de tes** ~**s** he asked after you; **aux dernières**~**s, il se porte bien** (fam) the last I heard he was doing fine; **il aura de mes**~**s!**

(fam) he'll be hearing from me!; **goûte ce petit vin, tu m'en diras des** ~**s** (fam) have a taste of this wine, it's really good!
(c) short story

nouvellement /nuvɛlmɑ̃/ *adv* recently

Nouvelle-Zélande /nuvɛlzelɑ̃d/ *pr nf* New Zealand

nouvelliste /nuvelist/ *nmf* short-story writer

novateur, -trice /nɔvatœʀ, tʀis/ **1** *adj* innovative
2 *nm,f* innovator, pioneer

⚹ **novembre** /nɔvɑ̃bʀ/ *nm* November

novice /nɔvis/ **1** *adj* inexperienced, green
2 *nmf* novice

noyade /nwajad/ *nf* drowning

noyau, *pl* ~**x** /nwajo/ *nm* (a) stone (GB), pit (US)
(b) small group; ~**x de résistance** pockets of resistance
(c) nucleus

noyauter /nwajote/ [1] *vtr* to infiltrate

noyé, ~e /nwaje/ *nm,f* drowned person

noyer¹ /nwaje/ [23] **1** *vtr* (gen) to drown; to flood ‹*village, engine*›; ~ **qn sous un flot de paroles** to talk sb's head off (colloq)
2 se noyer *v refl* (+ *v être*) to drown; (suicide) to drown oneself; **mourir noyé** to drown
IDIOM se ~ **dans un verre d'eau** to make a mountain out of a molehill

noyer² /nwaje/ *nm* walnut (tree)

⚹ **nu, ~e** /ny/ **1** *adj* ‹*person*› naked; ‹*wall, tree, coastline*› bare; ‹*truth*› plain; **pieds** ~**s** barefoot; **torse** ~ stripped to the waist
2 *nm* (in art) nude
3 à nu *phr* **être à** ~ to be exposed; **mettre son cœur à** ~ to open one's heart

⚹ **nuage** /nɥaʒ/ *nm* cloud; **sans** ~**s** ‹*sky*› cloudless; ‹*happiness*› unclouded; ~ **de lait** dash of milk
IDIOM descendre de son ~ to come back to earth

nuageux, -euse /nɥaʒø, øz/ *adj* ‹*sky*› cloudy

nuance /nɥɑ̃s/ *nf* (a) (of colour) shade
(b) (of meaning) nuance; **sans** ~ ‹*commentary*› clearcut; ‹*personality*› straightforward
(c) slight difference; **à cette** ~ **près que** with the small reservation that
(d) (Mus) nuance

nuancer /nɥɑ̃se/ [12] *vtr* (a) to qualify ‹*opinion*›; to modify ‹*view of situation*›; **peu nuancé** unsubtle
(b) to moderate ‹*remarks, statements*›

nucléaire /nyklɛɛʀ/ **1** *adj* nuclear
2 *nm* **le** ~ nuclear energy; nuclear technology

nudité /nydite/ *nf* (a) nakedness, nudity
(b) (of place, wall) bareness

⚹ indicates a very frequent word

nuée /nɥe/ *nf* (of insects) swarm; (of people) horde

nues /ny/ *nf pl* tomber des ~ (fam) to be flabbergasted (colloq); **porter qn aux ~** to praise sb to the skies

nui /nɥi/ ▶ NUIRE

nuire /nɥiʀ/ [69] **1 nuire à** *v+prep* to harm ‹*person*›; to be harmful to ‹*health, interests, reputation*›; to damage ‹*crops*›
2 se nuire *v refl* (+ *v être*) (a) to do each other a lot of harm
(b) to do oneself a lot of harm

nuisance /nɥizɑ̃s/ *nf* nuisance

nuisible /nɥizibl/ *adj* ‹*substance, waste*› dangerous; ‹*influence*› harmful; **insecte ~** (insect) pest; ~ **à** detrimental to

✓ **nuit** /nɥi/ *nf* night; **cette ~** last night; tonight; **voyager de ~** to travel by night; **avant la ~** before dark; **à la tombée de la ~** at nightfall; **il fait ~** it's dark; **il faisait ~ noire** it was pitch dark; **il se perd dans la ~ des temps** it is lost in the mists of time
■ ~ **blanche** sleepless night; ~ **bleue** *night of terrorist bomb attacks*
IDIOMS **c'est le jour et la ~** they're as different as chalk and cheese; **attends demain pour donner ta réponse: la ~ porte conseil** wait till tomorrow to give your answer: sleep on it first

nuitée /nɥite/ *nf* (in a hotel) overnight stay

✓ **nul, nulle** /nyl/ **1** *adj* (a) (fam) ‹*person*› hopeless; ‹*piece of work*› worthless; ‹*film*› trashy (colloq)
(b) (Law) ‹*contract*› void; ‹*will*› invalid; ‹*elections*› null and void; ‹*vote*› spoiled
(c) (Sport) **match ~** tie, draw (GB); nil-all draw (GB)
(d) ‹*difference*› nil
(e) ~ **homme/pays** no man/country; ~ **autre que vous** no-one else but you
2 *nm,f* (fam) idiot (colloq); **c'est un ~** he's a dead loss (colloq)
3 *pron* no-one
4 nulle part *phr* nowhere

nullement /nylmɑ̃/ *adv* not at all

nullité /nylite/ *nf* (a) (Law) nullity; **frapper de ~** to render void
(b) (of argument) invalidity; (of book, film) (fam) worthlessness
(c) (fam) (person) idiot (colloq)

numéraire /nymeʀɛʀ/ *nm* cash

numéral, ~e, *mpl* **-aux** /nymeʀal, o/ **1** *adj* numeral
2 *nm* numeral

numération /nymeʀasjɔ̃/ *nf* (Math) numeration
■ ~ **globulaire** blood count

numérique /nymeʀik/ *adj* (gen) numerical; ‹*display*› digital; **clavier ~** keypad

numériser /nymeʀize/ *vtr* to digitize

✓ **numéro** /nymeʀo/ *nm* (a) number; ~ **de téléphone** telephone number
(b) (magazine) issue; **suite au prochain ~** to be continued
(c) (in show) act
(d) (fam) **quel ~!** what a character!
■ ~ **d'abonné** customer's number; ~ **d'appel gratuit** freefone number (GB), toll-free number (US); ~ **vert** ▶ NUMÉRO D'APPEL GRATUIT
IDIOM **tirer le bon ~** to be lucky

numérotation /nymeʀɔtasjɔ̃/ *nf* numbering

numéroter /nymeʀɔte/ [1] *vtr* to number

numerus clausus /nymeʀysklozys/ *nm inv* quota

nunuche /nynyʃ/ *adj* (fam) bird-brained (colloq), silly

nu-pied, *pl* ~**s** /nypje/ *nm* sandal

nuptial, ~e, *mpl* **-iaux** /nypsjal, o/ *adj* ‹*mass*› nuptial; ‹*room*› bridal; **cérémonie ~e** wedding

nuque /nyk/ *nf* nape (of the neck)

nurse /nœʀs/ *nf* nanny (GB), nurse

nutritif, -ive /nytʀitif, iv/ *adj* ‹*skin cream*› nourishing; ‹*value*› nutritive

nutrition /nytʀisjɔ̃/ *nf* nutrition

nymphe /nɛ̃f/ *nf* nymph

nymphéa /nɛ̃fea/ *nm* waterlily

nymphomane /nɛ̃fɔman/ *adj, nf* nymphomaniac

- -

O o

- -

✓ **o, O** /o/ *nm inv* o, O

oasis /ɔazis/ *nf inv* oasis

✓ **obéir** /ɔbeiʀ/ [3] *v+prep* (a) to obey; ~ **à** to obey ‹*order*›
(b) ‹*brakes, vehicle*› to respond

obéissance /ɔbeisɑ̃s/ *nf* obedience

obéissant, ~e /ɔbeisɑ̃, ɑ̃t/ *adj* obedient

obélisque /ɔbelisk/ *nm* obelisk

obèse /ɔbɛz/ *adj* obese

objecter /ɔbʒɛkte/ [1] *vtr* (a) (suggest) to put forward ‹*argument, idea*›
(b) (excuse) ~ **un mal de tête pour refuser une invitation** to give a headache as an excuse for refusing an invitation

objectif, -ive /ɔbʒɛktif, iv/ **1** *adj* objective
2 *nm* **(a)** objective
(b) lens
(c) target
objection /ɔbʒɛksjɔ̃/ *nf* objection
objectivité /ɔbʒɛktivite/ *nf* objectivity

objet /ɔbʒɛ/ **1** *nm* **(a)** object; **~ fragile**
fragile item; **~s personnels** personal
possessions
(b) (of debate, research) subject; (of hatred,
desire) object; **faire l'~ de** to be the subject
of ‹*inquiry, research*›; to be subjected to
‹*surveillance*›; to be the object of ‹*desire,
hatred*›
(c) purpose, object; '**~: réponse à votre lettre
du…**' 're: your letter of…'
(d) (Law) **~ d'un litige** matter at issue
2 **-objet** (*combining form*) as an object;
femme-~ woman as an object
■ **~s trouvés** lost property; **~ volant non identifié, ovni** unidentified flying object, UFO

obligataire /ɔbligatɛʀ/ (Fin) *adj* ‹*market,
issue*›; **bond emprunt ~** bond issue

obligation /ɔbligasjɔ̃/ *nf* **(a)** obligation,
responsibility; duty
(b) necessity; **se voir** *or* **se trouver dans l'~
de faire** to be forced to do
(c) (Econ) bond
(d) (Law) obligation
■ **~s militaires, OM** military service

obligatoire /ɔbligatwaʀ/ *adj* **(a)** compulsory
(b) (fam) inevitable

obligatoirement /ɔbligatwaʀmɑ̃/ *adv*
inevitably, necessarily

obligé, ~e **1** *pp* ▶ OBLIGER
2 *pp adj* **(a)** (constrained) **se voir ~ de faire**
to be forced to do
(b) (indebted) **être ~ à qn de** to be obliged *or*
grateful to sb for
(c) (necessary) essential; **un passage ~ (pour)**
(figurative) a prerequisite (for)
3 *nm,f* **(a)** **être l'~ de qn** to be obliged *or*
indebted to sb
(b) (in law) obligor

obligeamment /ɔbliʒamɑ̃/ *adv* obligingly
obligeance /ɔbliʒɑ̃s/ *nf* **avoir l'~ de** to be
kind enough to
obligeant, ~e /ɔbliʒɑ̃, ɑ̃t/ *adj* obliging; kind

obliger /ɔbliʒe/ [13] **1** *vtr* **(a)** **~ qn à
faire** to force sb to do; ‹*rules*› to make it
compulsory for sb to do; ‹*duty*› to compel sb
to do; **je suis obligé de partir** I have to go
(b) **~ qn** to oblige sb
2 **s'obliger** *v refl* (+ *v être*) **s'~ à faire** to
force oneself to do

oblique /ɔblik/ *adj* slanting; sidelong;
oblique

obliquement /ɔblikmɑ̃/ *adv* at an angle;
diagonally

oblitération /ɔbliteʀasjɔ̃/ *nf* (of stamp)
cancelling (GB); **(cachet d')~** postmark

oblitérer /ɔbliteʀe/ [14] *vtr* to cancel, to
obliterate ‹*stamp*›

oblong, -ongue /ɔblɔ̃, ɔ̃g/ *adj* oblong
obnubiler /ɔbnybile/ [1] *vtr* to obsess
obscène /ɔpsɛn/ *adj* obscene
obscur, ~e /ɔpskyʀ/ *adj* **(a)** dark
(b) obscure
(c) lowly
(d) vague

obscurcir /ɔpskyʀsiʀ/ [3] **1** *vtr* **(a)** to
make [sth] dark ‹*place*›
(b) to obscure ‹*view*›
2 **s'obscurcir** *v refl* (+ *v être*) **(a)** ‹*sky,
place*› to darken
(b) ‹*situation*› to become confused

obscurément /ɔpskyʀemɑ̃/ *adv* **(a)** ‹*feel*›
vaguely
(b) ‹*live*› in obscurity

obscurité /ɔpskyʀite/ *nf* darkness
obsédant, ~e /ɔpsedɑ̃, ɑ̃t/ *adj* ‹*memory,
dream, music*› haunting; ‹*rhythm*› insistent
obsédé, ~e /ɔpsede/ *nm,f* **~ (sexuel)** sex
maniac

obséder /ɔpsede/ [14] *vtr* ‹*memory, dream*›
to haunt; ‹*idea, problem*› to obsess
obsèques /ɔpsɛk/ *nf pl* funeral
obséquieux, -ieuse /ɔpsekjø, øz/ *adj*
obsequious

observateur, -trice /ɔpsɛʀvatœʀ,
tʀis/ **1** *adj* observant
2 *nm,f* observer; (Comput) **~ passif** lurker

observation /ɔpsɛʀvasjɔ̃/ *nf* **(a)** observation
(b) observation, remark; comment
(c) reproach

observatoire /ɔpsɛʀvatwaʀ/ *nm*
(a) observatory
(b) look-out post

observer /ɔpsɛʀve/ [1] **1** *vtr* **(a)** to watch,
to observe
(b) to notice, to observe ‹*phenomenon,
reaction*›
(c) to observe ‹*rules, treaty*›; to keep to ‹*diet*›;
to maintain ‹*strategy*›; **~ le silence** to keep
quiet
2 **s'observer** *v refl* (+ *v être*) **(a)** to watch
each other
(b) to keep a check on oneself

obsession /ɔpsesjɔ̃/ *nf* obsession
obsolète /ɔpsɔlɛt/ *adj* obsolete
obstacle /ɔpstakl/ *nm* **(a)** obstacle
(b) (in horseriding) fence
obstétricien, -ienne /ɔpstetʀisjɛ̃,
ɛn/ *nm,f* obstetrician
obstétrique /ɔpstetʀik/ *nf* obstetrics
obstination /ɔpstinasjɔ̃/ *nf* obstinacy
obstiné, ~e /ɔpstine/ **1** *pp* ▶ OBSTINER
2 *pp adj* **(a)** stubborn
(b) dogged

obstinément /ɔpstinemɑ̃/ *adv*
obstinately

✓ indicates a very frequent word

obstiner: s'**obstiner** /ɔpstine/ [1] *v refl*
(+ *v être*) to persist

obstruction /ɔpstryksjɔ̃/ *nf* obstruction

obstruer /ɔpstrye/ [1] **1** *vtr* to obstruct
2 s'**obstruer** *v refl* (+ *v être*) to get
blocked

obtempérer /ɔptɑ̃peʁe/ [14] *v+prep* to
comply; ∼ **à** to comply with ‹order›

✦ **obtenir** /ɔptəniʁ/ [36] *vtr* to get, to obtain

obtention /ɔptɑ̃sjɔ̃/ *nf* getting, obtaining

obturation /ɔptyʁasjɔ̃/ *nf* (a) blocking (up)
(b) **vitesse d'**∼ shutter speed

obturer /ɔptyʁe/ [1] *vtr* to block up

obtus, ∼**e** /ɔpty, yz/ *adj* obtuse

obus /ɔby/ *nm inv* shell

✦ **occasion** /ɔkazjɔ̃/ *nf* (a) occasion; **à l'**∼
some time; **à** *or* **en plusieurs** ∼**s** on several
occasions; **les grandes** ∼**s** special occasions
(b) opportunity, chance; **être l'**∼ **de qch** to
give rise to sth
(c) second-hand buy
(d) bargain

occasionnel, -**elle** /ɔkazjɔnɛl/ *adj*
occasional

occasionner /ɔkazjɔne/ [1] *vtr* to cause

occident /ɔksidɑ̃/ *nm* (a) west
(b) **l'Occident** the West

✦ **occidental**, ∼**e**, *mpl* -**aux** /ɔksidɑtal,
o/ *adj* western
Occidental, ∼**e**, *mpl* -**aux** /ɔksidɑtal,
o/ *nm,f* Westerner

occitan /ɔksitɑ̃/ *nm* langue d'oc

occulte /ɔkylt/ *adj* (a) occult
(b) secret

occulter /ɔkylte/ [1] *vtr* (a) to eclipse
(b) to obscure ‹issue›; to conceal ‹truth›

occultisme /ɔkyltism/ *nm* occultism

occupant, ∼**e** /ɔkypɑ̃, ɑ̃t/ **1** *adj*
occupying
2 *nm,f* (of house) occupier; (of vehicle)
occupant

occupation /ɔkypasjɔ̃/ *nf* (a) (pastime)
occupation
(b) occupation, job
(c) occupancy
(d) (of country, factory) occupation

occupé, ∼**e** /ɔkype/ **1** *pp* ▶ OCCUPER
2 *pp adj* (a) ‹person, life› busy
(b) ‹seat› taken; ‹phone› engaged (GB), busy;
‹toilet› engaged
(c) ‹country› occupied

✦ **occuper** /ɔkype/ [1] **1** *vtr* (a) to live in,
to occupy ‹flat, house›; to be in ‹shower, cell›;
to sit in ‹seat›
(b) to take up ‹space, time›
(c) to occupy ‹person, mind›; **ça m'occupe!** it
keeps me busy!; **le sujet qui nous occupe** the
matter which we are dealing with
(d) to have ‹employment›; to hold ‹job, office›
(e) ‹strikers, army› to occupy ‹place›; ∼ **les
locaux** to stage a sit-in

2 s'**occuper** *v refl* (+ *v être*) (a) to keep
oneself busy *or* occupied
(b) **s'**∼ **de** to see to, to take care of ‹dinner,
tickets›; to be dealing with ‹file, matter›; to
take care of ‹child, animal, plant›; to attend
to ‹customer›; to be in charge of ‹finance,
library›; **occupe-toi de tes affaires** (fam) *or*
de ce qui te regarde! (fam) mind your own
business! (colloq)

occurrence /ɔkyʁɑ̃s/ *nf* (a) case,
instance; **en l'**∼ in this case
(b) occurrence

OCDE /osedeø/ *nf* (*abbr* = **Organisation
de coopération et de
développement économiques**)
OECD

océan /ɔseɑ̃/ *nm* ocean

océanique /ɔseanik/ *adj* oceanic

océanographe /ɔseanɔgʁaf/ *nmf*
oceanographer

ocre /ɔkʁ/ *adj inv*, *nm* ochre (GB)

octante /ɔktɑ̃t/ *adj inv*, *pron* (in Belgian,
Canadian, Swiss, French) eighty

octave /ɔktav/ *nf* octave

octet /ɔktɛt/ *nm* (a) (Comput) byte
(b) (in physics) octet

✦ **octobre** /ɔktɔbʁ/ *nm* October

octogénaire /ɔktɔʒenɛʁ/ *nmf*
octogenarian

octogonal, ∼**e**, *mpl* -**aux** /ɔktɔgɔnal,
o/ *adj* octagonal

octroi /ɔktʁwa/ *nm* (a) granting
(b) octroi

octroyer /ɔktʁwaje/ [23] *vtr* ∼ **à qn** to
grant sb ‹pardon, favour›; to allocate sb [sth]
‹budget›

oculaire /ɔkylɛʁ/ *adj* troubles ∼**s** eye
trouble; **témoin** ∼ eyewitness

oculiste /ɔkylist/ *nmf* oculist,
ophthalmologist

ode /ɔd/ *nf* ode

✦ **odeur** /ɔdœʁ/ *nf* smell

odieux, -**ieuse** /ɔdjø, øz/ *adj* horrible

odorant, ∼**e** /ɔdɔʁɑ̃, ɑ̃t/ *adj* which has a
smell

odorat /ɔdɔʁa/ *nm* sense of smell

OECE /oeseø/ *nf* (*abbr* = **Organisation
européenne de coopération
économique**) OEEC

œdème /edɛm/ *nm* (Med) oedema

œdipe /edip/ *nm* Oedipus complex

✦ **œil**, *pl* **yeux** /œj, jø/ *nm* eye; **ouvrir l'**∼ to
keep one's eyes open; **fermer les yeux sur
qch** to turn a blind eye to sth; **acheter qch
les yeux fermés** to buy sth with complete
confidence; **avoir l'**∼ **à tout** to be vigilant;
jeter un ∼ **à** *or* **sur qch** to have a quick look
at sth; **aux yeux de tous** openly; **jeter un
coup d'**∼ **à qch** to glance at sth; **avoir le
coup d'**∼ to have a good eye; **regarder qch
d'un** ∼ **neuf** to see sth in a new light; **voir** ⋯⋙

qch d'un mauvais ~ to take a dim view of
sth; **à mes yeux** in my opinion
■ ~ **de verre** glass eye
IDIOMS mon ~! (fam) my eye! (colloq), my
foot! (colloq); **à l'~** (fam) for nothing, for free
(colloq); **faire les gros yeux à qn** to glare at sb;
dévorer qn/qch des yeux to gaze longingly at
sb/sth; **faire les yeux doux à qn** to make eyes
at sb; **tourner de l'~** (fam) to faint; **cela me
sort par les yeux** (fam) I've had it up to here
(colloq); **avoir bon pied bon ~** to be as fit as a
fiddle; **sauter aux yeux** to be obvious

œillade /œjad/ nf **(a)** wink
(b) glance

œillère /œjɛʀ/ nf blinker

œillet /œjɛ/ nm **(a)** carnation
(b) (in shoe, tarpaulin) eyelet; (in belt) hole; (made
of metal) grommet

œilleton /œjtɔ̃/ nm (in door) peephole

œnologie /enɔlɔʒi/ nf oenology

œsophage /ezɔfaʒ/ nm oesophagus

œstrogène /ɛstʀɔʒɛn/ nm oestrogen

œuf /œf, pl ø/ nm egg; **~s de cabillaud** cod's
roe
■ ~ **à la coque** boiled egg; ~ **dur** hard-boiled
egg; ~ **sur le plat** fried egg; **~s brouillés**
scrambled eggs

♂ **œuvre** /œvʀ/ nf **(a)** (artistic, literary) work; **~s
complètes** complete works
(b) être à l'~ to be at work; **voir qn à l'~** to
see sb in action; **mettre en ~** to implement
‹reform›; to display ‹ingenuity›; **tout mettre
en ~ pour faire** to make every effort to do
■ ~ **d'art** work of art; ~ **de bienfaisance** or de
charité charity

off /ɔf/ adj inv (fam) **voix ~** voice-over

offensant, **~e** /ɔfɑ̃sɑ̃, ɑ̃t/ adj offensive
(pour to)

offense /ɔfɑ̃s/ nf insult

offenser /ɔfɑ̃se/ [1] **1** vtr to offend
2 s'offenser v refl (+ v être) to take
offence (GB)

offensif, -ive¹ /ɔfɑ̃sif, iv/ adj (Mil)
offensive

offensive² /ɔfɑ̃siv/ nf (Mil figurative)
offensive

offert, -e /ɔfɛʀ, ɛʀt/ ▶ OFFRIR

office /ɔfis/ **1** nm **(a) faire ~ de table** to
serve as a table
(b) ~ **religieux** service
(c) butlery
2 d'office phr **d'~** without consultation;
nos propositions ont été rejetées d'~ our
proposals were dismissed out of hand;
commis d'~ ‹lawyer› appointed by the court
■ ~ **du tourisme** tourist information office

♂ **officiel, -ielle** /ɔfisjɛl/ **1** adj official; **être
en visite officielle** to be on a state visit
2 nm official

♂ indicates a very frequent word

officier¹ /ɔfisje/ [2] vi to officiate

♂ **officier²** /ɔfisje/ nm officer

officieusement /ɔfisjøzmɑ̃/ adv
unofficially

officieux, -ieuse /ɔfisjø, øz/ adj
unofficial

officine /ɔfisin/ nf dispensary; pharmacy

offrande /ɔfʀɑ̃d/ nf offering

offrant /ɔfʀɑ̃/ **1** pres p ▶ OFFRIR
2 nm **vendre qch au plus ~** to sell sth to
the highest bidder

offre /ɔfʀ/ nf **(a)** offer; **répondre à une ~
d'emploi** to reply to a job advertisement
(b) (Econ) supply
■ ~ **d'achat** bid; ~ **publique d'achat, OPA**
takeover bid

♂ **offrir** /ɔfʀiʀ/ [4] **1** vtr **(a)** ~ **qch à qn** to
give sth to sb
(b) to buy **(à qn** for sb)
(c) to offer ‹choice›; to offer ‹resignation›; to
present ‹problems›
2 s'offrir v refl (+ v être) **(a) s'~** to buy
oneself ‹flowers›; **ils ne peuvent pas s'~ le
théâtre** they can't afford to go to the theatre
(GB); **s'~ un jour de vacances** to give oneself
a day off
(b) ‹solution› to present itself; **s'~ en
spectacle** to make an exhibition of oneself

offshore **1** nm **faire de l'~** offshoring
2 adj offshore

offusquer /ɔfyske/ [1] **1** vtr to offend
2 s'offusquer v refl (+ v être) to be
offended

ogive /ɔʒiv/ nf (Archit) rib

ogre /ɔgʀ/ nm ogre

♂ **oh** /o/ excl oh!; ~ **hisse!** heave-ho!

oie /wa/ nf goose; ~ **blanche** naïve young
girl

oignon /ɔɲɔ̃/ nm **(a)** onion
(b) (of flower) bulb
IDIOM occupe-toi de tes ~s (fam) mind your
own business (colloq)

♂ **oiseau**, pl **~x** /wazo/ nm bird; **un (drôle
d')~** an oddball (colloq)
IDIOM trouver l'~ rare (fam) to find the one
person in a million

oiseau-mouche, pl **oiseaux-
mouches** /wazomuʃ/ nm hummingbird

oiseleur /wazlœʀ/ nm bird-catcher

oisellerie /wazɛlʀi/ nf bird shop

oisif, -ive /wazif, iv/ **1** adj idle
2 nm,f idler; **les ~s** the idle rich

oisillon /wazijɔ̃/ nm fledgling

oisiveté /wazivte/ nf idleness
IDIOM l'~ est mère de tous les vices (Proverb)
the devil makes work for idle hands

olé: olé olé /ɔleɔle/ phr (fam) ‹joke›
naughty

oléagineux, -euse **1** adj oleaginous
2 nm inv oleaginous plant

oléiculture /ɔleikyltyʀ/ nf olive-growing

oléoduc /ɔleɔdyk/ nm (oil) pipeline

olfactif, -ive /ɔlfaktif, iv/ adj olfactory

oligo-élément, pl ∼s /ɔligoelemɑ̃/ nm trace element

olivâtre /ɔlivɑtʀ/ adj olive-greenish; sallow

olive /ɔliv/ nf olive

oliverale /ɔlivʀɛ/ nf olive grove

olivier /ɔlivje/ nm (a) olive tree
(b) olive wood

olympiade ⊡ nf Olympiad
⊡ **olympiades** nf pl Olympics

olympique /ɔlɛ̃pik/ adj Olympic

ombilic /ɔ̃bilik/ nm umbilicus, navel

ombrage /ɔ̃bʀaʒ/ nm shade
IDIOMS porter ∼ à qn to offend sb; prendre ∼ de qch to take umbrage at sth

ombrager /ɔ̃bʀaʒe/ [13] vtr to shade

ombrageux, -euse /ɔ̃bʀaʒø, øz/ adj tetchy

♂ **ombre** /ɔ̃bʀ/ nf (a) shade; tu leur fais de l'∼ you're (standing) in their light; (figurative) you put them in the shade; rester dans l'∼ de qn to be in sb's shadow
(b) shadow
(c) darkness
(d) laisser certains détails dans l'∼ to be deliberately vague about certain details
(e) hint; une ∼ de tristesse passa dans son regard a look of sadness crossed his/her face
■ ∼ chinoise shadow puppet; ∼ à paupières eye shadow
IDIOM jeter une ∼ au tableau to spoil the picture

ombrelle /ɔ̃bʀɛl/ nf parasol, sunshade

OMC /ɔɛmse/ nf (abbr = **Organisation Mondiale du Commerce**) WTO, World Trade Organization

omelette /ɔmlɛt/ nf omelette

omettre /ɔmɛtʀ/ [60] vtr to leave out, to omit

omission /ɔmisjɔ̃/ nf omission

omnibus /ɔmnibys/ nm inv slow or local train

omniprésent, -e /ɔmnipʀezɑ̃, ɑ̃t/ adj omnipresent

omnisports /ɔmnispɔʀ/ adj inv salle ∼ sports hall; club ∼ (multi-)sports club

omnivore /ɔmnivɔʀ/ nmf omnivore

omoplate /ɔmɔplat/ nf shoulder blade

OMS /ɔɛmɛs/ nf (abbr = **Organisation mondiale de la santé**) WHO, World Health Organization

♂ **on** /ɔ̃/ pron (a) ∼ a refait la route the road was resurfaced; ∼ a prétendu que it was claimed that; il pleut des cordes, comme ∼ dit it's raining cats and dogs, as they say
(b) we; mon copain et moi, ∼ va en Afrique my boyfriend and I are going to Africa
(c) you; alors, ∼ se promène? so you're taking a stroll then?
(d) ∼ fait ce qu'∼ peut! one does what one

can!; toi, ∼ ne t'a rien demandé nobody asked you for your opinion; ∼ ne m'a pas demandé mon avis they didn't ask me for my opinion

once /ɔ̃s/ nf ounce

♂ **oncle** /ɔ̃kl/ nm uncle

onctueux, -euse /ɔ̃ktɥø, øz/ adj
(a) smooth, creamy
(b) unctuous

onde /ɔ̃d/ nf wave; grandes ∼s long wave; sur les ∼s on the air

ondée /ɔ̃de/ nf shower

on-dit /ɔ̃di/ nm inv les ∼ hearsay

ondoyant, ∼e /ɔ̃dwajɑ̃, ɑ̃t/ adj rippling; lithe; swaying

ondoyer /ɔ̃dwaje/ [23] vi to undulate; to sway

ondulant, ∼e /ɔ̃dylɑ̃, ɑ̃t/ adj swaying; undulating

ondulation /ɔ̃dylasjɔ̃/ nf (a) undulation; swaying
(b) curves; wave

ondulé, ∼e /ɔ̃dyle/ adj ‹hair, shape› wavy; ‹cardboard› corrugated

onéreux, -euse /ɔneʀø, øz/ adj expensive

ONG /ɔɛ̃ʒe/ nf (abbr = **organisation non gouvernementale**) NGO

ongle /ɔ̃gl/ nm nail
IDIOM jusqu'au bout des ∼s through and through

onglet /ɔ̃glɛ/ nm (a) tab; avec ∼s with thumb-index
(b) (Culin) prime cut of beef

onirique /ɔniʀik/ adj dream-like

onomatopée /ɔnɔmatɔpe/ nf onomatopoeia

ont /ɔ̃/ ▶ AVOIR¹

ONU /ɔny, ɔɛny/ nf (abbr = **Organisation des Nations unies**) UN, UNO

onyx /ɔniks/ nm inv onyx

onze /ɔ̃z/ adj inv, pron, nm inv eleven

onzième /ɔ̃zjɛm/ ⊡ adj eleventh
⊡ nf (Sch) first year of primary school, age 6–7

OPA /ɔpea/ nf (abbr = **offre publique d'achat**) takeover bid

opaque /ɔpak/ adj (a) opaque
(b) (figurative) ‹text› opaque; ‹night› dark; ‹wood, fog› impenetrable

OPEP /ɔpɛp/ nf (abbr = **Organisation des pays producteurs de pétrole**) OPEC

opéra /ɔpeʀa/ nm (a) opera
(b) opera house

opérateur, -trice /ɔpeʀatœʀ, tʀis/ nm,f operator; ∼ de saisie keyboarder

♂ **opération** /ɔpeʀasjɔ̃/ nf (a) ∼ (chirurgicale) operation, surgery
(b) calculation
(c) (Tech) operation

⋯⟶

O

(d) process
(e) transaction
■ ∼ **escargot** convoy protest
opératoire /ɔpeʀatwaʀ/ *adj* **(a)** ⟨*technique*⟩
surgical; ⟨*risk*⟩ in operating
(b) operative
opercule /ɔpɛʀkyl/ *nm* **(a)** (Bot, Zool)
operculum
(b) lid
opéré, ∼e /ɔpeʀe/ *nm,f* person who has
had an operation
✧ **opérer** /ɔpeʀe/ [14] **1** *vtr* **(a)** to operate
on; ∼ **qn de l'appendicite** to remove sb's
appendix; **se faire ∼** to have an operation, to
have surgery
(b) to bring about ⟨*change*⟩
2 *vi* **(a)** (Med) to operate
(b) ⟨*cure, charm*⟩ to work
(c) to proceed
(d) ⟨*thief*⟩ to operate
opérette /ɔpeʀɛt/ *nf* operetta, light opera
ophtalmologiste /ɔftalmɔlɔʒist/ *nmf*
ophthalmologist
opiner /ɔpine/ [1] *vi* ∼ **du bonnet** *or* **de la
tête** to nod in agreement
opiniâtre /ɔpinjɑtʀ/ *adj* ⟨*resistance*⟩
dogged; ⟨*work*⟩ relentless; ⟨*person*⟩ tenacious
✧ **opinion** /ɔpinjɔ̃/ *nf* **(a)** opinion; **mon ∼ est
faite** my mind is made up
(b) **l'∼ (publique)** public opinion
opium /ɔpjɔm/ *nm* opium
opportun, ∼e /ɔpɔʀtœ̃, yn/ *adj*
appropriate
opportuniste /ɔpɔʀtynist/ *nmf*
opportunist
opportunité /ɔpɔʀtynite/ *nf*
(a) appropriateness
(b) opportunity
opposant, ∼e /ɔpozɑ̃, ɑ̃t/ *nm,f* opponent
opposé, ∼e /ɔpoze/ **1** *adj* **(a)** ⟨*direction*⟩
opposite
(b) ⟨*opinion*⟩ opposite; ⟨*parties, sides*⟩
opposing; ⟨*interests*⟩ conflicting
(c) opposed
2 **à l'opposé** *phr* **(a)** à l'∼ **de mes frères**
in contrast to my brothers
(b) **il est parti à l'∼** he went off in the
opposite direction
✧ **opposer** /ɔpoze/ [1] **1** *vtr* **(a)** to put up
⟨*resistance, argument*⟩
(b) ∼ **à** to match *or* pit [sb] against ⟨*person,
team*⟩
(c) ⟨*problem*⟩ to divide ⟨*people*⟩
(d) to compare
2 **s'opposer** *v refl* (+ *v être*) **(a)** **s'∼ à qch**
to be opposed to sth
(b) **s'∼ à** to stand in the way of ⟨*change*⟩
(c) to contrast
(d) ⟨*ideas, opinions*⟩ to conflict; ⟨*people*⟩ to
disagree
(e) ⟨*teams*⟩ to confront each other

✧ **opposition** /ɔpozisjɔ̃/ *nf* **(a)** opposition;
par ∼ à in contrast with *or* to
(b) **faire ∼ à un chèque** to stop a cheque (GB)
or check (US)
oppressant, ∼e /ɔpʀesɑ̃, ɑ̃t/ *adj*
oppressive
oppresser /ɔpʀese/ [1] *vtr* to oppress; **se
sentir oppressé** to feel breathless
oppression /ɔpʀesjɔ̃/ *nf* oppression
opprimer /ɔpʀime/ [1] *vtr* to oppress
⟨*people*⟩
opter /ɔpte/ [1] *vi* to opt
opticien, -ienne /ɔptisjɛ̃, ɛn/ *nm,f*
optician
optimal, ∼e, *mpl* **-aux** /ɔptimal, o/ *adj*
optimum
optimiser /ɔptimize/ [1] *vtr* to optimize
optimisme /ɔptimism/ *nm* optimism
optimiste /ɔptimist/ *adj* optimistic
option /ɔpsjɔ̃/ *nf* option; **en ∼** optional
optique /ɔptik/ **1** *adj* **(a)** (Anat) optic
(b) optical
2 *nf* **(a)** optics
(b) perspective
opulence /ɔpylɑ̃s/ *nf* opulence
or¹ /ɔʀ/ *conj* and yet; **∼, ce jour-là, il… now,
on that particular day, he…
✧ **or²** /ɔʀ/ **1** *adj inv* gold; ⟨*hair*⟩ golden
2 *nm* **(a)** gold; **en ∼** gold; ⟨*husband*⟩
marvellous (GB); ⟨*opportunity*⟩ golden
(b) gilding
oracle /ɔʀakl/ *nm* oracle
orage /ɔʀaʒ/ *nm* storm
orageux, -euse /ɔʀaʒø, øz/ *adj* stormy
oraison /ɔʀɛzɔ̃/ *nf* prayer; ∼ **funèbre**
funeral oration
oral, ∼e, *mpl* **-aux** /ɔʀal, o/ **1** *adj* **(a)** oral
(b) (Med) **par voie ∼e** orally
2 *nm* (Sch) oral (examination)
oralement /ɔʀalmɑ̃/ *adv* **(a)** (Med) orally
(b) verbally
orange¹ /ɔʀɑ̃ʒ/ *adj inv* orange; ⟨*light*⟩
amber (GB), yellow (US)
orange² /ɔʀɑ̃ʒ/ *nf* orange
orangeade /ɔʀɑ̃ʒad/ *nf* orangeade
oranger /ɔʀɑ̃ʒe/ *nm* orange tree
orangerie /ɔʀɑ̃ʒʀi/ *nf* orangery
orateur, -trice /ɔʀatœʀ, tʀis/ *nm,f*
(a) speaker
(b) orator
orbite /ɔʀbit/ *nf* **(a)** orbit
(b) eye-socket
orchestral, ∼e, *mpl* **-aux** /ɔʀkɛstʀal,
o/ *adj* orchestral
orchestration /ɔʀkɛstʀasjɔ̃/ *nf*
orchestration
orchestre /ɔʀkɛstʀ/ *nm* **(a)** orchestra
(b) band
(c) orchestra stalls (GB), orchestra (US)

✧ indicates a very frequent word

O

orchestrer /ɔʀkɛstʀe/ [1] *vtr* to orchestrate

orchidée /ɔʀkide/ *nf* orchid

⚘ **ordinaire** /ɔʀdinɛʀ/ **1** *adj* (a) ordinary; ‹*quality*› standard; ‹*reader, tourist*› average; **journée peu ~** unusual day
(b) **très ~** ‹*meal, wine*› very average; ‹*person*› very ordinary
2 *nm* **sortir de l'~** to be out of the ordinary
3 **à l'ordinaire, d'ordinaire** *phr* usually

ordinal, ~e, *mpl* **-aux** /ɔʀdinal, o/ *adj* ordinal

⚘ **ordinateur** /ɔʀdinatœʀ/ *nm* computer

ordination /ɔʀdinasjɔ̃/ *nf* ordination

ordonnance /ɔʀdɔnɑ̃s/ *nf* prescription

⚘ **ordonner** /ɔʀdɔne/ [1] *vtr* (a) to order
(b) to put [sth] in order
(c) to ordain

⚘ **ordre** /ɔʀdʀ/ *nm* (a) (command) order; **j'ai des ~s** I'm acting under orders; **à vos ~s!** (Mil) yes, sir!; **jusqu'à nouvel ~** until further notice
(b) (sequence) order; **par ~ alphabétique** in alphabetical order
(c) tidiness, orderliness
(d) (orderly state) order; **rappeler qn à l'~** to reprimand sb; **tout est rentré dans l'~** everything is back to normal; **rétablir l'~ (public)** to restore law and order
(e) nature; **c'est dans l'~ des choses** it's in the nature of things; **de l'~ de 30%** in the order of 30% (GB), on the order of 30% (US); **de premier ~** first-rate
(f) (in religion) order; **entrer dans les ~s** to take (holy) orders
(g) **libellez le chèque à l'~ de X** make the cheque (GB) *or* check (US) payable to X
■ **~ du jour** agenda

ordure /ɔʀdyʀ/ **1** *nf* filth
2 **ordures** *nf pl* refuse (GB), garbage (US)

ordurier, -ière /ɔʀdyʀje, ɛʀ/ *adj* filthy

orée /ɔʀe/ *nf* (a) edge
(b) (figurative) start

⚘ **oreille** /ɔʀɛj/ *nf* (a) ear; **n'écouter que d'une ~** to half-listen; **ouvre-bien les ~s!** listen carefully
(b) hearing; **avoir l'~ fine** to have keen hearing
(c) **à l'abri des ~s indiscrètes** where no-one can hear
IDIOM **tirer les ~s à qn** to tell sb off

oreiller /ɔʀeje/ *nm* pillow

oreillons /ɔʀejɔ̃/ *nm pl* mumps

ores: d'ores et déjà /dɔʀzedeʒa/ *phr* already

orfèvre /ɔʀfɛvʀ/ *nmf* goldsmith; **être ~ en la matière** to be an expert in the field

orfèvrerie /ɔʀfɛvʀəʀi/ *nf* (a) goldsmith's art
(b) goldsmith's and silversmith's

organe /ɔʀgan/ *nm* organ

organigramme /ɔʀganigʀam/ *nm* organization chart

organique /ɔʀganik/ *adj* organic

⚘ **organisation** /ɔʀganizasjɔ̃/ *nf* organization

⚘ **organiser** /ɔʀganize/ [1] **1** *vtr* to organize
2 **s'organiser** *v refl* (+ *v être*)
(a) ‹*opposition*› to get organized
(b) to organize oneself
(c) ‹*fight, help*› to be organized

⚘ **organisme** /ɔʀganism/ *nm* (a) body
(b) organism
(c) organization, body

orgasme /ɔʀgasm/ *nm* orgasm

orge /ɔʀʒ/ *nf* barley

orgie /ɔʀʒi/ *nf* orgy

orgue /ɔʀg/ *nm* (Mus) organ

orgueil /ɔʀgœj/ *nm* pride

orgueilleux, -euse /ɔʀgœjø, øz/ *adj* overproud

orient /ɔʀjɑ̃/ *nm* (a) east
(b) **l'Orient** the East

⚘ **oriental, ~e,** *mpl* **-aux** /ɔʀjɑ̃tal, o/ *adj* eastern; oriental

Oriental, ~e, *mpl* **-aux** /ɔʀjɑ̃tal, o/ *nm,f* Asian; **les Orientaux** Asians

orientation /ɔʀjɑ̃tasjɔ̃/ *nf* (a) (of house) aspect; (of aerial) angle
(b) (of inquiry) direction
(c) (Sch) **changer d'~** to change courses

orienter /ɔʀjɑ̃te/ [1] **1** *vtr* (a) to adjust ‹*aerial, lamp*›
(b) **~ la conversation sur** to bring the conversation around to
(c) to direct ‹*person*›
(d) (Sch) to give [sb] career advice
2 **s'orienter** *v refl* (+ *v être*) (a) to get *or* find one's bearings
(b) **s'~ vers** ‹*person*› to turn toward(s); **s'~ vers les carrières scientifiques** to go in for a career in science

orifice /ɔʀifis/ *nm* (a) orifice
(b) (of pipe) mouth; (of tube) neck

originaire /ɔʀiʒinɛʀ/ *adj* ‹*plant, animal*› native; **famille ~ d'Asie** Asian family

⚘ **original, ~e,** *mpl* **-aux** /ɔʀiʒinal, o/ **1** *adj*
(a) original
(b) eccentric
2 *nm* original

originalité /ɔʀiʒinalite/ *nf* originality

⚘ **origine** /ɔʀiʒin/ *nf* origin; **être d'~ modeste** to come from a modest background; **dès l'~** right from the start; **à l'~** originally

originel, -elle /ɔʀiʒinɛl/ *adj* original

orme /ɔʀm/ *nm* (a) elm (tree)
(b) elm (wood)

ornement /ɔʀnəmɑ̃/ *nm* (a) ornament
(b) decorative detail

orner /ɔʀne/ [1] *vtr* to decorate

ornière /ɔʀnjɛʀ/ *nf* rut

O

ornithologie /ɔʀnitɔlɔʒi/ *nf* ornithology

ornithorynque /ɔʀnitɔʀɛ̃k/ *nm* (duck-billed) platypus, duckbill (US)

orphelin, ~e /ɔʀfəlɛ̃, in/ *nm,f* orphan

orphelinat /ɔʀfəlina/ *nm* orphanage

orque /ɔʀk/ *nm or f* killer whale

orteil /ɔʀtɛj/ *nm* toe; **gros ~** big toe

orthodoxe /ɔʀtɔdɔks/ *adj, nmf* Orthodox

orthographe /ɔʀtɔgʀaf/ *nf* spelling

orthographier /ɔʀtɔgʀafje/ [2] *vtr* to spell

orthopédie /ɔʀtɔpedi/ *nf* orthopedics

orthophoniste /ɔʀtɔfɔnist/ *nmf* speech therapist

ortie /ɔʀti/ *nf* (stinging) nettle

orvet /ɔʀvɛ/ *nm* slowworm, blindworm

os /ɔs, *pl* o/ *nm inv* bone; **en chair et en ~** in the flesh
IDIOMS **il y a un ~** (fam) there's a hitch; **tomber sur un ~** (fam) to come across a snag; **être trempé jusqu'aux ~** (fam) to be soaked to the skin (colloq)

osciller /ɔsile/ [1] *vi* (a) ‹*pendulum*› to swing; ‹*boat*› to rock; ‹*head*› to roll from side to side
(b) ‹*currency*› to fluctuate
(c) to vacillate

osé, ~e /oze/ *adj* (a) risqué
(b) ‹*behaviour*› daring; ‹*words*› outspoken

oseille /ozɛj/ *nf* (a) sorrel
(b) (fam) dough (colloq), money

Ⓒ **oser** /oze/ [1] *vtr* to dare; **si j'ose dire** if I may say so

osier /ozje/ *nm* (a) (tree) osier
(b) wicker, osier

osmose /ɔsmoz/ *nf* osmosis

ossature /ɔsatyʀ/ *nf* skeleton; **~ du visage** bone structure

ossements /ɔsmɑ̃/ *nm pl* remains

osseux, -euse /ɔsø, øz/ *adj* (a) bony
(b) ‹*disease*› bone

ostentatoire /ɔstɑ̃tatwaʀ/ *adj* ostentatious

ostéopathe /ɔsteɔpat/ *nmf* osteopath

ostracisme /ɔstʀasism/ *nm* ostracism

ostréiculture /ɔstʀeikyltyʀ/ *nf* oyster farming

otage /ɔtaʒ/ *nm* hostage

OTAN /ɔtɑ̃/ *nf* (*abbr* = **Organisation du traité de l'Atlantique Nord**) NATO

otarie /ɔtaʀi/ *nf* eared seal, otary

ôter /ote/ [1] ① *vtr* (a) to take off ‹*clothes, glasses*›; to remove ‹*bones, stain*›
(b) **~ qch à qn** to take sth away from sb
(c) (in mathematics) **4 ôté de 9, il reste 5** 9 minus *or* take away 4 leaves 5
② **s'ôter** *v refl* (+ *v être*) **s'~ qch de l'esprit** to get sth out of one's mind *or* head

otite /ɔtit/ *nf* inflammation of the ear

 Ⓒ indicates a very frequent word

oto-rhino-laryngologiste, *pl* **~s** /otoʀinolaʀɛ̃gɔlɔʒist/ *nmf* ENT specialist

Ⓒ **ou** /u/ *conj* or; **~ (bien)... ~ (bien)...** either... or...

Ⓒ **où** /u/ ① *adv* where; **je l'ai perdu je ne sais ~** I've lost it somewhere or other; **par ~ êtes-vous passés pour venir?** which way did you come?; **~ en êtes-vous?** where have you got to?; **~ allons-nous?** what are things coming to!
② *rel pron* (a) where; **le quartier ~ nous habitons** the area we live in; **d'~ s'élevait de la fumée** out of which smoke was rising; **~ qu'ils aillent** wherever they go
(b) **la misère ~ elle se trouvait** the poverty in which she was living; **au train** *or* **à l'allure ~ vont les choses** (at) the rate things are going; **le travail s'est accumulé, d'~ ce retard** there is a backlog of work, hence the delay
(c) when; **le matin ~ je l'ai rencontré** the morning I met him

ouate /wat/ *nf* (a) cotton wool (GB), cotton (US)
(b) wadding

oubli /ubli/ *nm* (a) **l'~ de qch** forgetting sth; (of duty) neglect of sth
(b) omission
(c) oblivion; **tomber dans l'~** to be completely forgotten

Ⓒ **oublier** /ublije/ [2] ① *vtr* (a) to forget ‹*name, date, fact*›; to forget about ‹*worries, incident*›; **se faire ~** to keep a low profile
(b) to leave out ‹*person, detail*›
(c) to neglect ‹*duty, friend*›
② **s'oublier** *v refl* (+ *v être*) (a) to be forgotten
(b) to leave oneself out

oubliettes /ublijɛt/ *nf pl* oubliette

oued /wɛd/ *nm* wadi

Ⓒ **ouest** /wɛst/ ① *adj inv* west; western
② *nm* (a) west
(b) **l'Ouest** the West

ouf /uf/ ① *nm* **faire ~** to breathe a sigh of relief
② *excl* phew!

Ⓒ **oui** /wi/ ① *adv* yes; **alors c'est ~?** so the answer is yes?; **découvrir si ~ ou non** to discover whether or not; **dire ~ à qch** to welcome sth; to agree to sth; **faire ~ de la tête** to nod; **lui, prudent? un lâche, ~!** him, cautious? a coward, more like! (colloq); **je crois que ~** I think so
② *nm inv* (a) yes
(b) 'yes' vote; **le ~ l'a emporté** the ayes have it
IDIOM **pour un ~ (ou) pour un non** ‹*get angry*› for the slightest thing; ‹*change one's mind*› at the drop of a hat

ouï, ~e /wi/ ▶ OUÏR

ouï-dire /widiʀ/ *nm inv* **par ~** by hearsay

ouïe /wi/ *nf* (a) hearing; **être tout ~** to be all ears
(b) (of fish) gill

ouïr /wiʀ/ [38] *vtr* (dated) to hear; **j'ai ouï dire que** word has reached me that

ouistiti /wistiti/ *nm* marmoset

ouragan /uʀagɑ̃/ *nm* hurricane

ourler /uʀle/ [1] *vtr* to hem

ourlet /uʀlɛ/ *nm* hem

ours /uʀs/ *nm inv* (a) bear
(b) **il est un peu ~** he's a bit surly
■ **~ blanc** polar bear; **~ en peluche** teddy bear; **~ polaire** ▶ OURS BLANC
IDIOM **vendre la peau de l'~ avant de l'avoir tué** (Proverb) to count one's chickens before they're hatched

ourse /uʀs/ *nf* she-bear

oursin /uʀsɛ̃/ *nm* (sea) urchin

ourson /uʀsɔ̃/ *nm* bear cub

✓ **outil** /uti/ *nm* tool; **~ de travail** work tool

outrage /utʀaʒ/ *nm* insult
■ **~ à** agent *verbal assault of a policeman*

outrager /utʀaʒe/ [13] *vtr* to offend

outrance /utʀɑ̃s/ *nf* **à ~** excessively

outrancier, -ière /utʀɑ̃sje, ɛʀ/ *adj* extreme

outre /utʀ/ ① *prep* in addition to
② *adv* **passer ~** to pay no heed
③ **outre mesure** *phr* unduly
④ **en outre** *phr* in addition

outre-Atlantique /utʀatlɑ̃tik/ *adv* across the Atlantic; **d'~** American

outre-Manche /utʀəmɑ̃ʃ/ *adv* across the Channel; **d'~** British

outremer /utʀəmɛʀ/ *adj inv, nm* ultramarine

outre-mer /utʀəmɛʀ/ *adv* overseas

outrer /utʀe/ [1] *vtr* (a) to outrage
(b) to exaggerate

outre-tombe /utʀətɔ̃b/ *adv* **une voix d'~** a voice from beyond the grave

✓ **ouvert, ~e** /uvɛʀ, ɛʀt/ ① *pp* ▶ OUVRIR
② *pp adj* (a) open; **grand ~** wide open; **être ~ aux idées nouvelles** to be open to new ideas
(b) ‹gas› on; ‹tap› running
(c) ‹question› open-ended

ouvertement /uvɛʀtəmɑ̃/ *adv* openly; blatantly

✓ **ouverture** /uvɛʀtyʀ/ *nf* (a) opening; **heures d'~** opening hours
(b) openness; **~ d'esprit** open-mindedness; **~ à l'Ouest** opening-up to the West
(c) (Mus) overture

ouvrable /uvʀabl/ *adj* ‹day› working; ‹hours› business

✓ **ouvrage** /uvʀaʒ/ *nm* (a) work
(b) book, work
(c) piece of work; **~ de broderie** piece of embroidery
IDIOM **avoir du cœur à l'~** to work with a will

ouvragé, ~e /uvʀaʒe/ *adj* finely wrought

ouvrant, ~e /uvʀɑ̃, ɑ̃t/ *adj* **toit ~** sunroof

ouvré, ~e /uvʀe/ *adj* **jour ~** working day

ouvre-boîtes /uvʀəbwat/ *nm inv* can-opener

ouvreur, -euse /uvʀœʀ, øz/ *nm,f* usher; usherette

✓ **ouvrier, -ière** /uvʀije, ɛʀ/ ① *adj* of the workers; **classe ouvrière** working class
② *nm,f* worker; workman

✓ **ouvrir** /uvʀiʀ/ [32] ① *vtr* (gen) to open; to undo ‹collar, shirt, zip›; to initiate ‹dialogue›; to open up ‹possibilities, market›; **ne pas ~ la bouche** not to say a word; **~ les bras à qn** to welcome sb with open arms; **~ l'esprit à qn** to open sb's mind
② *vi* (a) to open the door; **ouvre-moi!** let me in!
(b) to open
(c) to be opened
③ **s'ouvrir** *v refl* (+ *v être*) (gen) to open; ‹shirt, dress› to come undone; ‹dialogue, process› to be initiated; ‹country, economy› to open up; ‹ground, scar› to open up; ‹person› to cut open ‹head›; **s'~ les veines** to slash one's wrists; **s'~ à qn** to open one's heart to sb

ovaire /ɔvɛʀ/ *nm* ovary

ovale /ɔval/ *adj, nm* oval

ovation /ɔvasjɔ̃/ *nf* (a) ovation
(b) accolade

ovationner /ɔvasjɔne/ [1] *vtr* to greet [sb/sth] with wild applause

ovni /ɔvni/ *nm* (*abbr* = **objet volant non identifié**) unidentified flying object, UFO

ovulation /ɔvylasjɔ̃/ *nf* ovulation

ovule /ɔvyl/ *nm* (a) (Anat) ovum
(b) (Bot) ovule

oxyde /ɔksid/ *nm* oxide; **~ de carbone** carbon monoxide

oxyder /ɔkside/ [1] *vtr*, **s'oxyder** *v refl* (+ *v être*) to oxidize

oxygène /ɔksiʒɛn/ *nm* (a) oxygen
(b) air

oxygéner /ɔksiʒene/ [14] ① *vtr* to oxygenate
② **s'oxygéner** *v refl* (+ *v être*) ‹person› to get some fresh air

ozone /ozon/ *nf* ozone; **la couche d'~** the ozone layer

O

Pp

p, P /pe/ *nm inv* p, P
PAC *nf* (*abbr* = **politique agricole commune**) CAP
pacha /paʃa/ *nm* pasha
pachyderme /paʃidɛʀm/ *nm* (Zool) pachyderm; **de ∼** (figurative) heavy
pacifier /pasifje/ [1] *vtr* to establish peace in
pacifique /pasifik/ **1** *adj* peaceful
2 *nmf* peace-loving person
Pacifique /pasifik/ *pr nm* **le ∼** the Pacific
pacifiste /pasifist/ *adj, nmf* pacifist
pacotille /pakɔtij/ *nf* **de la ∼** cheap rubbish
PACS *nm* (*abbr* = **pacte civil de solidarité**) contract of civil union
pacser: se pacser /pakse/ [1] *v refl* (+ *v être*) to sign a PACS
pacte /pakt/ *nm* pact
PAF /paf/ **1** *nm: abbr* ▶ PAYSAGE
2 *nf: abbr* ▶ POLICE
pagaie /pagɛ/ *nf* (Naut) paddle
pagaille **1** *nf* mess; **semer la ∼** to cause chaos
2 **en pagaille** *phr* in a mess
paganisme /paganism/ *nm* paganism
pagayer /pageje/ [21] *vi* to paddle
page¹ /paʒ/ *nm* page (boy)
⚜ **page²** /paʒ/ *nf* page; **en première ∼** on the front page; **tourner la ∼** (figurative) to turn over a new leaf
■ **∼ d'accueil** (Comput) home page; **∼ de publicité** commercial break
IDIOM **être à la ∼** to be up to date
pagination /paʒinasjɔ̃/ *nf* pagination
paginer /paʒine/ [1] *vtr* to paginate
pagne /paɲ/ *nm* **(a)** loincloth
(b) grass skirt
pagode /pagɔd/ *nf* pagoda
paie /pɛ/ *nf* pay; **bulletin** *or* **fiche de ∼** payslip
IDIOM **ça fait une ∼ que je ne l'ai pas vu** (fam) it's ages since I saw him (colloq)
paiement /pɛmɑ̃/ *nm* payment
païen, -ïenne /pajɛ̃, ɛn/ *adj, nm,f* pagan
paillard, ∼e /pajaʀ, aʀd/ *adj* bawdy
paillasse /pajas/ *nf* **(a)** straw mattress
(b) lab bench
(c) draining board
paillasson /pajasɔ̃/ *nm* doormat

⚜ indicates a very frequent word

paille /pɑj/ **1** *adj inv* **jaune ∼** straw yellow
2 *nf* straw; **∼ de fer** steel wool
IDIOMS **être sur la ∼** (fam) to be penniless; **tirer à la courte ∼** to draw lots
paillette /pajɛt/ *nf* **(a)** sequin, spangle (US); **robe à ∼s** sequined *or* spangled (US) dress
(b) glitter
(c) savon en ∼s soap flakes
⚜ **pain** /pɛ̃/ *nm* **(a)** bread; **des miettes de ∼** breadcrumbs
(b) loaf; **un petit ∼** a (bread) roll
(c) ∼ de viande meat loaf
(d) (of soap) bar
■ **∼ blanc** white bread; **∼ de campagne** farmhouse bread; **∼ complet** wholemeal bread (GB), wholewheat bread (US); **∼ d'épices** gingerbread; **∼ grillé** toast; **∼ au lait** milk roll; **∼ de mie** sandwich loaf; **∼ de seigle** rye bread; **∼ de son** bran loaf
IDIOMS **se vendre comme des petits ∼s** to sell like hot cakes; **ça ne mange pas de ∼** (fam) it doesn't cost anything; **je ne mange pas de ce ∼-là** (fam) I won't have anything to do with it
pair, ∼e¹ /pɛʀ/ **1** *adj* ‹number› even
2 *nm* **(a)** peer; **c'est une cuisinière hors ∼** she's an excellent cook
(b) aller *or* **marcher de ∼ avec qch** to go hand in hand with sth
3 **au pair** *phr* **travailler au ∼** to work as an au pair
paire² /pɛʀ/ *nf* pair; **donner une ∼ de gifles à qn** to box sb's ears
IDIOM **les deux font la ∼!** they're two of a kind!
paisible /pɛzibl/ *adj* peaceful, quiet, calm
paisiblement /pɛzibləmɑ̃/ *adv* peacefully
paître /pɛtʀ/ [74] *vi* to graze
IDIOM **envoyer ∼ qn** (fam) to send sb packing (colloq)
⚜ **paix** /pɛ/ *nf inv* peace; **avoir la ∼** to get some peace; **laisser qn en ∼** to leave sb alone; **la∼!** (fam) be quiet!
pakistanais, ∼e /pakistanɛ, ɛz/ *adj* Pakistani
palabrer /palabʀe/ [1] *vi* to discuss endlessly
palace /palas/ *nm* luxury hotel
⚜ **palais** /palɛ/ *nm inv* **(a)** palate
(b) palace
(c) (Law) **∼ (de justice)** law courts
■ **∼ des sports** sports centre (GB)
palan /palɑ̃/ *nm* hoist
pale /pal/ *nf* (of propeller, oar) blade
pâle /pɑl/ *adj* pale; **vert ∼** pale green

palefrenier ⸱⸱⸱❯ panorama ⸱⸱⸱⸱

IDIOM faire ~ figure à côté de to pale into insignificance beside

palefrenier, -ière /palfRənje, εR/ *nm,f* groom

paléolithique /paleɔlitik/ *adj, nm* Paleolithic

paléontologie /paleɔ̃tɔlɔʒi/ *nf* paleontology

palet /palε/ *nm* **(a)** (in ice hockey) puck **(b)** quoit

paletot /palto/ *nm* jacket

IDIOM **tomber sur le ~ de qn** (fam) to lay into sb (colloq)

palette /palεt/ *nf* **(a)** palette **(b)** range; **une ~ d'activités** a range of activities **(c)** (of pork, mutton) ≈ shoulder

pâleur /pɑlœR/ *nf* paleness; pallor

palier /palje/ *nm* **(a)** landing; **mon voisin de ~** my neighbour (GB) on the same floor **(b)** level; plateau **(c)** (in diving) ~ **(de décompression)** (decompression) stage

palière /paljεR/ *adj f* **porte ~** entry door

pâlir /pɑliR/ [3] *vi* **(a)** to fade **(b)** to grow pale

palissade /palisad/ *nf* fence

palliatif /paljatif/ *nm* palliative

pallier /palje/ [?] *vtr* to compensate for

palmarès /palmaRεs/ *nm inv* **(a)** honours (GB) list; list of (award) winners **(b)** record of achievements **(c)** hit parade **(d)** bestsellers list

palme /palm/ *nf* **(a)** palm leaf **(b)** palm (tree) **(c)** (for diver) flipper **(d)** (Mil) ≈ bar **(e)** prize

palmé, ~e /palme/ *adj* **(a)** ‹feet› webbed **(b)** ‹leaf› palmate

palmier /palmje/ *nm* palm (tree)

palombe /palɔ̃b/ *nf* wood pigeon

palourde /paluRd/ *nf* clam

palpable /palpabl/ *adj* palpable; tangible

palper /palpe/ [1] *vtr* **(a)** (Med) to palpate **(b)** to feel

palpitant, ~e /palpitɑ̃, ɑ̃t/ *adj* thrilling

palpitation /palpitasjɔ̃/ *nf* **(a)** (Med) palpitation **(b)** twitching

palpiter /palpite/ [1] *vi* ‹heart› to beat; to flutter; ‹vein› to pulse

paludisme /palydism/ *nm* malaria

pâmer: se pâmer /pɑme/ [1] *v refl* (+ *v être*) (liter) **se ~ devant qch** to swoon over sth

pamphlet /pɑ̃flε/ *nm* satirical tract

pamphlétaire /pɑ̃fletεR/ *nmf* pamphleteer

pamplemousse /pɑ̃pləmus/ *nm* grapefruit

pan /pɑ̃/ **1** *nm* **(a)** (of cliff, house) section; (of life) part **(b)** (of tower) side; **~s d'un manteau** coat-tails **2** *excl* *also onomatopoeic* bang!; thump!; whack!

pan- /pɑ̃, pan/ *pref* Pan; **~-russe** Pan-Russian; **~-européen** Pan-European

panacée /panase/ *nf* panacea

panache /panaʃ/ *nm* **(a)** panache **(b)** plume

panaché, ~e /panaʃe/ **1** *adj* ‹bouquet, salad› mixed; ‹tulip, ivy› variegated **2** *nm* shandy (GB), shandygaff (US)

panacher /panaʃe/ [1] *vtr* to mix

panama /panama/ *nm* panama (hat)

panaris /panaRi/ *nm inv* whitlow

pancarte /pɑ̃kaRt/ *nf* **(a)** notice (GB), sign (US) **(b)** placard (GB), sign (US)

pancréas /pɑ̃kReas/ *nm inv* pancreas

panda /pɑ̃da/ *nm* panda

pandémie /pɑ̃demi/ *nf* pandemic

paner /pane/ [1] *vtr* to coat with breadcrumbs

panier /panje/ *nm* **(a)** basket **(b)** (in dishwasher) rack **(c)** (Sport) basket ■ **~ à linge** linen basket; **~ à salade** salad shaker; Black Maria (GB), paddy wagon (US) IDIOMS **être un ~ percé** (fam) to spend money like water; **ils sont tous à mettre dans le même ~** (fam) they are all about the same; **le dessus du ~** (fam) the pick of the bunch; **mettre au ~** to throw [sth] out; to get rid of [sth]

panique /panik/ *nf* panic; **semer** *or* **jeter la ~** to spread panic; **être pris de ~** to be panic-stricken

paniquer /panike/ [1] *vi* (fam) to panic

panne /pan/ *nf* (of vehicle, machine) breakdown; (of engine) failure; **~ de courant** power failure; **tomber en ~ sèche** *or* **d'essence** to run out of petrol (GB) *or* gas (US); **être en ~ de** (fam) to be out of ‹coffee›; to have run out of ‹ideas›

panneau, *pl* **~x** /pano/ *nm* **(a)** sign; board **(b)** notice board (GB), bulletin board (US) **(c)** panel ■ **~ de configuration** (Comput) control panel; **~ indicateur** signpost; **~ publicitaire** hoarding (GB), billboard; **~ de signalisation routière** road sign; **~ solaire** solar panel IDIOM **tomber dans le ~** (fam) to fall for it (colloq)

panonceau, *pl* **~x** /panɔ̃so/ *nm* sign; board

panoplie /panɔpli/ *nf* **(a)** outfit **(b)** display of weapons

panorama /panɔRama/ *nm* **(a)** panorama ⸱⸱⸱❯

(b) (of art, culture) survey

panoramique /panɔʀamik/ *adj* (a) ‹view, visit› panoramic
(b) ‹windscreen› wrap-around
(c) ‹screen› wide

panse /pɑ̃s/ *nf* (a) (of cow) paunch
(b) (fam) belly (colloq)
(c) (of jug) belly

pansement /pɑ̃smɑ̃/ *nm* dressing; ∼ (adhésif) plaster (GB), Band-Aid®

panser /pɑ̃se/ [1] *vtr* to dress ‹wound›; to put a dressing on ‹arm, leg›

✎ **pantalon** /pɑ̃talɔ̃/ *nm* trousers (GB), pants (US); ∼ de pyjama pyjama (GB) *or* pajama (US) bottoms

panthère /pɑ̃tɛʀ/ *nf* panther

pantin /pɑ̃tɛ̃/ *nm* puppet

pantois, ∼e /pɑ̃twa, az/ *adj* flabbergasted

pantomime /pɑ̃tɔmim/ *nf* (a) mime
(b) mime show

pantouflard, ∼e /pɑ̃tuflaʀ, aʀd/ *adj* (fam) qu'est-ce que tu es ∼! what a stay-at-home you are!

pantoufle /pɑ̃tufl/ *nf* slipper

panure /panyʀ/ *nf* breadcrumbs

PAO /peao/ *nf* (a) *abbr* ▶ PRODUCTION
(b) *abbr* ▶ PUBLICATION

paon /pɑ̃/ *nm* peacock

paonne /pan/ *nf* peahen

✎ **papa** /papa/ *nm* dad (colloq), daddy (colloq), father; fils/fille à ∼ spoiled little rich kid (colloq)

pape /pap/ *nm* (a) pope
(b) (figurative) high priest

paperasse /papʀas/ *nf* (fam) (a) bumph (GB) (colloq), documents
(b) paperwork

papeterie /papɛtʀi/ *nf* (a) stationer's (shop), stationery shop (GB) *or* store (US)
(b) stationery
(c) papermaking industry
(d) paper mill

papi /papi/ *nm* (fam) granddad (colloq), grandpa (colloq)

✎ **papier** /papje/ *nm* (a) paper
(b) ∼s (d'identité) (identity) papers *or* documents
(c) (fam) (newspaper) article, piece (colloq)
■ ∼ alu (fam), ∼ (d')aluminium aluminium (GB) *or* aluminum (US) foil, kitchen foil; ∼ brouillon rough paper (GB), scrap paper; ∼ cadeau gift wrap; ∼ d'emballage wrapping paper; ∼ hygiénique toilet paper; ∼ journal newsprint; ∼ à lettres writing paper; ∼ peint wallpaper; ∼ de verre sandpaper; ∼s gras litter
IDIOM être dans les petits ∼s de qn (fam) to be in sb's good books; ▶ MUSIQUE

✎ indicates a very frequent word

papier-calque, *pl* **papiers-calque** /papjekalk/ *nm* tracing paper

papillon /papijɔ̃/ *nm* (a) butterfly; ∼ de nuit moth
(b) (brasse) ∼ butterfly (stroke)

papillonner /papijɔne/ [1] *vi* (a) to flit about
(b) to flirt incessantly

papillote /papijɔt/ *nf* (a) (Culin) foil parcel
(b) (for hair) curlpaper

papoter /papɔte/ [1] *vi* (fam) to chatter

paprika /papʀika/ *nm* paprika

papy ▶ PAPI

Pâque /pɑk/ *nf* la ∼ juive Passover

paquebot /pakbo/ *nm* liner

pâquerette /pɑkʀɛt/ *nf* daisy
IDIOM être au ras des ∼s (fam) to be very basic

Pâques /pɑk/ *nm, nf pl* Easter

✎ **paquet** /pakɛ/ *nm* (a) packet (GB), package (US); (of cigarettes, coffee) packet (GB), pack (US)
(b) parcel
(c) (of clothes) bundle
(d) (fam) masses
(e) (fam) packet (GB) (colloq), bundle (US) (colloq)
■ ∼ de muscles (fam) muscleman
IDIOM mettre le ∼ (fam) to pull out all the stops

paquet-cadeau, *pl* **paquets-cadeaux** /pakɛkado/ *nm* gift-wrapped present

✎ **par** /paʀ/ ① *prep* (a) elle est arrivée ∼ la droite she came from the right; le peintre a terminé *or* fini ∼ la cuisine the painter did the kitchen last
(b) ∼ le passé in the past; ∼ une belle journée d'été on a beautiful summer's day; ils sortent même ∼ moins 40° they go outdoors even when it's minus 40°
(c) per; ∼ jour/an a day/year; ∼ personne per person
(d) by; payer ∼ carte de crédit to pay by credit card; être pris ∼ son travail to be taken up with one's work; deux ∼ deux ‹work› in twos; ‹walk› two by two
(e) in; ∼ étapes in stages; ∼ endroits in places
(f) l'accident est arrivé ∼ sa faute it was his/her fault that the accident happened; ∼ jalousie out of jealousy
(g) through; tu peux me faire passer le livre ∼ ta sœur you can get the book to me via your sister; entre ∼ le garage come in through the garage
② de par *phr* (formal) (a) voyager de ∼ le monde to travel all over the world
(b) de ∼ leurs origines by virtue of their origins

parabole /paʀabɔl/ *nf* (a) parable
(b) parabola

parachever /paʀaʃve/ [16] *vtr* **(a)** to complete
(b) to put the finishing touches to
parachutage /paʀaʃytaʒ/ *nm* airdrop
parachute /paʀaʃyt/ *nm* parachute
parachuter /paʀaʃyte/ [1] *vtr* to parachute
parachutisme /paʀaʃytism/ *nm* parachuting
parachutiste /paʀaʃytist/ *nmf*
(a) parachutist
(b) paratrooper
parade /paʀad/ *nf* **(a)** (Mil) parade
(b) (in fencing) parry
(c) (by animal) display
parader /paʀade/ [1] *vi* to strut about
paradis /paʀadi/ *nm inv* **(a)** heaven
(b) paradise
■ ~ **terrestre** Garden of Eden
IDIOM tu ne l'emporteras pas au ~ (fam) you'll live to regret it
paradisiaque /paʀadizjak/ *adj* heavenly
paradoxal, ~e, *mpl* -aux /paʀadɔksal, o/ *adj* paradoxical
paradoxe /paʀadɔks/ *nm* paradox
paraffine /paʀafin/ *nf* **(a)** paraffin (GB), kerosene (US)
(b) paraffin wax
parages /paʀaʒ/ *nm pl* neighbourhood (GB); **elle est dans les** ~ she is around somewhere
paragraphe /paʀagʀaf/ *nm* paragraph
paraître /paʀɛtʀ/ [73] **1** *vi* **(a)** to come out, to be published; **'à** ~**'** 'forthcoming titles'
(b) to appear, to seem, to look
(c) to appear; to show; **elle ne laisse rien** ~ **de ses sentiments** she doesn't let her feelings show at all; ~ **en public** to appear in public; ~ **à son avantage** to look one's best
2 *v impers* **il paraît qu'il a menti** apparently he lied; **oui, il paraît** so I hear
parallèle¹ /paʀalɛl/ **1** *adj* **(a)** parallel
(b) ‹market› unofficial; ‹medicine› alternative
2 *nm* parallel
parallèle² /paʀalɛl/ *nf* parallel line
parallèlement /paʀalɛlmɑ̃/ *adv* **(a)** ~ **à** parallel to
(b) at the same time
paralyser /paʀalize/ [1] *vtr* **(a)** (Med) to paralyse (GB)
(b) to paralyse (GB) [sth]; to bring [sth] to a halt
paralysie /paʀalizi/ *nf* paralysis
paralytique /paʀalitik/ *adj, nmf* paralytic
paramédical, ~e, *mpl* -aux /paʀamedikal, o/ *adj* paramedical
paramètre /paʀamɛtʀ/ *nm* parameter; ~**s** (Comput) settings
paranoïaque /paʀanɔjak/ *adj, nmf* paranoiac

paranormal, ~e, *mpl* -aux /paʀanɔʀmal, o/ *adj* paranormal
parapente /paʀapɑ̃t/ *nm* **(a)** paraglider
(b) paragliding
parapharmacie /paʀafaʀmasi/ *nf* toiletries and vitamins
paraphe /paʀaf/ *nm* **(a)** initials
(b) signature
paraphrase /paʀafʀɑz/ *nf* paraphrase
paraplégique /paʀapleʒik/ *adj, nmf* paraplegic
parapluie /paʀaplɥi/ *nm* umbrella
parascolaire /paʀaskɔlɛʀ/ *adj* extracurricular
parasitaire /paʀazitɛʀ/ *adj* parasitic(al)
parasite /paʀazit/ **1** *adj* ‹organism› parasitic(al); ‹idea› intrusive
2 *nm* **(a)** parasite
(b) (on TV, radio) ~**s** interference
parasol /paʀasɔl/ *nm* beach umbrella; sun umbrella
paratonnerre /paʀatɔnɛʀ/ *nm* lightning rod
paravent /paʀavɑ̃/ *nm* screen
⚡ **parc** /paʀk/ *nm* **(a)** park
(b) playpen
(c) (for animals) pen
(d) (of facilities) (total) number; (of capital goods) stock; ~ **automobile** fleet of cars; (nationwide) number of cars (on the road); ~ **immobilier** housing stock
■ ~ **d'attractions** amusement *or* theme park; ~ **de loisirs** theme park; ~ **national** national park; ~ **naturel** nature park
⚡ **parce: parce que** /paʀs(ə)k(ə)/ *phr* because
parcelle /paʀsɛl/ *nf* **(a)** plot (of land)
(b) **une** ~ **de bonheur** a bit of happiness
parchemin /paʀʃəmɛ̃/ *nm* parchment
par-ci /paʀsi/ *adv* ~ **par-là** here and there
parcimonie /paʀsimɔni/ *nf* parsimony
parcmètre /paʀkmɛtʀ/ *nm* parking meter
⚡ **parcourir** /paʀkuʀiʀ/ [26] *vtr* **(a)** to travel all over ‹country›; ~ **la ville** to go all over town
(b) to cover ‹distance›
(c) to glance through ‹letter›; to scan ‹horizon›
parcours /paʀkuʀ/ *nm inv* **(a)** (of bus, traveller) route; (of river) course; ~ **fléché** waymarked trail
(b) (Sport) course; ~ **de golf** round of golf
(c) career; **son** ~ (of artist) the development of his/her art; **incident de** ~ hitch
par-delà /paʀdəla/ *prep* beyond
par-derrière /paʀdɛʀjɛʀ/ *adv* **(a)** **passer** ~ to go round (GB) *or* to the back; **ils m'ont attaqué** ~ they attacked me from behind
(b) **critiquer qn** ~ to criticize sb behind his/her back

p

par-dessous /paʀdəsu/ *prep, adv*
underneath

pardessus /paʀdəsy/ *nm inv* overcoat

par-dessus /paʀdəsy/ **1** *adv* (a) pose
ton sac dans un coin et mets ton manteau ∼
put your bag in a corner and put your coat
on top of it
(b) le mur n'est pas haut, passe ∼ the wall
isn't high, climb over it
2 *prep* (a) saute ∼ le ruisseau jump over
the stream
(b) ce que j'aime ∼ tout what I like best
of all

par-devant /paʀdəvɑ̃/ *adv* (a) passer ∼ to
come round by the front
(b) il te fait des sourires ∼ mais dit du mal
de toi dans ton dos he's all smiles to your
face but says nasty things about you behind
your back

pardon /paʀdɔ̃/ *nm* (a) forgiveness; pardon;
je te demande ∼ I'm sorry
(b) ∼! sorry!; ∼ madame/monsieur, je
cherche... excuse me please, I'm looking
for...

pardonnable /paʀdɔnabl/ *adj* forgivable;
ils ne sont pas ∼s it's unforgivable of them

pardonner /paʀdɔne/ [1] **1** *vtr* to forgive;
pardonnez-moi, mais... excuse me, but...
2 *vi* ne pas ∼ ‹illness, error› to be fatal

pare-balles /paʀbal/ *adj inv* bulletproof

pare-brise /paʀbʀiz/ *nm inv* windscreen
(GB), windshield (US)

pare-chocs /paʀʃɔk/ *nm inv* bumper
(GB), fender (US)

pare-feu, *pl* **pare-feu** or **pare-feux**
/paʀfø/ *nm* (a) (outdoor) firebreak
(b) (Comput) firewall

ꝺ **pareil**, **-eille** /paʀɛj/ **1** *adj* (a) similar;
c'est toujours ∼ avec toi it's always the same
with you; à nul autre ∼ without equal
(b) such; je n'ai jamais dit une chose pareille
I never said any such thing
2 *nm,f* equal; d'un dynamisme sans ∼
incredibly dynamic; pour moi c'est du ∼ au
même (fam) it makes no difference to me
3 *adv* (fam) faire ∼ to do the same

ꝺ **parent**, **∼e** /paʀɑ̃, ɑ̃t/ **1** *adj* ‹languages›
similar; ∼ avec ‹person› related to
2 *nm,f* (a) relative, relation
(b) (Zool) parent
3 *nm* (a) parent
(b) ∼s forebears
■ ∼ pauvre poor relation

parental, **∼e**, *mpl* **-aux** /paʀɑ̃tal, o/ *adj*
parental

parenté /paʀɑ̃te/ *nf* (a) (between people)
blood relationship
(b) (between stories) connection

parenthèse /paʀɑ̃tɛz/ *nf* (a) bracket;
ouvrir une∼ (figurative) to digress; entre ∼s
(figurative) incidentally

(b) interlude

parer /paʀe/ [1] **1** *vtr* (a) to ward off
(b) to protect
(c) to adorn
(d) ∼ qn/qch de qch to attribute sth to sb/
sth
2 **parer à** *v+prep* ∼ à toute éventualité
to be prepared for all contingencies; ∼ au
plus pressé to deal with the most urgent
matters first

pare-soleil /paʀsɔlɛj/ *nm inv* visor

paresse /paʀɛs/ *nf* laziness

paresser /paʀese/ [1] *vi* to laze (around)

paresseux, **-euse** /paʀɛsø, øz/ **1** *adj*
lazy
2 *nm,f* lazy person
3 *nm* (Zool) sloth

parfaire /paʀfɛʀ/ [10] *vtr* to complete
‹education, works›; to perfect ‹technique›

ꝺ **parfait**, **∼e** /paʀfɛ, ɛt/ **1** *adj* (a) perfect
(b) ‹likeness› exact; ‹discretion› absolute
(c) ‹tourist› archetypal; ‹example› classic
2 *nm* (in grammar) perfect

ꝺ **parfaitement** /paʀfɛtmɑ̃/ *adv* ‹happy,
capable› perfectly; ‹tolerate, accept› fully

ꝺ **parfois** /paʀfwa/ *adv* sometimes

parfum /paʀfœ̃/ *nm* (a) perfume
(b) (of flower, fruit) scent; (of bath salts)
fragrance; (of wine) bouquet; (of coffee) aroma
(c) flavour (GB)
IDIOM mettre qn au ∼ (fam) to put sb in the
picture

parfumé, **∼e** /paʀfyme/ **1** *pp*
▶ PARFUMER
2 *pp adj* (a) ‹flower› sweet-scented; ‹fruit,
air› fragrant
(b) ‹handkerchief› scented
(c) ‹glace ∼e au café coffee-flavoured (GB)
ice cream

parfumer /paʀfyme/ [1] **1** *vtr* (a) les
fleurs parfument la pièce the room is
fragrant with flowers
(b) to put scent on ‹handkerchief›; to put
scent in ‹bath›
(c) to flavour (GB)
2 **se parfumer** *v refl* (+ *v être*) (a) to
wear perfume
(b) to put perfume on

parfumerie /paʀfymʀi/ *nf* perfumery

pari /paʀi/ *nm* (a) bet
(b) betting
(c) gamble

parier /paʀje/ [2] *vtr* to bet; il y a fort or
gros à ∼ que it's a safe bet that; je l'aurais
parié! I knew it!

Paris /paʀi/ *pr n* Paris

parisien, **-ienne** /paʀizjɛ̃, ɛn/ *adj*
Parisian, Paris

parité /paʀite/ *nf* parity; à ∼ at parity

parjure /paʀʒyʀ/ *nm* perjury

ꝺ indicates a very frequent word

parking /paʀkiŋ/ *nm* car park (GB), parking lot (US)

par-là /paʀla/ *adv* **par-ci ~** here and there

parlant, ~e /paʀlɑ̃, ɑ̃t/ *adj* **(a)** ‹gesture› eloquent; ‹evidence, figure› which speaks for itself
(b) le cinéma **~** the talkies (colloq); un film **~** a talking picture

Parlement /paʀləmɑ̃/ *nm* Parliament

parlementaire /paʀləmɑ̃tɛʀ/ ⓵ *adj* parliamentary
⓶ *nmf* **(a)** Member of Parliament
(b) negotiator

parlementer /paʀləmɑ̃te/ [1] *vi* to negotiate

parler /paʀle/ [1] ⓵ *vtr* **(a)** to speak; **~** (l')italien to speak Italian
(b) ~ affaires/politique to talk (about) business/politics
⓶ **parler à** *v+prep* **~ à qn** to talk *or* speak to sb
⓷ **parler de** *v+prep* **(a) ~ de qn/qch** to talk about sb/sth; to mention sb/sth; **~ de tout et de rien, ~ de choses et d'autres** to talk about this and that; **les journaux en ont parlé** it was in the papers; **faire ~ de soi** to get oneself talked about; to make the news; **qui parle de vous expulser?** who said anything about throwing you out?; **ta promesse, parlons-en!** some promise!; **n'en parlons plus!** let's drop it; **that's the end of it; on m'a beaucoup parlé de vous** I've heard a lot about you
(b) ~ de ‹book, film› to be about
⓸ *vi* to talk, to speak; **parle plus fort** speak up, speak louder; **~ en connaissance de cause** to know what one is talking about; **une prime? tu parles!** (fam) a bonus? you must be joking! (colloq); **il s'écoute ~** he loves the sound of his own voice
⓹ **se parler** *v refl* (+ *v être*) **(a)** to talk *or* speak (to each other)
(b) to be on speaking terms
(c) ‹language, dialect› to be spoken
IDIOM trouver à qui ~ to meet one's match

parloir /paʀlwaʀ/ *nm* (in school) visitors' room; (in prison) visiting room; (in convent) parlour (GB)

parme /paʀm/ *adj inv, nm* mauve

Parmentier /paʀmɑ̃tje/ *pr n* **hachis ~** cottage pie, shepherd's pie

parmi /paʀmi/ *prep* **(a)** among, amongst
(b) demain il sera ~ nous he'll be with us tomorrow
(c) choisir ~ huit destinations to choose from eight destinations

parodie /paʀɔdi/ *nf* **(a)** parody
(b) mockery

parodier /paʀɔdje/ [2] *vtr* to parody

paroi /paʀwa/ *nf* **(a)** (of tunnel) side; (of cave) wall; (of tube, pipe) inner surface
(b) (of house) wall

(c) ~ rocheuse rock face
(d) (Anat) wall

paroisse /paʀwas/ *nf* parish

paroissial, ~e, *mpl* **-iaux** /paʀwasjal, o/ *adj* parish

parole /paʀɔl/ *nf* **(a)** speech; **avoir la ~ facile** to have the gift of the gab (colloq)
(b) laisser la ~ à qn to let sb speak; **temps de ~** speaking time
(c) word; **~s en l'air** empty words; **une ~ blessante** a hurtful remark
(d) (promise) word; **donner sa ~** to give one's word; **~ d'honneur!** cross my heart!, I promise!; **ma ~!** (upon) my word!
(e) words; **c'est ~ d'évangile** it's gospel truth; **~s** words, lyrics; **film sans ~s** silent film

parolier, -ière /paʀɔlje, ɛʀ/ *nm,f* **(a)** lyric writer
(b) librettist

paroxysme /paʀɔksism/ *nm* (of pleasure) paroxysm; (of battle) climax; (of ridiculousness) height

parpaing /paʀpɛ̃/ *nm* breeze-block, cinder block

parquer /paʀke/ [1] *vtr* **(a)** to pen ‹cattle›
(b) to coop up ‹people›
(c) to park ‹car›

parquet /paʀkɛ/ *nm* **(a)** parquet (floor)
(b) (Law) **le ~** ≈ the prosecution

parrain /paʀɛ̃/ *nm* **(a)** godfather
(b) (of candidate) sponsor; (of organization) patron

parrainer /paʀene/ [1] *vtr* **(a)** to be patron of ‹organization›
(b) to sponsor ‹programme, race›

parricide /paʀisid/ *nm* parricide

parsemer /paʀsəme/ [16] *vtr* **une pelouse parsemée de fleurs** a lawn dotted with flowers

part /paʀ/ ⓵ *nf* **(a)** (of cake) slice; (of meat, rice) helping; (of market, legacy) share; **avoir sa ~ de misères** to have one's (fair) share of misfortunes
(b) proportion; **une grande ~ de** a high proportion *or* large part of; **pour une bonne ~ to** a large *or* great extent; **à ~ entière** ‹member› full; ‹science› in its own right
(c) share; **faire sa ~ de travail** to do one's share of the work; **prendre ~ à** to take part in; **il m'a fait ~ de ses projets** he told me about his plans
(d) de toute(s) ~(s) from all sides; **de ~ et d'autre** on both sides, on either side; **de ~ en ~** ‹pierce› right *or* straight through
(e) pour ma/notre ~ for my/our part; **d'une ~..., d'autre ~...** on (the) one hand... on the other hand...; **prendre qch en mauvaise ~** to take sth badly
⓶ **à part** *phr* **(a)** ‹file› separately; **mettre qch à ~** to put sth to one side; **prendre qn à ~** to take sb aside; **une salle à ~** a separate ···:>

room; **blague à ~** joking aside
(b) être un peu à ~ *‹person›* to be out of the
ordinary; **un cas à ~** a special case
(c) apart from; **à ~ ça** apart from that
③ **de la part de** *phr* **(a)** de la **~** de
‹write, act› on behalf of
(b) de la **~** de qn from sb; **donne-leur le
bonjour de ma ~** say hello to them for me;
de leur ~, rien ne m'étonne nothing they do
surprises me
IDIOM faire la ~ des choses to put things in
perspective

partage /paʀtaʒ/ *nm* **(a)** dividing, sharing;
recevoir qch en ~ to be left sth (in a will)
(b) distribution
(c) sharing, division; **régner sans ~** to
reign absolutely; **une victoire sans ~** a total
victory
(d) division, partition

partagé, ~e /paʀtaʒe/ ① *pp* ▶ PARTAGER
② *pp adj* **(a)** *‹opinion, unions›* divided
(b) *‹reactions, feelings›* mixed
(c) être ~ to be torn
(d) *‹grief›* shared; **les torts sont ~s** they are
both to blame
(e) *‹affection›* mutual

◆ **partager** /paʀtaʒe/ [13] ① *vtr* **(a)** to share;
faire ~ qch à qn to let sb share in sth; **il sait
nous faire ~ ses émotions** he knows how to
get his feelings across
(b) to divide *‹country, room›*
(c) to divide [sth] (up), to split *‹inheritance,
work›*
② **se partager** *v refl* (+ *v être*) **(a)** to
share *‹money, work, responsibility›*
(b) to be divided, to be split
(c) *‹costs, responsibility›* to be shared; *‹cake›*
to be cut (up)

partance /paʀtɑ̃s/ *nf* **en ~** about to take
off; about to sail; about to leave; **être en ~
pour** *or* **vers** to be bound for

partenaire /paʀtənɛʀ/ *nmf* partner; **qui
était le ~ d'Arletty?** who played opposite
Arletty?
■ **~s sociaux** ≈ unions and management

partenariat /paʀtənaʀja/ *nm* partnership

parterre /paʀtɛʀ/ *nm* **(a)** (in garden) bed
(b) stalls (GB), orchestra (US)

◆ **parti, ~e¹** /paʀti/ ① *adj* (fam) **être ~** to be
tight (colloq)
② *nm* **(a)** group; party; **les ~s de
l'opposition** the opposition parties
(b) option; **prendre ~** to commit oneself;
prendre le ~ de qn to side with sb
(c) (dated) **bon ~** suitable match
■ **~ pris** bias
IDIOMS prendre son ~ de qch to come to
terms with sth; **tirer ~ de** to take advantage
of [sth]; to turn [sth] to good account

partial, ~e, *mpl* **-iaux** /paʀsjal, o/ *adj*
biased (GB)

partialité /paʀsjalite/ *nf* bias

participant, ~e /paʀtisipɑ̃, ɑ̃t/ *nm,f*
participant

participation /paʀtisipasjɔ̃/ *nf*
(a) participation; involvement
(b) contribution; **~ aux frais** (financial)
contribution
(c) (Fin) stake, holding

participe /paʀtisip/ *nm* participle; **~
passé** past participle

◆ **participer** /paʀtisipe/ [1] *v+prep* **(a) ~
à** to participate in, to take part in; to be
involved in
(b) ~ à to contribute to

particularisme /paʀtikylaʀism/ *nm*
distinctive identity

particularité /paʀtikylaʀite/ *nf*
(a) special feature
(b) (of disease, situation) particular nature

particule /paʀtikyl/ *nf* particle; **nom à ~**
aristocratic name

◆ **particulier, -ière** /paʀtikylje, ɛʀ/ ① *adj*
(a) particular
(b) *‹rights, privileges, role›* special; *‹example,
objective›* specific
(c) *‹car, secretary›* private
(d) *‹case, situation›* unusual; *‹talent,
effort›* special; *‹habits›* odd; *‹accent, style›*
distinctive, unusual; **c'est quelqu'un de très
~** he's/she's somebody out of the ordinary;
he's/she's weird
② **en particulier** *phr* **(a)** in private
(b) individually
(c) in particular, particularly
③ *nm* (simple) **~** private individual

◆ **particulièrement** /paʀtikyljɛʀmɑ̃/ *adv*
(a) particularly, exceptionally
(b) in particular

◆ **partie²** /paʀti/ ① *adj f* ▶ PARTI 1
② *nf* **(a)** part; (of amount, salary) proportion,
part; **~ de corps** body part; **la majeure ~
des gens** most people; **en ~** partly, in part;
faire ~ des premiers to be among the first;
cela fait ~ de leurs avantages that's one of
their advantages
(b) line (of work); **il est de la ~** it's in his
line (of work)
(c) game; **faire une ~** to have a game; **gagner
la ~** to win the game; (figurative) to win the
day; **j'espère que tu seras de la ~** I hope
you can come; **ce n'est que ~ remise** maybe
next time
(d) (in contract, negotiations) party; **les ~s
en présence** the parties involved; **être ~
prenante dans** to be actively involved in
(e) (Mus) part
■ **~ civile** plaintiff; **~ de pêche** fishing trip; **~
de plaisir** fun
IDIOMS avoir affaire à forte ~ to have a
tough opponent; **prendre qn à ~** to take sb
to task

partiel, -ielle /paʀsjɛl/ *adj* *‹payment›* part;
‹destruction, agreement› partial

◆ indicates a very frequent word

partir /paʀtiʀ/ [30] **1** *vi* (+ *v être*) **(a)** to leave, to go; ~ **à pied** to leave on foot; ~ **en courant** to run off; ~ **sans laisser d'adresse** to disappear without trace; ~ **loin/à Paris** to go far away/to Paris; ~ **en week-end** to go away for the weekend; ~ **à la pêche** to go fishing; ~ **en tournée** to set off on tour (GB) *or* on a tour; ~ **en retraite** to retire

(b) ‹*vehicle, train*› to leave; ‹*plane*› to take off; ‹*motor*› to start; **les coureurs sont partis** the runners are off; **à vos marques, prêts, partez!** on your marks, get set, go!

(c) ‹*bullet*› to be fired; ‹*cork*› to shoot out; ‹*capsule*› to shoot off; ‹*retort*› to slip out; **le coup de feu est parti** the gun went off; **il était tellement énervé que la gifle est partie toute seule** he was so angry that he slapped him/her before he could stop himself

(d) ‹*path, road*› to start; ~ **favori** to start favourite (GB); ~ **battu d'avance** to be doomed from the start; ~ **de rien** to start from nothing; **c'est parti!** go!; **et voilà, c'est parti, il pleut!** (fam) here we go, it's raining!; **être bien parti** to have got (GB) *or* gotten (US) off to a good start; **être bien parti pour gagner** to seem all set to win; **c'est mal parti** (fam) things don't look too good

(e) ~ **de** to start from ‹*idea*›; ~ **du principe que** to work on the assumption that; ~ **d'une bonne intention** to be well-meant

(f) ‹*stain*› to come out; ‹*smell*› to go; ‹*enamel, button*› to come off

(g) ‹*parcel, application*› to be sent (off)

(h) **quand il est parti on ne l'arrête plus** (fam) once he starts *or* gets going there's no stopping him

2 **à partir de** *phr* from; **à** ~ **de 16 heures/de 2 000 euros** from 4 o'clock onwards/2,000 euros; **à** ~ **du moment où** as soon as; as long as; **fabriqué à** ~ **d'un alliage** made from an alloy

partisan, ~**e** /paʀtizɑ̃, an/ **1** *adj*

(a) partisan

(b) ~ **de qch/de faire** in favour (GB) of sth/ of doing; **être** ~ **du moindre effort** (fam) to be lazy

2 *nm,f* (gen) supporter, partisan; (Mil) partisan

partition /paʀtisjɔ̃/ *nf* (Mus) score

partout /paʀtu/ *adv* **(a)** everywhere; **avoir mal** ~ to ache all over; **un peu** ~ **dans le monde** more or less all over the world; ~ **où je vais** wherever I go

(b) (Sport) **trois (points** *or* **buts)** ~ three all

IDIOM fourrer son nez ~ (fam) to stick one's nose into everything (colloq)

parure /paʀyʀ/ *nf* **(a)** finery

(b) set of jewels

parution /paʀysjɔ̃/ *nf* publication

parvenir /paʀvəniʀ/ [36] *v*+*prep* (+ *v être*)

(a) ~ **à** to reach ‹*place, person*›; **faire** ~ **qch à qn** to send sth to sb; to get sth to sb

(b) ~ **à** to reach ‹*agreement*›; to achieve ‹*balance*›

(c) ~ **à faire** to manage to do

parvenu, ~**e** /paʀvəny/ *nm,f* upstart

parvis /paʀvi/ *nm inv* (of church) square

pas¹ /pa/ *adv* **(a)** **je ne prends** ~ **de sucre** I don't take sugar; **ils n'ont** ~ **le téléphone** they haven't got a phone; **je ne pense** ~ I don't think so; **elle a aimé le film, mais lui** ~ she liked the film but he didn't

(b) (in expressions, exclamations) ~ **du tout** not at all; ~ **le moins du monde** not in the least; ~ **tant que ça,** ~ **plus que ça** not all that much; ~ **d'histoires!** I don't want any arguments *or* fuss!; ~ **de chance!** hard luck!; ~ **possible!** I can't believe it!; ~ **vrai?** (fam) isn't that so?

pas² /pa/ *nm inv* **(a)** step; **marcher à** ~ **feutrés** to walk softly; **faire ses premiers** ~ to take one's first steps; **faire le premier** ~ to make the first move; **suivre qn à** ~ to follow sb everywhere; **de là à dire qu'il s'en fiche** (fam), **il n'y a qu'un** ~ there's only a fine line between that and saying he doesn't care; **j'habite à deux** ~ **(d'ici)** I live very near here; **l'hiver arrive à grands** ~ winter is fast approaching; **apprendre les** ~ **du tango** to learn how to tango

(b) pace; **marcher d'un bon** ~ to walk at a brisk pace; **marcher au** ~ to march; (on horseback) to walk; **'roulez au** ~' 'dead slow' (GB), '(very) slow' (US); **mettre qn au** ~ to bring sb to heel; **partir au** ~ **de course** to rush off; **j'y vais de ce** ~ I'm on my way now

(c) footstep

(d) footprint; **revenir sur ses** ~ to retrace one's steps

IDIOMS se tirer d'un mauvais ~ to get out of a tight corner; **sauter le** ~ to take the plunge; **prendre le** ~ **sur qch** to overtake sth

pascal, ~**e**, *mpl* ~**s** *or*-**aux** /paskal, o/ *adj* ‹*weekend*› Easter; ‹*candle, lamb*› paschal

pas-de-porte /padpɔʀt/ *nm inv* key money

passable /pasabl/ *adj* **(a)** ‹*film*› fairly good; ‹*results*› reasonable

(b) (Sch) fair

passablement /pasabləmɑ̃/ *adv* ‹*drunk, annoyed*› rather; ‹*drink, worry*› quite a lot

passade /pasad/ *nf* fad

passage /pasaʒ/ *nm* **(a)** traffic; **interdire le** ~ **des camions dans la ville** to ban lorries from (driving through) the town

(b) stay; **ton** ~ **dans la ville a été bref** your stay in the town was brief

(c) **attendre le** ~ **du boulanger** to wait for the baker's van to come; **je peux te prendre au** ~ I can pick you up on the way; **des hôtes de** ~ short-stay guests; **se servir au** ~ to help oneself; (figurative) to take a cut (of the profits); to pocket some of the profits

(d) '~ **interdit, voie privée**' 'no entry, private road'; **pour céder le** ~ **à l'ambulance** in order to let the ambulance go past

⋯⋗

(e) chaque ∼ de votre chanson à la radio every time your song is played on the radio
(f) way, path; **prévoir le ∼ de câbles** to plan the route of cables
(g) ∼ **(de qch) à qch** transition (from sth) to sth
(h) alley; passageway
(i) (in novel) passage; (in film) sequence
■ ∼ **à l'acte** acting out; ∼ **à niveau** level crossing (GB), grade crossing (US); ∼ **pour piétons** pedestrian crossing; ∼ **à tabac** beating; ∼ **à vide** bad patch; unproductive period

passager, -ère /pasaʒe, ɛʀ/ **1** *adj* ‹situation, crisis› temporary; ‹feeling› passing; ‹shower› brief; ‹unease› slight, short-lived
2 *nm,f* passenger; ∼ **clandestin** stowaway

passant, ∼e /pasɑ̃, ɑ̃t/ **1** *adj* ‹street› busy
2 *nm,f* passer-by
3 *nm* (on belt, watchstrap) loop

passation /pasasjɔ̃/ *nf* ∼ **des pouvoirs** transfer of power

passe¹ /pɑs/ *nm* (fam) (a) master key
(b) pass

passe² /pɑs/ *nf* (a) (Sport) pass
(b) **être dans une ∼ difficile** to be going through a difficult patch; **être en ∼ de faire** to be (well) on the way to doing

✦ **passé, ∼e** /pase/ **1** *pp* ▶ PASSER
2 *pp adj* (a) ‹years, experiences› past; ∼ **de mode** dated
(b) **l'année passée** last year
(c) ‹colour, material› faded
3 *nm* (a) past
(b) past (tense)
4 *prep* after; ∼ **8 heures il s'endort dans son fauteuil** come eight o'clock he goes to sleep in his armchair
■ ∼ **antérieur** past anterior; ∼ **composé** present perfect; ∼ **simple** past historic

passéisme /paseism/ *nm* attachment to the past

passe-montagne, *pl* ∼**s** /pasmɔ̃taɲ/ *nm* balaclava

passe-partout /paspaʀtu/ *adj inv* ‹expression› catch-all; ‹garment› for all occasions

passe-passe /paspas/ *nm inv* **tour de ∼** conjuring trick; (figurative) sleight of hand

passeport /paspɔʀ/ *nm* passport

✦ **passer** /pase/ [1] **1** *vtr* (a) to cross ‹river, border›; to go through ‹door, customs›; to get over ‹hedge, obstacle›; **il m'a fait ∼ la frontière** he got me across the border; ∼ **qch à la douane** to get sth through customs
(b) to go past, to pass; **quand vous aurez passé le feu, tournez à droite** turn right after the lights; **le malade ne passera pas la nuit** the patient won't last the night
(c) ∼ **le doigt sur la table** to run one's finger over the table-top; ∼ **la tête à la fenêtre** to

stick one's head out of the window
(d) to pass ‹object›; to pass [sth] on ‹instructions, disease›; ∼ **sa colère sur ses collègues** to take one's anger out on one's colleagues
(e) to lend; to give
(f) (on phone) **tu peux me ∼ Chris?** can you put Chris on?; **je vous le passe** I'm putting you through
(g) to take, to sit (GB) ‹examination›; to have ‹interview›; **faire ∼ un test à qn** to give sb a test
(h) to spend ‹time›; **dépêche-toi, on ne va pas y ∼ la nuit!** (fam) hurry up, or we'll be here all night!
(i) **elle leur passe tout** she lets them get away with murder
(j) to skip ‹page, paragraph›; **je vous passe les détails** I'll spare you the details
(k) ∼ **l'aspirateur** to vacuum
(l) to filter ‹coffee›; to strain ‹fruit juice, sauce›; to purée ‹vegetables›
(m) to slip [sth] on ‹garment, ring›; to slip into ‹dress›
(n) to play ‹record, cassette›; to show ‹film, slides›; to place ‹ad›
(o) to enter into ‹agreement›; to place ‹order›
(p) (Aut) ∼ **la troisième** to go into third gear
(q) (Games) ∼ **son tour** to pass
2 *vi* (+ *v être*) (a) to go past *or* by, to pass; ∼ **sur un pont** to go over a bridge; **le facteur n'est pas encore passé** the postman (GB) *or* mailman (US) hasn't been yet; ∼ **à côté de** ‹person› to pass; ‹road› to run alongside; ∼ **à pied/à bicyclette** to walk/cycle past
(b) **je ne fais que** ∼ I've just popped in (GB) *or* dropped by for a minute; ∼ **dans la matinée** ‹plumber› to come by in the morning; ∼ **prendre qn/qch** to pick sb/sth up
(c) to go; **passons au salon** let's go into the lounge; **les contrebandiers sont passés en Espagne** the smugglers have crossed into Spain
(d) to get through; **tu ne passeras pas, c'est trop étroit** you'll never get through, it's too narrow; **il m'a fait signe de** ∼ he waved me on; **vas-y, ça passe!** go on, there's plenty of room!; ∼ **par-dessus bord** to fall overboard; **il est passé par la fenêtre** he fell out of the window; he got in through the window
(e) ∼ **par** to go through; ∼ **par le standard** to go through the switchboard; **je ne sais jamais ce qui te passe par la tête** I never know what's going on in your head
(f) (fam) **il accuse le patron, ses collègues, bref, tout le monde y ∼** he's accusing the boss, his colleagues—basically, everyone in sight; **que ça te plaise ou non, il va falloir y** ∼ whether you like it or not, there's no alternative; **on ne peut pas faire autrement que d'en ∼ par là** there is no other way around it
(g) ∼ **sur** to pass over ‹question, mistake›;

~ **à côté d'une question** to miss the point; **laisser ~ une occasion** to miss an opportunity
(h) soit dit en ~ incidentally
(i) ‹*comments, speech*› to go down well; ‹*law, measure, candidate*› to get through; ‹*attitude, doctrine*› to be accepted; **j'ai mangé quelque chose qui n'est pas passé** I ate something which didn't agree with me; **que je sois critiqué, passe encore, mais calomnié, non!** criticism is one thing, but I draw the line at slander; ~ **au premier tour** to be elected in the first round; ~ **dans la classe supérieure** to move up to the year above; **(ça) passe pour cette fois** (fam) I'll let it go this time
(j) ~ **à l'ennemi** to go over to the enemy; ~ **de main en main** to be passed around; ~ **constamment d'un sujet à l'autre** to flit from one subject to another; ~ **à un taux supérieur** to go up to a higher rate
(k) ~ **pour un imbécile** to look a fool; ~ **pour un génie** to pass as a genius; **il passe pour l'inventeur de l'ordinateur** he's supposed to have invented computers; **il se fait ~ pour mon frère** he passes himself off as my brother
(l) ‹*pain, crisis*› to pass; **quand l'orage sera or aura passé** when the storm is over; **ça passera** ‹*bad mood*› it'll pass; ‹*hurt*› you'll get over it; ~ **de mode** to go out of fashion; **faire ~ à qn l'envie de faire** to cure sb of the desire to do; **ce médicament fait ~ les maux d'estomac** this medicine relieves stomach ache
(m) ‹*performer, group*› (on stage) to be appearing; (on TV, radio) to be on; ‹*show, film*› to be on; ‹*music*› to be playing
(n) ~ **avant/après** to come before/after; **il fait ~ sa famille avant ses amis** he puts his family before his friends
(o) (fam) **où étais-tu passé?** where did you get to?; **où est passé mon livre?** where has my book got to?
(p) ‹*time*› to pass, to go by; **je ne vois pas le temps** ~ I don't know where the time goes
(q) ~ **de père en fils** to be handed down from father to son; **l'expression est passée dans la langue** the expression has become part of the language
(r) to be promoted to; **elle est passée maître dans l'art de mentir** she's an accomplished liar
(s) (fam) **y** ~ to die
(t) ‹*colour, material*› to fade
(u) ‹*coffee*› to filter
(v) ~ **en marche arrière** to go into reverse; **la troisième passe mal** third gear is a bit stiff
(w) (in bridge, poker) to pass
(x) passer à to turn to; ~ **à l'étape suivante** to move on to the next stage; **nous allons ~ au vote** let's vote now
(y) passer en or **y** ‹*money, amount*› to go on or into; ‹*product, material*› to go into
3 se passer *v refl* (+ *v être*) **(a)** to

happen; **tout s'est passé très vite** it all happened very fast; **tout se passe comme si le yen avait été dévalué** it's as if the yen had been devalued
(b) to take place; **la scène se passe au Viêt Nam** the scene is set in Vietnam
(c) ‹*examination, negotiations*› to go; **ça ne se passera pas comme ça!** I won't leave it at that!
(d) ‹*period*› to go by, to pass; **deux ans se sont passés depuis** that was two years ago
(e) se ~ **de** to do without ‹*object, activity, person*›; to go without ‹*meal, sleep*›; **se** ~ **de commentaires** to speak for itself
(f) se ~ **la langue sur les lèvres** to run one's tongue over one's lips; **se** ~ **la main sur le front** to put a hand to one's forehead
(g) ils se sont passé des documents they exchanged some documents
IDIOM **qu'est-ce qu'elle nous a passé!** (fam) she really went for us! (colloq)

passerelle /pasʀɛl/ *nf* **(a)** footbridge
(b) link
(c) (to boat) gangway; (to plane) steps

passe-temps /pastɑ̃/ *nm inv* pastime, hobby

passeur, -euse /pasœʀ, øz/ *nm,f*
(a) ferryman/ferrywoman
(b) smuggler; (for drugs) courier

passible /pasibl/ *adj* (Law) ~ **de** ‹*crime*› punishable by, ‹*person*› liable to

passif, -ive /pasif, iv/ **1** *adj* passive
2 *nm* **(a)** passive (voice)
(b) debit; **mettre qch au** ~ **de qn** to count sth amongst sb's failures

✓ **passion** /pasjɔ̃/ *nf* passion

passionnant, ~e /pasjɔnɑ̃, ɑ̃t/ *adj* exciting, fascinating, riveting

passionné, ~e /pasjɔne/ **1** *adj* ‹*love*› passionate; ‹*debate, argument*› impassioned; **être** ~ **de** or **pour qch** to have a passion for sth
2 *nm,f* enthusiast

passionnel, -elle /pasjɔnɛl/ *adj* ‹*debate*› impassioned; ‹*crime*› of passion

passionner /pasjɔne/ [1] **1** *vtr* **(a)** to fascinate; **la botanique le passionne** he has a passion for botany
(b) to inflame ‹*debate*›
2 se passionner *v refl* (+ *v être*) to have a passion (**pour** for)

passivité /pasivite/ *nf* passivity

passoire /paswaʀ/ *nf* **(a)** colander
(b) strainer

pastel /pastɛl/ **1** *adj inv* ‹*shade*› pastel
2 *nm* pastel

pastèque /pastɛk/ *nf* watermelon

pasteur /pastœʀ/ *nm* **(a)** minister, pastor
(b) priest
(c) shepherd

pasteuriser /pastœʀize/ [1] *vtr* to pasteurize

pastiche /pastiʃ/ nm pastiche

pastille /pastij/ nf (a) pastille, lozenge; ∼ contre la toux cough drop
(b) ∼ de menthe peppermint
(c) spot
(d) (of cloth, rubber) patch; (of plastic) disc

pastoral, ∼e¹, mpl -aux /pastɔʀal, o/ adj pastoral

pastorale² /pastɔʀal/ nf (Mus) pastoral

patachon /pataʃɔ̃/ nm (fam) mener une vie de ∼ to live in the fast lane

patata /patata/ excl (fam) ▶ PATATI

patate /patat/ nf (fam) (a) spud (colloq); ∼ douce sweet potato
(b) blockhead (colloq), idiot

patati /patati/ excl (fam) ∼, patata and so on and so forth

pataud, ∼e /pato, od/ adj clumsy

patauger /patoʒe/ [13] vi (a) to splash about; to paddle
(b) to flounder

pâte /pat/ ① nf (a) pastry; dough; batter
(b) paste
② **pâtes** nf pl ∼s (alimentaires) pasta
■ ∼ d'amandes marzipan; ∼s de fruit(s) fruit jellies; ∼ à modeler Plasticine®; ∼ à tartiner spread
IDIOM mettre la main à la ∼ to pitch in

pâté /pate/ nm (a) pâté
(b) pie; ∼ en croûte ≈ pie
(c) ∼ de maisons block (of houses)
(d) (ink)blot
(e) sandcastle

pâtée /pate/ nf dog food; cat food; swill

patelin /patlɛ̃/ nm (fam) small village

patente /patɑ̃t/ nf: licence (GB) to exercise a trade or profession

patère /pateʀ/ nf peg, hook

paternalisme /patɛʀnalism/ nm paternalism

paternaliste /patɛʀnalist/ adj paternalistic

paternel, -elle /patɛʀnɛl/ adj (a) paternal
(b) fatherly

paternité /patɛʀnite/ nf (a) fatherhood; (Law) paternity
(b) authorship

pâteux, -euse /patø, øz/ adj (a) ⟨substance⟩ doughy; ⟨gruel⟩ mushy
(b) ⟨voice⟩ thick

pathétique /patetik/ adj moving

pathologique /patɔlɔʒik/ adj pathological

patiemment /pasjamɑ̃/ adv patiently

patience /pasjɑ̃s/ nf patience
IDIOM prendre son mal en ∼ to resign oneself to one's fate

♂ **patient, ∼e** /pasjɑ̃, ɑ̃t/ adj, nm,f patient

patienter /pasjɑ̃te/ [1] vi to wait

patin /patɛ̃/ nm (a) skate
(b) (Tech) (on helicopter) skid; (on sledge) runner
■ ∼ à glace ice skate; ice-skating; ∼ à roulettes roller skate; roller-skating

patinage /patinaʒ/ nm skating

patine /patin/ nf patina; finish, sheen

patiner /patine/ [1] ① vtr to apply a finish to
② vi (a) to skate
(b) (Aut) ⟨wheel⟩ to spin; ⟨clutch⟩ to slip; faire ∼ l'embrayage to slip the clutch
③ **se patiner** v refl (+ v être) to acquire a patina

patineur, -euse /patinœʀ, øz/ nm,f skater

patinoire /patinwaʀ/ nf ice rink

pâtir /patiʀ/ [3] vi ∼ de to suffer as a result of

pâtisserie /patisʀi/ nf (a) cake shop, pâtisserie
(b) pastry, cake

pâtissier, -ière /patisje, ɛʀ/ nm,f confectioner, pastry cook

patois /patwa/ nm inv patois, dialect

patraque /patʀak/ adj (fam) être ∼ to be under the weather (colloq)

patriarche /patʀijaʀʃ/ nm patriarch

patrie /patʀi/ nf homeland, country

patrimoine /patʀimwan/ nm (a) (of person, family) patrimony; (of firm) capital
(b) heritage
■ ∼ génétique gene pool

patriote /patʀijɔt/ ① adj patriotic
② nmf patriot; en ∼ patriotically

patriotisme /patʀijɔtism/ nm patriotism

patron, -onne /patʀɔ̃, ɔn/ ① nm,f boss (colloq)
② nm (sewing) pattern
■ ∼ de pêche skipper, master

patronal, ∼e, mpl -aux /patʀɔnal, o/ adj ⟨organization⟩ employers'

patronat /patʀɔna/ nm employers

patronne ▶ PATRON 1

patronner /patʀɔne/ [1] vtr to sponsor

patronyme /patʀɔnim/ nm patronymic

patrouille /patʀuj/ nf patrol

patrouiller /patʀuje/ [1] vi to be on patrol

patte /pat/ nf (a) paw; foot; donner la ∼ to give its paw; retomber sur ses ∼s to fall on its feet
(b) (fam) leg, foot; tu es toujours dans mes ∼s you are always getting under my feet; marcher à quatre ∼s to walk on all fours; to crawl; traîner la ∼ to limp
(c) (fam) hand; bas les ∼s! (fam) keep your hands to yourself!; hands off! (colloq)
(d) tab; (on shelving unit) lug; (on garment) flap
(e) sideburn
■ ∼s d'éléphant flares; ∼ folle (fam) gammy leg (GB), game leg (US); ∼s de mouche spidery scrawl
IDIOMS faire ∼ de velours ⟨cat⟩ to draw in

its claws; ‹person› to switch on the charm; **montrer ~ blanche** to prove one is acceptable; **se tirer dans les ~s** to pull dirty tricks on each other

patte-d'oie, pl **pattes-d'oie** /patdwɑ/ nf
(a) crow's-foot
(b) junction

pâturage /pɑtyʀaʒ/ nm pasture

pâture /pɑtyʀ/ nf **(a)** feed; **être jeté en ~** (figurative) to be thrown to the lions
(b) pasture

paume /pom/ nf palm (of the hand)

paumé, -e /pome/ adj (fam) **(a)** ‹person› mixed up (GB), out of it (US) (colloq)
(b) ‹place› godforsaken

paumer /pome/ [1] (fam) **1** vtr, vi to lose
2 **se paumer** v refl (+ v être) to get lost

paupière /popjɛʀ/ nf eyelid

paupiette /popjɛt/ nf **~ de veau** stuffed escalope of veal

pause /poz/ nf **(a)** break; **faire une ~ to** take a break
(b) (in process) pause
(c) (Mus) rest

◊ **pauvre** /povʀ/ **1** adj **(a)** poor
(b) sparse; **~ en sucre** low in sugar; lacking sugar
(c) **un ~ type** (fam) a poor guy (colloq); a dead loss (colloq)
2 nmf (fam) **le/la ~!** poor thing!, poor man/ woman!
3 nm **un ~** a poor man; **~ d'esprit** half-wit

pauvrement /povʀamɑ̃/ adv poorly

pauvresse /povʀɛs/ nf poor wretch, pauper

pauvreté /povʀəte/ nf **(a)** poverty
(b) shabbiness

pavage /pavaʒ/ nm paving

pavaner: se pavaner /pavane/ [1] v refl (+ v être) to strut (about)

pavé /pave/ nm cobblestone; **se retrouver sur le ~** to find oneself out on the street
IDIOMS **lancer un ~ dans la mare** to set the cat among the pigeons; **tenir le haut du ~** to head the field

paver /pave/ [1] vtr to lay [sth] with cobblestones

pavillon /pavijɔ̃/ nm **(a)** (detached) house
(b) (for exhibition) pavilion; (of hospital) wing
(c) (of ear) auricle
(d) (of loudspeaker) horn
(e) (Naut) flag

pavillonnaire /pavijɔnɛʀ/ adj **zone ~** residential area; **banlieue ~** suburb consisting of houses (as opposed to high-rise buildings)

pavoiser /pavwaze/ [1] vi (fam) to crow

pavot /pavo/ nm poppy

payable /pɛjabl/ adj payable; **~ à la commande** cash with order

payant, -e /pɛjɑ̃, ɑ̃t/ adj **(a)** ‹person› paying

(b) ‹show› not free
(c) (fam) lucrative, profitable

paye /pɛj/ ▸ PAIE

payement /pɛjmɑ̃/ ▸ PAIEMENT

◊ **payer** /peje/ [21] **1** vtr **(a)** to pay; to pay for; **il est payé pour le savoir!** he knows that to his cost!; **faire ~ qch à qn** to charge sb for sth; **~ qch à qn** (fam) to buy sb sth
(b) to pay for ‹mistake, carelessness›
2 vi **(a)** ‹efforts, sacrifice› to pay off; ‹profession, activity› to pay
(b) (fam) to be funny
3 **se payer** v refl (+ v être) **(a)** ‹service, goods› to have to be paid for
(b) (fam) to treat oneself to ‹holiday›; to get ‹cold, bad mark›; to get landed with ‹job›; **se ~ un arbre** to crash into a tree
IDIOMS **se ~ du bon temps** (fam) to have a good time; **se ~ la tête de qn** (fam) to take the mickey out of sb (GB) (colloq), to razz sb (US) (colloq)

◊ **pays** /pei/ nm **(a)** country
(b) **la Bourgogne est le ~ du bon vin** Burgundy is the home of good wine; **gens du ~** local people
IDIOM **voir du ~** to do some travelling (GB)

◊ **paysage** /peizaʒ/ nm landscape, scenery
■ **~ audiovisuel français, PAF** French radio and TV scene

paysager, -ère /peizaʒe, ɛʀ/ adj
(a) environmental
(b) ‹garden› landscaped

paysagiste /peizaʒist/ nmf **(jardinier) ~** landscape gardener

◊ **paysan, -anne** /peizɑ̃, an/ **1** adj ‹life› rural; ‹ways› peasant; ‹soup, bread› country
2 nm,f **(a)** ≈ small farmer
(b) (derogatory) peasant

paysannerie /peizanʀi/ nf small farmers; peasantry

Pays-Bas /peibɑ/ pr nm pl **les ~** The Netherlands

PC /pese/ nm **(a)** (Pol) (abbr = **parti communiste**) CP, Communist Party
(b) (abbr = **personal computer**) PC

PCF /peseɛf/ nm (abbr = **parti communiste français**) French Communist Party

PCV /peseve/ nm (abbr = **paiement contre vérification**) reverse charge call (GB), collect call (US)

PDG /pedeʒe/ nm (abbr = **président-directeur général**) CEO, chief executive officer

péage /peaʒ/ nm **(a)** toll
(b) tollbooth

◊ **peau**, pl **~x** /po/ nf **(a)** skin; **n'avoir que la ~ sur les os** to be all skin and bone
(b) leather; **gants de ~** leather gloves
(c) peel
(d) (fam) life; **risquer sa ~** to risk one's life; **faire la ~ à qn** to kill sb; **vouloir la ~ de qn** ⋯⟩

to want sb dead
IDIOMS être bien dans sa ∼ (fam) to feel good
about oneself; **avoir qn dans la ∼** (fam) to
be crazy about sb (colloq); **prendre une balle
dans la ∼** (fam) to be shot

peaufiner /pofine/ [1] *vtr* to put the
finishing touches to ‹*work, text*›

Peau-Rouge, *pl* **Peaux-Rouges**
/poʀuʒ/ *nmf* Red Indian

⚘ **pêche** /pɛʃ/ *nf* (a) peach
(b) fishing; **aller à la ∼** to go fishing
(c) (fam) clout (colloq)
(d) (fam) **avoir la ∼** to be feeling great
■ **∼ à la ligne** angling

péché /peʃe/ *nm* sin; **ce serait un ∼ de
rater ça** (fam) it would be a crime to miss
that; **le chocolat, c'est mon ∼ mignon** I've
got a weakness for chocolate

pécher /peʃe/ [14] *vi* to sin; **∼ par excès
de confiance** to be overconfident; **le roman
pèche sur un point** the novel has one
shortcoming

pêcher¹ /pɛʃe/ [1] **1** *vtr* to go fishing for
2 *vi* to fish; **∼ à la mouche** to fly-fish; **∼ à
la ligne** to angle

pêcher² /pɛʃe/ *nm* peach tree

pécheresse /peʃʀɛs/ *nf* sinner

pêcherie /pɛʃʀi/ *nf* (a) fish factory
(b) fishing ground

pécheur /peʃœʀ/ *nm* sinner

pêcheur /pɛʃœʀ/ *nm* fisherman

pectoral, *pl* **-aux** /pɛktɔʀal, o/ *nm*
pectoral muscle

pécule /pekyl/ *nm* savings, nest egg (colloq)

pécuniaire /pekynjɛʀ/ *adj* financial

pédagogie /pedagɔʒi/ *nf* (a) education,
pedagogy
(b) teaching skills
(c) teaching method

pédagogique /pedagɔʒik/ *adj* ‹*activity*›
educational; ‹*system*› education; ‹*method*›
teaching

pédagogue /pedagɔg/ *nmf* educationalist

pédale /pedal/ *nf* pedal
IDIOM perdre les ∼s (fam) to lose one's grip

pédaler /pedale/ [1] *vi* to pedal

pédalier /pedalje/ *nm* (of bicycle) chain
transmission; (of piano) pedals

pédalo® /pedalo/ *nm* pedalo (GB), pedal
boat

pédant, **∼e** /pedɑ̃, ɑ̃t/ *adj* pedantic

pédérastie /pedeʀasti/ *nf* (a) pederasty
(b) homosexuality

pédestre /pedɛstʀ/ *adj* **randonnée ∼**
ramble

pédiatre /pedjatʀ/ *nmf* paediatrician

pédiatrie /pedjatʀi/ *nf* paediatrics

⚘ indicates a very frequent word

pédicure /pedikyʀ/ *nmf* chiropodist (GB),
podiatrist (US)

pedigree /pedigʀe/ *nm* pedigree

pédologue /pedɔlɔg/ *nmf* pedologist

pédophilie /pedɔfili/ *nf* paedophilia

pédopornographie /pedopɔʀnɔgʀafi/ *nf*
child pornography

pègre /pɛgʀ/ *nf* underworld

peigne /pɛɲ/ *nm* comb

peigner /peɲe/ [1] **1** *vtr* to comb ‹*hair,
wool*›
2 se peigner *v refl* (+ *v être*) to comb
one's hair

peignoir /pɛɲwaʀ/ *nm* dressing gown (GB),
robe (US); **∼ de bain** bathrobe

peinard, **∼e** /penaʀ, aʀd/ *adj* (fam) ‹*job*›
cushy (colloq); ‹*place*› snug

⚘ **peindre** /pɛ̃dʀ/ [55] **1** *vtr* (a) to paint
(b) to depict
2 *vi* to paint

⚘ **peine** /pɛn/ **1** *nf* (a) sorrow, grief; **avoir de
la ∼** to feel sad; **faire de la ∼ à qn** ‹*person*› to
hurt sb; ‹*event, remark*› to upset sb
(b) effort, trouble; **c'est ∼ perdue** it's a
waste of effort; **il n'est pas au bout de ses
∼s** his troubles are far from over; he's still
got a long way to go; **ce n'est pas la ∼ de
crier** there's no need to shout; **pour ta ∼** for
your trouble
(c) difficulty; **sans ∼** easily; **avec ∼** with
difficulty
(d) (Law) penalty, sentence; **∼ de prison**
prison sentence; '**défense de fumer sous ∼
d'amende**' 'no smoking, offenders will be
fined'
2 à peine *phr* hardly; **il était à ∼ arrivé
qu'il pensait déjà à repartir** no sooner had
he arrived than he was thinking of leaving
again
■ **∼ capitale** capital punishment; **∼ de cœur**
heartache; **∼ de mort** death penalty

peiner /pene/ [1] **1** *vtr* to sadden, to upset
2 *vi* ‹*person*› to struggle; ‹*car*› to labour
(GB)

peint, **∼e** /pɛ̃, ɛ̃t/ ▶ PEINDRE

peintre /pɛ̃tʀ/ *nm* painter

⚘ **peinture** /pɛ̃tyʀ/ *nf* (a) paint
(b) paintwork
(c) painting; **je ne peux pas le voir en ∼** (fam)
I can't stand the sight of him
(d) portrayal

peinturlurer /pɛ̃tyʀlyʀe/ [1] *vtr* to daub

péjoratif, **-ive** /peʒɔʀatif, iv/ *adj*
pejorative

Pékin /pekɛ̃/ *pr n* Beijing, Peking

PEL /peəɛl/ *nm*: *abbr* ▶ PLAN

pelage /pəlaʒ/ *nm* coat, fur

pelé, **∼e** /pəle/ *adj* ‹*animal*› mangy; ‹*hill*›
bare

pêle-mêle /pɛlmɛl/ *adv* higgledy-piggledy

peler /pəle/ [17] **1** *vtr* to peel

2 *vi* **(a)** ‹*skin, nose*› to peel
(b) (fam)~ **(de froid)** to freeze

pèlerin /pɛlʀɛ̃/ *nm* pilgrim

pèlerinage /pɛlʀinaʒ/ *nm* pilgrimage

pélican /pelikɑ̃/ *nm* pelican

pelisse /pəlis/ *nf* fur-trimmed coat, pelisse

pelle /pɛl/ *nf* shovel; spade; **à la** ~ (fam) by the dozen
■ ~ **à tarte** cake slice

pelleteuse /pɛltøz/ *nf* mechanical digger

pellicule /pelikyl/ **1** *nf* film
2 **pellicules** *nf pl* dandruff

pelote /p(ə)lɔt/ *nf* (of wool) ball

peloton /p(ə)lɔtɔ̃/ *nm* **(a)** platoon; ~ **d'exécution** firing squad
(b) (in cycling) pack; **dans le** ~ **de tête** in the leading pack

pelotonner: se pelotonner /p(ə)lɔtɔne/ [1] *v refl* (+ *v être*) **(a)** to snuggle up
(b) to huddle up

pelouse /p(ə)luz/ *nf* lawn; '~ **interdite**' 'keep off the grass'

peluche /p(ə)lyʃ/ *nf* **(a)** plush; **jouet en** ~ cuddly toy (GB), stuffed animal (US)
(b) fluff

pelucher /p(ə)lyʃe/ [1] *vi* to become fluffy

pelure /p(ə)lyʀ/ *nf* (of vegetable, fruit) peel; (of onion) skin

pelvis /pɛlvis/ *nm inv* pelvis

pénal, ~**e**, *mpl* **-aux** /penal, o/ *adj* criminal

pénaliser /penalize/ [1] *vtr* to penalize

pénalité /penalite/ *nf* penalty

penaud, ~**e** /pəno, od/ *adj* sheepish

penchant /pɑ̃ʃɑ̃/ *nm* **(a)** fondness
(b) weakness
(c) tendency

penché, ~**e** /pɑ̃ʃe/ **1** *pp* ▶ PENCHER
2 *pp adj* ‹*tree*› leaning; ‹*writing*› slanting

☞ **pencher** /pɑ̃ʃe/ [1] **1** *vtr* to tilt; to tip [sth] up; ~ **la tête en avant** to bend one's head forward(s)
2 *vi* **(a)** ‹*tower, tree*› to lean; ‹*boat*› to list; ‹*picture*› to slant
(b) ~ **pour** to incline toward(s) ‹*theory*›; to be in favour (GB) of ‹*solution*›
3 **se pencher** *v refl* (+ *v être*) **(a)** to lean
(b) to bend down
(c) **se** ~ **sur** to look into ‹*problem*›

pendable /pɑ̃dabl/ *adj* **jouer un tour** ~ **à qn** to play a rotten trick on sb

pendaison /pɑ̃dɛzɔ̃/ *nf* hanging

☞ **pendant** /pɑ̃dɑ̃/ **1** *prep* for; **je t'ai attendu** ~ **des heures** I waited for you for hours; ~ **combien de temps avez-vous vécu à Versailles?** how long did you live in Versailles?; **il a été malade** ~ **tout le trajet** he was sick throughout the journey; ~ **ce temps(-là)** meanwhile
2 **pendant que** *phr* while

pendeloque /pɑ̃dlɔk/ *nf* pendant, drop (on earring)

pendentif /pɑ̃dɑ̃tif/ *nm* pendant

penderie /pɑ̃dʀi/ *nf* **(a)** wardrobe
(b) walk-in cupboard (GB) *or* closet

pendouiller /pɑ̃duje/ [1] *vi* (fam) to dangle down

pendre /pɑ̃dʀ/ [6] **1** *vtr* **(a)** to hang ‹*person*›
(b) to hang ‹*picture, curtains*›; to hang up ‹*clothes*›
2 *vi* **(a)** ‹*object, clothes*› to hang; ‹*arms, legs*› to dangle
(b) ‹*strips, lock of hair*› to hang down; ‹*cheek, breasts*› to sag
3 **se pendre** *v refl* (+ *v être*) **(a)** to hang oneself
(b) **se** ~ **à** to hang from ‹*branch*›; **se** ~ **au cou de qn** to throw one's arms around sb's neck
IDIOM **ça te pend au nez** (fam) you've got it coming to you

pendu, ~**e** /pɑ̃dy/ **1** *pp* ▶ PENDRE
2 *pp adj* **(a)** ‹*person*› hanged
(b) ‹*object*› hung, hanging; **être** ~ **aux lèvres de qn** to hang on sb's every word; **être toujours** ~ **au téléphone** to spend all one's time on the telephone
3 *nm,f* hanged man/woman

pendulaire /pɑ̃dylɛʀ/ *adj* pendular

pendule¹ /pɑ̃dyl/ *nm* pendulum

pendule² /pɑ̃dyl/ *nf* clock
IDIOM **remettre les** ~**s à l'heure** to set the record straight

pénétrant, ~**e** /penetʀɑ̃, ɑ̃t/ *adj* ‹*wind*› penetrating; ‹*cold*› piercing; ‹*comment*› shrewd; ‹*mind, look*› penetrating

pénétration /penetʀasjɔ̃/ *nf* penetration

pénétré, ~**e** /penetʀe/ **1** *pp* ▶ PÉNÉTRER
2 *pp adj* earnest, intense; **être** ~ **de** to be imbued with ‹*feeling*›

☞ **pénétrer** /penetʀe/ [14] **1** *vtr* **(a)** ‹*rain*› to soak *or* seep into ‹*ground*›; ‹*sun*› to penetrate ‹*foliage*›
(b) to fathom ‹*secret, thoughts*›
(c) to penetrate
(d) ‹*idea, fashion*› to reach ‹*group*›
2 *vi* ~ **dans** to enter, to get into; to penetrate; **faire** ~ **la pommade en massant doucement** rub the ointment into your skin

pénible /penibl/ *adj* ‹*effort*› painful; ‹*work*› hard; ‹*journey*› difficult; ‹*person*› tiresome

péniblement /penibləmɑ̃/ *adv* ‹*walk*› with difficulty; ‹*reach*› barely

péniche /peniʃ/ *nf* barge

pénicilline /penisilin/ *nf* penicillin

péninsulaire /penɛ̃sylɛʀ/ *adj* peninsular

péninsule /penɛ̃syl/ *nf* peninsula

pénis /penis/ *nm inv* penis

pénitence /penitɑ̃s/ *nf* **(a)** penance
(b) punishment

pénitencier /penitɑ̃sje/ *nm* prison

pénitentiaire /penitɑ̃sjɛr/ *adj*
⟨institution⟩ penal; ⟨regime⟩ prison

pénombre /penɔ̃br/ *nf* half-light

pensable /pɑ̃sabl/ *adj* thinkable; **ce n'est pas ~** it's unthinkable

pense-bête, *pl* **pense-bêtes** /pɑ̃sbɛt/ *nm* reminder

⚡ **pensée** /pɑ̃se/ *nf* **(a)** thought; **être perdu dans ses ~s** to be lost in thought
(b) mind; **nous serons avec vous par la ~** we'll be with you in spirit
(c) thinking
(d) (Bot) pansy

⚡ **penser** /pɑ̃se/ [1] **1** *vtr* **(a)** to think; **~ du bien de qn** to think well of sb; **je n'en pense rien** I have no opinion about it; **c'est bien ce que je pensais!** I thought as much!; **tu penses vraiment ce que tu dis?** do you really mean what you're saying?; **tout porte à ~ que** there's every indication that; **vous pensez si j'étais content!** you can imagine how pleased I was!; **'il s'est excusé?'—'penses-tu!'** 'did he apologize?'—'you must be joking!'
(b) **ça me fait ~ qu'il faut que je leur écrive** that reminds me that I must write to them
(c) **~ faire** to be thinking of doing, to intend to do
(d) to think [sth] up ⟨plan, device⟩
2 **penser à** *v+prep* **(a)** **~ à** to think of, to think about; **ne pensez plus à rien** empty your mind; **sans ~ à mal** without meaning any harm; **tu n'y penses pas!** you can't be serious!; **n'y pensons plus!** let's forget about it!
(b) **~ à** to remember; **il me fait ~ à mon père** he reminds me of my father
(c) **~ à faire** to be thinking of doing
3 *vi* to think; **je lui ai dit ma façon de ~!** I gave him/her a piece of my mind!; **~ tout haut** to think out loud

penseur /pɑ̃sœr/ *nm* thinker

pensif, -ive /pɑ̃sif, iv/ *adj* pensive, thoughtful

pension /pɑ̃sjɔ̃/ *nf* **(a)** pension
(b) boarding house
(c) boarding school
■ **~ alimentaire** alimony; **~ complète** full board; **~ de famille** family hotel

pensionnaire /pɑ̃sjɔnɛr/ *nmf* **(a)** (in hotel) resident
(b) (in prison) inmate
(c) (Sch) boarder

pensionnat /pɑ̃sjɔna/ *nm* boarding school

pensionné, ~e /pɑ̃sjɔne/ *nm,f* pensioner

pensivement /pɑ̃sivmɑ̃/ *adv* pensively

pentagone /pɛ̃tagɔn/ *nm* pentagon

pente /pɑ̃t/ *nf* slope; **toit en ~** sloping roof
IDIOMS **être sur la mauvaise ~** ⟨person⟩ to be going astray; ⟨company⟩ to be going down-

hill; **remonter la ~** to get back on one's feet

Pentecôte /pɑ̃tkot/ *nf* Pentecost; **à la ~** at Whitsun

pénurie /penyri/ *nf* shortage

pépé /pepe/ *nm* (fam) **(a)** grandpa (colloq)
(b) old man

pépère /pepɛr/ *adj* (fam) ⟨life⟩ cushy (colloq); ⟨place⟩ nice

pépin /pepɛ̃/ *nm* **(a)** pip; **sans ~s** seedless
(b) (fam) slight problem
(c) (fam) umbrella

pépinière /pepinjɛr/ *nf* (for trees, plants) nursery

pépite /pepit/ *nf* nugget

péquenaud, ~e /pɛkno, od/ *nm,f* (fam) country bumpkin (colloq)

perçant, ~e /pɛrsɑ̃, ɑ̃t/ *adj* **(a)** ⟨cry, voice⟩ shrill; ⟨gaze⟩ piercing
(b) ⟨vision⟩ sharp

percée /pɛrse/ *nf* **(a)** opening
(b) breakthrough

perce-neige /pɛrsənɛʒ/ *nm inv or nf inv* snowdrop

perce-oreille, *pl* **~s** /pɛrsɔrɛj/ *nm* earwig

percepteur /pɛrsɛptœr/ *nm* tax inspector

perceptible /pɛrsɛptibl/ *adj* **(a)** ⟨sound⟩ perceptible
(b) ⟨tax⟩ payable

perception /pɛrsɛpsjɔ̃/ *nf* **(a)** tax office
(b) perception

percer /pɛrse/ [12] **1** *vtr* **(a)** to pierce ⟨body, surface⟩; to burst ⟨abscess, eardrum⟩
(b) to make ⟨door⟩; to bore ⟨tunnel⟩; to build ⟨road⟩; **~ un trou dans** to make a hole in
(c) to pierce ⟨silence, air⟩; to break through ⟨clouds⟩
(d) to penetrate ⟨secret⟩; **~ qn à jour** to see through sb
(e) **~ ses dents** to be teething
2 *vi* **(a)** ⟨sun⟩ to break through; ⟨plant⟩ to come up; ⟨tooth⟩ to come through
(b) (Mil, Sport) to break through
(c) ⟨actor⟩ to become known

perceuse /pɛrsøz/ *nf* drill

percevable /pɛrsəvabl/ *adj* ⟨tax⟩ payable

⚡ **percevoir** /pɛrsəvwar/ [5] *vtr* **(a)** to collect ⟨tax⟩; to receive ⟨rent⟩
(b) to perceive ⟨change⟩; to feel ⟨vibration⟩; **être perçu comme** to be seen as

perche /pɛrʃ/ *nf* **(a)** (gen) pole; (of ski tow) T-bar; (for microphone) boom
(b) (fam) **(grande) ~** beanpole (colloq)
(c) (Zool) perch
IDIOM **tendre la ~ à qn** to throw sb a line

perché, ~e /pɛrʃe/ *pp adj* perched; **voix haut ~e** high-pitched voice; **ma valise est ~e en haut de l'armoire** my suitcase is on top of the wardrobe

percher /pɛrʃe/ [1] **1** *vtr* **~ qch sur une étagère** to stick sth up on a shelf

p

2 *vi* to perch; to roost
3 **se percher** *v refl* (+ *v être*) to perch
perchoir /pɛɾʃwaɾ/ *nm* **(a)** perch
(b) (Pol, fam) Speaker's Chair
perclus, **∼e** /pɛɾkly, yz/ *adj* crippled
percolateur /pɛɾkɔlatœɾ/ *nm* (espresso) coffee machine
percussions /pɛɾkysjɔ̃/ *nf pl* **les ∼** percussion instruments; percussion section; drums
percutant, **∼e** /pɛɾkytɑ̃, ɑ̃t/ *adj* ‹criticism› hard-hitting; ‹slogan› punchy (colloq)
percuter /pɛɾkyte/ [1] **1** *vtr* ‹car, driver› to hit
2 *vi* **∼ contre** ‹vehicle› to crash into; ‹shell› to explode against
3 **se percuter** *v refl* (+ *v être*) to collide
perdant, **∼e** /pɛɾdɑ̃, ɑ̃t/ **1** *adj* losing; **être ∼** to have lost out
2 *nm,f* loser
perdition /pɛɾdisjɔ̃/ *nf* **(a)** **lieu de ∼** den of iniquity
(b) **en ∼** ‹ship› in distress
⚡ **perdre** /pɛɾdɾ/ [6] **1** *vtr* **(a)** to lose; **∼ de vue** to lose sight of; **leurs actions ont perdu 9%** their shares have dropped 9%
(b) to shed ‹leaves, flowers›
(c) to miss ‹chance›
(d) to waste ‹day, years›; **perdre son temps** to waste one's time
(e) **je perds mes chaussures** my shoes are too big; **je perds mon pantalon** my trousers are falling down
(f) to bring [sb] down; **cet homme te perdra** that man will be your undoing
2 *vi* to lose; **j'y perds** I lose out
3 **se perdre** *v refl* (+ *v être*) **(a)** to get lost; **se ∼ dans ses pensées** to be lost in thought
(b) ‹tradition› to die out
IDIOM **∼ la raison** *or* **l'esprit** to go out of one's mind
perdrix /pɛɾdɾi/ *nf inv* partridge
perdu, **∼e** /pɛɾdy/ **1** *pp* ▶ PERDRE
2 *pp adj* **(a)** lost; **chien ∼** stray dog; **balle ∼e** stray bullet; **c'est ∼ d'avance** it's hopeless
(b) ‹day, opportunity› wasted; **c'est du temps ∼** it's a waste of time
(c) ‹harvest› ruined; **il est ∼** there's no hope for him
(d) ‹person› lost
3 *adj* remote, isolated
IDIOMS **se lancer à corps ∼ dans** to throw oneself headlong into; **ce n'est pas ∼ pour tout le monde** somebody will do all right out of it
⚡ **père** /pɛɾ/ *nm* father; **Dupont ∼** Dupont senior; **le∼ Dupont** (fam) old Dupont (colloq)
■ **le ∼ Noël** Santa Claus
péremption /peɾɑ̃psjɔ̃/ *nf* **date de ∼** use-by date

péremptoire /peɾɑ̃ptwaɾ/ *adj* peremptory
pérenne /peɾɛn/ *adj* perennial
perfection /pɛɾfɛksjɔ̃/ *nf* perfection
perfectionnement /pɛɾfɛksjɔnmɑ̃/ *nm* improvement
perfectionner /pɛɾfɛksjɔne/ [1] **1** *vtr* to perfect ‹technique›; to refine ‹art›
2 **se perfectionner** *v refl* (+ *v être*) to improve
perfectionniste /pɛɾfɛksjɔnist/ *adj, nmf* perfectionist
perfide /pɛɾfid/ *adj* perfidious, treacherous
perfidie /pɛɾfidi/ *nf* perfidy, treachery
perforation /pɛɾfɔɾasjɔ̃/ *nf* perforation
perforer /pɛɾfɔɾe/ [1] *vtr* **(a)** to pierce; to perforate
(b) to punch; **carte perforée** punch card
performance /pɛɾfɔɾmɑ̃s/ *nf* **(a)** result, performance
(b) achievement
performant, **∼e** /pɛɾfɔɾmɑ̃, ɑ̃t/ *adj* ‹car, equipment› high-performance; ‹person, technique› efficient; ‹company› competitive
perfusion /pɛɾfyzjɔ̃/ *nm* (Med) drip (GB), IV (US)
péricliter /peɾiklite/ [1] *vi* to be going downhill
péridurale /peɾidyɾal/ *nf* epidural
péril /peɾil/ *nm* peril, danger; **à ses risques et ∼s** at his/her own risk; **il n'y a pas ∼ en la demeure** what's the hurry?
périlleux, **-euse** /peɾijø, øz/ *adj* perilous
périmé, **∼e** /peɾime/ *adj* **(a)** out-of-date; **son passeport est ∼** his/her passport has expired
(b) ‹idea, custom› outdated
périmètre /peɾimɛtɾ/ *nm* **(a)** perimeter
(b) area
périnée /peɾine/ *nm* perineum
⚡ **période** /peɾjɔd/ *nf* period; era
périodique /peɾjɔdik/ **1** *adj* **(a)** ‹fever› recurring
(b) **serviette ∼** sanitary towel (GB), sanitary napkin (US)
2 *nm* periodical
péripétie /peɾipesi/ *nf* **(a)** incident
(b) event
(c) adventure
(d) **les ∼s d'une intrigue** the twists and turns of a plot
périphérie /peɾifeɾi/ *nf* periphery
périphérique /peɾifeɾik/ **1** *adj* (gen) peripheral; ‹area› outlying; **radio ∼** broadcasting station situated outside the territory to which it transmits
2 *nm* ring road (GB), beltway (US)
périphrase /peɾifɾaz/ *nf* circumlocution
périple /peɾipl/ *nm* journey; voyage
périr /peɾiɾ/ [3] *vi* to die, to perish

p

périscolaire /peʀiskɔlɛʀ/ *adj*
extracurricular

périscope /peʀiskɔp/ *nm* periscope

périssable /peʀisabl/ *adj* perishable

Péritel® /peʀitɛl/ *nf* **prise** ~ scart socket;
scart plug

perle /pɛʀl/ *nf* **(a)** pearl; ~ **fine** real pearl
(b) (figurative) gem; ~ **rare** real treasure
(c) (fam) howler (colloq)

perler /pɛʀle/ [1] *vi* ‹*drop, tear*› to appear

permanence /pɛʀmanɑ̃s/ **1** *nf*
(a) permanence
(b) persistence
(c) ~ **téléphonique** manned line; **assurer** *or*
tenir une ~ to be on duty; to hold a surgery
(GB), to have office hours (US)
(d) permanently manned office
(e) (Sch) (private) study room (GB), study
hall (US)
2 **en permanence** *phr* **(a)** permanently
(b) constantly

⚡ **permanent, ~e¹** /pɛʀmanɑ̃, ɑ̃t/ *adj*
(a) ‹*staff, exhibition*› permanent; ‹*committee*›
standing
(b) ‹*tension, danger*› constant; ‹*show*›
continuous

permanente² /pɛʀmanɑ̃t/ *nf* perm

perméable /pɛʀmeabl/ *adj* permeable

⚡ **permettre** /pɛʀmɛtʀ/ [60] **1** *vtr* **(a)** ~
à qn de faire to allow sb to do, to give sb
permission to do; **(vous) permettez!** j'étais
là avant! excuse me! I was here first!; **il est
menteur comme c'est pas permis** (fam) he's
an incredible liar
(b) ~ **à qn de faire** to allow *or* enable sb to
do, to give sb the opportunity to do; **leurs
moyens ne le leur permettent pas** they can't
afford it; **autant qu'il est permis d'en juger** as
far as one can tell
2 **se permettre** *v refl* (+ *v être*) **(a)** je
peux me ~ **ce genre de plaisanterie avec
lui** I can get away with telling him that kind
of joke; **se** ~ **de faire** to take the liberty of
doing
(b) je ne peux pas me ~ **d'acheter une
nouvelle voiture** I can't afford to buy a new
car

permis, ~e /pɛʀmi, iz/ **1** *pp*
▶ PERMETTRE
2 *pp adj* permitted
3 *nm inv* permit, licence (GB)
■ ~ **de conduire** driving licence (GB), driver's
license (US); ~ **de séjour** residence permit; ~
de travail work permit

permission /pɛʀmisjɔ̃/ *nf* **(a)** permission
(b) (Mil) leave; **partir en** ~ to go on leave

permutable /pɛʀmytabl/ *adj*
interchangeable

permuter /pɛʀmyte/ [1] *vtr* to switch [sth]
around ‹*letters, labels*›

⚡ indicates a very frequent word

pernicieux, -ieuse /pɛʀnisjø, øz/ *adj*
pernicious

Pérou /peʀu/ *pr nm* Peru
IDIOM ce n'est pas le ~ it's not a fortune

perpendiculaire /pɛʀpɑ̃dikylɛʀ/ *adj, nf*
perpendicular

perpète /pɛʀpɛt/ *nf* (fam) **être condamné à**
~ (prisoners' slang) to get life (colloq); **habiter à**
~ to live miles away

perpétrer /pɛʀpetʀe/ [14] *vtr* to perpetrate

perpétuel, -elle /pɛʀpetɥɛl/ *adj*
perpetual

perpétuellement /pɛʀpetɥɛlmɑ̃/ *adv*
constantly, perpetually

perpétuer /pɛʀpetɥe/ [1] *vtr* to perpetuate

perpétuité /pɛʀpetɥite/ *nf* perpetuity; **à**
~ (Law) ‹*imprisonment*› life; ‹*imprisonment*›
life

perplexe /pɛʀplɛks/ *adj* perplexed, baffled

perplexité /pɛʀplɛksite/ *nf* perplexity

perquisition /pɛʀkizisjɔ̃/ *nf* search

perquisitionner /pɛʀkizisjɔne/ [1] *vtr* to
search ‹*house*›

perron /peʀɔ̃/ *nm* flight of steps

perroquet /peʀɔkɛ/ *nm* parrot

perruche /peʀyʃ/ *nf* budgerigar (GB),
parakeet (US)

perruque /peʀyk/ *nf* wig

persan, ~e /pɛʀsɑ̃, an/ *adj* Persian

perse /pɛʀs/ *adj* Persian

persécuter /pɛʀsekyte/ [1] *vtr* to
persecute

persécution /pɛʀsekysjɔ̃/ *nf* persecution

persévérance /pɛʀseveʀɑ̃s/ *nf*
perseverance

persévérer /pɛʀseveʀe/ [14] *vi* **(a)** to
persevere
(b) to persist

persienne /pɛʀsjɛn/ *nf* (louvred (GB))
shutter

persiflage /pɛʀsiflaʒ/ *nm* mockery

persifleur, -euse /pɛʀsiflœʀ, øz/ *adj*
‹*tone, comment*› mocking

persil /pɛʀsi(l)/ *nm* parsley

persistance /pɛʀsistɑ̃s/ *nf* persistence

persistant, ~e /pɛʀsistɑ̃, ɑ̃t/ *adj* ‹*heat,
problem*› continuing; ‹*smell, snow*› lingering;
‹*cough, symptom*› persistent

persister /pɛʀsiste/ [1] *vi* ‹*symptom, pain*›
to persist; ‹*inflation*› to continue; **je persiste
à croire que** I still think that

perso /pɛʀso/ *adj* (colloq) personal

⚡ **personnage** /pɛʀsɔnaʒ/ *nm* **(a)** character
(b) figure; **un** ~ **public** a public figure

personnaliser /pɛʀsɔnalize/ [1] *vtr* to
add a personal touch to

⚡ **personnalité** /pɛʀsɔnalite/ *nf*
(a) personality
(b) important person

personne¹ /pɛRsɔn/ *pron* anyone, anybody; no-one, nobody; ∼ **n'est parfait** nobody's perfect

⚜ **personne²** /pɛRsɔn/ *nf* person; **dix** ∼**s** ten people; **les** ∼**s âgées** the elderly; **bien fait de sa** ∼ good-looking; **le respect de la** ∼ respect for the individual; **il s'en occupe en** ∼ he's dealing with it personally; **c'est la cupidité en** ∼ he/she is greed personified ■ ∼ **à charge** dependant; ∼ **civile** *or* **morale** artificial person, legal entity

⚜ **personnel, -elle** /pɛRsɔnɛl/ ① *adj*
(a) ⟨*friend, effects*⟩ personal; ⟨*papers*⟩ private
(b) individual
(c) selfish
(d) ⟨*pronoun*⟩ personal
② *nm* staff; workforce; employees, personnel

personnellement /pɛRsɔnɛlmɑ̃/ *adv* personally

personnifier /pɛRsɔnifje/ [2] *vtr* to personify

⚜ **perspective** /pɛRspɛktiv/ *nf* (a) (in art) perspective
(b) view
(c) perspective, angle
(d) prospect

perspicace /pɛRspikas/ *adj* perceptive

perspicacité /pɛRspikasite/ *nf* insight, perspicacity

persuader /pɛRsɥade/ [1] *vtr* to persuade

persuasif, -ive /pɛRsɥazif, iv/ *adj* persuasive

persuasion /pɛRsɥazjɔ̃/ *nf* persuasion

⚜ **perte** /pɛRt/ *nf* (a) loss; **à** ∼ **de vue** as far as the eye can see
(b) waste
(c) ruin; **courir** *or* **aller à sa** ∼ to be heading for a fall

pertinemment /pɛRtinamɑ̃/ *adv*
(a) perfectly well
(b) pertinently

pertinence /pɛRtinɑ̃s/ *nf* pertinence

pertinent, -e /pɛRtinɑ̃, ɑ̃t/ *adj* pertinent

perturbant, -e /pɛRtyRbɑ̃, ɑ̃t/ *adj* disturbing

perturbation /pɛRtyRbasjɔ̃/ *nf*
(a) disruption
(b) disturbance
(c) upheaval

perturber /pɛRtyRbe/ [1] *vtr* to disrupt ⟨*traffic, market, meeting*⟩; to interfere with ⟨*development*⟩; to disturb ⟨*sleep*⟩

pervenche /pɛRvɑ̃ʃ/ *nf* (a) periwinkle
(b) (fam) (female) traffic warden (GB), meter maid (US) (colloq)

pervers, -e /pɛRvɛR, ɛRs/ ① *adj*
(a) wicked
(b) perverted
(c) ⟨*effect*⟩ pernicious
② *nm,f* pervert

perversion /pɛRvɛRsjɔ̃/ *nf* perversion

perversité /pɛRvɛRsite/ *nf* perversity

pervertir /pɛRvɛRtiR/ [3] *vtr* to corrupt

pesant, -e /pəzɑ̃, ɑ̃t/ *adj* (a) heavy
(b) cumbersome
(c) ⟨*atmosphere, silence*⟩ oppressive
IDIOM **valoir son** ∼ **d'or** to be worth its weight in gold

pesanteur /pəzɑ̃tœR/ *nf* (a) (of style) heaviness; (of bureaucracy) inertia
(b) gravity

pèse-personne, *pl* ∼**s** /pɛzpɛRsɔn/ *nm* bathroom scales

⚜ **peser** /pəze/ [16] ① *vtr* (a) to weigh
(b) to weigh up; ∼ **ses mots** to choose one's words carefully; **tout bien pesé** all things considered
② *vi* (a) to weigh; **je pèse 70 kg** I weigh 70 kg; ∼ **lourd** to weigh a lot
(b) to carry weight; ∼ **dans/sur une décision** to have a decisive influence in/on a decision
(c) ∼ **sur** ⟨*suspicion*⟩ to hang over ⟨*person*⟩
(d) ⟨*tax, debts*⟩ to weigh [sb/sth] down ⟨*person, country*⟩
(e) ⟨*person, decision*⟩ to influence (greatly) ⟨*policy*⟩

peseta /pezeta/ *nf* peseta

pessimisme /pesimism/ *nm* pessimism

pessimiste /pesimist/ ① *adj* pessimistic
② *nmf* pessimist

peste /pɛst/ *nf* (a) plague
(b) (fam) pest (colloq)
IDIOM **je me méfie de lui comme de la** ∼ (fam) I don't trust him an inch

pester /pɛste/ [1] *vi* ∼ **contre qn/qch** to curse sb/sth

pesticide /pɛstisid/ *nm* pesticide

pet /pɛ/ *nm* (fam) fart (colloq)

pétale /petal/ *nm* petal

pétanque /petɑ̃k/ *nf* petanque

pétarader /petaRade/ [1] *vi* to backfire

pétard /petaR/ *nm* banger (GB), firecracker (US); **les cheveux en** ∼ spiky hair, bed hair; **être en** ∼ (fam) to be hopping mad (GB) (colloq), to be real mad (US) (colloq)

péter /pete/ [14] *vi* (a) (pop) to fart (colloq)
(b) (fam) ⟨*balloon*⟩ to burst; ⟨*situation*⟩ to blow up; ⟨*thread*⟩ to snap

pétillant, -e /petijɑ̃, ɑ̃t/ *adj* sparkling

pétiller /petije/ [1] *vi* ⟨*drink*⟩ to fizz; ⟨*firewood*⟩ to crackle; ⟨*eyes*⟩ to sparkle

⚜ **petit, -e** /p(ə)ti, it/ ① *adj* (a) small, little; short; **une toute** ∼**e pièce** a tiny room; **se faire tout** ∼ (figurative) to try to make oneself inconspicuous
(b) ⟨*walk, distance*⟩ short
(c) young, little; **c'est notre** ∼ **dernier** he's our youngest
(d) ⟨*eater*⟩ light; ⟨*wage*⟩ low; ⟨*cry, worry*⟩ little; ⟨*hope*⟩ slight; ⟨*detail, defect*⟩ minor; ⟨*job*⟩ modest

⋯⋙

(e) une ~e trentaine de personnes under thirty people

2 *adv* **tailler ~** to be small-fitting; **~ à ~** little by little

■ **~ ami** boyfriend; **~ bois** kindling; **~ coin** (fam) (euphemistic) loo (GB) (colloq), bathroom (US); **~ déjeuner** breakfast; **~ noir** (fam) coffee; **~ nom** (fam) first name; **~ pois** (garden) pea, petit pois; **~ pot** jar of baby food; **~ rat** (de l'Opéra) *pupil at Paris Opéra's ballet school*; **~ salé** streaky salted pork; **~e amie** girlfriend; **~e annonce** classified advertisement; **~e nature** weakling; **~e reine** cycling; **~e voiture** toy car; **~s chevaux** ≈ ludo

petit-beurre, *pl* **petits-beurre** /p(ə)tibœʀ/ *nm* petit beurre biscuit

petit-cousin, **petite-cousine**, *mpl* **petits-cousins** /p(ə)tikuzɛ̃, p(ə)titkuzin/ *nm,f* second cousin

petite-fille, *pl* **petites-filles** /p(ə)titfij/ *nf* granddaughter

petitesse /p(ə)titɛs/ *nf* **(a)** pettiness
(b) small size

petit-fils, *pl* **petits-fils** /p(ə)tifis/ *nm* grandson

pétition /petisjɔ̃/ *nf* petition

petit-lait /p(ə)tilɛ/ *nm* **ça se boit comme du~!** (fam) it slips down nicely!

petit-nègre /p(ə)tinɛgʀ/ *nm inv* (fam) pidgin French

petits-enfants /p(ə)tizɑ̃fɑ̃/ *nm pl* grandchildren

pétrifiant, **~e** /petʀifjɑ̃, ɑ̃t/ *adj* petrifying

pétrifier /petʀifje/ [2] *vtr* **(a)** to petrify
(b) (figurative) to transfix

pétrin /petʀɛ̃/ *nm* dough trough
IDIOM **être dans le ~** to be in a fix (colloq)

pétrir /petʀiʀ/ [3] *vtr* **(a)** to knead ‹dough›
(b) to mould (GB), to mold (US) ‹personality›

pétrole /petʀɔl/ *nm* oil, petroleum

pétrolette /petʀɔlɛt/ *nf* (fam) moped

pétrolier, **-ière** /petʀɔlje, ɛʀ/ **1** *adj* oil
2 *nm* oil tanker

pétulant, **~e** /petylɑ̃, ɑ̃t/ *adj* exuberant

♂ **peu** /pø/

■ **Note** See the entries *avant, depuis, d'ici* and *sous* for the use of *peu* with these words.

1 *adv* **(a)** not much; **il parle ~** he doesn't talk much; **elle gagne très ~** she earns very little; **deux semaines c'est trop ~** two weeks isn't long enough; **si ~ que ce soit** however little; **très~ pour moi!** (fam) thanks, but no thanks!
(b) not very; **assez ~ connu** little-known; **elle n'est pas ~ fière** she's more than a little proud

2 *pron* few, not many

3 **de peu** *phr* only just

4 **peu de** *quantif* **~ de mots** few words; **~ de temps** little time

5 *nm* **le ~ de** the little ‹trust, freedom›; the

♂ indicates a very frequent word

---

few ‹books, friends›; the lack of ‹interest›

6 **un peu** *phr* **(a)** a little, a bit; **reste encore un ~** stay a little longer; **parle un ~ plus fort** speak a little louder; **un ~ plus de** a few more ‹books›; **a little more** ‹time›; **un ~ beaucoup** more than a bit
(b) just; **répète un~ pour voir!** (fam) you just try saying that again!; **pour un ~ ils se seraient battus** they very nearly had a fight

7 **peu à peu** *phr* gradually, little by little

8 **pour peu que** *phr* if; **pour ~ qu'il ait bu, il va nous raconter sa vie** one drink, and he'll tell us his life story

peuplade /pœplad/ *nf* small tribe

♂ **peuple** /pœpl/ *nm* people

peuplement /pœpləmɑ̃/ *nm* population

peupler /pœple/ [1] **1** *vtr* **(a)** to populate ‹country›; to stock ‹forest, pond›
(b) ‹animals, plants› to colonize ‹region›; ‹students› to fill ‹street›
2 **se peupler** *v refl* (+ *v être*) to fill up

peuplier /pøplije/ *nm* poplar

♂ **peur** /pœʀ/ *nf* fear; fright; scare; **être mort** *or* **vert** (fam) **de ~** to be scared to death; **une ~ panique s'empara de lui** he was panicstricken; **avoir ~** to be afraid; **j'en ai bien ~** I'm afraid so; **faire ~ à qn** to frighten sb; **maigre à faire ~** terribly thin

peureusement /pœʀøzmɑ̃/ *adv* fearfully

peureux, **-euse** /pœʀø, øz/ *adj* fearful

♂ **peut-être** /pøtɛtʀ/ *adv* perhaps, maybe

phalange /falɑ̃ʒ/ *nf* phalanx

phallocrate /falɔkʀat/ *nm* male chauvinist

phalloïde /falɔid/ *adj* **amanite ~** death cap

phallus /falys/ *nm inv* phallus

pharaon /faʀaɔ̃/ *nm* pharaoh

phare /faʀ/ *nm* **(a)** headlight
(b) lighthouse

pharmacie /faʀmasi/ *nf* **(a)** chemist's (shop) (GB), drugstore (US), pharmacy
(b) medicine cabinet
(c) (science) pharmacy

pharmacien, **-ienne** /faʀmasjɛ̃, ɛn/ *nm,f* (dispensing) chemist (GB), pharmacist

pharyngite /faʀɛ̃ʒit/ *nf* pharyngitis

pharynx /faʀɛ̃ks/ *nm inv* pharynx

♂ **phase** /faz/ *nf* **(a)** stage
(b) phase

phénoménal, **~e**, *mpl* **-aux** /fenɔmenal, o/ *adj* phenomenal

♂ **phénomène** /fenɔmɛn/ *nm*
(a) phenomenon
(b) (fam) **c'est un ~** he/she's quite a character

philanthropie /filɑ̃tʀɔpi/ *nf* philanthropy

philatélie /filateli/ *nf* stamp collecting

philatéliste /filatelist/ *nmf* philatelist

♂ **philosophe** /filɔzɔf/ *nmf* philosopher

♂ **philosophie** /filɔzɔfi/ *nf* philosophy

philosophique /filɔzɔfik/ *adj* philosophical

phobie /fɔbi/ *nf* phobia

phonétique /fɔnetik/ **1** *adj* phonetic
2 *nf* phonetics

phonographe /fɔnɔgʀaf/ *nm* gramophone (GB), phonograph (US)

phoque /fɔk/ *nm* (a) seal
(b) sealskin

phosphate /fɔsfat/ *nm* phosphate

phosphore /fɔsfɔʀ/ *nm* phosphorus

phosphorescent, **~e** /fɔsfɔʀesɑ̃, ɑ̃t/ *adj* phosphorescent

⚜ **photo** /fɔto/ *nf* (a) photography
(b) photo
■ ~ **d'identité** passport photo

photocomposition /fɔtokɔ̃pozisjɔ̃/ *nf* filmsetting (GB), photocomposition (US)

photocopie /fɔtokɔpi/ *nf* photocopy

photocopier /fɔtokɔpje/ [2] *vtr* to photocopy

photocopieur /fɔtokɔpjœʀ/ *nm* photocopier

photocopieuse /fɔtokɔpjøz/ *nf* photocopier

photogénique /fɔtoʒenik/ *adj* photogenic

photographe /fɔtogʀaf/ *nmf* photographer

photographie /fɔtogʀafi/ *nf*
(a) photography
(b) photograph, picture

photographier /fɔtogʀafje/ [2] *vtr* to photograph, to take a photo of

photographique /fɔtogʀafik/ *adj* photographic

photomaton® /fɔtomatɔ̃/ *nm* photo booth

photosynthèse /fɔtosɛ̃tɛz/ *nf* photosynthesis

photothèque /fɔtotɛk/ *nf* picture library

⚜ **phrase** /fʀaz/ *nf* (a) sentence
(b) phrase; **avoir une ~ malheureuse** to say the wrong thing; **~ toute faite** stock phrase
(c) (Mus) phrase

phréatique /fʀeatik/ *adj* **nappe ~** ground water

physicien, **-ienne** /fizisjɛ̃, ɛn/ *nm,f* physicist

physiologie /fizjɔlɔʒi/ *nf* physiology

physiologique /fizjɔlɔʒik/ *adj* physiological

physionomie /fizjɔnɔmi/ *nf* (a) face
(b) (figurative) (of country) face; (of area) appearance, look

physiothérapie /fizjoteʀapi/ *nf* physiotherapy (GB), physical therapy (US)

⚜ **physique¹** /fizik/ **1** *adj* physical
2 *nm* (a) physical appearance
(b) physique; **avoir un ~ séduisant** to look attractive
IDIOM **avoir le ~ de l'emploi** to look the part

physique² /fizik/ *nf* physics

piaf /pjaf/ *nm* (fam) little bird

piaffer /pjafe/ [1] *vi* (a) ‹horse› to paw the ground
(b) ‹person› to be impatient; **~ d'impatience** to be champing at the bit

piailler /pjaje/ [1] *vi* ‹bird› to chirp

pianiste /pjanist/ *nmf* pianist

piano /pjano/ **1** *nm* piano; **jouer qch au ~** to play sth on the piano
2 *adv* (Mus) piano
■ ~ **à queue** grand piano

pianoter /pjanɔte/ [1] *vi* to tinkle on the piano

PIB /peibe/ *nm: abbr* ▶ PRODUIT

pic /pik/ **1** *nm* (a) peak
(b) pick
(c) woodpecker
2 **à pic** *phr* ‹cliff› sheer; ‹ravine› very steep
IDIOM **tomber à ~** to come just at the right time

pichenette /piʃnɛt/ *nf* flick

pichet /piʃɛ/ *nm* jug (GB), pitcher

pick-up /pikœp/ *nm inv* (fam) record player

picorer /pikɔʀe/ [1] *vi* ‹bird› to peck about

picotement /pikɔtmɑ̃/ *nm* tingling; tickling

picoter /pikɔte/ [1] **1** *vtr* to sting ‹eyes, nose, skin›; to tickle ‹throat›
2 *vi* ‹throat› to tickle; ‹eyes› to sting

pie /pi/ *nf* (a) magpie
(b) (fam) chatterbox (colloq)

⚜ **pièce** /pjɛs/ **1** *nf* (a) room
(b) coin; **~ de monnaie** coin
(c) play; **~ de théâtre** play
(d) bit, piece; **en ~s** in bits; **mettre qn/qch en ~s** to pull sb/sth to pieces
(e) part; **~ de rechange** spare part
(f) patch
(g) document; **juger sur ~s** to judge on the actual evidence; **c'est inventé de toutes ~s** (figurative) it's a complete fabrication
(h) piece, item; (in chess set, puzzle) piece; **~ de collection** collector's item; **on n'est pas aux ~s** (fam) we're not in a sweat-shop
2 **-pièces** (*combining form*) (a) **un trois-~s cuisine** a three-roomed apartment with kitchen
(b) **un deux-~s** a two-piece swimsuit
■ ~ **à conviction** exhibit; **~ détachée** spare part; **en ~s détachées** in kit form; dismantled; **~ d'identité** identity papers; **~ maîtresse** showpiece; key element; **~ montée** layer cake

piécette /pjesɛt/ *nf* small coin

⚜ **pied** /pje/ *nm* (a) foot; **être ~s nus** to be barefoot(ed); **sauter à ~s joints** to jump with one's feet together; (figurative) to jump in with both feet; **coup de ~** kick; **à ~** on foot; **promenade à ~** walk; **taper du ~** to stamp one's foot; to tap one's foot; **de la tête aux ~s** from head to foot; **portrait en ~** full-length portrait; **avoir conscience de là où on met** ···⟶

les ~s (fam) to know what one is letting
oneself in for; **sur un ~ d'égalité** on an equal
footing
(b) (of hill, stairs) foot, bottom; (of glass) stem;
(of lamp) base; (of camera) stand
(c) (of celery, lettuce) head; **~ de vigne** vine
(d) (measurement) foot
■ **~ à coulisse** calliper rule
IDIOMS **être sur ~** ‹person› to be up and
about; ‹business› to be up and running;
mettre sur ~ to set up; **j'ai ~ l** I can touch the
bottom; **perdre ~** to go out of one's depth; to
lose ground; **être à ~ d'œuvre** to be ready to
get down to work; **elle joue au tennis comme
un ~** (fam) she's hopeless at tennis; **faire un
~ de nez à qn** to thumb one's nose at sb;
faire du ~ à qn to play footsy with sb (colloq);
faire des ~s et des mains (fam) **pour obtenir**
to work really hard at getting; **ça lui fera les
~s** (fam) that will teach him a lesson; **c'est
le ~** (fam) that's terrific (colloq); **mettre à ~ to**
suspend; **lever le ~** (fam) to slow down
pied-à-terre /pjetatɛR/ *nm inv* pied-à-
terre
pied-bot, *pl* **pieds-bots** /pjebo/ *nm*
person with a club foot
piédestal, *pl* **-aux** /pjedɛstal, o/ *nm*
pedestal
pied-noir, *pl* **pieds-noirs** /pjenwaR/ *nmf*
(fam) French colonial born in Algeria
piège /pjɛʒ/ *nm* **(a)** trap; **il s'est laissé
prendre au ~** he walked into the trap
(b) pitfall
piéger /pjeʒe/ [15] *vtr* **(a)** to trap ‹animal,
criminal›
(b) to trick, to trap ‹person›
(c) to booby-trap ‹letter, parcel, car›
piercing /pirsiŋ/ *nm* **le ~** body piercing;
elle a un ~ au nombril she has a pierced
navel
⚑ **pierre** /pjɛR/ *nf* stone; rock; **poser la
première ~** to lay the foundation stone
IDIOMS **jeter la ~ à qn** to accuse sb; **faire
d'une ~ deux coups** to kill two birds with
one stone
pierreries /pjɛRRi/ *nf pl* gems
pierreux, -euse /pjɛRø, øz/ *adj* stony
piété /pjete/ *nf* piety; **de ~** devotional
piétiner /pjetine/ [1] **1** *vtr* **(a)** to trample
[sth] underfoot
(b) to trample on
2 *vi* **(a)** **~ d'impatience** to hop up and
down with impatience
(b) to shuffle along; to trudge along
(c) to make no headway
piéton, -onne /pjetɔ̃, ɔn/ **1** *adj*
pedestrianized
2 *nm, f* pedestrian
piétonnier, -ière /pjetɔnje, ɛR/ *adj*
pedestrianized

piètre /pjɛtR/ *adj* ‹actor, writer› very
mediocre; ‹health, results› very poor; **c'est
une ~ consolation** that's small comfort
pieu, *pl* **~x¹** /pjø/ *nm* stake
pieuvre /pjœvR/ *nf* octopus
pieux², pieuse /pjø, øz/ *adj* **(a)** pious,
religious
(b) ‹affection, silence› reverent
■ **~ mensonge** white lie
pif /pif/ *nm* (fam) **(a)** nose, conk (GB) (colloq),
schnozzle (US) (colloq)
(b) intuition; **j'ai eu du ~** I had a hunch
(colloq); **au ~** ‹measure› roughly; ‹decide› just
like that
pige /piʒ/ *nf* **travailler à la ~, faire des ~s** to
do freelance work
pigeon /piʒɔ̃/ *nm* **(a)** pigeon
(b) (fam) sucker (colloq)
■ **~ voyageur** carrier pigeon
pigeonnier /piʒɔnje/ *nm* pigeon house;
pigeon loft; dovecote
piger /piʒe/ [13] *vtr* (fam) to understand
pigiste /piʒist/ *nmf* freelance
pigment /pigmɑ̃/ *nm* pigment
pigmenter /pigmɑ̃te/ [1] *vtr* to alter the
pigmentation of
pignon /piɲɔ̃/ *nm* **(a)** gable
(b) gearwheel
(c) pine kernel
IDIOM **avoir ~ sur rue** to be well-established
pilaf /pilaf/ *nm* pilau; **riz ~** pilau rice
pile¹ /pil/ *adv* (fam) **(a)** **s'arrêter ~** to stop
dead
(b) exactly; **à 10 heures et demie ~** at ten-
thirty sharp; **~ à l'heure** right on time; **tu
tombes ~** you're just the person I wanted
to see
pile² /pil/ *nf* **(a)** pile; stack
(b) **~ (électrique)** battery; **à ~s** battery-
operated
(c) pier
(d) (of coin) **le côté ~** the reverse side; **jouer à
~ ou face** to play heads or tails
■ **~ bouton** button battery; **~ solaire** solar cell
piler /pile/ [1] **1** *vtr* to grind; to crush
2 *vi* (fam) ‹car› to pull up short; ‹driver› to
slam on the brakes
pileux, -euse /pilø, øz/ *adj* **système ~**
hair
pilier /pilje/ *nm* **(a)** pillar
(b) (figurative) mainstay
(c) (in rugby) prop forward
pillage /pijaʒ/ *nm* pillage, plundering;
looting
pillard, ~e /pijaR, aRd/ *nm, f* looter;
pillager
piller /pije/ [1] *vtr* to pillage ‹town›; to loot
‹shop›; to plunder ‹temple›
pilleur, -euse /pijœR, øz/ *nm, f* looter;
plunderer
pilon /pilɔ̃/ *nm* **(a)** pestle

(b) (of poultry) drumstick

pilonnage /pilɔnaʒ/ *nm* (Mil) bombardment

pilotage /pilɔtaʒ/ *nm* piloting

pilote /pilɔt/ **1** *nm* pilot

2 **(-)pilote** (*combining form*) **projet(-)~** pilot project; **hôpital(-)~** experimental hospital

■ **~ automobile** racing driver

piloter /pilɔte/ [1] *vtr* to pilot ‹plane, ship›; to drive ‹car›

pilotis /pilɔti/ *nm inv* stilts

pilule /pilyl/ *nf* pill

IDIOMS **avaler la ~** (fam) to grin and bear it; **faire passer la ~** (fam) to sweeten the pill

pilule du lendemain /pilyl dy lɑ̃dəmɛ̃/ *nf* morning-after pill

pimbêche /pɛ̃bɛʃ/ *nf* stuck-up madam (colloq)

piment /pimɑ̃/ *nm* **(a)** hot pepper

(b) spice

■ **~ rouge** hot red pepper, chilli; **~ vert** green chilli pepper

pimpant, ~e /pɛ̃pɑ̃, ɑ̃t/ *adj* spruce, smart

pin /pɛ̃/ *nm* pine (tree); **pomme de ~** pine cone

pinailler /pinaje/ [1] *vi* (pop) to split hairs

pince /pɛ̃s/ *nf* **(a)** (pair of) pliers; (pair of) tongs

(b) (in garment) dart; **un pantalon à ~s** pleat front trousers (GB) *or* pants (US)

(c) (of crab) pincer, claw

■ **~ à cheveux** hair grip; **~ coupante** wire cutters; **~ à dessin** bulldog clip; **~ à épiler** tweezers; **~ à linge** clothes peg (GB), clothes-pin (US); **~ à sucre** sugar tongs; **~ à vélo** bicycle clip

pincé, ~e[1] /pɛ̃se/ *adj* ‹smile› tight-lipped; **prendre un air ~** to become stiff *or* starchy

pinceau, pl ~x /pɛ̃so/ *nm* (paint) brush

pincée[2] /pɛ̃se/ **1** *adj f* ▶ PINCÉ

2 *nf* (of pepper, salt) pinch

pincement /pɛ̃smɑ̃/ *nm* pinch; **avoir un ~ de cœur** to feel a twinge of sadness

pince-monseigneur, pl pinces-monseigneur /pɛ̃smɔ̃sɛɲœʀ/ *nf* jemmy, slim jim

pince-nez /pɛ̃sne/ *nm inv* pince-nez

pincer /pɛ̃se/ [12] **1** *vtr* **(a)** ‹person› to pinch; ‹crab› to nip

(b) (fam) to nab (colloq), to catch ‹thief›

(c) **~ les lèvres** to purse one's lips

(d) to pluck ‹string›

(e) ‹wind, cold› to sting ‹face›

2 **se pincer** *v refl* (+ *v être*) to pinch oneself; **se ~ le nez** to hold one's nose; **elle s'est pincée en refermant le tiroir** she caught her fingers closing the drawer

IDIOM **en ~ pour qn** (fam) to be stuck on sb (colloq)

pince-sans-rire /pɛ̃ssɑ̃ʀiʀ/ *nmf inv* **c'est un ~** he has a deadpan sense of humour (GB)

pincettes /pɛ̃sɛt/ *nf pl* **il n'est pas à prendre avec des ~** (fam) he's like a bear with a sore head (colloq)

pinède /pinɛd/ *nf* pine forest

pingouin /pɛ̃gwɛ̃/ *nm* **(a)** auk

(b) penguin

ping-pong® *pl ~s* /piŋpɔ̃ŋ/ *nm* table tennis, ping-pong®

pingre /pɛ̃gʀ/ *adj* stingy, niggardly

pingrerie /pɛ̃gʀəʀi/ *nf* stinginess

pin-pon /pɛ̃pɔ̃/ *nm:* *sound of a two-tone siren*

pin's /pins/ *nm inv* lapel badge

pintade /pɛ̃tad/ *nf* guinea fowl

pintadeau, pl ~x /pɛ̃tado/ *nm* young guinea fowl

pinte /pɛ̃t/ *nf* **(a)** pint (GB) (= 0,57 litre)

(b) ≈ quart (US) (= 0,94 litre)

(c) pot, tankard

pinter: se pinter /pɛ̃te/ [1] *v refl* (+ *v être*) (fam) to get plastered (colloq) *or* drunk

pin-up /pinœp/ *nf inv* (fam) glamour (GB) girl

pioche /pjɔʃ/ *nf* **(a)** mattock; pickaxe (GB), pickax (US)

(b) (Games) stack

piocher /pjɔʃe/ [1] *vtr* **(a)** to dig [sth] over ‹soil›

(b) (Games) to take [sth] from the stack ‹card›

piolet /pjɔlɛ/ *nm* ice axe (GB), ice pick (US)

pion, pionne /pjɔ̃, pjɔn/ **1** *nm,f* (fam, Sch) *student paid to supervise pupils*

2 *nm* **(a)** (in games) counter; (in chess) pawn; (in draughts) draught (GB), checker (US)

(b) (figurative) pawn

pionnier, -ière /pjɔnje, ɛʀ/ *adj, nm,f* pioneer

pipe /pip/ *nf* pipe

IDIOM **casser sa ~** (fam) to kick the bucket (colloq)

pipeau, pl ~x /pipo/ *nm* (reed-)pipe

IDIOMS **c'est du ~** (fam) it's no great shakes (colloq); **c'est pas du ~** (fam) it's for real (colloq)

pipelette /piplɛt/ *nf* (fam) gossip(monger)

piper /pipe/ [1] *vtr* **(a)** (fam) **ne pas ~ (mot)** not to say a word

(b) to load ‹dice›

pipi /pipi/ *nm* (fam) pee (colloq); wee-wee (colloq)

pipole /pipɔl/ *nmf* (fam) celeb (colloq)

piquant, ~e /pikɑ̃, ɑ̃t/ **1** *adj* **(a)** ‹stem, thistle› prickly; ‹naib› sharp

(b) ‹mustard, sauce› hot; ‹cheese› sharp

2 *nm* **(a)** (of stem, thistle) prickle; (of hedgehog, cactus) spine; (of barbed wire) spike, barb

(b) (of story) spiciness; (of situation) piquancy

pique[1] /pik/ *nm* (Games) spades

pique[2] /pik/ *nf* **(a)** cutting remark   ····⫶⫸

(b) pike; (of picador) lance

piqué, ∼e /pike/ *adj* ⟨*wood*⟩ worm-eaten; ⟨*linen, mirror, fruit*⟩ spotted; ⟨*paper*⟩ foxed

pique-assiette /pikasjɛt/ *nmf inv* (fam) sponger (colloq)

pique-nique, *pl* **∼s** /piknik/ *nm* picnic

piquer /pike/ [1] **1** *vtr* **(a)** to sting; to bite; to prick

(b) (fam) to give [sb] an injection; **faire ∼ un animal** to have an animal put down

(c) ⟨*mildew, rust*⟩ to spot ⟨*linen, mirror*⟩; to fox ⟨*paper, book*⟩

(d) ses yeux la piquaient her eyes were stinging; **ça me pique partout** I'm itchy all over

(e) (fam) to pinch (GB) (colloq), to steal ⟨*book, idea*⟩; to borrow ⟨*pencil, pullover*⟩

(f) to catch; **ils se sont fait ∼ à tricher pendant l'examen** they got caught cheating in the exam

(g) ∼ qn au vif to cut sb to the quick

(h) to arouse ⟨*curiosity*⟩

(i) (fam) **∼ un fou rire** to have a fit of the giggles; **∼ une crise de nerfs** to throw a fit (colloq); **∼ un cent mètres** to break into a run

(j) ∼ une tête to dive

2 *vi* **(a)** ⟨*beard*⟩ to be bristly; ⟨*wool*⟩ to be scratchy; ⟨*throat, eyes*⟩ to sting

(b) ⟨*bird*⟩ to swoop down; ⟨*plane*⟩ to dive; **∼ du nez** ⟨*person*⟩ to nod off; ⟨*plane*⟩ to go into a nosedive

(c) (fam) **arrête de ∼ dans le plat** stop picking (things out of the dish)

3 se piquer *v refl* (+ *v être*) **(a)** to prick oneself; **se ∼ aux orties** to get stung by nettles

(b) to inject oneself

(c) se ∼ de pouvoir réussir seul to claim that one can manage on one's own

IDIOMS quelle mouche t'a piqué? (fam) what's got into you? (colloq); **son article n'était pas piqué des hannetons** (fam) his/her article didn't pull any punches

piquet /pikɛ/ *nm* **(a)** stake

(b) peg

(c) (in skiing) gate pole

(d) (of sunshade) pole

(e) picket; **∼ de grève** (strike) picket, picket line

piquette /pikɛt/ *nf* (fam) plonk (GB) (colloq), cheap wine

piqûre /pikyʀ/ *nf* **(a)** injection, shot

(b) (of thorn, pin) prick; (of nettle, bee) sting; (of mosquito) bite

(c) stitch; stitching

pirate /piʀat/ *nm* pirate
■ **∼ de l'air** hijacker, skyjacker

pirater /piʀate/ [1] *vtr* to pirate

piraterie /piʀatʀi/ *nf* piracy
■ **∼ aérienne** hijacking, skyjacking; **∼ informatique** computer hacking

---

ᕯ indicates a very frequent word

ᕯ **pire** /piʀ/ **1** *adj* **(a)** worse (**que** than)

(b) worst; **les ∼s mensonges** the most wicked lies

2 *nm* **le ∼** the worst; **au ∼** at the very worst

pirogue /piʀɔg/ *nf* dugout canoe

pirouette /piʀwɛt/ *nf* pirouette; **s'en tirer par une ∼** to dodge the question skilfully (GB)

pis /pi/ **1** *adj inv* worse

2 *adv* worse; **tant ∼** too bad

3 *nm inv* (of cow) udder

pis-aller /pizale/ *nm inv* makeshift solution

pisciculteur, -trice /pisikyltœʀ, tʀis/ *nm,f* fish farmer

pisciculture /pisikyltyʀ/ *nf* fish farming

piscine /pisin/ *nf* swimming pool

pisse /pis/ *nf* (pop) piss (slang)

pissenlit /pisɑ̃li/ *nm* dandelion
IDIOM manger les ∼s par la racine (pop) to be pushing up the daisies (colloq)

pisser /pise/ (pop) [1] **1** *vtr* **∼ le sang** ⟨*person, nose, injury*⟩ to pour with blood

2 *vi* to pee (colloq), to piss (slang)
IDIOMS il pleut comme vache qui pisse it's pissing down (slang); **laisse ∼!** forget it!

pissotière /pisɔtjɛʀ/ *nf* (fam) street urinal

pistache /pistaʃ/ *nf* pistachio

ᕯ **piste** /pist/ *nf* **(a)** trail; **être sur une fausse ∼** to be on the wrong track

(b) (in police investigation) lead

(c) (in stadium) track; (in horseracing) racecourse (GB), racetrack (US); (in motor racing) racetrack; (in circus) ring; (in skiing) slope; (in cross-country skiing) trail; **∼ de danse** dance floor; **entrer en ∼** (at circus) to come into the ring; (figurative) to enter the fray

(d) track, path; (in desert) trail

(e) (in airport) runway

(f) (on record, cassette) track
■ **∼ cyclable** cycle lane; cycle path

pister /piste/ [1] *vtr* to trail, to track

pistil /pistil/ *nm* pistil

pistolet /pistɔlɛ/ *nm* **(a)** pistol, gun; **tirer au ∼** to fire a pistol

(b) (Tech) gun; **∼ à peinture** spray gun

pistolet-mitrailleur, *pl* **pistolets-mitrailleurs** /pistɔlɛmitʀajœʀ/ *nm* submachine gun

piston /pistɔ̃/ *nm* **(a)** (Tech) piston

(b) (fam) contacts; **avoir du ∼** to have connections in the right places

pistonner /pistɔne/ [1] *vtr* (fam) to pull strings for

pitance /pitɑ̃s/ *nf* fare

piteusement /pitøzmɑ̃/ *adv* pitifully, pathetically

piteux, -euse /pitø, øz/ *adj* **(a)** ⟨*results*⟩ poor, pitiful

(b) ⟨*air*⟩ crestfallen

pitié /pitje/ *nf* pity; mercy; **prendre qn en ∼** to take pity on sb; **il fait ∼** he's a pitiful sight; **par ∼, tais-toi!** for pity's sake, be quiet!

piton /pitɔ̃/ *nm* **(a)** hook **(b)** (in climbing) piton **(c)** (of mountain) peak

pitoyable /pitwajabl/ *adj* **(a)** pitiful **(b)** pathetic

pitoyablement /pitwajabləmɑ̃/ *adv* **(a)** pitifully **(b)** *‹fail›* miserably; *‹sing›* pathetically

pitre /pitʀ/ *nm* clown, buffoon

pitrerie /pitʀəʀi/ *nf* clowning

pittoresque /pitɔʀɛsk/ *adj* picturesque; colourful (GB)

pivert /pivɛʀ/ *nm* green woodpecker

pivoine /pivwan/ *nf* peony

pivot /pivo/ *nm* **(a)** (Tech) pivot **(b)** (of economy, strategy, group) linchpin; (of plot) kingpin **(c)** (Sport) (player) pivot, post **(d)** (of tooth) post and core

pivotant, ∼e /pivɔtɑ̃, ɑ̃t/ *adj* *‹chair›* swivel; *‹sign›* pivoting; *‹door›* revolving

pivoter /pivɔte/ [1] *vi* *‹person, animal, panel›* to pivot; *‹door›* to revolve; *‹chair›* to swivel

PJ /peʒi/ *nf* **(a)** (*abbr* = **police judiciaire**) *detective division of the French police force* **(b)** (*abbr* = **pièce(s) jointe(s)**) enc

PL (*written abbr* = **poids lourd**) HGV (GB), heavy truck (US)

placard /plakaʀ/ *nm* **(a)** cupboard; **mettre au ∼** (figurative) to put [sth] on ice *‹plan›*; to shunt [sb] aside *‹person›* **(b)** poster, bill

placarder /plakaʀde/ [1] *vtr* **(a)** to post, to stick **(b)** to cover [sth] with posters

place /plas/ *nf* **(a)** room, space **(b)** (in theatre, cinema, bus) seat; **payer sa ∼** (in cinema, theatre) to pay for one's ticket; (on train) to pay one's fare **(c)** place; **remettre qch à sa ∼** to put sth back in its place; **être en bonne ∼ pour gagner** to be well-placed *or* in a good position to win; **la ∼ d'un mot dans une phrase** the position of a word in a sentence; **sur ∼** to/on the scene; on the spot; **il faut savoir rester à sa ∼** you must know your place; **tenir une grande ∼ dans la vie de qn** to play a large part in sb's life **(d)** **à la ∼ de** instead of, in place of; **(si j'étais) à ta ∼** if I were in your position **(e)** **en ∼** *‹system, structure›* in place; *‹troops›* in position; *‹leader, party, regime›* ruling; **ne plus tenir en ∼** to be restless; **mettre en ∼** to put [sth] in place *‹programme›*; to put [sth] in position *‹team›*; to establish, to set up *‹network, institution›* **(f)** (in town) square; **la ∼ du village** the village square

(g) (Econ) market; **∼ financière** financial market **(h)** job; **perdre sa ∼** to lose one's job **(i)** **être dans la ∼** to be on the inside; **avoir un pied dans la ∼** to have a foot in the door

placé, ∼e /plase/ **1** *pp* ▸ PLACER **2** *pp adj* **(a)** (located) **être ∼** *‹object, tap, window›* to be; *‹chair, table, statue›* to be placed; *‹person›* (gen) to be; (at the theatre, cinema) to be sitting; **être bien/mal ∼** *‹building, shop›* to be well/badly situated; *‹person›* (at table, at a function) to have a good/bad place **(b)** (in a hierarchy) **être bien ∼ sur une liste** to have a good position on the list; **il est bien ∼ pour le poste** he's a likely candidate for the job; **avoir des amis haut ∼s** to have friends in high places **(c)** **être bien/mal ∼ pour faire** (to succeed) to be well/badly placed to do; (to know, judge) to be in a (good)/in no position to do

placebo /plasebo/ *nm* placebo

placement /plasmɑ̃/ *nm* **(a)** investment **(b)** **assurer le ∼ des diplômés** to ensure that graduates find employment **(c)** (of child) fostering

placenta /plasɛ̃ta/ *nm* placenta

placer /plase/ [12] **1** *vtr* **(a)** to put, to place *‹object›*; to seat *‹person›*; **∼ sa confiance en qn** to put one's trust in sb; **∼ ses espoirs en qn** to pin one's hopes on sb; **mal placé** *‹pride›* misplaced **(b)** to place, to find a job for *‹person›* **(c)** to invest *‹money›* **(d)** to slip in *‹remark, anecdote›*; **je n'arrive pas à en ∼ une** (fam) **avec elle!** I can't get a word in edgeways (GB) *or* edgewise (US) with her! **(e)** to place [sb] in care *‹child›* **2** **se placer** *v refl* (+ *v être*) **(a)** **se ∼ près de** to sit next to **(b)** **se ∼ premier** to come first

placeur, -euse /plasœʀ, øz/ *nm,f* usher/usherette

placide /plasid/ *adj* placid, calm

placier, -ière /plasje, ɛʀ/ *nm,f* **(a)** sales representative **(b)** market superintendent

plafond /plafɔ̃/ *nm* **(a)** ceiling; (of tent, vehicle, tunnel) roof **(b)** ceiling, limit

plafonnement /plafɔnmɑ̃/ *nm* **(a)** setting a ceiling on *‹pay›*; setting a limit on *‹spending›* **(b)** (on pay) ceiling (**de** on); (on spending) limitation (**de** of)

plafonnier /plafɔnje/ *nm* (gen) flush-fitting ceiling light; (in car) interior light

plage /plaʒ/ *nf* beach ∎ **∼ arrière** rear window shelf; **∼ horaire** time slot

plagiaire /plaʒjɛʀ/ *nmf* plagiarist

plagiat /plaʒja/ *nm* plagiarism

plagier /plaʒje/ [2] *vtr* to plagiarize

plaid /plɛd/ *nm* tartan rug (GB), plaid blanket (US)

plaidant, ∼e /plɛdɑ̃, ɑ̃t/ *adj* litigant

plaider /plede/ [1] **1** *vtr* to plead ‹case› **2** *vi* **(a)** to plead
(b) ∼ **en faveur de qn** ‹circumstances› to speak in favour (GB) of sb

plaidoirie /plɛdwaʀi/ *nf* plea

plaidoyer /plɛdwaje/ *nm* **(a)** speech for the defence (GB)
(b) plea

plaie /plɛ/ *nf* **(a)** wound; sore; cut
(b) (fam) **cet enfant, quelle**∼! (fam) that child is such a pain! (colloq)

plaignant, ∼e /plɛɲɑ̃, ɑ̃t/ *nm,f* plaintiff

⚜ **plaindre** /plɛ̃dʀ/ [54] **1** *vtr* to pity **2 se plaindre** *v refl* (+ *v être*) **(a)** to complain
(b) ‹injured person› to moan

plaine /plɛn/ *nf* plain

plain-pied: **de plain-pied** /dəplɛ̃pje/ *phr* **une maison de** ∼ a single-storey (GB) *or* single-story (US) house

plainte /plɛ̃t/ *nf* **(a)** (gen, Law) complaint
(b) moan, groan

plaintif, -ive /plɛ̃tif, iv/ *adj* plaintive

plaintivement /plɛ̃tivmɑ̃/ *adv* plaintively, dolefully

⚜ **plaire** /plɛʀ/ [59] **1 plaire à** *v+prep* **(a)** elle plaît aux hommes men find her attractive; elle m'a plu tout de suite I liked her straight away
(b) mon travail me plaît I like my job; un modèle qui plaît beaucoup a very popular model
2 se plaire *v refl* (+ *v être*) **(a)** ‹people, couple› to like each other
(b) ils se plaisent ici they like it here
(c) il se plaît à dire qu'il est issu du peuple he likes to say that he's a son of the people
3 *v impers* **s'il te plaît, s'il vous plaît** please

plaisamment /plɛzamɑ̃/ *adv* **(a)** agreeably
(b) amusingly

plaisance /plɛzɑ̃s/ *nf* **la navigation de** ∼ boating; **bateau de** ∼ pleasure boat

plaisancier, -ière /plɛzɑ̃sje, ɛʀ/ *nm,f* amateur sailor

plaisant, ∼e /plɛzɑ̃, ɑ̃t/ *adj* **(a)** pleasant
(b) amusing, funny

plaisanter /plɛzɑ̃te/ [1] *vi* to joke

plaisanterie /plɛzɑ̃tʀi/ *nf* joke

⚜ **plaisir** /plɛziʀ/ *nm* pleasure; **prendre un malin** ∼ **à faire** to take a wicked delight in doing; **faire** ∼ **à qn** to please sb; **faites-moi le** ∼ **de vous taire!** would you please shut up! (colloq); **faire durer le** ∼ to make the pleasure

⚜ indicates a very frequent word

last; (ironic) to prolong the agony

⚜ **plan** /plɑ̃/ *nm* **(a)** (of town, underground) map; (in building) plan, map
(b) (for building) plan; **tirer des** ∼**s** to draw up plans
(c) (of machine) blueprint
(d) (of essay, book) outline, framework
(e) (in cinematography) shot; **premier** ∼ foreground
(f) level; **au premier** ∼ **de l'actualité** at the forefront of the news; **sur le** ∼ **politique** from a political point of view
(g) plan; **c'est le bon** ∼ (fam) it's a good idea
■ ∼ **d'eau** artificial lake; ∼ **d'épargne** savings plan; ∼ **d'épargne-logement**, **PEL** *savings scheme entitling depositor to a cheap mortgage*
IDIOMS **laisser qn en** ∼ (fam) to leave sb in the lurch; **laisser qch en** ∼ (fam) to leave sth unfinished

⚜ **planche** /plɑ̃ʃ/ *nf* **(a)** (gen) plank; (for kneading dough) board; **faire la** ∼ to float on one's back
(b) plate
■ ∼ **à roulettes** (Sport) skateboard; ∼ **de salut** lifeline; ∼ **à voile** windsurfing board
IDIOMS **monter sur les** ∼**s** to go on the stage; **avoir du pain sur la** ∼ (fam) to have one's work cut out

plancher¹ /plɑ̃ʃe/ [1] *vi* (students' slang) to work

plancher² /plɑ̃ʃe/ *nm* **(a)** floor
(b) (Econ) floor; **atteindre un** ∼ to bottom out

planchiste /plɑ̃ʃist/ *nmf* windsurfer

plancton /plɑ̃ktɔ̃/ *nm* plankton

plané /plane/ *adj m* **vol** ∼ glide; **faire un vol** ∼ (figurative) to go flying

planer /plane/ [1] *vi* **(a)** ‹plane, bird› to glide
(b) **laisser** ∼ **le doute** to allow uncertainty to persist
(c) (fam) to have one's head in the clouds

planétaire /planetɛʀ/ *adj* planetary; (figurative) global

⚜ **planète** /planɛt/ *nf* planet

planeur /planœʀ/ *nm* **(a)** glider
(b) gliding

planifier /planifje/ [2] *vtr* to plan

planning /planiŋ/ *nm* (controversial) (fam) schedule
■ ∼ **familial** family planning service

planque /plɑ̃k/ *nf* (fam) (for person) hideout

planquer /plɑ̃ke/ [1] (fam) **1** *vtr* to hide ‹person›; to hide [sth] away ‹object›
2 se planquer *v refl* (+ *v être*) to hide

plan-séquence, *pl* **plans-séquences** /plɑ̃sekɑ̃s/ *nm* sequence shot

plant /plɑ̃/ *nm* young plant

plantaire /plɑ̃tɛʀ/ *adj* (Anat) plantar; **voûte** ∼ arch of the foot

plantation /plɑ̃tasjɔ̃/ *nf* **(a)** plantation
(b) (of flowers) bed; (of vegetables) patch

plante /plɑ̃t/ *nf* (a) plant; ~ **verte** houseplant; ~ **grasse** succulent
(b) ~ **(des pieds)** sole (of the foot)
planter /plɑ̃te/ [1] **1** *vtr* (a) to plant ‹flowers, shrub›
(b) to drive in ‹stake›; to knock in ‹nail›; ~ **un couteau dans** to stick a knife into
(c) to pitch ‹tent›; ~ **le décor** to set the scene
(d) ~ **(là)** to drop ‹tool›; to abandon ‹car›
2 se planter *v refl* (+ *v être*) (a) (fam) aller se ~ **devant qch** to go and stand in front of sth
(b) (fam) to crash
(c) (fam) to get it wrong; **il s'est planté en histoire** he made a mess of the history exam
plantureux, -euse /plɑ̃tyʀø, øz/ *adj* ‹bosom› ample; ‹woman› buxom
plaque /plak/ *nf* (of ice) patch; (on skin) blotch; (of glass) plate; (of marble) slab; (on door of surgery) brass plate; (of policeman) badge
■ ~ **d'égout** manhole cover; ~ **d'immatriculation** number plate (GB), license plate (US)
IDIOM **être à côté de la** ~ (fam) to be completely mistaken
plaqué, ~e /plake/ *adj* ~ **or** gold-plated
plaquer /plake/ [1] **1** *vtr* (a) ~ **qn contre qch** to pin sb against sth
(b) (fam) to leave ‹job, spouse›
2 se plaquer *v refl* (+ *v être*) se ~ **contre un mur** to flatten oneself against a wall
plaquette /plakɛt/ *nf* (a) (of butter) packet
(b) (of pills) ≈ blister strip
■ ~ **de frein** brake shoe
plastic /plastik/ *nm* plastic explosive
plasticage /plastikaʒ/ *nm* bomb attack (de on)
plastifier /plastifje/ [2] *vtr* to coat [sth] with plastic
plastique¹ /plastik/ *nm* plastic
plastique² /plastik/ *nf* (of object, statue) formal beauty; (of person) physique
plastiquer /plastike/ [1] *vtr* to carry out a bomb attack on
plastron /plastrɔ̃/ *nm* shirt front
plat, ~e /pla, plat/ **1** *adj* (a) flat
(b) ‹boat› flat-bottomed; ‹watch, lighter› slimline; ‹hair› limp
(c) ‹style, description› lifeless
2 *nm* (a) dish
(b) course
3 à plat *phr* (a) poser qch à ~ to lay sth down flat; à ~ **ventre** flat on one's stomach; **tomber à** ~ ‹joke› to fall flat
(b) ‹tyre› flat; ‹battery› flat (GB), dead
(c) (fam) **être à** ~ ‹person› to be run down
■ ~ **de résistance** main course
IDIOMS **mettre les pieds dans le** ~ (fam) to put one's foot in it; **faire tout un** ~ **de qch** (fam) to make a big deal about sth
platane /platan/ *nm* plane tree
plateau, ** *pl* ~x** /plato/ *nm* (a) tray

(b) ~ **de tournage** film set
(c) (in geography) plateau
(d) (of weighing scales) pan
plate-bande, ** *pl* **plates-bandes /platbɑ̃d/ *nf* border, flower bed
platée /plate/ *nf* (fam) plateful (de of)
plate-forme, ** *pl* **plates-formes /platfɔʀm/ *nf* platform; ~ **pétrolière** oil rig
platine¹ /platin/ *adj inv, nm* platinum
platine² /platin/ *nf* (record player) turntable
platitude /platityd/ *nf* platitude
platonique /platɔnik/ *adj* platonic
plâtre /plɑtʀ/ *nm* (a) plaster
(b) (Med) plaster cast
IDIOM **essuyer les** ~**s** to put up with the initial problems
plâtrer /plɑtʀe/ [1] *vtr* (a) to plaster ‹wall›
(b) (Med) ~ **le bras de qn** to put sb's arm in plaster
plâtreux, -euse /plɑtʀø, øz/ *adj* chalky
plâtrier, -ière /plɑtʀije, ɛʀ/ *nm,f* plasterer
plausible /plozibl/ *adj* plausible
playback /plɛbak/ *nm inv* miming, lip syncing; **chanter en** ~ to lip-sync (a song)
plébiscite /plebisit/ *nm* plebiscite
plébisciter /plebisite/ [1] *vtr* (a) to elect [sb] with a huge majority
(b) to vote overwhelmingly in favour (GB) of
pléiade /plejad/ *nf* galaxy, pleiad
plein, ~e /plɛ̃, plɛn/ **1** *adj* (a) full
(b) **un** ~ **panier** a basketful; **prendre à** ~**es mains** to pick up a handful of ‹earth, sand, coins›
(c) ‹brick, wall› solid; ‹cheeks, face› plump; ‹shape› rounded
(d) ‹power, effect› full; ‹satisfaction, confidence› complete
(e) ‹day, month› whole, full; ‹moon› full
(f) **en** ~**e poitrine/réunion/forêt** (right) in the middle of the chest/meeting/forest; **en** ~ **jour** in broad daylight; **en** ~ **été** at the height of summer
(g) (Zool) **pleine** ‹animal› pregnant; ‹cow› in calf
(h) (fam) sloshed (colloq), drunk
(i) **veste** ~**e peau** jacket made out of full skins
2 *adv* (a) **avoir des billes** ~ **les poches** to have one's pockets full of marbles; **il a des idées** ~ **la tête** he's full of ideas
(b) **être orienté** ~ **sud** to face due south
3 *nm* **faire le** ~ **de** to fill up with ‹water, petrol›; **le** ~**, s'il vous plaît** fill it up, please
4 plein de (fam) *quantif* ~ **de** lots of, loads (colloq) of
5 à plein *phr* fully
6 tout plein *phr* (fam) really
IDIOM **en avoir** ~ **le dos** (fam) to be fed up
plein-air /plɛnɛʀ/ *nm inv* (Sch) (outdoor) games
pleinement /plɛnmɑ̃/ *adv* fully

plein-emploi /plɛnɑ̃plwɑ/ *nm inv* full employment

plein-temps, *pl* **pleins-temps** /plɛ̃tɑ̃/ *nm* full-time job

plénier, -ière /plenje, ɛʀ/ *adj* plenary

pléonasme /pleɔnasm/ *nm* pleonasm

ᕤ **pleurer** /plœʀe/ [1] **1** *vtr* to mourn ‹friend›
2 *vi* (a) to cry, to weep
(b) ‹eyes› to water
(c) ~ sur qn/qch to shed tears over sb/sth; **arrête de** ~ **sur ton sort!** stop feeling sorry for yourself!
(d) (fam) ‹person› to whine
IDIOM **elle n'a plus que ses yeux pour** ~ all she can do is cry

pleureur /plœʀœʀ/ *adj m* **saule** ~ weeping willow

pleureuse /plœʀøz/ *nf* (hired) mourner

pleurnicher /plœʀniʃe/ [1] *vi* (fam) to snivel

pleurnicheur, -euse /plœʀniʃœʀ, øz/ *nm,f* (fam) sniveller

pleurs /plœʀ/ *nm pl* tears; **en** ~ in tears

pleuvoir /pløvwaʀ/ [39] **1** *v impers* to rain; **il pleut** it's raining; **il pleut à torrents** it's pouring with rain
2 *vi* ‹blows, bombs› to rain down

pli /pli/ *nm* (a) (gen) fold; (in trousers) crease; (in skirt) pleat
(b) (Games) trick
(c) letter; **sous** ~ **cacheté** in a sealed envelope
IDIOMS **ça ne fait pas un** ~ (fam) there's no doubt about it; **c'est un** ~ **à prendre** it's something you've got to get used to

pliage /plijaʒ/ *nm* folding

pliant, ~**e 1** *adj* folding
2 *nm* folding stool, campstool

plier /plije/ [2] **1** *vtr* (a) to fold; to fold up
(b) to bend ‹stem, arm›
(c) to submit
2 *vi* (a) ‹tree, branch, joint› to bend; ‹plank, floor› to sag
(b) to give in
3 **se plier** *v refl* (+ *v être*) (a) to fold
(b) **se** ~ **à** to submit to
IDIOM **être plié (en deux** *or* **quatre)** (fam) to be doubled up with laughter

plinthe /plɛ̃t/ *nf* skirting board (GB), baseboard (US)

plisser /plise/ [1] **1** *vtr* (a) to pleat ‹cloth›
(b) to crease ‹garment›
(c) ~ **le front** to knit one's brows; ~ **les yeux** to screw up one's eyes
2 *vi* ‹stocking› to wrinkle; ‹skirt› to be creased

pliure /plijyʀ/ *nf* fold; **la** ~ **du genou** the back of the knee

ᕤ indicates a very frequent word

plomb /plɔ̃/ *nm* (a) lead; **sans** ~ ‹petrol› unleaded; **soleil de** ~ burning sun; **ciel de** ~ leaden sky
(b) (in hunting) **un** ~ a lead pellet; **du** ~ lead shot
(c) fuse
IDIOMS **avoir du** ~ **dans l'aile** (fam) to be in a bad way (colloq); **cela va leur mettre du** ~ **dans la cervelle** (fam) that will knock some sense into them

plombage /plɔ̃baʒ/ *nm* (in dentistry) filling

plomber /plɔ̃be/ [1] *vtr* to fill ‹tooth›

plombier /plɔ̃bje/ *nm* plumber

plonge /plɔ̃ʒ/ *nf* (fam) washing up (GB), dishwashing (US)

plongée /plɔ̃ʒe/ *nf* (a) (skin) diving
(b) scuba diving
(c) snorkelling (GB); ~ **sous-marine** deep-sea diving; **faire de la** ~ to go diving

plongeoir /plɔ̃ʒwaʀ/ *nm* (a) diving-board
(b) springboard

plongeon /plɔ̃ʒɔ̃/ *nm* (a) dive
(b) fall

ᕤ **plonger** /plɔ̃ʒe/ [13] **1** *vtr* to plunge
2 *vi* (a) to dive
(b) ‹bird› to swoop down
3 **se plonger** *v refl* (+ *v être*) (a) to plunge
(b) to bury oneself

plongeur, -euse /plɔ̃ʒœʀ, øz/ *nm,f* (a) diver
(b) dishwasher

plot /plo/ *nm* (a) (electrical) contact
(b) (of wood) block

plouc /pluk/ *nm* (fam) country bumpkin (colloq)

plouf 1 *nm inv* splash; **faire un** ~ to go splash
2 *excl* splash!

ployer /plwaje/ [23] *vi* ‹branch, person› to bend; ~ **sous un fardeau** to be weighed down by a burden

plu /ply/ ▶ PLAIRE, PLEUVOIR

ᕤ **pluie** /plɥi/ *nf* (a) rain; **sous une** ~ **battante** in driving rain
(b) (of missiles, insults) hail; (of sparks, compliments) shower
■ ~**s acides** acid rain
IDIOMS **il n'est pas né de la dernière** ~ (fam) he wasn't born yesterday (colloq); **faire la** ~ **et le beau temps** to call the shots (colloq)

plume /plym/ *nf* (a) (Zool) feather
(b) (pen) nib; **écrire au fil de la** ~ to write as the thoughts come into one's head
IDIOM **voler dans les** ~**s de qn** (fam) to fly at sb

plumeau, *pl* ~**x** /plymo/ *nm* (a) feather duster
(b) tuft

plumer /plyme/ [1] *vtr* to pluck ‹bird›

plumier /plymje/ *nm* pencil box

ⵊ **plupart, la plupart** /laplypaʀ/ *nf inv* la ∼ des gens most people; la ∼ du temps most of the time, mostly

pluridisciplinaire /plyʀidisiplinɛʀ/ *adj* multidisciplinary

pluriel, -elle /plyʀjɛl/ **1** *adj* plural **2** *nm* plural

ⵊ **plus¹** /ply, plys, plyz/ **1** *prep* plus **2** *adv* (a) (comparative) more; (superlative) le ∼ the most; il travaille ∼ (que moi) he works more (than I do); ∼ j'y pense, moins je comprends the more I think about it, the less I understand; ∼ ça va as time goes on; qui ∼ est furthermore; de ∼ en ∼ more and more; ∼ petit smaller; le ∼ petit the smallest; trois heures ∼ tôt three hours earlier; deux fois ∼ cher twice as expensive; il est on ne peut ∼ désagréable he's as unpleasant as can be; il est ∼ ou moins artiste he's an artist of sorts; il a été ∼ ou moins poli he wasn't particularly polite (b) (in negative constructions) elle ne fume ∼ she doesn't smoke any more; il n'y a ∼ d'œufs there are no more eggs; ∼ jamais ça! never again!; ∼ que trois jours avant Noël! only three days to go until Christmas! **3** **plus de** *quantif* deux fois ∼ de livres que twice as many books as; il a gagné le ∼ d'argent he won the most money; les gens de ∼ de 60 ans people over 60 **4** **au plus** *phr* at the most **5** **de plus** *phr* (a) furthermore, what's more (b) donnez-moi deux pommes de ∼ give me two more apples; une fois de ∼ once more **6** **en plus** *phr* en ∼ (de cela) on top of that; les taxes en ∼ plus tax

plus² /plys/ *nm inv* (a) le signe ∼ the plus sign (b) (fam) plus (colloq)

ⵊ **plusieurs** /plyzjœʀ/ **1** *adj* several; une ou ∼ personnes one or more people **2** *pron* ∼ ont déjà signé several people have already signed

plus-value, *pl* ∼s /plyvaly/ *nf* (a) (of property) increase in value; (sales profit) capital gain (b) surcharge (c) (Econ) surplus value

ⵊ **plutôt** /plyto/ *adv* rather; instead; passe ∼ le matin call round (GB) *or* come by (US) in the morning preferably; ∼ mourir! I'd rather die!; demande ∼ à Corinne ask Corinne instead; dis ∼ que tu n'as pas envie de le faire why don't you just say that you don't want to do it?; la nouvelle a été ∼ bien accueillie the news went down rather well

pluvieux, -ieuse /plyvjø, øz/ *adj* wet, rainy

PME /peɛmə/ *nf pl* (*abbr* = **petites et moyennes entreprises**) small and medium-sized enterprises, SMEs

PMI /peɛmi/ *nf pl* (*abbr* = **petites et moyennes industries**) small and medium-sized industries

PMU /peɛmy/ *nm* (*abbr* = **Pari mutuel urbain**) *French state-controlled betting system*

PNB /peɛnbe/ *nm* (*abbr* = **produit national brut**) gross national product, GNP

pneu /pnø/ *nm* tyre (GB), tire (US)

pneumatique /pnømatik/ *adj* inflatable

pneumonie /pnømɔni/ *nf* pneumonia ■ ∼ atypique SARS

ⵊ **poche¹** /pɔʃ/ *nm* (livre de) ∼ paperback

ⵊ **poche²** /pɔʃ/ *nf* (a) (in garment, bag) pocket; en ∼ in one's pocket; il avait 200 euros en ∼ he had 200 euros on him; s'en mettre plein *or* se remplir les ∼s (fam) to line one's pockets; faire les ∼s de qn to pick sb's pocket (b) ∼ de gaz/d'air gas/air pocket (c) avoir des ∼s sous les yeux to have bags under one's eyes (d) (Zool) (of kangaroo) pouch ■ ∼ revolver hip pocket **IDIOMS** c'est dans la ∼ (fam) it's in the bag (colloq); en être de sa ∼ (fam) to be out of pocket; ne pas avoir les yeux dans sa ∼ (fam) not to miss a thing (colloq); connaître un endroit comme sa ∼ (fam) to know a place like the back of one's hand

pocher /pɔʃe/ [1] *vtr* (Culin) to poach

pochette /pɔʃɛt/ *nf* (a) (for pencils) case; (for credit cards) wallet; (for make-up, glasses) pouch; (for document) folder; (for record) sleeve (b) (of matches) book (c) clutch bag

pochoir /pɔʃwaʀ/ *nm* stencil

podcaster /pɔdkaste/ *vi* to podcast

podium /pɔdjɔm/ *nm* podium

poêle¹ /pwal/ *nm* (a) stove (b) (on coffin) pall

poêle² /pwal/ *nf* frying pan

ⵊ **poème** /pɔɛm/ *nm* poem; c'est tout un ∼ (fam) it's quite something

ⵊ **poésie** /pɔezi/ *nf* (a) poetry (b) poem

ⵊ **poète** /pɔɛt/ *nm* (a) poet (b) dreamer

poétique /pɔetik/ *adj* poetic

ⵊ **poids** /pwɑ/ *nm inv* (a) weight; peser son ∼ to be very heavy; adversaire de ∼ opponent to be reckoned with (b) burden; être un ∼ pour qn to be a burden on sb; avoir un ∼ sur la conscience to have a guilty conscience (c) influence (d) des ∼ en laiton brass weights (e) (in athletics) shot; lancer le ∼ to put the shot ■ ∼ et haltères weightlifting; ∼ lourd (Sport) heavyweight; heavy truck ⋯⋗

p

IDIOM avoir or **faire deux ~ deux mesures** to have double standards

poignant, **~e** /pwaɲɑ̃, ɑ̃t/ adj **(a)** poignant **(b)** heart-rending, harrowing

poignard /pwaɲaʀ/ nm dagger; **coup de ~** stab

poignarder /pwaɲaʀde/ [1] vtr to stab

poigne /pwaɲ/ nf **avoir de la ~** to have a strong grip; **homme à ~** strong man

poignée /pwaɲe/ nf **(a)** handful **(b)** (of door, drawer, bag) handle; (of sword) hilt ■ **~ de main** handshake

poignet /pwaɲe/ nm **(a)** wrist **(b)** (of shirt) cuff

poil /pwal/ nm **(a)** (on body, animal) hair; **à ~** (pop) stark naked; **caresser dans le sens du ~** to stroke [sth] the way the fur lies; **à ~** butter [sb] up (colloq); **ça marche au ~** (fam) it works like a dream **(b)** (fam) (of irony) touch; (of commonsense) shred; **à un ~ près** by a whisker **(c)** (of cloth) nap; (of brush) bristle ■ **~ à gratter** itching powder

IDIOMS être de bon/mauvais ~ (fam) to be in a good/bad mood; **hérisser le ~ de qn** (fam) to put sb's back up (colloq); **avoir un ~ dans la main** (fam) to be bone idle

poilu, **~e** /pwaly/ adj hairy

poinçon /pwɛ̃sɔ̃/ nm **(a)** (tool) punch **(b)** (on gold) die, stamp; hallmark

poinçonner /pwɛ̃sɔne/ [1] vtr **(a)** to punch, to clip **(b)** to hallmark

poinçonneur, **-euse** /pwɛ̃sɔnœʀ, øz/ nm,f ticket-puncher

poindre /pwɛ̃dʀ/ [56] vi ‹day› to break

poing /pwɛ̃/ nm fist; **coup de ~** punch; **montrer le ~** to shake one's fist; **être pieds et ~s liés** (figurative) to have one's hands tied **IDIOM dormir à ~s fermés** to sleep like a log

⚐ **point** /pwɛ̃/ **1** nm **(a)** point; **un ~ de rencontre** a meeting point; **~ de vente** (sales) outlet **(b)** (at sea) position; **faire le ~** to take bearings; (figurative) to take stock of the situation **(c) être sur le ~ de faire** to be just about to do; **au ~ où j'en suis, ça n'a pas d'importance!** I'm past caring! **(d) il m'agace au plus haut ~** he annoys me intensely; **je ne le pensais pas bête à ce ~** I didn't think he was that stupid; **à tel ~ que** to such an extent that; **douloureux au ~ que** so painful that **(e)** (on agenda) item, point; **un ~ de détail** a minor point; **en tout ~, en tous ~s** in every respect or way **(f)** dot; **un ~ de colle** a spot of glue; **un ~ de rouille** a speck of rust; **~ d'intersection** point of intersection

(g) (Games, Sport) point; **compter les ~s** to keep (the) score **(h)** (Sch) mark (GB), point (US); **être un bon ~ pour** to be a plus point for **(i)** full stop (GB), period (US); **mettre un ~ final à qch** (figurative) to put a stop to sth; **tu vas te coucher un ~ c'est tout!** (fam) you're going to bed and that's final! **(j)** (Med) pain; **avoir un ~ à la poitrine** to have a pain in one's chest **(k)** (in sewing, knitting) stitch **2 à point** phr **(a) à ~ nommé** just at the right moment **(b) à ~** ‹meat› medium rare **3 au point** phr **être au ~** ‹system, machine› to be well designed; ‹show› to be well put together; **mettre au ~** to perfect ‹system, method›; to develop ‹vaccine, machine›; **faire la mise au ~** (in photography) to focus; **faire une mise au ~** (figurative) to set the record straight ■ **~ argent** cash point; **~ chaud** trouble or hot spot; **~ de côté** (pain) stitch; **~ de départ** starting point; **nous revoilà à notre ~ de départ** (figurative) we're back to square one; **~ d'eau** water tap (GB) or faucet (US); **~ d'exclamation** exclamation mark (GB) or point (US); **~ faible** weak point; **~ fort** strong point; **~ d'interrogation** question mark; **~ de mire** (Mil) target; (figurative) focal point; **~ mort** neutral; **être au ~ mort** (in car) to be in neutral; ‹business, trade› to be at a standstill; **~ noir** (Med) blackhead; (of situation) problem; **~ de repère** landmark; point of reference; **~ de suture** (Med) stitch; **~ de vue** point of view; viewpoint; **du ~ de vue du sens** as far as meaning is concerned; **~s de suspension** suspension points; **~ zéro** ground zero **IDIOM être mal en ~** to be in a bad way

pointage /pwɛ̃taʒ/ nm **(a)** (on list) ticking off (GB), checking off (US) **(b)** (of employee) clocking in

pointe /pwɛ̃t/ **1** nf **(a)** (of knife) point; (of shoe) toe; (of hair) end; (of railing) spike; (of spear) tip; **en ~** pointed **(b) de ~** ‹technology› advanced, state-of-the-art; ‹sector, industry› high-tech; **à la ~ du progrès** state-of-the-art **(c)** high; **une vitesse de ~ de 200 km/h** a maximum or top speed of 200 km/h; **heure de ~** rush hour; **aux heures de ~** at peak time **(d)** (of garlic) touch; (of accent) hint **(e)** blocked shoe **2 pointes** nf pl **faire des ~s** to dance on points ■ **~ du pied** tiptoe

pointer /pwɛ̃te/ [1] **1** vtr **(a)** to tick off (GB), to check off (US) ‹names, figures›; to check ‹list› **(b)** to point ‹weapon›; **~ le doigt vers** to point at; **~ son nez** (fam) to show one's face **2** vi **(a)** ‹employee› to clock in; **~ à l'agence pour l'emploi** to sign on at the

---

⚐ indicates a very frequent word

unemployment office
(b) ‹sun, plant› to come up; ‹day› to break
3 **se pointer** v refl (+ v être) (fam) to
turn up
pointillé, ∼e /pwɛtije/ **1** adj dotted
2 nm dotted line
pointilleux, -euse /pwɛtijø, øz/ adj
‹person› fussy, pernickety
pointu, ∼e /pwɛty/ adj **(a)** (gen) pointed;
‹scissors› with a sharp point
(b) ‹check› close, thorough
(c) ‹question, approach› precise
pointure /pwɛtyʀ/ nf (of glove, shoe) size
point-virgule, pl **points-virgules**
/pwɛviʀgyl/ nm semicolon
poire /pwaʀ/ nf **(a)** pear
(b) (fam) sucker (colloq)
IDIOMS **couper la ∼ en deux** to split the
difference; **garder une ∼ pour la soif** to save
something for a rainy day
poireau, pl **∼x** /pwaʀo/ nm leek
poirier /pwaʀje/ nm **(a)** pear (tree)
(b) **faire le ∼** to do a headstand
pois /pwa/ nm inv **(a)** (Bot, Culin) pea; **petit ∼**
(garden) pea, petit pois
(b) dot; **à ∼** polka dot, spotted
■ **∼ cassé** split pea; **∼ chiche** chickpea
poison /pwazɔ̃/ nm poison
poisse /pwas/ nf (fam) **(a)** rotten luck (colloq)
(b) drag (colloq)
poisseux, -euse /pwasø, øz/ adj
‹hands, table› sticky; ‹atmosphere› muggy;
‹restaurant› greasy
⚜ **poisson** /pwasɔ̃/ nm fish; **les ∼s d'eau
douce/de mer** freshwater/saltwater fish
■ **∼ rouge** goldfish
IDIOM **être comme un ∼ dans l'eau** to be in
one's element
poissonnerie /pwasɔnʀi/ nf fishmonger's
(shop) (GB), fish shop (US)
poissonnier, -ière /pwasɔnje, ɛʀ/ nm,f
fishmonger (GB), fish vendor (US)
Poissons /pwasɔ̃/ pr nm pl Pisces
poitrail /pwatʀaj/ nm breast
poitrine /pwatʀin/ nf **(a)** chest; **tour de ∼**
chest size
(b) breasts; **tour de ∼** bust size
■ **∼ fumée** ≈ smoked streaky bacon
⚜ **poivre** /pwavʀ/ nm pepper
poivré, ∼e /pwavʀe/ adj ‹sauce› peppery
poivrer /pwavʀe/ [1] vtr to add pepper to
poivron /pwavʀɔ̃/ nm sweet pepper,
capsicum
poivrot, ∼e /pwavʀo, ɔt/ nm,f (fam) drunk
poker /pɔkɛʀ/ nm poker; **coup de ∼** gamble
polaire /pɔlɛʀ/ adj polar; arctic
polar /pɔlaʀ/ nm (fam) detective novel
polariser /pɔlaʀize/ [1] vtr, **se
polariser** v refl (+ v être) **(a)** to polarize
(b) to focus

pôle /pol/ nm **(a)** pole
(b) centre (GB)
polémique /pɔlemik/ nf debate
poli, ∼e /pɔli/ **1** pp ▶ POLIR
2 pp adj ‹metal, style› polished
3 adj polite
4 nm shine
⚜ **police** /pɔlis/ nf **(a)** police; police force
(b) security service
(c) **faire la ∼** to keep order
(d) (in insurance) policy
■ **∼ judiciaire, PJ** detective division of the
French police force; **∼ de l'air et des frontières, PAF** border police; **∼ des mœurs** or
mondaine vice squad; **∼ secours** ≈ emergency services
⚜ **policier, -ière** /pɔlisje, ɛʀ/ **1** adj (gen)
police; ‹novel› detective
2 nm policeman; **femme ∼** policewoman
poliment /pɔlimɑ̃/ adv politely
polir /pɔliʀ/ [3] vtr to polish ‹stone, metal›
polisson, -onne /pɔlisɔ̃, ɔn/ nm,f naughty
child
politesse /pɔlitɛs/ nf politeness; **rendre la
∼ à qn** to return the compliment
politicien, -ienne /pɔlitisjɛ̃, ɛn/ nm,f
politician
politique¹ /pɔlitik/ adj (gen) political;
‹behaviour, act› calculating
⚜ **politique²** /pɔlitik/ nf **(a)** politics; **faire de
la ∼** ‹militant› to be involved in politics
(b) policy; **notre ∼ des prix** our pricing
policy
IDIOMS **pratiquer la ∼ de l'autruche** to stick
one's head in the sand; **pratiquer la ∼ du pire**
to envisage the worst-case scenario
politiser /pɔlitize/ [1] vtr to politicize
pollen /pɔl(l)ɛn/ nm pollen
polluant, ∼e /pɔl(l)ɥɑ̃/ **1** adj polluting
2 nm pollutant
polluer /pɔl(l)ɥe/ [1] vtr to pollute
pollution /pɔl(l)ysjɔ̃/ nf pollution
polo /pɔlo/ nm **(a)** polo shirt
(b) (Sport) polo
polochon /pɔlɔʃɔ̃/ nm (fam) bolster; **bataille
de ∼s** pillow fight
Pologne /pɔlɔɲ/ pr nf Poland
polonais, ∼e /pɔlɔnɛ/ **1** adj Polish
2 nm (language) Polish
Polonais, ∼e nm,f Pole
poltronnerie /pɔltʀɔnʀi/ nf cowardice
polycopier /pɔlikɔpje/ [2] vtr to duplicate
polyculture /pɔlikyltyʀ/ nf mixed
farming
polygame /pɔligam/ adj polygamous
polyglotte /pɔliglɔt/ adj, nmf polyglot
Polytechnique /pɔliteknik/ nf: Grande
École of Science and Technology
polyvalence /pɔlivalɑ̃s/ nf **(a)** versatility
(b) (of employee) flexibility

polyvalent, ~e /pɔlivalɑ̃, ɑ̃t/ *adj*
‹equipment› multipurpose; ‹employee› who
does several jobs

pommade /pɔmad/ *nf* (Med) ointment
IDIOM **passer de la ~ à qn** (fam) to butter sb
up (colloq)

✧ **pomme** /pɔm/ *nf* (a) apple
(b) (of watering can) rose; (of shower) shower-
head; (of walking stick) pommel, knob
(c) (fam) mug (GB) (colloq), sucker (colloq); **ça
va encore être pour ma ~** I'm in for it again
(colloq)
■ **~ d'Adam** Adam's apple; **~ de pin** pine
cone; **~ de terre** potato; **~s frites** chips (GB),
(French) fries
IDIOM **tomber dans les ~s** (fam) to faint

pommeau, *pl* **~x** /pɔmo/ *nm* knob;
pommel

pommette /pɔmɛt/ *nf* cheekbone

pommier /pɔmje/ *nm* apple tree

pompe /pɔ̃p/ *nf* (a) pump
(b) (pop) shoe
(c) pomp
(d) (Sport, fam) press-up (GB), push-up
■ **~ à essence** petrol pump (GB), gas pump
(US); **~s funèbres** undertaker's (GB), funeral
director's (GB), funeral parlor (US)
IDIOM **avoir un coup de ~** (fam) to be knackered (GB) (slang) *or* pooped (colloq)

pomper /pɔ̃pe/ [1] *vtr* (a) to pump ‹liquid,
air›
(b) (students' slang) to copy
IDIOM **~ l'air à qn** (fam) to get on sb's nerves

pompette /pɔ̃pɛt/ *adj* (fam) tipsy (colloq),
drunk

pompeux, -euse /pɔ̃pø, øz/ *adj* pompous

pompier, -ière /pɔ̃pje, ɛʀ/ ① *adj*
pompous
② *nm* fireman, firefighter; **appeler les ~s**
to call the fire brigade (GB) *or* department
(US)

pompiste /pɔ̃pist/ *nmf* petrol (GB) *or* gas
(US) pump attendant

pompon /pɔ̃pɔ̃/ *nm* (on hat) pompom,
bobble; (on slipper) pompom
IDIOM **décrocher le ~** (fam) to win first prize

pomponner: se pomponner
/pɔ̃pɔne/ [1] *v refl* (+ *v être*) to get dolled up

ponce /pɔ̃s/ *nf* **pierre ~** pumice stone

poncer /pɔ̃se/ [12] *vtr* (a) (Tech) to sand
(b) to pumice

ponceuse /pɔ̃søz/ *nf* sander

ponction /pɔ̃ksjɔ̃/ *nf* (a) (Med) puncture
(b) levy

ponctualité /pɔ̃ktɥalite/ *nf* punctuality

ponctuation /pɔ̃ktɥasjɔ̃/ *nf* punctuation

ponctuel, -elle /pɔ̃ktɥɛl/ *adj* (a) ‹person›
punctual
(b) ‹action› limited; ‹problem› isolated

✧ indicates a very frequent word

ponctuer /pɔ̃ktɥe/ [1] *vtr* to punctuate

pondéré, ~e /pɔ̃deʀe/ *adj* (a) ‹person›
levelheaded
(b) ‹factor› weighted

pondre /pɔ̃dʀ/ [6] *vtr* (a) to lay ‹egg›
(b) (fam) to churn out (colloq) ‹poetry, articles›

poney /pɔnɛ/ *nm* pony

✧ **pont** /pɔ̃/ ① *nm* (a) bridge
(b) link, tie; **couper les ~s** to break off all
contact
(c) extended weekend (*including days
between a public holiday and a weekend*)
(d) deck
② **ponts** *nm pl* **~s (et chaussées)**
highways department
■ **~ aérien** airlift; **~ à péage** toll bridge
IDIOMS **coucher sous les ~s** to sleep rough,
to be a tramp; **il coulera beaucoup d'eau
sous les ~s avant que...** it will be a long
time before...; **faire un ~ d'or à qn** to offer sb
a large sum to accept a job

pontife /pɔ̃tif/ *nm* (a) pontiff; **le souverain
~** the pope
(b) (fam) pundit (colloq)

pontificat /pɔ̃tifika/ *nm* pontificate

pontifier /pɔ̃tifje/ [2] *vi* to pontificate

pont-levis, *pl* **ponts-levis** /pɔ̃ləvi/ *nm*
drawbridge

ponton /pɔ̃tɔ̃/ *nm* (a) landing stage
(b) pontoon

pope /pɔp/ *nm* pope, orthodox priest

popote /pɔpɔt/ *nf* (fam) cooking

populace /pɔpylas/ *nf* **la ~** the masses

✧ **populaire** /pɔpylɛʀ/ *adj* (a) ‹suburb›
working-class; ‹art, novel› popular; ‹edition›
cheap; ‹restaurant› basic; **classe ~** working
class
(b) ‹tradition› folk; **culture ~** folklore
(c) popular
(d) ‹revolt› popular; ‹will› of the people
(e) ‹expression, term› vulgar
(f) **République ~** People's Republic

popularité /pɔpylaʀite/ *nf* popularity

✧ **population** /pɔpylasjɔ̃/ *nf* population

populeux, -euse /pɔpylø, øz/ *adj* densely
populated, populous

popup ① *nm* (Comput) pop-up
advertisement
② *adj* (Comput) pop-up

porc /pɔʀ/ *nm* (a) pig, hog (US)
(b) pork
(c) pigskin

porcelaine /pɔʀsəlɛn/ *nf* porcelain, china

porcelet /pɔʀsəlɛ/ *nm* piglet

porc-épic, *pl* **~s** /pɔʀkepik/ *nm*
porcupine

porche /pɔʀʃ/ *nm* porch

porcherie /pɔʀʃəʀi/ *nf* pigsty

porcin, ~e /pɔʀsɛ̃, in/ *adj* porcine

pore /pɔʀ/ *nm* pore

poreux, -euse /pɔʀø, øz/ *adj* porous

porno /pɔʀno/ *adj, nm* (fam) porn (colloq)

pornographique /pɔʀnɔgʀafik/ *adj* pornographic

⚓ **port** /pɔʀ/ *nm* **(a)** harbour (GB)
(b) haven
(c) wearing; carrying
(d) bearing
(e) (transport) carriage; postage
■ ~ **d'attache** port of registry; home base; ~ **de pêche** fishing harbour (GB); ~ **de plaisance** marina
IDIOM **arriver à bon** ~ to arrive safe and sound

portable /pɔʀtabl/ ⟦1⟧ *adj* portable; **ordinateur** ~ laptop computer
⟦2⟧ *nm* mobile (phone) (GB); cellular phone, cellphone (US)

portail /pɔʀtaj/ *nm* (of park) gate; (of church) great door

portant, ~e /pɔʀtɑ̃, ɑ̃t/ *adj* **(a)** ‹wall› load bearing
(b) bien ~ in good health
IDIOM **à bout** ~ at point-blank range

portatif, -ive /pɔʀtatif, iv/ *adj* portable

⚓ **porte** /pɔʀt/ *nf* **(a)** door; gate; **devant la** ~ **de l'hôpital** outside the hospital; **aux** ~**s du désert** at the edge of the desert; **ouvrir sa** ~ **à qn** to let sb in; **c'est la** ~ **ouverte à la criminalité** it's an open invitation to crime; **mettre à la** ~ to expel; to fire; **ce n'est pas la** ~ **à côté** (fam) it's quite far
(b) gateway; **la victoire leur ouvre la** ~ **de la finale** the victory clears the way to the final for them
(c) (in airport) gate
(d) (car) door
■ ~ **battante** swing door; ~ **d'écluse** lock gate; ~ **d'entrée** front door; main entrance; ~ **de service** service entrance; ~ **de sortie** exit; escape route
IDIOMS **prendre la** ~ to leave; **entrer par la petite/grande** ~ to start at the bottom/top

porté, ~e¹ /pɔʀte/ *adj* **être** ~ **sur qch** to be keen on sth

porte-à-faux /pɔʀtafo/ *nm inv* **être en** ~ ‹wall› to be out of plumb; ‹construction› to be cantilevered; ‹person› to be in an awkward position

porte-à-porte /pɔʀtapɔʀt/ *nm inv*
(a) door-to-door selling
(b) door-to-door canvassing

porte-avions /pɔʀtavjɔ̃/ *nm inv* aircraft carrier

porte-bagages /pɔʀt(ə)bagaʒ/ *nm inv* carrier; luggage rack; roof rack

porte-bébé /pɔʀt(ə)bebe/ *nm inv* baby carrier

porte-bonheur /pɔʀt(ə)bɔnœʀ/ *nm inv* lucky charm

porte-clés, porte-clefs /pɔʀt(ə)kle/ *nm inv* key ring

porte-documents /pɔʀt(ə)dɔkymɑ̃/ *nm inv* briefcase, attaché case

portée² /pɔʀte/ ⟦1⟧ *adj f* ▸ PORTÉ
⟦2⟧ *nf* **(a)** range; **être à** ~ **de main** *or* **à la** ~ **de la main** to be within reach; to be to hand
(b) c'est à la ~ **de n'importe qui** anybody can do it; anybody can understand it; **se mettre à la** ~ **de qn** to come down to sb's level
(c) impact
(d) (of kittens) litter
(e) (Mus) staff, stave (GB)

porte-fenêtre, *pl* **portes-fenêtres** /pɔʀt(ə)fənɛtʀ/ *nf* French window

portefeuille /pɔʀt(ə)fœj/ ⟦1⟧ *adj* **jupe** ~ wrap-over skirt
⟦2⟧ *nm* **(a)** wallet (GB), billfold (US)
(b) portfolio

porte-jarretelles /pɔʀt(ə)ʒaʀtɛl/ *nm inv* suspender belt (GB), garter belt (US)

portemanteau, *pl* ~**x** /pɔʀt(ə)mɑ̃to/ *nm*
(a) coat rack
(b) coat stand
(c) coat hanger

portemine /pɔʀt(ə)min/ *nm* propelling (GB) *or* mechanical (US) pencil

porte-monnaie /pɔʀt(ə)mɔnɛ/ *nm inv* purse (GB), coin purse (US)

porte-parapluies /pɔʀt(ə)paʀaplɥi/ *nm inv* umbrella stand

porte-parole /pɔʀt(ə)paʀɔl/ *nm inv* spokesperson, spokesman/spokeswoman

porte-plume /pɔʀt(ə)plym/ *nm inv* penholder

⚓ **porter** /pɔʀte/ [1] ⟦1⟧ *vtr* **(a)** to carry
(b) ~ **qch quelque part** to take sth somewhere; ~ **qch à qn** to take sb sth
(c) ‹wall, chair› to carry, to bear ‹weight›
(d) to wear ‹dress, contact lenses›; to have ‹moustache›
(e) to have ‹initials, date, name›; to bear ‹seal›; **il porte bien son nom** the name suits him
(f) to bear ‹flowers›
(g) ~ **qch à** to bring sth up to, to put sth up to ‹rate, number›; ~ **la température de l'eau à 80°C** to heat the water to 80°C
(h) ~ **son regard vers** to look at; **si tu portes la main sur elle** if you lay a finger on her; ~ **un jugement sur qch** to pass judgment on sth
(i) ~ **qch sur un registre** to enter sth on a register; **se faire** ~ **malade** to report sick; ~ **plainte** to lodge a complaint
(j) tout nous porte à croire que... everything leads us to believe that...
(k) ~ **bonheur** *or* **chance** to be lucky
⟦2⟧ **porter sur** *v+prep* ‹debate› to be about; ‹measure› to concern; ‹ban› to apply to
⟦3⟧ *vi* **une voix qui porte** a voice that carries; **le coup a porté** the blow hit home
⟦4⟧ **se porter** *v refl* (+ *v être*) **(a) se** ~ ⋯⟶

bien/mal ⟨person⟩ to be well/ill; ⟨business⟩ to be going well/badly
(b) se ~ **sur** ⟨suspicion⟩ to fall on; ⟨infection⟩ to spread to

porte-savon /pɔʀt(ə)savɔ̃/ nm inv soapdish

porte-serviettes /pɔʀt(ə)sɛʀvjɛt/ nm inv towel rail

porteur, -euse /pɔʀtœʀ, øz/ **1** adj
(a) être ~ **d'un virus** to carry a virus
(b) mur ~ load-bearing wall
(c) ⟨market, sector⟩ expanding
(d) ⟨current, wave, frequency⟩ carrier
2 nm,f holder, bearer
3 nm **(a)** porter; messenger
(b) (of cheque) bearer; ~ **d'actions** shareholder
■ ~ **sain** (Med) symptom-free carrier

porte-voix /pɔʀt(ə)vwɑ/ nm inv megaphone

portier /pɔʀtje/ nm porter

portière /pɔʀtjɛʀ/ nf (of car) door

portillon /pɔʀtijɔ̃/ nm gate

portion /pɔʀsjɔ̃/ nf **(a)** (Culin) portion; helping
(b) part, portion; (of road) stretch
IDIOM **réduire qn à la ~ congrue** to give sb the strict minimum

portique /pɔʀtik/ nm **(a)** portico
(b) (in gym) frame
(c) swing frame

porto /pɔʀto/ nm port

portoricain, ~e /pɔʀtoʀikɛ̃, ɛn/ adj Puerto Rican

portrait /pɔʀtʀɛ/ nm **(a)** portrait
(b) description, picture
(c) tu es tout le ~ de ton père you're the spitting image of your father
(d) (fam) face; **se faire tirer le ~** to have one's photo taken

portrait-robot, pl **portraits-robots** /pɔʀtʀɛʀɔbo/ nm photofit®, identikit®

portuaire /pɔʀtɥɛʀ/ adj port

portugais, ~e /pɔʀtygɛ, ɛz/ **1** adj Portuguese
2 nm (language) Portuguese

Portugal /pɔʀtygal/ pr nm Portugal

pose /poz/ nf **(a)** (of window) putting in; (of cupboard) fitting; (of carpet) laying
(b) pose; **prendre une ~** to strike a pose
(c) (in photography) exposure

posé, ~e /poze/ adj ⟨air, person⟩ composed; ⟨gesture, voice⟩ controlled

posément /pozemɑ̃/ adv calmly, carefully

ⸯ **poser** /poze/ [1] **1** vtr **(a)** to put down ⟨book, glass⟩
(b) to put in ⟨window⟩; to install ⟨radiator⟩; to fit ⟨lock⟩; to lay ⟨tiling, cable⟩; to plant ⟨bomb⟩; to put up ⟨wallpaper, curtains⟩
(c) to assert ⟨theory⟩; ~ **sa candidature à un**

poste to apply for a job; ~ **une addition** to write a sum down
(d) to ask ⟨question⟩; to set ⟨riddle⟩; **ça ne pose aucun problème** that's no problem at all
(e) (Mus) to place ⟨voice⟩
2 vi **(a)** to pose
(b) to put on airs
3 **se poser** v refl (+ v être) **(a)** ⟨bird, insect⟩ to settle
(b) ⟨plane⟩ to land
(c) ⟨eyes⟩ to fall
(d) se ~ **en** to claim to be; to present oneself as
(e) se ~ **des questions** to ask oneself questions
(f) ⟨problem, case⟩ to arise; **la question ne se pose pas** there's no question of it; it goes without saying

poseur, -euse /pozœʀ, øz/ nm,f poser (colloq)
■ ~ **de bombes** bomber; ~ **de moquette** carpet fitter

ⸯ **positif, -ive** /pozitif, iv/ adj **(a)** ⟨reply⟩ affirmative
(b) ⟨interview⟩ constructive; ⟨outcome⟩ positive
(c) ⟨reaction⟩ favourable (GB)
(d) ⟨person, attitude⟩ positive
(e) ⟨number⟩ positive

ⸯ **position** /pozisjɔ̃/ nf **(a)** position; **en ~ horizontale** horizontally; **placer qn dans une ~ difficile** to put sb in a difficult or an awkward position
(b) (in ranking) place, position
(c) position, stance; **prendre ~ sur un problème** to take a stand on an issue; **camper sur ses ~s** to stand one's ground
(d) (bank) balance

positivement /pozitivmɑ̃/ adv ⟨answer⟩ positively; ⟨react, judge⟩ favourably (GB)

posologie /pozɔlɔʒi/ nf dosage

possédant, ~e /posedɑ̃, ɑ̃t/ nm,f **les ~s** the rich, the wealthy

possédé, ~e /posede/ nm,f **les ~s** the possessed

ⸯ **posséder** /posede/ [14] vtr **(a)** to own, to possess ⟨property, army⟩; to hold ⟨responsibility⟩
(b) to have ⟨skill, quality⟩
(c) to speak [sth] fluently; to have a thorough knowledge of [sth]
(d) ⟨anger, pain⟩ to overwhelm
(e) (fam) il nous a bien possédés he really had us there (colloq)

possesseur /posɛsœʀ/ nm (of property) owner; (of diploma) holder; (of passport) bearer

possessif, -ive /posesif, iv/ adj possessive

possession /posesjɔ̃/ nf possession

ⸯ **possibilité** /posibilite/ **1** nf
(a) possibility
(b) opportunity; ~ **d'embauche** job

ⸯ indicates a very frequent word

opportunity

2 **possibilités** *nf pl* **(a)** (of person) abilities; (of device) potential uses
(b) resources

✧ **possible** /pɔsibl/ **1** *adj* **(a)** possible; **dès que ~** as soon as possible; **tout le courage ~** the utmost courage; **tous les cas ~s et imaginables** every conceivable case; **le plus cher ~** ‹sell› at the highest possible price; **autant que ~** as much as possible; **il n'y a pas d'erreur ~, c'est lui** it's him, without a shadow of a doubt; **tout est ~** anything is possible; **pas~!** (fam) I don't believe it!; **'tu vas acheter une voiture?'—'~'** 'are you going to buy a car?'—'maybe'
(b) (fam) **il a une chance pas ~** he's incredibly lucky

2 *nm* **faire (tout) son ~** to do one's best

post(-) /pɔst/ *pref* post(-)

postal, ~e, *mpl* **-aux** /pɔstal, o/ *adj* ‹van› post office (GB), mail (US); ‹services› postal

poste¹ /pɔst/ *nm* **(a)** position, job; post; **~s vacants** *or* **à pourvoir** vacancies
(b) (Sport) position
(c) post; **~ (de travail)** work station; **il est toujours fidèle au ~** you can always rely on him
(d) ~ de police police station
(e) ~ de radio radio set
(f) (tele)phone; extension
(g) shift
(h) (in accountancy) item
■ **~ d'aiguillage** signal box; **~ de douane** customs post; **~ de pilotage** flight deck; **~ de secours** first-aid station

✧ **poste²** /pɔst/ *nf* post office; **envoyer par la ~** to send [sth] by post (GB), to mail (US)
■ **~ aérienne** airmail, **~ restante** poste restante (GB), general delivery (US)

✧ **poster¹** /pɔste/ [1] **1** *vtr* **(a)** to post (GB), to mail (US)
(b) to post ‹guard›; to put [sb] in place ‹spy›
2 se poster *v refl* (+ *v être*) **se ~ devant** to station oneself in front of

poster² /pɔstɛʀ/ *nm* poster

postérieur, ~e /pɔsteʀjœʀ/ *adj* **(a)** ‹date› later; ‹event› subsequent; **un écrivain ~ à Flaubert** a writer who came after Flaubert
(b) ‹part, section› posterior; ‹legs› hind

postérité /pɔsteʀite/ *nf* posterity; **passer à la ~** ‹person› to go down in history; ‹work› to become part of the cultural heritage

posthume /pɔstym/ *adj* posthumous

postiche /pɔstiʃ/ **1** *adj* ‹beard› false
2 *nm* **(a)** hairpiece; toupee; wig
(b) false moustache (GB) *or* mustache (US)
(c) false beard

postier, -ière /pɔstje, ɛʀ/ *nm,f* postal worker

postillon /pɔstijɔ̃/ *nm* (fam) drop of saliva

postillonner /pɔstijɔne/ [1] *vi* (fam) to spit (saliva)

post-scriptum /pɔstskʀiptɔm/ *nm inv* postscript

postsynchroniser /pɔstsɛ̃kʀɔnize/ [1] *vtr* to dub, to add the soundtrack to

postulant, ~e /pɔstylɑ̃, ɑ̃t/ *nm,f* candidate

postulat /pɔstyla/ *nm* premise; postulate

postuler /pɔstyle/ [1] *vi* to apply

posture /pɔstyʀ/ *nf* **(a)** posture
(b) position

pot /po/ *nm* **(a)** container; jar; carton, tub; (earthenware) pot; jug; **un ~ de peinture** a tin of paint
(b) (chamber) pot
(c) (fam) drink
(d) (fam) do (GB) (colloq), drinks party
(e) avoir du ~ to be lucky
■ **~ catalytique** catalytic converter; **~ d'échappement** (Aut) silencer (GB), muffler (US); exhaust
IDIOMS **payer les ~s cassés** to pick up the pieces; **tourner autour du ~** (fam) to beat about the bush

potable /pɔtabl/ *adj* **(a)** **eau ~** drinking water
(b) (fam) decent

potage /pɔtaʒ/ *nm* soup

potager /pɔtaʒe/ *nm* kitchen garden

pot-au-feu /pɔtofø/ *nm inv* **(a)** boiled beef (with vegetables)
(b) boiling beef

pot-aux-roses, *pl* **pots-aux-roses** /potoʀoz/ *nm* (figurative) skeleton in the closet

pot-de-vin, *pl* **pots-de-vin** /podvɛ̃/ *nm* bribe, backhander (GB) (colloq)

pote /pɔt/ *nm* (fam) mate (GB) (colloq), pal (US) (colloq)

poteau, *pl* **~x** /pɔto/ *nm* post; goalpost
■ **~ électrique** electricity pole (*supplying domestic power lines*)

potelé, ~e /pɔtle/ *adj* chubby

potence /pɔtɑ̃s/ *nf* gallows

potentiel, -ielle /pɔtɑ̃sjɛl/ **1** *adj* potential
2 *nm* potential

poterie /pɔtʀi/ *nf* **(a)** pottery
(b) piece of pottery

potiche /pɔtiʃ/ *nf* vase

potier, -ière /pɔtje, ɛʀ/ *nm,f* potter

potin /pɔtɛ̃/ *nm* (fam) **(a)** gossip
(b) din (colloq)

potion /posjɔ̃/ *nf* potion

potiron /pɔtiʀɔ̃/ *nm* pumpkin (GB), winter squash (US)

pot-pourri, *pl* **pots-pourris** /popuʀi/ *nm* **(a)** (Mus) medley
(b) potpourri

pou, *pl* **~x** /pu/ *nm* louse
IDIOMS **chercher des ~x** (fam) to nitpick (colloq); **être laid comme un ~** (fam) to be as ugly as sin

p

poubelle /pubɛl/ *nf* (inside) bin (GB), trash can (US); (outside) dustbin (GB), garbage can (US)

pouce /pus/ *nm* (a) thumb
(b) big toe
(c) inch; **ne pas bouger d'un ~** not to budge an inch
IDIOMS **se tourner** *or* **rouler les ~s** (fam) to twiddle one's thumbs; **manger sur le ~** to have a quick bite to eat; **donner un coup de ~ à qn** to help sb get started

poudre /pudʀ/ *nf* (gen) powder; **~ (à canon)** gunpowder; **~ à récurer** scouring powder
IDIOMS **mettre le feu aux ~s** to bring things to a head; **jeter de la ~ aux yeux** to try to impress

poudrer /pudʀe/ [1] *vtr* to powder

poudreux, -euse /pudʀø, øz/ *adj* powdery

poudrier /pudʀije/ *nm* powder compact

poudrière /pudʀijɛʀ/ *nf* (a) powder magazine
(b) (figurative) time bomb

pouf /puf/ *nm* (a) pouffe
(b) **faire ~** to fall with a soft thud

pouffer /pufe/ [1] *vi* **~ (de rire)** to burst out laughing

pouilleux, -euse /pujø, øz/ *adj* (a) (fam) seedy
(b) flea-ridden

poulailler /pulaje/ *nm* (a) henhouse; hen run
(b) hens
(c) (fam) (in theatre) **le ~** the Gods (GB), the gallery

poulain /pulɛ̃/ *nm* (a) colt; foal
(b) protégé

poularde /pulaʀd/ *nf* fattened chicken

poule /pul/ *nf* (a) hen
(b) boiling fowl
(c) (fam) **ma ~** my pet (colloq) (GB), honey (US) (colloq)
■ **~ d'eau** moorhen; **~ faisane** hen pheasant; **~ mouillée** (fam) wimp (colloq); **~ naine** bantam; **~ au pot** boiled chicken
IDIOMS **quand les ~s auront des dents** (fam) pigs might fly; **tuer la ~ aux œufs d'or** to kill the goose that lays the golden egg

ℱ **poulet** /pulɛ/ *nm* chicken
■ **~ d'élevage** ≈ battery chicken; **~ fermier** ≈ free-range chicken

pouliche /puliʃ/ *nf* filly

poulie /puli/ *nf* pulley

poulpe /pulp/ *nm* octopus

pouls /pu/ *nm inv* pulse

poumon /pumɔ̃/ *nm* lung; **~ d'acier** *or* **artificiel** iron lung; **à pleins ~s** ‹shout› at the top of one's voice; ‹breathe› deeply

poupe /pup/ *nf* stern; **avoir le vent en ~** to sail *or* run before the wind; (figurative) to have the wind in one's sails

poupée /pupe/ *nf* doll

poupon /pupɔ̃/ *nm* (a) tiny baby

(b) baby doll

pouponner /pupɔne/ [1] *vi* (fam) to play the doting father/mother

ℱ **pour¹** /puʀ/ *prep* (a) (in order) to; **~ faire** to do; in order to do; **pour ne pas faire** so as not to do; **c'était ~ rire** *or* **plaisanter** it was a joke; **~ que** so that; **~ ainsi dire** so to speak
(b) for; **le train ~ Paris** the train for Paris *or* to Paris; **ce sera prêt ~ vendredi?** will it be ready by Friday?; **~ toujours** forever; **le bébé c'est ~ quand?** when is the baby due?; **se battre ~ une femme** to fight over a woman; **c'est fait ~ étudié ~!** (fam) that's what it's for; **je suis ~** (fam) I'm in favour (GB)
(c) about; as regards; **se renseigner ~** to find out about; **~ l'argent** as regards the money, as for the money; **~ moi, il a tort** as far as I am concerned, he's wrong
(d) elle a **~ ambition d'être pilote** her ambition is to be a pilot
(e) elle avait **~ elle de savoir écouter** she had the merit of being a good listener
(f) **~ autant que je sache** as far as I know; **~ être intelligente, ça elle l'est!** she really is intelligent!
(g) j'ai mis **~ 40 euros d'essence** I've put in 40 euros' worth of petrol (GB) *or* gas (US); **merci ~ tout** thank you for everything; **je n'y suis ~ rien** I had nothing to do with it; **je n'en ai pas ~ longtemps** it won't take long
(h) dix **~ cent** ten per cent; **une cuillère de vinaigre ~ quatre d'huile** one spoonful of vinegar to four of oil; **~ une large part** to a large extent

pour² /puʀ/ *nm* **le ~ et le contre** the pros and the cons

pourboire /puʀbwaʀ/ *nm* tip

pourcentage /puʀsɑ̃taʒ/ *nm* (a) percentage
(b) commission
(c) cut (colloq)

pourchasser /puʀʃase/ [1] *vtr* (a) to hunt ‹animal, criminal›
(b) to pursue ‹person›

pourparlers /puʀpaʀle/ *nm pl* talks; **être en ~** ‹people› to be engaged in talks

pourpre /puʀpʀ/ *adj, nm* crimson

ℱ **pourquoi** /puʀkwa/ **1** *adv, conj* why; **~ donc?** but why?; **~ pas** *or* **non?** why not?; **~ pas un week-end à Paris?** what *or* how about a weekend in Paris?; **va donc savoir ~!** God knows why!
2 *nm inv* **le ~ et le comment** the why and the wherefore

pourri, ~e /puʀi/ **1** *pp* ▶ POURRIR
2 *pp adj* (a) (gen) rotten; ‹vegetation› rotting
(b) (fam) ‹weather, car› rotten (colloq); ‹person› crooked (colloq)
3 *nm* rotten part; **ça sent le ~** it smells rotten

pourrir /puʀiʀ/ [3] **1** *vtr* (a) to rot ‹wood›

ℱ indicates a very frequent word

(b) to spoil ‹person›
(c) (fam) to spoil [sb] rotten (colloq)
2 *vi* **(a)** ‹food› to go bad
(b) ‹wood› to rot
(c) ‹person› to rot; ‹situation› to deteriorate
pourriture /puʀityʀ/ *nf* **(a)** rot, decay
(b) corruption, rottenness
poursuite /puʀsɥit/ *nf* **(a)** pursuit; être à
la ∼ de to be in pursuit of
(b) chase
(c) continuation
(d) ∼ **(judiciaire)** (judicial) proceedings
⚹ **poursuivre** /puʀsɥivʀ/ [62] **1** *vtr* **(a)** to
chase
(b) ‹person› to hound; ‹nightmare› to haunt;
∼ qn de ses assiduités to force one's
attentions on sb
(c) to seek (after) ‹honours, truth›; to pursue
‹goal›
(d) to continue ‹journey, studies›; to pursue
‹talks›
(e) (Law) ∼ qn (en justice *or* devant les
tribunaux) to sue sb
2 *vi* to continue; ∼ sur un sujet to
continue talking on a subject
3 **se poursuivre** *v refl* (+ *v être*) ‹talks,
conflict, journey› to continue
⚹ **pourtant** /puʀtã/ *adv* though; et ∼ and
yet; techniquement ∼, le film est parfait
technically, however, the film is perfect
pourtour /puʀtuʀ/ *nm* **(a)** perimeter;
circumference
(b) surrounding area
pourvoir /puʀvwaʀ/ [40] **1** *vtr* **(a)** to fill
‹post›
(b) ∼ qn de to endow sb with
2 **pourvoir à** *v+prep* to provide for
3 **se pourvoir** *v refl* (+ *v être*) se ∼ de
to provide oneself with ‹currency›; to equip
oneself with ‹boots›
pourvoyeur, -euse /puʀvwajœʀ,
øz/ *nm,f* ∼ de source of ‹jobs, funding›
pourvu, ∼e /puʀvy/ **1** *pp* ▸ POURVOIR
2 **pourvu que** *phr* **(a)** provided (that),
as long as
(b) let's hope; ∼ que ça dure! let's hope it
lasts!
pousse /pus/ *nf* **(a)** (Bot) shoot
(b) growth
poussé, ∼e¹ /puse/ **1** *pp* ▸ POUSSER
2 *pp adj* ‹inquiry› thorough; ‹studies›
advanced
poussée² /puse/ *nf* **(a)** (of water, crowd)
pressure; (of wind) force
(b) thrust
(c) (Med) attack; ∼ de fièvre sudden high
temperature
(d) (in price) (sharp) rise; (in racism, violence)
upsurge
⚹ **pousser** /puse/ [1] **1** *vtr* **(a)** to push
‹wheelbarrow, person›; to move *or* shift [sth]
(out of the way), to push [sth] aside; ∼ une
porte to push a door to; to push a door open;

∼ qn du coude to give sb a dig *or* to nudge
sb with one's elbow
(b) ∼ qn à faire to encourage sb to do; to
urge sb to do; ‹hunger, despair› to drive sb
to do; ∼ à la consommation to encourage
people to buy more; to encourage people to
drink more
(c) to push ‹pupil›; to keep [sb] at it
‹employee›; to drive [sth] hard ‹car›
(d) to push ‹product, protégé›
(e) to pursue ‹studies, research›; c'est ∼ un
peu loin la plaisanterie that's taking the joke
a bit far
(f) to let out ‹cry›; to heave ‹sigh›
2 *vi* **(a)** ‹child› to grow; ‹plant› to grow; to
sprout; ‹tooth› to come through; ‹buildings›
to spring up; je fais ∼ des légumes I grow
vegetables; se laisser ∼ les cheveux to grow
one's hair
(b) ∼ plus loin tô go on further
(c) (fam) to overdo it, to go too far
3 **se pousser** *v refl* (+ *v être*) to move
over
IDIOM à la va comme je te pousse (fam) any
old how
poussette /pusɛt/ *nf* pushchair (GB),
stroller (US)
poussière /pusjɛʀ/ *nf* **(a)** dust; tomber en
∼ to crumble away; to fall to bits
(b) speck of dust
IDIOM 10 euros/20 ans et des ∼s (fam) just
over 10 euros/20 years
poussiéreux, -euse /pusjeʀø, øz/ *adj*
(a) dusty
(b) outdated, fossilized
poussin /pusɛ̃/ *nm* chick
poussoir /puswaʀ/ *nm* (push) button
poutre /putʀ/ *nf* **(a)** beam
(b) girder
⚹ **pouvoir¹** /puvwaʀ/ [49] **1** *v aux* **(a)** to be
able to; peux-tu soulever cette boîte? can
you lift this box?; dès que je pourrai as soon
as I can; je n'en peux plus I've had it (colloq);
tout peut arriver anything could happen;
il ne peut pas ne pas gagner he's bound to
win; on peut toujours espérer there's no
harm in wishing; qu'est-ce que cela peut
(bien) te faire? (fam) what business is it of
yours?
(b) to be allowed to; est-ce que je peux me
servir de ta voiture? can I use your car?; on
peut dire que it can be said that; on peut ne
pas faire l'accord the agreement is optional
(c) pouvez-vous/pourriez-vous me tenir la
porte s'il vous plaît? can you/could you hold
the door (open) for me please?
(d) puisse cette nouvelle année exaucer vos
vœux les plus chers may the new year bring
you everything you could wish for; s'il croit
que je vais payer il peut toujours attendre if
he thinks I'm going to pay he's got another
think coming; ce qu'il peut être grand! how
tall he is!

⋯⋗

2 *vtr* **que puis-je pour vous?** what can I do for you?; **je fais ce que je peux** I'm doing my best

3 *v impers* **il peut faire très froid en janvier** it can get very cold in January; **ce qu'il a pu pleuvoir!** you wouldn't believe how much it rained!

4 **il se peut** *v impers* **il se peut que les prix augmentent en juin** prices may *or* might rise in June; **cela se pourrait qu'il soit fâché** he might be angry

5 **on ne peut plus** *phr* **il est on ne peut plus timide** he is as shy as can be

6 **on ne peut mieux** *phr* **ils s'entendent on ne peut mieux** they get on extremely well

IDIOM autant que faire se peut as far as possible

pouvoir² /puvwaʀ/ *nm* **(a)** (gen) power; **~ d'achat** purchasing power; **avoir le ~ de faire** to be able to do, to have the power to do; **je n'ai pas le ~ de décider** it's not up to me to decide

(b) (Pol) power; **avoir tous ~s** to have *or* exercise full powers; **le ~ en place** the government in power

■ **le ~ judiciaire** the judiciary; **~ législatif** legislative power; **~s publics** authorities

pragmatisme /pʀagmatism/ *nm* pragmatism

praire /pʀɛʀ/ *nf* clam

prairie /pʀɛʀi/ *nf* meadow

praline /pʀalin/ *nf* sugared (GB) *or* sugar-coated (US) almond

praliné, ~e /pʀaline/ **1** *adj* praline

2 *nm* praline

praticable /pʀatikabl/ *adj* ‹road› passable

praticien, -ienne /pʀatisjɛ̃, ɛn/ *nm,f*
(a) general practitioner, GP
(b) practitioner

pratiquant, ~e /pʀatikɑ̃, ɑ̃t/ *adj* practising (GB); **être très ~** to be very devout

◆ **pratique** /pʀatik/ **1** *adj* practical; ‹device› handy; ‹place, route› convenient

2 *nf* **(a)** **la ~ des arts martiaux est très répandue** many people practise (GB) martial arts; **cela nécessite de longues heures de ~** it takes hours of practice; **avoir une bonne ~ de l'anglais** to have a good working knowledge of English
(b) practical experience
(c) practice; **mettre qch en ~** to put sth into practice
(d) **les ~s religieuses** religious practices

pratiquement /pʀatikmɑ̃/ *adv* **(a)** in practice
(b) practically, virtually; **~ jamais** hardly ever

◆ **pratiquer** /pʀatike/ [1] **1** *vtr* **(a)** to play ‹tennis›; to do ‹yoga›; to take part in ‹activity›; to practise (GB) ‹language›; **il est croyant**

mais ne pratique pas he believes in God but doesn't practise (GB) his religion
(b) to use ‹method, blackmail›; to pursue ‹policy›; to charge ‹rate of interest›
(c) to carry out ‹examination, graft›

2 **se pratiquer** *v refl* (+ *v être*) ‹sport› to be played; ‹technique, policy, strategy› to be used; ‹price, tariff› to be charged

pré /pʀe/ *nm* meadow

pré- /pʀe/ *pref* pre(-); **~-accord** preliminary agreement

pré-affranchi /pʀeafʀɑ̃ʃi/ *adj* postage-paid

préalable /pʀealabl/ **1** *adj* ‹notice› prior; ‹study› preliminary
2 *nm* precondition; preliminary
3 **au préalable** *phr* first, beforehand

préalablement /pʀealabləmɑ̃/ *adv* beforehand

préambule /pʀeɑ̃byl/ *nm* **(a)** preamble
(b) forewarning

préau, *pl* ~x /pʀeo/ *nm* (of school) covered playground; (of prison) exercise yard

préavis /pʀeavi/ *nm inv* notice

précaire /pʀekɛʀ/ *adj* ‹existence› precarious; ‹job› insecure; ‹construction› flimsy

précariser /pʀekaʀize/ [1] *vtr* **~ l'emploi** to casualize labour (GB)

précarité /pʀekaʀite/ *nf* precariousness; **la ~ de l'emploi** job insecurity

précaution /pʀekosjɔ̃/ *nf* precaution; caution; **par ~** as a precaution

précédemment /pʀesedamɑ̃/ *adv* previously

◆ **précédent, ~e** /pʀesedɑ̃, ɑ̃t/ **1** *adj* previous
2 *nm,f* **le ~, la ~e** the previous one
3 *nm* precedent; **sans ~** unprecedented

précéder /pʀesede/ [14] *vtr* **(a)** ‹person› to go in front of, to precede; ‹vehicle› to be in front of
(b) **il m'avait précédé de cinq minutes** he'd got there five minutes ahead of me
(c) ‹paragraph, crisis› to precede; **la semaine qui a précédé votre départ** the week before you left

précepte /pʀesɛpt/ *nm* precept

précepteur, -trice /pʀesɛptœʀ, tʀis/ *nm,f* (private) tutor

prêcher /pʀeʃe/ [1] **1** *vtr* **(a)** to preach
(b) to advocate
2 *vi* to preach
IDIOM ~ le faux pour savoir le vrai to tell a lie in order to get at the truth

précieusement /pʀesjøzmɑ̃/ *adv* carefully

◆ **précieux, -ieuse** /pʀesjø, øz/ *adj*
(a) ‹stone, book› precious; ‹piece of furniture› valuable
(b) ‹information› very useful; ‹collaborator›

p

◆ indicates a very frequent word

valued
(c) ‹friendship, right› precious; ‹friend› very dear
(d) ‹style, language› precious
précipice /pʀesipis/ nm precipice
précipitamment /pʀesipitamɑ̃/ adv hurriedly
précipitation /pʀesipitasjɔ̃/ **1** nf haste
2 **précipitations** nf pl rainfall, precipitation
précipité, ~e /pʀesipite/ adj **(a)** rapid
(b) hasty, precipitate
précipiter /pʀesipite/ [1] **1** vtr **(a)** ~ qn **dans le vide** (from roof) to push sb off; (out of window) to push sb out
(b) to hasten ‹departure, decision›; to precipitate ‹event›; ~ **les choses** to rush things
2 **se précipiter** v refl (+ v être) **(a)** **il s'est précipité dans le vide** he jumped off
(b) to rush; **se ~ au secours de qn** to rush to sb's aid, **se ~ sur** to rush at ‹person›; to rush for ‹object›
(c) to rush
(d) ‹action› to move faster
⚔ **précis, ~e** /pʀesi, iz/ **1** adj
(a) ‹programme, criterion› specific; ‹idea, date› definite; ‹moment› particular
(b) ‹person, gesture› precise; ‹figure, data› accurate; ‹place› exact
2 nm inv handbook
⚔ **précisément** /pʀesizemɑ̃/ adv precisely
⚔ **préciser** /pʀesize/ [1] **1** vtr **(a)** to add; **faut-il le** or **est-il besoin de ~** needless to say
(b) to state; ~ **ses intentions** to state one's intentions
(c) to specify; **pouvez-vous ~?** could you be more specific?
(d) to clarify ‹ideas›
2 **se préciser** v refl (+ v être) **(a)** ‹danger, future› to become clearer; ‹plan, trip› to take shape
(b) ‹shape, reality› to become clear
précision /pʀesizjɔ̃/ nf **(a)** precision
(b) accuracy; **localiser avec ~** to pinpoint; **instrument de ~** precision instrument
(c) detail
précité, ~e /pʀesite/ adj aforementioned
précoce /pʀekɔs/ adj **(a)** precocious
(b) ‹season› early
(c) ‹senility› premature
précompte /pʀekɔ̃t/ nm deduction; ~ **de l'impôt** deduction of tax at source
préconçu, ~e /pʀekɔ̃sy/ adj preconceived
préconiser /pʀekɔnize/ [1] vtr to recommend
précuit, ~e /pʀekɥi, it/ adj precooked
précurseur /pʀekyʀsœʀ/ **1** adj m precursory; **signes ~s de l'orage** signs that herald a storm
2 nm pioneer; ~ **de** precursor of
prédateur /pʀedatœʀ/ nm **(a)** predator

(b) hunter-gatherer
prédécesseur /pʀedesesœʀ/ nm predecessor
prédestiner /pʀedɛstine/ [1] vtr to predestine
prédicateur, -trice /pʀedikatœʀ, tʀis/ nm,f preacher
prédiction /pʀediksjɔ̃/ nf prediction
prédilection /pʀedilɛksjɔ̃/ nf predilection, liking; **de ~** favourite (GB)
prédire /pʀediʀ/ [65] vtr to predict
prédisposer /pʀedispoze/ [1] vtr to predispose
prédominant, ~e /pʀedɔminɑ̃, ɑ̃t/ adj predominant
prédominer /pʀedɔmine/ [1] vi to predominate
préétablir /pʀeetabliʀ/ [3] vtr to pre-establish
préexister /pʀeɛgziste/ [1] vi to pre-exist
préfabriqué /pʀefabʀike/ nm
(a) prefabricated material
(b) prefab (colloq)
préface /pʀefas/ nf preface
préfacer /pʀefase/ [12] vtr to write a or the preface to
préfectoral, ~e, mpl -aux /pʀefɛktɔʀal, o/ adj ‹level, authorization› prefectorial; ‹administration, building› prefectural
préfecture /pʀefɛktyʀ/ nf **(a)** prefecture
(b) main city of a French department
■ ~ **de police** police headquarters (in some large French cities)
préférable /pʀefeʀabl/ adj preferable
préféré, ~e /pʀefeʀe/ adj, nm,f favourite (GB)
préférence /pʀefeʀɑ̃s/ nf preference; **achète cette marque de ~** if you can, buy this brand
préférentiel, -ielle /pʀefeʀɑ̃sjɛl/ adj preferential
⚔ **préférer** /pʀefeʀe/ [14] vtr to prefer; **j'aurais préféré ne jamais l'apprendre** I wish I'd never found out
préfet /pʀefɛ/ nm prefect
préfigurer /pʀefigyʀe/ [1] vtr to prefigure
préfixe /pʀefiks/ nm prefix
préhistoire /pʀeistwaʀ/ nf prehistory
préjudice /pʀeʒydis/ nm harm, damage; ~ **moral** moral wrong; **porter ~ à qn** to harm sb; **au ~ de qn** to the detriment of sb
préjugé /pʀeʒyʒe/ nm prejudice; ~**(s) en faveur de qn** bias in favour (GB) of sb
préjuger /pʀeʒyʒe/ [13] vtr, **préjuger de** v+prep to prejudge
prélasser: se prélasser /pʀelase/ [1] v refl (+ v être) to lounge
prélat /pʀela/ nm prelate
prélavage /pʀelavaʒ/ nm prewash
prêle /pʀɛl/ nf (Bot) horsetail

p

prélèvement /pʁɛlɛvmɑ̃/ *nm* (a) sampling; sample; **faire un ~ de sang** to take a blood sample
(b) **faire un ~ bancaire de 100 euros** to make a debit of 100 euros
■ **~ automatique** direct debit; **~ à la source** deduction at source

prélever /pʁelve/ [16] *vtr* (a) to take a sample of ⟨blood, water⟩; to remove ⟨organ⟩
(b) to debit
(c) to deduct ⟨tax⟩
(d) to take ⟨percentage⟩

préliminaire /pʁeliminɛʁ/ **1** *adj* preliminary
2 préliminaires *nm pl* preliminaries

prélude /pʁelyd/ *nm* prelude

préluder /pʁelyde/ [1] *v+prep* **~ à** to be a prelude to

prématuré, **-e** /pʁematyʁe/ **1** *adj* premature
2 *nm,f* premature baby

préméditation /pʁemeditasjɔ̃/ *nf* premeditation

préméditer /pʁemedite/ [1] *vtr* to premeditate

⚐ **premier**, **-ière¹** /pʁəmje, ɛʁ/ **1** *adj*
(a) first; (dans) **les ~s temps** at first
(b) ⟨artist, power⟩ leading; ⟨student⟩ top; **être ~** to be top; to be first; **c'est le ~ prix** it's the cheapest
(c) ⟨impression⟩ first, initial
(d) ⟨quality⟩ prime; ⟨objective⟩ primary
2 *nm,f* first; **je préfère le ~** I prefer the first one; **arriver le ~** to come first; **être le ~ de la classe** to be top of the class
3 *nm* (a) first floor (GB), second floor (US)
(b) first; **le ~ de l'an** New Year's Day
(c) first arrondissement
4 en premier *phr* first
■ **~ âge** ⟨clothes⟩ for babies up to six months; **~ de cordée** (Sport) leader; **~ ministre** prime minister; **le ~ venu** just anybody; the first person to come along; **~s secours** first aid

première² /pʁəmjɛʁ/ **1** ▶ PREMIER 1, 2
2 *nf* (a) first; **~ mondiale** world first
(b) première
(c) (Sch) *sixth year of secondary school, age 16–17*
(d) (Aut) first (gear)
(e) (fam) first class
3 de première *phr* (fam) first-rate

premièrement /pʁəmjɛʁmɑ̃/ *adv*
(a) firstly, first
(b) for a start, for one thing

prémisse /pʁemis/ *nf* premise, premiss (GB)

prémolaire /pʁemɔlɛʁ/ *nf* premolar

prémonition /pʁemɔnisjɔ̃/ *nf* premonition

⚐ indicates a very frequent word

prémonitoire /pʁemɔnitwaʁ/ *adj* premonitory

prémunir /pʁemyniʁ/ [3] **1** *vtr* to protect
2 se prémunir *v refl* (+ *v être*) to protect oneself

prenant, **~e** /pʁənɑ̃, ɑ̃t/ *adj* ⟨film⟩ fascinating; ⟨voice⟩ captivating; ⟨work⟩ absorbing

⚐ **prendre** /pʁɑ̃dʁ/ [52]
peu /pø/
■ **Note** *Prendre* is very often translated by *to take* but see the entry below for a wide variety of usages. – for translations of certain fixed phrases such as *prendre froid, prendre soin de, prendre parti* etc, refer to the entries FROID, SOIN, PARTI.

1 *vtr* (a) to take; **~ un vase dans le placard** to take a vase out of the cupboard; **prenez donc une chaise** take a seat; **~ un congé** to take time off; **~ le train/l'avion** to take the train/plane; **on m'a pris tous mes bijoux** I had all my jewellery (GB) *or* jewelry (US) stolen; **la guerre leur a pris deux fils** they lost two sons in the war; **~ les mensurations de qn** to take sb's measurements; **~ les choses comme elles sont** to take things as they come; **ne le prends pas mal** don't take it the wrong way; **je vous ai pris pour quelqu'un d'autre** I thought you were someone else
(b) **~ un accent** to pick up an accent; to put on an accent
(c) to bring; **n'oublie pas de ~ des bottes** don't forget to bring a pair of boots
(d) to get ⟨food, petrol⟩; **~ de l'argent au distributeur** to get some money out of the cash dispenser
(e) to have ⟨drink, meal⟩; to take ⟨medicine⟩; **aller ~ une bière** to go for a beer
(f) to choose ⟨topic, question⟩
(g) to charge; **il prend 15% au passage** (fam) he takes a cut of 15%
(h) to take up ⟨space, time⟩
(i) to take [sb] on; to engage [sb]
(j) to pick [sb/sth] up; **~ les enfants à l'école** to collect the children from school
(k) to catch; **elle s'est fait ~ en train de voler** she got caught stealing
(l) (fam) **qu'est-ce qui te prend?** what's the matter with you?; **ça te/leur prend souvent?** are you/they often like this?
(m) to involve ⟨spectator, reader⟩; **être pris par un livre/film** to get involved in a book/film
(n) to get ⟨slap, sunburn⟩; to catch ⟨cold⟩
(o) **il est très gentil quand on sait le ~** he's very nice when you know how to handle him
(p) to take [sth] down ⟨address⟩
(q) **où a-t-il pris qu'ils allaient divorcer?** where did he get the idea they were going to get divorced?
(r) to take over ⟨management, power⟩; to assume ⟨control⟩; **je prends ça sur moi** I'll

see to it; **elle a pris sur elle de leur parler** she took it upon herself to talk to them
(s) to put on ‹weight›; to gain ‹lead›
(t) to take on ‹lease›; to take ‹job›
(u) to take on ‹rival›
(v) to take, to seize ‹town›; to capture ‹ship, tank›; to take ‹chesspiece, card›
2 *vi* **(a)** ~ **à gauche/vers le nord** to go left/north
(b) ‹wood› to catch; ‹fire› to break out
(c) ‹jelly, glue› to set; ‹mayonnaise› to thicken
(d) ‹strike, innovation› to be a success; ‹idea, fashion› to catch on; ‹dye, cutting› to take
(e) ~ **sur son temps libre pour traduire un roman** to translate a novel in one's spare time
(f) ~ **sur soi** to take a hold on oneself, to get a grip on oneself
(g) (fam) **ça ne prend pas!** it won't work!
(h) (fam) **c'est toujours moi qui prends!** I'm always the one who gets it in the neck! (colloq); **il en a pris pour 20 ans** he got 20 years
3 **se prendre** *v refl* (+ *v être*) **(a) en Chine le thé se prend sans sucre** in China they don't put sugar in their tea
(b) les mauvaises habitudes se prennent vite bad habits are easily picked up
(c) se ~ **par la taille** to hold each other around the waist
(d) se ~ **les doigts dans la porte** to catch one's fingers in the door
(e) (fam) **il s'est pris une gifle** he got a slap in the face
(f) se ~ **à faire** to find oneself doing; **se** ~ **de sympathie pour qn** to take to sb
(g) pour qui est-ce que tu te prends? who do you think you are?
(h) s'en ~ **à** to attack ‹person, press›; to take it out on [sb]; to go for [sb]
(i) savoir s'y ~ **avec** to have a way with ‹children›
(j) il faut s'y ~ **à l'avance pour avoir des places** you have to book ahead to get seats; **tu t'y es pris trop tard** you left it too late; **il s'y est pris à plusieurs fois** he tried several times; **elle s'y prend mal** she goes about it the wrong way
IDIOM **c'est à** ~ **ou à laisser** take it or leave it
preneur, -euse /pʀənœʀ, øz/ *nm,f* **il n'y a pas** ~ there are no takers; **trouver** ~ to attract a buyer; to find a buyer
prénom /pʀenɔ̃/ *nm* first name, forename
prénommer /pʀenɔme/ [1] **1** *vtr* to name, to call
2 **se prénommer** *v refl* (+ *v être*) to be called
prénuptial, ~e, *pl* **-iaux** /pʀenypsjal, o/ *adj* prenuptial; prior to marriage
préoccupant, ~e /pʀeɔkypɑ̃, ɑ̃t/ *adj* worrying
préoccupation /pʀeɔkypasjɔ̃/ *nf* worry
préoccuper /pʀeɔkype/ [1] **1** *vtr* **(a)** to worry; **avoir l'air préoccupé** to look worried
(b) to preoccupy

(c) to concern
2 **se préoccuper** *v refl* (+ *v être*) **se** ~ **de** to be concerned about ‹situation›; to think about ‹future›
préparateur, -trice /pʀepaʀatœʀ, tʀis/ *nm,f* ~ **en pharmacie** pharmacist's assistant
préparatifs /pʀepaʀatif/ *nm pl* preparations
préparation /pʀepaʀasjɔ̃/ *nf*
(a) preparation
(b) training
préparatoire /pʀepaʀatwaʀ/ *adj* preliminary
✔ **préparer** /pʀepaʀe/ [1] **1** *vtr* **(a)** (gen) to prepare; to make ‹meal›; to get [sth] ready ‹clothes, file›; to plan ‹holidays, future›; to draw up ‹plan›; to hatch ‹plot›; **il est en train de** ~ **le dîner** he's getting dinner ready; **des plats préparés** ready meals
(b) ~ **qn à qch** (gen) to prepare sb for sth; to coach sb for sth ‹race, examination›; **essaie de la** ~ **avant de lui annoncer la nouvelle** try and break the news to her gently
2 **se préparer** *v refl* (+ *v être*) **(a)** to get ready
(b) to prepare
(c) ‹storm, trouble› to be brewing; ‹changes› to be in the offing; **un coup d'État se prépare dans le pays** a coup d'état is imminent in the country
(d) se ~ **une tasse de thé** to make (GB) *or* fix (US) oneself a cup of tea
prépondérance /pʀepɔ̃deʀɑ̃s/ *nf* predominance
prépondérant, ~e /pʀepɔ̃deʀɑ̃, ɑ̃t/ *adj* predominant
préposé, ~e /pʀepoze/ *nm,f* **(a)** official; ~ **des douanes** customs official; ~ **au vestiaire** cloakroom attendant
(b) postman/postwoman (GB), mailman/mailwoman (US)
préposition /pʀepozisjɔ̃/ *nf* preposition
prépuce /pʀepys/ *nm* foreskin
préretraite /pʀeʀətʀɛt/ *nf* early retirement
prérogative /pʀeʀɔgativ/ *nf* prerogative; ~ **de qn/qch sur** primacy of sb/sth over
✔ **près** /pʀɛ/ **1** *adv* **(a)** close; **ce n'est pas tout** ~ it's quite a way; **se raser de** ~ to have a close shave
(b) ça pèse 10 kg, à quelques grammes ~ it weighs 10 kg, give or take a few grams; **à ceci** *or* **cela** ~ **que** except that; **il m'a remboursé au centime** ~ he paid me back to the very last penny; **gagner à deux voix** ~ to win by two votes; **à une exception** ~ with only one exception
2 **près de** *phr* **(a)** near; **être** ~ **du but** to be close to achieving one's goal; **j'aimerais être** ~ **de toi** I'd like to be with you
(b) near, nearly; **je ne suis pas** ~ **de recommencer** I'm not about to do that again; **le problème n'est pas** ~ **d'être résolu** the ····➤

p

problem is nowhere near solved
(c) close; **ils sont très ∼ l'un de l'autre** they
are very close
(d) nearly, almost; **cela coûte ∼ de
1 000 euros** it costs nearly 1,000 euros
3 de près *phr* closely; **se suivre de ∼**
‹*competitors*› to be close together; ‹*siblings*›
to be close in age
4 à peu près *phr* **∼ vide** practically
empty; **∼ 200 euros** about 200 euros; **à peu
∼ de la même façon** in much the same way
présage /pRezaʒ/ *nm* **(a)** omen
(b) harbinger
(c) prediction
présager /pRezaʒe/ [13] *vtr* ‹*event*› to
presage; ‹*person*› to predict; **laisser ∼** to
suggest
presbyte /pRɛsbit/ *adj* longsighted (GB),
farsighted (US)
presbytère /pRɛsbitɛR/ *nm* presbytery
presbytie /pRɛsbisi/ *nf* longsightedness
(GB), farsightedness (US)
préscolaire /pReskɔlɛR/ *adj* preschool
prescription /pRɛskRipsjɔ̃/ *nf*
prescription; ‘**se conformer aux ∼s du
médecin**’ ‘to be taken in accordance with
doctor's instructions’
prescrire /pRɛskRiR/ [67] *vtr* **(a)** (Med) to
prescribe
(b) to stipulate
présélection /pReselɛksjɔ̃/ *nf*
(a) shortlisting
(b) (Tech) presetting
présélectionner /pReselɛksjɔne/ [1] *vtr*
(a) to shortlist
(b) to preselect; to preset
ᵈ **présence** /pRezɑ̃s/ *nf* (gen) presence; (at
work) attendance; **il fait de la ∼, c'est tout**
he's present and not much else; **les forces
en ∼ dans le conflit** the forces involved in
the conflict; **il a besoin d'une ∼** he needs
company; **avoir beaucoup de ∼ (sur scène)**
to have great stage presence
■ **∼ d'esprit** presence of mind
ᵈ **présent, ∼e¹** /pRezɑ̃, ɑ̃t/ **1** *adj*
(a) present; **M. Maquanne, ici ∼**
Mr Maquanne, who is here with us; **avoir
qch ∼ à l'esprit** to have sth in mind ‹*advice*›;
to have sth fresh in one's mind ‹*memory*›
(b) actively involved; **un chanteur très ∼ sur
scène** a singer with a strong stage presence
2 *nm,f* **la liste des ∼s** the list of those
present
3 *nm* **(a) le ∼** the present
(b) (in grammar) present (tense)
(c) gift, present
4 à présent *phr* at present; now
présentable /pRezɑ̃tabl/ *adj* presentable
présentateur, -trice /pRezɑ̃tatœR,
tRis/ *nm,f* presenter; newsreader (GB),
newscaster (US)

ᵈ **présentation** /pRezɑ̃tasjɔ̃/ *nf*
(a) introduction; **faire les ∼s** to make the
introductions
(b) appearance
(c) (of dish, letter) presentation; (of products)
display
(d) show, showing; **∼ de mode** fashion show
(e) (of programme) presentation
(f) (of card, ticket) production; (of cheque)
presentation
(g) presentation, exposé
présente² /pRezɑ̃t/ **1** *adj f* ▸ PRÉSENT 1
2 *nf* **(a) par la ∼** hereby
(b) ▸ PRÉSENT 2
ᵈ **présenter** /pRezɑ̃te/ [1] **1** *vtr* **(a)** to
introduce; to present
(b) to show ‹*ticket, card, menu*›
(c) to present ‹*programme, show, collection*›;
to display ‹*goods*›
(d) to present ‹*receipt, bill*›; to submit
‹*estimate, report*›; to introduce ‹*proposal,
bill*›; **∼ une liste pour les élections** to
put forward a list (of candidates) for the
elections
(e) to present ‹*situation, budget, theory*›;
to set out ‹*objections, point of view*›; **∼ qn
comme (étant) un monstre** to portray sb as
a monster
(f) to offer ‹*condolences*›; **∼ des excuses** to
apologize
(g) to involve ‹*risk, difficulty*›; to show
‹*differences*›; to offer ‹*advantage*›; to have
‹*aspect, feature*›
2 *vi* **∼ bien** to have a smart appearance
3 se présenter *v refl* (+ *v être*) **(a) il
faut se ∼ à la réception** you must go to
reception; **présentez-vous à 10 heures** come
at 10 o'clock
(b) to introduce oneself
(c) se ∼ à to take ‹*examination*›; to stand for
‹*election*›
(d) ‹*opportunity*› to arise; ‹*solution*› to
emerge
(e) se ∼ en, se ∼ sous forme de ‹*product*› to
come in the form of
(f) l'affaire se présente bien things are
looking good
présentoir /pRezɑ̃twaR/ *nm* **(a)** display
stand *or* unit
(b) display shelf
préservatif /pRezɛRvatif/ *nm* condom
préservation /pRezɛRvasjɔ̃/ *nf*
protection; preservation
préserver /pRezɛRve/ [1] *vtr* **(a)** to preserve
(b) to protect
présidence /pRezidɑ̃s/ *nf* **(a)** presidency;
chairmanship
(b) presidential palace
ᵈ **président** /pRezidɑ̃/ *nm* president;
chairman
■ **∼ de la République** President of the
Republic

président-directeur, *pl* **présidents-
directeurs** /pRezidɑ̃diRɛktœR/ *nm* **∼**

ᵈ indicates a very frequent word

général chairman and managing director (GB), chief executive officer

présidente /pʀezidɑ̃t/ *nf* (a) president; chairwoman, chairperson; chairman (b) First Lady

présidentiel, -ielle /pʀezidɑ̃sjɛl/ *adj* presidential

présidentielles /pʀezidɑ̃sjɛl/ *nf pl* presidential election

présider /pʀezide/ [1] *vtr* (a) to chair (b) to be the president of; to be the chairman/chairwoman of; to preside over

présomption /pʀezɔ̃psjɔ̃/ *nf* (a) (Law) presumption
(b) assumption
(c) **plein de ~** presumptuous

présomptueux, -euse /pʀezɔ̃ptɥø, øz/ *adj* arrogant; presumptuous

⚜ **presque** /pʀɛsk/ *adv* almost, nearly; **il y a trois ans ~ jour pour jour** it's nearly three years to the day; **c'était le bonheur ou ~** it was as close to happiness as one can get; **il ne reste ~ rien** there's hardly anything left

presqu'île /pʀɛskil/ *nf* peninsula

pressant, ~e /pʀɛsɑ̃, ɑ̃t/ *adj* ‹need› pressing; ‹appeal› urgent; ‹salesman› insistent

⚜ **presse** /pʀɛs/ *nf* (a) press; newspapers; **avoir bonne ~** to be well thought of (b) (gen) press; (printing) press; **mettre sous ~** to send [sth] to press; **'sous ~'** 'in preparation'

pressé, ~e /pʀese/ *adj* (a) ‹person› in a hurry; ‹steps› hurried
(b) **~ de faire** keen to do
(c) ‹business› urgent; **parer au plus ~** to do the most urgent thing(s) first

presse-ail /pʀɛsaj/ *nm inv* garlic press

presse-citron /pʀɛssitʀɔ̃/ *nm inv* lemon squeezer

pressentiment /pʀɛsɑ̃timɑ̃/ *nm* premonition

pressentir /pʀɛsɑ̃tiʀ/ [30] *vtr* to have a premonition about

presse-papiers /pʀɛspapje/ *nm inv* paperweight

⚜ **presser** /pʀese/ [1] **1** *vtr* (a) **~ qn de faire** to urge sb to do
(b) to press ‹debtor›; to harry ‹enemy›
(c) ‹hunger, necessity› to drive [sb] on
(d) to increase ‹rhythm›; **~ le pas** *or* **mouvement** to hurry
(e) to press ‹button›
(f) to squeeze ‹hand, object›
(g) to squeeze ‹orange, sponge›; to press ‹grapes›
(h) to press ‹record›
2 *vi* ‹matter› to be pressing; ‹work› to be urgent; **le temps presse** time is running out
3 se presser *v refl* (+ *v être*) (a) **se ~ autour de qn/qch** to press around sb/sth
(b) to hurry up

(c) to flock

pressing /pʀɛsiŋ/ *nm* dry-cleaner's

⚜ **pression** /pʀɛsjɔ̃/ *nf* (a) (gen) pressure; **~ artérielle** blood pressure; **sous ~** under pressure; pressurized; **faire ~ sur** to press on ‹surface›; to put pressure on ‹person›
(b) snap (fastener)

pressoir /pʀɛswaʀ/ *nm* (a) pressing shed (b) press; **~ à pommes** cider press

pressurer /pʀɛsyʀe/ [1] *vtr* (a) to press ‹fruit, seeds›
(b) (fam) (exploiter) to milk (colloq)

pressuriser /pʀɛsyʀize/ [1] *vtr* to pressurize

prestance /pʀɛstɑ̃s/ *nf* **avoir de la ~** to have great presence

prestataire /pʀɛstatɛʀ/ *nm* (a) **~ de service** (service) contractor, service provider
(b) recipient (*of a state benefit*)

prestation /pʀɛstasjɔ̃/ *nf* (a) benefit
(b) provision; **~ de service** (provision of a) service
(c) service
(d) performance; **~ télévisée** televised appearance

prestidigitation /pʀɛstidiʒitasjɔ̃/ *nf* conjuring

prestige /pʀɛstiʒ/ *nm* prestige; **le ~ de l'uniforme** the glamour (GB) of a uniform

prestigieux, -ieuse /pʀɛstiʒjø, øz/ *adj* prestigious

présumé, ~e /pʀezyme/ *adj* alleged

présumer /pʀezyme/ [1] **1** *vtr* to presume; **le présumé terroriste** the alleged terrorist
2 présumer de *v+prep* **(trop) ~ de ses forces** to overestimate one's strength

présupposer /pʀesypoze/ [1] *vtr* to presuppose

⚜ **prêt, ~e** /pʀɛ, pʀɛt/ **1** *adj* ready; **être fin ~** to be all set; **il est ~ à tout** he will stop at nothing
2 *nm* (a) **le service de ~ de la bibliothèque** the library loans service
(b) loan
■ **~ immobilier** property loan; **~ personnalisé** personal loan

prêt-à-porter /pʀɛtapɔʀte/ *nm* ready-to-wear

prétendant, ~e /pʀetɑ̃dɑ̃, ɑ̃t/ **1** *nm,f* (a) candidate
(b) pretender
2 *nm* suitor

⚜ **prétendre** /pʀetɑ̃dʀ/ [6] **1** *vtr* to claim; **à ce qu'il prétend** according to him; **on le prétend très spirituel** he is said to be very witty
2 prétendre à *v+prep* to claim ‹damages›; to aspire to ‹job›
3 se prétendre *v refl* (+ *v être*) **il se** ⸱⸱⸱⸳

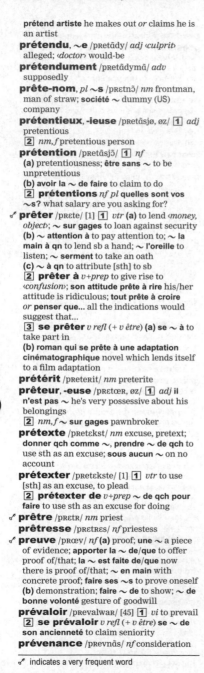

prétend artiste he makes out or claims he is an artist

prétendu, ~e /pʀetɑ̃dy/ adj ‹culprit› alleged; ‹doctor› would-be

prétendument /pʀetɑ̃dymɑ̃/ adv supposedly

prête-nom, pl ~s /pʀɛtnɔ̃/ nm frontman, man of straw; **société ~** dummy (US) company

prétentieux, -ieuse /pʀetɑ̃sjø, øz/ ① adj pretentious
② nm,f pretentious person

prétention /pʀetɑ̃sjɔ̃/ ① nf
(a) pretentiousness; **être sans ~** to be unpretentious
(b) **avoir la ~ de faire** to claim to do
② **prétentions** nf pl **quelles sont vos ~s?** what salary are you asking for?

♂ **prêter** /pʀete/ [1] ① vtr (a) to lend ‹money, object›; **~ sur gages** to loan against security
(b) **~ attention à** to pay attention to; **~ la main à qn** to lend sb a hand; **~ l'oreille to** listen; **~ serment** to take an oath
(c) **~ à qn** to attribute [sth] to sb
② **prêter à** v+prep to give rise to ‹confusion›; **son attitude prête à rire** his/her attitude is ridiculous; **tout prête à croire or penser que...** all the indications would suggest that...
③ **se prêter** v refl (+ v être) (a) **se ~ à** to take part in
(b) **roman qui se prête à une adaptation cinématographique** novel which lends itself to a film adaptation

prétérit /pʀeteʀit/ nm preterite

prêteur, -euse /pʀetœʀ, øz/ ① adj **il n'est pas ~** he's very possessive about his belongings
② nm,f **~ sur gages** pawnbroker

prétexte /pʀetɛkst/ nm excuse, pretext; **donner qch comme ~, prendre ~ de qch** to use sth as an excuse; **sous aucun ~** on no account

prétexter /pʀetɛkste/ [1] ① vtr to use [sth] as an excuse, to plead
② **prétexter de** v+prep **~ de qch pour faire** to use sth as an excuse for doing

♂ **prêtre** /pʀɛtʀ/ nm priest

prêtresse /pʀɛtʀɛs/ nf priestess

♂ **preuve** /pʀœv/ nf (a) proof; **une ~** a piece of evidence; **apporter la ~ de/que** to offer proof of/that; **la ~ est faite de/que** now there is proof of/that; **~ en main** with concrete proof; **faire ses ~s** to prove oneself
(b) demonstration; **faire ~ de** to show; **~ de bonne volonté** gesture of goodwill

prévaloir /pʀevalwaʀ/ [45] ① vi to prevail
② **se prévaloir** v refl (+ v être) **se ~ de son ancienneté** to claim seniority

prévenance /pʀevnɑ̃s/ nf consideration

♂ indicates a very frequent word

prévenant, ~e /pʀevnɑ̃, ɑ̃t/ adj considerate

♂ **prévenir** /pʀevniʀ/ [36] vtr (a) to tell
(b) to call ‹doctor, police›
(c) to warn
(d) to prevent ‹disaster›
(e) to anticipate ‹wishes›
IDIOM **mieux vaut ~ que guérir** (Proverb) prevention is better than cure

préventif, -ive /pʀevɑ̃tif, iv/ adj preventive

prévention /pʀevɑ̃sjɔ̃/ nf prevention; **faire de la ~** to take preventive action

prévenu, ~e /pʀevny/ nm,f (Law) defendant

prévisible /pʀevizibl/ adj predictable

prévision /pʀevizjɔ̃/ nf (a) forecasting; **en ~ de** in anticipation of
(b) prediction; forecast; **~s météorologiques** weather forecast

prévisionnel, -elle /pʀevizjɔnɛl/ adj projected

prévisionniste /pʀevizjɔnist/ nmf forecaster

♂ **prévoir** /pʀevwaʀ/ [42] vtr (a) to predict ‹change›; to foresee ‹event, victory›; to anticipate ‹reaction›; to forecast ‹result, weather›; **c'était à ~!** that was predictable!
(b) to plan ‹meeting, journey, building›; to set the date for ‹return, move›; (Law) to make provision for ‹case, eventuality›; **ce n'était pas prévu!** that wasn't meant to happen!; **remplissez le formulaire prévu à cet effet** fill in the appropriate form; **tout a été prévu** all the arrangements have been made
(c) to make sure one takes ‹coat, umbrella›
(d) to expect ‹visitor, shortage, strike›
(e) to allow ‹sum of money, time›

prévoyance /pʀevwajɑ̃s/ nf foresight

prévoyant, ~e /pʀevwajɑ̃, ɑ̃t/ adj far-sighted

prévu, ~e /pʀevy/ ▶ PRÉVOIR

♂ **prier** /pʀije/ [2] ① vtr (a) **~ qn de faire** to ask sb to do; **je vous prie d'excuser mon retard** I'm so sorry I'm late; **je vous prie de vous taire** will you kindly be quiet; **elle ne s'est pas fait ~** she didn't have to be asked twice
(b) to pray to ‹god›; **~ que** to pray that
② vi to pray

♂ **prière** /pʀijɛʀ/ nf (a) prayer; **faire sa ~** to say one's prayers
(b) request; plea, entreaty; **~ de ne pas fumer** no smoking please

prieuré /pʀijœʀe/ nm (a) priory
(b) priory church

primaire /pʀimɛʀ/ ① adj (a) primary
(b) ‹person› limited; ‹reasoning› simplistic
② nm (a) (Sch) **le ~** primary education
(b) (Econ) **le ~** the primary sector
(c) **le ~** the palaeozoic era

primate /pʀimat/ nm primate

primauté /pʀimote/ nf primacy

prime /pʀim/ **1** adj (a) de ~ abord at first, initially
(b) A ~ A prime
2 nf (a) bonus; free gift
(b) allowance
(c) subsidy
(d) (in insurance) premium
■ ~ d'ancienneté seniority bonus; ~ de risque danger money

primer /pʀime/ [1] **1** vtr (a) to take precedence over, to prevail over
(b) to award a prize to
2 primer sur v+prep (controversial) ▶ PRIMER 1A
3 vi pour moi, c'est la qualité qui prime what counts for me is quality

primeur /pʀimœʀ/ **1** nf avoir la ~ de l'information to be the first to hear sth
2 primeurs nf pl early fruit and vegetables

primevère /pʀimvɛʀ/ nf primrose

primitif, -ive /pʀimitif, iv/ adj (gen) primitive; ‹budget› initial; ‹project, state› original

primoaccédant /pʀimoaksedɑ̃/ nmf first-time buyer

primordial, ~e, mpl -iaux /pʀimɔʀdjal, o/ adj essential, vital

◦ᵖ **prince** /pʀɛ̃s/ nm prince
IDIOM être bon ~ to be magnanimous

princesse /pʀɛ̃sɛs/ nf princess
IDIOM aux frais de la ~ (fam) at the company's expense; at sb's expense

◦ᵖ **princier, -ière** /pʀɛ̃sje, ɛʀ/ adj ‹title, tastes, sum› princely; ‹luxury› dazzling

◦ᵖ **principal, ~e, mpl -aux** /pʀɛ̃sipal, o/ **1** adj (a) ‹factor› main; ‹task› principal
(b) ‹country, role› leading
(c) ‹inspector› chief
2 nm (a) le ~ the main thing
(b) (Sch) principal

principalement /pʀɛ̃sipalmɑ̃/ adv mainly

principauté /pʀɛ̃sipote/ nf principality

◦ᵖ **principe** /pʀɛ̃sip/ **1** nm (a) principle; par ~ on principle
(b) assumption
(c) (concept) principle; quel est le ~ de la machine à vapeur? how does a steam engine work?
2 en principe phr (a) as a rule
(b) in theory

printanier, -ière /pʀɛ̃tanje, ɛʀ/ adj ‹sun› spring; ‹weather› spring-like

◦ᵖ **printemps** /pʀɛ̃tɑ̃/ nm inv (a) spring
(b) (fam) mes 60 ~ my 60 summers

prion /pʀjɔ̃/ nm prion

priori ▶ A PRIORI

prioritaire /pʀijɔʀitɛʀ/ adj ‹file, project› priority; être ~ to have priority

priorité /pʀijɔʀite/ nf priority; avoir la ~ to have right (GB) or the right (US) of way

pris, ~e¹ /pʀi, pʀiz/ **1** pp ▶ PRENDRE
2 pp adj (a) busy; j'ai les mains ~es I've got my hands full; les places sont toutes ~es all the seats are taken
(b) ‹nose› stuffed up; ‹lungs› congested
(c) ~ de overcome with; ~ de panique panic-stricken

◦ᵖ **prise²** /pʀiz/ nf (a) storming; la ~ de la Bastille the storming of the Bastille
(b) catching; une belle ~ a fine catch
(c) (in judo, wrestling) hold
(d) n'offrir aucune ~ to have no handholds; to have no footholds; avoir ~ sur qn to have a hold over sb; donner ~ à to lay oneself open to
(e) socket (GB), outlet (US); ~ multiple (multiplug) adaptor; trailing socket
■ ~ de bec (fam) row, argument; ~ en charge (of expenses) payment; ~ de conscience realization; ~ de contact initial contact; ~ de courant socket (GB), outlet (US); ~ d'eau water supply point; ~ de sang blood test; ~ de vue shooting; shot
IDIOM être aux ~s avec des difficultés to be grappling with difficulties

priser /pʀize/ [1] vtr (a) to hold [sth] in esteem
(b) ~ (du tabac) to take snuff

prisme /pʀism/ nm prism

◦ᵖ **prison** /pʀizɔ̃/ nf prison; condamné à trois ans de ~ sentenced to three years' imprisonment

◦ᵖ **prisonnier, -ière** /pʀizɔnje, ɛʀ/ **1** adj il est ~ he is a prisoner
2 nm,f prisoner

privatif, -ive /pʀivatif, iv/ adj private

privation /pʀivasjɔ̃/ nf (a) (of rights) deprivation
(b) want; s'imposer des ~s to make sacrifices

privatisation /pʀivatizasjɔ̃/ nf privatization

privatiser /pʀivatize/ [1] vtr to privatize

◦ᵖ **privé, ~e** /pʀive/ **1** pp ▶ PRIVER
2 pp adj ~ de deprived of; tu seras ~ de dessert! you'll go without dessert!
3 adj (gen) private; ‹interview› unofficial
4 nm (a) (Econ) private sector
(b) (Sch) le ~ private schools
(c) en ~ in private

◦ᵖ **priver** /pʀive/ [1] **1** vtr ~ qn/qch de to deprive sb/sth of; ~ qn de sorties to forbid sb to go out
2 se priver v refl (+ v être) pourquoi se ~? why deprive ourselves?; se ~ de qch/de faire to go or do without sth/doing

privilège /pʀivilɛʒ/ nm privilege

privilégié, ~e /pʀivileʒje/ **1** pp
▶ PRIVILÉGIER
2 pp adj (a) privileged

⋯▹

(b) fortunate

(c) ‹moment, links› special; ‹treatment› preferential

privilégier /pʀivileʒje/ [2] vtr (a) to favour (GB)

(b) to give priority to

✒ **prix** /pʀi/ nm inv (a) price; à or au ∼ coûtant at cost price; acheter qch à ∼ d'or to pay a small fortune for sth; il faut être prêt à y mettre le ∼ you have to be prepared to pay for it; mettre qch à ∼ à 50 euros to start the bidding for sth at 50 euros

(b) (figurative) price; à tout ∼ at all costs; attacher beaucoup de ∼ à to value [sth] highly ‹friendship›

(c) prize

pro(-) /pʀo/ pref pro(-)

probabilité /pʀɔbabilite/ nf (a) probability, likelihood

(b) les ∼s probability theory

probable /pʀɔbabl/ adj probable, likely

✒ **probablement** /pʀɔbabləmã/ adv probably

probant, ∼e /pʀɔbã, ãt/ adj ‹argument, demonstration› convincing; ‹force, proof› conclusive

probatoire /pʀɔbatwaʀ/ adj examen ∼ assessment test; épreuve ∼ aptitude test

probité /pʀɔbite/ nf integrity, probity

problématique /pʀɔblematik/ adj ‹situation› problematic; ‹outcome› uncertain

✒ **problème** /pʀɔblɛm/ nm problem

✒ **procédé** /pʀɔsede/ nm (a) process

(b) practice (GB); échange de bons ∼s exchange of courtesies

✒ **procéder** /pʀɔsede/ [14] ① procéder à v+prep to carry out ‹check, survey›; to undertake ‹reform›; ∼ à un tirage au sort/un vote to hold a draw/a vote

② procéder de v+prep to be a product of

③ vi to go about things; ∼ par élimination to use a process of elimination

✒ **procédure** /pʀɔsedyʀ/ nf (a) proceedings

(b) procedure

✒ **procès** /pʀɔsɛ/ nm inv (a) trial

(b) lawsuit, case; intenter un ∼ à qn to sue sb

(c) indictment; faire le ∼ de qn/qch to put sb/sth in the dock

IDIOM sans autre forme de ∼ without further ado

processeur /pʀɔsesœʀ/ nm processor

procession /pʀɔsesjõ/ nf procession

✒ **processus** /pʀɔsesys/ nm inv (a) process

(b) (Med) evolution

procès-verbal, pl **-aux** /pʀɔsɛvɛʀbal, o/ nm (a) (of meeting) minutes

(b) statement of offence (GB)

✒ indicates a very frequent word

✒ **prochain**, ∼e /pʀɔʃɛ̃, ɛn/ ① adj (a) next; en juin ∼ next June; à la∼e! (fam) see you! (colloq)

(b) ‹meeting› coming, forthcoming; ‹departure, war› imminent; un jour ∼ one day soon

② nm fellow man; aime ton ∼ love thy neighbour (GB)

prochainement /pʀɔʃɛnmã/ adv soon

✒ **proche** /pʀɔʃ/ ① adj (a) nearby; ∼ de close to, near

(b) ‹departure› imminent; la victoire est ∼ victory is at hand; la fin est ∼ the end is (drawing) near

(c) ‹event› recent; ‹memory› real, vivid

(d) similar; ∼ de ‹figure, language› close to; ‹attitude› verging on

(e) ‹people› close; (on form) (plus) ∼ parent next of kin

② nm (a) close relative

(b) close friend

Proche-Orient /pʀɔʃɔʀjã/ pr nm le ∼ the Near East

proclamation /pʀɔklamasjõ/ nf proclamation

proclamer /pʀɔklame/ [1] vtr (a) to proclaim

(b) to declare

procréer /pʀɔkʀee/ [11] vi to procreate

procuration /pʀɔkyʀasjõ/ nf (a) power of attorney

(b) proxy; proxy form

procurer /pʀɔkyʀe/ [1] ① vtr to bring; to give

② se procurer v refl (+ v être) (a) to obtain

(b) to buy

procureur /pʀɔkyʀœʀ/ nm prosecutor

prodige /pʀɔdiʒ/ nm (a) prodigy

(b) feat; faire des ∼s to work wonders; ∼ technique technical miracle

prodigieux, -ieuse /pʀɔdiʒjø, øz/ adj ‹quantity› prodigious; ‹person› wonderful

prodigue /pʀɔdig/ adj (a) extravagant

(b) être ∼ de to be lavish with

prodiguer /pʀɔdige/ [1] vtr (a) to give lots of ‹advice›

(b) to give ‹treatment, first aid›

producteur, -trice /pʀɔdyktœʀ, tʀis/ ① adj pays ∼ de pétrole oil-producing country

② nm,f producer

productif, -ive /pʀɔdyktif, iv/ adj ‹work› productive; ‹investment› profitable

✒ **production** /pʀɔdyksjõ/ nf (a) (gen) production; (of energy) generation

(b) (gen) products, goods

■ ∼ assistée par ordinateur, PAO computer aided manufacturing, CAM

productivité /pʀɔdyktivite/ nf productivity

produire /pʀɔdɥiʀ/ [69] **1** *vtr* (a) (gen) to produce; **cette usine produit peu** this factory has a low output; **un artiste/écrivain qui produit beaucoup** a prolific artist/writer
(b) to bring in ‹*money, wealth*›; to yield ‹*interest*›
(c) to produce, to have ‹*effect, result*›; to create, to make ‹*impression*›; to cause ‹*sensation, emotion*›
2 se produire *v refl* (+ *v être*) (a) ‹*event*› to occur, to happen
(b) ‹*singer*› to perform

produit /pʀɔdɥi/ *nm* (a) product; **des ~s** goods, products; **~s alimentaires** foodstuffs; **~s agricoles** agricultural produce
(b) income; yield, return; profit; **vivre du ~ de sa terre** to live off the land; **le ~ de la vente** the proceeds of the sale
(c) (of research) result; (of activity) product
■ **~ chimique** chemical; **~ d'entretien** cleaning product, household product; **~ intérieur brut, PIB** gross domestic product, GDP; **~ national brut, PNB** gross national product, GNP

proéminent, ~e /pʀɔeminɑ̃, ɑ̃t/ *adj* prominent

profanateur, -trice /pʀɔfanatœʀ, tʀis/ *nm,f* profaner

profanation /pʀɔfanasjɔ̃/ *nf* desecration; defilement; debasement

profane /pʀɔfan/ **1** *adj* secular
2 *nmf* (a) layman/laywoman
(b) nonbeliever
3 *nm* **le ~ et le sacré** the sacred and the profane

profaner /pʀɔfane/ [1] *vtr* to desecrate ‹*temple*›; to defile ‹*memory*›; to debase ‹*institution*›

proférer /pʀɔfeʀe/ [14] *vtr* to hurl ‹*insults*›; to make ‹*threats*›; to utter ‹*words*›

professer /pʀɔfese/ [1] *vtr* to profess

professeur /pʀɔfesœʀ/ *nm* (in school) teacher; (in higher education) lecturer (GB), professor (US); (holding university chair) professor; **~ des écoles** primary school teacher

profession /pʀɔfesjɔ̃/ *nf* (a) occupation; profession; **exercer la ~ d'infirmière** to be a nurse by profession; **être sans ~** to have no occupation
(b) declaration, profession
■ **~ libérale** profession

professionnalisme /pʀɔfesjɔnalism/ *nm* professionalism

professionnel, -elle /pʀɔfesjɔnɛl/ **1** *adj* (a) ‹*qualifications*› professional; ‹*life, environment*› working; ‹*disease*› occupational; ‹*training*› vocational
(b) ‹*player*› professional
2 *nm,f* professional; **le salon est réservé aux ~s** the fair is restricted to people in the trade

professionnellement /pʀɔfesjɔnɛlmɑ̃/ *adv* professionally

professoral, ~e, *mpl* **-aux** /pʀɔfesɔʀal, o/ *adj* professorial

profil /pʀɔfil/ *nm* profile; **être de ~** to be in profile; **se mettre de ~** to turn sideways

profiler /pʀɔfile/ [1] **1** *vtr* **la tour profile sa silhouette dans le ciel** the tower is silhouetted *or* outlined against the sky
2 se profiler *v refl* (+ *v être*) ‹*shape*› to stand out; ‹*problem*› to emerge; ‹*events*› to approach

profit /pʀɔfi/ *nm* (a) benefit, advantage; **au ~ des handicapés** in aid of the handicapped; **mettre à ~** to make the most of ‹*free time, course*›; to turn [sth] to good account ‹*situation*›; to make good use of ‹*idea*›
(b) profit; **être une source de ~ pour** to be a source of wealth for

profitable /pʀɔfitabl/ *adj* (a) beneficial
(b) profitable

profiter /pʀɔfite/ [1] **1 profiter à** *v+prep* **~ à qn** to benefit sb
2 profiter de *v+prep* to use ‹*advantage*›; to make the most of ‹*holiday, situation*›; to take advantage of ‹*visit, weakness, person*›
3 *vi* (fam) ‹*person*› to grow; ‹*plant*› to thrive

profiteur, -euse /pʀɔfitœʀ, øz/ *nm,f* profiteer

profond, ~e /pʀɔfɔ̃, ɔ̃d/ **1** *adj* (a) deep; **peu ~** shallow
(b) ‹*boredom*› acute; ‹*sigh*› heavy; ‹*feeling, sleep, colour*› deep
(c) ‹*change, ignorance*› profound
(d) ‹*mind, remark*› profound; ‹*gaze*› penetrating
(e) **la France ~e** provincial France; **l'Amérique ~e** small-town America
2 *adv* deeply, deep down

profondément /pʀɔfɔ̃demɑ̃/ *adv* (a) ‹*dig*› deep
(b) deeply; greatly; profoundly; **détester ~** to loathe

profondeur /pʀɔfɔ̃dœʀ/ *nf* (a) depth; **avoir une ~ de 3 mètres** to be 3 metres (GB) deep
(b) (of feeling) depth; (of remark, work) profundity; **en ~** ‹*analysis*› in-depth; ‹*work*› thorough

profusion /pʀɔfyzjɔ̃/ *nf* profusion; abundance

progéniture /pʀɔʒenityʀ/ *nf* progeny

progiciel /pʀɔʒisjɛl/ *nm* software package

programmateur, -trice /pʀɔgʀamatœʀ, tʀis/ **1** *nm,f* programme (GB) planner
2 *nm* timer

programmation /pʀɔgʀamasjɔ̃/ *nf* programming

programme /pʀɔgʀam/ *nm* (a) programme (GB)
(b) (of action) plan; (of work) programme (GB); **c'est tout un ~!** (humorous) that'll take some doing!
(c) (Sch) syllabus

···>

p

(d) (Comput) program

programmer /pRɔgRame/ [1] *vtr* **(a)** to schedule ‹*broadcast*›; to plan ‹*work*›
(b) (Comput) to program

programmeur, -euse /pRɔgRamœR, øz/ *nm,f* (computer) programmer

⚜ **progrès** /pRɔgRɛ/ *nm inv* **(a)** progress; **les ~ de la médecine** advances in medicine; **être en ~** ‹*person*› to be making progress; ‹*results*› to be improving
(b) increase; **être en ~ de 10%** to be up by 10%
(c) (of illness) progression

progresser /pRɔgRese/ [1] *vi* **(a)** to rise; to increase; **~ de 3%** ‹*rate*› to rise by 3%; ‹*party*› to gain 3%
(b) ‹*politician*› to make gains; ‹*illness*› to spread; ‹*crime*› to be on the increase
(c) ‹*pupil, inquiry, country*› to make progress; ‹*relations*› to improve; ‹*technology*› to progress
(d) ‹*climber*› to make progress; ‹*army*› to advance

progressif, -ive /pRɔgResif, iv/ *adj* progressive

progression /pRɔgRɛsjɔ̃/ *nf* **(a)** progress; advance; spread; increase
(b) (in mathematics, music) progression

progressiste /pRɔgResist/ *adj* progressive

prohibé, ~e /pRɔibe/ *adj* ‹*goods, substance, weapon*› prohibited; ‹*trade, action*› illegal; **port d'arme ~** illegal possession of a firearm

prohiber /pRɔibe/ [1] *vtr* to prohibit

prohibitif, -ive /pRɔibitif, iv/ *adj* **(a)** ‹*price*› prohibitive
(b) ‹*law*› prohibition

prohibition /pRɔibisjɔ̃/ *nf* prohibition

proie /pRwa/ *nf* prey; **être en ~ à l'angoisse** to be racked by anxiety; **pays en ~ à la guerre civile** country in the grip of civil war

projecteur /pRɔʒɛktœR/ *nm* **(a)** searchlight; floodlight; **être sous les ~s** to be in the spotlight
(b) projector

projectile /pRɔʒɛktil/ *nm* missile; projectile

projection /pRɔʒɛksjɔ̃/ *nf* **(a)** **l'éruption commença par une ~ de cendres** the eruption began with a discharge of ashes
(b) **le cuisinier a reçu des ~s d'huile bouillante** the cook got spattered with scalding oil
(c) projection; showing; **salle de ~** screening room

projectionniste /pRɔʒɛksjɔnist/ *nmf* projectionist

⚜ **projet** /pRɔʒɛ/ *nm* **(a)** plan; **en ~, à l'état de ~** at the planning stage

⚜ indicates a very frequent word

(b) project
(c) (rough) draft
(d) (in architecture) execution plan
■ **~ de loi** (government) bill

projeter /pRɔʒte/ [20] *vtr* **(a)** to throw; **le choc l'a projeté par terre** the shock sent him hurtling to the ground
(b) to cast ‹*shadow*›
(c) to show ‹*film*›
(d) to plan (**de faire** to do)

prolétaire /pRɔletɛR/ *adj, nmf* proletarian

prolétariat /pRɔletaRja/ *nm* proletariat

proliférer /pRɔlifeRe/ [14] *vi* to proliferate

prolifique /pRɔlifik/ *adj* prolific

prolixe /pRɔliks/ *adj* verbose, prolix

prologue /pRɔlɔg/ *nm* prologue

prolongation /pRɔlɔ̃gasjɔ̃/ *nf* continuation; extension; (Sport) extra time

prolongé, ~e /pRɔlɔ̃ʒe/ *adj* ‹*effort*› sustained; ‹*stay*› extended; ‹*exhibition*› prolonged

prolongement /pRɔlɔ̃ʒmã/ *nm* **(a)** (of road, stay) extension
(b) **la rue Berthollet se trouve dans le ~ de la rue de la Glacière** Rue de la Glacière becomes Rue Berthollet

prolonger /pRɔlɔ̃ʒe/ [13] **1** *vtr* to extend ‹*stay*›; to prolong ‹*meeting, life*›
2 **se prolonger** *v refl* (+ *v être*) **(a)** to persist; to go on
(b) ‹*street*› **se ~ jusqu'à** to go as far as

⚜ **promenade** /pRɔmnad/ *nf* **(a)** walk; ride; drive
(b) walkway; promenade

⚜ **promener** /pRɔmne/ [16] **1** *vtr* **(a)** to take [sb] out ‹*person*›; to take [sth] out for a walk ‹*animal*›; **ça te promènera** (fam) it'll get you out
(b) to carry ‹*object*›
(c) to show [sb] around
2 **se promener** *v refl* (+ *v être*) to go for a walk/drive/ride

promeneur, -euse /pRɔmnœR, øz/ *nm,f* walker

promesse /pRɔmɛs/ *nf* **(a)** promise; **avoir la ~ de qn** to have sb's word; **tenir ses ~s** to keep one's promises
(b) **~ de vente** agreement to sell
■ **~ en l'air** *or* **de Gascon** *or* **d'ivrogne** empty *or* idle promise

prometteur, -euse /pRɔmɛtœR, øz/ *adj* promising

⚜ **promettre** /pRɔmɛtR/ [60] **1** *vtr* **(a)** **~ qch à qn** to promise sb sth; **je te promets qu'il le regrettera** he'll regret it, I guarantee you
(b) **une soirée qui promet bien des surprises** an evening that holds a few surprises in store
2 *vi* **(a)** ‹*pupil*› to show promise; **un film qui promet** a film which sounds interesting
(b) (fam) **cet enfant promet!** that child is

going to be a handful!; **ça promet!** that
promises to be fun!
③ **se promettre** *v refl* (+ *v être*) **(a)** to
promise oneself
(b) se ∼ de faire to resolve to do
promiscuité /pʀɔmiskɥite/ *nf* lack of
privacy
promontoire /pʀɔmɔ̃twaʀ/ *nm*
promontory
promoteur, -trice /pʀɔmɔtœʀ, tʀis/ *nm,f*
∼ **(immobilier)** property developer
promotion /pʀɔmɔsjɔ̃/ *nf* **(a)** promotion
(b) (special) offer; **en ∼ on** (special) offer
promotionnel, -elle /pʀɔmɔsjɔnɛl/ *adj*
promotional
promouvoir /pʀɔmuvwaʀ/ [43] *vtr* to
promote
prompt, ∼e /pʀɔ̃, pʀɔ̃t/ *adj ‹reaction›*
prompt; *‹gesture, glance›* swift; *‹return›*
sudden
promulguer /pʀɔmylge/ [1] *vtr* to
promulgate
prôner /pʀone/ [1] *vtr* to advocate
pronom /pʀɔnɔ̃/ *nm* pronoun
pronominal, ∼e, *mpl* **-aux** /pʀɔnɔminal,
o/ *adj* pronominal
prononcé, ∼e /pʀɔnɔ̃se/ *adj ‹accent, taste›*
strong; *‹wrinkles›* deep; **avoir un goût ∼ pour**
to be particularly fond of
⚜ **prononcer** /pʀɔnɔ̃se/ [12] ① *vtr* **(a)** to
pronounce *‹word›*
(b) to mention *‹name›*; to say *‹phrase›*
(c) to deliver *‹speech›*
(d) to pronounce *‹death penalty›*; **∼ le
divorce** to grant a divorce
② **se prononcer** *v refl* (+ *v être*) **(a)** to be
pronounced
(b) se ∼ contre/en faveur de qch to declare
oneself against/in favour (GB) of sth; **se ∼
sur qch** to give one's opinion on sth
prononciation /pʀɔnɔ̃sjasjɔ̃/ *nf*
pronunciation
pronostic /pʀɔnɔstik/ *nm* **(a)** forecast
(b) prediction
(c) (medical) prognosis
pronostiquer /pʀɔnɔstike/ [1] *vtr* (in sport)
to forecast *‹result›*; to herald *‹defeat, victory›*
propagande /pʀɔpagɑ̃d/ *nf* propaganda
propagateur, -trice /pʀɔpagatœʀ,
tʀis/ *nm,f* proponent
propagation /pʀɔpagasjɔ̃/ *nf* spread;
propagation
propager /pʀɔpaʒe/ [13] ① *vtr* to spread
‹rumour, disease›; to propagate *‹species,
sound›*
② **se propager** *v refl* (+ *v être*) to spread;
to propagate
propane /pʀɔpan/ *nm* propane
propension /pʀɔpɑ̃sjɔ̃/ *nf* propensity
prophète /pʀɔfɛt/ *nm* prophet
prophétie /pʀɔfesi/ *nf* prophecy

prophétiser /pʀɔfetize/ [1] *vtr* to
prophesy
propice /pʀɔpis/ *adj* favourable (GB);
trouver le moment ∼ to find the right
moment
proportion /pʀɔpɔʀsjɔ̃/ *nf* proportion;
en ∼, ils sont mieux payés they are
proportionately better paid; **être sans ∼
avec** to be out of (all) proportion to; **toutes
∼s gardées** relatively speaking
proportionnel, -elle¹ /pʀɔpɔʀsjɔnɛl/ *adj*
proportional
proportionnelle² /pʀɔpɔʀsjɔnɛl/ *nf*
proportional representation
proportionner /pʀɔpɔʀsjɔne/ [1] *vtr* **∼
qch à qch** to make sth proportional to sth;
proportionné à proportional to
⚜ **propos** /pʀɔpo/ ① *nm inv* **(a)** à ∼, je...
by the way, I...; **à ∼ de** about; **à ∼ de qui?**
about who?; **à ce ∼, je voudrais...** in this
connection, I would like...
(b) à ∼ at the right moment; **mal à ∼** at
(just) the wrong moment
② *nm pl* comments; **'∼ recueillis par J.
Brun'** 'interview by J. Brun'
⚜ **proposer** /pʀɔpoze/ [1] ① *vtr* **(a)** to
suggest
(b) to offer *‹drink, dish›*
(c) to put forward *‹solution›*; to propose
‹strategy›
② **se proposer** *v refl* (+ *v être*) **(a) se ∼
pour faire** to offer to do
(b) se ∼ de faire to intend to do
⚜ **proposition** /pʀɔpozisjɔ̃/ *nf* **(a)** suggestion
(b) proposal
(c) clause
■ **∼ de loi** ≈ bill
⚜ **propre** /pʀɔpʀ/ ① *adj* **(a)** clean; **nous voilà
∼s!** (figurative) we're in a fine mess now!
(b) tidy, neat
(c) *‹person, life›* decent; **des affaires pas très
∼s** unsavoury (GB) business
(d) own; **ma ∼ voiture** my own car; **ce sont
tes ∼s paroles** you said so yourself; those
were your very words
(e) of one's own; **chaque pays a des lois
qui lui sont ∼s** each country has its own
particular laws
(f) *‹baby›* toilet-trained; *‹animal›*
housetrained (GB), housebroken (US)
② **propre à** *phr* **(a)** ∼ à peculiar to
(b) ∼ à faire likely to do; liable to do
(c) ∼ à appropriate for; **produit déclaré
∼ à la consommation** product fit for
consumption
③ *nm* **(a) mettre qch au ∼** to make a fair
copy of sth
(b) c'est du ∼! (ironic) that's very nice!
**(c) le ∼ de cette nouvelle technologie est de
faire** what is peculiar to this new technology
is that it does; **∼ à rien** good-for-nothing
proprement /pʀɔpʀəmɑ̃/ *adv* **(a)** purely; **à
∼ parler** strictly speaking ┅┅⊹

(b) absolutely
(c) really
(d) literally; **l'air est devenu ~ irrespirable** the air has become literally unbreathable
(e) specifically
(f) well and truly; **le professeur l'a ~ remis à sa place** he was well and truly put in his place by the teacher
(g) neatly
(h) ‹*earn living*› honestly; ‹*live*› decently

propreté /pʀɔpʀəte/ nf (a) cleanliness; **d'une ~ douteuse** not very clean
(b) honesty

⚜ **propriétaire** /pʀɔpʀijetɛʀ/ nmf (a) owner; **un petit ~** a small-scale property owner; **ils sont ~s de leur maison** they own their own house; **faire le tour du ~** to look round (GB) *or* around the house
(b) landlord/landlady

⚜ **propriété** /pʀɔpʀijete/ nf (a) ownership
(b) property; **~ privée** private property
(c) (of substance) property
(d) (of term) aptness
■ **~ artistique et littéraire** copyright

propulser /pʀɔpylse/ [1] vtr to propel

propulseur /pʀɔpylsœʀ/ **1** adj m propellent
2 nm engine; **~ (de fusée)** (rocket) engine
■ **~ à hélice** propeller

propulsion /pʀɔpylsjɔ̃/ nf propulsion; **à ~ nucléaire** nuclear-powered

prorata /pʀɔʀata/ nm inv proportion

proroger /pʀɔʀɔʒe/ [13] vtr (a) to defer ‹*date*›; to renew ‹*passport*›
(b) to adjourn ‹*meeting*›

prosaïque /pʀɔzaik/ adj prosaic

proscription /pʀɔskʀipsjɔ̃/ nf
(a) proscription
(b) banishment; **frapper qn de ~** to banish sb

proscrire /pʀɔskʀiʀ/ [67] vtr to ban; to banish

proscrit, ~e /pʀɔskʀi, it/ nm,f outcast

prose /pʀoz/ nf (a) prose; **poème en ~** prose poem
(b) (humorous) distinctive prose

prosélytisme /pʀɔzelitism/ nm proselytizing

prospecter /pʀɔspɛkte/ [1] vtr (a) to canvass
(b) to prospect

prospecteur, -trice /pʀɔspɛktœʀ, tʀis/ nm,f (a) canvasser
(b) prospector

prospectif, -ive /pʀɔspɛktif, iv/ adj long-term

prospection /pʀɔspɛksjɔ̃/ nf (a) canvassing
(b) prospecting

prospectus /pʀɔspɛktys/ nm inv leaflet

⚜ indicates a very frequent word

prospère /pʀɔspɛʀ/ adj thriving; prosperous

prospérer /pʀɔspeʀe/ [14] vi to thrive; to prosper

prospérité /pʀɔspeʀite/ nf prosperity

prostate /pʀɔstat/ nf prostate (gland)

prosternation /pʀɔstɛʀnasjɔ̃/ nf
(a) prostration
(b) (figurative) self-abasement

prosternement /pʀɔstɛʀnəmɑ̃/ nm
(a) prostrate position
(b) prostration

prosterner: se prosterner /pʀɔstɛʀne/ [1] v refl (+ v être) (a) to prostrate oneself
(b) (figurative) to grovel

prostitué /pʀɔstitɥe/ nm (male) prostitute

prostituée /pʀɔstitɥe/ nf prostitute

prostituer: se prostituer /pʀɔstitɥe/ [1] v refl (+ v être) to prostitute oneself

prostitution /pʀɔstitysjɔ̃/ nf prostitution

prostration /pʀɔstʀasjɔ̃/ nf prostration

protagoniste /pʀɔtagɔnist/ nmf protagonist

protecteur, -trice /pʀɔtɛktœʀ, tʀis/ **1** adj (a) protective
(b) patronizing
2 nm,f protector

⚜ **protection** /pʀɔtɛksjɔ̃/ nf (a) protection; **être sous haute ~** to be under tight security; **de ~** ‹*screen, measures*› protective; ‹*zone, system*› protection
(b) protective device
■ **~ sociale** social welfare system

protectionnisme /pʀɔtɛksjɔnism/ nm protectionism

protectionniste /pʀɔtɛksjɔnist/ adj, nmf protectionist

protégé, ~e /pʀɔteʒe/ nm,f protégé

⚜ **protéger** /pʀɔteʒe/ [15] **1** vtr to protect
2 **se protéger** v refl (+ v être) to protect oneself

protège-slip, pl **~s** /pʀɔtɛʒslip/ nm panty-liner

protège-tibia, pl **~s** /pʀɔtɛʒtibja/ nm shinpad

protéine /pʀɔtein/ nf protein

protestant, ~e /pʀɔtɛstɑ̃, ɑ̃t/ adj, nm,f Protestant

protestantisme /pʀɔtɛstɑ̃tism/ nm Protestantism

protestataire /pʀɔtɛstatɛʀ/ nmf protester

protestation /pʀɔtɛstasjɔ̃/ nf protest

protester /pʀɔtɛste/ [1] **1** protester **de** v+prep **~ de son innocence** to protest one's innocence
2 vi to protest

prothèse /pʀɔtɛz/ nf prosthesis; artificial limb; dentures; ~ **auditive** hearing aid

prothésiste /pʀɔtezist/ nmf prosthetist

protocolaire /pʀɔtɔkɔlɛʀ/ adj formal; official; **question** ~ question of protocol

protocole /pʀɔtɔkɔl/ nm **(a)** formalities; protocol
(b) ~ **d'accord** draft agreement

prototype /pʀɔtɔtip/ nm prototype

protubérance /pʀɔtybeʀɑ̃s/ nf protuberance

protubérant, ~**e** /pʀɔtybeʀɑ̃, ɑ̃t/ adj protruding

prou /pʀu/ adv **peu ou** ~ more or less

proue /pʀu/ nf prow, bow(s)

prouesse /pʀuɛs/ nf feat; (ironic) exploit

♂ **prouver** /pʀuve/ [1] 1 vtr **(a)** to prove
(b) to show
(c) to demonstrate
2 **se prouver** v refl (+ v être) **(a)** to prove to oneself
(b) ils se sont prouvé qu'ils s'aimaient they proved their love for each other
IDIOM **n'avoir plus rien à** ~ to have proved oneself

provenance /pʀɔvnɑ̃s/ nf origin; **en** ~ **de** from

provençal, ~**e**, mpl **-aux** /pʀɔvɑ̃sal, o/ adj Provençal; **à la** ~**e** (Culin) (à la) provençale

provenir /pʀɔvniʀ/ [36] vi **(a)** to come (**de** from); **provenant de** from
(b) to stem (**de** from)

proverbe /pʀɔvɛʀb/ nm proverb

proverbial, ~**e**, mpl **-iaux** /pʀɔvɛʀbjal, o/ adj proverbial

providence /pʀɔvidɑ̃s/ 1 nf **(a)** salvation
(b) providence
2 **(-)providence** (combining form) **État(-)**~ welfare state

providentiel, **-ielle** /pʀɔvidɑ̃sjɛl/ adj providential

♂ **province** /pʀɔvɛ̃s/ nf **(a)** province
(b) la ~ the provinces; **ville de** ~ provincial town

provincial, ~**e**, mpl **-iaux** /pʀɔvɛ̃sjal, o/ adj, nm,f provincial

proviseur /pʀɔvizœʀ/ nm headteacher (GB) or principal (US) (of a lycée)

provision /pʀɔvizjɔ̃/ 1 nf **(a)** stock; supply
(b) deposit; credit (balance)
2 **provisions** nf pl food shopping

provisoire /pʀɔvizwaʀ/ adj provisional; temporary

provisoirement /pʀɔvizwaʀmɑ̃/ adv provisionally

provocant, ~**e** /pʀɔvɔkɑ̃, ɑ̃t/ adj provocative

provocateur, **-trice** /pʀɔvɔkatœʀ, tʀis/ nm,f agitator

provocation /pʀɔvɔkasjɔ̃/ nf provocation

♂ **provoquer** /pʀɔvɔke/ [1] vtr **(a)** to cause ‹accident›; to provoke ‹reaction, anger›; ~ **l'accouchement** to induce labour (GB)
(b) to provoke; ~ **qn en duel** to challenge sb to a duel
(c) (sexually) to arouse

proxénète /pʀɔksenɛt/ nm procurer, pimp

proxénétisme /pʀɔksenetism/ nm procuring

proximité /pʀɔksimite/ nf **(a)** nearness, proximity; **à** ~ nearby; **à** ~ **de** near
(b) imminence; **à cause de la** ~ **de Noël** because it is/was so close to Christmas

prude /pʀyd/ adj prudish

prudemment /pʀydamɑ̃/ adv **(a)** carefully
(b) cautiously

prudence /pʀydɑ̃s/ nf caution; **avec** ~ cautiously; with caution; **par** ~ as a precaution; **redoubler de** ~ to be doubly careful

prudent, ~**e** /pʀydɑ̃, ɑ̃t/ adj **(a)** careful; **ce n'est pas** ~ **de faire** it isn't safe to do
(b) cautious
(c) wise

prud'homme /pʀydɔm/ nm **Conseil des** ~**s** ≈ industrial tribunal (GB), labor relations board (US)

prune /pʀyn/ nf **(a)** plum
(b) plum brandy
IDIOM **pour des** ~**s** (fam) for nothing

pruneau, pl ~**x** /pʀyno/ nm prune

prunelle /pʀynɛl/ nf **(a)** sloe; ≈ sloe gin
(b) (of eye) pupil

prunier /pʀynje/ nm plum tree

Prusse /pʀys/ pr nf Prussia

PS /pɛɛs/ nm (abbr = **post-scriptum**) PS

psalmodier /psalmɔdje/ [2] vi to chant psalms

psaume /psom/ nm psalm

pseudo- /psødo/ pref pseudo; ~**-équilibre** so-called balance; ~**-savant** self-styled scientist

pseudonyme /psødɔnim/ nm pseudonym

psy /psi/ nmf (fam) shrink (colloq), therapist

psychanalyse /psikanaliz/ nf psychoanalysis

psychanalyser /psikanalize/ [1] vtr to psychoanalyse (GB)

psyché /psiʃe/ nf **(a)** cheval glass
(b) psyche

psychiatrie /psikjatʀi/ nf psychiatry

psychiatrique /psikjatʀik/ adj psychiatric

psychique /psiʃik/ adj mental

psychisme /psiʃism/ nm psyche

psychologie /psikɔlɔʒi/ nf **(a)** psychology
(b) (psychological) insight

psychologique /psikɔlɔʒik/ adj psychological

p

psychologue /psikɔlɔg/ **1** *adj* être ~ to understand people very well
2 *nmf* psychologist
psychopathe /psikɔpat/ *nmf* psychopath
psychose /psikoz/ *nf* (a) psychosis
(b) ~ **de la guerre** obsessive fear of war
psychosomatique /psikosɔmatik/ *adj* psychosomatic
psychothérapeute /psikoteʀapøt/ *nmf* psychotherapist
psychothérapie /psikoteʀapi/ *nf* psychotherapy
PTT /petete/ *nf pl* (*abbr* = **Administration des postes et télécommunications et de la télédiffusion**) *former French postal and telecommunications service*
pu /py/ ▶ POUVOIR¹
puant, ~**e** /pɥɑ̃, ɑ̃t/ *adj* (a) stinking; smelly
(b) (fam) **un type** ~ an incredibly arrogant guy (colloq)
puanteur /pɥɑ̃tœʀ/ *nf* stench
pub /pyb/ (fam) *abbr* ▶ PUBLICITÉ
pubère /pybɛʀ/ *adj* pubescent
puberté /pybɛʀte/ *nf* puberty
pubis /pybis/ *nm inv* pubes; pubis
❧ **public, -ique** /pyblik/ **1** *adj* public; ‹*education*› state (GB), public (US); ‹*company*› state-owned; **la dette publique** the national debt
2 *nm* (a) public; '**interdit au** ~' 'no admittance'; '**avis au** ~' 'public notice'
(b) audience; spectators; **tous** ~**s** for all ages
(c) readership
(d) **avoir un** ~ to have a following
(e) **le** ~ the public sector
❧ **publication** /pyblikasjɔ̃/ *nf* publication
■ ~ **assistée par ordinateur, PAO** desktop publishing, DTP
publicitaire /pyblisitɛʀ/ **1** *adj* ‹*campaign*› advertising; ‹*gift*› promotional
2 *nmf* **il/elle est** ~ he/she's in advertising
3 *nm* advertising agency
publicité /pyblisite/ *nf* (a) advertising; **faire de la** ~ **pour** to advertise
(b) (*also* **pub** (fam)) advertisement, advert (GB), ad (colloq)
(c) publicity; **faire une mauvaise** ~ **à qn/qch** to give sb/sth a bad press
■ ~ **comparative** knocking copy (colloq); ~ **mensongère** misleading advertising
❧ **publier** /pyblije/ [2] *vtr* to publish
publiquement /pyblikmɑ̃/ *adv* publicly
puce /pys/ *nf* (a) flea
(b) (silicon) chip; ~ **à mémoire** memory chip
IDIOMS ça m'a mis la ~ **à l'oreille** that set me thinking; **secouer les** ~ **à qn** (fam) to bawl sb out (colloq)

puceau, *pl* ~**x** /pyso/ *adj m* (fam) **il est encore** ~ he's still a virgin
pucelle /pysɛl/ *adj f* (fam) **être** ~ to be a virgin
puceron /pysʀɔ̃/ *nm* aphid
pudeur /pydœʀ/ *nf* (a) sense of modesty; **sans** ~ shamelessly
(b) decency; sense of propriety
pudibond, ~**e** /pydibɔ̃, ɔ̃d/ *adj* prudish
pudique /pydik/ *adj* (a) modest
(b) discreet
pudiquement /pydikmɑ̃/ *adv*
(a) modestly
(b) discreetly
puer /pɥe/ [1] **1** *vtr* to stink of
2 *vi* to stink; **il puait des pieds** his feet stank
puéricultrice /pɥeʀikyltʀis/ *nf* pediatric nurse
puériculture /pɥeʀikyltyʀ/ *nf* childcare
puéril, ~**e** /pɥeʀil/ *adj* childish; puerile
❧ **puis** /pɥi/ *adv* (a) then; **des poires et** ~ **des pêches** pears and peaches; **et** ~ **quoi encore!** (fam) what next?
(b) **il va être en colère? et** ~ (**après**)? (fam) so what if he's angry!
puisard /pɥizaʀ/ *nm* soakaway (GB), sink hole (US)
puiser /pɥize/ [1] *vtr* ~ **qch dans qch** to draw sth from sth
❧ **puisque**, (**puisqu'** *before vowel or mute h*) /pɥisk(ə)/ *conj* since; ~ **c'est comme ça, je m'en vais** if that's how it is, I'm off
❧ **puissance** /pɥisɑ̃s/ *nf* (a) power; **la** ~ **militaire** military strength *or* might
(b) (country) power; **une grande** ~ a superpower
(c) (of light) intensity; (of sound) volume
(d) (in algebra) power; **dix** ~ **trois** ten to the power (of) three
❧ **puissant**, ~**e** /pɥisɑ̃, ɑ̃t/ **1** *adj* powerful; strong
2 **puissants** *nm pl* **les** ~**s** the powerful
puits /pɥi/ *nm* (a) well; ~ **de pétrole** oil well
(b) shaft
■ ~ **de science** fount of knowledge
❧ **pull** /pyl/ *nm* (fam) sweater
pull-over, *pl* ~**s** /pylɔvɛʀ/ *nm* sweater
pullulement /pylylmɑ̃/ *nm* (a) proliferation
(b) multitude
pulluler /pylyle/ [1] *vi* (a) to proliferate
(b) **les touristes pullulent dans la région** the area is swarming with tourists
pulmonaire /pylmɔnɛʀ/ *adj* ‹*disease*› lung; ‹*artery*› pulmonary
pulpe /pylp/ *nf* (of fruit) pulp; (of potato) flesh
pulpeux, -euse /pylpø, øz/ *adj* ‹*body, lips*› luscious; ‹*fruit*› fleshy
pulsation /pylsasjɔ̃/ *nf* beat; ~**s cardiaques** heartbeat; heartbeats

---

❧ indicates a very frequent word

pulsion /pylsjɔ̃/ *nf* impulse, urge
pulvérisation /pylveʀizasjɔ̃/ *nf* (a) (liquid) spraying
(b) (of solid) pulverization (GB)
pulvériser /pylveʀize/ [1] *vtr* (a) to spray
(b) to pulverize
(c) to shatter (colloq) ‹record›
puma /pyma/ *nm* puma
punaise /pynɛz/ *nf* (a) drawing pin (GB), thumbtack (US)
(b) (Zool) bug
punaiser /pynɛze/ [1] *vtr* (fam) to pin *or* tack (US) [sth] up
punch¹ /pɔ̃ʃ/ *nm* (drink) punch
punch² /pœnʃ/ *nm* (a) punch
(b) energy; avoir du ∼ ‹slogan› to be punchy (colloq); ‹person› to have drive
punching-ball, *pl* ∼s /pœnʃiŋbol/ *nm* punchball (GB), punching bag (US)
punir /pyniʀ/ [3] *vtr* to punish
punitif, -ive /pynitif, iv/ *adj* punitive
punition /pynisjɔ̃/ *nf* (a) punishment
(b) il n'a pas fait sa ∼ he hasn't done the task he was given as punishment
pupille¹ /pypij/ *nmf* ward; ∼ de l'État child in care; ∼ de la Nation war orphan
pupille² /pypij/ *nf* (of eye) pupil
pupitre /pypitʀ/ *nm* (a) control panel; console
(b) music stand; music rest
(c) desk
(d) lectern
pupitreur, -euse /pypitʀœʀ, øz/ *nm,f* computer operator
⚹ **pur, ∼e** /pyʀ/ ① *adj* (a) (gen) pure; ‹diamond› flawless; ‹voice, sky› clear
(b) ‹truth› pure; ‹coincidence, madness› sheer; en ∼e perte to no avail; c'est de la paresse ∼e et simple it's laziness, pure and simple; ∼ et dur hardline
(c) ‹tradition› true; un ∼ produit de a typical product of; à l'état ∼ ‹genius› sheer
② *nm,f* virtuous person
purée /pyʀe/ *nf* purée; ∼ (de pommes de terre) mashed potatoes
∎ ∼ de pois pea souper (GB), fog
purement /pyʀmɑ̃/ *adv* purely
pureté /pyʀte/ *nf* purity

purgatif, -ive /pyʀgatif, iv/ *adj* purgative
purgatoire /pyʀgatwaʀ/ *nm* le ∼ purgatory
purge /pyʀʒ/ *nf* (a) purgative
(b) purge
purger /pyʀʒe/ [13] *vtr* (a) (Med) to purge
(b) to bleed ‹radiator›; to drain ‹pipe›; to purify ‹metal›
(c) (Law) to serve ‹sentence›
purificateur /pyʀifikatœʀ/ *nm* ∼ d'atmosphère *or* d'air air purifier
purification /pyʀifikasjɔ̃/ *nf* purification
purifier /pyʀifje/ [2] *vtr* to purify; to cleanse
purin /pyʀɛ̃/ *nm* slurry
puriste /pyʀist/ *nmf* purist
puritain, ∼e /pyʀitɛ̃, ɛn/ ① *adj* puritanical; Puritan
② *nm,f* puritan; Puritan
pur-sang /pyʀsɑ̃/ *nm inv* thoroughbred
pus /py/ *nm inv* pus
pustule /pystyl/ *nf* pustule
putois /pytwa/ *nm inv* (a) polecat
(b) skunk (fur)
putréfaction /pytʀefaksjɔ̃/ *nf* putrefaction; en état de ∼ decomposing
putsch /putʃ/ *nm* putsch
putt /pœt/ *nm* putt
putter /pœte/ *vtr* to putt
puzzle /pœzl, pyzl/ *nm* jigsaw puzzle
PV /peve/ *nm* (fam) (*abbr* = **procès-verbal**) fine; parking ticket; speeding ticket
PVC /pevese/ *nm* (*abbr* = **chlorure de polyvinyle**) PVC
pygmée /pigme/ *nmf* pygmy
pyjama /piʒama/ *nm* (pair of) pyjamas (GB), (pair of) pajamas (US)
pylône /pilon/ *nm* pylon; (for radio, TV transmitter) mast; (of bridge) tower
pyramide /piʀamid/ *nf* pyramid
pyrénéen, -éenne /piʀeneɛ̃, ɛn/ *adj* Pyrenean
pyrex® /piʀɛks/ *nm inv* Pyrex®
pyrogravure /piʀogʀavyʀ/ *nf* pokerwork
pyromane /piʀɔman/ *nmf* pyromaniac; (Law) arsonist
python /pitɔ̃/ *nm* python

Qq

q, Q /ky/ *nm inv* q, Q

qcm /kyseɛm/ *nm* (*abbr* = **questionnaire à choix multiple**) multiple-choice questionnaire, mcq

QG /kyʒe/ *nm: abbr* ▶ QUARTIER

QI /kyi/ *nm: abbr* ▶ QUOTIENT

qu' ▶ QUE

quadragénaire /kwadʀaʒenɛʀ/ *nmf* forty-year-old

quadrature /kwadʀatyʀ/ *nf* quadrature; **c'est la ~ du cercle** it's like squaring the circle

quadriennal, **~e**, *mpl* **-aux** / kwadʀijɛnal, o/ *adj* (a) ‹plan› four-year (b) quadrennial

quadrillage /kadʀijaʒ/ *nm* cross-ruling

quadrillé, **~e** /kadʀije/ *adj* ‹paper› squared

quadriller /kadʀije/ [1] *vtr* (a) ‹police› to spread one's net over
(b) to cross-rule ‹paper›

quadrimoteur /k(w)adʀimɔtœʀ/ *nm* four-engined plane

quadrupède /k(w)adʀypɛd/ *adj, nm* quadruped

quadruple /k(w)adʀypl/ *nm* **le ~ de cette quantité** four times this amount

quadruplé, **~e** /k(w)adʀyple/ *nm,f* quadruplet, quad

quai /kɛ/ *nm* (a) quay; **le navire est à ~** the ship has docked
(b) (of river) bank
(c) (station) platform
■ **~ d'embarquement** loading dock; **Quai des Orfèvres** *criminal investigation department of the French police force*; **Quai d'Orsay** French Foreign Office

qualificatif, **-ive** /kalifikatif, iv/ **1** *adj* qualifying
2 *nm* (a) (in grammar) qualifier
(b) term, word

qualification /kalifikasjɔ̃/ *nf*
(a) qualification
(b) skills; **sans ~** unskilled

qualifié, **~e** /kalifje/ *adj* ‹staff, labour› skilled; qualified

qualifier /kalifje/ [2] **1** *vtr* (a) to describe
(b) to qualify
2 se qualifier *v refl* (+ *v être*) (Sport) to qualify

qualitatif, **-ive** /kalitatif, iv/ *adj* qualitative

⚜ **qualité** /kalite/ *nf* (a) quality; **de première ~** of the highest quality; **avoir beaucoup de ~s** to have many qualities
(b) **en (sa) ~ de représentant** in his/her capacity as a representative; **nom, prénom et ~** surname, first name and occupation

⚜ **quand** /kɑ̃, kɑ̃t/ **1** *conj* (a) when; **~ il arrivera, vous lui annoncerez la nouvelle** when he gets here, you can tell him the news; **~ je pense que ma fille va avoir dix ans!** to think that my daughter's almost ten!; **~ je vous le disais!** I told you so!
(b) whenever; **~ il pleut plus de trois jours la cave est inondée** whenever it rains for more than three days, the cellar floods
(c) even if; **~ (bien même) la terre s'écroulerait, il continuerait à dormir** he'd sleep through an earthquake
2 *adv* when; **de ~ date votre dernière réunion?** when was your last meeting?; **depuis ~ habitez-vous ici?** how long have you been living here?; **à~ la semaine de 30 heures?** (fam) when will we get a 30-hour working week?
3 quand même *phr* still; **ils ne veulent pas de moi, mais j'irai ~ même!** they don't want me, but I'm still going!; **~ même, tu exagères!** (fam) come on, that's going too far!

⚜ **quant**: **quant à** /kɑ̃ta/ *phr* (a) as for; **la France, ~ à elle,...** as for France, it...
(b) about, concerning

quantifier /kɑ̃tifje/ [2] *vtr* to quantify

quantitatif, **-ive** /kɑ̃titatif, iv/ *adj* quantitative

⚜ **quantité** /kɑ̃tite/ *nf* (a) quantity, amount
(b) **des ~s de** scores of ‹people›; a lot of ‹things›; **du pain/vin en ~** plenty of bread/wine

quarantaine /kaʀɑ̃tɛn/ *nf* (a) **une ~** about forty (b) **être en ~** to be in quarantine; to be ostracized

quarante /kaʀɑ̃t/ *adj inv, pron, nm inv* forty

quarante-cinq /kaʀɑ̃tsɛ̃k/ *adj inv, pron, nm inv* forty-five
■ **~ tours** single

quarantième /kaʀɑ̃tjɛm/ *adj* fortieth

⚜ **quart** /kaʀ/ *nm* (a) quarter; **un ~ d'heure** a quarter of an hour; **les trois ~s du temps** (fam) most of the time
(b) quarter-litre (GB) bottle; quarter-litre (GB) pitcher
(c) (Naut) **être de ~** to be on watch
■ **~ de cercle** quadrant; **~ de tour** 90° turn; **faire qch au ~ de tour** (fam) to do sth immediately

---

⚜ indicates a very frequent word

⚲ quartier /kaʀtje/ *nm* **(a)** area, district; **de ~** ‹cinema, grocer› local **(b)** quarter; **un ~ de pommes** a slice of apple; **un ~ d'orange** an orange segment **(c)** (of moon) quarter **(d)** (Mil) **~s** quarters; **avoir ~ libre** to be off duty; to have time off ■ **~ général, QG** headquarters, HQ **IDIOM ne pas faire de ~** to show no mercy

quart-monde /kaʀmɔd/ *nm inv* underclass

quartz /kwaʀts/ *nm* quartz

quasi /kazi/ ⟦1⟧ *adv* almost ⟦2⟧ **quasi-** (*combining form*) **~-indifférence** virtual indifference; **la ~-totalité de** almost all of; **à la ~-unanimité** almost unanimously

quasiment /kazimã/ *adv* (fam) practically

quaternaire /kwatɛʀnɛʀ/ *adj, nm* Quaternary

quatorze /katɔʀz/ *adj inv, pron, nm inv* fourteen **IDIOM chercher midi à ~ heures** (fam) to complicate matters

quatorzième /katɔʀzjɛm/ *adj* fourteenth

quatrain /katʀɛ̃/ *nm* quatrain

⚲ quatre /katʀ/ *adj inv, pron, nm inv* four **IDIOMS faire les ~ volontés de qn** to give in to sb's every whim; **être tiré à ~ épingles** to be dressed up to the nines (colloq); **ne pas y aller par ~ chemins** not to beat about the bush; **je vais leur parler entre ~ yeux** I'm going to talk to them face to face; **monter un escalier ~ à ~** to go up the stairs four at a time; **être entre ~ planches** (fam) to be six feet under

quatre-heures /katʀœʀ/ *nm inv* afternoon snack (*for children*)

quatre-quarts /kat(ʀə)kaʀ/ *nm inv* pound cake

quatre-vingt(s) /katʀəvɛ̃/ *adj, pron, nm* eighty

quatre-vingt-dix /katʀəvɛ̃dis/ *adj inv, pron, nm inv* ninety

quatre-vingt-dixième /katʀəvɛ̃dizjɛm/ *adj* ninetieth

quatre-vingtième /katʀəvɛ̃tjɛm/ *adj* eightieth

quatrième /katʀijɛm/ ⟦1⟧ *adj* fourth ⟦2⟧ *nf* **(a)** (Sch) *third year of secondary school, age 13–14* **(b)** (Aut) fourth (gear) ■ **le ~ âge** very old people **IDIOM en ~ vitesse** (fam) in double quick time (colloq)

quatuor /kwatɥɔʀ/ *nm* quartet

⚲ que (**qu'** *before vowel or mute h*) /kə/ ⟦1⟧ *conj* **(a)** that; **je pense qu'il a raison** I think he's right; **je veux ~ tu m'accompagnes** I want you to come with me **(b)** so (that); **approche, ~ je te regarde** come closer so I can look at you **(c)** whether; **~ cela vous plaise ou non** whether you like it or not **(d)** **si vous venez et ~ vous ayez le temps** if you come and (if you) have the time **(e)** **il n'était pas sitôt parti qu'elle appela la police** no sooner had he left than she called the police **(f)** **~ tout le monde sorte!** everyone must leave!; **~ ceux qui n'ont pas compris le disent** let anyone who hasn't understood say so; **qu'il crève!** (pop) let him rot! (colloq) **(g)** than; as; **plus gros ~ moi** fatter than me; **aussi grand ~ mon frère** as tall as my brother ⟦2⟧ *pron* what; **~ dire?** what can you say?; **je ne sais pas ce qu'il a dit** I don't know what he said; **qu'est-ce que c'est que ça?** what's that? ⟦3⟧ *rel pron* that; who(m); which; **je n'aime pas la voiture ~ tu as achetée** I don't like the car (that) you've bought ⟦4⟧ *adv* **~ c'est joli** it's so pretty; **~ de monde** what a lot of people

Québec /kebɛk/ ⟦1⟧ *pr nm* **le ~** Quebec ⟦2⟧ *pr n* Quebec

québécols, ~e /kebekwa, az/ *adj* of Quebec

Québécois, ~e /kebekwa, az/ *nm,f* Quebecois, Quebecker

⚲ quel, quelle /kɛl/ ⟦1⟧ *det* who; what; which; **je me demande quelle est la meilleure solution** I wonder what the best solution is; **de ces deux médicaments, ~ est le plus efficace?** which of these two medicines is more effective? ⟦2⟧ *adj* **(a)** what; which; **quelle heure est-il?** what time is it?; **dans ~ tlroir l'as-tu mis?** which drawer did you put it in?; **~ âge as-tu?** how old are you? **(b)** what; how; **quelle coïncidence!** what a coincidence! **(c)** **quelle que soit la route que l'on prenne** whatever *or* whichever road we take; **~ que soit le vainqueur** whoever the winner may be

quelconque /kɛlkɔk/ ⟦1⟧ *adj* ‹person› ordinary; ordinary-looking; ‹novel, actor› poor; ‹restaurant› second-rate; ‹place› characterless ⟦2⟧ *adj* any; **si pour une raison ~** if for some reason or other; **si le livre avait un intérêt ~** if the book was in any way interesting

quelle ▶ QUEL

⚲ quelque /kɛlk/ ⟦1⟧ *quantif* some; a few; any; **depuis ~ temps** for some time; **je voudrais ajouter ~s mots** I'd like to add a few words; **ça dure trois heures et ~** it lasts over three hours; **si pour ~ raison que ce soit** if for whatever reason ⟦2⟧ *adv* **(a)** **les ~ deux mille spectateurs** the two thousand odd spectators **(b)** however; **~ admirable que soit son attitude** however admirable his/her attitude may be   ⋯⟩

③ **quelque chose** *pron* something; anything; **il y a ~ chose qui ne va pas** something's wrong; **si ~ chose leur arrive** if anything should happen to them; **il a ~ chose de son grand-père** he's got a look of his grandfather about him; **ça me dit ~ chose** it rings a bell

④ **quelque part** *phr* somewhere; anywhere

⑤ **quelque peu** *phr* somewhat

✧ **quelquefois** /kɛlkəfwɑ/ *adv* sometimes

quelques-uns, quelques-unes /kɛlkəzœ̃, yn/ *pron* some, a few

quelqu'un /kɛlkœ̃/ *pron* someone, somebody; anyone, anybody; **~ d'autre** someone else; **c'est ~ de compétent** he/she is competent

quémander /kemɑ̃de/ [1] *vtr* to beg

qu'en-dira-t-on /kɑ̃diʁatɔ̃/ *nm inv* gossip

quenelle /kənɛl/ *nf*: dumpling made of flour and egg, flavoured with meat or fish

quenotte /kənɔt/ *nf* (fam) toothy-peg (colloq), tooth

quenouille /kənuj/ *nf* distaff

querelle /kəʁɛl/ *nf* (a) quarrel; **chercher ~ à qn** to pick a quarrel with sb
(b) dispute

quereller: se quereller /kəʁele/ [1] *v refl* (+ *v être*) to quarrel

✧ **question** /kɛstjɔ̃/ *nf* (a) question; **je ne me suis jamais posé la ~** I've never really thought about it; **pose-leur la ~** ask them
(b) matter, question; issue; **~ d'habitude!** it's a matter of habit; **en ~** in question; at issue; **(re)mettre en ~** to reappraise; to reassess; **se remettre en ~** to take a new look at oneself; **la ~ n'est pas là** that's not the point; **il est ~ d'elle dans l'article** she's mentioned in the article; **il n'est pas ~ que tu partes** you can't possibly leave; **pas ~!** no way! (colloq)
(c) (fam) **~ santé, ça va** where health is concerned, things are OK

questionnaire /kɛstjɔnɛʁ/ *nm* questionnaire

questionner /kɛstjɔne/ [1] *vtr* to question

quête /kɛt/ *nf* (a) collection; **faire la ~** to take the collection; to pass the hat round; to collect for charity
(b) search; **la ~ du Graal** the quest for the Holy Grail

quêter /kete/ [1] *vi* to take the collection; **~ pour une œuvre** to collect for a charity

quetsche /kwɛtʃ/ *nf* (sweet purple) plum

✧ **queue** /kø/ *nf* (a) tail
(b) (of flower) stem; (of apple) stalk (GB), stem (US)
(c) (of pot) handle
(d) (Sport) cue
(e) (of procession) tail(-end); (of train) rear, back; **ils arrivent en ~ (de peloton) des**

grandes entreprises they come at the bottom of the league table of companies
(f) faire la ~ to queue (up) (GB), to stand in a queue (GB), to stand in line (US)
IDIOMS une histoire sans ~ ni tête (fam) a cock and bull story; **la ~ basse** with one's tail between one's legs; **il n'y en avait pas la ~ d'un(e)** (fam) there were none to be seen; **faire une ~ de poisson à qn** to cut in front of sb; **finir en ~ de poisson** to fizzle out

queue-de-cheval, *pl* **queues-de-cheval** /kødʃəval/ *nf* ponytail

queue-de-pie, *pl* **queues-de-pie** /kødpi/ *nf* (fam) tails, tailcoat

queux /kø/ *nm inv* (dated) **maître ~** chef

✧ **qui** /ki/ ① *pron* who; whom; **~ veut-elle voir?** who does she want to speak to?
② *rel pron* (a) who; that; which; **est-ce vous ~ venez d'appeler?** was it you who called just now?; **ce ~ me plaît chez lui** what I like about him
(b) **~ que vous soyez** whoever you are; **je n'ai jamais frappé ~ que ce soit** I've never hit anybody

quiche /kiʃ/ *nf* quiche, flan

quiconque /kikɔ̃k/ ① *rel pron* whoever, anyone who
② *pron* anyone, anybody

quiétude /kjetyd/ *nf* tranquillity

quignon /kiɲɔ̃/ *nm* crusty end (of a loaf)

quille /kij/ *nf* (a) skittle
(b) (Naut) keel
IDIOM être reçu comme un chien dans un jeu de ~s (fam) to be given a very unfriendly welcome

quincaillerie /kɛ̃kajʁi/ *nf* (a) hardware shop (GB) *or* store (US)
(b) hardware
(c) hardware business

quinconce /kɛ̃kɔ̃s/ *nm* **en ~** in staggered rows

quinquagénaire /kɛ̃kaʒenɛʁ/ *nmf* fifty-year-old

quinquennal, ~e, *mpl* -aux /kɛ̃kenal, o/ *adj* (a) *φplan* five-year
(b) five-yearly

quintal, *pl* **-aux** /kɛ̃tal, o/ *nm* quintal

quinte /kɛ̃t/ *nf* (a) (Mus) fifth
(b) **une ~ (de toux)** a coughing fit

quintette /kɛ̃tɛt/ *nm* quintet

quintuple /kɛ̃typl/ *nm* **le ~ de cette quantité** five times the amount

quintuplé, ~e /kɛ̃typle/ *nm,f* quintuplet, quin (GB), quint (US)

quinzaine /kɛ̃zɛn/ *nf* (a) fortnight (GB), two weeks; **sous ~** within 2 weeks
(b) **une ~** about fifteen

✧ **quinze** /kɛ̃z/ *adj inv, pron, nm inv* fifteen

quinzième /kɛ̃zjɛm/ *adj* fifteenth

quiproquo /kipʁoko/ *nm* misunderstanding

✧ indicates a very frequent word

quittance /kitãs/ *nf* (a) receipt
(b) bill

quitte /kit/ 1 *adj* (a) **nous sommes ~s, je suis ~ avec lui** we're quits
(b) **en être ~ pour la peur/un rhume** to get off with a fright/a cold
2 **quitte à** *phr* **~ à aller à Londres, autant que ce soit pour quelques jours** if you're going to London anyway, you might as well go for a few days
■ **~ ou double** double or quits

✧ **quitter** /kite/ [1] 1 *vtr* (a) to leave ‹place, person, road›
(b) to leave ‹job, organization›; **~ la scène** to give up acting; **il ne l'a pas quittée des yeux de tout le repas** he didn't take his eyes off her throughout the meal; **ne quittez pas** hold the line
(c) ‹company› to move from ‹street›; to move out of ‹building›
(d) **un grand homme nous a quittés** a great man has passed away
(e) to take off ‹garment, hat›
2 **se quitter** *v refl* (+ *v être*) to part; **ils ne se quittent plus** they're inseparable now

qui-vive /kiviv/ *nm inv* **être sur le ~** to be on the alert

✧ **quoi** /kwɑ/ 1 *pron* (a) what; **à ~ penses-tu?** what are you thinking about?; **à ~ bon recommencer?** what's the point of starting again?
(b) **~ qu'elle puisse en dire** whatever she may say; **~ qu'il en soit** be that as it may
2 *rel pron* **il n'y a rien sur ~ vous puissiez fonder vos accusations** there's nothing on which to base your accusations; **à ~ il a répondu** to which he replied; **après ~ ils sont partis** after which they left; **(il n'y a) pas de ~!** my pleasure; **il n'y a pas de ~ se fâcher** there's no reason to get angry; **il n'a (même) pas de ~ s'acheter un livre** he hasn't (even) got enough money to buy a book

✧ **quoique** (**quoiqu'** *before vowel or mute h*) /kwak(ə)/ *conj* although, though; **nous sommes mieux ici qu'à Paris, ~** we're better off here than in Paris, but then (again)

quota /kɔta/ *nm* quota (**sur** on)

quote-part, *pl* **quotes-parts** /kɔtpaʀ/ *nf* share

✧ **quotidien, -ienne** /kɔtidjɛ̃, ɛn/ 1 *adj*
(a) daily
(b) everyday
2 *nm* (a) daily (paper)
(b) everyday life

quotidiennement /kɔtidjɛnmɑ̃/ *adv* every day, daily

quotient /kɔsjɑ̃/ *nm* quotient
■ **~ intellectuel, QI** intelligence quotient, IQ

Rr

r, R /ɛʀ/ *nm inv* r, R

rab /ʀab/ *nm* (fam) (a) extra; **faire du ~** to do extra hours
(b) **demander du ~** to ask for seconds

rabâcher /ʀabɑʃe/ [1] 1 *vtr* to keep repeating
2 *vi* to keep harping on

rabais /ʀabɛ/ *nm inv* discount

rabaisser /ʀabese/ [1] 1 *vtr* to belittle
2 **se rabaisser** *v refl* (+ *v être*) to demean oneself

rabat /ʀaba/ *nm* (of bag, table, pocket) flap

rabat-joie /ʀabaʒwa/ *adj inv* **être ~** to be a killjoy

rabattre /ʀabatʀ/ [61] 1 *vtr* (a) ‹person› to shut ‹lid›; to put *or* fold up ‹foldaway seat, tray›
(b) to turn [sth] down ‹collar, sheet›
(c) ‹player› to smash ‹ball›
(d) **~ le gibier** to beat the undergrowth for game
2 **se rabattre** *v refl* (+ *v être*) (a) ‹lid› to shut; ‹leaf of table› to fold up
(b) ‹driver, vehicle› to pull back in
(c) **se ~ sur** to make do with

rabbin /ʀabɛ̃/ *nm* rabbi; **grand ~** chief rabbi

râblé, ~e /ʀable/ *adj* (a) ‹animal› sturdy
(b) ‹person› stocky

rabot /ʀabo/ *nm* (tool) plane

raboter /ʀabote/ [1] *vtr* to plane

rabougri, ~e /ʀabugʀi/ *adj* ‹tree› stunted

rabrouer /ʀabʀue/ [1] *vtr* to snub

racaille /ʀakaj/ *nf* scum

raccommoder /ʀakɔmɔde/ [1] *vtr* (a) to darn ‹socks›
(b) (fam) to reconcile ‹people›

raccompagner /ʀakɔ̃paɲe/ [1] *vtr* **~ qn chez lui** to walk/to drive sb (back) home

raccord /ʀakɔʀ/ *nm* (a) (in wallpaper) join
(b) (in painting) touch-up
(c) (in film) link shot

raccordement /ʀakɔʀdəmɑ̃/ *nm* link road

raccorder /ʀakɔʀde/ [1] *vtr* to connect

raccourci /ʀakuʀsi/ *nm* (road) shortcut

raccourcir /ʀakuʀsiʀ/ [3] 1 *vtr* (a) (gen) to shorten ⋯⟩

(b) to cut ‹text, speech›
2 *vi* ‹days› to get shorter, to draw in
IDIOM tomber sur qn à bras raccourcis (fam)
to lay into sb
raccrocher /ʀakʀɔʃe/ [1] 1 *vtr* to hang
[sth] back up
2 *vi* to hang up
3 **se raccrocher** *v refl* (+ *v être*) **se ~**
à to grab hold of ‹raib›; (figurative) to cling to
‹person, excuse›
◦ **race** /ʀas/ *nf* **(a)** race
(b) (Zool) breed; **chien de ~** pedigree (dog)
racheter /ʀaʃte/ [18] 1 *vtr* **(a)** to buy
[sth] back
(b) to buy some more ‹wine›
(c) to buy new ‹sheets›
(d) to buy out ‹company, factory›; **je rachète**
votre voiture 1 000 euros I'll buy your car off
you for 1,000 euros
(e) to redeem ‹sinner›
2 **se racheter** *v refl* (+ *v être*) to redeem
oneself
rachitique /ʀaʃitik/ *adj* ‹animal, plant,
person› scrawny
rachitisme /ʀaʃitism/ *nm* rickets
racial, **~e**, *mpl* **-iaux** /ʀasjal, o/ *adj* racial;
émeutes ~es race riots
racine /ʀasin/ *nf* root
racisme /ʀasism/ *nm* racism
raciste /ʀasist/ *adj, nmf* racist
racket /ʀakɛt/ *nm* extortion racket;
racketeering
raclée /ʀɑkle/ *nf* (fam) hiding (colloq)
racler /ʀɑkle/ [1] 1 *vtr* **(a)** to scrape [sth]
clean ‹plate›
(b) to scrape off ‹rust›
(c) to scrape against
2 **se racler** *v refl* (+ *v être*) **se ~ la gorge**
to clear one's throat
raclette /ʀɑklɛt/ *nf* **(a)** raclette (*Swiss
cheese dish*)
(b) scraper
racolage /ʀakɔlaʒ/ *nm* touting (**de** for);
soliciting (**de** for)
racoler /ʀakɔle/ [1] *vtr* ‹prostitute› to solicit
racontar /ʀakɔ̃taʀ/ *nm* (fam) **des ~s** idle
gossip
◦ **raconter** /ʀakɔ̃te/ [1] *vtr* to tell ‹story›; to
describe ‹incident›; **~ qch à qn** to tell sb sth;
qu'est-ce que tu racontes? what are you
talking about?
racornir /ʀakɔʀniʀ/ [3] *vtr*, **se racornir**
v refl (+ *v être*) **(a)** to harden
(b) to shrivel (up)
radar /ʀadaʀ/ *nm* radar; **~ automatique**
speed camera
rade /ʀad/ *nf* harbour (GB); **rester en ~**
(fam) ‹person› to be left stranded
radeau, *pl* **~x** /ʀado/ *nm* raft
radiateur /ʀadjatœʀ/ *nm* radiator; **~**
électrique electric heater

radiation /ʀadjasjɔ̃/ *nf* radiation
radical, **~e**, *mpl* **-aux** /ʀadikal, o/ *adj*,
nm,f radical
radicalement /ʀadikalmɑ̃/ *adv* radically;
completely
radier /ʀadje/ [2] *vtr* **~ un médecin** to
strike off a doctor (GB), to take away a
doctor's license (US); **~ un avocat** to disbar
a lawyer
radieux, **-ieuse** /ʀadjø, øz/ *adj* **(a)** ‹sun›
dazzling
(b) ‹weather› glorious
(c) ‹face, smile› radiant; ‹person› radiant
with joy
radin, **~e** /ʀadɛ̃, in/ *adj* (fam) stingy (colloq)
radinerie /ʀadinʀi/ *nf* (fam) stinginess
(colloq)
radio[1] /ʀadjo/ 1 *adj inv* ‹contact, signal›
radio
2 *nm* radio operator
◦ **radio**[2] /ʀadjo/ *nf* **(a)** radio
(b) X-ray
radioactivité /ʀadjoaktivite/ *nf*
radioactivity
radiocassette /ʀadjokasɛt/ *nm* radio
cassette player
radio-crochet /ʀadjokʀɔʃɛ/ *nm*: *singing
competition on the radio*
radiodiffuser /ʀadjodifyze/ [1] *vtr* to
broadcast
radiographie /ʀadjɔgʀafi/ *nf*
(a) radiography
(b) X-ray (photograph)
radiologue /ʀadjɔlɔg/ *nmf* radiologist
radiophonique /ʀadjofɔnik/ *adj* radio
radio-réveil, *pl* **radios-réveils**
/ʀadjoʀevɛj/ *nm* clock radio
radioscopie /ʀadjɔskɔpi/ *nf* fluoroscopy
radiothérapie /ʀadjoteʀapi/ *nf*
radiotherapy
radis /ʀadi/ *nm inv* radish; **je n'ai plus un ~**
(fam) I haven't got a penny
radoter /ʀadɔte/ [1] *vi* **(a)** to talk nonsense
(b) to repeat oneself
radoucir: **se radoucir** /ʀadusiʀ/ [3] *v
refl* (+ *v être*) ‹person› to soften up; ‹weather›
to turn milder
radoucissement /ʀadusismɑ̃/ *nm* **la**
météo annonce un ~ the forecast is for
milder weather
rafale /ʀafal/ *nf* **(a)** (of wind, rain) gust; (of
snow) flurry
(b) (of gunfire) burst
raffermir /ʀafɛʀmiʀ/ [3] *vtr* **(a)** to tone
‹skin›; to tone up ‹muscles›
(b) to strengthen ‹position›; to steady
‹market›
raffinage /ʀafinaʒ/ *nm* refining
raffiné, **~e** /ʀafine/ *adj* refined; ‹food›
sophisticated

◦ indicates a very frequent word

r

raffinement /ʀafinmɑ̃/ *nm* **(a)** refinement
(b) elegance

raffiner /ʀafine/ [1] *vtr* to refine

raffinerie /ʀafinʀi/ *nf* refinery; ~ **de pétrole** oil refinery

raffoler /ʀafɔle/ [1] *v+prep* ~ **de** to be crazy about (colloq)

raffut /ʀafy/ *nm* (fam) **(a)** racket (colloq)
(b) stink (colloq), row

rafiot /ʀafjo/ *nm* (fam) boat, (old) tub (colloq)

rafistoler /ʀafistɔle/ [1] *vtr* (fam) to patch up

rafle /ʀɑfl/ *nf* **(a)** raid
(b) roundup

rafler /ʀɑfle/ [1] *vtr* (fam) **(a)** to make off with, to swipe (colloq)
(b) to walk off with ‹medal, reward›

rafraîchir /ʀafʀɛʃiʀ/ [3] **1** *vtr* ‹rain› to cool ‹atmosphere›; **le thé glacé te rafraîchira** the iced tea will cool you down
2 se rafraîchir *v refl* (+ *v être*) ‹weather› to get cooler; ‹person› to refresh oneself
IDIOM ~ **la mémoire de qn** (fam) to refresh sb's memory

rafraîchissant, ~e /ʀafʀɛʃisɑ̃, ɑ̃t/ *adj* refreshing

rafraîchissement /ʀafʀɛʃismɑ̃/ *nm* refreshment

ragaillardir /ʀagajaʀdiʀ/ [3] *vtr* to cheer [sb] up

rage /ʀaʒ/ *nf* **(a)** rabies
(b) rage; **être fou de** ~ to be in a mad rage; **faire** ~ ‹disease› to be rife; ‹epidemic, fire› to rage
■ ~ **de dents** raging toothache

rageant, ~e /ʀaʒɑ̃, ɑ̃t/ *adj* (fam) infuriating

rageusement /ʀaʒøzmɑ̃/ *adv* furiously; angrily

ragot /ʀago/ *nm* (fam) malicious gossip

ragoût /ʀagu/ *nm* stew, ragout

rai /ʀɛ/ *nm* ~ **de lumière** ray of light

raï /ʀaj/ *nm*: *music from the Maghreb with Western influences*

raid /ʀɛd/ *nm* **(a)** (Mil) raid
(b) (Sport) trek

raide /ʀɛd/ *adj* **(a)** (gen) stiff; ‹hair› straight; ‹rope› taut
(b) steep
(c) (fam) **je trouve ça un peu** ~ that's a bit steep
IDIOMS **être** ~ **comme un piquet** to be stiff as a ramrod; **tomber** ~ to be flabbergasted

raideur /ʀɛdœʀ/ *nf* **(a)** stiffness
(b) steepness

raidir /ʀediʀ/ [3] **1** *vtr* to tense ‹arm, body›
2 se raidir *v refl* (+ *v être*) ‹body› to tense up; **se** ~ **contre la douleur** to brace oneself against pain

raie /ʀɛ/ *nf* **(a)** (in hair) parting (GB), part (US)
(b) scratch

(c) (Zool) skate

rail /ʀaj/ *nm* rail, track
■ ~ **de sécurité** crash barrier

raillerie /ʀɑjʀi/ *nf* mockery

rainette /ʀɛnɛt/ *nf* tree frog

rainure /ʀenyʀ/ *nf* groove

raisin /ʀɛzɛ̃/ *nm* grapes; ~**s secs** raisins

⚘ **raison** /ʀɛzɔ̃/ *nf* **(a)** reason; ~ **d'agir** reason for action; **en** ~ **d'une panne** owing to a breakdown; **à plus forte** ~ even more so, especially; **avec** ~ justifiably; **comme de** ~ as one might expect
(b) avoir ~ to be right; **donner** ~ **à qn** to agree with sb
(c) reason; **se rendre à la** ~ to see reason; **ramener qn à la** ~ to bring sb to his/her senses; **se faire une** ~ **de qch** to resign oneself to sth; **plus que de** ~ more than is sensible; **avoir** ~ **de qn/qch** to get the better of sb/sth; **à** ~ **de** at the rate of

raisonnable /ʀɛzɔnabl/ *adj* reasonable; moderate; sensible

raisonné, ~e /ʀɛzɔne/ **1** *pp* ▶ RAISONNER
2 *pp adj* **(a)** ‹attitude› cautious; ‹decision› carefully thought out
(b) ‹enthusiasm› measured

raisonnement /ʀɛzɔnmɑ̃/ *nm* reasoning; **selon le même** ~ by the same token; **il tient le** ~ **suivant** his argument is as follows; **je ne tiens pas le même** ~ I look at it differently

raisonner /ʀɛzɔne/ [1] **1** *vtr* to reason with
2 *vi* to think
3 se raisonner *v refl* (+ *v être*) ‹person› to be more sensible, to pull oneself together

rajeunir /ʀaʒœniʀ/ [3] **1** *vtr* **(a)** to make [sb] look/feel younger
(b) ~ **qn** to make sb out to be younger
(c) to bring *or* inject new blood into
2 *vi* to look/to feel younger

rajeunissement /ʀaʒœnismɑ̃/ *nm*
(a) **nous avons enregistré un** ~ **de la population** we see that the population is getting younger
(b) modernization
(c) updating
(d) rejuvenation

rajouter /ʀaʒute/ [1] *vtr* to add; **en** ~ (fam) to exaggerate

rajuster /ʀaʒyste/ [1] *vtr* to straighten ‹clothing›

râle /ʀɑl/ *nm* **(a)** rale
(b) groan
(c) death rattle

ralenti, ~e /ʀalɑ̃ti/ **1** *pp* ▶ RALENTIR
2 *pp adj* ‹gesture, rhythm, growth› slower
3 *nm* slow motion

ralentir /ʀalɑ̃tiʀ/ [3] *vtr*, *vi*, **se ralentir** *v refl* (+ *v être*) to slow down

ralentissement /ʀalɑ̃tismɑ̃/ *nm*
(a) slowing down ⋯⟶

r

(b) tailback

ralentisseur /ʀalɑ̃tisœʀ/ nm speed ramp

râler /ʀɑle/ [1] vi **(a)** (fam) to moan (colloq); **ça me fait ~** it annoys me
(b) to groan

râleur, -euse /ʀɑlœʀ, øz/ nm,f (fam) moaner (colloq)

ralliement /ʀalimɑ̃/ nm rallying

rallier /ʀalje/ [2] **1** vtr **~ qn à sa cause** to win sb over
2 se rallier v refl (+ v être) **se ~ à** to rally to ‹republicans›; to come round to ‹opinion›

rallonge /ʀalɔ̃ʒ/ nf **(a)** extension cord, extension lead (GB)
(b) (of table) leaf

rallonger /ʀalɔ̃ʒe/ [13] **1** vtr to extend; to lengthen
2 vi **les jours rallongent** the days are drawing out

rallye /ʀali/ nm (car) rally

ramadan /ʀamadɑ̃/ nm Ramadan; **faire le ~** to keep Ramadan

ramage /ʀamaʒ/ **1** nm (of bird) song
2 ramages nm pl foliage pattern

ramassage /ʀamasaʒ/ nm **car de ~** (for employees) works or company bus; (for pupils) school bus

ramassé, ~e /ʀamase/ **1** pp ▶ RAMASSER
2 pp adj **(a)** stocky, squat
(b) être ~ sur soi-même to be hunched up

✓ **ramasser** /ʀamase/ [1] **1** vtr to collect; to pick up; to dig up ‹potatoes›; **se faire ~ dans une rafle** (fam) to get picked up in a (police) raid
2 se ramasser v refl (+ v être) **(a)** to huddle up
(b) (fam) to come a cropper (colloq); **se faire ~ à un examen** to fail an exam

ramassis /ʀamasi/ nm inv (derogatory) (of people) bunch; (of ideas, objects) jumble

rambarde /ʀɑ̃baʀd/ nf guardrail

rame /ʀam/ nf **(a)** oar
(b) (of paper) ream
(c) une ~ de métro a metro train

rameau, pl **~x** /ʀamo/ nm (Bot) branch

✓ **ramener** /ʀamne/ [16] **1** vtr **(a) ~ l'inflation à 5%** to reduce inflation to 5 per cent
(b) to restore ‹order›; **~ qn à la réalité** to bring sb back to reality; **~ qn à la vie** to bring sb round; **~ toujours tout à soi** always to relate everything to oneself
(c) to take [sb/sth] back
(d) to bring back; to return
2 se ramener v refl (+ v être) **se ~ à** to come down to, to boil down to

ramequin /ʀamkɛ̃/ nm ramekin

ramer /ʀame/ [1] vi to row

rameur, -euse /ʀamœʀ, øz/ nm,f rower

rameuter /ʀamøte/ [1] vtr to round up

ramification /ʀamifikasjɔ̃/ nf **(a)** network
(b) ramification

ramifier: se ramifier /ʀamifje/ [2] v refl (+ v être) ‹stem, nerve› to branch; ‹branch› to divide

ramollir /ʀamɔliʀ/ [3] **1** vtr to soften
2 se ramollir v refl (+ v être) **(a)** to become soft
(b) (fam) ‹person› to get soft

ramollissement /ʀamɔlismɑ̃/ nm softening

ramoner /ʀamɔne/ [1] vtr to sweep ‹chimney›

ramoneur /ʀamɔnœʀ/ nm chimney sweep

rampant, ~e /ʀɑ̃pɑ̃, ɑ̃t/ adj **(a)** ‹animal› crawling; ‹plant› creeping
(b) ‹inflation› creeping

rampe /ʀɑ̃p/ nf **(a)** banister; hand-rail
(b) (in theatre) **la ~** the footlights
■ **~ d'accès** (for motorway) sliproad (GB), entrance ramp (US); (of building) ramp

ramper /ʀɑ̃pe/ [1] vi **(a)** to crawl
(b) to creep

ramure /ʀamyʀ/ nf **(a)** (of tree) branches
(b) antlers

rancard /ʀɑ̃kaʀ/ nm (pop) **(a)** (rendezvous) date
(b) (information) tip

rancart /ʀɑ̃kaʀ/ nm (fam) **mettre au ~** to shunt [sb] aside

rance /ʀɑ̃s/ adj rancid

rancœur /ʀɑ̃kœʀ/ nf resentment

rançon /ʀɑ̃sɔ̃/ nf **(a)** ransom
(b) la ~ de la gloire the price of fame

rancune /ʀɑ̃kyn/ nf **(a)** resentment
(b) grudge; **sans ~!** no hard feelings

rancunier, -ière /ʀɑ̃kynje, ɛʀ/ adj **être ~** to be a person who holds grudges

randonnée /ʀɑ̃dɔne/ nf hiking

randonneur, -euse /ʀɑ̃dɔnœʀ, øz/ nm,f hiker, rambler

✓ **rang** /ʀɑ̃/ nm **(a)** row; (in necklace) strand; **se mettre en ~s** ‹children› to get into (a) line
(b) (Mil, figurative) rank; **sortir du ~** to rise or come up through the ranks; **serrer les ~s** to close ranks
(c) (in a hierarchy) rank; **être au 5e ~ mondial des exportateurs** to be the 5th largest exporter in the world; **acteur de second ~** second-rate actor; **des personnes de son ~** people of one's own station

rangé, ~e¹ /ʀɑ̃ʒe/ **1** pp ▶ RANGER¹
2 pp adj ‹life› orderly; ‹person› well-behaved

rangée² /ʀɑ̃ʒe/ nf row

rangement /ʀɑ̃ʒmɑ̃/ nm **(a) c'est un maniaque du ~** he's obsessively tidy
(b) storage space

✓ **ranger¹** /ʀɑ̃ʒe/ [13] **1** vtr **(a)** to put away; **où ranges-tu tes verres?** where do you keep

✓ indicates a very frequent word

the glasses?
(b) to arrange, to put into order; **~ un animal dans les mammifères** to class an animal as a mammal
(c) to tidy
2 **se ranger** *v refl* (+ *v être*) **(a)** to line up
(b) ⟨vehicle, driver⟩ to pull over
(c) se ~ à l'avis de qn to go along with sb
(d) to settle down

ranger² /ʀɑ̃dʒɛʀ/ *nm* **(a)** ranger
(b) heavy-duty boot

ranimer /ʀanime/ [1] *vtr* **(a)** to revive ⟨person⟩
(b) to rekindle ⟨fire, hope⟩; to stir up ⟨quarrel⟩

rapace /ʀapas/ **1** *adj* ⟨person⟩ rapacious
2 *nm* bird of prey

rapacité /ʀapasite/ *nf* **(a)** (of animal) ferocity
(b) (of trader) greed

rapatrié, ~e /ʀapatʀije/ *nm,f* repatriate (de from)

rapatrier /ʀapatʀije/ [2] *vtr* to repatriate

râpe /ʀɑp/ *nf* (Culin) grater

râper /ʀɑpe/ [1] *vtr* to grate ⟨cheese, carrot⟩; **c'est râpé** (figurative) (fam) it's off (colloq)

rapetisser /ʀap(ə)tise/ [1] *vi* to shrink

râpeux, -euse /ʀɑpø, øz/ *adj* rough

raphia /ʀafja/ *nm* raffia

◈ **rapide** /ʀapid/ **1** *adj* quick, rapid; fast
2 *nm* **(a)** rapids; **descendre un ~** to shoot the rapids
(b) (train) express

◈ **rapidement** /ʀapidmɑ̃/ *adv* quickly; fast

rapidité /ʀapidite/ *nf* speed

rapiécer /ʀapjese/ [14] *vtr* to patch

rappel /ʀapɛl/ *nm* **(a)** reminder; **~ à l'ordre** call to order
(b) (lettre de) ~ reminder
(c) back pay
(d) (of ambassador) recall; (of actors) curtain call
(e) (Med) booster

◈ **rappeler** /ʀaple/ [19] **1** *vtr* **(a)** **~ qch à qn** to remind sb of sth; **rappelons-le** let's not forget; **~ qn à l'ordre** to call sb to order
(b) to call [sb] back
(c) (on phone) to call *or* to ring [sb] back
2 **se rappeler** *v refl* (+ *v être*) to remember

rappliquer /ʀaplike/ [1] *vi* (fam) **(a)** to turn up (colloq)
(b) to come back

◈ **rapport** /ʀapɔʀ/ **1** *nm* **(a)** connection, link; **être sans ~ avec, n'avoir aucun ~ avec** to have nothing to do with
(b) **~s** relations; **avoir *or* entretenir de bons ~s avec qn** to be on good terms with sb
(c) être en ~ avec qn to be in touch with sb
(d) sous tous les ~s in every respect
(e) report

(f) return, yield; **immeuble de ~** block of flats (GB) *or* apartment block (US) that is rented out
(g) ratio; **bon ~ qualité prix** good value for money
2 **par rapport à** *phr* **(a)** compared with; **par ~ au dollar** against the dollar
(b) le nombre de voitures par ~ au nombre d'habitants the number of cars per head of the population
(c) with regard to, toward(s); **l'attitude de la population par ~ à l'immigration** people's attitudes to immigration
■ **~ de force** power struggle; **~s sexuels** sexual relations

◈ **rapporter** /ʀapɔʀte/ [1] **1** *vtr* **(a)** to bring back; to take back
(b) to bring in ⟨income⟩; **~ 10%** to yield *or* to return 10%
(c) to report; **on m'a rapporté que** I was told that
2 *vi* **(a)** to bring in money
(b) (fam) to tell tales
3 **se rapporter** *v refl* (+ *v être*) **se ~ à** to relate to, to bear a relation to

rapproché, ~e /ʀapʀɔʃe/ **1** *pp*
▶ RAPPROCHER
2 *pp adj* close together

rapprochement /ʀapʀɔʃmɑ̃/ *nm*
(a) rapprochement
(b) connection

◈ **rapprocher** /ʀapʀɔʃe/ [1] **1** *vtr* **(a)** to move [sth] closer
(b) to bring [sth] forward(s) ⟨date⟩
(c) to bring [sb] (closer) together ⟨people⟩
(d) to compare
2 **se rapprocher** *v refl* (+ *v être*) to get closer, to get nearer; **leurs peintures se rapprochent des fresques antiques** their paintings are similar to classical frescoes

rapt /ʀapt/ *nm* kidnapping (GB), abduction

raquette /ʀakɛt/ *nf* **(a)** (for tennis) racket; (for table-tennis) bat (GB), paddle (US)
(b) snowshoe

◈ **rare** /ʀɑʀ/ *adj* **(a)** (not common) (gen) rare; ⟨job⟩ unusual; ⟨intelligence⟩ exceptional; **il est ~ qu'il vienne en train** it's unusual for him to come by train
(b) (not numerous) few, rare; ⟨visits⟩ infrequent; (not abundant) (gen) scarce; ⟨hair⟩ thin; ⟨vegetation⟩ sparse; **se faire ~** ⟨product⟩ to become scarce; **vous vous faites ~ ces temps-ci** you are not around much these days

raréfier /ʀaʀefje/ [2] **1** *vtr* **(a)** to rarefy ⟨air, gas⟩
(b) to make [sth] rare
2 **se raréfier** *v refl* (+ *v être*) ⟨air⟩ to become thinner; ⟨gas⟩ to rarefy; ⟨food, money⟩ to become scarce; ⟨species⟩ to become rare

rarement /ʀaʀmɑ̃/ *adv* rarely, seldom

rareté /ʀaʀte/ *nf* shortage, scarcity; rarity

rarissime /ʀɑʀisim/ adj extremely rare

ras, ~e /ʀɑ, ʀɑz/ **1** adj ‹hair› close-cropped; ‹fur› short; **à poil ~** ‹animal› short-haired; ‹carpet› short-piled; **en ~e campagne** in (the) open country; **une cuillère à café ~e** a level teaspoonful; **à ~ bord** to the brim
2 adv short; **couper (à) ~** to cut [sth] very short ‹hair, lawn›
3 **au ras de** phr **au ~ du sol** at ground level
IDIOM **faire table ~e de** to make a clean sweep of

RAS /ɛʀɑɛs/ (abbr = **rien à signaler**) nothing to report

rasade /ʀɑzad/ nf (a) glassful
(b) swig (colloq)

rasage /ʀɑzaʒ/ nm (a) (action) shaving
(b) (result) shave

ras-de-cou /ʀɑdku/ nm inv (a) crew-neck sweater
(b) choker

rase-mottes /ʀɑzmɔt/ nm inv **faire du ~, voler en ~** to fly low

raser /ʀɑze/ [1] **1** vtr (a) to shave; to shave off; **~ de près** to give [sb] a close shave
(b) to demolish; to raze [sth] to the ground
(c) ‹bullet› to graze; ‹plane, bird› to skim
2 **se raser** v refl (+ v être) to shave
IDIOM **~ les murs** to hug the walls

ras-le-bol /ʀɑlbɔl/ nm inv (fam) discontent

rasoir /ʀɑzwaʀ/ **1** adj inv (fam) boring
2 nm **~ mécanique** razor; **~ électrique** electric shaver

rassasier /ʀɑsazje/ [2] **1** vtr ‹food› to fill [sb] up
2 **se rassasier** v refl (+ v être) to eat one's fill

rassemblement /ʀɑsɑ̃bləmɑ̃/ nm (a) rally
(b) gathering
(c) meeting

✸ **rassembler** /ʀɑsɑ̃ble/ [1] **1** vtr to gather [sb/sth] together ‹people›; to round up ‹sheep, herd›; to unite ‹citizens, nation›; to gather ‹information, proof›; **~ ses forces** to summon up one's strength
2 **se rassembler** v refl (+ v être) (a) to gather
(b) to assemble

rasseoir: se rasseoir /ʀɑswaʀ/ [41] v refl (+ v être) to sit down (again)

rasséréner /ʀɑseʀene/ [14] vtr to calm [sb] down ‹person›

rassis, ~e /ʀɑsi, iz/ adj ‹bread› stale

rassurant, ~e /ʀɑsyʀɑ̃, ɑ̃t/ adj reassuring

rassurer /ʀɑsyʀe/ [1] **1** vtr to reassure
2 **se rassurer** v refl (+ v être) to reassure oneself; **rassure-toi** don't worry; **je suis rassuré** I'm relieved

rat /ʀɑ/ nm (a) rat

✸ indicates a very frequent word

(b) skinflint, cheapskate (colloq)

ratatiner: se ratatiner /ʀatatine/ [1] vpr
(a) ‹fruit› to shrivel
(b) ‹face, person› to become wizened

ratatouille /ʀatatuj/ nf ratatouille

rate /ʀat/ nf (a) (Zool) female rat
(b) (Anat) spleen

raté, ~e /ʀate/ **1** pp ▶ RATER
2 pp adj (a) ‹actor, painter› failed; **une vie ~e** a wasted life
(b) ‹opportunity› missed
3 nm,f (person) failure
4 **ratés** nm pl (in negotiations, system) hiccups

râteau, pl ~x /ʀɑto/ nm rake

râtelier /ʀɑtəlje/ nm hayrack
IDIOM **manger à tous les ~s** to run with the hare and hunt with the hounds

rater /ʀate/ [1] **1** vtr (a) to fail ‹exam›; to spoil ‹sauce›; **elle a raté son coup** (fam) she has failed
(b) to miss ‹train, target›
2 vi ‹plan› to fail; **il dit toujours des bêtises, ça ne rate jamais** (fam) he can always be relied upon to say something stupid

ratifier /ʀatifje/ [2] vtr (a) to ratify ‹treaty, contract›
(b) to confirm ‹plan, proposal›

ration /ʀasjɔ̃/ nf (a) ration
(b) share

rationaliser /ʀasjɔnalize/ [1] vtr to rationalize

rationnel, -elle /ʀasjɔnɛl/ adj rational

rationnement /ʀasjɔnmɑ̃/ nm rationing

rationner /ʀasjɔne/ [1] **1** vtr to ration ‹petrol›; to impose rationing on ‹population›
2 **se rationner** v refl (+ v être) to cut down

ratisser /ʀatise/ [1] vtr (a) to rake over; to rake up
(b) to comb ‹area›

raton /ʀatɔ̃/ nm young rat
■ **~ laveur** racoon

rattachement /ʀataʃmɑ̃/ nm (a) (of country) unification
(b) (of person) **demander son ~ à** to ask to be posted to

rattacher /ʀataʃe/ [1] vtr (a) to attach ‹region›; to post ‹employee›
(b) to retie; to fasten [sth] again
(c) **plus rien ne la rattache à Lyon** she no longer has any ties with Lyons

rattrapage /ʀatʀapaʒ/ nm (a) (Econ) adjustment
(b) catching up; **cours de ~** remedial lesson

rattraper /ʀatʀape/ [1] **1** vtr (a) to catch up with ‹competitor›
(b) to catch ‹fugitive›
(c) to make up for ‹lost time, deficit›; to make up ‹points, distance›; **~ son retard** to catch up

(d) to put right ‹error›; to smooth over ‹blunder›; to save ‹situation›
(e) to catch ‹object›
2 **se rattraper** *v refl* (+ *v être*) **(a)** to redeem oneself
(b) to make up for it
(c) (Sch) to catch up
(d) to make up one's losses
(e) se ~ **de justesse** to stop oneself just in time; **se ~ à une branche** to save oneself by catching hold of a branch

rature /RatyR/ *nf* crossing-out; deletion
raturer /RatyRe/ [1] *vtr* to cross out
rauque /Rok/ *adj* **(a)** husky
(b) hoarse
ravage /Rava3/ *nm* **les ~s de la guerre** the ravages of war; **faire des ~s** to wreak havoc; ‹epidemic› to take a terrible toll; **tu vas faire des ~s avec ta mini-jupe** (humorous) you'll knock them dead in that mini-skirt
ravagé, ~e /Rava3e/ *adj* (fam) crazy
ravager /Rava3e/ [13] *vtr* **(a)** ‹fire, war› to devastate, to ravage
(b) ‹disease› to ravage ‹face›; ‹grief› to tear [sb] apart
ravalement /Ravalmã/ *nm* **(a)** cleaning
(b) refacing
(c) (figurative) facelift
ravaler /Ravale/ [1] *vtr* **(a)** to clean; to reface; to renovate ‹building›
(b) to revamp ‹image›
(c) to suppress ‹anger›; **~ ses larmes** to hold back one's tears
ravier /Ravje/ *nm* small dish (for hors-d'œuvre)
ravigoter /Ravigote/ [1] *vtr* (fam) ‹fresh air› to invigorate; ‹drink› to perk [sb] up
ravin /Ravɛ̃/ *nm* ravine
ravir /RaviR/ [3] *vtr* **(a)** to delight; **ça te va à ~** it really suits you
(b) to steal
raviser: se raviser /Ravize/ [1] *v refl* (+ *v être*) to change one's mind
ravissant, ~e /Ravisã, ãt/ *adj* beautiful
ravisseur, -euse /RavisœR, øz/ *nm,f* kidnapper (GB), abductor
ravitaillement /Ravitajmã/ *nm* supplies
ravitailler /Ravitaje/ [1] **1** *vtr* **(a)** to provide [sb] with fresh supplies ‹town›
(b) to refuel
2 **se ravitailler** *v refl* (+ *v être*) to obtain fresh supplies
raviver /Ravive/ [1] *vtr* to rekindle; to revive
rayé, ~e /Reje/ **1** *pp* ▶ RAYER
2 *pp adj* **(a)** ‹fabric› striped
(b) ‹record› scratched
rayer /Reje/ [21] *vtr* **(a)** to cross [sth] out; '**~ la mention inutile**' 'delete whichever does not apply'
(b) **la ville a été rayée de la carte** the town

was wiped off the map
(c) to scratch
⚐ **rayon** /Rejɔ̃/ *nm* **(a)** radius; **dans un ~ de 10 km** within a 10 km radius; **~ d'action** range; (figurative) sphere of activity
(b) ray; beam; **les ~s X** X-rays; **être soigné aux ~s** to undergo radiation treatment
(c) (of wheel) spoke
(d) shelf; **~ de bibliothèque** (book)shelf
(e) (in big store) department; (in small shop) section; **tous nos modèles sont en ~** all our styles are on display
(f) (fam) **c'est mon ~** that's my department (colloq); **il en connaît un ~ à ce sujet** he knows a lot about it
rayonnage /Rejɔnaʒ/ *nm* shelves
rayonnant, ~e /Rejɔnã, ãt/ *adj* radiant
rayonne /Rejɔn/ *nf* rayon
rayonnement /Rejɔnmã/ *nm* **(a)** radiation
(b) radiance
(c) (of country) influence
rayonner /Rejɔne/ [1] *vi* **(a)** ‹light, heat› to radiate
(b) ‹star› to shine
(c) ‹person› to glow
(d) ‹city› to exert its influence
(e) ‹soldiers› to patrol; ‹tourists› to tour around
(f) ‹streets› to radiate
rayure /RejyR/ *nf* **(a)** stripe
(b) scratch
raz-de-marée /Radmare/ *nm inv* tidal wave
razzia /Razja/ *nf* raid
ré /Re/ *nm inv* (Mus) (note) D; (in sol-fa) re
réabonner /Reabɔne/ [1] *vtr* **~ qn** to renew sb's subscription (à to)
réaccoutumer /Reakutyme/ [1] *vtr* **~ qn à qch** to get sb used to sth again
réacheminer /Reaʃ(ə)mine/ *vt* to redirect
réacteur /ReaktœR/ *nm* **(a)** **~ (nucléaire)** (nuclear) reactor
(b) jet engine
⚐ **réaction** /Reaksjɔ̃/ *nf* **(a)** reaction; response
(b) **avion à ~** jet aircraft
réactionnaire /ReaksjɔnɛR/ *adj, nmf* reactionary
réactualiser /Reaktɥalize/ [1] *vtr* (gen) to update; to relaunch ‹debate›
réadapter: se réadapter /Readapte/ [1] *v refl* to readjust (à qch to sth)
réaffirmer /ReafiRme/ [1] *vtr* to reaffirm, to reassert
réagir /ReaʒiR/ [3] *vi* to react; to respond
réalisable /Realizabl/ *adj* feasible; workable
réalisateur, -trice /RealizatœR, tRis/ *nm,f* director
⚐ **réalisation** /Realizasjɔ̃/ *nf* **(a)** (of dream) fulfilment (GB)

⋯⟶

r

(b) (of study) carrying out
(c) achievement
(d) (of film) production

ꝰ **réaliser** /Realize/ [1] **1** *vtr* (a) to fulfil
(GB) ‹*ambition*›; to achieve ‹*ideal, feat*›
(b) to make ‹*model*›; to carry out ‹*survey, study*›
(c) to direct ‹*film*›
(d) to realize
2 **se réaliser** *v refl* (+ *v être*) (a) ‹*dream*›
to come true; ‹*predictions*› to be fulfilled
(b) se ~ (dans qch) to find fulfilment (GB)
(in sth)

réalisme /Realism/ *nm* realism

réaliste /Realist/ *adj* (gen) realistic; (in art)
realist

ꝰ **réalité** /Realite/ *nf* la ~ reality; en ~ in
reality; tenir compte des ~s to take the facts
into consideration

réanimation /Reanimasjɔ̃/ *nf* (a) (service
de) ~ intensive care (unit)
(b) resuscitation

réapparaître /Reaparɛtr/ [73] *vi* ‹*sun*› to
come out again; ‹*illness*› to recur

réapprovisionner /Reaprɔvizjɔne/ [1] *vtr*
to restock ‹*shop*›

réarmer /Rearme/ [1] *vtr* (a) to rearm
(b) to reload ‹*gun*›

réassortir /Reasɔrtir/ [3] *vtr* to replenish

rébarbatif, -ive /Rebarbatif, iv/ *adj* off-
putting; forbidding

rebâtir /R(ə)batir/ [3] *vtr* to rebuild

rebattre /R(ə)batr/ [61] *vtr* ~ les oreilles
de qn avec une histoire to go on (and on)
about something

rebattu, ~e /R(ə)baty/ **1** *pp* ▸ REBATTRE
2 *pp adj* ‹*joke, story*› hackneyed

rebelle /Rəbɛl/ **1** *adj* (a) rebel
(b) rebellious
(c) ‹*curl, lock of hair*› stray; ‹*stain*› stubborn
2 *nmf* rebel

rebeller: se rebeller /Rəbɛle/ [1] *v refl*
(+ *v être*) to rebel

rébellion /Rebɛljɔ̃/ *nf* rebellion

rebiffer: se rebiffer /R(ə)bife/ [1] *vpr*
(fam) to rebel

rebiquer /R(ə)bike/ [1] *vi* (fam) to stick up

reboiser /R(ə)bwaze/ [1] *vtr* to reafforest

rebond /R(ə)bɔ̃/ *nm* (a) bounce
(b) recovery

rebondi, ~e /R(ə)bɔ̃di/ *adj* (a) ‹*shape*›
round, rounded; ‹*cheek*› chubby; ‹*stomach*›
fat; ‹*buttocks*› rounded
(b) (figurative) ‹*wallet*› bulging

rebondir /R(ə)bɔ̃dir/ [3] *vi* (a) to bounce
(b) to start up again; to take a new turn

rebondissement /R(ə)bɔ̃dismɑ̃/ *nm*
(of controversy) sudden revival; (in trial) new
development

ꝰ indicates a very frequent word

rebord /R(ə)bɔr/ *nm* (a) ledge; ~ de fenêtre
windowsill
(b) rim
(c) edge

rebours, à rebours /aR(ə)bur/ *phr*
‹*count, walk*› backward(s)

rebouteux, -euse /R(ə)butø, øz/ *nm,f*
(fam) bonesetter

rebrousse-poil: à rebrousse-poil
/aR(ə)bruspwal/ *phr* the wrong way

rebrousser /R(ə)bruse/ [1] *vtr* ~ chemin
to turn back

rébus /Rebys/ *nm inv* rebus

rebut /R(ə)by/ *nm* rubbish; mettre qch au ~
to throw sth on the scrapheap

rebuter /R(ə)byte/ [1] *vtr* (a) to disgust; to
repel
(b) to put [sb] off

récalcitrant, ~e /Rekalsitrɑ̃, ɑ̃t/ *adj*
recalcitrant

recaler /R(ə)kale/ [1] *vtr* (fam) to fail
‹*candidate*›

récapitulatif /Rekapitylatif/ *nm*
summary of the main points

récapituler /Rekapityle/ [1] *vtr* to sum up

receler /Rəs(ə)le, Rsəle/ [17] *vtr* (a) ~ des
marchandises to possess stolen goods
(b) to contain

receleur, -euse /R(ə)s(ə)lœr, Rsəlœr,
øz/ *nm,f* possessor of stolen goods

récemment /Resamɑ̃/ *adv* recently

recensement /R(ə)sɑ̃smɑ̃/ *nm* (a) census
(b) inventory

recenser /R(ə)sɑ̃se/ [1] *vtr* (a) to take a
census of ‹*population*›
(b) to list ‹*objects*›

ꝰ **récent, ~e** /Resɑ̃, ɑ̃t/ *adj* recent; ‹*house*›
new

recentrer /Rəsɑ̃tre/ [1] *vtr*, **se
recentrer** *v refl* (+ *v être*) to refocus

récépissé /Resepise/ *nm* receipt

réceptacle /Resɛptakl/ *nm* container; ~ à
verre bottle bank

récepteur /Resɛptœr/ *nm* receiver

réceptif, -ive /Resɛptif, iv/ *adj* receptive

réception /Resɛpsjɔ̃/ *nf* (a) reception
(b) welcome
(c) s'occuper de la ~ des marchandises to
take delivery of the goods

réceptionner /Resɛpsjɔne/ [1] *vtr* (a) to
take delivery of ‹*goods*›
(b) to catch ‹*ball*›

réceptionniste /Resɛpsjɔnist/ *nmf*
receptionist

récession /Resesjɔ̃/ *nf* recession

recette /R(ə)sɛt/ *nf* (a) ~ (de cuisine)
recipe
(b) formula, recipe
(c) takings; faire ~ to bring in money;

(figurative) to be a success; **les ∼s et (les) dépenses** receipts and expenses

receveur, -euse /Rəs(ə)vœR, øz/ *nm,f* (on bus) conductor

■ ∼ **des postes** postmaster

🖋 **recevoir** /RəsvwaR, R(ə)səvwaR/ [5] *vtr*
(a) to receive, to get; **il a reçu une tuile sur la tête** he got hit on the head by a tile; **je n'ai d'ordre à ∼ de personne** I don't take orders from anyone
(b) to welcome ⟨*guests*⟩; **être bien reçu** to be well received; to get a good reception; **ils reçoivent beaucoup** they do a lot of entertaining; **Laval reçoit Caen** (Sport) Laval is playing host to Caen
(c) to see ⟨*patients*⟩
(d) to receive ⟨*radio signal*⟩
(e) (Sch) to pass ⟨*candidate*⟩; **être reçu à un examen** to pass an exam

rechange, de rechange /dəR(ə)ʃɑ̃ʒ/ *phr* ⟨*part*⟩ spare; ⟨*solution*⟩ alternative

réchapper /Reʃape/ [1] *v+prep* ∼ **de** to come through ⟨*illness, accident*⟩

recharge /R(ə)ʃaRʒ/ *nf* refill; reload

rechargeable /R(ə)ʃaRʒabl/ *adj* ⟨*lighter, pen*⟩ refillable; ⟨*battery, appliance*⟩ rechargeable

recharger /R(ə)ʃaRʒe/ [13] *vtr* to reload; to refill; to recharge ⟨*battery*⟩

réchaud /Reʃo/ *nm* stove; ∼ **électrique** electric ring (GB), hotplate

réchauffé, ∼e /Reʃofe/ 1 *pp*
▶ RÉCHAUFFER
2 *pp adj* ⟨*joke, story*⟩ hackneyed
3 *nm* **c'est du ∼** there's nothing new about it

réchauffement /Reʃofmɑ̃/ *nm* warming (up); **le ∼ de la planète** global warming

réchauffer /Reʃofe/ [1] 1 *vtr* (a) (Culin) to reheat, to heat [sth] up
(b) to warm up ⟨*person, hands, room*⟩
2 **se réchauffer** *v refl* (+ *v être*) to warm up

rêche /Rɛʃ/ *adj* ⟨*hands, fabric*⟩ rough

🖋 **recherche** /R(ə)ʃɛRʃ/ *nf* (a) research
(b) search; **être à la ∼ de** to be looking for
(c) ∼ **de** pursuit of ⟨*happiness*⟩
(d) **sans ∼** without affectation
■ ∼ **d'emploi** job-hunting

recherché, ∼e /R(ə)ʃɛRʃe/ 1 *pp*
▶ RECHERCHER
2 *pp adj* (a) sought-after
(b) in demand
(c) ⟨*dress*⟩ meticulous; ⟨*style*⟩ original
(d) ⟨*aim*⟩ intended

🖋 **rechercher** /R(ə)ʃɛRʃe/ [1] *vtr* (a) to look for; **il est recherché par la police** he's wanted by the police; **'recherchons vendeuse qualifiée'** 'qualified sales assistant (GB) *or* clerk (US) required'
(b) to seek ⟨*security*⟩; to fish for ⟨*compliments*⟩

rechigner /R(ə)ʃiɲe/ [1] 1 *v+prep* ∼ **à faire** to balk at doing
2 *vi* to grumble

rechute /Rəʃyt/ *nf* relapse

rechuter /R(ə)ʃyte/ [1] *vi* (a) (Med) to have a relapse
(b) (Econ) ⟨*price, currency*⟩ to fall again

récidive /Residiv/ *nf* (a) (Law) second offence (GB)
(b) (figurative) repetition
(c) (Med) recurrence

récidiver /Residive/ [1] *vi* (Law) to reoffend

récidiviste /Residivist/ *nmf* second offender, recidivist; habitual offender

récif /Resif/ *nm* reef

récipient /Resipjɑ̃/ *nm* container

réciprocité /ResipRɔsite/ *nf* reciprocity

réciproque /ResipRɔk/ 1 *adj* reciprocal
2 *nf* reverse; **la ∼ est vraie** the reverse is true

réciproquement /ResipRɔkmɑ̃/ *adv* **et ∼** and vice versa

🖋 **récit** /Resi/ *nm* (a) story
(b) narrative

récital /Resital/ *nm* recital

récitation /Resitasjɔ̃/ *nf* **apprendre une ∼** to learn a text (off) by heart

réciter /Resite/ [1] *vtr* to recite

réclamation /Reklamasjɔ̃/ *nf* (a) complaint
(b) claim; **sur ∼** on request

réclame /Reklam/ *nf* (a) publicity
(b) advertisement
(c) **'en ∼'** 'on offer' (GB), 'on sale'

🖋 **réclamer** /Reklame/ [1] 1 *vtr* to ask for ⟨*person, thing, money*⟩; to call for ⟨*reform, inquiry*⟩; to claim ⟨*compensation*⟩; **travail qui réclame de l'attention** work that requires attention
2 **se réclamer** *v refl* (+ *v être*) **se ∼ de** ⟨*person, group*⟩ to claim to be representative of

reclasser /Rəklase/ [1] *vtr* (a) to reclassify ⟨*documents*⟩
(b) to redeploy

reclus, ∼e /Rəkly, yz/ *adj* reclusive; **vivre ∼** to live as a recluse

réclusion /Reklyzjɔ̃/ *nf* (a) (Law) imprisonment
(b) reclusion

recoin /Rəkwɛ̃/ *nm* corner; (figurative) recess

récolte /Rekɔlt/ *nf* harvest; crop

récolter /Rekɔlte/ [1] *vtr* (a) to harvest ⟨*corn*⟩; to dig up ⟨*potatoes*⟩
(b) ⟨*bee*⟩ to collect ⟨*pollen*⟩; ⟨*person*⟩ to win ⟨*points*⟩; to collect ⟨*information*⟩

recommandable /Rəkɔmɑ̃dabl/ *adj* **un individu peu ∼** a disreputable individual

recommandation /Rəkɔmɑ̃dasjɔ̃/ *nf* recommendation

r

recommandé, **~e** /Rəkɔmɑ̃de/ ① *pp*
▶ RECOMMANDER
② *pp adj* ‹letter› registered

ⵏ **recommander** /Rəkɔmɑ̃de/ [1] ① *vtr*
(a) to advise
(b) to recommend
② **se recommander** *v refl* (+ *v être*) **se ~ de qn** to give sb's name as a reference

recommencement /Rəkɔmɑ̃smɑ̃/ *nm*
l'histoire est un éternel ~ history is constantly repeating itself

recommencer /Rəkɔmɑ̃se/ [12] *vtr* (a) to start [sth] again
(b) to do [sth] again

récompense /Rekɔ̃pɑ̃s/ *nf* (a) reward
(b) award

récompenser /Rekɔ̃pɑ̃se/ [1] *vtr* to reward

réconciliation /Rekɔ̃siljasjɔ̃/ *nf* reconciliation

réconcilier /Rekɔ̃silje/ [2] ① *vtr* ~ **Pierre avec Paul** to bring Pierre and Paul back together; ~ **morale et politique** to reconcile morality with politics
② **se réconcilier** *v refl* (+ *v être*) ‹friends› to make up; ‹nations› to be reconciled

reconduction /R(ə)kɔ̃dyksjɔ̃/ *nf* renewal

reconduire /R(ə)kɔ̃dɥiR/ [69] *vtr* (a) to see [sb] out; ~ **qn chez lui** to take sb home
(b) to extend ‹strike, ceasefire›; to renew ‹mandate›

réconfort /Rekɔ̃fɔR/ *nm* comfort

réconfortant, **~e** /Rekɔ̃fɔRtɑ̃, ɑ̃t/ *adj*
(a) comforting
(b) cheering
(c) fortifying

réconforter /Rekɔ̃fɔRte/ [1] *vtr* (a) to comfort; to console
(b) ~ **qn** to cheer sb up
(c) to fortify

ⵏ **reconnaissance** /R(ə)kɔnɛsɑ̃s/ *nf*
(a) gratitude; **en ~ de** in appreciation of
(b) recognition
(c) (of wrongs) admission, admitting; (of qualities) recognition, recognizing
(d) (Mil) reconnaissance

reconnaissant, **~e** /R(ə)kɔnɛsɑ̃, ɑ̃t/ *adj* grateful

ⵏ **reconnaître** /R(ə)kɔnɛtR/ [73] ① *vtr*
(a) to recognize ‹person›
(b) to identify; **je reconnais bien là leur générosité** it's just like them to be so generous
(c) to admit ‹facts, errors›
(d) to recognize ‹trade union, regime›; ~ **un enfant** to recognize a child legally
(e) to acknowledge
② **se reconnaître** *v refl* (+ *v être*) **se ~ à qch** to be recognizable by sth

reconnu, **~e** /R(ə)kɔny/ ① *pp*
▶ RECONNAÎTRE
② *pp adj* ‹fact› recognized

reconquérir /R(ə)kɔ̃keRiR/ [35] *vtr* to reconquer, to recover ‹territory›; (figurative) to regain ‹esteem›; to win back ‹person, right›

reconstituer /R(ə)kɔ̃stitɥe/ [1] *vtr* to reform ‹association›; to reconstruct ‹crime›; to recreate ‹era, decor›; to piece [sth] together again ‹broken object›; to build up again ‹reserves›

reconstitution /R(ə)kɔ̃stitysjɔ̃/ *nf* (of crime, event) reconstruction

reconstruire /R(ə)kɔ̃stRɥiR/ [69] *vtr* (a) to reconstruct
(b) to rebuild

reconversion /R(ə)kɔ̃vɛRsjɔ̃/ *nf* (of worker) redeployment; (of region) redevelopment; (of economy) restructuring; (of factory) conversion

reconvertir /R(ə)kɔ̃vɛRtiR/ [3] ① *vtr* to redeploy ‹staff›; to convert ‹factory›; to adapt ‹equipment›
② **se reconvertir** *v refl* (+ *v être*) ‹staff› to switch to a new type of employment; ‹company› to switch to a new type of production

recopier /R(ə)kɔpje/ [2] *vtr* (a) to copy out
(b) to write up ‹notes›

record /R(ə)kɔR/ ① *adj inv* record
② *nm* (Sport, figurative) record

recoudre /R(ə)kudR/ [76] *vtr* (a) to sew [sth] back on ‹button›
(b) (Med) to stitch up ‹wound›

recoupement /R(ə)kupmɑ̃/ *nm* crosscheck

recouper /R(ə)kupe/ [1] ① *vtr* to cut [sth] again ‹hair, hedge›; to recut ‹garment›
② **se recouper** *v refl* (+ *v être*)
(a) ‹versions› to tally; ‹results› to add up
(b) ‹lines› to intersect

recourbé, **~e** /R(ə)kuRbe/ *adj* (gen) curved; ‹nose, beak› hooked

recourir /R(ə)kuRiR/ [26] *v+prep* ~ **à** to use ‹remedy›; to resort to ‹strategy›

recours /R(ə)kuR/ *nm inv* (a) recourse; resort; **sans autre ~ que** with no other way out but; **avoir ~ à** to have recourse to ‹remedy›; to resort to ‹strategy›; to go to ‹expert›
(b) (Law) appeal

recouvrement /R(ə)kuvRəmɑ̃/ *nm* (of tax, contributions) collection; (of sum, debt) recovery

recouvrer /R(ə)kuvRe/ [1] *vtr* to recover; to collect ‹tax›

recouvrir /R(ə)kuvRiR/ [32] *vtr* (a) to cover
(b) to re-cover
(c) to hide, to conceal

recracher /R(ə)kRaʃe/ [1] *vtr* to spit out

récréation /RekReasjɔ̃/ *nf* (a) playtime (GB), break (GB), recess (US)
(b) recreation

ⵏ indicates a very frequent word

recréer /R(ə)kRee/ [11] *vtr* to recreate
récrier: **se récrier** /RekRije/ [2] *v refl* (+ *v être*) to exclaim
récrimination /RekRiminasjɔ̃/ *nf* recrimination
récriminer /RekRimine/ [1] *vi* to rail
recroqueviller: **se recroqueviller** /R(ə)kRɔkvije/ [1] *v refl* (+ *v être*) **(a)** ‹person› to huddle up
(b) ‹leaf, petal› to shrivel up
recrudescence /R(ə)kRydesɑ̃s/ *nf* (of violence, interest) fresh upsurge; (of bombing, demands) new wave; (of fire) renewed outbreak
recrudescent, **~e** /R(ə)kRydesɑ̃, ɑ̃t/ *adj* être ~ to be on the increase
recrue /RəkRy/ *nf* recruit
recrutement /R(ə)kRytmɑ̃/ *nm* recruitment
recruter /R(ə)kRyte/ [1] *vtr* to recruit
rectangle /Rɛktɑ̃gl/ *nm* rectangle
rectangulaire /Rɛktɑ̃gylɛR/ *adj* rectangular
recteur /RɛktœR/ *nm* (Sch, Univ) chief education officer
rectificatif, **-ive** /Rɛktifikatif, iv/ *nm* **(a)** (in newspaper) correction
(b) (to law) amendment
rectification /Rɛktifikasjɔ̃/ *nf* correction; rectification; adjustment
rectifier /Rɛktifje/ [2] *vtr* to correct, to rectify; to adjust
rectiligne /Rɛktiliɲ/ *adj* straight
recto /Rɛkto/ *nm* front, ~ **verso** on both sides
rectorat /RɛktɔRa/ *nm* ≈ local education authority (GB), ≈ board of education (US)
rectum /Rɛktɔm/ *nm* rectum
reçu, **~e** /R(ə)sy/ [1] *pp* ▶ RECEVOIR
[2] *pp adj* ‹candidate› successful
[3] *nm* receipt
recueil /R(ə)kœj/ *nm* collection; anthology
recueillement /Rəkœjmɑ̃/ *nm*
(a) contemplation
(b) reverence
recueilli, **~e** /Rəkœji/ [1] *pp* ▶ RECUEILLIR
[2] *pp adj* ‹air› rapt; ‹person› rapt in prayer; ‹crowd, silence› reverential
ℐ **recueillir** /RəkœjiR/ [27] [1] *vtr* **(a)** to collect ‹donations, anecdotes›; to gather ‹evidence, testimonies›
(b) to get ‹votes, news›; to gain ‹consensus›; to win ‹praise›
(c) to collect ‹water, resin›; to gather ‹honey›
(d) to take in ‹orphan›
(e) to record ‹impressions, opinions›
[2] **se recueillir** *v refl* (+ *v être*) to engage in private prayer
recul /R(ə)kyl/ *nm* **(a)** detachment; avec le ~ with hindsight, in retrospect; prendre du ~ to stand back
(b) (in production) drop, fall; (of doctrine) decline

(c) (of army) pulling back; (of tide, floodwaters) recession; avoir un mouvement de ~ to recoil; feu de ~ reversing light
reculé, **~e** /R(ə)kyle/ *adj* remote
reculer /R(ə)kyle/ [1] [1] *vtr* **(a)** to move back ‹object›
(b) (in car) to reverse (GB), to back up
(c) to put off ‹event, decision›; to put back ‹date›
[2] *vi* **(a)** ‹person› to move back; to stand back; ‹driver, car› to reverse (GB), to back up
(b) ‹army› to pull or to draw back
(c) ‹forest› to be gradually disappearing; ‹river› to go down; ‹sea› to recede
(d) ‹currency, exports› to fall; ‹doctrine› to decline; faire ~ le chômage to reduce unemployment
(e) to back down; ne ~ devant rien to stop at nothing
[3] **se reculer** *v refl* (+ *v être*) (gen) to move back; to stand back
reculons: **à reculons** /aR(ə)kylɔ̃/ *phr* aller à ~ to go backward(s)
récupérable /RekypeRabl/ *adj*
(a) ‹material› reusable
(b) ‹object› which can be made good again
(c) ‹delinquent› who can be rehabilitated
récupération /RekypeRasjɔ̃/ *nf* **(a)** salvage; recycling
(b) recovery
(e) appropriation
récupérer /RekypeRe/ [14] [1] *vtr* **(a)** to get back ‹money, strength›
(b) to retrieve
(c) to salvage ‹scrap iron›; to reclaim ‹rags›
(d) to save ‹boxes›
(e) to make up ‹days›
(f) to appropriate ‹ideas›
[2] *vi* to recover
récurer /RekyRe/ [1] *vtr* to scour; to scrub
récurrent, **~e** /RekyRɑ̃, ɑ̃t/ *adj* recurrent
récuser /Rekyze/ [1] [1] *vtr* to challenge ‹jury›
[2] **se récuser** *v refl* (+ *v être*) ‹judge› to decline to act in a case
recyclable /R(ə)siklabl/ *adj* recyclable
recyclage /R(ə)siklaʒ/ *nm* **(a)** recycling
(b) retraining
recycler /R(ə)sikle/ [1] [1] *vtr* **(a)** to recycle ‹material›
(b) ~ le personnel to retrain the staff
[2] **se recycler** *v refl* (+ *v être*) **(a)** to retrain
(b) to change jobs
rédacteur, **-trice** /Redaktœr, tris/ *nm,f*
(a) author, writer
(b) editor
rédaction /Redaksjɔ̃/ *nf* **(a)** writing
(b) editing
(c) editorial offices
(d) editorial staff
(e) (Sch) essay (GB), theme (US)

r

reddition /ʀɛdisjɔ̃/ nf surrender

rédemption /ʀedɑ̃psjɔ̃/ nf redemption

redescendre /ʀədesɑ̃dʀ/ [6] **1** vtr (gen) to take [sb/sth] back down; ‹person› to go/ come back down ‹stairs›
2 vi (+ v être) to go (back) down; to go down again

redevable /ʀədvabl, ʀ(ə)dəvabl/ adj être ~ de qch à qn to owe sth to sb; être ~ de l'impôt to be liable for tax

redevance /ʀədvɑ̃s, ʀ(ə)dəvɑ̃s/ nf (a) (gen) charge; (for television) licence (GB) fee; (for telephone) rental charge
(b) royalty

rédhibitoire /ʀedibitwaʀ/ adj ‹cost› prohibitive; ‹obstacle› insurmountable

rediffuser /ʀ(ə)difyze/ [1] vtr to repeat, to rerun ‹programme›

◦ᶠ **rédiger** /ʀediʒe/ [13] vtr to write ‹article›; to write up ‹notes›; to draft ‹contract›

redingote /ʀ(ə)dɛ̃gɔt/ nf (for man) frock coat; (for woman) fitted coat

redire /ʀədiʀ/ [65] vtr to repeat; **trouver quelque chose à ~ à qch** to find fault with sth

redite /ʀ(ə)dit/ nf (needless) repetition

redondance /ʀ(ə)dɔ̃dɑ̃s/ nf redundancy

redondant, **~e** /ʀ(ə)dɔ̃dɑ̃, ɑ̃t/ adj
(a) superfluous
(b) redundant

redonner /ʀ(ə)dɔne/ [1] vtr ~ qch à qn to give sb sth again

redorer /ʀ(ə)dɔʀe/ [1] vtr to regild; ~ son blason ‹person› to restore one's image

redoublant, **~e** /ʀ(ə)dublɑ̃, ɑ̃t/ nm,f student repeating a year

redoublement /ʀ(ə)dubləmɑ̃/ nm intensification

redoubler /ʀ(ə)duble/ [1] **1** vtr (Sch) ~ **une classe** to repeat a year
2 **redoubler de** v+prep ~ **de prudence** to be twice as careful; **la tempête a redoublé de violence** the storm has become even fiercer
3 vi **(a)** to repeat a year
(b) to intensify

redoutable /ʀ(ə)dutabl/ adj ‹weapon, exam› formidable; ‹disease› dreadful

redouter /ʀ(ə)dute/ [1] vtr to fear

redressement /ʀədʀɛsmɑ̃/ nm **maison de ~** reformatory

redresser /ʀ(ə)dʀɛse/ [1] **1** vtr **(a)** to straighten (up); to put [sth] up again; ~ **la tête** to lift one's head up
(b) to put [sth] back on its feet ‹economy›; to turn [sth] around ‹company›; to aid the recovery of ‹currency›
(c) to straighten up ‹glider, steering wheel›; ~ **la barre** to right the helm; (figurative) to put things back on an even keel

(d) to rectify ‹error›
2 **se redresser** v refl (+ v être) **(a)** to stand up; to sit up; to stand up straight; to sit up straight
(b) ‹economy, plant› to recover; ‹country› to get back on its feet

redresseur /ʀədʀɛsœʀ/ nm ~ **de torts** righter of wrongs

réductible /ʀedyktibl/ adj ‹costs› which can be reduced or cut

réduction /ʀedyksjɔ̃/ nf **(a)** discount, reduction; ~ **étudiants** concession for students
(b) cutting, reducing
(c) reduction, cut; ~s **d'effectifs** staff cuts
(d) (of statue) small replica

◦ᶠ **réduire** /ʀedɥiʀ/ [68] **1** vtr **(a)** to reduce; to cut ‹tax›; to cut down on ‹staff, spending›
(b) to reduce ‹photograph›; to scale down ‹drawing›; to cut ‹text›
(c) ~ **qch en poudre** to crush sth to powder; **être réduit en cendres** ‹city› to be reduced to ashes; ‹dreams› to turn to ashes
(d) ~ **à** to reduce to; **voilà à quoi j'en suis réduit!** this is what I've been reduced to!
(e) to reduce ‹sauce›
2 vi ‹sauce› to reduce; ‹spinach› to shrink
3 **se réduire** v refl (+ v être) **(a)** ‹costs› to be reduced; ‹imports› to be cut
(b) **cela se réduit à bien peu de chose** it doesn't amount to very much

réduit, **~e** /ʀedɥi, it/ **1** pp ▶ RÉDUIRE
2 pp adj **(a)** ‹rate, speed› reduced, lower; ‹time› shorter; ‹activity› reduced; ‹group› smaller; **visibilité ~e** restricted visibility
(b) ‹means, choice› limited; ‹group› small
(c) ‹size› small
3 nm cubbyhole

rééditer /ʀeedite/ [1] vtr to reprint ‹book›

rééducation /ʀeedykasjɔ̃/ nf
(a) physiotherapy; ~ **de la parole** speech therapy
(b) rehabilitation

rééduquer /ʀeedyke/ [1] vtr to restore normal functioning to ‹limb›; to rehabilitate

◦ᶠ **réel**, **réelle** /ʀeɛl/ **1** adj (gen) real; ‹fact› true
2 nm **le ~** the real

◦ᶠ **réellement** /ʀeɛlmɑ̃/ adv really

réembaucher /ʀeɑ̃boʃe/ [1] vtr to take [sb] on again

réemployer /ʀeɑ̃plwaje/ [23] vtr to reinvest ‹funds›; to re-employ ‹staff›

rééquilibrer /ʀeekilibʀe/ [1] vtr **(a)** (Aut) to balance ‹wheels›
(b) to balance ‹budget›

réévaluer /ʀeevalɥe/ [1] vtr **(a)** to revalue ‹currency›; to revise ‹tax›
(b) to reappraise

réexpédier /ʀeɛkspedje/ [2] vtr **(a)** to forward, to redirect
(b) to send [sth] back

◦ᶠ indicates a very frequent word

réf (*written abbr* = **référence**) ref

refaire /RəfɛR/ [10] **1** *vtr* (a) to do [sth] again ‹*exercise*›; to make [sth] again ‹*journey, mistake*›; **~ le même chemin** to go back the same way; **~ un numéro de téléphone** to redial a number
(b) **je vais ~ de la soupe** I'll make some more soup
(c) **vouloir ~ le monde** to want to change the world; **se faire ~ le nez** to have one's nose re-modelled (GB); **~ sa vie** to start all over again
(d) to redo ‹*roof*›; to redecorate ‹*room*›; to resurface ‹*road*›
2 se refaire *v refl* (+ *v être*) (a) **se ~ une santé** to recuperate; **se ~ une beauté** to redo one's make-up
(b) **se ~ à** to get used to [sth] again
(c) **on ne se refait pas** a person can't change

réfection /Refɛksjɔ̃/ *nf* repairing

réfectoire /RefɛktwaR/ *nm* refectory; (Mil) mess

⟋ référence /RefeRɑ̃s/ **1** *nf* (a) reference; **en** *or* **par ~ à** in reference to; **faire ~ à** to refer to; **lui? ce n'est pas une ~!** who, him? well, he's not much of an example!
(b) reference number
2 références *nf pl* references

référendum /RefeRɛ̃dɔm/ *nm* referendum

référer /RefeRe/ [14] **1 référer à** *v+prep* **en ~ à** to consult
2 se référer *v refl* (+ *v être*) (a) **se ~ à** to refer to
(b) **se ~ à** to consult

refermer /R(ə)fɛRme/ [1] **1** *vtr* (a) to close
(b) to close [sth] again
2 se refermer *v refl* (+ *v être*) ‹*door*› to close; ‹*wound*› to close up

réfléchi, ~e /Refleʃi/ *adj* (a) ‹*person*› reflective, thoughtful
(b) ‹*decision*› considered; ‹*action*› well-considered; **c'est tout ~** my mind is made up
(c) ‹*image*› reflected
(d) ‹*verb*› reflexive

⟋ réfléchir /RefleʃiR/ [3] **1** *vtr* to reflect ‹*heat*›
2 réfléchir à *v+prep* to think about
3 *vi* to think; **mais réfléchis donc un peu!** use your brain!
4 se réfléchir *v refl* (+ *v être*) to be reflected

réflecteur /ReflɛktœR/ *nm* reflector

reflet /R(ə)flɛ/ *nm* (a) reflection
(b) glint; shimmer; sheen; **cheveux châtains aux ~s roux** brown hair with auburn highlights

refléter /R(ə)flete/ [14] **1** *vtr* to reflect; **son visage reflétait son émotion** his/her emotion showed in his/her face
2 se refléter *v refl* (+ *v être*) to be reflected

réflexe /Reflɛks/ **1** *adj* reflex

2 *nm* (a) reflex
(b) reaction; **manquer de ~** to be slow to react; **par ~** automatically
■ **~ conditionné** conditioned reflex

⟋ réflexion /Reflɛksjɔ̃/ *nf* (a) thought, reflection
(b) thinking, reflection; **~ faite** *or* **à la ~, je n'irai pas** on second thoughts, I won't go; **donner matière à ~** to be food for thought
(c) remark, comment; **s'attirer des ~s** to attract criticism
(d) study; **document de ~** discussion paper
(e) (of image) reflection

refluer /R(ə)flɥe/ [1] *vi* ‹*liquid*› to flow back

reflux /R(ə)fly/ *nm inv* ebb tide

refonte /R(ə)fɔ̃t/ *nf* (a) overhaul
(b) (of contract) rewriting

reforestation /R(ə)fɔRɛstasjɔ̃/ *nf* reafforestation

réformateur, -trice /RefɔRmatœR, tRis/ *nm,f* reformer

⟋ réforme /RefɔRm/ *nf* (a) reform
(b) (Mil) discharge
(c) **la Réforme** the Reformation

réformé, ~e /RefɔRme/ *nm,f* Calvinist

reformer /R(ə)fɔRme/ [1] *vtr* to re-form

réformer /RefɔRme/ [1] *vtr* (a) to reform
(b) (Mil) to declare [sb] unfit for service ‹*conscript*›; to discharge ‹*soldier*›

refoulé, ~e /R(ə)fule/ *nm,f* repressed *or* inhibited person

refoulement /R(ə)fulmɑ̃/ *nm* (a) (of impulse) repression
(b) pushing back; turning back; driving back; forcing back

refouler /R(ə)fule/ [1] *vtr* (a) to suppress ‹*memory*›; to repress ‹*tendency*›; to hold back ‹*tears*›
(b) to force [sth] back ‹*liquid*›; to push back ‹*enemy*›; to turn back ‹*immigrant*›

réfractaire /RefRaktɛR/ *adj* (a) **~ à** resistant to ‹*influence*›; impervious to ‹*music*›
(b) refractory

réfracter /RefRakte/ [1] *vtr* to refract

réfraction /RefRaksjɔ̃/ *nf* refraction

refrain /R(ə)fRɛ̃/ *nm* (a) chorus
(b) (old) refrain

réfréner /R(ə)fRene/, **réfréner** /Refrene/ [14] *vtr* to curb

réfrigérant, ~e /RefRiʒeRɑ̃, ɑ̃t/ *adj* cooling

réfrigérateur /RefRiʒeRatœR/ *nm* refrigerator

réfrigérer /RefRiʒeRe/ [14] *vtr* to refrigerate ‹*food*›; to cool ‹*place*›

refroidir /RəfRwadiR/ [3] **1** *vtr* (a) to cool down; to cool
(b) **~ qn** to dampen sb's spirits
2 *vi* (a) to cool down
(b) to get cold
3 se refroidir *v refl* (+ *v être*) ‹*weather*› ···⟩

r

to get colder; ⟨joint⟩ to stiffen up; ⟨person⟩ to get cold

refroidissement /ʀəfʀwadismɑ̃/ *nm*
(a) drop in temperature
(b) cooling
(c) (Med) chill

refuge /ʀ(ə)fyʒ/ *nm* (a) refuge
(b) (mountain) refuge
(c) (for animals) sanctuary
(d) traffic island

réfugié, **~e** /ʀefyʒje/ *nm,f* refugee; **~ économique** economic refugee

réfugier: se réfugier /ʀefyʒje/ [2] *v refl* (+ *v être*) to take refuge

refus /ʀ(ə)fy/ *nm inv* refusal; **ce n'est pas de ~** (fam) I wouldn't say no (colloq)
■ **~ de priorité** failure to give way

⚜ **refuser** /ʀ(ə)fyze/ [1] **1** *vtr* (a) (gen) to refuse; to turn down ⟨offer⟩; **~ de faire** to refuse to do
(b) to reject ⟨budget, manuscript, racism⟩; to refuse to accept ⟨fact⟩; to turn away ⟨spectator⟩

2 se refuser *v refl* (+ *v être*) (a) **ça ne se refuse pas** it's too good to pass up (colloq); I wouldn't say no (colloq)
(b) to deny oneself ⟨pleasure⟩; **on ne se refuse rien!** (fam) you're certainly not stinting yourself!
(c) **se ~ à** to refuse to accept ⟨evidence⟩; to refuse to adopt ⟨solution⟩

réfuter /ʀefyte/ [1] *vtr* to refute

regagner /ʀ(ə)ɡaɲe/ [1] *vtr* (a) to get back to ⟨place⟩
(b) to regain ⟨esteem⟩

regain /ʀ(ə)ɡɛ̃/ *nm* **~ de** rise in ⟨inflation⟩; revival of ⟨interest⟩; resurgence of ⟨violence⟩

régal /ʀeɡal/ *nm* (a) culinary delight; **c'est un ~!** it's delicious!
(b) (figurative) delight; **un ~ pour les yeux** a feast for the eyes

régalade /ʀeɡalad/ *nf* **boire à la ~** to drink without letting one's lips touch the bottle

régaler: se régaler /ʀeɡale/ [1] *v refl* (+ *v être*) (a) **je me régale** it's delicious; **les enfants se sont régalés avec ton dessert** the children really enjoyed your dessert
(b) (figurative) **se ~ avec** to enjoy [sth] thoroughly ⟨film⟩; **se ~ de** to love ⟨anecdote⟩

⚜ **regard** /ʀ(ə)ɡaʀ/ **1** *nm* (a) look; **porter son ~ sur qch** to look at sth; **détourner le ~** to look away; **j'ai croisé son ~** our eyes met; **à l'abri des ~s indiscrets** far from prying eyes
(b) expression; **son ~ triste** his/her sad expression; **sous le ~ amusé de qn** under the amused eye of sb; **jeter un ~ noir à qn** to give sb a black look
(c) **le ~ des autres** other people's opinion; **porter un ~ nouveau sur qch** to take a fresh look at sth

2 au regard de *phr* (formal) **au ~ de la**

loi in the eyes of the law

3 en regard *phr* **avec une carte en ~** with a map on the opposite page

regardant, **~e** /ʀəɡaʀdɑ̃, ɑ̃t/ *adj* **ne pas être très ~** not to be very particular *or* fussy

⚜ **regarder** /ʀ(ə)ɡaʀde/ [1] **1** *vtr* (a) to look at ⟨person, scene, landscape⟩; **~ qch méchamment/fixement/longuement** to glare/stare/gaze at sth; **~ qn en face** to look sb in the face; **~ la réalité** *or* **les choses en face** to face facts; **~ qn de haut** to look down one's nose at sb
(b) to watch ⟨film, TV⟩; **regarde bien comment je fais** watch what I do carefully
(c) to look at ⟨watch, map⟩; to have a look at ⟨tyres, oil⟩; **~ qch dans** to look sth up in ⟨dictionary⟩; **~ si** to have a look and see if
(d) to look at ⟨situation⟩; **~ pourquoi/si/qui** to see why/if/who
(e) (fam) to concern ⟨person⟩; **ça ne vous regarde pas** it's none of your business
(f) **elle ne regarde que ses intérêts** she thinks only of her own interests

2 regarder à *v+prep* to think about; **ne pas ~ à la dépense** to spare no expense; **à y ~ de plus près** on closer examination

3 *vi* to look; **~ en l'air/par terre** to look up/down; **regarde où tu mets les pieds** watch where you put your feet

4 se regarder *v refl* (+ *v être*) (a) to look at oneself
(b) to look at one another

régate /ʀeɡat/ *nf* regatta

régence /ʀeʒɑ̃s/ *nf* (a) regency
(b) **la Régence** the Regency

régénérer /ʀeʒeneʀe/ [14] **1** *vtr* (a) to regenerate
(b) to reactivate

2 se régénérer *v refl* (+ *v être*) (a) ⟨cells⟩ to regenerate
(b) (figurative) to regain one's strength

régent, **~e** /ʀeʒɑ̃, ɑ̃t/ *nm,f* regent

régenter /ʀeʒɑ̃te/ [1] *vtr* (a) to rule
(b) to regulate

régie /ʀeʒi/ *nf* (a) state control; local government control
(b) **~ d'État** state-owned company
(c) stage management; production department
(d) central control room

regimber /ʀ(ə)ʒɛ̃be/ [1] *vi* (a) ⟨person⟩ to balk (**contre** at)
(b) ⟨horse⟩ to jib

⚜ **régime** /ʀeʒim/ *nm* (a) diet; **être au ~** to be on a diet
(b) (Pol) system (of government); government; regime
(c) (in administration) system, regime; **~ de faveur** preferential treatment
(d) (Law) **~ matrimonial** marriage settlement
(e) (of engine) (running) speed; **tourner à plein ~** ⟨engine⟩ to run at top speed; ⟨factory⟩ to work at full capacity

---

⚜ indicates a very frequent word

(f) (of bananas) bunch

régiment /ʀeʒimɑ̃/ *nm* regiment

ᵍ **région** /ʀeʒjɔ̃/ *nf* region; area

régional, **~e**, *mpl* **-aux** /ʀeʒjɔnal, o/ *adj* regional

régionalisme /ʀeʒjɔnalism/ *nm* regionalism

régir /ʀeʒiʀ/ [3] *vtr* to govern

régisseur /ʀeʒisœʀ/ *nm* **(a)** (of estate) steward, manager
(b) stage manager

registre /ʀ(ə)ʒistʀ/ *nm* **(a)** register; **les ~s de la police** police records
(b) (of novel) style
(c) (of language, voice) register; **cet acteur a un ~ limité** this actor has a limited range

réglable /ʀeglabl/ *adj* **(a)** adjustable
(b) payable

réglage /ʀeglaʒ/ *nm* regulating; setting; adjustment

ᵍ **règle** /ʀɛgl/ ⨍1⨍ *nf* **(a)** ruler
(b) rule; **~s de sécurité** safety regulations; **respecter les ~s du jeu** to play by the rules; **dans les ~s de l'art** by the rule book; **en ~ générale** as a rule
⨍2⨍ **règles** *nf pl* period
⨍3⨍ **en règle** *phr* ‹request› formal; ‹papers, accounts› in order; **subir un interrogatoire en ~** to be given a grilling; **pour passer la frontière, il faut être en ~** to cross the border, your papers must be in order

réglé, **~e** /ʀegle/ *adj* **(a)** ruled, lined
(b) ‹life› well-ordered
(c) **l'affaire est ~e** the matter is settled

ᵍ **règlement** /ʀɛgləmɑ̃/ *nm* **(a)** regulations, rules
(b) payment
(c) settlement
∎ **~ de comptes** settling of scores

réglementaire /ʀɛgləmɑ̃tɛʀ/ *adj* ‹uniform› regulation; ‹format› prescribed; ‹procedure› statutory

réglementation /ʀɛgləmɑ̃tasjɔ̃/ *nf*
(a) rules, regulations
(b) regulation, control

réglementer /ʀɛgləmɑ̃te/ [1] *vtr* to regulate

ᵍ **régler** /ʀegle/ [14] *vtr* **(a)** to settle ‹debt›; to pay ‹bill›; to pay for ‹purchase, work›; **avoir des comptes à ~ avec qn** (figurative) to have a score to settle with sb; **~ son compte à qn** (fam) to sort sb out
(b) to settle, to sort out ‹problem›
(c) to settle ‹details, terms›
(d) to adjust ‹height›; to regulate ‹speed›; to tune ‹engine›; to set ‹pressure›
(e) **~ sa conduite sur celle de qn** to model one's behaviour (GB) on sb's
(f) to rule (lines on) ‹paper›

réglisse /ʀeglis/ *nf* liquorice (GB), licorice (US)

régnant, **~e** /ʀeɲɑ̃, ɑ̃t/ *adj* ‹dynasty› reigning; ‹ideology› prevailing

règne /ʀɛɲ/ *nm* **(a)** reign; rule
(b) (figurative) reign
(c) (in biology) kingdom

régner /ʀeɲe/ [14] *vi* **(a)** ‹sovereign› to reign, to rule
(b) ‹boss› to be in control; **~ en maître sur** to reign supreme over
(c) ‹confusion, fear› to reign; ‹smell› to prevail; **la confiance règne!** (ironic) there's trust for you!; **faire ~** to give rise to ‹insecurity›; to impose ‹order›

regonfler /ʀ(ə)gɔ̃fle/ [1] *vtr* **(a)** to reinflate ‹tyre›; to blow [sth] up again ‹balloon›
(b) (fam) to increase ‹staff›; to boost ‹sales, profits›

regorger /ʀ(ə)gɔʀʒe/ [13] *vi* **~ de** ‹shop› to be packed with; ‹region› to have an abundance of

régresser /ʀegʀese/ [1] *vi* **(a)** ‹waters› to recede; ‹unemployment› to go down
(b) ‹industry› to be in decline
(c) ‹epidemic› to die out

régressif, **-ive** /ʀegʀesif, iv/ *adj* regressive

régression /ʀegʀesjɔ̃/ *nf* **(a)** decline
(b) regression

regret /ʀəgʀɛ/ *nm* regret; **j'apprends avec ~ que** I'm sorry to hear that; **j'ai le ~ de vous annoncer** I regret to inform you

regrettable /ʀəgʀetabl/ *adj* regrettable

ᵍ **regretter** /ʀəgʀete/ [1] *vtr* **(a)** to be sorry about, to regret ‹situation, action›; **je regrette de ne pas pouvoir t'aider** I'm sorry I can't help you
(b) to regret ‹decision›; **~ d'avoir fait** to regret doing; **je ne regrette rien** I have no regrets
(c) to miss ‹person, place›; **notre regretté collègue** (formal) our late colleague

regroupement /ʀ(ə)gʀupmɑ̃/ *nm*
(a) grouping; pooling; bringing together
(b) merger
(c) getting [sb/sth] back together; rounding up

regrouper /ʀ(ə)gʀupe/ [1] ⨍1⨍ *vtr* **(a)** to group [sth] together; to bring [sth] together; to pool ‹interests›; **~ deux chapitres en un seul** to merge two chapters into one
(b) to reassemble ‹pupils›; to round up ‹animals›
⨍2⨍ **se regrouper** *v refl* (+ *v être*)
(a) ‹companies› to group together; ‹malcontents› to gather
(b) ‹runners› to bunch together again

régularisation /ʀegylaʀizasjɔ̃/ *nf* **(a)** (of situation) sorting out, regularization
(b) (of watercourse) regulation

régulariser /ʀegylaʀize/ [1] *vtr* **(a)** to sort out, to regularize ‹position, situation›
(b) to regulate ‹flow›; to stabilize ‹price,

r

market

régularité /ʀegylaʀite/ *nf* (a) regularity
(b) (of rhythm, production, progress) steadiness;
(of features) regularity; (of writing) neatness; (of
surface) evenness; (of quantity) consistency
(c) legality

régulateur, -trice /ʀegylatœʀ,
tʀis/ ① *adj* regulating
② *nm* regulator

régulation /ʀegylasjɔ̃/ *nf* regulation,
control

régulier, -ière /ʀegylje, ɛʀ/ *adj* (a) (gen)
regular; *‹flow, rise, effort›* steady; *‹quality›*
consistent; *‹thickness›* even; *‹writing›* neat;
‹life› (well-)ordered; **vol** ~ scheduled flight
(b) *‹person›* honest; *‹papers, ballot›* in order;
‹government› legitimate
(c) *‹verb›* regular

régulièrement /ʀegyljɛʀmɑ̃/ *adv*
(a) regularly
(b) steadily
(c) evenly
(d) normally

régurgiter /ʀegyʀʒite/ [1] *vtr* to
regurgitate

réhabiliter /ʀeabilite/ [1] ① *vtr* (a) to
rehabilitate
(b) to renovate
② **se réhabiliter** *v refl* (+ *v être*) to
redeem oneself

réhabituer /ʀeabitɥe/ [1] *vtr* to
reaccustom (**qn à qch** sb to sth; **qn à faire** sb
to doing)

rehausser /ʀəose/ [1] *vtr* (a) to raise
(b) to enhance *‹prestige›*
(c) to set off *‹pattern›*

réimplanter /ʀeɛ̃plɑ̃te/ [1] *vtr* to re-
establish *‹factory, industry›*

réimprimer /ʀeɛ̃pʀime/ [1] *vtr* to reprint

rein /ʀɛ̃/ ① *nm* kidney; ~ **artificiel** kidney
machine
② **reins** *nm pl* **les** ~**s** the small of the
back; **une serviette autour des** ~**s** a towel
around one's waist

réincarner: se réincarner
/ʀeɛ̃kaʀne/ [1] *v refl* (+ *v être*) to be
reincarnated

reine /ʀɛn/ *nf* (a) queen
(b) (figurative) **être la** ~ **des imbéciles** (fam) to
be a prize idiot

reine-claude, *pl* **reines-claudes**
/ʀɛnklod/ *nf* greengage

reinette /ʀɛnɛt/ *nf* rennet apple

réinscrire: se réinscrire /ʀeɛ̃skʀiʀ/ [67] *v
refl* (+ *v être*) to re-enrol (GB)

réinsérer /ʀeɛ̃seʀe/ [14] *vtr* (a) to
reintegrate
(b) to reinsert

réinstaller /ʀeɛ̃stale/ [1] ① *vtr* to put
[sth] back

ꙸ indicates a very frequent word

② **se réinstaller** *v refl* (+ *v être*) **se** ~
dans un fauteuil to settle (oneself) back into
an armchair

réintégrer /ʀeɛ̃tegʀe/ [14] *vtr* (a) to return
to *‹place, group, system›*
(b) ~ **qn (dans ses fonctions)** to reinstate sb

réitérer /ʀeiteʀe/ [14] *vtr* to repeat

rejaillir /ʀ(ə)ʒajiʀ/ [3] *vi* (a) *‹liquid›* to
splash back; to spurt back
(b) ~ **sur qn** *‹success›* to reflect on sb;
‹scandal› to affect sb adversely

rejaillissement /ʀ(ə)ʒajismɑ̃/ *nm* (of
scandal) adverse effect; (of success) reflection

rejet /ʀ(ə)ʒɛ/ *nm* (a) (gen) rejection; (of
complaint) dismissal; (of motion) defeat; (of
request) denial
(b) (of waste) discharge; disposal; ~**s** waste

ꙸ **rejeter** /ʀəʒte, ʀʒəte/ [20] ① *vtr* (a) to
reject *‹advice, candidacy, outsider›*; to turn
down *‹offer›*; to deny *‹request›*; to set aside
‹decision›
(b) ~ **qch sur qn** to shift sth onto sb *‹blame›*
(c) *‹factory›* to discharge *‹waste›*; to eject
‹smoke›
(d) *‹person, company›* to dispose of *‹waste›*;
‹sea› to wash up *‹body, debris›*
(e) ~ **[qch] en arrière** to throw back *‹head,
hair›*
② **se rejeter** *v refl* (+ *v être*) **se** ~ **la faute**
to blame each other

rejeton /ʀəʒ(ə)tɔ̃, ʀʒətɔ̃/ *nm* (a) offshoot
(b) (fam) offspring

ꙸ **rejoindre** /ʀ(ə)ʒwɛ̃dʀ/ [56] ① *vtr* (a) to
meet up with
(b) to catch up with
(c) to join; to rejoin
(d) to get to; to get back to, to return to
(e) ~ **qn sur qch** to concur with sb on sth
② **se rejoindre** *v refl* (+ *v être*) *‹people›* to
meet up; *‹roads›* to meet

rejouer /ʀ(ə)ʒwe/ [1] *vtr* (gen) to play [sth]
again; to replay *‹match, point›*

réjoui, ~e /ʀeʒwi/ *adj* cheerful

réjouir /ʀeʒwiʀ/ [3] ① *vtr* (a) to delight
‹person›; to gladden *‹heart›*
(b) to amuse
② **se réjouir** *v refl* (+ *v être*) to rejoice; **se** ~
de to be delighted at *‹news›*; to be delighted
with *‹success›*

réjouissance /ʀeʒwisɑ̃s/ ① *nf* rejoicing
② **réjouissances** *nf pl* celebrations;
quel est le programme des ~**s?** (fam) what
delights are in store for us?

réjouissant, ~e /ʀeʒwisɑ̃, ɑ̃t/ *adj*
(a) heartening, delightful
(b) amusing

relâche /ʀ(ə)lɑʃ/ *nf* (a) (of theatre, cinema)
closure; **faire** ~ to be closed
(b) break, rest; **sans** ~ relentlessly

relâchement /ʀ(ə)lɑʃmɑ̃/ *nm* (a) (of
discipline, effort) slackening; (of morals)
loosening

(b) (of muscle) slackening

relâcher /ʀ(ə)laʃe/ [1] **1** *vtr* **(a)** to loosen ‹*hold*›

(b) to release ‹*captive*›

(c) to relax ‹*discipline*›; ∼ **son attention to** let one's attention wander; ∼ **ses efforts to** let up

2 se relâcher *v refl* (+ *v être*) **(a)** ‹*hold, tie*› to loosen; ‹*muscle*› to relax

(b) ‹*effort*› to slacken; ‹*zeal*› to flag; ‹*pupil*› to grow slack

relais /ʀ(ə)lɛ/ *nm inv* **(a)** intermediary; **prendre le** ∼ **(de qn/qch)** to take over (from sb/sth)

(b) (Sport) relay

(c) restaurant; hotel

(d) (Tech) relay; ∼ **hertzien** radio relay station

relance /ʀ(ə)lɑ̃s/ *nf* (of industry, idea) revival; (of economy) reflation; (in inflation) rise; **mesures de** ∼ reflationary measures

relancer /ʀ(ə)lɑ̃se/ [12] *vtr* **(a)** to throw [sth] again ‹*ball*›; to throw [sth] back (again) ‹*ball*›

(b) to restart ‹*engine*›; to relaunch ‹*company*›; to revive ‹*idea*›; to reopen ‹*debate*›; to boost ‹*investment*›; to reflate ‹*economy*›

(c) ‹*creditor*› to chase [sb] up; ‹*person*› to pester

relater /ʀ(ə)late/ [1] *vtr* (formal) to recount

⚹ **relatif, -ive¹** /ʀ(ə)latif, iv/ **1** *adj* relative; **le risque est très** ∼ there is relatively little risk

2 *nm* relative (pronoun)

⚹ **relation** /ʀ(ə)lasjɔ̃/ **1** *nf* **(a)** connection

(b) acquaintance; ∼**s d'affaires** business acquaintances

(c) relationship; **avoir de bonnes** ∼**s avec qn** to have a good relationship with sb; **entrer en** ∼ **avec qn** to get into touch with sb

2 relations *nf pl* relations

∎ ∼**s extérieures** foreign affairs; ∼**s publiques** public relations

relative² /ʀ(ə)lativ/ **1** *adj f* ▶ RELATIF 1

2 *nf* relative (clause)

relativement /ʀ(ə)lativmɑ̃/ **1** *adv* relatively

2 relativement à *phr* in relation to

relativiser /ʀ(ə)lativize/ [1] *vtr* to put [sth] into perspective

relativité /ʀ(ə)lativite/ *nf* relativity

relax /ʀəlaks/ *adj inv* (fam) ‹*person*› laid-back (colloq); ‹*clothes*› casual; ‹*party*› informal

relaxant, -e /ʀəlaksɑ̃, ɑ̃t/ *adj* relaxing

relaxation /ʀəlaksasjɔ̃/ *nf* relaxation

relaxer /ʀəlakse/ [1] **1** *vtr* **(a)** to discharge ‹*defendant*›

(b) to relax ‹*muscle, person*›

2 se relaxer *v refl* (+ *v être*) to relax

relayer /ʀ(ə)leje/ [21] **1** *vtr* **(a)** to take over from, to relieve

(b) to relay ‹*broadcast*›

2 se relayer *v refl* (+ *v être*) **(a)** to take turns

(b) to take over from each other

reléguer /ʀ(ə)lege/ [14] *vtr* (gen) to relegate; to consign ‹*object*›; ∼ **qn/qch au second plan** to push sb/sth into the background

relent /ʀ(ə)lɑ̃/ *nm* **(a)** lingering odour (GB)

(b) (figurative) whiff

relève /ʀ(ə)lɛv/ *nf* **(a)** **la** ∼ **s'effectue à 20 heures** the changeover takes place at 8 pm; **la** ∼ **de la garde** the changing of the guard; **prendre la** ∼ to take over

(b) relief; relief team

relevé, -e /ʀəlve, ʀləve/ **1** *adj* spicy

2 *nm* **(a)** noting down; **faire le** ∼ **de** to list ‹*mistakes*›; to make a note of ‹*expenses*›; to read ‹*meter*›

(b) ∼ **bancaire** bank statement; ∼ **d'identité bancaire, RIB** *bank account details for direct debits*

⚹ **relever** /ʀəlve, ʀləve/ [16] **1** *vtr* **(a)** to pick up ‹*person, stool*›; to put [sth] back up (again)

(b) to raise ‹*lever*›

(c) ∼ **la tête** to raise one's head; to look up; (figurative) to refuse to accept defeat

(d) to turn up ‹*collar*›; to lift ‹*skirt*›; to wind up ‹*car window*›; to raise ‹*sail, blind*›; ∼ **ses cheveux** to put one's hair up

(e) to note, to notice; to point out; ∼ **la moindre inexactitude** to seize on the slightest inaccuracy

(f) to take down ‹*date, name*›; to take ‹*prints*›; ∼ **le compteur** to read the meter

(g) to take in ‹*exam papers*›

(h) to react to ‹*remark*›; ∼ **le défi/un pari to** take up the challenge/a bet

(i) to rebuild ‹*wall*›; to put [sth] back on its feet ‹*country, economy*›

(j) to raise ‹*standard, price*›; to increase ‹*productivity*›

(k) to relieve ‹*team*›; ∼ **la garde** to change the guard

(l) to spice up ‹*dish, story*›

(m) ∼ **qn de ses fonctions** to relieve sb of their duties

2 relever de *v+prep* **(a)** ∼ **de** ‹*department*› to come under ‹*Ministry*›; **cela ne relève pas de mes fonctions** that's not part of my duties

(b) **cela relève de la gageure** this comes close to being impossible

3 se relever *v refl* (+ *v être*) **(a)** to pick oneself up; to get up again

(b) **se** ∼ **automatiquement** to be raised automatically

(c) ‹*blind*› to be raised

(d) **se** ∼ **de** to recover from

relief /ʀəljɛf/ *nm* **(a)** relief; (on medal, coin) raised pattern; **en** ∼ ‹*globe of the world*› in relief; ‹*letters*› raised; **cinéma en** ∼ three-dimensional cinema; **mettre qch en** ····⟩

r

~ to accentuate sth; **un** ~ **accidenté** a hilly
landscape
(b) depth; **l'effet de** ~ the effect of depth
relier /Rəlje/ [2] *vtr* **(a)** to link; to link up; to
link together; to join up; to connect
(b) to bind ‹*book*›; **relié cuir** leather-bound
religieuse¹ /Rəliʒjøz/ ⚑ *adj f* ▶
RELIGIEUX 1
⚑ *nf* **(a)** nun
(b) (Culin) religieuse
religieusement /Rəliʒjøzmɑ̃/ *adv*
(a) religiously
(b) ‹*listen*› with rapt attention
(c) ‹*get married*› in church
𝄢 **religieux, -ieuse²** /Rəliʒjø, øz/ ⚑ *adj*
(a) religious; ‹*school, wedding*› church;
‹*music*› sacred
(b) (figurative) ‹*silence*› reverent
⚑ *nm* monk
𝄢 **religion** /R(ə)liʒjɔ̃/ *nf* **(a)** religion
(b) faith
(c) entrer en ~ to enter the Church
reliquaire /R(ə)likɛR/ *nm* reliquary
reliquat /R(ə)lika/ *nm* (of sum) remainder;
(of account) balance
relique /R(ə)lik/ *nf* relic
relire /R(ə)liR/ [66] *vtr* to reread; to read
[sth] over
reliure /Rəljyr/ *nf* **(a)** binding
(b) bookbinding
reloger /R(ə)lɔʒe/ [13] *vtr* to rehouse
relooking /Rəlukiŋ/ *nm* makeover
reluire /R(ə)lɥiR/ [69] *vi* to shine; to glisten
IDIOM **il sait passer la brosse à** ~ he's a real
flatterer
reluisant, ~**e** /R(ə)lɥizɑ̃, ɑ̃t/ *adj* shiny;
glistening; **peu** ~ (figurative) far from brilliant
remâcher /R(ə)mɑʃe/ [1] *vtr* **(a)** to chew
[sth] again
(b) (fam) to ruminate over ‹*problem, past*›
remaniement /R(ə)manimɑ̃/ *nm*
modification; revision; reorganization
remanier /R(ə)manje/ [2] *vtr* to modify; to
redraft; to reorganize; to reshuffle
remarier: se remarier /R(ə)maRje/ [2] *v*
refl (+ *v être*) to remarry
remarquable /R(ə)maRkabl/ *adj*
(a) remarkable
(b) striking
(c) noteworthy
remarquablement /R(ə)
maRkabləmɑ̃/ *adv* remarkably
𝄢 **remarque** /R(ə)maRk/ *nf* **(a)** remark; **faire**
des ~**s** to comment
(b) (written) comment
(c) critical remark, criticism
remarqué, ~**e** /R(ə)maRke/ *adj* ‹*initiative*›
noteworthy; ‹*increase*› noticeable

𝄢 **remarquer** /R(ə)maRke/ [1] ⚑ *vtr* **(a)** to
point out
(b) to observe
(c) to notice; **remarque, ce n'est pas très**
important mind you, it's not very important;
se faire ~ to draw attention to oneself
(d) ~ **un visage dans la foule** to spot a face
in the crowd
⚑ **se remarquer** *v refl* (+ *v être*) **(a)** to
attract attention
(b) to show
remballer /Rɑ̃bale/ [1] *vtr* to pack [sth]
up again
rembarrer /Rɑ̃baRe/ [1] *vtr* (fam) to send
[sb] packing (colloq)
remblai /Rɑ̃blɛ/ *nm* **(a)** embankment; **route**
en ~ raised road
(b) filling in; banking up
(c) (terre de) ~ (for railway, road) ballast; (for
ditch) fill; (for excavation) backfill
rembobiner /Rɑ̃bɔbine/ [1] *vtr* to rewind
rembourrer /Rɑ̃buRe/ [1] *vtr* to stuff
‹*chair*›; to pad ‹*shoulders*›
remboursable /Rɑ̃buRsabl/ *adj* ‹*loan,*
debt› repayable; ‹*ticket, medicine, treatment*›
refundable
remboursement /Rɑ̃buRsəmɑ̃/ *nm*
(a) repayment
(b) refund
(c) reimbursement
rembourser /Rɑ̃buRse/ [1] *vtr* **(a)** to pay
off, to repay ‹*loan, debt*›
(b) to give a refund to ‹*customer*›; to refund
the price of ‹*item*›
(c) to reimburse ‹*expenses, employee*›; ~ **un**
ami to pay a friend back
rembrunir: se rembrunir /
Rɑ̃bRyniR/ [3] *v refl* (+ *v être*) ‹*face*› to darken,
to cloud over
remède /R(ə)mɛd/ *nm* medicine; remedy,
cure
■ ~ **de bonne femme** folk remedy; ~ **de cheval**
strong medicine
IDIOM **aux grands maux les grands** ~**s**
desperate times call for desperate measures
remédier: se remédier /R(ə)medje/ [2] *v+prep* ~ **à** to
remedy
remembrement /R(ə)mɑ̃bRəmɑ̃/ *nm*
regrouping of lands
remémorer: se remémorer /R(ə)
memɔRe/ [1] *v refl* (+ *v être*) to recall, to
recollect
remerciement /R(ə)mɛRsimɑ̃/ *nm*
thanks; **je n'ai pas eu un seul** ~ I didn't get a
word of thanks; **lettre de** ~ thank-you letter
𝄢 **remercier** /R(ə)mɛRsje/ [2] *vtr* **(a)** to
thank; **je vous remercie** thank you
(b) (ironic) to dismiss
𝄢 **remettre** /R(ə)mɛtR/ [60] ⚑ *vtr* **(a)** ~ **qch**
dans/sur to put sth back in/on; ~ **qch en**
mémoire à qn to remind sb of sth
(b) ~ **à qn** to hand [sth] over to sb ‹*keys*›; to

𝄢 indicates a very frequent word

hand [sth] in to sb ‹letter›; to present [sth] to sb ‹reward›
(c) ∼ qch droit or d'aplomb to put sth straight again
(d) to postpone ‹visit›
(e) to put [sth] on again ‹heating›; to play [sth] again ‹record›
(f) ∼ une vis to put a new screw in
(g) to add some more ‹salt›; to add another ‹nail›
(h) to put [sth] back on ‹coat›
(i) (Med) to put [sth] back in place ‹joint›
(j) ‹medicine› to make [sb] feel better
(k) ∼ qn/le visage de qn to remember sb/sb's face
(l) (fam) ∼ ça to start again; on s'est bien amusé, quand est-ce qu'on remet ça? that was fun, when are we going to do it again?
2 **se remettre** v refl (+ v être) **(a)** se ∼ à un endroit to go or get back to a place
(b) se ∼ au travail to go back to work; se ∼ au dessin to start drawing again
(c) se ∼ en jean to wear jeans again
(d) se ∼ de to recover from ‹illness›; to get over ‹shock›
(e) s'en ∼ à qn to leave it to sb; s'en ∼ à la décision de qn to accept sb's decision
(f) se ∼ avec qn to get back together with sb
réminiscence /Reminisɑ̃s/ nf
(a) reminiscence
(b) recollection
remise /R(ə)miz/ nf **(a)** attendre la ∼ des clés to wait for the keys to be handed over; ∼ des prix prizegiving; ∼ des médailles medals ceremony
(b) discount
(c) une ∼ de peine a remission
(d) ∼ de fonds remittance of funds
(e) (at a bank) paying-in slip
(f) shed
remiser /R(ə)mize/ [1] vtr to put [sth] away (dans in)
rémission /Remisjɔ̃/ nf remission; sans ∼ ‹punish› mercilessly; ‹rain› without stopping
remmener /Rɑ̃mne/ [16] vtr to take [sb] back
remodeler /Rəmɔdle/ [17] vtr to restructure; to reshape; to replan
remontant /R(ə)mɔ̃tɑ̃/ nm pick-me-up (colloq), tonic
remontée /R(ə)mɔ̃te/ nf **(a)** climb up; la ∼ de la Saône en péniche going up the Saône by barge
(b) (in price) rise; (in violence) increase
■ ∼ mécanique (Sport) ski lift
remonte-pente, pl ∼s /R(ə)mɔ̃tpɑ̃t/ nm ski-tow
⚹ **remonter** /Rəmɔ̃te/ [1] **1** vtr (+ v avoir)
(a) ∼ qch to take sth back up/upstairs; to bring sth back up/upstairs
(b) to put [sth] back up; ∼ un seau d'un puits to pull a bucket up from a well
(c) to raise ‹shelf, blind›; to wind [sth] back

up ‹car window›; to roll up ‹sleeves›; to turn up ‹collar›; to pull up ‹socks›
(d) to go/to come back up; to climb back up; to drive back up
(e) to sail up ‹river›; to go up ‹road›; ∼ une filière or piste to follow a trail
(f) ∼ qn or le moral de qn to cheer sb up
(g) to put [sth] back together again; to put [sth] back ‹wheel›
(h) to wind [sth] up; être remonté à bloc (fam) to be full of energy
(i) to revive ‹play, show›
2 vi (+ v être) **(a)** ‹person› to go/to come back up; ‹tide› to come in again; ‹price, temperature› to rise again; ∼ sur to step back onto ‹pavement›; to climb back onto ‹wall›; ∼ à la surface ‹diver› to surface; ‹oil, object› to rise to the surface; ∼ dans les sondages to move up in the opinion polls
(b) ∼ dans le temps to go back in time, ∼ à ‹historian› to go back to; ‹event› to date back to; faire ∼ to trace (back) ‹origins›
(c) ‹skirt› to ride up
(d) les odeurs d'égout remontent dans la maison the smell from the drains reaches our house
3 **se remonter** v refl (+ v être) se ∼ le moral to cheer oneself up; to cheer each other up
remontoir /R(ə)mɔ̃twaR/ nm winder
remontrance /Rəmɔ̃trɑ̃s/ nf reprimand
remontrer /Rəmɔ̃tRe/ [1] vi en ∼ à qn to teach sb a thing or two
remords /RəmɔR/ nm inv remorse
remorquage /RəmɔRkaʒ/ nm towing
remorque /RəmɔRk/ nf **(a)** towrope; prendre en ∼ to tow ‹car›
(b) trailer
remorquer /RəmɔRke/ [1] vtr to tow ‹vehicle›
remorqueur /RəmɔRkœR/ nm tug
remous /R(ə)mu/ nm inv **(a)** eddy
(b) backwash; wash
(c) (of ideas) turmoil; (in crowd) stir
rempailler /Rɑ̃paje/ [1] vtr to reseat ‹chair›
rempart /Rɑ̃paR/ nm **(a)** rampart; battlements; les ∼s de la ville the city walls
(b) defence (GB)
remplaçable /Rɑ̃plasabl/ adj replaceable
remplaçant, **-e** /Rɑ̃plasɑ̃, ɑ̃t/ nm,f
(a) (gen) substitute; (at school) supply (GB) or substitute (US) teacher; (actor) stand-in
(b) successor
remplacement /Rɑ̃plasmɑ̃/ nm replacement; faire des ∼s ‹teacher› to do supply (GB) or substitute (US) teaching; ‹temp› to do temporary work; produit de ∼ substitute
⚹ **remplacer** /Rɑ̃plase/ [12] vtr **(a)** to stand in for, to cover for ‹colleague›
(b) to replace; on peut ∼ le vinaigre par du jus de citron you can use lemon juice

⋯⟩

instead of vinegar

◆ **remplir** /ʀɑ̃pliʀ/ [3] *vtr* **(a)** to fill (up) ⟨*container*⟩; to fill in ⟨*form*⟩; ∼ **qch à moitié** to half fill sth; ∼ **qn de joie** to fill sb with joy; **une vie bien remplie** a full life
(b) to carry out ⟨*role, mission*⟩; to fulfil (GB) ⟨*duty, role*⟩

remplissage /ʀɑ̃plisaʒ/ *nm* **(a)** filling
(b) (derogatory) **faire du** ∼ to pad out one's work

remplumer: se remplumer /ʀɑ̃plyme/ [1] *v refl* (fam) (financially) to get back on one's feet; (physically) to put some weight back on

rempocher /ʀɑ̃pɔʃe/ [1] *vtr* to put [sth] back in one's pocket

remporter /ʀɑ̃pɔʀte/ [1] *vtr* to win ⟨*seat, title, victory*⟩; ∼ **un vif succès** to be a great success

rempoter /ʀɑ̃pɔte/ [1] *vtr* to repot

remuant, ∼e /ʀ(ə)mɥɑ̃, ɑ̃t/ *adj* **(a)** rowdy
(b) boisterous; energetic

remue-ménage /ʀ(ə)mymenaʒ/ *nm inv*
(a) commotion
(b) bustle

remuer /ʀ(ə)mɥe/ [1] **1** *vtr* **(a)** to move ⟨*hand, head*⟩; to wiggle ⟨*toe, hips*⟩; to wag ⟨*tail*⟩
(b) to shake ⟨*object*⟩
(c) to move ⟨*object*⟩
(d) to stir ⟨*soup*⟩; to toss ⟨*salad*⟩
(e) to turn over ⟨*earth*⟩; to poke ⟨*ashes*⟩
(f) (figurative) to rake up ⟨*past*⟩; to stir up ⟨*memories*⟩
(g) to upset ⟨*person*⟩
2 *vi* ⟨*person*⟩ to move; ⟨*leaves*⟩ to flutter; ⟨*boat*⟩ to bob up and down
3 **se remuer** *v refl* (+ *v être*) (fam) **(a)** to get a move on (colloq)
(b) **se** ∼ **pour obtenir** to make an effort to get

rémunérateur, -trice /ʀemyneʀatœʀ, tʀis/ *adj* lucrative

rémunération /ʀemyneʀasjɔ̃/ *nf* pay; payment

rémunérer /ʀemyneʀe/ [14] *vtr* to pay ⟨*person*⟩; to pay for ⟨*work*⟩

renâcler /ʀ(ə)nɑkle/ [1] *vi* **(a)** ⟨*person*⟩ to show reluctance
(b) ⟨*animal*⟩ to snort

renaissance /ʀ(ə)nɛsɑ̃s/ *nf* rebirth; revival

Renaissance /ʀ(ə)nɛsɑ̃s/ *nf* Renaissance

renaître /ʀ(ə)nɛtʀ/ [74] *vi* (+ *v être*) **(a)** to come back to life
(b) ⟨*hope, desire*⟩ to return; **faire** ∼ **l'espoir** to bring new hope

rénal, ∼e, *mpl* **-aux** /ʀenal, o/ *adj* ⟨*artery*⟩ renal; ⟨*infection*⟩ kidney

renard /ʀ(ə)naʀ/ *nm* **(a)** fox

◆ indicates a very frequent word

renarde /ʀ(ə)naʀd/ *nf* vixen

renardeau, *pl* ∼**x** /ʀ(ə)naʀdo/ *nm* fox cub

renchérir /ʀɑ̃ʃeʀiʀ/ [3] *vi* **(a)** to add; ∼ **sur ce que dit qn** to add something to what sb says
(b) to go one step further
(c) to raise the bidding

◆ **rencontre** /ʀɑ̃kɔ̃tʀ/ *nf* **(a)** meeting; encounter; **faire la** ∼ **de qn** to meet sb
(b) (Sport) match (GB), game (US); ∼ **d'athlétisme** athletics meeting (GB), track meet (US)
∎ ∼ **au sommet** summit meeting

◆ **rencontrer** /ʀɑ̃kɔ̃tʀe/ [1] **1** *vtr* **(a)** to meet ⟨*person*⟩; ∼ **qn sur son chemin** to come across sb
(b) to encounter, to meet with ⟨*problem, opposition*⟩
(c) to come across ⟨*object, word*⟩
(d) to meet ⟨*player, team*⟩
2 **se rencontrer** *v refl* (+ *v être*) **(a)** to meet
(b) ⟨*quality, object, person*⟩ to be found

rendant /ʀɑ̃dɑ̃/ ▶ RENDRE

rendement /ʀɑ̃dmɑ̃/ *nm* **(a)** (from land, investment) yield; (of machine, worker) output
(b) (of factory) productivity; (of machine, worker) efficiency
(c) (of sportsman, pupil) performance

rendez-vous /ʀɑ̃devu/ *nm inv*
(a) appointment; date; **sur** ∼ by appointment; **j'ai** ∼ **avec un ami** I'm meeting a friend; **le soleil n'était pas au** ∼ the sun didn't shine
(b) meeting
(c) gathering; meeting place

rendormir: se rendormir /ʀɑ̃dɔʀmiʀ/ [30] *v refl* (+ *v être*) to go back to sleep

◆ **rendre** /ʀɑ̃dʀ/ [6] **1** *vtr* **(a)** (gen) to give back, to return; to repay, to pay back ⟨*loan*⟩; to return ⟨*greeting, invitation, goods*⟩; ∼ **la pareille à qn** to pay sb back; **il la déteste mais elle le lui rend bien** he hates her and she feels the same about him
(b) ∼ **la santé/vue à qn** to restore sb's health/sight
(c) ∼ **qch possible** to make sth possible; ∼ **qn fou** to drive sb mad
(d) to hand in ⟨*homework*⟩
(e) ⟨*land*⟩ to yield ⟨*crop, quantity*⟩
(f) to convey ⟨*atmosphere, nuance*⟩; **ça ne rendra rien en couleurs** it won't come out in colour (GB)
(g) (fam) to bring up ⟨*food, bile*⟩
(h) to pronounce ⟨*sentence*⟩; to return ⟨*verdict*⟩
(i) les tomates rendent de l'eau (à la cuisson) tomatoes give out water during cooking
2 *vi* **(a)** ⟨*land*⟩ to be productive; ⟨*plant*⟩ to produce a good crop
(b) (fam) to throw up (colloq)
3 **se rendre** *v refl* (+ *v être*) **(a) se** ∼ **à**

Rome/en ville to go to Rome/to town
(b) se ~ indispensable/malade to make
oneself indispensable/ill
(c) to give oneself up; to surrender
(d) se ~ à qch to bow to ‹argument›
IDIOM **~ l'âme** or **l'esprit** to pass away
rendu, -e /Rɑ̃dy/ ▶ RENDRE
rêne /Rɛn/ nf rein
renfermé, ~e /Rɑ̃fɛRme/ **1** pp
▶ RENFERMER
2 pp adj ‹person› withdrawn; ‹feeling›
hidden
3 nm **odeur de ~** musty smell
renfermer /Rɑ̃fɛRme/ [1] **1** vtr to contain
2 se renfermer v refl (+ v être) to
become withdrawn
renflé, ~e /Rɑ̃fle/ adj ‹vase› rounded;
‹dome› bulbous; ‹stomach› bulging
renflement /Rɑ̃fləmɑ̃/ nm bulge
renflouer /Rɑ̃flue/ [1] vtr **(a)** to raise ‹ship›
(b) to bail out ‹person, company›
renfoncement /Rɑ̃fɔ̃smɑ̃/ nm recess; **~**
de porte doorway
💧 **renforcer** /Rɑ̃fɔRse/ [12] **1** vtr to
reinforce; to strengthen
2 se renforcer v refl (+ v être) ‹power› to
increase; ‹control› to become tighter; ‹team,
numbers› to grow; ‹sector› to grow stronger
renfort /Rɑ̃fɔR/ nm **(a)** (Mil) reinforcement
(b) support, annoncé à grand ~ de publicité
well-publicized
(c) (Sport) substitute
renfrogné, ~e /Rɑ̃fRɔɲe/ adj sullen
renfrogner: se renfrogner
/Rɑ̃fRɔɲe/ [1] v refl (+ v être) to become sullen
rengaine /Rɑ̃gɛn/ nf **c'est toujours la**
même ~ (figurative) it's the same old thing
every time
rengainer /Rɑ̃gene/ [1] vtr to sheathe
‹sword›; to put [sth] back in its holster
‹pistol›
rengorger: se rengorger /Rɑ̃gɔRʒe/ [13] v
refl (+ v être) ‹bird› to puff out its breast;
‹person› to swell with conceit
reniement /R(ə)nimɑ̃/ nm disavowal
renier /Rənje/ [2] **1** vtr to renounce
‹religion, opinion›; to disown ‹child, work,
friend›
2 se renier v refl (+ v être) to go back on
what one has said or promised
reniflement /R(ə)nifləmɑ̃/ nm **(a)** sniffing
(b) sniff
renifler /R(ə)nifle/ [1] vtr, vi to sniff
renne /Rɛn/ nm reindeer
renom /Rənɔ̃/ nm **(a)** fame
(b) reputation
renommé, ~e¹ /Rənɔme/ adj famous
renommée² /Rənɔme/ nf **(a)** reputation
(b) fame
renoncement /R(ə)nɔ̃smɑ̃/ nm
renunciation

💧 **renoncer** /R(ə)nɔ̃se/ [12] v+prep to give up;
~ à to give up; to abandon; to renounce; **~ à**
faire to abandon the idea of doing
renonciation /R(ə)nɔ̃sjasjɔ̃/ nf giving up
renouer /Rənwe/ [1] **1** vtr **(a)** to retie
‹laces›
(b) to pick up the thread of ‹conversation›
2 ~ avec v+prep to get back in touch
with ‹person›; to revive ‹tradition›; to go back
to ‹past›
renouveau, pl ~x /Rənuvo/ nm revival
renouveler /Rənuvle/ [19] **1** vtr **(a)** (gen)
to renew; to repeat ‹suggestion, experience›;
to replace ‹equipment, team›; to change
‹water›
(b) to revitalize ‹genre, style›
2 se renouveler v refl (+ v être) **(a) une**
pièce où l'air ne se renouvelle pas a room
which isn't aired
(b) ‹artist› to try out new ideas
(c) ‹experience› to be repeated
renouvellement /Rənuvɛlmɑ̃/ nm
(a) renewal
(b) replacement
(c) revitalization
rénovateur, -trice /RenɔvatœR,
tRis/ nm, f reformer
rénovation /Renɔvasjɔ̃/ nf renovation
rénover /Renɔve/ [1] vtr **(a)** to renovate
‹area, house›; to restore ‹furniture›
(b) to reform ‹institution, policy›; to revamp
‹project›
💧 **renseignement** /Rɑ̃sɛɲmɑ̃/ **1** nm
(a) information; **est-ce que je peux vous**
demander un ~? can I ask you something?;
~s pris upon investigation; **'pour tous ~s,**
s'adresser à…' 'all enquiries to…'
(b) (Mil) intelligence
2 renseignements nm pl
(a) information
(b) directory enquiries (GB) or assistance
(US)
renseigner /Rɑ̃seɲe/ [1] **1** vtr **~ qn** to
give information to sb
2 se renseigner v refl (+ v être) to find
out, to enquire; to make enquiries
rentabilisation /Rɑ̃tabilizasjɔ̃/ nf **la ~**
de l'entreprise est notre premier objectif
our primary aim is to make the company
profitable
rentabiliser /Rɑ̃tabilize/ [1] vtr to secure
a return on ‹investment›; to make a profit on
‹product›; to make [sth] profitable ‹business›
rentabilité /Rɑ̃tabilite/ nf **(a)** profitability
(b) return
rentable /Rɑ̃tabl/ adj profitable
rente /Rɑ̃t/ nf **(a)** private income
(b) annuity; **~ viagère** life annuity
(c) government stock
rentrée /Rɑ̃tRe/ nf **(a)** (general) return to
work (after the slack period of the summer
break in France); **~ (des classes** or **scolaire)** ⋯💧

r

start of the (new) school year; **mon livre sera publié à la ~** my book will be published in the autumn (GB) *or* fall (US)
(b) return (to work)
(c) comeback; **~ politique** political comeback
(d) receipts; **~ (d'argent)** income; takings
■ **~ parlementaire** reassembly of Parliament

ⅾ **rentrer** /Rɑ̃tRe/ [1] **1** *vtr* **(a)** to bring [sth] in; to take [sth] in
(b) to raise ⟨*landing gear*⟩; to draw in ⟨*claws*⟩; **rentrez le ventre!** hold your stomach in!
(c) to tuck ⟨*shirt*⟩ **(dans** into)
2 *vi* (+ *v être*) **(a)** to go in; to get in; to fit; **~ dans un arbre** (fam) to hit a tree
(b) ~ dans to go back into; to come back into
(c) ~ (chez soi) to get (*or* go *or* come) back (home); to return (home)
(d) ~ dans ses frais to recoup one's money
(e) ⟨*money*⟩ to come in
(f) faire ~ qch dans la tête de qn to get sth into sb's head
IDIOM il m'est rentré dedans (pop) he bumped *or* ran into me; he crashed into me

renversant, ~e /Rɑ̃vɛRsɑ̃, ɑ̃t/ *adj* astounding, astonishing

renverse /Rɑ̃vɛRs/ *nf* **tomber à la ~** to fall flat on one's back

renversement /Rɑ̃vɛRsəmɑ̃/ *nm*
(a) reversal
(b) overthrow; removal from office

renverser /Rɑ̃vɛRse/ [1] **1** *vtr* **(a)** to knock over; to knock down
(b) to spill
(c) to turn [sth] upside down
(d) to reverse
(e) to overthrow; to vote [sb/sth] out of office
2 **se renverser** *v refl* (+ *v être*) ⟨*boat*⟩ to capsize; ⟨*bottle*⟩ to fall over; ⟨*liquid*⟩ to spill

renvoi /Rɑ̃vwa/ *nm* **(a)** expulsion; dismissal
(b) return; **~ d'un colis** return of a parcel
(c) postponement
(d) cross-reference
(e) belch, burp (colloq)

ⅾ **renvoyer** /Rɑ̃vwaje/ [24] *vtr* **(a)** to throw [sth] back ⟨*ball*⟩; to reflect ⟨*light, heat*⟩; to echo ⟨*sound*⟩
(b) to return ⟨*mail*⟩
(c) to send [sb] back; **~ qn chez lui** to send sb home
(d) to expel; to dismiss
(e) to postpone ⟨*debate*⟩; to adjourn ⟨*case*⟩
(f) ~ à to refer to

réorganisation /ReɔRganizasjɔ̃/ *nf* reorganization

réorienter /ReɔRjɑ̃te/ [1] *vtr* to reorientate ⟨*pupil, student*⟩ **(vers** toward(s)); to reshape ⟨*policy*⟩

réouverture /ReuvɛRtyR/ *nf* reopening

repaire /R(ə)pɛR/ *nm* den; hideout

ⅾ indicates a very frequent word

ⅾ **répandre** /Repɑ̃dR/ [6] **1** *vtr* **(a)** to spread ⟨*substance*⟩; to pour ⟨*liquid*⟩; to spill ⟨*liquid*⟩
(b) to scatter ⟨*seeds, rubbish*⟩
(c) to spread ⟨*news, religion*⟩; to give off ⟨*heat, smoke, smell*⟩
2 **se répandre** *v refl* (+ *v être*) to spread

répandu, ~e /Repɑ̃dy/ *adj* widespread

réparable /Reparabl/ *adj* **(a)** ⟨*object*⟩ repairable
(b) ⟨*mistake*⟩ which can be put right

reparaître /R(ə)paRɛtR/ [73] *vi* **(a)**
▶ RÉAPPARAÎTRE
(b) ⟨*magazine*⟩ to be back in print

réparateur, -trice /RepaRatœR, tRis/ **1** *adj* refreshing
2 *nm,f* engineer (GB), fixer (US)

réparation /RepaRasjɔ̃/ *nf* **(a)** repairing, mending; repair
(b) compensation
(c) redress

réparer /RepaRe/ [1] *vtr* **(a)** to repair, to mend, to fix
(b) to put [sth] right ⟨*error*⟩; to make up for ⟨*oversight*⟩
(c) to compensate for ⟨*damage*⟩

reparler /R(ə)paRle/ [1] *vtr* **(a) ~ de** to discuss [sth] again **(à qn, avec qn** with sb)
(b) ~ à qn to be back on speaking terms with sb

repartie /Reparti/ *nf* rejoinder; **elle a de la ~** she always has a ready reply

repartir /R(ə)paRtiR/ [30] *vi* (+ *v être*) **(a)** to leave (again); to go back
(b) ⟨*person*⟩ to set off again; ⟨*machine*⟩ to start again; ⟨*sector*⟩ to pick up again
(c) ~ à zéro to start again from scratch

répartir /RepaRtiR/ [3] **1** *vtr* **(a)** to share [sth] out; to split ⟨*profits, expenses*⟩; to distribute ⟨*weight*⟩
(b) to spread ⟨*payments*⟩
2 **se répartir** *v refl* (+ *v être*) **(a)** to share out, to split
(b) ⟨*work, votes*⟩ to be split; **se ~ en** ⟨*people, objects*⟩ to divide (up) into

répartition /RepaRtisjɔ̃/ *nf* **(a)** sharing out; dividing up
(b) distribution

ⅾ **repas** /R(ə)pɑ/ *nm inv* meal

repassage /R(ə)pasaʒ/ *nm* ironing

repasser /R(ə)pase/ [1] **1** *vtr* **(a)** to iron
(b) to cross [sth] again ⟨*river, border*⟩
(c) to take [sth] again ⟨*exam*⟩
(d) to pass [sth] again ⟨*tool, salt*⟩; **je te repasse Jean** (on phone) I'll put you back on to Jean
(e) (fam) **~ qch à qn** to give sb sth ⟨*cold*⟩
2 *vi* (+ *v être*) **(a)** to go past again; **si tu repasses à Lyon, viens me voir** if you're ever back in Lyons, come and see me
(b) ⟨*film*⟩ to be showing again
(c) quand elle fait la vaisselle, je dois ~ derrière elle I always have to do the dishes

again after she's done them

repêchage /ʀ(ə)pɛʃaʒ/ nm (a) recovery (*from water*)
(b) épreuve de ~ resit (GB), retest (US)

repêcher /ʀ(ə)peʃe/ [1] vtr to recover; to fish out

repeindre /ʀ(ə)pɛdʀ/ [55] vtr to repaint

repenser /ʀ(ə)pɑ̃se/ [1] **1** vtr to rethink
2 repenser à v+prep to think back to ‹childhood›; to think again about ‹anecdote›

repenti, ~**e** /ʀ(ə)pɑ̃ti/ adj repentant

repentir¹: se repentir /ʀ(ə)pɑ̃tiʀ/ [30] v refl (+ v être) (a) to regret
(b) to repent

repentir² /ʀ(ə)pɑ̃tiʀ/ nm repentance

repérable /ʀ(ə)peʀabl/ adj that can be spotted

repérage /ʀ(ə)peʀaʒ/ nm (Mil) location (de of)

répercussion /ʀepɛʀkysjɔ̃/ nf repercussion

répercuter /ʀɔpɛʀkyte/ [1] **1** vtr (a) to pass [sth] on ‹increase›
(b) to send back ‹sound›
2 se répercuter v refl (+ v être) ‹sound› to echo; ‹increase› to be reflected (**sur** in)

repère /ʀ(ə)pɛʀ/ nm (a) marker; (reference) mark
(b) (event) landmark; (date) reference point

repérer /ʀ(ə)peʀe/ [14] **1** vtr (a) (fam) to spot; ~ **les lieux** to check out a place
(b) to locate ‹target›
2 se repérer v refl (+ v être) to get one's bearings

répertoire /ʀepɛʀtwaʀ/ nm (a) notebook with thumb index
(b) ~ **téléphonique** telephone book
(c) repertoire

répertorier /ʀepɛʀtɔʀje/ [2] vtr (a) to list; to index
(b) to identify

☞ **répéter** /ʀepete/ [14] **1** vtr (a) to repeat; ~ **qch à qn** to say sth to sb again; **je te répète que tu as tort** I'm telling you, you're wrong
(b) to rehearse ‹play›; to rehearse for ‹concert›
2 se répéter v refl (+ v être) (a) to repeat oneself
(b) **j'ai beau me** ~ **que…** no matter how often I tell myself that…
(c) ‹incident› to be repeated

répétitif, -ive /ʀepetitif, iv/ adj repetitive

répétition /ʀepetisjɔ̃/ nf (a) repetition
(b) rehearsal; ~ **générale** dress rehearsal

repeupler /ʀ(ə)pœple/ [1] vtr (a) to repopulate
(b) to restock
(c) to reforest

repiquer /ʀ(ə)pike/ [1] vtr to transplant ‹rice›; to prick out ‹seedlings›

répit /ʀepi/ nm respite

replacer /ʀ(ə)plase/ [12] vtr ~ **qch dans son contexte** to set sth back in context

replanter /ʀ(ə)plɑ̃te/ [1] vtr (a) to transplant
(b) to replant

replâtrer /ʀ(ə)plɑtʀe/ [1] vtr (a) to replaster
(b) to patch up ‹group›

replet, -ète /ʀəplɛ, ɛt/ adj plump, chubby

repli /ʀ(ə)pli/ nm (a) double fold
(b) fold
(c) (Mil) withdrawal
(d) ~ **sur soi(-même)** withdrawal

replier /ʀ(ə)plije/ [2] **1** vtr (a) to fold up ‹map›
(b) to fold [sth] back ‹sheet›
(c) to fold up ‹deckchair, fan›; to close ‹umbrella, penknife›
(d) **elle replia ses jambes** she tucked her legs under her; ~ **ses ailes** ‹bird› to fold its wings
2 se replier v refl (+ v être) (a) ‹blade› to fold up
(b) ‹army› to withdraw
(c) **se** ~ **sur soi-même** ‹person› to become withdrawn

réplique /ʀeplik/ nf (a) retort, rejoinder; **il a la** ~ **facile** he's always ready with an answer
(b) line; **donner la** ~ **à qn** to play opposite sb
(c) replica; **elle est la** ~ **de sa mère** she is the image of her mother

répliquer /ʀeplike/ [1] **1** vtr to retort
2 répliquer à v+prep to argue with ‹person›; to respond to ‹criticism›
3 vi (a) to answer back
(b) to retaliate, to respond

répondant, ~e /ʀepɔ̃dɑ̃, ɑ̃t/ nm,f referee; (Law) surety, guarantor

répondeur /ʀepɔ̃dœʀ/ nm ~ **(téléphonique)** (telephone) answering machine

☞ **répondre** /ʀepɔ̃dʀ/ [6] **1** vtr to answer, to reply; **il m'a été répondu que…** I was told that…; **qu'as-tu à** ~**?** what's your answer?
2 répondre à v+prep (a) ~ **à** to reply to, to answer ‹person, question, letter›; to answer ‹phone›
(b) ~ **à** to talk back to
(c) ~ **à** to answer, to meet ‹needs›; to fulfil (GB) ‹wishes›; to fit ‹description›; to come up to ‹expectations›
(d) ~ **à** to respond to ‹appeal, criticism›; to return ‹greeting›; ~ **à un sourire** to smile back; **les freins ne répondent plus** the brakes have failed
3 répondre de v+prep ~ **de qn** to vouch for sb; ~ **de ses actes** to answer for one's actions

☞ **réponse** /ʀepɔ̃s/ nf (a) answer, reply
(b) response

report /ʀəpɔʀ/ nm (a) adjournment; postponement; deferment ⋯▸

r

(b) transfer

reportage /ʀ(ə)pɔʀtaʒ/ *nm* (a) report
(b) reporting

reporter¹ /ʀ(ə)pɔʀte/ [1] **1** *vtr* (a) to put
back ‹date›; to postpone ‹event›; to defer
‹judgment›
(b) to carry forward ‹result›; to copy out
‹name›
(c) to take [sth] back ‹goods›
(d) to transfer ‹affection›; ~ **son agressivité
sur qn** to take one's aggression out on sb
2 se reporter *v refl* (+ *v être*) **se ~ à** to
refer to; to think back to

reporter² /ʀəpɔʀtɛʀ/ *nm* reporter

⚜ **repos** /ʀəpo/ *nm inv* rest; **mon jour de ~**
my day off

reposant, ~**e** /ʀəpozɑ̃, ɑ̃t/ *adj* peaceful,
restful; soothing; relaxing

repose-pieds /ʀ(ə)pozpje/ *nm inv*
footrest

⚜ **reposer** /ʀəpoze/ [1] **1** *vtr* (a) to rest;
avoir le visage reposé to look rested; **lire qch
à tête reposée** to read sth at one's leisure
(b) to put [sth] down ‹phone›; to put [sth]
down again
(c) to ask [sth] again ‹question›
2 *vi* (a) to rest; '**ici repose le Dr Grunard**'
'here lies Dr Grunard'; **laisser ~ la terre**
to rest the land; '**laisser ~ la pâte**' 'let the
dough stand'
(b) ~ **sur** to be based on; **la poutre repose
sur...** the beam is supported by...
3 se reposer *v refl* (+ *v être*) (a) to have
a rest, to rest
(b) **se ~ sur qn** to rely on sb

repose-tête /ʀəpoztɛt/ *nm inv* head rest

repoussant, ~**e** /ʀəpusɑ̃, ɑ̃t/ *adj* hideous

repousser /ʀ(ə)puse/ [1] **1** *vtr* (a) to
push [sth] to ‹door›; to push back ‹object›
(b) to push away ‹object›; to push back ‹lock
of hair›
(c) to push *or* drive back ‹crowd, animal›;
(Mil) to repel ‹attack›
(d) to dismiss ‹objection›; to decline ‹help›; to
turn down ‹request›
(e) to revolt
(f) to postpone ‹event›; to move [sth] back
‹date›
2 *vi* to grow again; to grow back

répréhensible /ʀepʀeɑ̃sibl/ *adj*
reprehensible

⚜ **reprendre** /ʀ(ə)pʀɑ̃dʀ/ [52] **1** *vtr* (a) ~
du pain/vin to have some more bread/wine;
j'en ai repris deux fois I had three helpings
(b) to pick [sth] up again ‹object, tool›; to take
[sth] back ‹present›; to collect ‹person, car›
(c) to take [sb] on again ‹employee›; ‹shop› to
take [sth] back ‹item›; **si on me reprend ma
vieille voiture** if I can trade in my old car
(d) to resume ‹walk, story›; to take up [sth]
again ‹studies›; to revive ‹play, tradition›; ~

le travail to go back to work; **tu reprends le
train à quelle heure?** what time is your train
back?; ~ **une histoire au début** to go back to
the beginning of a story
(e) to take over ‹business, shop›
(f) **on ne me reprendra plus à lui rendre
service!** you won't catch me doing him/her
any favours (GB) again!
(g) ~ **confiance** to regain one's confidence
(h) to alter ‹clothes›
(i) to take up ‹idea, thesis, policy›
(j) to repeat ‹argument›; to take up ‹slogan,
news›
(k) to correct ‹pupil›; ~ **le travail de qn** to
correct sb's work
(l) **mon mal de dents m'a repris** my
toothache has come back
2 *vi* (a) ‹business› to pick up again; ‹plant›
to recover
(b) to start again
(c) '**c'est étrange**,' **reprit-il** 'it's strange,' he
continued
3 se reprendre *v refl* (+ *v être*) (a) to
correct oneself
(b) to pull oneself together
(c) **s'y ~ à trois fois pour faire** to make three
attempts to do *or* at doing

représailles /ʀ(ə)pʀezɑj/ *nf pl* reprisals;
retaliation

⚜ **représentant**, ~**e** /ʀ(ə)pʀezɑ̃tɑ̃, ɑ̃t/ *nm,f*
(a) representative
(b) ~ **(de commerce)** sales representative

représentatif, -ive /ʀəpʀezɑ̃tatif, iv/ *adj*
representative

⚜ **représentation** /ʀəpʀezɑ̃tasjɔ̃/ *nf*
(a) representation
(b) performance
(c) commercial travelling (GB); ~ **exclusive**
sole agency

⚜ **représenter** /ʀəpʀezɑ̃te/ [1] **1** *vtr* (a) (in
painting) to depict; to portray
(b) to represent; to mean; **les enfants
représentent les deux tiers de la population**
children make up two thirds of the
population
(c) to represent ‹person, company›
(d) to perform ‹play›
2 se représenter *v refl* (+ *v être*) (a) to
imagine ‹scene›
(b) ‹opportunity› to arise again
(c) **se ~ à un examen** to retake an
examination

répressif, -ive /ʀepʀesif, iv/ *adj*
repressive

répression /ʀepʀesjɔ̃/ *nf* suppression

réprimande /ʀepʀimɑ̃d/ *nf* reprimand

réprimander /ʀepʀimɑ̃de/ [1] *vtr* to
reprimand

réprimer /ʀepʀime/ [1] *vtr* to suppress; to
repress ‹desire›

repris /ʀ(ə)pʀi/ *nm inv* ~ **de justice** ex-
convict

⚜ indicates a very frequent word

reprise /RəpRiz/ *nf* **(a)** (of work, negotiations) resumption; (of play, film) rerun; **à plusieurs** *or* **maintes** ~**s** on several occasions, repeatedly
(b) (of demand, production) increase; (of business) revival; (of economy) upturn
(c) (of goods) return, taking back; trade-in; (of company) takeover
(d) key money
(e) (Aut) acceleration
(f) mend; darn
(g) (in boxing) round; (in football) start of the second half

repriser /RəpRize/ [1] *vtr* to mend; to darn

réprobation /RepRɔbasjɔ̃/ *nf* disapproval

reproche /R(ə)pRɔʃ/ *nm* reproach; **j'ai un ou deux** ~**s à vous faire** I've one or two criticisms to make; **sans** ~ beyond reproach

reprocher /RəpRɔʃe/ [1] **1** *vtr* **(a)** ~ **qch à qn** to criticize *or* reproach sb for sth; **on ne peut rien lui** ~ he's/she's beyond reproach; **elle me reproche de ne jamais lui écrire** she complains that I never write to her
(b) **les faits qui lui sont reprochés** the charges against him/her
2 se reprocher *v refl* (+ *v être*) **se** ~ **qch** to blame *or* reproach oneself for sth

reproducteur, -trice /RəpRɔdyktœR, tRis/ *adj* **(a)** reproductive
(b) ‹animal› breeding

reproduction /R(ə)pRɔdyksjɔ̃/ *nf*
(a) reproduction
(b) reproduction, copy; **droit de** ~ copyright

reproduire /R(ə)pRɔduiR/ [69] **1** *vtr* (gen) to reproduce; to recreate ‹conditions›
2 se reproduire *v refl* (+ *v être*)
(a) ‹humans, plants› to reproduce
(b) ‹situation› to recur

réprouver /RepRuve/ [1] *vtr* to condemn

reptile /Rɛptil/ *nm* reptile

repu, ~e /Rəpy/ *adj* full

républicain, ~e /Repyblikɛ̃, ɛn/ *adj, nm,f* republican

républíque /Repyblik/ *nf* republic; **on est en** ~ it's a free country

répudier /Repydje/ [2] *vtr* **(a)** to repudiate ‹spouse›
(b) to renounce ‹right, faith›

répugnance /Repyɲɑ̃s/ *nf* **(a)** revulsion
(b) reluctance; **avec** ~ reluctantly

répugnant, ~e /Repyɲɑ̃, ɑ̃t/ *adj*
(a) revolting
(b) disgusting
(c) loathsome

répugner /Repyɲe/ [1] *v+prep* **(a)** ~ **à** ‹food› to disgust ‹person›
(b) ~ **à** ‹person› to be averse to ‹work›; ~ **à faire** to be reluctant to do

répulsion /Repylsjɔ̃/ *nf* repulsion

réputation /Repytasjɔ̃/ *nf* reputation; **se faire une** ~ to make a name for oneself

réputé, ~e /Repyte/ *adj* **(a)** ‹company› reputable; ‹writer› of repute; ‹product› well-known; ~ **pour qch** renowned for sth; **l'avocat le plus** ~ **de Paris** the best lawyer in Paris
(b) ~ **cher** reputed to be expensive

requérir /RəkeRiR/ [35] *vtr* **(a)** to request
(b) to require

requête /Rəkɛt/ *nf* **(a)** request
(b) (Law) petition

requiem /Rekwijɛm/ *nm inv* requiem

requin /R(ə)kɛ̃/ *nm* (Zool, figurative) shark

requis, ~e /Rəki, iz/ **1** *pp* ▶ REQUÉRIR
2 *pp adj* ‹patience› necessary; ‹age› required

réquisition /Rekizisjɔ̃/ *nf* requisitioning

réquisitionner /Rekizisjone/ [1] *vtr* **(a)** to requisition
(b) to commandeer ‹premises›; to conscript ‹workers›

réquisitoire /RekizitwaR/ *nm* closing speech for the prosecution

RER /ɛRəɛR/ *nm* (*abbr* = **réseau express régional**) *rapid-transit rail system in the Paris region*

rescapé, ~e /Rɛskape/ **1** *adj* surviving
2 *nm,f* survivor

rescousse: à la rescousse /alaRɛskus/ *phr* **aller à la** ~ **de qn** to go to sb's rescue

✍ **réseau, pl** ~**x** /Rezo/ *nm* network

réseautage /Rezotaʒ/ *nm* networking; ~ **social** social networking

réservation /RezɛRvasjɔ̃/ *nf* reservation, booking (GB)

✍ **réserve** /RezɛRv/ *nf* **(a)** reservation; **sous** ~ **de changement** subject to alteration; **'sous (toute)** ~**'** (in a programme) 'to be confirmed'
(b) stock; **des** ~ **s de sucre** a stock of sugar; ~**(s) d'argent** money in reserve
(c) (Econ) ~**s de charbon** coal reserves; ~**s d'eau** water supply
(d) (of person, manner) reserve
(e) stockroom
(f) (in museum) storeroom
(g) ~ **naturelle** nature reserve
(h) ~ **indienne** Indian reservation
(i) (Mil) **officier de** ~ reserve officer

réservé, ~e /RezɛRve/ **1** *pp* ▶ RÉSERVER
2 *pp adj* **(a)** ‹fishing› private
(b) ~ **à la clientèle** for patrons only; **voie** ~**e aux autobus** bus lane; **'tous droits** ~**s'** 'all rights reserved'
(c) ‹person› reserved

✍ **réserver** /RezɛRve/ [1] **1** *vtr* **(a)** to reserve, to book (GB) ‹seat, ticket›
(b) to put aside ‹goods›
(c) to set aside ‹money, time›
(d) ~ **un bon accueil à qn** to give sb a warm welcome; **sans savoir ce que l'avenir nous réserve** without knowing what the future ⋯⟶

r

has in store for us
(e) ~ **son jugement** to reserve judgment
2 **se réserver** *v refl* (+ *v être*) **se ~ les meilleurs morceaux** to save the best bits for oneself; **se ~ le droit de faire** to reserve the right to do; **il se réserve pour la candidature à la présidence** he's saving himself for the presidential race

réserviste /Rezɛrvist/ *nmf* reservist
réservoir /Rezɛrvwar/ *nm* **(a)** tank
(b) reservoir
résidant, ~e /Rezidã, ãt/ *adj* resident
résidence /Rezidãs/ *nf* **(a)** residence
(b) place of residence; **assigné à ~** under house arrest
■ **~ principale/secondaire** main/second home; **~ universitaire** (university) hall of residence (GB), residence hall (US)
résident, ~e /Rezidã, ãt/ *nm,f* resident
résidentiel, -ielle /Rezidãsjɛl/ *adj* residential
résider /Rezide/ [1] *vi* **(a)** to live
(b) **~ dans qch** to lie in sth
résidu /Rezidy/ *nm* **(a)** residue
(b) remnant
(c) waste
résignation /Reziɲasjɔ̃/ *nf* resignation (à to)
résigner: se résigner /Reziɲe/ [1] *v refl* (+ *v être*) to resign oneself
résiliation /Reziljasjɔ̃/ *nf* (of contract) termination
résilier /Rezilje/ [2] *vtr* to terminate ‹*contract*›
résine /Rezin/ *nf* resin
résineux /Rezinø/ *nm* conifer
ℐ **résistance** /Rezistãs/ *nf* **(a)** resistance; **manquer de ~** ‹*person*› to lack stamina
(b) (in electricity) (gen) resistance; (of household appliance) element
résistant, ~e /Rezistã, ãt/ **1** *adj*
(a) ‹*person*› tough, resilient; ‹*plant*› hardy
(b) ‹*metal*› resistant; ‹*fabric, garment*› hard-wearing
2 *nm,f* Resistance fighter
ℐ **résister** /Reziste/ [1] *v+prep* (gen) to resist;
~ à to resist ‹*offer*›; to stand ‹*strain*›; to withstand ‹*pressure*›; to get through ‹*ordeal*›; **le mur n'a pas résisté** the wall collapsed; **~ à l'épreuve du temps** to stand the test of time; **il ne supporte pas qu'on lui résiste** he doesn't like it when people stand up to him
résolu, ~e /Rezɔly/ **1** *pp* ▶ RÉSOUDRE
2 *pp adj* resolute, determined
résolument /Rezɔlymã/ *adv* resolutely
résolution /Rezɔlysjɔ̃/ *nf* **(a)** (gen, Pol) resolution
(b) resolve
(c) solution

résonance /Rezɔnãs/ *nf* (gen) resonance
résonner /Rezɔne/ [1] *vi* **(a)** ‹*step, laughter*› to ring out; ‹*cry, echo*› to resound; ‹*cymbals*› to clash
(b) ‹*room*› to echo; **~ de** to resound with
résorber /Rezɔrbe/ [1] **1** *vtr* to absorb ‹*deficit, surplus*›; to reduce ‹*inflation*›
2 **se résorber** *v refl* (+ *v être*) **(a)** ‹*deficit*› to be reduced
(b) (Med) to be resorbed
résorption /Rezɔrpsjɔ̃/ *nf* (of unemployment, inflation) reduction (**de** of)
ℐ **résoudre** /Rezudr/ [75] **1** *vtr* to solve ‹*equation, problem*›; to resolve ‹*crisis*›
2 **se résoudre** *v refl* (+ *v être*) **se ~ à faire** to resolve or make up one's mind to do; **être résolu à faire** to be determined to do
ℐ **respect** /Rɛspɛ/ *nm* (gen) respect; **manquer de ~ à qn** to be disrespectful to sb; **le ~ de soi** self-respect
IDIOMS sauf votre ~ with all due respect; **tenir qn en ~** to keep sb at bay
respectabilité /Rɛspɛktabilite/ *nf* respectability
respectable /Rɛspɛktabl/ *adj* respectable
ℐ **respecter** /Rɛspɛkte/ [1] **1** *vtr* (gen) to respect; to treat [sth] with respect; to honour (GB) ‹*commitment*›; **faire ~ l'ordre/la loi** to enforce order/the law
2 **se respecter** *v refl* (+ *v être*) to respect oneself; **tout homme qui se respecte** any self-respecting man
respectif, -ive /Rɛspɛktif, iv/ *adj* respective
respectueux, -euse /Rɛspɛktɥø, øz/ *adj* respectful; **~ de la loi** law-abiding; **salutations respectueuses** yours faithfully
respirable /Rɛspirabl/ *adj* **(a)** breathable
(b) ‹*atmosphere, mood*› bearable
respiration /Rɛspirasjɔ̃/ *nf* **(a)** breathing; **avoir une ~ difficile** to have breathing difficulties
(b) breath; **retenir sa ~** to hold one's breath
respiratoire /Rɛspiratwar/ *adj* respiratory
respirer /Rɛspire/ [1] **1** *vtr* **(a)** to breathe in ‹*air, dust*›
(b) to smell ‹*perfume*›
(c) ‹*person, place*› to exude
2 *vi* **(a)** to breathe
(b) (figurative) to catch one's breath; **laisse-moi ~** let me get my breath back
resplendir /Rɛsplãdir/ [3] *vi* **(a)** ‹*light*› to shine brightly; ‹*snow*› to sparkle
(b) **~ de santé** to be glowing with health
resplendissant, ~e /Rɛsplãdisã, ãt/ *adj*
(a) ‹*light*› brilliant
(b) ‹*beauty*› radiant
responsabiliser /Rɛspɔ̃sabilize/ [1] *vtr* to give [sb] a sense of responsibility
ℐ **responsabilité** /Rɛspɔ̃sabilite/ *nf* (gen) responsibility; (Law) liability; **avoir la ~ de** to be

---
ℐ indicates a very frequent word

responsible for; **engageant la ∼ de la société** for which the company is liable

∎ **∼ civile** (in insurance) personal liability

ℱ **responsable** /ʀɛspɔ̃sabl/ **1** *adj*
(a) ⟨*person, error*⟩ responsible
(b) accountable; (Law) liable
(c) **être ∼ de qn/qch** to be in charge of sb/sth
(d) ⟨*person, attitude, act*⟩ responsible
2 *nmf* (a) (gen) person in charge; (of shop, project) manager; (of party) leader; (of department) head
(b) **les ∼s de la catastrophe** the people responsible for the catastrophe
(c) **le grand ∼ c'est le tabac** smoking is the main cause

resquiller /ʀɛskije/ [1] *vi* (fam) (on train) not to pay the fare; (at show) to sneak in (colloq)

resquilleur, -euse /ʀɛskijœʀ, øz/ *nm,f* (fam) fare dodger

ressac /ʀəsak/ *nm* backwash

ressaisir: se ressaisir /ʀ(ə)sɛziʀ/ [3] *v refl* (+ *v être*) to pull oneself together

ressasser /ʀ(ə)sase/ [1] *vtr* to brood over ⟨*failure*⟩; to dwell on ⟨*misfortunes*⟩

ressemblance /ʀ(ə)sɑ̃blɑ̃s/ *nf*
(a) resemblance, likeness
(b) (between things) similarity

ressemblant, ∼e /ʀ(ə)sɑ̃blɑ̃, ɑ̃t/ *adj* un portrait ∼ a portrait which is a good likeness

ℱ **ressembler** /ʀ(ə)sɑ̃ble/ [1]
1 ressembler à *v+prep* to look like, to resemble; to be like
2 se ressembler *v refl* (+ *v être*) (a) to look alike
(b) to be alike

ressemeler /ʀ(ə)səmle/ [19] *vtr* to resole

ressentiment /ʀ(ə)sɑ̃timɑ̃/ *nm* resentment

ℱ **ressentir** /ʀ(ə)sɑ̃tiʀ/ [30] **1** *vtr* to feel
2 se ressentir *v refl* (+ *v être*) **se ∼ de** to feel the effects of; to suffer from

resserrer /ʀ(ə)seʀe/ [1] **1** *vtr* (a) to tighten ⟨*knot, screw, grip*⟩
(b) **resserrez les rangs!** close up a bit!
(c) to tighten up on ⟨*discipline, supervision*⟩
2 se resserrer *v refl* (+ *v être*) (a) ⟨*road*⟩ to narrow
(b) ⟨*friendship*⟩ to become stronger
(c) ⟨*link, knot, grip*⟩ to tighten
(d) ⟨*gap*⟩ to close
(e) ⟨*group of people*⟩ to draw closer together
(f) ⟨*discipline*⟩ to become stricter

resservir /ʀ(ə)seʀviʀ/ [30] **1** *vtr* (a) to serve [sth] (up) again
(b) to give [sb] another helping
2 se resservir *v refl* (+ *v être*) to take another helping

ressort /ʀ(ə)sɔʀ/ *nm* (a) (Tech) spring
(b) **avoir du ∼** to have resilience
(c) **être du ∼ de qn** to be within sb's province; (Law) to fall within the jurisdiction of ⟨*court*⟩; **en premier ∼** in the first resort

ressortir /ʀ(ə)sɔʀtiʀ/ [30] **1** *vtr* (a) to take [sth] out again
(b) to bring [sth] out again; to dig out (colloq) ⟨*affair, scandal*⟩
2 *vi* (+ *v être*) (a) ⟨*person*⟩ to go out again
(b) ⟨*bullet*⟩ to come out
(c) to stand out; **voici ce qui ressort de l'étude** the results of the study are as follows; **faire ∼** to bring to light ⟨*contradiction*⟩; ⟨*make-up*⟩ to accentuate ⟨*eyes*⟩
(d) ⟨*film, record*⟩ to be re-released
3 *v impers* (+ *v être*) **il ressort que** it emerges that

ressortissant, ∼e /ʀ(ə)sɔʀtisɑ̃, ɑ̃t/ *nm,f* national

ressouder /ʀ(ə)sude/ [1] *vtr* to solder [sth] again

ℱ **ressource** /ʀ(ə)suʀs/ *nf* (a) resource; **les ∼s énergétiques** energy resources
(b) option; **en dernière ∼** as a last resort
(c) **avoir de la ∼** (fam) to be resourceful
(d) **∼s means**; **être sans ∼s** to have no means of support

ressourcer: se ressourcer /ʀ(ə)suʀse/ [12] *v refl* (+ *v être*) to recharge one's batteries

ressusciter /ʀesysite/ [1] **1** *vtr* (a) to revive ⟨*tradition*⟩; to resurrect ⟨*past*⟩
(b) to raise [sb] from the dead; (figurative) to bring [sb] back to life
2 *vi* ⟨*dead person*⟩ to rise from the dead

restant, ∼e /ʀɛstɑ̃, ɑ̃t/ **1** *adj* remaining
2 *nm* (a) **le ∼** the remainder; the rest
(b) **un ∼ de poulet** some left-over chicken

restaurant /ʀɛstɔʀɑ̃/ *nm* restaurant

∎ **∼ universitaire, RU** university canteen (GB), cafeteria

restaurateur, -trice /ʀɛstɔʀatœʀ, tʀis/ *nm,f* (a) restaurant owner
(b) restorer

restauration /ʀɛstɔʀasjɔ̃/ *nf* (a) catering; **∼ rapide** fast-food industry
(b) restoration

restaurer /ʀɛstɔʀe/ [1] **1** *vtr* (a) to feed
(b) to restore
2 se restaurer *v refl* (+ *v être*) to have something to eat

ℱ **reste** /ʀɛst/ **1** *nm* **le ∼** the rest; the remainder; **un ∼ de tissu** some left-over material; **au ∼, du ∼** besides
2 restes *nm pl* (a) remains
(b) leftovers
IDIOMS sans demander son ∼ without further ado; **être en ∼ avec qn** to feel indebted to sb; **pour ne pas être en ∼** so as not to be outdone

ℱ **rester** /ʀɛste/ [1] (+ *v être*) **1** *vi* (a) to stay, to remain; **que ça reste entre nous!** this is strictly between you and me!
(b) to remain; **restez assis!** remain seated!; ···⟩

r

don't get up!; ~ **sans manger** to go without food; ~ **paralysé** to be left paralysed; ~ **les bras croisés** (figurative) to stand idly by
(c) to be left, to remain
(d) ‹*memory, work of art*› to live on
(e) ~ **sur une bonne impression** to be left with a good impression
(f) en ~ **à** to go no further than; **je compte bien ne pas en** ~ **là** I won't let the matter rest there; **restons-en là pour le moment** let's leave it at that for now
2 *v impers* **il reste une minute** there is one minute left; **il ne me reste plus que lui** he's all I've got left; **il reste que, il n'en reste pas moins que** the fact remains that

restituer /ʀɛstitɥe/ [1] *vtr* **(a)** to restore
(b) to reconstruct ‹*text*›; to reproduce ‹*sound*›

restitution /ʀɛstitysjɔ̃/ *nf* **(a)** return; restoration
(b) reproduction

restreindre /ʀɛstʀɛ̃dʀ/ [55] **1** *vtr* to curb, to cut back on; to limit; to restrict
2 se restreindre *v refl* (+ *v être*)
(a) ‹*possibilities*› to become restricted; ‹*influence*› to wane
(b) se ~ **(dans ses dépenses)** to cut back (on one's expenses)

restreint, ~**e** /ʀɛstʀɛ̃, ɛ̃t/ *adj* ‹*public, vocabulary*› limited; ‹*team*› small

restrictif, -ive /ʀɛstʀiktif, iv/ *adj* restrictive

restriction /ʀɛstʀiksjɔ̃/ *nf* **(a)** restriction; ~**s salariales** wage restraints; **sans** ~ freely
(b) sans ~ ‹*approve*› without reservations; ‹*support*› unreservedly

restructurer /ʀəstʀyktyʀe/ [1] *vtr* to restructure; to redevelop ‹*area*›

🖋 **résultat** /ʀezylta/ *nm* (gen) result; (of research) results, findings; (of negotiations, inquiry) result, outcome; **sans** ~ without success

résulter /ʀezylte/ [1] **1 résulter de** *v+prep* to be the result of, to result from
2 *v impers* **il résulte de ce que vous venez de dire que...** it follows from what you have just said that...; **il en résulte que...** as a result...

résumé /ʀezyme/ *nm* summary, résumé; **en** ~ to sum up; **faire un** ~ **de qch (à qn)** to give (sb) a rundown of *or* on sth

résumer /ʀezyme/ [1] **1** *vtr* **(a)** to summarize ‹*text*›
(b) to sum up ‹*news*›
2 se résumer *v refl* (+ *v être*) **(a)** to sum up
(b) se ~ **à** to come down to

résurgence /ʀezyʀʒɑ̃s/ *nf* resurgence; revival

resurgir /ʀ(ə)syʀʒiʀ/ [3] *vi* to reappear

résurrection /ʀezyʀɛksjɔ̃/ *nf*
(a) resurrection

🖋 indicates a very frequent word

(b) revival
(c) rebirth

rétablir /ʀetabliʀ/ [3] **1** *vtr* **(a)** to restore; ~ **la circulation** to get the traffic moving again
(b) to re-establish ‹*truth, facts*›
(c) ~ **qn dans ses fonctions** to reinstate sb in his/her job
2 se rétablir *v refl* (+ *v être*) **(a)** to recover
(b) ‹*calm*› to return; ‹*situation*› to return to normal

rétablissement /ʀetablismɑ̃/ *nm*
(a) restoration
(b) re-establishment
(c) recovery

rétamer /ʀetame/ [1] (fam) **1** *vtr* (tire) to wear [sb] out; (beat) to hammer (colloq)
2 se rétamer *v refl* (+ *v être*) to fall, to come a cropper (colloq)

retape /ʀ(ə)tap/ *nf* (pop) **faire de la** ~ **pour qch** to beat the drum for sth

retaper /ʀ(ə)tape/ [1] *vtr* (fam) **(a)** to do up ‹*house*›
(b) to put [sb] on his/her feet again

retard /ʀ(ə)taʀ/ *nm* **(a)** lateness
(b) delay; **avoir du** ~ to be late; **nous sommes en** ~ **sur l'emploi du temps** we're behind schedule; **prendre du** ~ to fall *or* get behind; **avoir du courrier en** ~ to have a backlog of mail; **sans** ~ without delay
(c) backwardness; **il a deux ans de** ~ (Sch) he's two years behind at school

retardataire /ʀ(ə)taʀdatɛʀ/ *nmf* latecomer

retardé, ~**e** /ʀətaʀde/ *adj* ‹*person*› backward

retardement, à retardement /aʀ(ə)taʀdəmɑ̃/ *phr* ‹*mechanism, device*› delayed-action; **bombe à** ~ time-bomb; ‹*act, get angry*› after the event

retarder /ʀ(ə)taʀde/ [1] **1** *vtr* **(a)** to make [sb] late; **être retardé** ‹*train*› to be delayed
(b) to hold [sb] up
(c) to put off, to postpone ‹*departure, operation*›
(d) to put back ‹*clock*›
2 *vi* ‹*clock*› to be slow

🖋 **retenir** /ʀət(ə)niʀ, ʀtəniʀ/ [36] **1** *vtr* **(a)** to keep ‹*person*›; ~ **qn prisonnier** to hold sb captive; ~ **qn à dîner** to ask sb to stay for dinner
(b) to hold [sb] up, to detain ‹*person*›
(c) to hold ‹*object, attention*›; to hold back ‹*hair, dog, crowd*›; to stop ‹*person*›; ~ **sa langue** to hold one's tongue; ~ **qn par la manche** to catch hold of sb's sleeve; **votre réclamation a retenu toute notre attention** your complaint is receiving our full attention
(d) to hold back ‹*tears*›; to hold ‹*breath*›; to stifle ‹*scream, yawn*›; to contain, to suppress

⟨anger⟩
(e) to retain ⟨heat, water, odour⟩
(f) to reserve, to book (GB) ⟨table, room⟩; to set ⟨date⟩
(g) to deduct ⟨sum⟩
(h) to remember; **toi, je te retiens!** (fam) I won't forget this!
(i) to accept ⟨argument, plan⟩; (Law) to uphold ⟨charge⟩
(j) (in mathematics) **je pose 5 et je retiens 2** I put down 5 and carry 2
2 se retenir v refl (+ v être) **(a)** to stop oneself; **se ~ à qch** to hang on to sth
(b) se ~ de pleurer to hold back the tears
(c) (fam) to control oneself

rétention /Retɑ̃sjɔ̃/ nf **(a)** (Med) retention
(b) withholding

retentir /R(ə)tɑ̃tiR/ [3] vi to ring out; to resound

retentissant, ~e /R(ə)tɑ̃tisɑ̃, ɑ̃t/ adj
(a) ⟨failure⟩ resounding; ⟨trial, film⟩ sensational
(b) ⟨cry, noise⟩ ringing; resounding

retentissement /R(ə)tɑ̃tismɑ̃/ nm (gen) effect; (of book, artist) impact

retenue /Rət(ə)ny/ nf **(a)** restraint; **perdre toute ~** to lose one's inhibitions; **boire sans ~** to drink to excess
(b) deduction
(c) (Sch) detention
(d) tu as oublié la ~ des dizaines you forgot to carry over from the tens column

réticence /Retisɑ̃s/ nf **(a)** reluctance
(b) ses ~s en ce qui concerne le passé his/ her reticence about the past

réticent, ~e /Retisɑ̃, ɑ̃t/ adj **(a)** hesitant
(b) reluctant

rétif, -ive /Retif, iv/ adj restive; rebellious

rétine /Retin/ nf retina

retiré, ~e /RətiRe/ adj **(a)** ⟨life⟩ secluded
(b) ⟨place⟩ remote

ℰ **retirer** /RətiRe/ [1] **1** vtr **(a)** to take off ⟨garment, piece of jewellery⟩
(b) to take out, to remove; **~ ses troupes d'un pays** to withdraw one's troops from a country
(c) to withdraw ⟨foot, hand⟩; **retire ta main** move your hand away
(d) to withdraw ⟨permission, privilege⟩; to take away ⟨right, property⟩; **~ un produit de la vente** to recall a product; **~ une pièce de l'affiche** to close a play
(e) to withdraw ⟨complaint, offer, support⟩; **je retire ce que j'ai dit** I take back what I said
(f) to collect, to pick up ⟨ticket, luggage⟩; to withdraw ⟨money⟩
(g) to get, to derive ⟨profit⟩; **il en retire 2 000 euros par an** he gets 2,000 euros a year out of it
2 se retirer v refl (+ v être) **(a)** to withdraw, to leave

(b) la mer se retire the tide is going out

retombées /Rətɔ̃be/ nf pl **(a)** ~ **radioactives** radioactive fallout
(b) effects, consequences
(c) (of invention) spin-offs

retomber /Rətɔ̃be/ [1] vi (+ v être) **(a)** to fall again; **~ en enfance** to regress to childhood
(b) ⟨person, cat, projectile⟩ to land; ⟨ball, curtain⟩ to come down; ⟨fog⟩ to set in again; **ça va te ~ sur le nez** (figurative) (fam) it'll come down on your head
(c) ⟨anger⟩ to subside; ⟨interest⟩ to wane
(d) ⟨currency, temperature⟩ to fall
(e) ~ sur qn ⟨responsibility⟩ to fall on sb; **faire ~ la responsabilité sur qn** to pass the buck to sb (colloq)

retordre /R(ə)tɔRdR/ [6] vtr **donner du fil à ~ à qn** to give sb a hard time

rétorquer /RetɔRke/ [1] vtr to retort

retors, ~e /RətɔR, ɔRs/ adj ⟨person⟩ crafty; ⟨argument⟩ devious

rétorsion /RetɔRsjɔ̃/ nf retaliation

retouche /R(ə)tuʃ/ nf alteration; (of photograph, picture) retouching

retoucher /R(ə)tuʃe/ [1] vtr to make alterations to; to touch up

ℰ **retour** /R(ə)tuR/ nm return; **(billet de) ~** return (ticket) (GB), round trip (ticket) (US); **au ~** on the way back; **être de ~ (à la maison)** to be back (home); **on attend le ~ au calme** people are waiting for things to calm down; **il connaît maintenant le succès et c'est un juste ~ des choses** he's successful now, and deservedly so; **elle s'engage, en ~, à payer la facture** she undertakes for her part to pay the bill; **'sans ~ ni consigne'** 'no deposit or return'; **par ~ du courrier** by return of post (GB), by the next mail (US)
■ **~ d'âge** change of life; **~ en arrière** flashback; **~ de bâton** (fam) backlash
IDIOM **être sur le ~** (fam) to be over the hill (colloq)

retournement /R(ə)tuRnəmɑ̃/ nm reversal; **un ~ de l'opinion publique** a turn around in public opinion

ℰ **retourner** /R(ə)tuRne/ [1] **1** vtr (+ v avoir) **(a)** to turn [sth] over; to turn ⟨mattress⟩
(b) to turn [sth] inside out
(c) to turn over ⟨earth⟩; to toss ⟨salad⟩
(d) to return ⟨compliment, criticism⟩; **~ la situation** to reverse the situation
(e) to turn [sth] upside down ⟨room⟩; ⟨news, film⟩ to shake ⟨person⟩
(f) to send [sth] back, to return
2 vi (+ v être) to go back, to return
3 se retourner v refl (+ v être) **(a)** to turn around
(b) to turn over; **il n'a pas arrêté de se ~ (dans son lit)** he kept tossing and turning
(c) (fam) to get organized
(d) se ~ contre qn ⟨person⟩ to turn against ⋯⋗

r

sb; ‹arguments› to backfire on sb
(e) elle s'est retourné le doigt she bent back her finger
(f) s'en ~ (chez soi) to go back (home)
④ *v impers* **j'aime savoir de quoi il retourne** I like to know what's going on
IDIOM ~ qn comme une crêpe (fam) to make sb change their mind completely

retracer /ʀətʀase/ [12] *vtr* **(a)** to redraw ‹line›
(b) to recount ‹event›

rétractable /ʀetʀaktabl/ *adj* retractable

rétracter /ʀetʀakte/ [1] *vtr*, **se rétracter** *v refl* (+ *v être*) to retract

retrait /ʀ(ə)tʀɛ/ ① *nm* (gen) withdrawal; (of suitcase, packet) collection; **~ du permis (de conduire)** disqualification from driving
② **en retrait** *phr* **maison en ~ de** house set back from ‹road›; **se tenir en ~** to stand back; **rester en ~** to stay in the background

ơ **retraite** /ʀ(ə)tʀɛt/ *nf* **(a)** retirement; **prendre sa ~** to retire
(b) pension
(c) (Mil) retreat
(d) (place) retreat; (of bandits) hiding place
■ **~ par capitalisation** loanback pension; **~ complémentaire** private pension

retraité, ~e /ʀətʀete/ *nm,f* retired person

retraiter /ʀətʀete/ [1] *vtr* to reprocess ‹plutonium›

retranché, ~e /ʀ(ə)tʀɑ̃ʃe/ *adj* entrenched

retranchement /ʀ(ə)tʀɑ̃ʃmɑ̃/ *nm* entrenchment; **pousser qn dans ses derniers ~s** to drive sb into a corner

retrancher /ʀ(ə)tʀɑ̃ʃe/ [1] ① *vtr* **(a)** to cut out ‹word›
(b) to subtract ‹amount›; to deduct ‹costs›
② **se retrancher** *v refl* (+ *v être*) (Mil, gen) to take up position; to entrench oneself

retransmettre /ʀətʀɑ̃smɛtʀ/ [60] *vtr*
(a) to broadcast; **retransmis par satellite** relayed by satellite
(b) to retransmit

retransmission /ʀətʀɑ̃smisjɔ̃/ *nf*
(a) broadcast
(b) relay
(c) retransmission

rétrécir /ʀetʀesiʀ/ [3] *vi*, **se rétrécir** *v refl* (+ *v être*) **(a)** to narrow
(b) to shrink

rétrécissement /ʀetʀesismɑ̃/ *nm*
(a) shrinkage
(b) narrowing
(c) contraction

rétribuer /ʀetʀibɥe/ [1] *vtr* to remunerate

rétribution /ʀetʀibysjɔ̃/ *nf* remuneration

rétro /ʀetʀo/ *nm* **(a)** nostalgic style
(b) retro fashions

rétroactif, -ive /ʀetʀoaktif, iv/ *adj* (Law, gen) retroactive

rétrograde /ʀetʀogʀad/ *adj* ‹person› reactionary; ‹policy, measure› retrograde

rétrograder /ʀetʀogʀade/ [1] ① *vtr* **(a)** to demote
(b) (Sport) to relegate
② *vi* (Aut) to change down (GB), to downshift (US)

rétrospectif, -ive¹ /ʀetʀɔspɛktif, iv/ *adj* retrospective

rétrospective² /ʀetʀɔspɛktiv/ *nf* (gen) retrospective; (of films) festival

rétrospectivement / ʀetʀɔspɛktivmɑ̃/ *adv* in retrospect; looking back

retroussé, ~e /ʀ(ə)tʀuse/ *adj* ‹nose› turned up; ‹lip› curling

retrousser /ʀ(ə)tʀuse/ [1] *vtr* to hitch up (GB), to hike up (US) ‹skirt›; to roll up ‹sleeves›

retrouvailles /ʀətʀuvɑj/ *nf pl* **(a)** reunion
(b) reconciliation

ơ **retrouver** /ʀətʀuve/ [1] ① *vtr* **(a)** to find ‹lost object›
(b) to find [sth] again ‹work, object›
(c) to regain ‹strength, health›
(d) to remember ‹name, tune›
(e) to be back in ‹place›
(f) to recognize ‹person, style›; **je retrouve sa mère en elle** I can see her mother in her
(g) to join, to meet ‹person›
② **se retrouver** *v refl* (+ *v être*) **(a)** to meet (again); **on s'est retrouvé en famille** the family got together; **comme on se retrouve!** fancy seeing you here!
(b) se ~ enceinte to find oneself pregnant; **se ~ sans argent** to be left penniless
(c) *se or* **s'y ~ dans** to find one's way around in ‹place, mess›; to follow, to understand ‹explanation›; **il y a trop de changements, on ne s'y retrouve plus** there are too many changes, we don't know if we're coming or going
(d) (fam) **s'y ~** to break even; (making profit) to do well
(e) ‹quality› to be found; ‹problem› to occur
(f) se ~ dans qn/qch to see *or* recognize oneself in sb/sth

rétroviseur /ʀetʀovizœʀ/ *nm* **(a)** rear-view mirror
(b) wing mirror (GB), outside rear-view mirror (US)

réunification /ʀeynifikasjɔ̃/ *nf* reunification

réunifier /ʀeynifje/ [2] ① *vtr* to reunify
② **se réunifier** *v refl* (+ *v être*) to be reunified

ơ **réunion** /ʀeynjɔ̃/ *nf* **(a)** meeting; **être en ~** ‹person› to be at a meeting
(b) gathering
(c) reunion
(d) (of different talents) combination; (of poems) collection

---

ơ indicates a very frequent word

(e) union

✧ **réunir** /ʀeyniʀ/ [3] **1** *vtr* **(a)** ‹*conference*› to bring together ‹*participants*›; ‹*organizer*› to get [sb] together ‹*participants*›
(b) to call [sb] together ‹*delegates*›; to convene ‹*assembly*›
(c) to have [sb] round (GB) *or* over
(d) to join ‹*edges*›
(e) to unite ‹*provinces*›
(f) ~ **les conditions nécessaires** to fulfil (GB) all the necessary conditions
(g) to raise ‹*funds*›
(h) to assemble ‹*elements, evidence*›; to gather [sth] together ‹*documents*›
(i) ‹*road, canal*› to connect
2 se réunir *v refl* (+ *v être*) to meet; to get together

✧ **réussir** /ʀeysiʀ/ [3] **1** *vtr* to achieve ‹*unification*›; to carry out [sth] successfully ‹*operation*›; to make a success of ‹*life*›
2 réussir à *v+prep* **(a)** ~ **à faire** to succeed in doing; ~ **à un examen** to pass an exam
(b) ~ **à qn** ‹*life, method*› to turn out well for sb; ‹*rest*› to do sb good
3 *vi* **(a)** to succeed
(b) ‹*attempt*› to be successful
(c) ‹*person*› to do well

réussite /ʀeysit/ *nf* (gen) success

revaloir /ʀ(ə)valwaʀ/ [45] *vtr* **je te revaudrai ça** (vengefully) I'll get even with you for that; (in gratitude) I'll return the favour (GB)

revalorisation /ʀ(ə)valɔʀizasjɔ̃/ *nf*
(a) (increase) **une** ~ **des salaires de 3%** a 3% wage increase
(b) (renewed esteem) **la** ~ **des enseignants** the enhanced prestige of teachers

revaloriser /ʀ(ə)valɔʀize/ [1] *vtr* **(a)** to increase ‹*salary*›; to revalue ‹*currency*›
(b) to reassert the value of ‹*traditions*›
(c) to renovate ‹*area*›

revanche /ʀ(ə)vɑ̃ʃ/ [1] *nf* **(a)** revenge
(b) (Sport) return match (GB) *or* game (US)
2 en revanche *phr* on the other hand

rêvasser /ʀɛvase/ [1] *vi* to daydream

✧ **rêve** /ʀɛv/ *nm* **(a)** dreaming
(b) dream; **fais de beaux** ~**s!** sweet dreams!
(c) ideal; **une maison de** ~ a dream house; **c'est le** ~ this is just perfect

rêvé, ~e /ʀeve/ *adj* ideal, perfect

revêche /ʀəvɛʃ/ *adj* ‹*manner, tone*› sour; ‹*person*› crabby

réveil /ʀevɛj/ *nm* **(a)** waking (up)
(b) (after anaesthetic) **j'ai eu des nausées au** ~ I felt nauseous when I regained consciousness
(c) (of movement) resurgence; (of pain) return; (of volcano) return to activity
(d) (Mil) reveille
(e) alarm clock

réveille-matin /ʀevɛjmatɛ̃/ *nm inv* alarm clock

✧ **réveiller** /ʀeveje/ [1] **1** *vtr* **(a)** to wake [sb] up, to wake
(b) to revive ‹*person*›; to awaken ‹*feeling*›; to arouse ‹*curiosity*›; to stir up ‹*memory*›
2 se réveiller *v refl* (+ *v être*) **(a)** to wake up; to awaken
(b) to regain consciousness
(c) ‹*volcano*› to become active again
(d) ‹*pain, appetite*› to come back; ‹*memory*› to be reawakened

réveillon /ʀevɛjɔ̃/ *nm* ~ **du Nouvel An** New Year's Eve party

réveillonner /ʀevɛjɔne/ [1] *vi* to celebrate Christmas Eve; to see the New Year in

révélateur, -trice /ʀevelatœʀ, tʀis/ **1** *adj* ‹*detail, fact*› revealing, telling
2 *nm* (in photography) developer

révélation /ʀevelasjɔ̃/ *nf* revelation

✧ **révéler** /ʀevele/ [14] **1** *vtr* **(a)** to reveal; to give away ‹*secret*›
(b) to show
(c) to discover ‹*artist*›
(d) (in photography) to develop
2 se révéler *v refl* (+ *v être*) **se** ~ **faux** to turn out to be wrong

revenant, ~e /ʀəv(ə)nɑ̃, ɑ̃t/ *nm,f* ghost

revendeur, -euse /ʀ(ə)vɑ̃dœʀ, øz/ *nm,f*
(a) stockist
(b) **un** ~ **de drogue** a drug dealer
(c) seller (of stolen goods)

revendicatif, -ive /ʀ(ə)vɑ̃dikatif, iv/ *adj* protest; **journée revendicative** day of protest

revendication /ʀ(ə)vɑ̃dikasjɔ̃/ *nf* (of workers) demand; (of country) claim

revendiquer /ʀ(ə)vɑ̃dike/ [1] *vtr* **(a)** to demand ‹*pay rise*›; to claim ‹*territory*›
(b) to claim responsibility for ‹*attack*›
(c) to proclaim ‹*origins*›

revendre /ʀ(ə)vɑ̃dʀ/ [6] *vtr* **(a)** to sell [sth] retail, to retail
(b) to resell ‹*car, house*›; to sell on ‹*stolen object*›; **avoir de l'énergie à** ~ to have energy to spare

✧ **revenir** /ʀəvniʀ, ʀvəniʀ/ [36] **1** *vi* **(a)** to come back; to come again
(b) ‹*person, animal, vehicle*› to come back, to return; ~ **de loin** (figurative) to have had a close shave; **mon chèque m'est revenu** my cheque (GB) *or* check (US) was returned
(c) ~ **à** to return to, to come back to ‹*method, story*›
(d) ‹*appetite, memory*› to come back; ‹*sun*› to come out again; ‹*season*› to return; ‹*idea, theme*› to recur; ~ **à la mémoire** *or* **l'esprit de qn** to come back to sb; **ça me revient!** now I remember!
(e) ~ **à 100 euros** to come to 100 euros; **ça revient cher** it works out expensive
(f) ~ **sur** to go back over ‹*question, past*›; to go back on ‹*decision, promise*›; to retract ‹*confession*›
(g) ~ **de** to get over ‹*illness, surprise*›; to ····❖

r

lose ‹illusion›; **la vie à la campagne, j'en suis revenu** as for life in the country, I've seen it for what it is; **je n'en reviens pas des progrès que tu as faits** (fam) I'm amazed at the progress you've made
(h) ~ **aux oreilles de qn** ‹remark› to reach sb's ears
(i) ~ **à qn** ‹property› to go to sb; ‹honour› to fall to sb; **ça leur revient de droit** it's theirs by right; **la décision revient au rédacteur** it is the editor's decision
(j) (Culin) **faire** ~ to brown
2 *v impers* **c'est à vous qu'il revient de trancher** it is for you to decide
IDIOM **il a une tête qui ne me revient pas** I don't like the look of him

✔ **revenu** /Rəv(ə)ny, Rvəny/ *nm* income; (of state) revenue
■ ~ **minimum d'insertion, RMI** *minimum benefit paid to those with no other source of income*

✔ **rêver** /Reve/ [1] **1** *vtr* **(a)** to dream
(b) to dream of ‹success, revenge›
2 *vi* to dream

réverbération /ReveRberasjɔ̃/ *nf* **(a)** glare
(b) reflection
(c) reverberation

réverbère /ReveRbeR/ *nm* street lamp *or* light

réverbérer /ReveRbere/ [14] **1** *vtr* to reflect
2 **se réverbérer** *v refl* (+ *v être*) ‹light, heat› to be reflected; ‹sound› to reverberate

révérence /ReveRɑ̃s/ *nf* **(a)** curtsey; bow
(b) reverence
IDIOM **tirer sa** ~ (fam) to take one's leave

révérencieux, -ieuse /ReveRɑ̃sjø, øz/ *adj* deferential (**envers** to); **attitude peu révérencieuse** irreverent attitude

révérend, ~e /ReveRɑ̃, ɑ̃d/ *nm,f*
(a) Father/Mother Superior
(b) reverend

révérer /ReveRe/ [14] *vtr* to revere

rêverie /REvRi/ *nf* **(a)** daydreaming
(b) daydream

revers /R(ə)veR/ *nm inv* **(a)** (of hand) back; (of cloth) wrong side; (of coin) reverse; **le** ~ **de la médaille** (figurative) the downside (colloq)
(b) (on jacket) lapel; (of trousers) turn-up (GB), cuff (US)
(c) (in tennis) backhand (stroke)
(d) setback

réversibilité /ReveRsibilite/ *nf* reversibility; (in law) reversion

réversible /ReveRsibl/ *adj* (gen) reversible

revêtement /R(ə)vɛtmɑ̃/ *nm* **(a)** (of road) surface
(b) coating; covering

revêtir /R(ə)vetiR/ [33] **1** *vtr* **(a)** to assume ‹gravity, solemnity›; to have ‹disadvantage›;

to take on ‹significance›; ~ **la forme de** to take the form of
(b) to put on ‹garment›
(c) ~ **qch de** to cover sth with ‹carpet, tiles›
2 **se revêtir** *v refl* (+ *v être*) **se** ~ **de** to put on ‹cloak›; to become covered with ‹snow›

rêveur, -euse /REvœR, øz/ **1** *adj* dreamy
2 *nm,f* dreamer

revient /R(ə)vjɛ̃/ *nm* **prix de** ~ cost price

revigorer /R(ə)vigɔRe/ [1] *vtr* to revive

revirement /R(ə)viRmɑ̃/ *nm* turnaround

réviser /Revize/ [1] *vtr* **(a)** to revise ‹position, prices›; to review ‹constitution›
(b) to overhaul ‹car, boiler›; to revise ‹manuscript›
(c) (Sch) to revise (GB), to review (US)

révision /Revizjɔ̃/ *nm* **(a)** revision; review
(b) (of car) service; (of manuscript) revision; (of accounts) audit
(c) (Sch) revision (GB), review (US)

revitaliser /R(ə)vitalize/ [1] *vtr* to revitalize

revivifier /R(ə)vivifje/ [2] *vtr* to revive; to revivify

revivre /R(ə)vivR/ [63] **1** *vtr* **(a)** to go over, to relive ‹event, past›; **faire** ~ **qch à qn** to bring back memories of sth to sb
(b) to live through [sth] again ‹war›
2 *vi* **(a)** to come alive again
(b) to be able to breathe again
(c) **faire** ~ to revive ‹tradition›

révocation /Revɔkasjɔ̃/ *nf* (of will) revocation; (of person) dismissal

revoici /R(ə)vwasi/ *prep* (fam) ~ **Marianne!** here's Marianne again!

revoilà /R(ə)vwala/ ▶ REVOICI

revoir¹ /R(ə)vwaR/ [46] *vtr* **(a)** to see [sb/ sth] again
(b) to go over ‹exercise, lesson›; to review ‹method›; to check through ‹accounts›

✔ **revoir²: au revoir** /ɔR(ə)vwaR/ *phr* goodbye

révoltant, ~e /Revɔltɑ̃, ɑ̃t/ *adj* appalling

révolte /Revɔlt/ *nf* **(a)** revolt
(b) rebellion

révolté, ~e /Revɔlte/ *adj* **(a)** (insubordinate) rebellious
(b) (shocked) appalled

révolter /Revɔlte/ [1] **1** *vtr* to appal (GB)
2 **se révolter** *v refl* (+ *v être*) **(a)** to rebel
(b) to be appalled

révolu, ~e /Revɔly/ *adj* **(a)** **ce temps est** ~ those days are over *or* past
(b) **avoir 12 ans** ~**s** to be over 12 years of age

✔ **révolution** /Revɔlysjɔ̃/ *nf* **(a)** revolution
(b) turmoil
(c) (of planet) revolution

révolutionnaire /RevɔlysjɔnɛR/ *adj, nmf* revolutionary

révolutionner /Revɔlysjɔne/ [1] *vtr* to revolutionize

✔ indicates a very frequent word

revolver /ʀevɔlvɛʀ/ *nm* **(a)** revolver
(b) handgun; **coup de** ∼ gunshot

révoquer /ʀevɔke/ [1] *vtr* **(a)** to revoke
‹will›
(b) to dismiss ‹person›

⚜ **revue** /ʀ(ə)vy/ *nf* **(a)** (gen) magazine;
(academic) journal
(b) (Mil) parade; **passer en** ∼ to review
‹troops›; to inspect ‹equipment›
(c) revue
(d) examination; **passer qch en** ∼ to go
over sth
■ ∼ **de presse** review of the papers

révulser /ʀevylse/ [1] **1** *vtr* to appal (GB)
2 se révulser *v refl* (+ *v être*) ‹eyes› to
roll (upward(s)); ‹face› to contort

révulsion /ʀevylsjɔ̃/ *nf* (Med, gen) revulsion

rez-de-chaussée /ʀɛdʃose/ *nm inv*
ground floor (GB), first floor (US)

RF (*written abbr* = **République
française**) French Republic

rhabiller: se rhabiller /ʀabije/ [1] *v refl*
(+ *v être*) to get dressed again
IDIOM il peut aller se ∼**!** (pop) he can go back
where he came from!

rhapsodie /ʀapsɔdi/ *nf* rhapsody

rhésus /ʀezys/ *nm inv* **(a) facteur** ∼ rhesus
factor
(b) rhesus monkey

rhétorique /ʀetɔʀik/ **1** *adj* rhetorical
2 *nf* rhetoric

Rhin /ʀɛ̃/ *pr nm* **le** ∼ the Rhine

rhinocéros /ʀinɔseʀɔs/ *nm inv* rhinoceros

rhubarbe /ʀybaʀb/ *nf* rhubarb

rhum /ʀɔm/ *nm* rum

rhumatisme /ʀymatism/ *nm* rheumatism

rhume /ʀym/ *nm* cold; ∼ **des foins** hay
fever

ri /ʀi/ ▶ **RIRE¹**

ribambelle /ʀibɑ̃bɛl/ *nf* (fam) (of children)
flock; (of friends) host; (of names) whole string

Ricain, ∼**e** /ʀikɛ̃, ɛn/ (fam) (offensive or
humorous) *nm,f* Yank (colloq)

ricaner /ʀikane/ [1] *vi* **(a)** to snigger
(b) to giggle

⚜ **riche** /ʀiʃ/ **1** *adj* (gen) rich; ‹person› rich,
wealthy; ‹library› well-stocked; ‹decor›
elaborate; **une** ∼ **idée** an excellent idea
2 *nmf* rich man/woman; **les** ∼**s** the rich

richement /ʀiʃmɑ̃/ *adv* richly, lavishly
‹furnished, decorated›

⚜ **richesse** /ʀiʃɛs/ **1** *nf* **(a)** wealth; **c'est
toute notre** ∼ it's all we have
(b) (of jewellery) magnificence; (of garment)
richness
(c) (of foodstuff) richness
(d) (of fauna, vocabulary) richness; (of
documentation) wealth
2 richesses *nf pl* wealth; ∼**s naturelles**
natural resources

richissime /ʀiʃisim/ *adj* (fam) fabulously
rich

ricin /ʀisɛ̃/ *nm* **huile de** ∼ castor oil

ricocher /ʀikɔʃe/ [1] *vi* ‹bullet› to ricochet
(**sur** off); (off an obstacle) to rebound (**sur** off)

ricochet /ʀikɔʃɛ/ *nm* (of bullet) ricochet; (of
stone) bounce; **faire des** ∼**s** to skim stones

rictus /ʀiktys/ *nm inv* (fixed) grin, rictus

ride /ʀid/ *nf* (on face, fruit) wrinkle; (on lake)
ripple

⚜ **rideau,** *pl* ∼**x** /ʀido/ *nm* **(a)** curtain
(b) (of shop) roller shutter
(c) (of flames) wall
■ ∼ **de fumée** blanket of smoke

rider /ʀide/ [1] **1** *vtr* **(a)** to wrinkle ‹face,
skin›
(b) to ripple ‹surface, lake›
2 se rider *v refl* (+ *v être*) **(a)** ‹skin› to
wrinkle
(b) ‹lake› to ripple

ridicule /ʀidikyl/ **1** *adj* **(a)** ridiculous
(b) ‹wage› ridiculously low, pathetic
2 *nm* **(a)** ridicule
(b) (of situation) absurdity

ridiculiser /ʀidikylize/ [1] **1** *vtr* to
ridicule; to wipe the floor with ‹competitor›
2 se ridiculiser *v refl* (+ *v être*) ‹person›
to make a fool of oneself

ridule /ʀidyl/ *nf* fine wrinkle

⚜ **rien¹** /ʀjɛ̃/ **1** *pron* **(a)** nothing; **il n'y a
plus** ∼ there's nothing left; ∼ **n'y fait!**
nothing's any good!; ∼ **d'autre** nothing
else; **'pourquoi?'—'pour** ∼**'** 'why?'—'no
reason'; **'merci'—'de** ∼**'** 'thank you'—'you're
welcome' *or* 'not at all'; **en moins de** ∼ in
no time at all; **ça ou** ∼, **c'est pareil** it makes
no odds; **c'est trois fois** ∼ (fam) it's next to
nothing
(b) ∼ **que la bouteille pèse deux kilos** the
bottle alone weighs two kilos; **elle voudrait
un bureau** ∼ **qu'à elle** (fam) she would like
an office all to herself; ∼ **que ça?** (fam) is
that all?; **ils habitent un château,** ∼ **que ça!**
(ironic) they live in a castle, no less! *or* if you
please!
(c) anything; **sans que j'en sache** ∼ without
my knowing anything about it
(d) (Sport, gen) nil; (in tennis) love
2 de rien (du tout) *phr* **un petit bleu de**
∼ **(du tout)** a tiny bruise
3 en rien *phr* at all, in any way
IDIOMS ∼ **à faire!** it's no good *or* use!; **ce
n'est pas** ∼**!** (exploit) it's quite something!;
(task) it's no joke!; (sum of money) it's not
exactly peanuts! (colloq)

rien² /ʀjɛ̃/ **1** *nm* **un** ∼ **le fâche** the
slightest thing annoys him; **se disputer pour
un** ∼ to quarrel over nothing; **les petits** ∼**s
qui rendent la vie agréable** the little things
which make life pleasant; **un/une** ∼ **du tout**
a worthless person
2 un rien *phr* (fam) a (tiny) bit

rieur, **rieuse** /ʁijœʁ, øz/ *adj* ‹person, tone›
cheerful; ‹face, eyes› laughing

rigide /ʁiʒid/ *adj* (a) rigid
(b) stiff

rigidité /ʁiʒidite/ *nf* rigidity

rigolade /ʁigɔlad/ *nf* (fam) (a) **quelle ∼!**
what a laugh! (colloq)
(b) joke
(c) **réparer ça, c'est de la ∼!** repairing this is
a piece of cake (colloq)

rigole /ʁigɔl/ *nf* (a) channel
(b) rivulet

rigoler /ʁigɔle/ [1] *vi* (fam) (a) to laugh
(b) to have fun
(c) to joke, to kid (colloq)

rigolo, **-ote** /ʁigɔlo, ɔt/ **1** *adj* (a) funny
(b) odd
2 *nm,f* (a) joker
(b) **c'est un petit ∼** he's quite a little
comedian

rigoriste /ʁigɔʁist/ *adj* ‹attitude›
unbending, rigoristic; ‹morals› strict

rigoureusement /ʁiguʁøzmɑ̃/ *adv*
completely; carefully

rigoureux, **-euse** /ʁiguʁø, øz/ *adj*
(a) ‹discipline, person› strict
(b) ‹climate, working conditions› harsh,
severe
(c) ‹research, demonstration› meticulous;
‹analysis› rigorous

rigueur /ʁigœʁ/ **1** *nf* (a) strictness
(b) harshness
(c) rigour (GB)
(d) (Econ) austerity
2 **de rigueur** *phr* obligatory
3 **à la rigueur** *phr* **à la ∼ je peux te
prêter 50 euros** at a pinch (GB) *or* in a pinch
(US) I can lend you 50 euros
IDIOM **tenir ∼ à qn de qch** to bear sb a
grudge for sth

rillettes /ʁijɛt/ *nf pl* ≈ potted meat

rime /ʁim/ *nf* rhyme

rimer /ʁime/ [1] *vi* (a) to rhyme
(b) **cela ne rime à rien** it makes no sense

rimmel® /ʁimɛl/ *nm* mascara

rinçage /ʁɛ̃saʒ/ *nm* (a) rinsing
(b) rinse

rince-doigts /ʁɛ̃sdwa/ *nm inv* (a) finger
bowl
(b) finger wipe

rincer /ʁɛ̃se/ [12] **1** *vtr* (a) to rinse
(b) to rinse [sth] out
2 **se rincer** *v refl* (+ *v être*) **se ∼ les
mains/les cheveux** to rinse one's hands/hair

ring /ʁiŋ/ *nm* (boxing) ring

ringard, **-e** /ʁɛ̃gaʁ, aʁd/ *adj* (fam) out of
date

riper /ʁipe/ [1] *vi* ‹foot› to slip; ‹bicycle› to
skid

riposte /ʁipɔst/ *nf* (a) reply, riposte
(b) response
(c) (Sport) (in fencing) riposte; (in boxing)
counter

riposter /ʁipɔste/ [1] **1** *vtr* to retort
2 *vi* (a) to retort; **∼ à qn/qch par to**
counter sb/sth with
(b) to respond
(c) (Mil) to return fire, to shoot back
(d) (in sport) to ripost

ripou, *pl* **∼x** /ʁipu/ *adj* (pop) crooked
(colloq), bent (colloq)

riquiqui /ʁikiki/ *adj inv* (fam) ‹room, car›
poky (colloq); ‹portion› measly (colloq)

⚡ **rire¹** /ʁiʁ/ [68] **1** *vi* (a) to laugh; **tu nous
feras toujours ∼!** you're a real scream!
(colloq)
(b) to have fun; **il faut bien ∼ un peu** you
need a bit of fun now and again; **fini de ∼**
the fun's over; **c'était pour ∼** it was a joke;
sans ∼ (fam) seriously; **laisse-moi ∼** (fam) ne
me fais pas ∼ (fam) don't make me laugh
(c) **∼ de qn/qch** to laugh at sb/sth
2 **se rire** *v refl* (+ *v être*) **se ∼ de qn**
(formal) to laugh at sb; **se ∼ des difficultés**
(formal) to make light of difficulties
IDIOMS **rira bien qui rira le dernier** (Proverb)
he who laughs last laughs longest; **être mort
de ∼** (fam) to be doubled up (with laughter)

rire² /ʁiʁ/ *nm* laughter; **un ∼** a laugh; **il a eu
un petit ∼** he chuckled
■ **∼s préenregistrés** canned laughter

ris /ʁi/ *nm inv* (a) (Culin) **∼ (de veau)** calf's
sweetbread
(b) (Naut) reef

risée /ʁize/ *nf* **être la ∼ de** to be the
laughing stock of

risette /ʁizɛt/ *nf* (fam) smile

risible /ʁizibl/ *adj* ridiculous, laughable

⚡ **risque** /ʁisk/ *nm* risk; **c'est sans ∼** it's safe;
à ∼s ‹group, loan› high-risk
■ **les ∼s du métier** occupational hazards

risqué, **∼e** /ʁiske/ *adj* (a) risky;
‹investment› high-risk
(b) ‹joke› risqué; ‹hypothesis› daring

⚡ **risquer** /ʁiske/ [1] **1** *vtr* (a) to face
‹accusation, condemnation›
(b) to risk ‹death, criticism›; **vas-y, tu ne
risques rien** go ahead, you're safe; (figurative)
go ahead, you've got nothing to lose; **∼ gros**
to take a major risk
(c) to risk ‹life, reputation, job›
(d) to venture ‹look, question›; to attempt
‹operation›; **∼ un œil** to venture a glance; **∼
le coup** (fam) to risk it
2 **risquer de** *v+prep* (a) **tu risques de te
brûler** you might burn yourself
(b) **il ne veut pas ∼ de perdre son travail** he
doesn't want to risk losing his job
3 **se risquer** *v refl* (+ *v être*) (a) to
venture; **je ne m'y risquerais pas!** I wouldn't
risk it

⚡ indicates a very frequent word

(b) se ~ à dire to dare to say
④ *v impers* **il risque de pleuvoir** it might
rain; **il risque d'y avoir du monde** there may
well be a lot of people there
IDIOM **~ le tout pour le tout** to stake *or* risk
one's all
risque-tout /ʀiskətu/ *adj inv* daredevil
rissoler /ʀisɔle/ [1] *vtr, vi* (Culin) to brown
ristourne /ʀistuʀn/ *nf* discount, rebate
rite /ʀit/ *nm* rite
rituel, -elle /ʀitɥɛl/ *adj, nm* ritual
rivage /ʀivaʒ/ *nm* shore
rival, ~e, *mpl* **-aux** /ʀival, o/ *adj, nm,f* rival
rivaliser /ʀivalize/ [1] *vi* **~ avec** to
compete with; **~ avec qch** to rival sth
rivalité /ʀivalite/ *nf* rivalry
rive /ʀiv/ *nf* **(a)** (of river) bank
(b) (of sea, lake) shore
river /ʀive/ [1] *vtr* to clinch ‹nail, rivet›; **être
rivé à** (figurative) to be tied to ‹one's work›;
avoir les yeux rivés sur to have one's eyes
riveted on
riverain, ~e /ʀivʀɛ̃, ɛn/ *nm,f* (of street)
resident; (beside river) riverside resident
rivet /ʀivɛ/ *nm* rivet
♂ **rivière** /ʀivjɛʀ/ *nf* river
■ **~ de diamants** diamond necklace
rixe /ʀiks/ *nf* brawl
riz /ʀi/ *nm* rice
rizière /ʀizjɛʀ/ *nf* paddy field
RMI /ɛʀɛmi/ *nm* (*abbr* = **revenu
minimum d'insertion**) *minimum benefit
paid to those with no other source of income*
RN /ɛʀɛn/ *nf* (*abbr* = **route nationale**)
≈ A road (GB), highway (US)
♂ **robe** /ʀɔb/ *nf* **(a)** (gen) dress
(b) (of lawyer) gown
(c) (of horse) coat; (of wine) colour (GB)
■ **~ de chambre** dressing gown, robe (US)
robinet /ʀɔbinɛ/ *nm* (for water) tap (GB),
faucet (US); (for gas) tap (GB), valve (US)
robot /ʀɔbo/ *nm* robot; **~ ménager** food
processor
robotique /ʀɔbɔtik/ *nf* robotics
robotisation /ʀɔbɔtizasjɔ̃/ *nf* automation
robotiser /ʀɔbɔtize/ [1] *vtr* to automate
robuste /ʀɔbyst/ *adj* robust, sturdy;
‹appetite› healthy; ‹faith› strong
robustesse /ʀɔbystɛs/ *nf* **(a)** robustness,
sturdiness
(b) soundness
roc /ʀɔk/ *nm* rock
rocade /ʀɔkad/ *nf* bypass; ring road (GB)
rocaille /ʀɔkaj/ *nf* **(a)** loose stones
(b) rock garden
rocailleux, -euse /ʀɔkajø, øz/ *adj*
(a) ‹terrain› rocky, stony
(b) ‹voice› harsh, grating

rocambolesque /ʀɔkãbɔlɛsk/ *adj*
fantastic, incredible
roche /ʀɔʃ/ *nf* rock
rocher /ʀɔʃe/ *nm* rock
rocheux, -euse /ʀɔʃø, øz/ *adj* rocky
rock /ʀɔk/ *nm* **(a)** rock (music)
(b) jive
rockeur, -euse /ʀɔkœʀ, øz/ *nm,f* **(a)** rock
musician
(b) rock fan
rococo /ʀɔkoko/ *adj inv* ‹art, style› rococo
rodage /ʀɔdaʒ/ *nm* (of vehicle, engine)
running in (GB), breaking in (US)
rodéo /ʀɔdeo/ *nm* rodeo
roder /ʀɔde/ [1] *vtr* **(a)** to run in (GB), to
break in (US) ‹engine›
(b) to polish up ‹show›; **être (bien) rodé**
‹department› to be running smoothly
rôder /ʀɔde/ [1] *vi* to prowl; **~ autour de qn**
to hang around sb
rôdeur, -euse /ʀɔdœʀ, øz/ *nm,f* prowler
rogne /ʀɔɲ/ *nf* (fam) **se mettre en ~** to get
mad (colloq)
rogner /ʀɔɲe/ [1] *vtr* **(a)** to trim ‹angle›; to
clip ‹nails›
(b) ~ sur to cut down on ‹budget›
rognon /ʀɔɲɔ̃/ *nm* (Culin) kidney
♂ **roi** /ʀwa/ *nm* king
■ **les ~ mages** the (Three) Wise Men
IDIOM **tirer les Rois** to eat Twelfth Night
cake
roitelet /ʀwatlɛ/ *nm* **(a)** wren
(b) kinglet
♂ **rôle** /ʀol/ *nm* **(a)** (for actor) part, role; **premier
~** lead, leading role
(b) (gen) role; (of heart, part of body) function,
role; **à tour de ~** in turn
IDIOM **avoir le beau ~** (fam) to have the easy
job
roller /ʀɔlɛʀ/ *nm* (skate) rollerblade; (activity)
rollerblading
♂ **romain, ~e¹** /ʀɔmɛ̃, ɛn/ *adj* **(a)** Roman
(b) l'Église ~e the Roman Catholic Church
(c) caractères ~s roman typeface
romaine² /ʀɔmɛn/ *nf* cos lettuce
♂ **roman, ~e** /ʀɔmɑ̃, an/ ① *adj* **(a)** ‹church,
style› Romanesque; (in England) Norman
(b) ‹language› Romance
② *nm* **(a)** novel; **~ courtois** courtly
romance
(b) (style) **le ~** the Romanesque
■ **~ policier** detective story
romance /ʀɔmɑ̃s/ *nf* **(a)** love song
(b) (literature) romance
romancer /ʀɔmɑ̃se/ [12] *vtr* **(a)** to
romanticize
(b) to fictionalize
romanche /ʀɔmɑ̃ʃ/ *nm, adj* Romans(c)h
romancier, -ière /ʀɔmɑ̃sje, ɛʀ/ *nm,f*
novelist

r

romand, ~e /ʀɔmɑ̃, ɑ̃d/ adj ‹Swiss person› French-speaking

romanesque /ʀɔmanɛsk/ 1 adj
(a) ‹person› romantic
(b) ‹narrative, story› fictional
2 nm (a) le ~ fiction
(b) le ~ d'une situation the fantastical aspect of a situation

roman-feuilleton, pl **romans-feuilletons** /ʀɔmɑ̃fœjtɔ̃/ nm serial

roman-fleuve, pl **romans-fleuves** /ʀɔmɑ̃flœv/ nm roman-fleuve, saga

roman-photo, pl **romans-photos** /ʀɔmɑ̃foto/ nm photo-story

romantique /ʀɔmɑ̃tik/ adj, nmf romantic

romantisme /ʀɔmɑ̃tism/ nm romanticism

romarin /ʀɔmaʀɛ̃/ nm rosemary

rombière /ʀɔ̃bjɛʀ/ nf (pop) une ~ an old bag (colloq)

rompre /ʀɔ̃pʀ/ [53] 1 vtr (gen) to break, to break off ‹relationship›; to upset ‹equilibrium›; to disrupt ‹harmony›; to end ‹isolation›
2 vi ~ avec to break with ‹habit, tradition›; to make a break from ‹past›; to break away from ‹background›; to break up with ‹fiancé›
3 se rompre v refl (+ v être) to break

rompu, ~e /ʀɔ̃py/ 1 pp ▶ ROMPRE
2 pp adj ~ (de fatigue) worn-out

romsteck /ʀɔmstɛk/ nm rump steak

ronce /ʀɔ̃s/ nf bramble

ronchon, **-onne** /ʀɔ̃ʃɔ̃, ɔn/ adj (fam) grumpy (colloq)

ronchonner /ʀɔ̃ʃɔne/ [1] vi (fam) to grumble

♂ **rond**, ~e¹ /ʀɔ̃, ʀɔ̃d/ 1 adj (a) ‹object, hole› round
(b) ‹writing› rounded; ‹face› round; ‹person› plump
(c) ‹number› round
(d) (fam) drunk
2 nm circle; faire des ~s dans l'eau to make ripples in the water
■ ~ de serviette napkin ring
IDIOM ouvrir des yeux ~s to be wide-eyed with astonishment

ronde² /ʀɔ̃d/ 1 adj f ▶ ROND 1
2 nf (a) round dance; entrer dans la ~ to join the dance
(b) (of policeman) patrol; (of soldiers) watch
(c) (Mus) semibreve (GB), whole note (US)
3 à la ronde phr around

rondelle /ʀɔ̃dɛl/ nf (a) slice
(b) (Tech) washer

rondement /ʀɔ̃dmɑ̃/ adv promptly

rondeur /ʀɔ̃dœʀ/ nf (a) roundness
(b) curve

rondin /ʀɔ̃dɛ̃/ nm log

rondouillard, ~e /ʀɔ̃dujaʀ, aʀd/ adj (fam) tubby (colloq)

rond-point, pl **ronds-points** /ʀɔ̃pwɛ̃/ nm roundabout (GB), traffic circle (US)

ronflant, ~e /ʀɔ̃flɑ̃, ɑ̃t/ adj (a) ‹stove› roaring
(b) ‹style› high-flown

ronflement /ʀɔ̃fləmɑ̃/ nm (a) snore
(b) (of engine) purr

ronfler /ʀɔ̃fle/ [1] vi ‹sleeper› to snore; ‹engine› to purr
(b) (fam) to be fast asleep

ronger /ʀɔ̃ʒe/ [13] 1 vtr (a) ‹mouse, dog› to gnaw; ‹worms› to eat into; ‹caterpillar› to eat away
(b) ‹acid, rust› to erode
(c) ‹disease› to wear down
2 se ronger v refl (+ v être) se ~ les ongles to bite one's nails
IDIOM se ~ les sangs (fam) to worry oneself sick

rongeur /ʀɔ̃ʒœʀ/ nm rodent

ronronnement /ʀɔ̃ʀɔnmɑ̃/ nm (of cat, engine) purring

ronronner /ʀɔ̃ʀɔne/ [1] vi to purr

roquet /ʀɔkɛ/ nm (a) yappy little dog
(b) (fam) bad-tempered little runt (colloq)

roquette /ʀɔkɛt/ nf (Mil) rocket

rosace /ʀozas/ nf (a) rosette
(b) rose window
(c) (decorative motif) rose

rosaire /ʀozɛʀ/ nm rosary

rosâtre /ʀozɑtʀ/ adj pinkish

rosbif /ʀɔsbif/ nm joint of beef (GB), roast of beef (US); (meal) roast beef

♂ **rose¹** /ʀoz/ adj (gen) pink; ‹cheeks› rosy
IDIOM la vie n'est pas ~ life isn't a bed of roses

rose² /ʀoz/ nf (Bot) rose
■ ~ des sables gypsum flower; ~ trémière hollyhock
IDIOMS envoyer qn sur les ~s (fam) to send sb packing (colloq); découvrir le pot aux ~s (fam) to find out what is going on

rosé /ʀoze/ nm rosé

roseau, pl ~x /ʀozo/ nm (Bot) reed

rosée /ʀoze/ nf dew

roseraie /ʀozʀɛ/ nf rose garden

rosier /ʀozje/ nm (Bot) rosebush, rose

rosir /ʀoziʀ/ [3] vi ‹sky› to turn pink; ‹face› to go pink

rosse /ʀɔs/ 1 adj (fam) nasty, mean
2 nf (a) nag (colloq)
(b) meanie (colloq), nasty person

rosser /ʀɔse/ [1] vtr (fam) to give [sb] a good thrashing; to beat ‹animal›

rosserie /ʀɔsʀi/ nf (a) nasty remark; mean trick
(b) meanness; nastiness

---

rossignol /ʀɔsiɲɔl/ *nm* nightingale

rot /ʀo/ *nm* (fam) burp (colloq); **faire un ~** to burp (colloq)

rotation /ʀɔtasjɔ̃/ *nf* (a) (movement) rotation (b) (Mil) turnaround (c) (of crops, staff, shift) rotation

roter /ʀɔte/ [1] *vtr* (fam) to burp (colloq), to belch

✧ **rôti** /ʀɔti/ *nm* (a) joint (b) roast

rotin /ʀɔtɛ̃/ *nm* rattan

rôtir /ʀɔtiʀ/ [3] *vtr* to roast ‹meat›; to toast, to grill ‹bread›

rôtisseur, -euse /ʀɔtisœʀ, øz/ *nm,f* seller of roast meat

rôtissoire /ʀɔtiswaʀ/ *nf* rotisserie, roasting spit

rotonde /ʀɔtɔ̃d/ *nf* (building) rotunda

rotondité /ʀɔtɔ̃dite/ *nf* roundness

rotule /ʀɔtyl/ *nf* (Anat) kneecap
IDIOM **être sur les ~s** (fam) to be on one's last legs

roturier, -ière /ʀɔtyʀje, ɛʀ/ *nm,f* commoner

rouage /ʀwaʒ/ *nm* (a) (of machine) (cog) wheel; **les ~s** the parts *or* works (b) (of administration) machinery; **les ~s bureaucratiques** the wheels of bureaucracy

roublard, ~e /ʀublaʀ, aʀd/ *adj* (fam) crafty, cunning

roublardise /ʀublaʀdiz/ *nf* (fam) craftiness, cunning

rouble /ʀubl/ *nm* rouble

roucouler /ʀukule/ [1] *vi* (a) ‹bird› to coo (b) ‹lovers› to bill and coo

roue /ʀu/ *nf* wheel; **~ dentée** cogwheel
■ **~ motrice** driving wheel; **~ de secours** spare wheel *or* tyre (GB), spare tire (US)
IDIOMS **être la cinquième ~ du carrosse** to feel unwanted; **pousser qn à la ~** to be behind sb; **faire la ~** ‹peacock› to spread its tail, to display; ‹person› to strut around; (in gymnastics) to do a cartwheel

rouer /ʀwe/ [1] *vtr* **~ qn de coups** to beat sb up

rouerie /ʀuʀi/ *nf* (a) cunning (b) cunning trick

rouet /ʀwɛ/ *nm* spinning wheel

✧ **rouge** /ʀuʒ/ 1 *adj* (a) (gen) red; ‹person, face› flushed (b) ‹beard, hair, fur› ginger (c) red-hot
2 *nmf* (communist) Red
3 *nm* (a) red; **le ~ lui monta au visage** he/she went red in the face (b) **~ à joues** blusher, rouge; **~ à lèvres** lipstick (c) **le feu est au ~** the (traffic) lights are red; **passer au ~** to jump the lights (GB) *or* a red light (d) (fam) red (wine); **gros ~** (fam) cheap red

wine; **un coup de ~** (fam) a glass of red wine
IDIOM **être ~ comme une tomate** *or* **une écrevisse** (from embarrassment) to be as red as a beetroot (GB) *or* a beet (US); (from running) to be red in the face

rougeâtre /ʀuʒɑtʀ/ *adj* reddish

rougeaud, ~e /ʀuʒo, od/ *adj* ‹person› ruddy-faced; ‹face, complexion› ruddy

rouge-gorge, *pl* **rouges-gorges** /ʀuʒɡɔʀʒ/ *nm* robin (redbreast)

rougeoiement /ʀuʒwamɑ̃/ *nm* red glow

rougeole /ʀuʒɔl/ *nf* measles

rougeoyer /ʀuʒwaje/ [23] *vi* ‹sun› to glow fiery red; ‹fire› to glow red

rouget /ʀuʒɛ/ *nm* red mullet, goatfish (US)

rougeur /ʀuʒœʀ/ *nf* (a) redness (b) redness; flushing (c) red blotch

rougir /ʀuʒiʀ/ [3] 1 *vtr* to redden
2 *vi* (a) to blush; to flush; to go red; **ne ~ de rien** to have no shame (b) ‹fruit, sky› to turn red (c) ‹metal› to become red hot

rougissant, ~e /ʀuʒisɑ̃, ɑ̃t/ *adj* ‹person› blushing; ‹sky› reddening

rouille /ʀuj/ 1 *adj inv* red-brown
2 *nf* rust

rouiller /ʀuje/ [1] 1 *vtr* to rust
2 *vi* to rust, to go rusty
3 **se rouiller** *v refl* (+ *v être*) to get rusty

roulade /ʀulad/ *nf* (Sport) roll

roulant, ~e /ʀulɑ̃, ɑ̃t/ *adj* **table ~e** trolley; **personnel ~** train crew

roulé /ʀule/ *nm* (Culin) roll

rouleau, *pl* **~x** /ʀulo/ *nm* (a) roll (b) breaker, roller (c) (Tech) roller (d) roller, curler
■ **~ compresseur** steamroller; **~ à pâtisserie** rolling pin

roulement /ʀulmɑ̃/ *nm* (a) (of thunder) rumble; (of drum) roll (b) (of capital) circulation (c) rotation; **travailler par ~** to work (in) shifts (d) (Tech) **~ à billes** ball bearing

✧ **rouler** /ʀule/ [1] 1 *vtr* (a) to roll ‹barrel, tyre›; to wheel ‹cart› (b) to roll up ‹carpet, sleeve, paper›; to roll ‹cigarette› (c) **~ les épaules** to roll one's shoulders (d) (fam) **~ qn** to cheat sb
2 *vi* (a) ‹ball, person› to roll (b) ‹vehicle› to go; **~ à gauche** to drive on the left; **les bus ne roulent pas le dimanche** the buses don't run on Sundays
3 **se rouler** *v refl* (+ *v être*) **se ~ dans** to roll in ‹grass, mud›

roulette /ʀulɛt/ *nf* (a) caster (b) roulette (c) (dentist's) drill

⋯⋗

IDIOM marcher comme sur des ∼s (fam) to go smoothly *or* like a dream

roulis /ʀuli/ *nm* (of boat) rolling; (of car, train) swaying

roulotte /ʀulɔt/ *nf* (horse-drawn) caravan (GB), trailer (US)

Roumanie /ʀumani/ *pr nf* Romania

roupie /ʀupi/ *nf* rupee

roupiller /ʀupije/ [1] *vi* (fam) to sleep

roupillon /ʀupijɔ̃/ *nm* (fam) snooze (colloq), nap

rouquin, ∼e /ʀukɛ̃, in/ *nm,f* (fam) redhead

rouspéter /ʀuspete/ [14] *vi* (fam) to grumble

rousse /ʀus/ ▸ ROUX

rousseur /ʀusœʀ/ *nf* (of hair, foliage) redness; (of shade) russet colour (GB)

roussi /ʀusi/ *nm* ça sent le ∼ there's a smell of burning; (figurative) there's trouble brewing

roussir /ʀusiʀ/ [3] **1** *vtr* to turn [sth] brown
2 *vi* (a) to go brown
(b) (Culin) faire ∼ to brown

routage /ʀutaʒ/ *nm* sorting and mailing

routard, ∼e /ʀutaʀ, aʀd/ *nm,f* (fam) backpacker

⚜ **route** /ʀut/ *nf* (a) road, highway (US); **tenir la** ∼ ‹car› to hold the road; (figurative) (fam) ‹argument› to hold water; ‹equipment› to be well-made
(b) road; **il y a six heures de** ∼ it's a six-hour drive; **faire de la** ∼ (fam) to do a lot of mileage
(c) route; ∼s **maritimes** sea routes
(d) way; **la** ∼ **sera longue** it will be a long journey; **j'ai changé d'avis en cours de** ∼ I changed my mind along the way; **être en** ∼ ‹person› to be on one's way; ‹dish› to be cooking; **être en** ∼ **pour** to be en route to; **faire fausse** ∼ to go off course; (figurative) to be mistaken; **se mettre en** ∼ to set off; **en** ∼! let's go!; **mettre en** ∼ to start ‹machine, car›; to get [sth] going ‹project›
■ ∼ **départementale** secondary road; ∼ **nationale** trunk road (GB), ≈ A road (GB), national highway (US)

routeur /ʀutœʀ/ *nm* router

routier, -ière /ʀutje, ɛʀ/ **1** *adj* road
2 *nm* (a) lorry driver (GB), truck driver
(b) transport café (GB), truck stop (US)

routine /ʀutin/ *nf* routine

routinier, -ière /ʀutinje, ɛʀ/ *adj* ‹person› set in one's ways; ‹work, life› routine

rouvrir: se rouvrir /ʀuvʀiʀ/ [32] *v refl* (+ *v être*) ‹door› to open (again); ‹wound› to open up (again)

roux, rousse /ʀu, ʀus/ **1** *adj* ‹leaves› russet; ‹hair› red; ‹person› red-haired; ‹fur›

ginger
2 *nm,f* red-haired person, redhead

royal, ∼e, *mpl* **-aux** /ʀwajal, o/ *adj*
(a) royal
(b) ‹present› fit for a king; ‹tip, salary› princely
(c) ‹indifference› supreme; ‹peace› blissful

royalement /ʀwajalmɑ̃/ *adv* (a) royally; **être payé** ∼ to be paid handsomely
(b) (fam) **il se moque** ∼ **de son travail** he really couldn't care less about his work

royaliste /ʀwajalist/ *adj, nmf* royalist
IDIOM être plus ∼ **que le roi** to be more Catholic than the pope

⚜ **royaume** /ʀwajom/ *nm* kingdom

Royaume-Uni /ʀwajomyni/ *pr nm* **le** ∼ the United Kingdom

royauté /ʀwajote/ *nf* (a) kingship
(b) monarchy

RSA *nm* (*abbr* = **Revenu de solidarité active**) additional top-up benefit given to those in low-paid employment

RSVP (*written abbr* = **répondez s'il vous plaît**) RSVP

ruade /ʀɥad/ *nf* (a) (by horse) buck
(b) (by person, party) attack

Ruanda /ʀwɑ̃da/ *pr nm* Rwanda

ruban /ʀybɑ̃/ *nm* ribbon; ∼ **adhésif** adhesive tape, sticky tape (GB)

rubéole /ʀybeɔl/ *nf* German measles

rubis /ʀybi/ *nm inv* (a) ruby
(b) ruby (red)

rubrique /ʀybʀik/ *nf* (a) (of newspaper) section; ∼ **mondaine** social column
(b) category

ruche /ʀyʃ/ *nf* (a) beehive
(b) hive of activity

rude /ʀyd/ *adj* (a) ‹job, day› hard, tough; ‹winter› harsh; ‹ordeal› severe
(b) ‹material, beard› rough
(c) ‹features› coarse
(d) **c'est un** ∼ **gaillard** he's a strapping fellow
(e) ‹opponent› tough

rudement /ʀydmɑ̃/ *adv* (a) roughly
(b) (fam) really

rudesse /ʀydes/ *nf* (a) harshness, severity
(b) coarseness

rudimentaire /ʀydimɑ̃tɛʀ/ *adj* (a) basic
(b) (Anat) rudimentary

rudiments /ʀydimɑ̃/ *nm pl* **avoir quelques** ∼ **de** to have a rudimentary knowledge of

rudoyer /ʀydwaje/ [23] *vtr* to bully

⚜ **rue** /ʀy/ *nf* street
IDIOMS ça ne court pas les ∼s (fam) it's pretty thin on the ground; **descendre dans la** ∼ to take to the street

ruée /ʀɥe/ *nf* rush; ∼ **vers l'or** gold rush

ruelle /ʀɥɛl/ *nf* alleyway, back street

ruer /ʀɥe/ [1] **1** *vi* ‹horse› to kick
2 **se ruer** *v refl* (+ *v être*) to rush
IDIOM ∼ **dans les brancards** to rebel

⚜ indicates a very frequent word

♂ **rugby** /ʀygbi/ *nm* rugby; ~ à treize rugby league; ~ à quinze rugby union

rugbyman, *pl* **rugbymen** /ʀygbiman, mɛn/ *nm* rugby player

rugir /ʀyʒiʀ/ [3] **1** *vtr* to bellow (out), to growl
2 *vi* ‹animal, engine› to roar; ‹wind› to howl

rugissement /ʀyʒismɑ̃/ *nm* (of animal, person) roar; (of wind) howling

rugosité /ʀygozite/ *nf* roughness

rugueux, -euse /ʀygø, øz/ *adj* rough

ruine /ʀɥin/ *nf* (a) (of building, person, reputation, company) ruin; (of civilization) collapse; (of hope) death; **en ~(s)** ruined; **ce n'est pas la ~** (fam) it's not that expensive
(b) ruin
(c) wreck

ruiner /ʀɥine/ [1] **1** *vtr* (a) to ruin ‹person, economy›; ~ **qn** to be a drain on sb's resources
(b) to destroy ‹health, happiness›
(c) to ruin ‹life›; to shatter ‹hopes›
2 **se ruiner** *v refl* (+ *v être*) to be ruined, to lose everything; to ruin oneself

ruineux, -euse /ʀɥinø, øz/ *adj* very expensive

ruisseau, *pl* ~**x** /ʀɥiso/ *nm* (a) stream, brook
(b) ~ **de larmes** stream of tears

ruisseler /ʀɥisle/ [19] *vi* (a) ‹water› to stream; ‹grease› to drip
(b) to be streaming; ~ **de sueur** to be dripping with sweat

ruissellement /ʀɥisɛlmɑ̃/ *nm* (of rain) streaming; (of grease) dripping

rumeur /ʀymœʀ/ *nf* (a) rumour (GB)
(b) (of voices, wind) murmur

ruminant /ʀyminɑ̃/ *nm* ruminant

ruminer /ʀymine/ [1] **1** *vtr* (a) to ruminate
(b) to brood on ‹misery›; to chew over (colloq) ‹idea, plan›
2 *vi* (a) to ruminate

(b) ‹person› to brood

rumsteck /ʀɔmstɛk/ *nm* rump steak

rupestre /ʀypɛstʀ/ *adj* (a) ‹plants› rock
(b) ‹paintings› cave, rock

rupture /ʀyptyʀ/ *nf* (a) (of relations) breaking-off
(b) breakdown
(c) break-up; **lettre de ~** letter ending a relationship
(d) (of dam, dyke) breaking; (of pipe) fracture

rural, ~e, *mpl* **-aux** /ʀyʀal, o/ *adj* ‹exodus, environment› rural; ‹road, life› country

ruse /ʀyz/ *nf* (a) trick, ruse; ~ **de guerre** (humorous) cunning stratagem
(b) cunning, craftiness

rusé, ~e /ʀyze/ *adj* cunning, crafty

ruser /ʀyze/ [1] *vi* (a) to be crafty
(b) ~ **avec** to trick ‹enemy, police›

rush, *pl* **rushes** /ʀœʃ/ **1** *nm* (in race) final burst
2 **rushes** *nm pl* (of film) rushes

russe /ʀys/ *adj, nm* Russian

Russie /ʀysi/ *pr nf* Russia

rustaud, ~e /ʀysto, od/ *adj* rustic

rusticité /ʀystisite/ *nf* rustic character

rustine® /ʀystin/ *nf* (puncture-repair) patch

rustique /ʀystik/ *adj* rustic, country

rustre /ʀystʀ/ **1** *adj* uncouth
2 *nm* lout

rut /ʀyt/ *nm* rutting season

rutilant, ~e /ʀytilɑ̃, ɑ̃t/ *adj* sparkling; gleaming

♂ **rythme** /ʀitm/ *nm* (a) rhythm; **marquer le ~** to beat time
(b) (of growth) rate; (of life) pace
■ ~ **cardiaque** heart rate

rythmer /ʀitme/ [1] *vtr* (a) to give rhythm to
(b) to regulate ‹life, work›

rythmique /ʀitmik/ *adj* rhythmic

Ss

s, S /ɛs/ *nm inv* s, S

s' (a) ► SE
(b) ► SI¹ 2

sa ► SON¹

sabbat /saba/ *nm* (a) Sabbath
(b) witches' Sabbath

sabbatique /sabatik/ *adj* (Univ) sabbatical

♂ **sable** /sɑbl/ *nm* sand; ~**s mouvants** quicksands

sablé, ~e /sable/ **1** *adj* **pâte ~e** shortcrust pastry
2 *nm* shortbread biscuit (GB) *or* cookie (US)

sabler /sable/ [1] *vtr* to grit ‹roadway›
IDIOM ~ **le champagne** to crack open some champagne

sablier /sablije/ *nm* hourglass; egg timer

sablonneux, -euse /sablɔnø, øz/ *adj* sandy

r
s

sabot /sabo/ nm (a) clog
(b) (Zool) hoof

sabotage /sabɔtaʒ/ nm sabotage

saboter /sabɔte/ [1] vtr to sabotage

saboteur, -euse /sabɔtœʀ, øz/ nm,f (of equipment) saboteur

sabre /sɑbʀ/ nm (a) sword
(b) sabre (GB)

sabrer /sɑbʀe/ [1] vtr (fam) to cut chunks out of ‹article›

✧ **sac** /sak/ nm (a) (gen) bag
(b) sack
(c) bag(ful), sack(ful)
(d) **mettre à** ~ to sack ‹city, region›; to ransack ‹shop, house›
■ ~ **de couchage** sleeping bag; ~ **à dos** rucksack, backpack; ~ **à main** handbag (GB), purse (US); ~ **postal** mail sack; ~ **à provisions** shopping bag, carry-all (US)
IDIOMS **l'affaire est dans le** ~ (fam) it's in the bag (colloq); **avoir plus d'un tour dans son** ~ to have more than one trick up one's sleeve; **vider son** ~ (fam) to get it off one's chest; **se faire prendre la main dans le** ~ to be caught red-handed; **mettre dans le même** ~ (fam) to lump together

saccade /sakad/ nf jerk

saccadé, ~e /sakade/ adj ‹movement› jerky; ‹rhythm› staccato; ‹voice› clipped

saccager /sakaʒe/ [13] vtr (a) to wreck, to devastate ‹region›; to vandalize ‹building›
(b) to sack

saccharine /sakaʀin/ nf saccharin

SACEM /sasɛm/ nf (abbr = **Société des auteurs, compositeurs et éditeurs de musique**) association of composers and music publishers to protect copyright and royalties

sacerdoce /sasɛʀdɔs/ nm priesthood

sachet /saʃɛ/ nm (of powder) packet; (of herbs, spices) sachet; ~ **de thé** tea bag

sacoche /sakɔʃ/ nf (a) bag
(b) (on bicycle) pannier (GB), saddlebag (US)

sacquer /sake/ [1] vtr (fam) (a) to sack (GB) (colloq), to fire (colloq)
(b) ‹teacher› to mark [sb] strictly
(c) **je ne peux pas le** ~ I can't stand the sight of him

sacre /sakʀ/ nm (of king) coronation; (of bishop) consecration

✧ **sacré, ~e** /sakʀe/ adj (a) ‹art, object, place› sacred; ‹cause› holy
(b) ‹rule, right› sacred
(c) (fam) **être un** ~ **menteur** to be a hell of a liar (colloq)
(d) (fam) ~ **Paul, va!** Paul, you old devil!
IDIOM **avoir le feu** ~ to be full of zeal

sacrement /sakʀəmɑ̃/ nm sacrament; **les derniers** ~s the last rites

sacrément /sakʀemɑ̃/ adv (fam) incredibly (colloq)

sacrer /sakʀe/ [1] vtr to crown ‹king›; to consecrate ‹bishop›

✧ **sacrifice** /sakʀifis/ nm sacrifice

sacrifier /sakʀifje/ [1] **1** vtr to sacrifice
2 sacrifier à v+prep to conform to ‹fashion›
3 se sacrifier v refl (+ v être) (a) to sacrifice oneself
(b) (fam) to make sacrifices

sacrilège /sakʀilɛʒ/ nm sacrilege

sacristie /sakʀisti/ nf (of catholic church) sacristy; (of protestant church) vestry

sacro-saint, ~e, mpl ~**s** /sakʀosɛ̃, ɛ̃t/ adj sacrosanct

sadique /sadik/ **1** adj sadistic
2 nmf sadist

sadisme /sadism/ nm sadism

sadomasochisme /sadomazɔʃism/ nm sadomasochism

safari /safaʀi/ nm safari

safran /safʀɑ̃/ adj inv, nm saffron

saga /saga/ nf saga

sagacité /sagasite/ nf sagacity, shrewdness

✧ **sage** /saʒ/ **1** adj (a) wise, sensible
(b) good, well-behaved
(c) ‹tastes, fashion› sober
2 nm (a) wise man, sage
(b) expert

sage-femme, pl **sages-femmes** /saʒfam/ nf midwife

sagement /saʒmɑ̃/ adv (a) wisely
(b) ‹sit, listen› quietly
(c) ‹dress› soberly

✧ **sagesse** /saʒɛs/ nf (a) wisdom, common sense; (of advice) soundness; **la voix de la** ~ the voice of reason
(b) good behaviour (GB)

Sagittaire /saʒitɛʀ/ pr nm Sagittarius

Sahara /saaʀa/ pr nm Sahara

saignant, ~e /sɛɲɑ̃, ɑ̃t/ adj (a) ‹meat› rare
(b) (figurative) (fam) ‹criticism› savage

saignée /sɛɲe/ nf (a) (Med) bloodletting, bleeding
(b) (in budget) hole
(c) (in tree) cut

saignement /sɛɲ(ə)mɑ̃/ nm bleeding

saigner /sɛɲe/ [1] **1** vtr (a) (Med) to bleed
(b) to kill ‹animal› by slitting its throat; ~ **un cochon** to stick a pig
2 vi to bleed; ~ **du nez** to have a nosebleed
IDIOMS ~ **qn à blanc** to bleed sb dry; **se** ~ **(aux quatre veines) pour qn** to make big sacrifices for sb

saillant, ~e /sajɑ̃, ɑ̃t/ adj (a) ‹jaw› prominent; ‹muscle, eyes› bulging; ‹angle› salient
(b) ‹fact, episode› salient

✧ indicates a very frequent word

S

saillie /saji/ *nf* (a) projection; **le balcon est en ~** the balcony juts out
(b) (Zool) covering

saillir /sajiʀ/ [28] *vi* (a) to jut out
(b) ‹*ribs, muscles*› to bulge

sain, ~e /sɛ̃, sɛn/ *adj* (gen) healthy, sound; ‹*wound*› clean; **~ d'esprit** sane; **~ de corps et d'esprit** sound in body and mind; **~ et sauf** ‹*return*› safe and sound

saindoux /sɛ̃du/ *nm inv* lard

sainement /sɛnmɑ̃/ *adv* (a) ‹*live*› healthily
(b) ‹*reason*› soundly

ꝯ **saint, ~e** /sɛ̃, sɛ̃t/ **1** *adj* (a) holy; **vendredi ~** Good Friday
(b) **~ Paul** Saint Paul
2 *nm,f* saint
■ **~e nitouche** goody-goody (colloq); **la Sainte Vierge** the Virgin Mary

Saint-Barthélémy /sɛ̃baʀtelemi/ *nf* **la ~** the St Bartholomew's Day massacre

saint-bernard /sɛ̃bɛʀnaʀ/ *nm inv* St Bernard

Saint-Esprit /sɛ̃tɛspʀi/ *pr nm* Holy Spirit

saInteté /sɛ̃te/ *nf* saintliness

saint-glinglin: à la saint-glinglin /alasɛ̃glɛ̃glɛ̃/ *phr* (fam) probably never; **rester/attendre jusqu'à la ~** to stay/to wait till the cows come home (colloq)

saint-honoré /sɛ̃tɔnɔʀe/ *nm inv*: cream-filled tart topped with choux and caramel

Saint-Jacques /sɛ̃ʒak/ *pr n* **coquille ~** scallop

Saint-Jean /sɛ̃ʒɑ̃/ *nf* **la ~** Midsummer Day

Saint-Sylvestre /sɛ̃silvɛstʀ/ *nf* **la ~** New Year's Eve

saisie /sezi/ *nf* (a) (gen, Law) seizure
(b) keyboarding; **~ de données** data capture

ꝯ **saisir** /seziʀ/ [3] **1** *vtr* (a) to grab; to seize; **~ au vol** to catch ‹*ball*›; **'affaire à ~'** 'amazing bargain'
(b) to understand
(c) to catch ‹*name, bits of conversation*›
(d) ‹*emotion, cold*› to grip ‹*person*›
(e) to strike, to impress ‹*person*›
(f) (Law) to seize ‹*property*›; **~ la justice d'une affaire** to refer a matter to a court
(g) (Comput) to capture ‹*data*›; to key ‹*text*›
2 se saisir *v refl* (+ *v être*) **se ~ de** to catch or grab hold of ‹*object*›

saisissant, ~e /sezisɑ̃, ɑ̃t/ *adj* (a) ‹*cold*› piercing
(b) ‹*effect, resemblance*› striking

ꝯ **saison** /sɛzɔ̃/ *nf* (gen) season; **en cette ~** at this time of year; **en toute ~** all (the) year round; **la haute/morte ~** the high/slack season; **prix hors ~** off-season prices

saisonnier, -ière /sɛzɔnje, ɛʀ/ **1** *adj* seasonal
2 *nm,f* (worker) seasonal worker

salace /salas/ *adj* salacious

ꝯ **salade** /salad/ *nf* (a) lettuce
(b) salad
(c) (fam) muddle; **raconter des ~s** to spin yarns (colloq)

saladier /saladje/ *nm* salad bowl

salaire /salɛʀ/ *nm* salary; wages

salaison /salɛzɔ̃/ *nf* salt meat

salamandre /salamɑ̃dʀ/ *nf* salamander

salant /salɑ̃/ *adj m* **marais ~** saltern

salarial, ~e, *mpl* **-iaux** /salaʀjal, o/ *adj*
(a) ‹*policy, rise*› wage
(b) **cotisation ~e** employee's contribution

salarié, ~e /salaʀje/ **1** *adj* ‹*worker*› wage-earning; ‹*job*› salaried
2 *nm,f* (a) wage earner
(b) salaried employee

salaud /salo/ *nm* (offensive) (pop) bastard (slang)

ꝯ **sale** /sal/ **1** *adj* (a) *after n* dirty
(b) *before n* (fam) ‹*person*› horrible; ‹*animal, illness, habit*› nasty; ‹*weather*› foul, horrible; ‹*work, place*› rotten; **~ menteur!** you dirty liar!; **il a une ~ tête** he looks dreadful; **faire une ~ tête** to look annoyed; **un ~ coup** a very nasty blow; **un ~ caractère** a foul temper
2 *nm* **mettre qch au ~** to put sth in the wash

salé, ~e /sale/ *adj* (a) salt, salty
(b) salted; ‹*snack*› savoury (GB)
(c) (fam) ‹*bill*› steep

salement /salmɑ̃/ *adv* (a) **manger ~** to be a messy eater
(b) (fam) badly, seriously

saler /sale/ [1] *vtr* (a) to salt ‹*food*›; **~ et poivrer** to add salt and pepper to
(b) to grit (GB), to salt (US) ‹*road*›

saleté /salte/ *nf* (a) dirtiness; dirt; filth; **ramasser les ~s** to pick up the rubbish (GB) or trash (US); **faire des ~s** to make a mess
(b) (fam) **c'est de la ~** ‹*gadget, goods*› it's rubbish; **c'est une vraie ~ ce virus!** it's a rotten bug!

salière /saljɛʀ/ *nf* saltcellar, saltshaker (US)

salir /saliʀ/ [3] **1** *vtr* (a) to dirty; to soil
(b) to sully ‹*reputation*›
2 *vi* ‹*industry, coal*› to pollute
3 se salir *v refl* (+ *v être*) to get dirty, to dirty oneself

salissant, ~e /salisɑ̃, ɑ̃t/ *adj* (a) ‹*colour*› which shows the dirt
(b) ‹*work*› dirty

salive /saliv/ *nf* saliva

saliver /salive/ [1] *vi* to salivate; **~ devant qch** to drool over sth

ꝯ **salle** /sal/ *nf* (a) (gen) room; hall; (in restaurant) (dining) room; (in hospital) ward; (in theatre) auditorium; **faire ~ comble** ‹*show*› to be packed; **en ~** ‹*sport*› indoor
(b) audience
■ **~ d'attente** waiting room; **~ de bains**

⋯⟫

S

bathroom; ~ **de cinéma** cinema (GB), movie theater (US); ~ **de classe** classroom; ~ **de concert** concert hall; ~ **d'eau** shower room; ~ **d'embarquement** departure lounge; ~ **des fêtes** village hall; community centre (GB); ~ **de garde** (in hospital) staff room; ~ **de gymnastique** gymnasium; ~ **de jeu(x)** (in casino) gaming room; (for children) playroom; ~ **à manger** dining room; dining-room suite; ~ **de séjour** living room; ~ **des ventes** auction room

◆ **salon** /salɔ̃/ *nm* **(a)** (gen) lounge; drawing room
(b) sitting-room suite; ~ **de jardin** garden furniture
(c) (trade) show; fair; exhibition; ~ **du livre** book fair
(d) (of intellectuals) salon
(e) (Comput) chatroom
■ ~ **de beauté** beauty salon; ~ **de coiffure** hairdressing salon; ~ **d'essayage** fitting room; ~ **de thé** tearoom

salopette /salɔpɛt/ *nf* overalls

salpêtre /salpɛtʀ/ *nm* saltpetre (GB)

salsifis /salsifi/ *nm inv* salsify

saltimbanque /saltɛ̃bɑ̃k/ *nmf* **(a)** street acrobat
(b) entertainer

salubre /salybʀ/ *adj* ‹lodgings› salubrious

salubrité /salybʀite/ *nf* (of air, climate) healthiness; (of dwelling) salubrity
■ ~ **publique** public health

saluer /salɥe/ [1] *vtr* **(a)** to greet ‹person›; ~ **qn de la tête** to nod to sb
(b) to say goodbye to ‹person›
(c) (Mil) to salute
(d) to welcome ‹decision, news›
(e) to pay tribute to ‹memory›

◆ **salut** /saly/ *nm* **(a)** greeting; ~! hello!, hi!; ~ **de la tête** nod
(b) salute
(c) salvation

salutaire /salytɛʀ/ *adj* ‹experience› salutary; ‹effect› beneficial; ‹air› healthy

salutation /salytasjɔ̃/ *nf* greeting

salvateur, -trice /salvatœʀ, tʀis/ *adj* saving

salve /salv/ *nf* **(a)** salvo; **tirer une** ~ **d'honneur** to fire a salute
(b) ~ **d'applaudissements** burst of applause

◆ **samedi** /samdi/ *nm* Saturday

SAMU /samy/ *nm* ‹abbr = **Service d'assistance médicale d'urgence**›
≈ mobile accident unit (GB), emergency medical service, EMS (US)

sanatorium /sanatɔʀjɔm/ *nm* sanatorium (GB), sanitarium (US)

sanctifier /sɑ̃ktifje/ [1] *vtr* to sanctify

sanction /sɑ̃ksjɔ̃/ *nf* (Law) penalty, sanction; disciplinary measure; (Sch) punishment

sanctionner /sɑ̃ksjɔne/ [1] *vtr* **(a)** to punish
(b) to give official recognition to ‹training›

sanctuaire /sɑ̃ktɥɛʀ/ *nm* **(a)** shrine
(b) sanctuary

sandale /sɑ̃dal/ *nf* sandal

sandwich, *pl* ~**s** *or* ~**es** /sɑ̃dwitʃ/ *nm* sandwich; **(pris) en** ~ sandwiched

◆ **sang** /sɑ̃/ *nm* **(a)** blood; **être en** ~ to be covered with blood; **se terminer dans le** ~ to end in bloodshed
(b) de ~ ‹brother, ties› blood; **être du même** ~ to be kin
IDIOMS **il a ça dans le** ~ it's in his blood; **mettre qch à feu et à** ~ to put sth to fire and sword; **mon** ~ **n'a fait qu'un tour** my heart missed a beat; I saw red; **se faire du mauvais** ~ (fam) to worry; **bon** ~! for God's sake! (colloq)

sang-froid /sɑ̃fʀwa/ *nm inv* composure; **garde ton** ~! keep calm!; **de** ~ in cold blood

sanglant, ~**e** /sɑ̃glɑ̃, ɑ̃t/ *adj* bloody

sangle /sɑ̃gl/ *nf* **(a)** (gen) strap
(b) (of saddle) girth
(c) (of seat, bed) webbing

sangler /sɑ̃gle/ [1] *vtr* to girth ‹horse›

sanglier /sɑ̃glije/ *nm* wild boar

sanglot /sɑ̃glo/ *nm* sob

sangloter /sɑ̃glɔte/ [1] *vi* to sob

sangsue /sɑ̃sy/ *nf* leech

sanguin, ~**e¹** /sɑ̃gɛ̃, in/ *adj* blood

sanguinaire /sɑ̃ginɛʀ/ *adj* ‹crime› bloody; ‹person› bloodthirsty

sanguine² /sɑ̃gin/ ① *adj f* ▶ SANGUIN
② *nf* **(a)** blood orange
(b) red chalk drawing

sanguinolent, ~**e** /sɑ̃ginɔlɑ̃, ɑ̃t/ *adj* blood-stained

sanisette® /sanizɛt/ *nf* automatic public toilet

sanitaire /sanitɛʀ/ ① *adj* ‹regulations› health; ‹conditions› sanitary
② **sanitaires** *nm pl* **les** ~**s** (in house) the bathroom; (in campsite) the toilet block

◆ **sans** /sɑ̃/ ① *adv* without
② *prep* **(a)** without; **un couple** ~ **enfant** a childless couple; ~ **cela** otherwise
(b) il est resté trois mois ~ **téléphoner** he didn't call for three months; **il est poli**, ~ **plus** he's polite, but that's as far as it goes
(c) on sera dix ~ **les enfants** there'll be ten of us not counting the children; **500 euros** ~ **l'hôtel** 500 euros not including accommodation
③ **sans que** *phr* without; **pars** ~ **qu'on te voie** leave without anyone seeing you
■ ~ **domicile fixe**, **SDF** of no fixed abode, NFA

sans-abri /sɑ̃zabʀi/ *nmf inv* **un** ~ a homeless person; **les** ~ the homeless

sans-emploi /sɑ̃zɑ̃plwa/ *nmf inv* unemployed person

◆ indicates a very frequent word

sans-faute /sɑ̃fot/ *nm inv* faultless performance

sans-gêne /sɑ̃ʒɛn/ *adj inv* bad-mannered

sans-papiers /sɑ̃papje/ *nm* illegal immigrant

santal /sɑ̃tal/ *nm* sandalwood

ᕈ **santé** /sɑ̃te/ *nf* health; **avoir la ∼** to enjoy good health; **se refaire une ∼** to build up one's strength; **avoir une petite ∼** to be frail; **à votre ∼!** cheers!; **à la ∼ de Janet!** here's to Janet!

santon /sɑ̃tɔ̃/ *nm* Christmas crib figure

saoul, ∼e ▶ soûl

saper /sape/ [1] **1** *vtr* to undermine
2 se saper *v refl* (+ *v être*) (fam) to dress

sapeur /sapœʀ/ *nm* sapper
IDIOM **fumer comme un ∼** to smoke like a chimney

sapeur-pompier, *pl* **sapeurs-pompiers** /sapœʀpɔ̃pje/ *nm* fireman

saphir /safiʀ/ *nm* (a) sapphire
(b) (on record player) stylus

sapin /sapɛ̃/ *nm* (a) fir tree; **∼ de Noël** Christmas tree
(b) deal

saquer /sake/ [1] (fam) ▶ sacquer

sarbacane /saʀbakan/ *nf* blowpipe

sarcasme /saʀkasm/ *nm* (a) sarcasm
(b) sarcastic remark

sarcastique /saʀkastik/ *adj* sarcastic

sarcophage /saʀkɔfaʒ/ *nm* sarcophagus

sardine /saʀdin/ *nf* (a) (Zool) sardine
(b) (fam) tent peg

sarment /saʀmɑ̃/ *nm* vine shoot

sarrasin /saʀazɛ̃/ *nm* buckwheat

sarrau /saʀo/ *nm* smock

sas /sɑs/ *nm inv* (a) airlock
(b) (on canal) lock
(c) (in bank) security double door system

satanique /satanik/ *adj* (a) ⟨smile, ruse⟩ fiendish
(b) ⟨cult⟩ Satanic

satellite /satelit/ *nm* satellite

satiété /sasjete/ **1** *nf* satiation, satiety
2 à satiété *phr* (a) **manger à ∼** to eat one's fill
(b) ⟨say, repeat⟩ ad nauseam

satin /satɛ̃/ *nm* satin

satiné, ∼e /satine/ *adj* ⟨fabric, cloth⟩ satiny; ⟨paint⟩ satin-finish

satire /satiʀ/ *nf* satire

satirique /satiʀik/ *adj* satirical

satisfaction /satisfaksjɔ̃/ *nf* satisfaction; **la ∼ de nos besoins** the fulfilment (GB) of our needs

ᕈ **satisfaire** /satisfɛʀ/ [10] **1** *vtr* (gen) to satisfy; to fulfil (GB) ⟨aspiration, requirement⟩
2 satisfaire à *v+prep* to fulfil (GB) ⟨obligation⟩; to meet ⟨norm, standard⟩

3 se satisfaire *v refl* (+ *v être*) **se ∼ de** to be satisfied with ⟨explanation⟩; to be content with ⟨low salary⟩

satisfaisant, ∼e /satisfəzɑ̃, ɑ̃t/ *adj*
(a) satisfactory
(b) satisfying

satisfait, ∼e /satisfɛ, ɛt/ *adj* ⟨customer, need, smile⟩ satisfied; ⟨desire⟩ gratified; ⟨person⟩ happy

saturation /satyʀasjɔ̃/ *nf* (of market) saturation; (in trains, hotels) overcrowding; (of network) overloading; **arriver à ∼** ⟨market, network⟩ to reach saturation point; ⟨person⟩ to have had as much as one can take

saturé, ∼e /satyʀe/ *adj* ⟨market⟩ saturated; ⟨profession⟩ overcrowded

saturer /satyʀe/ [1] *vtr* to saturate

satyre /satiʀ/ *nm* (a) satyr
(b) lecher

sauce /sos/ *nf* (Culin) sauce; **(r)allonger la ∼** (figurative) (fam) to spin things out
IDIOM **mettre qch à toutes les ∼s** to adapt sth to any purpose

saucière /sosjɛʀ/ *nf* sauceboat

saucisse /sosis/ *nf* sausage; **chair à ∼** sausage meat
■ **∼ de Francfort** frankfurter

saucisson /sosisɔ̃/ *nm* (slicing) sausage; **∼ à l'ail** garlic sausage; **∼ sec** ≈ salami

ᕈ **sauf¹** /sof/ **1** *prep* (a) except, but
(b) **∼ contrordre** failing an order to the contrary; **∼ avis contraire** unless otherwise stated, **∼ erreur de ma part** if I'm not mistaken
2 sauf si *phr* unless
3 sauf que *phr* except that

sauf², sauve /sof, sov/ *adj* (a) safe; **laisser la vie sauve à qn** to spare sb's life
(b) ⟨honour, reputation⟩ intact

sauf-conduit, *pl* **∼s** /sofkɔ̃dɥi/ *nm* safe-conduct

sauge /soʒ/ *nf* sage

saugrenu, ∼e /sogʀəny/ *adj* crazy, potty (GB) (colloq)

saule /sol/ *nm* willow

saumâtre /somɑtʀ/ *adj* ⟨water⟩ brackish; ⟨taste⟩ bitter and salty

saumon /somɔ̃/ *nm* salmon

saumure /somyʀ/ *nf* brine

sauna /sona/ *nm* sauna

saupoudrer /sopudʀe/ [1] *vtr* (a) to sprinkle
(b) (figurative) to give [sth] sparingly

saur /sɔʀ/ *adj m* **hareng ∼** kippered herring

ᕈ **saut** /so/ *nm* (a) jump; **faire un petit ∼** to skip; **au ∼ du lit** first thing in the morning
(b) (Sport) **le ∼** jumping
(c) (fam) **faire un ∼ chez qn** to pop in and see sb
■ **∼ à la corde** skipping; **∼ à l'élastique** bungee jumping; **∼ en hauteur** high jump; **∼ à la perche** pole vault; **∼ périlleux** mid-air ⋯⋗

somersault

saute /sot/ *nf* ~ **de température** sudden change in temperature; ~ **d'humeur** mood swing

sauté, ~e /sote/ [1] *adj* (Culin) sautéed [2] *nm* (Culin) ~ **d'agneau** sautéed lamb

saute-mouton /sotmutɔ̃/ *nm inv* leapfrog

⚜ **sauter** /sote/ [1] [1] *vtr* (a) to jump ‹distance, height›; to jump over ‹stream›
(b) to skip ‹meal, paragraph›; to leave out ‹details›; (Sch) ~ **une classe** to skip a year
(c) to miss ‹word, turn›
[2] *vi* (a) to jump; ~ **à pieds joints** to jump with one's feet together; ~ **à la corde** to skip (GB), to jump rope (US); **faire** ~ **un enfant sur ses genoux** to dandle a child on one's knee; ~ **sur qn** to pounce on sb; ~ **à la gorge de qn** to go for sb's throat; ~ **au cou de qn** to greet sb with a kiss
(b) ~ **dans un taxi** to jump *or* hop into a taxi
(c) ~ **d'un sujet à l'autre** to skip from one subject to another
(d) (fam) **faire** ~ **une réunion** to cancel a meeting; **faire** ~ **une contravention** to get out of paying a parking ticket
(e) ‹bicycle chain, fan belt› to come off
(f) **faire** ~ **une serrure** to force a lock; **faire** ~ **les boutons** to burst one's buttons
(g) ‹bridge, building› to be blown up, to go up; **faire** ~ **les plombs** to blow the fuses
(h) (Culin) **faire** ~ to sauté ‹onions›
IDIOMS ~ **aux yeux** to be blindingly obvious; **et que ça saute!** (fam) make it snappy! (colloq); ~ **au plafond** (fam) to jump for joy; to hit the roof (colloq); to be staggered

sauterelle /sotʁɛl/ *nf* grasshopper

sauterie /sotʁi/ *nf* party

sautillant, ~e /sotijã, ãt/ *adj* ‹rhythm, gait› bouncy; ‹bird› hopping

sautiller /sotije/ [1] *vi* (a) ‹bird› to hop
(b) ‹child› to skip along; to jump up and down

⚜ **sauvage** /sovaʒ/ [1] *adj* (a) ‹animal, plant› wild; ‹tribe› primitive
(b) ‹behaviour› savage, wild; ‹struggle› fierce
(c) unsociable
(d) illegal
[2] *nmf* (a) savage
(b) unsociable person, loner

sauvagement /sovaʒmã/ *adv* savagely

sauvageon, -onne /sovaʒɔ̃, ɔn/ *nm,f* wild child

sauvagerie /sovaʒʁi/ *nf* savagery

sauve ▶ SAUF²

sauvegarde /sovgaʁd/ *nf* (of heritage, peace, values) maintenance; (of rights) protection

sauvegarder /sovgaʁde/ [1] *vtr* (a) to safeguard
(b) (Comput) to save; to back [sth] up ‹file›

sauve-qui-peut /sovkipø/ *nm inv* stampede

―――――――――――――――
⚜ indicates a very frequent word

⚜ **sauver** /sove/ [1] [1] *vtr* (a) (gen) to save; ~ **la vie à qn** to save sb's life; **elle est sauvée** ‹ill person› she has pulled through (colloq)
(b) to salvage ‹goods›
(c) **ce qui le sauve à mes yeux, c'est sa générosité** his redeeming feature for me is his generosity
[2] **se sauver** *v refl* (+ *v être*) (a) to escape; to run away; (from danger) to run
(b) (fam) **il faut que je me sauve** I've got to rush off now
IDIOMS ~ **la situation** to save the day; **sauve qui peut!** run for your life!

sauvetage /sovtaʒ/ *nm* rescue; **cours de** ~ life-saving training

sauveteur /sovtœʁ/ *nm* rescuer

sauvette: **à la sauvette** /alasovɛt/ *phr*
(a) ‹prepare, sign› in a rush
(b) ‹film, record› on the sly

sauveur /sovœʁ/ *nm* saviour (GB)

savamment /savamã/ *adv* (a) learnedly, eruditely
(b) skilfully (GB)

savane /savan/ *nf* savannah

savant, ~e /savã, ãt/ [1] *adj* (a) ‹person› learned, erudite
(b) ‹study› scholarly; ‹calculation› complicated
(c) ‹manoeuvre› clever; ‹direction› skilful (GB)
(d) ‹animal› performing
[2] *nm,f* scholar
[3] *nm* scientist

savate /savat/ *nf* (fam) (a) old slipper
(b) old shoe

saveur /savœʁ/ *nf* flavour (GB); **sans** ~ tasteless

⚜ **savoir¹** /savwaʁ/ [47] [1] *vtr* (a) to know ‹truth, answer›; **vous n'êtes pas sans** ~ **que...** you are no doubt aware that...; **va** *or* **allez** ~! who knows!; **est-ce que je sais, moi!** how should I know!; **pour autant que je sache** as far as I know; **comment l'as-tu su?** how did you find out?; **je l'ai su par elle** she told me about it; **ne** ~ **que faire pour...** to be at a loss as to how to...; **sachant que** knowing that; given that; **qui vous savez** you-know-who; **je ne sais qui** somebody or other; **tu en sais des choses!** you really know a thing or two!
(b) ~ **faire** to know how to do; **je sais conduire** I can drive; ~ **écouter** to be a good listener; **elle sait y faire avec les hommes** she knows how to handle men
[2] **se savoir** *v refl* (+ *v être*) **ça se saurait** people would know about it
[3] **à savoir** *phr* that is to say
IDIOM **ne pas** ~ **où donner de la tête** not to know whether one is coming or going

savoir² /savwaʁ/ *nm* (a) learning
(b) knowledge
(c) body of knowledge

savoir-faire /savwaʁfɛʁ/ *nm inv* know-how

savoir-vivre /savwaʀvivʀ/ *nm inv* manners

savon /savɔ̃/ *nm* (a) soap; ~ **de Marseille** household soap
(b) (bar of) soap
IDIOM passer un ~ **à qn** (fam) to give sb a telling-off

savonner /savɔne/ [1] *vtr* to soap

savonnette /savɔnɛt/ *nf* small cake of soap

savourer /savuʀe/ [1] *vtr* to savour (GB)

savoureux, -euse /savuʀø, øz/ *adj* ‹dish› tasty; ‹anecdote› juicy

saxophone /saksɔfɔn/ *nm* saxophone

saxophoniste /saksɔfɔnist/ *nmf* saxophonist

scabreux, -euse /skabʀø, øz/ *adj* obscene

scalp /skalp/ *nm* (a) scalp
(b) scalping

scalpel /skalpɛl/ *nm* scalpel

scalper /skalpe/ [1] *vtr* to scalp

scandale /skɑ̃dal/ *nm* scandal; **faire (un** *or* **du)** ~ (gen) to cause a scandal; ‹person› to cause a fuss; **la presse à** ~ the gutter press; **c'est un** ~! it's scandalous!

scandaleux, -euse /skɑ̃dalø, øz/ *adj* scandalous, outrageous

scandaliser /skɑ̃dalize/ [1] **1** *vtr* to outrage
2 se scandaliser *v refl* (+ *v être*) to be shocked

scander /skɑ̃de/ [1] *vtr* (a) to scan
(b) to chant ‹slogan, name›

scandinave /skɑ̃dinav/ *adj* Scandinavian

scanneur /skanœʀ/ *nm* scanner

scaphandre /skafɑ̃dʀ/ *nm* (a) deep-sea diving suit
(b) spacesuit

scaphandrier /skafɑ̃dʀije/ *nm* deep-sea diver

scarabée /skaʀabe/ *nm* (a) beetle
(b) scarab

scarlatine /skaʀlatin/ *nf* scarlet fever

scatologie /skatɔlɔʒi/ *nf* scatology

sceau, *pl* ~**x** /so/ *nm* (a) seal; **sous le** ~ **du secret** in strictest secrecy
(b) stamp, hallmark

scélérat, ~**e** /selɛʀa, at/ *nm,f* villain

scellé /sele/ *nm* seal; **apposer les** ~**s** to affix seals

sceller /sele/ [1] *vtr* (a) to seal
(b) to fix [sth] securely ‹shelf, bar›

scénario /senaʀjo/ *nm* (a) screenplay, script
(b) scenario; ~ **catastrophe** nightmare scenario

scénariste /senaʀist/ *nmf* scriptwriter

scène /sɛn/ *nf* (a) (in theatre) stage; **entrer en** ~ to come on
(b) scene; **la** ~ **se passe à Paris** the scene is set in Paris
(c) quitter la ~ to give up the stage; **mettre en** ~ to stage ‹play›; to direct ‹film›
(d) scene; **occuper le devant de la** ~ (figurative) to be in the news
(e) **faire une** ~ to throw a fit (colloq)
(f) scene; ~**s de panique** scenes of panic
■ ~ **de ménage** domestic dispute

scepticisme /sɛptisism/ *nm* scepticism (GB), skepticism (US)

sceptique /sɛptik/ **1** *adj* sceptical (GB), skeptical (US); **laisser qn** ~ to leave sb unconvinced
2 *nmf* sceptic (GB), skeptic (US)

sceptre /sɛptʀ/ *nm* sceptre (GB)

schéma /ʃema/ *nm* (a) diagram
(b) outline
(c) pattern

schématique /ʃematik/ *adj* (a) ‹vision, argument› simplistic
(b) schematic

schématiser /ʃematize/ [1] *vtr* to simplify

schizophrénie /skizɔfʀeni/ *nf* schizophrenia

sciatique /sjatik/ **1** *adj* nerf ~ sciatic nerve
2 *nf* **avoir une** ~ to have sciatica

scie /si/ *nf* saw; ~ **sauteuse** jigsaw

sciemment /sjamɑ/ *adv* knowingly

science /sjɑ̃s/ *nf* (a) science
(b) knowledge
■ ~**s naturelles** ≈ biology (*sg*); ~**s occultes** black arts; **Sciences Po** (fam) *Institute of Political Science*

science-fiction /sjɑ̃sfiksjɔ̃/ *nf* science fiction

scientifique /sjɑ̃tifik/ **1** *adj* scientific
2 *nmf* scientist

scier /sje/ [2] *vtr* (a) to saw
(b) (fam) to stun

scierie /siʀi/ *nf* sawmill

scinder /sɛ̃de/ [1] **1** *vtr* to split ‹group›
2 se scinder *v refl* (+ *v être*) to split up

scintillant, ~**e** /sɛ̃tijɑ, ɑ̃t/ *adj* twinkling

scintiller /sɛ̃tije/ [1] *vi* ‹diamond› to sparkle; ‹star› to twinkle; ‹water› to glisten

scission /sisjɔ̃/ *nf* (a) split, schism
(b) fission

sciure /sjyʀ/ *nf* ~ **(de bois)** sawdust

sclérose /skleʀoz/ *nf* (a) (Med) sclerosis
(b) fossilization, ossification
■ ~ **en plaques** multiple sclerosis, MS

scléroser /skleʀoze/ [1] **1** *vtr* (Med) to sclerose
2 se scléroser *v refl* (+ *v être*) (a) ‹institution, person› to become fossilized
(b) (Med) ‹tissue› to become hardened

scolaire /skɔlɛʀ/ *adj* ‹holidays, book› school; ‹reform, publication› educational; ‹failure› academic; **établissement** ~ school

scolarisation /skɔlaʀizasjɔ̃/ nf schooling

scolariser /skɔlaʀize/ [1] vtr to send [sb] to school

scolarité /skɔlaʀite/ nf (a) schooling; **durant ma ~** when I was at school; **la ~ obligatoire** compulsory education
(b) (in university) registrar's office

scoliose /skɔljoz/ nf scoliosis

scooter /skutœʀ/ nm (motor) scooter

score /skɔʀ/ nm (a) (Sch, Sport) score; **~ nul** draw (GB), tie (US)
(b) results

scorie /skɔʀi/ nf (a) scoria
(b) slag

scorpion /skɔʀpjɔ̃/ nm (Zool) scorpion

Scorpion /skɔʀpjɔ̃/ pr nm Scorpio

scotch, pl **~es** /skɔtʃ/ nm (a) Scotch (whisky)
(b) ® Sellotape® (GB), Scotch® tape (US)

scotcher /skɔtʃe/ [1] vtr to Sellotape® (GB), to Scotch-tape® (US)

scout, **~e** /skut/ 1 adj scout
2 nm,f boy scout/girl scout

scribe /skʀib/ nm scribe

scribouillard, **~e** /skʀibujaʀ, aʀd/ nm,f (fam) pen pusher (GB) (colloq), pencil pusher (US)

script /skʀipt/ nm (a) **écrire en ~** to print
(b) script

scripte /skʀipt/ nmf continuity man/girl

scrupule /skʀypyl/ nm scruple

scrupuleusement /skʀypyløzmɑ̃/ adv scrupulously

scrupuleux, **-euse** /skʀypylø, øz/ adj scrupulous; **peu ~** unscrupulous

scrutateur, **-trice** /skʀytatœʀ, tʀis/ adj searching

scruter /skʀyte/ [1] vtr to scan ‹horizon›; to scrutinize ‹object›; to examine ‹ground, person›

scrutin /skʀytɛ̃/ nm (a) ballot; **dépouiller le ~** to count the votes
(b) polls; **jour du ~** polling day; **mode de ~** electoral system
■ **~ majoritaire** election by majority vote

sculpter /skylte/ [1] vtr to sculpt, to carve

sculpteur /skyltœʀ/ nm sculptor

sculptural, **~e**, mpl **-aux** /skyltyʀal, o/ adj ‹art› sculptural; ‹shape, beauty› statuesque

sculpture /skyltyʀ/ nf sculpture; **la ~ sur bois** woodcarving

SDF /ɛsdeɛf/ ▶ SANS

✝ **se** (**s'** before vowel or mute h) /sə, s/ pron
(a) oneself; himself; herself; itself; **il ~ regarde** he's looking at himself
(b) each other; **ils ~ regardaient** they were looking at each other

---

✝ indicates a very frequent word

(c) **~ ronger les ongles** to bite one's nails; **il ~ lave les pieds** he's washing his feet
(d) **elle ~ comporte honorablement** she behaves honourably (GB); **l'écart ~ creuse** the gap is widening
(e) **les exemples ~ comptent sur les doigts de la main** the examples can be counted on the fingers of one hand
(f) **comment ~ fait-il que...?** how come...?, how is it that...?

✝ **séance** /seɑ̃s/ nf (a) (of court, parliament) session; (of committee) meeting; **~ tenante** immediately
(b) (in cinema) show
■ **~ de spiritisme** séance

seau, pl **~x** /so/ nm bucket, pail

sébile /sebil/ nf begging bowl

sec, **sèche** /sɛk, sɛʃ/ 1 adj (a) ‹weather, hair› dry; ‹fruit› dried
(b) ‹wine, cider› dry; **boire son gin ~** to like one's gin straight
(c) ‹person, statement› terse; ‹letter› curt
(d) ‹noise› sharp
2 nm **être à ~** ‹river› to have dried up; (figurative) ‹person› to have no money
3 adv (a) **se briser ~** to snap
(b) (fam) ‹rain, drink› a lot
IDIOM **aussi ~** (fam) immediately

sécateur /sekatœʀ/ nm clippers

sécession /sesesjɔ̃/ nf secession

sèche /sɛʃ/ ▶ SEC 1

sèche-cheveux /sɛʃʃəvø/ nm inv hairdrier (GB), blow-dryer

sèche-linge /sɛʃlɛ̃ʒ/ nm inv tumble-drier (GB), tumble-dryer

sèchement /sɛʃmɑ̃/ adv drily, coldly

sécher /seʃe/ [1] 1 vtr (a) (gen) to dry
(b) (fam) to skip ‹class›
2 vi ‹hair, clothes› to dry; ‹mud› to dry up; **fleur séchée** dried flower; **mettre des vêtements à ~** to hang clothes up to dry

sécheresse /seʃʀɛs/ nf (a) drought
(b) dryness
(c) curt manner

séchoir /seʃwaʀ/ nm (a) clothes airer, clothes horse
(b) tumble-drier (GB), tumble-dryer

✝ **second**, **~e¹** /səgɔ̃, ɔ̃d/ 1 adj (a) (in sequence, series) second; **chapitre ~** chapter two; **en ~ lieu** secondly; **dans un ~ temps...** subsequently...; **c'est à prendre au ~ degré** it is not to be taken literally
(b) (in hierarchy) second; **de ~ ordre** second-rate; **politicien de ~ plan** minor politician; **jouer un ~ rôle** (in theatre) to play a supporting role; **jouer les ~s rôles** (figurative) to play second fiddle
2 nm,f second one
3 nm (a) second-in-command
(b) second floor (GB), third floor (US)
4 **en second** phr ‹arrive, leave› second

secondaire /səgɔ̃dɛʀ/ 1 adj (a) secondary

(b) minor
(c) (Sch) **école** ~ secondary school (GB), high school (US)
(d) **effets** ~s side effects
2 *nm* (Sch) secondary school (GB) *or* high school (US) education

seconde² /səgɔ̃d/ 1 *adj f* ▶ SECOND 1
2 *nf* **(a)** ▶ SECOND 2
(b) second; **en une fraction de** ~ in a split second
(c) (Sch) *fifth year of secondary school, age 15–16*
(d) **billet de** ~ second-class ticket
(e) (Aut) second (gear)

seconder /səgɔ̃de/ [1] *vtr* ‹*person*› to assist

secouer /səkwe/ [1] 1 *vtr* **(a)** to shake ‹*bottle, branch, person*›; to shake out ‹*rug, umbrella*›; ~ **la tête** to shake one's head; **être un peu secoué** (in car, plane) to have rather a bumpy ride
(b) to shake off ‹*dust, snow, yoke*›
(c) ‹*crisis*› to shake ‹*person, country*›
(d) (fam) to get [sb] going (colloq)
2 **se secouer** *v refl* (+ *v être*) **(a)** to give oneself a shake
(b) (fam) to pull oneself together
(c) (fam) to wake up, to get moving (colloq)

secourable /səkuʀabl/ *adj* ‹*person*› helpful

secourir /səkuʀiʀ/ [26] *vtr* **(a)** to help
(b) to rescue
(c) to give first aid to

secourisme /səkuʀism/ *nm* first aid

secouriste /səkuʀist/ *nmf* first-aid worker

⚜ **secours** /səkuʀ/ 1 *nm inv* help; **au** ~**!** help!; **appeler** *or* **crier au** ~ to shout for help; **porter** ~ **à qn** to help sb; **le** ~ **en mer** sea rescue operations; **de** ~ ‹*wheel*› spare; ‹*exit*› emergency; ‹*kit*› first-aid; ‹*team*› rescue; ‹*battery*› back-up
2 *nm pl* **(a)** rescuers; reinforcements
(b) relief supplies; supplies; **premiers** ~ first aid

secousse /səkus/ *nf* jolt; ~ **(sismique)** (earth) tremor

⚜ **secret, -ète** /səkʀɛ, ɛt/ 1 *adj* **(a)** secret
(b) ‹*person*› secretive
2 *nm* **(a)** secret; **ne pas avoir de** ~s **pour qn** to have no secrets from sb; **il n'en fait pas un** ~ he makes no secret of it
(b) secrecy; **mettre qn dans le** ~ to let sb in on the secret; **en** ~ in secret; **encore une de ces gaffes dont il a le** ~ another of those blunders that only he knows how to make
(c) solitary confinement
■ ~ **bancaire** bank confidentiality; ~ **de fabrication** industrial secret; ~ **de Polichinelle** open secret; ~ **professionnel** professional confidentiality

⚜ **secrétaire** /s(ə)kʀetɛʀ/ 1 *nmf* secretary
2 *nm* (piece of furniture) secretaire (GB), secretary (US)
■ ~ **de direction** personal assistant; ~ **d'État** (in France) minister; (in Great Britain, America) Secretary of State; ~ **de rédaction** sub-editor (GB), copy-editor

secrétariat /s(ə)kʀetaʀja/ *nm*
(a) secretarial work
(b) secretariat

secrète ▶ SECRET 1

secrètement /səkʀɛtmɑ̃/ *adv* secretly

sécréter /sekʀete/ [14] *vtr* **(a)** to secrete ‹*sap, bile*›
(b) to exude ‹*liquid*›

sécrétion /sekʀesjɔ̃/ *nf* secretion

sectaire /sɛktɛʀ/ *adj, nmf* sectarian

secte /sɛkt/ *nf* sect; faction

⚜ **secteur** /sɛktœʀ/ *nm* **(a)** (Econ) sector; ~ **tertiaire** service sector; ~ **d'activité** sector
(b) area, territory; (Mil) sector
(c) (electrical) **le** ~ the mains; **appareil fonctionnant sur** ~ mains-operated appliance; **panne de** ~ power failure

⚜ **section** /sɛksjɔ̃/ *nf* **(a)** section; (of party, trade union) branch; (of book) part
(b) (Sch) stream (GB), track (US)
■ ~ **d'autobus** fare stage

sectionner /sɛksjɔne/ [1] *vtr* **(a)** to sever
(b) to divide up ‹*organization*›

sectoriel, -ielle /sɛktɔʀjɛl/ *adj* sectoral

sectorisation /sɛktɔʀizasjɔ̃/ *nf* division

sectoriser /sɛktɔʀize/ [1] *vtr* to divide [sth] into sectors

Sécu /seky/ *nf* National Health Service

séculaire /sekylɛʀ/ *adj* **(a)** ‹*tradition*› ancient
(b) ‹*house, tree*› hundred-year-old

séculier, -ière /sekylje, ɛʀ/ *adj* secular

secundo /səgɔ̃do/ *adv* secondly

sécurisé, ~e /sekyʀize/ 1 *pp* ▶ SÉCURISER
2 *pp adj* secure; (Comput) **une ligne** ~**e** a secure line

sécuriser /sekyʀize/ [1] *vtr* **(a)** to reassure
(b) to make [sb] feel secure

⚜ **sécurité** /sekyʀite/ *nf* **(a)** security; ~ **de l'emploi** job security; **de** ~ ‹*system*› security; ‹*reasons*› of security
(b) safety; **se sentir en** ~ to feel secure *or* safe
■ ~ **routière** road safety; ~ **sociale** *French national health and pensions organization*

sédatif /sedatif/ *nm* sedative

sédentaire /sedɑ̃tɛʀ/ *adj* sedentary

sédentariser /sedɑ̃taʀize/ [1] *vtr* to settle

sédentarité /sedɑ̃taʀite/ *nf* (of population) settled way of life; (of job) sedentary nature

sédiment /sedimɑ̃/ *nm* sediment

sédimentation /sedimɑ̃tasjɔ̃/ *nf* sedimentation

séducteur, -trice /sedyktœʀ, tʀis/ 1 *adj* seductive, attractive ⋯ ◊

S

2 *nm,f* **(a)** charmer
(b) seducer/seductress

séduction /sedyksjɔ̃/ *nf* **(a)** charm
(b) seduction; **pouvoir de** ∼ (of person)
power of seduction; (of money) lure; (of words)
seductive power

séduire /sedɥiʀ/ [1] *vtr* **(a)** ‹person› to
captivate, to charm
(b) to appeal to ‹person›
(c) ‹person› to win over
(d) to seduce

séduisant, ∼**e** /sedɥizɑ̃, ɑ̃t/ *adj* ‹person›
attractive; ‹idea› appealing

segment /sɛgmɑ̃/ *nm* segment

segmenter /sɛgmɑ̃te/ [1] *vtr*, **se**
segmenter *v refl* (+ *v être*) to segment

ségrégation /segʀegasjɔ̃/ *nf* segregation

seiche /sɛʃ/ *nf* cuttlefish

seigle /sɛgl/ *nm* rye; **pain de** ∼ rye bread

◆ **seigneur** /sɛɲœʀ/ *nm* lord; **être grand** ∼ to
be full of largesse
■ ∼ **de la guerre** warlord
IDIOM à tout ∼ **tout honneur** (Proverb) credit
where credit is due

Seigneur /sɛɲœʀ/ *nm* Lord; ∼! Good Lord!

seigneurial, ∼**e**, *mpl* **-iaux** /sɛɲœʀjal,
o/ *adj* ‹home› stately; ‹manner› lordly

◆ **sein** /sɛ̃/ *nm* **(a)** (Anat) breast; **les** ∼**s nus**
topless; **nourrir (son enfant) au** ∼ to breast-
feed (one's baby)
(b) au ∼ **de** within

séisme /seism/ *nm* earthquake, seism

seize /sɛz/ *adj inv, pron, nm inv* sixteen

seizième /sɛzjɛm/ *adj* sixteenth

◆ **séjour** /seʒuʀ/ *nm* **(a)** stay; ∼**s à l'étranger**
(on CV) time spent abroad
(b) (salle de) ∼ living room
(c) un ∼ **champêtre** a rural retreat
■ ∼ **linguistique** language study vacation

séjourner /seʒuʀne/ [1] *vi* **(a)** ‹person› to
stay
(b) ‹liquid› to remain; ‹snow› to lie

◆ **sel** /sɛl/ *nm* **(a)** salt; **gros** ∼ coarse salt
(b) (figurative) **la situation ne manque pas de**
∼ the situation has a certain piquancy
■ ∼**s de bain** bath salts

sélect, ∼**e** /selɛkt/ *adj* (fam) ‹club, bar›
exclusive; ‹clientele› select

sélecteur, -trice **1** *adj* selective
2 *nm* **(a)** (Comput) selector
(b) (Aut) gear lever (GB), gearshift (US)

sélectif, -ive /selɛktif, iv/ *adj* selective

sélection /selɛksjɔ̃/ *nf* (gen) selection; (for
a job) selection process; ∼ **à l'entrée** selective
entry

sélectionner /selɛksjɔne/ [1] *vtr* to select

self-service, *pl* ∼**s** /sɛlfsɛʀvis/ *nm* self-
service restaurant

◆ indicates a very frequent word

selle /sɛl/ **1** *nf* saddle; **remis en** ∼ ‹player,
regime› firmly (re)established
2 **selles** *nf pl* (Med) stools

seller /sele/ [1] *vtr* to saddle

sellette /selɛt/ *nf* **être sur la** ∼ to be in the
hot seat

◆ **selon** /səlɔ̃/ *prep* **(a)** according to; ∼ **moi, il**
va pleuvoir in my opinion, it's going to rain;
∼ **les termes du président** in the President's
words; **l'idée** ∼ **laquelle** the idea that
(b) depending on ‹time, circumstances›; **la**
situation varie ∼ **les régions** the situation
varies from region to region; **c'est** ∼ (fam) it
all depends

semailles /səmɑj/ *nf pl* **(a)** sowing season
(b) seeds
(c) faire les ∼ to sow

◆ **semaine** /s(ə)mɛn/ *nf* **(a)** week
(b) week's wages
IDIOM vivre à la petite ∼ to live from day
to day

sémantique /semɑ̃tik/ **1** *adj* semantic
2 *nf* semantics

◆ **semblable** /sɑ̃blabl/ **1** *adj* **(a)** similar
(b) identical
2 *nmf* fellow creature; **eux et leurs** ∼**s**
they and their kind

semblant /sɑ̃blɑ̃/ *nm* **un** ∼ **de légalité** a
semblance of legality; **faire** ∼ **d'être triste** to
pretend to be sad

◆ **sembler** /sɑ̃ble/ [16] **1** *vi* to seem
2 *v impers* **il semble bon de faire** it seems
appropriate to do; **le problème est réglé à**
ce qu'il me semble the problem has been
solved, or so it seems to me; **faites comme**
bon vous semble do whatever you think
best; **elle a, semble-t-il, refusé** apparently,
she refused

semelle /s(ə)mɛl/ *nf* sole
■ ∼ **compensée** wedge heel; ∼ **intérieure**
insole
IDIOM être dur comme de la ∼ (fam) to be as
tough as old boots (GB) (colloq) *or* leather (US)

semence /s(ə)mɑ̃s/ *nf* seed

semer /s(ə)me/ [16] *vtr* **(a)** to sow ‹seeds›
(b) to sow ‹discord, doubt›; to spread
‹confusion, panic›
(c) to scatter ‹objects›; **semé de difficultés**
plagued with difficulties; **ciel semé d'étoiles**
star-spangled sky; **on récolte ce qu'on a**
semé as you sow so shall you reap
(d) (fam) to drop ‹purse, keys›
(e) (fam) to shake off ‹pursuer›

semestre /s(ə)mɛstʀ/ *nm* (Sch) semester

semestriel, -ielle /səmɛstʀijɛl/ *adj*
(a) twice-yearly; half-yearly
(b) (at university) ‹exam› end-of-semester (GB),
final (US); ‹class› one-semester

semeur, -euse /səmœʀ, øz/ *nm,f* sower;
∼ **de troubles** troublemaker

semi /səmi/ *pref* ∼**-automatic**
semiautomatic; ∼**-liberté** relative freedom;

∼-remorque articulated lorry (GB), tractor-trailer (US)

semi-échec, *pl* ∼**s** /səmieʃɛk/ *nm* partial failure

sémillant, ∼**e** /semijã, ãt/ *adj* spirited

séminaire /seminɛʀ/ *nm* (a) seminar
(b) seminary

séminariste /seminaʀist/ *nm* seminarist

sémiologie /semjɔlɔʒi/ *nf* semiology

sémiotique /semjɔtik/ **1** *adj* semiotic
2 *nf* semiotics

semis /s(ə)mi/ *nm inv* (a) sowing
(b) seedling
(c) seedbed

semonce /səmɔ̃s/ *nf* reprimand; **coup de ∼** warning shot

semoule /səmul/ *nf* semolina; **sucre ∼** caster sugar

sempiternel, -elle /sãpitɛʀnɛl/ *adj* perpetual

sénat /sena/ *nm* senate

sénateur /senatœʀ/ *nm* senator

sénile /senil/ *adj* senile

sénilité /senilite/ *nf* senility

⚔ **sens** /sãs/ **1** *nm inv* (a) direction, way; **dans le ∼ de la largeur** widthways, across; **être dans le bon ∼** to be the right way up; **retourner un problème dans tous les ∼** to consider a problem from every angle; **courir dans tous les ∼** to run all over the place; **∼ dessus dessous** upside down; (figurative) very upset; **aller dans le bon ∼** ⟨reforms⟩ to be a step in the right direction; **le ∼ de l'histoire** the tide of history; **nous travaillons dans ce ∼** that's what we are working toward(s)
(b) meaning; **le ∼ figuré d'un mot** the figurative sense of a word; **employer un mot au ∼ propre** to use a word literally; **cela n'a pas de ∼** it doesn't make sense; it's absurd
(c) sense; **retrouver l'usage de ses ∼** to regain consciousness; **avoir le ∼ pratique** to be practical; **ne pas avoir le ∼ du ridicule** not to realize when one looks silly; **avoir le ∼ des affaires** to have a flair for business; **n'avoir aucun ∼ des réalités** to live in a dream world
2 *nm pl* senses; **plaisirs des ∼** sensual pleasures
■ **∼ giratoire** roundabout (GB), traffic circle (US); **∼ interdit** no-entry sign; one-way street; **∼ obligatoire** one-way sign; **∼ unique** one-way sign; one-way street

⚔ **sensation** /sãsasjɔ̃/ *nf* feeling, sensation; **aimer les ∼s fortes** to like one's thrills; **la décision a fait ∼** the decision caused a sensation; **un journal à ∼** a tabloid

sensationnel, -elle /sãsasjɔnɛl/ *adj*
(a) (fam) fantastic (colloq)
(b) sensational, astonishing

sensé, ∼**e** /sãse/ *adj* sensible

sensément /sãsemã/ *adv* sensibly

sensibilisation /sãsibilizasjɔ̃/ *nf*
(a) **campagne de ∼** awareness campaign
(b) (Med) sensitizing

sensibiliser /sãsibilize/ [1] *vtr* (a) **∼ le public à un problème** to increase public awareness of an issue
(b) (Med) to sensitize

sensibilité /sãsibilite/ *nf* (a) sensibility
(b) (in photography) sensitivity

⚔ **sensible** /sãsibl/ *adj* (a) (gen) sensitive; **être ∼ aux compliments** to like compliments; **je suis ∼ au fait que** I am aware that; **un être ∼** a sentient being; **je suis très ∼ au froid** I really feel the cold
(b) ⟨skin⟩ sensitive; (because of injury) tender; ⟨limb⟩ sore; **j'ai la gorge ∼** I often get a sore throat
(c) ⟨rise, difference⟩ appreciable; ⟨effort⟩ real; **la différence est à peine ∼** the difference is hardly noticeable

sensiblement /sãsibləmã/ *adv* (a) ⟨reduce, increase⟩ appreciably, noticeably; ⟨different⟩ perceptibly
(b) ⟨alike⟩ roughly

sensiblerie /sãsibləʀi/ *nf* sentimentality

sensitif, -ive /sãsitif, iv/ *adj* sensory

sensoriel, -ielle /sãsɔʀjɛl/ *adj* sensory; **organe ∼** sense organ

sensualité /sãsɥalite/ *nf* sensuality

sensuel, -elle /sãsɥɛl/ *adj* sensual

sentence /sãtãs/ *nf* (a) sentence
(b) maxim

sentencieux, -ieuse /sãtãsjø, øz/ *adj* sententious

senteur /sãtœʀ/ *nf* scent

senti, ∼**e** /sãti/ *adj* **bien ∼** ⟨words⟩ well-chosen; ⟨answer⟩ blunt; ⟨speech⟩ forthright

sentier /sãtje/ *nm* path, track; **hors des ∼s battus** off the beaten track

⚔ **sentiment** /sãtimã/ *nm* feeling; **il est incapable de ∼** he's incapable of emotion; **faire du ∼** to sentimentalize; **prendre qn par les ∼s** to appeal to sb's better nature; **les beaux** *or* **bons ∼s** fine sentiments; **être animé de mauvais ∼s** to have bad intentions; **∼s affectueux** *or* **amicaux** best wishes

sentimental, ∼**e**, *mpl* **-aux** /sãtimãtal, o/ *adj* sentimental; romantic; **vie ∼e** lovelife

sentinelle /sãtinɛl/ *nf* sentry

⚔ **sentir** /sãtiʀ/ [30] **1** *vtr* (a) to smell
(b) to feel; **je ne sens rien** I can't feel anything; **je ne sens plus mes pieds** my feet are numb
(c) to be conscious of ⟨importance⟩; to feel ⟨beauty, force⟩; to appreciate ⟨difficulties⟩; to sense ⟨danger, disapproval⟩; **je sens qu'il est sincère** I feel that he's sincere; **je te sens inquiet** I can tell you're worried; **se faire ∼** ⟨need⟩ to be felt
2 *vi* (a) to smell; **ça sent l'ail** it smells of garlic

⋯∴

S

(b) le poisson commence à ∼ the fish is beginning to smell
(c) to smack of; **ciel nuageux qui sent l'orage** cloudy sky that heralds a storm
3 **se sentir** v refl (+ v être) **(a)** to feel; **se ∼ mieux** to feel better
(b) ‹effect› to be felt
IDIOM je ne peux pas le ∼ I can't stand him

seoir () /swaʀ/ [41] **1** **seoir à** vtr ‹dress› to suit
2 v impers **il sied de faire** it is appropriate to do

sépale /sepal/ nm sepal

séparable /sepaʀabl/ adj separable

séparation /sepaʀasjɔ̃/ nf **(a)** (gen, Law) separation
(b) (between gardens) boundary; (figurative) boundary, dividing line
■ ∼ **de biens** (Law) matrimonial division of property; ∼ **de corps** (Law) judicial separation

séparatisme /sepaʀatism/ nm separatism

séparé, ∼**e** /sepaʀe/ adj **(a)** **vivre ∼** to live apart
(b) separate

séparément /sepaʀemɑ̃/ adv separately

⚲ **séparer** /sepaʀe/ [1] **1** vtr **(a)** (gen) to separate; to pull [sb] apart ‹fighters›; **c'est un malentendu qui les a séparés** they parted because of a misunderstanding
(b) to distinguish between ‹concepts, areas›
(c) to divide; **tout les sépare** they are worlds apart
2 **se séparer** v refl (+ v être) **(a)** ‹guests› to part; ‹partners, lovers› to split up
(b) se ∼ de to leave ‹friend, group›; to split up with; (Law) to separate from ‹husband, wife›
(c) se ∼ de to let [sb] go ‹employee›; to part with ‹personal possession›
(d) to divide; **la route se sépare (en deux)** the road forks

sépia /sepja/ adj inv sepia

⚲ **sept** /sɛt/ adj inv, pron, nm inv seven
■ **les ∼ Familles** (Games) Happy Families
IDIOM **tourne ∼ fois ta langue dans ta bouche avant de parler** think before you speak

septante /sɛptɑ̃t/ adj inv, pron seventy

⚲ **septembre** /sɛptɑ̃bʀ/ nm September

septennat /sɛptena/ nm seven-year term (of office)

septentrional, ∼**e**, mpl **-aux** /sɛptɑ̃tʀijɔnal, o/ adj northern

septicémie /sɛptisemi/ nf blood-poisoning

septième /sɛtjɛm/ **1** adj seventh
2 nf (Sch) fifth year of primary school, age 10–11

■ le ∼ art cinematography

septuagénaire /sɛptɥaʒenɛʀ/ adj **être ∼** to be in one's seventies

septuor /sɛptɥɔʀ/ nm septet

sépulture /sepyltyʀ/ nf **(a)** grave
(b) burial

séquelle /sekɛl/ nf **(a)** after-effect
(b) repercussion
(c) consequence

séquence /sekɑ̃s/ nf sequence

séquestrer /sekɛstʀe/ [1] vtr (gen) to hold ‹hostage›; (Law) to confine [sb] illegally

sera /səʀa/ ▶ ÊTRE¹

serai /səʀe/ ▶ ÊTRE¹

seraient /səʀɛ/ ▶ ÊTRE¹

sérail /seʀaj/ nm **(a)** seraglio
(b) innermost circle

serais /səʀe/ ▶ ÊTRE¹

serait /səʀe/ ▶ ÊTRE¹

seras /səʀa/ ▶ ÊTRE¹

serein, ∼**e** /səʀɛ̃, ɛn/ adj ‹sky› clear; ‹person, face› serene; ‹criticism› objective

sereinement /səʀɛnmɑ̃/ adv ‹look› serenely; ‹speak› calmly; ‹judge› dispassionately

sérénade /seʀenad/ nf **(a)** serenade
(b) (fam) racket (colloq), din

sérénité /seʀenite/ nf **(a)** (of face, mind) serenity; (of person) equanimity
(b) (of judge, verdict) impartiality
(c) (of sky, weather) calmness

serez /səʀe/ ▶ ÊTRE¹

serf, **serve** /sɛʀ, sɛʀv/ nm,f serf

sergent /sɛʀʒɑ̃/ nm (Mil) (in army) ≈ sergeant

⚲ **série** /seʀi/ nf **(a)** series; **catastrophes en ∼** a series of catastrophes
(b) **numéro de ∼** serial number; ∼ **limitée** limited edition; **modèle de ∼** (gen) mass-produced model; (car) production model; **numéro hors ∼** special issue
(c) set, collection
(d) (on television) series
(e) (Sport) division
■ ∼ **noire** series of disasters

sérieusement /seʀjøzmɑ̃/ adv seriously; considerably

⚲ **sérieux**, **-ieuse** /seʀjø, øz/ **1** adj
(a) serious; **être ∼ dans son travail** to be serious about one's work; **avoir des lectures sérieuses** to read serious books
(b) ‹situation, threat› serious; ‹clue, lead› important; ‹offer› genuine; **'pas ∼ s'abstenir'** 'genuine enquiries only'
(c) reliable
(d) responsible; **cela ne fait pas très ∼** that doesn't make a very good impression
(e) ‹effort, need› real; ‹progress› considerable; ‹handicap› serious
2 nm seriousness; **garder son ∼** to keep a straight face; **perdre son ∼** to start to laugh; **se prendre au ∼** to take oneself seriously

---

⚲ indicates a very frequent word

seriez /səʀje/ ▶ ÊTRE¹

sérigraphie /seʀigʀafi/ *nf* **(a)** silkscreen printing
(b) silkscreen print

serin /səʀɛ̃/ *nm* (Zool) canary

seriner /səʀine/ [1] *vtr* (fam) ~ **qch à qn** to drum sth into sb

seringue /səʀɛ̃g/ *nf* syringe

serions /səʀjɔ̃/ ▶ ÊTRE¹

serment /sɛʀmɑ̃/ *nm* **(a)** oath; **prêter** ~ to take the oath
(b) vow
■ **un** ~ **d'ivrogne** an empty promise

sermon /sɛʀmɔ̃/ *nm* **(a)** sermon
(b) lecture

sermonner /sɛʀmɔne/ [1] *vtr* to lecture, to give [sb] a talking-to

séronégatif, -ive /seʀonegatif, iv/ *adj* HIV negative

serons /səʀɔ̃/ ▶ ÊTRE¹

seront /səʀɔ̃/ ▶ ÊTRE¹

séropositif, -ive /seʀopozitif, iv/ *adj*
(a) (gen) seropositive
(b) HIV positive

séropositivité /seʀopozitivite/ *nf* (HIV antibody) seropositivity

serpe /sɛʀp/ *nf* billhook

serpent /sɛʀpɑ̃/ *nm* (Zool) snake; ~ **à sonnette** rattlesnake

serpenter /sɛʀpɑ̃te/ [1] *vi* ‹road, river› to wind

serpentin /sɛʀpɑ̃tɛ̃/ *nm* streamer

serpillière /sɛʀpijɛʀ/ *nf* floorcloth

serre /sɛʀ/ *nf* **(a)** greenhouse
(b) talon, claw

serré, ~e /seʀe/ **1** *adj* **(a)** ‹screw, nut› tight; ‹skirt, trousers› tight; **trop serré** too tight
(b) ‹grass› thick; ‹writing› cramped
(c) ‹deadline, budget› tight; ‹bend› sharp; ‹control› strict; ‹struggle› hard; ‹debate› heated; ‹match› close
(d) ‹coffee› very strong
2 *adv* ‹write› in a cramped hand; ‹knit› tightly; **il va falloir jouer** ~ **si...** we can't take any chances if...

serre-livres /sɛʀlivʀ/ *nm inv* book end

serrement /sɛʀmɑ̃/ *nm* **(a)** ~ **de main** handshake
(b) avoir *or* **ressentir un** ~ **de cœur** to feel a pang

◆ **serrer** /seʀe/ [1] **1** *vtr* **(a)** to grip ‹steering wheel, rope›; ~ **qn/qch dans ses bras** to hug sb/sth; ~ **la main de qn** to shake hands with sb; ~ **les poings** to clench one's fists; **ça me serre le cœur de voir ça** it wrings my heart to see that
(b) to tighten ‹knot, screw›; to turn [sth] off tightly ‹tap›; **sans** ~ ‹attach, screw› loosely
(c) ‹shoes, clothes› to be too tight
(d) ~ **à droite** to get *or* stay in the right-hand

lane; ~ **qn de près** to be hot on sb's tail
(e) to push [sth] closer together ‹objects, tables›; to squeeze ‹person›; **être serrés** to be packed together
(f) to cut ‹expenses, prices›
2 se serrer *v refl* (+ *v être*) **(a)** to squeeze up; **ils se sont serrés les uns contre les autres** they huddled together
(b) se ~ **dans une jupe** to squeeze oneself into a skirt; **nous nous sommes serré la main** we shook hands
(c) avoir la gorge qui se serre to have a lump in one's throat

serrure /seʀyʀ/ *nf* lock; **trou de** ~ keyhole

serrurerie /seʀyʀʀi/ *nf* locksmith's

serrurier /seʀyʀje/ *nm* locksmith

sertir /sɛʀtiʀ/ [3] *vtr* to set ‹stone›

sérum /seʀɔm/ *nm* serum; ~ **de vérité** truth drug

servage /sɛʀvaʒ/ *nm* serfdom

servante /sɛʀvɑ̃t/ *nf* maidservant

serve ▶ SERF

serveur, -euse /sɛʀvœʀ, øz/ *nm,f* waiter/waitress

servi, ~e /sɛʀvi/ **1** *pp* ▶ SERVIR
2 *pp adj* **(a) 'prends de la viande'—'merci je suis déjà** ~' 'have some meat'—'I already have some, thank you'
(b) (fam) **nous voulions du soleil, nous sommes** ~**s** we wanted some sunshine and we've certainly got it

serviable /sɛʀvjabl/ *adj* obliging, helpful

◆ **service** /sɛʀvis/ **1** *nm* **(a)** favour (GB); **rendre un** ~ **à qn** to do sb a favour (GB)
(b) (in transport) service; ~ **de bus** bus service
(c) être en ~ ‹lift› to be in working order; ‹motorway› to be open; ‹bus› to be running
(d) rendre ~ **à qn** ‹machine› to be a help to sb; ‹shop› to be convenient (for sb)
(e) service; **être au** ~ **de son pays** to serve one's country; **travailler au** ~ **de la paix** to work for peace; **'à votre** ~!' 'don't mention it!', 'not at all!'; **avoir 20 ans de** ~ **dans une entreprise** to have been with a firm 20 years; **être de** *or* **en** ~ to be on duty; **état de** ~(s) record of service; **pharmacie de** ~ duty chemist
(f) (at table) service; **faire le** ~ to serve; to act as waiter
(g) (domestic) service; **entrer au** ~ **de qn** to go to work for sb; **prendre qn à son** ~ to take sb on; **escalier de** ~ backstairs
(h) department; ~ **du personnel** personnel department; ~ **des urgences** casualty department (GB), emergency room (US); **les** ~**s de sécurité** the security services; **chef de** ~ (in administration) section head; (in hospital) senior consultant
(i) (Mil) ~ **(militaire)** military *or* national service
(j) set; **un** ~ **à thé** a tea set; ~ **de table** dinner service
(k) (in church) service ⋯▸

S

(l) (Sport) service, serve; **être au ~** to serve

2 **services** *nm pl* services; **se passer des ~s de qn** to dispense with sb's services

■ **~ après-vente** after-sales service; **~ d'ordre** stewards; **~ de presse** press office; press and publicity department; **~ public** public service

serviette /sɛʀvjɛt/ *nf* **(a)** **~ (de toilette)** towel; **~ (de table)** (table) napkin

(b) briefcase

■ **~ de bain** bath towel; **~ hygiénique** sanitary towel (GB), sanitary napkin (US)

serviette-éponge, *pl* **serviettes-éponges** /sɛʀvjɛtepɔ̃ʒ/ *nf* terry towel

servile /sɛʀvil/ *adj* servile; slavish

servilement /sɛʀvilmɑ̃/ *adv* ‹obey, imitate› slavishly; ‹flatter› obsequiously

servilité /sɛʀvilite/ *nf* servility

ˢ **servir** /sɛʀviʀ/ [30] **1** *vtr* **(a)** to serve; **qu'est-ce que je vous sers (à boire)?** what would you like to drink?; **tu es mal servi** you haven't got much; **'Madame est servie'** 'dinner is served, Madam'; **au moment de ~** before serving

(b) ‹situation› to help ‹person, cause›; to serve ‹interests›; ‹person› to further ‹ambition›

(c) to deal ‹cards›

2 **servir à** *v+prep* **(a)** **~ à qn** to be used by sb; **~ à qch** to be used for sth; **les exercices m'ont servi à comprendre la règle** the exercises helped me to understand the rule

(b) to come in useful; **cela ne sert à rien de faire** there's no point in doing

3 **servir de** *v+prep* **~ d'intermédiaire à qn** to act as an intermediary for sb; **~ d'arme** to be used as a weapon

4 *vi* **(a)** (Mil) **~ dans** to serve in

(b) (Sport) to serve

(c) il a servi dix ans chez nous he was in our service for ten years

(d) ‹object› to be used

5 **se servir** *v refl* (+ *v être*) **(a)** (at table) to help oneself; **se ~ un verre de vin** to pour oneself a glass of wine

(b) (in shop) to serve oneself

(c) se ~ de qn/qch to use sb/sth; **se ~ d'une situation** to make use of a situation

(d) (Culin) to be served

serviteur /sɛʀvitœʀ/ *nm* servant

servitude /sɛʀvityd/ *nf* **(a)** servitude

(b) (figurative) constraint

ses ▶ SON¹

sésame /sezam/ *nm* sesame

session /sesjɔ̃/ *nf* **(a)** session

(b) examination session; **~ de rattrapage** retakes

(c) course

set /sɛt/ *nm* (Sport) set

■ **~ de table** place mat

ˢ indicates a very frequent word

seuil /sœj/ *nm* **~ (de la porte)** doorstep; doorway, threshold

ˢ **seul**, **~e** /sœl/ **1** *adj* **(a)** alone, on one's own; **vous êtes ~ dans la vie?** are you single?; **elle veut vous parler ~ à ~** *or* **~e à ~(e)** she wants to speak to you in private; **parler tout ~** to talk to oneself

(b) by oneself, on one's own; **il a mangé un poulet à lui tout ~** he ate a whole chicken all by himself; **ça va tout ~** it's really easy; things are running smoothly

(c) only; **la ~e et unique personne** the one and only person; **pas un ~ client** not a single customer; **l'espion et l'ambassadeur sont une ~e et même personne** the spy and the ambassador are one and the same person; **d'une ~e pièce** in one piece; **à la ~e idée de faire** at the very idea of doing; **ils ont parlé d'une ~e voix** they were unanimous; **elle ~e pourrait vous le dire** only she could tell you

(d) lonely; **c'est un homme ~** he's a lonely man

2 *nm,f* **le ~, la ~e** the only one; **les ~s, les ~es** the only ones; **ils sont les ~s à croire que...** they're alone in thinking that...

ˢ **seulement** /sœlmɑ̃/ *adv* **(a)** only; **nous étions ~ deux** there were only the two of us; **'nous étions dix'—'~?'** 'there were ten of us'—'is that all?'; **elle revient ~ demain** she's not coming back until tomorrow

(b) c'est possible, ~ je veux y réfléchir it's possible, only *or* but I'd like to think about it

(c) si ~ if only

sève /sɛv/ *nf* **(a)** sap

(b) (figurative) vigour (GB)

sévère /sevɛʀ/ *adj* ‹look, tone, punishment› severe; ‹person, upbringing› strict; ‹selection› rigorous; ‹judgment› harsh; ‹losses› heavy

sévèrement /sevɛʀmɑ̃/ *adv* severely; harshly; strictly

sévérité /severite/ *nf* **(a)** strictness, harshness

(b) sternness, severity

sévices /sevis/ *nm pl* physical abuse

sévir /seviʀ/ [3] *vi* **(a)** to clamp down

(b) ‹storm, war› to rage; ‹poverty› to be rife

(c) (figurative) ‹doctrine› to hold sway; ‹phenomenon› to be rife

sevrage /səvʀaʒ/ *nm* weaning

sevrer /səvʀe/ [16] *vtr* to wean

sexagénaire /sɛksaʒenɛʀ/ *nmf* sixty-year-old

ˢ **sexe** /sɛks/ *nm* **(a)** sex; **indépendamment du ~, de l'ethnie, de l'âge** irrespective of gender, race or age; **un bébé de ~ féminin** a female baby

(b) genitals

sexiste /sɛksist/ *adj, nmf* sexist

sexologue /sɛksɔlɔg/ *nmf* sex therapist

sextuor /sɛkstyɔʀ/ *nm* sextet

sextuplé, **~e** /sɛkstyple/ *nm,f* sextuplet

sexualité /sɛksɥalite/ *nf* sexuality

sexué, **~e** /sɛksɥe/ *adj* sexed; sexual

sexuel, -elle /sɛksɥɛl/ *adj* (gen) sexual; ‹education, gland› sex

seyant, **~e** /sɛjɑ̃, ɑ̃t/ *adj* becoming

SF /ɛsɛf/ *nf* (*abbr* = **science-fiction**) sci-fi

SFP /ɛsɛfpe/ *nf* (*abbr* = **Société française de production et de création audiovisuelles**) *French TV and video production company*

shaker /ʃekœʁ/ *nm* cocktail shaker

shampooing /ʃɑ̃pwɛ̃/ *nm* shampoo

shampouiner /ʃɑ̃pwine/ [1] *vtr* to shampoo

shampouineur, -euse /ʃɑ̃pwinœʁ, øz/ *nm,f*: *trainee hairdresser (who washes hair)*

shérif /ʃeʁif/ *nm* sheriff

shetland /ʃɛtlɑ̃d/ *nm* (a) Shetland wool
(b) Shetland pony

shoot /ʃut/ *nm* (a) (Sport) shot
(b) (fam) (of drug) fix (colloq)

shooter /ʃute/ [1] **1** *vi* to shoot
2 **se shooter** *v refl* (+ *v être*) (fam) to shoot up (colloq)

short /ʃɔʁt/ *nm* shorts

si¹ /si/ **1** *adv* (a) yes; 'tu ne le veux pas?'—'~!' 'don't you want it?'— 'yes I do!'; il n'ira pas, moi ~ he won't go, but I will
(b) so; c'est un homme ~ agréable he's such a pleasant man; ~ bien que so; so much so that; rien n'est ~ beau qu'un coucher de soleil there's nothing so beautiful as a sunset; est-elle ~ bête qu'on le dit? is she as stupid as people say (she is)?
2 *conj* (**s'** *before il or ils*) (a) if; ~ j'étais riche if I were rich; ~ j'avais su! if only I'd known!; vous pensez ~ j'étais content! you can imagine how happy I was!; ~ ce n'est (pas) toi, qui est-ce? if it wasn't you, who was it?; il n'a rien pris avec lui ~ ce n'est un livre he didn't take anything with him apart from a book; à quoi servent ces réunions ~ ce n'est à nous faire perdre notre temps? what purpose do these meetings serve other than to waste our time?; ~ tant est qu'une telle distinction ait un sens if such a distinction makes any sense
(b) ~ tu venais avec moi? how about coming with me?
(c) whereas

si² /si/ *nm inv* (Mus) (note) B; (in sol-fa) ti

siamois, **~e** /sjamwa, az/ **1** *adj* (a) ‹cat› Siamese
(b) des frères ~ male Siamese twins
2 *nm inv* (a) (language) Siamese
(b) Siamese cat

sibylle /sibil/ *nf* sibyl

SICAV /sikav/ *nf* (*abbr* = **société d'investissement à capital variable**) unit trust, mutual fund

sida /sida/ *nm* (*abbr* = **syndrome immunodéficitaire acquis**) Aids

side-car, *pl* **~s** /sidkaʁ/ *nm* (a) sidecar
(b) motorcycle combination

sidéral, **~e**, *mpl* **-aux** /sideʁal, o/ *adj* sidereal

sidérer /sideʁe/ [14] *vtr* (fam) (astonish) to stagger (colloq)

sidérurgie /sideʁyʁʒi/ *nf* steel industry

sidérurgique /sideʁyʁʒik/ *adj* steel

siècle /sjɛkl/ *nm* (a) century; au Vᵉ ~ après J.-C. in the 5th century AD; d'ici la fin du ~ by the turn of the century; il y a des ~s (fam) que je ne suis venu ici I haven't been here for ages
(b) age; le ~ de Louis XIV the age of Louis XIV

sied ▶ SEOIR

siège /sjɛʒ/ *nm* (a) seat
(b) ~ (social) (of company) head office; (of organization) headquarters
(c) (of MP) seat
(d) (Mil) siege
(e) (Anat) seat

siéger /sjeʒe/ [15] *vi* (a) to sit
(b) to be in session
(c) to have its headquarters

sien, sienne /sjɛ̃, sjɛn/ **1** *det* cette maison est sienne à présent the house is now his/hers
2 **le sien, la sienne, les siens, les siennes** *pron* his/hers; être de retour parmi les ~s to be back with one's family; to be back among one's own friends; faire des siennes ‹person› to be up to mischief; ‹computer› to act up

sieste /sjɛst/ *nf* nap, siesta

sifflant, **~e** /siflɑ̃, ɑ̃t/ *adj* (a) hissing; wheezing
(b) sibilant

sifflement /sifləmɑ̃/ *nm* (of person, train) whistle; (of kettle, wind) whistling; (of bird, insect) chirping; (of snake) hissing

siffler /sifle/ [1] **1** *vtr* (a) to whistle ‹tune›; to whistle for ‹dog›; to whistle at ‹person›
(b) ‹referee› to blow one's whistle for ‹foul›
(c) to hiss, to boo
2 *vi* (a) (gen) to whistle; ‹projectile› to whistle through the air; ‹bird› to chirp; ‹snake› to hiss
(b) to blow one's whistle

sifflet /siflɛ/ *nm* (a) whistle; coup de ~ whistle
(b) (of train) whistle; (of kettle) whistling
(c) hiss, boo
IDIOM couper le ~ à qn (fam) to shut sb up (colloq)

sifflotement /siflɔtmɑ̃/ *nm* whistling

siffloter /siflɔte/ [1] *vi* to whistle away to oneself

sigle /sigl/ *nm* acronym

S

signal, pl **-aux** /siɲal, o/ nm signal
■ ~ **d'alarme** alarm signal; ~ **sonore** (on answerphone) tone
signalement /siɲalmɑ̃/ nm description
⚥ **signaler** /siɲale/ [1] **1** vtr (a) ~ **qch à qn** to point sth out to sb; to inform sb of sth
(b) ~ **à qn que** to remind sb that
(c) to indicate ‹roadworks, danger›
(d) to report ‹fact›
2 **se signaler** v refl (+ v être) **se ~ par qch** to distinguish oneself by sth
signalétique /siɲaletik/ adj descriptive; **fiche ~** specification sheet
signalisation /siɲalizasjɔ̃/ nf
(a) signalling (GB)
(b) signals
■ ~ **routière** roadsigns and markings
signaliser /siɲalize/ [1] vtr to signpost ‹road›; to mark out and light ‹runway›
signataire /siɲatɛʀ/ nmf signatory
signature /siɲatyʀ/ nf (a) signature
(b) signing
⚥ **signe** /siɲ/ nm sign; ~ **astral** star sign; ~ **précurseur** omen; ~ **distinctif** or **particulier** distinguishing feature; **c'était un ~ du destin** it was fate; ~**s de ponctuation** punctuation marks; **faire ~ à qn** to wave to sb; (figurative) to get in touch with sb; **d'un ~ de la main/tête, elle m'a montré la cuisine** she pointed to/nodded her head in the direction of the kitchen; **faire ~ que oui** to indicate agreement
IDIOM **il n'a pas donné ~ de vie depuis six mois** there's been no sign of him for six months
⚥ **signer** /siɲe/ [1] **1** vtr to sign; **il signe son troisième roman** he's written his third novel
2 **se signer** v refl (+ v être) to cross oneself
signet /siɲɛ/ nm (Comput) bookmark; **créer un ~ sur** to bookmark ‹site›
signifiant, ~**e** /siɲifjɑ̃, ɑ̃t/ adj significant
significatif, -ive /siɲifikatif, iv/ adj significant
signification /siɲifikasjɔ̃/ nf (a) meaning
(b) importance
signifié /siɲifje/ nm signified
⚥ **signifier** /siɲifje/ [1] vtr (a) to mean
(b) ~ **qch à qn** to inform sb of sth
⚥ **silence** /silɑ̃s/ nm (a) silence; **'un peu de ~ s'il vous plaît'** 'quiet please'; **passer qch sous ~** to say nothing about sth
(b) (Mus) rest
silencieusement /silɑ̃sjøzmɑ̃/ adv silently
silencieux, -ieuse /silɑ̃sjø, øz/ **1** adj silent; quiet
2 nm (a) (on gun) silencer
(b) (on exhaust) silencer (GB), muffler (US)
silex /silɛks/ nm inv flint; **en** or **de ~** flint

⚥ indicates a very frequent word

silhouette /silwɛt/ nf (a) silhouette; outline
(b) figure; shape
silice /silis/ nf silica
silicium /silisjɔm/ nm silicon
silicone /silikon/ nf silicone
sillage /sijaʒ/ nm (a) (of ship) wake; (of plane) vapour (GB) trail; slipstream
(b) (of person) wake
sillon /sijɔ̃/ nm (a) furrow
(b) line
(c) fissure
(d) groove
sillonner /sijone/ [1] vtr (a) ‹roads› to criss-cross; ‹police› to patrol; ~ **la France en voiture** to drive all over France
(b) to furrow
silo /silo/ nm silo
simagrée /simagre/ nf play-acting
simiesque /simjɛsk/ adj ape-like
similaire /similɛʀ/ adj similar
similarité /similaʀite/ nf similarity
similicuir /similikɥiʀ/ nm imitation leather
similitude /similityd/ nf similarity
⚥ **simple** /sɛ̃pl/ **1** adj (a) (gen) simple; **c'est (bien) ~, il ne fait plus rien** he simply doesn't do anything any more
(b) ‹decor› plain; ‹person, air› unaffected
(c) ‹origins› modest
(d) ‹worker› ordinary; **c'est un ~ avertissement** it's just a warning; **le ~ fait de poser la question** the mere fact of asking the question; **par ~ curiosité** out of pure curiosity; **sur ~ présentation du passeport** on presentation of one's passport
(e) ‹ice-cream cone, knot› single
2 nm (a) **le prix varie du ~ au double** the price can turn out to be twice as high
(b) (Sport) ~ **dames/messieurs** ladies'/men's singles
■ ~ **d'esprit** simple-minded
⚥ **simplement** /sɛ̃pləmɑ̃/ adv (a) simply, merely, just; **vas-y, ~ fais attention** you can go, only be careful
(b) ‹dress, live› simply
(c) easily
simplet, -ette /sɛ̃plɛ, ɛt/ adj simple
simplicité /sɛ̃plisite/ nf (a) simplicity; **c'est d'une ~ enfantine** it's so easy a child could do it
(b) (of person) unpretentiousness; (of thing) simplicity; **avec ~** simply
simplification /sɛ̃plifikasjɔ̃/ nf simplification
simplifier /sɛ̃plifje/ [2] **1** vtr to simplify
2 **se simplifier** v refl (+ v être) **se ~ la vie** to make life easier for oneself
simpliste /sɛ̃plist/ adj simplistic
simulacre /simylakʀ/ nm (a) pretence (GB); ~ **de procès** mock trial

(b) sham; ∼ **de justice** travesty of justice

simulateur, -trice /simylatœr, tʀis/ **1** *nm,f* **(a)** shammer, faker
(b) malingerer
2 *nm* (Tech) simulator

simulation /simylasjɔ̃/ *nf* **(a)** simulation
(b) malingering

simuler /simyle/ [1] *vtr* to feign; to simulate

simultané, ∼e /simyltane/ *adj* simultaneous

sincère /sɛ̃sɛʀ/ *adj* (gen) sincere; ‹friend› true; ‹emotion, offer› genuine; ‹opinion› honest

sincèrement /sɛ̃sɛʀmɑ̃/ *adv* **(a)** ‹think› really; ‹regret, thank, speak› sincerely
(b) frankly

sincérité /sɛ̃seʀite/ *nf* sincerity; honesty; genuineness

sinécure /sinekyʀ/ *nf* sinecure

sine qua non /sinekwanɔn/ *phr* **condition** ∼ sine qua non

singe /sɛ̃ʒ/ *nm* **(a)** monkey; ape; **les grands** ∼**s** the apes
(b) mimic; **faire le** ∼ to clown around

singer /sɛ̃ʒe/ [13] *vtr* to ape; to feign

singeries /sɛ̃ʒʀi/ *nf pl* antics; **faire des** ∼ to monkey around; to pull funny faces

singulariser: se singulariser /sɛ̃gylaʀize/ [1] *v refl* (+ *v être*) to draw attention to oneself

singularité /sɛ̃gylaʀite/ *nf* **(a)** peculiarity, singularity
(b) uniqueness

singulier, -ière /sɛ̃gylje, ɛʀ/ **1** *adj*
(a) peculiar, unusual
(b) combat ∼ single combat
2 *nm* **(a)** singular
(b) singularity

singulièrement /sɛ̃gyljɛʀmɑ̃/ *adv*
(a) oddly
(b) radically

sinistre /sinistʀ/ **1** *adj* sinister; ‹place, future› bleak; ‹evening› dreary
2 *nm* disaster; accident; blaze

sinistré, ∼e /sinistʀe/ **1** *adj* stricken; **région** ∼**e** disaster area
2 *nm,f* disaster victim

✧ **sinon** /sinɔ̃/ **1** *conj* **(a)** otherwise, or else
(b) except, apart from
(c) not to say; **c'est devenu difficile** ∼ **impossible** it has become difficult if not impossible
2 sinon que *phr* except that, other than that

sinueux, -euse /sinɥø, øz/ *adj* sinuous; winding; tortuous

sinus /sinys/ *nm inv* sinus

sinusite /sinyzit/ *nf* sinusitis

siphon /sifɔ̃/ *nm* **(a)** (gen) siphon
(b) U-bend

siphonné, ∼e /sifɔne/ *adj* (fam) nuts (colloq), crazy (colloq)

sire /siʀ/ *nm* Sire

sirène /siʀɛn/ *nf* **(a)** (gen) siren; (of boat) foghorn
(b) mermaid, siren
■ ∼ **d'alarme** fire alarm

sirop /siʀo/ *nm* **(a)** syrup (GB), sirup (US); cordial
(b) (medicine) syrup (GB), sirup (US), mixture; ∼ **pectoral** cough mixture

siroter /siʀɔte/ [1] *vtr* (fam) to sip

sirupeux, -euse /siʀypø, øz/ *adj* syrupy (GB), sirupy (US)

sis, ∼e /si, siz/ *adj* located

sismique /sismik/ *adj* seismic

sismographie /sismɔgʀafi/ *nf* seismography

✧ **site** /sit/ *nm* **(a)** area; ∼ **touristique** place of interest; ∼ **archéologique** archaeological site
(b) site
■ ∼ **de bavardage** (Comput) chatroom; ∼ **de réseau social** social networking site; ∼ **vierge** green-field site; ∼ **Web** Web site

sitôt /sito/ **1** *adv* ∼ **rentrés** as soon as we/ they get back; as soon as we/they got back; **je n'y retournerai pas de** ∼ I won't go back there in a hurry (colloq)
2 *conj* ∼ **que** as soon as
IDIOM ∼ **dit,** ∼ **fait** no sooner said than done

✧ **situation** /sitɥasjɔ̃/ *nf* **(a)** situation
(b) job, position
(c) location
■ ∼ **de famille** marital status

✧ **situer** /sitɥe/ [1] **1** *vtr* **(a)** (in space and time) to place; **l'hôtel est bien situé** the hotel is in a good location
(b) ∼ **une histoire en 2001/à Palerme** to set a story in 2001/in Palermo
2 se situer *v refl* (+ *v être*) **(a) se** ∼ **à Paris en 1900** to be set in Paris in 1900
(b) politiquement, je me situe plutôt à gauche politically, I'm more to the left

✧ **six** /sis, *but before consonant* si, *and before vowel or mute h* siz/ *adj inv, pron, nm inv* six

sixième /sizjɛm/ **1** *adj* sixth
2 *nf* (Sch) *first year of secondary school, age 11–12*

skaï® /skaj/ *nm* imitation leather

skate-board, *pl* ∼**s** /skɛtbɔʀd/ *nm*
(a) skateboard
(b) skateboarding

sketch, *pl* ∼**es** /skɛtʃ/ *nm* sketch

ski /ski/ *nm* **(a)** ski
(b) le ∼ skiing
■ ∼ **de fond** cross-country skiing; ∼ **nautique** water skiing; ∼ **de piste** downhill skiing

skier /skje/ [2] *vi* to ski

skieur, -ieuse /skjœʀ, øz/ *nm,f* skier

slalom /slalɔm/ *nm* slalom

S

slalomer /slalɔme/ [1] vi **(a)** (Sport) to slalom
(b) (figurative) to zigzag

slave /slav/ adj Slavonic

Slave /slav/ nmf Slav

slip /slip/ nm **(a)** underpants
(b) slipway

slogan /slɔgɑ̃/ nm slogan

slow /slo/ nm slow dance

smala /smala/ nf (fam) tribe (colloq)

SME /ɛsɛmə/ nm: abbr ▶ SYSTÈME

SMIC /smik/ nm (abbr = **salaire minimum interprofessionel de croissance**) guaranteed minimum wage

smicard, **∼e** /smikaʀ, -aʀd/ nm,f: person on the minimum wage

smoking /smɔkiŋ/ nm dinner jacket (GB), tuxedo

SNCF /ɛsɛnseɛf/ nf (abbr = **Société nationale des chemins de fer français**) French national railway company

snob /snɔb/ **1** adj ‹person› stuck-up (colloq); ‹restaurant› posh
2 nmf snob; **c'est un ∼** he's a snob

snober /snɔbe/ [1] vtr to snub

snobisme /snɔbism/ nm snobbery

sobre /sɔbʀ/ adj **(a)** ‹person› abstemious; sober; temperate; ‹life› simple
(b) ‹style› plain, sober

sobrement /sɔbʀəmɑ̃/ adv soberly; in moderation; ‹live› frugally

sobriété /sɔbʀijete/ nf sobriety, temperance; restraint; moderation

sobriquet /sɔbʀike/ nm nickname

soc /sɔk/ nm ploughshare (GB), plowshare (US)

sociabilité /sɔsjabilite/ nf sociability

sociable /sɔsjabl/ adj **(a)** sociable
(b) social

⚬ᷤ **social**, **∼e**, mpl **-iaux** /sɔsjal, o/ **1** adj
(a) social; **le milieu ∼ de qn** sb's social background
(b) **conflit ∼** industrial dispute
2 nm **le ∼** social issues

socialement /sɔsjalmɑ̃/ adv socially; **être ∼ pris en charge** to be in the care of the social services

socialiser /sɔsjalize/ [1] vtr **(a)** to socialize
(b) to collectivize

socialisme /sɔsjalism/ nm socialism

socialiste /sɔsjalist/ adj, nmf socialist

sociétaire /sɔsjetɛʀ/ nmf member

⚬ᷤ **société** /sɔsjete/ nf **(a)** society; **la haute ∼** high society
(b) company; **∼ de nettoyage** cleaning company
(c) (formal) **rechercher la ∼ de qn** to seek sb's company

socioculturel, **-elle** /sɔsjokyltyʀɛl/ adj sociocultural; **centre ∼** recreation centre (GB)

socio-démocrate, pl **∼s** **1** adj social democratic
2 nmf social democrat

socio-éducatif, **-ive**, mpl **∼s** /sɔsjoedykatif, iv/ adj socioeducational

sociologie /sɔsjɔlɔʒi/ nf sociology

sociologue /sɔsjɔlɔg/ nmf sociologist

socioprofessionnel, **-elle** /sɔsjopʀɔfɛsjɔnɛl/ adj social and occupational

socle /sɔkl/ nm pedestal, plinth; base; stand

socque /sɔk/ nm clog

socquette /sɔkɛt/ nf ankle sock, anklet (US)

soda /sɔda/ nm fizzy drink (GB), soda (US)

sodium /sɔdjɔm/ nm sodium

sodomiser /sɔdɔmize/ [1] vtr to sodomize, to bugger

⚬ᷤ **sœur** /sœʀ/ nf sister; **∼ jumelle** twin sister

sofa /sɔfa/ nm sofa

⚬ᷤ **soi** /swa/ pron **(a)** **autour de ∼** around one; **laisser la porte se refermer derrière ∼** to let the door shut behind one; **trouver en ∼ les ressources nécessaires** to find the necessary inner resources; **garder qch pour ∼** to keep sth to oneself
(b) **la logique n'est pas un objectif en ∼** logic is not an end in itself; **cela va de ∼** it goes without saying

soi-disant /swadizɑ̃/ **1** adj inv **(a)** self-styled
(b) (controversial) so-called
2 adv supposedly; **elle a ∼ la migraine** she has a migraine, or so she says

soie /swa/ nf **(a)** silk
(b) bristle

soient /swa/ ▶ ÊTRE¹

soierie /swaʀi/ nf **(a)** silk
(b) silk industry

soif /swaf/ nf **(a)** thirst; **avoir ∼** to be thirsty
(b) **∼ de** thirst for; hunger for; lust for; **avoir ∼ d'affection** to crave affection

soignant, **∼e** /swaɲɑ̃, ɑ̃t/ adj medical; **médecin ∼** doctor, GP

soigné, **∼e** /swaɲe/ **1** pp ▶ SOIGNER
2 pp adj **(a)** ‹nails› well-manicured; ‹hair, clothes› immaculate
(b) ‹publication› carefully produced; ‹work› meticulous; **peu ∼** ‹work› careless

soigner /swaɲe/ [1] **1** vtr **(a)** ‹doctor› to treat
(b) to look after ‹person, customer›
(c) to take care over ‹appearance›; to look after ‹hands›
2 **se soigner** v refl (+ v être) **(a)** to treat oneself; to look after oneself
(b) ‹illness› to be treatable

⚬ᷤ indicates a very frequent word

s

(c) to take care over one's appearance

soigneusement /swaɲøzmɑ̃/ *adv*
carefully; meticulously; neatly

soigneux, -euse /swaɲø, øz/ *adj*
(a) ‹work› conscientious; ‹examination›
careful
(b) ‹person› neat, tidy

soi-même /swamɛm/ *pron* oneself

✷ **soin** /swɛ̃/ ① *nm* (a) care; prendre ~ de
qch to take care of sth; prendre ~ de qn/sa
santé to look after sb/one's health; prendre
~ de sa petite personne to coddle oneself;
laisser à qn le ~ de faire to leave it to sb
to do
(b) product; ~ antipelliculaire dandruff
treatment
② **soins** *nm pl* (a) (Med) treatment; care;
recevoir des ~s to receive treatment; ~s
dentaires dental care; les premiers ~s à
donner aux brûlés first-aid treatment for
burns; ~s à domicile homecare
(b) care; ~s corporels *or* du corps body care
(c) 'aux bons ~s de' 'care of', 'c/o'
IDIOM être aux petits ~s pour qn to attend
to sb's every need

✷ **soir** /swaʀ/ *nm* evening; night; le ~ du 3, le
3 au ~ on the evening of the 3rd; il sort tous
les samedis ~ he goes out every Saturday
night; 6 heures du ~ 6 pm; à ce ~! see you
tonight!

✷ **soirée** /swaʀe/ *nf* (a) evening; dans *or*
pendant la ~, en ~ in the evening
(b) party; aller dans une ~ to go to a party
(c) evening performance *or* show

sois /swa/ ▶ ÊTRE¹

✷ **soit¹** /swa/ ① ▶ ÊTRE¹
② *conj* (a) ~, ~ either, or; ~ du fromage,
~ un gâteau either cheese, or a cake
(b) that is, ie; toutes mes économies, ~
200 euros all my savings, ie *or* that is,
200 euros
(c) (in mathematics) ~ un triangle ABC let ABC
be a triangle

soit² /swat/ *adv* very well; je me suis
trompé, ~, mais là n'est pas la question
all right, so I was wrong, but that's not the
point

soixantaine /swasɑ̃tɛn/ *nf* (a) une ~
about sixty
(b) avoir la ~ to be about sixty

soixante /swasɑ̃t/ *adj inv, pron, nm inv*
sixty

soixante-dix /swasɑ̃tdis/ *adj inv, pron,
nm inv* seventy

soixante-dixième /swasɑ̃tdizjɛm/ *adj*
seventieth

soixantième /swasɑ̃tjɛm/ *adj* sixtieth

soja /sɔʒa/ *nm* soya bean (GB), soybean (US);
sauce de ~ soy sauce

✷ **sol** /sɔl/ *nm* (a) ground; floor
(b) soil
(c) (Mus) (note) G; (in sol-fa) soh

solaire /sɔlɛʀ/ *adj* ‹energy› solar; ‹engine›
solar-powered; ‹cream› sun

✷ **soldat** /sɔlda/ *nm* soldier, serviceman

solde¹ /sɔld/ ① *nm* balance; faire le ~ d'un
compte to settle an account
② **en solde** *phr* acheter une veste en ~
to buy a jacket in a sale
③ **soldes** *nm pl* sales; sale

solde² /sɔld/ *nf* (Mil) pay; avoir qn à sa ~
(figurative) to have sb in one's pay

solder /sɔlde/ [1] ① *vtr* (a) to sell off
‹merchandise›
(b) to settle the balance of ‹account›
② **se solder** *v refl* (+ *v être*) se ~ par qch
to end in sth

solderie /sɔldəʀi/ *nf* discount shop

sole /sɔl/ *nf* (Zool) sole

✷ **soleil** /sɔlɛj/ *nm* sun; ~ de minuit midnight
sun; en plein ~ ‹sit› in (the) hot sun; ‹leave
something› in direct sunlight; quand il y a du
~ when it's sunny; attraper un coup *or* des
coups de ~ to get sunburned

solennel, -elle /sɔlanɛl/ *adj* (gen) solemn;
‹appeal, declaration› formal

solennité /sɔlanite/ *nf* solemnity

solfège /sɔlfɛʒ/ *nm* (a) music theory; ~
chanté sol-fa
(b) music theory book

✷ **solidaire** /sɔlidɛʀ/ *adj* (a) ‹team, group›
united
(b) (Tech) ‹parts› interdependent

solidariser: se solidariser
/sɔlidaʀize/ [1] *v refl* (+ *v être*) se ~ avec qn/
qch to stand by sb/sth

solidarité /sɔlidaʀite/ *nf* solidarity

✷ **solide** /sɔlid/ ① *adj* (a) ‹food, matter› solid
(b) ‹house, friendship› solid; ‹shoes, bag›
sturdy; ‹link, fastening, blade› strong;
‹position, base› firm
(c) ‹person, constitution, heart› strong;
avoir la tête ~ (figurative) to have one's head
screwed on (right)
(d) ‹business, experience, reason› sound;
‹guarantee› firm
② *nm* (a) solid; manger du ~ to eat solids
(b) ce qu'il te dit, c'est du ~ what he says
is sound
(c) les meubles anciens, c'est du ~ antique
furniture is solidly built

solidement /sɔlidmɑ̃/ *adv* ‹attach,
establish› firmly; ‹barricaded› securely; un
rapport ~ documenté a well-documented
report

solidifier /sɔlidifje/ [2] *vtr*, **se
solidifier** *v refl* (+ *v être*) to solidify

solidité /sɔlidite/ *nf* (a) (of construction)
solidity; (of machine) strength; (of link)
firmness; (of clothes) hard-wearing quality;
d'une grande ~ well-built; sturdy; strong;
hard-wearing
(b) (of argument) soundness

S

soliloque /sɔlilɔk/ nm soliloquy

soliste /sɔlist/ nmf soloist

solitaire /sɔlitɛR/ **1** adj (a) ‹person, life› solitary; ‹old age, childhood› lonely; **navigateur ~** single-handed yachtsman
(b) ‹house› isolated
2 nmf solitary person, loner; **en ~** ‹live› alone; ‹sail› single-handed
3 nm (a) (diamond) solitaire
(b) rogue boar
(c) (Games) solitaire

solitude /sɔlityd/ nf (a) solitude
(b) loneliness

solliciter /sɔlisite/ [1] vtr (a) (formal) to seek ‹interview, post, advice›
(b) to approach ‹person, organization›; to canvass ‹customer, voter›; **être très sollicité** to be assailed by requests; to be very much in demand

sollicitude /sɔlisityd/ nf concern, solicitude

solstice /sɔlstis/ nm solstice

soluble /sɔlybl/ adj soluble

ƒ **solution** /sɔlysjɔ̃/ nf (a) solution, solving; resolution
(b) solution; **une ~ de facilité** an easy way out
(c) (in chemistry) solution

solutionner /sɔlysjɔne/ [1] vtr to solve

solvabilité /sɔlvabilite/ nf (a) solvency
(b) creditworthiness

solvable /sɔlvabl/ adj solvent; creditworthy

solvant /sɔlvɑ̃/ nm solvent

somatiser /sɔmatize/ [1] vtr to have a psychosomatic reaction to

ƒ **sombre** /sɔ̃bR/ adj (a) dark; **il fait ~** it's dark
(b) ‹thought, future› dark, black; ‹conclusion› depressing; ‹air, person› solemn
(c) before n (colloq) ‹idiot› absolute; ‹affair› murky

sombrer /sɔ̃bRe/ [1] vi (a) ‹ship› to sink
(b) **~ dans** ‹person› to sink into ‹despair, alcoholism›

sommaire /sɔmɛR/ **1** adj ‹explanation› cursory; ‹description› rough; ‹installation, meal› rough and ready; ‹execution› summary
2 nm (a) contents; **au ~ de notre numéro de juillet** featured in our July issue
(b) (fam) **au ~:** **un débat sur le chômage** a debate on unemployment is on the programme (GB)

sommairement /sɔmɛRmɑ̃/ adv summarily

sommation /sɔmasjɔ̃/ nf (from police) warning; (from guard) challenge

somme[1] /sɔm/ nm nap, snooze (colloq)

ƒ **somme**[2] /sɔm/ nf (a) sum, amount
(b) sum total; **la ~ de nos connaissances**

---

the sum total of our knowledge; **il a fourni une grosse ~ de travail** he did a great deal of work; **en ~, ~ toute** all in all

ƒ **sommeil** /sɔmɛj/ nm sleep; **avoir le ~ agité** to sleep fitfully; **avoir le ~ léger** to be a light sleeper

sommeiller /sɔmeje/ [1] vi (a) to doze
(b) to lie dormant

sommelier, -ière /sɔməlje, ɛR/ nm,f wine waiter, sommelier

sommer /sɔmme/ [1] vtr **~ qn de faire** to command sb to do

sommes /sɔm/ ▶ ÊTRE[1]

ƒ **sommet** /sɔmɛ/ nm (a) (of mountain) peak; summit
(b) (gen) top; (of wave) crest; (of curve, career) peak
(c) (of glory, stupidity) height; **atteindre des ~s** ‹prices, sales› to peak
(d) summit; **conférence au ~** summit meeting
(e) (of triangle, angle) apex; (of cone) vertex

sommier /sɔmje/ nm (bed) base

somnambule /sɔmnɑ̃byl/ **1** adj **être ~** to sleepwalk
2 nmf sleepwalker

somnifère /sɔmnifɛR/ **1** adj soporific
2 nm (a) soporific
(b) sleeping pill

somnolence /sɔmnɔlɑ̃s/ nf drowsiness

somnolent, ~e /sɔmnɔlɑ̃, ɑ̃t/ adj
(a) drowsy
(b) ‹town› sleepy; ‹industry, country› lethargic

somnoler /sɔmnɔle/ [1] vi (a) to drowse
(b) ‹town› to be sleepy; ‹industry, country› to be lethargic

somptueux, -euse /sɔ̃ptɥø, øz/ adj sumptuous

somptuosité /sɔ̃ptɥozite/ nf sumptuousness

ƒ **son**[1], **sa**, pl **ses** /sɔ̃, sa, sɛ/ det his/her/its; **ses enfants** his/her children; **ses pattes** its paws; **elle a ~ lundi** she's off on Monday; she gets Mondays off; **~ étourdie de sœur** (fam) his/her absent-minded sister

son[2] /sɔ̃/ nm (a) sound; **ingénieur du ~** sound engineer
(b) volume; **baisser le ~** to turn the volume down
(c) bran; **pain au ~** bran loaf
■ **~ et lumière** son et lumière

sonar /sɔnaR/ nm sonar

sonate /sɔnat/ nf sonata

sondage /sɔ̃daʒ/ nm (a) poll; survey
(b) (Med) catheterization; probe
(c) (Naut) sounding

sonde /sɔ̃d/ nf (a) (Med) catheter; probe
(b) sounding lead; sounding line
(c) drill
(d) taster

ƒ indicates a very frequent word

sonder /sɔ̃de/ [1] *vtr* **(a)** to poll; to survey;
to sound out
(b) to probe
(c) (Med) to catheterize; to probe
(d) (Naut) to sound

songe /sɔ̃ʒ/ *nm* dream

⚥ **songer** /sɔ̃ʒe/ [13] *v+prep* ~ à qch/à faire to
think of sth/of doing; **tu n'y songes pas!** you
can't be serious!

songeur, -euse /sɔ̃ʒœR, øz/ *adj* pensive

sonnant, ~**e** /sɔnɑ̃, ɑ̃t/ *adj* **à trois heures**
~**es** on the stroke of three

sonné, ~**e** /sɔne/ 1 *pp* ▸ SONNER
2 *pp adj* **(a)** groggy; shattered
(b) **elle a quarante ans bien** ~**s** (fam) she's
well into her forties

⚥ **sonner** /sɔne/ [1] 1 *vtr* **(a)** to ring ‹bell›
(b) ‹clock› to strike ‹hour›; ‹person› to sound
‹retreat, alarm›; to ring out ‹vespers›
(c) to ring for; **on ne t'a pas sonné!** (fam) did
anyone ask you?
(d) (fam) ‹blow› to make [sb] dizzy; ‹news› to
stagger
2 **sonner de** *v+prep* to sound ‹horn›; to
play ‹bagpipes›
3 *vi* **(a)** ‹bell, phone› to ring; ‹hour› to
strike; ‹alarm clock› to go off; ‹alarm,
trumpet› to sound; **leur dernière heure a
sonné** their last hour has come
(b) ‹word, expression› to sound

sonnerie /sɔnRi/ *nf* **(a)** ringing; chimes;
système qui déclenche une ~ system that
sets off an alarm
(b) (of horn) sounding
(c) (of mobile phone) ringtone

sonnet /sɔnɛ/ *nm* sonnet

sonnette /sɔnɛt/ *nf* bell; doorbell; **tirer
la** ~ **d'alarme** to pull the emergency cord;
(figurative) to sound the alarm

sonore /sɔnɔR/ *adj* **(a)** ‹laugh, kiss, slap›
resounding
(b) resonant; echoing; hollow-sounding
(c) ‹vibrations› sound; **le volume** ~ **est
tel que…** the noise level is so high that…;
effets ~**s** sound effects; **un document** ~ a
recording
(d) ‹consonant› voiced

sonorisation /sɔnɔRizasjɔ̃/ *nf* public
address system, PA system

sonorité /sɔnɔRite/ *nf* **(a)** (of instrument,
voice) tone; **les** ~**s de l'italien** the sound of
Italian
(b) (of hi-fi) sound quality
(c) resonance

sont /sɔ̃/ ▸ ÊTRE¹

sophistication /sɔfistikasjɔ̃/ *nf*
sophistication

sophistiqué, ~**e** /sɔfistike/ *adj*
(a) sophisticated
(b) artificial, mannered

sophrologie /sɔfRɔlɔʒi/ *nf* relaxation
therapy

soporifique /sɔpɔRifik/ *adj*, *nm* soporific

soprano /sɔpRano/ *nmf* soprano

sorbet /sɔRbɛ/ *nm* sorbet

sorcellerie /sɔRsɛlRi/ *nf* witchcraft;
sorcery

sorcier /sɔRsje/ 1 *adj m* (fam) **ce n'est
(pourtant) pas** ~**l** (but) it's dead easy (colloq)
2 *nm* **(a)** wizard; sorcerer
(b) witch doctor

sorcière /sɔRsjɛR/ *nf* witch; sorceress

sordide /sɔRdid/ *adj* squalid; sordid

sornettes /sɔRnɛt/ *nf pl* tall stories

⚥ **sort** /sɔR/ *nm* **(a)** lot; **être satisfait de son** ~
to be satisfied with one's lot
(b) fate; **le** ~ **est contre moi** I'm ill-fated; **tirer
qch au** ~ to draw lots for sth
(c) curse, spell; **jeter un** ~ **à qn** to put a
curse on sb; **le** ~ **en est jeté** the die is cast

sortable /sɔRtabl/ *adj* **mon mari n'est pas**
~ I can't take my husband anywhere

⚥ **sorte** /sɔRt/ 1 *nf* sort, kind
2 **de la sorte** *phr* in this way
3 **de sorte que** *phr* **(a)** so that
(b) **la toile est peinte de** ~ **que…** the canvas
is painted in such a way that…
(c) **de** ~ **que je n'ai pas pu venir** with the
result that I couldn't come
4 **en quelque sorte** *phr* in a way
5 **en sorte de** *phr* **fais en** ~ **d'être à
l'heure** try to be on time
6 **en sorte que** *phr* **fais en** ~ **que tout
soit en ordre** make sure everything is tidy

⚥ **sortie** /sɔRti/ *nf* **(a)** exit; **je t'attendrai à la**
~ I'll wait for you outside (the building); **à la**
~ **de la ville** on the outskirts of the town; on
the edge of the town
(b) **à ma** ~ **du tribunal** when I left the court;
se retrouver à la ~ **de l'école** to meet after
school; **à la** ~ **de l'hiver** at the end of winter
(c) **faire une** ~ **fracassante** to make a
dramatic exit; **la** ~ **de la récession/crise** the
end of the recession/crisis
(d) outing; **faire une** ~ **avec l'école** to go on
a school outing; **ce soir, c'est mon soir de**
~ tonight is my night out; **priver qn de** ~ to
keep sb in, to ground sb (colloq)
(e) (of new product) launching; (of film) release;
(of book) publication; (of fashion collection)
showing
(f) (Tech) output; **faire une** ~ **sur imprimante**
to print
■ ~ **des artistes** stage-door; ~ **d'autoroute**
motorway exit (GB), highway exit (US); ~ **de
bain** bathrobe

sortilège /sɔRtilɛʒ/ *nm* spell

⚥ **sortir¹** /sɔRtiR/ [30] 1 *vtr* **(a)** to take [sb/
sth] out ‹person, dog›
(b) to get [sb/sth] out; ~ **les mains de ses
poches** to take one's hands out of one's
pockets; ~ **la poubelle** to put the bin (GB) *or*
the garbage (US) *or* the trash (US) out; ~ **sa
langue** to stick one's tongue out
(c) (fam) to chuck (colloq) [sb] out ‹person›; to
send [sb] out ‹pupil›

⋯⋱

S

(d) ~ qn de to get sb out of ‹situation›
(e) to bring out ‹book›; to release ‹film›; to show ‹collection›
(f) to turn out ‹book, record, film, product›
(g) to bring [sth] out ‹newspaper›
(h) (fam) to come out with (colloq) ‹remarks›; ~ une blague to crack a joke
2 vi (+ v être) **(a)** to go out; to come out; ~ déjeuner to go out for lunch; être sorti to be out; ~ en courant to run out; faire ~ qn to get sb outside; laisser ~ qn to allow sb out
(b) to go out; ~ avec qn to go out with sb; inviter qn à sortir to ask sb out
(c) ~ de to leave; ~ de chez qn to leave sb's house; sortez d'ici! get out of here!; ~ de son lit to get out of bed; ~ tout chaud du four to be hot from the oven; ~ de chez le médecin to come out of the doctor's
(d) ~ d'un rêve to wake up from a dream; ~ de la récession to pull out of the recession; ~ de l'hiver to reach the end of winter
(e) ~ à peine de l'enfance to be just emerging from childhood; ~ d'une guerre to emerge from a war
(f) ‹water, smoke, cork› to come out; faire ~ to squeeze [sth] out ‹juice›; to eject ‹cassette›
(g) ‹bud, insect› to come out; ‹tooth› to come through
(h) to stick out
(i) ‹film, book, new model› to come out; ~ tous les jours/tous les mois ‹paper› to be published daily/monthly
(j) ~ de ‹person, product› to come from; ~ de Berkeley to have graduated from Berkeley; d'où sors-tu à cette heure? (fam) where have you been?
(k) ~ du sujet ‹remark› to be beside the point; cela sort de mes fonctions that's not within my authority
(l) ‹number› to come up
(m) (Comput) to exit
3 se sortir v refl (+ v être) **(a)** se ~ de la pauvreté to escape from poverty; s'en ~ to get out of it; to get over it; s'en ~ vivant to escape with one's life
(b) s'en ~ to pull through; to cope; to manage; s'en ~ à peine to scrape a living

sortir² /sɔʀtiʀ/ nm au ~ de at the end of

SOS /ɛsoɛs/ nm **(a)** SOS
(b) emergency service; ~ médecins emergency medical service
(c) helpline; ~ enfants battus child abuse helpline

sosie /sozi/ nm double; c'est ton ~! he/ she's the spitting image of you!

sot, sotte /so, sɔt/ **1** adj silly
2 nm,f silly thing; petit ~! you silly thing!

sottement /sɔtmɑ̃/ adv foolishly, stupidly

sottise /sɔtiz/ nf **(a)** silliness, foolishness
(b) silly remark; dire des ~s to talk rubbish
(c) faire des ~s ‹children› to be naughty

⚥ indicates a very frequent word

⚥ **sou** /su/ nm **(a)** (fam) penny (GB), cent (US); il est près de ses ~s he's a penny-pincher; c'est une affaire de gros ~s there's big money involved
(b) (fam) il n'a pas un ~ de bon sens he hasn't got a scrap of common sense
(c) (former unit of French currency) sou

soubassement /subasmɑ̃/ nm **(a)** (of building, pillar) base
(b) bedrock

soubresaut /subʀəso/ nm start; jolt

soubrette /subʀɛt/ nf maid

souche /suʃ/ nf **(a)** (tree) stump; (vine) stock
(b) stock; de ~ paysanne of peasant stock
(c) (of chequebook) stub
IDIOM dormir comme une ~ to sleep like a log

⚥ **souci** /susi/ nm **(a)** se faire du ~ to worry
(b) problem; j'ai d'autres ~s (en tête) I've got other things to worry about
(c) (formal) avoir le ~ de qch to care about sth; avoir le ~ de faire to be anxious to do; dans le seul ~ de faire plaisir with the sole intention of pleasing
(d) marigold

soucier: se soucier /susje/ **[2]** v refl (+ v être) to care (de about); sans se ~ de qch/ faire without concerning oneself with sth/ doing

soucieux, -ieuse /susjø, øz/ adj worried

soucoupe /sukup/ nf saucer
■ ~ volante flying saucer

⚥ **soudain, -e** /sudɛ̃, ɛn/ **1** adj sudden
2 adv suddenly, all of a sudden

soudainement /sudɛnmɑ̃/ adv suddenly

soude /sud/ nf ~ caustique caustic soda

souder /sude/ **[1]** **1** vtr **(a)** to weld
(b) to join ‹edges›; to bind [sb] together ‹people›
2 se souder v refl (+ v être) ‹vertebrae› to fuse; ‹bone› to knit together

soudoyer /sudwaje/ **[23]** vtr to bribe

soudure /sudyʀ/ nf weld, join; welding

soufflant, -e /suflɑ̃, ɑ̃t/ adj **(a)** machine ~e blowing apparatus
(b) (fam) stunning

⚥ **souffle** /sufl/ nm **(a)** breath; couper le ~ à qn to wind sb; (figurative) to take sb's breath away; (en) avoir le ~ coupé to be winded; (figurative) to be speechless; être à bout de ~ ‹person› to be out of breath; ‹country, economy› to be running out of steam; donner un second or nouveau ~ à qn/ qch to put new life into sb/sth; avoir du ~ ‹saxophonist› to have good lungs; ‹singer› to have a powerful voice; ‹sportsman› to be fit; (figurative) ‹person› to have staying power
(b) breathing
(c) breeze; pas un ~ d'air not a breath of air
(d) spirit; ~ révolutionnaire revolutionary spirit

(e) inspiration
(f) (from fan, explosion) blast
(g) (Med) ~ au cœur heart murmur
soufflé, ~e /sufle/ 1 *adj* (fam)
flabbergasted
2 *nm* (Culin) soufflé
souffler /sufle/ [1] 1 *vtr* (a) to blow out
‹candle›
(b) to blow ‹air, smoke, dust›
(c) to whisper ‹words›; ~ qch à l'oreille de
qn to whisper sth in sb's ear; ~ la réplique à
un acteur to prompt an actor
(d) to suggest ‹idea›
(e) to blow ‹glass›; to blast ‹metal›
(f) ‹explosion› to blow out ‹window›; to blow
up ‹building›
(g) (fam) to flabbergast
2 *vi* (a) ‹wind› to blow; le vent souffle fort
there's a strong wind
(b) ‹person› to get one's breath back; ‹horse›
to get its wind back
(c) to puff; suant et soufflant huffing and
puffing
(d) ‹person, animal› to blow; ~ dans une
trompette to blow into a trumpet
(e) to tell sb the answer; on ne souffle pas!
no prompting!
IDIOM ~ comme un bœuf *or* un phoque *or*
une locomotive to puff and pant
soufflerie /sufləri/ *nf* (a) blower; blower
house
(b) glassblower; glassblowing company
soufflet /sufle/ *nm* (a) bellows
(b) gusset
souffleur, -euse /suflœr, øz/ *nm,f*
(a) prompter
(b) ~ (de verre) glassblower
✦ **souffrance** /sufrãs/ *nf* suffering
souffrant, ~e /sufrã, ãt/ *adj* unwell
souffre-douleur /sufrədulœr/ *nm inv*
punch-bag (GB), punching-bag (US)
✦ **souffrir** /sufrir/ [4] 1 *vtr* (a) ~ tout de qn
to put up with anything from sb; il ne souffre
pas la critique he can't take criticism
(b) cette affaire ne peut ~ aucun retard this
matter brooks no delay
2 *vi* (a) ‹person› to suffer; ~ de to suffer
from; ma cheville me fait ~ my ankle hurts;
est-ce qu'il souffre? is he in pain?; faire ~
‹person› to make [sb] suffer; ‹situation› to
upset; ~ du racisme to be a victim of racism
(b) ‹crops, economy› to be badly affected;
‹country, city› to suffer
soufre /sufr/ *nm* sulphur (GB), sulfur (US)
souhait /swe/ *nm* wish
IDIOM à vos ~s! bless you!
souhaitable /swetabl/ *adj* desirable
✦ **souhaiter** /swete/ [1] *vtr* (a) to hope for
(b) ~ qch à qn to wish sb sth; ~ la
bienvenue à qn to welcome sb; je vous
souhaite d'obtenir très bientôt votre diplôme
I hope you get your degree very soon

(c) il souhaite se rendre là-bas en voiture he
would like to go by car
souiller /suje/ [1] *vtr* (a) to soil, to make
[sth] dirty; être souillé de to be stained with
(b) to defile ‹place, person›; to sully ‹memory›
souillon /sujɔ̃/ *nf* slattern
souillure /sujyr/ *nf* stain
souk /suk/ *nm* (a) souk
(b) (fam) mess; racket (colloq)
soûl, ~e /su, sul/ 1 *adj* drunk
2 **tout son soûl** *phr* ‹drink, eat› one's
fill
soulagement /sulaʒmã/ *nm* relief
soulager /sulaʒe/ [13] *vtr* (gen) to relieve;
to ease ‹conscience›; le comprimé m'a
soulagé the tablet made me feel better; tu
m'as soulagé d'un grand poids you've taken
a great weight off my shoulders
soûlant, ~e /sulã, ãt/ *adj* (fam) elle est ~e!
she makes my head spin!
soûler /sule/ [1] 1 *vtr* (a) ‹person› to get
[sb] drunk; ‹alcohol› to make [sb] drunk
(b) ‹perfume› to intoxicate
(c) (fam) tu me soûles avec tes histoires
you're making my head spin!
2 **se soûler** *v refl* (+ *v être*) to get drunk
soulèvement /sulɛvmã/ *nm* uprising
✦ **soulever** /sulve/ [16] 1 *vtr* (a) to lift
‹object›; to raise ‹dust›; ~ qn/qch de terre to
pick sb/sth up
(b) to arouse ‹enthusiasm, anger›; to stir up
‹crowd›; to raise ‹problems›
2 **se soulever** *v refl* (+ *v être*) (a) to raise
oneself up
(b) to rise up
IDIOM ça me soulève le cœur it turns my
stomach; it makes me sick
soulier /sulje/ *nm* shoe
IDIOM être dans ses petits ~s to feel
uncomfortable
✦ **souligner** /suliɲe/ [1] *vtr* (a) to underline
‹word›; to outline ‹eyes›
(b) to emphasize
✦ **soumettre** /sumɛtr/ [60] 1 *vtr* (a) to
bring [sb/sth] to heel ‹person, group, region›;
to subdue ‹rebels›
(b) ~ qn/qch à to subject sb/sth to
(c) to submit
(d) ~ un produit à une température élevée to
subject a product to a high temperature
2 **se soumettre** *v refl* (+ *v être*) (a) to
submit
(b) se ~ à to accept ‹rule›
soumis, ~e /sumi, iz/ 1 *pp* ▶ SOUMETTRE
2 *pp adj* submissive
soumission /sumisjɔ̃/ *nf* submission
soupape /supap/ *nf* valve
soupçon /supsɔ̃/ *nm* (a) suspicion
(b) (fam) (of milk, wine) drop; (of salt) pinch; (of
flavour) hint
soupçonner /supsɔne/ [1] *vtr* to suspect

S

soupçonneux, -euse /supsɔnø, øz/ adj
suspicious, mistrustful

soupe /sup/ nf (a) soup; à la~! (fam)
(humorous) grub's up! (colloq)
(b) (fam) slush
■ ~ **populaire** soup kitchen
IDIOMS être ~ **au lait** (fam) to be quick-
tempered; **cracher dans la** ~ (fam) to look a
gift horse in the mouth

soupente /supɑ̃t/ nf (a) loft, garret
(b) cupboard under the stairs

souper¹ /supe/ [1] vi to have late dinner

souper² /supe/ nm late dinner, supper

soupeser /supəze/ [16] vtr (a) to feel the
weight of
(b) to weigh up ⟨arguments⟩

soupière /supjɛR/ nf soup tureen

soupir /supiR/ nm sigh

soupirail, pl **-aux** /supiRaj, o/ nm cellar
window

soupirer /supiRe/ [1] vi to sigh

souple /supl/ adj (a) ⟨body⟩ supple; ⟨stalk⟩
flexible; ⟨hair⟩ soft
(b) ⟨step, style⟩ flowing; ⟨shape⟩ smooth
(c) ⟨rule⟩ flexible

souplesse /suplɛs/ nf (a) (of stalk)
flexibility; (of hair) softness; (of body)
suppleness
(b) (of step) litheness; (of gesture) grace; (of
car) smoothness; (of style) fluidity
(c) (of rule) flexibility

✧ **source** /suRs/ nf (a) spring
(b) source; **prendre sa** ~ **dans** or **à** ⟨river⟩
to rise in or at; **citer ses** ~s to give one's
sources
IDIOMS **ça coule de** ~ it's obvious; **retour
aux** ~s return to basics

sourcil /suRsi/ nm eyebrow

sourciller /suRsije/ [1] vi to raise one's
eyebrows; **sans** ~ without batting an eyelid
(GB) or eyelash (US)

sourd, ~e /suR, suRd/ **1** adj (a) deaf; ~ **à**
deaf to ⟨pleas⟩
(b) ⟨noise⟩ dull; ⟨voice⟩ muffled
(c) ⟨pain⟩ dull
(d) ⟨consonant⟩ voiceless, surd
2 nm,f deaf person; **les** ~s the deaf
IDIOMS **faire la** ~e **oreille** to turn a deaf
ear; **comme un** ~ ⟨shout⟩ at the top of one's
voice; ⟨hit, strike⟩ like one possessed; **ce n'est
pas tombé dans l'oreille d'un** ~ it didn't go
unheard

sourdine /suRdin/ nf (Mus) mute; (on piano)
soft pedal; **écouter la radio en** ~ to have the
radio on quietly

sourd-muet, sourde-muette, pl
sourds-muets, sourdes-muettes
/suRmɥɛ, suRdmɥɛt/ **1** adj deaf and dumb
2 nm,f deaf-mute

souriant, ~e /suRjɑ̃, ɑ̃t/ adj smiling

souriceau, pl **~x** /suRiso/ nm young
mouse

souricière /suRisjɛR/ nf (a) mousetrap
(b) trap

✧ **sourire¹** /suRiR/ [68] vi (a) to smile; ~
jusqu'aux oreilles to grin from ear to ear
(b) ~ **à qn** ⟨fate, fortune⟩ to smile on sb

✧ **sourire²** /suRiR/ nm smile; **le** ~ **aux lèvres**
with a smile on one's face

souris /suRi/ nf inv mouse

sournois, ~e /suRnwa, az/ adj ⟨person,
look⟩ sly; ⟨behaviour⟩ underhand; ⟨pain⟩
insidious

✧ **sous** /su/ prep (a) under, underneath; **un
journal** ~ **le bras** a newspaper under one's
arm; ~ **la pluie** in the rain
(b) under; ~ **le numéro 4757** under number
4757
(c) during; ~ **la présidence de Mitterrand**
during Mitterrand's presidency
(d) within; ~ **peu** before long
(e) ~ **traitement** undergoing treatment; ~
antibiotiques on antibiotics; **travailler** ~
Windows® (Comput) to work in Windows®

sous-alimenté, ~e, mpl ~s
/suzalimɑ̃te/ adj undernourished

sous-bois /subwɑ/ nm inv undergrowth

sous-catégorie, pl ~s /sukategɔRi/ nf
subcategory

sous-chef, pl ~s /suʃɛf/ nm second-
in-command

souscripteur, -trice /suskRiptœR,
tRis/ nm,f subscriber (**de** to)

souscription /suskRipsjɔ̃/ nf
(a) subscription
(b) ~ **d'un contrat d'assurances** taking out
an insurance policy

souscrire /suskRiR/ [67] **1** vtr to take out
⟨insurance⟩; to sign ⟨contract⟩; to subscribe
⟨sum of money⟩
2 souscrire à v+prep to subscribe to

souscrit, ~e **1** pp ▶ SOUSCRIRE
2 pp adj (a) subscribed
(b) subscript

sous-cutané, ~e, mpl ~s /sukytane/ adj
subcutaneous

sous-développé, ~e, mpl ~s
/sudevlɔpe/ adj underdeveloped

sous-directeur, -trice, mpl ~s
/sudiRɛktœR, tRis/ nm,f assistant manager

sous-direction, pl ~s /sudiRɛksjɔ̃/ nf
division; ~ **des affaires économiques et
financières** economic and financial affairs
division

sous-effectif, pl ~s /suzefɛktif/ nm
understaffing; **ils sont en** ~ they're
understaffed

sous-employer /suzɑ̃plwaje/ [23] vtr to
underemploy

sous-entendre /suzɑ̃tɑ̃dR/ [6] vtr to
imply

S

sous-entendu, ~e, *mpl* ~s
/suzãtãdy/ **1** *pp* ▶ SOUS-ENTENDRE
2 *pp adj* understood
3 *nm* innuendo

sous-équipé, ~e, *mpl* ~s /suzekipe/ *adj*
underequipped

sous-estimer /suzestime/ [1] *vtr* to
underestimate

sous-évaluer /suzevalɥe/ [1] *vtr* to
underestimate; to undervalue

sous-fifre, *pl* ~s /sufifʀ/ *nm* (fam)
underling

sous-jacent, ~e, *mpl* ~s /suʒasã, ãt/ *adj*
(a) ‹idea, problem, tension› underlying
(b) subjacent

sous-lieutenant, *pl* ~s /suljøtnã/ *nm* (in
the army) ≈ second lieutenant; (in the air force)
≈ pilot officer

sous-louer /sulwe/ [1] *vtr* to sublet; to
sublease

sous-main /sumɛ̃/ **1** *nm inv* desk blotter
2 **en sous-main** *phr* secretly

sous-marin, ~e, *mpl* ~s /sumaʀɛ̃,
in/ **1** *adj* submarine, underwater; deep-sea
2 *nm* (a) submarine
(b) (fam) spy

sous-marque, *pl* ~s /sumaʀk/ *nf* sub-
brand

sous-officier, *pl* ~s /suzɔfisje/ *nm*
noncommissioned officer

sous-ordre, *pl* ~s /suzɔʀdʀ/ *nm* suborder

sous-payer /supeje/ [21] *vtr* to underpay

sous-préfecture, *pl* ~s /supʀefɛktyʀ/
nf: administrative subdivision of a
department in France

sous-produit, *pl* ~s /supʀɔdɥi/ *nm*
(a) by-product
(b) second-rate product

sous-prolétariat, *pl* ~s /supʀɔletaʀja/ *nm*
underclass

sous-pull, *pl* ~s /supyl/ *nm* thin polo-
neck jumper

soussigné, ~e /susiɲe/ *adj*, *nm,f*
undersigned

sous-sol, *pl* ~s /susɔl/ *nm* (a) basement
(b) subsoil

sous-tasse, *pl* ~s /sutas/ *nf* saucer

sous-titrage, *pl* ~s /sutitʀaʒ/ *nm*
subtitling

sous-titre, *pl* ~s /sutitʀ/ *nm* subtitle

sous-titrer /sutitʀe/ [1] *vtr* to subtitle

soustraction /sustʀaksjɔ̃/ *nf* subtraction

soustraire /sustʀɛʀ/ [58] **1** *vtr* (a) to
subtract
(b) to steal
(c) to take away ‹person›; ~ qn/qch à la vue
de qn to hide sb/sth from sb
(d) to shield ‹person›; ~ qn à la mort to save
sb's life
2 **se soustraire** *v refl* (+ *v être*) (a) se ~
à to escape from

(b) se ~ à la justice to escape justice

sous-traitance, *pl* ~s /sutʀɛtãs/ *nf*
subcontracting; **travail donné en** ~ work
contracted out

sous-traiter /sutʀɛte/ *vtr* to subcontract

sous-verre /suvɛʀ/ *nm inv* (a) clip-frame
(b) coaster

sous-vêtement, *pl* ~s /suvɛtmã/ *nm*
underwear

soutane /sutan/ *nf* cassock

soute /sut/ *nf* hold; ~ à bagages baggage
hold

soutenable /sutnabl/ *adj* (a) bearable;
pas ~ unbearable
(b) tenable

soutenance /sutnãs/ *nf* viva (voce) (GB),
orals (US)

soutènement /sutɛnmã/ *nm* retaining
structure; (in mine) props

souteneur /sutnœʀ/ *nm* pimp (colloq),
procurer

✦ **soutenir** /sutniʀ/ [36] **1** *vtr* (a) (gen) to
support ‹person, team, currency›; ~ à bout
de bras to keep [sb/sth] afloat ‹person,
project›; ~ qn contre qn to side with sb
against sb; ~ le moral de qn to keep sb's
spirits up
(b) to maintain ‹contrary›; to defend
‹paradox›; to uphold ‹opinion›
(c) to keep [sb] going
(d) to keep [sth] going ‹conversation›; to keep
up ‹effort, pace›
(e) to withstand ‹shock, attack, stares›; to
bear ‹comparison›
(f) ~ sa thèse to have one's viva (voce) (GB)
or defense (US)
2 **se soutenir** *v refl* (+ *v être*) to support
each other

soutenu, ~e /sutny/ **1** *pp* ▶ SOUTENIR
2 *pp adj* ‹effort, activity› sustained;
‹attention› close; ‹rhythm› steady
3 *adj* (a) ‹market› firm; ‹colour› deep;
‹language› formal
(b) (Mus) ‹note› sustained

souterrain, ~e /sutɛʀɛ̃, ɛn/ **1** *adj*
(a) underground
(b) économie ~e black economy
2 *nm* underground passage, tunnel

✦ **soutien** /sutjɛ̃/ *nm* support

soutien-gorge, *pl* **soutiens-gorge**
/sutjɛ̃gɔʀʒ/ *nm* bra

soutirer /sutiʀe/ [1] *vtr* ~ qch à qn to
squeeze sth out of sb ‹money›; to extract sth
from sb ‹confession›

souvenance /suvnãs/ *nf* à ma ~ as far as
I recall; **avoir** ~ de qch to remember sth

souvenir[1]: **se souvenir** /suvniʀ/ [36] *v
refl* (+ *v être*) **se** ~ **de qn/qch** to remember
sb/sth

✦ **souvenir**[2] /suvniʀ/ *nm* (a) memory;
garder un bon ~ **de qch** to have happy
memories of sth; **ne pas avoir** ~ **de** to have ⋯⟶

S

no recollection of
(b) memory; **s'effacer du** ~ **de qn** to fade
from sb's memory
(c) souvenir; memento; **en** ~ as a souvenir;
as a memento; as a keepsake; **boutique de**
~**s** souvenir shop (GB) *or* store (US)
(d) mon bon ~ **à** remember me to

✓ **souvent** /suvɑ̃/ *adv* often

souverain, ~e /suvʀɛ̃, ɛn/ **1** *adj*
(a) ‹state› sovereign; ‹authority› supreme
(b) ‹happiness, scorn› supreme
(c) ‹remedy› sovereign; ‹advice, virtue›
sterling
(d) ‹person› haughty
2 *nm,f* sovereign, monarch

souverainement /suvʀɛnmɑ̃/ *adv* **votre
attitude me déplaît** ~ I dislike your attitude
intensely

souveraineté /suvʀɛnte/ *nf* sovereignty

soviet /sɔvjɛt/ *nm* soviet; **Soviet suprême**
Supreme Soviet

soviétique /sɔvjetik/ *adj* Soviet

soyeux, -euse /swajø, øz/ *adj* silky

soyez /swaje/ ▶ ÊTRE¹

soyons /swajɔ̃/ ▶ ÊTRE¹

SPA /ɛspea/ *nf* (abbr = **Société
protectrice des animaux**) society for
the prevention of cruelty to animals

spacieux, -ieuse /spasjø, øz/ *adj*
spacious

spaghetti /spageti/ *nm inv* **des** ~
spaghetti

sparadrap /spaʀadʀa/ *nm* **(a)** surgical *or*
adhesive tape
(b) (sticking) plaster (GB), Band-aid®

spartiate /spaʀsjat/ *adj, nmf* Spartan

spasme /spasm/ *nm* spasm

spasmophilie /spasmɔfili/ *nf*
spasmophilia

spatial, ~e, *mpl* **-iaux** /spasjal, o/ *adj*
(a) spatial
(b) space; **vaisseau** ~ spaceship

spatule /spatyl/ *nf* **(a)** spatula
(b) filling-knife

speaker, speakerine /spikœʀ,
spikʀin/ *nm,f* announcer

✓ **spécial, ~e,** *mpl* **-iaux** /spesjal, o/ *adj*
(a) special
(b) odd

spécialement /spesjalmɑ̃/ *adv*
(a) specially
(b) especially; **pas** ~ not especially

spécialiser: se spécialiser
/spesjalize/ [1] *v refl* (+ *v être*) to specialize

spécialiste /spesjalist/ *nmf* specialist

spécialité /spesjalite/ *nf* speciality (GB),
specialty (US)

spécificité /spesifisite/ *nf* **(a)** specificity
(b) characteristic

(c) uniqueness

spécifier /spesifje/ [2] *vtr* to specify

spécifique /spesifik/ *adj* specific

spécimen /spesimɛn/ *nm* **(a)** specimen
(b) (free) sample
(c) (fam) odd specimen (colloq)

✓ **spectacle** /spɛktakl/ *nm* **(a)** sight;
se donner *or* **s'offrir en** ~ to make an
exhibition of oneself
(b) show; ~ **de danse** dance show; **'~s'**
'entertainment'; **film à grand** ~ spectacular
(c) show business

spectaculaire /spɛktakylɛʀ/ *adj*
spectacular

spectateur, -trice /spɛktatœʀ, tʀis/ *nm,f*
(a) member of the audience
(b) spectator

spectre /spɛktʀ/ *nm* **(a)** ghost
(b) spectre (GB)
(c) ~ **lumineux** spectrum of light

spéculateur, -trice /spekylatœʀ,
tʀis/ *nm,f* speculator

spéculatif, -ive /spekylatif, iv/ *adj*
speculative

spéculation /spekylasjɔ̃/ *nf* **(a)** (Econ)
speculation; ~ **sur** speculation in
(b) (gen) speculation (**sur** on, about)

spéculer /spekyle/ [1] *vi* to speculate; ~ **à
la hausse/baisse** to bull/bear

spéléologie /speleɔlɔʒi/ *nf* **(a)** caving,
potholing (GB), spelunking (US)
(b) speleology

spermatozoïde /spɛʀmatozɔid/ *nm*
spermatozoon

sperme /spɛʀm/ *nm* sperm

sphère /sfɛʀ/ *nf* sphere

sphérique /sferik/ *adj* spherical

sphincter /sfɛ̃ktɛʀ/ *nm* sphincter

sphinx /sfɛ̃ks/ *nm inv* **(a)** Sphinx
(b) hawkmoth

spirale /spiʀal/ *nf* spiral

spiritisme /spiʀitism/ *nm* spiritualism

spiritualité /spiʀitɥalite/ *nf* spirituality

✓ **spirituel, -elle** /spiʀitɥɛl/ *adj* **(a)** spiritual
(b) witty

spiritueux, -euse /spiʀitɥø, øz/ *nm inv*
spirit

splendeur /splɑ̃dœʀ/ *nf* (of scenery, site)
splendour (GB); (of era, reign) glory

splendide /splɑ̃did/ *adj* splendid;
stunning

spolier /spɔlje/ [2] *vtr* to despoil (**de** of)

spongieux, -ieuse /spɔ̃ʒjø, øz/ *adj*
spongy

sponsoriser /spɔ̃sɔʀize/ [1] *vtr* to sponsor

spontané, ~e /spɔ̃tane/ *adj* spontaneous

spontanéité /spɔ̃taneite/ *nf* spontaneity

sporadique /spɔʀadik/ *adj* sporadic

spore /spɔʀ/ *nf* spore

✓ indicates a very frequent word

⚡ **sport** /spɔʀ/ *nm* sport; sports; **aller aux ∼s d'hiver** to go on a winter sports holiday (GB) *or* vacation (US)

sportif, -ive /spɔʀtif, iv/ **1** *adj* (a) ⟨*event*⟩ sports; **je ne suis pas ∼** I'm not the sporty type
(b) ⟨*appearance*⟩ athletic, sporty (colloq)
2 *nm, f* sportsman/sportswoman; **c'est un ∼** he's athletic

spot /spɔt/ *nm* (a) spotlight
(b) ∼ **(publicitaire)** commercial

squale /skwal/ *nm* shark

square /skwaʀ/ *nm* small public garden

squash /skwaʃ/ *nm* squash

squatter¹ /skwate/ [1] *vtr* to squat in

squatter² /skwatœʀ/ *nm* squatter

squelette /skəlɛt/ *nm* (a) skeleton
(b) (fam) bag of bones (colloq)
(c) framework

squelettique /skəlɛtik/ *adj* ⟨*person, legs*⟩ scrawny; ⟨*tree*⟩ skeletal; ⟨*report*⟩ sketchy

SRAS /ɛsɛʀaɛs/ *nm* (*abbr* = **syndrome respiratoire aigu sévère**) SARS

stabiliser /stabilize/ [1] **1** *vtr* to stabilize; to consolidate
2 se stabiliser *v refl* (+ *v être*) ⟨*unemployment*⟩ to stabilize; ⟨*person*⟩ to become stable

stabilité /stabilite/ *nf* stability

stable /stabl/ *adj* stable

stade /stad/ *nm* (a) (Sport) stadium
(b) stage; **à ce ∼** at this stage

stage /staʒ/ *nm* (a) professional training
(b) work experience; ∼ **pratique** period of work experience
(c) course; **suivre un ∼ de formation** to go on a training course

stagiaire /staʒjɛʀ/ *nmf* (a) trainee
(b) student teacher

stagnation /stagnasjɔ̃/ *nf* stagnation

stagner /stagne/ [1] *vi* to stagnate

stalactite /stalaktit/ *nf* stalactite

stalagmite /stalagmit/ *nf* stalagmite

stalle /stal/ *nf* stall

stand /stɑ̃d/ *nm* stand; stall
■ ∼ **de tir** shooting range; shooting gallery

standard /stɑ̃daʀ/ **1** *adj inv* standard
2 *nm* switchboard

standardisation /stɑ̃daʀdizasjɔ̃/ *nf* standardization

standardiste /stɑ̃daʀdist/ *nmf* switchboard operator

standing /stɑ̃diŋ/ *nm* (a) de ∼ ⟨*apartment*⟩ luxury
(b) standard of living

star /staʀ/ *nf* star

starter /staʀtɛʀ/ *nm* (Aut) choke

station /stasjɔ̃/ *nf* (a) station; taxi-rank (GB), taxi stand; **c'est à deux ∼s d'ici** it's two stops from here

(b) ∼ **(de radio)** (radio) station
(c) ∼ **balnéaire** seaside resort; ∼ **thermale** spa
(d) ∼ **debout** *or* **verticale** upright posture *or* position
(e) stop, pause

stationnaire /stasjɔnɛʀ/ *adj* (a) stationary
(b) stable

stationnement /stasjɔnmɑ̃/ *nm* parking

stationner /stasjɔne/ [1] *vi* to park

station-service, *pl* **stations-service** /stasjɔsɛʀvis/ *nf* service *or* filling station

statique /statik/ *adj* static

statistique /statistik/ *nf* (a) statistics
(b) statistic

statue /staty/ *nf* statue

statuer /statɥe/ [1] *vi* to give a ruling

statuette /statɥɛt/ *nf* statuette

statu quo /statykwo/ *nm inv* status quo

stature /statyʀ/ *nf* (a) stature
(b) height

⚡ **statut** /staty/ *nm* (a) statute
(b) status

statutaire /statytɛʀ/ *adj* statutory

steak /stɛk/ *nm* steak; **un ∼ haché** a hamburger

sténodactylo /stenodaktilo/ **1** *nmf* shorthand typist (GB), stenographer (US)
2 *nf* shorthand typing (GB), stenography (US)

sténographier /stenɔgʀafje/ [2] *vtr* to take [sth] down in shorthand

sténotypiste /stenɔtipist/ *nmf* stenotypist

steppe /stɛp/ *nf* steppe

stéréo /steʀeo/ *adj inv*, *nf* stereo

stéréophonique /steʀeɔfɔnik/ *adj* stereophonic

stéréotype /steʀeɔtip/ *nm* (a) stereotype
(b) cliché

stérile /steʀil/ *adj* (gen) sterile; ⟨*land*⟩ barren; ⟨*discussion*⟩ fruitless

stérilet /steʀilɛ/ *nm* coil, IUD

stériliser /steʀilize/ [1] *vtr* to sterilize

stérilité /steʀilite/ *nf* (a) sterility; barrenness
(b) fruitlessness

sterling /stɛʀliŋ/ *adj inv* sterling; **livre ∼** pound sterling

sternum /stɛʀnɔm/ *nm* breastbone, sternum

stéthoscope /stetɔskɔp/ *nm* stethoscope

stigmate /stigmat/ *nm* (a) scar
(b) mark

stimulant, ∼e /stimylɑ̃, ɑ̃t/ *adj* invigorating; bracing; stimulating

stimulation /stimylasjɔ̃/ *nf* stimulation

stimuler /stimyle/ [1] **1** *vtr* (a) to stimulate ⟨*organ, function*⟩
(b) to spur [sb] on ···>

S

2 *vi* **(a)** to be bracing
(b) (fam) to act as a spur
stimulus, *pl* **stimuli** /stimylys, stimyli/ *nm* stimulus
stipuler /stipyle/ [1] *vtr* to stipulate
stock /stɔk/ *nm* stock; **avoir qch en ~** to have sth in stock
stockage /stɔkaʒ/ *nm* **(a)** stocking; stockpiling
(b) (Comput) storage
stocker /stɔke/ [1] *vtr* **(a)** to stock
(b) to stockpile
(c) to store ‹*data*›
stoïque /stɔik/ *adj* stoical
stop /stɔp/ *nm* **(a)** stop sign
(b) (fam) hitch-hiking (colloq); **prendre qn en ~** to give sb a lift (GB) *or* ride (US)
stopper /stɔpe/ [1] 1 *vtr* **(a)** to stop; to halt ‹*development*›
(b) to mend
2 *vi* to stop
store /stɔR/ *nm* **(a)** blind
(b) awning
strabisme /strabism/ *nm* squint
strapontin /strapɔ̃tɛ̃/ *nm* foldaway seat
stratagème /strataʒɛm/ *nm* stratagem
strate /strat/ *nf* stratum
⚜ **stratégie** /strateʒi/ *nf* strategy
stratégique /strateʒik/ *adj* strategic
stratifié, ~e /stratifje/ *adj* **(a)** stratified
(b) laminated
stratosphère /stratɔsfɛR/ *nf* stratosphere
stress /strɛs/ *nm inv* stress
stressant, ~e /strɛsɑ̃, ɑ̃t/ *adj* stressful
stresser /strɛse/ [1] *vtr* to put [sb] on edge; to put [sb] under stress
strict, ~e /strikt/ *adj* **(a)** (gen) strict; **au sens ~** in the strict sense of the word
(b) ‹*hairstyle, outfit*› severe
strident, ~e /stridɑ̃, ɑ̃t/ *adj* ‹*noise*› piercing; ‹*voice*› strident
strie /stri/ *nf* **(a)** streak
(b) groove
(c) (in geology) **des ~s** striation
strip-tease /striptiz/ *nm* striptease
strophe /strɔf/ *nf* stanza, verse
⚜ **structure** /stryktyR/ *nf* **(a)** structure
(b) organization; **~ d'accueil** shelter, refuge
structurer /stryktyRe/ [1] *vtr* to structure
stuc /styk/ *nm* stucco
studieux, -ieuse /stydjø, øz/ *adj* ‹*pupil*› studious; ‹*holiday*› study
studio /stydjo/ *nm* **(a)** studio flat (GB), studio apartment (US)
(b) studio
stupéfaction /stypefaksjɔ̃/ *nf* stupefaction
stupéfait, ~e /stypefɛ, ɛt/ *adj* astounded

stupéfiant, ~e /stypefjɑ̃, ɑ̃t/ 1 *adj* stunning
2 *nm* drug, narcotic
stupéfier /stypefje/ [2] *vtr* to astound
stupeur /stypœR/ *nf* **(a)** astonishment
(b) (Med) stupor
stupide /stypid/ *adj* stupid
stupidité /stypidite/ *nf* stupidity
⚜ **style** /stil/ *nm* **(a)** style; **~ de vie** lifestyle; **c'est bien ton ~ de faire** it's just like you to do
(b) meubles de ~ (reproduction) period furniture
(c) speech form; **~ indirect** indirect *or* reported speech
stylé, ~e /stile/ *adj* well-trained
styliser /stilize/ [1] *vtr* to stylize
styliste /stilist/ *nmf* fashion designer
⚜ **stylo** /stilo/ *nm* (fountain) pen; **~ bille** ball-point pen; **~ feutre** felt-tip pen
su¹, ~e /sy/ ▶ SAVOIR¹
su² /sy/ *nm* **au vu et au ~ de tous** openly
suaire /sɥɛR/ *nm* shroud
suant, ~e /sɥɑ̃, ɑ̃t/ *adj* **(a)** sweaty
(b) (fam) deadly dull
suave /sɥav/ *adj* ‹*perfume, music, smile*› sweet; ‹*voice*› mellifluous; ‹*person, manner*› suave
subalterne /sybaltɛRn/ *nmf* subordinate; (Mil) low-ranking officer, subaltern
subconscient /sybkɔ̃sjɑ̃/ *nm* subconscious
subdiviser /sybdivize/ [1] *vtr* to subdivide
⚜ **subir** /sybiR/ [3] *vtr* **(a)** to be subjected to ‹*violence, pressure*›; to suffer ‹*defeat, damage*›
(b) to take ‹*examination*›; to have ‹*operation, test*›; **~ l'influence de qn** to be under sb's influence
(c) to put up with
(d) to undergo
subit, ~e /sybi, it/ *adj* sudden
subitement /sybitmɑ̃/ *adv* suddenly
subjectif, -ive /sybʒɛktif, iv/ *adj* subjective
subjectivité /sybʒɛktivite/ *nf* subjectivity
subjonctif /sybʒɔ̃ktif/ *nm* subjunctive
subjuguer /sybʒyge/ [1] *vtr* **(a)** to captivate, to enthral (GB)
(b) to subjugate
sublime /syblim/ *adj* sublime
sublimer /syblime/ [1] *vtr*, *vi* to sublimate
submerger /sybmɛRʒe/ [13] *vtr* **(a)** to submerge
(b) to flood ‹*market, switchboard*›
(c) ‹*crowd, emotion*› to overwhelm
(d) ~ qn de travail to inundate sb with work
subodorer /sybɔdɔRe/ [1] *vtr* to detect
subordination /sybɔRdinasjɔ̃/ *nf* subordination

⚜ indicates a very frequent word

S

subordonné, **~e¹** /sybɔʀdɔne/ *nm,f* subordinate

subordonnée² /sybɔʀdɔne/ *nf* subordinate clause; **~ relative** relative clause

subordonner /sybɔʀdɔne/ [1] *vtr* **(a) être subordonné à qn** to be subordinate to sb **(b) être subordonné à qch** to be subject to sth

suborner /sybɔʀne/ [1] *vtr* to bribe ‹*witness*›

subreptice /sybʀɛptis/ *adj* surreptitious

subside /sybsid/ *nm* **(a)** grant **(b)** allowance

subsidiaire /sybzidjɛʀ/ *adj* subsidiary; **question ~** tiebreaker

subsistance /sybzistɑ̃s/ *nf* subsistence; **(moyens de) ~** means of support

subsister /sybziste/ [1] *vi* **(a)** to remain **(b)** ‹*custom*› to survive **(c) ça leur suffit à peine pour ~** it's barely enough for them to live on

substance /sypstɑ̃s/ *nf* substance

substantif /sypstɑ̃tif/ *nm* noun, substantive

substituer /sypstitɥe/ [1] **1** *vtr* to substitute **2 se substituer** *v refl* (+ *v être*) **se ~ à** to take the place of

substitut /sypstity/ *nm* substitute

substitution /sypstitysjɔ̃/ *nf* substitution; **produit de ~, du sucre** sugar substitute

subterfuge /syptɛʀfyʒ/ *nm* ploy, subterfuge

subtil, **~e** /syptil/ *adj* subtle; skilful (GB)

subtiliser /syptilize/ [1] *vtr* **~ qch à qn** to steal sth from sb

subtilité /syptilite/ *nf* subtlety

subvenir /sybvəniʀ/ [36] *v+prep* **~ à** to meet ‹*expenses, needs*›; **~ aux besoins de sa famille** to provide for one's family

subvention /sybvɑ̃sjɔ̃/ *nf* **(a)** grant **(b)** subsidy

subventionner /sybvɑ̃sjɔne/ [1] *vtr* to subsidize

subversif, **-ive** /sybvɛʀsif, iv/ *adj* subversive

subversion /sybvɛʀsjɔ̃/ *nf* subversion

suc /syk/ *nm* (of fruit) juice; (of plant) sap; **~s digestifs** *or* **gastriques** gastric juices

succédané /syksedane/ *nm* substitute, ersatz

succéder /syksede/ [14] **1 succéder à** *v+prep* **(a) ~ à** to succeed ‹*person*› **(b) ~ à** to follow **2 se succéder** *v refl* (+ *v être*) to succeed *or* follow one another

⚘ **succès** /syksɛ/ *nm inv* success; **avoir du ~, être un ~** to be a success; ‹*record*› to be a hit; **à ~** ‹*actor, film*› successful

successeur /syksesœʀ/ *nm* successor

successif, **-ive** /syksesif, iv/ *adj* successive

succession /syksesjɔ̃/ *nf* **(a)** series, succession **(b)** (Law) succession; **prendre la ~ de** to succeed **(c)** inheritance, estate

succinct, **~e** /syksɛ̃, ɛ̃t/ *adj* ‹*essay*› succinct; ‹*speech*› brief; ‹*meal*› frugal

succomber /sykɔ̃be/ [1] *vi* **(a)** to die **(b)** to give way, to yield; **~ sous le poids to** collapse under the weight **(c) ~ à** to succumb to ‹*charm, despair*›; to give in to ‹*temptation*›

succulent, **~e** /sykylɑ̃, ɑ̃t/ *adj* delicious

succursale /sykyʀsal/ *nf* branch, outlet

sucer /syse/ [12] *vtr* to suck

sucette /sysɛt/ *nf* lollipop, lolly (GB) (colloq)

suçoter /sysɔte/ [1] *vtr* to suck

sucre /sykʀ/ *nm* **(a)** sugar **(b)** sugar lump
■ **~ cristallisé** granulated sugar; **~ glace** icing sugar (GB), powdered sugar (US); **~ en poudre** caster sugar (GB), superfine sugar (US); **~ roux** brown sugar
IDIOM **casser du ~ sur le dos de qn** to run sb down, to badmouth sb (colloq)

sucré, **~e** /sykʀe/ *adj* sweet; sweetened

sucrer /sykʀe/ [1] *vtr* to put sugar in, to sweeten

sucrerie /sykʀəʀi/ *nf* **(a)** sugar refinery **(b)** **~s** sweets (GB), candy (US)

sucrier /sykʀije/ *nm* sugar bowl

⚘ **sud** /syd/ **1** *adj inv* south; southern **2** *nm* **(a)** south; **exposé au ~** south-facing **(b) le Sud** the South

sudation /sydasjɔ̃/ *nf* sweating

sud-est /sydɛst/ **1** *adj inv* southeast; southeastern **2** *nm* southeast; **le Sud-Est asiatique** South East Asia

sudiste /sydist/ *adj, nmf* Confederate

sud-ouest /sydwɛst/ **1** *adj inv* southwest; southwestern **2** *nm* southwest

Suède /sɥɛd/ *pr nf* Sweden

suédois, **~e** /sɥedwa, az/ **1** *adj* Swedish **2** *nm* (language) Swedish

Suédois, **~e** /sɥedwa, az/ *nm,f* Swede

suer /sɥe/ [1] **1** *vi* to sweat; **~ sang et eau** to sweat blood and tears **2** *vi* to sweat; **faire ~ qn** (fam) to bore sb stiff (colloq)

sueur /sɥœʀ/ *nf* sweat; **j'en avais des ~s froides** I was in a cold sweat about it

suffi /syfi/ ▶ SUFFIRE

⚘ **suffire** /syfiʀ/ [64] **1** *vi* to be enough; **un rien suffit à le mettre en colère** it only takes the slightest thing to make him lose his temper **2 se suffire** *v refl* (+ *v être*) **se ~ (à** ⋯⋗

soi-même) to be self-sufficient
3 *v impers* **il suffit de me téléphoner** all you have to do is phone me; **il suffit d'une lampe pour éclairer la pièce** one lamp is enough to light the room; **il suffit que je sorte sans parapluie pour qu'il pleuve!** every time I go out without my umbrella, it's guaranteed to rain; **ça suffit (comme ça)!** that's enough!

suffisamment /syfizamɑ̃/ *adv* enough

suffisance /syfizɑ̃s/ *nf* self-importance

suffisant, **~e** /syfizɑ̃, ɑ̃t/ *adj* **(a)** sufficient
(b) self-important

suffixe /syfiks/ *nm* suffix

suffocant, **~e** /syfɔkɑ̃, ɑ̃t/ *adj*
(a) suffocating
(b) staggering

suffocation /syfɔkasjɔ̃/ *nf* suffocation; choking

suffoquer /syfɔke/ [1] **1** *vtr* to suffocate
2 *vi* **(a)** to suffocate
(b) to choke

suffrage /syfʀaʒ/ *nm* suffrage; **~s exprimés** recorded votes

suggérer /sygʒeʀe/ [14] *vtr* to suggest

suggestif, **-ive** /sygʒɛstif, iv/ *adj*
‹*music*› evocative; ‹*pose*› suggestive; ‹*dress*› provocative

suggestion /sygʒɛstjɔ̃/ *nf* suggestion

suicidaire /sɥisidɛʀ/ *adj* suicidal

suicide /sɥisid/ *nm* suicide

suicider: **se suicider** /sɥiside/ [1] *v refl* (+ *v être*) to commit suicide

suie /sɥi/ *nf* soot

suinter /sɥɛ̃te/ [1] *vi* **(a)** ‹*liquid*› to seep; to ooze
(b) ‹*walls*› to sweat; ‹*wound*› to weep

suis /sɥi/ ▸ ÊTRE¹

suisse /sɥis/ **1** *adj* Swiss
2 *nm* **(a)** Swiss Guard
(b) verger

Suisse /sɥis/ *pr nf* Switzerland

ꝋ **suite** /sɥit/ **1** *nf* **(a)** rest; **la ~ des événements** what happens next
(b) (of story) continuation; (of series) next instalment (GB); (of meal) next course
(c) sequel
(d) result; **les ~s** (of action) the consequences; (of incident) the repercussions; (of illness) the after-effects
(e) **donner ~ à** to follow up ‹*complaint*›; to deal with ‹*order*›; **rester sans ~** ‹*plan*› to be dropped
(f) **faire ~ à** to follow upon ‹*incident*›; **prendre la ~ de qn** to take over from sb
(g) **avoir de la ~ dans les idées** to be single-minded
(h) (of incidents) series; (of successes) run
(i) (hotel) suite
(j) (of monarch) suite

(k) (Mus) suite
2 **de suite** *phr* in succession, in a row; **et ainsi de ~** and so on
3 **par la suite** *phr* **(a)** afterward(s)
(b) later
4 **par suite de** *phr* due to
5 **à la suite de** *phr* **(a)** following
(b) behind
6 **suite à** *phr* **~ à votre lettre** with reference to your letter

suivant¹ /sɥivɑ̃/ *prep* **(a)** in accordance with ‹*tradition*›; **~ leur habitude** as they usually do
(b) depending on
(c) according to

ꝋ **suivant²**, **~e** /sɥivɑ̃, ɑ̃t/ **1** *adj*
(a) following
(b) next
2 *nm,f* **le ~** the following one; the next one
3 **le suivant, la suivante** *phr* as follows

suivi, **~e** /sɥivi/ **1** *pp* ▸ SUIVRE
2 *pp adj* **(a)** ‹*work*› steady; ‹*effort*› sustained; ‹*correspondence*› regular
(b) ‹*policy*› coherent
3 *nm* **(a)** monitoring
(b) follow-up; **~ des malades** follow-up care for patients

ꝋ **suivre** /sɥivʀ/ [62] **1** *vtr* **(a)** to follow ‹*person, car*›; **suivez le guide!** this way, please!
(b) to follow, to come after ‹*period, incident*›; **'à ~'** 'to be continued'
(c) to follow ‹*route, coast*›; ‹*road*› to run alongside ‹*railway line*›; **~ le droit chemin** to keep to the straight and narrow
(d) to follow ‹*example*›; to obey ‹*impulse*›
(e) to follow ‹*lesson, match*›; to follow the progress of ‹*pupil, patient*›; **~ l'actualité** to keep up with the news
(f) to do ‹*course*›
(g) to follow ‹*explanation, logic*›; **je vous suis** I'm with you
(h) to keep pace with [sb/sth]
2 *vi* **faire ~ son courrier** to have one's mail forwarded; **faire ~** please forward
3 **se suivre** *v refl* (+ *v être*) **(a)** ‹*numbers, pages*› to be in order; ‹*cards*› to be consecutive
(b) to happen one after the other
4 *v impers* **comme suit** as follows

ꝋ **sujet**, **-ette** /syʒɛ, ɛt/ **1** *adj* **être ~ à** to be prone to ‹*migraine*›
2 *nm* **(a)** subject; **un ~ d'actualité** a topical issue; **c'est à quel ~?** what is it about?; **au ~ de** about
(b) (Sch) question; **~ libre** topic of one's own choice; **hors ~** off the subject
(c) cause; **c'est un ~ d'étonnement** it is amazing
(d) **c'est un brillant ~** he's a brilliant student
(e) (of kingdom) subject

sulfate /sylfat/ *nm* sulphate (GB), sulfate (US)

ꝋ indicates a very frequent word

sulfureux, **-euse** /sylfyʀø, øz/ *adj*
‹*vapour*› sulphurous (GB), sulfurous (US);
‹*bath*› sulphur (GB), sulfur (US)

sultan /syltɑ̃/ *nm* sultan

sultane /syltan/ *nf* sultana

summum /sɔm(m)ɔm/ *nm* height

sumo /sumo, symo/ *nm inv* sumo wrestling

sunnisme /syn(n)ism/ *nm* Sunnism

sunnite /syn(n)it/ *adj, nmf* Sunni

super¹ /sypɛʀ/ *pref* super

⚹ **super²** /sypɛʀ/ **1** *adj inv* (fam) great (colloq)
  2 *nm* four-star (petrol) (GB), super

superbe /sypɛʀb/ *adj* superb, magnificent

superbement /sypɛʀbəmɑ̃/ *adv*
  (a) superbly
  (b) haughtily

supercarburant /sypɛʀkaʀbyʀɑ̃/ *nm*
  four-star petrol (GB), super

supercherie /sypɛʀʃəʀi/ *nf* (a) deception
  (b) hoax

supérette /sypeʀɛt/ *nf* minimarket

superficie /sypɛʀfisi/ *nf* area

superficiel, **-ielle** /sypɛʀfisjɛl/ *adj* (gen)
  superficial; ‹*layer*› surface

superflu, **~e** /sypɛʀfly/ *adj* (a) superfluous
  (b) unnecessary

⚹ **supérieur**, **~e** /sypeʀjœʀ/ **1** *adj* (a) ‹*jaw,
  lip, floor*› upper
  (b) ‹*ranks, classes*› upper
  (c) higher (à than); ‹*size*› bigger (à than);
  ‹*length*› longer (à than)
  (d) ‹*work, quality*› superior (à to)
  (e) ‹*air, tone*› superior
  2 *nm,f* (a) superior; **~ hiérarchique**
  immediate superior
  (b) (in monastery, convent) Superior
  3 *nm* higher education

supérieurement /sypeʀjœʀmɑ̃/ *adv*
  exceptionally

supériorité /sypeʀjɔʀite/ *nf* superiority

superlatif, **-ive** /sypɛʀlatif, iv/ **1** *adj*
  superlative
  2 *nm* superlative

⚹ **supermarché** /sypɛʀmaʀʃe/ *nm*
  supermarket

superposer /sypɛʀpoze/ [1] *vtr* (a) to
  stack [sth] (up); **lits superposés** bunk beds
  (b) to superimpose ‹*drawings*›

superposition /sypɛʀpozisjɔ̃/ *nf*
  superposition

superproduction /sypɛʀpʀɔdyksjɔ̃/ *nf*
  blockbuster (colloq)

superpuissance /sypɛʀpɥisɑ̃s/ *nf*
  superpower

superstitieux, **-ieuse** /sypɛʀstisjø,
  øz/ *adj* superstitious

superstition /sypɛʀstisjɔ̃/ *nf* superstition

superviser /sypɛʀvize/ [1] *vtr* to
  supervise

supplanter /syplɑ̃te/ [1] *vtr* to supplant

suppléant, **~e** /sypleɑ̃, ɑ̃t/ *nm,f*
  replacement; (for judge) deputy; (for teacher)
  supply (GB) *or* substitute (US) teacher; (for
  doctor) locum

suppléer /syplee/ [11] *v+prep* **~ à** to make
  up for, to compensate for

supplément /syplemɑ̃/ *nm* (a) extra
  charge; supplement; **le vin est en ~** the wine
  is extra
  (b) **~ d'informations** additional information
  (c) (newspaper) supplement

supplémentaire /syplemɑ̃tɛʀ/ *adj*
  additional, extra; **train ~** relief train

suppliant, **~e** /syplijɑ̃, ɑ̃t/ *adj* ‹*voice*›
  pleading; ‹*look*› imploring

supplice /syplis/ *nm* torture

supplicier /syplisje/ [2] *vtr* (a) to torture
  (b) to execute

supplier /syplije/ [2] *vtr* to beg, to beseech

support /sypɔʀ/ *nm* (a) support; **servir de
  ~ à qch** to serve as a support for sth
  (b) (for ornaments) stand
  (c) back-up; **~ audiovisuel** audio-visual aid

supportable /sypɔʀtabl/ *adj* bearable

⚹ **supporter¹** /sypɔʀte/ [1] **1** *vtr* (a) to
  support, to bear the weight of ‹*structure*›
  (b) to bear ‹*costs*›
  (c) to put up with ‹*misery, behaviour, person*›;
  to bear ‹*suffering*›; ‹*plant*› to withstand
  ‹*cold*›; **elle ne supporte pas d'attendre** she
  can't stand waiting
  2 **se supporter** *v refl* (+ *v être*) **ils ne
  peuvent plus se ~** they can't stand each
  other any more

supporter² /sypɔʀtœʀ/ *nmf* supporter

supporteur, **-trice** /sypɔʀtœʀ, -tʀis/ *nm,f*
  supporter

⚹ **supposer** /sypoze/ [1] *vtr* (a) to suppose
  (b) to assume
  (c) to presuppose

supposition /sypozisjɔ̃/ *nf* supposition

suppositoire /sypozitwaʀ/ *nm*
  suppository

suppôt /sypo/ *nm* **~ de Satan** fiend

suppression /sypʀesjɔ̃/ *nf* removal;
  abolition; withdrawal; suppression;
  elimination; breaking; ending; deletion; **~s
  d'emplois** job cuts

supprimer /sypʀime/ [1] *vtr* (a) to cut
  ‹*job*›; to stop ‹*aid, vibration*›; to abolish ‹*tax,
  law*›; to remove ‹*effect, obstacle*›; to do away
  with ‹*class*›; to withdraw ‹*licence*›; to break
  ‹*monopoly*›; to suppress ‹*evidence*›; to cut out
  ‹*sugar, salt*›; to delete ‹*word*›; **~ un train** to
  cancel a train
  (b) to eliminate ‹*person*›

suppurer /sypyʀe/ [1] *vi* to suppurate

supputer /sypyte/ [1] *vtr* to calculate, to
  work out

supranational, **~e**, *mpl* **-aux**
  /sypʀanasjɔnal, o/ *adj* supranational

S

suprématie /sypʀemasi/ *nf* supremacy

suprême /sypʀɛm/ *adj* supreme

❖ **sur¹** /syʀ/ *prep* **(a)** on; ~ **la table** on the table; **prends un verre** ~ **la table** take a glass from the table; **appliquer la lotion** ~ **vos cheveux** apply the lotion to your hair; **la clé est** ~ **la porte** the key is in the door; **écrire** ~ **du papier** to write on paper; **elle est** ~ **la photo** she's in the photograph
(b) over; **un pont** ~ **la rivière** a bridge across *or* over the river
(c) une table d'un mètre ~ **deux** a table that measures one metre (GB) by two; ~ **150 hectares** over an area of 150 hectares
(d) se diriger ~ **Valence** to head for Valence
(e) ‹*debate, essay, thesis*› on; ‹*poem*› about
(f) être ~ **une affaire** to be involved in a business deal
(g) une personne ~ **dix** one person out of *or* in ten; **un mardi** ~ **deux** every other Tuesday
(h) faire proposition ~ **proposition** to make one offer after another
(i) ils se sont quittés ~ **ces mots** with these words, they parted; ~ **le moment** at the time; ~ **ce, je vous laisse** with that, I must leave you

sur², ~**e** /syʀ/ *adj* (slightly) sour

❖ **sûr**, ~**e** /syʀ/ **1** *adj* **(a)** ‹*information, service, person*› reliable; ‹*opinion, investment*› sound; **d'une main** ~**e** with a steady hand
(b) safe
(c) certain; **c'est** ~ **et certain** it's definite; **à coup** ~ definitely
(d) sure; **j'en suis** ~ **et certain** I'm positive; **il est** ~ **de lui** he's self-confident; **j'en étais** ~**!** I knew it!
2 *adv* **bien** ~ **(que oui)** of course
IDIOM **être** ~ **de son coup** (fam) to be confident of success

surabondance /syʀabɔ̃dɑ̃s/ *nf* overabundance

surabonder /syʀabɔ̃de/ [1] *vi* to abound

surajouter: se surajouter / syʀaʒute/ [1] *v refl* to be added on (**à** to)

suranné, ~**e** /syʀane/ *adj* ‹*ideas*› outmoded; ‹*style*› outdated

surcharge /syʀʃaʀʒ/ *nf* excess load, overload; **une** ~ **de travail** extra work

surchargé, ~**e** /syʀʃaʀʒe/ *adj* ‹*day*› overloaded; ‹*class*› overcrowded

surcharger /syʀʃaʀʒe/ [13] *vtr* to overload; ~ **qn de travail** to overburden sb with work

surchauffer /syʀʃofe/ [1] *vtr* to overheat

surclasser /syʀklase/ [1] *vtr* to outclass

surconsommation /syʀkɔ̃sɔmasjɔ̃/ *nf* (Econ) overconsumption; ~ **de médicaments** excessive drug consumption

surcroît /syʀkʀwa/ *nm* increase; **un** ~ **de travail** extra work; **de** ~ moreover

surdité /syʀdite/ *nf* deafness

surdoué, ~**e** /syʀdwe/ *adj* (exceptionally) gifted

sureau, *pl* ~**x** /syʀo/ *nm* elder (tree)

sureffectif /syʀefɛktif/ *nm* excess staff

surélever /syʀelve/ [16] *vtr* to raise the height of ‹*house, road*›

sûrement /syʀmɑ̃/ *adv* **(a)** most probably
(b) ~ **pas** certainly not
(c) safely

surenchère /syʀɑ̃ʃɛʀ/ *nf* **(a)** higher bid
(b) faire de la ~ to try to go one better

surenchérir /syʀɑ̃ʃeʀiʀ/ [3] *vi* **(a)** to make a higher bid
(b) to chime in

surendetté, ~**e** /syʀɑ̃dete/ *adj* deeply in debt; overextended

surendettement /syʀɑ̃dɛtmɑ̃/ *nm* excessive debt

surestimer /syʀɛstime/ [1] **1** *vtr* to overvalue ‹*property*›; to overrate ‹*qualities*›
2 **se surestimer** *v refl* (+ *v être*) to rate oneself too highly

sûreté /syʀte/ *nf* **(a)** (of place, person) safety; (of country) security
(b) (of judgment) soundness; (of gesture) steadiness
(c) (on gun) safety catch; (on door) safety lock

surévaluer /syʀevalɥe/ [1] *vtr* to overvalue ‹*currency*›; to overestimate ‹*cost*›

surexciter /syʀɛksite/ [1] *vtr* to overexcite

surf /sœʀf/ *nm* surfing

❖ **surface** /syʀfas/ *nf* **(a)** surface; **de** ~ ‹*installations*› above ground; ‹*friendliness*› superficial; **faire** ~ to surface
(b) surface area; **en** ~ in area

surfait, ~**e** /syʀfɛ, ɛt/ *adj* overrated

surfer /sœʀfe/ [1] *vi* **(a)** to go surfing
(b) (Comput) ~ **sur l'Internet** to surf the Internet

surfiler /syʀfile/ [1] *vtr* to oversew

surgelé, ~**e** /syʀʒəle/ *adj* deep-frozen; **les produits** ~**s** frozen food

surgeler /syʀʒəle/ [17] *vtr* to deep-freeze

surgénérateur /syʀʒeneʀatœʀ/ *nm* fast-breeder reactor

surgir /syʀʒiʀ/ [3] *vi* ‹*person*› to appear suddenly; ‹*difficulty*› to crop up; **faire** ~ **la vérité** to bring the truth to light

surhomme /syʀɔm/ *nm* superman

surhumain, ~**e** /syʀymɛ̃, ɛn/ *adj* superhuman

surimpression /syʀɛ̃pʀesjɔ̃/ *nf* double exposure; **en** ~ superimposed

surinformation /syʀɛ̃fɔʀmasjɔ̃/ *nf* surfeit of information

sur-le-champ /syʀləʃɑ̃/ *adv* right away

❖ indicates a very frequent word

S

surlendemain /syʀlɑ̃d(ə)mɛ̃/ *nm* le ~ two days later

surligner /syʀliɲe/ [1] *vtr* to highlight

surligneur /syʀliɲœʀ/ *nm* highlighter (pen)

surmenage /syʀmənaʒ/ *nm* overwork

surmener /syʀmene/ [16] **1** *vtr* to overwork
2 **se surmener** *v refl* (+ *v être*) to push oneself too hard

surmontable /syʀmɔ̃tabl/ *adj* surmountable

surmonter /syʀmɔ̃te/ [1] *vtr* to overcome

surmultiplié, ~e /syʀmyltiplije/ *adj* vitesse ~e overdrive

surnager /syʀnaʒe/ [13] *vi* to float

surnaturel, -elle /syʀnatyʀɛl/ *adj*
(a) supernatural
(b) eerie

surnom /syʀnɔ̃/ *nm* nickname

surnombre /syʀnɔ̃bʀ/ *nm* en ~ ‹objects› surplus; ‹staff› excess; ‹passenger› extra

surnommer /syʀnɔme/ [1] *vtr* to nickname

surnuméraire /syʀnymeʀɛʀ/ *adj*, *nmf* supernumerary

surpasser /syʀpase/ [1] **1** *vtr* to surpass
2 **se surpasser** *v refl* (+ *v être*) to surpass oneself, to excel oneself

surpeuplé, ~e /syʀpœple/ *adj*
(a) overpopulated
(b) overcrowded

surplace /syʀplas/ *nm inv* faire du ~ (in traffic jam) to be stuck; (in work, inquiry) to be getting nowhere; (in cycling) to do a track stand

surplomb /syʀplɔ̃/ *nm* en ~ overhanging

surplomber /syʀplɔ̃be/ [1] *vtr* to overhang

surplus /syʀply/ *nm inv* (of goods) surplus

surpopulation /syʀpɔpylasjɔ̃/ *nf* overpopulation

surprenant, ~e /syʀpʀənɑ̃, ɑ̃t/ *adj* surprising; amazing

✦ **surprendre** /syʀpʀɑ̃dʀ/ [52] **1** *vtr* (a) to surprise
(b) to take [sb] by surprise; se laisser ~ par la pluie to get caught in the rain
(c) to catch ‹thief›
(d) to overhear ‹conversation›; to intercept ‹smile›
2 *vi* ‹behaviour› to be surprising; ‹show› to surprise; ‹person› to surprise people

surprise /syʀpʀiz/ *nf* surprise; créer la ~ to cause a stir; il m'a fait la ~ de venir me voir he came to see me as a surprise; avoir la bonne ~ d'apprendre que to be pleasantly surprised to hear that; voyage sans ~ uneventful trip; gagner sans ~ to win as expected

surproduction /syʀpʀɔdyksjɔ̃/ *nf* overproduction

surqualifié, ~e /syʀkalifje/ *adj* overqualified

surréalisme /syʀ(ʀ)ealism/ *nm* surrealism

surréaliste /syʀ(ʀ)ealist/ **1** *adj*
(a) surrealist
(b) ‹landscape, vision› surreal
2 *nmf* surrealist

surrégénérateur /syʀʀeʒeneʀatœʀ/ *nm* fast-breeder reactor

sursaut /syʀso/ *nm* (a) start; en ~ with a start
(b) (of energy, enthusiasm) sudden burst; (of pride, indignation) flash; dans un dernier ~ in a final spurt of effort

sursauter /syʀsote/ [1] *vi* to jump, to start

sursis /syʀsi/ *nm inv* (a) respite
(b) (Law) suspended sentence
(c) (Mil) deferment of military service

surtaxe /syʀtaks/ *nf* surcharge

surtaxer /syʀtakse/ [1] *vtr* to surcharge

✦ **surtout** /syʀtu/ *adv* above all; ~ quand/que especially when/as; ~ pas! certainly not!

surveillance /syʀvɛjɑ̃s/ *nf* (a) watch; (police) surveillance; déjouer la ~ de qn to escape detection by sb
(b) supervision; sous ~ médicale under medical supervision

surveillant, ~e /syʀvɛjɑ̃, ɑ̃t/ *nm,f*
(a) (Sch) supervisor
(b) ~ de prison prison warder (GB) or guard
(c) store detective

surveiller /syʀveje/ [1] **1** *vtr* (a) (gen) to watch; to keep watch on ‹building›
(b) to supervise ‹work, pupils›; to monitor ‹progress›
(c) ~ sa santé to take care of one's health
2 **se surveiller** *v refl* (+ *v être*) to watch oneself

survenir /syʀvəniʀ/ [36] *vi* (+ *v être*) ‹death, storm› to occur; ‹difficulty, conflict› to arise

survêtement /syʀvɛtmɑ̃/ *nm* tracksuit

survie /syʀvi/ *nf* survival

survivant, ~e /syʀvivɑ̃, ɑ̃t/ *nm,f* survivor

survivre à /syʀvivʀ/ [63] **1** **survivre à** *v+prep* ‹person› to survive ‹event, injuries›; to outlive ‹person›; ‹work, influence› to outlast ‹person›
2 *vi* to survive

survol /syʀvɔl/ *nm* (a) flying over
(b) synopsis

survoler /syʀvɔle/ [1] *vtr* (a) to fly over ‹place›
(b) to do a quick review of ‹problem›

survolté, ~e /syʀvɔlte/ *adj* (fam) overexcited

sus: en sus /ɑ̃sys/ *phr* être en ~ to be extra; en ~ de on top of; in addition to

susceptibilité /sysɛptibilite/ *nf* touchiness

susceptible /sysɛptibl/ *adj* (a) touchy ⋯▸

(b) ∼ **de faire** likely to do

susciter /sysite/ [1] *vtr* **(a)** to spark off ‹*reaction, debate*›; to create ‹*problem*› **(b)** to arouse ‹*enthusiasm, interest*›; to give rise to ‹*fear*›

susmentionné, ∼**e** *adj* aforementioned

suspect, ∼**e** /syspɛ, ɛkt/ **1** *adj* suspicious; ‹*information, logic*› dubious; ‹*foodstuff, honesty*› suspect; ‹*person*› suspicious-looking
2 *nm,f* suspect

suspecter /syspɛkte/ [1] *vtr* to suspect

suspendre /syspɑ̃dʀ/ [6] **1** *vtr* **(a)** to hang up; **être suspendu aux lèvres de qn** to be hanging on sb's every word
(b) to suspend ‹*programme, payment*›; to end ‹*strike*›; to adjourn ‹*session, inquiry*›
(c) to suspend ‹*official, athlete*›
2 se suspendre *v refl* (+ *v être*) to hang; **se** ∼ **à une corde** to hang from a rope

suspens: en suspens /ɑ̃syspɑ̃/ *phr* **(a) laisser qch en** ∼ to leave sth unresolved ‹*question*›; to leave sth unfinished ‹*work*›
(b) tenir qn en ∼ to keep sb in suspense

suspense /syspɛns/ *nm* suspense; **film/roman à** ∼ thriller

suspension /syspɑ̃sjɔ̃/ *nf* **(a)** (gen, Tech) suspension
(b) (of aid, work) suspension; (of session, trial) adjournment
(c) en ∼ ‹*particles*› in suspension
(d) pendant, ceiling light

suspicieux, -ieuse /syspisjø, øz/ *adj* suspicious

suspicion /syspisjɔ̃/ *nf* suspicion

sustenter: se sustenter /systɑ̃te/ [1] *v refl* (+ *v être*) to have a little snack

susurrer /sysyʀe/ [1] *vtr, vi* to whisper

suture /sytyʀ/ *nf* suture; **point de** ∼ stitch

suzerain, ∼**e** /syzʀɛ̃, ɛn/ *nm,f* suzerain

svelte /svɛlt/ *adj* slender

sveltesse /svɛltɛs/ *nf* slenderness

SVP (*written abbr* = **s'il vous plaît**) please

syllabe /sil(l)ab/ *nf* syllable

sylviculture /silvikyltyʀ/ *nf* forestry

symbiose /sɛ̃bjoz/ *nf* symbiosis

ꜰ **symbole** /sɛ̃bɔl/ *nm* **(a)** symbol
(b) creed

symbolique /sɛ̃bɔlik/ *adj* **(a)** symbolic
(b) ‹*gesture*› token; ‹*price*› nominal

symboliser /sɛ̃bɔlize/ [1] *vtr* to symbolize

symétrie /simetʀi/ *nf* symmetry

symétrique /simetʀik/ *adj* **(a)** ‹*design, face*› symmetrical
(b) ‹*relation*› symmetric

sympa /sɛ̃pa/ *adj inv* (fam) nice

sympathie /sɛ̃pati/ *nf* **(a) avoir de la** ∼ **pour qn** to like sb
(b) sympathy; **croyez à toute ma** ∼ you have

my deepest sympathy

sympathique /sɛ̃patik/ *adj* nice; pleasant

sympathisant, ∼**e** /sɛ̃patizɑ̃, ɑ̃t/ *nm,f* sympathizer

sympathiser /sɛ̃patize/ [1] *vi* to get on well

symphonie /sɛ̃fɔni/ *nf* symphony

symphonique /sɛ̃fɔnik/ *adj* symphonic

symptomatique /sɛ̃ptɔmatik/ *adj* symptomatic

symptôme /sɛ̃ptom/ *nm* symptom

synagogue /sinagɔg/ *nf* synagogue

synchronique /sɛ̃kʀɔnik/ *adj* synchronic

synchronisation /sɛ̃kʀɔnizasjɔ̃/ *nf* synchronization

synchroniser /sɛ̃kʀɔnize/ [1] *vtr* to synchronize

syncope /sɛ̃kɔp/ *nf* **(a)** fainting fit; **tomber en** ∼ to faint
(b) (Mus) syncopation

syndic /sɛ̃dik/ *nm* property manager

syndical, ∼**e**, *mpl* **-aux** /sɛ̃dikal, o/ *adj* (trade) union

syndicalisme /sɛ̃dikalism/ *nm* **(a)** trade unionism
(b) union activities

syndicaliste /sɛ̃dikalist/ *nmf* union activist

syndicat /sɛ̃dika/ *nm* **(a)** trade union (GB), labor union (US)
(b) (employers') association
■ ∼ **d'initiative** tourist information office

syndiqué, ∼**e** /sɛ̃dike/ *adj* **être** ∼ to be a union member

syndrome /sɛ̃dʀom/ *nm* syndrome
■ ∼ **de la classe économique** economy class syndrome; ∼ **immunodéficitaire acquis** acquired immunodeficiency syndrome

synergie /sinɛʀʒi/ *nf* synergy (**entre** between)

synonyme /sinɔnim/ **1** *adj* synonymous
2 *nm* synonym; **dictionnaire de** ∼**s** ≈ thesaurus

syntaxe /sɛ̃taks/ *nf* syntax

synthèse /sɛ̃tɛz/ *nf* **(a)** synthesis
(b) produit de ∼ synthetic product
(c) images de ∼ computer-generated images

synthétique /sɛ̃tetik/ *adj* **(a)** synthetic
(b) ‹*vision*› global

synthétiseur /sɛ̃tetizœʀ/ *nm* synthesizer

syphilis /sifilis/ *nf inv* syphilis

systématique /sistematik/ *adj* systematic

ꜰ **système** /sistɛm/ *nm* **(a)** system; ∼ **de canaux** canal system *or* network
(b) ∼ **pileux** hair
■ **le** ∼ **D** (fam) resourcefulness; ∼ **monétaire européen, SME** European Monetary System, EMS
IDIOM taper sur le ∼ **de qn** (fam) to get on sb's nerves

ꜰ indicates a very frequent word

Tt

t, T /te/ *nm inv* t, T; **en (forme de) T** T-shaped

t' ▶ TE

ta ▶ TON¹

tabac /taba/ *nm* **(a)** tobacco
(b) tobacconist's (GB), smoke shop (US)
(c) (fam) big hit
■ ~ **blond** Virginia tobacco; ~ **brun** dark tobacco; ~ **à priser** snuff
IDIOM **passer qn à** ~ (fam) to beat sb up

tabagie /tabaʒi/ *nf* **c'est une vraie** ~ **ici!** it's really smoky in here!

tabagisme /tabaʒism/ *nm* tobacco addiction
■ ~ **passif** passive smoking

tabernacle /tabɛrnakl/ *nm* tabernacle

♂ **table** /tabl/ *nf* **(a)** table; **mettre** *or* **dresser la** ~ to set *or* lay the table; **nous étions toujours à** ~ **quand…** we were still eating when…; **passer** *or* **se mettre à** ~ to sit down at the table; (figurative) (fam) to spill the beans (colloq)
(b) ~ **des négociations** negotiating table
(c) ~ **de logarithmes** log table
■ ~ **basse** coffee table; ~ **de chevet** bedside table (GB), night stand (US); ~ **d'écoute** wire-tapping set; **être mis sur** ~ **d'écoute** to have one's phone tapped; ~ **des matières** (table of) contents, ~ **de mixage** mixing desk; ~ **de nuit** ▶ TABLE DE CHEVET; ~ **ronde** round table
IDIOM **mettre les pieds sous la** ~ to let others wait on you

♂ **tableau**, *pl* ~**x** /tablo/ *nm* **(a)** picture; painting
(b) (description) picture; **en plus, il était ivre, tu vois un peu le**~**!** (fam) on top of that he was drunk, you can just imagine!
(c) table, chart
(d) (Sch) blackboard
(e) (displaying information) (gen) board; (for trains) indicator board; ~ **horaire** timetable
(f) (in play) short scene
■ ~ **d'affichage** notice board; ~ **de bord** (in car) dashboard; (on plane, train) instrument panel; ~ **de chasse** (in hunting) total number of kills; (figurative) list of conquests
IDIOM **jouer sur les deux** ~**x** to hedge one's bets

tablée /table/ *nf* table; **une grande** ~ a large party

tabler /table/ [1] *vi* ~ **sur** to bank on (colloq)

tablette /tablɛt/ *nf* **(a)** (of chocolate) bar; (of chewing-gum) stick
(b) shelf

tablier /tablije/ *nm* **(a)** apron
(b) roadway

IDIOM **rendre son** ~ to give in (GB) *or* give (US) one's notice

tabloïd /tabloid/ *adj, nm* tabloid

tabou /tabu/ 1 *adj* **(a)** taboo
(b) sacred
2 *nm* taboo

tabouret /taburɛ/ *nm* stool

tac /tak/ *nm* **répondre du** ~ **au** ~ to answer as quick as a flash

tache /taʃ/ *nf* **(a)** stain; ~ **d'humidité** damp patch
(b) (figurative) stain, blot; **sans** ~ ‹reputation› spotless
(c) (on fruit) mark; (on skin) blotch, mark
(d) (of colour) spot; patch
■ ~**s de rousseur** freckles
IDIOM **faire** ~ **d'huile** to spread like wildfire

♂ **tâche** /taʃ/ *nf* task, job; **tu ne me facilites pas la** ~**!** you're not making my job any easier!; **les** ~**s ménagères** household chores

tacher /taʃe/ [1] 1 *vtr* **(a)** ‹substance› to stain; ‹person› to get a stain on ‹garment›
(b) to tarnish, to stain ‹reputation›
2 *vi* to stain; **ça ne tache pas** it doesn't stain

tâcher /taʃe/ [1] *v+prep* ~ **de faire** to try to do

tacheté /taʃte/ *adj* ‹fur› speckled

tacite /tasit/ *adj* tacit

taciturne /tasityrn/ *adj* taciturn

tacler /takle/ *vtr* (Sport) to tackle

tact /takt/ *nm* tact; **avec** ~ tactfully

tactile /taktil/ *adj* ‹sense› tactile

tactique /taktik/ 1 *adj* (gen, Mil) tactical
2 *nf* tactic; **la** ~ tactics

taie /tɛ/ *nf* ~ **(d'oreiller)** pillowcase; ~ **(de traversin)** bolstercase

taillader /tajade/ [1] *vtr* to slash

♂ **taille** /taj/ *nf* **(a)** waist, waistline
(b) size; **de grande/petite** ~ large/small; **de** ~ ‹problem, ambition› considerable; ‹event, question› very important; **être de** ~ **à faire** to be up to *or* capable of doing
(c) (of garment) size; '~ **unique**' 'one size'; **essaie la** ~ **au-dessus** try the next size up
(d) height; **être de grande/petite** ~ to be tall/short
(e) (of tree, shrub) pruning; (of hedge) clipping, trimming; (of diamond, glass) cutting

taillé, ~**e** 1 *pp* ▶ TAILLER
2 *pp adj* **(a)** ~ **en athlète** built like an athlete
(b) **être** ~ **pour faire** to be cut out to do
(c) **cristal** ~ cut glass

taille-crayons /tajkʀɛjɔ̃/ *nm inv* pencil sharpener

tailler /taje/ [1] **1** *vtr* (a) to cut ‹glass, marble›; to sharpen ‹pencil›; to prune ‹tree, shrub›; to trim ‹hair, beard›
(b) to cut ‹steak›; to carve ‹sculpture›; to cut out ‹garment›; **taillé sur mesure** ‹garment› custom-made; (figurative) ‹role› tailor-made; ‹role› tailor-made
2 *vi* ~ **grand/petit** ‹garment› to be cut on the large/small side
3 **se tailler** *v refl* (+ *v être*) (a) to carve out [sth] for oneself ‹career, empire›; to make [sth] for oneself ‹reputation›
(b) (pop) to beat it (colloq)

tailleur /tajœʀ/ *nm* (a) (woman's) suit
(b) tailor; **s'asseoir en** ~ to sit down cross-legged
■ ~ **de pierre** stone-cutter

taillis /taji/ *nm inv* (a) undergrowth
(b) coppice

tain /tɛ̃/ *nm* **miroir sans** ~ two-way mirror

ꝰ **taire** /tɛʀ/ [59] **1** *vtr* (a) not to reveal ‹name, secret›; to hush up ‹truth›
(b) to keep [sth] to oneself ‹sadness, resentment›
2 *vi* **faire** ~ to make [sb] be quiet ‹pupils›; to silence ‹opponent, media›; to put a stop to ‹rumours›
3 **se taire** *v refl* (+ *v être*) (a) ‹person› to be silent
(b) ‹person› to stop talking; ‹bird, journalist› to fall silent; **tais-toi!** be quiet!
(c) ‹noise› to stop; ‹orchestra› to fall silent

talc /talk/ *nm* talc, talcum powder

ꝰ **talent** /talɑ̃/ *nm* talent; **de** ~ talented

talentueux, -euse /talɑ̃tɥø, øz/ *adj* talented

talisman /talismɑ̃/ *nm* talisman

talkie-walkie, *pl* **talkies-walkies** /tokiwoki/ *nm* walkie-talkie

taloche /talɔʃ/ *nf* (fam) clout (colloq)

talon /talɔ̃/ *nm* (a) (of foot, shoe) heel
(b) (of cheque, ticket) stub
(c) (in cards) pile
■ ~ **aiguille** stiletto heel
IDIOM **être sur les** ~**s de qn** to be hard *or* hot on sb's heels

talonner /talɔne/ [1] *vtr* (a) ~ **qn** to be hot on sb's heels
(b) ‹person› to badger ‹person›; ‹hunger, anxiety› to torment ‹person›

talonnette /talɔnɛt/ *nf* lift (in a shoe)

talus /taly/ *nm inv* (a) embankment
(b) bank, slope

tamanoir /tamanwaʀ/ *nm* anteater

tambouille /tɑ̃buj/ *nf* (fam) grub (colloq)

tambour /tɑ̃buʀ/ *nm* drum; **mener qch** ~ **battant** to deal with sth briskly

tambourin /tɑ̃buʀɛ̃/ *nm* tambourine

tambouriner /tɑ̃buʀine/ [1] *vi* ~ **à la porte de qn** to hammer on sb's door

tamis /tami/ *nm inv* sieve

Tamise /tamiz/ *pr nf* **la** ~ the Thames

tamiser /tamize/ [1] *vtr* to sieve, to sift ‹sand, flour›; to filter ‹light, colours›

tampon /tɑ̃pɔ̃/ *nm* (a) (in office) stamp; ~ **(encreur)** (ink) pad
(b) (for sponging) (gen) pad; (Med) swab; ~ **à récurer** scouring pad
(c) ~ **hygiénique** tampon

tamponner /tɑ̃pɔne/ [1] *vtr* (a) to swab ‹wound, cut›; to mop ‹forehead›
(b) to stamp ‹document›
(c) to crash into ‹vehicle›

tamponneuse /tɑ̃pɔnøz/ *adj f* **auto** ~ bumper car, dodgem (GB)

tam-tam, *pl* ~**s** /tamtam/ *nm* tomtom

tanche /tɑ̃ʃ/ *nf* tench

tandem /tɑ̃dɛm/ *nm* (a) tandem
(b) (figurative) duo

ꝰ **tandis: tandis que** /tɑ̃di(s)k(ə)/ *phr* while

tangent, ~**e¹** /tɑ̃ʒɑ̃, ɑ̃t/ *adj* (a) tangent, tangential
(b) (fam) **elle a été reçue, mais c'était** ~ she got through, but only by the skin of her teeth (colloq)

tangente² /tɑ̃ʒɑ̃t/ *nf* tangent

tangible /tɑ̃ʒibl/ *adj* tangible

tanguer /tɑ̃ge/ [1] *vi* ‹ship, plane› to pitch

tanière /tanjɛʀ/ *nf* (a) den
(b) lair

tank /tɑ̃k/ *nm* tank

tanner /tane/ [1] *vtr* (a) to tan ‹leather, hides›
(b) ‹sun› to make [sth] leathery ‹face, skin›

tannerie /tanʀi/ *nf* (a) tannery
(b) tanning

ꝰ **tant** /tɑ̃/ **1** *adv* (a) (so) much; **il a** ~ **insisté que…** he was so insistent that…; **vous m'en direz** ~**!** (fam) you don't say!; **le moment** ~ **attendu** the long-awaited moment
(b) **n'aimer rien** ~ **que…** to like nothing so much as…; ~ **bien que mal** ‹repair, lead› after a fashion; ‹manage› more or less; **essayer** ~ **bien que mal de s'adapter** to be struggling to adapt
(c) ~ **que** as long as; **je ne partirai pas** ~ **qu'il ne m'aura pas accordé un rendez-vous** I won't leave until he's given me an appointment; **traite-moi de menteur** ~ **que tu y es!** (fam) go ahead and call me a liar!
(d) (replacing number) **gagner** ~ **par mois** to earn so much a month
2 tant de *quantif* Loulou, Pivachon et ~ **d'autres** Loulou, Pivachon and so many others; ~ **de travail** so much work
3 (in phrases) ~ **pis** too bad; ~ **mieux** so much the better; ~ **mieux pour toi** good for you; ~ **et plus** a great deal; a great many; ~

et si bien que so much so that; **s'il avait un** ∼ **soit peu de bon sens** if he had the slightest bit of common sense; ∼ **qu'à faire, autant repeindre toute la pièce** we may as well repaint the whole room while we're at it; **en** ∼ **que** as; **en** ∼ **que tel** as such; **si** ∼ **est qu'il puisse y aller** that is if he can go at all; **je ne l'aime pas** ∼ **que ça** I don't like him/her all that much

⚹ **tante** /tɑ̃t/ nf aunt

⚹ **tantôt** /tɑ̃to/ adv sometimes

taon /tɑ̃/ nm horsefly

tapage /tapaʒ/ nm **(a)** din, racket (colloq)
  (b) furore (GB), furor (US)
  (c) hype; ∼ **médiatique** media hype
■ ∼ **nocturne** disturbance of the peace at night

tapageur, -euse /tapaʒœʀ, øz/ adj
  (a) ⟨person⟩ rowdy
  (b) ⟨luxury⟩ showy; ⟨campaign⟩ hyped up

tapant, ∼e /tapɑ̃, ɑ̃t/ adj **à trois heures** ∼**es** at three o'clock sharp or on the dot

tape /tap/ nf pat; slap

tape-à-l'œil /tapalœj/ adj inv (fam) ⟨colour⟩ loud; ⟨jewellery, decor⟩ garish

taper /tape/ [1] **1** vtr **(a)** to hit ⟨person, dog⟩
  (b) to type ⟨letter⟩
  2 taper sur v+prep to hit; ∼ **sur l'épaule de qn** to tap sb on the shoulder
  3 vi **(a)** ∼ **des mains** to clap one's hands; ∼ **à la porte** to knock at the door; **le soleil tape aujourd'hui** (fam) the sun is beating down today
  (b) ∼ **(à la machine)** to type
  4 se taper v refl (+ v être) **(a)** (fam) **se** ∼ **dessus** to knock each other about
  (b) c'est à se ∼ **la tête contre les murs** (figurative) it's enough to drive you up the wall
  (c) (fam) to get stuck with (colloq) ⟨chore, person⟩
IDIOM **elle m'a tapé dans l'œil** (fam) I thought she was striking

tapette /tapɛt/ nf **(a)** carpet beater
  (b) fly swatter
  (c) mousetrap

tapeur, -euse /tapœʀ, øz/ nm,f (fam) scrounger (colloq)

tapioca /tapjɔka/ nm tapioca

tapir¹: se tapir /tapiʀ/ [3] v refl (+ v être)
  (a) ⟨person, animal⟩ to hide
  (b) to crouch

tapir² /tapiʀ/ nm (Zool) tapir

⚹ **tapis** /tapi/ nm inv rug; carpet; mat; **mettre qch sur le** ∼ (figurative) to bring sth up; **mettre** or **envoyer qn au** ∼ to throw sb
■ ∼ **de bain(s)** bathmat; ∼ **roulant** moving walkway; (for luggage) carousel; (in factory, supermarket) conveyor belt

tapisser /tapise/ [1] vtr **(a)** to wallpaper; to decorate ⟨room⟩; to cover ⟨armchair⟩
  (b) ⟨snow⟩ to carpet ⟨ground⟩; ⟨residue⟩ to line

⟨bottom of container⟩

tapisserie /tapisʀi/ nf **(a)** tapestry
  (b) wallpaper
  (c) tapestry work
IDIOM **faire** ∼ to be a wallflower

tapissier, -ière /tapisje, ɛʀ/ nm,f
  (a) upholsterer
  (b) tapestry-maker

tapoter /tapɔte/ [1] vtr to tap ⟨table, object⟩; to pat ⟨cheeks, back⟩

taquin, ∼e /takɛ̃, in/ adj ⟨person⟩ teasing

taquiner /takine/ [1] vtr ⟨person⟩ to tease

tarabiscoté, ∼e /tarabiskɔte/ adj ⟨design⟩ over-ornate; ⟨reasoning⟩ convoluted

tarama /taʀama/ nm taramasalata

taratata /taʀatata/ excl (fam) nonsense!, rubbish! (colloq)

⚹ **tard** /taʀ/ **1** adv late, **plus** ∼ later; **bien plus** ∼ much later (on); **au plus** ∼ at the latest; **pas plus** ∼ **qu'hier** only yesterday
  2 sur le tard phr ⟨marry⟩ late in life

tarder /taʀde/ [1] **1** vi **(a)** ∼ **à faire** to take a long time doing; to put off or delay doing
  (b) ⟨reaction⟩ to be a long time coming; **les enfants ne vont pas** ∼ the children won't be long
  2 v impers **il me tarde de la revoir** I'm longing to see her again

tardif, -ive /taʀdif, iv/ adj late; belated

tardivement /taʀdivmɑ̃/ adv ⟨arrive⟩ late; ⟨react⟩ rather belatedly

tare /taʀ/ nf **(a)** tare
  (b) defect

taré, ∼e /taʀe/ adj (fam) crazy (colloq)

targette /taʀʒɛt/ nf bolt

targuer: se targuer /taʀge/ [1] v refl (+ v être) to claim, to boast

tarif /taʀif/ nm **(a)** (gen) rate; (on bus, train) fare; (for consultation) fee; **payer plein** ∼ to pay full price; to pay full fare; ∼ **de nuit** night-time rate
  (b) price list
■ ∼ **douanier** customs tariff

tarification /taʀifikasjɔ̃/ nf price setting; tariff

tarir /taʀiʀ/ [23] **1** vtr to dry up ⟨source, well⟩; to sap ⟨strength⟩
  2 vi **ne pas** ∼ **d'éloges sur qn/qch** to be full of praise for sb/sth
  3 se tarir v refl (+ v être) to dry up

tarot /taʀo/ nm tarot ⟨card game⟩

tartare /taʀtaʀ/ adj **(a)** Tartar
  (b) (Culin) **sauce** ∼ tartare sauce

tarte /taʀt/ nf **(a)** (Culin) tart
  (b) (pop) wallop (colloq)
IDIOM **c'est pas de la** ∼ (fam) it's no picnic (colloq)

tartelette /taʀtəlɛt/ nf ⟨small⟩ tart

tartine /taʀtin/ nf **(a)** slice of bread and butter
  (b) (fam) **il en a écrit une** ∼ he wrote reams ⋯⟩

about it

tartiner /taʀtine/ [1] *vtr* to spread

tartre /taʀtʀ/ *nm* (in kettle) scale; (on teeth) tartar

tartufe /taʀtyf/ *nm* hypocrite

tas /tɑ/ **1** *nm inv* **(a)** (gen) heap, pile; **en ~** ‹put, place› in a heap *or* pile; **~ de ferraille** scrap heap; (figurative) (fam) wreck
(b) (fam) **un ~, des ~** loads (colloq)
2 dans le tas *phr* (fam) **tirer dans le ~** to fire into the crowd
3 sur le tas *phr* **apprendre sur le ~** to learn on the job; **grève sur le ~** sit-down strike

tasse /tɑs/ *nf* cup; **~ à thé** teacup
IDIOM **boire la ~** (fam) to swallow a mouthful of water (when swimming)

tassement /tɑsmɑ̃/ *nm* contraction; **~ de vertèbres** compression of the vertebrae

tasser /tɑse/ [1] **1** *vtr* to press down ‹earth›; to pack down ‹hay›; to pack ‹clothes, people› (**dans** into); **il a la cinquantaine bien tassée** (fam) he's well over fifty
2 se tasser *v refl* (+ *v être*) **(a)** (with age) to shrink
(b) (in train, car) ‹people› to squash up
(c) (fam) ‹rumour, conflict› to die down

tata /tata/ *nf* (fam) auntie

tâter /tɑte/ [1] **1** *vtr* to feel; **~ le sol du pied** to test the ground
2 se tâter *v refl* (+ *v être*) (fam) **je me tâte** I'm thinking about it
IDIOM **~ le terrain** to put out feelers

tatillon, -onne /tatijɔ̃, ɔn/ *adj* nit-picking

tâtonnement /tɑtɔnmɑ̃/ *nm* **~s dans l'obscurité** groping around in the dark; **les ~s des chercheurs** tentative research; **après dix années de ~s** after ten years of trial and error

tâtonner /tɑtɔne/ [1] *vi* to grope about *or* around

tâtons: à tâtons /atɑtɔ̃/ *phr* **avancer à ~** to feel one's way along

tatouage /tatwaʒ/ *nm* tattoo

tatouer /tatwe/ [1] *vtr* to tattoo

tatoueur, -euse /tatwœʀ, øz/ *nm,f* tattooist

taudis /todi/ *nm inv* **(a)** hovel
(b) pigsty

taule /tol/ *nf* (pop) prison

taupe /top/ *nf* **(a)** (Zool) mole
(b) moleskin

taupinière /topinjɛʀ/ *nf* **(a)** molehill
(b) (mole) tunnels

taureau, *pl* ~x /tɔʀo/ *nm* (Zool) bull
IDIOM **prendre le ~ par les cornes** to take the bull by the horns

Taureau /tɔʀo/ *pr nm* Taurus

tauromachie /tɔʀɔmaʃi/ *nf* bullfighting

ſ indicates a very frequent word

ſ **taux** /to/ *nm inv* **(a)** (gen) rate; **~ de chômage** unemployment rate
(b) (Med) (of alcohol, albumen, sugar) level; (of bacteria, sperm) count

taxation /taksasjɔ̃/ *nf* **(a)** taxation
(b) assessment

taxe /taks/ *nf* tax; **boutique hors ~s** duty-free shop (GB) *or* store (US); **1 000 euros toutes ~s comprises** 1,000 euros inclusive of tax
■ **~ de douane** customs duty; **~ foncière** property tax; **~ d'habitation** ≈ council tax (GB) *(paid by residents to cover local services)*; **~ à la valeur ajoutée** value added tax

taxer /takse/ [1] *vtr* **(a)** (Econ) to tax
(b) **~ qn de laxisme** to accuse sb of being lax

taxi /taksi/ *nm* taxi, cab (US)

taxidermiste /taksidɛʀmist/ *nmf* taxidermist

Tchad /tʃad/ *pr nm* Chad

tchador /tʃadɔʀ/ *nm* chador

tchao /tʃao/ *excl* (fam) bye! (colloq), see you! (colloq)

tchater /tʃate/ *vi* to chat (online)

tchèque /tʃɛk/ **1** *adj* Czech; **République ~** Czech Republic
2 *nm* (Ling) Czech

tchin(-tchin) /tʃin(tʃin)/ *excl* (fam) cheers!

TD /tede/ *nm pl abbr* (fam) (*abbr*= **travaux dirigés**) (Sch) practical

ſ **te** (**t'** before vowel or mute h) /t(ə)/ *pron*
(a) (direct or indirect object) you
(b) (reflexive pronoun) yourself; **va ~ laver les mains** go and wash your hands

té /te/ *nm* T-square; **en ~** T-shaped

technicien, -ienne /tɛknisjɛ̃, ɛn/ *nm,f*
(a) technician
(b) technical expert
(c) engineer
■ **~ de surface** cleaner

ſ **technique¹** /tɛknik/ **1** *adj* technical
2 *nm* technical subjects

ſ **technique²** /tɛknik/ *nf* **(a)** technique
(b) technology

technocrate /tɛknɔkʀat/ *nmf* technocrat

ſ **technologie** /tɛknɔlɔʒi/ *nf* technology

teck /tɛk/ *nm* teak; **en ~** teak

teckel /tɛkɛl/ *nm* dachshund

tee-shirt, *pl* ~s /tiʃœʀt/ *nm* T-shirt

teigne /tɛɲ/ *nf* **(a)** (Med) ringworm
(b) moth
(c) (fam) **être méchant comme une ~** to be a nasty (GB) *or* real (US) piece of work

teigneux, -euse /tɛɲø, øz/ *adj* (fam) cantankerous

teindre /tɛ̃dʀ/ [73] **1** *vtr* to dye; to stain
2 se teindre *v refl* (+ *v être*) to dye one's hair

teint, ~e¹ /tɛ̃, tɛ̃t/ **1** *pp* ▶ TEINDRE
2 *pp adj* dyed; stained

3 *nm* complexion; **avoir le ~ rose** or **frais** to have a healthy glow to one's cheeks

teinte² /tɛ̃/ *nf* **(a)** shade
(b) colour (GB)

teinter /tɛ̃te/ [1] **1** *vtr* **(a)** to tint; to stain; to dye
(b) ~ qch de to tinge sth with
2 se teinter *v refl* (+ *v être*) **se ~ de** to become tinged with

teinture /tɛ̃tyʀ/ *nf* dye; (for wood) stain

teinturerie /tɛ̃tyʀʀi/ *nf* (dry-)cleaner's

teinturier, -ière /tɛ̃tyʀje, ɛʀ/ *nm,f* **(a)** dry-cleaner
(b) dyer

⚡ tel, telle /tɛl/ *adj* **(a)** such; **une telle conduite** such behaviour (GB)
(b) like; **~ père, ~ fils** like father like son
(c) telle est la vérité that is the truth; **comme ~, en tant que ~** as such; **ses affaires étaient restées telles quelles** his/her things were left as they were
(d) avec un ~ enthousiasme with such enthusiasm; **de telle sorte** or **façon** or **manière que** in such a way that; so that
(e) admettons qu'il arrive ~ jour, à telle heure suppose that he arrives on such and such a day, at such and such a time

télé /tele/ *adj inv, nf* (fam) TV

télé-achat /teleaʃa/ *nm* teleshopping

téléchargeable /teleʃaʀʒabl/ *adj* (Comput) downloadable; uploadable

téléchargement /teleʃaʀʒmɑ̃/ *nm* (Comput) download; upload

télécharger /teleʃaʀʒe/ *vt* (Comput) to download; to upload

télécommande /telekɔmɑ̃d/ *nf* remote control

télécommander /telekɔmɑ̃de/ [1] *vtr*
(a) to operate [sth] by remote control; **voiture télécommandée** remote-controlled car
(b) (figurative) to mastermind

télécommunication /telekɔmynikasjɔ̃/ *nf* telecommunications

téléconférence /telekɔ̃feʀɑ̃s/ *nf*
(a) conference call
(b) teleconference

télécopie /telekɔpi/ *nf* fax

télécopier /telekɔpje/ [2] *vtr* to fax

télécopieur /telekɔpjœʀ/ *nm* fax machine, fax

télé-crochet /telekʀɔʃɛ/ *nm: singing competition on the television*

télédiffuser /teledifyze/ [1] *vtr* to broadcast

télé-enseignement, *pl* **~s** /teleɑ̃sɛɲəmɑ̃/ *nm* distance learning

téléfilm /telefilm/ *nm* TV film, TV movie

télégramme /telegʀam/ *nm* telegram

télégraphier /telegʀafje/ [1] *vtr* to telegraph

télégraphique /telegʀafik/ *adj* ‹pole, message› telegraph; ‹style› telegraphic

téléguidage /telegidaʒ/ *nm* radio control

téléguider /telegide/ [1] *vtr* **(a)** to control [sth] by radio
(b) (figurative) to mastermind

télématique /telematik/ **1** *adj* ‹service, network› viewdata (GB), videotex®
2 *nf* telematics

téléobjectif /teleɔbʒɛktif/ *nm* telephoto lens

télépathie /telepati/ *nf* telepathy

téléphérique /teleferik/ *nm* cable car

⚡ téléphone /telefɔn/ *nm* phone
■ **~ arabe** (fam) grapevine, bush telegraph; **~ portable** mobile phone (GB), cellphone (US)
~ portatif pocket car phone; **le ~ rouge** hotline; **~ satellite** satphone, satellite phone

téléphoner /telefɔne/ [1] *vi* to phone; to make a phone call; **~ à qn** to phone sb

téléphonique /telefɔnik/ *adj* (tele)phone

télé réalité /teleʀealite/ *nf* reality TV

télescope /telɛskɔp/ *nm* telescope

télescoper /telɛskɔpe/ [1] **1** *vtr* ‹truck, juggernaut› to crush ‹car›
2 se télescoper *v refl* (+ *v être*)
(a) ‹vehicles› to collide
(b) ‹notions, tendencies› to overlap

télescopique /telɛskɔpik/ *adj* telescopic

téléscripteur /telɛskʀiptœʀ/ *nm* teleprinter, teletypewriter

télésiège /telesjɛʒ/ *nm* chair lift

téléski /teleski/ *nm* ski tow

téléspectateur, -trice /telespɛktatœʀ, tʀis/ *nm,f* viewer

télésurveillance /telesyʀvɛjɑ̃s/ *nf* electronic surveillance

télétransmission /teletʀɑ̃smisjɔ̃/ *nf* transmission

télétravail /teletʀavaj/ *nm* teleworking

télévente /televɑ̃t/ *nf* telesales

télévisé, ~e /televize/ *adj* television; televised

téléviseur /televizœʀ/ *nm* television (set)

⚡ télévision /televizjɔ̃/ *nf* television, TV
■ **~ numérique terrestre, TNT** digital terrestrial television, DTT

télex /telɛks/ *nm inv* telex; **par ~** by telex

télexer /telɛkse/ [1] *vtr* to telex

⚡ tellement /tɛlmɑ̃/ **1** *adv* (modifying an adjective or adverb) so; (modifying a verb or comparative) so much; **pas ~** not much; **il n'aime pas ~ lire** he doesn't like reading much; **j'ai de la peine à suivre ~ c'est compliqué** it's so complicated that I find it hard to follow
2 tellement de *quantif* (fam) **il y a ~ de choses à voir** there's so much to see; **il a eu ~ de chance** he was so lucky; **il y en a ~ qui aimeraient le faire** so many people would like to do it

téméraire /temeʀɛʀ/ *adj ‹person, plan›* reckless; *‹judgment›* rash; **courageux mais pas ∼** brave but not foolhardy

témérité /temeʀite/ *nf* recklessness; rashness; **avoir la ∼ de faire** to have the temerity to do

✧ **témoignage** /temwaɲaʒ/ *nm* (a) story (b) account; **∼s recueillis auprès de** accounts given by (c) evidence; testimony; **des ∼s contradictoires/qui concordent** conflicting/ corroborating evidence (d) **∼ d'amitié** (gift) token of friendship; **les ∼s de sympathie** expressions of sympathy

✧ **témoigner** /temwaɲe/ [1] **1** *vtr* (a) (Law) **'il était toujours poli', témoignent les voisins** neighbours (GB) say he was always polite; **témoigner que** to testify that (b) **∼ de l'affection** to show affection **2 témoigner de** *v+prep* (a) **∼ de** to show (b) **∼ du courage de qn** to vouch for sb's courage **3** *vi* (Law) to give evidence

✧ **témoin** /temwɛ̃/ *nm* (a) (gen, Law) witness; **∼ oculaire** eyewitness (b) (at duel) second (c) (Tech) indicator *or* warning light

tempe /tɑ̃p/ *nf* temple

tempérament /tɑ̃peʀamɑ̃/ *nm* disposition; **avoir du ∼** to have a strong character

tempérance /tɑ̃peʀɑ̃s/ *nf* temperance

température /tɑ̃peʀatyʀ/ *nf* temperature

tempéré, ∼e /tɑ̃peʀe/ *adj* temperate

tempérer /tɑ̃peʀe/ [14] *vtr* to temper; to moderate *‹argument›*

tempête /tɑ̃pɛt/ *nf* (a) gale; storm (b) uproar; **déclencher une ∼ de protestations** to trigger a wave of protest

tempêter /tɑ̃pɛte/ [1] *vi* to rage

✧ **temple** /tɑ̃pl/ *nm* (a) (gen) temple; (protestant) church (b) (figurative) temple

tempo /tɛmpo/ *nm* (Mus) tempo

temporaire /tɑ̃pɔʀɛʀ/ *adj* temporary

temporel, -elle /tɑ̃pɔʀɛl/ *adj* (gen) temporal

temporisateur, -trice **1** *adj* temporizing **2** *nm,f* temporizer

temporiser /tɑ̃pɔʀize/ [1] *vi* to stall

✧ **temps** /tɑ̃/ *nm inv* (a) weather; **un beau ∼** fine weather; **le ∼ est à la pluie** it looks like rain; **quel ∼ fait-il?** what's the weather like?; **par tous les ∼** in all weathers (b) time; **le ∼ arrangera les choses** time will take care of everything; **peu de ∼ avant** shortly before; **en peu de ∼** in a short time;

dans peu de ∼ shortly; **dans quelque ∼** before long; **pendant ce ∼(-là)** meanwhile; **qu'as-tu fait tout ce ∼(-là)?** what have you been doing all this time?; **en un rien de ∼** in no time at all; **les trois quarts du ∼** most of the time; **le ∼ de ranger mes affaires et j'arrive** just let me put my things away and I'll be with you; **on a (tout) le ∼** we've got (plenty of) time; **avoir dix** *or* **cent fois le ∼** to have all the time in the world; **laisser à qn le ∼ de faire** to give sb time to do; **mettre** *or* **prendre du ∼** to take time; **beaucoup de ∼** a long time; **tu y as mis le ∼!, tu en as mis du ∼!** you (certainly) took your time!; **le ∼ passe vite** time flies; **faire passer le ∼** to while away the time; **avoir du ∼ à perdre** to have time on one's hands; **c'est du ∼ perdu, c'est une perte de ∼** it's a waste of time; **le ∼ presse!** time is short!; **j'ai trouvé le ∼ long** (the) time seemed to drag; **finir dans les ∼** to finish in time; **à ∼** *‹leave, finish›* in time; **juste à ∼** just in time; **de ∼ en ∼, de ∼ à autre** from time to time; **il était ∼!** (impatiently) (and) about time too!; (with relief) just in the nick of time!; **en ∼ utile** in time; **en ∼ voulu** in due course; at the right time; **ne durer qu'un ∼** to be short-lived (c) **au** *or* **du ∼ des Grecs** in the time of the Greeks; **au** *or* **du ∼ où** in the days when; **le bon vieux ∼** the good old days; **ces derniers ∼** recently; **ces ∼-ci** lately; **de mon ∼** in my day; **dans le ∼** in those days; **en ∼ normal** usually; **en d'autres ∼** at any other time (d) stage; **en deux ∼** in two stages; **dans un premier ∼** first; **dans un deuxième ∼** subsequently; **dans un dernier ∼** finally (e) (of verb) tense (f) **avoir un travail à ∼ partiel/plein** to have a part-/full-time job (g) (Sport) time; **il a réalisé le meilleur ∼** he got the best time; **améliorer son ∼ d'une seconde** to knock a second off one's time (h) (of engine) stroke (i) (Mus) time; **mesure à deux ∼** two-four time

■ **∼ d'antenne** airtime; **∼ fort** (Mus) forte; (figurative) high point; **∼ mort** slack period; **∼ universel** Greenwich Mean Time, GMT IDIOMS **au ∼ pour moi!** my mistake!; **par les ∼ qui courent** with things as they are; **se payer du bon ∼** (fam) to have a whale of a time

tenable /tənabl/ *adj* (a) bearable; **la situation n'est pas ∼** the situation is unbearable (b) (defendable) tenable (c) **les élèves ne sont pas ∼s aujourd'hui** the pupils are being impossible today

tenace /tənas/ *adj* (a) *‹stain, headache›* stubborn; *‹perfume›* long-lasting; *‹fog, cough, memory›* persistent (b) *‹person›* tenacious; persistent; *‹will›* tenacious

ténacité /tenasite/ *nf* tenacity; persistence

✧ indicates a very frequent word

tenaille /tənɑj/ *nf* pincers

tenailler /tənɑje/ [1] *vtr* **il était tenaillé par le remords** he was racked with remorse

tenancier, -ière /tənɑ̃sje, ɛʀ/ *nm,f* (of café) landlord/landlady; (of hotel, casino) manager/manageress

tenant, ~**e** /tənɑ̃, ɑ̃t/ [1] *nm,f* (Sport) ~ **du titre** titleholder
[2] *nm* **d'un seul** ~ all in one piece
IDIOM **les** ~**s et les aboutissants de qch** the ins and outs of sth

⚹ **tendance** /tɑ̃dɑ̃s/ *nf* **(a)** tendency
(b) (in politics) tendency; **toutes** ~**s politiques confondues** across party lines
(c) trend

tendancieux, -ieuse /tɑ̃dɑ̃sjø, øz/ *adj* biased (GB), tendentious

tendeur /tɑ̃dœʀ/ *nm* **(a)** (of tent) guy rope
(b) (for roof rack) elastic strap

tendon /tɑ̃dɔ̃/ *nm* tendon

⚹ **tendre¹** /tɑ̃dʀ/ [6] [1] *vtr* **(a)** to tighten ‹rope, cable›; to stretch ‹elastic, skin›; to extend ‹spring›; ~ **le bras** to reach out; ~ **les bras à qn** to greet sb with open arms; ~ **la main** to reach out; to hold out one's hand; ~ **la main à qn** to hold one's hand out to sb; (figurative) to lend sb a helping hand
(b) to spread ‹cloth, sheet›
(c) to set ‹trap›; to put up ‹clothes line›
(d) ~ **qch à qn** to hold sth out to sb
[2] **tendre à** *v+prep* ~ **à faire** to tend to do
[3] *vi* **(a)** ~ **vers** to strive for
(b) ~ **vers** to approach ‹value›; to tend to ‹zero›
[4] **se tendre** *v refl* (+ *v être*) **(a)** to tighten
(b) to become strained

⚹ **tendre²** /tɑ̃dʀ/ [1] *adj* **(a)** ‹wood, fibre› soft; ‹skin, vegetables› tender
(b) ‹shoot, grass› new; ~ **enfance** earliest childhood
(c) ‹pink, green› soft
(d) ‹person› loving; ‹love, smile, words› tender; ‹temperament› gentle; **ne pas être** ~ **avec qn/qch** to be hard on sb/sth
(e) ‹husband, wife› dear
[2] *nmf* soft-hearted person

tendrement /tɑ̃dʀəmɑ̃/ *adv* tenderly

tendresse /tɑ̃dʀɛs/ *nf* **(a)** tenderness
(b) affection

tendu, ~**e** /tɑ̃dy/ [1] *pp* ▶ TENDRE¹
[2] *pp adj* ‹rope› tight
[3] *adj* ‹person, meeting› tense

ténèbres /tenɛbʀ/ *nf pl* **les** ~ darkness

ténébreux, -euse /tenebʀø, øz/ *adj*
(a) dark
(b) obscure

teneur /tənœʀ/ *nf* **(a)** (of solid) content; (of gas, liquid) level
(b) (of report) import

ténia /tenja/ *nm* tapeworm

⚹ **tenir** /təniʀ/ [36] [1] *vtr* **(a)** to hold; ~ **qn par la main** to hold sb's hand; **tiens!** (giving

sth to sb) here you are!; **tiens, regarde!** hey, look!; **si je le tenais!** if I could get my hands on him!
(b) to keep [sb] under control; **il nous tient** he's got a hold on us
(c) (Mil) to hold ‹hill, bridge, city›
(d) to hold ‹captive, animal›; **je te tiens!** I've caught you!
(e) to have ‹information›
(f) to hold ‹job›; to run ‹shop, house, business›; to be in charge of ‹switchboard, reception›
(g) to keep; '~ **hors de portée des enfants**' 'keep out of reach of children'
(h) ~ **sa tête droite** to hold one's head upright; ~ **les yeux baissés** to keep one's eyes lowered
(i) to hold down ‹load, cargo›; to hold up ‹trousers, socks›
(j) to keep to ‹itinerary›
(k) ~ **la mer** ‹ship› to be seaworthy; ~ **le coup** to hold out; ~ **le choc** ‹person› to stand the strain
(l) ‹object› to take up ‹room›; ‹person› to hold ‹role, position›
(m) ~ **qn/qch pour responsable** to hold sb/sth responsible; ~ **qn pour mort** to give sb up for dead
[2] **tenir à** *v+prep* **(a)** ~ **à** to be fond of, to like; ~ **à la vie** to value one's life
(b) **j'y tiens** I insist; ~ **à ce que qn fasse** to insist that sb should do
[3] **tenir de** *v+prep* ~ **de qn** to take after sb
[4] *vi* **(a)** ‹rope, shelf, dam› to hold; ‹stamp, glue› to stick; ‹bandage, structure› to stay in place; ‹hairstyle› to stay tidy
(b) ~ **(bon)** (gen) to hang on; (Mil) to hold out
(c) **la neige tient** the snow is settling; **les fleurs n'ont pas tenu** the flowers didn't last long
(d) ‹theory› to hold good; ‹alibi› to stand up
(e) ‹people, objects› to fit; ~ **à six dans une voiture** to fit six into a car; **mon article tient en trois pages** my article takes up only three pages
[5] **se tenir** *v refl* (+ *v être*) **(a)** **se** ~ **la tête à deux mains** to hold one's head in one's hands
(b) **se** ~ **par le bras** to be arm in arm; **se** ~ **par la main** to hold hands
(c) **se** ~ **à qch** to hold onto sth; **tiens-toi** *or* **tenez-vous bien** (figurative) (fam) prepare yourself for a shock
(d) **se** ~ **accroupi** to be squatting; **se** ~ **au milieu** to be standing in the middle; **se** ~ **prêt** to be ready
(e) to behave; **se** ~ **bien/mal** to behave well/badly
(f) **se** ~ **bien/mal** to have (a) good posture/ (a) bad posture; **tiens-toi droit!** stand up straight!
(g) ‹demonstration, exhibition› to be held
(h) ‹argument, book› to hold together; **ça se** ⋯⟩

tient it makes sense

(i) tenez-vous le pour dit! (fam) I don't want to have to tell you again!

(j) s'en ~ à to keep to; **s'en ~ aux ordres** to stick to orders; **ne pas savoir à quoi s'en ~** not to know what to make of it

6 *v impers* **il ne tient qu'à toi de partir** it's up to you to decide whether to leave; **qu'à cela ne tienne!** never mind!

tennis /tenis/ **1** *nm inv* tennis; **~ de table** table tennis

2 *nm inv or nf inv* tennis shoe

tennisman, *pl* **tennismen** /tenisman, mɛn/ *nm* (male) tennis player

ténor /tenɔʀ/ *nm* tenor

tension /tãsjɔ̃/ *nf* **(a)** (of cable, muscle) tension

(b) (Med) **~ (artérielle)** blood pressure; **être sous ~** to be under stress

(c) (in electricity) tension; **basse ~** low voltage; **sous ~** ‹wire› live; ‹machine› switched on

(d) (between people) tension

tentacule /tãtakyl/ *nm* tentacle

tentateur, -trice /tãtatœʀ, tʀis/ *nm,f* tempter/temptress

tentation /tãtasjɔ̃/ *nf* temptation

⚜ **tentative** /tãtativ/ *nf* attempt; **~ de meurtre** (gen) murder attempt; (Law) attempted murder

tente /tãt/ *nf* tent

⚜ **tenter** /tãte/ [1] *vtr* **(a)** to attempt; **~ sa chance** to try one's luck; **~ le tout pour le tout** to risk one's all

(b) to tempt; **cela ne la tente guère** that doesn't appeal to her very much; **laisse-toi ~!** be a devil!; **~ le diable** to court disaster

tenture /tãtyʀ/ *nf* **(a)** curtain; **~s** draperies

(b) fabric wall covering

tenu, ~e¹ /təny/ **1** *pp* ▸ TENIR

2 *pp adj* **(a) bien/mal ~** ‹child› well/badly cared for; ‹house› well/badly kept

(b) ~ de faire required to do; **~ à** bound by

tenue² /təny/ *nf* **(a) ~ (vestimentaire)** dress, clothes; **être en ~ légère** to be scantily dressed; **en ~** (Mil) uniformed

(b) avoir de la ~ to have good manners; **un peu de ~!** mind your manners!

(c) posture

ter /tɛʀ/ *adv* **(a)** (in address) ter; **15 ~ rue du Rocher** 15 ter rue du Rocher

(b) three times

térébenthine /teʀebãtin/ *nf* turpentine

tergal® /tɛʀgal/ *nm* Terylene®

tergiversation /tɛʀʒiveʀsasjɔ̃/ *nf* equivocation

tergiverser /tɛʀʒiveʀse/ [1] *vi* **(a)** to dither

(b) to shilly-shally

⚜ **terme** /tɛʀm/ **1** *nm* **(a)** term, word

(b) end; **mettre un ~ à qch** to put an end

to sth; **toucher à son ~** to come to an end; **arriver à ~** ‹period, contract› to expire; **accoucher avant ~** to give birth prematurely

(c) passé ce ~ vous paierez des intérêts after this date, you will pay interest; **à moyen ~** ‹loan› medium-term

(d) trouver un moyen ~ to find a compromise

2 **termes** *nm pl* terms; **~s de l'échange** terms of trade; **en bons ~s** on good terms

terminaison /tɛʀminɛzɔ̃/ *nf* ending

terminal, ~e¹, *mpl* **-aux** /tɛʀminal, o/ **1** *adj* ‹year› final; **phase ~e** (of operation) concluding phase; (of illness) terminal phase

2 *nm* terminal

terminale² /tɛʀminal/ *nf* (Sch) final year (*of secondary school*)

⚜ **terminer** /tɛʀmine/ [1] **1** *vtr* to finish; to end; **être terminé** to be over

2 *vi* to finish; **en ~ avec** to be through with; **pour ~** in conclusion

3 **se terminer** *v refl* **(a)** to end

(b) se ~ par ‹word, number, object› to end in

terminologie /tɛʀminɔlɔʒi/ *nf* terminology

terminus /tɛʀminys/ *nm inv* (of train) end of the line; (of bus) terminus

termite /tɛʀmit/ *nm* termite

ternaire /tɛʀnɛʀ/ *adj* (in maths, physics) ternary; (Mus) compound

terne /tɛʀn/ *adj* ‹hair, life› dull; ‹colour› drab; ‹eyes, expression› lifeless

ternir /tɛʀniʀ/ [3] **1** *vtr* **(a)** to tarnish ‹metal›; to fade ‹fabric›

(b) to tarnish ‹image, reputation›

2 **se ternir** *v refl* (+ *v être*) to tarnish

⚜ **terrain** /tɛʀɛ̃/ *nm* **(a)** (gen) ground; (Mil) field

(b) plot of land

(c) land

(d) (for football, rugby, cricket) pitch (GB), field; ground; (for volley-ball, handball, tennis) court; (in golf) course

(e) (figurative) **nous ne vous suivrons pas sur ce ~** we won't go along with you there; **un ~ d'entente** common ground; **travailler sur le ~** to do fieldwork; **~ favorable** (Med) predisposing factors; (in sociology) favourable (GB) environment; **déblayer le ~** to clear the ground; **préparer le ~** to pave the way; **tâter le ~** to put out feelers

■ **~ d'atterrissage** landing strip; **~ d'aviation** airfield; **~ de camping** campsite; **~ de jeu(x)** playground; **~ de sport(s)** sports ground; **~ vague** wasteland

terrasse /tɛʀas/ *nf* **(a)** terrace; **s'installer à la ~ d'un café** to sit at a table outside a café

(b) flat roof

(c) large balcony

terrassement /tɛʀasmã/ *nm* excavation; **faire des travaux de ~** to carry out excavation work

---

⚜ indicates a very frequent word

terrasser /tɛʀase/ [1] *vtr* ‹*illness*› to strike down; **terrassé par** (by heat, grief) prostrated by

terrassier /tɛʀasje/ *nm* building labourer (GB)

⚘ **terre** /tɛʀ/ ① *nf* **(a)** ground; **sous ~** underground
(b) earth; soil; **sortir de ~** ‹*plant*› to come up
(c) land; **le retour à la ~** the movement back to the land; **aller à ~** to go ashore; **s'enfoncer à l'intérieur de ~s** to go deep inland
(d) earth; **il croit que la ~ entière est contre lui** he thinks the whole world is against him; **redescends sur ~!** come back to earth!
(e) **de la ~ (glaise)** clay; **un pot en ~** an earthenware pot
(f) (in electricity) earth (GB), ground (US)
② **terre à terre** *phr* ‹*question*› basic; ‹*conversation, person*› pedestrian
③ **par terre** *phr* on the ground; on the floor; **c'est à se rouler par ~** (fam) it's hilarious; **ça a fichu tous nos projets par ~** (fam) it messed up all our plans (colloq)
■ **~ d'asile** country of refuge; **~ battue** trodden earth; **sur ~ battue** on a clay court
IDIOM avoir les pieds sur ~ (fam) to have one's feet firmly planted on the ground

Terre /tɛʀ/ *nf* Earth; **sur la ~** on Earth

terreau, *pl* **~x** /tɛʀo/ *nm* compost; **~ de feuilles** leaf mould (GB), leaf mold (US)

terre-plein, *pl* **terres-pleins** /tɛʀplɛ̃/ *nm* (of road) central reservation (GB), median strip (US)

terrer: se terrer /tɛʀe/ [1] *v refl* (+ *v être*)
(a) ‹*rabbit*› to disappear into its burrow; ‹*fox*› to go to earth
(b) ‹*fugitive*› to hide

terrestre /tɛʀɛstʀ/ *adj* **(a)** ‹*surface, diameter*› of the Earth
(b) ‹*animals*› land
(c) ‹*war, transport*› land; **la vie/le paradis ~** life/heaven on earth

terreur /tɛʀœʀ/ *nf* terror; **c'est ma grande ~** it's my greatest fear

⚘ **terrible** /tɛʀibl/ *adj* **(a)** (gen) terrible; ‹*thirst, desire*› tremendous; **il est~, il ne veut jamais avoir tort** (fam) it's terrible the way he never wants to admit that he's wrong
(b) (fam) terrific (colloq)

terriblement /tɛʀibləmɑ̃/ *adv* terribly; **il a ~ grandi** he's grown an awful lot

terrien, -ienne /tɛʀjɛ̃, ɛn/ *adj* **propriétaire ~** landowner

terrier /tɛʀje/ *nm* **(a)** (gen) hole; **un ~ de renard** a fox's earth
(b) (Zool) terrier

terrifiant, ~e /tɛʀifjɑ̃, ɑ̃t/ *adj* terrifying

terrifier /tɛʀifje/ [2] *vtr* to terrify

terrine /tɛʀin/ *nf* (gen) terrine; (round) earthenware bowl

⚘ **territoire** /tɛʀitwaʀ/ *nm* territory
■ **~ d'outre-mer, TOM** French overseas (administrative) territory

territorial, ~e, mpl -iaux /tɛʀitɔʀjal, o/ *adj* **(a)** ‹*waters, integrity*› territorial
(b) ‹*administration*› divisional; regional

terroir /tɛʀwaʀ/ *nm* land; **vin du ~** local wine

terroriser /tɛʀɔʀize/ [1] *vtr* **(a)** to terrorize
(b) to terrify

terrorisme /tɛʀɔʀism/ *nm* terrorism

terroriste /tɛʀɔʀist/ *adj, nmf* terrorist

tertiaire /tɛʀsjɛʀ/ *adj* **(a)** (Econ) ‹*sector, industry*› service
(b) (in geology) Tertiary

tertio /tɛʀsjo/ *adv* thirdly

tes ▸ TON¹

tesson /tesɔ̃/ *nm* shard, fragment

test /tɛst/ *nm* test; **~ (de dépistage) du sida** Aids test; **faire passer des ~s à qn** (gen) to give sb tests; (Med) to carry out tests on sb

testament /tɛstamɑ̃/ *nm* (Law) will; (figurative) legacy

testamentaire /tɛstamɑ̃tɛʀ/ *adj* of a will

tester /tɛste/ [1] *vtr* to test

testicule /tɛstikyl/ *nm* testicle

tétanos /tetanos/ *nm inv* tetanus

têtard /tɛtaʀ/ *nm* (Zool) tadpole

⚘ **tête** /tɛt/ *nf* **(a)** head; **en pleine ~** (right) in the head; **~ baissée** ‹*rush*› headlong; **la ~ en bas** ‹*hang*› upside down; **se laver la ~** to wash one's hair; **au-dessus de nos ~s** overhead; **être tombé sur la ~** (figurative) (fam) to have gone off one's rocker (colloq); **ma ~ est mise à prix** there's a price on my head; **vouloir la ~ de qn** to want sb's head; to be after sb's head; **risquer sa ~** to risk one's neck (colloq); **des ~s vont tomber** (figurative) heads will roll
(b) face; **une bonne/sale ~** a nice/nasty face; **tu en fais une ~!** what a face!; **quelle ~ va-t-il faire?** how's he going to react?; **il (me) fait la ~** he's sulking; **il a une ~ à tricher** he looks like a cheat; **tu as une ~ à faire peur, aujourd'hui!** you look dreadful today!
(c) **de ~** ‹*quote, recite*› from memory; ‹*calculate*› in one's head; **tu n'as pas de ~!** you have a mind like a sieve!; **avoir qch en ~ to have sth in mind**; **où avais-je la ~?** whatever was I thinking of?; **ça (ne) va pas, la~?** (fam) are you out of your mind or what?; **mets-lui ça dans la ~** drum it into him/her; **passer par la ~ de qn** ‹*idea*› to cross sb's mind; **monter la ~ à Pierre contre Paul** to turn Pierre against Paul; **j'ai la ~ qui tourne** my head's spinning; **monter à la ~ de qn** ‹*alcohol, success*› to go to sb's head; **il a encore toute sa ~ (à lui)** he's still got all his faculties; **n'en faire qu'à sa ~** to go one's own way; **tenir ~ à qn** to stand up to sb
(d) (person) **avoir ses ~s** to have one's favourites (GB); **un dîner en ~ à ~** an intimate dinner for two; **par ~** (gen) a head, each; (in statistics) per capita
(e) (measurement) head; **avoir une ~ d'avance sur qn** to be a short length in front of sb

(f) il a été nommé à la ~ du groupe he was appointed head of the group; **prendre la ~ des opérations** to take charge of operations; **être à la ~ d'une immense fortune** to be the possessor of a huge fortune
(g) top; **être en ~** (of list, category) to be at the top; (in election, race, survey) to be in the lead; **en ~ de phrase** at the beginning of a sentence
(h) (of train) front; (of convoy) head; (of tree, mast) top; (of screw, nail) head; **en ~ de file** first in line
(i) (Sport) (in football) **faire une ~** to head the ball
(j) (Mil) (of missile) warhead
(k) ~ de lecture (in tape recorder, video recorder) head
■ **~ en l'air** scatterbrain; **~ brûlée** daredevil; **~ à claques** (fam) pain (colloq); **~ de linotte**
▶ TÊTE EN L'AIR; **~ de mort** skull; death's head; skull and crossbones; **~ de mule** (fam) mule; **être une vraie ~ de mule** (fam) to be as stubborn as a mule; **~ de Turc** (fam) whipping boy
IDIOMS j'en mettrais ma ~ à couper I'd swear to it; **en avoir par-dessus la ~** (fam) to be fed up to the back teeth (colloq); **ça me prend la ~** (fam) it's a real drag (colloq)

tête-à-queue /tɛtakø/ *nm inv* **faire un ~** to slew round *or* around

tête-à-tête /tɛtatɛt/ *nm inv* **(a)** tête-à-tête
(b) private meeting

tête-bêche /tɛtbɛʃ/ *adv* **(a)** top-to-tail
(b) head-to-tail

tétée /tete/ *nf* **(a)** feeding
(b) feed

téter /tete/ [14] **1** *vtr* to suck at ‹breast›; to feed from ‹bottle›; to suck ‹milk›
2 *vi* to suckle; **donner à ~ à** to feed ‹baby›

tétine /tetin/ *nf* **(a)** teat (GB), nipple (US)
(b) dummy (GB), pacifier (US)
(c) (of animal) teat

têtu, ~e /tety/ *adj* stubborn

♂ **texte** /tɛkst/ *nm* **(a)** text; '**~ intégral**' 'unabridged'
(b) (Law) **~ de loi** bill; law

textile /tɛkstil/ **1** *adj* textile
2 *nm* **(a)** textile industry
(b) ~s synthétiques synthetic fibres (GB)

texto **1** (fam) ▶ TEXTUELLEMENT
2 *nm* text message

textphone /tɛkstfɔn/ *nm* textphone

textuellement /tɛkstɥɛlmã/ *adv* ‹recount› word for word

texture /tɛkstyʀ/ *nf* **(a)** (of fabric, material) texture
(b) (of novel) structure

TGV /teʒeve/ *nm* (*abbr* = **train à grande vitesse**) TGV, high-speed train

thé /te/ *nm* **(a)** tea

♂ indicates a very frequent word

(b) tea party

théâtral, ~e, mpl -aux /teɑtʀal, o/ *adj*
(a) ‹performance› stage; ‹season, company› theatre (GB); ‹production, technique› theatrical; **l'œuvre ~e de Racine** the plays of Racine
(b) ‹gesture› histrionic; ‹tone› melodramatic

♂ **théâtre** /teatʀ/ *nm* theatre (GB); **le ~ antique** Greek classical drama; **de ~** ‹actor, director, ticket› theatre (GB); ‹decor, costume› stage; **coup de ~** coup de théâtre; (figurative) dramatic turn of events; **faire du ~** (as profession) to be an actor; (at school) to do drama; **être le ~ d'affrontements** (figurative) to be the scene of fighting
■ **~ de Boulevard** farce

théière /tejɛʀ/ *nf* teapot

théine /tein/ *nf* theine

thématique **1** *adj* thematic
2 *nf* themes

♂ **thème** /tɛm/ *nm* **(a)** topic, subject; (of film) theme
(b) (translation) prose
(c) (Mus) theme
■ **~ astral** birth chart

théologie /teɔlɔʒi/ *nf* theology

théorème /teɔʀɛm/ *nm* theorem

théoricien, -ienne /teɔʀisjɛ̃, ɛn/ *nm,f* theoretician

♂ **théorie** /teɔʀi/ *nf* theory; **en ~** in theory

théorique /teɔʀik/ *adj* theoretical

thérapeute /teʀapøt/ *nmf* therapist

thérapeutique /teʀapøtik/ *adj* ‹effect› therapeutic; **choix ~** choice of treatment

thérapie /teʀapi/ *nf* **(a)** (Med) treatment
(b) (in psychology) therapy

thermal, ~e, mpl -aux /tɛʀmal, o/ *adj* ‹spring› thermal; **station ~e** spa

thermalisme /tɛʀmalism/ *nm*
(a) balneology
(b) hydrotherapy industry

thermes /tɛʀm/ *nm pl* **(a)** (Roman) thermae
(b) thermal baths

thermique /tɛʀmik/ *adj* thermal

thermo /tɛʀmo/ *pref* thermo; **~nucléaire** thermonuclear

thermomètre /tɛʀmɔmɛtʀ/ *nm* thermometer

thermostat /tɛʀmɔsta/ *nm* thermostat

thèse /tɛz/ *nf* **(a)** (for doctorate) thesis (GB), dissertation (US)
(b) thesis, argument
(c) avancer la ~ de l'accident to put forward the theory that it was an accident

thon /tɔ̃/ *nm* tuna

thonier *nm* tuna boat

thoracique /tɔʀasik/ *adj* **cage ~** ribcage

thorax /tɔʀaks/ *nm inv* thorax

thym /tɛ̃/ *nm* thyme

thyroïde /tiʀɔid/ *adj, nf* thyroid

tibia /tibja/ *nm* shinbone, tibia

tic /tik/ *nm* **(a)** tic; **être plein de** ∼**s** to be constantly twitching
(b) ∼ **de langage** verbal tic
ticket /tikɛ/ *nm* (for train, platform) ticket; ∼ **de caisse** till receipt (GB), sales slip (US); ∼ **modérateur** *patient's contribution towards the cost of medical treatment*
ticket-restaurant®, *pl* **tickets-restaurant** /tikɛʀɛstɔʀɑ̃/ *nm* luncheon voucher, meal ticket
tic-tac /tiktak/ *nm inv* **faire** ∼ to tick
tiède /tjɛd/ *adj* **(a)** lukewarm; warm; mild
(b) (figurative) lukewarm
tièdement /tjɛdmɑ̃/ *adv* half-heartedly
tiédeur /tjedœʀ/ *nf* **(a)** (of season) mildness; (of air, room) warmth
(b) (figurative) half-heartedness
tiédir /tjediʀ/ [3] *vi* **(a) faire** ∼ to warm *or* heat (up); **laisser** ∼ to allow [sth] to cool
(b) ‹feelings› to cool; ‹enthusiasm› to wane
tien, tienne /tjɛ̃, tjɛn/ **le tien, la tienne, les tiens, les tiennes** *pron* yours; **un métier comme le** ∼ a job like yours; **à la tienne!** cheers!; (ironic) good luck to you!
tiens ▶ TENIR
tierce¹ /tjɛʀs/ ▶ TIERS 1
tiercé /tjɛʀse/ *nm* (Games) **jouer au** ∼ to bet on the horses
tiers, tierce² /tjɛʀ, tjɛʀs/ **1** *adj* third; **un pays** ∼ (gen) another country; a non-member country; **une tierce personne** a third party
2 *nm inv* **(a)** third; **le** ∼**/les deux** ∼ **du travail** one third/two thirds of the work
(b) (person) outsider; (Law) third party
■ **le Tiers État** the Third Estate
tiers-monde /tjɛʀmɔ̃d/ *nm* Third World
tiers-mondisme /tjɛʀmɔ̃dism/ *nm* support for the Third World
tiers-mondiste **1** *adj* in support of the Third World
2 *nmf* supporter of the Third World
tige /tiʒ/ *nf* (of plant) stem, stalk
tigre /tigʀ/ *nm* (Zool) tiger
tigré, ∼**e** /tigʀe/ *adj* **(a)** striped
(b) spotted
tigresse /tigʀɛs/ *nf* (Zool, figurative) tigress
tilleul /tijœl/ *nm* **(a)** limetree
(b) limewood
(c) lime-blossom tea
tilt /tilt/ *nm* (fam) **ça a fait** ∼ **(dans mon esprit)** (fam) the penny dropped (colloq)
timbale /tɛ̃bal/ *nf* **(a)** (metal) tumbler
(b) (Mus) kettledrum; ∼**s** timpani
(c) (Culin) timbale
timbre /tɛ̃bʀ/ *nm* **(a)** stamp
(b) postmark
(c) (of voice) tone, timbre
(d) (Med) patch
timbre-poste, *pl* **timbres-poste** /tɛ̃bʀəpɔst/ *nm* postage stamp
timbrer /tɛ̃bʀe/ [1] *vtr* to stamp

timide /timid/ *adj* ‹person› shy, timid; ‹criticism› timid; ‹success› limited
timidement /timidmɑ̃/ *adv* shyly; timidly; (without conviction) half-heartedly
timidité /timidite/ *nf* shyness
timoré, ∼**e** /timɔʀe/ *adj* timorous
tintamarre /tɛ̃tamaʀ/ *nm* din; **faire du** ∼ to make a din
tintement /tɛ̃tmɑ̃/ *nm* chiming; tinkling
tinter /tɛ̃te/ [1] *vi* ‹bells› to chime; ‹doorbell› to ring; ‹small bell› to tinkle; ‹glass, coins› to clink; ‹keys› to jingle; (Mus) ‹triangle› to ring
tintinnabuler /tɛ̃tinabyle/ [1] *vi* to tinkle
tipi /tipi/ *nm* te(e)pee
tique /tik/ *nf* (Zool) tick
tiquer /tike/ [1] *vi* (fam) to wince; **sans** ∼ without batting an eyelid (GB) *or* eyelash (US)
tir /tiʀ/ *nm* **(a)** (Mil) fire; **déclencher le** ∼ to open fire
(b) (Sport) shooting
(c) ∼ **de grenades** grenade firing
(d) (in games, sports) (with ball) shot
(e) shooting
tirade /tiʀad/ *nf* **(a)** declamation
(b) tirade
tirage /tiʀaʒ/ *nm* **(a)** ∼ **(au sort)** draw; **désigner par** ∼ **(au sort)** to draw ‹name, winner›
(b) impression
(c) edition; ∼ **limité** limited edition
(d) (of book) run; (of newspaper) circulation
tiraillement /tiʀajmɑ̃/ *nm* **(a)** pulling, tugging
(b) nagging pain; ∼**s d'estomac** hunger pangs
(c) friction
tirailler /tiʀaje/ [1] *vtr* to tug (at), to pull (at) ‹rope, sleeve›; **être tiraillé entre son travail et sa famille** to be torn between one's work and one's family
tire-au-flanc /tiʀoflɑ̃/ *nm inv* (fam) shirker, skiver (colloq)
tire-bouchon, *pl* ∼**s** /tiʀbuʃɔ̃/ *nm* corkscrew; **en** ∼ ‹tail› curly
tire-d'aile: à tire-d'aile /atiʀdɛl/ *phr* in a flurry of wings; (figurative) hurriedly
tirelire /tiʀliʀ/ *nf* piggy bank
⚹ **tirer** /tiʀe/ [1] **1** *vtr* **(a)** to pull ‹vehicle›; to pull up ‹chair, armchair›; to pull away ‹rug›
(b) to pull ‹hair›; to pull on ‹rope›; to tug at ‹sleeve›; ∼ **qn par le bras** to pull sb's arm
(c) ∼ **ses cheveux en arrière** to pull back one's hair; **avoir les traits tirés** to look drawn
(d) to draw ‹bolt, curtain›; to pull down ‹blind›; to close ‹door, shutter›
(e) to fire off ‹bullet, grenade›; to fire ‹missile›; to shoot ‹arrow›
(f) (Sport) ∼ **un penalty** to take a penalty
(g) ∼ **(au sort)** to draw ‹card, name, winner›; to draw for ‹partner›
····⟩

(h) (in astrology) ∼ **les cartes à qn** to tell the cards for sb
(i) to draw ‹wine›; to withdraw ‹money›; ∼ **qch de sa poche** to pull sth out of one's pocket
(j) ∼ **le pays de la récession** to get the country out of recession; **tire-moi de là!** get me out of this!
(k) ∼ **qch de qn** to get sth from sb ‹information, confession›; ∼ **qch de qch** to draw sth from sth ‹strength, resources›; to derive sth from sth ‹pride, satisfaction›; to make sth out of sth ‹money›
(l) ∼ **de qch** to base [sth] on sth ‹story, film›; to get [sth] from sth ‹name›
(m) to print ‹book, negative›; to run off ‹proofs, copies›
(n) to draw ‹line›
(o) (fam) **plus qu'une semaine à** ∼ only one more week to go
(p) ∼ **un chèque** to draw a cheque (GB) or check (US)

2 vi **(a)** to pull; ∼ **sur qch** to pull on sth; to tug at sth
(b) (with firearm) to shoot; to fire
(c) (in football) to shoot; (in handball, basketball) to take a shot
(d) ∼ **(au sort)** to draw lots
(e) **la cheminée tire bien** the chimney draws well
(f) ∼ **à mille exemplaires** ‹periodical› to have a circulation of one thousand
(g) ∼ **sur le jaune/l'orangé** ‹colour› to be yellowish/orangy

3 **se tirer** v refl (+ v être) **(a)** se ∼ **de** to come through ‹situation, difficulties›
(b) se ∼ **une balle** to shoot oneself; **se** ∼ **dessus** to shoot at one another
(c) (fam) **s'en** ∼ to cope; (from accident) to escape; (from illness) to pull through; **s'en** ∼ **à bon prix** to get off lightly

tiret /tiRɛ/ nm dash

tirette /tiRɛt/ nf pull tab; cord

tireur, -euse /tiRœʀ, øz/ nm,f **(a)** (Mil, Sport) marksman/markswoman
(b) gunman

tiroir /tiRwaR/ nm (in piece of furniture) drawer; **à** ∼**s** (figurative) ‹novel, play› episodic
IDIOM racler les fonds de ∼ to scrape some money together

tiroir-caisse, pl **tiroirs-caisses** /tiRwaRkɛs/ nm cash register

tisane /tizan/ nf herbal tea, tisane

tison /tizɔ̃/ nm (fire) brand

tisonnier /tizɔnje/ nm poker

tissage /tisaʒ/ nm **(a)** weaving
(b) weave

tisser /tise/ [1] vtr **(a)** ‹person, machine› to weave
(b) ‹spider› to spin ‹web›

tisserand, ∼**e** /tisRɑ̃, ɑ̃d/ nm,f weaver

tissu /tisy/ nm **(a)** material, fabric
(b) (Anat) ∼ **osseux** bone tissue
(c) (of intrigue) web; (of lies) pack; (of insults) string; ∼ **social** social fabric

titan /titɑ̃/ nm titan; **de** ∼ titanic

titane /titan/ nm titanium

titiller /titije/ [1] vtr to titillate

◌ **titre** /titR/ nm **(a)** (of book, film, chapter) title; (in newspaper) headline; **avoir pour** ∼ to be entitled; **les** ∼**s de l'actualité** the headlines
(b) (rank) title; ∼ **mondial** world title; ∼ **nobiliaire** or **de noblesse** title; **le** ∼ **d'ingénieur** the status of qualified engineer; **en** ∼ ‹professor, director› titular; ‹supplier› appointed; ‹mistress, rival› official; ∼**s universitaires** university qualifications
(c) **à juste** ∼ quite rightly; **à** ∼ **d'exemple** as an example; **à** ∼ **définitif** on a permanent basis; **à** ∼ **privé** in a private capacity; **à** ∼ **gracieux** free; **à** ∼ **indicatif** as a rough guide; **à quel** ∼ **a-t-il été invité?** why was he invited?
(d) (Law) deed; ∼ **de propriété** title deed
(e) (on stock exchange) security
(f) (Econ) item; ∼ **budgétaire** budgetary item
(g) (of solution) titre (GB); (of wines, spirits) strength; (of precious metal) fineness
■ ∼ **de gloire** claim to fame; ∼ **interbancaire de paiement, TIP** bank account details to make a payment by direct debit; ∼ **de séjour** residence permit; ∼ **de transport** ticket

titré, ∼**e** /titRe/ adj titled; **être** ∼ to be titled

tituber /titybe/ [1] vi to stagger

titulaire /titylɛR/ **1** adj (gen) permanent; ‹lecturer› tenured
2 nmf **(a)** (gen) permanent staff member; tenured lecturer (GB) or professor (US)
(b) holder; **être** ∼ **de** to hold ‹degree, post›; to have ‹bank account›

titularisation /titylaRizasjɔ̃/ nf confirmation in a post; (Univ) granting of tenure

titulariser /titylaRize/ [1] vtr to give permanent status to ‹staff›; to grant tenure to ‹professor›

toast /tost/ nm toast

toboggan /tɔbɔgɑ̃/ nm **(a)** slide
(b) ® flyover (GB), overpass (US)
(c) (Tech) (for rubble) chute

toc /tɔk/ **1** nm (fam) **c'est du** ∼ it's fake
2 excl ∼**!** ∼**!** knock! knock!

tocsin /tɔksɛ̃/ nm alarm (bell), tocsin

toge /tɔʒ/ nf **(a)** (of academic) gown; (of judge) robe
(b) toga

◌ **toi** /twa/ pron **(a)** you; ∼, **ne dis rien** don't say anything; **elle est plus âgée que** ∼ she's older than you; **à** ∼ (in game) your turn; **c'est à** ∼ it's yours; **c'est à** ∼ **de choisir** it's your turn to choose; it's up to you to choose
(b) yourself; **reprends-**∼ pull yourself

◌ indicates a very frequent word

together

⚡ **toile** /twal/ *nf* **(a)** cloth; ~ **de lin** linen (cloth); **de la grosse** ~ canvas **(b)** (in art) canvas; painting; ~ **de maître** master painting **(c)** (Naut) canvas **(d)** (Comput) (World Wide) Web ■ ~ **d'araignée** spider's web; cobweb; ~ **cirée** oilcloth; ~ **de jute** hessian; ~ **de tente** canvas; tent

toilettage /twalɛtaʒ/ *nm* (of animal) grooming

toilette /twalɛt/ **1** *nf* **(a)** **faire sa** ~ ‹person› to have a wash; ‹animal› to wash itself; **faire la** ~ **d'un mort** to lay out a corpse **(b)** outfit; **en grande** ~ all dressed up **2 toilettes** *nf pl* toilet (GB), bathroom (US)

toiletter /twalete/ [1] *vtr* to groom ‹dog›

toi-même /twamɛm/ *pron* yourself

toise /twaz/ *nf* height gauge

toiser /twaze/ [1] *vtr* to look [sb] up and down

toit /twa/ *nm* roof ■ **le** ~ **du Monde** the roof of the world; ~ **ouvrant** sunroof **IDIOM crier qch sur (tous) les** ~**s** to shout sth from the rooftops

toiture /twatyʀ/ *nf* **(a)** roof **(b)** roofing

tôle /tol/ *nf* **(a)** sheet metal **(b)** metal sheet *or* plate **(c)** (pop) ▶ TAULE

tolérable /tɔleʀabl/ *adj* bearable; tolerable

tolérance /tɔleʀɑ̃s/ *nf* **(a)** tolerance; indulgence **(b)** **ce n'est pas un droit, c'est une** ~ it isn't legal but it is tolerated **(c)** (of medicine, noise) tolerance

tolérant, ~**e** /tɔleʀɑ̃, ɑ̃t/ *adj* tolerant

tolérer /tɔleʀe/ [14] *vtr* to tolerate

tôlerie /tolʀi/ *nf* sheet-metal working; sheet-metal trade; sheet-metal works

tollé /tɔle/ *nm* outcry, hue and cry

TOM /tɔm/ *nm: abbr* ▶ TERRITOIRE

⚡ **tomate** /tɔmat/ *nf* **(a)** tomato **(b)** tomato plant **(c)** *pastis with a dash of grenadine*

tombal, ~**e**, *mpl* -**aux** /tɔ̃bal, o/ *adj* **inscription** ~**e** gravestone inscription

tombant, ~**e** /tɔ̃bɑ̃, ɑ̃t/ *adj* ‹shoulders› sloping; ‹moustache, eyelids› drooping; ‹ears› floppy

tombe /tɔ̃b/ *nf* **(a)** grave **(b)** gravestone

tombeau, *pl* ~**x** /tɔ̃bo/ *nm* **(a)** tomb; **mettre qn au** ~ to lay sb in their grave **(b)** **c'est un** ~ ‹person› he/she will keep quiet

tombée /tɔ̃be/ *nf* **à la** ~ **du jour** at close of day; **la** ~ **de la nuit** nightfall

⚡ **tomber**[1] /tɔ̃be/ [1] **1** *vi* (+ *v être*) **(a)** (gen) to fall; ‹person, chair› to fall over; ‹tree, wall› to fall down; (from height) ‹person, vase› to fall off; ‹hair, teeth› to fall out; ‹plaster, covering› to come off; ~ **du lit/de ma poche** to fall out of bed/out of my pocket; **le vent a fait** ~ **une tuile du toit** the wind blew a tile off the roof; **se laisser** ~ **dans un fauteuil** to flop into an armchair; **laisser** ~ **un gâteau sur le tapis** to drop a cake on the carpet **(b)** ‹rain, snow, theatre curtain› to fall; ‹fog› to come down; **qu'est-ce que ça tombe!** (fam) it's pouring down!; **la foudre est tombée sur un arbre** the lightning struck a tree **(c)** ‹price, temperature› to fall; ‹anger› to subside; ‹fever› to come down; ‹wind› to drop; ‹day› to draw to a close; ‹conversation› to die down; **faire** ~ to bring down ‹price, temperature›; to dampen ‹enthusiasm›; **je tombe de sommeil** I can't keep my eyes open **(d)** ‹dictator, regime, city› to fall; ‹obstacle› to vanish; **faire** ~ to bring down ‹regime, dictator›; (figurative) to break down ‹barriers› **(e)** ‹belly› to sag; ‹shoulders› to slope **(f)** ‹lock of hair› to fall; ~ **bien/mal** ‹garment, curtain› to hang well/badly **(g)** ~ **dans un piège** (figurative) to fall into a trap; ~ **sous le coup d'une loi** to fall within the provisions of a law; ~ **aux mains** *or* **entre les mains de qn** ‹document, power› to fall into sb's hand; ~ **malade/amoureux** to fall ill/in love **(h)** ‹decision, verdict› to be announced; ‹news› to break; ‹reply› to be given **(i)** ~ **sur** to come across ‹stranger, object›; to run into ‹friend›; ~ **sur la bonne page** to hit on the right page; **si tu prends cette rue, tu tomberas sur la place** if you follow that street, you'll come to the square **(j)** **c'est tombé juste au bon moment** it came just at the right time; **tu ne pouvais pas mieux** ~! you couldn't have come at a better time!; you couldn't have done better!; **tu tombes mal, j'allais partir** you're unlucky, I was just about to leave; **il faut toujours que ça tombe sur moi!** (fam) (decision, choice) why does it always have to be me?; (misfortune) why does it always have to happen to me? **(k)** ‹birthday› to fall on ‹day› **(l)** **laisser** ~ to give up ‹job, activity›; to drop ‹plan, habit›; **laisse** ~! forget it!; **laisser** ~ **qn** to drop sb; to let sb down **(m)** ~ **sur qn** ‹soldiers, thugs› to fall on sb; ‹raiders, police› to descend on sb **2** *vtr* to take off ‹clothes›

tomber[2] /tɔ̃be/ *nm* hang; **ce velours a un beau** ~ this velvet hangs well

tombeur /tɔ̃bœʀ/ *nm* (fam) lady-killer

tombola /tɔ̃bɔla/ *nf* tombola (GB), lottery

tome[1] /tɔm/ *nm* **(a)** volume **(b)** part, book

tome[2] /tɔm/ ▶ TOMME

tomme /tɔm/ *nf* tomme *or* tome (cheese)

tommette /tɔmɛt/ *nf* hexagonal floor tile

♂ **ton¹**, **ta**, *pl* **tes** /tɔ̃, ta, te/ *det* your; **un de tes amis** a friend of yours

ton² /tɔ̃/ *nm* (a) pitch; tone; ~ **grave/ aigu** low/high pitch; **d'un** ~ **dédaigneux** scornfully; **baisser le** ~ to lower one's voice; (figurative) to moderate one's tone; **eh bien, si tu le prends sur ce** ~ well, if you're going to take it like that
(b) (in linguistics) tone; **langue à** ~**s** tone language
(c) **donner le** ~ to set the tone; to set the fashion; **de bon** ~ in good taste
(d) (Mus) pitch; key; tone; (instrument) pitch pipe
(e) (of colour) shade; ~ **sur** ~ in matching tones

tonalité /tɔnalite/ *nf* (a) (Mus) key; tonality
(b) (of vowel) tone
(c) (of voice) tone
(d) (of colours) tonality
(e) dialling tone (GB), dial tone (US)

tondeuse /tɔ̃dœz/ *nf* (a) (for sheep) shears
(b) (for cutting hair) clippers
(c) ~ **(à gazon)** lawnmower

tondre /tɔ̃dʀ/ [6] *vtr* to shear ‹*sheep*›; to clip ‹*dog*›; to mow ‹*lawn*›; ~ **qn** to shave sb's head

tongs /tɔ̃g/ *nf pl* flip-flops, thongs (US)

tonicité /tɔnisite/ *nf* (a) bracing effect
(b) tone

tonifiant, ~**e** /tɔnifjɑ̃, ɑ̃t/ *adj* (a) ‹*climate, air*› bracing
(b) ‹*exercise, lotion*› toning

tonifier /tɔnifje/ [2] *vtr* to tone up

tonique¹ /tɔnik/ *adj* (a) ‹*drink*› tonic; (figurative) ‹*air*› bracing; ‹*book*› stimulating
(b) **lotion** ~ toning lotion
(c) ‹*accent*› tonic

tonique² /tɔnik/ *nf* (Mus) tonic

tonitruant, ~**e** /tɔnitʀyɑ̃, ɑ̃t/ *adj* booming

tonitruer /tɔnitʀye/ [1] *vi* to thunder

tonnage /tɔnaʒ/ *nm* tonnage

tonnant, ~**e** /tɔnɑ̃, ɑ̃t/ *adj* booming; thunderous

tonne /tɔn/ *nf* (1,000 kg) tonne, metric ton; **des** ~**s de choses à faire** (fam) loads of things to do (colloq)

tonneau, *pl* ~**x** /tɔno/ *nm* (a) barrel
(b) (of car) somersault
(c) (of plane) barrel roll
(d) (Naut) ton
IDIOM **du même** ~ (fam) of the same kind

tonnelle /tɔnɛl/ *nf* arbour (GB)

tonner /tɔne/ [1] *vi*, *v impers* to thunder

tonnerre /tɔnɛʀ/ *nm* (a) thunder; **un coup de** ~ a clap of thunder; (figurative) a thunderbolt
(b) (of cannons, artillery) thundering; **un** ~ **d'applaudissements** thunderous applause

─────────

♂ indicates a very frequent word

(c) (fam) **ça marche du** ~ it's going fantastically well

tonsure /tɔ̃syʀ/ *nf* (of monk) tonsure

tonte /tɔ̃t/ *nf* (a) (des moutons) shearing
(b) fleece

tonton /tɔ̃tɔ̃/ *nm* (fam) uncle; ~ **Pierre** Uncle Pierre

tonus /tɔnys/ *nm inv* (a) (of person) energy, dynamism
(b) (of muscle) tone, tonus

top /tɔp/ *nm* pip, beep; **donner le** ~ **de départ** to give the starting signal

topaze /tɔpaz/ *nf* topaz

toper /tɔpe/ [1] *vi* **topons là!** let's shake on it!

topo /tɔpo/ *nm* (fam) short talk; short piece; **c'est toujours le même** ~ it's always the same old story (colloq)

topographie /tɔpɔgʀafi/ *nf* topography

toquade /tɔkad/ *nf* (fam) (a) (for thing) passion
(b) (on person) crush (colloq)

toque /tɔk/ *nf* (a) (of woman) toque; (of chef) chef's hat; (of judge) hat; ~ **en fourrure** fur cap
(b) (of jockey) cap

toqué, ~**e** /tɔke/ *adj* (fam) crazy (colloq)

torche /tɔʀʃ/ *nf* torch
■ ~ **électrique** torch (GB), flashlight

torcher /tɔʀʃe/ [1] *vtr* (fam) (a) to wipe
(b) to dash off (colloq) ‹*article, report*›; to cobble [sth] together

torchis /tɔʀʃi/ *nm inv* cob (for walls)

torchon /tɔʀʃɔ̃/ *nm* (a) (gen) cloth; ~ **(de cuisine)** tea towel (GB), dish towel (US)
(b) (newspaper) (derogatory) rag (colloq)
(c) (fam) messy piece of work
IDIOM **le** ~ **brûle** (fam) it's war

tordant, ~**e** /tɔʀdɑ̃, ɑ̃t/ *adj* (fam) hilarious

tordre /tɔʀdʀ/ [6] **1** *vtr* (a) to twist ‹*arm, wrist*›; to wring ‹*neck*›
(b) to bend ‹*nail, bar, bumper*›
(c) to wring out ‹*washing*›
2 **se tordre** *v refl* (+ *v être*) (a) ‹*person*› **se** ~ **la cheville** to twist one's ankle; **se** ~ **de douleur** to writhe in pain
(b) ‹*bumper*› to bend

tordu, ~**e** /tɔʀdy/ *adj* (a) ‹*nose, legs*› crooked; ‹*branches, trunk, iron bar*› twisted
(b) (figurative) ‹*idea*› weird, strange; ‹*logic, reasoning*› twisted

tornade /tɔʀnad/ *nf* tornado

torpeur /tɔʀpœʀ/ *nf* torpor

torpille /tɔʀpij/ *nf* torpedo

torpiller /tɔʀpije/ [1] *vtr* to torpedo

torréfier /tɔʀefje/ [2] *vtr* to roast

torrent /tɔʀɑ̃/ *nm* torrent; **pleuvoir à** ~**s** to rain very heavily

torrentiel, **-ielle** /tɔʀɑ̃sjɛl/ *adj* torrential

torride /tɔʀid/ *adj* torrid; ‹*sun*› scorching

tors, torse¹ /tɔʀ, tɔʀs/ *adj* (gen) twisted

torsade /tɔʀsad/ *nf* (a) twist, coil
(b) cable stitch
(c) (in architecture) cable moulding (GB), cable molding (US)

torsader /tɔʀsade/ [1] *vtr* to twist; **une colonne torsadée** a cable column

torse² /tɔʀs/ *nm* (a) (gen) chest; **se mettre ~ nu** to strip to the waist
(b) (Anat) torso

torsion /tɔʀsjõ/ *nf* (a) twisting
(b) torsion

tort /tɔʀ/ ⟨1⟩ *nm* (a) **avoir ~** to be wrong; **j'aurais bien ~ de m'inquiéter!** it would be silly of me to worry!; **être en ~** to be in the wrong; **donner ~ à qn** ⟨*referee, judge*⟩ to blame sb; ⟨*facts*⟩ to prove sb wrong
(b) fault; **les ~s sont partagés** there are faults on both sides; **avoir des ~s envers qn** to have wronged sb
(c) mistake; **j'ai eu le ~ de croire** I made the mistake of believing him
(d) **faire du ~ à qn/qch** to harm sb/sth
⟨2⟩ **à tort** *phr* ⟨*accuse*⟩ wrongly; **à ~ et à travers** ⟨*spend*⟩ wildly; **parler à ~ et à travers** to talk a lot of nonsense

torticolis /tɔʀtikɔli/ *nm inv* stiff neck

tortillard /tɔʀtijaʀ/ *nm* (fam) small local train

tortiller /tɔʀtije/ [1] ⟨1⟩ *vtr* to twist ⟨*fibres, strands*⟩; **to twiddle** ⟨*handkerchief*⟩
⟨2⟩ **se tortiller** *v refl* (+ *v être*) to wriggle

tortionnaire /tɔʀsjɔnɛʀ/ *nmf* torturer

tortue /tɔʀty/ *nf* (a) (sea) turtle
(b) tortoise (GB), turtle (US)
(c) (butterfly) tortoiseshell

tortueux, -euse /tɔʀtɥø, øz/ *adj* (a) ⟨*road, staircase*⟩ winding
(b) (figurative) ⟨*behaviour*⟩ devious; ⟨*mind, reasoning*⟩ tortuous

torture /tɔʀtyʀ/ *nf* torture

torturer /tɔʀtyʀe/ [1] ⟨1⟩ *vtr* (a) to torture ⟨*person*⟩
(b) ⟨*thought, feeling*⟩ to torment
(c) to distort ⟨*text*⟩; **style torturé** tortured style
⟨2⟩ **se torturer** *v refl* (+ *v être*) to torment oneself; **se ~ l'esprit** to rack one's brains

torve /tɔʀv/ *adj* ⟨*look*⟩ menacing, baleful

♂ **tôt** /to/ *adv* (a) ⟨*start*⟩ early; **~ le matin** early in the morning
(b) soon, early; **le plus ~ serait le mieux** the sooner the better; **~ ou tard** sooner or later; **on ne m'y reprendra pas de si ~** I won't do that again in a hurry

♂ **total, ~e,** *mpl* **-aux** /tɔtal, o/ ⟨1⟩ *adj* complete, total
⟨2⟩ *nm* total
⟨3⟩ **au total** *phr* **au ~ cela fait 350 euros** altogether that comes to 350 euros

♂ **totalement** /tɔtalmã/ *adv* totally, completely

totaliser /tɔtalize/ [1] *vtr* (a) to total ⟨*profits*⟩
(b) to have a total of ⟨*points, votes*⟩

totalitaire /tɔtalitɛʀ/ *adj* (a) ⟨*regime, state*⟩ totalitarian
(b) ⟨*doctrine*⟩ all-embracing

totalitarisme /tɔtalitaʀism/ *nm* totalitarianism

totalité /tɔtalite/ *nf* **la ~ du personnel** all the staff; **la ~ des dépenses** the total expenditure; **nous vous rembourserons en ~** we will refund you in full

totem /tɔtɛm/ *nm* (a) totem
(b) totem pole

toubib /tubib/ *nm* (fam) doctor, quack (colloq)

toucan /tukã/ *nm* toucan

touchant, ~e /tuʃã, ãt/ *adj* moving; touching

touche /tuʃ/ *nf* (a) (gen) button; (on keyboard) key; (on stringed instrument) fret
(b) (of paintbrush) stroke; (of paint) dash; (of artist) touch
(c) (Sport) sideline, touchline; **mettre qn sur la ~** (figurative) to push sb aside
(d) (in fencing) hit
(e) (in fishing) bite
■ **~ dièse** hash key; **~ étoile** star key

touche-à-tout /tuʃatu/ *adj inv* **être ~ to** be into everything; to be a jack of all trades

♂ **toucher¹** /tuʃe/ [1] ⟨1⟩ *vtr* (a) **~ (de la main)** to touch ⟨*object, surface, person*⟩; **~ du bois** (superstitiously) to touch wood; **~ le front de qn** to feel sb's forehead
(b) to be touching ⟨*wall, ceiling, bottom of sth*⟩; **~ le sol** to land
(c) to hit ⟨*opponent, car, kerb*⟩
(d) to touch, to move ⟨*person*⟩; **ça me touche beaucoup** I am very touched
(e) ⟨*event, crisis*⟩ to affect ⟨*person, country*⟩; ⟨*storm*⟩ to hit ⟨*region, city*⟩
(f) ⟨*country, house*⟩ to be next to
(g) ⟨*person*⟩ to get ⟨*money*⟩; to cash ⟨*cheque*⟩
⟨2⟩ **toucher à** *v+prep* (a) **~ à** to touch ⟨*object*⟩; **~ à tout** to be into everything; (figurative) to be a jack of all trades; **avec son air de ne pas y ~, c'est un malin** (fam) he looks as if butter wouldn't melt in his mouth, but he's a sly one
(b) **~ à** to concern ⟨*activity, issue*⟩
(c) **~ à** to infringe on ⟨*right, freedom*⟩
(d) **~ à** to get on to ⟨*problem*⟩
⟨3⟩ **se toucher** *v refl* (+ *v être*) ⟨*houses, gardens*⟩ to be next to each other

toucher² /tuʃe/ *nm* (a) **le ~** touch, the sense of touch
(b) (of pianist) touch

touche-touche: à touche-touche /atuʃtuʃ/ *phr* (fam) **être à ~** ⟨*cars*⟩ to be bumper to bumper; ⟨*people*⟩ to be on top of each other (colloq)

touffe /tuf/ *nf* (of hair, grass) tuft

touffu, ~e /tufy/ adj (a) ‹eyebrows, beard›
bushy; ‹vegetation› dense; ‹bush› thick; **au
poil** ~ with thick fur
(b) ‹text› dense

touiller /tuje/ [1] vtr (fam) to stir ‹sauce›

☞ **toujours** /tuʒuʀ/ adv (a) always; **comme** ~
as always; **de** ~ ‹friend› very old; ‹friendship›
long-standing; ~ **plus vite** faster and faster
(b) still; **il n'est** ~ **pas levé?** is he still not
up?
(c) anyway; **on peut** ~ **essayer** we can
always try; **c'est** ~ **ça de pris** or **de gagné**
that's something at least; ~ **est-il que** the
fact remains that

toupet /tupɛ/ nm (a) (fam) cheek (colloq),
nerve (colloq)
(b) (of hair) tuft; quiff (GB), forelock (US)

toupie /tupi/ nf top; **faire tourner une** ~ to
spin a top

☞ **tour¹** /tuʀ/ nm (a) (gen) turn; (around axis)
revolution; **donner un** ~ **de clé** to turn the
key; **faire un** ~ **de manège** to have a go on
the merry-go-round; **faire un** ~ **sur soi-même**
‹dancer› to spin around; ‹planet› to rotate;
fermer qch à double ~ to double-lock sth; **à**
~ **de bras** (fam) ‹invest, buy up› left, right and
centre (GB) (colloq), left and right (US) (colloq)
(b) **faire le** ~ **de qch** (gen) to go around sth;
to drive around sth; **la nouvelle a vite fait
le** ~ **du village** the news spread rapidly
through the village
(c) (of pond) edges; (of pipe, tree trunk)
circumference; (of head, hips) measurement;
(standard measurement) size
(d) walk, stroll; (on bicycle) ride; (in car) drive,
spin; **je suis allé faire un** ~ **à Paris** I went
to Paris
(e) look; **faire le** ~ **d'un problème** to have a
look at a problem; **faire le** ~ **de ses relations**
to go through one's acquaintances; **ce
roman, on en a vite fait le** ~ (fam) there's not
much to this novel
(f) (gen) turn; (in competition) round; **à qui le**
~? whose turn is it?; **chacun son** ~ each
one in his turn; **il perd plus souvent qu'à
son** ~ he loses more often than he would
like; he loses more often than he should; ~ **à**
~ by turns; in turn
(g) ~ **de scrutin** ballot, round of voting
(h) trick; **jouer un** ~ **à qn** to play a trick on
sb; **ça te jouera des** ~**s** it's going to get you
into trouble one of these days
(i) trick; ~ **de cartes** card trick; ~ **d'adresse**
feat of skill
(j) (in situation) turn; **donner un** ~ **nouveau à
qch** to give a new twist to sth
(k) (Tech) lathe
■ ~ **de chant** song recital; ~ **de garde** turn of
duty; ~ **de potier** potter's wheel; ~ **de rein(s)**
back strain

tour² /tuʀ/ nf (a) tower

(b) tower block (GB), high rise (US)
(c) (in chess) rook, castle
(d) siege-tower

tourbe /tuʀb/ nf peat

tourbière /tuʀbjɛʀ/ nf peat bog

tourbillon /tuʀbijɔ̃/ nm (a) whirlwind;
whirlpool; ~ **de poussière** whirl of dust
(b) (of memories) swirl; (of reforms) whirlwind

tourbillonner /tuʀbijɔne/ [1] vi ‹snow,
leaves› to swirl, to whirl; ‹dancers› to twirl

tourelle /tuʀɛl/ nf (of building, tank) turret;
(of submarine) conning tower

tourisme /tuʀism/ nm tourism
■ ~ **culturel** heritage tourism; ~ **vert** countryside holidays

touriste /tuʀist/ nmf tourist

touristique /tuʀistik/ adj ‹brochure,
menu, season› tourist; ‹influx› of tourists;
‹town, area› which attracts tourists

tourment /tuʀmɑ̃/ nm torment

tourmente /tuʀmɑ̃t/ nf (a) storm
(b) turmoil

tourmenté, ~e /tuʀmɑ̃te/ adj (a) ‹person,
face› tormented; ‹soul› tortured
(b) ‹era, life› turbulent
(c) ‹landscape› rugged

tourmenter /tuʀmɑ̃te/ [1] **1** vtr (a) to
worry
(b) to torment
(c) ‹creditors› to harass
2 se tourmenter v refl (+ v être) to
worry

tournage /tuʀnaʒ/ nm (a) shooting,
filming
(b) film set

tournant, ~e /tuʀnɑ̃, ɑ̃t/ **1** adj ‹seat›
swivel; ‹sprinkler› rotating; ‹door› revolving
(b) ‹presidency› rotating; ‹strike› staggered
2 nm (a) (in road) bend
(b) turning point
(c) turn; **au** ~ **du siècle** at the turn of the
century
(d) change of direction

tourné, ~e¹ /tuʀne/ adj (a) ~ **vers** ‹eyes,
look, person› turned toward(s); ‹activity,
policy› oriented toward(s); ~ **vers le
passé/l'avenir** backward-/forward-looking;
porte ~**e vers la mer** gate facing the sea
(b) **bien** ~ ‹compliment, letter› nicely
phrased
(c) ‹milk› off

tourne-disque, pl ~**s** /tuʀnədisk/ nm
record player

tournée² /tuʀne/ nf (a) (of postman) round
(b) (of team, singer) tour
(c) (fam) (of drinks) round

tournemain: en un tournemain
/ɑ̃nœ̃tuʀnəmɛ̃/ phr in no time

☞ **tourner** /tuʀne/ [1] **1** vtr (a) to turn; ~ **la
tête vers** to turn to look at; ~ **les yeux vers**
to look at

(b) to shoot ‹film›
(c) to get around ‹difficulty, law›
(d) to phrase ‹letter, criticism›
(e) ~ qn/qch en dérision to deride sb/sth
(f) ~ et retourner qch dans son esprit to
mull sth over
(g) to stir ‹sauce›; to toss ‹salad›
2 *vi* **(a)** (gen) to turn; ‹planet› to rotate;
‹rotating door› to revolve; ‹dancer› to spin;
faire ~ to turn; to spin; **faire** ~ **les tables** (in
spiritualism) to do table-turning
(b) ~ **autour de** (gen) to turn around; ‹planet›
to revolve around; ‹plane› to circle
(c) ~ **(en rond)** ‹person› to go round and
round; ‹driver› to drive round and round; ~
en rond (figurative) ‹discussion› to go round
in circles
(d) ~ **autour de** ‹sum of money› to be
(somewhere) in the region of
(e) ‹engine, factory› to run; ~ **rond** ‹engine›
to run smoothly; ‹business› to be doing well;
faire ~ to run ‹business, company›; **mon frère
ne tourne pas rond depuis quelque temps**
(fam) my brother has been acting strangely
for some time
(f) les choses ont bien/mal tourné pour lui
things turned out well/badly for him
(g) ‹director› to shoot; ~ **(dans un film)**
‹actor› to make a film (GB) *or* movie (US)
(h) ‹milk, meat› to go off
(i) ~ **autour de qn** to hang around sb
3 **se tourner** *v refl* (+ *v être*) **(a) se** ~
vers qn/qch to turn to sb/sth
(b) se ~ **vers qn/qch** to turn toward(s) sb/
sth
(c) to turn around
tournesol /tuʀnəsɔl/ *nm* sunflower
tournevis /tuʀnəvis/ *nm inv* screwdriver
tourniquet /tuʀnikɛ/ *nm* **(a)** turnstile
(b) revolving stand
(c) sprinkler
tournoi /tuʀnwɑ/ *nm* tournament
tournoyer /tuʀnwaje/ [23] *vi* **(a)** ‹leaves,
papers› to swirl around; ‹vultures› to wheel;
‹flies› to fly around in circles
(b) ‹dancers› to whirl; **faire** ~ to twirl ‹stick,
skirt›
tournure /tuʀnyʀ/ *nf* **(a)** turn; **prendre** ~
‹plan› to take shape
(b) ~ **(de phrase)** turn of phrase
■ ~ **d'esprit** frame of mind
tourte /tuʀt/ *nf* pie; ~ **à la viande** meat pie
tourteau, *pl* ~**x** /tuʀto/ *nm* (Culin, Zool)
crab
tourtereau, *pl* ~**x** /tuʀtəʀo/ **1** *nm* (Zool)
young turtle dove
2 **tourtereaux** *nm pl* (humorous)
lovebirds
tourterelle /tuʀtəʀɛl/ *nf* turtle dove
tous ▸ TOUT
Toussaint /tusɛ̃/ *nf* **la** ~ All Saints' Day
tousser /tuse/ [1] *vi* ‹person› to cough
toussotement /tusɔtmɑ̃/ *nm* cough;
splutter

toussoter /tusɔte/ [1] *vi* ‹person› to have a
slight cough; ‹engine› to splutter
⚡ **tout** /tu/, ~**e** /tut/, *mpl* **tous** /tu/ *adj*, /tus/
pron, *fpl* **toutes** /tut/

──────────

■ **Note** You will find translations for expressions
such as *à tout hasard*, *tout compte fait*, *tout neuf*
etc, at the entries HASARD, COMPTE, NEUF etc.

──────────

1 *pron* **(a) tout** everything; all; anything; ~
est prétexte à querelle(s) any pretext will do
to start a quarrel; ~ **n'est pas perdu** all is
not lost; **en** ~ in all; in every respect; **en** ~
et pour ~ all told; ~ **bien compté** *or* **pesé** *or*
considéré all in all
(b) tous /tus/, **toutes** all; all of them/you/
you; **tous ensemble** all together; **est-ce que
ça conviendra à tous?** will it suit everybody?
2 *adj* **(a) bois** ~ **ton lait** drink all your
milk; ~ **le reste** everything else; ~ **le monde**
everybody; **manger** ~ **un pain** to eat a whole
loaf; **il a plu** ~**e la journée** it rained all day
(long)
(b) c'est ~ **un travail** it's quite a job
(c) all; everything; anything; ~ **ce qui
compte** all that matters; ~ **ce qu'il dit n'est
pas vrai** not all of what he says is true; **être**
~ **ce qu'il y a de plus serviable** to be most
obliging
(d) any; **à** ~ **moment** at any time;
constantly; ~ **autre que lui/toi aurait
abandonné** anybody else would have given
up
(e) en ~**e franchise** in all honesty; **il aurait** ~
intérêt à placer cet argent it would be in his
best interests to invest this money
(f) il a souri pour ~**e réponse** his only reply
was a smile
(g) tous, toutes all, every; **j'ai** ~**es les
raisons de me plaindre** I have every reason
to complain; **nous irons tous les deux** we'll
both go; **je les prends tous les trois** I'm
taking all three
(h) tous/toutes les every; **tous les deux
jours** every other day; **tous les combien?**
how often?
3 *adv* **(a)** very, quite; all; **être** ~ **étonné** to
be very surprised; ~ **seul** all by oneself; ~
en haut right at the top; **la colline est** ~ **en
fleurs** the hill is a mass of flowers; **veste** ~
cuir all leather jacket
(b) ~ **prêt** ready-made
(c) while; although; **il lisait** ~ **en marchant**
he was reading as he walked; **elle le
défendait** ~ **en le sachant coupable** she
defended him although she knew he was
guilty
(d) ~ **malin/roi qu'il est, il...** he may be
clever/a king, but he...
4 **du tout** *phr* **(pas) du** ~ not at all
5 *nm* (*pl* ~**s**) whole; **le** ~ the (whole) lot; the
main thing; **former un** ~ to make up *or* form
a whole
6 **Tout-** (*combining form*) **le Tout-Paris/
-Londres** the Paris/London smart set
■ ~ **à coup** suddenly; ~ **d'un coup** suddenly; ⋯⟶

t

all at once; ~ **à fait** quite, absolutely; ~ **à l'heure** in a moment; a little while ago, just now; **à ~ à l'heure!** see you later!; ~ **de même** all the same, even so; ~ **de même!** really!; ~ **de suite** at once

IDIOM être ~ yeux ~ oreilles to be very attentive

tout-à-l'égout /tutalegu/ *nm inv* main drainage, main sewer

◆ **toutefois** /tutfwa/ *adv* however

toute-puissance /tutpɥisãs/ *nf* omnipotence; supremacy

toutou /tutu/ *nm* (fam) doggie (colloq), dog

tout-petit, *pl* ~**s** /tup(ə)ti/ *nm* **(a)** baby
(b) toddler

Tout-Puissant /tupɥisã/ *nm* **le ~** the Almighty, God Almighty

tout-venant /tuv(ə)nã/ *nm inv* all and sundry

toux /tu/ *nf inv* cough

toxicité /tɔksisite/ *nf* toxicity

toxicodépendance /tɔksikodepãdãs/ *nf* drug dependency

toxicologie /tɔksikɔlɔʒi/ *nf* toxicology

toxicomane /tɔksikɔman/ *nmf* drug addict

toxicomanie /tɔksikɔmani/ *nf* drug addiction

toxine /tɔksin/ *nf* toxin

toxique /tɔksik/ *adj* toxic, poisonous

TP /tepe/ *nm pl: abbr* ▶ TRAVAIL

trac /tʀak/ *nm* (fam) (of actor) stage fright; (before exam, conference) nerves; **avoir le ~** (gen) to feel nervous; ‹actor, performer› to have stage fright

traçage /tʀasaʒ/ *nm* **(a)** marking out; laying-out
(b) (Comput) tracing

tracas /tʀaka/ *nm inv* **(a)** trouble
(b) problems; ~ **quotidiens** everyday problems
(c) worries; **se faire du ~ pour qn/qch** to worry about sb/sth

tracasser /tʀakase/ [1] **1** *vtr* to bother ‹person›
2 se tracasser *v refl* (+ *v être*) to worry

tracasserie /tʀakasʀi/ *nf* **(a)** hassle (colloq)
(b) harassment

◆ **trace** /tʀas/ *nf* **(a)** trail; **suivre qn à la ~** to track sb; (figurative) to follow sb's trail
(b) ~**s** tracks; ~**s d'ours/de ski** bear's/ski tracks; ~**s de pas** footprints; **sur les ~s de Van Gogh** in the footsteps of Van Gogh
(c) (of burn) mark; (of wound) scar; (of paint) mark; (of blood, dampness) trace; ~**s de doigts** fingermarks; ~**s de coups** bruises
(d) (of activity) sign; (of presence) trace; **des ~s d'effraction** signs of a break-in

◆ indicates a very frequent word

tracé /tʀase/ *nm* **(a)** (of town) layout; (of road) plan
(b) (of road, railway) route; (of river) course; (of border, coast) line
(c) (on graph, in sketch) line

tracer /tʀase/ [12] *vtr* **(a)** to draw ‹line, map, portrait›; (on graph) to plot ‹curve›; to write ‹word, letters›
(b) **à 15 ans son avenir était déjà tout tracé** at 15, his/her future was already mapped out
(c) ~ **le chemin à qn** (figurative) to show sb the way

trachée /tʀaʃe/ *nf* windpipe

trachée-artère, *pl* **trachées-artères** /tʀaʃeaʀtɛʀ/ *nf* windpipe, trachea

trachéite /tʀakeit/ *nf* tracheitis

tract /tʀakt/ *nm* pamphlet, tract

tractation /tʀaktasjɔ̃/ *nf* negotiation

tracter /tʀakte/ [1] *vtr* ‹vehicle› to tow ‹trailer›; ‹cable› to pull up ‹cable car›

tracteur /tʀaktœʀ/ *nm* tractor

traction /tʀaksjɔ̃/ *nf* **(a)** traction; **à ~ mécanique** mechanically drawn
(b) (Tech) tension
■ ~ **arrière** (Aut) rear-wheel drive; ~ **avant** (Aut) front-wheel drive

◆ **tradition** /tʀadisjɔ̃/ *nf* **(a)** tradition
(b) legend; **la ~ veut que...** legend has it that...

traditionaliste /tʀadisjɔnalist/ *adj, nmf* traditionalist

◆ **traditionnel, -elle** /tʀadisjɔnɛl/ *adj* traditional

traducteur, -trice /tʀadyktœʀ, tʀis/ *nm,f* translator

◆ **traduction** /tʀadyksjɔ̃/ *nf* translation; **faire des ~s** to do translation work

◆ **traduire** /tʀadɥiʀ/ [69] **1** *vtr* **(a)** to translate
(b) ‹word, artist, book› to convey; ‹rebellion, violence› to be the expression of; ‹price rise› to be the result of
(c) (Law) ~ **qn en justice** to bring sb to justice
2 se traduire *v refl* (+ *v être*) **(a)** ‹joy, fear› to show
(b) ‹crisis, instability› to result; **se ~ par un échec** to result in failure

traduisible /tʀadɥizibl/ *adj* translatable

trafic /tʀafik/ *nm* **(a)** traffic; ~ **d'armes** arms dealing; ~ **de drogue** drug trafficking
(b) ~ **(routier)** (road) traffic; ~ **aérien** air traffic

trafiquant, ~**e** /tʀafikã, ãt/ *nm,f* trafficker, dealer; ~ **de drogue** drugs dealer

trafiquer /tʀafike/ [1] *vtr* **(a)** to fiddle with ‹car, meter›
(b) (fam) **je me demande ce qu'il trafique** I wonder what he's up to

tragédie /tʀaʒedi/ *nf* tragedy

tragédien, **-ienne** /tʀaʒedjɛ̃, ɛn/ *nm,f*
tragic actor

tragique /tʀaʒik/ **1** *adj* tragic
2 *nm* tragedy

trahir /tʀaiʀ/ [3] **1** *vtr* **(a)** to betray; to
break ‹promise›
(b) ‹writing, words› to betray ‹thoughts›
(c) ‹translator, words› to misrepresent
(d) ‹strength, legs› to fail ‹person›
2 **se trahir** *v refl* (+ *v être*) to give oneself
away, to betray oneself

trahison /tʀaizɔ̃/ *nf* **(a)** treachery; ∼ **de**
qn/qch betrayal of sb/sth
(b) treason

✣ **train** /tʀɛ̃/ **1** *nm* **(a)** train; **par le** *or* **en** ∼
‹travel› by train
(b) (convoy) train; ∼ **de péniches** train of
barges
(c) series (**de** of)
(d) pace; **aller bon** ∼ to walk briskly;
(figurative) ‹rumours› to be flying around;
‹sales› to be going well; ‹conversation› to
flow easily; **au** ∼ **où vont les choses** (at) the
rate things are going; **à fond de** ∼ (fam) at
top speed
(e) (Zool) ∼ **de derrière** hindquarters; ∼ **de**
devant forequarter
2 **en train** *phr* **(a)** **être en** ∼ to be full of
energy
(b) **mettre en** ∼ to get [sth] started ‹process›
(c) **être en** ∼ **de faire** to be (busy) doing;
j'étais en ∼ **de dormir** I was sleeping
■ ∼ **d'atterrissage** undercarriage; ∼ **électrique**
(toy) train set; ∼ **de vie** lifestyle

traînant, ∼**e** /tʀɛnɑ̃, ɑ̃t/ *adj* shuffling; **voix**
∼**e** drawl

traînard, ∼**e** /tʀɛnaʀ, aʀd/ *nm,f* (fam)
slowcoach, slowpoke; straggler

traînasser /tʀɛnase/ [1] *vi* (fam) **(a)** to loaf
about (colloq)
(b) to take ages

traîne /tʀɛn/ *nf* **(a)** (of dress) train
(b) seine (net)
IDIOM être à la ∼ to lag behind

traîneau, *pl* ∼**x** /tʀɛno/ *nm* **(a)** sleigh
(b) (of vacuum cleaner) cylinder

traînée /tʀɛne/ *nf* **(a)** streak; ∼ **de sang**
streak of blood
(b) trail

traîner /tʀɛne/ [1] **1** *vtr* **(a)** to drag [sb/
sth] (along) ‹person, suitcase›; to drag [sth]
across the floor ‹chair›
(b) (fam) to lug [sth] around (colloq) ‹object›; to
drag [sth] around ‹object›
(c) ∼ **qn chez le médecin** to drag sb off to
the doctor's
(d) **il traîne un rhume depuis deux semaines**
for two weeks now he's had a cold that he
can't shake off; ∼ **les pieds** to drag one's feet
2 *vi* **(a)** ∼ **dans les rues** to hang around on
the streets; **j'ai traîné au lit** I slept in
(b) to take forever; **ne traîne pas, on doit**
terminer à 4 heures get a move on (colloq),

we've got to finish at four
(c) to dawdle
(d) ‹building work, illness› to drag on
(e) ∼ **par terre** ‹skirt› to trail on the ground;
‹curtains› to trail on the floor
(f) ∼ **derrière qch** to be trailing behind sth
(g) ‹clothes, toys› to be lying about *or* around;
laisser ∼ **qch** to leave sth lying about *or*
around
3 **se traîner** *v refl* (+ *v être*) **(a)** ‹injured
person› **se** ∼ **par terre** to drag oneself along
the ground
(b) **se** ∼ **jusqu'à la cuisine** to drag oneself
through to the kitchen
(c) ‹train› to crawl along; ‹negotiations› to
drag on
IDIOMS ∼ **la jambe** *or* **la patte** (fam) to limp;
∼ **ses guêtres** (fam) *or* **ses bottes** (fam) to
knock around (colloq)

train(-)train /tʀɛ̃tʀɛ̃/ *nm inv* (derogatory)
(fam) daily routine

traire /tʀɛʀ/ [58] *vtr* to milk ‹cow, goat›

trait¹, ∼**e** /tʀɛ, ɛt/ ▸ **TRAIRE**

✣ **trait**² /tʀɛ/ **1** *nm* **(a)** line; stroke; **souligner**
un mot d'un ∼ **rouge** to underline a word
in red; ∼ **pour** ∼ ‹replica› line for line;
‹reproduce› line by line
(b) (of style, book) feature; (of person) trait;
∼ **caractéristique** characteristic; ∼ **de**
caractère trait, characteristic
(c) ∼ **d'humour** *or* **d'esprit** witticism; ∼ **de**
génie stroke of genius
(d) **avoir** ∼ **à** to relate to
(e) **d'un (seul)** ∼ (gen) in one go
(f) **de** ∼ ‹animal› draught (GB), draft (US)
2 **traits** *nm pl* features
■ ∼ **d'union** hyphen; (figurative) link
IDIOM tirer un ∼ **sur qch** to put sth firmly
behind one

traitant /tʀɛtɑ̃/ *adj m* **médecin** ∼ doctor,
GP

✣ **traite** /tʀɛt/ **1** *nf* **(a)** (Econ) draft, bill
(b) **la** ∼ **des Blanches** the white slave trade
(c) milking; **la** ∼ **des vaches** milking cows
2 **d'une traite** *phr* **d'une (seule)** ∼
‹recite› in one breath; ‹drink› in one go

traité /tʀɛte/ *nm* **(a)** (Law) treaty; ∼
commercial trade agreement
(b) treatise

✣ **traitement** /tʀɛtmɑ̃/ *nm* **(a)** (Med)
treatment
(b) salary
(c) handling; **il faut accélérer le** ∼ **des**
demandes applications must be dealt with
more quickly
(d) (of data) processing
(e) (Tech) (of water, waste) processing; (of wood)
treatment
■ ∼ **de faveur** preferential treatment; ∼ **de**
texte word-processing (package)

✣ **traiter** /tʀɛte/ [1] **1** *vtr* **(a)** to treat ‹person,
animal, object›
(b) (Med) to treat ‹sick person, infection›   ⋯⋯⟶

(c) to deal with ‹question, problem›
(d) to treat ‹wood, textile›; to process ‹waste›
(e) to process ‹data›
(f) ~ qn de qch to call sb sth
2 **traiter de** v+prep to deal with
3 vi to negotiate, to do (GB) or make a deal
4 **se traiter** v refl (+ v être) ils se sont traités de tous les noms they called each other all sorts of names

traiteur /tʀɛtœʀ/ nm caterer

traître, traîtresse /tʀɛtʀ, tʀɛtʀɛs/ nm,f traitor; en ~ by surprise

traîtrise /tʀɛtʀiz/ nf **(a)** act of treachery
(b) (of person) treachery

trajectoire /tʀaʒɛktwaʀ/ nf **(a)** (of bullet, missile) trajectory
(b) (of planet, satellite) path
(c) career

trajet /tʀaʒɛ/ nm **(a)** journey, trip; (by sea) crossing
(b) route

trame /tʀam/ nf **(a)** (of fabric) weft
(b) (of story) framework

tramer: se tramer /tʀame/ [1] v refl (+ v être) ‹plot› to be hatched

trampoline /tʀɑ̃pɔlin/ nm trampoline

tramway /tʀamwɛ/ nm **(a)** tram (GB), streetcar (US)
(b) tramway (GB), streetcar line (US)

tranchant, ~e /tʀɑ̃ʃɑ̃, ɑ̃t/ **1** adj
(a) sharp
(b) ‹person› forthright; ‹tone› curt
2 nm (of blade) sharp edge, cutting edge

tranche /tʀɑ̃ʃ/ nf **(a)** (of bread, meat, cheese) slice; (of lard, bacon) rasher
(b) (of operation) phase; (in timetable) period, time slot
(c) (of book, coin) edge
■ ~ d'âge age bracket

tranché, ~e¹ /tʀɑ̃ʃe/ **1** pp ▶ TRANCHER
2 pp adj ‹salmon› pre-sliced
3 adj **(a)** ‹opinion, position, reply› cut-and-dried; ‹inequalities› marked
(b) ‹colours› bold

tranchée² /tʀɑ̃ʃe/ nf **(a)** (Mil) trench
(b) (of road) cutting

trancher /tʀɑ̃ʃe/ [1] **1** vtr to slice, to cut ‹bread, meat›; to cut through ‹rope›; to cut [sth] off ‹head›; to slit ‹throat›
2 vi **(a)** ‹colour, outline› to stand out
(b) to come to a decision

✔ **tranquille** /tʀɑ̃kil/ adj **(a)** quiet; calm; peaceful; tiens-toi ~! keep still!; be quiet!; il s'est tenu ~ pendant quelques mois he behaved himself for a few months
(b) être ~ to be or feel easy in one's mind; sa mère n'est pas ~ quand il sort his mother worries when he goes out
(c) avoir la conscience ~ to have a clear conscience

✔ indicates a very frequent word

tranquillement /tʀɑ̃kilmɑ̃/ adv **(a)** elle dort ~ she's sleeping peacefully; j'aimerais pouvoir travailler ~ I wish I could work in peace
(b) quietly
(c) nous avons marché ~ we walked along at a leisurely pace
(d) nous étions ~ en train de discuter we were chatting away happily

tranquillisant, ~e /tʀɑ̃kiliz ɑ̃, ɑ̃t/ **1** adj reassuring, comforting
2 nm tranquillizer (GB)

tranquilliser /tʀɑ̃kilize/ [1] vtr to reassure

tranquillité /tʀɑ̃kilite/ nf **(a)** calmness; calm
(b) ~ (d'esprit) peace of mind

transaction /tʀɑ̃zaksjɔ̃/ nf transaction

transalpin, ~e /tʀɑ̃zalpɛ̃, in/ adj
(a) transalpine
(b) Italian

transat¹ /tʀɑ̃zat/ nm (fam) **(a)** deckchair
(b) baby chair

transat² /tʀɑ̃zat/ nf (Sport) transatlantic race

transatlantique /tʀɑ̃zatlɑ̃tik/ adj transatlantic

transborder /tʀɑ̃sbɔʀde/ [1] vtr to transship ‹goods›; to transfer ‹passengers›

transbordeur /tʀɑ̃sbɔʀdœʀ/ nm
(a) transporter bridge
(b) traverser
(c) ferry

transcendant, ~e /tʀɑ̃sɑ̃dɑ̃, ɑ̃t/ adj
(a) (in philosophy) transcendent
(b) (fam) wonderful

transcender /tʀɑ̃sɑ̃de/ [1] vtr to transcend

transcription /tʀɑ̃skʀipsjɔ̃/ nf transcription

transcrire /tʀɑ̃skʀiʀ/ [67] vtr to transcribe

transe /tʀɑ̃s/ nf trance

transférer /tʀɑ̃sfeʀe/ [14] vtr **(a)** (gen) to transfer; to relocate ‹offices›
(b) (Law) to transfer, to convey ‹property›

transfert /tʀɑ̃sfɛʀ/ nm **(a)** (of person, data, money, property) transfer; (of offices) relocation
(b) (psychological) transference

transfigurer /tʀɑ̃sfigyʀe/ [1] vtr to transform

transformable /tʀɑ̃sfɔʀmabl/ adj convertible

transformateur /tʀɑ̃sfɔʀmatœʀ/ nm transformer

transformation /tʀɑ̃sfɔʀmasjɔ̃/ nf transformation; (of mineral, energy) conversion

✔ **transformer** /tʀɑ̃sfɔʀme/ [1] **1** vtr **(a)** to alter ‹garment, façade›; to change ‹person, landscape›
(b) ~ qn/qch en (gen) to turn sb/sth into; to transform sb/sth into; ~ un garage en

bureau to convert a garage into an office
2 **se transformer** *v refl* (+ *v être*)
(a) ‹person› to transform oneself; to be transformed
(b) se ∼ en ‹embryo, larva, bud› to turn into
transfrontalier, -ière /tʀɑ̃sfʀɔ̃talje, ɛʀ/ *adj* cross-border
transfuge /tʀɑ̃sfyʒ/ **1** *nmf* defector
2 *nm* (Mil) deserter
transfusé, ∼e /tʀɑ̃sfyze/ **1** *pp*
▶ TRANSFUSER
2 *pp adj* ‹blood› transfused; ‹person› who has been given a blood transfusion
transfuser /tʀɑ̃sfyze/ [1] *vtr* to give a blood transfusion to
transfusion /tʀɑ̃sfyzjɔ̃/ *nf* transfusion
transgresser /tʀɑ̃sgʀɛse/ [1] *vtr* to break ‹law, rule, taboo›; to defy ‹ban›
transhumance /tʀɑ̃zymɑ̃s/ *nf* transhumance, seasonal migration of livestock to summer pastures
transi, ∼e /tʀɑ̃zi/ **1** *pp* ▶ TRANSIR
2 *pp adj* chilled; ∼ de peur paralysed (GB) with fear; un amoureux ∼ a bashful lover
transiger /tʀɑ̃ziʒe/ [13] *vi* to compromise
transir /tʀɑ̃ziʀ/ [3] *vtr* to chill; to paralyse (GB)
transistor /tʀɑ̃zistɔʀ/ *nm* transistor
transit /tʀɑ̃zit/ *nm* transit; en ∼ in transit
transitaire **1** *adj* transit; pays ∼ transit point
2 *nmf* forwarding agent
transiter /tʀɑ̃zite/ [1] *vi* ∼ par ‹goods, passengers› to pass through, to go via
transitif, -ive /tʀɑ̃zitif, iv/ *adj* transitive
transition /tʀɑ̃zisjɔ̃/ *nf* transition
transitoire /tʀɑ̃zitwaʀ/ *adj* transitional
translucide /tʀɑ̃slysid/ *adj* translucent
transmanche /tʀɑ̃smɑ̃ʃ/ *adj inv* cross-Channel
transmetteur /tʀɑ̃smɛtœʀ/ *nm* transmitter
♂ **transmettre** /tʀɑ̃smɛtʀ/ [60] **1** *vtr* **(a)** to pass [sth] on, to convey ‹information, order, news›; to pass [sth] on ‹story, knowledge›; to pass [sth] down ‹culture, fortune›; transmets-leur mes félicitations give them my congratulations
(b) to transmit ‹image, signal, data›
(c) to broadcast ‹news, programme›
(d) to hand [sth] on ‹property, land›; to hand over ‹power›
(e) (Med) to transmit ‹virus, illness›
2 **se transmettre** *v refl* (+ *v être*) **(a)** to pass [sth] on to each other ‹message, data›
(b) ‹signals, data› to be transmitted
(c) ‹tradition, culture› to be handed down; ‹story› to be passed on
(d) ‹virus, illness› to be transmitted
transmissible /tʀɑ̃smisibl/ *adj* transmissible, transmittable

transmission /tʀɑ̃smisjɔ̃/ *nf*
(a) transmission, passing on; la ∼ des connaissances the communication of knowledge
(b) (of data, signals) transmission
(c) (of programme) broadcasting
(d) (of tradition, secret, culture) handing down; (of fortune, property) transfer
(e) (Aut, Med) transmission
■ ∼ de pensées thought transference
transparaître /tʀɑ̃spaʀɛtʀ/ [73] *vi* to show through; laisser ∼ ‹face, words› to betray; ‹person› to let [sth] show ‹emotions›
transparence /tʀɑ̃spaʀɑ̃s/ *nf* **(a)** (of glass, fabric) transparency; (of water) clearness; on voyait ses jambes en ∼ (à travers sa jupe) you could see her legs through her skirt
(b) (of skin) translucency; (of colour) limpidity
(c) (of person) transparency; (of policy) openness
transparent, ∼e /tʀɑ̃spaʀɑ̃, ɑ̃t/ **1** *adj*
(a) transparent; ‹water› clear
(b) ‹complexion› translucent
(c) ‹person› transparent
2 *nm* (for overhead projector) transparency
transpercer /tʀɑ̃spɛʀse/ [12] *vtr*
(a) ‹sword, arrow› to pierce ‹body›; ‹bullet› to go through
(b) ‹rain› to go through
(c) ‹pain› to shoot through
transpiration /tʀɑ̃spiʀasjɔ̃/ *nf*
(a) sweating, perspiration
(b) sweat
(c) (Bot) transpiration
transpirer /tʀɑ̃spiʀe/ [1] *vi* **(a)** to sweat, to perspire
(b) ‹secret› to leak out
transplantation /tʀɑ̃splɑ̃tasjɔ̃/ *nf*
(a) transplant; ∼ d'organes organ transplants
(b) transplantation
transplanter /tʀɑ̃splɑ̃te/ [1] *vtr* to transplant
♂ **transport** /tʀɑ̃spɔʀ/ **1** *nm* transport, transportation (US)
2 **transports** *nm pl* ∼s en commun public transport *or* transportation (US)
transportable /tʀɑ̃spɔʀtabl/ *adj* transportable; il n'est pas ∼ (injured person) he cannot be moved
transporter /tʀɑ̃spɔʀte/ [1] *vtr* **(a)** to carry ‹person, object›; to transport ‹passengers, goods›; être transporté à l'hôpital to be taken to hospital
(b) to carry ‹pollen, virus, disease›
(c) être transporté dans un monde féerique to be transported to a magical world
transporteur /tʀɑ̃spɔʀtœʀ/ *nm* carrier; ∼ aérien air carrier; ∼ routier road haulier (GB), road haulage contractor (GB), trucking company (US)
transposer /tʀɑ̃spoze/ [1] *vtr* to transpose

transsexuel, -elle /tʀɑ̃sɛksɥɛl/ *adj, nm,f* transsexual

transsibérien, -ienne [1] *adj* trans-Siberian
[2] *nm* **le Transsibérien** the Trans-Siberian Railway

transvaser /tʀɑ̃svaze/ [1] *vtr* to decant ‹liquid›

transversal, ~e, *mpl* **-aux** /tʀɑ̃svɛʀsal, o/ *adj* transverse; **rue ~e** side street

trapèze /tʀapɛz/ *nm* **(a)** (Sport) trapeze
(b) (in geometry) trapezium (GB), trapezoid (US)

trapéziste /tʀapezist/ *nmf* trapeze artist

trappe /tʀap/ *nf* (gen) trap door

trappeur /tʀapœʀ/ *nm* trapper

trapu, ~e /tʀapy/ *adj* ‹man, outline› stocky

traquenard /tʀaknaʀ/ *nm* trap

traquer /tʀake/ [1] *vtr* (gen) to track down; ‹photographer› to hound ‹film star›

traumatisant, ~e /tʀomatizɑ̃, ɑ̃t/ *adj* traumatic

traumatiser /tʀomatize/ [1] *vtr* to traumatize

traumatisme /tʀomatism/ *nm* **(a)** (Med) traumatism
(b) (psychological) trauma

✐ **travail,** *pl* **-aux** /tʀavaj, o/ [1] *nm* **(a)** (gen) work; job; **se mettre au ~** to get down to work; **avoir du ~** to have work to do; **les gros travaux** the heavy work; **(félicitations) c'est du beau ~!** you've done a great job on that!; **qu'est-ce que c'est que ce ~?** what do you call this?; **ne me téléphone pas à mon ~** don't call me at work; **chercher du/un ~** to look for work/a job; **être sans ~** to be out of work; **le ~ temporaire** temporary work; **le ~ de nuit** nightwork
(b) (Econ) labour (GB); **entrer dans le monde du ~** to enter the world of work
(c) le ~ musculaire muscular effort
(d) le ~ de working with *or* in ‹metal, wood, stone›
(e) workmanship; **un ~ superbe** a superb piece of workmanship
(f) (of water, erosion) action
(g) (of wine) fermentation; (of wood) warping
(h) (of woman in childbirth) labour (GB)
[2] **travaux** *nm pl* **(a)** (gen) work; (on road) roadworks (GB), roadwork (US); **faire faire des travaux dans sa maison** to have work done in one's house
(b) (of researcher) work
(c) (of commission) deliberations
(d) les travaux agricoles agricultural work; **travaux de couture** needlework
■ **~ à la chaîne** assembly-line work; **~ à domicile** working at *or* from home; **~ au noir** (gen) *work for which no earnings are declared*; (holding two jobs) moonlighting; **travaux manuels** handicrafts; **travaux pratiques, TP**

✐ indicates a very frequent word

practical work; lab work; **travaux publics, TP** civil engineering

travaillé, ~e /tʀavaje/ [1] [1] *pp* ▶ TRAVAILLER
[2] *pp adj* ‹jewel› finely-worked; ‹carving› elaborate; ‹gold, silver› wrought; ‹style› polished

✐ **travailler** /tʀavaje/ [1] [1] *vtr* **(a)** to work on ‹style, school subject, voice, muscles›; to practise (GB) ‹sport, instrument›
(b) to work ‹wood, metal›; (Culin) to knead ‹dough›; to cultivate ‹land›
(c) ~ qn ‹idea, affair› to be on sb's mind; ‹jealousy, pain› to plague sb; **un doute me travaillait** I had a nagging doubt
[2] **travailler à** *v+prep* to work on ‹project, essay›; to work toward(s) ‹objective›
[3] *vi* **(a)** ‹person, machine, muscles› to work; **faire ~ son cerveau** to apply one's mind; **~ en équipes** to work shifts
(b) ‹shop, hotel, shopkeeper› to do business; **~ à perte** ‹company, business› to run at a loss
(c) nous voulons la paix et c'est dans ce sens que nous travaillons we want peace and we are working toward(s) it
(d) ‹athlete› to train; ‹musician› to practise (GB)
(e) ‹wood› to warp

✐ **travailleur, -euse** /tʀavajœʀ, øz/ [1] *adj*
(a) ‹pupil› hardworking
(b) ‹classes› working
[2] *nm,f* worker

travailliste /tʀavajist/ [1] *adj* Labour
[2] *nmf* Labour MP

travée /tʀave/ *nf* **(a)** row
(b) (Tech) span

travelling /tʀavliŋ/ *nm* (in cinema) tracking; tracking shot

✐ **travers** /tʀavɛʀ/ [1] *nm inv* **(a)** foible, quirk
(b) (Naut) beam
(c) (Culin) **~ de porc** sparerib
[2] **à travers** *phr* **(a)** ‹see, look› through
(b) ‹walk› across; **voyager à ~ le monde** to travel all over the world
(c) voyager à ~ le temps to travel through time
(d) through; **à ~ ces informations** through this information
[3] **au travers** *phr* through; **passer au ~ de** (figurative) to escape ‹inspection›
[4] **de travers** *phr* **(a)** askew; **ta veste est boutonnée de ~** your jacket is buttoned up wrongly; **il a le nez de ~** he has a twisted nose; **j'ai avalé de ~** it went down the wrong way; **regarder qn de ~** to give sb filthy looks
(b) wrong; **comprendre de ~** to misunderstand
[5] **en travers** *phr* across; **un bus était en ~ de la route** a bus was stuck across the road; **se mettre en ~ de la route** ‹people› to stand in the middle of the road; **rester en ~ de la gorge de qn** (fam) to be hard to swallow

traverse /tʀavɛʀs/ *nf* (on railway line) sleeper (GB), tie (US)

traversée /tʀavɛʀse/ *nf* **(a)** crossing; **la ∼ du désert** crossing the desert; (figurative) (of company) a difficult period
(b) (of city) **évitez la ∼ de Paris** avoid going through Paris

⚡ **traverser** /tʀavɛʀse/ [1] *vtr* **(a)** to cross ⟨road, bridge, border, town, ocean, room⟩; to go through ⟨town, forest, tunnel⟩; to make one's way through ⟨group, crowd⟩; **il traversa le jardin en courant** he ran across the garden (GB) *or* yard (US)
(b) ⟨river⟩ to run through ⟨region⟩; ⟨road⟩ to go through ⟨region⟩; ⟨bridge, river⟩ to cross ⟨railway line, town⟩
(c) ⟨rain⟩ to soak through ⟨clothes⟩; **la balle lui a traversé le bras** the bullet went right through his/her arm
(d) to go through ⟨crisis⟩; to live through ⟨war⟩
(e) ∼ **l'esprit de qn** to cross sb's mind

traversin /tʀavɛʀsɛ̃/ *nm* bolster

travesti, ∼**e** /tʀavɛsti/ 1 *pp* ▶ TRAVESTIR
2 *pp adj* in disguise; **rôle** ∼ role played by a member of the opposite sex
3 *nm* **(a)** transvestite
(b) (actor) actor playing a female role; (in cabaret) drag artist (colloq)

travestir /tʀavɛstiʀ/ |3| 1 *vtr* **(a)** to dress [sb] up ⟨person⟩
(b) to distort ⟨truth⟩
2 **se travestir** *v refl* (+ *v être*) **(a)** to dress up
(b) to cross-dress

trébucher /tʀebyʃe/ [1] *vi* to stumble

trèfle /tʀɛfl/ *nm* **(a)** clover
(b) (Games) (card) club; (suit) clubs
(c) shamrock

tréfonds /tʀefɔ̃/ *nm inv* **le** ∼ **de** the very depths of

treillage /tʀɛjaʒ/ *nm* **(a)** trellis
(b) lattice fence

treille /tʀɛj/ *nf* **(a)** (vine) arbour (GB)
(b) climbing vine

treillis /tʀɛji/ *nm inv* **(a)** (Mil) fatigues
(b) canvas
(c) trellis; ∼ **métallique** wire grille

treize /tʀɛz/ *adj inv, pron, nm inv* thirteen

treizième /tʀɛzjɛm/ *adj* thirteenth

tréma /tʀema/ *nm* diaeresis; **i** ∼ i diaeresis

tremblant, ∼**e** /tʀɑ̃blɑ̃, ɑ̃t/ *adj* **(a)** ⟨person, hands⟩ shaking
(b) ⟨voice⟩ trembling
(c) ⟨image, light⟩ flickering; ⟨sound⟩ tremulous

tremble /tʀɑ̃bl/ *nm* aspen

tremblement /tʀɑ̃bləmɑ̃/ *nm* **(a)** (of person, hands) shaking, trembling; (of lips) trembling
(b) (of voice) trembling
(c) (of leaves) quivering
■ ∼ **de terre** earthquake

trembler /tʀɑ̃ble/ [1] *vi* **(a)** ⟨person, legs⟩ to shake, to tremble
(b) ⟨voice⟩ to tremble; ⟨sound, note⟩ to waver
(c) ⟨building, floor⟩ to shake
(d) (be afraid) to tremble; ∼ **pour qn** to fear for sb
(e) ⟨light, image⟩ to flicker
(f) ⟨leaves⟩ to quiver

trembloter /tʀɑ̃blɔte/ [1] *vi* **(a)** ⟨person, hands⟩ to tremble slightly
(b) ⟨voice⟩ to tremble

trémolo /tʀemɔlo/ *nm* **(a)** (of voice) quaver
(b) (of instrument) tremolo

trémousser: se trémousser /tʀemuse/ [1] *v refl* (+ *v être*) **(a)** to fidget
(b) to wiggle around

trempe /tʀɑ̃p/ *nf* **avoir la** ∼ **d'un dirigeant** to have the makings of a leader

trempé, ∼**e** /tʀɑ̃pe/ 1 *pp* ▶ TREMPER
2 *pp adj* **(a)** ⟨person, garments⟩ soaked (through); ⟨grass⟩ sodden
(b) (Tech) ⟨steel⟩ tempered; ⟨glass⟩ toughened

tremper /tʀɑ̃pe/ [1] 1 *vtr* **(a)** ⟨rain, person⟩ to soak ⟨person, garment⟩
(b) to dip; **j'ai juste trempé mes lèvres** I just had a sip
(c) to soak ⟨hands⟩
(d) (Tech) to temper
2 *vi* **(a)** ⟨clothes, vegetables⟩ to soak; **faire** ∼ **qch** to soak sth
(b) (fam) ∼ **dans qch** to be mixed up in sth

tremplin /tʀɑ̃plɛ̃/ *nm* **(a)** springboard
(b) (ski jump; water-ski) jump

trentaine /tʀɑ̃tɛn/ *nf* **(a)** **une** ∼ about thirty
(b) **avoir la** ∼ to be about thirty

⚡ **trente** /tʀɑ̃t/ *adj inv, pron, nm inv* thirty

trente-et-un /tʀɑ̃teœ̃/ *nm* **être sur son** ∼ (fam) to be dressed up to the nines

trentenaire /tʀɑ̃tənɛʀ/ *adj* ⟨person⟩ in his/her thirties; ⟨tree, building⟩ around thirty years old

trente-six /tʀɑ̃tsis/ *adj inv, pron, nm inv* thirty-six
IDIOM voir ∼ **chandelles** (fam) to see stars

trente-trois /tʀɑ̃tʀwa/ *adj inv, pron, nm inv* thirty-three
■ ∼ **tours** LP

trentième /tʀɑ̃tjɛm/ *adj* thirtieth

trépas /tʀepɑ/ *nm* (dated) demise

trépidant, ∼**e** /tʀepidɑ̃, ɑ̃t/ *adj* ⟨rhythm, speed⟩ pulsating; ⟨life⟩ hectic; ⟨story⟩ exciting

trépied /tʀepje/ *nm* (gen) tripod

trépigner /tʀepiɲe/ [1] *vi* (with anger, impatience) to stamp one's feet

⚡ **très** /tʀɛ/ *adv* very; ∼ **connu** very well-known; **être** ∼ **amoureux** to be very much in love; ∼ **en avance** very early; ∼ **volontiers** gladly; **'tu vas bien?'**—**'non, pas** ∼**'** 'are you well?'—'no, not terribly'; **elle a** ∼ **envie de** ⋯⟶

partir she's dying to leave (colloq)

✐ **trésor** /tʀezɔʀ/ nm **(a)** treasure
(b) déployer des ～s d'inventivité to show
infinite inventiveness
(c) (person) **mon ～ precious**

trésorerie /tʀezɔʀʀi/ nf **(a)** funds; cash
(b) (of company) accounts
(c) government finance

trésorier, -ière /tʀezɔʀje, ɛʀ/ nm,f
treasurer

tressaillement /tʀɛsajmɑ̃/ nm **(a)** (from
surprise, fear) start; (of hope, pleasure) quiver;
(from pain) wince
(b) (of person, muscle, animal) twitch; (of machine,
ground) vibration

tressaillir /tʀɛsajiʀ/ [28] vi **(a)** (with surprise)
to start; (with pleasure) to quiver
(b) ⟨person, muscle⟩ to twitch

tresse /tʀɛs/ nf **(a)** plait (GB), braid (US)
(b) (of thread) braid

tresser /tʀɛse/ [1] vtr to plait (GB), to braid
(US) ⟨hair, threads⟩; to weave ⟨straw, string⟩

tréteau, pl ～x /tʀeto/ nm trestle

treuil /tʀœj/ nm winch

trêve /tʀɛv/ nf **(a)** (Mil) truce
(b) respite; ～ **de plaisanteries!** that's enough
joking!

tri /tʀi/ nm sorting; sorting out; **centre de ～**
(postal) sorting office; **faire le ～ de** to sort
⟨mail⟩; to sort out ⟨documents, clothes⟩; **faire
un ～ parmi des choses** to select among
things

triage /tʀijaʒ/ nm **gare de ～** marshalling
(GB) yard

triangle /tʀijɑ̃gl/ nm triangle
■ **～ des Bermudes** Bermuda Triangle

triangulaire /tʀijɑ̃gylɛʀ/ adj
(a) triangular
(b) ⟨agreement, partnership⟩ three-way

triathlon /tʀiatlɔ̃/ nm triathlon

tribal, ～e, mpl **-aux** /tʀibal, o/ adj tribal

tribord /tʀibɔʀ/ nm starboard

tribu /tʀiby/ nf tribe

tribulations /tʀibylasjɔ̃/ nf pl tribulations

tribun /tʀibœ̃/ nm **(a)** tribune
(b) great orator

✐ **tribunal,** pl **-aux** /tʀibynal, o/ nm (Law)
court; **traîner qn devant les tribunaux** to take
sb to court

tribune /tʀibyn/ nf **(a)** (in stadium) stand; (in
court) gallery
(b) (of speaker) platform, rostrum
(c) (in newspaper) comments column

tribut /tʀiby/ nm tribute

tributaire /tʀibytɛʀ/ adj **être ～ de**
⟨country, person⟩ to depend on

tricentenaire /tʀisɑ̃tnɛʀ/ adj three-
hundred-year-old

triche /tʀiʃ/ nf (fam) **c'est de la ～** that's
cheating

tricher /tʀiʃe/ [1] vi to cheat; ～ **sur son âge**
to lie about one's age

tricherie /tʀiʃʀi/ nf cheating

tricheur, -euse /tʀiʃœʀ, øz/ nm,f cheat

tricolore /tʀikɔlɔʀ/ adj **(a)** three-coloured
(GB); **feux ～s** traffic lights
(b) (fam) French; **l'équipe ～** the French team

tricot /tʀiko/ nm **(a)** knitting; **faire du ～**
to knit
(b) knitwear; **en ～** knitted

tricoter /tʀikɔte/ [1] vtr to knit; **tricoté (à
la) main** handknitted

tricycle /tʀisikl/ nm tricycle

trident /tʀidɑ̃/ nm trident

tridimensionnel, -elle
/tʀidimɑ̃sjɔnɛl/ adj three-dimensional

triennal, ～e, mpl **-aux** /tʀijenal, o/ adj
(a) ⟨mandate⟩ three-year
(b) ⟨vote⟩ three-yearly

trier /tʀije/ [2] vtr **(a)** to sort ⟨mail⟩
(b) to sort [sth] out ⟨information⟩; to select
⟨clients⟩
IDIOM ～ **sur le volet** to handpick

trifouiller /tʀifuje/ [1] vi (fam) ～ **dans** to
rummage through; to tinker with

trilingue /tʀilɛ̃g/ adj trilingual

trilogie /tʀilɔʒi/ nf trilogy

trimbal(l)er /tʀɛ̃bale/ [1] vtr (fam) to lug
[sth] around; to drag [sb] around

trimer /tʀime/ [1] vi (fam) to slave away

trimestre /tʀimɛstʀ/ nm **(a)** (period)
quarter; (Sch) term
(b) quarterly income; quarterly payment

trimestriel, -ielle /tʀimɛstʀijɛl/ adj (gen)
quarterly; ⟨exam⟩ end-of-term

trimoteur /tʀimɔtœʀ/ nm three-engined
plane

tringle /tʀɛ̃gl/ nf **(a)** (gen) rail
(b) (Tech) rod

trinité /tʀinite/ nf trinity

trinquer /tʀɛ̃ke/ [1] vi to clink glasses; ～ **à
qch** to drink to sth

trio /tʀi(j)o/ nm trio

triomphal, ～e, mpl **-aux** /tʀijɔ̃fal, o/ adj
triumphant

triomphalisme /tʀijɔ̃falism/ nm
triumphalism

triomphant, ～e /tʀijɔ̃fɑ̃, ɑ̃t/ adj
triumphant

triomphateur, -trice /tʀijɔ̃fatœʀ,
tʀis/ adj triumphant

triomphe /tʀijɔ̃f/ nm triumph; **faire un ～ à
qn** to give sb a triumphal reception

triompher /tʀijɔ̃fe/ [1] **1 triompher de**
v+prep to triumph over ⟨enemy⟩; to overcome
⟨resistance⟩
2 vi **(a)** ⟨fighter⟩ to triumph; ⟨truth⟩ to
prevail

✐ indicates a very frequent word

(b) to be triumphant

tripartisme /tʀipaʀtism/ *nm* tripartite *or* three-party system

tripatouiller /tʀipatuje/ [1] *vtr* (fam) to fiddle with (colloq) ‹object›; to paw (colloq) ‹person›

triperie /tʀipʀi/ *nf* **(a)** tripe shop
(b) tripe trade

tripes /tʀip/ *nf pl* **(a)** (Culin) tripe
(b) (fam) guts, innards

triplace /tʀiplas/ *adj* three-seater

triple /tʀipl/ **1** *adj* triple; **l'avantage est** ~ the advantages are threefold; **en** ~ **exemplaire** in triplicate; ~ **idiot!** (fam) prize idiot! (colloq)
2 *nm* **coûter le** ~ to cost three times as much

triplé, ~**e** /tʀiple/ *nm,f* triplet

triplement /tʀipləmɑ̃/ *adv* **(a)** in three respects
(b) trebly

tripler /tʀiple/ [1] **1** *vtr* to treble ‹quantity, price›
2 *vi* to treble (**de** in)

triporteur /tʀipɔʀtœʀ/ *nm* delivery tricycle

tripot /tʀipo/ *nm* **(a)** gambling joint (colloq)
(b) dive (colloq)

tripotée /tʀipote/ *nf* (fam) **(a)** (good) hiding (colloq)
(b) une ~ de hordes of

tripoter /tʀipote/ [1] *vtr* (fam) to fiddle with ‹object›

trique /tʀik/ *nf* cudgel; **battre à coups de** ~ to cudgel
IDIOM être maigre *or* **sec comme un coup de** ~ to be as thin as a rake

trisaïeul, ~**e** /tʀizajœl/ *nm,f* great-great-grandfather/grandmother

trisannuel, -elle /tʀizanɥɛl/ *adj* triennial

trisomie /tʀizɔmi/ *nf* trisomy; ~ 21 Down's Syndrome

trisomique /tʀizɔmik/ *adj* **enfant** ~ Down's Syndrome child

ꝫ **triste** /tʀist/ *adj* **(a)** (gen) sad; ‹town, existence› dreary; ‹weather, day› gloomy; ‹colour› drab
(b) ‹end, business, reputation› dreadful; ‹show, state› sorry; ‹character› unsavoury (GB); **c'est la** ~ **vérité** unfortunately, that's the truth of the matter; **faire la** ~ **expérience de qch** to learn about sth to one's cost

tristement /tʀistəmɑ̃/ *adv* sadly

tristesse /tʀistɛs/ *nf* (gen) sadness; (of place, evening) dreariness; (of weather, day) gloominess

triton /tʀitɔ̃/ *nm* (Zool) **(a)** (mollusc) triton
(b) newt

triturer /tʀityʀe/ [1] *vtr* to fiddle with ‹button›; to knead] ‹dough›
IDIOM se ~ **la cervelle** (fam) *or* **les méninges**

(fam) to rack one's brains (colloq)

trivial, ~**e**, *mpl* **-iaux** /tʀivjal, o/ *adj*
(a) coarse
(b) ordinary, everyday; ‹style› mundane

trivialité /tʀivjalite/ *nf* **(a)** coarseness
(b) triteness, triviality
(c) platitude

troc /tʀɔk/ *nm* barter; **faire du** ~ to barter

troène /tʀoɛn/ *nm* privet

troglodyte /tʀɔglɔdit/ *nm* cave-dweller

trogne /tʀɔɲ/ *nf* (fam) mug (colloq), face

trognon /tʀɔɲɔ̃/ *nm* (of apple) core

ꝫ **trois** /tʀwɑ/ *adj inv, pron, nm inv* three
IDIOMS être haut comme ~ **pommes** to be kneehigh to a grasshopper; **jamais deux sans** ~ bad luck comes in threes

trois-huit /tʀwaɥit/ *nm pl* system of three eight-hour shifts

ꝫ **troisième** /tʀwazjɛm/ **1** *adj* third
2 *nf* **(a)** (Sch) *fourth year of secondary school, age 14–15*
(b) (Aut) third (gear)
■ **le** ~ **âge** the elderly

troisièmement /tʀwazjɛmmɑ̃/ *adv* thirdly

trois-mâts /tʀwamɑ/ *nm inv* three-master

trois-quarts /tʀwakaʀ/ **1** *nm inv*
(a) three-quarter-length coat
(b) (rugby player) three quarter
2 **de trois-quarts** *phr* ‹portrait› three-quarter-length

trombe /tʀɔ̃b/ *nf* **(a)** (caused by whirlwind) waterspout; **partir en** ~ to go hurtling off
(b) ~**s d'eau** masses of water; torrential rain

trombone /tʀɔ̃bɔn/ *nm* **(a)** trombone
(b) trombonist
(c) paperclip

trompe /tʀɔ̃p/ *nf* **(a)** (Zool) (of elephant) trunk; (of insect) proboscis
(b) (Mus) horn

trompe-la-mort /tʀɔ̃plamɔʀ/ *nmf inv* daredevil

trompe-l'œil /tʀɔ̃plœj/ *nm inv* **(a)** (painting) trompe l'œil
(b) (figurative) smokescreen

ꝫ **tromper** /tʀɔ̃pe/ [1] **1** *vtr* **(a)** (gen) to deceive; to be unfaithful to ‹husband, wife›; ~ **les électeurs** to mislead the voters
(b) ~ **la vigilance de qn** to slip past sb's guard
(c) **pour** ~ **l'attente** to while away the time
2 **se tromper** *v refl* (+ *v être*) **(a)** to be mistaken; **se** ~ **sur qn** to be wrong about sb; **il ne faut pas s'y** ~, **qu'on ne s'y trompe pas** make no mistake about it
(b) to make a mistake; **se** ~ **de bus** to take the wrong bus

tromperie /tʀɔ̃pʀi/ *nf* deceit

trompette¹ /tʀɔ̃pɛt/ *nm* (in army) bugler

trompette² /tʀɔ̃pɛt/ *nf* trumpet

trompettiste /tʀɔ̃petist/ *nmf* trumpet (player)

trompeur, -euse /tʀɔ̃pœʀ, øz/ *adj* ‹promise› misleading; ‹appearance› deceptive

tronc /tʀɔ̃/ *nm* **(a)** (of tree, body) trunk; (of column) shaft
(b) collection box
■ **~ commun** (of species) common origin; (of disciplines) (common) core curriculum

tronche /tʀɔ̃ʃ/ *nf* (pop) mug (colloq), face

tronçon /tʀɔ̃sɔ̃/ *nm* section

tronçonneuse /tʀɔ̃sɔnøz/ *nf* chain saw

trône /tʀon/ *nm* throne

trôner /tʀone/ [1] *vi* **le professeur trônait au milieu de ses étudiants** the professor was holding court among his students; **~ sur** ‹photograph› to have pride of place on

tronquer /tʀɔ̃ke/ [1] *vtr* to truncate

✎ **trop** /tʀo/ **1** *adv* too; too much; **beaucoup** *or* **bien ~ lourd** far *or* much too heavy; **j'ai ~ mangé** I've had too much to eat; **j'ai ~ dormi** I've slept too long; **nous sommes ~ peu nombreux** there are too few of us; **12 francs c'est ~ peu** 12 francs is too little; **ce serait ~ beau!** one should be so lucky!; **c'est ~ bête!** how stupid!; **~ enthousiaste** overenthusiastic; **~ c'est ~!** enough is enough!; **c'était ~ drôle** it was so funny
2 **trop de** *quantif* **~ de pression/ meubles** too much pressure/furniture; **~ de livres/monde** too many books/people
3 **de trop, en trop** *phr* **il y a une assiette en ~** there's one plate too many; **il y a 12 euros de ~** there's 12 euros too much; **ta remarque était de ~** your remark was uncalled for; **se sentir de ~** to feel one is in the way

trophée /tʀofe/ *nm* trophy

tropical, ~e, *mpl* **-aux** /tʀopikal, o/ *adj* tropical

tropique /tʀopik/ *nm* tropic

trop-perçu, *pl* **~s** /tʀopɛʀsy/ *nm* **(a)** excess payment
(b) overpayment of tax; **remboursement d'un ~** tax refund

trop-plein, *pl* **~s** /tʀoplɛ̃/ *nm* **(a)** (of energy) excess
(b) (Tech) (from bath) overflow

troquer /tʀoke/ [1] *vtr* (gen) **~ qch contre qch** to swap sth for sth, to barter sth for sth

troquet /tʀokɛ/ *nm* (fam) bar

trot /tʀo/ *nm* trot

trotte /tʀot/ *nf* (fam) **ça fait une ~** it's a fair walk

trotter /tʀote/ [1] *vi* **(a)** ‹horse, rider› to trot
(b) ‹person, mouse› to scurry (about)
(c) (figurative) **~ dans la tête** ‹thought› to go through one's mind; ‹music› to go through one's head

trotteur /tʀotœʀ/ *nm* **(a)** trotter
(b) ‹shoe with a low, broad heel›

trotteuse /tʀotøz/ *nf* (on watch) second hand

trottiner /tʀotine/ [1] *vi* **(a)** ‹horse› to jog
(b) ‹person, mouse› to scurry along

trottinette /tʀotinɛt/ *nf* scooter

✎ **trottoir** /tʀotwaʀ/ *nm* pavement (GB), sidewalk (US); **le bord du ~** the kerb (GB) *or* curb (US)

✎ **trou** /tʀu/ *nm* **(a)** hole
(b) (in timetable) (gen) gap; (in budget) deficit; (in savings) hole
(c) (fam) **~ (perdu)** dump (colloq)
■ **~ d'aération** airhole; **~ d'air** air pocket; **~ de mémoire** memory lapse; **~ normand** *glass of spirits between courses to aid digestion*; **~ de serrure** keyhole

troublant, ~e /tʀublɑ̃, ɑ̃t/ *adj* **(a)** disturbing; disconcerting
(b) (sexually) unsettling

✎ **trouble** /tʀubl/ **1** *adj* **(a)** ‹liquid› cloudy; ‹glasses› smudgy
(b) ‹picture, outline› blurred
(c) ‹feeling› confused; ‹business, milieu› shady
2 *adv* **je vois ~** my eyes are blurred
3 *nm* **(a)** unrest; **~s ethniques** ethnic unrest
(b) trouble; **jeter le ~** to stir up trouble
(c) confusion; embarrassment
(d) emotion; **ressentir un ~** to feel a thrill of emotion
(e) (Med) **~s** disorders
■ **~ obsessionnel compulsif, TOC** (Med) obsessive compulsive disorder, OCD

trouble-fête /tʀublfɛt/ *nmf inv* spoilsport

troubler /tʀuble/ [1] **1** *vtr* **(a)** to make [sth] cloudy ‹liquid›; to blur ‹sight, picture›
(b) to disturb ‹sleep, person›; to disrupt ‹plans›; **en ces temps troublés** in these troubled times
(c) to disconcert ‹person›
2 **se troubler** *v refl* (+ *v être*) **(a)** ‹person› to become flustered
(b) ‹liquid› to become cloudy; **ma vue se troubla** my eyes became blurred

trouée /tʀue/ *nf* **(a)** gap
(b) (Mil) breach

trouer /tʀue/ [1] *vtr* to make a hole (*or* holes) in; to wear a hole (*or* holes) in; **semelle trouée** sole with a hole (*or* holes) in it

troufion /tʀufjɔ̃/ *nm* (pop) soldier

trouillard, ~e (pop) **1** *adj* cowardly
2 *nm,f* chicken (colloq), coward

trouille /tʀuj/ *nf* (pop) **avoir la ~** to be scared

✎ **troupe** /tʀup/ *nf* **(a)** (Mil) troops
(b) (of actors) company; (on tour) troupe
(c) (of deer) herd; (of birds) flock; (of tourists)

✎ indicates a very frequent word

troop; (of children) band

troupeau, pl ~x /tʀupo/ nm (of buffalo, cattle) herd; (of sheep) flock; (of geese) gaggle

trousse /tʀus/ nf **(a)** (little) case
(b) kit
■ ~ **d'écolier** pencil case; ~ **de médecin** doctor's bag; ~ **de secours** first-aid kit; ~ **de toilette** toilet bag
IDIOM **être aux ~s de qn** to be hot on sb's heels

trousseau, pl ~x /tʀuso/ nm **(a)** (of keys) bunch
(b) (of bride) trousseau; (of baby) clothes

trouvaille /tʀuvɑj/ nf **(a)** (object) find
(b) bright idea, brainwave

trouvé, ~e /tʀuve/ **1** pp ▶ TROUVER
2 pp adj **réplique bien ~e** neat riposte; **tout ~** ‹solution› ready-made; ‹culprit› obvious

⚡ **trouver** /tʀuve/ [1] **1** vtr **(a)** (gen) to find; ~ **qch par hasard** to come across sth; ~ **un intérêt à qch** to find sth interesting; ~ **à redire** to find fault; ~ **le moyen de faire** to manage to do; **j'ai trouvé!** I've got it!; **tu as trouvé ça tout seul?** (ironic) did you work that out all by yourself?; **si tu continues tu vas me~!** (fam) don't push your luck!; ~ **du plaisir à faire** to get pleasure out of doing; **aller ~ qn** to go and see sb
(b) **je trouve ça drôle** I think it's funny; **j'ai trouvé bon de vous prévenir** I thought it right to warn you; **je me demande ce qu'elle te trouve!** I wonder what she sees in you!; **je te trouve bien calme, qu'est-ce que tu as?** you're very quiet, what's the matter?
2 **se trouver** v refl (+ v être) **(a)** to be; **se ~ à Rome** to be in Rome; **se ~ dans l'impossibilité de faire** to be unable to do
(b) to feel; **j'ai failli me ~ mal** I nearly passed out
(c) **il se trouve beau** he thinks he's good-looking
(d) to find ‹excuse›
3 v impers **il se trouve qu'elle ne leur avait rien dit** as it happened, she hadn't told them anything; **si ça se trouve ça te plaira** (fam) you might like it

truand /tʀyɑ̃/ nm **(a)** gangster
(b) crook

trublion /tʀyblijɔ̃/ nm troublemaker

⚡ **truc** /tʀyk/ nm **(a)** (fam) knack; trick; **avoir un ~ pour gagner de l'argent** to know a good way of making money; **un ~ du métier** a trick of the trade
(b) thing; **il y a un tas de ~s à faire dans la maison** there are loads of things to do in the house (colloq); **il y a un ~ qui ne va pas** there's something wrong
(c) (fam) thingummy (colloq), whatsit (colloq)
(d) (person) what's-his-name/what's-her-name, thingy (colloq)

trucage /tʀykaʒ/ nm (in cinema) special effect

truchement /tʀyʃmɑ̃/ nm **par le ~ de qch** through sth; **par le ~ de qn** through the intervention of sb

truculent, ~e /tʀykylɑ̃, ɑ̃t/ adj earthy

truelle /tʀyɛl/ nf trowel

truffe /tʀyf/ nf **(a)** (Culin) truffle
(b) (of dog) nose

truffer /tʀyfe/ [1] vtr **ta lettre est truffée de fautes** your letter is riddled with mistakes

truie /tʀɥi/ nf sow

truite /tʀɥit/ nf trout

truquage ▶ TRUCAGE

truquer /tʀyke/ [1] vtr **(a)** to fiddle (colloq) ‹accounts›
(b) to mark ‹cards›
(c) to fix ‹elections, match›

trust /tʀœst/ nm trust

tsar /tsaʀ/ nm tsar

tsé-tsé /tsetse/ nf inv (**mouche**) ~ tsetse (fly)

tsigane ▶ TZIGANE

TTC (abbr = **toutes taxes comprises**) inclusive of tax

⚡ **tu** /ty/ pron you
IDIOM **être à ~ et à toi avec qn** to be on familiar terms with sb

tuant, ~e /tɥɑ̃, ɑ̃t/ adj (fam) exhausting

tuba /tyba/ nm **(a)** (Mus) tuba
(b) (of swimmer) snorkel

tube /tyb/ **1** nm **(a)** tube; pipe
(b) (fam) (song) hit
2 **à pleins tubes** phr (fam) **mettre le son à pleins ~s** to turn the sound right up (colloq)
■ ~ **cathodique** cathode ray tube; ~ **digestif** digestive tract; ~ **à essai** test tube

tubercule /tybɛʀkyl/ nm **(a)** (Bot) tuber
(b) (Anat) tuberosity

tuberculeux, **-euse** /tybɛʀkylø, øz/ adj tubercular; **être ~** to have TB

tuberculose /tybɛʀkyloz/ nf tuberculosis, TB

tubulaire /tybylɛʀ/ adj tubular

TUC /tyk/ nm pl (abbr = **travaux d'utilité collective**) paid community service (for the young unemployed)

tué /tɥe/ nm person killed; **sept ~s, cinq blessés** seven people killed, five injured

⚡ **tuer** /tɥe/ [1] **1** vtr **(a)** (gen) to kill
(b) (fam) to wear [sb] out
2 **se tuer** v refl (+ v être) **(a)** (accidentally) to be killed
(b) to kill oneself
(c) **se ~ au travail** to work oneself to death

tuerie /tyʀi/ nf killings

tue-tête: à tue-tête /atytɛt/ phr at the top of one's voice

tueur, **-euse** /tɥœʀ, øz/ nm,f **(a)** killer
(b) slaughterman/slaughterwoman
■ ~ **à gages** hired or professional killer

t

tuile /tɥil/ *nf* **(a)** tile
(b) (fam) blow; **quelle ∼!** what a blow!
(c) (Culin) *thin almond biscuit*
tulipe /tylip/ *nf* tulip
tuméfier /tymefje/ [2] *vtr* to make [sth]
swell up
tumeur /tymœʀ/ *nf* tumour (GB)
tumulte /tymylt/ *nm* **(a)** uproar
(b) turmoil
tumultueux, -euse /tymyltɥø, øz/ *adj*
turbulent; tempestuous; stormy
tungstène /tœ̃gstɛn/ *nm* tungsten
tunique /tynik/ *nf* tunic
tunisien, -ienne /tynizjɛ̃, ɛn/ *adj*
Tunisian
tunnel /tynɛl/ *nm* tunnel; **le ∼ sous la
Manche** the Channel Tunnel
IDIOM voir le bout du ∼ to see light at the
end of the tunnel
turban /tyʀbɑ̃/ *nm* turban
turbin /tyʀbɛ̃/ *nm* (pop) daily grind (colloq),
work
turbine /tyʀbin/ *nf* turbine
turboréacteur /tyʀboʀeaktœʀ/ *nm*
turbojet (engine)
turbot /tyʀbo/ *nm* turbot
turbulence /tyʀbylɑ̃s/ *nf* **(a)** turbulence
(b) unruliness
(c) unrest
turbulent, ∼e /tyʀbylɑ̃, ɑ̃t/ *adj* ‹child›
unruly; ‹class› rowdy; ‹teenager› rebellious;
être ∼ en classe to be disruptive in class
turc, turque /tyʀk/ ① *adj* Turkish
② *nm* (language) Turkish
Turc, Turque /tyʀk/ *nm,f* Turk
turfiste /tœʀfist/ *nmf* racegoer, punter
(colloq)
turlupiner /tyʀlypine/ [1] *vtr* (fam) to
bother
turpitude /tyʀpityd/ *nf* **(a)** turpitude,
depravity
(b) base act; low remark
turque ▶ TURC 1
Turquie /tyʀki/ *pr nf* Turkey
turquoise /tyʀkwaz/ *adj inv, nf* turquoise

tutelle /tytɛl/ *nf* guardianship
tuteur, -trice /tytœʀ, tʀis/ ① *nm,f*
(a) (Law) guardian
(b) tutor
② *nm* (Bot) stake
tutoiement /tytwamɑ̃/ *nm* using the 'tu'
form
tutoyer /tytwaje/ [23] *vtr* to address [sb]
using the 'tu' form
tutu /tyty/ *nm* tutu
tuyau, *pl* ∼**x** /tɥijo/ *nm* **(a)** (Tech) pipe
(b) (fam) tip (colloq)
■ **∼ d'arrosage** hose; **∼ d'échappement**
exhaust
tuyauterie /tɥijotʀi/ *nf* (Tech) piping
TVA /tevea/ *nf* (*abbr* = **taxe à la valeur
ajoutée**) VAT
tympan /tɛ̃pɑ̃/ *nm* eardrum
⚜ **type** /tip/ ① *nm* **(a)** type, kind; **plusieurs
accidents de ce ∼** several accidents of this
kind
(b) (classic) example; **elle est le ∼ même de
la femme d'affaires** she's the classic example
of a business woman
(c) (physical) type
(d) (fam) guy (colloq); **sale ∼!** swine! (colloq);
brave ∼ nice chap (colloq)
② **(-)type** (*combining form*) typical,
classic
typer /tipe/ [1] *vtr* to portray [sb] as a type;
to play [sb] as a type
typhoïde /tifɔid/ *adj, nf* typhoid
typhon /tifɔ̃/ *nm* typhoon
typique /tipik/ *adj* typical
typiquement /tipikmɑ̃/ *adv* typically;
une famille ∼ américaine a typically
American family
typographie /tipɔgʀafi/ *nf* typography
typographique /tipɔgʀafik/ *adj*
typographical
tyran /tiʀɑ̃/ *nm* tyrant
tyrannie /tiʀani/ *nf* tyranny
tyrannique /tiʀanik/ *adj* tyrannical
tyranniser /tiʀanize/ [1] *vtr* to tyrannize
tzigane /dzigan, tsigan/ ① *adj, nmf* gypsy
② *nm* (language) Romany

Uu

u, **U** /y/ *nm inv* u, U; **en (forme de) U** U-shaped

ubac /ybak/ *nm* north-facing side

ubiquité /ybikɥite/ *nf* ubiquity; **je n'ai pas le don d'~!** I can't be everywhere at once!

ubuesque /ybyɛsk/ *adj* grotesque

ulcère /ylsɛR/ *nm* ulcer

ulcérer /ylseRe/ [14] *vtr* **(a)** to sicken, to revolt
(b) (Med) to ulcerate

ulcéreux, -euse /ylseRø, øz/ *adj* ‹wound› ulcerated

ULM /yɛlɛm/ *nm inv* (*abbr* – **ultraléger motorisé**) microlight; microlighting; **faire de l'~** to go microlighting

ultérieur, ~e /ylteRjœR/ *adj* subsequent; **une date ~e** a later date

ultérieurement /ylteRjœRmɑ̃/ *adv*
(a) subsequently
(b) later

ultimatum /yltimatɔm/ *nm* ultimatum

ultime /yltim/ *adj* **(a)** final
(b) ultimate

ultra /yltRa/ *adj*, *nmf* extremist

ultraconfidentiel, -ielle /yltRakɔ̃fidɑ̃sjɛl/ *adj* top secret

ultrafin, ~e /yltRafɛ̃, in/ *adj* ‹slice› wafer-thin; ‹stocking› sheer; ‹fibre› ultra-fine

ultraléger, -ère /yltRaleʒe, ɛR/ *adj* ‹material, cigarette› ultra light; ‹clothing, fabric, equipment› very light

ultramoderne /yltRamɔdɛRn/ *adj* (gen) ultramodern; ‹system, technology› state-of-the-art

ultrarapide /yltRaRapid/ *adj* high-speed

ultrasecret, -ète /yltRasəkRɛ, ɛt/ *adj* top secret

ultrasensible /yltRasɑ̃sibl/ *adj* ‹person› hypersensitive; ‹film› ultrasensitive; ‹issue› highly sensitive

ultrason /yltRasɔ̃/ *nm* ultrasound

ultraviolet, -ette /yltRavjɔlɛ, ɛt/ ⓵ *adj* ultraviolet
⓶ *nm* ultraviolet ray; **séance d'~s** session on a sunbed

ululer /ylyle/ [1] *vi* to hoot

♂ **un, une¹** /œ̃(n), yn/ ⓵ *det* (*pl* **des**) **(a)** a, an; one; **un homme** a man; **une femme** a woman; **avec ~ sang-froid remarquable** with remarkable self-control; **il n'y avait pas ~ arbre** there wasn't a single tree; **~ accident est vite arrivé** accidents soon happen
(b) **il y avait des roses et des lis** there were roses and lilies; **il y a des gens qui trichent** there are some people who cheat
(c) **il fait ~ froid** *or* **~ de ces froids!** it's so cold!; **elle m'a donné une de ces gifles!** she gave me such a slap!; **il y a ~ monde aujourd'hui!** there are so many people today!
⓶ *pron* (*pl* **uns**, **unes**) one; **(l')~ de** *or* **d'entre nous** one of us; **les ~s pensent que...** some think that...
⓷ *adj* one, a, an; **trente et une personnes** thirty-one people; **~ jour sur deux** every other day
⓸ *nm, f* one; **~ par personne** one each; **les deux villes n'en font plus qu'une** the two cities have merged into one; **~ à** *or* **par ~** one by one
⓹ *nm* one; **page ~** page one
IDIOMS **fière comme pas une** extremely proud; **il est menteur comme pas ~** he's the biggest liar; **~ pour tous et tous pour ~** all for one and one for all

unanime /ynanim/ *adj* unanimous

unanimement /ynanimmɑ̃/ *adv*
(a) ‹adopted, elected› unanimously
(b) (figurative) ‹admired› universally

unanimité /ynanimite/ *nf* unanimity; **à l'~** ‹elected› unanimously; **à l'~ moins deux voix** with only two votes against; **faire l'~** to have unanimous support *or* backing

une² /yn/ ⓵ *det, pron, adj* ▸ UN 1, 2, 3, 4
⓶ *nf* **la ~** the front page; **être à la ~** to be in the headlines

♂ **uni, ~e** /yni/ ⓵ *pp* ▸ UNIR
⓶ *pp adj* **(a)** ‹family› close-knit; ‹couple› close; ‹people, rebels› united
(b) ‹fabric, colour› plain
(c) ‹surface› smooth, even

unicité /ynisite/ *nf* uniqueness

unidirectionnel, -elle /ynidiRɛksjɔnɛl/ *adj* ‹transmitter› unidirectional; ‹receiver› one-way

unième /ynjɛm/ *adj* first; **vingt et ~** twenty-first

unification /ynifikasjɔ̃/ *nf* unification

unifier /ynifje/ [2] ⓵ *vtr* **(a)** to unify ‹country, market›
(b) to standardize ‹procedure, system›
⓶ **s'unifier** *v refl* (+ *v être*) ‹countries, groups› to unite

uniforme /ynifɔRm/ ⓵ *adj* (gen) uniform; ‹buildings, streets, existence› monotonous; ‹regulation› across-the-board
⓶ *nm* uniform; **en ~** uniformed

uniformément /ynifɔRmemɑ̃/ *adv* uniformly

uniformiser /ynifɔʀmize/ [1] *vtr* to standardize ‹rate›; to make [sth] uniform ‹colour›

uniformité /ynifɔʀmite/ *nf* (of tastes) uniformity; (of life, buildings) monotony

unijambiste /yniʒɑ̃bist/ ⓵ *adj* être ∼ to have only one leg ⓶ *nmf* one-legged person

unilatéral, ∼e, *mpl* -aux /ynilateʀal, o/ *adj* unilateral; ‹parking› on one side only

unilingue /ynilɛ̃g/ *adj* unilingual, monolingual

uninominal, ∼e, *mpl* -aux /yninɔminal, o/ *adj* (Pol) ‹ballot› for a single candidate

✔ **union** /ynjɔ̃/ *nf* (a) union
(b) association; ∼ **de consommateurs** consumers' association
(c) marriage
■ ∼ **libre** cohabitation; ∼ **sportive**, US sports club; **Union européenne** European Union
IDIOM l'∼ **fait la force** (Proverb) united we stand, divided we fall

✔ **unique** /ynik/ *adj* (a) only; **il est l'**∼ **témoin** he's the only witness; **être fille** *or* **fils** ∼ to be an only child
(b) single; **parti** ∼ single party; **système à parti** ∼ one-party system; **'prix** ∼**'** 'all at one price'
(c) unique; **une occasion** ∼ a unique opportunity; ∼ **en son genre** ‹person, object› one of a kind; ‹event› one-off (GB), one-shot (US)
(d) (fam) **ce type est** ∼**!** that guy's priceless! (colloq)

✔ **uniquement** /ynikmɑ̃/ *adv* (gen) only; **en vente** ∼ **par correspondance** available by mail order only; **c'était** ∼ **pour te taquiner** it was only to tease you; **il pense** ∼ **à s'amuser** all he thinks about is having fun; ∼ **dans un but commercial** purely for commercial ends

✔ **unir** /yniʀ/ [3] ⓵ *vtr* (a) to unite ‹people, country›; **des hommes unis par les mêmes idées** men brought together by the same ideas
(b) to combine ‹qualities, resources›
(c) to join [sb] in matrimony
⓶ **s'unir** *v refl* (+ *v être*) (a) to unite
(b) to marry

unisexe /yniseks/ *adj* unisex

unisson /ynisɔ̃/ *nm* unison; **à l'**∼ (Mus) in unison; (figurative) in accord

unitaire /yniteʀ/ *adj* ‹cost› unit

✔ **unité** /ynite/ *nf* (a) unity; **film qui manque d'**∼ film lacking in cohesion; **il y a** ∼ **de vues entre eux** they share the same viewpoint
(b) unit; ∼ **monétaire** unit of currency; **20 euros l'**∼ 20 euros each; **vendre qch à l'**∼ to sell sth singly
■ ∼ **centrale (de traitement)** (Comput) central

processing unit, CPU; ∼ **de disque** (Comput) disk drive

✔ **univers** /yniveʀ/ *nm inv* (a) universe
(b) whole world
(c) world; **l'**∼ **de Kafka** Kafka's world

universaliser /yniveʀsalize/ [1] *vtr* to universalize

universalité /yniveʀsalite/ *nf* universality

✔ **universel**, **-elle** /yniveʀsɛl/ *adj* ‹language, theme› universal; ‹history› world; ‹remedy› all-purpose

universitaire /yniveʀsiteʀ/ ⓵ *adj* ‹town› university; ‹work› academic ⓶ *nmf* academic

✔ **université** /yniveʀsite/ *nf* university (GB), college (US)
■ ∼ **d'été** summer school

uns ▶ UN 2

Untel, **Unetelle** /œtɛl, yntɛl/ *nm,f* **Monsieur** ∼ Mr so-and-so; **Madame Unetelle** Mrs so-and-so

urbain, ∼e /yʀbɛ̃, ɛn/ *adj* (a) urban; **vie** ∼e city life
(b) (formal) urbane

urbanisation /yʀbanizasjɔ̃/ *nf* urbanization

urbaniser /yʀbanize/ [1] *vtr* to urbanize ‹region›; **zone urbanisée** built-up area

urbanisme /yʀbanism/ *nm* town planning (GB), city planning (US)

urbaniste /yʀbanist/ *nmf* town planner (GB), city planner (US)

urée /yʀe/ *nf* urea

urètre /yʀetʀ/ *nm* urethra

urgence /yʀʒɑ̃s/ *nf* (a) urgency; **il y a** ∼ it's urgent, it's a matter of urgency; **d'**∼ ‹act› immediately; ‹summon› urgently; ‹measures, treatment› emergency; **de toute** *or* **d'extrême** ∼ as a matter of great urgency; **transporter qn d'**∼ **à l'hôpital** to rush sb to hospital (GB) *or* to the hospital (US); **en** ∼ as a matter of urgency
(b) (Med) **une** ∼ an emergency; **le service des** ∼**s, les** ∼**s** the casualty department

urgent, ∼e /yʀʒɑ̃, ɑ̃t/ *adj* urgent

urinaire /yʀineʀ/ *adj* urinary; **appareil** ∼ urinary tract

urinal, *pl* **-aux** /yʀinal, o/ *nm* urinal

urine /yʀin/ *nf* urine

uriner /yʀine/ [1] *vi* to urinate

urinoir /yʀinwaʀ/ *nm* urinal

urne /yʀn/ *nf* (a) ∼ **(électorale)** ballot box; **se rendre aux** ∼**s** to go to the polls
(b) urn

urologie /yʀɔlɔʒi/ *nf* urology

urologue /yʀɔlɔg/ *nmf* urologist

URSS /yɛʀɛsɛs, yʀs/ *pr nf* (*abbr* = **Union des Républiques socialistes soviétiques**) USSR

urticaire /yʀtikeʀ/ *nf* hives

✔ indicates a very frequent word

uruguayen, -enne /yʀygwejɛ̃, ɛn/ adj
Uruguayan

us /ys/ nm pl **les ∼ et coutumes** the ways
and customs

US /yɛs/ nf (abbr = **union sportive**)
sports club

USA /yɛsa/ nm pl (abbr = **United States
of America**) USA

⚹ **usage** /yzaʒ/ nm **(a)** use; **à l'∼, par l'∼**
with use; **en ∼** in use; **faire ∼ de** to use
‹product›; to exercise ‹authority›; **faire bon/
mauvais ∼ de qch** to put sth to good/bad
use; **faire de l'∼** ‹garment› to last; **à ∼ privé**
for private use; **à ∼s multiples** ‹appliance›
multipurpose; **il a perdu l'∼ d'un œil/l'∼
de la parole** he's lost the use of one eye/
the power of speech; **hors d'∼** ‹garment›
unwearable; ‹machine› out of order
(b) (in a language) usage; **en ∼** in usage
(c) custom; **l'∼ est de faire** the custom is to
do; it's usual practice to do; **entrer dans l'∼**
‹word› to come into common use; ‹behaviour›
to become common practice; **d'∼** ‹politeness›
customary; ‹precautions› usual
■ **∼ de faux** (Law) use of false documents;
faux et ∼ de faux forgery and use of false
documents

usagé, ∼e /yzaʒe/ adj **(a)** ‹garment› well-
worn; ‹tyre› old
(b) ‹syringe› used

usager /yzaʒe/ nm (of service) user; (of
language) speaker; **∼ de la route** road-user

usant, ∼e /yzɑ̃, ɑ̃t/ adj exhausting,
wearing

usé, ∼e /yze/ [1] pp ▶ USER
[2] pp adj ‹object› worn; ‹person› worn-down;
‹heart, eyes› worn-out; ‹joke› hackneyed; **∼
jusqu'à la corde** ‹carpet› threadbare; ‹tyre›
worn down to the tread; (figurative) ‹joke›
hackneyed

⚹ **user** /yze/ [1] [1] vtr to wear out ‹shoes›;
to wear down ‹person›; **les piles sont usées**
the batteries have run down or out; **∼ ses
vêtements jusqu'à la corde** to wear one's
clothes out; **∼ sa santé** to ruin one's health
[2] **user de** v+prep (gen) to use; to exercise
‹right›; to take ‹precautions›; **∼ de diplomatie**
to be diplomatic
[3] **s'user** v refl (+ v être) **(a)** ‹shoes› to
wear out
(b) ‹person› s'**∼ à la tâche** or **au travail** to
wear oneself out with overwork; s'**∼ la
santé** to ruin one's health

usinage /yzinaʒ/ nm **(a)** (with a machine tool)
machining
(b) (industrial production) manufacture

usine /yzin/ nf factory, plant
■ **∼ de traitement** recycling plant; **∼**
métallurgique ironworks; **∼ sidérurgique**
steelworks

usiner /yzine/ [1] vtr **(a)** to machine
(b) to manufacture

usité, ∼e /yzite/ adj commonly used

ustensile /ystɑ̃sil/ nm utensil

usuel, -elle /yzɥɛl/ adj ‹object› everyday;
‹word› common

usufruit /yzyfʀɥi/ nm (Law) usufruct

usufruitier, -ière /yzyfʀɥitje, ɛʀ/ nm,f
tenant for life

usure /yzyʀ/ nf **(a)** (of clothes) wear and
tear; (of tyre, machine) wear; **résister à l'∼** to
wear well
(b) (of energy, enemy) wearing down
(c) **∼ du temps** wearing effect of time
(d) usury

usurier, -ière /yzyʀje, ɛʀ/ nm,f usurer

usurpateur, -trice /yzyʀpatœʀ,
tʀis/ nm,f usurper

usurpation /yzyʀpasjɔ̃/ nf usurpation

usurper /yzyʀpe/ [1] vtr to usurp

ut /yt/ nm (Mus) C

utérus /yteʀys/ nm inv womb

⚹ **utile** /ytil/ [1] adj (gen) useful; **être ∼**
‹person, book› to be helpful; ‹umbrella› to
come in handy; **il est ∼ de signaler** it's
worth pointing out; **il n'a pas jugé ∼ de me
prévenir** he didn't think it necessary to let
me know; **en quoi puis-je vous être ∼?** how
can I help you?
[2] nm **joindre l'∼ à l'agréable** to mix
business with pleasure

utilement /ytilmɑ̃/ adv ‹intervene›
effectively; ‹occupy oneself› usefully

utilisable /ytilizabl/ adj usable

⚹ **utilisateur, -trice** /ytilizatœʀ, tʀis/ nm,f
user

⚹ **utilisation** /ytilizasjɔ̃/ nf use

⚹ **utiliser** /ytilize/ [1] vtr (gen) to use; to make
use of ‹resources›

utilitaire /ytilitɛʀ/ adj ‹role› practical;
‹object› functional, utilitarian; ‹vehicle›
commercial

utilité /ytilite/ nf **(a)** usefulness; **d'une
grande ∼** ‹book, machine› very useful;
‹person› very helpful; **d'aucune ∼** of no use
(b) use; **je n'en ai pas l'∼** I have no use for it

utopie /ytɔpi/ nf **(a)** Utopia
(b) wishful thinking

utopique /ytɔpik/ adj utopian

UV /yve/ nm pl (abbr = **ultraviolets**)
ultraviolet rays; **séance d'∼** session on a
sunbed

uvule /yvyl/ nf uvula

Vv

v, V /ve/ *nm inv* v, V; **en (forme de) V**
V-shaped; **pull en V** V-necked sweater

va /va/ ▶ ALLER¹

⚹ **vacance** /vakɑ̃s/ **1** *nf* vacancy
2 **vacances** *nf pl* holiday (GB), vacation
(US); **être en ~s** to be on holiday (GB) *or*
vacation (US)
■ **~s scolaires** (Sch) school holidays (GB) *or*
vacation (US)

vacancier, -ière /vakɑ̃sje, ɛʀ/ *nm,f*
holidaymaker (GB), vacationer (US)

vacant, ~e /vakɑ̃, ɑ̃t/ *adj* vacant

vacarme /vakaʀm/ *nm* din, racket (colloq)

vacataire /vakatɛʀ/ *nmf* **(a)** temporary
employee
(b) supply teacher (GB), substitute teacher
(US)

vaccin /vaksɛ̃/ *nm* (Med) vaccine

vaccination /vaksinasjɔ̃/ *nf* vaccination

vacciner /vaksine/ [1] *vtr* **(a)** to vaccinate
(b) (humorous) **je suis vacciné!** (fam) I've
learned my lesson!

vache /vaʃ/ **1** *adj* (fam) mean, nasty
2 *nf* **(a)** cow
(b) cowhide
■ **~ à eau** water bottle; **~ à lait** (figurative)
money-spinner (colloq); **années de ~s mai-
gres** lean years
IDIOM **parler français comme une ~ espag-
nole** (fam) to speak very bad French

vachement /vaʃmɑ̃/ *adv* (fam) really

vacherie /vaʃʀi/ *nf* (fam) **(a)** meanness
(b) bitchy remark (colloq)
(c) dirty trick
(d) c'est une vraie ~ ce virus this virus is a
damned nuisance (colloq)

vachette /vaʃɛt/ *nf* **(a)** young cow
(b) calfskin

vacillant, ~e /vasijɑ̃, ɑ̃t/ *adj* **(a)** ‹legs›
unsteady; ‹person› unsteady on one's legs;
‹light, flame› flickering
(b) ‹power, majority› shaky

vaciller /vasije/ [1] *vi* **(a)** ‹person› to be
unsteady on one's legs; ‹legs› to be unsteady
(b) ‹person, object› to sway; ‹light, flame› to
flicker
(c) ‹health› to fail; ‹majority› to weaken

vadrouille /vadʀuj/ *nf* (fam) stroll; **être en
~** to be wandering about

vadrouiller /vadʀuje/ [1] *vi* (fam) to
wander around

────────────

⚹ indicates a very frequent word

va-et-vient /vaevjɛ̃/ *nm inv* **(a)** comings
and goings; **faire le ~** to go to and fro; to go
back and forth
(b) two-way switch

vagabond, ~e /vagabɔ̃, ɔ̃d/ **1** *adj* ‹dog›
stray; ‹mood› ever-changing
2 *nm,f* vagrant

vagabondage /vagabɔ̃daʒ/ *nm*
(a) wandering
(b) (Law) vagrancy

vagabonder /vagabɔ̃de/ [1] *vi* to wander

vagin /vaʒɛ̃/ *nm* vagina

vagissement /vaʒismɑ̃/ *nm* wail

vague¹ /vag/ **1** *adj* vague; **ce sont de ~s
parents** they're distant relatives
2 *nm* **(a)** **il regardait dans le ~** he was
staring into space
(b) avoir du ~ à l'âme to feel melancholic

⚹ **vague²** /vag/ *nf* wave; **faire des ~s** ‹wind›
to make ripples; (figurative) ‹scandal› to cause
a stir
■ **~ de chaleur** heatwave; **~ de froid** cold spell
IDIOM **être au creux de la ~** to be at a low
ebb

vaguement /vagmɑ̃/ *adv* vaguely

vaillamment /vajamɑ̃/ *adv* courageously,
valiantly

vaillance /vajɑ̃s/ *nf* courage; **avec ~**
courageously

vaillant, ~e /vajɑ̃, ɑ̃t/ *adj* **(a)** courageous
(b) strong

⚹ **vain, ~e** /vɛ̃, vɛn/ **1** *adj* **(a)** futile; **mes
efforts ont été ~s** my efforts were in vain
(b) ‹promises› empty; ‹hopes› vain
(c) ‹person› vain
2 **en vain** *phr* in vain

⚹ **vaincre** /vɛ̃kʀ/ [57] **1** *vtr* **(a)** to defeat
‹opponent›
(b) to overcome ‹prejudices, complex›; to beat
‹unemployment, illness›
2 *vi* to win

vaincu, ~e /vɛ̃ky/ ▶ VAINCRE

vainement /vɛnmɑ̃/ *adv* in vain

vainqueur /vɛ̃kœʀ/ **1** *adj m* victorious
2 *nm* victor; winner; prizewinner;
conqueror

vais /vɛ/ ▶ ALLER¹

⚹ **vaisseau**, *pl* **~x** /veso/ *nm* **(a)** (Anat, Bot)
vessel
(b) (Naut) vessel; warship
■ **~ spatial** spaceship

vaisselier /vesəlje/ *nm* dresser

vaisselle /vesɛl/ *nf* **(a)** crockery, dishes
(b) dishes; **faire la ~** to do the dishes

val, *pl* ~**s** *or* **vaux** /val, vo/ *nm* valley
IDIOM **être toujours par monts et par vaux** to
be always on the move
valable /valabl/ *adj* **(a)** ‹*explanation*› valid;
‹*solution*› viable
(b) ‹*document*› valid
(c) (fam) ‹*work, project*› worthwhile
valdinguer /valdɛ̃ge/ [1] *vi* (fam) to go
flying (colloq)
valet /valɛ/ *nm* **(a)** manservant
(b) (in cards) jack
■ ~ **de chambre** valet; ~ **de ferme** farm hand;
~ **de nuit** rack, valet (US)
ᵩ **valeur** /valœʀ/ *nf* **(a)** value; **prendre de la** ~
to go up in value; **les objets de** ~ valuables
(b) (of person, artist) worth; (of work) value,
merit; (of method, discovery) value; **attacher
de la** ~ **à qch** to value sth; **mettre qch en** ~
to emphasize ‹*fact, talent*›; to set off ‹*eyes,
painting*›; **se mettre en** ~ to make the best of
oneself; to show oneself to best advantage
(c) validity
(d) value; **nous n'avons pas les mêmes** ~**s**
we don't share the same values
(e) (on stock exchange) security; ~**s** securities,
stock, stocks and shares
■ ~ **sûre** gilt-edged security (GB), blue chip;
(figurative) safe bet; ~**s mobilières** securities
valeureux, -euse /valœʀø, øz/ *adj*
valorous (dated)
validation /validasjɔ̃/ *nf* **(a)** validation
(b) stamping
valide /valid/ *adj* **(a)** valid
(b) able-bodied; fit
valider /valide/ [1] *vtr* to stamp ‹*ticket*›;
faire ~ to have [sth] recognized ‹*diploma*›
validité /validite/ *nf* validity
valise /valiz/ *nf* suitcase; **faire ses** ~**s** to
pack
IDIOM **avoir des** ~**s sous les yeux** (fam) to
have bags under one's eyes
vallée /vale/ *nf* valley
vallon /valɔ̃/ *nm* dale, small valley
vallonné, -e /valɔne/ *adj* ‹*landscape*›
undulating; ‹*country*› hilly
ᵩ **valoir** /valwaʀ/ [45] **1** *vtr* ~ **qch à qn** to
earn sb sth ‹*praise, criticism*›; to win sb sth
‹*friendship*›; to bring sb sth ‹*problems*›
2 *vi* **(a)** ~ **une fortune/cher** to be worth a
fortune/a lot; **ça vaut combien?** how much
is it worth?; ~ **de l'or** (figurative) to be very
valuable
(b) **que vaut ce film/vin?** what's that film/
wine like?; **il ne vaut pas mieux que son
frère** he's no better than his brother; **ne
rien** ~ to be rubbish; to be useless; to be
worthless; **la chaleur ne me vaut rien** the
heat doesn't suit me; **ça ne me dit rien qui
vaille** I don't like the sound of it
(c) to be as good as; **ton travail vaut bien/
largement le leur** your work is just as good/
every bit as good as theirs; **rien ne vaut la**

soie nothing beats silk
(d) to be worth; **le musée vaut le détour** the
museum is worth a detour; **ça vaut la peine**
or **le coup** (fam) it's worth it
(e) ‹*rule, criticism*› to apply
(f) **faire** ~ to put [sth] to work ‹*money*›; to
point out ‹*necessity*›; to emphasize ‹*quality*›;
to assert ‹*right*›; **faire** ~ **que** to point out
that; **se faire** ~ to push oneself forward
3 **se valoir** *v refl* (+ *v être*) to be the same
4 *v impers* **il vaut mieux faire, mieux vaut
faire** it's better to do; **il vaut mieux que tu y
ailles** you'd better go
valorisation /valɔʀizasjɔ̃/ *nf* **(a)** (of
product) promotion
(b) (of region, resources) development
valoriser /valɔʀize/ [1] *vtr* **(a)** to
promote ‹*product*›; to make [sth] attractive
‹*profession, course*›
(b) to develop ‹*region, resources*›
valse /vals/ *nf* waltz
valse-hésitation, *pl* **valses-
hésitations** /valsezitasjɔ̃/ *nf* shilly-
shallying (colloq)
valser /valse/ [1] *vi* to waltz
valseur, -euse /valsœʀ, øz/ *nm,f* waltzer
valu, ~e /valy/ ▶ VALOIR
valve /valv/ *nf* valve
vamp /vɑ̃p/ *nf* (fam) vamp
vampire /vɑ̃piʀ/ *nm* **(a)** vampire
(b) (figurative) bloodsucker
(c) (Zool) vampire bat
vampiriser /vɑ̃piʀize/ [1] *vtr* (figurative) to
cannibalize
van /vɑ̃/ *nm* **(a)** horsebox (GB), horse-car
(US)
(b) van
vandale /vɑ̃dal/ *nmf* vandal
vandalisme /vɑ̃dalism/ *nm* vandalism
vanille /vanij/ *nf* vanilla; **une gousse de** ~
a vanilla pod
vanité /vanite/ *nf* **(a)** vanity; **tirer** ~ **de qch**
to pride oneself on sth
(b) (of efforts) futility; (of promise) emptiness;
(of undertaking) uselessness
vaniteux, -euse /vanitø, øz/ *adj* vain
vanne /van/ *nf* **(a)** gate; sluice gate;
floodgate
(b) (fam) dig (colloq)
IDIOM **fermer les** ~**s** (fam) to cut funding
vanner /vane/ [1] *vtr* (fam) to tire [sb] out
vannerie /vanʀi/ *nf* basket-making; **objets
en** ~ wickerwork
vantardise /vɑ̃taʀdiz/ *nf* **(a)** boastfulness
(b) boast
vanter /vɑ̃te/ [1] **1** *vtr* to praise, to extol
2 **se vanter** *v refl* (+ *v être*) **(a)** to boast
(b) **se** ~ **de faire** to pride oneself on doing
va-nu-pieds /vanypje/ *nmf inv* tramp,
bum (US) (colloq)

v

vapeur /vapœʀ/ ① nf steam; **bateau à** ~ steamboat; **renverser la** ~ (figurative) to backpedal; **faire cuire qch à la** ~ to steam sth
② **vapeurs** nf pl fumes

vaporeux, -euse /vapɔʀø, øz/ adj diaphanous

vaporisateur /vapɔʀizatœʀ/ nm spray

vaporisation /vapɔʀizasjɔ̃/ nf spraying

vaporiser /vapɔʀize/ [1] vtr to spray

vaquer /vake/ [1] v+prep ~ **à ses occupations** to attend to one's business

varappe /vaʀap/ nf rock-climbing

varappeur, -euse /vaʀapœʀ, øz/ nm,f rock climber

varech /vaʀɛk/ nm kelp

vareuse /vaʀøz/ nf (a) jersey
(b) (Mil) uniform jacket

variable /vaʀjabl/ ① adj (a) variable
(b) ‹weather› changeable; ‹mood› unpredictable
② nf variable

variante /vaʀjɑ̃t/ nf variant

variation /vaʀjasjɔ̃/ nf variation; **connaître de fortes** ~**s** to fluctuate considerably

varice /vaʀis/ nf varicose vein

varicelle /vaʀisɛl/ nf chicken pox

varié, ~e /vaʀje/ adj (a) varied
(b) various

varier /vaʀje/ [2] ① vtr to vary; **pour** ~ **les plaisirs** just for a (pleasant) change
② vi to vary; **l'inflation varie de 4% à 6%** inflation fluctuates between 4% and 6%

variété /vaʀjete/ ① nf (a) variety; **une grande** ~ **d'articles** a wide range of items
(b) (Bot) variety
(c) sort
② **variétés** nf pl **spectacle de** ~**s** variety show; **les** ~**s françaises** French popular music

variole /vaʀjɔl/ nf smallpox

Varsovie /vaʀsɔvi/ pr n Warsaw

vas /va/ ▶ ALLER¹

vase¹ /vɑz/ nm vase
IDIOM c'est la goutte d'eau qui fait déborder le ~ it's the last straw

vase² /vɑz/ nf silt, sludge

vasectomie /vazɛktɔmi/ nf vasectomy

vaseux, -euse /vɑzø, øz/ adj (a) muddy
(b) (fam) **je me sens plutôt** ~ I'm not really with it (colloq)
(c) (fam) ‹speech, explanation› woolly

vasistas /vazistas/ nm inv louvre (GB) window

vasque /vask/ nf (a) (of fountain) basin
(b) bowl

vassal, ~e, mpl -aux /vasal, o/ nm,f vassal

◆ **vaste** /vast/ adj (a) ‹estate, sector› vast; ‹market› huge
(b) ‹audience, choice› large
(c) ‹fraud› massive; ‹campaign› extensive; ‹movement, attack› large-scale; ‹work› wide-ranging

va-t-en-guerre /vatɑ̃gɛʀ/ nm inv warmonger

va-tout /vatu/ nm inv **jouer/tenter son** ~ to stake/to risk everything

vaudeville /vodvil/ nm light comedy; **tourner au** ~ to turn into a farce

vaudou /vodu/ adj inv, nm voodoo

vaurien, -ienne /voʀjɛ̃, ɛn/ nm,f (a) rascal
(b) lout, yobbo (GB) (colloq), hoodlum (colloq)

vautour /votuʀ/ nm vulture

vautrer: se vautrer /votʀe/ [1] v refl (+ v être) (a) **se** ~ **sur** to sprawl on
(b) **se** ~ **dans un fauteuil** to loll in an armchair

va-vite: à la va-vite /alavavit/ phr in a rush

veau, pl ~**x** /vo/ nm (a) calf
(b) (Culin) veal
(c) calfskin

vecteur /vɛktœʀ/ nm (a) vector
(b) (figurative) vehicle
(c) (of disease) carrier

vécu, ~e /veky/ ① pp ▶ VIVRE
② pp adj ‹drama, story› real-life
③ nm personal experiences

vedette /vədɛt/ nf (a) star; **avoir la** ~ to have top billing
(b) (Naut) launch

végétal, ~e, mpl -aux /veʒetal, o/ ① adj vegetable
② nm vegetable

végétalien, -ienne /veʒetaljɛ̃, ɛn/ adj, nm,f vegan

végétarien, -ienne /veʒetaʀjɛ̃, ɛn/ adj, nm,f vegetarian

végétatif, -ive /veʒetatif, iv/ adj vegetative

végétation /veʒetasjɔ̃/ ① nf vegetation
② **végétations** nf pl (Med) adenoids

végéter /veʒete/ [14] vi ‹person› to vegetate; ‹project› to stagnate

véhémence /veemɑ̃s/ nf vehemence

◆ **véhicule** /veikyl/ nm vehicle
■ ~ **utilitaire** commercial vehicle

véhiculer /veikyle/ [1] vtr to carry ‹people, goods, substance›; ~ **une image** to promote an image

◆ **veille** /vɛj/ nf (a) **la** ~ the day before; **la** ~ **au soir** the night before; **à la** ~ **de** on the eve of
(b) **être en état de** ~ to be awake
(c) vigil

veillée /veje/ nf (a) evening; **à la** ~ in the evening
(b) vigil; ~ **funèbre** wake

◆ indicates a very frequent word

⚔ **veiller** /veje/ [1] **1** *vtr* to watch over ‹ill person›; to keep watch over ‹dead person›

2 veiller à *v+prep* to look after ‹health›; ~ **à ce que** to see to it that, to make sure that

3 veiller sur *v+prep* to watch over ‹child›

4 *vi* **(a)** to stay up
(b) to be on watch
(c) to be watchful
IDIOM ~ **au grain** to be on one's guard

veilleur /vejœʀ/ *nm,f* ~ **de nuit** night watchman

veilleuse /vɛjøz/ *nf* **(a)** night light
(b) pilot light
(c) side light (GB), parking light (US)

veinard, ~e /venaʀ, aʀd/ *nm,f* (fam) lucky devil (colloq)

veine /vɛn/ *nf* **(a)** vein
(b) (in wood) grain
(c) (of coal) seam
(d) inspiration; **dans la même** ~ in the same vein; **en** ~ **de générosité** in a generous mood
(e) (fam) luck; **il a de la** ~ he's lucky

veiné, ~e /vene/ *adj* ‹skin, hand, marble› veined; ‹wood› grained

veinure /venyʀ/ *nf* (in wood) grain; (in marble) veining

vêler /vɛle/ [1] *vi* ‹cow› to calve

velléité /vɛlleite/ *nf* **(a)** vague desire
(b) vague attempt

⚔ **vélo** /velo/ *nm* (fam) bike; **faire du** ~ to cycle
■ ~ **d'appartement** exercise bike; ~ **tout terrain, VTT** mountain bike

vélo-cross /velokʀɔs/ *nm inv* **(a)** cyclo-cross
(b) cyclo-cross bike

vélomoteur /velomɔtœʀ/ *nm* moped

velours /vəluʀ/ *nm inv* **(a)** velvet
(b) corduroy
IDIOMS **une main de fer dans un gant de** ~ an iron fist in a velvet glove; **faire patte de** ~ to switch on the charm

velouté, ~e /vəlute/ **1** *adj* ‹skin, voice› velvety; ‹wine› smooth
2 *nm* **(a)** (Culin) ~ **de champignons** cream of mushroom soup
(b) softness; smoothness

velu, ~e /vəly/ *adj* **(a)** hairy
(b) (Bot) villous

vénal, ~e, mpl -aux /venal, o/ *adj* ‹person› venal; ‹behaviour› mercenary

vendable /vɑ̃dabl/ *adj* saleable (GB)

vendange /vɑ̃dɑ̃ʒ/ *nf* grape harvest

vendanger /vɑ̃dɑ̃ʒe/ [13] **1** *vtr* to harvest ‹grapes›; to pick the grapes from ‹vine›
2 *vi* to harvest the grapes

vendeur, -euse /vɑ̃dœʀ, øz/ *nm,f* **(a)** shop assistant (GB), salesclerk (US)
(b) salesman/saleswoman
■ ~ **ambulant** pedlar (GB), peddler (US); ~ **de journaux** news vendor

⚔ **vendre** /vɑ̃dʀ/ [6] **1** *vtr* **(a)** to sell; ~ **à crédit** to sell on credit; ~ **en gros** to wholesale; ~ **au détail** to retail; **'à** ~**'** 'for sale'
(b) to betray ‹person›; to sell ‹secrets›

2 se vendre *v refl* (+ *v être*) **(a)** to be sold
(b) **se** ~ **bien** to sell well
(c) to sell oneself; **se** ~ **à l'ennemi** to sell out to the enemy

⚔ **vendredi** /vɑ̃dʀədi/ *nm* Friday; ~ **saint** Good Friday

vendu, ~e /vɑ̃dy/ **1** *pp* ▶ VENDRE
2 *pp adj* bribed
3 *nm,f* traitor

vénéneux, -euse /venenø, øz/ *adj* poisonous

vénérable /veneʀabl/ *adj* ‹person› venerable; ‹tree, object› ancient

vénération /veneʀasjɔ̃/ *nf* veneration

vénérer /veneʀe/ [14] *vtr* to venerate; to revere

vénérien, -ienne /veneʀjɛ̃, ɛn/ *adj* venereal

vengeance /vɑ̃ʒɑ̃s/ *nf* revenge

venger /vɑ̃ʒe/ [13] **1** *vtr* to avenge
2 se venger *v refl* (+ *v être*) to get one's revenge; **se** ~ **sur qn/qch** to take it out on sb/sth

vengeur, vengeresse /vɑ̃ʒœʀ, vɑ̃ʒʀɛs/ *adj* vengeful; avenging; vindictive

véniel, -ielle /venjɛl/ *adj* ‹sin› venial

venimeux, -euse /vənimø, øz/ *adj* venomous

venin /vənɛ̃/ *nm* venom

⚔ **venir** /vəniʀ/ [36] **1** *v aux* **(a)** ~ **de faire** to have just done; **elle vient de partir** she's just left; **'vient de paraître'** (of book) 'new!'
(b) ~ **aggraver la situation** to make the situation worse
(c) **le ballon est venu rouler sous mes pieds** the ball rolled up to my feet
(d) **s'il venait à pleuvoir** if it should rain
2 *vi* (+ *v être*) **(a)** to come; ~ **de** to come from; ~ **après/avant** to come after/before; **allez, viens!** come on!; **viens voir** come and see; **j'en viens** I've just been there; **je viens de sa part** he/she sent me to see you; **faire** ~ **qn** to send for sb; to get sb to come; **faire** ~ **le médecin** to call the doctor; **ça ne m'est jamais venu à l'idée** it never crossed my mind; **dans les jours à** ~ in the next few days
(b) **en** ~ **à** to come to; **en** ~ **aux mains** to come to blows

⚔ **vent** /vɑ̃/ *nm* **(a)** wind; ~ **d'est** east wind; ~ **du large** seaward wind; **grand** ~ gale, strong wind; **il fait** *or* **il y a du** ~ it's windy; **en plein** ~ exposed to the wind; in the open; **passer en coup de** ~ (figurative) to rush through; **faire du** ~ (with fan) to create a breeze; ~ **favorable, bon** ~ favourable (GB) wind; **avoir le** ~ **en poupe** to sail *or* run before the wind; ⋯▶

(figurative) to have the wind in one's sails; **coup de ~** fresh gale
(b) un ~ de liberté a wind of freedom; **un ~ de folie** a wave of madness
(c) (euphemistic) wind
IDIOMS **c'est du ~!** it's just hot air!; **du ~!** (fam) get lost! (colloq); **quel bon ~ vous amène?** to what do I owe the pleasure (of your visit)?; **être dans le ~** to be trendy; **avoir ~ de qch** to get wind of sth; **contre ~s et marées** come hell or high water; against all odds

◆ **vente** /vɑ̃t/ *nf* sale; **en ~ libre** (gen) freely available; *‹medicines›* available over the counter; **mettre qch en ~** to put [sth] up for sale
■ **~ par correspondance** mail order selling; **~ au détail** retailing; **~ aux enchères** auction (sale); **~ en gros** wholesaling

ventilateur /vɑ̃tilatœʀ/ *nm* fan; ventilator
ventilation /vɑ̃tilasjɔ̃/ *nf* ventilation (system)
ventiler /vɑ̃tile/ [1] *vtr* **(a)** to ventilate
(b) to break down *‹expenses, profits›*
(c) to assign *‹staff›*; to allocate *‹tasks, equipment›*
ventouse /vɑ̃tuz/ *nf* **(a)** suction pad (GB), suction cup (US); **faire ~** to stick
(b) plunger
(c) (Med) cupping glass
ventral, ~e, *mpl* **-aux** /vɑ̃tʀal, o/ *adj* ventral; **parachute ~** lap-pack parachute
◆ **ventre** /vɑ̃tʀ/ *nm* **(a)** stomach; **avoir mal au ~** to have stomach ache; **ça me donne mal au ~ de voir ça** (figurative) (fam) it makes me sick to see that sort of thing
(b) (of animal) (under)belly
(c) ne rien avoir dans le ~ (fam) to have no guts (colloq); **avoir la peur au ~** to feel sick with fear
(d) (of pot, boat, plane) belly
IDIOM **courir ~ à terre** to run flat out
ventricule /vɑ̃tʀikyl/ *nm* ventricle
ventriloque /vɑ̃tʀilɔk/ *nmf* ventriloquist
ventripotent, ~e /vɑ̃tʀipɔtɑ̃, ɑ̃t/ *adj* (fam) portly, fat-bellied
ventru, ~e /vɑ̃tʀy/ *adj* *‹man›* paunchy, pot-bellied; *‹pot, piece of furniture›* rounded; *‹wall›* bulging
venu, ~e¹ /vəny/ **1** *pp* ▸ VENIR
2 *pp adj* **bien ~** apt; **mal ~** badly timed; **il serait mal ~ de le leur dire** it wouldn't be a good idea to tell them
3 *nm,f* **nouveau ~** newcomer
venue² /vəny/ *nf* visit; **~ au monde** birth
vêpres /vɛpʀ/ *nf pl* vespers
ver /vɛʀ/ *nm* worm; woodworm; maggot
■ **~ à soie** silkworm; **~ solitaire** tapeworm; **~ de terre** earthworm
IDIOM **tirer les ~s du nez à qn** (fam) to worm

◆ indicates a very frequent word

information out of sb
véracité /veʀasite/ *nf* truthfulness
véranda /veʀɑ̃da/ *nf* veranda
verbal, ~e, *mpl* **-aux** /vɛʀbal, o/ *adj* verbal; verb
verbaliser /vɛʀbalize/ [1] *vi* to record an offence (GB)
verbe /vɛʀb/ *nm* **(a)** verb
(b) language; **avoir le ~ haut** to be arrogant in one's speech
verdâtre /vɛʀdɑtʀ/ *adj* greenish
verdeur /vɛʀdœʀ/ *nf* sprightliness
verdict /vɛʀdikt/ *nm* verdict
verdir /vɛʀdiʀ/ [3] *vi* **(a)** (gen) to turn green; *‹copper›* to tarnish
(b) to turn pale
verdoyant, ~e /vɛʀdwajɑ̃, ɑ̃t/ *adj* green
verdure /vɛʀdyʀ/ *nf* **(a)** greenery
(b) green vegetables
véreux, -euse /veʀø, øz/ *adj* **(a)** *‹fruit›* worm-eaten
(b) *‹politician, lawyer›* bent (colloq), crooked
verge /vɛʀʒ/ *nf* **(a)** penis
(b) switch, birch
vergé /vɛʀʒe/ *nm* laid paper
verger /vɛʀʒe/ *nm* orchard
vergeture /vɛʀʒətyʀ/ *nf* stretch mark
verglacé, ~e /vɛʀɡlase/ *adj* icy
verglas /vɛʀɡla/ *nm inv* black ice
vergogne: sans vergogne /sɑ̃vɛʀɡɔɲ/ *phr* shamelessly
véridique /veʀidik/ *adj* true
vérifiable /veʀifjabl/ *adj* **être facilement ~** to be easy to check *or* verify
vérification /veʀifikasjɔ̃/ *nf* (on equipment, identity) check; (of alibi, fact) verification
◆ **vérifier** /veʀifje/ [2] **1** *vtr* to check; to verify
2 se vérifier *v refl* (+ *v être*) *‹hypothesis, theory›* to be borne out
◆ **véritable** /veʀitabl/ *adj* real; true; genuine
véritablement /veʀitabləmɑ̃/ *adv* really
◆ **vérité** /veʀite/ *nf* **(a)** truth; **l'épreuve de ~** the acid test; **à la ~** to tell the truth
(b) énoncer des ~s premières to state the obvious
(c) sincerity
verlan /vɛʀlɑ̃/ *nm*: *French slang formed by inverting the syllables*
vermeil, -eille /vɛʀmɛj/ **1** *adj* **(a)** bright red
(b) *‹wine›* ruby
2 *nm* vermeil
vermicelle /vɛʀmisɛl/ *nm* **du ~, des ~s** vermicelli
vermifuge /vɛʀmifyʒ/ *nm* wormer
vermillon /vɛʀmijɔ̃/ *adj inv* bright red
vermine /vɛʀmin/ *nf* **(a)** vermin
(b) (figurative) scum
vermoulu, ~e /vɛʀmuly/ *adj* worm-eaten

verni, ∼**e** /vɛʀni/ **1** *pp* ▶ VERNIR

  2 *pp adj* varnished; patent-leather; glazed

  3 *adj* (fam) lucky; **il n'est pas** ∼ he's unlucky

vernir /vɛʀniʀ/ [3] **1** *vtr* to varnish; to glaze

  2 se vernir *v refl* (+ *v être*) **se** ∼ **les ongles** to paint one's nails

vernis /vɛʀni/ *nm inv* (a) varnish; glaze

  (b) (figurative) veneer; **si on gratte le** ∼**, on voit que...** if you scratch the surface, you'll see that...

  ■ ∼ **à ongles** nail varnish (GB) *or* polish

vernissage /vɛʀnisaʒ/ *nm* (a) (of art exhibition) preview, private view

  (b) varnishing; glazing

vernissé, ∼**e** /vɛʀnise/ *adj* (a) glazed

  (b) glossy

✦ **verre** /vɛʀ/ *nm* (a) glass; **de** *or* **en** ∼ glass; **un** ∼ **à eau/vin** a water/wine glass; ∼**s et couverts** glassware and cutlery; **lever son** ∼ **à la santé de qn** to raise one's glass to sb

  (b) glass, glassful; **un** ∼ **d'eau/de vin** a glass of water/wine

  (c) drink

  (d) lens; ∼ **grossissant** magnifying glass

  ■ ∼ **de contact** contact lens; ∼ **à pied** stemmed glass

verrerie /vɛʀʀi/ *nf* (a) glassmaking

  (b) glassworks, glass factory

verrière /vɛʀjɛʀ/ *nf* (a) glass roof

  (b) glass wall

verroterie /vɛʀɔtʀi/ *nf* glass jewellery (GB) *or* jewelry (US)

verrou /vɛʀu/ *nm* bolt

  IDIOM **être sous les** ∼**s** to be behind bars

verrouillage /vɛʀujaʒ/ *nm* bolting; locking; locking mechanism

  ■ ∼ **central** *or* **centralisé (des portes)** central locking

verrouiller /vɛʀuje/ [1] *vtr* to bolt ⟨*window, door*⟩; to lock ⟨*car door, gun*⟩

verrue /vɛʀy/ *nf* wart; ∼ **plantaire** verruca

✦ **vers¹** /vɛʀ/ *prep*

  ■ **Note** When *vers* is part of an expression such as *se tourner vers, tendre vers* etc, you will find the translation at the entries TOURNER, TENDRE¹ 3 etc.

  – See below for other uses of *vers*.

  (a) toward(s); **se déplacer de la gauche** ∼ **la droite** to move from left to right

  (b) near, around; about; toward(s); ∼ **cinq heures** at about five o'clock; ∼ **le soir** toward(s) evening

vers² /vɛʀ/ *nm inv* line (of verse)

versant /vɛʀsɑ̃/ *nm* side

versatile /vɛʀsatil/ *adj* unpredictable, volatile

verse: **à verse** /avɛʀs/ *phr* **il pleut à** ∼ it's pouring down

Verseau /vɛʀso/ *pr nm* Aquarius

versement /vɛʀsəmɑ̃/ *nm* (a) payment; ∼ **comptant** cash payment

  (b) instalment (GB)

  (c) deposit; **faire un** ∼ **sur son compte** to pay money into one's account

✦ **verser** /vɛʀse/ [1] **1** *vtr* (a) to pour

  (b) to pay ⟨*sum, pension*⟩

  (c) to shed ⟨*tear, blood*⟩

  (d) ∼ **une pièce à un dossier** to add a document to a file

  2 *vi* (a) to overturn

  (b) to lapse

  (c) ⟨*jug*⟩ to pour

verset /vɛʀsɛ/ *nm* (in Bible, Koran) verse

verseur, -euse /vɛʀsœʀ, øz/ *adj* pouring; **flacon** ∼ bottle with a pouring spout

versifier /vɛʀsifje/ [2] *vtr* to put [sth] into verse

✦ **version** /vɛʀsjɔ̃/ *nf* (a) translation (*into one's own language*)

  (b) version

  ■ ∼ **originale**, **vo** (of film) original version

verso /vɛʀso/ *nm* back; **voir au** ∼ see over(leaf)

✦ **vert**, ∼**e** /vɛʀ, vɛʀt/ **1** *adj* (a) green; **être** ∼ **de peur** to be white with fear

  (b) ⟨*fruit*⟩ green, unripe; ⟨*wine*⟩ immature

  (c) sprightly

  (d) (*before n*) ⟨*reprimand*⟩ sharp, stiff

  2 *nm* green

  3 verts *nm pl* **les** ∼**s** the Greens

  IDIOM **avoir la main** ∼**e** to have green fingers (GB) *or* a green thumb (US)

vert-de-gris /vɛʀdəgʀi/ **1** *adj inv* blue-green

  2 *nm inv* verdigris

vertébral, ∼**e**, *mpl* **-aux** /vɛʀtebʀal, o/ *adj* vertebral

vertèbre /vɛʀtɛbʀ/ *nf* vertebra

vertébré /vɛʀtebʀe/ *nm* vertebrate

vertement /vɛʀtəmɑ̃/ *adv* sharply

vertical, ∼**e¹**, *mpl* **-aux** /vɛʀtikal, o/ *adj* vertical; upright

verticale² /vɛʀtikal/ *nf* vertical

verticalement /vɛʀtikalmɑ̃/ *adv*

  (a) vertically

  (b) (in crossword) down

vertige /vɛʀtiʒ/ *nm* (a) dizziness; vertigo; **avoir le** ∼ to suffer from vertigo; to feel dizzy

  (b) **avoir des** ∼**s** to have dizzy *or* giddy spells

vertigineux, -euse /vɛʀtiʒinø, øz/ *adj* dizzy, giddy; breathtaking; staggering

✦ **vertu** /vɛʀty/ **1** *nf* (a) virtue; **de petite** ∼ of easy virtue

  (b) (of plant, remedy) property

  2 en vertu de *phr* by virtue of ⟨*law*⟩; in accordance with ⟨*agreement*⟩

vertueux, -euse /vɛʀtɥø, øz/ *adj* virtuous

verve /vɛʀv/ *nf* eloquence

verveine /vɛʀvɛn/ *nf* verbena (tea)

vésicule /vezikyl/ nf vesicle; ~ biliaire
gall bladder

vespéral, ~e, mpl -aux /vɛspeʀal, o/ adj
evening

vessie /vesi/ nf bladder
IDIOM prendre des ~s pour des lanternes
(fam) to think the moon is made of green
cheese

veste /vɛst/ nf jacket; ~ de survêtement
tracksuit top
IDIOM retourner sa ~ (fam) to change sides

vestiaire /vɛstjɛʀ/ nm (in gym) changing
room (GB), locker room; (in theatre)
cloakroom; laisser sa fierté au ~ to forget
one's pride

vestibule /vɛstibyl/ nm hall; foyer (GB),
lobby

vestige /vɛstiʒ/ nm (a) relic; des ~s
archéologiques archaeological remains
(b) vestige

vestimentaire /vɛstimãtɛʀ/ adj tenue ~
way of dressing; mode ~ fashion

veston /vɛstɔ̃/ nm (man's) jacket

◆ **vêtement** /vɛtmã/ nm piece of clothing;
des ~s clothes; '~s pour hommes'
'menswear'; ~s de sport sportswear

vétéran /veteʀã/ nm veteran

vétérinaire /veteʀinɛʀ/ [1] adj veterinary
[2] nmf veterinary surgeon (GB),
veterinarian (US)

vétille /vetij/ nf trifle

vêtir /vɛtiʀ/ [33] [1] vtr to dress ‹person,
doll›
[2] se vêtir v refl (+ v être) to dress
(oneself)

veto /veto/ nm veto; mettre or opposer son
~ à qch to veto sth

vêtu, ~e /vɛty/ ▶ VÊTIR

vétuste /vetyst/ adj (a) dilapidated
(b) outdated

vétusté /vetyste/ nf dilapidation (de of),
run-down state (de of); outdated state (de of)

veuf, **veuve** /vœf, vœv/ [1] adj widowed
[2] nm,f widower/widow

veule /vøl/ adj weak, spineless

veuvage /vœvaʒ/ nm widowhood

veuve ▶ VEUF

vexant, ~e /vɛksã, ãt/ adj hurtful
(b) tiresome, vexing

vexation /vɛksasjɔ̃/ nf humiliation

vexer /vɛkse/ [1] [1] vtr (a) to offend
(b) to annoy
[2] se vexer v refl (+ v être) to take offence
(GB)

via /vja/ prep via; through

viabilité /vjabilite/ nf (a) viability
(b) (of road) suitability for vehicles

viable /vjabl/ adj (a) viable

(b) ‹project› feasible; ‹situation› bearable,
tolerable

viaduc /vjadyk/ nm viaduct

viager /vjaʒe/ nm life annuity

◆ **viande** /vjãd/ nf meat; ~ de bœuf/mouton
beef/mutton
■ ~ des Grisons dried beef

vibrant, ~e /vibʀã, ãt/ adj (a) vibrating
(b) ‹voice› resonant; ‹speech› vibrant; ‹praise›
glowing; ‹plea› impassioned; ‹crowd› excited

vibration /vibʀasjɔ̃/ nf vibration;
traitement par ~s vibromassage

vibrer /vibʀe/ [1] vi (a) to vibrate
(b) ‹voice› to quiver; ‹heart› to thrill

vibromasseur /vibʀomasœʀ/ nm
vibrator

vicaire /vikɛʀ/ nm curate

vice /vis/ nm (a) vice; vivre dans le ~ to
lead a dissolute life
(b) vice; mon ~, c'est le tabac my vice is
smoking
(c) fault, defect; ~ de fabrication
manufacturing defect

vice-président, ~e, mpl ~s
/vispʀezidã, ãt/ nm,f (of state) vice-president;
(of committee, company) vice-chair(man), vice-
president (US)

vice-roi, pl ~s /visʀwa/ nm viceroy

vice(-)versa /visvɛʀsa/ adv vice versa

vichy /viʃi/ nm (a) gingham
(b) vichy water

vicier /visje/ [2] vtr to pollute ‹air›; to
contaminate ‹blood›

vicieux, -ieuse /visjø, øz/ adj (a) lecherous;
il faut être ~ pour aimer ça you've got to be
perverted to like that
(b) ‹person› sly; ‹attack› well-disguised;
‹question› trick; ‹argument› deceitful
(c) un cercle ~ a vicious circle

vicinal, ~e, mpl -aux /visinal, o/ adj
chemin ~ byroad

vicomte /vikɔ̃t/ nm viscount

vicomtesse /vikɔ̃tɛs/ nf viscountess

◆ **victime** /viktim/ nf (a) victim, casualty;
être ~ d'un infarctus to suffer a heart attack
(b) sacrificial victim

◆ **victoire** /viktwaʀ/ nf (gen) victory; (Sport) win

victorien, -ienne /viktɔʀjɛ̃, ɛn/ adj
Victorian

victorieux, -ieuse /viktɔʀjø, øz/ adj
‹army› victorious; ‹athlete› winning; ‹smile›
of victory

victuailles /viktɥaj/ nf pl provisions,
victuals

vidange /vidãʒ/ nf (a) emptying
(b) oil change; huile de ~ waste oil
(c) (of washing machine) waste pipe

vidanger /vidãʒe/ [13] [1] vtr (a) to empty,
to drain ‹tank, ditch›
(b) to drain off ‹liquid›
[2] vi ‹washing machine› to empty

_____

◆ indicates a very frequent word

V

✧ vide /vid/ **1** *adj* **(a)** empty; ‹*tape, page*› blank; ‹*flat*› vacant; **tu l'as loué ∼ ou meublé?** are you renting it unfurnished or furnished?

(b) ‹*mind, day*› empty; ‹*look*› vacant

2 *nm* **(a)** space; **sauter** *or* **se jeter dans le ∼** to jump; (figurative) to leap into the unknown; **parler dans le ∼** to talk to oneself; to talk at random

(b) vacuum; void; **emballé sous ∼** vacuum-packed; **faire le ∼ autour de soi** to drive everybody away; **j'ai besoin de faire le ∼ dans ma tête** I need to forget about everything

(c) emptiness; **le ∼ de l'existence** the emptiness of life

(d) gap; **combler un** *or* **le ∼** to fill in a gap; (figurative) to fill a gap

3 à vide *phr* **(a)** empty

(b) with no result

vidéaste /videast/ *nmf* video director

vide-greniers /vidgRənje/ *nm inv* bric-a-brac sale

vidéo /video/ **1** *adj inv* video

2 *nf* video; **tourner un film en ∼** to make a video

vidéocassette /videokasɛt/ *nf* videotape

vidéoclip /videoklip/ *nm* (music) video

vidéoclub /videoklœb/ *nm* video store

vidéoconférence /videokɔ̃feRɑ̃s/ *nf*
(a) videoconference
(b) videoconferencing

vidéodisque /videodisk/ *nm* videodisc

vide-ordures /vidɔRdyR/ *nm inv* rubbish (GB) *or* garbage (US) chute

vidéothèque /videotɛk/ *nf* **(a)** video library
(b) video collection

vide-poches /vidpɔʃ/ *nm inv* tidy

vider /vide/ [1] **1** *vtr* **(a)** to empty; to drain ‹*tank, pond*›

(b) to empty [sth] (out) ‹*water, rubbish*›

(c) (fam) to throw [sb] out (colloq)

(d) (Culin) to gut ‹*fish*›; to draw ‹*game*›

(e) (fam) to wear [sb] out; to drain

2 se vider *v refl* (+ *v être*) to empty; **en été, Paris se vide de ses habitants** in the summer all Parisians leave town

videur, -euse /vidœR, øz/ *nm,f* (fam) bouncer

✧ vie /vi/ *nf* (gen) life; **être en ∼** to be alive; **il y a laissé sa ∼** that was how he lost his life; **donner la ∼ à qn** to bring sb into the world; **la ∼ est chère** the cost of living is high; **mode de ∼** lifestyle; **notre ∼ de couple** our relationship; **donner de la ∼ à une fête** to liven up a party; **sans ∼** lifeless

■ **∼ active** working life

IDIOMS **c'est la belle ∼!** this is the life!; **avoir la ∼ dure** ‹*prejudices*› to be ingrained; **mener la ∼ dure à qn** to make life hard for sb; **faire la ∼** (fam) to have a wild time; to

live it up (colloq); **à la ∼, à la mort!** till death us do part!

vieil ⊳ VIEUX

vieillard, ∼e /vjɛjaR, aRd/ *nm,f* old man/woman; **les ∼s** old people

vieille ⊳ VIEUX

vieillesse /vjɛjɛs/ *nf* (of person) old age; (of building, tree) great age

vieilli, ∼e /vjeji/ **1** *pp* ⊳ VIEILLIR

2 *pp adj* **(a)** old-looking

(b) ‹*equipment*› outdated; ‹*expression*› dated

(c) vin **∼ en fût** wine matured in the cask

vieillir /vjejiR/ [3] **1** *vtr* **(a)** ‹*hairstyle*› to make [sb] look older

(b) ‹*illness*› to age ‹*person*›

2 *vi* **(a)** to get older; **je vieillis** I'm getting old; **j'ai vieilli** I'm older; **notre population vieillit** we have an ageing population

(b) ‹*body, building*› to show signs of age; ‹*person*› to age; **il vieillit mal** he's losing his looks

(c) ‹*wine*› to mature

(d) ‹*work*› to become outdated

3 se vieillir *v refl* (+ *v être*) **(a)** to make oneself look older

(b) to make oneself out to be older

vieillissant, ∼e /vjejisɑ̃, ɑ̃t/ *adj* ageing

vieillissement /vjejismɑ̃/ *nm* ageing

vieillot, -otte /vjejo, ɔt/ *adj* quaint; old-fashioned

viennois, ∼e /vjɛnwa, az/ *adj* **(a)** (in Austria) Viennese; (in France) of Vienne

(b) (Culin) ‹*chocolate, coffee*› Viennese

viennoiserie /vjɛnwazRi/ *nf* Viennese pastry

✧ vierge /vjɛRʒ/ **1** *adj* **(a)** virgin

(b) blank; unused; clean

(c) ‹*wool*› new; ‹*olive oil*› virgin

2 *nf* virgin

Vierge /vjɛRʒ/ **1** *nf* **(a)** **la (Sainte) ∼** the (Blessed) Virgin

(b) madonna

2 *pr nf* Virgo

Viêt Nam /vjɛtnam/ *pr nm* Vietnam

vietnamien, -ienne /vjɛtnamjɛ̃, ɛn/ **1** *adj* Vietnamese

2 *nm* (language) Vietnamese

✧ vieux (**vieil** before vowel or mute *h*), **vieille,** *mpl* **vieux** /vjø, vjɛj/ **1** *adj* old; **être ∼ avant l'âge** to be old before one's time; **une institution vieille de 100 ans** a 100-year-old institution; **il est très vieille France** he's a gentleman of the old school

2 *nm,f* **(a)** old person; **un petit ∼** a little old man; **les ∼** old people; **mes ∼** (fam) my parents

(b) (fam) **mon pauvre ∼** you poor old thing

3 *adv* **vivre ∼** to live to a ripe old age; **il s'habille ∼** he dresses like an old man

4 *nm* **prendre un coup de ∼** to age; **faire du neuf avec du ∼** to revamp things

■ **vieille fille** old maid; **∼ beau** ageing Romeo;

~ **garçon** old bachelor; ~ **jeu** old-fashioned; ~ **rose** dusty pink
IDIOM ~ **comme le monde,** ~ **comme Hérode** as old as the hills

✧ **vif, vive¹** /vif, viv/ **1** adj (a) ⟨colour, light⟩ bright
(b) ⟨person⟩ lively, vivacious; ⟨imagination⟩ vivid
(c) ⟨protests⟩ heated; ⟨opposition⟩ fierce; **sa réaction a été un peu vive** he/she reacted rather strongly
(d) ⟨contrast⟩ sharp; ⟨interest, desire⟩ keen; ⟨pain⟩ acute; ⟨success⟩ notable
(e) ⟨pace, movement⟩ brisk; **à vive allure** ⟨drive⟩ at high speed; **avoir l'esprit** ~ to be very quick
(f) ⟨cold, wind⟩ biting; ⟨edge⟩ sharp; **air** ~ fresh air; **cuire à feu** ~ to cook over a high heat
(g) **de vive voix** in person
2 nm à ~ ⟨flesh⟩ bared; ⟨knee⟩ raw; ⟨wire⟩ exposed; **avoir les nerfs à** ~ to be on edge; **la plaie est à** ~ it's an open wound; **piquer qn au** ~ to cut sb to the quick

vigie /viʒi/ nf (Naut) (a) lookout
(b) crow's nest

vigilance /viʒilɑ̃s/ nf vigilance; **échapper à la** ~ **de qn** to escape sb's attention

vigilant, ~**e** /viʒilɑ̃, ɑ̃t/ adj ⟨person⟩ vigilant; ⟨eye⟩ watchful

vigile /viʒil/ nm (a) night watchman
(b) security guard

Vigipirate /viʒipiRat/ nm: government public security measures

vigne /viɲ/ nf (a) vine
(b) vineyard
■ ~ **vierge** Virginia creeper

vigneron, -onne /viɲ(ə)Rɔ̃, ɔn/ nm,f winegrower

vignette /viɲɛt/ nf (a) detachable label on medicines for reimbursement by social security
(b) tax disc (GB)
(c) label
(d) vignette

vignoble /viɲɔbl/ nm vineyard

vigoureux, -euse /viguRø, øz/ adj
(a) ⟨person, handshake⟩ vigorous; ⟨athlete, body⟩ strong; ⟨plant⟩ sturdy
(b) ⟨resistance, style⟩ vigorous

vigueur /vigœR/ **1** nf (a) vigour (GB)
(b) strength
2 **en vigueur** phr ⟨law, system⟩ in force; ⟨regime, conditions⟩ current; **entrer en** ~ to come into force

VIH /veiaʃ/ nm (abbr = **virus immunodéficitaire humain**) HIV

viking /vikiŋ/ adj Viking

vil, ~**e** /vil/ adj ⟨person⟩ base; ⟨deed⟩ vile, base

vilain, ~**e** /vilɛ̃, ɛn/ **1** adj (a) ugly

(b) (fam) ⟨germ, creature⟩ nasty; ⟨child⟩ naughty
(c) ⟨fault⟩ bad; ⟨word⟩ dirty
2 nm,f naughty boy/girl

vilenie /vileni/ nf (a) baseness (**de** of)
(b) vile or base act

villa /villa/ nf (a) ≈ detached house
(b) villa

✧ **village** /vilaʒ/ nm village

villageois, ~**e** /vilaʒwa, az/ nm,f villager

✧ **ville** /vil/ nf (a) town; city; **la vieille** ~ the old town; **aller en** ~ to go into town
(b) town or city council
■ ~ **d'eau(x)** spa town; ~ **franche** free city; ~ **nouvelle** new town

ville-dortoir, pl **villes-dortoirs** /vildɔRtwaR/ nf dormitory town (GB)

villégiature /vileʒjatyR/ nf holiday (GB), vacation (US)

✧ **vin** /vɛ̃/ nm wine; ~ **blanc/rouge** white/red wine; ~ **de pays** or **de terroir** quality wine produced in a specific region; **couper son** ~ to add water to one's wine
■ ~ **d'appellation d'origine contrôlée** appellation contrôlée wine ⟨with a guarantee of origin⟩; ~ **cuit** wine which has undergone heating during maturation; ~ **d'honneur** reception
IDIOMS avoir le ~ **gai/triste** to get happy/ maudlin after one has had a few drinks; **mettre de l'eau dans son** ~ to mellow; **quand le** ~ **est tiré, il faut le boire** (Proverb) once you have started something, you have to see it through

✧ **vinaigre** /vinɛgR/ nm vinegar
IDIOM tourner au ~ to turn sour

vinaigrette /vinɛgRɛt/ nf French dressing

vinasse /vinas/ nf (fam) plonk (GB) (colloq), cheap wine

vindicatif, -ive /vɛ̃dikatif, iv/ adj vindictive

✧ **vingt** /vɛ̃, vɛ̃t/ **1** adj inv twenty
2 pron twenty; (Sch) **j'ai eu** ~ **sur** ~ ≈ I got full marks (GB) or full credit (US)
3 nm inv twenty

vingtaine /vɛ̃tɛn/ nf **une** ~ about twenty

vingtième /vɛ̃tjɛm/ adj twentieth

vinicole /vinikɔl/ adj ⟨sector, region⟩ wine-producing; ⟨cellar, trade⟩ wine

vinyle /vinil/ nm vinyl

viol /vjɔl/ nm (a) rape
(b) (of law, temple) violation

violacé, ~**e** /vjɔlase/ adj purplish

violation /vjɔlasjɔ̃/ nf (a) (of law, territory) violation
(b) (of agreement, confidentiality) breach
■ ~ **de domicile** forcible entry ⟨into a person's home⟩

violemment /vjɔlamɑ̃/ adv violently

✧ **violence** /vjɔlɑ̃s/ nf (a) violence; ~ **verbale** verbal abuse; **par la** ~ through violence; with violence; **se faire** ~ to force oneself

---

✧ indicates a very frequent word

(b) act of violence; ~s à l'enfant child abuse

⚘ **violent**, ~e /vjɔlɑ̃, ɑ̃t/ *adj* violent; ‹colour› harsh

violenter /vjɔlɑ̃te/ [1] *vtr* to assault sexually

violer /vjɔle/ [1] *vtr* **(a)** to rape; **se faire** ~ to be raped
(b) to desecrate ‹tomb›; ~ l'intimité de qn to invade sb's privacy
(c) to infringe ‹law›

violet, -ette¹ /vjɔlɛ, ɛt/ ① *adj* purple ② *nm* purple

violette² /vjɔlɛt/ *nf* violet

violeur /vjɔlœʀ/ *nm* rapist

violon /vjɔlɔ̃/ *nm* violin
■ ~ d'Ingres hobby
IDIOM **accorder ses** ~s to agree on which line to take

violoncelle /vjɔlɔ̃sɛl/ *nm* cello

violoncelliste /vjɔlɔ̃selist/ *nmf* cellist

violoniste /vjɔlɔnist/ *nmf* violinist

vipère /vipɛʀ/ *nf* viper; **avoir une langue de** ~ to have a wicked tongue

virage /viʀaʒ/ *nm* **(a)** bend
(b) change of direction
(c) (in skiing) turn

virago /viʀago/ *nf* virago

viral, ~e, *mpl* -aux /viʀal, o/ *adj* viral

virement /viʀmɑ̃/ *nm* transfer; **faire un** ~ to make a transfer
■ ~ automatique standing order

virer /viʀe/ [1] ① *vtr* **(a)** to transfer ‹money›
(b) (fam) to fire ‹employee›; **se faire** ~ to get fired
② **virer à** *v+prep* ~ au rouge to turn red
③ *vi* **(a)** ‹vehicle› to turn; ~ de bord (figurative) to do a U-turn, to do a flip-flop (US)
(b) to change colour (GB); ‹colour› to change

virevolter /viʀvɔlte/ [1] *vi* to twirl

virginité /viʀʒinite/ *nf* virginity

virgule /viʀgyl/ *nf* **(a)** comma; **à la** ~ près down to the last comma
(b) (decimal) point

viril, ~e /viʀil/ *adj* manly, virile; masculine

virilité /viʀilite/ *nf* virility

virtualité /viʀtɥalite/ *nf* **(a)** virtuality
(b) potentiality

virtuel, -elle /viʀtɥɛl/ *adj* **(a)** potential
(b) (in science) virtual

virtuellement /viʀtɥɛlmɑ̃/ *adv*
(a) virtually
(b) potentially

virtuose /viʀtɥoz/ ① *adj* virtuoso
② *nmf* **(a)** (Mus) virtuoso
(b) master

virtuosité /viʀtɥozite/ *nf* **(a)** (Mus) virtuosity
(b) brilliance

virulence /viʀylɑ̃s/ *nf* virulence

virulent, ~e /viʀylɑ̃, ɑ̃t/ *adj* virulent

virus /viʀys/ *nm inv* **(a)** (Med, Comput) virus
(b) bug (colloq), craze

vis /vis/ *nf inv* screw
IDIOM **serrer la** ~ à qn to tighten the screws on sb

visa /viza/ *nm* visa
■ ~ de censure (censor's) certificate

⚘ **visage** /vizaʒ/ *nm* face; **à** ~ **découvert** openly

vis-à-vis /vizavi/ ① *nm inv* **(a)** maison sans ~ house with an open outlook
(b) assis en ~ sitting opposite each other
(c) (Sport) opponent
(d) meeting, encounter
② **vis-à-vis de** *phr* **(a)** ~ de qch in relation to sth; ~ de qn toward(s) sb
(b) beside

viscéral, ~e, *mpl* -aux /viseʀal, o/ *adj*
(a) réaction ~e gut reaction
(b) visceral

viscéralement /viseʀalmɑ̃/ *adv* violently, virulently

viscère /visɛʀ/ *nm* **(a)** internal organ
(b) les ~s viscera

viscosité /viskozite/ *nf* viscosity

visée /vize/ *nf* **(a)** aim
(b) design
(c) sighting; aiming

⚘ **viser** /vize/ [1] ① *vtr* **(a)** to aim at ‹target›; to aim for ‹heart, middle›
(b) to aim for ‹job, results›; to aim at ‹market›
(c) ‹law, campaign› to be aimed at; ‹remark, allusion› to be meant for
② **viser à** *v+prep* ~ à qch/à faire to aim at sth/to do
③ *vi* to aim; ~ (trop) haut (figurative) to set one's sights (too) high

viseur /vizœʀ/ *nm* **(a)** viewfinder
(b) (of gun) sight

visibilité /vizibilite/ *nf* visibility

⚘ **visible** /vizibl/ *adj* **(a)** visible
(b) obvious

visiblement /vizibləmɑ̃/ *adv* visibly

visière /vizjɛʀ/ *nf* **(a)** (of cap) peak
(b) eyeshade

⚘ **vision** /vizjɔ̃/ *nf* **(a)** eyesight, vision
(b) view; ~ globale global view
(c) sight
(d) avoir des ~s to see things, to have visions

visionnaire /vizjɔnɛʀ/ *adj*, *nmf* visionary

visionner /vizjɔne/ [1] *vtr* to view ‹film, slides›

visionneuse /vizjɔnøz/ *nf* viewer

⚘ **visite** /vizit/ *nf* visit; call; **rendre** ~ à qn to pay sb a call; **avoir de la** ~ to have visitors
■ ~ de contrôle (Med) follow-up visit; ~ médicale medical (examination)

⚘ **visiter** /vizite/ [1] *vtr* **(a)** to visit ‹museum, town›
(b) to view ‹apartment›

⋯▷

(c) to visit ‹patient›

visiteur, -euse /vizitœʀ, øz/ *nm,f* visitor

vison /vizɔ̃/ *nm* (a) mink
(b) mink (coat)

visqueux, -euse /viskø, øz/ *adj*
(a) viscous, viscid
(b) sticky, gooey (colloq)

visser /vise/ [1] *vtr* (a) to screw [sth] on
(b) être vissé sur sa chaise to be glued to one's chair

visualisation /vizɥalizasjɔ̃/ *nf*
visualization; (Comput) display

visualiser /vizɥalize/ [1] *vtr* to visualize

visuel, -elle /vizɥɛl/ *adj* visual

vital, ~e, *mpl* **-aux** /vital, o/ *adj* vital

vitalité /vitalite/ *nf* vitality; energy

vitamine /vitamin/ *nf* vitamin

vitaminé, ~e /vitamine/ *adj* with added vitamins

  ơ **vite** /vit/ *adv* (a) quickly; ~! quick!; ça ira ~ it'll soon be over; it won't take long; on a pris un verre ~ fait (fam) we had a quick drink
(b) j'ai parlé trop ~ I spoke too hastily; I spoke too soon; c'est ~ dit! that's easy to say!

  ơ **vitesse** /vitɛs/ *nf* (a) speed; partir à toute ~ to rush away; à deux ~s ‹system› two-tier; faire de la ~ to drive fast; prendre qn de ~ to outstrip sb; en ~ quickly; in a rush
(b) gear
IDIOM à la ~ grand V, en quatrième ~ at top speed

viticole /vitikɔl/ *adj* wine; wine-producing

viticulteur, -trice /vitikyltœʀ, tʀis/ *nm,f* wine grower

viticulture /vitikyltyʀ/ *nf* wine-growing

vitrage /vitʀaʒ/ *nm* windows; double ~ double glazing

vitrail, *pl* **-aux** /vitʀaj, o/ *nm* stained glass window

vitre /vitʀ/ *nf* (a) windowpane
(b) pane of glass
(c) (of car, train) window

vitrerie /vitʀəʀi/ (a) glazier's
(b) glasswork

vitrier /vitʀije/ *nm* glazier

vitrifier /vitʀifje/ [2] *vtr* (a) to varnish ‹floor›
(b) (Tech) to vitrify

vitrine /vitʀin/ *nf* (a) (shop (GB) *or* store (US)) window; faire les ~s to go window-shopping
(b) display cabinet (GB), curio cabinet (US)
(c) (show)case

vitriol /vitʀijɔl/ *nm* vitriol

vitupérer /vitypeʀe/ [14] *vi* to rail

vivable /vivabl/ *adj* bearable; ce n'est pas ~ ici it is impossible to live here

vivace /vivas/ *adj* enduring

ơ indicates a very frequent word

vivacité /vivasite/ *nf* (a) (of person) vivacity; (of feeling) intensity
(b) (of intelligence) keenness; (of reaction, movement) swiftness; avec ~ ‹move, react› swiftly
(c) (of memory, colour, impression) vividness; (in eyes) spark; (of light) brightness

  ơ **vivant, ~e** /vivɑ̃, ɑ̃t/ **1** *adj* (a) living; il est ~ he is alive; un homard ~ a live lobster
(b) ‹person, style› lively; ‹description› vivid
(c) être encore ~ ‹custom› to be still alive
2 *nm* (a) living being; les ~s the living
(b) du ~ de mon père while my father was alive

vive² /viv/ **1** *adj f* ▶ VIF 1
2 *nf* weever

vivement /vivmɑ̃/ *adv* ‹encourage, react› strongly; ‹contrast, speak› sharply; ‹move, feel, regret› deeply; ‹rise› swiftly

vivier /vivje/ *nm* (a) fishpond
(b) fish-tank

vivifiant, ~e /vivifjɑ̃, ɑ̃t/ *adj*
(a) invigorating
(b) stimulating

vivifier /vivifje/ [2] *vtr* to invigorate

vivisection /vivisɛksjɔ̃/ *nf* vivisection

vivoter /vivɔte/ [1] *vi* to struggle along

  ơ **vivre** /vivʀ/ [63] **1** *vtr* (a) to live through ‹era›; to go through ‹difficult times›; to experience ‹love›
(b) to cope with ‹divorce, failure, change›
2 *vi* (a) to live; ~ vieux to live to a great age; vive la révolution! long live the revolution!; ~ à la campagne to live in the country; être facile à ~ to be easy to live with; to be easy to get on with; ~ avec son temps to move with the times; se laisser ~ to take things easy; apprendre à ~ à qn (fam) to teach sb some manners (colloq); ~ aux dépens de qn to live off sb
(b) ‹fashion› to last; avoir vécu ‹person› to have seen a great deal of life; (humorous) ‹object› to have had its day
(c) ‹town› to be full of life
IDIOM qui vivra verra what will be will be

vivres /vivʀ/ *nm pl* (a) food, supplies
(b) couper les ~ à qn to cut off sb's allowance

vizir /viziʀ/ *nm* vizier; le Grand ~ the Grand Vizier

vo /veo/ *nf*: *abbr* ▶ VERSION

vocable /vɔkabl/ *nm* term

vocabulaire /vɔkabylɛʀ/ *nm* vocabulary

vocal, ~e, *mpl* **-aux** /vɔkal, o/ *adj* vocal

vocalement /vɔkalmɑ̃/ *adv* vocally

vocalise /vɔkaliz/ *nf* singing exercise

vocation /vɔkasjɔ̃/ *nf* (a) vocation, calling
(b) purpose; région à ~ agricole farming area

vociférer /vɔsifeʀe/ [14] *vtr*, *vi* to shout

vodka /vɔdka/ *nf* vodka

vœu, *pl* ~**x** /vø/ *nm* **(a)** wish; **faire un** ~ to make a wish
(b) New Year's greetings; **adresser ses** ~**x à qn** to wish sb a happy New Year
(c) vow; **faire** ~ **de pauvreté** to take a vow of poverty

vogue /vɔg/ *nf* fashion, vogue

voguer /vɔge/ [1] *vi* ‹ship› to sail
IDIOM et vogue la galère! come what may!

✓ **voici** /vwasi/ **1** *prep* here is, this is; here are, these are; ~ **mes clés** here are my keys; ~ **un mois** a month ago; ~ **bientôt deux mois qu'elle travaille chez nous** she's been working with us for nearly two months
2 **voici que** *phr* all of a sudden

✓ **voie** /vwa/ *nf* **(a)** way; **montrer la** ~ **à qn** to show sb the way; **ouvrir la** ~ **à** to pave the way for; **être sur la bonne** ~ ‹person› to be on the right track; **les travaux sont en bonne** ~ the work is progressing; **par** ~ **de conséquence** consequently; **espèce en** ~ **de disparition** endangered species
(b) channels; **par des** ~ **détournées** by roundabout means
(c) lane; **route à trois** ~**s** three-lane road
(d) (of railway) track; **le train entre en gare** ~ **2** the train is arriving at platform 2
(e) **par** ~ **buccale** *or* **orale** orally
■ ~ **aérienne** air route; ~ **ferrée** railway track (GB), railroad track (US); ~ **de garage** siding; **mettre qn sur une** ~ **de garage** (figurative) to shunt sb onto the sidelines; **Voie lactée** Milky Way; ~ **privée** private road; ~ **publique** public highway; ~ **rapide** expressway; ~ **sans issue** dead end; no through road; ~**s respiratoires** respiratory tract

✓ **voilà** /vwala/ **1** *prep* here is, this is; here are, these are; **voici mon fils et** ~ **ma fille** this is my son and this is my daughter; **me** ~**!** I'm coming!; **le** ~ **qui se remet à rire!** there he goes again laughing!; ~ **tout** that's all; ~ **un mois** a month ago
2 **en voilà** *phr* **tu veux des fraises? en** ~ you'd like some strawberries? here you are
3 **voilà que** *phr* (fam) **et** ~ **qu'une voiture arrive** and the next thing you know, a car pulls up
4 *excl* ~**! j'arrive!** (I'm) coming!; **(et)** ~**! il remet ça!** there he goes again!
IDIOM il a de l'argent, en veux-tu en ~**!** he has as much money as he could wish for!

voilage /vwalaʒ/ *nm* net curtain (GB), sheer curtain (US)

voile[1] /vwal/ *nm* **(a)** veil; **lever le** ~ **sur qch** to bring sth out in the open
(b) voile
■ ~ **islamique** yashmak; ~ **du palais** soft palate, velum

✓ **voile**[2] /vwal/ *nf* (Naut) **(a)** sail; **faire** ~ **vers** to sail toward(s)
(b) sailing

voilé, ~**e** /vwale/ *adj* **(a)** ‹person, object› veiled

(b) ‹sun, sky› hazy; ‹eyes› misty; ‹voice› with a catch in it; ‹photo› fogged
(c) ‹threat, criticism› veiled
(d) ‹wheel› buckled

voiler /vwale/ [1] **1** *vtr* **(a)** to veil ‹landscape, sun›; ‹person, fact› to conceal ‹event, fact›
(b) to buckle ‹wheel›
(c) to mist ‹eyes›
(d) to cover ‹face, nudity›; to veil ‹statue›
2 **se voiler** *v refl* (+ *v être*) **(a)** ‹sky› to cloud over; ‹sun› to become hazy; ‹eyes› to become misty
(b) ‹person› to wear a veil
IDIOM se ~ **la face** to look the other way

voilette /vwalɛt/ *nf* veil

voilier /vwalje/ *nm* **(a)** sailing boat (GB), sailboat (US)
(b) yacht, sailing ship

voilure /vwalyʀ/ *nf* sails; **une** ~ **de 500m²** 500m² of sail

✓ **voir** /vwaʀ/ [46] **1** *vtr* **(a)** to see; **faire** ~ **qch à qn** to show sb sth; **laisser** ~ **qch** to show sth; ~ **si/pourquoi** to find out *or* to see if/why; **on l'a vue entrer** she was seen going in; **je le vois** *or* **verrais bien enseignant** I can just see him as a teacher; **aller** ~ **qn** to go to see sb; **le film est à** ~ the film is worth seeing; ~ **du pays** to see the world; **on voit bien qu'elle n'a jamais travaillé!** you can tell she's never worked!; **on n'a jamais vu ça!** it's unheard of!
(b) **avoir quelque chose à** ~ **avec** to have something to do with
2 **voir à** *v+prep* to see to; **voyez à ce que tout soit prêt** see to it that everything is ready
3 *vi* **(a)** ~, **y** ~ to be able to see; ~ **double** to see double
(b) ~ **clair dans qch** to have a clear understanding of sth; **il faut** ~ we'll have to see
4 **se voir** *v refl* (+ *v être*) **(a)** to see oneself
(b) ‹stain› to show; **la tour se voit de loin** the tower can be seen from far away; **ça ne s'est jamais vu!** it's unheard of!
(c) **se** ~ **obligé** *or* **dans l'obligation de faire** to find oneself forced to do
(d) to see each other; **ils ne peuvent pas se** ~ **(en peinture** (fam)**)** they can't stand each other
IDIOMS ne pas ~ **plus loin que le bout de son nez** to see no further than the end of one's nose; **j'en ai vu d'autres** I've seen worse; **en faire** ~ **à qn** to give sb a hard time

✓ **voire** /vwaʀ/ *adv* or even, not to say

voirie /vwaʀi/ *nf* road, rail and waterways network

✓ **voisin**, ~**e** /vwazɛ̃, in/ **1** *adj* **(a)** ‹house, town› neighbouring (GB); ‹lake, forest› nearby; ‹room› next; **les régions** ~**es de la Manche** the regions bordering the English Channel
(b) ‹date, result› close (**de** to)

⋯▸

(c) ‹feelings, ideas› similar; ‹species› (closely) related

2 nm, f neighbour (GB); **ma ~e de palier** the woman across the landing; **mon ~ de table** the man next to me at table

voisinage /vwazinaʒ/ nm **(a)** neighbourhood (GB); **entretenir des rapports de bon ~** to maintain neighbourly (GB) relations

(b) proximity; **vivre dans le ~ d'une usine** to live close to a factory

✶ **voiture** /vwatyʀ/ nf **(a)** car, automobile (US)
(b) carriage (GB), car (US); **en ~!** all aboard!
■ **~ à bras** hand-drawn cart; **~ de tourisme** saloon (car) (GB), sedan (US)

voiture-balai, pl **voitures-balais** /vwatyʀbalɛ/ nf support vehicle

voiture-lit, pl **voitures-lits** /vwatyʀli/ nf sleeper, sleeping car (US)

✶ **voix** /vwa/ nf inv **(a)** (gen) voice; **élever la ~** to raise one's voice; **à ~ haute** out loud; **rester sans ~** to be speechless; **à portée de ~** within earshot; **faire entendre sa ~** (figurative) to make oneself heard
(b) vote
(c) à la ~ active/passive in the active/ passive voice

✶ **vol** /vɔl/ **1** nm **(a)** (of bird, plane) flight; **prendre son ~** to fly off; **à ~ d'oiseau** as the crow flies; **il y a trois heures de ~** it's a three-hour flight; **de ~** ‹conditions› flying; ‹plan› flight
(b) un ~ de a flock of ‹birds›; a cloud of ‹insects›; **de haut ~** (figurative) ‹diplomat› high-flying; ‹burglar› big-time
(c) theft, robbery
2 au vol phr **attraper une balle au ~** to catch a ball in mid-air; **saisir des bribes de conversation au ~** to catch snatches of conversation
■ **~ à l'arraché** bag snatching; **~ avec effraction** burglary; **~ à l'étalage** shoplifting; **~ à la tire** pickpocketing

volage /vɔlaʒ/ adj fickle

volaille /vɔlɑj/ nf **(a)** poultry
(b) fowl

volant, ~e /vɔlɑ̃, ɑ̃t/ **1** adj flying
2 nm **(a)** steering wheel; **être au ~** to be at the wheel; **un brusque coup de ~** a sharp turn of the wheel; **un as du ~** an ace driver; **la sécurité au ~** safe driving
(b) flounce; **à ~s** flounced
(c) shuttlecock

volatil, ~e¹ /vɔlatil/ adj volatile

volatile² /vɔlatil/ nm **(a)** fowl
(b) bird

volatiliser: se volatiliser /vɔlatilize/ [1] v refl (+ v être) **(a)** to volatilize
(b) (humorous) to vanish into thin air

volcan /vɔlkɑ̃/ nm volcano

✶ indicates a very frequent word

volcanique /vɔlkanik/ adj **(a)** ‹region› volcanic
(b) ‹temperament› explosive

volée /vɔle/ **1** nf **(a)** (of birds) flock, flight
(b) (of blows, stones) volley; **donner une ~ à qn** to give sb a good thrashing
(c) flight (of stairs)
(d) (Sport) volley
2 à toute volée phr **les cloches sonnaient à toute ~** the bells were pealing out

✶ **voler** /vɔle/ [1] **1** vtr **(a) ~ qch à qn** to steal sth from sb; **tu ne l'as pas volé!** (figurative) it serves you right!
(b) ~ qn to rob sb; **~ le client** to rip the customer off (colloq)
2 vi **(a)** to fly; **~ au secours de qn** to rush to sb's aid
(b) ~ en éclats ‹window› to shatter

volet /vɔlɛ/ nm **(a)** shutter
(b) (of leaflet, brochure) (folding) section; (of plan) part, component
(c) (of film, series) instalment (GB)

voleter /vɔlte/ [20] vi to flutter

voleur, -euse /vɔlœʀ, øz/ **1** adj **être ~** ‹child› to be a thief; ‹shopkeeper› to be dishonest
2 nm, f thief; swindler
IDIOM se sauver comme un ~ to slip away like a thief in the night

volière /vɔljɛʀ/ nf aviary

volley(-ball) /vɔlɛ(bol)/ nm volleyball

volontaire /vɔlɔ̃tɛʀ/ **1** adj **(a)** ‹work› voluntary; ‹omission› deliberate
(b) ‹person, air› determined; ‹child› self-willed
2 nmf volunteer; **se porter ~** to volunteer

✶ **volonté** /vɔlɔ̃te/ **1** nf **(a)** will; **bonne ~** goodwill; **aller contre la ~ de qn** to go against sb's wishes; **manifester la ~ de faire** to show one's willingness to do
(b) willpower; **avoir une ~ de fer** to have an iron will
2 à volonté phr **(a)** 'vin/pain à ~' 'unlimited wine/bread'
(b) ‹modifiable› as required

volontiers /vɔlɔ̃tje/ adv **(a)** gladly; **j'irais ~ à Paris** I'd love to go to Paris; **'tu me le prêtes?'—'~'** 'will you lend it to me?'— 'certainly'
(b) ‹admit› readily

volt /vɔlt/ nm volt

voltage /vɔltaʒ/ nm voltage

volte-face /vɔlt(ə)fas/ nf inv **(a) faire ~** to turn around
(b) (figurative) volte-face, U-turn

voltige /vɔltiʒ/ nf **(haute) ~** acrobatics

voltiger /vɔltiʒe/ [13] vi **(a)** to flutter
(b) to go flying

volubilité /vɔlybilite/ nf volubility

✶ **volume** /vɔlym/ nm (gen) volume; **donner du ~ à ses cheveux** to give one's hair body; **~ sonore** sound level

volumineux, -euse /vɔlyminø, øz/ adj
voluminous, bulky

volupté /vɔlypte/ nf voluptuousness

voluptueux, -euse /vɔlyptɥø, øz/ adj
voluptuous

volute /vɔlyt/ nf (on pillar, column) volute; (of
violin) scroll; (of smoke) curl

vomi /vɔmi/ nm (fam) vomit

vomir /vɔmiʀ/ [3] **1** vtr to bring up ‹meal›;
to vomit ‹bile›

2 vi ‹person› to be sick

vomissement /vɔmismã/ nm vomiting

vont /võ/ ▸ ALLER¹

vorace /vɔʀas/ adj voracious

voracité /vɔʀasite/ nf voracity,
voraciousness

vos ▸ VOTRE

votant, ~e /vɔtã, ãt/ nm,f voter

vote /vɔt/ nm (a) voting; (of law) passing
(b) vote

⚔ **voter** /vɔte/ [1] **1** vtr to vote ‹budget›;
to pass ‹parliamentary bill›; to vote for
‹amnesty›

2 vi to vote; **~ blanc** to cast a blank vote

⚔ **votre, pl vos** /vɔtʀ, vo/ det your; **c'est pour
~ bien** it's for your own good; **à ~ arrivée**
when you arrive; when you arrived

vôtre /votʀ/ **1** det mes biens sont ~s all I
have is yours; **'amicalement ~'** 'best wishes'

2 **le vôtre, la vôtre, les vôtres** pron
yours; **à la ~!** (fam) cheers!

vouer /vwe/ [1] **1** vtr (a) **~ une
reconnaissance éternelle à qn** to be
eternally grateful to sb; **~ un véritable culte
à qn** to worship sb
(b) to doom; **film voué à l'échec** film doomed
to failure
(c) **~ sa vie à qch** to devote one's life to sth

2 **se vouer** v refl (+ v être) (a) **se ~ à qch**
to devote oneself to sth
(b) **ils se vouent une haine féroce** they hate
each other intensely

⚔ **vouloir¹** /vulwaʀ/ [48] **1** vtr (a) (gen) to
want; **qu'est-ce qu'ils nous veulent encore?**
(fam) what do they want now?; **il en veut
2 000 euros** he wants 2,000 euros for it;
comme le veut la loi as the law requires;
que veux-tu boire? what do you want to
drink?; **je voudrais un kilo de poires** I'd
like a kilo of pears; **je comprends très
bien que tu ne veuilles pas répondre** I can
quite understand that you may not wish
to reply; **sans le ~** ‹knock over, reveal› by
accident; ‹annoy› without meaning to; **que
tu le veuilles ou non** whether you like it or
not; **elle fait ce qu'elle veut de son mari** she
twists her husband around her little finger;
je ne vous veux aucun mal I don't wish you
any harm; **tu ne voudrais pas me faire croire
que…** you're not trying to tell me that…; **tu
voudrais que je leur fasse confiance?** do you
expect me to trust them?; **comment veux-**

tu que je le sache? how should I know?;
j'aurais voulu t'y voir! (fam) I'd like to have
seen you in the same position!; **tu l'auras
voulu!** it'll be all your own fault!
(b) **voulez-vous fermer la fenêtre?** would you
mind closing the window?; **voudriez-vous
avoir l'obligeance de faire** (formal) would you
be so kind as to do; **veuillez patienter** (on
phone) please hold the line; **si vous voulez
bien me suivre** if you'd like to follow me;
veux-tu te taire! will you be quiet!; **ils ont
bien voulu nous prêter leur voiture** they
were kind enough to lend us their car; **je
veux bien te croire** I'm quite prepared to
believe you; **je veux bien qu'il soit malade
mais…** I know he's ill, but…; **'ce n'est pas
cher'—'si on veut!'** 'it's not expensive'—'or
so you say!'
(c) **~ dire** to mean; **qu'est-ce que ça veut dire?**
what does that mean?; what's all this about?
(d) **comme le veut la tradition** as tradition
has it

2 **en vouloir** v+prep (a) **en ~ à qn** to
bear a grudge against sb; **je leur en veux de
m'avoir trompé** I hold it against them for
not being honest with me; **ne m'en veux pas**
please forgive me
(b) **en ~ à qch** to be after sth

3 **se vouloir** v refl (+ v être) (a) ‹person›
to like to think of oneself as; ‹book, method›
to be meant to be
(b) **s'en ~** to be cross (GB) or mad (US)
with oneself; **s'en ~ de** to regret; **je m'en
serais voulu de ne pas vous avoir prévenu** I
would never have forgiven myself if I hadn't
warned you

IDIOM ~ c'est pouvoir (Proverb) where there's
a will there's a way

vouloir² /vulwaʀ/ nm will

voulu, ~e /vuly/ **1** pp ▸ VOULOIR¹

2 pp adj (a) required; **on n'obtient jamais
les renseignements ~s** you never get the
information you want; **en temps ~** in time;
au moment ~ at the right time
(b) ‹omission› deliberate; ‹meeting› planned

⚔ **vous** /vu/ pron (a) you; **je sais que ce n'est
pas ~** I know it wasn't you; **c'est ~ qui
avez gagné** you have won; **~ aussi, ~ avez
l'air malade** you don't look very well either;
ce sont des amis à ~? are they friends of
yours?; **c'est à ~** it's yours, it belongs to you;
it's your turn
(b) yourself; yourselves; **allez ~ laver les
mains** go and wash your hands; **pensez à ~
deux** think of yourselves

vous-même, pl vous-mêmes
/vumɛm/ pron (a) yourself; **vous me l'avez
dit ~** you told me yourself
(b) **allez-y ~s** go yourselves; **vous verrez par
~s** you'll see for yourselves

voûte /vut/ nf (gen) vault; (of porch)
archway; (of tunnel) roof; (figurative) (of leaves,
branches) arch

⋯⋗

■ **la ~ céleste** the sky; the heavens; **~ du palais** roof of the mouth; **~ plantaire** arch of the foot

voûté, ~e /vute/ *adj* **(a)** ‹cellar› vaulted **(b)** ‹back› bent; **il est ~** he has a stoop

voûter /vute/ [1] 1 *vtr* **(a)** (in architecture) to vault ‹room› **(b)** to give [sb] a stoop

2 **se voûter** *v refl* (+ *v être*) ‹person› to develop a stoop; ‹back› to become bent

vouvoiement /vuvwamɑ̃/ *nm* using the 'vous' *or* polite form

vouvoyer /vuvwaje/ [23] *vtr* to address [sb] using the 'vous' form

❡ **voyage** /vwajaʒ/ *nm* trip; journey; **partir en ~** to go on a trip; **le ~ aller** the outward journey; **aimer les ~s** to love travelling (GB)

■ **~ d'affaires** business trip; **être en ~ d'affaires** to be on a business trip; **~ d'études** study trip; **~ de noces** honeymoon; **~ organisé** package tour (GB)

voyager /vwajaʒe/ [13] *vi* to travel

❡ **voyageur, -euse** /vwajaʒœr, øz/ *nm,f* **(a)** passenger; '**réservé aux ~s munis de billets**' 'ticketholders only' **(b)** traveller (GB)

■ **~ de commerce** travelling (GB) salesman

voyagiste /vwajaʒist/ *nmf* tour operator

voyance /vwajɑ̃s/ *nf* clairvoyance

voyant, ~e /vwajɑ̃, ɑ̃t/ 1 *adj* ‹colour› loud 2 *nm,f* **(a)** clairvoyant **(b)** sighted person 3 *nm* light; **~ d'huile** (Aut) oil warning light

voyelle /vwajɛl/ *nf* vowel

voyeur, -euse /vwajœr, øz/ *nm,f* voyeur

voyeurisme /vwajœrism/ *nm* voyeurism

voyou /vwaju/ *nm* lout

vrac: en vrac /ɑ̃vrak/ *phr* **(a)** loose, unpackaged **(b)** in bulk **(c) jeter ses idées en ~ sur le papier** to jot down one's ideas as they come

❡ **vrai, ~e** /vrɛ/ 1 *adj* true; real, genuine; **il n'y a rien de ~ dans ses déclarations** there's no truth in his statements; **la ~e raison de mon départ** the real reason for my leaving; **des ~s jumeaux** identical twins; **plus ~ que nature** ‹picture, scene› larger than life 2 *nm* truth; **il y a du ~ dans ce que tu dis** there's some truth in what you say; **être dans le ~** to be in the right; **pour de ~** for real; **à ~ dire, à dire ~** to tell the truth 3 *adv* **faire ~** to look real; **son discours sonne ~** his speech has the ring of truth

❡ **vraiment** /vrɛmɑ̃/ *adv* really

vraisemblable /vrɛsɑ̃blabl/ *adj* ‹excuse› convincing; ‹scenario› plausible; ‹hypothesis› likely; **il est ~ que** it is likely that

❡ indicates a very frequent word

vraisemblablement /vrɛsɑ̃blabləmɑ̃/ *adv* probably

vraisemblance /vrɛsɑ̃blɑ̃s/ *nf* (of hypothesis) likelihood; (of situation, explanation) plausibility

vrille /vrij/ *nf* **(a)** spiral; (of airplane) tailspin; **descendre en ~** ‹airplane› to go into a spiral dive **(b)** (Bot) tendril **(c)** (Tech) gimlet

vrombir /vrɔ̃bir/ [3] *vi* ‹engine› to roar; **faire ~ un moteur** to rev up an engine

VRP /veɛrpe/ *nm* (*abbr* = **voyageur représentant placier**) representative, rep (colloq)

VTC /vetese/ *nm* (*abbr* = **vélo tous chemins**) hybrid bike

VTT /vetete/ ▶ VÉLO

vu, ~e¹ /vy/ 1 *pp* ▶ VOIR 2 *pp adj* **(a)** être **bien/mal ~** ‹person› to be/not to be well thought of; **c'est bien ~ de faire cela** it's good form to do that; **ce serait plutôt mal ~** it wouldn't go down well **(b) bien ~!** I good point!; **c'est tout ~** my mind is made up **(c) ~?** got it? (colloq) 3 *prep* in view of 4 **vu que** *phr* in view of the fact that

❡ **vue²** /vy/ *nf* **(a)** sight; **avoir une bonne ~** to have good eyesight; **don de double ~** gift of second sight; **perdre qn de ~** (figurative) to lose touch with sb; **à ~** ‹shoot› on sight; ‹fly plane› without instruments; ‹payable› on demand **(b)** view; **à ma ~, il s'enfuit** he took to his heels when he saw me; **avoir ~ sur le lac** to look out onto the lake **(c)** (opinion) view; **~s** views; **~ optimiste des choses** optimistic view of things **(d) avoir des ~s sur qn/qch** to have designs on sb/sth **(e) en ~** in sight; ‹person› prominent; **mettre une photo bien en ~** to display a photo prominently; **c'est quelqu'un de très en ~** he's/she's very much in the public eye; **j'ai un terrain en ~** I have a plot of land in mind; **I've got my eye on a piece of land; en ~ de faire** with a view to doing

■ **~ d'ensemble** overall view

IDIOMS **à ~ d'œil** *or* **de nez** (fam) at a rough guess; **vouloir en mettre plein la ~ à qn** to try to dazzle sb

vulcanologue /vylkanɔlɔg/ *nmf* volcanologist

vulgaire /vylgɛr/ *adj* **(a)** vulgar, coarse **(b)** common, ordinary; **c'est un ~ employé** he's just a lowly employee

vulgairement /vylgɛrmɑ̃/ *adv* **(a)** ‹speak› coarsely **(b)** commonly

vulgarisation /vylgarizasjɔ̃/ *nf* popularization; **revue de ~ scientifique**

scientific magazine for the general public
vulgariser /vylgaʀize/ [1] **1** *vtr* to popularize; to bring [sth] into general use **2** **se vulgariser** *v refl* (+ *v être*) ‹*technology*› to become generally accessible;

‹*expression*› to come into general use
vulgarité /vylgaʀite/ *nf* vulgarity, coarseness
vulnérable /vylneʀabl/ *adj* vulnerable
vulve /vylv/ *nf* vulva

w, W /dubləve/ *nm inv* (a) (letter) w, W
(b) W (*written abbr* = **watt**) 60 W 60 W
wagon /vagɔ̃/ *nm* (a) wagon (GB), car (US); (for passengers) carriage (GB), car (US)
(b) wagonload (GB), carload (US)
■ ~ **à bestiaux** cattle truck (GB), cattle car (US); ~ **de marchandises** goods wagon (GB), freight car (US)
wagon-bar, *pl* **wagons-bars** /vagɔ̃baʀ/ *nm* buffet car
wagon-citerne, *pl* **wagons-citernes** /vagɔ̃sitɛʀn/ *nm* tanker
wagon-lit, *pl* **wagons-lits** /vagɔ̃li/ *nm* sleeper, sleeping car (US)
wagonnet /vagɔnɛ/ *nm* trolley (GB), cart (US)

wagon-restaurant, *pl* **wagons-restaurants** /vagɔ̃ʀɛstɔʀɑ̃/ *nm* restaurant car (GB), dining car (US)
wallon, -onne /walɔ̃, ɔn/ **1** *adj* Walloon **2** *nm* (language) Walloon
Wallonie /walɔni/ *pr nf* Walloon area of Belgium
waters /watɛʀ/ *nm pl* (fam) toilets
watt-heure, *pl* **watts-heures** /watœʀ/ *nm* watt-hour
WC /(dublə)vese/ *nm pl* toilet; **aller aux** ~ to go to the toilet
webmestre /wɛbmɛstʀ/ *nmf* webmaster
winchester /winʃɛstɛʀ/ *nf* Winchester® rifle
wishbone /wiʃbon/ *nm* (Naut, Sport) wishbone boom

X x

x, X /iks/ *nm inv* x, X; **il y a x temps que c'est fini** it's been over for ages; **porter plainte contre X** (Law) to take an action against person or persons unknown; **film classé X** X-rated film (GB) *or* movie (US)
xénophobe /gzenɔfɔb/ **1** *adj* xenophobic

2 *nmf* xenophobe
xénophobie /gzenɔfɔbi/ *nf* xenophobia
xérès /kseʀɛs/ *nm inv* sherry
xylographe /ksilɔgʀaf/ *nm* xylographer
xylophène® /ksilɔfɛn/ *nm* wood preservative

y¹, Y /igʀɛk/ *nm inv* y, Y
♂ **y²** /i/ *pron* (a) it; **tu t'** ~ **attendais?** were you expecting it?; **il n'** ~ **connaît rien** he knows nothing about it; **j'** ~ **pense parfois** I sometimes think about it; **elle n'** ~ **peut rien** there's nothing she can do about it; **j'** ~ **viens**

I'm coming to that; **rien n'** ~ **fait** it's no use; **je n'** ~ **comprends rien** I don't understand a thing; **tu** ~ **as gagné** you got the best deal; **plus difficile qu'il n'** ~ **paraît** harder than it seems
(b) there; **j'** ~ **ai mangé une fois** I ate there ⸱⸱⸱➔

once; **n'~ va pas** don't go
(c) il ~ a there is/are; **du vin? il n'~ en a
plus** wine? there's none left; **il n'~ a qu'à
téléphoner** just phone
IDIOM ~ **mettre du sien** to work at it

ya(c)k /'jak/ *nm* yak

yaourt /'jauʀ(t)/ *nm* yoghurt

yaourtière /'jauʀtjɛʀ/ *nf* yoghurt-maker

yéménite /'jemenit/ *adj* Yemeni

yen /'jɛn/ *nm* yen

yéti /'jeti/ *nm* yeti

⚹ **yeux** ▶ ŒIL

yoga /'jɔga/ *nm* yoga

yole /'jɔl/ *nf* skiff

yougoslave /'jugɔslav/ *adj* Yugoslavian

youpi /'jupi/ *excl* (fam) yippee!

youyou /'juju/ *nm* **(a)** ululation
(b) dinghy

Zz

z, Z /zɛd/ *nm inv* z, Z

zaïrois, ~e /zaiʀwa, az/ *adj* Zairean

zambien, -ienne /zɑ̃bjɛ̃, ɛn/ *adj* Zambian

zapper /zape/ [1] *vi* to flick through the TV
channels

zèbre /zɛbʀ/ *nm* **(a)** zebra
(b) (figurative) (fam) bloke (GB) (colloq), guy
(colloq)

zébré, ~e /zebʀe/ *adj* ‹fabric› zebra-
striped; ~ **de** streaked with

zébrure /zebʀyʀ/ *nf* stripe

zébu /zeby/ *nm* zebu

zèle /zɛl/ *nm* zeal, enthusiasm; **faire du ~** *or*
de l'excès de ~ to be overzealous

zélé, ~e /zele/ *adj* enthusiastic, zealous

zénith /zenit/ *nm* zenith; **à son ~** ‹career›
at its height

zéphyr /zefiʀ/ *nm* zephyr

⚹ **zéro** /zeʀo/ ❶ *adj* ~ **heure** midnight,
twenty-four hundred (hours); **il sera
exactement ~ heure vingt minutes dix
secondes** the time will be twelve twenty and
ten seconds precisely; **j'ai eu ~ faute dans
ma dictée** I didn't make a single mistake
in my dictation; **niveau/croissance ~** zero
level/growth
❷ *nm* **(a)** zero, nought (GB); **avoir un ~ en
latin** to get zero *or* nought in Latin; **remettre
un compteur à ~** to reset a counter to zero;
avoir le moral à ~ (figurative) to be down in
the dumps (colloq); **c'est beau à regarder
mais question goût c'est ~** (fam) it's nice to
look at, but no marks for flavour (GB)
(b) (in sport) (gen) nil (GB), zero; (in tennis) love;
trois (buts) à ~ three nil
■ ~ **de conduite** (Sch) bad mark for behaviour
(GB)
IDIOMS **partir de ~** to start from scratch;
tout reprendre à ~ to start all over again

zeste /zɛst/ *nm* **un ~ de citron** the zest of
a lemon

zézayer /zezeje/ [21] *vi* to lisp

zibeline /ziblin/ *nf* sable

zieuter /zjøte/ [1] *vtr* (fam) to get a load of
(colloq), to take a look at

zigoto /zigoto/ *nm* (fam) guy (colloq); **faire le
~** to clown around

zigue /zig/ *nm* (fam) guy (colloq)

zigzag /zigzag/ *nm* zigzag; **route en ~**
winding road; **faire des ~s** to zigzag (**parmi**
through); **partir en ~** to zigzag off

zinc /zɛ̃g/ *nm* **(a)** zinc; **toiture de** *or* **en ~**
tin roofing
(b) (fam) counter, bar

zingueur /zɛ̃gœʀ/ *nm* roofer

zinzin ❶ *adj inv* (crazy) cracked (colloq)
❷ *nm* thingamajig (colloq)

zip /zip/ *nm* zip (GB), zipper (US)

zippé, ~e /zipe/ *adj* zip-up

zipper /zipe/ *vt* (Comput) to zip

zizanie /zizani/ *nf* ill-feeling, discord

zizi /zizi/ *nm* (fam) willy (GB) (colloq), penis

zodiac® /zɔdjak/ *nm* inflatable dinghy

zodiaque /zɔdjak/ *nm* zodiac

zona /zona/ *nm* shingles

zonage /zonaʒ/ *nm* zoning

zonard, ~e /zonaʀ, aʀd/ *nm,f* (fam)
dropout (colloq)

⚹ **zone** /zon/ *nf* **(a)** zone, area; ~ **interdite** off-
limits area; (on signpost) no entry
(b) la ~ (fam) the slum belt; **de seconde ~**
second-rate
■ ~ **d'activités** business park; ~ **artisanale**
small industrial estate (GB) *or* park; ~ **bleue**
restricted parking zone; ~ **industrielle** industrial estate (GB) *or* park; ~ **de saisie** (Comput)
input box

zoner /zone/ [1] *vi* (fam) to hang about
(colloq)

zoo /zo/ *nm* zoo

zoologie /zɔɔlɔʒi/ *nf* zoology

zoom /zum/ *nm* **(a)** zoom lens
(b) zoom

⚹ indicates a very frequent word

zouave /zwav/ *nm* **(a)** (fam) clown, comedian; **faire le ~** to clown around (colloq) **(b)** (soldier) zouave

zoulou, **~e** /zulu/ *adj* Zulu

zozo /zozo/ *nm* (fam) ninny (GB) (colloq), jerk (colloq)

zozoter /zɔzɔte/ [1] *vi* to lisp

zut /zyt/ *excl* (fam) damn! (colloq)

• •

**Calendar
Culture
Letters**

French traditions, festivals, and holidays

1 January
le jour de l'an (New Year's Day) is a public holiday and a day of family celebration, with a large lunch, traditionally featuring seafood.

6 January
la Fête des Rois (Epiphany or Twelfth night). Around this time, most families have a *galette des Rois*, a puff pastry cake filled with *frangipane* (almond paste). The cake contains a *fève*, literally a bean, as this is what was originally used. Nowadays the *fève* takes the form of a tiny plastic or ceramic figure. The person who gets the *fève* in their portion becomes the king or queen and puts on the cardboard crown which comes with the cake.

2 February
la Chandeleur (Candlemas) is celebrated in the Church but is not a public holiday. However, it is traditional to eat *crêpes* (pancakes) on this day.

14 February
la Saint Valentin (St Valentine's Day). As in many other countries, people celebrate a romantic relationship with gifts of flowers or chocolates.

1 April
le premier avril (April Fool's Day). The French take advantage of this occasion to play tricks on one another, calling out *poisson d'avril!* (literally 'April fish').

1 May
La Fête du Travail (International Labour Day) is a public holiday.

8 May
le 8 mai or **la Fête de la Victoire** is a public holiday commemorating Victory in Europe (VE day) on 8 May 1945.

24 June
la Saint-Jean (Midsummer's Day). In many areas, bonfires (*les feux de la Saint-Jean*) are lit on Midsummer's Night. People are supposed to jump over these, re-enacting a pagan custom intended to ward off the cold of winter.

14 July
la Fête Nationale (**le 14 juillet**) is usually called Bastille Day in English and is a public holiday in France. It commemorates the taking of the Bastille prison in Paris and the liberation of its prisoners by the people of Paris in 1789, one of the first events of the Revolution. All over France there are parades on the day of the 14th and firework displays and *bals* (local dances) either on the night of the 13th or of the 14th.

15 August
l'Assomption (Feast of the Assumption) is a Catholic festival and a public holiday. Many people in France are either setting off on holiday around the 15th or else returning home, so this is traditionally a very busy time on the roads.

1 November
la Toussaint (All Saints' Day) is a public holiday and the day when people remember their dead relatives and friends, although properly speaking it is All Souls' Day the following day that is set aside for this in the Church. People take flowers to the cemetery, particularly chrysanthemums, as these are in bloom at this time. Because of this association, it is best to avoid taking chrysanthemums as a gift for someone. Schoolchildren have a two-week holiday around this time.

11 November
L'Armistice; le 11 novembre is a public holiday to commemorate the end of World War I in 1918, and a day of remembrance for those who died in the two world wars and in subsequent conflicts. All towns and villages hold parades in which war

veterans accompany local officials and a brass band to lay wreaths on the war memorial. In Paris, the President lays a wreath on the tomb of the unknown soldier beneath the Arc de Triomphe on the Champs-Élysées.

8 December
la Fête de l'Immaculée Conception (Feast of the Immaculate Conception). In the city of Lyons, this is celebrated as **la Fête de la Lumière** (Festival of Light) said to commemorate the Virgin Mary's intervention to prevent the plague reaching Lyons in the Middle Ages. People put rows of candles in coloured glass jars on the outsides of their windowsills, so that all the buildings in the centre of the city are illuminated.

24 December
la veille de Noël (Christmas Eve) is the time when most people exchange presents. Traditionally, the evening is the time for *le réveillon de Noël*, a large meal often starting with seafood, oysters being particularly popular. Turkey is generally eaten as a main course, sometimes with chestnut stuffing. A variety of cheeses will be followed by *la bûche de Noël*, a delicious rolled sponge in the form of a snow-covered log, filled with chocolate, coffee or even Grand Marnier flavoured buttercream. Many people go to church to celebrate *la messe de minuit* (Midnight Mass).

25 December
Noël (Christmas) is a public holiday and a day of eating and drinking, often with relatives. French people do not usually send Christmas cards, the custom being to send wishes for the coming year to more distant friends and relatives during the month of January.

26 December
There is no particular name in French for the day after Christmas Day and it is not a public holiday.

31 December
la Saint-Sylvestre (New Year's Eve). Many people have parties to celebrate *le réveillon de la Saint-Sylvestre* (New Year's Eve Party). Once again, food

plays a major part and, as at Christmas, this is a time to splash out on luxury foods such as *foie gras*. There will often be dancing and the New Year will be welcomed in with champagne.

Movable feasts

Mardi gras Shrove Tuesday, the last day of carnival before the beginning of Lent on Ash Wednesday. Traditionally, *crêpes* (pancakes) are eaten for supper. In many areas of France, sugared fritters are eaten between *la fête des Rois* and *mardi gras*. These are called *bugnes* in and around Lyons and *oreillettes* farther south.

le vendredi saint Good Friday is celebrated in the Church, but is not a public holiday.

Pâques An important Christian festival, Easter is celebrated throughout France; *le lundi de Pâques* (Easter Monday) is a public holiday. Easter Sunday, *le dimanche de Pâques*, is for many people the occasion for a big family lunch. Easter hunts are organised for children, with chocolate eggs, rabbits, hens, or fish traditionally hidden in the family garden.

l'Ascension The celebration of Ascension Day takes place (usually on a Thursday) 40 days after Easter. It is a Catholic festival and a public holiday in France.

la Pentecôte The Catholic feast is celebrated seven weeks after Easter, with the following Monday traditionally a public holiday in France. Between 2004 and 2007 **le lundi de Pentecôte** reverted to a normal working day for economic reasons, but the public holiday was reinstated for certain members of society (for example, schoolchildren and teachers) in 2008.

la Fête des Mères (Mother's Day) is the Sunday after *Pentecôte*. This is another occasion for a big family meal, with presents for the mother. **La Fête des Pères** (Father's Day) is celebrated in similar fashion two weeks later.

Calendar

A–Z of French Life and Culture

Académie française A learned body, founded by Cardinal Richelieu in 1635, whose main role nowadays is to monitor new developments in the French language. It is not always taken entirely seriously by the public at large. Its 40 members are elected for life on the basis of their contribution to scholarship or literature, and are known as '*les Immortels*'.

Agence France Presse ▶ PRESSE

agrégation This qualification, attained through competitive examination or CONCOURS, entitles the holder to teach at the highest level in secondary and tertiary education.

Air France Created in 1933, the French national airline merged in 2004 with KLM Royal Dutch Airlines to become the world's largest airline group by turnover. The French state no longer holds a majority stake in the group. The company once operated five supersonic Concorde jets, but the last ever Air France Concorde passenger flight was from New York to Paris on 31 May 2003.

Alliance Française A private organization that aims to spread awareness of French language and culture. It has centres in cities throughout the world, providing language classes and a variety of cultural activities.

Allocations familiales Known colloquially as *les allocs*, *les allocations familiales* (family allowances) are paid to any French family with two or more children. A range of other *allocations* (benefits) are also available: for single parents, to help with childcare, to pay towards housing, etc.

Alps, The A mountain range that runs north to south along the border between France, Switzerland, and Italy. It is 350 km (219 miles) long and 50–60 km (31–37.5 miles) wide. The highest peak in western Europe, Mont Blanc (4,810 m [15,776 ft]) lies in the Alps, straddling the French/Italian border. The Alpine region is home to many popular ski resorts.

Alsace Lying on the frontier of Germany and Switzerland in the northeast of France, Alsace has long been the object of territorial disputes between Germany and France. French during the RÉVOLUTION, German after the Franco-German war (1871), French in 1918, German in 1940, the region has been French again since 1945. Since 1949, Strasbourg, the capital of Alsace, has been the seat of the CONSEIL DE L'EUROPE. Alsatian white wines are highly regarded, as is its traditional cabbage dish, *choucroute* (*sauerkraut*).

année scolaire School holidays are fixed nationally, and each *académie* (local education authority or school district) falls into one of three zones, so that the starts and ends of holidays are staggered. The year lasts from early September to late June, and main breaks occur in early November (*la Toussaint*), at Christmas and New Year, in February and in Spring.

ANPE (*Agence Nationale pour l'emploi*) The national agency providing services for the unemployed as well as for employers seeking workers. In order to qualify for unemployment benefits (*allocations chômage*), job hunters must have been unemployed for at least six months. Benefits, paid by the ASSEDIC (*Association pour l'emploi dans l'industrie et le commerce*), are calculated according to the last salary earned by the job seeker and the duration of his/her period of unemployment. In the initial period of unemployment, a job seeker receives a high percentage of his/her last salary. This figure is gradually reduced to the point where the job seeker no longer qualifies for benefits and is known as a *chômeur/-euse en fin de droits*. In December 2008, ANPE and ASSEDIC merged to create a single organization called *Pôle Emploi*.

antisémitisme ► RACISME

Arc de Triomphe This Paris monument stands at the centre of the radiating spokes formed by 12 avenues including the CHAMPS-ÉLYSÉES. It was commissioned by NAPOLÉON to commemorate his victories, and completed in 1836. In 1921 it became a war memorial, and the site of the tomb of the 'unknown soldier'; a flame is lit there every evening in memory of those who have fallen in battle.

architecture Since the 1970s, the French state has promoted several major architectural projects, particularly in Paris, including the 1977 Pompidou Centre (also known as BEAUBOURG), the glass pyramid of the Louvre designed by American architect I. M. Pei and built in 1989, the Grande Arche de la Défense in western Paris, and the Institut du Monde Arabe, designed by Jean Nouvel. In 2004 the Millau viaduct, the tallest in the world, was opened by the French president, Jacques Chirac. Designed by English architect Lord Norman Foster, the 2.5 km (1.6 mile) long, 340 m (1,122 ft) high structure was dubbed 'the bridge in the clouds'.

Ariane The name of the European Space Agency's rockets, produced and operated by the private company Arianespace and launched from Kourou in French Guiana (Guyane française). The Ariane rockets have been used to put commercial satellites into space, but have met with mixed fortunes. Ariane 5-ECA, whose maiden flight ended in an explosion, successfully launched Superbird 7 in August 2008.

Armistice ► FRENCH TRADITIONS, FESTIVALS, AND HOLIDAYS

arrondissement A subdivision of a DÉPARTEMENT. Each *arrondissement* has a *sous-préfet* representing the state administration at local level.

Culture

In Paris, Lyons, and Marseilles, an arrondissement is a subdivision of the COMMUNE, and has its own *maire* and local council.

ARTE A TV channel, run jointly by France and Germany, which provides a high standard of cultural programmes.

Assemblée Nationale The lower house of the French parliament, in which 577 DÉPUTÉS are elected for a five-year term. A member, who must be at least 23 years old, has to be elected by at least 50 per cent of the votes cast and, if necessary, a second round of voting is held to ensure this. Party affiliation is indicated by a *député*'s allocation to a seat within a left–right gradation in the semi-circular chamber. The Assemblée Nationale passes laws, votes on the budget, and questions MINISTRES (who cannot be *députés*).

Astérix ► BANDE DESSINÉE

autoroutes France has an extensive motorway system, which is largely financed by tolls calculated according to the distance travelled and the vehicle type. Tickets are obtained and tolls paid at *péages* (tollgates). The speed limit for standard vehicles is 130 km/h (approx. 80 mph) and 110 km/h (approx. 70 mph) in wet weather.

Avignon Historic town in the southeast of France. Surrounded by 17th-century city walls, the centre of Avignon is dominated by the 14th-century Pope's Palace (the Popes lived here from 1309 to 1403). The 12th-century Saint-Bénezet Bridge, which spans the River RHÔNE here and which has mostly collapsed, is familiar from the song, '*Sur le pont d'Avignon*', but the town is now probably best known for its annual theatre festival, held since 1947, and one of the main cultural events of the year.

baccalauréat Known informally as *le bac*, this is an examination sat in the final year of the LYCÉE (*la terminale*), so usually at age 17 or 18. Students sit exams in a fairly broad range of subjects in a particular category: the '*bac S*' places the emphasis on the sciences, for example, whilst the '*bac L*' has a literary bias. Some categories cater for students specializing in more job-based subjects such as agriculture. The final result is given as a single overall mark or grade out of 20, although the scores for individual subjects are also given. It is common to use *le bac* as a point of reference in job adverts, so that *bac + 4* would mean a person who had completed four years of full-time study after the bac, with appropriate diplomas to show for it.

bachelier Holder of the BACCALAURÉAT, entitled to enrol for university courses.

bande dessinée plays a significant cultural role in France. More than a comic book or entertainment for youth, it is a form of popular literature known as the *neuvième art* (the 'ninth art', films being the 'seventh' and TV the 'eighth') and celebrated annually at the *Festival d'Angoulême*. Cartoon characters such as Astérix, Lucky Luke, and TINTIN are household names, and older comic books are often collectors' items.

banlieue The *banlieue* are the suburbs around main cities, and particularly the poorer residential areas around city centres, which have expanded dramatically in recent decades. The term often has a pejorative connotation, and evokes images of concrete tower blocks ('*grands ensembles*'), urban decay, and crime. The *cités* (deprived estates) are often difficult areas to live in. The government – along with the *banlieusards* (those who live there) – is trying to find ways to rehabilitate the *banlieue*.

Basque A people that has – since prehistoric times – inhabited le Pays Basque (the Basque region), an area that borders the coast of the Bay of Biscay and lies on the slopes of the Pyrenees mountains, encompassing parts of both France and Spain. Around 2.1 million Basques live in the region, the majority in Spain. The town of Bayonne is the largest city in the French Basque region (le Pays Basque français); every year a carnival (*une feria*) is held there, featuring bullfights and swordstick dancing. The Basque language, Euskara, is said to be the earliest European language; the Basque name for their country is Euzkadi. *Les Basques* have long sought autonomy from France and Spain; in Spain the region now has some autonomy, with responsibility for education, health care, policing, and taxation. In France, however, the region does not have any autonomous status, nor is Basque recognized as an official language, though it is taught in some schools.

bateaux-mouches The *bateaux-mouches* are large riverboats that transport (mainly) tourists along the River SEINE on sightseeing tours. Some also have restaurants on board. The boats were first introduced on the River Saône in Lyons in 1863; they were built in 'the flies' quarter' and the name stuck (*une mouche* is a fly). The boats' pointed noses and two large windows at the front also make them look like flies.

BCBG An abbreviation, which is a term in its own right, for '*bon chic bon genre*'. It describes a social type and the associated lifestyle, dress code, and linguistic mannerisms: someone who is essentially conventionally *bourgeois* or upper middle-class in their values and tastes. It is not necessarily intended as a compliment.

BCD *La Bibliothèque et Centre de Documentation* is a library and resource centre that exists in all French secondary schools, and is where pupils prepare school work. *Documentalistes* are the people responsible for the centres; they work in partnership with the schoolteachers.

Beaubourg Designed by the English architect Richard Rogers and the Italian Renzo Piano, the Centre National d'Art et de Culture Georges Pompidou (named after the former president of France) took its name from the district where it stands, though it is more often known as the Pompidou Centre. With its colourful ventilation pipes, and escalators in clear tubes (all on the exterior of the building), the centre was controversial when it was opened in 1977. Nowadays, as host to contemporary art exhibitions – and 800,000 visitors a year – it is an accepted addition to the Parisian scene. The terrace in front of the building is popular with street entertainers, and there are superb views of MONTMARTRE and Sacré-Cœur from the top of the building.

Bercy Though it's the name of a district in southeastern Paris, Bercy is primarily associated, if not synonymous, with the Ministry of Finance which is located there. Bercy is also home to a large stadium and concert complex, the Palais Omnisports Paris Bercy or POPB, and to a multiplex cinema and shopping area known as Bercy Village.

PLACE
CHARLES DE GAULI

Beur (fem. Beurette) A term in VERLAN derived from the French word *Arabe,* which refers to the French-born children of North African immigrants (primarily Algerian but also Tunisian and Moroccan). The *jeunes Beurs* have been at the heart of anti-racist activity in recent years, but equally at the centre of ethnic tensions in the suburbs (BANLIEUE) of major French cities. Educated within the French school system, many Beurs feel set apart from both French and Arabic culture. Beur artists express this sense of 'in-between-ness' through music, cinema, and literature in works such as *La Haine* (Hate; 1995), a film by Mathieu Kassovitz, which looks at the alienation felt by a Jew, an Arab, and a black African living in a housing project in Paris, and Leïla Houari's *Zeida de nulle part* (Zeida from Nowhere, 1985), a book that explores the hopes and dreams of a young *Maghrébine*. The term is not used so frequently now as it has been in the past. *See also* MAGHRÉBINS.

Bison Futé Symbolized by a little Native American, *Bison Futé* is a creation of the *Centre National d'Information Routière*, the French traffic information service, which reports on travel conditions nationwide, particularly during holiday periods when traffic is heaviest, and recommends alternative routes (*les itinéraires 'bis'*) for travellers keen to avoid traffic jams. The *Bison Futé* traffic tips are broadcast across the full range of media (radio, TV, the national press, the internet, and MINITEL) and appear at regular intervals on the road system itself. Information is updated constantly to reflect actual traffic conditions, enabling motorists to choose the best time to travel. Allied to *Bison Futé* is a colour-coding system to mark the relative intensity of traffic at any time (green, red, yellow, and black), which is a key factor in staggering holiday traffic on the roads.

Culture

Bleus, Les The French national football team, who wear a blue strip, are known as *Les Bleus*. Supporters shout, '*Allez les Bleus*' ('Come on, Blues !') to urge them on. The team entered footballing legend in 1998 when they won the World Cup at home, beating Brazil in the final. Zinedine Zidane (known as Zizou), who captained the team and scored two goals in their 3–0 victory, achieved iconic status in France. The French rugby union team is also known as *Les Bleus*.

Bordeaux A region in the southwest of France that borders the Atlantic Ocean. Its historical capital of the same name is also one of the main commercial centres in the southwest of France. Bordeaux is probably best known for its world-famous wines.

boules A type of bowls, also known as *pétanque*, played all over France using metal balls and a jack known as a *cochonnet*. *Terrains de boules* (playing areas) are set aside for the game in many towns and villages, though one of the beauties of the game is that it can be played virtually anywhere. So a family lunch in the summer will often end in a game of *boules* (*une partie de boules*). There are some regional variations, notably in the size and form of the playing area and the size of the bowls.

Bourse There are seven stock exchanges (*bourse de valeurs*) in France, where dealing is carried out by *agents de change*. Most operations on the Paris Bourse are computerized. The index of the 40 most quoted prices is the CAC-40 (*compagnie des agents de change-40*).

brasserie The original meaning of *brasserie* is 'brewery', and although the word is still used in this sense, it has also come to mean a type of bar-restaurant, usually serving simple, traditional French food at reasonable prices. Most brasseries offer a set-price menu (*prix fixe*), especially at lunchtime.

Bretagne Known in English as Brittany, this northwestern peninsula is lapped by the English Channel and the Atlantic Ocean. Prehistoric chambers and standing stones bear witness to the presence of peoples who later resisted the Romans. In the fifth and sixth centuries, the Celtic Bretons (from what is now Great Britain) sought refuge here, and it was only in the 16th century that Brittany was unified with France. Rennes, Brest, and Lorient are the main cities; agriculture, fishing, and tourism the main economic activities. Folklore is still very important, as is the use of the BRETON language.

Breton The ancient Celtic language of Brittany (BRETAGNE). It is related to Welsh, Irish, Scottish Gaelic, and Cornish. Recent decades have seen a revival of interest in the language going hand in hand with the assertion of a regional cultural identity and a movement for independence from France. Breton is fairly widely spoken and is taught in secondary schools in the region, although it is not recognized as an official language in France. *See also* LANGUES.

brevet This usually designates a type of vocational qualification such as the *brevet d'études professionnelles*, or *BEP*, which is awarded after two years of practically oriented coursework at a LYCÉE *professionnel*, or the *brevet de technicien supérieur*, or *BTS*, taken after the BACCALAURÉAT and representing two years of study in a specific vocational field. The *brevet des collèges* is a general educational qualification taken at around the age of 15 at the end of study in a COLLÈGE.

bureau de tabac Tobacconists can be individual shops or be found in a *bar-tabac* or *café-tabac*. They are also often combined with a newsagent's (*marchand de journaux*). They are licensed to sell tobacco and cigarettes, and also have a state licence to sell stamps, LOTO and other game tickets, and certain official documents. The red cigar-shaped sign that marks the *tabac* is known as a '*carotte*'.

café Since 1910 the number of traditional cafés or bistros in France has dropped from 510,000 to 57,000, and Paris has even been invaded by branches of Starbucks and McDonalds. In Paris the Café de Flore (which played host to famous French writers and philosophers such as Jean-Paul Sartre and Simone de Beauvoir), Les Deux Magots (a favourite of Pablo Picasso's) and Café de la Gare (opened by Coluche and Depardieu as a theatre) are among many famous cafés with a long history. Parisian waiters often still dress in traditional style, with black waistcoats and long white aprons.

Camargue The Camargue lies at the delta of the RHÔNE, near the Mediterranean, in the far south of France. Around 85,000 hectares (209,950 acres) have been designated as a nature reserve. Its protected species include the famous black bulls, white horses, and pink flamingoes. In the southeast corner of the Camargue are salt marshes, which have been worked since ancient times. Every year Gypsies make a May pilgrimage to Saintes-Maries de la Mer, a little port in the middle of the Camargue, to meet and attend religious ceremonies.

Canal Plus A privately owned French television channel. Viewers pay a subscription to view. One of its most popular programmes is *Les Guignols de l'Info*, which uses puppets to satirize French politicians and other well-known public figures.

Cannes film festival The first Cannes film festival (*Association Française du Festival International du Film*) took place in 1946 at the glamorous Côte d'Azur resort. Now many in the film industry travel from around the world to see and be seen at the May festival, which showcases films 'showing talent deserving encouragement'. The *Palme d'Or* (Golden Palm) is awarded for the best feature film.

canton An administrative unit of French local government which contains several communes. It elects a member of the CONSEIL GÉNÉRAL. Also, a state in the Swiss federation. Each of the 26 Swiss cantons has its own constitution, elected assemblies, and courts.

CAPES is a teaching qualification, awarded by competitive examination or CONCOURS, which is normally required to teach in a COLLÈGE or LYCÉE. Those who gain the qualification are known as *capésiens* and are committed to at least five years' service in a state school.

carnet de notes is a pupil's school report book, in which teachers enter test and exam results and write notes for parents to summarize students' progress. This is also where all communication passing between parents and the school is archived, as well as any detentions.

carte bancaire There are more than 30 million credit cards in France. The '*Carte bleue*' (blue card) was the first credit card to be introduced in France, in 1967, and used to be the most ubiquitous, but nowadays Mastercard, Eurocard, and Visa are also commonly used.

carte grise; certificat d'immatriculation The registration document for a motor vehicle. It is an offence not to carry it when driving the vehicle, and police checks are frequent. Up to 15 April 2009 vehicles were registered in the DÉPARTEMENT in which the owner lived, so numbers had to be changed if the owner moved to a different area.

carte nationale d'identité Although not obligatory, most French citizens possess a national identity card, obtained from their local MAIRIE, PRÉFECTURE, or police station. It is accepted as a travel document by all EU countries and is valid for 10 years.

cassoulet This meat and bean dish from the southwest of France (especially Toulouse) is named after the earthenware pot in which it is served. It consists of white beans baked slowly in goose or duck fat, along with meat such as duck or goose confit, lamb, and Toulouse sausages.

Catalan The language spoken by 25 per cent of people in Spain and by some people in the Perpignan area of southwest France. It is taught in schools in the area but is not recognized as an official language in France. *See also* LANGUES.

CE *Cycle* or *cours élémentaire* (*CE*) is the programme for the two years of primary school for children aged 7 to 9 (*CE1* and *CE2*).

Césars Prizes awarded annually for achievements in the film industry; the French equivalent of the Oscars.

Chambre des députés ▶ ASSEMBLÉE NATIONALE

champagne An alcoholic drink inextricably linked with indulgence and celebration, champagne is the produce of a particular region of northeast France, comprising the DÉPARTEMENTS of Aube, Marne, Ardennes, and Haute-Marne. Wine production in the region dates back to Roman times, but it was not until the 17th century that sparkling wine was deliberately produced in Champagne (the monk, Dom Pérignon, was one of the first to develop the process). Champagne is now a protected brand: only sparkling wine produced in this region can bear the name. In the 19th century, 6,000 hectares (14,830 acres) of vines destroyed by the phylloxera aphid had to be replaced with American vinestocks; World War II also wreaked havoc in the region. The industry has since boomed, however, and around 300 million bottles of champagne are now sold each year.

champignons Refers to any mushroom-like fungi, whether edible or not. Hunting for edible mushrooms is a popular leisure activity and many varieties are highly prized. Advice on whether they are edible or not can usually be obtained from a PHARMACIE.

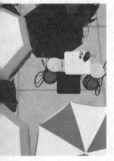

Champs-Elysées The world-famous avenue in central Paris, known for its luxury shops, hotels, and clubs. At one end stands the ARC DE TRIOMPHE, the scene of the remembrance ceremony each year for the Armistice of 1918.

Chandeleur ▶ FRENCH TRADITIONS, FESTIVALS AND HOLIDAYS

chanson à textes ▶ CHANSON FRANÇAISE

chanson française Often referred to as '*chanson à textes*', *la chanson française* is characterized by two main features: the lyrics must be meaningful and the song must be sung in French. The genre was popularized by singers such as Maurice Chevalier and Joséphine Baker during World War II, Edith Piaf and Juliette Gréco in the 1950s and 1960s, and Johnny Hallyday from the 1970s onward. In the 1960s, the lyrics of singer-poets such as Georges Brassens and Jacques Brel reinvigorated the genre; their texts are often studied in schools today. *La chanson française* was taken through the 1980s and beyond by singers such as Patricia Kaas and Alain Souchon, and today MC Solaar, the rap singer, and Corneille (soul) have brought it into the 21st century.

charcuterie A shop or supermarket counter selling a wide variety of pork products. As well as cuts of pork, *charcutiers* usually sell sausages and various types of raw and cooked ham, pâtés, and a selection of *saucissons*. Most *charcuteries* also offer a variety of salads, savoury pastries, and dishes that can be reheated at home or on the premises. *Charcuteries* offering a catering service usually advertise themselves as *charcutier-traiteur* (*traiteur* means 'caterer'). *La charcuterie* is also used to refer to pork products such as ham and *saucisson*.

Culture

chasse *La chasse* (hunting) is a widely practised sport in France, particularly among older people. Legislation as to the rights of hunters to hunt over privately owned land varies according to the region and the amount of land concerned. During the hunting season, it is advisable not to stray from public footpaths in the countryside on the days of the week when hunting is permitted. *CPNT* (*Chasse, Pêche, Nature et Traditions*) [Hunting, Fishing, Nature, and Traditions] is a single-issue party representing the interests of hunters in the ASSEMBLÉE NATIONALE.

châteaux A distinctive feature of the French countryside are the châteaux: the castles, palaces, mansions, and stately homes that can be seen throughout the region. Many are old castles dating from the Middle Ages and called '*châteaux forts*'. Later, unfortified palaces were built: the most famous are the '*châteaux de la Loire*', such as Amboise and Chenonceau, which were built in the Renaissance period. One of the largest châteaux in France is Versailles. Rebuilt for Louis XIV in the 17th century, today it has 3 million visitors each year. Two other châteaux – the Grand and Petit Trianon – stand in its grounds, as does Marie-Antoinette's hamlet, built in the style of Normandy cottages.

Culture

chômage ▶ ANPE

CHU *Centre Hospitalier Universitaire* is a teaching hospital attached to the medical faculty of a university.

CIDJ (*Centre d'Informations et de Documentation pour la Jeunesse*) is where pupils and students often go in order to find information related to youth issues as well as information about careers and studies in general.

cinéma Cinema has always been a popular medium in France; it was in Paris in December 1895 that the Lumière brothers first demonstrated their *cinématographe*, showing moving pictures to a paying audience. In the 1920s, French filmmakers such as Louis Delluc and Jean Cocteau experimented with avant-garde cinema, while in the 1930s Jean Renoir produced masterpieces such as *La Grande Illusion*. Marcel Carné's epic tale, *Les Enfants du Paradis,* followed in 1945. In 1959, Jean-Luc Godard's *À Bout de Souffle* established him at the forefront of the *nouvelle vague*, the 'new wave', along with François Truffaut. *Cinéma Beur* (from the slang word meaning second-generation North Africans) arrived in the 1980s with Rachid Bouchareb, and has since coexisted with *cinéma du look*. Visually impressive, with non-naturalistic photography, intense colours, and romantic stories filmed in the studio, the best-known example of the genre is *Le Fabuleux destin d'Amélie Poulain* (2001), which grossed more than $33 million at the box office.

Cinquième Republique ▶ RÉPUBLIQUE

classe de neige A period, generally a week, that a school class, usually of under-twelves, spends in a mountain area. Ski tuition is integrated with normal schoolwork.

Code Napoléon A civil code introduced by the French emperor NAPOLÉON BONAPARTE in 1804 and named Code Napoléon in 1807. It still underpins the legal systems of France and many other European countries. The code attempted to unify the customs of northern and southern France, and was a combination of rational and traditional principles. It includes key concepts such as equality for all in the eyes of the law, and no recognition of privilege. The code was adopted in most of continental Europe, and survived Napoleon's downfall in 1815.

cohabitation is when a president and a prime minister from opposing political parties (PARTIS POLITIQUES) rule the country together. This can happen because there are separate elections for the National Assembly and the presidency. It last occurred from 1997 to 2002, when the socialists won a majority of seats in the National Assembly, so socialist Lionel Jospin was appointed prime minister in the government of the right-wing president, Jacques Chirac.

collège A state school for pupils between the ages of 11 and 15, between the ÉCOLE PRIMAIRE and LYCÉE. The organization of the school and the curriculum followed are laid down at national level.

colonie de vacances A holiday village or summer camp for children. Originally a means of giving poor city children a break in the country, these are still largely state-subsidized. They are known informally as '*colo*'.

Comédie Française The oldest national theatre company, this society of French actors was founded in 1680. Its repertoire is mainly classical. Molière's plays have been performed more than 30,000 times by the Comédie; Shakespeare is one of the few foreign authors who is also regularly performed. Every 15 January, on the anniversary of Molière's birth in 1622, a bust of him is brought on stage so that actors can pay homage to the writer.

commune The smallest administrative unit of French local government. Each has its own MAIRIE and CONSEIL MUNICIPAL, and with other communes forms a CANTON.

concours A competitive examination that is used to determine entry into many areas of the public services, including teaching, as well as to the most prestigious institutes of higher education.

conduite accompagnée Learner drivers who are 16 years old and have passed the theory (*code de la route*) part of the driving test in a state-approved driving school are allowed to practise driving a vehicle accompanied by a qualified driver aged 28 or over who has a clean driving licence. Such drivers can only drive at a maximum of 110 km/h (69 mph) on AUTOROUTES and must have a white sticker with a red A (for *apprenant*, or 'learner') affixed to the car.

conseil de classe A committee representing each class in a COLLÈGE or LYCÉE consisting of the class teachers, two elected parent members, and two elected class members. It is chaired by the head teacher. The *conseil de classe* meets regularly to discuss the progress of the class and any problems that may have arisen.

Conseil de l'Europe The Council of Europe was founded in 1949. Its headquarters are in Strasbourg, the capital of ALSACE, and it has 45 member states, all of whom are committed to democracy and human rights. The Council's main purpose is to draft treaties and legislation; these are sent to member countries for ratification by individual national legislatures. The 1950 Convention for the Protection of Human Rights and Fundamental Freedoms set up the European Court of Human Rights, which hears cases brought by individuals. Member states must adhere to the court's rulings or face expulsion from the Council.

conseil général The body of representatives elected every six years to implement public policy in each DÉPARTEMENT.

conseil municipal The *conseil municipal* is the local council elected for a six-year term by the inhabitants of a COMMUNE. The *conseil municipal* then elects the mayor (*le maire*). It is responsible for the management of local public services and amenities.

conseil régional Each member of a *conseil régional* is elected for a term of six years to represent a DÉPARTEMENT. The *conseillers régionaux* then appoint a president and an executive team.

conservatoires Many towns play host to these academies, which dispense specialist teaching in music and drama. There are 20 in Paris alone. Prizes are given to the best pupils.

Corse, La Island situated off the southeast of mainland France in the Mediterranean. Italian for many centuries, the island was sold to France in 1767. Ajaccio in the south and Bastia in the north are the main towns of the two DÉPARTEMENTS making up La Corse. The economic activities are agriculture, fishing, and tourism. Corsica enjoys special status and has an assembly with additional powers, though since the late 1970s there have been sometimes violent protests against the French government by those wanting complete independence from France.

Côte d'Azur The Côte d'Azur (literally 'Azure Coast') is the name for the French Riviera, the coastal region in the south of France that borders the Mediterranean and extends from south of Marseilles to the border with Italy. It became very famous in the 1920s as many foreigners – English aristocrats in particular – fell in love with its wild coastline. The towns of Nice, Cannes, and Monte Carlo are well known for attracting rich and famous holidaymakers.

couscous A North African dish introduced into France by the MAGHRÉBINS. The name comes from the granulated wheat-flour, or couscous, that forms the basis for the dish; this is served with a vegetable stew and various accompaniments, such as *merguez* (spicy sausages), chicken, mutton, or fish.

CP The *cycle préparatoire* or *cours préparatoire* is the first year of primary school, starting a child's formal education off at the statutory age of six. Most children will already have attended an ÉCOLE MATERNELLE.

CRS *Compagnies républicaines de sécurité* are special police units trained in public order techniques and riot control. They also police the AUTOROUTES and support mountain rescue and lifeguard work. *See also* MAI 1968.

décentralisation The tendency for the government in Paris to order the affairs of the rest of the country has been questioned for decades. A 1982 bill covering the rights and freedoms of COMMUNES, DÉPARTEMENTS, and RÉGIONS gave them much more autonomy. There is a slow movement to increase the decentralization of power; advocates of this are called *décentralisateurs*.

Déclaration des Droits de l'Homme et du Citoyen In August 1789 the French Assembly produced the 'Declaration of the Rights of Man and of the Citizen', which was adopted and signed under pressure by Louis XVI. It established the importance of recognizing human rights in all circumstances. The first article states: 'Men are born and remain free and equal in rights.' These principles have informed many conventions since.

de Gaulle, Charles One of the key figures in recent French political history, General Charles de Gaulle's striking profile is instantly recognizable. Having served in the army during World War I, de Gaulle's attempt to modernize it met with little success. When France fell to German forces in June 1940, de Gaulle travelled to Britain. From there he rallied his 'Free French' volunteers and resistance fighters within France; he entered Paris with the liberating forces in 1944. Politically sidelined for some years, he came back to power during the Algerian War and became the first president of the Cinquième RÉPUBLIQUE (Fifth Republic) from 1958

to 1969. The increased presidential powers he instituted at that time are
still in force.

département An administrative unit of government in France. Each
département has a number and this appears as the first two digits in
postcodes for addresses within the area, and as the two-digit number at the
end of the registration plates of vehicles registered before 15 April 2009.

député An elected member of the ASSEMBLÉE NATIONALE.

Disneyland Resort Paris (was EuroDisney) opened near Paris in 1992
amid great controversy, with many people fearing that French culture
would be undermined by this American intruder. However, the many
visitors do not seem to share this concern; after a slow start, the theme
park now attracts more than 12 million people a year to the 'lands', studios,
and costumed parades familiar from its counterparts in the United States.

DOM-TOM Acronym for *Département d'outre-mer* and
Territoire d'outre-mer, the French overseas territories. The
DÉPARTEMENTS have the status of a RÉGION. At present there are
four: Guadeloupe, Guyane, Martinique, and Réunion. The
territoires, which include Nouvelle-Calédonie (New Caledonia)
and Tahiti, are constitutionally part of the French republic, and
citizens have French nationality.

école libre Private sector school education, provided
predominantly by the Catholic Church.

école maternelle A school providing free nursery education
from age two to six. Many children start at two and virtually all
children attend between the ages of four and six, which is the
statutory school starting age and the time at which children move into the
ÉCOLE PRIMAIRE.

école primaire A primary school for children between the ages of six, the
statutory minimum age for starting school, and 11.

école secondaire Secondary education in France consists of two phases:
COLLÈGE (11 to 15 years) and LYCÉE (15/16 to 17/18 years).

EDF-GDF *Électricité de France-Gaz de France* was the utility combining
electricity generation and distribution of gas and electricity. It was split
into two entities in January 2008: *ErDF* owned by *EDF*, and *GrDF* owned by
GDF Suez, now a private gobal company.

Eiffel Tower Built by Gustave Eiffel for the Paris World Exhibition in
1889, La Tour Eiffel was the highest in the world until 1930. The tower has
three lifts and 1,665 steps and – with 6 million visitors per year – is one of
the biggest attractions in Paris.

Élysée ► PALAIS DE L'ÉLYSÉE

Culture

Emmaüs A charitable organization founded in 1954 by Abbé Pierre, a Catholic priest and well-known public figure who died in 2007. The organization, which has wide public support, aims to help the underprivileged. It has centres throughout France, run by volunteers, who collect and sell secondhand furniture, clothes, and bric-à-brac.

énergie nucléaire Nearly 86 per cent of French electricity is produced by nuclear power; only the United States produces more. There are more nuclear sites in France than in any other European country. Defenders of nuclear power argue that, because of its policy, France creates much less CO_2 than most industrialized countries. However, disposal of nuclear waste remains a problem.

Entente Cordiale A colonial-era agreement signed by the British and French on 8 April 1904, which aimed to settle long-standing disputes between the UK and France in countries such as Morocco, Egypt, Siam, Madagascar, the New Hebrides, West and Central Africa, and Newfoundland. But it also represented a shift from a history overshadowed by conflict and rivalry to a sustained era of *rapprochement* and alliance. In 2004 many Franco-British events were held to celebrate the 100th anniversary of its signing.

L'Équipe ► PRESSE

EuroDisney ► DISNEYLAND RESORT PARIS

faculté More usually known as *la fac*, this is how students describe their university, in particular the location. So 'to go to university' would be '*aller à la fac.*'

festivals All year round there are theatre, music, dance, contemporary art, circus, and street festivals, but the majority take place in the summer months between June and September. The most popular are: Vienne for Jazz, La Rochelle for Francofolies (featuring CHANSONS FRANÇAISES), Orange and Aix-en-Provence for opera, Avignon for theatre, Chalon-sur-Saône for street performances, Arles for photography and dance, La Côte-St-André for Berlioz, Lyons for advertising and contemporary art. In Brittany the Festival Interceltique is becoming more and more popular. *See also* FÊTE DE LA MUSIQUE.

Fête de la Musique, created in 1982, is celebrated each year on the summer solstice, 21 June. It is now a major musical event all over France. In Paris amateur and professional musicians alike dust off their instruments and set up in any spare spot, from courtyards to châteaux, parks to doorways. The night echoes to every imaginable style of music as musicians play to large crowds.

Fête Nationale ► FRENCH TRADITIONS, FESTIVALS, AND HOLIDAYS

Culture

Figaro, Le ▶ PRESSE

FNAC A large chain of bookshops that also sells music, software, phones, and photographic equipment. They also run a booking system – in-store and via the internet – for all cultural events in France.

France 2 (FR2) is the main publicly owned television channel, which aims to provide a wide range of quality programmes.

France 3 (FR3), a state-owned TV channel, is regionally based and required to promote regional diversity and cover a wide range of beliefs and opinions.

France Télécom Orange is one of the world's leading telecommunications companies, providing mobile telephony and internet broadband services amongst other high-tech products..

Francophonie Invented by a French geographer in 1880, the word describes the French-speaking world – that is, countries where French is spoken as the official language or a language of culture. In 2005 this comprised 51 countries plus five associated ones. Five hundred million people live in Francophone countries, but only 120 million are actually Francophones (French-speaking).

Franglais can mean either French characterized by excessive use of English words, or the mixing of French and English (either intentionally, for fun, or unintentionally). There has been a long battle in France since World War II to preserve the national language from corruption by foreign words, particularly Americanisms. This has been only partially successful. The government's support of French cinema and the dubbing industry has gone some way to protecting the language. The use of French is officially monitored and regulated by the ACADÉMIE FRANÇAISE.

Front National ▶ PARTIS POLITIQUES

gastronomie The art or science of good eating is an enduring passion in France. It can be traced through the long history of some Parisian restaurants – *L'Auberge de la Mère Poulard* dates from 1888, Maxim's dates from 1893; through its tradition of great French chefs from Marie-Antoine Carême (1784–1833) to Paul Bocuse (1926–); through its world-famous culinary academy, *Le Cordon Bleu*, established in 1895; and through the great variety of its regional dishes, from *bouillabaisse* to *pâté de foie gras*. As in the rest of Europe, chefs strive to gain 'chefs' hats' (the mark of excellence from the *Gault Millau Guide*), and stars (the supreme accolade being three) from the *Michelin Guide*.

Gaule, La The region that now comprises modern France was once occupied by a Celtic tribe known as the Gauls. Between 57 and 52 BC, Julius

Culture

Caesar and the Roman army conquered La Gaule. The Gauls saw many changes in their way of life: Roman buildings such as Le Pont du Gard and the amphitheatre at Nîmes were erected; wine was drunk in preference to beer; their own gods were replaced by Roman ones. In 486 AD the Romans were expelled from Gaul by Clovis (465–511), ruler of the Franks, and the country was renamed 'France' after its new occupiers.

gendarmerie nationale A section of the military which provides police services outside the major towns.

gîte rural A farmhouse or other building in the country that has been turned into a holiday cottage. Houses displaying the official *gîtes de France* sign must conform to certain standards.

GR or *grandes randonnées* are long-distance footpaths, maintained by the *Fédération française de randonnée pédestre*. *GR* (major hiking routes) are marked by white and red or yellow and red signs; *PR* (*petites randonnées*) are marked by yellow signs. GR20 is a famous route across Corsica.

grande école A prestigious higher education establishment admitting students on the results of a CONCOURS. They have different areas of specialization, and competition for entry is fierce, as they are widely believed to offer the highest level of education available and thus a guarantee of subsequent career success.

grottes There are many prehistoric *grottes*, or caves, in France, relics of the cave-dwelling peoples who settled in the south of France nearly a million years ago. La grotte Chauvet, in the Ardèche in southeastern France, was discovered by amateur speleologists. It is famous for its more than 300 animal paintings and engravings dating back to the Paleolithic era, between 32,000 and 30,000 years ago. The cave is closed to the public, but a reproduction is being built for visitors at La Mathe. La grotte de Lourdes is a place of pilgrimage; in 1858 a young girl claimed to have seen the Virgin Mary here.

Guyane ▶ DOM-TOM

Harki From the Arab *harka*, meaning movement, this is the name given to Algerian soldiers who fought on the French side against those Algerians seeking independence from 1954 to 1962. Around 50,000–70,000 *Harkis* were killed in Algeria. Since the 1990s there has been a greater recognition of the role they played on behalf of France.

haute couture The *Chambre Syndicale de la Couture Parisienne* was founded in 1868 by Charles Worth (1825–95), who was actually born in England but became a highly successful Parisian designer. This association of *haute-couture* ('high-tailoring') houses defined the art of *couture*.

Nowadays *haute couture* is a term regulated by the government. Each year the *Chambre Syndicale de la Haute Couture* decides which houses qualify to carry the *haute-couture* label; they have to meet strict criteria in terms of design, production, and presentation of fashion shows. *Haute-couture* clothes are the product of many hours of work, and are therefore extremely expensive. Famous French designers include Christian Dior (1905–57), Yves St Laurent (1936–2008), and Jean-Paul Gaultier (1952–).

l'Hexagone Because of the shape of the map of France, which resembles a six-sided figure, France is often referred to as 'the Hexagon'. *L'Hexagone* refers to mainland France, excluding its islands and other dependencies. *See also* DOM-TOM.

HLM An abbreviation of *habitation à loyer modéré*. A type of public housing, usually an apartment in an estate, available for a relatively low rent with an option to buy as long as the property is retained for a minimum of five years. *HLMs* are built and managed either by public bodies, by the private sector supported by state loans, or by cooperatives. About 13 million people live in *HLMs*.

hôtel de ville ▶ MAIRIE

immatriculation ▶ PLAQUE D'IMMATRICULATION

immigration Of the 62 million people who live in France, about 4 million (around 7 per cent) are immigrants (*les immigrés*). Immigration used to be dominated by Europeans (54 per cent of those entering France in 1975 were from Europe), but today most immigrants are Algerians, Moroccans, Tunisians, people from the African colonies, Turks, and Asians (from the former colonies of Vietnam, Laos, and Cambodia). To work in France, incomers have to obtain *une carte de séjour* from the authorities. This is not always easy, particularly for non-EU citizens. People in illegal situations are called '*sans papiers*' (literally, 'without papers'). There are believed to be about 1 million '*sans papiers*' in the country. *See also* RACISME.

Islam ▶ RELIGION

justice The French Minister of Justice is called *Le Garde des Sceaux* (*un sceau* is a stamp, or seal). Barristers, or *avocats*, plead at the bar (*le barreau*). Solicitors, known as *notaires*, are very involved in local life, as they deal with property. You may sometimes need to go to see the *notaire*, even when you are just looking for a place to rent.

laïcité The concept of *laïcité* has been a fundamental principle in French society since the RÉVOLUTION, which separated religion from the functions of government – though the Church and State were only formally separated in 1905. *Laïcité* literally means secularism, but implies a free expression of religion, although religion is not accorded any special status. The issue has been hotly debated recently in France, after a Muslim girl was expelled from her school for wearing a *hijab*, or veil. In 2004, a law was passed forbidding the wearing of notable religious symbols in a move designed to protect the secular state.

langues French is the official language of France, though regional languages are now also taught in some schools. Since 1951 it has been possible to take some part of the BACCALAURÉAT in BRETON, CATALAN, or OCCITAN, and since 1974 in Corsican. There are six principal regional languages spoken in France: Breton (Britanny), Alsatian (ALSACE), Occitan (or *langue d'Oc*, spoken in 32 French DÉPARTEMENTS in the south); Catalan (south); and Corsican (French Riviera and Corsica). Up to 76 languages are spoken in France and the DOM-TOM, 29 in Nouvelle-Calédonie (New Caledonia) alone.

Latin Quarter ► QUARTIER LATIN

Légion d'honneur Instituted in 1802 by NAPOLÉON BONAPARTE to honour military exploits, this is now the system of honours awarded by the state for meritorious achievement. There are five grades of distinction, of which the basic rank is *chevalier* and the highest is *grand-croix*. The award is in the gift of the president, who is the *grand maître*.

Libération ► PRESSE

Liberté, Egalité, Fraternité This rousing cry for 'liberty, equality, and fraternity' was first invoked during the RÉVOLUTION of 1789. It summarizes the driving principles behind French society. The motto can be seen on objects such as stamps or coins. It is also frequently emblazoned on the façades of town halls and schools.

licence The first level of university degree, awarded after a three-year course. *See* UNIVERSITÉ.

livret de famille An official family record book, recording births, marriages, and deaths, which is given to married and unmarried parents alike and is often used to verify family links.

Loire The Loire is the name of a DÉPARTEMENT in Rhône-Alpes around St-Étienne; it is also the longest river in France, running for 1,020 km (637.5 miles) from the Cévennes region to the Atlantic Ocean. In the 15th century, the river was an ideal way to transport goods; in addition the beautiful forests, ideal for hunting, encouraged kings and nobles to build castles nearby (*les* CHÂTEAUX *de la Loire*).

LOTO The French national lottery, played using special machines that can be found in BUREAUX DE TABAC throughout France.

Louvre Originally a medieval fortress, then the palace of the kings of France, the Louvre became a museum after the French RÉVOLUTION. In 1989 the architect I. M. Pei added the glass pyramid to create an underground entrance. The *Mona Lisa* (*La Joconde*) by Leonardo da Vinci is probably the most famous of some 3,150 paintings displayed in the museum. It also houses around 350,000 Egyptian, Greek and Roman antiquities, as well as many other exhibits dating from classical times to the early 19th century. More than 8 million people visit the Louvre each year.

Luxembourg ▶ PALAIS DU LUXEMBOURG

lycée A school providing the last three years of secondary education after the COLLÈGE. The first year is *la seconde* at the age of 15/16, going through *la première*, and ending with *la terminale* at age 17/18, when students sit the BACCALAURÉAT. As well as those *lycées* that provide a conventional education, there are a number of different types of *lycée* offering a more vocationally based education.

M6 A popular, privately owned commercial TV company.

magasins Opening and closing times of shops (*les magasins*) vary according to the type of shop and the location. Department stores (*les grands magasins*) are generally open all day from 9 a.m. to 7 p.m. In larger towns, most other shops, with the exception of small food shops, are also open all day. Privately owned food shops such as butchers and fishmongers generally open at 8 a.m. and do not close in the evening until 7 or 7.30 p.m. They usually close, however, between midday and 2 or 3 p.m. In small towns, all the shops generally close for two or three hours in the middle of the day. In both small and large towns, all types of food shops tend to be open on Sunday mornings until midday. In smaller towns many shops are closed on Mondays.

Maghrébins About 1.3 million people of Maghreb origin (from France's ex-colonial territories of Morocco, Algeria, and Tunisia) live and work in France. They came to work in France during the '*trente glorieuses*', the three decades of postwar boom (1945–75). Many worked in car factories. Their children are known as BEURS in VERLAN.

Mai 1968: les événements Following disputes with university authorities and the police, students all over France went on strike. The government's attempts to suppress dissent using the CRS riot police made the situation much worse; street battles followed, and the students ripped cobbles up from the roads to form barricades. Ten million French workers joined the students in their protest and the country was paralysed for nearly two weeks. In response, President Charles DE GAULLE dissolved the ASSEMBLÉE NATIONALE and called new elections. The revolutionary fervour of the protesters subsided and de Gaulle was re-elected, though in return he promised major reforms in education.

Culture

mairie Administrative headquarters of the CONSEIL MUNICIPAL and the office of the *maire*, who is the local representative of state authority, officiating at marriages and supervising local elections. The *maire*'s powers can be quite extensive, especially in the larger towns, while the position can also be held on a part-time basis. The *maire*'s office is also known as the *hôtel de ville* (town hall) in larger towns.

Mans, Le town midway between Paris and the Atlantic coast, Le Mans is renowned for its 24-hour endurance motor car race, held every year.

marchés All towns in France have a weekly market with stalls selling a variety of produce, and some areas in big cities have a market every day. Many stalls are run by local people selling their own produce. Despite having access to supermarkets, many people still do much of their shopping *au marché*.

mariage Church weddings are not legally recognized in France, Belgium, or Switzerland (although they are in Quebec), so all couples must be married legally in a civil ceremony, whether or not they want a church wedding (which usually takes place afterwards but can be up to several weeks later). In France, the civil ceremony is a relatively short affair held in the *mairie* (town hall), and conducted by the mayor or his/her deputy. The couple vow to be responsible for the moral instruction and education of their future family, and are presented with a LIVRET DE FAMILLE. If the couple are holding a church ceremony then that is often the 'public' wedding, with the civil marriage usually a private family affair. Guests are often invited to the *vin d'honneur*, which begins the reception, where they can simply toast the newlyweds with a glass of champagne without staying on for a meal. For those who do stay, celebrations can continue for days, particularly in rural areas. The traditional wedding cake is the *pièce montée* or *croquembouche*, a magnificent tower of custard-filled choux buns coated in caramel. The legal age for getting married in France is 18 for men and 15 for women; in Belgium, Switzerland, and Quebec it is 18 for both parties (although it is possible to marry younger with parental consent). Same-sex marriage has been legally possible in Belgium since 2003, and in Quebec since 2004.

Marianne The symbolic female figure often used to represent the French Republic (la RÉPUBLIQUE française). There are statues of her in public places all over France, frequently in town halls, and she also appears on the standard French stamp. She is often depicted wearing a Phrygian bonnet, a pointed cap which became one of the symbols of liberty of the 1789 RÉVOLUTION. Actresses Brigitte Bardot, Catherine Deneuve, and Laetitia Casta are among the well-known figures who have been used to represent the modern-day Marianne.

Marseillaise, La The popular name for the French national anthem, composed by Claude-Joseph Rouget de Lisle in 1792. It was adopted as a marching song by a group of republican volunteers from Marseilles, and it marked their entry into Paris. Many rock and jazz adaptations exist; there is even a reggae version, written in 1979 by Serge Gainsbourg.

Matignon L'Hôtel Matignon in the rue de Varenne in Paris is the official residence and office of the prime minister (PREMIER MINISTRE). (Hôtel is used here in the sense of a large private town house, which would have been its original use in the 18th century.) *Matignon* is effectively a synonym for the prime ministerial office, like 'Downing Street' in the UK.

Médecins du monde A charitable organization that provides medical and humanitarian aid in areas stricken by war, famine, or natural disaster.

Médecins sans frontières A charitable organization that sends medical teams anywhere in the world (hence their title) in order to cope with the effects on people of war and natural disasters.

MEDEF Known until 1998 as *le CNPF* (*Conseil national du patronat français*), *le MEDEF* (*Mouvement des entreprises de France*) is an umbrella organization representing the majority of employers' interest groups, large and small.

Métro (Chemin de fer métropolitain) The first line (Line 1) on the Parisian *métro* was completed in 1900. Now there are 16 lines (1–14 and 3b and 7b) in this underground rail system. It is run by RATP. The RER, a rapid-transit rail network, is linked to the *métro*. Many of the distinctive and charming Art Nouveau entrances to the underground, created by the architect Hector Guimard (1867–1942) in the early 1900s, still survive. Other main cities in France such as Lyons, Marseilles, and Lille also have underground railway systems. Rennes is the smallest town in the world to have its own métro system.

ministre Appointed by the PRÉSIDENT DE LA RÉPUBLIQUE on the advice of the PREMIER MINISTRE, a *ministre* heads a department of state and becomes a member of the *conseil des ministres*. The title *ministre d'État* is a recognition that the ministry is of greater than normal significance. In the *Cinquième* RÉPUBLIQUE, a DÉPUTÉ has to resign his or her seat in order to take office as a *ministre*.

Minitel A computer terminal available from France Télécom that gave users access to the Télétel network. This can now be accessed via the Internet. Télétel/Minitel offers a huge variety of services, including the telephone directory, train schedules, etc.

MJC (Maison des jeunes et de la culture) Founded in 1944, these youth clubs are established in most towns. They offer cultural, scientific, social, and sporting activities. They are subsidized partly by the COMMUNE or by associations, and partly by the State.

Monaco Situated on the southern coast of France, near the border with Italy, Monaco is just 1.95 sq km in area. A principality under the protection of France, it was ruled by Prince Rainier III of the Grimaldi family from 1949 until his death in 2005, when he was succeeded by his son Albert II. Monaco is a tax haven, famous for its Casino, its expensive yacht-filled marina, and many very chic boutiques.

Monde, Le ▶ PRESSE

Montmartre The 18th ARRONDISSEMENT of Paris, Montmartre is the highest point of the city. Its 130 m (426 ft) summit is topped by the basilica of Sacré Cœur. Montmartre has a strong association with artists: Renoir, Monet, and Van Gogh were among those who frequented the area in the early 20th century. Today it is a busy tourist attraction that still retains its village-like atmosphere.

Moulin Rouge Created in 1889, the Moulin Rouge cabaret became famous for the can-can dance performed by its beautiful stars, and was immortalized in the paintings of artist Toulouse-Lautrec. Edith Piaf and Joséphine Baker are among the many famous names who have sung there. The 2001 film, *Moulin Rouge*, starring Nicole Kidman and Ewan McGregor, vividly recreated its early *demi-monde* atmosphere.

Musée national A museum directly under the control of the MINISTRE *de la Culture*, for example the LOUVRE or Musée d'Orsay in Paris. These museums are generally closed on Tuesdays.

Napoléon Bonaparte French politician and military leader, Napoléon (1769–1821) was emperor of France from 1804 to 1815. As a general, he waged wars throughout Europe and North Africa; as a politician he instituted a number of important political and social changes, including reorganizing the Treasury, setting up the Bank of France, creating LYCÉES, and establishing the CODE NAPOLÉON. He married and divorced Joséphine de Beauharnais; his marriage to Marie Louise, daughter of the Emperor Francis I, resulted in the birth of a son (Napoléon) in 1811. His failure in the Peninsular War and a disastrous campaign in Russia signalled a reversal in his military fortunes, which was compounded by his defeat at Waterloo in 1815. He died in exile on the island of St Helena.

Notre Dame The Gothic cathedral of Notre Dame was built between 1163 and 1345 and stands on the Île de la Cité in the centre of the River SEINE. With its dramatic gargoyles, flying buttresses and stunning stained-glass rose windows, it is one of Paris's main tourist attractions. *Notre-Dame de Paris* (also known as *The Hunchback of Notre Dame*), by the French

Culture

Romantic writer Victor Hugo (1802–85), is set around the cathedral and tells the story of the deformed bell-ringer Quasimodo and his love for the beautiful Esméralda.

Occitan The old language of the southern half of France (*langue d'Oc*). It is still spoken in a number of different dialects by an estimated four million people, and recent years have seen an immense revival of interest in promoting its survival. It can now be learned in many schools in the south, although it has no status as an official language in France. *See also* LANGUES.

OGM Only some very specific varieties of *organismes génétiquement modifiés* or genetically modified foods can be sold and consumed in France. The French Ministry of Agriculture is closely monitoring the use and consumption of genetically modified foods (*la biovigilance*) in order to assess any possible side effects.

Ouest-France ▶ PRESSE

PACS *Le pacte civil de solidarité* (contract of civil union), established in November 1999, is designed to safeguard the common interests of partners living together either in mixed or same-sex couples. The PACS does not apply to under-18s, to couples who are blood relatives, or those already in another marriage or relationship. It entails certain obligations on the part of the couple who sign the 'pact', such as a commitment to mutual support and maintenance and shared responsibility for joint expenses. In return, couples are given certain rights, for example over joint property, accommodation, etc.

Palais Bourbon A large 18th-century residence on the Left Bank of the River SEINE that is now the seat of the ASSEMBLÉE NATIONALE.

Palais de l'Élysée The official residence and office of the French president, situated just off the CHAMPS-ÉLYSÉES in Paris.

Palais des Congrès A huge conference centre. Several large cities have one of these, notably Paris and Lyons. As well as supplying luxury conference facilities, they have a large amount of exhibition space, and auditoriums where concerts and performances are held.

Palais du Luxembourg A 17th-century palace in the Jardin du Luxembourg in Paris. It is now the seat of the SÉNAT.

Pâques ▶ FRENCH TRADITIONS, FESTIVALS, AND HOLIDAYS

Partis politiques In general, French political parties reflect a basic left/right divide. On the left, the main parties are the *Parti Socialiste* (*PS*) and the *Parti Communiste Française* (*PCF*), while the principal party on the right is the *Union pour un Mouvement Populaire* (UMP), with the

Mouvement Démocrate for the centre. There are in addition more extreme groups at both ends of the political spectrum; such as Jean-Marie Le Pen's extreme right *Front National* (*FN*). Beyond the general left/right divide, the ecological movement is represented by *Les Verts* and *Génération Écologie*.

Pei, I. M. ▶ ARCHITECTURE, LOUVRE

pelote The most popular sport in the Basque region, there are several variations on pelota, or *la pelote basque*. The European version is thought to derive from 'real' tennis. It can be played just using the hand, with rackets, with a wooden bat (*pala*) or with a wicker basket that propels the ball (*cesta*). It can be played against a wall or between two teams separated by a net, and the ball can reach speeds of around 160 km/h (100 mph).

périphérique *Le périphérique* (*le périph*) is the ring road or beltway that runs round the central area of Paris. It is often blocked with traffic jams.

Other major cities in France have ring roads which are also often congested, particularly during the rush hour, '*l'heure de pointe*'.

permis de conduire A driving licence can be issued to a person over the age of 18 who has passed both parts of the driving test, the theory and the practical. The first part is the theory test (*code de la route*) and consists of 40 questions about the highway code. This can be sat from the age of 16 upwards and gives the right to the CONDUITE ACCOMPAGNÉE. The practical driving test has to be taken within two years of the theory test. It is compulsory to carry your driving licence when driving a vehicle.

pétanque ▶ BOULES

pharmacie Pharmacies in France used to sell only medicines and closely related products such as toiletries and some brands of perfume. However, these days they often sell a wider range of goods. Pharmacists generally play an active paramedical role, and people will often consult a pharmacist rather than a doctor in the case of minor ailments, or accidents such as snake bites. Pharmacies are easily spotted by the green cross, lit up when the pharmacy is open. A *pharmacie de garde* (duty chemist) can dispense medicines outside normal opening hours as part of a local rota.

plaque d'immatriculation A vehicle's registration plate for vehicles registered before 15 April 2009. The last two figures indicate the number of the DÉPARTEMENT in which the owner lives.

PMU The PMU (*pari mutuel urbain*) sign can be seen outside many BUREAUX DE TABAC. It indicates a state-regulated horse-race betting outlet. The most popular form of betting is the *tiercé*, in which punters have to predict the first three places in a given race.

Pôle Emploi ▶ ANPE

police There are three principal police forces: the *police municipale*, responsible for routine local policing such as traffic offences, who are locally organized and not armed; the *police nationale*, who are nationally organized and generally armed; and the GENDARMERIE NATIONALE, which is a branch of the military.

Pompidou Centre ▶ BEAUBOURG

pompiers There are around 240,000 '*sapeurs-pompiers*', or firemen, in France, of whom more than 200,000 are volunteer non-professionals. *Les sapeurs-pompiers* play a unique role in modern France. They deal with fires, but also have teams of highly trained paramedics who are constantly on call to deal with all manner of emergencies, including traffic accidents. Unless there is a crime involved, in emergencies people tend to call *les pompiers* by dialling 18.

Poste, La is in charge of all mail and parcel deliveries. *Les facteurs* and *les factrices* (postmen and -women) deliver the mail. In 2006 *La Banque Postale* was created as a bank subsidiary of *La Poste*. It now has nearly 30 million customers.

préfecture The administrative headquarters of a DÉPARTEMENT. *Le préfet* is the most senior official responsible for representing the state within the *département*.

premier ministre The chief minister of the government, appointed by the PRÉSIDENT DE LA RÉPUBLIQUE and responsible for the overall management of government affairs.

président de la République The president is head of state and is elected for a term of five years. Under the terms of the constitution of the *Cinquième* RÉPUBLIQUE, the president plays a strong executive role in the governing of the country.

Presse Also referred to as *le quatrième pouvoir*, the press plays a central role in French cultural life. The best-known and most respected French newspaper is *Le Monde*, which provides in-depth coverage of national and international news. In its new format, it publishes more photographs than in the past. National newspapers reflect the main political trends in public life (*Le Figaro* is associated with the right, while *Libération* is a left-wing publication, and so on). There are also several large-circulation regional newspapers (e.g. *Ouest-France*), as well as specialist publications like *L'Équipe*, the sports daily. France publishes more than 15,000 weekly and monthly magazines. The main French press agency is *l'Agence France Presse* (*AFP*).

Prix Goncourt A literary prize awarded every November for a novel

Culture

published in that year. The event attracts considerable media coverage and speculation.

Quai d'Orsay The *ministère des Affaires étrangères* (Ministry of Foreign Affairs) is situated here, so journalists often use Quai d'Orsay to mean the ministry.

Quartier Latin As the location of France's oldest university, the Sorbonne, the Latin Quarter still bustles with students. Situated on the Left Bank of the SEINE, it is a lively district, full of a range of new and second-hand bookshops (*librairies*), ethnic restaurants, and markets. Many of the cafés and bistros have played host to major literary and artistic figures of the 20th century, such as Jean-Paul Sartre and Pablo Picasso, and the legacy of its past lives on. Other attractions include the remains of Gallo-Roman baths, and the Panthéon, in which many of France's great and good have been laid to rest.

Québec was founded in 1608 by the French explorer, Samuel de Champlain. It is Canada's largest province and Quebec City is its capital. Montreal is the largest city in the province. Eighty per cent of the inhabitants of Quebec – *un(e) Québécois(e)* – speak French. In 1995, a referendum on independence from Canada was held: those living in Quebec voted 50.6 per cent against independence and 49.4 per cent in favour. *Les Québécois* speak French with a recognizable accent, and certain words are unique to the province.

racisme As in many other countries, racism has remained an issue in France into the 21st century. In the 2002 elections, *Le Front National* made strong gains before being defeated in the second round of voting; the party leader, Jean-Marie Le Pen, has been widely criticized for his xenophobic and anti-Semitic pronouncements. Since the 1980s, rising racial tensions, particularly but not exclusively in LA BANLIEUE, have aided the party's growing influence. Debates about immigration, integration, assimilation, and the right to difference have dominated the news in recent years. Anti-racist movements such as SOS RACISME aim to reverse the trend towards extremism.

radio There are three types of radio station in France: public stations run by the state-owned RADIO FRANCE; commercial stations such as *Europe 1*, *RTL*, *Radio Monte Carlo*, which are financed by advertising and which broadcast from border areas; and privately owned local stations (originally known as *radios libres*), which began to develop following a change in broadcasting laws in 1982.

Radio France The state-owned radio broadcasting company runs stations covering a range of interests, including *France Info*, which features 24-hour news, *France Culture*, which covers cultural and social topics, and *France Musique*, featuring classical, jazz, and world music.

RATP The Paris public transport authority, with a monopoly over the provision of bus, métro, and tram services. It is jointly responsible with the SNCF for running the RER (the *Réseau Express Régional*; *see* MÉTRO).

région The largest administrative unit in France, consisting of a number of DÉPARTEMENTS. Each has its own CONSEIL RÉGIONAL (regional council), which has responsibilities in education and economic planning.

religion Historically and culturally, France is a Catholic country, but the Catholic Church is no longer so influential as it once was. In 1970, 75 per cent of babies were baptised, but by 2000 the figure had dropped to 20 per cent. With 5 million Muslims, more than any other European country, Islam is the second religion in France.

rentrée The week at the beginning of September when the new school year starts and around which much of French administrative life revolves. The preceding weeks see intensive advertising of associated merchandise, from books and stationery to clothes and sports equipment. Many stores and supermarkets have a range of special purchases at bargain prices. *La rentrée littéraire* marks the start of the literary year and *la rentrée parlementaire* signals the return of members of parliament after the recess.

repas Traditionally the midday meal was the big meal of the day, and for people who live in country areas this is still largely the case. Even in big cities many people continue to eat a big meal in the middle of the day, either in a family restaurant near their place of work, or by buying a freshly cooked hot dish from a CHARCUTERIE. However, people living and working in the larger cities are tending more and more to have a snack lunch and to eat their main meal in the evening. In either case, the main meal virtually always consists of a number of courses, typically a starter such as pâté, *saucisson*, or *crudités*, then meat or fish with a vegetable dish, followed by cheese and dessert. Cheese is virtually always eaten, as one might expect in a country that boasts such a huge variety and number of cheeses, and is always served before the dessert. In town and country alike, Sunday is the day for a big family meal in the middle of the day, and the pâtisseries are usually crowded on Sunday mornings as people queue up to buy a large tart or gâteau for dessert.

République France is a republic; the first republic was declared in 1792 after the French Revolution. Its new constitution was based on the DÉCLARATION DES DROITS DE L'HOMME ET DU CITOYEN. The *Cinquième République* (Fifth Republic) is now in force; it was established by DE GAULLE in 1958 after 80 per cent of French people voted in favour of a new constitution.

Résistance The Resistance movement fought military occupation by German forces in France (1940–44). After France signed an armistice with

Germany in June 1940, acts of resistance were organized by students and miners; armed resistance came from communists and socialists who had been forced into hiding, and from Belgian, Polish, Dutch, and Spanish fighters. These men and women formed themselves into '*maquis*' units. Despite the terrible risks involved, there were many resistance groups. They carried out ambushes and acts of sabotage, such as derailing trains, attacking German garrisons, and blowing up bridges. During the D-day landings in June 1944, they helped Allied troops liberate their country. Many memorials recall the courage and determination of these fighters.

restaurants France is famed for the quality of its restaurants, from the small family-run businesses to the grand establishments. It is always possible to find restaurants and BRASSERIES offering set-price menus (*menus à prix fixe*), which are generally good value for money. A basket of bread is usually included in the price of the meal, and most restaurants will have several inexpensive house wines, available in *pichets* (jugs) of a

quarter, half, and one litre. Service is included in the bill, although many people do leave a tip if the meal and the service have been good.

restos du coeur A charitable organization, *les restos (restaurants) du coeur* are widely publicized by virtue of having been set up by a much-loved humourist called Coluche. He died in a motorcycle accident in 1986. *Les restos du coeur* serve meals to the poor and homeless, particularly in winter.

Révolution (française); Révolution de 1789 By 1789 administrative and revenue reforms were long overdue in France; the 'third estate' (middle-classes) set up a National Assembly demanding change. Louis XVI's indecisive response led to the storming of the Bastille prison on 14 July, and the DÉCLARATION DES DROITS DE L'HOMME ET DU CITOYEN. By the following year a new constitution had been set up, and in 1792 the National Convention, which had replaced the National Assembly, abolished the monarchy. Louis XVI was executed on 21 January 1793. The Revolution's major legacies were the establishment of individual rights and a nationalist pride: the right to vote, civil equality, the Constitution, the TRICOLORE, and the MARSEILLAISE were some of its many products.

Rhône Department of France around Lyons, and a major French river. The Rhône is 812 km (507.5 miles) long and flows from Switzerland through the mountains of the Jura and down to Lyons. There it is joined by the Saône, its main tributary. It then continues south to its delta in the CAMARGUE. The world-famous Côtes du Rhone vineyards line the valley from Vienne, south of Lyons, to AVIGNON, producing wines such as Crozes-Hermitage and Châteauneuf du Pape.

RMI (*Revenu minimum d'insertion*) Introduced in 1988, the *RMI* is an allowance designed to support the poorest members of society by bringing them above the poverty line and allowing them access to various social security benefits.

roller *Le roller*, or rollerblading, is a very popular sport in France, with an estimated five million practitioners. In Paris on Friday evenings rollerbladers stream through the streets; up to 12,000 people can take part in these impressive displays.

route départementale These are signalled on French road maps as 'D' followed by a number, and are marked in yellow. They are roads maintained by the DÉPARTEMENT and are secondary roads, not intended for fast travel. Many of them have stretches marked in green on maps to highlight areas or views of particular interest.

route nationale A *route nationale* forms part of the state-maintained road network, outside the AUTOROUTES but providing fast roads for travel between towns and cities. They are signalled by 'N' followed by the road number and are marked in red on French road maps.

SAMU A 24-hour service coordinated by each DÉPARTEMENT to send mobile medical services and staff to accident scenes and emergencies. SAMU stands for *le Service d'Aide Médicale d'Urgence*.

sans papiers ▶ IMMIGRATION

SARL Acronym for *société à responsabilité limité*. A private limited company. All such companies are officially registered at the Chamber of Commerce. In situations where such a company goes bankrupt, the director is not personally liable for debts unless he has committed fraud.

SDF Abbreviation of *sans domicile fixe* ('of no fixed abode'), describing those living on the streets, below the poverty line. In winter the authorities in Paris and other major cities provide dormitories where people can sleep, but space is limited. *SDF*s often sleep in MÉTRO stations. There are estimated to be about 50,000 homeless people in Paris alone. See also RESTOS DU COEUR.

Sécu An abbreviation of *Sécurité sociale*, the national system for provision of sickness, maternity, child, unemployment, old-age, and housing benefits. All workers make contributions. However, the social-security budget deficit in France is large and the government is trying to find ways to reduce it (for instance, by getting people to make a small contribution to the price of seeing their doctor).

Seine The river that flows through the centre of Paris. Its source is northwest of Dijon, and it flows into the sea between Le Havre and Honfleur. It is an important commercial route, carrying cargo from Paris to the coast,

Culture

Culture

and a major tourist attraction. The banks of the river in Paris became a UNESCO World Heritage Site in 1991. Since 2002, for two months in the summer, two miles of the Right Bank have been transformed from dual carriageway into a 'beach' – 'Paris Plage' – complete with tons of sand, palm trees, sunbeds, and parasols.

Sénat The upper house of parliament which meets in the PALAIS DU LUXEMBOURG. It consists of 343 elected *sénateurs*. It votes on laws and the state budget.

SIDA The *Syndrome Immunodéficitaire Acquis*, or AIDS. The first case occurred in France in 1981. Nowadays death from AIDS has decreased enormously in France due to effective treatment and prevention, helped by campaign groups such as SIDACTION.

SMIC *Salaire Minimum Interprofessionnel de Croissance*: the basic minimum legal wage fixed annually by decree. People earning the SMIC are known as *smicards*. Those under the age of 18 can be paid less than the minimum wage.

SNCF *La Société Nationale des Chemins de Fer Français*. The state-owned rail company, founded in 1937, which also has access to private finance. Its remit covers the full range of rail transport services from small local trains to the high-speed TGV.

Solaar MC ▶ CHANSON FRANÇAISE

Sorbonne ▶ QUARTIER LATIN

syndicats Although it plays a less central role than it did in the first half of the 20th century, with only 10 per cent of employees unionized, the trade union movement is still a significant actor in French public life and has considerable power and influence. Major unions include the *CGC (Confédération générale des cadres)* and the *CGT (Confédération générale du travail)*. There is also an employers' association, the MEDEF.

tabac ▶ BUREAU DE TABAC

télécarte A phone card for use in telephone kiosks, widely available from FRANCE TÉLÉCOM, *bureaux de poste*, BUREAUX DE TABAC, and *marchands de journaux*.

télé realité *La télé réalité* (reality TV), imported from abroad, has enjoyed great success recently in France. The first reality TV show, *Loft Story*, known as 'Big Brother' in other countries, was shown on the French channel M6 in 2001. To the horror of the cultural élite, the show attracted record numbers of viewers. TF1 responded by launching a whole series of similar reality shows, the most successful being *Star Academy* (creating a pop star) and *Koh-Lanta*, where players are stranded on a desert island. Many others have followed.

TF1 *Télévision Française 1* was originally a state-controlled television station, but is now privately owned. *TF1* has an obligation to ensure that 50 per cent of its programmes are of French origin.

TGV *Le train à grande vitesse* is a high-speed electric train operated by the SNCF. In March 2007 the new TGV broke the world rail speed record hitting 574 km/h (356 mph).

Tintin A comic-book character invented by the Belgian cartoonist Hergé in 1929. Tintin's adventures with the irrepressible Captain Haddock are still bestsellers and have been translated into more than 40 languages. *See also* BANDE DESSINÉE.

TOM (territoires d'outre mer ▶ DOM-TOM

Tour de France Probably the most famous cycle race in the world, the Tour de France takes place over a different route each year but always ends around 14 July on the CHAMPS-ÉLYSÉES. The race was inaugurated in 1903 by Henri Desgrange, editor of the sports newspaper *L'Auto*, in order to boost circulation above that of a rival publication.

travail (work) People cannot officially work below the age of 16. In 2000, the working week was reduced to 35 hours (in companies with more than 20 employees), which is now the shortest in Europe. French workers get five weeks' paid holiday per year. Retirement is fixed at the age of 60, but people can take early retirement, known as '*préretraite*'. Those who have children under the age of three can choose to take *un congé parental d'éducation* (parental child-rearing leave). Many French women and men work *à mi-temps* (part-time) or *à temps partiel* (partial time, generally four days a week). One quarter of the workforce is employed by the French state. Unemployment, at around 8 per cent, is among the highest in Europe.

(le drapeau) tricolore The name of the French flag, so called because it is made up of three colours: blue, white, and red, arranged in vertical stripes. The flag was adopted during the RÉVOLUTION and was intended to represent the ideals: LIBERTÉ, EGALITÉ, FRATERNITÉ.

troisième âge Nowadays called *les séniors*, *le troisième âge* (the elderly) refers to people who are retired (generally over 60). The '*université du troisième âge*', created in 1973, offers over-60s the chance to study a wide range of subjects for a minimal fee.

Tuileries These central Parisian gardens originally housed a palace begun in 1564. Later Louis XV lived there while Versailles was being built. The palace was eventually destroyed during the period of the Commune in

1871. The site takes its name from the tile kilns that used to stand here (*une tuilerie* is a tile factory). The gardens were designed in 1664 by Le Nôtre, who also designed the gardens at Versailles. The Tuileries now host the Orangerie and Jeu de Paume art galleries.

UDF *Union pour la Démocratie Française*, or *UDF*, was a political grouping that allowed various centre-right parties to work together at times of elections. In 2007 it was fully integrated within the *Mouvement Démocrate* (*le MoDem*).

UMP *Union pour un Mouvement Populaire* (*UMP*) is a French political party of the centre right. Renamed after the 2002 election, it was formed from the *Rassemblement pour la République* or *RPR* (Jacques Chirac's party), and Chirac supporters from the *Démocratie Libérale (DL)*, and *L'Union pour la Démocratie Française (UDF)*.

Union Européenne The European Union, previously known as the European Community, was founded on 1 November 1993. Its aim is to further political, economic, and social cooperation between members. There are now 27 countries in the union. Twelve member countries, including France, have undergone monetary union and adopted a common currency, the euro. They were joined by Slovenia in 2007, and Malta and Cyprus in 2008.

Université There are 90 universities in France. The State subsidises the French universities but there are also independent establishments, mainly Catholic universities, in Lyons, Paris, Toulouse, Angers, and Lille. The university system now has three levels: LICENCE (BACCALAURÉAT +3), *master* (*Bac* +5), and *doctorat* (*Bac* +8). Some universities have a special reputation for certain subjects (historically the most renowned is the Sorbonne). To enter university students have to have the *baccalauréat*. Fees for the year are minimal, except for private education. The most popular course is humanities, followed by sciences, medicine, and sport.

Variété française ▶ CHANSON FRANÇAISE

vendanges The grape harvests (*les vendanges*) are traditionally held in September, though the harvest can often begin at the end of August and finish in October, depending on the maturity of the grapes, the region, and the weather. *Les vendanges tardives* (late harvests) make sweet wines such as Sauternes. Now widely mechanized, harvesting is still done by hand in Beaujolais and CHAMPAGNE.

verlan A form of French slang that reverses the order of syllables in many common words, rendering them more or less incomprehensible to the uninitiated. For example, the term itself is derived from the word *l'envers*, the syllables of which are reversed to create *vers-l'en*, which in turn becomes *verlan*. Single syllable words are also converted, so *femme* becomes *meuf*, *mec* becomes *keum*, etc. A recent coinage for *énervé* ('irritated') is *vénère*. Originally used as an anti-authoritarian weapon by French youth and others, *verlan* is now commonly heard in everyday speech in France. Some words have been through the process twice: *beur*, for example, has now been reversed back to '*reub*' or '*reubeu*'.

Verts, Les ▶ PARTIS POLITIQUES

Vichy After the German invasion of France in June 1940, Vice-Premier Marshal Henri Pétain signed an armistice with Hitler, which divided France into occupied and unoccupied sectors, and allowed Pétain to set up a government in the spa town of Vichy, central France. The Vichy government became a German tool, deporting French Jews to Germany and substituting the motto *Travail, Famille, Patrie* (Work, Family, Country) for *Liberté, Egalité, Fraternité*. In response, the British cut off diplomatic relations with Vichy France and allowed General DE GAULLE to rally his Free French forces from London. When the Allies invaded North Africa in November 1942, Hitler annulled the armistice of 1940 and invaded Vichy France anyway. After the war, many members of the Vichy government were arrested and some executed. Pétain was sentenced to life imprisonment.

Vigipirate An emergency plan to reinforce police and military security, bringing an increased uniformed presence to public places at times of potential disorder, such as terrorist attacks, etc.

Villette, La In the heart of Paris's 19th ARRONDISSEMENT is the Parc La Villette, the largest green space in the city. It is home to the Cité des Sciences et de l'Industrie, a modern science museum, the Cité de la Musique, which stages concerts and exhibitions, and the Conservatoire National Supérieur de Musique et de Danse de Paris. La Grande Halle, on the southern edge of the park, is used for exhibitions and the Villette Jazz Festival. The park also contains theme gardens, the Zenith rock venue, and the Theâtre Paris Villette.

VTT *Vélo tout terrain* or *VTT* is the French for mountain bike. Mountain biking is a popular French sport, particularly among younger people. The signposted tracks are called Parcours *VTT*.

Zidane ▶ BLEUS, LES

Culture

Letter-writing in French

Holiday postcard

- *Beginnings (informal):* Cher *is used for a man,* Chère *for a woman. A letter to two males or to a male and female begins with* Chers. *For two female correspondents:* Chères Madeleine et Hélène. *For friends and relatives:* Chers amis, Chers cousins, *etc. For a family:* Chers tous.

- *Address: On an envelope Mr, Mrs and Miss can be abbreviated to M., Mme, Mlle, although the full forms are considered preferable in more formal letters. There is no direct equivalent for Ms. If you do not know a woman's marital status use* Madame (Mme).

  Road names such as rue, avenue, place *are not generally given capital letters.*

  The name of the town comes after the postcode and on the same line.

Letters

14.7.2010

Cher Alexandre,

Grosses bises d'Edimbourg! Cela fait trois jours que nous sommes ici et nous n'avons pas encore vu la pluie! Espérons que ça va durer. La vieille ville est très belle et du château on a une vue splendide jusqu'à l'estuaire. Et en Normandie, comment ça va?

A bientôt pour des retrouvailles parisiennes,

Marie et Dominique

M. A. Pilnard

38 rue Glacière

75013 Paris

- *Endings (informal):* Bien amicalement, Amitiés; A bientôt = *see you soon.*

Letter-writing in French

. . . .

Christmas and New Year wishes (informal)

- On most personal letters French speakers do not put their address at the top of the letter. The date is given preceded by le. For the first day of the month le 1er is used. Generally, the name of the town in which the letter is written is placed before the date.

① The tradition of Christmas cards is much less widespread in France than in Great Britain. While Christmas greetings may be sent, it is more customary to send best wishes for the New Year in January.

② In the year 2010/2011 etc. = en l'an 2010/2011 etc., but bonne année 2010/2011

le 18 décembre 2010①

Chers Steve et Michelle,

Nous vous souhaitons un Joyeux Noël① et une très bonne année 2011②! En espérant que cette nouvelle année vous apportera tout ce que vous désirez et que nous trouverons une occasion pour nous revoir!

Bises à vous deux,

Gérard

New Year wishes (formal)

le 5 janvier 2011

Je vous ① présente mes meilleurs vœux pour l'année 2011. Que cette année vous apporte, à vous et à votre famille, bonheur et prospérité.

Pierre Carlier

① Note the use of the formal form vous.

Letters

. . . .

Invitation (informal)

Invitations to parties are usually by word of mouth, but for more formal events such as weddings, invitations are sent out.

① *Note the use of the informal form* tu *betweeen good friends.*

Paris, le 28/04/09

Cher Denis,

Que fais-tu ① cet été? Pascal et moi avons décidé d'inviter tous les copains d'Orléans à nous rejoindre dans notre maison de Dordogne pour le weekend du 16 juillet. Il y aura fête au village avec bal populaire et feu d'artifice. Le petit vin du pays n'est pas mal non plus!

Nous comptons sur toi pour venir trinquer avec nous,

Bises,

Martine

■ *Endings (informal):* Bises *(= lots of love) is very informal and is appropriate for very good friends and family. Alternatives for close friends and family include* Bien à toi, Bons baisers *or affectionately* Je t'embrasse. *If the letter is addressed to more than one person use* Bien à vous *or* Je vous embrasse.

. . . .
Invitation (formal)

Christine et Félix Prévost
81 rue Esque moise
59000 Lille

　　　　　　　　　　Lille, le 28 avril 2009

Chers amis,

Nous avons l'immense plaisir de vous
annoncer le mariage de notre fils Victor et
de mademoiselle Stéphanie Heusdens.

La cérémonie aura lieu à l'Hôtel de Ville à
15 heures le samedi 11 juin. Vous recevrez
bientôt un faire-part et une invitation à
dîner mais nous tenions à vous prévenir
suffisamment tôt pour que vous puissiez
arranger votre voyage. Nous espérons qu'il
vous sera possible de vous joindre à nous.

Amicalement, ①

Christine et Félix

Letters

■ *In a more formal letter, especially where a reply is generally required, the sender's address is written on the left-hand side of the page. An alternative is in the centre of the page, particularly on printed stationery.*

① *Endings: Alternatives could be* Amitiés, Bien amicalement.

Accepting an invitation

Emilie Joly
2 rue de la Pompe
75016 Paris

le 16 mars 2009

Chère Madame Dubois,

Je vous ① remercie de bien vouloir me recevoir pour les deux premières semaines de juillet. Je serai très heureuse de vous revoir ainsi que Natalie, bien entendu. Nous avons passé un si bon séjour linguistique à Manchester l'été dernier que nous avions très envie de nous retrouver. Mes parents ne pouvant m'envoyer en Angleterre cette année, c'est avec un immense plaisir que j'accepte votre invitation.

Je vous prie de bien vouloir accepter, Madame, l'expression de mes sentiments les meilleurs.

Emilie

- In a more formal social letter where the correspondent is known personally by name it can be used in the opening greeting.

- The title of the person receiving the letter must be repeated in the closing formula. These formulas are more elaborate than in English, with a number of possible variations. Some of these are shown in the following letters in this section.

① Since the letter is from a young person to the mother of a friend, she uses the formal vous form and writes to her as Madame Dubois. Madame Dubois would address Emilie using tu.

Letters

Letter-writing in French

. . . .

Replying to a job advertisement

- *Address: The sender's address may be written or printed in the middle of the page or on the left-hand side. The address of the person receiving the letter is on the right-hand side or beneath the sender's address if it is in the central position. Where the name or job title of the person is known it is used in their address.*

- *Beginnings (formal): the standard opening for a business letter when the recipient is not personally known to you is Monsieur, Madame, Mademoiselle or Messieurs in the case of general correspondence to a company.*

  If the person holds a very important position this can be used, e.g. Monsieur le Maire, Madame le Consul.

Alexander Smith
5, Winchester Drive
Stoke Gifford
Bristol BS34 8DP

Bristol, le 4 février 2009

Madame la Directrice
MEDIAPHOT
6 rue de la Victoire
62100 Calais

Madame,

L'annonce parue en page 13 dans 'Courrier Photo' concernant un poste de tireur m'a vivement interessé. Je suis actuellement photographe indépendant mais je serais heureux de travailler à nouveau au sein d'une équipe d'entreprise. Je pense posséder l'expérience et les qualités requises pour vous donner toute satisfaction dans ce poste, comme vous pourrez le constater au vu de mon CV. Je suis de nationalité britannique mais je me débrouille bien en français. Je souhaite travailler à Calais car je vais prochainement me marier avec une Calaisienne.

Je me tiens à votre disposition pour un entretien éventuel, et vous prie d'agréer, Madame, l'expression de mes sentiments distingués.

A. Smith

P.J. ① : un CV avec photo ②

Letters

- *Endings (formal): the form of address used in the opening should be inserted into the closing formula e.g. Madame, Monsieur le Maire, etc*

  ① *P.J. (pièce(s) jointe(s)) = enclosures (encl).*

  ② *In France prospective employers generally request a handwritten letter (lettre manuscrite) and a photograph to accompany an application or curriculum vitae.*

· ·

Curriculum Vitae

David Baker
67 Whiteley Avenue
St George
Bristol
BS5 6TW
Grande-Bretagne

Téléphone +44 (0)117 945 3421; Fax +44 (0)117 945 7225

e-mail dbaker@hotmail.com

Nationalité britannique

Né ① le 30.06.1988 à Londres

FORMATION ET DIPLÔMES

2004: GCSEs dans sept matières (équivalent à un niveau de fin de Seconde) John Radcliffe School, Croydon

2006: 'A Levels' en Mathématiques, Informatique, Allemand et Français (équivalent au Baccalauréat)

EXPERIENCE PROFESSIONNELLE

2007: Stage de quatre mois à Sempo-Informatik, Francfort au département médias

2008: Contrat de formation de six mois à MEDIALAB, Paris (conception d'images de synthèse)

DIVERS

Très bonne connaissance de l'outil informatique

Allemand et français courants

Permis de conduire

---

① *The feminine form* née *is used for a woman.*

■ *Where appropriate a heading* 'Situation de famille' *could give relevant personal details e.g.* marié/e, deux/trois enfants etc.; divorcé/e, deux enfants; célibataire.

• •

Seeking a job as an au pair

Sally Paledra
5 Avon Crescent
Kenilworth
Warwickshire
CV8 2PQ

le 3 mars 2009

Madame,

Vos coordonnées m'ont été communiquées par l'agence 'Au Pair International', qui m'a demandé de vous écrire directement. Je suis en effet à la recherche d'un emploi au pair pour une période de neuf à dix mois à partir de septembre prochain.

J'aime beaucoup les enfants et ils apprécient également ma compagnie. J'ai une grande expérience du baby-sitting. J'ai aussi fait un stage d'un mois dans une crèche privée ①.

Je suis enthousiaste, discrète et je sais prendre des initiatives.
J'ai étudié le français au lycée pendant cinq ans et je connais un peu la France pour y avoir passé des vacances à plusieurs reprises. J'ai aussi mon permis de conduire.

Dans l'espoir d'une réponse positive de votre part, je vous prie d'agréer, Madame, l'expression de mes salutations respectueuses.

S. Paledra

P.J. : un CV avec photo

Letters

① *Or be more specific, e.g.* pour des enfants de 3 mois à 3 ans.

■ *To supply references:* Vous trouverez également ci-joint les adresses de personnes pouvant fournir une lettre de recommandation *or* pouvant me recommander.

. . . .

Booking a hotel room

Miss Sylvia Daley
The Willows
49 North Terrace
Kings Barton
Nottinghamshire
NG8 4LQ
England

Hôtel Beauséjour
Chemin des Mimosas
06100 Grasse

le 8 avril 2009

Madame,

J'ai bien reçu le dépliant de votre hôtel et je vous en remercie.

Je souhaite réserver une chambre calme avec salle de bains, en pension complète ① pour la période du 10 au 19 juin. Pour les arrhes, je vous prie de m'informer de leur montant et des modalités de paiement possibles depuis la Grande-Bretagne.

En vous remerciant d'avance, je vous prie de croire, Madame, en mes sentiments les meilleurs.

S. Daley

① Or une chambre avec douche en demi-pension or avec petit déjeuner. *The term en suite does not exist for bathroom facilities in French.*

. . . .

Cancelling a reservation

Mrs J. Warrington
Downlands
Steyning
West Sussex   Hôtel des Voyageurs
BN44 6LZ   9 cours Gambetta

                                               91940 Les Ulis

                                               le 15 février 2009

Monsieur,

Je suis au regret de devoir annuler la réservation de chambre pour deux personnes pour la nuit du 24 au
25 mars, que j'avais effectuée par téléphone le 18 janvier dernier. ①

Je vous remercie de votre compréhension et vous prie d'agréer, Monsieur, l'expression de mes sentiments
distingués.

J. Warrington

---

① If reasons for the cancellation are specified these could include: pour raisons de santé/de
   famille, en raison d'un décès dans la famille, etc.

Sending   File   Edit   View Text   Mail   Attach   User   Tools Window
an e-mail

                 Fichier Edition Vue   Texte   Message Rattacher Agent   Outil Fenêtre

Fichier Edition Vue Texte Message Rattacher

To: toothild@scene.co.uk
Cc: itumoran@ecosse.ac.uk
Subject: tu es connectée?

Cher Daniel,

J'ai bien reçu ton mél①. Je suis ravie que nous puissons communiquer
par Internet. N'oublie pas de joindre à ton prochain message le fichier sur
l'argot que tu m'as promis!

Salut, ②

Clare

---

① Note that mél is an abbreviated form of message électronique. To send an attachment = joindre
   un fichier.

② Endings (informal): An alternative could be A bientôt or simply Bises to a close friend in an
   informal context.

Letters

Letters

Opening an online bank account

Banque Exemplaire en ligne

Formulaire de demande d'accès à l'e-banking

Veuillez remplir vos coordonnées ci-dessous, puis cliquez sur **'envoyer'**.
Les champs marqués d'un * sont obligatoires.

Cliquez ici si vous avez besoin **d'aide**

Regardez notre **démo interactive** ou consultez les questions les plus fréquemment posées par nos clients ici : **FAQ**.

Vos coordonnées

* Titre   * Prénom   * Nom

* Date de naissance   Numéro de téléphone   Téléphone portable

jj   mm   aaaa

* Domicile légal   * Code postal

Address e-mail

*Banque Exemplaire en ligne, ainsi que d'autres sociétés du Groupe Exemplaire, aimeraient vous contacter par e-mail au sujet de nos produits et services susceptibles de vous intéresser. Si vous ne désirez **pas** recevoir ces informations, veuillez cocher cette case.* ☐

* Votre compte – obligatoire

Si vous êtes déjà titulaire d'un compte courant auprès de la Banque Exemplaire, veuillez fournir les données relatives à votre compte. Si vous n'êtes pas titulaire d'un compte courant auprès de la Banque Exemplaire, veuillez remplir votre numéro de carte de crédit.

◉   Code agence   ▼   Numéro de compte

ou

◯   Numéro de carte de crédit   Code de sécurité   **Qu'est-ce que mon code de sécurité ?**

* Etes-vous titulaire d'autres comptes auprès de la Banque Exemplaire ou de sociétés du Groupe Exemplaire?   **Oui** ☐ **Non** ☐

Qu'est-ce que c'est ?

* Votre mot de passe

Veuillez saisir votre mot de passe pour accéder au service e-banking de la Banque Exemplaire

Saisissez votre mot de passe   *(de 8 à 16 caractères – uniquement minuscules et chiffres)*

Confirmez votre mot de passe

Ne révélez pas votre mot de passe à autrui. Utilisez-le uniquement pour votre compte Banque Exemplaire en ligne.

* Conditions légales

☐ Je confirme avoir lu et compris les **conditions générales** de la Banque Exemplaire et j'accepte de m'y soumettre.

Buying train tickets online

Achetez vos billets en ligne avec **Europtrains**

| Billets | Horaires | Plans, destinations & itineraries |

De
Sélectionnez une gare ▼   voir toutes les gares

À
Sélectionnez une gare ▼   voir toutes les gares

Date de départ
Jun ▼ 17 ▼ 2009 ▼   **Heure** Toutes les heures ▼
calendrier

Date de retour
(à ignorer en cas d'aller simple)
Jun ▼ 18 ▼ 2009 ▼   **Heure** Toutes les heures ▼
calendrier

Dates flexibles? ☐

Nombre de passagers   Adultes ▼   Enfants ▼   Etudiants ▼   Seniors ▼

RECHERCHE

1e classe ☐
2e classe ☐

Offre Spéciale

Economisez 25%
en réservant en ligne
à partir du 1er juillet 2009

• **Aller simple Londres–Bruxelles: moitié prix**

Cliquez ici pour en savoir plus

• **Aller-retour Londres–Paris à partir de 50€ seulement**

Cliquez ici pour plus de détails

Etudiants achetez votre abonnement rail et économisez à chaque voyage
Pour plus de détails, veuillez téléphoner.
Offre soumise à conditions

Mon compte
Nom de utilisateur
Mot de passe
Retenir mon mot de passe ☐
Mot de passe oublié?
Inscrivez-vous ici

Autres options
Voyageurs d'affaires
Voyages en groupe
Voyager avec un fauteuil roulant
Voyager à vélo

Modifier une réservation
Annuler une réservation
Recevoir vos billets

Autres offres spéciales
Abonnements rail
Hôtels
Assurance voyage

plan du site | à propos de nous | FAQ | contactez-nous

Letters

SMS (electronic text messaging)

The basic principles governing French SMS abbreviations are similar to those governing English SMS. Certain words or syllables can be represented by letters or numbers that sound the same but take up less space. Also, points, accents and other diacritics are generally omitted altogether. For example, the syllables '-pé' and '-té' can be replaced by the letters P and T, the word 'sans' by '100', and the conjunction 'que' by 'ke'. Another way of shortening words is simply to omit certain letters, especially vowels. For example, 'bonjour' becomes 'bjr' and 'quand' becomes 'qd'.

As in English, 'emoticons' are very popular, and some of the more established ones are included in the table below.

Glossary of French SMS abbreviations

Abbreviation	Full word	Abbreviation	Full word	Emoticons*	
1mn	juste une minute	kfé	café	:-)	sourire
		ki	qui	;-)	clin d'œil
100	sans	koi29	quoi de neuf	:-(	pas content,
5pa	sympa	l8	lui		déçu
6né	cinéma	L	elle	:-D	je rigole
@+	à plus tard	mat1	matin	:-X	motus et
@2m1	à demain	MDR	mort de rire		bouche
ap	après	MSG	message		cousue
aprM, AM	après-midi	pb	problème	:-|	indifférent
bi1to	bientôt	pk	pourquoi	:'(	je pleure
bjr	bonjour	pr	pour	|I	endormi
bsr	bonsoir	qd	quand	:|	hmmm...
C	c'est	ri1	rien	:-o	oh!
cad	c'est à dire	rstp	réponds s'il	:-@	hurlant
dak	d'accord		te plaît	:-P	lapsus (ma
d1ngue	dingue	seur	sœur		langue a
dzolé	désolé	slt cv?	salut ça va?		fourché)
entouK	en tout cas	strC	stressé	0:-)	un ange
fet	fête	svp	s'il vous	:-*	bisou
frR	frère		plaît	:[	abattu
G	j'ai	tjr	toujours	@-`-,—	une rose
IR	hier	TOK	t'es OK?		
jamé	jamais	TOQP	t'es	*NB: the '-' which depicts the	
jenémar	j'en ai marre		occupé?	nose is often omitted or	
je t'M	je t'aime	Vlo	vélo	replaced by an 'o' eg. :) or	
ke	que	vs	vous	:o)	
kekina	qu'est-ce qu'il ya?	we	week-end		

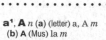

a¹, A *n* (a) (letter) a, A *m*
(b) **A** (Mus) la *m*

⚬ **a², an** *det* un/une

> ■ **Note** The determiner or indefinite article *a* or
> *an* is translated by *un + masculine noun* and by
> *une + feminine noun*: *a tree* = un arbre; *a chair*
> = une chaise. There are, however, some cases
> where the article is not translated:
> — with professions and trades: *her mother is a
> teacher* = sa mère est professeur;
> — with other nouns used in apposition: *he's a
> widower* = il est veuf;
> — with *what a*: *what a pretty house* = quelle jolie
> maison.
> — When expressing prices in relation to weight,
> the definite article *le/la* is used in French: *ten eu-
> ros a kilo* = dix euros le kilo. In other expressions
> where *a/an* means *per* the French translation is
> *par. twice a day* = deux fois par jour; but: *50 kilo-
> metres an hour* = 50 kilomètres/heure.

A2 level *n* (GB) *seconde moitié des épreuves
pour les A levels*

aback *adv* **to be taken** ～ être déconcerté/-e

⚬ **abandon** *vtr* abandonner ‹*person, hope*›;
renoncer à ‹*activity, attempt*›

abbey *n* abbaye *f*

abbreviate *vtr* abréger (**to** en)

abbreviation *n* abréviation *f*

abdomen *n* abdomen *m*

abduct *vtr* enlever

abide *vi* (*prét, pp* **abode** *ou* ～**d**) **to** ～ **by**
respecter ‹*rule, decision*›

⚬ **ability** *n* (a) (capability) capacité *f*; **to the best
of one's** ～ de son mieux
(b) (talent) talent *m*

⚬ **able** *adj*

> ■ **Note** *to be able to* meaning *can* is usually
> translated by the verb *pouvoir*. *I was not able to
> help him* = je ne pouvais pas l'aider.
> — When *to be able to* implies the acquiring of
> skill, *savoir* is used: *he's nine and he's still not
> able to read* = il a neuf ans et il ne sait toujours
> pas lire.

(a) **to be** ～ **to do** pouvoir faire; **she was** ～ **to
play the piano at the age of four** elle savait
jouer du piano à quatre ans
(b) ‹*lawyer, teacher*› compétent/-e; ‹*child*›
doué/-e

able-bodied *adj* robuste, fort/-e

abnormal *adj* anormal/-e

abnormality *n* anomalie *f*

aboard ① *adv* à bord
② *prep* à bord de ‹*plane*›; dans ‹*train*›; ～
ship à bord

abolish *vtr* abolir ‹*law, right*›; supprimer
‹*service, allowance*›

abolition *n* (of law, right) abolition *f*; (of
service) suppression *f*

abominable *adj* abominable

aborigine *n* aborigène *mf*

abort *vtr* faire avorter ‹*foetus*›; abandonner
‹*computer program*›

abortion *n* avortement *m*; **to have an** ～ se
faire avorter

abortive *adj* ‹*attempt, project*› avorté/-e;
‹*coup, raid*› manqué/-e

⚬ **about** ① *adj* **to be** ～ **to do** être sur le point
de faire
② *adv* (a) environ, à peu près; ～ **an hour**
environ une heure; **it's** ～ **the same** c'est à
peu près pareil; **at** ～ **6 pm** vers 18 h; **it's just**
～ **ready** c'est presque prêt
(b) **there was no-one** ～ il n'y avait personne;
there is a lot of flu ～ il y a beaucoup de
grippes en ce moment; **he's somewhere** ～ il
est dans les parages
③ *prep* (a) (concerning) **a book** ～ **France** un
livre sur la France; **what's it** ～? (of book, film)
ça parle de quoi?; **may I ask what it's** ～?
pourriez-vous me dire de quoi il s'agit?; **it's**
～ **my son** c'est au sujet de mon fils
(b) **there's something odd** ～ **him** il a
quelque chose de bizarre; **what I like** ～ **her
is her honesty** ce que j'aime chez elle c'est
sa franchise
(c) (around) **to wander** ～ **the streets** errer
dans les rues
(d) **how** *or* **what** ～ **some tea?** et si on
prenait un thé?; **how** ～ **going into town?** et
si on allait en ville?
(e) **what** ～ **the legal costs?** et les frais de
justice?; **what** ～ **you?** et toi?
IDIOMS **it's** ～ **time (that) somebody made an
effort** il serait temps que quelqu'un fasse un
effort; ～ **time too!** ce n'est pas trop tôt! (fam)

about-face *n* volte-face *f inv*

⚬ **above** ① *prep* au-dessus de; ～ **the painting**
au-dessus du tableau; ～ **it** au-dessus;
children ～ **the age of 12** les enfants âgés de
plus de 12 ans; ～ **all else** par-dessus tout;
to hear sth ～ **the shouting** entendre qch au
milieu des cris
② *adj* **the** ～ **items** les articles
susmentionnés *or* figurant ci-dessus
③ *adv* (a) au-dessus; **a desk with a shelf** ～
un bureau avec une étagère au-dessus; **the
apartment** ～ l'appartement du dessus
(b) (in text) **see** ～ voir ci-dessus
(c) (more) plus; **children of 12 and** ～ les
enfants âgés de 12 ans et plus

⋯⇒

a

④ **above all** phr surtout

above-mentioned adj susmentionné/-e

abrasive adj ‹person, manner› mordant/-e

abreast adv **to walk three ~** marcher à trois de front; **to keep ~ of** se tenir au courant de

abroad adv à l'étranger; **from ~** de l'étranger

abrupt adj brusque

ABS n (abbr = **anti-lock braking system**) ABS; **~ brakes** freins mpl ABS

abscess n abcès m

abseiling n (GB) descente f en rappel

⚲ **absence** n absence f

absent adj absent/-e **(from** de)

absentee n absent/-e m/f

absentee ballot n bulletin de vote m d'un (électeur) absent

absent-minded adj distrait/-e

absolute adj absolu/-e

⚲ **absolutely** adv absolument

absorb vtr absorber; **~ed in one's work** plongé/-e dans son travail

absorbent adj absorbant/-e

abstain vi s'abstenir **(from** de)

abstract adj abstrait/-e

absurd adj absurde, ridicule

abundant adj abondant/-e

⚲ **abuse** ① n (a) (maltreatment) mauvais traitement m; (sexual) sévices mpl (sexuels) (b) (of alcohol, power) abus m; **drug ~** usage m des stupéfiants
(c) (insults) injures fpl
② vtr (a) (hurt) maltraiter; (sexually) abuser de ‹woman›; exercer des sévices sexuels sur ‹child›
(b) abuser de ‹position, power, trust›
(c) (insult) injurier

abusive adj ‹person› grossier/-ière; ‹words› injurieux/-ieuse

abyss n abîme m

⚲ **academic** ① n universitaire mf
② adj (a) ‹career, book› universitaire; ‹year› académique
(b) (theoretical) théorique

academy n (school) école f; (learned society) académie f

accelerate vi accélérer

accelerator n accélérateur m

accent n accent m

accentuate vtr souligner

⚲ **accept** vtr (gen) accepter; (tolerate) admettre

acceptable adj acceptable

acceptance n acceptation f

⚲ **access** ① n accès m; **to have ~ to** avoir accès à ‹information, funds, place›
② vtr accéder à ‹database, information›

⚲ indicates a very frequent word

accessible adj accessible **(to** à)

accessory n accessoire m; (on car) extra m

⚲ **accident** n accident m; **car/road ~** accident de voiture/de la route; **by ~** accidentellement; (by chance) par hasard

accidental adj (a) ‹death› accidentel/-elle
(b) ‹mistake› fortuit/-e

accidentally adv (a) (by accident) accidentellement
(b) (by chance) par hasard

accident-prone adj sujet/-ette aux accidents

accommodate vtr (a) (put up) loger
(b) (hold, provide space for) contenir
(c) (adapt to) s'adapter à ‹change, view›
(d) (satisfy) satisfaire ‹need›

accommodating adj accommodant/-e **(to** envers)

accommodation n (also **~s** (US)) logement m

accommodation officer n responsable mf de l'hébergement

⚲ **accompany** vtr accompagner

accomplice n complice mf

accomplish vtr accomplir ‹task, mission›; réaliser ‹objective›

accomplishment n réussite f

accord n accord m; **of my own ~** de moi-même

accordance: in accordance with phr ‹act› conformément à ‹rules, instructions›; ‹be› conforme à ‹law, agreement›

according: according to phr (a) ‹act› selon ‹law, principles›; **~ to plan** comme prévu
(b) d'après ‹newspaper, person›

accordingly adv en conséquence

accordion n accordéon m

accost vtr (approach) aborder; (sexually) accoster

⚲ **account** ① n (a) (in bank, post office, shop) compte m **(at, with** à); **in my ~** sur mon compte
(b) **to take sth into ~, to take ~ of sth** tenir compte de qch
(c) (description) compte-rendu m
(d) **on ~ of** à cause de; **on no ~** sous aucun prétexte; **on my ~** à cause de moi
② **accounts** n pl (a) (records) comptabilité f, comptes mpl
(b) (department) (service m) comptabilité f
■ **account for** (a) (explain) expliquer ‹fact, behaviour›; justifier ‹expense›
(b) (represent) représenter ‹proportion, percentage›

accountable adj responsable **(to** devant; **for** de)

accountancy n comptabilité f

accountant n comptable mf

account holder n titulaire mf

account manager n responsable mf de clientèle

account number n numéro m de compte

accumulate 1 vtr accumuler
2 vi s'accumuler

accuracy n (of figures, watch) justesse f; (of map, aim) précision f; (of forecast) exactitude f

accurate adj ‹figures, watch, information› juste; ‹report, map, forecast› exact/-e

accurately adv ‹calculate› exactement; ‹report› avec exactitude; ‹assess› précisément

accusation n accusation f

◆ **accuse** vtr accuser (of de)

accused n the ~ l'accusé/-e m/f

accuser n accusateur/-trice m/f

accustomed adj (a) to be ~ to sth/to doing avoir l'habitude de qch/de faire
(b) (usual) habituel/-elle

ace n as m

ache 1 n douleur f (in à)
2 vi ‹person› avoir mal; **my back** ~s j'ai mal au dos

◆ **achieve** vtr atteindre ‹aim›; atteindre à ‹perfection›; obtenir ‹result›; réaliser ‹ambition›

◆ **achievement** n réussite f

aching adj ‹body, limbs› douloureux/-euse

acid n, adj acide m

acid rain n pluies fpl acides

◆ **acknowledge** vtr admettre ‹fact›; reconnaître ‹error, problem, authority›; accuser réception de ‹letter›

acknowledgement 1 n (a) (of error, guilt) aveu m
(b) (confirmation of receipt) accusé m de réception
2 **acknowledgements** n pl (in book) remerciements mpl

acne n acné f

acorn n gland m

acoustic adj acoustique

acoustic guitar n guitare f sèche

acoustics n pl the ~ are good l'acoustique f est bonne

acquaintance n connaissance f (with de)

acquainted adj to be ~ se connaître; **to get** or **become** ~ **with sb** faire la connaissance de qn; **to get** or **become** ~ **with sth** découvrir qch

acquiesce vi accepter; **to** ~ **in sth** donner son accord tacite à qch

◆ **acquire** vtr acquérir ‹expertise›; obtenir ‹information›; faire l'acquisition de ‹possessions›; acheter ‹company›

acquit vtr (p prés etc **-tt-**) (Law) acquitter; **to be** ~**ted** être disculpé/-e (of de)

acre n acre f, ≈ demi-hectare m

acrobat n acrobate mf

acrobatics n pl acrobaties fpl

◆ **across** 1 prep (a) a journey ~ **the desert** un voyage à travers le désert; **the bridge** ~ **the river** le pont qui traverse la rivière; **to go** or **travel** ~ **sth** traverser qch; **she leaned** ~ **the table** elle s'est penchée au-dessus de la table
(b) (on the other side of) de l'autre côté de; ~ **the street (from me)** de l'autre côté de la rue
2 adv **to help sb** ~ aider qn à traverser; **to go** ~ **to sb** aller vers qn; **to look** ~ **at sb** regarder dans la direction de qn
3 **across from** phr en face de

acrylic n acrylique m

◆ **act** 1 n (a) acte m; **an** ~ **of kindness** un acte de bonté
(b) (Law) loi f; **Act of Parliament** loi votée par le Parlement
(c) (in show) numéro m
(d) **to put on an** ~ jouer la comédie
2 vtr jouer ‹part, role›
3 vi (a) (take action) agir
(b) (behave) agir, se comporter
(c) ‹actor› jouer, faire du théâtre
(d) (pretend) jouer la comédie, faire semblant
(e) (take effect) ‹drug› agir
(f) **to** ~ **as** ‹person, object› servir de
■ **act out** jouer ‹role, part›; réaliser ‹fantasy›

acting 1 n (performance) jeu m, interprétation f; (occupation) métier m d'acteur; **I've done some** ~ j'ai fait du théâtre
2 adj ‹director, manager› intérimaire

◆ **action** n (a) (gen) action f; (steps) mesures fpl; **to take** ~ agir, prendre des mesures (**against** contre); **to put a plan into** ~ mettre un projet à exécution
(b) (fighting) action f, combat m; **killed in** ~ tué/-e au combat
(c) (in filming) action f; ~**!** moteur!

action film n film m d'action

action group n groupe m de pression

action-packed adj ‹film› plein/-e d'action; ‹holiday› bien rempli/-e

action replay n (GB) répétition f d'une séquence

activate vtr faire démarrer ‹system›; actionner ‹switch›; déclencher ‹alarm›

◆ **active** adj ‹person, life› actif/-ive; ‹volcano› en activité

activist n activiste mf

◆ **activity** n activité f

activity holiday n (GB) ≈ vacances fpl sportives

◆ **actor** n acteur m, comédien m

actress n actrice f, comédienne f

◆ **actual** adj ‹circumstances› réel/réelle; ‹words› exact/-e; **in** ~ **fact** en fait; **the** ~ **problem** le problème lui-même

◆ **actually** adv (a) (in fact) en fait; **their profits have** ~ **risen** en fait, leurs bénéfices ont augmenté; ~**, I don't feel like it** à vrai dire je n'en ai pas envie

⋯⋫

a

(b) (really) vraiment; **yes, it ~ happened!** mais oui, c'est vraiment arrivé!

acupuncture *n* acupuncture *f*

acute *adj* (a) ‹*anxiety, pain*› vif/vive; ‹*boredom*› profond/-e
(b) ‹*illness*› aigu/aiguë
(c) ‹*mind*› pénétrant/-e
(d) ‹*accent, angle*› aigu/aiguë

⚷ **ad** *n* (*abbr* = **advertisement**) (a) (small) ~ (petite) annonce *f* (**for** pour)
(b) (on radio, TV) pub *f* (fam) (**for** pour)

AD (*abbr* = **Anno Domini**) ap J.-C.

adamant *adj* catégorique (**about** sur); **he is ~ that** il maintient que

adapt [1] *vtr* adapter (**to** à; **for** pour; **from** de)
[2] *vi* ‹*person*› s'adapter (**to** à)

adaptable *adj* souple

adapter, **adaptor** *n* adaptateur *m*

⚷ **add** *vtr* (a) ajouter, rajouter (**onto, to** à)
(b) (*also* ~ **together**) additionner ‹*numbers*›; **to ~ sth to** ajouter qch à ‹*figure, total*›
■ **add up**: [1] *vi* ~ **up** ‹*facts, figures*› s'accorder; **to ~ up to** s'élever à ‹*total*›
[2] *vtr* ~ **up [sth]** additionner ‹*cost, numbers*›

adder *n* (snake) vipère *f*

addict *n* (a) (drug-user) toxicomane *mf*
(b) (of TV, coffee) accro *mf* (fam) (**of** de)

addicted *adj* **to be ~** (to alcohol, drugs) avoir une dépendance (**to** à); (to TV, coffee) être accro (fam) (**to** de)

addiction *n* dépendance *f* (**to** à)

addictive *adj* ‹*drug, substance*› qui crée une dépendance; **to be ~** ‹*chocolate, power*› être comme une drogue

⚷ **addition** [1] *n* (a) (to list, house) ajout *m*
(b) (in mathematics) addition *f*
[2] **in addition** *phr* en plus

⚷ **additional** *adj* supplémentaire

additive *n* additif *m*

add-on *adj* supplémentaire

⚷ **address** [1] *n* adresse *f*; **to change (one's) ~** changer d'adresse
[2] *vtr* (a) mettre l'adresse sur ‹*parcel, letter*›; **to ~ sth to sb** adresser qch à qn
(b) (speak to) s'adresser à ‹*group*›
(c) (aim) adresser ‹*remark, complaint*› (**to** à)

address book *n* carnet *m* d'adresses

adenoids *n pl* végétations *fpl* (adénoïdes)

adept *adj* expert/-e (**at** en)

adequate *adj* (a) (sufficient) suffisant/-e
(b) (satisfactory) satisfaisant/-e

adhere *vi* adhérer (**to** à)

adhesive [1] *n* colle *f*, adhésif *m*
[2] *adj* collant/-e; **~ tape** papier *m* collant, Scotch® *m*

adjacent *adj* contigu/contiguë; **~ to sth** attenant à qch

⚷ indicates a very frequent word

adjective *n* adjectif *m*

adjourn *vtr* ajourner ‹*trial*› (**for** pour; **until** à)

adjudicate *vtr* juger ‹*contest*›; examiner ‹*case, claim*›

adjust [1] *vtr* régler ‹*component, level, position, speed*›; ajuster ‹*price, rate*›; rajuster ‹*clothing*›; modifier ‹*figures*›
[2] *vi* ‹*person*› s'adapter (**to** à)

adjustable *adj* réglable

adjustment *n* (a) (of rates) rajustement *m* (**of** de); (of controls, machine) réglage *m* (**of** de)
(b) (mental) adaptation *f* (**to** à)
(c) (modification) modification *f*; **to make ~s to** apporter des modifications à ‹*system, machine*›

ad-lib *vtr*, *vi* (*p prés etc* **-bb-**) improviser

administer *vtr* (*also* **administrate**) gérer ‹*company, affairs, estate*›; gouverner ‹*territory*›

⚷ **administration** *n* (gen) administration *f*; (paperwork) travail *m* administratif

administrative *adj* administratif/-ive

administrator *n* administrateur/-trice *m/f*

admirable *adj* admirable

admiral *n* amiral *m*

admiration *n* admiration *f* (**for** pour)

admire *vtr* admirer

admirer *n* admirateur/-trice *m/f*

admission *n* (a) (entry) entrée *f*, admission (**to** dans); **'no ~'** 'entrée interdite'
(b) (fee) (droit *m* d')entrée *f*
(c) (confession) aveu *m*; **an ~ of guilt** un aveu de culpabilité

admissions office *n* (Univ) service *m* d'inscriptions

⚷ **admit** *vtr* (*p prés etc* **-tt-**) (a) reconnaître, admettre ‹*mistake, fact*›; **to ~ that...** reconnaître que...; **to ~ to** reconnaître, admettre ‹*mistake, fact*›
(b) (confess) reconnaître ‹*guilt*›; **to ~ to sth/doing** avouer qch/avoir fait
(c) (let in) laisser entrer ‹*person*› (**into** dans); **to be ~ted to hospital** être hospitalisé/-e

admittance *n* accès *m*, entrée *f*; **'no ~'** 'accès interdit au public'

admittedly *adv* il est vrai, il faut en convenir

adolescent [1] *n* adolescent/-e *m/f*
[2] *adj* (a) (gen) adolescent/-e; ‹*crisis, rebellion*› d'adolescent; ‹*problem*› des adolescents
(b) (childish) puéril/-e

⚷ **adopt** *vtr* adopter

adopted *adj* ‹*child*› adopté/-e; ‹*son, daughter*› adoptif/-ive

adoption *n* adoption *f*

adorable *adj* adorable

adore vtr adorer (**doing** faire)

adoring adj ‹husband› épris/-e; ‹fan› passionné/-e

adrenalin(e) n adrénaline f

Adriatic (Sea) pr n the ~ la mer f Adriatique, l'Adriatique f

adrift adj, adv ‹person, boat› à la dérive; **to come** ~ se détacher (**of, from** de)

ADSL n (abbr = **asymmetrical digital subscriber line**) ADSL f

✓ **adult** ① n adulte mf
② adj (gen) adulte; ‹life› d'adulte; ‹film, magazine› pour adultes

adultery n adultère m (**with** avec)

adulthood n âge m adulte

advance ① n (a) (forward movement) avance f, (progress) progrès m
(b) (sum of money) avance f, acompte m (**on** sur)
(c) **to make** ~**s to sb** (gen) faire des démarches auprès de qn; (sexually) faire des avances à qn
② vtr (a) avancer ‹sum of money›
(b) faire avancer ‹career, research›; servir ‹cause, interests›
③ vi (a) (move forward) ‹person› avancer, s'avancer (**on, towards** vers); (Mil) ‹army› avancer (**on** sur)
(b) (progress) progresser, faire des progrès
④ **in advance** phr à l'avance

advanced adj ‹course, class› supérieur/-e; ‹student, stage› avancé/-e; ‹equipment, technology› de pointe, perfectionné/-e

advance warning n préavis m

✓ **advantage** n (a) avantage m; **it is to our ~ to do** il est dans notre intérêt de faire
(b) (asset) atout m
(c) **to take** ~ **of** utiliser, profiter de ‹situation, offer, service›; exploiter ‹person›

advantageous adj avantageux/-euse

advent n (gen) apparition f (**of** de); **Advent** (prior to Christmas) l'Avent m

adventure n aventure f

adventure holiday n vacances fpl 'aventure'

adventurous adj aventureux/-euse

adverb n adverbe m

adverse adj ‹reaction, conditions, publicity› défavorable; ‹effect, consequences› négatif/-ive

advert n (GB) (colloq) (in paper) annonce f; (small ad) petite annonce f; (on TV, radio) pub f (fam), spot m publicitaire

advertise ① vtr faire de la publicité pour ‹product, event, service›; mettre or passer une annonce pour ‹car, house, job›
② vi (a) (for publicity) faire de la publicité
(b) (in small ads) passer une annonce

advertisement n (a) (for product, event) publicité f (**for** pour); **a good/bad** ~ **for** une bonne/mauvaise publicité pour
(b) (to sell house, get job) annonce f; (in small ads) petite annonce f

advertising n publicité f

advertising agency n agence f de publicité

advertising campaign n campagne f publicitaire

✓ **advice** n conseils mpl (**on** sur; **about** à propos de); **a piece of** ~ un conseil; **it was good** ~ c'était un bon conseil

advisable adj **it is** ~ **to do** il est recommandé de faire

✓ **advise** vtr (a) conseiller, donner des conseils à (**about** sur); **to** ~ **sb to do** conseiller à qn de faire; **to** ~ **sb against doing** déconseiller à qn de faire
(b) recommander ‹rest, course of action›
(c) (inform) **to** ~ **sb (of)** aviser qn (de)

adviser, advisor n conseiller/-ère m/f (**to** auprès de)

advisory service n service m d'aide et de conseil

Aegean (Sea) pr n the ~ la mer Égée

aerial ① n antenne f
② adj aérien/-ienne

aerobics n aérobic m

aeroplane n (GB) avion m

aerosol n bombe f aérosol

aesthetic, esthetic (US) adj esthétique

✓ **affair** n (a) affaire f; **state of** ~**s** situation f
(b) (relationship) liaison f (**with** avec)

✓ **affect** vtr (a) (have effect on) avoir une incidence sur ‹price›; affecter, avoir des conséquences pour ‹career, environment›; affecter, toucher ‹region, population›; influer sur ‹decision, outcome›
(b) (emotionally) émouvoir
(c) (Med) atteindre ‹person›; affecter ‹health, heart›

affection n affection f (**for sb** pour qn)

affectionate adj affectueux/-euse

affinity n (a) (attraction) attirance f (**with, for** pour)
(b) (resemblance) ressemblance f

affinity card n carte f de fidélité

affluence n richesse f

✓ **afford** vtr (a) (financially) **to be able to** ~ **sth** avoir les moyens d'acheter qch; **if I can** ~ **it** si j'ai les moyens; **I can't** ~ **to pay the rent** je n'ai pas les moyens de payer le loyer
(b) (spare) **to be able to** ~ disposer de ‹time›
(c) (risk) **to be able to** ~ **sth/to do** se permettre qch/de faire; **he can't** ~ **to wait** il ne peut pas se permettre d'attendre

affordable adj ‹price› abordable

afield adv **far** ~ loin; **further** ~ plus loin

afloat adj, adv **to stay** ~ ‹person, object› rester à la surface (de l'eau); ‹boat› rester à flot

✓ **afraid** adj (a) (scared) **to be** ~ avoir peur (**of** de; **to do, of doing** de faire)   ⋯⋗

(b) (anxious) she was ～ (that) there would be an accident elle craignait un accident; **I'm ～ it might rain** je crains qu'il (ne) pleuve
(c) I'm ～ I can't come je suis désolé mais je ne peux pas venir; **I'm ～ so/not** je crains que oui/non

afresh *adv* à nouveau

Africa *pr n* Afrique *f*; **to ～** en Afrique

ᵈ **African** **1** *n* Africain/-e *m/f*
2 *adj* africain/-e; *‹elephant›* d'Afrique

African-American *n* Afro-américain/-e *m/f*

Afro-Caribbean *adj* antillais/-e

ᵈ **after** **1** *adv* après; **soon** *or* **not long ～** peu après; **the year ～** l'année suivante *or* d'après; **the day ～** le lendemain
2 *prep* **(a)** après; **shortly ～ the strike** peu après la grève; **～ that** après (cela); **the day ～ tomorrow** après-demain; **to tidy up ～ sb** ranger derrière qn; **to ask ～ sb** demander des nouvelles de qn; **～ you!** après vous!
(b) that's the house they're ～ c'est la maison qu'ils veulent acheter; **the police are ～ him** il est recherché par la police
(c) year ～ year tous les ans; **it was one disaster ～ another** on a eu catastrophe sur catastrophe
(d) we called her Kate ～ my mother nous l'avons appelée Kate comme ma mère
(e) (US) **it's twenty ～ eleven** il est onze heures vingt
3 *conj* **(a)** (in the past) après avoir *or* être (+ *pp*), après que (+ *indicative*); **～ he had consulted Bill, he left** après avoir consulté Bill, il est parti; **～ he had changed she brought him to the office** après qu'il se fut changé, elle le conduisit au bureau; **～ we married/he left** après notre mariage/son départ
(b) (in the future) quand, une fois que
(c) why did he do that ～ we'd warned him? pourquoi a-t-il fait ça alors que nous l'avions prévenu?
4 after all *phr* après tout

after-effect *n* (Med) contrecoup *m*; (figurative) répercussion *f*

aftermath *n* conséquences *fpl*; **in the ～ of** à la suite de *‹war, scandal, election›*

afternoon *n* après-midi *m or f inv*; **in the ～** (dans) l'après-midi; **on Friday ～(s)** le vendredi après-midi; **good ～!** bonjour!

after-sales service *n* service *m* après-vente

after-shave *n* après-rasage *m*

aftershock *n* secousse *f* secondaire

after-sun *adj* après-soleil *inv*

aftertaste *n* arrière-goût *m*

afterthought *n* pensée *f* après coup

afterwards, **afterward** (US) *adv* **(a)** (after) après; **straight ～** tout de suite après

ᵈ indicates a very frequent word

(b) (later) plus tard

ᵈ **again** *adv* encore

■ **Note** When used with a verb, *again* is often translated by adding the prefix *re* to the verb in French: *to start again* = recommencer; *to marry again* = se remarier; *I'd like to read that book again* = j'aimerais relire ce livre; *she never saw them again* = elle ne les a jamais revus. You can check *re*+ verbs by consulting the French side of the dictionary.
— For other uses of *again*, see below.

sing it ～! chante-le encore!; **once ～** encore une fois; **yet ～ he refused** il a encore refusé; **when you are well ～** quand tu seras rétabli; **I'll never go there ～** je n'y retournerai jamais; **～ and ～** à plusieurs reprises

ᵈ **against** *prep* contre; **～ the wall** contre le mur; **I'm ～ it** je suis contre; **to be ～ doing** être contre l'idée de faire; **the pound fell ～ the dollar** la livre a baissé par rapport au dollar; **～ a background of** sur un fond de; **～ the light** à contre-jour

ᵈ **age** **1** *n* **(a)** âge *m*; **to come of ～** atteindre la majorité; **to be under ～** (Law) être mineur/-e
(b) (era) ère *f*, époque *f* (of de); **the video ～** l'ère de la vidéo; **in this day and ～** à notre époque
(c) (colloq) **it's ～s since I've played golf** ça fait une éternité que je n'ai pas joué au golf; **I've been waiting for ～s** j'attends depuis des heures
2 *vtr, vi* vieillir

aged *adj* **(a) ～ between 20 and 25** âgé/-e de 20 à 25 ans; **a boy ～ 12** un garçon de 12 ans
(b) (old) âgé/-e

age group *n* tranche *f* d'âge

ageism *n* discrimination *f* en raison de l'âge

ᵈ **agency** *n* agence *f*

ᵈ **agenda** *n* ordre *m* du jour

ᵈ **agent** *n* agent *m* (**for sb** de qn)

aggravate *vtr* (make worse) aggraver; (annoy) exaspérer

aggression *n* (gen) agression *f*; (of person) agressivité *f*

aggressive *adj* agressif/-ive

aggro *n* (colloq) (violence) violence *f*; (hostility) hostilité *f*

agile *adj* agile

agitate *vi* faire campagne (**for** pour)

agitated *adj* agité/-e, inquiet/-iète

AGM *n* (*abbr* = **annual general meeting**) assemblée *f* générale annuelle

agnostic *n, adj* agnostique *mf*

ᵈ **ago** *adv* **three weeks ～** il y a trois semaines; **long ～** il y a longtemps; **how long ～?** il y a combien de temps?; **not long ～** il y a peu de temps

agonize *vi* se tourmenter (**over, about** à propos de)

agonizing *adj* ‹*pain, death*› atroce; ‹*choice*› déchirant/-e

agony *n* (physical) douleur *f* atroce; (mental) angoisse *f*

agony aunt *n* journaliste *mf* responsable du courrier du cœur

agony column *n* courrier *m* du cœur

⚡ **agree** ① *vtr* (*prét, pp* **agreed**) (a) (concur) être d'accord (**that** sur le fait que)
(b) (admit) convenir (**that** que)
(c) (consent) **to** ∼ **to do** accepter de faire; **she** ∼**d to speak to me** elle a accepté de me parler
(d) (settle on, arrange) se mettre d'accord sur ‹*date, price*›; **to** ∼ **to do** convenir de faire
② *vi* (*prét, pp* **agreed**) (a) (hold same opinion) être d'accord (**with** avec; **about, on** sur; **about doing** pour faire); **'I** ∼**!'** 'je suis bien d'accord!'
(b) (reach mutual understanding) se mettre d'accord (**about, on** sur)
(c) (consent) accepter; **to** ∼ **to** consentir à ‹*suggestion, terms*›
(d) (hold with, approve) **to** ∼ **with** approuver ‹*belief, idea, practice*›
(e) (tally) ‹*stories, statements, figures*› concorder (**with** avec)
(f) (suit) **to** ∼ **with sb** ‹*climate*› être bon/ bonne pour qn; ‹*food*› réussir à qn
(g) (in grammar) s'accorder (**with** avec; **in** en)
③ **agreed** *pp adj* convenu/-e; **is that** ∼**d?** c'est entendu?

agreeable *adj* agréable

⚡ **agreement** *n* (a) accord *m* (**to do** pour faire); **to reach an** ∼ parvenir à un accord
(b) (undertaking) engagement *m*
(c) (contract) contrat *m*
(d) (in grammar) accord *m*

agricultural *adj* agricole

agriculture *n* agriculture *f*

aground *adv* **to run** ∼ s'échouer

⚡ **ahead** ① *adv* (a) ‹*run*› en avant; **to send sb on** ∼ envoyer qn en éclaireur; **to send one's luggage on** ∼ faire envoyer ses bagages; **a few kilometres** ∼ à quelques kilomètres
(b) (in time) **in the months** ∼ pendant les mois à venir
(c) (in leading position) **to be** ∼ **in the polls** être en tête des sondages; **to be 30 points** ∼ avoir 30 points d'avance
② **ahead of** *phr* (a) (in front of) devant ‹*person, vehicle*›; **to be three metres** ∼ **of sb** avoir trois mètres d'avance sur qn
(b) **to be** ∼ **of sb** (in polls, ratings) avoir un avantage sur qn; **to be** ∼ **of the others** ‹*pupil*› être plus avancé/-e que les autres

⚡ **aid** ① *n* aide *f* (**from** de; **to, for** à); **in** ∼ **of** au profit de ‹*charity*›
② *adj* ‹*organization*› d'entraide
③ *vtr* aider ‹*person*› (**to do** à faire); faciliter ‹*digestion, recovery*›

aid agency *n* organisation *f* humanitaire

---

aide *n* aide *mf*, assistant/-e *m/f*

Aids *n* (*abbr* = **Acquired Immune Deficiency Syndrome**) sida *m*

Aids awareness *n* sensibilisation *f* au problème du sida

Aids sufferer *n* sidéen/-éenne *m/f*

Aids virus *n* virus *m* du sida

aid worker *n* travailleur *m* humanitaire

⚡ **aim** ① *n* (a) (purpose) but *m*
(b) (with weapon) **to take** ∼ **at sb/sth** viser qn/qch
② *vtr* (a) **to be** ∼**ed at sb** ‹*campaign, product, remark*› viser qn
(b) braquer ‹*gun, camera*› (**at** sur); lancer ‹*ball, stone*› (**at** sur)
③ *vi* **to** ∼ **for sth, to** ∼ **at sth** viser qch; **to** ∼ **at doing, to** ∼ **to do** avoir l'intention de faire

⚡ **air** ① *n* (a) air *m*; **in the open** ∼ en plein air, au grand air; **to let the** ∼ **out of sth** dégonfler qch; **he threw the ball up into the** ∼ il a jeté le ballon en l'air
(b) **to travel by** ∼ voyager par avion
(c) (on radio, TV) **to be/go on the** ∼ être/ passer à l'antenne
② *vtr* (a) aérer ‹*garment, room, bed*›
(b) exprimer ‹*opinion, view*›; **to** ∼ **one's grievances** exposer ses griefs
IDIOMS **to put on** ∼**s** se donner de grands airs; **to vanish into thin** ∼ se volatiliser

air ambulance *n* avion *m* sanitaire

airbag *n* airbag *m*

air bed *n* (GB) matelas *m* pneumatique

air-conditioned *adj* climatisé/-e

air-conditioning *n* climatisation *f*, air *m* conditionné

⚡ **aircraft** *n* (*pl* ∼) avion *m*, aéronef *m*

aircrew *n* équipage *m* d'un avion

airfare *n* tarif *m* d'avion

airfield *n* aérodrome *m*, terrain *m* d'aviation

air force *n* armée *f* de l'air, forces *fpl* aériennes

air-freshener *n* désodorisant *m* d'atmosphère

air gun *n* fusil *m* à air comprimé

airhead *n* (colloq) évaporé/-e *m/f*

air hostess *n* hôtesse *f* de l'air

airline *n* compagnie *f* aérienne

airmail *n* poste *f* aérienne; **by** ∼ par avion

airplane *n* (US) avion *m*

⚡ **airport** *n* aéroport *m*

air raid *n* attaque *f* aérienne, raid *m* (aérien)

airstrike *n* frappe *f* aérienne

air terminal *n* (at airport) aérogare *f*; (in town) terminal *m*

airtight *adj* étanche à l'air

air-traffic controller *n* contrôleur/-euse *m/f* aérien/-ienne, aiguilleur *m* du ciel

a

air travel *n* voyages *mpl* aériens
airwaves *n pl* ondes *fpl*
airy *adj* (a) ‹room› clair/-e et spacieux/-ieuse
(b) ‹manner› désinvolte, insouciant/-e
aisle *n* (a) (in church) (side passage) bas-côté
m; (centre passage) allée *f* centrale
(b) (in train, plane) couloir *m*; (in cinema, shop)
allée *f*
ajar *adj, adv* entrouvert/-e, entrebâillé/-e
alarm ① *n* (a) (warning) alarme *f*; **smoke ~**
détecteur *m* de fumée
(b) (fear) frayeur *f*; (concern) inquiétude *f*
② *vtr* inquiéter ‹person›
alarm clock *n* réveille-matin *m*, réveil *m*
alarmed *adj* (a) (afraid) effrayé/-e
(b) (equipped with warning device) ‹door›
équipé/-e d'un système d'alarme
✦ **album** *n* album *m*
✦ **alcohol** *n* alcool *m*; **~-free** sans alcool; **~
content** teneur *f* en alcool
alcoholic ① *n* alcoolique *mf*
② *adj* ‹drink› alcoolisé/-e; ‹stupor› alcoolique
alcoholism *n* alcoolisme *m*
alcopop *n* soda *m* alcoolisé
alcove *n* renfoncement *m*
ale *n* bière *f*
alert ① *n* alerte *f*
② *adj* (a) (lively) ‹child› éveillé/-e; ‹adult›
alerte
(b) (attentive) vigilant/-e
③ *vtr* (a) alerter ‹authorities›
(b) **to ~ sb to** mettre qn en garde contre
‹danger›; attirer l'attention de qn sur ‹fact,
situation›
A levels *n pl* (GB Sch) ≈ baccalauréat *m*
algebra *n* algèbre *f*
Algeria *pr n* Algérie *f*
alias ① *n* (Comput) alias *m*
② *adv* alias
alibi *n* (a) (Law) alibi *m*
(b) (excuse) excuse *f*
alien *n* (a) (gen, Law) étranger/-ère *m/f* (**to** à)
(b) (from space) extraterrestre *mf*
alienate *vtr* éloigner ‹supporters,
colleagues›
alight ① *adj* **to set sth ~** mettre le feu
à qch
② *vi* ‹passenger› descendre (**from** de)
alike ① *adj* (identical) pareil/-eille; (similar)
semblable; **to look ~** se ressembler
② *adv* ‹dress, think› de la même façon
alimony *n* pension *f* alimentaire
✦ **alive** *adj* (a) vivant/-e, en vie; **to be burnt ~**
être brûlé/-e vif/vive
(b) **to come ~** ‹party, place› s'animer;
‹history› prendre vie
(c) **to be ~** ‹tradition› être vivant/-e;

‹interest› être vif/vive
(d) **~ with** grouillant/-e de ‹insects›
alkaline *adj* alcalin/-e
✦ **all**

■ **Note** When *all* is used as a pronoun, it is
generally translated by *tout*.
— When *all* is followed by a *that* clause, *all that*
is translated by *tout ce que*: *after all (that) we've
done* = après tout ce que nous avons fait.
— When referring to a specified group of people
or objects, the translation of *all* reflects the number and gender of the people or objects referred
to; *tous* is used for a group of people or objects
of masculine or mixed or unspecified gender and
toutes for a group of feminine gender: *we were
all delighted* = nous étions tous ravis; *'where
are the cups?'—'they're all in the kitchen'* = 'où
sont les tasses?'—'elles sont toutes dans la
cuisine'. ▶ 1
— In French, determiners agree in gender and
number with the noun that follows: *all the time*
= tout le temps; *all the family* = toute la famille;
all men = tous les hommes; *all the books* = tous
les livres; *all women* = toutes les femmes; *all the
chairs* = toutes les chaises. ▶ 2
— As an adverb meaning *completely*, *all* is
generally translated by *tout*: *he was all alone* = il
était tout seul; *the girls were all excited* = les filles
étaient tout excitées.
— However, when the adjective that follows is
in the feminine and begins with a consonant
the translation is *toute/toutes*: *she was all alone*
= elle était toute seule; *the girls were all alone*
= les filles étaient toutes seules. ▶ 3a
— For more examples and particular usages see
the entry below.

① *pron* tout; **that's ~ I want** c'est tout ce que
je veux; **I spent it ~, I spent ~ of it** j'ai tout
dépensé; **~ of our things** toutes nos affaires
② *det* tout/toute (+*sg*); tous/toutes (+*pl*); **~ those
who came** (men, mixed group) tous ceux qui sont
venus; (women) toutes celles qui sont venues; **~
his life** toute sa vie; **~ the time** tout le temps
③ *adv* (a) tout; **she's ~ wet** elle est toute mouillée;
~ in white tout en blanc; **~ along the canal** tout
le long du canal; **to be ~ for sth** être tout à fait
pour qch; **tell me ~ about it!** raconte-moi tout!
(b) (Sport) **(they are) six ~** (il y a) six partout
④ **all along** *phr* ‹know› depuis le début,
toujours
⑤ **all the** *phr* **~ the more difficult** d'autant
plus difficile; **~ the better!** tant mieux!
⑥ **all too** *phr* ‹easy, often› bien trop
⑦ **at all** *phr* **not at ~!** (acknowledging thanks)
de rien!; (answering query) pas du tout!; **it is
not at ~ certain** ce n'est pas du tout certain;
nothing at ~ rien du tout
⑧ **of all** *phr* **the easiest of ~** le plus facile;
first of ~ pour commencer
all clear *n* **to give sb the ~** donner le feu
vert à qn (**to do** pour faire); ‹doctor› déclarer
qn guéri/-e
allegation *n* allégation *f*

✦ indicates a very frequent word

allege *vtr* to ∼ that (claim) prétendre que (+ *conditional*); (publicly) déclarer que (+ *conditional*); **it was** ∼**d that** il a été dit que

alleged *adj* présumé/e

allegedly *adv* prétendument

allegiance *n* allégeance *f*

allergic *adj* allergique (**to** à)

allergist *n* allergologue *mf*

allergy *n* allergie *f* (**to** à)

alleviate *vtr* soulager ‹*boredom, pain*›; réduire ‹*overcrowding, stress*›

alley *n* (walkway) allée *f*; (for vehicles) ruelle *f*

alliance *n* alliance *f*

allied *adj* ‹*group*› allié/-e

all-important *adj* essentiel/-ielle

all-inclusive *adj* ‹*fee, price*› tout compris

all-in-one *adj* ‹*garment*› d'une seule pièce

all-night *adj* ‹*party, meeting*› qui dure toute la nuit; ‹*service*› ouvert/-e toute la nuit; ‹*radio station*› qui émet 24 heures sur 24

allocate *vtr* affecter ‹*funds*› (**for, to** à); accorder ‹*time*› (**to** à); assigner ‹*tasks*› (**to** à)

allot *vtr* (*p prés etc* -**tt**-) attribuer ‹*money*› (**to** à); **in the** ∼**ted time** dans le temps imparti

allotment *n* (GB) parcelle *f* de terre

all-out *adj* ‹*strike*› total/-e; ‹*attack*› en règle; ‹*effort*› acharné/-e

all over ① *adj* fini/-e; **when it's** ∼ quand tout sera fini
② *adv* (everywhere) partout; **to be trembling** ∼ trembler de partout
③ *prep* partout dans ‹*room, town*›; ∼ **China** partout en Chine

allow *vtr* (a) (authorize) permettre à, autoriser ‹*person, organization*› (**to do** faire); **it isn't** ∼**ed** c'est interdit; **she isn't** ∼**ed to go out** elle n'a pas le droit de sortir
(b) (let) laisser; **he** ∼**ed the situation to get worse** il a laissé la situation s'aggraver
(c) (enable) **to** ∼ **sb/sth to do** permettre à qn/qch de faire; **it would** ∼ **the company to expand** cela permettrait à la société de s'agrandir
(d) (allocate) prévoir; **to** ∼ **two days for the job** prévoir deux jours pour faire le travail
(e) ‹*referee*› accorder ‹*goal*›; ‹*insurer*› agréer ‹*claim*›
(f) (condone) tolérer ‹*rudeness, swearing*›
■ **allow for** tenir compte de

allowance *n* (a) (gen) allocation *f*; (from employer) indemnité *f*
(b) (tax) ∼ abattement *m* fiscal
(c) (spending money) (for child) argent *m* de poche; (for student) argent *m* (pour vivre); (from trust, guardian) rente *f*
(d) **your baggage** ∼ **is 40 kg** vous avez droit à 40 kg de bagages
(e) **to make** ∼(**s**) **for sth** tenir compte de qch; **to make** ∼(**s**) **for sb** essayer de comprendre qn

alloy wheel *n* jante *f* en alliage léger

all right, alright ① *adj* ‹*film, garment, place*› pas mal (fam); **is my hair** ∼? ça va à mes cheveux?; **are you** ∼? ça va?; **I'm** ∼ **thanks** ça va merci; **is it** ∼ **if...?** est-ce que ça va si...?
② *adv* (a) (giving agreement) d'accord
(b) ‹*work*› comme il faut; ‹*see, hear*› bien

all-round (GB), **all-around** (US) *adj* ‹*athlete*› complet/-ète; ‹*improvement*› général/-e

all-rounder *n* **to be a good** ∼ être bon/ bonne en tout

all-time *adj* ‹*record*› absolu/-e; **the** ∼ **greats** (people) les grands *mpl*; ∼ **high record** *m* absolu

all told *adv* en tout

allusion *n* allusion *f* (**to** à)

ally ① *n* (*pl* -**ies**) allié/-e *m/f*
② *v refl* **to** ∼ **oneself with** s'allier avec

almond *n* (a) (nut) amande *f*
(b) (*also* ∼ **tree**) amandier *m*

almost *adv* (a) (practically) presque; **we're** ∼ **there** nous sommes presque arrivés; **it's** ∼ **dark** il fait presque nuit
(b) **he** ∼ **died/forgot** il a failli mourir/ oublier

alone ① *adj* seul/-e; **all** ∼ tout seul/toute seule; **to leave sb** ∼ laisser qn seul/-e; (in peace) laisser qn tranquille; **leave that bike** ∼! ne touche pas à ce vélo!
② *adv* (a) ‹*work, live, travel*› seul/-e
(b) **for this reason** ∼ rien que pour cette raison

IDIOM to go it ∼ (colloq) faire cavalier seul

along

> ■ **Note** When *along* is used as a preposition meaning *all along* it can usually be translated by *le long de*: *there were trees along the road* = il y avait des arbres le long de la route. For particular usages see the entry below.
> — *along* is often used after verbs of movement. If the addition of *along* does not change the meaning of the verb, *along* will not be translated: *as he walked along* = tout en marchant.

① *adv* **to push sth** ∼ pousser qch; **to be running** ∼ courir; **I'll be** ∼ **in a second** j'arrive tout de suite
② *prep* (a) (all along) le long de; **there were chairs** ∼ **the wall** il y avait des chaises contre le mur
(b) **to walk** ∼ **the beach** marcher sur la plage; **to look** ∼ **the shelves** chercher dans les rayons; **halfway** ∼ **the path** à mi-chemin
③ **along with** *phr* (accompanied by) accompagné/-e de; (at same time as) en même temps que

alongside ① *prep* (a) (all along) le long de
(b) **to draw up** ∼ **sb** ‹*vehicle*› s'arrêter à la hauteur de qn
② *adv* à côté

aloud *adv* ‹*read*› à haute voix; ‹*think*› tout haut

a

alphabet *n* alphabet *m*

alphabetically *adv* par ordre alphabétique

alpine *adj* (*also* **Alpine**) alpin/-e

Alps *pr n pl* the ~ les Alpes *fpl*

✓ **already** *adv* déjà; **it's 10 o'clock** ~ il est déjà 10 heures; **he's** ~ **left** il est déjà parti

alright = ALL RIGHT

Alsatian *n* (GB) (dog) berger *m* allemand

✓ **also** *adv* aussi

alter ⓵ *vtr* (a) changer ‹*person*›; (radically) transformer ‹*person*›; changer ‹*opinion, rule, timetable*›; modifier ‹*amount, document*›; affecter ‹*value, climate*›
  (b) retoucher ‹*dress, shirt*›
  ⓶ *vi* changer

alteration ⓵ *n* modification *f* (**to, in** de)
  ⓶ **alterations** *n pl* (building work) travaux *mpl*

alternate ⓵ *adj* (a) (successive) ‹*chapters, layers*› en alternance
  (b) (every other) **on** ~ **days** un jour sur deux
  (c) (US) (other) autre
  ⓶ *vtr* **to** ~ **sth and** *or* **with sth** alterner qch et qch
  ⓷ *vi* ‹*people*› se relayer; ‹*colours, patterns, seasons*› alterner (**with** avec)

alternately *adv* alternativement

✓ **alternative** ⓵ *n* (from two) alternative *f*, autre possibilité *f*; (from several) possibilité *f*; **to have no** ~ ne pas avoir le choix
  ⓶ *adj* (a) ‹*date, flight, plan*› autre; ‹*accommodation, product*› de remplacement; ‹*solution*› de rechange
  (b) (unconventional) alternatif/-ive

alternatively *adv* sinon; ~, **you can book by phone** vous avez aussi la possibilité de réserver par téléphone

alternative medicine *n* médecines *fpl* parallèles *or* douces

✓ **although** *conj* bien que (+ *subjunctive*); ~ **he is shy** bien qu'il soit timide

altitude *n* altitude *f*

alto *n* (*pl* -**tos**) (voice) (of female) contralto *m*; (of male) haute-contre *f*

altogether *adv* (a) (completely) complètement; **not** ~ **true** pas complètement vrai
  (b) (in total) en tout; **how much is that** ~? ça fait combien en tout?

aluminium (GB), **aluminum** (US) *n* aluminium *m*

aluminium foil *n* papier *m* aluminium

✓ **always** *adv* toujours; **he's** ~ **complaining** il n'arrête pas de se plaindre

Alzheimer's disease *n* maladie *f* d'Alzheimer

am *adv* (*abbr* = **ante meridiem**) **three** ~ trois heures (du matin)

✓ indicates a very frequent word

amalgamate ⓵ *vtr* (merge) fusionner ‹*companies, schools*› (**with** avec; **into** en)
  ⓶ *vi* ‹*company, union*› fusionner (**with** avec)

amateur ⓵ *n* amateur *m*
  ⓶ *adj* ‹*sportsperson, musician*› amateur; ‹*sport*› en amateur

amaze *vtr* surprendre; (stronger) stupéfier

amazed *adj* stupéfait/-e; **I'm** ~ (**that**) ça m'étonne que (+ *subjunctive*)

amazement *n* stupéfaction *f*

✓ **amazing** *adj* extraordinaire

Amazon *pr n* Amazone *m*

ambassador *n* ambassadeur *m*

amber *n* (a) (resin, colour) ambre *m*
  (b) (GB) (traffic signal) orange *m*

ambiguous *adj* ambigu/ambiguë

ambition *n* ambition *f* (**to do** de faire)

ambitious *adj* ambitieux/-ieuse

ambulance *n* ambulance *f*; ~ **crew** équipe *f* d'ambulanciers/-ières

ambush ⓵ *n* embuscade *f*
  ⓶ *vtr* tendre une embuscade à

amenable *adj* ~ **to** ‹*person*› sensible à ‹*reason, advice*›

amend *vtr* amender ‹*law*›; modifier ‹*document*›

amendment *n* (to law) amendement *m* (**to** à); (to contract) modification *f* (**to** à)

amends *n pl* **to make** ~ se racheter; **to make** ~ **for** réparer ‹*damage*›; **to make** ~ **to sb** (financially) dédommager qn

amenities *n pl* (of hotel) équipements *mpl*; (of house, sports club) installations *fpl*

America *pr n* Amérique *f*

✓ **American** ⓵ *n* (a) (person) Américain/-e *m/f*
  (b) (*also* ~ **English**) américain *m*
  ⓶ *adj* américain/-e; ‹*embassy*› des États-Unis

American Indian *n* Indien/-ienne *m/f* d'Amerique du Nord

amiable *adj* aimable (**to** avec)

amicable *adj* (friendly) amical/-e; **an** ~ **settlement** un arrangement à l'amiable

amiss ⓵ *adj* **there is something** ~ il y a quelque chose qui ne va pas
  ⓶ *adv* **to take sth** ~ prendre qch de travers

ammunition *n* munitions *fpl*

amnesty *n* amnistie *f*

✓ **among, amongst** *prep* (a) (amidst) parmi; ~ **the crowd** parmi la foule; **to be** ~ **friends** être entre amis
  (b) (one of) ~ **the world's poorest countries** un des pays les plus pauvres du monde; **she was** ~ **those who survived** elle faisait partie des survivants; **to be** ~ **the first** être dans les premiers
  (c) (between) entre

✓ **amount** *n* (of goods, food) quantité *f*; (of people, objects) nombre *m*; (of money) somme *f*; **a large ~ of** beaucoup de; **the full ~** le montant total

■ **amount to** (a) (*be*) s'élever à ‹*total*›
(b) (be equivalent to) revenir à ‹*confession, betrayal*›; **it ~s to the same thing** cela revient au même

amp *n* (a) (*abbr* = **ampere**) ampère *m*
(b) (colloq) (*abbr* = **amplifier**) ampli *m* (fam)

amphetamine *n* amphétamine *f*

ample *adj* (a) ‹*provisions, resources*› largement suffisant/-e (**for** pour); **there's ~ room** il y a largement la place
(b) ‹*proportions, bust*› généreux/-euse

amplifier *n* amplificateur *m*

amputate *vtr* amputer; **to ~ sb's leg** amputer qn de la jambe

amuse [1] *vtr* (a) (cause laughter) amuser; **to be ~d at** *or* **by** s'amuser de
(b) (entertain) ‹*game, story*› distraire
(c) (occupy) ‹*activity, hobby*› occuper
[2] *v refl* **to ~ oneself** (a) (entertain) se distraire
(b) (occupy) s'occuper

amusement *n* (a) (mirth) amusement *m* (**at** face à)
(b) (diversion) distraction *f*

amusement arcade *n* (GB) salle *f* de jeux électroniques

amusement park *n* parc *m* d'attractions

amusing *adj* amusant/-e

an ▶ A²

anachronism *n* anachronisme *m*

anaemic *adj* (Med) anémique

anaesthetic (GB), **anesthetic** (US) *n, adj* anesthésique *m*

anaesthetize (GB), **anesthetize** (US) *vtr* anesthésier

analogy *n* analogie *f*

✧ **analyse** (GB), **analyze** (US) *vtr* analyser

✧ **analysis** *n* analyse *f*

analytic(al) *adj* analytique

anarchist *n, adj* anarchiste *mf*

anarchy *n* anarchie *f*

anatomy *n* anatomie *f*

ancestor *n* ancêtre *mf*

anchor *n* ancre *f*; **to drop ~** jeter l'ancre

anchovy *n* anchois *m*

✧ **ancient** *adj* (dating from BC) antique; (very old) ancien/-ienne; **~ Greek** grec ancien; **~ Greece** la Grèce antique; **~ monument** monument *m* historique

✧ **and** *conj* et; **cups ~ plates** des tasses et des assiettes; **he stood up ~ went out** il s'est levé et il est sorti; **come ~ see** viens voir; **two hundred ~ sixty-two** deux cent soixante-deux; **faster ~ faster** de plus en plus vite

Andorra *pr n* Andorre *f*

angel *n* ange *m*

✧ **anger** [1] *n* colère *f* (**at** devant; **towards** contre)
[2] *vtr* mettre [qn] en colère ‹*person*›

angle [1] *n* angle *m*
[2] *vi* (a) (fish) pêcher (à la ligne)
(b) (colloq) **to ~ for sth** chercher à obtenir qch

Anglo-French *adj* anglo-français/-e, franco-britannique

angrily *adv* ‹*react, speak*› avec colère

✧ **angry** *adj* ‹*person, expression*› furieux/-ieuse; ‹*scene, words*› de colère; **to be ~** (**at** *or* **with sb**) être en colère (contre qn); **to get ~** se fâcher; **to make sb ~** mettre qn en colère

✧ **animal** [1] *n* animal *m*, bête *f*
[2] *adj* animal/-e

animal activist *n* militant/-e *m/f* pour les droits des animaux

animal experiment *n* expérience *f* sur les animaux

animal rights *n pl* droits *mpl* des animaux

animal testing *n* expérimentation *f* animale

animated *adj* animé/-e

animator *n* (cartoonist) animateur/-trice *m/f*

ankle *n* cheville *f*

ankle chain *n* chaîne *f* de cheville

ankle sock *n* socquette *f*

annex [1] *n* (*also* **annexe** (GB)) annexe *f*
[2] *vtr* annexer ‹*territory, land, country*› (**to** à)

annihilate *vtr* anéantir

anniversary *n* anniversaire *m* (**of** de)

annotate *vtr* annoter

✧ **announce** *vtr* annoncer (**that** que)

announcement *n* (a) (spoken) annonce *f*
(b) (written) avis *m*; (of birth, death) faire-part *m inv*

announcer *n* (on TV) speaker/-erine *m/f*; **radio ~** présentateur/-trice *m/f* de radio

annoy *vtr* ‹*person*› (by behaviour) agacer; (by opposing wishes) contrarier; ‹*noise*› gêner

annoyance *n* agacement *m* (**at** devant), contrariété *f* (**at** à cause de)

annoyed *adj* contrarié/-e (**at, by** par); (stronger) agacé/-e, fâché/-e (**at, by** par); **~ with sb** fâché/-e contre qn

annoying *adj* agaçant/-e (**to do** de faire)

✧ **annual** [1] *n* (a) (book) album *m* (annuel)
(b) (plant) plante *f* annuelle
[2] *adj* annuel/-elle

annually *adv* ‹*earn, produce*› par an; ‹*do, inspect*› tous les ans

anomaly *n* anomalie *f*

anonymous *adj* anonyme

anorak *n* anorak *m*

anorexia (nervosa) *n* anorexie *f* mentale

a

♂ **another**

■ **Note** *Another* is translated by *un autre* or *une autre* according to the gender of the noun it refers to: *another book* = un autre livre; *another chair* = une autre chaise.

— Note that *en* is always used with *un/une autre* in French to represent a noun that is understood: *that cake was delicious, can I have another (one)?* = ce gâteau était délicieux, est-ce que je peux en prendre un autre? For more examples and particular usages, see the entry below.

1 *det* **(a)** (an additional) un/-e autre, encore un/-e; **would you like ~ drink?** est-ce que tu veux un autre verre?; **I've broken ~ plate** j'ai encore cassé une assiette; **that will cost you ~ £5** cela vous coûtera 5 livres sterling de plus; **in ~ five weeks** dans cinq semaines **(b)** (a different) un/-e autre; **~ time** une autre fois; **he has ~ job now** il a un nouveau travail maintenant
2 *pron* un/-e autre; **she had ~** elle en a pris un/-e autre; **one after ~** l'un/l'une après l'autre; **in one way or ~** d'une façon ou d'une autre

♂ **answer 1** *n* (gen) réponse *f* (**to** à); (to problem, puzzle) solution *f* (**to** à); **there's no ~** (to door) il n'y a personne; (on phone) ça ne répond pas; **the right/wrong ~** la bonne/ mauvaise réponse
2 *vtr* répondre à; **to ~ the door** aller *or* venir ouvrir la porte; **to ~ the phone** répondre au téléphone
3 *vi* **(a)** répondre; **to ~ to** répondre *or* correspondre à
(b) (be accountable) **to ~ to sb** être responsable devant qn
■ **answer back** répondre
■ **answer for** répondre de ‹*action, person*›; **they have a lot to ~ for!** ils ont beaucoup de comptes à rendre!

answerable *adj* responsable (**to sb** devant qn; **for sth** de qch)

answering machine, **answerphone** *n* répondeur *m* (téléphonique)

ant *n* fourmi *f*

antagonize *vtr* (annoy) contrarier; (stronger) éveiller l'hostilité de

Antarctic 1 *pr n* **the ~** l'Antarctique *m*
2 *adj* antarctique

antelope *n* antilope *f*

antenatal *adj* prénatal/-e

antenatal class *n* (GB) cours *m* de préparation à l'accouchement

antenna *n* (*pl* -**ae** *ou* -**as**) antenne *f*

anthropology *n* anthropologie *f*

anti 1 *prep* contre
2 **anti(-)** *pref* anti(-)

antibacterial *adj* antibactérien/-ienne

♂ indicates a very frequent word

antibiotic *n* antibiotique *m*; **on ~s** sous antibiotiques

anticipate *vtr* **(a)** (foresee) prévoir, s'attendre à ‹*problem, delay*›; **as ~d** comme prévu
(b) (guess in advance) anticiper ‹*needs, result*›
(c) (pre-empt) devancer ‹*person, act*›

anticipation *n* **(a)** (excitement) excitation *f*; (pleasure in advance) plaisir *m* anticipé
(b) (expectation) prévision *f* (**of** de)

anticlimax *n* déception *f*

anticlockwise *adj, adv* (GB) dans le sens inverse des aiguilles d'une montre

antidepressant *n* antidépresseur *m*

antidote *n* antidote *m* (**to, for** contre, à)

anti-globalization *n* antimondialisme *m*

antihistamine *n* antihistaminique *m*

antique 1 *n* (object) objet *m* ancien *or* d'époque; (furniture) meuble *m* ancien *or* d'époque
2 *adj* ancien/-ienne

antique shop *n* magasin *m* d'antiquités

anti-Semitism *n* antisémitisme *m*

antiseptic *n, adj* antiseptique *m*

antisocial *adj* **(a)** **~ behaviour** comportement *m* incorrect; (criminal behaviour) comportement *m* délinquant
(b) (reclusive) sauvage

anti-theft *adj* ‹*lock, device*› antivol *inv*

anti-virus software *n* logiciel *m* antivirus

antiwar *adj* anti-guerre

antlers *n pl* bois *mpl* de cerf

anxiety *n* **(a)** (worry) grandes inquiétudes *fpl* (**about** à propos de; **for** pour); **to be in a state of ~** être angoissé/-e
(b) (eagerness) désir *m* ardent (**to do** de faire)
(c) (in psychology) anxiété *f*

anxiety attack *n* crise *f* d'angoisse

anxious *adj* **(a)** (worried) très inquiet/-iète (**about** à propos de; **for** pour); **to be ~ about doing** s'inquiéter de faire
(b) ‹*moment, time*› angoissant/-e
(c) (eager) très désireux/-euse (**to do** de faire)

anxiously *adv* **(a)** (worriedly) avec inquiétude
(b) (eagerly) avec impatience

♂ **any**

■ **Note** When *any* is used as a determiner in questions and conditional sentences it is translated by *du, de l', de la* or *des* according to the gender and number of the noun that follows: *is there any soap?* = y a-t-il du savon?; *is there any flour?* = y a-t-il de la farine?; *are there any questions?* = est-ce qu'il y a des questions?
— In negative sentences *any* is translated by *de* or *d'* (before a vowel or mute 'h'): *we don't have any money* = nous n'avons pas d'argent.
— When *any* is used as a pronoun in negative sentences and in questions it is translated by *en*:

we don't have any = nous n'en avons pas; *have you got any?* = est-ce que vous en avez?
— For more examples and other uses see the entry below.

1 *det* **(a)** (in questions, conditional sentences) du/de l'/de la/des; **is there ∼ tea?** est-ce qu'il y a du thé?; **if you have ∼ money** si vous avez de l'argent
(b) (with negative) de, d'; **I don't need ∼ advice** je n'ai pas besoin de conseils
(c) (no matter which) n'importe quel/quelle, tout; **∼ pen will do** n'importe quel stylo fera l'affaire; **you can have ∼ cup you like** vous pouvez prendre n'importe quelle tasse; **I'm ready to help in ∼ way I can** je suis prêt à faire tout ce que je peux pour aider; **come round and see me ∼ time** passe me voir quand tu veux
2 *pron, quantif* **(a)** (in questions, conditional sentences) **have you got ∼?** est-ce que vous en avez?; **have ∼ of you got a car?** est-ce que l'un/-e d'entre vous a une voiture?
(b) (with negative) en; **he hasn't got ∼** il n'en a pas; **there is hardly ∼ left** il n'en reste presque pas; **she doesn't like ∼ of them** (people) elle n'aime aucun d'entre eux/elles; (things) elle n'en aime aucun/-e
(c) (no matter which) n'importe lequel/laquelle; **'which colour would you like?'—'∼'** 'quelle couleur veux-tu?'—'n'importe laquelle'; **∼ of these pens** n'importe lequel de ces stylos; **∼ of them could do it** n'importe qui d'entre eux/elles pourrait le faire
3 *adv* **have you got ∼ more of these?** est-ce que vous en avez d'autres?; **do you want ∼ more wine?** voulez-vous encore du vin?; **he doesn't live here ∼ more** il n'habite plus ici

anybody *pron* (*also* **anyone**) **(a)** (in questions, conditional sentences) quelqu'un; **is there ∼ in the house?** est-ce qu'il y a quelqu'un dans la maison?; **if ∼ asks, tell them I've gone out** si quelqu'un me cherche, dis que je suis sorti
(b) (with negative) personne; **there wasn't ∼ in the house** il n'y avait personne dans la maison; **I didn't have ∼ to talk to** il n'y avait personne avec qui j'aurais pu parler
(c) (no matter who) n'importe qui; **∼ could do it** n'importe qui pourrait le faire; **∼ who wants to, can go** tous ceux qui le veulent, peuvent y aller; **∼ can make a mistake** ça arrive à tout le monde de faire une erreur; **∼ would think you were deaf** c'est à croire que tu es sourd

anyhow *adv* **(a)** = ANYWAY A
(b) (carelessly) n'importe comment

✔ **anyone** = ANYBODY

✔ **anything** *pron* **(a)** (in questions, conditional sentences) quelque chose; **is there ∼ to be done?** peut-on faire quelque chose?
(b) (with negative) rien; **she didn't say ∼** elle n'a rien dit; **he didn't have ∼ to do** il n'avait rien à faire; **don't believe ∼ he says** ne crois

pas un mot de ce qu'il dit
(c) (no matter what) tout; **∼ is possible** tout est possible; **she'll eat ∼** elle mange tout; **he was ∼ but happy** il n'était pas du tout heureux

anytime *adv* (*also* **any time**) n'importe quand; **∼ after 2 pm** n'importe quand à partir de 14 heures; **∼ you like** quand tu veux; **he could arrive ∼ now** il pourrait arriver d'un moment à l'autre

✔ **anyway** *adv* **(a)** (*also* **anyhow**) (in any case) de toute façon
(b) (all the same) quand même; **I don't really like hats, but I'll try it on ∼** je n'aime pas vraiment les chapeaux, mais je vais quand même l'essayer; **thanks ∼** merci quand même
(c) (at any rate) en tout cas; **we can't go out, not yet ∼** nous ne pouvons pas sortir, pas pour l'instant en tout cas
(d) (well) **'∼, we arrived at the station…'** 'bref, nous sommes arrivés à la gare…'

✔ **anywhere** *adv* **(a)** (in questions, conditional sentences) quelque part; **we're going to Spain, if ∼** si on va quelque part, ce sera en Espagne
(b) (with negative) nulle part; **you can't go ∼** tu ne peux aller nulle part; **there isn't ∼ to sit** il n'y a pas de place pour s'asseoir; **you won't get ∼ if you don't pass your exams** tu n'arriveras à rien si tu ne réussis pas tes examens; **crying isn't going to get you ∼** ça ne t'avancera à rien de pleurer
(c) (no matter where) n'importe où; **∼ you like** où tu veux; **∼ in England** partout en Angleterre

✔ **apart** **1** *adj, adv* **(a) trees planted 10 metres ∼** des arbres plantés à 10 mètres d'intervalle
(b) (separated) séparé/-e; **we hate being ∼** nous détestons être séparés; **they need to be kept ∼** il faut les garder séparés
(c) (to one side) **he stood ∼ (from the group)** il se tenait à l'écart (du groupe)
2 **apart from** *phr* **(a)** (separate from) à l'écart de; **it stands ∼ from the other houses** elle est à l'écart des autres maisons; **he lives ∼ from his wife** il vit séparé de sa femme
(b) (leaving aside) en dehors de, à part; **∼ from being illegal, it's also dangerous** (mis) à part que c'est illégal, c'est aussi dangereux

apartheid *n* apartheid *m*

✔ **apartment** *n* appartement *m*

apartment block *n* immeuble *m*

apartment house *n* (US) résidence *f*

apathetic *adj* (by nature) amorphe; (from illness, depression) apathique

apex *n* (*pl* **-exes, -ices**) sommet *m*

APEX *n* (*abbr* = **Advance Purchase Excursion**) APEX *m*

apologetic *adj* ⟨gesture, letter⟩ d'excuse; **to be ∼ (about)** s'excuser (de)

apologize *vi* s'excuser (**to sb** auprès de qn; **for sth** de qch; **for doing** d'avoir fait)

apology *n* excuses *fpl* (**for sth** pour qch; **for doing** pour avoir fait); **to make an ~** s'excuser

apostrophe *n* apostrophe *f*

appal (GB), **appall** (US) *vtr* ((GB) *p prés etc* -**ll**-) (shock) scandaliser; (horrify, dismay) horrifier

appalling *adj* (a) ‹*crime, conditions*› épouvantable
(b) ‹*manners, joke, taste*› exécrable; ‹*noise, weather*› épouvantable

apparatus *n* (gen) appareil *m*; (in gym) agrès *mpl*

✧ **apparent** *adj* (a) (seeming) ‹*contradiction, willingness*› apparent/-e
(b) (clear) évident/-e; **for no ~ reason** sans raison apparente

✧ **apparently** *adv* apparemment

✧ **appeal** ① *n* (a) (gen, Law) appel *m* (**for** à; **on behalf of** en faveur de)
(b) (attraction) charme *m*; (interest) intérêt *m*
② *vi* (a) (Law) faire appel (**against** de)
(b) (Sport) **to ~ to** demander l'arbitrage de ‹*referee*›; **to ~ against** contester ‹*decision*›
(c) **to ~ for** lancer un appel à ‹*order, tolerance*›; faire appel à ‹*witnesses*›; **to ~ for help** demander de l'aide
(d) (attract) **to ~ to sb** ‹*idea*› tenter qn; ‹*person*› plaire à qn; ‹*place*› attirer qn

appeal fund *n* fonds *m* d'aide

appealing *adj* (a) (attractive) ‹*child*› attachant/-e; ‹*idea*› séduisant/-e; ‹*modesty*› charmant/-e
(b) ‹*look*› suppliant/-e

✧ **appear** *vi* (a) (become visible) apparaître
(b) (turn up) arriver
(c) (seem) **to ~ to be/to do** ‹*person*› avoir l'air d'être/de faire; **to ~ depressed** avoir l'air déprimé; **it ~s that** il semble que
(d) ‹*book, article, name*› paraître
(e) **to ~ on stage** paraître en scène; **to ~ on TV** passer à la télévision
(f) (Law) **to ~ in court** comparaître devant le tribunal

✧ **appearance** *n* (a) (arrival) (of person, vehicle) arrivée *f*; (of development, invention) apparition *f*; **to put in an ~** faire une apparition
(b) (on TV, in play, film) passage *m*
(c) (look) (of person) apparence *f*; (of district, object) aspect *m*; **to judge** *or* **go by ~s** se fier aux apparences

appendicitis *n* appendicite *f*

appendix *n* (*pl* -**ixes, -ices**) appendice *m*; **to have one's ~ removed** se faire opérer de l'appendicite

appetite *n* appétit *m*

appetite suppressant *n* anorexigène *m*

appetizer *n* (biscuit, olive etc) amuse-gueule *m inv*; (starter) hors-d'œuvre *m*

appetizing *adj* appétissant/-e

applaud *vtr, vi* applaudir

applause *n* applaudissements *mpl*; **there was a burst of ~** les applaudissements ont éclaté

apple *n* pomme *f*

applecore *n* trognon *m* de pomme

applet *n* (Comput) applet *m*, applette *f*

apple tree *n* pommier *m*

appliance *n* appareil *m*; **household ~** appareil électroménager

applicant *n* (for job, membership) candidat/-e *m/f* (**for** à); (for passport, benefit, loan) demandeur/-euse *m/f* (**for** de); (for citizenship) postulant/-e *m/f* (**for** à)

✧ **application** *n* (a) (for job) candidature *f* (**for** à); (for membership, passport, loan) demande *f* (**for** de)
(b) (of ointment) application *f* (**to** à)
(c) (of law, penalty, rule) application *f*

application form *n* (gen) formulaire *m* de demande; (for job) formulaire *m* de candidature; (for membership) demande *f* d'inscription

✧ **apply** ① *vtr* (gen) appliquer; exercer ‹*pressure*› (**to** sur)
② *vi* (a) **to ~ (for)** faire une demande (de) ‹*passport, loan, visa, permit*›; poser sa candidature à ‹*job*›; **to ~ to** faire une demande d'inscription à ‹*college*›
(b) (be valid) ‹*definition, term*› s'appliquer (**to** à); ‹*ban, rule, penalty*› être en vigueur
③ *v refl* **to ~ oneself** s'appliquer

✧ **appoint** *vtr* nommer ‹*person*› (**to sth** à qch; **to do** pour faire; **as** comme); fixer ‹*date, place*›

appointment *n* (a) (meeting) rendez-vous *m* (**at** chez; **with** avec; **to do** pour faire); **business ~** rendez-vous *m* d'affaires; **to make an ~** prendre rendez-vous
(b) (to post) nomination *f*

appraisal *n* évaluation *f*

✧ **appreciate** ① *vtr* (a) apprécier ‹*help, effort*›; être sensible à ‹*favour*›; être reconnaissant/-e de ‹*kindness, sympathy*›; **I'd ~ it if you could reply soon** je vous serais reconnaissant de répondre sans tarder
(b) (realize) se rendre (bien) compte de, être conscient/-e de
(c) (enjoy) apprécier ‹*music, art, food*›
② *vi* ‹*object*› prendre de la valeur; ‹*value*› monter

appreciation *n* (a) (gratitude) remerciement *m* (**for** pour)
(b) (enjoyment) appréciation *f* (**of** de)
(c) (increase) hausse *f* (**of, in** de)

appreciative *adj* (a) (grateful) reconnaissant/-e (**of** de)
(b) (admiring) admiratif/-ive

✧ indicates a very frequent word

apprehensive *adj* inquiet/-iète; **to be ~ about sth/doing** appréhender qch/de faire

apprentice *n* apprenti/-e *m/f* (**to** de)

apprenticeship *n* apprentissage *m*

ℱ **approach** ① *n* (a) (route of access) voie *f* d'accès
(b) (arrival) approche *f*
(c) (to problem) approche *f*
(d) **to make ~es to sb** faire des démarches auprès de qn
② *vtr* (a) (draw near to) s'approcher de ‹*person, place*›; (verge on) approcher de
(b) (deal with) aborder ‹*problem, subject*›
(c) **to ~ sb (about sth)** s'adresser à qn (au sujet de qch); (more formally) faire des démarches auprès de qn (pour qch)
③ *vi* ‹*person, car*› (s')approcher; ‹*event, season*› approcher

approachable *adj* abordable, d'un abord facile

ℱ **appropriate** ① *adj* (a) ‹*behaviour, choice, place*› approprié/-e (**for** pour); ‹*dress, gift*› qui convient (*after n*) (**for** à); ‹*punishment*› juste (**for** à); ‹*name*› bien choisi/-e
(b) (relevant) ‹*authority*› compétent/-e
② *vtr* s'approprier ‹*property, document*›; affecter ‹*funds, land*› (**for** à)

appropriately *adv* (a) ‹*behave, speak*› avec à-propos; ‹*dress*› convenablement
(b) ‹*designed, chosen, sited*› judicieusement

approval *n* approbation *f* (**of** de; **to do** pour faire); **on ~** à l'essai

ℱ **approve** ① *vtr* approuver ‹*product, plan*›; accepter ‹*person*›
② *vi* **to ~ of sb/sth** apprécier qn/qch; **he doesn't ~ of drinking** il est contre l'alcool

approving *adj* approbateur/-trice

approximate *adj* approximatif/-ive

ℱ **approximately** *adv* (a) (about) environ; **at ~ four o'clock** vers quatre heures
(b) ‹*equal, correct*› à peu près

apricot *n* (fruit) abricot *m*

ℱ **April** *n* avril *m*

April Fools' Day *n* le premier avril

apron *n* tablier *m*

apt *adj* ‹*choice, description*› heureux/-euse; ‹*title, style*› approprié/-e (**to, for** à)

aptitude *n* aptitude *f*

aquarium *n* (*pl* **-iums, -ia**) aquarium *m*

Aquarius *n* Verseau *m*

aquarobics *n* aquagym *f*

aquatic *adj* (gen) aquatique; ‹*sport*› nautique

aqueduct *n* aqueduc *m*

Arab ① *n* (person) Arabe *mf*
② *adj* arabe

Arabic ① *n* (language) arabe *m*
② *adj* arabe; ‹*lesson, teacher*› d'arabe

Arab-Israeli *adj* israélo-arabe

arbitrary *adj* arbitraire

arbitration *n* arbitrage *m*; **to go to ~** ≈ aller aux prud'hommes.

arcade *n* arcade *f*; **shopping ~** galerie *f* marchande

arch ① *n* arche *f*
② *vtr* arquer; **to ~ one's back** ‹*person*› cambrer le dos; ‹*cat*› faire le dos rond
③ **arch(-)** *pref* par excellence; **~-enemy** ennemi/-e *m/f* juré/-e; **~-rival** grand rival

archaeologist (GB), **archeologist** (US) *n* archéologue *mf*

archaeology (GB), **archeology** (US) *n* archéologie *f*

archery *n* tir *m* à l'arc

architect *n* architecte *mf*

architecture *n* architecture *f*

archive *n* archive *f*

Arctic ① *pr n* **the ~** l'Arctique *m*
② *adj* arctique

ardent *adj* ‹*defence, opposition, lover*› passionné/-e; ‹*supporter*› fervent/-e

ℱ **area** *n* (a) (region) région *f*; (of city) zone *f*; (district) quartier *m*; **in the London ~** dans la région de Londres; **residential ~** zone *f* résidentielle
(b) (in building) **dining ~** coin *m* salle-à-manger; **no-smoking ~** zone *f* non-fumeurs; **waiting ~** salle *f* d'attente
(c) (of knowledge) domaine *m*; (of business) secteur *m*
(d) (in geometry) aire *f*; (of land) superficie *f*

area code *n* indicatif *m* de zone

arena *n* arène *f*

Argentina *pr n* Argentine *f*

ℱ **argue** ① *vtr* (debate) discuter (de), débattre (de); **to ~ that** (maintain) soutenir que
② *vi* (a) (quarrel) se disputer (**with** avec; **about, over** sur, pour)
(b) (debate) discuter (**about** de)
(c) (put one's case) argumenter (**for** en faveur de; **against** contre)

ℱ **argument** *n* (a) (quarrel) dispute *f* (**about** à propos de); **to have an ~** se disputer
(b) (discussion) débat *m*, discussion *f*
(c) (case) argument *m* (**for** en faveur de; **against** contre)

argumentative *adj* ergoteur/-euse

Aries *n* Bélier *m*

ℱ **arise** *vi* (*prét* **arose**, *pp* **arisen**) (a) ‹*problem*› survenir; ‹*question*› se poser; **if the need ~s** si le besoin se fait sentir
(b) (be the result of) résulter (**from** de)

aristocrat *n* aristocrate *mf*

arithmetic *n* arithmétique *f*

ℱ **arm** ① *n* bras *m*; (of chair) accoudoir *m*; **~ in ~** bras dessus bras dessous; **to have sth over/under one's ~** avoir qch sur/sous le bras; **to fold one's ~s** croiser les bras
② **arms** *n pl* (weapons) armes *fpl*
③ *vtr* (Mil) armer

⋯⋗

IDIOM **to keep sb at ∼'s length** tenir qn à distance

armaments *n pl* armements *mpl*

armband *n* (for swimmer) bracelet *m* de natation; (for mourner) crêpe *m* de deuil

armchair *n* fauteuil *m*

armed *adj* armé/-e (**with** de); ‹*raid, robbery*› à main armée

armed forces, armed services *n pl* forces *fpl* armées

armour (GB), **armor** (US) *n* armure *f*

armoured (GB), **armored** (US) *adj* blindé/-e

armour-plated (GB), **armor-plated** (US) *adj* ‹*vehicle*› blindé/-e; ‹*ship*› cuirassé/-e

armpit *n* aisselle *f*

arms control *n* contrôle *m* des armements

arms race *n* course *f* aux armements

arms treaty *n* traité *m* sur le contrôle des armements

ॳ **army** ① *n* armée *f*; **to join the ∼** s'engager ② *adj* militaire

aroma *n* arôme *m*

aromatherapist *n* aromathérapeute *mf*

aromatherapy *n* aromathérapie *f*

ॳ **around** ① *adv* (a) (approximately) environ, à peu près; **at ∼ 3 pm** vers 15 heures
(b) (in the vicinity) **to be (somewhere) ∼** être dans les parages; **are they ∼?** est-ce qu'ils sont là?
(c) (in circulation) **CDs have been ∼ for years** ça fait des années que les CD existent; **one of the most gifted musicians ∼** un des musiciens les plus doués du moment
(d) **all ∼** tout autour; **the only garage for miles ∼** le seul garage à des kilomètres à la ronde; **to ask sb (to come) ∼** dire à qn de passer
② *prep* (a) autour de ‹*fire, table*›; **the villages ∼ Dublin** les villages des environs de Dublin; **clothes scattered ∼ the room** des vêtements éparpillés partout dans la pièce; **(all) ∼ the world** partout dans le monde; **to walk ∼ the town** se promener dans la ville; **the people ∼ here** les gens d'ici
(b) (at) vers; **∼ midnight** vers minuit

arouse *vtr* éveiller ‹*interest, suspicion*›; exciter ‹*anger, jealousy*›; **to be ∼d** ‹*person*› être excité/-e

arrange ① *vtr* (a) disposer ‹*chairs, ornaments*›; arranger ‹*room, hair, clothes*›; arranger, disposer ‹*flowers*›
(b) (organize) organiser ‹*party, meeting, holiday*›; fixer ‹*date, appointment*›; **to ∼ to do** s'arranger pour faire
(c) convenir de ‹*loan*›
② *vi* **to ∼ for sth** prendre des dispositions pour qch; **to ∼ for sb to do** prendre des dispositions pour que qn fasse

ॳ **arrangement** *n* (a) (of objects, chairs) disposition *f*; (of flowers) composition *f*
(b) (agreement) entente *f*, accord *m*; **to come to an ∼** s'arranger
(c) (preparations) **∼s** préparatifs *mpl*; **to make ∼s to do** s'arranger pour faire

array *n* gamme *f*

arrears *n pl* arriéré *m*; **I am in ∼ with my payments** j'ai du retard dans mes paiements

ॳ **arrest** ① *n* arrestation *f*; **to be under ∼** être en état d'arrestation
② *vtr* arrêter

arrival *n* arrivée *f*; **on sb's ∼** à l'arrivée de qn

arrival(s) lounge *n* salon *m* d'arrivée

arrivals board *n* tableau *m* d'arrivée

arrival time *n* heure *f* d'arrivée

ॳ **arrive** *vi* (a) arriver (**at** à; **from** de)
(b) **to ∼ at** parvenir à ‹*decision, solution*›

arrogant *adj* arrogant/-e

arrow *n* flèche *f*

arse *n* (GB) (slang) cul

arson *n* incendie *m* criminel

arsonist *n* pyromane *mf*

ॳ **art** *n* art *m*; **I'm bad at ∼** je suis mauvais en dessin

artefact *n* objet *m* (fabriqué)

artery *n* artère *f*

art exhibition *n* (paintings) exposition *f* de tableaux; (sculpture) exposition *f* de sculpture

art gallery *n* (museum) musée *m* d'art; (commercial) galerie *f* d'art

arthritis *n* arthrite *f*

artichoke *n* artichaut *m*

ॳ **article** *n* article *m* (**about, on** sur)

artificial *adj* artificiel/-ielle

artificial limb *n* prothèse *f*, membre *m* artificiel

artificial respiration *n* respiration *f* artificielle

artillery *n* artillerie *f*

artisan *n* artisan *m*

ॳ **artist** *n* artiste *mf*

artistic *adj* ‹*talent*› artistique; ‹*temperament, person*› artiste

arts *n pl* (a) (culture) **the ∼** les arts *mpl*
(b) (Univ) lettres *fpl*
(c) **∼ and crafts** artisanat *m*

art school *n* école *f* des beaux-arts

arts student *n* étudiant/-e *m/f* en lettres

art student *n* étudiant/-e *m/f* des beaux-arts

ॳ **as** ① *conj* (a) comme; **∼ you know** comme vous le savez; **∼ usual** comme d'habitude; **do ∼ I say** fais ce que je te dis; **leave it ∼ it is** laisse-le tel quel; **∼ she was coming down the stairs** comme elle descendait l'escalier; **∼ she grew older** au fur et à mesure qu'elle vieillissait; **∼ a child, he…** (quand il était) enfant, il…

ॳ indicates a very frequent word

(b) (because, since) comme, puisque; ~ **you were out, I left a note** comme *or* puisque tu étais sorti, j'ai laissé un petit mot **(c)** (although) **strange ~ it may seem** aussi curieux que cela puisse paraître; **try ~ he might, he could not forget it** il avait beau essayer, il ne pouvait pas oublier **(d) the same...~ le/la même...que; I've got a jacket the same ~ yours** j'ai la même veste que toi **(e) so ~ to do** pour faire, afin de faire ② *prep* comme, en; **dressed ~ a sailor** habillé/-e en marin; **he works ~ a pilot** il travaille comme pilote; **a job ~ a teacher** un poste d'enseignant/-e; **to treat sb ~ an equal** traiter qn en égal ③ *adv* (in comparisons) **he is ~ intelligent ~ you** il est aussi intelligent que toi; **~ fast ~ you can** aussi vite que possible; **he's twice ~ strong ~ me** il est deux fois plus fort que moi, **I have ~ much** *or* **~ many ~ she has** j'en ai autant qu'elle; **~ much ~ possible** autant que possible; **~ little ~ possible** le moins possible; **~ soon ~ possible** dès que possible; **he has a house in Nice ~ well ~ an apartment in Paris** il a une maison à Nice ainsi qu'un appartement à Paris ④ **as for** *phr* quant à, pour ce qui est de ⑤ **as of** *phr* à partir de ⑥ **as if** *phr* comme (si); **it looks ~ if we've lost** on dirait que nous avons perdu ⑦ **as long as** *phr* du moment que (+ *indicative*), pourvu que (+ *subjunctive*) ⑧ **as such** *phr* en tant que tel

asbestos *n* amiante *m*

ASBO *n* (GB) (*abbr* = **anti-social behaviour order**) ordre *m* sur le comportement antisocial

ascend *vtr* gravir ⟨*steps, hill*⟩

ascent *n* ascension *f*

ascertain *vtr* établir (**that** que)

ash *n* **(a)** cendre *f* **(b)** (*also* ~ **tree**) frêne *m*

ashamed *adj* honteux/-euse; **to be ~** avoir honte (**of** de; **to do** de faire; **that** que (+ *subjunctive*))

ashen *adj* ⟨*complexion*⟩ terreux/-euse

ashore *adv* **to go ~** débarquer; **washed ~** rejeté/-e sur le rivage

ashtray *n* cendrier *m*

Asia *pr n* Asie *f*

Asian ① *n* (from Far East) Asiatique *mf*; (in UK) personne *f* originaire du sous-continent indien ② *adj* asiatique

aside ① *n* **to say sth in an ~** dire qch en aparté ② *adv* **to stand ~** s'écarter; **to put sth ~** (save) mettre qch de côté; (in shop) réserver qch; **to take sb ~** prendre qn à part ③ **aside from** *phr* à part

ask ① *vtr* **(a)** demander; **to ~ a question** poser une question; **to ~ sb sth** demander qch à qn; **to ~ sb to do** demander à qn de faire **(b)** (invite) inviter ⟨*person*⟩ (**to** à); **to ~ sb to dinner** inviter qn à dîner ② *vi* **(a)** (request) demander **(b)** (make enquiries) se renseigner; **to ~ about sb** s'informer au sujet de qn ③ *v refl* **to ~ oneself** se demander ■ **ask after** demander des nouvelles de ⟨*person*⟩ ■ **ask for:** ① ¶ ~ **for [sth]** demander ⟨*drink, money, help*⟩ ② ¶ ~ **for [sb]** demander à voir; (on phone) demander à parler à

askance *adv* **to look ~ at sb/sth** considérer qn/qch avec méfiance

askew *adj, adv* de travers

asking price *n* prix *m* demandé

asleep *adj* **to be ~** dormir; **to fall ~** s'endormir; **to be sound** *or* **fast ~** dormir à poings fermés

asparagus *n* asperge *f*

aspect *n* **(a)** aspect *m* **(b)** (of house) orientation *f*

asphalt *n* bitume *m*

aspic *n* aspic *m*

aspiration *n* aspiration *f* (**to** à)

aspire *vi* aspirer (**to** à; **to do** à faire)

aspirin *n* aspirine® *f*

ass *n* **(a)** (donkey) âne *m* **(b)** (colloq) (fool) idiot/-e *m/f* **(c)** (US) (slang) cul *m*

assassin *n* assassin *m*

assassinate *vtr* assassiner

assassination *n* assassinat *m*

assault ① *n* **(a)** (Law) agression *f* (**on** sur) **(b)** (Mil) assaut *m* (**on** de) ② *vtr* **(a)** (Law) agresser; **to be indecently ~ed** être victime d'une agression sexuelle **(b)** (Mil) assaillir

assemble ① *vtr* **(a)** (gather) rassembler **(b)** (construct) assembler; **easy to ~** facile à monter ② *vi* ⟨*passengers, marchers*⟩ se rassembler; ⟨*parliament, team, family*⟩ se réunir

assembly *n* **(a)** (gen) assemblée *f* **(b)** (Sch) rassemblement *m* **(c)** (of components, machines) assemblage *m*

assembly line *n* chaîne *f* de montage

assent ① *n* assentiment *m* (**to** à) ② *vi* donner son assentiment (**to** à)

assert *vtr* **(a)** (state) affirmer (**that** que); **to ~ oneself** s'affirmer **(b)** revendiquer ⟨*right, claim*⟩

assertion *n* déclaration *f* (**that** selon laquelle)

assertive *adj* assuré/-e

assess *vtr* **(a)** évaluer ⟨*person, problem*⟩; estimer ⟨*damage, value*⟩ ⋯⟩

(b) fixer ‹tax›
(c) (Sch) contrôler ‹pupil›

❡ **assessment** n (a) (evaluation) appréciation f (of de); (of damage, value) estimation f (of de)
(b) (for tax) imposition f
(c) (Sch) contrôle m

❡ **asset** n atout m; ~s (private) avoir m; (of company) actif m

assign vtr (a) assigner ‹resources› (to à)
(b) to ~ a task to sb confier une tâche à qn
(c) (attribute) attribuer (to à)
(d) (appoint) nommer (to à)

assignment n (a) (specific duty) mission f
(b) (academic) devoir m

assimilate ⒈ vtr assimiler
⒉ vi s'assimiler (into dans)

❡ **assist** ⒈ vtr (a) (help) aider; (in organization) assister (to do, in doing à faire)
(b) (facilitate) faciliter ‹development, process›
⒉ vi aider (in doing à faire); to ~ in prendre part à ‹operation, rescue›

❡ **assistance** n aide f (to à); (more formal) assistance f (to à)

assistant ⒈ n (a) (helper) assistant/-e m/f; (in hierarchy) adjoint/-e m/f
(b) (also **shop** ~) vendeur/-euse m/f
(c) (GB) (**foreign language**) ~ (in school) assistant/-e m/f; (in university) lecteur/-trice m/f
⒉ adj ‹editor, manager› adjoint/-e

❡ **associate** ⒈ n associé/-e m/f
⒉ vtr (a) associer ‹idea, memory› (with à)
(b) to be ~d with ‹person› faire partie de ‹movement, group›; être mêlé/-e à ‹shady deal›
⒊ vi to ~ with sb fréquenter qn

association n association f

assorted adj ‹objects, colours› varié/-e; ‹foodstuffs› assorti/-e

assortment n (of objects, colours) assortiment m (of de); (of people) mélange m (of de)

❡ **assume** vtr (a) (suppose) supposer (that que)
(b) prendre ‹control, identity, office›; assumer ‹responsibility›; affecter ‹expression, indifference›; **under an** ~**d name** sous un nom d'emprunt

assumption n supposition f

assurance n assurance f

assure vtr assurer; **to** ~ **sb that** assurer à qn que

asterisk n astérisque m

asthma n asthme m

asthmatic n, adj asthmatique mf

astonish vtr surprendre, étonner

astonished adj étonné/-e (by, at par; to do de faire)

astonishing adj étonnant/-e

astonishment n étonnement m

❡ indicates a very frequent word

astound vtr stupéfier

astounding adj incroyable

astray adv (a) **to go** ~ (go missing) se perdre
(b) **to lead sb** ~ (confuse) induire qn en erreur; (corrupt) détourner qn du droit chemin

astride ⒈ adv à califourchon
⒉ prep à califourchon sur

astrologer, astrologist n astrologue mf

astrology n astrologie f

astronaut n astronaute mf

astronomer n astronome mf

astronomic, astronomical adj astronomique

astronomy n astronomie f

astute adj astucieux/-ieuse

asylee n bénéficiaire mf du droit d'asile

asylum n asile m; **lunatic** ~ asile de fous

asylum-seeker n demandeur/-euse m/f d'asile

❡ **at** prep

■ **Note** at is often translated by à: at the airport = à l'aéroport; at midnight = à minuit; at the age of 50 = à l'âge de 50 ans.
— Remember that à + le always becomes au and à + les always becomes aux (au bureau, aux bureaux).
— When at means at the house, shop etc of, it is translated by chez: at Amanda's = chez Amanda; at the hairdresser's = chez le coiffeur.
— For examples and other usages, see the entry below.
— At is used with many verbs, adjectives and nouns (look at, good at, at last) etc. For translations consult the appropriate verb, adjective or noun entry.

(a) à; ~ **school** à l'école; ~ **4 o'clock** à quatre heures; ~ **Easter** à Pâques; ~ **night** la nuit; ~ **the moment** en ce moment
(b) chez; ~ **my house** chez moi; ~ **home** à la maison, chez soi

atheist n, adj athée mf

Athens pr n Athènes

athlete n athlète mf

athlete's foot n mycose f

athletic adj athlétique

athletics n (GB) athlétisme m; (US) sports mpl

Atlantic ⒈ pr n **the** ~ l'Atlantique m
⒉ adj ‹coast› atlantique

atlas n atlas m

ATM n (abbr = **automated teller machine**) guichet m automatique

atmosphere n (a) (air) atmosphère f
(b) (mood) ambiance f; (bad) atmosphère f

atom n atome m

atom bomb n bombe f atomique

atomic adj atomique, nucléaire

atrocious ⋯⋗ autograph ⋯⋯

atrocious *adj* atroce

atrocity *n* atrocité *f*

at sign *n* (Comput) arobase *m*

⋇ **attach** *vtr* attacher (**to** à)

attaché *n* attaché/-e *m/f*

attaché case *n* attaché-case *m*

attached *adj* (a) (fond) **to be** ∼ **to** être attaché/-e à

(b) *‹document›* ci-joint/-e

attachment *n* (a) (affection) attachement *m*

(b) (device) accessoire *m*

(c) (in e-mail) pièce-jointe *f*

⋇ **attack** ① *n* (a) (gen) attaque *f* (**on** contre); (criminal) agression *f* (**against, on** contre); (terrorist) attentat *m*

(b) (of illness) crise *f* (**of** de)

② *vtr* (a) (gen) attaquer; (criminally) agresser *‹victim›*

(b) s'attaquer à *‹task, problem›*

attacker *n* (gen) agresseur *m*; (Mil, Sport) attaquant/-e *m/f*

⋇ **attempt** ① *n* (a) tentative *f* (**to do** de faire); **to make an** ∼ **to do** *or* **at doing** tenter de faire

(b) **to make an** ∼ **on sb's life** attenter à la vie de qn

② *vtr* tenter (**to do** de faire); ∼**ed murder** tentative de meurtre

⋇ **attend** ① *vtr* assister à *‹ceremony, meeting›*; aller à *‹church, school›*; suivre *‹class, course›*

② *vi* être présent/-e

■ **attend to** s'occuper de *‹person, problem›*

attendance *n* présence *f* (**at** à)

attendant *n* (in cloakroom, museum, car park) gardien/-ienne *m/f*; (at petrol station) pompiste *mf*; (at pool) surveillant/-e *m/f*

attendee *n* participant/-e *m/f*

⋇ **attention** *n* (a) attention *f*; **to draw** ∼ **to sth** attirer l'attention sur qch

(b) (Mil) **to stand to** *or* **at** ∼ être au garde-à-vous; ∼! garde-à-vous!

attention deficit disorder *n* troubles *mpl* chroniques de l'attention

attentive *adj* (alert) attentif/-ive; (solicitous) attentionné/-e (**to** à)

attic *n* grenier *m*; **the toys are in the** ∼ les jouets sont au grenier

attic room *n* mansarde *f*

⋇ **attitude** *n* attitude *f* (**to, towards** (GB) à l'égard de)

attorney *n* (US) avocat *m*

⋇ **attract** *vtr* attirer

attraction *n* (a) (favourable feature) attrait *m* (**of** de; **for** pour)

(b) (entertainment, sight) attraction *f*

(c) (sexual) attirance *f* (**to** pour)

attractive *adj* *‹person, offer›* séduisant/-e; *‹child›* charmant/-e; *‹place›* attrayant/-e

attribute ① *n* attribut *m*

② *vtr* attribuer (**to** à)

aubergine *n* (GB) aubergine *f*

auburn *adj* auburn *inv*

auction ① *n* enchères *fpl*

② *vtr* (*also* ∼ **off**) vendre [qch] aux enchères

auctioneer *n* commissaire-priseur *m*

auction house *n* société *f* de commissaires-priseurs

audacity *n* audace *f*

audible *adj* audible

⋇ **audience** *n* (in cinema, concert, theatre) public *m*, salle *f*; (of radio programme) auditeurs *mpl*; (of TV programme) téléspectateurs *mpl*

audience ratings *n pl* indice *m* d'écoute

audio *adj* audio *inv*

audiobook *n* livre-cassette *m*

audiovisual, AV *adj* audiovisuel/-elle

audit ① *n* audit *m*

② *vtr* auditer, vérifier

audition ① *n* audition *f* (**for** pour)

② *vtr, vi* auditionner (**for** pour)

auditor *n* (a) commissaire *m* aux comptes

(b) (US) (student) auditeur/-trice *m/f*

auditorium *n* (*pl* **-iums** *ou* **-ia**) salle *f*

augur *vi* **to** ∼ **well** être de bon augure

⋇ **August** *n* août *m*

aunt *n* tante *f*

au pair *n* (jeune) fille *f* au pair

aura *n* (*pl* **-ras** *ou* **-rae**) (of place) atmosphère *f*; (of person) aura *f*

aural *adj* (a) (gen) auditif/-ive

(b) (Sch) *‹comprehension, test›* oral/-e

auspicious *adj* prometteur/-euse

austere *adj* austère

austerity *n* austérité *f*

Australia *pr n* Australie *f*

⋇ **Australian** ① *n* Australien/-ienne *m/f*

② *adj* australien/-ienne; *‹embassy›* d'Australie

Austria *pr n* Autriche *f*

Austrian ① *n* Autrichien/-ienne *m/f*

② *adj* autrichien/-ienne; *‹embassy›* d'Autriche

authentic *adj* authentique

⋇ **author** *n* auteur *m*

authoritarian *adj* autoritaire

authoritative *adj* (a) (forceful) autoritaire

(b) (reliable) *‹work›* qui fait autorité; *‹source›* bien informé/-e

⋇ **authority** *n* (a) autorité *f*; **the authorities** les autorités

(b) (permission) autorisation *f*

authorization *n* autorisation *f*

authorize *vtr* autoriser (**to do** à faire)

autism *n* autisme *m*

autobiographical *adj* autobiographique

autobiography *n* autobiographie *f*

Autocue® *n* prompteur *m*

autograph ① *n* autographe *m* ⋯⋗

2 *vtr* dédicacer

automatic 1 *n* (a) (washing machine) machine *f* à laver automatique
(b) (car) voiture *f* (à changement de vitesse) automatique
(c) (gun) automatique *m*
2 *adj* automatique

automatically *adv* automatiquement

automatic pilot *n* (device) pilote *m* automatique

automation *n* automatisation *f*

automobile *n* (US) automobile *f*

autonomy *n* autonomie *f*

autopsy *n* autopsie *f*

ꝏ **autumn** *n* automne *m*; in ∼ en automne

auxiliary *n, adj* auxiliaire *mf*

availability *n* (of option, service) existence *f*; **subject to** ∼ (of holidays, rooms, theatre seats) dans la limite des places disponibles

ꝏ **available** *adj* disponible (**for** pour; **to** à)

avalanche *n* avalanche *f*

avarice *n* cupidité *f*

avenge *vtr* venger

avenue *n* (a) (street, road) avenue *f*
(b) (path, driveway) allée *f*

ꝏ **average** 1 *n* moyenne *f* (**of** de); **on** (**the**) ∼ en moyenne; **above/below** (**the**) ∼ au-dessus de/au-dessous de la moyenne
2 *adj* moyen/-enne
3 *vtr* faire en moyenne

averse *adj* opposé/-e (**to** à); **to be** ∼ **to doing** répugner à faire

aversion *n* aversion *f* (**to** pour)

avert *vtr* éviter; **to** ∼ **one's eyes from sth** détourner les yeux de qch

aviary *n* volière *f*

aviation *n* aviation *f*

avid *adj* ⟨collector, reader⟩ passionné/-e; **to be** ∼ **for sth** être avide de qch

avocado *n* (*also* ∼ **pear**) avocat *m*; avocat *m*

ꝏ **avoid** *vtr* (gen) éviter; esquiver ⟨issue, question⟩; **to** ∼ **doing** éviter de faire

await *vtr* attendre

awake 1 *adj* (not yet asleep) éveillé/-e; **wide** ∼ bien réveillé/-e; **the noise kept me** ∼ le bruit m'a empêché de dormir
2 *vtr* (*prét* **awoke** *ou* **awaked** (littér), *pp* **awoken** *ou* **awaked** (littér)) réveiller ⟨person⟩
3 *vi* (*prét* **awoke** *ou* **awaked** (littér), *pp* **awoken** *ou* **awaked** (littér)) ⟨person⟩ se réveiller

ꝏ **award** 1 *n* (prize) prix *m* (**for** de)

2 *vtr* décerner ⟨prize⟩; attribuer ⟨grant⟩; accorder ⟨points, penalty⟩

award ceremony *n* cérémonie *f* de remise de prix

award-winning *adj* ⟨book, film⟩ primé/-e; ⟨writer⟩ lauréat/-e

ꝏ **aware** *adj* (conscious) conscient/-e (**of** de); (informed) au courant (**of** de)

awareness *n* conscience *f* (**of** de; **that** que)

ꝏ **away**

■ **Note** *away* often appears after a verb in English to show that an action is continuous or intense. If *away* does not change the basic meaning of the verb only the verb is translated: *he was snoring away* = il ronflait.

---

1 *adj* (Sport) ⟨goal, match, win⟩ à l'extérieur; **the** ∼ **team** les visiteurs *mpl*
2 *adv* (a) **to be** ∼ être absent/-e (**from** de); **to be** ∼ **on business** être en voyage d'affaires; **to be** ∼ **from home** ne pas être chez soi, être absent/-e de chez soi; **she's** ∼ **in Paris** elle est à Paris; **to crawl** ∼ partir en rampant; **3 km** ∼ à 3 km; **London is two hours** ∼ Londres est à deux heures d'ici; **my birthday is two months** ∼ mon anniversaire est dans deux mois
(b) (Sport) ⟨play⟩ à l'extérieur

awe *n* crainte *f* mêlée d'admiration; **to listen in** ∼ écouter impressionné/-e; **to be in** ∼ **of sb** avoir peur de qn

awe-inspiring *adj* impressionnant/-e

awful *adj* (a) affreux/-euse, atroce; (in quality) exécrable
(b) **I feel** ∼ (ill) je ne me sens pas bien du tout; (guilty) je culpabilise
(c) (colloq) **an** ∼ **lot** (**of**) énormément (de)

awfully *adv* extrêmement

awkward *adj* (a) ⟨tool⟩ peu commode; ⟨shape, design⟩ difficile
(b) (clumsy) ⟨person, gesture⟩ maladroit/-e
(c) ⟨issue, choice⟩ difficile; **at an** ∼ **time** au mauvais moment
(d) (embarrassing) ⟨question⟩ embarrassant/-e; ⟨situation⟩ délicat/-e; ⟨silence⟩ gêné/-e
(e) (uncooperative) ⟨person⟩ difficile (**about** à propos de)

awning *n* (on shop) banne *f*, auvent *m*; (on tent, house) auvent *m*; (on market stall) bâche *f*

awry 1 *adj* de travers *inv*
2 *adv* **to go** ∼ mal tourner

axe, ax (US) 1 *n* hache *f*
2 *vtr* virer (fam) ⟨employee⟩; supprimer ⟨jobs⟩; abandonner ⟨plan⟩

axis *n* (*pl* **axes**) axe *m*

axle *n* essieu *m*

Bb

b, **B** n (a) (letter) b, B m
(b) B (Mus) si m

BA n (abbr = **Bachelor of Arts**) (degree) diplôme m universitaire de lettres

babe n (colloq) super nana f (fam)

⚘ **baby** 1 n bébé m
2 adj ‹clothes, food› pour bébés; ‹brother, sister› petit/-e (before n); ~ **seal** bébé phoque

babysit vi faire du babysitting

babysitter n baby-sitter mf

babysitting n baby-sitting m

baccalaureate n European/International Baccalaureate baccalauréat m européen/international

bachelor n célibataire m

Bachelor of Arts n (person) licencié/-e m/f ès lettres

⚘ **back** 1 n (a) (of person, animal) dos m; to turn one's ~ on sb/sth tourner le dos à qn/qch; behind sb's ~ dans le dos de qn
(b) (of page, cheque, hand, envelope, coat) dos m; (of vehicle, plane, building, head) arrière m; (of chair, sofa) dossier m; (of cupboard, drawer, fridge, bus) fond m; the ones at the ~ couldn't see ceux qui étaient derrière ne pouvaient pas voir; the steps at the ~ of the building l'escalier à l'arrière de l'immeuble; at the ~ of the drawer au fond du tiroir; at the ~ of the plane/bus à l'arrière de l'avion/au fond du bus; in the ~ (of the car) à l'arrière
(c) (Sport) arrière m; left ~ arrière gauche
2 adj ‹paw, wheel› arrière; ‹bedroom› du fond; ‹page› dernier/-ière (before n); ‹garden, gate› de derrière
3 adv (a) to be ~ être de retour; I'll be ~ in five minutes je reviens dans cinq minutes; to come ~ rentrer (from de); to come ~ home rentrer chez soi
(b) to give/put sth ~ rendre/remettre qch; to phone ~ rappeler; I'll write ~ (to him) je lui répondrai
(c) ‹look, jump, lean› en arrière
(d) ~ in 1964/April en 1964/avril
(e) to travel to London and ~ faire un aller-retour à Londres
4 vtr (a) (support) soutenir ‹candidate, bill›; apporter son soutien à ‹project›; justifier ‹claim› (with à l'aide de); financer ‹venture›
(b) to ~ the car into the garage rentrer la voiture au garage en marche arrière
(c) (bet on) parier sur ‹favourite, winner›
5 **back and forth** phr to go or travel ~ and forth (commute) faire la navette (between entre); to go or walk ~ and forth faire des allées et venues (between entre); to sway ~ and forth se balancer

■ **back away** reculer; to ~ away from s'éloigner de ‹person›; chercher à éviter ‹confrontation›

■ **back down** céder

■ **back out**: 1 ¶ ~ out (a) ‹car, driver› sortir en marche arrière
(b) ‹person› se désister; to ~ out of annuler ‹deal›
2 ¶ ~ [sth] out: to ~ the car out of the garage faire sortir la voiture du garage en marche arrière

■ **back up** confirmer ‹claims, theory›; soutenir ‹person›; (Comput) sauvegarder

backache n to have ~ avoir mal au dos

backbencher n (GB Pol) député m (sans portefeuille ministériel)

backbone n colonne f vertébrale

back button n (Comput) bouton m retour

back cover n dos m

backdate vtr antidater ‹cheque, letter›

back door n (of car) portière f arrière; (of building) porte f de derrière

backdrop n toile f de fond

backer n (a) (supporter) allié/-e m/f
(b) (of project) commanditaire m; (of business) bailleur m de fonds

backfire vi (a) ‹scheme› avoir l'effet inverse; to ~ on sb se retourner contre qn
(b) ‹car› pétarader

backgammon n jaquet m

⚘ **background** 1 n (a) (of person) (social) milieu m; (family) origines fpl; (professional) formation f
(b) (of events, situation) contexte m; against a ~ of violence dans un climat de violence; to remain in the ~ rester au second plan; voices in the ~ des voix en bruit de fond
(c) (of painting, photo, scene) arrière-plan m; in the ~ à l'arrière-plan
2 adj (a) ‹information› sur les origines de la situation; ~ **reading** lectures fpl complémentaires
(b) ‹music, lighting› d'ambiance; ‹noise› de fond

backhand n (Sport) revers m

backhander n (colloq) (bribe) pot-de-vin m

backing n (a) (support) soutien m
(b) (reverse layer) revêtement m intérieur

backing singer n chanteur/-euse m/f d'accompagnement

backing vocals n pl chœurs mpl

backlash n réaction f violente (against contre)

backlog *n* retard *m*; **I've got a huge ~ (of work)** j'ai plein de travail en retard

back number *n* ancien numéro *m*

backpack ① *n* sac *m* à dos
② *vi* **to go ~ing** partir en voyage avec son sac à dos

backpacker *n* routard/-e *m/f*

back pay *n* rappel *m* de salaire

back-pedal *vi* (*p prés etc* **-ll-** (GB), **-l-** (US)) (figurative) faire marche arrière

back rest *n* dossier *m*

back seat *n* siège *m* arrière; **to take a ~** (figurative) s'effacer

backside *n* (colloq) derrière *m* (fam)

backstage *adv* dans les coulisses

backstreet ① *n* petite rue *f*
② *adj* ‹*loanshark, abortionist*› clandestin/-e

backstroke *n* dos *m* crawlé

back to back *adv* **to stand ~** ‹*two people*› se mettre dos à dos

back to front *adj, adv* à l'envers

backtrack *vi* rebrousser chemin; (figurative) faire marche arrière

backup ① *n* (gen) soutien *m*; (Mil) renforts *mpl*; (Comput) sauvegarde *f*
② *adj* ‹*copy, disk, file*› de sauvegarde

backward ① *adj* (a) ‹*look, step*› en arrière
(b) ‹*nation*› arriéré/-e
(c) ‹*person*› arriéré/-e
② *adv* (*also* **backwards**) (a) ‹*walk*› à reculons; ‹*lean, step, fall*› en arrière; **to move ~** reculer; **to walk ~ and forward** faire des allées et venues
(b) ‹*count*› à rebours; ‹*play*› à l'envers

backwards = BACKWARD 2

backwater *n* village *m* tranquille, trou *m* (fam)

backyard *n* (a) (GB) (courtyard) arrière-cour *f*
(b) (US) (back garden) jardin *m* de derrière

bacon *n* bacon *m*, ≈ lard *m*; **~ and egg(s)** des œufs au bacon

bacteria *n pl* bactéries *fpl*

✧ **bad** ① *n* **the good and the ~** le bon et le mauvais; **there is good and ~ in everyone** il y a du bon et du mauvais dans chacun
② *adj* (*comp* **worse**, *superl* **worst**) (a) (gen) mauvais/-e (*before n*) ‹*joke*› stupide; ‹*language*› grossier/-ière; **to be ~ at** être mauvais/-e en ‹*subject*›; **not ~** (colloq) pas mal (fam); **too ~!** (sympathetic) pas de chance!; (hard luck) tant pis!; **it will look ~** cela fera mauvais effet; **to feel ~** avoir mauvaise conscience (**about** à propos de)
(b) (serious) ‹*accident, injury, mistake*› grave; **a ~ cold** un gros rhume
(c) **it's ~ for you** *or* **your health** c'est mauvais pour la santé

(d) **to have a ~ back** souffrir du dos; **to have a ~ chest** être malade des poumons; **to be in a ~ way** (colloq) aller très mal
(e) ‹*fruit*› pourri/-e; **to go ~** pourrir

badge *n* (gen) badge *m*; (official) insigne *m*

badly *adv* (*comp* **worse**, *superl* **worst**)
(a) ‹*begin, behave, sleep*› mal; ‹*made, worded*› mal; **to go ~** ‹*exam, interview*› mal se passer; **to do ~** ‹*candidate, company*› obtenir de mauvais résultats; **to take sth ~** mal prendre qch
(b) ‹*suffer*› beaucoup; ‹*affect*› sérieusement; ‹*hurt, damaged*› gravement
(c) **to want/need sth ~** avoir très envie de/grand besoin de qch

badly behaved *adj* désobéissant/-e

badly off *adj* pauvre

bad-mannered *adj* ‹*person*› mal élevé/-e

badminton *n* badminton *m*

bad-tempered *adj* (temporarily) irrité/-e; (habitually) irritable

baffle *vtr* rendre [qn] perplexe, confondre

baffled *adj* perplexe (**by** devant)

✧ **bag** ① *n* sac *m* (**of** de)
② **bags** *n pl* bagages *mpl*; **to pack one's ~s** faire ses bagages; (figurative) faire ses valises
IDIOM to have ~s under one's eyes avoir des valises sous les yeux (fam)

baggage *n* bagages *mpl*

baggage allowance *n* franchise *f* de bagages

baggage reclaim *n* réception *f* des bagages

baggy *adj* large, ample

bagpipes *n* cornemuse *f*

bail *n* caution *f*; **to be (out) on ~** être libéré/-e sous caution
■ **bail out**: ① **~ out** (of plane) sauter
② **~ [sb] out** (gen) tirer [qn] d'affaire ‹*person*›; (Law) payer la caution pour ‹*person*›

bailiff *n* huissier *m*

bait *n* appât *m*

bake ① *vtr* faire cuire [qch] au four ‹*dish, vegetable*›; faire ‹*bread, cake*›
② *vi* (a) (make bread) faire du pain; (make cakes) faire de la pâtisserie
(b) (cook) ‹*food*› cuire

baked beans *n pl* haricots *mpl* blancs à la sauce tomate

baked potato *n* pomme *f* de terre en robe des champs (au four)

baker *n* boulanger/-ère *m/f*

bakery *n* boulangerie *f*

✧ **balance** ① *n* (a) équilibre *m* (**between** entre); **to lose one's ~** perdre l'équilibre; **the right ~** le juste milieu
(b) (scales) balance *f*; **to hang in the ~** être en jeu
(c) (of account) solde *m*; **to pay the ~** verser le surplus

---

✧ indicates a very frequent word

2 *vtr* **(a)** mettre [qch] en équilibre ‹*ball, plate*› **(on** sur**)**
(b) (*also* ~ **out**) (compensate for) compenser, équilibrer
(c) (counterbalance) contrebalancer ‹*weights*›
(d) (adjust) équilibrer ‹*diet, budget*›; **to** ~ **the books** dresser le bilan
3 *vi* **(a)** ‹*person*› se tenir en équilibre **(on** sur**)**; ‹*object*› tenir en équilibre **(on** sur**)**
(b) (*also* ~ **out**) s'équilibrer
(c) ‹*books, figures*› être en équilibre
4 balanced *pp adj* ‹*person, view, diet*› équilibré/-e; ‹*article, report*› objectif/-ive

balance of payments *n* balance *f* des paiements
balance of power *n* équilibre *m* des forces
balance of trade *n* balance *f* du commerce extérieur
balance sheet *n* bilan *m*
balcony *n* **(a)** (in house, hotel) balcon *m*
(b) (in theatre) deuxième balcon *m*
bald *adj* **(a)** ‹*man, head*› chauve
(b) ‹*tyre*› lisse
Bali *pr n* Bali *f*, **in** ~ à Bali
Balkan **1 Balkans** *pr n pl* **the** ~**s** les Balkans *mpl*
2 *adj* balkanique
◆ **ball** **1** *n* **(a)** (gen) balle *f*; (in football, rugby) ballon *m*; (in billiards) bille *f*
(b) (of dough, clay) boule *f* **(of** de**)**; (of wool, string) pelote *f* **(of** de**)**
(c) (dance) bal *m*
2 balls *n pl* (slang) **(a)** (testicles) couilles *fpl* (pop)
(b) (rubbish) conneries *fpl* (pop)
ballet *n* ballet *m*
ball gown *n* robe *f* de bal
balloon *n* **(a)** ballon *m*
(b) (*also* **hot air** ~) montgolfière *f*
ballot **1** *n* **(a)** scrutin *m*
(b) (*also* ~ **paper**) bulletin *m* de vote
2 *vtr* consulter [qn] (par vote) **(on** sur**)**
ballot box *n* urne *f* (électorale)
ballpark figure *n* (colloq) chiffre *m* approximatif
ballpoint (pen) *n* stylo *m* (à) bille
ballroom *n* salle *f* de danse
ballroom dancing *n* danse *f* de salon
Baltic *adj* **the** ~ **Sea** la mer *f* Baltique
ban **1** *n* interdiction *f* **(on** de**)**
2 *vtr* (*p prés etc* **-nn-**) (gen) interdire; suspendre ‹*athlete*›; **to** ~ **sb from doing** interdire à qn de faire
banal *adj* banal/-e
banana *n* banane *f*
◆ **band** *n* **(a)** (of people) groupe *m* **(of** de**)**; (of musicians) (rock) groupe (de rock); (municipal) fanfare *f*; **jazz** ~ orchestre *m* de jazz
(b) (strip) bande *f*
(c) (GB) (of age, income tax) tranche *f*

(d) (around arm) brassard *m*; **(hair)** ~ bandeau *m*
■ **band together** se réunir **(to do** pour faire**)**
bandage **1** *n* bandage *m*
2 *vtr* bander ‹*head, limb, wound*›
bandit *n* bandit *m*
bandwagon *n*
IDIOM **to jump** *or* **climb on the** ~ prendre le train en marche
bang **1** *n* **(a)** (of explosion) détonation *f*, boum *m*; (of door, window) claquement *m*
(b) (knock) coup *m*
2 *adv* ~ **in the middle** en plein centre
3 *vtr* **(a)** taper sur ‹*drum, saucepan*›; **to** ~ **sth down on the table** poser bruyamment qch sur la table; **to** ~ **one's head** se cogner la tête **(on** contre**)**; **to** ~ **one's fist on the table** taper du poing sur la table
(b) (slam) claquer ‹*door, window*›
4 *vi* ‹*door, shutter*› claquer
IDIOM ~ **goes** (colloq) **my holiday/my promotion** je peux dire adieu à mes vacances/mon avancement
■ **bang into**: ¶ ~ **into [sb/sth]** heurter
bangle *n* bracelet *m*
banish *vtr* bannir **(from** de**)**
banister, bannister (GB) *n* rampe *f* (d'escalier)
◆ **bank** **1** *n* **(a)** banque *f*
(b) (of river, lake) rive *f*; (of major river) bord *m*; (of canal) berge *f*
(c) (mound) talus *m*; (of snow) congère *f*; (of flowers) massif *m*; (of fog, mist) banc *m*
2 *vi* **to** ~ **with the National** avoir un compte (bancaire) à la Nationale
■ **bank on** compter sur ‹*person*› **(to do** pour faire**)**; **to** ~ **on doing** escompter faire
bank account *n* compte *m* bancaire
bank card *n* carte *f* bancaire
bank charges *n pl* frais *mpl* bancaires
bank clerk *n* employé/-e *m/f* de banque
banker *n* banquier/-ière *m/f*
banker's draft *n* traite *f* bancaire
banker's order *n* virement *m* bancaire
bank holiday *n* (GB) jour *m* férié; (US) jour *m* de fermeture des banques
banking *n* **(a)** (business) opérations *fpl* bancaires
(b) (profession) la banque
banking hours *n pl* heures *fpl* d'ouverture des banques
bank manager *n* directeur/-trice *m/f* d'agence bancaire
banknote *n* billet *m* de banque
bank robber *n* cambrioleur/-euse *m/f* de banque
bank robbery *n* cambriolage *m* de banque
bankroll *vtr* (colloq) financer

b

bankrupt *adj* ‹person› ruiné/-e; ‹economy› en faillite; **to go ~** faire faillite

bankruptcy *n* faillite *f*

bank statement *n* relevé *m* de compte

banner *n* banderole *f*

baptism *n* baptême *m*

baptize *vtr* baptiser

✐ **bar** ① *n* (a) (of metal, wood) barre *f*; (on cage, window) barreau *m*
(b) (pub) bar *m*; (counter) comptoir *m*
(c) **~ of soap** savonnette *f*; **~ of chocolate** tablette *f* de chocolat
(d) (Law) (profession) **the ~** le barreau
(e) (Sport) barre *f*
(f) (Mus) mesure *f*
② *prep* sauf; **all ~ one** tous sauf un seul/une seule
③ *vtr* (*p prés etc* **-rr-**) (a) barrer ‹way, path›; **to ~ sb's way** barrer le passage à qn
(b) (ban) exclure ‹person› (**from sth** de qch); **to ~ sb from doing** interdire à qn de faire

barbaric *adj* barbare

barbecue *n* barbecue *m*

barbed wire, **barbwire** (US) *n* (fil *m* de fer) barbelé *m*

barber *n* coiffeur *m* (pour hommes)

Barcelona *pr n* Barcelone *f*

bar chart *n* histogramme *m*

bar code *n* code *m* à barres

bare ① *adj* (gen) nu/-e; ‹cupboard, room› vide; **with one's ~ hands** à mains nues; **the ~ minimum** le strict nécessaire
② *vtr* **to ~ one's teeth** montrer les dents

bareback *adv* ‹ride› à cru

barefoot ① *adj* **to be ~** être nu-pieds
② *adv* ‹run, walk› pieds nus

✐ **barely** *adv* à peine

bargain ① *n* (a) (deal) marché *m* (**between** entre)
(b) (good buy) affaire *f*
② *vi* (a) (for deal) négocier (**with** avec)
(b) (over price) marchander (**with** avec)
■ **bargain for**, **bargain on** s'attendre à

bargaining ① *n* négociations *fpl*
② *adj* ‹position, power› de négociation

barge ① *n* péniche *f*; (for freight) chaland *m*
② *vi* **to ~ past sb** passer devant qn en le bousculant
■ **barge in** (enter noisily) faire irruption; (interrupt) interrompre brutalement

bark ① *n* (a) (of tree) écorce *f*
(b) (of dog) aboiement *m*
② *vi* aboyer (**at sb/sth** après qn/qch)

barley *n* orge *f*

barmaid *n* serveuse *f* de bar

barman *n* (*pl* **~men**) barman *m*

barn *n* (for crops) grange *f*; (for cattle) étable *f*

baron *n* baron *m*

barracks *n* caserne *f*

barrage *n* (gen) barrage *m*; (Mil) tir *m* de barrage

barrel *n* (a) (for beer, wine) tonneau *m*, fût *m*; (for oil) baril *m*
(b) (of gun) canon *m*

barricade *n* barricade *f*

barrier *n* barrière *f*

barrier cream *n* crème *f* protectrice

barring *prep* à moins de

barrister *n* (GB) avocat/-e *m/f*

barter *vi* (exchange) faire du troc; (haggle) marchander

✐ **base** ① *n* (gen, Mil) base *f*; (of tree, lamp) pied *m*
② *adj* ignoble
③ *vtr* fonder (**on** sur); **the film is ~d on a true story** le film est tiré d'une histoire vraie; **to be ~d in Paris** ‹person, company› être basé/-e à Paris

baseball *n* base-ball *m*

basement *n* sous-sol *m*; **in the ~** au sous-sol

bash ① *n* (colloq) (*pl* **-es**) (a) (blow) coup *m*
(b) (attempt) tentative *f*; **to have a ~ at sth**, **to give sth a ~** s'essayer à qch
(c) (party) grande fête *f*
② *vtr* cogner ‹person›; rentrer dans ‹tree, wall, kerb›
■ **bash into**: ¶ **~ into [sth]** rentrer dans

bashful *adj* timide

✐ **basic** *adj* (a) (gen) essentiel/-ielle; ‹problem, principle› fondamental/-e
(b) (elementary) ‹knowledge, skill› élémentaire; ‹wage, training› de base

✐ **basically** *adv* fondamentalement

basics *n pl* essentiel *m*; **to get down to ~** aborder l'essentiel

basil *n* basilic *m*

basin *n* (a) (bowl) bol *m*
(b) (in bathroom) lavabo *m*; (portable) cuvette *f*

✐ **basis** *n* (*pl* **-ses**) base *f* (**for**, de); **on a regular/temporary ~** régulièrement/à titre provisoire

basket *n* panier *m*

basketball *n* (game) basket(-ball) *m*; (ball) ballon *m* de basket

bass *n* basse *f*

bass drum *n* grosse caisse *f*

bass guitar *n* basse *f*

bastard *n* (slang) (a) (illegitimate child) bâtard/-e *m/f*
(b) (unpleasant man) salaud *m* (pop)

baste *vtr* (Culin) arroser

bastion *n* bastion *m*

bat ① *n* (a) (in cricket, baseball) batte *f*; (in table tennis) raquette *f*
(b) (Zool) chauve-souris *f*
② *vi* (*p prés etc* **-tt-**) (be batsman) être le batteur; (handle a bat) manier la batte

---

✐ indicates a very frequent word

batch n (of loaves) fournée f; (of goods) lot m

bated adj with ~ breath en retenant son souffle

bath ⟨1⟩ n bain m; (GB) (tub) baignoire f; **to have a** ~ prendre un bain
⟨2⟩ **baths** n pl (a) (for swimming) piscine f
(b) (in spa) thermes mpl
⟨3⟩ vtr (GB) baigner

bathe ⟨1⟩ vtr laver ‹wound› (in dans; with à)
⟨2⟩ vi (a) (swim) se baigner
(b) (US) (take bath) prendre un bain
(c) **to be** ~**d in** ruisseler de ‹sweat›; être inondé/-e de ‹light›

bather n baigneur/-euse m/f

bathing n baignade f

bathing cap n bonnet m de bain

bathing costume n costume m de bain

bath mat n tapis m de bain

bathrobe n sortie f de bain

bathroom n (a) salle f de bains
(b) (US) (lavatory) toilettes fpl

bathroom cabinet n armoire f de toilette

bathroom scales n pl pèse-personne m

bath towel n serviette f de bain

bathtub n baignoire f

baton n (GB) (policeman's) matraque f; (traffic policeman's) bâton m; (Mus) baguette f; (in relay race) témoin m

batsman n batteur m

batter ⟨1⟩ n pâte f
⟨2⟩ vtr battre

battered adj (a) ‹kettle, hat› cabossé/-e, ‹suitcase› très abîmé/-e
(b) ‹wife› battu/-e

battery n pile f; (in car) batterie f

battery charger n chargeur m de batteries

battery farming n élevage m en batterie

battery powered adj à piles

✔ **battle** ⟨1⟩ n bataille f; (figurative) lutte f
⟨2⟩ vi (gen, Mil) combattre (**with sb** contre qn); **to** ~ **for sth/to do** lutter pour qch/pour faire

battlefield n champ m de bataille

battleship n cuirassé m

bawdy adj ‹song› grivois/-e; ‹person› paillard/-e

bawl vi (weep) brailler; (shout) hurler

bay ⟨1⟩ n (a) (on coast) baie f
(b) (also ~ **tree**) (Bot) laurier(-sauce) m
(c) **loading/parking** ~ aire f de chargement/stationnement
⟨2⟩ vi ‹dog› aboyer (**at** contre, après)
IDIOM to hold sb/sth at ~ tenir qn/qch à distance

bay leaf n feuille f de laurier

bayonet n baïonnette f

BC (abbr = **Before Christ**) av. J.-C.

Bcc n (abbr = **Blind carbon copy**) copie f invisible

✔ **be**

■ **Note** for translations of there is, there are, here is and here are, see the entries THERE and HERE.

⟨1⟩ vi (p prés **being**, 3ᵉ pers sg prés **is**, prét **was**, pp **been**) (a) être; **she is French** elle est française; **we are late** nous sommes en retard; **he is a doctor/widower** il est médecin/veuf; **it is Monday** c'est lundi; **it's me!** c'est moi!; ~ **good!** sois sage!
(b) (physical and mental states) avoir; **I am cold/hot** j'ai froid/chaud; **are you hungry/thirsty?** as-tu faim/soif?; **his hands were cold** il avait froid aux mains
(c) (weather) faire; **it is cold/windy** il fait froid/du vent; **it is 40°** il fait 40°
(d) (health) aller; **how are you?** (polite) comment allez-vous?; (more informally) comment vas-tu?; (very informally) ça va?; **how is your son?** comment va votre fils?;
▶ WELL¹, FINE, BETTER
(e) (visit) **I've never been to Sweden** je ne suis jamais allé en Suède; **have you ever been to Africa?** tu es déjà allé en Afrique?; **has the postman been?** est-ce que le facteur est passé?
(f) (age) avoir; **how old are you?** quel âge as-tu?; **I am 23** j'ai 23 ans
(g) (in mathematics) faire; **2 plus 2 is 4** 2 et 2 font 4
(h) (cost) coûter; **how much is it?** combien ça coûte?
(i) (phrases) **so** ~ **it** d'accord; **if I were you** à ta place
⟨2⟩ v aux (a) (in passives) être; **the doors have been repainted** les portes ont été repeintes, on a repeint les portes; **it is said that…** on dit que…
(b) (in continuous tenses) **we are going to London tomorrow** nous allons à Londres demain; **it is raining** il pleut; **he is reading** il lit, il est en train de lire; ▶ FOR, SINCE
(c) (with infinitive) devoir; **you are to do it at once** tu dois le faire tout de suite; **they are to** ~ **married** ils vont se marier; **it was to** ~ **expected** il fallait s'y attendre; **it was nowhere to** ~ **found** il était introuvable
(d) (in tag questions) **it's a lovely house, isn't it?** c'est une très belle maison, n'est-ce pas?; **they're not in the garden, are they?** ils ne sont pas dans le jardin, par hasard?; **today is Tuesday, isn't it?** c'est bien mardi aujourd'hui?
(e) (in short answers) **'you are not going out'—'yes I am!'** 'tu ne sors pas'—'si!'; **'are you English?'—'yes, I am'** 'vous êtes anglais?'—'oui', 'oui, je suis anglais'

✔ **beach** n plage f

beach ball n ballon m de plage

beach buggy n buggy m

beacon n (a) (on runway) balise f   ⋯‥

(b) (lighthouse) phare *m*

(c) (*also* **radio** ∼) radiobalise *f*

bead *n* **(a)** perle *f*; **(string of)** ∼**s** collier *m*

(b) (of sweat, dew) goutte *f*

beak *n* bec *m*

beam ⓵ *n* **(a)** (of light, torch) rayon *m*; (of car lights, lighthouse) faisceau *m*

(b) (wooden) poutre *f*

⓶ *vtr* transmettre ⟨*signal*⟩

⓷ *vi* rayonner

bean *n* haricot *m*

beansprout *n* germe *m* de soja

✦ **bear** ⓵ *n* ours *m*

⓶ *vtr* (*prét* **bore**, *pp* **borne**) **(a)** (carry) porter; **to** ∼ **a resemblance to** ressembler à; **to** ∼ **no relation to** n'avoir aucun rapport avec; **to** ∼ **sth in mind** tenir compte de qch

(b) (endure) supporter; **I can't** ∼ **to watch** je ne veux pas voir ça

(c) (stand up to) résister à ⟨*scrutiny, inspection*⟩

(d) (yield) donner ⟨*fruit, crop*⟩; ⟨*investment*⟩ rapporter ⟨*interest*⟩

⓷ *vi* (*prét* **bore**, *pp* **borne**) **(a) to** ∼ **left/ right** ⟨*person*⟩ prendre à gauche/à droite

(b) to bring pressure to ∼ **on sb** exercer une pression sur qn

■ **bear out** confirmer ⟨*claim, story*⟩; appuyer ⟨*person*⟩

■ **bear up** ⟨*person*⟩ tenir le coup; ⟨*structure*⟩ résister

■ **bear with**: ∼ **with [sb]** être indulgent/-e avec; ∼ **with me for a minute** pardonnez-moi un instant

bearable *adj* supportable

beard *n* barbe *f*

bearded *adj* barbu/-e

bearer *n* (of news, gift, letter) porteur/-euse *m/f*; (of passport) titulaire *mf*

bearing *n* **(a)** (of person) allure *f*

(b) to have no/little ∼ **on sth** n'avoir aucun rapport/avoir peu de rapport avec qch

(c) to take a compass ∼ faire un relevé au compas

bearings *n pl* **to get one's** ∼ se repérer

beast *n* **(a)** (animal) bête *f*

(b) (colloq) (person) brute *f*

✦ **beat** ⓵ *n* **(a)** (of drum, heart) battement *m*

(b) (rhythm) rythme *m*

(c) (of policeman) ronde *f*

⓶ *vtr* (*prét* **beat**, *pp* **beaten**) **(a)** battre; **to** ∼ **sb with a stick** donner des coups de bâton à qn; **to** ∼ **sb at tennis** battre qn au tennis; **to** ∼ **time** (Mus) battre la mesure; **she beat me to it** elle a été plus rapide que moi

(b) it ∼**s walking** c'est mieux que marcher; **you can't** ∼ **Italian shoes** rien ne vaut les chaussures italiennes

⓷ *vi* (*prét* **beat**, *pp* **beaten**) ⟨*waves, rain*⟩ battre (**against** contre); ⟨*person*⟩ cogner (**at, on** à); ⟨*heart, drum, wings*⟩ battre

■ **beat back** repousser ⟨*group, flames*⟩

■ **beat down** ⟨*rain*⟩ tomber à verse (**on** sur); ⟨*sun*⟩ taper (**on** sur)

■ **beat off** repousser ⟨*attacker*⟩

■ **beat up** tabasser (fam) ⟨*person*⟩

beating *n* **(a)** (punishment) raclée *f* (fam), correction *f*

(b) (of drum, heart, wings) battement *m*

beautician *n* esthéticien/-ienne *m/f*

✦ **beautiful** *adj* beau/belle (*before n*); ⟨*weather, shot*⟩ superbe; **a** ∼ **place** un bel endroit

■ **Note** the irregular form *bel* of the adjective *beau, belle* is used before masculine nouns beginning with a vowel or a mute 'h'.

beautifully *adv* **(a)** ⟨*play, write*⟩ admirablement

(b) ⟨*furnished*⟩ magnifiquement; ∼ **dressed** habillé/-e avec beaucoup de goût

✦ **beauty** *n* beauté *f*

beauty parlour (GB), **beauty parlor** (US) *n* salon *m* de beauté

beauty queen *n* reine *f* de beauté

beauty salon *n* salon *m* de beauté

beauty spot *n* **(a)** (on skin) grain *m* de beauté; (fake) mouche *f*

(b) (place) beau site *m or* coin *m*

beaver *n* castor *m*

✦ **because** ⓵ *conj* parce que

⓶ **because of** *phr* à cause de

beckon ⓵ *vtr* faire signe à; **to** ∼ **sb in** faire signe à qn d'entrer

⓶ *vi* faire signe; **to** ∼ **to sb to do** faire signe à qn de faire

✦ **become** ⓵ *vi* (*pp* **become**) devenir; **to** ∼ **ill** tomber malade

⓶ *v impers* (*pp* **become**) **what has** ∼ **of your brother?** qu'est-ce que ton frère est devenu?

becoming *adj* ⟨*behaviour*⟩ convenable; ⟨*garment, haircut*⟩ seyant/-e

✦ **bed** *n* **(a)** lit *m*; **to go to** ∼ aller au lit

(b) (of flowers) parterre *m*

(c) (of sea) fond *m*; (of river) lit *m*

bed and breakfast, **B and B** *n* chambre *f* avec petit déjeuner, ≈ chambre *f* d'hôte

bedclothes *n pl* couvertures *fpl*

bedraggled *adj* dépenaillé/-e

bedridden *adj* alité/-e, cloué/-e au lit

bedroom *n* chambre *f* (à coucher)

bedside *n* chevet *m*

bedsit, **bedsitter** *n* (GB) chambre *f* meublée

bedspread *n* dessus *m* de lit

bedtime *n* **it's** ∼ c'est l'heure d'aller se coucher

bee *n* abeille *f*

beech *n* hêtre *m*

beef *n* bœuf *m*; **roast** ∼ rôti *m* de bœuf

beefburger *n* hamburger *m*

✦ indicates a very frequent word

beehive *n* ruche *f*

beeline *n*
IDIOM to make a ~ for se diriger tout droit vers

beep ① *n* (of electronic device) bip *m*; (of car) coup *m* de klaxon®
② *vi* ‹device› faire bip *or* bip-bip; ‹car› klaxonner

beer *n* bière *f*

bee sting *n* piqûre *f* d'abeille

beet *n* betterave *f*

beetle *n* scarabée *m*

beetroot *n* (GB) betterave *f*

ℱ **before** ① *prep* (a) avant; **the day ~ yesterday** avant-hier; **the day ~ the exam** la veille de l'examen
(b) (in front of) devant
(c) (US) (in telling time) **ten ~ six** six heures moins dix
② *adj* précédent/-e, d'avant; **the day ~** la veille; **the week ~** la semaine précédente
③ *adv* (a) (beforehand) avant; **long ~** bien avant; (previously) auparavant; **two months ~** deux mois auparavant
(b) (already) déjà; **have you been to India ~?** est-ce que tu es déjà allé en Inde?; **I've never seen him ~ in my life** c'est la première fois que je le vois; **you never told me ~** tu ne m'as jamais dit ça
④ *conj* avant de (+ *infinitive*), avant que (+ *subj*); **~ I go, I would like to say that** avant de partir, je voudrais dire que; **~ he goes, I must remind him that** avant qu'il parte, il faut que je lui rappelle que

beforehand *adv* (ahead of time) à l'avance; (earlier) auparavant, avant

befriend *vtr* (look after) prendre [qn] sous son aile; (make friends with) se lier d'amitié avec

beg ① *vtr* (*p prés etc* -**gg**-) demander (from à); **to ~ sb for sth** demander qch à qn; **I ~ your pardon** je vous demande pardon
② *vi* (*p prés etc* -**gg**-) ‹person› mendier (from à); ‹dog› faire le beau; **to ~ for help** demander de l'aide

beggar *n* mendiant/-e *m/f*

ℱ **begin** ① *vtr* (*p prés* -**nn**-, *prét* **began**, *pp* **begun**) commencer ‹journey, meeting, meal, game› (with par, avec); provoquer ‹debate, dispute›; lancer ‹campaign, trend›; déclencher ‹war›; **to ~ doing** commencer à faire
② *vi* (*p prés* -**nn**-, *prét* **began**, *pp* **begun**) commencer; **to ~ with sth** commencer par qch; **to ~ again** recommencer
③ **to begin with** *phr* (at first) au début, au départ; (firstly) d'abord, premièrement

beginner *n* débutant/-e *m/f*

ℱ **beginning** *n* début *m*, commencement *m*; **in** *or* **at the ~** au départ, au début; **to go back to the ~** reprendre au début

beginnings *n pl* (of person, business) débuts *mpl*; (of movement) origines *fpl*

behalf: (**on ~ of** (GB), **in ~ of** (US)) *phr* ‹act, speak› au nom de, pour; ‹phone, write› de la part de; ‹negotiate› pour le compte de

behave ① *vi* se comporter, se conduire (towards envers)
② *v refl* **to ~ oneself** bien se comporter; **~ yourself!** tiens-toi bien!

ℱ **behaviour** (GB), **behavior** (US) *n* (gen) comportement *m* (towards envers); (Sch) conduite *f*; **to be on one's best ~** bien se tenir

behead *vtr* décapiter

ℱ **behind** ① *n* (colloq) derrière *m* (fam)
② *adj* **to be ~ with** avoir du retard dans ‹work›; **to be too far ~** avoir trop de retard
③ *adv* ‹follow on› derrière; ‹look, glance› en arrière; **the car ~** la voiture de derrière
④ *prep* (a) derrière; **~ my back** derrière le dos; (figurative) derrière mon dos; **~ the scenes** en coulisses
(b) (supporting) **to be (solidly) ~ sb** soutenir qn (à fond)

beige *n*, *adj* beige *m*

Beijing *pr n* Pékin, Bei-jing

ℱ **being** *n* (a) (human) ~ être *m* (humain)
(b) **to come into ~** prendre naissance

Beirut *pr n* Beyrouth

Belarus *pr n* Bélarus *f*

belch ① *n* renvoi *m*, rot *m*
② *vtr* (*also* ~ **out**) vomir, cracher ‹smoke, fire›
③ *vi* avoir un renvoi

belfry *n* beffroi *m*, clocher *m*

Belgian ① *n* Belge *mf*
② *adj* belge; ‹embassy› de Belgique

Belgium *pr n* Belgique *f*

belie *vtr* démentir

ℱ **belief** *n* (a) (opinion) conviction *f* (about sur, à propos de)
(b) (confidence) confiance *f*, foi *f* (in dans)
(c) (religious faith) foi *f*

believable *adj* crédible

ℱ **believe** ① *vtr* croire; **I don't ~ you!** ce n'est pas vrai!
② *vi* **to ~ in** croire à ‹promises, ghosts›; croire en ‹God›

believer *n* (in God) croyant/-e *m/f*; (in progress, liberty) adepte *mf* (in de)

belittle *vtr* rabaisser

bell *n* (in church) cloche *f*; (handbell) clochette *f*; (on toy, cat) grelot *m*; (on bicycle) sonnette *f*; **door ~** sonnette *f*
IDIOM that name rings a ~ ce nom me dit quelque chose

belligerent ① *n* belligérant *m*
② *adj* ‹person› agressif/-ive; ‹country› belligérant/-e

bellow *vi* ‹bull› mugir (with de); ‹person› hurler

bellows n pl soufflet m

belly n ventre m

bellyache n (colloq) mal m au ventre

bellybutton n (colloq) nombril m

◊ **belong** vi to ~ to ‹property› appartenir à ‹person›; ‹person› faire partie de ‹club, society, set›; where do these books ~? où vont ces livres?

belongings n pl affaires fpl; **personal** ~ effets mpl personnels

beloved n, adj bien-aimé/-e m/f

◊ **below** [1] prep au-dessous de; ~ **freezing** au-dessous de zéro; ~ **the surface** sous la surface

[2] adv **the apartment** ~ l'appartement du dessous; **the people (in the street)** ~ les gens en bas (dans la rue); **the village** ~ le village en contrebas; **100 metres** ~ 100 mètres plus bas; **see** ~ (on page) voir ci-dessous

belt [1] n (gen) ceinture; (Tech) courroie f

[2] vtr (colloq) (hit) flanquer une beigne à (fam) ‹person›

IDIOMS **to tighten one's** ~ se serrer la ceinture; **that was below the** ~ c'était un coup bas

■ **belt out**: ~ **out** [sth], ~ [sth] **out** chanter [qch] à pleins poumons ‹song›

■ **belt up** (a) (colloq) (shut up) la fermer (fam), se taire

(b) (Aut) attacher sa ceinture de sécurité

bemused adj perplexe

bench n (a) (gen) banc m; (workbench) établi m

(b) (also **Bench**) (Law) (judges collectively) magistrature f (assise); (judges hearing a case) Cour f

benchmark [1] n (a) (gen) point m de référence

(b) (Comput) test m de performance

[2] vtr évaluer les performances de ‹computer system›

bend [1] n (in road) tournant m, virage m; (in river) courbe f

[2] vtr (prét, pp **bent**) plier ‹arm, leg›; pencher ‹head›; tordre ‹pipe, nail, wire›

[3] vi (prét, pp **bent**) (a) ‹road, path› tourner; ‹branch› ployer

(b) ‹person› se pencher; **to** ~ **forward** se pencher en avant

■ **bend down**, **bend over** se pencher

beneath [1] prep (a) sous; ~ **the calm exterior** sous des apparences calmes

(b) **it is** ~ **you to do** c'est indigne de toi de faire

[2] adv en dessous; **the apartment** ~ l'appartement en dessous

benefactor n bienfaiteur m

beneficial adj ‹effect, influence› bénéfique; ‹change› salutaire

beneficiary n bénéficiaire mf

◊ indicates a very frequent word

◊ **benefit** [1] n (a) (advantage) avantage m (**from** de)

(b) (financial aid) allocation f; **to be on** ~**(s)** (GB) toucher les allocations

[2] adj ‹concert, match› de bienfaisance

[3] vtr (p prés etc **-t-**) profiter à ‹person›; être avantageux/-euse pour ‹group, nation›

[4] vi (p prés etc **-t-**) profiter; **to** ~ **from** tirer profit de; **to** ~ **from doing** gagner à faire

IDIOM **to give sb the** ~ **of the doubt** accorder à qn le bénéfice du doute

benevolent adj bienveillant/-e

benign adj (a) ‹person, smile› bienveillant/-e

(b) (Med) bénin/-igne

bent adj (a) ‹nail, wire, stick› tordu/-e; ‹person› (stooped) courbé/-e

(b) **to be** ~ **on doing** vouloir à tout prix faire

bereaved adj endeuillé/-e, en deuil

bereavement n deuil m

berry n baie f

berserk adj **to go** ~ être pris/-e de folie furieuse

berth [1] n (a) (bunk) couchette f

(b) (at dock) mouillage m

[2] vtr faire mouiller ‹ship›

[3] vi ‹ship› venir à quai

IDIOM **to give sb/sth a wide** ~ (colloq) éviter qn/qch

beset adj **a country** ~ **by strikes** un pays en proie aux grèves

◊ **beside** prep (a) (next to) à côté de; ~ **the sea** au bord de la mer

(b) (in comparison with) par rapport à

IDIOMS **to be** ~ **oneself (with anger)** être hors de soi; **to be** ~ **oneself (with joy)** être fou/folle de joie

besides [1] adv (a) (moreover) d'ailleurs

(b) (in addition) en plus, aussi

[2] prep en plus de

besiege vtr (Mil) assiéger; (figurative) assaillir

besotted adj follement épris/-e (**with** de)

best [1] n **the** ~ le meilleur/la meilleure m/f; **the** ~ **of friends** les meilleurs amis/ meilleures amies du monde; **at** ~ au mieux; **to make the** ~ **of sth** s'accommoder de qch; **to do one's** ~ **to do** faire de son mieux or faire (tout) son possible pour faire; **all the** ~**!** (good luck) bonne chance!; (cheers) à ta santé!

[2] adj (superlative of **good**) meilleur/-e; **the** ~ **book I've ever read** le meilleur livre que j'aie jamais lu; **my** ~ **dress** ma plus belle robe

[3] adv (superlative of **well**) le mieux; ~ **of all** mieux que tout

best friend n meilleur ami/meilleure amie m/f

best man n témoin m

bestow vtr accorder ‹honour› (**on** à); conférer ‹title› (**on** à)

bestseller n bestseller m

best-selling *adj* ‹*product*› le/la plus vendu/-e; **the ~ novelist of 1999** le romancier qui s'est vendu le plus en 1999

bet 1 *n* pari *m*; (in casino) mise *f*
2 *vtr* (*p prés etc* **-tt-**, *prét*, *pp* **bet** *ou* ~**ted**) parier (on sur)
3 *vi* (*p prés etc* **-tt-**, *prét*, *pp* **bet** *ou* ~**ted**) parier (on sur); (in casino) miser

betray *vtr* trahir

betrayal *n* trahison *f*

better

━ **Note** When *better* is used as an adjective, it is translated by *meilleur* or *mieux* depending on the context (see 2 below, and note that *meilleur* is the comparative form of *bon*, *mieux* the comparative form of *bien*).

1 *n* **the ~ of the two** le meilleur/la meilleure *or* le/la mieux des deux; **so much the ~** tant mieux
2 *adj* (*comparative of* **good**) meilleur/-e; **this wine is ~** ce vin est meilleur; **to get ~** ‹*situation, weather*› s'améliorer; ‹*ill person*› aller mieux; **things are getting ~** ça va mieux; **to be ~** ‹*patient, cold*› aller mieux; **to be a ~ swimmer than sb** nager mieux que qn; **to be ~ at** être meilleur/-e en ‹*subject, sport*›; **it's ~ than nothing** c'est mieux que rien; **the bigger/sooner the ~** le plus grand/vite possible; **the less said about that the ~** mieux vaut ne pas parler de ça
3 *adv* (*comparative of* **well**) mieux; **you had ~ do, you'd ~ do** (advising) tu ferais mieux de faire; (warning) tu as intérêt à faire; **we'd ~ leave** on ferait mieux de partir
4 *vtr* améliorer
IDIOMS for ~ (**or**) **for worse** advienne que pourra; (in wedding vow) pour le meilleur et pour le pire; **to get the ~ of** triompher de ‹*opponent*›; **his curiosity got the ~ of him** sa curiosité a pris le dessus; **to go one ~** faire encore mieux (**than** que); **to think ~ of it** changer d'avis

better off *adj* (a) (more wealthy) plus riche (**than** que)
(b) (in better situation) mieux

betting *n* paris *mpl*

betting shop *n* (GB) bureau *m* de PMU

between 1 *prep* (a) entre; **~ you and me, ~ ourselves** entre nous; **~ now and next year** d'ici l'année prochaine
(b) **they drank the whole bottle ~** (**the two of**) **them** ils ont bu toute la bouteille à eux deux
2 *adv* (*also* **in ~**) (in space) au milieu, entre les deux; (in time) entre-temps; **the two main roads and the streets (in) ~** les deux rues principales et les petites rues situées entre elles; **neither red nor orange, but somewhere in ~** ni rouge ni orange mais entre les deux

beverage *n* boisson *f*, breuvage *m*

beware 1 *excl* prenez garde!, attention!
2 *vi* se méfier (**of** de); **~ of…** attention à…

bewildered *adj* ‹*person*› déconcerté/-e (**at, by** par); ‹*look*› perplexe

bewildering *adj* déconcertant/-e

bewitch *vtr* ensorceler

beyond 1 *prep* (a) (in space and time) au-delà de
(b) **~ one's means** au-dessus de ses moyens; **~ all hope** au-delà de toute espérance; **~ one's control** hors de son contrôle; **he is ~ help** on ne peut rien faire pour lui; **it's ~ me** ça me dépasse
(c) (other than) en dehors de, à part
2 *adv* au-delà
3 *conj* à part (+ *infinitive*)
IDIOM to be in the back of ~ être au bout du monde

bias 1 *n* (*pl* **-es**) (a) (prejudice) parti *m* pris
(b) (tendency) tendance *f*
2 *vtr* (*p prés etc* **-s-** *ou* **-ss-**) **to ~ sb against/in favour of** prévenir qn contre/en faveur de

biased, biassed *adj* ‹*person*› partial/-e; ‹*report*› manquant d'objectivité; **to be ~** ‹*person*› avoir des partis pris; **to be ~ against** avoir un préjugé défavorable envers

bib *n* (baby's) bavoir *m*; (of apron, dungarees) bavette *f*

Bible *n* Bible *f*

biblical *adj* biblique

bibliography *n* bibliographie *f*

bicarbonate of soda *n* bicarbonate *m* de soude

bicentenary, bicentennial *n* bicentenaire *m*

biceps *n* (*pl* ~) biceps *m*

bicker *vi* se chamailler (**about** au sujet de)

bickering *n* chamailleries *fpl*

bicycle 1 *n* bicyclette *f*, vélo *m*; **on a/by ~** à bicyclette
2 *adj* ‹*pump*› à bicyclette; ‹*bell, lamp*› de bicyclette; ‹*race*› cycliste

bicycle clip *n* pince *f* à vélo

bicycle lane *n* piste *f* cyclable

bid 1 *n* (a) (at auction) enchère *f* (**for** sur; **of** de)
(b) (for contract) soumission *f*
(c) (attempt) tentative *f* (**to do** pour faire)
2 *vtr* (*p prés* **-dd-**, *prét* **bade** *ou* **bid**, *pp* **bidden** *ou* **bid**) (a) offrir ‹*money*› (**for** pour)
(b) (say) **to ~ sb good morning** dire bonjour à qn
3 *vi* (*p prés* **-dd-**, *prét* **bade** *ou* **bid**, *pp* **bidden** *ou* **bid**) (at auction) enchérir (**for** sur); (for contract) soumissionner (**for** pour)

bidder *n* (at auction) enchérisseur/-euse *m/f*; **to go to the highest ~** être adjugé/-e au plus offrant/-e

bidding *n* (at auction) enchères *fpl*

bide *vi*
IDIOM to ~ one's time attendre le bon moment

bidet *n* bidet *m*

bifocals *n pl* verres *mpl* à double foyer

ᒯ **big** *adj* (gen) grand/-e (*before n*); (bulky, fat) gros/grosse (*before n*); ⟨meal⟩ copieux/-ieuse; **to get ~(ger)** (taller) grandir; (fatter) grossir; **a ~ book** (thick) un gros livre; (large-format) un grand livre; **his ~ brother** son grand frère, son frère aîné; **a ~ mistake** une grave erreur; **to be in ~ trouble** être dans le pétrin (fam); **to have ~ ideas, to think ~** voir grand

bigamy *n* bigamie *f*

big business *n* **(a)** les grandes entreprises *fpl*
(b) to be ~ rapporter gros

big dipper *n* (GB) (at fair) montagnes *fpl* russes

big game *n* gros gibier *m*

bigheaded *adj* (colloq) prétentieux/-ieuse

bigmouth *n* (colloq) **he's such a ~!** il ne sait pas tenir sa langue!

big name *n* (in music, art) grand nom *m*; (in film, sport) star *f*; **to be a ~** être connu/-e (**in** dans le monde de)

bigoted *adj* intolérant/-e, sectaire

bigotry *n* intolérance *f*, sectarisme *m*

big screen *n* grand écran *m*

big shot *n* (colloq) gros bonnet *m* (fam)

big toe *n* gros orteil *m*

big top *n* (tent) grand chapiteau *m*

bike *n* (cycle) vélo *m*; (motorbike) moto *f*

biker *n* (colloq) motard *m* (fam)

bikini *n* bikini® *m*

bilingual *adj* bilingue

ᒯ **bill** 1 *n* **(a)** (in restaurant) addition *f*; (for services, electricity) facture *f*; (from hotel, doctor, dentist) note *f*
(b) (Pol) projet *m* de loi
(c) (poster) affiche *f*
(d) (US) **dollar ~** billet *m* d'un dollar
(e) (beak) bec *m*
2 *vtr* **to ~ sb for sth** facturer qch à qn
IDIOM **to fit** *or* **fill the ~** faire l'affaire

billboard *n* panneau *m* d'affichage

billet *vtr* cantonner (**on, with** chez)

billiards *n* billard *m*

ᒯ **billion** *n* (a thousand million) milliard *m*; (GB) (a million million) billion *m*

billionaire *n* milliardaire *mf*

billow *vi* ⟨clouds, smoke⟩ s'élever en tourbillons
■ **billow out** ⟨skirt, sail⟩ se gonfler; ⟨steam⟩ s'élever

billy goat *n* bouc *m*

bimbo *n* (colloq) ravissante idiote *f* (derogatory)

bin *n* (GB) (for rubbish) poubelle *f*

bind *vtr* (*prét, pp* **bound**) **(a)** (tie up) attacher (**to** à)
(b) to be bound by être tenu/-e par ⟨law, oath⟩

(c) (*also* **~ together**) unir ⟨people, community⟩
(d) relier ⟨book⟩

binder *n* (for papers, lecture notes) classeur *m*

binding 1 *n* reliure *f*
2 *adj* ⟨agreement, contract⟩ qui engage

binge *n* (colloq) **to go on a ~** faire la noce

binge-drinking *n*: habitude de consommer une quantité excessive de boissons alcooliques en un temps très court

bingo *n* bingo *m*

bin liner *n* (GB) sac *m* poubelle

binoculars *n pl* jumelles *fpl*

biochemist *n* biochimiste *mf*

biochemistry *n* biochimie *f*

biodegradable *adj* biodégradable

biodiesel *n* biodiesel *m*

biodiversity *n* diversité *f* biologique

bioengineering *n* génie *m* biologique

biographical *adj* biographique

biography *n* biographie *f*

biological *adj* biologique

biological clock *n* horloge *f* biologique

biological warfare *n* guerre *f* biologique

biologist *n* biologiste *mf*

biology *n* biologie *f*

biopsy *n* biopsie *f*

biotechnology *n* biotechnologie *f*

birch *n* bouleau *m*

ᒯ **bird** *n* **(a)** (Zool) oiseau *m*
(b) (GB) (colloq) (girl) nana *f* (fam)
IDIOM **to kill two ~s with one stone** faire d'une pierre deux coups

bird flu *n* grippe *f* aviaire

bird of prey *n* oiseau *m* de proie

bird's eye view *n* vue *f* d'ensemble

birdsong *n* chant *m* des oiseaux

bird-watching *n* **to go ~** observer les oiseaux

biro® *n* (GB) (*pl* **~s**) stylo-bille *m*, bic® *m*

ᒯ **birth** *n* naissance *f* (**of** de)

birth certificate *n* certificat *m* de naissance

birth control *n* (in society) contrôle *m* des naissances; (by couple) contraception *f*

ᒯ **birthday** *n* anniversaire *m*; **Happy Birthday!** Bon *or* Joyeux Anniversaire!

birthday party *n* (for child) goûter *m* d'anniversaire; (for adult) soirée *f* d'anniversaire

birthing pool *n* piscine *f* d'accouchement

birthmark *n* tache *f* de naissance

birth mother *n* mère *f* biologique

birthplace *n* lieu *m* de naissance

birthrate *n* taux *m* de natalité

birth sign *n* signe *m* du zodiaque

ᒯ indicates a very frequent word

biscuit n (a) (GB) biscuit m, petit gâteau m
(b) (US) pain m au lait

bisexual n, adj bisexuel/-elle m/f

bishop n (a) évêque m
(b) (in chess) fou m

◆ **bit** [1] n (a) (gen) morceau m (of de); (of paper, string, land) bout m (of de); (of book, film) passage m
(b) (colloq) a ~ (of) un peu (de); a little ~ un petit peu
(c) (of horse) mors m
[2] **a bit** phr (colloq) un peu; a ~ early un peu trop tôt; she isn't a ~ like me elle ne me ressemble pas du tout
IDIOMS ~ by ~ petit à petit; ~s and pieces (fragments) morceaux mpl; (belongings) affaires fpl

bitch n (a) (dog) chienne f
(b) (colloq derogatory) garce f (fam)

bite [1] n (a) morsure f; (from insect) piqûre f
(b) (mouthful) bouchée f; to have a ~ to eat manger un morceau
[2] vtr (prét **bit**, pp **bitten**) ‹animal, person› mordre; ‹insect› piquer; to ~ one's nails se ronger les ongles
[3] vi (prét **bit**, pp **bitten**) ‹fish› mordre
■ **bite off**: ~ off [sth], ~ [sth] off arracher [qch] d'un coup de dent

biting adj (a) ‹wind› cinglant/-e
(b) ‹comment› mordant/-e

bitter adj (gen) amer/-ère; ‹wind› glacial/-e; ‹disappointment, truth› cruel/-elle
IDIOM to the ~ end jusqu'au bout

bitterly adv ‹complain, speak› amèrement; ‹regret› profondément; it's ~ cold il fait un froid terrible

bitterness n amertume f

bizarre adj bizarre

◆ **black** [1] n (a) (colour) noir m
(b) (also **Black**) (person) Noir/-e m/f
(c) to be in the ~ être créditeur/-trice
[2] adj (a) (gen) noir/-e; ‹night› obscur/-e; ‹tea› nature; to turn ~ noircir
(b) (also **Black**) ‹community, culture› noir/-e
■ **black out** ‹person› s'évanouir

black and white [1] n noir et blanc m
[2] adj ‹TV, camera film› noir et blanc inv; ‹movie, photography› (en) noir et blanc inv

blackberry n mûre f

blackbird n merle m

blackboard n tableau m (noir); on the ~ au tableau

black box n boîte f noire

blackcurrant n cassis m

blacken vtr noircir

black eye n œil m poché

blackhead n point m noir

black ice n verglas m

blacklist [1] n liste f noire
[2] vtr mettre [qn] à l'index

blackmail [1] n chantage m

[2] vtr faire chanter ‹victim›

blackmailer n maître-chanteur m

black market n on the ~ au marché noir

blackout n (a) (power cut) panne f de courant; (in wartime) black-out m
(b) (faint) étourdissement m

Black Sea pr n mer f Noire

black sheep n brebis f galeuse

blacksmith n forgeron m

black tie n (on invitation) '~' 'tenue f de soirée'

bladder n vessie f

blade n (of knife, sword, axe) lame f; (of fan, propeller, oar) pale f; (of grass) brin m

◆ **blame** [1] n responsabilité f (for de)
[2] vtr I ~ you c'est ta faute; to ~ sb for sth reprocher qch à qn; to ~ sth on sb tenir qn responsable de qch; to be to ~ for sth être responsable de qch
[3] v refl to ~ oneself for sth se sentir responsable de qch

blameless adj irréprochable

blancmange n blanc-manger m

bland adj ‹food, flavour› fade; ‹person› terne

blank [1] n (a) (empty space) blanc m; my mind's a ~ j'ai la tête vide
(b) (cartridge) cartouche f à blanc
[2] adj (a) ‹paper, page› blanc/blanche; ‹screen› vide, ‹cassette› vierge
(b) ‹expression› ébahi/-e; my mind went ~ j'ai eu un trou de mémoire
■ **blank out**: ~ [sth] out, ~ out [sth] rayer [qch] de sa mémoire

blank cheque (GB), **blank check** (US) n chèque m en blanc; (figurative) carte f blanche

blanket n (a) couverture f
(b) (of snow) couche f; (of cloud, fog) nappe f

blare
■ **blare out**: [1] ¶ ~ out ‹music, radio› jouer à plein volume
[2] ¶ ~ out [sth] déverser ‹music›

blasphemous adj ‹person› blasphémateur/-trice; ‹statement› blasphématoire

blasphemy n blasphème m

blast [1] n (a) (explosion) explosion f
(b) (of air) souffle m
(c) at full ~ ‹play music› à plein volume
[2] vtr (blow up) faire sauter; to ~ a hole in the wall percer un mur à l'explosif
■ **blast off** ‹rocket› décoller

blast-off n lancement m

blatant adj ‹lie, disregard› éhonté/-e; ‹abuse› flagrant/-e

blatantly adv ouvertement; to be ~ obvious sauter aux yeux

blaze [1] n (fire) incendie m; (in hearth) feu m, flambée f; in a ~ of publicity sous les feux des médias
[2] vtr to ~ a trail faire œuvre de pionnier ⋯›

③ *vi* (also ~ **away**) (a) ‹fire, house› brûler
(b) ‹lights› briller

blazer *n* blazer *m*

blazing *adj* (violent) ‹argument› violent/-e;
‹fire› ronflant/-e; ‹building, car› embrasé/-e

bleach ① *n* (a) (disinfectant) eau *f* de javel
(b) (for hair) décolorant *m*
② *vtr* décolorer ‹hair›; blanchir ‹linen›

bleak *adj* ‹landscape› désolé/-e; ‹weather›
maussade; ‹outlook, future› sombre

bleary *adj* ‹eyes› bouffi/-e; to be ~-eyed
avoir les yeux bouffis

bleat *vi* ‹sheep, goat› bêler

bleed ① *vtr* (prét, pp **bled**) to ~ **sb dry**
saigner qn à blanc
② *vi* (prét, pp **bled**) saigner; my finger's
~ing j'ai le doigt qui saigne

bleep ① *n* (signal) bip *m*, bip-bip *m*
② *vtr* to ~ **sb** appeler qn (au bip), biper qn

bleeper *n* (GB) bip *m*

blemish *n* (gen) imperfection *f*; (on fruit)
tache *f*; (pimple) bouton *m*

blend ① *n* mélange *m* (of de)
② *vtr* mélanger ‹ingredients, colours, styles›
③ *vi* to ~ **(together)** ‹colours, tastes, styles›
se fondre; to ~ **with** ‹colours, tastes, sounds›
se marier à; ‹smells› se mêler à
■ **blend in**: ① ¶ ~ in s'harmoniser (**with**
avec)
② ¶ ~ **[sth] in** incorporer ‹ingredient›

blender *n* mixeur *m*, mixer *m*

bless *vtr* bénir; ~ **you!** (after sneeze) à vos
souhaits!; to be ~ed with jouir de ‹health,
beauty›

blessing *n* (a) bénédiction *f*
(b) (good thing) bienfait *m*; a ~ **in disguise** un
bienfait caché

blight *n* (on society) plaie *f* (on de); urban ~
délabrement *m* urbain

blind ① *n* (a) the ~ les aveugles *mpl*
(b) (on window) store *m*
② *adj* ‹person› aveugle; to go ~ perdre la
vue; ~ **in one eye** borgne
③ *vtr* (a) ‹injury, accident› rendre aveugle
(b) ‹sun, light› éblouir
(c) ‹pride, love› aveugler
IDIOM to turn a ~ **eye** fermer les yeux (to
sur)

blind alley *n* voie *f* sans issue

blind date *n* rendez-vous *m* avec un/-e
inconnu/-e

blindfold ① *n* bandeau *m*
② *adj* (also ~**ed**) aux yeux bandés
③ *adv* les yeux bandés
④ *vtr* bander les yeux à ‹person›

blinding *adj* ‹light› aveuglant/-e; ‹headache›
atroce

blindly *adv* ‹obey, follow› aveuglément

─────────────
✍ indicates a very frequent word

blindness *n* cécité *f*; (figurative)
aveuglement *m*

blind spot *n* (a) (in eye) point *m* aveugle
(b) (in car, on hill) angle *m* mort

blink *vi* ‹person› cligner des yeux; ‹light›
clignoter

blinker *n* (a) (Aut) clignotant *m*
(b) ~s œillères *fpl*

blinkered *adj* ‹attitude, approach› borné/-e

blip *n* (on screen) spot *m*; (on graph) accident *m*
(d'une courbe)

bliss *n* bonheur *m* parfait

blissfully *adv* ~ **happy** au comble du
bonheur; ~ **ignorant** dans la plus parfaite
ignorance

blister ① *n* (on skin) ampoule *f*
② *vi* ‹skin, paint› cloquer

blister pack *n* blister *m*, habillage *m*
transparent

blithely *adv* (nonchalantly) avec insouciance;
(cheerfully) allègrement

blitz ① *n* bombardement *m* aérien
② *vtr* bombarder

blizzard *n* tempête *f* de neige; (in Arctic
regions) blizzard *m*

bloated *adj* ‹face, body› bouffi/-e; ‹stomach›
ballonné/-e

blob *n* (a) (drop) grosse goutte *f*
(b) (shape) forme *f* floue

✍ **block** ① *n* (a) (slab) bloc *m*
(b) ~ **of flats** immeuble *m* (d'habitation);
office ~ immeuble de bureaux
(c) (of houses) pâté *m* de maisons
(d) (for butcher, executioner) billot *m*
② *vtr* bloquer ‹exit, road, ball›; boucher
‹drain, hole, artery, view›; to have a ~ed
nose avoir le nez bouché
■ **block out**: ~ **out [sth]**, ~ **[sth] out** (a) (hide)
boucher ‹view›; cacher ‹light, sun›
(b) (suppress) refouler ‹memory, problem›

blockade ① *n* blocus *m*
② *vtr* bloquer, faire le blocus de ‹port›

blockage *n* obstruction *f*

blockbook *vtr* louer [qch] en groupe
‹seats›

blockbuster *n* (colloq) (a) (book) livre *m* à
succès, bestseller *m*
(b) (film) superproduction *f*

block capitals, **block letters** *n pl* in
~ (on form) en caractères *mpl* or capitales *fpl*
d'imprimerie

blog ① *n* blog *m*
② *vi* bloguer

blogger *n* blogger *m*

bloke *n* (colloq) type *m* (fam), mec *m* (fam)

blonde ① *n* blonde *f*
② *adj* blond/-e

✍ **blood** *n* sang *m*
IDIOM in cold ~ de sang-froid

blood bank *n* banque *f* du sang

bloodcurdling *adj* à vous figer le sang dans les veines

blood donor *n* donneur/-euse *m/f* de sang

blood group *n* groupe *m* sanguin

blood pressure *n* tension *f* artérielle; high ~ hypertension *f*

blood relation *n* parent/-e *m/f* par le sang

bloodshed *n* effusion *f* de sang

bloodshot *adj* injecté/-e de sang

blood sport *n* sport *m* sanguinaire

bloodstained *adj* taché/-e de sang

bloodstream *n* sang *m*

blood test *n* analyse *f* de sang

bloodthirsty *adj* sanguinaire

blood type *n* groupe *m* sanguin

bloody ⒈ *adj* (a) ‹hand, body› ensanglanté/-e; ‹battle› sanglant/-e
(b) (GB) (colloq) sacré/-e (*before n*); ~ **fool!** espèce d'idiot!
⒉ *adv* (GB) (slang) sacrément (fam)

bloom ⒈ *n* (flower) fleur *f*; in ~ en fleur
⒉ *vi* (a) (be in flower) être fleuri/-e; (come into flower) fleurir
(b) to be ~ing with health être resplendissant/-e de santé

blossom ⒈ *n* (flower) fleur *f*; (flowers) fleurs *fpl*
⒉ *vi* fleurir; (figurative) s'épanouir

blot ⒈ *n* (gen) tache *f*; (of ink) pâté *m*; (figurative) ombre *f*
⒉ *vtr* (*p prés etc* **-tt-**) (a) (dry) sécher [qch] au buvard ‹ink›
(b) (stain) tacher

■ **blot out** effacer ‹memories›; masquer ‹view›

blotch *n* (on skin) plaque *f* rouge; (of ink, colour) tache *f*

blotchy *adj* ‹complexion› marbré/-e

blotting paper *n* papier *m* buvard

blouse *n* chemisier *m*

ꞏ **blow** ⒈ *n* coup *m*
⒉ *vtr* (*prét* **blew**, *pp* **blown**) (a) the wind blew the door shut un coup de vent a fermé la porte; to be blown off course ‹ship› être dévié/-e par le vent
(b) ‹person› faire ‹bubble, smoke ring›; souffler ‹glass›; to ~ one's nose se moucher; to ~ one's whistle donner un coup de sifflet
(c) ‹explosion› faire ‹hole› (in dans); to be blown to pieces *or* bits by être réduit/-e en poussière par
(d) faire sauter ‹fuse›; griller ‹light bulb›
⒊ *vi* (*prét* **blew**, *pp* **blown**) (a) ‹wind› souffler; ‹person› souffler (into dans; on sur)
(b) to ~ in the wind ‹flag, clothes› voler au vent
(c) ‹fuse› sauter; ‹bulb› griller; ‹tyre› éclater

■ **blow away**: ⒈ ¶ ~ away s'envoler
⒉ ¶ ~ [sth] away, ~ away [sth] ‹wind› emporter ‹object›

■ **blow down** ‹wind› faire tomber ‹tree›

■ **blow off**: ⒈ ¶ ~ off ‹hat› s'envoler
⒉ ¶ ~ [sth] off ‹wind› emporter ‹hat›; ‹explosion› emporter ‹roof›

■ **blow out** souffler ‹candle›; éteindre ‹flames›

■ **blow over** ‹storm› s'apaiser; ‹affair› être oublié/-e

■ **blow up**: ⒈ ¶ ~ up ‹building› sauter; ‹bomb› exploser
⒉ ¶ ~ [sb/sth] up (a) faire sauter ‹building, person›; faire exploser ‹bomb›
(b) gonfler ‹tyre›
(c) agrandir ‹photograph›

blow-dry ⒈ *n* brushing *m*
⒉ *vtr* to ~ sb's hair faire un brushing à qn

blowout *n* (a) (electrical) court-circuit *m*
(b) (of tyre) crevaison *f*
(c) (colloq) (meal) gueuleton *m* (fam)

blowtorch *n* lampe *f* à souder

blubber ⒈ *n* (of whale) graisse *f* de baleine
⒉ *vi* (US) (cry) (colloq) pleurer comme un veau

bludgeon *vtr* to ~ sb to death tuer qn à coups de matraque

ꞏ **blue** ⒈ *n* bleu *m*
⒉ *adj* (a) bleu/-e
(b) (colloq) ‹movie› porno (fam); ‹joke› cochon/-onne (fam)
IDIOM to appear/happen out of the ~ apparaître/se passer à l'improviste

bluebell *n* jacinthe *f* des bois

blueberry *n* (US) myrtille *f*

blue cheese *n* (fromage *m*) bleu *m*

blue chip *adj* ‹company, share› de premier ordre

blue collar worker *n* ouvrier *m*, col *m* bleu

blue jeans *n pl* jean *m*

blueprint *n* bleu *m*; (figurative) projet *m* (**for** pour; **for doing** pour faire)

blues *n pl* (a) (Mus) the ~ le blues *m*
(b) (colloq) to have the ~ avoir le cafard (fam)

bluff *vtr, vi* bluffer (fam)
IDIOM to call sb's ~ prendre qn au mot

blunder ⒈ *n* bourde *f*
⒉ *vi* (a) (make mistake) faire une bourde
(b) (move clumsily) to ~ into sth se cogner à qch

blunt ⒈ *adj* (a) ‹knife, scissors› émoussé/-e; ‹pencil› mal taillé/-e; ‹instrument› contondant/-e
(b) ‹person, manner› abrupt/-e; ‹criticism› direct/-e
⒉ *vtr* émousser ‹knife›

bluntly *adv* franchement

blur ⒈ *n* image *f* floue
⒉ *vtr* (*p prés etc* **-rr-**) brouiller

blurb *n* (on book cover) texte *m* de présentation; (derogatory) baratin *m*

blurred *adj* indistinct/-e; ‹image, idea› flou/-e; ‹memory› confus/-e; to have ~ vision ⋯⋗

avoir des troubles de la vue

blurt
■ **blurt out** laisser échapper ‹truth, secret›

blush vi rougir (**at** devant; **with** de)

blusher n fard m à joues

blustery adj ~ **wind** bourrasque f

blu-tak® n patafix® m

BMI n (abbr = **body mass index**) IMC m

BO n (colloq) (abbr = **body odour**) odeur f corporelle; **he's got ~** il sent mauvais

boar n (also **wild ~**) sanglier m

♂ **board** [1] n **(a)** (plank) planche f; **bare ~s** plancher nu
(b) (committee) conseil m; **~ of directors** conseil d'administration
(c) (for chess, draughts) tableau m
(d) (in classroom) tableau m (noir)
(e) (notice board) panneau m d'affichage; (to advertise) panneau m
(f) (Comput) plaquette f
(g) (accommodation) **full ~** pension f complète; **half ~** demi-pension f; **~ and lodging** le gîte et le couvert
[2] vtr monter à bord de ‹plane, ship›; monter dans ‹bus, train›; ‹pirates› aborder ‹vessel›
[3] **on board** phr à bord
IDIOMS **above ~** légal/-e; **across the ~** à tous les niveaux
■ **board up** boucher [qch] avec des planches ‹window›; barricader [qch] avec des planches ‹house›

boarder n **(a)** (lodger) pensionnaire m
(b) (school pupil) interne mf

board game n jeu m de société (à damier)

boarding n embarquement m

boarding card n carte f d'embarquement

boarding school n école f privée avec internat

board meeting n réunion f du conseil d'administration

boardroom n salle f du conseil

boast [1] n vantardise f
[2] vtr s'enorgueillir de
[3] vi se vanter (**about** de)

boastful adj vantard/-e

♂ **boat** n (gen) bateau m; (sailing) voilier m; (rowing) barque f; (liner) paquebot m
IDIOM **to be in the same ~** (colloq) être tous/ toutes dans la même galère

boater n (hat) canotier m

boathouse n abri m à bateaux

boating [1] n navigation f de plaisance
[2] adj ‹accident, enthusiast› de bateau; ‹trip› en bateau

boatyard n chantier m de construction de bateaux

bob [1] n (haircut) coupe f au carré
[2] vi (p prés etc **-bb-**) (also **~ up and**

---

down) ‹boat, float› danser

bobsled, **bobsleigh** n bobsleigh m

bode vi **to ~ well/ill** être de bon/mauvais augure

bodily adj ‹function› physiologique; ‹fluid› organique

♂ **body** n **(a)** (of person, animal) corps m
(b) (corpse) corps m, cadavre m
(c) (of car) carrosserie f
(d) (of water) étendue f
(e) (organization) organisme m
(f) (of wine) corps m; (of hair) volume m

bodybuilder n culturiste mf

body-building n culturisme m

bodyguard n garde m du corps

body language n langage m corporel

body mass index n indice m de masse corporelle

body part n partie f de corps

body piercing n piercing m

body warmer n gilet m matelassé

bodywork n carrosserie f

bog n **(a)** (marshy ground) marais m
(b) (also **peat ~**) tourbière f
IDIOM **to get ~ged down in sth** s'enliser dans qch

boggle vi **the mind ~s!** c'est époustouflant!

bog-standard adj (colloq) ordinaire

bogus adj ‹doctor, document› faux/fausse (before n); ‹claim› bidon inv; ‹company› factice

bohemian adj ‹lifestyle› de bohème; ‹person› bohème

boil [1] n **(a)** **to bring sth to the ~** porter qch à ébullition
(b) (on skin) furoncle m
[2] vtr faire bouillir; **to ~ an egg** faire cuire un œuf
[3] vi bouillir; **the kettle is ~ing** l'eau bout (dans la bouilloire); **to make sb's blood ~** faire sortir qn de ses gonds
■ **boil down to** (figurative) se ramener à
■ **boil over** déborder

boiled egg n œuf m à la coque

boiled potatoes n pl pommes fpl de terre à l'anglaise

boiler n chaudière f

boiler suit n (GB) bleu m de travail

boiling adj ‹liquid› bouillant/-e; **it's ~!** (colloq) il fait une chaleur infernale!

boiling point n point m d'ébullition; (figurative) point m limite

boisterous adj ‹adult, game› bruyant/-e; ‹child› turbulent/-e

bold adj **(a)** (daring) ‹person› intrépide; ‹attempt, plan› audacieux/-ieuse
(b) (cheeky) ‹person› effronté/-e
(c) ‹colour› vif/vive; ‹design› voyant/-e; **~ print** caractères mpl gras

bollard n balise f

bolster [1] n traversin m

---

2 *vtr* (*also* ~ **up**) soutenir

bolt **1** *n* (a) (lock) verrou *m*
(b) ~ **of lightning** coup *m* de foudre
2 *vtr* (a) (lock) verrouiller
(b) (*also* ~ **down**) engloutir ‹*food*›
3 *vi* ‹*horse*› s'emballer; ‹*person*› détaler (fam)
4 **bolt upright** *phr* droit/-e comme un i
IDIOM a ~ **out of the blue** un coup de tonnerre

⚜ **bomb** **1** *n* bombe *f*
2 *vtr* bombarder ‹*town, house*›
bombard *vtr* bombarder (**with** de)
bomb blast *n* explosion *f*
bomb disposal unit *n* équipe *f* de déminage *m*
bomber *n* (a) (plane) bombardier *m*
(b) (terrorist) poseur/-euse *m/f* de bombes
bomber jacket *n* blouson *m* d'aviateur
bombing *n* bombardement *m*; (by terrorists) attentat *m* à la bombe
bomb scare *n* alerte *f* à la bombe
bombshell *n* obus *m*; (figurative) bombe *f*
bombsite *n* zone *f* touchée par une explosion
Bomb Squad *n* brigade *f* antiterroriste
bona fide *adj* ‹*attempt*› sincère; ‹*member*› vrai/-e (*before n*); ‹*contract*› de bonne foi
bond **1** *n* (a) (link) liens *mpl* (**of** de, **between** entre)
(b) (in finance) obligation *f*, **savings** ~ bon *m* d'épargne
2 *vtr* (stick) faire adhérer
3 *vi* ‹*person*› s'attacher (**with** à)
⚜ **bone** **1** *n* os *m*; (of fish) arête *f*
2 *vtr* désosser ‹*joint, chicken*›; enlever les arêtes de ‹*fish*›
IDIOMS ~ **of contention** sujet *m* de dispute; **to have a** ~ **to pick with sb** avoir un compte à régler avec qn
bone china *n* porcelaine *f* tendre *or* à l'os
bone dry *adj* complètement sec/sèche
bone idle *adj* flemmard/-e
bone-marrow transplant *n* greffe *f* de moelle osseuse
bonfire *n* (of rubbish) feu *m* de jardin; (for celebration) feu *m* de joie
Bonfire Night *n* (GB) la soirée du 5 novembre (*fêtée avec feux de joie et feux d'artifice*)
bonnet *n* (a) (hat) bonnet *m*
(b) (GB Aut) capot *m*
bonus *n* (a) (payment) prime *f*
(b) (advantage) avantage *m*
bony *adj* ‹*person, body*› anguleux/-euse; ‹*finger, arm*› osseux/-euse
boo **1** *n* huée *f*
2 *excl* (to give sb a fright) hou!; (to jeer) hou! hou!
3 *vtr* (3ᵉ pers sg prés **boos**, prét, pp **booed**) huer ‹*actor, speaker*›

4 *vi* (3ᵉ pers sg prés **boos**, prét, pp **booed**) pousser des huées
booby trap **1** *n* (a) mécanisme *m* piégé
(b) (practical joke) traquenard *m*
2 *vtr* (*p prés etc* **-pp-**) piéger
booing *n* huées *fpl*
⚜ **book** **1** *n* (a) livre *m* (**about** sur; **of** de); **history** ~ livre d'histoire
(b) (exercise book) cahier *m*
(c) (of cheques, tickets, stamps) carnet *m*; ~ **of matches** pochette *f* d'allumettes
2 **books** *n pl* (accounts) livres *mpl* de comptes
3 *vtr* (a) réserver ‹*table, room, taxi, ticket*›; faire les réservations pour ‹*holiday*›; **to be fully** ~**ed** être complet/-ète
(b) ‹*policeman*› dresser un procès-verbal *or* un P.V. (fam) à ‹*motorist, offender*›; (US) (arrest) arrêter ‹*suspect*›
(c) ‹*referee*› donner un carton jaune à ‹*player*›
4 *vi* réserver
IDIOMS **to be in sb's good** ~**s** être dans les petits papiers de qn (fam); **to be in sb's bad** ~**s** ne pas avoir la cote avec qn
bookcase *n* bibliothèque *f*
book club *n* club *m* du livre
booking *n* (GB) réservation *f*
booking form *n* bon *m* de réservation
booking office *n* (GB) bureau *m* de location
bookkeeping *n* comptabilité *f*
booklet *n* brochure *f*
booklist *n* liste *f* de livres
bookmaker *n* bookmaker *m*
bookmark **1** *n* (for page) marque-pages *m*, signet *m*; (Comput) signet *m*
2 *vtr* créer un signet sur ‹*website*›
bookseller *n* libraire *mf*
bookshelf *n* (*pl* **-shelves**) (single) étagère *f*; (in bookcase) rayon *m*
bookshop, **book store** (US) *n* librairie *f*
book token *n* (GB) chèque-livre *m*
bookworm *n* mordu/-e *m/f* (colloq) de la lecture
boom **1** *n* (a) (of cannon, thunder) grondement *m*; (of drum) boum *m*; (of explosion) détonation *f*; ~! badaboum!
(b) (Econ) boom *m*; (in prices, sales) explosion *f* (**in** de)
2 *vi* (a) ‹*cannon, thunder*› gronder; ‹*voice*› retentir
(b) ‹*economy*› prospérer; ‹*exports, sales*› monter en flèche; **business is** ~**ing** les affaires vont bien
boon *n* (a) (asset) aide *f* précieuse (**to** à)
(b) (stroke of luck) aubaine *f* (**for** pour)
boost **1** *n* **to give sb/sth a** ~ encourager qn/stimuler qch
2 *vtr* stimuler ‹*economy, sales*›; encourager ‹*investment*›; augmenter ‹*profit*›; **to** ~ **sb's** ···⁖

confidence redonner confiance à qn; **to ~ morale** remonter le moral

booster n (Med) vaccin m de rappel

boot n (a) botte f; (of climber, hiker) chaussure f; (for workman, soldier) brodequin m; **football ~** (GB); chaussure f de football
(b) (GB) (of car) coffre m
■ **boot up**: **~ [sth] up, ~ up [sth]** amorcer ‹computer›

booth n (in language lab) cabine f; (at fair) baraque f; **polling ~** isoloir m; **telephone ~** cabine f (téléphonique)

bootlace n lacet m (de chaussure)

booze n (colloq) bibine f (fam); (wine only) pinard m (fam)

✔ **border** 1 n (a) (frontier) frontière f; **to cross the ~** passer la frontière
(b) (edge) bord m
(c) (flower bed) plate-bande f
2 vtr (a) ‹road, land› longer ‹lake, forest›; ‹country› border ‹ocean›; avoir une frontière commune avec ‹country›
(b) (surround) border
3 adj frontalier/-ière
■ **border on**: **~ on [sth]** (a) ‹country› être limitrophe de; ‹garden, land› toucher
(b) (verge on) friser ‹rudeness, madness›

border dispute n différend m frontalier

borderline n frontière f, limite f (**between** entre); **a ~ case** un cas limite

bore 1 n (a) (person) raseur/-euse m/f (fam)
(b) (situation) **what a ~!** quelle barbe!
(c) (of gun) calibre m
2 vtr (a) ennuyer ‹person›
(b) (drill) percer ‹hole›; creuser ‹well, tunnel›

bored adj ‹expression› ennuyé/-e; **to be** or **get ~** s'ennuyer (**with** de)
IDIOM **to be ~ stiff** or **~ to tears** s'ennuyer à mourir

boredom n ennui m

boring adj ennuyeux/-euse

✔ **born** adj né/-e; **to be ~** naître; **she was ~ in May** elle est née en mai

born-again adj né/-e de nouveau

borough n arrondissement m urbain

borrow vtr emprunter (**from** à)

borrower n emprunteur/-euse m/f

borrowing n emprunt m

Bosnia pr n Bosnie f

Bosnian adj bosniaque, bosnien/-ienne; **~ Serb/Muslim** Serbe/Musulman de Bosnie

bosom n poitrine f; **in the ~ of one's family** au sein de sa famille; **~ friend** ami/-e m/f intime

✔ **boss** n (colloq) patron/-onne m/f, chef m
■ **boss about** (colloq) **boss around** (colloq) mener [qn] par le bout du nez ‹person›

bossy adj (colloq) autoritaire

✔ indicates a very frequent word

botanic(al) adj botanique; **~ gardens** jardin m botanique

botany n botanique f

botch vtr (colloq) bâcler

✔ **both** 1 det **~ sides of the road** les deux côtés de la rue; **~ children came** les enfants sont venus tous les deux; **~ her parents** ses deux parents
2 conj **~ here and abroad** ici comme à l'étranger
3 pron, quantif (of things) les deux; **let's take ~ of them** prenons les deux; **~ of you are wrong** vous avez tort tous les deux

✔ **bother** 1 n (a) (inconvenience) ennui m, embêtement m (fam); **without any ~** sans aucune difficulté
(b) (GB) (colloq) (trouble) ennuis mpl; **to be in a spot of ~** avoir des ennuis
2 vtr (a) (worry) tracasser; **don't let it ~ you** ne te tracasse pas avec ça
(b) (disturb) déranger; **I'm sorry to ~ you** je suis désolé de vous déranger
3 vi (a) (take trouble) **please don't ~** s'il te plaît, ne te dérange pas; **don't ~ doing** ce n'est pas la peine de faire
(b) (worry) **it's not worth ~ing about** ça ne vaut pas la peine qu'on s'en occupe

✔ **bottle** 1 n (gen) bouteille f; (for perfume, medicine) flacon m; (for baby) biberon m
2 vtr (a) embouteiller ‹milk, wine›
(b) (GB) mettre [qch] en conserve ‹fruit›
3 **bottled** pp adj ‹beer, gas› en bouteille; **~d water** eau f minérale
■ **bottle up** étouffer ‹anger, grief›

bottle bank n réceptacle m à verre

bottle feed vtr nourrir [qn] au biberon

bottleneck n (a) (traffic jam) embouteillage m
(b) (narrow part of road) rétrécissement m de la chaussée

bottle-opener n décapsuleur m

bottle top n capsule f (de bouteille)

✔ **bottom** 1 n (a) (of hill, steps, wall) pied m; (of page, list) bas m; (of bag, bottle, hole, river, sea, garden) fond m; (of boat) carène f; (of vase, box) dessous m; (of league) dernière place f; **at the ~ of the pile** sous le tas; **to be ~ of the class** être dernier/-ière de la classe
(b) (colloq) (buttocks) derrière m (fam)
2 adj ‹layer, shelf› du bas; ‹sheet› de dessous; ‹bunk› inférieur/-e; ‹division, half› dernier/-ière (before n)
3 (colloq) **bottoms** n pl pyjama **~s** pantalon m de pyjama; **bikini ~s** bas m de maillot de bain
IDIOM **to get to the ~ of a matter** découvrir le fin fond d'une affaire

bottom line n (decisive factor) **the ~ is that** la vérité c'est que; **that's the ~** ça c'est le vrai problème

boulder n rocher m

bounce 1 n (a) (of ball) rebond m

(b) (of mattress, material) élasticité *f*; (of hair) souplesse *f*

2 *vtr* faire rebondir ‹ball›

3 *vi* **(a)** ‹ball, object› rebondir (**off** sur; **over** au dessus de); **to ~ up and down on sth** ‹person› sauter sur qch

(b) (colloq) ‹cheque› être sans provision

■ **bounce back** (after illness) se remettre; (in career) faire un retour en force

bouncer *n* (colloq) videur *m*

bound 1 **bounds** *n pl* limites *fpl*; **to be out of ~s** être interdit/-e d'accès

2 *adj* **(a) to be ~ to do sth** aller sûrement faire qch; **it was ~ to happen** cela devait arriver

(b) (obliged) (by promise, rules, terms) tenu/-e (**by** par; **to do** de faire)

(c) ~ for ‹person, bus, train› en route pour; ‹aeroplane› à destination de

3 *vi* bondir; **to ~ into the room** entrer dans la pièce en coup de vent

boundary *n* (gen) limite *f* (**between** entre); (of sports field) limites *fpl* du terrain

bouquet *n* bouquet *m*

bourgeois *adj* bourgeois/-e

bout *n* **(a)** (of fever, malaria) accès *m*; (of insomnia) crise *f*; **drinking ~** soûlerie *f*

(b) (in boxing) combat *m*

(c) (period of activity) période *f*

boutique *n* boutique *f*

bow¹ *n* **(a)** (weapon) arc *m*

(b) (for violin) archet *m*

(c) (knot) nœud *m*

bow² 1 *n* **(a)** (movement) salut *m*; **to take a ~** saluer

(b) (of ship) avant *m*, proue *f*

2 *vtr* baisser ‹head›; courber ‹branch›; incliner ‹tree›

3 *vi* **(a)** saluer; **to ~ to sb** saluer qn

(b) to ~ to pressure céder à la pression

bowel *n* intestin *m*; **the ~s of the earth** les entrailles *fpl* de la terre

bowl 1 *n* (for food) bol *m*; (for salad) saladier *m*; (for soup) assiette *f* creuse; (for washing) cuvette *f*; (of lavatory) cuvette *f*

2 *vtr* lancer ‹ball›

3 *vi* **(a)** lancer; **to ~ to sb** lancer la balle à qn

(b) (US) (go bowling) aller au bowling

■ **bowl over (a)** (knock down) renverser ‹person›

(b) to be ~ed over (by news) être stupéfait/-e; (by beauty, generosity) être bouleversé/-e

bowlegged *adj* ‹person› aux jambes arquées

bowler *n* (in cricket) lanceur *m*

(b) (also **~ hat**) chapeau *m* melon

bowling *n* (also **tenpin ~**) bowling *m*

bowling alley *n* bowling *m*

bowling green *n* terrain *m* de boules (sur gazon)

bowls *n* jeu *m* de boules (sur gazon)

bow tie *n* nœud-papillon *m*

⚡ **box** 1 *n* **(a)** (cardboard) boîte *f*; (crate) caisse *f*; **~ of matches** boîte d'allumettes

(b) (on page, form) case *f*

(c) (in theatre) loge *f*; (in stadium) tribune *f*

(d) (also **PO Box**) boîte *f* postale

2 *vtr* **(a)** (pack) mettre [qch] en caisse

(b) to ~ sb's ears gifler qn

3 *vi* (Sport) boxer

boxer *n* **(a)** (fighter) boxeur *m*

(b) (dog) boxer *m*

boxer shorts *n pl* caleçon *m* (court)

boxing *n* boxe *f*

Boxing Day *n* (GB) lendemain *m* de Noël

box number *n* numéro *m* de boîte postale

box office *n* guichet *m*

⚡ **boy** *n* garçon *m*

boy band *n* boys band *m*

boycott 1 *n* boycottage *m* (**against, of, on** de)

2 *vtr* boycotter

boyfriend *n* (petit) copain *m* or ami *m*

bra *n* soutien-gorge *m*

brace 1 *n* **(a)** (for teeth) appareil *m* dentaire

(b) (for broken limb) attelle *f*

2 **braces** *n pl* (GB) bretelles *fpl*

3 *vtr* ‹person› arc-bouter ‹body, back› (**against** contre)

4 *v refl* **to ~ oneself** (physically) s'arc-bouter; (mentally) se préparer (**for** à; **to do** à faire)

bracelet *n* bracelet *m*

bracing *adj* vivifiant/-e, tonifiant/-e

bracken *n* fougère *f*

bracket 1 *n* **(a)** (round) parenthèse *f*; (square) crochet *m*; **in ~s** entre parenthèses *or* crochets

(b) (for shelf) équerre *f*; (for lamp) applique *f*

(c) (category) **age ~** tranche *f* d'âge

2 *vtr* **(a)** (put in brackets) (round) mettre [qch] entre parenthèses; (square) mettre [qch] entre crochets

(b) (also **~ together**) mettre [qn] dans le même groupe ‹people›

brag *vi* (*p prés etc* **-gg-**) se vanter (**to** auprès de; **about** de)

braid *n* **(a)** (of hair) tresse *f*, natte *f*

(b) (trimming) galon *m*

⚡ **brain** *n* cerveau *m*; **~s** cervelle *f*

brainchild *n* grande idée *f*

brain damage *n* lésions *fpl* cérébrales

brain dead *adj* dans un coma dépassé

brain drain *n* fuite *f* des cerveaux

brain surgery *n* neurochirurgie *f*

brain teaser *n* (colloq) casse-tête *m inv*

brainwash *vtr* faire subir un lavage de cerveau à

brainwashing n (of prisoners) lavage m de cerveau; (of public) bourrage m (fam) de crâne
brainwave n idée f géniale, illumination f
brainy adj (colloq) doué/-e
braise vtr braiser
brake ⟦1⟧ n frein m
⟦2⟧ vi freiner
brake pad n plaquette f de frein
bramble n (a) ronce f
(b) (GB) (berry) mûre f
bran n son m
⚜ **branch** n (a) (of tree) branche f; (of road, railway) embranchement m
(b) (of shop) succursale f; (of bank) agence f; (of company) filiale f
■ **branch off** bifurquer
■ **branch out** se diversifier
⚜ **brand** ⟦1⟧ n marque f
⟦2⟧ vtr (a) marquer (au fer) ⟨animal⟩
(b) to ~ sb as sth désigner qn comme qch
branded adj ⟨goods⟩ de marque inv
brandish vtr brandir
brand leader n leader m du marché
brand name n marque f déposée
brand-new adj tout neuf/toute neuve
brandy n eau-de-vie f; (cognac) cognac m
brash adj ⟨person, manner⟩ bravache
brass n (a) (metal) laiton m, cuivre m jaune
(b) (also ~ **section**) (Mus) cuivres mpl
brass band n fanfare f
brat n (colloq) marmot m (fam), môme mf (fam)
bravado n bravade f
brave ⟦1⟧ n (Indian) brave m
⟦2⟧ adj (gen) courageux/-euse; ⟨smile⟩ brave;
to put on a ~ **face** faire bonne contenance
⟦3⟧ vtr braver
bravely adv courageusement
bravery n courage m, bravoure f
brawl ⟦1⟧ n bagarre f
⟦2⟧ vi se bagarrer (**with** avec)
bray vi ⟨donkey⟩ braire; ⟨person⟩ brailler
brazen adj éhonté/-e
■ **brazen out**: ~ it out payer d'audace
Brazil pr n Brésil m
breach ⟦1⟧ n (a) (of rule) infraction f (**of** à); (of discipline, duty) manquement m (**of** à); (of copyright) violation f; **to be in** ~ **of** enfreindre ⟨law⟩; violer ⟨agreement⟩
(b) (gap) brèche f
⟦2⟧ vtr faire une brèche dans ⟨defence⟩
breach of contract n rupture f de contrat
breach of the peace n atteinte f à l'ordre public
bread n pain m
bread and butter n tartine f de pain beurré; (figurative) gagne-pain m
breadbin n (GB) boîte f or huche f à pain

breadboard n planche f à pain
breadcrumbs n pl miettes fpl de pain; (Culin) chapelure f
breadline n **to be on the** ~ être au seuil de l'indigence
bread roll n petit pain m
breadth n largeur f; (figurative) (of experience, knowledge) étendue f
breadwinner n soutien m de famille
⚜ **break** ⟦1⟧ n (a) (gap) (in wall) brèche f; (in row, line) espace m; (in circuit) rupture f
(b) (pause) (gen) pause f; (at school) récréation f; **to take a** ~ faire une pause; **the Christmas** ~ les vacances de Noël; **to have a** ~ **from work** arrêter de travailler; **a** ~ **with the past** une rupture avec le passé
(c) (also **commercial** ~) page f de publicité
(d) **a lucky** ~ un coup de veine (fam)
⟦2⟧ vtr (prét **broke**, pp **broken**) (a) (gen) casser, briser ⟨seal⟩; rompre ⟨silence, monotony, spell⟩; **to** ~ **one's leg** se casser la jambe
(b) enfreindre ⟨law⟩; **to** ~ **one's promise** manquer à sa promesse
(c) dépasser ⟨speed limit⟩; battre ⟨record⟩
(d) ⟨branches⟩ freiner ⟨fall⟩; ⟨hay⟩ amortir ⟨fall⟩
(e) débourrer ⟨horse⟩
(f) (in tennis) **to** ~ **sb's serve** faire le break
(g) **to** ~ **the news to sb** apprendre la nouvelle à qn
⟦3⟧ vi (prét **broke**, pp **broken**) (a) (gen) se casser; ⟨arm, bone, leg⟩ se fracturer; ⟨bag⟩ se déchirer; **to** ~ **in two** se casser en deux
(b) ⟨waves⟩ se briser
(c) ⟨good weather⟩ se gâter; ⟨heatwave⟩ cesser
(d) ⟨storm, scandal, story⟩ éclater
(e) **to** ~ **with sb** rompre les relations avec qn; **to** ~ **with tradition** rompre avec la tradition
(f) ⟨boy's voice⟩ muer
■ **break away** (a) se détacher (**from** de)
(b) (escape) échapper
■ **break down**: ⟦1⟧ ¶ ~ **down** (a) ⟨car, machine⟩ tomber en panne
(b) ⟨person⟩ s'effondrer, craquer (fam); **to** ~ **down in tears** fondre en larmes
⟦2⟧ ¶ ~ **[sth] down** (a) enfoncer ⟨door⟩; (figurative) faire tomber ⟨barriers⟩; vaincre ⟨resistance⟩
(b) (analyse) ventiler ⟨cost, statistics⟩; décomposer ⟨data, findings⟩ (**into** par)
■ **break even** rentrer dans ses frais
■ **break free** s'échapper
■ **break in**: ⟦1⟧ ¶ ~ **in** (a) ⟨thief⟩ entrer (par effraction); ⟨police⟩ entrer de force
(b) (interrupt) interrompre
⟦2⟧ ¶ ~ **[sth] in** débourrer ⟨horse⟩; assouplir ⟨shoe⟩
■ **break into** (a) entrer dans [qch] (par effraction) ⟨building⟩; forcer ⟨safe⟩
(b) entamer ⟨new packet, savings⟩
(c) **to** ~ **into song/into a run** se mettre à

⚜ indicates a very frequent word

chanter/courir
■ **break off**: 1 ¶ ~ off (a) ‹end› se casser; ‹handle, piece› se détacher
(b) ‹speaker› s'interrompre
2 ¶ ~ [sth] off (a) casser ‹branch, piece›
(b) rompre ‹engagement›; interrompre ‹conversation›
■ **break out** (a) ‹epidemic, fire› se déclarer; ‹fight, riot, storm› éclater; **to ~ out in a rash** avoir une éruption de boutons
(b) ‹prisoner› s'échapper **(of** de)
■ **break up** 1 ¶ ~ up (a) ‹couple› se séparer
(b) ‹crowd, cloud› se disperser; ‹meeting› se terminer
(c) (GB Sch) **schools ~ up on Friday** les cours finissent vendredi
2 ¶ ~ [sth] up démanteler ‹drugs ring›; séparer ‹couple›; désunir ‹family›; briser ‹marriage›; mettre fin à ‹demonstration›

breakaway n ‹faction, group, state› séparatiste

breakdown n (a) (of vehicle, machine) panne f
(b) (of communications, negotiations) rupture f; (of discipline, order) effondrement m
(c) **to have a (nervous) ~** faire une dépression (nerveuse)
(d) (of figures, statistics) ventilation f

breakfast n petit déjeuner m

breakfast television n télévision f à l'heure du petit déjeuner

break-in n cambriolage m

breaking point n (figurative) **to be at ~** être à bout

breakneck adj ‹pace, speed› fou/folle, insensé/-e

breakthrough n (gen) percée f; (in negotiations, investigation) progrès m

break-up n (of alliance, relationship) rupture f; (of political party, family, group) éclatement m; (of marriage) échec m

breakwater n brise-lames m inv

breast n (a) (woman's) sein m; (chest) poitrine f
(b) (Culin) (of poultry) blanc m, filet m

breast-feed vtr, vi (prét, pp **-fed**) allaiter

breast stroke n brasse f

✧ **breath** n (a) souffle m; **out of ~** à bout de souffle; **to hold one's ~** retenir sa respiration; (figurative) retenir son souffle
(b) (from mouth) haleine f; (visible) respiration f; **to have bad ~** avoir (une) mauvaise haleine
IDIOM **to take sb's ~ away** couper le souffle à qn

breathalyse (GB), **breathalyze** (US) vtr faire subir un alcootest à ‹driver›

Breathalyzer® n alcootest m

breathe 1 vtr (a) respirer ‹oxygen›
(b) souffler ‹germs› **(on** sur)
(c) **don't ~ a word!** pas un mot!
2 vi (a) ‹person, animal› respirer; **to ~**

heavily souffler fort, haleter
(b) ‹wine› s'aérer
■ **breathe in**: 1 ¶ ~ in inspirer
2 ¶ ~ [sth] in inhaler
■ **breathe out**: 1 ¶ ~ out expirer
2 ¶ ~ out, ~ [sth] out exhaler

breather n pause f; **take a ~** faire une pause

breathing n respiration f

breathing space n (a) (respite) répit m
(b) (postponement) délai m

breathless adj ‹runner› hors d'haleine; ‹asthmatic› haletant/-e

breathtaking adj ‹feat, skill› stupéfiant/-e; ‹scenery› à vous couper le souffle

breath test 1 n alcootest m
2 vtr faire subir un alcootest à ‹driver›

breed 1 n race f
2 vtr (prét, pp **bred**) élever ‹animals›; (figurative) engendrer
3 vi (prét, pp **bred**) se reproduire
4 **bred** pp adj ill-/well-~ mal/bien élevé/-e

breeder n (of animals) éleveur m

breeding n (a) (of animals) reproduction f
(b) (good manners) bonnes manières fpl

breeding ground n (figurative) foyer m **(for** de)

breeze 1 n brise f
2 vi **to ~ in/out** entrer/sortir d'un air dégagé; **to ~ through an exam** réussir un examen sans difficulté

brevity n brièveté f

brew 1 vtr brasser ‹beer›; préparer ‹tea›; **freshly ~ed coffee** du café fraîchement passé
2 vi (a) ‹beer› fermenter; ‹tea› infuser
(b) ‹storm, crisis› se préparer

brewer n brasseur m

brewery n brasserie f

bribe 1 n pot-de-vin m
2 vtr soudoyer ‹police›; suborner ‹witness›; acheter ‹servant, voter›

bribery n corruption f

bric-a-brac sale n vide-greniers m inv

brick n brique f

bricklayer n maçon m

bridal adj ‹gown› de mariée; ‹car› des mariés; ‹suite› nuptial/-e

bride n (jeune) mariée f; **the ~ and groom** les (jeunes) mariés mpl

bridegroom n jeune marié m

bridesmaid n demoiselle f d'honneur

bridge 1 n (a) pont m (**over** sur; **across** au-dessus de); (figurative) (link) rapprochement m
(b) (on ship) passerelle f
(c) (of nose) arête f; (of spectacles) arcade f
(d) (on guitar, violin) chevalet m
(e) (for teeth) bridge m
(f) (game) bridge m

⋯⊱

2 *vtr* **(a) to ∼ a gap in [sth]** combler un vide dans ‹*conversation*›; combler un trou dans ‹*budget*›
(b) (span) enjamber ‹*two eras*›

bridle **1** *n* bride *f*
2 *vtr* brider
3 *vi* se cabrer (**at** contre; **with** sous l'effet de)

bridle path *n* piste *f* cavalière

❡ **brief** **1** *n* **(a)** (GB) (remit) attributions *fpl*; (role) tâche *f*
(b) (Law) dossier *m*
2 **briefs** *n pl* slip *m*
3 *adj* bref/brève; **in ∼** en bref
4 *vtr* (inform) informer (**on** de); (instruct) donner des instructions à (**on sur**)

briefcase *n* serviette *f*; (without handle) porte-documents *m inv*

briefing *n* briefing *m* (**on** sur)

briefly *adv* **(a)** (gen) brièvement; ‹*look, pause*› un bref instant
(b) (in short) en bref

brigade *n* brigade *f*

❡ **bright** *adj* **(a)** ‹*colour*› vif/vive; ‹*garment*› aux couleurs vives; ‹*sunshine*› éclatant/-e; ‹*room, day*› clair/-e; ‹*star, eye, metal*› brillant/-e
(b) (clever) intelligent/-e; **a ∼ idea** une idée lumineuse
(c) to look on the ∼ side voir le bon côté des choses

brighten
■ **brighten up**: **1** ❡ **∼ up (a)** ‹*person*› s'égayer (**at** à); ‹*face*› s'éclairer (**at** à)
(b) ‹*weather*› s'éclaircir
2 ❡ **∼ [sth] up** égayer ‹*room, decor*›

brightly *adv* **(a)** ‹*dressed*› de couleurs vives
(b) ‹*shine, burn*› d'un vif éclat

brightness *n* **(a)** (of colour, light, smile) éclat *m*
(b) (of room) clarté *f*

bright spark *n* (GB) (colloq) petit/-e futé/-e *m/f* (fam)

brilliance *n* éclat *m*

❡ **brilliant** *adj* **(a)** ‹*student, career, success*› brillant/-e
(b) (bright) éclatant/-e
(c) (GB) (colloq) (fantastic) super (fam), génial/-e (fam); **to be ∼ at sth** être doué/-e en qch

brilliantly *adv* **(a)** (very well) brillamment
(b) (very brightly) ‹*shine*› avec éclat

brim *n* bord *m*

brine *n* **(a)** (sea water) eau *f* de mer
(b) (for pickling) saumure *f*

❡ **bring** *vtr* (*prét, pp* **brought**) **(a)** apporter ‹*present, object, message*›; amener ‹*person, animal, car*›; **to ∼ sth with one** apporter qch;

to ∼ sb/sth into the room faire entrer qn/ qch dans la pièce
(b) apporter ‹*happiness, rain, change, hope*›; **to ∼ a smile to sb's face** faire sourire qn
■ **bring about** provoquer ‹*change, disaster*›; entraîner ‹*success, defeat*›
■ **bring along** apporter ‹*object*›; amener, venir avec ‹*friend, partner*›
■ **bring back (a)** rapporter ‹*souvenir*› (**from** de); **to ∼ back memories** ranimer des souvenirs
(b) rétablir ‹*custom*›; restaurer ‹*monarchy*›
■ **bring down (a)** renverser ‹*government*›
(b) réduire ‹*inflation, expenditure*›; faire baisser ‹*price, temperature*›
(c) (shoot down) abattre
■ **bring forward** avancer ‹*date*›
■ **bring in** rapporter ‹*money, interest*›; introduire ‹*legislation, measure*›; rentrer ‹*harvest*›; faire appel à ‹*expert, army*›
■ **bring off** réussir ‹*feat*›; conclure ‹*deal*›
■ **bring on (a)** provoquer ‹*attack, migraine*›
(b) faire entrer ‹*substitute player*›
■ **bring out (a)** sortir ‹*edition, new model*›
(b) (highlight) faire ressortir ‹*flavour, meaning*›
■ **bring round (a)** (revive) faire revenir [qn] à soi
(b) (convince) convaincre
■ **bring up (a)** aborder, parler de ‹*subject*›
(b) vomir, rendre ‹*food*›
(c) élever ‹*child*›; **well brought up** bien élevé/-e

brink *n* bord *m*

brisk *adj* **(a)** (efficient) ‹*manner, tone*› vif/vive; ‹*person*› efficace
(b) (energetic) ‹*trot*› rapide; **at a ∼ pace** à vive allure
(c) ‹*business, trade*› florissant/-e; **business was ∼** les affaires marchaient bien
(d) ‹*air*› vivifiant/-e; ‹*wind*› vif/vive

bristle **1** *n* (gen) poil *m*; (on pig) soie *f*
2 *vi* **(a)** ‹*hairs*› se dresser
(b) ‹*person*› se hérisser (**at** à; **with** de)

Britain *pr n* (also **Great ∼**) Grande-Bretagne *f*

❡ **British** **1** *n pl* **the ∼** les Britanniques *mpl*
2 *adj* britannique; **the ∼ embassy** l'ambassade *f* de Grande-Bretagne

British Isles *pr n pl* îles *fpl* Britanniques

Briton *n* Britannique *mf*

Brittany *pr n* Bretagne *f*

brittle *adj* ‹*twig*› cassant/-e; ‹*nails, hair*› fragile

broach *vtr* aborder ‹*subject*›

❡ **broad** *adj* **(a)** (wide) large; **to have ∼ shoulders** être large d'épaules
(b) ‹*meaning*› large; ‹*outline*› général/-e
(c) ‹*accent*› fort/-e (*before n*); **in ∼ daylight** en plein jour

❡ indicates a very frequent word

broadband *adj* à haut débit

broad-based *adj* ‹approach, campaign› global/-e; ‹education› généralisé/-e

broad bean *n* fève *f*

broadcast [1] *n* émission *f*
[2] *vtr* (*prét, pp* ~ *ou* ~**ed**) diffuser ‹programme› (**to** à)
[3] *vi* (*prét, pp* ~ *ou* ~ed) ‹station, channel› émettre (**on** sur)

broadcaster *n* animateur/-trice *m/f*

broadcasting *n* (field) communication *f* audiovisuelle; (action) diffusion *f*; **to work in** ~ travailler dans l'audiovisuel

broaden [1] *vtr* étendre ‹appeal, scope›; élargir ‹horizons, knowledge›; **travel** ~**s the mind** les voyages ouvrent l'esprit
[2] *vi* s'élargir

broadminded *adj* ‹person› large d'esprit; ‹attitude› libéral/-e

broadsheet *n* journal *m* de grand format

brocade *n* brocart *m*

broccoli *n* (Bot) brocoli *m*; (Culin) brocolis *mpl*

brochure *n* (booklet) brochure *f*, (leaflet) dépliant *m*; (for hotel) prospectus *m*

broil *vtr* (US) faire griller ‹meat›

broke *adj* (colloq) ‹person› fauché/-e (fam)

broken *adj* (a) (gen) cassé/-e; ‹glass, window, line› brisé/-e; ‹radio, machine› détraqué/-e
(b) ‹man, woman› brisé/-e
(c) ‹French› mauvais/-e (*before n*)

broken-down *adj* ‹machine› en panne

broken-hearted *adj* **to be** ~ avoir le cœur brisé

broken home *n* famille *f* désunie

broken marriage *n* foyer *m* désuni

broker *n* courtier *m*; **insurance** ~ courtier *m* d'assurance; **real-estate** ~ (US) agent *m* immobilier

brolly *n* (GB) (colloq) parapluie *m*

bronchitis *n* bronchite *f*

bronze *n* bronze *m*

brooch *n* broche *f*

brood [1] *n* (of birds) couvée *f*; (of mammals) nichée *f*
[2] *vi* (a) (ponder) broyer du noir; **to** ~ **about** ressasser, ruminer ‹problem›
(b) ‹bird› couver

brook *n* ruisseau *m*

broom *n* balai *m*

broth *n* bouillon *m*

brothel *n* maison *f* close

↗ **brother** *n* frère *m*

brother-in-law *n* beau-frère *m*

brotherly *adj* fraternel/-elle

brow *n* (a) (forehead) front *m*; (eyebrow) sourcil *m*

(b) (of hill) sommet *m*

↗ **brown** [1] *n* (of object) marron *m*; (of hair, skin, eyes) brun *m*
[2] *adj* (a) ‹shoes, leaves, paint, eyes› marron *inv*; ‹hair› châtain *inv*; **light/dark** ~ marron clair/foncé
(b) (tanned) bronzé/-e; **to go** ~ bronzer
[3] *vtr* faire roussir ‹sauce›; faire dorer ‹meat, onions›
[4] *vi* ‹meat, potatoes› dorer

brown bread *n* pain *m* complet

brown envelope *n* enveloppe *f* kraft

Brownie *n* jeannette *f*

brown paper *n* papier *m* kraft

brown rice *n* riz *m* complet

brown sugar *n* sucre *m* brun, cassonade *f*

browse *vi* (a) (in shop) regarder
(b) (graze) brouter

■ **browse through** feuilleter ‹book›

browser *n* navigateur *m*

bruise [1] *n* (on skin) bleu *m*, ecchymose *f* (**on** sur); (on fruit) tache *f* (**on** sur)
[2] *vtr* meurtrir ‹person›; taler, abîmer ‹fruit›; **to** ~ **one's arm** se faire un bleu sur le bras

brunette *n* brune *f*

brunt *n* **to bear the** ~ **of** être le plus touché/ la plus touchée par ‹disaster›; subir tout le poids de ‹anger›

brush [1] *n* (a) (for hair, clothes, shoes) brosse *f*; (small, for sweeping up) balayette *f*; (broom) balai *m*; (for paint) pinceau *m*
(b) **to have a** ~ **with death** frôler la mort; **to have a** ~ **with the law** avoir des démêlés avec la justice
[2] *vtr* brosser ‹carpet, clothes›; **to** ~ **one's hair/teeth** se brosser les cheveux/les dents
[3] *vi* **to** ~ **against** frôler; **to** ~ **past sb** frôler qn en passant

■ **brush aside** repousser ‹criticism, person›

■ **brush up (on)** se remettre à ‹subject›

brushwood *n* (firewood) brindilles *fpl*; (brush) broussailles *fpl*

brusque *adj* brusque (**with** avec)

Brussels *pr n* Bruxelles

Brussels sprout *n* chou *m* de Bruxelles

brutal *adj* brutal/-e

brutality *n* brutalité *f* (**of** de)

brute [1] *n* (a) (man) brute *f*
(b) (animal) bête *f*
[2] *adj* ‹strength› simple (*before n*); **by** ~ **force** par la force

BSc *n* (GB Univ) (*abbr* = **Bachelor of Science**) diplôme *m* universitaire en sciences

BSE *n* (*abbr* = **Bovine Spongiform Encephalopathy**) ESB *f*, encéphalopathie *f* spongiforme bovine

b

bubble ⓵ *n* bulle *f* (in dans); **to blow ∼s**
faire des bulles
⓶ *vi* ⟨*fizzy drink*⟩ pétiller; ⟨*boiling liquid*⟩
bouillonner; **to ∼ (over) with** déborder de
⟨*enthusiasm, ideas*⟩
bubble bath *n* bain *m* moussant
bubblewrap *n* bulle-pack® *m*
buck ⓵ *n* (a) (US) (colloq) dollar *m*
(b) (male animal) mâle *m*
⓶ *vi* ⟨*horse*⟩ ruer
IDIOM to pass the ∼ refiler (fam) la responsabilité à quelqu'un d'autre
bucket *n* seau *m* (of de)
buckle ⓵ *n* boucle *f*
⓶ *vtr* (a) attacher, boucler ⟨*belt, shoe*⟩
(b) (damage) gondoler
⓷ *vi* (a) ⟨*metal, surface*⟩ se gondoler; ⟨*wheel*⟩
se voiler
(b) ⟨*belt, shoe*⟩ s'attacher, se boucler
(c) ⟨*knees, legs*⟩ céder
bud ⓵ *n* (of leaf) bourgeon *m*; (of flower)
bouton *m*
⓶ *vi* (*p prés etc* **-dd-**) (a) (develop leaf buds)
bourgeonner; (develop flower buds) boutonner
(b) ⟨*flower, breast*⟩ pointer
Buddha *pr n* Bouddha *m*
Buddhism *n* bouddhisme *m*
Buddhist *n, adj* bouddhiste *mf*
budding *adj* ⟨*athlete, champion*⟩ en herbe;
⟨*talent, career, romance*⟩ naissant/-e
buddy *n* (colloq) copain *m*, pote *m* (fam)
budge ⓵ *vtr* (a) (move) bouger
(b) (persuade) faire changer d'avis à
⓶ *vi* (a) (move) bouger (**from, off** de)
(b) (give way) changer d'avis (**on** sur)
■ **budge over** (colloq), **budge up** (colloq)
se pousser
budgerigar *n* perruche *f*
☞ **budget** ⓵ *n* budget *m* (**for** pour)
⓶ *vi* **to ∼ for** budgétiser ses dépenses en
fonction de ⟨*increase, needs*⟩
buff *n* (a) (colloq) (enthusiast) mordu/-e *m/f*
(b) (colour) chamois *m*
buffalo *n* (*pl* **-oes** *or collect* **∼**) (GB) buffle
m; (US) bison *m*
buffer *n* tampon *m*
buffet¹ *n* buffet *m*
buffet² *vtr* ⟨*wind*⟩ ballotter ⟨*ship*⟩; battre
⟨*coast*⟩
buffoon *n* bouffon/-onne *m/f*
bug ⓵ *n* (a) (colloq) (insect) (gen) bestiole *f*;
(bedbug) punaise *f*
(b) (*also* **stomach ∼**) (colloq) ennuis *mpl*
gastriques
(c) (germ) microbe *m*
(d) (fault) (gen) défaut *m*; (Comput) bogue *f or*
m, bug *m*
(e) (hidden microphone) micro *m* caché
⓶ *vtr* (*p prés etc* **-gg-**) (a) poser des micros

dans ⟨*room, building*⟩; **the room is ∼ged** il y
a un micro (caché) dans la pièce
(b) (colloq) (annoy) embêter ⟨*person*⟩
buggy *n* (a) (GB) (pushchair) poussette *f*
(b) (US) (pram) landau *m*
(c) (carriage) boghei *m*
bugle *n* clairon *m*
☞ **build** ⓵ *n* (of person) carrure *f*
⓶ *vtr* (*prét, pp* **built**) (gen) construire;
édifier ⟨*church, monument*⟩; bâtir ⟨*career,*
future⟩; fonder ⟨*empire*⟩; créer ⟨*software,*
interface⟩; **to be well built** ⟨*person*⟩ être bien
bâti/-e
⓷ *vi* (*prét, pp* **built**) construire; **to ∼ on**
tirer parti de ⟨*popularity, success*⟩
■ **build up:** ⓵ ¶ **∼ up** ⟨*gas, deposits*⟩
s'accumuler; ⟨*traffic*⟩ s'intensifier; ⟨*business,*
trade⟩ se développer; ⟨*tension, excitement*⟩
monter
⓶ ¶ **∼ [sth] up** accumuler ⟨*wealth*⟩;
établir ⟨*trust*⟩; constituer ⟨*collection*⟩; créer
⟨*business*⟩; établir ⟨*picture, profile*⟩; se faire
⟨*reputation*⟩; affermir ⟨*muscles*⟩; **to ∼ oneself**
up, to ∼ up one's strength prendre des forces
builder *n* (contractor) entrepreneur *m* en
bâtiment; (worker) ouvrier/-ière *m/f* du
bâtiment
☞ **building** *n* (gen) bâtiment *m*; (with offices,
apartments) immeuble *m*; (palace, church)
édifice *m*
building contractor *n* entrepreneur *m*
en bâtiment
building site *n* chantier *m* (de
construction)
building society *n* (GB) société *f*
d'investissement et de crédit immobilier
build-up *n* (a) (in traffic, pressure)
intensification *f* (of de); (in weapons,
stocks) accumulation *f* (of de); (in tension)
accroissement *m* (of de)
(b) (publicity) **the ∼ to sth** les préparatifs de qch
built-in *adj* ⟨*wardrobe*⟩ encastré/-e;
(figurative) intégré/-e
built-up *adj* ⟨*region*⟩ urbanisé/-e; **∼ area**
agglomération *f*
bulb *n* (a) (electric) ampoule *f* (électrique)
(b) (of plant) bulbe *m*
Bulgaria *pr n* Bulgarie *f*
Bulgarian ⓵ *n* (a) (person) Bulgare *mf*
(b) (language) bulgare *m*
⓶ *adj* bulgare
bulge ⓵ *n* (in clothing, carpet) bosse *f*; (in pipe,
tube) renflement *m*; (in tyre) hernie *f*; (in wall)
bombement *m*; (in cheek) gonflement *m*
⓶ *vi* ⟨*bag, pocket, cheeks*⟩ être gonflé/-e;
⟨*wallet*⟩ être bourré/-e; ⟨*surface*⟩ se
boursoufler; ⟨*stomach*⟩ ballonner; **his eyes**
were bulging les yeux lui sortaient de la tête
bulimia (nervosa) *n* boulimie *f*
bulimic *n, adj* boulimique *mf*
bulk *n* (a) (of package, correspondence) volume
m; (of building, vehicle) masse *f*; **the ∼ of** la

☞ indicates a very frequent word

majeure partie de
(b) in ~ ‹buy, sell› en gros; ‹transport› en vrac

bulk-buying n achat m en gros

bulky adj ‹person› corpulent/-e; ‹package› volumineux/-euse; ‹book› épais/-aisse

bull n (ox) taureau m; (elephant, whale) mâle m

bull bar n pare-buffle(s) m

bulldog n bouledogue m

bulldozer n bulldozer m, bouteur m

bullet n balle f

bulletin n bulletin m; **news** ~ bulletin d'informations

bulletin board n (gen) tableau m d'affichage; (Comput) messagerie f électronique

bulletproof adj ‹glass, vehicle, door› blindé/-e

bulletproof vest n gilet m pare-balles inv

bullfight n corrida f

bullfighter n torero m

bullfighting n (gen) corridas fpl; (art) tauromachie f

bullion n lingots mpl

bullock n bœuf m

bullring n arène f

bull's-eye n mille m

bully ⓵ n (child) petite brute f; (adult) tyran m
⓶ vtr intimider; (stronger) tyranniser

bum n (colloq) (a) (GB) (buttocks) derrière m (fam)
(b) (US) (vagrant) clochard m

bumbag n (sacoche f) banane f

bumblebee n bourdon m

bumf, bumph n (GB) (colloq) paperasserie f (fam)

bump ⓵ n (a) (lump) (on body) bosse f (on à); (on road) bosse f (on, in sur)
(b) (jolt) secousse f
(c) (sound) bruit m sourd
⓶ vtr cogner (against, on contre); to ~ one's head se cogner la tête
■ **bump into** ⓵ rentrer dans ‹person, object›
⓶ (meet) tomber sur (fam) ‹person›

bumper ⓵ n pare-chocs m inv
⓶ adj ‹crop, sales, year› record (after n); ‹edition› exceptionnel/-elle

bumper car n auto f tamponneuse

bumpkin n (colloq) (also **country** ~) péquenaud/-e m/f (fam)

bumpy adj ‹road› accidenté/-e; ‹wall› irrégulier/-ière; ‹landing› agité/-e

bun n (a) (cake) petit pain m sucré
(b) (hairstyle) chignon m

bunch n (of flowers) bouquet m; (of vegetables) botte f; (of grapes) grappe f; (of bananas) régime m; (of keys) trousseau m, (of people) groupe m

bundle ⓵ n (of clothes) ballot m; (of papers, notes) liasse f; (of books) paquet m; (of straw) botte f; ~ **of sticks** fagot m de bois; ~ **of nerves** boule f de nerfs
⓶ vtr **to** ~ **sb/sth into** fourrer (fam) qn/ qch dans

bundled software n ensemble m de logiciels complémentaires (livré avec un ordinateur)

bungalow n pavillon m (sans étage)

bungee jumping n saut m à l'élastique

bungle vtr rater (fam) ‹attempt, burglary›

bunion n oignon m

bunk n (a) (on ship, train) couchette f
(b) (also ~ **bed**) lits mpl superposés
■ **bunk off** (colloq) **to** ~ **off school** sécher l'école

bunker n (a) (Mil) bunker m
(b) (in golf) bunker m
(c) (for coal) soute f

bunny n (a) (also ~ **rabbit**) (Jeannot) lapin m
(b) (also ~ **girl**) hôtesse f

bunting n guirlandes fpl

buoy ⓵ n (gen) bouée f; (for marking) balise f (flottante)
⓶ vtr (also ~ **up**) (a) revigorer ‹person, morale›
(b) stimuler ‹prices, economy›
(c) (keep afloat) maintenir à flot

buoyant adj (a) ‹object› qui flotte
(b) ‹person› vif/vive; ‹mood, spirits› enjoué/-e; ‹step› allègre
(c) ‹market, prices› ferme; ‹economy› en expansion

burden ⓵ n fardeau m (**to sb** pour qn)
⓶ vtr (a) (also ~ **down**) encombrer (**with** de)
(b) (figurative) (with work, taxes) accabler (**with** de); **I don't want to** ~ **you with my problems** je ne veux pas vous ennuyer avec mes problèmes

bureau n (pl ~**s** ou ~**x**) (a) (office) bureau m
(b) (US) (government department) service m
(c) (GB) (desk) secrétaire m
(d) (US) (chest of drawers) commode f

bureaucracy n bureaucratie f

bureaucrat n bureaucrate mf

bureaucratic adj bureaucratique

burgeoning adj ‹talent, love, industry, crime› croissant/-e; ‹population, industries› en plein essor

burger n hamburger m

burger bar n fast-food m

burglar n cambrioleur/-euse m/f

burglar alarm n sonnerie f d'alarme

burglary n (gen) cambriolage m; (Law) vol m avec effraction

burgle vtr cambrioler

burgundy ① **Burgundy** pr n Bourgogne f

② n (a) (also **Burgundy**) (wine) bourgogne m

(b) (colour) (couleur f) bordeaux m

burial n enterrement m

burka n burqa f

burly adj ‹person› solidement charpenté/-e

Burma pr n Birmanie f

ɔ̆ **burn** ① n brûlure f

② vtr (prét, pp **burned** ou **burnt** (GB)) (gen) brûler; laisser brûler ‹food›

③ vi (prét, pp **burned** ou **burnt** (GB)) brûler

■ **burn down**: ① ¶ ~ down ‹house› être détruit/-e par le feu

② ¶ ~ [sth] down réduire [qch] en cendres ‹house›

■ **burn up** brûler ‹calories›; dépenser ‹energy›

burner n (on cooker) brûleur m; (for CDs etc.) graveur m

IDIOM to put sth on the back ~ mettre qch en veilleuse

burning ① n there's a smell of ~ ça sent le brûlé

② adj (a) (on fire) en flammes, en feu; (alight) ‹candle, lamp, fire› allumé/-e

(b) ‹desire› brûlant/-e; ‹passion› ardent/-e

burnt-out adj ‹building, car› calciné/-e; ‹person› usé/-e (par le travail)

burp (colloq) ① n rot m (fam), renvoi m

② vi ‹person› roter (fam); ‹baby› faire son rot (fam)

burrow ① n terrier m

② vi ‹animal› creuser un terrier; to ~ into/ under sth creuser dans/sous qch

bursary n (GB) (grant) bourse f (d'études)

burst ① n (of flame) jaillissement m; (of gunfire) rafale f; (of activity, enthusiasm) accès m; a ~ of laughter un éclat de rire; a ~ of applause un tonnerre d'applaudissements

② vtr (prét, pp **burst**) (gen) crever; rompre ‹blood vessel›; to ~ its banks ‹river› déborder

③ vi (prét, pp **burst**) (gen) crever; ‹pipe› éclater; ‹dam› rompre; to be ~ing with health/pride déborder de santé/fierté

■ **burst into** (a) faire irruption dans ‹room›

(b) to ~ into flames s'enflammer; to ~ into tears fondre en larmes

■ **burst out**: to ~ out laughing éclater de rire; to ~ out crying fondre en larmes

■ **burst through** rompre ‹barricade›; to ~ through the door entrer violemment

bury vtr enterrer

ɔ̆ **bus** n (pl **buses**) autobus m, bus m; (long-distance) autocar m, car m; **by** ~ en (auto)bus, par le bus; **on the** ~ dans le bus

bus conductor n receveur m d'autobus

bus driver n conducteur/-trice m/f d'autobus

bush n (a) buisson m

(b) (bushland) the ~ la brousse f

IDIOM don't beat about the ~ cessez de tourner autour du pot

bushfire n feu m de brousse

bushy adj ‹hair, tail› touffu/-e; ‹beard› épais/-aisse; ‹eyebrows› broussailleux/-euse

ɔ̆ **business** ① n (a) (commerce) affaires fpl; to go into ~ se lancer dans les affaires; she's gone to Brussels on ~ elle est allée à Bruxelles en voyage d'affaires; to mix ~ with pleasure joindre l'utile à l'agréable; he's in the insurance ~ il travaille dans les assurances

(b) (company, firm) affaire f, entreprise f; (shop) commerce m, boutique f; small ~es les petites entreprises

(c) let's get down to ~ passons aux choses sérieuses; to go about one's ~ vaquer à ses occupations

(d) (concern) that's her ~ ça la regarde; it's none of your ~! ça ne te regarde pas!; mind your own ~! (colloq) occupe-toi de tes affaires! (fam)

② adj ‹address, letter, transaction› commercial/-e; ‹meeting› d'affaires

IDIOMS she means ~! elle ne plaisante pas!; to work like nobody's ~ (colloq) travailler d'arrache-pied

business associate n associé/-e m/f

business card n carte f de visite

business class n (on plane) classe f affaires

business hours n pl (in office) heures fpl de bureau; (of shop) heures fpl d'ouverture

businesslike adj sérieux/-ieuse

businessman n (pl **-men**) homme m d'affaires

business park n parc m d'affaires or d'activités

business plan n projet m commercial

business school n école f de commerce

business studies n pl études fpl de commerce

business trip n voyage m d'affaires

businesswoman n (pl **-women**) femme f d'affaires

busker n (GB) musicien/-ienne m/f ambulant/-e

bus lane n couloir m d'autobus

bus pass n carte f de bus

bus shelter n abribus® m

bus station n gare f routière

bus stop n arrêt m de bus

bust ① n (a) (breasts) poitrine f

(b) (statue) buste m

② adj (colloq) (a) (broken) fichu/-e (fam)

(b) (bankrupt) to go ~ faire faillite

bustle ① n (activity) affairement m (of de); hustle and ~ grande animation f

② vi ‹person, crowd› s'affairer; to ~ in/out entrer/sortir d'un air affairé

bustling adj ‹street, shop, town› animé/-e

ɔ̆ indicates a very frequent word

busy ⓵ *adj* **(a)** ⟨person⟩ occupé/-e (with avec; **doing** à faire)

(b) ⟨shop⟩ où il y a beaucoup de monde; ⟨junction, airport⟩ où le trafic est intense; ⟨road⟩ très fréquenté/-e; ⟨street, town⟩ animé/-e; ⟨day, week⟩ chargé/-e

(c) (engaged) ⟨line⟩ occupé/-e

⓶ *v refl* **to ~ oneself doing** s'occuper à faire

busybody *n* (colloq) **he's a real ~** il se mêle de tout

but ⓵ *conj* mais

⓶ *prep* sauf; **anybody ~ him** n'importe qui sauf lui; **nobody ~ me knows how to do it** il n'y a que moi qui sache le faire; **he's nothing ~ a coward** ce n'est qu'un lâche; **the last ~ one** l'avant-dernier

⓷ *adv* **one can't help ~ admire her** on ne peut pas s'empêcher de l'admirer

⓸ **but for** *phr* **~ for you, I would have died** sans toi je serais mort; **he would have gone ~ for me** si je n'avais pas été là il serait parti

butane *n* butane *m*

butcher ⓵ *n* boucher *m*; **~'s (shop)** boucherie *f*

⓶ *vtr* abattre ⟨animal⟩; massacrer ⟨people⟩

butchery *n* **(a)** (trade) boucherie *f*

(b) (slaughter) massacre *m*

butler *n* maître *m* d'hôtel, majordome *m*

butt ⓵ *n* **(a)** (of rifle) crosse *f*; (of cigarette) mégot *m* (fam)

(b) (US) (buttocks) derrière *m* (fam)

(c) **to be the ~ of sb's jokes** être la cible des blagues de qn

⓶ *vtr* ⟨person⟩ donner un coup de tête à; ⟨animal⟩ donner un coup de corne à

■ **butt in** interrompre

butter ⓵ *n* beurre *m*

⓶ *vtr* beurrer ⟨bread⟩

■ **butter up** (colloq): **~ [sb] up, ~ up [sb]** passer de la pommade à (fam)

buttercup *n* bouton d'or *m*

butterfingers *n* empoté/-e *m/f*

butterfly *n* papillon *m*

IDIOM **to have butterflies (in one's stomach)** avoir le trac (fam)

butterfly stroke *n* brasse *f* papillon

buttock *n* fesse *f*

button ⓵ *n* **(a)** (on coat, switch) bouton *m*

(b) (US) (badge) badge *m*

(c) (Comput) bouton *m*

⓶ *vi* ⟨dress⟩ se boutonner

■ **button up** boutonner ⟨garment⟩

buttonhole ⓵ *n* **(a)** (on garment) boutonnière *f*

(b) (GB) (flower) (fleur *f* de) boutonnière *f*

⓶ *vtr* (colloq) accrocher (fam) ⟨person⟩

buttress *n* **(a)** contrefort *m*; (figurative) soutien *m*

(b) (*also* **flying ~**) arc-boutant *m*

buxom *adj* ⟨woman⟩ à la poitrine généreuse

buy ⓵ *n* **a good ~** une bonne affaire

⓶ *vtr* (*prét, pp* **bought**) acheter (**from sb** à qn); **to ~ sth from the supermarket/from the baker's** acheter qch au supermarché/chez le boulanger; **to ~ sb sth** acheter qch à qn; **to ~ some time** gagner du temps

■ **buy off** acheter ⟨person, witness⟩

■ **buy out** racheter la part de ⟨co-owner⟩

■ **buy up** acheter systématiquement ⟨shares, property⟩

buyer *n* acheteur/-euse *m/f*

buyout *n* rachat *m* d'entreprise

buzz ⓵ *n* **(a)** (of insect) bourdonnement *m*

(b) (colloq) (phone call) **to give sb a ~** passer un coup de fil à qn

(c) (colloq) (thrill) **it gives me a ~** (from alcohol) ça me fait planer (fam); **to get a ~ out of doing** prendre son pied (fam) en faisant

⓶ *vtr* **to ~ sb** appeler qn au bip, biper qn

⓷ *vi* ⟨bee, fly⟩ bourdonner; ⟨buzzer⟩ sonner

buzzard *n* buse *f*

buzzer *n* (gen) sonnerie *f*; (on pocket) bip *m*

buzzword *n* (colloq) mot *m* à la mode

by ⓵ *prep* **(a)** (with passive verbs) par; **he was bitten ~ a snake** il a été mordu par un serpent

(b) (with present participle) en; **~ working extra hours** en faisant des heures supplémentaires; **to learn French ~ listening to the radio** apprendre le français en écoutant la radio; **to begin ~ doing** commencer par faire

(c) (by means of) par; **to pay ~ cheque** payer par chèque; **~ mistake/accident** par erreur/accident; **to travel to Rome ~ Venice** aller à Rome en passant par Venise; **to travel ~ bus/train** voyager en bus/train; **~ bicycle** à bicyclette, en vélo; **~ candlelight** ⟨dine⟩ aux chandelles; ⟨read⟩ à la bougie

(d) (from) à; **I could tell ~ the look on her face that** rien qu'à la regarder je savais que

(e) (near) à côté de, près de; **~ the window** à côté de la fenêtre; **~ the sea** au bord de la mer

(f) (showing authorship) de; **a film ~ Claude Chabrol** un film de Claude Chabrol; **who is it ~?** c'est de qui?

(g) (in time expressions) avant; **~ midnight** avant minuit; **~ this time next week** d'ici la semaine prochaine; **~ the time she had got downstairs he was gone** le temps qu'elle descende, il était parti; **he should be here ~ now** il devrait être déjà là

(h) (according to) selon; **to play ~ the rules** jouer selon les règles; **~ my watch** à ma montre

(i) (showing amount) de; **prices have risen ~ 20%** les prix ont augmenté de 20%; **he's taller than me ~ two centimetres** il fait deux centimètres de plus que moi

(j) (in measurements) sur; **20 metres ~ 10 metres** 20 mètres sur 10

(k) (showing rate, quantity) à; **paid ~ the hour** ⋯>

payé à l'heure
(l) little ∼ little peu à peu; **day** ∼ **day** jour après jour; **one** ∼ **one** un par un, une par une; ∼ **oneself** tout seul/toute seule; **to go** *or* **pass** ∼ **sb/sth** passer devant qn/qch
(m) (in compass directions) quart; **south** ∼ **south-west** sud quart sud-ouest
2 *adv* **(a)** (past) **to go** ∼ passer; **the people walking** ∼ les gens qui passent/passaient, les passants; **as time goes** ∼ avec le temps
(b) (near) près; **he lives close** ∼ il habite tout près
(c) (aside) **to put money** ∼ mettre de l'argent de côté
by(e)-election *n* (GB) élection *f* partielle
by(e)law *n* arrêté *m* municipal

bye *excl* (colloq) (*also* ∼**-bye**) au revoir!
bygone *adj* ‹*days, years, scene*› d'antan; **a** ∼ **era** une époque révolue
IDIOM to let ∼**s be** ∼**s** enterrer le passé
bypass **1** *n* **(a)** (road) rocade *f*
(b) (pipe, channel) by-pass *m inv*
(c) (in electricity) dérivation *f*
(d) (*also* ∼ **operation**) (Med) pontage *m*
2 *vtr* contourner ‹*town, city*›
by-product *n* dérivé *m*; (figurative) effet *m* secondaire
bystander *n* spectateur/-trice *m/f*
byte *n* (Comput) octet *m*
byword *n* **to be a** ∼ **for** être synonyme de

Cc

c, C *n* **(a)** (letter) c, C *m*
(b) C (Mus) do *m*
cab *n* **(a)** (taxi) taxi *m*
(b) (for driver) cabine *f*
cabbage *n* chou *m*
cab-driver *n* chauffeur *m* de taxi
cabin *n* **(a)** (hut) cabane *f*; (in holiday camp) chalet *m*
(b) (in boat, plane) cabine *f*
cabin crew *n* personnel *m* de bord
cabinet *n* **(a)** (cupboard) petit placard *m*; **display** ∼ vitrine *f*; **cocktail** ∼ meuble *m* bar
(b) (GB Pol) cabinet *m*
cabinet minister *n* (GB) ministre *m*
cable **1** *n* câble *m*
2 *adj* ‹*channel, network*› câblé/-e
cable car *n* téléphérique *m*
cable TV *n* télévision *f* par câble
cab-rank, cab stand *n* station *f* de taxis
cackle *vi* ‹*hen*› caqueter; ‹*person*› (talk) caqueter; (laugh) ricaner
CAD *n* (*abbr* = **computer-aided design**) CAO *f*
CADCAM *n* (*abbr* = **computer-aided design and computer-aided manufacture**) CFAO *f*
caddy *n* caddie *m*
cadet *n* (Mil) élève *mf* officier
cadge *vtr* (colloq) **to** ∼ **sth off** *or* **from sb** taper (fam) qch à qn ‹*cigarette, money*›; **to** ∼ **a meal/a lift** se faire inviter/emmener en voiture

⚐ **indicates a very frequent word**

Caesarean, Caesarian *n* (*also* ∼ **section**) césarienne *f*
café *n* **(a)** ≈ snack-bar *m*; **pavement** ∼, **sidewalk** ∼ café *m*
(b) (US) bistro *m*
cafeteria *n* (gen) cafétéria *f*; (Sch) cantine *f*; (Univ) restaurant *m* universitaire
caffein(e) *n* caféine *f*; ∼**-free** décaféiné/-e
cage **1** *n* cage *f*
2 *vtr* mettre [qch] en cage ‹*animal*›; **a** ∼**d animal** un animal en cage
cagoule *n* (GB) K-way® *m*
cahoots *n pl* (colloq) **to be in** ∼ être de mèche (fam) **(with)** (avec)
Cairo *pr n* Le Caire
cajole *vtr* cajoler
cake *n* **(a)** (Culin) gâteau *m*; (sponge) génoise *f*
(b) (of soap, wax) pain *m*
IDIOM it's a piece of ∼ (colloq) c'est du gâteau (fam)
cake shop *n* ≈ pâtisserie *f*
calcium *n* calcium *m*
⚐ **calculate** *vtr* **(a)** calculer ‹*cost, distance, price*›
(b) évaluer ‹*effect, probability*›
(c) **to be** ∼**d to do** avoir été conçu/-e pour faire
calculated *adj* ‹*crime*› prémédité/-e; ‹*attempt, insult*› délibéré/-e; ‹*risk*› calculé/-e
calculating *adj* ‹*manner, person*› calculateur/-trice
calculation *n* calcul *m*
calculator *n* calculatrice *f*, calculette *f*
calendar *n* calendrier *m*
calf *n* (*pl* **calves**) **(a)** (Zool) veau *m*
(b) (*also* ∼**skin**) vachette *f*

(c) (Anat) mollet *m*

calibre (GB), **caliber** (US) *n* calibre *m*

California *pr n* Californie *f*

⚡ **call** ⊡ *n* **(a)** (*also* **phone** ~) appel *m* (téléphonique) (**from** de); **to make a** ~ appeler, téléphoner

(b) (cry) (human) appel *m* (**for** à); (animal) cri *m*

(c) (summons) appel *m*

(d) (visit) visite *f*

(e) (demand) demande *f* (**for** de)

(f) (need) **there's no** ~ **for sth** il n'y a pas de raison pour qch

(g) (Sport) décision *f*

(h) to be on ~ ‹*doctor*› être de garde; ‹*engineer*› être de service

⊡ *vtr* **(a)** (gen) appeler; **what is he** ~**ed?** comment s'appelle-t-il?; **the boss** ~**ed me into his office** le chef m'a fait venir dans son bureau

(b) organiser ‹*strike*›; convoquer ‹*meeting*›; fixer ‹*election*›

(c) (waken) réveiller ‹*person*›

(d) (describe as) **to** ~ **sb stupid** traiter qn d'imbécile; **I wouldn't** ~ **it spacious** je ne dirais pas que c'est spacieux

⊡ *vi* **(a)** (gen) appeler; **who's** ~**ing?** qui est à l'appareil?

(b) (visit) passer; **to** ~ **at** passer chez ‹*person, shop*›; passer à ‹*bank, library*›; ‹*train*› s'arrêter à ‹*town, station*›

■ **call back**: ⊡ ¶ ~ **back** (on phone) rappeler

⊡ ¶ ~ **[sb] back** rappeler ‹*person*›

■ **call for (a)** ¶ ~ **for [sth]** (shout) appeler ‹*ambulance, doctor*›; **to** ~ **for help** appeler à l'aide

(b) (demand) réclamer

(c) (require) exiger ‹*treatment, skill*›; nécessiter ‹*change*›

■ **call in**: ⊡ ¶ ~ **in** (visit) passer

⊡ ¶ ~ **[sb] in** faire entrer ‹*client, patient*›; faire appel à ‹*expert*›

■ **call off** abandonner ‹*investigation*›; annuler ‹*deal, wedding*›; rompre ‹*engagement*›

■ **call on (a)** (visit) rendre visite à ‹*relative, friend*›; visiter ‹*patient, client*›

(b) to ~ **on sb to do** demander à qn de faire

■ **call out**: ⊡ ¶ ~ **out** appeler; (louder) crier

⊡ ¶ ~ **[sb] out (a)** appeler ‹*doctor, troops*›

(b) ‹*union*› lancer un ordre de grève à ‹*members*›

⊡ ¶ ~ **[sth] out** appeler ‹*name, number*›

■ **call up**: ⊡ ¶ ~ **up** appeler

⊡ ¶ ~ **[sb/sth] up (a)** (on phone) appeler

(b) (Mil) appeler [qn] sous les drapeaux ‹*soldier*›

call box *n* (GB) cabine *f* téléphonique; (US) poste *m* téléphonique

call centre *n* centre *m* d'appels

caller *n* **(a)** (on phone) personne *f* qui appelle

(b) (visitor) visiteur/-euse *m/f*

callous *adj* inhumain/-e

call-out charge *n* frais *mpl* de déplacement

calm ⊡ *n* calme *m*; (in adversity) sang-froid *m*

⊡ *adj* calme; **keep** ~**!** du calme!

⊡ *vtr* calmer

■ **calm down**: ⊡ ¶ ~ **down** se calmer

⊡ ¶ ~ **[sb/sth] down** calmer

calmly *adv* ‹*act, speak*› calmement; ‹*sleep, smoke*› tranquillement

Calor gas® *n* (GB) butane *m*

calorie *n* calorie *f*

camcorder *n* caméscope® *m*

camel *n* chameau *m*

⚡ **camera** *n* **(a)** (for photos) appareil *m* photo

(b) (for movies) caméra *f*

camera crew *n* équipe *f* de télévision

cameraman *n* (*pl* **-men**) cadreur *m*, cameraman *m*

camisole *n* caraco *m*

camouflage ⊡ *n* camouflage *m*

⊡ *vtr* camoufler (**with** avec)

⚡ **camp** ⊡ *n* camp *m*

⊡ *vi* camper; **to go** ~**ing** faire du camping

⚡ **campaign** ⊡ *n* campagne *f*

⊡ *vi* faire campagne (**for** pour; **against** contre)

campaigner *n* militant/-e *m/f* (**for** pour; **against** contre); (Pol) candidat/-e *m/f* en campagne (électorale)

camp bed *n* lit *m* de camp

camper *n* **(a)** (person) campeur/-euse *m/f*

(b) (*also* ~ **van**) camping-car *m*

campfire *n* feu *m* de camp

camping *n* camping *m*; **to go** ~ faire du camping

campsite *n* terrain *m* de camping, camping *m*

campus *n* (*pl* **-puses**) campus *m*

⚡ **can**[1] *modal aux* (*prét, cond* **could**, *nég au prés* **cannot, can't**) **(a)** (be able to) pouvoir; ~ **you come?** est-ce que tu peux venir?, peux-tu venir?; **we will do all we** ~ nous ferons tout ce que nous pouvons *or* tout notre possible

(b) (know how to) savoir; **she** ~ **swim** elle sait nager; **I can't drive** je ne sais pas conduire; **he** ~ **speak French** il parle français

(c) (permission, requests, offers, suggestions) pouvoir; ~ **we park here?** est-ce que nous pouvons nous garer ici?; **you can't turn right** vous ne pouvez pas *or* vous n'avez pas le droit de tourner à droite; ~ **you do me a favour?** peux-tu *or* est-ce que tu peux me rendre un service?

(d) (with verbs of perception) ~ **they see us?** est-ce qu'ils nous voient?; **I can't feel a thing** je ne sens rien; **she can't understand English** elle ne comprend pas l'anglais

(e) (in expressions) **you can't be hungry!** tu ne peux pas avoir faim!; **you can't be serious!** tu veux rire!; **this can't be right** il doit y avoir une erreur; ~ **you believe it!** tu te rends compte?; **what** ~ **she want from me?** qu'est-ce qu'elle peut bien me vouloir?

can² 1 *n* (of food) boîte *f*; (of drink) cannette *f*; (aerosol) bombe *f*; (for petrol) bidon *m*; (of paint) pot *m*
2 *vtr* (*p prés etc* **-nn-**) mettre [qch] en conserve

Canada *pr n* Canada *m*

Canadian 1 *n* Canadien/-ienne *m/f*
2 *adj* canadien/-ienne; ‹*embassy*› du Canada

canal *n* canal *m*

canal boat, **canal barge** *n* péniche *f*

Canaries *pr n pl* (*also* **Canary Islands**)
the ∼ les Canaries *fpl*

cancel *vtr* (gen) annuler; mettre une opposition à ‹*cheque*›

cancellation *n* annulation *f*

∮ **cancer** *n* cancer *m*; **to have** ∼ avoir un cancer; **lung** ∼ cancer du poumon

Cancer *n* Cancer *m*

cancer patient *n* cancéreux/-euse *m/f*

cancer research *n* cancérologie *f*

candid *adj* franc/franche

∮ **candidate** *n* candidat/-e *m/f*

candle *n* bougie *f*; (in church) cierge *m*

candlelight *n* lueur *f* de bougie

candlelit dinner *n* dîner *m* aux chandelles

candlestick *n* bougeoir *m*; (ornate) chandelier *m*

candy *n* (US) (sweets) bonbons *mpl*; (sweet) bonbon *m*

candyfloss *n* (GB) barbe *f* à papa

cane *n* (a) (material) rotin *m*; ∼ **furniture** meubles en rotin
(b) (of sugar, bamboo) canne *f*
(c) (for walking) canne *f*; (for plant) tuteur *m*; (GB) (for punishment) badine *f*

canine *n* canine *f*

canister *n* boîte *f* métallique; **a tear gas** ∼ une bombe lacrymogène

cannabis *n* cannabis *m*

canned *adj* (a) ‹*food*› en boîte
(b) (colloq) ‹*laughter*› enregistré/-e

cannibal *n* cannibale *mf*

cannon *n* (*pl* ∼ *ou* ∼**s**) canon *m*

canoe 1 *n* (gen) canoë *m*; (dugout) pirogue *f*; (Sport) canoë-kayac *m*
2 *vi* faire du canoë

canoeing *n* **to go** ∼ faire du canoë-kayac

can-opener *n* ouvre-boîtes *m inv*

cantankerous *adj* acariâtre

canteen *n* (a) (GB) (dining room) cantine *f*
(b) (Mil) (flask) bidon *m*; (mess tin) gamelle *f*
(c) **a** ∼ **of cutlery** une ménagère

canter *vi* ‹*rider*› faire un petit galop; ‹*horse*› galoper

canvas *n* toile *f*

---

canvass *vtr* (a) **to** ∼ **voters** faire du démarchage électoral auprès des électeurs
(b) **to** ∼ **opinion on sth** sonder l'opinion au sujet de qch
(c) (for business) prospecter ‹*area*›

canvasser *n* agent *m* électoral

canyon *n* cañon *m*

canyoning *n* canyoning *m*

cap 1 *n* (a) casquette *f*; **baseball** ∼ casquette de baseball
(b) (of pen) capuchon *m*; (of bottle) capsule *f*
(c) (for tooth) couronne *f*
2 *vtr* (*p prés etc* **-pp-**) (a) (limit) imposer une limite budgétaire à ‹*local authority*›; plafonner ‹*budget*›
(b) (cover) couronner (**with** de)
IDIOM **to** ∼ **it all** pour couronner le tout

capability *n* (a) (capacity) capacité *f* (**to do** de faire)
(b) (aptitude) aptitude *f*; **outside my capabilities** au-delà de mes compétences

∮ **capable** *adj* (a) (competent) compétent/-e
(b) (able) capable (**of** de)

∮ **capacity** *n* (a) (of box, bottle) contenance *f*; (of building) capacité *f* d'accueil; **full to** ∼ comble
(b) (of factory) capacité *f* de production
(c) (role) **in my** ∼ **as a doctor** en ma qualité de médecin
(d) (ability) **to have a** ∼ **for** avoir des facilités pour ‹*learning, mathematics*›; **a** ∼ **for doing** une aptitude à faire

cape *n* (a) (cloak) cape *f*
(b) (on coast) cap *m*

caper *n* (a) (Culin) câpre *f*
(b) (colloq) (scheme) combine *f*
(c) (colloq) (antic) pitrerie *f*

Cape Town *pr n* Le Cap

∮ **capital** 1 *n* (a) (letter) majuscule *f*
(b) (*also* ∼ **city**) capitale *f*
(c) (money) capital *m*
2 *adj* (a) ‹*letter*› majuscule; ∼ **A** A majuscule
(b) (Law) ‹*offence*› capital/-e

capital expenditure *n* dépenses *fpl* d'investissement

capital investment *n* dépenses *fpl* d'investissement

capitalism *n* capitalisme *m*

capitalist *n*, *adj* capitaliste *mf*

capitalize *vi* **to** ∼ **on** tirer parti de ‹*situation, advantage*›

capital punishment *n* peine *f* capitale

capitulate *vi* capituler (**to** devant)

Capricorn *n* Capricorne *m*

capsize *vi* chavirer

captain 1 *n* capitaine *m*
2 *vtr* être le capitaine de ‹*team*›; commander ‹*ship, platoon*›

caption *n* légende *f*

captivate *vtr* captiver, fasciner

captive n captif/-ive m/f
captivity n captivité f
captor n (of person) geôlier/-ière m/f
◈ **capture** **1** n (of person, animal) capture f; (of stronghold) prise f
2 vtr **(a)** capturer ‹person, animal›; prendre ‹stronghold›
(b) saisir ‹likeness›; rendre ‹feeling›
◈ **car** **1** n **(a)** (Aut) voiture f
(b) (on train) wagon m; **restaurant ~** wagon-restaurant m
2 adj ‹industry, insurance› automobile; ‹journey, chase› en voiture; ‹accident› de voiture
caramel n caramel m
carat n carat m; **18 ~ gold** or 18 carats
caravan **1** n caravane f; (horse-drawn) roulotte f
2 vi (p près etc **-nn-**) **to go ~ning** (GB) faire du caravanage
caravan site n camping m pour caravanes
carbohydrate n hydrate m de carbone
car bomb n bombe f dissimulée dans une voiture
carbon n carbone m
carbon copy n copie f carbone; (figurative) réplique f exacte
carbon dioxide n dioxyde m de carbone
carbon footprint n empreinte f écologique
carbon monoxide n monoxyde m de carbone
carbon neutral adj neutre en carbone
car boot sale n (GB) brocante f (d'objets apportés dans le coffre de sa voiture)
carburettor (GB), **carburetor** (US) n carburateur m
◈ **card** n carte f
IDIOM **to play one's ~s right** bien jouer son jeu (fam)
cardboard n carton m
cardboard box n (boîte f en) carton m
cardboard city n: zone urbaine où les sans-abri logent dans des cartons
card game n partie f de cartes
cardiac adj cardiaque
cardiac arrest n arrêt m du cœur
cardigan n cardigan m
card key n carte f magnétique
cardphone n téléphone m à carte
card trick n tour m de cartes
◈ **care** **1** n **(a)** (attention) attention f, soin m; **to take ~ to do** prendre soin de faire; **'take ~!'** (be careful) 'fais attention!'; (goodbye) 'à bientôt!'; **'handle with ~'** 'fragile'
(b) (looking after) (of person, animal) soins mpl; (of car, plant, clothes) entretien m (**of** de); **to take ~ of** (deal with) s'occuper de ‹child, client,

garden, details›; (be careful with) prendre soin de ‹machine, car›; (keep in good condition) entretenir ‹car, teeth›; (look after) garder ‹shop, watch›; **to take ~ of oneself** (look after oneself) prendre soin de soi; (cope) se débrouiller tout seul/toute seule; (defend oneself) se défendre
(c) (Med) soins mpl
(d) (GB) **to be in ~** ‹child› être (placé/-e) en garde
(e) (worry) souci m
2 vi **(a)** (be concerned) **to ~ about** s'intéresser à ‹art, environment›; se soucier du bien-être de ‹pupils, the elderly›; **I don't ~!** ça m'est égal!; **she couldn't ~ less about…** elle se moque or se fiche (fam) complètement de…; complètement de…; **I'm past caring** je m'en moque
(h) (love) **to ~ about sb** aimer qn
■ **care for: 1** ¶ **~ for [sth] (a)** (like) aimer; **would you ~ for a drink?** voulez-vous boire quelque chose?
(b) (maintain) entretenir ‹car, garden›; prendre soin de ‹skin, plant›
2 ¶ **~ for [sb/sth]** s'occuper de ‹child, animal›; soigner ‹patient›
care assistant n aide-soignant/-e m/f
◈ **career** n carrière f
career break n interruption f de carrière
careers adviser, careers officer n conseiller/-ère m/f d'orientation
careers office n service m d'orientation professionnelle
carefree adj insouciant/-e
careful adj ‹person, driving› prudent/-e; ‹planning, preparation› minutieux/-ieuse; ‹research, examination› méticuleux/-euse; **to be ~ to do** or **about doing** prendre soin de faire; **to be ~ with sth** faire attention à qch; **be ~!** (fais) attention!
◈ **carefully** adv ‹walk, open, handle› prudemment; ‹write› soigneusement; ‹listen, read, look› attentivement
caregiver n (US) personne ayant un parent handicapé ou malade à charge
careless adj ‹person› négligent/-e, imprudent/-e; ‹work› bâclé/-e; ‹writing› négligé/-e; ‹driving› négligent/-e; **~ mistake** faute d'étourderie; **it was ~ of me to do** ça a été de la négligence de ma part de faire
carelessness n négligence f
carer n (GB) (relative) personne ayant un parent handicapé ou malade à charge; (professional) aide f familiale, aidant/-e m/f
caress vtr caresser
caretaker n concierge mf
care worker n assistant/-e m/f social/-e
car ferry n ferry m
cargo n (pl **~es** ou **~s**) chargement m
cargo ship n cargo m
car hire n location f de voitures

car hire company n société f de location de voitures

Caribbean pr n the ∼ (sea) la mer des Antilles or des Caraïbes

caricature n caricature f

caring adj (a) (loving) ‹parent› affectueux/-euse
(b) (compassionate) ‹person, attitude› compréhensif/-ive; ‹society› humain/-e

carjacking n vol m de voiture (avec agression du conducteur)

carnage n carnage m

carnation n œillet m

carnival n (a) carnaval m
(b) (US) (funfair) fête f foraine

carol n chant m de Noël

carousel n (a) (merry-go-round) manège m
(b) (for luggage, slides) carrousel m

car park n (GB) parc m de stationnement

carpenter n menuisier m

carpentry n menuiserie f

carpet n (fitted) moquette f; (loose) tapis m

carpet sweeper n balai m mécanique

car phone n téléphone m de voiture

car radio n autoradio m

carriage n (a) (ceremonial) carrosse m
(b) (of train) wagon m, voiture f
(c) (of goods) transport m; ∼ **paid** port m payé
(d) (of typewriter) chariot m

carriageway n chaussée f

carrier n (a) (transport company) transporteur m; (airline) compagnie f aérienne
(b) (of disease) porteur/-euse m/f
(c) (also ∼ **bag**) (GB) sac m (en plastique)

carrot n carotte f

◇ᵉ **carry** ① vtr (a) ‹person› porter; **to** ∼ **sth in/out** apporter/emporter qch
(b) ‹vehicle, pipe, vein› transporter; ‹tide, current› emporter
(c) comporter ‹warning›
(d) comporter ‹risk, responsibility›; être passible de ‹penalty›
(e) ‹bridge, road› supporter ‹load, traffic›
(f) faire voter ‹bill›; **the motion was carried by 20 votes to 13** la motion l'a emporté par 20 votes contre 13
(g) (Med) être porteur/-euse de ‹disease, virus›
(h) (in mathematics) retenir
(i) (hold) porter ‹head›
② vi ‹sound, voice› porter
IDIOM to get carried away (colloq) s'emballer (fam), se laisser emporter
■ **carry forward** reporter ‹balance, total›
■ **carry off** (gen) emporter; remporter ‹prize›; **to** ∼ **it off** l'emporter
■ **carry on:** ① ¶ ∼ **on (a)** (continue) continuer (**doing** à faire)

◇ᵉ indicates a very frequent word

(b) (behave) se conduire
② ¶ ∼ **on [sth]** maintenir ‹tradition›; poursuivre ‹activity, discussion›
■ **carry out** réaliser ‹study›; effectuer ‹experiment, reform, attack, repairs›; exécuter ‹plan, orders›; mener ‹investigation, campaign›; accomplir ‹mission›; remplir ‹duties›; mettre [qch] à exécution ‹threat›; tenir ‹promise›

carryall n (US) fourre-tout m inv

carrycot n (GB) porte-bébé m

carry-on n (colloq) cirque m (fam)

carryout n repas m à emporter

car seat n siège-auto m

carsick adj to be ∼ avoir le mal de la route

cart ① n charrette f
② vtr (colloq) (also ∼ **around**, ∼ **about**) (colloq) trimballer (fam) ‹bags›

cartel n cartel m; **drug** ∼ cartel m de la drogue

car theft n vol m de voitures

carton n (of juice, milk) carton m, brique f; (of yoghurt, cream) pot m; (of cigarettes) cartouche f; (US) (for house removals) carton m

cartoon n (a) (film) dessin m animé
(b) (drawing) dessin m humoristique; (comic strip) bande f dessinée

cartridge n (for pen, gun, video) cartouche f; (for camera) chargeur m

cartwheel n to do a ∼ faire la roue

carve ① vtr (a) tailler, sculpter ‹wood, stone, figure› (out of dans)
(b) graver ‹letters, name› (onto sur)
(c) découper ‹meat›
② vi découper
■ **carve out (a)** se faire ‹niche, name›; se tailler ‹reputation, market›
(b) creuser ‹gorge, channel›
■ **carve up:** ¶ ∼ **up [sth]**, ∼ **[sth] up** partager ‹proceeds›; morceler ‹estate, territory›

carving n sculpture f

carving knife n couteau m à découper

car wash n lavage m automatique

◇ᵉ **case¹** ① n (a) (gen) cas m; **in that** ∼ en ce cas, dans ce cas-là; **in 7 out of 10** ∼**s** 7 fois sur 10, dans 7 cas sur 10; **a** ∼ **in point** un cas d'espèce, un exemple typique
(b) (Law) affaire f; procès m; **the** ∼ **for the Crown** (GB), **the** ∼ **for the State** (US) l'accusation f; **the** ∼ **for the defence** la défense
(c) (argument) arguments mpl
② **in any case** phr (a) (besides, anyway) de toute façon
(b) (at any rate) en tout cas
③ **in case** phr au cas où (+ conditional); **just in** ∼ au cas où
④ **in case of** phr en cas de ‹fire, accident›

case² n (a) (suitcase) valise f; (crate, chest) caisse f
(b) (display cabinet) vitrine f

(c) (for spectacles, binoculars, weapon) étui *m*; (for camera, watch) boîtier *m*

CASE *n* (*abbr* = **computer-aided software engineering**) CPAO *f*

case study *n* étude *f* de cas

⚘ **cash** ① *n* **(a)** (notes and coin) espèces *fpl*, argent *m* liquide; **to pay in ~** payer en espèces; **I haven't got any ~ on me** je n'ai pas d'argent liquide
(b) (money in general) argent *m*
(c) (payment) comptant *m*; **discount for ~** remise *f* pour paiement comptant
② *vtr* encaisser ‹cheque›
■ **cash in:** ① **to ~ in on** tirer profit de, profiter de
② ¶ **~ [sth] in** se faire rembourser, réaliser ‹bond, policy›; (US) encaisser ‹check›

cash-and-carry *n* libre-service *m* de vente en gros

cash card *n* carte *f* de retrait

cash desk *n* caisse *f*

cash dispenser *n* (*also* **cashpoint**) distributeur *m* automatique de billets de banque, billetterie *f*

cashew nut *n* cajou *m*

cash flow *n* marge *f* brute d'auto-financement, MBA *f*

cashier *n* caissier/-ière *m/f*

cashless *adj* ‹society› sans argent liquide

cashmere *n* (lainage *m* en) cachemire *m*

cash on delivery, COD *n* envoi *m* contre remboursement

cashpoint = CASH DISPENSER

cash register *n* caisse *f* enregistreuse

casino *n* casino *m*

cask *n* fût *m*, tonneau *m*

casserole *n* **(a)** (container) daubière *f*, cocotte *f*
(b) (GB) (food) ragoût *m* cuit au four

cassette *n* cassette *f*

cassette deck *n* platine *f* à cassettes

cassette player *n* lecteur *m* de cassettes

cast ① *n* **(a)** (list of actors) distribution *f*; (actors) acteurs *mpl*
(b) (*also* **plaster ~**) (Med) plâtre *m*
(c) (mould) moule *m*
② *vtr* (*prét*, *pp* **cast**) **(a)** jeter, lancer ‹stone, fishing line›; projeter ‹shadow›; **to ~ doubt on** émettre des doutes sur; **to ~ light on** éclairer; **to ~ a spell on** jeter un sort à
(b) jeter ‹glance› (at sur)
(c) distribuer les rôles de ‹play, film›; **she was cast as Blanche** elle a joué Blanche
(d) couler ‹plaster, metal›
(e) to ~ one's vote voter

castaway *n* naufragé/-e *m/f*

caste *n* caste *f*

caster sugar *n* (GB) sucre *m* en poudre

casting *n* distribution *f*

casting vote *n* voix *f* prépondérante

cast iron *n* fonte *f*; **a ~ alibi** un alibi en béton (fam)

castle *n* **(a)** château *m*
(b) (in chess) tour *f*

cast-offs *n pl* vêtements *mpl* dont on n'a plus besoin, vieux vêtements

castrate *vtr* castrer

casual *adj* **(a)** (informal) ‹clothes, person› décontracté/-e
(b) ‹acquaintance, relationship› de passage; **~ sex** relations *fpl* sexuelles non suivies
(c) ‹attitude, gesture, remark› désinvolte
(d) ‹glance› superficiel/-ielle
(e) ‹work› (temporary) temporaire; (occasional) occasionnel/-elle

casualize *vtr* **to ~ labour** précariser l'emploi

casually *adv* **(a)** ‹enquire, remark› d'un air détaché
(b) ‹dressed› simplement

casualty ① *n* **(a)** (person) victime *f*
(b) (hospital ward) urgences *fpl*; **in ~** aux urgences
② **casualties** *n pl* (soldiers) pertes *fpl*; (civilians) victimes *fpl*

casual wear *n* vêtements *mpl* sport

⚘ **cat** *n* (domestic) chat *m*; (female) chatte *f*; **the big ~s** les grands félins *mpl*
IDIOMS **to let the ~ out of the bag** vendre la mèche; **to rain ~s and dogs** pleuvoir des cordes

catalogue, catalog (US) *n* catalogue *m*

catalyst *n* catalyseur *m*

catalytic converter *n* pot *m* catalytique

catapult *n* (hand-held) lance-pierres *m inv*

catarrh *n* catarrhe *m*

catastrophe *n* catastrophe *f*

⚘ **catch** ① *n* **(a)** (on purse, door) fermeture *f*
(b) (drawback) piège *m*
(c) (act of catching) prise *f*; **to play ~** jouer à la balle
(d) (in fishing) pêche *f*; (one fish) prise *f*
② *vtr* (*prét*, *pp* **caught**) **(a)** ‹person› attraper ‹ball, fish, person›; **to ~ hold of sth** attraper qch; **to ~ sb's attention** *or* **eye** attirer l'attention de qn; **to ~ sight of sb/sth** apercevoir qn/qch
(b) (take by surprise) prendre, attraper; **to ~ sb doing** surprendre qn en train de faire; **we got caught in the rain** nous avons été surpris par la pluie
(c) prendre ‹bus, plane›
(d) (grasp) prendre ‹hand, arm›; agripper ‹branch, rope›; captiver, éveiller ‹interest›
(e) (hear) saisir (fam), comprendre
(f) to ~ one's fingers in se prendre les doigts dans ‹drawer, door›; **to get one's shirt caught on** accrocher sa chemise à ‹nail›; **to get caught in** se prendre dans ‹barbed wire, thorns›

⋯⋗

(g) attraper ‹cold, disease, flu›
(h) to ∼ fire prendre feu, s'enflammer
3 vi (prét, pp **caught**) **(a) to ∼ on** ‹shirt› s'accrocher à ‹nail›; ‹wheel› frotter contre ‹frame›
(b) ‹wood, fire› prendre
■ **catch on (a)** (become popular) devenir populaire **(with** auprès de)
(b) (understand) comprendre, saisir
■ **catch out (a)** (take by surprise) prendre [qn] de court; (doing something wrong) prendre [qn] sur le fait
(b) (trick) attraper, jouer un tour à
■ **catch up**: **1** **¶ ∼ up** (in race) regagner du terrain; **to ∼ up on** rattraper ‹work, sleep›; se remettre au courant de ‹news›
2 **¶ ∼ [sb/sth] up** rattraper
catch-22 situation n situation f inextricable
catching adj contagieux/-ieuse
catchphrase n formule f favorite, rengaine f
catchy adj ‹tune› entraînant/-e; ‹slogan› accrocheur/-euse
categorical adj catégorique
categorize vtr classer **(by** d'après)
ϙ **category** n catégorie f
cater vi **(a)** ‹caterer› organiser des réceptions
(b) to ∼ for (GB) or **to** (US) accueillir ‹children, guests›; pourvoir à ‹needs›; ‹programme› s'adresser à ‹audience›
caterer n traiteur m
catering n (provision) approvisionnement m; (trade, industry, career) restauration f
caterpillar n chenille f
cathedral n cathédrale f
Catholic n, adj catholique mf
Catholicism n catholicisme m
catnap vi (p prés etc **-pp-**) faire un somme, sommeiller
Catseye® n (GB) plot m rétroréfléchissant
cattle n bétail m
catwalk n podium m; **∼ show** défilé m de mode
cauliflower n chou-fleur m
ϙ **cause** **1** n cause f **(of** de); **there is ∼ for concern** il y a des raisons de s'inquiéter; **to have ∼ to do** avoir des raisons de faire; **with good ∼** à juste titre
2 vtr causer, occasionner ‹damage, grief, problem›; provoquer ‹chaos, disease, controversy›; entraîner ‹suffering›; amener ‹confusion›; **to ∼ sb problems** causer des problèmes à qn; **to ∼ trouble** créer des problèmes
caustic adj caustique
caution **1** n **(a)** (care) prudence f
(b) (wariness) circonspection f
(c) (warning) avertissement m

ϙ indicates a very frequent word

2 vtr **(a)** (warn) avertir **(that** que)
(b) (Sport) donner un avertissement à ‹player›
IDIOM **to throw** or **cast ∼ to the wind(s)** oublier toute prudence
cautionary adj ‹look, gesture› d'avertissement; **a ∼ tale** un conte moral
cautious adj **(a)** (careful) prudent/-e
(b) (wary) ‹person, reception, response› réservé/-e; ‹optimism› prudent/-e
cave n grotte f
■ **cave in (a)** ‹tunnel, roof› s'effondrer
(b) ‹person› céder
caveman n (pl **-men**) homme m des cavernes
caviar(e) n caviar m
caving n spéléologie f; **to go ∼** faire de la spéléologie
cavity n cavité f
cavort vi faire des cabrioles
caw vi croasser
cc n (abbr = **cubic centimetre**) cm³
CCTV n (abbr = **closed-circuit television**) télévision f en circuit fermé
CD n (abbr = **compact disc**) CD m
CD player, **CD system** n platine f laser
CD-ROM n CD-ROM m, disque m optique compact
cease vtr, vi cesser
cease-fire n cessez-le-feu m inv
cedar n cèdre m
cede vtr, vi céder **(to** à)
cedilla n cédille f
ceiling n plafond m
ϙ **celebrate** **1** vtr fêter; (more formally) célébrer
2 vi faire la fête
celebrated adj célèbre **(for** pour)
celebration n **(a)** (celebrating) célébration f
(b) (party) fête f
(c) (public festivities) **∼s** cérémonies fpl
celebrity **1** n célébrité f
2 adj ‹guest› célèbre; ‹panel› de célébrités
celery n céleri m
celibate adj (chaste) chaste
ϙ **cell** n cellule f
cellar n cave f
cello n violoncelle m
cellphone, **cellular phone** n
(a) radiotéléphone m
(b) téléphone m portable
cellulite n cellulite f
Celsius adj Celsius inv
Celt n Celte mf
Celtic adj celtique, celte
cement n ciment m
cement mixer n bétonnière f
cemetery n cimetière m
censor **1** n censeur mf

2 *vtr* censurer
censorship *n* censure *f* (of de)
censure **1** *n* censure *f*
    2 *vtr* critiquer
census *n* recensement *m*
cent *n* (of dollar) cent *m*; (of euro) cent *m*,
    centime *m* [d'euro]
centenary *n* centenaire *m*
center (US) = CENTRE
centigrade *adj* in degrees ~ en degrés
    Celsius
centimetre (GB), **centimeter** (US) *n*
    centimètre *m*
✓ **central** *adj* (a) central/-e; ~ **London** le
    centre de Londres
    (b) (in the town centre) situé/-e en centre-ville
    (c) (key) principal/-e
Central America *pr n* Amérique *f*
    centrale
central heating *n* chauffage *m* central
centralize *vtr* centraliser
central locking *n* verrouillage *m* central
    or centralisé
central reservation *n* (GB Aut) terre-
    plein *m* central
✓ **centre** (GB), **center** (US) **1** *n* centre
    m; **in the** ~ au centre; **town** ~, **city** ~
    centre-ville *m*; **the** ~ **of attention** le centre
    de l'attention; **the** ~ **of power** le siège du
    pouvoir; **shopping/sports** ~ centre *m*
    commercial/sportif
    2 *vtr*, *vi* centrer
    ■ **centre around**, **centre on** ‹activities,
    person› se concentrer sur; ‹people, industry›
    se situer autour de ‹town›; ‹life, thoughts› être
    centré/-e sur ‹person, work›
centre-forward *n* (Sport) avant-centre *m*
centre ground *n* centre *m*; **to occupy the**
    ~ être au centre
centre-half *n* (Sport) demi-centre *m*
centrepiece (GB), **centerpiece** (US)
    n (of table) décoration *f* centrale; (of exhibition)
    clou *m*
centre-stage: **to take/occupy** ~ devenir/
    être le point de mire
✓ **century** *n* siècle *m*; **in the 20th** ~ au XXᵉ
    siècle; **at the turn of the** ~ au début du siècle
ceramic *adj* en céramique
ceramics *n* céramiques *fpl*
cereal *n* céréale *f*; **breakfast** ~ céréales
    pour le petit déjeuner
cerebral palsy *n* paralysie *f* motrice
    centrale
ceremony *n* cérémonie *f*; **to stand on** ~
    faire des cérémonies
cert *n* (colloq) **it's a (dead)** ~! (colloq) ça ne
    fait pas un pli! (fam)
✓ **certain** *adj* (a) (sure) certain/-e, sûr/-e
    (**about, of** de); **I'm** ~ (**of it**) j'en suis certain
    or sûr; **absolutely** ~ sûr et certain; **I'm** ~

that I checked je suis sûr d'avoir vérifié; **I'm**
    ~ **that he refused** je suis sûr qu'il a refusé
    (b) (specific) ‹amount, number, conditions›
    certain/-e (*before n*); ~ **people** certains *mpl*;
    to a ~ **extent** dans une certaine mesure
✓ **certainly** *adv* certainement
certainty *n* certitude *f*
certificate *n* (gen) certificat *m*; (of birth,
    death, marriage) acte *m*; **18-**~ **film** film interdit
    aux moins de 18 ans
certified *adj* certifié/-e
certified mail *n* (US) **to send by** ~
    envoyer en recommandé
certified public accountant *n* (US)
    expert-comptable *m*
certify *vtr* (a) (confirm) certifier
    (b) (authenticate) authentifier
cervical cancer *n* cancer *m* du col de
    l'utérus
cervical smear *n* frottis *m* vaginal
CFC *n* (*abbr* = **chlorofluorocarbon**)
    CFC *m*
chafe *vi* frotter (**on, against** sur)
✓ **chain** **1** *n* (a) (metal links) chaîne *f*
    (b) (on lavatory) chasse *f* (d'eau)
    (c) (on door) chaîne *f* de sûreté
    (d) (of shops, hotels) chaîne *f* (of de)
    (e) (of events) série *f*; (of ideas) enchaînement
    m
    2 *vtr* enchaîner ‹person, animal›; **to** ~ **a**
    bicycle to sth attacher une bicyclette à qch
    avec une chaîne
chain reaction *n* réaction *f* en chaîne
chain saw *n* tronçonneuse *f*
chain-smoke *vi* (colloq) fumer comme un
    sapeur (fam), fumer sans arrêt
chain-smoker *n* gros fumeur/grosse
    fumeuse *m/f*
chain store *n* (single shop) magasin *m*
    faisant partie d'une chaîne; (retail group)
    magasin *m* à succursales multiples
✓ **chair** **1** *n* (a) (gen) chaise *f*; (armchair) fauteuil *m*
    (b) (chairperson) président/-e *m/f*
    (c) (Univ) chaire *f* (**of, in** de)
    2 *vtr* présider ‹meeting›
chair lift *n* télésiège *m*
✓ **chairman** *n* président/-e *m/f*; **Mr Chairman**
    monsieur le Président; **Madam Chairman**
    madame la Présidente
chairperson *n* président/-e *m/f*
chalet *n* (mountain) chalet *m*; (in holiday camp)
    bungalow *m*
chalk *n* craie *f*
✓ **challenge** **1** *n* (a) défi *m*; **to take up a** ~
    relever un défi
    (b) (challenging task) challenge *m*; **to rise to the**
    ~ relever le challenge
    2 *vtr* (a) défier ‹person› (**to** à; **to do** de faire)
    (b) débattre ‹ideas›; contester ‹statement,
    authority›
challenger *n* challenger *m* (**for** de)

challenging adj (a) ‹work› stimulant/-e
(b) ‹look› provocateur/-trice

chamber 1 n chambre f
2 **chambers** n pl (Law) cabinet m; (GB Pol) **the upper/lower** ∼ la Chambre des lords/des communes

chambermaid n femme f de chambre

chamber music n musique f de chambre

Chamber of Commerce n chambre f de commerce et d'industrie

chameleon n caméléon m

champagne n, adj champagne m inv

✓ **champion** n champion/-ionne m/f

championship n championnat m

✓ **chance** 1 n (a) (opportunity) occasion f; **to have** or **get the** ∼ **to do** avoir l'occasion de faire; **you've missed your** ∼ tu as laissé passer l'occasion
(b) (likelihood) chance f; **there is a** ∼ **that she'll get a job in Paris** il y a des chances qu'elle trouve un travail à Paris; **she has a good** ∼ elle a de bonnes chances
(c) (luck) hasard m; **by** ∼ par hasard
(d) (risk) risque m; **to take a** ∼ prendre un risque
(e) (possibility) chance f; **not to stand a** ∼ n'avoir aucune chance; **by any** ∼ par hasard
2 vtr **to** ∼ **doing** courir le risque de faire; **to** ∼ **it** tenter sa chance
IDIOM no ∼**!** (colloq) pas question! (fam)

chancellor n (head of government) chancelier/-ière m/f; (Univ) président m

Chancellor of the Exchequer n (GB) Chancelier m de l'Échiquier

chandelier n lustre m

✓ **change** 1 n (a) (gen) changement m; (adjustment) modification f; **the** ∼ **in the schedule** la modification du programme; ∼ **of plan** changement de programme; **a** ∼ **of clothes** des vêtements de rechange; **a** ∼ **for the better** un changement en mieux; **that makes a nice** ∼ ça change agréablement; **she needs a** ∼ elle a besoin de se changer les idées; **to need a** ∼ **of air** avoir besoin de changer d'air; **for a** ∼ pour changer
(b) (cash) monnaie f; **small** ∼ petite monnaie; **she gave me 10 euros** ∼ elle m'a rendu 10 euros; **have you got** ∼ **for 50 euros?** pouvez-vous me changer un billet de 50 euros?
2 vtr (a) (alter) changer; (in part) modifier; **to** ∼ **sb/sth into** transformer qn/qch en; **to** ∼ **one's mind** changer d'avis; **to** ∼ **one's mind about doing** abandonner l'idée de faire; **to** ∼ **colour** changer de couleur
(b) (exchange) changer de ‹clothes, name, car, job, TV channel›; (in shop) échanger ‹item› (for pour); **to** ∼ **places** (seats) changer de place (with avec)
(c) (replace) changer ‹battery, tyre›; **to** ∼ **a bed**

changer les draps
(d) changer ‹cheque, currency› (into, for en)
3 vi (a) ‹situation, person› changer; ‹wind› tourner; **the lights** ∼**d from red to orange** les feux sont passés du rouge à l'orange
(b) (into different clothes) se changer; **to** ∼ **into** passer ‹garment›; **to** ∼ **out of** ôter, enlever ‹garment›
(c) (from bus, train) changer
4 **changed** pp adj ‹man, woman› autre (before n)
■ **change round** déplacer ‹large objects›; changer [qn/qch] de place ‹workers, objects, words›

changeable adj ‹condition, weather› changeant/-e; ‹price› variable

changeover n passage m (to à)

changing adj ‹colours, environment› changeant/-e; ‹attitude, world› en évolution

changing room n (at sports centre) vestiaire m; (US) (in shop) cabine f d'essayage

✓ **channel** 1 n (a) (TV station) chaîne f; (radio band) canal m
(b) (groove) rainure f
(c) (in sea, river) chenal m
(d) **through the proper** ∼**s** par la voie normale; **to go through official** ∼**s** passer par la voie officielle
2 vtr (p prés etc **-ll-** (GB), **-l-** (US)) canaliser (to, into dans)

Channel pr n **the (English)** ∼ la Manche

channel ferry n ferry m trans-Manche

channel-hop vi (p prés etc **-pp-**) zapper (fam)

Channel Islands pr n pl îles fpl Anglo-Normandes

Channel Tunnel pr n tunnel m sous la Manche

chant 1 n (a) (of crowd) chant m scandé
(b) (of devotees) mélopée f
2 vi ‹crowd› scander des slogans; ‹choir, monks› psalmodier

chaos n (gen) pagaille f (fam); (economic, cosmic) chaos m; **in a state of** ∼ ‹house› sens dessus dessous; ‹country› en plein chaos

chaotic adj désordonné/-e

chap 1 n (GB) (colloq) type m (fam)
2 vtr (p prés etc **-pp-**) gercer; ∼**ped lips** lèvres gercées

chapel n chapelle f

chaperone 1 n chaperon m
2 vtr chaperonner

chaplain n aumônier m

✓ **chapter** n chapitre m; **in** ∼ **3** au chapitre 3

✓ **character** n (a) (gen) caractère m
(b) (in book, play, film) personnage m (from de)
(c) (a real) ∼ un sacré numéro (fam); **a local** ∼ une figure locale

characteristic 1 n (gen) caractéristique f; (of person) trait m de caractère

---

✓ indicates a very frequent word

2 *adj* caractéristique (of de)
characterize *vtr* (a) (depict) dépeindre (as comme)
(b) (typify) caractériser; **to be ~d by** se caractériser par
character reference *n* références *fpl*
charade *n* comédie *f*
charades *n pl* (game) charades *fpl*
charcoal 1 *n* (a) (fuel) charbon *m* de bois
(b) (for drawing) fusain *m*
2 *adj* (*also* ~ **grey**) (gris) anthracite *inv*
◆ **charge** 1 *n* (a) (fee) frais *mpl*; additional *or* extra ~ supplément *m*; **to reverse the ~s** (on phone) appeler en PCV
(b) (accusation) accusation *f* (of de); (Law) inculpation *f*; **murder** ~ inculpation d'assassinat; **to press ~s against sth** engager des poursuites contre qch
(c) (attack) charge *f* (**against** contre)
(d) **to be in** ~ (gen) être responsable (of de); (Mil) commander; **the person in** ~ le/la responsable; **to take** ~ prendre les choses en main
(e) (child) enfant *mf* dont on s'occupe; (pupil) élève *mf*; (patient) malade *mf*
(f) (explosive, electrical) charge *f*
2 *vtr* (a) prélever *‹commission›*; percevoir *‹interest›* (**on** sur); **to** ~ **sb for sth** faire payer qch à qn; **how much do you** ~? vous prenez combien?; **I** ~ **£20 an hour je prends 20 livres sterling de l'heure**
(b) **to** ~ **sth to** mettre qch sur *‹account›*
(c) *‹police›* inculper *‹suspect›* (**with** de)
(d) (rush at) charger *‹enemy›*; *‹bull›* foncer sur *‹person›*
(e) charger *‹battery›*
3 *vi* **to** ~ **into/out of** se précipiter dans/de *‹room›*
charge account *n* (US) compte-client *m*
charge card *n* (credit card) carte *f* de crédit; (store card) carte *f* d'achat
char-grilled *adj* *‹steak›* grillé/-e au charbon de bois
charisma *n* charisme *m*
charismatic *adj* charismatique
charitable *adj* *‹person, act, explanation›* charitable (**to** envers); *‹organization›* caritatif/-ive
charity *n* (a) (virtue) charité *f*
(b) (organization) organisation *f* caritative; **to give to/collect money for** ~ donner à/collecter des fonds pour des œuvres de bienfaisance
charity shop *n* magasin *m* d'articles d'occasion (*vendus au profit d'une œuvre de bienfaisance*)
charity work *n* travail *m* bénévole (*au profit d'une œuvre de bienfaisance*)
charm *n* (a) charme *m*
(b) lucky ~ porte-bonheur *m inv*
charming *adj* *‹person, place›* charmant/-e; *‹child, animal›* adorable

charred *adj* carbonisé/-e
chart 1 *n* (a) (graph) graphique *m*
(b) (table) tableau *m*
(c) (map) carte *f*
(d) **the** ~**s** le hit-parade
2 *vtr* (a) (on map) tracer *‹route›*
(b) enregistrer *‹progress›*
charter 1 *n* charte *f*
2 *vtr* affréter *‹plane›*
chartered accountant, CA *n* (GB) ≈ expert-comptable *m*
charter flight *n* (GB) vol *m* charter
chase 1 *n* poursuite *f* (**after** de)
2 *vtr* (a) pourchasser *‹person, animal›*; **to** ~ **sb/sth up** *or* **down the street** courir après qn/qch dans la rue
(b) (*also* ~ **after**) courir après *‹woman, man, success›*
■ **chase away, chase off** chasser *‹person, animal›*
chassis *n* (*pl* ~) châssis *m*
chastity *n* chasteté *f*
chat 1 *n* conversation *f*; **to have a** ~ bavarder (**with** avec; **about** sur)
2 *vi* (*p prés etc* -**tt**-) bavarder (**with, to** avec)
■ **chat up** (GB) (colloq) draguer (fam)
chatline *n* réseau *m* téléphonique; (sexual) ≈ téléphone *m* rose
chatroom *n* site *m* de bavardage, salon *m* virtuel
chat show *n* (GB) talk-show *m*
chatter 1 *n* (of person) bavardage *m*; (of birds) gazouillis *m*
2 *vi* *‹person›* bavarder; *‹birds›* gazouiller; **her teeth were** ~**ing** elle claquait des dents
chatterbox *n* moulin *m* à paroles (fam)
chatty *adj* *‹person›* ouvert/-e; *‹letter›* vivant/-e
chauffeur 1 *n* chauffeur *m*; **a** ~**-driven car** une voiture avec chauffeur
2 *vtr* conduire
chauvinist *n, adj* (a) (gen) chauvin/-e *m/f*
(b) (*also* **male** ~) macho *m* (fam)
◆ **cheap** *adj* (a) bon marché *inv*; **to be** ~ être bon marché, ne pas coûter cher *inv*; ~**er** moins cher/-ère
(b) (shoddy) de mauvaise qualité
(c) *‹joke›* facile; *‹trick›* sale (*before n*)
cheapen *vtr* rabaisser
cheaply *adv* *‹produce, sell›* à bas prix; **to eat** ~ manger pour pas cher
cheap rate *adj, adv* à tarif réduit
cheat 1 *n* tricheur/-euse *m/f*
2 *vtr* tromper; **to feel** ~**ed** se sentir lésé/-e; **to** ~ **sb (out) of** dépouiller qn de
3 *vi* tricher (**in** à); **to** ~ **at cards** tricher aux cartes; **to** ~ **on sb** tromper qn
Chechnya *pr n* Tchétchénie *f*
◆ **check** 1 *n* (a) (for quality, security) contrôle *m* (**on** sur)
(b) (medical) examen *m*

⋯▷

(c) (restraint) frein *m* (**on** à)
(d) (in chess) ∼! échec au roi!; **in** ∼ en échec
(e) (*also* ∼ **fabric**) tissu *m* à carreaux (*also* ∼ **pattern**) carreaux *mpl*
(f) (US) (cheque) chèque *m*
(g) (US) (bill) addition *f*
(h) (US) (receipt) ticket *m*
(i) (US) (tick) croix *f*
2 *adj* ‹shirt, skirt› à carreaux
3 *vtr* **(a)** (gen) vérifier; contrôler ‹ticket, area, work›; prendre ‹temperature›; examiner ‹watch, map, pocket›
(b) (curb) contrôler ‹prices, inflation›; freiner ‹growth›; maîtriser ‹emotions›
4 *vi* **(a)** vérifier; **to** ∼ **with sb** demander à qn; **to** ∼ **for** dépister ‹problems›; chercher ‹leaks, flaws›
(b) to ∼ **into** arriver à ‹hotel›
■ **check in:** 1 ¶ ∼ **in** (at airport) enregistrer; (at hotel) arriver (**at** à)
2 ¶ ∼ **[sb/sth] in** enregistrer ‹baggage, passengers›
■ **check off** cocher ‹items›
■ **check out:** 1 ¶ ∼ **out** (leave) partir; **to** ∼ **out of** quitter ‹hotel›
2 ¶ ∼ **[sth] out** vérifier ‹information›; examiner ‹package, building›; se renseigner sur ‹club, scheme›
■ **check up on** faire une enquête sur ‹person›; vérifier ‹story, details›
checkbook *n* (US) carnet *m* de chèques, chéquier *m*
checkered (US) = CHEQUERED
checkers (US) = CHEQUERS
check-in *n* enregistrement *m*
checking account *n* (US) compte *m* courant
checklist *n* liste *f* de contrôle
checkmate *n* échec *m* et mat
checkout *n* caisse *f*
checkout assistant *n* caissier/-ière *m/f*
checkpoint *n* poste *m* de contrôle
checkroom *n* (US) (cloakroom) vestiaire *m*; (for baggage) consigne *f*
checkup *n* **(a)** (at doctor's) examen *m* médical, bilan *m* de santé; **to have a** ∼ passer *or* se faire faire un examen médical
(b) (at dentist's) visite *f* de routine
cheek *n* **(a)** (of face) joue *f*; ∼ **to** ∼ joue contre joue
(b) culot *m* (fam); **what a** ∼! quel culot!
cheekbone *n* pommette *f*
cheeky *adj* ‹person› effronté/-e, insolent/-e; ‹question› impoli/-e; ‹grin› espiègle, coquin/-e
cheer 1 *n* acclamation *f*; **to get a** ∼ être acclamé/-e
2 **cheers** *excl* **(a)** (toast) à la vôtre! (fam); (to close friend) à la tienne! (fam)

ᵟ indicates a very frequent word

(b) (GB) (colloq) (thanks) merci!
(c) (GB) (colloq) (goodbye) salut!
3 *vtr, vi* applaudir
■ **cheer up:** 1 ¶ ∼ **up** reprendre courage; ∼ **up!** courage!
2 ¶ ∼ **[sb] up** remonter le moral ‹person›
3 ¶ ∼ **[sth] up** égayer ‹room›
cheerful *adj* ‹person, mood, music› joyeux/-euse; ‹tone› enjoué/-e; ‹colour› gai/-e
cheerleader *n* majorette *f*
cheese *n* fromage *m*; ∼ **sandwich** sandwich *m* au fromage
cheeseboard *n* (object) plateau *m* à fromage; (selection) plateau *m* de fromages
cheetah *n* guépard *m*
chef *n* chef *m* cuisinier
chemical 1 *n* produit *m* chimique
2 *adj* chimique
chemist *n* **(a)** (GB) pharmacien/-ienne *m/f*; ∼'s **(shop)** pharmacie *f*
(b) (scientist) chimiste *mf*
chemistry *n* chimie *f*
chemotherapy *n* chimiothérapie *f*
cheque (GB), **check** (US) *n* chèque *m*; **to make out** *or* **write a** ∼ **for £20** faire un chèque de 20 livres sterling
chequebook (GB), **checkbook** (US) *n* chéquier *m*, carnet *m* de chèques
cheque card *n* (GB) carte *f* de garantie bancaire
chequered (GB), **checkered** (US) *adj*
(a) ‹cloth› à damiers
(b) ‹career, history› en dents de scie
chequers (GB), **checkers** (US) *n* jeu *m* de dames
cherish *vtr* caresser ‹hope›; chérir ‹memory, person›
cherry 1 *n* **(a)** (fruit) cerise *f*
(b) (*also* ∼ **tree**) cerisier *m*
2 *adj* (*also* ∼-**red**) rouge cerise *inv*
chess *n* échecs *mpl*; **a game of** ∼ une partie d'échecs
chessboard *n* échiquier *m*
chess set *n* jeu *m* d'échecs
ᵟ **chest** *n* **(a)** (of person) poitrine *f*; ∼ **measurement** tour *m* de poitrine
(b) (furniture) coffre *m*; ∼ **of drawers** commode *f*
(c) (crate) caisse *f*
IDIOM **to get something off one's** ∼ (colloq) vider son sac (fam)
chestnut 1 *n* **(a)** (nut) marron *m*, châtaigne *f*
(b) (*also* ∼ **tree**) (horse) marronnier *m* (d'Inde); (sweet) châtaignier *m*
2 *adj* ‹hair› châtain *inv*; **a** ∼ **horse** un (cheval) alezan
chew *vtr* mâcher ‹food, gum›; mordiller ‹pencil›; ronger ‹bone›
chewing gum *n* chewing-gum *m*

chewy *adj* difficile à mâcher

chick *n* (fledgling) oisillon *m*; (of fowl) poussin *m*

chicken *n* (a) (fowl) poulet *m*, poule *f*
(b) (meat) poulet *m*
(c) (colloq) (coward) poule *f* mouillée
■ **chicken out** (colloq) se dégonfler (fam)

chicken pox *n* varicelle *f*

chicken wire *n* grillage *m* (à mailles fines)

chickpea *n* pois *m* chiche

chicory *n* (a) (vegetable) endive *f*
(b) (in coffee) chicorée *f*

⚘ **chief** ① *n* chef *m*
② *adj* (a) ⟨reason⟩ principal/-e
(b) ⟨editor⟩ en chef

chief executive *n* directeur *m* général

chiefly *adv* notamment, surtout

chief of police *n* ≈ préfet *m* de police

Chief of Staff *n* (Mil) chef *m* d'état-major; (of White House) secrétaire *m* général

chiffon *n* mousseline *f*

chilblain *n* engelure *f*

⚘ **child** *n* (*pl* **children**) enfant *mf*; **when I was a ~** quand j'étais enfant

child abuse *n* mauvais traitements *mpl* infligés à un enfant; (sexual) sévices *mpl* sexuels exercés sur l'enfant

childbirth *n* accouchement *m*

childcare *n* (nurseries etc) structures *fpl* d'accueil pour les enfants d'âge préscolaire; (bringing up children) éducation *f* des enfants

childcare facilities *n pl* crèche *f*

childhood ① *n* enfance *f*; **in (his) early ~** dans sa prime enfance
② *adj* ⟨friend, memory⟩ d'enfance; ⟨illness⟩ infantile

childish *adj* puéril/-e

childless *adj* sans enfants

childlike *adj* enfantin/-e

childminder *n* (GB) nourrice *f*

child pornography *n* pédopornographie *f*

children's home *n* maison *f* d'enfants

Chile *pr n* Chili *m*

chill ① *n* (a) (coldness) fraîcheur *f*; **there is a ~ in the air** le fond de l'air est frais; **to send a ~ down sb's spine** donner des frissons à qn
(b) (illness) coup *m* de froid
② *adj* (a) ⟨wind⟩ frais/fraîche
(b) ⟨reminder, words⟩ brutal/-e
③ *vtr* (a) mettre [qch] à refroidir ⟨dessert, soup⟩; rafraîchir ⟨wine⟩
(b) (make cold) faire frissonner ⟨person⟩; **to ~ sb's** *or* **the blood** glacer le sang à qn
④ *vi* ⟨dessert⟩ refroidir; ⟨wine⟩ rafraîchir
■ **chill out** (colloq) décompresser (fam); **~ out!** laisse faire!

chilli, **chili** *n* (a) (also **~ pepper**) piment *m* rouge
(b) (also **~ powder**) chili *m*
(c) (also **~ con carne**) chili *m* con carne

chilly *adj* froid; **it's ~** il fait froid

chime *n* carillon *m*

chimney *n* (*pl* **-neys**) cheminée *f*

chimpanzee *n* chimpanzé *m*

chin *n* menton *m*

china ① *n* porcelaine *f*
② *adj* ⟨cup, plate⟩ en porcelaine

China *pr n* Chine *f*

⚘ **Chinese** ① *n* (a) (person) Chinois/-oise *m/f*
(b) (language) chinois *m*
② *adj* chinois/-oise; ⟨embassy⟩ de Chine

chink *n* (a) (in wall) fente *f*; (in curtain) entrebâillement *m*
(b) (sound) tintement *m*

chip ① *n* (a) (fragment) fragment *m* (of de); (of wood) copeau *m*; (of glass) éclat *m*
(b) (in wood, china) ébréchure *f*
(c) (microchip) puce *f* (électronique)
② **chips** *n pl* (a) (GB) (fried potatoes) frites *fpl*
(b) (US) (crisps) chips *fpl*
③ *vtr* (*p prés etc* **-pp-**) ébrécher ⟨glass, plate⟩; écailler ⟨paint⟩; **to ~ a tooth** se casser une dent
IDIOM **to have a ~ on one's shoulder** être amer/-ère
■ **chip in** (GB) (colloq) (financially) donner un peu d'argent

chipboard *n* aggloméré *m*

chip shop *n* marchand *m* de frites

chiropodist *n* pédicure *mf*

chiropractor *n* chiropraticien/-ienne *m/f*, chiropracteur *m*

chirp *vi* ⟨bird⟩ pépier

chisel ① *n* ciseau *m*
② *vtr* (*p prés etc* **-ll-**, **-l-** (US)) ciseler

chitchat *n* (colloq) bavardage *m*

chivalry *n* (a) (courtesy) galanterie *f*

chive *n* ciboulette *f*

chlorine *n* chlore *m*

choc-ice *n* (GB) esquimau *m*

chock-a-block *adj* plein à craquer

chocolate ① *n* chocolat *m*
② *adj* ⟨sweets⟩ en chocolat; ⟨biscuit, cake, ice cream⟩ au chocolat

⚘ **choice** *n* choix *m* (**between, of** entre); **to make a ~** faire un choix, choisir; **to be spoilt for ~** avoir l'embarras du choix; **out of** *or* **from ~** par choix

choir *n* (of church, school) chorale *f*; (professional) chœur *m*

choirboy *n* petit chanteur *m*, jeune choriste *m*

choke ① *n* (Aut) starter *m*
② *vtr* (a) (throttle) étrangler ⟨person⟩ ⋯⟩

(b) ‹fumes, smoke› étouffer
3 vi s'étouffer
■ **choke back** étouffer ‹cough, sob›; **to ~ back one's tears** retenir ses larmes
cholera n choléra m
cholesterol n cholestérol m
◌ **choose** 1 vtr (prét **chose**, pp **chosen**)
(a) (select) choisir (**from** parmi)
(b) (decide) décider (**to do** de faire)
2 vi (prét **chose**, pp **chosen**) **(a)** (select) choisir (**between** entre)
(b) (prefer) **to ~ to do** préférer faire
choosy adj difficile (**about** en ce qui concerne)
chop 1 n (Culin) côtelette f; **pork ~** côtelette f de porc
2 vtr (p prés etc **-pp-**) **(a)** (also ~ **up**) couper ‹wood›; couper, émincer ‹vegetable, meat›; hacher ‹parsley, onion›; **to ~ sth finely** hacher qch
(b) réduire ‹service, deficit›
IDIOM **to ~ and change** ‹person› changer d'avis comme de chemise
■ **chop down** abattre ‹tree›
■ **chop off** couper ‹branch, end›; trancher ‹head, hand, finger›
chopping board n planche f à découper
chopping knife n couteau m de cuisine
choppy adj ‹sea, water› agité/-e
chopstick n baguette f (chinoise)
chord n accord m
chore n tâche f; **to do the ~s** faire le ménage
choreograph vtr chorégraphier
chorus n **(a)** (singers) chœur m
(b) (piece of music) chœur m
(c) (refrain) refrain m
Christ pr n le Christ, Jésus-Christ
christen vtr baptiser
christening n baptême m
◌ **Christian** 1 n chrétien/-ienne m/f
2 adj chrétien/-ienne; ‹attitude› charitable
Christianity n christianisme m
Christian name n nom m de baptême
◌ **Christmas** n ~ (**day**) (jour m de) Noël; **at ~** à Noël; **Merry ~!, Happy ~!** Joyeux Noël!
Christmas card n carte f de Noël
Christmas eve n veille f de Noël
Christmas tree n sapin m de Noël
chrome n chrome m
chronic adj **(a)** ‹illness› chronique
(b) ‹liar› invétéré/-e; ‹problem, shortage› chronique
chronicle n chronique f
chronological adj chronologique
chubby adj ‹child, finger› potelé/-e; ‹cheek› rebondi/-e; ‹face› joufflu/-e; ‹adult› rondelet/-ette

chuck vtr (colloq) **(a)** (also ~ **away**) balancer (fam), jeter
(b) larguer (fam) ‹boyfriend, girlfriend›
chuckle vi glousser; **to ~ at sth** rire de qch
chuffed adj (GB) (colloq) vachement (fam) content/-e (**about, at, with** de)
chum n (colloq) copain/copine m/f (fam), pote m (fam)
chunk n **(a)** (of meat, fruit) morceau m; (of wood) tronçon m; (of bread) quignon m; **pineapple ~s** ananas m en morceaux
(b) (of population, text, day) partie f (**of** de)
◌ **church** 1 n (pl ~**es**) (Catholic, Anglican) église f; (Protestant) temple m
2 adj ‹bell, choir, steeple› d'église; ‹fête› paroissial/-e; ‹wedding› religieux/-ieuse
churchgoer n pratiquant/-e m/f
church hall n salle f paroissiale
churchyard n cimetière m
churn 1 n **(a)** (for butter) baratte f
(b) (GB) (for milk) bidon m
2 vtr **to ~ butter** baratter
■ **churn out** pondre [qch] en série ‹novels›; produire [qch] en série ‹goods›
■ **churn up** faire des remous dans ‹water›
chute n **(a)** (slide) toboggan m
(b) (for rubbish) vide-ordures m inv
(c) (for toboggan) piste f de toboggan
cicada n cigale f
cider n cidre m
cigar n cigare m
cigarette 1 n cigarette f
2 adj ‹ash, smoke› de cigarette; ‹case, paper› à cigarettes
cigarette lighter n (portable) briquet m; (in car) allume-cigares m inv
cinder n (glowing) braise f; (ash) cendre f
Cinderella pr n Cendrillon
cinecamera n caméra f (d'amateur)
cine film n pellicule f cinématographique
cinema n cinéma m
cinemagoer n (regular) cinéphile mf, amateur m de cinéma; (spectator) spectateur/-trice m/f
cinnamon n cannelle f
◌ **circle** 1 n **(a)** (gen) cercle m; **to go round in ~s** tourner en rond; **to have ~s under one's eyes** avoir les yeux cernés
(b) (in theatre) balcon m; **in the ~** au balcon
2 vtr **(a)** ‹plane› tourner autour de ‹airport›; ‹person, animal, vehicle› faire le tour de ‹building›; tourner autour de ‹person, animal›
(b) (surround) encercler
3 vi tourner en rond (**around** autour de)
circuit n **(a)** (gen) circuit m
(b) (lap) tour m
circuit breaker n disjoncteur m
circular 1 n (newsletter) circulaire f; (advertisement) prospectus m

---

◌ indicates a very frequent word

2 adj ‹object› rond/-e; ‹argument› circulaire

circulate **1** vtr faire circuler
2 vi **(a)** (gen) circuler
(b) (at party) **let's ~ on va aller faire connaissance

circulation n **(a)** (gen) circulation f
(b) (of newspaper) tirage m

circulation figures n pl chiffres mpl de tirage

circumcision n (of boy) circoncision f; (of girl) excision f

circumference n circonférence f

circumflex n accent m circonflexe

✧ **circumstances** n pl **(a)** circonstances fpl; **in** or **under the ~** dans ces circonstances; **under no ~** en aucun cas
(b) (financial position) situation f

circumstantial adj ‹evidence› indirect/-e

circus n cirque m

CIS pr n (abbr – **Commonwealth of Independent States**) CEI f

cistern n (of lavatory) réservoir m de chasse d'eau; (in loft or underground) citerne f

✧ **citizen** n **(a)** (of state) citoyen/-enne m/f; (when abroad) ressortissant/-e m/f
(b) (of town) habitant/-e m/f

citizenship n nationalité f

citrus fruit n agrume m

✧ **city** n (grande) ville f; **the City** (GB) la City

city centre (GB), **city center** (US) n centre-ville m

civic adj ‹administration, official› municipal/-e; ‹pride, responsibility› civique

civic centre (GB), **civic center** (US) n centre m municipal (culturel et administratif)

✧ **civil** adj **(a)** ‹case, court, offence› civil/-e
(b) (polite) courtois/-e

civil engineering n génie m civil

civilian n civil/-e m/f

civilization n civilisation f

civilized adj civilisé/-e

civil law n droit m civil

civil liberty n libertés fpl individuelles

civil partnership n union f civile (entre partenaires de même sexe)

civil rights n pl droits mpl civils

civil servant n fonctionnaire mf

civil service n fonction f publique

civil war n guerre f civile

✧ **claim** **1** n **(a)** (demand) revendication f
(b) (in insurance) (against a person) réclamation f; (for fire, theft) demande f d'indemnisation
(c) (for welfare benefit) demande f d'allocation
(d) (assertion) affirmation f
2 vtr **(a)** (maintain) prétendre
(b) revendiquer ‹money, property, responsibility, right›
(c) faire une demande de ‹benefit›; faire une demande de remboursement de ‹expenses›

3 vi **(a)** **to ~ for damages** faire une demande pour dommages et intérêts
(b) (apply for benefit) faire une demande d'allocation

claimant n **(a)** (for benefit, compensation) demandeur/-euse m/f (**to** à)
(b) (to title, estate) prétendant/-e m/f (**to** à)

claim form n déclaration f de sinistre

clairvoyant n voyant/-e m/f, extralucide mf

clam n palourde f
■ **clam up** ne plus piper mot (**on sb** à qn)

clammy adj moite

clamour (GB), **clamor** (US) **1** n (shouting) clameur f
2 vi **(a)** (demand) **to ~ for sth** réclamer qch; **to ~ for sb to do sth** réclamer à qn de faire
(b) (rush, fight) se bousculer (**for** pour avoir; **to do** pour faire)

clamp **1** n **(a)** (on bench) valet m
(b) (also **wheel~**) sabot m de Denver
2 vtr **(a)** cramponner ‹two parts›; (at bench) fixer [qch] à l'aide d'un valet (**onto** à)
(b) serrer ‹jaw, teeth›
(c) (also **wheel~**) mettre un sabot de Denver à ‹car›
■ **clamp down**: **~ down on** faire de la répression contre ‹crime›; mettre un frein à ‹extravagance›

clampdown n mesures fpl de répression (**on sb** contre qn; **on sth** de qch)

clan n clan m

clandestine adj clandestin/-e

clang **1** n tracas m, bruit m métallique
2 vi ‹gate› claquer avec un son métallique; ‹bell› retentir

clap **1** n **to give sb a ~** applaudir qn; **a ~ of thunder** un coup de tonnerre
2 vtr (p prés etc **-pp-**) **to ~ one's hands** battre or taper des mains, frapper dans ses mains
3 vi (p prés etc **-pp-**) applaudir

clapping n applaudissements mpl

claret n **(a)** (wine) bordeaux m (rouge)
(b) (colour) bordeaux m

clarification n éclaircissement m, clarification f

clarify vtr éclaircir, clarifier

clarinet n clarinette f

clarity n clarté f

clash **1** n **(a)** (confrontation) affrontement m
(b) (of cultures, interests, personalities) conflit m
(c) **a ~ of cymbals** un coup de cymbales
2 vtr entrechoquer ‹bin lids›; frapper ‹cymbals›
3 vi **(a)** (fight, disagree) s'affronter; **to ~ with sb** (fight) se heurter à qn; (disagree) se quereller avec qn (**on, over** au sujet de)
(b) (be in conflict) ‹interests, beliefs› être incompatibles
(c) (coincide) ‹meetings› avoir lieu en même ···⟶

temps (**with** que)
(d) ⟨*colours*⟩ jurer

ᵍ **clasp** *n* (on bracelet, bag, purse) fermoir *m*; (on belt) boucle *f*

ᵍ **class** **1** *n* (gen) classe *f*; (lesson) cours *m* (in de); **to be in a ~ of one's own** être hors catégorie; **to travel first/second ~** voyager en première/deuxième classe **first/second ~ degree** ≈ licence *f* avec mention très bien/bien
2 *vtr* classer

class conscious *adj* soucieux/-ieuse des distinctions sociales

classic *n, adj* classique *m*

classical *adj* classique

classics *n* lettres *fpl* classiques

classification *n* (a) (category) classification *f*, catégorie *f*
(b) (categorization) classement *m*

classified **1** *n* (*also* ~ **ad**) petite annonce *f*
2 *adj* (secret) confidentiel/-ielle

classify *vtr* (a) (file) classer
(b) (declare secret) classer [qch] confidentiel/-ielle

classmate *n* camarade *mf* de classe

classroom *n* salle *f* de classe

classroom assistant *n* aide-éducateur/-trice *m/f*

class system *n* système *m* de classes

classy *adj* (colloq) ⟨*person, dress*⟩ qui a de la classe; ⟨*car, hotel*⟩ de luxe; ⟨*actor, performance*⟩ de grande classe

clatter **1** *n* cliquetis *m*; (loud) fracas *m*
2 *vi* ⟨*typewriter*⟩ cliqueter; ⟨*dishes*⟩ s'entrechoquer

clause *n* (a) (in grammar) proposition *f*
(b) (in contract, treaty) clause *f*; (in will, act of Parliament) disposition *f*

claustrophobia *n* claustrophobie *f*

claw *n* (a) (gen) griffe *f*; (of bird of prey) serre *f*; (of crab, lobster) pince *f*
(b) (on hammer) arrache-clou *m*, pied-de-biche *m*

clay *n* argile *f*

ᵍ **clean** **1** *adj* (a) (gen) propre; ⟨*air, water*⟩ pur/-e; **my hands are ~** j'ai les mains propres; **~ and tidy** d'une propreté irréprochable; **a ~ sheet of paper** une feuille blanche
(b) ⟨*joke*⟩ anodin/-e
(c) ⟨*reputation*⟩ sans tache; ⟨*record, licence*⟩ vierge
(d) (Sport) ⟨*tackle*⟩ sans faute; ⟨*hit*⟩ précis/-e
(e) (neat) ⟨*lines, profile*⟩ pur/-e
2 *vtr* nettoyer; **to ~ one's teeth** se brosser les dents

▪ **clean out** nettoyer [qch] à fond ⟨*cupboard, room*⟩

▪ **clean up**: **1** ¶ ~ **up** (a) tout nettoyer
(b) (wash oneself) se débarbouiller
2 ¶ ~ **[sth] up** nettoyer

clean-cut *adj* ⟨*image, person*⟩ soigné/-e

cleaner *n* (a) (woman) femme *f* de ménage; (man) agent *m* de nettoyage
(b) (detergent) produit *m* de nettoyage
(c) (shop) **cleaner's** pressing *m*

cleaning *n* (domestic) ménage *m*; (commercial) nettoyage *m*, entretien *m*

cleaning product *n* produit *m* d'entretien

cleanliness *n* propreté *f*

cleanse *vtr* nettoyer ⟨*skin, wound*⟩

cleanser *n* (a) (for face) démaquillant *m*
(b) (household) produit *m* d'entretien

clean-shaven *adj* **he's ~** il n'a ni barbe ni moustache

ᵍ **clear** **1** *adj* (a) (transparent) ⟨*glass, liquid*⟩ transparent/-e; ⟨*blue*⟩ limpide; ⟨*lens, varnish*⟩ incolore; ⟨*honey*⟩ liquide; **~ soup** consommé *m*
(b) (distinct) ⟨*image, outline*⟩ net/nette; ⟨*sound, voice*⟩ clair/-e
(c) (comprehensible) ⟨*description, instruction*⟩ clair/-e; **to make sth ~ to sb** faire comprendre qch à qn; **is that ~?** est-ce que c'est clair?
(d) (obvious) ⟨*need, sign*⟩ évident/-e; ⟨*advantage*⟩ net/nette (*before n*); ⟨*majority*⟩ large (*before n*); **it is ~ that** il est clair que
(e) (not confused) ⟨*idea, memory*⟩ clair/-e; ⟨*plan*⟩ précis/-e; **to keep a ~ head** garder les idées claires
(f) (empty) ⟨*view*⟩ dégagé/-e; ⟨*table*⟩ débarrassé/-e; ⟨*space*⟩ libre
(g) ⟨*conscience*⟩ tranquille
(h) ⟨*skin*⟩ net/nette; ⟨*sky*⟩ sans nuage; ⟨*day, night*⟩ clair/-e; **on a ~ day** par temps clair/-e
2 *adv* **to jump ~ of sth** éviter qch en sautant sur le côté; **to pull sb ~ of** extraire qn de ⟨*wreckage*⟩; **to stay** *or* **steer ~ of** éviter ⟨*town centre, troublemakers*⟩
3 *vtr* (a) enlever ⟨*rubbish, papers, mines*⟩; dégager ⟨*snow*⟩ (**from, off** de)
(b) déboucher ⟨*drains*⟩; débarrasser ⟨*table, room*⟩; vider ⟨*desk*⟩; évacuer ⟨*area, building*⟩; effacer ⟨*screen*⟩; défricher ⟨*land*⟩; **to ~ one's throat** se racler la gorge; **to ~ a path through sth** se frayer un chemin à travers qch
(c) dissiper ⟨*fog, smoke*⟩; disperser ⟨*crowd*⟩
(d) s'acquitter de ⟨*debt*⟩
(e) ⟨*bank*⟩ compenser ⟨*cheque*⟩
(f) innocenter ⟨*accused*⟩ (**of** de); **to ~ one's name** blanchir son nom
(g) approuver ⟨*request*⟩; **to ~ sth with sb** obtenir l'accord de qn pour qch
(h) franchir ⟨*hurdle, wall*⟩
(i) **to ~ customs** passer à la douane
4 *vi* (a) ⟨*liquid, sky*⟩ s'éclaircir
(b) ⟨*smoke, fog, cloud*⟩ se dissiper
(c) ⟨*air*⟩ se purifier
(d) ⟨*rash*⟩ disparaître

ᵍ indicates a very frequent word

(e) «cheque» être compensé/-e
■ **clear away**: 1 ¶ ∼ **away** débarrasser
2 ¶ ∼ **[sth] away** balayer «leaves»; enlever
«rubbish»; ranger «papers, toys»
■ **clear up**: 1 ¶ ∼ **up (a)** (tidy up) faire du
rangement
(b) «weather» s'éclaircir; «infection» disparaître
2 ¶ ∼ **[sth] up** ranger «mess, room, toys»;
ramasser «litter»
résoudre «problem»; dissiper
«misunderstanding»
clearance n (a) (of rubbish) enlèvement m;
land ∼ défrichement m du terrain
(b) (permission) autorisation f
(c) (also ∼ **sale**) liquidation f
clear-cut adj «plan, division» précis/-e;
«difference» net/nette (before n); «problem,
rule» clair/-e
clear-headed adj lucide
clearing n (glade) clairière f
ℐ **clearly** adv (a) «speak, hear, think, write»
clairement; «see» bien; «visible» bien; «labelled»
clairement
(b) (obviously) manifestement
clear-out n (colloq) **to have a** ∼ faire du
rangement
cleavage n décolleté m
cleaver n fendoir m
clef n clef f, **in the treble** ∼ en clef de fa
cleft adj «chin» marqué/-e d'un sillon;
«palate» fendu/-e
clench vtr serrer
clergy n clergé m
clergyman n (pl **-men**) ecclésiastique m
clerical adj (a) (of clergy) clérical/-e
(b) «staff» de bureau; ∼ **work** travail m de
bureau
clerk n (a) (in office, bank) employé/-e m/f
(b) (GB) (to lawyer) ≈ clerc m; (in court)
greffier/-ière m/f
(c) (US) (in hotel) réceptionniste mf; (in shop)
vendeur/-euse m/f
clever adj (a) (intelligent) intelligent/-e
(b) (ingenious) «solution, gadget, person»
astucieux/-ieuse, futé/-e
(c) (skilful) habile, adroit/-e
cliché n cliché m, lieu m commun
clichéd adj «expression» rebattu/-e; «idea,
technique» éculé/-e; «art, music» bourré/-e
(fam) de clichés
click 1 n (a) (of machine, lock) déclic m
(b) (of fingers, heels, tongue) claquement m
(c) (Comput) clic m
2 vtr **to** ∼ **one's fingers** faire claquer ses
doigts; **to** ∼ **one's heels** claquer des talons
3 vi «camera, lock» faire un déclic; «door»
faire un petit bruit sec; **to** ∼ **on** cliquer sur
«icon»
ℐ **client** n client/-e m/f
clientele n clientèle f

cliff n (by sea) falaise f; (inland) escarpement
m
climate n climat m
climate change n changement m
climatique
climax n (of war, conflict) paroxysme m; (of
plot, speech, play) point m culminant; (of career)
apogée m
ℐ **climb** 1 n (up hill) escalade f; (up tower)
montée f; (up mountain) ascension f
2 vtr grimper «hill»; faire l'ascension de
«mountain»; escalader «lamppost, wall»;
grimper à «ladder, tree»; monter «staircase»
3 vi (a) «person» grimper; **to** ∼ **down**
descendre «rock face»; **to** ∼ **over** enjamber
«stile»; passer par-dessus «fence, wall»;
escalader «debris, rocks»; **to** ∼ **up** grimper à
«ladder, tree»; monter «steps»
(b) «aircraft» monter
(c) «road» monter
(d) (increase) monter
■ **climb down** revenir sur sa décision
climber n grimpeur/-euse m/f, alpiniste mf
climbing n escalade f
clinch vtr (a) **to** ∼ **a deal** conclure une
affaire
(b) décider de «argument»
cling vi (prét, pp **clung**) (a) **to** ∼ **(on) to sb/**
sth se cramponner à qn/qch; **to** ∼ **together**
se cramponner l'un à l'autre
(b) «clothes» coller (**to** à)
(c) «smell» résister
clingfilm n (GB) scellofrais® m
clinic n centre m médical
ℐ **clinical** adj (a) «medicine» clinique;
«approach» objectif/-ive
(b) (unfeeling) froid/-e
clink 1 vtr faire tinter «glass, keys»; **to** ∼
glasses with trinquer avec
2 vi «glass, keys» tinter
clip 1 n (a) (on earring) clip m; (for hair)
barrette f
(b) (from film) extrait m
2 vtr (p prés etc **-pp-**) (a) tailler «hedge»;
couper «nails, moustache»; tondre «dog, sheep»
(b) accrocher «microphone» (**to** à); fixer
«brooch» (**to** à)
IDIOM to ∼ **sb's wings** rogner les ailes à qn
clipart n clip-art m
clipboard n (gen) porte-bloc m inv à pince;
(Comput) presse-papiers m inv
clip frame n sous-verre m inv
clip-ons n pl clips mpl
clippers n pl (for nails) coupe-ongles m inv;
(for hair, hedge) tondeuse f
clipping n (from paper) coupure f de presse
cloak 1 n cape f
2 vtr (a) ∼**ed in** enveloppé/-e dans
«darkness»; enveloppé/-e de «secrecy»
(b) (disguise) masquer
cloakroom n (a) (for coats) vestiaire m ⋯⋯

(b) (GB) (lavatory) toilettes *fpl*

clock *n* (large) horloge *f*; (small) pendule *f*; (Sport) chronomètre *m*; **to put the ~s forward/back one hour** avancer/reculer les pendules d'une heure; **to work around the ~** travailler 24 heures sur 24

■ **clock off** (GB) pointer (à la sortie)

■ **clock on** (GB) pointer

clock radio *n* radio-réveil *m*

clock tower *n* beffroi *m*

clockwise *adj, adv* dans le sens des aiguilles d'une montre

clockwork *adj* ⟨*toy*⟩ mécanique
IDIOM **to go like ~** aller comme sur des roulettes

clog *n* sabot *m*

cloister *n* cloître *m*

clone ① *n* clone *m*
② *vtr* cloner

cloning *n* clonage *m*

⚘ **close¹** ① *adj* (a) (near) proche (**to** de), voisin/-e (**to** de)
(b) ⟨*relative, friend*⟩ proche; ⟨*resemblance*⟩ frappant/-e
(c) ⟨*contest, result*⟩ serré/-e
(d) ⟨*scrutiny*⟩ minutieux/-ieuse; ⟨*supervision*⟩ étroit/-e; **to pay ~ attention to sth** faire une attention toute particulière à qch; **to keep a ~ watch** *or* **eye on sb/sth** surveiller étroitement qn/qch
(e) ⟨*print, formation*⟩ serré/-e
(f) ⟨*weather*⟩ lourd/-e; **it's ~** il fait lourd
② *adv* **to live quite ~ (by)** habiter tout près; **to move sth ~r** approcher qch; **to follow ~ behind sb** suivre de près; **to hold sb ~** serrer qn; **~ together** serrés les uns contre les autres; **Christmas is ~** Noël approche
③ **close by** *phr* près de ⟨*wall, bridge*⟩; **the ambulance is ~ by** l'ambulance n'est pas loin
④ **close to** *phr* (a) (near) près de
(b) (on point of) au bord de ⟨*tears, hysteria*⟩; **to be ~ to doing** être sur le point de faire
(c) (almost) près de; **to come ~ to doing** faillir faire
IDIOM **it was a ~ call** (colloq) *or* **shave** (colloq) *or* **thing** je l'ai/tu l'as *etc* échappé belle

⚘ **close²** ① *n* fin *f*
② *vtr* (a) fermer ⟨*door, book*⟩
(b) fermer ⟨*border, port*⟩; barrer ⟨*road*⟩; interdire l'accès à ⟨*area*⟩
(c) mettre fin à ⟨*meeting*⟩; fermer ⟨*account*⟩
(d) **to ~ the gap** réduire l'écart
(e) conclure ⟨*deal*⟩
③ *vi* (a) ⟨*airport, polls, shop*⟩ fermer; ⟨*door, container, eyes, mouth*⟩ se fermer
(b) (cease to operate) fermer définitivement
(c) ⟨*meeting, play*⟩ prendre fin; **to ~ with** se terminer par ⟨*song*⟩
(d) ⟨*currency, index*⟩ clôturer (**at** à)
(e) ⟨*gap*⟩ se réduire

⚘ indicates a very frequent word

④ **closed** *pp adj* fermé/-e; **behind ~d doors** à huis clos

■ **close down**: ① **¶~ down** fermer définitivement
② **¶~ [sth] down** fermer [qch] définitivement

■ **close up**: ① **¶~ up (a)** ⟨*flower, wound*⟩ se refermer; ⟨*group*⟩ se serrer
(b) ⟨*shopkeeper*⟩ fermer
② **¶~ [sth] up (a)** fermer ⟨*shop*⟩
(b) boucher ⟨*hole*⟩

closed-circuit television, CCTV *n* télévision *f* en circuit fermé

close-fitting *adj* ⟨*garment*⟩ ajusté/-e, près du corps

close-knit *adj* ⟨*family, group*⟩ très uni/-e

⚘ **closely** *adv* ⟨*follow, watch*⟩ de près; ⟨*resemble*⟩ beaucoup; **to be ~ related** ⟨*people*⟩ être proches parents

close-run *adj* très serré/-e

closet ① *n* (US) (cupboard) placard *m*; (for clothes) penderie *f*
② *adj* ⟨*alcoholic, fascist*⟩ inavoué/-e

close-up ① *n* gros plan *m*; **in ~** en gros plan
② **close up** *adv* (**from**) **~** de près

closing ① *n* fermeture *f*
② *adj* ⟨*minutes, words*⟩ dernier/-ière (*before n*); ⟨*scene, stage*⟩ final/-e; ⟨*speech*⟩ de clôture

closing date *n* date *f* limite (**for** de)

closing-down sale, closing-out sale (US) *n* liquidation *f*

closing time *n* heure *f* de fermeture

closure *n* fermeture *f*

clot ① *n* caillot *m*
② *vtr, vi* (*p prés etc* **-tt-**) coaguler, cailler

cloth *n* (a) (fabric) tissu *m*
(b) (for polishing, dusting) chiffon *m*; (for floor) serpillière *f*; (for drying dishes) torchon *m*; (for table) nappe *f*

⚘ **clothes** *n pl* vêtements *mpl*; **to put on/take off one's ~** s'habiller/se déshabiller

clothes brush *n* brosse *f* à habits

clotheshanger *n* cintre *m*

clothes line *n* corde *f* à linge

clothes peg *n* pince *f* à linge

clothes shop *n* magasin *m* de vêtements

clothing *n* vêtements *mpl*; **an item** *or* **article of ~** un vêtement

cloud ① *n* nuage *m*; **to cast a ~ over sth** jeter une ombre sur qch
② *vtr* (a) ⟨*steam, breath*⟩ embuer ⟨*mirror*⟩; ⟨*tears*⟩ brouiller ⟨*vision*⟩
(b) obscurcir ⟨*judgment*⟩; brouiller ⟨*memory*⟩; **to ~ the issue** brouiller les cartes
IDIOM **to be living in ~-cuckoo-land** croire au père Noël

■ **cloud over** ⟨*sky*⟩ se couvrir (de nuages); ⟨*face*⟩ s'assombrir

cloudy *adj* (a) ⟨*weather*⟩ couvert/-e
(b) ⟨*liquid*⟩ trouble

clout n **(a)** (blow) claque f, coup m
(b) (influence) influence f (**with** auprès de, sur)

clove n **(a)** (spice) clou m de girofle
(b) (of garlic) gousse f

clover n trèfle m

clown n clown m
■ **clown around** (GB) faire le clown or le pitre

⚥ **club** n **(a)** (association) club m
(b) (colloq) (nightclub) boîte f de nuit
(c) (in cards) trèfle m
(d) (for golf) club m
(e) (weapon) massue f
■ **club together** cotiser

club car n (US) wagon-bar m de première classe

club class n classe f club or affaires

cluck vi ‹hen› glousser

clue n indication f (**to, as to** quant à); (in police investigation) indice m (**to** quant à); (in crossword) définition f; **I haven't (got) a** ∼

clued-up adj (colloq) calé/-e (fam) (**about** sur)

clueless adj (colloq) nul/nulle (fam) (**about** en)

clump n (of flowers, grass) touffe f; (of trees) massif m; (of earth) motte f

clumsiness n (carelessness) maladresse f; (awkwardness) gaucherie f; (of system) côté m peu pratique

clumsy adj ‹person, attempt› maladroit/-e; ‹object› grossier/-ière; ‹animal› pataud/-e; ‹tool› peu maniable; ‹style› lourd/-e

cluster 1 n (of flowers, berries) grappe f; (of people, islands, trees) groupe m; (of houses) ensemble m; (of diamonds) entourage m; (of stars) amas m
2 vi ‹people› se rassembler (**around** autour de)

clutch 1 n (Aut) embrayage m
2 vtr tenir fermement
■ **clutch at** tenter d'attraper ‹branch, rail, person›; saisir ‹arm›

clutch bag n pochette f

clutches n pl **to fall into the** ∼ of tomber sous les griffes or la patte (fam) de

clutter 1 n désordre m
2 vtr (also ∼ **up**) encombrer

Co n (abbr = **company**) Cie

c/o prep (abbr = **care of**) chez

⚥ **coach** 1 n **(a)** (bus) (auto)car m
(b) (GB) (of train) wagon m
(c) (Sport) entraîneur/-euse m/f
(d) (for drama, voice) répétiteur/-trice m/f
(e) (horse-drawn) carrosse m
2 vtr **(a)** (Sport) entraîner ‹team›
(b) (teach) **to** ∼ **sb** donner des leçons particulières à qn (**in** en)

coach station n gare f routière

coach trip n excursion f en autocar

coal n charbon m

IDIOM to haul sb over the ∼**s** (colloq) passer un savon à qn (fam)

coalfield n bassin m houiller

coal fire n cheminée f (où brûle un feu de charbon)

coalition n coalition f

coalmine n mine f de charbon

coalminer n mineur m

coarse adj **(a)** ‹texture› grossier/-ière; ‹skin› épais/-aisse; ‹sand, salt› gros/grosse (before n)
(b) ‹manners› grossier/-ière; ‹language, joke› cru/-e

coast 1 n côte f; **off the** ∼ près de la côte
2 vi ‹car, bicycle› descendre en roue libre

coastal adj côtier/-ière

coaster n (mat) dessous-de-verre m inv

coastguard n **(a)** (person) garde-côte m
(b) (organization) gendarmerie f maritime

coastline n littoral m

coat 1 n **(a)** (garment) manteau m
(b) (of dog, cat) pelage m; (of horse, leopard) robe f
(c) (layer) couche f
2 vtr **to** ∼ **sth with** enduire qch de ‹paint, adhesive›; couvrir qch de ‹dust, oil›; enrober qch de ‹breadcrumbs, chocolate, sauce›

coat hanger n cintre m

coat of arms n blason m, armoiries fpl

coat rack n portemanteau m

coax vtr cajoler; **to** ∼ **sb into doing** persuader qn (gentiment) de faire

cobbler n cordonnier m

cobblestones n pl pavés mpl

cobweb n toile f d'araignée

cocaine n cocaïne f

cock 1 n **(a)** (rooster) coq m
(b) (male bird) (oiseau m) mâle m
2 vtr **(a)** **to** ∼ **an eyebrow** hausser les sourcils; **to** ∼ **a leg** ‹dog› lever la patte; **to** ∼ **an ear** dresser l'oreille
(b) (tilt) pencher
(c) (Mil) armer ‹gun›

cock-and-bull story n histoire f abracadabrante or à dormir debout

cockatoo n cacatoès m

cockerel n jeune coq m

cockle n coque f

cockpit n cockpit m, poste m de pilotage

cockroach n cafard m

cocktail n cocktail m

cocktail bar n bar m

cocky adj impudent/-e

cocoa n cacao m; (drink) chocolat m

coconut n noix f de coco

cocoon n cocon m

cod n (pl ∼) morue f

COD n (abbr = **cash on delivery**) envoi m contre remboursement

code [1] n (a) (gen) code m
 (b) (also **dialling** ∼) indicatif m
 [2] vtr coder
codeine n codéine f
code name n nom m de code
codeword n (password) mot m de passe
coeducational adj mixte
coeliac adj cœliaque
coerce vtr exercer des pressions sur; **to** ∼
sb into doing contraindre qn à faire
coexist vi coexister (**with** avec)
⚜ **coffee** [1] n café m; **a black/white** ∼ un
café (noir)/au lait
 [2] adj ‹dessert› au café; ‹cup, filter, spoon›
à café
coffee break n pause(-)café f
coffee pot n cafetière f
coffee table n table f basse
coffin n cercueil m
cog n (tooth) dent f d'engrenage; (wheel)
pignon m
cohabit vi cohabiter (**with** avec)
coherent adj cohérent/-e
coil [1] n (a) (of rope, barbed wire) rouleau m;
(of electric wire) bobine f; (of hair) boucle f; (of
snake) anneau m
 (b) (contraceptive) stérilet m
 [2] vtr (also ∼ **up**) enrouler ‹hair, rope,
wire›
 [3] vi s'enrouler (**round** autour de)
coin [1] n pièce f (de monnaie); **a pound** ∼
une pièce d'une livre
 [2] vtr forger ‹term›
coin box n (pay phone) cabine f
(téléphonique) à pièces
coincide vi coïncider (**with** avec)
coincidence n coïncidence f, hasard m;
it is a ∼ **that** c'est par coïncidence que; **by** ∼
par hasard
coincidental adj fortuit/-e
coin operated adj qui marche avec des
pièces
coke n (a) (fuel) coke m
 (b) (colloq) (cocaine) coke f (fam)
Coke® n coca m
colander n passoire f
⚜ **cold** [1] n (a) (chilliness) froid m; **to feel the** ∼
être sensible au froid, être frileux/-euse
 (b) (Med) rhume m; **to have a** ∼ être
enrhumé/-e, avoir un rhume
 [2] adj (a) (chilly) froid; **to be** or **feel** ∼
‹person› avoir froid; **the room was** ∼ il faisait
froid dans la pièce; **it's** or **the weather's** ∼ il
fait froid; **to go** ∼ ‹food, water› se refroidir
 (b) ‹manner› froid/-e; **to be** ∼ **to** or **towards**
sb être froid/-e avec qn
IDIOMS **in** ∼ **blood** de sang-froid; **to be out**
∼ être sans connaissance

⚜ indicates a very frequent word

cold-blooded adj ‹animal› à sang froid;
‹killer› sans pitié
cold calling n démarchage m par
téléphone
coldness n froideur f
cold shoulder n **to give sb the** ∼ snober
qn, battre froid à qn
cold sore n bouton m de fièvre
cold sweat n **to bring sb out in a** ∼
donner des sueurs froides à qn
cold turkey n (colloq) (treatment) sevrage m;
(reaction) réaction f de manque; **to be** ∼ être
en manque
Cold War n guerre f froide
coleslaw n salade f à base de chou cru
colic n coliques fpl
collaborate vi collaborer (**on** à; **with**
avec)
collaboration n collaboration f
collaborator n collaborateur/-trice m/f
collapse [1] n (a) (of regime, economy)
effondrement m (**of, in** de)
 (b) (of deal, talks) échec m
 (c) (of company) faillite f (**of** de)
 (d) (of person) (physical) écroulement m;
(mental) effondrement m
 (e) (of building, bridge) effondrement m; (of
tunnel, wall) écroulement m
 (f) (Med) (of lung) collapsus m
 [2] vi (a) ‹regime, economy› s'effondrer;
‹deal, talks› échouer
 (b) ‹company› faire faillite
 (c) ‹person› s'écrouler
 (d) ‹building, bridge› s'effondrer; ‹tunnel,
wall› s'écrouler; ‹chair› s'affaisser (**under**
sous)
 (e) (Med) ‹lung› se dégonfler
 (f) (fold) ‹bike, pushchair› se plier
collapsible adj pliant/-e
collar n (a) (on garment) col m
 (b) (for animal) collier m
IDIOM **to get hot under the** ∼ se mettre en
rogne (fam)
collarbone n clavicule f
collar size n encolure f
collate vtr collationner
⚜ **colleague** n collègue mf
⚜ **collect** [1] adv (US) **to call sb** ∼ appeler
qn en PCV
 [2] vtr (a) ramasser ‹wood, litter, rubbish›;
rassembler ‹information›; recueillir
‹signatures›
 (b) (as hobby) collectionner, faire collection
de ‹stamps, coins›
 (c) ‹objects› prendre, ramasser ‹dust›
 (d) percevoir ‹rent›; encaisser ‹fares,
money›; recouvrer ‹debt›; toucher ‹pension›;
percevoir ‹tax, fine›
 (e) faire la levée de ‹mail, post›
 (f) (pick up) aller chercher ‹person›; récupérer
‹keys, book›

3 vi **(a)** ‹dust, leaves› s'accumuler; ‹people› se rassembler
(b) to ∼ for charity faire la quête pour des bonnes œuvres
4 **collected** pp adj **(a)** ‹person› calme
(b) (assembled) the ∼ed works of Dickens les œuvres complètes de Dickens

✧ **collection** n **(a)** (of coins, records) collection f; (anthology) recueil m; art ∼ collection f (de tableaux)
(b) (money) collecte f (for pour); (in church) quête f
(c) (of mail) levée f

collective adj collectif/-ive
collective ownership n copropriété f
collector n **(a)** (of coins, stamps) collectionneur/-euse m/f
(b) (of taxes) percepteur m; (of rent, debts) encaisseur m
collector's item n pièce f de collection
✧ **college** n établissement m d'enseignement supérieur; (school, part of university) collège m; (US Univ) faculté f; to go to ∼, to be at or in (US) ∼ faire des études supérieures
college of further education, CFE n (GB) école ouverte aux adultes et aux jeunes pour terminer un cycle d'études secondaires
collide vi ‹vehicle, plane› entrer en collision (with avec)
collie n (dog) colley m
colliery n houillère f
collision n collision f
colloquial adj familier/-ière
colon n **(a)** (Anat) côlon m
(b) (punctuation) deux points mpl
colonel n colonel m
colonialist n, adj colonialiste mf
colonization n colonisation f
colonize vtr coloniser
colonizer n colon m
colony n colonie f
✧ **colour** (GB), **color** (US) **1** n **(a)** couleur f; what ∼ is it? de quelle couleur est-il/elle?; to put ∼ into sb's cheeks redonner des couleurs à qn
(b) (dye) (for food) colorant m; (for hair) teinture f
2 vtr **(a)** (with paints, crayons) colorier; (with food dye) colorer
(b) (prejudice) fausser ‹judgment›
3 vi ‹person› rougir
IDIOMS to be off ∼ ne pas être en forme; to show one's true ∼s se montrer sous son vrai jour
colour blind adj daltonien/-ienne
coloured (GB), **colored** (US) adj ‹pen, paper, bead› de couleur; ‹picture› en couleur; ‹light, glass› coloré/-e
colour film n (for camera) pellicule f couleur

colourful (GB), **colorful** (US) adj
(a) ‹dress, shirt› aux couleurs vives
(b) ‹story, life› haut en couleur; ‹character› pittoresque
colouring (GB), **coloring** (US) n **(a)** (of animal) couleurs fpl; (of person) teint m
(b) (for food) colorant m
colour scheme n couleurs fpl, coloris m
colour supplement n supplément m illustré
colour television n télévision f (en) couleur
colt n poulain m
✧ **column** n **(a)** (pillar) colonne f
(b) (on page, list) colonne f
(c) (newspaper article) rubrique f; sports ∼ rubrique sportive
columnist n journaliste mf
coma n coma m; in a ∼ dans le coma
comatose adj (Med) comateux/-euse; (figurative) abruti/-e
comb **1** n peigne m
2 vtr to ∼ sb's hair peigner qn; to ∼ one's hair se peigner
combat **1** n combat m
2 vtr (p prés etc **-tt-**) lutter contre, combattre
combat jacket n veste f de treillis
✧ **combination** n combinaison f
✧ **combine** **1** n groupe m
2 vtr **(a)** combiner ‹activities, colours, items› (with avec); associer ‹ideas, aims› (with à); to ∼ forces (merge) s'allier; (cooperate) collaborer
(b) (Culin) mélanger (with avec)
3 vi **(a)** ‹activities, colours, elements› se combiner
(b) ‹people, groups› s'associer; ‹firms› fusionner
combined adj **(a)** (joint) ∼ operation collaboration f; a ∼ effort une collaboration
(b) (total) ‹salary, age› total/-e
(c) ‹effects› combiné/-e
combine harvester n moissonneuse batteuse f
✧ **come** vi (prét **came**, pp **come**)
(a) ‹person, day› venir; ‹bus, news, winter, war› arriver; ‹dustman, postman› passer; to ∼ down descendre ‹stairs, street›; to ∼ up monter ‹stairs, street›; to ∼ into entrer dans ‹house, room›; when the time ∼s lorsque le moment sera venu; (I'm) coming! j'arrive!; to ∼ to sb for venir demander [qch] à qn ‹money, advice›; don't ∼ any closer ne vous approchez pas (plus); to ∼ as a shock/surprise être un choc/une surprise
(b) (reach) to ∼ up/down to ‹water› venir jusqu'à; ‹dress, curtain› arriver à
(c) (happen) how ∼? comment ça se fait?; to take things as they ∼ prendre les choses comme elles viennent; ∼ what may advienne que pourra

⋯▸

C

(d) (begin) to ∼ to do finir par faire
(e) to ∼ from ⟨person⟩ être originaire de, venir de ⟨city, country⟩; ⟨word, legend⟩ venir de ⟨language, country⟩; ⟨stamps, painting⟩ provenir de ⟨place⟩; ⟨smell, sound⟩ venir de ⟨place⟩
(f) (in order) to ∼ after suivre, venir après; to ∼ before (in time, list, queue) précéder; (in importance) passer avant; to ∼ first/last (in race) arriver premier/dernier
(g) when it ∼s to sth/to doing lorsqu'il s'agit de qch/de faire
(h) to ∼ true se réaliser; to ∼ undone se défaire
■ **come across**: ☐1 ¶ ∼ across ⟨meaning, message⟩ passer; ⟨feelings⟩ transparaître; ∼ across as donner l'impression d'être ⟨liar, expert⟩; paraître ⟨honest⟩
☐2 ¶ ∼ across [sth] tomber sur ⟨article⟩
■ **come along (a)** ⟨bus, person⟩ arriver; ⟨opportunity⟩ se présenter
(b) (hurry up) ∼ along! dépêche-toi!
(c) (attend) venir (to à)
(d) (progress) ⟨pupil⟩ faire des progrès; ⟨book, work, project⟩ avancer; ⟨painting, tennis⟩ progresser
■ **come apart (a)** (accidentally) ⟨book, box⟩ se déchirer; ⟨toy, camera⟩ se casser
(b) (intentionally) ⟨components⟩ se séparer; ⟨machine⟩ se démonter
■ **come around** (US) = COME ROUND
■ **come away** partir
■ **come back (a)** (return) revenir (from de; to à); (to one's house) rentrer
(b) ⟨law, system⟩ être rétabli/-e; ⟨trend⟩ revenir à la mode
■ **come down (a)** ⟨person, lift, blind⟩ descendre; ⟨curtain⟩ tomber
(b) ⟨price, inflation, temperature⟩ baisser; ⟨cost⟩ diminuer
(c) ⟨snow, rain⟩ tomber
(d) ⟨ceiling, wall⟩ s'écrouler; ⟨hem⟩ se défaire
(e) to ∼ down with attraper ⟨flu⟩
■ **come forward (a)** (step forward) s'avancer
(b) (volunteer) se présenter
■ **come in (a)** (enter) entrer **(through** par)
(b) ⟨tide⟩ monter
(c) to ∼ in useful être utile
(d) to ∼ in for criticism ⟨person⟩ être critiqué/-e; ⟨plan⟩ faire l'objet de nombreuses critiques
■ **come into (a)** hériter de ⟨money⟩; entrer en possession de ⟨inheritance⟩
(b) luck doesn't ∼ into it ce n'est pas une question de hasard
■ **come off (a)** ⟨button, handle⟩ se détacher; ⟨lid⟩ s'enlever; ⟨paint⟩ s'écailler
(b) ⟨ink⟩ s'effacer; ⟨stain⟩ partir
(c) ⟨plan, trick⟩ réussir
■ **come on (a)** ∼ on! allez!
(b) ⟨person, patient⟩ faire des progrès; ⟨bridge, novel⟩ avancer; ⟨plant⟩ pousser

(c) ⟨light⟩ s'allumer; ⟨heating, fan⟩ se mettre en route
(d) ⟨actor⟩ entrer en scène
■ **come out (a)** ⟨person, animal, vehicle⟩ sortir **(of** de); ⟨star⟩ apparaître; ⟨sun, moon⟩ se montrer
(b) (strike) faire la grève; to ∼ out on strike faire la grève
(c) ⟨contact lens, tooth⟩ tomber; ⟨contents⟩ sortir; ⟨cork⟩ s'enlever
(d) ⟨water, smoke⟩ sortir **(through** par)
(e) ⟨stain⟩ s'en aller, partir
(f) ⟨magazine, novel⟩ paraître; ⟨album, film, product⟩ sortir
(g) ⟨details, facts⟩ être révélé/-e; ⟨results⟩ être connu/-e
(h) ⟨photo, photocopy⟩ être réussi/-e
(i) to ∼ out with sortir ⟨excuse⟩; raconter ⟨nonsense⟩; to ∼ straight out with it le dire franchement
(j) ⟨homosexual⟩ déclarer publiquement son homosexualité
■ **come over**: ¶ ∼ over venir **(to do** faire); what's ∼ over you? qu'est-ce qui te prend?
■ **come round** (GB), **come around** (US) **(a)** (regain consciousness) reprendre connaissance
(b) (visit) venir
(c) (change mind) changer d'avis
■ **come through**: ☐1 ¶ ∼ through **(a)** (survive) s'en tirer
(b) ⟨heat, ink⟩ traverser; ⟨light⟩ passer
☐2 ¶ ∼ through [sth] se tirer de ⟨crisis⟩; survivre à ⟨operation, ordeal⟩
■ **come to**: ☐1 ¶ ∼ to reprendre connaissance
☐2 ¶ ∼ to [sth] ⟨shopping⟩ revenir à; ⟨bill, total⟩ s'élever à; that ∼s to £40 cela fait 40 livres sterling; it may not ∼ to that nous n'en arriverons peut-être pas là
■ **come under: (a)** to ∼ under threat être menacé/-e
(b) (be classified under) être classé/-e dans le rayon ⟨reference, history⟩
■ **come up (a)** ⟨problem, issue⟩ être soulevé/-e; ⟨name⟩ être mentionné/-e
(b) ⟨opportunity⟩ se présenter; something urgent has ∼ up j'ai quelque chose d'urgent à faire
(c) ⟨sun, moon⟩ sortir; ⟨daffodils⟩ sortir
(d) (in law) ⟨case⟩ passer au tribunal
(e) to ∼ up against se heurter à ⟨problem⟩
(f) to ∼ up with trouver ⟨answer, idea⟩
comeback n come-back m; to make a ∼ ⟨person⟩ faire un come-back; ⟨trend⟩ revenir à la mode
comedian n (male) comique m
comedienne n actrice f comique
comedy n comédie f
comet n comète f
comeuppance n (colloq) to get one's ∼ avoir ce qu'on mérite

⚲ indicates a very frequent word

comfort [1] *n* (a) confort *m*; to live in ~ vivre dans l'aisance; home ~s le confort du foyer
(b) (consolation) réconfort *m*, consolation *f*
[2] *vtr* consoler; (stronger) réconforter

ơ **comfortable** *adj* (a) ⟨chair, clothes, journey⟩ confortable; ⟨temperature⟩ agréable
(b) ⟨person⟩ à l'aise

comfortably *adv* (gen) confortablement; (easily) facilement, aisément; to be ~ off être à l'aise

comforting *adj* réconfortant/-e

comic [1] *n* (a) = COMEDIAN
(b) (magazine) bande *f* dessinée
[2] *adj* comique

comical *adj* cocasse, comique

comic strip *n* bande *f* dessinée

coming [1] *n* arrivée *f*; ~s and goings allées et venues *fpl*
[2] *adj* ⟨election, event⟩ prochain/-e (*before n*); ⟨months, weeks⟩ à venir

comma *n* virgule *f*

ơ **command** [1] *n* (a) (order) ordre *m*
(b) (military control) commandement *m*; to be in ~ commander
(c) (of language) maîtrise *f*; to be in ~ of the situation avoir la situation en main
(d) (Comput) commande *f*
[2] *vtr* (a) ordonner à ⟨person⟩ (to do de faire)
(b) inspirer ⟨affection, respect⟩
(c) (Mil) commander ⟨regiment⟩

commander *n* (gen) chef *m*; (Mil) commandant *m*

commanding *adj* ⟨manner, voice⟩ impérieux/-ieuse; ⟨presence⟩ imposant/-e

commanding officer, CO *n* commandant *m*

commando *n* (*pl* -os, -oes) commando *m*

commemorate *vtr* commémorer

commence *vtr*, *vi* commencer

commend *vtr* louer (on pour)

ơ **comment** [1] *n* (a) (public) commentaire *m* (on sur); (in conversation) remarque *f* (on sur); (written) annotation *f*
(b) to be a ~ on en dire long sur
[2] *vi* faire des commentaires (on sur)

commentary *n* commentaire *m* (on de)

commentator *n* (sports) commentateur/-trice *m/f*; (current affairs) journaliste *mf*

commerce *n* commerce *m*

ơ **commercial** [1] *n* annonce *f* publicitaire
[2] *adj* commercial/-e

commercial break *n* publicité *f*

commercial traveller *n* voyageur *m* de commerce

commiserate *vi* compatir (with avec; about, over à propos de)

ơ **commission** [1] *n* (a) (fee) commission *f*
(b) (order) commande *f* (for de)

(c) (committee) commission *f* (on sur)
[2] *vtr* (a) commander ⟨work⟩ (from à); to ~ sb to do charger qn de faire
(b) (Mil) to be ~ed (as) an officer être nommé/-e officier

commissioner *n* (a) (gen) membre *m* d'une commission
(b) (GB) (in police) ≈ préfet *m* de police
(c) (in the EC) membre *m* de la Commission européenne

ơ **commit** *vtr* (*p prés etc* -tt-) (a) commettre ⟨crime, error, sin⟩; to ~ suicide se suicider
(b) to ~ oneself s'engager (to à)
(c) consacrer ⟨money, time⟩ (to à)

ơ **commitment** *n* (a) (obligation) engagement *m* (to do à faire)
(b) (sense of duty) attachement *m* (to à)

committed *adj* (a) (devoted) ⟨parent, teacher⟩ dévoué/-e; ⟨Christian, Socialist⟩ fervent/-e; to be ~ to/to doing se consacrer à/à faire
(b) (with commitments) pris/-e

ơ **committee** *n* comité *m*; (to investigate, report) commission *f*

commodity *n* article *m*; (food) denrée *f*

ơ **common** [1] *n* terrain *m* communal
[2] **Commons** *n pl* (GB Pol) the Commons les Communes *fpl*
[3] *adj* (a) (frequent) courant/-e, fréquent/-e; in ~ use d'un usage courant
(b) (shared) commun/-e (to à); in ~ en commun; it is ~ knowledge c'est de notoriété publique
(c) the ~ people le peuple; a ~ criminal un criminel ordinaire
(d) (low-class) commun/-e; it looks/sounds ~ ça fait commun

common-law husband *n* concubin *m*

common-law marriage *n* concubinage *m*

common-law wife *n* concubine *f*

commonly *adv* communément

Common Market *n* Marché *m* commun

commonplace *adj* (common) commun/-e; (trite) banal/-e

common room *n* salle *f* de détente

common sense *n* bon sens *m*, sens *m* commun

Commonwealth *n* the ~ le Commonwealth

Commonwealth of Independent States *pr n* Communauté *f* des États indépendants

commotion *n* (a) (noise) vacarme *m*, brouhaha *m*
(b) (disturbance) émoi *m*, agitation *f*

communal *adj* ⟨property, area, showers⟩ commun/-e; ⟨garden⟩ collectif/-ive; ⟨life⟩ communautaire

commune *n* communauté *f*

communicate ① *vtr* communiquer
‹*ideas, feelings*› (**to** à); transmettre
‹*information*› (**to** à)
② *vi* communiquer

✶ **communication** *n* communication *f*

communication cord *n* (GB) sonnette
f d'alarme

communications *n pl* (GB)
communications *fpl*, liaison *f*

communications company *n* société
f de communications

communication studies *n pl* études
fpl en communication

communion *n* communion *f*

communism *n* communisme *m*

communist *n, adj* communiste *mf*

✶ **community** *n* communauté *f*

community care *n* soins *mpl* en dehors
du milieu hospitalier

community centre (GB),
community center (US) *n* maison *f* de
quartier

community service *n* travail *m*
d'intérêt public

commute *vi* **to ~ between Oxford and
London** faire le trajet entre Oxford et
Londres tous les jours

commuter *n* navetteur/-euse *m/f*,
migrant/-e *m/f* journalier/-ière

compact ① *n* poudrier *m*
② *adj* compact/-e

compact disc *n* disque *m* compact

companion *n* compagnon/compagne *m/f*

companionship *n* compagnie *f*

✶ **company** *n* (a) (firm) société *f*; **airline ~**
compagnie *f* aérienne
(b) **theatre ~** troupe *f* de théâtre, compagnie
f théâtrale
(c) (Mil) compagnie *f*
(d) (companionship) compagnie *f*; **to keep sb ~**
tenir compagnie à qn
(e) (visitors) visiteurs *mpl*

company car *n* voiture *f* de fonction

company director *n* directeur/-trice
m/f général/-e

company pension scheme *n* régime
m de retraite de l'enterprise

company secretary *n* secrétaire *mf*
général/-e

comparable *adj* comparable (**to, with** à)

comparative *adj* (a) (in grammar)
comparatif/-ive
(b) (relative) relatif/-ive; **in ~ terms** en termes
relatifs
(c) ‹*study*› comparatif/-ive

comparatively *adv* relativement

✶ **compare** ① *vtr* comparer (**with, to** avec, à)
② *vi* être comparable (**with** à)

✶ indicates a very frequent word

③ **compared with** *prep phr* **~d with sb/
sth** par rapport à qn/qch
④ *v refl* **to ~ oneself with** *or* **to** se
comparer à

✶ **comparison** *n* comparaison *f*; **in** *or* **by ~
with** par rapport à

compartment *n* compartiment *m*

compass *n* boussole *f* (*also* **ship's ~**)
compas *m*; compas *m*; **the points of the ~** les
points *mpl* cardinaux

compasses *n pl* **(a pair of) ~** un compas

compassion *n* compassion *f* (**for** pour)

compassionate *adj* compatissant/-e; **on
~ grounds** pour raisons *fpl* personnelles

compatible *adj* compatible (**with** avec)

compel *vtr* (*p prés etc* **-ll-**) contraindre (**to
do** à faire), obliger (**to do** à faire)

compelling *adj* ‹*reason, argument*›
convaincant/-e; ‹*speaker*› fascinant/-e

compensate ① *vtr* dédommager,
indemniser
② *vi* **to ~ for** compenser

compensation *n* (a) (gen) compensation
f (**for** de)
(b) (financial) indemnisation *f*

✶ **compete** ① *vi* (a) (gen) rivaliser; **to ~
against** *or* **with** rivaliser avec (**for** pour
obtenir)
(b) (commercially) ‹*companies*› se faire
concurrence; **to ~ with** faire concurrence à
(**for** pour obtenir)
(c) (in sport) être en compétition (**against,
with** avec); **to ~ in** participer à ‹*Olympics,
race*›
② **competing** *pres p adj* rival/-e

competence *n* (a) (ability) compétence *f*
(b) (skill) compétences *fpl*

competent *adj* compétent/-e, capable

✶ **competition** *n* (a) (gen) concurrence *f*
(b) (contest) concours *m*; (race) compétition *f*
(c) (competitors) concurrence *f*

competitive *adj* (a) ‹*person*› qui a
l'esprit de compétition; ‹*environment*›
compétitif/-ive
(b) ‹*price, product*› compétitif/-ive
(c) ‹*sport*› de compétition

competitor *n* concurrent/-e *m/f*

compilation *n* (a) (collection) compilation *f*
(b) (act of compiling) (of reference book) rédaction
f; (of dossier) constitution *f*

compile *vtr* (a) dresser ‹*list, catalogue*›;
établir ‹*report*›
(b) (Comput) compiler

complacent *adj* suffisant/-e; **to be ~
about** être trop confiant/-e de ‹*success,
future*›

✶ **complain** *vi* se plaindre (**to** à; **about** de; **of**
de); (officially) se plaindre (**to** auprès de)

✶ **complaint** *n* plainte *f*; (official) réclamation
f; **there have been ~s about the noise** on
s'est plaint du bruit; **to have grounds** *or*

cause for ∼ avoir lieu de se plaindre
complement 1 *n* complément *m*
2 *vtr* compléter
complementary *adj* complémentaire
(**to** de)
complementary medicine *n*
médecine *f* parallèle
❧ **complete** 1 *adj* (a) complet/-ète
(b) (finished) achevé/-e
2 *vtr* (a) (finish) terminer ⟨building, course, exercise⟩; achever ⟨task, journey⟩
(b) compléter ⟨collection, phrase⟩
(c) remplir ⟨form⟩
❧ **completely** *adv* complètement
completion *n* achèvement *m*
❧ **complex** 1 *n* complexe *m*; **sports** ∼
complexe sportif; **he's got a** ∼ **about his weight** son poids le complexe
2 *adj* complexe
complexion *n* teint *m*
complexity *n* complexité *f*
compliance *n* conformité (**with** à)
compliant *adj* conciliant/-e
complicate *vtr* compliquer
complicated *adj* compliqué/-e
complication *n* (a) (problem) inconvénient *m*, problème *m*
(b) (Med) complication *f*
compliment 1 *n* compliment *m*; **to pay sb a** ∼ faire un compliment à qn
2 *vtr* complimenter, faire des compliments à
complimentary *adj* (a) ⟨remark⟩
flatteur/-euse
(b) (free) gratuit/-e
compliments *n pl* compliments *mpl*
(**to** à)
comply *vi* **to** ∼ **with** se conformer à ⟨orders⟩; respecter, observer ⟨rules⟩
❧ **component** *n* (gen) composante *f*; (in car, machine) pièce *f*; (electrical) composant *m*
compose *vtr* (a) (gen) composer; ∼**d of** composé/-e de
(b) **to** ∼ **oneself** se ressaisir
composed *adj* calme
composer *n* compositeur/-trice *m/f*
composition *n* (a) (gen) composition *f*
(b) (essay) rédaction *f* (**about, on** sur)
compost *n* compost *m*
composure *n* calme *m*
compound 1 *n* (a) (enclosure) enceinte *f*
(b) (in chemistry) composé *m* (**of** de)
(c) (word) mot *m* composé
2 *adj* (a) (gen) composé/-e
(b) (Med) ⟨fracture⟩ multiple
comprehend *vtr* comprendre
comprehensible *adj* compréhensible, intelligible
comprehension *n* compréhension *f*
comprehensive 1 *n* (*also* ∼ **school**)
(GB Sch) école *f* (publique) secondaire

2 *adj* ⟨report, list⟩ complet/-ète, détaillé/-e; ⟨knowledge⟩ étendu/-e; ∼ **insurance policy**
assurance *f* tous risques
compress 1 *n* compresse *f*
2 *vtr* comprimer
comprise *vtr* comprendre; **to be** ∼**d of**
être composé/-e de
compromise 1 *n* compromis *m*
2 *vtr* compromettre
3 *vi* transiger, arriver à un compromis; **to** ∼ **on sth** trouver un compromis sur qch
compromising *adj* compromettant/-e
compulsive *adj* (a) (inveterate) invétéré/-e; (psychologically) compulsif/-ive
(b) (fascinating) fascinant/-e
compulsory *adj* obligatoire
❧ **computer** *n* ordinateur *m*
computer-aided design, CAD *n*
conception *f* assistée par ordinateur, CAO *f*
computer-aided learning, CAL *n*
enseignement *m* assisté par ordinateur
computer crime *n* piratage *m*
informatique
computer dating *n* organisation *f* de
rencontres (en utilisant un ordinateur)
computer game *n* jeu *m* informatique
computer graphics *n* infographie *f*
computer hacker *n* pirate *m*
informatique
computerize *vtr* mettre [qch] sur
ordinateur ⟨accounts⟩; informatiser ⟨list⟩
computer literate *adj* **to be** ∼ avoir des
notions d'informatique
computer program *n* programme *m*
informatique
computer programmer *n*
programmeur/-euse *m/f*
computer science *n* informatique *f*
computer scientist *n* informaticien/
-ienne *m/f*
computing *n* informatique *f*
comrade *n* camarade *mf*
comradeship *n* camaraderie *f*
con (colloq) 1 *n* escroquerie *f*, arnaque *f*
(pop)
2 *vtr* (*p prés etc* **-nn-**) tromper, rouler
(fam), arnaquer (pop)
conceal *vtr* dissimuler (**from** à)
concede 1 *vtr* concéder
2 *vi* céder
conceit *n* suffisance *f*
conceited *adj* ⟨person⟩ vaniteux/-euse;
⟨remark⟩ suffisant/-e
conceive *vtr, vi* concevoir
❧ **concentrate** 1 *vtr* concentrer ⟨effort⟩;
employer ⟨resources⟩; centrer ⟨attention⟩
2 *vi* (a) ⟨person⟩ se concentrer (**on** sur); **to** ∼ **on doing** s'appliquer à faire
(b) **to** ∼ **on** ⟨film, journalist⟩ s'intéresser
surtout à

ᵍ **concentration** n concentration f (on
  sur); **to lose one's ~** se déconcentrer
concentration camp n camp m de
  concentration
ᵍ **concept** n concept m
conception n conception f
ᵍ **concern** ① n (a) (worry) inquiétude
  f (**about** à propos de); **to cause ~** être
  inquiétant/-e
  (b) (preoccupation) préoccupation f;
  environmental ~s des préoccupations
  écologiques
  (c) (company) entreprise f; **a going ~** une
  affaire rentable
  ② vtr (a) (worry) inquiéter
  (b) (affect, interest) concerner, intéresser;
  to whom it may ~ à qui de droit; (in letter)
  Monsieur; **as far as the pay is ~ed** en ce qui
  concerne le salaire
  (c) (be about) ‹book, programme› traiter de;
  ‹fax, letter› concerner
concerned adj (a) (anxious) inquiet/-ète
  (**about** à propos de); **to be ~ for sb** se faire
  du souci pour qn
  (b) (involved) concerné/-e; **all (those) ~** toutes
  les personnes concernées
concerning prep concernant
concert n concert m
concerted adj ‹action, campaign›
  concerté/-e; **to make a ~ effort to do** faire un
  sérieux effort pour faire
concert hall n salle f de concert
concertina ① n concertina m
  ② vi se plier en accordéon
concerto n (pl **-tos** ou **-tia**) concerto m
concession n (a) (compromise) concession
  f (**on** sur; **to** à)
  (b) (discount) réduction f; '**~s**' 'tarif réduit'
conciliatory adj ‹gesture, terms›
  conciliant/-e; ‹measures› conciliatoire
concise adj concis/-e
ᵍ **conclude** ① vtr conclure
  ② vi ‹story, event› se terminer (**with** par,
  sur); ‹speaker› conclure (**with** par)
concluding adj final/-e
ᵍ **conclusion** n (a) (end) fin f
  (b) (opinion, resolution) conclusion f
conclusive adj concluant/-e
concoct vtr concocter
concrete ① n béton m
  ② adj (a) ‹block› de béton; ‹base› en béton
  (b) (real) concret/-ète
concuss vtr **to be ~ed** être
  commotionné/-e
concussion n commotion f cérébrale
condemn ① vtr (a) (gen) condamner
  (b) déclarer [qch] inhabitable ‹building›
  ② **condemned** pp adj ‹cell› des
  condamnés à mort; **~ed man/woman**

condamné/-e m/f à mort
condensation n (on walls) condensation f;
  (on windows) buée f
condense ① vtr condenser
  ② vi se condenser
condensed milk n lait m concentré
  sucré
condescend vtr **to ~ to do** condescendre
  à faire
condescending adj condescendant/-e
ᵍ **condition** n (a) (gen) condition f; **on ~ that
  you come** à condition que tu viennes
  (b) (state) état m, condition f; **to be in good/
  bad ~** ‹house, car› être en bon/mauvais état
  (c) (disease) maladie f
conditional adj conditionnel/-elle
conditioner n après-shampooing m,
  démêlant m
condolences n pl condoléances fpl
condom n préservatif m
condominium n (also **~ unit**) (US)
  appartement m (dans une copropriété)
condone vtr tolérer
conducive adj **~ to** favorable à
ᵍ **conduct** ① n conduite f (**towards** envers)
  ② vtr (a) mener ‹business, campaign›
  (b) mener ‹experiment, inquiry›; célébrer
  ‹ceremony›
  (c) (Mus) diriger ‹orchestra›
  (d) conduire ‹electricity, heat›
conductor n (a) (Mus) chef m d'orchestre
  (b) (on bus) receveur m; (on train) chef m de
  train
conductress n receveuse f
cone n (a) (shape) cône m
  (b) (also **ice-cream ~**) cornet m
  (c) (for traffic) balise f
confectioner n (of sweets) confiseur/-euse
  m/f; (of cakes) pâtissier-confiseur m; **~'s**
  (shop) pâtisserie-confiserie f
confectionery n (sweets) confiserie f;
  (cakes) pâtisserie f
confer ① vtr (p prés etc **-rr-**) conférer
  (**on** à)
  ② vi (p prés etc **-rr-**) conférer (**about** de;
  with avec)
ᵍ **conference** n (academic, business)
  conférence f; (political) congrès m
confess ① vtr (a) avouer (**that** que)
  (b) confesser ‹sins›
  ② vi avouer; **to ~ to a crime** avouer (avoir
  commis) un crime
confession n (a) (gen, Law) aveu m (**of** de)
  (b) (in religion) confession f; **to go to ~** se
  confesser
confetti n confettis mpl
confide vi **to ~ in** se confier à ‹person›
ᵍ **confidence** n (a) (faith) confiance f (**in** en);
  to have (every) ~ in sb/sth avoir (pleine)
  confiance en qn/qch

ᵍ indicates a very frequent word

(b) (in politics) **vote of** ~ vote *m* de confiance; **motion of no** ~ motion *f* de censure
(c) (self-assurance) assurance *f*, confiance *f* en soi
(d) to tell sb sth in ~ dire qch à qn confidentiellement

confidence trick *n* escroquerie *f*

confident *adj* **(a)** (sure) sûr/-e, confiant/-e
(b) (self-assured) assuré/-e, sûr/-e de soi

confidential *adj* confidentiel/-ielle

configure *vtr* configurer

confine *vtr* **(a)** confiner ‹*person*› (**in, to** dans); enfermer ‹*animal*› (**in** dans)
(b) (limit) limiter (**to** à)

confined *adj* (gen) confiné/-e; ‹*space*› restreint/-e

confinement *n* (in prison) détention *f*

ⱷ **confirm** *vtr* confirmer; **to** ~ **receipt of sth** accuser réception de

confirmation *n* confirmation *f*

confirmed *adj* ‹*smoker, liar*› invétéré/-e; ‹*bachelor, sinner*› endurci/-e

confiscate *vtr* confisquer (**from** à)

ⱷ **conflict** ⏴1⏵ *n* conflit *m*
⏴2⏵ *vi* être en contradiction (**with** avec)

conflicting *adj* contradictoire

conform ⏴1⏵ *vtr* conformer (**to** à)
⏴2⏵ *vi* ‹*person*› se conformer (**with, to** à)

conformist *n, adj* conformiste *mf*

confront *vtr* affronter ‹*danger, enemy*›; faire face à ‹*problem*›

confrontation *n* affrontement *m*

confrontational *adj* provocateur/-trice

ⱷ **confuse** *vtr* **(a)** (bewilder) troubler ‹*person*›
(b) (mistake) confondre (**with** avec)
(c) (complicate) compliquer ‹*argument*›; **to** ~ **the issue** compliquer les choses

confused *adj* ‹*person*› troublé/-e; ‹*account, thoughts, mind*› confus/-e; **to get** ~ s'embrouiller

confusing *adj* déroutant/-e, peu clair/-e

confusion *n* confusion *f*

congeal *vi* ‹*fat*› se figer; ‹*blood*› se coaguler

congenial *adj* agréable

congenital *adj* congénital/-e

congested *adj* **(a)** ‹*road*› embouteillé/-e; ‹*district*› surpeuplé/-e
(b) ‹*lungs*› congestionné/-e

congestion *n* **(a)** traffic ~ embouteillages *mpl*
(b) (of lungs) congestion *f*

congestion charge *n* péage *m* urbain

conglomerate *n* conglomérat *m*

congratulate *vtr* féliciter (**on** de)

congratulations *n pl* félicitations *fpl*; ~ **on the birth of your new baby** félicitations à l'occasion de la naissance de votre bébé

congregate *vi* se rassembler

congregation *n* assemblée *f* des fidèles

ⱷ **congress** *n* congrès *m* (**on** sur)

Congress *n* (US) Congrès *m*

congressman *n* (*pl* **-men**) (US) membre *m* du Congrès

conifer *n* conifère *m*

conjugal *adj* conjugal/-e

conjugate ⏴1⏵ *vtr* conjuguer
⏴2⏵ *vi* ‹*verb*› se conjuguer

conjunctivitis *n* conjonctivite *f*

conjure *vi* faire des tours de prestidigitation
▪ **conjure up** évoquer ‹*image*›

conjurer *n* prestidigitateur/-trice *m/f*

con man *n* arnaqueur *m* (pop), escroc *m*

ⱷ **connect** *vtr* **(a)** raccorder ‹*end, hose*› (**to** à); accrocher ‹*coach*› (**to** à)
(b) ‹*road, railway*› relier ‹*place, road*› (**to, with** à)
(c) brancher ‹*appliance*› (**to** à)
(d) raccorder ‹*phone, subscriber*›

connected *adj* **(a)** ‹*idea, event*› lié/-e (**to, with** avec); **everything** ~ **with music** tout ce qui se rapporte à la musique
(b) (in family) apparenté/-e (**to** à)

connecting *adj* **(a)** ‹*flight*› de correspondance
(b) ‹*room*› attenant/-e

ⱷ **connection** *n* **(a)** (link) (between events) rapport *m*; (of person) lien *m* (**between** entre; **with** avec); **in** ▪ **with** au sujet de, à propos de
(b) (contact) relation *f*; **to have useful** ~**s** avoir des relations
(c) (to mains) branchement *m*
(d) (to telephone network) raccordement *m*; (to number) mise *f* en communication (**to** avec); **bad** ~ mauvaise communication *f*
(e) (in travel) correspondance *f*
(f) (Comput) connexion *f*; **Internet** ~ connexion Internet

connive *vi* **to** ~ **at** contribuer délibérément à; **to** ~ (**with sb**) **to do** être de connivence *or* de mèche (fam) (avec qn) pour faire

connoisseur *n* connaisseur/-euse *m/f*

connotation *n* connotation *f* (**of** de)

conquer *vtr* conquérir ‹*territory, people*›; vaincre ‹*enemy, unemployment*›

conqueror *n* conquérant/-e *m/f*

conquest *n* conquête *f*

conscience *n* conscience *f*; **they have no** ~ ils n'ont aucun sens moral **to have a guilty** ~ avoir mauvaise conscience; **to have a clear** ~ avoir la conscience tranquille

conscientious *adj* consciencieux/-ieuse

conscientious objector, CO *n* objecteur *m* de conscience

conscious *adj* **(a)** (aware) conscient/-e (**of** de; **that** du fait que)
(b) (deliberate) ‹*decision*› réfléchi/-e; ‹*effort*› consciencieux/-ieuse
(c) (awake) réveillé/-e

consciousness *n* **to lose/regain** ~ perdre/reprendre connaissance

conscript n appelé m

conscription n (system) conscription f

consecrate vtr consacrer

consecutive adj consécutif/-ive

consensus n consensus m (**among** au sein de; **about** quant à; **on** sur)

consent [1] n consentement m; **age of ~** âge m légal; **by common** or **mutual ~** d'un commun accord
[2] vi consentir (**to** à); **to ~ to sb doing** consentir à ce que qn fasse

⚜️ **consequence** n (a) conséquence f; **as a ~ of** du fait de ‹change, process›; à la suite de ‹event›
(b) (importance) importance f

consequently adv par conséquent

conservation n (a) (of nature) protection f (**of** de); **energy ~** maîtrise f de l'énergie
(b) (of heritage) conservation f

conservation area n zone f protégée

conservationist n défenseur m des ressources naturelles

conservative [1] n conservateur/-trice m/f
[2] adj (a) ‹party› conservateur/-trice
(b) ‹taste, style› classique

Conservative Party n (GB) parti m conservateur

conservatory n (a) (for plants) jardin m d'hiver
(b) (academy) conservatoire m

conserve [1] n confiture f
[2] vtr (a) protéger ‹forest›; sauvegarder ‹wildlife›; conserver ‹remains, ruins›
(b) économiser ‹resources›; ménager ‹energy›

⚜️ **consider** vtr (a) (give thought to) considérer ‹options, facts›; examiner ‹evidence, problem›; étudier ‹offer›
(b) (take into account) prendre [qch] en considération ‹risk, cost›; songer à ‹person›; faire attention à ‹person's feelings›
(c) (envisage) **to ~ doing** envisager de faire; **to ~ sb/sth as sth** penser à qn/qch comme qch
(d) (regard) **to ~ that** considérer or estimer que; **to ~ oneself (to be) a genius** se considérer comme un génie

considerable adj considérable

considerate adj ‹person› attentionné/-e; ‹behaviour› courtois/-e; **to be ~ towards sb** avoir des égards pour qn

⚜️ **consideration** n (a) considération f (**for** envers); **to give sth careful ~** réfléchir longuement à qch; **to take sth into ~** prendre qch en considération; **out of ~** par considération
(b) (fee) **for a ~** moyennant finance

considering prep, conj étant donné, compte tenu de

⚜️ indicates a very frequent word

consign vtr expédier ‹goods› (**to** à)

consignment n (sending) expédition f; (goods) lot m, livraison f

⚜️ **consist** vi **to ~ of** se composer de; **to ~ in** résider dans; **to ~ in doing** consister à faire

consistency n (a) (texture) consistance f
(b) (of view, policy) cohérence f

⚜️ **consistent** adj (a) ‹growth, level, quality› régulier/-ière
(b) ‹attempts, demands› répété/-e
(c) ‹argument› cohérent/-e; **~ with** en accord avec ‹account, belief›

consistently adv (invariably) systématiquement; (repeatedly) à maintes reprises

consolation n consolation f (**to** pour)

console [1] n (a) (control panel) console f
(b) (for hi-fi) meuble m hi-fi; (for video) meuble m vidéo
[2] vtr consoler (**for**, on de; **with** avec)

consolidate vtr (a) consolider ‹position›
(b) réunir ‹resources›; fusionner ‹companies›

consonant n consonne f

consortium n (pl -**tiums** ou -**tia**) consortium m

conspicuous adj ‹feature, sign› visible; ‹garment› voyant/-e; **to be ~** se remarquer

conspiracy n conspiration f

conspirator n conspirateur/-trice m/f

conspire vi conspirer; **to ~ to do** ‹people› conspirer en vue de faire; ‹events› conspirer à faire

constable n (GB) agent m de police

⚜️ **constant** adj ‹problem, reminder, threat› permanent/-e; ‹care, temperature› constant/-e; ‹disputes, questions› incessant/-e; ‹attempts› répété/-e; ‹companion› éternel/-elle

constantly adv constamment

constellation n constellation f

constipated adj constipé/-e

constipation n constipation f

constituency n (district) circonscription f électorale; (voters) électeurs mpl

constituent n (a) (Pol) électeur/-trice m/f
(b) (of character) trait m; (of event, work of art) élément m

constitute vtr constituer

constitution n constitution f

constitutional adj constitutionnel/-elle

constraint n contrainte f

constrict vtr comprimer ‹flow, blood vessel›; gêner ‹breathing, movement›

⚜️ **construct** vtr construire (**of** avec; **in** en)

⚜️ **construction** n construction f

construction site n chantier m

construction worker n ouvrier/-ière m/f du bâtiment

constructive adj constructif/-ive

consul *n* consul *m*

consulate *n* consulat *m*

consult ① *vtr* consulter (**about** sur)
② *vi* s'entretenir (**about** sur; **with** avec)

consultancy *n* (*also* ~ **firm**) cabinet-conseil *m*

consultant *n* (a) (expert) consultant/-e *m/f*, conseiller/-ère *m/f* (**on**, **in** en)
(b) (GB) (doctor) spécialiste *mf*

consultation *n* (for advice) consultation *f* (**about** sur); (for discussion) entretien *m* (**about** sur); **after** ~ **with** après avoir consulté

consumables *n pl* consommables *mpl*

consume *vtr* (a) (use up) consommer ‹*fuel, food, drink*›
(b) **to be** ~**d by** *or* **with** être dévoré/-e par ‹*envy*›; brûler de ‹*desire*›; être rongé/-e par ‹*guilt*›

ℰ **consumer** *n* consommateur/-trice *m/f*; (of electricity, gas) abonné/-e *m/f*

consumer advice *n* conseils *mpl* au consommateurs

consumer goods *n pl* biens *mpl* de consommation

consumer protection *n* défense *f* du consommateur

consumer society *n* société *f* de consommation

consummate *vtr* consommer ‹*marriage*›

consumption *n* consommation *f*

ℰ **contact** ① *n* (a) (gen) contact *m* (**between** entre; **with** avec); **to be in/make** ~ être en/se mettre en contact
(b) (acquaintance) connaissance *f*; (professional) contact *m*
② *vtr* contacter, se mettre en rapport avec

contact lens *n* lentille *f* *or* verre *m* de contact

contactless *adj* ‹*card*› sans contacts

contagious *adj* contagieux/-ieuse

ℰ **contain** *vtr* (a) contenir ‹*amount, ingredients*›; contenir, comporter ‹*information, mistakes*›
(b) (curb) maîtriser ‹*blaze*›; enrayer ‹*epidemic*›; limiter ‹*costs, problem*›; retenir ‹*flood*›

container *n* (for food, liquids) récipient *m*; (for plants) bac *m*; (for waste, for transporting) conteneur *m*

contaminate *vtr* contaminer

contamination *n* contamination *f*

contemplate *vtr* (a) (consider) envisager (**doing** de faire)
(b) (look at) contempler

ℰ **contemporary** ① *n* contemporain/-e *m/f*
② *adj* (present-day) contemporain/-e; (up-to-date) moderne; (of same period) de l'époque

contempt *n* mépris *m* (**for** de); **to hold sb/ sth in** ~ mépriser qn/qch; ~ **of court** (Law) outrage *m* à magistrat

contemptible *adj* méprisable

contemptuous *adj* méprisant/-e

contend ① *vtr* soutenir (**that** que)
② *vi* (a) (deal with) **to** ~ **with** affronter
(b) (compete) **to** ~ **with sb for sth** disputer qch à qn

contender *n* (a) (in competition) concurrent/-e *m/f*
(b) (for post) candidat/-e *m/f* (**for** à)

ℰ **content** ① *n* (a) (quantity) teneur *f*
(b) (of book, essay) fond *m*
② *adj* satisfait/-e (**with** de)

contented *adj* ‹*person*› content/-e (**with** de); ‹*feeling*› de bien-être

contention *n* (a) (opinion) assertion *f*
(b) (dispute) dispute *f*

contentment *n* contentement *m*

contents *n pl* (gen) contenu *m*; (of house, for insurance) biens *mpl* mobiliers; **list** *or* **table of** ~ table *f* des matières

contest ① *n* (a) (competition) concours *m*
(b) (struggle) lutte *f*
② *vtr* (a) contester ‹*decision, will*›
(b) (compete for) disputer ‹*match*›

contestant *n* (in competition, game) concurrent/-e *m/f*; (in fight) adversaire *mf*; (for job, in election) candidat/-e *m/f*

ℰ **context** *n* contexte *m*

continent *n* (a) continent *m*
(b) **the Continent** (GB); l'Europe *f* continentale

continental *adj* (a) continental/-e
(b) (GB) ‹*holiday*› en Europe continentale

continental breakfast *n* petit déjeuner *m* (*avec café, pain, beurre et confiture*)

continental quilt *n* (GB) couette *f*

contingency *n* imprévu *m*

contingency fund *n* fonds *m* de secours

contingency plan *n* plan *m* de réserve

continual *adj* continuel/-elle

continually *adv* continuellement

continuation *n* (a) (gen) continuation *f*
(b) (of story) suite *f*; (of route) prolongement *m*

ℰ **continue** ① *vtr* continuer
② *vi* ‹*person*› continuer (**doing, to do** à *or* de faire); ‹*noise, debate, strike*› se poursuivre; **to** ~ **with** continuer, poursuivre ‹*task, treatment*›

continuity *n* continuité *f*

continuous *adj* (a) ‹*growth, decline, noise*› continu/-e; ‹*care*› constant/-e; ‹*line*› ininterrompu/-e; ~ **assessment** (GB); contrôle *m* continu
(b) ‹*tense*› progressif/-ive

continuously *adv* (without a break) sans interruption; (repeatedly) continuellement

contort *vtr* tordre

contortion *n* contorsion *f*

contour *n* (a) (outline) contour *m*   ⋯⟐

(b) (*also* ~ **line**) courbe *f* hypsométrique *or* de niveau

contraband *n* contrebande *f*

contraception *n* contraception *f*

contraceptive ⟨1⟩ *n* contraceptif *m*
⟨2⟩ *adj* contraceptif/-ive

⚘ **contract** ⟨1⟩ *n* contrat *m*
⟨2⟩ *vtr* **(a)** (gen) contracter
(b) to be ~ed to do être tenu/-e par contrat de faire
⟨3⟩ *vi* **(a)** to ~ to do s'engager par contrat à faire
(b) ⟨*muscle, wood*⟩ se contracter

contraction *n* contraction *f*

contract killer *n* tueur/-euse *m/f* à gages

contractor *n* **(a)** (business) entrepreneur/-euse *m/f*
(b) (worker) contractuel/-elle *m/f*

contradict *vtr, vi* contredire

contradiction *n* contradiction *f*

contradictory *adj* contradictoire (**to** à)

contraflow *n* (GB) circulation *f* à sens alterné

contraindication *n* contre-indication *f*

contrary ⟨1⟩ *n* contraire *m*; **on the** ~ (bien) au contraire; **unless you hear anything to the** ~ sauf contrordre
⟨2⟩ *adj* **(a)** ⟨*idea, view*⟩ contraire
(b) ⟨*person*⟩ contrariant/-e
⟨3⟩ **contrary to** *phr* contrairement à

⚘ **contrast** ⟨1⟩ *n* contraste *m*; **in** ~ **to sth, by** ~ **with sth** par contraste avec qch; **in** ~ **to sb** à la différence de qn; **by** *or* **in** ~ par contre
⟨2⟩ *vtr* **to** ~ **X with Y** faire ressortir le contraste (qui existe) entre X et Y
⟨3⟩ *vi* contraster (**with** avec)

contrasting *adj* ⟨*examples*⟩ opposé/-e; ⟨*colour*⟩ contrasté/-e; ⟨*views*⟩ très différent/-e

⚘ **contribute** ⟨1⟩ *vtr* **(a)** verser ⟨*sum*⟩ (**to** à); **to** ~ **£5m** contribuer pour 5 millions de livres sterling
(b) (to gift, charity) donner (**to** à; **towards** pour)
(c) apporter ⟨*ideas*⟩ (**to** à); écrire ⟨*article*⟩ (**to** pour)
⟨2⟩ *vi* **(a)** **to** ~ **to** *or* **towards** contribuer à ⟨*change, decline*⟩
(b) (to community life, research) participer (**to** à); (to programme, magazine) collaborer (**to** à)
(c) **to** ~ **to** cotiser à ⟨*pension fund*⟩
(d) (to charity) donner (**to** à)

⚘ **contribution** *n* **(a)** (to tax, pension, profits, cost) contribution *f* (**towards** à)
(b) (to charity, campaign) don *m*; **to make a** ~ faire un don (**to** à)
(c) **sb's** ~ le rôle que qn a joué dans ⟨*success, undertaking*⟩; ce que qn a apporté à ⟨*science, sport*⟩
(d) (to programme) participation *f*; (to magazine) article *m*

⚘ indicates a very frequent word

contributor *n* (to charity) donateur/-trice *m/f*; (in discussion) participant/-e *m/f*; (to magazine, book) collaborateur/-trice *m/f*

con trick *n* (colloq) escroquerie *f*, duperie *f*

contrive *vtr* (arrange) organiser; **to** ~ **to do** parvenir à faire

contrived *adj* **(a)** ⟨*incident, meeting*⟩ non fortuit/-e
(b) ⟨*plot*⟩ tiré/-e par les cheveux; ⟨*style, effect*⟩ étudié/-e

⚘ **control** ⟨1⟩ *n* **(a)** (gen) contrôle *m* (**of** de); (of operation, project) direction *f* (**of** de); (of life, emotion, self) maîtrise *f* (**of, over** de); **to be in** ~ **of** contrôler ⟨*territory*⟩; diriger ⟨*operation, organization*⟩; maîtriser ⟨*problem*⟩; avoir le contrôle de ⟨*ball, vehicle*⟩; **to be in** ~ (of oneself) se maîtriser; **to bring** *or* **keep [sth] under** ~ maîtriser; **to lose** ~ (**of sth**) perdre le contrôle (de qch)
(b) (on vehicle, equipment) commande *f*; (on TV) bouton *m* de réglage; **to be at the** ~s être aux commandes
⟨2⟩ *vtr* (*p prés etc* **-ll-**) **(a)** dominer ⟨*organization, situation*⟩; contrôler ⟨*territory*⟩; diriger ⟨*traffic, project*⟩; être majoritaire dans ⟨*company*⟩
(b) maîtriser ⟨*person, animal, inflation, fire*⟩; endiguer ⟨*epidemic*⟩; dominer ⟨*emotion*⟩; retenir ⟨*laughter*⟩; **to** ~ **oneself** se contrôler
(c) commander ⟨*machine*⟩; manœuvrer ⟨*boat, vehicle*⟩; piloter ⟨*plane*⟩; contrôler ⟨*ball*⟩
(d) régler ⟨*speed, temperature*⟩; contrôler ⟨*immigration, prices*⟩

control panel *n* (on plane) tableau *m* de bord; (on machine) tableau *m* de contrôle; (on TV) (panneau *m* de) commandes *fpl*; (on computer) panneau *m* de configuration

control room *n* poste *m* de commande; (TV) (salle *f* de) régie *f*

control tower *n* tour *f* de contrôle

controversial *adj* (gen) controversé/-e; (open to criticism) qui prête à controverse

controversy *n* controverse *f*

conundrum *n* énigme *f*

convalesce *vi* se remettre

convene *vtr* organiser ⟨*meeting*⟩; convoquer ⟨*group*⟩

convenience *n* avantage *m* (**of doing** de faire); (of device, food, shop) commodité *f*; **for (the sake of)** ~ pour raisons de commodité; **at your** ~ quand cela vous conviendra

convenience foods *n pl* plats *mpl* (tout) préparés

convenient *adj* **(a)** ⟨*place, time*⟩ pratique; **to be** ~ **for sb** convenir à qn
(b) (useful, practical) pratique, commode
(c) ⟨*shops*⟩ situé/-e tout près; ⟨*chair*⟩ à portée de main

convent *n* couvent *m*

convention *n* **(a)** (gen) convention *f*
(b) (social norms) convenances *fpl*, conventions *fpl*

conventional adj (gen) conventionnel/
-elle; ‹person› conformiste; ‹medicine›
traditionnel/-elle

converge vi converger

conversant adj to be ~ with être versé/-e
dans

⚐ **conversation** n conversation f

converse vi converser (with avec; in en)

conversion n (of currency, measurement)
conversion f (from de; into en); (of building)
aménagement m (to, into en); (to new
beliefs) conversion f (from de; to à); (in rugby)
transformation f

conversion rate n taux m de change

convert ① n converti/-e m/f (to à)
② vtr (a) (change into sth else) transformer;
(modify) adapter
(b) convertir ‹currency, measurement› (from
de; to, into en)
(c) aménager ‹building, loft› (to, into en)
(d) (to new beliefs) convertir (to à; from de)
(e) (in rugby) transformer ‹try›
③ vi (a) ‹sofa, device› être convertible (into
en)
(b) ‹person› se convertir (to à; from de)

convertible n décapotable f

convex adj convexe

convey vtr (a) ‹person› transmettre
‹information› (to à); exprimer ‹condolences,
feeling, idea› (to à)
(b) ‹words, images› traduire ‹mood,
impression›
(c) ‹vehicle› transporter; ‹pipes› amener

conveyancing n rédaction f des actes de
propriété

conveyor belt n (in factory) transporteur
m à bande or à courroie; (for luggage) tapis
m roulant

convict ① n (imprisoned criminal) détenu/-e
m/f; (deported criminal) bagnard m
② vtr reconnaître or déclarer [qn] coupable
(of de; of doing d'avoir fait)

conviction n (a) (Law) condamnation f
(for pour)
(b) (belief) conviction f (that que)

convince vtr convaincre ‹person› (to do
de faire)

convincing adj ‹account, evidence›
convaincant/-e; ‹victory, lead› indiscutable

convoy n convoi m

convulsion n convulsion f

coo vi roucouler

cook ① n cuisinier/-ière m/f
② vtr faire cuire ‹vegetables, pasta, eggs›;
préparer ‹meal› (for pour)
③ vi ‹person› cuisiner, faire la cuisine;
‹vegetable, meat, meal› cuire

cook-chill foods n pl plats mpl
préparés, plats mpl cuisinés

cooker n (GB) cuisinière f

cookery book n (GB) livre de cuisine

cookie n (a) (biscuit) gateau m sec, biscuit m

(b) (Comput) cookie m

cooking n cuisine f

cooking apple n pomme f à cuire

cooking chocolate n chocolat m
pâtissier

⚐ **cool** ① n (a) (coldness) fraîcheur f
(b) (colloq) (calm) sang-froid m; to keep one's
~ (not get angry) ne pas s'énerver; (stay calm)
garder son sang-froid; to lose one's ~ (get
angry) s'énerver; (panic) perdre son sang-froid
② adj (a) ‹day, drink, water, weather› frais/
fraîche; ‹dress› léger/-ère; ‹colour› froid/-e
(b) (calm) calme
(c) (unfriendly) froid/-e
(d) (casual) décontracté/-e, cool inv (fam)
(e) (colloq) (trendy) branché/-e (fam)
③ vtr (a) refroidir ‹soup›; rafraîchir ‹wine,
room›
(b) calmer ‹anger, ardour›
④ vi (a) (get colder) refroidir
(b) ‹enthusiasm› faiblir; ‹friendship› se
dégrader
■ **cool down** ‹engine, water› refroidir;
‹person, situation› se calmer

cool bag n sac m isotherme

cool box n (GB) glacière f

cooling-off period n (in industrial relations)
délai m de conciliation; (in contract) délai m
de réflexion

coop n poulailler m
■ **coop up**: ¶ ~ [sb/sth] up enfermer, cloîtrer

cooperate vi coopérer (with avec; in à; in
doing pour faire)

cooperation n coopération f (on à)

cooperative ① n (a) (organization)
coopérative f
(b) (US) (apartment house) immeuble m en
copropriété
② adj coopératif/-ive

coordinate ① n (on map, graph)
coordonnée f
② vtr coordonner (with avec)

coordinates n pl (clothes) ensemble m

coordination n coordination f

coordinator n coordinateur/-trice m/f

cope vi s'en sortir (fam), se débrouiller; to
~ with s'occuper de ‹person, work›; faire
face à ‹demand, disaster, problem›; supporter
‹death, depression, difficult person›

Copenhagen pr n Copenhague

copious adj (a) (plentiful) ‹supply›
abondant/-e
(b) (generous) ‹quantity, serving› copieux/
-ieuse

cop-out n (colloq) (excuse) excuse f bidon
(fam)

copper n (a) (metal) cuivre m
(b) (GB) (colloq) (coin) petite monnaie f
(c) (GB) (colloq) (policeman) flic m (fam)
(d) (colour) couleur f cuivre

⚐ **copy** ① n (a) (gen) copie f

···⟋

(b) (of book, newspaper, report) exemplaire m
[2] *vtr* copier (**from** sur)
[3] *vi* copier
■ **copy down**, **copy out** recopier ‹quote, address›

copyright n copyright m, droit m d'auteur

coral n corail m

cord [1] n cordon m
[2] **cords** n pl (colloq) (also **corduroys**) pantalon m en velours (côtelé)

cordial [1] n **(a)** (fruit drink) sirop m de fruits
(b) (US) (liqueur) liqueur m
[2] adj cordial/-e (**to**, **with** avec)

cordless adj ‹telephone, kettle› sans fil

cordon n cordon m
■ **cordon off** boucler ‹street, area›; contenir ‹crowd›

corduroy n velours m côtelé

✓ **core** n **(a)** (of apple) trognon m
(b) (of problem) cœur m
(c) rotten to the ∼ pourri/-e jusqu'à l'os;
English to the ∼ anglais/-e jusqu'au bout des ongles
(d) (of nuclear reactor) cœur m
(e) (small group) noyau m; **hard** ∼ noyau dur

core curriculum n tronc m commun

Corfu pr n Corfou f

cork n **(a)** (substance) liège m
(b) (object) bouchon m

corkscrew n tire-bouchon m

corn n **(a)** (GB) (wheat) blé m
(b) (US) (maize) maïs m
(c) (on foot) cor m

cornea n (pl ∼s ou **-neae**) cornée f

✓ **corner** [1] n **(a)** (gen) coin m; **the house on the** ∼ la maison qui fait l'angle; **at the** ∼ **of the street** au coin de la rue; **to go round the** ∼ tourner au coin de la rue; **just around the** ∼ (nearby) tout près; (around the bend) juste après le coin; **out of the** ∼ **of one's eye** du coin de l'œil
(b) (bend) virage m
(c) (in boxing) coin m (de repos); (in football, hockey) corner m
[2] vtr **(a)** acculer ‹animal, enemy›; coincer (fam) ‹person›
(b) accaparer ‹market›
IDIOMS in a tight ∼ dans une impasse; **to cut** ∼**s** (financially) faire des économies

corner shop n petite épicerie f

cornerstone n pierre f angulaire

cornflour n farine f de maïs

cornflower n bleuet m, barbeau m

corn on the cob n maïs m en épi

Cornwall pr n (comté m de) Cornouailles f

corny adj (colloq) ‹joke› (old) éculé/-e; (feeble) faiblard/-e (fam); ‹film, story› à la guimauve

coronary n infarctus m

coronation n couronnement m

✓ indicates a very frequent word

coroner n coroner m

corporal n (gen) caporal m; (in artillery) brigadier m

corporal punishment n châtiment m corporel

✓ **corporate** adj **(a)** ‹accounts, funds› appartenant/-e à une société; ‹clients, employees› d'une société (or de sociétés)
(b) ‹action› commun/-e; ‹decision› collectif/-ive

corporate identity, **corporate image** n image f de marque (d'une société)

corporate raider n raider m (organisateur d'OPA)

corporation n (grande) société f

corps n corps m

corpse n cadavre m

✓ **correct** [1] adj **(a)** ‹amount, answer, decision› correct/-e; ‹figure, time› exact/-e
(b) ‹behaviour› correct/-e, convenable
[2] vtr corriger

correcting fluid n liquide m correcteur

correction n correction f

correspond vi **(a)** (match) concorder, correspondre (**with** à)
(b) (be equivalent) être équivalent/-e (**to** à)
(c) (exchange letters) correspondre (**with** avec; **about** au sujet de)

correspondence n correspondance f

correspondence course n cours m par correspondance

correspondent n **(a)** (journalist) journaliste mf; (abroad) correspondant/-e m/f
(b) (letter writer) correspondant/-e m/f

corresponding adj (matching) correspondant/-e; (similar) équivalent/-e

corridor n **(a)** couloir m
(b) (of land) corridor m

corroborate vtr corroborer

corrode [1] vtr corroder
[2] vi se corroder

corrosion n corrosion f

corrugated adj ondulé/-e

corrugated iron n tôle f ondulée

corrupt [1] adj corrompu/-e
[2] vtr corrompre

corruption n corruption f

Corsica pr n Corse f

cosh n (GB) matraque f

cosmetic [1] n produit m de beauté
[2] adj (figurative) superficiel/-ielle

cosmetic surgery n chirurgie f esthétique

cosmonaut n cosmonaute mf

cosmopolitan n, adj cosmopolite mf

✓ **cost** [1] n **(a)** (price) coût m, prix m (**of** de); (expense incurred) frais mpl; **at** ∼ au prix coûtant
(b) (figurative) prix m; **at all** ∼**s** à tout prix; **he knows to his** ∼ **that** il a appris à ses dépens que

2 *vtr* (a) (*prét pp* **cost**) coûter; **how much does it ~?** combien ça coûte?; **the TV will ~ £100 to repair** la réparation de la télé coûtera 100 livres sterling
(b) (*prét pp* **costed**) (estimate price of) calculer le prix de revient de ‹*product*›; calculer le coût de ‹*project, work*›

co-star **1** *n* co-vedette *f*
2 *vtr* **a film ~ring X and Y** un film avec X et Y

cost-cutting *n* réduction *f* des frais

cost-effective *adj* rentable

costly *adv* coûteux/-euse

cost of living *n* coût *m* de la vie

cost price *n* (for producer) prix *m* de revient; (for consumer) prix *m* coûtant

costume *n* (a) (clothes) costume *m*
(b) (*also* **swimming ~**) (GB) maillot *m* de bain

costume jewellery (GB), **costume jewelry** (US) *n* bijoux *mpl* fantaisie

cosy (GB), **cozy** (US) *adj* (comfortable) douillet/-ette; (intimate) intime; **it's ~ here** on est bien ici

cot *n* (a) (GB) (for baby) lit *m* de bébé
(b) (US) (bed) lit *m* de camp

cot death *n* (GB) mort *f* subite du nourrisson

cottage *n* maisonnette *f*; (thatched) chaumière *f*

cottage cheese *n* fromage *m* blanc à gros grains

cotton *n* (a) (plant, material) coton *m*
(b) (thread) fil *m* de coton

cotton bud *n* Coton Tige® *m*

cotton wool *n* ouate *f* (de coton)

couch *n* (a) (sofa) canapé *m*
(b) (doctor's) lit *m*; (psychoanalyst's) divan *m*

couch potato *n* (colloq) pantouflard/-e *m/f* (fam) (*qui passe son temps devant la télé*)

cough **1** *n* toux *f*; **to have a ~** tousser
2 *vi* tousser

cough mixture *n* (sirop *m*) antitussif *m*

could *modal aux* (a) (be able to) pouvoir; **I couldn't move** je ne pouvais pas bouger; **she couldn't come yesterday** elle n'a pas pu venir hier
(b) (know how to) savoir; **he couldn't swim** il ne savait pas nager; **she ~ speak four languages** elle parlait quatre langues
(c) (permission, requests, suggestions) pouvoir; **we ~ only go out at weekends** nous ne pouvions sortir *or* nous n'avions le droit de sortir que le week-end; **~ I speak to Annie?** est-ce que je pourrais parler à Annie?; **~ you help me?** pourrais-tu m'aider?
(d) (with verbs of perception) **I couldn't see a thing** je n'y voyais rien; **they couldn't understand me** ils ne me comprenaient pas; **we ~ hear them laughing** on les entendait rire
(e) **you ~ have died** tu aurais pu mourir;

they ~ have warned us ils auraient pu nous prévenir; **I ~ be wrong** je me trompe peut-être; **if only I ~ start again** si seulement je pouvais tout recommencer

council *n* conseil *m*; **the town ~** le conseil municipal; **the Council of Europe** le Conseil de l'Europe

council estate *n* lotissement *m* de logements sociaux

council house *n* habitation *f* à loyer modéré

council housing *n* logements *mpl* sociaux

councillor, councilor (US) *n* conseiller/-ère *m/f*

council scheme *n* (Scotland) ▶ COUNCIL ESTATE

council tax *n* (GB) ≈ impôts *mpl* locaux

counsel **1** *n* (lawyer) avocat/-e *m/f*
2 *vtr* conseiller ‹*person*› (**about, on** sur)

counselling (GB), **counseling** (US) *n* (advice) assistance *f*; (psychological) aide *f* psychosociale; **debt ~** assistance aux personnes endettées; **bereavement ~** aide psychosociale aux personnes endeuillées

counsellor, counselor (US) *n* conseiller/-ère *m/f*

count **1** *n* (a) (numerical record) décompte *m*; (at election) dépouillement *m*; **at the last ~** au dernier décompte; **to keep (a) ~ of** tenir compte de; **to lose ~** ne plus savoir où on en est dans ses calculs; **to be out for the ~** (colloq) être KO (fam)
(b) (level) taux *m*; **cholesterol ~** taux de cholestérol
(c) (figure) chiffre *m*
(d) (Law) chef *m* d'accusation; **on three ~s** pour trois chefs d'accusation
(e) (nobleman) comte *m*
2 *vtr* (a) (number) ‹*points, people, objects*›; énumérer ‹*reasons, causes*›; **~ing the children** en comptant les enfants; **not ~ing my sister** sans compter ma sœur
(b) (consider) **to ~ sb as sth** considérer qn comme qch
3 *vi* compter; **it's the thought that ~s** c'est l'intention qui compte
■ **count against** jouer contre ‹*person*›
■ **count on** compter sur ‹*person, event*›; **don't ~ on it!** ne comptez pas dessus!
■ **count up** calculer ‹*cost, hours*›; compter ‹*money, boxes*›

countdown *n* compte *m* à rebours (**to** avant)

counter **1** *n* (a) (in shop, snack bar) comptoir *m*; (in bank, post office) guichet *m*; (in pub, bar) bar *m*
(b) (in game) jeton *m*
2 *vtr* répondre à ‹*threat*›; neutraliser ‹*effet*›; parer ‹*blow*›; enrayer ‹*inflation*›
3 *vi* riposter (**with sth** par qch)
4 **counter to** *phr* (gen) contrairement à; ⋯⃗

‹be, go, run› à l'encontre de

counteract vtr contrebalancer ‹influence›; contrecarrer ‹negative effects›

counter-attack n contre-attaque f (against sur)

counter-clockwise adj, adv (US) dans le sens inverse des aiguilles d'une montre

counterfeit **1** adj ‹signature, note› contrefait/-e; ~ **money** fausse monnaie f **2** vtr contrefaire

counterfoil n talon m, souche f

counterpart n (of person) homologue mf; (of company, institution) équivalent m

counter-productive adj contre-productif/-ive

countersign vtr contresigner

countertop n (US) plan m de travail

countess n comtesse f

countless adj ~ **letters** un nombre incalculable de lettres; **on** ~ **occasions** je ne sais combien de fois

⚬ **country** n (a) pays m; **developing/third world** ~ pays en voie de développement/du tiers monde; ~ **of birth** pays natal (b) (countryside) campagne f; **in the** ~ à la campagne; **open** ~ rase campagne; **across** ~ à travers la campagne

country club n club m de loisirs

country dancing n danse f folklorique

country house n manoir m

country music n country music f

countryside n campagne f

⚬ **county** n comté m

county council n (GB) ≈ conseil m régional

coup n (a) (also ~ **d'état**) coup m d'État (b) **to pull off a** ~ réussir un beau coup

⚬ **couple** n (a) couple m (b) **a** ~ (**of**) (two) deux; (a few) deux ou trois; **a** ~ **of times** deux ou trois fois

coupon n (a) (voucher) bon m; **petrol** ~ (GB) bon d'essence (b) (in ad) coupon m; **reply** ~ coupon-réponse m

courage n courage m

courageous adj courageux/-euse

courgette n courgette f

courier n (a) (also **travel** ~) accompagnateur/-trice m/f (b) (for parcels, documents) coursier m; (for drugs) transporteur m

⚬ **course** **1** n (a) (gen) cours m (of de); **in the** ~ **of** au cours de; **in the** ~ **of time** avec le temps; **in due** ~ en temps utile; ~ **of action** moyen m d'action, parti m (b) (route) cours m; (of boat, plane) cap m; **to be on** ~ ‹boat, plane› tenir le cap; **to go off** ~ ‹ship› dévier de son cap; **to change** ~ (gen)

changer de direction; ‹boat, plane› changer de cap (c) (classes) cours m (**in** en; **of** de) (d) (Med) **a** ~ **of treatment** un traitement (e) (Sport) (in golf) terrain m de golf m; (in racing) champ m de courses (f) (part of meal) plat m; **the main** ~ le plat principal; **five-**~ **meal** repas m de cinq plats **2 of course** phr bien sûr, évidemment

course book n méthode f

coursework n devoirs mpl (de contrôle continu)

⚬ **court** **1** n (a) (Law) cour f, tribunal m; **to go to** ~ aller devant les tribunaux (**over** pour); **to take sb to** ~ poursuivre qn en justice (b) (for tennis, squash) court m; (for basketball) terrain m (c) (of sovereign) cour f (d) (courtyard) cour f **2** vtr courtiser ‹woman, voters›

court case n procès m, affaire f

courteous adj courtois/-e (**to** envers)

courtesy n courtoisie f

courthouse n (Law) palais m de justice

court-martial vtr (p prés etc **-ll-**) faire passer [qn] en cour martiale

courtroom n salle f d'audience

courtyard n cour f

cousin n cousin/-e m/f

cove n (bay) avise f

⚬ **cover** **1** n (a) (lid) couvercle m; (for duvet, typewriter, cushion, furniture) housse f; (of record) pochette f; (blanket) couverture f (b) (shelter) abri m; **to take** ~ se mettre à l'abri; **under** ~ à l'abri (c) (for teacher, doctor) remplacement m (d) (insurance) assurance f (**for** pour; **against** contre) **2** vtr (a) (gen) couvrir (**with** avec); recouvrir ‹cushion, sofa, surface, person, cake› (**with** de) (b) (deal with) ‹article, speaker› traiter; ‹journalist› couvrir (c) (insure) assurer, couvrir (**for, against** contre; **for doing** pour faire) ■ **cover for** remplacer ‹employee› ■ **cover up**: **1 to** ~ **up for** couvrir ‹friend› **2** ¶ ~ **[sth] up** recouvrir ‹object›; dissimuler ‹mistake, truth›; étouffer ‹scandal›

⚬ **coverage** n (gen) couverture f; **newspaper** ~ couverture par les journaux; **live** ~ reportage m en direct

cover charge n prix m de couvert

covering n (a) (for wall, floor) revêtement m (b) (layer of snow, moss) couche f

covering letter n lettre f d'accompagnement

cover note n (from insurance company) attestation f d'assurance

---

⚬ indicates a very frequent word

covert adj ‹operation› secret/-ète; ‹glance› furtif/-ive; ‹threat› voilé/-e

cover-up n opération f de camouflage

cover version n version f

covetous adj cupide

cow n vache f

coward n lâche mf

cowardice n lâcheté f

cowardly adj lâche

cowboy n (a) (US) cowboy m
(b) (incompetent worker) fumiste m

cower vi se recroqueviller

cox ⟦1⟧ n barreur m
⟦2⟧ vtr, vi barrer

coy adj (a) ‹smile, look› de fausse modestie
(b) (reticent) réservé/-e (**about** à propos de)

cozy (US) = cosy

crab n crabe m

crack ⟦1⟧ n (a) (in rock) fissure f; (in varnish, ground) craquelure f; (in wall, cup, bone) fêlure f
(b) (in door) entrebâillement m; (in curtains) fente f
(c) (also ~ **cocaine**) crack m
(d) (noise) craquement m
(e) (colloq) (attempt) essai m, tentative f; **to have a ~ at doing** essayer de faire
⟦2⟧ adj ‹player› de première; ‹troops, shot› d'élite
⟦3⟧ vtr (a) fêler ‹bone, wall, cup›
(b) casser ‹nut, egg›; **to ~ a safe** fracturer un coffre-fort; **to ~ sth open** ouvrir qch; **to ~ one's head open** se fendre le crâne
(c) déchiffrer ‹code›
(d) faire claquer ‹whip›; faire craquer ‹knuckles, joints›
⟦4⟧ vi (a) ‹bone, cup, wall, ice› se fêler; ‹varnish› se craqueler; ‹skin› se crevasser; ‹ground› se fendre
(b) ‹person› craquer (fam)
(c) ‹knuckles, twig› craquer; ‹whip› claquer
(d) ‹voice› se casser
▪ **crack down** prendre des mesures énergiques, sévir (**on** contre)

crackdown n mesure f sévère (**on** contre); **the ~ on drugs** l'action f antidrogue

cracker n (a) (biscuit) cracker m, biscuit m salé
(b) (for Christmas) diablotin m

crackle ⟦1⟧ n crépitement m
⟦2⟧ vi ‹fire, radio› crépiter; ‹hot fat› grésiller

cradle ⟦1⟧ n berceau m
⟦2⟧ vtr bercer ‹baby›; tenir [qch] délicatement ‹object›

craft n (a) (skill) métier m
(b) (craftwork) artisanat m; **arts and ~s** artisanat (d'art)
(c) (boat) embarcation f

craftsman n artisan m

crafty adj astucieux/-ieuse

crag n rocher m escarpé

cram ⟦1⟧ vtr (p prés etc -mm-) **to ~ sth into** enfoncer or fourrer (fam) qch dans ‹bag, car›; **~med full** plein à craquer
⟦2⟧ vi (p prés etc -mm-) ‹student› bachoter (**for** pour)

cramp ⟦1⟧ n crampe f
⟦2⟧ vtr gêner

cramped adj ‹house, office› exigu/-uë

cranberry n canneberge f

crane n grue f

crank n (a) (colloq) (freak) fanatique mf, fana mf (fam)
(b) (handle) manivelle f

crash ⟦1⟧ n (a) (noise) fracas m
(b) (accident) accident m; **car ~** accident de voiture; **train ~** catastrophe f ferroviaire
(c) (of stock market) krach m
⟦2⟧ vtr **to ~ one's car** avoir un accident de voiture
⟦3⟧ vi (a) ‹car, plane› s'écraser; ‹vehicles, planes› se rentrer dedans, se percuter; **to ~ into sth** rentrer dans or percuter qch
(b) ‹share prices› s'effondrer
▪ **crash out** (colloq) (go to sleep) pioncer (pop); (collapse) s'écrouler (fam)

crash course n cours m intensif

crash diet n régime m d'amaigrissement intensif

crash helmet n casque m

crash landing n atterrissage m en catastrophe

crass adj grossier/-ière; **~ ignorance** ignorance f crasse

crate n (for bottles, china) caisse f; (for fruit, vegetables) cageot m

crater n (of volcano) cratère m; (caused by explosion) entonnoir m

cravat n foulard m (pour homme)

crave vtr (also ~ **for**) avoir un besoin maladif de ‹drug›; avoir soif de ‹affection›; avoir envie de ‹food›

crawl ⟦1⟧ n (a) (in swimming) crawl m
(b) **at a ~** au pas; **to go at a ~** ‹vehicle› rouler au pas
⟦2⟧ vi (a) ‹insect, snake, person› ramper
(b) ‹baby› marcher à quatre pattes
(c) ‹vehicle› rouler au pas
(d) ‹time› se traîner
(e) **to be ~ing with** fourmiller de ‹insects, tourists›
(f) (colloq) (flatter) faire du lèche-bottes (fam) (**to** à)

crayfish n (a) (freshwater) écrevisse f
(b) (spiny lobster) langouste f

crayon n (wax) craie f grasse; (pencil) crayon m de couleur

craze n vogue f; **to be the latest ~** faire fureur

crazy adj (colloq) (gen) fou/folle; ‹idea› insensé/-e; **~ about** fou/folle de ‹person›; ····⟩

passionné/-e de ⟨activity⟩

crazy golf n (GB) mini-golf m

creak vi ⟨hinge⟩ grincer; ⟨floorboard⟩ craquer

cream ⓵ n crème f; strawberries and ∼ fraises à la crème
⓶ adj (a) (couleur) crème inv
(b) ⟨cake, bun⟩ à la crème
∎ **cream off**: ∼ off [sth], ∼ [sth] off prélever ⟨best pupils⟩; ramasser ⟨profits⟩

cream cheese n fromage m à tartiner

cream soda n soda m parfumé à la vanille

crease ⓵ n (intentional) pli m; (accidental) faux pli m
⓶ vtr froisser ⟨paper, cloth⟩
⓷ vi ⟨cloth⟩ se froisser

⚘ **create** vtr (gen) créer; provoquer ⟨interest⟩; poser ⟨problem⟩; faire ⟨good impression⟩

⚘ **creation** n création f

⚘ **creative** adj (a) ⟨person⟩ créatif/-ive
(b) ⟨process, imagination⟩ créateur/-trice

creator n créateur/-trice m/f (of de)

creature n (a) (living being) créature f
(b) (animal) animal m

crèche n (GB) (nursery) crèche f; (in shopping centre) halte-garderie f; **workplace** ∼ crèche f d'entreprise

credentials n pl (a) (reputation) qualifications fpl
(b) (reference) pièce f d'identité

credibility n crédibilité f

credible adj crédible

⚘ **credit** ⓵ n (a) (merit) mérite m (for de); **to get/take the** ∼ se voir attribuer/s'attribuer le mérite (for de); **to be a** ∼ **to sb/sth** faire honneur à qn/qch
(b) (in business) crédit m; **to buy sth on** ∼ acheter qch à crédit; **to be in** ∼ être créditeur/-trice
⓶ vtr (a) **to** ∼ **sb with** attribuer à qn ⟨achievement⟩
(b) créditer ⟨account⟩ (with de)

credit card n carte f de crédit

credit crunch n crise f du crédit

credit facilities n pl facilités fpl de crédit

credit note n avoir m

creditor n créancier/-ière m/f

credits n pl générique m

creditworthy adj solvable

credulous adj crédule, naïf/naïve

creed n (religious persuasion) croyance f; (opinions) principes mpl, credo m

creek n (a) (GB) crique f
(b) (US) (stream) ruisseau m

creep vi (prét, pp **crept**) (a) **to** ∼ **in/out** ⟨person⟩ entrer/sortir à pas de loup; **to** ∼ **under sth** se glisser sous qch; **to** ∼ **along**

⚘ indicates a very frequent word

⟨vehicle⟩ avancer lentement; ⟨insect, cat⟩ ramper
(b) ⟨plant⟩ grimper

creeper n (in jungle) liane f; (climbing plant) plante f grimpante

creepy adj (colloq) qui donne la chair de poule

creepy-crawly n (colloq) bestiole f (fam)

cremate vtr incinérer

cremation n (a) (ceremony) crémation f
(b) (practice) incinération f

crematorium n (pl **-oria** ou **-oriums**) (GB) crématorium m

crepe, crêpe n crêpe m

crescent n croissant m

crescent moon n croissant m de (la) lune

cress n cresson m

crest n (a) (ridge) crête f
(b) (coat of arms) armoiries fpl

Crete pr n Crète f

Creutzfeldt-Jacob disease, CJD n maladie f de Creutzfeldt-Jacob

crevice n fissure f

⚘ **crew** n (a) (on ship, plane) équipage m
(b) (on film, radio) équipe f

crewcut n coupe f (de cheveux) en brosse

crew neck sweater n pull m ras du cou

crib ⓵ n (cot) lit m d'enfant
⓶ vi (p prés etc **-bb-**) copier (from sur)

crick n a ∼ **in one's neck** un torticolis

cricket n (a) (insect) grillon m
(b) (game) cricket m

cricketer n joueur m de cricket

⚘ **crime** n (a) (minor) délit m; (serious) crime m (against contre)
(b) (phenomenon) criminalité f

⚘ **criminal** n, adj criminel/-elle m/f

criminal record n casier m judiciaire; **to have a/no** ∼ avoir un casier judiciaire chargé/vierge

crimson ⓵ n cramoisi m
⓶ adj pourpre

cringe vi (a) (in fear) avoir un mouvement de recul
(b) (with embarrassment) avoir envie de rentrer sous terre

cripple ⓵ n impotent/-e m/f
⓶ vtr (a) estropier; ∼**d for life** infirme à vie
(b) paralyser ⟨country, industry⟩

⚘ **crisis** n (pl **-ses**) crise f (in dans; over à cause de)

crisp adj ⟨biscuit⟩ croustillant/-e; ⟨fruit⟩ croquant/-e; ⟨garment⟩ frais/fraîche; ⟨banknote, snow⟩ craquant/-e; ⟨air⟩ vif/vive; ⟨manner⟩ brusque

crispbread n pain m grillé suédois

crisps n pl (also **potato** ∼) chips fpl

575

crisscross ⋯⊹ cruiser ⋯⋯

crisscross 1 adj ‹pattern› en croisillons
2 vi s'entrecroiser
criterion n (pl **-ia**) critère m (**for** de)
◊ **critic** n (a) (reviewer) critique m
(b) (opponent) détracteur/-trice m/f
◊ **critical** adj ‹point, condition, remark›
critique; ‹stage› crucial/-e; ‹moment› décisif/
-ive; **to be ∼ of sb/sth** critiquer qn/qch
critically adv (a) ‹examine› d'un œil
critique
(b) ‹ill› très gravement
◊ **criticism** n critique f
criticize vtr, vi critiquer
croak vi ‹frog› coasser
Croatia pr n Croatie f
crochet vtr faire [qch] au crochet; **a ∼(ed)
sweater** un pull au crochet
crockery n vaisselle f
crocodile n crocodile m
croissant n croissant m
crony n (petit/-e) copain/copine m/f
crook n (a) (person) escroc m
(b) (shepherd's) houlette f
(c) (of arm) creux m
IDIOM **by hook or by ∼** coûte que coûte
crooked adj (a) ‹line› brisé/-e; ‹picture,
teeth, beam› de travers
(b) (colloq) (dishonest) malhonnête
crop n (a) (produce) culture f; (harvest) récolte
f
(b) (whip) cravache f
■ **crop up** ‹matter, problem› surgir; ‹name›
être mentionné/-e; ‹opportunity› se présenter
◊ **cross** 1 n (a) croix f; **to put a ∼ against**
cocher ‹name, item›
(b) (hybrid) croisement m
2 adj (angry) fâché/-e (**with** contre); **to get
∼** se fâcher
3 vtr (a) (gen) traverser; franchir ‹border,
line›; **it ∼ed his mind that** il lui est venu à
l'esprit or l'idée que; **to ∼ one's legs** croiser
les jambes
(b) (intersect) couper
(c) barrer ‹cheque›
4 vi se croiser
■ **cross off, cross out** barrer, rayer ‹name,
item›
cross-border adj trans-frontalier/-ière
cross-Channel adj trans-Manche
cross-check vtr, vi revérifier
cross-country n (a) (running) cross m
(b) (skiing) ski m de fond
cross cultural adj inter-culturel/-elle
cross-examine vtr (gen) interroger; (Law)
faire subir un contre-interrogatoire à
cross-eyed adj ‹person› atteint/-e de
strabisme; **to be ∼** loucher, avoir un
strabisme
crossfire n feux mpl croisés; **to get caught
in the ∼** être pris/-e entre deux feux

crossing n (a) (journey) traversée f
(b) (on road) passage m clouté; (level crossing)
passage m à niveau
cross-legged adv ‹sit› en tailleur
cross-purposes n pl **we are at ∼** il y a
un malentendu; (disagreement) nous sommes
en désaccord
cross-reference n renvoi m (**to** à)
crossroads n (pl ∼) carrefour m
cross-section n échantillon m (**of** de)
crosswalk n (US) passage m (pour)
piétons
crossword n (also ∼ **puzzle**) mots mpl
croisés
crotch n (a) (of body) entrecuisse m
(b) (in trousers) entrejambe m
crotchet n (GB) noire f
crouch vi (also ∼ **down**) s'accroupir; (to
spring) ‹animal› se ramasser
crow 1 n corbeau m
2 vi (a) (exult) exulter
(b) (prét **-ed** ou **crew**) ‹cock› chanter
IDIOM **as the ∼ flies** à vol d'oiseau
crowbar n pince-monseigneur f
◊ **crowd** 1 n foule f; (watching sport, play)
spectateurs mpl
2 vtr (a) entasser ‹people, furniture› (**into**
dans)
(b) encombrer ‹room, house› (**with** de)
3 vi **to ∼ into** s'entasser dans ‹room, lift,
vehicle›
crowded adj (a) ‹place› plein/-e de monde;
(jam-packed) bondé/-e; **to be ∼ with** être
plein/-e de
(b) ‹schedule› chargé/-e
crowd-puller n (event) grosse attraction f
crown 1 n (a) (of monarch) couronne f
(b) (of hill) crête f; (of head) crâne m
(c) (on tooth) couronne f
2 vtr couronner
Crown court n (GB) ≈ cour f d'assises
crown jewels n pl joyaux mpl de la
Couronne
crown prince n prince m héritier
crow's nest n nid m de pie
◊ **crucial** adj crucial/-e
crucifix n crucifix m
crude adj (a) ‹method› rudimentaire;
‹estimate› approximatif/-ive
(b) ‹joke› grossier/-ière; ‹person› vulgaire
(c) (unprocessed) brut/-e; **∼ oil** pétrole m brut
cruel adj cruel/-elle
cruelty n cruauté f (**to** envers)
cruise 1 n croisière f; **to go on a ∼** faire
une croisière
2 vtr ‹driver, taxi› parcourir ‹street, city›
3 vi ‹ship› croiser; ‹plane› voler
cruise missile n missile m de croisière
cruiser n (a) (cabin cruiser) petit bateau m
de croisière
(b) (Mil) croiseur m

crumb n miette f

crumble 1 vtr émietter ‹bread›
2 vi (a) ‹rock› s'effriter; ‹building› se délabrer
(b) ‹relationship, economy› se désagréger; ‹opposition› s'effondrer

crummy adj (colloq) (a) (substandard) minable (fam)
(b) (unwell) **to feel ∼** se sentir patraque (fam)

crumple vtr froisser ‹paper›; **to ∼ sth into a ball** rouler qch en boule

crunch vtr croquer ‹apple, biscuit›
IDIOM **when** or **if it comes to the ∼** au moment crucial

crunchy adj croquant/-e

crusade n croisade f

crush 1 n bousculade f
2 vtr (a) écraser ‹can, fruit, person, vehicle› (**against** contre); broyer ‹arm, leg›; piler ‹ice›
(b) écraser ‹enemy, uprising›; étouffer ‹protest›
(c) chiffonner ‹garment, fabric›

crushing adj ‹defeat, weight› écrasant/-e; ‹blow› percutant/-e; **a ∼ setback** un revers cuisant

crust n (gen) croûte f; **the earth's ∼** l'écorce f terrestre

crutch n béquille f

crux n **the ∼ of the matter** le point crucial

◦ **cry** 1 n cri m
2 vi pleurer (**about** à cause de); **to ∼ with laughter** rire aux larmes
■ **cry out** (a) (with pain, grief) pousser un cri or des cris
(b) (call) crier, s'écrier
■ **cry off** (cancel) se décommander

cryogenics n cryogénie f

crypt n crypte f

cryptic adj ‹remark› énigmatique; ‹crossword› crypté/-e

crystal n cristal m

crystal ball n boule f de cristal

crystal clear adj (a) ‹water› cristallin/-e
(b) (obvious) clair/-e comme de l'eau de roche

CS gas n gaz m lacrymogène

cub n (Zool) petit m

Cuba pr n Cuba f

cubby-hole n (colloq) cagibi m (fam)

cube 1 n (gen) cube m; **ice ∼** glaçon m
2 vtr couper [qch] en cubes ‹meat›

cubic adj (a) cubique
(b) ‹metre, centimetre› cube

cubicle n (in changing room) cabine f; (in public toilets) cabinet m

cuckoo n coucou m

cucumber n concombre m

cuddle 1 n câlin m; **to give sb a ∼** faire un câlin à qn

2 vtr câliner

cuddly toy n (GB) peluche f

cue n (a) (line) réplique f; (action) signal m
(b) (Sport) queue f de billard

cuff n (a) poignet m
(b) (US) (on trousers) revers m
IDIOM **off the ∼** au pied levé

cuff link n bouton m de manchette

cul-de-sac n impasse f, cul-de-sac m

culinary adj culinaire

cull 1 n massacre m
2 vtr massacrer ‹seals, whales›

culminate vtr aboutir (**in** à)

culottes n pl jupe-culotte f

culprit n coupable mf

cult 1 n culte m; (contemporary religion) secte f
2 adj **a ∼ film** un film-culte; **to be a ∼ figure** faire l'objet d'un culte

cultivate vtr cultiver

◦ **cultural** adj culturel/-elle

cultural attaché n attaché/-e m/f culturel/-elle

◦ **culture** n culture f

cultured adj cultivé/-e

culture shock n choc m culturel

culture vulture n (colloq) fana mf de culture

cumbersome adj encombrant/-e

cumulative adj cumulatif/-ive

cunning 1 n (of person) ruse f; (nastier) fourberie f
2 adj (a) ‹person› rusé/-e; (nastier) fourbe
(b) ‹trick› habile; ‹device› astucieux/-ieuse

◦ **cup** 1 n (a) tasse f
(b) (trophy) coupe f
2 vtr (p prés etc **-pp-**) **to ∼ sth in one's hands** prendre qch dans le creux de ses mains

cupboard n placard m

curable adj guérissable

curate n vicaire m

curator n conservateur/-trice m/f

curb 1 n (a) restriction f (**on** à)
(b) (US) (sidewalk) bord m du trottoir
2 vtr refréner ‹desires›; limiter ‹powers›; juguler ‹spending›; restreindre ‹consumption›

curdle vi ‹milk› se cailler; ‹sauce› tourner

cure 1 n remède m (**for** à)
2 vtr (a) (gen) guérir (**of** de)
(b) (Culin) (dry) sécher; (salt) saler; (smoke) fumer

cure-all n panacée f (**for** contre)

curfew n couvre-feu m; **ten o'clock ∼** couvre-feu à partir de dix heures

curio n curiosité f, objet m rare

curiosity n curiosité f (**about** sur, au sujet de); **out of ∼** par curiosité

◦ indicates a very frequent word

curious ⋯⟩ cut ⋯⟩

curious *adj* curieux/-ieuse

curiously *adv* ‹silent, detached›
étrangement; ~ **enough** chose assez curieuse

curl ① *n* boucle *f*
② *vtr* friser ‹hair›
③ *vi* (a) ‹hair› friser
(b) (*also* ~ **up**) ‹paper› (se) gondoler; ‹edges, leaf› se racornir
■ **curl up** ‹person› se pelotonner; ‹cat› se mettre en rond; **to** ~ **up in bed** se blottir dans son lit

curler *n* bigoudi *m*

curly *adj* ‹hair› (tight curls) frisé/-e; (loose curls) bouclé/-e; ‹tail, eyelashes› recourbé/-e

currant *n* raisin *m* de Corinthe

currency *n* monnaie *f*, devise *f*

current ① *n* courant *m*
② *adj* ‹leader, situation, policy› actuel/-elle; ‹year, research› en cours

current account *n* (GB) compte *m* courant

current affairs *n* actualité *f*

currently *adv* actuellement, en ce moment

curriculum *n* (*pl* **-lums** *ou* **-la**)
programme *m*; **in the** ~ au programme

curriculum vitae *n* curriculum vitae *m*

curry ① *n* curry *m*; **chicken** ~ curry de poulet
② *vtr* **to** ~ **favour** chercher à se faire bien voir (**with sb** de qn)

curse ① *n* (a) (scourge) fléau *m*
(b) (swearword) juron *m*
(c) (spell) malédiction *f*
② *vtr* maudire
③ *vi* jurer (**at** après)

cursor *n* curseur *m*

curt *adj* sec/sèche

curtail *vtr* (restrict) mettre une entrave à; (cut back) réduire

curtain *n* rideau *m*

curtsey ① *n* (*pl* **-eys** *ou* **-ies**) révérence *f*
② *vi* (*prét, pp* **-seyed** *ou* **-sied**) faire la révérence (**to** à)

curve ① *n* courbe *f*
② *vi* ‹line, wall› s'incurver; ‹road, railway› faire une courbe

cushion ① *n* coussin *m*
② *vtr* amortir

cushy *adj* (colloq) peinard/-e (fam)

custard *n* (GB) (creamy) ≈ crème *f* anglaise

custodial sentence *n* peine *f* de prison

custodian *n* (of collection) gardien/-ienne *m/f*; (in museum) conservateur/-trice *m/f*

custody *n* (a) (detention) détention *f*; **to take sb into** ~ arrêter qn
(b) (of child) garde *f*

custom *n* (a) (tradition) coutume *f*, usage *m*
(b) (customers) clientèle *f*

customary *adj* habituel/-elle; (more formal) coutumier/-ière

◆ **customer** *n* client/-e *m/f*

customer services *n* service *m* clientèle

customize *vtr* fabriquer [qch] sur commande ‹car›

custom-made *adj* ‹clothes› fait/-e sur mesure

customs *n* douane *f*; **to go through** ~ passer à la douane

customs duties *n pl* droits *mpl* de douane

customs hall *n* douane *f*

customs officer, customs official *n* douanier/-ière *m/f*

◆ **cut** ① *n* (a) (incision) entaille *f*; (in surgery) incision *f*
(b) (wound) coupure *f*
(c) (hairstyle) coupe *f*
(d) (colloq) (share) part *f*
(e) (reduction) réduction *f* (**in** de); **job** ~**s** suppression *f* d'emplois; **a** ~ **in salary** une baisse de salaire
② *vtr* (*p prés* **-tt-**, *prét, pp* **cut**) (a) (gen) couper; **to** ~ **oneself** se couper; **to** ~ **one's finger** se couper le doigt; **to have one's hair cut** se faire couper les cheveux
(b) tailler ‹gem, suit, marble›; ‹locksmith› faire ‹key›
(c) (edit) couper ‹article, film›; supprimer ‹scene›
(d) (reduce) réduire ‹cost, inflation, list› (**by** de); baisser ‹price›
(e) **to** ~ **a tooth** percer une dent
(f) (record) faire, graver ‹album›
(g) (Comput) couper ‹text›
③ *vi* (*p prés* **-tt-**, *prét, pp* **cut**) (a) (with knife, scissors) couper; **to** ~ **into** entamer ‹cake›; couper ‹fabric, paper›; inciser ‹flesh›
(b) **to** ~ **down a sidestreet** couper par une petite rue
IDIOM **to** ~ **sb dead** ignorer complètement qn
■ **cut back**: ① ¶ ~ **back** faire des économies
② ¶ ~ **[sth] back** (a) (reduce) réduire (**to** à)
(b) (prune) tailler
■ **cut down**: ① ¶ ~ **down** réduire sa consommation; **to** ~ **down on smoking** fumer moins
② ¶ ~ **[sth] down** (a) (chop down) abattre
(b) (reduce) réduire
■ **cut off** (a) couper ‹hair, piece, corner›; enlever ‹excess, crusts›; amputer ‹limb›
(b) (disconnect) couper ‹mains service›
(c) **to** ~ **off sb's allowance** couper les vivres à qn
(d) **to** ~ **sb off** (on phone) couper qn; (interrupt) interrompre qn
(e) **to feel** ~ **off** se sentir isolé/-e
■ **cut out**: ① ¶ ~ **out** ‹engine, fan› s'arrêter
② ¶ ~ **[sth] out** (a) découper ‹article, picture› (**from** dans)
(b) (colloq) ~ **it out!** ça suffit!

⋯⟩

■ **cut short** abréger ‹*holiday, discussion*›
■ **cut up** couper
cut and paste *n* couper-coller *m*
cutback *n* réduction *f*; ~s in réductions dans le budget de ‹*defence, health*›; **government** ~s réductions budgétaires du gouvernement
cute *adj* (colloq) **(a)** mignon/-onne
(b) (US) (clever) malin/-igne
cutlery *n* couverts *mpl*
cutlet *n* côtelette *f*
cut-off ⬛1⬛ *n* (upper limit) limite *f*
⬛2⬛ **cut-offs** *n pl* jean *m* coupé
cut-price (GB), **cut-rate** (US) *adj* à prix réduit
cut-throat *adj* ‹*competition*› acharné/-e; **a ~ business** un milieu très dur
cutting ⬛1⬛ *n* **(a)** (from newspaper) coupure *f* (**from** de)
(b) (in film-making) montage *m*
⬛2⬛ *adj* ‹*tone*› cassant/-e; ‹*remark*› désobligeant/-e
cutting edge *n* **to be at the ~ of** être à l'avant-garde de
CV, cv *n* (*abbr* = **curriculum vitae**) cv, CV *m*
cyanide *n* cyanure *m*
cyber attack *n* cyberattaque *f*
cybercafe *n* cybercafé *m*

cyberculture *n* cyberculture *f*
cyberspace *n* cyberespace *m*
✧ **cycle** ⬛1⬛ *n* **(a)** cycle *m*
(b) (bicycle) vélo *m*
⬛2⬛ *vi* faire du vélo
cycle lane *n* piste *f* cyclable
cycle race *n* course *f* cycliste
cycling *n* cyclisme *m*
cycling shorts *n pl* cuissard *m*
cyclist *n* (gen) cycliste *mf*; (Sport) coureur/-euse *m/f* cycliste
cyclone *n* cyclone *m*
cygnet *n* jeune cygne *m*
cylinder *n* **(a)** (in engine) cylindre *m*
(b) (of gas) bouteille *f*
(c) (*also* **hot water ~**) (GB) ballon *m* d'eau chaude
cynic *n* cynique *mf*
cynical *adj* cynique
cynicism *n* cynisme *m*
Cyprus *pr n* Chypre *f*
cyst *n* kyste *m*
Czech ⬛1⬛ *n* **(a)** (person) Tchèque *mf*
(b) (language) tchèque *m*
⬛2⬛ *adj* tchèque
Czech Republic *pr n* République *f* tchèque

D d

d, D *n* **(a)** (letter) d, D *m*
(b) D (Mus) ré *m*
dab ⬛1⬛ *n* (of paint) touche *f*; (of butter) petit morceau *m*
⬛2⬛ *vtr* tamponner ‹*stain*› (**with** de); **to ~ one's eyes** se tamponner les yeux
dabble *v*
■ **dabble in** faire [qch] en amateur ‹*painting, politics*›
dachshund *n* teckel *m*
✧ **dad, Dad** *n* (colloq) papa *m* (fam); père *m*
daddy, Daddy *n* (colloq) papa *m* (fam)
daffodil *n* jonquille *f*
daft *adj* (colloq) bête
dagger *n* poignard *m*
IDIOM **to look ~s at sb** fusiller qn du regard
✧ **daily** ⬛1⬛ *n* (*pl* **dailies**) (newspaper) quotidien *m*
⬛2⬛ *adj* **(a)** ‹*visit, routine*› quotidien/-ienne; **on a ~ basis** tous les jours
(b) ‹*wage, rate*› journalier/-ière
⬛3⬛ *adv* quotidiennement; **twice ~** deux fois

✧ indicates a very frequent word

par jour
dainty *adj* ‹*porcelain, handkerchief*› délicat/-e; ‹*shoe, hand, foot*› mignon/-onne
dairy ⬛1⬛ *n* **(a)** (on farm) laiterie *f*; (shop) crémerie *f*
(b) (company) société *f* laitière
⬛2⬛ *adj* ‹*butter*› fermier/-ière; ‹*cow, farm, product, cream*› laitier/-ière
daisy *n* (common) pâquerette *f*; (garden) marguerite *f*
IDIOM **to be as fresh as a ~** être frais/fraîche comme un gardon
dam *n* barrage *m*
✧ **damage** ⬛1⬛ *n* **(a)** (gen) dégâts *mpl* (**to** causés à)
(b) (Med) **brain ~** lésions *fpl* cérébrales
(c) (figurative) **to do ~ to** porter atteinte à; **the ~ is done** le mal est fait
⬛2⬛ *vtr* **(a)** endommager ‹*building*›; nuire à ‹*environment, health*›; **to ~ one's eyesight** s'abîmer les yeux
(b) porter atteinte à ‹*reputation*›
damages *n pl* (Law) dommages-intérêts *mpl*

damaging *adj* (to reputation, person) préjudiciable (**to** à, pour); ‹*effect*› préjudiciable; (to health, environment) nuisible (**to** pour)

damn (colloq) **1** *n* **not to give a ~ about** sb/ sth se ficher (fam) éperdument de qn/qch
2 *adj* (also **damned**) ‹*key, car*› fichu/-e (fam) (*before n*)
3 *excl* merde! (fam), zut! (fam)

damp **1** *n* humidité *f*
2 *adj* ‹*clothes, house*› humide; ‹*skin*› moite

dampen *vtr* (a) humecter ‹*cloth*›
(b) refroidir ‹*enthusiasm*›

damson *n* prune *f* (de Damas)

⚜ **dance** **1** *n* (gen) danse *f*; (social occasion) soirée *f* dansante
2 *vi* (a) ‹*person*› danser (**with** avec)
(b) ‹*eyes*› briller (**with** de)
■ **dance about**, **dance up and down** sautiller sur place

dancer *n* danseur/-euse *m/f*

dancing *n* danse *f*

dandruff *n* pellicules *fpl*

⚜ **danger** *n* danger *m* (**of** de; **to** pour); **to be in ~** être en danger; **to be in ~ of doing** risquer de faire

danger list *n* **on the ~** dans un état critique

⚜ **dangerous** *adj* dangereux/-euse (**for** pour; **to do** de faire)
IDIOM **to be on ~ ground** avancer en terrain miné

dangerously *adv* (gen) dangereusement; ‹*ill*› gravement; **to live ~** prendre des risques

danger signal *n* signal *m* de danger

dangle **1** *vtr* balancer ‹*puppet, keys*›; laisser pendre ‹*legs*›
2 *vi* ‹*puppet, keys*› se balancer (**from** à); ‹*earrings*› pendiller; ‹*legs*› pendre

Danish **1** *n* (language) danois *m*
2 *adj* (gen) danois/-e; ‹*embassy*› du Danemark

dare **1** *n* défi *m*
2 *modal aux* oser; **to ~ (to) do** oser faire; **I ~ say** c'est bien possible
3 *vtr* **to ~ sb to do** défier qn de faire; **I ~ you!** chiche que tu ne le fais pas! (fam)

daredevil *n, adj* casse-cou *mf inv*

daring *adj* (a) (courageous, novel) audacieux/ -ieuse
(b) ‹*suggestion, dress*› osé/-e

⚜ **dark** **1** *n* **in the ~** dans le noir *or* l'obscurité; **before ~** avant la (tombée de la) nuit; **after ~** après la tombée de la nuit
2 *adj* (a) ‹*room, alley, day, sky*› sombre; **it is getting ~** il commence à faire noir *or* nuit; **it's ~** il fait noir *or* nuit
(b) ‹*colour, suit*› sombre; **a ~ blue dress** une robe bleu foncé
(c) ‹*hair, complexion*› brun/-e
(d) ‹*secret, thought*› noir/-e (*before n*)

IDIOMS **to be in the ~** être dans le noir; **to leave sb in the ~** laisser qn dans l'ignorance; **to keep sb in the ~ about sth** cacher qch à qn

darken **1** *vtr* (a) obscurcir ‹*sky, landscape*›; assombrir ‹*house*›
(b) foncer ‹*colour*›
2 *vi* (a) ‹*sky, room*› s'obscurcir
(b) (in colour) foncer; ‹*skin*› brunir

dark glasses *n pl* lunettes *fpl* noires

darkness *n* obscurité *f*; **in ~** dans l'obscurité

darkroom *n* chambre *f* noire

dark-skinned *adj* basané/-e

darling *n* (a) (my) **~** (to loved one) chéri/-e *m/f*; (to child) mon chou (fam); (to acquaintance) mon cher/ma chère *m/f*
(b) (kind, lovable person) amour *m*, ange *m*

darn *vtr* repriser

dart *n* fléchette *f*; **to play ~s** jouer aux fléchettes

dartboard *n* cible *f*

dash **1** *n* (a) (rush) course *f* folle; **it was a mad ~** on a dû se presser
(b) (small amount) (of liquid) goutte *f*; (of powder) pincée *f*; (of colour) touche *f*
(c) (punctuation) tiret *m*
2 *vtr* (a) **to ~ sb/sth against** projeter qn/ qch contre ‹*rocks*›
(b) anéantir ‹*hopes*›
3 *vi* se précipiter (**into** dans); **to ~ out of** sortir en courant de ‹*shop, room*›
■ **dash off**: **1** ¶ **~ off** se sauver
2 ¶ **~ [sth] off** écrire [qch] en vitesse

dashboard *n* tableau *m* de bord

⚜ **data** *n pl* données *fpl*

database *n* base *f* de données

data entry *n* introduction *f* de données

data processing *n* (procedure) traitement *m* des données; (career) informatique *f*; (department) service *m* informatique

data protection *n* protection *f* de l'information

data security *n* sécurité *f* des données

data storage device *n* périphérique *m* de stockage

⚜ **date** **1** *n* (a) date *f*; **~ of birth** date de naissance; **what's the ~ today?** on est le combien aujourd'hui?; **at a later ~**, **at some future ~** plus tard
(b) (on coin) millésime *m*
(c) (meeting) rendez-vous *m*; **to have a lunch ~** être pris/-e à déjeuner
(d) **who's your ~ for tonight?** avec qui sors-tu ce soir?
(e) (fruit) datte *f*
2 *vtr* (a) (gen) dater
(b) sortir avec ‹*person*›
3 *vi* **to ~ from** *or* **back to** ‹*building*› dater de; ‹*problem, friendship*› remonter à
4 **to date** *phr* à ce jour, jusqu'ici

dated adj ‹clothes, style› démodé/-e; ‹idea, custom› dépassé/-e; ‹language› vieilli/-e; **the film seems** ∼ **now** le film a mal vieilli

date rape n viol m (au cours d'une sortie en tête à tête)

dating agency n club m de rencontres

✓ **daughter** n fille f

daughter-in-law n (pl **daughters-in-law**) belle-fille f, bru f

daunting adj ‹task, prospect› décourageant/-e; ‹person› intimidant/-e

dawdle vi (colloq) flâner, traînasser (fam)

dawn ⎡1⎤ n aube f; **at** ∼ à l'aube; **at the crack of** ∼ à l'aube

⎡2⎤ vi **(a)** ‹day› se lever

(b) it ∼**ed on me that** je me suis rendu compte que; **it suddenly** ∼**ed on her why** elle a soudain compris pourquoi

dawn raid n descente f de police très tôt le matin

✓ **day** n **(a)** jour m; **what** ∼ **is it today?** quel jour sommes-nous aujourd'hui?; **every** ∼ tous les jours; **every other** ∼ tous les deux jours; **from** ∼ **to** ∼ ‹live› au jour le jour; ‹change› d'un jour à l'autre; **the** ∼ **when** or **that** le jour où; **the** ∼ **after** le lendemain; **the** ∼ **before** la veille; **the** ∼ **before yesterday** avant-hier; **the** ∼ **after tomorrow** après-demain

(b) (with emphasis on duration) journée f; **all** ∼ toute la journée; **during the** ∼ pendant la journée

(c) (age, period) époque f; **in those** ∼**s** à cette époque; **these** ∼**s** ces temps-ci

IDIOMS **those were the** ∼**s** c'était le bon temps; **that'll be the** ∼**!** je voudrais voir ça!; **to call it a** ∼ s'arrêter là; **to save the** ∼ sauver la situation

daybreak n aube f

day-care n (for children) service m de garderie

daydream ⎡1⎤ n rêves mpl

⎡2⎤ vi rêvasser

daylight n **(a)** (light) jour m, lumière f du jour; **it was still** ∼ il faisait encore jour

(b) (dawn) lever m du jour, point m du jour

daylight robbery n (colloq) **it's** ∼**!** c'est de l'arnaque! (fam)

day nursery n garderie f

day release n formation f permanente

day return n (GB) aller-retour m valable une journée

daytime n journée f

day-to-day adj quotidien/-ienne

day-trip n excursion f pour la journée

daze n **in a** ∼ (from news) ahuri/-e; (from blow) étourdi/-e; (from drugs) hébété/-e

dazed adj (by news) ahuri/-e; (by blow) étourdi/-e

✓ indicates a very frequent word

dazzle vtr éblouir; **to** ∼ **sb with** éblouir qn par ‹beauty, knowledge›

dazzling adj éblouissant/-e

D-day n **(a)** (important day) jour m J

(b) (Mil) le 6 juin 1944 (jour du débarquement des Alliés en Normandie)

✓ **dead** ⎡1⎤ n **(a) the** ∼ les morts mpl

(b) at ∼ **of night** en pleine nuit; **in the** ∼ **of winter** en plein hiver

⎡2⎤ adj mort/-e; **the** ∼ **man/woman** le mort/ la morte; **a** ∼ **body** un cadavre; **to drop (down)** ∼ tomber raide mort/-e; **the phone went** ∼ la ligne a été coupée

⎡3⎤ adv (GB) ‹certain, straight› absolument; ∼ **on time** pile (fam) à l'heure; ∼ **easy** (colloq) simple comme bonjour (fam); **they were** ∼ **lucky!** (colloq) ils ont eu du pot! (fam); ∼ **tired** (colloq) crevé/-e (fam), claqué/-e (fam); **to be** ∼ **set on doing** être tout à fait décidé/-e à faire; **to stop** ∼ s'arrêter net

deaden vtr calmer ‹pain›; amortir ‹blow›; assourdir ‹sound›

dead end ⎡1⎤ n impasse f

⎡2⎤ **dead-end** adj ‹job› sans perspectives

dead heat n (in athletics) arrivée f ex-aequo; (in horseracing) dead-heat m inv

deadline n date f or heure f limite, délai m; **to meet a** ∼ respecter un délai

deadlock n impasse f; **to reach (a)** ∼ aboutir à une impasse

dead loss n (colloq) **to be a** ∼ être nul/ nulle (fam)

deadly ⎡1⎤ adj **(a)** ‹poison, enemy› mortel/-elle

(b) in ∼ **earnest** avec le plus grand sérieux

⎡2⎤ adv ‹dull, boring› terriblement

deadpan adj ‹humour› pince-sans-rire inv

✓ **deaf** ⎡1⎤ n **the** ∼ les sourds mpl, les malentendants mpl

⎡2⎤ adj **(a)** sourd/-e; **to go** ∼ devenir sourd/-e

(b) to turn a ∼ **ear to** faire la sourde oreille à, rester sourd/-e à

deaf aid n (GB) prothèse f auditive

deafening adj assourdissant/-e

deaf without speech adj sourd-muet/ sourde-muette

✓ **deal** ⎡1⎤ n **(a)** (agreement) accord m; (in business) affaire f; (with friend) marché m; **it's a** ∼**!** marché conclu!

(b) a great or **good** ∼ beaucoup **(of** de)

⎡2⎤ vtr (prét, pp **dealt**) **(a)** porter ‹blow› **(to** à)

(b) distribuer ‹cards›; donner ‹hand›

⎡3⎤ vi (prét, pp **dealt**) **to** ∼ **in** être dans le commerce de ‹commodity, shares›

■ **deal with (a)** s'occuper de ‹problem, request›

(b) traiter de ‹topic›

dealer n **(a)** (in business) marchand/-e m/f; (large-scale) négociant/-e m/f

(b) (on stock exchange) opérateur/-trice *m/f*
(c) (in drugs) revendeur/-euse *m/f* de drogue,
dealer *m* (fam)
(d) (in cards) donneur/-euse *m/f*
dealing ① *n* **(a)** (trading) vente *f*; **foreign
exchange** ~ opérations *fpl* de change; **share**
~ transactions *fpl* boursières
(b) (trafficking) trafic *m*; **drug** ~ le trafic de
drogue
② **dealings** *n pl* relations *fpl* (**with** avec)
dear ① *n* (my) ~ mon chéri/ma chérie *m/f*;
(more formal) mon cher/ma chère *m/f*
② *adj* **(a)** (gen) cher/chère; **he's my ~est
friend** c'est mon meilleur ami; **to hold sb/sth
~** être attaché/-e à qn/qch, chérir qn/qch
(b) (in letter) cher/chère; **Dear Sir/Madam**
Monsieur, Madame; **Dear Sirs** Messieurs;
Dear Mr Jones Cher Monsieur; **Dear Mr and
Mrs Jones** Cher Monsieur, Chère Madame;
Dear Anne and Paul Chers Anne et Paul
③ *excl* **oh ~!** (dismay, surprise) oh mon Dieu!;
(less serious) aïe!, oh là là!
⚜ **death** *n* mort *f*; (more formally) décès *m*;
to drink/to work oneself to ~ se tuer en
buvant/au travail
IDIOMS **to be at ~'s door** être à l'article de
la mort; **to frighten sb to ~** faire une peur
bleue à qn (fam); **to be bored to ~** (colloq)
s'ennuyer à mourir; **I'm sick to ~ of this!**
(colloq) j'en ai par-dessus la tête!
death camp *n* camp *m* de la mort
death penalty *n* peine *f* de mort
death row *n* quartier *m* des condamnés
à mort
death sentence *n* condamnation *f* à mort
death threat *n* menaces *fpl* de mort
death toll *n* nombre *m* de morts
death trap *n* **to be a ~** être très
dangereux/-euse
debar *vtr* (*p prés etc* **-rr-**) **to be ~red from
doing** ne pas avoir le droit de faire
debatable *adj* discutable
⚜ **debate** *n* débat *m* (**on, about** sur); (informal
discussion) discussion *f* (**about** à propos de); **to
hold a ~ on** débattre de *‹issue›*
debauchery *n* débauche *f*
debit ① *n* débit *m*
② *vtr* débiter *‹account›* (**with** de)
debit card *n* carte *f* bancaire (*sans
paiement différé*)
debrief *vtr* interroger; **to be ~ed**
‹diplomat, agent› rendre compte (oralement)
d'une mission; *‹defector, freed hostage›* être
interrogé/-e
debris *n* (of plane) débris *mpl*; (of building)
décombres *mpl*; (rubbish) déchets *mpl*
⚜ **debt** *n* dette *f* (**to** envers); **to get into ~**
s'endetter
debt collector *n* agent *m* de
recouvrement
debtor *n* débiteur/-trice *m/f*

debug *vtr* (*p prés etc* **-gg-**) déboguer
‹software›
debut *n* débuts *mpl*
⚜ **decade** *n* décennie *f*
decadent *adj* décadent/-e
decaffeinated *adj* décaféiné/-e
decanter *n* (for wine, port) carafe *f* (à
décanter); (for whisky) flacon *m* à whisky
decathlon *n* décathlon *m*
decay ① *n* **(a)** (of vegetation, body)
pourriture *f*; (of building) délabrement *m*
(b) **tooth ~** carie *f* dentaire
(c) (of society) décadence *f*
② *vi ‹timber, vegetation›* pourrir; *‹tooth›* se
carier; *‹building›* se détériorer
deceased ① *n* **the ~** le défunt/la défunte
m/f
② *adj* décédé/-e, défunt/-e
deceit *n* malhonnêteté *f*
deceitful *adj* malhonnête
deceive ① *vtr* **(a)** tromper, duper *‹friend›*;
to be ~d être dupe
(b) tromper *‹spouse, lover›*
② *v refl* **to ~ oneself** se faire des illusions
⚜ **December** *n* décembre *m*
decency *n* **(a)** (good manners) politesse *f*
(b) (propriety) convenances *fpl*
decent *adj* **(a)** *‹family, man, woman›*
comme il faut, bien *inv* (fam); **it's ~ of him**
c'est très gentil à lui
(b) (adequate) convenable
(c) (good) *‹camera, education, result›* bon/
bonne (*before n*); *‹profit›* appréciable; **to
make a ~ living** bien gagner sa vie
(d) *‹behaviour, clothes, language›* décent/-e,
correct/-e
decentralize *vtr* décentraliser
deception *n* duplicité *f*
deceptive *adj* trompeur/-euse
⚜ **decide** ① *vtr* **(a)** **to ~ to do** décider de
faire; (after much hesitation) se décider à faire
(b) (settle) régler *‹matter›*; décider de *‹fate,
outcome›*
② *vi* décider; **to ~ against** écarter *‹plan,
idea›*; **to ~ between** choisir, faire un choix
entre *‹applicants, books›*
■ **decide on (a)** se décider pour *‹hat,
wallpaper›*; fixer *‹date›*
(b) décider de *‹course of action, size, budget›*
deciduous *adj ‹tree›* à feuilles caduques
decimal *adj ‹system, currency›* décimal/-e;
~ **point** virgule *f*
decipher *vtr* déchiffrer
⚜ **decision** *n* décision *f*; **to make** *or* **take a ~**
prendre une décision
decision-maker *n* décideur/-euse *m/f*
decision-making *n* **to be good/bad at ~**
savoir/ne pas savoir prendre des décisions
decisive *adj* **(a)** *‹manner, tone›* ferme
(b) *‹battle, factor›* décisif/-ive; *‹argument›*
concluant/-e

d

deck n (a) (on ship) pont m; **on ~** sur le pont; **below ~(s)** sur le pont inférieur
(b) (US) (terrace) terrasse f
(c) **~ of cards** jeu m de cartes
IDIOM **to clear the ~s** déblayer le terrain

deckchair n chaise f longue, transat m

declaration n déclaration f

⚜ **declare** vtr (a) déclarerannoncer (**that** que); annoncer ‹intention, support›
(b) déclarer ‹war› (**on** à); proclamer ‹independence›
(c) déclarer ‹income›

⚜ **decline** ① n (a) (waning) déclin m (**of** de); **to be in ~** être sur le déclin
(b) (drop) baisse f (**in, of** de); **to be on the** or **in ~** être en baisse
② vi (a) (drop) ‹demand, quality› baisser (**by** de); ‹support› être en baisse
(b) (wane) être sur le déclin
(c) (refuse) refuser

decode vtr décoder ‹code, message, signal›

decompose vi se décomposer

decompress vtr décomprimer, décompresser

decor n décoration f; (in theatre) décor m

decorate ① vtr (a) décorer ‹cake, tree› (**with** de, avec)
(b) **to ~ a room** (paint) peindre une pièce; (paper) tapisser une pièce
② vi faire des travaux de décoration

decoration n décoration f

decorative adj décoratif/-ive

decorator n peintre m, décorateur/-trice m/f

decoy ① n leurre m
② vtr attirer [qn] dans un piège

⚜ **decrease** ① n diminution f (**in** de); (in price) baisse f (**in** de)
② vi ‹population› diminuer; ‹price, popularity, rate› baisser, diminuer

decreasing adj décroissant/-e

decree n (a) (order) décret m
(b) (judgment) jugement m, arrêt m

decrepit adj ‹building› délabré/-e; ‹horse, old person› décrépit/-e

decriminalize vtr décriminaliser, légaliser

dedicate vtr dédier ‹book› (**to** à); consacrer ‹life› (**to** à)

dedicated adj ‹teacher, mother, fan› dévoué/-e; ‹worker› zélé/-e

dedication n (a) (devotion) dévouement m (**to** à); **~ to duty** dévouement
(b) (in a book, on music programme) dédicace f

deduce vtr déduire (**that** que)

deduct vtr prélever ‹subscription, tax› (**from** sur); déduire ‹sum› (**from** de)

deduction n (a) (from wages) retenue f (**from** sur); (of tax) prélèvement m

(b) (conclusion) déduction f, conclusion f

deed n (a) (action) action f; **to do one's good ~ for the day** faire sa bonne action or sa BA (fam)
(b) (for property) acte m de propriété

⚜ **deep** ① adj (a) (gen) profond/-e; ‹snow› épais/épaisse; **a ~-pile carpet** une moquette de haute laine; **how ~ is the lake?** quelle est la profondeur du lac?; **the lake is 13 m ~** le lac fait 13 m de profondeur
(b) (dark) ‹colour› intense; ‹tan› prononcé/-e; **~ blue eyes** des yeux d'un bleu profond
(c) **to be ~ in thought** être plongé/-e dans ses pensées; **to be ~ in conversation** être en grande conversation
② adv (a) ‹dig, bury, cut› profondément
(b) **~ down** or **inside she was frightened** dans son for intérieur elle avait peur

deep-(fat-)fryer n friteuse f

deepen ① vtr (a) creuser ‹channel›
(b) approfondir ‹knowledge, understanding›
② vi (a) ‹concern, love› augmenter; ‹knowledge› s'approfondir; ‹crisis› s'aggraver; ‹mystery› s'épaissir; ‹silence› se faire plus profond
(b) ‹voice› devenir plus grave
(c) ‹colour› foncer
③ **deepening** pres p adj ‹mystery, need, rift› croissant/-e; ‹crisis› de plus en plus grave; ‹confusion› de plus en plus grand/-e

deep-freeze n congélateur m

deep-fry vtr faire frire

⚜ **deeply** adv profondément

deep-rooted adj ‹anxiety, prejudice› profondément enraciné/-e

deep-sea adj ‹diver, diving› sous-marin/-e; ‹fisherman, fishing› hauturier/-ière

deep-vein thrombosis n thrombose f veineuse profonde, phlébite f

deer n (pl ~) (red) cerf m; (roe) chevreuil m; (fallow) daim m; (doe) biche f

de-escalate vtr faire baisser ‹tension, violence›; désamorcer ‹crisis›

deface vtr abîmer ‹wall›; couvrir [qch] d'inscriptions, dégrader ‹monument›

default ① vi ne pas régler ses échéances
② **by default** phr par défaut; **to win by ~** gagner par forfait

defeat ① n défaite f; **to admit ~** ‹team, troops› concéder la défaite; ‹person› avouer son échec
② vtr (a) vaincre ‹enemy›; battre ‹team, opposition, candidate›; **the government was ~ed** le gouvernement a été mis en échec
(b) rejeter ‹bill, proposal›
(c) **it ~s me** ça me dépasse

defeatist n, adj défaitiste mf

defect ① n (flaw) défaut m; (minor) imperfection f; **a speech ~** un défaut d'élocution
② vi faire défection; **to ~ to the West** passer à l'Ouest

⚜ indicates a very frequent word

defective ⋯✧ delinquent ⋯⋯

defective *adj* défectueux/-euse

defector *n* transfuge *mf* (**from** de)

✧ **defence** (GB), **defense** (US) *n* (gen, Law, Sport) défense *f*; **in her** ~ à sa décharge

defenceless (GB), **defenseless** (US) *adj* ‹*person, animal*› sans défense; ‹*town, country*› sans défenses

✧ **defend** *vtr* défendre ‹*fort, freedom, interests, title*›; justifier ‹*behaviour, decision*›

defendant *n* accusé/-e *m/f*

defender *n* défenseur *m*

defensive *adj* ‹*reaction, behaviour*› de défense; **to be (very)** ~ être sur la défensive

defer [1] *vtr* (*p prés etc* **-rr-**) reporter ‹*meeting, decision*› (**until** à); remettre [qch] à plus tard ‹*departure*›; différer ‹*payment*›
[2] *vi* (*p prés etc* **-rr-**) **to** ~ **to sb** s'incliner devant qn

deference *n* déférence *f*; **in** ~ **to** par déférence pour

defiance *n* attitude *f* de défi

defiant *adj* ‹*person*› rebelle; ‹*behaviour*› provocant/-e

deficiency *n* (**a**) (shortage) insuffisance *f* (**of, in** de); (of vitamins) carence *f* (**of** en)
(**b**) (weakness) faiblesse *f*

deficient *adj* déficient/-e (**in** en)

deficit *n* déficit *m*

✧ **define** *vtr* définir

definite *adj* ‹*plan, amount*› précis/-e; ‹*feeling, improvement, increase*› net/nette; ‹*decision, agreement*› ferme; **a** ~ **answer** une réponse claire et nette; **nothing is** ~ **yet** rien n'est encore sûr; **to be** ~ (sure) être certain/-e (**about** de); (unyielding) être formel/-elle (**about** sur)

✧ **definitely** *adv* sans aucun doute; **he** ~ **said he wasn't coming** il a bien dit qu'il ne viendrait pas

✧ **definition** *n* définition *f*

definitive *adj* définitif/-ive

deflate *vtr* dégonfler

deflationary *adj* déflationniste

deflect *vtr* (**a**) défléchir, dévier ‹*missile*›
(**b**) détourner ‹*blame, criticism, attention*›

deformed *adj* déformé/-e; (from birth) difforme

defraud *vtr* escroquer ‹*client, employer*›; frauder ‹*tax office*›

defrost [1] *vtr* décongeler ‹*food*›; dégivrer ‹*refrigerator*›
[2] *vi* ‹*refrigerator*› dégivrer; ‹*food*› décongeler

deft *adj* adroit/-e de ses mains, habile

defunct *adj* défunt/-e

defuse *vtr* désamorcer

defy *vtr* (**a**) défier ‹*authority, person*›
(**b**) **to** ~ **sb to do** mettre qn au défi de faire
(**c**) défier ‹*description*›; résister à ‹*efforts*›

degenerate [1] *adj* dégénéré/-e

[2] *vi* dégénérer

degrade *vtr* humilier ‹*person*›

degrading *adj* ‹*conditions, film*› dégradant/-e; ‹*job*› avilissant/-e; ‹*treatment*› humiliant/-e

✧ **degree** *n* (**a**) (measurement) degré *m*
(**b**) (from university) diplôme *m* universitaire; **first** *or* **bachelor's** ~ ≈ licence *f*
(**c**) **to such a** ~ **that** à tel point que; **to a** ~, **to some** ~ dans une certaine mesure; **by** ~**s** petit à petit
(**d**) (US) **first** ~ **murder** homicide *m* volontaire avec préméditation

degree ceremony *n* (GB Univ) cérémonie *f* de remise des diplômes

degree course *n* (GB Univ) programme *m* d'études universitaires

dehydrated *adj* déshydraté/-e; ‹*milk*› en poudre; **to become** ~ se déshydrater

de-icer *n* dégivrant *m*

deign *vtr* **to** ~ **to do** condescendre à faire, daigner faire

deity *n* divinité *f*

dejected *adj* découragé/-e

delay [1] *n* (gen) retard *m* (**of** de; **to, on** sur); **a few minutes'** ~ un délai de quelques minutes; **without (further)** ~ sans (plus) tarder
[2] *vtr* (**a**) différer ‹*decision, publication*›; **to** ~ **doing** attendre pour faire
(**b**) retarder ‹*train, arrival, post*›

delayed *adj* **to be** ~ être retardé/-e

delegate [1] *n* délégué/-e *m/f*
[2] *vtr* déléguer ‹*responsibility, task*› (**to** à)

delegation *n* délégation *f*

delete *vtr* supprimer (**from** de); (with pen) barrer; (on computer) effacer

delete key *n* touche *f* effacement

deliberate *adj* (**a**) (intentional) délibéré/-e; **it was** ~ il/elle l'a fait *etc* exprès
(**b**) (measured) ‹*movement*› mesuré/-e

deliberately *adv* ‹*do, say*› exprès; ‹*sarcastic, provocative*› délibérément

delicacy *n* (**a**) (of object, situation) délicatesse *f*; (of mechanism) sensibilité *f*
(**b**) (food) (savoury) mets *m* raffiné/-e; (sweet) friandise *f*

delicate *adj* (gen) délicat/-e; ‹*features*› fin/-e

delicatessen *n* (**a**) (shop) épicerie *f* fine
(**b**) (US) (eating-place) restaurant-traiteur *m*

delicious *adj* délicieux/-ieuse

delight [1] *n* joie *f*, plaisir *m*; **to take** ~ **in sth/in doing** prendre plaisir à qch/à faire
[2] *vtr* ravir ‹*person*› (**with** par)

delighted *adj* ravi/-e (**at, by, with** de; **to do** de faire); ~ **to meet you** enchanté

delightful *adj* charmant/-e

delinquency *n* délinquance *f*

delinquent *n, adj* délinquant/-e *m/f*

delirious *adj* to be ∼ délirer

ᵈ **deliver** ① *vtr* (a) livrer ‹goods, groceries›
(to à); distribuer ‹mail› (to à); remettre ‹note›
(to à)
(b) mettre au monde ‹baby›; délivrer ‹baby
animal›
(c) faire ‹speech›; donner ‹ultimatum›; rendre
‹verdict›
② *vi* ‹tradesman› livrer; ‹postman›
distribuer le courrier

ᵈ **delivery** *n* (a) (of goods, milk) livraison *f*; (of
mail) distribution *f*; on ∼ à la livraison
(b) (of baby) accouchement *m*

delude *vtr* tromper; to ∼ oneself se faire
des illusions

deluge *n* déluge *m*

delusion *n* illusion *f*

ᵈ **demand** ① *n* (a) (gen) demande *f* (for de);
on ∼ (gen) à la demande; ‹payable› à vue; to
be in ∼ être très demandé/-e
(b) (pressure) exigence *f*
② *vtr* (a) (request) demander ‹reform›;
(forcefully) exiger ‹ransom›; réclamer ‹inquiry›
(b) (require) demander ‹skill, time, patience›
(of sb de qn); (more imperatively) exiger

demanding *adj* (a) ‹person› exigeant/-e
(b) ‹work, course› ardu/-e; ‹schedule›
chargé/-e

demean *v refl* to ∼ oneself s'abaisser

demeaning *adj* humiliant/-e

demented *adj* fou/folle

dementia *n* démence *f*

demerara (sugar) *n* sucre *m* roux
cristallisé

demilitarize *vtr* démilitariser

demister *n* (GB) dispositif *m* antibuée

demo *n* (colloq) (*pl* -mos) (a) (protest) manif
f (fam)
(b) (sample version) démo *f* (fam), version *f* de
démonstration

demobilize *vtr* démobiliser

ᵈ **democracy** *n* démocratie *f*

democrat *n* démocrate *mf*

democratic *adj* démocratique

demolish *vtr* démolir

demolition *n* démolition *f*

demon *n* démon *m*

ᵈ **demonstrate** ① *vtr* (a) démontrer
‹theory, truth›
(b) manifester ‹concern, support›; montrer
‹skill›
(c) faire la démonstration de ‹machine,
product›; to ∼ how to do montrer comment
faire
② *vi* manifester (for en faveur de; against
contre)

demonstration *n* (a) (march)
manifestation *f* (against contre; for en faveur
de)

(b) (of machine, theory) démonstration *f*

demonstrative *adj* démonstratif/-ive

demonstrator *n* manifestant/-e *m/f*

demoralize *vtr* démoraliser

demote *vtr* rétrograder

den *n* (a) (of lion) antre *m*; (of fox) tanière *f*
(b) (room) tanière *f*

denial *n* (of accusation, rumour) démenti *m*;
(of guilt, rights, freedom) négation *f*; to be in ∼
refuser d'admettre qch

denim ① *n* jean *m*; ∼s jean *m*
② *adj* ‹jacket, skirt› en jean; ∼ **jeans** jean *m*

Denmark *pr n* Danemark *m*

denomination *n* (a) (name) dénomination *f*
(b) (faith) confession *f*
(c) (value) valeur *f*

denounce *vtr* (a) (inform on, criticize)
dénoncer
(b) (accuse) accuser

dense *adj* dense

density *n* densité *f*

dent ① *n* (in metal) bosse *f*
② *vtr* cabosser ‹car›

dental *adj* dentaire

dental floss *n* fil *m* dentaire

dental surgeon *n* chirurgien-dentiste *m*

dental surgery *n* (GB) (premises) cabinet
m dentaire

dentist *n* dentiste *mf*

dentistry *n* médecine *f* dentaire

dentures *n pl* dentier *m*

ᵈ **deny** *vtr* (a) démentir ‹rumour›; nier
‹accusation›; to ∼ doing *or* having done nier
avoir fait
(b) to ∼ sb sth refuser qch à qn

deodorant *n* (personal) déodorant *m*; (for
room) déodorisant *m*

depart *vi* (a) partir (from de; for pour)
(b) (deviate) to ∼ from s'éloigner de

ᵈ **department** *n* (a) (of company) service *m*
(b) (governmental) ministère *m*; (administrative)
service *m*; **social services** ∼ services
sociaux
(c) (in store) rayon *m*; **toy** ∼ rayon jouets
(d) (in hospital) service *m*
(e) (in university) département *m*
(f) (in school) section *f*

departmental *adj* ‹head, meeting› de
service

department store *n* grand magasin *m*

departure *n* (of person, train) départ *m*; (from
truth, regulation) entorse *f* (from à); (from policy,
tradition) rupture *f* (from par rapport à)

departure gate *n* porte *f* de départ

departures board *n* tableau *m* des
départs

departure time *n* heure *f* de départ

ᵈ **depend** *vi* to ∼ on dépendre de, compter
sur (for pour); to ∼ on sb/sth to do compter
sur qn/qch pour faire; that ∼s cela dépend;

ᵈ indicates a very frequent word

~ing on the season suivant la saison

dependable adj ‹person› digne de confiance; ‹machine› fiable

dependant n personne f à charge

dependence, dependance (US) n
(a) (reliance) dépendance f (on vis-à-vis de)
(b) (addiction) dépendance f (on à)

dependent adj ‹relative› à charge; **to be ~ (up)on** (gen) dépendre de; (financially) vivre à la charge de

depict vtr (visually) représenter; (in writing) dépeindre (**as** comme)

depiction n peinture f, représentation f

deplete vtr réduire

deplorable adj déplorable

deplore vtr déplorer

deploy vtr déployer

depopulation n dépeuplement m

deport vtr expulser (**to** vers)

deportation n expulsion f

depose vtr déposer

deposit ☐1 n (a) (to bank account) dépôt m; **on ~** en dépôt
(b) (on house, hire purchase goods) versement m initial (**on** sur); (on holiday, goods) acompte m, arrhes fpl
(c) (against damage, breakages) caution f
(d) (on bottle) consigne f
(e) (of silt, mud) dépôt m; (of coal, mineral) gisement m
☐2 vtr déposer ‹money›; **to ~ sth with sb** confier qch à qn

deposit account n (GB) compte m de dépôt

depot n (a) (gen) dépôt m
(b) (US) (station) (bus) gare f routière; (rail) gare f ferroviaire

depress vtr (a) déprimer ‹person›
(b) appuyer sur ‹button›
(c) faire baisser ‹prices›; affaiblir ‹trading›

depressed adj (a) ‹person› déprimé/-e
(b) ‹region, industry› en déclin

depressing adj déprimant/-e

depression n dépression f; **to suffer from ~** être dépressif/-ive

deprivation n (poverty) privations fpl

deprive vtr priver (**of** de)

deprived adj ‹area, family› démuni/-e; ‹childhood› malheureux/-euse

depth ☐1 n (a) (of hole, water) profondeur f; (of layer) épaisseur f; **to be out of one's ~** (in water) ne plus avoir pied; (in situation) être complètement perdu/-e
(b) (of colour, emotion) intensité f; (of crisis) gravité f
(c) (of knowledge) étendue f; (of analysis, novel) profondeur f; **to examine sth in ~** examiner qch en détail
☐2 **depths** n pl (of sea) profondeurs fpl; **in the ~s of winter** au plus profond de l'hiver; **to be in the ~s of despair** toucher le fond

du désespoir

deputize vi **to ~ for sb** remplacer qn

deputy ☐1 n (a) (aide) adjoint/-e m/f; (replacement) remplaçant/-e m/f
(b) (politician) député m
☐2 adj adjoint/-e

deputy chairman n vice-président m

deputy president n vice-président m

derail vtr faire dérailler

deranged adj dérangé/-e

deregulate vtr libérer ‹prices›; déréguler ‹market›

derelict adj ‹building› délabré/-e

derision n moqueries fpl

derive vtr tirer ‹benefit, income› (**from** de)

derogatory adj désobligeant/-e (**about** envers); ‹term› péjoratif/-ive

descend ☐1 vtr descendre ‹steps, slope, path›
☐2 vi (a) ‹person, plane› descendre (**from** de)
(b) ‹rain, darkness, mist› tomber (**on, over** sur)
(c) **to ~ on sb** débarquer chez qn (fam)
(d) **to be ~ed from** descendre de

descendant n descendant/-e m/f (**of** de)

descent n (a) descente f (**on, upon** sur)
(b) (extraction) descendance f

✔ **describe** vtr décrire

✔ **description** n description f (**of** de); (for police) signalement m (**of** de)

descriptive adj descriptif/-ive

desecrate vtr profaner ‹altar, shrine›

desert ☐1 n désert m
☐2 vtr abandonner ‹person› (**for** pour); déserter ‹cause›; abandonner ‹post›
☐3 vi ‹soldier› déserter
IDIOM **to get one's just ~s** avoir ce qu'on mérite

desert boot n bottine f en croûte de cuir, clarks® f inv

deserted adj désert/-e

deserter n déserteur m (**from** de)

desert island n île f déserte

✔ **deserve** vtr mériter (**to do** de faire)

deserving adj ‹winner› méritant/-e; ‹cause› louable

✔ **design** ☐1 n (a) (development) (of object, appliance) conception f; (of building, room) agencement m; (of clothing) création f
(b) (drawing, plan) plan m (**for** de)
(c) (art of designing) design m; (fashion) stylisme m
(d) (pattern) motif m; **a leaf ~** un motif de feuilles
(e) (subject of study) arts mpl appliqués
☐2 vtr (a) concevoir ‹building, appliance›; **to be ~ed for sth/to do** être conçu/-e pour qch/ pour faire
(b) ‹designer› créer ‹costume, garment›; dessiner ‹building, appliance›

designate *vtr* **to ∼ sb (as) sth** désigner qn (comme) qch; **to ∼ sth (as) sth** classer qch (comme) qch; **to ∼ sth for** destiner qch à

designer ⟦1⟧ *n* (gen) concepteur/-trice *m/f*; (of furniture, in fashion) créateur/-trice *m/f*; (of sets) décorateur/-trice *m/f*; **costume ∼** costumier/-ière *m/f*
⟦2⟧ *adj* **∼ clothes, ∼ labels** vêtements *mpl* griffés; **∼ label** griffe *f*

design fault *n* faute *f* de conception

desirable *adj* (a) ⟨outcome, solution⟩ souhaitable; ⟨area, position⟩ convoité/-e; ⟨job, gift⟩ séduisant/-e
(b) (sexually) désirable

⚜ **desire** ⟦1⟧ *n* désir *m* (**for** de); **to have no ∼ to do** n'avoir aucune envie de faire
⟦2⟧ *vtr* désirer; **it leaves a lot to be ∼d** cela laisse beaucoup à désirer

⚜ **desk** *n* (a) bureau *m*; **writing ∼** secrétaire *m*
(b) (in classroom) (pupil's) table *f*; (teacher's) bureau *m*
(c) **reception ∼** réception *f*; **information ∼** bureau *m* de renseignements; **cash ∼** caisse *f*

desktop *n* (also **∼ computer**) ordinateur *m* de bureau

desktop publishing, DTP *n* micro-édition *f*, PAO *f*

desolate *adj* désolé/-e

despair ⟦1⟧ *n* désespoir *m*; **in** *or* **out of ∼** de désespoir
⟦2⟧ *vi* désespérer (**of** de; **of doing** de faire)

desperate *adj* ⟨person, plea, situation⟩ désespéré/-e; ⟨criminal⟩ prêt/-e à tout; **to be ∼ for** avoir désespérément besoin de ⟨affection, help⟩; attendre désespérément ⟨news⟩

desperately *adv* (a) ⟨plead, look, fight⟩ désespérément; **to need sth ∼** avoir très besoin de qch
(b) ⟨poor⟩ terriblement; ⟨ill⟩ très gravement

desperation *n* désespoir *m*

despicable *adj* méprisable

despise *vtr* mépriser

⚜ **despite** *prep* malgré

despondent *adj* abattu/-e, découragé/-e

despot *n* despote *m*

dessert *n* dessert *m*

dessertspoon *n* cuillère *f* à dessert

dessert wine *n* vin *m* doux

destabilize *vtr* déstabiliser

destination *n* destination *f*

destined *adj* (a) destiné/-e (**for, to** à; **to do** à faire)
(b) (bound for) **∼ for Paris** à destination de Paris

destiny *n* destin *m*, destinée *f*

destitute *adj* sans ressources

⚜ *indicates a very frequent word*

⚜ **destroy** *vtr* (a) détruire ⟨building, evidence⟩; briser ⟨career, person⟩
(b) (kill) abattre ⟨animal⟩; détruire, anéantir ⟨population, enemy⟩

⚜ **destruction** *n* destruction *f*

destructive *adj* destructeur/-trice

detach *vtr* détacher (**from** de)

detachable *adj* ⟨coupon, section, strap⟩ détachable; ⟨lever, collar⟩ amovible

detached *adj* détaché/-e

detached house *n* maison *f* (individuelle)

detachment *n* détachement *m*

⚜ **detail** ⟦1⟧ *n* détail *m*; **in (more) ∼** (plus) en détail; **to go into ∼s** entrer dans les détails; **to have an eye for ∼** prêter attention aux détails
⟦2⟧ *vtr* exposer [qch] en détail ⟨plans⟩; énumérer ⟨items⟩

detain *vtr* (a) (delay) retenir
(b) (keep in custody) placer [qn] en détention

detainee *n* détenu/-e *m/f*

⚜ **detect** *vtr* déceler ⟨error, traces⟩; détecter ⟨crime, leak, sound⟩; sentir ⟨mood⟩

detectable *adj* discernable

detection *n* (of disease, error) détection *f*; **crime ∼** la lutte contre la criminalité; **to escape ∼** ⟨criminal⟩ ne pas être découvert/-e; ⟨error⟩ ne pas être décelé/-e

detective *n* ≈ inspecteur/-trice *m/f* (de police); **private ∼** détective *m*

detective story *n* roman *m* policier

detector *n* détecteur *m*

detention *n* (a) (confinement) détention *f*
(b) (in school) retenue *f*, colle *f* (fam)

detention centre *n* centre *m* de détention pour mineurs

deter *vtr* (*p prés etc* **-rr-**) dissuader (**from doing** de faire)

detergent *n* détergent *m*

deteriorate *vi* se détériorer

determination *n* détermination *f*

⚜ **determine** *vtr* déterminer; **to ∼ how** établir comment

determined *adj* ⟨person⟩ fermement décidé/-e (**to do** à faire); ⟨air⟩ résolu/-e

deterrent *n* (gen) moyen *m* de dissuasion; (Mil) force *f* de dissuasion

detest *vtr* détester (**doing** faire)

detonate *vtr* faire exploser ⟨bomb⟩

detour *n* détour *m*

detox (colloq) ⟦1⟧ *n* **to be in ∼** être en cure de désintoxication
⟦2⟧ *adj* ⟨centre, treatment⟩ de désintoxication

detract *vi* **to ∼ from** porter atteinte à ⟨success, value⟩; nuire à ⟨image⟩; diminuer ⟨pleasure⟩

detriment *n* **to the ∼ of** au détriment de

detrimental *adj* nuisible (**to** à)

deuce *n* (in tennis) ∼! égalité!

devaluation *n* (of currency) dévaluation *f*

devastated *adj* ‹land, region› ravagé/-e; ‹person› anéanti/-e

devastation *n* dévastation *f*

◌′ **develop** ⏩ ① *vtr* **(a)** attraper ‹illness›; prendre ‹habit›; présenter ‹symptom›
(b) élaborer ‹plan›; mettre au point ‹technique›; développer ‹argument›
(c) développer ‹mind, business, market›
(d) mettre en valeur ‹land, site›; aménager ‹city centre›
(e) (in photography) développer
② *vi* **(a)** (evolve) ‹child, society, country, plot› se développer; ‹skills› s'améliorer; **to** ∼ **into** devenir
(b) (come into being) ‹friendship, difficulty› naître; ‹crack› se former; ‹illness› se déclarer
(c) (progress, advance) ‹friendship› se développer; ‹difficulty, illness› s'aggraver; ‹crack, fault› s'accentuer; ‹game, story› se dérouler
(d) (in size) ‹town, business› se développer

developer *n* (also **property** ∼) promoteur *m* (immobilier); promoteur *m* (immobilier)

developing country *n* pays *m* en voie de développement

◌′ **development** *n* **(a)** (gen) développement *m*
(b) (of product) mise *f* au point; (of housing, industry) création *f*
(c) (of land) mise *f* en valeur; (of site, city centre) aménagement *m*
(d) (innovation) progrès *m*; **major** ∼**s** des découvertes *fpl* majeures (**in** dans le domaine de)
(e) (event) changement *m*; **recent** ∼**s in Europe** les derniers événements en Europe

deviate *vi* **(a)** (from norm) s'écarter (**from** de)
(b) (from course) dévier (**from** de)

◌′ **device** *n* **(a)** (household) appareil *m*
(b) (Tech) dispositif *m*
(c) (also **explosive** ∼, **incendiary** ∼) engin *m* explosif
(d) (means) moyen *m* (**for doing, to do** de *or* pour faire)
IDIOM to be left to one's own ∼**s** être laissé/-e à soi-même

devil *n* **(a)** (also **Devil**) **the** ∼ le Diable
(b) (evil spirit) démon *m*
IDIOM speak of the ∼! quand on parle du loup (on en voit la queue)! (fam)

devil's advocate *n* avocat *m* du diable

devious *adj* retors/-e

devise *vtr* concevoir ‹scheme, course›; inventer ‹product, machine›

devoid *adj* ∼ **of** dépourvu/-e de

devolution *n* **(a)** (of powers) transfert *m* (**from** de; **to** à)
(b) (policy) régionalisation *f*

devote *vtr* consacrer (**to** à; **to doing** à faire); **to** ∼ **oneself** se consacrer (**to** à)

devoted *adj* ‹person, animal› dévoué/-e (**to** à); ‹fan› fervent/-e

devotion *n* (to person, work) dévouement *m* (**to** à); (to cause) attachement *m* (**to** à); (to God) dévotion *f* (**to** à)

devour *vtr* dévorer

devout *adj* ‹Catholic, prayer› fervent/-e; ‹person› pieux/pieuse

dew *n* rosée *f*

diabetes *n* diabète *m*

diabetic *n*, *adj* diabétique *mf*

diagnose *vtr* diagnostiquer

diagnosis *n* (*pl* **-ses**) diagnostic *m*

diagonal ⏩ ① *n* diagonale *f*
② *adj* diagonal/-e

diagonally *adv* en diagonale

diagram *n* schéma *m*; (in mathematics) figure *f*

dial ⏩ ① *n* cadran *m*
② *vtr* (*p prés etc* **-ll-** (GB), **-l-** (US)) faire, composer ‹number›; appeler ‹person›; **to** ∼ **999** (for police, ambulance) ≈ appeler police secours; (for fire brigade) ≈ appeler les pompiers

dialect *n* dialecte *m*

dialling code *n* (GB) indicatif *m*

dialling tone (GB), **dial tone** (US) *n* tonalité *f*

dialogue *n* dialogue *m*

dialogue box *n* boîte *f* de dialogue

dialysis *n* (*pl* **-lyses**) dialyse *f*

diameter *n* diamètre *m*

diamond *n* **(a)** (gem) diamant *m*
(b) (shape) losange *m*
(c) (in cards) carreau *m*

diaper *n* (US) couche *f* (de bébé)

diaphragm *n* diaphragme *m*

diarrhoea (GB), **diarrhea** (US) *n* diarrhée *f*

diary *n* **(a)** (for appointments) agenda *m*; **to put sth in one's** ∼ noter qch dans son agenda
(b) (journal) journal *m* intime

dice ⏩ ① *n* (*pl* ∼) (object) dé *m*; (game) dés *mpl*
② *vtr* couper [qch] en cubes ‹vegetable, meat›

dictate ⏩ ① *vtr* **(a)** dicter ‹letter›
(b) imposer ‹terms› (**to** à); déterminer ‹outcome›
② *vi* **(a)** **to** ∼ **to one's secretary** dicter une lettre (*or* un texte) à sa secrétaire
(b) **to** ∼ **to sb** imposer sa volonté à qn

dictation *n* dictée *f*

dictator *n* dictateur *m*

dictatorship *n* dictature *f*

dictionary *n* dictionnaire *m*

◌′ **die** *vi* (*p prés* **dying**, *prét*, *pp* **died**) mourir (**of, from** de); **to be dying** être mourant/-e, se mourir; **to be dying to do** mourir d'envie de ···⊹

d

faire; **to be dying for** avoir une envie folle de
■ **die down** ‹*emotion, row*› s'apaiser;
‹*fighting*› s'achever; ‹*storm*› se calmer;
‹*laughter*› diminuer; ‹*applause*› se calmer
■ **die out** ‹*species*› disparaître

diesel *n* (a) (*also* ∼ **fuel**, ∼ **oil**) gazole *m*
(b) (*also* ∼ **car**) diesel *m*

diesel engine *n* (moteur *m*) diesel *m*

diet *n* (a) (normal food) alimentation *f* (of à
base de)
(b) (slimming food) régime *m*; **to go on a** ∼ se
mettre au régime

dietician *n* diététicien/-ienne *m/f*

differ *vi* (a) (be different) différer (from de;
in par)
(b) (disagree) différer (on sur; from sb de qn)

✓ **difference** *n* (a) différence *f* (in, of de); **to
tell the** ∼ **between** faire la différence entre;
it won't make any ∼ ça ne changera rien; **it
makes no** ∼ **to me** cela m'est égal
(b) (disagreement) différend *m* (over à propos
de; with avec); **a** ∼ **of opinion** une divergence
d'opinion

✓ **different** *adj* différent/-e (**from, to** (GB);
than (US) de)

differentiate ① *vtr* différencier (**from**
de)
② *vi* (a) (tell the difference) faire la différence
(**between** entre)
(b) (show the difference) faire la distinction
(**between** entre)

differently *adv* (in another way) autrement
(**from** que); (in different ways) différemment
(**from** de)

✓ **difficult** *adj* difficile; **to find it** ∼ **to do**
avoir du mal à faire; **to be** ∼ **to get on with**
être difficile à vivre

✓ **difficulty** *n* difficulté *f*; **to have** ∼ **(in)**
doing avoir du mal à faire

diffident *adj* ‹*person*› qui manque
d'assurance; ‹*smile, gesture*› timide

dig ① *n* (a) (with elbow) coup *m* de coude (**in**
dans)
(b) (colloq) (jibe) **to take a** ∼ **at sb** lancer une
pique (fam) à qn
(c) (in archaeology) fouilles *fpl*; **to go on a** ∼
aller faire des fouilles
② **digs** *n pl* (GB) chambre *f* (meublée)
③ *vtr* (*p prés* -**gg**-; *pp* **dug**) (a) creuser
‹*hole, tunnel, grave*› (**in** dans)
(b) bêcher ‹*garden*›; fouiller ‹*site*›
(c) extraire ‹*coal*› (**out of** de)
④ *vi* (*p prés* -**gg**-; *pp* **dug**) ‹*miner*› creuser;
‹*archaeologist*› fouiller; ‹*gardener*› bêcher
■ **dig up** (a) déterrer ‹*body, treasure, scandal*›;
arracher ‹*roots, weeds*›; excaver ‹*road*›
(b) bêcher ‹*garden*›

digest *vtr* digérer ‹*food*›; assimiler ‹*facts*›

digestion *n* digestion *f*

digit *n* (a) (number) chiffre *m*

(b) (finger) doigt *m*; (toe) orteil *m*

✓ **digital** *adj* ‹*display, recording*› numérique;
‹*watch*› à affichage numérique; ‹*camera, TV*›
numérique

digitize *vtr* numériser

dignified *adj* ‹*person*› digne; ‹*manner*›
empreint/-e de dignité

dignity *n* dignité *f*

digress *vi* faire une digression; **to** ∼ **from**
s'écarter de

dilapidated *adj* délabré/-e

dilate ① *vtr* dilater
② *vi* se dilater

dilemma *n* dilemme *m* (about à propos de);
to be in a ∼ être pris/-e dans un dilemme

diligent *adj* appliqué/-e

dilute *vtr* diluer (**with** avec)

dim ① *adj* (a) ‹*room*› sombre
(b) ‹*light*› faible; **to grow** ∼ baisser
(c) ‹*outline*› vague
(d) ‹*memory*› vague (**before** *n*)
(e) (colloq) (stupid) bouché/-e (fam)
② *vtr* (*p prés etc* -**mm**-) baisser ‹*light,
headlights*›; mettre [qch] en veilleuse ‹*lamp*›

dime *n* (US) (pièce *f* de) dix cents *mpl*
IDIOM they're a ∼ **a dozen** (colloq) on en
trouve à la pelle (fam)

dimension *n* dimension *f*

-dimensional *combining form* **three**∼ à
trois dimensions

dime store *n* (US) bazar *m*

diminish *vtr, vi* diminuer

dimple *n* fossette *f*

din *n* vacarme *m*

dine *vi* dîner

diner *n* (a) (person) dîneur/-euse *m/f*
(b) (US) (restaurant) café-restaurant *m*

dinghy *n* (a) (*also* **sailing** ∼) dériveur *m*
(b) (inflatable) canot *m*

dingy *adj* ‹*colour*› défraîchi/-e; ‹*place*›
minable

dining car *n* wagon-restaurant *m*

dining room *n* (in house) salle *f* à manger;
(in hotel) salle *f* de restaurant

✓ **dinner** *n* (a) dîner *m*; **to go out to** ∼ dîner
dehors; **to have** ∼ dîner
(b) (banquet) dîner *m* (**for** en l'honneur de)

dinner hour *n* (GB Sch) heure *f* du
déjeuner

dinner jacket, DJ *n* smoking *m*

dinner party *n* dîner *m*

dinnertime *n* heure *f* du dîner

dinosaur *n* dinosaure *m*

dip ① *n* (a) (in ground, road) creux *m*
(b) (bathe) baignade *f*
(c) (in prices, rate, sales) (mouvement *m* de)
baisse *f* (**in** dans)
(d) (Culin) sauce *f*
② *vtr* (*p prés etc* -**pp**-) (a) tremper (**in, into**
dans)

✓ indicates a very frequent word

(b) (GB Aut) baisser ‹*headlights*›; ∼**ped headlights** codes *mpl*
[3] *vi* (*p prés etc* **-pp-**) **(a)** ‹*bird, plane*› piquer
(b) ‹*land, road*› être en pente
(c) to ∼ **into** puiser dans ‹*savings*›; parcourir ‹*novel*›

diploma *n* diplôme *m* (**in** en)
diplomacy *n* diplomatie *f*
diplomat *n* diplomate *mf*
diplomatic *adj* diplomatique; **to be** ∼ avoir du tact
dipstick *n* jauge *f* de niveau d'huile
✔ **direct** [1] *adj* (gen) direct/-e; ‹*person*› franc/franche
[2] *adv* directement; **to fly** ∼ prendre un vol direct
[3] *vtr* **(a)** (address, aim) adresser ‹*appeal, criticism*› (**at** à; **against** contre); cibler ‹*campaign*› (**at** sur); orienter ‹*effort, resource*› (**to, towards** vers)
(b) (control) diriger ‹*company, project*›; régler ‹*traffic*›
(c) diriger ‹*attack, light*› (**at** vers)
(d) réaliser ‹*film, programme*›; mettre [qch] en scène ‹*play*›; diriger ‹*actor, opera*›
(e) (show route) **to** ∼ **sb to sth** indiquer le chemin de qch à qn
[4] *vi* (in cinema, radio, TV) faire de la réalisation; (in theatre) faire de la mise en scène

direct debit *n* prélèvement *m* automatique
✔ **direction** [1] *n* direction *f*; **in the right/ wrong** ∼ dans la bonne/mauvaise direction; **to go in the opposite** ∼ aller en sens inverse; **from all** ∼**s** de tous les côtés
[2] **directions** *n pl* **(a)** (for route) indications *fpl*; **to ask for** ∼**s** demander son chemin (**from** à)
(b) (for use) instructions *fpl* (**as to, about** sur); ∼**s for use** mode *m* d'emploi
✔ **directly** *adv* **(a)** ‹*connect, challenge, go*› directement; ‹*point*› droit; ‹*above*› juste
(b) (at once) ∼ **after** aussitôt après; ∼ **before** juste avant
(c) (very soon) d'ici peu
(d) (frankly) ‹*speak*› franchement
direct mail *n* mailing *m*, publipostage *m*
✔ **director** *n* **(a)** (of company) (sole) directeur/-trice *m/f*; (on board) administrateur/-trice *m/f*
(b) (of play, film) metteur *m* en scène; (of orchestra) chef *m* d'orchestre; (of choir) chef *m* des chœurs
directory *n* **(a)** (*also* **telephone** ∼) annuaire *m*
(b) (for business use) répertoire *m* d'adresses; **street** ∼ répertoire *m* des rues
(c) (Comput) répertoire *m*
directory assistance (US), **directory enquiries** *n pl* (GB) (service

m des) renseignements *mpl*
direct speech *n* style *m* direct
dirt *n* **(a)** (on clothing, in room) saleté *f*; (on body, cooker) crasse *f*; (in carpet, engine, filter) saletés *fpl*
(b) (soil) terre *f*; (mud) boue *f*
dirt track *n* chemin *m* de terre battue
dirty [1] *adj* **(a)** ‹*face, clothing, street*› sale; ‹*work*› salissant/-e; **to get** ∼ se salir; **to get sth** ∼ salir qch
(b) ‹*needle*› qui a déjà servi; ‹*wound*› infecté/-e
(c) (colloq) ‹*book, joke*› cochon/-onne (fam); ‹*mind*› mal tourné/-e
(d) (colloq) ‹*trick*› sale (*before n*)
[2] *vtr* salir
IDIOM **to give sb a** ∼ **look** regarder qn d'un sale œil

disability *n* infirmité *f*; **mental/physical** ∼ handicap *m* mental/physique
disable *vtr* **(a)** ‹*accident*› rendre [qn] infirme
(b) immobiliser ‹*machine*›
(c) (Comput) désactiver
disabled [1] *n* **the** ∼ les handicapés *mpl*
[2] *adj* handicapé/-e
disabled access *n* voie *f* d'accès pour handicapés
disadvantage *n* inconvénient *m*; **to be at a** ∼ être désavantagé/-e
disadvantaged *adj* défavorisé/-e
disagree *vi* **(a)** ne pas être d'accord (**with** avec; **on, about** sur); **we often** ∼ nous avons souvent des avis différents
(b) ‹*facts, accounts, result*› être en désaccord (**with** avec)
(c) to ∼ **with sb** ‹*food*› ne pas réussir à qn
disagreeable *adj* désagréable
disagreement *n* **(a)** (difference of opinion) désaccord *m* (**about, on** sur)
(b) (argument) différend *m* (**about, over** sur)
disallow *vtr* **(a)** (Sport) refuser ‹*goal*›
(b) (gen, Law) rejeter ‹*claim, decision*›
✔ **disappear** *vi* disparaître
disappearance *n* disparition *f* (**of** de)
disappoint *vtr* décevoir
disappointed *adj* déçu/-e (**about, with sth** par qch)
disappointing *adj* décevant/-e
disappointment *n* déception *f*; **to be a** ∼ **to sb** décevoir qn
disapproval *n* désapprobation *f* (**of** de)
disapprove *vi* **to** ∼ **of** désapprouver ‹*person, lifestyle*›; être contre ‹*smoking*›
disapproving *adj* désapprobateur/-trice
disarm *vtr, vi* désarmer
disarmament *n* désarmement *m*
disaster *n* catastrophe *f*; (long-term) désastre *m*

disaster area n région f sinistrée; (figurative) catastrophe f

disaster fund n fonds m de soutien

disaster movie n film m catastrophe

disaster victim n sinistré/-e m/f

disastrous adj désastreux/-euse

disbelief n incrédulité f

✓ **disc, disk** (US) n (a) (gen, Mus) disque m (b) identity ∼ plaque f d'identité; tax ∼ vignette f (automobile)

discard vtr (a) (get rid of) se débarrasser de ‹possessions›; mettre [qch] au rebut ‹furniture› (b) (drop) abandonner ‹plan, policy›; laisser tomber ‹person›

discerning adj perspicace

discharge ⟨1⟩ n (a) (of patient) renvoi m au foyer (b) (of gas, smoke) émission f; (of liquid) écoulement m; (of waste) déversement m (c) (from eye, wound) sécrétions fpl ⟨2⟩ vtr (a) renvoyer ‹patient›; décharger ‹accused›; to be ∼d from hospital être autorisé/-e à quitter l'hôpital; to be ∼d from the army être libéré/-e de l'armée (b) renvoyer ‹employee› (c) émettre ‹gas›; déverser ‹sewage› (d) (Med) to ∼ pus suppurer

discipline ⟨1⟩ n discipline f ⟨2⟩ vtr (a) (control) discipliner (b) (punish) punir

disciplined adj discipliné/-e

disclaim vtr nier

disclaimer n démenti m

disclose vtr révéler ‹information›

disclosure n révélation f (of de)

disco n discothèque f

discomfort n (a) (physical) sensation f pénible (b) (embarrassment) sentiment m de gêne

disconcerting adj (worrying) troublant/-e; (unnerving) déconcertant/-e

disconnect vtr débrancher ‹pipe, fridge›; couper ‹telephone›; décrocher ‹carriage›

discontent n mécontentement m

discontented adj mécontent/-e

discontinue vtr supprimer ‹service›; arrêter ‹production›; cesser ‹visits›

discount ⟨1⟩ n remise f (on sur); to give sb a ∼ faire une remise à qn ⟨2⟩ vtr écarter ‹idea, possibility›; ne pas tenir compte de ‹advice, report›

discount store n solderie f

discourage vtr décourager

✓ **discover** vtr découvrir (that que)

discovery n découverte f

discredit vtr discréditer ‹person, organization›; mettre en doute ‹report, theory›

✓ indicates a very frequent word

discreet adj discret/-ète

discrepancy n divergence f

discretion n discrétion f; to use one's ∼ agir à sa discrétion

discriminate vi (a) (act with bias) établir une discrimination (against envers; in favour of en faveur de) (b) (distinguish) to ∼ between faire une or la distinction entre

discrimination n discrimination f

discus n disque m

✓ **discuss** vtr (talk about) discuter de; (in writing) examiner

✓ **discussion** n discussion f; (in public) débat m

disdainful adj dédaigneux/-euse

✓ **disease** n maladie f

disembark vtr, vi débarquer

disenchanted adj désabusé/-e

disengage vtr dégager (from de)

disfigure vtr défigurer

disgrace ⟨1⟩ n honte f; to be in ∼ (officially) être en disgrâce ⟨2⟩ vtr déshonorer ‹team, family›

disgraceful adj scandaleux/-euse

disguise ⟨1⟩ n déguisement m; in ∼ déguisé/-e ⟨2⟩ vtr déguiser ‹person, voice›; camoufler ‹blemish›; cacher ‹emotion, fact›

disgust ⟨1⟩ n (physical) dégoût m; (moral) écœurement m (at devant) ⟨2⟩ vtr (physically) dégoûter; (morally) écœurer

disgusting adj (physically) répugnant/-e; (morally) écœurant/-e

dish n (a) plat m; to do the ∼es faire la vaisselle (b) (also satellite ∼) antenne f parabolique

■ **dish out** distribuer ‹advice, compliments, money›; servir ‹food›

dishcloth n (for washing) lavette f; (for drying) torchon m (à vaisselle)

dishevelled adj ‹person› débraillé/-e; ‹hair› décoiffé/-e; ‹clothes› en désordre

dishonest adj malhonnête

dishonesty n (financial) malhonnêteté f; (moral) mauvaise foi f

dishonour (GB), **dishonor** (US) n déshonneur m

dishtowel n torchon m

dishwasher n (machine) lave-vaisselle m inv; (person) plongeur/-euse m/f

disillusioned adj désabusé/-e; to be ∼ with perdre ses illusions sur

disinfect vtr désinfecter

disinfectant n désinfectant m

disintegrate vi se désagréger

disinterested adj impartial/-e

disk n (a) (Comput) disque m (b) (US) = DISC

disk drive (unit) n unité f de disques

dislike [1] n aversion f (**for** pour); **to take a ~ to sb** prendre qn en aversion
[2] vtr ne pas aimer (**doing** faire)

dislocate vtr **to ~ one's shoulder** se démettre l'épaule

dislodge vtr déplacer ‹rock, tile, obstacle›

disloyal adj déloyal/-e (**to** envers)

dismal adj ‹place, sight› lugubre
(b) (colloq) ‹failure, attempt› lamentable

dismantle vtr (a) démonter ‹construction›
(b) démanteler ‹organization›

dismay n consternation f (**at** devant)

✧ **dismiss** vtr (a) écarter ‹idea, suggestion›; exclure ‹possibility›
(b) chasser ‹thought, worry›
(c) licencier ‹employee›; démettre [qn] de ses fonctions ‹director, official›
(d) (end interview with) congédier ‹person›; (send out) ‹teacher› laisser sortir ‹class›
(e) (Law) **the case was ~ed** il y a eu non-lieu

dismissal n (of employee) licenciement m; (of manager, minister) destitution f

dismissive adj dédaigneux/-euse

disobedient adj désobéissant/-e

disobey [1] vtr désobéir à ‹person›; enfreindre ‹law›
[2] vi ‹person› désobéir

disorder n (a) (lack of order) désordre m
(b) (disturbances) émeutes fpl
(c) (Med) (malfunction) troubles mpl; (disease) maladie f

disorganized adj désorganisé/-e

disorientate vtr désorienter

disown vtr renier ‹person›; désavouer ‹document›

dispassionate adj (impartial) objectif/-ive (**about** au sujet de)

dispatch [1] n (report) dépêche f
[2] vtr envoyer ‹person› (**to** à); expédier ‹letter, parcel› (**to** à)

dispel vtr (p prés etc **-ll-**) dissiper ‹doubt, fear, myth›

dispensary n (GB) (in hospital) pharmacie f; (in chemist's) officine f

dispense vtr (a) ‹machine› distribuer ‹drinks, money›
(b) ‹chemist› préparer ‹medicine, prescription›
(c) (exempt) dispenser (**from sth** de qch; **from doing** de faire)
■ **dispense with** (a) se passer de ‹services, formalities›
(b) abandonner ‹policy›
(c) (make unnecessary) rendre inutile

dispenser n distributeur m

disperse [1] vtr disperser ‹crowd, fumes›
[2] vi (a) ‹crowd› se disperser
(b) ‹mist› se dissiper

displaced person n personne f déplacée

✧ **display** [1] n (a) (in shop) étalage m; (of furniture, vehicles) exposition f; **window ~** vitrine f; **to be on ~** être exposé/-e
(b) (demonstration) (of art, craft) démonstration f; (of dance, sport) exhibition f; **air ~** fête f aéronautique
(c) (of emotion) démonstration f; (of strength) déploiement m; (of wealth) étalage m
(d) (Aut, Comput) écran m
[2] vtr (a) (show, set out) afficher ‹information, poster›; exposer ‹object›
(b) (reveal) faire preuve de ‹intelligence, interest, skill›; révéler ‹emotion, vice, virtue›
(c) (flaunt) faire étalage de ‹beauty, knowledge, wealth›; exhiber ‹legs, chest›

displeased adj mécontent/-e (**with, at** de)

disposable adj (a) (throwaway) jetable
(b) (available) disponible

disposal n (a) (of waste product) élimination f; **for ~** à jeter
(b) (of company, property) vente f
(c) **to be at sb's ~** être à la disposition de qn

dispose v
■ **dispose of** (a) se débarrasser de ‹body, rubbish›; détruire ‹evidence›; désarmer ‹bomb›
(b) écouler ‹stock›; vendre ‹car, shares›

disproportionate adj disproportionné/-e (**to** par rapport à)

disprove vtr réfuter

dispute [1] n (a) (quarrel) (between individuals) dispute f; (between groups) conflit m (**over, about** à propos de)
(b) (controversy) controverse f (**over, about** sur)
[2] vtr contester ‹claim, figures›
(b) se disputer ‹property, title›

disqualify vtr (a) (gen) exclure; **to ~ sb from doing** interdire à qn de faire
(b) (Sport) disqualifier
(c) (GB Aut) **to ~ sb from driving** retirer le permis de conduire à qn

disregard [1] n (for problem, person) indifférence f (**for sth** à qch; **for sb** envers qn); (for danger, life, law) mépris m (**for** de)
[2] vtr (a) ne pas tenir compte de ‹problem, evidence, remark›; fermer les yeux sur ‹fault›; mépriser ‹danger›
(b) ne pas respecter ‹law, instruction›

disrepair n délabrement m; **to fall into ~** se délabrer

disreputable adj ‹person› peu recommandable; ‹place› mal famé/-e

disrespect n manque m de respect (**for** envers)

disrespectful adj ‹person› irrespectueux/-euse (**to, towards** envers)

disrupt vtr perturber ‹traffic, trade, meeting›; bouleverser ‹lifestyle, schedule, routine›; interrompre ‹power supply›

disruption n (disorder) perturbations fpl; (of schedule) bouleversement m

disruptive adj perturbateur/-trice

dissatisfaction n mécontentement m

dissatisfied adj mécontent/-e (**with** de)

dissect vtr disséquer

dissertation n (GB Univ) mémoire m (**on** sur)

dissident n, adj dissident/-e m/f

dissimilar adj dissemblable; ∼ **to** différent/-e de

dissolve ① vtr (a) ‹acid, water› dissoudre ‹solid, grease›
(b) faire dissoudre ‹tablet, powder› (**in** dans)
(c) dissoudre ‹assembly, parliament, partnership›
② vi (a) ‹tablet› se dissoudre (**in** dans; **into** en)
(b) ‹hope› s'évanouir; ‹outline, image› disparaître
(c) **to** ∼ **into tears** fondre en larmes

dissuade vtr dissuader (**from doing** de faire)

⚡ **distance** n distance f (**between** entre; **from** de; **to** à); **to keep one's** ∼ garder ses distances (**from** avec); **in the** ∼ au loin; **it's within walking** ∼ on peut y aller à pied

distance learning n enseignement m à distance

distant adj (a) (remote) éloigné/-e
(b) (faint) ‹memory, prospect› lointain/-e
(c) (cool) ‹person› distant/-e

distaste n dégoût m

distinct adj (gen) distinct/-e (**from** de); ‹resemblance, preference, progress› net/nette (before n); ‹advantage› indéniable

distinction n (a) (gen) distinction f
(b) (Univ) mention f très bien

distinctive adj caractéristique (**of** de)

distinguish vtr distinguer (**from** de); **to be** ∼**ed by** se caractériser par

distinguished adj (a) (elegant) distingué/-e
(b) (famous) éminent/-e

distinguishing adj distinctif/-ive

distort vtr déformer

distract vtr distraire; **to** ∼ **sb from doing** empêcher qn de faire

distracting adj gênant/-e

distraction n (a) (from concentration) distraction f
(b) (diversion) diversion f

distraught adj éperdu/-e

distress ① n (a) (emotional) désarroi m; **to cause sb** ∼ faire de la peine à qn
(b) (physical) souffrance f
(c) ‹ship› **in** ∼ en détresse
② vtr faire de la peine à ‹person›; (stronger) bouleverser ‹person› (**to do** de faire)

distressed adj (upset) peiné/-e (**at, by** par); (stronger) bouleversé/-e (**at, by** par)

⚡ indicates a very frequent word

distressing adj ‹case, event, idea› pénible; ‹news› navrant/-e; ‹sight› affligeant/-e

distribute vtr (a) (share out) distribuer ‹films, supplies, money› (**to** à; **among** entre)
(b) (spread out) répartir ‹load, tax burden›

⚡ **distribution** n distribution f

distributor n distributeur m (**for sth** de qch)

⚡ **district** n (in country) région f; (in city) quartier m; (administrative) district m

district attorney n (US) représentant m du ministère public

distrust vtr se méfier de

disturb vtr (a) (interrupt) déranger ‹person›; troubler ‹silence, sleep›
(b) (upset) troubler ‹person›; (concern) inquiéter ‹person›

disturbance n (a) (interruption, inconvenience) dérangement m
(b) (riot) troubles mpl; (fight) altercation f

disturbed adj (a) ‹sleep› agité/-e
(b) ‹child› perturbé/-e

disturbing adj ‹portrayal› troublant/-e; ‹book, film› perturbant/-e; ‹report, increase› inquiétant/-e

disused adj désaffecté/-e

ditch ① n fossé m
② vtr laisser tomber ‹friend›; abandonner ‹idea, vehicle›; plaquer (fam) ‹girlfriend, boyfriend›

dither vi tergiverser (**about, over** sur)

ditto adv idem

dive ① n (a) (by swimmer) plongeon m
(b) (of plane, bird) piqué m
② vi (prét ∼**d** (GB), **dove** (US)) (a) ‹person› plonger (**off, from** de; **down to** jusqu'à)
(b) (as hobby) faire de la plongée

diver n plongeur/-euse m/f; (deep-sea) scaphandrier m

diverge vi diverger; **to** ∼ **from** s'écarter de

diverse adj (varied) divers/-e; (different) différent/-e

diversify vi se diversifier

diversion n (a) (distraction) diversion f (**from** à)
(b) (of river, money) détournement m
(c) (of traffic) déviation f

diversity n diversité f

divert vtr (a) détourner ‹water›; dévier ‹traffic›; dérouter ‹flight› (**to** sur); détourner ‹funds› (**to** au profit de)
(b) (distract) détourner

⚡ **divide** ① vtr (a) (also ∼ **up**) partager ‹food, money, time, work›
(b) (separate) séparer (**from** de)
(c) (split) diviser ‹friends, group›
(d) (in mathematics) diviser (**by** par)
② vi ‹road› bifurquer; ‹river, train› se séparer en deux; ‹group› (into two) se séparer en deux; ‹cell, organism› se diviser

dividend n dividende m

dividing line n ligne f de démarcation
diving n (from board) plongeon m; (under sea) plongée f sous-marine
diving board n plongeoir m
diving suit n scaphandre m
ⓢ **division** n (gen) division f
divisive adj ‹policy› qui sème la discorde; **to be socially** ~ créer des inégalités sociales
divorce 1 n divorce m
2 vtr **to** ~ **sb** divorcer de or d'avec qn; **they're** ~d ils ont divorcé; **she's** ~d elle est divorcée
divorcee n divorcé/-e m/f
DIY n (GB) (abbr = **do-it-yourself**) bricolage m
dizzy adj ‹height› vertigineux/-euse; **to make sb** ~ donner le vertige à qn; **to feel** ~ avoir la tête qui tourne
DJ n (abbr = **disc jockey**) DJ mf
DNA n (abbr = **deoxyribonucleic acid**) ADN m
ⓢ **do** 1 v aux (3ᵉ pers sg prés **does**, prét **did**, pp **done**) (a) (gen) ~ **you like Mozart?** est-ce que tu aimes Mozart?, aimes-tu Mozart?; **I don't smoke** je ne fume pas; **don't shut the door** ne ferme pas la porte; ~ **sit down** asseyez-vous; **I** ~ **like your dress** j'aime beaucoup ta robe; **he lives in London, doesn't he?** il habite à Londres, n'est-ce pas?; **Lola didn't phone,** ~ **she?** Lola n'a pas téléphoné par hasard?; **don't** ~ **that!** ne fais pas ça!; **he said he'd tell her and he did** il a dit qu'il le lui dirait et il l'a fait; **so/neither does he** lui aussi/non plus
(b) (in short answers) **'I love peaches'—'so** ~ **I'** 'j'adore les pêches'—'moi aussi'; **'who wrote it?'—'I did'** 'qui l'a écrit?'—'moi'; **'shall I tell him?'—'no don't'** 'est-ce que je le lui dis?'— 'non'; **'he knows the President'—'does he?'** 'il connaît le Président'—'vraiment?'; **'Tim didn't say that'** — **'yes he did'** 'Tim n'a pas dit ça' — 'si'
2 vtr (3ᵉ pers sg prés **does**, prét **did**, pp **done**) (a) (gen) faire; **to** ~ **the cooking/one's homework** faire la cuisine/ses devoirs; **to** ~ **sth again** refaire qch; **to** ~ **sb's hair** coiffer qn; **to** ~ **one's teeth** se brosser les dents; **what have you done to your hair?** qu'est-ce que vous avez fait à vos cheveux?; **what has he done with the newspaper?** qu'est-ce qu'il a fait du journal?; **to** ~ **60** ‹car, driver› faire du 60 à l'heure
(b) (colloq) (cheat) **we've been done** on s'est fait avoir; **to** ~ **sb out of £5** refaire (fam) qn de 5 livres sterling
3 vi (3ᵉ pers sg prés **does**, prét **did**, pp **done**) (a) (behave) faire; ~ **as you're told** (by me) fais ce que je te dis; (by others) fais ce qu'on te dit
(b) (serve purpose) faire l'affaire; **that box will** ~ cette boîte fera l'affaire
(c) (be acceptable) **this really won't** ~! (of

situation, attitude) ça ne peut pas continuer comme ça!; (of work) c'est franchement mauvais!
(d) (be enough) ‹amount of money› suffire
(e) (get on) ‹person› s'en sortir; ‹business› marcher
(f) (in health) **mother and baby are both** ~ing **well** la mère et l'enfant se portent bien; **the patient is** ~ing **well** le malade est en bonne voie
IDIOMS **how** ~ **you do** enchanté; **well done!** bravo!; **it doesn't** ~ **to be** ce n'est pas une bonne chose d'être; **it was all I could** ~ **not to laugh** je me suis retenu pour ne pas rire; **she does nothing but moan** elle ne fait que se plaindre
■ **do away with** se débarrasser de
■ **do up** (a) (fasten) nouer ‹laces›; remonter ‹zip›; ~ **up your buttons** boutonne-toi
(b) (wrap) faire ‹parcel›
(c) (renovate) restaurer ‹house›
■ **do with** (a) **what's it (got) to** ~ **with you?** en quoi est-ce que ça te regarde?; **it has nothing to** ~ **with you** cela ne vous concerne pas
(b) (tolerate) supporter
(c) (need) **I could** ~ **with a holiday** j'aurais bien besoin de partir en vacances
(d) (finish) **it's all over and done with** c'est bien fini
■ **do without** se passer de ‹person, advice›
dock 1 n (a) (in port) dock m; (for repairing ship) cale f
(b) (US wharf) appontement m
(c) (GB Law) banc m des accusés
2 vi arriver au port
dockworker n docker m
dockyard n chantier m naval
ⓢ **doctor** 1 n (a) (Med) médecin m, docteur m
(b) (Univ) docteur m
2 vtr frelater ‹food, wine›; falsifier ‹figures›; altérer ‹document›
doctorate n doctorat m
docudrama n docudrame m
ⓢ **document** n document m
documentary n documentaire m (**about, on** sur)
dodge 1 n (GB) (colloq) (trick) combine f (fam)
2 vtr esquiver ‹bullet, blow, question›
dodgem (car) n (GB) auto f tamponneuse
dodgy adj (colloq) (untrustworthy) louche (fam); (risky) ‹decision, plan› risqué/-e; ‹situation, moment› délicat/-e
ⓢ **dog** n (a) chien m; (female) chienne f
(b) (male fox, wolf) mâle m
IDIOM **to go to the** ~s ‹company, country› aller à vau-l'eau
dog collar n (a) collier m de chien
(b) (clerical) col m romain
dog-eared adj écorné/-e
dogged adj ‹attempt› obstiné/-e; ‹person, refusal› tenace; ‹resistance› opiniâtre

d

doghouse n (US) niche f (à chien)
IDIOM **to be in the ~** être tombé/-e en disgrâce
dogmatic adj dogmatique (**about** sur)
dog paddle n nage f à la manière d'un chien
dogsbody n (GB) (colloq) bonne f à tout faire
doh n (Mus) do m, ut m
doing n this is her ~ c'est son ouvrage; **it takes some ~**! ce n'est pas facile du tout!
dole n (GB) allocation f de chômage; **on the ~** au chômage
■ **dole out** (colloq) distribuer
doll n poupée f
✓ **dollar** n dollar m
dollar bill n billet m d'un dollar
dolphin n dauphin m
domain n domaine m (**of** de)
dome n dôme m
✓ **domestic** adj (a) ⟨market, flight⟩ intérieur/-e; ⟨crisis, issue⟩ de politique intérieure
(b) ⟨life, harmony⟩ familial/-e; ⟨dispute⟩ conjugal/-e; ⟨violence⟩ dans la famille
domestic appliance n appareil m électroménager
domesticate vtr domestiquer
dominant adj dominant/-e
✓ **dominate** vtr, vi dominer
domineering adj autoritaire
domino n domino m; **to play ~es** jouer aux dominos
donate vtr faire don de (**to** à)
donation n don m (**of** de; **à** to)
done ① adj ⟨food⟩ cuit/-e; **well ~** bien cuit/-e
② excl (deal) marché conclu!
IDIOM **it's not the ~ thing** ça ne se fait pas
donkey n âne m
donor n (a) (of organ) donneur/-euse m/f
(b) (of money) donateur/-trice m/f
donor card n carte f de donneur d'organes
doodle vi gribouiller
doom n (of person) perte f; (of country) catastrophe f
doomed adj condamné/-e; **to be ~ to failure** être voué/-e à l'échec
✓ **door** n (in building) porte f (**to** de); (in car, train) porte f, portière f; **behind closed ~s** à huis clos
doorbell n sonnette f
doorman n portier m
doormat n paillasson m
doorstep n pas m de porte
door-to-door adj ⟨canvassing⟩ à domicile; **~ selling** porte à porte m inv

✓ indicates a very frequent word

doorway n (a) (frame) embrasure f
(b) (entrance) porte f, entrée f
dope ① n (colloq) (a) cannabis m
(b) (fool) imbécile m/f (fam)
② vtr (Sport) doper ⟨horse, athlete⟩; (gen) droguer ⟨person⟩
dope test n (Sport) contrôle m antidopage
dormant adj ⟨emotion, talent⟩ latent/-e
(b) ⟨volcano⟩ en repos
dormitory n (a) (GB) dortoir m
(b) (US Univ) résidence f, foyer m
dormitory town n ville f dortoir
dormouse n (pl **dormice**) muscardin m
dose n dose f (**of** de); **a ~ of flu** une bonne grippe
IDIOM **he's all right in small ~s** il est supportable à doses homéopathiques
dot n (gen) point m; (on fabric) pois m
IDIOM **at ten on the ~** à dix heures pile
dot-com ① n (**also ~ company**) société f Internet or virtuelle, société f dot-com
② adj ⟨shares⟩ des sociétés Internet or virtuelles; ⟨millionaire⟩ du commerce électronique
dot-com bubble n bulle f Internet
dote vi **to ~ on sb/sth** adorer qn/qch
dotted line n pointillé m
✓ **double** ① n (a) (drink) double m
(b) (of person) sosie m; (in film, play) doublure f
② **doubles** n pl double m; **mixed ~s** double mixte
③ adj double; **with a ~ 'n'** avec deux 'n'; **two ~ four (244)** deux cent quarante-quatre
④ adv (a) **~ the amount** deux fois plus
(b) **to see ~** voir double
(c) ⟨fold, bend⟩ en deux
⑤ vtr doubler ⟨amount, dose⟩; multiplier [qch] par deux ⟨number⟩
⑥ vi (a) ⟨sales, prices, salaries⟩ doubler
(b) **to ~ for sb** (actor) doubler qn
(c) **the sofa ~s as a bed** le canapé fait aussi lit
IDIOM **on** or **at the ~** au plus vite
■ **double back** rebrousser chemin
double act n duo m
double-barrelled name n (GB) ≈ nom m à particule
double bass n contrebasse f
double bed n lit m double, grand lit m
double-breasted adj ⟨jacket⟩ croisé/-e
double-check vtr vérifier [qch] à nouveau
double chin n double menton m
double-click vi double-cliquer
double cream n (GB) ≈ crème f fraîche
double-cross vtr (colloq) doubler, trahir ⟨person⟩
double-decker n (GB) (bus) autobus m à impériale or à deux étages; (sandwich) sandwich m double
double door n porte f à deux battants

double Dutch *n* (colloq) baragouinage *m* (fam)

double glazing *n* double vitrage *m*

double-park *vi* se garer en double file

double room *n* chambre *f* pour deux personnes

double standard *n* to have ∼s faire deux poids deux mesures

double take *n* to do a ∼ avoir une réaction à retardement

double vision *n* to have ∼ voir double

double yellow line(s) *n* (*pl*) (GB Aut) *marquage au sol interdisant le stationnement*

⚹ **doubt** ⟦1⟧ *n* doute *m*; **there is no ∼ (that)** il ne fait aucun doute que; **to have no ∼ (that)** être certain/-e que; **to be in ∼** ⟨*person*⟩ être dans le doute; ⟨*outcome*⟩ être incertain/-e; **if** *or* **when in ∼** dans le doute; **without (a) ∼** sans aucun doute

⟦2⟧ *vtr* douter de ⟨*fact, ability, honesty, person*⟩; **I ∼ it!** j'en doute!; **I ∼ if he'll come** je doute qu'il vienne

doubtful *adj* (a) (unsure) incertain/-e
(b) ⟨*character, activity, taste*⟩ douteux/-euse

dough *n* (Culin) pâte *f*

doughnut, donut (US) *n* beignet *m*

douse, dowse *vtr* éteindre ⟨*fire*⟩; tremper ⟨*person*⟩; **to ∼ sth with petrol** arroser qch d'essence

dove *n* colombe *f*

Dover *pr n* Douvres

dowdy *adj* ⟨*person*⟩ mal fagoté/-e; ⟨*clothes*⟩ sans chic

⚹ **down¹**

■ **Note** When used to indicate vague direction, *down* often has no explicit translation in French: *to go down to London* = aller à Londres; *down in Brighton* = à Brighton.
— For examples and further usages, see the entry below.

⟦1⟧ *adv* (a) **to go** *or* **come ∼** descendre; **to fall ∼** tomber; **to sit ∼ on the floor** s'asseoir par terre; **to pull ∼ a blind** baisser un store; **∼ below** en bas; **the telephone lines are ∼** les lignes téléphoniques sont coupées; **face ∼** ⟨*fall*⟩ face contre terre; ⟨*lie*⟩ à plat ventre; (in water) le visage dans l'eau

(b) (lower) **profits are well ∼ on last year's** les bénéfices sont nettement inférieurs à ceux de l'année dernière; **to get one's weight ∼** maigrir; **I'm ∼ to my last cigarette** il ne me reste plus qu'une cigarette

(c) (Sport) **to be two sets ∼** ⟨*tennis player*⟩ perdre par deux sets

(d) (as deposit) **to pay £40 ∼** payer 40 livres sterling comptant

⟦2⟧ *prep* **to go ∼ the street** descendre la rue; **to run ∼ the hill** descendre la colline en courant; **to go ∼ town** aller en ville; **they live ∼ the road** ils habitent un peu plus loin dans la rue

⟦3⟧ *adj* (a) (colloq) **to feel ∼** être déprimé/-e
(b) ⟨*escalator*⟩ qui descend
(c) ⟨*computer*⟩ en panne
IDIOMS **it's ∼ to you to do it** c'est à toi de le faire; **∼ with tyrants!** à bas les tyrans!

down² *n* duvet *m*

down-and-out *n* clochard/-e *m/f*

downbeat *adj* (a) (pessimistic) pessimiste
(b) (laidback) décontracté/-e

downfall *n* chute *f*; **drink proved to be his ∼** c'est la boisson qui a causé sa perte

downhearted *adj* abattu/-e

downhill *adv* **to go ∼** ⟨*person, vehicle*⟩ descendre; **he's going ∼** (declining) il est sur le déclin

downhill skiing *n* ski *m* de piste

download *vtr* (Comput) télécharger

downmarket *adj* ⟨*products*⟩ bas de gamme *inv*; ⟨*area*⟩ populaire; ⟨*newspaper, programme*⟩ grand public *inv*

down payment *n* acompte *m*

downplay *vtr* minimiser l'importance de

downpour *n* averse *f*

downright ⟦1⟧ *adj* ⟨*insult*⟩ véritable (*before n*); ⟨*refusal*⟩ catégorique; ⟨*liar*⟩ fieffé/-e (*before n*)
⟦2⟧ *adv* ⟨*stupid, rude*⟩ carrément

downsize *vi* réduire les effectifs

Down's syndrome *n* trisomie *f* 21

downstairs ⟦1⟧ *adj* ⟨*room*⟩ en bas; **the ∼ flat** (GB) *or* **apartment** (US) l'appartement du rez-de-chaussée
⟦2⟧ *adv* en bas; **to go** *or* **come ∼** descendre (l'escalier)

downstream *adj*, *adv* en aval (**of** de); **to go ∼** descendre le courant

down-to-earth *adj* pratique; **she's very ∼** (practical) elle a les pieds sur terre; (unpretentious) elle est très simple

downtown *adj* (US) ⟨*store, hotel*⟩ du centre ville

downtrodden *adj* tyrannisé/-e

downturn *n* (in economy, career) déclin *m* (**in** de); (in demand, profits) chute *f* (**in** de)

down under *adv* (colloq) en Australie

downward ⟦1⟧ *adj* ⟨*movement*⟩ vers le bas; **∼ trend** (Econ) tendance *f* à la baisse
⟦2⟧ *adv* = DOWNWARDS

downwards *adv* (*also* **downward**) vers le bas; **to slope ∼** descendre en pente (**to** vers)

doze *vi* somnoler
■ **doze off** (momentarily) s'assoupir; (to sleep) s'endormir

dozen *n* (a) (twelve) douzaine *f*; **a ∼ eggs** une douzaine d'œufs; **£1 a ∼** une livre sterling la douzaine
(b) (several) **∼s of** des dizaines de ⟨*people, things, times*⟩

drab *adj* terne

draft ① *n* **(a)** (of letter, speech) brouillon
m; (of novel, play) ébauche *f*; (of contract, law)
avant-projet *m*
(b) (on bank) traite *f* (**on** sur)
(c) (US) (conscription) service *m* militaire
(d) (US) = DRAUGHT
② *vtr* **(a)** faire le brouillon de ‹*letter,
speech*›; rédiger ‹*contract, law*›
(b) (US) (conscript) incorporer (**into** dans)
(c) (GB) (transfer) détacher (**to** auprès de;
from de)
■ **draft in** faire venir, amener ‹*police, troops*›
draft dodger *n* (US Mil) insoumis *m*
draftsman (US) = DRAUGHTSMAN
drag ① *n* **(a)** (fam) **what a ~!** quelle barbe!
(fam)
(b) ‹*person*› **in ~** en travesti
② *adj* **(a)** ‹*artist*› de spectacle de travestis
(b) ‹*racing*› de dragsters
③ *vtr* (*p prés etc* **-gg-**) **(a)** (trail) traîner;
(pull) tirer ‹*boat, sledge*›; **to ~ sth along the
ground** traîner qch par terre; **to ~ one's feet**
traîner les pieds; (figurative) faire preuve de
mauvaise volonté (**on** quant à); **don't ~ my
mother into this** ne mêle pas ma mère à ça
(b) draguer ‹*river, lake*›
(c) (Comput) glisser
④ *vi* (*p prés etc* **-gg-**) **(a)** ‹*hours, days*›
traîner; ‹*story, plot*› traîner en longueur
(b) (trail) **to ~ in** ‹*hem, belt*› traîner dans
‹*mud*›
(c) to ~ on tirer une bouffée de ‹*cigarette*›
■ **drag on** traîner en longueur
drag and drop *n* glisser-lâcher *m*
drain ① *n* **(a)** (in street) canalisation *f*; (in
building) canalisation *f* d'évacuation; (pipe)
descente *f* d'eau; (ditch) fossé *m* d'écoulement
(b) (of people, skills, money) hémorragie *f*;
to be a ~ on sb's resources épuiser les
ressources de qn
② *vtr* **(a)** drainer ‹*land*›
(b) épuiser ‹*resources*›
(c) vider ‹*glass*›
(d) (Culin) égoutter ‹*pasta, vegetables*›
③ *vi* **(a)** ‹*liquid*› s'écouler (**out of, from** de;
into dans)
(b) ‹*dishes, food*› s'égoutter
drainage *n* (of land) drainage *m*; (system)
tout-à-l'égout *m inv*
draining board *n* égouttoir *m*
drainpipe *n* descente *f*
drake *n* canard *m* (mâle)
drama *n* (genre) théâtre *m*; (acting, directing)
art *m* dramatique; (play, dramatic event) drame
m; TV/radio ~ dramatique *f*; **to make a ~
out of sth** faire tout un drame de qch
dramatic *adj* ‹*art, effect, event*›
dramatique; ‹*change, landscape*›
spectaculaire; ‹*entrance*› théâtral/-e
dramatist *n* auteur *m* dramatique

✦ indicates a very frequent word

dramatize *vtr* **(a)** (for stage) adapter [qch]
à la scène; (for screen) adapter [qch] à l'écran;
(for radio) adapter [qch] pour la radio
(b) (make dramatic) donner un caractère
dramatique à; (excessively) dramatiser
drape ① *n* (US) rideau *m*
② *vtr* draper (**in, with** de)
drastic *adj* ‹*policy, measure*› draconien/
-ienne; ‹*reduction, remedy*› drastique; ‹*effect*›
catastrophique; ‹*change*› radical/-e
drastically *adv* ‹*change, reduce*›
radicalement; ‹*reduce, limit*› sévèrement
draught (GB), **draft** (US) *n* **(a)** (cold air)
courant *m* d'air
(b) on ~ ‹*beer*› à la pression
draughts *n* (GB) jeu *m* de dames; **to play ~**
jouer aux dames
draughtsman (GB), **draftsman** (US) *n*
dessinateur/-trice *m/f*
draughty (GB), **drafty** (US) *adj* plein/-e de
courants d'air
✦ **draw** ① *n* **(a)** (in lottery) tirage *m* (au sort)
(b) (Sport) match *m* nul; **it was a ~** (in race) ils
sont arrivés ex aequo
② *vtr* (*prét* **drew**, *pp* **drawn**) **(a)** faire
‹*picture, plan*›; dessiner ‹*person, object*›;
tracer ‹*line*›
(b) (pull) ‹*animal, engine*› tirer
(c) tirer ‹*conclusion*› (**from** de)
(d) (attract) attirer ‹*crowd*› (**to** vers);
susciter ‹*reaction*›; **to ~ sb into** mêler qn à
‹*conversation*›; entraîner qn dans ‹*argument,
battle*›
(e) retirer ‹*money*› (**from** de); tirer ‹*cheque*›
(**on** sur); toucher ‹*wages, pension*›
(f) (in lottery) tirer [qch] au sort ‹*ticket*›
(g) sortir ‹*sword, knife*›; **to ~ a gun on sb**
sortir un pistolet et le braquer sur qn
③ *vi* (*prét* **drew**, *pp* **drawn**) **(a)** (make
picture) dessiner
(b) to ~ ahead (of sb/sth) (in race) gagner
du terrain (sur qn/qch); (in contest, election)
prendre de l'avance (sur qn/qch); **to ~
alongside** ‹*boat*› accoster; **to ~ near** ‹*time*›
approcher; **to ~ level** se retrouver au même
niveau
(c) (in match) faire match nul
IDIOMS to ~ the line fixer des limites; **to ~
the line at doing** se refuser à faire
■ **draw away** (move off) s'éloigner (**from** de);
(move ahead) prendre de l'avance (**from** sur)
■ **draw in**: ① ¶ ~ **in (a)** ‹*days, nights*›
raccourcir
(b) ‹*bus*› arriver; ‹*train*› entrer en gare
② ¶ ~ **[sth] in** rentrer ‹*stomach, claws*›
■ **draw out**: ① ¶ ~ **out** ‹*train, bus*› partir;
the train drew out of the station le train a
quitté la gare
② ¶ ~ **[sth] out (a)** (remove) tirer ‹*purse,
knife*› (**of** de); retirer ‹*nail, cork*› (**of** de)
(b) (withdraw) retirer ‹*money*›
(c) (prolong) faire durer
③ ¶ ~ **[sb] out** faire sortir [qn] de sa

coquille
- **draw up (a)** établir ‹contract›; dresser, établir ‹list, report›
  (b) approcher ‹chair› (**to** de)
drawback *n* inconvénient *m*
drawer *n* tiroir *m*
drawing *n* dessin *m*
drawing board *n* planche *f* à dessin
drawing pin *n* punaise *f*
drawing room *n* salon *m*
drawl *n* voix *f* traînante
drawn *adj* **(a) to look** ~ avoir les traits tirés
  (b) ‹game, match› nul/nulle
dread *vtr* appréhender (**doing** de faire); (stronger) redouter (**doing** de faire)
dreadful *adj* épouvantable, affreux/-euse
dreadfully *adv* ‹disappointed› terriblement; ‹suffer› affreusement; ‹behave› abominablement; **I'm** ~ **sorry** je suis navré
✔ **dream** ① *n* rêve *m*
  ② *adj* ‹house, car, vacation› de rêve
  ③ *vtr* (*prét, pp* **dreamt**, ~**ed**) rêver (**that** que)
  ④ *vi* (*prét, pp* **dreamt**, ~**ed**) rêver; **he dreamt about** *or* **of sth/doing** il a rêvé de qch/qu'il faisait; **I wouldn't** ~ **of selling the house** il ne me viendrait jamais à l'esprit de vendre la maison
- **dream up** concevoir ‹idea›; imaginer ‹character, plot›
dreamer *n* **(a)** (inattentive person) rêveur/-euse *m/f*
  (b) (idealist) idéaliste *mf*
dreary *adj* ‹weather, landscape, life› morne; ‹person› ennuyeux/-euse
dredge *vtr* draguer ‹river›
dregs *n pl* (of wine) lie *f*; (of coffee) marc *m*
drench *vtr* (in rain, sweat) tremper (**in** de)
✔ **dress** ① *n* **(a)** (garment) robe *f*
  (b) (clothes) tenue *f*; **formal** ~ tenue habillée
  ② *vtr* **(a)** habiller ‹person›; **to get** ~**ed** s'habiller; **to be** ~**ed in** être vêtu/-e de
  (b) assaisonner ‹salad›; préparer ‹meat, fish›
  (c) panser ‹wound›
- **dress up** (smartly) s'habiller; (in fancy dress) se déguiser (**as** en)
dress circle *n* premier balcon *m*
dresser *n* **(a) to be a stylish** ~ s'habiller avec chic
  (b) (for dishes) buffet *m*
  (c) (US) (for clothes) commode-coiffeuse *f*
dressing *n* **(a)** (Med) pansement *m*
  (b) (sauce) assaisonnement *m*
  (c) (US) (stuffing) farce *f*
dressing gown *n* (GB) robe *f* de chambre
dressing room *n* loge *f*
dressing table *n* coiffeuse *f*
dressmaker *n* couturière *f*
dress rehearsal *n* (répétition *f*) générale *f*

dress sense *n* **to have** ~ s'habiller avec goût
dribble ① *n* (of liquid) filet *m*; (of saliva) bave *f*
  ② *vi* **(a)** ‹liquid› dégouliner (**on, onto** sur; **from** de); ‹person› baver
  (b) (Sport) dribbler
dried *adj* ‹fruit, herb› sec/sèche; ‹flower, vegetable› séché/-e; ‹milk, egg› en poudre
drier *n* séchoir *m*
drift ① *n* **(a) the** ~ **of the current** le sens du courant
  (b) (of snow) congère *f*; (of leaves) tas *m*
  (c) (meaning) sens *m* (général)
  ② *vi* **(a)** ‹boat› dériver; ‹balloon› voler à la dérive; ‹smoke, fog› flotter
  (b) ‹snow› former des congères *fpl*; ‹leaves› s'amonceler
  (c) to ~ **through life** errer sans but dans la vie
- **drift apart** ‹friends› se perdre de vue; ‹lovers› se détacher progressivement l'un de l'autre
driftwood *n* bois *m* flotté
drill ① *n* **(a)** (for wood, masonry) perceuse *f*; (for oil) trépan *m*; (for mining) foreuse *f*; (for teeth) roulette *f*
  (b) (Mil) exercice *m*
  (c) fire ~ exercice *m* d'évacuation en cas d'incendie
  ② *vtr* **(a)** percer ‹hole, metal›; passer la roulette à ‹tooth›
  (b) (Mil) entraîner ‹soldiers›
  ③ *vi* **(a)** (in wood, masonry) percer un trou (**into** dans); **to** ~ **for sth** faire des forages pour trouver qch
  (b) (Mil) ‹soldiers› faire de l'exercice
✔ **drink** ① *n* boisson *f*; **to have a** ~ boire quelque chose; (alcoholic) prendre un verre
  ② *vtr* (*prét* **drank**, *pp* **drunk**) boire (**from** dans)
  ③ *vi* (*prét* **drank**, *pp* **drunk**) boire (**from** dans); **don't** ~ **and drive** ne conduisez pas si vous avez bu
drinkable *adj* (safe) potable; (nice) buvable
drink-driving *n* (GB) conduite *f* en état d'ivresse
drinking water *n* eau *f* potable
drip ① *n* **(a)** (drop) goutte *f* (qui tombe)
  (b) (GB Med) **to be on a** ~ être sous perfusion
  ② *vi* (*p prés etc* **-pp-**) **(a)** ‹liquid› tomber goutte à goutte; **to** ~ **from** *or* **off** dégouliner de
  (b) ‹tap, branches› goutter; ‹washing› s'égoutter
✔ **drive** ① *n* **(a) to go for a** ~ aller faire un tour (en voiture); **it's a 40 km** ~ il y a 40 km de route
  (b) (campaign) campagne *f* (**against** contre; **for, towards** pour; **to do** pour faire)
  (c) (motivation) dynamisme *m*   ⋯⋗

(d) (Comput) entraînement *m* de disques
(e) (Aut) transmission *f*
(f) (*also* ∼**way**) allée *f*
(g) (Sport) drive *m*
② *vtr* (*prét* **drove**, *pp* **driven**) **(a)** conduire ‹*vehicle, passenger*›; piloter ‹*racing car*›; **I** ∼ **15 km every day** je fais 15 km en voiture chaque jour; **to** ∼ **sth into** rentrer qch dans ‹*garage, space*›
(b) (compel) pousser ‹*person*› (**to do** à faire)
(c) (power, propel) actionner ‹*engine, pump*›
(d) to ∼ **a nail through sth** enfoncer un clou dans qch
③ *vi* (*prét* **drove**, *pp* **driven**) conduire; **to** ∼ **along** rouler; **to** ∼ **to work** aller au travail en voiture; **to** ∼ **into** entrer dans ‹*car park*›; rentrer dans ‹*tree*›
■ **drive back (a)** repousser ‹*people, animals*›
(b) ramener ‹*passenger*›
drive-by shooting *n* attaque *f* criminelle (*exécutée d'une voiture en marche*)

⚬ **driver** *n* **(a)** conducteur/-trice *m/f*; ∼**s** (motorists) automobilistes *mfpl*
(b) (of taxi) chauffeur *m*
driver's license *n* (US) permis *m* de conduire
driving ① *n* conduite *f*
② *adj* ‹*rain*› battant/-e; ‹*wind, hail*› cinglant/-e
driving force *n* (person) force *f* agissante (**behind** de); (money, ambition) moteur *m* (**behind** de)
driving instructor *n* moniteur/-trice *m/f* d'auto-école
driving lesson *n* leçon *f* de conduite
driving licence *n* (GB) permis *m* de conduire
driving school *n* auto-école *f*
driving seat *n* place *f* du conducteur
IDIOM **to be in the** ∼ être aux commandes
driving test *n* examen *m* du permis de conduire; **to take/pass one's** ∼ passer/ réussir son permis (de conduire)
drizzle ① *n* bruine *f*
② *vi* bruiner
drone *n* **(a)** (of engine) ronronnement *m*; (of insects) bourdonnement *m*
(b) (Zool) faux bourdon *m*
drool *vi* baver; **to** ∼ **over sb/sth** s'extasier sur qn/qch
droop *vi* ‹*eyelids, head, shoulders*› tomber; ‹*plant*› commencer à se faner
⚬ **drop** ① *n* **(a)** (of liquid) goutte *f*
(b) (decrease) baisse *f* (**in** de); **a 5%** ∼ **in sth** une baisse de 5% de qch
(c) (fall) **there's a** ∼ **of 100 m** il y a un dénivelé de 100 m; **a steep** ∼ **on either side** une pente abrupte de chaque côté; **a sheer** ∼ un à-pic
(d) (delivery) (from aircraft) largage *m*

─────────────

⚬ indicates a very frequent word

② *vtr* (*p prés etc* **-pp-**) **(a)** (by accident) laisser tomber; (on purpose) lâcher
(b) ‹*aircraft*› parachuter ‹*person, supplies*›; larguer ‹*bomb*›
(c) (*also* ∼ **off**) déposer ‹*person, object*›
(d) (lower) baisser ‹*eyes, voice, level, price*›
(e) to ∼ **a hint about sth** faire allusion à qch; **to** ∼ **sb a line** envoyer un mot à qn
(f) laisser tomber ‹*friend, school subject*›; renoncer à ‹*habit, idea*›
③ *vi* (*p prés etc* **-pp-**) **(a)** (fall) ‹*object*› tomber; ‹*person*› (deliberately) se laisser tomber; **the plane** ∼**ped to an altitude of 1,000 m** l'avion est descendu à une altitude de 1 000 m
(b) the cliff ∼**s into the sea** la falaise tombe dans la mer
(c) (decrease) baisser; **to** ∼ (**from sth**) **to sth** tomber (de qch) à qch
IDIOM **a** ∼ **in the ocean** une goutte d'eau dans la mer
■ **drop in** passer; **to** ∼ **in on sb** passer voir qn
■ **drop off (a)** (fall off) tomber
(b) ∼ **off (to sleep)** s'endormir
(c) (decrease) diminuer
■ **drop out (a)** (fall out) tomber (**of** de)
(b) (from race) se désister; (from project) se retirer; (from school, university) abandonner ses études; (from society) se marginaliser
drop-dead *adv* (colloq) ∼ **gorgeous** super beau/belle (fam)
drop-down menu *n* menu *m* déroulant
dropout *n* marginal/-e *m/f*
droppings *n pl* (of mouse, sheep) crottes *fpl*; (of horse) crottin *m*; (of bird) fiente *f*
drop shot *n* (Sport) amorti *m*
drought *n* sécheresse *f*
drown ① *vtr* **(a)** noyer ‹*person, animal*›
(b) (*also* ∼ **out**) couvrir ‹*sound*›
② *vi* se noyer
IDIOM **to** ∼ **one's sorrows** noyer son chagrin dans l'alcool
drowning *n* noyade *f*
drowsy *adj* à moitié endormi/-e; **to feel** ∼ avoir envie de dormir
⚬ **drug** ① *n* **(a)** (Med) médicament *m*; **to be on** ∼**s** prendre des médicaments
(b) (narcotic) drogue *f*; **to be on** *or* **to take** ∼**s** (gen) se droguer; ‹*athlete*› se doper
② *vtr* (*p prés etc* **-gg-**) administrer des somnifères à ‹*person*›
drug abuse *n* consommation *f* de stupéfiants
drug addict *n* toxicomane *mf*
drug addiction *n* toxicomanie *f*
drugged *adj* ‹*person*› drogué/-e; ‹*drink*› additionné/-e d'un narcotique
drug habit *n* accoutumance *f* à la drogue
drug mule *n* mule *f*
drugs raid *n* opération *f* antidrogue
drugstore *n* (US) drugstore *m*

drug-taking n usage m de stupéfiants; (in sport) dopage m

drug test n (Sport) contrôle m antidopage

drug user n toxicomane mf

drum ⓵ n (a) (Mus) tambour m
(b) (barrel) bidon m; (larger) baril m
⓶ **drums** n pl batterie f; **to play** ~**s** jouer de la batterie
⓷ vtr (p prés etc **-mm-**) **to** ~ **one's fingers** tambouriner des doigts (**on** sur); **to** ~ **sth into sb** enfoncer qch dans le crâne de qn (fam)
▪ **drum up** trouver ‹business›; racoler ‹customers›

drummer n (in army) tambour m; (jazz or pop) batteur m; (classical) percussionniste mf

drumstick n (a) (Mus) baguette f de tambour
(b) (of chicken, turkey) pilon m

drunk ⓵ n (also **drunkard**) ivrogne m
⓶ adj ivre; **to get** ~ s'enivrer (**on** de)

drunken adj ‹person› ivre; ‹party› bien arrosé/-e; ‹sleep› éthylique; ‹state› d'ivresse

dry ⓵ adj (a) sec/sèche; **to keep sth** ~ tenir qch au sec; **on** ~ **land** sur la terre ferme; **a** ~ **day** un jour sans pluie
(b) ‹wit, person, remark› pince-sans-rire inv; ‹book› aride
⓶ vtr faire sécher ‹clothes, washing›; sécher ‹meat, produce›; **to** ~ **the dishes** essuyer la vaisselle; **to** ~ **one's hands** se sécher les mains
⓷ vi ‹clothes, washing› sécher
▪ **dry out** (a) ‹cloth› sécher; ‹plant› se dessécher
(b) (colloq) ‹alcoholic› se faire désintoxiquer
▪ **dry up** ⓵ (a) ¶ ~ up ‹river, well› s'assécher
(b) (run out) se tarir
(c) (dry the dishes) essuyer la vaisselle
⓶ ¶ ~ [**sth**] up essuyer ‹dishes›

dry-clean vtr **to have sth** ~**ed** faire nettoyer qch (chez le teinturier)

dry-cleaner's n teinturerie f

dryer n séchoir m

DTP n (abbr = **desktop publishing**) PAO f

dual adj double

dual carriageway n (GB) route f à quatre voies

dual nationality n double nationalité f

dub vtr (p prés etc **-bb-**) (into foreign language) doubler (**into** en); ~**bed film** film doublé

dubious adj ‹reputation, answer› douteux/ -euse; ‹claim› suspect/-e

duchess n duchesse f

duck ⓵ n (pl ~**s**, collect ~) canard m
⓶ vtr (a) **to** ~ **one's head** baisser vivement la tête
(b) (dodge) esquiver ‹blow›
(c) se dérober de ‹responsibility›
⓷ vi baisser vivement la tête; ‹boxer›

esquiver un coup; **to** ~ **behind** se cacher derrière

duckling n caneton m

duct n (a) (for air, water) conduit m; (for wiring) canalisation f
(b) (Anat, Med) conduit m

dud adj (colloq) ‹banknote› faux/fausse (before n); ‹cheque› en bois (fam); ‹book, movie› nul/nulle (fam)

due ⓵ n dû m; **I must give her her** ~, **she…** il faut lui rendre cette justice, elle…
⓶ adj (a) (payable) **to be/fall** ~ arriver/venir à échéance; **the rent is** ~ **on the 6th** le loyer doit être payé le 6; **the balance** ~ le solde dû
(b) (owed) **the respect** ~ **to him** le respect auquel il a droit, le respect qu'on lui doit
(c) **we are** ~ **(for) a wage increase soon** nos salaires doivent bientôt être augmentés
(d) **after** ~ **consideration** après mûre réflexion; **in** ~ **course** (at the proper time) en temps voulu; (later) plus tard
(e) **to be** ~ **to do** devoir faire; **to be** ~ **(in)** ‹train, bus› être attendu/-e; ‹person› devoir arriver
⓷ adv **to face** ~ **north** ‹building› être orienté/-e plein nord; **to go** ~ **south** aller droit vers le sud
⓸ **due to** phr en raison de; **to be** ~ **to** ‹delay, cancellation› être dû/due à; ~ **to unforeseen circumstances** pour des raisons indépendantes de notre volonté

dues n pl (for membership) cotisation f; (for import, taxes) droits mpl

duet n duo m

duffel bag n sac m (de) marin

duffel coat n duffle-coat m

duke n duc m

dull ⓵ adj (a) ‹person, book› ennuyeux/ -euse; ‹life, journey› monotone; ‹appearance› triste; ‹weather› maussade
(b) ‹eye, colour, complexion› terne
⓶ vtr ternir ‹shine›; émousser ‹blade, pain›

duly adv (in proper fashion) dûment; (as expected, as arranged) comme prévu

dumb adj (a) muet/muette; **to be struck** ~ rester muet/muette (**with** de)
(b) (colloq) (stupid) ‹person› bête; ‹question, idea› idiot/-e

dumb down vtr abaisser le niveau intellectuel de ‹course, programme›

dumbfounded adj abasourdi/-e

dummy ⓵ n (a) (model) mannequin m
(b) (GB) (for baby) tétine f
⓶ adj faux/fausse

dummy run n (trial) essai m

dump ⓵ n (a) (for rubbish) décharge f publique
(b) (Mil) **arms** ~ dépôt m d'armes
(c) (colloq) (town, village) trou m (fam); (house) baraque f (fam) minable
⓶ vtr (a) jeter ‹refuse›; ensevelir ‹nuclear waste›; déverser ‹sewage› ⋯⋗

d
e

(b) (colloq) plaquer (fam) ‹*boyfriend*›; se débarrasser de ‹*car*›
IDIOM to be down in the ~s (colloq) avoir le cafard (fam)

dumper (truck), dump truck *n* tombereau *m*

dunce *n* cancre *m* (**at, in** en)

dune *n* dune *f*

dung *n* (for manure) fumier *m*

dungarees *n pl* (fashionwear) salopette *f*; (workwear) bleu *m* de travail

Dunkirk *pr n* Dunkerque

duo *n* (*pl* **~s**) duo *m*

duplicate ① *n* (of document) double *m* (**of** de); (of painting, cassette) copie *f*
② *adj* **(a)** ‹*cheque, receipt*› en duplicata; **a ~ key** un double de clé
(b) (in two parts) ‹*form, invoice*› en deux exemplaires
③ *vtr* **(a)** (copy) faire un double de ‹*document*›; copier ‹*painting, cassette*›
(b) (photocopy) photocopier

durable *adj* ‹*material*› résistant/-e; ‹*equipment*› solide; ‹*friendship, tradition*› durable

duration *n* durée *f*

duress *n* **under ~** sous la contrainte

✦ **during** *prep* pendant, au cours de

dusk *n* nuit *f* tombante, crépuscule *m*; **at ~** à la nuit tombante

dust ① *n* poussière *f*
② *vtr* épousseter ‹*furniture*›; saupoudrer ‹*cake*› (**with** de, avec)

dustbin *n* (GB) poubelle *f*

dust cover *n* (on book) jaquette *f*; (on furniture) housse *f* (de protection)

duster *n* chiffon *m* (à poussière)

dustman *n* (GB) éboueur *m*

dustpan *n* pelle *f* (à poussière)

dusty *adj* poussiéreux/-euse

Dutch ① *n* **(a)** (people) **the ~** les Néerlandais *mpl*

(b) (language) néerlandais *m*
② *adj* (gen) néerlandais/-e; ‹*embassy*› des Pays-Bas
IDIOMS to go ~ (colloq) payer chacun sa part; **to go ~ with sb** (colloq) faire fifty-fifty avec qn (fam)

✦ **duty** *n* **(a)** (obligation) devoir *m* (**to** envers); **in the course of ~** (Mil) en service; (gen) dans l'exercice de ses fonctions
(b) (task) fonction *f*; **to take up one's duties** prendre ses fonctions
(c) (work) service *m*; **to be on/off ~** (Mil, Med) être/ne pas être de service; (Sch) être/ne pas être de surveillance
(d) (tax) taxe *f*; **customs duties** droits *mpl* de douane

duty-free *adj, adv* hors taxe(s)

duvet *n* (GB) couette *f*

duvet cover *n* housse *f* de couette

DVD *n* (*abbr* = **digital video disc**) DVD *m*

DVT *n* (*abbr* = **deep-vein thrombosis**) TVP *f*

dwarf *n, adj* nain/naine *m/f*

dwell
■ **dwell on** (talk about) s'étendre sur; (think about) s'attarder sur

dwindle *vi* diminuer

dye ① *n* teinture *f*
② *vtr* teindre; **to ~ sth red** teindre qch en rouge; **to ~ one's hair** se teindre les cheveux

dying *adj* ‹*person, animal*› mourant/-e; ‹*art*› en voie de disparition

dyke *n* **(a)** (on coast) digue *f*; (beside ditch) remblai *m*
(b) (GB) (ditch) fossé *m*

dynamic *adj* dynamique

dynamite *n* dynamite *f*

dynamo *n* **(a)** dynamo *f*
(b) (colloq) **he's a real ~** il déborde d'énergie

dysentery *n* dysenterie *f*

dysfunctional *adj* dysfonctionnel/-elle

dyslexia *n* dyslexie *f*

dyslexic *n, adj* dyslexique *mf*

Ee

e, E *n* **(a)** (letter) e, E *m*
(b) E (Mus) mi *m*
(c) E (drug) ecstasy *m*

✦ **each** ① *det* ‹*person, group, object*› chaque *inv*; **~ morning** chaque matin, tous les matins; **~ one** chacun/-e
② *pron* chacun/-e *m/f*; **~ of you** chacun/-e de vous, chacun/-e d'entre vous; **oranges at**

30p ~ des oranges à 30 pence (la) pièce

✦ **each other** *pron*
■ **Note** *each other* is very often translated by using a reflexive pronoun (*nous, vous, se, s'*).

(*also* **one another**) they know **~** ils se connaissent; **to help ~** s'entraider; **kept apart from ~** séparés l'un de l'autre

eager *adj* ‹*person, acceptance*› enthousiaste; ‹*face*› où se lit l'enthousiasme; ‹*student*› plein

✦ indicates a very frequent word

d'enthousiasme; ~ **to do** (keen) désireux/
-euse de faire; (impatient) pressé/-e de faire;
~ **for sth** avide de qch; **to be ~ to please**
chercher à faire plaisir

eagle n aigle m

⚬ **ear** n **(a)** oreille f
(b) (of wheat, corn) épi m
IDIOM to play it by ~ improviser

earache n **to have ~** (GB) or **an ~** avoir
une otite

eardrum n tympan m

earl n comte m

⚬ **early** ⟦1⟧ adj **(a)** (one of the first) ‹years,
novels› premier/-ière (before n); ~ **man** les
premiers hommes
(b) ‹delivery› rapide; ‹vegetable, fruit›
précoce; **to have an ~ lunch/night** déjeuner/
se coucher tôt; **in ~ childhood** dans la petite
or première enfance; **at an ~ age** à un très
jeune âge; **to be in one's ~ thirties** avoir
entre 30 et 35 ans; **at the earliest** au plus tôt;
in the ~ spring au début du printemps; **in
the ~ afternoon** en début d'après-midi
⟦2⟧ adv **(a)** tôt; **to get up ~** se lever tôt or de
bonne heure; **it's too ~** il est trop tôt; **as I
said earlier** comme je l'ai déjà dit
(b) (sooner than expected) en avance; **I'm a bit ~**
je suis un peu en avance

early retirement n retraite f anticipée

earmark vtr désigner ‹person, money, site›

⚬ **earn** vtr **(a)** ‹person› gagner ‹money›;
‹investment› rapporter ‹interest›; **to ~ a** or
one's living gagner sa vie
(b) to ~ sb's respect se faire respecter de qn

earner n salarié/-e m/f

earnest ⟦1⟧ n **in ~** ‹speak› sérieusement;
‹begin› vraiment, pour de bon
⟦2⟧ adj ‹person› sérieux/-ieuse; ‹wish›
sincère

earning power n capacité f de gain

earnings n pl (of person) salaire m, revenu
m (from de); (of company) gains mpl (from de);
(from shares) (taux m de) rendement m

earphones n pl (over ears) casque m; (in
ears) écouteurs mpl

earring n boucle f d'oreille

⚬ **earth** ⟦1⟧ n **(a)** terre f
(b) (colloq) **how/where/who on ~...?**
comment/où/qui donc or diable (fam) ...?;
nothing on ~ would persuade me to come je
ne viendrais pour rien au monde
⟦2⟧ vtr (GB) mettre [qch] à la terre

earthenware n faïence f

earthquake n tremblement m de terre

earth tremor n secousse f sismique

earwig n perce-oreille m

ease ⟦1⟧ n **(a)** (lack of difficulty) facilité f
(b) to feel/to be at ~ se sentir/être à l'aise;
to put sb's mind at ~ rassurer qn (about à
propos de)
⟦2⟧ vtr **(a)** atténuer ‹pain, tension, pressure›;

réduire ‹congestion›; diminuer ‹burden›
(b) faciliter ‹communication, transition›
(c) to ~ sth into introduire qch délicatement
dans
⟦3⟧ vi ‹tension, pain, pressure› s'atténuer;
‹rain› diminuer
∎ **ease off** ‹business› ralentir; ‹demand› se
réduire; ‹traffic, rain› diminuer; ‹person›
relâcher son effort
∎ **ease up** ‹tense person, storm› se calmer;
‹authorities› relâcher la discipline; **to ~ up
on sb/on sth** être moins sévère envers qn/
pour qch

easel n chevalet m

⚬ **easily** adv facilement; **it's ~ the best** c'est
de loin le meilleur; **she could ~ die** elle
pourrait bien mourir

⚬ **east** ⟦1⟧ n **(a)** (compass direction) est m
(b) the East (Orient) l'Orient m; (part of country)
l'Est m
⟦2⟧ adj (gen) est inv; ‹wind› d'est
⟦3⟧ adv ‹move› vers l'est; ‹live, lie› à l'est
(of de)

Easter ⟦1⟧ n Pâques m; **at ~** à Pâques;
Happy ~ Joyeuses Pâques
⟦2⟧ adj ‹Sunday, egg› de Pâques

eastern adj **(a)** ‹coast› est inv; ‹town,
accent› de l'est; **Eastern Europe** l'Europe de
l'Est; ~ **France** l'est de la France
(b) (also **Eastern**) (oriental) oriental/-e

East Timor pr n Timor m oriental

⚬ **easy** ⟦1⟧ adj **(a)** ‹job, question, life, victim›
facile; **it's ~ to do** c'est facile à faire; **it's ~
to make a mistake** il est facile de se tromper;
it isn't ~ to do ce n'est pas facile à faire;
it isn't ~ to park il n'est pas facile de se
garer; **to make it** or **things easier** faciliter les
choses (for pour)
(b) (relaxed) ‹smile, grace› décontracté/-e;
‹style› plein/-e d'aisance; **at an ~ pace** d'un
pas tranquille
(c) (colloq) **I'm ~** ça m'est égal
⟦2⟧ adv **(a) to take it** or **things ~** ne pas s'en
faire
(b) (colloq) **to go ~ on** or **with** y aller
doucement avec

easygoing adj ‹person› accommodant/-e;
‹manner, attitude› souple

easy terms n pl facilités fpl de paiement

⚬ **eat** ⟦1⟧ vtr (prét **ate**, pp **eaten**) manger
‹food›; prendre ‹meal›
⟦2⟧ vi (prét **ate**, pp **eaten**) manger
∎ **eat out** aller au restaurant

eating disorder n trouble m du
comportement alimentaire

eating habits n pl habitudes fpl
alimentaires

eavesdrop vi (p prés etc **-pp-**) écouter
aux portes

ebb ⟦1⟧ n reflux m
⟦2⟧ vi ‹tide› descendre; ‹enthusiasm› décliner

ebony n **(a)** (wood) ébène f   ⋯⋗

(b) (colour) noir *m* d'ébène
e-book *n* e-book *m*
EC *n* (*abbr* = **European Commission**) CE *f*
e-cash *n* argent *m* électronique, argent *m* virtuel
eccentric *n*, *adj* excentrique *mf*
ECG *n* (*abbr* = **electrocardiogram**) ECG *m*.
echo ⊞ *n* (*pl* ∼**es**) écho *m*
  ⊡ *vtr* **(a)** répercuter ‹*sound*›
  (b) reprendre ‹*ideas, opinions*›
  ⊟ *vi* retentir, résonner
eclipse ⊞ *n* éclipse *f* (**of** de)
  ⊡ *vtr* éclipser
eco-friendly *adj* qui ne nuit pas à l'environnement
ecological *adj* écologique
ecological footprint *n* empreinte *f* écologique
ecologist *n*, *adj* écologiste *mf*
ecology *n* écologie *f*
e-commerce *n* commerce *m* électronique
◌ **economic** *adj* (gen) économique; (profitable) rentable
economical *adj* ‹*person*› économe; ‹*machine, method*› économique
economic refugee *n* réfugié/-e *mf* économique
economics *n* (science) économie *f*; (subject of study) sciences *fpl* économiques; (financial aspects) aspects *mpl* économiques (**of** de)
economist *n* économiste *mf*
economize *vtr, vi* économiser
◌ **economy** *n* économie *f*
economy class *n* classe *f* économique
economy class syndrome *n* syndrome *m* de la classe économique
economy drive *n* campagne *f* de restriction
eco-warrior *n* éco-guerrier/-ière *m*/*f*
ecstasy *n* **(a)** extase *f*
  (b) (drug) ecstasy *m*
eczema *n* eczéma *m*
Eden *pr n* Éden *m*, paradis *m* terrestre
◌ **edge** ⊞ *n* **(a)** (outer limit) bord *m*; (of wood, clearing) lisière *f*; **the film had us on the** ∼ **of our seats** le film nous a tenus en haleine
  (b) (of blade) tranchant *m*
  (c) (of book, plank) tranche *f*
  (d) **to be on** ∼ ‹*person*› être énervé/-e
  ⊡ *vi* **to** ∼ **forward** avancer doucement; **to** ∼ **towards** s'approcher à petits pas de
edgeways, edgewise *adv* ‹*move*› latéralement; ‹*lay, put*› sur le côté
  IDIOM I can't get a word in ∼ je n'arrive pas à placer un mot
edible *adj* comestible

Edinburgh *pr n* Édimbourg
edit *vtr* **(a)** (in publishing) éditer
  (b) (cut) couper ‹*text, version*›
  (c) monter ‹*film, programme*›
edition *n* édition *f*
◌ **editor** *n* (of newspaper) rédacteur/-trice *m*/*f* en chef (**of** de); (of book, manuscript) correcteur/-trice *m*/*f*; (of writer, works, anthology) éditeur/-trice *m*/*f*; (of film) monteur/-euse *m*/*f*
editorial ⊞ *n* éditorial *m* (**on** sur)
  ⊡ *adj* **(a)** (in journalism) de la rédaction, rédactionnel/-elle
  (b) (in publishing) éditorial/-e
educate *vtr* **(a)** ‹*teacher*› instruire; ‹*parent*› assurer l'instruction de; **to be** ∼**d in Paris** faire ses études à Paris
  (b) informer ‹*public*› (**about, in** sur)
educated *adj* ‹*person, classes*› instruit/-e; ‹*accent*› élégant/-e
◌ **education** *n* **(a)** éducation *f*, instruction *f*; **health** ∼ hygiène *f*
  (b) (formal schooling) études *fpl*; **to have had a university** *or* **college** ∼ avoir fait des études supérieures
  (c) (national system) enseignement *m*
educational *adj* **(a)** ‹*establishment*› d'enseignement
  (b) ‹*game, programme*› éducatif/-ive; ‹*talk*› instructif/-ive
EEC *n* (*abbr* = **European Economic Community**) CEE *f*
eel *n* anguille *f*
eerie *adj* ‹*silence, place*› étrange et inquiétant/-e
◌ **effect** ⊞ *n* **(a)** effet *m* (**of** de; **on** sur); **to take** ∼ ‹*price increases*› prendre effet; ‹*pills, anaesthetic*› commencer à agir; **to come into** ∼ ‹*law, rate*› entrer en vigueur; **she dresses like that for** ∼ elle s'habille comme ça pour faire de l'effet
  (b) (repercussions) répercussions *fpl* (**of** de; **on** sur)
  ⊡ **effects** *n pl* effets *mpl*
  ⊟ *vtr* effectuer ‹*repair, sale, change*›
  ⊠ **in effect** *phr* en fait, en réalité
◌ **effective** *adj* efficace
◌ **effectively** *adv* **(a)** (efficiently) efficacement
  (b) (in effect) en fait, en réalité
effeminate *adj* efféminé/-e
efficiency *n* (of person, method, organization) efficacité *f* (**in doing** à faire); (of machine) rendement *m*
efficient *adj* **(a)** ‹*person, management*› efficace (**at doing** pour ce qui est de faire)
  (b) ‹*machine*› économique
◌ **effort** *n* effort *m*; **to make the** ∼ faire l'effort; **to spare no** ∼ ne pas ménager ses efforts; **to be worth the** ∼ en valoir la peine; **it is an** ∼ **to do** il est pénible de faire

---

◌ indicates a very frequent word

EFL n (abbr = **English as a Foreign Language**) anglais m langue étrangère

✧ **eg** (abbr = **exempli gratia**) par ex

egalitarian adj égalitaire

✧ **egg** n œuf m
■ **egg on** pousser ‹person›

eggcup n coquetier m

eggplant n (US) aubergine f

egg white n blanc m d'œuf

egg yolk n jaune m d'œuf

ego n (a) amour-propre m; **it boosted his ~** ça lui a redonné confiance en lui-même
(b) (in psychology) moi m, ego m

egoism n égoïsme m

egoist n égoïste mf

egotist n égotiste mf

Egypt pr n Égypte f

EHIC n (abbr = **European Health Insurance Card**) CEAM f

Eid al-Adha pr n Aïd el-Kebir

eiderdown n édredon m

Eid-ul-Fitr pr n Aïd el-Fitr

✧ **eight** n, pron, det huit m inv

eighteen n, pron, det dix-huit m inv

eighteenth ⅟ n (a) (in order) dix-huitième mf
(b) (of month) dix-huit m inv
(c) (fraction) dix-huitième m
② adj, adv dix-huitième

eighth ⅟ n (a) (in order) huitième mf
(b) (of month) huit m inv
(c) (fraction) huitième m
② adj, adv huitième

eighties n pl (a) (era) **the ~** les années fpl quatre-vingt
(b) (age) **to be in one's ~** avoir entre quatre-vingts et quatre-vingt-dix ans

eightieth n, adj, adv quatre-vingtième mf

eighty n, pron, det quatre-vingts m

eighty-one n, pron, det quatre-vingt-un m

Éire pr n Éire f, République f d'Irlande

✧ **either** ⅟ pron, quantif (a) (one or other) l'un/-e ou l'autre; **take ~** (of them) prends l'un/-e ou l'autre; **I don't like ~** (of them) je n'aime ni l'un/-e ni l'autre; **'which book do you want?'—'~'** 'quel livre veux-tu?'— 'n'importe'
(b) (both) **~ of the two is possible** les deux sont possibles
② det (a) (one or other) n'importe lequel/ laquelle; **take ~ road** prenez n'importe laquelle des deux routes; **I can't see ~ child** je ne vois aucun de ces deux enfants
(b) (both) **in ~ case** dans un cas comme dans l'autre; **~ way, it will be difficult** de toute manière, ce sera difficile
③ adv non plus; **I can't do it ~** je ne peux pas le faire non plus
④ conj (a) (as alternatives) **~...or...** soit... soit..., (ou)...ou...

(b) (in the negative) **I wouldn't believe ~ Patrick or Emily** je ne croirais ni Patrick ni Emily

eject ⅟ vtr (a) ‹machine, system› rejeter ‹waste›; ‹volcano› cracher ‹lava›
(b) faire sortir ‹cassette›
(c) expulser ‹troublemaker›
② vi ‹pilot› s'éjecter

eject button n touche f d'éjection

eke
■ **eke out** faire durer ‹income, supplies› (**by** à force de; **by doing** en faisant); **to ~ out a living** essayer de joindre les deux bouts

elaborate ⅟ adj ‹excuse› compliqué/-e; ‹network, plan› complexe; ‹design› travaillé/-e; ‹painting, sculpture› ouvragé/-e
② vtr élaborer ‹theory›
③ vi entrer dans les détails; **to ~ on** s'étendre sur ‹proposal›; développer ‹remark›

elapse vi s'écouler

elastic n, adj élastique m

elasticated adj élastique

elastic band n élastique m

elated adj transporté/-e de joie

elbow n coude m

elbow grease n huile f de coude (fam)

elbowroom n (room to move) espace m vital; (figurative) marge f de manœuvre

elder ⅟ n (a) (older person) aîné/-e m/f; (of tribe, group) ancien m
(b) (tree) sureau m
② adj aîné/-e; **the ~ girl** l'aînée f, la fille aînée

elderly ⅟ n **the ~** les personnes fpl âgées
② adj ‹person, population› âgé/-e

eldest ⅟ n aîné/-e m/f
② adj aîné/-e; **the ~ child** l'aîné/-e

✧ **elect** vtr (a) (by vote) élire (**from, from among** parmi)
(b) (choose) choisir (**to do** de faire)

✧ **election** n élection f, scrutin m; **to win an ~** gagner aux élections

election campaign n campagne f électorale

electoral adj électoral/-e

electorate n électorat m, électeurs mpl

electric adj électrique

electrical adj électrique

electric blanket n couverture f chauffante

electrician n électricien/-ienne m/f

electricity n électricité f; **to turn off/on the ~** couper/rétablir le courant (électrique)

electric shock n décharge f électrique

electrify vtr (a) électrifier ‹railway›
(b) électriser ‹audience›

electrocute vtr électrocuter

electronic adj électronique

electronic engineer n électronicien/ -ienne m/f

electronic organizer n ordinateur m
de poche

electronic publishing n éditique f

electronics n électronique f

electronic tagging n marquage m
électronique (des criminels)

elegant adj ⟨person, clothes, gesture⟩
élégant/-e; ⟨manners⟩ distingué/-e;
⟨restaurant⟩ chic

ᵒᶠ **element** n (a) élément m; **an ∼ of luck** une
part de chance
(b) (in heater, kettle) résistance f

elementary adj (a) (basic) élémentaire
(b) ⟨school⟩ primaire; ⟨teacher⟩ de primaire

elephant n éléphant m

elevate vtr élever (**to** au rang de)

elevated adj ⟨language, rank, site⟩ élevé/-e;
⟨railway, canal⟩ surélevé/-e

elevator n (a) (US) (lift) ascenseur m
(b) (hoist) élévateur m

eleven n, pron, det onze m inv

eleventh ① n (a) (in order) onzième mf
(b) (of month) onze m inv
(c) (fraction) onzième m
② adj, adv onzième

elf n (pl **elves**) lutin m

eligible adj **to be ∼ for** avoir droit à
⟨allowance, benefit, membership⟩; **to be ∼ to
do** être en droit de faire

ᵒᶠ **eliminate** vtr (gen) éliminer; écarter
⟨suspect⟩

elimination n élimination f; **by a process
of ∼** en procédant par élimination

élite ① n élite f
② adj ⟨group, minority⟩ élitaire;
⟨restaurant, club⟩ réservé/-e à l'élite; ⟨squad⟩
d'élite

elm n orme m

elongated adj allongé/-e

elope vi s'enfuir (**with** avec)

eloquent adj éloquent/-e

ᵒᶠ **else** ① adv d'autre; **somebody/nothing ∼**
quelqu'un/rien d'autre; **something ∼** autre
chose; **somewhere** or **someplace** (US) ∼
ailleurs; **how ∼ can we do it?** comment le
faire autrement?; **what ∼ would you like?**
qu'est-ce que tu voudrais d'autre?
② **or else** phr sinon

ᵒᶠ **elsewhere** adv ailleurs

elusive adj ⟨person, animal, happiness⟩
insaisissable; ⟨prize, victory⟩ hors d'atteinte

emaciated adj ⟨person, feature⟩ émacié/-e;
⟨limb, body⟩ décharné/-e; ⟨animal⟩ étique

ᵒᶠ **e-mail, email** ① n (medium) e-mail m,
courrier m électronique, courriel m; (item of
mail) e-mail m, message m électronique
② vtr envoyer un e-mail à ⟨person⟩; envoyer
[qch] par e-mail ⟨document⟩

ᵒᶠ indicates a very frequent word

e-mail address n adresse f électronique

emancipate vtr émanciper

emancipation n émancipation f

embalm vtr embaumer

embankment n (a) (for railway, road)
remblai m
(b) (by river) quai m, digue f

embargo n embargo m

embark vi (a) (on ship) s'embarquer (**for**
pour)
(b) **to ∼ on** entreprendre ⟨journey⟩; se lancer
dans ⟨career, process, project⟩

embarkation n embarquement m

embarrass vtr plonger [qn] dans
l'embarras; **to be/to feel ∼ed** être/se sentir
gêné/-e

embarrassing adj embarrassant/-e

embarrassment n confusion f, gêne
f (**about, at** devant); **to my ∼** à ma grande
confusion

embassy n ambassade f

embedded adj (a) ⟨software⟩ embarqué/-e
(b) ⟨journalist⟩ intégré/-e

embers n pl braises f pl

embezzle vtr détourner ⟨funds⟩ (**from** de)

emblem n emblème m

embody vtr incarner ⟨virtue, evil, ideal⟩

embrace ① n étreinte f
② vtr (a) (hug) étreindre
(b) (include) comprendre
③ vi s'étreindre

embroider ① vtr (a) broder (**with** de)
(b) embellir ⟨story, truth⟩
② vi broder, faire de la broderie

embroidery n broderie f

embryo n embryon m

emerald n (a) (stone) émeraude f
(b) (colour) émeraude m

ᵒᶠ **emerge** vi (a) ⟨person, animal⟩ sortir (**from**
de)
(b) ⟨problem, result⟩ se faire jour; ⟨pattern⟩ se
dégager; ⟨truth⟩ apparaître

ᵒᶠ **emergency** ① n (gen) cas m d'urgence;
(Med) urgence f; **in an ∼, in case of ∼** en cas
d'urgence; **it's an ∼** c'est urgent
② adj ⟨plan, repairs, call, stop⟩ d'urgence;
⟨brakes, vehicle⟩ de secours

emergency exit n sortie f de secours

emergency landing n atterrissage m
d'urgence

emergency services n pl (police) ≈
police f secours; (ambulance) service m d'aide
médicale d'urgence; (fire brigade) (sapeurs-)
pompiers mpl

emergency worker n secouriste mf

emigrant n (about to leave) émigrant/-e m/f;
(settled elsewhere) émigré/-e m/f

emigrate vi émigrer

emission n émission f (**from** provenant de)

emit vtr émettre

emoticon n (Comput) émoticône f, smiley m (fam)

⚹ **emotion** n émotion f

⚹ **emotional** adj ‹problem› émotif/-ive; ‹reaction› émotionnel/-elle; ‹tie, response› affectif/-ive; ‹speech› passionné/-e; **to feel ~** être ému/-e (**about** par); **she's rather ~** elle est assez émotive

emotionally adv ‹speak, react› avec émotion; **~ deprived** privé/-e d'affection; **~ disturbed** caractériel/-ielle

emotive adj ‹issue› qui soulève les passions; ‹word› chargé/-e de connotations

empathize vi **to ~ with** s'identifier à ‹person›

emperor n empereur m

emphasis n (pl **-ses**) accent m; **to lay** or **put the ~ on sth** mettre l'accent sur qch

⚹ **emphasize** vtr mettre l'accent sur ‹policy, need›; mettre [qch] en valeur ‹eyes›

emphatic adj ‹statement› catégorique; ‹voice, manner› énergique; **to be ~ about** insister sur

empire n empire m

⚹ **employ** vtr **(a)** employer ‹person, company› (as en qualité de); **to be ~ed** avoir un emploi **(b)** (use) utiliser ‹machine, tool›; employer ‹tactics, technique›; recourir à ‹measures›

employable adj capable de faire un travail

⚹ **employee** n salarié/-e m/f

⚹ **employer** n employeur/-euse m/f

⚹ **employment** n travail m, emploi m

employment agency n bureau m de recrutement

empower vtr (legally) **to ~ sb to do** autoriser qn à faire; (politically) donner à qn le pouvoir de faire

empress n impératrice f

⚹ **empty** **1** adj **(a)** ‹street› désert/-e; ‹desk› libre; ‹container› vide; ‹page› vierge **(b)** ‹promise, threat› en l'air; ‹gesture› vide de sens; ‹life› vide **2** vtr, vi = EMPTY OUT **■ empty out**: **1** ¶ **~ out** ‹building, container› se vider; ‹contents› se répandre **2** ¶ **~ [sth] out** vider ‹container, drawer›; verser ‹liquid›

empty-handed adj ‹arrive, leave› les mains vides; ‹return› bredouille inv

emulate vtr imiter

emulsion n émulsion f

⚹ **enable** vtr **(a) to ~ sb to do** permettre à qn de faire **(b)** faciliter ‹growth›; favoriser ‹learning›

enamel n émail m

enchant vtr enchanter

enchanting adj enchanteur/-eresse

encircle vtr ‹troops, police› encercler; ‹fence, wall› entourer; ‹belt, bracelet› enserrer

enclose vtr **(a)** (gen) entourer (**with, by** de); (with fence, wall) clôturer (**with, by** avec) **(b)** (in letter) joindre (**with, in** à); **please find ~d a cheque for £10** veuillez trouver ci-joint un chèque de dix livres sterling

enclosure n **(a)** (for animals) enclos m; (for racehorses) paddock m; (for officials) enceinte f **(b)** (fence) clôture f

encompass vtr inclure, comprendre

encore **1** n bis m; **to play an ~** jouer un bis **2** excl **~!** bis!

encounter **1** n (gen) rencontre f (**with** avec); (Mil) affrontement m **2** vtr rencontrer ‹opponent, resistance, problem›; essuyer ‹setback›; croiser ‹person›

⚹ **encourage** vtr **(a)** encourager (**to do** à faire) **(b)** stimuler ‹investment›; favoriser ‹growth›

encouragement n encouragement m

encouraging adj encourageant/-e

encroach vi **to ~ on** ‹person› empiéter sur; ‹sea, vegetation› gagner du terrain sur ‹land›

encrypt vtr crypter

encyclop(a)edia n encyclopédie f

⚹ **end** **1** n **(a)** (final part) fin f; **'The End'** 'Fin'; **to put an ~ to sth** mettre fin à qch; **to come to an ~** se terminer; **in the ~ I went home** finalement je suis rentré chez moi; **for days on ~** pendant des jours et des jours **(b)** (extremity) bout m, extrémité f; **at the ~ of, on the ~ of** au bout de; **at the ~ of the garden** au fond du jardin; **the third from the ~** le/la troisième avant la fin; **to stand sth on (its) ~** mettre qch debout **(c)** (aim) but m; **to this ~** dans ce but; **a means to an ~** un moyen d'arriver à ses fins **(d)** (Sport) **to change ~s** changer de côté **2** vtr mettre fin à; **to ~ sth with** terminer qch par; **to ~ it all** en finir avec la vie **3** vi ‹day, book› se terminer (**in, with** par); ‹contract, agreement› expirer **■ end up** finir par devenir ‹president›; finir par être ‹rich›; **to ~ up doing** finir par faire

endanger vtr mettre [qch] en danger ‹health, life›; compromettre ‹career, prospects›

endangered species n espèce f menacée

endearing adj ‹person, habit› attachant/-e; ‹smile› engageant/-e

endeavour, endeavor (US) **1** n tentative f (**to do** de faire) **2** vtr **to ~ to do** (do one's best) faire tout son possible pour faire; (find a means) trouver un moyen de faire

ending n fin f, dénouement m

endive n (GB) chicorée f; (US) endive f

endless adj ‹patience, choice› infini/-e; ‹supply› inépuisable; ‹list, search, meeting› ⋯⟫

interminable

endorse *vtr* donner son aval à ‹*policy*›; appuyer ‹*decision*›; approuver ‹*product*›; endosser ‹*cheque*›

endow *vtr* doter (**with** de)

end result *n* résultat *m* final

endurance *n* endurance *f*

endure ①︎ *vtr* endurer ‹*hardship*›; supporter ‹*behaviour, person*›; subir ‹*attack, defeat*› ②︎ *vi* durer

ᴄ **enemy** ①︎ *n* (*pl* **-mies**) ennemi/-e *m/f* ②︎ *adj* ‹*forces, aircraft, territory*› ennemi/-e; ‹*agent*› de l'ennemi

energetic *adj* énergique

ᴄ **energy** *n* énergie *f*

energy policy *n* politique *f* énergétique

energy-saving *adj* qui permet de faire des économies d'énergie

enforce *vtr* appliquer ‹*rule, policy*›; faire respecter ‹*law, court order*›

ᴄ **engage** ①︎ *vtr* (**a**) **to be** ~**d in** se livrer à ‹*activity*›; **to** ~ **sb in conversation** engager la conversation avec qn (**b**) passer ‹*gear*›; **to** ~ **the clutch** embrayer ②︎ *vi* **to** ~ **in** se livrer à ‹*activity*›; se lancer dans ‹*research*›

engaged *adj* (**a**) **to be** ~ être fiancé/-e (**to** à); **to get** ~ se fiancer (**to** à) (**b**) ‹*WC, phone*› occupé/-e

engaged tone *n* (GB) tonalité *f* 'occupé'

engagement *n* (**a**) (appointment) rendez-vous *m inv* (**b**) (before marriage) fiançailles *fpl*

engagement ring *n* bague *f* de fiançailles

ᴄ **engine** *n* (**a**) (gen) moteur *m*; (in ship) machines *fpl* (**b**) locomotive *f*; **steam** ~ locomotive à vapeur

engine driver *n* mécanicien *m*

engineer ①︎ *n* (graduate) ingénieur *m*; (in factory) mécanicien *m* monteur; (repairer) technicien *m*; (on ship) mécanicien *m* ②︎ *vtr* (**a**) (plot) manigancer (**b**) (build) construire

engineering *n* ingénierie *f*; **civil** ~ génie *m* civil

England *pr n* Angleterre *f*

ᴄ **English** ①︎ *n* (**a**) (people) **the** ~ les Anglais (**b**) (language) anglais *m* ②︎ *adj* ‹*language, food*› anglais/-e; ‹*lesson, teacher*› d'anglais; ‹*team*› d'Angleterre

English Channel *pr n* **the** ~ la Manche

Englishman *n* (*pl* **-men**) Anglais *m*

English-speaking *adj* anglophone

Englishwoman *n* (*pl* ~**women**) Anglaise *f*

engrave *vtr* graver

ᴄ indicates a very frequent word

engraving *n* gravure *f*

engrossed *adj* **to be** ~ **in** être absorbé/-e par, être plongé/-e dans

engulf *vtr* engloutir

ᴄ **enhance** *vtr* améliorer ‹*prospects, status*›; mettre [qch] en valeur ‹*appearance, qualities*›

enigma *n* énigme *f*

enigmatic *adj* énigmatique

ᴄ **enjoy** ①︎ *vtr* (**a**) aimer (**doing** faire); **I didn't** ~ **the party** je ne me suis pas amusé à la soirée (**b**) (have) jouir de ‹*good health, popularity*› ②︎ *v refl* **to** ~ **oneself** s'amuser

enjoyable *adj* agréable

enjoyment *n* plaisir *m*

enlarge ①︎ *vtr* agrandir ②︎ *vi* (**a**) ‹*pupil, pores*› se dilater; ‹*tonsils*› enfler (**b**) **to** ~ **on** s'étendre sur ‹*subject*›; développer ‹*idea*›

enlighten *vtr* éclairer (**on** sur)

enlightening *adj* instructif/-ive

enlightenment *n* (edification) instruction *f*; (clarification) éclaircissement *m*; **the (Age of) Enlightenment** le Siècle des lumières

enlist ①︎ *vtr* recruter; **to** ~ **sb's help** s'assurer l'aide de qn ②︎ *vi* s'enrôler, s'engager

enmity *n* inimitié *f* (**towards** envers)

enormity *n* énormité *f*

enormous *adj* (gen) énorme; ‹*effort*› prodigieux/-ieuse

ᴄ **enough**

■ **Note** When *enough* is used as a pronoun and if the sentence does not specify what it is enough of, the pronoun *en*, meaning of *it/of them*, must be added before the verb in French: *will there be enough?* = est-ce qu'il y en aura assez?

①︎ *pron, quantif* assez; **have you had** ~ **to eat?** avez-vous assez mangé?; **more than** ~ largement assez; **is that** ~**?** ça suffit?; **I've had** ~ **of him** j'en ai assez de lui ②︎ *adv* assez; **curiously** ~**,...** aussi bizarre que cela puisse paraître... ③︎ *det* assez de; **have you got** ~ **chairs?** avez-vous assez de chaises?

enquire ①︎ *vtr* demander ②︎ *vi* se renseigner (**about** sur); **to** ~ **after sb** demander des nouvelles de qn

enquiring *adj* ‹*look, voice*› interrogateur/-trice; ‹*mind*› curieux/-ieuse

enquiry *n* demande *f* de renseignements; **to make enquiries** demander des renseignements (**about** sur); ▶ INQUIRY

enrage *vtr* rendre [qn] furieux/-ieuse

enrich *vtr* enrichir

enrol, enroll ①︎ *vtr* (*p prés etc* **-ll-**) (gen) inscrire; (Mil) enrôler ②︎ *vi* (*p prés etc* **-ll-**) (gen) s'inscrire (**in, on** à); (Mil) s'engager (**in** dans)

enrolment, **enrollment** (US) n (gen) inscription f (**in**, **on** à); (Mil) enrôlement m

ensuing adj ‹period› qui suivit; ‹event› qui s'ensuivit

en suite adj attenant/-e

✍ **ensure** vtr garantir; **to** ~ **that…** s'assurer que…

entail vtr impliquer ‹travel, work›; entraîner ‹expense›; nécessiter ‹effort›

✍ **enter** [1] vtr (a) entrer dans ‹room, house, phase, period, profession, army›; participer à ‹race, competition›; entrer à ‹parliament›; **to** ~ **sb's mind** or **head** venir à l'idée or à l'esprit de qn
(b) engager ‹horse› (**for** dans); présenter ‹poem, picture› (**for** à)
(c) inscrire ‹figure, fact› (**in** dans); (in diary) noter ‹appointment› (**in** dans); (in computer) entrer ‹data›
[2] vi (a) (come in) entrer
(b) **to** ~ **for** s'inscrire à ‹exam›; s'inscrire pour ‹race›
■ **enter into** entrer en ‹conversation›; entamer ‹negotiations›; passer ‹contract›

enterprise n (a) (gen) entreprise f
(b) (initiative) esprit m d'initiative

enterprising adj ‹person› entreprenant/-e; ‹plan› audacieux/-ieuse

entertain [1] vtr (a) (keep amused) divertir; (make laugh) amuser; (keep occupied) distraire, occuper
(b) (play host to) recevoir ‹guests›
(c) entretenir ‹idea›; nourrir ‹doubt, ambition, illusion›
[2] vi recevoir

entertainer n (comic) comique mf; (performer, raconteur) amuseur/-euse m/f

entertaining [1] adj divertissant/-e
[2] n **they do a lot of** ~ ils reçoivent beaucoup

entertainment n (a) divertissement m, distractions fpl
(b) (event) spectacle m

entertainment industry n industrie f du spectacle

enthusiasm n enthousiasme m (**for** pour)

enthusiast n (for sport, DIY) passionné/-e m/f; (for music, composer) fervent/-e m/f

enthusiastic adj (gen) enthousiaste; ‹discussion› exalté/-e; ‹worker, gardener› passionné/-e

entice vtr (with offer, charms, prospects) attirer; (with food, money) appâter

✍ **entire** adj entier/-ière; **the** ~ **family** toute la famille, la famille entière

✍ **entirely** adv ‹destroy, escape› entièrement; ‹different, unnecessary› complètement

entirety n ensemble m, totalité f

✍ **entitle** vtr **to** ~ **sb to sth** donner droit à qch à qn; **to be** ~**d to sth** avoir droit à qch; **to be** ~**d to do** avoir le droit de faire

entitlement n droit m

entity n entité f

entrance [1] n (gen) entrée f; **to gain** ~ **to** être admis/-e à or dans ‹club, university›
[2] vtr transporter, ravir

entrance examination n (GB Sch, Univ) examen m d'entrée; (for civil service) concours m d'entrée

entrance fee n droit m d'entrée

entrance hall n (in house) vestibule m; (in public building) hall m

entrance requirements n pl diplômes mpl requis

entrant n (in competition) participant/-e m/f; (in exam) candidat/-e m/f

entreat vtr implorer, supplier (**to do** faire)

entreaty n prière f, supplication f

entrepreneur n entrepreneur/-euse m/f

entrust vtr confier; **to** ~ **sb with sth**, **to** ~ **sth to sb** confier qch à qn

✍ **entry** n (a) (gen) entrée f; **to gain** ~ **to** or **into** s'introduire dans ‹building›; accéder à ‹computer file›; '**no** ~' (on door) 'défense d'entrer'; (in one way street) 'sens interdit'
(b) (in diary) note f; (in ledger) écriture f
(c) (for competition) œuvre f présentée à un concours

entry form n (for membership) fiche f d'inscription; (for competition) bulletin m de participation

entry phone n interphone m

envelope n enveloppe f

envious adj envieux/-ieuse; **to be** ~ **of sb/sth** envier qn/qch

✍ **environment** n (physical, cultural) environnement m; (social) milieu m

✍ **environmental** adj ‹conditions, changes› du milieu; ‹concern, issue› lié/-e à l'environnement, écologique; ‹protection, pollution› de l'environnement; ~ **disaster** catastrophe f écologique

environmental health n hygiène f publique

environmentally adv ~ **safe**, ~ **sound** qui ne nuit pas à l'environnement; ~ **friendly product** produit qui respecte l'environnement

environmental studies n pl (GB Sch) études fpl géographiques et biologiques de l'environnement

envisage vtr (anticipate) prévoir (**doing** de faire); (visualize) envisager (**doing** de faire)

envoy n envoyé/-e m/f

envy [1] n envie f; (long-term) jalousie f
[2] vtr **to** ~ **sb sth** envier qch à qn

enzyme n enzyme f

epic [1] n (gen) épopée f; (film) film m à grand spectacle; (novel) roman-fleuve m
[2] adj épique

epidemic [1] n épidémie f   ⋯⋗

e

2 *adj* épidémique

epidural *n* péridurale *f*

epilepsy *n* épilepsie *f*

epileptic *n, adj* épileptique *mf*

ℱ **episode** *n* épisode *m*

epitome *n* épitomé *m*; **the ∼ of kindness** la bonté incarnée

epitomize *vtr* personnifier, incarner

epoch *n* époque *f*

ℱ **equal** **1** *n* égal/-e *m/f*
  2 *adj* (a) égal/-e (**to** à); **∼ opportunities/ rights** égalité *f* des chances/des droits
  (b) **to be ∼ to** être à la hauteur de ‹task›
  3 *adv* ‹finish› à égalité
  4 *vtr* égaler

equality *n* égalité *f*; **∼ of opportunity** égalité des chances

equalize *vi* égaliser

ℱ **equally** *adv* ‹divide, share› en parts égales; **∼ difficult** tout aussi difficile; **∼, we might say that…** de même, on pourrait dire que…

equate *vtr* (identify) assimiler (**with, to** à); (compare) comparer (**with, to** à)

equation *n* équation *f*

equator *n* équateur *m*

equilibrium *n* (*pl* **-riums** *ou* **-ria**) équilibre *m*

equip *vtr* (*p prés etc* **-pp-**) équiper (**for** pour; **with** de)

ℱ **equipment** *n* (gen) équipement *m*; (office, electrical, photographic) matériel *m*; **a piece** *or* **item of ∼** un article

equivalent **1** *n* équivalent *m*
  2 *adj* équivalent/-e

ℱ **era** *n* (in history, geology) ère *f*; (in politics, fashion) époque *f*

eradicate *vtr* éliminer ‹poverty, crime›; éradiquer ‹disease›

erase *vtr* effacer

eraser *n* (rubber) gomme *f*; (for blackboard) brosse *f* feutrée

erect **1** *adj* ‹posture› droit/-e; ‹tail, ears› dressé/-e
  2 *vtr* ériger ‹building›; monter ‹scaffolding, tent, screen›

erection *n* (gen) érection *f*; (of building) construction *f*; (edifice) édifice *m*

ermine *n* hermine *f*

erode *vtr* éroder ‹rock, metal›; saper ‹confidence›

erosion *n* érosion *f*

erotic *adj* érotique

err *vi* (a) (make mistake) faire erreur
  (b) **to ∼ on the side of caution** pécher par excès de prudence

errand *n* commission *f*, course *f*; **to run an ∼ for sb** aller faire une commission pour qn

ℱ indicates a very frequent word

erratic *adj* ‹behaviour, person, driver› imprévisible; ‹moods› changeant/-e

ℱ **error** *n* (in spelling, grammar, typing) faute *f*; (in calculation, on computer) erreur *f*

erupt *vi* (a) ‹volcano› entrer en éruption
  (b) ‹violence› éclater

eruption *n* (of volcano) éruption *f*; (of violence, anger) explosion *f*

escalate *vi* ‹conflict, violence› s'intensifier; ‹prices› monter en flèche; ‹unemployment› augmenter rapidement

escalator *n* escalier *m* mécanique, escalator® *m*

escapade *n* frasque *f*

ℱ **escape** **1** *n* fuite *f*, évasion (**from** de; **to** vers) *f*; **to have a narrow** *or* **lucky ∼** l'échapper belle
  2 *vtr* échapper à
  3 *vi* (a) ‹person› s'enfuir, s'évader (**from** de); ‹animal› s'échapper (**from** de); (figurative) s'évader; **to ∼ with one's life** s'en sortir vivant
  (b) (leak) fuir

escape clause *n* clause *f* dérogatoire

escape key *n* touche *f* d'échappement

escape route *n* (in case of fire etc) plan *m* d'évacuation; (for fugitives) itinéraire *m* d'évasion

escapism *n* évasion *f* (du réel)

escort **1** *n* (a) (for security) escorte *f*; **police ∼** escorte de police
  (b) (companion) compagnon/compagne *m/f*
  (c) (in agency) hôtesse *f*; **∼ agency** agence *f* d'hôtesses
  2 *vtr* (a) (for security) escorter; **to ∼ sb in/ out** faire entrer/sortir qn sous escorte
  (b) (to a function) accompagner; (home) raccompagner

ℱ **especially** *adv* (a) (above all) surtout, en particulier; **him ∼** lui en particulier; **∼ as it's so hot** d'autant plus qu'il fait si chaud
  (b) (on purpose) exprès, spécialement
  (c) (unusually) particulièrement

espresso *n* (*pl* **∼s**) express *m inv*

essay *n* (a) (Sch) rédaction *f* (**on, about** sur); (extended) dissertation *f* (**on** sur)
  (b) (literary) essai *m* (**on** sur)

essence *n* essence *f*

ℱ **essential** **1** *n* **a car is not an ∼** une voiture n'est pas indispensable; **the ∼s** l'essentiel *m*
  2 *adj* ‹role, feature, element› essentiel/-ielle; ‹ingredient, reading› indispensable; ‹difference› fondamental/-e; **it is ∼ that we agree** il est indispensable que nous soyons d'accord

essentially *adv* essentiellement

essential oil *n* huile *f* essentielle

ℱ **establish** *vtr* (gen) établir; fonder ‹company›

establishment *n* (a) (gen) établissement *m*

(b) (shop, business) maison *f*
(c) the Establishment l'ordre *m* établi
⚘ **estate** *n* **(a)** (stately home and park) domaine *m*, propriété *f*
  (b) = HOUSING ESTATE
  (c) (assets) biens *mpl*
  (d) (*also* ∼ **car**) (GB) break *m*
estate agency *n* (GB) agence *f* immobilière
estate agent *n* (GB) agent *m* immobilier
esteem *n* estime *f*
⚘ **estimate** ⏢1 *n* **(a)** estimation *f*
  (b) (quote for client) devis *m*
  ⏢2 *vtr* évaluer ⟨*value, size, distance*⟩; **to** ∼ **that** estimer que
  ⏢3 **estimated** *pp adj* ⟨*cost, figure*⟩ approximatif/-ive; **an** ∼**d 300 people** environ 300 personnes
estimator *n* (US) métreur *m*
Estonia *pr n* Estonie *f*
estranged *adj* ∼ **from sb** séparé/-e de qn; **her** ∼ **husband** son mari dont elle est séparée
⚘ **etc** *adv* (*written abbr* = **et cetera**) etc
etching *n* eau-forte *f*
eternal *adj* ⟨*life*⟩ éternel/-elle; ⟨*chatter, optimist*⟩ perpétuel/-elle
ethical *adj* ⟨*problem, objection*⟩ moral/-e; ⟨*investment, theory*⟩ éthique
ethics *n* (code) moralité *f*; **professional** ∼ déontologie *f*
ethnic *adj* ethnique
ethnic cleansing *n* purification *f* ethnique
ethnic minority *n* minorité *f* ethnique
etiquette *n* **(a)** (social) bienséance *f*, étiquette *f*
  (b) (professional, diplomatic) protocole *m*
euphemism *n* euphémisme *m*
euphoria *n* euphorie *f*
euro *n* euro *m*
Euro- *pref* euro-
eurocheque *n* Eurochèque *m*
Eurocrat *n* eurocrate *mf*
Euro-MP *n* député *m* européen
Europe *pr n* Europe *f*
⚘ **European** ⏢1 *n* Européen/-éenne *m/f*
  ⏢2 *adj* européen/-éenne
European Commission *n* Commission *f* européenne
European Monetary System, EMS *n* système *m* monétaire européen, SME *m*
European Monetary Union, EMU *n* Union *f* monétaire européenne
European Union, EU *n* Union *f* européenne, UE *f*
eurosceptic *n* eurosceptique *mf*
Eurozone *n* Eurozone *f*
euthanasia *n* euthanasie *f*

evacuate *vtr* évacuer
evacuee *n* évacué/-e *m/f*
evade *vtr* esquiver ⟨*blow*⟩; éluder ⟨*problem*⟩
evaluate *vtr* évaluer
evaluation *n* évaluation *f*
evaporate *vi* ⟨*liquid*⟩ s'évaporer
evaporated milk *n* lait *m* condensé non sucré
evasion *n* (of responsibility) dérobade *f* (**of** à); **tax** ∼ évasion *f* fiscale
evasive *adj* ⟨*answer*⟩ évasif/-ive; ⟨*look*⟩ fuyant/-e
eve *n* veille *f*; **on the** ∼ **of** à la veille de
⚘ **even**[1] ⏢1 *adv* **(a)** (gen) même; **he didn't** ∼ **try** il n'a même pas essayé; **don't tell anyone, not** ∼ **Bob** ne dis rien à personne, pas même à Bob; ∼ **if/when** même si/quand
  (b) (with comparative) encore; ∼ **colder** encore plus froid
  ⏢2 **even so** *phr* quand même
  ⏢3 **even though** *phr* bien que (+ *subjunctive*)
even[2] *adj* ⟨*surface, voice, temper*⟩ égal/-e; ⟨*teeth, hemline*⟩ régulier/-ière; ⟨*temperature*⟩ constant/-e; ⟨*number*⟩ pair/-e; **to get** ∼ **with sb** rendre à qn la monnaie de sa pièce
⚘ **evening** *n* soir *m*; (with emphasis on duration) soirée *f*; **in the** ∼ le soir; **all** ∼ toute la soirée; **every** ∼ tous les soirs
evening class *n* cours *m* du soir
evening dress *n* (formal clothes) tenue *f* de soirée
⚘ **event** *n* **(a)** événement *m*
  (b) (eventuality) cas *m*; **in the** ∼ **of a fire** en cas d'incendie; **in any** ∼ de toute façon
  (c) (in athletics) épreuve *f*
eventful *adj* mouvementé/-e
⚘ **eventually** *adv* finalement; **to do sth** ∼ finir par faire qch
⚘ **ever** ⏢1 *adv* **(a)** jamais; **no-one will** ∼ **forget** personne n'oubliera jamais; **hardly** ∼ rarement, presque jamais; **has he** ∼ **lived abroad?** est-ce qu'il a déjà vécu à l'étranger?; **do you** ∼ **make mistakes?** est-ce qu'il t'arrive de te tromper?; **he's happier than he's** ∼ **been** il n'a jamais été aussi heureux; **more beautiful than** ∼ plus beau/belle que jamais
  (b) (always) toujours; **as cheerful as** ∼ toujours aussi gai; **the same as** ∼ toujours le même; **they lived happily** ∼ **after** ils vécurent toujours heureux
  ⏢2 **ever since** *phr* depuis; ∼ **since we arrived** depuis notre arrivée
evergreen *n* arbre *m* à feuilles persistantes
everlasting *adj* éternel/-elle
⚘ **every** ⏢1 *det* **(a)** (each) chaque; ∼ **time** chaque fois; ∼ **house in the street** toutes les maisons de la rue; **I've read** ∼ **one of her books** j'ai lu tous ses livres ⋯⟫

(b) (emphatic) **there is ~ chance that you'll have a place** il y a toutes les chances que tu aies une place; **to have ~ right to complain** avoir tous les droits de se plaindre
(c) (indicating frequency) **~ day** tous les jours; **~ Thursday** tous les jeudis; **once ~ few days** tous les deux ou trois jours
2 **every other** phr **~ other day** tous les deux jours; **~ other Sunday** un dimanche sur deux
IDIOM **~ now and then, ~ so often** de temps en temps

⚹ **everybody** pron (also **everyone**) tout le monde

everyday adj ‹life› quotidien/-ienne; ‹clothes› de tous les jours; **in ~ use** d'usage courant

⚹ **everyone** = EVERYBODY

⚹ **everything** pron tout

everywhere adv partout

evict vtr expulser (**from** de)

eviction n expulsion f

⚹ **evidence** n **(a)** (proof) preuves fpl (**that** que; **of, for** de; **against** contre)
(b) (testimony) témoignage m (**from** de); **to give ~** témoigner, déposer (**for sb** en faveur de qn; **against sb** contre qn)
(c) (trace) trace f (**of** de)

evident adj manifeste

evidently adv **(a)** (apparently) apparemment
(b) (patently) manifestement

evil 1 n mal m
2 adj ‹person, forces› malfaisant/-e; ‹act› diabolique; ‹spirit› maléfique; ‹smell› nauséabond/-e

⚹ **evolution** n évolution f (**from** à partir de)

evolve vi évoluer

ewe n brebis f

ex- pref ex-, ancien/-ienne (**before** n)

exact adj exact/-e; **to be (more) ~** plus précisément

⚹ **exactly** adv exactement

exaggerate vtr, vi exagérer

exaggeration n exagération f

exam n examen m

examination n examen m (**in** de); **French ~** examen m de français; **to take/pass an ~** passer/réussir un examen; **to have an ~** (Med) passer un examen médical

examination paper n sujets mpl d'examen

⚹ **examine** vtr examiner

examiner n examinateur/-trice m/f

⚹ **example** n exemple m; **for ~** par exemple; **to set a good ~** donner l'exemple; **to make an ~ of sb** punir qn pour l'exemple

excavate 1 vtr fouiller ‹site›; creuser ‹tunnel›

2 vi faire des fouilles

exceed vtr dépasser (**by** de)

excel vi exceller (**at, in** en; **at** or **in doing** à faire)

⚹ **excellent** adj excellent/-e

⚹ **except** 1 prep sauf; **everybody ~ Lisa** tout le monde sauf Lisa, tout le monde à l'exception de or excepté Lisa; **who could have done it ~ him?** qui aurait pu le faire sinon lui?
2 **except for** phr à part, à l'exception de

⚹ **exception** n **(a)** exception f (**for** pour); **with the ~ of** à l'exception de
(b) **to take ~ to** prendre [qch] comme une insulte

exceptional adj exceptionnel/-elle

excess 1 n excès m (**of** de)
2 adj **~ weight** excès m de poids; **~ baggage** excédent m de bagages

excessive adj excessif/-ive

⚹ **exchange** 1 n **(a)** échange m; **in ~** en échange (**for** de); **~ visit** voyage m d'échange
(b) (in banking) change m; **the ~ rate** le taux de change
(c) (also **telephone ~**) central m (téléphonique)
2 vtr échanger (**for** contre; **with** avec)

exchange control n contrôle m des changes

Exchange Rate Mechanism, ERM n système m monétaire européen

Exchequer pr n (GB) **the ~** l'Échiquier m, le ministère des finances

excite vtr exciter

excited adj (gen) excité/-e; ‹voice, conversation› animé/-e

excitement n excitation f

⚹ **exciting** adj passionnant/-e

exclaim vtr s'exclamer

exclamation mark, exclamation point (US) n point m d'exclamation

exclude vtr exclure (**from** de)

excluding prep à l'exclusion de; **~ VAT** TVA non comprise

exclusion zone n zone f interdite

exclusive 1 n (report) exclusivité f
2 adj **(a)** ‹club› fermé/-e; ‹hotel› de luxe; ‹district› huppé/-e
(b) ‹story, rights› exclusif/-ive; ‹interview› en exclusivité; **~ of meals** les repas non compris

excruciating adj ‹pain› atroce

excursion n (organized) excursion f

excuse 1 n excuse f (**for sth** à qch; **for doing** pour faire; **to do** pour faire); **to make ~s** trouver des excuses; **an ~ to leave early** un bon prétexte pour partir tôt; **there's no ~ for such behaviour** ce genre de conduite est inexcusable
2 vtr **(a)** excuser ‹person› (**for doing** de faire, d'avoir fait); **~ me!** (apology) excusez-moi!,

---

⚹ indicates a very frequent word

pardon!; (beginning an enquiry) excusez-moi; (pardon) pardon?
(b) (exempt) dispenser **(from sth** de qch; **from doing** de faire)
ex-directory adj sur la liste rouge
execute vtr exécuter
execution n exécution f
executioner n bourreau m
✔ **executive** ① n (a) cadre m; **sales** ⁓ cadre m commercial
(b) (committee) exécutif m, comité m exécutif; **party** ⁓ bureau m du parti
② adj (a) ‹post› de cadre
(b) ‹power› exécutif/-ive
exemplify vtr illustrer, exemplifier
exempt ① adj exempt/-e **(from** de)
② vtr exempter **(from** de)
exemption n exemption f; (from exam) dispense f
✔ **exercise** ① n exercice m
② vtr (a) exercer ‹body›; faire travailler ‹limb, muscles›
(b) faire preuve de ‹control, restraint›; exercer ‹power, right›
③ vi faire de l'exercice
exercise bike n (at home) vélo m d'appartement; (in gym) vélo m d'entraînement
exercise book n cahier m
exert vtr exercer ‹pressure, influence› **(on** sur); **to** ⁓ **oneself** se fatiguer
exfoliator n (Cosmet) exfoliant m
exhale vi ‹person› expirer
exhaust ① n (a) (also ⁓ **pipe**) pot m d'échappement
(b) (also ⁓ **fumes**) gaz mpl d'échappement
② vtr épuiser; ⁓**ed** épuisé/-e
exhaustion n épuisement m
exhibit ① n (a) œuvre f exposée
(b) (US) (exhibition) exposition f
② vtr exposer ‹work of art›; manifester ‹preference, sign›
✔ **exhibition** n exposition f; **art** ⁓ exposition; **to make an** ⁓ **of oneself** se donner en spectacle
exhibition centre (GB), **exhibition center** (US) n palais m des expositions
exhilarating adj ‹game› stimulant/-e; ‹experience› exaltant/-e; ‹speed› enivrant/-e
exile ① n (a) (person) exilé/-e m/f
(b) (expulsion) exil m **(from** de); **in** ⁓ en exil
② vtr exiler **(de from)**
✔ **exist** vi exister
✔ **existence** n existence f **(of** de)
existing adj ‹laws, order› existant/-e; ‹policy, management› actuel/-elle
exit ① n sortie f; **'no** ⁓' 'interdit'
② vi sortir
exodus n exode m
exotic adj exotique

✔ **expand** ① vtr développer ‹business, network, range›; élargir ‹horizon, knowledge›; étendre ‹empire›; gonfler ‹lungs›
② vi ‹business, sector, town› se développer; ‹economy› être en expansion; ‹metal› se dilater
expanse n étendue f
expansion n développement m **(in** de; **into** dans); (of economy) expansion f; (of population) accroissement m
expatriate n, adj expatrié/-e m/f
✔ **expect** ① vtr (a) s'attendre à ‹event, victory, defeat, trouble›; **to** ⁓ **the worst** s'attendre au pire; **to** ⁓ **sb to do** s'attendre à ce que qn fasse; **I** ⁓ **(that) I'll lose** je m'attends à perdre; **more than** ⁓**ed** plus que prévu
(b) s'attendre à ‹sympathy, help› **(from** de la part de)
(c) attendre ‹baby, guest›
(d) (require) demander, attendre ‹hard work› **(from** de); **I** ⁓ **you to be punctual** je vous demande d'être ponctuel
(e) (GB) (suppose) **I** ⁓ **so** je pense que oui; **I** ⁓ **he's tired** il doit être fatigué
② vi (a) **to** ⁓ **to do** s'attendre à faire
(b) (require) **I** ⁓ **to see you there** je compte bien vous y voir
(c) (be pregnant) **to be** ⁓**ing** attendre un enfant
expectant adj (a) ‹look› plein d'attente
(b) ‹mother› futur/-e ‹before n›
✔ **expectation** n (a) (prediction) prévision f; **against all** ⁓**(s)** à l'encontre des prévisions générales
(b) (hope) aspiration f, attente f; **to live up to sb's** ⁓**s** répondre à l'attente de qn
expedient adj (a) (appropriate) opportun/-e
(b) (advantageous) politique
expedition n expédition f; **to go on an** ⁓ partir en expédition
expel vtr (p prés etc **-ll-**) (gen) expulser; renvoyer ‹pupil›
expenditure n dépense f
✔ **expense** ① n (a) (cost) frais mpl; (money spent) dépense f; **at one's own** ⁓ à ses propres frais; **to go to great** ⁓ dépenser beaucoup d'argent **(to do** pour faire); **to spare no** ⁓ ne pas regarder à la dépense
(b) **at the** ⁓ **of** au détriment de ‹health, public, safety›; **at sb's** ⁓ ‹laugh, joke› aux dépens de qn
② **expenses** n pl frais mpl
expense account n frais mpl de représentation
✔ **expensive** adj (gen) cher/chère; ‹holiday, mistake› coûteux/-euse; ‹taste› de luxe
✔ **experience** ① n expérience f
② vtr connaître ‹loss, problem›; éprouver ‹emotion›
experienced adj (gen) expérimenté/-e; ‹eye› entraîné/-e

e

ℐ **experiment** ⟨1⟩ *n* expérience *f* (in en; on sur)
　　⟨2⟩ *vi* expérimenter, faire des essais
experimental *adj* expérimental/-e
experimentation *n* expériences *fpl*
ℐ **expert** ⟨1⟩ *n* spécialiste *mf* (in en, de), expert *m* (in en)
　　⟨2⟩ *adj* ⟨*opinion, advice*⟩ autorisé/-e; ⟨*witness*⟩ expert/-e; ⟨*eye*⟩ exercé/-e; **an ∼ cook** un cordon bleu
expertise *n* compétences *fpl*; (very specialized) expertise *f* (in dans le domaine de)
expire *vi* ⟨*deadline, offer*⟩ expirer; ⟨*period*⟩ arriver à terme; **my passport has ∼d** mon passeport est périmé
expiry date *n* (of credit card, permit) date *f* d'expiration
ℐ **explain** *vtr* expliquer (that que; to à)
ℐ **explanation** *n* explication *f* (of de; for à)
explicit *adj* explicite
explode ⟨1⟩ *vtr* (a) faire exploser ⟨*bomb*⟩
　　(b) pulvériser ⟨*theory, rumour, myth*⟩
　　⟨2⟩ *vi* (gen) exploser; ⟨*boiler, building, ship*⟩ sauter
exploit ⟨1⟩ *n* exploit *m*
　　⟨2⟩ *vtr* exploiter
exploitation *n* exploitation *f*
ℐ **explore** ⟨1⟩ *vtr* explorer
　　⟨2⟩ *vi* **to go exploring** partir en exploration
explorer *n* explorateur/-trice *m/f*
explosion *n* explosion *f*
explosive ⟨1⟩ *n* explosif *m*
　　⟨2⟩ *adj* ⟨*device, force*⟩ explosif/-ive; ⟨*substance*⟩ explosible
export ⟨1⟩ *n* (process) exportation *f* (of de); (product) produit *m* d'exportation
　　⟨2⟩ *vtr, vi* exporter
exporter *n* exportateur/-trice *m/f* (of de)
ℐ **expose** *vtr* (a) exposer (to à)
　　(b) (make public) révéler ⟨*identity*⟩; dénoncer ⟨*person, scandal*⟩
　　(c) **to ∼ oneself** commettre un outrage à la pudeur
ℐ **exposure** *n* (a) (of secret, crime) révélation *f*
　　(b) (to light, sun, radiation) exposition *f* (to à)
　　(c) **to die of ∼** mourir de froid
　　(d) (*also* **∼ time**) temps *m* de pose
　　(e) (picture) pose *f*
ℐ **express** ⟨1⟩ *n* rapide *m*
　　⟨2⟩ *adj* ⟨*letter, parcel*⟩ exprès; ⟨*delivery, train*⟩ rapide
　　⟨3⟩ *adv* **to send sth ∼** envoyer qch en exprès
　　⟨4⟩ *vtr* exprimer; **to ∼ oneself** s'exprimer
ℐ **expression** *n* expression *f*
expressive *adj* expressif/-ive
exquisite *adj* exquis/-e
ℐ **extend** ⟨1⟩ *vtr* (a) agrandir ⟨*house*⟩; prolonger ⟨*runway*⟩; élargir ⟨*range*⟩; **∼ed family** famille *f* étendue

(b) prolonger ⟨*visit, visa*⟩
(c) étendre ⟨*arm, leg*⟩; tendre ⟨*hand*⟩
　　⟨2⟩ *vi* s'étendre (**as far as** jusqu'à; **from** de)
extension *n* (a) (on cable, table) rallonge *f*; (to house) addition *f*
　　(b) (phone) poste *m* supplémentaire; **∼ (number)** (numéro *m* de) poste *m*
　　(c) (of deadline) délai *m* supplémentaire
extension lead *n* rallonge *f*
extensive *adj* (a) ⟨*network*⟩ vaste (*before n*); ⟨*list*⟩ long/longue (*before n*); ⟨*tests*⟩ approfondi/-e; ⟨*changes*⟩ important/-e
　　(b) ⟨*damage, loss*⟩ grave, considérable; ⟨*burns*⟩ grave
ℐ **extent** *n* (a) (of area, problem, power) étendue *f*; (of damage) ampleur *f*
　　(b) (degree) mesure *f*; **to a certain/great ∼** dans une certaine/large mesure
exterior ⟨1⟩ *n* extérieur *m* (of de)
　　⟨2⟩ *adj* extérieur/-e (**to** à)
exterminate *vtr* éliminer ⟨*vermin*⟩; exterminer ⟨*people, race*⟩
external *adj* (gen) extérieur/-e (**to** à); ⟨*surface, injury, examiner*⟩ externe
extinct *adj* ⟨*species*⟩ disparu/-e; ⟨*volcano*⟩ éteint/-e; **to become ∼** ⟨*species, animal, plant*⟩ disparaître
extinguish *vtr* éteindre ⟨*fire, cigarette*⟩
extinguisher *n* extincteur *m*
ℐ **extra** ⟨1⟩ *n* (a) (feature) option *f*; **the sunroof is an ∼** le toit ouvrant est en option
　　(b) (actor) figurant/-e *m/f*
　　⟨2⟩ *adj* supplémentaire; **an ∼ £1,000** 1 000 livres sterling de plus
　　⟨3⟩ *adv* **∼ careful** encore plus prudent (que d'habitude); **you have to pay ∼** il faut payer un supplément
extra charge *n* supplément *m*
extract ⟨1⟩ *n* extrait *m* (from de)
　　⟨2⟩ *vtr* (a) extraire (from de)
　　(b) arracher ⟨*promise*⟩ (from à)
extra-curricular *adj* parascolaire
extraordinary *adj* extraordinaire
extraterrestrial *n, adj* extraterrestre *mf*
extra time *n* (in sport) prolongation *f*; **to go into ∼** jouer les prolongations
extravagance *n* (a) (trait) prodigalité *f*
　　(b) (luxury) luxe *m*
extravagant *adj* (a) ⟨*person*⟩ dépensier/-ière; ⟨*way of life*⟩ dispendieux/-ieuse; **to be ∼ with sth** gaspiller qch
　　(b) (luxurious) luxueux/-euse
extra virgin olive oil *n* huile *f* d'olive extra vierge
extreme ⟨1⟩ *n* extrême *m*; **to go to ∼s** pousser les choses à l'extrême
　　⟨2⟩ *adj* (gen) extrême; ⟨*view, measure, reaction*⟩ extrémiste
ℐ **extremely** *adv* extrêmement
extreme sports *n pl* sports *mpl* extrêmes

ℐ indicates a very frequent word

extremism *n* extrémisme *m*

extrovert *n, adj* extraverti/-e *m/f*

⚡ **eye** ⓵ *n* (a) œil *m*; **with blue** ∼**s** aux yeux bleus; **in front of** *or* **before your (very)** ∼**s** sous vos yeux; **to keep an** ∼ **on sb/sth** surveiller qn/qch; **to have one's** ∼ **on** (watch) surveiller ⟨*person*⟩; (want) avoir envie de ⟨*house*⟩; viser ⟨*job*⟩; **to catch sb's** ∼ attirer l'attention de qn; **as far as the** ∼ **can see** à perte de vue; **to have an** ∼ **for** avoir le sens de ⟨*detail*⟩
(b) (of needle) chas *m*
⓶ *vtr* regarder
IDIOMS an ∼ **for an** ∼ œil pour œil; **to make** ∼**s at sb** faire les yeux doux à qn; **to see** ∼ **to** ∼ **with sb (about sth)** partager le point de vue de qn (au sujet de qch)

eyeball *n* globe *m* oculaire

eyebrow *n* sourcil *m*

eyebrow pencil *n* crayon *m* à sourcils

eye-catching *adj* ⟨*design, poster*⟩ attrayant/-e; ⟨*advertisement, headline*⟩ accrocheur/-euse

eyedrops *n pl* gouttes *fpl* pour les yeux

eyelash *n* cil *m*

eyelid *n* paupière *f*

eye liner *n* eye-liner *m*

eye shadow *n* fard *m* à paupières

eyesight *n* vue *f*

eye test *n* examen *m* de la vue

eyewitness *n* témoin *m* oculaire

e-zine *n* magazine *m* électronique, e-zine *m*

Ff

f, F *n* (a) (letter) f, F *m*
(b) F (Mus) fa *m*

fable *n* fable *f*

fabric *n* (a) (cloth) tissu *m*
(b) (of building) structure *f*; **the** ∼ **of society** le tissu social

fabricate *vtr* (a) inventer [qch] de toutes pièces ⟨*story, evidence*⟩
(b) fabriquer ⟨*document*⟩

fabric softener *n* assouplissant *m*

fabulous *adj* (a) fabuleux/-euse
(b) (colloq) (wonderful) sensationnel/-elle (fam)

façade, facade *n* façade *f* (of de)

⚡ **face** ⓵ *n* (a) (of person) visage *m*, figure *f*; (of animal) face *f*; **to slam the door/laugh in sb's** ∼ claquer la porte/rire au nez de qn; **to pull** *or* **make a** ∼ faire une grimace; (in disgust) faire la grimace
(b) **to lose** ∼ perdre la face; **to save** ∼ sauver la face
(c) (of clock, watch) cadran *m*; (of coin) côté *m*; (of planet) surface *f*; (of cliff, mountain) face *f*; (of playing card) face *f*; ∼ **up/down** à l'endroit/ l'envers
⓶ *vtr* (a) (look towards) ⟨*person*⟩ faire face à; ⟨*building, room*⟩ donner sur; **to** ∼ **south** ⟨*person*⟩ regarder au sud; ⟨*building*⟩ être orienté/-e au sud
(b) se trouver face à ⟨*challenge, crisis*⟩; se trouver menacé/-e de ⟨*defeat, redundancy*⟩; affronter ⟨*rival, team*⟩; **to be** ∼**d with** se trouver confronté/-e à ⟨*problem, decision*⟩
(c) (acknowledge) ∼ **the facts, you're finished!** regarde la réalité en face, tu es fini!; **let's** ∼ **it, nobody's perfect** admettons-le, personne n'est parfait
(d) (tolerate prospect) **I can't** ∼ **doing** je n'ai

pas le courage de faire; **he couldn't** ∼ **the thought of eating** l'idée de manger lui était insupportable
(e) revêtir ⟨*façade, wall*⟩ (**with** de)
⓷ **in the face of** *phr* (a) en dépit de ⟨*difficulties*⟩
(b) face à, devant ⟨*opposition, enemy, danger*⟩
⓸ **face to face** *adv* ⟨*be seated*⟩ face à face; **to come** ∼ **to** ∼ **with** se retrouver face à; **to talk to sb** ∼ **to** ∼ parler à qn en personne
■ **face up to** faire face à ⟨*problem, responsibilities*⟩

faceless *adj* anonyme

face-lift *n* lifting *m*; **to have a** ∼ se faire faire un lifting; **to give [sth] a** ∼ rénover ⟨*building*⟩; réaménager ⟨*town centre*⟩

face mask *n* masque *m* de beauté

facet *n* facette *f*

facetious *adj* ⟨*remark*⟩ facétieux/-ieuse; ⟨*person*⟩ farceur/-euse

face-to-face ⓵ *adj* **a** ∼ **discussion, a** ∼ **meeting** un face-à-face *inv*
⓶ **face to face** *adv* ▶ FACE 4

face value *n* (of coin) valeur *f* nominale; **to take [sth] at** ∼ prendre [qch] au pied de la lettre; **to take sb at** ∼ juger qn sur les apparences

facilitate *vtr* faciliter ⟨*progress, talks*⟩; favoriser ⟨*development*⟩

⚡ **facility** ⓵ *n* (a) (building) complexe *m*, installation *f*
(b) (ease) facilité *f*
(c) (feature) fonction *f*
⓶ **facilities** *n pl* (equipment) équipement *m*; (infrastructure) infrastructure *f*; **facilities** ⋯⟩

for the disabled installations *fpl* pour les handicapés; **parking facilities** parking *m*

facsimile *n* (gen) fac-similé *m*; (sculpture) reproduction *f*

⚡ **fact** *n* fait *m*; **~s and figures** les faits et les chiffres; **to know for a ~** that savoir de source sûre que; **due to the ~** that étant donné que; **in ~, as a matter of ~** en fait; **to be based on ~** être fondé/-e sur des faits réels

IDIOMS **to know the ~s of life** savoir comment les enfants viennent au monde; **the (hard) ~s of life** les réalités de la vie

fact-finding *adj* ⟨mission, tour⟩ d'information

faction *n* (group) faction *f*

⚡ **factor** *n* facteur *m*; **common ~** point *m* commun; (in mathematics) facteur commun; **protection ~** indice *m* de protection

factory *n* usine *f*

factory farming *n* élevage *m* industriel

factory shop *n* magasin *m* d'usine

factory worker *n* ouvrier/-ière *m/f* (d'usine)

fact sheet *n* bulletin *m* d'informations

factual *adj* ⟨evidence⟩ factuel/-elle; ⟨account, description⟩ basé/-e sur les faits; **~ programme** reportage *m*

faculty *n* (*pl* **-ties**) **(a)** (ability) faculté *f* (**for** de)
(b) (GB Univ) faculté *f*
(c) (US Univ, Sch) (staff) corps *m* enseignant

fad *n* **(a)** (craze) engouement *m* (**for** pour)
(b) (whim) (petite) manie *f*

fade ① *vtr* décolorer
② *vi* ⟨fabric⟩ se décolorer, se défraîchir; ⟨colour⟩ passer; ⟨lettering, smile, memory⟩ s'effacer; ⟨flowers⟩ se faner; ⟨image⟩ s'estomper; ⟨sound⟩ s'affaiblir; ⟨interest, excitement⟩ s'évanouir; ⟨hearing, light⟩ baisser

■ **fade away** ⟨sound⟩ s'éteindre; ⟨sick person⟩ dépérir

faded *adj* ⟨clothing⟩ décoloré/-e; ⟨jeans⟩ délavé/-e; ⟨photo⟩ jauni/-e; ⟨flower⟩ fané/-e

faeces, **feces** (US) *n pl* matières *fpl* fécales

⚡ **fail** ① *n* (in exam) échec *m*
② *vtr* **(a)** échouer à ⟨exam, driving test⟩; échouer en ⟨subject⟩; coller (fam) ⟨candidate, pupil⟩
(b) (omit) **to ~ to do** manquer de faire; **to ~ to mention that…** omettre de signaler que…
(c) (be unable) **to ~ to do** ne pas réussir à faire
(d) ⟨person⟩ laisser tomber ⟨friend⟩; ⟨courage⟩ manquer à ⟨person⟩; ⟨memory⟩ faire défaut à ⟨person⟩
③ *vi* **(a)** (not succeed) ne pas réussir; ⟨exam candidate, attempt, plan⟩ échouer; ⟨crop⟩ être mauvais/-e; **if all else ~s** en dernier recours

(b) ⟨eyesight, hearing, light⟩ baisser; ⟨health⟩ décliner
(c) ⟨brakes⟩ lâcher; ⟨power⟩ être coupé/-e; ⟨heart⟩ lâcher
④ **without fail** *phr* ⟨arrive, do⟩ sans faute; ⟨happen⟩ à coup sûr

failing ① *n* défaut *m*
② *prep* **~ that**, **~ this** sinon

⚡ **failure** *n* **(a)** (lack of success) échec *m* (**in** à)
(b) (person) raté/-e *m/f* (fam); (venture or event) échec *m*
(c) (of engine, machine) panne *f*
(d) (Med) défaillance *f*
(e) (omission) **~ to comply with the rules** non-respect *m* de la réglementation; **~ to pay** non-paiement *m*

faint ① *adj* **(a)** ⟨smell, accent, breeze⟩ léger/-ère; ⟨sound, voice, protest⟩ faible; ⟨markings⟩ à peine visible; ⟨recollection⟩ vague; **I haven't the ~est idea** je n'en ai pas la moindre idée
(b) **to feel ~** se sentir mal, défaillir
② *vi* s'évanouir (**from** sous l'effet de)

fainthearted *n* **the ~** (cowardly) les timorés *mpl*; (over-sensitive) les natures *fpl* sensibles

⚡ **fair** ① *n* (funfair, market) foire *f*; (for charity) kermesse *f*; **trade ~** foire commerciale
② *adj* **(a)** (just) ⟨arrangement, person, trial, wage⟩ équitable (**to** pour); ⟨comment, decision, point⟩ juste; **it's only ~ that she should be first** ce n'est que justice qu'elle soit la première; **it isn't ~** ce n'est pas juste
(b) (quite good) assez bon/bonne
(c) **a ~ number of** un bon nombre de; **the house was a ~ size** la maison était de bonne taille
(d) ⟨weather⟩ beau/belle (**before** *n*); ⟨wind⟩ favorable
(e) ⟨hair⟩ blond/-e; ⟨complexion⟩ clair/-e
(f) **with her own ~ hands** de ses blanches mains; **the ~ sex** le beau sexe
③ *adv* ⟨play⟩ franc jeu

IDIOM **to win ~ and square** remporter une victoire indiscutable

fairground *n* champ *m* de foire

fair-haired *adj* blond/-e

⚡ **fairly** *adv* **(a)** (quite, rather) assez; ⟨sure⟩ pratiquement
(b) (justly) ⟨obtain, win⟩ honnêtement

fair-minded *adj* impartial/-e

fairness *n* **(a)** (of person) équité *f*; (of judgment) impartialité *f*; **in all ~** en toute justice
(b) (of complexion) blancheur *f*; (of hair) blondeur *f*

fair play *n* **to have a sense of ~** jouer franc jeu, être fair-play; **to ensure ~** faire respecter les règles du jeu

fairy *n* fée *f*

fairy story, **fairy tale** *n* conte *m* de fées

⚡ **faith** *n* **(a)** (confidence) confiance *f*; **I have no ~ in her** elle ne m'inspire pas confiance; **in**

⚡ indicates a very frequent word

good ∼ en toute bonne foi
(b) (belief) foi *f* (in en); **the Muslim** ∼ la foi
musulmane
faithful 1 *n* **the** ∼ les fidèles *mpl*
2 *adj* fidèle **(to** à)
faithfully *adv* fidèlement; **yours** ∼ (in letter)
veuillez agréer, Monsieur/Madame, mes/nos
salutations distinguées
faith healer *n* guérisseur *m*
faith healing *n* guérison *f* par la foi
fake 1 *n* **(a)** (jewel, work of art, note) faux *m*
(b) (person) imposteur *m*
2 *adj* faux/fausse (*before n*)
3 *vtr* contrefaire ‹*signature, document*›;
falsifier ‹*results*›; feindre ‹*emotion, illness*›
4 *vi* faire semblant
falcon *n* faucon *m*
Falklands *pr n pl* (*also* **Falkland**
Islands) **the** ∼ les îles *fpl* Malouines
✓ᶠ **fall** 1 *n* **(a)** (gen) chute *f* (**from** de); (in
wrestling) tombé *m*
(b) (decrease) baisse *f* (**in** de); (more drastic)
chute *f* (**in** de)
(c) (in pitch) descente *f*
(d) (of government) chute *f*; (of monarchy)
renversement *m*
(e) (US) (autumn) automne *m*
2 **falls** *n pl* chutes *fpl*
3 *vi* (*prét* **fell**, *pp* **fallen**) **(a)** (gen)
tomber (**from, off, out of** de; **into** dans); **to** ∼
10 metres tomber de 10 mètres; **to** ∼ **down**
tomber dans ‹*hole, stairs*›; **to** ∼ **on** *or* **to the**
floor *or* **the ground** tomber par terre; **to** ∼ **at**
sb's feet se jeter aux pieds de qn; **to** ∼ **from**
power tomber
(b) ‹*quality, standard, level*› diminuer;
‹*temperature, price, production, number*›
baisser (**by** de); **to** ∼ **to/from** descendre à/de
■ **fall apart (a)** ‹*bike, table*› être délabré/-e;
‹*shoes*› être usé/-e; ‹*car, house*› tomber en
ruine
(b) ‹*country*› se désagréger; ‹*person*› craquer
(fam)
■ **fall back** reculer; (Mil) se replier
■ **fall back on** avoir recours à ‹*savings,
parents*›
■ **fall behind** prendre du retard; **to** ∼
behind with (GB) *or* **in** (US) prendre du retard
dans ‹*work, project*›; être en retard pour
‹*payments, rent*›
■ **fall down (a)** ‹*person, poster*› tomber; ‹*tent,
scaffolding*› s'effondrer
(b) (GB) ‹*argument, comparison*› faiblir
■ **fall for:** 1 ¶ ∼ **for [sth]** se laisser prendre
à ‹*trick, story*›
2 ¶ ∼ **for [sb]** tomber amoureux/-euse de
■ **fall in (a)** ‹*walls, roof*› s'écrouler,
s'effondrer
(b) ‹*soldiers*› former les rangs
■ **fall off (a)** ‹*person, hat, label*› tomber
(b) ‹*attendance, sales, output*› diminuer;
‹*quality*› baisser; ‹*support*› retomber
■ **fall open** ‹*book*› tomber ouvert/-e; ‹*robe*›

s'entrebâiller
■ **fall out (a)** tomber; **his hair is** ∼**ing out** il
perd ses cheveux
(b) (quarrel) se brouiller (**over** à propos de;
with avec)
■ **fall over:** 1 ¶ ∼ **over** ‹*person*› tomber (par
terre); ‹*object*› se renverser
2 ¶ ∼ **over [sth]** trébucher sur ‹*object*›
■ **fall through** ‹*plans, deal*› échouer
fallacy *n* erreur *f*
fallible *adj* faillible
fallout *n* retombées *fpl*
false *adj* faux/fausse
false alarm *n* fausse alerte *f*
false bottom *n* (in bag, box) double fond *m*
falsely *adv* **(a)** (wrongly) faussement;
(mistakenly) à tort
(b) ‹*smile, laugh*› avec affectation
false pretences *n pl* **on** *or* **under** ∼ en
utilisant un subterfuge; (by an action) par des
moyens frauduleux
false start *n* faux départ *m*
false teeth *n pl* dentier *m*
falsify *vtr* falsifier
falsity *n* fausseté *f*
falter *vi* **(a)** ‹*person, courage*› faiblir
(b) (when speaking) ‹*person*› bafouiller; ‹*voice*›
trembloter
(c) (when walking) ‹*person*› chanceler; ‹*footstep*›
hésiter
faltering *adj* ‹*economy, demand*› en déclin;
‹*voice*› hésitant/-e
fame *n* renommée *f* (**as** en tant que); ∼ **and**
fortune la gloire et la fortune
✓ᶠ **familiar** *adj* familier/-ière (**to** à); **her face**
looked ∼ **to me** son visage m'était familier;
that name sounds ∼ ce nom me dit quelque
chose; **it's a** ∼ **story** c'est un scénario connu;
to be ∼ **with sth** connaître qch
familiarity *n* familiarité *f* (**with** avec)
familiarize 1 *vtr* **to** ∼ **sb with**
familiariser qn avec
2 *v refl* **to** ∼ **oneself with** se familiariser
avec ‹*system, work*›; s'habituer à ‹*person,
place*›
✓ᶠ **family** *n* famille *f*; **this must run in the** ∼ ça
doit être de famille
family name *n* nom *m* de famille
family planning *n* planning *m* familial
family tree *n* arbre *m* généalogique
family unit *n* cellule *f* familiale
famine *n* famine *f*
famished *adj* (colloq) **I'm** ∼ je meurs de
faim
✓ᶠ **famous** *adj* (gen) célèbre (**for** pour); ‹*school,
university*› réputé/-e (**for** pour)
✓ᶠ **fan** 1 *n* **(a)** (of jazz) mordu/-e *m/f* (fam); (of
star, actor) fan *mf* (fam); (Sport) supporter *m*
(b) (for cooling) (mechanical) ventilateur *m*;
(hand-held) éventail *m*   ⋯>

2 *vtr* (*p prés etc* **-nn-**) attiser ‹*fire*›; **to ~ one's face** s'éventer le visage

■ **fan out**: 1 ¶ **~ out** ‹*police, troops*› se déployer (en éventail)

2 ¶ **~ [sth] out** ouvrir [qch] en éventail ‹*cards, papers*›

fanatic *n* fanatique *mf*

fanaticism *n* fanatisme *m*

fan belt *n* courroie *f* de ventilateur

fancy 1 *n* (a) (liking) **to take sb's ~** ‹*object*› faire envie à qn; **to take a ~ to sb** s'attacher à qn; (sexually) (GB) s'enticher de qn

(b) (whim) caprice *m*; **as the ~ takes me** comme ça me prend

(c) (fantasy) imagination *f*; **a flight of ~** une lubie

2 *adj* ‹*equipment*› sophistiqué/-e; ‹*food, hotel, restaurant*› de luxe; ‹*paper, box*› fantaisie *inv*; ‹*clothes*› chic

3 *vtr* (a) (colloq) (want) avoir (bien) envie de ‹*food, drink, object*›; **what do you ~ for lunch?** qu'est-ce qui te plairait pour le déjeuner?

(b) (GB) (colloq) **she fancies him** elle s'est entichée de lui

(c) **~ seeing you here!** (colloq) tiens donc, toi ici?

(d) (Sport) voir [qn/qch] gagnant ‹*athlete, horse*›

fancy dress *n* (GB) déguisement *m*; **in ~** déguisé/-e

fancy dress party *n* bal *m* costumé

fang *n* (of dog, wolf) croc *m*; (of snake) crochet *m* (à venin)

fan mail *n* lettres *fpl* envoyées par des admirateurs

fantasize *vi* fantasmer (**about** sur); **to ~ about doing** rêver de faire

fantastic *adj* (a) (colloq) (wonderful) merveilleux/-euse, super *inv* (fam)

(b) (unrealistic) ‹*story*› invraisemblable

(c) (colloq) (huge) ‹*profit*› fabuleux/-euse; ‹*speed, increase*› vertigineux/-euse

(d) (magical) fantastique

fantasy *n* (a) (dream) rêve *m*; (in psychology) fantasme *m*

(b) (fiction) fantastique *m*

fanzine *n* magazine *m* des fans, fanzine *m*

FAQ *n* (*abbr* = **frequently asked questions**) FAQ *f*, foire *f* aux questions

✍ **far** 1 *adv* (a) (in space) loin; **~ off, ~ away** au loin; **is it ~ to York?** est-ce que York est loin d'ici?; **how ~ is it to Leeds?** combien y a-t-il (de kilomètres) jusqu'à Leeds?; **how ~ is Glasgow from London?** Glasgow est à quelle distance de Londres?; **as ~ as** jusqu'à

(b) (in time) **as ~ back as 1965** déjà en 1965; **as ~ back as he can remember** d'aussi loin qu'il s'en souvienne; **the holidays are not ~ off** c'est bientôt les vacances

(c) (very much) bien; **~ better** bien mieux; **~ too fast** bien trop vite

(d) **how ~ have they got?** où en sont-ils?; **as ~ as possible** autant que possible, dans la mesure du possible; **as ~ as we know** pour autant que nous le sachions; **as ~ as I am concerned** quant à moi

(e) **to go too ~** aller trop loin; **to push sb too ~** pousser qn à bout

2 *adj* (a) **the ~ north/south (of)** l'extrême nord/sud (de); **the ~ east/west (of)** tout à fait à l'est/l'ouest (de)

(b) autre; **at the ~ end of the room** à l'autre bout de la pièce; **on the ~ side of the wall** de l'autre côté du mur

(c) (of party) **the ~ right/left** l'extrême droite/gauche

3 **by far** *phr* de loin

4 **far from** *phr* loin de; **~ from satisfied** loin d'être satisfait/-e

5 **so far** *phr* (a) (up till now) jusqu'ici, jusqu'à présent; **so ~, so good** pour l'instant tout va bien

(b) (up to a point) **you can only trust him so ~** tu ne peux pas lui faire entièrement confiance

IDIOMS **not to be ~ off** *or* **out** *or* **wrong** ne pas être loin du compte; **~ and wide** partout; **to be a ~ cry from** être bien loin de; **she will go ~** elle ira loin; **this wine won't go very ~** on ne va pas aller loin avec ce vin

faraway *adj* lointain/-e

farce *n* farce *f*

farcical *adj* ridicule

fare *n* (on bus, underground) prix *m* du ticket; **half/full ~** demi-/plein tarif *m*

Far East *pr n* Extrême-Orient *m*

farewell *n* adieu *m*

far-fetched *adj* tiré/-e par les cheveux (fam)

✍ **farm** 1 *n* ferme *f*

2 *vtr* cultiver, exploiter ‹*land*›

■ **farm out**: **~ out [sth]** sous-traiter ‹*work*› (**to** à)

✍ **farmer** *n* (gen) fermier *m*; (in official terminology) agriculteur *m*; (arable) cultivateur *m*; **pig ~** éleveur *m* de porcs

farmers' market *n* marché *m* de producteurs

farming *n* (profession) agriculture *f*; (of land) exploitation *f*; **sheep ~** élevage *m* de moutons

farmyard *n* cour *f* de ferme

far-off *adj* lointain/-e

far-reaching *adj* ‹*effect*› considérable; ‹*change, reform*› radical/-e; ‹*plan, proposal*› d'une portée considérable

far-sighted *adj* (a) (prudent) ‹*person, policy*› prévoyant/-e

(b) (US) ‹*person*› presbyte

farther *adj, adv* (*comparative of* **far**) = FURTHER 1A, B 2B

✍ indicates a very frequent word

farthest = FURTHEST

fascinate *vtr* (interest) passionner; (stronger) fasciner

fascinating *adj* ‹book, discussion› passionnant/-e; ‹person› fascinant/-e

fascination *n* passion *f* (**with, for** pour)

fascism *n* fascisme *m*

fascist *n, adj* fasciste *mf*

⚜ **fashion** ⟨1⟩ *n* (a) mode *f* (**for** de); **in ~** à la mode; **to go out of ~** se démoder, passer de mode; **to be all the ~** faire fureur
(b) (manner) façon *f*, manière *f*; **after a ~** plus ou moins bien
⟨2⟩ *vtr* façonner ‹clay, wood› (**into** en); fabriquer ‹object› (**out of, from** de)

fashionable *adj* ‹clothes› à la mode (**among, with** parmi); ‹resort, restaurant› chic (**among, with** parmi)

fashion designer *n* modéliste *mf*; (world-famous) grand couturier *m*

fashion house *n* maison *f* de couture

fashion model *n* mannequin *m*

fashion show *n* présentation *f* de collection

⚜ **fast** ⟨1⟩ *n* jeûne *m*
⟨2⟩ *adj* (a) rapide; **to be a ~ reader/runner** lire/courir vite
(b) (ahead of time) **my watch is ~** ma montre avance; **you're five minutes ~** ta montre avance de cinq minutes
⟨3⟩ *adv* (a) vite, rapidement; **how ~ can you run?** est-ce que tu cours vite?
(b) ‹hold› ferme; ‹stuck› bel et bien; ‹shut› bien; **to be ~ asleep** dormir à poings fermés

fasten ⟨1⟩ *vtr* (a) fermer ‹lid, case›; attacher ‹belt, necklace›; boutonner ‹coat›
(b) fixer ‹notice, shelf› (**to** à; **onto** sur); attacher ‹lead, rope› (**to** à)
⟨2⟩ *vi* ‹box› se fermer; ‹necklace, skirt› s'attacher

fastener *n* (gen) attache *f*; (hook) agrafe *f*; (clasp) fermoir *m*

fast food *n* restauration *f* rapide

fast food restaurant *n* fast-food *m*, restovite *m*

fast-forward ⟨1⟩ *n* avance *f* rapide
⟨2⟩ *vtr* faire avancer rapidement ‹tape›

fast-growing *adj* en pleine expansion

fast lane *n* voie *f* de dépassement

fast track ⟨1⟩ *n* promotion *f* accélérée
⟨2⟩ **fast-track** *vtr* former [qn] de façon accélérée

fat ⟨1⟩ *n* (a) (in diet) matières *fpl* grasses; **animal ~s** graisses *fpl* animales
(b) (on meat) gras *m*
(c) (for cooking) matière *f* grasse
(d) (in body) graisse *f*
⟨2⟩ *adj* (a) ‹person, animal, body, bottom› gros/grosse (*before n*); **to get ~** grossir
(b) ‹wallet› rebondi/-e; ‹envelope, file, magazine› épais/épaisse

(c) ‹profit, cheque› gros/grosse (*before n*)

fatal *adj* ‹accident, injury› mortel/-elle (**to** pour); ‹flaw, mistake› fatal/-e; ‹decision› funeste; ‹day, hour› fatidique

fatalist *n* fataliste *mf*

fatality *n* (person killed) mort *m*

fatally *adv* (a) ‹wounded› mortellement
(b) ‹flawed› irrémédiablement

fate *n* sort *m*

fateful *adj* ‹decision› fatal/-e; ‹day› fatidique

fat-free *adj* sans matières grasses

⚜ **father** ⟨1⟩ *n* père *m*
⟨2⟩ *vtr* engendrer ‹child›

Father Christmas *n* (GB) le père Noël

father-in-law *n* (*pl* ~s-in-law) beau-père *m*

fatherly *adj* paternel/-elle

fathom ⟨1⟩ *n* brasse *f* anglaise (= 1.83 m)
⟨2⟩ *vtr* (also ~ **out** (GB)) comprendre

fatigue *n* (a) (of person) épuisement *m*
(b) **metal ~** fatigue *f* du métal
(c) (US Mil) corvée *f*

fatten *vtr* (also ~ **up**) engraisser ‹animal›; faire grossir ‹person›

fattening *adj* ‹food, drink› qui fait grossir

fatty *adj* ‹tissue, deposit› graisseux/-euse; ‹food, meat› gras/grasse

fatuous *adj* stupide

faucet *n* (US) robinet *m*

⚜ **fault** ⟨1⟩ *n* (a) (flaw) défaut *m* (**in** dans); **he's always finding ~** il trouve toujours quelque chose à redire
(b) (responsibility) faute *f*; **to be sb's ~** être (de) la faute de qn; **it's my own ~** c'est de ma faute
(c) (in tennis) ~! faute!
(d) (in earth) faille *f*
⟨2⟩ *vtr* prendre [qn/qch] en défaut; **it cannot be ~ed** c'est irréprochable

faultless *adj* ‹performance, manners› impeccable; ‹taste› irréprochable

faulty *adj* ‹wiring, machine› défectueux/-euse

fauna *n* (*pl* ~s *ou* -ae) faune *f*

faux pas *n* (*pl* ~) impair *m*

⚜ **favour** (GB), **favor** (US) ⟨1⟩ *n* (a) (kindness) service *m*; **to do sb a ~** rendre service à qn; **to return a** *or* **the ~** rendre la pareille
(b) **to be in sb's ~** ‹situation› être avantageux/-euse pour qn; ‹financial rates, wind› être favorable à qn
(c) **to win/lose ~ with sb** s'attirer/perdre les bonnes grâces de qn
⟨2⟩ *vtr* (a) (prefer) être pour ‹method, solution›; être partisan de ‹political party›
(b) (benefit) ‹circumstances› favoriser ‹person›; ‹law› privilégier ‹person›
⟨3⟩ **in favour of** *phr* (a) (on the side of) en faveur de; **to be in ~ of sb/sth** être pour qn/qch
(b) (to the advantage of) **to work in sb's ~** ⋯⫶

avantager qn; **to decide in sb's** ~ (Law)
donner gain de cause à qn
(c) (out of preference for) ‹reject› au profit de
favourable (GB), **favorable** (US) adj
‹conditions, impression, reply› favorable **(to**
à); ‹result, sign› bon/bonne **(before** n)
favourably (GB), **favorably** (US) adv
‹speak, write› en termes favorables; ‹look on›
d'un œil favorable; **to compare** ~ **with sth**
soutenir la comparaison avec qch
ℐ **favourite** (GB), **favorite** (US) ⓵ n (gen)
préféré/-e m/f; (Sport) favori/-ite m/f
⓶ adj préféré/-e, favori/-ite
favouritism (GB), **favoritism** (US) n
favoritisme m
fawn ⓵ n (Zool) faon m
⓶ vtr **to** ~ **on sb** flagorner qn
fax ⓵ n (pl ~**es**) **(a)** (also ~ **message**)
télécopie f, fax m
(b) (also ~ **machine**) télécopieur m, fax m
⓶ vtr télécopier, faxer ‹document›; envoyer
une télécopie or un fax à
fax number n numéro m de télécopie or
de fax
faze vtr (colloq) dérouter
ℐ **fear** ⓵ n **(a)** (fright) peur f
(b) (apprehension) crainte f **(for** pour)
(c) (possibility) **there's no** ~ **of him** or **his
being late** il n'y a pas de danger qu'il soit
en retard
⓶ vtr craindre; **to** ~ **the worst** craindre le
pire, s'attendre au pire
⓷ vi **to** ~ **for sb/sth** craindre pour qn/qch
fearless adj sans peur, intrépide
feasible adj **(a)** ‹project› réalisable
(b) ‹excuse, explanation› plausible
feast ⓵ n (meal) festin m; (religious) fête f
⓶ vi se régaler **(on** de)
feat n exploit m; **it was no mean** ~ cela
n'a pas été une mince affaire; **a** ~ **of
engineering** une prouesse technologique
feather n plume f
ℐ **feature** ⓵ n **(a)** (distinctive characteristic) trait
m, caractéristique f
(b) (aspect) aspect m, côté m
(c) (of face) trait m
(d) (of car, computer, product) accessoire m
(e) (report) (in paper) article m de fond **(on**
sur); (on TV, radio) reportage m **(on** sur)
⓶ vtr ‹film, magazine› présenter ‹story,
star›; ‹advert, poster› représenter ‹person›
⓷ vi **(a)** (figure) figurer
(b) ‹performer› jouer **(in** dans)
feature film n long métrage m
ℐ **February** n février m
ℐ **federal** adj fédéral/-e
federation n fédération f
fed up adj (colloq) **to be** ~ en avoir marre
(fam) **(of** de)

ℐ **fee** n **(a)** (for service) honoraires mpl; **school**
~**s** frais mpl de scolarité
(b) (for admission) droit m d'entrée; (for
membership) cotisation f
feeble adj (gen) faible; ‹excuse› peu
convaincant/-e; ‹joke, attempt› médiocre
ℐ **feed** ⓵ n (for animals) ration f de nourriture;
(for baby) (breast) tétée f; (bottle) biberon m
⓶ vtr (prét, pp **fed**) **(a)** nourrir ‹animal,
plant, person› **(on** de); donner à manger à
‹pet›; ravitailler ‹army›
(b) (supply) alimenter ‹machine›; mettre des
pièces dans ‹meter›; faire passer ‹ball› **(to** à);
to ~ **sth into** mettre or introduire qch dans
feedback n **(a)** (from people) remarques fpl
(on sur; **from** de la part de)
(b) (on hi-fi) réaction f parasite
feeding bottle n biberon m
ℐ **feel** ⓵ n **(a)** (atmosphere) atmosphère f
(b) (sensation) sensation f
(c) to get the ~ **of** se faire à ‹controls,
system›; **to have a** ~ **for language** bien savoir
manier la langue
⓶ vtr (prét, pp **felt**) **(a)** éprouver ‹affection,
desire, pride›; ressentir ‹hostility, obligation,
effects›
(b) (believe) **to** ~ **(that)** estimer que
(c) sentir ‹blow, draught, heat›; ressentir
‹ache, stiffness, effects›
(d) (touch) tâter ‹washing, cloth›; palper
‹patient, shoulder, parcel›; **to** ~ **one's way**
avancer à tâtons; (figurative) tâter le terrain
(e) avoir conscience de ‹presence, tension›
⓷ vi (prét, pp **felt**) **(a)** se sentir ‹sad, happy,
nervous, safe, ill, tired›; être ‹sure, surprised›;
avoir l'impression d'être ‹trapped, betrayed›;
to ~ **afraid/ashamed** avoir peur/honte; **to**
~ **hot/thirsty** avoir chaud/soif; **to** ~ **as if** or
as though avoir l'impression que; **she isn't**
~**ing herself today** elle n'est pas dans son
assiette aujourd'hui (fam)
(b) (seem) être ‹cold, smooth›; avoir l'air
‹eerie›; **it** ~**s odd** ça fait drôle; **it** ~**s like
(a) Sunday** on se croirait un dimanche
(c) (want) **to** ~ **like sth** avoir envie de qch; **I** ~
like a drink je prendrais bien un verre
(d) to ~ **(around** or **about) in** fouiller dans
‹bag, pocket, drawer›; **to** ~ **along** tâtonner le
long de ‹edge, wall›
■ **feel for:** ⓵ ¶ ~ **(around) for [sth]** chercher
[qch] à tâtons
⓶ ¶ ~ **for [sb]** plaindre
■ **feel up to:** ¶ ~ **up to (doing) sth** se sentir
d'attaque (fam) or assez bien pour (faire) qch
feelgood adj optimiste; **to play on the**
~ **factor** essayer de créer un sentiment de
bien-être
ℐ **feeling** n **(a)** (emotion) sentiment m; **to hurt
sb's** ~**s** blesser qn
(b) (opinion, belief) sentiment m; ~**s are
running high** les esprits s'échauffent
(c) (sensitivity) sensibilité f; **to speak with
great** ~ parler avec beaucoup de passion

ℐ indicates a very frequent word

(d) (impression) impression *f*; **I had a ∼ you'd say that** je sentais que tu allais dire ça; **I've got a bad ∼ about this** j'ai le pressentiment que cela va mal se passer

(e) (physical sensation) sensation *f*; **a dizzy ∼** une sensation de vertige

fee-paying *adj* ‹*school*› payant/-e

feign *vtr* feindre ‹*innocence, surprise*›; simuler ‹*illness, sleep*›

fell ⟨1⟩ *n* montagne *f*
⟨2⟩ *vtr* abattre ‹*tree*›; assommer ‹*person*›
IDIOM **in one ∼ swoop** d'un seul coup

✧ **fellow** ⟨1⟩ *n* **(a)** (colloq) (man) type *m* (fam), homme *m*
(b) (of society, association) membre *m* (**of** de)
(c) (GB) (lecturer) membre *m* (du corps enseignant) d'un collège universitaire
(d) (US) (researcher) universitaire *mf* titulaire d'une bourse de recherche
⟨2⟩ *adj* **her ∼ teachers** ses collègues professeurs; **a ∼ Englishman** un compatriote anglais

fellowship *n* **(a)** (companionship) camaraderie *f*
(b) (association) association *f*

felony *n* crime *m*

felt *n* feutre *m*

felt-tip (pen) *n* feutre *m*

✧ **female** ⟨1⟩ *n* **(a)** (Bot, Zool) femelle *f*
(b) (woman) femme *f*
⟨2⟩ *adj* **(a)** (Bot, Zool) femelle; **∼ rabbit** lapine *f*
(b) ‹*population, role*› féminin/-e; ‹*voice*› de femme; **∼ student** étudiante *f*
(c) ‹*plug, socket*› femelle

feminine ⟨1⟩ *n* féminin *m*
⟨2⟩ *adj* féminin/-e

feminist *n, adj* féministe *mf*

fence ⟨1⟩ *n* **(a)** clôture *f*
(b) (in showjumping) obstacle *m*; (in horseracing) haie *f*
⟨2⟩ *vtr* clôturer ‹*area, garden*›
IDIOM **to sit on the ∼** ne pas prendre position

fencing *n* escrime *f*

fend *vi* **to ∼ for oneself** se débrouiller (tout seul/toute seule)

■ **fend off** repousser ‹*attacker*›; parer ‹*blow*›; écarter ‹*question*›

fender *n* **(a)** (for fire) garde-cendre *m*
(b) (US Aut) aile *f*

fennel *n* fenouil *m*

fern *n* fougère *f*

ferocious *adj* ‹*animal*› féroce; ‹*attack*› sauvage; ‹*heat*› accablant/-e

ferret *n* furet *m*

■ **ferret about** fureter, fouiller (**in** dans)

ferry ⟨1⟩ *n* (long-distance) ferry *m*; (over short distances) bac *m*
⟨2⟩ *vtr* transporter ‹*passenger, goods*›

fertile *adj* ‹*land, imagination*› fertile; ‹*human, animal, egg*› fécond/-e

fertility treatment *n* traitement *m* contre la stérilité

fertilize *vtr* fertiliser ‹*land*›; féconder ‹*animal, plant, egg*›

fertilizer *n* engrais *m*

fervent *adj* ‹*admirer*› fervent/-e

fester *vi* ‹*wound, sore*› suppurer

✧ **festival** *n* (gen) fête *f*; (arts event) festival *m*

festivity *n* réjouissance *f*

fetch *vtr* **(a)** aller chercher; **∼!** (to dog) rapporte!
(b) ‹*goods*› rapporter; **to ∼ a good price** rapporter un bon prix; **these vases can ∼ up to £600** le prix de ces vases peut atteindre 600 livres sterling

fetching *adj* ravissant/-e

fête *n* (church, village) kermesse *f* (paroissiale)

fetus (US) = FOETUS

feud ⟨1⟩ *n* querelle *f*
⟨2⟩ *vi* se quereller

feudal *adj* féodal/-e

fever *n* fièvre *f*; **to have a ∼** avoir de la fièvre; **gold ∼** la fièvre de l'or

feverish *adj* ‹*person, eyes*› fiévreux/-euse; ‹*dreams*› délirant/-e; ‹*excitement, activity*› fébrile

fever pitch *n* **to bring a crowd to ∼** déchaîner une foule; **our excitement had reached ∼** notre excitation était à son comble

✧ **few**

■ **Note** When *a few* is used as a pronoun and if the sentence does not specify what it refers to, the pronoun *en* (= *of them*) must be added before the verb in French: *there were only a few* = il n'y en avait que quelques-uns/quelques-unes.

⟨1⟩ *det* **(a)** (not many) peu de; **∼ visitors/letters** peu de visiteurs/lettres
(b) (couple of) **every ∼ days** tous les deux ou trois jours; **the first ∼ weeks** les premières semaines

⟨2⟩ *pron, quantif* peu; **∼ of us succeeded** peu d'entre nous ont réussi

⟨3⟩ **a few** *det, quantif, pron* **(a)** (as determiner, quantifier) quelques; **a ∼ people** quelques personnes; **quite a ∼ people** pas mal (fam) de gens, un bon nombre de personnes; **a ∼ of the soldiers** quelques soldats; **a ∼ of us** un certain nombre d'entre nous
(b) (as pronoun) quelques-uns/quelques-unes; **I would like a ∼ more** j'en voudrais quelques-uns/quelques-unes de plus; **I only need a ∼** il ne m'en faut que quelques-uns/quelques-unes
IDIOM **they are ∼ and far between** ils sont rarissimes

fewer ⟨1⟩ *det* moins de; **∼ and ∼ pupils** de moins en moins d'élèves
⟨2⟩ *pron* (*comparative of* **few**) moins; **∼** ⋯▸

than 50 people moins de 50 personnes; **no ∼ than** pas moins de

fewest *det* le moins de

fiancé *n* fiancé *m*

fiancée *n* fiancée *f*

fibre (GB), **fiber** (US) *n* (a) (gen) fibre *f*
(b) (in diet) fibres *fpl*

fibreglass (GB), **fiberglass** (US) *n* fibres *fpl* de verre

fibre optic (GB), **fiber optic** (US) *adj* ‹cable› à fibres optiques; ‹link› par fibres optiques

fickle *adj* ‹lover, friend› inconstant/-e; ‹fate, public opinion› changeant/-e; ‹weather› capricieux/-ieuse

fiction *n* (a) (genre) le roman
(b) (invention) fiction *f*

fictional *adj* ‹character, event› imaginaire

fictionalize *vtr* romancer

fictitious *adj* (a) (false) ‹name, address› fictif/-ive
(b) (imaginary) imaginaire

fiddle ⊞ *vtr* (colloq) falsifier ‹tax return, figures›
⊡ *vi* (a) (fidget) **to ∼ with sth** tripoter qch
(b) (adjust) **to ∼ with** tourner ‹knobs, controls›

fidelity *n* fidélité *f* (**of** de; **to** à)

fidget *vi* ne pas tenir en place

☞ **field** ⊞ *n* (a) (gen) champ *m* (**of** de); (sports ground) terrain *m*; **football ∼** terrain de football
(b) (of knowledge) domaine *m* (**of** de)
⊡ *adj* (a) ‹hospital› de campagne
(b) ‹test, study› sur le terrain; ‹work› de terrain

field day *n* (a) (school trip) sortie *f* (éducative)
(b) (US) (sports day) journée *f* sportive
IDIOM to have a ∼ (gen) s'amuser comme un fou/une folle; ‹press, critics› jubiler; (make money) ‹shopkeepers› faire d'excellentes affaires

field trip *n* (one day) sortie *f* éducative; (longer) voyage *m* d'études

fieldwork *n* travail *m* de terrain

fierce *adj* ‹animal, expression, person› féroce; ‹battle, storm› violent/-e; ‹competition› acharné/-e; ‹flames, heat› intense

fiercely *adv* ‹oppose› avec acharnement; ‹fight› sauvagement; ‹shout› violemment; ‹burn› avec intensité; ‹competitive, critical› extrêmement; ‹determined, loyal› farouchement

fifteen *n, pron, det* quinze *m inv*

fifteenth ⊞ *n* (a) (in order) quinzième *mf*
(b) (of month) quinze *m inv*
(c) (fraction) quinzième *m*
⊡ *adj, adv* quinzième

fifth ⊞ *n* (a) (in order) cinquième *mf*

☞ indicates a very frequent word

(b) (of month) cinq *m*
(c) (fraction) cinquième *m*
⊡ *adj, adv* cinquième

fifties *n pl* (a) (era) **the ∼** les années *fpl* cinquante
(b) (age) **to be in one's ∼** avoir entre cinquante et soixante ans

fiftieth *n, adj, adv* cinquantième *mf*

fifty *n, pron, det* cinquante *m inv*

fifty-fifty ⊞ *adj* **to have a ∼ chance** avoir une chance sur deux (**of doing** de faire)
⊡ *adv* **to share sth ∼** partager qch moitié-moitié; **to go ∼** faire moitié-moitié

fig *n* figue *f*

☞ **fight** ⊞ *n* (a) (gen) bagarre *f* (**between** entre; **over** pour); (Mil) bataille *f* (**between** entre; **for** pour); (in boxing) combat *m* (**between** entre)
(b) (struggle) lutte *f* (**against** contre; **for** pour, **to do** pour faire)
(c) (argument) dispute *f* (**over** au sujet de; **with** avec)
⊡ *vtr* (*prét, pp* **fought**) (a) se battre contre ‹person›
(b) lutter contre ‹disease, opponent, emotion, proposal›; combattre ‹fire›; mener ‹campaign, war› (**against** contre); **to ∼ one's way through** se frayer un passage dans ‹crowd›
⊟ *vi* (*prét, pp* **fought**) (a) (gen, Mil) se battre
(b) (campaign) lutter
(c) (argue) se quereller (**over** à propos de)
■ **fight back**: ⊞ ¶ **∼ back** se défendre
⊡ ¶ **∼ back [sth]** refréner ‹tears, fear, anger›
■ **fight off**: ⊞ ¶ **∼ off [sth], ∼ [sth] off** se libérer de ‹attacker›; repousser ‹attack›
⊡ ¶ **∼ off [sth]** lutter contre ‹illness›; rejeter ‹criticism, proposal›

fighter *n* (a) (Sport) boxeur *m*
(b) (determined person) lutteur/-euse *m/f*
(c) (*also* **∼ plane**) avion *m* de chasse

fighting ⊞ *n* (gen) bagarre *f*; (Mil) combat *m*
⊡ *adj* (a) ‹unit, force› de combat
(b) ‹talk› agressif/-ive

fighting chance *n* **to have a ∼** avoir de bonnes chances

fighting fit *adj* **to be ∼** être en pleine forme

figment *n* **a ∼ of your imagination** un produit de ton imagination

figurative *adj* figuré/-e

☞ **figure** ⊞ *n* (a) chiffre *m*; **a four-∼ number** un nombre de quatre chiffres; **in double ∼s** à deux chiffres
(b) (person) personnage *m*; **well-known ∼** personnalité *f* célèbre; **father ∼** image *f* du père
(c) (body shape) ligne *f*; **to lose one's ∼** prendre de l'embonpoint
(d) (diagram, shape) figure *f*

2 *vi* (appear) figurer (**in** dans)
▪ **figure out** trouver ‹*answer, reason*›; **to ~ out who/why** arriver à comprendre qui/pourquoi
figurehead *n* (symbolic leader) représentant/-e *m/f* nominal/-e; (of ship) figure *f* de proue
figure of speech *n* figure *f* de rhétorique
figure skating *n* patinage *m* artistique
⚹ **file** **1** *n* **(a)** (for papers) (gen) dossier *m*; (cardboard) chemise *f*; (binder) classeur *m*
(b) (record) dossier *m* (**on** sur)
(c) (Comput) fichier *m*
(d) (tool) lime *f*
(e) **in single ~** en file indienne
2 *vtr* **(a)** classer ‹*invoice, letter, record*› (**under** sous)
(b) déposer ‹*application, complaint*› (**with** auprès de); **to ~ a lawsuit** (**against sb**) intenter *or* faire un procès (à qn)
(c) limer ‹*wood, metal*›; **to ~ one's nails** se limer les ongles
3 *vi* **they ~d into/out of the classroom** ils sont entrés dans/sortis de la salle l'un après l'autre
file cabinet (US), **filing cabinet** *n* classeur *m* à tiroirs
file sharing *n* partage *m* de fichiers
⚹ **fill** **1** *vtr* **(a)** remplir ‹*container, page*› (**with** de); garnir ‹*cushion, pie, sandwich*› (**with** de); ‹*dentist*› plomber ‹*tooth, cavity*›
(b) ‹*crowd, sound*› remplir ‹*room, street*›; ‹*smoke, protesters*› envahir ‹*building, room*›; occuper ‹*time, day, hours*›; ‹*emotion, thought*› remplir ‹*mind, person*›
(c) boucher ‹*crack, hole, void*› (**with** avec)
(d) répondre à ‹*need*›
(e) ‹*company, university*› pourvoir ‹*post, vacancy*›
(f) ‹*applicant*› occuper ‹*post, vacancy*›
(g) ‹*wind*› gonfler ‹*sail*›
2 *vi* se remplir (**with** de)
▪ **fill in**: **1 to ~ in for sb** remplacer qn
2 ¶ **~ [sth] in** remplir ‹*form*›; donner ‹*detail, name, date*›
3 ¶ **~ [sb] in** mettre [qn] au courant (**on** de)
▪ **fill out**: **1** ¶ **~ out** ‹*person*› prendre du poids; ‹*face*› s'arrondir
2 ¶ **~ [sth] out** remplir ‹*form*›; faire ‹*prescription*›
▪ **fill up**: **1** ¶ **~ up** ‹*bath, theatre, bus*› se remplir (**with** de)
2 ¶ **~ [sth] up** remplir ‹*kettle, box, room*› (**with** de)
filler *n* **(a)** (for car body) mastic *m*; (for wall) reboucheur *m*
(b) (TV show) bouche-trou *m*
fillet **1** *n* filet *m*; **~ steak** filet *m* de bœuf
2 *vtr* enlever les arêtes de, fileter ‹*fish*›
filling **1** *n* **(a)** (of sandwich, baked potato) garniture *f*; (for peppers, meat) farce *f*

(b) (for tooth) plombage *m*
2 *adj* ‹*food, dish*› bourratif/-ive (fam)
filling station *n* station-service *f*
⚹ **film** **1** *n* **(a)** (movie) film *m*
(b) (for camera) pellicule *f*
(c) (layer) pellicule *f*
2 *vtr* filmer
3 *vi* tourner
film fan *n* cinéphile *mf*
film festival *n* festival *m* de cinéma
film industry *n* industrie *f* cinématographique
filming *n* tournage *m*
film set *n* plateau *m* de tournage
film star *n* vedette *f* de cinéma
film studio *n* studio *m* de cinéma
filter **1** *n* filtre *m*
2 *vtr* filtrer ‹*liquid, gas*›; faire passer ‹*coffee*›
3 *vi* **to ~ into** ‹*light, sound, water*› pénétrer dans ‹*area*›
filth *n* **(a)** (dirt) crasse *f*
(b) (vulgarity) obscénités *fpl*; (swearing) grossièretés *fpl*
filthy *adj* **(a)** (dirty) crasseux/-euse; (revolting) répugnant/-e
(b) ‹*language*› ordurier/-ière; ‹*mind*› mal tourné/-e
(c) (GB) ‹*look*› noir/-e
fin *n* (of fish, seal) nageoire *f*; (of shark) aileron *m*
⚹ **final** **1** *n* (Sport) finale *f*
2 *adj* **(a)** (last) dernier/-ière
(b) ‹*decision*› définitif/-ive; ‹*result*› final/-e
finale *n* finale *f*
finalist *n* finaliste *mf*
finalize *vtr* conclure ‹*contract*›; arrêter ‹*plan, details*›; faire la dernière mise au point de ‹*article*›; fixer ‹*timetable, route*›
⚹ **finally** *adv* **(a)** (eventually) finalement, enfin
(b) (lastly) finalement, pour finir
(c) (definitively) définitivement
finals *n pl* (GB Univ) examens *mpl* de fin d'études, (US Univ) examens *mpl* de fin de semestre
⚹ **finance** **1** *n* **(a)** (gen) finance *f*
(b) (funds) fonds *mpl* (**for** pour; **from** auprès de)
2 *vtr* financer ‹*project*›
finance company *n* société *f* de financement
finances *n pl* situation *f* financière
⚹ **financial** *adj* financier/-ière
financial year *n* (GB) exercice *m*, année *f* budgétaire
⚹ **find** **1** *n* **(a)** (gen) découverte *f*
(b) (good buy) trouvaille *f*
2 *vtr* (*prét, pp* **found**) **(a)** trouver; **I can't ~ my keys** je ne trouve pas mes clés; **I couldn't ~ the time** je n'ai pas eu le temps
(b) (experience) éprouver ‹*pleasure,*
⋯▶

satisfaction⟩ (in dans)
(c) (Law) to ~ that conclure que; to ~ sb
guilty déclarer qn coupable
■ **find out**: ⌊1⌋ ~ out se renseigner; if he ever
~s out si jamais il l'apprend
⌊2⌋ ¶ ~ [sth] out découvrir ⟨fact, answer,
name, cause, truth⟩
⌊3⌋ ¶ ~ out who/why/where trouver qui/
pourquoi/où
⌊4⌋ ¶ ~ out about [sth] (a) (learn by chance)
découvrir ⟨plan, affair, breakage⟩
(b) (research) faire des recherches sur ⟨subject⟩
◈ **findings** n pl conclusions fpl
◈ **fine** ⌊1⌋ n (gen) amende f; (for traffic offence)
contravention f
⌊2⌋ adj (a) (very good) excellent/-e
(b) (satisfactory) bon/bonne (before n); that's ~
très bien; '~, thanks' 'très bien, merci'
(c) (nice) ⟨weather, day⟩ beau/belle (before n)
(d) (delicate) fin/-e
(e) (subtle) ⟨adjustment, detail, distinction⟩
subtil/-e
(f) (refined) ⟨lady, clothes⟩ beau/belle (before n)
(g) (commendable) ⟨person⟩ merveilleux/-euse
⌊3⌋ adv ⟨get along, come along, do⟩ très bien
⌊4⌋ vtr (gen) condamner [qn] à une amende;
(for traffic offence) donner une contravention à
fine art n beaux-arts mpl
IDIOM she's got cheating down to a ~ elle
est passée maître dans l'art de tricher
fine-tune vtr ajuster
◈ **finger** ⌊1⌋ n doigt m
⌊2⌋ vtr toucher ⟨fruit, goods⟩; tripoter (fam)
⟨necklace⟩
IDIOM to keep one's ~s crossed croiser les
doigts (for sb pour qn)
finger-nail n ongle m
fingerprint n empreinte f digitale
fingertip n bout m du doigt
finicky adj ⟨person⟩ difficile (about pour);
⟨job, task⟩ minutieux/-ieuse
◈ **finish** ⌊1⌋ n (pl ~es) (a) (end) fin f
(b) (Sport) arrivée f
(c) (of wood, car) finition f; (of fabric, leather)
apprêt m
⌊2⌋ vtr (a) finir, terminer ⟨chapter, sentence,
task⟩; terminer, achever ⟨building, novel⟩; to
~ doing finir de faire
(b) (leave) finir ⟨work, school⟩
(c) (consume) finir ⟨cigarette, drink, meal⟩
(d) (put an end to) briser ⟨career⟩
⌊3⌋ vi (gen) finir; ⟨speaker⟩ finir de parler;
⟨conference, programme, term⟩ finir, se
terminer; ⟨holidays⟩ se terminer
■ **finish off** finir, terminer ⟨letter, meal, task⟩
■ **finish up**: ⌊1⌋ ~ up finir
⌊2⌋ ¶ ~ [sth] up finir ⟨milk, paint, cake⟩
finishing line (GB), **finish line** (US) n
ligne f d'arrivée
finishing touch n to put the ~(es) to sth
mettre la dernière main à qch

◈ indicates a very frequent word

finite adj (gen) fini/-e; ⟨resources⟩ limité/-e
Finland pr n Finlande f
Finn n Finlandais/-e m/f
Finnish ⌊1⌋ n (language) finnois m
⌊2⌋ adj ⟨culture, food, politics⟩
finlandais/-e; ⟨ambassador, embassy⟩ de
Finlande
(b) ⟨grammar⟩ finnois/-e; ⟨teacher, lesson⟩ de
finnois
fir n (also ~ **tree**) sapin m
◈ **fire** ⌊1⌋ n (a) feu m; to set ~ to sth mettre le
feu à qch; to be on ~ être en feu; to catch ~
prendre feu; to sit by the ~ s'asseoir près du
feu or au coin du feu
(b) (blaze) incendie m; to start a ~ provoquer
un incendie
(c) to open ~ on sb ouvrir le feu sur qn
⌊2⌋ excl (a) (raising alarm) au feu!
(b) (Mil) feu!
⌊3⌋ vtr (a) décharger ⟨gun, weapon⟩; tirer
⟨shot⟩; lancer ⟨arrow, missile⟩; to ~ questions
at sb bombarder qn de questions
(b) (dismiss) renvoyer, virer (fam) ⟨person⟩
⌊4⌋ vi tirer (at, on sur)
fire alarm n alarme f incendie
firearm n arme f à feu
firebomb ⌊1⌋ n bombe f incendiaire
⌊2⌋ vtr incendier ⟨building⟩
fire brigade n pompiers mpl
fire engine n voiture f de pompiers
fire escape n escalier m de secours
fire exit n sortie f de secours
fire extinguisher n extincteur m
firefighter n pompier m
fireguard n pare-étincelles m inv
fireman n pompier m
fireplace n cheminée f
fireproof adj ⟨door, clothing⟩ ignifugé/-e
fire service n (sapeurs-)pompiers mpl
fire station n caserne f de pompiers
firewood n bois m à brûler
firework n feu m d'artifice
firing n (of guns) tir m
firing line n to be in the ~ (Mil) être dans
la ligne de tir; (under attack) faire l'objet de
violentes critiques
firing squad n peloton m d'exécution
◈ **firm** ⌊1⌋ n entreprise f, société f
⌊2⌋ adj (a) ⟨mattress, fruit, handshake⟩ ferme
(b) ⟨basis, grasp⟩ solide
(c) ⟨offer, intention, refusal⟩ ferme; ⟨evidence⟩
concret/-ète
(d) ⟨person, leadership⟩ ferme (with sb avec
qn)
⌊3⌋ adv to stand ~ tenir bon
◈ **first** ⌊1⌋ n (a) (gen) premier/-ière m/f (to do
à faire)
(b) (of month) premier m inv; the ~ of May le
premier mai
(c) (also ~-**class honours degree**) (GB)

Univ) ≈ licence *f* avec mention très bien
2 *adj* premier/-ière (*before n*); **the ~ three pages** les trois premières pages; **at ~ glance** *or* **sight** à première vue; **I'll ring ~ thing in the morning** je vous appellerai en tout début de matinée
3 *adv* (a) ‹*arrive, leave*› le premier/la première; **women and children ~** les femmes et les enfants d'abord; **to come ~** ‹*contestant*› terminer premier/première (**in** à); ‹*career, family*› passer avant tout
(b) (to begin with) d'abord; **~ of all** tout d'abord
(c) (for the first time) pour la première fois; **I ~ met him in Paris** je l'ai rencontré pour la première fois à Paris
4 **at first** *phr* au début
IDIOM ~ things ~ chaque chose en son temps
first aid *n* (a) (treatment) premiers soins *mpl*
(b) (as skill) secourisme *m*
first-aid kit *n* trousse *f* de secours
first class *adj* (a) ‹*hotel, ticket*› de première (classe)
(b) ‹*stamp, mail*› (au) tarif rapide
(c) (GB) ‹*degree*› avec mention très bien
(d) (excellent) excellent/-e
first cousin *n* (male) cousin *m* germain; (female) cousine *f* germaine
first floor *n* (GB) premier étage *m*; (US) rez-de-chaussée *m*
first form *n* (GB Sch) (classe *f* de) sixième *f*
first grade *n* (US Sch) cours *m* préparatoire
firsthand *adj, adv* de première main
firstly *adv* premièrement
first name *n* prénom *m*
first night *n* première *f*
first-rate *adj* excellent/-e
first-time buyer *n* personne *f* qui achète sa première maison
⚔ **fish** **1** *n* (*pl* ~, ~**es**) poisson *m*
2 *vi* pêcher; **to ~ for trout** pêcher la truite; **to ~ for compliments** rechercher les compliments
■ **fish out**: **~ out [sth]** (a) (from bag, pocket) sortir
(b) (from water) repêcher
fish and chips *n* poisson *m* frit avec des frites
fish and chip shop *n* (GB) friterie *f*
fishbowl *n* bocal *m* (à poissons)
fisherman *n* pêcheur *m*
fish finger *n* (GB) bâtonnet *m* de poisson
fishing *n* pêche *f*; **to go ~** aller à la pêche
fishing boat *n* bateau *m* de pêche
fishing rod *n* canne *f* à pêche
fish market *n* halle *f* aux poissons
fishmonger *n* (GB) poissonnier/-ière *m/f*; **~'s (shop)** poissonnerie *f*
fishnet *adj* ‹*stockings*› à résille

fish stick *n* (US) bâtonnet *m* de poisson
fish tank *n* aquarium *m*
fishy *adj* (a) ‹*smell, taste*› de poisson
(b) (colloq) (suspect) louche (fam)
fist *n* poing *m*
⚔ **fit** **1** *n* (a) (Med) crise *f*, attaque *f*
(b) (of anger, passion, panic) accès *m*; **~ of coughing** quinte *f* de toux; **to have sb in ~s** (colloq) donner le fou rire à qn
(c) (of garment) **to be a good ~** être à la bonne taille; **to be a tight ~** être juste
2 *adj* (a) ‹*person*› (in trim) en forme; **to get ~** retrouver la forme
(b) **to be ~ for** (worthy of) être digne de ‹*person, hero, king*›; (capable of) être capable de faire ‹*job*›; **not ~ for human consumption** impropre à la consommation; **to see** *or* **think ~ to do** juger bon de faire; **to be in no ~ state to do** ne pas être en état de faire
3 *vtr* (*prét* **fitted**, **fit** (US), *pp* **fitted**)
(a) ‹*garment*› être à la taille de; ‹*shoe*› être à la pointure de; ‹*key*› aller dans ‹*lock*›; aller dans ‹*envelope, space*›
(b) **to ~ sth in** *or* **into** trouver de la place pour qch dans ‹*room, house, car*›
(c) (install) mettre [qch] en place ‹*lock, door, kitchen, shower*›
(d) correspondre à ‹*description, requirements*›
4 *vi* (*prét* **fitted**, **fit** (US), *pp* **fitted**)
(a) ‹*garment*› être à ma/ta/sa taille, aller; ‹*shoes*› être à ma/ta/sa pointure, aller; ‹*key, lid, sheet*› aller
(b) ‹*toys, books*› tenir (**into** dans); **will the table ~ in that corner?** y a-t-il de la place pour la table dans ce coin?
(c) **to ~ with** correspondre à ‹*story, facts*›
IDIOM in ~s and starts par à-coups
■ **fit in**: **1** **¶ ~ in** (a) ‹*key, object*› aller; **will you all ~ in?** (into car, room) est-ce qu'il y a de la place pour vous tous?
(b) (figurative) ‹*person*› s'intégrer (**with** à); **I'll ~ in with your plans** j'accorderai mes projets avec les vôtres
2 **~ [sb/sth] in** caser ‹*objects*›; caser ‹*game, meeting*›; trouver le temps pour voir ‹*patient, colleague*›
fitness *n* (physical) forme *f*
fitted *adj* ‹*wardrobe*› encastré/-e; ‹*kitchen*› intégré/-e
fitted carpet *n* moquette *f*
fitting **1** *n* (a) (part) installation *f*
(b) (for clothes, hearing aid) essayage *m*
2 *adj* ‹*description*› adéquat/-e; ‹*memorial, testament*› qui convient
fitting room *n* salon *m* d'essayage
⚔ **five** *n, pron, det* cinq *m inv*
five-a-side *n* (*also* **~ football**) football *m* à cinq (joueurs)
⚔ **fix** **1** *n* (a) (difficulty) **to be in a ~** être dans le pétrin (fam)
(b) (colloq) (dose of drugs) shoot *m* (fam)

⸭

2 *vtr* **(a)** fixer ‹*date, venue, price, limit*›; déterminer ‹*position*›
(b) arranger ‹*meeting, visit*›; préparer ‹*drink, meal*›; **to ~ one's hair** se donner un coup de peigne; **how are we ~ed for time/money?** qu'est-ce qu'on a comme temps/argent? (fam)
(c) (mend) réparer
(d) fixer ‹*handle, shelf*› (**on** sur; **to** à)
(e) fixer ‹*attention*› (**on** sur); tourner ‹*thoughts*› (**on** vers)
(f) (colloq) truquer ‹*contest, election*›
3 fixed *pp adj* ‹*gaze, income, price*› fixe; ‹*expression*› figé/-e; ‹*menu*› à prix fixe
■ **fix up** organiser ‹*holiday, meeting*›; décider de ‹*date*›

fixed-term contract *n* contrat *m* à durée déterminée

fixture *n* **(a)** installation *f*; **~s and fittings** équipements *mpl*
(b) (Sport) rencontre *f*

fizzle
■ **fizzle out** ‹*interest, romance*› s'éteindre; ‹*campaign, project*› faire fiasco; ‹*story*› se terminer en queue de poisson

fizzy *adj* gazeux/-euse

flabby *adj* ‹*skin, muscle*› flasque; ‹*person*› aux chairs flasques

flag 1 *n* drapeau *m*
2 *vi* (*p prés etc* **-gg-**) ‹*interest*› faiblir; ‹*strength*› baisser; ‹*conversation*› languir; ‹*athlete*› flancher (fam)
■ **flag down** faire signe de s'arrêter à ‹*person*›; héler ‹*taxi*›

flagpole *n* mât *m*

flagrant *adj* flagrant/-e

flagstone *n* dalle *f*

flair *n* **(a)** (talent) don; **to have a ~ for** être doué/-e pour ‹*languages*›
(b) (style) classe *f*

flake 1 *n* (of snow) flocon *m*
2 *vi* (*also* **~ off**) ‹*plaster, stone*› s'effriter; ‹*skin*› peler

flamboyant *adj* ‹*person*› haut/-e en couleur; ‹*lifestyle*› exubérant/-e; ‹*colour, clothes*› voyant/-e; ‹*gesture*› extravagant/-e

flame *n* flamme *f*; **in ~s** en flammes; **to go up in ~s** s'enflammer; **to burst into ~s** s'embraser

flamer *n* (Internet) auteur *m* d'un message injurieux

flaming 1 *n* (Internet) envoi *m* de messages injurieux
2 *adj* **(a)** ‹*vehicle, building*› en flammes
(b) ‹*row*› violent/-e

flamingo *n* (*pl* **~s** *ou* **-oes**) flamant *m* (rose)

flammable *adj* inflammable

flan *n* (savoury) quiche *f*, tarte *f*; (sweet) tarte *f*

flank 1 *n* flanc *m*
2 *vtr* **to be ~ed by** ‹*person*› être flanqué/-e

par; ‹*place*› être bordé/-e par

flannel *n* **(a)** (wool) flanelle *f*; (cotton) pilou *m*
(b) (*also* **face ~**) (GB) ≈ gant *m* de toilette

flap 1 *n* **(a)** (on pocket, envelope, tent) rabat *m*; (on table) abattant *m*
(b) (of wings) battement *m*
2 *vtr* (*p prés etc* **-pp-**) ‹*wing*› battre; ‹*sail, flag*› claquer; ‹*clothes*› voleter

flare 1 *n* **(a)** (on runway) balise *f* lumineuse; (distress signal) fusée *f* (de détresse); (Mil) (on target) fusée *f* éclairante
(b) (of match, lighter) lueur *f*
2 *vi* **(a)** ‹*firework, match*› jeter une brève lueur
(b) ‹*skirt*› s'évaser; ‹*nostrils*› se dilater
■ **flare up (a)** ‹*fire*› s'embraser
(b) ‹*violence*› éclater; ‹*person*› s'emporter
(c) ‹*illness*› réapparaître; ‹*pain*› se réveiller

flares *n pl* pantalon *m* à pattes d'éléphant

flash 1 *n* **(a)** (of torch, headlights) lueur *f* soudaine; (of jewels, metal) éclat *m*; **a ~ of lightning** un éclair
(b) in *or* **like a ~** en un clin d'œil
(c) (on camera) flash *m*
2 *vtr* **(a) to ~ one's headlights (at)** faire un appel de phares (à)
(b) lancer ‹*look, smile*› (**at** à)
(c) (transmit) faire apparaître ‹*message*›
(d) (colloq) (show) ‹*person*› montrer [qch] rapidement ‹*card, money*›
(e) (*also* **~ about**, **around**) exhiber ‹*credit card*›; étaler ‹*money*›
3 *vi* ‹*light*› clignoter; ‹*eyes*› lancer des éclairs; **to ~ on and off** clignoter
■ **flash by**, **flash past** ‹*person, bird*› passer comme un éclair; ‹*landscape*› défiler

flashback *n* **(a)** (in film) flash-back *m* (**to** à)
(b) (memory) souvenir *m*

flashing *adj* ‹*light, sign*› clignotant/-e

flash light *n* lampe *f* de poche

flashy *adj* (colloq) ‹*car, dress, tie*› tape-à-l'œil *inv*; ‹*jewellery*› clinquant/-e

flask *n* thermos® *f or m inv*; (hip) ~ flasque *f*

flat 1 *n* **(a)** (GB) appartement *m*; **one-bedroom ~** deux pièces *m inv*
(b) the ~ of le plat de ‹*hand, sword*›
2 *adj* **(a)** (gen) plat/-e; ‹*nose, face*› aplati/-e
(b) ‹*tyre, ball*› dégonflé/-e; **to have a ~ tyre** avoir un pneu à plat
(c) ‹*refusal, denial*› catégorique
(d) ‹*fare, fee*› forfaitaire; ‹*charge, rate*› fixe
(e) ‹*beer*› éventé/-e
(f) (GB) ‹*car battery*› à plat; ‹*battery*› usé/-e
(g) (Mus) ‹*note*› bémol *inv*; ‹*voice, instrument*› faux/fausse
3 *adv* **(a)** ‹*lay, lie*› à plat; **~ on one's back** sur le dos
(b) in 10 minutes ~ en 10 minutes pile
(c) ‹*sing*› faux

✧ indicates a very frequent word

IDIOM to fall ∼ ⟨joke⟩ tomber à plat; ⟨party⟩ tourner court; ⟨plan⟩ tomber à l'eau

flatmate n (GB) colocataire mf

flat out adv (colloq) ⟨drive⟩ à fond de train; ⟨work⟩ d'arrache-pied

flat rate ☐1 n taux m fixe
   ☐2 **flat-rate** adj ⟨fee, tax⟩ forfaitaire

flatten ☐1 vtr (a) ⟨rain⟩ coucher ⟨crops, grass⟩; abattre ⟨fence⟩; ⟨bombing⟩ raser ⟨building⟩
(b) (smooth out) aplanir ⟨surface⟩; aplatir ⟨metal⟩
(c) (crush) écraser ⟨fruit, object⟩
   ☐2 v refl **to ∼ oneself** s'aplatir (**against** contre)

flatter vtr flatter (**on** sur)

flattering adj flatteur/-euse

flattery n flatterie f

flaunt vtr étaler ⟨wealth⟩; faire étalage de ⟨charms, knowledge⟩

flavour (GB), **flavor** (US) ☐1 n goût m; (subtler) saveur f; **full of ∼** savoureux/-euse
   ☐2 vtr (gen) donner du goût à; (add specific taste) parfumer (**with** à)

flavouring (GB), **flavoring** (US) n (for sweet taste) parfum m; (for meat, fish) assaisonnement m

flaw n défaut m

flawed adj défectueux/-euse

flea n puce f

flea market n marché m aux puces

fleck ☐1 n (of colour, light) tache f; (of foam) flocon m; (of blood, paint) petite tache f; (of dust) particule f
   ☐2 vtr ∼**ed with** ⟨fabric⟩ moucheté/-e de ⟨colour⟩

fledg(e)ling n oisillon m

flee vtr, vi (prét, pp **fled**) fuir

fleece n toison f; ∼**-lined** fourré/-e

fleet n (a) (of ships) flotte f; (of small vessels) flottille f
(b) (of vehicles) (on road) convoi m

fleeting adj ⟨memory, pleasure⟩ fugace; ⟨moment⟩ bref/brève (before n); ⟨glance⟩ rapide

Flemish ☐1 n (a) **the ∼** les Flamands mpl
(b) (language) flamand m
   ☐2 adj flamand/-e

flesh n chair f

fleshy adj charnu/-e

flex ☐1 n (GB) fil m
   ☐2 vtr faire jouer ⟨muscle⟩; fléchir ⟨limb⟩

flexibility n souplesse f, flexibilité f

flexible adj (a) ⟨arrangement, plan⟩ flexible
(b) ⟨person⟩ souple (**about** en ce qui concerne)

flexitime (GB), **flextime** (US) n horaire m flexible or souple

flick ☐1 n (with finger) chiquenaude f; (with whip, cloth) petit coup m
   ☐2 vtr (a) (with finger) donner une chiquenaude à; (with tail, cloth) donner un petit

coup à; **he ∼ed his ash on the floor** il a fait tomber sa cendre par terre
(b) appuyer sur ⟨switch⟩

flicker vi ⟨fire, light⟩ vaciller, trembloter; ⟨image⟩ clignoter; ⟨eye, eyelid⟩ cligner
■ **flick through** feuilleter ⟨book⟩

flick knife n (GB) couteau m à cran d'arrêt

✦ **flight** n (a) (gen) vol m (**to** vers; **from** de); **we took the next ∼ (out)** nous avons pris l'avion suivant
(b) (escape) fuite f (**from** devant); **to take ∼** prendre la fuite
(c) **a ∼ of steps** une volée de marches; **six ∼s (of stairs)** six étages
(d) **a ∼ of fancy** une invention

flight attendant n (male) steward m; (female) hôtesse f de l'air

flight bag n bagage m à main

flight path n route f de vol

flimsy adj ⟨fabric⟩ léger/-ère; ⟨structure⟩ peu solide; ⟨excuse⟩ piètre (before n); ⟨evidence⟩ mince

flinch vi tressaillir; **without ∼ing** sans broncher; **to ∼ from doing** hésiter à faire

fling ☐1 n (a) (colloq) (spree) bon temps m
(b) (affair) aventure f
   ☐2 vtr (prét, pp **flung**) lancer
   ☐3 v refl **to ∼ oneself** se jeter (**across** en travers de; **over** par dessus)
■ **fling away:** ∼ [sth] away jeter qch
■ **fling open** ouvrir [qch] brusquement ⟨door⟩; ouvrir [qch] tout grand ⟨window⟩

flint n (a) (rock) silex m
(b) (in lighter) pierre f à briquet

flip ☐1 n (somersault) tour m
   ☐2 vtr (p prés etc **-pp-**) (a) lancer ⟨coin⟩; faire sauter ⟨pancake⟩
(b) basculer ⟨switch⟩
■ **flip through** feuilleter ⟨book⟩

flipchart n tableau m de conférence, paperboard m

flip-flop n (a) (sandal) tong f
(b) (US) (about-face) volte-face f inv

flippant adj ⟨remark, person⟩ désinvolte; ⟨tone, attitude⟩ cavalier/-ière

flipper n (a) (Zool) nageoire f
(b) (for swimmer) palme f

flirt ☐1 n flirteur/-euse m/f
   ☐2 vi flirter; **to ∼ with** flirter avec ⟨person⟩; jouer avec ⟨danger⟩; caresser ⟨idea⟩

flirtatious adj charmeur/-euse, dragueur/-euse (fam derogatory)

flit vi (p prés etc **-tt-**) (a) (**also ∼ about**) ⟨bird, moth⟩ voleter; ⟨person⟩ aller d'un pas léger
(b) **a look of panic ∼ted across his face** une expression de panique lui traversa le visage

float ☐1 n (a) (on net) flotteur m; (on line) bouchon m
(b) (GB) (swimmer's aid) planche f; (US) (life jacket) gilet m de sauvetage
(c) (carnival vehicle) char m   ····⟩

2 *vtr* **(a)** ‹*person*› faire flotter ‹*boat, logs*›
(b) émettre ‹*shares, loan*›; lancer [qch] en
Bourse ‹*company*›; laisser flotter ‹*currency*›
3 *vi* **(a)** flotter; **to ~ on one's back**
‹*swimmer*› faire la planche; **the boat was
~ing out to sea** le bateau voguait vers le
large; **to ~ up into the air** s'envoler
(b) ‹*currency*› flotter
■ **float off** ‹*boat*› dériver; ‹*balloon*› s'envoler
floating *adj* **(a)** ‹*bridge*› flottant/-e
(b) ‹*population*› instable
floating voter *n* électeur *m* indécis
flock **1** *n* (of sheep, goats) troupeau *m*; (of
birds) volée *f*
2 *vi* ‹*animals, people*› affluer (**around**
autour de; **into** dans); **to ~ together** ‹*people*›
s'assembler; ‹*animals*› se rassembler
flog *vtr* (*p prés etc* **-gg-**) (beat) flageller
flood **1** *n* **(a)** inondation *f*
(b) a ~ of un flot de ‹*people, memories*›; un
déluge de ‹*letters, complaints*›; **to be in ~s of
tears** verser des torrents de larmes
2 *vtr* **(a)** inonder ‹*area*›; faire déborder
‹*river*›
(b) ‹*light*› inonder
(c) inonder ‹*market*› (**with** de)
(d) (Aut) noyer ‹*engine*›
3 *vi* **(a)** ‹*river*› déborder
(b) to ~ into sth ‹*light*› inonder qch; ‹*people*›
envahir qch; **to ~ over sb** ‹*emotion*› envahir
qn
floodgate *n* vanne *f*
floodlight **1** *n* projecteur *m*; **under ~s**
(Sport) en nocturne
2 *vtr* (*prét, pp* **floodlit**) illuminer
‹*building*›; éclairer ‹*stage*›
✧ **floor** **1** *n* **(a)** (of room) (wooden) plancher *m*,
parquet *m*; (stone) sol *m*; (of car, lift) plancher
m; **dance ~** piste *f* de danse; **on the ~** par
terre
(b) (of stock exchange) parquet *m*; (of debating
chamber) auditoire *m*; (of factory) atelier *m*
(c) (storey) étage *m*; **on the first ~** (GB) au
premier étage; (US) au rez-de-chaussée
2 *vtr* **(a)** terrasser ‹*attacker, boxer*›
(b) ‹*question*› décontenancer ‹*candidate*›
IDIOM to wipe the ~ with sb battre qn à
plates coutures
floorboard *n* latte *f*, planche *f*
floor cloth *n* serpillière *f*
floor show *n* spectacle *m* (*de cabaret*)
flop **1** *n* (failure) fiasco *m* (fam)
2 *vi* (*p prés etc* **-pp-**) **(a) to ~ (down)**
s'effondrer
(b) (colloq) ‹*play, film*› faire un four (fam);
‹*project, venture*› être un fiasco (fam)
floppy *adj* ‹*ears*› pendant/-e; ‹*hat*› à bords
tombants
floppy disk *n* disquette *f*
flora *n* flore *f*

───────────────

✧ indicates a very frequent word

floral *adj* ‹*design, fabric*› à fleurs;
‹*arrangement*› floral/-e
Florida *pr n* Floride *f*
florist *n* (person) fleuriste *mf*; (shop) fleuriste
m
floss *n* fil *m* dentaire
flotsam *n* ~ **and jetsam** épaves *fpl*
flounce **1** *n* (frill) volant *m*
2 *vi* **to ~ in/off** entrer/partir dans un
mouvement d'indignation
flounder *vi* **(a)** ‹*animal, person*› se débattre
(in dans)
(b) (falter) ‹*speaker*› bredouiller; ‹*economy*›
stagner; ‹*career, company*› piétiner
flour *n* farine *f*
flourish **1** *n* **(a)** (gesture) geste *m* théâtral;
with a ~ ‹*do*› de façon théâtrale
(b) (in style) fioriture *f*
2 *vtr* brandir ‹*ticket, document*›
3 *vi* prospérer
flourishing *adj* ‹*garden, industry*›
florissant/-e; ‹*business, town*› prospère
flout *vtr* se moquer de ‹*convention, rules*›
✧ **flow** **1** *n* **(a)** (of liquid) écoulement *m*; (of
blood, electricity, water) circulation *f*; (of refugees,
words) flot *m*; (of information) circulation *f*; **in
full ~** ‹*speaker*› en plein discours; **traffic ~**
circulation *f*
(b) (of tide) flux *m*
2 *vi* **(a)** ‹*liquid*› couler (**into** dans); **the river
~s into the sea** le fleuve se jette dans la mer
(b) ‹*conversation, words*› couler; ‹*wine, beer*›
couler à flots
(c) ‹*blood, electricity*› circuler (**through,
round** dans)
(d) ‹*hair, dress*› flotter
flowchart *n* organigramme *m*
✧ **flower** **1** *n* fleur *f*; **to be in ~** être en fleur
2 *vi* **(a)** ‹*flower, tree*› fleurir
(b) ‹*love, person*› s'épanouir
flower arranging *n* décoration *f* florale
flower bed *n* parterre *m* de fleurs
flowering **1** *n* floraison *f* (**of** de)
2 *adj* (producing blooms) à fleurs; (in bloom)
en fleurs
flower pot *n* pot *m* de fleurs
flower shop *n* fleuriste *m*
flowery *adj* ‹*design*› à fleurs; ‹*language,
speech*› fleuri/-e
flu *n* grippe *f*
fluctuate *vi* fluctuer (**between** entre)
flue *n* (of chimney) conduit *m*; (of stove, boiler)
tuyau *m*
fluency *n* aisance *f*
fluent *adj* **(a) her French is ~** elle parle
couramment français; **in ~ English** dans un
anglais parfait
(b) ‹*speech*› éloquent/-e; ‹*style*› coulant/-e
fluently *adv* couramment

fluff ☐1 *n* (on clothes) peluche *f*; (on carpet) poussière *f*; (under furniture) mouton *m*, flocon *m* de poussière
☐2 *vtr* (a) (*also* ~ **up**) hérisser ‹*feathers*›; faire bouffer ‹*hair*›
(b) (colloq) rater ‹*cue, exam*›

fluffy *adj* (a) ‹*toy*› en peluche; ‹*hair*› bouffant/-e
(b) (light) ‹*mixture*› léger/-ère; ‹*egg white, rice*› moelleux/-euse

fluid *n, adj* fluide *m*

fluid ounce *n* once *f* liquide ((GB) = *0.028 l*; (US) = *0.030 l*)

fluke *n* coup *m* de veine (fam); **by a** (**sheer**) ~ (tout à fait) par hasard

fluorescent *adj* fluorescent/-e

fluoride *n* fluorure *m*

flurry *n* (a) (gust) rafale *f*
(b) (bustle) agitation *f* soudaine; **a** ~ **of activity** un tourbillon d'activité
(c) (of complaints, enquiries) vague *f*

flush ☐1 *n* (a) (blush) rougeur *f*
(b) (surge) **a** ~ **of** un élan de ‹*pleasure, pride*›; un accès de ‹*anger, shame*›
(c) (of toilet) chasse *f* d'eau
☐2 *vtr* **to** ~ **the toilet** tirer la chasse (d'eau); **to** ~ **sth down the toilet** faire partir qch dans les toilettes
☐3 *vi* (a) (redden) rougir (**with** de)
(b) **the toilet doesn't** ~ la chasse d'eau ne fonctionne pas
■ **flush out** débusquer ‹*sniper, spy*›; **to** ~ **sb/ sth out of** faire sortir qn/qch de ‹*shelter*›

flushed *adj* (a) ‹*cheeks*› rouge (**with** de); **to be** ~ avoir les joues rouges
(b) ~ **with** rayonnant/-e de ‹*pride*›

fluster ☐1 *n* agitation *f*
☐2 *vtr* énerver; **to look** ~**ed** avoir l'air énervé

flute *n* flûte *f*

flutter ☐1 *n* (of wings, lashes) battement *m*
☐2 *vtr* (a) **the bird** ~**ed its wings** l'oiseau battait des ailes
(b) agiter ‹*fan, handkerchief*›; **to** ~ **one's eyelashes** battre des cils
☐3 *vi* (a) **the bird's wings** ~**ed** l'oiseau battit des ailes
(b) ‹*flag*› flotter; ‹*clothes, curtains*› s'agiter; ‹*eyelids, lashes*› battre
(c) (*also* ~ **down**) ‹*leaves*› tomber en voltigeant
(d) ‹*heart*› palpiter (**with** de); ‹*pulse*› battre faiblement

flux *n* **in** (**a state of**) ~ dans un état de perpétuel changement

ᴒ **fly** ☐1 *n* mouche *f*
☐2 **flies** *n pl* (of trousers) braguette *f*
☐3 *vtr* (*prét* **flew**, *pp* **flown**) (a) piloter ‹*aircraft, balloon*›; faire voler ‹*kite*›
(b) (transport) emmener [qn] par avion ‹*person*›
(c) ‹*bird, aircraft*› parcourir ‹*distance*›

(d) ‹*ship*› arborer ‹*flag*›
☐4 *vi* (*prét* **flew**, *pp* **flown**) (a) ‹*bird, insect, aircraft, kite*› voler; **to** ~ **over** *or* **across sth** survoler qch
(b) ‹*passenger*› voyager en avion, prendre l'avion; ‹*pilot*› piloter, voler; **to** ~ **from Rome to Athens** aller de Rome à Athènes en avion
(c) ‹*sparks, insults*› voler; **to** ~ **open** s'ouvrir brusquement; **to go** ~**ing** (colloq) ‹*person*› faire un vol plané, valdinguer (fam); **to** ~ **into a rage** se mettre en colère
(d) (*also* ~ **past**, ~ **by**) ‹*time, holidays*› passer très vite, filer (fam)
(e) ‹*flag, scarf, hair*› flotter; **to** ~ **in the wind** flotter au vent
■ **fly away** s'envoler

fly-by-night *adj* ‹*company*› douteux/-euse; ‹*person*› irresponsable

fly-drive *adj* avec formule avion plus voiture

flying ☐1 *n* **to be afraid of** ~ avoir peur de l'avion
☐2 *adj* (a) ‹*insect, machine*› volant/-e; ‹*object, broken glass*› qui vole; **to take a** ~ **leap** sauter avec élan
(b) ‹*visit*› éclair *inv*
IDIOMS **with** ~ **colours** ‹*pass*› haut la main; **to get off to a** ~ **start** prendre un très bon départ

fly-on-the-wall *adj* ‹*film*› pris/-e sur le vif

flyover *n* (a) (GB) pont *m* routier
(b) (US) (aerial display) défilé *m* aérien

fly spray *n* bombe *f* insecticide

FM *n* (*abbr* = **frequency modulation**) FM *f*

foal *n* poulain *m*

foam ☐1 *n* (a) (on sea, from mouth) écume *f*; (on drinks) mousse *f*
(b) (chemical) mousse *f*
(c) (*also* ~ **rubber**) mousse *f*
☐2 *vi* (a) (*also* ~ **up**) ‹*beer*› mousser; ‹*sea*› se couvrir d'écume; **to** ~ **at the mouth** écumer; (figurative) écumer de rage
(b) ‹*horse*› suer

foam bath *n* bain *m* moussant

fob *n* (pocket) gousset *m*; (chain) chaîne *f*
■ **fob off** se débarrasser de ‹*enquirer, customer*›; rejeter ‹*enquiry*›

focal point *n* (a) (in optics) foyer *m*
(b) (of village, building) point *m* de convergence (**of** de; **for** pour)
(c) (main concern) point *m* central

ᴒ **focus** ☐1 *n* (*pl* -**es**, **foci**) (a) (focal point) foyer *m*; **in** ~ au point; **to go out of** ~ ‹*device*› se dérégler; ‹*image*› devenir flou
(b) (device on lens) mise *f* au point
(c) (of attention, interest) centre *m*
(d) (emphasis) accent *m*
☐2 *vtr* (*p prés etc* -**s-** *ou* -**ss-**) (a) concentrer ‹*ray*› (**on** sur); fixer ‹*eyes*› (**on** sur)
(b) mettre [qch] au point, régler ‹*lens, camera*› ⋯⟩

3 *vi* (*p prés etc* **-s-** *ou* **-ss-**) to ~ on ⟨*photographer*⟩ cadrer sur; ⟨*eyes, attention*⟩ se fixer sur; ⟨*report*⟩ se concentrer sur
4 **focused** *pp adj* ⟨*person*⟩ déterminé/-e

fodder *n* fourrage *m*

foe *n* ennemi/-e *m/f*

foetus, fetus (US) *n* fœtus *m*

fog **1** *n* brouillard *m*
2 *vtr* (*p prés etc* **-gg-**) (*also* ~ **up**) ⟨*steam*⟩ embuer ⟨*glass*⟩; ⟨*light*⟩ voiler ⟨*film*⟩

foggy *adj* ⟨*day, weather*⟩ brumeux/-euse; **it's** ~ **il y a du brouillard**

foghorn *n* corne *f* de brume

foible *n* petite manie *f*

foil **1** *n* papier *m* d'aluminium; **silver ~** papier argenté
2 *vtr* contrecarrer ⟨*person*⟩; déjouer ⟨*attempt*⟩

foist *vtr* to ~ sth on sb repasser qch à qn

fold **1** *n* (a) (in fabric, paper, skin) pli *m*
(b) (for sheep) parc *m*
2 *vtr* (a) plier ⟨*paper, shirt, chair*⟩; replier ⟨*wings*⟩
(b) croiser ⟨*arms*⟩; joindre ⟨*hands*⟩
3 *vi* (a) ⟨*chair*⟩ se plier
(b) (fail) ⟨*play*⟩ quitter l'affiche; ⟨*company*⟩ fermer
IDIOM **to return to the ~** rentrer au bercail
■ **fold back** rabattre ⟨*shutters, sheet, sleeve*⟩
■ **fold in** incorporer ⟨*sugar, flour*⟩
■ **fold up** plier ⟨*newspaper, chair*⟩

folder *n* (a) (for papers) chemise *f*
(b) (for artwork) carton *m*

folding *adj* ⟨*bed, table, chair*⟩ pliant/-e; ⟨*door*⟩ en accordéon

foliage *n* feuillage *m*

⸱ **folk** **1** *n* (people) gens *mpl*
2 *adj* (a) (traditional) ⟨*tale, song*⟩ folklorique
(b) (modern) ⟨*music*⟩ folk *inv*
(c) ⟨*hero*⟩ populaire

folklore *n* folklore *m*

⸱ **follow** **1** *vtr* (gen) suivre; poursuivre ⟨*career*⟩; **~ed by** suivi/-e de
2 *vi* (a) suivre; **to ~ in sb's footsteps** suivre les traces de qn; **there's ice cream to ~** ensuite il y a de la glace; **the results were as ~s** les résultats ont été les suivants
(b) (understand) suivre; **I don't ~** je ne suis pas
(c) **it ~s that** il s'ensuit que
■ **follow through** mener [qch] à terme ⟨*project*⟩; aller jusqu'au bout de ⟨*idea*⟩
■ **follow up** donner suite à ⟨*letter, threat, offer*⟩ (**with** par); suivre ⟨*story, lead*⟩

follower *n* (a) (of thinker, artist) disciple *m*; (of political leader) partisan/-e *m/f*
(b) (of team) supporter *m*

following **1** *n* (of religion, cult) adeptes *mfpl*; (of party, political figure) partisans/-anes *mpl/fpl*; (of soap opera, show) public *m*; (of sports team) supporters *mpl*

2 *adj* suivant/-e
3 *prep* suite à, à la suite de

follow-up **1** *n* (a) (film, record, single, programme) suite *f* (**to** à)
(b) (of patient, socialwork case) suivi *m*
2 *adj* (a) (supplementary) ⟨*work*⟩ de suivi; ⟨*check*⟩ de contrôle; ⟨*discussion, article*⟩ complémentaire; ⟨*letter*⟩ de rappel
(b) (of patient, ex-inmate) ⟨*visit*⟩ de contrôle

folly *n* folie *f*

fond *adj* (a) ⟨*embrace, farewell*⟩ affectueux/-euse; ⟨*eyes, smile*⟩ tendre; ~ **memories** de très bons souvenirs
(b) ⟨*wish, ambition*⟩ cher/chère
(c) **to be ~ of sb** aimer beaucoup qn; **to be ~ of sth** aimer qch

fondle *vtr* caresser

⸱ **food** *n* nourriture *f*, alimentation *f*; **frozen** ~ aliments surgelés; **Chinese ~** la cuisine chinoise; **that's ~ for thought** ça donne à réfléchir

food aid *n* aide *f* alimentaire

foodie *n* (colloq) amateur *m* de bonne bouffe (fam)

food poisoning *n* intoxication *f* alimentaire

food processor *n* robot *m* ménager

foodstuff *n* denrée *f* alimentaire

fool **1** *n* (a) idiot/-e *m/f* (**to do** de faire); **you stupid ~!** (colloq) espèce d'idiot/-e!; **to make sb look a ~** faire passer qn pour un/-e idiot/-e; **to act the ~** faire l'imbécile
(b) (jester) fou *m*
2 *vtr* tromper, duper

foolhardy *adj* téméraire

foolish *adj* (a) ⟨*person*⟩ bête (**to do** de faire)
(b) ⟨*grin, expression*⟩ stupide; **to feel ~** se sentir ridicule
(c) ⟨*decision, question, remark*⟩ idiot/-e

foolproof *adj* (a) ⟨*method, plan*⟩ infaillible
(b) ⟨*machine*⟩ d'utilisation très simple

⸱ **foot** **1** *n* (*pl* **feet**) (a) (of person) pied *m*; (of animal) patte *f*; (of sock, chair) pied *m*; **on ~** à pied; **from head to ~** de la tête aux pieds; **to put one's ~ down** faire acte d'autorité; (Aut) accélérer
(b) (measurement) pied *m* (= *0.3048 m*)
(c) (of mountain) pied *m* (**of** de); **at the ~ of** au pied de ⟨*bed*⟩; à la fin de ⟨*list, letter*⟩; en bas de ⟨*page, stairs*⟩
2 *vtr* to ~ **the bill** payer la facture (**for** de, **pour**)
IDIOMS **to be under sb's feet** être dans les jambes de qn; **rushed off one's feet** débordé/-e; **to put one's ~ in it** (colloq) faire une gaffe; **to stand on one's own two feet** se débrouiller tout seul/toute seule

footage *n* film *m*, pellicule *f*; **some ~ of** des images de

foot and mouth (disease) *n* fièvre *f* aphteuse

⸱ indicates a very frequent word

⚬ **football** *n* **(a)** (game) (GB) football *m*; (US)
football *m* américain
(b) (ball) ballon *m* de football
footballer *n* (GB) joueur/-euse *m/f* de
football
foot brake *n* (Aut) frein *m* (à pied)
footbridge *n* passerelle *f*
foothold *n* prise *f* (de pied); **to gain a ~**
«company» prendre pied; «ideology» s'imposer
footing *n* **(a)** (basis) **on a firm ~** sur une
base solide; **to be on an equal ~ with sb** être
sur un pied d'égalité avec qn
(b) (grip for feet) **to lose one's ~** perdre pied
footlights *n pl* rampe *f*
footloose *adj* libre comme l'air
footnote *n* note *f* de bas de page
foot passenger *n* passager *m* sans
véhicule
footpath *n* (in countryside) sentier *m*; (in town)
trottoir *m*
footprint *n* empreinte *f* (de pied)
footstep *n* pas *m*
footstool *n* repose-pied *m*
footwear *n* chaussures *fpl*
⚬ **for** *prep* **(a)** (gen) pour; **~ sb** pour qn; **he
cooked dinner ~ us** il nous a préparé
à manger; **what's it ~?** c'est pour quoi
faire?, ça sert à quoi?; **to go ~ a swim** aller
nager; **that's ~ us to decide** c'est à nous de
décider; **she's the person ~ the job** elle est
la personne qu'il faut pour le travail; **the
reason ~ doing** la raison pour laquelle on
fait; **if it weren't ~ her...** sans elle...; **'~ sale'**
'à vendre'; **it is impossible ~ me to stay** il
m'est impossible de rester
(b) «work, play» pour; «MP» de; **the minister ~
education** le ministre de l'éducation
(c) (on behalf of) pour; **to be pleased ~ sb** être
content/e pour qn; **say hello to him ~ me**
dis-lui bonjour de ma part
(d) (in time expressions) (with a completed action
in the past) pendant; (with an incomplete action
started in the past) depuis; **I waited ~ two hours**
j'ai attendu pendant deux heures; **I have/had
been waiting ~ an hour** j'attends/j'attendais
depuis une heure; **I'm going to Tokyo ~ five
weeks** je vais à Tokyo pour cinq semaines;
the best show I've seen ~ years le meilleur
spectacle que j'aie vu depuis des années;
we've been together ~ two years ça fait
deux ans que nous sommes ensemble; **she's
off to Paris ~ the weekend** elle va à Paris
pour le week-end; **to stay ~ a year** rester
un an; **to be away ~ a year** être absent/-e
pendant un an; **I was in Paris ~ two weeks**
j'ai passé deux semaines à Paris; **the car
won't be ready ~ another six weeks** la
voiture ne sera pas prête avant six semaines;
it's time ~ bed c'est l'heure d'aller au lit
(e) (indicating distance) pendant; **to drive ~
miles** rouler pendant des kilomètres; **the last
shop ~ 30 miles** le dernier magasin avant

50 kilomètres
(f) (indicating cost, value) pour; **it was sold ~
£100** ça s'est vendu (pour) 100 livres sterling;
a cheque ~ £20 un chèque de 20 livres
sterling
(g) (in favour of) **to be ~** être pour «peace,
divorce»; **the argument ~ recycling**
l'argument en faveur du recyclage
(h) T ~ Tom T comme Tom; **what's the
French ~ 'boot'?** comment dit-on 'boot' en
français?
(i) ~ one thing... and ~ another...
premièrement... et deuxièmement...; **I, ~
one, agree with her** en tout cas moi, je suis
d'accord avec elle
forbid *vtr* (*p prés* **-dd-**, *prét* **forbad(e)**, *pp*
forbidden) défendre, interdire; **to ~ sb to
do** défendre *or* interdire à qn de faire; **to ~
sb sth** défendre *or* interdire qch à qn; **God
~!** Dieu m'en/l'en *etc* garde!
forbidden *adj* «subject, fruit» défendu/-e;
«place» interdit/-e; **smoking is ~** il est
interdit de fumer
forbidding *adj* «building» intimidant/-e;
«landscape» inhospitalier/-ière; «expression»
rébarbatif/-ive
⚬ **force** ① *n* force *f*; **by ~** par la force; **the
police ~** la police; **a ~ 10 gale** un vent de
force 10
② **forces** *n pl* (*also* **armed ~s**) **the ~s**
les forces *fpl* armees
③ *vtr* forcer (**to do** à faire)
④ **in force** *phr* **(a)** (in large numbers) en
force
(b) «law, prices, ban» en vigueur
■ **force on: ~ [sth] on sb** imposer [qch] à qn,
forcer qn à accepter [qch]
forced *adj* «smile, landing» forcé/-e;
«conversation» peu naturel/-elle
force-feed *vtr* (*prét*, *pp* **-fed**) gaver
«animal, bird»; alimenter [qn] de force
«person»
forceful *adj* «person, behaviour» énergique;
«attack, speech» vigoureux/-euse
ford ① *n* gué *m*
② *vtr* **to ~ a river** passer une rivière à gué
fore *n* **to the ~** en vue, en avant; **to come to
the ~** «person, issue» s'imposer à l'attention;
«quality» ressortir
forearm *n* avant-bras *m inv*
foreboding *n* pressentiment *m*
forecast ① *n* **(a)** (*also* **weather ~**)
météo *f* (fam), bulletin *m* météorologique
(b) (outlook) (gen) pronostics *mpl*; (Econ)
prévisions *fpl*
② *vtr* (*prét*, *pp* **-cast**) prévoir (**that** que)
forecaster *n* **(a)** (of weather) spécialiste *mf*
de la météorologie
(b) (economic) conjoncturiste *mf*
forecourt *n* (of shop) parking *m*; (of garage)
aire *f* de stationnement; (of station) cour *f* de
la gare

forefinger n index m

forefront n at or in the ～ of à la pointe de ‹change, research, debate›; au premier plan de ‹campaign, struggle›

foregone adj it is a ～ conclusion c'est couru d'avance

foreground n premier plan m

forehand n (Sport) coup m droit

forehead n front m

⚡ **foreign** adj (a) ‹country, imports, policy› étranger/-ère; ‹market› extérieur/-e; ‹trade, travel› à l'étranger
(b) (alien) ‹concept› étranger/-ère (to à)

foreign affairs n pl affaires fpl étrangères

foreign body n corps m étranger

foreign correspondent n correspondant/-e m/f à l'étranger

foreigner n étranger/-ère m/f

foreign exchange n devises fpl

foreign exchange market n marché m des changes

foreign minister, foreign secretary (GB) n ministre m des Affaires étrangères

Foreign Office, FO n (GB) ministère m des Affaires étrangères

foreman n (a) (supervisor) contremaître m
(b) (Law) président m (d'un jury)

foremost ⓵ adj premier/-ière (before n), plus grand
⓶ adv first and ～ avant tout

forename n prénom m

forensic evidence n résultats mpl des expertises médico-légales

forensic science n médecine f légale

forensic scientist n médecin m légiste

forensic tests n pl expertises fpl médico-légales

forerunner n (person) précurseur m; (institution, invention, model) ancêtre m

foresee vtr (prét **foresaw**, pp **foreseen**) prévoir

foreseeable adj prévisible

foreshadow vtr annoncer

foresight n prévoyance f (to do de faire)

foreskin n prépuce m

⚡ **forest** n forêt f

forester n forestier/-ière m/f

forest fire n incendie m de forêt

forestry n (science) sylviculture f

foretaste n avant-goût m (of de)

foretell vtr (prét, pp **foretold**) prédire

⚡ **forever** adv pour toujours; to go on ～ ‹pain, noise, journey› durer une éternité; the desert seemed to go on ～ le désert semblait ne pas avoir de limites; she is ～ complaining elle est toujours en train de se plaindre

foreword n avant-propos m inv

forfeit ⓵ n gage m
⓶ vtr perdre ‹right, liberty›

forge ⓵ n forge f
⓶ vtr (a) forger ‹metal›
(b) contrefaire ‹banknotes, signature›; a ～d passport un faux passeport
(c) forger ‹alliance›; établir ‹identity, link›
⓷ vi to ～ ahead accélérer; to ～ ahead with aller de l'avant dans ‹plan›

forger n (of documents) faussaire m; (of artefacts) contrefacteur/-trice m/f; (of money) faux-monnayeur m

forgery n contrefaçon f

⚡ **forget** ⓵ vtr (prét **-got**, pp **-gotten**) oublier (that que; to do de faire)
⓶ vi (prét **-got**, pp **-gotten**) oublier
■ **forget about** oublier

forgetful adj distrait/-e

forget-me-not n myosotis m

forgive vtr (prét **-gave**, pp **-given**) pardonner à ‹person›; pardonner ‹act, remark›; to ～ sb sth pardonner qch à qn; to ～ sb for doing pardonner à qn d'avoir fait

forgiveness n pardon m

forgo vtr (prét **-went**, pp **-gone**) renoncer à

fork ⓵ n (a) (for eating) fourchette f
(b) (tool) fourche f
(c) (in river, on bicycle) fourche f; (in railway) embranchement m; (in road) bifurcation f
⓶ vi (also ～ **off**) bifurquer
■ **fork out** (colloq) casquer (fam) (for pour)

forked lightning n éclair m ramifié

forklift truck n (GB) (also **forklift** (US)) chariot m élévateur à fourche

forlorn adj (a) (sad) ‹appearance› malheureux/-euse
(b) (desperate) ‹attempt› désespéré/-e

⚡ **form** ⓵ n (a) (gen) forme f; in the ～ of sous forme de; to be in good ～ être en bonne or pleine forme; it is bad ～ (to do) cela ne se fait pas (de faire); as a matter of ～ pour la forme
(b) (document) formulaire m; blank ～ formulaire vierge
(c) (GB Sch) classe f; in the first ～ ≈ en sixième
⓶ vtr (a) former ‹queue, circle, barrier› (from avec); nouer ‹friendship, relationship›; to ～ part of faire partie de
(b) se faire ‹impression, opinion›
(c) former ‹personality, tastes, ideas, attitudes›
⓷ vi se former

formal adj (a) (official) ‹agreement, complaint, invitation› officiel/-ielle
(b) (not casual) ‹language› soutenu/-e; ‹occasion› solennel/-elle; ‹manner› cérémonieux/-ieuse; ‹clothing› habillé/-e
(c) ‹training› professionnel/-elle;

⚡ indicates a very frequent word

formal dress ⋯⟶ fourteenth ⋯⋯

‹qualification› reconnu/-e

formal dress *n* tenue *f* de soirée

formality *n* (a) (legal or social convention) formalité *f*
(b) (of occasion, manner) solennité *f*; (of language) caractère *m* soutenu

formally *adv* (a) (officially) officiellement
(b) (not casually) cérémonieusement

format ①️ *n* format *m*
②️ *vtr* (*p prés etc* **-tt-**) (Comput) formater

 ⚑ **formation** *n* formation *f*

⚑ **former** ①️ *n* the ～ (singular noun) celui-là/celle-là *m/f*; (plural noun) ceux-là/celles-là *mpl/fpl*
②️ *adj* (a) *‹era, life›* antérieur/-e; *‹size, state›* initial/-e, original/-e; **he's a shadow of his ～ self** il n'est plus que l'ombre de lui-même
(b) *‹leader, husband, champion›* ancien/-ienne (*before n*)
(c) (first of two) premier/-ière (*before n*)

formerly *adv* autrefois

formidable *adj* (a) (intimidating) redoutable
(b) (awe-inspiring) impressionnant/-e

formula *n* (*pl* **-lae** *ou* **～s**) (a) formule *f* (**for** de; **for doing** pour faire)
(b) (baby milk) lait *m* en poudre

fort *n* fort *m*

forte *n* **to be sb's ～** être le fort de qn

forth *adv* **from this day ～** à partir d'aujourd'hui; **from that day ～** à dater de ce jour; ▶ BACK, SO

forthcoming *adj* (a) *‹event, book›* prochain/-e (*before n*)
(b) **she wasn't very ～ about it** elle était peu disposée à en parler

forthright *adj* direct/-e

forties *n pl* (a) (era) **the ～** les années *fpl* quarante
(b) (age) **to be in one's ～** avoir entre quarante et cinquante ans

fortieth *n, adj, adv* quarantième *mf*

fortified *adj ‹place›* fortifié/-e; **～ wine** vin *m* doux; **～ with vitamins** vitaminé/-e

fortify *vtr* fortifier

fortnight *n* (GB) quinze jours *mpl*; **the first ～ in August** la première quinzaine d'août

fortnightly *adj ‹meeting, visit›* qui a lieu toutes les deux semaines; *‹magazine›* publié/-e toutes les deux semaines

fortunate *adj* heureux/-euse

fortunately *adv* heureusement

fortune *n* (a) fortune *f*; **to make a ～** faire fortune
(b) **to have the good ～ to do** avoir la chance *or* le bonheur de faire
(c) **to tell sb's ～** dire la bonne aventure à qn

fortune-teller *n* diseur/-euse *m/f* de bonne aventure

forty *n, pron, det* quarante *m inv*

⚑ **forward** ①️ *n* (Sport) avant *m*

②️ *adj* (a) (bold) effronté/-e
(b) (towards the front) *‹movement›* en avant; **to be too far ～** *‹seat›* être trop en avant
(c) (advanced) avancé/-e; **he's no further ～** il n'est pas plus avancé
③️ *adv* (*also* **forwards**) **to step ～** faire un pas en avant; **to fall ～** tomber en avant; **to go** *or* **walk ～** avancer; **to move sth ～** avancer qch; **a way ～** une solution
④️ *vtr* (a) expédier *‹goods›*; envoyer *‹parcel›*
(b) (send on) faire suivre, réexpédier *‹mail›*

forwarding address *n* nouvelle adresse *f* (pour faire suivre le courrier)

forward-looking *adj ‹company, person›* tourné/-e vers l'avenir

forward planning *n* planification *f* à long terme

forwards – FORWARD 3

fossil *n* fossile *m*

fossil fuel *n* combustible *m* fossile

foster ①️ *adj ‹child, parent›* adoptif/-ive
②️ *vtr* (a) (encourage) encourager *‹attitude›*; promouvoir *‹activity›*
(b) prendre [qn] en placement *‹child›*

foster family *n* famille *f* de placement

foster home *n* foyer *m* de placement

foul ①️ *n* (Sport) faute *f* (**by** de; **on** sur)
②️ *adj* (a) *‹smell, air›* fétide; *‹taste›* infect/-e
(b) *‹weather, day›* épouvantable; **to be in a ～ mood** être d'une humeur massacrante (fam); **to have a ～ temper** avoir un sale caractère
(c) *‹language›* ordurier/-ière
(?) *adv* **to taste ～** avoir un goût infect
④️ *vtr* (a) polluer *‹environment›*; souiller *‹pavement›*
(b) (Sport) commettre une faute contre *‹player›*

foul-mouthed *adj* grossier/-ière

foul play *n* acte *m* criminel; (in sport) jeu *m* irrégulier

foul-up *n* (colloq) cafouillage *m* (fam)

found *vtr* fonder (**on** sur)

foundation *n* (a) (founding) fondation *f*
(b) **～s** (of building) fondations *fpl*
(c) (*also* **～ cream**) fond *m* de teint

foundation course *n* (GB Univ) année *f* de préparation à des études supérieures

founder *n* fondateur/-trice *m/f*

foundry *n* fonderie *f*

fountain *n* fontaine *f*

fountain pen *n* stylo *m* (à encre)

⚑ **four** *n, pron, det* quatre *m inv*
IDIOM **on all ～s** à quatre pattes

four-by-four *n* quatre-quatre *m inv*

four-letter word *n* mot *m* grossier

four-star ①️ *n* (*also* **～ petrol**) (GB) super(carburant) *m*
②️ *adj ‹hotel, restaurant›* quatre étoiles

fourteen *n, pron, det* quatorze *m inv*

fourteenth ①️ *n* (a) (in order) quatorzième *mf*

(b) (of month) quatorze *m inv*
(c) (fraction) quatorzième *m*
⟦2⟧ *adj, adv* quatorzième
⚹ **fourth** ⟦1⟧ *n* **(a)** (in order) quatrième *mf*
(b) (of month) quatre *m inv*
(c) (fraction) quatrième *m*
(d) (*also* ~ **gear**) (Aut) quatrième *f*
⟦2⟧ *adj, adv* quatrième
four-wheel drive (vehicle) *n*
quatre-quatre *m inv*
fowl *n* volaille *f*
fox *n* renard *m*
foxhound *n* fox-hound *m*
fox hunting *n* chasse *f* au renard
fraction *n* fraction *f* (of de)
fracture ⟦1⟧ *n* fracture *f*
⟦2⟧ *vtr* fracturer ⟨bone, rock⟩
⟦3⟧ *vi* ⟨bone⟩ se fracturer
fragile *adj* fragile
fragment *n* (of rock, manuscript) fragment *m*;
(of glass, china) morceau *m*
fragrance *n* parfum *m*
fragrant *adj* odorant/-e
frail *adj* ⟨person⟩ frêle; ⟨health, hope⟩
précaire
⚹ **frame** ⟦1⟧ *n* **(a)** (of building, boat, roof)
charpente *f*; (of car) châssis *m*; (of bicycle,
racquet) cadre *m*; (of bed) sommier *m*; (of tent)
armature *f*
(b) (of picture, window) cadre *m*; (of door)
encadrement *m*
(c) (body) corps *m*
⟦2⟧ **frames** *n pl* (of spectacles) monture *f*
⟦3⟧ *vtr* **(a)** encadrer ⟨picture, face⟩
(b) formuler ⟨question⟩
frame of mind *n* état *m* d'esprit; **to be in
the right/wrong** ~ **for doing** être/ne pas être
d'humeur à faire
framework *n* structure *f*; (figurative) cadre
m
franc *n* franc *m*
France *pr n* France *f*
franchise *n* **(a)** (right to vote) droit *m* de vote
(b) (commercial) franchise *f*
francophile *n, adj* francophile *mf*
frank *adj* franc/franche
Frankfurt *pr n* Francfort
frankly *adv* franchement
frantic *adj* **(a)** ⟨activity⟩ frénétique
(b) ⟨effort, search⟩ désespéré/-e; **to be** ~ **with**
worry être fou/folle d'inquiétude
frantically *adv* **(a)** (wildly) frénétiquement
(b) (desperately) désespérément
fraternal *adj* fraternel/-elle
fraternity *n* fraternité *f*
fraud *n* fraude *f*
fraudulent *adj* ⟨practice, use⟩
frauduleux/-euse; ⟨signature, cheque⟩

⚹ indicates a very frequent word

falsifié/-e; ⟨earnings⟩ illicite
fraught *adj* ⟨situation, atmosphere⟩
tendu/-e; ⟨person⟩ accablé/-e (**with** de); **to be**
~ **with** être lourd/-e de ⟨danger, difficulty⟩
fray *vi* ⟨material, rope⟩ s'effilocher
frayed *adj* ⟨nerves⟩ à bout; **tempers were** ~
les gens s'énervaient
frazzle *n* (colloq) **to burn sth to a** ~ calciner
qch; **to be worn to a** ~ être lessivé/-e (fam)
freak ⟦1⟧ *n* **(a)** (strange person) original/-e *m/f*
(b) (at circus) phénomène *m*; ~ **show**
exhibition *f* de monstres
(c) (unusual occurrence) aberration *f*; **a** ~ **of**
nature une bizarrerie de la nature
(d) (fam) (enthusiast) mordu/-e *m/f* (fam), fana
mf (fam)
⟦2⟧ *adj* ⟨accident, storm⟩ exceptionnel/-elle
■ **freak out** (colloq) (get angry) piquer une
crise (fam); (go mad) flipper (fam)
freckle *n* tache *f* de rousseur
⚹ **free** ⟦1⟧ *adj* **(a)** (gen) libre; **to be** ~ **to do**
être libre de faire; **to set [sb/sth]** ~ libérer
⟨person⟩; rendre la liberté à ⟨animal⟩
(b) (*also* ~ **of charge**) gratuit/-e;
'**admission**' '~' 'entrée gratuite'
(c) to be ~ **with** être prodigue de ⟨advice⟩;
to be very ~ **with money** dépenser sans
compter
⟦2⟧ *adv* **(a)** ⟨run, roam⟩ librement, en toute
liberté; **to go** ~ ⟨hostage⟩ être libéré/-e;
⟨criminal⟩ circuler en toute liberté
(b) (without paying) gratuitement
⟦3⟧ *vtr* **(a)** (gen) libérer; (from wreckage)
dégager
(b) débloquer ⟨money, resources⟩
⟦4⟧ **-free** *combining form* **smoke/sugar-**~
sans fumée/sucre; **interest-**~ sans intérêt
⟦5⟧ **for free** *phr* gratuitement
IDIOMS to have a ~ **hand** avoir carte
blanche (**in** pour); **to be a** ~ **agent** pouvoir
agir à sa guise; ~ **and easy** décontracté/-e
freebee, freebie *n* (colloq) (free gift)
cadeau *m*; (newspaper) journal *m* gratuit; (trip)
voyage *m* gratuit
⚹ **freedom** *n* liberté *f* (**to do** de faire); ~
of the press liberté de la presse; ~ **of
information** libre accès *m* à l'information
freedom fighter *n* combattant *m* de la
liberté
freefall *n* chute *f* libre
Freefone® *n* (*also* **Freephone**®) numéro
m vert d'appel gratuit
free-for-all *n* mêlée *f* générale
free gift *n* cadeau *m*
free kick *n* coup *m* franc
freelance ⟦1⟧ *n* (*also* **freelancer**)
free-lance *mf*
⟦2⟧ *adv* ⟨work⟩ en free-lance
freely *adv* (gen) librement; ⟨spend, give⟩
sans compter; ⟨admit⟩ volontiers

free market n (also ~ **economy**) économie f de marché

Freephone® = FREEFONE

freepost n (GB) port m payé

free-range adj ‹chicken› élevé/-e en plein air; ‹eggs› de poules élevées en plein air

free speech n liberté f d'expression

freestyle n (in swimming) nage f libre; (in skiing) figures fpl libres; (in wrestling) lutte f libre

free trade n libre-échange m

freeware n freeware m, graticiel m

freeway n (US) autoroute f

free will n libre arbitre m; **of one's (own)** ~ de plein gré

freeze ① n (a) (in weather) gelées fpl
(b) (Econ) gel m (on de)
② vtr (prét **froze**, pp **frozen**) (a) congeler ‹food›; ‹cold weather› geler ‹liquid, pipes›
(b) (Econ) bloquer, geler ‹prices, wages, assets›
(c) (anaesthetize) insensibiliser ‹gum, skin›
③ vi (prét **froze**, pp **frozen**) (a) ‹water, pipes› geler; ‹food› se congeler
(b) (feel cold) geler; **to be freezing to death** mourir de froid
(c) (not move) ‹person, blood, smile› se figer
④ v impers geler

freeze-dried adj lyophilisé/-e

freeze frame n arrêt m sur image

freezer n congélateur m

freezer compartment n freezer m

freezing ① n zéro m; **below** ~ en-dessous de zéro
② adj **I'm** ~ je suis gelé; **it's** ~ **in here** on gèle ici

freezing cold adj ‹room, wind› glacial/-e; ‹water› glacé/-e

freight n (a) (goods) fret m, marchandises fpl
(b) (transport system) transport m
(c) (cost) (frais mpl de) port m

freighter n (a) (ship) cargo m
(b) (plane) avion-cargo m

✔ **French** ① n (a) (people) **the** ~ les Français mpl
(b) (language) français m
② adj ‹culture, food, politics› français/-e; ‹teacher, lesson› de français; ‹ambassador, embassy› de France

French fries n pl frites fpl

Frenchman n (pl **-men**) Français m

French-speaking adj francophone

French toast n pain m perdu

French window n porte-fenêtre f

Frenchwoman n (pl **-women**) Française f

frenetic adj ‹activity› frénétique; ‹lifestyle› trépidant/-e

frenzied adj ‹activity› frénétique; ‹attempt› désespéré/-e

frenzy n frénésie f, délire m

✔ **frequency** n fréquence f (of de)

frequent adj (a) (common) ‹expression› courant/-e
(b) (happening often) fréquent/-e; **to make** ~ **use of sth** se servir souvent or fréquemment de qch

✔ **frequently** adv souvent, fréquemment

fresco n (pl **-oes**) fresque f

✔ **fresh** adj (a) frais/fraîche; **to smell** ~ avoir une odeur fraîche; ~ **orange juice** jus d'orange pressée; **while it is still** ~ **in your mind** tant que tu l'as tout frais à l'esprit
(b) ‹evidence, attempt› nouveau/-elle (before n); ‹linen› propre; **to make a** ~ **start** prendre un nouveau départ
(c) ‹approach, outlook› (tout) nouveau/ (toute) nouvelle (before n)
(d) **to feel** or **be** ~ ‹person› être plein/-e d'entrain
(e) (colloq) (cheeky) impertinent/-e; **to be** ~ **with sb** être un peu familier/-ière avec qn

fresh air n air m frais; **to get some** ~ prendre l'air, s'oxygéner

freshen
■ **freshen up** faire un brin de toilette

freshly adv fraîchement; ~ **ironed/washed** qui vient d'être repassé/lavé

fresh water n eau f douce

fret vi (p prés etc **-tt-**) (a) (be anxious) s'inquiéter (**over, about** pour, au sujet de)
(b) (cry) pleurer

Freudian slip n lapsus m

friction n (a) (rubbing) frottement m
(b) (conflict) conflits mpl (**between** entre); **to cause** ~ être cause de friction

✔ **Friday** n vendredi m

fridge n (GB) frigo m (fam), réfrigérateur m

fridge-freezer n réfrigérateur-congélateur m

✔ **friend** n ami/-e m/f (**of** de); **to make** ~**s** se faire des amis; **to make** ~**s with sb** devenir ami/-e m/f avec qn

friendly ① adj ‹person, attitude, argument, match› amical/-e; ‹animal› affectueux/-euse; ‹government, nation› ami (after n); **to be** ~ **with sb** être ami/-e m/f avec qn
② **-friendly** combining form
environment-~ qui ne nuit pas à l'environnement; **user-**~ d'utilisation facile, convivial/-e

friendly fire n (Mil) feu m allié

friendship n amitié f

fries n pl (US) (colloq) frites fpl

fright n peur f; **to take** ~ prendre peur, s'effrayer; **to give sb a** ~ faire peur à qn, effrayer qn

frighten vtr faire peur à, effrayer

frightened adj **to be** ~ avoir peur (**of** de; **to do** de faire)

frightening adj effrayant/-e

frightful adj (a) (inducing horror) abominable, épouvantable
(b) (colloq) (bad) ⟨prospect, mistake⟩ terrible; ⟨headache⟩ affreux/-euse

frill n (on dress) volant m; (on shirt) jabot m

fringe n (a) frange f; **on the ~s of society** en marge de la société
(b) (in theatre) **the ~** théâtre m alternatif

fringe benefits n pl avantages mpl sociaux or en nature

frisk vtr fouiller ⟨person⟩

fritter n beignet m
■ **fritter away** gaspiller ⟨time, money⟩

frivolous adj frivole

frizzy adj ⟨hair⟩ crépu/-e

frog n grenouille f
IDIOM **to have a ~ in one's throat** avoir un chat dans la gorge

frogman n homme-grenouille m

frogs' legs n pl cuisses fpl de grenouille

⚡ **from** prep

■ Note from is often translated by de: from Rome = de Rome; from the sea = de la mer.
— Remember that de + le always becomes du (from the office = du bureau), and de + les always becomes des (from the United States = des États-Unis).
— For examples and particular usages, see the entry below.

(a) de; **where is he ~?** d'où est-il?, d'où vient-il?; **she comes ~ Oxford** elle vient d'Oxford; **paper ~ Denmark** du papier provenant du Danemark; **a flight ~ Nice** un vol en provenance de Nice; **a friend ~ Chicago** un ami (qui vient) de Chicago; **a colleague ~ Japan** un collègue japonais; **a man ~ the council** un homme qui travaille pour le conseil municipal; **a letter ~ Tim** une lettre (de la part) de Tim; **who is it ~?** c'est de la part de qui?; **alcohol can be made ~ a wide range of products** on peut faire de l'alcool à partir de produits très variés; **10 km ~ the sea** à 10 km de la mer; **15 years ~ now** dans 15 ans, d'ici 15 ans
(b) **~ ... to...** de ... à...; **the journey ~ A to B** le voyage de A à B; **the road ~ A to B** la route qui va de A à B; **open ~ 2 pm to 5 pm** ouvert de 14 à 17 heures; **~ June to August** du mois de juin au mois d'août; **to rise ~ 10 to 17%** passer de 10 à 17%; **~ start to finish** du début à la fin; **everything ~ paperclips to wigs** tout, des trombones aux perruques; **~ day to day** de jour en jour
(c) (starting from) à partir de; **~ today/May** à partir d'aujourd'hui/du mois de mai; **wine ~ £5 a bottle** du vin à partir de 5 livres sterling la bouteille; **~ then on** dès lors; **~ the age of**

8 depuis l'âge de 8 ans
(d) (based on) **~ a short story** d'après un conte; **to speak ~ experience** parler d'expérience
(e) (among) **to choose** or **pick ~** choisir parmi
(f) (in mathematics) **10 ~ 27 leaves 17** 27 moins 10 égale 17
(g) (because of) **I know her ~ work** je la connais car on travaille ensemble; **~ what I saw/he said** d'après ce que j'ai vu/ce qu'il a dit

⚡ **front** [1] n (a) (of house) façade f; (of shop) devanture f; (of cupboard, box, sweater, building) devant m; (of book) couverture f; (of card, coin, banknote) recto m; (of car, boat) avant m; (of fabric) endroit m; **to button at the ~** se boutonner sur le devant; **on the ~ of the envelope** au recto de l'enveloppe
(b) (of train, queue) tête f; (of auditorium) premier rang m; **at the ~ of the line** en tête de la file; **to sit at the ~ of the class** s'asseoir au premier rang de la classe; **I'll sit in the ~** je vais m'asseoir devant; **at the ~ of the coach** à l'avant du car
(c) (GB) (promenade) front m de mer, bord m de mer; **on the sea ~** au bord de la mer
(d) (Mil) front m
(e) (in weather) front m
(f) (façade) façade f; **it's just a ~** ce n'est qu'une façade
[2] adj ⟨entrance⟩ côté rue; ⟨garden, window⟩ de devant; ⟨bedroom⟩ qui donne sur la rue; ⟨wheel⟩ avant; ⟨seat⟩ (in cinema) au premier rang; (in vehicle) de devant; ⟨leg, paw, tooth⟩ de devant; ⟨view⟩ de face
[3] vtr (a) (colloq) être à la tête de ⟨band⟩
(b) présenter ⟨TV show⟩
[4] vi **to ~ onto** (GB) or **on** (US) donner sur
[5] **in front** phr ⟨walk⟩ devant; **the car in ~** la voiture de devant; **the people in ~** les gens qui sont devant; **to be in ~** (in race) être en tête; **I'm 30 points in ~** j'ai 30 points d'avance
[6] **in front of** phr devant

front bench n (GB Pol) (seats) rangs mpl du gouvernement

front door n porte f d'entrée

frontier n frontière f

front line n (a) (Mil) front m
(b) (exposed position) **to be in the ~** être en première ligne

front page [1] n première page f
[2] **front-page** adj ⟨picture, story⟩ à la une (fam); **the ~ headlines** les gros titres, la manchette

frost n gel m

frostbite n gelures fpl

frosted adj ⟨nail varnish⟩ nacré/-e; ⟨glass⟩ dépoli/-e, opaque

frosty adj (a) ⟨morning⟩ glacial/-e; ⟨windscreen⟩ couvert/-e de givre; **it was a ~ night** il gelait cette nuit-là
(b) (unfriendly) glacial/-e

froth n (on beer, champagne) mousse f; (on water) écume f; (around mouth) écume f

frown vi froncer les sourcils; **to ~ at sb** regarder qn en fronçant les sourcils
■ **frown on, frown upon** désapprouver, critiquer

frozen adj (a) ‹food› congelé/-e
(b) ‹lake, pipe, ground› gelé/-e; **I'm ~** je suis gelé; **to be ~ stiff** être transi/-e de froid

⚜ **fruit** n (pl for collective ~) fruit m; **a piece of ~** un fruit

fruit cake n cake m

fruition n **to come to ~** se réaliser; **to bring sth to ~** réaliser qch

fruit juice n jus m de fruits

fruit machine n machine f à sous

fruit salad n salade f de fruits

fruity adj ‹wine, fragrance› fruité/-e

frustrate vtr frustrer ‹person›; réduire [qch] à néant ‹effort›; contrarier ‹plan›; entraver ‹attempt›

frustrated adj frustré/-e

frustrating adj (a) (irritating) énervant/-e
(b) (unsatisfactory) frustrant/-e

frustration n frustration f (**at, with** quant à)

fry ① vtr (prét, pp **fried**) faire frire
② **fried** pp adj **fried fish** poisson m frit; **fried food** friture f; **fried eggs** œufs mpl au plat; **fried potatoes** pommes fpl de terre sautées

frying pan n (GB) poêle f (à frire)

⚜ **fuel** ① n (for heating) combustible m; (for car, plane) carburant m
② vtr (p prés etc **-ll-** (GB), **-l-** (US))
(a) alimenter ‹engine›
(b) ravitailler ‹plane›
(c) aggraver ‹tension›; attiser ‹hatred›

fuel tank n (of car) réservoir m

fugitive n fugitif/-ive m/f, fuyard/-e m/f

fulfil (GB), **fulfill** (US) vtr (p prés etc **-ll-**)
(a) réaliser ‹ambition›; répondre à ‹desire, need›; **to feel ~led** se sentir comblé/-e
(b) remplir ‹duty, conditions, contract›

fulfilment (GB), **fulfillment** (US) n
(a) (satisfaction) épanouissement m
(b) **the ~ of** la réalisation de ‹ambition, need›

⚜ **full** ① adj (a) (gen) plein/-e (**of** de); ‹hotel, flight, car park› complet/-ète; ‹theatre› comble; **I'm ~ (up)** je n'en peux plus
(b) (busy) ‹day, week› chargé/-e, bien rempli/-e; **a very ~ life** une vie très remplie
(c) (complete) ‹name, breakfast, story› complet/-ète; ‹price, control› total/-e; ‹responsibility› entier/-ière; ‹support› inconditionnel/-elle
(d) ‹member› à part entière
(e) ‹employment, bloom› plein/-e (before n); **at ~ volume** à plein volume; **at ~ speed** à toute vitesse; **to get ~ marks** (GB); obtenir la note maximale
(f) (for emphasis) ‹hour, kilo, month› bon/bonne (before n)

(g) (rounded) ‹cheeks› rond/-e; ‹figure› fort/-e; ‹skirt, sleeve› ample
② adv **to know ~ well that** savoir fort bien que; **with the heating up ~** avec le chauffage à fond
③ **in full** phr ‹pay› intégralement; **to write sth in ~** écrire qch en toutes lettres

full blast adv (colloq) **the TV was on (at) ~** la télé marchait à pleins tubes (fam)

full-blown adj (a) ‹disease› déclaré/-e; ‹epidemic› extensif/-ive
(b) ‹crisis, war› à grande échelle

full board n (in hotel) pension f complète

full-cream milk n (GB) lait m entier

full-length adj ‹coat, curtain› long/longue; ‹mirror› en pied; **a ~ film** un long métrage

full moon n pleine lune f

full name n nom m et prénom m

full price adj, adv au prix fort

full-scale adj (a) ‹drawing› grandeur f nature
(b) ‹investigation› approfondi/-e
(c) ‹alert› général/-e; ‹crisis› généralisé/-e

full-size(d) adj grand format inv

full stop n (GB) point m

full time ① n (Sport) fin m du match
② **full-time** adj (a) (Sport) ‹score› final/-e
(b) ‹job, student› à plein temps
③ adv ‹study, work› à plein temps

⚜ **fully** adv (a) ‹understand› très bien; ‹recover› complètement; ‹dressed› entièrement; ‹awake, developed› complètement; **to be ~ qualified** avoir obtenu tous ses diplômes
(b) ‹open› à fond; **~ booked** complet/-ète

fully-fledged adj ‹member› à part entière; ‹lawyer› diplômé/-e

fumble vtr mal attraper ‹ball›
■ **fumble about** (in dark) tâtonner (**to do** pour faire); **to ~ about in** fouiller dans ‹bag›

fume vi (a) ‹chemical, mixture› fumer
(b) (colloq) **to be fuming** être furibond/-e (fam)

fumes n pl émanations fpl; **petrol ~** (GB), **gas ~** (US) vapeurs fpl d'essence

⚜ **fun** n plaisir m, amusement m; **to have ~** s'amuser (**doing** en faisant; **with** avec); **windsurfing is ~** c'est amusant de faire de la planche à voile; **for ~** pour s'amuser; **she is great ~ to be with** on s'amuse beaucoup avec elle
IDIOM to make ~ of or **poke ~ at sb/sth** se moquer de qn/qch

⚜ **function** ① n (a) (gen) fonction f
(b) (reception) réception f; (ceremony) cérémonie f (officielle)
② vi (a) (work properly) fonctionner
(b) **to ~ as** ‹object› faire fonction de, servir de; ‹person› jouer le rôle de

functional adj (a) (in working order) opérationnel/-elle
(b) ‹furniture, design› fonctionnel/-elle

function key n touche f de fonction

ⳍ **fund** ⟦1⟧ *n* fonds *m*; **relief** ~ caisse *f* de
secours; **disaster** ~ collecte *f* en faveur des
sinistrés
⟦2⟧ **funds** *n pl* fonds *mpl*, capitaux *mpl*; **to
be in** ~**s** avoir de l'argent
⟦3⟧ *vtr* financer ‹*company, project*›

fundamental *adj* ‹*issue*› fondamental/-e;
‹*error, importance*› capital/-e; ‹*concern*›
principal/-e

fundamentalist *n, adj* (gen)
fondamentaliste *mf*; (religious) intégriste *mf*

ⳍ **funding** *n* financement *m*

fund-raising *n* collecte *f* de fonds

funeral *n* enterrement *m*, obsèques *fpl*

funeral home (US), **funeral parlour**
n entreprise *f* de pompes funèbres

fun fair *n* fête *f* foraine

fungus *n* (*pl* **-gi**) (a) (mushroom)
champignon *m*
(b) (mould) moisissure *f*

fun-loving *adj* ‹*person*› qui aime s'amuser

funnel *n* (a) (for liquids) entonnoir *m*
(b) (on ship) cheminée *f*

ⳍ **funny** *adj* (amusing) drôle, amusant/-e; (odd)
bizarre; **to feel** ~ (colloq) se sentir tout/-e
chose (fam)

fur ⟦1⟧ *n* (of animal) poils *mpl*; (for garment)
fourrure *f*
⟦2⟧ *adj* ‹*collar, coat*› de fourrure

furious *adj* (a) furieux/-ieuse (**with, at**
contre); **he's** ~ **about it** cela l'a rendu
furieux
(b) ‹*debate, struggle*› acharné/-e; ‹*storm*›
déchaîné/-e; **at a** ~ **rate** à un rythme effréné

furnace *n* (boiler) chaudière *f*; (in foundry)
fourneau *m*; (for forging) four *m*

furnish *vtr* meubler ‹*room, apartment*›

furnishings *n pl* ameublement *m*

furniture *n* mobilier *m*, meubles *mpl*;
a piece of ~ un meuble

furry *adj* ‹*toy*› en peluche; ‹*kitten*› au poil
touffu

ⳍ **further** ⟦1⟧ *adv* (*comparative of* **far**)
(a) (gen) (*also* **farther**) plus loin (**than** que);
how much ~ **is it?** c'est encore loin?; ~
back/forward plus en arrière/en avant; ~
away *or* **off** plus loin; ~ **on** encore plus loin
(b) (in time) (*also* **farther**) ~ **back than 1964**
avant 1964; **we must look** ~ **ahead** nous
devons regarder plus vers l'avenir
(c) **I haven't read** ~ **than page twenty** je n'ai
pas lu au-delà de la page vingt; **prices fell**

(**even**) ~ les prix ont baissé encore plus
⟦2⟧ *adj* (*comparative of* **far**) (a) (additional)
a ~ **500 people** 500 personnes de plus; ~
changes d'autres changements; **without** ~
delay sans plus attendre
(b) (*also* **farther**) ‹*side, end*› autre
⟦3⟧ *vtr* (a) (GB) **to** ~ **the lights** faire sauter
‹*career, plan*›; servir ‹*cause*›

further education *n* (GB Univ) ≈
enseignement *m* professionnel

furthest ⟦1⟧ *adj* (*superlative of* **far**) le plus
éloigné/la plus éloignée
⟦2⟧ *adv* (*also* **the** ~) le plus loin

furtive *adj* ‹*glance, movement*› furtif/-ive;
‹*behaviour*› suspect/-e

fury *n* fureur *f*; **to be in a** ~ être en fureur

fuse, fuze (US) ⟦1⟧ *n* fusible *m*; **to blow a**
~ faire sauter un fusible; (get angry) piquer
une crise (fam)
⟦2⟧ *vtr* (a) (GB) **to** ~ **the lights** faire sauter
les plombs
(b) (join) fondre [qch] ensemble ‹*metals*›

fuse box *n* boîte *f* à fusibles

fuselage *n* fuselage *m*

fuse wire *n* fusible *m*

fuss ⟦1⟧ *n* (a) (agitation) remue-ménage *m*
inv; **to make a** ~ faire des histoires; **to make
a** ~ **about sth** faire toute une histoire à
propos de qch
(b) **to kick up a** ~ **about sth** (colloq) piquer
une crise à propos de qch (fam)
(c) (attention) **to make a** ~ **of** être aux
petits soins avec *or* pour ‹*person*›; caresser
‹*animal*›
⟦2⟧ *vi* (a) (worry) se faire du souci (**about**
pour)
(b) (show attention) **to** ~ **over sb** (colloq) être
aux petits soins avec *or* pour qn

fussy *adj* **to be** ~ **about one's food/about
details** être maniaque sur la nourriture/sur
les détails

futile *adj* (a) (vain) vain/-e
(b) (inane) futile

ⳍ **future** ⟦1⟧ *n* (a) avenir *m*; **in the** ~ dans
l'avenir; **in** ~ à l'avenir
(b) (*also* ~ **tense**) futur *m*
⟦2⟧ *adj* ‹*generation, developments,
investment, earnings*› futur/-e; ‹*prospects*›
d'avenir; ‹*queen, king*› futur/-e (*before n*); **at
some** ~ **date** à une date ultérieure

fuze (US) = FUSE

fuzzy *adj* (a) ‹*hair, beard*› crépu/-e
(b) ‹*image*› flou/-e; ‹*idea, mind*› confus/-e

Gg

g, G n **(a)** (letter) g, G m
(b) G (Mus) sol m
(c) g (*written abbr* = **gram**) g
gab n (colloq)
IDIOM **to have the gift of the** ~ (colloq) avoir
du bagou(t) (fam)
gadget n gadget m
gaffe n bévue f
gag ① n **(a)** (on mouth) bâillon m
(b) (colloq) (joke) blague f (fam)
② vtr (*p prés etc* **-gg-**) bâillonner ‹person›
③ vi (*p prés etc* **-gg-**) avoir un haut-le-cœur
gage (US) = GAUGE
◦' **gain** ① n **(a)** (financial) gain m, profit m
(b) (increase) augmentation f (**in** de)
(c) (advantage) gain m; (advances) progrès m
(**in** de)
② vtr **(a)** (gen) gagner; acquérir ‹experience›
(**from** de); obtenir ‹advantage› (**from** grâce
à); **we have nothing to** ~ nous n'avons rien
à gagner
(b) to ~ **speed** prendre de la vitesse *or* de
l'élan; **to** ~ **weight** prendre du poids
③ vi **(a)** (increase) **to** ~ **in popularity** gagner
en popularité; **to** ~ **in value** prendre de la
valeur
(b) (profit) **she hasn't** ~**ed by it** cela ne lui a
rien rapporté
■ **gain on** rattraper ‹person, vehicle›
galaxy n galaxie f
gale n vent m violent
gallery n **(a)** (gen) galerie f
(b) (art) ~ musée m (d'art)
(c) (in theatre) dernier balcon m
Gallic adj (French) français/-e
galling adj vexant/-e
gallon n gallon m ((GB) = *4.546 l*; (US)
= *3.785 l*)
gallop ① n galop m
② vi galoper
galore adv ‹prizes, bargains› à profusion;
‹drinks, sandwiches› à volonté, à gogo (fam)
galvanize vtr galvaniser ‹group,
community›; relancer ‹campaign›; **to** ~ **sb
into doing** pousser qn à faire
gambit n **(a)** tactique f
(b) (in chess) gambit m
gamble ① n pari m; **it's a** ~ c'est risqué
② vtr **(a)** jouer ‹money›
(b) (figurative) miser (**on** sur)
③ vi (at cards, on shares) jouer; (on horses)
parier; (figurative) miser (**on** sur)
gambler n joueur/-euse m/f
gambling n jeu m (d'argent)

◦' **game** ① n **(a)** jeu m; **to play a** ~ jouer à un
jeu; **to have a** ~ **of** faire une partie de
(b) (match) match m (**of** de); (in tennis) jeu m
(c) (Culin) gibier m
② **games** n pl **(a)** (GB Sch) sport m
(b) (*also* **Games**) (sporting event) Jeux mpl
IDIOM **to give the** ~ **away** vendre la mèche
gamekeeper n garde-chasse m
game plan n stratégie f
game reserve n (for hunting) réserve f de
chasse; (for protection) réserve f naturelle
games console n console f de jeux vidéo
game show n jeu m télévisé
games room n salle f de jeux
games software n logiciel m de jeux,
ludiciel m
gaming n on-line ~ jeux mpl en ligne
gaming zone n (on Internet) salle f de jeux
en ligne
gammon n jambon m
gang n **(a)** (of criminals) gang m; (of youths,
friends) bande f
(b) (of workmen, prisoners) équipe f
■ **gang up** se coaliser (**on, against** contre)
gangland n ≈ le Milieu
gang leader n chef m de bande
gangmaster n gangmaster m, chef m
d'équipe (d'ouvriers saisonniers)
gang-rape n viol m collectif
gangster n gangster m
gangway n **(a)** (to ship) passerelle f
(b) (GB) (in bus, cinema) allée f
◦' **gap** n **(a)** (gen) trou m (**in** dans); (between
planks, curtains) interstice m (**in** entre); (between
cars) espace m (**in** entre); (in cloud) trouée f
(**in** dans)
(b) (of time) intervalle m; (in conversation)
silence m
(c) (discrepancy) écart m (**between** entre);
a 15-year age ~ une différence d'âge de
15 ans
(d) (in knowledge) lacune f (**in** dans)
(e) (in market) créneau m
gape vi **(a)** (stare) rester bouche bée; **to** ~ **at**
sb/sth regarder qn/qch bouche bée
(b) to ~ **open** ‹chasm› s'ouvrir tout grand;
‹wound› être béant/-e; ‹garment› bâiller
gaping adj ‹person› bouche bée; ‹wound,
hole› béant/-e
gap year n: année d'interruption des études
entre le lycée et l'université
garage n garage m
garbage n **(a)** (US) (refuse) ordures fpl
(b) (nonsense) âneries fpl, bêtises fpl

garbage can n (US) poubelle f

garbage truck n (US) camion m des éboueurs

garbled adj ‹account, instructions› confus/-e

ᶜᵉ **garden** ① n jardin m
② vi jardiner, faire du jardinage

garden centre (GB), **garden center** (US) n jardinerie f

gardener n jardinier/-ière m/f

gardening n jardinage m

gargle vi se gargariser (**with** avec)

garish adj tape-à-l'œil inv

garland n guirlande f

garlic n ail m

garment n vêtement m

garnish ① n garniture f
② vtr garnir (**with** de)

garter n (a) (for stocking) jarretière f; (for socks) fixe-chaussette m
(b) (US) (suspender) jarretelle f

ᶜᵉ **gas** ① n (a) (fuel) gaz m
(b) (anaesthetic) anesthésie f
(c) (US) (petrol) essence f
② vtr (p prés etc **-ss-**) gazer

gas chamber n chambre f à gaz

gas cooker n cuisinière f à gaz

gas fire n (appareil m de) chauffage m à gaz

gash ① n entaille f
② vtr entailler

gas mask n masque m à gaz

gasoline n (US) essence f

gas oven n four m à gaz

gasp ① n halètement m
② vi (a) (for air) haleter
(b) to ∼ (**in amazement**) avoir le souffle coupé (par la surprise)

gas pedal n (US) accélérateur m

gas station n (US) station-service f

gastro-enteritis n gastro-entérite f

gate n (of field, level crossing) barrière f; (in town, prison, airport, garden) porte f; (of courtyard, palace) portail m; **at the** ∼ à l'entrée

gatecrash vtr (colloq) (without paying) resquiller (fam) à; (without invitation) se pointer (fam) sans invitation à

gatecrasher n (colloq) (at concert) resquilleur/-euse m/f; (at party) intrus/-e m/f

ᶜᵉ **gather** ① n (in garment) fronce f
② vtr (a) cueillir ‹fruit, flowers›; ramasser ‹fallen fruit, wood›; recueillir ‹information›; rassembler ‹courage, strength›; **to** ∼ **speed** prendre de la vitesse
(b) to ∼ **that...** déduire que...; **I** ∼ (**that**) **he was there** d'après ce que j'ai compris il était là
(c) (in sewing) faire des fronces à
③ vi ‹people, crowd› se rassembler; ‹family›

se réunir; ‹clouds› s'amonceler

gathering n réunion f; **social/family** ∼ réunion entre amis/de famille

gaudy adj tape-à-l'œil inv

gauge, gage (US) ① n (a) (of gun, screw) calibre m; (of metal, wire) épaisseur f
(b) (of railway) écartement m (des voies)
(c) (measuring instrument) jauge f; **fuel** ∼ jauge d'essence
② vtr (a) mesurer ‹diameter›; jauger ‹distance, quantity›; calibrer ‹gun›
(b) évaluer ‹mood, reaction›

gaunt adj décharné/-e

gauze n (fabric) gaze f; (wire) grillage m

ᶜᵉ **gay** ① n homosexuel/-elle m/f, gay mf
② adj (a) homosexuel/-elle
(b) (happy) gai/-e; ‹laughter› joyeux/-euse

Gaza strip pr n bande f de Gaza

gaze ① n regard m
② vi **to** ∼ **at sb/sth** regarder qn/qch; (in wonder) contempler qn/qch

GCSE n (abbr = **General Certificate of Secondary Education**) (pl ∼s) (GB) certificat m d'études secondaires

gear n (a) (equipment) matériel m
(b) (clothes) fringues fpl (fam); **football** ∼ tenue f de football
(c) (Aut) vitesse f; **to be in third** ∼ être en troisième; **to put a car in** ∼ passer la vitesse; **you're not in** ∼ tu es au point mort
■ **gear up** se préparer; **to be** ∼**ed up** être prêt/-e (**for** pour)

gearbox n boîte f de vitesses

gearstick (GB), **gearshift** (US) n levier m de vitesses

gear wheel n pignon m

gel ① n gel m
② vi (p prés etc **-ll-**) (a) (Culin) prendre
(b) (figurative) prendre forme

gem n (jewel) pierre f précieuse

Gemini n Gémeaux mpl

gender n (a) (of word) genre m
(b) (of person, animal) sexe m

gene n gène m

genealogy n généalogie f

gene library n génothèque f

gene pool n patrimoine m héréditaire

ᶜᵉ **general** ① n général m
② adj général/-e
③ **in general** phr (usually) en général; (overall) dans l'ensemble

general election n élections fpl législatives

generalization n généralisation f (**about** sur)

generalize vtr, vi généraliser (**about** à propos de)

general knowledge n culture f générale

ᶜᵉ indicates a very frequent word

generally *adv* **(a)** (usually) en général, généralement; ∼ **speaking...** en règle générale...
(b) (overall) **the quality is** ∼ **good** dans l'ensemble la qualité est bonne
(c) ⟨*talk*⟩ d'une manière générale

general practitioner, GP *n* (médecin *m*) généraliste *mf*

general public *n* (grand) public *m*

general-purpose *adj* à usages multiples

general strike *n* grève *f* générale

generate *vtr* produire ⟨*power, heat, income, waste*⟩; créer ⟨*employment*⟩; susciter ⟨*interest, tension, ideas*⟩; entraîner ⟨*profit, publicity*⟩

generation *n* **(a)** génération *f*; **the younger/older** ∼ la jeune/l'ancienne génération
(b) (of electricity, data) production *f*

generation gap *n* fossé *m* des générations

generator *n* (of electricity) générateur *m*; (in hospital, on farm) groupe *m* électrogène

generosity *n* générosité *f*

generous *adj* (gen) généreux/-euse; ⟨*size*⟩ grand/-e (*before n*); ⟨*hem*⟩ bon/bonne (*before n*)

gene therapy *n* thérapie *f* génique

genetic *adj* génétique

genetically modified, GM *adj* génétiquement modifié/-e

genetic engineering *n* génie *m* génétique

genetic fingerprinting *n* empreintes *fpl* génétiques

genetics *n* génétique *f*

genetic testing *n* tests *mpl* de dépistage génétique

Geneva *pr n* Genève

genial *adj* cordial/-e

genitals *n pl* organes *mpl* génitaux

genius *n* (*pl* ∼**es** *ou* **-ii** (liter)) génie *m*

genome *n* génome *m*

gentle *adj* (gen) doux/douce; ⟨*hint, reminder*⟩ discret/-ète; ⟨*pressure, touch, breeze*⟩ léger/-ère; ⟨*exercise*⟩ modéré/-e

gentleman *n* (*pl* **-men**) **(a)** (man) monsieur *m*
(b) (well-bred) gentleman *m*

gently *adv* (gen) doucement; ⟨*treat, cleanse*⟩ avec douceur; ⟨*cook*⟩ à feu doux; ⟨*speak*⟩ gentiment; **to break the news** ∼ annoncer la nouvelle avec ménagement

gents *n pl* (toilets) toilettes *fpl*; (on sign) 'Messieurs'

genuine *adj* ⟨*reason, motive*⟩ vrai/-e (*before n*); ⟨*work of art*⟩ authentique; ⟨*jewel, substance*⟩ véritable; ⟨*person, effort, interest*⟩ sincère; ⟨*buyer*⟩ sérieux/-ieuse

genuinely *adv* (really and truly) vraiment; (in reality) réellement

geoengineering *n* géoingénierie *f*

geography *n* géographie *f*

geology *n* géologie *f*

geometry *n* géométrie *f*

gerbil *n* gerbille *f*

geriatric *adj* ⟨*hospital, ward*⟩ gériatrique

germ *n* **(a)** (microbe) microbe *m*
(b) (seed) germe *m*

German ⟦1⟧ *n* **(a)** (person) Allemand/-e *m/f*
(b) (language) allemand *m*
⟦2⟧ *adj* ⟨*custom, food*⟩ allemand/-e; ⟨*ambassador, embassy*⟩ d'Allemagne; ⟨*teacher, course*⟩ d'allemand

German measles *n* rubéole *f*

Germany *pr n* Allemagne *f*

germinate ⟦1⟧ *vtr* faire germer
⟦2⟧ *vi* germer

germ warfare *n* guerre *f* bactériologique

gesticulate *vi* gesticuler

gesture ⟦1⟧ *n* geste *m* (**of** de)
⟦2⟧ *vi* faire un geste; **to** ∼ **at** *or* **towards sth** désigner qch d'un geste; **to** ∼ **to sb** faire signe à qn

get

■ Note This much-used verb has no multi-purpose equivalent in French and therefore is very often translated by choosing a synonym: *to get lunch = to prepare lunch = préparer le déjeuner.*

— When *get* is used to express the idea that a job is done not by you but by somebody else (*to get a room painted*), *faire* is used in French followed by an infinitive (*faire repeindre une pièce*).

— When *get* has the meaning of *become* and is followed by an adjective (*to get rich*), *devenir* is sometimes useful but check the appropriate entry (RICH) as a single verb often suffices (*s'enrichir*).

— The phrasal verbs (*get around, get down, get on* etc) are listed separately at the end of the entry GET.

— For examples and further uses of *get* see the entry below.

⟦1⟧ *vtr* (*p prés* **-tt-**, *prét* **got**, *pp* **got, gotten** (US)) **(a)** (receive) recevoir ⟨*letter, grant*⟩; recevoir, percevoir ⟨*salary, pension*⟩; capter ⟨*channel*⟩
(b) (inherit) **to** ∼ **sth from sb** hériter qch de qn ⟨*article, money*⟩; tenir qch de qn ⟨*trait*⟩
(c) (obtain) obtenir ⟨*permission, divorce*⟩; trouver ⟨*job*⟩
(d) (buy) acheter ⟨*item, newspaper*⟩ (**from** chez); avoir ⟨*ticket*⟩; **to** ∼ **sb sth, to** ∼ **sth for sb** (as gift) acheter qch à qn
(e) (acquire) se faire ⟨*reputation*⟩
(f) (achieve) obtenir ⟨*grade*⟩
(g) (fetch) chercher ⟨*person, help*⟩; **to** ∼ **sb sth, to** ∼ **sth for sb** aller chercher qch pour qn
(h) (move) **to** ∼ **sb/sth downstairs** faire descendre qn/qch
(i) (help progress) **this is** ∼**ting us nowhere** ça ne nous avance à rien; **where will that** ∼ ⋯⟶

you? à quoi ça t'avancera?

(j) (deal with) **I'll ∼ it** (of phone) je réponds; (of doorbell) j'y vais

(k) (prepare) préparer ‹*breakfast, lunch*›

(l) (take hold of) attraper ‹*person*› **(by** par)

(m) (colloq) (oblige to give) **to ∼ sth out of sb** faire sortir qch à qn ‹*money*›; obtenir qch de qn ‹*truth*›

(n) (contract) attraper ‹*cold, disease*›; **he got measles from his sister** sa sœur lui a passé la rougeole

(o) (catch) prendre ‹*bus, train*›

(p) (have) **to have got** avoir ‹*object, money, friend*›; **I've got a headache** j'ai mal à la tête; **to ∼ the idea that** se mettre dans la tête que

(q) to ∼ a surprise être surpris/-e; **to ∼ a shock** avoir un choc; **to ∼ a bang on the head** recevoir un coup sur la tête

(r) (as punishment) prendre ‹*five years*›; avoir ‹*fine*›

(s) (understand, hear) comprendre

(t) (colloq) (annoy) **what ∼s me is…** ce qui m'agace c'est que…

(u) to ∼ to like sb finir par apprécier qn; **how did you ∼ to hear of…?** comment avez-vous entendu parler de…?; **we got to know them last year** on a fait leur connaissance l'année dernière

(v) (have opportunity) **to ∼ to do** avoir l'occasion de faire, pouvoir faire

(w) (must) **to have got to do** devoir faire ‹*homework, chore*›; **it's got to be done** il faut le faire; **you've got to realize that…** il faut que tu te rendes compte que…

(x) (make) **to ∼ sb to pay** faire payer qn; **to ∼ sb to tell the truth** faire dire la vérité à qn

(y) (ask) **to ∼ sb to wash the dishes** demander à qn de faire la vaisselle

(z) to ∼ the car repaired faire réparer la voiture; **to ∼ one's hair cut** se faire couper les cheveux; **to ∼ the car going** faire démarrer la voiture; **to ∼ one's socks wet** mouiller ses chaussettes; **to ∼ one's finger trapped** se coincer le doigt; **to ∼ a dress made** se faire faire une robe

2 *vi* (*p prés* **-tt-**, *prét* **got**, *pp* **got**, **gotten** (US)) **(a)** (become) devenir ‹*suspicious, old*›; **it's ∼ting late** il se fait tard

(b) (forming passive) **to ∼ killed** se faire tuer; **to ∼ hurt** être blessé/-e

(c) (become involved in) **to ∼ into** (colloq) se mettre à ‹*hobby*›; commencer dans ‹*profession*›; **to ∼ into a fight** se battre

(d) (arrive) **to ∼ there** arriver; **to ∼ to the airport** arriver à l'aéroport; **how did you ∼ here?** comment est-ce que tu es venu?; **where did you ∼ to?** où est-ce que tu étais passé?

(e) (progress) **I'm ∼ting nowhere with this essay** je n'avance pas dans cette dissertation; **now we're ∼ting somewhere** il y a du progrès

---

⚜ indicates a very frequent word

(f) (put on) **to ∼ into** mettre, enfiler ‹*pyjamas*›

■ **get about (a)** (move) se déplacer

(b) (travel) voyager

■ **get across (a)** traverser ‹*river, road*›

(b) faire passer ‹*message*› **(to** à)

■ **get ahead** (make progress) progresser

■ **get along (a) how are you ∼ting along?** (in job, school) comment ça se passe?

(b) ‹*people*› bien s'entendre **(with** avec)

■ **get around** **1** ¶ **∼ around** (a) = GET ABOUT

(b) (manage to do) **she'll ∼ around to visiting us eventually** elle va bien finir par venir nous voir; **I haven't got around to it yet** je n'ai pas encore eu le temps de m'en occuper

2 ¶ **∼ around [sth]** contourner ‹*problem, law*›

■ **get at** (colloq) **(a)** (reach) atteindre ‹*object*›; découvrir ‹*truth*›

(b) (criticize) être après ‹*person*›

(c) (insinuate) **what are you ∼ting at?** où est-ce que tu veux en venir?

■ **get away (a)** (leave) partir

(b) (escape) s'échapper

(c) to ∼ away with a crime échapper à la justice; **you won't ∼ away with it!** tu ne vas pas t'en tirer comme ça!

■ **get away from (a)** quitter ‹*place*›; échapper à ‹*person*›

(b) there's no ∼ting away from it on ne peut pas le nier

■ **get back**: **1** ¶ **∼ back (a)** (return) rentrer; (after short time) revenir

(b) (move backwards) reculer

2 ¶ **∼ back to [sth] (a)** (return to) rentrer à ‹*house, city*›; revenir à ‹*office, point*›; **when we ∼ back to London** à notre retour à Londres; **to ∼ back to sleep** se rendormir; **to ∼ back to normal** redevenir normal

(b) (return to earlier stage) revenir à ‹*main topic, former point*›

3 ¶ **∼ back to [sb]** revenir à; **I'll ∼ back to you** (on phone) je vous rappelle

4 ¶ **∼ [sth] back** (regain) récupérer ‹*lost object*›; reprendre ‹*strength*›; **she got her money back** elle a été remboursée

■ **get by (a)** (pass) passer

(b) (survive) s'en sortir **(on, with** avec)

■ **get down**: **1** ¶ **∼ down (a)** (descend) descendre **(from, out of** de)

(b) (on floor) (crouch) se baisser; **to ∼ down on one's knees** s'agenouiller

(c) to ∼ down to se mettre à ‹*work*›; **to ∼ down to doing** se mettre à faire

2 ¶ **∼ down [sth]** descendre ‹*slope*›

3 ¶ **∼ [sth] down** (from height) descendre

4 ¶ **∼ [sb] down** (depress) déprimer

■ **get in**: **1** ¶ **∼ in (a)** (to building) entrer; (to vehicle) monter

(b) (return home) rentrer

(c) (arrive) arriver

(d) (penetrate) pénétrer

(e) ‹*party*› passer; ‹*candidate*› être élu/-e

(f) (Sch, Univ) ‹*applicant*› être admis/-e

2 ¶ **∼ [sth] in** (buy) acheter

■ **get into** (a) (enter) entrer dans ‹building›; monter dans ‹vehicle›
(b) (as member) devenir membre de; (as student) être admis/-e à
(c) (squeeze into) rentrer dans ‹garment, size›

■ **get off**: ⊡1 ¶ ~ **off** (a) (from bus) descendre (at à)
(b) (start on journey) partir
(c) (leave work) finir
(d) (colloq) (escape punishment) s'en tirer (**with** avec)
(e) **to ~ off to a good start** prendre un bon départ; **to ~ off to sleep** s'endormir
⊡2 ¶ ~ **off** [sth] (a) descendre de ‹wall, bus›
(b) s'écarter de ‹subject›
⊡3 ¶ ~ [sth] **off** (a) (send off) envoyer ‹letter›;
(b) (remove) enlever

■ **get on**: ⊡1 ¶ ~ **on** (a) (climb aboard) monter
(b) (GB) (like each other) bien s'entendre
(c) (fare) **how did you ~ on?** comment est-ce que ça s'est passé?; **how are you ~ting on?** comment est-ce que tu t'en sors?
(d) (GB) (approach) **he's ~ting on for 40** il approche des quarante ans; **it's ~ting on for midnight** il est presque minuit
⊡2 ¶ ~ **on** [sth] monter dans ‹vehicle›
⊡3 ¶ ~ [sth] **on** mettre ‹garment, lid›; monter ‹tyre›

■ **get on with**: ⊡1 **to ~ on with one's work** continuer à travailler
⊡2 ¶ **to ~ on with** [sb] (GB) s'entendre avec ‹person›

■ **get out** ⊡1 ¶ ~ **out** (a) (exit) sortir (**through**, **by** par); ~ **out!** va-t-en!
(b) (alight) descendre
(c) ‹prisoner› être libéré/-e
(d) ‹news› être révélé/-e
⊡2 ¶ ~ [sth] **out** (a) (take out) sortir (**of** de)
(b) retirer ‹cork›
(c) enlever ‹stain›
(d) emprunter ‹library book›

■ **get out of** (a) sortir de ‹building›; descendre de ‹vehicle›; être libéré/-e de ‹prison›; quitter ‹profession›
(b) **to ~ out of doing** s'arranger pour ne pas faire; **I'll try to ~ out of it** j'essaierai de me libérer
(c) perdre ‹habit›
(d) **what do you ~ out of your job?** qu'est-ce que ton travail t'apporte?; **what will you ~ out of it?** qu'est-ce que vous en retirerez?

■ **get over** (a) traverser ‹stream, bridge›; passer au-dessus de ‹wall›
(b) se remettre de ‹illness, shock›; **I can't ~ over it** (amazed) je n'en reviens pas
(c) surmonter ‹problem›; **to ~ sth over with** en finir avec qch

■ **get round** (GB): ⊡1 ¶ ~ **round** = GET AROUND
⊡2 ¶ ~ **round** [sb] (colloq) persuader [qn]

■ **get through**: ⊡1 (a) ¶ ~ **through** (squeeze through) passer
(b) **to ~ through to sb** (on phone) avoir qn au téléphone; (make oneself understood) se faire comprendre

(c) ‹news, supplies› arriver
(d) ‹examinee› réussir
⊡2 ¶ ~ **through** [sth] (a) terminer ‹book›; finir ‹meal, task›; réussir à ‹exam›
(b) (use) manger ‹food›; dépenser ‹money›

■ **get together**: ⊡1 ¶ ~ **together** se réunir (**about**, **over** pour discuter de)
⊡2 ¶ ~ [sb/sth] **together** réunir ‹people›; former ‹company›

■ **get up**: ⊡1 ¶ ~ **up** (a) (from bed, chair) se lever (**from** de)
(b) (on ledge, wall) monter
(c) ‹storm› se préparer; ‹wind› se lever
(d) **what did you ~ up to?** (enjoyment) qu'est-ce que tu as fait de beau?; (mischief) qu'est-ce que tu as fabriqué? (fam)
⊡2 ¶ ~ **up** [sth] (a) arriver en haut de ‹hill, ladder›
(b) augmenter ‹speed›

get-together n réunion f (entre amis)

ghastly adj horrible

gherkin n cornichon m

ghetto n (pl ~**s** ou ~**es**) ghetto m

ghetto blaster n (colloq) (gros) radiocassette m portable

ghost n fantôme m

giant ⊡1 n géant m
⊡2 adj géant/-e

gibberish n charabia m

giddy adj (a) **to feel ~** avoir la tête qui tourne
(b) ‹height, speed› vertigineux/-euse

⚹ **gift** n (a) (present) cadeau m (**to** à); **to give sb a ~** faire or offrir un cadeau à qn
(b) (donation) don m
(c) (talent) don m; **to have a ~ for doing** avoir le don de faire; **to have the ~ of the gab** avoir du bagou(t) (fam)

gifted adj doué/-e

gift shop n magasin m de cadeaux

gift token, **gift voucher** n (GB) chèque-cadeau m

gift wrap n papier m cadeau

gig n (colloq) concert m de rock

gigantic adj gigantesque

giggle ⊡1 n petit rire m; **to get the ~s** attraper le fou rire
⊡2 vi rire

gilt ⊡1 n dorure f
⊡2 adj ‹frame, paint› doré/-e

gimmick n (scheme) truc m (fam); (object) gadget m

gin n gin m; ~ **and tonic** gin tonic m

ginger n (a) (Bot, Culin) gingembre m
(b) (colour) roux m

ginger-haired adj roux/rousse

⚹ **girl** n (a) (child) fille f; (teenager) jeune fille f; **baby ~** petite fille f, bébé m; **little ~** petite fille f, fillette f
(b) (daughter) fille f

girl band n girls band m

girlfriend n (female friend) amie f; (sweetheart) (petite) amie f

girl guide (GB), **girl scout** (US) n éclaireuse f

giro n (GB) (system) système m de virement bancaire; (cheque) mandat m

gist n essentiel m (of de)

⚹ **give** ⟦1⟧ n élasticité f

⟦2⟧ vtr (prét **gave**, pp **given**) (gen) donner (**to** à); transmettre ‹message› (**to** à); transmettre, passer ‹illness› (**to** à); laisser ‹seat› (**to** à); accorder ‹grant› (**to** à); faire ‹injection, massage› (**to** à); faire ‹speech›; **to ~ sb sth** donner qch à qn; (politely, as a gift) offrir qch à qn; **to ~ sb pleasure** faire plaisir à qn; **~ him my best (wishes)** transmets-lui mes amitiés; **she gave him a drink** elle lui a donné à boire; **to ~ sb enough room** laisser suffisamment de place à qn

⟦3⟧ vi (prét **gave**, pp **given**) ‹mattress, sofa› s'affaisser; ‹shelf, floorboard› fléchir; ‹branch› ployer

IDIOMS **~ or take an inch (or two)** à quelques centimètres près; **to ~ and take** faire des concessions; **to ~ as good as one gets** rendre coup pour coup; **to ~ it all one's got** (colloq) (y) mettre le paquet

■ **give away**: ⟦1⟧ ¶ **~ [sth] away (a)** donner ‹item, sample›
(b) révéler ‹secret›
(c) laisser échapper ‹match, goal, advantage› (**to** au bénéfice de)
⟦2⟧ ¶ **~ [sb] away (a)** (betray) ‹expression, fingerprints› trahir; ‹person› dénoncer (**to** à); **to ~ oneself away** se trahir
(b) (in marriage) conduire [qn] à l'autel

■ **give back** rendre (**to** à)

■ **give in**: ⟦1⟧ ¶ **~ in (a)** (yield) céder (**to** à)
(b) (stop trying) abandonner; **I ~ in—tell me!** je donne ma langue au chat (fam)—dis-le-moi!
⟦2⟧ ¶ **~ [sth] in** rendre ‹work›; remettre ‹ticket, key›

■ **give off** émettre ‹signal, radiation, light›; dégager ‹heat, fumes›

■ **give out**: ⟦1⟧ ¶ **~ out** ‹strength› s'épuiser; ‹engine› tomber en panne
⟦2⟧ ¶ **~ [sth] out** (distribute) distribuer (**to** à)

■ **give up**: ⟦1⟧ ¶ **~ up** abandonner; **to ~ up on** laisser tomber ‹diet, crossword, pupil, patient›; ne plus compter sur ‹friend, partner›
⟦2⟧ ¶ **~ up [sth] (a)** renoncer à ‹habit, title, claim›; sacrifier ‹free time›; quitter ‹job›; **to ~ up smoking/drinking** cesser de fumer/de boire
(b) abandonner ‹search, hope, struggle›; renoncer à ‹idea›
(c) céder ‹seat, territory›
⟦3⟧ ¶ **~ [sb] up (a)** (hand over) livrer (**to** à); **to ~ oneself up** se livrer (**to** à)
(b) laisser tomber ‹lover›

■ **give way (a)** (collapse) s'effondrer; ‹fence,

⚹ indicates a very frequent word

‹cable› céder; **his legs gave way** ses jambes se sont dérobées sous lui
(b) (GB) (when driving) céder le passage (**to** à)
(c) (yield) céder; **to ~ way to** faire place à

give-and-take n concessions fpl mutuelles

giveaway n **to be a ~** être révélateur/-trice

given ⟦1⟧ adj (a) ‹point, level, number› donné/-e; ‹volume, length› déterminé/-e; **at any ~ moment** à n'importe quel moment
(b) **to be ~ to sth/to doing** avoir tendance à qch/à faire; **I am not ~ to doing** je n'ai pas l'habitude de faire
⟦2⟧ prep (a) (in view of) **~ (the fact) that** étant donné que
(b) (with) avec ‹training, proper care›

given name n prénom m

⚹ **glad** adj content/-e, heureux/-euse (**about** de; **that** que; **to do** de faire); **he was only too ~ to help me** il ne demandait qu'à m'aider

gladly adv (willingly) volontiers; (with pleasure) avec plaisir

glamorize vtr peindre [qn/qch] sous de belles couleurs

glamorous adj ‹person, image, look› séduisant/-e; ‹older person› élégant/-e; ‹dress› splendide; ‹occasion› brillant/-e; ‹job› prestigieux/-ieuse

glamour, glamor (US) n (of person) séduction f; (of job) prestige m; (of travel, cars) fascination f

⚹ **glance** ⟦1⟧ n coup m d'œil
⟦2⟧ vi **to ~ at** jeter un coup d'œil à; **to ~ around the room** parcourir la pièce du regard

■ **glance off** ‹bullet, stone› ricocher sur or contre

glancing adj ‹blow, kick› oblique

gland n glande f; **to have swollen ~s** avoir des ganglions

glandular fever n mononucléose f infectieuse

glare ⟦1⟧ n (a) (angry look) regard m furieux
(b) (from lights) lumière f éblouissante
⟦2⟧ vi ‹person› lancer un regard furieux (**at** à)

glaring adj (a) ‹mistake, injustice› flagrant/-e
(b) ‹light› éblouissant/-e

⚹ **glass** ⟦1⟧ n (a) verre m; **wine ~** verre à vin; **a ~ of wine** un verre de vin
(b) (mirror) miroir m
⟦2⟧ adj ‹bottle, shelf› en verre; ‹door› vitré/-e
⟦3⟧ **glasses** n pl lunettes fpl

glass ceiling n: niveau professionnel que la discrimination empêche certains groupes sociaux de dépasser

glassy-eyed adj (from drink, illness) aux yeux vitreux; (hostile) au regard glacial

glaze ⟦1⟧ n (a) (on pottery) vernis m

(b) (Culin) nappage *m*; (icing) glaçage *m*
2 *vtr* **(a)** vernisser ‹*pottery*›
(b) (Culin) glacer

glazed *adj* ‹*door*› vitré/-e; **to have a ∼ look in one's eyes** avoir les yeux vitreux

gleam **1** *n* (of light) lueur *f*; (of sunshine) rayon *m*; (of gold, polished surface) reflet *m*
2 *vi* ‹*light*› luire; ‹*knife, leather, surface*› reluire; ‹*eyes*› briller

gleaming *adj* **(a)** ‹*eyes, light*› brillant/-e; ‹*leather, surface*› reluisant/-e
(b) (clean) étincelant/-e (de propreté)

glide *vi* ‹*skater, boat*› glisser (**on, over** sur); (in air) planer

glider *n* planeur *m*

gliding *n* vol *m* à voile

glimpse **1** *n* **(a)** vision *f* fugitive (**of** de); **to catch a ∼ of sth** entrevoir qch
(b) (insight) aperçu *m* (**of, at** de)
2 *vtr* entrevoir

glisten *vi* ‹*eyes, hair, surface*› luire; ‹*water*› scintiller

glitch *n* (colloq) (gen) pépin *m* (fam); (Comput) problème *m* technique

glitter **1** *n* **(a)** (substance) paillettes *fpl*
(b) (sparkle) éclat *m*
2 *vi* scintiller

gloat *vi* jubiler (**at, over** à l'idée de)

✺ **global** *adj* **(a)** (world-wide) mondial/-e
(b) (comprehensive) global/-e

global warming *n* réchauffement *m* de la planète

globe *n* **(a)** **the ∼** le globe
(b) (model) globe *m* terrestre

gloom *n* **(a)** (darkness) obscurité *f*
(b) (despondency) morosité *f* (**about, over** à propos de)

gloomy *adj* **(a)** (dark) sombre
(b) ‹*expression, person, voice*› lugubre; ‹*weather*› morose; ‹*news, outlook*› déprimant/-e

glorify *vtr*, glorifier

glorious *adj* **(a)** ‹*view, weather*› magnifique; ‹*holiday*› merveilleux/-euse
(b) (illustrious) glorieux/-ieuse

glory **1** *n* **(a)** (honour) gloire *f*
(b) (splendour) splendeur *f*
2 *vi* **to ∼ in** être très fier/fière de

gloss *n* **(a)** (shine) lustre *m*
(b) (paint) laque *f*

■ **gloss over** (pass rapidly over) glisser sur; (hide) dissimuler

glossary *n* glossaire *m*

glossy *adj* ‹*hair, material*› luisant/-e; ‹*photograph*› brillant/-e; ‹*brochure*› luxueux/-euse

glossy magazine *n* magazine *m* illustré (de luxe)

glove *n* gant *m*

glove compartment *n* boîte *f* à gants

glow **1** *n* **(a)** (from fire) rougeoiement *m*; (of candle) lueur *f*
(b) (of complexion) éclat *m*
2 *vi* **(a)** ‹*metal, embers*› rougeoyer; ‹*lamp, cigarette*› luire
(b) **to ∼ with health** resplendir de santé; **to ∼ with pride** rayonner de fierté

glower *vi* lancer des regards noirs (**at** à)

glowing *adj* **(a)** ‹*ember*› rougeoyant/-e; ‹*face, cheeks*› (from exercise) rouge; (from pleasure) radieux/-ieuse
(b) ‹*account, terms*› élogieux/-ieuse

glue **1** *n* colle *f*
2 *vtr* coller; **to ∼ sth on** *or* **down** coller qch
3 **glued** (colloq) *pp adj* **to be ∼d to the TV** être collé/-e devant la télé (fam); **to be ∼d to the spot** être cloué/-e sur place

glue sniffer *n* sniffeur/-euse *m/f* (fam) de colle

glue-sniffing *n* inhalation *f* de colle

glut *n* surabondance *f*, excès *m*

glutton *n* glouton/-onne *m/f*

glycerin(e) *n* glycérine *f*

GMT *n* (*abbr* = **Greenwich Mean Time**) TU

gnash *vtr* **to ∼ one's teeth** grincer des dents

gnaw **1** *vtr* ronger ‹*bone, wood*›
2 *vi* **(a)** **to ∼ at** *or* **on sth** ronger qch
(b) **to ∼ at sb** ‹*hunger, remorse, pain*› tenailler qn

GNP *n* (= **gross national product**) PNB *m*

GNVQ *n* (*abbr* = **General National Vocational Qualification**) ≈ baccalauréat *m* professionnel

✺ **go**

■ **Note As an intransitive verb**
— *go* as a simple intransitive verb is translated by *aller*: *where are you going?* = où vas-tu?; *Sasha went to London last week* = Sasha est allé à Londres la semaine dernière.
— Note that *aller* conjugates with *être* in compound tenses. For the conjugation of *aller*, see the French verb tables.
— The verb *go* produces a great many phrasal verbs (*go up, go down, go out, go back* etc). Many of these are translated by a single verb in French (*monter, descendre, sortir, retourner* etc). The phrasal verbs are listed separately at the end of the entry GO.
As an auxiliary verb
— When *go* is used as an auxiliary to show intention, it is also translated by *aller*: *I'm going to buy a car* = je vais acheter une voiture; *I was going to talk to you about it* = j'allais t'en parler.

1 *vi* (*3* pers sg prés **goes**, *prét* **went**, *pp* **gone**) **(a)** aller (**from** de; **to** à, en); **to ∼ to Paris/to California** aller à Paris/en Californie; **to ∼ to town/to the country** aller en ville/à la campagne; **they went home** ils sont rentrés chez eux; **to ∼ on holiday** partir ⋯⋗

en vacances; **to ~ for a drink** aller prendre un verre; **~ and ask her** va lui demander; **to ~ to school/work** aller à l'école/au travail; **to ~ to the doctor's** aller chez le médecin; **let's ~, let's get ~ing** allons-y
(b) (leave) partir; **I'm ~ing** je m'en vais
(c) (become) **to ~ red** rougir; **to ~ white** blanchir; **to ~ mad** devenir fou/folle
(d) to ~ unnoticed passer inaperçu/-e; **the question went unanswered** la question est restée sans réponse; **to ~ free** être libéré/-e
(e) (become impaired) **his memory is going** il perd la mémoire; **my voice is going** je n'ai plus de voix; **the battery is going** la pile est presque à plat
(f) (of time) passer, s'écouler
(g) (operate, function) ‹*vehicle, machine, clock*› marcher, fonctionner; **to get [sth] going** mettre [qch] en marche; **to keep going** ‹*business*› se maintenir; ‹*machine*› continuer à marcher; ‹*person*› continuer
(h) (belong, be placed) aller; **where do these plates ~?** où vont ces assiettes?; **it won't ~ into the box** ça ne rentre pas dans la boîte; **five into four won't ~** quatre n'est pas divisible par cinq
(i) (be about to) **to be going to do** aller faire; **it's going to snow** il va neiger
(j) (turn out) passer; **how did the party ~?** comment s'est passée la soirée?; **it went well/badly** ça s'est bien/mal passé
(k) (make sound, perform action or movement) (gen) faire; ‹*bell, alarm*› sonner; **she went like this with her fingers** elle a fait comme ça avec ses doigts
(l) (take one's turn) **you ~ next** c'est ton tour après, c'est à toi après; **you ~ first** après vous
(m) (match) **those two colours don't ~ together** ces deux couleurs ne vont pas ensemble
2 *vtr* (*3ᵉ pers sg prés* **goes**, *prét* **went**, *pp* **gone**) faire ‹*distance, number of miles*›
3 *n* (*pl* **goes**) (GB) (turn) tour *m*; (try) essai *m*; **whose ~ is it?** à qui le tour?; (in game) à qui de jouer?
4 to go *phr* **there are three days/pages to ~** il reste encore trois jours/pages
IDIOMS to make a ~ of sth réussir qch; **she's always on the ~** elle n'arrête jamais; **in one ~** d'un seul coup; **it goes without saying that** il va sans dire que; **as the saying goes** comme dit le proverbe; **anything goes** tout est permis

■ **go about** s'attaquer à ‹*task*›; **to ~ about one's business** vaquer à ses occupations
■ **go ahead** ‹*event*› avoir lieu; **~ ahead!** vas-y!; **they are going ahead with the project** ils ont décidé de mettre le projet en route
■ **go along** aller; **to make sth up as one goes along** inventer qch au fur et à mesure
■ **go along with** être d'accord avec ‹*person, view*›; accepter ‹*plan*›

■ **go around (a)** se promener, circuler; **they ~ around everywhere together** ils vont partout ensemble
(b) ‹*rumour*› courir
■ **go away** partir; **~ away!** va-t-en!
■ **go back (a)** (return) retourner; (turn back) rebrousser chemin; **to ~ back to sleep** se rendormir; **to ~ back to work** se remettre au travail
(b) (date back) remonter (**to** à)
(c) (revert) revenir (**to** à)
■ **go back on** revenir sur ‹*promise, decision*›
■ **go by: 1 ¶ ~ by** ‹*person*› passer; **as time goes by** avec le temps
2 ¶ ~ by [sth] juger d'après ‹*appearances*›; **to ~ by the rules** suivre le règlement
■ **go down 1 ¶ ~ down (a)** (descend) (gen) descendre; ‹*sun*› se coucher; **to ~ down on one's knees** se mettre à genoux
(b) to ~ down well/badly être bien/mal reçu/-e
(c) ‹*price, temperature, standard*› baisser
(d) ‹*swelling*› désenfler; ‹*tyre*› se dégonfler
(e) (Comput) tomber en panne
2 ¶ ~ down [sth] descendre ‹*hill*›
■ **go for: 1 ¶ ~ for [sb/sth] (a)** (colloq) (be keen on) aimer
(b) (apply to) **the same goes for him!** c'est valable pour lui aussi!
2 ¶ ~ for [sb] (a) (attack) attaquer
(b) he has a lot going for him il a beaucoup de choses pour lui
3 ¶ ~ for [sth] (a) essayer d'obtenir ‹*honour, victory*›; **she's going for the world record** elle vise le record mondial; **~ for it!** (colloq) vas-y, fonce! (fam)
(b) (choose) choisir, prendre
■ **go in (a)** (enter) entrer; (go back in) rentrer
(b) ‹*troops*› attaquer
(c) ‹*sun*› se cacher
■ **go in for (a)** (be keen on) aimer
(b) s'inscrire à ‹*exam, competition*›
■ **go into (a)** (enter) entrer dans ‹*building*›; se lancer dans ‹*business, profession*›
(b) (examine) étudier ‹*question*›
(c) a lot of work went into this project beaucoup de travail a été investi dans ce projet
■ **go off: 1 ¶ ~ off (a)** ‹*bomb*› exploser
(b) ‹*alarm clock*› sonner; ‹*fire alarm*› se déclencher
(c) ‹*person*› partir, s'en aller
(d) (GB) ‹*milk, cream*› tourner; ‹*meat*› s'avarier; ‹*butter*› rancir; ‹*performer, athlete*› perdre sa forme
(e) ‹*lights, heating*› s'éteindre
(f) (happen, take place) **the concert went off very well** le concert s'est très bien passé
2 ¶ ~ off [sb/sth] (GB) n'aimer plus
■ **go on: 1 ¶ ~ on (a)** (happen) se passer; **how long has this been going on?** depuis combien de temps est-ce que ça dure?
(b) (continue on one's way) poursuivre son chemin
(c) (continue) continuer; **the list goes on and on** la liste est infinie

---

⚡ indicates a very frequent word

(d) (of time) (elapse) **as time went on, they…**
avec le temps, ils…; **as the evening went on**
au fur et à mesure que la soirée avançait
(e) to ~ on about sth ne pas arrêter de
parler de qch
(f) (proceed) passer; **let's ~ on to the next
item** passons au point suivant; **he went on to
say that…** puis il a dit que…
(g) ‹heating, lights› s'allumer
(h) ‹actor› entrer en scène
2 ¶ **~ on [sth]** se fonder sur ‹evidence,
information›; **that's all we've got to ~ on**
c'est tout ce que nous savons avec certitude
■ **go on at** s'en prendre à ‹person›
■ **go out (a)** (leave, depart) sortir; **to ~ out for a
drink** aller prendre un verre
(b) to ~ out with sb sortir avec qn
(c) ‹tide› descendre
(d) ‹fire, light› s'éteindre
■ **go over**: **1** ¶ **~ over** (cross over) aller (**to**
vers)
2 ¶ **~ over [sth] (a)** passer [qch] en revue
‹details, facts›; vérifier ‹accounts, figures›;
relire ‹article›
(b) (exceed) dépasser ‹limit, sum›
■ **go round** (GB): **1** ¶ **~ round (a)** ‹wheel›
tourner
(b) to ~ round to see sb aller voir qn
(c) ‹rumour› circuler
(d) (make detour) faire un détour
2 ¶ **~ round [sth]** faire le tour de ‹shops,
house, museum›
■ **go through**: **1** ¶ **~ through** ‹law› passer;
‹business deal› être conclu/-e
2 ¶ **~ through [sth] (a)** endurer, subir
‹experience›; passer par ‹stage, phase›; **she's
gone through a lot** elle a beaucoup souffert
(b) (check) examiner
(c) (search) fouiller ‹belongings›
(d) (perform) remplir ‹formalities›
(e) (use up) dépenser ‹money›; consommer
‹food, drink›
■ **go through with** réaliser ‹plan›; **I can't ~
through with it** je ne peux pas le faire
■ **go under** couler
■ **go up**: **1** ¶ **~ up (a)** (ascend) monter; **to ~
up to bed** monter se coucher
(b) ‹price, temperature› monter; ‹figures›
augmenter; ‹curtain› se lever (**on** sur)
2 ¶ **~ up [sth]** monter, gravir ‹hill›
■ **go without**: **1** ¶ **~** without s'en passer
2 ¶ **~ without [sth]** se passer de
go-ahead n (colloq) **to give sb the ~** donner
le feu vert à qn; **to get the ~** recevoir le feu
vert
⚡ **goal** n but m
goalkeeper n gardien m de but
goalpost n poteau m de but
goat n chèvre f
gobble **1** vtr (also ~ **down**, ~ **up**)
engloutir
2 vi ‹turkey› glouglouter
gobbledygook n (colloq) charabia m (fam)

go-between n intermédiaire mf
gobsmacked adj (GB) (colloq)
estomaqué/-e (fam)
⚡ **god** n dieu m; **God** Dieu m
godchild n filleul/-e m/f
goddaughter n filleule f
goddess n déesse f
godfather n parrain m
godmother n marraine f
godparent n parrain/marraine m/f; **the
~s** le parrain et la marraine
godsend n aubaine f
godson n filleul m
goggles n pl lunettes fpl; (for swimming)
lunettes fpl de plongée
going **1** n (a) (departure) départ m
(b) (progress) **that's good ~!** c'est rapide!; **it
was slow ~** (on journey) ça a été long, (at work)
ça n'avançait pas vite; **to be heavy ~** ‹book›
être difficile à lire; ‹work, conversation› être
laborieux/-ieuse
(c) when the **~ gets tough** quand les choses
vont mal; **she finds her new job hard ~** elle
trouve que son nouveau travail est difficile;
they got out while the ~ was good ils s'en
sont tirés (fam) avant qu'il ne soit trop tard
2 adj **(a)** ‹price› actuel/-elle, en cours; **the
~ rate** le tarif en vigueur
(b) ~ concern affaire f qui marche
(c) it's the best model ~ c'est le meilleur
modèle sur le marché
goings-on n pl (colloq) (events) événements
mpl; (activities) activités fpl; (behaviour)
conduite f
go-kart n kart m
gold **1** n or m
2 adj ‹jewellery, tooth› en or; ‹coin, ingot,
ore, wire› d'or
IDIOMS as good as ~ sage comme une image; **to be worth one's weight in ~** valoir son
pesant d'or
gold dust n poudre f d'or; **to be like ~** être
une denrée rare
golden adj **(a)** (made of gold) en or, d'or
(b) (gold coloured) doré/-e, d'or; **~ hair**
cheveux mpl blonds dorés
(c) ‹age, days› d'or; **a ~ opportunity** une
occasion en or
golden handshake n prime f de départ
golden rule n règle f d'or
goldfish n (pl -fish ou -fishes) poisson
m rouge
gold medal n médaille f d'or
gold mine n mine f d'or
gold-plated adj plaqué/-e or
gold rush n ruée f vers l'or
goldsmith n orfèvre m
golf n golf m; **to play ~** faire du golf
golf club n (place) club m de golf; (stick)
crosse f de golf
golf course n (terrain m de) golf m

golfer n joueur/-euse m/f de golf, golfeur/-euse m/f

gone adj **(a)** (departed) parti/-e; (dead) disparu/-e
(b) (past) **it's ～ six o'clock** il est six heures passées

gong n gong m

✿ **good** ❶ n **(a)** (virtue) bien m; **～ and evil** le bien et le mal; **to be up to no ～** mijoter qch (fam); **to come to no ～** mal tourner
(b) (benefit) bien m; **it'll do you ～** ça te fera du bien; **it didn't do my migraine any ～** ça n'a pas arrangé ma migraine
(c) (use) **it's no ～ crying** ça ne sert à rien de pleurer; **what ～ would it do me?** à quoi cela me servirait-il?

❷ adj (comp **better**, superl **best**) **(a)** (gen) bon/bonne (before n); **it's a ～ film** c'est un bon film; **it was a ～ party** c'était une soirée réussie; **the ～ weather** le beau temps; **she's a ～ swimmer** elle nage bien; **to be ～ at** être bon/bonne en ‹Latin, physics›; être bon/bonne à ‹badminton, chess›; **to be ～ with** savoir comment s'y prendre avec ‹children, animals›; aimer ‹figures›; **to have a ～ time** bien s'amuser; **it's ～ to see you again** je suis content de vous revoir; **I don't feel too ～** je ne me sens pas très bien; **the ～ thing is that…** ce qui est bien c'est que…; **to taste ～** avoir bon goût; **to smell ～** sentir bon; **we had a ～ laugh** on a bien ri; **to wait/walk for a ～ hour** attendre/marcher une bonne heure
(b) (well-behaved) ‹child, dog› sage; **be ～!** sois sage!
(c) (high quality) ‹hotel› bon/bonne (before n); ‹coat, china› beau/belle (before n); ‹degree› avec mention
(d) (kind) ‹person› gentil/-ille; (virtuous) ‹man, life› vertueux/-euse; **to do sb a ～ turn** rendre service à qn; **would you be ～ enough to do** auriez-vous la gentillesse de faire
(e) (beneficial) **to be ～ for** faire du bien à ‹person, plant›; être bon/bonne pour ‹health, business, morale›
(f) (fortunate) **it's a ～ job** or **thing (that)** heureusement que; **it's a ～ job** or **thing too!** tant mieux!; ▶ BETTER, BEST

❸ excl (expressing pleasure, satisfaction) c'est bien!; (with relief) tant mieux!; (to encourage, approve) très bien!

❹ **as good as** phr quasiment; **to be as ～ as new** être comme neuf/neuve

❺ **for good** phr pour toujours
IDIOMS **～ for you!** bravo!; **it's too ～ to be true** c'est trop beau pour être vrai

good afternoon phr bonjour

goodbye phr au revoir

good evening phr bonsoir

good-for-nothing n bon/bonne m/f à rien

good-humoured (GB), **good-humored** (US) adj ‹crowd, discussion› détendu/-e;

‹rivalry› amical/-e; ‹remark, smile› plaisant/-e; **to be ～** ‹person› avoir bon caractère

good-looking adj beau/belle (before n)

good morning phr bonjour

good-natured adj ‹person› agréable; ‹animal› placide

goodness ❶ n **(a)** (quality, virtue) bonté f
(b) (nourishment) **to be full of ～** être plein/-e de bonnes choses
❷ excl (also **～ gracious!**) mon Dieu!
IDIOM for **～'** sake! pour l'amour de Dieu!

goodnight phr bonne nuit

goods n pl articles mpl, marchandise f

goods train n (GB) train m de marchandises

goodwill n **(a)** (kindness) bonne volonté f
(b) (of business) clientèle f

google® ❶ vtr googler
❷ vi chercher sur (le moteur de recherche) Google®

goose n (pl **geese**) oie f

gooseberry n groseille f à maquereau
IDIOM **to be a** or **play ～** tenir la chandelle

goose pimples n pl chair f de poule

gorge ❶ n gorge f
❷ v refl **to ～ oneself** se gaver (**on** de)

gorgeous adj **(a)** (colloq) ‹food, scenery› formidable (fam); ‹kitten, baby› adorable; ‹weather, day, person› splendide
(b) (sumptuous) somptueux/-euse

gorilla n gorille m

gorse n ajoncs mpl

gory adj sanglant/-e

gosh excl (colloq) ça alors! (fam)

go-slow n (GB) grève f perlée

gospel n Évangile m

gospel music n gospel m

gossip ❶ n **(a)** (malicious) commérages mpl (**about** sur); (not malicious) nouvelles fpl (**about** sur)
(b) (person) commère f
❷ vi bavarder; (more maliciously) faire des commérages (**about** sur)

gossip column n échos mpl

got: to have got phr **(a)** **to have ～** avoir
(b) **I've ～ to go** il faut que j'y aille

gouge ❶ n rainure f
❷ vtr **(a)** (dig) creuser ‹hole› (**in** dans)
(b) (US) (colloq) (overcharge) estamper (fam)
■ **gouge out:** ¶ **～ out [sth]**, **～ [sth] out** creuser ‹pattern›; enlever ‹bad bit›; **to ～ sb's eyes out** arracher les yeux à qn

gourd n **(a)** (container) gourde f
(b) (fruit) calebasse f

gout n goutte f

govern ❶ vtr **(a)** gouverner ‹country, state, city›; administrer ‹colony, province›
(b) (control) régir ‹use, conduct, treatment›
(c) (determine) déterminer ‹decision›; régler ‹flow, speed›
❷ vi ‹parliament, president› gouverner

✿ indicates a very frequent word

governess n (pl ~es) gouvernante f

governing adj ‹party› au pouvoir; ‹class›
dirigeant/-e; **the ~ principle** l'idée directrice

✶ **government** ⃞1 n gouvernement m; **(the
state)** l'État m; **in ~** au pouvoir
⃞2 adj ‹minister, plan› du gouvernement;
‹department, majority, policy›
gouvernemental/-e; ‹expenditure, borrowing›
de l'État; ‹funds› public/-ique

governmental adj gouvernemental/-e

governor n (of state, colony, bank)
gouverneur m; (of prison) directeur m; (of
school) membre m du conseil d'établissement

gown n (dress) robe f; (of judge, academic) toge
f; (of surgeon) blouse f

GP n (abbr = **general practitioner**)
(médecin m) généraliste mf

GPS n (abbr = **global positioning
system**) GPS

✶ **grab** ⃞1 vtr (p prés etc **-bb-**) empoigner
‹money, object›; saisir ‹arm, person,
opportunity›; **to ~ hold of** se saisir de
⃞2 vi (p prés etc **-bb-**) **to ~ at** se jeter sur

grace n (a) (gen) grâce f; **sb's saving ~** ce
qui sauve qn
(b) to give sb two days' ~ accorder un délai
de deux jours à qn
(c) (prayer) (before meal) bénédicité m; (after
meal) grâces fpl
IDIOM **to be full of airs and ~s** prendre des
airs

graceful adj ‹dancer, movement›
gracieux/-ieuse; ‹person› élégant/-e

✶ **grade** ⃞1 n (a) (quality) qualité f; **high-/
low-~** de qualité supérieure/inférieure
(b) (mark) note f (in en)
(c) (rank) échelon m
(d) (US) (class) classe f
⃞2 vtr (by quality) classer (**according to**
selon); (by size) calibrer (**according to** selon)

grade school n (US) école f primaire

gradient n pente f, inclinaison f

gradual adj (a) ‹change, increase›
progressif/-ive
(b) ‹slope› doux/douce

gradually adv (slowly) peu à peu; (by
degrees) progressivement

graduate ⃞1 n diplômé/-e m/f
⃞2 vi (a) terminer ses études (**at** from à);
(US Sch) ≈ finir le lycée
(b) (progress) **to ~ (from sth) to** passer (de
qch) à

graduate training scheme n
programme m de formation professionnelle
pour étudiants diplômés

graduation n (also ~ **ceremony**)
(cérémonie f de) remise f des diplômes

graffiti n graffiti mpl

graffiti artist n tagger m

graft ⃞1 n greffe f; **skin ~** greffe de la peau
⃞2 vtr greffer (**onto** sur)

grain n (a) (of rice, wheat, sand, salt) grain m
(b) (crops) céréales fpl
(c) (figurative) (of truth, comfort) brin m
(d) (in wood, stone) veines fpl; (in leather, paper,
fabric) grain m
IDIOM **it goes against the ~** c'est contre tous
mes/nos/leurs principes

gram(me) n gramme m

grammar n grammaire f

grammar school n (GB) ≈ lycée m (à
recrutement sélectif)

grammatical adj (a) ‹error› de
grammaire
(b) (correct) grammaticalement correct

granary n grenier m

granary bread n pain m aux céréales

grand adj ‹building, ceremony› grandiose;
on a ~ scale à très grande échelle; **the
Grand Canyon** le Grand Cañon m; **to play the
~ lady** jouer à la grande dame

grandchild n (girl) petite-fille f; (boy) petit-fils
m; **his grandchildren** ses petits-enfants mpl

granddaughter n petite-fille f

grandeur n (of scenery) majesté f; (of
building) caractère m grandiose

grandfather n grand-père m

grandfather clock n horloge f comtoise

grandma n (colloq) mémé f (fam), mamy f
(fam), mamie f (fam)

grandmother n grand-mère f

grandpa n (colloq) pépé m (fam), papy m
(fam), papi m (fam)

grandparents n pl grands-parents mpl

grand piano n piano m à queue

grand slam® n grand chelem m

grandson n petit-fils m

grandstand n tribune f

grand total n total m

granite n granit(e) m

granny n (colloq) mémé f (fam)

✶ **grant** ⃞1 n (gen) subvention f; (for study)
bourse f
⃞2 vtr (a) accorder ‹permission›; accéder à
‹request›
(b) to ~ sb [sth] accorder [qch] à qn
‹interview, leave, visa›; concéder [qch] à qn
‹citizenship›
(c) to ~ that reconnaître que
IDIOMS **to take sth for ~ed** considérer qch
comme allant de soi; **he takes his mother for
~ed** il croit que sa mère est à son service

granulated adj ‹sugar› cristallisé/-e

granule n (of sugar, salt) grain m; (of coffee)
granule m

grape n grain m de raisin; **a bunch of ~s**
une grappe de raisin

grapefruit n pamplemousse m

grapeseed oil n huile f de pépins de
raisin

g

grapevine n (in vineyard) pied m de vigne; (in greenhouse, garden) vigne f
 IDIOM **to hear sth on the ~** apprendre qch par le téléphone arabe
graph n graphique m
graphic adj (a) ‹art, display, technique› graphique
 (b) ‹account› (pleasantly described) vivant/-e; (gory) cru/-e
graphic design n graphisme m
graphic designer n graphiste mf
graphics n pl (a) (on screen) visualisation f graphique
 (b) **computer ~** infographie f
 (c) (in film, TV) images fpl; (in book) illustrations fpl
graphics card n carte f graphique
graphics interface n interface f graphique
graph paper n papier m millimétré
grasp ① n (a) (hold, grip) prise f
 (b) (understanding) maîtrise f
 ② vtr (a) empoigner ‹rope, hand›; saisir ‹opportunity›
 (b) (comprehend) saisir, comprendre
 ③ vi **to ~ at** tenter de saisir
grasping adj cupide
grass n herbe f; (lawn) pelouse f
 IDIOM **the ~ is greener (on the other side of the fence)** on croit toujours que c'est mieux ailleurs
grass court n court m en gazon
grasshopper n sauterelle f
grassroots ① n pl **the ~** le peuple
 ② adj ‹movement› populaire; ‹support› de base
grate ① n grille f de foyer
 ② vtr râper ‹carrot, cheese›
 ③ vi (a) ‹metal object› grincer (**on** sur)
 (b) (annoy) agacer; **that ~s** ça m'agace
grateful adj reconnaissant/-e (**to** à; **for** de)
grater n râpe f
gratify vtr faire plaisir à ‹person›; satisfaire ‹desire›; **to be gratified** être satisfait/-e
grating ① n (bars) grille f
 ② adj ‹noise› grinçant/-e; ‹voice› désagréable
gratitude n reconnaissance f (**to, towards** envers; **for** de)
gratuitous adj gratuit/-e
grave ① n tombe f
 ② adj (a) ‹illness› grave; ‹risk› sérieux/-ieuse; ‹danger› grand/-e (before n)
 (b) (solemn) sérieux/-ieuse
gravel n (coarse) graviers mpl; (fine) gravillons mpl
gravestone n pierre f tombale
graveyard n cimetière m
gravitate vi **to ~ to(wards)** graviter vers

✐ indicates a very frequent word

gravity n (a) pesanteur f; **centre of ~** centre m de gravité
 (b) (of situation) gravité f
gravy n sauce f (au jus de rôti)
gravy boat n saucière f
gray (US) = GREY
graze ① n écorchure f
 ② vtr (a) **to ~ one's knee** s'écorcher le genou (**on, against** sur)
 (b) (touch lightly) frôler
 ③ vi ‹sheep› brouter; ‹cow› paître
grease ① n graisse f
 ② vtr graisser
greasy adj ‹hair, skin, food› gras/grasse; ‹overalls› graisseux/-euse
✐ **great** adj (a) (gen) grand/-e (before n); ‹number, increase› important/-e; ‹heat› fort/-e (before n); **a ~ deal (of)** beaucoup (de); **with ~ difficulty** avec beaucoup de mal
 (b) (colloq) ‹book, party, weather› génial/-e (fam), formidable (fam); ‹opportunity› formidable (fam); **to feel ~** se sentir en pleine forme; **~!** génial!
great aunt n grand-tante f
great big adj (très) grand/-e (before n), énorme
Great Britain pr n Grande-Bretagne f
great grandchild n (girl) arrière-petite-fille f; (garçon) arrière-petit-fils m
great grandfather n arrière-grand-père m
great grandmother n arrière-grand-mère f
great-great grandchild n (girl) arrière-arrière-petite-fille f; (boy) arrière-arrière-petit-fils m
greatly adv ‹admire, regret› beaucoup, énormément; ‹surprised, distressed› très, extrêmement; ‹improved, changed› considérablement
greatness n (of achievement) importance f; (of person) grandeur f
great uncle n grand-oncle m
Greece pr n Grèce f
greed n (a) (for money, power) avidité f (**for** de)
 (b) (also **greediness**) (for food) gourmandise f
greedy adj (a) (for food) gourmand/-e; (stronger) goulu/-e; ‹look› avide; **a ~ pig** (colloq) un goinfre (fam)
 (b) (for money, power) avide (**for** de)
Greek ① n (a) (person) Grec/Grecque m/f
 (b) (language) grec m
 ② adj ‹government, island› grec/grecque; ‹embassy› de Grèce
 IDIOM **it's all ~ to me** c'est du chinois pour moi
✐ **green** ① n (a) (colour) vert m
 (b) **village ~** terrain m communal
 (c) (in bowling) boulingrin m; (in golf) green m

(d) (person) écologiste *mf*; **the Greens** les Verts

2 greens *n pl* (GB) légumes *mpl* verts

3 *adj* **(a)** (in colour) vert/-e
(b) ‹*countryside*› verdoyant/-e
(c) (colloq) (naïve) naïf/naïve
(d) (inexperienced) novice
(e) ‹*policies, candidate, issues*› écologiste; ‹*product*› écologique

green card *n* **(a)** (driving insurance) carte *f* verte (internationale)
(b) (US) (residence and work permit) carte *f* de séjour

greenery *n* verdure *f*

greenfield site *n* terrain *m* vert

greengrocer *n* marchand *m* de fruits et légumes

greenhouse *n* serre *f*

greenhouse effect *n* effet *m* de serre

Greenland *pr n* Groenland *m*

greet *vtr* **(a)** (say hello to) saluer
(b) to be ~ed with *or* **by** provoquer ‹*dismay, amusement*›

greeting **1** *n* salutation *f*
2 greetings *n pl* **Christmas ~s** vœux *mpl* de Noël; **Season's ~s** meilleurs vœux

greetings card (GB), **greeting card** (US) *n* carte *f* de vœux

grey (GB), **gray** (US) **1** *n* gris *m*
2 *adj* **(a)** (in colour) gris/-e
(b) (grey-haired) **to go** *or* **turn ~** grisonner
(c) (dull) ‹*existence, day*› morne; ‹*person, town*› terne
■ **grey out: to be ~ed out** (Comput) être en grisé

grey area *n* zone *f* floue

grey-haired *adj* aux cheveux gris

greyhound *n* lévrier *m*

grid *n* **(a)** grille *f*
(b) (GB) (network) réseau *m*

gridlock *n* embouteillage *m*, bouchon *m*

grief *n* chagrin *m*
IDIOMS **to come to ~** ‹*person*› (have an accident) avoir un accident; (fail) échouer; ‹*business*› péricliter; **good ~!** mon Dieu!

grief-stricken *adj* accablé/-e de douleur

grievance *n* griefs *mpl* (**against** contre)

grieve *vi* **to ~ for** *or* **over** pleurer ‹*person*›

grievous bodily harm, GBH *n* (Law) coups *mpl* et blessures *fpl*

grill **1** *n* gril *m*
2 *vtr* **(a)** faire griller ‹*meat, fish*›
(b) (colloq) (interrogate) mettre [qn] sur la sellette (fam)

grille *n* (gen) grille *f*; (on car) calandre *f*

grim *adj* **(a)** ‹*news, town, future*› sinistre; ‹*sight, conditions*› effroyable; ‹*reality*› dur/-e
(b) ‹*struggle*› acharné/-e; ‹*resolve*› terrible
(c) ‹*face*› grave

grimace **1** *n* grimace *f* (**of** de)
2 *vi* (involuntary) faire une grimace (**with, in**

de); (pull a face) faire la grimace

grime *n* (of city) saleté *f*; (on object, person) crasse *f*

grimy *adj* ‹*city*› noir/-e; ‹*hands, window*› crasseux/-euse

✓ **grin** **1** *n* sourire *m*
2 *vi* (*p prés etc* **-nn-**) sourire (**at** à; **with** de)

grind **1** *n* (colloq) boulot *m* (fam) *or* travail *m* monotone
2 *vtr* (*prét, pp* **ground**) moudre ‹*corn, coffee beans*›; écraser ‹*grain*›; hacher ‹*meat*›; **to ~ one's teeth** grincer des dents
3 *vi* (*prét, pp* **ground**) ‹*machine*› grincer; **to ~ to a halt** ‹*machine*› s'arrêter; ‹*vehicle*› s'arrêter avec un grincement de freins; ‹*factory, production*› s'immobiliser

grindstone *n* meule *f or* pierre *f* à aiguiser
IDIOM **to keep** *or* **have one's nose to the ~** travailler sans relâche

grip **1** *n* **(a)** prise *f* (**on** sur)
(b) to lose one's ~ on reality perdre contact avec la réalité; **to come to ~s with sth** en venir aux prises avec qch; **get a ~ on yourself! ressaisis-toi!**
(c) (of tyre) adhérence *f*
2 *vtr* (*p prés etc* **-pp-**) **(a)** (grab) agripper; (hold) serrer
(b) ‹*tyres*› adhérer à ‹*road*›; ‹*shoes*› accrocher à ‹*ground*›
(c) (captivate) captiver

gripping *adj* captivant/-e

grisly *adj* ‹*story, sight*› horrible; ‹*remains*› macabre

gristle *n* cartilage *m*

grit **1** *n* **(a)** (on lens) grains *mpl* de poussière; (sandy dirt) grains *mpl* de sable
(b) (GB) (for roads) sable *m*
2 *vtr* (*p prés etc* **-tt-**) (GB) sabler ‹*road*›
IDIOM **to ~ one's teeth** serrer les dents

grizzly *n* (also **~ bear**) grizzli *m*

groan **1** *n* (of pain, despair) gémissement *m*; (of disgust, protest) grognement *m*
2 *vi* (in pain) gémir; (in disgust, protest) grogner

grocer *n* (person) épicier/-ière *m/f*; **~'s (shop)** épicerie *f*

groceries *n pl* provisions *fpl*

grocery *n* (also **~ shop** (GB), **~ store**) épicerie *f*

groggy *adj* groggy; **to feel ~** avoir les jambes en coton (fam)

groin *n* aine *f*

groom **1** *n* **(a)** (bridegroom) **the ~** le jeune marié
(b) (for horse) palefrenier/-ière *m/f*
2 *vtr* **(a)** panser ‹*horse*›
(b) to ~ sb for préparer à qn ‹*exam, career*›

groove *n* (gen) rainure *f*; (on record) sillon *m*; (on screw) fente *f*

grope **1** *vtr* (sexually) tripoter (fam)
2 *vi* **to ~ for sth** chercher qch à tâtons

gross ⬚1 *n* (*pl* ~) grosse *f*
  ⬚2 *adj* (a) ⟨*income, profit*⟩ brut/-e
  (b) ⟨*error, exaggeration*⟩ grossier/-ière;
  ⟨*abuse, inequality*⟩ choquant/-e; ⟨*injustice*⟩
  flagrant/-e
  (c) ⟨*behaviour*⟩ vulgaire; ⟨*language*⟩ cru/-e
  (d) (colloq) (revolting) dégoûtant/-e
  (e) (colloq) (obese) obèse
  ⬚3 *vtr* ⟨*business, company*⟩ faire un bénéfice
  brut de

grossly *adv* ⟨*misleading, irresponsible*⟩
  extrêmement; ⟨*underpaid*⟩ scandaleusement;
  ~ **overweight** obèse

gross national product, GNP *n*
  produit *m* national brut, PNB *m*

grotesque *n, adj* grotesque *m*

grotto *n* (*pl* ~s *ou* ~es) grotte *f*

grotty *adj* (colloq) minable (fam); **to feel** ~ se
  sentir tout chose (fam)

⚡ **ground** ⬚1 *n* (a) sol *m*, terre *f*; **on the** ~
  par terre; **above** ~ en surface; **below** ~
  sous terre
  (b) (area, territory) terrain *m*; **a piece of** ~ un
  terrain
  (c) (sportsground) terrain *m*
  ⬚2 **grounds** *n pl* (a) (garden) parc *m* (of de)
  (b) (reasons) ~s **for sth** motifs *mpl* de qch;
  ~s **for doing** motifs pour faire; **on the** ~s
  that en raison du fait que
  ⬚3 *pp adj* ⟨*coffee, pepper*⟩ moulu/-e
  ⬚4 *vtr* (a) immobiliser ⟨*aircraft*⟩
  (b) ⟨*ship*⟩ **to be** ~**ed** s'échouer
  IDIOMS **to gain** ~ gagner du terrain (**on**,
  over sur); **to hold one's** ~ tenir bon; **to go to**
  ~ se terrer; **that suits me down to the** ~ ça
  me convient parfaitement

ground floor *n* rez-de-chaussée *m inv*; **on**
  the ~ au rez-de-chaussée

grounding *n* bases *fpl* (**in** en, de)

groundnut oil *n* huile *f* d'arachide

ground rules *n pl* grands principes *mpl*;
  to change the ~ modifier les règles du jeu

groundsheet *n* tapis *m* de sol

ground troops *n pl* troupes *fpl* terrestres

groundwork *n* travail *m* préparatoire
  (**for** à)

ground zero *n* (New York) point *m* zéro

⚡ **group** ⬚1 *n* groupe *m*; **in** ~s en groupes
  ⬚2 *vtr* grouper
  ⬚3 *vi* ~ **together** ⟨*people*⟩ se grouper

group booking *n* réservation *f* de groupe

group therapy *n* thérapie *f* de groupe

group work *n* travail *m* en groupes

grouse *n* (*pl* ~) tétras *m*

grove *n* bosquet *m*; **lemon** ~ verger *m* de
  citronniers

grovel *vi* (*p prés etc* **-ll-** (GB), **-l-** (US))
  ramper (**to, before** devant)

⚡ indicates a very frequent word

⚡ **grow** ⬚1 *vtr* (*prét* **grew**, *pp* **grown**)
  (a) cultiver ⟨*plant, crop*⟩
  (b) laisser pousser ⟨*beard, nails*⟩; **to** ~ **5 cm**
  ⟨*person*⟩ grandir de 5 cm; ⟨*plant*⟩ pousser
  de 5 cm
  ⬚2 *vi* (*prét* **grew**, *pp* **grown**) (a) ⟨*person*⟩
  grandir (**by** de); ⟨*plant, hair*⟩ pousser (**by** de)
  (b) ⟨*population, tension*⟩ augmenter (**by**
  de); ⟨*company, economy*⟩ se développer;
  ⟨*opposition, support, problem*⟩ devenir plus
  important; ⟨*crisis*⟩ s'aggraver
  (c) devenir ⟨*hotter, stronger*⟩; **to** ~ **old**
  vieillir; **to** ~ **impatient** s'impatienter; **I grew**
  to like him j'ai appris à l'aimer
  ■ **grow apart** s'éloigner l'un de l'autre
  ■ **grow on** it ~s **on you** on finit par l'aimer;
  he's ~**ing on me** je commence à le trouver
  plus sympathique
  ■ **grow out of** (a) **he's grown out of his suit**
  son costume est devenu trop petit pour lui
  (b) **he'll** ~ **out of it** (of habit) ça lui passera
  ■ **grow up** (gen) grandir; **when I** ~ **up** quand
  je serai grand

grower *n* (of fruit) producteur/-trice *m/f*; (of
  crops) cultivateur/-trice *m/f*

growl ⬚1 *n* grondement *m*
  ⬚2 *vi* ⟨*dog*⟩ gronder

grown-up ⬚1 *n* adulte *mf*, grande
  personne *f*
  ⬚2 *adj* adulte

⚡ **growth** *n* (a) (gen) croissance *f* (**in, of**
  de); (of hair, nails) pousse *f*; (of economy)
  expansion *f* (**in, of** de); (in numbers, productivity)
  augmentation *f* (**in** de)
  (b) (tumour) grosseur *f*, tumeur *f*

growth area *n* secteur *m* en expansion

growth industry *n* industrie *f* en
  expansion

growth rate *n* taux *m* de croissance

grubby *adj* malpropre

grudge ⬚1 *n* **to bear sb a** ~ en vouloir
  à qn
  ⬚2 *vtr* **to** ~ **sb their success** en vouloir à qn
  de sa réussite; **to** ~ **doing** rechigner à faire

grudgingly *adv* ⟨*admit*⟩ avec réticence

gruelling, grueling (US) *adj*
  exténuant/-e

gruesome *adj* horrible

gruff *adj* bourru/-e

grumble *vi* ⟨*person*⟩ ronchonner (**at sb**
  après qn; **to** auprès de); **to** ~ **about** se
  plaindre de

grumpy *adj* grincheux/-euse

grunge *n* (colloq) (dirt) crasse *f*; (style) grunge
  m

grunt ⬚1 *n* grognement *m*
  ⬚2 *vi* grogner

G-string *n* (garment) string *m*

guarantee ⬚1 *n* garantie *f*
  ⬚2 *vtr* garantir

◆ **guard** 1 *n* **(a)** (for person) surveillant/-e *m/f*; (for place, object, at prison) gardien/-ienne *m/f*; (soldier) garde *m*
(b) (military duty) garde *f*, surveillance *f*; **to be on ∼** être de garde
(c) to catch sb off ∼ prendre qn au dépourvu
(d) (GB) (on train) chef *m* de train
2 *vtr* **(a)** (protect) surveiller ⟨place, object⟩; protéger ⟨person⟩
(b) surveiller ⟨hostage, prisoner⟩
(c) garder ⟨secret⟩

guard dog *n* chien *m* de garde

guarded *adj* circonspect/-e (**about** à propos de)

guardian *n* **(a)** (gen) gardien/-ienne *m/f* (**of** de)
(b) (of child) tuteur/-trice *m/f*

guardian angel *n* ange *m* gardien

Guernsey *pr n* Guernesey *f*

guerrilla *n* guérillero *m*

guerrilla war *n* guérilla *f*

◆ **guess** 1 *n* supposition *f*, conjecture *f*; **at a (rough) ∼ I would say that...** au hasard je dirais que...; **it's anybody's ∼!** les paris sont ouverts!
2 *vtr* **(a)** deviner; **∼ what!** tu sais quoi! (fam)
(b) (suppose) supposer
3 *vi* deviner; **to keep sb ∼ing** ne pas satisfaire la curiosité de qn

guesswork *n* conjecture *f*

◆ **guest** *n* (in one's home) invité/-e *m/f*; (at hotel) client/-e *m/f*; **be my ∼!** je vous en prie!

guesthouse *n* pension *f* de famille

guest room *n* chambre *f* d'amis

guestworker *n* travailleur immigré/travailleuse immigrée *m/f*

guidance *n* conseils *mpl* (**from** de)

guide 1 *n* **(a)** (person, book) guide *m* (**to** de)
(b) (idea) indication *f*; **as a rough ∼** à titre d'indication
(c) (*also* **Girl Guide**) guide *f*
2 *vtr* guider (**to** vers)

guide book *n* guide *m*

guide dog *n* chien *m* d'aveugle

guided tour *n* visite *f* guidée

guideline *n* (rough guide) indication *f*; (in political context) directive *f*; (advice) conseils *mpl*

guild *n* (medieval) guilde *f*; (modern) association *f*

guillotine *n* **(a)** guillotine *f*
(b) (for paper) massicot *m*

guilt *n* culpabilité *f*

◆ **guilty** *adj* coupable; **to feel ∼** culpabiliser; **to feel ∼ about** se sentir coupable vis-à-vis de

guinea-pig *n* **(a)** (Zool) cochon *m* d'Inde
(b) (in experiment) cobaye *m*

guitar *n* guitare *f*

guitarist *n* guitariste *mf*

gulch *n* (US) ravin *m*

gulf *n* **(a)** golfe *m*; **the Gulf** la région *f* du Golfe
(b) (figurative) fossé *m* (**between** qui sépare)

Gulf States *pr n pl* **the ∼** (in Middle East) les États *mpl* du Golfe

Gulf War *pr n* guerre *f* du Golfe

gull *n* mouette *f*

gullible *adj* crédule

gully *n* ravin *m*

gulp 1 *n* (of liquid) gorgée *f*; (of air) bouffée *f*, goulée *f*; (of food) bouchée *f*
2 *vtr* (*also* **∼ down**) engloutir ⟨food, drink⟩
3 *vi* avoir la gorge serrée

gum *n* **(a)** (in mouth) gencive *f*
(b) (*also* **chewing ∼**) chewing-gum *m*
(c) (adhesive) colle *f*; (resin) gomme *f*

◆ **gun** *n* (weapon) arme *f* à feu, (revolver) revolver *m*; (rifle) fusil *m*; (cannon) canon *m*; **to fire a ∼** tirer
IDIOMS **to jump the ∼** agir prématurément; **to stick to one's ∼s** (colloq) s'accrocher (fam)
■ **gun down** abattre, descendre

gunfire *n* (from hand-held gun) coups *mpl* de feu; (from artillery) fusillade *f*

gun laws *n pl* législation *f* sur les armes à feu

gun licence *n* permis *m* de port d'armes

gunman *n* homme *m* armé

gunpoint *n* **to hold sb up at ∼** tenir qn sous la menace d'une arme

gunpowder *n* poudre *f*

gunshot *n* coup *m* de feu

gunshot wound *n* blessure *f* par balle

gurgle 1 *n* (of water) gargouillement *m*; (of baby) gazouillis *m*
2 *vi* ⟨water⟩ gargouiller; ⟨baby⟩ gazouiller

guru *n* gourou *m*

gush *vi* jaillir

gust *n* rafale *f*

gusto *n* **with ∼** avec enthousiasme

gut 1 *n* (colloq) bide *m* (fam)
2 *adj* ⟨feeling, reaction⟩ viscéral/-e, instinctif/-ive
3 *vtr* (*p prés etc* **-tt-**) ⟨fire⟩ ravager ⟨building⟩

guts *n pl* (colloq) **(a)** (of human) tripes *fpl* (fam); (of animal) entrailles *fpl*
(b) (courage) cran *m* (fam)

gutsy *adj* (colloq) (spirited) fougueux/-euse; (brave) courageux/-euse

gutter *n* (on roof) gouttière *f*; (in street) caniveau *m*

gutter press *n* presse *f* à sensation

◆ **guy** *n* (colloq) type *m* (fam); **a good/bad ∼** (in films) un bon/méchant

Guy Fawkes Day *n* (GB) le 5 novembre (*anniversaire de la Conspiration des Poudres*)

guzzle *vtr* (colloq) engloutir
gym *n* **(a)** (*abbr* = **gymnasium**) salle *f* de gym, gymnase *m*
(b) (*abbr* = **gymnastics**) gym *f* (fam)
gymnasium *n* (*pl* ∼**s** *ou* **-ia**) gymnase *m*
gymnast *n* gymnaste *mf*

gymnastics *n pl* gymnastique *f*
gym shoe *n* tennis *f*
gynaecologist (GB), **gynecologist** (US) *n* gynécologue *mf*
gypsy *n* (gen) bohémien/-ienne *m/f*; (Central European) tzigane *mf*; (Spanish) gitan/-e *m/f*

H h

h, H *n* h, H *m*
habit *n* **(a)** habitude *f*; **to get into/out of the** ∼ **of doing** prendre/perdre l'habitude de faire; **out of** ∼ par habitude
(b) (addiction) accoutumance *f*
(c) (of monk, nun) habit *m*
habitable *adj* habitable
habitat *n* habitat *m*
habit-forming *adj* **to be** ∼ créer une accoutumance
habitual *adj* ‹*behaviour, reaction*› habituel/-elle; ‹*drinker, smoker, liar*› invétéré/-e
habitual offender *n* récidiviste *mf*
hack **1** *n* (colloq) (writer) écrivaillon *m*; (journalist) journaliste *m/f* qui fait la rubrique des chiens écrasés
2 *vtr* tailler dans ‹*bushes*› (**with** à coups de); **to** ∼ **sb/sth to pieces** tailler qn/qch en pièces
3 *vi* **(a) to** ∼ **through sth** tailler dans qch
(b) (Comput) (colloq) pirater (fam); **to** ∼ **into** s'introduire dans ‹*system*›
hacker *n* **(computer)** ∼ pirate *m* informatique
hacking *n* (Comput) piratage *m* (fam) informatique
hackles *n pl* (on dog) poils *mpl* du cou; **the dog's** ∼ **began to rise** le chien se hérissait
hackneyed *adj* ‹*joke*› éculé/-e; ‹*subject*› rebattu/-e; ∼ **phrase** cliché *m*
haddock *n* (*pl* ∼**s** *ou* ∼) églefin *m*
haemophilia (GB), **hemophilia** (US) *n* hémophilie *f*
haemophiliac (GB), **hemophiliac** (US) *n, adj* hémophile *mf*
haemorrhage (GB), **hemorrhage** (US) **1** *n* hémorragie *f*
2 *vi* faire une hémorragie
haemorrhoids (GB), **hemorrhoids** (US) *n pl* hémorroïdes *fpl*
haggard *adj* ‹*appearance, person*› exténué/-e; ‹*face, expression*› défait/-e

haggle *vi* marchander; **to** ∼ **over sth** discuter du prix de qch
Hague *pr n* **The** ∼ La Haye
hail **1** *n* grêle *f*
2 *vtr* **(a)** héler ‹*person, taxi, ship*›
(b) (praise) **to** ∼ **sb as** acclamer qn comme; **to** ∼ **sth as sth** saluer qch comme qch
3 *v impers* grêler
hailstone *n* grêlon *m*
hailstorm *n* averse *f* de grêle
❧ **hair** *n* **(a)** (on head) cheveux *mpl*; (on body) poils *mpl*; (of animal) poil *m*; **to have one's** ∼ **done** se faire coiffer; **long-**∼**ed** ‹*person*› aux cheveux longs; ‹*animal*› à poil long
(b) (individually) (on head) cheveu *m*; (on body) poil *m*
IDIOM to split ∼**s** couper les cheveux en quatre
hairband *n* bandeau *m*
hairbrush *n* brosse *f* à cheveux
haircut *n* coupe *f* (de cheveux)
hairdo *n* (colloq) coiffure *f*
hairdresser *n* coiffeur/-euse *m/f*
hairdrier *n* (hand-held) sèche-cheveux *m inv*; (hood) casque *m*
hair gel *n* gel *m* coiffant
hairgrip *n* (GB) pince *f* à cheveux
hairpin bend *n* virage *m* en épingle à cheveux
hair-raising *adj* ‹*adventure, tale*› à vous faire dresser les cheveux sur la tête
hair remover *n* crème *f* dépilatoire
hair-slide *n* (GB) barrette *f*
hairspray *n* laque *f*
hair straighteners *n pl* fer *m* à défriser
hairstyle *n* coiffure *f*
hairy *adj* (gen) poilu/-e
halal *adj* ‹*meat*› hallal *inv*
❧ **half** **1** *n* (*pl* **halves**) **(a)** moitié *f*; **to cut sth in** ∼ couper qch en deux
(b) (fraction) demi *m*; **four and a** ∼ quatre et demi
(c) (GB) (half pint) demi-pinte *f*
2 *adj* ∼ **an hour** une demi-heure; **a** ∼**-litre**, ∼ **a litre** un demi-litre; **two and a** ∼ **cups**

❧ indicates a very frequent word

deux tasses et demie

3 *pron* **(a)** la moitié *f*; ~ **of the students** la moitié des étudiants
(b) (in time) demi/-e *m/f*; **an hour and a** ~ une heure et demie; ~ **past two** (GB) deux heures et demie
4 *adv* à moitié; **to** ~ **close sth** fermer qch à moitié; **it's** ~ **the price** c'est moitié moins cher; **I** ~ **expected it** je m'y attendais plus ou moins
IDIOM **to go halves with sb** partager avec qn

halfback *n* (Sport) demi *m*

half-board *n* demi-pension *f*

half-brother *n* demi-frère *m*

half day *n* demi-journée *f*

half fare *n* demi-tarif *m*

half-hearted *adj* peu enthousiaste

half-heartedly *adv* sans conviction

half hour *n* demi-heure *f*; **on the** ~ à la demie

half-mast *n* **at** ~ en berne

half-moon *n* **(a)** demi-lune *f*
(b) (of fingernail) lunule *f*

half price *adv*, *adj* à moitié prix

half-sister *n* demi-sœur *f*

half term *n* (GB Sch) vacances *fpl* de la mi-trimestre

half-time *n* (Sport) mi-temps *f*; **at** ~ à la mi-temps

halfway *adv* **(a)** à mi-chemin (**between** entre; **to** de); ~ **up** *or* **down** à mi-hauteur de ‹*stairs, tree*›; ~ **down the page** à mi-page
(b) (in time) ~ **through** au milieu

halfway house *n* (rehabilitation centre) centre *m* de réadaptation

🔊 **hall** *n* **(a)** (in house) entrée *f*; (in hotel, airport) hall *m*; (for public events) (grande) salle *f*
(b) (country house) manoir *m*

hallelujah *excl* alléluia!

hallmark **1** *n* **(a)** (GB) (on metal) poinçon *m*
(b) (typical feature) caractéristique *f*
2 *vtr* poinçonner; **to be** ~**ed** porter un poinçon

hall of residence *n* résidence *f* universitaire

Halloween *n*: *la veille de la Toussaint*

hallucinate *vi* avoir des hallucinations

hallucination *n* hallucination *f*

hallway *n* entrée *f*

halo *n* (*pl* ~**s** *ou* ~**es**) **(a)** auréole *f*
(b) (in astronomy) halo *m*

halt **1** *n* (stop) arrêt *m*; **to come to a** ~ ‹*vehicle, troops*› s'arrêter; ‹*work*› être interrompu/-e; **to call a** ~ **to sth** mettre fin à qch
2 *vtr* arrêter
3 *vi* s'arrêter

halterneck *n*, *adj* dos *m inv* nu

halve **1** *vtr* réduire [qch] de moitié ‹*number, rate*›; couper [qch] en deux ‹*carrot, cake*›
2 *vi* ‹*number, rate, time*› diminuer de moitié

ham *n* jambon *m*

hamburger *n* **(a)** (burger) hamburger *m*
(b) (US) (ground beef) pâté *m* de viande

hammer **1** *n* marteau *m*
2 *vtr* **(a)** marteler ‹*metal, table*›; **to** ~ **sth into** enfoncer qch dans ‹*wall, fence*›
(b) **to** ~ **sth into sb** faire entrer qch dans la tête de qn; **to** ~ **home a message** bien faire comprendre un message
(c) (colloq) (defeat) battre [qn] à plates coutures
3 *vi* (pound) tambouriner (**on**, **at** contre)
■ **hammer out**: ~ **out** [sth], ~ [sth] **out** (negotiate) parvenir à [qch] après maintes discussions ‹*agreement, policy, formula*›

hamper **1** *n* panier *m* à pique-nique
2 *vtr* entraver ‹*movement, career, progress*›

hamster *n* hamster *m*

hamstring *n* tendon *m* du jarret

🔊 **hand** **1** *n* **(a)** main *f*; **he had a pencil in his** ~ il avait un crayon à la main; **to hold sb's** ~ tenir qn par la main; **to make sth by** ~ faire qch à la main; **the letter was delivered by** ~ la lettre a été remise en mains propres; **to give sb a (helping)** ~ donner un coup de main à qn; **to have sth to** ~ avoir qch sous la main; **to be on** ~ ‹*person*› être disponible; **to get out of** ~ devenir incontrôlable; **to take sb/sth in** ~ prendre qn/qch en main ‹*situation, person*›
(b) (cards) jeu *m*
(c) (worker) ouvrier/-ière *m/f*; (crew member) membre *m* de l'équipage
(d) (on clock, dial) aiguille *f*
(e) **on the one** ~…, **on the other** ~… d'une part…, d'autre part…
2 *vtr* **to** ~ **sth to sb** donner qch à qn
3 **hand in hand** *phr* ‹*run, walk*› la main dans la main; **to go** ~ **in** ~ aller de pair (**with** avec)
4 **out of hand** *phr* ‹*reject*› d'emblée
IDIOMS **to have one's** ~**s full** avoir assez à faire; **to try one's** ~ **at sth** s'essayer à; **to know sth like the back of one's** ~ connaître qch comme sa poche
■ **hand down** passer ‹*object, clothes*› (**to sb** à qn); transmettre ‹*property*›
■ **hand in** remettre ‹*form*› (**to** à); rendre ‹*homework, keys*›
■ **hand out** distribuer ‹*food, leaflets*›
■ **hand over**: **1** ¶ ~ **over to [sb]** passer l'antenne à ‹*reporter*›; passer la main à ‹*deputy, successor*›
2 ¶ ~ [sth] **over** rendre ‹*weapon*›; céder ‹*business*›; remettre ‹*keys, money*›
3 ¶ ~ [sb] **over** livrer ‹*prisoner*›

handbag *n* sac *m* à main

hand baggage *n* bagages *mpl* à main

handball n (Sport) handball m
handbook n manuel m; (technical) livret m
technique
handbrake n frein m à main
handcuffs n pl menottes fpl
handful n (a) (fistful) poignée f
(b) (of people) poignée f; (of buildings, objects)
petit nombre m
(c) (colloq) **to be a** ~ être épuisant/-e
handgun n arme f de poing
hand-held adj ‹camera› de reportage; ‹tool›
à main; ‹device› portatif/-ive; ‹computer› de
poche
hand-held device n (Comput) terminal m
mobile de poche
handicap ☐1 n handicap m
☐2 vtr (p prés etc **-pp-**) handicaper
handicapped adj ‹person› handicapé/-e;
mentally/physically ~ **children** des enfants
handicapés mentaux/physiques
handicrafts n pl (Sch) travaux mpl
manuels
handiwork n ouvrage m
handkerchief n mouchoir m
⚡ **handle** ☐1 n (on door, drawer, bag) poignée
f; (on bucket, cup, basket) anse f; (on frying pan)
queue f; (on saucepan, cutlery, hammer, spade)
manche m; (on wheelbarrow, pump) bras m
☐2 vtr (a) manipuler ‹explosives, food›;
manier ‹gun›; '~ **with care**' 'fragile'
(b) (manage) manier ‹horse›; manœuvrer
‹car›; **to know how to** ~ **children** savoir s'y
prendre avec les enfants
(c) (deal with) faire face à ‹crisis›; supporter
‹stress›; ‹department, lawyer› s'occuper de
‹enquiries, case›
handlebars n pl guidon m
handling n (a) (holding, touching) (of food,
waste) manipulation f; (of tool, weapon)
maniement m
(b) (way of dealing) **her** ~ **of the theme** sa
façon de traiter le thème; **their** ~ **of the
economy** leur gestion de l'économie
handling charge n (a) (for goods) frais
mpl de manutention
(b) (administrative) frais mpl administratifs
hand luggage n bagages mpl à main
handmade adj fait/-e à la main
handout n (a) (charitable) don m
(b) (leaflet) prospectus m
handpick vtr (a) cueillir [qch] à la main
‹grapes›
(b) trier [qn] sur le volet ‹staff›
handshake n poignée f de main
handsome adj beau/belle (before n)
hands-on adj ‹experience, manager› de
terrain; ‹control› direct/-e; ‹approach›
pragmatique
handstand n (Sport) équilibre m

⚡ indicates a very frequent word

handwriting n écriture f
handwritten adj manuscrit/-e
handy adj ‹book, skill› utile; ‹tool, pocket,
size› pratique; ‹shop› bien situé/-e; **to keep/
have [sth]** ~ garder/avoir [qch] sous la main
‹keys, passport›
handyman n bricoleur m
⚡ **hang** ☐1 n **to get the** ~ **of sth** (colloq) piger
qch (fam)
☐2 vtr (prét, pp **hung**) (a) (from hook, coat
hanger) accrocher (**from** à; **by** par; **on** à);
(from string, rope) suspendre (**from** à); (peg up)
étendre ‹washing› (**on** sur)
(b) poser ‹wallpaper›
(c) pendre ‹criminal, victim›
☐3 vi (prét, pp **hung**) (a) (on hook) être
accroché/-e; (from height) être suspendu/-e; (on
washing line) être étendu/-e
(b) ‹arm, leg› pendre
(c) ‹curtain, garment› tomber
(d) ‹person› être pendu/-e (**for** pour)
☐4 v refl (prét, pp **hanged**) **to** ~ **oneself** se
pendre (**from** à)
■ **hang around** (colloq) (a) (also ~ **about**)
(wait) attendre; (aimlessly) traîner
(b) **to** ~ **around with sb** passer son temps
avec qn
■ **hang back** (in fear) rester derrière;
(figurative) être réticent/-e
■ **hang down** (gen) pendre; ‹hem› être
défait/-e
■ **hang on**: ☐1 ~ **on** (a) (hold on) **to** ~ **on** (**to
sth**) s'accrocher (à qch)
(b) (wait) attendre
(c) (colloq) (survive) tenir (fam); ~ **on in there!**
(colloq) tiens bon!
☐2 ¶ ~ **on [sth]** (depend on) dépendre de
■ **hang out** ☐1 ¶ ~ **out** (a) (protrude) dépasser
(b) (colloq) (live) crécher (fam)
(c) (colloq) (sit around) traîner (fam)
☐2 ¶ ~ **[sth] out** étendre ‹washing›; sortir
‹flag›
■ **hang up**: ☐1 ¶ ~ **up** (on phone) raccrocher;
to ~ **up on sb** raccrocher au nez de qn
☐2 ¶ ~ **[sth] up** (on hook) accrocher; (on
hanger) suspendre; (on line) étendre
hangar n hangar m
hanger-on n (colloq) parasite m
hang-glider n deltaplane m
hanging n (a) (of person) pendaison f
(b) (curtain) rideau m; (on wall) tenture f
hangover n (from drink) gueule f de bois (fam)
hang-up n (colloq) complexe m, problème m
hanker vi **to** ~ **after** or **for sth** rêver de qch
hanky, hankie n (colloq) m mouchoir m
haphazard adj peu méthodique
⚡ **happen** vi (a) (occur) arriver, se passer,
se produire; **what's** ~**ing?** qu'est-ce qui se
passe?; **to** ~ **again** se reproduire; **whatever**
~**s** quoi qu'il arrive
(b) (occur by chance) **if you** ~ **to see her, say
hello** si par hasard tu la vois, salue-la de ma

part; **as it ~ed, the weather that day was bad** il s'est trouvé qu'il faisait mauvais ce jour-là

happily adv **(a)** (cheerfully) joyeusement; **a ~ married man** un mari heureux; **they all lived ~ ever after** ils vécurent heureux jusqu'à la fin de leurs jours
(b) (willingly) ⟨admit⟩ volontiers
(c) (luckily) heureusement

happiness n bonheur m

⚘ **happy** adj **(a)** heureux/-euse (about de; that que + subjunctive); **to be ~ with sth** être satisfait/-e de qch; **to keep a child ~** amuser un enfant; **to be ~ to do** être heureux/-euse de faire
(b) (in greetings) **Happy Birthday!** Bon anniversaire!; **Happy Christmas!** Joyeux Noël!; **Happy New Year!** Bonne année!

happy ending n heureux dénouement m
happy medium n juste milieu m

harangue vtr (p prés **haranguing**) (about politics) haranguer; (moralize) sermonner

harass 1 vtr harceler
2 **harassed** pp adj excédé/-e

harassment n (general) harcèlement m; (in the workplace) mobbing m

harbour (GB), **harbor** (US) 1 n port m
2 vtr nourrir ⟨suspicion, illusion⟩; receler ⟨criminal⟩

⚘ **hard** 1 adj **(a)** (firm) dur/-e; **to go ~** durcir
(b) (difficult) ⟨problem, question, task⟩ dur/-e, difficile; ⟨choice, decision, life⟩ difficile; **it's ~ to do** c'est dur or difficile à faire; **to find it ~ to do** avoir du mal à faire; **it was ~ work** ça a été dur or difficile; **to be a ~ worker** être travailleur/-euse
(c) (severe) ⟨person, look, words⟩ dur/-e, sévère; ⟨blow⟩ dur/-e, terrible; ⟨winter⟩ rude; **to be ~ on sb** ⟨person⟩ être dur/-e envers qn; **~ luck!** pas de chance!; **no ~ feelings!** sans rancune!
(d) ⟨evidence, fact⟩ solide
(e) ⟨liquor⟩ fort/-e; ⟨drug⟩ dur/-e
(f) ⟨water⟩ dur/-e, calcaire
2 adv ⟨push, hit, cry⟩ fort; ⟨work⟩ dur; ⟨study, think⟩ sérieusement; ⟨look, listen⟩ attentivement; **to try ~** (mentally) faire beaucoup d'efforts; (physically) essayer de toutes ses forces

hard and fast adj ⟨rule, distinction⟩ absolu/-e

hardback (book) n livre m relié
hardboard n aggloméré m
hard-boiled egg n œuf m dur
hard copy n (Comput) tirage m
hard core 1 n (group, demonstrators) noyau m dur
2 **hard-core** adj **(a)** (established) ⟨supporter, opponent, protest⟩ irréductible
(b) (extreme) ⟨pornography, video⟩ hard inv (fam)

hard court n court m en dur

hard disk n disque m dur
hard-earned adj ⟨cash⟩ durement gagné/-e
harden 1 vtr **(a)** (faire) durcir ⟨glue, wax⟩
(b) endurcir ⟨person⟩ (to à); durcir ⟨attitude⟩; **to ~ one's heart** s'endurcir (to à)
2 vi **(a)** ⟨glue, wax, skin⟩ durcir
(b) ⟨voice, stance⟩ se durcir

hardened adj ⟨criminal⟩ endurci/-e; ⟨drinker⟩ invétéré/-e

hard hat n (helmet) casque m; (for riding) bombe f
hard-hearted adj insensible
hard-hitting adj ⟨speech, criticism⟩ musclé/-e; ⟨report⟩ très critique

hard labour (GB), **hard labor** (US) n travaux mpl forcés

hardliner n jusqu'au-boutiste mf; (political) partisan/-e m/f de la ligne dure

⚘ **hardly** adv **(a)** (barely) ⟨begin, know, see⟩ à peine; **~ had they set off when** à peine étaient-ils partis que
(b) (not really) **one can ~ expect that** on ne peut guère s'attendre à ce que; **it's ~ likely** c'est peu probable; **it's ~ surprising** ce n'est guère étonnant; **I can ~ believe it!** j'ai peine à le croire!
(c) **~ any/ever/anybody** presque pas/jamais/personne; **he ~ ever writes** il n'écrit presque jamais

hard of hearing adj **to be ~** entendre mal
hard-pressed, hard-pushed adj en difficulté; (for time) pressé/-e; **to be ~ to do** avoir du mal à faire

hardship n **(a)** (difficulty) détresse f; (poverty) privations fpl
(b) (ordeal) épreuve f

hard shoulder n bande f d'arrêt d'urgence
hard up adj (colloq) fauché/-e (fam)
hardware n **(a)** (gen) articles mpl de quincaillerie
(b) (Comput) matériel m (informatique)
(c) (Mil) équipement m

hardware shop, hardware store n quincaillerie f
hard-working adj travailleur/-euse
hardy adj ⟨person⟩ robuste; ⟨plant⟩ résistant/-e
hare n lièvre m
haricot n (GB) (also **~ bean**) (dried) haricot m blanc; (fresh) haricot m vert

harm 1 n mal m; **to do sb ~** faire du mal à qn; **to do ~ to sth** endommager qch; **out of ~'s way** en sûreté
2 vtr faire du mal à ⟨person⟩; endommager ⟨crops, lungs⟩; nuire à ⟨population⟩

harmful adj ⟨chemical, ray⟩ nocif/-ive; ⟨behaviour, gossip⟩ nuisible (to pour)

harmless adj **(a)** ⟨chemical, virus⟩ inoffensif/-ive (to pour); ⟨growth⟩ bénin/ ⋯⋗

bénigne
(b) ⟨*person*⟩ inoffensif/-ive; ⟨*fun, joke*⟩ innocent/-e

harmonica *n* harmonica *m*

harmonious *adj* harmonieux/-ieuse

harmonize **1** *vtr* harmoniser
2 *vi* jouer en harmonie (**with** avec)

harmony *n* harmonie *f*

harness **1** *n* harnais *m*
2 *vtr* **(a)** harnacher ⟨*horse*⟩
(b) (attach) atteler ⟨*animal*⟩ (**to** à)
(c) exploiter ⟨*power, energy*⟩

harp *n* harpe *f*
■ **harp on** (colloq) rabâcher (fam) toujours la même chose sur ⟨*issue, event*⟩

harpoon *n* harpon *m*

harrowing *adj* ⟨*experience*⟩ atroce; ⟨*film, image*⟩ déchirant/-e

harsh *adj* **(a)** ⟨*punishment, measures*⟩ sévère; ⟨*tone, regime, person*⟩ dur/-e; ⟨*conditions*⟩ difficile
(b) ⟨*light, colour*⟩ cru/-e; ⟨*sound*⟩ rude, dur/-e à l'oreille

harshly *adv* ⟨*treat, speak*⟩ durement; ⟨*punish*⟩ sévèrement

harvest **1** *n* (of wheat, fruit) récolte *f*; (of grapes) vendange *f*
2 *vtr* moissonner ⟨*corn*⟩; récolter ⟨*vegetables*⟩; cueillir ⟨*fruit*⟩; vendanger ⟨*grapes*⟩

has-been *n* (colloq) homme fini/femme finie *m/f*

hassle (colloq) **1** *n* complications *fpl*; **it was a real** ~ c'était enquiquinant (fam)
2 *vtr* talonner (**about** à propos de)

haste *n* hâte *f*; **to act in** ~ agir à la hâte

hasten **1** *vtr* accélérer ⟨*destruction*⟩; précipiter ⟨*departure, death, decline*⟩
2 *vi* se hâter; **to** ~ **to do** s'empresser de faire

hasty *adj* ⟨*talks, marriage, departure*⟩ précipité/-e; ⟨*meal*⟩ rapide; ⟨*note*⟩ écrit/-e à la hâte; ⟨*decision*⟩ inconsidéré/-e; ⟨*conclusion*⟩ hâtif/-ive

hat *n* chapeau *m*

hatch **1** *n* **(a)** (on aircraft) panneau *m* mobile; (in boat) écoutille *f*; (in car) portière *f*
(b) (*also* **serving** ~) passe-plats *m inv*
2 *vtr* **(a)** faire éclore ⟨*eggs*⟩
(b) tramer ⟨*plot, scheme*⟩
3 *vi* ⟨*chicks, fish eggs*⟩ éclore

hatchback *n* voiture *f* avec hayon

hatchet *n* hachette *f*

✧ **hate** **1** *n* haine *f*
2 *vtr* **(a)** (dislike) détester; (violently) haïr
(b) (not enjoy) avoir horreur de ⟨*sport, food*⟩; **to** ~ **doing** avoir horreur de faire
(c) (in apology) **to** ~ **to do** être désolé/-e de faire

✧ indicates a very frequent word

hate mail *n* lettres *fpl* d'injures

hatred *n* haine *f* (**of** de; **for** pour)

hat trick *n* triplé *m*

haughty *adj* ⟨*person*⟩ hautain/-e; ⟨*manner*⟩ altier/-ière

haul **1** *n* **(a)** (taken by criminals) butin *m*
(b) (found by police, customs) saisie *f*; **arms** ~ saisie d'armes
(c) **it's a long** ~ la route est longue
(d) (of fish) pêche *f*
2 *vtr* (drag) tirer

haulage *n* **(a)** (transport) transport *m* routier
(b) (cost) frais *mpl* de transport

haunch *n* hanche *f*

haunt **1** *n* lieu *m* de prédilection
2 *vtr* hanter

haunted *adj* ⟨*house*⟩ hanté/-e; ⟨*face, look*⟩ tourmenté/-e

haunting *adj* (gen) lancinant/-e; ⟨*memory*⟩ obsédant/-e

✧ **have** **1** *vtr* **(a)** (possess) avoir; **she has (got) a dog** elle a un chien; **I haven't (got) enough time** je n'ai pas assez de temps
(b) (with noun object) **to** ~ **a wash** se laver; **to** ~ **a sandwich** manger un sandwich; **to** ~ **a whisky** boire un whisky; **to** ~ **a cigarette** fumer une cigarette; **to** ~ **breakfast** prendre le petit déjeuner; **to** ~ **lunch** déjeuner; **I had some more cake** j'ai repris du gâteau
(c) (receive, get) recevoir ⟨*letter*⟩; **I've had no news from him** je n'ai pas eu de nouvelles de lui; **to let sb** ~ **sth** donner qch à qn
(d) (hold) faire ⟨*party*⟩; tenir ⟨*meeting*⟩; organiser ⟨*competition, exhibition*⟩; avoir ⟨*conversation*⟩
(e) (exert, exhibit) avoir ⟨*effect, influence*⟩; avoir ⟨*courage, courtesy*⟩ (**to do** de faire)
(f) (spend) passer; **to** ~ **a nice day** passer une journée agréable; **to** ~ **a good time** s'amuser; **to** ~ **a hard time** traverser une période difficile; **to** ~ **a good holiday** (GB) *or* vacation (US) passer de bonnes vacances
(g) (*also* ~ **got**) **I've got letters to write** j'ai du courrier à faire; **I've got a lot of work to do** j'ai beaucoup de travail
(h) (suffer) avoir; **to** ~ **(the) flu/a heart attack** avoir la grippe/une crise cardiaque; **to** ~ **toothache** avoir mal aux dents; **he had his car stolen** il s'est fait voler sa voiture; **she has had her windows broken** on lui a cassé ses vitres
(i) to ~ **the car fixed** faire réparer la voiture; **to** ~ **the house painted** faire peindre la maison; **to** ~ **one's hair cut** se faire couper les cheveux; **to** ~ **an injection** se faire faire une piqûre
(j) (cause to become) **she had them completely baffled** elle les a complètement déroutés; **I had it finished by 5 o'clock** je l'avais fini avant 5 heures
(k) (allow) tolérer; **I won't** ~ **this kind of behaviour!** je ne tolérerai pas ce comportement!

(I) (give birth to) ‹*woman*› avoir ‹*child*›; ‹*animal*› mettre bas, avoir ‹*young*›

2 *modal aux* (must) **I ~ to leave early** il faut que je parte, je dois partir; **something has (got) to be done** il faut faire quelque chose; **you don't ~ to leave so early** tu n'as pas besoin de *or* tu n'es pas obligé de partir si tôt

3 *v aux* **(a)** avoir; (with movement and reflexive verbs) être; **she has lost her bag** elle a perdu son sac; **she has already left** elle est déjà partie; **he has hurt himself** il s'est blessé; **having finished his breakfast, he went out** après avoir fini son petit déjeuner, il est sorti **(b)** (in tags, short answers) **you've seen the film, haven't you?** tu as vu le film, n'est-ce pas?; **you haven't seen the film, ~ you?** tu n'as pas vu le film?; **you haven't seen my bag, ~ you?** tu n'as pas vu mon sac, par hasard?; '**~ you seen him?**'—'**yes, I ~**' 'est-ce que tu l'as vu?'—'oui'; '**you've never met him**'—'**yes I ~!**' 'tu ne l'as jamais rencontré'—'mais si!' **(c)** (if) **had I known, I wouldn't have bought it** si j'avais su, je ne l'aurais pas acheté

IDIOMS **I've had it (up to here) with…** (colloq) j'en ai marre de… (fam); **to ~ it in for sb** (colloq) avoir qn dans le collimateur (fam); **she doesn't ~ it in her to do** elle est incapable de faire; **to ~ it out with sb** s'expliquer avec qn; **the ~s and the ~-nots** les riches et les pauvres

■ **have on (a)** porter ‹*coat, skirt*›; **he had (got) nothing on** il n'avait rien sur lui **(b) to ~ sth on** (be busy) avoir qch de prévu **(c) to ~ sb on** (colloq) faire marcher qn (fam)

haven *n* **(a)** (safe place) refuge *m* **(for** pour) **(b)** (harbour) port *m*

havoc *n* dévastation *f*; **to wreak ~** provoquer des dégâts; (figurative) tout mettre sens dessus dessous

Hawaii *pr n* Hawaï *m*

hawk *n* faucon *m*

hawthorn *n* aubépine *f*

hay *n* foin *m*

hay fever *n* rhume *m* des foins

haystack *n* meule *f* de foin
IDIOM **it is/was like looking for a needle in a ~** autant chercher une aiguille dans une botte de foin

haywire *adj* (colloq) **(a)** (faulty) **to go ~** ‹*plan*› dérailler; ‹*machinery*› se détraquer **(b)** (crazy) détraqué/-e (fam)

hazard **1** *n* risque *m* (**to** pour); **a health ~** un risque pour la santé **2** *vtr* hasarder ‹*opinion, guess*›

hazardous *adj* dangereux/-euse

haze *n* (mist) brume *f*; (of smoke, dust) nuage *m*

hazel **1** *n* noisetier *m* **2** *adj* ‹*eyes*› (couleur de) noisette *inv*

hazelnut *n* noisette *f*

hazy *adj* ‹*weather, morning*› brumeux/-euse; ‹*sunshine*› voilé/-e; ‹*idea, memory*› vague (*before n*)

he *pron* il; **~'s seen us** il nous a vus; **there ~ is** le voilà; **she lives in Oxford but ~ doesn't** elle habite Oxford mais lui non; **~'s a genius** c'est un génie; **~ and I** lui et moi

head **1** *n* **(a)** (gen) tête *f*; **from ~ to foot** *or* **toe** de la tête aux pieds; **to stand on one's ~** faire le poirier; **£10 a ~** *or* **per ~** 10 livres sterling par personne **(b)** (of family, church) chef *m*; (of organization) responsable *mf*, directeur/-trice *m/f*; **~ of State** chef d'État **2 heads** *n pl* (of coin) face *f*; '**~s or tails?**' 'pile ou face?' **3** *adj* **(a)** ‹*injury*› à la tête **(b)** (chief) ‹*cashier, cook, gardener*› en chef **4** *vtr* **(a)** être en tête de ‹*list, queue*›; être à la tête de ‹*firm, team*›; mener ‹*expedition, inquiry*› **(b) ~ed writing paper** papier *m* à lettres à en-tête **(c)** (steer) diriger ‹*vehicle*› (**towards** vers) **(d)** (Sport) **to ~ the ball** faire une tête **5** *vi* **where was the train ~ed** *or* **~ing?** où allait le train?; **to ~ home** rentrer; **he's ~ing this way!** il vient par ici!

IDIOMS **to go to sb's ~** monter à la tête de qn; **to keep/lose one's ~** garder/perdre son sang-froid; **off the top of one's ~** ‹*say, answer*› sans réfléchir

■ **head for (a)** se diriger vers ‹*place*› **(b)** courir à ‹*defeat*›; courir vers ‹*trouble*›

headache *n* mal *m* de tête; **to have a ~** avoir mal à la tête

headband *n* bandeau *m*

headbutt *vtr* donner un coup de tête à

head cold *n* rhume *m* de cerveau

headdress *n* (of feathers) coiffure *f*; (of lace) coiffe *f*

header *n* **(a)** (colloq) (dive) **to take a ~** piquer une tête (fam) **(b)** (in sport) tête *f*

headfirst *adv* ‹*fall, plunge*› la tête la première; ‹*rush into*› tête baissée

head-hunt *vtr* (seek to recruit) (chercher à) recruter

head-hunter *n* chasseur *m* de têtes

heading *n* (of article, column) titre *m*; (of subject area, topic) rubrique *f*; (on notepaper, letter) en-tête *m*

headlamp, headlight *n* (of car) phare *m*

headline *n* (in paper) gros titre *m*; **to hit the ~s** faire la une (fam); **the front-page ~** la manchette; **the news ~s** les grands titres (de l'actualité)

headlong **1** *adj* **a ~ dash** une ruée **2** *adv* ‹*fall*› la tête la première; ‹*run*› à toute vitesse

head office *n* siège *m* social

head-on *adj* ‹*crash, collision*› de front

headphones *n pl* casque *m*

headquarters *n pl* (gen) siège *m* social; (Mil) quartier *m* général

head rest n (gen) appui-tête m; (Aut) repose-tête m inv

head start n to have a ~ avoir une longueur d'avance (over sur)

headstone n pierre f tombale

headstrong adj ‹person› têtu/-e; ‹attitude› obstiné/-e

head teacher n directeur/-trice m/f

headway n to make ~ avancer, faire des progrès

heady adj ‹wine, mixture› capiteux/-euse; ‹perfume› entêtant/-e; ‹experience› grisant/-e

heal ① vtr guérir ‹person, injury›
② vi ‹wound, cut› se cicatriser; the fracture has ~ed l'os s'est ressoudé

healer n guérisseur/-euse m/f

healing ① n guérison f
② adj ‹power› curatif/-ive; ‹effect› salutaire; the ~ process le rétablissement

✍ **health** n santé f; in good/bad ~ en bonne/ mauvaise santé; here's to your ~! à votre santé!

health club n club m de remise en forme

health farm n: établissement pour cures d'amaigrissement, de rajeunissement

health food n aliments mpl naturels, aliments mpl diététiques

healthily adv sainement

health insurance n assurance f maladie

Health Service n (a) (GB for public) services mpl de santé
(b) (US) (Univ) infirmerie f

✍ **healthy** adj ‹person, dog› en bonne santé; ‹livestock, plant, lifestyle, diet› sain/-e; ‹air› salutaire; ‹appetite› robuste; ‹economy› sain/-e; ‹profit› excellent/-e

heap ① n (a) (pile) tas m
(b) (colloq) ~s of plein de
② vtr (a) (pile) entasser
(b) to ~ sth on sb couvrir qn de qch ‹praise›; accabler qn de qch ‹scorn›

heaped adj a ~ spoonful une bonne cuillerée

✍ **hear** ① vtr (prét, pp **heard**) (a) (gen) entendre; to make oneself heard se faire entendre; (figurative) faire entendre sa voix
(b) apprendre ‹news, rumour›
(c) (listen to) écouter ‹lecture, broadcast›; ‹judge› entendre ‹case, evidence›
② vi (prét, pp **heard**) entendre; to ~ about entendre parler de
IDIOM ~! ~! bravo!
■ **hear from** avoir des nouvelles de ‹person›
■ **hear of** entendre parler de; I won't ~ of it! il n'en est pas question!

✍ **hearing** n (a) (sense) ouïe f, audition f; his ~ is not very good il n'a pas l'oreille très fine
(b) (before court) audience f

hearing aid n prothèse f auditive

hearing-impaired adj malentendant/-e

hearsay n ouï-dire m inv, on-dit m inv

hearse n corbillard m

✍ **heart** n (a) (gen) cœur m; by ~ ‹learn, know› par cœur; to take sth to ~ prendre qch à cœur; right in the ~ of London en plein cœur de Londres; the ~ of the matter le fond du problème
(b) (in cards) ~(s) cœur m
IDIOMS to have one's ~ set on sth vouloir qch à tout prix; to take/lose ~ prendre/ perdre courage

heartache n chagrin m

heart attack n crise f cardiaque, infarctus m

heartbeat n battement m de cœur

heartbreaking adj ‹sight, story› navrant/-e; ‹cry, appeal› déchirant/-e

heartbroken adj to be ~ avoir le cœur brisé

heart disease n maladies fpl cardiaques

heartening adj encourageant/-e

heart failure n arrêt m du cœur

heartfelt adj sincère

hearth n foyer m; ~ rug petit tapis m

heartless adj ‹person› sans cœur; ‹attitude, treatment› cruel/-elle

heartthrob n (colloq) idole f

heart-to-heart n to have a ~ (with sb) parler à cœur ouvert (avec qn)

heart transplant n greffe f du cœur

hearty adj ‹welcome, greeting› cordial/-e; ‹person› jovial/-e; ‹laugh› franc/franche; ‹appetite› solide; ‹approval› chaleureux/-euse

✍ **heat** ① n (a) chaleur f; in this ~ par cette chaleur; in the ~ of the moment dans le feu de l'action
(b) (Sport) (round) épreuve f éliminatoire; (in athletics) série f
(c) (Zool) to be on or in ~ être en chaleur
② vtr chauffer ‹house, pool›; faire chauffer ‹food, oven›
■ **heat up** faire chauffer ‹food›; (reheat) faire réchauffer

heated adj (a) ‹water, pool› chauffé/-e
(b) ‹debate, argument› animé/-e

heater n appareil m de chauffage

heathen n, adj (irreligious) païen/-ienne m/f; (uncivilized) barbare m/f

heather n bruyère f

heating n chauffage m

heat stroke n coup m de chaleur (avec collapsus)

heatwave n vague f de chaleur

heave ① vtr (prét, pp **heaved**; (Naut) **hove**) (lift) hisser; (pull) traîner péniblement; (throw) lancer (at sur); to ~ a sigh pousser un soupir

---

✍ indicates a very frequent word

2 *vi* (*prét, pp* **heaved**; (Naut) **hove**)
(a) ‹*sea, ground*› se soulever et s'abaisser
(b) (pull) tirer de toutes ses forces
(c) (retch) avoir un haut-le-cœur; (vomit) vomir

heaven *n* ciel *m*, paradis *m*; **thank ~(s)!**
Dieu soit loué!; **good ~s!** grands dieux!

heavenly *adj* (a) ‹*choir, body*› céleste;
‹*peace*› divin/-e
(b) (fam) (wonderful) divin/-e

heavily *adv* (a) ‹*lean, fall*› lourdement;
‹*sleep, sigh*› profondément; ‹*breathe*› (noisily)
bruyamment; (with difficulty) péniblement; **~
underlined** souligné/-e d'un gros trait
(b) ‹*rain*› très fort; ‹*snow, invest, smoke,
drink, rely*› beaucoup; ‹*bleed*› abondamment;
‹*taxed, armed*› fortement

⚹ **heavy** *adj* (gen) lourd/-e; ‹*shoes, frame*›
gros/grosse (*before n*); ‹*line, features*›
épais/épaisse; ‹*blow, fighting*› violent/-e;
‹*rain, frost, perfume, accent*› fort/-e; ‹*snow*›
abondant/-e; ‹*traffic*› dense; ‹*gunfire*›
nourri/-e; ‹*bleeding*› abondant/-e; ‹*sentence,
fine*› sévère; ‹*cold*› gros/grosse (*before n*);
with a ~ heart le cœur gros; **to be a ~
sleeper** avoir le sommeil lourd; **to be a ~
drinker** boire beaucoup

heavy-handed *adj* maladroit/-e

heavy metal *n* hard rock *m*

heavyweight *n* (a) (boxer) poids *m* lourd
(b) (figurative) (colloq) grosse légume *f* (fam)

Hebrew **1** *n* (a) (person) Hébreu *m*
(b) (language) hébreu *m*
2 *adj* ‹*language*› hébraïque; ‹*person*›
hébreu/hébraïque

heckle **1** *vtr* interpeller
2 *vi* chahuter

hectic *adj* ‹*activity*› intense; ‹*day, life,
schedule*› mouvementé/-e

hedge **1** *n* haie *f*
2 *vi* se dérober
IDIOM **to ~ one's bets** se couvrir

hedge fund *n* fonds *m* spéculatif

hedgehog *n* hérisson *m*

hedgerow *n* haie *f*

heed **1** *n* **to take ~ of sb** tenir compte de
ce que dit qn; **to take ~ of sth** tenir compte
de qch
2 *vtr* tenir compte de ‹*warning, advice*›

heel *n* talon *m*
IDIOMS **to fall head over ~s in love with sb**
tomber éperdument amoureux de qn; **to be
hot on sb's ~s** talonner qn

heel bar *n* talon-minute *m*

hefty *adj* ‹*person*› costaud (fam); ‹*object*›
pesant/-e; ‹*blow*› puissant/-e; ‹*sum*›
considérable

heifer *n* génisse *f*

height *n* (a) (of person) taille *f*; (of table, tower,
tree) hauteur *f*
(b) (of plane) altitude *f*; **to be scared of ~s**
avoir le vertige

(c) (peak) **at the ~ of the season** en pleine
saison; **at the ~ of** au plus fort de ‹*storm,
crisis*›; **the ~ of** le comble de ‹*luxury,
stupidity, cheek*›; **to be the ~ of fashion** être
le dernier cri

heighten **1** *vtr* intensifier ‹*emotion*›;
augmenter ‹*tension, suspense*›; accentuer
‹*effect*›
2 *vi* ‹*tension*› monter

heir *n* héritier/-ière *m/f* (**to** de)

heiress *n* héritière *f*

heirloom *n* héritage *m*; **a family ~** un objet
de famille

helicopter *n* hélicoptère *m*

hell *n* (a) enfer *m*; **to make sb's life ~** rendre
la vie infernale à qn
(b) (colloq) **a ~ of a shock** un choc terrible;
a ~ of a lot worse nettement pire; **oh, what
the ~!** tant pis!; **why the ~...?** pourquoi...,
bon Dieu? (fam); **what the ~ is he doing?**
qu'est-ce qu'il fait, bon Dieu? (fam)
IDIOMS **for the ~ of it** (colloq) par plaisir; **to
raise ~** (colloq) faire une scène (**with sb** à qn)

hello *excl* (a) (greeting) bonjour!; (on the phone)
allô!
(b) (in surprise) tiens!

helm *n* barre *f*; **at the ~** à la barre

helmet *n* casque *m*

⚹ **help** **1** *n* aide *f*; (in emergency) secours *m*;
with the ~ of à l'aide de ‹*stick, knife*›; avec
l'aide de ‹*person*›; **it's/she's a (great) ~** ça/
elle aide beaucoup; **to cry for ~** appeler au
secours
2 *excl* au secours!
3 *vtr* (a) aider (**to do** à faire); **to ~ each
other** s'entraider; **to ~ sb across** aider qn
à traverser
(b) (serve) **to ~ sb to** servir [qch] à qn ‹*food,
wine*›; **to ~ oneself** se servir
(c) (prevent) **I couldn't ~ laughing** je n'ai pas
pu m'empêcher de rire; **it can't be ~ed!** on
n'y peut rien!; **he can't ~ being stupid!** ce
n'est pas de sa faute s'il est stupide!
4 *vi* aider; **he never ~s with the
housework** il n'aide jamais à faire le
ménage; **this map doesn't ~ much** cette
carte n'est pas d'un grand secours
■ **help out**: **1** ¶ **~ out** aider, donner un
coup de main (fam)
2 ¶ **~ [sb] out** aider, donner un coup de
main à (fam); (financially) dépanner (fam)

help desk *n* service *m* d'assistance
technique téléphonique

helper *n* aide *mf*, assistant/-e *m/f*; (for
handicapped person) aide *f* sociale

helpful *adj* ‹*person*› serviable; ‹*advice,
suggestion*› utile

helping *n* portion *f*

helpless *adj* (a) (powerless) ‹*person*›
impuissant/-e; (because of infirmity, disability)
impotent/-e
(b) (defenceless) ‹*person*› sans défense

h

helpline *n* service *m* d'assistance (téléphonique)

hem *n* ourlet *m*
■ **hem in** cerner ⟨*person*⟩

hemisphere *n* hémisphère *m*

hemp *n* chanvre *m*

hen *n* (chicken) poule *f*; (female bird) femelle *f*

hence *adv* (a) (for this reason) (*before noun*) d'où; (*before adjective*) donc
(b) (from now) d'ici

henchman *n* acolyte *m*

henna *n* henné *m*

hen night *n* soirée *f* passée entre femmes (*avant le mariage de l'une d'elles*)

hen-pecked *adj* ~ **husband** mari *m* mené par le bout du nez

hepatitis *n* hépatite *f*

✐ **her**

■ **Note** In French determiners agree in gender and number with the noun that follows. So *her*, when used as a determiner, is translated by *son* + masculine singular noun (son chien), by *sa* + feminine singular noun (sa maison) BUT by *son* + feminine noun beginning with a vowel or mute 'h' (son assiette) and by *ses* + plural noun (ses enfants).
— When *her* is stressed, *à elle* is added after the noun: HER *house* = sa maison à elle.

1 *pron* (a) (direct object) la, l'; **I saw** ~ je l'ai vue; **he gave** ~ **the book** il lui a donné le livre; **catch** ~**!** attrape-la!; **give it to** ~ donne-le-lui
(b) (after preposition, to be) elle; **it's for** ~ c'est pour elle; **it's** ~ c'est elle **2** *det* son/sa/ses

herald 1 *n* héraut *m*
2 *vtr* (*also* ~ **in**) annoncer

heraldry *n* héraldique *f*

herb *n* herbe *f*; **mixed** ~**s** ≈ herbes de Provence

herbal tea *n* tisane *f*, infusion *f*

herd 1 *n* troupeau *m*
2 *vtr* rassembler ⟨*animals*⟩; **to** ~ **people into a room** conduire des gens dans une pièce
IDIOM to follow the ~ être un mouton de Panurge

✐ **here** *adv*

■ **Note** When *here* is used to indicate the location of an object, a point etc close to the speaker, it is generally translated by *ici*: **come and sit here** = viens t'asseoir ici.
— When the location is not so clearly defined, *là* is the usual translation: **he's not here at the moment** = il n'est pas là pour l'instant.
— *voici* is used to translate *here is* and *here are* when the speaker is drawing attention to an object, a place, a person etc physically close to him or her.
— For examples and particular usages, see the entry below.

✐ indicates a very frequent word

(a) ici; **near** ~ près d'ici; **come over** ~ venez par ici; ~ **and there** par endroits; ~ **they are/she comes!** les/la voici!; ~ **are my keys** voici mes clés; ~ **you are** tiens, tenez
(b) (indicating presence, arrival) **she's not** ~ **right now** elle n'est pas là pour le moment; ~ **we are at last** nous voilà enfin; **we get off** ~ c'est là qu'on descend; **now that summer's** ~ maintenant que c'est l'été; ~**'s our chance** voilà notre chance
IDIOMS ~**'s to our success!** à notre succès!; ~**'s to you!** à la tienne!

hereabout (US), **hereabouts** (GB) *adv* par ici

hereafter 1 *n* **the** ~ l'au-delà *m*
2 *adv* (Law) ci-après

here and now *n* **the** ~ (present) le présent

hereby *adv* par la présente

hereditary *adj* héréditaire

heresy *n* hérésie *f*

heritage *n* patrimoine *m*; ~ **tourism** tourisme culturel

hermit *n* ermite *m*

hernia *n* (*pl* ~**s** *ou* ~**e**) hernie *f*

✐ **hero** *n* (*pl* ~**es**) héros *m*

heroic *adj* héroïque

heroin *n* héroïne *f*

heroin addict *n* héroïnomane *mf*

heroine *n* héroïne *f*

heroism *n* héroïsme *m*

heron *n* héron *m*

hero-worship 1 *n* culte *m* du héros, adulation *f*
2 *vtr* (*p prés etc* -**pp**-, -**p**- (US)) aduler

herring *n* hareng *m*

hers *pron*

■ **Note** In French, possessive pronouns reflect the gender and number of the noun they are standing for; *hers* is translated by *le sien*, *la sienne*, *les siens*, *les siennes*, according to what is being referred to.

my car is red but ~ **is blue** ma voiture est rouge mais la sienne est bleue; **the green pen is** ~ le stylo vert est à elle; **which house is** ~**?** laquelle est sa maison?; **I'm a friend of** ~ c'est une amie à moi; **it's not** ~ ce n'est pas à elle

✐ **herself** *pron* (a) (reflexive) se, s'; **she's hurt** ~ elle s'est blessée
(b) (after preposition) elle, elle-même; **for** ~ pour elle, pour elle-même; **(all) by** ~ toute seule
(c) (emphatic) elle-même; **she made it** ~ elle l'a fait elle-même
(d) **she's not** ~ **today** elle n'est pas dans son assiette aujourd'hui

hesitant *adj* hésitant/-e; **to be** ~ **about doing** hésiter à faire

hesitate *vi* hésiter (over sur; to do à faire)

hesitation *n* hésitation *f*

heterosexual *n, adj* hétérosexuel/-elle *m/f*

hexagon *n* hexagone *m*

✔ **hey** *excl* (colloq) (call for attention) hé!, eh!; (in protest) dis donc!

heyday *n* (gen) âge *m* d'or; (of person) beaux jours *mpl*

HGV *n* (GB) (*abbr* = **heavy goods vehicle**) PL *m*, poids *m* lourd

hi *excl* (colloq) salut! (fam)

hibernate *vi* hiberner

hiccup, hiccough *n* (a) hoquet *m*; **to have (the)** ~**s** avoir le hoquet (b) (setback) anicroche *f*

hidden *adj* caché/-e

✔ **hide** ⟦1⟧ *n* (skin) peau *f*; (leather) cuir *m*
⟦2⟧ *vtr* (*prét* **hid**, *pp* **hidden**) cacher ‹object, person› (from à); dissimuler ‹feeling› (from à)
⟦3⟧ *vi* (*prét* **hid**, *pp* **hidden**) se cacher

hide and seek (GB), **hide-and-go-seek** (US) *n* cache-cache *m inv*

hideaway *n* retraite *f*

hideous *adj* ‹person, monster, object› hideux/-euse; ‹noise› affreux/-euse

hiding *n* (a) **to go into** ~ se cacher; **to come out of** ~ sortir de sa cachette (b) (beating) correction *f*

hiding place *n* cachette *f*

hierarchy *n* hiérarchie *f*

hieroglyph, hieroglyphic *n* hiéroglyphe *m*

hi-fi *n* (a) (set of equipment) chaîne *f* hi-fi *inv* (b) (*abbr* = **high fidelity**) hi-fi *f inv*

✔ **high** ⟦1⟧ *n* (a) **to reach a new** ~ atteindre son niveau le plus élevé
(b) (colloq) **to be on a** ~ être en pleine euphorie
⟦2⟧ *adj* (a) (gen) haut/-e; **how** ~ **is the cliff?** quelle est la hauteur de la falaise?; **it is 50 m** ~ ça fait 50 m de haut
(b) ‹number, price, volume› élevé/-e; ‹wind› violent/-e; ‹hope› grand/ e (*before n*); **at** ~ **speed** à grande vitesse; **to have a** ~ **temperature** avoir de la fièvre; ~ **in** riche en ‹fat, iron›
(c) ‹quality, standard, rank› supérieur/-e; **friends in** ~ **places** des amis haut placés
(d) ‹ideal, principle› noble
(e) ‹pitch, voice› aigu/aiguë; ‹note› haut/-e
(f) (colloq) (on drug) défoncé/-e (fam); (happy) ivre de joie
⟦3⟧ *adv* haut

highbrow *n, adj* intellectuel/-elle *m/f*

high chair *n* chaise *f* de bébé

high-class *adj* ‹hotel, shop, car› de luxe; ‹goods› de première qualité; ‹area› de grand standing

high court *n* cour *f* suprême

high-definition TV, HDTV *n* télévision *f* à haute définition

higher education *n* enseignement *m* supérieur

high fashion *n* haute couture *f*

high-flier *n* jeune loup *m*

high-handed *adj* despotique

high heels *n pl* hauts talons *mpl*

high jump *n* (Sport) saut *m* en hauteur

Highlands *pr n pl* Highlands *mpl*, Hautes-Terres *fpl* (d'Écosse)

✔ **highlight** ⟦1⟧ *n* (a) (in hair) (natural) reflet *m*; (artificial) mèche *f* (b) (of match, event) point *m* culminant; (of year, evening) point *m* fort
⟦2⟧ **highlights** *n pl* (on radio, TV) résumé *m*
⟦3⟧ *vtr* (*prét*, *pp* **-lighted**) (a) (with pen) surligner
(b) (emphasize) mettre l'accent sur

highlighter *n* (pen) surligneur *m*

✔ **highly** *adv* ‹dangerous, intelligent› extrêmement; ~ **unlikely** fort peu probable; **to think** ~ **of sb** penser beaucoup de bien de qn

highly-paid *adj* très bien payé/-e

highly-strung *adj* très tendu/ e

Highness *n* **His or Her (Royal)** ~ Son Altesse *f*

high-pitched *adj* ‹voice, sound› aigu/aiguë

high point *n* point *m* culminant

high-powered *adj* ‹car, engine› de grande puissance; ‹person› dynamique; ‹job› de haute responsabilité

high-profile *adj* ‹politician, group› bien en vue; ‹visit› qui fait beaucoup de bruit

high-ranking *adj* de haut rang

high rise (building) *n* tour *f* (d'habitation)

high school *n* (US Sch) ≈ lycée *m*; (GB Sch) établissement *m* secondaire

high-speed *adj* ‹train› à grande vitesse

high street (GB) *n* (*also* **High Street**) (in town) rue *f* principale; (in village) grand-rue *f*

high-street shop *n* boutique *f* appartenant à une chaîne

high street spending *n* dépenses *fpl* de consommation courante

high-tech *adj* ‹industry› de pointe; ‹equipment, car› ultramoderne

high tide *n* marée *f* haute

highway *n* (GB) route *f* nationale; (US) autoroute *f*

Highway Code *n* (GB) Code *m* de la Route

hijack *vtr* détourner ‹plane›

hijacker *n* (of plane) pirate *m* (de l'air); (of bus, truck) pirate *m* (de la route)

hijacking *n* détournement *m*

hike ① *n* randonnée *f*; **to go on a** ~ faire une randonnée
② *vtr* (*also* ~ **up**) augmenter ‹*rate, price*›

hiker *n* randonneur/-euse *m/f*

hiking *n* randonnée *f*

hilarious *adj* désopilant/-e, hilarant/-e

hill *n* colline *f*; (hillside) coteau *m*; (incline) pente *f*, côte *f*

hillside *n* on the ~ à flanc de coteau

hilltop *n* sommet *m* de colline

hilly *adj* vallonné/-e

ᵈ **him** *pron* **(a)** (direct object) le, l'; **I know** ~ je le connais; **catch** ~! attrape-le!; **I gave** ~ **the book** je lui ai donné le livre; **phone** ~! téléphone-lui!
(b) (after preposition, to be) lui; **it's for** ~ c'est pour lui; **it's** ~ c'est lui

Himalayas *pr n pl* **the** ~ (les montagnes *fpl* de) l'Himalaya *m*

ᵈ **himself** *pron* **(a)** (reflexive) se, s' (indirect object) lui; **he's hurt** ~ il s'est blessé
(b) (after preposition) lui, lui-même; **for** ~ pour lui, pour lui-même; **(all) by** ~ tout seul
(c) (emphatic) lui-même; **he made it** ~ il l'a fait lui-même
(d) he's not ~ **today** il n'est pas dans son assiette aujourd'hui

hinder *vtr* entraver ‹*development, career*›; freiner ‹*progress, efforts*›

hind legs *n pl* pattes *fpl* de derrière

hindrance *n* entrave *f*; **to be a** ~ **to sb/sth** gêner qn/qch

hindsight *n* **with (the benefit of)** ~ avec le recul, rétrospectivement

Hindu ① *n* Hindou/-e *m/f*
② *adj* hindou/-e

hinge ① *n* charnière *f*; (lift-off) gond *m*
② *vi* (*p prés* **hingeing**) **to** ~ **on** dépendre de

hint ① *n* **(a)** (remark) allusion *f* (**about** à); **to drop** ~s faire des allusions
(b) (clue) indication *f*; (piece of advice) conseil *m*
(c) (of spice, accent) pointe *f*; (of colour) touche *f*; (of smile) ébauche *f*; (of irony) soupçon *m*
② *vtr* **to** ~ **that** laisser entendre que (**to** à)
③ *vi* faire des allusions; **to** ~ **at** faire allusion à

hip ① *n* hanche *f*
② *adj* (colloq) ‹*person*› branché/-e
③ *excl* ~ ~ **hurrah!** hip hip hip hourra!

hippie, hippy *n, adj* hippie *mf*

hippopotamus, hippo *n* (*pl* **-muses** *ou* **-mi**) hippopotame *m*

ᵈ **hire** ① *n* location *f*; **for** ~ ‹*boat, skis*› à louer; ‹*taxi*› libre
② *vtr* louer ‹*equipment, vehicle*›; engager ‹*person*›

ᵈ indicates a very frequent word

hire purchase, HP *n* achat *m* à crédit; **on** ~ à crédit

ᵈ **his**

■ **Note** In French determiners agree in gender and number with the noun that follows. So *his*, when used as a determiner, is translated by *son* + masculine singular noun (son chien), by *sa* + feminine singular noun (sa maison) BUT by *son* + feminine noun beginning with a vowel or mute 'h' (son assiette) and by *ses* + plural noun (ses enfants).
— When *his* is stressed, *à lui* is added after the noun: HIS house = sa maison à lui.
— In French possessive pronouns reflect the gender and number of the noun they are standing for. When used as a possessive pronoun, *his* is translated by *le sien, la sienne, les siens* or *les siennes* according to what is being referred to.

① *det* son/sa/ses
② *pron* **all the drawings were good but** ~ **was the best** tous les dessins étaient bons mais le sien était le meilleur; **the blue car is** ~ la voiture bleue est à lui; **it's not** ~ ce n'est pas à lui; **which house is** ~? laquelle est sa maison?; **I'm a colleague of** ~ je suis un/-e de ses collègues

hiss ① *n* sifflement *m*
② *vi* ‹*person, steam, snake*› siffler; ‹*cat*› cracher; ‹*fat*› grésiller

historian *n* historien/-ienne *m/f*

ᵈ **historic(al)** *adj* historique

ᵈ **history** *n* **(a)** histoire *f*; **to make** ~ entrer dans l'histoire
(b) (past experience) antécédents *mpl*; **to have a** ~ **of violence** avoir un passé violent

ᵈ **hit** ① *n* **(a)** (blow, stroke) coup *m*
(b) (success) (play, film) succès *m*; (record) tube *m* (fam); **to be a big** ~ avoir un succès fou
(c) (Comput) (visit to Website) hit *m* (fam), visite *f* (à un site Web); (occurences in search) occurence *f*
② *vtr* (*p prés* **-tt-**, *prét, pp* **hit**) **(a)** (strike) frapper ‹*person, ball*›; **to** ~ **one's head on sth** se cogner la tête contre qch
(b) atteindre ‹*target, enemy*›
(c) (collide with) heurter ‹*wall*›; ‹*vehicle*› renverser ‹*person*›
(d) (affect adversely) affecter, toucher
(e) (reach) arriver à ‹*motorway*›; rencontrer ‹*traffic, bad weather*›; ‹*figures, weight*› atteindre ‹*level*›
IDIOM to ~ **it off with sb** bien s'entendre avec qn

■ **hit back**: ① ¶ ~ **[sb] back** rendre un coup à
② ¶ ~ **[sth] back** renvoyer ‹*ball*›

hit-and-run *adj* ‹*accident*› où le chauffeur a pris la fuite

hitch ① *n* problème *m*, pépin *m* (fam)
② *vtr* **(a)** attacher ‹*trailer*› (**to** à)
(b) (colloq) **to** ~ **a lift** faire du stop (fam)
③ *vi* (colloq) faire du stop (fam)

hitchhike vi faire du stop (fam); **to ~ to Paris** aller à Paris en stop (fam)

hitchhiker n auto-stoppeur/-euse m/f

hitchhiking n auto-stop m

hit man n tueur m à gages

hit parade n palmarès m, hit-parade m

hit single n tube m (fam)

HIV n (abbr = **human immunodeficiency virus**) (virus m) VIH m; **~ positive** séropositif/-ive; **~ negative** séronégatif/-ive

hive n ruche f; **a ~ of activity** une vraie ruche

hoard ⃞1 n (of treasure) trésor m; (of provisions) provisions fpl; (of miser) magot m (fam)
⃞2 vtr amasser ‹objects, money, food›

hoarding n (GB) (a) (billboard) panneau m publicitaire
(b) (fence) palissade f

hoarse adj ‹voice› rauque; **to be ~** être enroué/-e

hoax ⃞1 n canular m
⃞2 adj ‹call, warning› bidon inv (fam)

hob n (GB) (on cooker) table f de cuisson

hobble vi boitiller

hobby n passe-temps m inv

hockey n (GB) hockey m; (US) hockey m sur glace; **~ stick** crosse f de hockey

hoe ⃞1 n houe f, binette f
⃞2 vtr biner ‹ground›; sarcler ‹flower beds›

hog ⃞1 n (US) (pig) porc m, verrat m
⃞2 vtr (colloq) (prét, pp **-gg-**) monopoliser
IDIOM **to go the whole ~** (colloq) (be extravagant) faire les choses en grand; (go to extremes) aller jusqu'au bout

hoist vtr hisser ‹flag, sail, heavy object›

✓ **hold** ⃞1 n (a) (grasp) prise f; **to get ~ of** attraper ‹rope, handle›
(b) **to get ~ of** se procurer ‹book, ticket›; découvrir ‹information›
(c) **to get ~ of sb** (contact) joindre qn; (find) trouver qn
(d) (control) emprise f (**on, over** sur); **to have a ~ on or over sb** avoir de l'emprise sur qn; **to get a ~ of oneself** se reprendre
(e) **to put a call on ~** mettre un appel en attente
(f) (in plane) soute f; (on boat) cale f
⃞2 vtr (prét, pp **held**) (a) tenir; **to ~ sth in one's hand** tenir qch à la main ‹brush, pencil›; (enclosed) tenir qch dans la main ‹coin, sweet›; **to ~ sb (in one's arms)** serrer qn dans ses bras; **to ~ sth in place** maintenir qch en place
(b) organiser ‹meeting, competition, reception›; célébrer ‹church service›; mener ‹inquiry›; faire passer ‹interview›
(c) (contain) ‹drawer, box, case› contenir ‹objects, possessions›
(d) avoir ‹opinion, belief›

(e) (keep against will) détenir ‹person›; **to ~ sb hostage** garder qn en otage
(f) détenir, avoir ‹power, record›; être titulaire de ‹degree›
(g) **to ~ sb's attention** retenir l'attention de qn; **to ~ sb responsible** tenir qn pour responsable
(h) (defend successfully) tenir ‹territory, city›; conserver ‹title, seat›; **to ~ one's own** bien se défendre
(i) (on phone) **can you ~ the line please?** ne quittez pas s'il vous plaît
⃞3 vi (prét, pp **held**) (a) ‹bridge, dam, rope› tenir
(b) ‹weather› se maintenir; ‹luck› durer
(c) (on phone) patienter
(d) **~ still!** tiens-toi tranquille!

▪ **hold against: to ~ sth against sb** reprocher qch à qn

▪ **hold back:** ⃞1 ¶**~ back** se retenir (**from doing** de faire)
⃞2 ¶**~ [sb/sth] back (a)** contenir ‹water, crowd, anger›; retenir ‹tears, person›
(b) entraver ‹development›

▪ **hold down (a)** tenir, maîtriser ‹person›
(b) garder ‹job›

▪ **hold on (a)** (wait) attendre; **'~ on...'** (on phone) 'ne quittez pas...'
(b) (grip) s'accrocher; **'~ on (tight)!'** 'tiens-toi (bien)!'

▪ **hold on to** s'agripper à ‹branch, rope, person›; (to prevent from falling) retenir ‹person›; serrer ‹object, purse›

▪ **hold out:** ⃞1 ¶**~ out** tenir bon; **to ~ out against** tenir bon devant ‹threat, changes›
⃞2 ¶**~ [sth] out** tendre ‹hand› (**to** à)

▪ **hold to: ~ sb to [sth]** faire tenir [qch] à qn ‹promise›

▪ **hold up (a)** soutenir ‹shelf›; tenir ‹trousers›
(b) (raise) lever; **to ~ one's hand up** lever la main
(c) (delay) retarder ‹person, flight›; ralentir ‹production, traffic›
(d) (rob) attaquer

holdall n fourre-tout m, sac m

holder n (of passport, degree, post, account) titulaire mf; (of ticket, record) détenteur/-trice m/f; (of title) tenant/-e m/f

holding n (share) participation f

hold-up n (a) (delay) retard m; (on road) embouteillage m, bouchon m
(b) (robbery) hold-up m

✓ **hole** n (a) (gen) trou m
(b) (GB) (in tooth) cavité f
(c) (of fox, rabbit) terrier m

hole-in-the-wall n (colloq) distributeur m automatique de billets de banque

✓ **holiday** n (a) (GB) (vacation) vacances fpl; **to go on ~** partir en vacances
(b) (GB) (time off work) congé m
(c) (public, bank) jour m férié

holiday home n résidence f secondaire

holiday job n (in summer) job m (fam) d'été

holidaymaker n (GB) vacancier/-ière m/f
holiday resort n lieu m de villégiature
Holland pr n Hollande f, Pays-Bas mpl
hollow 1 n creux m
2 adj ‹object, cheeks› creux/creuse; ‹words›
faux/fausse, vain/-e; **a ~ laugh** un rire forcé;
to sound ~ sonner faux
holly n houx m
holocaust n holocauste m; **the Holocaust**
l'Holocauste m
hologram n hologramme m
holster n étui m de revolver
holy adj (gen) saint/-e; ‹water› bénit/-e
Holy Bible n Sainte Bible f
Holy Land pr n Terre f Sainte
Holy Spirit n Saint-Esprit m
homage n hommage m; **to pay ~ to** rendre
hommage à
⚬ **home** 1 n (a) (house) maison f; (country)
pays m natal; **broken ~** foyer désuni; **to
leave ~** quitter la maison
(b) (institution) maison f; **to put sb in a ~**
mettre qn dans un établissement spécialisé
(c) (Sport) **to play at ~** jouer à domicile
2 adj (a) ‹life› de famille; ‹comforts› du
foyer
(b) ‹market, affairs› intérieur/-e; ‹news›
national/-e
(c) (Sport) ‹match, win› à domicile; ‹team›
qui reçoit
3 adv (a) ‹come, go› (to house) à la maison,
chez soi; (to country) dans son pays
(b) **to bring sth ~ to sb** faire comprendre or
voir qch à qn; **to strike ~** toucher juste
4 **at home** phr (a) ‹be, work, stay› à la
maison, chez soi
(b) (Sport) ‹play› à domicile
(c) (at ease) ‹feel› à l'aise (**with** avec); **make
yourself at ~** fais comme chez toi
home address n adresse f personnelle
home cooking n bonne cuisine f
familiale
home economics n (Sch) cours m
d'économie domestique
home help n (GB) aide f familiale
homeland n pays m d'origine, patrie f
homeland security n sécurité f des
frontières
homeless n **the ~** les sans-abri mpl
homely adj (a) (GB) (cosy, welcoming)
accueillant/-e
(b) (GB) (unpretentious) simple
(c) (US) (plain) ‹person› sans attraits
homemade adj fait/-e maison, maison inv
Home Office n ministère m de l'Intérieur
homeopathic adj homéopathique
home owner n propriétaire mf
home page n page f d'accueil

⚬ indicates a very frequent word

home rule n gouvernement m autonome
Home Secretary n Ministre m de
l'Intérieur
home shopping n téléachat m
homesick adj **to be ~** (for country) avoir le
mal du pays
home town n ville f natale
home video n vidéo f d'amateur
homeward adv ‹travel ~(s)› rentrer; **to
be ~ bound** être sur le chemin de retour
homework n (a) (Sch) devoirs mpl
(b) (research) **to do some ~ on** faire quelques
recherches au sujet de
homeworker n travailleur/-euse m/f à
domicile
homeworking n travail m à domicile
homicidal adj homicide
homicide n (a) (murder) homicide m
(b) (person) meurtrier/-ière m/f
homogenous adj homogène
homosexual n, adj homosexuel/-elle m/f
homosexuality n homosexualité f
honest adj ‹answer, account› sincère;
‹person› (truthful, trustworthy) honnête; **to be ~
with sb** être franc/franche avec qn; **to be ~,
I don't care** à dire vrai, ça m'est égal
honestly adv (a) (truthfully) honnêtement
(b) (really) vraiment
(c) (sincerely) franchement
honesty n honnêteté f
honey n (a) miel m
(b) (colloq) (dear) chéri/-e m/f
honeycomb n (in hive) rayon m de miel; (for
sale) gâteau m de miel
honeymoon n lune f de miel; **to go on ~**
partir en voyage de noces
honeysuckle n chèvrefeuille m
Hong Kong pr n Hongkong m
honk vtr **to ~ one's horn** donner un coup
de klaxon®
honor (US) = HONOUR
honorable (US) = HONOURABLE
honorary adj honoraire
⚬ **honour** (GB), **honor** (US) 1 n
(a) honneur m; **in ~ of** en l'honneur de
(b) (in titles) **Your Honour** Votre Honneur
2 vtr honorer ‹person, cheque, contract›;
tenir ‹promise, commitment›
honourable (GB), **honorable** (US) adj
(gen) honorable; ‹person, intention› honnête
honours degree n: licence réservée aux
meilleurs étudiants
hood n (a) (of coat) capuchon m; (balaclava)
cagoule f
(b) (on cooker) hotte f
(c) (GB) (on car, pram) capote f
(d) (US Aut) (bonnet) capot m
(e) (US) (colloq) (gangster) truand m
hoof n (pl **~s** ou **hooves**) sabot m
hook 1 n (a) (on wall, for picture) crochet m

(b) (on fishing line) hameçon *m*
(c) (fastener) agrafe *f*; ~**s and eyes** agrafes *fpl*
(d) to take the phone off the ~ décrocher le téléphone
(e) (in boxing) crochet *m*; **left** ~ crochet du gauche
2 *vtr* accrocher (**on, onto** à)
IDIOM **to get sb off the** ~ tirer qn d'affaire
hooked *adj* **(a)** ‹*nose, beak*› crochu/-e
(b) to be ~ **on** se camer (fam) à ‹*drugs*›; être mordu/-e (fam) de ‹*films, computer games*›
hooligan *n* vandale *m*, voyou *m*; **soccer** ~ hooligan *m*
hoop *n* (ring) cerceau *m*; (in croquet) arceau *m*
hooray *excl* hourra!
hoot 1 *n* (of owl) (h)ululement *m*; (of car) coup *m* de klaxon®
2 *vtr* **to** ~ **one's horn** donner un coup de klaxon®
3 *vi* ‹*owl*› (h)ululer; ‹*car*› klaxonner; ‹*person, crowd*› (derisively) huer; **to** ~ **with laughter** éclater de rire
hoover *vtr* (GB) **to** ~ **a room** passer l'aspirateur dans une pièce
Hoover® *n* (GB) aspirateur *m*
hop 1 *n* (of frog, rabbit, child) bond *m*; (of bird) sautillement *m*
2 **hops** *n pl* houblon *m*
3 *vi* (*p prés etc* **-pp-**) ‹*person*› sauter; (on one leg) sauter à cloche-pied; ‹*bird*› sautiller; **to** ~ **into bed/off a bus** sauter dans son lit/d'un bus
⚔ **hope** 1 *n* espoir *m* (**of** de); **to raise sb's** ~**s** faire naître l'espoir chez qn; **to give up** ~ abandonner tout espoir; **to have no** ~ **of sth** n'avoir aucune chance de qch
2 *vtr* espérer (**that** que); **to** ~ **to do** espérer faire; **I (do)** ~ **so/not** j'espère (bien) que oui/ que non
3 *vi* espérer; **to** ~ **for a reward** espérer avoir une récompense; **let's** ~ **for the best** espérons que tout se passera bien
hopeful *adj* ‹*person, expression*› plein/-e d'espoir; ‹*attitude, mood*› optimiste; ‹*sign, situation*› encourageant/-e
hopefully *adv* **(a)** (with luck) avec un peu de chance
(b) (with hope) ‹*say*› avec optimisme
hopeless *adj* **(a)** ‹*attempt, case, struggle*› désespéré/-e; **it's** ~**!** inutile!
(b) (colloq) (incompetent) nul/nulle (fam)
hopelessness *n* **(a)** (despair) désespoir *m*
(b) (futility) futilité *f* (**of doing** de faire)
hopscotch *n* marelle *f*
horizon *n* horizon *m*; **on the** ~ à l'horizon; (figurative) en vue
horizontal *adj* horizontal/-e
hormone *n* hormone *f*
hormone replacement therapy, **HRT** *n* hormonothérapie *f* substitutive
horn *n* **(a)** (of animal, snail) corne *f*

(b) (Mus) cor *m*
(c) (of car) klaxon® *m*; (of ship) sirène *f*
hornet *n* frelon *m*
horoscope *n* horoscope *m*
horrendous *adj* épouvantable
horrible *adj* **(a)** (unpleasant) ‹*place, clothes, smell*› affreux/-euse; ‹*weather, food, person*› épouvantable; **to be** ~ **to sb** être méchant/-e avec qn
(b) (shocking) ‹*death, crime*› horrible
horrid *adj* affreux/-euse
horrific *adj* atroce
horrify *vtr* horrifier
horrifying *adj* ‹*experience, sight*› horrifiant/-e; ‹*behaviour*› effroyable
horror *n* horreur *f* (**at** devant); **to have a** ~ **of sth/of doing** avoir horreur de qch/de faire
horror film *n* film *m* d'épouvante
horror story *n* histoire *f* d'épouvante
⚔ **horse** *n* cheval *m*
IDIOM **from the** ~**'s mouth** de source sûre
∎ **horse about, horse around** chahuter
horseback *n* **on** ~ à cheval
horseback riding *n* (US) équitation *f*
horse chestnut *n* (tree) marronnier *m* (d'Inde); (fruit) marron *m* (d'Inde)
horsefly *n* taon *m*
horsepower *n* puissance *f* (en chevaux)
horse race *n* course *f* de chevaux
horseracing *n* courses *fpl* de chevaux, courses *fpl* hippiques
horseradish sauce *n* sauce *f* au raifort
horseriding *n* équitation *f*
horseshoe *n* fer *m* à cheval
horseshow *n* concours *m* hippique
horticulture *n* horticulture *f*
hose, hosepipe (GB) *n* (gen) tuyau *m*; (for garden) tuyau *m* d'arrosage; (fire) ~ lance *f* à incendie
hospice *n* établissement *m* de soins palliatifs
hospitable *adj* hospitalier/-ière (**to** envers)
⚔ **hospital** *n* hôpital *m*; **to be taken to** ~ être hospitalisé/-e; **in** ~ à l'hôpital
hospitality *n* hospitalité *f*
hospitalize *vtr* hospitaliser
⚔ **host** 1 *n* **(a)** (gen) hôte *m*
(b) (on radio, TV) animateur/-trice *m/f*
(c) (multitude) foule *f* (**of** de)
2 *vtr* organiser ‹*party*›; animer ‹*show*›
hostage *n* otage *m*; **to hold sb** ~ garder qn en otage
host country *n* pays *m* hôte *or* d'accueil
hostel *n* (for workers, refugees) foyer *m*; (youth) ~ auberge *f* de jeunesse
hostess *n* hôtesse *f*
hostile *adj* hostile (**to** à)
hostility *n* hostilité *f* (**towards** à l'égard de)

hot *adj* (a) (gen) chaud/-e; **it's ∼ here** il fait chaud ici; **to be** *or* **feel ∼** ‹person› avoir chaud; **to go ∼ and cold** (with fever) être fiévreux/-euse; (with fear) avoir des sueurs froides
(b) (Culin) ‹mustard, spice› fort/-e; ‹sauce, dish› épicé/-e
(c) **to be ∼ on sb's trail** être sur les talons de qn

hot air balloon *n* montgolfière *f*
hotbed *n* foyer *m* (**of** de)
hot dog *n* hot dog *m*
hotel *n* hôtel *m*
hotelier, hotelkeeper *n* (GB) hôtelier/ -ière *m/f*
hot-headed *adj* ‹person› impétueux/-euse
hotline *n* (a) (for orders, tickets) ligne *f* ouverte, permanence *f* téléphonique
(b) (Mil, Pol) téléphone *m* rouge
hotplate *n* plaque *f* de cuisson
hot seat *n*
IDIOM **to be in the ∼** être sur la sellette
hotshot *n* gros bonnet *m* (fam)
hot spot *n* (colloq) (a) (trouble spot) point *m* chaud
(b) (sunny country) pays *m* chaud
hot-tempered *adj* colérique
hot water bottle *n* bouillotte *f*
hound ① *n* chien *m* de chasse
② *vtr* harceler, traquer ‹person›
■ **hound out** chasser (**of** de)
hour *n* heure *f*; **£10 per ∼** 10 livres sterling (de) l'heure; **to be paid by the ∼** être payé/-e à l'heure; **60 km an hour** 60 km à l'heure; **in the early ∼s** au petit matin
hourly ① *adj* horaire
② *adv* ‹arrive, phone› toutes les heures
house ① *n* (a) (gen) maison *f*; **at my/his ∼** chez moi/lui; **to go to sb's ∼** aller chez qn; **on the ∼** aux frais de la maison
(b) (in theatre) (audience) assistance *f*; (auditorium) salle *f*; (performance) séance *f*
(c) (music) house music *f*
② *vtr* loger ‹person›; abriter ‹collection›
houseboat *n* péniche *f* aménagée
housebound *adj* confiné/-e chez soi
house call *n* visite *f* à domicile
household ① *n* maison *f*; (in survey) ménage *m*; **head of the ∼** chef *m* de famille
② *adj* ‹expenses› du ménage; ‹chore› ménager/-ère
household appliance *n* appareil *m* électroménager
householder *n* (a) (occupier) occupant/-e *m/f*
(b) (owner) propriétaire *mf*
household name *n* **he's a ∼** il est célèbre
house husband *n* homme *m* au foyer

housekeeper *n* gouvernante *f*
housekeeping *n* (money) argent *m* du ménage
House of Commons *n* (GB) Chambre *f* des communes
House of Lords *n* (GB) Chambre *f* des lords, Chambre *f* haute
House of Representatives *n* (US) Chambre *f* des représentants
houseplant *n* plante *f* d'intérieur
house-proud *adj* fier/fière de son intérieur
Houses of Parliament *n pl* (GB) Parlement *m* Britannique
house-to-house *adj* ‹search› de maison en maison
house-trained *adj* (GB) propre
house-warming (party) *n* pendaison *f* de crémaillère
housewife *n* (*pl* **-wives**) femme *f* au foyer; ménagère *f*
housework *n* travaux *mpl* ménagers; **to do the ∼** faire le ménage
housing *n* logements *mpl*
housing estate *n* (GB) cité *f*
hover *vi* ‹eagle› planer; ‹helicopter› faire du surplace; **to ∼ around sb/sth** tourner autour de qn/qch
hovercraft *n* (*pl* ∼) aéroglisseur *m*
how ① *adv* (a) (gen) comment; **∼ are you?** comment allez-vous?; **∼'s your brother?** comment va ton frère?; **∼ are things?** comment ça va?; **∼ do you do!** enchanté!; **to know ∼ to do** savoir faire
(b) (in number, quantity questions) **∼ much is this?** combien ça coûte?; **∼ much do you weigh?** combien pèses-tu?; **∼ many people?** combien de personnes?; **∼ many times** combien de fois; **∼ long will it take?** combien de temps cela va-t-il prendre?; **∼ tall are you?** combien mesures-tu?; **∼ far is it?** c'est à quelle distance?; **∼ old is she?** quel âge a-t-elle?; **∼ soon can you get here?** dans combien de temps peux-tu être ici?
(c) (in exclamations) **∼ wonderful/awful!** c'est fantastique/affreux!; **∼ clever of you!** comme c'est intelligent de ta part!
② (colloq) **how come** *phr* **∼ come?** pourquoi?; **∼ come you always get the best place?** comment ça se fait que tu aies toujours la meilleure place?
however *adv* (a) (nevertheless) toutefois, cependant
(b) *adv* (no matter how) **∼ hard I try, I can't** j'ai beau essayer, je n'y arrive pas; **∼ difficult the task is** aussi difficile que soit la tâche; **∼ small she may be** si petite soit-elle; **∼ much it costs** quel qu'en soit le prix; **∼ long it takes** quel que soit le temps que ça prendra; **∼ you like** comme tu veux
howl ① *n* hurlement *m*
② *vi* hurler

✓ indicates a very frequent word

HQ *n* (Mil) (*abbr* = **headquarters**) QG *m*
HTML *n* (*abbr* = **HyperText Markup Language**) HTML *m*
hub *n* (of wheel) moyeu *m*; (figurative) centre *m*
hubcap *n* enjoliveur *m*
huddle *vi* to ~ **around** se presser autour de ‹fire, radio›; to ~ **together** se serrer les uns contre les autres
hue *n* (a) (colour) couleur *f*, teinte *f*
(b) ~ **and cry** tollé *m*
huff (colloq) **1** *n* **in a** ~ vexé/-e
2 *vi* souffler
hug **1** *n* étreinte *f*; **to give sb a** ~ serrer qn dans ses bras
2 *vtr* (*p prés etc* **-gg-**) (a) (embrace) serrer [qn] dans ses bras
(b) **to** ~ **the coast/kerb** serrer la côte/le trottoir
⚹ **huge** *adj* ‹object, garden, city, country› immense; ‹person, animal› gigantesque; ‹appetite, success› énorme; ‹debts, sum› gros/ grosse (*before n*)
hugely *adv* (a) (emphatic) extrêmement
(b) ‹increase, vary› considérablement; ‹enjoy› énormément
hull *n* (of ship, plane) coque *f*; (of tank) carcasse *f*
hum **1** *n* (of insect, traffic, voices) bourdonnement *m*; (of machinery) ronronnement *m*
2 *vi* (*p prés etc* **-mm-**) ‹person› fredonner; ‹insect, aircraft› bourdonner; ‹machine› ronronner
⚹ **human** **1** *n* humain *m*
2 *adj* ‹body, behaviour› humain/-e; ‹characteristic, rights› de l'homme
human being *n* être *m* humain
humane *adj* ‹person› humain/-e; ‹act› d'humanité
human interest story *n* histoire *f* vécue
humanitarian *adj* humanitaire
humanity *n* humanité *f*
human nature *n* nature *f* humaine
human resources manager *n* responsable *mf* de la gestion des ressources humaines
humble *adj* (gen) modeste; ‹person› humble
humid *adj* ‹climate› humide; ‹weather› lourd/-e
humidity *n* humidité *f*
humiliate *vtr* humilier
humiliating *adj* humiliant/-e
humiliation *n* humiliation *f*
humorous *adj* (a) ‹story, book› humoristique
(b) ‹person, look› plein/-e d'humour
humour (GB), **humor** (US) **1** *n* (a) (wit) humour *m*; **a good sense of** ~ le sens de l'humour

(b) (mood) humeur *f*; **to be in good/bad** ~ être de bonne/mauvaise humeur
2 *vtr* amadouer ‹person›
hump *n* bosse *f*
hunch **1** *n* intuition *f*
2 *vtr* **to** ~ **one's shoulders** rentrer les épaules
hunched *adj* ‹back, figure› voûté/-e; ‹shoulders› rentré/-e
⚹ **hundred** **1** *n* cent *m*; **two** ~ deux cents; **two** ~ **and one** deux cent un; **in nineteen** ~ en mille neuf cents; **in nineteen** ~ **and three** en mille neuf cent trois; ~**s of times** des centaines de fois
2 *pron, det* cent; **two** ~ **euros** deux cents euros; **two** ~ **and five euros** deux cent cinq euros; **about a** ~ **people** une centaine de personnes
hundredth *n, adj, adv* centième *mf*
hundredweight *n* (GB) = 50.80 *kg*; (US) = 45.36 *kg*
Hungarian **1** *n* (a) (person) Hongrois/-e *m/f*
(b) (language) hongrois *m*
2 *adj* hongrois/-e
Hungary *pr n* Hongrie *f*
hunger *n* faim *f*
hunger strike *n* grève *f* de la faim
hung-over *adj* (colloq) **to be** ~ avoir la gueule de bois (fam)
hungry *adj* **to be** ~ avoir faim; **to make sb** ~ donner faim à qn; ~ **for** assoiffé/-e de ‹success, power›
hunk *n* (a) (of bread, cheese) gros morceau *m*
(b) (colloq) (man) beau mec *m* (fam)
hunt **1** *n* (a) (for animals) chasse *f* (**for** à)
(b) (search) recherche *f* (**for** de)
2 *vtr* rechercher ‹person›; chasser ‹animal›
3 *vi* (a) (for prey) chasser
(b) (search) **to** ~ **for sth** chercher [qch] partout ‹object, person›
hunter *n* (person) chasseur/-euse *m/f*
hunting *n* chasse *f* (**of** à); **to go** ~ aller à la chasse
hunt saboteur *n* opposant/-e *m/f* à la chasse au renard
hurdle *n* (a) (Sport) haie *f*
(b) (obstacle) obstacle *m*
hurl *vtr* (a) (throw) lancer (**at** sur)
(b) (shout) **to** ~ **insults at sb** accabler qn d'injures
hurrah, hurray *n, excl* hourra *m*
hurricane *n* ouragan *m*
hurry **1** *n* hâte *f*, empressement *m*; **to be in a** ~ être pressé/-e (**to do** de faire); **to leave in a** ~ partir à la hâte
2 *vtr* terminer [qch] à la hâte ‹meal, task›; bousculer ‹person›
3 *vi* se dépêcher (**over doing** de faire); **to** ~ **out** sortir précipitamment
■ **hurry up** se dépêcher; ~ **up!** dépêche-toi!

h

✓ **hurt** ① *adj* (gen) blessé/-e; **to feel ~** être peiné/-e
② *vtr* (*prét, pp* **hurt**) (a) (injure) **to ~ oneself** se blesser, se faire mal; **to ~ one's back** se blesser *or* se faire mal au dos
(b) (cause pain to) faire mal à; **you're ~ing my arm** vous me faites mal au bras
(c) (emotionally) blesser; (offend) froisser; **to ~ sb's feelings** blesser quelqu'un
③ *vi* (*prét, pp* **hurt**) (a) (be painful) faire mal; **my throat ~s** j'ai mal à la gorge
(b) (emotionally) blesser
hurtful *adj* blessant/-e
hurtle *vi* **to ~ down sth** dévaler qch; **to ~ along a road** foncer sur une route
✓ **husband** *n* mari *m*; (on form) époux *m*
hush ① *n* silence *m*
② *excl* chut!
■ **hush up**: ① ¶ **~ [sth] up** étouffer ‹affair›
② ¶ **~ [sb] up** faire taire ‹person›
hush-hush *adj* (colloq) très confidentiel/-ielle
hustle ① *n* **~ (and bustle)** (lively) effervescence *f*; (tiring) agitation *f*
② *vtr* pousser, bousculer ‹person›
hut *n* (gen) cabane *f*; (dwelling) hutte *f*; (on beach) cabine *f* (de plage)
hutch *n* (for rabbits) clapier *m*
hybrid bike *n* vélo *m* tous chemins, VTC *m*
hydrant *n* (*also* **fire ~**) bouche *f* d'incendie
hydraulic *adj* hydraulique
hydroelectricity *n* hydroélectricité *f*
hydrofoil *n* (a) (craft) hydroptère *m*
(b) (foil) aile *f* portante

hydrogen *n* hydrogène *m*
hyena *n* hyène *f*
hygiene *n* hygiène *f*
hygienic *adj* hygiénique
hymn *n* cantique *m*
hype *n* (colloq) battage *m* publicitaire
■ **hype up** faire du battage pour ‹film, star, book›; gonfler ‹story›
hyper *adj* (colloq) surexcité/-e
hyperactive *adj* hyperactif/-ive
hyperlink *n* lien *m* (hypertext)
hypermarket *n* (GB) hypermarché *m*
hypertext *n* hypertext *m*
hyperventilate *vi* être en hyperventilation
hyphen *n* trait *m* d'union
hypnosis *n* hypnose *f*
hypnotherapy *n* hypnothérapie *f*
hypnotist *n* hypnotiseur *m*
hypnotize *vtr* hypnotiser
hypoallergenic *adj* hypoallergénique
hypocrisy *n* hypocrisie *f*
hypocrite *n* hypocrite *mf*
hypocritical *adj* hypocrite
hypodermic *adj* hypodermique
hypothermia *n* hypothermie *f*
hypothesis *n* (*pl* **-theses**) hypothèse *f*
hysteria *n* hystérie *f*
hysterical *adj* (a) ‹person, behaviour› hystérique
(b) (colloq) (funny) délirant/-e
hysterics *n* (a) (fit) crise *f* de nerfs; **to have ~** avoir une crise de nerfs
(b) (laughter) **to be in ~** rire aux larmes

I i

i, I¹ *n* i, I *m*
✓ **I²** *pron* je, j'; **I am called Frances** je m'appelle Frances; **I closed the door** j'ai fermé la porte; **he's a student but I'm not** il est étudiant mais moi pas; **he and I went to the cinema** lui et moi sommes allés au cinéma
IBAN *n* (*abbr* = **Internation Bank Account Number**) IBAN *m*
✓ **ice** ① *n* glace *f*; (on roads) verglas *m*; (in drink) glaçons *mpl*
② *vtr* glacer ‹cake›
③ **iced** *pp adj* ‹water› avec des glaçons; **~d tea** thé glacé
■ **ice over** ‹windscreen, river› se couvrir de glace

✓ indicates a very frequent word

iceberg *n* iceberg *m*
icebox *n* (a) (GB) (freezer compartment) freezer *m*
(b) (US) (fridge) réfrigérateur *m*
ice-cold *adj* glacé/-e
ice cream *n* glace *f*
ice-cube *n* glaçon *m*
ice hockey *n* hockey *m* sur glace
Iceland *pr n* Islande *f*
Icelandic ① *n* (language) islandais *m*
② *adj* ‹people, customs› islandais/-e
ice rink *n* patinoire *f*
ice-skate ① *n* patin *m* à glace
② *vi* faire du patin à glace
ice-skating *n* patinage *m* sur glace

icicle n stalactite f (de glace)

icing n glaçage m

icing sugar n (GB) sucre m glace

icon n icône f

iconize vtr (Comput) iconiser

icy adj (a) ‹road› verglacé/-e
(b) ‹wind› glacial/-e; ‹hands› glacé/-e
(c) ‹look, reception› glacial/-e

ID n pièce f d'identité

ID card n carte f d'identité

✓ **idea** n idée f (about, on sur); I have no ~ je
n'ai aucune idée; to have no ~ why/how ne
pas savoir pourquoi/comment; I've an ~ that
he might be lying j'ai dans l'idée qu'il ment

ideal ☐1 n idéal m
☐2 adj idéal/-e

idealism n idéalisme m

idealist n idéaliste mf

idealistic adj idéaliste

idealize vtr idéaliser

ideally adv (a) (preferably) ~, the tests
should be free l'idéal serait que les examens
soient gratuits; ~, we'd like to stay l'idéal
pour nous, ce serait de rester
(b) (perfectly) ~ situated idéalement situé/-e

identical adj identique (to, with à)

identical twin n vrai jumeau/vraie
jumelle m/f

identification n (a) identification f (with
à)
(b) (proof of identity) pièce f d'identité

identify ☐1 vtr identifier (as comme étant;
to à); to ~ sb/sth with sb/sth identifier qn/
qch à qn/qch
☐2 vi to ~ with s'identifier à

identikit n (also **Identikit**®)
portrait-robot m

✓ **identity** n identité f

identity bracelet n gourmette f

identity card n carte f d'identité

identity parade n (GB) séance f
d'identification

identity theft n vol m d'identité

ideological adj idéologique

ideology n idéologie f

idiom n (a) (phrase) idiome m
(b) (language) (of speakers) parler m; (of theatre,
sport) langue f; (of music) style m

idiomatic adj idiomatique

idiosyncrasy n particularité f

idiosyncratic adj particulier/-ière

idiot n idiot/-e m/f

idiotic adj bête

idle ☐1 adj (a) (lazy) ‹person›
paresseux/-euse
(b) ‹boast, threat› vain/-e; ‹curiosity›
oiseux/-euse; ‹chatter› inutile
(c) (without occupation) ‹person› oisif/-ive; ‹day,
hour, moment› de loisir

(d) ‹dock, mine› à l'arrêt; ‹machine› arrêté/-e
☐2 vi ‹engine› tourner au ralenti
■ **idle away** passer [qch] à ne rien faire
‹day, time›

idol n idole f

idolize vtr adorer ‹friend, parent›; idolâtrer
‹star›

idyllic adj idyllique

✓ **ie** (abbr = **that is**) c-à-d

✓ **if** ☐1 conj (a) si; ~ I won a lot of money,
I would travel si je gagnais beaucoup
d'argent, je voyagerais; ~ I had known,
I would have told you si j'avais su, je te
l'aurais dit; ~ I were you, I... (moi) à ta
place, je...; ~ not sinon; I wonder ~ they
will come je me demande s'ils vont venir; do
you mind ~ I smoke? cela vous dérange si je
fume?; what ~ he died? et s'il mourait?
(b) (although) bien que; it's a good shop, ~ a
little expensive c'est un bon magasin, bien
qu'un peu cher
☐2 **if only** phr (a) (I wish) si seulement; ~
only I had known! si (seulcment) j'avais su!
(b) ~ only because (of) ne serait-ce qu'à
cause de; ~ only for a moment ne serait-ce
que pour un instant

iffy adj (colloq) (dubious) suspect/-e

igloo n igloo m, iglou m

ignite ☐1 vtr faire exploser ‹fuel›;
enflammer ‹material›
☐2 vi ‹petrol, gas› s'enflammer; ‹rubbish,
timber› prendre feu

ignition n (a) (system) allumage m
(b) (also ~ **switch**) contact m

ignition key n clé f de contact

ignorance n ignorance f

ignorant adj (of a subject) ignorant/-e; to be
~ about tout ignorer de ‹subject›; to be ~ of
ignorer ‹possibilities›

✓ **ignore** vtr ignorer ‹person›; ne pas relever
‹mistake, remark›; ne pas tenir compte
de ‹feeling, fact›; ne pas suivre ‹advice›; se
désintéresser complètement de ‹problem›

ill ☐1 n mal m; to wish sb ~ souhaiter du
mal à qn
☐2 adj malade; I feel ~ je ne me sens pas
bien; to be taken ~, to fall ~ tomber malade
☐3 adv he is ~ suited to the post il n'est
guère fait pour ce poste; to speak ~ of sb
dire du mal de qn

ill at ease adj gêné/-e, mal à l'aise

✓ **illegal** ☐1 n (US) immigrant/-e m/f
clandestin/-e
☐2 adj (gen) illégal/-e; ‹parking› illicite;
‹immigrant› clandestin/-e; (Sport)
irrégulier/-ière

illegally adv illégalement

illegible adj illisible

illegitimate adj illégitime

ill-equipped adj mal équipé/-e

ill-fitting adj ‹garment, shoe› qui va mal

ill-health n mauvaise santé f

illicit adj illicite

ill-informed adj mal informé/-e

illiterate n, adj analphabète mf

❧ **illness** n maladie f

illogical adj illogique

ill-treatment n mauvais traitements mpl

illuminate vtr éclairer

illuminated adj ‹sign› lumineux/-euse

illumination n (lighting) éclairage m

illuminations n pl (GB) illuminations fpl

illusion n illusion f; to have no ∼s about sth ne pas se faire d'illusions sur qch; to be or to labour under the ∼ that s'imaginer que

illustrate vtr illustrer

illustration n illustration f

illustrator n illustrateur/-trice m/f

ill will n rancune f

❧ **image** n (gen) image f; (of company, personality) image f de marque; **he is the (spitting)** ∼ **of you** c'est toi tout craché

image-conscious adj conscient/-e de son image de marque

image maker n professionnel/-elle m/f de l'image de marque

image processing n traitement m de l'image

imagery n images fpl

imaginary adj imaginaire

imagination n imagination f

imaginative adj ‹person, performance› plein d'imagination; ‹mind› imaginatif/-ive; ‹solution, device› ingénieux/-ieuse

❧ **imagine** vtr (a) (visualize, picture) (s')imaginer; **to** ∼ **being rich/king** s'imaginer riche/roi; **you must have** ∼**d it** ce doit être un effet de ton imagination
(b) (suppose) supposer, imaginer (**that** que)

imbalance n déséquilibre m

imbecile n, adj imbécile mf

imitate vtr imiter

imitation ⒈ n imitation f
⒉ adj ‹snow› artificiel/-ielle; ∼ **fur** imitation f fourrure; ∼ **jewel** faux bijou m; ∼ **leather** similicuir m

imitator n imitateur/-trice m/f

immaculate adj ‹dress, manners› impeccable; ‹performance› parfait/-e

immaterial adj (a) (unimportant) sans importance
(b) (intangible) immatériel/-ielle

immature adj (a) ‹plant› qui n'est pas arrivé à maturité
(b) (childish) immature; **don't be so** ∼! ne te conduis pas comme un enfant!

❧ **immediate** adj (a) ‹effect, reaction› immédiat/-e; ‹thought› premier/-ière (before n)
(b) ‹concern, goal› premier/-ière (before n);

(c) ‹vicinity› immédiat/-e; **his** ∼ **family** ses proches; **in the** ∼ **future** dans l'avenir proche

❧ **immediately** adv immédiatement; ∼ **after/before** juste avant/après

immense adj immense

immerse vtr plonger (**in** dans)

immersion course n (GB) cours m avec immersion linguistique

immigrant n, adj (recent) immigrant/-e m/f; (established) immigré/-e m/f

immigration n immigration f

immigration control n (system) contrôle m de l'immigration

imminent adj imminent/-e

immobile adj immobile

immobilize vtr paralyser ‹traffic, organization›; immobiliser ‹engine, patient, limb›

immobilizer n système m antidémarrage

immoral adj immoral/-e

immorality n immoralité f

immortal n, adj immortel/-elle m/f

immortality n immortalité f

immortalize vtr immortaliser

immune adj (a) (Med) ‹person› immunisé/-e (**to** contre); ‹reaction, system› immunitaire
(b) (oblivious) ∼ **to** insensible à
(c) **to be** ∼ **from** être à l'abri de ‹attack, arrest›; être exempté/-e de ‹tax›

immunity n immunité f (**to, against** contre)

immunize vtr immuniser

❧ **impact** n (a) (effect) impact m (**on** sur); **to make an** ∼ faire de l'effet
(b) (of hammer, vehicle) choc m; (of bomb, bullet) impact m; **on** ∼ au moment de l'impact

impair vtr affecter ‹performance›; diminuer ‹ability›; affaiblir ‹hearing, vision›; détériorer ‹health›

impaired adj ‹hearing, vision› affaibli/-e; **his speech is** ∼ il a des problèmes d'élocution

impart vtr (a) transmettre ‹knowledge, enthusiasm› (**to** à); communiquer ‹information› (**to** à)
(b) donner ‹atmosphere›

impartial adj ‹advice, judge› impartial/-e; ‹account› objectif/-ive

impassable adj ‹obstacle› infranchissable; ‹road› impraticable

impassive adj impassible

impatience n (a) (eagerness) impatience f (**to do** de faire)
(b) (irritation) agacement m (**with** à l'égard de; **at** devant)

impatient adj (a) (eager) ‹person› impatient/-e; ‹gesture, tone› d'impatience; **to be** ∼ **to do** être impatient/-e or avoir hâte de faire
(b) (irritable) agacé/-e (**at** par); **to be/get** ∼

impeach ⋯⟶ improvement

with sb s'impatienter contre qn

impeach *vtr* mettre [qn] en accusation

impeccable *adj* ‹behaviour› irréprochable; ‹appearance› impeccable

impede *vtr* entraver

impending *adj* imminent/-e

impenetrable *adj* impénétrable

imperative ⨍1⨍ *n* impératif *m*
⨍2⨍ *adj* ‹need› urgent/-e; ‹tone› impérieux/-ieuse

imperceptible *adj* imperceptible

imperfect ⨍1⨍ *n* imparfait *m*
⨍2⨍ *adj* ‹goods› défectueux/-euse; ‹logic, knowledge› imparfait/-e; **the ~ tense** l'imparfait *m*

imperial *adj* (a) (gen) impérial/-e
(b) (GB) ‹measure› conforme aux normes britanniques

imperious *adj* impérieux/-ieuse

impersonal *adj* impersonnel/-elle

impersonate *vtr* (imitate) imiter; (pretend to be) se faire passer pour ‹police officer›

impersonator *n* imitateur/-trice *m/f*

impertinent *adj* impertinent/-e (**to** envers)

impervious *adj* (to charm, suffering) indifférent/-e (**to** à); (to demands) imperméable (**to** à)

impetuous *adj* ‹person› impétueux/-euse; ‹action› impulsif/-ive

impetus *n* (a) impulsion *f* (**to** à)
(b) (momentum) élan *m*; **to gain/lose ~** prendre/perdre de l'élan

impinge *vi* **to ~ on** (restrict) empiéter sur; (affect) affecter

implacable *adj* implacable

implant ⨍1⨍ *n* implant *m*
⨍2⨍ *vtr* implanter (**in** dans)

implausible *adj* peu plausible

✶ **implement** ⨍1⨍ *n* (gen) instrument *m*; (tool) outil *m*; **farm ~s** outillage *m* agricole
⨍2⨍ *vtr* exécuter ‹contract, decision, idea›; mettre [qch] en application ‹law›

implementation *n* (of contract, idea) exécution *f*; (of law, policy) mise *f* en application; (Comput) implémentation *f*

implicate *vtr* impliquer (**in** dans)

implication *n* (a) (possible consequence) implication *f*
(b) (suggestion) insinuation *f*

implicit *adj* (a) (implied) implicite (**in** dans)
(b) ‹faith, trust› absolu/-e

imply *vtr* (a) ‹person› (insinuate) insinuer (**that** que); (make known) laisser entendre (**that** que)
(b) (mean) ‹argument› impliquer; ‹term, word› laisser supposer (**that** que)

impolite *adj* impoli/-e (**to** envers)

import ⨍1⨍ *n* importation *f*
⨍2⨍ *vtr* importer (**from** de; **to** en)

✶ **importance** *n* importance *f*

✶ **important** *adj* important/-e; **it is ~ that** il est important que (+ *subjunctive*); **his children are very ~ to him** ses enfants comptent beaucoup pour lui

importer *n* importateur/-trice *m/f*

✶ **impose** ⨍1⨍ *vtr* imposer ‹embargo, rule› (**on sb** à qn; **on sth** sur qch); infliger ‹sanction› (**on** à); **to ~ a fine on sb** frapper qn d'une amende; **to ~ a tax on tobacco** imposer le tabac
⨍2⨍ *vi* s'imposer; **to ~ on sb's kindness** abuser de la bonté de qn

imposing *adj* ‹person› imposant/-e; ‹sight› impressionnant/-e

✶ **impossible** ⨍1⨍ *n* **the ~** l'impossible *m*
⨍2⨍ *adj* impossible; **to make it ~ for sb to do** mettre qn dans l'impossibilité de faire

impotent *adj* impuissant/-e

impound *vtr* emmener [qch] à la fourrière ‹vehicle›; confisquer ‹goods›

impractical *adj* ‹suggestion, idea› peu réaliste; **to be ~** ‹person› manquer d'esprit pratique

imprecise *adj* imprécis/-e

impress ⨍1⨍ *vtr* (a) impressionner ‹person› (**with** par; **by doing** en faisant); **they were ~ed** ça leur a fait bonne impression
(b) **to ~ sth (up)on sb** faire bien comprendre qch à qn
⨍2⨍ *vi* faire bonne impression

impression *n* (a) (gen) impression *f*; **to be under** *or* **have the ~ that** avoir l'impression que; **to make a good/bad ~** faire bonne/mauvaise impression (**on** sur)
(b) (imitation) imitation *f*; **to do ~s** faire des imitations

impressionable *adj* influençable

✶ **impressive** *adj* (gen) impressionnant/-e; ‹building, sight› imposant/-e

imprint ⨍1⨍ *n* empreinte *f*
⨍2⨍ *vtr* (a) (fix) graver (**on** dans)
(b) (print) imprimer (**on** sur)

imprison *vtr* emprisonner

imprisonment *n* emprisonnement *m*

improbable *adj* (unlikely to happen) improbable; (unlikely to be true) invraisemblable

impromptu *adj* impromptu/-e

improper *adj* (dishonest) irrégulier/-ière; (indecent) indécent/-e; (incorrect) impropre, abusif/-ive

✶ **improve** ⨍1⨍ *vtr* (gen) améliorer; augmenter ‹chances›; **to ~ one's mind** se cultiver (l'esprit)
⨍2⨍ *vi* (a) s'améliorer
(b) **to ~ on** améliorer ‹score›; renchérir sur ‹offer›

✶ **improvement** *n* (a) amélioration *f* (**in, of, to** de); **the new edition is an ~ on the old one** la nouvelle édition est bien meilleure ⋯⟶

que l'ancienne

(b) (in house) aménagement *m*; **home** ~**s** aménagements *mpl* du domicile

improvise ① *vtr* improviser; **an** ~**d table** une table de fortune
② *vi* improviser

impudent *adj* insolent/-e, impudent/-e

impulse *n* impulsion *f*; **to have a sudden** ~ **to do** avoir une envie soudaine de faire; **on (an)** ~ sur un coup de tête

impulse buy *n* achat *m* d'impulsion

impulsive *adj* (spontaneous) spontané/-e; (rash) impulsif/-ive

impure *adj* impur/-e

⚹ **in** ① *prep* **(a)** (inside) dans; ~ **the box** dans la boîte; ~ **the newspaper** dans le journal; ~ **the school/town** dans l'école/la ville; ~ **school/town** à l'école/en ville; ~ **the country(side)** à la campagne; ~ **the photo** sur la photo; **chicken** ~ **a white wine sauce** du poulet à la sauce au vin blanc; ~ **Rome** à Rome; ~ **France/Spain** en France/Espagne; ~ **Canada/the United States** au Canada/aux États-Unis

(b) (showing occupation, activity) dans; ~ **insurance** dans les assurances; **to be** ~ **politics** faire de la politique; **to be** ~ **the team** faire partie de l'équipe

(c) (present in) chez; **it's rare** ~ **cats** c'est rare chez les chats; **he hasn't got it** ~ **him to succeed** il n'est pas fait pour réussir

(d) (showing manner, medium) en; ~ **Greek** en grec; ~ **B flat** en si bémol; ~ **a skirt** en jupe; **dressed** ~ **black** habillé/-e en noir; ~ **pencil/ink** au crayon/à l'encre; **to speak** ~ **a whisper** chuchoter; ~ **pairs** par deux; ~ **a circle** en cercle; ~ **the rain** sous la pluie

(e) (as regards) **rich** ~ **minerals** riche en minéraux; **deaf** ~ **one ear** sourd/-e d'une oreille; **10 cm** ~ **length** 10 cm de long

(f) (because of) dans; ~ **his hurry** dans sa précipitation; ~ **the confusion** dans la mêlée

(g) (with present participle) en; ~ **accepting** en acceptant; ~ **doing so** en faisant cela

(h) (with superlatives) de; **the tallest tower** ~ **the world** la plus grande tour du monde

(i) (in ratios) **a gradient of 1** ~ **4** une pente de 25%; **a tax of 20 pence** ~ **the pound** une taxe de 20 pence par livre sterling; **to have a one** ~ **five chance** avoir une chance sur cinq

(j) (with numbers) **she's** ~ **her twenties** elle a entre vingt et trente ans; **to cut sth** ~ **three** couper qch en trois; **the temperature was** ~ **the thirties** il faisait dans les trente degrés

(k) (during) ~ **May** en mai; ~ **1963** en 1963; ~ **summer** en été; ~ **the night** pendant la nuit; ~ **the morning(s)** le matin; **at four** ~ **the morning** à quatre heures du matin; ~ **the twenties** dans les années 20

(l) (within) ~ **ten minutes** en dix minutes; **I'll be back** ~ **half an hour** je serai de retour

---

⚹ indicates a very frequent word

dans une demi-heure

(m) (for) depuis; **it hasn't rained** ~ **weeks** il n'a pas plu depuis des semaines

② *adv* **(a) to come** ~ entrer; **to run** ~ entrer en courant; **to ask** *or* **invite sb** ~ faire entrer qn

(b) (at home) **to be** ~ être là; **to stay** ~ rester à la maison

(c) (arrived) **the train is** ~ le train est en gare; **the ferry is** ~ le ferry est à quai

(d) the tide is ~ c'est marée haute

(e) (Sport) **the ball is** ~ la balle est bonne

(f) (in supply) **we don't have any** ~ nous n'en avons pas en stock; **to get some beer** ~ aller chercher de la bière

③ *adj* (colloq) **to be** ~, **to be the** ~ **thing** être à la mode

④ **in and out** *phr* **to come** ~ **and out** entrer et sortir; **to weave** ~ **and out of** se faufiler entre ⟨traffic, tables⟩

IDIOM **he's** ~ **for a shock/surprise** il va avoir un choc/être surpris

inability *n* incapacité *f* (**to do** de faire)

inaccessible *adj* (out of reach) inaccessible; (hard to understand) peu accessible (**to** à)

inaccuracy *n* **(a)** (of report, estimate) inexactitude *f*
(b) (error) inexactitude *f*

inaccurate *adj* inexact/-e

inactive *adj* inactif/-ive

inadequate *adj* insuffisant/-e (**for** pour)

inadvisable *adj* inopportun/-e, à déconseiller

inane *adj* ⟨person, conversation⟩ idiot/-e; ⟨programme⟩ débile (fam)

inanimate *adj* inanimé/-e

inappropriate *adj* **(a)** ⟨behaviour⟩ inconvenant/-e, peu convenable; ⟨remark⟩ inopportun/-e
(b) ⟨advice, word⟩ qui n'est pas approprié

inarticulate *adj* **(a) to be** ~ ne pas savoir s'exprimer
(b) ⟨mumble⟩ inarticulé/-e; ⟨speech⟩ inintelligible

inasmuch *phr* (insofar as) dans la mesure où; (seeing as) vu que

inattentive *adj* ⟨pupil⟩ inattentif/-ive

inaudible *adj* inaudible

inauguration *n* (of exhibition) inauguration *f*; (of president) investiture *f*

in-between *adj* intermédiaire

inbuilt *adj* intrinsèque

Inc *n abbr* (US) ≈ SA

incapable *adj* incapable (**of doing** de faire)

incapacitate *vtr* ⟨accident, illness⟩ immobiliser

incendiary device *n* engin *m* incendiaire

incense *n* encens *m*

incensed *adj* outré/-e (**at** de; **by** par)
incentive *n* (a) **to give sb the** ~ **to do** donner envie à qn de faire; **there is no** ~ **for people to save** rien n'incite les gens à faire des économies
(b) (*also* **cash** ~) prime *f*
incentive scheme *n* système *m* de primes d'encouragement
incessant *adj* incessant/-e
incessantly *adv* sans cesse
incest *n* inceste *m*
incestuous *adj* incestueux/-euse
✐ **inch** *n* (*pl* ~**es**) (a) pouce *m* (= 2.54 cm)
(b) ~ **by** ~ petit à petit; **to come within an** ~ **of winning** passer à deux doigts de la victoire
incidence *n* **the** ~ **of** la fréquence de ‹thefts, deaths›; **high/low** ~ **of sth** taux élevé/ faible de qch
✐ **incident** *n* incident *m*
incidental *adj* ‹detail, remark› secondaire
incidentally *adv* (by the way) à propos; (by chance) par la même occasion
incident room *n* bureau *m* des enquêteurs
incinerate *vtr* incinérer
incite *vtr* **to** ~ **violence** inciter à la violence; **to** ~ **sb to do** pousser *or* inciter qn à faire
inclination *n* inclination *f*
incline ① *vtr* (a) incliner ‹head›
(b) **to be** ~**d to do** avoir tendance à faire; **if you feel so** ~**d** si l'envie vous en prend
② *vi* (a) (tend) **to** ~ **to** *or* **towards** tendre vers
(b) ‹road, tower› s'incliner
✐ **include** *vtr* inclure, comprendre; **all the ministers, Blanc** ~**d** tous les ministres, Blanc inclu; **breakfast is** ~**d in the price** le petit déjeuner est compris
including *prep* (y) compris; **£50** ~ **VAT** 50 livres sterling TVA comprise; ~ **service** service compris; ~ **July** y compris juillet; **not** ~ **July** sans compter juillet
inclusive *adj* inclus/-e; ‹price› forfaitaire; **all-**~ tout compris
incoherent *adj* incohérent/-e
✐ **income** *n* revenus *mpl*, revenu *m*
income bracket *n* tranche *f* de revenu
income tax *n* impôt *m* sur le revenu
incoming *adj* ‹call, mail› qui vient de l'extérieur; ‹government› nouveau/-elle; ‹tide› montant/-e
incomparable *adj* sans pareil/-eille
incompatible *adj* incompatible
incompetent *adj* ‹doctor, government› incompétent/-e; ‹work, performance› mauvais/-e (*before n*)
incomplete *adj* (a) ‹work, building› inachevé/-e

(b) ‹set› incomplet/-ète
incomprehensible *adj* ‹reason› incompréhensible; ‹speech› inintelligible
inconceivable *adj* inconcevable
inconclusive *adj* ‹meeting› sans conclusion véritable; ‹evidence› peu concluant/-e
incongruous *adj* ‹sight› déconcertant/-e; ‹appearance› surprenant/-e
inconsiderate *adj* ‹person› peu attentif/ -ive à autrui; ‹remark› maladroit/-e; **to be** ~ **towards sb** manquer d'égards envers qn
inconsistent *adj* ‹work› inégal/-e; ‹behaviour› changeant/-e; ‹argument› incohérent/-e; ‹attitude› inconsistant/-e; **to be** ~ **with** être en contradiction avec
inconspicuous *adj* ‹person› qui passe inaperçu/-e; ‹place, clothing› discret/-ète
inconvenience ① *n* (a) (trouble) dérangement *m*; **to put sb to great** ~ causer beaucoup de dérangement à qn
(b) (disadvantage) inconvénient *m*
② *vtr* déranger
inconvenient *adj* ‹location, arrangement› incommode; ‹time› inopportun/-e
incorporate *vtr* (a) (make part of) incorporer (**into** dans)
(b) (contain) comporter
(c) **Smith and Brown Incorporated** Smith et Brown SA
incorrect *adj* incorrect/-e (**to do** de faire)
incorrigible *adj* incorrigible
✐ **increase** ① *n* (a) (in amount) augmentation *f* (**in**, **of** de); **a 5%** ~ une augmentation de 5%
(b) (in degree) accroissement *m*; **to be on the** ~ être en progression
② *vtr* augmenter (**by** de; **to** jusqu'à)
③ *vi* augmenter (**by** de); **to** ~ **in value** prendre de la valeur; **to** ~ **in size** s'agrandir
increased *adj* ‹demand, risk› accru/-e
increasing *adj* ‹number› croissant/-e
✐ **increasingly** *adv* de plus en plus
incredible *adj* incroyable
incredulous *adj* incrédule
incriminating *adj* ‹statement, document› compromettant/-e; ‹evidence› incriminant/-e
incubator *n* (for child) couveuse *f*; (for eggs, bacteria) incubateur *m*
incur *vtr* (*p prés etc* **-rr-**) contracter ‹debts›; subir ‹loss›; encourir ‹expense, risk, wrath›
incurable *adj* (a) ‹disease› incurable
(b) ‹optimist, romantic› incorrigible
incursion *n* (gen) intrusion *f*; (Mil) incursion *f*
indebted *adj* **to be** ~ **to sb** (under an obligation) être redevable à qn; (grateful) être reconnaissant/-e à à qn
indecent *adj* (a) (improper) indécent/-e
(b) (unreasonable) ‹haste› malséant/-e

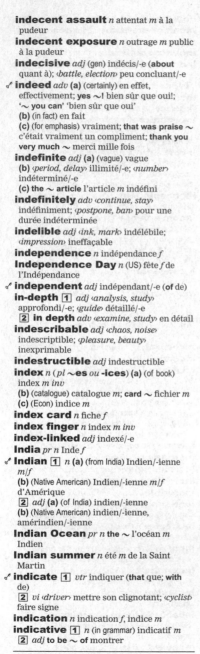

indecent assault n attentat m à la pudeur

indecent exposure n outrage m public à la pudeur

indecisive adj (gen) indécis/-e (about quant à); ‹battle, election› peu concluant/-e

ⅆ **indeed** adv (a) (certainly) en effet, effectivement; **yes** ∼! bien sûr que oui!; '∼ **you can**' 'bien sûr que oui'
(b) (in fact) en fait
(c) (for emphasis) vraiment; **that was praise** ∼ c'était vraiment un compliment; **thank you very much** ∼ merci mille fois

indefinite adj (a) (vague) vague
(b) ‹period, delay› illimité/-e; ‹number› indéterminé/-e
(c) **the** ∼ **article** l'article m indéfini

indefinitely adv ‹continue, stay› indéfiniment; ‹postpone, ban› pour une durée indéterminée

indelible adj ‹ink, mark› indélébile; ‹impression› ineffaçable

independence n indépendance f

Independence Day n (US) fête f de l'Indépendance

ⅆ **independent** adj indépendant/-e (**of** de)

in-depth ⟦1⟧ adj ‹analysis, study› approfondi/-e; ‹guide› détaillé/-e
⟦2⟧ **in depth** adv ‹examine, study› en détail

indescribable adj ‹chaos, noise› indescriptible; ‹pleasure, beauty› inexprimable

indestructible adj indestructible

index n (pl ∼**es** ou **-ices**) (a) (of book) index m inv
(b) (catalogue) catalogue m; **card** ∼ fichier m
(c) (Econ) indice m

index card n fiche f

index finger n index m inv

index-linked adj indexé/-e

India pr n Inde f

ⅆ **Indian** ⟦1⟧ n (a) (from India) Indien/-ienne m/f
(b) (Native American) Indien/-ienne m/f d'Amérique
⟦2⟧ adj (a) (of India) indien/-ienne
(b) (Native American) indien/-ienne, amérindien/-ienne

Indian Ocean pr n **the** ∼ l'océan m Indien

Indian summer n été m de la Saint Martin

ⅆ **indicate** ⟦1⟧ vtr indiquer (**that** que; **with** de)
⟦2⟧ vi ‹driver› mettre son clignotant; ‹cyclist› faire signe

indication n indication f, indice m

indicative ⟦1⟧ n (in grammar) indicatif m
⟦2⟧ adj **to be** ∼ **of** montrer

indicator n (a) (pointer) aiguille f
(b) (board) tableau m
(c) (on car) clignotant m

indict vtr inculper

indictment n (a) (Law) acte m d'accusation
(b) (criticism) mise f en accusation

indie adj (colloq) (Mus) indépendant/-e

indifference n indifférence f

indifferent adj (a) (uninterested) indifférent/-e (**to, as to** à)
(b) (mediocre) médiocre

indigenous adj indigène (**to** à)

indigestion n indigestion f; **to have** ∼ avoir des brûlures d'estomac

indignant adj indigné/-e (**at** de; **about, over** par)

indigo n, adj indigo m inv

indirect adj indirect/-e

indirectly adv indirectement

indirect speech n discours m indirect

indiscreet adj indiscret/-ète

indiscretion n (lack of discretion) manque m de discrétion; (act) indiscrétion f

indiscriminate adj (a) (random) sans distinction
(b) ‹person› sans discernement

indispensable adj indispensable

indisputable adj ‹champion› indiscuté/-e; ‹fact› indiscutable

indistinct adj ‹sound, markings› indistinct/-e; ‹memory› confus/-e; ‹photograph› flou/-e

ⅆ **individual** ⟦1⟧ n individu m
⟦2⟧ adj (a) ‹effort, freedom, portion› individuel/-elle; ‹comfort, attitude› personnel/-elle; ‹tuition› particulier/-ière
(b) (separate) **each** ∼ **article** chaque article (individuellement)
(c) (idiosyncratic) particulier/-ière

individuality n individualité f

individually adv (personally, in person) individuellement; (one at a time) séparément

indoctrinate vtr endoctriner

Indonesia pr n Indonésie f

indoor adj ‹pool, court› couvert/-e; ‹lavatory› à l'intérieur; ‹photography, shoes› d'intérieur; ‹sports facilities› en salle

indoors adv à l'intérieur, dans la maison; ∼ **and outdoors** dedans et dehors; **to go** ∼ rentrer

induce vtr (a) (persuade) persuader (**to do** de faire); (stronger) inciter (**to** à; **to do** à faire)
(b) (bring about) provoquer

induction course n stage m d'introduction

induction loop n boucle f magnétique

indulge ⟦1⟧ vtr (a) céder à ‹whim, desire›
(b) gâter ‹child›; céder à ‹adult›
⟦2⟧ vi **to** ∼ **in** se livrer à ‹speculation›; se complaire dans ‹nostalgia›; se laisser tenter

---

ⅆ indicates a very frequent word

par ⟨food⟩
3 *v refl* **to ~ oneself** se faire plaisir

indulgence *n* (a) (tolerance) indulgence *f*
(**towards** envers; **for** pour)
(**b**) **~ in food** gourmandise *f*, **it's my one ~**
c'est mon péché mignon

indulgent *adj* indulgent/-e (**to, towards**
pour, envers)

ℐ **industrial** *adj* (gen) industriel/-ielle;
⟨accident⟩ du travail

industrial action *n* (GB) (strike) grève *f*

industrial estate *n* zone *f* industrielle

industrialize *vtr* industrialiser

industrial relations *n pl* relations *fpl*
entre les patrons et les ouvriers

industrial waste *n* déchets *mpl*
industriels

industrious *adj* diligent/-e

ℐ **industry** *n* (a) industrie *f*; **the oil ~**
l'industrie du pétrole
(**b**) (diligence) zèle *m* (au travail)

inedible *adj* ⟨meal⟩ immangeable; ⟨plants⟩
non comestible

ineffective *adj* inefficace

ineffectual *adj* ⟨person⟩ incapable; ⟨policy⟩
inefficace; ⟨attempt⟩ infructueux/-euse

inefficiency *n* (lack of organization)
manque *m* d'organisation; (incompetence)
incompétence *f*; (of machine, method)
inefficacité *f*

inefficient *adj* (disorganized) mal
organisé/-e; (incompetent) incompétent/-e; (not
effective) inefficace

ineligible *adj* **to be ~** (for job) ne pas
remplir les conditions pour poser sa
candidature (**for** à); (for election) être
inéligible; (for pension, benefit) ne pas avoir
droit (**for** à)

inequality *n* inégalité *f*

inert *adj* inerte

inertia *n* inertie *f*

inevitable *adj* inévitable (**that** que +
subjunctive)

inexcusable *adj* inexcusable (**that** que +
subjunctive)

inexhaustible *adj* inépuisable

inexpensive *adj* pas cher/chère

inexperienced *adj* inexpérimenté/-e

inexplicable *adj* inexplicable

infallible *adj* infaillible

infamous *adj* ⟨person⟩ tristement célèbre;
⟨crime⟩ infâme

infancy *n* (a) petite enfance *f*
(**b**) (figurative) débuts *mpl*; **in its ~** à ses
débuts

infant *n* (baby) bébé *m*; (child) petit enfant *m*

infantry *n* infanterie *f*, fantassins *mpl*

infant school *n* ≈ école *f* maternelle

infatuated *adj* **to be ~ with** être entiché/-e
de

infatuation *n* engouement *m* (**with** pour)

infect *vtr* contaminer ⟨person, blood, food⟩;
infecter ⟨wound⟩

ℐ **infection** *n* infection *f*

infectious *adj* (a) ⟨disease⟩
infectieux/-ieuse; ⟨person⟩ contagieux/-ieuse
(**b**) ⟨laughter⟩ communicatif/-ive

infer *vtr* ⟨p prés etc **-rr-**⟩ déduire

inferior **1** *n* inférieur/-e *m/f*
2 *adj* (a) ⟨goods, work⟩ de qualité inférieure
(**b**) ⟨position⟩ inférieur/-e; **to make sb feel ~**
donner un sentiment d'infériorité à qn

inferiority *n* infériorité *f* (**to** vis-à-vis de)

inferiority complex *n* complexe *m*
d'infériorité

inferno *n* brasier *m*

infertile *adj* ⟨land⟩ infertile; ⟨person⟩ stérile

infertility *n* stérilité *f*

infest *vtr* infester (**with** de)

infidelity *n* infidélité *f*

infighting *n* conflits *mpl* internes

infiltrate *vtr* infiltrer ⟨organization, group⟩

infinite *adj* infini/-e

infinitely *adv* infiniment

infinitive *n* infinitif *m*; **in the ~** à l'infinitif

infinity *n* infini *m*

infirmary *n* (a) (hospital) hôpital *m*
(**b**) (in school, prison) infirmerie *f*

inflamed *adj* (Med) enflammé/-e

inflammable *adj* inflammable

inflammation *n* inflammation *f*

inflatable *adj* ⟨mattress, dinghy⟩
pneumatique; ⟨toy⟩ gonflable

inflate *vtr* gonfler ⟨tyre, dinghy⟩

inflation *n* inflation *f*

inflexible *adj* (a) ⟨person, attitude⟩
inflexible; ⟨system⟩ rigide
(**b**) ⟨material⟩ rigide

inflict *vtr* infliger ⟨pain, presence, defeat⟩
(**on** à); causer ⟨damage⟩ (**on** à)

ℐ **influence** **1** *n* influence *f*; **to be** *or* **have
an ~ on** avoir une influence sur; **to drive
while under the ~ of alcohol** conduire en
état d'ébriété
2 *vtr* influencer ⟨person⟩ (**in** dans); influer
sur ⟨decision, choice, result⟩; **to be ~d by sb/
sth** se laisser influencer par qn/qch

influential *adj* influent/-e

influenza *n* grippe *f*

influx *n* afflux *m*

info *n* (colloq) renseignements *mpl*, tuyaux
mpl (fam)

ℐ **inform** **1** *vtr* informer, avertir (**of, about**
de; **that** du fait que); **to keep sb ~ed** tenir qn
informé/-e *or* au courant (**of, as to** de)
2 *vi* **to ~ on** *or* **against** dénoncer

informal *adj* (a) ⟨person⟩ sans façons;
⟨manner, style⟩ simple; ⟨language⟩
familier/-ière; ⟨clothes⟩ de tous les jours

⋯⟶

(b) ‹visit› privé/-e; ‹invitation› verbal/-e;
‹discussion, interview› informel/-elle
⚜ **information** n **(a)** renseignements mpl,
informations fpl **(on, about** sur**); a piece of**
~ un renseignement, une information
(b) (US) (service m des) renseignements mpl
information desk, information
office n bureau m des renseignements
information pack n documentation f
information superhighway n
autoroutes fpl de l'information
information technology, IT n
informatique f
informative adj instructif/-ive
informer n indicateur/-trice m/f
infrared adj infrarouge
infrastructure n infrastructure f
infringe ① vtr enfreindre ‹rule›; ne pas
respecter ‹rights›
② vi to ~ **on** or **upon** empiéter sur ‹rights›
infringement n (of rule) infraction f (**of** à);
(of rights) violation f
infuriating adj exaspérant/-e
ingenious adj ingénieux/-ieuse,
astucieux/-ieuse
ingenuity n ingéniosité f
ingenuous adj ingénu/-e, candide
ingot n lingot m
ingrained adj ‹dirt› bien incrusté/-e;
‹habit, hatred› enraciné/-e
ingratitude n ingratitude f
ingredient n (Culin) ingrédient m; (figurative)
élément m (**of** de)
inhabit vtr **(a)** habiter ‹house, region, planet›
(b) vivre dans ‹fantasy world›
inhabitant n habitant/-e m/f
inhale ① vtr aspirer, inhaler
② vi (breathe in) inspirer; (smoke) avaler la
fumée
inhaler n inhalateur m
inherent adj inhérent/-e (**to** à)
inherit vtr hériter de ‹money, property,
title›; **to** ~ **sth from sb** hériter qch de qn
inheritance n héritage m; **to come into an**
~ faire un héritage
inhibit vtr inhiber ‹person, reaction›;
entraver ‹activity, progress›
inhibited adj inhibé/-e, refoulé/-e
inhibition n inhibition f; **to get rid of one's**
~**s** se libérer de ses inhibitions
inhospitable adj inhospitalier/-ière
in-house adj interne
inhuman adj inhumain/-e
inhumanity n inhumanité f (**to** envers)
⚜ **initial** ① n initiale f
② adj initial/-e; ~ **letter** initiale f
③ vtr (p prés etc **-ll-** (GB), **-l-** (US))
parapher, parafer

⚜ indicates a very frequent word

⚜ **initially** adv au départ
initiate ① n initié/-e m/f
② vtr **(a)** mettre en œuvre ‹project,
reform›; amorcer ‹talks›; entamer, engager
‹proceedings›
(b) (teach) **to** ~ **sb into** initier qn à
⚜ **initiative** n initiative f; **on one's own** ~ de
son propre chef
inject vtr injecter ‹vaccine› (**into** dans); **to**
~ **sb (with sth)** faire une injection or une
piqûre (de qch) à qn
injection n **(a)** (Med) piqûre f
(b) (Tech) injection f
⚜ **injure** vtr **(a)** blesser ‹person›; **to** ~ **one's**
hand se blesser la main
(b) nuire à, compromettre ‹health,
reputation›
injured ① n the ~ les blessés mpl
② adj **(a)** (gen) blessé/-e
(b) (Law) the ~ **party** la partie lésée
⚜ **injury** n blessure f; **head injuries** blessures
à la tête
injury time n (Sport) arrêts mpl de jeu
injustice n injustice f
ink n encre f; **in** ~ à l'encre
inkjet printer n imprimante f à jet
d'encre
inkling n petite idée f; **to have an** ~ **that**
avoir l'idée que
inland ① adj intérieur/-e
② adv ‹travel, lie› à l'intérieur des terres
Inland Revenue n (GB) service m des
impôts britannique
in-laws n pl (parents) beaux-parents mpl;
(other relatives) belle-famille f, parents mpl
par alliance
inmate n (of mental hospital) interné/-e m/f;
(of prison) détenu/-e m/f
inn n **(a)** (hotel) auberge f
(b) (pub) pub m
inner adj intérieur/-e
inner city ① n the ~ les quartiers mpl
déshérités
② **inner-city** n ‹problems› des quartiers
déshérités; ‹area› déshérité/-e
innermost adj sb's ~ **thoughts** les
pensées les plus intimes de qn
innocence n innocence f
innocent n, adj innocent/-e m/f
innovation n innovation f
innovative adj innovateur/-trice
innovator n innovateur/-trice m/f
innuendo n (pl ~**s** ou ~**es**) (veiled slights)
insinuations fpl; (sexual references) allusions
fpl grivoises
inoculation n vaccination f, inoculation f
inoffensive adj inoffensif/-ive
in-patient n malade mf hospitalisé/-e
input n **(a)** (of money) apport m; (of energy)
alimentation f (**of** en)

(b) (contribution) contribution *f*
(c) (Comput) (data) données *fpl* d'entrée *or* à traiter
inquest *n* enquête *f* (**on, into** sur)
inquire = ENQUIRE
◦ **inquiry** *n* enquête *f* (**into** sur); **murder** ∼ enquête criminelle; ▸ ENQUIRY
inquisitive *adj* curieux/-ieuse
insane *adj* (gen) fou/folle; (Law) aliéné/-e
insanitary *adj* insalubre, malsain/-e
insanity *n* (gen) folie *f*; (Law) aliénation *f* mentale
insatiable *adj* insatiable
inscription *n* inscription *f*
insect *n* insecte *m*; ∼ **bite** piqûre *f* d'insecte
insecticide *n, adj* insecticide *m*
insect repellent *n* insectifuge *m*, produit *m* anti-insecte
insecure *adj* **(a)** ‹person› qui manque d'assurance
(b) ‹job› précaire; ‹investment› risqué/-e
insecurity *n* **(a)** (psychological) manque *m* d'assurance
(b) (of position, situation) insécurité *f*
insensitive *adj* ‹person› (tactless) sans tact; (unfeeling) insensible (**to** à); ‹remark› indélicat/-e
inseparable *adj* inséparable (**from** de)
insert *vtr* insérer (**in** dans)
◦ **inside** ⓵ *n* intérieur *m*; **to overtake on the** ∼ (in Europe, US) doubler à droite; (in GB, Australia) doubler à gauche; **people on the** ∼ les gens qui sont dans la place
⓶ *prep* (US) ∼ **of (a)** à l'intérieur de; ∼ **the box** à l'intérieur de *or* dans la boîte; **to be** ∼ **(the house)** être à l'intérieur (de la maison)
(b) (under) ∼ **(of) an hour** en moins d'une heure
⓷ *adj* **(a)** ‹cover, pocket› intérieur/-e; ‹toilet› à l'intérieur
(b) ‹information› de première main
(c) **the** ∼ **lane** (of road) (in Europe, US) la voie de droite; (in GB, Australia) la voie de gauche; (of athletics track) le couloir intérieur
⓸ *adv* (indoors) à l'intérieur; **to look** ∼ regarder à l'intérieur *or* dedans; **to go** *or* **come** ∼ entrer; **to bring sth** ∼ rentrer ‹chairs›
⓹ **inside out** *phr* ∼ à l'envers; **to turn sth** ∼ **out** retourner qch; **to know sb/sth** ∼ **out** connaître qn/qch à fond
insider dealing *n* délit *m* d'initié
insides *n pl* (colloq) (of human) intestin *m*, estomac *m*, boyaux *mpl* (fam)
insight *n* **(a)** (glimpse, understanding) aperçu *m*, idée *f* (**into** de)
(b) (intuition) perspicacité *f*, intuition *f*
insignificant *adj* ‹cost, difference› négligeable; ‹person, detail› insignifiant/-e
insincere *adj* peu sincère; **to be** ∼ manquer de sincérité

insinuate *vtr* insinuer (**that** que)
insinuation *n* insinuation *f*
insipid *adj* fade
◦ **insist** ⓵ *vtr* **(a)** (demand) insister (**that** pour que)
(b) (maintain) affirmer (**that** que)
⓶ *vi* insister; **to** ∼ **on** exiger ‹punctuality, silence›; **to** ∼ **on doing** vouloir à tout prix faire, tenir à faire
insistent *adj* **to be** ∼ insister (**about** sur; **that** pour que + *subjunctive*)
insofar: **insofar as** *phr* ∼ **as** dans la mesure où
insole *n* semelle *f* (intérieure)
insolent *adj* insolent/-e
insomnia *n* insomnie *f*
inspect *vtr* examiner [qch] de près ‹document, product›; contrôler, vérifier ‹accounts›; inspecter ‹school, factory, pitch, wiring›; contrôler ‹passport, ticket, baggage›
inspection *n* (gen) inspection *f*; (of ticket, passport) contrôle *m*; **on closer** ∼ en y regardant de plus près
inspector *n* **(a)** (gen) inspecteur/-trice *m/f*
(b) (GB) **police** ∼ inspecteur *m* de police
(c) (GB) (on bus) contrôleur/-euse *m/f*
inspiration *n* inspiration *f* (**for** pour)
◦ **inspire** *vtr* inspirer; **to be** ∼**d by sth** s'inspirer de qch
inspired *adj* ‹person› inspiré/-e; ‹idea› lumineux/-euse; **an** ∼ **guess** une heureuse inspiration
inspiring *adj* ‹person, speech› enthousiasmant/-e; ‹thought› exaltant/-e
◦ **instal(l)** *vtr* **(a)** installer ‹equipment, software›; poser ‹windows›
(b) **to** ∼ **sb in office** installer qn
installation *n* installation *f*
instalment (GB), **installment** (US) *n* versement *m* partiel; **in** ∼**s** en plusieurs versements
◦ **instance** *n* exemple *m*; **for** ∼ par exemple
instant ⓵ *n* instant *m*; **come here this** ∼! viens ici tout de suite!
⓶ *adj* **(a)** ‹access, effect, rapport, success› immédiat/-e; ‹solution› instantané/-e
(b) ‹coffee, soup› instantané/-e
instant camera *n* polaroïd® *m*
instantly *adv* immédiatement
◦ **instead** ⓵ *adv* **we didn't go home—we went to the park** ∼ au lieu de rentrer nous sommes allés au parc; **let's take a taxi** ∼ prenons plutôt un taxi; **I was going to phone but wrote** ∼ j'allais téléphoner mais finalement j'ai écrit; **her son went** ∼ son fils y est allé à sa place
⓶ **instead of** *phr* ∼ **of sth/of doing** au lieu de qch/de faire; **use oil** ∼ **of butter** utilisez de l'huile à la place du beurre; ∼ **of sb** à la place de qn
instep *n* cou-de-pied *m*

instigate *vtr* lancer ‹attack›; engager ‹proceedings›

instill (GB), **instill** (US) *vtr* (*p prés etc* **-ll-**) inculquer ‹attitude› (**in** à); donner ‹confidence› (**in** à)

instinct *n* instinct *m* (**for** de)

instinctive *adj* instinctif/-ive

ᵈ **institute** ① *n* institut *m*
② *vtr* instituer

ᵈ **institution** *n* (**a**) (gen) institution *f*; financial ∼ organisme *m* financier
(**b**) (home, hospital) établissement *m* spécialisé

institutionalize *vtr* (**a**) (place in care) placer [qn] dans un établissement spécialisé; (in mental hospital) interner
(**b**) (establish officially) institutionnaliser; ∼d ‹racism, violence› institutionnalisé/-e

instruct *vtr* (**a**) **to** ∼ **sb to do** donner l'ordre à qn de faire; **to be** ∼**ed to do** recevoir l'ordre de faire
(**b**) (teach) instruire; **to** ∼ **sb in** enseigner [qch] à qn ‹subject›

instruction *n* instruction *f*; ∼**s for use** mode *m* d'emploi

instruction book *n* livret *m* de l'utilisateur

instructor *n* (**a**) (in sports, driving) moniteur/-trice *m/f* (**in** de); (military) instructeur *m*
(**b**) (US) professeur *m*

ᵈ **instrument** *n* instrument *m*; **to play an** ∼ jouer d'un instrument

instrumental ① *n* instrumental *m*
② *adj* (**a**) **to be** ∼ **in sth/in doing** contribuer à qch/à faire
(**b**) (Mus) instrumental/-e

instrument panel *n* tableau *m* de bord

insufficient *adj* **there are** ∼ **copies** il n'y a pas assez d'exemplaires; **to be** ∼ **for** être insuffisant/-e pour

insulate *vtr* isoler ‹roof, room, wire›

insulation *n* isolation *f*

insulin *n* insuline *f*

insult ① *n* insulte *f*
② *vtr* insulter

ᵈ **insurance** *n* assurance *f* (**against** contre; **for** pour); **to take out** ∼ **against sth** s'assurer contre qch

insurance policy *n* (police *f* d')assurance *f*

insure *vtr* assurer (**against** contre)

intact *adj* intact/-e

intake *n* (**a**) (consumption) consommation *f*
(**b**) (Sch, Univ) (admissions) admissions *fpl*
(**c**) **an** ∼ **of breath** une inspiration *f*

intangible *adj* insaisissable

integral *adj* intégral/-e; ‹part› intégrant/-e; ∼ **to** intrinsèque à

integrate ① *vtr* (**a**) (incorporate, absorb) intégrer (**into** dans; **with** à)

(**b**) (combine) combiner ‹systems›
② *vi* ‹person› s'intégrer (**with** à; **into** dans)

integration *n* intégration *f* (**with** à)

integrity *n* intégrité *f*

intellect *n* (**a**) (mental capacity) intelligence *f*
(**b**) (person) esprit *m*

intellectual *n, adj* intellectuel/-elle *m/f*

ᵈ **intelligence** *n* (**a**) intelligence *f* (**to do** de faire)
(**b**) (gen, Mil) (information) renseignements *mpl*
(**c**) (Mil) (secret service) services *mpl* de renseignements

intelligent *adj* intelligent/-e

intelligible *adj* intelligible (**to** à)

ᵈ **intend** *vtr* vouloir; **to** ∼ **to do, to** ∼ **doing** avoir l'intention de faire; **to be** ∼**ed for** être destiné/-e à ‹person›; être prévu/-e pour ‹purpose›

intense *adj* (**a**) (gen) intense
(**b**) ‹person› sérieux/-ieuse

intensify ① *vtr* intensifier
② *vi* s'intensifier

intensive *adj* intensif/-ive

intensive care *n* **in** ∼ en réanimation

intensive care unit *n* service *m* de soins intensifs

intent *adj* ‹person, expression› absorbé/-e; ∼ **on doing** résolu/-e à faire
IDIOM **to all** ∼**s and purposes** quasiment, en fait

ᵈ **intention** *n* intention *f* (**to do, of doing** de faire)

intentional *adj* intentionnel/-elle

intentionally *adv* intentionnellement, exprès

interact *vi* ‹two factors, phenomena› agir l'un sur l'autre; ‹people› communiquer; (Comput) dialoguer

interactive *adj* interactif/-ive

intercept *vtr* intercepter

interchange ① *n* (**a**) (road junction) échangeur *m*
(**b**) (exchange) échange *m*
② *vtr* échanger

interchangeable *adj* interchangeable

intercom *n* interphone® *m*

intercourse *n* rapports *mpl* (sexuels)

ᵈ **interest** ① *n* (**a**) (gen) intérêt *m* (**in** pour); **to hold sb's** ∼ retenir l'attention de qn; **it's in your (own)** ∼(**s**) **to do** il est dans ton intérêt de faire; **to have sb's best** ∼**s at heart** vouloir le bien de qn
(**b**) (hobby) centre *m* d'intérêt
(**c**) (on loan, from investment) intérêts *mpl* (**on** de)
② *vtr* intéresser (**in** à)

interested *adj* ‹expression, onlooker› intéressé/-e; **to be** ∼ **in** s'intéresser à ‹subject, activity›; **I am** ∼ **in doing** ça m'intéresse de faire

ᵈ indicates a very frequent word

interest-free adj sans intérêt

ℱ **interesting** adj intéressant/-e

interest rate n taux m d'intérêt

interface ① n interface f
② vtr connecter, relier

interfere vi (a) to ~ in se mêler de ‹affairs›; she never ~s elle ne se mêle jamais de ce qui ne la regarde pas
(b) (intervene) intervenir
(c) to ~ with ‹person› toucher, traficoter (fam) ‹machine›
(d) to ~ with ‹activity› empiéter sur ‹family life›

interference n (on radio) parasites mpl

interfering adj ‹person› envahissant/-e

interim ① n in the ~ entre-temps
② adj ‹arrangement, government› provisoire; ‹post, employee› intérimaire

interior ① n (a) intérieur m
(b) Secretary/Department of the Interior (US); ministre m/ministère m de l'Intérieur
② adj intérieur/-e

interior decorator n décorateur/-trice m/f

interlink vtr to be ~ed être lié/-e (with à)

interlock vi ‹pipes› s'emboîter; ‹mechanisms› s'enclencher; ‹fingers› s'entrelacer

interlude n (interval) intervalle m; (during play, concert) entracte m

intermediary n, adj intermédiaire mf

intermediate adj (a) (gen) intermédiaire
(b) (Sch) ‹course› de niveau moyen; ‹level› moyen/-enne

intermission n entracte m

intern ① n (US) (a) (Med) interne mf
(b) (gen) stagiaire mf
② vtr (Mil) interner

ℱ **internal** adj (a) (gen) interne
(b) (within country) intérieur/-e

ℱ **international** adj international/-e

internationally adv ‹known, respected› dans le monde entier

internee n interné/-e m/f

ℱ **Internet** n Internet m; on the ~ sur Internet

Internet access n accès m Internet

Internet kiosk n borne f d'accès public à Internet

Internet service provider, ISP n fournisseur m d'accès Internet

Internet user n internaute mf

interpret ① vtr interpréter (as comme)
② vi faire l'interprète

interpreter n interprète mf

interrogate vtr interroger

interrogation n interrogatoire m

interrogative n interrogatif m; in the ~ à la forme interrogative

interrupt vtr, vi interrompre

interruption n interruption f

intersect ① vtr croiser
② vi ‹roads› se croiser; to ~ with croiser

intersection n intersection f

interstate n (US) (also ~ **highway**) autoroute f (inter-États)

interval n (a) intervalle m; at regular ~s à intervalles réguliers; at four-hourly ~s toutes les quatre heures; at 100 metre ~s à 100 mètres d'intervalle
(b) (GB) (in theatre) entracte m

intervene vi intervenir (on behalf of en faveur de)

ℱ **intervention** n intervention f (on behalf of en faveur de)

ℱ **interview** ① n (a) (also **job** ~) entretien m
(b) (in newspaper) interview f
② vtr (a) faire passer un entretien à ‹candidate›
(b) ‹journalist› interviewer ‹celebrity›; ‹police› interroger ‹suspect›

interviewee n (a) (for job) candidat/-e m/f
(b) (on TV, radio) personne f interviewée

interviewer n (a) (for job) personne f faisant passer l'entretien
(b) (on radio, TV, in press) intervieweur/-euse m/f

interwar adj the ~ years l'entre-deux-guerres m

intestine n intestin m

intimacy n intimité f

intimate adj (a) (gen) intime; to be on ~ terms with sb être intime avec qn
(b) ‹knowledge› approfondi/-e

intimidate vtr intimider

intimidating adj ‹behaviour, person› intimidant/-e; ‹obstacle, sight, size› impressionnant/-e; ‹prospect› redoutable

ℱ **into** prep (a) ‹put, go, disappear› dans ‹place›; to run ~ a wall rentrer dans un mur; to bang ~ sb/sth heurter qn/qch; to go ~ town/~ the office aller en ville/au bureau; to get ~ a car monter dans une voiture; to get ~ bed se mettre au lit
(b) ‹transform› en; to change dollars ~ euros changer des dollars en euros; to translate sth ~ French traduire qch en français
(c) to continue ~ the 18th century continuer jusqu'au XVIIIᵉ siècle; well ~ the afternoon jusque tard dans l'après-midi
(d) (colloq) (keen on) to be ~ sth être fana de qch (fam); to be ~ drugs se droguer
(e) (in division) 8 ~ 24 goes 3 times or is 3 24 divisé par 8 égale 3

intolerable adj intolérable, insupportable

intolerance n intolérance f (of, towards vis-à-vis de; to à)

intolerant *adj* intolérant/-e (**of, towards** vis-à-vis de; **with** envers)

intoxicated *adj* ivre

intoxicating *adj* ‹*drink*› alcoolisé/-e; ‹*effect, substance*› toxique

intranet *n* intranet

intransitive *adj* intransitif/-ive

intravenous *adj* intraveineux/-euse

intravenous drug user *n* usager *m* de drogues par voie intraveineuse

in-tray *n* corbeille *f* arrivée

intrepid *adj* intrépide

intricate *adj* ‹*mechanism, pattern, plot*› compliqué/-e; ‹*problem*› complexe

intrigue ⎡1⎤ *n* intrigue *f*
⎡2⎤ *vtr* intriguer; **she was** ~**d by his story** son histoire l'intriguait

intriguing *adj* ‹*person, smile*› fascinant/-e; ‹*story*› curieux/-ieuse, intéressant/-e

✦ **introduce** *vtr* (a) présenter ‹*person*› (**as** comme; **to** à); **may I** ~ **my son?** je vous présente mon fils; **to** ~ **sb to** initier qn à ‹*painting, drugs*›
(b) introduire ‹*law, reform, word, product, change*› (**in, into** dans)
(c) (on TV, radio) présenter ‹*programme*›

✦ **introduction** *n* (a) (of person) présentation *f*; **letter of** ~ lettre de recommandation
(b) (of liquid, system, law) introduction *f* (**into** dans)
(c) (to speech, book) introduction *f*

introductory *adj* (a) ‹*speech, paragraph*› préliminaire; ‹*course*› d'initiation
(b) ‹*offer*› de lancement

introvert *n* introverti/-e *m/f*

intrude *vi* (a) **to** ~ **in** s'immiscer dans ‹*affairs, conversation*›
(b) **to** ~ **(on sb's privacy)** être importun/-e

intruder *n* intrus/-e *m/f*

intrusive *adj* ‹*question, cameras*› indiscret/-ète; ‹*phone call, presence*› importun/-e

intuition *n* intuition *f* (**about** concernant)

intuitive *adj* intuitif/-ive

inundate *vtr* inonder ‹*land*›; submerger ‹*organization, market*›

invade *vtr* envahir

invader *n* envahisseur/-euse *m/f*

invalid ⎡1⎤ *n* (sick person) malade *mf*; (disabled person) infirme *mf*
⎡2⎤ *adj* ‹*claim, passport*› pas valable; ‹*contract, marriage*› nul/nulle

invaluable *adj* ‹*assistance, experience*› inestimable; ‹*person, service*› précieux/-ieuse

invasion *n* invasion *f*; ~ **of (sb's) privacy** atteinte *f* à la vie privée (de qn)

invent *vtr* inventer

invention *n* invention *f*

inventive *adj* inventif/-ive

inventor *n* inventeur/-trice *m/f*

inventory *n* (a) inventaire *m*
(b) (US) stock *m*

inverted commas *n pl* (GB) guillemets *mpl*; **in** ~ entre guillemets

✦ **invest** ⎡1⎤ *vtr* investir, placer ‹*money*›; consacrer ‹*time, energy*› (**in** à)
⎡2⎤ *vi* (a) investir; **to** ~ **in shares** placer son argent en valeurs
(b) (buy) **to** ~ **in sth** s'acheter qch

✦ **investigate** *vtr* (a) enquêter sur ‹*crime, case*›; faire une enquête sur ‹*person*›
(b) (study) examiner ‹*possibility, report*›

✦ **investigation** *n* (a) (inquiry) enquête *f* (**of,** **into** sur)
(b) (of accounts, reports) vérification *f*

✦ **investment** *n* (financial) investissement *m*, placement *m*

investment manager *n* gérant/-e *m/f* de porte-feuille

✦ **investor** *n* investisseur/-euse *m/f* (**in** dans); (in shares) actionnaire *mf*

invigilate *vtr* surveiller ‹*examination*›

invisible *adj* invisible

invisible ink *n* encre *f* sympathique

invitation *n* invitation *f*

invitation card *n* carton *m* (d'invitation)

✦ **invite** *vtr* inviter ‹*person*›; **to** ~ **sb for a drink** inviter qn à prendre un verre; **to** ~ **sb in** inviter qn à entrer; **to** ~ **sb over** *or* **round (to one's house)** inviter qn chez soi

inviting *adj* ‹*room*› accueillant/-e; ‹*meal*› appétissant/-e; ‹*prospect*› alléchant/-e

invoice ⎡1⎤ *n* facture *f*
⎡2⎤ *vtr* envoyer une facture à ‹*customer*›; **to** ~ **sb for sth** facturer qch à qn

✦ **involve** *vtr* (a) (entail) impliquer, nécessiter ‹*effort, travel*›; entraîner ‹*problems*›
(b) (cause to participate) faire participer ‹*person*› (**in** à); **to be** ~**d in** participer à, être engagé/-e dans ‹*business, project*›; être mêlé/-e à ‹*scandal, robbery*›
(c) (affect) concerner, impliquer ‹*person, animal, vehicle*›
(d) (engross) **to get** ~**d in** se laisser prendre par, se plonger dans ‹*film, book, work*›
(e) **to get** ~**d with sb** avoir une liaison avec qn

involved *adj* (a) (complicated) ‹*explanation*› compliqué/-e
(b) ‹*person, group*› (implicated) impliqué/-e; (affected) concerné/-e
(c) (necessary) ‹*effort*› à fournir; **because of the expense** ~ à cause de la dépense que cela entraîne

involvement *n* (a) (in activity, task) participation *f* (**in** à); (in enterprise, politics) engagement *m* (**in** dans)
(b) (with group) liens *mpl*; (with person) relations *fpl*

✦ indicates a very frequent word

inward ⟦1⟧ *adj* ⟨*satisfaction*⟩
personnel/-elle; ⟨*relief, calm*⟩ intérieur/-e
⟦2⟧ *adv* ((GB) *also* **inwards**) (open, move,
grow) vers l'intérieur
inward-looking *adj* replié/-e sur soi-
même
inwards (GB) = INWARD 2
in-your-face *adj* (colloq) agressif/-ive
iodine *n* (element) iode *m*; (antiseptic) teinture
f d'iode
IOU *n* reconnaissance *f* de dette
IQ *n* (*abbr* = **intelligence quotient**)
QI *m*
Iran *pr n* Iran *m*
Iraq *pr n* Iraq *m*
irate *adj* furieux/-ieuse (about au sujet de)
Ireland *pr n* Irlande *f*
⚔ **Irish** ⟦1⟧ *n* (a) (people) the ~ les Irlandais
mpl
(b) (language) irlandais *m*
⟦2⟧ *adj* irlandais/-e
Irishman *n* (*pl* **-men**) Irlandais *m*
Irish Republic *pr n* République *f*
d'Irlande
Irish sea *pr n* mer *f* d'Irlande
Irishwoman *n* (*pl* **-women**) Irlandaise *f*
iron ⟦1⟧ *n* (a) (metal) fer *m*; **scrap ~** ferraille
f
(b) (for clothes) fer *m* (à repasser)
⟦2⟧ *vtr* repasser ⟨*clothes*⟩
ironic(al) *adj* ironique
ironing *n* repassage *m*
ironing board *n* planche *f* à repasser
ironmonger *n* quincaillier/-ière *m/f*; **~'s**
(shop) quincaillerie *f*
irony *n* ironie *f*
irrational *adj* ⟨*behaviour*⟩ irrationnel/-elle;
⟨*fear, hostility*⟩ sans fondement; **he's rather**
~ il n'est pas très raisonnable
irregular *adj* (a) irrégulier/-ière
(b) (US) ⟨*merchandise*⟩ de second choix
irregularity *n* irrégularité *f*
irrelevant *adj* (a) ⟨*remark*⟩ hors de propos;
⟨*fact*⟩ qui n'est pas pertinent; ⟨*question*⟩ sans
rapport avec le sujet
(b) (unimportant) **the money's ~** ce n'est pas
l'argent qui compte
irreligious *adj* irréligieux/-ieuse
irreparable *adj* irréparable
irreplaceable *adj* irremplaçable
irrepressible *adj* ⟨*high spirits*⟩
irrépressible; ⟨*person*⟩ infatigable
irresistible *adj* irrésistible
irrespective: **irrespective of** *phr* sans
tenir compte de ⟨*age, class*⟩; sans distinction
de ⟨*race*⟩
irresponsible *adj* irresponsable
irreversible *adj* ⟨*process, decision*⟩
irréversible; ⟨*disease*⟩ incurable

irritable *adj* irritable
irritable bowel syndrome *n*
colopathie *f* fonctionnelle
irritate *vtr* irriter
irritating *adj* irritant/-e
Islam *n* Islam *m*
Islamic *adj* islamique
Islamist *adj* islamiste
⚔ **island** *n* (a) île *f*; (small) îlot *m*
(b) (*also* **traffic ~**) refuge *m*
islander *n* insulaire *mf*, habitant/-e *m/f*
d'une île (or de l'île)
Isle of Man *pr n* île *f* de Man
isolate *vtr* isoler (from de)
isolation *n* isolement *m*
Israel *pr n* Israël (*never with article*)
Israeli ⟦1⟧ *n* Israélien/-ienne *m/f*
⟦2⟧ *adj* israélien/-ienne
⚔ **issue** ⟦1⟧ *n* (a) problème *m*, question *f*; **to**
make an ~ (out) of faire une histoire de; **at**
~ en question
(b) (of stamps, shares) émission *f*; (of book)
publication *f*
(c) (journal, magazine) numéro *m*; **back ~**
vieux numéro *m*
⟦2⟧ *vtr* (a) (allocate) distribuer; **to ~ sb with**
sth fournir qch à qn
(b) délivrer ⟨*declaration*⟩; émettre ⟨*order,*
warning⟩
(c) émettre ⟨*stamps, shares*⟩; publier ⟨*book*⟩
⚔ **it** *pron* (a) (subject pronoun) il, elle; **'where is**
the chair?' — 'it's in the kitchen' 'où est la
chaise?' — 'elle est dans la cuisine'; **it's a**
good film c'est un bon film
(b) (object pronoun) le, la l'; **I want ~** je le/la
veux
(c) (after a preposition) **about/from/of ~** en; **in/**
to ~ y; **I've heard about ~** j'en ai entendu
parler; **he went to ~** il y est allé
(d) (in questions) **who is ~?** qui est-ce?, qui
c'est? (fam); **where is ~?** (of object) où est-il/
elle?; (of place) où est-ce?, où est-ce que c'est?,
c'est où? (fam); **what is ~?** (of object, noise)
qu'est-ce que c'est?, c'est quoi? (fam); (what's
happening?) qu'est-ce qui se passe?; (what is the
matter?) qu'est-ce qu'il y a?
(e) (impersonal uses) **it's raining/snowing** il
pleut/neige; **~ is easy to learn English** il
est facile d'apprendre l'anglais; **~ doesn't**
matter ç ne fait rien; **it's time to eat** c'est
l'heure de manger; **~'s me** c'est moi
IT *n* (*abbr* = **information technology**)
informatique *f*
Italian ⟦1⟧ *n* (a) (person) Italien/-ienne *m/f*
(b) (language) italien *m*
⟦2⟧ *adj* (gen) italien/-ienne; ⟨*embassy*⟩ d'Italie
italics *n pl* italique *m*; **in ~** en italique
Italy *pr n* Italie *f*
itch ⟦1⟧ *n* démangeaison *f*
⟦2⟧ *vi* avoir des démangeaisons; **my back**
is ~ing j'ai le dos qui me démange; **these** ···⟩

socks make me ∼ ces chaussettes me grattent

itchy *adj* (colloq) **I feel** ∼ **all over** ça me gratte partout

IDIOM **to have** ∼ **feet** (colloq) avoir la bougeotte (fam)

✧ **item** *n* **(a)** article *m*; ∼**s of clothing** vêtements *mpl*; **news** ∼ article *m*
(b) (on agenda) point *m*

itemize *vtr* détailler; ∼**d bill** facture *f* le détaillée

itinerary *n* itinéraire *m*

✧ **its** *det* son/sa/ses

■ **Note** In French determiners agree in number and gender with the noun that follows. *its* is translaged by *son + masculine noun*: *its nose* = son nez; by *sa + feminine noun*: *its tail* = sa queue; BUT by *son + feminine noun beginning with a vowel or mute 'h'*: *its ear* = son oreille; and by *ses + plural noun*: *its ears* = ses oreilles.

✧ **itself** *pron* **(a)** (reflexive) se, s'; **the cat hurt** ∼ le chat s'est fait mal
(b) (emphatic) lui-même/elle-même; **the house** ∼ **was pretty** la maison elle-même était jolie; **he was kindness** ∼ c'était la bonté même *or* personnifiée
(c) (after prepositions) **the heating comes on by** ∼ le chauffage se met en marche tout seul; **learning French is not difficult in** ∼ l'apprentissage du français n'est pas difficile en soi

IVF *n* (*abbr* = **in vitro fertilization**) fécondation *f* in vitro

ivory *n, adj* ivoire *m*

ivy *n* lierre *m*

Jj

j, J *n* j, J *m*

jab 1 *n* **(a)** (GB) (vaccination) vaccin *m*; (injection) piqûre *f*
(b) (in boxing) direct *m*
2 *vtr* **to** ∼ **sth into sth** planter qch dans qch

jabber *vi* (chatter) jacasser; (in foreign language) baragouiner

jack *n* **(a)** (for car) cric *m*
(b) (in cards) valet *m* (**of** de)
(c) (in bowls) cochonnet *m*
IDIOM **to be a** ∼ **of all trades** être un/-e touche-à-tout *inv*
■ **jack in** (GB) (colloq): ∼ **in [sth]**, ∼ **[sth] in** plaquer (fam), laisser tomber ‹*job*›

jackal *n* chacal *m*

jackdaw *n* choucas *m*

jacket *n* **(a)** (garment) veste *f*; (man's) veste *f*, veston *m*
(b) (*also* **dust** ∼) jaquette *f*
(c) (US) (of record) pochette *f*

jacket potato *n* pomme *f* de terre en robe des champs (au four)

jack-in-the-box *n* diable *m* à ressort

jackknife *vi* ‹*lorry*› se mettre en portefeuille

jackpot *n* **to hit the** ∼ (win prize) gagner le gros lot; (have great success) faire un tabac (fam)

jade *n* **(a)** (stone) jade *m*
(b) (*also* ∼ **green**) vert *m* jade

jaded *adj* **(a)** (exhausted) fatigué/-e
(b) (bored) ‹*person, palate*› blasé/-e

jagged *adj* ‹*rock, cliff*› déchiqueté/-e; ‹*tooth, blade*› ébréché/-e; ‹*knife, saw*› dentelé/-e

jail 1 *n* prison *f*
2 *vtr* mettre [qn] en prison

jam 1 *n* **(a)** confiture *f*; **apricot** ∼ confiture d'abricots
(b) (of traffic) embouteillage *m*
(c) (in machine, system) blocage *m*
(d) (colloq) (difficulty) pétrin *m* (fam); **to be in a** ∼ être dans le pétrin (fam)
(e) (*also* ∼ **session**) bœuf *m* (fam), jam-session *f*
2 *vtr* (*p prés etc* **-mm-**) **(a) to** ∼ **one's foot on the brake** freiner à bloc
(b) (wedge) coincer; **the key's** ∼**med** la clé s'est coincée
(c) (block) enrayer ‹*mechanism*›; coincer ‹*lock, door, system*›
(d) (*also* ∼ **up**) cars ∼**med (up) the roads** les routes étaient embouteillées
(e) (cause interference in) brouiller ‹*frequency*›
3 *vi* (*p prés etc* **-mm-**) **(a)** ‹*mechanism*› s'enrayer; ‹*lock, door*› se coincer
(b) (Mus) improviser

Jamaica *pr n* Jamaïque *f*

jam-packed *adj* bondé/-e; **to be** ∼ **with sth** être bourré/-e de qch

jangle 1 *n* (of bells, pots) tintement *m*; (of keys) cliquetis *m*
2 *vi* ‹*bells*› tinter; ‹*bangles, keys*› cliqueter

janitor *n* (US) gardien *m*

✧ **January** *n* janvier *m*

Japan *pr n* Japon *m*

✧ indicates a very frequent word

◂ **Japanese** ① n (a) (person) Japonais/-e m/f
(b) (language) japonais m
② adj ‹culture, food, politics› japonais/-e; ‹teacher, lesson› de japonais; ‹ambassador, embassy› du Japon

jar ① n (a) pot m; (large) bocal m; (earthenware) jarre f
(b) (jolt) secousse f, choc m
② vtr (p prés etc -**rr**-) (a) ébranler, secouer; to ~ one's shoulder se cogner l'épaule
(b) (US) to ~ sb into action pousser qn à agir
③ vi (p prés etc -**rr**-) (a) ‹music, voice› rendre un son discordant; to ~ on sb's nerves agacer qn
(b) (clash) ‹colours› jurer; ‹note› sonner faux

jargon n jargon m

jasmine n jasmin m

jaundice n jaunisse f

jaundiced adj (cynical) négatif/-ive

javelin n javelot m

jaw n mâchoire f

jawbone n mâchoire f

jawline n menton m

jay n geai m

jazz ① n jazz m
② adj ‹musician, singer› de jazz; ~ band jazz-band m
IDIOM and all that ~ et tout le bataclan (fam)
■ **jazz up** (colloq) rajeunir ‹dress›; égayer ‹room›

jazzy adj (a) ‹colour› voyant/-e; ‹pattern, dress› bariolé/-e
(b) ‹music› jazzy inv

jealous adj jaloux/-ouse (of de); to make sb ~ rendre qn jaloux

jealousy n jalousie f

jeans n pl jean m; a pair of ~ un jean

Jeep® n jeep® f

jeer ① n huée f
② vtr huer
③ vi se moquer; to ~ at sb ‹crowd› huer qn; ‹individual› railler qn

jeering n huées fpl

jellied adj en aspic; ~ eels anguilles fpl en gelée

Jell-o® n (US) gelée f de fruits

jelly n (a) (savoury) gelée f; (sweet) gelée f de fruits
(b) (jam) gelée f

jellyfish n (pl ~ ou ~**es**) méduse f

jeopardize vtr compromettre ‹career, plans›; mettre [qch] en péril ‹lives, troops›

jeopardy n in ~ en péril, menacé/-e

jerk ① n (a) (jolt) (of vehicle) secousse f; (of muscle, limb) tressaillement m, (petit) mouvement m brusque; with a ~ of his head d'un brusque mouvement de la tête
(b) (colloq) (idiot) abruti m
② vtr tirer brusquement ‹object›
③ vi ‹person, limb, muscle› tressaillir

jerky ① n (also **beef** ~) (US) bœuf m séché
② adj ‹movement› saccadé/-e; ‹style, phrase› haché/-e

jersey n (a) (sweater) pull-over m
(b) (for sports) maillot m
(c) (fabric) jersey m

Jersey pr n Jersey f

Jerusalem pr n Jérusalem

jest ① n plaisanterie f; in ~ pour plaisanter
② vi plaisanter

jester n bouffon m

Jesuit n, adj jésuite m

Jesus ① pr n Jésus; ~ **Christ** Jésus-Christ
② excl (slang) ~ (**Christ**)! nom de Dieu! (fam)

jet ① n (a) (also ~ **plane**) jet m, avion m à réaction
(b) (of water, flame) jet m
(c) (on hob) brûleur m; (of engine) gicleur m
(d) (stone) jais m
② vi to ~ off to s'envoler pour

jet black adj de jais inv

jet engine n moteur m à réaction, réacteur m

jetfoil n hydroglisseur m

jetlag n décalage m horaire

jetlagged adj to be ~ souffrir du décalage horaire

jet setter n to be a ~ faire partie du jet-set

jet-skiing n jet-ski m

jettison vtr (from ship) jeter [qch] par-dessus bord; (from plane) larguer

jetty n (of stone) jetée f; (of wood) appontement m

Jew n juif/juive m/f

jewel n (a) (gem) pierre f précieuse; (piece of jewellery) bijou m; (in watch) rubis m
(b) (person) perle f; (town, object) joyau m

jeweller (GB), **jeweler** (US) n (person) bijoutier/-ière m/f; ~'s (shop) bijouterie f

jewellery (GB), **jewelry** (US) n (gen) bijoux mpl; (in shop, workshop) bijouterie f; a piece of ~ un bijou

Jewish adj juif/juive

jib n (a) (sail) foc m
(b) (of crane) flèche f

jibe n moquerie f

jiffy n in a ~ en un clin d'œil

Jiffy bag® n enveloppe f matelassée

jig n gigue f

jiggle ① vtr agiter
② vi (also ~ **about**, ~ **around**) gigoter; (impatiently) se trémousser

jigsaw n (a) (also ~ **puzzle**) puzzle m
(b) (saw) scie f sauteuse

jilt vtr abandonner, plaquer (fam)

jingle ① n (a) (of bells) tintement m; (of keys) cliquetis m

⋯▷

(b) (verse) ritournelle *f*; (for advert) refrain *m* publicitaire, sonal *m*
2 *vi* ‹keys, coins› cliqueter

jingoist *n, adj* chauvin/-e *m/f*

jinx *n* **(a)** (curse) sort *m*; **to put a ~ on** jeter un sort à; **there's a ~ on me** j'ai la poisse (fam)
(b) (unlucky person, object) **it's a ~** ça porte la poisse

jitters *n pl* **to have the ~** ‹person, stock market› être nerveux/-euse; ‹actor› avoir le trac

⚬ **job** **1** *n* **(a)** (employment) emploi *m*; (post) poste *m*; **to get a ~** trouver un emploi; **a teaching ~** un poste d'enseignant; **what's her ~?** qu'est-ce qu'elle fait (comme travail)?
(b) (role) fonction *f*; **it's my ~ to do** c'est à moi de faire
(c) (duty) travail *m*; **she's only doing her ~** elle fait son travail
(d) (task) travail *m*; **to find a ~ for sb to do** trouver du travail pour qn
(e) (assignment) tâche *f*
(f) to make a good ~ of sth faire du bon travail avec qch
(g) (colloq) **quite a ~** toute une affaire (fam) **(to do, doing** de faire)
2 *adj* ‹advert, offer› d'emploi; ‹pages› des emplois
IDIOM that'll do the ~ ça fera l'affaire

job centre *n* (GB) bureau *m* des services nationaux de l'emploi

job creation scheme *n* (GB) plan *m* pour la création d'emplois

job description *n* description *f* de poste

job-hunting *n* chasse *f* à l'emploi

jobless *n* **the ~** les sans-emplois *mpl*

jobseeker's allowance *n* allocation *f* chômage

jobshare *n* poste *m* partagé

job sharing *n* partage *m* de poste

jockey *n* jockey *m*

jockey shorts *n pl* (US) slip *m* (d'homme)

jockstrap *n* (colloq) suspensoir *m*

jodhpurs *n pl* jodhpurs *mpl*

jog **1** *n* **(a)** (with elbow) coup *m* de coude
(b) at a ~ au petit trot (fam)
(c) (Sport) **to go for a ~** aller faire un jogging
(d) (US) (in road) coude *m*
2 *vtr* (*p prés etc* **-gg-**) (with elbow) donner un coup de coude à; **to ~ sb's memory** rafraîchir la mémoire de qn
3 *vi* (*p prés etc* **-gg-**) **to go ~ging** faire du jogging

jogger *n* joggeur/-euse *m/f*

jogging *n* jogging *m*

⚬ **join** **1** *n* raccord *m*
2 *vtr* **(a)** devenir membre de ‹organization,

⚬ *indicates a very frequent word*

team›; adhérer à ‹club›; s'inscrire à ‹library›; entrer dans ‹firm›; s'engager dans ‹army›; **to ~ a union** se syndiquer
(b) se mettre dans ‹queue›
(c) (meet up with) rejoindre ‹person›; **may I ~ you?** (sit down) puis-je me joindre à vous?
(d) (connect) réunir, joindre ‹ends, pieces›; assembler ‹parts›; relier ‹points, towns› (**to** à)
(e) ‹road› rejoindre ‹motorway›; ‹river› se jeter dans ‹sea›
3 *vi* **(a)** (become member) (of party, club) adhérer; (of group, class) s'inscrire
(b) ‹pieces› se joindre; ‹wires› se raccorder; ‹roads› se rejoindre

■ **join in**: **1** **¶ ~ in** participer
2 **¶ ~ in [sth]** participer à ‹talks, game›; prendre part à ‹strike, demonstration, bidding›; **to ~ in the fun** se joindre à la fête

■ **join up**: **1** **¶ ~ up (a)** (enlist) s'engager
(b) (meet up) ‹people› se retrouver; ‹roads, tracks› se rejoindre
2 **¶ ~ [sth] up** relier ‹characters, dots›

joiner *n* menuisier/-ière *m/f*

⚬ **joint** **1** *n* **(a)** (Anat) articulation *f*; **to be out of ~** ‹shoulder› être déboîté/-e
(b) (in carpentry) assemblage *m*; (in metalwork) joint *m*
(c) (of meat) rôti *m*
(d) (colloq) (place) endroit *m*; (café) boui-boui *m* (fam)
(e) (colloq) (cannabis) joint *m* (fam)
2 *adj* ‹action› collectif/-ive; ‹programme, session› mixte; ‹measures, procedure› commun/-e; ‹winner› ex aequo *inv*; ‹talks› multilatéral/-e

joint account *n* compte *m* joint

joint effort *n* collaboration *f*

joint honours *n pl* (GB Univ) licence *f* combinée

jointly *adv* conjointement; **to be ~ owned by** être la copropriété de

joint owner *n* copropriétaire *mf*

joint venture *n* **(a)** (Econ) coentreprise *f*
(b) (gen) projet *m* en commun

joke **1** *n* **(a)** plaisanterie *f*, blague *f* (fam); **to tell a ~** raconter une blague; **to play a ~ on sb** jouer un tour à qn; **it's no ~ doing** ce n'est pas facile de faire
(b) (person) guignol *m*; (event, situation) farce *f*
2 *vi* plaisanter, blaguer (fam); **you must be joking!** tu veux rire!

joker *n* **(a)** (prankster) farceur/-euse *m/f*
(b) (in cards) joker *m*

jolly **1** *adj* ‹person› enjoué/-e; ‹tune› joyeux/-euse
2 *vtr* **to ~ sb along** amadouer qn

jolt **1** *n* **(a)** (jerk) secousse *f*
(b) (shock) choc *m*
2 *vtr* secouer ‹passenger›
3 *vi* ‹vehicle› cahoter

Jordan *pr n* (country) Jordanie *f*

jostle *vi* se bousculer (**for** pour; **to do pour** faire)

jot *v*
■ **jot down** noter ‹*ideas, names*›

journal *n* (**a**) (diary) journal *m*
(**b**) (periodical) revue *f*; (newspaper) journal *m*

journalism *n* journalisme *m*

✍ **journalist** *n* journaliste *mf*

✍ **journey** *n* (long) voyage *m*; (short or habitual) trajet *m*; **bus** ~ trajet en bus; **to go on a** ~ partir en voyage

jowl *n* (jaw) mâchoire *f*; (fleshy fold) bajoue *f*

joy *n* (**a**) (delight) joie *f* (**at** devant)
(**b**) (pleasure) plaisir *m*; **the** ~ **of doing** le plaisir de faire
IDIOM **to be full of the** ~**s of spring** être en pleine forme

joyrider *n* jeune chauffard *m* en voiture volée

joyriding *n* rodéo *m* à la voiture volée

joystick *n* (in plane) manche *m* à balai; (for video game) manette *f*

jubilant *adj* ‹*person*› exultant/-e; ‹*crowd*› en liesse; ‹*expression, mood*› réjoui/-e

jubilee *n* jubilé *m*

Judaism *n* judaïsme *m*

✍ **judge** **1** *n* (**a**) (in court) juge *m*
(**b**) (at competition) (gen) membre *m* du jury; (Sport) juge *m*
(**c**) **to be a good** ~ **of character** savoir juger les gens
2 *vtr* (**a**) juger ‹*person*›
(**b**) faire partie du jury de ‹*show, competition*›
(**c**) estimer ‹*distance, age*›; prévoir ‹*outcome, reaction*›
(**d**) (consider) juger, estimer
3 *vi* juger; **judging by** or **from**... à en juger d'après...

✍ **judgment**, **judgement** *n* jugement *m*

judicial *adj* (gen) judiciaire; ‹*decision*› jurisprudentiel/-ielle

judiciary *n* (**a**) (system of courts) système *m* judiciaire
(**b**) (judges) magistrature *f*

judo *n* judo *m*

jug *n* (**a**) (GB) (earthenware) pichet *m*; (pot-bellied) cruche *f*; (glass) carafe *f*; (for cream, milk, water) pot *m*
(**b**) (US) (flagon) cruche *f*

juggernaut *n* (GB) poids *m* lourd

juggle *vi* jongler (**with** avec)

juggler *n* jongleur/-euse *m/f*

jugular *n*, *adj* jugulaire *f*

juice *n* (**a**) (from fruit, meat) jus *m*; **fruit** ~ jus de fruit
(**b**) (sap) suc *m*
(**c**) **gastric** ~**s** sucs digestifs or gastriques

juicy *adj* (**a**) ‹*fruit*› juteux/-euse
(**b**) (colloq) ‹*story*› croustillant/-e

jukebox *n* juke-box *m*

✍ **July** *n* juillet *m*

jumble *n* (**a**) (of papers, objects) tas *m*; (of ideas) fouillis *m*; (of words) fatras *m*
(**b**) (GB) (items for sale) bric-à-brac *m*, vieux objets *mpl*
■ **jumble up** mélanger ‹*letters, shapes*›

jumble sale *n* (GB) vente *f* de charité

jumbo *n* (*also* ~ **jet**) gros-porteur *m*

✍ **jump** **1** *n* (**a**) (leap) saut *m*, bond *m*; **parachute** ~ saut en parachute
(**b**) (in horse race) obstacle *m*
(**c**) (in price, wages) bond *m* (**in** dans)
2 *vtr* (**a**) sauter ‹*obstacle, ditch*›
(**b**) **to** ~ **the lights** griller (fam) le feu (rouge); **to** ~ **the queue** passer devant tout le monde
(**c**) **to** ~ **ship** ne pas rejoindre son bâtiment
3 *vi* (**a**) (leap) sauter; **to** ~ **across** or **over sth** franchir qch d'un bond; **to** ~ **up and down** sautiller; (in anger) trépigner de colère
(**b**) (start in surprise) sursauter
(**c**) ‹*prices, rate*› monter en flèche
(**d**) **to** ~ **at** sauter sur ‹*opportunity*›; accepter [qch] avec enthousiasme ‹*offer*›
■ **jump back** ‹*person*› faire un bond en arrière; ‹*lever*› lâcher brusquement
■ **jump down** ‹*person*› sauter (**from** de)
■ **jump on**: **1** ¶ ~ **on [sth]** sauter dans ‹*bus, train*›; sauter sur ‹*bicycle, horse*›
2 ¶ ~ **on [sb]** sauter sur qn
■ **jump out** ‹*person*› sauter; **to** ~ **out of** sauter par ‹*window*›; sauter de ‹*bed, train*›
■ **jump up** ‹*person*› se lever d'un bond

jumper *n* (**a**) (GB) (sweater) pull *m*, pull-over *m*
(**b**) (US) (pinafore) robe *f* chasuble

jump leads *n pl* câbles *mpl* de démarrage

jump-start *vtr* faire démarrer [qch] avec des câbles ‹*car*›

jump suit *n* combinaison *f*

jumpy *adj* (colloq) ‹*person*› nerveux/-euse; ‹*market*› instable

junction *n* (**a**) (of two roads) carrefour *m*; (on motorway) échangeur *m*
(**b**) (of railway lines) nœud *m* ferroviaire; (station) gare *f* de jonction

✍ **June** *n* juin *m*

jungle *n* jungle *f*

junior **1** *n* (**a**) (younger person) cadet/-ette *m/f*
(**b**) (low-ranking worker) subalterne *mf*
(**c**) (GB Sch) élève *mf* du primaire
(**d**) (US Univ) ≈ étudiant/-e *m/f* de premier cycle; (in high school) ≈ élève *mf* de première
2 *adj* (**a**) ‹*colleague, rank, position*› subalterne
(**b**) (Sport) ‹*race, team*› des cadets; ‹*player*› jeune
(**c**) (*also* **Junior**) Mortimer ~ Mortimer fils or junior

junior high school *n* (US) ≈ collège *m*

junior minister *n* secrétaire *m* d'État

junior school n (GB) école f (primaire)
junk n **(a)** (rubbish) camelote f (fam)
(b) (second-hand) bric-à-brac m
(c) (boat) jonque f
junk food n nourriture f industrielle
junkie n (colloq) drogué/-e m/f
junk mail n prospectus mpl
junk shop n boutique f de bric-à-brac
junkyard n (for scrap) dépotoir m; (for old cars) cimetière f de voitures
junta n junte f
Jupiter pr n Jupiter f
jurisdiction n **(a)** (gen) compétence f (over sur)
(b) (Law) juridiction f (over sur)
juror n juré m
jury n jury m
jury box n banc m des jurés
jury duty (US), **jury service** (GB) n to do ∼ faire partie d'un jury
✧ **just¹** 1 adv **(a)** to have ∼ done venir (juste) de faire; **he had only ∼ left** il venait tout juste de partir
(b) (immediately) juste; ∼ **before/after** juste avant/après
(c) (slightly) ∼ **over/under 20 kg** un peu plus/moins de 20 kg
(d) (only, merely) juste; ∼ **for fun** juste pour rire; ∼ **two days ago** il y a juste deux jours; **he's ∼ a child** ce n'est qu'un enfant
(e) (purposely) exprès; **he did it ∼ to annoy us** il l'a fait exprès pour nous embêter
(f) (barely) tout juste; ∼ **on time** tout juste à l'heure; **he's ∼ 20** il a tout juste 20 ans; **I (only) ∼ caught the train** j'ai eu le train de justesse
(g) (simply) tout simplement; ∼ **tell the truth** dis la vérité, tout simplement; **she ∼ won't listen** elle ne veut tout simplement pas écouter; **'∼ a moment'** 'un instant'
(h) (exactly) exactement; **that's ∼ what I want** c'est exactement ce que je veux; **it's ∼ right** c'est parfait; **she looks ∼ like her father** c'est son père tout craché (fam); **it's ∼ like him to forget** c'est bien de lui d'oublier
(i) (possibly) **it might** or **could ∼ be true** il se peut que ce soit vrai

(j) (at this or that very moment) **to be ∼ doing** être en train de faire; **to be ∼ about to do** être sur le point de faire; **he was ∼ leaving** il partait
(k) (positively, totally) vraiment; **that's ∼ wonderful** c'est vraiment merveilleux
(l) (in requests) **if you could ∼ hold this box** si vous pouvez tenir cette boîte
(m) (equally) ∼ **as big as**… (tout) aussi grand que…
(n) (with imperative) donc; ∼ **you dare!** essaie donc voir!; ∼ **imagine!** imagine donc!
2 **just about** phr presque; ∼ **about everything** à peu près tout; **I can ∼ about see it** je peux tout juste le voir
3 **just as** phr ∼ **as he came** juste au moment où il est arrivé
4 **just now** phr en ce moment; **I saw him ∼ now** je viens juste de le voir
just² adj ‹person, decision› juste; ‹demand› justifié/-e; ‹claim, criticism› légitime
✧ **justice** n **(a)** (fairness) justice f; **the portrait doesn't do her ∼** le portrait ne l'avantage pas
(b) (the law) justice f; **to bring sb to ∼** traduire qn en justice
Justice Department n (US) ministère m de la justice
Justice of the Peace n juge m de paix
justifiable adj (that is justified) légitime; (that can be justified) justifiable
justification n raison f; **to have some ∼ for doing** avoir des raisons de faire
justified adj justifié/-e; **to feel ∼ in doing** se sentir en droit de faire
✧ **justify** vtr justifier
jut vi (p prés etc **-tt-**) (also ∼ **out**) avancer en saillie (**into** dans); ‹balcony› faire saillie (**over** sur)
juvenile n (gen) jeune mf; (Law) mineur/-e m/f
juvenile delinquency n délinquance f juvénile
juvenile delinquent n jeune délinquant/-e m/f
juvenile offender n délinquant/-e m/f mineur/-e
juxtapose vtr juxtaposer (**with** à)

✧ indicates a very frequent word

K k

k, K *n* k, K *m*
kale *n* (*also* **curly** ∼) chou *m* frisé
kaleidoscope *n* kaléidoscope *m*
kangaroo *n* kangourou *m*
karaoke *n* karaoké *m*
karate *n* karaté *m*
Kashmir *pr n* Cachemire *m*
kayak *n* kayak *m*
kebab *n* (*also* **shish** ∼) chiche-kebab *m*
kedgeree *n* (GB) pilaf *m* de poisson
keel *n* quille *f*
■ **keel over** ‹*boat*› chavirer; ‹*person*›
s'écrouler; ‹*tree*› s'abattre
keen *adj* (a) (eager) ‹*artist, footballer,
supporter*› enthousiaste; ‹*student*› assidu/-e;
to be ∼ **on** tenir à ‹*plan, project*›; être
chaud/-e pour (fam) ‹*idea*›; être passionné/-e
de ‹*activity*›; **to be** ∼ **on doing** *or* **to do** tenir à
faire; **to be** ∼ **on sb** en pincer (fam) pour qn
(b) ‹*appetite, interest*› vif/vive; ‹*eye,
intelligence*› vif/vive; ‹*sight*› perçant/-e;
‹*hearing, sense of smell*› fin/-e
(c) ‹*competition*› intense
⚬ **keep** ① *n* (a) pension *f*; **to pay for one's** ∼
payer une pension
(b) (tower) donjon *m*
② *vtr* (*prét, pp* **kept**) (a) (retain) garder
‹*receipt, money, letter, seat*›; **to** ∼ **sb/sth clean**
garder qn/qch propre; **to** ∼ **sth warm** garder
qch au chaud; **to** ∼ **sb warm** protéger qn
du froid; **to** ∼ **sb waiting** faire attendre qn;
to ∼ **sb talking** retenir qn; **to** ∼ **an engine
running** laisser un moteur en marche
(b) (detain) retenir; **I won't** ∼ **you a minute** je
n'en ai pas pour longtemps
(c) tenir ‹*shop*›; élever ‹*chickens*›
(d) (sustain) **to** ∼ **[sth] going** entretenir
‹*conversation, fire*›; maintenir ‹*tradition*›;
I'll make you a sandwich to ∼ **you going** je
te ferai un sandwich pour que tu tiennes
le coup
(e) (store) mettre, ranger; **where do you** ∼
your cups? où rangez-vous vos tasses?
(f) (support) faire vivre, entretenir ‹*family*›
(g) tenir ‹*accounts, diary*›
(h) **to** ∼ **sth from sb** taire *or* cacher qch à qn;
to ∼ **sth to oneself** garder qch pour soi
(i) (prevent) **to** ∼ **sb from doing** empêcher qn
de faire
(j) tenir ‹*promise*›; garder ‹*secret*›; se rendre à
‹*appointment*›
(k) (Mus) **to** ∼ **time** battre la mesure
③ *vi* (*prét, pp* **kept**) (a) (continue) **to** ∼
doing continuer à *or* de faire, ne pas arrêter
de faire; **to** ∼ **going** ‹*person*› continuer

(b) (remain) **to** ∼ **out of the rain** se protéger
de la pluie; **to** ∼ **warm** se protéger du froid;
to ∼ **calm** rester calme; **to** ∼ **silent** garder
le silence
(c) ‹*food*› se conserver, se garder
(d) ‹*news, business*› attendre
(e) **'how are you** ∼**ing?'** 'comment
allez-vous?'; **she's** ∼**ing well** elle va bien
④ *v refl* **to** ∼ **oneself to oneself** ne pas être
sociable
⑤ **for keeps** *phr* pour de bon, pour
toujours
■ **keep away**: ① ¶ ∼ **away** ne pas
s'approcher (**from** de)
② ¶ ∼ **[sth/sb] away** empêcher [qch/qn] de
s'approcher
■ **keep back**: ① ¶ ∼ **back** ne pas
s'approcher (**from** de)
② ¶ ∼ **[sb/sth] back (a)** empêcher [qn] de
s'approcher ‹*crowd*› (**from** de); ‹*dam*› retenir
‹*water*›
(b) (retain) garder ‹*money*›; conserver ‹*food*›
■ **keep down**: ¶ ∼ **[sth] down**, ∼ **down [sth]**
limiter ‹*number, speed, inflation*›; limiter
l'augmentation de ‹*prices, unemployment*›
■ **keep off**: ① ¶ ∼ **off [sth] (a)** ne pas
marcher sur ‹*grass*›
(b) éviter ‹*alcohol*›; s'abstenir de parler de
‹*subject*›
② ¶ ∼ **[sth] off** éloigner ‹*insects*›; **this
plastic sheet will** ∼ **the rain off** cette housse
en plastique protège de la pluie
■ **keep on**: ① ¶ ∼ **on doing** continuer à
faire; **to** ∼ **on about** ne pas arrêter de parler
de; **to** ∼ **on at sb** harceler qn (**to do** pour qu'il
fasse)
② ¶ ∼ **[sb] on** garder
■ **keep out** ① ¶ ∼ **out of [sth] (a)** ne
pas entrer dans ‹*house*›; **'**∼ **out!'** 'défense
d'entrer'
(b) rester à l'abri de ‹*sun, danger*›
(c) ne pas se mêler de ‹*argument*›; **to** ∼ **out
of sb's way** (not hinder) ne pas gêner qn; (avoid
seeing) éviter qn
② ¶ ∼ **[sb/sth] out** ne pas laisser entrer
‹*person, animal*›
■ **keep to** ne pas s'écarter de ‹*road*›;
respecter, s'en tenir à ‹*facts*›; respecter ‹*law,
rules*›
■ **keep up**: ① ¶ ∼ **up** ‹*car, runner, person*›
suivre
② ¶ ∼ **[sth] up (a)** tenir ‹*trousers*›
(b) continuer ‹*attack, studies*›; entretenir
‹*correspondence, friendship*›; maintenir
‹*membership, tradition, pace*›
③ ¶ ∼ **[sb] up** ‹*noise*› empêcher [qn] de
dormir   ····⟫

k

■ **keep up with** (a) aller aussi vite que ‹person›; suivre ‹class›; ‹wages› suivre ‹inflation›; faire face à ‹demand›
(b) suivre ‹fashion, developments›

keeper n (curator) conservateur/-trice m/f; (guard) gardien/-ienne m/f

keep fit n gymnastique f d'entretien

keeping n (a) (custody) in sb's ~ à la garde de qn; **to put sb/sth in sb's** ~ confier qn/qch à qn
(b) (conformity) **in** ~ **with** conforme à ‹law, tradition›; **to be in** ~ **with** correspondre à ‹image, character›; s'harmoniser avec ‹surroundings›

keg n (for liquid) fût m; (for gunpowder) baril m

kennel n (a) (GB) (for dog) niche f
(b) (establishment) chenil m

Kenya pr n Kenya m; **in** ~ au Kenya

kerb n (GB) bord m du trottoir

kernel n (of nut, fruitstone) amande f

kerosene, kerosine n (a) (US) (paraffin) pétrole m (lampant)
(b) (fuel) kérosène m

kestrel n (faucon m) crécerelle f

kettle n bouilloire f; **to put the** ~ **on** mettre l'eau à chauffer

kettledrum n timbale f

ɗ **key** ① n (a) clé f; **a front-door** ~ une clé de maison; **a set** or **bunch of** ~s un jeu de clés; **under lock and** ~ sous clé; **radiator** ~ clavette f à radiateur
(b) (on computer, piano) touche f; (on oboe, flute) clé f
(c) (vital clue) clé f, secret m (**to** de)
(d) (on map) légende f; (to abbreviations, symbols) liste f; (for code) clé f
(e) (to test, riddle) solutions fpl; (Sch) corrigé m
(f) (Mus) ton m, tonalité f; **to sing in/off** ~ chanter juste/faux
② adj ‹figure, role› clé; ‹point› capital/-e
③ vtr (a) (also ~ **in**) saisir ‹data›
(b) (adapt) adapter (**to** à)

keyboard n clavier m

keyboards n pl synthétiseur m

keyed-up adj (excited) excité/-e; (tense) tendu/-e

keyhole n trou m de serrure

keyhole surgery n chirurgie f endoscopique

keynote speech n discours m programme

key-ring n porte-clés m inv

keyword n mot m clé

khaki adj kaki inv

kibbutz n (pl ~**es** ou ~**im**) kibboutz m

ɗ **kick** ① n (a) (of person, horse) coup m de pied; (of donkey, cow) coup m de sabot; (of swimmer) battement m de pieds; (of footballer) tir m

(b) (colloq) (thrill) **to get a** ~ **out of doing** prendre plaisir à faire
(c) (of firearm) recul m
② vtr (once) ‹person› donner un coup de pied à ‹person›; donner un coup de pied dans ‹door, ball, tin can›; ‹horse› botter ‹person›; ‹donkey, cow› donner un coup de sabot à ‹person›; (repeatedly) ‹person› donner des coups de pied à ‹person›; donner des coups de pieds dans ‹object›; **to** ~ **sb on the leg** ‹person, horse› donner à qn un coup de pied à la jambe; ‹donkey, cow› donner à qn un coup de sabot dans la jambe
③ vi ‹person› (once) donner un coup de pied; (repeatedly) donner des coups de pied; ‹swimmer› faire des battements de pieds; ‹cow› ruer; ‹horse› botter
IDIOMS **to** ~ **the habit** (colloq) (of drug addiction) décrocher (fam); (of smoking) arrêter de fumer; **I could have** ~**ed myself** je me serais donné des claques (fam)
■ **kick around, kick about** donner des coups de pied dans, s'amuser avec ‹ball›
■ **kick off** (a) (Sport) donner le coup d'envoi
(b) (colloq) (start) commencer
■ **kick out:** ① ¶ ~ **out** ‹animal› ruer
② ¶ ~ **[sb] out** (colloq) virer (fam)

kick-off n (Sport) coup m d'envoi

kick-start ① n (also ~**-starter**) kick m
② vtr (a) faire démarrer [qch] au pied ‹motorbike›
(b) relancer ‹economy›

ɗ **kid** ① n (a) (colloq) (child) enfant mf, gosse mf (fam); (youth) gamin/-e m/f (fam)
(b) (young goat) chevreau/-ette m/f
(c) (goatskin) chevreau m
② vtr (colloq) (p prés etc -**dd**-) charrier (fam) (**about** à propos de)
③ vi (colloq) (p prés etc -**dd**-) rigoler (fam); **no** ~**ding!** sans blague! (fam)
④ v refl (colloq) **to** ~ **oneself** se faire des illusions

kidnap vtr (p prés etc -**pp**-) enlever

kidnapper n ravisseur/-euse m/f

kidnapping n enlèvement m

kidney n (a) (Anat) rein m
(b) (Culin) rognon m

kidney bean n haricot m rouge

kidney machine n rein m artificiel; **to be on a** ~ être sous dialyse

ɗ **kill** ① n mise f à mort
② vtr (a) tuer ‹person, animal›; **they** ~**ed each other** ils se sont entre-tués; **even if it** ~**s me!** (colloq) même si je dois y laisser ma peau! (fam); **my feet are** ~**ing me** (colloq) j'ai mal aux pieds
(b) mettre fin à, étouffer ‹rumour›; ‹editor› supprimer ‹story›
(c) faire disparaître ‹pain›; ôter ‹appetite›
(d) (spend) **to** ~ **time** tuer le temps (**by doing** en faisant)
③ vi ‹person, animal, drug› tuer
④ v refl **to** ~ **oneself** se suicider

ɗ indicates a very frequent word

killer n (person) meurtrier m; (animal) tueur/-euse m/f; **heroin is a ~** l'héroïne tue

killer whale n épaulard m

killing n (of individual) meurtre m (**of** de); (of animal) mise f à mort (**of** de)

killjoy n rabat-joie mf inv

kiln n four m

kilo n kilo m

kilobyte, **KB** n kilo-octet m, Ko m

kilogram(me) n kilogramme m

kilometre (GB), **kilometer** (US) n kilomètre m

kilowatt n kilowatt m

⚜ **kind** ▢1 n (a) (sort, type) sorte f, genre m, type m; **this ~ of person** ce genre de personne; **all ~s of people** toutes sortes de personnes; **what ~ of dog is it?** qu'est-ce que c'est comme chien?; **what ~ of person is she?** comment est-elle?, quel genre de personne est-ce?; **this is one of a ~** il/elle est unique en son genre
(b) (in vague descriptions) **a ~ of** une sorte de; **I heard a ~ of rattling noise** j'ai entendu comme un cliquetis
(c) (classified type) espèce f, genre m; **one's own ~** les gens de son espèce
▢2 adj ‹person, gesture, words› gentil/-ille; ‹act› bon/bonne (before n); **to be ~ to sb** être gentil/-ille avec qn; **to be ~ to animals** bien traiter les animaux; **that's very ~ of you** c'est très gentil or aimable de votre part; **would you be ~ enough to pass me the salt?** auriez-vous l'amabilité de me passer le sel?
▢3 **in kind** phr ‹pay› en nature
▢4 **kind of** phr (colloq) **he's ~ of cute** il est plutôt mignon; **I ~ of like him** en fait, je l'aime bien; **'is it interesting?'—'~ of'** 'est-ce que c'est intéressant?'—'assez'

kindergarten n jardin m d'enfants

kind-hearted adj ‹person› de cœur

kindle vtr (a) allumer ‹fire›
(b) attiser ‹desire, passion›; susciter ‹interest›

kindly ▢1 adj ‹person› gentil/-ille; ‹smile› bienveillant/-e
▢2 adv (a) (in a kind way) avec gentillesse; **to speak ~ of sb** dire du bien de qn
(b) (obligingly) gentiment; **would you ~ do/refrain from doing** auriez-vous l'amabilité de faire/de ne pas faire
(c) (favourably) **to take ~ to** apprécier

kindness n gentillesse f, bonté f

kindred spirit n âme f sœur

kinetics n cinétique f

⚜ **king** n (a) (monarch) roi m; **King Charles** le roi Charles
(b) (in chess, cards) roi m; (in draughts, checkers) dame f

kingdom n (a) (country) royaume m
(b) (Bot, Zool) règne m; **the animal ~** le règne animal

kingfisher n martin-pêcheur m

king-size(d) adj ‹packet› géant/-e; ‹portion, garden› énorme; **~ bed** grand lit m; **~ cigarettes** cigarettes fpl extra-longues

kink n (in rope, tube) nœud m; **the hosepipe has a ~ in it** le tuyau d'arrosage est tordu

kiosk n (a) (stand) kiosque m
(b) (GB) (phone box) cabine f

kipper n (GB) hareng m fumé et salé, kipper m

⚜ **kiss** ▢1 n baiser m; **to give sb a ~** embrasser qn, donner un baiser à qn
▢2 vtr embrasser, donner un baiser à ‹person›; **to ~ sb on** embrasser qn sur ‹cheek, lips›; **we ~ed each other** nous nous sommes embrassés
▢3 vi s'embrasser

kiss of life n (GB) bouche-à-bouche m inv; **to give sb the ~** faire le bouche-à-bouche à qn

kit n (a) (implements) trousse f
(b) (gear, clothes) affaires fpl; **football ~** affaires de football
(c) (for assembly) kit m
(d) (Mil) paquetage m
■ **kit out** équiper (with de)

kitbag n (for sport) sac m de sport; (for travel) sac m de voyage; (Mil) sac m de soldat

⚜ **kitchen** n cuisine f

kitchen foil n papier m d'aluminium

kitchen roll n essuie-tout m inv

kitchen sink n évier m

kitchen unit n élément m de cuisine

kite n cerf-volant m; **to fly a ~** faire voler un cerf-volant

kitten n chaton m

kitty n cagnotte f

kiwi fruit n kiwi m

kleptomaniac n, adj kleptomane mf

knack n (a) (dexterity) tour m de main (**of doing** pour faire); **to get the ~** attraper le tour de main; **to lose the ~** perdre la main
(b) (talent) don m (**for doing** de faire)

knapsack n sac m à dos

knave n (in cards) valet m

knead vtr pétrir ‹dough›; masser ‹flesh›

⚜ **knee** ▢1 n genou m; **on (one's) hands and ~s** à quatre pattes
▢2 vtr donner un coup de genou à ‹person›
IDIOM to go weak at the ~s avoir les jambes qui flageolent

kneecap n rotule f

knee-deep adj **the water was ~** l'eau arrivait aux genoux

kneel vi (also ~ **down**) (prét, pp **kneeled**, **knelt**) se mettre à genoux; **to be ~ing** être à genoux

knee-length adj ‹skirt› qui s'arrête au genou; ‹boots› haut/-e; ‹socks› long/longue

knickers n pl (GB) petite culotte f

knick-knack n bibelot m

knife [1] *n* (*pl* **knives**) couteau *m*
[2] *vtr* donner un coup de couteau à; **to be ~d** recevoir un coup de couteau
knife-edge *n* **to be (living) on a ~** ‹person› être au bord de l'abîme
knife-point *n* **at ~** sous la menace d'un couteau
knight [1] *n* (gen) chevalier *m*; (in chess) cavalier *m*
[2] *vtr* (GB) anoblir ‹person› (**for** pour)
knighthood *n* titre *m* de chevalier
knit [1] *vtr* (*prét*, *pp* **knitted**, **knit**) tricoter ‹sweater, hat›; **~ted** en tricot
[2] *vi* (*prét*, *pp* **knitted**, **knit**) (a) tricoter
(b) ‹broken bones› se souder
knitting *n* tricot *m*
knitwear *n* tricots *mpl*
knob *n* (a) (of door) bouton *m*; (on bannister) boule *f*
(b) (control button) bouton *m*
knobbly (GB), **knobby** (US) *adj* ‹fingers› noueux/-euse; ‹knees› saillant/-e
❖ **knock** [1] *n* (a) (blow) coup *m* (**on** sur; **with** de); **a ~ at the door** un coup à la porte; **~! ~!** toc! toc!
(b) (setback) coup *m*; **to take a ~** en prendre un coup
[2] *vtr* (a) (strike) cogner ‹object›; **to ~ one's head on sth** se cogner la tête contre qch; **to ~ sb unconscious** assommer qn; **to ~ sth off** *or* **out of sth** faire tomber qch de qch
(b) (colloq) (criticize) dénigrer
[3] *vi* (a) ‹branch, engine, object› cogner (**on**, **against** contre); ‹person› frapper (**at**, **on** à)
(b) (collide) **to ~ into** *or* **against sth** heurter qch
■ **knock down** (a) (deliberately) jeter [qn] à terre ‹person›; défoncer ‹door›; démolir ‹building›; (accidentally) renverser ‹person, object›; abattre ‹fence›
(b) ‹buyer› faire baisser ‹price›; ‹seller› baisser ‹price›
■ **knock off**: [1] **¶ ~ off** arrêter de travailler
[2] (a) **¶ ~ [sb/sth] off**, **~ off [sb/sth]** (cause to fall) faire tomber ‹person, object›
(b) (colloq) (reduce) **to ~ £10 off the price of sth** réduire le prix de qch de 10 livres
(c) (colloq) **~ it off!** ça suffit!
■ **knock out** (a) casser ‹tooth›
(b) (make unconscious) ‹person, blow› assommer; ‹drug› endormir; ‹boxer› mettre [qn] au tapis ‹opponent›
(c) (Sport) éliminer ‹opponent, team›
■ **knock over** renverser ‹person, object›
knockabout *n* (Sport) échange *m* de balles
knockdown *adj* ‹price› sacrifié/-e
knocker *n* heurtoir *m*
knocking *n* (at door) coups *mpl*; (in engine) cognement *m*
knock-kneed *adj* cagneux/-euse

knock-on effect *n* implications *fpl*
knock-out [1] *n* (in boxing) knock-out *m*
[2] *adj* (a) (Sport) ‹competition› avec tours éliminatoires
(b) (colloq) ‹pills› sédatif/-ive
knot [1] *n* (a) nœud *m*; **to tie a ~** faire un nœud; **to tie sth in a ~** nouer qch
(b) (in wood) nœud *m*
(c) (group) petit groupe *m* (**of** de)
[2] *vtr* (*p prés etc* **-tt-**) nouer (**together** ensemble)
❖ **know** [1] *vtr* (*prét* **knew**, *pp* **known**) (gen) savoir; (be acquainted or familiar with) connaître ‹place, person, way›; **to ~ why/ how** savoir pourquoi/comment; **to ~ how to do** savoir faire; **to ~ sb by sight** connaître qn de vue; **to get to ~ sb** faire connaissance avec qn; **he ~s all about it** il est au courant; **I knew it!** j'en étais sûr!
[2] *vi* (*prét* **knew**, *pp* **known**) savoir; **as you ~** comme vous le savez; **to ~ about** (have information) être au courant de ‹event›; (have skill) s'y connaître en ‹computing, engines›; **to ~ of** (from experience) connaître; (from information) avoir entendu parler de; **to let sb ~ of** *or* **about** tenir qn au courant de
IDIOM **to be in the ~** être bien informé/-e
know-all *n* (colloq) (GB) je-sais-tout *mf inv*
know-how *n* (colloq) savoir-faire *m inv*
knowing *adj* ‹look, smile› entendu/-e
❖ **knowledge** *n* (a) (awareness) connaissance *f*; **to my ~** à ma connaissance; **without sb's ~** à l'insu de qn
(b) (factual wisdom) connaissances *fpl*; (of specific field) connaissance *f*; **technical ~** connaissances techniques
knowledgeable *adj* ‹person› savant/-e; **to be ~ about** s'y connaître en ‹subject›
known *adj* ‹authority, danger› reconnu/-e; ‹cure› connu/-e
knuckle *n* (a) (of person) jointure *f*, articulation *f*
(b) (Culin) (of lamb, mutton) manche *m* de gigot; (of pork, veal) jarret *m*
■ **knuckle down** (colloq) s'y mettre (sérieusement)
knuckle-duster *n* coup-de-poing *m* américain
koala (bear) *n* koala *m*
Koran *n* Coran *m*
Korea *pr n* Corée *f*
kosher *adj* (a) ‹food, restaurant› casher
(b) (colloq) (not illegal) **it's ~** c'est réglo (fam)
Kosovan [1] *n* Kosovar/-e *m/f*
[2] *adj* kosovar/-e
Kosovo *pr n* Kosovo *m*
Kurd *n* Kurde *mf*
Kurdish *adj* kurde
Kurdistan *pr n* Kurdistan *m*
Kuwait *pr n* Koweït *m*
Kyrgyzstan *pr n* Kirghizistan *m*

L l

l, L n l, L m

lab n labo m (fam)

lab coat n blouse f blanche

label [1] n (a) (on clothing, jar) étiquette f
(b) (also **record** ~) label m
(c) (Comput) label m
[2] vtr (p prés etc **-ll-** (GB), **-l-** (US))
(a) étiqueter ‹clothing, jar›
(b) classer, étiqueter (derogatory) ‹person› (as comme)

labor (US) = LABOUR

laboratory n laboratoire m

laborer (US) = LABOURER

labor union n (US) syndicat m

⚬ **labour** (GB), **labor** (US) [1] n (a) (work) travail m
(b) (also ~ **force**) main-d'œuvre f
(c) (Med) accouchement m; **to be in** ~ être en train d'accoucher
[2] vi travailler (at à; on sur; to do pour faire)
IDIOM **to** ~ **the point** insister lourdement

Labour [1] n (GB) parti m travailliste
[2] adj travailliste

labourer (GB), **laborer** (US) n ouvrier/-ière m/f du bâtiment

Labour Party n (GB) parti m travailliste

labour-saving adj ‹feature, system› qui facilite le travail; ~ **device** appareil m ménager

labyrinth n labyrinthe m, dédale m

lace [1] n (a) (fabric) dentelle f
(b) (on shoe, boot, dress) lacet m; (on tent) cordon m
[2] vtr (a) lacer ‹shoes›
(b) **to** ~ **a drink with sth** mettre qch dans une boisson

lace-up (shoe) n chaussure f à lacet

⚬ **lack** [1] n manque m (of de); **through** ~ **of** par manque de
[2] vtr manquer de
[3] vi **to be** ~**ing** manquer; **to be** ~**ing in** manquer de

lacklustre (GB), **lackluster** (US) adj terne

lacquer n (a) (for hair) laque f
(b) (varnish) laque f

lacy adj en or de dentelle

lad n (colloq) (boy) garçon m

ladder [1] n (a) (for climbing) échelle f
(b) (GB) (in stockings) échelle f, maille f filée
[2] vtr, vi filer

laddish adj (colloq) macho inv (fam)

ladle n (Culin) louche f

⚬ **lady** [1] n (pl **ladies**) (a) (woman) dame f; **ladies and gentlemen** mesdames et messieurs; **a little old** ~ une petite vieille; **she's a real** ~ elle est très distinguée
(b) (in titles) **Lady Churchill** Lady Churchill
[2] **ladies** n pl toilettes fpl; (on sign) 'Dames'

ladybird n coccinelle f

ladylike adj ‹behaviour› distingué/-e

lag [1] n (also **time** ~) décalage m
[2] vtr (p prés etc **-gg-**) calorifuger ‹pipe, tank›; isoler ‹roof›
■ **lag behind**: [1] ¶ ~ **behind** ‹person, prices› être à la traîne
[2] ¶ ~ **behind [sb/sth]** traîner derrière ‹person›; être en retard sur ‹rival, product›

lager n bière f blonde

lager lout n (GB) voyou m (qui se soûle à la bière)

lagoon n lagune f

laidback adj (colloq) décontracté/-e

laid up adj **to be** ~ être alité/-e

lake n lac m

lamb n agneau m; **leg of** ~ gigot m d'agneau

lamb's wool n laine f d'agneau, lambswool m

lame adj boiteux/-euse

lament [1] n lamentation f
[2] vtr se lamenter sur ‹fate, misfortune›

lamentable adj déplorable

laminated adj ‹plastic› stratifié/-e; ‹wood› contreplaqué/-e; ‹card› plastifié/-e

lamp n lampe f

lamppost n réverbère m

lampshade n abat-jour m

lance vtr percer ‹boil, abscess›

⚬ **land** [1] n (a) (terrain, property) terrain m; (very large) terres fpl
(b) (farmland) terre f
(c) (country) pays m
(d) (not sea) terre f; **dry** ~ terre ferme; **to reach** ~ toucher terre; **by** ~ par voie de terre
[2] vtr (a) ‹pilot› poser ‹aircraft›; faire atterrir ‹space capsule›
(b) prendre ‹fish›
(c) (colloq) décrocher (fam) ‹job, contract, prize›
(d) (colloq) **to be** ~**ed with sb/sth** se retrouver avec qn/qch sur les bras
[3] vi (a) ‹aircraft, passenger› atterrir
(b) ‹ship› accoster
(c) ‹person, animal, object› atterrir; ‹ball›   ⋯⟶

toucher le sol; **most of the paint** ∼**ed on me** presque toute la peinture m'est tombée dessus

landing n (a) (at turn of stairs) palier m; (storey) étage m
(b) (from boat) (of people) débarquement m; (of cargo) déchargement m
(c) (by plane) atterrissage m (**on** sur)

landing card n carte f de débarquement

landing gear n train m d'atterrissage

landing strip n piste f d'atterrissage

landlady n (owner) propriétaire f; (live-in) logeuse f; (of pub) patronne f

landlord n (owner) propriétaire m; (live-in) logeur m; (of pub) patron m

landmark n (for bearings) point m de repère; (major step) étape f importante

land mine n mine f antipersonnel

landowner n propriétaire mf foncier/-ière

landscape n paysage m

landscape gardener n jardinier/-ière m/f paysagiste

landslide n (a) glissement m de terrain
(b) (also ∼ **victory**) victoire f écrasante

lane n (a) (in country) chemin m, petite route f; (in town) ruelle f
(b) (of road) voie f, file f; (air, sea) couloir m; (Sport) couloir m

⚹ **language** n (a) (system in general) langage m
(b) (of a particular nation) langue f; **the French** ∼ la langue française
(c) (of a particular group, style) langage m; **legal** ∼ langage juridique; **bad** or **foul** ∼ langage grossier
(d) (Comput) langage m

language barrier n obstacle m or barrière f de la langue

language laboratory, **language lab** n laboratoire m de langues

languish vi (remain neglected) ‹person› languir; ‹object› traîner

lank adj ‹hair› plat/-e

lantern n lanterne f

lap n (a) (of person) genoux mpl; **in one's** ∼ sur les genoux
(b) (Sport) (of track) tour m de piste; (of racecourse) tour m de circuit
IDIOM **in the** ∼ **of luxury** dans le plus grand luxe
■ **lap up** (a) laper ‹milk, water›
(b) boire [qch] comme du petit lait ‹compliment, flattery›

lap belt n ceinture f ventrale

lapel n revers m

lapse ⟨1⟩ n (a) (slip) défaillance f; **a** ∼ **in concentration** un relâchement de l'attention
(b) (interval) intervalle m, laps m de temps
⟨2⟩ vi (a) ‹contract, membership› expirer; ‹insurance› prendre fin

(b) **to** ∼ **into** se mettre à parler ‹jargon, German›; tomber dans ‹coma›; prendre ‹bad habits›

laptop n (also ∼ **computer**) portable m

lard n saindoux m

larder n garde-manger m inv

⚹ **large** ⟨1⟩ adj (gen) grand/-e (before n); ‹appetite, piece, person, nose› gros/grosse (before n); ‹amount› important/-e; ‹crowd, family› nombreux/-euse
⟨2⟩ **at large** phr (a) ‹prisoner, criminal› en liberté
(b) ‹society, population› en général, dans son ensemble
IDIOM **by and** ∼ en général

large-scale adj à grande échelle

lark n (a) (Zool) alouette f
(b) (colloq) (fun) **for a** ∼ pour rigoler (fam)

laryngitis n laryngite f

larynx n larynx m

lasagne n lasagnes fpl

laser ⟨1⟩ n laser m
⟨2⟩ adj ‹beam, disc› laser inv; ‹printer› à laser

laser treatment n thérapie f au laser

lash ⟨1⟩ n (a) (eyelash) cil m
(b) (whipstroke) coup m de fouet
⟨2⟩ vtr fouetter ‹person, animal›; ‹rain› cingler ‹windows›
■ **lash out** ‹person› devenir violent/-e; **to** ∼ **out at sb** (physically) frapper qn; (verbally) invectiver qn

⚹ **last** ⟨1⟩ pron **the** ∼ le dernier/la dernière m/f (**to do** à faire); **the** ∼ **but one** l'avant-dernier/-ière; **the night before** ∼ (evening) avant-hier soir; (night) la nuit d'avant-hier; **the week before** ∼ il y a deux semaines
⟨2⟩ adj dernier/-ière (before n); ∼ **week/year** la semaine/l'année dernière; ∼ **Christmas** à Noël l'an dernier; **over the** ∼ **ten years** durant ces dix dernières années; ∼ **night** (evening) hier soir; (night-time) la nuit dernière
⟨3⟩ adv (a) (to come in ∼ ‹runner, racing car› arriver en dernier; **the girls left** ∼ les filles sont parties les dernières; **to leave sth till** ∼ s'occuper de qch en dernier (lieu); ∼ **of all** en dernier lieu
(b) **she was** ∼ **here in 1976** la dernière fois qu'elle est venue ici, c'était en 1976
⟨4⟩ vi (a) durer; **it's too good to** ∼! c'est trop beau pour que ça dure!; **he won't** ∼ **long here** il ne tiendra pas longtemps ici
(b) ‹fabric› faire de l'usage; ‹perishables› se conserver
⟨5⟩ **at last** adv enfin

last-ditch adj ‹attempt, stand› désespéré/-e, ultime

lasting adj ‹effect, impression› durable; ‹relationship› sérieux/-ieuse

lastly adv enfin, finalement

last-minute adj de dernière minute

⚹ indicates a very frequent word

last name n nom m de famille
last rites n pl derniers sacrements mpl
latch n (fastening) loquet m; (spring lock) serrure f (de sûreté)
■ **latch on to** (colloq) s'accrocher à ‹object, person›; exploiter ‹idea›
✔ **late** ⟦1⟧ adj (a) ‹arrival› tardif/-ive; **to be ~ (for sth)** être en retard (pour qch); **to make sb ~** retarder qn; **to be ~ with the rent** payer son loyer avec du retard; **dinner will be a bit ~** le dîner sera retardé
(b) ‹hour, supper, date› tardif/-ive; **to have a ~ night** (aller) se coucher tard; **to be in one's ~ fifties** approcher de la soixantaine; **in ~ January** (à la) fin janvier; **in the ~ 50s** à la fin des années 50
(c) (deceased) feu/-e (formal); **my ~ wife** ma pauvre femme
⟦2⟧ adv (a) ‹arrive, start, finish› en retard; **to be running ~** ‹person› être en retard; ‹train, bus› avoir du retard; **to start three months ~** commencer avec trois mois de retard
(b) ‹get up, open, close› tard; ‹marry› sur le tard; **~ last night/in the evening** tard hier soir/dans la soirée
latecomer n retardataire mf
late developer n **to be a ~** ‹child› être lent/-e
lately adv ces derniers temps
late-night adj ‹film› dernier/-ière (before n); ‹session› en nocturne; **it's ~ shopping on Thursdays** les magasins restent ouverts tard le jeudi
✔ **later** ⟦1⟧ adj ‹date› ultérieur/-e; ‹model, novel› postérieur/-e
⟦2⟧ adv plus tard; **~ on** plus tard; **six months ~** six mois après; **to leave no ~ than 6 am** partir au plus tard à 6 heures; **see you ~!** à tout à l'heure!
latest ⟦1⟧ adj dernier/-ière (before n)
⟦2⟧ **at the latest** phr au plus tard
latex n latex m
lathe n tour m
lather n mousse f
Latin ⟦1⟧ n (language) latin m
⟦2⟧ adj latin/-e
Latin America pr n Amérique f latine
Latin American adj latino-américain/-e
latitude n latitude f
✔ **latter** n **the ~** ce dernier/cette dernière m/f; **ces derniers/ces dernières** mpl/fpl
Latvia pr n Lettonie f
✔ **laugh** ⟦1⟧ n rire m; **to like a good ~** aimer bien rire; **to get a ~** faire rire; **for a ~** (colloq) pour rigoler (fam)
⟦2⟧ vi rire (about, over de); **to ~ at sb/sth** rire de qn/qch; **the children ~ed at the clown** le clown a fait rire les enfants; **he's afraid of being ~ed at** il a peur qu'on se moque de lui
■ **laugh off** choisir de rire de ‹criticism, insult›

laughable adj ridicule
laughing stock n risée f
laughter n rires mpl
✔ **launch** ⟦1⟧ n (a) (for patrolling) vedette f; (for pleasure) bateau m de plaisance
(b) (of new boat, rocket) lancement m; (of lifeboat) mise f à l'eau; (of campaign, product) lancement m
⟦2⟧ vtr (a) mettre [qch] à l'eau ‹dinghy, lifeboat›; lancer ‹new ship, missile, rocket›
(b) (start) lancer ‹campaign, career, product›; ouvrir ‹investigation›
launch pad, launching pad n aire f de lancement
launder vtr (a) laver ‹clothes›
(b) blanchir ‹money›
launderette (GB), **laundromat** (US) n laverie f automatique
laundry n (a) (place) (commercial) blanchisserie f; (in hotel, house) laverie f
(b) (linen) linge m; **to do the ~** faire la lessive
laurel n laurier m
lava n lave f
lavatory n toilettes fpl
lavender n lavande f
lavish ⟦1⟧ adj ‹party, lifestyle› somptueux/-euse
⟦2⟧ vtr prodiguer ‹money, affection› (on à)
lavishly adv ‹decorated› luxueusement; ‹spend› sans compter; ‹entertain› généreusement
✔ **law** n (a) (gen) loi f; **to obey/break the ~** respecter/enfreindre la loi; **to be against the ~** être interdit/-e; **by ~** conformément à la loi
(b) (Univ) droit m; **to study ~** faire son droit
law-abiding adj respectueux/-euse des lois
law and order n ordre m public
law court n tribunal m
law firm n cabinet m d'avocats
lawful adj ‹owner, strike› légal/-e; ‹conduct› licite; ‹wife, husband› légitime
lawless adj ‹society› anarchique; ‹area, town› tombé/-e dans l'anarchie
lawn n pelouse f
lawnmower n tondeuse f (à gazon)
law school n faculté f de droit
lawsuit n procès m
✔ **lawyer** n (who practises law) avocat/-e m/f; (expert in law) juriste mf
lax adj relâché/-e
laxative n laxatif m
✔ **lay** ⟦1⟧ adj (a) (non-specialist) **~ person** profane mf
(b) ‹preacher, member› laïque
⟦2⟧ vtr (prét, pp **laid**) (a) (place) poser ‹object, card› (in dans; on sur); (spread out) étaler ‹rug, newspaper› (on sur); (arrange) disposer (on sur); **to ~ the table (for)** mettre ⋯⋗

la table (pour)
(b) (prepare) préparer ⟨plan, trail⟩; poser ⟨basis, foundation⟩; tendre ⟨trap⟩
(c) (Zool) pondre ⟨egg⟩
3 vi (prét, pp **laid**) ⟨bird⟩ pondre
■ **lay down (a)** coucher ⟨baby, patient⟩; étaler ⟨rug, cards⟩; poser ⟨book, implement⟩; déposer ⟨weapon⟩
(b) to ~ down one's life for sacrifier sa vie pour
(c) établir ⟨rule⟩; poser ⟨condition⟩
■ **lay off** (temporarily) mettre [qn] en chômage technique; (permanently) licencier
■ **lay on** prévoir ⟨meal, transport⟩; organiser ⟨trip⟩
■ **lay out (a)** disposer ⟨goods, food⟩; étaler ⟨map, garment, fabric⟩
(b) concevoir ⟨building, advert⟩; mettre [qch] en page ⟨letter⟩; monter ⟨page⟩
layabout n (colloq) fainéant/-e m/f (fam)
lay-by n (GB) aire f de repos
⚹ **layer** **1** n couche f
2 vtr **(a)** couper [qch] en dégradé ⟨hair⟩
(b) disposer [qch] en couches ⟨cheese, potatoes⟩
layman n profane m
lay-off n (permanent) licenciement m; (temporary) mise f en chômage technique
layout n (of page, book, computer screen) mise f en page; (of advert, article) présentation f; (of building) agencement m; (of town) plan m; (of garden) dessin m
laze vi (also ~ **about**, ~ **around**) paresser
lazily adv ⟨move, wonder⟩ nonchalamment; ⟨lie, float⟩ mollement; ⟨flow, bob⟩ doucement
laziness n paresse f
lazy adj ⟨person⟩ paresseux/-euse; ⟨day, holiday⟩ paisible; ⟨movement, pace⟩ lent/-e
⚹ **lead¹** **1** n **(a) to be in the ~** être en tête; **to go into the ~** passer en tête
(b) (initiative) **to take the ~** prendre l'initiative; **to follow sb's ~** suivre l'exemple de qn
(c) (clue) piste f
(d) (leading role) rôle m principal
(e) (wire) fil m
(f) (GB) (for dog) laisse f
2 adj ⟨guitarist⟩ premier/-ière (before n); ⟨role, singer⟩ principal/-e
3 vtr (prét, pp **led**) **(a)** (guide, escort) mener, conduire ⟨person⟩ (**to sth** à qch; **to sb** auprès de qn); **to ~ sb away** éloigner qn (**from** de)
(b) (bring) ⟨path, sign⟩ mener (**to** à)
(c) (cause) **to ~ sb to do** amener qn à faire
(d) mener ⟨army, team, attack, strike⟩; diriger ⟨orchestra, research⟩
(e) (conduct, have) mener ⟨active life⟩; **to ~ a life of luxury** vivre dans le luxe
4 vi (prét, pp **led**) **(a) to ~ to** ⟨path⟩ mener à; ⟨door⟩ s'ouvrir sur; ⟨exit, trapdoor⟩ donner

⚹ indicates a very frequent word

accès à
(b) (result in) **to ~ to** entraîner ⟨complication, discovery, accident⟩
(c) ⟨runner, car, company⟩ être en tête; ⟨team, side⟩ mener; **to ~ by 15 seconds** avoir 15 secondes d'avance
(d) (in walk) aller devant; (in action, discussion) prendre l'initiative; (in dancing) conduire
■ **lead up to (a)** (precede) précéder ⟨event⟩
(b) (build up to) amener ⟨topic⟩
lead² n plomb m; (in pencil) mine f
leaded petrol (GB), **leaded gasoline** (US) n essence f au plomb
⚹ **leader** n **(a)** (of nation) chef m d'État, dirigeant/-e m/f; (of gang) chef m; (of party) leader m; (of trade union) secrétaire mf; (of strike, movement) meneur/-euse m/f
(b) (in competition) premier/-ière m/f; (horse) cheval m de tête; (in market, field) leader m
⚹ **leadership** n dirigeants mpl, direction f; **under the ~ of** sous la direction de
leadership contest, **leadership election** n (Pol) élection f à la direction du parti
leadership qualities n pl qualités fpl de leader
lead-free adj sans plomb
leading adj **(a)** ⟨lawyer, politician⟩ éminent/-e, important/-e; ⟨company, bank⟩ important/-e; ⟨brand⟩ dominant/-e
(b) ⟨role⟩ (main) majeur/-e; (in theatre) principal/-e
(c) (Sport) ⟨driver, car⟩ en tête de course; ⟨team⟩ en tête du classement
leading edge **1** n **at the ~ of** à la pointe de ⟨technology⟩
2 **leading-edge** adj ⟨technology⟩ de pointe
lead story n histoire f à la une (fam)
⚹ **leaf** n (pl **leaves**) **(a)** (of plant) feuille f
(b) (of book) page f
IDIOM **to turn over a new ~** tourner la page
■ **leaf through** feuilleter ⟨papers, book⟩
leaflet n (gen) dépliant m; (advertising) prospectus m
⚹ **league** n **(a)** (alliance) ligue f; **to be in ~ with sb** être de mèche avec qn (fam)
(b) (GB Sport) (competition) championnat m; (association) ligue f
(c) they're not in the same ~ ils ne sont pas comparables
league table n classement m
leak **1** n fuite f
2 vtr divulguer ⟨information, document⟩
3 vi **(a)** ⟨container, roof⟩ fuir; ⟨boat⟩ faire eau
(b) ⟨liquid, gas⟩ s'échapper (**from** de)
leaky adj ⟨container, pipe⟩ qui fuit; ⟨boat⟩ qui prend l'eau
⚹ **lean** **1** adj **(a)** ⟨body, face⟩ mince; ⟨meat⟩ maigre
(b) ⟨year, times⟩ difficile

2 *vtr* (*prét, pp* **leaned** *ou* **leant**) appuyer (**against** contre)

3 *vi* (*prét, pp* **leaned** *ou* **leant**) ‹*wall, building*› pencher; **to ~ against sth** ‹*bicycle, ladder*› être appuyé/-e contre qch; ‹*person*› s'appuyer à qch; (with back) s'adosser à qch; **to ~ out of the window** se pencher par la fenêtre

■ **lean back** se pencher en arrière

■ **lean forward** se pencher en avant

■ **lean on**: **1** ¶ **~ on [sth]** s'appuyer sur ‹*stick*›; s'accouder à ‹*windowsill*›

2 ¶ **~ on [sb]** (as support) s'appuyer sur ‹*person*›; (depend on) compter sur ‹*person*›; (pressurize) faire pression sur ‹*person*›

■ **lean over**: **~ over [sth]** se pencher par-dessus [qch]

leap **1** *n* (a) (jump) saut *m*, bond *m*

(b) (step in process) bond *m* (en avant)

(c) (in price) bond *m* (**in** dans)

2 *vi* (*prét, pp* **leapt, leaped**) (a) ‹*person, animal*› bondir, sauter; **to ~ to one's feet, to ~ up** se lever d'un bond; **to ~ across** *or* **over sth** franchir qch d'un bond

(b) ‹*heart*› bondir (**with** de)

(c) (*also* **~ up**) ‹*price*› grimper (**by** de)

■ **leap at**: **~ at [sth]** sauter sur ‹*chance, offer*›

■ **leap up** (a) (jump to one's feet) bondir sur ses pieds

(b) ‹*price, rate*› grimper

leapfrog *n* saute-mouton *m*

leap year *n* année *f* bissextile

✎ **learn** **1** *vtr* (*prét, pp* **learned** *ou* **learnt**) (gen) apprendre; acquérir ‹*skills*› (**from** de); **to ~ (how) to do** apprendre à faire; **to ~ that** apprendre que

2 *vi* (*prét, pp* **learned** *ou* **learnt**) apprendre; **to ~ about sth** apprendre qch; **to ~ from one's mistakes** tirer la leçon de ses erreurs

learned *adj* ‹*person, book*› érudit/-e; ‹*journal*› spécialisé/-e; ‹*society*› savant/-e

learner *n* (beginner) débutant/-e *m/f*; **to be a fast/slow ~** apprendre/ne pas apprendre vite

learner driver *n* élève *mf* d'auto-école

✎ **learning** *n* (a) (knowledge) érudition *f*

(b) (process) apprentissage *m*

learning curve *n* courbe *f* d'apprentissage

learning difficulties *n pl* (of schoolchildren) difficultés *fpl* scolaires; (of adults) difficultés *fpl* d'apprentissage

lease **1** *n* bail *m*

2 *vtr* louer [qch] à bail ‹*house*›; louer ‹*car*›

leaseholder *n* locataire *mf* à bail

leash *n* laisse *f*

leasing **1** *n* (by company) crédit-bail *m*; (by individual) location *f* avec option d'achat

2 *adj* ‹*company, scheme*› de leasing

✎ **least** **1** *det* **the ~** le moins de; (in negative constructions) le *or* la moindre; **they have**

the **~ money** ce sont eux qui ont le moins d'argent; **I haven't the ~ idea** je n'en ai pas la moindre idée

2 *pron* **the ~** le moins; **we have the ~** c'est nous qui en avons le moins; **it was the ~ I could do!** c'est la moindre des choses!

3 *adv* (a) (with adjective or noun) **the ~** le/ la moins; (with plural noun) les moins; **the ~ wealthy families** les familles les moins riches

(b) (with verbs) le moins *inv*; **I like that one (the) ~** c'est celui-là que j'aime le moins; **nobody liked it, ~ of all John** personne ne l'aimait, John encore moins que les autres

4 **at least** *phr* (at the minimum) au moins; **she's at ~ 40** elle a au moins 40 ans; **they could at ~ have phoned!** ils auraient au moins pu téléphoner!; **he's gone to bed—at ~ I think so** il est allé se coucher—du moins, je pense

5 **in the least** *phr* **not in the ~** pas du tout

IDIOM **last but not ~, last but by no means ~** enfin et surtout

leather **1** *n* cuir *m*

2 *adj* ‹*garment, object*› de cuir, en cuir

✎ **leave** **1** *n* congé *m*; **three days' ~** trois jours de congé

2 *vtr* (*prét, pp* **left**) (a) (depart from) partir de ‹*house, station etc*›; (more permanently) quitter ‹*country, city etc*›; (go out of) sortir de ‹*room, building*›; **he left home early** il est parti tôt de chez lui; **to ~ school** quitter l'école

(b) (forget) oublier ‹*child, object*›

(c) (quitter) ‹*partner*›

(d) laisser ‹*instructions, tip*› (**for** pour; **with** à); **to ~ sb sth** laisser qch à qn; **to ~ sb/sth in sb's care** confier qn/qch à qn

(e) laisser ‹*food, drink, gap*›; **to ~ sth lying around** laisser traîner qch; **to ~ sth tidy** laisser qch en ordre

(f) **to ~ sth to sb** laisser [qch] à qn ‹*job, task*›; **to ~ it (up) to sb to do** laisser à qn le soin de faire; **to ~ sb to it** laisser qn se débrouiller; **~ it to** *or* **with me** je m'en occupe

(g) ‹*oil, wine*› faire ‹*stain*›; ‹*cup, plate*› laisser ‹*stain, mark*›

(h) (postpone) laisser ‹*task, homework*›; **~ it till tomorrow** laisse ça pour demain

(i) (bequeath) léguer (**to sb** à qn)

3 *vi* (*prét, pp* **left**) partir (**for** pour)

■ **leave behind** (a) (go faster than) distancer ‹*person, competitor*›; **to be** *or* **get left behind** (physically) se faire distancer; (intellectually) ne pas suivre; (in business) se laisser distancer

(b) ‹*traveller*› laisser [qch] derrière soi ‹*town, country*›; ‹*person*› quitter ‹*family, husband*›; en finir avec ‹*past*›

(c) (forget) oublier, laisser ‹*object, child, animal*›

■ **leave out** (a) (accidentally) oublier ‹*word, ingredient, person*›; (deliberately) omettre ‹*name, ···⟩*

fact; ne pas mettre ⟨*ingredient, object*⟩; tenir [qn] à l'écart ⟨*person*⟩; **to ∼ sb out of** exclure qn de ⟨*group*⟩
(b) (outdoors) laisser [qch] dehors
leaving ① *n* départ *m*
② *adj* ⟨*party, present*⟩ d'adieu
Lebanon *pr n* (**the**) ∼ (**le**) Liban *m*
lecherous *adj* lubrique
lectern *n* (in church) lutrin *m*; (for lecture notes) pupitre *m*
lecture ① *n* conférence *f* (**on** sur); (GB Univ) cours *m* magistral (**on** sur)
② *vtr* **(a)** (GB Univ) donner des cours à ⟨*class*⟩
(b) (scold) faire la leçon à ⟨*person*⟩
③ *vi* **(a)** (gen) donner une conférence (**on** sur)
(b) (GB Univ) **to ∼ in sth** enseigner qch (à l'université)
lecture notes *n pl* notes *fpl* de cours
lecturer *n* **(a)** (speaker) conférencier/-ière *m/f*
(b) (GB Univ) enseignant/-e *m/f* (du supérieur)
(c) (US Univ) ≈ chargé *m* de cours
lecture theatre *n* amphithéâtre *m*
ledge *n* **(a)** (shelf) rebord *m*
(b) (on mountain) saillie *f* (rocheuse)
ledger *n* registre *m* de comptabilité, grand livre *m*
leech *n* sangsue *f*
leek *n* poireau *m*
leer *vi* **to ∼ at sb/sth** lorgner qn/qch (fam)
leeway *n* liberté *f* de manœuvre
⚥ **left** ① *n* gauche *f*; **on the ∼** sur la gauche; (politically) à gauche
② *adj* **(a)** ⟨*eye, hand, shoe*⟩ gauche
(b) (remaining) **to be ∼** rester; **there are/we have five minutes ∼** il reste/il nous reste cinq minutes; **I've got one ∼** il m'en reste un
③ *adv* ⟨*go, look, turn*⟩ à gauche
left-hand *adj* ⟨*side*⟩ de gauche
left-hand drive *n* voiture *f* avec la conduite à gauche
left-handed *adj* gaucher/-ère
left-luggage (office) *n* (GB) consigne *f*
left-luggage lockers *n pl* consigne *f* automatique
leftovers *n pl* restes *mpl*
left wing ① *n* **the ∼** la gauche *f*
② **left-wing** *adj* ⟨*attitude*⟩ de gauche; **they are very ∼** ils sont très à gauche
⚥ **leg** *n* **(a)** (of person, horse) jambe *f*; (of other animal) patte *f*
(b) (of furniture) pied *m*
(c) (Culin) (of lamb) gigot *m*; (of poultry, pork, frog) cuisse *f*
(d) (of trousers) jambe *f*
(e) (of journey, race) étape *f*

⚥ indicates a very frequent word

IDIOM to pull sb's ∼ faire marcher qn
legacy *n* **(a)** (Law) legs *m*
(b) (figurative) héritage *m*; (of war) séquelles *fpl*
⚥ **legal** *adj* **(a)** ⟨*document, system*⟩ juridique; ⟨*costs*⟩ de justice; **to take ∼ advice** consulter un avocat
(b) ⟨*heir, right, separation*⟩ légal/-e; ⟨*owner, claim*⟩ légitime
legal action *n* **to take ∼ against sb** intenter un procès à qn
legal aid *n* aide *f* juridique
legal holiday *n* (US) jour *m* férié
legalize *vtr* légaliser
legally *adv* ⟨*valid, void*⟩ juridiquement; **this contract is ∼ binding** ce contrat vous engage; ⟨*act*⟩ légalement
legal proceedings *n pl* poursuites *fpl* judiciaires
legal tender *n* monnaie *f* légale
legend *n* légende *f* (**of** de)
legendary *adj* légendaire
leggings *n pl* (for baby) collant *m*; (for woman) caleçon *m*
legible *adj* lisible
Legionnaire's disease *n* légionellose *f*
⚥ **legislation** *n* législation *f*
legitimate *adj* **(a)** (justifiable) ⟨*action, question, request*⟩ légitime; ⟨*excuse*⟩ valable
(b) (lawful) ⟨*organization*⟩ régulier/-ière; ⟨*child, heir, owner*⟩ légitime
legitimize *vtr* (legalize) légaliser; (justify) justifier
leisure ① *n* loisirs *mpl*; **to do sth at (one's) ∼** prendre son temps pour faire qch
② *adj* ⟨*centre, facilities*⟩ de loisirs
leisure centre *n* centre *m* de loisirs
leisure time *n* loisirs *mpl*, temps *m* libre
leisure wear *n* vêtements *mpl* de sport
lemon *n* (fruit) citron *m*
lemonade *n* (fizzy) limonade *f*; (still) citronnade *f*; (US) (fresh) citron *m* pressé
lemon juice *n* jus *m* de citron; (GB) (drink) citron *m* pressé
lemon tea *n* thé *m* au citron
lemon tree *n* citronnier *m*
lend *vtr* (*pp, prét* **lent**) **(a)** (loan) prêter ⟨*object, money*⟩; **to ∼ sb sth, to ∼ sth to sb** prêter qch à qn; **to ∼ a hand** donner un coup de main
(b) (give) conférer ⟨*quality, credibility*⟩ (**to** à); prêter ⟨*support*⟩; **to ∼ weight to sth** donner du poids à qch
lender *n* prêteur/-euse *m/f*
lending *n* prêt *m*
⚥ **length** ① *n* **(a)** longueur *f*; **what ∼ is the plank?** de quelle longueur est la planche?; **to be 50 cm in ∼** faire 50 cm de long
(b) (of book, film, list) longueur *f*; (of event, prison sentence) durée *f*; **∼ of time** temps *m*
(c) (of string, carpet, wood) morceau *m*; (of fabric)

≈ métrage *m*; (of pipe, track) tronçon *m*; **dress** ~ hauteur *f* de robe
(d) (Sport) longueur *f*
2 **at length** *phr* longuement
IDIOM to go to great ~s to do se donner beaucoup de mal pour faire

lengthen **1** *vtr* rallonger ‹*garment*› **(by** de, par); prolonger ‹*shelf, road*› **(by** de, par); prolonger ‹*stay*›
2 *vi* ‹*queue, list*› s'allonger; ‹*days*› rallonger

lengthy *adj* long/longue

lenient *adj* ‹*person*› indulgent/-e **(with** pour); ‹*punishment*› léger/-ère

lens *n* (in optical instruments) lentille *f*; (in spectacles) verre *m*; (in camera) objectif *m*; (contact) lentille *f*

lens cap *n* bouchon *m* d'objectif

Lent *n* carême *m*

lentil *n* lentille *f*

Leo *pr n* Lion *m*

leopard *n* léopard *m*

leotard *n* justaucorps *m inv*

leper *n* lépreux/-euse *m/f*

leprosy *n* lèpre *f*

lesbian *n* lesbienne *f*

✓ **less** **1** *det* moins de; ~ **beer** moins de bière; **I have** ~ **money than him** j'ai moins d'argent que lui
2 *pron* moins; **I have** ~ **than you** j'en ai moins que toi; ~ **than ten** moins de dix; **in** ~ **than three hours** en moins de trois heures; **even** ~ encore moins
3 *adv* moins; **I read** ~ **these days** je lis moins à présent; **the more I see him, the** ~ **I like him** plus je le vois, moins je l'aime
4 *prep* moins; ~ **15% discount** moins 15% de remise; ~ **tax** avant impôts
5 **less and less** *phr* de moins en moins

lessen *vtr* diminuer ‹*influence, feelings*›; réduire ‹*cost*›; atténuer ‹*impact, pain*›

lesser **1** *adj* moindre; **to a** ~ **extent** à un moindre degré
2 *adv* moins; ~ **known** moins connu

✓ **lesson** *n* cours *m*, leçon *f*; **Spanish** ~ cours d'espagnol; **driving** ~ leçon de conduite; **I'm going to teach him a** ~**!** je vais lui donner une bonne leçon!

✓ **let¹**

■ **Note** When *let* is used with another verb to make a suggestion (*let's do it at once*), the first person plural of the appropriate verb can generally be used to express this in French: *faisons-le tout de suite*. (Note that the verb alone translates *let us do* and no pronoun appears in French.)
— In the spoken language, however, French speakers will use the much more colloquial *on* + present tense or *si on* + imperfect tense: *let's go!* = allons-y *or* on y va!; *let's go to the cinema tonight* = si on allait au cinéma ce soir?
— These translations can also be used for suggestions in the negative: *let's not take* or *don't*

let's take the bus—let's walk = on ne prend pas le bus, on y va à pied *or* ne prenons pas le bus, allons-y à pied.
— When *let* is used to mean *allow*, it is generally translated by the verb *laisser*. For more examples and particular usages, see the entry below.

vtr (*p prés* **-tt-**, *prét, pp* **let**) **(a)** (in suggestions, commands) ~**'s get out of here!** sortons d'ici!; ~**'s not** *or* **don't** ~**'s** (GB) **talk about that!** n'en parlons pas!
(b) (allow) **to** ~ **sb do** laisser qn faire; ~ **me explain** laisse-moi t'expliquer; **don't** ~ **it get you down** ne te laisse pas abattre; **she wanted to go but they wouldn't** ~ **her** elle voulait y aller mais ils ne l'ont pas laissée faire; **to** ~ **one's hair grow** se laisser pousser les cheveux
■ **let down**: **1** ¶ ~ **[sb] down (a)** (disappoint) laisser tomber [qn]; **to feel let down** être déçu/-e
(b) (embarrass) faire honte à [qn]
2 ¶ ~ **[sth] down (a)** (GB) dégonfler ‹*tyre*›
(b) rallonger ‹*garment*›
■ **let go**: **1** ¶ ~ **go** lâcher prise; **to** ~ **go of sb/sth** lâcher qn/qch
2 ¶ ~ **[sb] go (a)** relâcher ‹*prisoner*›
(b) lâcher ‹*person, arm*›
(c) licencier ‹*employee*›
(d) to ~ **oneself go** se laisser aller
3 ¶ ~ **[sth] go** lâcher ‹*rope, bar*›
■ **let in**: **1** ¶ ~ **[sth] in** ‹*roof, window*› laisser passer ‹*rain*›; ‹*shoes*› prendre ‹*water*›; ‹*curtains*› laisser passer ‹*light*›
2 ¶ ~ **[sb] in (a)** (show in) faire entrer; (admit) laisser entrer
(b) to ~ **oneself in for** aller au devant de ‹*trouble*›
■ **let off**: **1** ¶ ~ **off [sth]** tirer ‹*fireworks*›; faire exploser ‹*bomb*›; faire partir ‹*gun*›
2 ¶ ~ **[sb] off (a)** (excuse) **to** ~ **sb off** dispenser qn de ‹*homework*›
(b) (leave unpunished) ne pas punir ‹*culprit*›
■ **let out**: **1** ¶ ~ **[sb] out** (US) ‹*school*› finir (at à)
2 ¶ ~ **out [sth] (a)** laisser échapper ‹*cry*›; **to** ~ **out a roar** beugler
(b) (GB) (reveal) révéler **(that** que)
3 ¶ ~ **[sth] out (a)** faire sortir ‹*animal*›; donner libre cours à ‹*anger*›
(b) élargir ‹*waistband*›
4 ¶ ~ **[sb] out** laisser sortir ‹*prisoner*› **(of** de); faire sortir ‹*pupils, employees*› **(of** de)
■ **let up** ‹*rain, wind*› se calmer; ‹*pressure*› s'arrêter; ‹*heat*› diminuer

let² *vtr* (*p prés* **-tt-**, *prét, pp* **let**) (*also* ~ **out** (GB)) **'to** ~**'** 'à louer'

letdown *n* déception *f*

lethal *adj* ‹*substance, gas, dose*› mortel/-elle; ‹*weapon*› meurtrier/-ière

lethargic *adj* léthargique; **to feel** ~ se sentir engourdi/-e

✓ **letter** *n* **(a)** lettre *f* **(to** pour; **from** de)
(b) (of alphabet) lettre *f*

letter bomb n lettre f piégée
letter box n boîte f à lettres
letterhead n en-tête m
letters page n courrier m des lecteurs
lettuce n salade f, laitue f
letup n accalmie f; (respite) pause f
leuk(a)emia n leucémie f
⚥ **level** 1 n (a) (gen) niveau m; **to be on the same ~ as sb** être du même niveau que qn; **at street ~** au niveau de la rue
(b) (of unemployment, illiteracy) taux m; (of spending) montant m; (of satisfaction, anxiety) degré m
(c) (in hierarchy) échelon m
2 adj (a) ⟨shelf, floor⟩ droit/-e; ⟨table⟩ horizontal/-e
(b) ⟨ground, surface, land⟩ plat/-e
(c) (Culin) ⟨teaspoonful⟩ ras/-e
(d) **to be ~** ⟨shoulders, windows⟩ être à la même hauteur; ⟨floor, building⟩ être au même niveau; **~ with the ground** au ras du sol
(e) **to remain ~** ⟨figures⟩ rester stable
3 adv **to draw ~** arriver à la même hauteur (**with** que)
4 vtr (p prés etc **-ll-** (GB), **-l-** (US))
(a) (destroy) raser ⟨village⟩
(b) lancer ⟨accusation⟩ (**at** contre); adresser ⟨criticism⟩ (**at** à); braquer ⟨gun⟩ (**at** sur)
(c) aplanir ⟨ground, surface⟩
IDIOMS **to be ~-pegging** être à égalité; **to ~ with sb** être honnête avec qn
■ **level off** ⟨prices, curve⟩ se stabiliser
level crossing n passage m à niveau
level-headed adj sensé/-e
lever n (Aut, Tech) levier m; (small) manette f
levy 1 n taxe f, impôt m
2 vtr prélever ⟨tax, duty⟩; imposer ⟨fine⟩
lewd adj ⟨joke, gesture, remark⟩ obscène; ⟨person⟩ lubrique
lexicon n lexique m
liability 1 n (a) (Law) responsabilité f
(b) (drawback) handicap m
2 **liabilities** n pl passif m, dettes fpl
liable adj (a) (likely) **to be ~ to do** risquer de faire; **it's ~ to rain** il risque de pleuvoir, il se peut qu'il pleuve
(b) (legally subject) **to be ~ to** être passible de ⟨fine⟩; **to be ~ for tax** ⟨person, company⟩ être imposable; ⟨goods⟩ être soumis/-e à l'impôt
liaise vi travailler en liaison (**with** avec)
liaison n liaison f
liar n menteur/-euse m/f
libel 1 n diffamation f
2 vtr (p prés etc **-ll-** (GB), **-l-** (US)) diffamer
libellous (GB), **libelous** (US) adj diffamatoire
liberal 1 n libéral/-e m/f
2 adj (a) (politically) libéral/-e

(b) ⟨amount⟩ généreux/-euse; ⟨person⟩ prodigue (**with** de)
Liberal n libéral/-e m/f
Liberal Democrat n (GB) libéral-démocrate mf
liberalism n libéralisme m
liberalize vtr libéraliser
liberate 1 vtr libérer (**from** de)
2 **liberated** pp adj ⟨lifestyle, woman⟩ libéré/-e
3 **liberating** pres p adj libérateur/-trice
liberation n libération f (**from** de); **women's ~** libération de la femme
liberty n liberté f
Libra n Balance f
librarian n bibliothécaire mf
⚥ **library** n bibliothèque f; **public ~** bibliothèque municipale; **mobile ~** (GB); bibliobus m
lice n pl poux mpl
⚥ **licence** (GB), **license** (US) n (a) (for trading) licence f
(b) (to drive, fish) permis m; (for TV) redevance f; **to lose one's (driving) ~** se faire retirer son permis (de conduire)
(c) (freedom) licence f
licence number n (of car) numéro m minéralogique or d'immatriculation
licence plate n plaque f minéralogique or d'immatriculation
license 1 n (US) = LICENCE
2 vtr (a) (authorize) autoriser (**to do** à faire)
(b) faire immatriculer ⟨vehicle⟩
licensed adj (a) ⟨restaurant⟩ qui a une licence de débit de boissons
(b) ⟨dealer, firm, taxi⟩ agréé/-e; ⟨pilot⟩ breveté/-e; ⟨vehicle⟩ en règle
licensing laws n pl (GB) lois fpl réglementant la vente des boissons alcoolisées
lick 1 n (a) coup m de langue
(b) **a ~ of paint** un petit coup de peinture
2 vtr (a) lécher; **to ~ one's lips** se lécher les babines
(b) (colloq) écraser ⟨team, opponent⟩; **to get ~ed** se faire écraser
IDIOM **to ~ one's wounds** panser ses blessures
licorice (US) = LIQUORICE
lid n (a) (cover) couvercle m
(b) (eyelid) paupière f
⚥ **lie** 1 n mensonge m; **to tell a ~** mentir
2 vi (a) (p prés **lying**, prét pp **lied**) (tell falsehood) mentir (**to sb** à qn, **about** à propos de); **he ~d about her** il a menti à son propos
(b) (p prés **lying**, prét **lay**, pp **lain**, also for c & d) ⟨person, animal⟩ (action) s'allonger; (state) être allongé/-e; ⟨objects⟩ être couché/-e; **he was lying on the bed** il était allongé sur le lit; **to ~ on one's back** s'allonger sur le dos; **~ still** ne bougez pas; **here ~s John Brown** ci-gît John Brown

---

⚥ indicates a very frequent word

(c) (be situated) être; **to ~ open** ‹book› être ouvert/-e; **that's where our future ~s** c'est là qu'est notre avenir; **to ~ before sb** ‹life, career› s'ouvrir devant qn; **what ~s ahead?** qu'est-ce qui nous attend?; **the house lay empty for years** la maison est restée vide pendant des années

(d) (can be found) résider; **their interests ~ elsewhere** leurs intérêts résident ailleurs; **to ~ in** ‹cause, secret, talent› résider dans; ‹popularity, strength, fault› venir de; **the responsibility ~s with them** ce sont eux qui sont responsables

IDIOMS **to ~ low** garder un profil bas; **to take it lying down** (colloq) se laisser faire
■ **lie around** traîner; **to leave sth lying around** laisser traîner qch
■ **lie down** (briefly) s'allonger; (for longer period) se coucher

lie detector n détecteur m de mensonge

lie-in n **to have a ~** faire la grasse matinée

lieu ① **in lieu** adv phr **one week's holiday in ~** une semaine de vacances pour compenser
② **in lieu of** prep phr à la place de

✍ **life** n (pl **lives**) **(a)** (gen) vie f; **that's ~!** c'est la vie!; **the first time in my ~** la première fois de ma vie; **a job for ~** un emploi à vie; **a friend for ~** un ami pour la vie; **for the rest of one's ~** pour le restant de ses jours; **full of ~** plein/-e de vie; **to come to ~** ‹shy person› sortir de sa réserve; ‹fictional character› prendre vie; ‹party› s'animer
(b) (of machine, product) durée f
(c) (Law) **to serve ~** être emprisonné/-e à vie; **to sentence sb to ~** condamner qn à perpétuité
IDIOM **to have the time of one's ~** s'amuser comme un fou/une folle

lifebelt n bouée f de sauvetage

lifeboat n canot m de sauvetage

life drawing n dessin m d'après modèle

life-expectancy n espérance f de vie; (of product) durée f probable

lifeguard n surveillant/-e m/f de baignade

life imprisonment n réclusion f à perpétuité

life insurance n assurance-vie f

lifejacket n gilet m de sauvetage

lifeless adj ‹body, object› inanimé/-e; ‹performance› peu vivant/-e; ‹voice› éteint/-e

lifelike adj très ressemblant/-e

lifeline n bouée f de sauvetage

lifelong adj ‹friendship, fear› de toute une vie; **to have had a ~ ambition to do** avoir toujours rêvé de faire

lifesaving n (gen) sauvetage m; (Med) secourisme m

life sentence n condamnation f à perpétuité

life-size adj grandeur nature inv

life span n durée f de vie

life story n vie f

lifestyle n style m de vie

life-support machine n **to be on a ~** être sous assistance respiratoire

lifetime n vie f; **in her ~** de son vivant; **the chance of a ~** une chance unique; **to seem like a ~** sembler une éternité

✍ **lift** ① n **(a)** (GB) (elevator) ascenseur m; (for goods) monte-charge m inv
(b) (ride) **she asked me for a ~** elle m'a demandé de la conduire; **can I give you a ~?** je peux te déposer quelque part?
(c) (colloq) (boost) **to give sb a ~** remonter le moral à qn
② vtr **(a)** (pick up) soulever ‹object, person›; **to ~ sth out of the box** sortir qch de la boîte
(b) (raise) lever ‹arm, head›
(c) (remove) lever ‹ban, sanctions›
(d) (boost) **to ~ sb's spirits** remonter le moral à qn
(e) (colloq) (steal) piquer (fam) **(from** dans)
③ vi ‹bad mood, headache› disparaître; ‹fog› se dissiper
■ **lift off:** ① ¶ **~ off** ‹rocket› décoller; ‹top, cover› s'enlever
② ¶ **~ [sth] off** enlever ‹cover, lid›
■ **lift up** soulever ‹book, suitcase, lid›; lever ‹head, veil, eyes›; relever ‹jumper, coat›

lift-off n lancement m

ligament n ligament m

✍ **light** ① n **(a)** (brightness) lumière f; **against the ~** à contre-jour
(b) (in building, machine) lumière f; (in street) réverbère m; (on ship) feu m; (on dashboard) voyant m (lumineux)
(c) (Aut) (headlight) phare m; (rearlight) feu m arrière; (inside car) veilleuse f
(d) (flame) **to set ~ to** mettre le feu à; **have you got a ~?** tu as du feu?
(e) (aspect) jour m; **to see sth in a different ~** voir qch sous un jour différent
(f) **to come to** or **be brought to ~** être découvert/-e
② **lights** n pl (traffic) **~s** feu m, feux mpl; **the ~s are red** le feu est au rouge
③ adj **(a)** (bright) **to get** or **grow ~er** ‹sky› s'éclaircir; **while it's still ~** pendant qu'il fait encore jour
(b) ‹colour, wood, skin› clair/-e; **~ blue** bleu clair inv
(c) ‹material, wind, clothing, meal› léger/-ère; ‹rain› fin/-e; ‹drinker› modéré/-e; **to be a ~ sleeper** avoir le sommeil léger
(d) ‹knock, footsteps› léger/-ère
(e) ‹work› peu fatigant/-e; ‹exercise› léger/-ère
(f) ‹music› léger/-ère; **a bit of ~ relief** un peu de divertissement; **some ~ reading** quelque chose de facile à lire
④ vtr (prét, pp **lit** ou **lighted**) **(a)** allumer ‹oven, cigarette, fire›; enflammer ‹paper›; craquer ‹match›
(b) ‹torch, lamp› éclairer

⋯›

■ **light up** ⟨*lamp*⟩ s'allumer; ⟨*face*⟩ s'éclairer; ⟨*eyes*⟩ briller de joie

light bulb *n* ampoule *f*

lighten ① *vtr* éclaircir ⟨*colour, hair, skin*⟩; détendre ⟨*atmosphere*⟩
② *vi* ⟨*sky, hair*⟩ s'éclaircir; ⟨*atmosphere*⟩ se détendre

light entertainment *n* variétés *fpl*

lighter *n* (for smokers) briquet *m*; (for gas cooker) allume-gaz *m inv*

lighter fuel *n* (gas) gaz *m* à briquet; (liquid) essence *f* à briquet

light-hearted *adj* ⟨*person*⟩ enjoué/-e; ⟨*book*⟩ humoristique

lighthouse *n* phare *m*

lighting *n* éclairage *m*

lightly *adv* (a) ⟨*touch, kiss, season*⟩ légèrement
(b) ⟨*undertake, dismiss*⟩ à la légère
(c) **to get off** ∼ s'en tirer à bon compte

lightning ① *n* (in sky) éclairs *mpl*; (striking sth) foudre *f*; **a flash of** ∼ un éclair; **struck by** ∼ frappé/-e par la foudre
② *adj* ⟨*visit, raid*⟩ éclair *inv*

light switch *n* interrupteur *m*

lightweight *adj* ⟨*garment*⟩ léger/-ère; ⟨*champion*⟩ des poids légers

light year *n* année-lumière *f*

꜒ **like¹** ① *prep* (a) (gen) comme; **to be** ∼ **sb/sth** être comme qn/qch; **to look** ∼ ressembler à; **big cities** ∼ **London** les grandes villes comme Londres *or* telles que Londres; **you know what she's** ∼! tu sais comment elle est!; **it was just** ∼ **a fairytale!** on aurait dit un conte de fée!; **it looks** ∼ **rain** on dirait qu'il va pleuvoir; **what's it** ∼? c'est comment?; **what was the weather** ∼? quel temps faisait-il?
(b) (typical of) **it's not** ∼ **her to be late** ça ne lui ressemble pas *or* ce n'est pas son genre d'être en retard; **that's just** ∼ **him!** c'est bien (de) lui!
② *conj* (a) (in the same way as) comme; ∼ **they used to** comme ils le faisaient autrefois
(b) (colloq) (as if) comme si; **he acts** ∼ **he owns the place** il se conduit comme s'il était chez lui
③ *n* **fires, floods and the** ∼ les incendies, les inondations et autres catastrophes de ce genre; **she won't speak to the** ∼**s of us!** (colloq) elle refuse de parler à des gens comme nous!

꜒ **like²** *vtr* (a) aimer bien ⟨*person*⟩; aimer (bien) ⟨*artist, food, music, style*⟩; **to** ∼ **doing** *or* **to do** aimer (bien) faire; **to** ∼ **A best** préférer A; **how do you** ∼ **living in London?** ça te plaît de vivre à Londres?; **she doesn't** ∼ **to be kept waiting** elle n'aime pas qu'on la fasse attendre
(b) (wish) vouloir, aimer; **I would** ∼ **a ticket**

꜒ indicates a very frequent word

je voudrais un billet; **I would** ∼ **to do** je voudrais *or* j'aimerais faire; **would you** ∼ **to come to dinner?** voudriez-vous venir dîner?; **we'd** ∼ **her to come** nous voudrions *or* aimerions qu'elle vienne; **if you** ∼ si tu veux; **you can do what you** ∼ tu peux faire ce que tu veux

likeable *adj* ⟨*person*⟩ sympathique; ⟨*novel, music*⟩ agréable

likelihood *n* probabilité *f*, chances *fpl*; **in all** ∼ selon toute probabilité

꜒ **likely** *adj* (a) (probable) probable; ⟨*explanation*⟩ plausible; **prices are** ∼ **to rise** les prix risquent d'augmenter; **it is** *or* **seems** ∼ **that she'll come** il est probable qu'elle viendra; **it is hardly** ∼ **that she'll come** il y a peu de chances qu'elle vienne; **a** ∼ **story!** à d'autres! (fam)
(b) (promising) ⟨*candidate*⟩ prometteur/-euse

like-minded *adj* du même avis

liken *vtr* comparer (**to** à)

likeness *n* (a) (similarity) ressemblance *f*; **family** ∼ air *m* de famille
(b) (picture) **to be a good** ∼ être ressemblant/-e

likewise *adv* (similarly) également, de même; (also) aussi, de même

liking *n* **to take a** ∼ **to sb** se prendre d'affection pour qn; **to be to sb's** ∼ plaire à qn

lilac *n, adj* lilas *m inv*

lily *n* lys *m inv*

lily of the valley *n* muguet *m*

limb *n* (a) (arm, leg) membre *m*
(b) (of tree) branche *f* (maîtresse)

limber *v*

■ **limber up** s'échauffer

limbo *n* (a) (state) les limbes *mpl*; **to be in** ∼ être dans les limbes
(b) (dance) limbo *m*

lime *n* (a) (calcium) chaux *f*
(b) (fruit) citron *m* vert
(c) (*also* ∼ **tree**) tilleul *m*

lime green *n, adj* citron *m* vert *inv*

lime juice *n* jus *m* de citron vert

limelight *n* vedette *f*; **to be in the** ∼ tenir la vedette

limestone *n* calcaire *m*

꜒ **limit** ① *n* limite *f*; **within** ∼**s** dans une certaine limite; **to push sb to the** ∼ pousser qn à bout
② *vtr* limiter (**to** à)

limitation *n* (a) (restriction) restriction *f* (**on** à)
(b) (shortcoming) limite *f*; **to know one's (own)** ∼**s** connaître ses propres limites

꜒ **limited** *adj* limité/-e

limited company *n* (GB) société *f* anonyme

limousine *n* limousine *f*

limp ① *n* **to have a** ∼ boiter

2 *adj* mou/molle

3 *vi* boiter; **to ~ in/away** entrer/s'éloigner en boitant

linchpin *n* (essential element) **the ~ of** ⟨*person*⟩ le pilier de

✦ line **1** *n* (a) (gen, Sport) ligne *f*; (shorter, thicker) trait *m*; (in drawing) trait *m*; **a straight ~** une ligne droite
(b) (of people, cars) file *f*; (of trees) rangée *f*; **to stand** *or* **wait in ~** faire la queue
(c) (on face) ride *f*
(d) (rope) corde *f*; (for fishing) ligne *f*; **to put the washing on the ~** étendre le linge
(e) (electric cable) ligne *f* (électrique)
(f) (phone connection) ligne *f*; **at the other end of the ~** au bout du fil; **the ~ went dead** la ligne a été coupée
(g) (rail route) ligne *f* (**between** entre); (rails) voie *f*
(h) (shipping company, airline) compagnie *f*
(i) (in genealogy) lignée *f*
(j) (in prose) ligne *f*; (in poetry) vers *m*; **to learn one's ~s** ⟨*actor*⟩ apprendre son texte
(k) **to fall into ~ with** s'aligner sur; **to bring sb into ~** ramener qn dans le rang; **to keep sb in ~** tenir qn en main
(l) (stance) **the official ~** la position officielle; **to take a firm ~ with sb** se montrer ferme avec qn
(m) (type of product) gamme *f*
(n) (Mil) enemy ~s lignes *fpl* ennemies
2 *vtr* doubler ⟨*garment*⟩ (**with** avec); tapisser ⟨*shelf*⟩ (**with** de); border ⟨*route*⟩
3 **in line with** *phr* en accord avec ⟨*policy, trend*⟩; **to increase in ~ with** augmenter proportionnellement à
■ line up: **1** ¶ **~ up** (side by side) se mettre en rang; (one behind the other) se mettre en file
2 ¶ **~ [sth] up** (a) (align) aligner (**with** sur)
(b) sélectionner ⟨*team*⟩

lined *adj* ⟨*face*⟩ ridé/-e; ⟨*paper*⟩ ligné/-e; ⟨*curtains*⟩ doublé/-e

line manager *n* responsable opérationnel/-elle *m/f*

linen *n* (a) (fabric) lin *m*
(b) (household) linge *m* de maison; (underwear) linge *m* de corps

linen basket *n* panier *m* à linge sale

linen cupboard (GB), **linen closet** (US) *n* armoire *f* à linge

line of fire *n* ligne *f* de tir

line of work *n* métier *m*

liner *n* paquebot *m* de grande ligne

linesman *n* (GB) (in tennis) juge *m* de ligne; (in football, hockey) juge *m* de touche

line-up *n* (Sport) équipe *f*; (personnel, pop group) groupe *m*

linger *vi* (a) ⟨*person*⟩ s'attarder; ⟨*gaze*⟩ s'attarder (**on** sur)
(b) ⟨*memory, smell*⟩ persister
(c) ⟨*doubt, suspicion*⟩ subsister

lingerie *n* lingerie *f*

linguist *n* linguiste *mf*

linguistic *adj* linguistique

linguistics *n* linguistique *f*

lining *n* doublure *f*

✦ link **1** *n* (a) (in chain) maillon *m*
(b) (connection by rail, road) liaison *f*
(c) (between facts, events) rapport *m* (**between** entre); (between people) lien *m* (**with** avec)
(d) (tie) relation *f*, lien *m*
(e) (in TV, radio, computing) liaison *f*
2 *vtr* (a) ⟨*road, cable*⟩ relier ⟨*places, objects*⟩; **to ~ A to B** *or* **A and B** relier A à B; **to ~ arms** ⟨*people*⟩ se donner le bras
(b) **to ~ sth to** *or* **with** lier qch à ⟨*inflation*⟩; établir un lien entre qch et ⟨*fact, crime, illness*⟩
(c) connecter ⟨*terminals*⟩
(d) (in TV, radio) établir une liaison entre ⟨*places*⟩ (**by** par)
3 **linked** *pp adj* ⟨*circles, symbols*⟩ entrelacé/-e; ⟨*issues, problems*⟩ lié/-e
■ link up: **1** ¶ **~ up** ⟨*firms*⟩ s'associer; **to ~ up with** s'associer avec ⟨*college, firm*⟩
2 ¶ **~ [sth] up** relier

link road *n* route *f* de raccordement

link-up *n* (a) (on TV, radio) liaison *f*
(b) (collaboration) association *f*

lino *n* lino *m*

lint *n* tissu *m* ouaté

lion *n* lion *m*

lion cub *n* lionceau *m*

lioness *n* lionne *f*

✦ lip *n* (a) lèvre *f*
(b) (of jug) bec *m*

liposuction *n* liposuccion *f*

lip-read *vi* (*prét, pp* **-read**) lire sur les lèvres de quelqu'un

lipsalve *n* baume *m* pour les lèvres

lip service *n* **to pay ~ to feminism** se dire féministe pour la forme

lipstick *n* rouge *m* à lèvres

liqueur *n* liqueur *f*

liquid *n, adj* liquide *m*

liquidate *vtr* liquider

liquidation *n* liquidation *f*

liquidizer *n* (GB Culin) mixeur *m*

liquor *n* alcool *m*

liquorice, licorice (US) *n* (a) (plant) réglisse *f*
(b) (substance) réglisse *m*

liquor store *n* (US) magasin *m* de vins et spiritueux

Lisbon *pr n* Lisbonne

lisp *n* zézaiement *m*; **to have a ~** zézayer

✦ list **1** *n* liste *f* (**of** de)
2 *vtr* (a) (gen) faire la liste de ⟨*objects, people*⟩; **to be ~ed in a directory** être repris/-e dans un répertoire

⋯⟫

(b) (Comput) lister
3 *vi* ‹*vessel*› donner de la bande
4 **listed** *pp adj* (GB) ‹*building*› classé; ‹*company*› coté/-e en Bourse

ℐ **listen** *vi* écouter; **to ~ to sb/sth** écouter qn/qch; **to ~ to reason** écouter la voix de la raison; **to ~ (out) for** guetter
■ **listen in** écouter (par indiscrétion)

listener *n* **(a) to be a good ~** savoir écouter
(b) (to radio) auditeur/-trice *m/f*

listeria *n* (bacteria) listéria *f*; (illness) listériose *f*

listing **1** *n* **(a)** inscription *f* (in dans); **Stock Exchange ~** liste *f* des sociétés cotées en Bourse
(b) (Comput) listing *m*
2 **listings** *n pl* pages *fpl* d'informations

listless *adj* ‹*person*› apathique

list price *n* prix *m* au catalogue

literacy *n* (in a population) taux *m* d'alphabétisation

literal *adj* **(a)** ‹*meaning*› littéral/-e
(b) ‹*translation*› mot à mot

literally *adv* ‹*mean*› littéralement; ‹*translate*› mot à mot; **to take sth ~** prendre qch au pied de la lettre; **(quite) ~** bel et bien

literary *adj* littéraire

literary criticism *n* critique *f* littéraire

literate *adj* **(a)** (able to read and write) **to be ~** savoir lire et écrire
(b) (cultured) ‹*person*› cultivé/-e

ℐ **literature** *n* **(a)** littérature *f*; **a work of ~** une œuvre littéraire
(b) (pamphlets, brochures) documentation *f*

lithe *adj* leste

Lithuania *pr n* Lituanie *f*

litigation *n* litiges *mpl*

litre, **liter** (US) *n* litre *m*

litter **1** *n* **(a)** (rubbish) détritus *mpl*; (substantial) ordures *fpl*; (paper) papiers *mpl*
(b) (of young) portée *f*; **to have a ~** mettre bas
(c) (for pet tray) litière *f*
2 *vtr* **to be ~ed with** ‹*ground*› être jonché/-e de

litter bin *n* poubelle *f*

ℐ **little**

■ **Note** When *a little* is used as a pronoun and if the sentence does not specify what it refers to, the pronoun *en* (= *of it*) must be added before the verb: *I have a little left* = il m'en reste un peu.

1 *adj* **(a)** (small) petit/-e (*before n*)
(b) (not much) peu de; **~ chance** peu de chances; **very ~ damage** très peu de dégâts; **there's so ~ time** il y a si peu de temps
2 *pron* **a ~** un peu; **I only ate a ~** je n'en ai mangé qu'un peu; **he remembers very ~** il ne se souvient pas bien; **there's ~ I can do** je ne peux pas faire grand-chose; **to do as ~**

as possible en faire le moins possible; **~ or nothing** quasiment rien
3 *adv* **(a)** (not much) peu; **I go there very ~** j'y vais très peu; **the next results were ~ better** les résultats suivants étaient à peine meilleurs; **~ more than an hour ago** il y a à peine plus d'une heure
(b) (not at all) **~ did they know that** ils étaient bien loin de se douter que
4 **a little (bit)** *phr* un peu; **a ~ (bit) anxious** un peu inquiet/-iète; **a ~ less/more** un peu moins/plus; **stay a ~ longer** reste encore un peu
5 **as little as** *phr* **for as ~ as 10 dollars a day** pour seulement 10 dollars par jour; **as ~ as £60** juste 60 livres sterling
IDIOM ~ by ~ petit à petit

little finger *n* petit doigt *m*, auriculaire *m*
IDIOM to wrap *or* **twist sb around one's ~** mener qn par le bout du nez

ℐ **live¹** *vi* **(a)** (gen) vivre; **as long as I ~**... tant que je vivrai...; **to ~ to regret sth** en venir à regretter qch; **long ~ democracy!** vive la démocratie!; **to ~ on** *or* **off** vivre de ‹*fruit, charity*›; vivre sur ‹*wage*›
(b) (dwell) ‹*person*› vivre, habiter (**with** avec); ‹*animal*› vivre; **they ~ at number 7** ils habitent au numéro 7; **to ~ in** vivre dans, habiter ‹*house, apartment*›; **easy to ~ with** facile à vivre
(c) (put up with) **to ~ with** accepter ‹*situation*›; supporter ‹*decor*›
IDIOM to ~ it up (colloq) mener la grande vie
■ **live in** ‹*maid*› être logé/-e et nourri/-e
■ **live on** ‹*reputation, tradition*› se perpétuer
■ **live up to** ‹*person*› répondre à ‹*expectations*›; être à la hauteur de ‹*reputation*›

live² **1** *adj* **(a)** (alive) vivant/-e
(b) ‹*broadcast*› en direct; ‹*performance*› sur scène; ‹*album*› enregistré/-e en public; **before a ~ audience** devant un public
(c) ‹*cable*› sous tension
2 *adv* ‹*appear, broadcast*› en direct

live-in *adj* ‹*maid, nanny*› qui est logé/-e et nourri/-e; **to have a ~ lover** vivre en concubinage

livelihood *n* gagne-pain *m*

lively *adj* **(a)** ‹*person*› plein/-e d'entrain; ‹*place, atmosphere, conversation*› animé/-e
(b) (fast) ‹*pace*› vif/vive; ‹*music, dance*› entraînant/-e

liven
■ **liven up**: **1** **¶ ~ up** s'animer
2 **¶ ~ [sth] up** animer ‹*event*›

liver *n* foie *m*

livery *n* **(a)** (uniform) livrée *f*
(b) (boarding horses) **at ~** en pension

livestock *n* bétail *m*

live wire *n* boute-en-train *m inv*

livid *adj* **(a)** (furious) furieux/-ieuse
(b) (in colour) ‹*face, scar*› livide

ℐ indicates a very frequent word

✓ **living** ① n **(a)** vie f; **to work for a ~** travailler pour gagner sa vie; **what do you do for a ~?** qu'est-ce que vous faites dans la vie?
(b) (lifestyle) vie f; **easy ~** une vie facile
② adj vivant/-e; **within ~ memory** de mémoire d'homme

living conditions n pl conditions fpl de vie

living expenses n pl frais mpl de subsistance

living room n salle f de séjour, salon m

living standards n pl niveau m de vie

living together n cohabitation f

living will n: déclaration écrite (de l'intéressé) refusant l'acharnement thérapeutique

lizard n lézard m

llama n lama m

load ① n **(a)** (gen) charge f; (on vehicle, animal) chargement m; (on ship, plane) cargaison f; (figurative) fardeau m; **three (lorry-)~s of sand** trois camions de sable
(b) (colloq) (a lot) **a (whole) ~ of people** des tas (fam) de gens; **that's a ~ of nonsense** (colloq) c'est vraiment n'importe quoi (fam)
② **loads** n pl (colloq) **~s of** (+ plural nouns) des tas (fam) de; **~s of times** plein de or des tas (fam) de fois; **we've got ~s of time** nous avons tout notre temps; **~s of work** un travail fou (fam)
③ vtr **(a)** (gen) charger ‹vehicle, gun› (with de); mettre un film dans ‹camera›
(b) (Comput) charger ‹program›
(c) to ~ sb with combler qn de ‹presents, honours›

loaded adj **(a)** ‹tray, lorry, gun› chargé/-e (with de)
(b) (colloq) (rich) bourré/-e de fric (fam)
(c) ‹question› tendancieux/-ieuse

loaf n (pl **loaves**) pain m; **a ~ of bread** un pain
■ **loaf about**, **loaf around** traînasser

loafer n **(a)** (shoe) mocassin m
(b) (idler) flemmard/-e m/f (fam)

✓ **loan** ① n (when borrowing) emprunt m; (when lending) prêt m; **to be on ~** être prêté/-e (**to** à)
② vtr (also **~ out**) prêter (**to** à)

loan shark n (colloq) usurier/-ière m/f

loath adj **to be ~ to do** répugner à faire

loathe vtr détester (**doing** faire)

loathsome adj répugnant/-e

lobby ① n **(a)** (of hotel) hall m; (of theatre) lobby m
(b) (also **~ group**) lobby m
② vi faire pression (**for** pour obtenir)

lobbying n lobbying m

lobe n lobe m

lobster n homard m

✓ **local** ① n **(a) the ~s** les gens mpl du coin
(b) (pub) pub m du coin

② adj (gen) local/-e; ‹library, shop› du quartier; ‹radio, news› régional/-e

local anaesthetic n anesthésique m local

local authority n (GB) autorités fpl locales

local call n communication f téléphonique locale

local election n élection f locale

local government n administration f locale

locality n **(a)** (neighbourhood) voisinage m
(b) (place) endroit m

localization n localisation f

localized adj localisé/-e

✓ **locate** vtr **(a)** (find) retrouver ‹object›; localiser ‹fault›
(b) (position) situer ‹site›

✓ **location** n endroit m; **on ~** ‹filmed› en extérieur

✓ **lock** ① n **(a)** (with key) serrure f; (with bolt) verrou m; **under ~ and key** sous clé
(b) (of hair) mèche f
(c) (on canal) écluse f
(d) (Comput) verrouillage m
② vtr fermer [qch] à clé
③ vi **(a)** ‹door, drawer› fermer à clé
(b) ‹steering wheel› se bloquer
■ **lock in** enfermer ‹person›; **to ~ oneself in** s'enfermer
■ **lock out:** **~ sb out** enfermer qn dehors; **to ~ oneself out** s'enfermer dehors
■ **lock together** ‹components, pieces› s'emboîter
■ **lock up:** ① ¶ **~ up** fermer
② ¶ **~ [sth] up** fermer [qch] à clé ‹house›
③ ¶ **~ [sb] up** enfermer ‹hostage›; mettre [qn] sous les verrous ‹killer›

locker n casier m, vestiaire m

locker room n vestiaire m

locket n médaillon m

locksmith n serrurier m

locomotive n locomotive f

locum n (GB) remplaçant/-e m/f

lodge ① n (small house) pavillon m; (for gatekeeper) loge f (du gardien)
② vtr **to ~ an appeal** faire appel; **to ~ a complaint** porter plainte; **to ~ a protest** protester
③ vi **(a)** ‹person› loger (**with** chez)
(b) ‹bullet› se loger; ‹small object› se coincer

lodger n (room only) locataire mf; (with meals) pensionnaire mf

lodgings n pl logement m

loft n **(a)** (attic) grenier m
(b) (US) (apartment) loft m

loft conversion n aménagement m de grenier

log ① n **(a)** (of wood) rondin m; (for burning) bûche f
(b) (of ship) journal m de bord; (of plane) ⋯➤

carnet *m* de vol

2 *vtr* (*p prés etc* **-gg-**) **(a)** (record) noter **(b)** (*also* ~ **up**) avoir à son actif ‹*miles*› **IDIOM to sleep like a** ~ dormir comme une souche

■ **log in**, **log on** ouvrir une session, se connecter

■ **log off**, **log out** clore une session, se déconnecter

log book *n* (of car) ≈ carte *f* grise; (written record) registre *m*

log cabin *n* cabane *f* en rondins

log fire *n* feu *m* de bois

loggerheads *n pl* **to be at** ~ être en désaccord (**with** avec)

logic *n* logique *f*

logical *adj* logique

logistics *n* logistique *f*

logo *n* logo *m*

log-off *n* fin *f* de connexion

log-on *n* début *m* de connexion

loin *n* (Culin) (GB) ≈ côtes *fpl* premières; (US) ≈ filet *m*

loiter *vi* (idly) traîner; (pleasurably) flâner; (suspiciously) rôder

loll *vi* ‹*person*› se prélasser; ‹*head*› tomber; ‹*tongue*› pendre

lollipop *n* sucette *f*

London *pr n* Londres

Londoner *n* Londonien/-ienne *m/f*

lone *adj* solitaire

loneliness *n* (of person) solitude *f*; (of place) isolement *m*

lonely *adj* ‹*person*› seul/-e; ‹*life*› solitaire; ‹*place*› isolé/-e

lonely hearts' column *n* petites annonces *fpl* (*de rencontre*)

loner *n* solitaire *mf*

lonesome *adj* (US) solitaire

⚘ **long** 1 *adj* (gen) long/longue; ‹*delay*› important/-e; ‹*grass*› haut/-e; **to be 20 minutes** ~ durer 20 minutes; **to be 20 metres** ~ avoir *or* faire 20 mètres de long; **to get** ~er ‹*days, list, queue*› s'allonger; ‹*grass, hair*› pousser; **she's been away a** ~ **time** elle est restée longtemps absente; **it's been a** ~ **time since…**; ça fait longtemps que…; **to take a** ~ **time** ‹*person*› être lent/-e; ‹*task*› prendre longtemps; **a** ~ **way off** loin; **we've come a** ~ **way** nous avons fait beaucoup de chemin

2 *adv* **(a)** (a long time) longtemps; **I won't be** ~ je n'en ai pas pour longtemps; **how** ~ **will you be?** tu en as pour combien de temps?; **how** ~ **did it take him?** il lui a fallu combien de temps?; **how** ~ **is the interval?** combien de temps dure l'entracte?; **I haven't got** ~ je n'ai pas beaucoup de temps; ~**er than he thought** plus de temps qu'il ne pensait;

before ~ (in past) peu après; (in future) dans peu de temps; **not for** ~ pas longtemps; ~ **after** longtemps après; **not** ~ **after** peu après; ~ **ago** il y a longtemps; ~ **before** bien avant; **he's no** ~er **head** il n'est plus chef; **I can't stay any** ~er je ne peux pas rester plus longtemps

(b) (for a long time) depuis longtemps; **those days are** ~ **gone** ce temps-là n'est plus

3 *vi* **to** ~ **for sth** avoir très envie de qch; **to** ~ **to do** rêver de faire

4 **as long as** *phr* (provided) du moment que (+ *indicative*), pourvu que (+ *subjunctive*)

IDIOMS ~ **time no see!** (colloq) ça fait une paye (fam) qu'on ne s'est pas vus!; **so** ~! (colloq) salut!

long-awaited *adj* longtemps attendu/-e

long-distance *adj* ‹*runner*› de fond; ‹*telephone call*› (within the country) interurbain/-e; ‹*lorry driver*› (GB); routier *m*

long-haired *adj* ‹*person*› aux cheveux longs; ‹*animal*› à poil long

longhand *n* **in** ~ écrit/-e à la main

long-haul *adj* ‹*flight, aircraft*› long-courrier *inv*

longing *n* **(a)** grand désir *m* (**for** de; **to do** de faire) **(b)** (nostalgia) nostalgie *f* (**for** de)

longitude *n* longitude *f*

long jump *n* (GB) saut *m* en longueur

long-life *adj* ‹*milk*› longue conservation *inv*; ‹*battery*› longue durée *inv*

long-range *adj* ‹*missile*› (à) longue portée; ‹*forecast*› à long terme

long-sighted *adj* presbyte

long-standing *adj* de longue date

long term 1 *n* **in the** ~ à long terme 2 **long-term** *adj*, *adv* à long terme

long-time *adj* de longue date

long-wave *n* grandes ondes *fpl*

long-winded *adj* verbeux/-euse

loo *n* (GB) (colloq) vécés *mpl* (fam), toilettes *fpl*

⚘ **look** 1 *n* **(a)** (glance) coup *m* d'œil; **to have** *or* **take a** ~ **at sth** jeter un coup d'œil à *or* sur qch; **to have** *or* **take a good** ~ **at** regarder [qch] de près; **to have a** ~ **inside/behind sth** regarder à l'intérieur de/derrière qch; **to have a** ~ **round** faire un tour dans ‹*park, town*›

(b) (search) **to have a (good)** ~ (bien) chercher

(c) (expression) regard *m*; **a** ~ **of sadness** un regard triste; **from the** ~ **on his face…** à son expression…

(d) (appearance) (of person) air *m*; (of building, scenery) aspect *m*

2 **looks** *n pl* ~**s aren't everything** il n'y a pas que la beauté qui compte; **he's losing his** ~**s** il n'est pas aussi beau qu'autrefois

3 *vi* **(a)** regarder (**into** dans; **over** par-dessus); **to** ~ **away** détourner le regard

or les yeux; **to ~ out of the window** regarder par la fenêtre

(b) (search) chercher, regarder

(c) (appear, seem) avoir l'air, paraître; **you ~ cold** tu as l'air d'avoir froid; **he ~s young for his age** il fait jeune pour son âge; **that makes you ~ younger** ça te rajeunit; **the picture will ~ good in the study** le tableau ira bien dans le bureau; **it doesn't ~ right** ça ne va pas; **things are ~ing good** les choses se présentent bien; **to ~ like sb/sth** ressembler à qn/qch; **what does the house ~ like?** comment est la maison?; **it ~s like rain** on dirait qu'il va pleuvoir

4 *vtr* **(a)** (gaze, stare) regarder; **to ~ sb in the eye** regarder qn dans les yeux

(b) (appear) **to ~ one's age** faire son âge; **she's 40 but she doesn't ~ it** elle a 40 ans mais elle ne les fait pas; **to ~ one's best** être à son avantage

■ **look after** soigner ‹patient›; garder ‹child›; s'occuper de ‹customer, plant, finances, shop›; surveiller ‹class, luggage›; entretenir ‹car›

■ **look around**: **1** ¶ **~ around (a)** (glance) regarder autour de soi

(b) to ~ around for sb/sth chercher qn/qch

(c) (in town) faire un tour

2 ¶ **~ around [sth]** visiter ‹church, town›

■ **look at (a)** regarder; (briefly) jeter un coup d'œil sur

(b) (examine) examiner ‹patient›; jeter un coup d'œil à ‹car›; étudier ‹problem, options›

(c) (see, view) voir ‹life, situation›; envisager ‹problem›

■ **look back (a)** (turn around) se retourner (**at** pour regarder)

(b) to ~ back on se tourner sur ‹past›; repenser à ‹experience›; **~ing back on it** rétrospectivement

■ **look down**: **1** ¶ **~ down** (from a height) regarder en bas

2 ¶ **~ down on [sb/sth] (a)** regarder [qch] d'en haut

(b) (condescendingly) mépriser

■ **look for** chercher ‹person, object›

■ **look forward to** attendre [qch] avec impatience; **she's ~ing forward to going on holiday** elle a hâte de partir en vacances; **I ~ forward to hearing from you** (in letter) j'espère avoir bientôt de tes nouvelles; (formal) dans l'attente de votre réponse, je vous prie d'agréer mes sincères salutations

■ **look into** examiner ‹matter›

■ **look on**: **1** ¶ **~ on** (watch) regarder; (be present) assister à

2 ¶ **~ on [sb/sth]** considérer ‹person, event› (**as** comme; **with** avec)

■ **look onto** ‹house› donner sur ‹street›

■ **look out**: **1** ¶ **~ out** (take care) faire attention (**for** à); (be wary) se méfier (**for** de); **~ out!** attention!

2 ¶ **~ out for [sb/sth]** guetter ‹person›; être à l'affût de ‹bargain, new talent›

■ **look round** **1** (look behind) se retourner;

(look about) regarder autour de soi

2 ¶ **~ round [sth]** visiter ‹town›; **to ~ round the shops** faire les magasins

■ **look through**: **1** ¶ **~ through [sth] (a)** parcourir ‹report›; feuilleter ‹magazine›

(b) fouiller dans ‹belongings›

2 ¶ **~ through [sb]** faire semblant de ne pas voir

■ **look to (a)** (rely on) compter sur [qn/qch]

(b) (turn to) se tourner vers ‹future, friends›

■ **look up**: **1** ¶ **~ up** (raise eyes) lever les yeux (**from** de); **things are ~ing up for us** les choses s'arrangent pour nous

2 ¶ **~ [sb/sth] up (a)** chercher ‹phone number, price› (**in** dans)

(b) passer voir ‹acquaintance›

3 ¶ **~ up to [sb]** admirer ‹person›

look-alike *n* sosie *m*

look-in *n* (GB) **to get a ~** avoir sa chance; **to give sb a ~** donner sa chance à qn

look-out *n* **(a) to be on the ~ for** rechercher ‹stolen vehicle›; être à l'affût de ‹bargain, new talent›; guetter ‹visitor›

(b) (place) poste *m* d'observation

loom **1** *n* métier *m* à tisser

2 *vi* **(a)** (*also* **~ up**) surgir (**out of** de; **over** au-dessus de)

(b) ‹war, crisis› menacer; ‹exam, interview› être imminent/-e; **to ~ large** ‹issue› peser lourd

loony *adj* (colloq) tartelu/-e (fam)

loop **1** *n* (gen, Comput) boucle *f*

2 *vtr* nouer

3 *vi* ‹road, path› faire une boucle

IDIOM to be in/out of the ~ être/ne pas être informé

loophole *n* lacune *f*

loose *adj* **(a)** ‹knot, screw› desserré/-e; ‹handle, tooth› branlant/-e; ‹button› qui se découd; ‹thread› décousu/-e; **to hang ~** ‹hair› être dénoué/-e; **~ connection** faux contact

(b) (free) **to break ~** ‹animal› s'échapper (**from** de); **to cut sb ~** détacher qn; **to let ~** libérer ‹animal, prisoner›

(c) ‹page› détaché/-e; **~ change** petite monnaie

(d) ‹jacket, trousers› ample; ‹collar› lâche

(e) ‹link, weave› lâche

(f) ‹translation, interpretation› assez libre; ‹wording› imprécis/-e; ‹connection, guideline› vague; ‹style› relâché/-e

(g) ‹morals› dissolu/-e

IDIOM to be at a ~ end (GB), **to be at ~ ends** (US) ne pas trop savoir quoi faire

loosely *adv* **(a)** ‹hold, wind, wrap› sans serrer; **his clothes hung ~ on him** il flottait dans ses vêtements

(b) ‹connected, organized› de façon souple

(c) ‹translate, describe› assez librement

loosely knit *adj* ‹group, structure› peu uni/-e

loosen *vtr* desserrer ‹*belt, strap, collar*›; dégager ‹*nail, post*›; relâcher ‹*grip, rope, control*›; dénouer ‹*hair*›
■ **loosen up (a)** (sport) s'échauffer
(b) (relax) se détendre

loot ① *n* butin *m*
② *vtr* piller ‹*shops*›

looter *n* pillard/-e *m/f*

lopsided *adj* ‹*object, smile*› de travers; ‹*argument, view*› irrationnel/-elle

✤ **lord** *n* **(a)** (ruler) seigneur *m* (**of** de)
(b) (peer) lord *m*; **the (House of) Lords** la Chambre des Lords; **my Lord** (to noble) Monsieur le comte/duc *etc*
IDIOM to ∼ it over sb (colloq) regarder qn de haut

Lord *n* **(a)** (in prayers) Seigneur *m*
(b) (colloq) (in exclamations) **good ∼!** grand Dieu!

Lord Mayor *n* lord-maire *m*

lordship *n* (*also* **Lordship**) **your/his ∼** (of noble) Monsieur; (of judge) Monsieur le Juge

lorry *n* (*pl* **-ies**) (GB) camion *m*

lorry driver *n* (GB) routier *m*, chauffeur *m* de poids lourd

✤ **lose** ① *vtr* (*prét, pp* **lost**) **(a)** (gen) perdre; **to ∼ one's way** se perdre; **to ∼ interest in sth** se désintéresser de qch
(b) ‹*clock*› retarder de ‹*minutes, seconds*›
(c) (get rid of) semer (fam) ‹*pursuer*›
② *vi* (*prét, pp* **lost**) **(a)** (gen) perdre
(b) ‹*clock*› retarder
■ **lose out** être perdant/-e

loser *n* (gen, Sport) perdant/-e *m/f*

✤ **loss** *n* perte *f* (**of** de); **to be at a ∼** (puzzled) être perplexe; (helpless) être perdu/-e

lost *adj* **(a)** ‹*person, animal*› perdu/-e; **to get ∼** ‹*person, animal*› se perdre; ‹*object*› s'égarer; **get ∼!** (colloq) fiche le camp! (fam)
(b) ‹*opportunity*› manqué/-e; ‹*cause*› perdu/-e; ‹*civilization*› disparu/-e; **to be ∼ on sb** passer au-dessus de la tête de qn; **to be ∼ for words** être interloqué/-e; **to be ∼ in** être plongé/-e dans ‹*book, thought*›

lost and found *n* objets *mpl* trouvés

lost property *n* (GB) objets *mpl* trouvés

✤ **lot**¹ ① *pron* **(a)** (great deal) **a ∼** beaucoup; **he spent a ∼** il a beaucoup dépensé, il a dépensé beaucoup d'argent; **to mean a ∼ to sb** avoir beaucoup d'importance pour qn
(b) (colloq) **the ∼** (le) tout
② *quantif* **a ∼ of money/time** beaucoup d'argent/de temps; **I see a ∼ of him** je le vois beaucoup
③ **lots** *quantif, pron* (colloq) **∼s (and ∼s) of** des tas (fam) de, beaucoup de; **∼s of things** des tas (fam) de choses
④ **a lot** *adv* beaucoup; **he's a ∼ better/worse** il va beaucoup mieux/plus mal; **this happens quite a ∼** cela arrive très souvent

lot² *n* **(a)** (destiny) sort *m*; (quality of life) condition *f*
(b) (US) parcelle *f* (de terrain)
(c) (at auction) lot *m*
(d) to draw ∼s tirer au sort
(e) (batch) fournée *f*

lotion *n* lotion *f*

lottery *n* loterie *f*

✤ **loud** ① *adj* **(a)** ‹*music, voice*› fort/-e; ‹*noise, scream*› grand/-e (*before n*); ‹*comment, laugh*› bruyant/-e; ‹*applause*› vif/vive
(b) ‹*colour*› criard/-e; ‹*person, behaviour*› exubérant/-e
② *adv* fort; **out ∼** à voix haute

loudly *adv* ‹*knock, talk*› bruyamment; ‹*scream*› fort; ‹*protest*› vivement

loudspeaker *n* (for announcements) haut-parleur *m*; (for hi-fi) enceinte *f*

lounge *n* **(a)** (in house, hotel) salon *m*
(b) (in airport) **departure ∼** salle *f* d'embarquement
(c) (*also* **cocktail ∼**) (US) bar *m*
■ **lounge about**, **lounge around** paresser

lousy *adj* (colloq) minable (fam); **a ∼ trick** un sale tour

lout *n* malotru *m* (fam)

loutish *adj* ‹*person*› grossier/-ière; ‹*behaviour*› de voyou

louvred (GB), **louvered** (US) *adj* ‹*doors*› à lamelles

lovable *adj* ‹*person*› sympathique; ‹*child*› adorable

✤ **love** ① *n* **(a)** amour *m*; **to be/fall in ∼** être/tomber amoureux/-euse (**with** de); **to make ∼** faire l'amour; **Andy sends his ∼** Andy t'embrasse; **with ∼ from Bob**, **∼ Bob** affectueusement, Bob
(b) (GB) (term of affection) mon chéri/ma chérie *m/f*
(c) (in tennis) zéro *m*
② *vtr* aimer; **to ∼ each other** s'aimer; **to ∼ doing** *or* **to do** aimer beaucoup faire; **'I'd ∼ to!'** 'avec plaisir!'
IDIOM ∼ at first sight le coup de foudre

love affair *n* liaison *f* (**with** avec; **between** entre)

loved one *n* être *m* cher

love-life *n* vie *f* amoureuse

lovely *adj* **(a)** (beautiful) ‹*colour, garden, woman*› beau/belle (*before n*), joli/-e (*before n*); **to look ∼** ‹*child, dress*› être ravissant/-e
(b) (pleasant) ‹*letter, person*› charmant/-e; ‹*meal, smell*› délicieux/-ieuse; ‹*idea, surprise*› bon/bonne (*before n*); ‹*present, weather*› magnifique

lover *n* **(a)** (male) amant *m*; (female) maîtresse *f*; **they are ∼s** ils sont amants
(b) (person in love) amoureux/-euse *m/f*
(c) (enthusiast) amateur *m*; **jazz ∼** amateur de jazz

loving adj (gen) tendre; ‹care› affectueux/-euse

⚡ **low** [1] n **(a)** (in weather) dépression f
(b) to be at or **have hit an all-time ~** être au plus bas
[2] adj **(a)** (gen) bas/basse; ‹speed› réduit/-e; ‹number, rate› faible (before n); ‹battery› presque à plat inv; **in a ~ voice** tout bas; **to be ~ on staff** manquer de personnel; **to be ~ in sugar** contenir peu de sucre
(b) ‹mark, quality› mauvais/-e (before n)
(c) (depressed) déprimé/-e
(d) ‹behaviour› ignoble
[3] adv **(a)** ‹aim› bas; ‹bend› très bas; ‹fly› à basse altitude
(b) (in importance) **it's very ~ (down) on the list** c'est tout à fait secondaire
(c) ‹speak, sing› bas; **to turn [sth] down ~** baisser ‹heating, light›
[4] vi ‹cow› meugler

low-alcohol adj peu alcoolisé/-e
lowbrow adj ‹person› peu intellectuel/-elle
low-budget adj à petit budget
low-calorie adj ‹diet› hypocalorique; ‹food› à faible teneur en calories
low-cost adj économique, bon marché
low-cut adj décolleté/-e
low-down adj (colloq) tuyau m (fam)
lower [1] adj inférieur/-e
[2] vtr **(a)** baisser ‹barrier, curtain, flag›, abaisser ‹ceiling›; **to ~ sb/sth** descendre qn/qch (**into** dans; **onto** sur)
(b) (reduce) baisser ‹prices, standards›; réduire ‹pressure, temperature›; abaisser ‹age limit›; **to ~ one's voice** baisser la voix
(c) affaler ‹sail›
[3] v refl **to ~ oneself (a)** s'abaisser
(b) to ~ oneself into s'asseoir précautionneusement dans ‹bath, armchair›
lower class n (pl ~es) **the ~(es)** la classe ouvrière
lower sixth n (GB Sch) ≈ classe f de première; **to be in the ~** être en première
low-fat adj ‹diet› sans matières grasses; ‹cheese› allégé/-e; ‹milk› écrémé/-e
low-income adj ‹family› à faible revenue; ‹bracket› des bas salaires
low-key adj ‹approach› discret/-ète; ‹meeting, talks› informel/-elle
low-level adj ‹bombing› à basse altitude; ‹talks› informel/-elle; ‹radiation› faible
low-lying adj à basse altitude
low-paid adj ‹job› faiblement rémunéré/-e; ‹worker› peu rémunéré/-e
low-priced adj à bas prix
low-profile adj discret/-ète
low-quality adj de qualité inférieure
low-risk adj à risque limité
low season n basse saison f
low-tech adj traditionnel/-elle
low tide n marée f basse

loyal adj ‹friend› loyal/-e (**to** envers); ‹customer› fidèle (**to** à)
loyalty n loyauté f (**to, towards** envers)
loyalty card n carte f de fidélité
lozenge n pastille f
LP n (disque m) 33 tours m
L-plate n (GB Aut) plaque f d'élève conducteur débutant accompagné
Ltd (GB) (abbr = **limited (liability)**) ≈ SARL
lubricant n lubrifiant m
lucid adj **(a)** (clear) clair/-e
(b) (sane) ‹person› lucide; ‹moment› de lucidité
luck n chance f; **good ~** chance f; **bad ~** malchance f; **to bring sb good/bad ~** porter bonheur/malheur à qn; **it's good ~** ça porte bonheur; **bad** or **hard ~!** pas de chance!; **good ~!** bonne chance!; **to be in/out of ~** avoir de la/ne pas avoir de chance
luckily adv heureusement (**for** pour)
⚡ **lucky** adj **(a)** (fortunate) **to be ~** avoir de la chance
(b) ‹charm, colour, number› porte-bonheur inv; **it's my ~ day!** c'est mon jour de chance!
lucrative adj lucratif/-ive
ludicrous adj grotesque
luggage n bagages mpl
luggage rack n porte-bagages m inv
lukewarm adj tiède
lull [1] n (in storm, fighting) accalmie f; (in conversation) pause f
[2] vtr **to ~ sb to sleep** endormir qn en le berçant; **to ~ sb into thinking that...** faire croire à qn que...; **to be ~ed into a false sense of security** se laisser aller à un sentiment de sécurité trompeur
lullaby n berceuse f
lumber [1] n (US) bois m de construction
[2] vtr (GB) (colloq) **to get** or **be ~ed with sb/ sth** se retrouver avec qn/qch sur les bras
[3] vi (also **~ along**) avancer d'un pas lourd; ‹vehicle› avancer péniblement
lumberjack n bûcheron/-onne m/f
luminous adj lumineux/-euse
lump [1] n **(a)** (gen) morceau m; (of soil, clay) motte f; (in sauce) grumeau m
(b) (on body) (from knock) bosse f (**on** sur)
(c) (tumour) grosseur f (**in, on** à)
[2] vtr **to ~ X and Y together** mettre X et Y dans le même panier (fam)
IDIOM to have a ~ in one's throat avoir la gorge serrée
lump sum n versement m unique
lunar adj ‹landscape› lunaire; ‹eclipse› de lune; ‹landing› sur la lune
lunatic n fou/folle m/f
⚡ **lunch** n déjeuner m; **to have ~** déjeuner; **to take sb out for ~** emmener qn déjeuner au restaurant; **to close for ~** fermer le midi

lunchbox n boîte f à sandwichs
lunchbreak n pause-déjeuner f
luncheon voucher, LV n ticket-repas m, ticket-restaurant® m
lunch hour n heure f du déjeuner
lunchtime n heure f du déjeuner
lung n poumon m
lunge vi bondir (at vers; forward en avant)
lurch vi ⟨person, vehicle⟩ tanguer; **to ~ forward** ⟨car⟩ faire un bond en avant
IDIOM **to leave sb in the ~** abandonner qn
lure 1 n (a) (attraction) attrait m (of de)
(b) (in hunting) leurre m
2 vtr attirer (into dans; with avec); **they ~d him out of his house** ils ont réussi à le faire sortir de chez lui par la ruse
lurid adj (a) ⟨colour⟩ criard/-e
(b) ⟨detail, past⟩ épouvantable
lurk vi **he was ~ing in the bushes** il était tapi dans les buissons; **to ~ in the garden** rôder dans le jardin
lurker n (Computing) observateur m passif/observatrice f passive

luscious adj ⟨food⟩ succulent/-e; ⟨woman⟩ pulpeux/-euse
lush adj ⟨vegetation⟩ luxuriant/-e; ⟨hotel, surroundings⟩ luxueux/-euse
lust 1 n (a) désir m; (deadly sin) luxure f
(b) (for power, blood) soif f (for de)
2 vi **to ~ for** or **after sb/sth** convoiter qn/qch
luvvy n (colloq) acteur/-trice m/f prétentieux/-ieuse
Luxembourg pr n Luxembourg m
luxurious adj ⟨apartment, lifestyle⟩ de luxe (never after v); **his apartment is ~** son appartement est luxueux
luxury 1 n luxe m
2 adj ⟨hotel, product, holiday⟩ de luxe
lychee n litchi m
lying n mensonges mpl
lynch vtr lyncher
lynch mob n lyncheurs mpl
lyrical adj lyrique; **to wax ~ (about sth)** disserter avec lyrisme (sur qch)
lyrics n pl paroles fpl
lyric-writer n parolier/-ière m/f

M m

m, M n m, M m
MA n (abbr = **Master of Arts**) diplôme m supérieur de lettres
macabre adj macabre
macaroni n macaronis mpl
mace n (a) (spice) macis m
(b) (ceremonial staff) masse f
Macedonia pr n Macédoine f
machete n machette f
✓ **machine** n machine f; **sewing ~ machine** à coudre; **by ~** à la machine
machine gun n mitrailleuse f
machine-readable adj ⟨data⟩ directement exploitable; ⟨passport⟩ vérifiable par ordinateur
machinery n (a) (equipment) machines fpl; (working parts) mécanisme m, rouages mpl; **a piece of ~** une machine
(b) (figurative) dispositifs mpl
macho adj macho (fam)
mackerel n maquereau m
mackintosh, macintosh n imperméable m
mad adj (a) ⟨person⟩ fou/folle (with de); ⟨dog⟩ enragé/-e; ⟨idea, scheme⟩ insensé/-e; **to go**

~ devenir fou/folle; **to drive sb ~** rendre qn fou
(b) (colloq) (angry) furieux/-ieuse; **to be ~ at** or **with sb** être très en colère contre qn; **to go ~** se mettre dans une colère folle
(c) (colloq) (enthusiastic) **~ about** or **on** fou/folle de (fam) ⟨person, hobby⟩
(d) ⟨panic⟩ infernal/-e; **the audience went ~** le public s'est déchaîné
IDIOM **to work like ~** travailler comme un fou/une folle
madam n madame f; **Dear Madam** (in letter) Madame
mad cow disease n maladie f de la vache folle
maddening adj ⟨person⟩ énervant/-e; ⟨delay, situation⟩ exaspérant/-e
made adj **a ~ man** un homme qui a réussi; **he's got it ~** (sure to succeed) sa réussite est assurée; (has succeeded) il n'a plus à s'en faire
Madeira pr n Madère
made-to-measure adj ⟨garment⟩ fait/-e sur mesure
made-up adj (a) (wearing make-up) maquillé/-e
(b) ⟨story⟩ fabriqué/-e
madly adv (a) (frantically) frénétiquement
(b) ⟨jealous⟩ follement; **~ in love (with sb)**

✓ indicates a very frequent word

follement *or* éperdument amoureux/-euse
(de qn)

madman *n* (colloq) fou *m* (fam), malade *m*
(fam)

madness *n* folie *f*; **it is** ~ **to do** c'est de la
folie de faire

Mafia *n* **the** ~ la Mafia

⚹ **magazine** *n* (a) revue *f*; (mainly photos)
magazine *m*; **fashion** ~ magazine de mode;
women's ~ journal *m* féminin
(b) (on radio, TV) magazine *m*
(c) (of gun, camera) magasin *m*

maggot *n* (in fruit) ver *m*; (for fishing) asticot
m

magic 1 *n* magie *f*
2 *adj* magique

magical *adj* magique

magic carpet *n* tapis *m* volant

magician *n* (wizard) magicien *m*; (entertainer)
illusionniste *m*

magistrate *n* magistrat *m*

magistrate's court *n* ≈ tribunal *m*
de police

magnanimous *adj* magnanime

magnate *n* magnat *m*; **oil** ~ magnat du
pétrole

magnesium *n* magnésium *m*

magnet *n* aimant *m*; (figurative) pôle *m*
d'attraction (**for** pour)

magnetic *adj* (a) ⟨rod⟩ aimanté/-e; ⟨field,
force, storm⟩ magnétique
(b) ⟨appeal⟩ irrésistible; **to have a** ~
personality avoir du charisme

magnetism *n* magnétisme *m*

magnificent *adj* magnifique

magnify *vtr* grossir

magnifying glass *n* loupe *f*

magnitude *n* ampleur *f* (**of** de)

magnolia *n* (a) (also ~ **tree**) magnolia *m*
(b) (colour) crème *m*

magpie *n* pie *f*

mahogany *n* acajou *m*

maid *n* (in house) bonne *f*; (in hotel) femme *f*
de chambre

maiden 1 *n* jeune fille *f*
2 *adj* ⟨flight, voyage, speech⟩ inaugural/-e

maiden name *n* nom *m* de jeune fille

mail 1 *n* (a) (postal service) poste *f*; **by** ~
par la poste
(b) (letters) courrier *m*
(c) (e-mail) courrier *m* électronique
2 *vtr* envoyer, expédier ⟨letter, parcel⟩ (**to** à)

mailbox *n* (for posting) boîte *f* aux lettres; (for
delivery) boîte *f* à lettres; (for e-mail) boîte *f* aux
lettres électronique

mailing *n* (for advertising) publipostage *m*,
mailing *m*

mailing list *n* fichier-clientèle *m*

mailman ((US)) *n* *pl* **-men** (US) facteur *m*

mail order 1 *n* **to buy (by)** ~ acheter par
correspondance

2 *adj* ⟨business, goods⟩ de vente *f* par
correspondance

maim *vtr* estropier

⚹ **main** 1 *n* (a) (pipe) canalisation *f*
(b) **the** ~**s** (of electricity) secteur *m*; (of water,
gas) le réseau de distribution; (of sewage) le
réseau d'évacuation
2 *adj* principal/-e

main course *n* plat *m* principal

mainframe *n* (also ~ **computer**)
ordinateur *m* central

mainland *n* territoire *m* continental; **on
the** ~ sur le continent

main line 1 *n* grande ligne *f*
2 *adj* ⟨station⟩ de grande ligne
3 **mainline** *vi* (colloq) se piquer

⚹ **mainly** *adv* surtout, essentiellement

main road *n* (in country) route *f* principale;
(in town) grande rue *f*

mainstream 1 *n* courant *m* dominant
2 *adj* (a) (conventional) traditionnel/-elle
(b) ~ **jazz** jazz mainstream

⚹ **maintain** *vtr* (a) (keep steady) maintenir
(b) subvenir aux besoins de ⟨family⟩;
entretenir ⟨army, house, property⟩
(c) continuer à affirmer ⟨innocence⟩; **to** ~
that soutenir que

maintenance *n* (a) (upkeep) entretien *m*
(**of** de)
(b) (GB Law) (alimony) pension *f* alimentaire

maisonette *n* duplex *m*

maize *n* maïs *m*

majestic *adj* majestueux/-euse

majesty *n* (a) (grandeur) majesté *f*
(b) **His/Her Majesty** sa Majesté

⚹ **major** 1 *n* (a) (Mil) commandant *m*
(b) (US Univ) matière *f* principale
(c) (Mus) ton *m* majeur
2 *adj* (a) ⟨event⟩ important/-e; ⟨role⟩
majeur/-e; ⟨significance⟩ capital/-e; **a** ~
operation, ~ **surgery** une grosse opération
(b) (main) principal/-e
(c) (Mus) majeur/-e; **in a** ~ **key** en majeur
3 *vi* (US Univ) **to** ~ **in** se spécialiser en

Majorca *pr n* Majorque *f*; **in** ~ à Majorque

⚹ **majority** *n* majorité *f* (**of** de); **to be in a** *or*
the ~ être en majorité

⚹ **make** 1 *n* marque *f*
2 *vtr* (*prét, pp* **made**) (a) (gen) faire; **to**
~ **the bed** faire le lit; **to** ~ **a noise** faire du
bruit; **to** ~ **a rule** établir une règle; **to** ~
room/the time (for sth) trouver de la place/
du temps (pour qch); **to** ~ **friends/enemies**
se faire des amis/des ennemis; **to** ~ **oneself
understood** se faire comprendre; **it's made
(out) of gold** c'est en or; **made in France**
fabriqué en France; **he was made treasurer**
on l'a fait trésorier; **to** ~ **a habit/an issue of**
sth faire de qch une habitude/une affaire;
it's been made into a film on en a fait *or* tiré
un film; **three and three** ~ **six** trois et trois
font six   ····⟫

(b) (with adjective) **to ~ sb happy/ill** rendre qn heureux/malade; **to ~ sb hungry** donner faim à qn; **to ~ sth better/bigger/worse** améliorer/agrandir/aggraver qch
(c) (with infinitive) **to ~ sb cry** faire pleurer qn; **I made her smile** je l'ai fait sourire; **to ~ sb pay the bill** faire payer l'addition à qn; **to ~ sb wait** faire attendre qn; **they made me do it** ils m'ont obligé *or* forcé; **it ~s her voice sound funny** ça lui donne une drôle de voix
(d) (earn) gagner ‹*salary*›; **to ~ a living** gagner sa vie; **to ~ a profit** réaliser des bénéfices; **to ~ a loss** subir des pertes
(e) (reach) arriver jusqu'à ‹*place, position*›; atteindre ‹*ranking, level*›; **we'll never ~ it** nous n'y arriverons jamais; **to ~ the front page** faire la une
(f) (estimate, say) **what time do you ~ it?** quelle heure as-tu?; **I ~ it five o'clock** il est cinq heures à ma montre; **let's ~ it five dollars** disons cinq dollars; **can we ~ it a bit later?** peut-on dire un peu plus tard?; **what do you ~ of it?** qu'en dis-tu?
(g) (cause success of) assurer la réussite de ‹*holiday, meal*›; **it really made my day** ça m'a rendu heureux pour la journée
IDIOMS **to ~ it** (colloq) (in career, life) y arriver; (to party, meeting) réussir à venir; **I can't ~ it** je ne peux pas venir
■ **make do** faire avec; **to ~ do with** se contenter de qch
■ **make for (a)** (head for) se diriger vers
(b) (help create) permettre, assurer
■ **make good**: **1** ¶ **~ good** réussir
2 ¶ **~ good [sth] (a)** réparer ‹*damage, omission*›; rattraper ‹*lost time*›; combler ‹*deficit*›
(b) tenir ‹*promise*›
■ **make out**: **1** ¶ **~ out** affirmer, prétendre **(that** que)
2 ¶ **~ [sb/sth] out (a)** (see, distinguish) distinguer
(b) (claim) **to ~ sth out to be easy/difficult** prétendre que qch est facile/difficile
(c) (understand) comprendre (if si); **I can't ~ him out** je n'arrive pas à le comprendre
(d) (write out) faire, rédiger; **to ~ out a cheque to sb** faire un chèque à qn; **it is made out to X** il est à l'ordre de X
■ **make up**: **1** ¶ **~ up (a)** (after quarrel) se réconcilier (**with** avec)
(b) to ~ up for rattraper ‹*lost time, lost sleep*›; compenser ‹*personal loss*›
2 ¶ **~ [sth] up (a)** inventer ‹*story, excuse*›
(b) (prepare) faire ‹*parcel, garment, bed*›; préparer ‹*prescription*›
(c) (constitute) faire; **to be made up of** être fait/-e *or* composé/-e de
(d) (compensate for) rattraper ‹*loss, time*›; combler ‹*deficit*›
make-believe *n* fantaisie *f*
makeover *n* transformation *f*

---

maker *n* (of clothes, food, appliance) fabricant *m*; (of cars, aircraft) constructeur *m*
makeshift *adj* improvisé/-e
make-up *n* **(a)** maquillage *m*; **to put on one's ~** se maquiller
(b) (character) caractère *m*
make-up bag *n* trousse *f* de maquillage
make-up remover *n* démaquillant *m*
making *n* (of film, programme) réalisation *f*; (of product) fabrication *f*; (of clothes) confection *f*; **his problems are of his own ~** ses ennuis sont de sa faute; **a disaster is in the ~** une catastrophe se prépare
IDIOM **to have all the ~s of** avoir tout pour faire
maladjusted *adj* inadapté/-e
malaria *n* paludisme *m*
Malaysia *pr n* Malaisie *f*
♂ **male** **1** *n* **(a)** (animal) mâle *m*
(b) (man) homme *m*
2 *adj* **(a)** ‹*plant, animal*› mâle
(b) ‹*population, role, trait*› masculin/-e; ‹*company*› des hommes; **a ~ voice** une voix d'homme; **~ student** étudiant *m*
(c) ‹*plug, socket*› mâle
male chauvinism *n* machisme *m*
male chauvinist *n* phallocrate *m*
male model *n* mannequin *m* homme *or* masculin
malevolent *adj* malveillant/-e
malformed *adj* ‹*limb, nose*› difforme; ‹*organ*› malformé/-e
malfunction **1** *n* **(a)** (poor operation) mauvais fonctionnement *m*
(b) (breakdown) défaillance *f*
2 *vi* mal fonctionner
malice *n* méchanceté *f* (**towards** à)
malicious *adj* ‹*comment, person*› malveillant/-e; ‹*act*› méchant/-e; ‹*lie*› calomnieux/-ieuse
malign *vtr* calomnier
malignant *adj* **(a)** ‹*look*› malveillant/-e; ‹*person*› malfaisant/-e
(b) (Med) malin/-igne
mall *n* **(a)** (shopping arcade) (in town) galerie *f* marchande; (in suburbs) (US) centre *m* commercial
(b) (US) (street) rue *f* piétonne
mallet *n* maillet *m*
malnutrition *n* sous-alimentation *f*
malpractice *n* **(a)** (gen, Law) malversations *fpl*
(b) (US Med) erreur *f* médicale
malt *n* **(a)** (grain) malt *m*
(b) (whisky) whisky *m* pur malt
(c) (US) (malted milk) lait *m* malté
Malta *pr n* Malte *f*
maltreat *vtr* maltraiter
mammal *n* mammifère *m*
mammoth **1** *n* mammouth *m*

2 *adj* ‹task› gigantesque; ‹organization› géant/-e

man **1** *n* (*pl* **men**) (a) homme *m*; an old ~ un vieillard; ~ **to** ~ d'homme à homme; ~ **and wife** mari et femme
(b) (mankind) l'humanité *f*
(c) (in chess) pièce *f*; (in draughts) pion *m*
2 *vtr* (*p prés etc* -**nn**-) (a) tenir ‹switchboard, desk›
(b) armer [qch] en hommes ‹ship›
IDIOM every ~ **for himself** chacun pour soi

manage **1** *vtr* (a) **to** ~ **to do** réussir à faire, se débrouiller (fam) pour faire
(b) diriger ‹project, finances, organization›; gérer ‹business, shop, hotel, estate›; gérer ‹money, time›
(c) (handle) savoir s'y prendre avec ‹person, animal›; manier ‹tool, boat›
2 *vi* se débrouiller

manageable *adj* ‹size, car› maniable; ‹problem› maîtrisable; ‹person, animal› docile

management *n* (a) (system, field) gestion *f*; **bad** ~ mauvaise gestion
(b) (managers) direction *f*; **top** ~ la haute direction **the** ~ **team** l'équipe dirigeante

management consultant *n* conseiller *m* en gestion

management trainee *n* apprenti manager *m*

manager *n* (of firm, bank) directeur/-trice *m/f*; (of shop) gérant/-e *m/f*; (of farm) exploitant/-e *m/f*; (of project) responsable *mf*, directeur/-trice *m/f*; (in show business) directeur/-trice *m/f* artistique; (Sport) manager *m*

manageress *n* (of firm, bank) directrice *f*; (of shop, hotel) gérante *f*; (of project) responsable *f*, directrice *f*; (in show business) directrice *f* artistique

managerial *adj* ‹experience› en gestion; ‹decision› de la direction; ~ **staff** les cadres *mpl*

managing director, MD *n* directeur/-trice *m/f* général/-e

mandarin *n* (a) (fruit) mandarine *f*; (tree) mandarinier *m*
(b) (person) mandarin *m*

mandate *n* (authority) autorité *f*; (Pol) mandat *m*

mane *n* crinière *f*

manger *n* mangeoire *f*

mangle *vtr* mutiler ‹body›; broyer ‹vehicle›

mango *n* (fruit) mangue *f*

mangrove *n* palétuvier *m*, manglier *m*

mangy *adj* ‹dog› galeux/-euse

manhandle *vtr* malmener, maltraiter

manhole *n* regard *m*

manhood *n* (a) âge *m* d'homme
(b) (masculinity) masculinité *f*

mania *n* manie *f*

maniac *n* (a) (colloq) fou/folle *m/f*
(b) (in psychology) maniaque *mf*

manic *adj* (a) (manic-depressive) maniaco-dépressif/-ive; (obsessive) obsessionnel/-elle
(b) (figurative) ‹activity, behaviour› frénétique

manicure **1** *n* manucure *f*
2 *vtr* **to** ~ **one's nails** se faire les ongles

manifest **1** *adj* manifeste, évident/-e
2 *vtr* manifester

manifesto *n* manifeste *m*, programme *m*

manipulate *vtr* manipuler

manipulative *adj* manipulateur/-trice

mankind *n* humanité *f*

manly *adj* viril/-e

man-made *adj* ‹fibre, fabric› synthétique; ‹lake› artificiel/-ielle; ‹tools› fait/-e à la main

manner **1** *n* (a) (way, method) manière *f*, façon *f*; **in this** ~ de cette manière *or* façon; **in a** ~ **of speaking** pour ainsi dire
(b) (way of behaving) attitude *f*; **she has an aggressive** ~ elle a une attitude agressive
(c) (sort, kind) sorte *f*, genre *m* (of de)
2 **manners** *n pl* (a) manières *fpl*; **to have good/bad** ~**s** avoir de bonnes/mauvaises manières; **it's bad** ~**s to do** il est mal élevé de faire
(b) (customs) mœurs *fpl*

mannerism *n* (habit) particularité *f*; (quirk) manie *f*

manoeuvre (GB), **maneuver** (US) **1** *n* manœuvre *f*
2 *vtr* (a) manœuvrer ‹vehicle, object›
(b) (figurative) manœuvrer ‹person›; faire dévier ‹discussion› (**to** vers)
3 *vi* manœuvrer

manor *n* (*also* ~ **house**) manoir *m*

manpower *n* main-d'œuvre *f*

mansion *n* (in countryside) demeure *f*; (in town) hôtel *m* particulier

manslaughter *n* homicide *m* involontaire

mantelpiece *n* (manteau *m* de) cheminée *f*

manual **1** *n* manuel *m*
2 *adj* ‹labour, worker› manuel/-elle; ‹gearbox, typewriter› mécanique

manufacture **1** *n* (gen) fabrication *f*; (of clothes) confection *f*; (of cars) construction *f* **2** *vtr* (gen) fabriquer; construire ‹cars›

manufacturer *n* (gen) fabricant *m* (**of** de); (of cars) constructeur *m*

manure *n* fumier *m*; **horse** ~ crottin *m* de cheval

manuscript *n* manuscrit *m*

many **1** *det* beaucoup de, un grand nombre de; ~ **people** beaucoup de gens, un grand nombre de personnes; ~ **times** de nombreuses fois, bien des fois; **for** ~ **years** pendant de nombreuses années; **how** ~ **people/times?** combien de personnes/fois?; ···>

too ~ trop de; **I have as ~ books as you (do)** j'ai autant de livres que toi; **so ~** tant de
2 *pron, quantif* (*comp* **more,** *superl* **most**) beaucoup; **not ~** pas beaucoup; **too ~** trop; **how ~?** combien?; **as ~ as you like** autant que tu veux; **I didn't know there were so ~** je ne savais pas qu'il y en avait autant; **~ (of them) were killed** beaucoup d'entre eux ont été tués

many-sided *adj* à multiples facettes

⚜ **map** *n* carte *f* (**of** de); (of town, underground) plan *m* (**of** de); **street ~** plan des rues
■ **map out** élaborer, mettre [qch] au point ⟨*plans, strategy*⟩; tracer ⟨*future*⟩

maple *n* érable *m*

mar *vtr* (*p prés etc* **-rr-**) gâcher

marathon 1 *n* marathon *m*
2 *adj* (**a**) (Sport) **~ runner** marathonien/-ienne *m/f*
(**b**) (massive) -marathon; **a ~ session** une séance-marathon

marble *n* (**a**) (stone) marbre *m*
(**b**) (Games) bille *f*; **to play ~s** jouer aux billes

march 1 *n* marche *f*
2 *vi* (**a**) (Mil) marcher au pas; **to ~ (for) 40 km** faire une marche de 40 km; **forward ~!** en avant, marche!
(**b**) (in protest) manifester (**against** contre; **for** pour)
(**c**) **to ~ along** (walk briskly) marcher d'un pas vif; **to ~ in** (angrily) entrer l'air furieux; **she ~ed up to his desk** elle s'est dirigée droit sur son bureau

⚜ **March** *n* mars *m*

marcher *n* (in demonstration) manifestant/-e *m/f*; (in procession) marcheur/-euse *m/f*

mare *n* (horse) jument *f*; (donkey) ânesse *f*

margarine *n* margarine *f*

margin *n* marge *f*; **by a narrow ~** de justesse, de peu

marginal *adj* marginal/-e

marginalize *vtr* marginaliser

marigold *n* souci *m*

marijuana *n* marijuana *f*

marinade *vtr* (*also* **marinate**) faire mariner; faire mariner

marine 1 *n* (**a**) (soldier) fusilier *m* marin; **the Marines** les marines *mpl*
(**b**) (navy) **the merchant ~** la marine marchande
2 *adj* ⟨*mammal, biology*⟩ marin/-e; ⟨*explorer, life*⟩ sous-marin/-e; ⟨*insurance, law*⟩ maritime

marital *adj* conjugal/-e

marital status *n* situation *f* de famille

marjoram *n* marjolaine *f*

⚜ **mark** 1 *n* (**a**) (gen) marque *f*; (stain) tache *f*
(**b**) **as a ~ of** en signe de ⟨*esteem, respect*⟩
(**c**) (Sch, Univ) note *f*

(**d**) **the high-tide ~** le maximum de la marée haute; **at gas ~ 7** à thermostat 7
(**e**) (Sport) **on your ~s!** à vos marques!
(**f**) (*also* **Deutschmark**) deutschmark *m*
2 *vtr* (**a**) (gen) marquer; (stain) tacher
(**b**) ⟨*arrow, sign, label*⟩ indiquer ⟨*position, road*⟩
(**c**) (Sch, Univ) corriger; **to ~ sb absent** noter qn absent
(**d**) (Sport) marquer
3 *vi* (**a**) ⟨*teacher*⟩ faire des corrections
(**b**) (stain) se tacher
(**c**) (Sport) marquer
IDIOMS **~ my words** crois-moi; **to ~ time** (Mil) marquer le pas; (figurative) (wait) attendre; (wait for right moment) attendre le bon moment

marked *adj* (**a**) ⟨*difference, increase, contrast*⟩ marqué/-e, net/nette (*before n*); ⟨*accent*⟩ prononcé/-e
(**b**) **he's a ~ man** on en veut à sa vie

marker *n* (**a**) (pen) marqueur *m*
(**b**) (tag) repère *m*

⚜ **market** 1 *n* (**a**) (gen, Econ) marché *m*
(**b**) (stock market) Bourse *f*
2 *vtr* (**a**) (sell) commercialiser, vendre
(**b**) (promote) lancer *or* mettre [qch] sur le marché

market day *n* jour *m* du marché

market economy *n* économie *f* de marché

market forces *n pl* forces *fpl* du marché

market gardening *n* culture *f* maraîchère

⚜ **marketing** *n* (**a**) (field) marketing *m*, mercatique *f*
(**b**) (department) service *m* de marketing

marketing strategy *n* stratégie *f* commerciale

market leader *n* (product) produit *m* vedette; (company) leader *m* du marché

marketplace *n* place *f* du marché

market research *n* étude *f* de marché

market town *n* bourg *m*

market trader *n* vendeur/-euse *m/f* sur un marché

market value *n* valeur *f* marchande

markings *n pl* (on animal) taches *fpl*; (on aircraft) marques *fpl*; **road ~** signalisation *f* horizontale

marksman *n* tireur *m* d'élite

marmalade *n* confiture *f or* marmelade *f* d'oranges

maroon 1 *n* bordeaux *m*
2 *vtr* **to be ~ed on an island** être bloqué/-e sur une île; **the ~ed sailors** les naufragés

marquee *n* (**a**) (GB) (tent) grande tente *f*; (of circus) chapiteau *m*
(**b**) (US) (canopy) (grand) auvent *m*

⚜ **marriage** *n* mariage *m* (**to** avec)

marriage certificate *n* extrait *m* d'acte de mariage

⚜ indicates a very frequent word

married *adj* ‹person› marié/-e (**to** à); ‹life›
conjugal/-e; **~ couple** couple *m*
marrow *n* (**a**) (in bone) moelle *f*
(**b**) (GB) (vegetable) courge *f*; **baby ~** (GB);
courgette *f*
marrowbone *n* os *m* à moelle
✔ **marry** ❶ *vtr* se marier avec, épouser
‹fiancé(e)›; ‹priest› marier ‹couple›; **to get
married** se marier (**to** avec); **will you ~ me?**
veux-tu m'épouser?
❷ *vi* se marier
Mars *pr n* Mars *f*
marsh *n* (*also* **marshland**); (terrain)
marécage *m*; (region) marais *m*
marshal ❶ *n* (**a**) (Mil) maréchal *m*
(**b**) (at rally, ceremony) membre *m* du service
d'ordre
(**c**) (US) (in fire service) capitaine *m* des
pompiers
❷ *vtr* (*p prés* **-ll-** (GB), **-l-** (US)) rassembler
martial *adj* ‹art, law› martial/-e; ‹spirit›
guerrier/-ière
martyr ❶ *n* martyr/-e *m/f*
❷ *vtr* martyriser
martyrdom *n* martyre *m*
marvel ❶ *n* merveille *f*
❷ *vi* s'étonner (**at** de), être émerveillé/-e
(**at** par)
marvellous (GB), **marvelous** (US)
adj merveilleux/-euse; **that's ~!** c'est
formidable!
marzipan *n* pâte *f* d'amandes
mascot *n* mascotte *f*; **lucky ~** porte-
bonheur *m inv*
masculine *adj* masculin/-e
masculinity *n* masculinité *f*
mash ❶ *n* (for animals) pâtée *f*
❷ *vtr* (*also* **~ up**) écraser
mashed potatoes *n pl* purée *f* de
pommes de terre
mask ❶ *n* masque *m*; (for eyes only) loup *m*
❷ *vtr* masquer
masking tape *n* ruban *m* adhésif
masochist *n*, *adj* masochiste *mf*
mason *n* (**a**) (in building) maçon *m*
(**b**) (**Mason** *also* **Free~**) franc-maçon *m*
masonry *n* maçonnerie *f*
masquerade ❶ *n* bal *m* masqué;
(figurative) mascarade *f*
❷ *vi* **to ~ as sb/sth** se faire passer pour
qn/qch
✔ **mass** ❶ *n* (**a**) masse *f* (**of** de); (of people)
foule *f* (**of** de); (of details) quantité *f* (**of** de)
(**b**) (in church) messe *f*
❷ **masses** *n pl* (**a**) the **~es** les masses *fpl*
(**b**) (GB) (colloq) **~es of work** beaucoup *or*
plein (fam) de travail; **~es of people** des tas
(fam) de gens
❸ *adj* ‹audience, movement, meeting,
tourism› de masse; ‹exodus, protest,
unemployment› massif/-ive; **~ hysteria**

hystérie *f* collective
❹ *vi* ‹troops› se regrouper; ‹bees› se masser;
‹clouds› s'amonceler
massacre ❶ *n* massacre *m*
❷ *vtr* massacrer
massage ❶ *n* massage *m*
❷ *vtr* masser
mass grave *n* charnier *m*
✔ **massive** *adj* (gen) énorme; ‹increase, cut›
massif/-ive
mass-marketing *n* commercialisation
f massive
mass media *n* (mass) médias *mpl*
mass murderer *n* auteur *m* d'un
massacre
mass production *n* fabrication *f* en
série
mast *n* (on ship, for flags) mât *m*; (for aerial)
pylône *m*
✔ **master** ❶ *n* (**a**) (gen) maître *m*
(**b**) (Sch) (primary) maître *m*, instituteur *m*;
(secondary) professeur *m*; (GB Univ) (of college)
principal *m*
(**c**) (*also* **~ copy**) original *m*
❷ *vtr* ‹chef, craftsman› maître (*before n*);
‹spy› professionnel/-elle
❸ *vtr* (**a**) maîtriser ‹subject›; posséder ‹art,
skill›
(**b**) dominer ‹feelings›; surmonter ‹phobia›
master key *n* passe-partout *m inv*
masterly *adj* magistral/-e
mastermind ❶ *n* cerveau *m* (**of, behind**
de)
❷ *vtr* organiser ‹robbery, event›
Master of Arts *n* diplôme *m* supérieur
de lettres
master of ceremonies *n* (in cabaret)
animateur/-trice *m/f*; (at banquet) maître *m*
des cérémonies
Master of Science *n* diplôme *m*
supérieur en sciences
masterpiece *n* chef-d'œuvre *m*
master plan *n* plan *m* d'ensemble
master's (degree) *n* ≈ maîtrise (**in** de)
mastery *n* maîtrise *f* (**of** de)
mat ❶ *n* (**a**) (on floor) (petit) tapis *m*; (for
wiping feet) paillasson *m*
(**b**) (on table) dessous-de-plat *m inv*; **place ~**
set *m* de table
❷ *vi* (*p prés etc* **-tt-**) ‹hair› s'emmêler;
‹wool› se feutrer; ‹fibres› s'enchevêtrer
✔ **match** ❶ *n* (**a**) (Sport) match *m*
(**b**) (matchstick) allumette *f*
(**c**) **to be a ~ for sb** être un adversaire à la
mesure de qn; **to be no ~ for sb** être trop
faible pour qn
❷ *vtr* (**a**) (gen) correspondre à; ‹colour, bag›
être assorti/-e à; **to ~ (up) the names to the
photos** trouver les noms qui correspondent
aux photos
(**b**) (equal) égaler ‹record, achievements›

⋯▸

3 *vi* ⟨*colours, clothes, curtains*⟩ être assortis/-ies; ⟨*components*⟩ aller ensemble; **with gloves to** ~ avec des gants assortis

matchbox *n* boîte *f* d'allumettes

match point *n* balle *f* de match

matchstick *n* allumette *f*

mate **1** *n* (a) (GB) (colloq) (friend) copain *m* (fam); (at work, school) camarade *mf*
(b) (Zool) (male) mâle *m*; (female) femelle *f*
(c) (assistant) aide *mf*
(d) (in navy) second *m*
2 *vtr* (a) accoupler ⟨*animal*⟩ (**with** à or avec)
(b) (in chess) faire mat
3 *vi* ⟨*animal*⟩ s'accoupler (**with** à, avec)

ⸯ **material** **1** *n* (a) (substance) (gen) matière *f*, substance *f*; (Tech) matériau *m*; **waste** ~ déchets *mpl*
(b) (fabric) tissu *m*, étoffe *f*
(c) (written matter) documentation *f*; **teaching** ~ matériel *m* pédagogique; **reading** ~ lecture *f*
(d) (potential) étoffe *f*; **she is star** ~ elle a l'étoffe d'une vedette
2 **materials** *n pl* (equipment) matériel *m*; **cleaning** ~s produits *mpl* d'entretien; **building** ~s matériaux de construction
3 *adj* matériel/-ielle

materialistic *adj* matérialiste

materialize *vi* (a) ⟨*hope, offer, plan, threat*⟩ se concrétiser; ⟨*event, situation*⟩ se réaliser; ⟨*idea*⟩ prendre forme
(b) (appear) ⟨*person, object*⟩ surgir; ⟨*spirit*⟩ se matérialiser

maternal *adj* maternel/-elle (**towards** avec)

maternity *n* maternité *f*

maternity leave *n* congé *m* de maternité

maternity unit *n* service *m* d'obstétrique

maternity ward *n* maternité *f*

math *n* (US) (colloq) math *fpl* (fam)

mathematical *adj* mathématique

mathematician *n* mathématicien/-ienne *m/f*

mathematics *n* mathématiques *fpl*

maths *n* (GB) (colloq) maths *fpl* (fam)

matinée *n* matinée *f*

mating season *n* saison *f* des amours

matriculate *vi* ⟨*student*⟩ s'inscrire

matrimony *n* mariage *m*

matrix *n* (*pl* **-trices**) matrice *f*

matron *n* (a) (GB) (in hospital) infirmière *f* en chef; (in school) infirmière *f*
(b) (of nursing home) directrice *f*
(c) (US) (warder) gardienne *f*

matt (GB), **matte** (US) *adj* ⟨*paint*⟩ mat/-e; ⟨*photograph*⟩ sur papier mat

ⸯ **matter** **1** *n* (a) (affair) affaire *f*; (requiring solution) problème *m*; (on agenda) point *m*;

it will be no easy ~ cela ne sera pas (une affaire) facile; **important** ~s **to discuss** des choses importantes à discuter; **private** ~ affaire privée; **a** ~ **for the police** un problème qui relève de la police; **that's another** ~ c'est une autre histoire; **the fact of the** ~ **is that** la vérité est que
(b) (question) question *f*; **a** ~ **of** une question de ⟨*opinion, principle, taste*⟩; **a** ~ **of life and death** une question de vie ou de mort
(c) (trouble) **is anything the** ~? y a-t-il un problème?; **what's the** ~? qu'est-ce qu'il y a?; **what's the** ~ **with Louise?** qu'est-ce qu'elle a, Louise?; **there's something the** ~ **with my car** ma voiture a un problème
(d) (substance) matière *f*; **vegetable** ~ matière végétale
(e) (printed ~) imprimés *mpl*; **advertising** ~ publicité *f*; **reading** ~ lecture *f*; **subject** ~ contenu *m*
(f) (Med) (pus) pus *m*
2 *vi* être important/-e; **it doesn't** ~ ça ne fait rien; **it doesn't** ~ **whether he comes or not** peu importe qu'il vienne ou pas
IDIOMS as a ~ **of course** automatiquement; **no** ~ **how late it is** peu importe l'heure; **as a** ~ **of fact** en fait; **for that** ~ d'ailleurs; **no** ~ **what (happens)** quoi qu'il arrive; **and to make** ~s **worse** et pour ne rien arranger

matter-of-fact *adj* ⟨*voice, tone*⟩ détaché/-e; ⟨*person*⟩ terre à terre

mattress *n* matelas *m*

mature **1** *adj* (a) ⟨*plant, animal*⟩ adulte
(b) ⟨*person*⟩ mûr/-e; ⟨*attitude, reader*⟩ adulte
(c) ⟨*hard cheese*⟩ fort/-e; ⟨*soft cheese*⟩ affiné/-e; ⟨*whisky*⟩ vieux/vieille
2 *vi* (a) (physically) ⟨*person, animal*⟩ devenir adulte
(b) (psychologically) ⟨*person*⟩ mûrir
(c) ⟨*wine*⟩ vieillir; ⟨*cheese*⟩ s'affiner
(d) ⟨*policy*⟩ arriver à échéance

mature student *n* personne *f* qui reprend des études (*après un temps au foyer ou dans la vie active*)

maul *vtr* ⟨*animal*⟩ lacérer

mauve *n, adj* mauve *m*

maverick *n, adj* nonconformiste *mf*

maxim *n* maxime *f*

maximize *vtr* maximiser ⟨*profit, sales*⟩; (Comput) agrandir

maximum **1** *n* (*pl* **-imums, -ima**) maximum *m*
2 *adj* maximum *inv*

maximum security prison *n* prison *f* de haute surveillance

ⸯ **may** *modal aux* (a) (expressing possibility) **it** ~ **rain** il pleuvra peut-être, il se peut qu'il pleuve; **she** ~ **not have seen him** elle ne l'a peut-être pas vu; **'are you going to accept?'—'I** ~'** 'tu vas accepter'—'peut-être'; **he** ~ **not come** il risque de ne pas venir; **be that as it** ~ quoi qu'il en soit; **come what** ~ advienne que pourra

---

ⸯ indicates a very frequent word

(b) (expressing permission) **you ~ sit down** vous pouvez vous asseoir; **~ I come in?** puis-je entrer?

(c) (wish) **~ he rest in peace** qu'il repose en paix

◦ **May** n mai m

◦ **maybe** adv peut-être; **~ they'll arrive early** peut-être qu'ils arriveront tôt

mayday n (distress signal) mayday m

May Day n premier mai m, fête f du travail

mayhem n (chaos) désordre m; (violence) grabuge m (fam)

mayor n maire m

mayoress n (wife of mayor) femme f du maire; (lady mayor) mairesse f

maze n (puzzle, in gardens) labyrinthe m; (of streets, corridors) dédale m

MBA n (abbr = **Master of Business Administration**) ≈ maîtrise f de gestion

MC n (abbr = **Master of Ceremonies**) (in cabaret) animateur/-trice m/f; (at banquet) maître m des cérémonies

◦ **me** pron **(a)** me, m'; **she knows ~** elle me connaît; **he loves ~** il m'aime
(b) (in imperatives, after prepositions and to be) moi; **give it to ~!** donne-le-moi!; **it's for ~** c'est pour moi; **it's ~** c'est moi

ME n (abbr = **myalgic encephalomyelitis**) encéphalomyélite f myalgique

meadow n **(a)** (field) pré m
(b) (also **~land**) prés mpl, prairies fpl
(c) (also **water ~**) prairie f inondable

meagre (GB), **meager** (US) adj maigre (before n)

◦ **meal** n **(a)** repas m; **to go out for a ~** aller (manger) au restaurant
(b) (from grain) farine f

◦ **mean** ❶ n moyenne f
❷ adj **(a)** ⟨person⟩ avare, radin/-e (fam); **he's ~ with money** il est près de ses sous
(b) (unkind, vicious) méchant/-e (**to** avec); **a ~ trick** un sale tour
(c) (average) ⟨weight, age⟩ moyen/-enne
(d) that's no ~ feat! ce n'est pas un mince exploit!
❸ vtr (prét, pp **meant**) **(a)** ⟨word, phrase, symbol⟩ signifier, vouloir dire; ⟨sign⟩ vouloir dire; **the name ~s nothing to me** ce nom ne me dit rien
(b) (intend) **to ~ to do** avoir l'intention de faire; **to be meant for sb** être destiné/-e à qn; **I didn't ~ to do it** je ne l'ai pas fait exprès; **she meant no offence** elle ne pensait pas à mal; **he doesn't ~ you any harm** il ne te veut aucun mal; **to ~ well** avoir de bonnes intentions; **he ~s what he says** (he is sincere) il est sérieux; (he is menacing) il ne plaisante pas; **without ~ing to** par inadvertance
(c) (entail) ⟨strike, law⟩ entraîner ⟨shortages, changes⟩

(d) (intend to say) vouloir dire; **what do you ~ by that remark?** qu'est-ce que tu veux dire par là?; **I know what you ~** je comprends
(e) (money) **~s a lot to him** l'argent compte beaucoup pour lui; **your friendship ~s a lot to me** ton amitié est très importante pour moi
(f) (be destined) **to be meant to do** être destiné/-e à faire; **it was meant to be** or **happen** cela devait arriver; **they were meant for each other** ils étaient faits l'un pour l'autre
(g) (be supposed to be) **he's meant to be/to be doing** il est censé être/faire

meander vi ⟨river, road⟩ serpenter

◦ **meaning** n (of word, remark, action, life) sens m; (of symbol, film, dream) signification f

meaningful adj **(a)** (significant) ⟨word, statement, result⟩ significatif/-ive
(b) (profound) ⟨relationship, comment, lyrics⟩ sérieux/-ieuse; ⟨experience⟩ riche
(c) (eloquent) ⟨look, smile⟩ entendu/-e; ⟨gesture⟩ significatif/-ive

meaningless adj **(a)** ⟨word, phrase⟩ dépourvu/-e de sens
(b) (pointless) ⟨act, sacrifice⟩ futile, vain/-e; ⟨violence⟩ insensé/-e

means ❶ n (pl **~**) moyen m (**of doing** de faire); **a ~ of** un moyen de ⟨communication, transport⟩; **by ~ of** au moyen de; **yes, by all ~** oui, certainement; **it is by no ~ certain** c'est loin d'être sûr
❷ n pl moyens mpl, revenus mpl; **to live within one's ~** vivre selon ses moyens

means test n enquête f sur les ressources

meantime adv (in the) **~** pendant ce temps; **for the ~** pour le moment

◦ **meanwhile** adv **(a)** (during this time) pendant ce temps
(b) (until then) en attendant
(c) (since then) entre-temps

measles n rougeole f

◦ **measure** ❶ n **(a)** (gen) mesure f; **to take ~s** prendre des mesures; **weights and ~s** les poids et mesures mpl
(b) (measuring device) instrument m de mesure
❷ vtr **(a)** mesurer; **to ~ four by five metres** mesurer quatre mètres sur cinq
(b) (compare) **to ~ sth against** comparer qch à
IDIOM for good ~ pour faire bonne mesure
■ **measure out** mesurer ⟨land, flour, liquid⟩; doser ⟨medicine⟩
■ **measure up** ⟨person⟩ avoir les qualités requises; **to ~ up to** être à la hauteur de ⟨expectations⟩; soutenir la comparaison avec ⟨achievement⟩

measurement n **(a)** (of room, object) dimension f
(b) (of person) **to take sb's ~s** prendre les mensurations de qn; **chest ~** tour m de poitrine; **leg ~** longueur f de jambe

m

measuring jug n verre m gradué
measuring tape n mètre m ruban
meat n viande f; **crab** ~ chair f de crabe
meat-eater n (animal) carnivore m; (person)
they're not great ~s ils ne mangent pas
beaucoup de viande
meaty adj (a) ‹flavour, smell› de viande
(b) ‹article, book› substantiel/-ielle
(c) ‹person, hand› épais/-aisse
Mecca pr n La Mecque
mechanic n mécanicien/-ienne m/f
mechanical adj mécanique
mechanical engineering n
construction f mécanique
mechanics n pl (a) (field) mécanique f
(b) (workings) mécanisme m
⚙ **mechanism** n mécanisme m (of de)
mechanization n mécanisation f
medal n médaille f; **gold** ~ médaille d'or
medallion n médaillon m
medallist (GB), **medalist** (US) n
médaillé/-e m/f; **gold** ~ médaillé/-e m/f d'or
meddle vi **to** ~ **in** se mêler de ‹affairs›; **to**
~ **with** toucher à ‹property›
⚙ **media** [1] n médias mpl
[2] adj ‹coverage, image, personality›
médiatique; ‹power, reaction, report› des
médias
median (strip) n (US) terre-plein m
central
media studies n pl communication f et
journalisme m
mediate [1] vtr négocier ‹settlement,
peace›
[2] vi ‹person› arbitrer; **to** ~ **in/between**
servir de médiateur dans/entre
mediator n médiateur/-trice m/f
⚙ **medical** [1] n (in school, army, for job) visite f
médicale; (private) examen m médical
[2] adj médical/-e
medical insurance n
assurance-maladie f
medical student n étudiant/-e m/f en
médecine
medicated adj (gen) médical/-e; ‹shampoo›
traitant/-e
medication n médicaments mpl
medicinal adj ‹property, use›
thérapeutique; ‹herb› médicinal/-e
⚙ **medicine** n (a) (field) médecine f
(b) (drug) médicament m (**for** pour)
**medicine cabinet, medicine
cupboard** n armoire f à pharmacie
medicine man n sorcier m guérisseur
medieval adj médiéval/-e
mediocre adj médiocre
mediocrity n (a) (state) médiocrité f
(b) (person) médiocre mf
meditate vtr, vi méditer

⚙ indicates a very frequent word

Mediterranean [1] pr n (a) **the** ~ (**sea**)
la (mer) Méditerranée
(b) (region) **the** ~ les pays méditerranéens
[2] adj méditerranéen/-éenne
medium [1] n (a) (pl **-iums** ou **-ia**)
(means) moyen m
(b) **to find** or **strike a happy** ~ trouver le
juste milieu
(c) (pl **-iums**) (spiritualist) médium m
[2] adj moyen/-enne
medium-dry adj ‹drink› demi-sec
medium-rare adj ‹meat› à point
medium-sized adj de taille moyenne
medley n (a) (Mus) pot-pourri m (**of** de)
(b) (mixture) mélange m
meek adj docile
⚙ **meet** [1] n (a) (Sport) rencontre f (sportive);
track ~ (US) rencontre f d'athlétisme
(b) (GB) (in hunting) rendez-vous m de
chasseurs
[2] vtr (prét, pp **met**) (a) rencontrer
‹person, team, enemy›
(b) (make acquaintance of) faire la connaissance
de ‹person›; **have you met each other?** vous
vous connaissez?
(c) (await) attendre; **she went to** ~ **them** elle
est allée les attendre or chercher; **to** ~ **sb
off** (GB) or **at** (US) **the plane** attendre qn à
l'aéroport
(d) répondre à, satisfaire à ‹criteria,
standards, needs›; payer ‹bills, costs›;
couvrir ‹debts›; faire face à ‹obligations,
commitments›; remplir ‹conditions›
(e) se montrer à la hauteur de ‹challenge›
[3] vi (prét, pp **met**) (a) ‹people, teams›
se rencontrer; ‹committee, parliament› se
réunir; **to** ~ **again** ‹people› se revoir
(b) (by appointment) ‹people› se retrouver
(c) (make acquaintance) ‹people› se connaître
(d) ‹lips, roads› se rencontrer; **their eyes met**
leurs regards se croisèrent
IDIOM to make ends ~ joindre les deux
bouts
■ **meet up** (colloq) se retrouver; **to** ~ **up with**
(colloq) retrouver ‹friend›
■ **meet with**: [1] ¶ ~ **with [sb]** rencontrer
‹person, delegation›
[2] ¶ ~ **with [sth]** rencontrer ‹opposition,
success, suspicion›; être accueilli/-e avec
‹approval›; subir ‹failure›
⚙ **meeting** n (a) (official) réunion f; **in a** ~ en
réunion
(b) (informal) rencontre f
(c) (GB Sport) **athletics** ~ rencontre f
d'athlétisme; **race** ~ réunion f de courses
meeting-place n (lieu m de)
rendez-vous m
meeting point n point m de rencontre
megabyte, MB n mégaoctet m, Mo m
megalomaniac n, adj mégalomane mf
megaphone n porte-voix m inv
megastore n mégastore m
melancholy [1] n mélancolie f

2 adj ⟨person⟩ mélancolique; ⟨music, occasion⟩ triste

mellow **1** adj (a) ⟨wine⟩ moelleux/-euse; ⟨flavour⟩ suave; ⟨tone⟩ mélodieux/-ieuse
(b) ⟨person⟩ détendu/-e; ⟨atmosphere⟩ serein/-e
2 vtr ⟨experience⟩ assagir ⟨person⟩
3 vi ⟨person, behaviour⟩ s'assagir

melodrama n mélodrame m

melodramatic adj mélodramatique

melody n mélodie f

melon n melon m

melt **1** vtr (a) faire fondre ⟨snow, plastic, butter⟩
(b) attendrir ⟨heart⟩
2 vi (a) fondre; to ~ in your mouth fondre dans la bouche
(b) to ~ into se fondre dans ⟨crowd⟩

meltdown n fusion f du cœur d'un réacteur

melting point n point m de fusion

 ♂ **member** n (a) membre m; to be a ~ of faire partie de ⟨group⟩; être membre de ⟨club, committee⟩; ~ of staff (gen) employé/-e m/f; (Sch, Univ) enseignant/-e m/f; ~ of the public (in street) passant/-e m/f; (in theatre, cinema) spectateur/-trice m/f ~ state m membre
(b) (also **Member**) (of parliament) député m
(c) (limb) membre m

Member of Congress, MC n (US) membre m du Congrès

Member of Parliament, MP n (GB) député m (for de)

Member of the European Parliament, MEP n (GB) député m au Parlement européen

membership n (a) (of club, organization) adhésion f (of à)
(b) (fee) cotisation f
(c) (members) membres mpl

membrane n membrane f

memento n (pl ~s ou ~es) souvenir m (of de)

memo n note f de service

memoirs n pl mémoires mpl

memo pad n bloc-notes m

memorable adj ⟨event⟩ mémorable; ⟨person, quality⟩ inoubliable

memorial **1** n mémorial m (to à)
2 adj commémoratif/-ive

memorize vtr apprendre [qch] par cœur

 ♂ **memory** n (a) mémoire f; from ~ de mémoire; to have a good ~ for faces être physionomiste; in (loving) ~ of à la mémoire de
(b) (recollection) souvenir m; childhood memories souvenirs d'enfance

memory stick n memory stick m

menace **1** n menace f
2 vtr menacer (with de, avec)

menacing adj menaçant/-e

mend **1** n to be on the ~ ⟨person⟩ être en voie de guérison; ⟨economy⟩ reprendre
2 vtr réparer ⟨object, road⟩; (stitch) raccommoder; (darn) repriser; that won't ~ matters ça n'arrangera pas les choses
3 vi ⟨injury⟩ guérir; ⟨person⟩ se rétablir
IDIOM to ~ one's ways s'amender

menial adj ⟨job⟩ subalterne; ⟨attitude⟩ servile; ~ tasks basses besognes

meningitis n méningite f

menopause n ménopause f

men's room n (US) toilettes fpl pour hommes

menstruation n menstruation f

menswear n prêt-à-porter m pour hommes

 ♂ **mental** adj (gen) mental/-e; ⟨ability, effort, energy⟩ intellectuel/-elle; ⟨hospital, institution⟩ psychiatrique

mental block n blocage m psychologique

mentality n mentalité f

mentally adv (a) ~ handicapped handicapé/-e mental; the ~ ill les malades mentaux
(b) ~ exhausted surmené/-e intellectuellement

mentholated adj au menthol

 ♂ **mention** **1** n mention f (of de); it got a ~ on the radio on en a parlé à la radio
2 vtr (a) faire mention de ⟨person, fact⟩; please don't ~ my name ne mentionnez pas mon nom; to ~ sb/sth to sb parler de qn/qch à qn; not to ~ sans parler de; without ~ing any names sans nommer personne; don't ~ it! je vous en prie!, je t'en prie!
(b) (acknowledge) citer ⟨name⟩

menu n menu m

menu bar n barre f de menu

MEP n (GB) (abbr = **Member of the European Parliament**) député m au Parlement européen

mercenary **1** n mercenaire mf
2 adj ⟨person⟩ intéressé/-e

merchandise n marchandises fpl

merchant n (selling in bulk) négociant m; (selling small quantities) marchand m

merchant bank n (GB) banque f d'affaires

merchant banker n cadre m d'une banque d'affaires

merchant navy (GB), **merchant marine** (US) n marine f marchande

merciful adj (a) ⟨person⟩ clément/-e (to, towards envers); ⟨act⟩ charitable
(b) ⟨occurrence⟩ heureux/-euse; a ~ release une délivrance

merciless adj ⟨ruler, criticism⟩ impitoyable (to, towards envers); ⟨heat⟩ implacable

mercury **1** n mercure m
2 **Mercury** pr n Mercure f

mercy *n* clémence *f*; **to have ~ on sb** avoir pitié de qn; **to beg for ~** demander grâce; **at the ~ of** à la merci de

mercy killing *n* (a) euthanasie *f* (b) (act) acte *m* d'euthanasie

mere *adj* (a) ⟨*coincidence, nonsense*⟩ pur/-e (*before n*); ⟨*formality*⟩ simple (*before n*); **he's a ~ child** ce n'est qu'un enfant; **the beach is a ~ 2 km from here** la plage n'est qu'à 2 km d'ici
(b) (very) ⟨*idea*⟩ simple (*before n*); **the ~ sight of her makes me nervous** rien que de la voir, ça rend nerveux

◦ **merely** *adv* simplement, seulement

merge ① *vtr* (a) **to ~ sth with** fusionner qch avec ⟨*company, group*⟩
(b) mélanger ⟨*colours, designs*⟩
② *vi* (a) (*also* **~ together**) ⟨*companies, departments*⟩ fusionner (**with** avec); ⟨*roads, rivers*⟩ se rejoindre
(b) ⟨*colours, sounds*⟩ se confondre

merger *n* fusion *f*

meringue *n* meringue *f*

merit ① *n* mérite *m*
② *vtr* mériter

mermaid *n* sirène *f*

merrily *adv* (a) (happily) joyeusement
(b) (unconcernedly) avec insouciance

merry *adj* (a) (happy) joyeux/-euse, gai/-e; **Merry Christmas!** joyeux Noël!
(b) (colloq) (tipsy) éméché/-e

merry-go-round *n* manège *m*

mesh ① *n* (a) (netting) (of string) filet *m*; (of metal) grillage *m*
(b) (net) mailles *fpl*
② *vi* (Tech) ⟨*cogs*⟩ s'engrener; **to ~ with** s'emboîter dans

mesmerize ① *vtr* hypnotiser
② **mesmerized** *pp adj* fasciné/-e, médusé/-e

mess ① *n* (a) désordre *m*; **what a ~!** quel désordre!, quelle pagaille! (fam); **to make a ~** ⟨*person*⟩ mettre du désordre; **this report is a ~!** ce rapport est fait n'importe comment!; **to make a ~ on the carpet** salir la moquette; **to make a ~ of the job** massacrer (fam) le travail
(b) (Mil) cantine *f*
② *vi* (colloq) (a) **to ~ with** toucher à ⟨*drugs*⟩
(b) **don't ~ with him** évite-le; **don't ~ with me** ne me cherche pas
■ **mess about** (colloq), **mess around** (colloq): ① ¶ **~ around** faire l'imbécile
② ¶ **~ [sb] around** traiter qn par-dessus la jambe (fam), prendre qn pour un imbécile
■ **mess up** (colloq): ① ¶ **~ up** (US) faire l'imbécile
② ¶ **~ [sth] up** (a) semer la pagaille dans ⟨*papers*⟩; mettre du désordre dans ⟨*kitchen*⟩
(b) (ruin) louper (fam) ⟨*exam*⟩; gâcher ⟨*chances, life*⟩

◦ **indicates a very frequent word**

③ ¶ **~ [sb] up** ⟨*drugs, alcohol*⟩ détruire; ⟨*experience*⟩ faire perdre les pédales à qn (fam)

◦ **message** *n* message *m* (**about** au sujet de)

message window *n* (Comput) feuille *f* de message

messaging *n* messagerie *f* électronique

messenger *n* messager/-ère *m/f*; (for hotel, company) garçon *m* de courses, coursier/-ière *m/f*

messy *adj* (a) ⟨*house*⟩ en désordre; ⟨*appearance*⟩ négligé/-e; ⟨*handwriting*⟩ peu soigné/-e
(b) ⟨*work, job*⟩ salissant/-e; **he's a ~ eater** il mange comme un cochon
(c) ⟨*lawsuit*⟩ compliqué/-e; **a ~ business** une sale affaire

◦ **metal** ① *n* métal *m*
② *adj* en métal

metallic *adj* ⟨*substance*⟩ métallique; ⟨*paint, finish*⟩ métallisé/-e; ⟨*taste*⟩ de métal

metaphor *n* métaphore *f*

mete *v*
■ **mete out** infliger ⟨*punishment*⟩; rendre ⟨*justice*⟩

meteor *n* météore *m*

meteorite *n* météorite *f*

meter ① *n* (a) compteur *m*; **gas ~** compteur de gaz
(b) (*also* **parking ~**) parcmètre *m*
(c) (US) = METRE
② *vtr* mesurer la consommation de ⟨*electricity, gas*⟩

◦ **method** *n* (a) (of teaching, contraception, training) méthode *f* (**for doing** pour faire); (of payment, treatment, production) mode *m* (**of** de)
(b) (orderliness) méthode *f*

methodical *adj* méthodique

Methodist *n, adj* méthodiste *mf*

methylated spirit(s) *n* alcool *m* à brûler

meticulous *adj* méticuleux/-euse

◦ **metre** (GB), **meter** (US) *n* mètre *m*

metric *adj* métrique

metropolitan *adj* (a) ⟨*area, population*⟩ urbain/-e; **~ New York** l'agglomération de New York
(b) **~ France** la France métropolitaine

mettle *n* courage *m*; **to be on one's ~** être sur la sellette; **to put sb on his ~** amener qn à montrer de quoi il est capable

Mexico *pr n* Mexique *m*

miaow ① *n* miaou *m*
② *vi* miauler

microbe *n* microbe *m*

microchip *n* puce *f*, circuit *m* intégré

microcosm *n* microcosme *m*

microfilm *n* microfilm *m*

microlighting *n* ULM *m*, ultra léger *m* motorisé

micromanage *vtr* microgérer

microphone *n* microphone *m*

microscope *n* microscope *m*

microwave ⟦1⟧ *n* ~ (oven) four *m* à micro ondes

⟦2⟧ *vtr* passer [qch] au four à micro-ondes

mid- *pref* in the ~20th century au milieu du vingtième siècle; ~afternoon milieu *m* de l'après-midi; (in) ~May (à la) mi-mai; he's in his ~forties il a environ quarante-cinq ans

midair ⟦1⟧ *adj* ‹collision› en plein vol

⟦2⟧ **in midair** *phr* (in mid-flight) en plein vol; (in the air) en l'air

midday *n* midi *m*

ℱ **middle** ⟦1⟧ *n* (a) milieu *m*; in the ~ of au milieu de; in the ~ of May à la mi-mai; to be in the ~ of doing être en train de faire; to split [sth] down the ~ partager [qch] en deux ‹bill, work›; diviser [qch] en deux ‹group, opinion›; in the ~ of nowhere en pleine brousse (fam)

(b) (waist) taille *f*

⟦2⟧ *adj* ‹door, shelf› du milieu; ‹size, difficulty› moyen/-enne; there must be a ~ way il doit y avoir une solution intermédiaire

middle-aged *adj* ‹person› d'âge mûr; ‹outlook, view› vieux jeu *inv*

Middle Ages *n pl* the ~ le Moyen Âge

middle class ⟦1⟧ *n* classe *f* moyenne

⟦2⟧ **middle-class** *adj* ‹person› de la classe moyenne; ‹attitude, view› bourgeois/-e

Middle East *pr n* Moyen-Orient *m*

middle-eastern *adj* du Moyen-Orient

middleman *n* intermédiaire *m*

middle-size(d) *adj* de taille moyenne

middleweight *n* poids *m* moyen

middling *adj* moyen/-enne; fair to ~ pas trop mal

midfield *n* milieu *m* du terrain

midge *n* moucheron *m*

midget *n* nain/-e *m/f*

midnight *n* minuit *m*

midriff *n* ventre *m*

midst *n* in the ~ of au beau milieu de; in the ~ of change/war en plein changement/ pleine guerre; in our ~ parmi nous

midsummer *n* milieu *m* de l'été

Midsummer('s) Day *n* la Saint-Jean

midtown *n* (US) centre-ville *m*

midway ⟦1⟧ *n* (US) attractions *fpl* foraines

⟦2⟧ *adj* ‹post, position› de mi-course; ‹stage, point› de mi-parcours

⟦3⟧ *adv* ~ between/along à mi-chemin entre/le long de; ~ through au milieu de

midweek ⟦1⟧ *adj* de milieu de semaine

⟦2⟧ *adv* en milieu de semaine

midwife *n* (*pl* **-wives**) sage-femme *f*; male ~ homme *m* sage-femme

midwinter *n* milieu *m* de l'hiver

ℱ **might¹** *modal aux* (*prét de* **may**, *nég* **might not**, **mightn't**) (a) (expressing possibility) peut-être; 'will you come?'—'I ~' 'tu viendras?'—'peut-être'; she ~ not have heard the news elle n'a peut-être pas entendu la nouvelle; I ~ lose my job je risque de perdre mon travail

(b) (expressing annoyance) you ~ have been killed! tu aurais pu te faire tuer!; I ~ have known! j'aurais dû m'en douter!

(c) I thought it ~ rain j'ai pensé qu'il risquait de pleuvoir; I thought you ~ say that je m'attendais à ce que tu dises ça; he said you ~ be hurt il a dit que tu serais peut-être blessé

(d) ~ I make a suggestion? puis-je me permettre de faire une suggestion?; it ~ be better to wait ce serait peut-être mieux d'attendre

might² *n* (a) (power) puissance *f*

(b) (physical strength) force *f*; with all his ~ de toutes ses forces

mighty *adj* puissant/-e

migrant ⟦1⟧ *n* (person) migrant/-e *m/f*; (bird) oiseau *m* migrateur; (animal) animal *m* migrateur

⟦2⟧ *adj* ‹labour› saisonnier/-ière; ‹bird, animal› migrateur/-trice

migrate *vi* (a) ‹person› émigrer

(b) ‹bird, animal› migrer

mike *n* (colloq) micro *m* (fam)

mild *adj* (a) ‹surprise› léger/-ère; ‹interest, irritation› modéré/-e

(b) ‹weather, winter› doux/douce; ‹climate› tempéré/-e

(c) ‹beer, taste, tobacco› léger/-ère; ‹cheese› doux/douce; ‹curry› peu épicé/-e

(d) ‹soap, detergent› doux/douce

(e) ‹infection› bénin/-igne; ‹attack, sedative› léger/-ère

(f) ‹person, voice› doux/douce

mildew *n* moisissure *f*

ℱ **mile** *n* (a) mile *m* (= *1,609 m*); it's 50 ~s away ≈ c'est à 80 kilomètres d'ici

(b) to walk for ~s marcher pendant des kilomètres; it's ~s away! c'est au bout du monde; to be ~s away (daydreaming) être complètement ailleurs; ~s from anywhere loin de tout; to stand out a ~ sauter aux yeux

mileage *n* (a) nombre *m* de miles

(b) (done by car) kilométrage *m*

(c) (miles per gallon) consommation *f*

milestone *n* borne *f* (milliaire); (figurative) étape *f* importante

militant ⟦1⟧ *n* (activist) agitateur/-trice *m/f*

⟦2⟧ *adj* militant/-e

militarize *vtr* militariser; ~d zone zone *f* militarisée

ℱ **military** ⟦1⟧ *n* the ~ (army) l'armée *f*; (soldiers) les militaires *mpl*

⟦2⟧ *adj* militaire

m

military service n service m militaire

militia n milice f

milk [1] n lait m; powdered ~ lait en poudre; full cream ~ lait entier; skimmed ~ lait écrémé
[2] vtr (a) traire ‹cow›
(b) (exploit) exploiter ‹situation, system›; to ~ sb dry saigner qn à blanc

milk chocolate n chocolat m au lait

milkman n laitier m

milkshake n milkshake m

milky adj (a) ‹drink› au lait
(b) ‹skin, liquid, colour› laiteux/-euse

Milky Way pr n Voie f lactée

mill [1] n (a) moulin m; water/pepper ~ moulin à eau/à poivre
(b) (factory) fabrique f; steel ~ aciérie f
[2] vtr moudre ‹flour, pepper›

millennium bug n bogue m de l'an 2000

millennium n (pl -niums ou -nia) millénaire m

milligram(me) n milligramme m

millimetre (GB), **millimeter** (US) n millimètre m

ꝺ **million** [1] n million m; ~s of des millions de
[2] adj a ~ people/pounds un million de personnes/de livres

millionaire n millionnaire mf

milometer n (GB) ≈ compteur m kilométrique

mime [1] n mime m; ~ show pantomime f
[2] vtr, vi mimer

mime artist n mime mf

mimic [1] n imitateur/-trice m/f
[2] vtr (p prés etc -ck-) imiter

mince [1] n (GB) viande f hachée; beef ~ bœuf m haché
[2] vtr hacher ‹meat›

ꝺ **mind** [1] n (a) esprit m; peace of ~ tranquillité d'esprit; it's all in the ~ c'est tout dans la tête (fam); to cross sb's ~ venir à l'esprit de qn; to have something on one's ~ être préoccupé/-e; to set sb's ~ at rest rassurer qn; nothing could be further from my ~ loin de moi cette pensée; to take sb's ~ off sth distraire qn de qch; my ~'s a blank j'ai un trou de mémoire; I can't get him out of my ~ je n'arrive pas à l'oublier; are you out of your ~? (colloq) tu es fou/folle? (fam)
(b) (brain) intelligence f; with the ~ of a two-year-old avec l'intelligence d'un enfant de deux ans
(c) (opinion) avis m; to my ~ à mon avis; to make up one's ~ about/to do se décider à propos de/à faire; to change one's ~ about sth changer d'avis sur qch; to keep an open ~ about sth réserver son jugement sur qch; to know one's own ~ avoir des idées bien à

soi; to speak one's ~ dire ce qu'on a à dire
[2] vtr (a) surveiller ‹manners, language›; faire attention à ‹hazard›
(b) I don't ~ ça m'est égal, ça ne me dérange pas; I don't ~ the cold le froid ne me dérange pas; I don't ~ cats, but I prefer dogs je n'ai rien contre les chats, mais je préfère les chiens; will they ~ us being late? est-ce qu'ils seront fâchés si nous sommes en retard?; would you ~ keeping my seat for me? est-ce que ça vous ennuierait de garder ma place?; I wouldn't ~ a glass of wine je prendrais volontiers un verre de vin; if you don't ~ si cela ne vous fait rien; never ~ (don't worry) ne t'en fais pas; (it doesn't matter) peu importe; he can't afford an apartment, never ~ a big house il ne peut pas se permettre un appartement encore moins une grande maison
(c) s'occuper de ‹animal, children›; tenir ‹shop›
[3] in mind phr I have something in ~ for this evening j'ai une idée pour ce soir; to bear sth in ~ (remember) ne pas oublier qch; (take into account) prendre qch en compte
IDIOMS to read sb's ~ lire dans les pensées de qn; to see sth in one's ~'s eye imaginer qch; to have a ~ of one's own savoir ce qu'on veut

mind-blowing adj (colloq) époustouflant/-e (fam)

mind-boggling adj (colloq) stupéfiant/-e

mindless adj ‹person, programme› bête; ‹work› abrutissant/-e; ‹vandalism› gratuit/-e; ‹task› machinal/-e

ꝺ **mine¹** pron

■ Note In French, possessive pronouns reflect the gender and number of the noun they are standing for. So mine is translated by le mien, la mienne, les miens, les miennes, according to what is being referred to.

his car is red but ~ is blue sa voiture est rouge mais la mienne est bleue; which (glass) is ~? lequel (de ces verres) est le mien or est à moi?; his children are older than ~ ses enfants sont plus âgés que les miens; the blue car is ~ la voiture bleue est à moi; she's a friend of ~ c'est une amie à moi; it's not ~ ce n'est pas à moi

mine² [1] n mine f
[2] vtr (a) extraire ‹gems, mineral›; exploiter ‹area›
(b) (Mil) miner ‹area›

minefield n champ m de mines; (figurative) terrain m miné

miner n mineur m

mineral [1] n (substance, class) minéral m; (for extraction) minerai m
[2] adj minéral/-e; ~ ore minerai m

mineral water n eau f minérale

mingle vi (a) to ~ with se mêler à ‹crowd, guests›

m

miniature ⋯⟶ mishandle ⋯⋯

(b) ‹sounds› se confondre (**with** à); ‹smells, feelings› se mêler (**with** à)

miniature 1 *n* miniature *f*
2 *adj* (gen) miniature; ‹dog, horse› nain/-e

minicab *n* (GB) taxi *m* (non agréé)

minidisc *n* minidisque *m*

minimalist *adj* minimaliste

minimum 1 *n* minimum *m* (**of** de)
2 *adj* minimum, minimal/-e

mining 1 *n* exploitation *f* minière
2 *adj* ‹industry, town› minier/-ière; ‹accident› de mine

mini-skirt *n* mini-jupe *f*

ℱ **minister** 1 *n* (**a**) (GB) ministre *m*; ∼ **of** *or* **for Defence, Defence** ∼ ministre de la Défense
(b) (clergyman) ministre *m* du culte
2 *vi* **to** ∼ **to** donner des soins à ‹person›; **to** ∼ **to sb's needs** pourvoir aux besoins de qn

minister of state *n* (GB) ministre *m* délégué

ministry *n* (GB) ministère *m*

mink *n* vison *m*

ℱ **minor** 1 *n* (Law) mineur/-e *m/f*
2 *adj* (gen, Mus) mineur/-e; ‹injury, burn› léger/-ère; ∼ **road** route secondaire

ℱ **minority** *n* minorité *f*; **to be in the** ∼ être en minorité

minstrel *n* ménestrel *m*

mint 1 *n* (**a**) (herb) menthe *f*
(b) (sweet) bonbon *m* à la menthe
(c) (for coins) hôtel *m* des Monnaies
2 *adj* **in** ∼ **condition** à l'état neuf
3 *vtr* (**a**) frapper ‹coin›
(b) forger ‹word, expression›

minuet *n* menuet *m*

minus 1 *n* (**a**) (in mathematics) moins *m*
(b) (drawback) inconvénient *m*
2 *adj* ‹symbol, button› moins; ‹number, quantity, value› négatif/-ive; ∼ **sign** signe moins
3 *prep* (**a**) moins; **what is 20** ∼ **8?** combien font 20 moins 8?; **it is** ∼ **15 (degrees)** il fait moins 15 (degrés)
(b) (without) sans

minuscule *adj* minuscule

ℱ **minute¹** 1 *n* minute *f*; **five** ∼**s past ten** dix heures cinq; **it's five** ∼**s' walk away** c'est à cinq minutes à pied; **the** ∼ **I heard the news** dès que j'ai appris la nouvelle; **any** ∼ **now** d'une minute à l'autre; **at the last** ∼ à la dernière minute
2 **minutes** *n pl* compte-rendu *m*

minute² *adj* ‹particle› minuscule; ‹quantity› infime; ‹risk, variation› minime

minute hand *n* aiguille *f* des minutes

miracle *n* miracle *m*; **to work** *or* **perform** ∼**s** faire des miracles

miraculous *adj* (**a**) ‹escape, recovery› miraculeux/-euse
(b) ‹speed, strength› prodigieux/-ieuse

mirror 1 *n* (**a**) (gen) miroir *m*, glace *f*; (Aut) rétroviseur *m*
(b) (figurative) reflet *m*
2 *vtr* refléter; **to be** ∼**ed in** se refléter dans

mirth *n* (laughter) hilarité *f*; (joy) joie *f*

misapprehension *n* malentendu *m*, erreur *f*; **to be (labouring) under a** ∼ se tromper

misappropriate *vtr* détourner ‹funds›

misbehave *vi* ‹child› se tenir mal; ‹adult› se conduire mal

miscalculation *n* erreur *f* de calcul; (figurative) mauvais calcul *m*

miscarriage *n* (**a**) (Med) fausse couche *f*; **to have a** ∼ faire une fausse couche
(b) (Law) **a** ∼ **of justice** une grave erreur judiciaire

miscellaneous *adj* divers/-e

mischief *n* espièglerie *f*; **to get into** *or* **make** ∼ faire des bêtises; **he's up to** ∼ il prépare quelque chose; **to be full of** ∼ être espiègle; **it keeps them out of** ∼ ça les occupe

mischievous *adj* ‹child, comedy, humour› espiègle; ‹smile, eyes› malicieux/-ieuse

misconception *n* idée *f* fausse

misdemeanour, misdemeanor (US) *n* délit *m*

miser *n* avare *mf*

miserable *adj* (**a**) ‹person, event, expression› malheureux/-euse; ‹thoughts› noir/-e; ‹weather› sale (*before n*); **to feel** ∼ avoir le cafard
(b) ‹amount› misérable; ‹wage, life› de misère; ‹attempt, failure, performance› lamentable

miserly *adj* ‹person› avare; ‹amount› maigre

misery *n* (**a**) (unhappiness) souffrance *f*; (gloom) abattement *m*; **to make sb's life a** ∼ faire de la vie de qn un enfer
(b) (misfortune) **the miseries of unemployment** le chômage et son cortège de misères
(c) (GB) (colloq) (child) pleurnicheur/-euse *m/f*; (adult) rabat-joie *m inv*

misfire *vi* (**a**) ‹gun, rocket› faire long feu; ‹engine› avoir des ratés
(b) ‹plan, joke› tomber à plat

misfit *n* marginal/-e *m/f*

misfortune *n* (unfortunate event) malheur *m*; (bad luck) malchance *f*

misgiving *n* crainte *f*; **to have** ∼**s about sth** avoir des craintes quant à qch; **to have** ∼**s about sb** avoir des doutes au sujet de qn

misguided *adj* ‹strategy, attempt› peu judicieux/-ieuse; ‹person› malavisé/-e

mishandle *vtr* (**a**) mal conduire ‹operation, meeting›; mal s'y prendre avec ‹person›
(b) (roughly) manier [qch] sans précaution ‹object›; malmener ‹person, animal›

m

mishap *n* incident *m*

mishear *vtr* (*prét, pp* **misheard**) mal entendre

misinform *vtr* mal renseigner

misinterpret *vtr* mal interpréter

misinterpretation *n* interprétation *f* erronée

misjudge *vtr* mal évaluer ‹*speed, distance*›; mal calculer ‹*shot*›; mal juger ‹*person*›

mislay *vtr* (*prét, pp* **mislaid**) égarer

mislead *vtr* (*prét, pp* **misled**) (deliberately) tromper; (unintentionally) induire [qn] en erreur

misleading *adj* ‹*impression, title, information*› trompeur/-euse; ‹*claim, statement, advertising*› mensonger/-ère

mismanage *vtr* mal diriger ‹*firm, project*›; mal gérer ‹*finances*›

misplace *vtr* égarer

misprint *n* coquille *f*, faute *f* typographique

mispronounce *vtr* mal prononcer

misread *vtr* (*prét, pp* **misread**) (read wrongly) mal lire; (misinterpret) mal interpréter ‹*actions*›

misrepresent *vtr* présenter [qn] sous un faux jour ‹*person*›; déformer ‹*views, facts*›

misrepresentation *n* (of facts) déformation *f*

⚥ **miss** **1** *n* **(a)** (in game) coup *m* manqué *or* raté

(b) to give [sth] a ~ (colloq) ne pas aller à ‹*film, lecture*›; se passer de ‹*dish, drink, meal*›

2 *vtr* **(a)** manquer ‹*target*›

(b) rater ‹*bus, plane, event, meeting*›; laisser passer ‹*chance*›; I ~ed the train by five minutes j'ai raté le train de cinq minutes

(c) ne pas saisir ‹*joke, remark*›

(d) sauter ‹*line, class*›; manquer ‹*school*›

(e) (avoid) échapper à ‹*death, injury*›; éviter ‹*traffic, bad weather, rush hour*›; he just ~ed being caught il a failli être pris

(f) I ~ you tu me manques; he ~ed Paris Paris lui manquait; I'll ~ coming to the office le bureau va me manquer

3 *vi* **(a)** (Games, Sport, Mil) rater son coup; ~ed! raté!

(b) ‹*engine*› avoir des ratés

■ **miss out**: **1** ¶ ~ out être lésé/-e

2 ¶ ~ out on [sth] laisser passer, louper (fam)

3 ¶ ~ [sb/sth] out sauter ‹*line, verse*›; omettre ‹*fact, point, person*›

Miss *n* Mademoiselle *f*; (written abbreviation) Mlle

misshapen *adj* ‹*leg*› difforme; ‹*object*› déformé/-e

missile *n* **(a)** (Mil) missile *m*

(b) (rock, bottle) projectile *m*

missing *adj* to be ~ manquer; to go ~ ‹*person, object*› disparaître; the ~ jewels/ child les bijoux disparus/l'enfant disparu; there are two books ~ il manque deux livres

⚥ **mission** *n* mission *f*

missionary *n* missionnaire *mf*

mist *n* brume *f*

■ **mist over, mist up** ‹*lens, window*› s'embuer

⚥ **mistake** **1** *n* (gen) erreur *f*; (in text, spelling, typing) faute *f*; to make a ~ se tromper; by ~ par erreur

2 *vtr* (*prét* **-took**, *pp* **-taken**) **(a)** to ~ sth for sth else prendre qch pour qch d'autre; to ~ sb for sb else confondre qn avec qn d'autre

(b) mal interpréter ‹*meaning*›

mistaken *adj* **(a)** to be ~ avoir tort; he was ~ in thinking it was over il avait tort de croire que c'était fini

(b) ‹*enthusiasm, generosity*› mal placé/-e

mistletoe *n* gui *m*

mistranslation *n* erreur *f* de traduction

mistreat *vtr* maltraiter

mistress *n* maîtresse *f*

mistrust **1** *n* méfiance *f* (of à l'égard de)

2 *vtr* se méfier de

misty *adj* ‹*conditions, morning*› brumeux/ -euse; ‹*lens, window*› embué/-e; ‹*photo*› flou/-e

misunderstand *vtr* (*prét, pp* **-stood**) mal comprendre; (completely) ne pas comprendre

misunderstanding *n* malentendu *m*

misunderstood *adj* to feel ~ se sentir incompris/-e

misuse **1** *n* (of equipment) mauvais usage *m*; (of word) usage *m* impropre; (of power, authority) abus *m*

2 *vtr* faire mauvais usage de ‹*equipment*›; mal employer ‹*word, resources*›; abuser de ‹*authority*›

mitigate *vtr* atténuer ‹*effects, distress, sentence*›; réduire ‹*risks*›; minimiser ‹*loss*›

mitre (GB), **miter** (US) *n* mitre *f*

mitten *n* moufle *f*

⚥ **mix** **1** *n* **(a)** (gen) mélange *m*

(b) (Mus) mixage *m*, mix *m*

2 *vtr* **(a)** (gen) mélanger (with avec; and à)

(b) préparer ‹*drink*›; malaxer ‹*cement, paste*›

(c) (Mus) mixer

3 *vi* **(a)** (also ~ **together**) se mélanger (with avec, à)

(b) (socialize) être sociable; to ~ with fréquenter

■ **mix up (a)** (confuse) confondre; to get two things/people ~ed up confondre deux choses/personnes

(b) (jumble up) mélanger, mêler ‹*papers, photos*›

(c) to get ~ed up in se trouver mêlé/-e à

⚥ indicates a very frequent word

mixed adj **(a)** ‹collection, programme, diet›
varié/-e; ‹nuts, sweets› assorti/-e; ‹salad›
composé/-e; ‹group, community› (socially, in
age) mélangé/-e; **of ∼ blood** de sang mêlé
(b) (for both sexes) mixte
(c) ‹reaction, feelings, reception› mitigé/-e

mixed ability adj (Sch) ‹class, teaching›
sans groupes de niveau

mixed race n **of ∼** métis/-isse

mixer n **(a)** (Culin) batteur m électrique
(b) (drink) boisson f nonalcoolisée

mixing n (combining) mélange m; (Mus)
mixage m

mixture n mélange m **(of** de)

mix-up n confusion f **(over** sur)

moan 1 n **(a)** (noise) gémissement m
(b) (colloq) (complaint) plainte f **(about** au sujet
de)
2 vi **(a)** (groan) gémir **(with** de)
(b) (colloq) (complain) râler (fam) **(about** contre)

moat n douve f

mob 1 n foule f **(of** de)
2 vtr **(p prés etc -bb-)** assaillir ‹person›;
envahir ‹place›

✧ **mobile** 1 n mobile m
2 adj **(a)** ‹object, population› mobile;
‹canteen› ambulant/-e
(b) to be ∼ (able to walk) pouvoir marcher;
(able to travel) pouvoir se déplacer

mobile phone n téléphone m portable,
portable m

mobilization n mobilisation f

mobilize vtr, vi mobiliser

mocha n **(a)** (coffee) moka m
(b) (flavour) arôme m de café et de chocolat

mock 1 n (GB Sch) examen m blanc
2 adj **(a)** ‹suede, ivory› faux/fausse (before
n); **∼ leather** similicuir m
(b) (feigned) simulé/-e; **in ∼ terror** en feignant
la terreur
3 vtr se moquer de ‹person, efforts, beliefs›
4 vi ‹person› se moquer

mockery n moquerie f

mod con n (GB) confort m (moderne)

mode n mode m

✧ **model** 1 n **(a)** (of car, appliance, garment)
modèle m
(b) (person) (artist's) modèle m; (fashion)
mannequin m
(c) (scale model) maquette f
(d) (perfect example) modèle m **(of** de)
2 adj **(a)** ‹railway, soldier, village›
miniature; ‹aeroplane, boat, car› modèle
réduit
(b) ‹husband, student, prison› modèle
3 vtr **(p prés etc -ll-, -l-** (US)) **(a)** modeler
‹clay, wax›
(b) ‹fashion model› présenter ‹garment›
4 vi **(p prés etc -ll-, -l-** (US)) **(a)** ‹artist's
model› poser
(b) ‹fashion model› travailler comme

mannequin

modelling (GB), **modeling** (US) n **(a)** (of
clothes) **to take up ∼** devenir mannequin;
have you done any ∼? as-tu déjà travaillé
comme mannequin?
(b) (Comput) modélisation f

modem n modem m

moderate 1 adj **(a)** (not extreme)
modéré/-e **(in** dans)
(b) ‹success, income› moyen/-enne
2 vtr modérer
3 vi se modérer

moderation n modération f **(in** dans); **in
∼** avec modération

✧ **modern** adj moderne; **the ∼ world** le
monde contemporain

modernize vtr moderniser

modern languages n pl langues fpl
vivantes

modest adj **(a)** modeste **(about** au sujet de)
(b) ‹gift, aim› modeste; ‹sum, salary›
modique

modesty n modestie f

modify vtr modifier

modular adj modulaire

module n module m

mogul n magnat m

Mohammed, Mahomet pr n Mahomet

moist adj ‹soil› humide; ‹cake› moelleux/
-euse; ‹hands› moite; ‹skin› bien hydraté/-e

moisten vtr humecter

moisture n humidité f

moisturizer n (lotion) lait m hydratant;
(cream) crème f hydratante

molar n, adj molaire f

mold (US) = MOULD

mole n **(a)** (Zool) taupe f
(b) (on skin) grain m de beauté

molecule n molécule f

molest vtr agresser [qn] sexuellement

mollycoddle vtr dorloter

molt (US) = MOULT

molten adj en fusion

✧ **moment** n **(a)** (instant) instant m; **in a ∼**
dans un instant; **at any ∼** à tout instant
(b) (point in time) moment m; **at the ∼** en ce
moment; **at the right ∼** au bon moment

momentarily adv **(a)** (for an instant)
momentanément
(b) (US) (very soon) dans un instant; (at any
moment) d'un moment à l'autre

momentary adj passager/-ère

momentous adj capital/-e

momentum n (gen) élan m; (in physics)
vitesse f

monarch n monarque m

monarchy n monarchie f

monastery n monastère m

✧ **Monday** n lundi m

monetary union n union f monétaire

⚬ **money** n argent m; **to make** ~ ‹person› gagner de l'argent; ‹business, project› rapporter de l'argent
IDIOMS **to get one's** ~'s **worth, to get a good run for one's** ~ en avoir pour son argent; **your** ~ **or your life!** la bourse ou la vie!

money belt n ceinture f porte-monnaie

moneybox n tirelire f

moneylender n prêteur/-euse m/f

moneymaker n (product) article m qui rapporte beaucoup; (activity) activité f lucrative

money order, MO n mandat m postal

mongrel n (chien m) bâtard m

monitor ① n (Comput, Med) moniteur m
② vtr (a) surveiller ‹results, patient, breathing›
(b) être à l'écoute de ‹broadcast›

monk n moine m

monkey n (a) (Zool) singe m
(b) (colloq) (rascal) galopin m (fam)

monochrome adj ‹film› en noir et blanc; ‹colour scheme› monochrome

monogamous adj monogame

monogamy n monogamie f

monologue, monolog (US) n monologue m

monopolize vtr (a) détenir le monopole de ‹market, supply›
(b) (figurative) monopoliser

monopoly n monopole m

monoski vi faire du monoski

monotonous adj monotone

monotony n monotonie f

monsoon n mousson f

monster n monstre m

monstrous adj (a) (ugly) monstrueux/-euse; ‹building› hideux/-euse
(b) (huge) énorme

⚬ **month** n mois m; **in two** ~s, **in two** ~s' **time** dans deux mois; **every other** ~ tous les deux mois; **in the** ~ **of June** au mois de juin

monthly ① n (journal) mensuel m
② adj mensuel/-elle; ~ **instalment** mensualité f
③ adv ‹pay, earn› au mois; ‹happen, visit, publish› tous les mois

Montreal pr n Montréal

monument n monument m

moo vi meugler

⚬ **mood** n (a) (humour) humeur f; **in a good/bad** ~ de bonne/mauvaise humeur; **to be in the** ~ **for doing** avoir envie de faire; **to be in no** ~ **for doing** ne pas être d'humeur à faire
(b) (bad temper) saute f d'humeur; **to be in a** ~ être de mauvaise humeur

mood swing n saute f d'humeur

⚬ indicates a very frequent word

moody adj (a) (unpredictable) d'humeur changeante, lunatique
(b) (sulky) de mauvaise humeur

moon n lune f
IDIOMS **to be over the** ~ être aux anges; **once in a blue** ~ tous les trente-six du mois (fam); **the man in the** ~ le visage de la Lune

moonlight ① n clair m de lune
② vi travailler au noir

moonlit adj éclairé/-e par la lune; **a** ~ **night** une nuit de lune

moor ① n lande f
② vtr amarrer ‹boat›
③ vi ‹boat› mouiller

moorings n pl amarres fpl

moorland n lande f

moose n (Canadian) orignal m; (European) élan m

mop ① n (a) (of cotton) balai m à franges; (of sponge) balai m éponge
(b) ~ **of hair** crinière f (fam)
② vtr (p prés etc **-pp-**) (a) laver [qch] à grande eau ‹floor›
(b) **to** ~ **one's face/brow** s'éponger le visage/le front
■ **mop up** éponger ‹milk, wine›

mope vi se morfondre
■ **mope about, mope around** traîner (comme une âme en peine)

moped n vélomoteur m

⚬ **moral** ① n morale f
② **morals** n pl moralité f
③ adj moral/-e

morale n moral m

morality n moralité f

moral majority n majorité f bien-pensante

morbid adj morbide

⚬ **more** ① adv (a) (comparative) plus (**than** que); ~ **expensive** plus cher/chère; ~ **easily** plus facilement
(b) (to a greater extent) plus, davantage; **you must rest** ~ il faut que tu te reposes davantage; **he is all the** ~ **angry because** il est d'autant plus en colère que
(c) (longer) **I don't work there any** ~ je n'y travaille plus
(d) (again) **once** ~ une fois de plus, encore une fois
(e) (else) **nothing** ~ rien de plus; **something** ~ autre chose
② det plus de; **I have** ~ **money than him** j'ai plus d'argent que lui; **some** ~ **books** quelques livres de plus; **there's no** ~ **bread** il n'y a plus de pain; **have some** ~ **beer!** reprenez de la bière!
③ pron, quantif (a) (larger amount or number) plus; **it costs** ~ il/elle coûte plus cher (**than** que); **he eats** ~ **than you** il mange plus que toi
(b) (additional amount) davantage; **I need** ~ **of them** il m'en faut plus; **I need** ~ **of it** il m'en faut davantage

4 **more and more** *phr* de plus en plus; ~ **and** ~ **work** de plus en plus de travail
5 **more or less** *phr* plus ou moins
6 **more than** *phr* **(a)** (greater amount or number) plus de; ~ **than 20 people** plus de 20 personnes; ~ **than half** plus de la moitié; ~ **than enough** plus qu'assez
(b) (extremely) ~ **than generous** plus que généreux

moreover *adv* de plus, qui plus est

◆ **morning** **1** *n* matin *m*; (with emphasis on duration) matinée *f*; **in the** ~ le matin; **on Monday** ~**s** le lundi matin; **(on) Monday** ~ lundi matin; **later this** ~ plus tard dans la matinée; **yesterday/tomorrow** ~ hier/demain matin
2 *excl* (good) ~! bonjour!

morning-after pill *n* pilule *f* du lendemain

Morocco *pr n* Maroc *m*

Morse (code) *n* morse *m*; **in** ~ en morse

morsel *n* morceau *m*

mortal *n, adj* mortel/-elle *m/f*

mortality *n* mortalité *f*

mortar *n* mortier *m*

mortgage *n* emprunt-logement *m* **(on** pour)

mortgage rate *n* taux *m* de l'emprunt-logement

mortuary *n* morgue *f*

mosaic *n* mosaïque *f*

Moscow *pr n* Moscou

Moslem = MUSLIM

mosque *n* mosquée *f*

mosquito *n* moustique *m*

mosquito repellent *n* anti-moustique *m*

moss *n* mousse *f*

◆ **most**

■ **Note** When used to form the superlative of adjectives, *most* is translated by *le plus* or *la plus* depending on the gender of the noun and by *les plus* with plural noun: *the most beautiful woman in the room* = la plus belle femme de la pièce; *the most expensive hotel in Paris* = l'hôtel le plus cher de Paris; *the most difficult problems* = les problèmes les plus difficiles. For examples and further uses, see the entry below.

---

1 *det* **(a)** (the majority of) la plupart de; ~ **people** la plupart des gens
(b) (in superlatives) le plus de; **she got the** ~ **votes** c'est elle qui a obtenu le plus de voix
2 *pron* **(a)** (the greatest number) la plupart (**of** de); (the largest part) la plus grande partie (**of** de); ~ **of the time** la plupart du temps; ~ **of us** la plupart d'entre nous; **for** ~ **of the day** pendant la plus grande partie de la journée; ~ **of the bread** presque tout le pain
(b) (all) **the** ~ **you can expect is...** tout ce que tu peux espérer c'est...

(c) (in superlatives) le plus; **John has got the** ~ c'est John qui en a le plus
3 *adv* **(a)** (in superlatives) **the** ~ **beautiful château in France** le plus beau château de France; ~ **easily** le plus facilement
(b) (very) très, extrêmement; ~ **encouraging** très *or* extrêmement encourageant; ~ **probably** très vraisemblablement
(c) (more than all the rest) le plus; **what annoyed him** ~ **(of all) was** ce qui l'ennuyait le plus c'était que
4 **at (the) most** *phr* au maximum, au plus
5 **for the most part** *phr* (most of them) pour la plupart; (most of the time) la plupart du temps; (chiefly) surtout, essentiellement
6 **most of all** *phr* par-dessus tout
IDIOM **to make the** ~ **of** tirer le meilleur parti de ‹situation, resources, abilities›; profiter de ‹opportunity, good weather›

◆ **mostly** *adv* **(a)** (chiefly) surtout, essentiellement; (most of them) pour la plupart
(b) (most of the time) la plupart du temps

MOT *n* (also ~ **test**) (GB) contrôle *m* technique des véhicules; contrôle *m* technique des véhicules

moth *n* papillon *m* de nuit; (in clothes) mite *f*

◆ **mother** **1** *n* mère *f*
2 *vtr* (coddle) dorloter

motherboard *n* carte *f* mère

motherhood *n* maternité *f*

mother-in-law *n* (*pl* **mothers-in-law**) belle-mère *f*

motherly *adj* maternel/-elle

mother-of-pearl *n* nacre *f*

Mother's Day *n* fête *f* des Mères

mother tongue *n* langue *f* maternelle

◆ **motion** **1** *n* **(a)** mouvement *m*; **to set [sth] in** ~ mettre [qch] en marche ‹machine›; mettre [qch] en route ‹plan›; déclencher ‹chain of events›
(b) (proposal) motion *f*
2 *vi* **to** ~ **to sb (to do)** faire signe á qn (de faire)

motionless *adj* immobile

motivate *vtr* motiver ‹person›

motivated *adj* **(a)** ‹person, pupil› motivé/-e
(b) **politically/racially** ~ ‹act› politique/raciste

motivation *n* motivation *f*

motive *n* (gen) motif *m* (**for, behind** de); (for crime) mobile *m* (**for** de)

motley *adj* ‹crowd, gathering› bigarré/-e; ‹collection› hétéroclite

motor **1** *n* moteur *m*
2 *adj* **(a)** ‹vehicle› automobile; ‹show› de l'automobile
(b) ‹mower› à moteur

motorbike *n* moto *f*

motorboat n canot m automobile

motorcycle n motocyclette f

motorcyclist n motocycliste mf

motor home n auto-caravane f

motorist n automobiliste mf

motor racing n course f automobile

motorway n (GB) autoroute f

mottled adj ‹skin, paper› marbré/-e; ‹hands› tacheté/-e

motto n devise f

mould (GB), **mold** (US) ① n (a) (Culin, figurative) moule m
(b) (fungi) moisissure f
② vtr modeler ‹plastic, clay, shape›; façonner ‹character, opinions› (**into** pour en faire)

mouldy (GB), **moldy** (US) adj moisi/-e; **to go** ∼ moisir

moult (GB), **molt** (US) vi ‹cat, dog› perdre ses poils; ‹bird› muer

mound n (a) (hillock) tertre m
(b) (heap) monceau m (**of** de)

mount ① vtr (a) monter sur ‹platform, horse›
(b) monter ‹jewel, picture, exhibit›
(c) organiser ‹demonstration›
② vi (a) ‹person, staircase› monter (**to** jusqu'à)
(b) ‹number, toll› augmenter; ‹concern› grandir
(c) (on horse) se mettre en selle

ℰ **mountain** n montagne f

mountain bike n vélo m tout-terrain, VTT m

mountaineer n alpiniste mf

mountaineering n alpinisme m

mountainous adj montagneux/-euse

mountain top n cime f

mourn ① vtr pleurer ‹person, death›
② vi ‹person› porter le deuil; **to** ∼ **for sb/ sth** pleurer qn/qch

mourning n deuil m

mouse n (pl **mice**) (Comput, Zool) souris f
■ **mouse over**: ¶ ∼ **over [sth]** passer la souris sur [qch]

mousemat n tapis m de souris

mouse pointer n pointeur m de la souris

moustache, mustache (US) n moustache f

ℰ **mouth** ① n (a) (of human, horse) bouche f; (of other animal) gueule f
(b) (of cave, tunnel) entrée f; (of river) embouchure f; (of volcano) bouche f
② vtr articuler silencieusement
IDIOM by word of ∼ de bouche à oreille

mouthful n (of food) bouchée f; (of liquid) gorgée f

mouth organ n harmonica m

ℰ indicates a very frequent word

mouth-to-mouth resuscitation n bouche-à-bouche m inv

mouthwash n eau f dentifrice

mouth-watering adj appétissant/-e

ℰ **move** ① n (a) (movement) mouvement m; (gesture) geste m
(b) (of residence) déménagement m; (of company) transfert m
(c) (in game) coup m; **it's your** ∼ c'est ton tour
(d) (step, act) manœuvre f; **a good/bad** ∼ une bonne/mauvaise idée; **to make the first** ∼ faire le premier pas
② vtr (a) déplacer ‹game piece, cursor, car, furniture›; transporter ‹patient, army›; **to** ∼ **sth (out of the way)** enlever qch
(b) ‹person› bouger ‹limb, head›; ‹wind, mechanism› faire bouger ‹leaf, wheel›
(c) (relocate) muter ‹staff›; transférer ‹office›; **to** ∼ **house** déménager
(d) (affect) émouvoir; **to be deeply** ∼**d** être très ému/-e
③ vi (a) (stir) bouger; ‹lips› remuer
(b) (travel) ‹vehicle› rouler; ‹person› avancer; ‹procession, army› être en marche; **to** ∼ **back** reculer; **to** ∼ **forward** s'avancer; **to** ∼ **away** s'éloigner
(c) (change home, location) déménager; **to** ∼ **to the countryside/to Japan** s'installer à la campagne/au Japon
(d) (change job) être muté/-e
(e) (act) agir
IDIOM to get a ∼ **on** (colloq) se dépêcher
■ **move about, move around** ‹person› (fidget) remuer; (move home) déménager
■ **move along:** ① ¶ ∼ **along** (stop loitering) circuler; (proceed) avancer; (squeeze up) se pousser
② ¶ ∼ **[sb/sth] along** faire circuler ‹onlookers, crowd›
■ **move away** s'éloigner; (move house) déménager
■ **move in** (a) (to house) emménager; **to** ∼ **in with sb** s'installer avec ‹friend, lover›
(b) (advance, attack) s'avancer (**on** sur)
■ **move on** ‹person, traveller› se mettre en route; ‹vehicle› repartir; **to** ∼ **on to** passer à ‹next item›
■ **move out** (of house) déménager; **to** ∼ **out of** quitter
■ **move over** se pousser
■ **move up** (a) (make room) se pousser
(b) (be promoted) être promu/-e

ℰ **movement** n mouvement m; (of hand, arm) geste m

ℰ **movie** (US) ① n film m
② **movies** n pl **the** ∼**s** le cinéma

movie camera n caméra f

movie star n vedette f de cinéma

movie theater n (US) cinéma m

moving adj (a) ‹vehicle› en marche; ‹parts, target› mobile; ‹staircase, walkway› roulant/-e
(b) ‹scene, speech› émouvant/-e

mow *vtr* (*pp* ∼**ed**, **mown**) tondre ‹grass, lawn›

mower *n* tondeuse *f* à gazon

MP *n* (GB) (*abbr* = **Member of Parliament**) député *m* (for de)

MP3 player *n* (lecteur *m*) MP3 *m*

◆ **Mr** *n* (*pl* **Messrs**) M., Monsieur

MRI *n* (*abbr* = **magnetic resonance imaging**) IRM *f*

◆ **Mrs** *n* Mme, Madame

Ms *n* ≈ Mme.

MSc *n* (*abbr* = **Master of Science**) diplôme *m* supérieur en sciences

◆ **much** ⟦1⟧ *adv* beaucoup; ∼ **more/less** beaucoup plus/moins; ∼ **smaller** beaucoup plus petit; **I don't read** ∼ je ne lis pas beaucoup; **we'd** ∼ **rather stay here** nous préférerions de beaucoup rester ici; **does it hurt** ∼? est-ce que ça fait très mal?; **we don't go out** ∼ nous ne sortons pas beaucoup *or* souvent; **it's** ∼ **the same** c'est à peu près pareil (**as** que); **too** ∼ trop; **very** ∼ beaucoup; **thank you very** ∼ merci beaucoup; **so** ∼ tellement; **as** ∼ autant (**as** que); **they hated each other as** ∼ **as ever** ils se détestaient toujours autant ⟦2⟧ *pron* beaucoup; **do you have** ∼ **left?** est-ce qu'il vous en reste beaucoup?; **we didn't eat** ∼ nous n'avons pas mangé grand-chose; **I don't see** ∼ **of them now** je ne les vois plus beaucoup maintenant; **so** ∼ tellement, tant; **we'd eaten so** ∼ **that** nous avions tellement mangé que; **too** ∼ trop; **it costs too** ∼ c'est trop cher; **twice as** ∼ deux fois plus; **as** ∼ **as possible** autant que possible; **how** ∼? combien?; **it's not** *or* **nothing** ∼ ce n'est pas grand-chose; **he's not** ∼ **to look at** il n'est pas très beau ⟦3⟧ *det* beaucoup de; **I haven't got** ∼ **time** je n'ai pas beaucoup de temps; **she didn't speak** ∼ **English** elle ne connaissait que quelques mots d'anglais; **too** ∼ **money** trop d'argent; **don't use so** ∼ **salt** ne mets pas tant de sel; **we paid twice as** ∼ nous avons payé deux fois plus; **how** ∼ **time have we got left?** combien de temps nous reste-t-il? ⟦4⟧ **much as** *phr* bien que (+ *subjunctive*) ⟦5⟧ **so much as** *phr* without so ∼ **as an apology** sans même s'excuser; **if you so** ∼ **as move** si tu fais le moindre mouvement

muck *n* saletés *fpl*; (mud) boue *f*
■ **muck about** (colloq), **muck around** (colloq): ⟦1⟧ ¶ ∼ **about** (fool about) faire l'imbécile; **to** ∼ **about with** traficoter (fam) ‹appliance›; toucher à ‹object› ⟦2⟧ ¶ ∼ **[sb] about** se ficher de (fam) qn
■ **muck in** mettre la main à la pâte (fam)

mud *n* boue *f*

muddle *n* (a) (mess) pagaille *f* (fam)
(b) (mix-up) malentendu *m* (over à propos de)
(c) **to get into a** ∼ ‹person› s'embrouiller
■ **muddle up**: ⟦1⟧ ¶ ∼ **[sth] up** (disorder)

semer la pagaille (fam) dans ⟦2⟧ ¶ ∼ **[sb] up** embrouiller les idées de; **to get [sth]** ∼**d up** s'embrouiller dans ‹dates, names›

muddled *adj* confus/-e

muddy *adj* ‹hand› couvert/-e de boue; ‹shoe, garment› crotté/-e; ‹road, water› boueux/-euse; ‹green, yellow› terne

mudguard *n* garde-boue *m inv*

muffle *vtr* assourdir ‹bell, drum›

muffler *n* (US) (for car) silencieux *m*

mug ⟦1⟧ *n* (a) grande tasse *f*
(b) (GB) (fool) poire *f* (fam); **it's a** ∼**'s game** c'est un attrape-nigaud ⟦2⟧ *vtr* (*p prés etc* **-gg-**) agresser; **to be** ∼**ged** se faire agresser

mugger *n* agresseur *m*

mugging *n* (attack) agression *f*; (crime) agressions *fpl*

muggy *adj* ‹room, day› étouffant/-e; ‹weather› lourd/-e

Muhammad *pr n* Mahomet

mule *n* mulet *m*, mule *f*
IDIOM **as stubborn as a** ∼ têtu/-e comme une mule

mull *v*
■ **mull over** retourner [qch] dans sa tête

mulled wine *n* vin *m* chaud

multicultural *adj* multiculturel/-elle

multidisciplinary *adj* pluridisciplinaire

multi-ethnic *adj* multi-ethnique

multi-function *adj* multifonctions *inv*

multigym *n* appareil *m* de musculation

multilateral *adj* multilatéral/-e

multimedia *n*, *adj* multimédia *m inv*

multinational *adj* multinational/-e

◆ **multiple** *n*, *adj* multiple *m*

multiple choice *adj* à choix multiple

multiple sclerosis, **MS** *n* sclérose *f* en plaques

multiplex *n* (Cinema) complexe *m* multi-salles

multiply ⟦1⟧ *vtr* multiplier (**by** par) ⟦2⟧ *vi* se multiplier

multipurpose *adj* ‹tool, gadget› à usages multiples; ‹area, organization› polyvalent/-e

multipurpose vehicle, **MPV** *n* monospace *m*

multi-racial *adj* multiracial/-e

multistorey *adj* (GB) ‹car park› à niveaux multiples; ‹building› à étages

multitrack *adj* multipiste *inv*

multitude *n* multitude *f*

mum, **Mum** *n* (GB) (colloq) maman *f*
IDIOM **to keep** ∼ ne pas piper mot

mumble *vtr*, *vi* marmonner

mumbo jumbo *n* (colloq) charabia *m* (fam)

mummy *n* (a) (*also* **Mummy**) (colloq) maman *f* ⋯⋗

(b) (embalmed body) momie f

mumps n oreillons mpl

munch vtr ⟨person⟩ mâcher; ⟨animal⟩ mâchonner

mundane adj terre-à-terre, quelconque

municipal adj municipal/-e

mural n (wall painting) peinture f murale; (in cave) peinture f rupestre

✧ **murder** ⟨1⟩ n meurtre m
⟨2⟩ vtr assassiner
IDIOM to get away with ∼ exercer ses talents en toute impunité

murderer n assassin m, meurtrier m

murderess n meurtrière f

murderous adj ⟨look⟩ assassin/-e; ⟨deeds, thoughts⟩ meurtrier/-ière

murky adj (a) ⟨light, water, colour⟩ glauque
(b) ⟨past⟩ trouble

murmur ⟨1⟩ n murmure m (of de)
⟨2⟩ vtr, vi murmurer

✧ **muscle** n muscle m
■ **muscle in** (colloq) s'imposer (on dans)

muscle strain n élongation f

muscular adj ⟨disease, tissue⟩ musculaire; ⟨person, body, limbs⟩ musclé/-e

museum n musée m

mushroom n (a) (Bot, Culin) champignon m
(b) (colour) beige m rosé

✧ **music** n musique f

✧ **musical** ⟨1⟩ n comédie f musicale
⟨2⟩ adj (a) ⟨person⟩ musicien/-ienne
(b) ⟨voice, laughter⟩ mélodieux/-ieuse; ⟨score⟩ musical/-e

musical instrument n instrument m de musique

musician n musicien/-ienne m/f

music video n clip m (vidéo)

musk n musc m

Muslim ⟨1⟩ n Musulman/-e m/f
⟨2⟩ adj musulman/-e

mussel n moule f

✧ **must** ⟨1⟩ modal aux (nég **must not**, **mustn't**) (a) (expressing obligation) I ∼ go je dois partir, il faut que je parte; he ∼ sit the exam in June il faut qu'il passe l'examen au mois de juin; you ∼ check your rear-view mirror first il faut regarder dans le rétroviseur d'abord; I ∼ say I was impressed je dois dire que j'ai été impressionné; we mustn't tell anyone il ne faut en parler à personne, nous ne devons en parler à personne
(b) (making deductions) they ∼ really detest each other ils doivent vraiment se détester; it ∼ be pleasant living there ça doit être

agréable de vivre là-bas; he ∼ have been surprised il a dû être surpris
⟨2⟩ n it's a ∼ c'est indispensable; this film is a ∼ ce film est à voir or à ne pas rater; a visit to the Louvre is a ∼ une visite au Louvre s'impose

mustache (US) = MOUSTACHE

mustard n moutarde f

muster vtr (also ∼ up) rassembler ⟨troops⟩; rallier ⟨support⟩; trouver ⟨energy, enthusiasm⟩
IDIOM to pass ∼ être acceptable

musty adj to smell ∼ sentir le moisi or le renfermé

mute adj muet/-ette

mutilate vtr mutiler

mutiny n mutinerie f

mutter vtr, vi marmonner

mutton n mouton m

mutual adj (a) (reciprocal) réciproque; the feeling is ∼ c'est réciproque
(b) ⟨friend, interests⟩ commun/-e; ⟨consent⟩ mutuel/-elle; by ∼ agreement d'un commun accord

mutual aid n entraide f

✧ **my**

■ **Note** In French, determiners agree in gender and number with the noun that follows. So *my* is translated by *mon* + masculine singular noun (mon chien), *ma* + feminine singular noun (ma maison) BUT by *mon* + feminine noun beginning with a vowel or mute 'h' (mon assiette) and by *mes* + plural noun (mes enfants).
— When *my* is stressed, *à moi* is added after the noun: MY *house* = ma maison à moi.

⟨1⟩ det mon/ma/mes
⟨2⟩ excl ∼ ∼! ça alors!

Myanmar pr n Myanmar m

✧ **myself** pron (a) (reflexive) me, m'; I've hurt ∼ je me suis fait mal
(b) (emphatic) moi-même; I saw it ∼ je l'ai vu moi-même; (all) by ∼ tout seul/toute seule
(c) (after prepositions) moi, moi-même; I feel proud of ∼ je suis fier de moi
(d) (expressions) I'm not much of a dog-lover ∼ personnellement je n'aime pas trop les chiens; I'm not ∼ today je ne suis pas dans mon assiette aujourd'hui

mysterious adj mystérieux/-ieuse

mystery n (a) mystère m
(b) (book) roman m policier

mystify vtr laisser [qn] perplexe

myth n mythe m

mythology n mythologie f

N n

n, N *n* n, N *m*

naff *adj* (GB) (colloq) ringard/-e (fam)

nag *vtr* (*p prés etc* **-gg-**) enquiquiner (fam)
(**about** au sujet de)

nagging *adj* (a) his ∼ wife sa mégère de
femme
(b) ⟨*pain, doubt*⟩ tenace

nail ①️ *n* (a) (on finger, toe) ongle *m*
(b) (Tech) clou *m*
②️ *vtr* clouer
▪ **nail down**: ①️ ¶ ∼ [sth] **down** clouer
②️ ¶ ∼ [sb] **down** coincer (fam) ⟨*person*⟩

nail-biting *adj* ⟨*match, finish*⟩ palpitant/-e;
⟨*wait*⟩ angoissant/-e

nailbrush *n* brosse *f* à ongles

nail file *n* lime *f* à ongles

nail varnish *n* vernis *m* à ongles

nail varnish remover *n* dissolvant *m*

naïve *adj* naïf/naïve

naked *adj* nu/-e

✧ **name** ①️ *n* (a) (gen) nom *m*; (of book, film)
titre *m*; **first** ∼ prénom *m*; **my** ∼ **is Louis** je
m'appelle Louis
(b) (reputation) réputation *f*
(c) (insult) **to call sb** ∼**s** injurier qn
②️ *vtr* (a) (call) appeler ⟨*person, area*⟩;
baptiser ⟨*boat*⟩; **they** ∼**d her after** (GB) *or* **for**
(US) **her mother** ils l'ont appelée comme sa
mère; **a boy** ∼**d Pascal** un garçon nommé
Pascal
(b) (cite) citer; ∼ **three American States** citez
trois États américains
(c) révéler ⟨*sources*⟩; révéler l'identité de
⟨*suspect*⟩; **to** ∼ ∼**s** donner des noms
(d) (state) indiquer ⟨*place, time*⟩; fixer ⟨*price,
terms*⟩

name-drop *vi* (*p prés etc* **-pp-**) citer des
gens célèbres (*qu'on prétend connaître*)

namely *adv* à savoir

namesake *n* homonyme *m*

nanny *n* (GB) bonne *f* d'enfants

nanny goat *n* chèvre *f*

nap ①️ *n* petit somme *m*; **afternoon** ∼
sieste *f*
②️ *vi* (*p prés etc* **-pp-**) sommeiller

nape *n* nuque *f*; **the** ∼ **of the neck** la nuque

napkin *n* serviette *f* (de table)

nappy *n* (GB) couche *f* (de bébé)

narcotic ①️ *n* (soporific) narcotique *m*;
(illegal drug) stupéfiant *m*
②️ *adj* narcotique

narked *adj* (colloq) en rogne (fam), en boule
(fam)

narration *n* récit *m*, narration *f*

narrative ①️ *n* (account) récit *m*;
(storytelling) narration *f*
②️ *adj* ⟨*prose, poem*⟩ narratif/-ive; ⟨*skill,
talent*⟩ de conteur

narrator *n* narrateur/-trice *m/f*

narrow ①️ *adj* (gen) étroit/-e; ⟨*views*⟩
étriqué/-e; ⟨*majority, margin*⟩ faible (*before*
n); **to have a** ∼ **lead** avoir une légère avance;
to have a ∼ **escape** l'échapper belle
②️ *vtr* (a) (limit) limiter (**to** à), **to** ∼ **the gap**
réduire l'écart
(b) rétrécir ⟨*road, path, arteries*⟩; **to** ∼ **one's
eyes** plisser les yeux
③️ *vi* (gen) se rétrécir; ⟨*gap, margin*⟩ se
réduire (**to** à)
▪ **narrow down** réduire ⟨*numbers, list,
choice*⟩ (**to** à); limiter ⟨*investigation, research*⟩
(**to** à)

narrowly *adv* (barely) de justesse

narrow-minded *adj* borné/-e

nasal *adj* ⟨*vowel*⟩ nasal/-e; ⟨*accent, voice*⟩
nasillard/-e

nasal spray *n* nébuliseur *m* (*pour le nez*)

nasty *adj* (a) ⟨*person, expression, remark*⟩
méchant/-e; ⟨*experience, surprise, feeling,
task*⟩ désagréable; ⟨*habit, smell, taste*⟩
mauvais/-e (*before n*); ⟨*trick*⟩ sale (*before n*);
⟨*cut, bruise*⟩ vilain/-e (*before n*); ⟨*accident*⟩
grave
(b) (ugly) affreux/-euse

✧ **nation** *n* nation *f*; (people) peuple *m*

✧ **national** ①️ *n* ressortissant/-e *m/f*
②️ *adj* national/-e; **the** ∼ **press** (GB) les
grands quotidiens *mpl*

national anthem *n* hymne *m* national

National Curriculum *n* (GB)
programme *m* scolaire national

National Front *n* (GB) *parti britannique
d'extrême droite*

National Health Service, NHS *n*
(GB) services *mpl* de santé britanniques,
≈ Sécurité *f* Sociale

National Insurance, NI *n* (GB) securité
f sociale britannique; ∼ **number** numéro *m*
de sécurité sociale

nationalism *n* nationalisme *m*

nationality *n* nationalité *f*

nationalize *vtr* nationaliser ⟨*industry*⟩

nationwide ①️ *adj* ⟨*appeal, coverage,
strike*⟩ sur l'ensemble du territoire;
⟨*campaign*⟩ national/-e; ⟨*survey, poll*⟩ à
l'échelle nationale
②️ *adv* dans tout le pays

native ①️ *n* autochtone *mf*; **to be a** ∼ **of**
être originaire de

····>

2 *adj* **(a)** ‹*land*› natal/-e; ‹*tongue*›
maternel/-elle; ∼ **German speaker** personne
f de langue maternelle allemande
(b) ‹*flora, fauna, peoples*› indigène

Native American *n, adj* amérindien/
-ienne *m/f*

Nativity *n* nativité *f*

NATO *n* (*abbr* = **North Atlantic Treaty
Organization**) OTAN *f*

⚜ **natural** *adj* **(a)** (gen) naturel/-elle
(b) ‹*gift, talent*› inné/-e; ‹*artist, storyteller*›
né/-e
(c) (unaffected) simple, naturel/-elle

naturalize *vtr* naturaliser ‹*person*›; **to be
∼d** se faire naturaliser

naturally *adv* **(a)** (obviously, of course)
naturellement
(b) (by nature) de nature; **politeness comes ∼
to him** il est d'un naturel poli
(c) ‹*behave, smile, speak*› avec naturel

⚜ **nature** *n* nature *f*; **let ∼ take its course**
laissez faire la nature; **it's not in her ∼ to
be aggressive** elle n'est pas agressive de
nature; **it is in the ∼ of things** il est dans
l'ordre des choses

nature conservancy *n* protection *f* de
la nature

nature reserve *n* réserve *f* naturelle

nature trail *n* sentier *m* écologique

naughty *adj* **(a)** (disobedient) vilain/-e
(b) (rude) ‹*joke, picture, story*› coquin/-e

nausea *n* nausée *f*

nauseating *adj* écœurant/-e

nauseous *adj* ‹*taste, smell*› écœurant/-e; **to
feel ∼** avoir la nausée

nautical *adj* nautique

naval *adj* ‹*battle, forces, base*› naval/-e;
‹*officer, recruit, uniform, affairs*› de la
marine

nave *n* nef *f*

navel *n* nombril *m*

navel ring *n* piercing *m* au nombril

navigate **1** *vtr* **(a)** parcourir ‹*seas*›
(b) piloter ‹*plane*›; gouverner ‹*ship*›
2 *vi* (in vessel, plane) naviguer; (in rally) faire
le copilote; (on journey) tenir la carte

navigation *n* navigation *f*

navigator *n* (in vessel, plane) navigateur/
-trice *m/f*; (in car) copilote *mf*

navy **1** *n* **(a)** (fleet) flotte *f*; (fighting force)
marine *f*
(b) (*also* ∼ **blue**) bleu *m* marine
2 *adj* (*also* ∼ **blue**) bleu marine *inv*

Nazi *n, adj* nazi/-e *m/f*

⚜ **near** **1** *adv* **(a)** (close) près; **to live quite ∼**
habiter tout près; **to move ∼er** s'approcher
davantage (**to** de); **to bring sth ∼er**
approcher qch
(b) (nearly) **as ∼ perfect as it could be**

⚜ indicates a very frequent word

aussi proche de la perfection que possible;
nowhere ∼ finished loin d'être fini
2 *prep* **(a)** ∼ près de; ∼ **here** près d'ici; ∼ **the
beginning of the article** presque au début de
l'article; **he's no ∼er (making) a decision** il
n'est pas plus décidé
(b) (in time) ∼**er the time** quand la date
approchera; **it's getting ∼ Christmas** Noël
approche
3 *adj* proche; **in the ∼ future** dans un
avenir proche; **the ∼est shops** les magasins
les plus proches
4 *vtr* approcher de; **to ∼ completion**
toucher à sa fin
5 **near enough** *phr* à peu près
6 **near to** *phr* **(a)** (in space) près de; ∼**er to**
plus près de
(b) (on point of) au bord de ‹*tears, collapse*›
(c) to come ∼ to doing faillir faire

nearby **1** *adj* ‹*person*› qui se trouve/
trouvait etc à proximité; ‹*town, village*› d'à
côté
2 *adv* tout près; ‹*park, stand, wait*› à
proximité

⚜ **nearly** *adv* presque; **I very ∼ gave up** j'ai
bien failli abandonner; **not ∼ as talented as**
loin d'être aussi doué que

near miss *n* **to have a ∼** ‹*planes*› frôler la
collision; ‹*cars*› faillir se percuter

near-sighted *adj* myope

neat **1** *adj* **(a)** ‹*person*› (in habits)
ordonné/-e; (in appearance) soigné/-e;
‹*room, house, desk*› bien rangé/-e; ‹*garden,
handwriting*› soigné/-e
(b) ‹*explanation, solution*› habile
(c) ‹*figure*› bien fait/-e; ‹*features*› régulier/
-ière
(d) ‹*alcohol, spirits*› sans eau
2 *adv* ‹*drink whisky*› sec, sans eau

neatly *adv* **(a)** (tidily) ‹*dress, fold, arrange*›
avec soin; ‹*write*› proprement
(b) (perfectly) ‹*illustrate, summarize*›
parfaitement; ‹*link*› habilement

⚜ **necessarily** *adv* (definitely) forcément;
(of necessity) nécessairement; **not ∼** pas
forcément

⚜ **necessary** *adj* (gen) nécessaire;
‹*qualification*› requis/-e; **if ∼, as ∼** si besoin
est; **it is ∼ for him to do** il faut qu'il fasse

necessitate *vtr* nécessiter

necessity *n* **(a)** (need) nécessité *f*; **from ∼**
par nécessité; **the ∼ for** le besoin de
(b) (essential item) **to be an absolute ∼** être
indispensable

⚜ **neck** *n* **(a)** (of person) cou *m*; (of horse, donkey)
encolure *f*
(b) (collar) col *m*; (neckline) encolure *f*
(c) (of bottle, vase, womb) col *m*
IDIOMS **to be ∼ and ∼** être à égalité; **to stick
one's ∼ out** (colloq) prendre des risques

necklace *n* collier *m*

neckline *n* encolure *f*

necktie *n* (US) cravate *f*

nectar *n* nectar *m*

nectarine *n* nectarine *f*, brugnon *m*

ơ **need** ☐1 *modal aux* **you needn't finish it today** tu n'es pas obligé de le finir aujourd'hui; **~ he reply?** est-ce qu'il faut qu'il réponde?, est-ce qu'il doit répondre?; **I needn't have hurried** ce n'était pas la peine de me dépêcher, ce n'était pas la peine que je me dépêche

☐2 *vtr* **(a)** (require) **to ~ sth/to do** avoir besoin de qch/de faire; **more money is ~ed** nous avons besoin de plus d'argent; **everything you ~** tout ce qu'il vous faut; **everything you ~ to know about computers** tout ce que vous devez savoir sur les ordinateurs

(b) (have to) **you'll ~ to work hard** il va falloir que tu travailles dur; **he didn't ~ to ask permission** il n'était pas obligé de demander la permission; **something ~ed to be done** il fallait faire quelque chose

☐3 *n* **(a)** (necessity) nécessité *f* (for de); **I can't see the ~ for it** je n'en vois pas la nécessité; **to feel the ~ to do** éprouver le besoin de faire; **there's no ~ to wait** inutile d'attendre; **there's no ~ to worry** ce n'est pas la peine de s'inquiéter; **there's no ~, I've done it** inutile, c'est fait; **if ~ be** s'il le faut, si nécessaire

(b) (want, requirement) besoin *m* (for de); **to be in ~ of sth** avoir besoin de qch

(c) (poverty) **to be in ~** être dans le besoin

needle ☐1 *n* aiguille *f*

☐2 *vtr* harceler

IDIOM **to have pins and ~s** avoir des fourmis

needless *adj* ‹anxiety, suffering› inutile; ‹intrusion, intervention› inopportun/-e

needlework *n* couture *f*

needy *adj* ‹person› nécessiteux/-euse; ‹sector, area› sans ressources

negate *vtr* (cancel out) réduire [qch] à néant

ơ **negative** ☐1 *n* **(a)** (of photo) négatif *m*

(b) (in grammar) négation *f*; **in the ~** à la forme négative

☐2 *adj* (gen) négatif/-ive; ‹effect, influence› néfaste

neglect ☐1 *n* **(a)** (of person) négligence *f*; (of building, garden) manque *m* d'entretien; (of health, appearance) manque *m* de soin

(b) (lack of interest) indifférence *f* (of à l'égard de)

☐2 *vtr* **(a)** ne pas s'occuper de ‹person, dog, plant›; ne pas entretenir ‹garden, house›; négliger ‹health, friend, work›

(b) (fail) **to ~ to do** négliger de faire

neglected *adj* (gen) négligé/-e; ‹garden, building› mal entretenu/-e; **to feel ~** se sentir délaissé/-e

negligence *n* négligence *f*

negligent *adj* ‹person, procedure› négligent/-e; ‹air, manner› nonchalant/-e

negligible *adj* négligeable

negotiable *adj* **(a)** ‹rate, terms› négociable

(b) ‹road, pass› praticable; ‹obstacle› franchissable

negotiate ☐1 *vtr* **(a)** (in business, diplomacy) négocier

(b) négocier ‹bend›; franchir ‹obstacle›

☐2 *vi* négocier (**with** avec; **for** pour obtenir)

☐3 **negotiated** *pp adj* ‹settlement, peace› négocié/-e

negotiation *n* négociation *f*; **to be under ~** être en cours de négociations

negotiator *n* négociateur/-trice *m/f*

neigh *vi* hennir

ơ **neighbour** (GB), **neighbor** (US) *n* voisin/-e *m/f*

neighbourhood (GB), **neighborhood** (US) *n* **(a)** (district) quartier *m*

(b) (vicinity) **in the ~** dans le voisinage

neighbouring (GB), **neighboring** (US) *adj* voisin/-e

ơ **neither** ☐1 *conj* **I have ~ the time nor the money** je n'ai ni le temps ni l'argent; **~ tea, nor milk** ni (le) thé, ni (le) lait; **'I can't sleep'—'~ can I'** 'je n'arrive pas à dormir'—'moi non plus'

☐2 *det* aucun/-e des deux; **~ book is suitable** aucun des deux livres ne convient; **~ girl replied** aucune des deux filles n'a répondu

☐3 *pron, quantif* ni l'un/-e ni l'autre *m/f*; **~ of them came** ni l'un ni l'autre n'est venu

neon ☐1 *n* néon *m*

☐2 *adj* ‹light, sign› au néon; ‹atom› de néon

nephew *n* neveu *m*

Neptune *pr n* (planet) Neptune *f*

nerve ☐1 *n* **(a)** (Anat) nerf *m*; (Bot) nervure *f*

(b) (courage) courage *m*; **to lose one's ~** perdre son courage

(c) (colloq) (cheek) culot *m* (fam); **you've got a ~!** tu as un sacré culot! (fam)

☐2 **nerves** *n pl* (gen) nerfs *mpl*; (stage fright) trac *m* (fam); **to get on sb's ~s** taper sur les nerfs de qn

nerve-(w)racking *adj* angoissant/-e

nervous *adj* **(a)** ‹person› (fearful) timide; (anxious) angoissé/-e; (highly strung) nerveux/-euse; ‹smile, laugh, habit› nerveux/-euse; **to be ~ about doing** avoir peur de faire; **to feel ~** (apprehensive) être angoissé/-e; (before performance) avoir le trac (fam); (afraid) avoir peur; (ill at ease) se sentir mal à l'aise

(b) (Anat, Med) nerveux/-euse

nervous breakdown *n* dépression *f* nerveuse

nervously *adv* nerveusement

nervous wreck *n* (colloq) boule *f* de nerfs (fam)

nest ☐1 *n* **(a)** (of bird, animal) nid *m*

(b) **~ of tables** tables *fpl* gigognes

☐2 *vi* ‹bird› faire son nid

nest egg *n* magot *m* (fam)

nestle vi (a) ⟨person, animal⟩ se blottir (against contre; under sous)
(b) ⟨village, house⟩ être niché/-e

net [1] n (gen) filet m; (in football) filets mpl
[2] adj (also **nett**) (gen) net/nette; ⟨loss⟩ sec/sèche
[3] vtr (p prés etc **-tt-**) (a) prendre [qch] au filet ⟨fish⟩
(b) (financially) ⟨person⟩ faire un bénéfice de; ⟨sale, export, deal⟩ rapporter

Net n Net m

netball n: sport d'équipe proche du basket joué par les femmes

net curtain n voilage m

Netherlands pr n the ~ les Pays-Bas mpl, la Hollande

netiquette n netiquette f

netspeak n jargon m Internet

netting n (of rope) filet m; (of metal, plastic) grillage m; (fabric) voile m

nettle n (also **stinging** ~) ortie f

🔹 **network** [1] n réseau m (of de)
[2] vtr (Comput) interconnecter
[3] vi tisser un réseau de relations

networking n (a) (Comput) interconnexion f
(b) (establishing contacts) ~ **is important** c'est important d'avoir des contacts

network television n (US) chaîne f nationale

neurosis n (pl **-oses**) névrose f

neurotic adj névrosé/-e

neuter [1] n neutre m
[2] adj neutre
[3] vtr châtrer ⟨animal⟩

neutral [1] n (Aut) **in/into** ~ au point mort
[2] adj neutre (about en ce qui concerne)

neutrality n neutralité f

neutralize vtr neutraliser

🔹 **never** adv (a) (not ever) **I** ~ **go to London** je ne vais jamais à Londres; **she** ~ **says anything** elle ne dit jamais rien; **it's now or** ~ c'est le moment ou jamais; ~ **again** plus jamais; ~ **lie to me again!** ne me mens plus jamais!
(b) (emphatic negative) **he** ~ **said a word** il n'a rien dit; **I** ~ **knew that** je ne le savais pas; **he** ~ **so much as apologized** il ne s'est même pas excusé

never-ending adj interminable

nevertheless adv (a) (all the same) quand même
(b) (nonetheless) pourtant, néanmoins

🔹 **new** adj nouveau/-elle (before n); (brand new) neuf/neuve; **I bought a** ~ **computer** (to replace old one) j'ai acheté un nouvel ordinateur; (a brand new model) j'ai acheté un ordinateur neuf; **as good as** ~ comme neuf; **to be** ~ **to** ne pas être habitué/-e à ⟨job, way of life⟩; **we're** ~ **to the area** nous sommes

nouveaux venus dans la région

New Age adj ⟨music, traveller⟩ New Age inv

newborn adj nouveau-né/-née

new build n nouvelle construction f

newcomer n (in place, job, club) nouveau venu/nouvelle venue m/f; (in sport, theatre, cinema) nouveau/-elle m/f

newfound adj tout nouveau/toute nouvelle

new look [1] n nouveau style m
[2] **new-look** adj ⟨product⟩ nouvelle version inv; ⟨car, team⟩ nouveau/-elle (before n); ⟨edition, show⟩ remanié/-e

newly adv ⟨arrived, built, formed, qualified⟩ nouvellement; ⟨washed⟩ fraîchement

newlyweds n pl jeunes mariés mpl

🔹 **news** n (a) nouvelle(s) f (pl); **a piece of** ~ une nouvelle; (in newspaper) une information; **have you heard the** ~? tu connais la nouvelle?
(b) (on radio, TV) **the** ~ les informations fpl, le journal m

news agency n agence f de presse

newsagent's n (GB) magasin m de journaux

news bulletin (GB), **newscast** (US) n bulletin m d'information

newscaster n présentateur/-trice m/f des informations

news conference n conférence f de presse

newsdealer n (US) marchand m de journaux

news editor n rédacteur/-trice m/f

newsgroup n forum m de discussion

news headlines n pl (on TV) titres mpl de l'actualité

news item n sujet m d'actualité

newsletter n bulletin m

🔹 **newspaper** n journal m

newsreader n (GB) présentateur/-trice m/f des informations

newsreel n actualités fpl

newsstand n kiosque m à journaux

New Year n le nouvel an m; **to see in the** ~ fêter la Saint-Sylvestre; **Happy** ~! bonne année!

New Year's day (GB), **New Year's** (US) n le jour m de l'an

New Year's Eve n la Saint-Sylvestre

New Zealand pr n Nouvelle-Zélande f

🔹 **next**

■ **Note** When *next* is used as an adjective, it is generally translated by *prochain* when referring to something which is still to come or happen and by *suivant* when it generally means *following*: *I'll be 40 next year* = j'aurai 40 ans l'année prochaine; *the next year, he went to Spain* = l'année suivante il est allé en Espagne.

🔹 indicates a very frequent word

— For examples and further usages see the entry below.

───────────

1 *pron* from one minute to the ~ d'un instant à l'autre; **the week after** ~ dans deux semaines

2 *adj* **(a)** prochain/-e, suivant/-e; **get the** ~ **train** prenez le prochain train; **he got on the** ~ **train** il a pris le train suivant; **'~!'** 'au suivant!'; **'you're** ~' 'c'est à vous'; **the** ~ **size (up)** la taille au-dessus; ~ **Thursday** jeudi prochain; **he's due to arrive in the** ~ **10 minutes** il devrait arriver d'ici 10 minutes; **this time** ~ **week** dans une semaine; **the** ~ **day** le lendemain

(b) ‹*room, street*› voisin/-e; ‹*building, house*› voisin/-e, d'à côté

3 *adv* **(a)** (afterwards) ensuite, après; **what happened** ~**?** que s'est-il passé ensuite?

(b) (on a future occasion) **when I** ~ **go there** la prochaine fois que j'irai

(c) (in order) **the** ~ **tallest is Patrick** ensuite c'est Patrick qui est le plus grand

4 **next to** *phr* **(a)** (almost) presque; ~ **to impossible** presque impossible; **to get sth for** ~ **to nothing** avoir qch pour quasiment rien; **in** ~ **to no time it was over** en un rien de temps c'était fini

(b) (beside, close to) à côté de; **two seats** ~ **to each other** deux sièges l'un à côté de l'autre; **to wear silk** ~ **to the skin** porter de la soie à même la peau

next door 1 *adj* (*also* **next-door**) d'à côté

2 *adv* ‹*live, move in*› à côté

next-door neighbour *n* voisin/-e *m/f* (d'à côté)

next of kin *n* **to be sb's** ~ être le parent le plus proche de qn

NGO *n* (*abbr* = **Non-Governmental Organization**) ONG *f*

nib *n* plume *f*

nibble *vi* ‹*animal*› mordiller; ‹*person*› grignoter

◈ **nice** *adj* **(a)** ‹*drive, holiday, place*› agréable; ‹*house, picture, outfit, weather*› beau/belle (*before n*); **did you have a** ~ **time?** tu t'es bien amusé?; ~ **to have met you** ravi d'avoir fait votre connaissance; **have a** ~ **day!** bonne journée!; **you look very** ~ tu es très chic

(b) (tasty) bon/bonne (*before n*); **to taste** ~ avoir bon goût

(c) ‹*person*› sympathique; **to be** ~ **to sb** être gentil/-ille avec qn

(d) ‹*neighbourhood, school*› comme il faut *inv*; **it is not** ~ **to tell lies** ce n'est pas bien de mentir

IDIOM ~ **one!** (in admiration) bravo!; (ironic) il ne manquait plus que ça!

nice-looking *adj* beau/belle (*before n*)

nicely *adv* **(a)** (kindly) gentiment

(b) (attractively) agréablement

(c) (politely) poliment

(d) (satisfactorily) bien; **that'll do** ~ cela fera

l'affaire

niche *n* (recess) niche *f*; (figurative) place *f*; (in the market) créneau *m*

niche market *n* marché *m* spécialisé

nick 1 *n* encoche *f* (in dans)

2 *vtr* **(a)** (cut) faire une entaille dans

(b) (GB) (colloq) (steal) piquer (fam)

3 (GB) (arrest) pincer (fam)

IDIOM just in the ~ **of time** juste à temps

nickel *n* **(a)** (US) pièce *f* de cinq cents

(b) (metal) nickel *m*

nickname 1 *n* surnom *m*

2 *vtr* surnommer

nicotine *n* nicotine *f*

nicotine patch *n* patch *m* à la nicotine

niece *n* nièce *f*

niggle (colloq) **1** *n* (complaint) remarque *f*; **I've a** ~ **at the back of my mind** il y a quelque chose qui me travaille

2 *vtr* (irritate) tracasser

niggling *adj* ‹*doubt, worry*› insidieux/-ieuse

◈ **night** *n* nuit *f*; (before going to bed) soir *m*; **at** ~ la nuit; **all** ~ **long** toute la nuit; **late at** ~ tard le soir; **he arrived last** ~ il est arrivé hier soir; **I slept badly last** ~ j'ai mal dormi cette nuit *or* la nuit dernière; **the** ~ **before** last avant-hier soir; **on Tuesday** ~s le mardi soir; **to get an early** ~ se coucher tôt; **a** ~ **at the opera** une soirée à l'opéra

nightclub *n* boîte *f* de nuit

nightclubbing *n* **to go** ~ aller en boîte (fam)

nightdress *n* chemise *f* de nuit

nightingale *n* rossignol *m*

nightlife *n* vie *f* nocturne

nightmare *n* cauchemar *m*; **to have a** ~ faire un cauchemar

night school *n* cours *mpl* du soir

night shelter *n* asile *m* de nuit

night shift *n* (period) **to be/work on the** ~ être/travailler de nuit; (workers) équipe *f* de nuit

nightshirt *n* chemise *f* de nuit (d'homme)

night spot *n* (colloq) boîte *f* de nuit

night-time *n* nuit *f*; **at** ~ la nuit

night watchman *n* veilleur *m* de nuit

nil *n* (gen) néant *m*; (Sport) zéro *m*

Nile *pr n* Nil *m*

nimble *adj* ‹*person*› agile; ‹*fingers*› habile

◈ **nine** *n, pron, det* neuf *m inv*

nineteen *n, pron, det* dix-neuf *m inv*

IDIOM to talk ~ **to the dozen** parler à n'en plus finir

nineteenth 1 *n* **(a)** (in order) dix-neuvième *mf*

(b) (of month) dix-neuf *m inv*

(c) (fraction) dix-neuvième *m*

2 *adj, adv* dix-neuvième

nineties *n pl* **(a)** (era) **the** ~ les années *fpl* quatre-vingt dix

⋯⫶

(b) (age) **to be in one's** ~ avoir entre quatre-vingt-dix et cent ans

ninetieth *n*, *adj*, *adv* quatre-vingt-dixième *mf*

nine-to-five *adj* ‹job, routine› de bureau

ninety *n*, *pron*, *det* quatre-vingt-dix *m inv*

ninth [1] *n* **(a)** (in order) neuvième *mf*
(b) (of month) neuf *m inv*
(c) (fraction) neuvième *m*
[2] *adj*, *adv* neuvième

nip [1] *n* (pinch) pincement *m*; (bite) morsure *f*; **there's a** ~ **in the air** il fait frisquet (fam)
[2] *vtr* (*p prés etc* -**pp**-) (pinch) pincer; (bite) donner un petit coup de dent à; (playfully) mordiller
[3] *vi* (*p prés etc* -**pp**-) (bite) mordre; (playfully) mordiller

nipple *n* mamelon *m*

nippy *adj* (colloq) **(a)** (cold) **it's a bit** ~ il fait frisquet (fam)
(b) (quick) ‹person› vif/vive; ‹car› rapide

nit *n* (egg) lente *f*; (larva) larve *f* de pou

nit-pick *vi* chercher la petite bête (fam), pinailler (fam)

nitrogen *n* azote *m*

nitty-gritty *n* (colloq) **to get down to the** ~ passer aux choses sérieuses

ꞏ **no** [1] *particle* non; ~ **thanks** non merci
[2] *det* **(a)** (none, not any) aucun/-e; **to have** ~ **money** ne pas avoir d'argent; **she has** ~ **talent** elle n'a aucun talent; **of** ~ **interest** sans intérêt
(b) (prohibiting) ~ **smoking** défense de fumer; ~ **parking** stationnement interdit; ~ **talking!** silence!
(c) (for emphasis) **he's** ~ **expert** ce n'est certes pas un expert; **this is** ~ **time to cry** ce n'est pas le moment de pleurer
(d) (hardly any) **in** ~ **time** en un rien de temps
[3] *adv* **it's** ~ **further/easier** ce n'est pas plus loin/facile; **I** ~ **longer work there** je n'y travaille plus; ~ **later than Wednesday** pas plus tard que mercredi

no., No. (written *abbr* = **number**) n°

nobility *n* noblesse *f*

noble *n*, *adj* noble *m*

ꞏ **nobody** [1] *pron* (also **no-one**) personne; ~ **saw her** personne ne l'a vue; **there was** ~ **in the car** il n'y avait personne dans la voiture; **I heard** ~ je n'ai entendu personne; ~ **but me** personne sauf moi
[2] *n* **to be a** ~ être insignifiant/-e

nocturnal *adj* nocturne

ꞏ **nod** [1] *n* **she gave him a** ~ elle lui a fait un signe de (la) tête; (as greeting) elle l'a salué d'un signe de tête; (indicating assent) elle a fait oui de la tête
[2] *vtr* (*p prés etc* -**dd**-) **to** ~ **one's head** faire un signe de tête; (to indicate assent) hocher la tête

ꞏ indicates a very frequent word

[3] *vi* (*p prés etc* -**dd**-) faire un signe de tête (**to** à); (in assent) faire oui de la tête

no-go area *n* quartier *m* chaud (*où la police etc ne s'aventure plus*)

no-hoper *n* (colloq) raté/-e *m/f* (fam)

ꞏ **noise** *n* bruit *m*; (shouting) tapage *m*; **to make a** ~ faire du bruit

noisy *adj* ‹person, place› bruyant/-e; ‹meeting, protest› tumultueux/-euse

nomad *n* nomade *mf*

nominal *adj* (gen) nominal/-e; ‹fee, sum› minime; ‹fine› symbolique

nominate *vtr* **(a)** (propose) proposer; **to** ~ **sb for a prize** sélectionner qn pour un prix
(b) (appoint) nommer (**to sth** à qch); **to** ~ **sb (as) chairman** nommer qn président

nomination *n* (as candidate) proposition *f* de candidat; (for award) sélection *f*; (appointment) nomination *f* (**to** à)

nominative *n*, *adj* nominatif *m*

nonaddictive *adj* qui ne crée pas de dépendance

nonalcoholic *adj* non alcoolisé/-e

nonbeliever *n* non-croyant/-e *m/f*

nonchalant *adj* nonchalant/-e

noncommittal *adj* évasif/-ive

noncompliance *n* (with standards) non-conformité *f* (**with** à); (with orders) non-obéissance *f* (**with** à)

nonconformist *adj* non conformiste

noncooperation *n* refus *m* de coopération

nondenominational *adj* ‹church› œcuménique; ‹school› laïque

nondescript *adj* ‹person, clothes› insignifiant/-e; ‹building› quelconque

ꞏ **none** *pron* **(a)** (not any) aucun/-e *m/f*; ~ **of us/them** aucun de nous/d'entre eux; ~ **of the wine was French** il n'y avait aucun vin français; ~ **of the milk had been drunk** on n'avait pas touché au lait; ~ **of the bread was fresh** tout le pain était rassis; **we have** ~ nous n'en avons pas; **there's** ~ **left** il n'y en a plus; ~ **of it was true** il n'y avait rien de vrai
(b) (nobody) personne; ~ **but him** personne sauf lui

nonentity *n* (person) personne *f* insignifiante

nonessentials *n pl* (objects) accessoires *mpl*; (details) accessoire *m sg*

nonetheless *adv* pourtant, néanmoins

nonexistent *adj* inexistant/-e

nonfiction *n* œuvres *fpl* non fictionnelles

no-nonsense *adj* ‹manner, attitude, policy› direct/-e; ‹person› franc/franche

nonplussed *adj* perplexe

non-profitmaking *adj* ‹organization› à but non lucratif

nonresident *n* non-résident/-e *m/f*

nonsense *n* (foolishness) absurdités *fpl*; **to talk/write** ~ dire/écrire n'importe quoi; ~!

balivernes! *fpl*; **I won't stand for this** ～ j'en ai assez de ces bêtises

nonsmoker *n* non-fumeur/-euse *m/f*

non-smoking *adj* non fumeur *inv*

nonstarter *n* **to be a** ～ ‹*plan, idea*› être voué/-e à l'échec

nonstick *adj* antiadhésif/-ive

nonstop [1] *adj* ‹*journey*› sans arrêt; ‹*train, flight*› direct/-e; ‹*noise*› incessant/-e [2] *adv* ‹*work, talk, drive, argue*› sans arrêt; ‹*fly*› sans escale

non-taxable *adj* non imposable

noodles *n pl* nouilles *fpl*

nook *n* coin *m*; **every** ～ **and cranny** tous les coins et recoins

noon *n* midi *m*; **at 12** ～ à midi

no-one = NOBODY 1

noose *n* (loop) nœud *m* coulant; (for hanging) corde *f*

✧ **nor** *conj* ～ **do I** moi non plus; ～ **can he** lui non plus; **he was not a cruel man,** ～ **a mean one** il n'était ni cruel, ni méchant; **she hasn't written,** ～ **has she telephoned** elle n'a pas écrit, et elle n'a pas téléphoné non plus

norm *n* norme *f* (**for** pour; **to do** de faire)

✧ **normal** [1] *n* normale *f*; **above/below** ～ au-dessus/en dessous de la norme [2] *adj* (gen) normal/-e; ‹*place, time*› habituel/-elle

normality *n* normalité *f*

✧ **normally** *adv* normalement

Normandy *pr n* Normandie *f*

✧ **north** [1] *n* (a) (compass direction) nord *m* (b) (part of world, country) **the North** le Nord [2] *adj* (gen) nord *inv*; ‹*wind*› du nord; **in** ～ **London** dans le nord de Londres [3] *adv* ‹*move*› vers le nord; ‹*lie, live*› au nord (**of** de)

North Africa *pr n* Afrique *f* du Nord

North America *pr n* Amérique *f* du Nord

northeast [1] *n* nord-est *m* [2] *adj* ‹*coast, side*› nord-est *inv*; ‹*wind*› de nord-est [3] *adv* ‹*move*› vers le nord-est; ‹*lie, live*› au nord-est (**of** de)

✧ **northern** *adj* ‹*coast*› nord *inv*; ‹*town, accent*› du nord; ‹*hemisphere*› Nord *inv*; ～ **England** le nord de l'Angleterre

Northern Ireland *pr n* Irlande *f* du Nord

North Pole *pr n* pôle *m* Nord

North Sea *pr n* **the** ～ la mer du Nord

northwest [1] *n* nord-ouest *m* [2] *adj* ‹*coast*› nord-ouest *inv*; ‹*wind*› de nord-ouest [3] *adv* ‹*move*› vers le nord-ouest; ‹*lie, live*› au nord-ouest (**of** de)

Norway *pr n* Norvège *f*

Norwegian [1] *n* (a) (person) Norvégien/-ienne *m/f* (b) (language) norvégien *m*

[2] *adj* norvégien/-ienne

✧ **nose** *n* nez *m*
IDIOMS **to look down one's** ～ **at sb/sth** prendre qn/qch de haut; **to turn one's** ～ **up at sth** faire le dégoûté/la dégoûtée devant qch; **to poke** *or* **stick one's** ～ **into sth** (colloq) fourrer son nez dans qch (fam)
■ **nose about, nose around** fouiner (**in** dans)

nosebleed *n* saignement *m* de nez

nose-dive *n* piqué *m*; **to go into a** ～ ‹*plane*› faire un piqué; (figurative) chuter

nose ring *n* piercing *m* au nez

nostalgia *n* nostalgie *f*

nostalgic *adj* nostalgique

nostril *n* (of person) narine *f*; (of horse) naseau *m*

nosy *adj* (colloq) fouineur/-euse (fam)

✧ **not** [1] *adv* (a) (with a verb) ne…pas; **she isn't at home** elle n'est pas chez elle; **we won't need a car** nous n'aurons pas besoin d'une voiture; **hasn't he seen it?** il ne l'a pas vu alors?; **I hope** ～ j'espère que non; **certainly** ～ sûrement pas; ～ **only** *or* **just** non seulement; **whether it rains or** ～ qu'il pleuve ou non; **why** ～? pourquoi pas?; ～ **everyone likes it** ça ne plaît pas à tout le monde; **it's** ～ **every day that** ce n'est pas tous les jours que; ～ **a sound was heard** on n'entendait pas un bruit; ～ **bad** pas mal
(b) (in question tags) **she's English, isn't she?** elle est anglaise, n'est-ce pas?; **he likes fish, doesn't he?** il aime le poisson, n'est-ce pas?
[2] ～ **at all** *phr* (in no way) pas du tout; (responding to thanks) de rien
[3] ～ **not that** *phr* ～ **that I know of** pas (autant) que je sache; **if she refuses,** ～ **that she will…** si elle refuse, je ne dis pas qu'elle le fera…

notable *adj* ‹*person*› remarquable; ‹*event, success, difference*› notable

notably *adv* (in particular) notamment; (markedly) remarquablement

notch [1] *n* entaille *f* [2] *vtr* encocher ‹*stick*›
■ **notch up** (colloq) remporter ‹*point, prize*›

✧ **note** [1] *n* (a) (gen) note *f*; (short letter) mot *m*; **to take** ～ **of** prendre note de (b) (Mus) (sound, symbol) note *f*; (piano key) touche *f* (c) (bank) ～ billet *m* [2] *vtr* noter [3] **of note** *phr* ‹*person*› éminent/-e, réputé/-e; ‹*development*› digne d'intérêt
IDIOM **to compare** ～**s** échanger ses impressions (**with** avec)
■ **note down** noter

notebook *n* carnet *m*

notebook pc *n* ordinateur *m* portable

noted *adj* ‹*intellectual, criminal*› célèbre; **to be** ～ **for** être réputé/-e pour

notepad *n* bloc-notes *m*

n

notepaper *n* papier *m* à lettres
noteworthy *adj* remarquable
✓ **nothing**

■ **Note** When *nothing* is used alone as a reply to a question in English, it is translated by *rien*: *'what are you doing?'—'nothing'* = 'que fais-tu?'—'rien'.
— *nothing* as a pronoun, when it is the subject of a verb, is translated by *rien ne* (+ verb or, in compound tenses, + auxiliary verb): *nothing changes* = rien ne change; *nothing has changed* = rien n'a changé.
— *nothing* as a pronoun, when it is the object of a verb, is translated by *ne…rien*; *ne* comes before the verb, and before the auxiliary in compound tenses, and *rien* comes after the verb or auxiliary: *I see nothing* = je ne vois rien; *I saw nothing* = je n'ai rien vu.
— When *ne rien* is used with an infinitive, the two words are not separated: *I prefer to say nothing* = je préfère ne rien dire.
— For more examples and particular usages, see the entry below.

1 *pron* **I knew ~ about it** je n'en savais rien; **we can do ~ (about it)** nous n'y pouvons rien; **~ much** pas grand-chose; **~ else** rien d'autre; **I had ~ to do with it!** je n'y étais pour rien!; **it's ~ to do with us** ça ne nous regarde pas; **to stop at ~** ne reculer devant rien (**to do** pour faire); **he means ~ to me** il n'est rien pour moi; **the names meant ~ to him** les noms ne lui disaient rien; **for ~** (free) gratuitement; (pointlessly) pour rien
2 *adv* **it is ~ like as difficult as** c'est loin d'être aussi difficile que; **she is** *or* **looks ~ like her sister** elle ne ressemble pas du tout à sa sœur
3 **nothing but** *phr* **he's ~ but a coward** ce n'est qu'un lâche; **they've done ~ but moan** ils n'ont fait que râler (fam); **it's caused me ~ but trouble** ça ne m'a valu que des ennuis

✓ **notice** **1** *n* (a) (written sign) pancarte *f*; (advertisement) annonce *f*; (announcing birth, marriage, death) avis *m*
(b) (attention) attention *f*; **to take ~** faire attention (**of** à); **to take no ~ (of)** ne pas faire attention (à)
(c) (notification) préavis *m*; **one month's ~** un mois de préavis; **until further ~** jusqu'à nouvel ordre; **at short ~** à la dernière minute; **to give in one's ~** donner sa démission
2 *vtr* remarquer ‹*absence, mark*›; **to get oneself ~d** se faire remarquer
noticeable *adj* visible
noticeboard *n* panneau *m* d'affichage
notification *n* notification *f*; (in newspaper) avis *m*; **to receive ~ that** être avisé/-e que

notify *vtr* notifier; **to ~ sb of** aviser qn de ‹*result, incident*›; avertir qn de ‹*intention*›; informer qn de ‹*birth, death*›
✓ **notion** *n* (a) (idea) idée *f*
(b) (understanding) notion *f*
notorious *adj* ‹*criminal, organization*› notoire; ‹*district*› mal famé/-e; ‹*case*› tristement célèbre
notoriously *adv* notoirement; **they're ~ unreliable** il est bien connu qu'on ne peut pas compter sur eux
notwithstanding **1** *adv* néanmoins
2 *prep* (in spite of) en dépit de; (excepted) exception faite de
nought *n* zéro *m*
noun *n* nom *m*, substantif *m*
nourish *vtr* nourrir (**with** avec; **on** de)
nourishment *n* nourriture *f*
✓ **novel** **1** *n* roman *m*
2 *adj* original/-e
novelist *n* romancier/-ière *m/f*
novelty *n* nouveauté *f* (**of doing** de faire)
✓ **November** *n* novembre *m*
novice *n* débutant/-e *m/f*; (in religious order) novice *mf*
✓ **now** **1** *conj* **~ (that)** maintenant que
2 *adv* (a) maintenant; **do it ~** fais-le maintenant; **right ~** tout de suite; **any time ~** d'un moment à l'autre; **(every) ~ and then** *or* **again** de temps en temps
(b) (with preposition) **you should have phoned him before ~** tu aurais dû lui téléphoner avant; **before** *or* **until ~** jusqu'à présent; **he should be finished by ~** il devrait avoir déjà fini; **between ~ and next Friday** d'ici vendredi prochain; **between ~ and then** d'ici là; **from ~ on(wards)** dorénavant
(c) (in the past) **it was ~ 4 pm** il était alors 16 heures; **by ~ it was too late** à ce moment-là, il était trop tard
(d) **~ there's a man I can trust!** ah! voilà un homme en qui on peut avoir confiance!; **careful ~!** attention!; **~ then, let's get back to work** bon, reprenons le travail
nowadays *adv* (these days) de nos jours; (now) actuellement
nowhere **1** *adv* nulle part; **I've got ~ else to go** je n'ai nulle part où aller; **there's ~ to sit down** il n'y a pas d'endroit pour s'asseoir; **all this talk is getting us ~** tout ce bavardage ne nous avance à rien; **flattery will get you ~!** tu n'arriveras à rien en me flattant
2 **nowhere near** *phr* loin de; **~ near sufficient** loin d'être suffisant/-e
noxious *adj* nocif/-ive
nozzle *n* (of hose, pipe) ajutage *m*; (of hoover) suceur *m*; (for icing) douille *f*
nuance *n* nuance *f*
✓ **nuclear** *adj* nucléaire
nuclear bomb *n* bombe *f* atomique

✓ indicates a very frequent word

n

nuclear deterrent *n* force *f* de dissuasion nucléaire

nuclear energy, **nuclear power** *n* énergie *f* nucléaire *or* atomique

nuclear power station *n* centrale *f* nucléaire

nuclear waste *n* déchets *mpl* nucléaires

nucleus *n* (*pl* **-clei**) noyau *m*

nude ① *n* nu/-e *m/f*; in the ～ nu/-e
② *adj* ‹person› nu/-e

nudge *vtr* (push) pousser du coude; (accidentally) heurter; (brush against) frôler

nudist *n*, *adj* nudiste *mf*

nugget *n* pépite *f*

nuisance *n* (gen) embêtement *m*; (Law) nuisance *f*; **what a ～!** que c'est agaçant!

nuisance call *n* appel *m* anonyme

null *adj* (Law) ～ **and void** nul et non avenu

nullify *vtr* invalider, annuler

numb ① *adj* (a) (from cold) engourdi/-e (with par); (from anaesthetic) insensible; **to go ～** s'engourdir
(b) (figurative) hébété/-e (with par)
② *vtr* ‹cold› engourdir; (Med) insensibiliser; **to ～ the pain** endormir la douleur

✧ **number** ① *n* (a) (gen) nombre *m*; (written figure) chiffre *m*; **a three-figure ～** un nombre à trois chiffres; **a ～ of** un certain nombre de
(b) (of bus, house, page, telephone) numéro *m*; **a wrong ～** un faux numéro
(c) (by performer) (act) numéro *m*; (song) chanson *f*
② *vtr* (a) (allocate number to) numéroter
(b) (amount to, include) compter
IDIOMS **his days are ～ ed** ses jours sont comptés; **to look after ～ one** penser avant tout à son propre intérêt

numberplate *n* (GB) plaque *f* minéralogique *or* d'immatriculation

numeracy *n* aptitude *f* au calcul

numeral *n* chiffre *m*

numerical *adj* numérique

✧ **numerous** *adj* nombreux/-euse

nun *n* religieuse *f*, bonne sœur *f*

✧ **nurse** ① *n* (a) (Med) infirmier/-ière *m/f*; **male ～** infirmier *m*
(b) = NURSEMAID
② *vtr* (a) soigner ‹person, cold›
(b) allaiter ‹baby›
(c) nourrir ‹grievance, hope›

nursemaid *n* nurse *f*, bonne *f* d'enfants

nursery *n* (a) (*also* **day ～**) crèche *f*; (in hotel, shop) garderie *f*
(b) (room) chambre *f* d'enfants
(c) (for plants) pépinière *f*

nursery rhyme *n* comptine *f*

nursery school *n* école *f* maternelle

nursing *n* profession *f* d'infirmier/-ière

nursing home *n* (a) (old people's) maison *f* de retraite; (convalescent) maison *f* de repos
(b) (GB) (maternity) clinique *f* obstétrique

nurture *vtr* (a) élever ‹child›; soigner ‹plant›
(b) nourrir ‹hope, feeling, talent›

nut *n* (a) (walnut) noix *f*; (hazel) noisette *f*; (almond) amande *f*; (peanut) cacahuète *f*
(b) (Tech) écrou *m*

nutcracker *n* casse-noisettes *m inv*

nutmeg *n* noix *f* de muscade

nutrition *n* (process) nutrition *f*, alimentation *f*; (science) diététique *f*

nutritional *adj* ‹value› nutritif/-ive; ‹composition, information› nutritionnel/-elle

nutritious *adj* nourrissant/-e

nutshell *n* (a) coquille *f* de noix *or* noisette
(b) (figurative) **in a ～** en un mot

nuzzle *vtr* frotter son nez contre
■ **nuzzle up: to ～ up against** *or* **to sb** se blottir contre qn

NVQ *n* (*abbr* = **National Vocational Qualification**) qualification *f* nationale professionnelle (*obtenue par formation continue ou initiale*)

nylon *n* nylon® *m*

nymph *n* nymphe *f*

Oo

o, **O** *n* (a) (letter) o, O *m*
(b) **O** (spoken number) zéro

oaf *n* (clumsy) balourd/-e *m/f*; (loutish) mufle *m*

oak ① *n* chêne *m*
② *adj* de *or* en chêne

OAP *n* (GB) (*abbr* = **old age pensioner**) retraité/-e *m/f*

oar *n* rame *f*

oasis *n* (*pl* **oases**) (in desert) oasis *f*; (figurative) havre *m*

oat *n* ～s avoine *f*
IDIOM **to sow one's wild ～s** jeter sa gourme

oath *n* (a) serment *m*; **under ～**, **on ～** (GB); sous serment
(b) (swearword) juron *m*

oatmeal *n* (a) (cereal) farine *f* d'avoine
(b) (US) (porridge) bouillie *f* d'avoine

obedience *n* obéissance *f* (**to** à)

obedient *adj* obéissant/-e

obese *adj* obèse

obesity n obésité f

obey [1] vtr obéir à ‹person, instinct›; se conformer à ‹instructions, law›
[2] vi ‹person› obéir

obituary n (also ~ **notice**) nécrologie f

✔ **object** [1] n (a) (item) objet m
(b) (goal) but m (of de)
(c) (focus) **to be the** ~ **of** être l'objet de
(d) (in grammar) complément m d'objet
[2] vtr objecter (**that** que)
[3] vi soulever des objections; **to** ~ **to** protester contre ‹attitude, comment›; **to** ~ **to doing** se refuser à faire; **I** ~ **to their behaviour** je trouve leur comportement inadmissible

objection n objection f (**to** à; **from** de la part de); **I've no** ~**(s)** je n'y vois pas d'inconvénient

objectionable adj ‹remark› désobligeant/-e; ‹behaviour, language› choquant/-e; ‹person› insupportable

objective [1] n objectif m
[2] adj objectif/-ive, impartial/-e

objectively adv objectivement

obligation n (a) (duty) devoir m (**towards, to** envers); **to be under (an)** ~ **to do** être obligé/-e de faire
(b) (commitment) obligation f (**to** envers; **to do** de faire)
(c) (debt) dette f

obligatory adj obligatoire (**to do** de faire)

oblige vtr (a) (compel) obliger (**to do** à faire)
(b) (be helpful) rendre service à
(c) **to be** ~**d to sb** être reconnaissant/-e à qn (**for** de)

obliging adj serviable

obliterate vtr effacer ‹trace, word, memory›; anéantir ‹landmark, city›

oblivion n oubli m

oblivious adj (unaware) inconscient/-e; **to be** ~ **of** or **to** ne pas être conscient/-e de

oblong [1] n rectangle m
[2] adj oblong/-ongue, rectangulaire

obnoxious adj odieux/-ieuse, exécrable

obscene adj obscène

obscure [1] adj obscur/-e; (indistinct) vague
[2] vtr obscurcir ‹truth›; cacher ‹view›; **to** ~ **the issue** embrouiller la question

observant adj observateur/-trice

✔ **observation** n observation f (**of** de); **to keep sb/sth under** ~ surveiller qn/qch

✔ **observe** vtr (a) (see, notice) observer (**that** que)
(b) ‹doctor, police› surveiller
(c) (remark) faire observer (**that** que)
(d) observer ‹law, custom›

observer n observateur/-trice m/f (**of** de)

obsess vtr obséder

obsession n obsession f

obsessive adj ‹person› maniaque; ‹neurosis› obsessionnel/-elle; ‹thought› obsédant/-e

obsolescence n (gen) désuétude f; **built-in** ~ obsolescence f planifiée

obsolete adj ‹technology› dépassé/-e; ‹custom, idea› démodé/-e; ‹word› désuet/-ète

obstacle n obstacle m; **to be an** ~ faire obstacle (**to** à)

obstacle course n (Mil) parcours m du combattant; (figurative) course f d'obstacles

obstacle race n course f d'obstacles

obstetrician n obstétricien/-ienne m/f

obstinate adj ‹person› têtu/-e (**about** en ce qui concerne); ‹behaviour, silence, effort› obstiné/-e; ‹resistance› acharné/-e

obstruct vtr cacher ‹view›; bloquer ‹road›; gêner ‹traffic, person, progress›; faire obstruction à ‹player›; entraver le cours de ‹justice›

obstruction n (a) (to traffic, progress) obstacle m; (in pipe) bouchon m
(b) (in sport) obstruction f

✔ **obtain** vtr obtenir

obtrusive adj ‹noise› gênant/-e; ‹person, behaviour› importun/-e

obtuse adj ‹person› obtus/-e; ‹remark› stupide

✔ **obvious** [1] n **to state the** ~ enfoncer les portes ouvertes
[2] adj évident/-e (**to** pour)

✔ **obviously** [1] adv manifestement; **she** ~ **needs help** il est évident qu'elle a besoin d'aide; **he's** ~ **lying** il est clair qu'il ment
[2] excl bien sûr!, évidemment!

✔ **occasion** n occasion f; **on one** ~ une fois; **to rise to the** ~ se montrer à la hauteur des circonstances; **on special** ~**s** dans les grandes occasions

occasional adj ‹event› qui a lieu de temps en temps; **the** ~ **letter** une lettre de temps en temps

occasionally adv de temps à autre; **very** ~ très rarement

occult n **the** ~ les sciences fpl occultes

occupant n (a) (of building, bed) occupant/-e m/f
(b) (of vehicle) passager/-ère m/f

occupation n (a) (Mil) occupation f (**of** of)
(b) (trade) métier m; (profession) profession f
(c) (activity) occupation f

occupational adj ‹accident› du travail; ‹risk› du métier; ‹safety› au travail

occupational hazard n **it's an** ~ ça fait partie des risques du métier

occupier n occupant/-e m/f

occupy vtr occuper; **to keep oneself occupied** s'occuper (**by doing** en faisant)

✔ indicates a very frequent word

occur *vi* (*p prés etc* **-rr-**) **(a)** (happen) se produire
(b) (be present) se trouver
(c) the idea ∼red to me that... l'idée m'est venue à l'esprit que...; **it didn't ∼ to me** ça ne m'est pas venu à l'idée

occurrence *n* **(a)** (event) fait *m*; **to be a rare ∼** se produire rarement
(b) (instance) occurrence *f*
(c) (of disease, phenomenon) cas *m*

ocean *n* océan *m*

o'clock *adv* **at one ∼** à une heure; **it's two ∼** il est deux heures

octagon *n* octogone *m*

octave *n* octave *f*

October *n* octobre *m*

octopus *n* (*pl* ∼**es** *ou* ∼) **(a)** (Zool) pieuvre *f*
(b) (Culin) poulpe *m*

OD *n, vi* (colloq) = OVERDOSE

odd ⟨1⟩ *adj* **(a)** (strange, unusual) ⟨*person, object, occurrence*⟩ bizarre
(b) ⟨*socks, gloves*⟩ dépareillés
(c) (miscellaneous) **some ∼ bits of cloth** quelques bouts de tissu
(d) ⟨*number*⟩ impair/-e
(e) to be the ∼ one out ⟨*person, animal, plant*⟩ être l'exception *f*; ⟨*drawing, word*⟩ être l'intrus *m*; (when selecting team) être sans partenaire
⟨2⟩ **-odd** *combining form* **sixty-∼ people/years** une soixantaine de personnes/d'années

oddity *n* (odd thing) bizarrerie *f*; (person) excentrique *mf*

odd job *n* (for money) petit boulot *m*; ∼**s** (in house, garden) petits travaux *mpl*

odd-job man *n* homme *m* à tout faire

odds *n pl* **(a)** (in betting) cote *f* (**on** sur)
(b) (chance, likelihood) chances *fpl*; **the ∼ are against his winning** il y a peu de chances qu'il gagne; **to win against the ∼** gagner contre toute attente
IDIOM at ∼ (in dispute) être en conflit; (inconsistent) en contradiction (**with** avec)

odds and ends *n pl* (GB) bricoles *fpl* (fam)

odour (GB), **odor** (US) *n* odeur *f*

of *prep*

■ **Note** In almost all its uses, the preposition *of* is translated by *de*. For exceptions, see the entry below.
— Remember that *de* + *le* always becomes *du* and that *de* + *les* always becomes *des*.
— When of *it* or *of them* are used for something already referred to, they are translated by *en*: *there's a lot of it* = il y en a beaucoup; *there are several of them* = il y en a plusieurs.
— Note, however, the following expressions used when referring to people: *there are six of them* = ils sont six; *there were several of them* = ils étaient plusieurs.

(a) (in most uses) de; **the leg ∼ the table** le pied de la table
(b) (made of) en; **a ring (made) ∼ gold** une bague en or
(c) a friend ∼ mine un ami à moi; **that's kind ∼ you** c'est très gentil de votre part *or* à vous; **some ∼ us/them** quelques-uns d'entre nous/d'entre eux

off ⟨1⟩ *adv* **(a)** (leaving) **to be ∼** partir, s'en aller; **it's time you were ∼** il est temps que tu partes; **I'm ∼** je m'en vais
(b) (at a distance) **to be 30 metres ∼** être à 30 mètres; **some way ∼** assez loin
(c) (ahead in time) **Easter is a month ∼** Pâques est dans un mois; **the exam is still several months ∼** l'examen n'aura pas lieu avant plusieurs mois
⟨2⟩ *adj* **(a)** (free) **Tuesday's my day ∼** je ne travaille pas le mardi; **to have the morning ∼** avoir la matinée libre
(b) (turned off) **to be ∼** ⟨*water, gas*⟩ être coupé/-e; ⟨*tap*⟩ être fermé/-e; ⟨*light, TV*⟩ être éteint/-e
(c) (cancelled) ⟨*match, party*⟩ annulé/-e
(d) (removed) **the lid is ∼** il n'y a pas de couvercle; **with her make-up ∼** sans maquillage; **25% ∼** 25% de remise
(e) (colloq) (bad) **to be ∼** ⟨*food*⟩ être avarié/-e; ⟨*milk*⟩ avoir tourné/-e
⟨3⟩ *prep* **(a)** (*also* **just ∼**) juste à côté de ⟨*kitchen*⟩; **∼ the west coast** au large de la côte ouest; **just ∼ the path** tout près du sentier
(b) it is ∼ the point là n'est pas la question
(c) (colloq) **to be ∼ one's food** ne pas avoir d'appétit
IDIOMS to feel a bit ∼ (colloq) ne pas être dans son assiette (fam); **to have an ∼ day** ne pas être dans un de ses bons jours

off-centre (GB), **off-center** (US) *adj* décentré/-e

off-chance *n* **just on the ∼** au cas où

off-colour *adj* (colloq) (unwell) patraque (fam)

offence (GB), **offense** (US) *n* **(a)** (crime) délit *m*
(b) (insult) **to cause ∼ to sb** offenser qn; **to take ∼ (at)** s'offenser (de)
(c) (Mil) offensive *f*

offend ⟨1⟩ *vtr* offenser ⟨*person*⟩
⟨2⟩ *vi* commettre une infraction (**against** à)

offender *n* **(a)** (Law) délinquant/-e *m/f*
(b) (culprit) coupable *mf*

offensive ⟨1⟩ *n* (Mil, Sport) offensive *f*
⟨2⟩ *adj* ⟨*remark*⟩ injurieux/-ieuse (**to** pour); ⟨*behaviour*⟩ insultant/-e; ⟨*language*⟩ grossier/-ière

offer ⟨1⟩ *n* **(a)** offre *f* (**to do** de faire); **job ∼** offre d'emploi
(b) (of goods) **to be on special ∼** être en promotion
⟨2⟩ *vtr* (gen) offrir; donner ⟨*advice, explanation, information*⟩; émettre ⟨*opinion*⟩; proposer ⟨*service*⟩; **to ∼ sb sth** offrir qch à qn; **to ∼ to do** se proposer pour faire
⟨3⟩ *vi* se proposer

O

offering n (gift) cadeau m; (sacrifice) offrande f

offhand ① adj désinvolte
② adv ∼, **I don't know** comme ça au pied levé je ne sais pas

✦ **office** n (a) (place) bureau m
(b) (position) fonction f, charge f; **public** ∼ fonctions fpl officielles; **to hold** ∼ ⟨president, mayor⟩ être en fonction; ⟨political party⟩ être au pouvoir

office block, **office building** n (GB) immeuble m de bureaux

✦ **officer** n (a) (in army, navy) officier m
(b) (also **police** ∼) policier m

office worker n employé/-e m/f de bureau

✦ **official** ① n fonctionnaire mf; (of party, union) officiel/-ielle m/f; (at town hall) employé/-e m/f
② adj officiel/-ielle

offing n **in the** ∼ en perspective

off-key adj faux/fausse

off-licence n (GB) magasin m de vins et de spiritueux

off-limits adj interdit/-e

off-line adj (Comput) (not on the Internet) hors ligne; ⟨processing⟩ en différé

off-load vtr (get rid of) écouler ⟨goods⟩; **to** ∼ **the blame onto sb** rejeter la responsabilité sur qn

off-message adj (Pol) **to be** ∼ être en désaccord avec la politique gouvernementale

off-peak adj ⟨electricity⟩ au tarif de nuit; ⟨travel⟩ en période creuse; ⟨call⟩ au tarif réduit

off-putting adj (GB) ⟨manner⟩ peu engageant/-e; **it was very** ∼ c'était déroutant

off-road vi rouler en tout terrain

off-road vehicle n véhicule m tout terrain

off-season adj ⟨cruise, holiday⟩ hors saison

offset vtr (p prés **-tt-**, prét, pp **offset**) compenser (**by** par); **to** ∼ **sth against sth** mettre qch et qch en balance

offshore ① adj (out to sea) au large, en mer; (towards the sea) de terre ∼ **breeze** brise f de terre
② adv offshore
③ vtr délocaliser
④ vi faire de l'offshore

offside ① n (GB) côté m conducteur
② adj (a) (GB) ⟨lane⟩ (in France) de gauche; (in UK) de droite
(b) (Sport) hors jeu inv

offspring n (pl ∼) progéniture f

offstage adj, adv dans les coulisses

off-the-cuff adj ⟨remark, speech⟩ impromptu/-e

off-the-peg adj ⟨garment⟩ de prêt-à-porter

off-the-shelf adj ⟨goods⟩ disponible en magasin; ⟨software⟩ fixe

off-the-wall adj (colloq) loufoque (fam)

off-white adj blanc cassé inv

✦ **often** adv souvent; **as** ∼ **as not**, **more** ∼ **than not** le plus souvent; **how** ∼ **do you meet?** vous vous voyez tous les combien?; **once too** ∼ une fois de trop; **every so** ∼ de temps en temps

✦ **oh** excl oh!; ∼ **dear!** oh là là!; ∼ **(really)?** ah bon?

✦ **oil** ① n (gen) huile f; (petroleum) pétrole m; **crude** ∼ pétrole brut; **engine** ∼ huile de moteur; **heating** ∼ fioul m
② vtr huiler

oil change n vidange f

oilcloth n toile f cirée

oil field n champ m pétrolifère

oil painting n peinture f à l'huile

oil refinery n raffinerie f de pétrole

oil rig n (offshore) plate-forme f pétrolière offshore; (on land) tour f de forage

oilseed rape n colza m

oilskins n pl (GB) ciré m

oil slick n marée f noire

oil well n puits m de pétrole

oily adj ⟨cloth, food, hair⟩ gras/grasse; ⟨dressing, substance⟩ huileux/-euse

ointment n pommade f

✦ **okay**, **OK** (colloq) ① n **to give sb/sth the** ∼ donner le feu vert à qn/qch
② adj **it's** ∼ **by me** ça ne me dérange pas; **is it** ∼ **if...?** est-ce que ça va si...?; **he's** ∼ (nice) il est sympa (fam); **I'm** ∼ aller bien; **I'm** ∼ ça va; **'how was the match?'—'**∼**'** 'comment as-tu trouvé le match?'—'pas mal'
③ adv ⟨cope, work out⟩ (assez) bien
④ particle (a) (giving agreement) d'accord
(b) (introducing topic) bien

✦ **old** adj (a) ⟨person⟩ vieux/vieille (before n), âgé/-e; ⟨object, tradition, song⟩ vieux/vieille (before n); **an** ∼ **man** un vieil homme, un vieillard; **an** ∼ **woman** une vieille femme, une vieille; **to get** ∼ vieillir; **how** ∼ **are you?** quel âge as-tu?; **I'm ten years** ∼ j'ai dix ans; **a six-year-**∼ **boy** un garçon (âgé) de six ans; **my** ∼**er brother** mon frère aîné; **I'm the** ∼**est** c'est moi l'aîné/-e
(b) (former, previous) ⟨address, school, job, system⟩ ancien/-ienne (before n); **in the** ∼ **days** autrefois

■ **Note** The irregular form vieil of the adjective vieux/vieille is used before masculine nouns beginning with a vowel or a mute 'h'.

old age n vieillesse f

old-age pensioner, **OAP** n (GB) retraité/-e m/f

old-fashioned adj ⟨person, ways⟩ vieux jeu inv; ⟨idea, attitude, garment, machine⟩

démodé/-e

old people's home n maison f de retraite

old wives' tale n conte m de bonne femme

olive ▢1 n (a) (fruit) olive f (b) (also ∼ **tree**) olivier m ▢2 adj ‹dress, eyes› vert olive inv; ‹complexion› olivâtre

olive green n, adj vert m olive inv

olive oil n huile f d'olive

Olympics n pl (also **Olympic Games**) jeux mpl Olympiques

ombudsman n médiateur m

omelette n omelette f

omen n présage m

ominous adj ‹cloud› menaçant/-e; ‹news› inquiétant/-e; ‹sign› de mauvais augure

omission n omission f

omit vtr (p prés etc **-tt-**) omettre (**from** de; **to do** de faire)

omnipotent adj omnipotent/-e

omnipresent adj omniprésent/-e

✧ **on** ▢1 prep (a) (position) sur ‹table, coast, motorway›; ∼ **the beach** sur la plage; ∼ **top of the piano** sur le piano; ∼ **the floor** par terre; **there's a stain** ∼ **it** il y a une tache dessus; **to live** ∼ **Park Avenue** habiter Park Avenue; **a studio flat** ∼ **Avenue Montaigne** un studio avenue Montaigne; **the paintings** ∼ **the wall** les tableaux qui sont au mur; **I've got no small change** ∼ **me** je n'ai pas de monnaie sur moi; **to have a smile** ∼ **one's face** sourire; **to hang sth** ∼ **a nail** accrocher qch à un clou; ∼ **a string** au bout d'une ficelle (b) (about, on the subject of) sur; ∼ **Africa** sur l'Afrique (c) **to be** ∼ faire partie de ‹team›; être membre de ‹committee› (d) (in expressions of time) ∼ **22 February** le 22 février; ∼ **Friday** vendredi; ∼ **Saturdays** le samedi; ∼ **my birthday** le jour de mon anniversaire; ∼ **sunny days** quand il fait beau (e) (immediately after) ∼ **his arrival** à son arrivée; ∼ **hearing the truth she…** quand elle a appris la vérité, elle… (f) (taking) **to be** ∼ **steroids** prendre des stéroïdes; **to be** ∼ **drugs** se droguer (g) (powered by) **to run** ∼ **batteries** fonctionner sur piles; **to run** ∼ **electricity** marcher à l'électricité (h) (indicating a medium) ∼ **TV** à la télé; ∼ **the news** aux informations; ∼ **video** en vidéo; ∼ **drums** à la batterie (i) (earning) **to be** ∼ **£20,000 a year** gagner 20 000 livres sterling par an; **to be** ∼ **a low income** avoir un bas salaire (j) (paid for by) **it's** ∼ **me** je t'invite (k) (indicating transport) **to travel** ∼ **the bus** voyager en bus; ∼ **the plane** dans l'avion; **to**

be ∼ **one's bike** être à vélo; **to leave** ∼ **the first train** prendre le premier train ▢2 adj (a) **while the meeting is** ∼ pendant la réunion; **I've got a lot** ∼ je suis très occupé; **the news is** ∼ **in 10 minutes** les informations sont dans 10 minutes; **what's** ∼? (on TV) qu'est-ce qu'il y a à la télé?; (at the cinema, theatre) qu'est-ce qu'on joue?; **there's nothing** ∼ il n'y a rien de bien (b) **to be** ∼ ‹TV, oven, light› être allumé/-e; ‹dishwasher, radio› marcher; ‹tap› être ouvert/-e; **the power is** ∼ il y a du courant (c) **to be** ∼ ‹lid› être mis/-e ▢3 adv (a) **to have nothing** ∼ être nu/-e; **to have make-up** ∼ être maquillé/-e; **with slippers** ∼ en pantoufles (b) **from that day** ∼ à partir de ce jour-là; **20 years** ∼ 20 ans plus tard; **to walk** ∼ continuer à marcher; **to go to Paris then** ∼ **to Marseilles** aller à Paris et de là à Marseille; **a little further** ∼ un peu plus loin ▢4 **on and off** phr de temps en temps ▢5 **on and on** phr **to go** ∼ **and** ∼ ‹speaker› parler pendant des heures; ‹speech› durer des heures; **to go** ∼ **and** ∼ **about** ne pas arrêter de parler de **IDIOM it's just** or **simply not** ∼ (GB) (out of the question) c'est hors de question; (not the done thing) ça ne se fait pas; (unacceptable) c'est inadmissible

on-board adj (in-car) embarqué/-e

✧ **once** ▢1 n **just this** ∼ pour cette fois; **for** ∼ pour une fois ▢2 adv (a) (one time) une fois; ∼ **and for all** une (bonne) fois pour toutes; ∼ **too often** une fois de trop; ∼ **a day** une fois par jour (b) (formerly) autrefois; ∼ **upon a time there was a king** il était une fois un roi ▢3 conj une fois que, dès que ▢4 **at once** phr (a) (immediately) tout de suite; **all at** ∼ tout d'un coup (b) (simultaneously) à la fois

once-over n (colloq) **to give sth the** ∼ jeter un rapide coup d'œil à qch; **to give sb the** ∼ évaluer qn au premier coup d'œil

oncoming adj ‹car, vehicle› venant en sens inverse

✧ **one** ▢1 det (a) (single) un/une; ∼ **car** une voiture; ∼ **dog** un chien; **to raise** ∼ **hand** lever la main (b) (unique, sole) seul/-e (before n); **my** ∼ **vice** mon seul vice; **my** ∼ **and only tie** ma seule et unique cravate; **the** ∼ **and only Edith Piaf** l'incomparable Edith Piaf (c) (same) même; **at** ∼ **and the same time** en même temps ▢2 pron (a) (indefinite) un/une m/f; **can you lend me** ∼? tu peux m'en prêter un/une?; ∼ **of them** (person) l'un d'eux/l'une d'elles; (thing) l'un/l'une m/f (b) (impersonal) (as subject) on; (as object) vous; ∼ **never knows** on ne sait jamais (c) (demonstrative) **the grey** ∼ le gris/la grise; ⋯⟶

o

this ～ celui-ci/celle-ci; **which** ～? lequel/
laquelle?; **that's the** ～ c'est celui-là/celle-là;
he's/she's the ～ **who** c'est lui/elle qui
(d) ～**-fifty** (in sterling) une livre cinquante
3 *n* (number) un *m*; (referring to feminine) une
f; ～ **o'clock** une heure; **in** ～**s and twos** par
petits groupes
4 **one by one** *phr* un par un/une par
une
IDIOMS **to be** ～ **up on sb** (colloq) avoir un
avantage sur qn; **to go** ～ **better than sb** faire
mieux que qn; **I for** ～ **think that** pour ma
part je crois que

one another *pron* (*also* **each other**)

■ **Note** *one another* is very often translated by
using a reflexive pronoun (*nous, vous, se, s'*).

they love ～ ils s'aiment; **to help** ～
s'entraider; **to worry about** ～ s'inquiéter
l'un pour l'autre; **kept apart from** ～ séparés
l'un de l'autre

one-off *adj* (GB) ‹*experiment*› unique;
‹*event, payment*› exceptionnel/-elle
one-parent family *n* famille *f*
monoparentale
one-piece *adj* ～ **swimsuit** maillot *m* de
bain une pièce
one's *det* son/sa/ses; ～ **books/friends** ses
livres/amis; **to wash** ～ **hands** se laver les
mains; **to do** ～ **best** faire de son mieux
oneself *pron* **(a)** (reflexive) se, s'; **to wash/cut**
～ se laver/couper
(b) (for emphasis) soi-même
(c) (after prepositions) soi; **sure of** ～ sûr/-e de
soi; **(all) by** ～ tout seul/toute seule
one-sided *adj* ‹*account*› partial/-e; ‹*contest*›
inégal/-e; ‹*deal*› inéquitable
one-time *adj* ancien/-ienne (*before n*)
one-to-one *adj* ‹*talk*› en tête à tête; ～
meeting tête-à-tête *m inv*; ～ **tuition** cours
mpl particuliers
one-way *adj* **(a)** ‹*traffic*› à sens unique; ～
street sens *m* unique
(b) ～ **ticket** aller *m* simple
ongoing *adj* ‹*process*› continu/-e; ‹*battle,
story*› continuel/-elle
onion *n* oignon *m*
⚹ **on-line** *adj* (Comput) (on the Internet) en ligne;
‹*mode*› connecté/-e; ‹*data processing*› en
direct
onlooker *n* spectateur/-trice *m/f*
⚹ **only** **1** *conj* mais, seulement; **I'd go** ～ **I'm
too old** j'irais bien mais je suis trop vieux
2 *adj* seul/-e; ～ **child** enfant unique
3 *adv* **(a)** (exclusively) ～ **in Italy can one…**
il n'y a qu'en Italie que l'on peut…; ～ **time
will tell** seul l'avenir nous le dira; **'men** ～**'**
'réservé aux hommes'
(b) (in expressions of time) ～ **yesterday** pas plus
tard qu'hier; **it seems like** ～ **yesterday** j'ai
l'impression que c'était hier

⚹ indicates a very frequent word

(c) (merely) **you** ～ **had to ask** tu n'avais qu'à
demander; **it's** ～ **fair** ce n'est que justice; **he**
～ **grazed his knees** il s'est juste égratigné
les genoux; ～ **half the money** juste la moitié
de l'argent
4 **only just** *phr* **(a)** (very recently) **to have**
～ **just done** venir juste de faire
(b) (barely) ～ **just wide enough** juste assez
large; ～ **just** (narrowly) de justesse
5 **only too** *phr* ～ **too well** trop bien; ～
too pleased trop content/-e
on-message *adj* (Pol) **to be** ～ être en
accord avec la politique gouvernementale
o.n.o. (GB) (*abbr* = **or nearest offer**) à
débattre
on-screen *adj* sur l'écran
onset *n* début *m* (of de)
onside *adj, adv* en jeu
on-site *adj* sur place
onslaught *n* attaque *f* (on contre)
on-target earnings, OTE *n pl* '～
£40,000' 'salaire plus commission pouvant
atteindre 40 000 livres sterling'
on-the-job *adj* ‹*training*› sur le lieu de
travail
on the spot *adv* ‹*decide*› sur-le-champ;
‹*killed*› sur le coup; **to be** ～ être sur place
⚹ **onto** *prep* (*also* **on to**) sur
IDIOM **to be** ～ **something** (colloq) être sur
une piste
onus *n* obligation *f*; **the** ～ **is on sb to do** il
incombe à qn de faire
onward **1** *adj* ～ **flight** correspondance *f*
(to à destination de)
2 *adv* (US) = ONWARDS
onwards *adv* (*also* **onward**) **to carry** ～
continuer; **from now** ～ à partir d'aujourd'hui;
from that day ～ à dater de ce jour
ooze **1** *vtr* **the wound** ～**d blood** du sang
suintait de la blessure
2 *vi* **to** ～ **with** ‹*person*› rayonner de ‹*charm,
sexuality*›
opal *n* opale *f*
opaque *adj* opaque
⚹ **open** **1** *n* **in the** ～ (outside) dehors, en plein
air; **to bring sth out into the** ～ mettre qch au
grand jour
2 *adj* **(a)** (gen) ouvert/-e; **to be half** ～ ‹*door*›
être entrouvert/-e; **the** ～ **air** le plein air; **in**
～ **country** en rase campagne; **on** ～ **ground**
sur un terrain découvert; **the** ～ **road** la
grand-route; **the** ～ **sea** la haute mer
(b) (not covered) ‹*car, carriage*› découvert/-e,
décapoté/-e
(c) ～ **to** exposé/-e à ‹*air, wind, elements*›; ～
to attack exposé/-e à l'attaque; **to lay oneself**
～ **to criticism** s'exposer (ouvertement) à la
critique
(d) ‹*access, competition*› ouvert/-e à tous;
‹*meeting*› public/-ique
(e) (candid) ‹*person*› franc/franche (**about** à
propos de)
(f) (blatant) ‹*hostility, contempt*› non

dissimulé/-e

(g) to leave the date ∼ laisser la date en suspens; **to keep an ∼ mind** réserver son jugement

⊡ *vtr* (gen) ouvrir; entamer ‹*discussions*›

⊡ *vi* **(a)** ‹*door, flower, curtain*› s'ouvrir; **to ∼ onto sth** ‹*door, window*› donner sur qch **(b)** ‹*shop, bar*› ouvrir; ‹*meeting, play*› commencer (**with** par)

(c) ‹*film*› sortir (sur les écrans)

▪ **open up** ⊡ ¶ **∼ up (a)** ‹*shop, branch*› ouvrir

(b) ‹*gap*› se creuser

(c) (figurative) ‹*person*› se confier

⊡ ¶ **∼ [sth] up** ouvrir

open-air *adj* ‹*pool, stage*› en plein air

open day *n* journée *f* portes ouvertes

opener *n* (for bottles) décapsuleur *m*; (for cans) ouvre-boîte *m*

open-heart surgery *n* (operation) opération *f* à cœur ouvert

✱ **opening** ⊡ *n* **(a)** (start) début *m*

(b) (of exhibition, shop) ouverture *f*; (of play, film) première *f*

(c) (gap) trouée *f*

(d) (opportunity) occasion *f* (**to do** de faire); (in market) débouché *m* (**for** pour); (for job) poste *m*

⊡ *adj* ‹*scene, move*› premier/-ière (*before n*); ‹*remarks*› préliminaire; ‹*ceremony*› d'inauguration

opening hours *n pl* heures *fpl* d'ouverture

open learning *n*: formule d'enseignement à distance ou dans un centre ouvert à tous

open market *n* marché *m* libre

open-minded *adj* **to be ∼** avoir l'esprit ouvert

open-necked *adj* ‹*shirt*› à col ouvert

open-plan *adj* ‹*office*› paysagé/-e

open ticket *n* billet *m* ouvert

Open University, OU *n* (GB Univ) *système d'enseignement universitaire par correspondance ouvert à tous*

opera *n* opéra *m*

opera glasses *n* jumelles *fpl* de théâtre

opera house *n* opéra *m*

✱ **operate** ⊡ *vtr* **(a)** faire marcher ‹*appliance, vehicle*›

(b) pratiquer ‹*policy, system*›

(c) (manage) gérer

⊡ *vi* **(a)** (do business) opérer

(b) (function) marcher

(c) (run) ‹*service*› fonctionner

(d) (Med) opérer; **to ∼ on** opérer ‹*person*›; **to ∼ on sb's leg** opérer qn à la jambe

operating instructions *n pl* mode *m* d'emploi

operating room (US), **operating theatre** (GB) *n* salle *f* d'opération

operating system *n* système *m* d'exploitation

✱ **operation** *n* **(a)** (gen, Med) opération *f*; **to have a heart ∼** se faire opérer du cœur **(b) to be in ∼** ‹*plan*› être en vigueur; ‹*machine*› fonctionner; ‹*oil rig, mine*› être en exploitation

operational *adj* **(a)** (ready to operate) opérationnel/-elle

(b) ‹*budget, costs*› d'exploitation

operative ⊡ *n* (worker) employé/-e *m/f*

⊡ *adj* en vigueur

operator *n* **(a)** (on telephone) standardiste *mf*

(b) (of radio, computer) opérateur *m*

(c) he's a smooth ∼ il sait s'y prendre

✱ **opinion** *n* opinion *f* (**about** de), avis *m* (**about, on** sur); **to have a high/low ∼ of sb/ sth** avoir une bonne/mauvaise opinion de qn/qch; **in my ∼** à mon avis

opinionated *adj* **to be ∼** avoir des avis sur tout

opinion poll *n* sondage *m* d'opinion

✱ **opponent** *n* (in contest) adversaire *mf*; (of regime) opposant/-e *m/f* (**of** à)

opportune *adj* ‹*moment*› opportun/-e

opportunist *n, adj* opportuniste *mf*

✱ **opportunity** *n* occasion *f* (**for** de); **to take the ∼ to do** profiter de l'occasion pour faire

✱ **oppose** ⊡ *vtr* s'opposer à ‹*plan, bill*›; **to be ∼d to sth/to doing** être contre qch/contre l'idée de faire

⊡ **opposing** *pres p adj* ‹*party, team*› adverse; ‹*view, style*› opposé/-e

⊡ **as opposed to** *phr* par opposition à

opposite ⊡ *n* contraire *m* (**to, of** de)

⊡ *adj* (gen) opposé/-e; ‹*building*› d'en face; ‹*page*› ci-contre; ‹*effect*› inverse; **at ∼ ends of** aux deux bouts de ‹*table, street*›

⊡ *adv* en face; **directly ∼** juste en face

⊡ *prep* en face de ‹*building, park, person*›

opposite number *n* (gen) homologue *m*; (Sport) adversaire *mf*

✱ **opposition** *n* opposition *f* (**to** à); **the Opposition** (in politics) l'opposition *f*

oppress *vtr* opprimer ‹*people, nation*›

oppressive *adj* **(a)** ‹*law*› oppressif/-ive

(b) ‹*heat, atmosphere*› oppressant/-e

opt *vi* **to ∼ for sth** opter pour qch; **to ∼ to do** choisir de faire

▪ **opt out** décider de ne pas participer (**of** à)

optical *adj* optique

optical illusion *n* illusion *f* d'optique

optician *n* (selling glasses) opticien/-ienne *m/f*; (eye specialist) (GB) optométriste *mf*

optimism *n* optimisme *m*

optimist *n* optimiste *mf*

optimistic *adj* optimiste (**about** quant à)

optimize *vtr* optimiser

optimum *n, adj* optimum *m*

ⵚ **option** *n* option *f* (**to do** de faire); **to have the ~ of doing** pouvoir choisir de faire; **I didn't have much ~** je n'avais guère le choix

optional *adj* facultatif/-ive; **~ extras** accessoires *mpl* en option

ⵚ **or** *conj* (a) (gen) ou; **black ~ white?** noir ou blanc?; **either here ~ at Dave's** soit ici soit chez Dave; **whether he likes it ~ not** que cela lui plaise ou non; **in a week ~ so** dans huit jours environ; **~ should I say** ou bien devrais-je dire
(b) (linking alternatives in the negative) **I can't come today ~ tomorrow** je ne peux venir ni aujourd'hui ni demain; **without food ~ lodgings** sans nourriture ni abri
(c) (otherwise) sinon, autrement

oral ⓵ *n* oral *m*
⓶ *adj* ‹examination, communication, contraceptive› oral/-e; ‹medicine› par voie orale

orange ⓵ *n* (a) (fruit) orange *f*
(b) (colour) orange *m*
⓶ *adj* orange *inv*

orange juice *n* jus *m* d'orange

orbit ⓵ *n* orbite *f*
⓶ *vtr* décrire une orbite autour de ‹sun, planet›

orchard *n* verger *m*

orchestra *n* orchestre *m*

orchestrate *vtr* orchestrer

orchid *n* orchidée *f*

ordain *vtr* (a) (decree) décréter (**that** que)
(b) ordonner ‹priest›

ordeal *n* épreuve *f*

ⵚ **order** ⓵ *n* (a) (gen) ordre *m*; **in alphabetical ~** dans l'ordre alphabétique; **to restore ~** rétablir l'ordre
(b) (command) ordre *m* (**to do** de faire); **to be under ~s to do** avoir (l')ordre de faire
(c) (in shop, restaurant) commande *f*
(d) (operational state) **in working ~** en état de marche; **to be out of ~** ‹phone line› être en dérangement; ‹lift, machine› être en panne
(e) (all right) **in ~** ‹documents› en règle; **that remark was way out of ~** cette remarque était tout à fait déplacée
(f) (also **religious ~**) ordre *m*
⓶ *vtr* (a) (command) ordonner; **to ~ sb to do** ordonner à qn de faire
(b) commander ‹goods, meal›; réserver ‹taxi› (**for** pour)
⓷ *vi* ‹diner, customer› commander
⓸ **in order that** *phr* (with the same subject) afin de (+ *infinitive*), pour (+ *infinitive*); (when subject of verb changes) afin que (+ *subjunctive*), pour que (+ *subjunctive*)
⓹ **in order to** *phr* pour, afin de
■ **order about, order around: to ~ people around** donner des ordres

ⵚ indicates a very frequent word

order form *n* bon *m or* bulletin *m* de commande

orderly ⓵ *n* (medical) aide-soignant/-e *m/f*
⓶ *adj* ‹queue› ordonné/-e; ‹pattern, row› régulier/-ière; ‹mind, system› méthodique; ‹crowd, demonstration› calme

ⵚ **ordinary** ⓵ *n* **to be out of the ~** sortir de l'ordinaire
⓶ *adj* (a) (normal) ‹family, life, person› ordinaire; ‹clothes› de tous les jours
(b) (average) ‹consumer, family› moyen/-enne
(c) (uninspiring) quelconque (derogatory)

ore *n* minerai *m*; **iron ~** minerai de fer

organ *n* (a) (gen) organe *m*
(b) (Mus) orgue *m*

organ donor *n* donneur/-euse *m/f* d'organes

organic *adj* ‹substance, development› organique; ‹produce, farming› biologique

organism *n* organisme *m*

ⵚ **organization** *n* (a) (group) organisation *f*; (government) organisme *m*; (voluntary) association *f*
(b) (arrangement) organisation *f* (**of** de)

ⵚ **organize** *vtr* organiser ‹event, time, life›; ranger ‹books, papers›

organized crime *n* grand banditisme *m*

organizer *n* (a) (person) organisateur/-trice *m/f*
(b) (also **personal ~**) (agenda *m*) organisateur *m*; **electronic ~** agenda *m* électronique

organ transplant *n* transplantation *f* d'organe

orgy *n* orgie *f*

orient ⓵ *n* **the Orient** l'Orient *m*
⓶ *vtr* (also **orientate**) orienter (**towards** vers)

oriental *adj* (gen) oriental/-e; ‹appearance, eyes› d'Oriental; ‹carpet› d'Orient

orienteering *n* course *f* d'orientation

ⵚ **origin** *n* origine *f*

ⵚ **original** ⓵ *n* original *m*
⓶ *adj* (a) (gen) original/-e
(b) (initial) ‹inhabitant, owner› premier/-ière (before *n*); ‹question, site› originel/-elle

originality *n* originalité *f*

ⵚ **originally** *adv* (a) (initially) au départ
(b) (in the first place) à l'origine

originate *vi* ‹custom, style, tradition› voir le jour; ‹fire› se déclarer; **to ~ from** ‹goods› provenir de

originator *n* (a) (of idea, rumour) auteur *m*
(b) (of invention, system) créateur/-trice *m/f*

ornament *n* (a) (trinket) bibelot *m*
(b) (ornamentation) ornement *m*

ornamental *adj* ‹plant› ornemental/-e; ‹lake› d'agrément; ‹motif› décoratif/-ive

ornate *adj* richement orné/-e

ornithology *n* ornithologie *f*

orphan *n* orphelin/-e *m/f*

orphanage *n* orphelinat *m*

orthodox *adj* orthodoxe

orthopaedic (GB), **orthopedic** (US) *adj* orthopédique

ostentatious *adj* ostentatoire

osteopath *n* ostéopathe *mf*

ostracize *vtr* ostraciser

ostrich *n* autruche *f*

✦ **other** ⓵ *adj* autre; **the ~ one** l'autre; **the ~ 25** les 25 autres; **~ people** les autres; **he was going the ~ way** il allait dans la direction opposée; **the ~ day** l'autre jour; **every ~ year** tous les deux ans; **every ~ Saturday** un samedi sur deux

⓶ *pron* **the ~s** les autres; **~s** (as subject) d'autres; (as object) les autres; **one after the ~** l'un après l'autre; **someone or ~** quelqu'un; **some book or ~** un livre, je ne sais plus lequel; **somehow or ~** d'une manière ou d'une autre

⓷ **other than** *phr* **~ than that** à part ça; **nobody knows ~ than you** tu es le seul à le savoir

✦ **otherwise** ⓵ *adv* autrement; **no woman, married or ~** aucune femme, mariée ou non ⓶ *conj* sinon; **it's quite safe, ~ I wouldn't do it** ce n'est pas dangereux du tout, sinon je ne le ferais pas

otter *n* loutre *f*

ouch *excl* aïe!

ought *modal aux* **I ~ to do/to have done** je devrais/j'aurais dû faire; **that ~ to fix it** ça devrait arranger les choses; **oughtn't we to ask?** ne croyez-vous pas que nous devrions demander?; **we ~ to say something** nous devrions dire quelque chose; **someone ~ to have accompanied her** quelqu'un aurait dû l'accompagner

ounce *n* once *f* (*= 28.35 g*)

✦ **our** *det* notre/nos

> ■ **Note** In French, determiners agree in gender and number with the noun that follows. So *our* is translated by *notre* + masculine or feminine singular noun (notre chien, notre maison) and *nos* + plural noun (nos enfants).
> — When *our* is stressed, *à nous* is added after the noun: OUR *house* = notre maison à nous.

ours *pron*

> ■ **Note** In French, possessive pronouns reflect the number and gender of the noun they are standing for. Thus *ours* is translated by *le nôtre*, *la nôtre* or *les nôtres* according to what is being referred to.

their children are older than ~ leurs enfants sont plus âgés que les nôtres; **which tickets are ~?** lesquels de ces billets sont les nôtres *or* à nous?; **a friend of ~** un ami à nous; **the blue car is ~** la voiture bleue est à nous; **it's not ~** ce n'est pas à nous

✦ **ourselves** *pron* **(a)** (reflexive) nous; **we've hurt ~** nous nous sommes fait mal **(b)** (emphatic) nous-mêmes; **we did it ~** nous l'avons fait nous-mêmes **(c)** (after prepositions) **for ~** pour nous, pour nous-mêmes; **(all) by ~** tout seuls/toutes seules

✦ **out**

> ■ **Note** When *out* is used as an adverb meaning *outside*, it often adds little to the sense of the phrase: *they're out in the garden* = *they're in the garden*. In such cases *out* will not usually be translated: *ils sont dans le jardin*.

⓵ *vtr* révéler l'homosexualité de ‹*person*›

⓶ *adv* **(a)** (outside) dehors; **to stay ~ in the rain** rester (dehors) sous la pluie; **~ there** dehors **(b)** (to go *or* walk ~) sortir; **I couldn't find my way ~** je ne trouvais pas la sortie; **when the tide is ~** à marée basse; **further ~** plus loin; **to invite sb ~ to dinner** inviter qn au restaurant **(c)** (absent) **to be ~** être sorti/-e **(d)** **to be ~** ‹*book, exam results*› être publié/-e **(c)** **to be ~** ‹*sun, moon, stars*› briller **(f)** **to be ~** ‹*fire, light*› être éteint/-e **(g)** (Sport) **to be ~** ‹*player*› être éliminé/-e; **'~!'** (of ball) 'out!' **(h)** (over) **before the week is ~** avant la fin de la semaine **(i)** (colloq) **to be ~ to do** être bien décidé/-e à faire; **he's just ~ for what he can get** c'est l'intérêt qui le guide

⓷ **out of** *phr* **(a)** **to go** *or* **walk** *or* **come ~ of** sortir de; **to jump ~ of the window** sauter par la fenêtre; **to take sth ~ of one's bag** prendre qch dans son sac **(b)** (expressing ratio) sur; **two ~ of every three** deux sur trois **(c)** hors de ‹*reach, sight*›; en dehors de ‹*city*›; à l'abri de ‹*sun*› **(d)** **to be (right) ~ of** ne plus avoir de ‹*item*› **IDIOM to be ~ of it** (colloq) être dans les vapes (fam)

out-and-out *adj* ‹*villain, liar*› fieffé/-e; ‹*supporter*› pur/-e et dur/-e; ‹*success, failure*› total/-e

outback *n* **the ~** la brousse (australienne)

outboard motor *n* moteur *m* hors-bord

outbreak *n* (of war) début *m*; (of violence, spots) éruption *f*; (of disease) déclaration *f*

outbuilding *n* dépendance *f*

outburst *n* accès *m*

outcast *n* exclu/-e *m/f*

✦ **outcome** *n* résultat *m*

outcry *n* tollé *m* (**about, against** contre)

outdated *adj* ‹*idea, practice, theory*› dépassé/-e; ‹*clothing*› démodé/-e

outdo *vtr* (*prét* **outdid**, *pp* **outdone**) surpasser

outdoor *adj* ‹*life, activity, sport*› de plein air; ‹*restaurant*› en plein air

outdoors *adv* ‹*sit, work, play*› dehors; ‹*live*› en plein air; ‹*sleep*› à la belle étoile; **to go ~** sortir

outer *adj* (a) (outside) extérieur/-e
(b) ‹*limit*› extrême

outer space *n* espace *m* (extra-atmosphérique)

outfit *n* tenue *f*

outgoing *adj* (a) (sociable) ouvert/-e et sociable
(b) ‹*government*› sortant/-e

outgoings *n pl* (GB) sorties *fpl* (de fonds)

outgrow *vtr* (*prét* **outgrew**, *pp* **outgrown**) (a) (grow too big for) devenir trop grand pour
(b) (grow too old for) se lasser de [qch] avec le temps; **he'll ~ it** ça lui passera

outlandish *adj* bizarre

outlast *vtr* durer plus longtemps que

outlaw ⒈ *n* hors-la-loi *m inv*
⒉ *vtr* déclarer illégal/-e ‹*practice, organization*›

outlay *n* dépenses *fpl* (**on** en)

outlet *n* (a) (for gas, air, water) tuyau *m* de sortie
(b) **retail ~** point *m* de vente
(c) (for emotion, talent) exutoire *m*
(d) (US) (socket) prise *f* de courant

outline ⒈ *n* (a) (silhouette) contour *m*
(b) (of plan, policy) grandes lignes *fpl*; (of essay) plan *m*
⒉ *vtr* exposer brièvement ‹*aims, plan, reasons*›

outlive *vtr* survivre à ‹*person*›

outlook *n* (a) (attitude) vue *f*
(b) (prospects) perspectives *fpl*

outlying *adj* (away from city centre) excentré/-e; (remote) isolé/-e

outnumber *vtr* être plus nombreux/-euses que

out-of-body experience *n* **to have an ~** faire une projection hors du corps

out-of-date *adj* ‹*ticket, passport*› périmé/-e; ‹*concept*› dépassé/-e

outpatient *n* malade *mf* externe; **~s' department** service *m* de consultation

outpost *n* avant-poste *m*

output *n* (yield) rendement *m*; (of factory) production *f*

outrage ⒈ *n* (a) (anger) indignation *f* (**at** devant)
(b) (atrocity) atrocité *f*
(c) (scandal) scandale *m*
⒉ *vtr* scandaliser ‹*public*›

outrageous *adj* scandaleux/-euse; ‹*remark*› outrancier/-ière

outright ⒈ *adj* ‹*control, majority*› absolu/-e; ‹*ban*› catégorique; ‹*victory, winner*› incontesté/-e
⒉ *adv* (gen) catégoriquement; ‹*killed*› sur le coup

outset *n* **at the ~** au début; **from the ~** dès le début

ᵍ **outside** ⒈ *n* (a) extérieur *m*; **on the ~** à l'extérieur
(b) (maximum) **at the ~** au maximum
⒉ *adj* extérieur/-e; **~ lane** (in GB) voie *f* de droite; (in US, Europe) voie *f* de gauche; (on athletics track) couloir *m* extérieur; **an ~ chance** une faible chance
⒊ *adv* dehors
⒋ *prep* (*also* **~ of**) (a) en dehors de ‹*city*›; de l'autre côté de ‹*boundary*›; à l'extérieur de ‹*building*›
(b) (in front of) devant ‹*house, shop*›

outsider *n* (a) (in community) étranger/-ère *m/f*
(b) (Sport) outsider *m*

outsize *adj* ‹*clothes*› grande taille

outskirts *n pl* périphérie *f*

outsource *vtr* (a) (subcontract) sous-traiter
(b) (to another country for cheaper labour) externaliser

outsourcing *n* (a) (subcontracting) sous-traitance
(b) (to another country for cheaper labour) externalisation

outspoken *adj* **to be ~** parler sans détour

outstanding *adj* (a) (praiseworthy) remarquable
(b) (striking) frappant/-e
(c) ‹*bill*› impayé/-e; ‹*work*› inachevé/-e; **~ debts** créances *fpl* à recouvrer

outstay *vtr* **to ~ one's welcome** s'éterniser

outstretched *adj* ‹*hand, arm*› tendu/-e; ‹*wings*› déployé/-e

outstrip *vtr* (*p prés etc* **-pp-**) dépasser ‹*person*›; excéder ‹*production, demand*›

outward ⒈ *adj* ‹*appearance, sign*› extérieur/-e; ‹*calm*› apparent/-e; **~ journey** aller *m*
⒉ *adv* ((GB) *also* **outwards**) vers l'extérieur

outwardly *adv* (apparently) en apparence

outwards (GB) = OUTWARD 2

outweigh *vtr* l'emporter sur

outwit *vtr* (*p prés etc* **-tt-**) être plus futé/-e que ‹*person*›

outworker *n* travailleur/-euse *m/f* à domicile

oval *n, adj* ovale *m*

ovary *n* ovaire *m*

ovation *n* ovation *f*; **to give sb a standing ~** se lever pour ovationner qn

oven *n* four *m*

oven glove *n* manique *f*

ᵍ **over**

■ **Note** *over* is often used with another preposition in English (*to, in, on*) without altering the meaning. In this case *over* is usually not

overact ⋯⊁ overlap ⋯⋯

translated in French: *to be over in France* = être en France; *to swim over to sb* = nager vers qn.

1 *prep* **(a)** par-dessus; **he jumped ~ it** il a sauté par-dessus; **to wear a sweater ~ one's shirt** porter un pull par-dessus sa chemise; **a bridge ~ the Thames** un pont sur la Tamise
(b) (across) **it's just ~ the road** c'est juste de l'autre côté de la rue; **~ here/there** par ici/là; **come ~ here!** viens (par) ici!
(c) (above) au-dessus de; **they live ~ the shop** ils habitent au-dessus de la boutique; **children ~ six** les enfants de plus de six ans; **temperatures ~ 40°** des températures supérieures à *or* au-dessus de 40°
(d) (in the course of) **~ the weekend** pendant le week-end; **~ the last few days** au cours de ces derniers jours; **~ the years** avec le temps; **~ Christmas** à Noël
(e) **to be ~** s'être remis/-e de *‹illness, operation›*; **to be ~ the worst** avoir passé le pire
(f) (by means of) **~ the phone** par téléphone; **~ the radio** à la radio
(g) (everywhere) **all ~ the house** partout dans la maison

2 *adj, adv* **(a)** (finished) **to be ~** *‹term, meeting›* être terminé/-e; *‹war›* être fini/-e
(b) (more) **children of six and ~** les enfants de plus de six ans
(c) **to invite** *or* **ask sb ~** inviter qn; **we had them ~ on Sunday** ils sont venus dimanche
(d) (on radio, TV) **~ to you** à vous; **now ~ to our Paris studios** nous passons l'antenne à nos studios de Paris
(e) (showing repetition) **five times ~** cinq fois de suite; **to start all ~ again** recommencer à zéro; **I had to do it ~** (US) j'ai dû recommencer; **I've told you ~ and ~ (again)...** je t'ai dit je ne sais combien de fois...

overact *vi* en faire trop

⚡ **overall 1** *n* (GB) (coat-type) blouse *f*; (child's) tablier *m*
2 overalls *n pl* (GB) combinaison *f*; (US) salopette *f*
3 *adj ‹cost›* global/-e; *‹improvement›* général/-e; *‹effect›* d'ensemble; *‹majority›* absolu/-e
4 *adv* **(a)** (in total) en tout
(b) (in general) dans l'ensemble

overawe *vtr* intimider

overbalance *vi ‹person›* perdre l'équilibre; *‹pile of objects›* s'écrouler

overboard *adv* par-dessus bord, à l'eau

overbook *vtr, vi* surréserver

overcast *adj ‹sky›* couvert/-e

overcharge *vtr* faire payer trop cher à

overcoat *n* pardessus *m*

overcome 1 *vtr (prét* **-came**, *pp* **-come)** battre *‹opponent›*; vaincre *‹enemy›*; surmonter *‹dislike, fear›*; **to be ~ with despair** succomber au désespoir
2 *vi (prét* **-came**, *pp* **-come)** triompher

overcook *vtr* trop cuire

overcrowded *adj ‹train, room›* bondé/-e; *‹city›* surpeuplé/-e; *‹class›* surchargé/-e

overcrowding *n* (in city, institution) surpeuplement *m*; (in transport) surencombrement *m*; **~ in classrooms** les classes surchargées

overdo *vtr (prét* **overdid**, *pp* **overdone)** **to ~ it** (when describing) exagérer; (when performing) forcer la note (fam); (when working) en faire trop (fam)

overdose, OD 1 *n* (large dose) surdose *f*; (lethal dose) (of medicine) dose *f* mortelle; (of drugs) overdose *f*; **to take an ~** absorber une dose excessive de médicaments
2 *vi* (on medicine) prendre une dose mortelle de médicaments; (on drugs) faire une overdose

overdraft *n* découvert *m*

overdrawn *adj* à découvert

overdressed *adj* trop habillé/-e

overdrive *n* **to go into ~** *‹person›* s'activer intensivement

overdue *adj ‹baby, work›* en retard (by de); *‹bill›* impayé/-e; **this measure is long ~** cette mesure aurait dû être prise il y a longtemps

overeat *vi (prét* **overate**, *pp* **overeaten)** manger à l'excès

overestimate *vtr* surestimer

overexcited *adj* surexcité/-e

overflow 1 *vtr ‹river›* inonder *‹banks›*
2 *vi* déborder (**into** dans; **with** de)

overflow car park *n* parking *m* de délestage

overgrown *adj ‹garden›* envahi/-e par la végétation

overhaul 1 *n* (of machine) révision *f*; (of system) restructuration *f*
2 *vtr* réviser *‹car, machine›*; restructurer *‹system›*

overhead 1 *adj ‹cable, railway›* aérien/-ienne
2 *adv* **(a)** (in sky) dans le ciel
(b) (above sb's head) au-dessus de ma/sa etc tête

overhead projector *n* rétroprojecteur *m*

overheads (GB), **overhead** (US) *n pl* frais *mpl* généraux

overhear *vtr (p prés, pp* **-heard)** entendre par hasard

overheat *vi ‹car, equipment›* chauffer

overindulge *vi* faire des excès

overjoyed *adj* fou/folle de joie (**at** devant)

overkill *n* (excess publicity) matraquage *m*

overland 1 *adj ‹route›* terrestre; *‹journey›* par route
2 *adv* par route

overlap *vi (p prés etc* **-pp-)** se chevaucher

overleaf *adv* au verso

overload *vtr* surcharger (**with** de)

overlook *vtr* (a) ‹*building, window*› donner sur
(b) (miss) ne pas voir ‹*detail, error*›; **to ~ the fact that** négliger le fait que
(c) (ignore) ignorer ‹*effect, need*›

overnight ① *adj* (a) ‹*journey, train*› de nuit; ‹*stop*› pour une nuit
(b) ‹*success*› immédiat/-e
② *adv* (a) **to stay ~** passer la nuit
(b) ‹*change, disappear, transform*› du jour au lendemain

overnight bag *n* petit sac *m* de voyage

overpass (US) *n* (a) (for cars) toboggan *m*
(b) (footbridge) passerelle *f*

overpopulated *adj* surpeuplé/-e

overpower *vtr* (a) maîtriser ‹*thief*›; vaincre ‹*army*›
(b) ‹*smell, smoke*› accabler

overpowering *adj* ‹*person*› intimidant/-e; ‹*desire, urge*› irrésistible; ‹*heat*› accablant/-e; ‹*smell*› irrespirable

overpriced *adj* **it's ~** c'est trop cher pour ce que c'est

overqualified *adj* surqualifié/-e

overrated *adj* ‹*person, work*› surfait/-e

overreact *vi* réagir de façon excessive

override *vtr* (*prét* **-rode**, *pp* **-ridden**) l'emporter sur ‹*consideration*›; passer outre à ‹*decision*›

overriding *adj* ‹*importance*› primordial/-e; ‹*priority*› numéro un

overrule *vtr* **to be ~d** ‹*decision*› être annulé/-e

overrun *vtr* (*p prés* **-nn-**, *prét* **overran**, *pp* **overrun**) (a) (invade) envahir ‹*country, site*›
(b) (exceed) dépasser ‹*time, budget*›

overseas ① *adj* (a) ‹*student, investor*› étranger/-ère
(b) ‹*trade, market*› extérieur/-e
② *adv* à l'étranger

overshadow *vtr* éclipser ‹*achievement*›

oversight *n* erreur *f*; **due to an ~** par inadvertance

oversimplify *vtr* simplifier [qch] à l'excès

oversleep *vi* (*prét, pp* **-slept**) se réveiller trop tard

overspend *vi* (*prét, pp* **-spent**) trop dépenser

overstay *vtr* **to ~ one's visa** dépasser la limite de validité de son visa

overstep *vtr* (*p prés etc* **-pp-**) dépasser ‹*bounds*›; **to ~ the mark** aller trop loin

overt *adj* évident/-e, manifeste

overtake *vtr, vi* (*prét* **-took**, *pp* **-taken**) dépasser

over-the-top, OTT *adj* (colloq) outrancier/-ière; **to go over the top** aller trop loin

overthrow *vtr* (*prét* **-threw**, *pp* **-thrown**) renverser ‹*government, system*›

overtime ① *n* heures *fpl* supplémentaires
② *adv* **to work ~** ‹*person*› faire des heures supplémentaires

overtone *n* sous-entendu *m*, connotation *f*

overture *n* ouverture *f*

overturn ① *vtr* (a) renverser ‹*car, chair*›; faire chavirer ‹*boat*›
(b) faire annuler ‹*decision, sentence*›
② *vi* ‹*car, chair*› se renverser; ‹*boat*› chavirer

overweight *adj* (a) ‹*person*› trop gros/grosse
(b) ‹*suitcase*› trop lourd/-e

overwhelm ① *vtr* (a) ‹*wave, avalanche*› submerger; ‹*enemy*› écraser
(b) ‹*shame, grief*› accabler
② **overwhelmed** *pp adj* (with letters, offers, kindness) submergé/-e (**with, by** de); (with shame, work) accablé/-e (**with, by** de); (by sight, experience) ébloui/-e (**by** par)

overwhelming *adj* ‹*defeat, victory, majority*› écrasant/-e; ‹*desire*› irrésistible; ‹*heat, sorrow*› accablant/-e; ‹*support*› massif/-ive

overwork *vi* se surmener

overworked *adj* surmené/-e

owe *vtr* devoir; **to ~ sth to sb** devoir qch à qn

owing ① *adj* à payer, dû/-e
② **owing to** *phr* en raison de

owl *n* hibou *m*; (with tufted ears) chouette *f*

ℱ **own** ① *adj* propre; **her ~ car** sa propre voiture
② *pron* **my ~** le mien, la mienne; **his/her ~** le sien, la sienne; **he has a room of his ~** il a sa propre chambre *or* une chambre à lui; **a house of our (very) ~** une maison (bien) à nous
③ *vtr* avoir ‹*car, house, dog*›; **she ~s three shops** elle est propriétaire de trois magasins; **who ~s that house?** à qui est cette maison?
IDIOMS **to get one's ~ back** se venger (**on sb** de qn); **on one's ~** tout seul/toute seule
■ **own up** avouer

ℱ **owner** *n* propriétaire *mf*; **car ~** automobiliste *mf*; **home ~** propriétaire *mf*

ownership *n* propriété *f*; (of land) possession *f*

ox *n* (*pl* **~en**) bœuf *m*

oxygen *n* oxygène *m*

oyster *n* huître *f*

ozone *n* ozone *m*

ozone layer *n* couche *f* d'ozone

ℱ indicates a very frequent word

Pp

p, P *n* p, P *m*

PA *n* (*abbr* = **personal assistant**) secrétaire *mf* de direction

⚘ pace 1 *n* (step) pas *m*; (rate) rythme *m*; (speed) vitesse *f*; **at a fast/slow ~** vite/ lentement; **at walking ~** au pas

2 *vi* **to ~ up and down** (impatiently) faire les cent pas; **to ~ up and down sth** arpenter ‹*cage, room*›

pacemaker *n* (a) (Med) stimulateur *m* cardiaque

(b) (athlete) lièvre *m*

Pacific *pr n* **the ~** le Pacifique; **the ~ Ocean** l'océan Pacifique

pacifist *n, adj* pacifiste *mf*

pacify *vtr* apaiser ‹*person*›; pacifier ‹*country*›

⚘ pack 1 *n* (a) (box) paquet *m*; (large box) boîte *f*; (bag) sachet *m*

(b) (group) bande *f*; (of hounds) meute *f*; **a ~ of lies** un tissu de mensonges

(c) (in rugby) pack *m*

(d) (of cards) jeu *m* de cartes

(e) (backpack) sac *m* à dos

2 *vtr* (a) (in suitcase) mettre [qch] dans une valise ‹*clothes*›; (in box, crate) emballer ‹*ornaments, books*›

(b) emballer ‹*box, crate*›; **to ~ one's suitcase** faire sa valise

(c) ‹*crowd*› remplir complètement ‹*church, theatre*›

(d) tasser ‹*snow, earth*›

3 *vi* (a) ‹*person*› faire ses valises

(b) **to ~ into** ‹*crowd*› s'entasser dans ‹*place*›

■ **pack up:** 1 ¶ **~ up** (a) ‹*person*› faire ses valises

(b) (colloq) (break down) ‹*TV, machine*› se détraquer (fam); ‹*car*› tomber en panne

2 ¶ **~ [sth] up, ~ up [sth]** (in boxes, crates) emballer

⚘ package 1 *n* (a) (parcel) paquet *m*, colis *m*

(b) (of proposals, measures, aid) ensemble *m* (of de)

(c) (Comput) progiciel *m*

2 *vtr* conditionner, emballer

package deal *n* offre *f* globale

package holiday (GB), **package tour** *n* voyage *m* organisé

packaging *n* conditionnement *m*

packed *adj* comble; **~ with** plein/-e de

packed lunch *n* panier-repas *m*

packet *n* (gen) paquet *m*; (sachet) sachet *m*

packing *n* (a) (packaging) emballage *m*

(b) **to do one's ~** faire ses valises

pact *n* pacte *m*

pad 1 *n* (a) (of paper) bloc *m*

(b) (for leg) jambière *f*

(c) (of paw) coussinet *m*; (of finger) pulpe *f*

(d) (*also* **launch ~**) rampe *f* de lancement

2 *vtr* (*p prés etc* **-dd-**) rembourrer ‹*chair, shoulders, jacket*› (with avec); capitonner ‹*walls*›

3 *vi* (*p prés etc* **-dd-**) **to ~ along/around** avancer/aller et venir à pas feutrés

■ **pad out** étoffer, délayer ‹*essay, speech*›

padded envelope *n* enveloppe *f* matelassée

padding *n* (stuffing) rembourrage *m*

paddle 1 *n* (a) (oar) pagaie *f*

(b) **to go for a ~** faire trempette *f*

2 *vi* (a) (row) pagayer

(b) (wade) patauger

(c) ‹*duck, swan*› barboter

paddling pool *n* (public) pataugeoire *f*; (inflatable) piscine *f* gonflable

padlock 1 *n* (on door) cadenas *m*; (for bicycle) antivol *m*

2 *vtr* cadenasser ‹*door, gate*›; mettre un antivol à ‹*bicycle*›

paediatrician (GB), **pediatrician** (US) *n* pédiatre *mf*

paedophile (GB), **pedophile** (US) *n* pédophile *mf*

pagan *n, adj* païen/païenne *m/f*

⚘ page 1 *n* (a) (in book) page *f*; **on ~ two** à la page deux

(b) (attendant) groom *m*; (US) coursier *m*

2 *vtr* (on pager) rechercher; (over loudspeaker) faire appeler

pageant *n* (play) reconstitution *f* historique; (carnival) fête *f* à thème historique

pageboy *n* (at wedding) garçon *m* d'honneur

pager *n* récepteur *m* d'appel

paid *adj* ‹*work, job*› rémunéré/-e; ‹*holiday*› payé/-e; **~ assassin** tueur *m* à gages

⚘ pain 1 *n* (a) douleur *f*; **to be in ~** souffrir; **period ~s** règles *fpl* douloureuses

(b) (colloq) (annoying person, thing) **he's/it's a ~** il est/c'est enquiquinant (fam); **he's a ~ in the neck** (colloq) il est casse-pieds (fam)

2 **pains** *n pl* **to be at ~s to do** prendre grand soin de faire; **to take great ~s over** *or* **with sth** se donner beaucoup de mal pour qch

painful *adj* douloureux/-euse; ‹*lesson, memory*› pénible

painkiller *n* analgésique *m*

painless *adj* (a) (pain-free) indolore

(b) (trouble-free) sans peine

painstaking adj minutieux/-ieuse

⚘ **paint** ① n peinture f

② **paints** n pl couleurs fpl

③ vtr **(a)** (gen) peindre; peindre le portrait de ‹person›; **to ~ one's nails** se vernir les ongles

(b) (depict) dépeindre

④ vi peindre

paintbox n boîte f de couleurs

paintbrush n pinceau m

painter n peintre m

⚘ **painting** n **(a)** (activity, art form) peinture f

(b) (work of art) tableau m; (unframed) toile f; (of person) portrait m

(c) (decorating) peintures fpl

⚘ **pair** n **(a)** (gen) paire f; **to be one of a ~** faire partie d'une paire; **in ~s** ‹work› en groupes de deux; **a ~ of scissors** une paire de ciseaux; **a ~ of trousers** un pantalon

(b) (couple) couple m

■ **pair off** (as a couple) se mettre ensemble; (for temporary purposes) se mettre par deux

■ **pair up** ‹dancers, lovers› former un couple; ‹competitors› faire équipe

paisley n tissu m à motifs cachemire

pajamas (US) = PYJAMAS

Pakistan pr n Pakistan m

Pakistani ① n Pakistanais/-e m/f

② adj pakistanais/-e

palace n palais m

palatable n ‹food› savoureux/-euse; ‹solution, idea› acceptable

palate n palais m

pale ① adj (gen) pâle; ‹light, dawn› blafard/-e; **to turn** or **go ~** pâlir

② vi pâlir; **to ~ into insignificance** devenir dérisoire

Palestine pr n Palestine f

Palestinian ① n Palestinien/-ienne m/f

② adj palestinien/-ienne

palette n palette f

pallet n (for loading) palette f

pallid adj ‹skin, light› blafard/-e

palm n **(a)** paume f; **in the ~ of one's hand** dans le creux de la main; **he read my ~** il m'a lu les lignes de la main

(b) (also ~ **tree**) palmier m

(c) (also ~ **leaf**) palme f

■ **palm off** (colloq): **to ~ sth off** faire passer qch (as pour); **to ~ sth off on sb**, **to ~ sb off with sth** refiler (fam) qch à qn

Palm Sunday n dimanche m des Rameaux

palmtop n (also ~ **computer**) ordinateur m de poche

palpable adj ‹fear, tension› palpable; ‹lie, error, nonsense› manifeste

palpitate vi palpiter (**with** de)

⚘ indicates a very frequent word

paltry adj ‹sum› dérisoire; ‹excuse› piètre (before n)

pamper vtr choyer ‹person, pet›

pamphlet n brochure f; (political) tract m

pan ① n (saucepan) casserole f

② vtr (p prés etc -**nn**-) **(a)** (colloq) (criticize) éreinter

(b) (in photography) faire un panoramique de

pancake n crêpe f

pancake day n mardi m gras

pandemonium n tohu-bohu m

pander vi **to ~ to** céder aux exigences de ‹person›; flatter ‹whim›

pane n vitre f, carreau m; **a ~ of glass** une vitre, un carreau

⚘ **panel** n **(a)** (of experts, judges) commission f; (on discussion programme) invités mpl; (on quiz show) jury m

(b) (section of wall) panneau m

(c) (of instruments, switches) tableau m

pang n **(a)** (emotional) serrement m de cœur; **a ~ of jealousy** une pointe de jalousie

(b) ~**s of hunger** crampes fpl d'estomac

panhandler n (US) (colloq) mendiant/-e m/f

panic ① n panique f, affolement m

② vtr (p prés etc -**ck**-) affoler ‹person, animal›; semer la panique dans ‹crowd›

③ vi (p prés etc -**ck**-) s'affoler

panic buying n achats mpl par crainte de la pénurie

panic-stricken adj pris/-e de panique

panorama n panorama m

pansy n pensée f

pant vi haleter

panther n **(a)** (leopard) panthère f

(b) (US) (puma) puma m

panties n pl (US) slip m (de femme)

pantomime n (GB) spectacle m pour enfants

pantry n garde-manger m inv

pants n pl **(a)** (US) (trousers) pantalon m

(b) (GB) (underwear) slip m

panty hose n (US) collant m

panty-liner n protège-slip m

⚘ **paper** ① n **(a)** (for writing, drawing) papier m; **a piece of ~** (scrap) un bout de papier; (clean sheet) une feuille (de papier); (for wrapping) un morceau de papier; **writing/tissue ~** papier à lettres/de soie

(b) (also **wall**~) papier m peint

(c) (newspaper) journal m

(d) (exam) épreuve f (**on** sur); (lecture) communication f (**on** sur)

(e) (exam) épreuve f (**on** de)

② **papers** n pl (documents) papiers mpl

③ adj ‹bag, hat, handkerchief, napkin› en papier; ‹plate, cup› en carton

④ vtr tapisser ‹room, wall›

paperback n livre m de poche

paperclip n trombone m

paper knife n coupe-papier m inv

paper round n he does a ~ il livre des journaux

paper shop n marchand m de journaux

paper towel n essuie-tout m inv

paperweight n presse-papier m inv

paperwork n (administration) travail m administratif; (documentation) documents mpl

par n (a) to be on a ~ with ‹performance› être comparable à; ‹person› être l'égal/-e de; to be up to ~ être à la hauteur; to be below or under ~ ‹performance› être en dessous de la moyenne; ‹person› ne pas se sentir en forme
(b) (in golf) par m

parachute ⒈ n parachute m
⒉ vi descendre en parachute

parachute drop n parachutage m

parachute jump n saut m en parachute

parachuting n parachutisme m

parade ⒈ n (a) (procession) parade f
(b) (Mil) défilé m
⒉ vtr (display) faire étalage de
⒊ vi défiler (through dans); to ~ up and down ‹soldier, model› défiler; ‹child› parader

parade ground n champ m de manœuvres

paradise n paradis m; in ~ au paradis

paradox n paradoxe m

paradoxical adj paradoxal/-e

paraffin n (a) (GB) (fuel) pétrole m
(b) (also ~ **wax**) paraffine f

paragliding n parapente m

paragon n modèle m (of de)

⚜ **paragraph** n paragraphe m

parallel ⒈ n (a) (gen) parallèle m
(b) (in mathematics) parallèle f
⒉ adj (a) (gen) parallèle (**to, with** à)
(b) (similar) analogue (**to, with** à)
⒊ adv ~ **to**, ~ **with** parallèlement à

Paralympics n pl (also **Paralympic Games**) jeux mpl paralympiques

paralyse (GB), **paralyze** (US) vtr paralyser

paralysis n paralysie f

paramedic n auxiliaire mf médical/-e

parameter n paramètre m

paramilitary ⒈ n membre m d'une organisation paramilitaire
⒉ adj paramilitaire

paramount adj to be ~, to be of ~ importance être d'une importance capitale

paranoid adj (Med) paranoïde; (gen) paranoïaque (**about** au sujet de)

paraphernalia n attirail m

paraphrase vtr paraphraser

parascending n parachutisme m ascensionnel

parasite n parasite m

paratrooper n parachutiste m

parcel n paquet m, colis m
IDIOM to be part and ~ of faire partie intégrante de
▪ **parcel up**: ~ up [sth], ~ [sth] up emballer

parcel bomb n colis m piégé

parched adj (a) (dry) desséché/-e
(b) (thirsty) to be ~ mourir de soif

parchment n (document) parchemin m; (paper) papier-parchemin m

pardon ⒈ n (a) (gen) pardon m
(b) (Law) (also **free** ~) grâce f
⒉ excl (what?) pardon?; (sorry!) pardon!
⒊ vtr (a) (gen) pardonner; ~ **me!** pardon!
(b) (Law) gracier ‹criminal›

⚜ **parent** n parent m

parental adj des parents, parental/-e

parent company n maison f mère

parenthood n (fatherhood) paternité f; (motherhood) maternité f

parenting n éducation f des enfants

parents' evening n réunion f pour les parents d'élèves

Paris pr n Paris

parish n (a) paroisse f
(b) (GB) (administrative) commune f

Parisian ⒈ n Parisien/-ienne m/f
⒉ adj parisien/-ienne

⚜ **park** ⒈ n (a) (public garden) jardin m public, parc m
(b) (estate) parc m
⒉ vtr garer ‹car›
⒊ vi ‹driver› se garer
⒋ **parked** pp adj en stationnement

park-and-ride n parking m relais

parking n stationnement m; 'No ~' 'stationnement interdit'

parking lot n (US) parking m

parking meter n parcmètre m

parking place, **parking space** n place f

parking ticket n (fine) contravention f, PV m (fam)

⚜ **parliament** n parlement m

parliamentary adj parlementaire

parlour (GB), **parlor** (US) n petit salon m

parody ⒈ n parodie f
⒉ vtr parodier ‹person, style›

parole n liberté f conditionnelle; on ~ en liberté conditionnelle

parrot n perroquet m

parry vtr (a) (Sport) parer
(b) éluder ‹question›

parsley n persil m

parsnip n panais m

⚜ **part** ⒈ n (a) (of whole) partie f; (of country) région f; to be (a) ~ of faire partie de; that's the best/hardest ~ c'est ça le meilleur/le plus dur; for the most ~ dans l'ensemble ⋯⊹

(b) (Tech) (component) pièce *f*; **spare** ~**s** pièces détachées

(c) (of serial) épisode *m*

(d) (role) rôle *m* (**in** dans); **to take** ~ participer (**in** à)

(e) (actor's role) rôle *m* (**of** de)

(f) (measure) mesure *f*

(g) (behalf) **on the** ~ **of** de la part de; **for my** ~ pour ma part

(h) (US) (in hair) raie *f*

2 *adv* en partie; ~ **French,** ~ **Chinese** moitié français, moitié chinois

3 *vtr* séparer ‹*two people*›; écarter ‹*legs*›; entrouvrir ‹*lips, curtains*›; **to** ~ **one's hair** se faire une raie

4 *vi* (a) (split up) se séparer; **to** ~ **from sb** quitter qn

(b) ‹*crowd, clouds*› s'ouvrir

■ **part with** se séparer de ‹*object*›; **to** ~ **with money** débourser

part exchange *n* (GB) reprise *f*; **to take sth in** ~ reprendre qch

partial *adj* (a) (not complete) partiel/-ielle

(b) (biased) partial/-e

(c) (fond) **to be** ~ avoir un faible pour

partially sighted *n* **the** ~ les malvoyants *mpl*

✔ **participant** *n* participant/-e *m/f* (**in** à)

✔ **participate** *vi* participer (**in** à)

participation *n* participation *f* (**in** à)

participle *n* participe *m*

particle *n* particule *f*

✔ **particular** **1** *adj* (a) (gen) particulier/-ière; **for no** ~ **reason** sans raison particulière

(b) (fussy) méticuleux/-euse; **to be** ~ **about** être exigeant/-e sur ‹*cleanliness, punctuality*›; prendre grand soin de ‹*appearance*›; être difficile pour ‹*food*›

2 in particular *phr* en particulier

✔ **particularly** *adv* (a) (in particular) en particulier

(b) (especially) spécialement

particulars *n pl* (information) détails *mpl*; (name, address) coordonnées *fpl*

parting *n* (a) séparation *f*

(b) (GB) (in hair) raie *f*

partisan *n* (gen, Mil) partisan *m*

partition **1** *n* (a) (in room, house) cloison *f*

(b) (of country) partition *f*

2 *vtr* (a) cloisonner ‹*area, room*›

(b) diviser ‹*country*›

partly *adv* en partie

✔ **partner** *n* (a) (professional) associé/-e *m/f* (**in** dans)

(b) (economic, political, sporting) partenaire *m*

(c) (married) époux/-se *m/f*; (unmarried) partenaire *mf*

partnership *n* association *f*; **to go into** ~ **with** s'associer à

✔ indicates a very frequent word

part of speech *n* partie *f* du discours

part-time *adj, adv* à temps partiel

✔ **party** *n* (a) (social event) fête *f*; (in evening) soirée *f*; (formal) réception *f*; **to have a** ~ faire une fête; **birthday** ~ (fête d')anniversaire *m*; **children's** ~ goûter *m* d'enfants

(b) (group) groupe *m*; (Mil) détachement *m*; **rescue** ~ équipe *f* de secouristes

(c) (in politics) parti *m*

(d) (Law) partie *f*

party dress *n* robe *f* de soirée; (for child) belle robe *f*

party line *n* (a) **the** ~ la ligne du parti

(b) (phone line) ligne *f* commune

party political broadcast *n*: émission *dans laquelle un parti expose sa politique*

✔ **pass** **1** *n* (a) (permit) laisser-passer *m inv*; (for journalists) coupe-file *m inv*; **travel** ~ carte *f* d'abonnement

(b) (Sch, Univ) (in exam) moyenne *f* (**in** en); **to get a** ~ être reçu/-e

(c) (Sport) (in ball games) passe *f*; (in fencing) botte *f*

(d) (in mountains) col *m*

2 *vtr* (a) (gen) passer ‹*plate, ball, time*›

(b) passer ‹*checkpoint, customs*›; passer devant ‹*building, area*›; dépasser ‹*vehicle, level, expectation*›; **to** ~ **sb in the street** croiser qn dans la rue

(c) ‹*person*› réussir ‹*test, exam*›; ‹*car, machine*› passer [qch] (avec succès) ‹*test*›

(d) adopter ‹*bill, motion*›

(e) admettre ‹*candidate*›

(f) prononcer ‹*sentence*›

3 *vi* (gen) passer; (in exam) réussir

IDIOM **to make a** ~ **at sb** faire du plat (fam) à qn

■ **pass around, pass round** faire circuler ‹*document, photos*›; faire passer ‹*food, plates*›

■ **pass away** décéder

■ **pass by** ‹*procession*› défiler; ‹*person*› passer

■ **pass down** transmettre (**from** de; **to** à)

■ **pass off** faire passer ‹*person, incident*› (**as** pour)

■ **pass on** transmettre ‹*condolences, message*›; passer ‹*clothes, cold*› (**to** à)

■ **pass out** (faint) perdre connaissance; (fall drunk) tomber ivre mort

■ **pass through** traverser

passable *adj* (a) ‹*standard, quality*› passable; ‹*knowledge, performance*› assez bon/bonne

(b) ‹*road*› praticable; ‹*river*› franchissable

passage *n* (a) (gen) passage

(b) (*also* ~**way**) (indoors) corridor *m*

(c) (journey) traversée *f*

✔ **passenger** *n* (in car, plane, ship) passager/-ère *m/f*; (in train, bus, on underground) voyageur/-euse *m/f*

passerby *n* (*pl* **passersby**) passant/-e *m/f*

passing *adj* **(a)** ‹*motorist, policeman*› qui passe/qui passait
(b) ‹*whim*› passager/-ère
(c) ‹*reference*› en passant *inv*
(d) ‹*resemblance*› vague (*before n*)

passion *n* passion *f*

passionate *adj* passionné/-e

passive ① *n* **the** ~ le passif, la voix passive
② *adj* passif/-ive

passkey *n* passe *m*

pass mark *n* moyenne *f*

Passover *n* Pâque *f* juive

passport *n* passeport *m*

password *n* mot *m* de passe

⚘ **past** ① *n* passé *m*; **in the** ~ dans le passé
② *adj* **(a)** (preceding) ‹*weeks, months*› dernier/-ière (*before n*); **in the** ~ **two years** dans les deux dernières années; **during the** ~ **few days** ces derniers jours
(b) (former) ‹*times, problems, experience*› passé/-e; ‹*president*› ancien/-ienne (*before n*); ‹*government*› précédent/-e; **in times** ~ autrefois, jadis
(c) **summer is** ~ l'été est fini; **that's all** ~ c'est du passé
③ *prep* **(a) to walk** *or* **go** ~ **sb/sth** passer devant qn/qch; **to drive** ~ **sth** passer devant qch (en voiture)
(b) (in time) **it's** ~ **6** il est 6 heures passées; **twenty** ~ **two** deux heures vingt; **half** ~ **two** deux heures et demie; **he is** ~ **70** il a 70 ans passés
(c) (beyond) après; ~ **the church** après l'église; **to be** ~ **caring** ne plus s'en faire
④ *adv* **to go** *or* **walk** ~ passer
IDIOMS to be ~ **it** (colloq) avoir passé l'âge; **to be** ~ **its best** ‹*food*› être un peu avancé/-e; ‹*wine*› être un peu éventé/-e; **I wouldn't put it** ~ **him (to do)** ça ne m'étonnerait pas de lui (qu'il fasse)

pasta *n* pâtes *fpl* (alimentaires)

paste ① *n* **(a)** (glue) colle *f*
(b) (mixture) pâte *f*
(c) (Culin) (fish, meat) pâte *m*; (vegetable) purée *f*
② *vtr* (gen, Comput) coller (**onto** sur; **into** dans; **together** ensemble)

pastel ① *n* pastel *m*
② *adj* ‹*colour, pink, shade*› pastel *inv*

pasteurize *vtr* pasteuriser

pastime *n* passe-temps *m inv*

pastor *n* pasteur *m*

pastoral *n* pastoral/-e; ‹*role, work*› de conseiller/-ère

pastrami *n* bœuf *m* fumé

pastry *n* **(a)** (mixture) pâte *f*
(b) (cake) pâtisserie *f*

past tense *n* passé *m*

pasture *n* pré *m*, pâturage *m*

pat ① *n* **(a)** (gentle tap) petite tape *f*
(b) (of butter) noix *f*

② *vtr* (*p prés etc* **-tt-**) tapoter ‹*hand*›; caresser ‹*dog*›
IDIOM to have sth off (GB) *or* **down** ~ connaître qch par cœur

patch ① *n* (*pl* ~**es**) **(a)** (in clothes) pièce *f*; (on tyre) rustine® *f*; (on eye) bandeau *m*
(b) (of snow, ice) plaque *f*; (of damp, rust, sunlight) tache *f*; (of fog) nappe *f*; (of blue sky) coin *m*
(c) (area of ground) zone *f*; (for planting) carré *m*; **a** ~ **of grass** un coin d'herbe
(d) (GB) (colloq) (territory) territoire *m*
(e) (colloq) (period) période *f*
② *vtr* rapiécer ‹*hole, trousers*›; réparer ‹*tyre*›
■ **patch up**: ① ¶ ~ **up [sth]**, ~ **[sth] up** soigner ‹*person*›; rapiécer ‹*hole, trousers*›; réparer ‹*ceiling, tyre*›; (figurative) rafistoler (fam) ‹*marriage*›
② ¶ ~ **up [sth]** résoudre ‹*differences*›

patchy *adj* ‹*colour, essay, quality*› inégal/-e; ‹*knowledge*› incomplet/-ète; ~ **cloud** nuages *mpl* épars

paté *n* pâté *m*; **salmon** ~ terrine *f* de saumon

patent ① *n* brevet *m* (**for, on** pour)
② *adj* (obvious) manifeste
③ *vtr* faire breveter

patent leather *n* (cuir *m*) verni *m*

paternal *adj* paternel/-elle

paternity *n* paternité *f*

paternity leave *n* congé *m* de paternité

⚘ **path** *n* **(a)** (track) (*also* ~**way**) chemin *m*; (narrower) sentier *m*; (in garden) allée *f*
(b) (course) (of projectile, vehicle, sun) trajectoire *f*; (of river) cours *m*; (of hurricane) itinéraire *m*
(c) (option) voie *f*

pathetic *adj* **(a)** (moving) pathétique
(b) (inadequate) misérable
(c) (colloq) (awful) lamentable

pathological *adj* ‹*fear, hatred*› pathologique; ‹*jealousy*› maladif/ive

pathology *n* pathologie *f*

patience *n* **(a)** patience *f* (**with** avec)
(b) (card game) réussite *f*

⚘ **patient** ① *n* patient/ e *m/f*
② *adj* patient (**with** avec)

patiently *adv* avec patience, patiemment

patio *n* **(a)** (terrace) terrasse *f*
(b) (courtyard) patio *m*

patio doors *n pl* porte-fenêtre *f*

patriot *n* patriote *mf*

patriotic *adj* ‹*mood, song*› patriotique; ‹*person*› patriote

patriotism *n* patriotisme *m*

patrol ① *n* patrouille *f*
② *vtr, vi* (*p prés etc* **-ll-**) patrouiller

patrol boat, **patrol vessel** *n* patrouilleur *m*

patrol car *n* voiture *f* de police

patron *n* **(a)** (of artist) mécène *m*; (of person) protecteur/-trice *m/f*; (of charity) bienfaiteur/-trice *m/f*

⋯⟶

(b) (client) client/-e *m/f* (of de)
patronage *n* (support) patronage *m*; ~ of
the arts mécénat *m*
patronize *vtr* **(a)** traiter [qn] avec
condescendance ‹*person*›
(b) fréquenter ‹*restaurant, cinema*›
patronizing *adj* condescendant/-e
patron saint *n* saint/-e *m/f* patron/-onne
patter [1] *n* **(a)** (of rain) crépitement *m*; ~ of
footsteps bruit *m* de pas rapides et légers
(b) (talk) baratin *m*
[2] *vi* ‹*child, mouse*› trottiner; ‹*rain*› crépiter
♂ **pattern** *n* **(a)** (design) dessin *m*, motif *m*
(b) (of behaviour) mode *m*; weather ~s
tendances *fpl* climatiques
(c) (in dressmaking) patron *m*; (in knitting)
modèle *m*
(d) (model, example) modèle *m*
patterned *adj* ‹*fabric*› à motifs
paunch *n* ventre *m*
pauper *n* indigent/-e *m/f*
pause [1] *n* **(a)** (silence) silence *m*
(b) (break) pause *f*
(c) (stoppage) interruption *f*
[2] *vi* **(a)** (stop speaking) marquer une pause
(b) (stop) s'arrêter; to ~ in interrompre
‹*activity*›; to ~ for thought faire une pause
pour réfléchir
(c) (hesitate) hésiter
pave *vtr* paver (with de); to ~ the way for
sb/sth ouvrir la voie à qn/qch
pavement *n* **(a)** (GB) (footpath) trottoir *m*
(b) (US) (roadway) chaussée *f*
pavement café *n* café *m* avec terrasse
pavilion *n* pavillon *m*
paving slab, **paving stone** *n* dalle *f*
paw [1] *n* patte *f*
[2] *vtr* to ~ the ground ‹*horse*› piaffer; ‹*bull*›
frapper le sol du sabot
pawn [1] *n* pion *m*
[2] *vtr* mettre [qch] au mont-de-piété
pawnbroker *n* prêteur/-euse *m/f* sur
gages
pawnshop *n* mont-de-piété *m*
♂ **pay** [1] *n* salaire *m*
[2] *vtr* (*prét, pp* **paid**) **(a)** payer (for pour);
to ~ cash payer comptant; to ~ sth into
verser qch sur ‹*account*›; all expenses paid
tous frais payés
(b) ‹*account*› rapporter ‹*interest*›
(c) (give) to ~ attention to faire attention à;
to ~ a tribute to sb rendre hommage à qn; to
~ sb a compliment faire des compliments à
qn; to ~ sb a visit rendre visite à qn
(d) (benefit) it would ~ him to do il y
gagnerait à faire; it doesn't ~ to do cela ne
sert à rien de faire
[3] *vi* (*prét, pp* **paid**) **(a)** ‹*person*› payer; to
~ for sth payer qch; you have to ~ to get

in l'entrée est payante; to ~ one's own way
payer sa part; the work doesn't ~ very well
le travail est mal payé
(b) ‹*business*› rapporter; ‹*activity*› payer; to
~ for itself ‹*business, purchase*› s'amortir
■ **pay back** rembourser ‹*person, money*›
■ **pay in** (GB) déposer ‹*cheque, sum*›
■ **pay off**: [1] ¶ ~ off être payant/-e
[2] ¶ ~ [sb] off **(a)** (dismiss) congédier
‹*worker*›
(b) (bribe) acheter le silence de ‹*person*›
[3] ¶ ~ [sth] off rembourser ‹*debt*›
■ **pay up** (colloq) ~ up payer
payable *adj* **(a)** (gen) payable
(b) to make a cheque ~ to faire un chèque
à l'ordre de
pay cheque (GB), **pay check** (US) *n*
chèque *m* de paie
payday *n* jour *m* de paie
payee *n* bénéficiaire *mf*
♂ **payment** *n* (gen) paiement *m*; (in settlement)
règlement *m*; (into account, of instalments)
versement *m*; monthly ~ mensualité *f*
pay-packet *n* enveloppe *f* de paie
pay phone *n* téléphone *m* public
payslip *n* bulletin *m* de salaire
pay television *n* télévision *f* à péage
pc, **PC** *n* (*abbr* = **personal computer**)
ordinateur *m* (personnel), PC *m*
PDF *n* (*abbr* = **Portable Document
Format**) PDF *m*
PE *n* (*abbr* = **physical education**)
éducation *f* physique
pea *n* pois *m*
♂ **peace** *n* paix *f*; to keep the ~ (between
countries, individuals) maintenir la paix; (in town)
‹*police*› maintenir l'ordre public; I need a bit
of ~ and quiet j'ai besoin d'un peu de calme;
to find ~ of mind trouver la paix
peaceful *adj* **(a)** (tranquil) paisible
(b) (without conflict) pacifique
peacefully *adv* **(a)** ‹*sleep*› paisiblement
(b) (without violence) pacifiquement
peace-keeping forces *n pl* forces *fpl*
de maintien de la paix
peacemaker *n* (Pol) artisan *m* de la paix;
(in family) conciliateur *m*
peace process *n* processus *m* de paix
peace talks *n pl* pourparlers *mpl* de paix
peacetime *n* temps *m* de paix
peach *n* pêche *f*
peacock *n* paon *m*
♂ **peak** [1] *n* **(a)** (of mountain) pic *m* (of de)
(b) (of cap) visière *f*
(c) (of inflation, demand, price) maximum *m* (in
dans; of de); (on a graph) sommet *m*
(d) (of career, empire) apogée *m* (of de); (of
fitness, form) meilleur *m* (of de); in the ~ of
condition en excellente santé; to be past its
or one's ~ avoir fait son temps
[2] *adj* ‹*figure, level, price*› maximum;
‹*fitness*› meilleur/-e

♂ indicates a very frequent word

3 *vi* culminer (**at** à)

peaked *adj* (a) ‹*cap, hat*› à visière; ‹*roof*› pointu/-e
(b) (US) pâlot/-otte

peak period *n* période *f* de pointe

peak rate *n* (for phone calls) tarif *m* rouge

peak time *n* (on TV) heures *fpl* de grande écoute; (for switchboard, traffic) heures *fpl* de pointe

peaky *adj* (colloq) pâlot/-otte

peal *n* (of bells) carillonnement *m*; (of thunder) grondement *m*; ~**s of laughter** éclats *mpl* de rire

peanut *n* (nut) cacahuète *f*; (plant) arachide *f*

peanut butter *n* beurre *m* de cacahuètes

pear *n* poire *f*

pearl **1** *n* perle *f*
2 *adj* ‹*necklace, brooch*› de perles; ‹*button*› en nacre

pear tree *n* poirier *m*

peasant *n* paysan/-anne *m/f*

peat *n* tourbe *f*

pebble *n* caillou *m*; (on beach) galet *m*

pecan *n* noix *f* de pecan

peck **1** *n* (a) (from bird) coup *m* de bec
(b) (colloq) **to give sb a** ~ (**on the cheek**) faire une bise à qn
2 *vtr* ‹*bird*› picorer ‹*food*›; donner un coup de bec à ‹*person, animal*›
3 *vi* (a) ‹*bird*› **to** ~ **at** picorer ‹*food*›
(b) (colloq) **to** ~ **at one's food** ‹*person*› chipoter

pecking order *n* ordre *m* hiérarchique

peckish *adj* (colloq) **to be** ~ avoir un petit creux (fam)

pectorals *n pl* (*also* **pecs** (colloq)) pectoraux *mpl*

peculiar *adj* (a) (odd) bizarre
(b) (to be) ~ **to** être particulier/-ière à *or* propre à

peculiarity *n* (a) (feature) particularité *f*
(b) (strangeness) bizarrerie *f*

pedal **1** *n* pédale *f*
2 *vi* (*p prés etc* **-ll-** (GB), **-l-** (US)) pédaler

pedal bin *n* (GB) poubelle *f* à pédale

pedal boat *n* pédalo® *m*

pedantic *adj* pédant/-e

peddle *vtr* colporter ‹*wares, ideas*›; **to** ~ **drugs** revendre de la drogue

peddler *n* (street vendor) colporteur *m*; **drug** ~ trafiquant *m*

pedestal *n* socle *m*, piédestal *m*; **to put sb on a** ~ mettre qn sur un piédestal

pedestrian **1** *n* piéton *m*
2 *adj* ‹*street, area*› piétonnier/-ière, piéton/-onne

pedestrian crossing *n* passage *m* pour piétons, passage *m* clouté

pedestrian precinct *n* (GB) zone *f* piétonne

pediatrician (US) = PAEDIATRICIAN

pedicure *n* **to have a** ~ se faire soigner les pieds

pedigree **1** *n* (a) (of animal) pedigree *m*; (of person) ascendance *f*
(b) (purebred animal) animal *m* avec pedigree
2 *adj* ‹*animal*› de pure race

pee *n* (colloq) pipi *m* (fam); **to have a** ~ faire pipi (fam)

peek *n* **to have a** ~ **at** jeter un coup d'œil furtif à

peel **1** *n* (gen) peau *f*; (of citrus fruit) écorce *f*; (of onion) pelure *f*; (peelings) épluchures *fpl*
2 *vtr* éplucher ‹*vegetable, fruit*›; décortiquer ‹*prawn*›; écorcer ‹*stick*›
3 *vi* ‹*skin*› peler; ‹*fruit, vegetable*› s'éplucher
■ **peel off:** **1** ¶ ~ **off** ‹*label*› se détacher; ‹*paint*› s'écailler; ‹*paper*› se décoller
2 ¶ ~ [sth] **off** enlever ‹*clothing, label*›

peeler *n* économe *m*

peelings *n pl* épluchures *fpl*

peep **1** *n* **to have a** ~ **at sth** jeter un coup d'œil à qch; (furtively) regarder qch à la dérobée
2 *vi* (a) jeter un coup d'œil (**over** par-dessus; **through** par); **to** ~ **at sb/sth** jeter un coup d'œil à qn/qch; (furtively) regarder qn/qch furtivement
(b) ‹*chick*› pépier

peephole *n* (in fence) trou *m*; (in door) judas *m*

peer **1** *n* (a) (equal) (in status) pair *m*; (in profession) collègue *m/f*
(b) (contemporary) (adult) personne *f* de la même génération; (child) enfant *m/f* du même âge
(c) (GB) (*also* ~ **of the realm**) pair *m*
2 *vi* **to** ~ **at** scruter, regarder attentivement

peerage *n* (GB Pol) pairie *f*; **to be given a** ~ être anobli/-e

peer group *n* (a) (of same status) pairs *mpl*
(b) (contemporaries) (adults) personnes *fpl* de la même génération; (children) enfants *mpl* du même âge

peer group pressure *n* pression *f* du groupe

peg *n* (a) (hook) patère *f*
(b) (GB) (*also* **clothes** ~) pince *f* à linge
(c) (of tent) piquet *m*
(d) (in carpentry) cheville *f*

pejorative *adj* péjoratif/-ive

Peking *pr n* Pékin

pelican *n* pélican *m*

pellet *n* (a) (of paper, wax, mud) boulette *f*
(b) (of shot) plomb *m*

pelmet *n* cantonnière *f*

pelt **1** *n* (fur) fourrure *f*; (hide) peau *f*
2 *vtr* bombarder (**with sth** de qch)
3 *vi* (a) (*also* ~ **down**) ‹*rain*› tomber à verse ⋯⋗

(b) (run) **to ~ along** courir à toutes jambes
pelvis n bassin m, pelvis m
pen n **(a)** (for writing) stylo m
(b) (for animals) parc m, enclos m
penal n ‹law, code, system› pénal/-e; ‹colony, institution› pénitentiaire
penalize vtr pénaliser
penalty n **(a)** (punishment) peine f, pénalité f; (fine) amende f
(b) (figurative) prix m **(for** de)
(c) (in soccer) penalty m; (in rugby) pénalité f
pence (GB) ▶ PENNY
pencil n crayon m; **in ~** au crayon
■ **pencil in: ~** [sth] **in, ~ in** [sth] écrire [qch] au crayon; **let's ~ in the second of May** disons le deux mai pour l'instant
pencil case n trousse f (à crayons)
pencil sharpener n taille-crayon m
pendant n (on necklace) pendentif m
pending ① adj **(a)** ‹case› en instance; ‹matter› en souffrance
(b) (imminent) imminent/-e
② prep en attendant
pendulum n pendule m, balancier m
penetrate vtr pénétrer; percer ‹cloud, silence, defences›; traverser ‹wall›; ‹spy› infiltrer ‹organization›
penetrating adj ‹cold, eyes, question› pénétrant/-e; ‹sound, voice› perçant/-e
pen friend n correspondant/-e m/f
penguin n pingouin m, manchot m
penicillin n pénicilline f
peninsula n péninsule f
penis n pénis m
penitent n, adj pénitent/-e m/f
penitentiary n (US) prison f
penknife n canif m
pennant n **(a)** (flag) fanion m; (on boat) flamme f
(b) (US Sport) championnat m
penniless adj sans le sou, sans ressources
penny n (pl-**ies** ou **pence** (GB)) **(a)** (GB) penny m; **a five pence** or **five p piece** une pièce de cinq pence; **a 25p stamp** un timbre-poste à 25 pence
(b) (US) cent m
IDIOMS **the ~ dropped** (colloq) ça a fait tilt (fam); **not to have a ~ to one's name** être sans le sou
pension n (from state) pension f; (from employer) retraite f
pensioner n retraité/-e m/f
pension scheme n plan m de retraite
pentagon n **(a)** pentagone m
(b) the Pentagon (US) le Pentagone m
Pentecost n Pentecôte f
penthouse n appartement m de grand standing

─────────────
ꞔ indicates a very frequent word

pent-up adj ‹energy, frustration› contenu/-e; ‹feelings› réprimé/-e
penultimate adj avant-dernier/-ière
ꞔ **people** ① n (nation) peuple m
② n pl **(a)** (in general) gens mpl; (specified or counted) personnes fpl; **old ~** les personnes âgées; **they're nice ~** ce sont des gens sympathiques; **there were a lot of ~** il y avait beaucoup de monde; **other ~'s property** le bien des autres
(b) (of a town) habitants mpl; (of a country) peuple m
(c) (citizens) **the ~** le peuple

■ **Note** gens is masculine plural and never countable. When counting people, you must use personnes rather than gens: three people = trois personnes.
— When used with gens, some adjectives such as vieux, bon, mauvais, petit, vilain placed before gens take the feminine form: les vieilles gens.

people carrier n monospace m
pep v ■ **pep up** remettre [qn] d'aplomb ‹person›; animer ‹party, team›
pepper n **(a)** (spice) poivre m
(b) (vegetable) poivron m
peppercorn n grain m de poivre
pepper mill n moulin m à poivre
peppermint n **(a)** (sweet) pastille f de menthe
(b) (plant) menthe f poivrée
pepper pot, **pepper shaker** n poivrier m
pep talk n (colloq) laïus m (fam) d'encouragement
ꞔ **per** prep par; **~ annum** par an; **~ head** par tête or personne; **80 km ~ hour** 80 km à l'heure; **£5 ~ hour** 5 livres sterling (de) l'heure; **as ~ your instructions** conformément à vos instructions
per capita adj, adv par personne
perceive vtr percevoir
ꞔ **per cent** n, adv pour cent m
ꞔ **percentage** n pourcentage m
perceptible adj perceptible (**to** à)
perception n **(a)** (by senses) perception f
(b) (view) **my ~ of him** l'idée que je me fais de lui
(c) (insight) perspicacité f
perceptive adj ‹person› perspicace; ‹analysis› fin/-e; ‹article› intelligent/-e
perch ① n **(a)** (gen) perchoir m
(b) (fish) perche f
② vi se percher (**on** sur)
percolator n cafetière f à pression
percussion n (Mus) percussions fpl
perennial adj **(a)** perpétuel/-elle
(b) ‹plant› vivace
ꞔ **perfect** ① n parfait m; **in the ~** au parfait
② adj (gen) parfait/-e (**for** pour); ‹moment,

name, place, partner, solution idéal/-e (**for** pour); *‹hostess›* exemplaire
[3] *vtr* perfectionner

perfection *n* perfection *f* (**of** de)

perfectionist *n, adj* perfectionniste *mf*

✓ **perfectly** *adv* (a) (totally) *‹clear, happy›* tout à fait
(b) (very well) *‹fit, illustrate›* parfaitement

perforate *vtr* perforer

✓ **perform** [1] *vtr* (a) exécuter *‹task›*; accomplir *‹duties›*; procéder à *‹operation›*
(b) jouer *‹play›*; chanter *‹song›*; exécuter *‹dance, trick›*
(c) célébrer *‹ceremony›*
[2] *vi* (a) *‹actor, musician›* jouer
(b) **to ∼ well/badly** *‹team›* bien/mal jouer; *‹interviewee›* faire bonne/mauvaise impression; *‹exam candidate, company›* avoir de bons/de mauvais résultats

✓ **performance** *n* (a) (rendition) interprétation *f* (**of** de)
(b) (concert, show, play) représentation *f* (**of** de); **to put on a ∼ of Hamlet** donner une représentation d'Hamlet
(c) (of team, sportsman) performance *f* (**in** à)
(d) (of duties) exercice *m* (**of** de); (of task) exécution *f* (**of** de)
(e) (of car, engine) performances *fpl*

performance artist *n* artiste *mf* de performances

performance indicators *n pl* tableau *m* de bord

performer *n* artiste *mf*

performing arts *n pl* arts *mpl* scéniques

perfume [1] *n* parfum *m*
[2] *vtr* parfumer

✓ **perhaps** *adv* peut-être; **∼ she's forgotten** elle a peut-être oublié

peril *n* péril *m*, danger *m*

perimeter *n* périmètre *m*

✓ **period** [1] *n* (a) (gen) période *f*; (era) époque *f*
(b) (US) (full stop) point *m*
(c) (menstruation) règles *fpl*
(d) (Sch) (lesson) cours *m*, leçon *f*; **to have a free ∼** ≈ avoir une heure de libre
[2] *adj* (of a certain era) *‹costume, furniture›* d'époque

periodical *n, adj* périodique *m*

peripheral *adj* *‹vision, suburb›* périphérique; *‹issue, investment›* annexe

periphery *n* périphérie *f*; **to remain on the ∼ of** rester à l'écart de *‹event, movement›*

periscope *n* périscope *m*

perish *vi* (a) (die) périr (**from** de)
(b) *‹food›* se gâter; *‹rubber›* se détériorer

perishables *n pl* denrées *fpl* périssables

perjure *v refl* **to ∼ oneself** faire un faux témoignage

perjury *n* faux témoignage *m*

perk *n* (colloq) avantage *m*

■ **perk up** *‹person›* se ragaillardir; *‹business, life, plant›* reprendre

perky *adj* guilleret/-ette

perm *n* permanente *f*; **to have a ∼** se faire faire une permanente

permanent [1] *n* (US) permanente *f*
[2] *adj* permanent/-e

permanently *adv* *‹happy, tired›* en permanence; *‹employed, disabled›* de façon permanente; *‹close, emigrate, settle›* définitivement

permeate *vtr* (a) *‹liquid, gas›* s'infiltrer dans; *‹odour›* pénétrer dans
(b) *‹ideas›* imprégner

permissible *adj* *‹level, conduct›* admissible; *‹error›* acceptable

permission *n* permission *f*; (official) autorisation *f*; **to get ∼ to do** obtenir la permission *or* l'autorisation de faire

permissive *adj* permissif/-ive

permit [1] *n* (a) permis *m*; **work ∼** permis *m* de travail
(b) (US Aut) permis *m* (de conduire)
[2] *vtr* (*p prés etc* **-tt-**) permettre; **to ∼ sb to do** permettre à qn de faire; **smoking is not ∼ted** il est interdit de fumer
[3] *vi* (*p prés etc* **-tt-**) permettre

pernickety (GB), **persnickety** (US) *adj* (colloq) (a) (detail-conscious) pointilleux/-euse (**about** sur)
(b) (choosy) tatillon/-onne (**about** quant à)

peroxide blonde *n* blonde *f* décolorée

perpendicular *adj* perpendiculaire

perpetrate *vtr* perpétrer *‹deed, fraud›*; monter *‹hoax›*

perpetrator *n* auteur *m* (**of** de)

perpetual *adj* *‹meetings, longing, turmoil›* perpétuel/-elle; *‹darkness, stench›* permanent/-e

perpetuate *vtr* perpétuer

perplexed *adj* perplexe

persecute *vtr* persécuter

persecution *n* persécution *f*

perseverance *n* persévérance *f*

persevere *vi* persévérer (**with, at** dans)

persist *vi* persister (**in** dans; **in doing** à faire)

persistence *n* persévérance *f*

persistent *adj* (a) (persevering) persévérant/-e; (obstinate) obstiné/-e (**in** dans)
(b) *‹rain, denial›* persistant/-e; *‹enquiries, noise, pressure›* continuel/-elle; *‹illness, fears, idea›* tenace

persistent offender *n* récidiviste *mf*

✓ **person** *n* (*pl* **people** *ou* **∼s** (soutenu)) personne *f*; **in ∼** en personne; **to have sth about one's ∼** avoir qch sur soi

personable *adj* *‹person›* qui présente bien

✓ **personal** [1] *n* (US) petite annonce *f* personnelle
[2] *adj* *‹opinion, life, call, matter›* ···⟩

p

personnel/-elle; ‹safety, choice, income, insurance› individuel/-elle; ‹service› personnalisé/-e; **to make a** ∼ **appearance** venir en personne (**at** à)

personal ad n petite annonce f personnelle

personal column n petites annonces fpl personnelles

personality n personnalité f

personal loan n emprunt m; (by bank etc) prêt m personnel

personally adv personnellement

personal organizer n ≈ agenda m

personal property n biens mpl personnels

personal stereo n baladeur m

personify vtr incarner ‹ideal›

personnel n (a) (staff, troops) personnel m (b) (department) service m du personnel

⚘ **perspective** n perspective f; **to keep things in** ∼ garder un sens de la mesure; **to put things into** ∼ relativiser les choses

perspex® n plexiglas® m

perspiration n (a) (sweat) sueur f (b) (sweating) transpiration f

perspire vi transpirer

persuade vtr (a) (influence) persuader; **to** ∼ **sb to do** persuader qn de faire (b) (convince) convaincre (**of** de; **that** que)

persuasion n (a) (persuading) persuasion f (b) (religion) confession f (c) (political views) conviction f

persuasive adj ‹person› persuasif/-ive; ‹argument, evidence› convaincant/-e

pert adj ‹person, manner› espiègle; ‹hat, nose› coquin/-e

pertinent adj pertinent/-e

perturb vtr perturber

perturbing adj troublant/-e

pervade vtr imprégner

perverse adj (a) (twisted) ‹person› retors/-e; ‹desire› pervers/-e (b) (contrary) ‹refusal, attempt, attitude› illogique; **to take a** ∼ **pleasure in doing** prendre un malin plaisir à faire

perversion n (a) (deviation) perversion f (b) (of facts, justice) travestissement m

pervert ① n pervers/-e m/f ② vtr (a) (corrupt) corrompre (b) (misrepresent) travestir ‹truth›; dénaturer ‹meaning›; **to** ∼ **the course of justice** entraver l'action de la justice

perverted adj (deviant) pervers/-e; (distorted) ‹idea› tordu/-e

pessimism n pessimisme m

pessimist n pessimiste mf

pessimistic adj pessimiste

⚘ indicates a very frequent word

pest n (a) (animal) animal m nuisible; (insect) insecte m nuisible (b) (colloq) (person) enquiquineur/-euse m/f (fam)

pester vtr harceler

pesticide n pesticide m

pet ① n (a) (animal) animal m de compagnie (b) (favourite) chouchou/chouchoute m/f (fam) ② adj (a) (favourite) favori/-ite (b) ∼ **dog** chien ③ vtr (p prés etc **-tt-**) caresser ‹animal› ④ vi (p prés etc **-tt-**) ‹people› échanger des caresses

petal n pétale m

peter v ▪ **peter out** ‹conversation› tarir; ‹supplies› s'épuiser

pet food n aliments mpl pour chiens et chats

pet hate (GB) n bête f noire

petition ① n pétition f ② vtr adresser une pétition à ‹person, body› ③ vi **to** ∼ **for divorce** demander le divorce

pet name n petit nom m

pet project n enfant m chéri (figurative)

petrified adj pétrifié/-e

petrol (GB) n essence f; **to fill up with** ∼ faire le plein (d'essence)

petrol can n bidon m à essence

petroleum n pétrole m

petrol station n (GB) station f d'essence

pet shop (GB), **pet store** (US) n animalerie f

petticoat n (full slip) combinaison m; (half slip) jupon m

petty adj ‹person, squabble› mesquin/-e; ‹detail› insignifiant/-e

petty cash n petite caisse f

petty crime n petite délinquance f

petty officer n ≈ maître m

petty theft n larcin m

pew n banc m (d'église)

pewter n étain m

PGCE n (abbr = **postgraduate certificate in education**) diplôme m de spécialisation dans l'enseignement

pharmaceutical adj pharmaceutique

pharmacist n pharmacien/-ienne m/f

pharmacy n pharmacie f

⚘ **phase** ① n phase f; **it's just a** ∼ **(he's/they're going through)** ça lui/leur passera ② vtr échelonner (**over** sur) ▪ **phase in** introduire [qch] progressivement ▪ **phase out** supprimer [qch] peu à peu

PhD n (abbr = **Doctor of Philosophy**) doctorat m

pheasant n faisan/-e m/f

phenomenal adj phénoménal/-e

phenomenon n (pl **-na**) phénomène m

phew *excl* (in relief) ouf!; (when too hot) pff!
philanthropist *n* philanthrope *mf*
philistine *n* béotien/-ienne *m/f*
philosopher *n* philosophe *mf*
philosophic(al) *adj* (a) ‹knowledge, question› philosophique
(b) (calm, stoical) philosophe (about à propos de)
philosophy *n* philosophie *f*
phobia *n* phobie *f*
⚜ **phone** ⊡ *n* téléphone *m*; **to be on the ~** (be talking) être au téléphone (**to sb** avec qn); (be subscriber) avoir le téléphone
⊡ *vtr* (also ~ **up**) passer un coup de fil à (fam), téléphoner à, appeler
⊡ *vi* (also ~ **up**) téléphoner; **to ~ for a taxi** appeler un taxi
phone book *n* annuaire *m* (téléphonique)
phone booth, phone box (GB) *n* cabine *f* téléphonique
phone call *n* coup *m* de fil (fam); (more formal) communication *f* (téléphonique)
phone card *n* (GB) télécarte *f*
phone-in *n* émission *f* à ligne ouverte
phone link *n* liaison *f* téléphonique
phone number *n* numéro *m* de téléphone
phoney (colloq) ⊡ *n* (a) (affected person) poseur/-euse *m/f*
(b) (impostor) charlatan *m*
⊡ *adj* ‹address, accent› faux/fausse (before *n*); ‹company, excuse› bidon *inv* (fam); ‹emotion› simulé/-e
phoney war *n* the ~ la drôle de guerre
phosphates *n pl* phosphates *mpl*
⚜ **photo** = PHOTOGRAPH 1
photo album *n* album *m* de photos
photo booth *n* photomaton® *m*
photo-call *n* séance *f* de photos
photocopier *n* photocopieuse *f*
photocopy ⊡ *n* photocopie *f*
⊡ *vtr* photocopier
photogenic *adj* photogénique
⚜ **photograph** ⊡ *n* (also **photo**) photo *f*; **in the ~** sur la photo; **to take a ~ of sb/sth** prendre qn/qch en photo
⊡ *vtr* photographier, prendre [qn/qch] en photo
photographer *n* photographe *mf*
photography *n* photographie *f*
photo opportunity *n* séance *f* de photos
photo session *n* séance *f* de photos
phrase ⊡ *n* expression *f*
⊡ *vtr* formuler ‹question, speech›
phrasebook *n* manuel *m* de conversation
⚜ **physical** ⊡ *n* (check-up) bilan *m* de santé
⊡ *adj* physique
physical fitness *n* forme *f* physique
physically handicapped *adj* **to be ~** être handicapé/-e *m/f* physique

physicist *n* physicien/-ienne *m/f*
physics *n* physique *f*
physiology *n* physiologie *f*
physiotherapy *n* kinésithérapie *f*
physique *n* physique *m*
pianist *n* pianiste *mf*
piano *n* piano *m*
⚜ **pick** ⊡ *n* (a) (tool) pioche *f*, pic *m*; (of climber) piolet *m*
(b) (choice) choix *m*; **to have one's ~ of** avoir le choix parmi; **take your ~** choisis
(c) **the ~ of the bunch** (singular) le meilleur/ la meilleure du lot
⊡ *vtr* (a) (choose) choisir (**from** parmi); (in sport) sélectionner ‹player› (**from** parmi); **to ~ a fight** chercher à se bagarrer (fam) (**with** avec); (quarrel) chercher querelle (**with** à)
(b) **to ~ one's way through** avancer avec précaution parmi ‹rubble, litter›
(c) cueillir ‹fruit, flowers›
(d) gratter ‹spot, scab›; **to ~ sth from** *or* **off** enlever qch de; **to ~ one's teeth/nose** se curer les dents/le nez
⊡ *vi* choisir
▪ **pick at** (a) ‹person› manger [qch] du bout des dents ‹food›; gratter ‹spot, scab›
(b) ‹bird› picorer ‹crumbs›
▪ **pick on** harceler, s'en prendre à ‹person›
▪ **pick out** (a) (select) choisir; (single out) repérer
(b) distinguer ‹landmark›; reconnaître ‹person in photo›; repérer ‹person in crowd›
▪ **pick up** ⊡ ¶ ~ **up** ‹business› reprendre; ‹weather, health› s'améliorer; ‹ill person› se rétablir
⊡ ~ **[sb/sth] up** (a) ¶ (lift up) ramasser ‹object, litter, toys›; relever ‹person›; **to ~ up the receiver** décrocher le téléphone; **to ~ oneself up** se relever
(b) prendre ‹passenger, cargo›; passer prendre ‹ticket, keys›; prendre, acheter ‹milk, paper›; **could you ~ me up?** est-ce que tu peux venir me chercher?
(c) apprendre ‹language›; prendre ‹habit, accent›; développer ‹skill›; **you'll soon ~ it up** tu t'y mettras vite
(d) trouver ‹trail, scent›; ‹radar› détecter la présence de ‹aircraft, person, object›; ‹radio receiver› capter ‹signal›
(e) gagner ‹point›; acquérir ‹reputation›; **to ~ up speed** prendre de la vitesse
(f) (resume) reprendre ‹conversation, career›
(g) ramasser ‹partner, prostitute›
pickaxe (GB), **pickax** (US) *n* pioche *f*
picket ⊡ *n* piquet *m* (de grève)
⊡ *vtr* installer un piquet de grève aux portes de ‹factory›
picking ⊡ *n* (of crop) cueillette *f*
⊡ **pickings** *n pl* (rewards) gains *mpl*
pickle ⊡ *n* (a) (preserves) conserves *fpl* au vinaigre
(b) (gherkin) cornichon *m*

⋯▷

2 *vtr* (in vinegar) conserver [qch] dans du vinaigre
IDIOM to be in a ~ être dans le pétrin (fam)
pick-me-up *n* remontant *m*
pickpocket *n* voleur *m* à la tire
pickup truck *n* (GB) pick-up *m inv*
picnic *n* pique-nique *m*; **to go for** *or* **on a ~** aller faire un pique-nique, pique-niquer
⚡ **picture** **1** *n* **(a)** (painting) peinture *f*, tableau *m*; (drawing) dessin *m*; (in book) illustration *f*; (in mind) image *f*
(b) (description) description *f*
(c) (snapshot) photo *f*, photographie *f*
(d) I get the ~ je vois; **to put sb in the ~** mettre qn au courant
(e) (film) film *m*
(f) (on TV screen) image *f*
2 *vtr* s'imaginer
picture card *n* figure *f* (carte)
picture frame *n* cadre *m*
picture hook *n* crochet *m* (à tableaux)
picturesque *adj* pittoresque
pie *n* tourte *f*; **meat ~** tourte à la viande
⚡ **piece** *n* **(a)** (gen) morceau *m*; (of string, ribbon) bout *m*; **a ~ of furniture** un meuble; **a ~ of luggage** une valise; **a ~ of advice** un conseil; **a ~ of information** un renseignement; **a ~ of luck** un coup de chance; **£20 a ~** 20 livres sterling pièce; **to fall to ~s** ‹object› tomber en morceaux; ‹argument› s'effondrer; **to go to ~s** (from shock) s'effondrer; (emotionally) craquer (fam); (in interview) paniquer complètement
(b) (of jigsaw, machine, model) pièce *f*; **to take sth to ~s** démonter qch
(c) (article) article *m* (on sur)
(d) (coin) **a 50p ~** une pièce de 50 pence
(e) (in chess) pièce *f*
IDIOM to give sb a ~ of one's mind dire ses quatre vérités à qn
▪ **piece together**: **~ [sth] together, ~ together [sth]** reconstituer ‹vase, letter›; assembler ‹puzzle›; reconstituer ‹facts›
piecemeal **1** *adj* (random) fragmentaire; (at different times) irrégulier/-ière
2 *adv* petit à petit
pie chart *n* diagramme *m* circulaire sectorisé, camembert *m* (fam)
pier *n* (at seaside) jetée *f* (sur pilotis); (landing stage) embarcadère *f*
pierce *vtr* (make hole in) percer; (penetrate) transpercer
piercing *adj* ‹scream, eyes› perçant/-e; ‹light› intense; ‹wind› glacial/-e, pénétrant/-e
pig *n* **(a)** (animal) porc *m*, cochon *m*
(b) (colloq) ‹person› (greedy) goinfre *m* (fam); (dirty) cochon/-onne *m/f* (fam); (nasty) sale type *m* (fam)
▪ **pig out** (colloq) se goinfrer (fam), s'empiffrer (fam) (**on** de)

⚡ indicates a very frequent word

pigeon *n* pigeon *m*
pigeonhole (GB) **1** *n* casier *m*
2 *vtr* étiqueter, cataloguer
pigeon-toed *adj* **to be ~** marcher les pieds en dedans
piggyback (ride) *n* **to give sb a ~** porter qn sur son dos *or* sur ses épaules
piggy bank *n* tirelire *f*
pigheaded *adj* entêté/-e, obstiné/-e
piglet *n* porcelet *m*, petit cochon *m*
pigment *n* pigment *m*
pigpen (US) = PIGSTY
pigskin *n* peau *f* de porc
pigsty, pigpen (US) *n* (*pl* **-sties**) porcherie *f*
pigtail *n* natte *f*
pike *n* (fish) brochet *m*
pile **1** *n* **(a)** (heap) tas *m* (of de); (stack) pile *f* (of de); **in a ~** en tas *or* en pile
(b) (of fabric, carpet) poil *m*
(c) (colloq) **~s of** des tas (fam) de ‹books, letters›; **~s of money** plein d'argent (fam)
2 **piles** *n pl* hémorroïdes *fpl*
3 *vtr* entasser (**on** sur; **into** dans)
▪ **pile up** ‹debts, problems, work› s'accumuler
pileup *n* carambolage *m*
pilfer **1** *vtr* dérober (**from** dans)
2 *vi* commettre des larcins
pilgrim *n* pèlerin *m* (**to** de)
pilgrimage *n* pèlerinage *m*
pill *n* **(a)** (gen) comprimé *m*, cachet *m*
(b) (contraceptive) **the ~** la pilule
pillage *vtr, vi* piller
pillar *n* pilier *m*
pillar box *n* (GB) boîte *f* aux lettres
pillion **1** *n* (*also* **~ seat**) siège *m* de passager
2 *adv* **to ride ~** monter en croupe
pillow *n* oreiller *m*
pillowcase *n* taie *f* d'oreiller
⚡ **pilot** **1** *n* pilote *m*
2 *adj* **(a)** ‹project, study› pilote; ‹series› expérimental/-e
(b) ‹error› de pilotage
pilot light *n* veilleuse *f*; (electric) voyant *m* lumineux
pilot scheme *n* projet-pilote *m*
pimp *n* proxénète *m*
pimple *n* bouton *m*
pimply *adj* boutonneux/-euse
pin **1** *n* **(a)** (for cloth, paper) épingle *f*
(b) **three-~ plug** prise *f* à trois fiches
(c) (for wood, metal) goujon *m*
(d) (Med) broche *f*
(e) (brooch) barrette *f*
2 *vtr* (*p prés etc* **-nn-**) **(a)** épingler ‹dress, hem, curtain›
(b) (trap) **to ~ sb to** coincer qn contre ‹wall, floor›
(c) (colloq) **to ~ sth on sb** mettre qch sur le

dos de qn ‹theft›
- **pin down**: ⊡ ¶ ~ [sb] down (a) (physically) immobiliser (to à)
  (b) (figurative) coincer; **to ~ sb down to a definite date** arriver à fixer une date ferme avec qn
  ⊡ ¶ ~ [sth] down identifier ‹concept, feeling›
- **pin up** accrocher ‹poster, notice› (on à)

PIN (number) n (abbr = **personal identification number**) code m confidentiel (pour carte bancaire)

pinafore n (a) (apron) tablier m
  (b) (dress) robe-chasuble f

pinball n flipper m

pincers n pl tenailles fpl

pinch ⊡ n (a) pincement m; **to give sb a ~** pincer qn
  (b) (of salt, spice) pincée f
  ⊡ vtr (a) (on arm, leg) pincer
  (b) ‹shoe› serrer
  (c) (colloq) (steal) faucher (fam) (from à)
  ⊡ vi ‹shoe› serrer
  IDIOM **to feel the ~** avoir de la peine à joindre les deux bouts

pine ⊡ n pin m
  ⊡ adj ‹furniture› en pin
  ⊡ vi ‹person› languir (for après); ‹animal› s'ennuyer (for de)

pineapple n ananas m

pinecone n pomme f de pin

ping-pong® n ping-pong® m

pink ⊡ n (a) (colour) rose m
  (b) (flower) œillet m mignardise
  ⊡ adj rose; **to go** or **turn ~** rosir; (blush) rougir (with de)

pinnacle n (a) (on building) pinacle m
  (b) (of rock) cime f (of de)
  (c) (figurative) apogée m (of de)

pinpoint vtr indiquer ‹problem, causes, location, site›; déterminer ‹time›

pinstripe(d) adj ‹fabric, suit› à fines rayures

pint n pinte f ((GB) = 0.57 l, (US) = 0.47 l); **a ~ of milk** ≈ un demi-litre de lait; **a ~ (of beer)** un demi

pinup n (woman) pin-up f (fam); (poster of star) affiche f de vedette; (star) idole f

pioneer ⊡ n pionnier m (of, in de)
  ⊡ vtr **to ~ the use of** être le premier/la première à utiliser

pious adj pieux/pieuse

pip n (a) (seed) pépin m
  (b) (on radio) top m
  IDIOM **to be ~ped at** or **to the post** se faire souffler la victoire

pipe ⊡ n (a) (for gas, water) tuyau m; (underground) conduite f
  (b) (smoker's) pipe f
  ⊡ **pipes** n pl (Mus) cornemuse f
  ⊡ vtr water is ~d across/to l'eau est acheminée par canalisation à travers/jusqu'à

- **pipe down** (colloq) faire moins de bruit
- **pipe up** ‹voice› se faire entendre

pipe-dream n chimère f

pipeline n oléoduc m; **to be in the ~** être prévu/-e

piping hot adj fumant/-e

pique n dépit m; **a fit of ~** un accès de dépit

pirate ⊡ n pirate m
  ⊡ adj ‹video, tape, radio› pirate (after n); ‹ship› de pirates
  ⊡ vtr pirater ‹tape, video, software›

pirouette n pirouette f

Pisa pr n Pise

Pisces n Poissons mpl

pistol n pistolet m

piston n piston m

pit ⊡ n (a) (in ground, in garage) fosse f; **gravel ~** carrière f de gravier
  (b) (mine) mine f
  (c) (in theatre) parterre m; **orchestra ~** fosse f d'orchestre
  (d) (US) (in fruit) noyau m
  ⊡ vtr (p prés etc -**tt**-) **to ~ sb against** opposer qn à ‹opponent›; **to ~ one's wits against sb** se mesurer à qn
  IDIOM **it's the ~s!** (colloq) c'est l'horreur!

pit bull terrier n pit bull m

pitch ⊡ n (a) (sportsground) terrain m; **football ~** terrain de foot(ball)
  (b) (of note, voice) hauteur f; (in music) ton m
  (c) (highest point) comble m
  (d) (sales talk) boniment m
  (e) (for street trader) emplacement m
  ⊡ vtr (a) (throw) jeter (**into** dans); (Sport) lancer
  (b) adapter ‹campaign, speech› (at à)
  (c) ‹singer› trouver ‹note›
  (d) planter ‹tent›; **to ~ camp** établir un camp
  ⊡ vi (a) ‹boat› tanguer
  (b) (US) (in baseball) lancer (la balle)
- **pitch in** (colloq) (eat) attaquer (fam); (help) donner un coup de main (fam)

pitch-black adj tout/-e noir/-e

pitcher n (a) (jug) cruche f
  (b) (US Sport) lanceur m

pitchfork n fourche f

pitfall n écueil m (of de)

pith n (a) (of fruit) peau f blanche
  (b) (of plant) moelle f

pitiful adj ‹cry, sight› pitoyable; ‹state› lamentable; ‹amount› ridicule

pitiless adj impitoyable

pittance n **to live on/earn a ~** vivre avec/gagner trois fois rien

pity ⊡ n (a) (compassion) pitié f (for pour); **out of ~** par pitié; **to take ~ on sb** avoir pitié de qn
  (b) (shame) dommage m; **what a ~!** quel dommage!
  ⊡ vtr plaindre

pivot 1 *vtr* faire pivoter ‹*lever*›; orienter
‹*lamp*›
2 *vi* (a) ‹*lamp, device*› pivoter (**on** sur)
(b) (figurative) ‹*outcome, success*› reposer (**on**
sur)

pixel *n* pixel *m*

pizza *n* pizza *f*

placard *n* (at protest march) pancarte *f*; (on
wall) affiche *f*

⚜ **place** 1 *n* (a) (location, position) endroit *m*;
in ∼s ‹*hilly, damaged, worn*› par endroits;
∼ **of birth/work** lieu *m* de naissance/travail;
∼ **of residence** domicile *m*; **to be in the
right** ∼ **at the right time** être là où il faut
quand il le faut; **to lose/find one's** ∼ (in
book) perdre/retrouver sa page; (in paragraph,
speech) perdre/retrouver le fil; **all over the** ∼
(everywhere) partout
(b) (home) **at Isabelle's** ∼ chez Isabelle; **your**
∼ **or mine?** chez toi ou chez moi?
(c) (on bus, at table, in queue) place *f*
(d) (on team, with firm, on course) place *f* (**on**
dans; **as** comme)
(e) (in competition, race) place *f*; **to finish in first**
∼ terminer premier/-ière *or* à la première
place; **in the first** ∼ (firstly, when listing)
premièrement; (most importantly, most notably)
tout d'abord, pour commencer
(f) (correct position) **everything is in its** ∼
tout est bien à sa place; **to hold sth in** ∼
maintenir qch en place; **in** ∼ ‹*law, system,
scheme*› en place; **to put sb in his/her** ∼
remettre qn à sa place
(g) (personal level or position) **it's not my** ∼ **to
do** ce n'est pas à moi de faire; **in his** ∼ à sa
place
(h) (moment) moment *m*; **in** ∼s ‹*funny, boring,
silly*› par moments
2 *vtr* (a) (gen) placer
(b) passer ‹*order*›; **to place a bet** parier (**on**
sur)
(c) (in competition, exam) classer
(d) (identify) situer ‹*person*›; reconnaître
‹*accent*›
3 **out of place** *phr* déplacé/-e; **to look
out of** ∼ ‹*building, person*› détonner

place mat *n* set *m* de table

placement *n* (*also* **work** ∼) stage *m*

place-name *n* nom *m* de lieu

placid *adj* placide

plagiarize *vtr, vi* plagier

plague 1 *n* (a) (bubonic) peste *f*
(b) (epidemic) épidémie *f*
(c) (of ants, locusts) invasion *f*
(d) (figurative) plaie *f*
2 *vtr* (a) **to be** ∼**d by** être en proie à
‹*doubts, difficulties*›
(b) (harass) harceler

plaice *n* (*pl* ∼) plie *f*, carrelet *m*

plaid *adj* écossais/-e

plain 1 *n* plaine *f*
2 *adj* (a) (simple) simple
(b) (of one colour) uni/-e; ‹*envelope*› sans
inscription; **a** ∼ **blue dress** une robe toute
bleue
(c) ‹*woman*› quelconque
(d) (obvious) évident/-e, clair/-e; **it's** ∼ **to see**
ça saute aux yeux
(e) ‹*common sense*› simple (*before n*);
‹*ignorance*› pur/-e et simple *after n*
(f) ‹*yoghurt, rice*› nature *inv*

plain chocolate *n* chocolat *m* à croquer

plain clothes *adj* ‹*policeman*› en civil

plainly *adv* (a) (obviously) manifestement
(b) ‹*see, remember*› clairement
(c) ‹*speak*› franchement
(d) ‹*dress, eat*› simplement; ‹*furnished*›
sobrement

plait *n* natte *f*

⚜ **plan** 1 *n* (gen) plan *m*; (definite aim) projet *m*
(**for** de; **to do** pour faire); **to go according to**
∼ se passer comme prévu
2 *vtr* (*p prés etc* **-nn-**) (a) (prepare, organize)
planifier ‹*future*›; organiser, préparer
‹*timetable, meeting, expedition*›; organiser
‹*day*›; faire un plan de ‹*career*›; faire le plan
de ‹*essay, book*›; préméditer ‹*crime*›
(b) (intend, propose) projeter ‹*visit, trip*›; **to** ∼
to do projeter de faire
(c) (design) concevoir
3 *vi* (*p prés etc* **-nn-**) prévoir; **to** ∼ **for sth**
prévoir qch; **to** ∼ **on doing** compter faire
■ **plan ahead** (vaguely) faire des projets; (look,
think ahead) prévoir

⚜ **plane** *n* (a) (aircraft) avion *m*
(b) (in geometry) plan *m*
(c) (tool) rabot *m*
(d) (*also* ∼ **tree**) platane *m*

⚜ **planet** *n* planète *f*

plank *n* planche *f*

planner *n* planificateur/-trice *m/f*; (in town
planning) urbaniste *mf*

⚜ **planning** *n* (a) (of industry, economy, work)
planification *f*; (of holiday, party) organisation *f*
(b) (in town) urbanisme *m*; (out of town)
aménagement *m* du territoire

planning permission *n* permis *m* de
construire

⚜ **plant** 1 *n* (a) (Bot) plante *f*
(b) (factory) usine *f*
2 *vtr* (a) planter ‹*seed, bulb, tree*›
(b) placer ‹*bomb, spy*›; **to** ∼ **drugs on sb**
cacher de la drogue sur qn pour l'incriminer
3 *v refl* **to** ∼ **oneself between/in front of** se
planter entre/devant

plantation *n* plantation *f*

plaque *n* (a) (on wall, monument) plaque *f*
(b) (on teeth) plaque *f* dentaire

plaster 1 *n* (a) (gen) plâtre *m*
(b) (GB) (*also* **sticking** ∼) sparadrap *m*
2 *vtr* (a) faire les plâtres de ‹*house*›
(b) (cover) couvrir (**with** de)

⚜ indicates a very frequent word

plaster cast n plâtre m
plasterer n plâtrier m
plastic ① n plastique m; (credit cards) cartes fpl de crédit
② adj ‹bag, toys, container› en plastique
plastic surgeon n chirurgien m esthétique
plastic surgery n chirurgie f plastique
⚔ **plate** ① (a) (dish) (for eating) assiette f; (for serving) plat m
(b) (sheet of metal) plaque f, tôle f
(c) (numberplate) plaque f minéralogique
(d) (illustration) planche f
(e) (in dentistry) dentier m
(f) (in earth's crust) plaque f
② -**plated** combining form **gold/silver-**~**d** plaqué/-e or/argent
plate glass n verre m à vitre
platform n (a) (for performance) estrade f; (at public meeting) tribune f
(b) (in scaffolding) plate-forme f
(c) (in politics) plate-forme f électorale
(d) (at station) quai m
(e) (Comput) plate-forme f
platform shoes n pl chaussures fpl à plateforme
platinum n platine m
platinum blonde n blonde f platine or platinée
platonic adj platonique
platoon n (of soldiers, police, firemen) section f; (in cavalry) peloton m
platter n (dish) plat m
plausible adj plausible, vraisemblable
⚔ **play** ① n (a) (in theatre) pièce f (**about** sur)
(b) (recreation) jeu m
(c) (Sport) (game) partie f; **out of** ~**/in** ~ ‹ball› hors jeu/en jeu
(d) (movement, interaction) jeu m; **to come into** ~ entrer en jeu; **a** ~ **on words** un jeu de mots
② vtr (a) jouer à ‹game, cards›; jouer ‹card›; **to** ~ **hide and seek** jouer à cache-cache; **to** ~ **a joke on sb** jouer un tour à qn
(b) jouer de ‹instrument›; jouer ‹tune, symphony, chord›; jouer à ‹venue›
(c) (in theatre) interpréter, jouer ‹role›
(d) mettre ‹tape, video, CD›
③ vi jouer
IDIOM **to** ~ **for time** essayer de gagner du temps
■ **play along**: **to** ~ **along with sb** entrer dans le jeu de qn
■ **play down** minimiser ‹effects, disaster›
■ **play out**: ~ **out** [sth] vivre ‹fantasy›
■ **play up** (colloq) ‹computer, person› faire des siennes (fam)
play-acting n comédie f, simagrées fpl
playboy n playboy m
⚔ **player** n (in sport, music) joueur/-euse m/f; (actor) comédien/-ienne m/f; **tennis** ~ joueur/-euse m/f de tennis

playful adj ‹remark› taquin/-e; ‹child, kitten› joueur/-euse
playground n cour f de récréation
playgroup n ≈ halte-garderie f
playhouse n théâtre m
playing card n carte f à jouer
playing field n terrain m de sport
playlist n liste f d'écoute
play-off n (GB) prolongation f; (US) match m crucial
playroom n salle f de jeux
playschool n ≈ halte-garderie f
plaything n jouet m
playtime n récréation f
playwright n auteur m dramatique
plaza n (a) (square) place f; **shopping** ~ centre m commercial
(b) (US) péage m
plc, PLC n (GB) (abbr – **public limited company**) SA
plea n (a) (gen) appel m (**for** à); (for money, food) demande f (**for** de)
(b) (Law) **to enter a** ~ **of guilty/not guilty** plaider coupable/non coupable
plead ① vtr (prét, pp **pleaded**, **pled** (US)) plaider
② vi (prét, pp **pleaded**, **pled** (US)) (a) **to** ~ **with sb** supplier qn
(b) (Law) plaider
pleasant adj agréable
⚔ **please** ① adv s'il vous plaît; **'may I?'—'**~ **do'** 'je peux?'—'oui, je vous en prie'
② vtr faire plaisir à ‹person›; **she is hard to** ~ elle est difficile (à contenter)
③ vi plaire; **do as you** ~ fais comme il te plaira, fais comme tu veux
pleased adj content/-e (**that** que + subjunctive; **about, at** de; **with** de); **to look** ~ **with oneself** avoir l'air content de soi; **I am** ~ **to announce that...** j'ai le plaisir d'annoncer que...; ~ **to meet you** enchanté
pleasing adj ‹appearance, colour, voice› agréable; ‹manner, personality› avenant/-e; ‹effect, result› heureux/-euse
pleasurable adj agréable
pleasure n plaisir m (**of** de; **of doing** de faire); **for** ~ par plaisir; **my** ~ (replying to request for help) avec plaisir; (replying to thanks) je vous en prie
pleat n pli m
pleated adj ‹skirt› plissé/-e; ‹trousers› à plis (after n)
pledge ① n (a) (promise) promesse f
(b) (money promised to charity) promesse f de don
② vtr promettre ‹allegiance, aid, support› (**to** à); **to** ~ **one's word** donner sa parole
plentiful adj abondant/-e
⚔ **plenty** quantif, pron ~ **of** beaucoup de; ~ **to do** beaucoup à faire

pliable adj ‹twig, plastic› flexible; ‹person› malléable

pliers n pl pinces fpl; **a pair of ~s** des pinces

plight n (a) (dilemma) situation f désespérée (b) (suffering) détresse f

plimsoll n (GB) chaussure f de tennis

plod v ■ **plod along** ‹walk› avancer d'un pas lent
■ **plod away** ‹work› travailler ferme, bosser (fam)

plodder n bûcheur/-euse m/f (fam)

plonk (colloq) ① n (wine) vin m ordinaire, pinard m (pop)
② vtr (also ~ **down**) planter ‹plate, bottle, box› (on sur)

✎ **plot** ① n (a) (conspiracy) complot m
(b) (of novel, film, play) intrigue f
(c) ~ **of land** parcelle f de terre; **a vegetable** ~ un carré de légumes
(d) (building site) terrain m à bâtir
② vtr (p prés etc **-tt-**) (a) (plan) comploter ‹murder, attack, return›; fomenter ‹revolution›
(b) (chart) relever [qch] sur une carte ‹course›
(c) (on graph) tracer [qch] point par point ‹curve, graph›
③ vi (p prés etc **-tt-**) conspirer (**against** contre)

plough (GB), **plow** (US) ① n charrue f
② vtr (a) labourer ‹land, field›; creuser ‹furrow›
(b) (invest) **to ~ money into** investir beaucoup d'argent dans ‹project, company›
■ **plough back**: ~ [sth] back, ~ back [sth] réinvestir ‹profits, money› (into dans)
■ **plough through** avancer péniblement dans ‹mud, snow›; ramer sur (fam) ‹book›

ploy n stratagème m (**to do** pour faire)

pluck ① n courage m, cran m (fam)
② vtr (a) cueillir ‹flower, fruit›
(b) plumer ‹chicken›
(c) (in music) pincer ‹strings›; pincer les cordes de ‹guitar›
(d) **to ~ one's eyebrows** s'épiler les sourcils
IDIOM **to ~ up one's courage** prendre son courage à deux mains

plucky adj courageux/-euse

plug ① n (a) (on appliance) prise f (de courant)
(b) (in bath, sink) bonde f
(c) (also **spark** ~) bougie f
(d) (in advertising) pub f (fam), publicité f (**for** pour)
② vtr (p prés etc **-gg-**) (a) boucher ‹hole› (**with** avec)
(b) (colloq) (promote) faire de la publicité pour ‹book, show, product›
(c) **to ~ sth into** brancher qch à
■ **plug in**: ① ¶ ~ **in** se brancher
② ¶ ~ [sth] **in** brancher ‹appliance›

plug and play n plug and play m (on branche et ça marche)

plughole n (GB) bonde f

plum ① n prune f
② adj (a) (colour) prune inv
(b) (colloq) **to get a ~ job** décrocher un boulot en or (fam)

plumb ① adv (a) (US) ‹crazy› complètement
(b) (colloq) ~ **in the middle** en plein milieu
② vtr sonder ‹depths›; **to ~ the depths of** toucher le fond de ‹despair, misery›

plumber n plombier m

plumbing n plomberie f

plummet vi chuter, dégringoler (fam)

plump adj ‹person, arm, leg› potelé/-e; ‹cheek, face› rond/-e, plein/-e

plunge ① vtr plonger (**into** dans)
② vi ‹road, cliff, waterfall› plonger; ‹bird, plane› piquer; ‹person› (dive) plonger; (fall) tomber (**from** de); ‹rate, value› chuter
IDIOM **to take the ~** se jeter à l'eau

plunger n ventouse f

plural ① n pluriel m; **in the ~** au pluriel
② adj ‹noun, adjective› au pluriel; ‹form, ending› du pluriel

✎ **plus** ① n avantage m
② adj **the ~ side** le côté positif; **50 ~** plus de 50; **the 65-~ age group** les personnes qui ont 65 ans et plus
③ prep plus; **15 ~ 12** 15 plus 12
④ conj et; **bedroom ~ bathroom** chambre et salle de bains

plus-fours n pl culotte f de golf

plus sign n signe m plus

Pluto pr n (planet) Pluton f

plutonium n plutonium m

ply ① vtr (a) vendre ‹wares›; **to ~ one's trade** exercer son métier
(b) **to ~ sb with food/drink** ne cesser de remplir l'assiette/le verre de qn
② vi ‹boat, bus› faire la navette (**between** entre)

plywood n contreplaqué m

pm adv (abbr = **post meridiem**) **two ~** deux heures de l'après-midi; **nine ~** neuf heures du soir

pneumatic drill n marteau m piqueur

pneumonia n pneumonie f

poach ① vtr (a) chasser [qch] illégalement ‹game›
(b) (Culin) faire pocher
② vi braconner

poacher n braconnier m

PO Box n boîte f postale

✎ **pocket** ① n (a) (in garment) poche f
(b) (in billiards) bourse f
② adj ‹diary, dictionary, edition› de poche
③ vtr empocher

pocketbook n (US) (wallet) portefeuille m; (handbag) sac m à main

✎ indicates a very frequent word

pocketknife n couteau m de poche
pocket money n argent m de poche
podcast [1] n podcast m (*fichier numérique téléchargeable audio ou vidéo*)
[2] vtr podcaster (*mettre à disposition sur un site internet des fichiers téléchargeables audio ou vidéo*)
podgy adj (colloq) grassouillet/-ette
podium n (*pl* -**iums, -ia**) (for speaker, conductor) estrade f; (for winner) podium m
ᐟ **poem** n poème m
poet n poète m
poetic adj poétique
poetry n poésie f; to write/read ~ écrire/lire des poèmes
poignant adj poignant/-e
ᐟ **point** [1] n (a) (of knife, needle, pencil) pointe f
(b) (location, position on scale) point m; (less specific) endroit m
(c) (extent, degree) point m; up to a ~ jusqu'à un certain point
(d) (moment) (precise) moment m; (stage) stade m; to be on the ~ of doing être sur le point de faire; at this ~ in her career à ce stade(-là) de sa carrière; at some ~ in the future plus tard; at one ~ à un moment donné
(e) (question, idea) point m; to make the ~ that faire remarquer que; you've made your ~ vous vous êtes exprimé; to make a ~ of doing (as matter of pride) mettre un point d'honneur à faire; (do deliberately) faire exprès
(f) (central idea) point m essentiel; to come straight to the ~ aller droit au fait; to keep or stick to the ~ rester dans le sujet; to miss the ~ ne pas comprendre; that's beside the ~ là n'est pas la question; to get the ~ comprendre; that's not the ~ il ne s'agit pas de cela
(g) (purpose) objet m; what's the ~ of doing…? à quoi bon faire…?; there's no ~ in doing ça ne sert à rien de faire; I don't see the ~ of doing je ne vois pas l'intérêt de faire
(h) (feature, characteristic) point m, côté m; her strong ~ son point fort
(i) (in scoring) point m; match ~ (in tennis) balle f de match
(j) (decimal point) virgule f
(k) (headland) pointe f
[2] vtr (a) (aim, direct) to ~ sth at sb braquer qch sur qn ‹camera, gun›; to ~ one's finger at sb montrer qn du doigt
(b) (show) to ~ the way to indiquer la direction de
(c) (in ballet, gym) to ~ one's toes faire des pointes
[3] vi (a) (indicate) indiquer or montrer (du doigt); to ~ at sb/sth montrer qn/qch du doigt
(b) ‹signpost, arrow, compass› indiquer; to be ~ing at sb ‹gun, camera› être braqué/-e sur qn
■ **point out** [1] montrer ‹place, person› (to à)

[2] faire remarquer ‹fact, discrepancy›
point-blank adv (a) ‹shoot› à bout portant
(b) ‹refuse, deny› catégoriquement
pointed adj (a) ‹hat, stick, chin› pointu/-e
(b) ‹remark› qui vise quelqu'un
pointer n (a) (piece of information) indication f
(b) (on projector screen) flèche f
(c) (Comput) pointeur m
pointless adj ‹request, activity› absurde; it's ~ to do/for me to do ça ne sert à rien de faire/que je fasse
point of view n point m de vue
poise n (a) (confidence) assurance f
(b) (physical elegance) aisance f
poised adj (a) (self-possessed) plein/-e d'assurance
(b) (elegant) plein/-e d'aisance
(c) (on the point of) to be ~ to do être sur le point de faire
poison [1] n poison m
[2] vtr empoisonner ‹person, environment, relationship›; ‹fumes› intoxiquer ‹person›
poisoning n empoisonnement m
poisonous adj (a) ‹chemicals, gas› toxique; ‹mushroom, berry› vénéneux/-euse; ‹snake, insect, bite› venimeux/-euse
(b) ‹rumour, propaganda› pernicieux/-ieuse
poke vtr (a) (jab, prod) pousser [qn] du bout du doigt ‹person›; donner un coup dans ‹pile, substance›; tisonner ‹fire›
(b) (push, put) to ~ sth into enfoncer qch dans ‹hole, pot›; to ~ one's head out of the window passer la tête par la fenêtre
■ **poke around, poke about** farfouiller (in dans)
■ **poke out:** [1] ¶ ~ out ‹elbow, toe, blade› dépasser
[2] ¶ ~ out [sth], ~ [sth] out sortir ‹head, nose, tongue›
poker n (a) (for fire) tisonnier m
(b) (cardgame) poker m
IDIOM (as) stiff as a ~ raide comme la justice
poker-faced adj ‹person› impassible
Poland pr n Pologne f
polar adj polaire
pole n (a) (stick) perche f; (for tent, flag) mât m; (for skiing) bâton m
(b) (of earth's axis) pôle m
Pole n Polonais/-e m/f
pole dancing n pole dancing m
pole star n étoile f polaire
pole vault n saut m à la perche
ᐟ **police** [1] n (a) (police force) the ~ la police
(b) (policemen) policiers mpl
[2] vtr maintenir l'ordre dans ‹area›
police constable, PC n agent m de police
Police Department, PD n (US) services mpl de police (d'une ville)
police force n police f

policeman n (pl **-men**) agent m de police
police officer n policier m
police station n poste m de police; (larger) commissariat m
policewoman n (pl **-women**) femme f policier
policing n (a) (maintaining law and order) maintien m de l'ordre
(b) (of demonstration, match) organisation f du service d'ordre
(c) (of measures) contrôle m de l'application
♂ **policy** n (a) (plan, rule) politique f (**on** sur)
(b) (in insurance) (cover) contrat m; (document) police f
policyholder n assuré/-e m/f
policy unit n comité m de conseillers politiques
polio n poliomyélite f
polish [1] n (a) (for wood, floor) cire f; (for shoes) cirage m; (for brass, silver) pâte f à polir; (for car) lustre m
(b) (shiny surface) éclat m
(c) (of manner, performance) élégance f
[2] vtr (a) cirer ‹shoes, furniture›; astiquer ‹leather, car, glass, brass›; polir ‹stone›
(b) (refine) soigner ‹performance, image›; affiner ‹style›
■ **polish off** (colloq) expédier (fam) ‹food, job›
Polish [1] n (language) polonais m
[2] adj polonais/-e
polished adj (a) ‹surface, wood› poli/-e; ‹floor, shoes› ciré/-e
(b) ‹manner› raffiné/-e
(c) ‹performance› (bien) rodé/-e
polite adj poli/-e (**to** avec)
politeness n politesse f
♂ **political** adj politique
politically correct, **PC** adj politiquement correct/-e
political prisoner n prisonnier/-ière m/f politique
♂ **politician** n homme/femme m/f politique
politicize vtr politiser
♂ **politics** n (a) (gen) politique f
(b) (subject) sciences fpl politiques
(c) (views) opinions fpl politiques
♂ **poll** [1] n (a) (vote casting) scrutin m, vote m; (election) élections fpl; **to go to the ~s** se rendre aux urnes
(b) (survey) sondage m (**on** sur)
[2] vtr (a) obtenir ‹votes›
(b) (canvass) interroger ‹group›
pollen n pollen m
polling booth n isoloir m
polling day n jour m des élections
polling station n bureau m de vote
poll tax n (GB) ≈ impôts mpl locaux
pollutant n polluant m
pollute vtr polluer

polluter n pollueur/-euse m/f
pollution n pollution f
polo n polo m
polo neck n (GB) col m roulé
poltergeist n esprit m frappeur
poly [1] n (GB) (Hist) (colloq) (abbr = **polytechnic**) établissement m d'enseignement supérieur
[2] **poly+** pref poly-
polystyrene n polystyrène m
polytechnic n (GB) (also **poly**) établissement m d'enseignement supérieur
polythene n (GB) polyéthylène m
pomegranate n grenade f
pompom, **pompon** n pompon m
pompous adj ‹person› plein/-e de suffisance; ‹air, speech, style› pompeux/-euse
pond n (large) étang m; (smaller) mare f; (in garden) bassin m
ponder vi réfléchir (**on** à); (more deeply) méditer (**on** sur)
pontiff n pontife m
pontoon n (a) (pier) ponton m
(b) (GB Games) vingt-et-un m
pony n poney m
ponytail n queue f de cheval
poodle n caniche m
♂ **pool** [1] n (a) (pond) étang m; (artificial) bassin m
(b) (also **swimming ~**) piscine f
(c) (of water, light) flaque f; **a ~ of blood** une mare de sang
(d) (kitty) cagnotte f; (in cards) mises fpl
(e) (of money, resources) pool m; (of ideas, experience) réservoir m
(f) (billiards) billard m américain
[2] **pools** n pl (GB) (also **football ~s**) ≈ loto m sportif
[3] vtr mettre [qch] en commun
pool table n table f de billard américain
♂ **poor** adj (a) ‹person, country› pauvre (**in** en)
(b) ‹quality, work, planning, weather, visibility› mauvais/-e (before n); ‹attendance› faible
(c) (deserving pity) pauvre (before n); **~ you!** mon/ma pauvre!
(d) ‹attempt, excuse› piètre (before n)
poorly adv (a) ‹live, dress, dressed› pauvrement
(b) ‹written, lit, paid› mal
pop [1] n (a) (sound) pan m; **to go ~** faire pan
(b) (colloq) (drink) soda m
(c) (music) musique f pop
(d) (each) **tickets were £5 a ~** les tickets étaient 5 livres sterling pièce
[2] adj ‹concert, group, music, song› pop; ‹record, singer› de pop
[3] vtr (p prés etc **-pp-**) (a) faire éclater ‹balloon, bubble›
(b) faire sauter ‹cork›
(c) (colloq) (put) **to ~ sth in(to)** mettre qch

dans ‹oven, cupboard, mouth›

4 vi (p prés etc **-pp-**) **(a)** ‹balloon› éclater;
‹cork, buttons› sauter
(b) ‹ears› se déboucher brusquement; **her
eyes were ∼ping out of her head** les yeux lui
sortaient de la tête
(c) (GB) (colloq) (go) **to ∼ into town/the bank**
faire un saut (fam) en ville/à la banque
■ **pop in** (GB) (colloq) passer
■ **pop out** (GB) (colloq) sortir
■ **pop round, pop over** (GB) passer
pope n pape m; **Pope Paul VI** le Pape Paul VI
poplar n peuplier m
poppy n pavot m; **wild ∼** coquelicot m
pop sock n mi-bas m
⚘ **popular** adj **(a)** ‹actor, politician› populaire
(**with, among** parmi); ‹hobby, sport›
répandu/-e (**with, among** chez); ‹food, dish›
prisé/-e (**with, among** par); ‹product, resort,
colour, design› en vogue (**with, among** chez);
John is very ∼ John a beaucoup d'amis
(b) (of or for the people) ‹music, movement,
press› populaire; ‹entertainment› grand
public inv; ‹science, history› de vulgarisation
popularity n popularité f (**of** de; **with**
auprès de)
popularize vtr (make fashionable)
généraliser; (make accessible) vulgariser
⚘ **population** n population f
pop-up menu n menu m déroulant or
contextuel
pop-up window n fenêtre m popup
porcelain n porcelaine f
porch n **(a)** (of house, church) porche m
(b) (US) (veranda) véranda f
porcupine n porc-épic m
pore n pore m
■ **pore over** être plongé/-e dans ‹book›;
étudier soigneusement ‹map›
pork n (viande f de) porc m
pornographic adj pornographique
pornography n pornographie f
porpoise n marsouin m
porridge n porridge m (bouillie de flocons
d'avoine)
port n **(a)** (harbour) port m; **in ∼** au port; **∼
of call** escale f; (figurative) arrêt m
(b) (drink) porto m
(c) (Comput) port m
portable adj portable
porter n **(a)** (in station, airport, hotel) porteur
m; (in hospital) brancardier m
(b) (GB) (doorman) (of hotel) portier m; (of
apartment block) gardien/-ienne m/f
(c) (US) (steward) employé m des wagons-lits
portfolio n **(a)** (case) porte-documents m
inv; (for drawings) carton m (à dessins)
(b) (sample) portfolio m
(c) (in politics, finance) portefeuille m
porthole n hublot m

portion n **(a)** (of house, machine, document,
country) partie f (**of** de)
(b) (share) (of money, blame) part f (**of** de)
(c) (at meal) portion f
portrait n portrait m
portray vtr **(a)** (depict) décrire ‹place, era,
event›; présenter ‹person, situation›
(b) ‹actor› interpréter ‹character›
(c) ‹artist› peindre ‹person›; ‹picture, artist›
représenter ‹scene›
Portugal pr n Portugal m
Portuguese **1** n **(a)** (person) Portugais/-e
m/f
(b) (language) portugais m
2 adj portugais/-e
pose **1** vtr poser ‹problem› (**for** pour);
présenter ‹challenge› (**to** à); représenter
‹threat, risk› (**to** pour); soulever ‹question›
(**about** de)
2 vi **(a)** ‹artist's model› poser; ‹performer›
prendre des poses
(b) to ∼ as se faire passer pour
(c) (posture) frimer (fam)
poser n (colloq) **(a)** (person) frimeur/
-euse m/f (fam)
(b) (puzzle) colle f (fam)
posh adj (colloq) ‹person› huppé/-e (fam);
‹house, area, clothes, car› chic; ‹voice›
distingué/-e
⚘ **position** **1** n **(a)** (gen) position f; **to be in
∼** (in place) être en place; (ready) être prêt/-e
(b) (situation, state) situation f; **to be in a ∼ to
do** être en mesure de faire
(c) (Sport) poste m; **what ∼ does he play?**
quel est son poste?
(d) (job) poste m
2 vtr poster ‹policemen, soldiers›; disposer
‹object›
⚘ **positive** adj **(a)** (affirmative) ‹answer,
reaction, result› positif/-ive
(b) (optimistic) ‹message, person, feeling, tone›
positif/-ive
(c) (constructive) ‹contribution, effect, progress›
positif/-ive; ‹advantage, good› réel/réelle
(before n)
(d) (sure) ‹identification, proof› formel/-elle;
‹fact› indéniable; **to be ∼** être sûr/-e (**about**
de; **that** que)
(e) (forceful) ‹action› catégorique
(f) (in mathematics, science) positif/-ive
(g) (extreme) ‹pleasure› pur/-e (before n);
‹disgrace, outrage, genius› véritable (before n)
positive discrimination n mesures fpl
antidiscriminatoires
possess vtr **(a)** posséder ‹property,
weapon, proof, charm›; avoir ‹power,
advantage›; (illegally) détenir ‹arms, drugs›
(b) (take control of) ‹anger, fury› s'emparer
de ‹person›; ‹devil› posséder ‹person›; **what
∼ed you to do that?** qu'est-ce qui t'a pris de
faire ça?
possession **1** n **(a)** (gen) possession f ⋯▷

(b) (Law) (illegal) détention *f* (**of** de)
② **possessions** *n pl* biens *mpl*

possessive ① *n* (in grammar) possessif *m*
② *adj* possessif/-ive (**towards** à l'égard de;
with avec)

✧ **possibility** *n* **(a)** (chance, prospect)
possibilité *f*
(b) (eventuality) éventualité *f*

✧ **possible** *adj* possible; **he did as much
as** ∼ il a fait tout son possible; **as far as** ∼
dans la mesure du possible; **as quickly as** ∼
le plus vite possible; **as soon as** ∼ dès que
possible

✧ **possibly** *adv* **(a)** (maybe) peut-être
(b) (for emphasis) **how could they** ∼
understand? comment donc pourraient-ils
comprendre?; **we can't** ∼ **afford it** nous n'en
avons absolument pas les moyens

✧ **post** ① *n* **(a)** (job) poste *m* (**as, of** de); **to
hold a** ∼ occuper un poste
(b) (GB) (postal system) poste *f*; (letters) courrier
m; (delivery) distribution *f*; **by return of** ∼ par
retour du courrier; **it was lost in the** ∼ cela
s'est égaré dans le courrier
(c) (Mil) poste *m*
(d) (pole) poteau *m*
② **post-** *pref* post-; **in** ∼**-1992 Europe** dans
l'Europe d'après 1992
③ *vtr* **(a)** (GB) (send by post) poster, expédier
[qch] (par la poste); (put in letterbox) mettre
[qch] à la poste
(b) (stick up) afficher ‹notice, poster›;
annoncer ‹details, results›
(c) (gen, Mil) (send abroad) affecter (**to** à)
(d) (station) poster ‹guard, sentry›

postage *n* affranchissement *m*; **including**
∼ **and packing** frais *mpl* d'expédition inclus;
∼ **free** franc de port ∼ **paid** pré-affranchi

postal *adj* ‹charges, district› postal/-e;
‹application› par la poste

postal order, **PO** *n* (GB) mandat *m* (**for**
de)

postbox *n* (GB) boîte *f* aux lettres

postcard *n* carte *f* postale

post code *n* (GB) code *m* postal

postdate *vtr* postdater

poster *n* (for information) affiche *f*; (decorative)
poster *m*

posterity *n* postérité *f*

poster paint *n* gouache *f*

postgraduate ① *n* ≈ étudiant/-e *m/f* de
troisième cycle
② *adj* ≈ de troisième cycle

posthumous *adj* posthume

postman *n* facteur *m*

postmark *n* cachet *m* de la poste

post-mortem *n* autopsie *f*

post-natal *adj* post-natal/-e

post office, **PO** *n* poste *f*

postpone *vtr* reporter, remettre (**until** à;
for de)

postscript *n* (in letter) post-scriptum *m inv*
(**to** à); (to book) postface *f* (**to** à)

posture ① *n* **(a)** (pose) posture *f*; (figurative)
(stance) position *f*
(b) (bearing) maintien *m*; **to have good/bad** ∼
se tenir bien/mal
② *vi* poser, prendre des poses

post-viral (fatigue) syndrome *n*
encéphalomyélite *f* myalgique

postwar *adj* d'après-guerre

pot ① *n* **(a)** (container) pot *m*
(b) (teapot) théière *f*; (coffee pot) cafetière *f*
(c) ∼**s and pans** casseroles *fpl*
(d) (piece of pottery) poterie *f*
② *vtr* (*p prés etc* **-tt-**) **(a)** mettre [qch] en
pot ‹jam›
(b) (in billiards) blouser ‹ball›
(c) mettre [qch] en pot ‹plant›
③ **potted** *pp adj* **(a)** ‹plant› en pot
(b) ‹biography, history› bref/brève (*before n*)
IDIOMS **to go to** ∼ ‹person› se laisser aller;
‹situation› aller à vau-l'eau; **to take** ∼ **luck**
(for meal) (GB) manger à la fortune du pot;
(gen) prendre ce que l'on trouve

potassium *n* potassium *m*

potato *n* (*pl* **-es**) pomme *f* de terre

potato chips (US), **potato crisps**
(GB) *n pl* chips *fpl*

potato peeler *n* épluche-légumes *m inv*

pot belly *n* bedaine *f*

potent *adj* **(a)** ‹symbol, drug› puissant/-e;
‹drink› fort/-e
(b) (sexually) viril/-e

✧ **potential** ① *n* potentiel *m* (**as** en tant
que; **for** de); **the** ∼ **to do** les qualités *fpl*
nécessaires pour faire; **to fulfil one's** ∼
montrer de quoi on est capable
② *adj* ‹buyer, danger, energy, market,
victim› potentiel/-ielle; ‹champion, rival› en
puissance; ‹investor› éventuel/-elle

pothole *n* fondrière *f*, nid *m* de poule

potholing *n* (GB) spéléologie *f*

pot plant *n* plante *f* d'appartement

potter *n* potier *m*

∎ **potter about**, **potter around** (GB) (do
odd jobs) bricoler (fam); (go about daily chores)
suivre son petit train-train (fam)

pottery *n* poterie *f*

potting compost *n* terreau *m*

potty (colloq) ① *n* pot *m* (d'enfant)
② *adj* (GB) ‹person› dingue (fam); ‹idea›
farfelu/-e (fam); **to be** ∼ **about** être toqué/-e
de (fam)

pouch *n* **(a)** (bag) petit sac *m*; (for tobacco)
blague *f* (à tabac); (for ammunition) étui *m* (à
munitions)
(b) (of marsupials) poche *f* ventrale

poultry *n* (birds) volailles *fpl*; (meat) volaille *f*

pounce *vi* bondir; **to** ∼ **on** ‹animal› bondir
sur ‹prey, object›; ‹person› se jeter sur ‹victim›

✧ indicates a very frequent word

⚬ pound ⓵ n (a) (weight measurement) livre f
(= 453.6 g); **two ∼s of apples** ≈ un kilo de
pommes
(b) (unit of currency) livre f
(c) (for dogs, cars) fourrière f
⓶ vtr **(a)** (Culin) piler ‹spices, grain›; aplatir
‹meat›
(b) ‹waves› battre ‹shore›
(c) ‹artillery› pilonner ‹city›
⓷ vi **(a) to ∼ on** marteler ‹door, wall›
(b) ‹heart› battre
(c) to ∼ up/down the stairs monter/
descendre l'escalier d'un pas lourd
(d) my head is ∼ing j'ai l'impression que ma
tête va éclater
pour ⓵ vtr **(a)** verser ‹liquid›; couler
‹cement, metal, wax›
(b) (also ∼ **out**) servir ‹drink›
(c) to ∼ money into investir des sommes
énormes dans
⓶ vi **(a)** ‹liquid› couler (à flots); **to ∼ into**
‹water, liquid› couler dans; ‹smoke, fumes› se
répandre dans; ‹light› inonder ‹room›; **tears**
∼ed down her face les larmes ruisselaient
sur son visage
(b) to ∼ into ‹people› affluer dans; **to ∼ out**
of ‹people, cars› sortir en grand nombre de
⓷ v impers **it's ∼ing (with rain)** il pleut à
verse
∎ **pour away** vider
∎ **pour in** ‹people› affluer; ‹letters, money›
pleuvoir; ‹water› entrer à flots
∎ **pour out**: ⓵ ¶ ∼ **out** ‹liquid, smoke,
crowd› se déverser; ‹people› sortir en grand
nombre
⓶ ¶ ∼ **[sth] out (a)** verser, servir ‹coffee,
wine›
(b) rejeter ‹fumes, sewage›; **to ∼ out one's**
troubles or **heart to sb** s'épancher auprès
de qn
pout vi faire la moue
poverty n pauvreté f; (more severe) misère f
poverty line n seuil m de pauvreté
poverty-stricken adj dans la misère
POW n (abbr = **prisoner of war**)
prisonnier/-ière m/f de guerre
powder ⓵ n poudre f
⓶ vtr **to ∼ one's face** se poudrer le visage
powdered adj ‹egg, milk, coffee› en poudre
powdery adj ‹snow› poudreux/-euse;
‹stone› friable
⚬ power ⓵ n (a) (control) pouvoir m; **to be in/**
come to ∼ être/accéder au pouvoir; **to be in**
sb's ∼ être à la merci de qn
(b) (influence) influence f (**over** sur)
(c) (capability) pouvoir m; **to do everything in**
one's ∼ faire tout ce qui est en son pouvoir
(**to do** pour faire)
(d) (also ∼**s**) (authority) attributions fpl
(e) (physical force) (of person, explosion) force f;
(of storm) violence f
(f) (Tech) énergie f; (current) courant m; **to**
switch on the ∼ mettre le courant
(g) (of vehicle, plane) puissance f; **to be running**

at full/half ∼ fonctionner à plein/mi-régime
(h) (in mathematics) **6 to the ∼ of 3** 6 puissance 3
(i) (country) puissance f
⓶ adj ‹drill, cable› électrique; ‹brakes›
assisté/-e
⓷ vtr faire marcher ‹engine›; propulser
‹plane, boat›
IDIOMS **to do sb a ∼ of good** faire à qn un
bien fou; **the ∼s that be** les autorités
powerboat n hors-bord m inv
power cut n coupure f de courant
⚬ powerful adj ‹person, engine, computer›
puissant/-e; ‹smell, emotion, voice,
government› fort/-e; ‹argument› solide
powerless adj impuissant/-e (**against** face
à); **to be ∼ to do** ne pas pouvoir faire
power line n ligne f à haute tension
power of attorney n procuration f
power plant (US), **power station** n
centrale f (électrique)
power sharing n partage m du pouvoir
power steering n direction f assistée
power user n (Comput) utilisateur/-trice
mf avancé/-e
PR n **(a)** (abbr = **public relations**)
relations fpl publiques
(b) (abbr = **proportional**
representation)
practical ⓵ n (exam) épreuve f pratique;
(lesson) travaux mpl pratiques
⓶ adj **(a)** (gen) pratique
(b) ‹plan› réalisable
practicality n **(a)** (of person) esprit m
pratique; (of equipment) facilité f d'utilisation
(b) (of scheme, idea, project) aspect m pratique
practical joke n farce f
practically adv **(a)** (almost) pratiquement
(b) (in practical way) d'une manière pratique
⚬ practice ⓵ n **(a)** (exercises) exercices mpl;
(experience) entraînement m; **to have had ∼**
in or **at sth/in** or **at doing sth** avoir déjà fait
qch; **to be out of ∼** être rouillé/-e (fam)
(b) (for sport) entraînement m; (for music,
drama) répétition f
(c) (procedure) pratique f, usage m; **it's**
standard ∼ to do il est d'usage de faire;
business ∼ usage en affaires
(d) (habit) habitude f
(e) (custom) coutume f
(f) (business of doctor, lawyer) cabinet m
(g) (not theory) pratique f; **in ∼** en pratique
⓶ adj ‹game, match› d'essai; ‹flight›
d'entraînement
⓷ vtr, vi (US) = PRACTISE
IDIOM ∼ **makes perfect** c'est en forgeant
qu'on devient forgeron (Proverb)
practise (GB), **practice** (US) ⓵ vtr
(a) travailler ‹song, speech, French›; s'exercer
à ‹movement, shot›; répéter ‹play›; **to ∼ the**
piano travailler le piano; **to ∼ doing** or **how**
to do s'entraîner à faire
(b) (use) pratiquer ‹restraint, kindness›;

⋯⟩

utiliser ‹*method*›
(c) exercer ‹*profession*›
(d) (observe) pratiquer ‹*custom, religion*›
 2 *vi* **(a)** (at instrument) s'exercer; (for sports)
s'entraîner; (for play, concert) répéter
(b) (work) exercer; **to ~ as** exercer la
profession de ‹*doctor, lawyer*›
practising (GB), **practicing** (US) *adj*
‹*Christian, Muslim*› pratiquant/-e; ‹*doctor,
lawyer*› en exercice; ‹*homosexual*› actif/-ive
practitioner *n* praticien/-enne *m/f*;
dental ~ dentiste *mf*
pragmatic *adj* pragmatique
pragmatist *n* pragmatiste *mf*
prairie *n* plaine *f* (herbeuse)
praise **1** *n* éloges *mpl*, louanges *fpl*
 2 *vtr* **(a)** faire l'éloge de ‹*person, book*› (**as**
en tant que)
(b) louer ‹*God*› (**for** pour)
praiseworthy *adj* digne d'éloges
pram *n* (GB) landau *m*
prance *vi* ‹*horse*› caracoler; ‹*person*›
sautiller
prank *n* farce *f*
prattle *vi* bavarder; ‹*children*› babiller; **to ~
on about sth** parler de qch à n'en plus finir
prawn *n* crevette *f* rose, bouquet *m*
pray *vi* prier (**for** pour)
prayer *n* prière *f*; **to say one's ~s** faire sa
prière
preach **1** *vtr* prêcher (**to** à)
 2 *vi* prêcher (**to** à); (figurative) sermonner
IDIOM **to practise what one ~es** prêcher
d'exemple
preacher *n* prédicateur *m*; (clergyman)
pasteur *m*
prearrange *vtr* fixer [qch] à l'avance
precarious *adj* précaire
precaution *n* précaution *f* (**against**
contre)
precautionary *adj* préventif/-ive
precede *vtr* précéder
precedence *n* **(a)** (in importance) priorité
f (**over** sur)
(b) (in rank) préséance *f* (**over** sur)
precedent *n* précédent *m*; **to set a ~** créer
un précédent
preceding *adj* précédent/-e
precinct *n* **(a)** (GB) (*also* **shopping ~**)
quartier *m* commerçant
(b) (GB) (*also* **pedestrian ~**) zone *f*
piétonne
(c) (US) (administrative district) circonscription *f*
precious *adj* **(a)** (valuable) précieux/-ieuse
(b) (held dear) ‹*person*› cher/chère (**to** à)
(c) (affected) précieux/-ieuse, affecté/-e
precipice *n* précipice *m*
précis *n* résumé *m*

ᕈ **indicates a very frequent word**

precise *adj* **(a)** (exact) précis/-e
(b) ‹*person, mind*› méticuleux/-euse
precisely *adv* **(a)** (exactly) exactement,
précisément; **at ten o'clock ~** à dix heures
précises
(b) (accurately) ‹*describe, record*› avec
précision
precision *n* précision *f*
preclude *vtr* exclure ‹*possibility*›;
empêcher ‹*action*›
precocious *adj* précoce
preconceived *adj* préconçu/-e
preconception *n* opinion *f* préconçue
precondition *n* condition *f* requise
precursor *n* (person) précurseur *m*; (sign)
signe *m* avant-coureur
predate *vtr* antidater ‹*cheque*›; ‹*discovery,
building*› être antérieur/-e à
predator *n* prédateur *m*
predecessor *n* prédécesseur *m*
predetermine *vtr* déterminer d'avance
predicament *n* situation *f* difficile
ᕈ **predict** *vtr* prédire
predictable *adj* prévisible
prediction *n* prédiction *f* (**that** selon
laquelle)
predispose *vtr* prédisposer
predominant *adj* prédominant/-e
predominantly *adv* principalement
predominate *vi* prédominer
pre-eminent *adj* éminent/-e
pre-empt *vtr* **(a)** anticiper ‹*question,
decision, move*›; devancer ‹*person*›
(b) (thwart) contrecarrer ‹*action, plan*›
pre-emptive *adj* préventif/-ive
preen *v refl* **to ~ oneself** ‹*bird*› se lisser les
plumes; ‹*person*› se pomponner
prefab *n* (bâtiment *m*) préfabriqué *m*
preface *n* (to book) préface *f*; (to speech)
préambule *m*
prefect *n* (GB Sch) élève *m/f* chargé/-e de la
surveillance
ᕈ **prefer** *vtr* **(a)** (like better) préférer, aimer
mieux; **I ~ painting to drawing** je préfère la
peinture au dessin; **to ~ it if** aimer mieux
que (+ *subjunctive*)
(b) (Law) **to ~ charges** ‹*police*› déférer [qn]
au parquet
preferable *adj* préférable (**to** à)
preferably *adv* de préférence
preference *n* préférence *f* (**for** pour)
preferential *adj* préférentiel/-ielle
prefigure *vtr* ‹*event*› préfigurer; ‹*person*›
être le précurseur de
prefix *n* (*pl* **-es**) préfixe *m*
pregnancy *n* (gen) grossesse *f*; (Zool)
gestation *f*
pregnant *adj* (gen) enceinte; (Zool) pleine;
to get sb ~ (colloq) faire un enfant à qn (fam)

preheat ⋯⟶ preserve ⋯⋯

preheat *vtr* préchauffer ‹oven›

prehistoric *adj* préhistorique

prejudice ☐1 *n* préjugé *m*; **racial/political ~** préjugés raciaux/en matière de politique
☐2 *vtr* **(a)** (bias) influencer; **to ~ sb against/in favour of** prévenir qn contre/en faveur de
(b) porter préjudice à ‹claim, case›; léser ‹person›; compromettre ‹chances›

prejudiced *adj* ‹person› plein/-e de préjugés; ‹account› partial/-e; ‹opinion› préconçu/-e

preliminary ☐1 *n* **(a)** (gen) **as a ~ to** en prélude à
(b) (Sport) épreuve *f* éliminatoire
☐2 **preliminaries** *n pl* préliminaires *mpl* (to à)
☐3 *adj* préliminaire

prelude *n* prélude *m* (to à)

premarital *adj* avant le mariage

premature *adj* ‹baby, action› prématuré/-e; ‹ejaculation, menopause› précoce

premeditate *vtr* préméditer

premier ☐1 *n* premier ministre *m*
☐2 *adj* premier/-ière (before n)

première ☐1 *n* première *f*
☐2 *vtr* donner [qch] en première ‹film, play›

premises *n pl* locaux *mpl*; **on the ~** sur place; **off the ~** à l'extérieur; **to leave the ~** quitter les lieux

premium *n* **(a)** (extra payment) supplément *m*
(b) (on stock exchange) prime *f* d'émission
(c) (in insurance) prime *f* (d'assurance)
(d) to be at a ~ valoir de l'or; **to set a (high) ~ on sth** mettre qch au (tout) premier plan

premium bond (GB) *n* obligation *f* à lots

premonition *n* prémonition *f*

prenatal *adj* prénatal/-e

prenuptial agreement *n* contrat *m* prénuptial

preoccupation *n* préoccupation *f*

preoccupied *adj* préoccupé/-e

preoccupy *vtr* (*prét, pp* **-pied**) préoccuper

prepaid *adj* payé/-e d'avance; **~ envelope** enveloppe *f* affranchie pour la réponse

preparation *n* préparation *f*; **~s** préparatifs *mpl*; **in ~ for sth** en vue de qch

preparatory *adj* ‹training, course, drawing› préparatoire; ‹meeting, report, investigations› préliminaire

preparatory school *n* **(a)** (GB) école *f* primaire privée
(b) (US) lycée *m* privé

ᵉ **prepare** ☐1 *vtr* préparer; **to ~ to do** se préparer à faire; **to ~ sb for** préparer qn à
☐2 *vi* **to ~ for** se préparer à ‹trip, talks, exam, war›; se préparer pour ‹party, ceremony, game›; **to ~ oneself** se préparer

ᵉ **prepared** *adj* **(a)** (willing) **to be ~ to do** être prêt/-e à faire

(b) (ready) **to be ~ for** être prêt/-e pour ‹event›; **to come ~** venir bien préparé/-e; **to be ~ for the worst** s'attendre au pire

preposition *n* préposition *f*

preposterous *adj* grotesque

prerequisite *n* **(a)** (gen) préalable *m* (of de; for à)
(b) (US Univ) unité *f* de valeur

prerogative *n* (official) prérogative *f*; (personal) droit *m*

preschool ☐1 *n* (US) école *f* maternelle
☐2 *adj* préscolaire

prescribe *vtr* **(a)** (Med, figurative) prescrire (for sb à qn; for sth pour qch)
(b) imposer ‹rule›

prescription *n* ordonnance *f*; **repeat ~** ordonnance renouvelable

prescription charges *n pl* frais *mpl* d'ordonnance

ᵉ **presence** *n* présence *f*

presence of mind *n* présence *f* d'esprit

ᵉ **present** ☐1 *n* **(a)** (gift) cadeau *m*; **to give sb a ~** offrir un cadeau à qn
(b) the ~ le présent; **for the ~** pour le moment, pour l'instant
(c) (also **~ tense**) présent *m*
☐2 *adj* **(a)** (attending) présent/-e; **to be ~ at** assister à
(b) (current) actuel/-elle; **up to the ~ day** jusqu'à ce jour
☐3 *vtr* **(a)** (gen) présenter; offrir ‹chance, opportunity›; **to be ~ed with a choice** se trouver face à un choix
(b) remettre ‹prize, certificate› (to à)
☐4 *v refl* **to ~ oneself** se présenter; **to ~ itself** ‹opportunity, thought› se présenter
☐5 **at present** *phr* (at this moment) en ce moment; (nowadays) actuellement

presentable *adj* présentable

ᵉ **presentation** *n* **(a)** (gen) présentation *f*
(b) (talk) exposé *m*
(c) (of gift, award) remise *f* (of de)
(d) (portrayal) représentation *f*

present-day *adj* actuel/-elle

presenter *n* présentateur/-trice *m/f*

presently *adv* (currently) à présent; (soon, in future) bientôt

present perfect *n* passé *m* composé

preservation *n* (of building, wildlife, peace) préservation *f* (of de); (of food) conservation *f* (of de); (of life) protection *f* (of de)

preservative *n* (for food) agent *m* de conservation; (for wood) revêtement *m* (protecteur)

preserve ☐1 *n* **(a)** (Culin) (jam) confiture *f*; (pickle) conserve *f*
(b) (territory) chasse *f* gardée (of de)
☐2 *vtr* **(a)** (save) préserver ‹land, building, tradition› (for pour); entretenir ‹wood, leather, painting›
(b) (maintain) préserver ‹peace, standards,

⋯⟶

rights»; maintenir «*order*»; garder «*humour, dignity, health*»
(c) conserver «*food*»

preset *vtr* (*prét*, *pp* -**set**) régler (à l'avance) «*timer, cooker*»; programmer «*video*»

preside *vi* présider; **to ~ at sth** présider qch; **to ~ over** présider «*conference, committee*»

presidency *n* présidence *f*

𝒻 **president** *n* (a) président·e *m/f*; **to run for ~** être candidat·e à la présidence
(b) (US) (managing director) président-directeur *m* général

presidential *adj* présidentiel/-ielle

𝒻 **press** ⬛1 *n* (a) **the ~, the Press** la presse *f*; **to get a good/bad ~** avoir bonne/mauvaise presse
(b) (*also* **printing ~**) presse *f*
(c) (device for flattening) presse *f*
⬛2 *vtr* (a) (push) appuyer sur; **to ~ sth in** enfoncer qch; **to ~ one's nose against sth** coller son nez contre qch
(b) (squeeze) presser «*fruit, flower*»; serrer «*arm, hand, person*»
(c) (iron) repasser «*clothes*»
(d) (urge) faire pression sur «*person*»; mettre [qch] en avant «*issue*»; **to ~ sb to do** presser qn de faire; **to ~ a point** insister
⬛3 *vi* (a) **to ~ (down)** appuyer
(b) «*crowd, person*» se presser (**forward** vers l'avant)
⬛4 *v refl* **to ~ oneself against** se plaquer contre «*wall*»; se presser contre «*person*»
■ **press for** faire pression pour obtenir «*change, release*»; **to be ~ed for** ne pas avoir beaucoup de «*time, cash*»
■ **press on** continuer; **to ~ on with** faire avancer «*reform, plan*»

press agency *n* agence *f* de presse

press conference *n* conférence *f* de presse

pressing *adj* (a) (urgent) urgent/-e
(b) «*invitation*» pressant/-e

press release *n* communiqué *m* de presse

press-stud *n* (GB) (bouton-)pression *m*

press-up *n* pompe *f* (fam)

𝒻 **pressure** *n* (a) (gen) pression *f*; **to put ~ on sb** faire pression sur qn; **to do sth under ~** faire qch sous la contrainte
(b) (of traffic, tourists) flux *m*

pressure cooker *n* cocotte-minute® *f*

pressure group *n* groupe *m* de pression

pressurize *vtr* (a) pressuriser «*cabin, suit, gas*»
(b) faire pression sur «*person*»; **he was ~d into going** on a fait pression sur lui pour qu'il y aille

prestige *n* prestige *m*

prestigious *adj* prestigieux/-ieuse

presumably *adv* sans doute

presume *vtr* (a) (suppose) supposer, présumer
(b) (dare) **to ~ to do** se permettre de faire

presumptuous *adj* présomptueux/-euse, arrogant/-e

presuppose *vtr* présupposer (**that** que)

pre-tax *adj* avant impôts *inv*

pretence (GB), **pretense** (US) *n* faux-semblant *m*; **to make a ~ of sth** feindre qch; **to make a ~ of doing** faire semblant de faire

pretend ⬛1 *vtr* **to ~ that** faire comme si; **to ~ to do** faire semblant de faire
⬛2 *vi* faire semblant

pretension *n* prétention *f*

pretentious *adj* prétentieux/-ieuse

preterite *n* prétérit *m*

pretext *n* prétexte *m*

𝒻 **pretty** ⬛1 *adj* joli/-e; **it was not a ~ sight** ce n'était pas beau à voir
⬛2 *adv* (colloq) (very) vraiment; (fairly) assez; **~ good** pas mal du tout

prevail *vi* (a) (win) prévaloir (**against** contre)
(b) (be common) prédominer
■ **prevail upon** persuader «*person*»

prevailing *adj* «*attitude, style*» qui prévaut; «*rate*» en vigueur; «*wind*» dominant/-e

prevalent *adj* (a) (widespread) répandu/-e
(b) (ruling) qui prévaut

prevaricate *vi* se dérober

𝒻 **prevent** *vtr* prévenir «*fire, illness, violence*»; éviter «*conflict, disaster, damage*»; faire obstacle à «*marriage*»; **to ~ sb from doing** empêcher qn de faire

preventable *adj* évitable

prevention *n* prévention *f*; **crime ~** lutte *f* contre la délinquance

preventive *adj* préventif/-ive

preview *n* (of film, play) avant-première *f*

𝒻 **previous** *adj* précédent/-e; (further back in time) antérieur/-e

𝒻 **previously** *adv* (before) auparavant, avant; (already) déjà

prewar *adj* d'avant-guerre *inv*

prey *n* proie *f*
■ **prey on** (a) (hunt) chasser
(b) (worry) **to ~ on sb's mind** préoccuper qn
(c) (exploit) exploiter «*fears, worries*»

𝒻 **price** ⬛1 *n* (a) (cost) prix *m*; **to go up in ~** augmenter; **to pay a high ~ for sth** payer qch cher; **at any ~** à tout prix
(b) (value) valeur *f*; **to put a ~ on** évaluer «*object, antique*»
⬛2 *vtr* fixer le prix de (**at** à)

price cut *n* baisse *f* du prix

price freeze *n* blocage *m* des prix

priceless *adj* (a) (extremely valuable) inestimable
(b) (colloq) (amusing) impayable (fam)

𝒻 indicates a very frequent word

price list *n* (in shop, catalogue) liste *f* des prix; (in bar, restaurant) tarif *m*

price rise *n* hausse *f* des prix

price tag *n* (label) étiquette *f*

price war *n* guerre *f* des prix

prick ☐1 *n* (of needle) piqûre *f*
☐2 *vtr* piquer; **to ~ one's finger** se piquer le doigt
☐3 *vi* piquer
■ **prick up: to ~ up one's ears** ‹person› dresser l'oreille; **the dog ~ed up its ears** le chien a dressé les oreilles

prickle ☐1 *n* (of hedgehog, plant) piquant *m*
☐2 *vi* ‹hairs› se hérisser (**with** de)

prickly *adj* (a) ‹bush, leaf› épineux/-euse; ‹animal› armé/-e de piquants; ‹thorn› piquant/-e
(b) (itchy) qui gratte
(c) (colloq) (touchy) irritable (**about** à propos de)

pride ☐1 *n* (a) fierté *f*; **to take ~ in** être fier/fière de ‹ability, achievement›; soigner ‹appearance, work›; **to be sb's ~ and joy** être la (grande) fierté de qn
(b) (self-respect) amour-propre *m*; (excessive) orgueil *m*
(c) (of lions) troupe *f*
☐2 *v refl* **to ~ oneself on sth/on doing** être fier/fière de qch/de faire
IDIOM **to have ~ of place** occuper la place d'honneur

priest *n* prêtre *m*; **parish ~** curé *m*

priesthood *n* (calling) prêtrise *f*; **to enter the ~** entrer dans les ordres

prig *n* béguele *mf*

prim *adj* (also **~ and proper**) ‹person, manner, appearance› guindé/-e; ‹expression› pincé/-e; ‹voice› affecté/-e; ‹clothing› très convenable

primarily *adv* (chiefly) essentiellement; (originally) à l'origine

primary ☐1 *n* (US) (also **~ election**) primaire *f*
☐2 *adj* (a) (main) principal/-e; ‹sense, meaning, stage› premier/-ière; **of ~ importance** de première importance
(b) (Sch) ‹teaching, education› primaire
(c) ‹industry, products› de base

primary colour (GB), **primary color** (US) *n* couleur *f* primaire

primary school *n* école *f* primaire

primary (school) teacher *n* (GB) instituteur/-trice *m/f*

primate *n* (a) (mammal) primate *m*
(b) (archbishop) primat *m* (**of** de)

prime ☐1 *n* **in one's ~** (professionally) à son apogée; (physically) dans la fleur de l'âge; **in its ~** à son apogée; **to be past its ~** avoir connu des jours meilleurs
☐2 *adj* (a) (chief) principal/-e; ‹importance› primordial/-e
(b) (good quality) ‹site› de premier ordre; ‹meat, cuts› de premier choix; **of ~ quality** de

première qualité
(c) (classic) ‹example› excellent/-e (*before n*)
☐3 *vtr* (a) (brief) préparer; **to ~ sb about** mettre qn au courant de; **to ~ sb to say** souffler à qn de dire
(b) (Mil, Tech) amorcer

⚜ **prime minister, PM** *n* Premier ministre *m*

prime mover *n* (person) promoteur/-trice *m/f*

prime number *n* nombre *m* premier

prime time *n* heures *fpl* de grande écoute *m*

primeval *adj* primitif/-ive

primitive ☐1 *n* primitif *m*
☐2 *adj* primitif/-ive

primrose *n* primevère *f* (jaune)

prince *n* prince *m*

princess *n* princesse *f*

principal ☐1 *n* (of senior school) proviseur *m*; (of junior school, college) directeur/-trice *m/f*
☐2 *adj* principal/-e

⚜ **principle** *n* principe *m*; **in ~** en principe; **on ~** par principe

print ☐1 *n* (a) (typeface) caractères *mpl*; **the small *or* fine ~** les détails; **in ~** disponible en librairie; **out of ~** épuisé/-e
(b) (etching) estampe *f*; (engraving) gravure *f*
(c) (of photo) épreuve *f*
(d) (of finger, hand, foot) empreinte *f*; (of tyre) trace *f*
(e) (fabric) tissu *m* imprimé
☐2 *vtr* (a) imprimer ‹book, banknote, pattern, design›
(b) (publish) publier
(c) faire développer ‹photos›
(d) (write) écrire [qch] en script
■ **print off** tirer ‹copies›
■ **print out** imprimer

printer *n* (person, firm) imprimeur *m*; (machine) imprimante *f*

printout *n* sortie *f* sur imprimante; (perforated) listing *m*

print-preview *vtr* prévisualiser

⚜ **prior** ☐1 *adj* (a) (previous) préalable; **~ notice** préavis *m*
(b) (more important) prioritaire
☐2 **prior to** *phr* avant

⚜ **priority** *n* priorité *f*

priory *n* prieuré *m*

prise *v* ■ **prise apart** séparer ‹layers, people›
■ **prise off** enlever [qch] en forçant ‹lid›
■ **prise open** ouvrir [qch] en forçant ‹door›

prism *n* prisme *m*

⚜ **prison** *n* prison *f*; **to put sb in ~** emprisonner qn

prison camp *n* camp *m* de prisonniers

prisoner *n* prisonnier/-ière *m/f*; (in jail) détenu/-e *m/f*

prison officer n surveillant/-e m/f de prison

prison sentence n peine f de prison

pristine adj immaculé/-e

privacy n (a) (private life) vie f privée; **to invade sb's** ~ s'immiscer dans la vie privée de qn
(b) (solitude) intimité f (**of** de)

✦ **private** 1 n simple soldat m
2 adj (a) ‹property, vehicle, meeting, life› privé/-e; ‹letter, phone call› personnel/-elle; ‹sale› de particulier à particulier; ‹place› tranquille; **room with** ~ **bath** chambre avec salle de bains particulière; **a** ~ **joke** une plaisanterie pour initiés
(b) ‹sector, education, school, hospital› privé/-e; ‹accommodation, lesson› particulier/-ière
3 **in private** phr en privé

private eye n (colloq) détective m privé

privately adv (a) (in private) en privé
(b) (not in public sector) dans le privé; ~**-owned** privé/-e

privatization n privatisation f

privatize vtr privatiser

privilege n privilège m

privileged adj ‹minority, life› privilégié/-e; ‹information› confidentiel/-ielle

✦ **prize** 1 n (a) (award) prix m; (in lottery) lot m; **first** ~ premier prix; (in lottery) gros lot
(b) (valued object) trésor m; (reward for effort) récompense f
2 adj (a) ‹vegetable, bull› primé/-e; ‹pupil› hors-pair inv
(b) ‹possession› précieux/-ieuse
(c) ‹idiot, example› parfait/-e (before n)

prize draw n (for charity) tombola f; (for advertising) tirage m au sort

prize-giving n remise f des prix

prize money n argent m du prix

prizewinner n (in lottery) gagnant/-e m/f; (of award) lauréat/-e m/f

✦ **pro** 1 n (a) (colloq) (professional) pro mf (fam)
(b) (advantage) **the** ~**s and cons** le pour et le contre; **the** ~**s and cons of sth** les avantages et les inconvénients de qch
2 prep (in favour of) pour

proactive adj ‹approach, role› dynamique

probability n (of desirable event) chances fpl; (of unwelcome event) risques mpl

probable adj probable

✦ **probably** adv probablement

probation n (a) (for adult) sursis m avec mise à l'épreuve; (for juvenile) mise f en liberté surveillée
(b) (trial period) période f d'essai

probationary adj (trial) ‹period, year› d'essai; (training) ‹period› probatoire

probation officer n (for juveniles) délégué/-e m/f à la liberté surveillée; (for adults) agent m de probation

probe 1 n (a) (investigation) enquête f
(b) (instrument) sonde f
2 vtr (Med, Tech) sonder (**with** avec)

probing adj ‹look› inquisiteur/-trice; ‹question› pénétrant/-e; ‹examination› très poussé/-e

✦ **problem** 1 n problème m
2 adj ‹child› difficile; ‹family› à problèmes

problematic(al) adj problématique

problem page n courrier m du cœur

✦ **procedure** n procédure f

✦ **proceed** vi (a) (set about) procéder; **to** ~ **with** poursuivre
(b) (be in progress) ‹project, work› avancer; ‹interview, talks, trial› se poursuivre
(c) ‹person, road› continuer; ‹vehicle› avancer

proceedings n pl (a) (meeting) réunion f; (ceremony) cérémonie f; (discussion) débats mpl
(b) (Law) poursuites fpl

proceeds n pl (of sale) produit m; (of event) recette f

✦ **process** 1 n (a) (gen) processus m (**of** de); **to be in the** ~ **of doing** être en train de faire; **in the** ~ en même temps
(b) (method) procédé m
2 vtr (a) traiter ‹applications, data›
(b) traiter ‹raw materials, chemical, waste›
(c) développer ‹film›
(d) (Culin) (mix) mixer; (chop) hacher

processing n traitement m; **the food** ~ **industry** l'industrie alimentaire

procession n (of demonstration, carnival) défilé m; (formal) cortège m; (religious) procession f

processor n (Comput) unité f centrale

proclaim vtr proclamer (**that** que)

proclamation n proclamation f

procrastinate vi atermoyer

procure vtr procurer; **to** ~ **sth for sb** procurer qch à qn; **to** ~ **sth for oneself** se procurer qch

prod 1 n (a) (poke) petit coup m
(b) (colloq) (reminder) **to give sb a** ~ secouer (fam) qn
2 vtr (p prés etc **-dd-**) (also ~ **at**) (with foot, instrument, stick) donner des petits coups à; (with finger) toucher

prodigy n prodige m

✦ **produce** 1 n produits mpl
2 vtr (a) (cause) produire ‹result, effect›; provoquer ‹reaction, change›
(b) ‹region, farmer, company› produire (**from** à partir de); ‹worker, machine› fabriquer
(c) (generate) produire ‹heat, sound, energy›; rapporter ‹profits›
(d) (present) produire ‹passport, report›; fournir ‹evidence, argument, example›; **to** ~ **sth from** sortir qch de ‹pocket, bag›

✦ indicates a very frequent word

(e) produire ⟨*show, film*⟩; (GB) mettre [qch] en scène ⟨*play*⟩
(f) (put together) préparer ⟨*meal*⟩; mettre au point ⟨*timetable, package, solution*⟩; éditer ⟨*brochure, guide*⟩

◇ **producer** *n* **(a)** (of produce) producteur *m*; (of machinery, goods) fabricant *m*
(b) (of film) producteur/-trice *m/f*; (GB) (of play) metteur *m* en scène

◇ **product** *n* produit *m*

◇ **production** *n* **(a)** (of crop, foodstuffs, metal) production *f* (**of** de); (of machinery, furniture, cars) fabrication (**of** de)
(b) (output) production *f*
(c) (of film, opera) production *f* (**of** de); (of play) mise *f* en scène (**of** de)

production line *n* chaîne *f* de fabrication

productive *adj* ⟨*factory, land, day*⟩ productif/-ive; ⟨*system, method, use*⟩ efficace; ⟨*discussion*⟩ fructueux/-euse

productivity *n* productivité *f*

profane *adj* **(a)** (blasphemous) impie
(b) (secular) profane

profession *n* profession *f*

◇ **professional** ① *n* professionnel/-elle *m/f*
② *adj* professionnel/-elle

professionalism *n* (of person, organization) professionnalisme *m*; (of performance, work) (haute) qualité *f*

professionally *adv* **(a)** (expertly) ⟨*designed*⟩ par un professionnel
(b) (in work situation) dans un cadre professionnel
(c) ⟨*play sport*⟩ en professionnel/-elle; **he sings** ∼ il est chanteur professionnel
(d) (to a high standard) de manière professionnelle

◇ **professor** *n* **(a)** (Univ) (chair holder) professeur *m* d'Université
(b) (US Univ) (teacher) professeur *m*

proficiency *n* (practical) compétence *f* (**in, at** en); (academic) niveau *m* (**in** en)

proficient *adj* compétent/-e

profile *n* (of face) profil *m*; (of body) silhouette *f*; **in** ∼ de profil; **to have/maintain a high** ∼ occuper/rester sur le devant de la scène

profiling *n* (gen, Med) typage *m*

◇ **profit** ① *n* **(a)** bénéfice *m*, profit *m*; **gross/ net** ∼ bénéfice brut/net
(b) (figurative) profit *m*
② *vtr* profiter à ⟨*person, group*⟩
③ *vi* **to** ∼ **by** *or* **from sth** tirer profit de qch

profitable *adj* rentable; (figurative) fructueux/-euse

profit margin *n* marge *f* bénéficiaire

profit sharing *n* intéressement *m* des salariés aux bénéfices

profound *adj* profond/-e

profuse *adj* ⟨*praise, thanks*⟩ profus/-e; ⟨*bleeding*⟩ abondant/-e

profusely *adv* ⟨*sweat, bleed*⟩ abondamment; **to apologize** ∼ se confondre en excuses

prognosis *n* **(a)** (Med) pronostic *m* (**on, about** sur)
(b) (prediction) pronostics *mpl*

◇ **program** ① *n* **(a)** (Comput) programme *m*
(b) (US) (on radio, TV) émission *f*
② *vtr, vi* programmer (**to do** pour faire)

◇ **programme** (GB), **program** (US) ① *n* **(a)** (broadcast) émission *f* (**about** sur)
(b) (schedule) programme *m*
(c) (for play, opera) programme *m*
② *vtr* programmer ⟨*machine*⟩ (**to do** pour faire)

programmer *n* programmeur/-euse *m/f*

◇ **progress** ① *n* **(a)** (advances) progrès *m*; **to make** ∼ ⟨*person*⟩ faire des progrès
(b) (of person, inquiry) progression *f*; (of talks, disease, career) évolution *f*; **to be in** ∼ ⟨*discussions, exam*⟩ être en cours
② *vi* progresser

progression *n* **(a)** (evolution) évolution *f*
(b) (improvement) progression *f*
(c) (series) suite *f*

progressive *adj* **(a)** (gen) progressif/-ive
(b) (forward-looking) ⟨*person, policy*⟩ progressiste; ⟨*school*⟩ parallèle

progress report *n* (on construction work) rapport *m* sur l'état des travaux; (on project) rapport *m* sur l'état du projet; (on patient) bulletin *m* de santé

prohibit *vtr* interdire; **to** ∼ **sb from doing** interdire à qn de faire

prohibition *n* interdiction *f* (**on, against** de)

prohibitive *adj* prohibitif/-ive

◇ **project** ① *n* **(a)** (scheme) projet *m* (**to do** pour faire)
(b) (Sch) dossier *m* (**on** sur); (Univ) mémoire *m* (**on** sur); **research** ∼ programme *m* de recherches
(c) (US) (state housing) (large) ≈ cité *f* HLM; (small) ≈ lotissement *m* HLM
② *vtr* **(a)** envoyer ⟨*missile*⟩; faire porter ⟨*voice*⟩
(b) projeter ⟨*guilt, anxiety*⟩ (**onto** sur)
(c) (estimate) prévoir
(d) projeter ⟨*image, slides*⟩

projecting *adj* saillant/-e

projector *n* projecteur *m*

pro-life *adj* contre l'avortement

proliferate *vi* proliférer

prolific *adj* (gen) prolifique; ⟨*decade*⟩ fécond/-e; ⟨*growth*⟩ rapide

prologue *n* prologue *m* (**to** de)

prolong *vtr* prolonger

promenade *n* (path) promenade *f*; (by sea) front *m* de mer

p

prominent adj (a) ⟨figure, campaigner⟩ très en vue; ⟨artist⟩ éminent/-e; **to play a ~ part in sth** jouer un rôle de premier plan dans qch
(b) ⟨place, feature⟩ proéminent/-e; ⟨ridge, cheekbone⟩ saillant/-e; ⟨eye⟩ exorbité/-e

promiscuity n (sexual) vagabondage m sexuel

promiscuous adj ⟨person⟩ aux mœurs légères

ꝺ **promise** [1] n promesse f; **to break one's ~** manquer à sa promesse; **she shows great ~** elle promet beaucoup
[2] vtr **to ~ to do** promettre de faire; **to ~ sb sth** promettre qch à qn
[3] vi promettre; **do you ~?** c'est promis?

promising adj ⟨situation, result, future⟩ prometteur/-euse; ⟨artist, candidate⟩ qui promet

ꝺ **promote** vtr (a) (in rank) promouvoir (**to** à)
(b) (advertise) faire de la publicité pour; (market) promouvoir
(c) (encourage) promouvoir
(d) (GB) (in football) **to be ~d from the fourth to the third division** passer de quatrième en troisième division

promotion n promotion f

promotional video n vidéo f publicitaire

prompt [1] adj rapide; **to be ~ to do** être prompt/-e à faire
[2] vtr (a) provoquer ⟨reaction, decision⟩; susciter ⟨concern, comment⟩; **to ~ sb to do** inciter qn à faire
(b) (remind) souffler à ⟨actor⟩

prompter n (a) (in theatre) souffleur/-euse m/f
(b) (US) (teleprompter) téléprompteur m

promptly adv (a) (immediately) immédiatement
(b) (without delay) rapidement
(c) (punctually) à l'heure; **~ at six o'clock** à six heures précises

prone adj (a) **to be ~ to** être sujet/-ette à ⟨colds⟩; être enclin/-e à ⟨depression⟩
(b) **to lie ~** être allongé/-e face contre terre

pronoun n pronom m

pronounce vtr prononcer
■ **pronounce on** se prononcer sur ⟨case, matter⟩

pronounced adj ⟨accent, tendency⟩ prononcé/-e; ⟨change, increase⟩ marqué/-e

pronunciation n prononciation f

proof n (a) (evidence) preuve f; **~ of identity** pièce f d'identité
(b) (in printing, photography) épreuve f
(c) (of alcohol) **to be 70% ~** ≈ titrer 40° d'alcool

proof of purchase n justificatif m d'achat

proofread vtr (prét, pp **-read**) corriger les épreuves de

prop [1] n étai m
[2] **props** n pl accessoires mpl
[3] vtr (p prés etc **-pp-**) (a) (also **~ up**) étayer
(b) **to ~ sb/sth against sth** appuyer qn/qch contre qch

propaganda n propagande f

propagate vi se propager

propel vtr (p prés etc **-ll-**) propulser

propeller n hélice f

ꝺ **proper** adj (a) (right) ⟨term, spelling⟩ correct/-e; ⟨order, tool, response⟩ bon/bonne (before n); ⟨clothing⟩ qu'il faut; **everything is in the ~ place** tout est à sa place
(b) (adequate) ⟨recognition, facilities⟩ convenable; ⟨education, training⟩ bon/bonne (before n); ⟨care⟩ requis/-e
(c) (respectable) ⟨person⟩ correct/-e; ⟨upbringing⟩ convenable
(d) (real, full) ⟨doctor, holiday, job⟩ vrai/-e (before n)
(e) (actual) **in the village ~** dans le village même

ꝺ **properly** adv (a) (correctly) correctement
(b) (fully) complètement; **I didn't have time to thank you ~** je n'ai pas eu le temps de vous remercier
(c) (adequately) convenablement

proper name, **proper noun** n nom m propre

ꝺ **property** n (a) (belongings) propriété f, biens mpl
(b) (real estate) biens mpl immobiliers
(c) (house) propriété f
(d) (characteristic) propriété f

property developer n promoteur m immobilier

property owner n propriétaire mf

prophecy n prophétie f

prophet n prophète m

ꝺ **proportion** [1] n (a) (of group, population) proportion f (**of** de); (of income, profit, work) part f (**of** de)
(b) (ratio) proportion f
(c) (harmony) **out of/in ~** hors de/en proportion
(d) (perspective) **to get sth out of all ~** faire tout un drame de qch; **to be out of all ~** être tout à fait disproportionné/-e (**to** par rapport à)
[2] **proportions** n pl dimensions fpl

proportional adj proportionnel/-elle

proportional representation, **PR** n représentation f proportionnelle

ꝺ **proposal** n (a) (suggestion) proposition f
(b) (of marriage) demande f en mariage

ꝺ **propose** [1] vtr proposer ⟨course of action, solution⟩; présenter ⟨motion⟩
[2] vi faire sa demande en mariage (**to** à)

ꝺ indicates a very frequent word

③ **proposed** pp adj ‹action, reform›
envisagé/-e
proposition ① n (a) (suggestion)
proposition f
(b) (assertion) assertion f
② vtr faire une proposition à ‹person›
proprietor n propriétaire mf (of de)
propriety n (a) (politeness) correction f
(b) (morality) décence f
proscribe vtr proscrire
prose n (a) prose f
(b) (GB) (translation) thème m
prosecute ① vtr poursuivre [qn] en
justice
② vi engager des poursuites
prosecution n (Law) (a) (accusation)
poursuites fpl (judiciaires)
(b) the ∼ le/les plaignant/-s; (state, Crown) le
ministère public
prosecutor n (Law) procureur m
✓ **prospect** ① n (a) (hope) espoir m, chance
f
(b) (outlook) perspective f
② **prospects** n pl perspectives fpl
prospective adj ‹buyer, candidate›
potentiel/-ielle; ‹husband, wife› futur/-e
(before n)
prospectus n brochure f
prosper vi prospérer
prosperity n prospérité f
prosperous adj prospère
prostate n (also ∼ gland) prostate f
prostitute ① n prostituée f; male ∼
prostitué m
② vtr prostituer ‹person, talent›
prostitution n prostitution f
prostrate adj to lie ∼ être allongé/-e de
tout son long; ∼ with grief accablé/-e de
chagrin
protagonist n protagoniste mf
✓ **protect** vtr (gen) protéger (against contre;
from de, contre); défendre ‹consumer,
interests› (against contre)
✓ **protection** n protection f
protection factor n indice m de
protection
protection racket n racket m
protective adj protecteur/-trice
protein n protéine f
✓ **protest** ① n (a) protestation f; in ∼ en
signe de protestation
(b) (demonstration) manifestation f
② vtr (a) to ∼ that protester que; to ∼
one's innocence protester de son innocence
(b) (US) (complain about) protester contre (to
auprès de)
③ vi (a) (complain) protester
(b) (demonstrate) manifester (against contre)
Protestant n, adj protestant/-e m/f

protester n manifestant/-e m/f
protocol n protocole m
prototype n prototype m (of de)
protrude vi (gen) dépasser; ‹teeth› avancer
protruding adj ‹rock› en saillie; ‹eyes›
globuleux/-euse; ‹ears› décollé/-e; ‹ribs›
saillant/-e; ‹chin› en avant
✓ **proud** adj (a) fier/fière (of de); ‹owner›
heureux/-euse (before n)
(b) ‹day, moment› grand/-e (before n)
✓ **prove** ① vtr prouver; (by demonstration)
démontrer; to ∼ a point montrer qu'on a
raison
② vi to ∼ to be s'avérer être
③ v refl to ∼ oneself faire ses preuves; to
∼ oneself (to be) se révéler
proverb n proverbe m
✓ **provide** vtr (a) (supply) fournir ‹opportunity,
evidence, jobs, meals› (for à); apporter
‹answer, support› (for à); assurer ‹service,
access, training, shelter› (for à)
(b) ‹clause, law› prévoir (that que)
■ **provide for** (a) envisager ‹eventuality,
expenses›
(b) subvenir aux besoins de ‹family›; to be
well ∼d for être à l'abri du besoin
provided, providing conj (also ∼ that)
à condition que (+ subjunctive)
province n province f; in the ∼s en
province
provincial adj (a) ‹newspaper, town› de
province; ‹life› provincial/-e
(b) (narrow) provincial/-e
✓ **provision** ① n (a) (of goods, equipment)
fourniture f (of de; to à); (of service)
prestation f; ∼ of food/supplies
approvisionnement m (to de)
(b) (for future) dispositions fpl
(c) (in agreement) clause f; (in bill, act)
disposition f
② **provisions** n pl (supplies) provisions fpl
provisional adj provisoire
provocative adj (a) ‹dress, remark›
provocant/-e
(b) ‹book› qui fait réfléchir
provoke vtr (a) (annoy) provoquer
(b) (cause) susciter ‹anger, complaints›;
provoquer ‹laughter, reaction›
prow n proue f
prowess n (a) (skill) prouesses fpl
(b) (bravery) vaillance f
prowl ① vtr to ∼ the streets rôder dans
les rues
② vi ‹animal, person› rôder
proximity n proximité f
proxy n (a) (person) mandataire mf
(b) by ∼ par procuration
prudent adj prudent/-e
prudish adj pudibond/-e, prude
prune ① n (Culin) pruneau m
② vtr (cut back) tailler; (thin out) élaguer
pry vi to ∼ into mettre son nez dans

p

PS *n* (*abbr* = **postscriptum**) PS *m*
psalm *n* psaume *m*
pseudonym *n* pseudonyme *m*
psych *v* ■ **psych up** (colloq): **to** ∼ **oneself up** se préparer (psychologiquement) (**for** pour)
psychiatric *adj* psychiatrique
psychiatrist *n* psychiatre *mf*
psychiatry *n* psychiatrie *f*
psychic *n* médium *m*, voyant/-e *m/f*
psychoanalysis *n* psychanalyse *f*
psychological *adj* psychologique
psychologist *n* psychologue *mf*
psychology *n* psychologie *f*
psychopath *n* psychopathe *mf*
psychotherapist *n* psychothérapeute *mf*
PTO (*abbr* = **please turn over**) TSVP
pub *n* (GB) pub *m*
puberty *n* puberté *f*
ᕗ **public** ⟦1⟧ *n* **the** ∼ le public
  ⟦2⟧ *adj* (gen) public/-ique; ‹*library, amenity*› municipal/-e; ‹*duty, spirit*› civique; **to be in the** ∼ **eye** occuper le devant de la scène
  ⟦3⟧ **in public** *phr* en public
public address (system) *n* (système *m* de) sonorisation *f*
public assistance *n* (US) aide *f* sociale
ᕗ **publication** *n* publication *f*
public company *n* société *f* anonyme par actions
public convenience *n* (GB) toilettes *fpl*
public holiday *n* (GB) jour *m* férié
publicity *n* publicité *f*; **to attract** ∼ attirer l'attention des médias
publicity campaign *n* (to sell product) campagne *f* publicitaire; (to raise social issue) campagne *f* de sensibilisation
publicity stunt *n* coup *m* publicitaire
publicize *vtr* (a) attirer l'attention du public sur ‹*issue, problem*›
  (b) rendre [qch] public ‹*information, facts*›
  (c) faire de la publicité pour ‹*show*›
publicly *adv* publiquement
public opinion *n* opinion *f* publique
public prosecutor *n* procureur *m* général
public relations, PR *n* relations *fpl* publiques
public school *n* (GB) école *f* privée; (US) école *f* publique
public sector *n* secteur *m* public
public transport *n* transports *mpl* en commun
ᕗ **publish** *vtr* publier ‹*book, letter, guide*›; éditer ‹*newspaper, magazine*›
publisher *n* (a) (person) éditeur/-trice *mf*
  (b) (*also* **publishing house**) maison *f* d'édition

ᕗ indicates a very frequent word

publishing *n* édition *f*
pudding *n* (a) (GB) (dessert course) dessert *m*
  (b) (cooked dish) pudding *m*
  (c) (GB) (sausage) **black/white** ∼ boudin *m* noir/blanc
puddle *n* flaque *f*
puff ⟦1⟧ *n* (of air, smoke, steam) bouffée *f*; (of breath) souffle *m*
  ⟦2⟧ *vtr* tirer sur ‹*pipe*›
  ⟦3⟧ *vi* (a) **to** ∼ **at** tirer des bouffées de ‹*cigarette, pipe*›
  (b) (pant) souffler
  ■ **puff out** (a) gonfler ‹*cheeks*›; ‹*bird*› hérisser ‹*feathers*›
  (b) **to** ∼ **out smoke** lancer des bouffées de fumée
  ■ **puff up:** ⟦1⟧ ¶ ∼ **up** ‹*feathers*› se hérisser; ‹*eye*› devenir bouffi/-e; ‹*rice*› gonfler
  ⟦2⟧ ¶ ∼ **[sth] up** hérisser ‹*feathers, fur*›; ∼**ed up with pride** rempli/-e d'orgueil
puff pastry *n* pâte *f* feuilletée
puffy *adj* bouffi/-e
ᕗ **pull** ⟦1⟧ *n* (a) (tug) coup *m*; **to give sth a** ∼ tirer sur qch
  (b) (attraction) force *f*; (figurative) attrait *m* (**of** de)
  (c) (colloq) (influence) influence *f* (**over, with** sur)
  ⟦2⟧ *vtr* (a) (gen) tirer; tirer sur ‹*cord, rope*›; **to** ∼ **sb/sth through** faire passer qn/qch par ‹*hole, window*›; **to** ∼ **sth out of** tirer qch de ‹*pocket, drawer*›; **to** ∼ **sb out of** retirer qn de ‹*wreckage*›; sortir qn de ‹*river*›
  (b) (colloq) sortir ‹*gun, knife*›; **to** ∼ **a gun on sb** menacer qn avec un pistolet
  (c) appuyer sur ‹*trigger*›
  (d) se faire une élongation à ‹*muscle*›
  (e) **to** ∼ **a face** faire la grimace
  ⟦3⟧ *vi* tirer (**at, on** sur)
  ■ **pull apart** (a) (dismantle) démonter
  (b) (destroy) ‹*child*› mettre en pièces; ‹*animal*› déchiqueter
  ■ **pull away:** ⟦1⟧ ¶ ∼ **away** ‹*car*› démarrer
  ⟦2⟧ ¶ ∼ **[sb/sth] away** éloigner ‹*person*›; retirer ‹*hand*›; **to** ∼ **sb/sth away from** écarter qn/qch de ‹*window, wall*›
  ■ **pull back** (a) ‹*troops*› se retirer (**from** de)
  (b) ‹*car, person*› reculer
  ■ **pull down** démolir ‹*building*›; baisser ‹*blind, trousers*›
  ■ **pull in** ‹*car, bus, driver*› s'arrêter
  ■ **pull off** (a) ôter ‹*coat, sweater*›; enlever ‹*shoes, lid, sticker*›
  (b) conclure ‹*deal*›; réaliser ‹*feat*›
  ■ **pull out:** ⟦1⟧ ¶ ∼ **out** (a) ‹*car, truck*› déboîter; **to** ∼ **out of sth** quitter qch ‹*station, drive*›
  (b) ‹*troops, participants*› se retirer (**of** de)
  ⟦2⟧ ¶ ∼ **[sth] out** (a) extraire ‹*tooth*›; enlever ‹*splinter*›; arracher ‹*weeds*›
  (b) (from pocket) sortir
  ■ **pull over:** ⟦1⟧ ¶ ∼ **over** ‹*motorist, car*› s'arrêter (sur le côté)

2 ¶ ~ **[sb/sth] over** ‹police› forcer [qn/qch] à se ranger sur le côté
■ **pull through** ‹accident victim› s'en tirer
■ **pull together**: **1** ¶ ~ **together** faire un effort
2 ¶ ~ **oneself together** se ressaisir
■ **pull up**: **1** ¶ ~ **up's** s'arrêter
2 ¶ ~ **up [sth]**, ~ **[sth] up (a)** (uproot) arracher
(b) lever ‹anchor›; remonter ‹trousers, socks›; prendre ‹chair›
3 ¶ ~ **[sb] up (a)** (lift) hisser
(b) (reprimand) réprimander
(c) arrêter ‹driver›

pull-down menu n (Comput) menu m déroulant
pulley n poulie f
pullover n pull-over m
pulp **1** n (soft centre) pulpe f; (crushed mass) pâte f
2 vtr écraser ‹fruit, vegetable›; réduire [qch] en pâte ‹wood, cloth›; mettre [qch] au pilon ‹newspapers, books›
pulp fiction n littérature f de gare
pulpit n chaire f
pulse n pouls m
pulse rate n pouls m
pulverize vtr pulvériser
pump **1** n **(a)** (for air) pompe f; bicycle ~ pompe à vélo
(b) (plimsoll) chaussure f de sport; (GB) (flat shoe) ballerine f; (US) (shoe with heel) chaussure f à talon
2 vtr **(a)** pomper ‹air, gas, water› (out of de)
(b) (colloq) (question) cuisiner (fam) ‹person›
(c) (Med) **to** ~ **sb's stomach** faire un lavage d'estomac à qn
3 vi ‹heart› battre violemment
■ **pump up** gonfler ‹tyre, air bed›
pumpkin n citrouille f
pun n jeu m de mots, calembour m
punch **1** n **(a)** (blow) coup m de poing
(b) (of style, performance) énergie f
(c) (drink) punch m
2 vtr **(a)** donner un coup de poing à ‹person›; **to** ~ **sb in the face** donner un coup de poing dans la figure de qn
(b) perforer ‹cards, tape›; (manually) poinçonner ‹ticket›
Punch-and-Judy show n ≈ (spectacle m de) guignol m
punchbag n (GB) sac m de sable
punch line n chute f
punch-up n (GB) (colloq) bagarre f
punctual adj ponctuel/-elle
punctually adv ‹start, arrive, leave› à l'heure
punctuation n ponctuation f
punctuation mark n signe m de ponctuation

puncture **1** n crevaison f; **we had a** ~ **on the way** on a crevé en chemin
2 vtr crever ‹tyre, balloon, air bed›; **to** ~ **a lung** se perforer un poumon
puncture (repair) kit n boîte f de rustines®
pundit n expert/-e m/f
pungent adj ‹flavour› relevé/-e; ‹smell› fort/-e; ‹gas, smoke› âcre
punish vtr punir
punishment n punition f; (stronger) châtiment m
punitive adj punitif/-ive
punk **1** n **(a)** (music) punk m
(b) (punk rocker) punk mf
(c) (US) (colloq) voyou m
2 adj punk inv
punnet n (GB) barquette f
punt n **(a)** (boat) barque f (à fond plat)
(b) (Irish pound) livre f irlandaise
puny adj ‹person, body› chétif/-ive
pup n **(a)** (also **puppy**) chiot m
(b) (seal, otter) petit m
✓ **pupil** n **(a)** (Sch) élève mf
(b) (in eye) pupille f
puppet n marionnette f
✓ **purchase** **1** n achat m
2 vtr acheter
purchasing power n pouvoir m d'achat
pure adj pur/-e
puree n purée f
purely adv purement
purge **1** n purge f
2 vtr purger ‹party, system› (of de); expier ‹sin›
purify vtr (gen) purifier; épurer ‹water, chemical›
purist n, adj puriste mf
purity n pureté f
purple **1** n violet m
2 adj (bluish) violet/-ette; (reddish) pourpre
✓ **purpose** **1** n **(a)** (aim) but m; **for the** ~ **of doing** dans le but de faire
(b) (also **strength of** ~) résolution f
2 **on** ~ phr exprès
purposely adv exprès, intentionnellement
purpose-made adj fait/-e spécialement (**for** pour)
purr **1** n (of cat, engine) ronronnement m
2 vi ‹cat, engine› ronronner
purse n (for money) porte-monnaie m inv; (US) (handbag) sac m à main
IDIOM to hold the ~-**strings** tenir les cordons de la bourse
purser n commissaire m de bord
✓ **pursue** vtr **(a)** (chase) poursuivre
(b) poursuivre ‹aim, ambition, studies›; mener ‹policy›; se livrer à ‹occupation, interest›; **to** ~ **a career** faire carrière (**in** dans)

p

pursuer *n* poursuivant/-e *m/f*

pursuit *n* (a) poursuite *f*; **in ~ of** à la poursuite de; **in hot ~** à vos/ses etc trousses (b) (hobby) passe-temps *m inv*; **artistic ~s** activités *fpl* artistiques

◢ **push** ⟨1⟩ *n* poussée *f*; **to give sb/sth a ~** pousser qn/qch
⟨2⟩ *vtr* (a) pousser ⟨person, car, pram⟩; appuyer sur ⟨button, switch⟩; **to ~ sb/sth away** repousser qn/qch; **she ~ed him down the stairs** elle l'a poussé dans l'escalier; **to ~ sb aside** écarter qn; **to ~ sb too far** pousser qn à bout
(b) (colloq) (promote) promouvoir ⟨policy, theory⟩
(c) (colloq) (sell) vendre ⟨drugs⟩
⟨3⟩ *vi* pousser; **to ~ past sb** bousculer qn
IDIOMS **at a ~** (GB) s'il le faut; **to ~ one's luck** aller un peu trop loin

■ **push around** (colloq) (bully) bousculer ⟨person⟩

■ **push for** faire pression en faveur de ⟨reform⟩

■ **push in:** ⟨1⟩ **~ in** resquiller
⟨2⟩ **¶ ~ [sth] in** enfoncer ⟨button, door, window⟩

■ **push over:** ⟨1⟩ **~ over!** (colloq) pousse-toi!
⟨2⟩ **¶ ~ [sb/sth] over** renverser ⟨person, table, car⟩

■ **push through** faire voter ⟨bill, legislation⟩; faire passer ⟨deal⟩

push-button *adj* ⟨telephone⟩ à touches

pushchair *n* (GB) poussette *f*

pusher *n* (colloq) (*also* **drug ~**) revendeur/-euse *m/f* de drogue

push-start *vtr* pousser [qch] pour le/la faire démarrer ⟨vehicle⟩

push-up *n* (Sport) pompe *f* (fam)

pushy *adj* (colloq) (ambitious) arriviste; **she's very ~** (assertive) elle s'impose

◢ **put** *vtr* (*p prés* **-tt-**, *prét, pp* **put**) (a) (place) mettre ⟨object, person⟩ (**in** dans; **on** sur); **to ~ sth through** glisser qch dans ⟨letterbox⟩; **to ~ sb through** envoyer qn à ⟨university⟩; faire passer qn par ⟨ordeal⟩; faire passer [qch] à qn ⟨test⟩; **to ~ one's hand to** porter la main à ⟨mouth⟩
(b) (devote, invest) **to ~ money/energy into sth** investir de l'argent/son énergie dans qch; **to ~ a lot into** s'engager à fond pour ⟨work, project⟩; sacrifier beaucoup à ⟨marriage⟩
(c) **to ~ money towards** donner de l'argent pour ⟨gift⟩; **~ it towards some new clothes** sers-t'en pour acheter des vêtements; **to ~ tax on sth** taxer qch
(d) (express) **to ~ it bluntly** pour parler franchement; **let me ~ it another way** laissez-moi m'exprimer différemment
IDIOM **I wouldn't ~ it past him!** ça ne m'étonnerait pas de lui!

■ **put across** communiquer ⟨idea, case⟩

■ **put away** (a) (tidy away) ranger
(b) (save) mettre [qch] de côté
(c) (colloq) avaler ⟨food⟩; descendre (fam) ⟨drink⟩

■ **put back** (a) (return) remettre; **to ~ sth back where it belongs** remettre qch à sa place
(b) remettre ⟨meeting⟩ (**to** à; **until** jusqu'à)
(c) retarder ⟨clock, watch⟩

■ **put down** ⟨1⟩ **¶ ~ [sth] down** (a) poser ⟨object⟩
(b) réprimer ⟨rebellion⟩
(c) (write down) mettre (par écrit)
(d) **to ~ sth down to** mettre qch sur le compte de; **to ~ sth down to the fact that** imputer qch au fait que
(e) (by injection) piquer ⟨animal⟩
(f) **to ~ down a deposit** verser des arrhes; **to ~ £50 down on sth** verser 50 livres sterling d'arrhes sur qch
⟨2⟩ **¶ ~ [sb] down** (a) déposer ⟨passenger⟩
(b) (humiliate) rabaisser

■ **put forward** (a) (propose) avancer ⟨theory, name⟩; soumettre ⟨plan⟩; présenter la candidature de ⟨person⟩
(b) (in time) avancer ⟨meeting, date, clock⟩ (**by** de; **to** à)

■ **put in:** ⟨1⟩ **¶ ~ in** (a) ⟨ship⟩ faire escale (**at** à; **in** dans)
(b) **to ~ in for** postuler pour ⟨job, promotion, rise⟩; demander ⟨transfer⟩
⟨2⟩ **¶ ~ [sth] in** (a) installer ⟨heating, units⟩
(b) (make) faire ⟨request, claim⟩; **to ~ in an appearance** faire une apparition
(c) passer ⟨time⟩
(d) (insert) mettre

■ **put off:** ⟨1⟩ **¶ ~ [sth] off** (a) (delay, defer) remettre [qch] (à plus tard)
(b) (turn off) éteindre ⟨light, radio⟩
⟨2⟩ **¶ ~ [sb] off** (a) décommander ⟨guest⟩; dissuader ⟨person⟩; **to be easily put off** se décourager facilement
(b) (repel) ⟨appearance, smell⟩ dégoûter; ⟨manner, person⟩ déconcerter

■ **put on** (a) mettre ⟨garment, make-up⟩
(b) allumer ⟨light, heating⟩; mettre ⟨record, music⟩; **to ~ the kettle on** mettre de l'eau à chauffer
(c) prendre ⟨weight, kilo⟩
(d) (produce) monter ⟨play, exhibition⟩
(e) (adopt) prendre ⟨accent, expression⟩; **he's ~ting it on** il fait semblant

■ **put out** (a) (extend) tendre ⟨hand⟩; **to ~ out one's tongue** tirer la langue
(b) éteindre ⟨fire, cigarette⟩
(c) sortir ⟨bin, garbage⟩; faire sortir ⟨cat⟩
(d) diffuser ⟨warning, statement⟩
(e) mettre ⟨food, towels⟩
(f) (dislocate) se démettre ⟨shoulder⟩
(g) (inconvenience) déranger ⟨person⟩; (annoy) contrarier ⟨person⟩

■ **put through** (a) (implement) faire passer ⟨bill, reform⟩
(b) passer ⟨caller⟩ (**to** à)

◢ indicates a very frequent word

■ **put together** (a) (assemble) assembler
⟨pieces, parts⟩; **to ~ sth back together**
reconstituer qch
(b) (place together) mettre ensemble
(c) établir ⟨list⟩; faire ⟨film, programme⟩
(d) construire ⟨argument⟩
■ **put up**: ⏹1 ¶ ~ **up [sth]** opposer
⟨resistance⟩; **to ~ up a fight** combattre
⏹2 ¶ ~ **[sth] up** (a) hisser ⟨flag, sail⟩; relever
⟨hair⟩; **to ~ up one's hand** lever la main
(b) mettre ⟨sign, plaque⟩; afficher ⟨list⟩
(c) dresser ⟨fence, tent⟩
(d) augmenter ⟨rent, prices, tax⟩; faire
monter ⟨temperature⟩
(e) (provide) fournir ⟨money⟩
⏹3 ¶ ~ **[sb] up** (a) (lodge) héberger
(b) **to ~ sb up to sth** pousser qn à qch
■ **put up with** supporter ⟨person, situation⟩

put-down n remarque f humiliante
putt ⏹1 n putt m
⏹2 vi putter
putty n mastic m
puzzle ⏹1 n (a) (mystery) mystère m
(b) (game) casse-tête m inv
⏹2 vtr déconcerter
puzzle book n livre m de jeux
puzzled adj perplexe
PVC n (abbr = **polyvinyl chloride**) PVC m
pygmy n pygmée mf
pyjamas (GB), **pajamas** (US) n pl
pyjama m; **a pair of ~** un pyjama
pylon n pylône m
pyramid n pyramide f
python n python m

Q q

q, **Q** n q, Q m
quack ⏹1 n (a) (of duck) coin-coin m inv
(b) (GB) (colloq) (doctor) toubib m (fam)
(c) (impostor) charlatan m
⏹2 vi cancaner
quadrangle n (a) (shape) quadrilatère m
(b) (courtyard) cour f carrée
quadruple ⏹1 n, adj quadruple m
⏹2 vtr, vi quadrupler
quadruplet n quadruplé/-e m/f
quagmire n bourbier m
quail ⏹1 n (pl ~**s** ou collect ~) caille f; ~'**s**
egg œuf m de caille
⏹2 vi trembler
quaint adj (a) (pretty) pittoresque
(b) (old-world) au charme vieillot
(c) (odd) bizarre
quake vi trembler
qualification n (a) (diploma, degree)
diplôme m (**in** en); (experience, skills)
qualification f
(b) (restriction) restriction f; **without ~** sans
réserves
qualified adj (a) (for job) (having diploma)
diplômé/-e; (having experience, skills) qualifié/-e
(b) (competent) (having authority) qualifié/-e
(**to do** pour faire); (having knowledge)
compétent/-e (**to do** pour faire)
(c) (modified) nuancé/-e, mitigé/-e
qualifier n (contestant) qualifié/-e m/f;
(match) éliminatoire f
⚹ **qualify** ⏹1 vtr (a) (modify) nuancer
⟨approval, opinion⟩; préciser ⟨statement,
remark⟩
(b) (entitle) **to ~ sb to do** donner à qn le droit

de faire
⏹2 vi (a) (get diploma, degree) obtenir son
diplôme (**as** dc, cn)
(b) (be eligible) remplir les conditions
(requises); **to ~ for** avoir droit à
⟨membership, legal aid⟩; **to ~ to do** avoir le
droit de faire
(c) (Sport) se qualifier
qualitative adj qualitatif/-ive
⚹ **quality** ⏹1 n qualité f
⏹2 adj de qualité
quality control n contrôle m de qualité
qualm n scrupule m
quandary n embarras m; (serious) dilemme
m
quantifiable adj facile à évaluer
quantify vtr quantifier
quantitative adj quantitatif/-ive
quantity n quantité f; **in ~** en grande
quantité
quantity surveyor n (GB) métreur m
quantum leap n saut m quantique;
(figurative) bond m prodigieux
quarantine ⏹1 n quarantaine f; **in ~** en
quarantaine
⏹2 vtr mettre [qn/qch] en quarantaine
quarrel ⏹1 n dispute f (**between** entre; **over**
au sujet de); **to have a ~** se disputer
⏹2 vi (p prés etc **-ll-** (GB), **-l-** (US)) (a) (argue)
se disputer
(b) (sever relations) se brouiller
(c) **to ~ with** contester ⟨claim, idea⟩; se
plaindre de ⟨price, verdict⟩
quarrelling (GB), **quarreling** (US) n
disputes fpl

p
q

quarrelsome *adj* ⟨person⟩ querelleur/
-euse; ⟨remark⟩ agressif/-ive

quarry ⚀ *n* (a) (in ground) carrière *f*
(b) (prey) proie *f*; (in hunting) gibier *m*
⚁ *vtr* extraire ⟨stone⟩

quarry tile *n* carreau *m* de terre cuite

quart *n* (GB) = *1.136 l* (US) = *0.946 l*

◦ᐟ **quarter** ⚀ *n* (a) (one fourth) quart *m*; **in a ~
of an hour** dans un quart d'heure
(b) (three months) trimestre *m*
(c) (district) quartier *m*
⚁ **quarters** *n pl* (Mil) quartiers *mpl*; (gen)
logement *m*
⚂ *pron* (a) (25%) quart *m*; **only a ~ passed**
seul le quart a réussi
(b) (in time phrases) **at (a) ~ to 11** (GB), **at a ~
of 11** (US) à onze heures moins le quart; **an
hour and a ~** une heure et quart
⚃ *adj* **a ~ century** un quart de siècle
⚄ *adv* **a ~ full** au quart plein; **~ the price**
quatre fois moins cher
⚅ *vtr* couper [qch] en quatre ⟨cake, apple⟩
⚆ **at close quarters** *phr* de près

quarterfinal *n* quart *m* de finale

quarterly ⚀ *adj* trimestriel/-ielle
⚁ *adv* tous les trois mois

quartermaster *n* (in army) intendant *m*;
(in navy) maître *m* de timonerie

quartet *n* quatuor *m*; **jazz ~** quartette *m*

quartz *n* quartz *m*

quash *vtr* rejeter ⟨proposal⟩; réprimer
⟨rebellion⟩

quasi(-) *pref* quasi (+ *adj*) quasi- (+ *n*)

quaver ⚀ *n* (a) (GB Mus) croche *f*
(b) (trembling) tremblement *m* (in dans)
⚁ *vi* trembloter

quay *n* quai *m*; **on the ~** sur le quai

quayside *n* quai *m*

queasiness *n* nausée *f*

queasy *adj* **to be** *or* **feel ~** avoir mal au
cœur

Quebec *pr n* Québec *m*; **in ~** (city) à
Québec; (province) au Québec

◦ᐟ **queen** *n* (a) (gen) reine *f*
(b) (in cards) dame *f*

queen bee *n* reine *f* des abeilles

queen mother *n* Reine mère *f*

Queen's Counsel, QC *n* (GB Law) avocat
m éminent

queer *adj* (a) (strange) étrange, bizarre
(b) (suspicious) louche, suspect

quell *vtr* étouffer ⟨anger, anxiety, revolt⟩

quench *vtr* étancher ⟨thirst⟩; étouffer
⟨desire⟩

querulous *adj* grincheux/-euse

query ⚀ *n* question *f* (about au sujet de);
a ~ from sb une question venant de qn
⚁ *vtr* mettre en doute; **to ~ whether**
demander si

◦ᐟ indicates a very frequent word

quest *n* quête *f*; **the ~ for sb/sth** la
recherche de qn/qch

◦ᐟ **question** ⚀ *n* (a) (gen) question *f* (about
sur); **to ask sb a ~** poser une question à
qn; **it's a ~ of doing** il s'agit de faire; **that's
another ~** c'est une autre affaire; **there was
never any ~ of you paying** il n'a jamais été
question que tu paies; **the person in ~** la
personne en question; **it's out of the ~ for
him to leave** il est hors de question qu'il
parte
(b) (doubt) doute *m*; **to call sth into ~** mettre
qch en doute; **it's open to ~** cela se discute
⚁ *vtr* (a) (interrogate) questionner ⟨suspect,
politician⟩
(b) (cast doubt upon) mettre en doute ⟨tactics,
methods⟩

questionable *adj* (a) (debatable)
discutable
(b) (dubious) douteux/-euse

questioner *n* interrogateur/-trice *m/f*

questioning *n* (of person) interrogation
f; **to bring sb in for ~** amener qn pour
interrogatoire

question mark *n* point *m* d'interrogation

questionnaire *n* questionnaire *m* (on sur)

queue ⚀ *n* (GB) (of people) queue *f*, file *f*
(d'attente); (of vehicles) file *f*; **to stand in a
~** faire la queue; **to join the ~** ⟨person⟩ se
mettre à la queue; ⟨car⟩ se mettre dans la file;
to jump the ~ (colloq) passer avant son tour
⚁ *vi* (also **~ up**) ⟨people⟩ faire la queue (for
pour); ⟨taxis⟩ attendre en ligne

queue-jump *vi* resquiller, passer avant
son tour

quibble *vi* chicaner (about, over sur)

◦ᐟ **quick** ⚀ *n* **to bite one's nails to the ~** se
ronger les ongles jusqu'au sang
⚁ *adj* (a) (speedy) ⟨pace, reply, profit, meal⟩
rapide; ⟨storm, shower⟩ bref/brève (before
n); **to have a ~ coffee** prendre un café en
vitesse; **to have a ~ wash** faire une toilette
rapide; **she's a ~ worker** elle travaille vite;
the ~est way to do le meilleur moyen de
faire; **to make a ~ recovery** se rétablir vite;
be ~ (about it)! dépêche-toi!
(b) (clever) ⟨child, student⟩ vif/vive d'esprit
(c) (prompt) ⟨reaction⟩ vif/vive; **to be a ~
learner** apprendre vite
⚂ *adv* **~!** vite!; **~ as a flash** avec la rapidité
de l'éclair
IDIOM to cut *or* **sting sb to the ~** piquer qn
au vif

quicken ⚀ *vtr* accélérer ⟨pace⟩; stimuler
⟨interest⟩
⚁ *vi* ⟨pace⟩ s'accélérer; ⟨anger⟩ s'intensifier

quick-fire *adj* rapide

quicklime *n* chaux *f* vive

◦ᐟ **quickly** *adv* (rapidly) vite, rapidement;
(without delay) sans tarder; **(come) ~!** (viens)
vite!

quick march *n* (Mil) ≈ pas *m* cadencé

quicksand *n* sables *mpl* mouvants;
(figurative) bourbier *m*

q

quicksilver n mercure m
quick-tempered adj coléreux/-euse
quick time n (US) marche f rapide
quid n (pl ~) (GB) (colloq) livre f (sterling)
⚘ **quiet** ⨿ n (a) (silence) silence m
(b) (peace) tranquillité f
(c) (colloq) (secret) **on the ~** discrètement
⨪ adj (a) (silent) ⟨church, person, room⟩
silencieux/-ieuse; **to keep ~** garder le
silence; **to go ~** se taire; **to keep sb ~** faire
taire ⟨dog, child⟩; **be ~** (stop talking) tais-toi;
(make no noise) ne fais pas de bruit
(b) (not noisy) ⟨voice⟩ bas/basse; ⟨engine⟩
silencieux/-ieuse; ⟨music⟩ doux/douce; **in a
~ voice** à voix basse; **to keep the children ~**
⟨activity⟩ tenir les enfants tranquilles
(c) (discreet) discret/-ete; **to have a ~ word
with sb** prendre qn à part pour lui parler
(d) (calm) ⟨village, holiday, night, life⟩
tranquille
(e) ⟨meal⟩ intime; ⟨wedding⟩ célébré/-e dans
l'intimité
(f) (secret) **to keep [sth] ~** ne pas divulguer
⟨plans⟩; garder [qch] secret/-ète ⟨engagement⟩
■ **quiet down** (US) ▶ QUIETEN DOWN
quieten vtr (a) (calm) calmer ⟨person,
animal⟩
(b) (silence) faire taire ⟨critics, children⟩
■ **quieten down** (GB): ⨿ ¶ **~ down** (a)
(become calm) ⟨person, activity⟩ se calmer
(b) (fall silent) se taire
⨪ ¶ **~ [sb/sth] down** (calm) calmer
(silence) faire taire
⚘ **quietly** adv (a) (not noisily) ⟨move⟩ sans bruit;
⟨cough, speak⟩ doucement
(b) (silently) ⟨play, read, sit⟩ en silence
(c) (calmly) calmement
quietness n (a) (silence) silence m
(b) (of voice) faiblesse f
(c) (of place) tranquillité f
quiff n (GB) (on forehead) toupet m; (on top of
head) houppe f
quill n (a) (feather) penne f; (stem of feather)
tuyau m de plume
(b) (on porcupine) piquant m
(c) (also ~ **pen**) plume f d'oie
quilt ⨿ n (a) (GB) (duvet) couette f
(b) (bed cover) dessus m de lit
⨪ vtr matelasser
quinine n quinine f
quintuplet n quintuplé/-e m/f
quip ⨿ n trait m d'esprit
⨪ vi (p prés etc **-pp-**) plaisanter
quirk n (of person) excentricité f; (of fate,
nature) caprice m
quit ⨿ vtr (p prés etc **-tt-**, prét, pp **quitted** ou
quit) démissionner de ⟨job⟩; quitter ⟨place,
person, profession⟩
⨪ vi (p prés etc **-tt-**, prét, pp **quitted** ou **quit**)
(a) (give up) arrêter (**doing** de faire)
(b) (resign) démissionner
⚘ **quite** adv (a) (completely) ⟨new, ready,
understand⟩ tout à fait; ⟨alone, empty,

exhausted⟩ complètement; ⟨impossible⟩
totalement; ⟨extraordinary⟩ vraiment; **I ~
agree** je suis tout à fait d'accord; **you're ~
right** vous avez entièrement raison; **it's ~ all
right** c'est sans importance; **are you ~ sure?**
en êtes-vous certain?; **~ clearly** ⟨see⟩ très
clairement
(b) (exactly) **not ~** pas exactement; **I don't ~
know** je ne sais pas du tout
(c) (rather) ⟨big, easily, often⟩ assez; **it's ~
small** ce n'est pas très grand; **it's ~ warm
today** il fait bon aujourd'hui; **it's ~ likely
that** il est très probable que; **I ~ like Chinese
food** j'aime assez la cuisine chinoise; **~ a
few** un bon nombre de ⟨people, examples⟩; **~
a lot of money** pas mal d'argent; **I've thought
about it ~ a bit** j'y ai pas mal réfléchi
(d) (as intensifier) **~ simply** tout simplement;
~ a difference une différence considérable;
that will be ~ a change for you ce sera un
grand changement pour toi; **she's ~ a
woman!** quelle femme!
(e) (expressing agreement) **~ (so)** c'est sûr
quits adj (colloq) **to be ~** être quitte (**with sb**
envers qn)
quiver ⨿ n (a) tremblement m
(b) (for arrows) carquois m
⨪ vi ⟨voice, lip, animal⟩ trembler (**with** de);
⟨leaves⟩ frémir; ⟨flame⟩ vaciller
quiz ⨿ n (pl **~zes**) (a) (game) jeu m
de questions-réponses, quiz m; (written, in
magazine) questionnaire m (**about** sur)
(b) (US Sch) interrogation f
⨪ vtr (p prés etc **-zz-**) questionner (**about**
au sujet de)
quiz game, **quiz show** n jeu m de
questions-réponses
quizzical adj interrogateur/-trice
quota n (a) (prescribed number, amount) quota
m (**of**, for de)
(b) (share) part f (**of** de); (officially allocated)
quote-part f
quotation n (a) (quote) citation f
(b) (estimate) devis m
quotation marks n pl (also **quotes**)
guillemets mpl; **in ~** entre guillemets
⚘ **quote** ⨿ n (a) (quotation) citation f (**from** de)
(b) (statement to journalist) déclaration f
(c) (estimate) devis m
⨪ **quotes** n pl = QUOTATION MARKS
⨫ vtr (a) citer ⟨person, passage, proverb⟩;
rapporter ⟨words⟩; rappeler ⟨reference
number⟩; **she was ~d as saying that...** elle
aurait dit que...
(b) (state) indiquer ⟨price, figure⟩; **they ~d us
£200** dans leur devis, ils ont demandé £200
sterling
(c) (on stock exchange) coter ⟨share, price⟩ (**at** à)
(d) (in betting) **to be ~d 6 to 1** être coté/-e 6
contre 1
⨬ vi (from text, author) faire des citations; **to
~ from Keats** citer Keats

q

Rr

r, **R** *n* r, R *m*

rabbi *n* rabbin *m*

rabbit *n* lapin *m*

rabid *adj* (a) (with rabies) enragé/-e
(b) (fanatical) fanatique

rabies *n* rage *f*

ơ **race** ① *n* (a) (gen, Sport) course *f*; **to have a ~** faire la course
(b) (ethnic group) race *f*
② *vtr* faire la course avec ‹person, car, horse› (**to** jusqu'à)
③ *vi* (a) (gen, Sport) courir; **to ~ in/away** entrer/partir en courant
(b) (hurry) se dépêcher (**to do** de faire)
(c) ‹heart› battre précipitamment; ‹engine› s'emballer

racehorse *n* cheval *m* de course

racer *n* (bike) vélo *m* de course

race relations *n pl* relations *fpl* inter-raciales

racetrack *n* (for horses) champ *m* de courses; (for cars) circuit *m*; (for dogs, cycles) piste *f*

racial *adj* racial/-e

racing *n* courses *fpl*

racing car *n* voiture *f* de course

racing cyclist *n* coureur/-euse *m/f* cycliste

racing driver *n* coureur/-euse *m/f* automobile

racism *n* racisme *m*

racist *n, adj* raciste *mf*

rack ① *n* (a) (for plates) égouttoir *m*; (for clothes) portant *m*; (for bottles) casier *m*
(b) = ROOF RACK
(c) (torture) chevalet *m*
② *vtr* ~**ed with** torturé/-e par ‹guilt›
IDIOM **to ~ one's brains** se creuser la cervelle (fam)

racket *n* (a) (*also* **racquet**) (Sport) raquette *f*
(b) (colloq) (noise) vacarme *m*
(c) (swindle) escroquerie *f*

racketeering *n* racket *m*

racquetball *n* (US) ≈ squash *m*

racy *adj* (a) (lively) plein/-e de verve
(b) (risqué) osé/-e

radar *n* radar *m*

radiant *adj* radieux/-ieuse

radiate *vtr* (a) rayonner de ‹happiness›; déborder de ‹confidence›
(b) émettre ‹heat›

ơ indicates a very frequent word

radiation *n* (medical, nuclear) radiation *f*; (rays) radiations *fpl*

radiation exposure *n* irradiation *f*

radiation sickness *n* maladie *f* des rayons

radiator *n* radiateur *m*

radical *n, adj* radical/-e *m/f*

ơ **radio** ① *n* (*pl* ~**s**) radio *f*; **on the ~** à la radio
② *adj* ‹signal› radio *inv*; ‹programme› de radio
③ *vtr* (3ᵉ *pers sg prés* ~**s**, *prét, pp* ~**ed**) **to ~ sth (to sb)** communiquer qch par radio (à qn)
④ *vi* (3ᵉ *pers sg prés* ~**s**, *prét, pp* ~**ed**) **to ~ for help** appeler au secours par radio

radioactive *adj* radioactif/-ive

radio alarm *n* radio-réveil *m*

radio announcer *n* speaker/-erine *m/f*

radio cassette (recorder) *n* radiocassette *f*

radiology *n* radiologie *f*

radio station *n* (channel) station *f* de radio; (installation) station *f* émettrice

radiotherapy *n* radiothérapie *f*

radish *n* radis *m*

radius *n* (*pl* -**dii** *ou* -**diuses**) rayon *m*

raffle *n* tombola *f*

raft *n* radeau *m*

rafter *n* chevron *m*

rag *n* (a) (cloth) chiffon *m*
(b) (colloq) (newspaper) torchon *m* (fam)

rage ① *n* (a) rage *f*, colère *f*; **to fly into a ~** entrer dans une colère noire
(b) (colloq) **to be (all) the ~** faire fureur
② *vi* (a) ‹storm, battle› faire rage
(b) ‹person› tempêter (**at, against** contre)

ragged *adj* (a) ‹garment› en loques; ‹cuff, collar› effiloché/-e; ‹person› dépenaillé/-e
(b) ‹outline› déchiqueté/-e

raging *adj* (a) ‹passion, argument› violent/-e; ‹thirst, pain› atroce; **a ~ toothache** une rage de dents
(b) ‹blizzard, sea› déchaîné/-e

rags *n pl* loques *fpl*; **in ~** en haillons

raid ① *n* raid *m* (**on** sur); (on bank) hold-up *m* (**on** de); (by police, customs) rafle *f* (**on** dans)
② *vtr* ‹military› faire un raid sur; ‹police› faire une rafle dans; ‹criminals› attaquer ‹bank›

raider *n* (a) (thief) pillard *m*
(b) (*also* **corporate ~**) raider *m*

rail n (a) (on balcony) balustrade f; (on tower) garde-fou m; (handrail) rampe f
(b) (for curtains) tringle f
(c) (for train) rail m; **by** ~ par chemin de fer
railing n (also ~s) grille f
railroad n (US) (a) (network) chemin m de fer
(b) (also ~ **track**) voie f ferrée
railroad car n (US) wagon m
railway n (GB) (a) (network) chemin m de fer
(b) (also ~ **line**) ligne f de chemin de fer
(c) (also ~ **track**) voie f ferrée
railway carriage n (GB) wagon m
railway station n (GB) gare f
✓ **rain** ⟦1⟧ n pluie f; **in the** ~ sous la pluie
⟦2⟧ v impers pleuvoir; **it's** ~**ing (hard)** il pleut (à verse)
rainbow n arc-en-ciel m
raincoat n imperméable m
raindrop n goutte f de pluie
rainfall n niveau m de précipitations
rain forest n forêt f tropicale
rainy adj ‹afternoon, climate› pluvieux/-ieuse
rainy season n saison f des pluies
✓ **raise** ⟦1⟧ n (US) (pay rise) augmentation f
⟦2⟧ vtr (a) (lift) lever ‹baton, barrier, curtain›; hisser ‹flag›; soulever ‹lid›; renflouer ‹sunken ship›; **to** ~ **one's hand/head** lever la main/tête
(b) (increase) augmenter ‹price, offer, salary› (from de; to à); élever ‹standard›; reculer ‹age limit›; **to** ~ **one's voice** (to be heard) parler plus fort; (in anger) hausser le ton; **to** ~ **the bidding** (in gambling) monter la mise; (at auction) monter l'enchère
(c) (cause) faire naître ‹fears›; soulever ‹dust›
(d) (mention) soulever ‹issue, objection›
(e) (bring up) élever ‹child, family›
(f) (breed) élever ‹livestock›
(g) (find) trouver ‹capital›
(h) (collect) lever ‹tax›; ‹person› collecter ‹money›
(i) (end) lever ‹ban›
(j) (give) **to** ~ **the alarm** donner l'alarme
raised adj ‹platform, jetty› surélevé/-e; ~ **voices** des éclats de voix
raisin n raisin m sec
rake ⟦1⟧ n râteau m
⟦2⟧ vtr ratisser ‹grass, leaves›
■ **rake up**: ~ **up [sth]**, ~ **[sth] up** ressusciter ‹grievance›; remuer ‹past›
rally ⟦1⟧ n (a) (meeting) rassemblement m
(b) (race) rallye m
(c) (in tennis) échange m
⟦2⟧ vtr rassembler ‹support, troops›
⟦3⟧ vi (a) ‹people› se rallier (**to** à)
(b) (recover) ‹patient› se rétablir
rallying call n cri m de ralliement
ram ⟦1⟧ n bélier m
⟦2⟧ vtr (p prés etc **-mm-**) (a) (crash into) rentrer dans, heurter
(b) (push) enfoncer

RAM n (Comput) (abbr = **random access memory**) RAM f
ramble n randonnée f, balade f
■ **ramble on** discourir (**about** sur)
rambler n randonneur/-euse m/f
rambling adj (a) ‹house› plein/-e de coins et de recoins
(b) ‹talk, article› décousu/-e
ramification n ramification f
ramp n rampe f; (GB) (to slow traffic) ralentisseur m; (up to plane) passerelle f; (US) (slip road) bretelle f
rampage n **to be** or **go on the** ~ tout saccager
rampant adj ‹crime, disease› endémique
rampart n rempart m
ram raid ⟦1⟧ n casse f à la voiture bélier
⟦2⟧ vtr dévaliser [qch] à l'aide d'une voiture bélier
ramshackle adj délabré/-e
ranch n ranch m
rancid adj rance; **to go** ~ rancir
random adj (fait/-e) au hasard
✓ **range** ⟦1⟧ n (a) (of prices, products) gamme f; (of activities) éventail m, choix m; (of radar, weapon) portée f (**of** de)
(b) (US) (prairie) prairie f
(c) (of mountains) chaîne f
(d) (stove) (wood) fourneau m
(e) (also **shooting** ~) champ m de tir
⟦2⟧ vi (a) (vary) varier (**between** entre)
(b) (cover) **to** ~ **over sth** couvrir qch
ranger n garde-forestier m
rank ⟦1⟧ n (a) (gen) rang m; (in military, police) grade m; **to break** ~s ‹soldiers› rompre les rangs; **to close** ~s serrer les rangs
(b) taxi ~ station f de taxis
⟦2⟧ adj (a) ‹outsider, beginner› complet/-ète
(b) ‹odour› fétide
⟦3⟧ vtr classer (**among** parmi)
⟦4⟧ vi se classer (**among** parmi)
rank and file n **the** ~ la base f
ranking n classement m
rankle vi **it still** ~s je ne l'ai pas encore digéré (fam)
ransack vtr fouiller ‹drawer› (**for** pour trouver); mettre [qch] à sac ‹house›
ransom n rançon f; **to hold sb to** (GB) or **for** (US) ~ garder qn en otage
rant vi déclamer; **to** ~ **and rave** tempêter
rap ⟦1⟧ n (a) (tap) coup m sec
(b) (music) rap m
⟦2⟧ vtr (p prés etc **-pp-**) frapper sur ‹table, door›
rape ⟦1⟧ n (a) (attack) viol m
(b) (plant) colza m
⟦2⟧ vtr violer
rapid adj rapide
rapidly adv rapidement
rapids n pl rapides mpl

r

rapist *n* violeur *m*

rapper *n* (Mus) rappeur/-euse *m/f*

rapport *n* bons rapports *mpl*

rapture *n* ravissement *m*; **to go into** ~**s about sth** s'extasier sur qch

rapturous *adj* ‹*delight*› extasié/-e; ‹*applause*› frénétique

⚹ **rare** *adj* **(a)** (uncommon) rare
(b) ‹*steak*› saignant/-e

rarely *adv* rarement

raring *adj* **to be** ~ **to do** être très impatient/-e de faire; **to be** ~ **to go** piaffer d'impatience

rarity *n* **(a) to be a** ~ ‹*occurrence*› être rare; ‹*plant*› être une plante rare; ‹*collector's item*› être une pièce rare
(b) (rareness) rareté *f*

rascal *n* coquin/-e *m/f*

rash **1** *n* **(a)** (on skin) rougeurs *fpl*
(b) (figurative) vague *f* (**of** de)
2 *adj* irréfléchi/-e

rasher *n* tranche *f*

raspberry *n* framboise *f*

rasping *adj* ‹*voice, sound*› râpeux/-euse

rat *n* rat *m*

⚹ **rate** **1** *n* **(a)** (speed) rythme *m*; **at this** ~ (figurative) à ce train-là
(b) (level) taux *m*; **the interest** ~ le taux d'intérêt
(c) (charge, fee) tarif *f*
(d) (in foreign exchange) cours *m*
2 rates *n pl* (GB) impôts *mpl* locaux;
business ~**s** ≈ taxe *f* professionnelle
3 *vtr* **(a)** (classify) **to** ~ **sb as sth** considérer qn comme qch; **to** ~ **sb among** classer qn parmi
(b) estimer ‹*honesty, friendship, person*›
IDIOM at any ~ en tout cas

ratepayer *n* (GB) contribuable *m/f*

⚹ **rather** *adv* **(a)** plutôt (**than** que); **I** ~ **like him** je le trouve plutôt sympathique; **it's** ~ **like an apple** ça ressemble un peu à une pomme
(b) (preferably) **I would (much)** ~ **do** je préférerais (de loin) faire (**than do** que faire); **I'd** ~ **not** j'aimerais mieux pas

ratify *vtr* ratifier

rating *n* cote *f*

ratings *n pl* indice *m* d'écoute, audimat® *m*

⚹ **ratio** *n* proportion *f*, rapport *m*

ration **1** *n* ration *f*
2 *vtr* rationner ‹*food*› (**to** à); limiter la ration de ‹*person*› (**to** à)

rational *adj* ‹*approach, argument*› rationnel/-elle; ‹*person*› sensé/-e

rationale *n* **(a)** (reasons) raisons *fpl* (**for** pour; **for doing** de faire)
(b) (logic) logique *f* (**behind** de)

rationalize *vtr* **(a)** (justify) justifier
(b) (GB) (streamline) rationaliser

⚹ indicates a very frequent word

rationing *n* rationnement *m*

rat race *n* foire *f* d'empoigne

rat run *n*: *petite rue servant de raccourci*

rattle **1** *n* **(a)** (of bottles, cutlery, chains) cliquetis *m*; (of window, engine) vibrations *fpl*
(b) (baby's) hochet *m*
2 *vtr* ‹*wind*› faire vibrer ‹*window*›; ‹*person*› s'acharner sur ‹*handle*›
3 *vi* ‹*bottles, cutlery, chains*› s'entrechoquer; ‹*window*› vibrer

rattlesnake *n* serpent *m* à sonnette, crotale *m*

raucous *adj* ‹*laugh*› éraillé/-e; ‹*person*› bruyant/-e

raunchy *adj* (colloq) ‹*performer, voice, song*› torride

ravage *vtr* ravager

rave **1** *n* (GB) (colloq) (party) bringue *f* (fam) (branchée)
2 *adj* (colloq) ‹*review*› dithyrambique
3 *vi* (enthusiastically) parler avec enthousiasme (**about** de); (when fevered) délirer

ravenous *adj* ‹*animal*› vorace; **to be** ~ avoir une faim de loup

ravine *n* ravin *m*

raving *adj* (fanatical) enragé/-e; **a** ~ **lunatic** un fou furieux/une folle furieuse

ravioli *n* ravioli *mpl*

ravishing *adj* ravissant/-e

raw *adj* **(a)** ‹*food*› cru/-e; ‹*rubber, sugar, data*› brut/-e; ‹*sewage*› non traité/-e
(b) (without skin) ‹*patch*› à vif
(c) (cold) ‹*weather*› froid/-e et humide
(d) (inexperienced) inexpérimenté/-e
IDIOM to get a ~ **deal** (colloq) être défavorisé/-e

raw material *n* matière *f* première

ray *n* rayon *m*; **a** ~ **of** une lueur de ‹*hope*›

raze *vtr* raser

razor *n* rasoir *m*

razor blade *n* lame *f* de rasoir

re¹ *n* (Mus) ré *m*

re² *prep* (abbr = **with reference to**) (about) au sujet de; (in letterhead) 'objet'

RE *n* (Sch) (abbr = **Religious Education**) éducation *f* religieuse

⚹ **reach** **1** *n* portée *f*; **out of** ~ hors de portée; **within (arm's)** ~ à portée de (la) main; **within easy** ~ ‹*place*› tout près
2 *vtr* **(a)** atteindre ‹*place, person, object, switch*›; ‹*sound, news, letter*› parvenir à ‹*person, place*›
(b) (come to) arriver à ‹*decision, understanding*›; **to** ~ **a verdict** (Law) rendre un verdict
(c) toucher ‹*audience, market*›
(d) (in height, length) arriver à ‹*floor, ceiling*›
3 *vi* **(a) to** ~ **up/down** lever/baisser le bras; **to** ~ **out** tendre le bras
(b) (extend) **to** ~ **(up/down) to** arriver jusqu'à

reaches *n pl* **the upper/lower** ~ (of river) la partie supérieure/inférieure

react *vi* réagir (**to** à; **against** contre)

✦ **reaction** *n* réaction *f*

reactionary *n*, *adj* réactionnaire *mf*

reactor *n* réacteur *m*

✦ **read** ① *vtr* (*prét*, *pp* **read**) **(a)** (gen) lire; **to** ~ **sb's mind** lire dans les pensées de qn
(b) (at university) faire des études de ‹*history, French*›
(c) relever ‹*meter*›
② *vi* (*prét*, *pp* **read**) lire (**to sb** à qn)
∎ **read out** lire [qch] à haute voix
∎ **read up**: **to** ~ **up on sth/sb** étudier qch/qn à fond

readable *adj* **(a)** (legible) lisible
(b) (enjoyable) agréable à lire

✦ **reader** *n* lecteur/-trice *m/f*

readily *adv* **(a)** (willingly) sans hésiter
(b) (easily) facilement

✦ **reading** *n* **(a)** lecture *f*
(b) (on meter) relevé *m* (**on** de); (on instrument) indication *f* (**on** de)
(c) (interpretation) interprétation *f* (**of** de)

reading glasses *n pl* lunettes *fpl* (pour lire)

reading list *n* liste *f* d'ouvrages recommandés

readjust ① *vtr* régler [qch] de nouveau
② *vi* ‹*person*› se réadapter (**to** à)

readvertise *vtr* refaire paraître une annonce pour ‹*post, item*›

✦ **ready** *adj* **(a)** (prepared) prêt/-e (**for** pour; **to do** à faire); **to get** ~ **se** préparer; **to get sth** ~ préparer qch; ~, **steady, go** à vos marques, prêts, partez!
(b) (willing) prêt/-e (**to do** à faire)

ready-made *adj* ‹*clothes*› de confection; ‹*excuse*› tout/-e fait/-e

ready-to-wear *adj* ‹*garment*› prêt-à-porter

✦ **real** *adj* **(a)** (not imaginary) véritable, réel/réelle; **in** ~ **life** dans la réalité
(b) (genuine) ‹*diamond, flower, leather*› vrai/-e (*before n*), authentique
(c) (proper) ‹*holiday, rest*› véritable, vrai/-e (*before n*)
(d) (for emphasis) ‹*charmer, pleasure*› vrai/-e (*before n*)

real estate *n* **(a)** (property) biens *mpl* immobiliers
(b) (US) (profession) immobilier *m*

realism *n* réalisme *m*

realist *n*, *adj* réaliste *mf*

realistic *adj* réaliste

✦ **reality** *n* réalité *f* (**of** de)

reality TV *n* télé *f* réalité

realization *n* prise *f* de conscience

✦ **realize** *vtr* **(a)** se rendre compte de; **to** ~ **that** se rendre compte que; **to make sb** ~ **sth** faire comprendre qch à qn
(b) réaliser ‹*idea, dream, goal*›; **to** ~ **one's**

potential développer ses capacités

reallocate *vtr* réattribuer

✦ **really** ① *adv* **(a)** (gen) vraiment
(b) (in actual fact) en fait, réellement; ~? (expressing disbelief) c'est vrai?
② *excl* (*also* **well** ~!) franchement!

real time *n* (Comput) temps *m* réel

realtor *n* (US) agent *m* immobilier

reap *vtr* **(a)** moissonner ‹*corn*›
(b) récolter ‹*benefits*›

reappear *vi* reparaître

reappearance *n* réapparition *f*

reapply *vi* reposer sa candidature (**for** à)

reappraise *vtr* réexaminer ‹*question*›; réévaluer ‹*writer, work*›

rear ① *n* **(a)** (of building, car, room) arrière *m*; (of procession, train) queue *f*
(b) (of person) derrière *m* (fam)
② *adj* **(a)** ‹*door, garden*› de derrière
(b) (of car) ‹*light, seat, wheel*› arrière *inv*
③ *vtr* élever ‹*child, animals*›; cultiver ‹*plants*›
④ *vi* (*also* ~ **up**) ‹*horse*› se cabrer

rearmament *n* réarmement *m*

rearrange *vtr* réaménager ‹*room*›; modifier ‹*plans*›; changer ‹*appointment*›

rear-view mirror *n* rétroviseur *m*

✦ **reason** ① *n* **(a)** (cause) raison *f* (**for, behind** de); **for no (good)** ~ sans raison valable; **to have** ~ **to do** avoir des raisons de faire; **the** ~ **why...** la raison pour laquelle...; **I'll tell you the** ~ **why** je vais te *or* vous dire pourquoi; **to have every** ~ **to do** avoir tout lieu de faire; **with good** ~ à juste titre
(b) (common sense) raison *f*; **to listen to** *or* **see** ~ entendre raison; **it stands to** ~ **that** il va sans dire que; **within** ~ dans la limite du raisonnable
② *vi* **to** ~ **with sb** raisonner qn

✦ **reasonable** *adj* **(a)** (sensible) raisonnable
(b) (moderately good) convenable

reasonably *adv* **(a)** (sensibly) raisonnablement
(b) (rather) assez

reasoning *n* raisonnement *m*

reassert *vtr* réaffirmer ‹*authority, claim*›

reassess *vtr* réexaminer, reconsidérer

reassurance *n* **(a)** (comfort) réconfort *m*
(b) (guarantee) garantie *f*

reassure *vtr* rassurer ‹*person*› (**about** sur)

reassuring *adj* rassurant/-e

rebate *n* remboursement *m*

rebel ① *n* rebelle *mf*
② *vi* (*p prés etc* **-ll-**) se rebeller

rebellion *n* rébellion *f*, révolte *f*

rebellious *adj* rebelle, insoumis/-e

rebuff ① *n* rebuffade *f*
② *vtr* rabrouer ‹*person*›; repousser ‹*advances*›

rebuild *vtr* (*prét*, *pp* **rebuilt**) reconstruire

r

rebuke ⟨1⟩ n réprimande f
⟨2⟩ vtr réprimander (**for** pour)
rebut vtr (p prés etc **-tt-**) réfuter
⟨ **recall** ⟨1⟩ n (memory) mémoire f
⟨2⟩ vtr (**a**) (remember) se souvenir de
(**b**) (summon back) rappeler
recapitulate vtr, vi récapituler
recapture vtr recapturer ⟨prisoner,
animal⟩; reprendre ⟨town⟩; recréer ⟨period,
atmosphere⟩
recede vi (gen) s'éloigner; ⟨hope, memory⟩
s'estomper
receding adj ⟨chin⟩ fuyant/-e; **he has a ~
hairline** son front se dégarnit
receipt ⟨1⟩ n (**a**) reçu m, récépissé m; (from
till) ticket m de caisse
(**b**) (act of receiving) réception f
⟨2⟩ **receipts** n pl (takings) recette f (**from**
de)
⟨ **receive** ⟨1⟩ vtr (**a**) (gen) recevoir; receler
⟨stolen goods⟩
(**b**) (greet) accueillir, recevoir ⟨visitor,
proposal, play⟩ (**with** avec); **to be well ~d** être
bien reçu/-e
⟨2⟩ **received** pp adj ⟨ideas, opinions⟩
reçu/-e
receiver n (**a**) (telephone) combiné m
(**b**) (radio or TV) (poste m) récepteur m
receivership n (GB) **to go into ~** être
placé/-e sous administration judiciaire
receiving n (crime) recel m
⟨ **recent** adj ⟨event, change, arrival, film⟩
récent/-e; ⟨acquaintance, development⟩
nouveau/-elle (before n); **in ~ years** au cours
des dernières années
⟨ **recently** adv récemment; **until ~** jusqu'à
ces derniers temps
reception n (**a**) (also ~ **desk**) réception f
(**b**) (gathering) réception f (**for sb** en l'honneur
de qn; **for sth** à l'occasion de qch)
(**c**) (welcome) accueil m (**for** de)
(**d**) (on radio, TV) réception f (**on** sur)
receptionist n réceptionniste mf
receptive adj réceptif/-ive (**to** à)
recess n (**a**) (in parliament) (holiday) vacances
fpl
(**b**) (US) (break) (in school) récréation f; (during
meeting) pause f
(**c**) (alcove) alcôve f, recoin m
recession n récession f
recharge vtr recharger
rechargeable adj rechargeable
recipe n recette f (**for** de)
recipient n (of letter) destinataire mf; (of
benefits, aid, cheque) bénéficiaire mf; (of prize,
award) lauréat/-e m/f
reciprocal adj réciproque
reciprocate ⟨1⟩ vtr retourner
⟨compliment⟩; payer [qch] de retour ⟨love⟩;

rendre ⟨affection⟩
⟨2⟩ vi rendre la pareille
recital n récital m
recite vtr, vi réciter
reckless adj imprudent/-e
recklessly adv ⟨act⟩ avec imprudence;
⟨promise, spend⟩ de manière inconsciente
reckon vtr (**a**) (judge) considérer (**that** que)
(**b**) (colloq) (think) **to ~ (that)** croire que
(**c**) calculer ⟨amount⟩
■ **reckon on** (colloq): ⟨1⟩ ¶ **~ on [sb/sth]**
compter sur
⟨2⟩ ¶ **~ on doing** compter faire
■ **reckon with** compter avec
reckoning n (estimation) estimation f;
(accurate calculation) calculs mpl
reclaim vtr (**a**) reconquérir ⟨coastal
land⟩; assécher ⟨marsh⟩; défricher ⟨forest⟩;
récupérer ⟨glass, metal⟩
(**b**) récupérer ⟨deposit, money⟩
reclaimable adj ⟨waste product⟩
récupérable
recline vi ⟨person⟩ s'allonger; ⟨seat⟩
s'incliner
reclining adj (**a**) ⟨figure⟩ allongé/-e
(**b**) ⟨seat⟩ inclinable; ⟨chair⟩ réglable
recluse n reclus/-e m/f
recognition n reconnaissance f; **in ~ of**
en reconnaissance de
recognizable adj reconnaissable
⟨ **recognize** vtr reconnaître (**by** à)
recoil vi reculer (**from** devant)
recollect ⟨1⟩ vtr se souvenir de, se
rappeler
⟨2⟩ vi se souvenir
recollection n souvenir m
⟨ **recommend** vtr (**a**) (commend)
recommander
(**b**) (advise) conseiller, recommander
recommendation n recommandation f;
to give sb a ~ recommander qn
recommended reading n livres mpl
conseillés or recommandés
recompense n (**a**) (reward) récompense
f (**for** de)
(**b**) (compensation) dédommagement m (**for**
pour)
reconcile vtr (**a**) réconcilier ⟨people⟩
(**b**) concilier ⟨attitudes, views⟩
(**c**) **to become ~d to sth** se résigner à qch
reconnaissance n reconnaissance f
reconnoitre (GB), **reconnoiter** (US)
⟨1⟩ vtr reconnaître
⟨2⟩ vi faire une reconnaissance
reconsider ⟨1⟩ vtr réexaminer
⟨2⟩ vi réfléchir
reconstruct vtr (**a**) (rebuild) reconstruire
⟨building⟩
(**b**) ⟨police⟩ faire une reconstitution de ⟨crime⟩

⟨ indicates a very frequent word

reconstruction *n* **(a)** (of building) reconstruction *f*
(b) (of crime) reconstitution *f*

⚬ **record** ❶ *n* **(a)** (of events) compte-rendu *m*; (of official proceedings) procès-verbal *m*; **to keep a ∼ of sth** noter qch; **to say sth off the ∼** dire qch en privé; **to set the ∼ straight** mettre les choses au clair
(b) (data) ∼s (historical, public) archives *fpl*; (personal, administrative) dossier *m*
(c) (history) (of individual) passé *m*; (of organization, group) réputation *f*
(d) (*also* **criminal** ∼) casier *m* judiciaire
(e) (Mus) disque *m*
(f) (of athlete) record *m* (**for, in** de)
❷ *adj* **(a)** ⟨*company, label*⟩ de disques
(b) ⟨*sales, time*⟩ record (*after n*); **to be at a ∼ high/low** être à son niveau le plus haut/bas
❸ *vtr* **(a)** (note) ⟨*detail, idea, opinion*⟩ noter
(b) (on disc, tape) enregistrer
(c) ⟨*instrument*⟩ enregistrer ⟨*temperature, rainfall*⟩

record book *n* livre *m* des records
recorded *adj* (on tape) enregistré/-e; (documented) ⟨*case, sighting*⟩ connu/-e
recorded delivery *n* (GB) **to send sth ∼** envoyer qch en recommandé
recorder *n* (Mus) flûte *f* à bec
record-holder *n* recordman/recordwoman *m/f*
recording *n* enregistrement *m*
record player *n* tourne-disque *m*
recourse *n* recours *m* (**to** à)

⚬ **recover** ❶ *vtr* **(a)** retrouver, récupérer ⟨*money, vehicle*⟩; récupérer ⟨*territory*⟩; (from water) repêcher, retrouver ⟨*body, wreck*⟩; **to ∼ one's strength** reprendre des forces
(b) (recoup) réparer, compenser ⟨*losses*⟩
❷ *vi* **(a)** (from illness) se remettre (**from** de); (from defeat) se ressaisir (**from** après)
(b) ⟨*economy*⟩ se redresser

recovery *n* **(a)** (getting better) rétablissement *m*, guérison *f*
(b) (of economy, company, market) reprise *f*
(c) (getting back) (of vehicle) rapatriement *m*; (of money) récupération *f*

recovery vehicle *n* camion *m* de dépannage
recreate *vtr* recréer
recreation *n* **(a)** (leisure) loisirs *mpl*
(b) (playtime) récréation *f*
recreational drug *n*: drogue que l'on prend de façon occasionnelle
recreational vehicle, RV *n* camping-car *m*
recrimination *n* récrimination *f*
recruit ❶ *n* recrue *f*
❷ *vtr* recruter (**from** dans)
recruiting officer *n* officier *m* recruteur
recruitment *n* recrutement *m*

rectangle *n* rectangle *m*
rectangular *adj* rectangulaire
rectify *vtr* rectifier
rector *n* pasteur *m*
recuperate *vi* se rétablir (**from** de), récupérer
recur *vi* (*p prés etc* **-rr-**) ⟨*event, error*⟩ se reproduire; ⟨*illness*⟩ réapparaître; ⟨*theme*⟩ revenir
recurrence *n* (of illness) récurrence *f*; (of symptom) réapparition *f*
recurrent *adj* récurrent/-e
recycle *vtr* recycler ⟨*paper, waste*⟩
recycling *n* recyclage *m*

⚬ **red** ❶ *n* **(a)** (colour) rouge *m*; **in ∼** en rouge
(b) **to be in the ∼** ⟨*person, account*⟩ être à découvert; ⟨*company*⟩ être en déficit
❷ *adj* rouge (**with** de); ⟨*hair*⟩ roux/rousse; **to go** *or* **turn ∼** rougir
IDIOM **to be caught ∼-handed** être pris/-e la main dans le sac (fam)

red alert *n* alerte *f* rouge
Red Crescent *n* Croissant-Rouge *m*
Red Cross *n* Croix-Rouge *f*
redcurrant *n* groseille *f*
redden *vtr, vi* rougir
redecorate *vtr* repeindre et retapisser, refaire
redeem *vtr* **(a)** retirer ⟨*pawned goods*⟩; rembourser ⟨*debt*⟩
(b) racheter ⟨*sinner*⟩; **her one ∼ing feature is...** ce qui la rachète, c'est...
redeploy *vtr* redéployer ⟨*troops*⟩; réaffecter ⟨*staff*⟩
redevelop *vtr* réaménager ⟨*site, town*⟩
red-faced *adj* (embarrassed) penaud/-e
redhead *n* roux/rousse *m/f*
red herring *n* faux problème *m*
red-hot *adj* ⟨*metal, coal*⟩ chauffé/-e au rouge
redial ❶ *vtr* refaire ⟨*number*⟩
❷ *vi* recomposer le numéro
redial facility *n* rappel *m* du dernier numéro composé
redirect *vtr* canaliser ⟨*resources*⟩; dévier ⟨*traffic*⟩; réexpédier ⟨*mail*⟩
rediscover *vtr* redécouvrir
red light area *n* quartier *m* chaud
redo *vtr* (*3ᵉ pers sg prés* **redoes**, *prét* **redid**, *pp* **redone**) refaire
red pepper *n* poivron *m* rouge
redress *vtr* **to ∼ the balance** rétablir l'équilibre
red tape *n* paperasserie *f*

⚬ **reduce** *vtr* **(a)** réduire ⟨*inflation, number, pressure, sentence*⟩ (**by** de); baisser ⟨*prices, temperature*⟩; **to ∼ speed** ralentir; **to ∼ sb to tears** faire pleurer qn; **to be ∼d to begging** en être réduit/-e à la mendicité ⋯∶

(b) (in cooking) faire réduire ‹sauce, stock›

ɔ̆ **reduction** n **(a)** (in inflation, pressure, number) réduction f (**in** de); (of weight, size) diminution f (**in** de)
(b) (discount) réduction f, rabais m

redundancy n **(a)** (unemployment) chômage m
(b) (dismissal) licenciement m

redundant adj **(a)** (GB) (dismissed) licencié/-e; (out of work) au chômage; **to be made** ∼ être licencié/-e
(b) (not needed) superflu/-e

reed n **(a)** (plant) roseau m
(b) (Mus) anche f

reef n récif m, écueil m

reek vi **to** ∼ **(of sth)** puer (qch)

reel 1 n bobine f; (for fishing) moulinet m
2 vi (sway) ‹person› tituber; **the blow sent him** ∼**ing** le coup l'a projeté en arrière
∎ **reel off** débiter ‹list, names›

re-elect vtr réélire

re-emerge vi ‹person, sun› réapparaître; ‹problem› resurgir

re-examine vtr réexaminer

refectory n réfectoire m

ɔ̆ **refer** 1 vtr (p prés etc **-rr-**) renvoyer ‹task, problem› (**to** à); **to** ∼ **sb to** ‹person› envoyer qn à ‹department›
2 vi (p prés etc **-rr-**) **(a)** (allude to) **to** ∼ **to** parler de, faire allusion à ‹person, topic, event›
(b) (relate, apply) **to** ∼ **to** ‹number, date, term› se rapporter à
(c) (consult) **to** ∼ **to** consulter ‹notes, article›

referee 1 n **(a)** arbitre m
(b) (GB) (giving job reference) personne f pouvant fournir des références
2 vtr, vi arbitrer

ɔ̆ **reference** 1 n **(a)** (allusion) référence f (**to** à), allusion f (**to** à)
(b) (consultation) **without** ∼ **to sb/sth** sans consulter qn/qch; **for future** ∼ pour information
(c) (in book, letter) référence f
(d) (testimonial) références fpl
2 **with reference to** phr **with** ∼ **to your letter** suite à votre lettre

reference book n ouvrage m de référence

reference number n numéro m de référence

referendum n (pl **-da**) référendum m

referral n (of matter, problem) renvoi m (**to** à)

refill 1 n (for ballpoint, lighter, perfume) recharge f
2 vtr recharger ‹pen, lighter›; remplir [qch] à nouveau ‹glass, bottle›

refine vtr **(a)** raffiner ‹oil, sugar›
(b) (improve) peaufiner ‹theory›

refined adj raffiné/-e

refinement n (elegance) raffinement m

refinery n raffinerie f

ɔ̆ **reflect** 1 vtr **(a)** refléter ‹image›; **to be** ∼**ed in sth** se refléter dans qch
(b) renvoyer, réfléchir ‹light, heat›
(c) (think) se dire
2 vi **(a)** (think) réfléchir (**on, upon** à)
(b) **to** ∼ **well/badly on sb** faire honneur/du tort à qn

reflection n **(a)** (image) reflet m (**of** de), image f (**of** de)
(b) (thought) réflexion f; **on** ∼ à la réflexion

reflector n (on vehicle) catadioptre m

reflex 1 n réflexe m
2 adj réflexe; **a** ∼ **action** un réflexe

reflexive verb n verbe m pronominal réfléchi

ɔ̆ **reform** 1 n réforme f
2 vtr réformer

reformation n réforme f; **the Reformation** la Réforme

refrain 1 n refrain m
2 vi se retenir; **to** ∼ **from doing** s'abstenir de faire

refresh vtr ‹bath, drink› rafraîchir; ‹rest› reposer; **to** ∼ **sb's memory** rafraîchir la mémoire à qn

refresher course n cours m de recyclage

refreshing adj ‹drink, shower› rafraîchissant/-e; ‹rest› réparateur/-trice

refreshments n pl (drinks) rafraîchissements mpl; **light** ∼ repas m léger

refrigerate vtr frigorifier

refrigerator n réfrigérateur m, frigidaire® m

refuel vi (p prés etc **-ll-** (GB), **-l-** (US)) se ravitailler en carburant

refuge n **(a)** (shelter, protection) refuge m (**from** contre); **to take** ∼ **from** s'abriter de ‹storm›
(b) (hostel) foyer m

refugee n réfugié/-e m/f

refugee camp n camp m de réfugiés

refund 1 n remboursement m
2 vtr rembourser

refurbish vtr rénover

refusal n refus m (**to do** de faire); (to application) réponse f négative

ɔ̆ **refuse**¹ 1 vtr refuser (**to do** de faire)
2 vi refuser

refuse² n (GB) (household) ordures fpl; (industrial) déchets mpl; (garden) déchets mpl de jardinage

refuse collector n (GB) éboueur m

refute vtr réfuter

regain vtr retrouver ‹health, strength, sight, composure›; reconquérir ‹power, seat›; reprendre ‹lead, control›; **to** ∼

ɔ̆ indicates a very frequent word

consciousness reprendre connaissance

regal *adj* royal/-e

regale *vtr* régaler (**with** de)

regalia *n pl* insignes *mpl*

ꝃ **regard** ① *n* **(a)** (consideration) égard *m*; **out of** ～ **for** par égard pour
(b) (esteem) estime *f* (**for** pour); **to hold sb/ sth in high** ～ avoir beaucoup d'estime pour qn/qch
(c) with *or* **in** ～ **to** en ce qui concerne; **in this** ～ à cet égard
② *vtr* considérer (**as** comme)

regarding *prep* concernant

regardless ① *prep* ～ **of** sans tenir compte de
② *adv* malgré tout

regards *n pl* amitiés *fpl*; **give them my** ～ transmettez-leur mes amitiés

regatta *n* régate *f*

regent *n* régent/-e *m/f*

reggae *n* reggae *m*

ꝃ **regime, régime** *n* régime *m*

regiment *n* régiment *m*

ꝃ **region** *n* région *f*; **(somewhere) in the** ～ **of £300** environ 300 livres sterling

ꝃ **regional** *adj* régional/-e

ꝃ **register** ① *n* registre *m*; (at school) cahier *m* des absences
② *vtr* **(a)** déclarer ‹birth, death›; faire immatriculer ‹vehicle›; faire enregistrer ‹luggage, company›; déposer ‹trademark, complaint›
(b) ‹instrument› indiquer ‹speed, temperature›; ‹person› exprimer ‹anger, disapproval›
(c) envoyer [qch] en recommandé ‹letter›
③ *vi* (for course, school, to vote) s'inscrire; (at hotel) se présenter

registered *adj* **(a)** ‹voter› inscrit/-e; ‹vehicle, student› immatriculé/-e; ‹charity› ≈ agréé/-e
(b) ‹letter› recommandé/-e; **by** ～ **post** en recommandé

registered trademark *n* marque *m* déposée

registrar *n* **(a)** (GB) (gen) officier *m* d'état civil; (medical) adjoint *m*
(b) (academic) responsable *mf* du bureau de la scolarité

registration *n* (of person) inscription *f*; (of trademark, patent) dépôt *m*; (of birth, death, marriage) déclaration *f*

registration number *n* numéro *m* d'immatriculation

registry office *n* (GB) bureau *m* de l'état civil; **to get married in a** ～ se marier civilement

regress *vi* régresser (**to** au stade de)

regret ① *n* regret *m* (**about** à propos de); **to have no** ～**s about doing** ne pas regretter d'avoir fait

② *vtr* (*p prés etc* **-tt-**) regretter (**that** que + *subjunctive*); **to** ～ **doing** regretter d'avoir fait; **l** ～ **to inform you that** j'ai le regret de vous informer que

regretfully *adv* à regret

regrettable *adj* regrettable (**that** que + *subjunctive*)

ꝃ **regular** ① *n* **(a)** (client, visitor) habitué/-e *m/f*
(b) (US) (petrol) ordinaire *m*
② *adj* **(a)** (gen) régulier/-ière; **to take** ～ **exercise** faire de l'exercice régulièrement
(b) (usual) ‹activity, customer, visitor› habituel/-elle; ‹viewer, listener› fidèle
(c) ‹army, soldier› de métier

regularity *n* régularité *f*

regularly *adv* régulièrement

regulate *vtr* **(a)** (gen, Econ) réguler
(b) (adjust) régler ‹mechanism›

ꝃ **regulation** ① *n* **(a)** (gen) règlement *m*; (for safety, fire) consigne *f*; **under the (new)** ～**s** selon la (nouvelle) réglementation; **against the** ～**s** contraire au règlement *or* aux normes
(b) (controlling) réglementation *f*
② *adj* ‹width, length, uniform› réglementaire

regurgitate *vtr* régurgiter; (figurative) ressortir

rehabilitate *vtr* réinsérer ‹handicapped person, ex-prisoner›; réhabiliter ‹addict, area›

rehabilitation centre (GB), **rehabilitation center** (US) *n* (for the handicapped) centre *m* de rééducation; (for addicts etc) centre *m* de réinsertion

rehearsal *n* répétition *f* (**of** de)

rehearse ① *vtr* répéter ‹scene›; préparer ‹speech, excuse›
② *vi* répéter (**for** pour)

reheat *vtr* réchauffer

rehouse *vtr* reloger

reign ① *n* règne *m*
② *vi* régner (**over** sur)

reimburse *vtr* rembourser

rein *n* rêne *f*

reincarnation *n* réincarnation *f*

reindeer *n* (*pl* ～) renne *m*

reinforce *vtr* renforcer

reinforced concrete *n* béton *m* armé

reinforcement *n* (support) renfort *m*; ～**s** (Mil) renforts

reinstate *vtr* réintégrer ‹employee›

reiterate *vtr* réitérer

ꝃ **reject** ① *n* marchandise *f* de deuxième choix
② *vtr* rejeter ‹advice, application, person, transplant›; refuser ‹candidate, manuscript›; démentir ‹claim, suggestion›

rejection n (gen) rejet m; (of candidate, manuscript) refus m

rejection letter n lettre f de refus

rejoice vi se réjouir (at, over de)

rejuvenate vtr rajeunir

rekindle vtr ranimer

relapse 1 n rechute f
2 vi (Med) rechuter (gen) to ~ into retomber dans

✎ **relate** 1 vtr (a) (connect) faire le rapprochement entre
(b) raconter ‹story› (to à)
2 vi to ~ to (have connection) se rapporter à; (communicate) s'entendre avec

✎ **related** adj (a) ‹person› apparenté/-e (by, through par; to à)
(b) (connected) ‹area, idea, incident› lié/-e (to à); drug-~ lié/-e à la drogue

✎ **relation** 1 n (a) (relative) parent/-e m/f; my ~s ma famille
(b) (connection) rapport m
2 **relations** n pl (dealings) relations fpl (with avec)

✎ **relationship** n (a) (between people) relations fpl; (with colleagues) rapports mpl
(b) (connection) rapport m (to, with avec)

✎ **relative** 1 n parent/-e m/f; my ~s ma famille
2 adj (a) (gen) relatif/-ive
(b) (respective) respectif/-ive

✎ **relatively** adv relativement; ~ speaking toutes proportions gardées

✎ **relax** 1 vtr décontracter ‹muscle›; assouplir ‹restrictions, discipline›; détendre ‹body›; relâcher ‹efforts, grip, concentration›
2 vi (a) ‹person› se détendre
(b) ‹grip› se relâcher; ‹jaw, muscle› se décontracter

relaxation n (a) (of person) détente f
(b) (of restrictions, discipline) assouplissement m (in de)

relaxed adj détendu/-e, décontracté/-e

relaxing adj ‹atmosphere, activity› délassant/-e; ‹vacation› reposant/-e

relay 1 n (a) (of workers) équipe f (de relais)
(b) (also ~ race) course f de relais
2 vtr (prét, pp ~ed) transmettre ‹message› (to à)

✎ **release** 1 n (a) (liberation) libération f
(b) (relief) soulagement m
(c) (for press) communiqué m
(d) (of film) sortie f
(e) (film, video, record) (also new ~) nouveauté f
2 vtr (a) libérer ‹prisoner›; dégager ‹accident victim›; relâcher ‹animal›; to ~ sb from dégager qn de ‹promise›
(b) faire jouer ‹catch, clasp›; déclencher ‹shutter›; desserrer ‹handbrake›; larguer ‹bomb›
(c) (let go) lâcher ‹object, arm, hand›

✎ indicates a very frequent word

(d) faire sortir ‹film, record›

relegate vtr (a) reléguer ‹person, object› (to à)
(b) (GB Sport) reléguer (to en)

relegation n relégation f

relent vi céder

relentless adj ‹pressure› implacable; ‹noise, activity› incessant/-e; ‹attack› acharné/-e

✎ **relevant** adj (a) ‹issue, facts, point› pertinent/-e; ‹information› utile; to be ~ to avoir rapport à
(b) (appropriate) ‹chapter› correspondant/-e; ‹period› en question

reliable adj ‹friend, witness› digne de confiance, fiable; ‹employee, firm› sérieux/-ieuse; ‹car, memory, account› fiable; ‹information, source› sûr/-e

reliant adj to be ~ on être dépendant/-e de

relic n relique f

✎ **relief** n (a) (from pain, distress) soulagement m
(b) (aid) aide f, secours m
(c) (in sculpture, geography) relief m

relief agency n organisation f humanitaire

relief fund n fonds m de secours

relief supplies n pl secours mpl

relief work n travail m humanitaire

relief worker n secouriste mf

relieve vtr (a) soulager ‹pain, suffering, tension›; dissiper ‹boredom›; remédier à ‹poverty, famine›; to be ~d être soulagé/-e
(b) to ~ sb of débarrasser qn de ‹coat, bag›; soulager qn de ‹burden›
(c) (help) secourir ‹troops, population›
(d) relever ‹worker, sentry›

✎ **religion** n religion f

✎ **religious** adj (gen) religieux/-ieuse; ‹person› croyant/-e; ‹war› de religion

relinquish vtr renoncer à ‹claim, right› (to en faveur de); céder ‹task, power› (to à)

relish 1 n (a) with ~ ‹eat, drink› avec un plaisir évident
(b) (Culin) condiment m
2 vtr savourer ‹food›; se réjouir de ‹prospect›

relocate 1 vtr muter
2 vi ‹company› déménager; (for cheaper labour) délocaliser; ‹employee› être muté/-e

relocation n délocalisation f

reluctance n réticence f (to do à faire)

reluctant adj ‹person› peu enthousiaste; to be ~ to do être peu disposé/-e à faire

reluctantly adv à contrecœur

✎ **rely** vi (a) (be dependent) to ~ on dépendre de ‹person, aid, industry›; reposer sur ‹method, technology, exports›
(b) (count) to ~ on sb/sth compter sur qn/qch (to do pour faire)

✎ **remain** vi rester; to ~ silent garder le silence

remainder *n* reste *m* (of de)

remains *n pl* restes *mpl*

remand [1] *n* **on ~** (in custody) en détention provisoire; (on bail) en liberté sous caution [2] *vtr* **to be ~ed in custody** être placé/-e en détention provisoire

remand centre *n* (GB) centre *m* de détention (provisoire)

remark [1] *n* remarque *f* [2] *vtr* **(a)** (comment) faire remarquer (**that** que; **to** à) **(b)** (notice) remarquer (**that** que)

remarkable *adj* remarquable

remarry *vi* se remarier

remedial *adj* (Sch) ‹*class*› de rattrapage

remedy [1] *n* remède *m* (**for** à, contre) [2] *vtr* remédier à

✶ **remember** [1] *vtr* **(a)** (recall) se souvenir de, se rappeler ‹*fact, name, place, event*›; se souvenir de ‹*person*›; **to ~ doing** se rappeler avoir fait, se souvenir d'avoir fait **(b)** (not forget) **to ~ to do** penser à faire, ne pas oublier de faire [2] *vi* se souvenir

✶ **remind** *vtr* rappeler; **to ~ sb of sb/sth** rappeler qn/qch à qn; **to ~ sb to do** rappeler à qn de faire

reminder *n* rappel *m* (**of** de; **that** du fait que)

reminisce *vi* évoquer ses souvenirs (**about** de)

reminiscent *adj* **to be ~ of sb/sth** faire penser à qn/qch

remiss *adj* négligent/-e

remission *n* **(a)** (of sentence, debt) remise *f* **(b)** (Med) rémission *f*

remit *n* attributions *fpl*

remnant *n* (gen) reste *m*; (of building, past) vestige *m*; (of fabric) coupon *m*

remorse *n* remords *m* (**for** de)

remote *adj* **(a)** ‹*area, village*› isolé/-e; ‹*ancestor, country*› éloigné/-e **(b)** (aloof) ‹*person*› distant/-e **(c)** (slight) ‹*chance*› vague, infime

remote control *n* télécommande *f*

remote-controlled *adj* télécommandé/-e

remotely *adv* ‹*resemble*› vaguement; **he's not ~ interested** ça ne l'intéresse pas du tout

removal *n* **(a)** (of furniture, parcel, rubbish) enlèvement *m*; (Med) ablation *f*; **stain ~** détachage *m* **(b)** (change of home) déménagement *m* (**from** de, **to** à)

✶ **remove** *vtr* **(a)** (gen, Med) enlever (**from** de); enlever, ôter ‹*clothes, shoes*›; supprimer ‹*threat*›; chasser ‹*doubt*›; **cousin once ~d** cousin au deuxième degré **(b)** **to ~ sb from office** démettre qn de ses fonctions

remover *n* déménageur *m*

remuneration *n* rémunération *f*

Renaissance *n* **the ~** la Renaissance

render *vtr* rendre

rendezvous [1] *n* (*pl* **~**) rendez-vous *m inv* [2] *vi* **to ~ with sb** rejoindre qn

renegade *n* renégat/-e *m/f*

renew *vtr* (gen) renouveler; renouer ‹*acquaintance*›; raviver ‹*courage*›; faire prolonger ‹*library book*›

renewal *n* (of contract, passport) renouvellement *m*; (of hostilities) reprise *f*; (of interest) regain *m*

renewed *adj* ‹*interest, optimism*› accru/-e; ‹*attack, call*› renouvelé/-e

renounce *vtr* (gen) renoncer à; renier ‹*faith, friend*›

renovate *vtr* rénover ‹*building*›

renovation *n* rénovation *f*; **~s** travaux *mpl* de rénovation

renowned *adj* célèbre (**for** pour)

rent [1] *n* loyer *m*; **for ~** à louer [2] *vtr* louer

rental *n* (of car, premises, equipment) location *f*; (of phone line) abonnement *m*

rent boy *n* jeune prostitué *m*

reoffend *vi* récidiver

reopen *vtr*, *vi* rouvrir

reorganize *vtr* réorganiser

rep *n* représentant/-e *m/f* (de commerce)

repair [1] *n* réparation *f*; **to be (damaged) beyond ~** ne pas être réparable; **to be in good/bad ~** être en bon/mauvais état [2] *vtr* réparer

repairman *n* réparateur *m*

repatriate *vtr* rapatrier

repatriation *n* rapatriement *m*

repay *vtr* (*prét, pp* **repaid**) rembourser ‹*person, sum*›; rendre ‹*hospitality, favour*›

repayment *n* remboursement *m* (**on** de)

repeal [1] *n* abrogation *f* (**of** de) [2] *vtr* abroger

✶ **repeat** [1] *n* (gen) répétition *f*; (on radio, TV) rediffusion *f*; (Mus) reprise *f* [2] *vtr* (gen) répéter; (Sch) redoubler ‹*year*›; rediffuser ‹*programme*›

repeated *adj* ‹*warnings, requests, attempts*› répété/-e; ‹*setbacks*› successif/-ive

repeatedly *adv* plusieurs fois, à plusieurs reprises

repel *vtr* (*p prés etc* **-ll-**) repousser

repellent *adj* repoussant/-e

repent *vi* se repentir

repercussion *n* répercussion *f*

repertoire *n* répertoire *m*

repetition *n* répétition *f*

repetitive *adj* répétitif/-ive

repetitive strain injury, **RSI** *n* microtraumatismes *mpl* répétés

r

replace *vtr* **(a)** (put back) remettre ‹lid, cork›; remettre [qch] à sa place ‹book, ornament›
(b) (provide replacement for) remplacer (**with** par)
replacement *n* **(a)** (person) remplaçant/-e *m/f* (**for** de)
(b) (act) remplacement *m*
(c) (spare part) pièce *f* de rechange
replay 1 *n* (Sport) match *m* rejoué
2 *vtr* rejouer
replenish *vtr* reconstituer ‹stocks›
replica *n* réplique *f*, copie *f* (**of** de)
reply 1 *n* réponse *f*
2 *vtr, vi* répondre
report 1 *n* **(a)** (written account) rapport *m* (**on** sur); (verbal account, minutes) compte-rendu *m*; (in media) communiqué *m*; (longer) reportage *m*
(b) (GB Sch) (also **school** ∼) bulletin *m* scolaire; (US Sch) (review) critique *f*
2 *vtr* **(a)** signaler ‹fact, event, theft, accident›; **to** ∼ **sth to sb** transmettre qch à qn ‹result, decision, news›
(b) (make complaint about) signaler ‹person›; se plaindre de ‹noise›
3 *vi* **(a) to** ∼ **on** faire un compte-rendu sur ‹talks, progress›; ‹reporter› faire un reportage sur ‹events›; ‹committee, group› faire son rapport sur
(b) (present oneself) se présenter; **to** ∼ **for duty** prendre son service
(c) to ∼ **to** être sous les ordres (directs) de ‹manager, superior›
report card *n* (US) bulletin *m* scolaire
reporter *n* journaliste *mf*, reporter *mf*
repose *n* repos *m*; **in** ∼ au repos
repossess *vtr* ‹bank› saisir ‹house›; ‹creditor› reprendre possession de ‹property›
repossession *n* saisie *f* immobilière
reprehensible *adj* répréhensible
represent *vtr* **(a)** (gen) représenter
(b) (present) présenter ‹person, event› (**as** comme)
representation *n* **(a)** représentation *f* (**of** de; **by** par)
(b) to make ∼**s to sb** faire des démarches *fpl* auprès de qn
representative 1 *n* **(a)** représentant/-e *m/f*
(b) (US) (politician) député *m*
2 *adj* représentatif/-ive (**of** de), typique (**of** de)
repress *vtr* réprimer ‹reaction, smile›; refouler ‹feelings›
reprieve 1 *n* **(a)** (Law) remise *f* de peine
(b) (delay) sursis *m*
(c) (respite) répit *m*
2 *vtr* accorder une remise de peine à ‹prisoner›

∼ indicates a very frequent word

reprimand 1 *n* réprimande *f*
2 *vtr* réprimander
reprisal *n* représailles *fpl*
reproach 1 *n* reproche *m*; **beyond** ∼ irréprochable
2 *vtr* reprocher à ‹person›; **to** ∼ **sb with** or **for sth** reprocher qch à qn
reprocessing plant *n* (also **nuclear** ∼) usine *f* de retraitement (des déchets nucléaires)
reproduce 1 *vtr* reproduire
2 *vi* se reproduire
reproduction *n* reproduction *f*
reproduction furniture *n* meubles *mpl* de style
reproductive *adj* reproducteur/-trice
reproof *n* réprimande *f*
reprove *vtr* réprimander (**for doing** de faire)
reptile *n* reptile *m*
republic *n* république *f*
republican 1 *n* républicain/-e *m/f*, Republican (US); Républicain/-e *m/f*
2 *adj* (also **Republican**) républicain/-e
repudiate *vtr* rejeter
repugnant *adj* répugnant/-e
repulse *vtr* repousser
repulsion *n* répulsion *f*
repulsive *adj* repoussant/-e
reputable *adj* de bonne réputation
reputation *n* réputation *f* (**as** de)
repute *n* **of** ∼ réputé/-e
reputed *adj* (gen) réputé/-e; (Law) putatif/-ive; **he is** ∼ **to be very rich** à ce que l'on dit il serait très riche
request 1 *n* **(a)** demande *f* (**for** de; **to** à), requête *f* (**for** de; **to** à); **on** ∼ sur demande
(b) (on radio) dédicace *f*
2 *vtr* demander (**from** à); **to** ∼ **sb to do** demander à qn de faire
require *vtr* **(a)** (need) avoir besoin de
(b) (necessitate) ‹job, situation› exiger ‹funds, qualifications›; **to be** ∼**d to do** être tenu/-e de faire
requirement *n* **(a)** (need) besoin *m*
(b) (condition) condition *f*
(c) (obligation) obligation *f* (**to do** de faire)
(d) (US Univ) matière *f* obligatoire
requisite *adj* exigé/-e, requis/-e
requisition *vtr* réquisitionner
reschedule *vtr* (change time) changer l'heure de; (change date) changer la date de
rescue 1 *n* **(a)** (aid) secours *m*; **to come/ go to sb's** ∼ venir/aller au secours de qn; **to come to the** ∼ venir à la rescousse
(b) (operation) sauvetage *m* (**of** de)
2 *vtr* **(a)** (save) sauver
(b) (aid) porter secours à
(c) (release) libérer
rescue worker *n* secouriste *mf*

research [1] *n* recherche *f* (**into, on** sur)
[2] *vtr* faire des recherches sur ‹topic›;
préparer ‹book, article›
research and development, R&D
n recherche-développement *f*, recherche *f* et
développement *m*
researcher *n* chercheur/-euse *m/f*; (in TV)
documentaliste *mf*
resemblance *n* ressemblance *f* (**between**
entre; **to** avec)
resemble *vtr* ressembler à; **to ~ each**
other se ressembler
resent *vtr* en vouloir à ‹person› (**for doing**
d'avoir fait); ne pas aimer ‹tone›
resentful *adj* plein/-e de ressentiment (**of**
sb envers qn)
resentment *n* ressentiment *m*
reservation *n* (a) (doubt) réserve *f*; **without**
~ sans réserve; **to have ~s about sth** avoir
des doutes sur qch
(b) (booking) réservation *f*
(c) (US) (Indian) **~** réserve *f* (indienne)
reservation desk *n* bureau *m* des
réservations
reserve [1] *n* (a) (stock) réserve *f*; **to keep**
sth in ~ tenir qch en réserve
(b) (reticence) réserve *f*
(c) (Mil) **the ~(s)** la réserve
(d) (Sport) remplaçant/-e *m/f*
(e) réserve *f*; **wildlife ~** réserve naturelle
[2] *vtr* réserver
reserved *adj* réservé/-e
reservoir *n* réservoir *m*
reset *vtr* (*p prés* **-tt-**, *prét, pp* **reset**) régler
‹machine›; remettre [qch] à l'heure ‹clock›
reshuffle *n* remaniement *m*
reside *vi* résider, habiter (**with** avec)
residence *n* résidence *f*
residence permit *n* permis *m* de séjour
resident [1] *n* (gen) résident/-e *m/f*;
(of street) riverain/-e *m/f*; (of guest house)
pensionnaire *mf*
[2] *adj* ‹population› local/-e; ‹staff, tutor› à
demeure
residential *adj* ‹area› résidentiel/-ielle;
‹staff› à demeure; ‹course› en internat; **to**
be in ~ care être pris en charge par une
institution
residue *n* résidu *m* (**of** de)
resign [1] *vtr* démissionner de ‹post, job›
[2] *vi* démissionner (**as** du poste de; **from** de)
[3] *v refl* **to ~ oneself** se résigner (**to** à)
resignation *n* (a) (from post) démission *f*
(**from** de; **as** du poste de)
(b) (patience) résignation *f*
resigned *adj* résigné/-e (**to** à)
resilient *adj* (morally) déterminé/-e;
(physically) résistant/-e
resin *n* résine *f*
resist [1] *vtr* résister à

[2] *vi* résister
resistance *n* résistance *f* (**to** à)
Resistance *n* **the ~** la Résistance
resistance fighter *n* résistant/-e *m/f*.
resistant *adj* (a) **heat-~** résistant/-e à la
chaleur; **water-~** imperméable
(b) (opposed) **~ to** réfractaire à
resit *vtr* (*prét, pp* **resat**) (GB) repasser
‹exam, test›
reskill *vtr* recycler
resolute *adj* ‹person› résolu/-e
resolution *n* résolution *f*; **to make a ~ to**
do prendre la résolution de faire
resolve [1] *n* détermination *f*
[2] *vtr* (a) (gen) résoudre
(b) (decide) **to ~ that** décider que; **to ~ to do**
résoudre de faire
resonant *adj* ‹voice› sonore
resort [1] *n* (a) recours *m*; **as a last ~** en
dernier recours
(b) **seaside ~** station *f* balnéaire; **ski ~**
station *f* de ski
[2] *vi* **to ~ to** recourir à
resound *vi* (a) ‹noise› retentir (**through**
dans)
(b) ‹place› retentir (**with** de)
resounding *adj* ‹cheers› retentissant/-e;
‹success› éclatant/-e
resource *n* ressource *f*
resource centre (GB), **resource**
center (US) *n* centre *m* de documentation
resourceful *adj* plein/-e de ressources,
débrouillard/-e (fam)
respect [1] *n* (a) (gen) respect *m*; **out of ~**
par respect (**for** pour); **with (all due) ~** sauf
votre respect; **with ~ to** par rapport à
(b) (aspect) égard *m*; **in many ~s** à bien des
égards
[2] **respects** *n pl* respects *mpl*; **to pay**
one's ~s to sb présenter ses respects à qn
[3] *vtr* respecter
respectable *adj* (a) ‹person, family›
respectable
(b) (adequate) ‹amount› respectable;
‹performance› honorable
respectful *adj* respectueux/-euse
respective *adj* respectif/-ive
respiration *n* respiration *f*
respirator *n* respirateur *m*
respiratory *adj* respiratoire
respite *n* répit *m* (**from** dans)
respond *vi* (a) (answer) répondre (**to** à; **with**
par)
(b) (react) réagir (**to** à)
response *n* (a) (answer) réponse *f* (**to** à); **in**
~ to en réponse à
(b) (reaction) réaction *f* (**to** à; **from** de)
responsibility *n* responsabilité *f* (**for** de);
to take ~ for sth prendre la responsabilité
de qch

r

⚡ **responsible** *adj* (a) (to blame) responsable
(for de)
(b) (in charge) ~ **for doing** chargé/-e de faire
(c) (trustworthy) responsable
(d) ⟨*job*⟩ à responsabilités

responsive *adj* réceptif/-ive

⚡ **rest** **1** *n* (a) (remainder) **the** ~ le reste (of
de); **for the** ~ **of my life** pour le restant de
mes jours
(b) (other people) **the** ~ **(of them)** les autres
(c) (repose) repos *m*; (break) pause *f*; **to have a**
~ se reposer
2 *vtr* (a) (lean) **to** ~ **sth on** appuyer qch sur
(b) reposer ⟨*legs*⟩; ne pas utiliser ⟨*injured
limb*⟩
3 *vi* (a) se reposer; **to** ~ **easy** être
tranquille; **to let the matter** ~ en rester là
(b) (be supported) **to** ~ **on** reposer sur
(c) **to** ~ **on** ⟨*decision*⟩ reposer sur
⟨*assumption*⟩
■ **rest with**: ~ **with [sb/sth]** être entre les
mains de

restart *vtr* (a) reprendre ⟨*talks*⟩
(b) remettre [qch] en marche ⟨*engine*⟩

⚡ **restaurant** *n* restaurant *m*

restaurant car *n* (GB) wagon-restaurant
m

restaurant owner *n* restaurateur/-trice
m/f

restful *adj* ⟨*holiday*⟩ reposant/-e; ⟨*place*⟩
paisible

restless *adj* ⟨*person*⟩ nerveux/-euse;
⟨*patient, sleep*⟩ agité/-e

restock *vtr* regarnir ⟨*shelf*⟩ (with en);
réapprovisionner ⟨*shop*⟩ (with en)

restoration *n* restauration *f*

restore *vtr* (a) restituer ⟨*property*⟩ (to à)
(b) rétablir ⟨*health, peace, monarchy*⟩; rendre
⟨*faculty*⟩; **to** ~ **sb to power** ramener qn au
pouvoir
(c) (repair) restaurer

restrain **1** *vtr* retenir ⟨*person*⟩; contenir
⟨*crowd*⟩; maîtriser ⟨*animal*⟩
2 *v refl* **to** ~ **oneself** se retenir

restrained *adj* ⟨*manner*⟩ calme; ⟨*reaction*⟩
modéré/-e; ⟨*person*⟩ posé/-e

restraint *n* (a) (moderation) modération *f*
(b) (restriction) restriction *f*; **wage** ~ contrôle
m des salaires
(c) (constraint) contrainte *f*

restrict *vtr* limiter ⟨*activity, choice, growth*⟩
(to à); restreindre ⟨*freedom*⟩; réserver ⟨*access,
membership*⟩ (to à)

restricted *adj* ⟨*growth, movement*⟩
limité/-e; ⟨*document*⟩ confidentiel/-ielle;
⟨*parking*⟩ réglementé/-e

restriction *n* limitation *f*

re-string *vtr* (*prét, pp* **re-strung**)
changer les cordes de ⟨*guitar*⟩; recorder
⟨*racket*⟩; renfiler ⟨*necklace*⟩

⚡ indicates a very frequent word

rest room *n* (US) toilettes *fpl*

⚡ **result** **1** *n* résultat *m* (of de); **as a** ~ **of** à
la suite de; **as a** ~ en conséquence
2 *vi* résulter; **to** ~ **in** avoir pour résultat

resume *vtr, vi* reprendre

résumé *n* (a) (summary) résumé *m*
(b) (US) (CV) curriculum vitae *m inv*

resumption *n* reprise *f* (of de)

resurface **1** *vtr* refaire (la surface de)
⟨*road*⟩
2 *vi* ⟨*submarine*⟩ faire surface; ⟨*person*⟩
refaire surface

resurrect *vtr* ressusciter

resurrection *n* résurrection *f*; **the
Resurrection** la Résurrection

resuscitate *vtr* (Med) réanimer

resuscitation *n* réanimation *f*

retail **1** *n* vente *f* au détail
2 *adv* au détail
3 *vi* **to** ~ **at** se vendre au détail à

retailer *n* détaillant *m*

retail price *n* prix *m* de détail

retail sales *n pl* ventes *fpl* au détail

retail trade *n* commerce *m* de détail

⚡ **retain** *vtr* garder ⟨*control, identity*⟩;
conserver ⟨*heat, title*⟩; retenir ⟨*water, fact*⟩

retaliate *vi* réagir

retaliation *n* représailles *fpl* (for de)

retarded *adj* retardé/-e

retch *vi* avoir des haut-le-cœur

rethink *n* **to have a** ~ y repenser

reticent *adj* réticent/-e; **to be** ~ **about sth**
être discret/-ète sur qch

retina *n* rétine *f*

retinue *n* escorte *f*

retire *vi* (a) (from work) prendre sa retraite
(b) (withdraw) se retirer (from de)

retired *adj* retraité/-e

retirement *n* retraite *f*

retirement age *n* âge *m* de la retraite

retirement home *n* maison *f* de retraite

retiring *adj* (shy) réservé/-e

retort **1** *n* riposte *f*
2 *vtr* rétorquer (**that** que)

retrace *vtr* **to** ~ **one's steps** revenir sur
ses pas

retract **1** *vtr* rétracter ⟨*statement, claws*⟩;
escamoter ⟨*landing gear*⟩
2 *vi* ⟨*landing gear*⟩ s'escamoter

retrain **1** *vtr* recycler ⟨*staff*⟩
2 *vi* ⟨*person*⟩ se recycler

retraining *n* recyclage *m*

retreat **1** *n* retraite *f*
2 *vi* ⟨*person*⟩ se retirer (**into** dans; **from**
de); ⟨*army*⟩ se replier (**to** sur); ⟨*flood water*⟩
reculer; **to** ~ **into a dream world** se réfugier
dans un monde imaginaire

retrial *n* nouveau procès *m*

retrieve *vtr* récupérer ‹object›; redresser ‹situation›; extraire ‹data›

retrograde *adj* rétrograde

retrospect: **in retrospect** *phr* rétrospectivement

retrospective ① *n* (also ∼ **exhibition** or ∼ **show**) rétrospective *f*
② *adj* (a) (gen) rétrospectif/-ive
(b) (Law) rétroactif/-ive

⚘ **return** ① *n* (a) (gen) retour *m* (**to** à; **from** de; **of** de); **by** ∼ **of post** par retour du courrier
(b) (on investment) rendement *m* (**on** de)
② *vtr* (a) (give back) rendre; (pay back) rembourser; **to** ∼ **sb's call** rappeler qn
(b) (bring back) rapporter (**to** à)
(c) (put back) remettre
(d) (send back) renvoyer; '∼ **to sender**' 'retour à l'expéditeur'
(e) (reciprocate) répondre à ‹love›
(f) (Mil) riposter à ‹fire›
(g) (Law) prononcer ‹verdict›
(h) rapporter ‹profit›
③ *vi* (a) (come back) revenir (**from** de); retourner (**to** à); (get back from abroad) rentrer (**from** de); (get back home) rentrer chez soi
(b) (resume) **to** ∼ **to** reprendre ‹activity›; **to** ∼ **to power** revenir au pouvoir
(c) (recur) ‹symptom, doubt› réapparaître
④ **in return** *phr* en échange (**for** de)
IDIOM **many happy** ∼**s!** bon anniversaire!

return fare *n* prix *m* d'un billet aller-retour

return flight *n* vol *m* de retour

return ticket *n* billet *m* aller-retour

return trip *n* retour *m*

reunification *n* réunification *f*

reunion *n* réunion *f*

reunite *vtr* réunir ‹family›; réunifier ‹party›

reuse *vtr* réutiliser

rev *vtr* (colloq) (*p prés etc* -**vv**- *also* ∼ **up**) monter le régime de ‹engine›

revalue *vtr* réévaluer

revamp *vtr* rajeunir ‹image›; réorganiser ‹company›; retaper (fam) ‹building›

⚘ **reveal** *vtr* (gen) révéler; dévoiler ‹truth, plan›; **to** ∼ **sth to sb** révéler qch à qn

revealing *adj* (a) ‹remark› révélateur/-trice
(b) ‹blouse› décolleté/-e

revel *vi* (*p prés etc* -**ll**- (GB), -**l**- (US)) **to** ∼ **in** sth/**in** doing se délecter de qch/à faire

revelation *n* révélation *f*

revenge ① *n* vengeance *f*; **to get one's** ∼ se venger (**for** de; **on** sur)
② *v refl* **to** ∼ **oneself** se venger

⚘ **revenue** *n* revenus *mpl*

reverberate *vi* résonner (**with** de; **through** dans, par); (figurative) se propager

revere *vtr* révérer

reverence *n* profond respect *m*

Reverend *n* (a) (Protestant) pasteur *m*
(b) (as title) **the** ∼ **Jones** le révérend Jones; ∼ **Mother** Révérende Mère

reverent *adj* ‹hush› religieux/-ieuse; ‹expression› de respect

reverie *n* rêverie *f*

reversal *n* (of policy, roles) renversement *m*; (of order, trend) inversion *f*; (of fortune) revers *m*

reverse ① *n* (a) (opposite) **the** ∼ le contraire
(b) (back) **the** ∼ (of coin) le revers; (of banknote) le verso; (of fabric) l'envers *m*
(c) (Aut) (also ∼ **gear**) marche *f* arrière
② *adj* (a) ‹effect› contraire; **in** ∼ **order** ‹answer questions› en commençant par le dernier/la dernière; ‹list› en commençant par la fin
(b) (Aut) ∼ **gear** marche *f* arrière
③ *vtr* inverser ‹trend, process›; renverser ‹roles›; faire rouler [qch] en marche arrière ‹car›; **to** ∼ **the charges** appeler en PCV
④ *vi* ‹driver› faire marche arrière
⑤ **in reverse** *phr* en sens inverse

reverse charge call *n* appel *m* en PCV

reversible *adj* réversible

revert *vi* **to** ∼ **to** reprendre ‹habit, name›; redevenir ‹wilderness›

⚘ **review** ① *n* (a) (reconsideration) révision *f* (of de); (report) rapport *m* (of sur)
(b) (of book, film) critique *f* (of de)
(c) (magazine) revue *f*
(d) (Mil) revue *f*
(e) (US Sch, Univ) révision *f*
② *vtr* (a) reconsidérer ‹situation›; réviser ‹attitude, policy›; passer [qch] en revue ‹troops›
(b) faire la critique de ‹book, film›
(c) (US Sch, Univ) réviser

reviewer *n* critique *m*

revise ① *vtr* (a) (alter) réviser, modifier ‹estimate, figures›; **to** ∼ **one's opinion of sb/ sth** réviser son jugement sur qn/qc
(b) (GB) (for exam) réviser ‹subject›
(c) (correct) revoir, réviser ‹text›
② *vi* (GB) ‹student› réviser

revision *n* révision *f*

revitalize *vtr* revitaliser

revival *n* (of economy) reprise *f*; (of interest) regain *m*; (of custom, language) renouveau *m*

revive ① *vtr* (a) ranimer ‹person›
(b) raviver ‹custom›; ranimer ‹interest, hopes›; relancer ‹movement, fashion›; revigorer ‹economy›
② *vi* (a) ‹person› reprendre connaissance
(b) ‹economy› reprendre

revoke *vtr* révoquer ‹will›; annuler ‹decision›

revolt ① *n* révolte *f* (**against** contre)
② *vtr* dégoûter, révolter
③ *vi* se révolter (**against** contre)

revolting *adj* (a) (physically) répugnant/-e; (morally) révoltant/-e   ⋯⟩

(b) (colloq) ⟨food⟩ infect/-e; ⟨person⟩ affreux/
-euse

revolution n (a) révolution f (in dans)
(b) (Aut, Tech) tour m

revolutionary n, adj révolutionnaire mf

revolutionize vtr révolutionner

revolve vi (a) (turn) tourner (around autour
de)
(b) to ~ around (be focused on) être axé/-e sur

revolving adj ⟨chair⟩ pivotant/-e; ⟨stage⟩
tournant/-e; ~ door porte f à tambour

revue n revue f

revulsion n dégoût m

reward ⟨1⟩ n récompense f; a £50 ~
50 livres sterling de récompense
⟨2⟩ vtr récompenser (for de, pour)

rewarding adj ⟨experience⟩
enrichissant/-e; ⟨job⟩ gratifiant/-e

rewind vtr (prét, pp **rewound**)
rembobiner ⟨tape, film⟩

rewind button n bouton m de retour en
arrière

rewire vtr refaire l'installation électrique
de ⟨building⟩

reword vtr reformuler

rework vtr retravailler ⟨theme, metal⟩

rewrite vtr (prét **rewrote**, pp
rewritten) ré(é)crire ⟨story, history⟩

rhapsody n rhapsodie f

rhetoric n rhétorique f

rhetorical adj rhétorique

rheumatism n rhumatisme m

Rhine pr n Rhin m

rhinoceros n (pl **-eroses, -eri** ou ~)
rhinocéros m

rhubarb n rhubarbe f

rhyme ⟨1⟩ n (a) (gen) rime f
(b) (poem) vers mpl; (children's) comptine f
⟨2⟩ vi rimer (with avec)

rhythm n rythme m

rhythmic(al) adj rythmique

rib n (a) (Anat, Culin) côte f
(b) (in umbrella) baleine f; (in plane, building)
nervure f

ribbon n ruban m

rib cage n cage f thoracique

rice n riz m

✓ **rich** ⟨1⟩ n the ~ les riches mpl
⟨2⟩ adj riche; to grow or get ~ s'enrichir; to
make sb ~ enrichir qn

riches n pl richesses fpl

richness n richesse f

rickety adj branlant/-e

rickshaw n pousse-pousse m inv

ricochet vi (prét, pp **ricocheted,
ricochetted**) ricocher (**off** sur)

✓ indicates a very frequent word

rid ⟨1⟩ vtr (p prés **-dd-**, prét, pp **rid**) to ~
sb/sth of débarrasser qn/qch de
⟨2⟩ pp adj to get ~ of se débarrasser de ⟨old
car, guests⟩; éliminer ⟨poverty⟩

riddance n
IDIOM good ~ (to bad rubbish)! bon débarras! (fam)

riddle ⟨1⟩ n (a) (puzzle) devinette f
(b) (mystery) énigme f
⟨2⟩ vtr to be ~d with être criblé/-e de
⟨bullets⟩; être rongé/-e par ⟨disease, guilt⟩

✓ **ride** ⟨1⟩ n (a) (in vehicle, on bike) trajet m (in,
on en, à); (for pleasure) tour m, promenade f;
to go for a ~ aller faire un tour; to give sb a
~ (US); emmener qn (en voiture)
(b) (on horse) promenade f à cheval
⟨2⟩ vtr (prét **rode**, pp **ridden**) (a) rouler à
⟨bike⟩; to ~ a horse monter à cheval; can you
~ a bike? sais-tu faire du vélo?
(b) (US) prendre ⟨bus, subway⟩; parcourir
⟨range⟩
(c) chevaucher ⟨wave⟩
⟨3⟩ vi (prét **rode**, pp **ridden**) (go horse-
riding) faire du cheval; to ~ in or on prendre
⟨bus⟩
IDIOM to take sb for a ~ rouler qn (fam)
■ **ride out** surmonter ⟨crisis⟩; survivre à
⟨recession⟩; to ~ out the storm surmonter la
crise
■ **ride up** (a) ⟨rider⟩ s'approcher (**to** de)
(b) ⟨skirt⟩ remonter

rider n (a) (on horse) cavalier/-ière m/f; (on
motorbike) motocycliste mf; (on bike) cycliste mf
(b) (to document) annexe f

ridge n (a) (along mountain top) arête f, crête f
(b) (on rock, metal surface) strie f; (in ploughed
land) crête f
(c) (on roof) faîte m, faîtage m

ridicule ⟨1⟩ n ridicule m
⟨2⟩ vtr tourner [qn/qch] en ridicule

ridiculous adj ridicule

riding n équitation f; to go ~ faire de
l'équitation

riding school n centre m équestre

rife adj to be ~ être répandu/-e

riffraff n populace f

rifle ⟨1⟩ n (firearm) fusil m
⟨2⟩ vtr vider ⟨wallet, safe⟩
■ **rifle through** fouiller dans

rift n (a) (disagreement) désaccord m;
(permanent) rupture f
(b) (in rock) fissure f; (in clouds) trouée f

rig ⟨1⟩ n (for oil) (on land) tour f de forage;
(offshore) plate-forme f pétrolière offshore
⟨2⟩ vtr (p prés etc **-gg-**) truquer ⟨election,
result⟩
■ **rig up** installer ⟨equipment⟩; improviser
⟨clothes line, shelter⟩

rigging n (a) (on ship) gréement m
(b) (of election, competition, result) truquage m

✓ **right** ⟨1⟩ n (a) (side, direction) droite f; on or to
your ~ à votre droite

(b) (in politics) (*also* **Right**) the ~ la droite
(c) (morally) bien *m*; ~ **and wrong** le bien et le mal
(d) (just claim) droit *m*; **to have a** ~ **to sth** avoir droit à qch; **civil** ~**s** droits civils
2 *adj* **(a)** (not left) droit/-e, de droite
(b) (morally) bien; **it is only** ~ **and proper** ce n'est que justice; **to do the** ~ **thing** faire ce qu'il faut
(c) (correct) ‹*choice, direction, size, answer*› bon/bonne (*before n*); ‹*word*› juste; ‹*time*› exact/-e; **to be** ~ ‹*person*› avoir raison; ‹*answer*› être juste
(d) (suitable) qui convient; **the** ~ **person for the job** la personne qu'il faut pour le poste; **to be in the** ~ **place at the** ~ **time** être là où il faut au bon moment
(e) (in good order) **the engine isn't quite** ~ le moteur ne fonctionne pas très bien; **I don't feel quite** ~ **these days** je ne me sens pas très bien ces jours-ci
(f) to put *or* **set** ~ corriger ‹*mistake*›; réparer ‹*injustice*›; arranger ‹*situation*›; réparer ‹*machine*›
(g) ‹*angle*› droit/-e; **at** ~ **angles to** à angle droit avec, perpendiculaire à
3 *adv* **(a)** (not left) à droite; **to turn/look** ~ tourner/regarder à droite
(b) (directly) droit, directement; **it's** ~ **in front of you** c'est droit *or* juste devant toi; **I'll be** ~ **back** je reviens tout de suite
(c) (exactly) ~ **in the middle of the room** en plein milieu de la pièce; ~ **now** (immediately) tout de suite; (US) (at this point in time) en ce moment
(d) (correctly) juste, comme il faut; **you're not doing it** ~ tu ne fais pas ça comme il faut; **to guess** ~ deviner juste
(e) (completely) tout; **go** ~ **back to the beginning** revenez tout au début; ~ **at the bottom** tout au fond; **to turn the central heating** ~ **up** mettre le chauffage central à fond
(f) (very well) bon; ~, **let's have a look** bon, voyons ça
4 *vtr* redresser
IDIOM by ~**s** normalement, en principe
right angle *n* angle *m* droit
right away *adv* tout de suite
righteous *adj* vertueux/-euse
rightful *adj* légitime
right-hand *adj* du côté droit; **on the** ~ **side** sur la droite
right-hand drive *n* conduite *f* à droite
right-handed *adv* ‹*person*› droitier/-ière; ‹*blow*› du droit
right-hand man *n* bras *m* droit
rightly *adv* **(a)** (accurately) correctement
(b) (justifiably) à juste titre; ~ **or wrongly** à tort ou à raison
(c) (with certainty) au juste; **I don't** ~ **know** je ne sais pas au juste
right-of-centre *adj* (Pol) centre droite *inv*

right of way *n* **(a)** (Aut) priorité *f*
(b) (over land) droit *m* de passage; '**no** ~' 'entrée *f* interdite'
right-on *adj* (colloq) **they're very** ~ ils s'appliquent à être idéologiquement corrects sur tout
right-thinking *adj* bien-pensant/-e
right wing **1** *n* **the** ~ la droite
2 **right-wing** *adj* ‹*attitude*› de droite; **they are very** ~ ils sont très à droite
rigid *adj* ‹*rules, person, material*› rigide; ‹*controls, timetable*› strict/-e
rigidly *adv* ‹*oppose*› fermement; ‹*control*› rigoureusement; ‹*stick to, apply*› strictement
rigorous *adj* rigoureux/-euse
rigour (GB), **rigor** (US) *n* rigueur *f*
rim *n* bord *m*; (on wheel) jante *f*
rind *n* **(a)** (on cheese) croûte *f*; (on bacon) couenne *f*
(b) (on fruit) peau *f*
✓ **ring** **1** *n* **(a)** anneau *m*; (with stone) bague *f*; **a diamond** ~ une bague de diamants; **a wedding** ~ une alliance
(b) (circle) cercle *m*; **to have** ~**s under one's eyes** avoir les yeux cernés
(c) (at door) coup *m* de sonnette; (of phone) sonnerie *f*
(d) (in circus) piste *f*; (in boxing) ring *m*
(e) (of smugglers, spies) réseau *m*
(f) (on cooker) (electric) plaque *f*; (gas) brûleur *m*
2 *vtr* (*prét* **rang**, *pp* **rung**) **(a)** sonner ‹*church bells*›; **to** ~ **the doorbell** *or* **bell** sonner
(b) (GB) (*also* ~ **up**) appeler
3 *vi* (*prét* **rang**, *pp* **rung**) **(a)** ‹*bell, phone, person*› sonner; **the doorbell rang** on a sonné à la porte
(b) ‹*footsteps, laughter*› résonner; **to** ~ **true** sonner vrai
(c) (GB) (phone) téléphoner; **to** ~ **for** appeler ‹*taxi*›
■ **ring off** (GB) raccrocher
■ **ring out** ‹*voice, cry*› retentir; ‹*bells*› sonner
ring binder *n* classeur *m* à anneaux
ringing *n* **(a)** (of bell, alarm) sonnerie *f*
(b) (in ears) bourdonnement *m*
ringleader *n* meneur/-euse *m/f*
ringlet *n* anglaise *f*
ringroad *n* (GB) périphérique *m*
ringtone *n* sonnerie *f*
rinse **1** *n* rinçage *m*
2 *vtr* rincer; (wash) laver
riot **1** *n* **(a)** émeute *f*, révolte *f*; **prison** ~ mutinerie *f*
(b) a ~ **of** une profusion de ‹*colours*›
2 *vi* ‹*crowd, demonstrators*› se soulever; ‹*prisoners*› se mutiner
IDIOM to run ~ ‹*crowd*› se déchaîner; ‹*imagination*› se débrider; ‹*plant*› proliférer
rioter *n* émeutier/-ière *m/f*; (in prison) mutin *m*

r

riot gear n tenue f antiémeutes

rioting n émeutes fpl, bagarres fpl

riot police n forces fpl antiémeutes

rip ⟦1⟧ vtr (p prés etc **-pp-**) déchirer; **to ~ sth out** arracher qch
⟦2⟧ vi (p prés etc **-pp-**) ⟨fabric⟩ se déchirer
■ **rip off:** ⟦1⟧ ¶ **~ off [sth], ~ [sth] off**
(a) arracher ⟨garment, roof⟩
(b) (colloq) (steal) rafler (fam) ⟨idea, design⟩
⟦2⟧ ¶ **~ [sb] off** arnaquer (pop)
■ **rip through: ~ through [sth]** ⟨bomb blast⟩ défoncer ⟨building⟩

RIP (abbr = **rest in peace**) qu'il/elle repose en paix

ripe adj ⟨fruit⟩ mûr/-e; ⟨cheese⟩ fait/-e

ripen ⟦1⟧ vtr mûrir ⟨fruit⟩; affiner ⟨cheese⟩
⟦2⟧ vi ⟨fruit⟩ mûrir; ⟨cheese⟩ se faire

rip-off n (colloq) arnaque f (pop)

ripple ⟦1⟧ n ondulation f
⟦2⟧ vi (a) ⟨water⟩ se rider; (making noise) clapoter
(b) ⟨hair, corn⟩ onduler; ⟨muscles⟩ saillir

 rise ⟦1⟧ n (a) (increase) augmentation f (in de); (in prices, pressure) hausse f (in de); (in temperature) élévation f (in de)
(b) (of person) ascension f; (of empire) essor m
(c) (slope) montée f
⟦2⟧ vi (prét **rose**, pp **risen**) (a) ⟨water, tension⟩ monter; ⟨price, temperature⟩ augmenter; ⟨voice⟩ devenir plus fort/-e; ⟨hopes⟩ grandir
(b) (get up) ⟨person⟩ se lever; **to ~ from the dead** ressusciter; **to ~ to the occasion** se montrer à la hauteur
(c) ⟨road⟩ monter; ⟨cliff⟩ s'élever
(d) ⟨sun, moon⟩ se lever
(e) ⟨dough⟩ lever
IDIOM **to give ~ to** donner lieu à ⟨rumours⟩; causer ⟨problem⟩

rising ⟦1⟧ n soulèvement m
⟦2⟧ adj (gen) en hausse; ⟨tension⟩ grandissant/-e; ⟨sun, moon⟩ levant/-e

 risk ⟦1⟧ n risque m; **to run a ~** courir un risque; **to take ~s** prendre des risques; **at ~** menacé/-e
⟦2⟧ vtr risquer; **to ~ doing** courir le risque de faire

risky adj ⟨decision, undertaking⟩ risqué/-e; ⟨share, investment⟩ à risques

risqué adj osé/-e

rite n rite m

ritual ⟦1⟧ n rituel m, rites mpl
⟦2⟧ adj rituel/-elle

rival ⟦1⟧ n (person) rival/-e m/f; (company) concurrent/-e m/f
⟦2⟧ adj ⟨team, business⟩ rival/-e; ⟨claim⟩ opposé/-e
⟦3⟧ vtr (p prés etc **-ll-** (GB), **-l-** (US)) rivaliser avec (in de)

rivalry n rivalité f (between entre)

 indicates a very frequent word

 river n (flowing into sea) fleuve m; (tributary) rivière f

riverbank n berge f; **along the ~** le long de la rivière

riverside ⟦1⟧ n berges fpl
⟦2⟧ adj ⟨pub⟩ au bord de la rivière

rivet ⟦1⟧ n rivet m
⟦2⟧ vtr (a) (Tech) riveter
(b) **to be ~ed by** être captivé/-e par; **to be ~ed to the spot** être cloué/-e sur place

riveting adj fascinant/-e

Riviera n **the Italian ~** la Riviera; **the French ~** la Côte d'Azur

 road n (a) route f; **the ~ to Leeds** la route de Leeds
(b) (street) rue f
(c) (figurative) voie f (to de); **to be on the right ~** être sur la bonne voie

roadblock n barrage m routier

road hump n ralentisseur m

road rage n violence f au volant

roadshow n (play, show) spectacle m de tournée; (publicity tour) tour m promotionnel

roadside n bord m de la route

roadsign n panneau m de signalisation

road tax disc n vignette f

roadworks n pl travaux mpl (routiers)

roadworthy adj en état de rouler

roam vtr parcourir ⟨countryside⟩; faire le tour de ⟨shops⟩; traîner dans ⟨streets⟩
■ **roam around** ⟨person⟩ vadrouiller (fam)

roaming n (mobile phone) itinérance f

roar ⟦1⟧ n (of lion) rugissement m; (of person) hurlement m; (of engine) vrombissement m; (of traffic) grondement m; **a ~ of laughter** un éclat de rire
⟦2⟧ vi ⟨lion⟩ rugir; ⟨person⟩ hurler; ⟨sea, wind⟩ mugir; ⟨fire⟩ ronfler; ⟨engine⟩ vrombir

roaring adj (a) ⟨engine, traffic⟩ grondant/-e; **a ~ fire** une belle flambée
(b) ⟨success⟩ fou/folle

roast ⟦1⟧ n (Culin) rôti m; (US) barbecue m
⟦2⟧ adj ⟨meat, potatoes⟩ rôti/-e; **~ beef** rôti m de bœuf, rosbif m
⟦3⟧ vtr rôtir ⟨meat, potatoes⟩; (faire) griller ⟨chestnuts⟩; torréfier ⟨coffee beans⟩

rob vtr (p prés etc **-bb-**) voler ⟨person⟩; dévaliser ⟨bank, train⟩; **to ~ sb of sth** voler qch à qn; (figurative) priver qn de qch

robber n voleur/-euse m/f

robbery n vol m

robe n (a) (ceremonial garment) robe f
(b) (US) (bath robe) peignoir m

robin n (also **~ redbreast**) rouge-gorge m

robot n robot m

robust adj robuste

 rock ⟦1⟧ n (a) (substance) roche f; **solid ~** roche dure
(b) (boulder) rocher m

(c) (*also* ∼ **music**) rock *m*
2 *vtr* (a) balancer ‹*cradle*›; bercer ‹*baby, boat*›
(b) ‹*tremor*› secouer ‹*town*›; ‹*scandal*› ébranler ‹*government*›
3 *vi* ‹*person*› se balancer; **to** ∼ **back and forth** se balancer d'avant en arrière
IDIOMS **on the** ∼**s** ‹*drink*› avec des glaçons; **to be on the** ∼**s** ‹*marriage*› aller à vau-l'eau
rock and roll *n* (*also* **rock'n'roll**) rock and roll *m*
rock bottom *n* **to hit** ∼ toucher le fond
rock climber *n* varappeur/-euse *m/f*
rock climbing *n* varappe *f*
rockery *n* (GB) rocaille *f*
rocket **1** *n* (a) (gen, Mil) fusée *f*
(b) (salad) roquette *f*
2 *vi* ‹*price, profit*› monter en flèche
rock face *n* paroi *f* rocheuse
rockfall *n* chute *f* de pierres
rocking chair *n* fauteuil *m* à bascule
rocking horse *n* cheval *m* à bascule
rock star *n* rock-star *f*
rocky *adj* (a) ‹*beach, path, road*› rocailleux/-euse; ‹*coast*› rocheux/-euse
(b) ‹*relationship, period*› difficile; ‹*business*› précaire
Rocky Mountains *pr n pl* (*also* **Rockies**) **the** ∼ les montagnes *fpl* Rocheuses
rod *n* (a) (gen, Tech) tige *f*; **curtain/stair** ∼ tringle *f* à rideaux/de marche
(b) (for punishment) baguette *f*
(c) (for fishing) canne *f* à pêche
rodent *n* rongeur *m*
roe *n* œufs *mpl* (de poisson)
roe deer *n* (male) chevreuil *m*; (female) chevrette *f*
rogue *n* (a) (rascal) coquin *m*
(b) (animal) solitaire *m*
⚥ **role** *n* rôle *m* (**of** de); **title** ∼ rôle-titre *m*
role model *n* modèle *m*
role-play *n* (Sch) jeu *m* de rôle; (for therapy) psychodrame *m*
⚥ **roll** **1** *n* (a) (of paper, cloth) rouleau *m*; (of banknotes) liasse *f*; (of flesh) bourrelet *m*; **a** ∼ **of film** une pellicule
(b) (bread) petit pain *m*; **cheese** ∼ **sandwich** *m* au fromage
(c) (of dice) lancer *m*
(d) (register) liste *f*; **to call the** ∼ faire l'appel
2 *vtr* (a) (gen) rouler; faire rouler ‹*dice*›; **to** ∼ **sth into a ball** faire une boulette de ‹*paper*›; faire une boule de ‹*clay, dough*›
(b) étirer ‹*dough*›
3 *vi* (a) ‹*person, animal*› rouler (**onto** sur); ‹*car, plane*› faire un tonneau; ‹*ship*› tanguer
(b) ‹*thunder*› gronder; ‹*drum*› rouler
(c) ‹*camera, press*› tourner
■ **roll about** (GB), **roll around** ‹*animal, person*› se rouler; ‹*marbles, tins*› rouler

■ **roll down** baisser ‹*blind, sleeve*›
■ **roll over** se retourner
■ **roll up** enrouler ‹*rug, poster*›; **to** ∼ **up one's sleeves** retrousser ses manches
roller *n* (a) (gen) rouleau *m*
(b) (curler) bigoudi *m*
rollerblade **1** *n* patin *m* en ligne; roller *m*
2 *vi* faire du patin en ligne; roller
roller blind *n* store *m*
roller coaster *n* montagnes *fpl* russes
roller-skate *n* patin *m* à roulettes
roller-skating *n* patinage *m* à roulettes; **to go** ∼ faire du patin à roulettes
rolling pin *n* rouleau *m* à pâtisserie
rollneck *n* col *m* roulé
ROM *n* (*abbr* = **read-only memory**) ROM *f*, mémoire *f* morte
Roman **1** *n* Romain/-e *m/f*
2 *adj* romain/-e
Roman Catholic *n, adj* catholique *mf*
romance *n* (a) (of era, place) charme *m*; (of travel) côté *m* romantique
(b) (love affair) histoire *f* d'amour; (love) amour *m*
(c) (novel) roman *m* d'amour; (film) film *m* d'amour
Romania *pr n* Roumanie *f*
Romanian **1** *n* (a) (person) Roumain/-e *m/f*
(b) (language) roumain *m*
2 *adj* roumain/-e
romantic **1** *n* romantique *mf*
2 *adj* (a) ‹*setting, story, person*› romantique
(b) ‹*attachment*› sentimental/-e
(c) ‹*novel, film*› d'amour
romantic fiction *n* (genre) romans *mpl* d'amour
romanticize *vtr* idéaliser
Romany *n* Tzigane *mf*, Romani *mf*
romp **1** *n* ébats *mpl*
2 *vi* s'ébattre
rompers *n pl* (*also* **romper suit**) barboteuse *f*
roof *n* (a) (on building) toit *m*
(b) (Anat) **the** ∼ **of the mouth** la voûte du palais
IDIOM **to go through** *or* **hit the** ∼ ‹*person*› sauter au plafond (fam); ‹*prices*› battre tous les records
roof rack *n* galerie *f*
rooftop *n* toit *m*
rook *n* (a) (bird) (corbeau *m*) freux *m*
(b) (in chess) tour *f*
⚥ **room** **1** *n* (a) pièce *f*; (bedroom) chambre *f*; (for working) bureau *m*; (for meetings, teaching, operating) salle *f*
(b) (space) place *f*; **to make** ∼ faire de la place
2 *vi* (US) loger (**with** chez)

roommate n (a) (in same room) camarade mf de chambre
(b) (US) (flatmate) compagnon/compagne m/f d'appartement
room service n service m de chambre
room temperature n température f ambiante; **at** ~ ⟨wine⟩ chambré/-e
roomy adj ⟨car, house⟩ spacieux/-ieuse; ⟨garment⟩ ample; ⟨bag, cupboard⟩ grand/-e (before n)
roost 1 n perchoir m
2 vi (in trees) percher (pour la nuit); (in attic) se nicher
IDIOM **to rule the** ~ faire la loi
rooster n coq m
✓ **root** 1 n (a) racine f; **to take** ~ ⟨plant⟩ prendre racine; ⟨idea, value⟩ s'établir; ⟨industry⟩ s'implanter
(b) (of problem) fond m; (of evil) origine f
2 vtr **to be** ~**ed in** être ancré/-e dans; **deeply-**~**ed** bien enraciné/-e; ~**ed to the spot** figé/-e sur place
■ **root around**, **root about** fouiller (in dans)
■ **root out** traquer ⟨corruption⟩; déloger ⟨person⟩
rootless adj sans racines
rope 1 n (gen, Sport) corde f; (of pearls) rang m
2 vtr attacher ⟨victim, animal⟩ (**to** à); encorder ⟨climber⟩
IDIOM **to know the** ~**s** connaître les ficelles (fam)
■ **rope in** (colloq): ~ [sb] **in**, ~ **in** [sb] (to help with task) embaucher (fam)
rope ladder n échelle f de corde
rosary n (prayer) rosaire m; (beads) chapelet m
rose n rose f
rosebud n bouton m de rose
rose bush n rosier m
rosemary n romarin m
rose-tinted adj
IDIOM **to see the world through** ~ **spectacles** voir la vie en rose
rosette n (for winner) cocarde f
roster n (also **duty** ~) tableau m de service
rostrum n (pl **-trums** ou **-tra**) estrade f
rosy adj ⟨cheek, light⟩ rose; **to paint a** ~ **picture** peindre un tableau favorable
rot 1 n pourriture f
2 vtr (p prés etc **-tt-**) pourrir
3 vi (p prés etc **-tt-**) (also ~ **away**) pourrir
rota n (GB) tableau m de service
rotary adj rotatif/-ive
rotate 1 vtr faire tourner ⟨blade⟩
2 vi ⟨blade, handle, wings⟩ tourner

rotation n rotation f
rote n **by** ~ par cœur
rotten adj (a) ⟨produce⟩ pourri/-e; ⟨teeth⟩ gâté/-e; ⟨smell⟩ de pourriture
(b) (corrupt) pourri/-e (fam)
(c) (colloq) (bad) ⟨weather⟩ pourri/-e; ⟨cook, driver⟩ exécrable
rouble n rouble m
rough 1 adj (a) ⟨material⟩ rêche; ⟨hand, skin, surface, rock⟩ rugueux/-euse; ⟨terrain⟩ cahoteux/-euse
(b) ⟨person, behaviour, sport⟩ brutal/-e, violent/-e; ⟨landing⟩ brutal/-e; ⟨area⟩ dur/-e
(c) ⟨description, map⟩ sommaire; ⟨figure, idea, estimate⟩ approximatif/-ive
(d) (difficult) dur, difficile; **a** ~ **time** une période difficile
(e) (crude) grossier/-ière
(f) (harsh) ⟨voice, taste, wine⟩ âpre
(g) (stormy) ⟨sea, crossing⟩ agité/-e
2 adv **to sleep** ~ dormir à la dure
IDIOM **to** ~ **it** vivre à la dure
roughage n fibres fpl
rough-and-ready adj ⟨person, manner⟩ fruste; ⟨conditions⟩ rudimentaire; ⟨method, system⟩ sommaire
roughen vtr rendre [qch] rêche or rugueux
roughly adv (a) ⟨calculate⟩ grossièrement; ~ **speaking** en gros; ~ **10%** à peu près 10%
(b) ⟨treat, hit⟩ brutalement
(c) ⟨make⟩ grossièrement
rough paper n feuille f de brouillon
roulette n roulette f
✓ **round** 1 adv (GB) (a) **all** ~ tout autour; **whisky all** ~! du whisky pour tout le monde!; **to go all the way** ~ faire tout le tour; **to go** ~ **and** ~ tourner en rond
(b) (to place, home) **to go** ~ **to sb's house** passer chez qn; **to ask sb** ~ dire à qn de passer à la maison; **to invite sb** ~ **for lunch** inviter qn à déjeuner (chez soi)
(c) **all year** ~ toute l'année; **this time** ~ cette fois-ci
2 prep (GB) (a) autour de ⟨table⟩; **to sit** ~ **the fire** s'asseoir au coin du feu
(b) **to go** ~ **the corner** tourner au coin de la rue; **just** ~ **the corner** tout près; **to go** ~ **an obstacle** contourner un obstacle
(c) **her sister took us** ~ **Oxford** sa sœur nous a fait visiter Oxford; **to go** ~ **the shops** faire les magasins
3 n (a) (of competition) manche f; (of golf, cards) partie f; (in boxing) round m; (in showjumping) parcours m; (in election) tour m; (of talks) série f; **a** ~ **of drinks** une tournée; **a** ~ **of ammunition** une cartouche; **a** ~ **of applause** une salve d'applaudissements; **a** ~ **of toast** un toast
(b) **to do one's** ~**s** ⟨postman, milkman⟩ faire sa tournée; ⟨doctor⟩ visiter ses malades; ⟨guard⟩ faire sa ronde; **to go** or **do the** ~**s** ⟨rumour, flu⟩ circuler

---

✓ indicates a very frequent word

(c) (shape) rondelle *f*
4 *adj* **(a)** rond/-e; **in ∼ figures, that's £100** si on arrondit, ça fait 100 livres sterling; **a ∼ dozen** une douzaine exactement
(b) to have ∼ shoulders avoir le dos voûté
5 *vtr* contourner ‹*headland*›; **to ∼ the corner** tourner au coin; **to ∼ a bend** prendre un virage
6 **round about** *phr* **(a)** (approximately) à peu près, environ
(b) (vicinity) **the people ∼ about** les gens des environs
■ **round off (a)** finir ‹*meal, evening*› **(with** par); conclure ‹*speech*›
(b) arrondir ‹*corner, figure*›
■ **round on: ∼ on [sb]** attaquer violemment; **she ∼ed on me** elle m'est tombée dessus (fam)
■ **round up (a)** regrouper ‹*people*›; rassembler ‹*livestock*›
(b) arrondir [qch] au chiffre supérieur ‹*figure*›

roundabout **1** *n* (GB) (in fairground) manège *m*; (in playground) tourniquet *m*; (for traffic) rond-point *m*
2 *adj* **to come by a ∼ way** faire un détour; **by ∼ means** par des moyens détournés; **a ∼ way of saying** une façon détournée de dire

rounders *n* (GB) ≈ baseball *m*

round-neck(ed) sweater *n* pull-over *m* ras de cou *inv*

round-the-clock *adj* 24 heures sur 24

round-the-world *adj* autour du monde

round trip *n* aller-retour *m*

roundup *n* **(a)** (herding) rassemblement *m* (**of** de)
(b) (by police) rafle *f*

rouse *vtr* réveiller ‹*person*›; susciter ‹*anger, interest*›

rousing *adj* ‹*speech*› galvanisant/-e; ‹*music*› exaltant/-e

rout **1** *n* déroute *f*, défaite *f*
2 *vtr* (Mil) mettre en déroute; (figurative) battre à plates coutures

✧ **route** **1** *n* chemin *m*, itinéraire *m*; (in shipping) route *f*; (in aviation) ligne *f*, (figurative) (to power) voie *f* (**to** de); **bus ∼** ligne d'autobus
2 *vtr* expédier, acheminer ‹*goods*›

router *n* (Comput) routeur *m*

routine **1** *n* **(a)** routine *f*
(b) (act) numéro *m*
2 *adj* **(a)** ‹*enquiry, matter*› de routine
(b) (uninspiring) routinier/-ière

routinely *adv* **(a)** ‹*check, review*› systématiquement
(b) ‹*tortured, abused*› régulièrement

routing number *n* (US) code *m* d'agence

✧ **row¹** **1** *n* **(a)** (of people, plants, stitches) rang *m* (**of** de); (of houses, seats, books) rangée *f* (**of** de)
(b) (succession) **six times in a ∼** six fois de suite; **the third week in a ∼** la troisième semaine d'affilée

2 *vtr* **to ∼ a boat up the river** remonter la rivière à la rame
3 *vi* (gen) ramer; (Sport) faire de l'aviron; **to ∼ across** traverser [qch] à la rame ‹*lake*›

row² **1** *n* **(a)** (quarrel) dispute *f* (**about** à propos de); (public) querelle *f*; **to have a ∼ with** se disputer avec
(b) (noise) tapage *m*
2 *vi* se disputer (**with** avec; **about, over** à propos de)

rowboat *n* (US) bateau *m* à rames

rowdy *adj* (noisy) tapageur/-euse; (in class) chahuteur/-euse

rowing *n* aviron *m*

rowing boat *n* (GB) bateau *m* à rames

✧ **royal** *adj* royal/-e

royal blue *n*, *adj* bleu *m* roi *inv*

Royal Highness *n* **His ∼** Son Altesse *f* royale; **Your ∼** Votre Altesse *f*

royalty *n* **(a)** (persons) membres *mpl* d'une famille royale
(b) (to author, musician) droits *mpl* d'auteur; (on patent) royalties *fpl*

rub **1** *n* **(a)** (massage) friction *f*
(b) (polish) coup *m* de chiffon
2 *vtr* (*p prés etc* **-bb-**) se frotter ‹*chin, eyes*›; frotter ‹*stain, surface*›; frictionner ‹*sb's back*›; **to ∼ sth into the skin** faire pénétrer qch dans la peau
3 *vi* (*p prés etc* **-bb-**) frotter
IDIOM **to ∼ sb up the wrong way** prendre qn à rebrousse-poil (fam)
■ **rub out** (erase) effacer
■ **rub in: ∼ [sth] in, ∼ in [sth]** faire pénétrer ‹*lotion*›; **there's no need to ∼ it in!** (colloq) inutile d'en rajouter! (fam)

rubber **1** *n* **(a)** (substance) caoutchouc *m*
(b) (GB) (eraser) gomme *f*
2 *adj* de *or* en caoutchouc

rubber band *n* élastique *m*

rubber glove *n* gant *m* en *or* de caoutchouc

rubber plant *n* caoutchouc *m*

rubber stamp *n* tampon *m*

rubber tree *n* hévéa *m*

rubbish **1** *n* **(a)** (refuse) déchets *mpl*; (domestic) ordures *fpl*; (on site) gravats *mpl*
(b) (inferior goods) camelote *f* (fam); **this book is ∼!** (colloq) ce livre est nul! (fam)
(c) (nonsense) bêtises *fpl*
2 *vtr* (GB) descendre [qn/qch] en flammes

rubbish bin *n* (GB) poubelle *f*

rubbish dump *n* (GB) décharge *f* (publique)

rubbish heap *n* tas *m* d'ordures

rubble *n* (after explosion) décombres *mpl*; (on site) gravats *mpl*

ruby **1** *n* **(a)** (gem) rubis *m*
(b) (*also* **∼ red**) rouge *m* rubis
2 *adj* **(a)** ‹*liquid, lips*› vermeil/-eille; **∼ wedding** noces *fpl* de vermeil

⋯⟶

(b) ⟨*bracelet, necklace*⟩ de rubis

rucksack *n* sac *m* à dos

rudder *n* (on boat) gouvernail *m*; (on plane) gouverne *f*

ruddy *adj* ⟨*cheeks*⟩ coloré/-e

rude *adj* **(a)** (impolite) ⟨*comment*⟩ impoli/-e; ⟨*person*⟩ mal élevé/-e; **to be ∼ to sb** être impoli/-e envers qn

(b) (indecent) ⟨*joke*⟩ grossier/-ière; **a ∼ word** un gros mot

rudimentary *adj* rudimentaire

rudiments *n pl* rudiments *mpl* (of de)

rueful *adj* ⟨*smile, thought*⟩ triste

ruff *n* (of lace) fraise *f*; (of fur, feathers) collier *m*

ruffle **1** *n* (at sleeve) manchette *f*; (at neck) ruche *f*; (on shirt front) jabot *m*

2 *vtr* **(a)** ébouriffer ⟨*hair, fur*⟩; hérisser ⟨*feathers*⟩; rider ⟨*water*⟩

(b) (disconcert) énerver; (upset) froisser

rug *n* **(a)** tapis *m*; (by bed) descente *f* de lit

(b) (GB) (blanket) couverture *f*

rugby *n* rugby *m*

rugby league *n* rugby *m* à 13

rugby union *n* rugby *m* à 15

rugged *adj* **(a)** ⟨*landscape*⟩ accidenté/-e; ⟨*coastline*⟩ déchiqueté/-e

(b) ⟨*man, features*⟩ rude

ruin **1** *n* ruine *f*

2 *vtr* **(a)** ruiner ⟨*economy, career*⟩; **to ∼ one's eyesight** s'abîmer la vue

(b) gâcher ⟨*holiday, meal*⟩; abîmer ⟨*clothes*⟩

IDIOM **to go to rack and ∼** se délabrer

ruined *adj* **(a)** (derelict) en ruines

(b) (spoilt) ⟨*holiday, meal*⟩ gâché/-e; ⟨*clothes, furniture*⟩ abîmé/-e; ⟨*reputation*⟩ ruiné/-e; (financially) ruiné/-e

⚹ **rule** **1** *n* **(a)** (of game, language) règle *f*; (of school, organization) règlement *m*; **against the ∼s** contraire aux règles *or* au règlement **(to do** de faire); **∼s and regulations** réglementation *f*; **as a ∼** généralement

(b) (authority) domination *f*, gouvernement *m*

(c) (for measuring) règle *f*

2 *vtr* **(a)** ⟨*ruler, law*⟩ gouverner; ⟨*monarch*⟩ régner sur; ⟨*party*⟩ diriger; ⟨*army*⟩ commander

(b) ⟨*factor*⟩ dicter ⟨*strategy*⟩; **to be ∼d by** ⟨*person*⟩ être mené/-e par ⟨*passions, spouse*⟩

(c) (draw) faire, tirer ⟨*line*⟩

(d) ⟨*court, umpire*⟩ **to ∼ that** décréter que

3 *vi* **(a)** ⟨*monarch, anarchy*⟩ régner

(b) ⟨*court, umpire*⟩ statuer

■ **rule out (a)** exclure ⟨*possibility, candidate*⟩ (of de); **to ∼ out doing** exclure de faire

(b) interdire ⟨*activity*⟩

ruler *n* **(a)** (leader) dirigeant/-e *m/f*

(b) (measure) règle *f*

ruling **1** *n* décision *f*

2 *adj* **(a)** (in power) dirigeant/-e

⚹ indicates a very frequent word

(b) (dominant) dominant/-e

rum *n* rhum *m*

rumble **1** *n* (of thunder, artillery, trucks) grondement *m*; (of stomach) gargouillement *m*

2 *vi* ⟨*thunder, artillery*⟩ gronder; ⟨*stomach*⟩ gargouiller

ruminate *vi* **(a)** (think) **to ∼ on** *or* **about** ruminer sur

(b) (Zool) ruminer

rummage *vi* fouiller (**through** dans)

rummy *n* rami *m*

rumour (GB), **rumor** (US) *n* rumeur *f*, bruit *m*

rumoured (GB), **rumored** (US) *adj* **it is ∼ that** il paraît que, on dit que

rump *n* **(a)** (*also* **∼ steak**) rumsteck *m*

(b) (of animal) croupe *f*

rumple *vtr* ébouriffer ⟨*hair*⟩; froisser ⟨*clothes, sheets, papers*⟩

⚹ **run** **1** *n* **(a)** course *f*; **a two-mile ∼** une course de deux miles; **to go for a ∼** aller courir; **to break into a ∼** se mettre à courir

(b) (flight) **on the ∼** en fuite; **to make a ∼ for it** fuir, s'enfuir

(c) (series) (of successes, failures) série *f*; (in printing) tirage *m*; **to have a ∼ of luck** être en veine

(d) (trip, route) trajet *m*

(e) (in cricket, baseball) point *m*

(f) (for rabbit, chickens) enclos *m*

(g) (in tights) échelle *f*

(h) (for skiing) piste *f*

(i) (in cards) suite *f*

2 *vtr* (*prét* **ran**, *pp* **run**) **(a)** courir ⟨*distance, marathon*⟩; **to ∼ a race** faire une course

(b) (drive) **to ∼ sb to the station** conduire qn à la gare

(c) (pass, move) **to ∼ one's hand over** passer la main sur; **to ∼ one's eye(s) over** parcourir rapidement

(d) (manage) diriger; **a well-/badly-run organization** une organisation bien/mal dirigée

(e) (operate) faire fonctionner ⟨*machine*⟩; faire tourner ⟨*motor*⟩; exécuter ⟨*program*⟩; entretenir ⟨*car*⟩; **to ∼ tests on** effectuer des tests sur

(f) (organize, offer) organiser ⟨*competition, course*⟩; mettre [qch] en place ⟨*bus service*⟩

(g) faire couler ⟨*bath*⟩; ouvrir ⟨*tap*⟩

(h) (enter) faire courir ⟨*horse*⟩; présenter ⟨*candidate*⟩

3 *vi* (*prét* **ran**, *pp* **run**) **(a)** ⟨*person, animal*⟩ courir; **to ∼ across/down sth** traverser/descendre qch en courant; **to ∼ for the bus** courir pour attraper le bus; **to ∼ come ∼ning** accourir (**towards** vers)

(b) (flee) fuir, s'enfuir; **to ∼ for one's life** s'enfuir pour sauver sa peau (fam)

(c) (colloq) (rush off) filer (fam)

(d) (function) ⟨*machine*⟩ marcher; **to leave the**

engine ∼ning laisser tourner le moteur
(e) (continue, last) ‹contract, lease› être valide
(f) ‹play, musical› tenir l'affiche (**for** pendant)
(g) (pass) **to** ∼ **past/through** ‹road, frontier, path› passer/traverser; **to** ∼ **(from) east to west** aller d'est en ouest
(h) (move) ‹sledge› glisser; ‹curtain› coulisser
(i) ‹bus, train› circuler
(j) (flow) couler; **tears ran down his face** les larmes coulaient sur son visage; **my nose is** ∼**ning** j'ai le nez qui coule
(k) ‹dye, garment› déteindre; ‹make-up› couler
(l) (as candidate) se présenter; **to** ∼ **for president** être candidat/-e à la présidence
IDIOMS **in the long** ∼ à long terme; **in the short** ∼ à brève échéance
■ **run about, run around** courir
■ **run away**: ① ¶ ∼ **away** s'enfuir; **to** ∼ **away from home** ‹child› faire une fugue
② ¶ ∼ **away with [sb/sth] (a)** (flee) partir avec
(b) rafler (fam) ‹prize, title›
■ **run down**: ① ¶ ∼ **down** ‹battery› se décharger; ‹watch› retarder
② ¶ ∼ **[sb/sth] down (a)** (in vehicle) renverser
(b) réduire ‹production, defences›; user ‹battery›
(c) (disparage) dénigrer
■ **run into (a)** heurter, rentrer dans (fam) ‹car, wall›
(b) (encounter) rencontrer ‹person, difficulty›
(c) (amount to) s'élever à ‹hundreds, millions›
■ **run off** partir en courant
■ **run out** ① ¶ ∼ **out (a)** ‹supplies, oil› s'épuiser; **time is** ∼**ning out** le temps manque
(b) ‹pen, machine› être vide
(c) ‹contract, passport› expirer
② ¶ ∼ **out of** ne plus avoir de ‹petrol, time, money, ideas›; **to be** ∼**ning out of** n'avoir presque plus de ‹petrol, time, money, ideas›
■ **run over** (in vehicle) (injure) renverser; (kill) écraser
■ **run through** parcourir ‹list, article›; répéter ‹scene, speech›
■ **run up** accumuler ‹debt›
■ **run up against** se heurter à ‹difficulty›
runaway adj ‹teenager› fugueur/-euse; ‹slave› fugitif/-ive; ‹horse› emballé/-e
rundown n récapitulatif m (**on** de)
run-down adj **(a)** (exhausted) fatigué/-e, à plat (fam)
(b) (shabby) décrépit/-e
rung n **(a)** (of ladder) barreau m
(b) (in hierarchy) échelon m
run-in n (colloq) prise f de bec (fam)
runner n **(a)** (person, animal) coureur m
(b) (horse) partant/-e m/f
(c) (messenger) estafette f
(d) (for door, seat) glissière f; (for drawer) coulisseau m; (on sled) patin m
(e) (on stairs) chemin m d'escalier
runner bean n (GB) haricot m d'Espagne

runner up n (pl ∼**s up**) second/-e m/f (**to** après)
running ① n **(a)** (sport, exercise) course f à pied
(b) (management) direction f (**of** de)
② adj **(a)** ‹water› courant/-e; ‹tap› ouvert/-e
(b) ‹five days› ∼ cinq jours de suite
IDIOM **to be in/out of the** ∼ être/ne plus être dans la course (**for** pour)
running battle n éternel conflit m
running commentary n commentaire m ininterrompu
running total n total m cumulé
runny adj ‹jam, sauce› liquide; ‹butter› fondu/-e; ‹omelette› baveux/-euse; **to have a** ∼ **nose** avoir le nez qui coule
run-of-the-mill adj ordinaire, banal/-e
runt n **(a)** (of litter) le plus faible m de la portée
(b) (weakling) avorton m
run-up n **(a)** (for a jump) course f d'élan; **to take a** ∼ prendre son élan pour sauter
(b) (preceding period) **the** ∼ **to** la dernière ligne droite avant
runway n piste f d'aviation
rupee n roupie f
rupture n rupture f
✔ **rural** adj (country) rural/-e; (pastoral) champêtre
ruse n stratagème m
✔ **rush** ① n **(a)** (surge) ruée f (**to do** pour faire); **to make a** ∼ **for sth** ‹crowd› se ruer vers qch; ‹individual› se précipiter vers qch
(b) (hurry) **to be in a** ∼ être pressé/-e (**to do** de faire); **to leave in a** ∼ partir en vitesse
(c) (of liquid, adrenalin) montée f; (of air) bouffée f
(d) (plant) jonc m
② vtr **(a)** **to** ∼ **sth to** envoyer qch d'urgence à; **to be** ∼**ed to the hospital** être emmené/-e d'urgence à l'hôpital
(b) expédier ‹task, speech›
(c) (hurry) bousculer ‹person›
(d) (charge at) sauter sur ‹person›; prendre d'assaut ‹building›
③ vi ‹person› (hurry) se dépêcher (**to do** de faire); (rush forward) se précipiter (**to do** pour faire); **to** ∼ **out of the room** se précipiter hors de la pièce; **to** ∼ **down the stairs/past** descendre l'escalier/passer à toute vitesse
■ **rush into**: ① **to** ∼ **into marriage/a purchase** se marier/acheter sans prendre le temps de réfléchir
② ¶ ∼ **[sb] into doing** bousculer [qn] pour qu'il/elle fasse
■ **rush out**: ¶ ∼ **out** sortir en vitesse
■ **rush through**: ① ¶ ∼ **through [sth]** expédier ‹task›
② ¶ ∼ **[sth] through** adopter en vitesse ‹legislation›; traiter en priorité ‹order, application›
rushed adj ‹attempt, letter› expédié/-e

r

rush hour n heures fpl de pointe
rusk n biscuit m pour bébés
russet adj roussâtre
Russia pr n Russie f
Russian ①️ n (a) (person) Russe mf
(b) (language) russe m
②️ adj ‹culture, food, politics› russe; ‹teacher, lesson› de russe; ‹embassy› de Russie
rust ①️ n rouille f
②️ vtr rouiller ‹metal›
③️ vi ‹metal› se rouiller
rustic adj rustique
rustle ①️ n (of paper, dry leaves) froissement m; (of leaves, silk) bruissement m
②️ vtr froisser ‹papers›

rusty adj rouillé/-e
rut n (a) (in ground) ornière f
(b) (routine) be in a ∼ être enlisé/-e dans la routine
(c) (Zool) the ∼ le rut
rutabaga n (US) rutabaga m
ruthless adj impitoyable (in dans)
RV n (US) (abbr = **recreational vehicle**) camping-car m, autocaravane f
Rwanda pr n Rwanda m
rye n (a) (cereal) seigle m
(b) (US) (also ∼ **whiskey**) whisky m à base de seigle
rye bread n pain m de seigle

Ss

s, S n s, S m
sabbath n (also **Sabbath**) (Jewish) sabbat m; (Christian) jour m du seigneur
sabbatical n congé m sabbatique
sabotage ①️ n sabotage m
②️ vtr saboter
saboteur n saboteur/-euse m/f
sabre, saber (US) n sabre m
sachet n sachet m
sack ①️ n (a) sac m
(b) to get the ∼ se faire mettre à la porte (fam)
②️ vtr (a) (colloq) mettre [qn] à la porte (fam) ‹employee›
(b) mettre [qch] à sac ‹town›
sacrament n sacrement m
sacred adj sacré/-e (to pour)
sacrifice ①️ n sacrifice m (to à; of de)
②️ vtr (a) (gen) sacrifier (to à)
(b) (to the gods) offrir [qch] en sacrifice (to à)
③️ v refl to ∼ oneself se sacrifier (for pour)
sacrilege n sacrilège m
sacrosanct adj sacro-saint/-e
✎ **sad** adj triste (that que + subjunctive); it makes me ∼ cela me rend triste
sadden vtr attrister
saddle ①️ n selle f
②️ vtr (a) seller ‹horse›
(b) to ∼ sb with mettre [qch] sur les bras de qn ‹responsibility, task›
saddle bag n sacoche f
sadist n sadique mf
sadistic adj sadique
sadness n tristesse f

─────────────────
✎ indicates a very frequent word

sae n (abbr = **stamped addressed envelope**) enveloppe f timbrée à votre/son adresse
safari n safari m
safari park n parc m zoologique (où les animaux vivent en semi-liberté)
✎ **safe** ①️ n coffre-fort m
②️ adj (a) (after ordeal, risk) ‹person› sain et sauf/saine et sauve; ‹object› intact/-e; ∼ **and sound** sain et sauf/saine et sauve
(b) (free from threat, harm) **to be** ∼ ‹person› être en sécurité; ‹document, valuables› être en lieu sûr; ‹company, job, reputation› ne pas être menacé/-e; **is the bike** ∼ **here?** est-ce qu'on peut laisser le vélo ici sans risque?; **have a** ∼ **journey!** bon voyage!
(c) (risk-free) ‹toy, level, method› sans danger; ‹place, vehicle› sûr/-e; ‹structure, building› solide; **it's not** ∼ c'est dangereux
(d) (prudent) ‹investment› sûr/-e; ‹choice› prudent/-e
(e) (reliable) **to be in** ∼ **hands** être en bonnes mains
IDIOMS **better** ∼ **than sorry!** mieux vaut prévenir que guérir!; **just to be on the** ∼ **side** simplement par précaution
safe bet n **it's a** ∼ c'est quelque chose de sûr
safe-conduct n laissez-passer m inv
safe-deposit box n coffre m (à la banque)
safeguard ①️ n garantie f (for pour; against contre)
②️ vtr protéger (against, from contre)
safe house n refuge m
safekeeping n **in sb's** ∼ à la garde de qn
safely adv (a) ‹come back› (of person) sans encombre; (of parcel, goods) sans dommage;

(of plane) ‹*land, take off*› sans problème;
I arrived ∼ je suis bien arrivé
(b) we can ∼ assume that… nous pouvons
être certains que…
(c) ‹*locked, hidden*› bien

safe sex *n* rapports *mpl* sexuels sans
risque

✔ **safety** *n* sécurité *f*; **in** ∼ en (toute) sécurité;
to reach ∼ parvenir en lieu sûr

safety belt *n* ceinture *f* de sécurité

safety net *n* filet *m* (de protection);
(figurative) filet *m* de sécurité

safety pin *n* épingle *f* de sûreté

sag *vi* (*p prés etc* **-gg-**) (a) ‹*beam, mattress*›
s'affaisser; ‹*tent, rope*› ne pas être bien
tendu/-e
(b) ‹*breasts*› pendre; ‹*flesh*› être flasque

saga *n* saga *f*

sage *n* (a) (herb) sauge *f*
(b) (wise person) sage *m*

Sagittarius *n* Sagittaire *m*

Sahara *pr n* Sahara *m*; **the** ∼ **desert** le
désert du Sahara

sail ① *n* (a) (of boat) voile *f*; **to set sail**
prendre la mer; **a ship in full** ∼ un navire
toutes voiles dehors
(b) (of windmill) aile *f*
② *vtr* (a) piloter ‹*ship, yacht*›
(b) traverser [qch] en bateau ‹*ocean,
channel*›
③ *vi* (a) ‹*person*› voyager en bateau; **to** ∼
around the world faire le tour du monde en
bateau
(b) ‹*ship*› **to** ∼ **across** traverser ‹*ocean*›; **the
boat** ∼**s at 10 am** le bateau part à 10 h
(c) (as hobby) **to go** ∼**ing** faire de la voile
■ **sail through** gagner [qch] facilement
‹*match*›; **to** ∼ **through an exam** réussir un
examen les doigts dans le nez (fam)

sailboard *n* planche *f* à voile

sailboarder *n* véliplanchiste *mf*

sailboat *n* (US) bateau *m* à voiles

sailing *n* voile *f*

sailing boat *n* bateau *m* à voiles

sailing ship *n* voilier *m*

sailor *n* marin *m*

saint *n* saint/-e *m/f*; **Saint Mark** saint Marc

sake *n* (a) **for the** ∼ **of clarity** pour la clarté;
for the ∼ **of argument** à titre d'exemple; **to
kill for the** ∼ **of killing** tuer pour le plaisir
de tuer; **for old times'** ∼ en souvenir du bon
vieux temps
(b) (benefit) **for the** ∼ **of sb, for sb's** ∼ par
égard pour qn; **for God's/heaven's** ∼**!** pour
l'amour de Dieu/du ciel!

salad *n* salade *f*; **ham** ∼ salade au jambon

salad bar *n* buffet *m* de crudités

salad bowl *n* saladier *m*

salad dressing *n* sauce *f* pour salade

salami *n* saucisson *m* sec

salary *n* salaire *m*

✔ **sale** *n* (a) (gen) vente *f* (of de; to à); **for sale** à
vendre; **on** ∼ (GB) en vente
(b) (at cut prices) solde *f*; **the sales** les soldes;
in the ∼(s) (GB), **on** ∼ (US); en solde

sale price *n* prix *m* soldé

sales assistant *n* (GB) vendeur/-euse
m/f

sales executive *n* cadre *m* commercial

salesman *n* (*pl* -**men**) (rep) représentant
m; (in shop) vendeur *m*

sales pitch *n* baratin *m* (fam) publicitaire

sales rep, sales representative *n*
représentant/-e *m/f*

saleswoman *n* (*pl* -**women**) (rep)
représentante *f*; (in shop) vendeuse *f*

saliva *n* salive *f*

salivate *vi* saliver

sallow *adj* cireux/-euse

salmon *n* (*pl* ∼) saumon *m*

salmonella *n* (*pl* -**æ** *ou* -**as**) salmonelle *f*

salon *n* salon *m*

saloon *n* (a) (GB) (*also* ∼ **car**) berline *f*
(b) (US) saloon *m*, bar *m*
(c) (on boat) salon *m*

salt ① *n* sel *m*
② *vtr* saler ‹*meat, fish, road, path*›

saltcellar *n* salière *f*

salty *adj* ‹*water, food, flavour*› salé/-e

salutary *adj* salutaire

salute ① *n* salut *m*
② *vtr, vi* saluer

salvage ① *n* (a) (rescue) sauvetage *m* (of
de)
(b) (goods rescued) biens *mpl* récupérés
② *vtr* (a) sauver ‹*cargo, materials,
belongings*› (from de); effectuer le sauvetage
de ‹*ship*›
(b) sauver ‹*marriage, reputation, game*›
(c) (for recycling) récupérer ‹*metal, paper*›

salvation *n* salut *m*

Salvation Army *n* Armée *f* du Salut

salve ① *n* baume *m*
② *vtr* **to** ∼ **one's conscience** soulager sa
conscience

Samaritan *n* **the Good** ∼ le bon
Samaritain; **the** ∼**s** les Samaritains *mpl*

✔ **same** ① *adj* même (as que); **to be the** ∼
être le/la même; **to look the** ∼ être pareil/
-eille; **to be the** ∼ **as sth** être comme qch;
it amounts *or* **comes to the** ∼ **thing** cela
revient au même; **it's all the** ∼ **to me** ça
m'est complètement égal; **if it's all the** ∼
to you si ça ne te fait rien; **at the** ∼ **time** en
même temps; **to remain** *or* **stay the** ∼ ne pas
changer
② **the same** *pron* la même chose (as
que); **I'll have the** ∼ je prendrai la même
chose; **to do the** ∼ **as sb** faire comme qn;
the ∼ **to you!** (in greeting) à toi aussi, à toi de ┈┊

même!; (of insult) toi-même! (fam)

3 **the same** adv ‹act, dress› de la même façon; **to feel the ~ as sb** penser comme qn **IDIOMS all the ~...**, **just the ~,...** tout de même,...; **thanks all the ~** merci quand même

same-day adj ‹service› effectué/-e dans la journée

same-sex adj de même sexe

⚹ **sample** **1** n (a) (of product, fabric) échantillon m
(b) (for analysis) prélèvement m
2 vtr (a) (taste) goûter (à) ‹food, wine›
(b) (test) essayer ‹products›; sonder ‹opinion, market›

sanatorium (GB), **sanitarium** (US) n (pl **-riums** ou **-ria** (GB)) sanatorium m

sanctimonious adj supérieur/-e

sanction **1** n sanction f; **to impose ~s** prendre des sanctions
2 vtr (permit) autoriser; (approve) sanctionner

sanctity n sainteté f

sanctuary n (a) (safe place) refuge m
(b) (holy place) sanctuaire m
(c) (for wildlife) réserve f; (for mistreated pets) refuge m

sand **1** n sable m
2 vtr (a) (also ~ **down**) poncer ‹floor›; frotter [qch] au papier de verre ‹woodwork›
(b) sabler ‹icy road›

sandal n sandale f

sand castle n château m de sable

sand dune n dune f

sandpaper **1** n papier m de verre
2 vtr poncer

sandpit n (quarry) sablière f; (for children) bac m à sable

sandstone n grès m

sandwich **1** n sandwich m; **cucumber ~** sandwich au concombre
2 vtr **to be ~ed between** ‹car, building, person› être pris/-e en sandwich entre

sandwich bar n sandwich bar m

sandwich course n (GB) cours m avec stage pratique

sandy adj (a) ‹beach› de sable; ‹path, soil› sablonneux/-euse
(b) ‹hair› blond roux inv; ‹colour› sable (inv after n)

sane adj (a) ‹person› sain/-e d'esprit
(b) ‹policy, judgment› sensé/-e

sanitarium (US) = SANATORIUM

sanitary adj (a) ‹engineer, installations› sanitaire
(b) (hygienic) hygiénique; (clean) propre

sanitary towel (GB), **sanitary napkin** (US) n serviette f hygiénique or périodique

⚹ indicates a very frequent word

sanitation n installations fpl sanitaires

sanity n équilibre m mental

Santa (Claus) pr n le père Noël

sap **1** n sève f
2 vtr (p prés etc **-pp-**) saper ‹strength, courage, confidence›

sapling n jeune arbre m

sapphire n (a) (stone) saphir m
(b) (colour) bleu m saphir

sarcasm n sarcasme m

sarcastic adj sarcastique

sardine n sardine f

Sardinia pr n Sardaigne f

sardonic adj ‹laugh, look› sardonique; ‹person, remark› acerbe

SARS n SRAS m

SAS n (GB) (abbr = **Special Air Service**) commandos mpl britanniques aéroportés

sash n (round waist) large ceinture f; (ceremonial) écharpe f

sassy adj (US) (colloq) culotté (fam)

Satan pr n Satan

satanic adj ‹rites› satanique; ‹pride, smile› démoniaque

satchel n cartable m (à bandoulière)

satellite n satellite m

satellite dish n antenne f parabolique

satellite TV n télévision f par satellite

satin **1** n satin m
2 adj ‹garment, shoe› de satin; **with a ~** finish satiné/-e

satire n satire f (on sur)

satiric(al) adj satirique

satirize vtr faire la satire de

satisfaction n satisfaction f

satisfactory adj satisfaisant/-e

satisfied adj (a) (pleased) satisfait/-e (with, about de)
(b) (convinced) convaincu/-e (by par; that que)

⚹ **satisfy** vtr (a) satisfaire ‹person, need, desires, curiosity›; assouvir ‹hunger›
(b) (persuade) convaincre ‹person, public opinion› (that que)
(c) (meet) satisfaire à ‹demand, requirements, conditions›

satisfying adj (a) ‹meal› substantiel/-ielle
(b) ‹job› qui apporte de la satisfaction
(c) ‹result, progress› satisfaisant/-e

satnav n GPS m

satphone n téléphone m satellite

saturate vtr saturer (with de)

saturated adj (wet) ‹person, clothes› trempé/-e; ‹ground› détrempé/-e

saturation point n point m de saturation; **to reach ~** arriver à saturation

⚹ **Saturday** n samedi m; **he has a ~ job** il a un petit boulot (fam) le samedi

Saturn pr n (planet) Saturne f

sauce n sauce f

saucepan n casserole f

saucer *n* soucoupe *f*

Saudi Arabia *pr n* Arabie *f* saoudite

sauna *n* sauna *m*

saunter *vi* (*also* ~ **along**) marcher d'un pas nonchalant; **to** ~ **off** s'éloigner d'un pas nonchalant

sausage *n* saucisse *f*

sausage roll *n* feuilleté *m* à la chair à saucisse

savage [1] *n* sauvage *mf*
[2] *adj* (gen) féroce; ⟨*blow, beating*⟩ violent/-e; ⟨*attack*⟩ sauvage; ⟨*criticism*⟩ virulent/-e
[3] *vtr* ⟨*dog*⟩ attaquer [qn/qch] sauvagement; ⟨*lion*⟩ déchiqueter

✓ **save** [1] *n* (Sport) arret *m* de but
[2] *vtr* (a) (rescue) sauver (**from** de); **to** ~ **sb's life** sauver la vie à qn
(b) (put by, keep) mettre [qch] de côté ⟨*money, food*⟩ (**to do** pour faire); garder ⟨*goods, documents*⟩ (**for** pour); sauvegarder ⟨*data, file*⟩; **to have money** ~**d** avoir de l'argent de côté; **to** ~ **sth for sb, to** ~ **sb sth** garder qch pour qn
(c) (economize on) économiser ⟨*money*⟩ (**by doing** en faisant); gagner ⟨*time, space*⟩ (**by doing** en faisant); **to** ~ **one's energy** ménager ses forces; **you'll** ~ **money** vous ferez des économies; **to** ~ **sb/sth (from) having to do** éviter à qn/qch de faire
(d) (Sport) arrêter
[3] *vi* (a) (put money by) = SAVE UP
(b) (economize) économiser, faire des économies; **to** ~ **on** faire des économies de ⟨*energy, paper*⟩
■ **save up** faire des économies; **to** ~ **up for** mettre de l'argent de côté pour s'acheter ⟨*car, house*⟩; mettre de l'argent de côté pour s'offrir ⟨*holiday*⟩

saver *n* épargnant/-e *m/f*

saving grace *n* bon côté *m*; **it's his** ~ c'est ce qui le sauve

savings *n pl* économies *fpl*

savings account *n* (GB) compte *m* d'épargne; (US) compte *m* rémunéré

savings bank *n* caisse *f* d'épargne

saviour (GB), **savior** (US) *n* sauveur *m*

savour (GB), **savor** [1] *n* saveur *f*
[2] *vtr* savourer

savoury (GB), **savory** (US) *adj* (not sweet) salé/-e; (appetizing) appétissant/-e

saw [1] *n* scie *f*
[2] *vtr* (*prét* **sawed**, *pp* **sawn** (GB), **sawed** (US)) scier; **to** ~ **through/down/off** scier

sawdust *n* sciure *f* (de bois)

sawn-off shotgun *n* (GB) fusil *m* à canon scié

saxophone *n* saxophone *m*

✓ **say** [1] *n* **to have one's** ~ dire ce qu'on a à dire (**on** sur); **to have a** ~/**no** ~ **in sth** avoir/ ne pas avoir son mot à dire sur qch; **to have no** ~ **in the matter** ne pas avoir voix au chapitre
[2] *vtr* (*prét, pp* **said**) (a) (gen) dire (**to** à); **'hello,' he said** 'bonjour,' dit-il; **to** ~ **(that)** dire que; **they** ~ **she's very rich, she is said to be very rich** on dit qu'elle est très riche; **to** ~ **sth about sb/sth** dire qch au sujet de qn/qch; **to** ~ **sth to oneself** se dire qch; **let's** ~ **no more about it** n'en parlons plus; **it goes without** ~**ing that** il va sans dire que; **that is to** ~ c'est-à-dire; **let's** ~ **there are 20** mettons *or* supposons qu'il y en ait 20; **how high would you** ~ **it is?** à ton avis, quelle en est la hauteur?, **I'd** ~ **she was about 25** je lui donnerais environ 25 ans
(b) ⟨*sign, clock, dial, gauge*⟩ indiquer
[3] *vi* (*prét, pp* **said**) stop when I ~ arrête quand je te le dirai; **he wouldn't** ~ il n'a pas voulu dire
IDIOMS **it** ~**s a lot for sb/sth** c'est tout à l'honneur de qn/qch; **there's a lot to be said for that method** cette méthode est très intéressante à bien des égards; **when all is said and done** tout compte fait, en fin de compte

saying *n* dicton *m*

scab *n* croûte *f*

scaffolding *n* échafaudage *m*

scald *vtr* ébouillanter

scalding *adj* brûlant/-e

✓ **scale** [1] *n* (a) (gen) échelle *f*; **pay** ~, **salary** ~ échelle des salaires; **on a** ~ **of 1 to 10** sur une échelle allant de 1 à 10
(b) (extent) (of disaster, success, violence) étendue *f* (**of** de); (of defeat, recession, task) ampleur *f* (**of** de); (of activity, operation) envergure *f* (**of** de)
(c) (on ruler, gauge) graduation *f*
(d) (for weighing) balance *f*
(e) (Mus) gamme *f*
(f) (on fish, insect) écaille *f*
[2] **scales** *n pl* balance *f*
[3] *vtr* (a) escalader ⟨*wall, mountain*⟩
(b) écailler ⟨*fish*⟩
■ **scale down**: ~ **[sth] down,** ~ **down [sth]** réduire l'échelle de ⟨*drawing*⟩; réduire ⟨*activity*⟩

scale drawing *n* dessin *m* à l'échelle

scale model *n* maquette *f* à l'échelle

scallop, scollop *n* coquille *f* Saint-Jacques

scalp [1] *n* cuir *m* chevelu
[2] *vtr* scalper

scam *n* (colloq) escroquerie *f*

scamper *vi* **to** ~ **about** *or* **around** ⟨*child, dog*⟩ gambader; ⟨*mouse*⟩ trottiner

scan [1] *n* (Med) (CAT) scanner *m*; (ultrasound) échographie *f*
[2] *vtr* (*p prés etc* **-nn-**) (a) lire rapidement ⟨*page, newspaper*⟩
(b) (examine) scruter ⟨*face, horizon*⟩

⋯⟶

S

(c) ‹beam of light, radar› balayer
(d) (Med) faire un scanner de ‹organ›
scandal n scandale m
scandalize vtr scandaliser
scandalous adj scandaleux/-euse
Scandinavia pr n Scandinavie f
scanner n (Comput, Med) scanner m; (for bar codes) lecteur m optique
scanty adj ‹meal, supply› maigre (before n); ‹information› sommaire; ‹knowledge› rudimentaire; ‹swimsuit› minuscule
scapegoat n bouc m émissaire (**for** de)
scar ⊡ n cicatrice f; (on face from knife) balafre f
⊡ vtr (p prés etc **-rr-**) marquer; (on face with knife) balafrer; **to ~ sb for life** laisser à qn une cicatrice permanente; (figurative) marquer qn pour la vie
scarce adj rare; **to become ~** se faire rare
scarcely adv à peine; **~ anybody believes it** presque personne ne le croit
scare ⊡ n **(a)** peur f; **to give sb a ~** faire peur à qn
(b) (alert) alerte f; **bomb ~** alerte à la bombe
⊡ vtr faire peur à
■ **scare away**, **scare off** faire fuir ‹animal, attacker›; (figurative) dissuader
scarecrow n épouvantail m
scared adj ‹animal, person› effrayé/-e; ‹look› apeuré/-e; **to be** or **feel ~** avoir peur; **to be ~ stiff** (colloq) avoir une peur bleue (fam)
scaremongering n alarmisme m
scarf n (pl **scarves**) (long) écharpe f; (square) foulard m
scarlet n, adj écarlate f
scarlet fever n scarlatine f
scary adj (colloq) qui fait peur
scathing adj ‹remark, tone, wit› cinglant/-e; ‹criticism› virulent/-e
scatter ⊡ vtr **(a)** (also **~ around**, **~ about**) répandre ‹seeds, earth›; éparpiller ‹books, papers, clothes›
(b) disperser ‹crowd, herd›
⊡ vi ‹people, animals, birds› se disperser
scatter-brained adj ‹person› étourdi/-e; ‹idea› farfelu/-e (fam)
scattered adj ‹houses, trees, population, clouds› épars/-e; ‹books, litter› éparpillé/-e; ‹support, resistance› clairsemé/-e
scatty adj (colloq) (GB) étourdi/-e
scavenge vi **to ~ for food** ‹bird, animal› chercher de la nourriture
scavenger n **(a)** (animal) charognard m
(b) (person) (for food) faiseur m de poubelles; (for objects) récupérateur m
scenario n (pl **~s**) (gen) cas m de figure; (of film, play) scénario m
⚘ **scene** n **(a)** (gen) scène f; **behind the ~s** dans les coulisses fpl; **you need a change of ~** tu as besoin de changer de décor
(b) (of crime, accident) lieu m; **at** or **on the ~**

sur les lieux
(c) (image, sight) image f
(d) (view) vue f
scenery n **(a)** (landscape) paysage m
(b) (in theatre) décors mpl
scent ⊡ n **(a)** (smell) odeur f
(b) (perfume) parfum m
(c) (of animal) fumet m; (in hunting) piste f
⊡ vtr **(a)** flairer ‹prey, animal›
(b) pressentir ‹danger, trouble›
(c) (perfume) parfumer ‹air›
sceptic (GB), **skeptic** (US) n sceptique mf
sceptical (GB), **skeptical** (US) adj sceptique
scepticism (GB), **skepticism** (US) n scepticisme m
schedule ⊡ n **(a)** (of work, events) programme m; (timetable) horaire m; **to be ahead of/behind ~** être en avance/en retard; **to arrive on/ahead of ~** ‹bus, train, plane› arriver à l'heure/en avance
(b) (list) liste f
⊡ vtr (plan) prévoir; (arrange) programmer
scheduled flight n vol m régulier
⚘ **scheme** ⊡ n **(a)** projet m, plan m (**to do**, **for doing** pour faire); **pension ~** régime m de retraite
(b) (plot) combine f (**to do** pour faire)
⊡ vi comploter
scheming n machinations fpl
schizophrenic adj schizophrénique
scholar n érudit/-e m/f
scholarship n bourse f (**to** pour)
⚘ **school** ⊡ n **(a)** école f; **at ~** à l'école
(b) (US) (university) université f
(c) (of fish) banc m
⊡ adj ‹holiday, outing, trip, uniform, year› scolaire
schoolbag n sac m de classe
schoolboy n (pupil) élève m; (primary) écolier m; (secondary) collégien m
schoolchild n écolier/-ière m/f
school fees n pl frais mpl de scolarité
schoolfriend n camarade mf de classe
schoolgirl n (pupil) élève f; (primary) écolière f; (secondary) collégienne f
schooling n scolarité f
school-leaver n (GB) jeune mf ayant fini sa scolarité
school leaving age n âge m de fin de scolarité
school lunch n repas m de la cantine scolaire
school report (GB), **school report card** (US) n bulletin m scolaire
schoolteacher n enseignant/-e m/f; (primary) instituteur/-trice m/f; (secondary) professeur m
schoolwork n travail m de classe

⚘ indicates a very frequent word

◆ **science** ⟦1⟧ *n* science *f*; **to study** ∼ étudier les sciences
  ⟦2⟧ *adj* ‹exam, subject› scientifique; ‹teacher, textbook› de sciences

science fiction *n* science-fiction *f*

◆ **scientific** *adj* scientifique

◆ **scientist** *n* scientifique *mf*

scissors *n pl* ciseaux *mpl*

scoff ⟦1⟧ *vtr* (GB) (colloq) (eat) engloutir (fam), bouffer (fam)
  ⟦2⟧ *vi* se moquer (**at** de)

scold *vtr* gronder (**for doing** pour avoir fait)

scoop ⟦1⟧ *n* (a) (for measuring) mesure *f*
  (b) (of ice cream) boule *f*
  (c) (in journalism) exclusivité *f*
  ⟦2⟧ *vtr* (colloq) décrocher (fam) ‹prize, sum of money, story›

scooter *n* (a) (child's) trottinette *f*
  (b) (motorized) scooter *m*

scope *n* (a) (opportunity) possibilité *f* (**for** de)
  (b) (of inquiry, report, book) portée *f*, (of plan) envergure *f*
  (c) (of person) compétences *fpl*

scorch ⟦1⟧ *n* (also ∼ **mark**) légère brûlure *f*
  ⟦2⟧ *vtr* ‹fire› brûler; ‹sun› dessécher ‹grass, trees›; griller ‹lawn›; ‹iron› roussir ‹fabric›

scorching *adj* (colloq) (also ∼ **hot**) ‹day› torride; ‹weather› caniculaire

◆ **score** ⟦1⟧ *n* (a) (Sport) score *m*; (in cards) marque *f*; **to keep (the)** ∼ marquer les points; (in cards) tenir la marque
  (b) (in exam, test) note *f*, résultat *m*
  (c) (Mus) (written music) partition *f*; (for film) musique *f* (de film)
  (d) (twenty) **a** ∼ vingt *m*, une vingtaine *f*
  (e) **on this** *or* **that** ∼ à ce sujet
  ⟦2⟧ *vtr* (a) marquer ‹goal, point›; remporter ‹victory, success›; **to** ∼ **9 out of 10** avoir 9 sur 10
  (b) (cut) entailler
  ⟦3⟧ *vi* (gain point) marquer un point; (obtain goal) marquer un but
  IDIOM **to settle a** ∼ régler ses comptes

scoreboard *n* tableau *m* d'affichage

scorn ⟦1⟧ *n* mépris *m* (**for** pour)
  ⟦2⟧ *vtr* (despise) mépriser; (reject) accueillir avec mépris ‹claim, suggestion›

scornful *adj* méprisant/-e

Scorpio *n* Scorpion *m*

Scot *n* Écossais/-e *m/f*

Scotch ⟦1⟧ *n* (also ∼ **whisky**) whisky *m*, scotch *m*
  ⟦2⟧ *adj* écossais/-e

Scotch tape® *n* (US) scotch® *m*

scot-free *adj* **to get off** ∼ (unpunished) s'en tirer sans être inquiété/-e; (unharmed) s'en sortir indemne

Scotland *pr n* Écosse *f*

Scottish *adj* écossais/-e

scour *vtr* (a) (scrub) récurer

(b) (search) parcourir ‹area, list› (**for** à la recherche de)

scourer *n* tampon *m* à récurer

scourge *n* fléau *m*

scout *n* (a) (also **boy** ∼) scout *m*
  (b) (Mil) éclaireur *m*
  (c) (also **talent** ∼) découvreur/-euse *m/f* de nouveaux talents
  ■ **scout around** explorer; **to** ∼ **around for sth** rechercher qch

scowl ⟦1⟧ *n* air *m* renfrogné
  ⟦2⟧ *vi* prendre un air renfrogné

scramble ⟦1⟧ *n* (a) (rush) course *f* (**for** pour; **to do** pour faire)
  (b) (climb) escalade *f*
  ⟦2⟧ *vtr* brouiller ‹signal›
  ⟦3⟧ *vi* **to** ∼ **up** escalader; **to** ∼ **down** dégringoler

scrambled egg *n* (also ∼**s**) œufs *mpl* brouillés

scrambling *n* (Sport) motocross *m*

scrap ⟦1⟧ *n* (a) (of paper, cloth) petit morceau *m*; (of news, information) fragment *m*
  (b) (old iron) ferraille *f*
  ⟦2⟧ **scraps** *n pl* (of food) restes *mpl*; (from butcher's) déchets *mpl*
  ⟦3⟧ *vtr* (*p prés etc* **-pp-**) (a) (colloq) abandonner ‹idea, plan, system›
  (b) détruire ‹aircraft, equipment›

scrapbook *n* album *m*

scrap dealer *n* ferrailleur *m*

scrape ⟦1⟧ *n* **to get into a** ∼ (colloq) s'attirer des ennuis
  ⟦2⟧ *vtr* (a) (clean) gratter ‹vegetables, shoes›
  (b) érafler ‹car, paintwork, furniture›; **to** ∼ **one's knees** s'écorcher les genoux
  ⟦3⟧ *vi* **to** ∼ **against sth** (rub) frotter contre qch; (scratch) érafler qch
  ■ **scrape by** (financially) s'en sortir à peine; (in situation) s'en tirer de justesse
  ■ **scrape in** (to university, class) entrer de justesse
  ■ **scrape out**: ¶ ∼ **out [sth]**, ∼ **[sth] out** nettoyer [qch] en grattant ‹saucepan›
  ■ **scrape through**: ⟦1⟧ ¶ ∼ **through** s'en tirer de justesse
  ⟦2⟧ ¶ ∼ **through [sth]** réussir de justesse à ‹exam, test›

scrap heap *n* **to be thrown on the** ∼ être mis/-e au rebut

scrap iron, **scrap metal** *n* ferraille *f*

scrap paper *n* papier *m* brouillon

scrap yard *n* chantier *m* de ferraille, casse *f*

scratch ⟦1⟧ *n* (a) (on skin) égratignure *f*; (from a claw, fingernail) griffure *f*
  (b) (on metal, furniture) éraflure *f*; (on record, glass) rayure *f*
  (c) (sound) grattement *m*
  (d) (colloq) **he/his work is not up to** ∼ il/son travail n'est pas à la hauteur
  (e) **to start from** ∼ partir de zéro   ⋯⫶

S

2 *vtr* **(a)** to ∼ one's initials on sth graver ses initiales sur qch
(b) ⟨*cat, person*⟩ griffer ⟨*person*⟩; ⟨*thorns, rose bush*⟩ égratigner ⟨*person*⟩; érafler ⟨*car, wood*⟩; rayer ⟨*record*⟩; ⟨*cat*⟩ se faire les griffes sur ⟨*furniture*⟩; ⟨*person*⟩ to ∼ sb's eyes out arracher les yeux à quelqu'un
(c) to ∼ sb's back gratter le dos de qn
3 *vi* se gratter

scratch card *n* jeu *m* de grattage

scrawl **1** *n* gribouillage *m*
2 *vtr, vi* gribouiller

scrawny *adj* ⟨*person, animal*⟩ décharné/-e

⚜ **scream** **1** *n* (of person, animal) cri *m* (perçant); (stronger) hurlement *m*; (of brakes) grincement *m*; (of tyres) crissement *m*
2 *vtr* crier
3 *vi* crier; (stronger) hurler

screech **1** *n* (of person, animal) cri *m* strident; (of tyres) crissement *m*
2 *vi* ⟨*person, animal*⟩ pousser un cri strident; ⟨*tyres*⟩ crisser

⚜ **screen** **1** *n* **(a)** (on TV, VDU, at cinema) écran *m*
(b) (furniture) paravent *m*
(c) (US) (in door) grille *f*
2 *vtr* **(a)** (at cinema) projeter; (on TV) diffuser
(b) (conceal) cacher; (protect) protéger (**from** de)
(c) (test) examiner le cas de ⟨*applicants, candidates*⟩; contrôler ⟨*baggage*⟩; to ∼ sb for cancer faire passer à qn des tests de dépistage du cancer

screening *n* **(a)** (showing) projection *f*; (on TV) diffusion *f*
(b) (of patients) examens *mpl* de dépistage
(c) (vetting) filtrage *m*

screenplay *n* scénario *m*

screen saver *n* économiseur *m* d'écran

screenwriter *n* scénariste *mf*

screw **1** *n* vis *f*
2 *vtr* visser (**into** dans; **onto** sur)
■ **screw up (a)** froisser ⟨*piece of paper, material*⟩; to ∼ up one's eyes plisser les yeux; to ∼ up one's face faire la grimace
(b) (colloq) faire foirer (fam) ⟨*plan, task*⟩

screwdriver *n* **(a)** (tool) tournevis *m*
(b) (cocktail) vodka-orange *f*

scribble *vtr, vi* griffonner, gribouiller

scrimp *vi* économiser; to ∼ and save se priver de tout

script *n* **(a)** (for film, radio, TV) script *m*; (for play) texte *m*
(b) (GB Sch, Univ) copie *f* (d'examen)

scripture *n* (*also* **Holy Scripture**, **Holy Scriptures**) (Christian) Écritures *fpl*; (other) textes *mpl* sacrés

scriptwriter *n* scénariste *mf*

scroll *n* rouleau *m*
■ **scroll down**: **1** ¶ ∼ down ⟨*person*⟩ faire défiler de haut en bas

2 ¶ ∼ down [sth] faire défiler [qch] de haut en bas ⟨*document*⟩
■ **scroll up**: **1** ¶ ∼ up ⟨*person*⟩ faire défiler de bas en haut
2 ∼ up [sth] faire défiler [qch] de bas en haut ⟨*document*⟩

scroll bar *n* barre *f* de défilement

scrounge *vtr* (colloq) to ∼ sth off sb piquer (fam) qch à qn ⟨*cigarette*⟩; taper (fam) qn de ⟨*money*⟩

scrounger *n* (colloq) parasite *m*

scrub **1** *n* **(a)** (clean) to give sth a (good) ∼ (bien) nettoyer qch
(b) (Bot) broussailles *fpl*
2 *vtr* (*p prés etc* **-bb-**) frotter ⟨*back, clothes*⟩; récurer ⟨*pan, floor*⟩; nettoyer ⟨*vegetable*⟩; to ∼ one's nails se brosser les ongles
■ **scrub up** ⟨*doctor*⟩ se stériliser les mains

scrubbing brush, **scrub brush** (US) *n* brosse *f* de ménage

scruff *n* by the ∼ of the neck par la peau du cou

scruffy *adj* ⟨*clothes, person*⟩ dépenaillé/-e; ⟨*flat, town*⟩ délabré/-e

scrum, **scrummage** *n* (in rugby) mêlée *f*

scrunchie *n* chouchou *m*

scruple *n* scrupule *m* (**about** vis-à-vis de)

scrupulous *adj* scrupuleux/-euse

scrutinize *vtr* scruter ⟨*face, motives*⟩; examiner [qch] minutieusement ⟨*document, plan*⟩; vérifier ⟨*accounts, votes*⟩

scrutiny *n* examen *m*

scuba diving *n* plongée *f* sous-marine

scuff **1** *n* (*also* ∼ **mark**) (on floor, furniture) rayure *f*; (on leather) éraflure *f*
2 *vtr* érafler ⟨*shoes*⟩; rayer ⟨*floor, furniture*⟩

scuffle *n* bagarre *f*

sculpt *vtr, vi* sculpter

sculptor *n* sculpteur *m*

sculpture *n* sculpture *f*

scum *n* **(a)** (on pond) écume *f*
(b) (on liquid) mousse *f*
(c) they're the ∼ of the earth c'est de la racaille

scuttle **1** *vtr* **(a)** saborder ⟨*ship*⟩
(b) faire échouer ⟨*talks, project*⟩
2 *vi* to ∼ away or off filer

scythe *n* faux *f inv*

⚜ **sea** **1** *n* mer *f*; beside *or* by the ∼ au bord de la mer; the open ∼ le large; by ∼ ⟨*travel*⟩ en bateau; ⟨*send*⟩ par bateau
2 *adj* ⟨*air, breeze*⟩ marin/-e; ⟨*bird, water*⟩ de mer; ⟨*crossing, voyage*⟩ par mer; ⟨*battle*⟩ naval/-e; ⟨*power*⟩ maritime

seafood *n* fruits *mpl* de mer

seafront *n* front *m* de mer

seagull *n* mouette *f*

sea horse *n* hippocampe *m*

seal **1** *n* **(a)** (Zool) phoque *m*

(b) (stamp) sceau *m*
(c) (on container) plomb *m*; (on package, letter) cachet *m*; (on door) scellés *mpl*
2 *vtr* **(a)** cacheter ⟨*document*⟩
(b) fermer, cacheter ⟨*envelope*⟩
(c) fermer [qch] hermétiquement ⟨*jar, tin*⟩; rendre [qch] étanche ⟨*window frame*⟩
(d) sceller ⟨*alliance, friendship*⟩ (**with** par); to
~ **sb's fate** décider du sort de qn
■ **seal off** isoler ⟨*ward*⟩; boucler ⟨*area, building*⟩; barrer ⟨*street*⟩

sea lion *n* lion *m* de mer

seam *n* (of garment) couture *f*

seamless *adj* ⟨*transition*⟩ sans heurts; ⟨*process, whole*⟩ continu/-e

seaplane *n* hydravion *m*

✓ **search** **1** *n* **(a)** (for person, object) recherches *fpl* (**for sb/sth** pour retrouver qn/qch); **in ~ of** à la recherche de
(b) (of place) fouille *f* (**of** de)
(c) (Comput) recherche *f*
2 *vtr* **(a)** fouiller ⟨*area, building*⟩; fouiller dans ⟨*cupboard, drawer, memory*⟩
(b) examiner (attentivement) ⟨*map, records*⟩
3 *vi* **(a)** chercher; **to ~ for** *or* **after sb/sth** chercher qn/qch; **to ~ through** fouiller dans ⟨*cupboard, bag*⟩; examiner ⟨*records, file*⟩
(b) (Comput) **to ~ for** rechercher ⟨*data, file*⟩
■ **search out**: ~ **[sb/sth] out**, ~ **out [sb/sth]** découvrir

search engine *n* moteur *m* de recherche

searching *adj* ⟨*look, question*⟩ pénétrant/-e

searchlight *n* projecteur *m*

search party *n* équipe *f* de secours

search warrant *n* mandat *m* de perquisition

sea salt *n* sel *m* de mer

seashell *n* coquillage *m*

seashore *n* (part of coast) littoral *m*; (beach) plage *f*

seasick *adj* **to feel ~** avoir le mal de mer

seaside **1** *n* **the ~** le bord de la mer
2 *adj* ⟨*hotel*⟩ en bord de mer; ⟨*town*⟩ maritime; ~ **resort** station *f* balnéaire

✓ **season** **1** *n* saison *f*; **strawberries are in/out of ~** c'est/ce n'est pas la saison des fraises; **the holiday ~** la période des vacances; **Season's greetings!** Joyeuses fêtes!
2 *vtr* (with spices) relever; (with condiments) assaisonner

seasonal *adj* ⟨*work, change*⟩ saisonnier/ -ière; ⟨*fruit, produce*⟩ de saison

seasoned *adj* ⟨*soldier*⟩ aguerri/-e; ⟨*traveller*⟩ grand/-e (*before n*); ⟨*campaigner, performer*⟩ expérimenté/-e; ⟨*dish*⟩ assaisonné/-e; **highly ~** relevé/-e, épicé/-e

seasoning *n* assaisonnement *m*

season ticket *n* (for travel) carte *f* d'abonnement; (for theatre, matches) abonnement *m*

✓ **seat** **1** *n* **(a)** (chair) siège *m*; (bench-type) banquette *f*
(b) (place) place *f*; **take** *or* **have a ~** asseyez-vous; **to book a ~** réserver une place
(c) (of trousers) fond *m*
2 *vtr* **(a)** placer ⟨*person*⟩
(b) **the car ~s five** c'est une voiture à cinq places; **the table ~s six** c'est une table de six couverts

seatbelt *n* ceinture *f* (de sécurité)

-seater *combining form* **a two~** (plane) un avion *m* à deux places; (car) un coupé; (sofa) un (canapé) deux places

seating *n* places *fpl* assises; **I'll organize the ~** je placerai les gens

sea urchin *n* oursin *m*

sea view *n* vue *f* sur la mer

seaweed *n* algue *f* marine

seaworthy *adj* en état de naviguer

secateurs *n pl* (GB) sécateur *m*

secluded *adj* retiré/-e

seclusion *n* isolement *m* (**from** à l'écart de)

✓ **second** **1** *n* **(a)** (in order) deuxième *mf*, second/-e *m/f*
(b) (unit of time) seconde *f*; (instant) instant *m*
(c) (of month) deux *m inv*
(d) (Aut) (*also* ~ **gear**) deuxième *f*, seconde *f*
(e) (defective article) article *m* qui a un défaut
(f) (*also* ~**-class honours degree**) (GB Univ) ≈ licence *f* avec mention bien
2 *adj* deuxième, second/-e; **to have a ~ helping** (of sth) reprendre (de qch); **to have a ~ chance to do sth** avoir une nouvelle chance de faire
3 *adv* **(a)** (in second place) deuxième; **to come** *or* **finish ~** arriver deuxième; **the ~ biggest building** le deuxième bâtiment de par sa grandeur
(b) (*also* **secondly**) deuxièmement
4 *vtr* (in debate) appuyer ⟨*proposal*⟩
IDIOMS **to be ~ nature** être automatique; **to be ~ to none** être sans pareil; **on ~ thoughts** à la réflexion; **to have ~ thoughts** avoir quelques hésitations *or* doutes

secondary *adj* secondaire

secondary school *n* ≈ école *f* secondaire

second class **1** *adv* ⟨*travel*⟩ en deuxième classe; ⟨*send*⟩ au tarif lent
2 **second-class** *adj* **(a)** ⟨*post, stamp*⟩ au tarif lent
(b) ⟨*carriage, ticket*⟩ de deuxième classe
(c) (second-rate) de qualité inférieure

second hand **1** *n* (on watch, clock) trotteuse *f*
2 **second-hand** *adj* ⟨*clothes, car*⟩ d'occasion; ⟨*news, information*⟩ de seconde main
3 *adv* ⟨*buy*⟩ d'occasion; ⟨*find out, hear*⟩ indirectement

secondly *adv* deuxièmement

S

second name n (surname) nom m de famille; (second forename) deuxième prénom m

second-rate adj de second ordre

seconds n pl (colloq) rab m (fam)

secrecy n secret m

secret ① n secret m; **to tell sb a ~** confier un secret à qn
② adj secret/-ète
③ **in secret** phr en secret

secretarial adj ‹skills, work› de secrétaire; ‹college› de secrétariat

♦ **secretary** n (a) (assistant) secrétaire mf (**to sb** de qn)
(b) **Foreign Secretary** (GB), **Secretary of State** (US); ministre m des Affaires étrangères

secretive adj ‹person, organization› secret/-ète; **to be ~ about sth** faire un mystère de qch

secretly adv secrètement

secret weapon n arme f secrète

sect n secte f

♦ **section** n (a) (of train, aircraft, town, book) partie f; (of pipe, tunnel, road) tronçon m; (of object, kit) élément m; (of fruit) quartier m; (of population) tranche f
(b) (of company, department) service m; (of library, shop) rayon m
(c) (of act, bill, report) article m; (of newspaper) rubrique f

♦ **sector** n secteur m

secular adj ‹politics, society, education› laïque; ‹belief, music› profane

♦ **secure** ① adj (a) ‹job, marriage, income› stable; ‹basis, base› solide
(b) ‹hiding place› sûr/-e
(c) ‹padlock, knot› solide; ‹structure, ladder› stable; ‹rope› bien attaché/-e; ‹door, window› bien fermé/-e; ‹line› sécurisé/-e
(d) **to feel ~** se sentir en sécurité
② vtr (a) obtenir ‹promise, release, right, victory›
(b) bien attacher ‹rope›; bien fermer ‹door, window›; stabiliser ‹ladder›
(c) protéger ‹house›; assurer ‹position, future›
(d) garantir ‹loan, debt› (**against, on** sur)

secure unit n (in children's home) section surveillée dans une maison de rééducation; (in psychiatric hospital) quartier m de haute sécurité

securities n pl titres mpl

♦ **security** ① n (a) sécurité f; **job ~** sécurité de l'emploi; **national ~** sûreté f de l'État
(b) (guarantee) garantie f (**on** sur)
② adj ‹camera, check, measures› de sécurité; ‹firm, staff› de surveillance

security code n code m de sécurité

security guard n garde m sécurité, vigile m

security leak n fuite f (d'information)

sedate ① adj ‹person› posé/-e; ‹lifestyle, pace› tranquille
② vtr mettre [qn] sous calmants ‹patient›

sedation n sédation f; **under ~** sous calmants

sedative n sédatif m, calmant m

seduce vtr séduire

seductive adj ‹person› séduisant/-e; ‹smile› aguicheur/-euse

♦ **see** ① vtr (prét **saw**, pp **seen**) (a) voir; **can you ~ him?** est-ce que tu le vois?; **I can't ~ him** je ne le vois pas; **to ~ the sights** faire du tourisme; **~ you next week!** à la semaine prochaine!; **to ~ sb as** considérer qn comme ‹friend, hero›; **it remains to be seen whether** or **if** reste à voir si
(b) (make sure) **to ~ (to it) that** veiller à ce que (+ subjunctive); **~ (to it) that the children are in bed by nine** veillez à ce que les enfants soient couchés à neuf heures
(c) (accompany) **to ~ sb to the station** accompagner qn à la gare; **to ~ sb home** raccompagner qn chez lui/elle
② vi (prét **saw**, pp **seen**) voir; **I can't ~** je ne vois rien; **I'll go and ~** je vais voir; **we'll just have to wait and ~** il ne nous reste plus qu'à attendre; **let's ~, let me ~** voyons (un peu)
■ **see off: to ~ sb off** dire au revoir à qn
■ **see out: to ~ sb out** raccompagner qn à la porte
■ **see through**: ① ¶ **~ through [sth]** déceler ‹deception, lie›
② ¶ **~ through [sb]** percer [qn] à jour
③ ¶ **~ [sth] through** mener [qch] à bonne fin
■ **see to** s'occuper de ‹arrangements›

♦ **seed** n (a) (gen) graine f; (fruit pip) pépin m; (for sowing) semences fpl; **to go to ~** ‹plant› monter en graine; ‹person› se ramollir; ‹organization, country› être en déclin
(b) (Sport) tête f de série

seedling n plant m

seedy adj ‹person› louche; ‹area, club› mal famé/-e

♦ **seek** vtr (prét, pp **sought**) (a) chercher ‹agreement, refuge, solution›; demander ‹advice, help, permission›
(b) ‹police, employer› rechercher ‹person›
■ **seek out** aller chercher, dénicher

♦ **seem** vi sembler; **it ~s that** il semble que (+ subjunctive); **it ~s to me that** il me semble que (+ indicative); **he ~s happy/disappointed** il a l'air heureux/déçu; **it ~s odd (to me)** ça me paraît bizarre; **he ~s to be looking for someone** on dirait qu'il cherche quelqu'un

seep vi suinter; **to ~ away** s'écouler; **to ~ through sth** ‹water, gas› s'infiltrer à travers

qch; ‹*light*› filtrer à travers qch

seesaw ① *n* tapecul *m*
  ② *vi* ‹*price, rate*› osciller

seethe *vi* (a) to ~ **with rage** bouillir de colère; **he was seething** il était furibond
(b) (teem) grouiller; **the streets were seething with tourists** les rues grouillaient de touristes

see-through *adj* transparent/-e

segment *n* segment *m*; (of orange) quartier *m*

segregate *vtr* (a) (separate) séparer (**from** de)
(b) (isolate) isoler (**from** de)

segregated *adj* ‹*education, society*› ségrégationniste; ‹*area, school*› où la ségrégation raciale (*or* religieuse) est en vigueur

segregation *n* ségrégation *f* (**from** de)

seize *vtr* (a) saisir; **to ~ hold of** se saisir de ‹*person*›; s'emparer de ‹*object*›
(b) s'emparer de ‹*territory, prisoner, power*›; prendre ‹*control*›
■ **seize up** ‹*engine*› se gripper; ‹*limb*› se bloquer

seizure *n* (a) (of territory, power) prise *f*; (of arms, drugs, property) saisie *f*
(b) (Med) attaque *f*

seldom *adv* rarement

⌀ **select** ① *adj* ‹*group*› privilégié/-e; ‹*hotel*› chic, sélect/-e; ‹*area*› chic, cossu/-e
  ② *vtr* sélectionner (**from, from among** parmi)

⌀ **selection** *n* sélection *f*

selective *adj* ‹*memory, recruitment*› sélectif/-ive; ‹*admission, education*› basé/-e sur la sélection; ‹*account*› tendancieux/-ieuse

⌀ **self** *n* (*pl* **selves**) moi *m*; **he's back to his old ~ again** il est redevenu lui-même

self-addressed envelope, **SAE** *n* enveloppe *f* à mon/votre etc adresse

self-adhesive *adj* autocollant/-e

self-assembly *adj* en kit

self-assured *adj* plein/-e d'assurance

self-catering *adj* ‹*flat*› avec cuisine; ~ **holiday** vacances *fpl* en location

self-centred (GB), **self-centered** (US) *adj* égocentrique

self-confessed *adj* avoué/-e

self-confidence *n* assurance *f*

self-confident *adj* ‹*person*› sûr/-e de soi; ‹*attitude*› plein/-e d'assurance

self-conscious *adj* (a) (shy) timide; **to be ~ about sth/about doing** être gêné/-e par qch/de faire
(b) ‹*style*› conscient/-e

self-contained *adj* ‹*flat*› indépendant/-e

self-control *n* sang-froid *m*

self-defence (GB), **self-defense** (US) *n* (gen) autodéfense *f*; (Law) légitime défense *f*

self-destructive *adj* autodestructeur/ -trice

self-determination *n* autodétermination *f*

self-disciplined *adj* autodiscipliné/-e

self-effacing *adj* effacé/-e

self-employed *adj* indépendant/-e; **to be ~** travailler à son compte

self-esteem *n* amour-propre *m*

self-evident *adj* évident/-e

self-explanatory *adj* explicite

self-expression *n* expression *f* de soi/de lui-même etc

self-governing *adj* autonome

self-image *n* image *f* de soi-même/de lui-même etc

self-important *adj* suffisant/-e

self-induced *adj* auto-infligé/-e

self-indulgent *adj* complaisant/-e

self-interested *adj* intéressé/-e

selfish *adj* égoïste (**to do** de faire)

selfishness *n* égoïsme *m*

selfless *adj* ‹*person*› dévoué/-e; ‹*devotion*› désintéressé/-e

self-pity *n* apitoiement *m* sur soi-même

self-portrait *n* autoportrait *m*

self-raising flour (GB), **self-rising flour** (US) *n* farine *f* à gateau

self-reliant *adj* autosuffisant/-e

self-respect *n* respect *m* de soi

self-respecting *adj* ‹*teacher, journalist, comedian*› qui se respecte

self-righteous *adj* satisfait/-e de soi-même

self-rule *n* autonomie *f*

self-sacrifice *n* abnégation *f*

self-satisfied *adj* satisfait/-e de soi-même

self-service ① *n* libre-service *m*
  ② *adj* ‹*cafeteria*› en libre-service

self-sufficient *adj* autosuffisant/-e

self-taught *adj* autodidacte

⌀ **sell** ① *vtr* (*prét, pp* **sold**) (a) vendre; **to ~ sth to sb, to ~ sb sth** vendre qch à qn; **to ~ sth for £5** vendre qch 5 livres sterling
(b) (promote sale of) faire vendre
(c) faire accepter ‹*idea, image, policy, party*›
  ② *vi* (*prét, pp* **sold**) (a) ‹*person, shop, dealer*› vendre (**to sb** à qn)
(b) ‹*goods, product, house, book*› se vendre
■ **sell off**: ¶ ~ **[sth] off**, ~ **off [sth]** liquider; (in sale) solder
■ **sell out** (a) ‹*merchandise*› se vendre; **we've sold out of tickets** tous les billets ont été vendus; **we've sold out** nous avons tout vendu; **the play has sold out** la pièce affiche complet
(b) (colloq) (betray one's principles) retourner sa veste (fam)

sell-by date *n* date *f* limite de vente
seller's market *n* marché *m* à la hausse
selling ① *n* vente *f*
　② *adj* ‹price› de vente
Sellotape® ① *n* scotch® *m*
　② **sellotape** *vtr* scotcher
sellout ① *n* the show was a ∼ le spectacle affichait complet
　② *adj* ‹performance› à guichets fermés
semen *n* sperme *m*
semester *n* (US) semestre *m*
semiautomatic *n, adj* semi-automatique *m*
semibreve *n* (GB Mus) ronde *f*
semicircle *n* demi-cercle *m*
semicolon *n* point-virgule *m*
semiconscious *adj* à peine conscient/-e
semidarkness *n* pénombre *f*, demi-jour *m*
semi-detached (house) *n* maison *f* jumelée
semifinal *n* demi-finale *f*
semifinalist *n* demi-finaliste *mf*
seminar *n* séminaire *m* (on sur)
semi-skimmed *adj* ‹milk› demi-écrémé/-e
senate *n* sénat *m*
senator *n* sénateur *m* (for de)
ᵈ **send** *vtr* (*prét, pp* **sent**) (a) envoyer; to ∼ sth to sb, to ∼ sb sth envoyer qch à qn; to ∼ sb home (from school, work) renvoyer qn chez lui/elle; to ∼ sb to prison mettre qn en prison; ∼ her my love! embrasse-la de ma part; ∼ them my regards transmettez-leur mes amitiés
　(b) to ∼ shivers down sb's spine donner froid dans le dos à qn; to ∼ sb to sleep endormir qn; it sent him into fits of laughter ça l'a fait éclater de rire
　IDIOM to ∼ sb packing (colloq) envoyer balader qn (fam)
■ **send away**: ① ¶ ∼ away for [sth] commander [qch] par correspondance
　② ¶ ∼ [sb/sth] away faire partir
　③ to ∼ an appliance away to be mended envoyer un appareil chez le fabricant pour le faire réparer
■ **send for** appeler ‹doctor, plumber›; demander ‹reinforcements›
■ **send in** envoyer ‹letter, form, troops›; faire entrer ‹visitor›; to ∼ in one's application poser sa candidature
■ **send off**: ① ¶ ∼ off for [sth] commander [qch] par correspondance
　② ¶ ∼ [sth] off envoyer, expédier ‹letter›
　③ ¶ ∼ [sb] off (Sport) expulser
■ **send on** expédier [qch] à l'avance ‹baggage›; faire suivre ‹letter, parcel›
■ **send out** (a) émettre ‹light, heat›

ᵈ indicates a very frequent word

　(b) faire sortir ‹pupil›
■ **send up** (GB) (colloq) (parody) parodier
sender *n* expéditeur/-trice *m/f*
send-off *n* adieux *mpl*
send-up *n* (GB) (colloq) parodie *f*
senile *adj* sénile
senile dementia *n* démence *f* sénile
ᵈ **senior** ① *n* (a) (gen) aîné/-e *m/f*; to be sb's ∼ être plus âgé/-e que qn
　(b) (GB Sch) élève *mf* dans les grandes classes; (US Sch) élève *mf* de terminale
　② *adj* (a) (older) ‹person› plus âgé/-e
　(b) ‹civil servant› haut/-e (before *n*); ‹partner› principal/-e; ‹officer, job, post› supérieur/-e
senior citizen *n* personne *f* du troisième âge
senior high school *n* (US Sch) ≈ lycée *m*
seniority *n* (in years) âge *m*; (in rank) statut *m* supérieur; (in years of service) ancienneté *f*
senior management *n* direction *f*
senior school *n* lycée *m*
sensation *n* sensation *f*; to cause *or* create a ∼ faire sensation
sensational *adj* sensationnel/-elle
sensationalist *adj* ‹headline, story, writer› à sensation
sensationalize *vtr* faire un reportage à sensation sur ‹event, story›
ᵈ **sense** ① *n* (a) (faculty, ability) sens *m*; a ∼ of humour/direction le sens de l'humour/de l'orientation; ∼ of hearing ouïe *f*; ∼ of sight vue *f*; ∼ of smell odorat *m*; ∼ of taste goût *m*; ∼ of touch toucher *m*; to lose all ∼ of time perdre toute notion du temps
　(b) (feeling) a ∼ of identity un sentiment d'identité; a ∼ of purpose le sentiment d'avoir un but
　(c) (common) ∼ bon sens *m*; to have the ∼ to do avoir le bon sens de faire
　(d) (meaning) sens *m*; (reason) there's no ∼ in doing cela ne sert à rien de faire; to make ∼ of sth comprendre qch; I can't make ∼ of this article je ne comprends rien à cet article; to make ∼ ‹sentence, film› avoir un sens
　② **senses** *n pl* to come to one's senses revenir à la raison
　③ *vtr* (a) deviner (that que); to ∼ danger sentir un danger
　(b) ‹machine› détecter
　IDIOMS to see ∼ entendre raison; to talk ∼ dire des choses sensées
senseless *adj* (a) ‹violence› gratuit/-e; ‹discussion› absurde; ‹act, waste› insensé/-e
　(b) to knock sb ∼ faire perdre connaissance à qn
sensible *adj* ‹person, attitude› raisonnable; ‹decision, solution› judicieux/-ieuse; ‹garment› pratique; ‹diet› intelligent/-e
sensitive *adj* (a) (gen) sensible (to à)
　(b) ‹person› (easily hurt) sensible, susceptible (to à)

(c) ‹situation› délicat/-e; ‹issue› difficile; ‹information› confidentiel/-ielle

sensitivity n sensibilité f (to à)

sensor n détecteur m

sensual adj sensuel/-elle

✧ **sentence** 1 n (a) (Law) peine f; **to serve a** ∼ purger une peine
(b) (in grammar) phrase f
2 vtr condamner (**to** à; **to do** à faire; **for** pour)

sentiment n (a) (feeling) sentiment m (**for** pour; **towards** envers)
(b) (opinion) opinion f

sentimental adj sentimental/-e

sentry n sentinelle f

✧ **separate** 1 adj (a) (independent, apart) ‹piece, section› à part; **she has a** ∼ **room** elle a une chambre à part; **the flat is** ∼ **from the rest of the house** l'appartement est indépendant du reste de la maison; **keep the knives** ∼ rangez les couteaux séparément; **keep the knives** ∼ **from the forks** séparez les couteaux des fourchettes
(b) (different) ‹sections, problems› différent/-e; ‹organizations, agreements› distinct/-e; **they have** ∼ **rooms** ils ont chacun leur chambre; **they asked for** ∼ **bills** (in restaurant) ils ont demandé chacun leur addition
2 vtr (a) séparer (**from** de)
(b) (sort out) répartir ‹people›; trier ‹objects, produce›
3 vi se séparer (**from** de)

separately adv séparément

separates n pl (garments) coordonnés mpl

separation n séparation f (**from** de)

separatist n, adj séparatiste mf

✧ **September** n septembre m

septic adj infecté/-e; **to go** or **turn** ∼ s'infecter

septic tank n fosse f septique

sequel n suite f (**to** à)

sequence n (a) (series) série f
(b) (order) ordre m; **in** ∼ dans l'ordre
(c) (in film) séquence f

Serbia pr n Serbie f

Serb, Serbian 1 n Serbe mf
2 adj serbe

serene adj serein/-e

sergeant n (a) (GB Mil) sergent m
(b) (US Mil) caporal-chef m
(c) (in police) ≈ brigadier m

serial n feuilleton m; **TV** ∼ feuilleton télévisé

serialize vtr adapter [qch] en feuilleton

serial killer n tueur m en série

serial number n numéro m de série

✧ **series** n (pl ∼) série f; **a drama** ∼ une série de fiction

✧ **serious** adj ‹person, expression, discussion, offer› sérieux/-ieuse; ‹accident, crime, crisis, problem› grave; ‹literature, actor› de qualité; ‹attempt, concern› réel/réelle; **to be** ∼ **about sth** prendre qch au sérieux; **to be** ∼ **about doing** avoir vraiment l'intention de faire

✧ **seriously** adv (a) ‹speak, think› sérieusement; **to take sb/sth** ∼ prendre qn/qch au sérieux
(b) ‹ill, injured› gravement; ‹underestimate› vraiment

seriousness n (a) (of person, film, study) sérieux m; (of tone, occasion, reply) gravité f; **in all** ∼ sérieusement
(b) (of illness, problem, situation) gravité f

sermon n sermon m

serrated adj dentelé/-e; ∼ **knife** couteau-scie m

serum n sérum m

servant n domestique mf

✧ **serve** 1 n (Sport) service m
2 vtr (a) servir ‹country, cause, public›; travailler au service de ‹employer, family›
(b) servir ‹customer, guest, meal, dish›; **to** ∼ **sb with sth** servir qch à qn
(c) (provide facility) ‹power station, reservoir› alimenter; ‹public transport, library, hospital› desservir
(d) (satisfy) servir ‹interests›; satisfaire ‹needs›
(e) **to** ∼ **a purpose** être utile; **to** ∼ **the** or **sb's purpose** faire l'affaire
(f) purger ‹prison sentence›
(g) (Law) délivrer ‹injunction› (**on sb** à qn); **to** ∼ **a summons on sb** citer qn à comparaître
(h) (Sport) servir
3 vi (a) (in shop) servir; (at table) faire le service
(b) **to** ∼ **on** être membre de ‹committee, jury›
(c) **to** ∼ **as sth** servir de qch
(d) (Mil) servir (**as** comme; **under** sous)
(e) (Sport) servir (**for** pour); **Bruno to** ∼ au service, Bruno
IDIOM it ∼**s you right!** ça t'apprendra!

server n (Sport, Comput) serveur m

✧ **service** 1 n (a) (gen) service m; (**accident and**) **emergency** ∼ service des urgences; **'out of** ∼' (on machine) 'en panne'
(b) (overhaul) révision f
(c) (ceremony) office m; **Sunday** ∼ office du dimanche; **marriage** ∼ cérémonie f nuptiale
2 **services** n pl (a) (also ∼ **area**) aire m de services
(b) (Mil) **the Services** les armées fpl
3 vtr faire la révision de ‹vehicle›; entretenir ‹machine, boiler›; **to have one's car** ∼**d** faire réviser sa voiture

service centre (GB), **service center** (US) n centre m de service après-vente

service charge n (a) (in restaurant) service m; **what is the** ∼? le service est de combien?
(b) (in banking) frais mpl de gestion de compte

service engineer n technicien m de maintenance

serviceman n (pl **-men**) militaire m

service provider n fournisseur m d'accès

service station n station-service f

servicewoman n (pl **-women**) femme f soldat

serving n portion f

serving dish n plat m (de service)

serving spoon n cuillère f de service

⚥ **session** n (a) (gen) séance f

(b) (of parliament) session f

(c) (US Sch) (term) trimestre m; (period of lessons) cours m

⚥ **set** ⟦1⟧ n (a) (of keys, tools) jeu m; (of golf clubs, chairs) série f; (of cutlery) service m; (of rules, instructions, tests) série f; a new ~ of clothes des vêtements neufs; they're sold in ~s of 10 ils sont vendus par lots de 10; a ~ of fingerprints des empreintes digitales; a ~ of traffic lights des feux mpl (de signalisation); a chess ~ un jeu d'échecs; a ~ of false teeth un dentier

(b) (Sport) (in tennis) set m

(c) TV or television ~ poste m de télévision

(d) (scenery) (for play) décor m; (for film) plateau m

(e) (GB Sch) groupe m

(f) (hair-do) mise f en plis

⟦2⟧ adj (a) ⟨pattern, procedure, rule, task⟩ bien déterminé/-e; ⟨time, price⟩ fixe; ⟨menu⟩ à prix fixe; ~ phrase expression f consacrée; to be ~ in one's ways avoir ses habitudes

(b) ⟨expression, smile⟩ figé/-e

(c) (Sch, Univ) ⟨text⟩ au programme

(d) (ready) prêt/-e (for pour; to do à faire)

(e) to be (dead) ~ against sth/doing être tout à fait contre qch/l'idée de faire; to be ~ on doing tenir absolument à faire

(f) ⟨jam, jelly, honey⟩ épais/épaisse; ⟨cement⟩ dur/-e; ⟨yoghurt⟩ ferme

⟦3⟧ vtr (p prés **-tt-**, prét, pp **set**) (a) (place) placer ⟨object⟩ (on sur); monter ⟨gem⟩ (in dans); a house ~ among the trees une maison située au milieu des arbres; to ~ the record straight mettre les choses au point; his eyes are ~ very close together ses yeux sont très rapprochés

(b) mettre ⟨table⟩; tendre ⟨trap⟩

(c) fixer ⟨date, deadline, price, target⟩; lancer ⟨fashion, trend⟩; donner ⟨tone⟩; établir ⟨precedent, record⟩; to ~ a good/bad example to sb montrer le bon/mauvais exemple à qn; to ~ one's sights on viser

(d) mettre [qch] à l'heure ⟨clock⟩; mettre ⟨alarm clock, burglar alarm⟩

(e) (start) to ~ sth going mettre qch en marche ⟨machine⟩; to ~ sb laughing/thinking faire rire/réfléchir qn

(f) donner ⟨homework, essay⟩; to ~ an exam préparer les sujets d'examen

⚥ indicates a very frequent word

(g) (in fiction, film) situer; the film is ~ in Munich le film se passe à Munich

(h) to ~ sth to music mettre qch en musique

(i) (Med) immobiliser ⟨broken bone⟩

(j) to have one's hair ~ se faire faire une mise en plis

⟦4⟧ vi (p prés **-tt-**, prét, pp **set**) (a) ⟨sun⟩ se coucher

(b) ⟨jam, concrete⟩ prendre; ⟨glue⟩ sécher

(c) ⟨fracture⟩ se ressouder

■ **set about** se mettre à ⟨work⟩; to ~ about (the job or task of) doing commencer à faire

■ **set apart** distinguer (from de)

■ **set aside** réserver ⟨area, room, time⟩ (for pour); mettre [qch] de côté ⟨money, stock⟩

■ **set back**: ⟦1⟧ ¶ ~ back [sth], ~ [sth] back (delay) retarder

⟦2⟧ ¶ ~ [sb] back coûter les yeux de la tête à (fam)

■ **set down**: ~ down [sth], ~ [sth] down (a) (establish) fixer ⟨conditions⟩

(b) (record) enregistrer ⟨fact⟩

■ **set in** ⟨infection⟩ se déclarer; ⟨depression⟩ s'installer

■ **set off**: ⟦1⟧ ¶ ~ off partir (for pour); to ~ off on a journey partir en voyage

⟦2⟧ ¶ ~ [sth] off (a) faire partir ⟨firework⟩; faire exploser ⟨bomb⟩; déclencher ⟨riot, panic, alarm⟩

(b) (enhance) mettre [qch] en valeur ⟨garment⟩

(c) to ~ sth off against profits/debts déduire qch des bénéfices/des dettes

⟦3⟧ ¶ ~ [sb] off faire pleurer ⟨baby⟩; she laughed and that ~ me off elle a ri et ça m'a fait rire à mon tour

■ **set on**: ⟦1⟧ ¶ ~ on [sb] attaquer qn

⟦2⟧ ¶ ~ [sth] on sb lâcher [qch] contre qn ⟨dog⟩

■ **set out**: ⟦1⟧ ¶ ~ out se mettre en route (for pour; to do pour faire); to ~ out to do ⟨person⟩ entreprendre de faire

⟦2⟧ ¶ ~ [sth] out (a) disposer ⟨goods, chairs, food⟩; préparer ⟨board game⟩

(b) présenter ⟨ideas, proposals⟩; formuler ⟨objections, terms⟩

■ **set up**: ⟦1⟧ to ~ up on one's own s'établir à son compte; to ~ up in business monter une affaire

⟦2⟧ ¶ ~ [sth] up (a) monter ⟨stand, stall⟩; assembler ⟨equipment, easel⟩; ériger ⟨roadblock⟩; to ~ up home s'installer

(b) préparer ⟨experiment⟩; (Sport) préparer ⟨goal, try⟩

(c) créer ⟨business, company⟩; implanter ⟨factory⟩; former ⟨support group, charity⟩; constituer ⟨committee⟩

(d) organiser ⟨meeting⟩; mettre [qch] en place ⟨procedures⟩

⟦3⟧ ¶ ~ [sb] up (a) she ~ her son up (in business) as a gardener elle a aidé son fils à s'installer comme jardinier

(b) that deal has ~ her up for life grâce à ce contrat elle n'aura plus à se soucier de rien

S

(c) (GB) (colloq) ‹police› tendre un piège à ‹criminal›; ‹friend› monter un coup contre ‹person›

setback n revers m (**for** pour)

settee n canapé m

ᵈ **setting** n **(a)** (location) cadre m
(b) (in jewellery) monture f
(c) (position on dial) position f (de réglage)

setting-up n (of scheme, business) création f; (of factory) implantation f

ᵈ **settle** ① vtr **(a)** installer ‹person, animal›
(b) calmer ‹stomach, nerves›
(c) régler ‹matter, business, dispute›; mettre fin à ‹conflict, strike›; régler, résoudre ‹problem›; décider ‹match›; **that's** ∼**d** voilà qui est réglé
(d) fixer ‹arrangements, price›
(e) to ∼ **one's affairs** mettre de l'ordre dans ses affaires
(f) régler ‹bill, debt, claim›
② vi **(a)** ‹dust› se déposer; ‹bird, insect› se poser
(b) (in new home) s'installer
(c) ‹contents, ground› se tasser
(d) ‹weather› se mettre au beau fixe
(e) (Law) régler; **to** ∼ **out of court** parvenir à un règlement à l'amiable

■ **settle down (a)** (get comfortable) s'installer (**on** sur; **in** dans)
(b) (calm down) ‹person› se calmer
(c) (marry) se ranger

■ **settle for:** ∼ **for sth** se contenter de qch

■ **settle in (a)** (move in) s'installer
(b) (become acclimatized) s'adapter

■ **settle up** (pay) payer

settlement n **(a)** (agreement) accord m
(b) (Law) règlement m
(c) (dwellings) village m; (colonial) territoire m

set-top box n décodeur m

ᵈ **seven** n, pron, det sept m inv

seventeen n, pron, det dix-sept m inv

seventeenth ① n **(a)** (in order) dix-septième mf
(b) (of month) dix-sept m inv
(c) (fraction) dix-septième m
② adj, adv dix-septième

seventh ① n **(a)** (in order) septième mf
(b) (of month) sept m inv
(c) (fraction) septième m
② adj, adv septième

seventies n pl **(a)** (era) **the** ∼ les années fpl soixante-dix
(b) (age) **to be in one's** ∼ avoir plus de soixante-dix ans

seventieth n, adj, adv soixante-dixième mf

seventy n, pron, det soixante-dix m inv

sever vtr **(a)** sectionner ‹limb, artery›; couper ‹rope, branch›
(b) rompre ‹link, relations›; couper ‹communications›

ᵈ **several** ① quantif ∼ **of you/us** plusieurs d'entre vous/d'entre nous

② det plusieurs; ∼ **books** plusieurs livres

ᵈ **severe** adj **(a)** ‹problem, damage, shortage, injury, depression, shock› grave; ‹weather, cold, winter› rigoureux/-euse
(b) (harsh) sévère (**with sb** avec qn)
(c) ‹haircut, clothes› austère

severely adv ‹damage› sévèrement; ‹affect, shock› durement; ‹disabled› gravement; ‹injured› grièvement; ‹beat› violemment

severity n (of problem, illness) gravité f; (of punishment, treatment) sévérité f; (of climate) rigueur f

sew ① vtr (prét **sewed**, pp **sewn**, **sewed**) coudre
② vi (prét **sewed**, pp **sewn**, **sewed**) coudre, faire de la couture

■ **sew up** recoudre ‹hole, tear›; faire ‹seam›; (re)coudre ‹wound›

sewage n eaux fpl usées

sewer n égout m

sewing n (activity) couture f; (piece of work) ouvrage m

sewing machine n machine f à coudre

ᵈ **sex** ① n **(a)** (gender) sexe m; **the opposite** ∼ le sexe opposé
(b) (intercourse) (one act) rapport m sexuel; (repeated) rapports mpl sexuels
② adj sexuel/-elle

sex change n **to have a** ∼ changer de sexe

sex discrimination n discrimination f sexuelle

sex education n éducation f sexuelle

sexism n sexisme m

sexist n, adj sexiste mf

sex object n objet m érotique

sex offender n délinquant/-e m/f sexuel/ -elle

ᵈ **sexual** adj sexuel/-elle

sexual abuse n violence f sexuelle

sexual harassment n harcèlement m sexuel

sexuality n sexualité f

sexually transmitted disease, STD n maladie f sexuellement transmissible, MST f

sexy adj (colloq) ‹person, clothing› sexy inv (fam); ‹book› érotique

shabby adj ‹person› habillé/-e de façon miteuse; ‹room, furnishings, clothing› miteux/-euse; ‹treatment› mesquin/-e

shack n cabane f

shade ① n **(a)** (shadow) ombre f; **in the** ∼ à l'ombre (**of** de)
(b) (of colour) ton m
(c) (also **lamp** ∼) abat-jour m inv
(d) (US) (also **window** ∼) store m
② vtr donner de l'ombre à; **to** ∼ **one's eyes (with one's hand)** s'abriter les yeux de la main

IDIOMS to put sb in the ∼ éclipser qn; **to put** ⋯⋯>

S

sth in the ∼ surpasser *or* surclasser qch

shadow ⓵ *n* ombre *f*; **to have** ∼**s under one's eyes** avoir les yeux cernés
⓶ *vtr* filer ‹person›

shadow cabinet *n* (GB) cabinet *m* fantôme

shadowy *adj* (dark) sombre; (indistinct) ‹outline› flou/-e; ‹form› indistinct/-e

shady *adj* (a) ‹place› ombragé/-e
(b) ‹deal, businessman› véreux/-euse

shaft *n* (a) (of tool) manche *m*; (of arrow) tige *f*; (in machine) axe *m*
(b) (passage, vent) puits *m*
(c) ∼ **of light** rai *m*; ∼ **of lightning** éclair *m*

shaggy *adj* ‹hair, beard, eyebrows› en broussailles; ‹animal› poilu/-e

✓ **shake** ⓵ *n* (a) **to give sb/sth a** ∼ secouer qn/qch
(b) (*also* **milk-**∼) milk-shake *m*
⓶ *vtr* (*prét* **shook**, *pp* **shaken**) (a) (gen) secouer; **to** ∼ **one's head** (in dismay) hocher la tête; (to say no) faire non de la tête; **to** ∼ **hands with sb, to** ∼ **sb's hand** serrer la main de qn, donner une poignée de main à qn
(b) ébranler ‹confidence, faith, resolve›; ‹event, disaster› secouer ‹person›
⓷ *vi* (*prét* **shook**, *pp* **shaken**) (a) (tremble); **to** ∼ **with** trembler de ‹fear, cold, emotion›; se tordre de ‹laughter›
(b) (shake hands) **'let's** ∼ **on it!'** 'serrons-nous la main!'
■ **shake off** se débarrasser de ‹cold, depression, habit, person›; se défaire de ‹feeling›
■ **shake up** (a) agiter ‹bottle, mixture›
(b) ‹experience, news› secouer ‹person›

shaken *adj* (shocked) choqué/-e

shake-up *n* réorganisation *f*; (Pol) remaniement *m*

shaky *adj* (a) ‹chair, ladder› branlant/-e; **I feel a bit** ∼ je me sens un peu flageolant
(b) ‹relationship, position› instable; ‹evidence, argument› peu solide; ‹knowledge, memory› peu sûr/-e; ‹regime› chancelant/-e; **my French is a bit** ∼ mon français est un peu hésitant

✓ **shall** *modal aux* (a) (in future tense) **I** ∼ *or* **I'll see you tomorrow** je vous verrai demain; **we** ∼ **not** *or* **shan't have a reply before Friday** nous n'aurons pas de réponse avant vendredi
(b) (in suggestions) ∼ **I set the table?** est-ce que je mets la table?; ∼ **we go to the cinema tonight?** et si on allait au cinéma ce soir?; **let's buy some peaches,** ∼ **we?** et si on achetait des pêches?

shallot *n* (a) (GB) échalote *f*
(b) (US) cive *f*

✓ indicates a very frequent word

shallow *adj* ‹container, water, grave› peu profond/-e; ‹breathing, character, response› superficiel/-ielle

shallows *n pl* bas-fonds *mpl*

sham ⓵ *n* (a) (person) imposteur *m*
(b) **it's (all) a** ∼ c'est de la comédie
⓶ *adj* ‹event› prétendu/-e ‹before n›; ‹object, building, idea› factice; ‹activity, emotion› feint/-e
⓷ *vi* (*p prés etc* **-mm-**) faire semblant

shambles *n* (colloq) pagaille *f* (fam)

shame ⓵ *n* (a) (gen) honte *f*
(b) **it's a (real) shame** c'est (vraiment) dommage; **it was a** ∼ **(that) she lost** c'est dommage qu'elle ait perdu
⓶ *vtr* (a) (embarrass) faire honte à
(b) (disgrace) déshonorer (**by doing** en faisant)

shameful *adj* honteux/-euse

shameless *adj* ‹person› éhonté/-e; ‹attitude› effronté/-e; ‹negligence› scandaleux/-euse

shampoo ⓵ *n* shampooing *m*
⓶ *vtr* (*prés* **-poos**, *prét*, *pp* **-pooed**) faire un shampooing à; **to** ∼ **one's hair** se faire un shampooing

shamrock *n* trèfle *m*

shandy, shandygaff (US) *n* panaché *m*

shantytown *n* bidonville *m*

✓ **shape** ⓵ *n* forme *f*; **a square** ∼ une forme carrée; **what** ∼ **is the room?** quelle forme a la pièce?; **to take** ∼ prendre forme; **to be in/out of** ∼ ‹person› être/ne pas être en forme; **to get in** ∼ se mettre en forme; **to knock sth into** ∼ mettre qch au point ‹project, idea, essay›
⓶ *vtr* (a) modeler ‹clay›; sculpter ‹wood›
(b) ‹person, event› déterminer ‹future, idea›; modeler ‹character›
■ **shape up** (a) (develop) ‹person› s'en sortir
(b) (meet expectations) être à la hauteur

-shaped *combining form* **star-/V-**∼ en forme d'étoile/de V

shapeless *adj* sans forme, informe

shapely *adj* ‹woman› bien fait/-e; ‹ankle› fin/-e; ‹leg› bien galbé/-e

✓ **share** ⓵ *n* (a) part *f* (**of** de); **to pay one's (fair)** ∼ payer sa part
(b) (in stock market) action *f*
⓶ *vtr* partager (**with** avec); **we** ∼ **an interest in animals** nous aimons tous les deux les animaux
⓷ *vi* **to** ∼ **in** prendre part à
■ **share out** (amongst selves) partager ‹food›; (amongst others) répartir ‹food› (**among, between** entre)

shared *adj* ‹house, interest› partagé/-e; ‹facilities› commun/-e

shareholder *n* actionnaire *mf*

share option scheme *n* plan *m* de participation par achat d'actions

shareware n shareware m, logiciel m contributif

shark n requin m

⚔ **sharp** ⒈ adj (a) ‹razor› tranchant/-e; ‹edge› coupant/-e; ‹blade, scissors, knife› bien aiguisé/-e
(b) ‹tooth, fingernail, end, needle› pointu/-e; ‹pencil› bien taillé/-e; ‹features› anguleux/-euse
(c) ‹angle› aigu/aiguë; ‹bend› brusque; ‹drop, incline› fort/-e; ‹fall, rise› brusque, brutal/-e
(d) ‹taste, smell› âcre; ‹fruit› acide
(e) ‹pain, cold› vif/vive; ‹cry› aigu/aiguë; ‹blow› sévère; ‹frost› intense
(f) ‹tongue› acéré/-e; ‹tone› acerbe
(g) ‹person, mind› vif/vive; ‹eyesight› perçant/-e
(h) ‹businessman› malin/-igne; ~ **operator** filou m
(i) ‹image› net/nette; ‹contrast› prononcé/-e
(j) (Mus) ‹note› dièse inv; (too high) aigu/aiguë
⒉ adv (a) ‹stop› net; **to turn ~ left** tourner brusquement vers la gauche
(b) (colloq) **at 9 o'clock ~** à neuf heures pile (fam)
(c) (Mus) ‹sing, play› trop haut

sharpen vtr aiguiser, affûter ‹blade, scissors›; tailler ‹pencil›

sharpener n taille-crayon m

sharply adv (a) ‹turn, rise, fall› brusquement, brutalement
(b) ‹speak› d'un ton brusque

shatter ⒈ vtr fracasser ‹window, glass›; rompre ‹peace, silence›; briser ‹hope›; démolir ‹nerves›
⒉ vi ‹window, glass› voler en éclats

shattered adj (a) ‹dream› brisé/-e; ‹life, confidence› anéanti/-e
(b) ‹person› (devastated) effondré/-e; (tired) (colloq) crevé/-e (fam), épuisé/-e

shave ⒈ n **to have a ~** se raser
⒉ vtr (pp ~**d** ou **shaven**) ‹barber› raser ‹person›; **to ~ one's beard off** se raser la barbe; **to ~ one's legs** se raser les jambes
⒊ vi (pp ~**d** ou **shaven**) se raser
IDIOM **that was a close ~!** je l'ai/il l'a etc échappé belle!

shaver n (also **electric ~**) rasoir m électrique

shaving ⒈ n (a) (action) rasage m
(b) ~**s** (of wood, metal) copeaux mpl
⒉ adj ‹cream, foam› à raser

shaving brush n blaireau m

shaving mirror n petit miroir m

shawl n châle m

⚔ **she** pron elle; ~**'s not at home** elle n'est pas chez elle; **here ~ is** la voici; **there ~ is** la voilà; ~**'s a beautiful woman** c'est une belle femme

sheaf n (pl **sheaves**) (of corn, flowers) gerbe f; (of papers) liasse f

shear vtr (prét **sheared**, pp **shorn**) tondre ‹grass, sheep›

shears n pl (a) (for garden) cisaille f
(b) (for sheep) tondeuse f

shed ⒈ n (in garden) remise f, abri m; (at factory site, port) hangar m
⒉ vtr (prét, pp **shed**) (a) verser ‹tears›; perdre ‹leaves, weight, antlers›; ‹lorry› déverser ‹load›; verser ‹blood›; **to ~ skin** muer
(b) répandre ‹light, happiness›

sheep n (pl ~) mouton m; (ewe) brebis f; **black ~** brebis f galeuse

sheep dog n chien m de berger

sheepish adj penaud/-e

sheepskin n peau f de mouton

sheer adj (a) ‹boredom, hypocrisy, stupidity› pur/-e (before n)
(b) ‹cliff› à pic
(c) ‹fabric› léger/-ère, fin/-e; ‹stockings› extra-fin/-e

sheet n (a) (of paper, stamps) feuille f; (of metal, glass) plaque f
(b) (for bed) drap m; **dust ~** housse f
(c) **fact ~** bulletin m d'informations
(d) (of ice) couche f; (of flame) rideau m

sheet lightning n éclair m en nappe

sheet metal n tôle f

sheik n cheik m

shelf n (pl **shelves**) (a) étagère f; (in oven) plaque f; (in shop, fridge) rayon m; (**a set of**) **shelves** une étagère
(b) (in rock, ice) corniche f

shelf-life n (of product) durée f de conservation; (of technology, pop music) durée f de vie

shell ⒈ n (a) (of egg, nut, snail) coquille f; (of crab, tortoise, shrimp) carapace f; **sea ~** coquillage m; **to come out of one's ~** sortir de sa coquille
(b) (bomb) obus m; (cartridge) cartouche f
(c) (of building) carcasse f
⒉ vtr (a) (Mil) pilonner ‹town, installation›
(b) (Culin) écosser ‹peas›; décortiquer ‹prawn, nut›
∎ **shell out** (colloq): ~ **out [sth]** débourser ‹sum› (**for** pour)

shellfish n pl (a) (Zool) crustacés mpl; (mussels, oysters) coquillages mpl
(b) (Culin) fruits mpl de mer

shelter ⒈ n (a) abri m; **to take ~ from** s'abriter de ‹weather›
(b) (for homeless) refuge m (**for** pour); (for refugee) asile m
⒉ vtr (a) (against weather) abriter (**from, against** de); (from truth) protéger (**from** de)
(b) donner refuge or asile à ‹refugee›
⒊ vi se mettre à l'abri; **to ~ from the storm** s'abriter de l'orage

sheltered accommodation n foyer-résidence m

S

shelving n (at home) étagères fpl; (in shop) rayons mpl

shepherd n berger m

shepherd's pie n hachis m Parmentier

sheriff n shérif m

sherry n xérès m, sherry m

Shia(h) 1 n chiisme m
2 adj chiite

shield 1 n (a) (Mil) bouclier m
(b) (on machine) écran m de protection; (around gun) pare-balles m inv
(c) (US) (policeman's badge) insigne m
2 vtr protéger; **to ~ one's eyes** se protéger les yeux

⚔ **shift** 1 n (a) (change) changement m (in de), modification f (in de)
(b) (at work) période f de travail; (group of workers) équipe f; **to work an eight-hour ~** faire les trois-huit
2 vtr (a) déplacer ⟨furniture, vehicle⟩; bouger, remuer ⟨arm⟩; changer ⟨theatre scenery⟩
(b) faire partir, enlever ⟨stain, dirt⟩
(c) rejeter ⟨blame, responsibility⟩ (onto sur); **to ~ attention away from a problem** détourner l'attention d'un problème
(d) (US Aut) **to ~ gear** changer de vitesse
3 vi (also ~ **about**) ⟨load⟩ bouger; **to ~ from one foot to the other** se dandiner d'un pied sur l'autre

shift key n touche f de majuscule

shiftless adj paresseux/-euse, apathique

shift work n travail m posté

shifty adj louche, sournois/-e

Shiism n chiisme m

Shiite 1 n chiite m
2 adj chiite

shimmer vi (a) ⟨jewels, water⟩ scintiller; ⟨silk⟩ chatoyer
(b) (in heat) ⟨landscape⟩ vibrer

shin, shinbone n tibia m

shine 1 n lustre m
2 vtr (a) (prét, pp **shone**) braquer ⟨headlights, spotlight, torch⟩ (on sur)
(b) (prét, pp **shined**) faire reluire ⟨silver⟩; cirer ⟨shoes⟩
3 vi (prét, pp **shone**) (a) ⟨hair, light, sun⟩ briller; ⟨brass, floor⟩ reluire; **the light is shining in my eyes** j'ai la lumière dans les yeux
(b) ⟨eyes⟩ briller (with de); ⟨face⟩ rayonner (with de)
(c) (excel) briller; **to ~ at** être brillant/-e en ⟨science, languages⟩
IDIOM **to take a ~ to sb** (colloq) s'enticher de qn (fam)
■ **shine through** ⟨talent⟩ éclater au grand jour

shingle 1 n (a) (on beach) galets mpl
(b) (on roof) bardeau m
2 **shingles** n pl (Med) zona m

shining adj (a) ⟨hair, metal, eyes⟩ brillant/-e

(b) ⟨face⟩ radieux/-ieuse
(c) ⟨example⟩ parfait/-e (before n)

shiny adj (a) ⟨metal, surface, hair⟩ brillant/-e
(b) ⟨shoes, wood⟩ bien ciré/-e

⚔ **ship** 1 n navire m; (smaller) bateau m; **passenger ~** paquebot m
2 vtr (p prés etc -**pp**-) transporter [qch] par mer

shipment n cargaison f

ship owner n armateur m

shipping n navigation f, trafic m maritime

shipping company n compagnie f maritime

shipwreck 1 n (event) naufrage m; (ship) épave f
2 vtr **to be ~ed** faire naufrage; **a ~ed sailor** un marin naufragé

shipyard n chantier m naval

shirk vtr esquiver ⟨task, duty⟩; fuir ⟨responsibility⟩

⚔ **shirt** n (man's) chemise f; (woman's) chemisier m; (for sport) maillot m

shirt-sleeve n manche f de chemise; **in one's ~s** en manches de chemise

shirty adj (GB) (colloq) **to get ~** prendre la mouche (fam)

shit excl (slang) merde! (pop)

shiver 1 n frisson m; **to give sb the ~s** donner froid dans le dos à qn
2 vi (with cold) grelotter (with de); (with fear) frémir (with de); (with disgust) frissonner (with de)

shoal n (of fish) banc m

⚔ **shock** 1 n (a) choc m; **to get or have a ~** avoir un choc; **to give sb a ~** faire un choc à qn; **to be in ~** être en état de choc
(b) (electrical) décharge f; **to get a ~** prendre une décharge
(c) (of collision) choc m; (of explosion) souffle m
(d) **a ~ of red hair** une tignasse rousse
2 vtr (distress) consterner; (scandalize) choquer

shock absorber n amortisseur m

shocking adj ⟨sight⟩ consternant/-e; ⟨news⟩ choquant/-e

shock wave n remous mpl; **to send ~s through the stock market** provoquer des remous à la Bourse

shoddy adj ⟨product⟩ de mauvaise qualité; ⟨work⟩ mal fait/-e

⚔ **shoe** 1 n chaussure f; (for horse) fer m
2 vtr (p prés **shoeing**, prét, pp **shod**) ferrer ⟨horse⟩

shoelace n lacet m de chaussure

shoe polish n cirage m

shoe shop n magasin m de chaussures

shoe size n pointure f

shoestring n (US) lacet m de chaussure
IDIOM **on a ~** (colloq) avec peu de moyens

S

⚔ indicates a very frequent word

shoo *vtr* (*also* ~ **away**) chasser

🗸 **shoot** ① *n* (Bot) pousse *f*

② *vtr* (*prét, pp* **shot**) **(a)** tirer ‹*bullet, arrow*› (**at** sur); lancer ‹*missile*› (**at** sur)
(b) tirer sur ‹*person, animal*›; (kill) abattre ‹*person, animal*›; **she shot him in the leg** elle lui a tiré dans la jambe; **to ~ sb dead** abattre qn; **to ~ oneself** se tirer une balle
(c) to ~ questions at sb bombarder qn de questions
(d) (film) tourner ‹*film, scene*›; prendre [qch] (en photo) ‹*subject*›
(e) mettre ‹*bolt*›
(f) to ~ the rapids franchir les rapides
(g) (US) jouer à ‹*pool*›

③ *vi* (*prét, pp* **shot**) **(a)** tirer (**at** sur)
(b) to ~ forward s'élancer à toute vitesse; **the car shot past** la voiture est passée en trombe
(c) (Sport) tirer, shooter

■ **shoot down** abattre, descendre (fam) ‹*plane, pilot*›

■ **shoot up** ① ‹*flames, spray*› jaillir; ‹*prices, profits*› monter en flèche
② ¶ ~ **up** [sth], ~ [sth] **up** (inject) (colloq) se shooter à (fam) ‹*heroin*›

shooting ① *n* **(a)** (killing) meurtre *m* (par arme à feu)
(b) (shots) coups *mpl* de feu, fusillade *f*
② *adj* ‹*pain*› lancinant/-e

shooting range *n* stand *m* de tir

shooting star *n* étoile *f* filante

shoot-out *n* (colloq) fusillade *f*

🗸 **shop** ① *n* **(a)** magasin *m*; (small, fashionable) boutique *f*; **to go to the ~s** aller faire les courses
(b) (US) (in department store) rayon *m*
(c) (workshop) atelier *m*
② *vi* (*p prés etc* **-pp-**) **to go ~ping** aller faire des courses; (browse) aller faire les magasins
IDIOM to talk ~ parler boutique

■ **shop around** (compare prices) faire le tour des magasins (**for** pour trouver); (compare courses, services etc) bien chercher

shopaholic *n* (colloq) accro *mf* (fam) du shopping

shop assistant *n* (GB) vendeur/-euse *m/f*

shopkeeper *n* commerçant/-e *m/f*

shoplifter *n* voleur/-euse *m/f* à l'étalage

shoplifting *n* vol *m* à l'étalage

shopping *n* courses *fpl*

shopping bag *n* sac *m* à provisions

shopping cart *n* (US) (in shop) caddie® *m*, chariot *m*; (online) panier *m*

shopping centre (GB), **shopping mall** (US) *n* centre *m* commercial

shopping trolley *n* caddie® *m*

shop-soiled *adj* (GB) ‹*garment*› sali/-e

shop steward *n* représentant/-e *m/f* syndical/-e

shop window *n* vitrine *f*

shopworn *adj* (US) ‹*garment*› sali/-e

shore *n* (of sea) côte *f*, rivage *m*; (of lake) rive *f*; **on** ~ à terre

🗸 **short** ① *n* **(a)** (drink) alcool *m* fort
(b) (film) court métrage *m*
② **shorts** *n pl* short *m*; (underwear) caleçon *m*
③ *adj* **(a)** ‹*stay, memory, period*› court/-e (*before n*); ‹*course*› de courte durée; ‹*conversation, speech, chapter*› bref/brève (*before n*); ‹*walk*› petit/-e (*before n*); **the days are getting ~er** les jours diminuent *or* raccourcissent
(b) ‹*hair, dress, distance, stick*› court/-e (*before n*)
(c) ‹*person*› petit/-e (*before n*)
(d) to be in ~ supply être difficile à trouver; **time is getting ~** le temps presse
(e) (lacking) **he is ~ of sth** il lui manque qch; **to be ~ on** ‹*person*› manquer de ‹*talent, tact*›; **to run ~ of** manquer de ‹*clothes, money, food*›
(f) Tom is ~ for Thomas Tom est le diminutif de Thomas
(g) (abrupt) **to be ~ with sb** être brusque avec qn
(h) ‹*pastry*› brisé/-e
④ *adv* ‹*stop*› net; **to stop ~ of doing** se retenir pour ne pas faire
⑤ **in short** *phr* bref
⑥ **short of** *phr* ~ **of doing** à moins de faire
IDIOMS to sell oneself ~ se sous-estimer; **to make ~ work of sth/sb** expédier qch/qn

shortage *n* pénurie *f*, manque *m* (**of** de)

shortbread, shortcake *n* sablé *m*

short-change *vtr* ne pas rendre toute sa monnaie à

short circuit ① *n* court-circuit *m*
② **short-circuit** *vtr* court-circuiter
③ **short-circuit** *vi* faire court-circuit

shortcomings *n pl* points *mpl* faibles

shortcut *n* raccourci *m*; **keyboard ~** raccourci clavier

shorten ① *vtr* abréger ‹*visit, life*›; raccourcir ‹*garment, talk*›; réduire ‹*time, list*›
② *vi* ‹*days*› diminuer

shortfall *n* (in budget, accounts) déficit *m*; (in earnings, exports) manque *m*

shorthand *n* sténographie *f*, sténo *f* (fam)

shorthand-typist *n* sténo-dactylo *f*

shortlist ① *n* liste *f* des candidats sélectionnés
② *vtr* sélectionner ‹*applicant*› (**for** pour)

short-lived *adj* **to be ~** ne pas durer longtemps

shortly *adv* **(a)** ‹*return*› bientôt; ‹*be published*› prochainement
(b) ~ **after(wards)/before** peu (de temps) après/avant
(c) (crossly) sèchement

shortsighted *adj* **(a)** myope ····⫶

S

(b) (figurative) ‹*person*› peu clairvoyant/-e;
‹*policy, decision*› à courte vue
short-sleeved *adj* à manches courtes
short-staffed *adj* **to be** ∼ manquer de
personnel
short story *n* nouvelle *f*
short term ① *n* **in the** ∼ dans l'immédiat
② **short-term** *adj* à court terme
shortwave *n* ondes *fpl* courtes
⚆ **shot** ① *n* **(a)** (from gun) coup *m* (de feu)
(b) (Sport) (in tennis, golf, cricket) coup *m*; (in
football) tir *m*
(c) (snapshot) photo *f* (**of** de)
(d) (in film-making) plan *m* (**of** de); **action** ∼
scène *f* d'action
(e) (injection) piqûre *f* (**of** de)
(f) to have a ∼ **at doing** essayer de faire
(g) (person) **a good** ∼ un bon tireur
② *adj* ‹*silk*› changeant/-e
shotgun *n* fusil *m*
shot put *n* (Sport) lancer *m* de poids
⚆ **should** *modal aux* (*conditional of* **shall**)
(a) ∼ **I call the doctor?** est-ce que je devrais
faire venir le médecin?; **why shouldn't I do
it?** pourquoi est-ce que je ne le ferais pas?;
she ∼ **learn to drive** elle devrait apprendre à
conduire; **shouldn't you be at school?** tu ne
devrais pas être à l'école?
(b) it shouldn't be difficult ça ne devrait pas
être difficile; **she** ∼ **have been here hours
ago** elle aurait dû arriver il y a plusieurs
heures déjà; **it shouldn't have cost so much**
ça n'aurait pas dû coûter si cher
(c) I ∼ **think she's about 40** à mon avis, elle
doit avoir à peu près 40 ans; **I shouldn't be
surprised** cela ne m'étonnerait pas
(d) ∼ **you require any further information,
please contact…** si vous souhaitez plus de
renseignements, adressez-vous à…
(e) I ∼ **think so!** je l'espère!; **I** ∼ **think not!**
j'espère bien que non!; **how** ∼ **I know?**
comment veux-tu que je le sache?; **flowers?
you shouldn't have!** des fleurs? il ne fallait
pas!
⚆ **shoulder** ① *n* épaule *f*
② *vtr* se charger de ‹*burden, expense, task*›;
endosser ‹*responsibility*›
IDIOM **to rub** ∼**s with sb** côtoyer qn
shoulder blade *n* omoplate *f*
shoulder-length *adj* ‹*hair*› mi-long/-ue
shoulder pad *n* épaulette *f*
⚆ **shout** ① *n* cri *m* (**of** de)
② *vtr* crier; (stronger) hurler
③ *vi* crier; **to** ∼ **at sb** crier après qn; **he
was** ∼**ing to me** il me criait quelque chose
■ **shout out** pousser un cri
shouting *n* cris *mpl*
shove ① *n* **to give sb/sth a** ∼ pousser
qn/qch
② *vtr* **(a)** (push) pousser (**against** contre); **to**

∼ **sth into sth** fourrer qch dans qch
(b) (jostle) bousculer ‹*person*›
③ *vi* pousser
■ **shove up** (colloq) se pousser
shovel ① *n* pelle *f*
② *vtr* (*p prés etc* **-ll-** (GB), **-l-** (US)) enlever
[qch] à la pelle ‹*leaves, snow*› (**off** de)
⚆ **show** ① *n* **(a)** spectacle *m*; (in cinema)
séance *f*; (on radio, TV) émission *f*; (of slides)
projection *f*
(b) (exhibition) exposition *f*; (of cars, boats)
salon *m*; (of fashion) défilé *m*; **flower/dog** ∼
exposition florale/canine
(c) (of feelings) semblant *m* (**of** de); (of strength)
démonstration *f* (**of** de); (of wealth) étalage
m (**of** de); **he made a** ∼ **of concern** il a
affiché sa sollicitude; **to be just for** ∼ être de
l'esbroufe (fam)
② *vtr* (*prét* **showed**, *pp* **shown**) **(a)**
montrer ‹*person, object, photo, feelings*› (**to**
à); présenter ‹*ticket*› (**to** à); ‹*TV channel,
cinema*› passer ‹*film*›; ‹*garment*› laisser
voir ‹*underclothes, stain*›; indiquer ‹*time,
direction*›; **to** ∼ **sb sth** montrer qch à qn;
that carpet ∼**s the dirt** cette moquette est
salissante
(b) (exhibit) présenter ‹*animal*›; exposer
‹*flower, vegetables*›
(c) (prove) démontrer ‹*truth, guilt*›
(d) to ∼ **sb to their seat** placer qn; **to** ∼ **sb
to their room** accompagner qn à sa chambre;
to ∼ **sb to the door** reconduire qn
③ *vi* (*prét* **showed**, *pp* **shown**) **(a)** ‹*stain,
label*› se voir; ‹*emotion*› se voir; (in eyes) se
lire
(b) ‹*film*› passer
IDIOM **to have nothing to** ∼ **for sth** ne rien
avoir tiré de qch
■ **show in**: ¶ ∼ **[sb] in** faire entrer
■ **show off**: ① ¶ ∼ **off** faire le fier/la fière
② ¶ ∼ **[sb/sth] off** faire admirer ‹*skill*›;
exhiber ‹*baby, car*›
■ **show out**: ¶ ∼ **[sb] out** accompagner [qn]
à la porte
■ **show round**: ¶ ∼ **[sb] round** faire visiter
■ **show up**: ① ¶ ∼ **up** (colloq) (arrive) se
montrer (fam)
② ¶ ∼ **up [sth]** révéler ‹*fault, mark*›
③ ¶ ∼ **[sb] up** faire honte à ‹*person*›
show business *n* industrie *f* du
spectacle
showcase *n* (for paintings, ideas) vitrine *f*;
(for new artist etc) tremplin *m*
showdown *n* confrontation *f*
shower ① *n* **(a)** (douche) douche *f*; **to have a** ∼
prendre une douche
(b) (of rain) averse *f*
② *vtr* **to** ∼ **sb with sth** couvrir qn de ‹*gifts,
compliments, praise*›
③ *vi* ‹*person*› prendre une douche
show house *n* maison-témoin *f*
showjumping *n* saut *m* d'obstacles
show-off *n* (colloq) m'as-tu-vu *mf inv* (fam)

⚆ indicates a very frequent word

S

show of hands n vote m à mains levées

showroom n exposition f; **to look at cars in a** ∼ regarder les voitures exposées

shrapnel n éclats mpl d'obus

shred ⟦1⟧ n (a) (of paper, fabric) lambeau m
(b) (of evidence, truth) parcelle f
⟦2⟧ vtr (p prés etc **-dd-**) déchiqueter ⟨paper⟩; râper ⟨vegetables⟩

shredder n (for paper) déchiqueteuse f

shrewd adj ⟨person⟩ habile; ⟨move, investment⟩ astucieux/-ieuse

shriek ⟦1⟧ n (a) (of pain, fear) cri m perçant, hurlement m; (of delight) cri m; ∼**s of laughter** éclats mpl de rire
(b) (of bird) cri m
⟦2⟧ vi crier, hurler (**in, with** de)

shrill adj ⟨voice, cry, laugh⟩ perçant/-e; ⟨whistle, tone⟩ strident/-e

shrimp n crevette f grise; (US) (prawn) crevette f rose

shrine n (a) (place) lieu m de pèlerinage
(b) (building) chapelle f
(c) (tomb) tombeau m

shrink ⟦1⟧ vtr (prét **shrank**, pp **shrunk** or **shrunken**) faire rétrécir ⟨fabric⟩; contracter ⟨wood⟩
⟦2⟧ vi (prét **shrank**, pp **shrunk** or **shrunken**) (a) ⟨fabric⟩ rétrécir; ⟨timber⟩ se contracter; ⟨dough, meat⟩ réduire; ⟨sales⟩ être en recul; ⟨resources⟩ s'amenuiser; ⟨old person, body⟩ se tasser
(b) **to** ∼ **from** se dérober devant ⟨conflict, responsibility⟩; **to** ∼ **from doing** hésiter à faire

shrinking adj ⟨population, market⟩ en baisse; ⟨audience⟩ qui s'amenuise

shrink-wrap vtr (p prés etc **-pp-**) emballer [qch] sous film plastique

shrivel ⟦1⟧ vtr ⟨sun, heat⟩ flétrir ⟨skin⟩; dessécher ⟨plant, leaf⟩
⟦2⟧ vi (p prés etc **-ll-** (GB), **-l-** (US)) (also ∼ **up**) ⟨fruit, vegetable⟩ se ratatiner; ⟨skin⟩ se flétrir; ⟨plant, meat⟩ se dessécher

shroud ⟦1⟧ n linceul m
⟦2⟧ vtr envelopper (**in** dans)

Shrove Tuesday n mardi m gras

shrub n arbuste m

shrubbery n massif m d'arbustes

♂ **shrug** ⟦1⟧ n haussement m d'épaules
⟦2⟧ vtr (p prés etc **-gg-**) **to** ∼ **one's shoulders** hausser les épaules
■ **shrug off** ignorer ⟨problem, rumour⟩

shudder ⟦1⟧ n (a) (of person) frisson m (**of** de)
(b) (of vehicle) secousse f
⟦2⟧ vi (a) ⟨person⟩ frissonner (**with** de)
(b) ⟨vehicle⟩ **to** ∼ **to a halt** avoir quelques soubresauts et s'arrêter

shuffle vtr (a) battre ⟨cards⟩
(b) brasser ⟨papers⟩
(c) **to** ∼ **one's feet** traîner les pieds

shun vtr (p prés etc **-nn-**) fuir ⟨people, publicity, temptation⟩; dédaigner ⟨work⟩

shunt ⟦1⟧ vtr aiguiller ⟨wagon, engine⟩ (**into** sur)
⟦2⟧ vi ⟨train⟩ changer de voie

♂ **shut** ⟦1⟧ adj fermé/-e; **her eyes were** ∼ elle avait les yeux fermés; **to slam the door** ∼ claquer la porte (pour bien la fermer); **to keep one's mouth** (colloq) ∼ se taire
⟦2⟧ vtr (p prés **-tt-**, prét, pp **shut**) fermer
⟦3⟧ vi (p prés **-tt-**, prét, pp **shut**) (a) ⟨door, book, box, mouth⟩ se fermer
(b) ⟨office, factory⟩ fermer
■ **shut down**: ⟦1⟧ ¶ ∼ **down** ⟨business⟩ fermer; ⟨machinery⟩ s'arrêter
⟦2⟧ ¶ ∼ **[sth] down** fermer ⟨business⟩; arrêter ⟨machinery⟩
■ **shut in**: ∼ **[sb/sth] in** enfermer
■ **shut off**: ∼ **[sth] off**, ∼ **off [sth]** couper ⟨supply, motor⟩
■ **shut out** (a) laisser [qn/qch] dehors ⟨animal, person⟩; éliminer ⟨noise⟩; **to be** ∼ **out** être à la porte
(b) empêcher [qch] d'entrer ⟨light⟩
■ **shut up**: ⟦1⟧ ¶ ∼ **up** (colloq) se taire (**about** au sujet de)
⟦2⟧ ¶ ∼ **[sb] up** (a) (colloq) (silence) faire taire ⟨person⟩
(b) (confine) enfermer ⟨person, animal⟩ (**in** dans)
⟦3⟧ ¶ ∼ **[sth] up**, ∼ **up [sth]** fermer ⟨house⟩

shutdown n fermeture f

shutter n (a) (wooden, metal) volet m; (on shop front) store m
(b) (on camera) obturateur m

shuttle ⟦1⟧ n (a) navette f
(b) (also ∼**cock**) volant m
⟦2⟧ vtr transporter ⟨passengers⟩

shuttle service n service m de navette

shy ⟦1⟧ adj ⟨person⟩ timide (**with, of** avec); ⟨animal⟩ farouche (**with, of** avec)
⟦2⟧ vi ⟨horse⟩ faire un écart (**at** devant)
■ **shy away** se tenir à l'écart (**from** de)

Siberia pr n Sibérie f

sibling n frère/sœur m/f

Sicily pr n Sicile f

♂ **sick** adj (a) (ill) malade; **worried** ∼ malade d'inquiétude
(b) (nauseous) **to be** ∼ vomir; **to feel** ∼ avoir mal au cœur
(c) ⟨joke, mind⟩ malsain/-e
(d) (disgusted) écœuré/-e, dégoûté/-e
(e) (colloq) **to be** ∼ **of sb/sth** en avoir assez or marre (fam) de qn/qch

sick bay n infirmerie f

sick building syndrome n syndrome m causé par un milieu de travail insalubre

sicken ⟦1⟧ vtr (disgust) écœurer
⟦2⟧ vi **to be** ∼**ing for sth** couver qch

sickening adj ⟨sight⟩ qui soulève le cœur; ⟨smell, cruelty⟩ écœurant/-e

S

sickie *n* (colloq) **to throw/pull/chuck a** ∼ se faire porter pâle (fam)

sick leave *n* congé *m* de maladie

sickly *adj* (a) ⟨*person, plant*⟩ chétif/-ive
(b) ⟨*smell, taste*⟩ écœurant/-e; ⟨*colour*⟩ fadasse; ∼ **sweet** douceâtre

sickness *n* (a) (illness) maladie *f*
(b) (nausea) nausée *f*; **bouts of** ∼ vomissements *mpl*

sick note *n* (colloq) (for school) mot *m* d'excuse; (for work) certificat *m* médical

sickpay *n* indemnité *f* de maladie

sickroom *n* infirmerie *f*

◆ **side** ① *n* (a) (gen) côté *m*; (of animal's body, hill) flanc *m*; (of lake, road) bord *m*; **on one's/ its** ∼ sur le côté; ∼ **by** ∼ côte à côte; **at** *or* **by the** ∼ **of** au bord de ⟨*lake, road*⟩; à côté de ⟨*building*⟩
(b) **to take** ∼**s** prendre position; **to change** ∼**s** changer de camp
(c) (Sport) (team) équipe *f*
② *adj* ⟨*door, window, entrance, view*⟩ latéral/-e
③ **on the side** *phr* **with salad on the** ∼ avec de la salade; **to work on the** ∼ (in addition) travailler à côté; (illegally) travailler au noir
■ **side with** se mettre du côté de ⟨*person*⟩

sideboard *n* buffet *m*

sideboards (GB), **sideburns** *n pl* pattes *fpl*

side effect *n* (of drug) effet *m* secondaire; (of action) répercussion *f*

side impact bars *n pl* (Aut) renforts *mpl* latéraux

sideline *n* (a) **as a** ∼ comme à-côté
(b) (Sport) ligne *f* de touche; **on the** ∼**s** sur la touche

sidelong *adj* ⟨*look*⟩ oblique

side plate *n* petite assiette *f*

side saddle *adv* en amazone

side show *n* attraction *f*

sidestep *vtr* (*p prés etc* **-pp-**) éviter ⟨*opponent*⟩; éluder ⟨*issue*⟩

side street *n* petite rue *f*

side stroke *n* brasse *f* indienne

sidetrack *vtr* fourvoyer ⟨*person*⟩; **to get** ∼**ed** se fourvoyer

sidewalk *n* (US) trottoir *m*

sideways ① *adj* ⟨*look, glance*⟩ de travers
② *adv* ⟨*move*⟩ latéralement; ⟨*look at*⟩ de travers

siding *n* voie *f* de garage

siege *n* siège *m*; **to lay** ∼ **to sth** assiéger qch

siesta *n* sieste *f*; **to have a** ∼ faire la sieste

sieve ① *n* (for draining) passoire *f*; (for sifting) tamis *m*
② *vtr* tamiser ⟨*flour*⟩

sift *vtr* (a) tamiser, passer [qch] au tamis ⟨*flour*⟩
(b) passer [qch] au crible ⟨*information*⟩
■ **sift through** trier ⟨*applications*⟩; fouiller (dans) ⟨*ashes*⟩

◆ **sigh** ① *n* soupir *m*
② *vi* soupirer, pousser un soupir; **to** ∼ **with relief** pousser un soupir de soulagement

◆ **sight** ① *n* (a) (gen) vue *f*; **at first** ∼ à première vue; **to catch** ∼ **of sb/sth** apercevoir qn/qch; **to lose** ∼ **of sb/sth** perdre qn/qch de vue; **I can't stand the** ∼ **of him!** je ne peux pas le voir (fam) (en peinture)!; **to be in** ∼ ⟨*land, border*⟩ être en vue; ⟨*peace, freedom*⟩ être proche; **to be out of** ∼ être caché/-e; **don't let her out of your** ∼! ne la quitte pas des yeux!
(b) (scene) spectacle *m*; **it was not a pretty** ∼! ce n'était pas beau à voir!
② **sights** *n pl* (a) attractions *fpl* touristiques (**of** de); **to see the** ∼**s** faire du tourisme
(b) (on rifle, telescope) viseur *m*
(c) **to set one's** ∼**s on sth** viser qch

sightseeing *n* tourisme *m*; **to go** ∼ faire du tourisme

sightseer *n* touriste *mf*

◆ **sign** ① *n* (a) (gen) signe *m*; **the pound** ∼ le symbole de la livre sterling
(b) (road sign) panneau *m* (**for** pour); (smaller) pancarte *f*; (outside shop) enseigne *f*
② *vtr, vi* signer
■ **sign on** (a) (GB) (for benefit) pointer au chômage
(b) (for course) s'inscrire (**for** à, dans)
■ **sign up** (a) (in forces) s'engager
(b) (for course) s'inscrire (**for** à, dans)

◆ **signal** ① *n* signal *m* (**for** de)
② *vtr* (*p prés etc* **-ll-** (GB), **-l-** (US)) **to** ∼ **(to sb) that** faire signe (à qn) que
③ *vi* (*p prés etc* **-ll-** (GB), **-l-** (US)) (a) (gesture) faire des signes
(b) (in car) mettre son clignotant

signature *n* signature *f*

signature tune *n* indicatif *m*

significance *n* (a) (importance) importance *f*
(b) (meaning) signification *f*

◆ **significant** *adj* ⟨*amount, impact*⟩ considérable; ⟨*event, role*⟩ important/-e; ⟨*name*⟩ significatif/-ive

signify *vtr* indiquer

sign language *n* code *m* *or* langage *m* gestuel

signpost *n* panneau *m* indicateur

Sikh *n*, *adj* sikh *mf*

◆ **silence** ① *n* silence *m*; **in** ∼ en silence
② *vtr* faire taire

silencer *n* (US) (for car) silencieux *m*

◆ **silent** *adj* (a) silencieux/-ieuse; **to be** ∼ se taire
(b) ⟨*disapproval, prayer*⟩ muet/muette
(c) ⟨*film*⟩ muet/muette

◆ indicates a very frequent word

silhouette *n* silhouette *f*
silicon chip *n* puce *f* électronique
silk *n* soie *f*
silky *adj* soyeux/-euse
sill *n* (of window) (interior) rebord *m*; (exterior) appui *m*
silly ① *adj* ‹person› idiot/-e; ‹question, game› stupide; ‹behaviour, clothes› ridicule
② *adv* **to drink oneself ~** s'abrutir d'alcool; **to bore sb ~** assommer qn
silo *n* (*pl* ~**s**) silo *m*
silt *n* limon *m*, vase *f*
silver ① *n* **(a)** (metal, colour) argent *m*
(b) (silverware) argenterie *f*
(c) (medal) médaille *f* d'argent
② *adj* ‹ring, coin› en argent
silver birch *n* bouleau *m* argenté
silver foil *n* (GB) papier *m* d'aluminium
silverware *n* argenterie *f*
SIM card *n* carte *f* SIM
⚡ **similar** *adj* similaire, analogue; **~ to** analogue à, comparable à
similarity *n* ressemblance *f* (**to, with** avec)
similarly *adv* de la même façon
simmer *vi* **(a)** ‹soup› cuire à feu doux, mijoter; ‹water› frémir
(b) ‹person› bouillonner (**with** de); ‹revolt, violence› couver
⚡ **simple** *adj* **(a)** (gen) simple; ‹dress, style› sobre
(b) (dimwitted) simplet/-ette (fam), simple d'esprit
simplicity *n* simplicité *f*
simplify *vtr* simplifier
simplistic *adj* simpliste
⚡ **simply** *adv* **(a)** ‹write, dress, live› simplement, avec simplicité; **to put it ~...** en deux mots...
(b) (merely) simplement
simulate *vtr* (feign) simuler ‹anger, illness›; affecter ‹interest›; (reproduce) simuler
simulator *n* simulateur *m*
simultaneous *adj* simultané/-e
sin ① *n* péché *m*, crime *m*
② *vi* (*p prés etc* -**nn**-) pécher (**against** contre)
⚡ **since** ① *prep* depuis; **I haven't seen him ~ then** je ne l'ai pas vu depuis; **I haven't been feeling well ~ Monday** je ne me sens pas bien depuis lundi; **I had been waiting ~ 9 o'clock** j'attendais depuis 9 heures
② *conj* **(a)** (from the time when) depuis que; **~ he's been away** depuis qu'il est absent; **ever ~ I married him** depuis que nous nous sommes mariés, depuis notre mariage; **I've known him ~ I was 12** je le connais depuis que j'ai 12 ans *or* depuis l'âge de 12 ans; **it's 10 years ~ we last met** cela fait 10 ans que nous ne nous sommes pas revus
(b) (because) comme; **~ you're so clever, do**

it yourself! puisque tu es tellement malin, fais-le toi-même!
③ *adv* **she has ~ qualified** depuis elle a obtenu son diplôme; **I haven't phoned her ~** je ne lui ai pas téléphoné depuis
sincere *adj* sincère
sincerely *adv* sincèrement; **Yours ~, Sincerely yours** (US); Veuillez agréer, Monsieur/Madame, l'expression de mes sentiments les meilleurs
sincerity *n* sincérité *f*
sinew *n* tendon *m*
⚡ **sing** ① *vtr* (*prét* **sang**, *pp* **sung**) chanter; **to ~ sb's praises** chanter les louanges de qn
② *vi* (*prét* **sang**, *pp* **sung**) chanter
Singapore *pr n* Singapour *f*
singe *vtr* (*p prés* **singeing**) brûler [qch] légèrement ‹hair, clothing›; (with iron) roussir ‹clothes›
singer *n* chanteur/-euse *m/f*
singing *n* chant *m*
⚡ **single** ① *n* **(a)** (*also* **~ ticket**) aller *m* simple
(b) (*also* **~ room**) chambre *f* pour une personne
(c) (record) 45 tours *m*
② *adj* **(a)** (sole) seul/-e (*before n*)
(b) (for one) ‹sheet, bed, person› pour une personne
(c) (unmarried) célibataire
(d) every ~ day tous les jours sans exception; **every ~ one of those people** chacune de ces personnes
■ **single out** choisir ‹person›
single cream *n* ≈ crème *f* fraîche liquide
single currency *n* monnaie *f* unique
single file *adv* en file indienne
single-handed(ly) *adv* tout seul/toute seule
single market *n* marché *m* unique
single-minded *adj* tenace, résolu/-e
single mother *n* mère *f* qui élève ses enfants seule
single-parent *adj* ‹family› monoparental/-e
singles *n pl* (Sport) **the women's/men's ~** le simple dames/messieurs
singles bar *n* bar *m* de rencontres pour célibataires
singles charts *n pl* palmarès *m* des 45 tours
single-sex *adj* non mixte
singlet *n* (GB) **(a)** (Sport) maillot *m*
(b) (vest) maillot *m* de corps
singular ① *n* singulier *m*
② *adj* singulier/-ière
sinister *adj* sinistre
sink ① *n* (in kitchen) évier *m*; (in bathroom) lavabo *m*

····⟶

2 *vtr* (*prét* **sank**, *pp* **sunk**) (a) couler ‹*ship*›
(b) forer ‹*oil well, shaft*›; creuser ‹*foundations*›; enfoncer ‹*post, pillar*› (into dans); **the dog sank its teeth into my arm** le chien a planté ses crocs dans mon bras
3 *vi* (*prét* **sank**, *pp* **sunk**) (a) ‹*ship, object, person*› couler
(b) ‹*sun*› baisser; ‹*cake*› redescendre; **to ~ to the floor** s'effondrer; **to ~ into a chair** s'affaler dans un fauteuil; **to ~ into a deep sleep** sombrer dans un profond sommeil
(c) ‹*building, wall*› s'effondrer; **to ~ into** s'enfoncer dans ‹*mud*›; sombrer dans ‹*anarchy, obscurity*›
■ **sink in** ‹*news*› faire son chemin

sinner *n* pécheur/-eresse *m/f*

sinus *n* (*pl ~es*) sinus *m inv*

sip **1** *n* petite gorgée *f*
2 *vtr* (*p prés etc* **-pp-**) boire [qch] à petites gorgées

siphon **1** *n* siphon *m*
2 *vtr* (*also* ~ **off**) siphonner ‹*petrol, water*›

◆ **sir** *n* (a) Monsieur; **Dear Sir** Monsieur
(b) (GB) (in titles) **Sir James** Sir James

siren *n* sirène *f*

sirloin *n* aloyau *m*

◆ **sister** *n* (a) (gen) sœur *f*
(b) (GB) (nurse) infirmière *f* chef

sister-in-law *n* (*pl* **sisters-in-law**) belle-sœur *f*

◆ **sit** **1** *vtr* (*prét, pp* **sat**) (GB) se présenter à, passer ‹*exam*›
2 *vi* (*prét, pp* **sat**) (a) s'asseoir (**at** à; **in** dans; **on** sur); **to be sitting** être assis/-e; **to ~ still** se tenir tranquille
(b) ‹*committee, court*› siéger
(c) **to ~ on** faire partie de ‹*committee, jury*›
(d) ‹*hen*› **to ~ on** couver ‹*eggs*›
■ **sit about**, **sit around** rester assis à ne rien faire
■ **sit down** s'asseoir (**at** à; **in** dans; **on** sur)
■ **sit in** ‹*observer*› assister (**on** à)
■ **sit up** se redresser; **to be ~ing up** être assis/-e; **~ up straight!** tiens-toi droit!

sitcom *n* (colloq) sitcom *m*

◆ **site** *n* (a) (*also* **building** ~) (before building) terrain *m*; (during building) chantier *m*
(b) (for tent) emplacement *m*; **caravan ~** (GB); terrain *m* de caravaning
(c) (archaeological) site *m*

sitting *n* (a) (session) séance *f*
(b) (in canteen) service *m*

sitting room *n* salon *m*

sitting target *n* cible *f* facile

situate *vtr* situer; **to be ~d** être situé/-e, se trouver

◆ indicates a very frequent word

◆ **situation** *n* situation *f*

sit-ups *n pl* abdominaux *mpl*

◆ **six** *n, pron, det* six *m inv*

sixteen *n, pron, det* seize *m inv*

sixteenth **1** *n* (a) (in order) seizième *mf*
(b) (of month) seize *m inv*
(c) (fraction) seizième *m*
2 *adj, adv* seizième

sixth **1** *n* (a) (in order) sixième *mf*
(b) (of month) six *m inv*
(c) (fraction) sixième *m*
2 *adj, adv* sixième

sixth form (GB Sch) *n* (lower) ≈ classes *fpl* de première; (upper) ≈ classes *fpl* de terminale

sixth form college *n* (GB) lycée *m* (*n'ayant que des classes de première et terminale*)

sixth sense *n* sixième sens *m*

sixties *n pl* (a) (era) **the ~** les années *fpl* soixante
(b) (age) **to be in one's ~** avoir entre soixante et soixante-dix ans

sixtieth *n, adj, adv* soixantième *mf*

◆ **sixty** *n, pron, det* soixante *m inv*

◆ **size** *n* (of person, paper, clothes) taille *f*; (of container, room, building, region) grandeur *f*; (of apple, egg, book, parcel) grosseur *f*; (of carpet, bed, machine) dimensions *fpl*; (of population, audience) importance *f*; (of class, company) effectif *m*; (of shoes, gloves) pointure *f*
IDIOM to cut sb down to ~ remettre qn à sa place, rabattre le caquet à qn (fam)
■ **size up** se faire une opinion de ‹*person*›; évaluer ‹*situation*›; mesurer ‹*problem*›

sizeable *adj* ‹*amount*› assez important/-e; ‹*house, field, town*› assez grand/-e

sizzle *vi* grésiller

skate **1** *n* (a) (ice) patin *m* à glace; (roller) patin *m* à roulettes
(b) (fish) raie *f*
2 *vi* patiner (**on, along** sur)

skateboard *n* skateboard *m*, planche *f* à roulettes

skateboarder *n* skateur/-euse *m/f*

skater *n* patineur/-euse *m/f*

skating *n* patinage *m*

skating rink *n* (ice) patinoire *f*; (roller-skating) piste *f* de patins à roulettes

skeleton *n* squelette *m*

skeleton key *n* passe-partout *m inv*

skeptic (US) = SCEPTIC

skeptical (US) = SCEPTICAL

skepticism (US) = SCEPTICISM

sketch **1** *n* (a) (drawing, draft) esquisse *f*; (hasty outline) croquis *m*; **rough ~** ébauche *f*
(b) (comic scene) sketch *m*
2 *vtr* faire une esquisse de; (hastily) faire un croquis de

sketchbook *n* carnet *m* à croquis

sketchpad *n* bloc *m* à dessin

sketchy *adj* ‹information, details› insuffisant/-e; ‹memory› vague

skewer ①‹ *n* (for kebab) brochette *f*; (for joint) broche *f*
②‹ *vtr* embrocher

ski ①‹ *n* ski *m*
②‹ *vi* (*prét, pp* **ski'd** *ou* **skied**) faire du ski; **to ~ down a slope** descendre une pente à skis

ski boot *n* chaussure *f* de ski

skid ①‹ *n* dérapage *m*
②‹ *vi* (*p prés etc* **-dd-**) déraper (**on** sur)

skier *n* skieur/-ieuse *m/f*

skiing *n* ski *m*; **to go ~** faire du ski

skiing holiday *n* vacances *fpl* de neige

ski jumping *n* saut *m* à skis

skilful (GB), **skillful** (US) *adj* habile, adroit/-e

ski lift *n* remontée *f* mécanique

✧ **skill** ①‹ *n* (a) (intellectual) habileté *f*, adresse *f*; (physical) dextérité *f*
(b) (special ability) (acquired) compétence *f*, capacités *fpl*; (practical) technique *f*
②‹ **skills** *n pl* (training) connaissances *fpl*

skilled *adj* (a) (trained) ‹labour, work› qualifié/-e
(b) (talented) consommé/-e

skim ①‹ *vtr* (*p prés etc* **-mm-**) (a) (remove cream) écrémer; (remove scum) écumer
(b) ‹plane, bird› raser, frôler ‹surface, treetops›
(c) **to ~ stones** faire des ricochets avec des cailloux
②‹ *vi* (*p prés etc* **-mm-**) **to ~ through** parcourir ‹book, article›; **to ~ over** passer rapidement sur ‹event, facts›

skim(med) milk *n* lait *m* écrémé

skimp *vi* **to ~ on** lésiner sur

skimpy *adj* ‹garment› minuscule; ‹portion, allowance, income› maigre (*before n*)

✧ **skin** ①‹ *n* peau *f*; (of onion) pelure *f*
②‹ *vtr* (*p prés etc* **-nn-**) (a) écorcher ‹animal›
(b) **to ~ one's knee** s'écorcher le genou
IDIOMS **to have a thick ~** être insensible; **to be** *or* **get soaked to the ~** être trempé/-e jusqu'aux os (fam); **by the ~ of one's teeth** de justesse

skin-deep *adj* superficiel/-ielle

skin diving *n* plongée *f* sous-marine

skinhead *n* (GB) (youth) skin(head) *m*

skinny *adj* (colloq) maigre

skint *adj* (colloq) (GB) fauché/-e (fam)

skintight *adj* moulant/-e

skip ①‹ *n* (a) (jump) petit bond *m*
(b) (GB) (container) benne *f*
②‹ *vtr* (*p prés etc* **-pp-**) sauter ‹page, lunch, school›
③‹ *vi* (*p prés etc* **-pp-**) (a) (once) bondir; (several times) sautiller

(b) (with rope) sauter à la corde

ski pants *n* fuseau *m* (de ski)

ski pass *n* forfait-skieur *m*

skipper *n* (of ship) capitaine *m*; (of fishing boat) patron *m*; (of yacht) skipper *m*

skipping rope *n* corde *f* à sauter

ski resort *n* station *f* de ski

skirt ①‹ *n* jupe *f*
②‹ *vtr* (a) contourner ‹wood, village, city›
(b) esquiver ‹problem›

skirting board *n* plinthe *f*

ski slope *n* piste *f*

ski suit *n* combinaison *f* de ski

skittle ①‹ *n* quille *f*
②‹ **skittles** *n pl* (jeu *m* de) quilles *fpl*

skive *vi* (GB) (*also* **~ off**) (colloq) (shirk) tirer au flanc (fam); (be absent) (from school) sécher l'école (fam); (from work) ne pas aller au boulot (fam)

skulk *vi* rôder; **to ~ out/off** sortir/s'éloigner furtivement

skull *n* crâne *m*

skunk *n* mouffette *f*

✧ **sky** *n* ciel *m*

skydiving *n* parachutisme *m* (en chute libre)

sky-high *adj* ‹prices, rates› exorbitant/-e

skyjacker *n* (colloq) pirate *m* de l'air

skylight *n* fenêtre *f* à tabatière

skyline *n* (in countryside) ligne *f* d'horizon; (in city) ligne *f* des toits

sky marshal *n* garde *m* armé (*à bord d'un avion*)

skyscraper *n* gratte-ciel *m inv*

slab *n* (of stone, wood, concrete) dalle *f*; (of meat, cheese, cake) pavé *m*; (of chocolate) tablette *f*

slack ①‹ *n* (in rope, cable) mou *m*
②‹ *adj* (a) ‹worker› peu consciencieux/-ieuse; ‹work› peu soigné/-e
(b) ‹period› creux/creuse (*after n*); ‹demand, sales› faible
(c) ‹cable, rope, body› détendu/-e
③‹ *vi* ‹worker› se relâcher dans son travail
▪ **slack off** ‹business, trade› diminuer; ‹rain› se calmer

slacken ①‹ *vtr* (a) donner du mou à ‹rope›; lâcher ‹reins›
(b) réduire ‹pace›
②‹ *vi* (a) ‹rope› se relâcher
(b) ‹activity, pace, speed, business› ralentir

slalom *n* slalom *m*

slam ①‹ *vtr* (*p prés etc* **-mm-**) ‹person› claquer ‹door›; ‹wind› faire claquer ‹door›; **to ~ the door in sb's face** claquer la porte au nez de qn; **to ~ the ball into the net** renvoyer brutalement la balle dans le filet
②‹ *vi* (*p prés etc* **-mm-**) ‹door› claquer (**against** contre); **to ~ shut** se refermer en claquant

S

slander n (gen) calomnie f (**on** sur); (Law) diffamation f orale

slang n argot m

slangy adj (colloq) argotique

slant 1 n (a) (perspective) point m de vue (**on** sur)
(b) (bias) tendance f
(c) (slope) pente f
2 vi ‹floor, ground› être en pente; ‹handwriting› pencher (**to** vers)

slanting adj ‹roof› en pente; **~ eyes** yeux mpl bridés

slap 1 n tape f (**on** sur); (stronger) claque f (**on** sur); **a ~ in the face** une gifle
2 vtr (p prés etc -**pp**-) donner une tape à ‹person, animal›; **to ~ sb in the face** gifler qn

slap bang adv (colloq) **he ran ~ into the wall** il s'est cogné en plein dans le mur en courant; **~ in the middle (of)** au beau milieu (de)

slapdash adj (colloq) ‹person› brouillon/-onne (fam); **in a ~ way** à la va-vite

slash 1 n (a) (wound) balafre f (**on** à)
(b) (in fabric, seat, tyre) lacération f; (in painting) entaille f; (in skirt) fente f
(c) (in printing) barre f oblique
2 vtr (a) balafrer ‹cheek›; faire une balafre à ‹person›; couper ‹throat›; ‹knife› entailler ‹face›; **to ~ one's wrists** se tailler les veines
(b) taillader ‹painting, fabric, tyres›; trancher ‹cord›
(c) (reduce) réduire [qch] (considérablement) ‹amount, spending›; sacrifier ‹prices›

slat n (of shutter, blind) lamelle f; (of bench, bed) lame f

slate 1 n ardoise f
2 vtr (a) couvrir [qch] d'ardoises ‹roof›
(b) (GB) (colloq) (criticize) taper sur (fam) (**for** pour)
IDIOM **to wipe the ~ clean** faire table rase

slaughter 1 n (a) (in butchery) abattage m
(b) (massacre) massacre m, boucherie f (fam)
2 vtr (a) abattre ‹animal›
(b) massacrer ‹people›
(c) (colloq) (defeat) écraser

slaughterhouse n abattoir m

Slav 1 n Slave mf
2 adj slave

slave 1 n esclave mf
2 vi (also **~ away**) travailler comme un forçat, trimer (fam)

slaver vi ‹person, animal› baver

slavery n esclavage m

slaw (US) = COLESLAW

slay vtr (prét **slew**, pp **slain**) faire périr ‹enemy›; pourfendre ‹dragon›

sleaze n (colloq) (pornography) pornographie f; (corruption) corruption f

sleazy adj (colloq) ‹club, area, character› louche; ‹story, aspect› scabreux/-euse; ‹café,

hotel› borgne

sled, **sledge** (GB) 1 n luge f; (sleigh) traîneau m
2 vi (p prés etc -**dd**-) faire de la luge

sledgehammer n masse f

sleek adj (a) ‹hair› lisse et brillant/-e; ‹animal› au poil lisse et brillant
(b) ‹shape› élégant/-e; ‹figure› mince et harmonieux/-ieuse

🗝 **sleep** 1 n sommeil m; **to go to ~** s'endormir; **to go back to ~** se rendormir; **to send** or **put sb to ~** endormir qn; **to have a ~** dormir; **my leg has gone to ~** (colloq) j'ai la jambe engourdie; **to put an animal to ~** faire piquer un animal
2 vi (prét, pp **slept**) dormir; **to ~ at a friend's house** coucher chez un ami
IDIOM **to ~ like a log** or **top** dormir comme une souche or un loir

■ **sleep in** (stay in bed late) faire la grasse matinée; (oversleep) dormir trop tard

■ **sleep on**: **to ~ on a decision** attendre le lendemain pour prendre une décision

sleeping bag n sac m de couchage

sleeping car n voiture-lit f, wagon-lit m

sleeping pill n somnifère m

sleepless adj **to have a ~ night** passer une nuit blanche

sleepover n **she's having a ~** elle invite des amies à coucher chez elle

sleepwalk vi marcher en dormant, être somnambule

sleepy adj ‹voice, village› endormi/-e, somnolent/-e; **to feel** or **be ~** avoir envie de dormir, avoir sommeil; **to make sb ~** ‹fresh air› donner envie de dormir à qn; ‹wine› endormir qn, assoupir qn

sleet n neige f fondue

sleeve n (a) (of garment) manche f
(b) (of record) pochette f
(c) (Tech) (inner) chemise f; (outer) gaine f
IDIOM **to have something up one's ~** avoir quelque chose en réserve

sleeveless adj sans manches

sleigh n traîneau m

sleight of hand n (a) (dexterity) dextérité f
(b) (trick) tour m de passe-passe

slender adj (a) ‹person› mince; ‹waist› fin/-e
(b) ‹income, means› modeste, maigre (before n)

sleuth n limier m, détective m

slew vi ‹vehicle› déraper; ‹mast› pivoter

slice 1 n (a) (of bread, meat) tranche f; (of cheese) morceau m; (of pie, tart) part m; (of lemon, cucumber, sausage) rondelle f
(b) (of profits) part f; (of territory, population) partie f
(c) (utensil) spatule f
2 vtr (a) couper [qch] (en tranches) ‹loaf, roast›; couper [qch] en rondelles ‹lemon, cucumber›

🗝 indicates a very frequent word

(b) fendre ‹air›
(c) (Sport) slicer, couper ‹ball›
3 *vi* **to ~ through** fendre ‹water, air›; trancher ‹timber, rope, meat›
sliced bread *n* pain *m* en tranches
slice of life *n* tranche *f* de vie
slick **1** *n* (*also* **oil ~**) (on water) nappe *f* de pétrole; (on shore) marée *f* noire
2 *adj* (a) ‹production› habile; ‹operation› mené/-e rondement
(b) (superficial) qui a un éclat plutôt superficiel
(c) ‹person› roublard/-e (fam); ‹answer› astucieux/-ieuse; ‹excuse› facile
(d) (US) (slippery) ‹road, surface› glissant/-e; ‹hair› lissé/-e
slide **1** *n* (a) (in playground) toboggan *m*
(b) (photographic) diapositive *f*
(c) (microscope plate) lame *f* porte-objet
(d) (GB) (*also* **hair ~**) barrette *f*
(e) (decline) baisse *f* (in de)
2 *vtr* (*prét, pp* **slid**) faire glisser
3 *vi* (*prét, pp* **slid**) (a) ‹car, person› glisser, partir en glissade (into dans; on sur); **to ~ in and out** ‹drawer› coulisser
(b) ‹prices, shares› baisser
slide projector *n* projecteur *m* de diapositives
slide rule (GB), **slide ruler** (US) *n* règle *f* à calcul
slide show *n* (at exhibition) diaporama *m*; (at lecture, at home) séance *f* de projection
sliding *adj* ‹door› coulissant/-e; ‹roof› ouvrant/-e
sliding scale *n* échelle *f* mobile
slight **1** *n* affront *m* (on à; from de la part de)
2 *adj* (a) (gen) léger/-ère (before n); ‹risk, danger› faible (before n); ‹pause, hesitation› petit/-e (before n); **not to have the ~est difficulty** ne pas avoir la moindre difficulté
(b) (in build) mince
3 *vtr* (a) (offend) offenser; (stronger) humilier
(b) (US) (underestimate) sous-estimer
⚬ᵒ **slightly** *adv* ‹fall, change› légèrement; ‹different, more, less› un peu
slim **1** *adj* ‹person, figure› mince; ‹ankle, leg› fin/-e, mince; ‹watch, calculator› plat/-e
2 *vi* (*p prés etc* **-mm-**) (GB) maigrir; **I'm ~ming** je fais un régime amaigrissant
slime *n* dépôt *m* gluant *or* visqueux; (of slug, snail) bave *f*
sling **1** *n* (a) (Med) écharpe *f*
(b) (for carrying baby) porte-bébé *m*; (for carrying load) élingue *f*
2 *vtr* (*prét, pp* **slung**) lancer ‹object, insult› (at à)
⚬ᵒ **slip** **1** *n* (a) (error) erreur *f*; **~ of the tongue** lapsus *m*
(b) (receipt) reçu *m*; (for salary) bulletin *m*; **~ of paper** bout *m* de papier
(c) (stumble) faux pas *m*

(d) (petticoat) (full) combinaison *f*; (half) jupon *m*
2 *vtr* (*p prés etc* **-pp-**) (a) (gen) glisser (into dans); **she ~ped the shirt over her head** (put on) elle a enfilé sa chemise; (take off) elle a retiré sa chemise
(b) ‹dog› se dégager de ‹leash›; ‹boat› filer ‹moorings›; **it had ~ped my mind (that)** j'avais complètement oublié (que); **to let ~ a remark** laisser échapper une remarque
(c) (Med) **to ~ a disc** se déplacer une vertèbre
3 *vi* (*p prés etc* **-pp-**) (a) **to ~ into** passer ‹dress, costume›; tomber dans ‹coma›
(b) **to ~ into/out of** se glisser dans/hors de ‹room, building›
(c) ‹person, vehicle› glisser (on sur; off de); ‹knife, razor, pen› glisser, déraper; **to ~ through sb's fingers** ‹money, opportunity› filer entre les doigts de qn
(d) (Aut) ‹clutch› patiner
slipknot *n* nœud *m* coulant
slip-on (shoe) *n* mocassin *m*
slipped disc *n* hernie *f* discale
slipper *n* pantoufle *f*
slippery *adj* glissant/-e
slip road *n* bretelle *f* d'accès
slipshod *adj* ‹person› négligent/-e; ‹appearance, work› négligé/-e, peu soigné/-e
slip-up *n* (colloq) bourde *f* (fam)
slit **1** *n* fente *f* (in dans)
2 *adj* ‹eyes› bridé/-e; ‹skirt› fendu/-e
3 *vtr* (*prét, pp* **slit**) (on purpose) faire une fente dans; (by accident) déchirer; **to ~ sb's throat** égorger qn; **to ~ one's wrists** s'ouvrir les veines
slither *vi* glisser
sliver *n* (of glass) éclat *m*; (of food) mince tranche *f*
slob *n* (colloq) (lazy) flemmard/-em/*f* (fam)
slog *vi* (colloq) (*p prés etc* **-gg-**) (*also* **~ away**) travailler dur, bosser (fam)
slogan *n* slogan *m*
slop **1** *vtr* renverser ‹liquid›
2 *vi* (*also* **~ over**) ‹liquid› déborder
slope **1** *n* pente *f*
2 *vi* être en pente (towards vers); ‹writing› pencher (to vers)
sloping *adj* ‹ground, roof› en pente; ‹ceiling› incliné/-e; ‹writing› penché/-e
sloppy *adj* (a) (colloq) ‹appearance› débraillé/-e; ‹work› peu soigné/-e
(b) (colloq) (over-emotional) sentimental/-e
slot **1** *n* (a) (for coin, ticket) fente *f*; (for letters) ouverture *f*; (groove) rainure *f*
(b) (in timetable, schedule) créneau *m*
2 *vtr* (*p prés etc* **-tt-**) **to ~ sth into a machine** insérer qch dans une machine
3 *vi* (*p prés etc* **-tt-**) **to ~ into sth** ‹coin, piece› s'insérer dans qch; **to ~ into place** *or* **position** s'encastrer

···⟩

■ **slot together** s'emboîter
sloth n (Zool) paresseux m
slot machine n (game) machine f à sous; (vending machine) distributeur m automatique
slouch vi être avachi/-e
Slovakia pr n Slovaquie f
Slovenia pr n Slovénie f
slovenly adj négligé/-e
ꝗ **slow** ⟦1⟧ adj (a) (gen) lent/-e
(b) ‹business, market› stagnant/-e
(c) (dull-witted) lent/-e (d'esprit)
(d) to be ∼ ‹clock, watch› retarder; to be 10 minutes ∼ retarder de 10 minutes
⟦2⟧ adv lentement
⟦3⟧ vtr, vi (also ∼ **down**) ralentir
ꝗ **slowly** adv lentement
slow motion n ralenti m; in ∼ au ralenti
slow-moving adj lent/-e
sludge n (a) (also **sewage** ∼) eaux fpl usées
(b) (mud) vase f
slug n limace f
sluggish adj (a) ‹person, animal› léthargique; ‹circulation› lent/-e
(b) ‹market, trade› qui stagne
sluice n (a) (also ∼ **gate**) vanne f
(b) (also ∼**way**) canal m
slum n (a) (area) quartier m pauvre
(b) (dwelling) taudis m
slumber ⟦1⟧ n sommeil m
⟦2⟧ vi sommeiller
slump ⟦1⟧ n (in trade, prices) effondrement m (in de)
⟦2⟧ vi (a) ‹demand, trade, price› chuter (from de, to à, by de); ‹economy, market› s'effondrer; ‹popularity› être en forte baisse
(b) ‹person, body› s'affaler (fam)
slur ⟦1⟧ n (a) (in speech) marmonnement m
(b) (Mus) liaison f
(c) (aspersion) calomnie f
⟦2⟧ vi (p prés etc **-rr-**) avoir du mal à articuler
⟦3⟧ **slurred** pp adj ‹voice, speech› inarticulé/-e
slush n neige f fondue
slush fund n caisse f noire
sly adj ‹person, animal› rusé/-e; ‹remark, smile› entendu/-e
IDIOM on the ∼ en douce (fam), en cachette
smack ⟦1⟧ n claque f; (on face) gifle f
⟦2⟧ vtr (on face) gifler ‹person›; taper ‹object› (on sur; against contre); she ∼ed him on the bottom elle lui a donné une tape sur les fesses
⟦3⟧ vi to ∼ of sentir
ꝗ **small** ⟦1⟧ n the ∼ of the back le creux du dos
⟦2⟧ adj (a) (gen) petit/-e (before n); ‹quantity, amount› faible (before n)
(b) to feel ∼ être dans ses petits souliers

(fam); to make sb feel or look ∼ humilier qn
⟦3⟧ adv ‹write› petit
small ad n (GB) petite annonce f
small change n petite monnaie f
small talk n banalités fpl; to make ∼ faire la conversation
ꝗ **smart** ⟦1⟧ adj (a) (elegant) ‹person, clothes› élégant/-e; ‹restaurant, hotel, street› chic
(b) (clever) malin/-e
(c) ‹blow› vif/vive; ‹rebuke› cinglant/-e; to walk at a ∼ pace marcher à vive allure
(d) (Comput) intelligent/-e
⟦2⟧ vi ‹cut, cheeks› brûler; his eyes were ∼ing from the smoke la fumée lui brûlait les yeux
smart bomb n bombe f intelligente
smart card n carte f à puce
smarten v ■ **smarten up** embellir ‹room›; to ∼ oneself up se faire beau
smash ⟦1⟧ n (a) (colloq) (also ∼**-up**) (accident) collision f
(b) (colloq) (also ∼ **hit**) tube m (fam)
(c) (in tennis) smash m
(d) (sound) fracas m
⟦2⟧ vtr (a) briser ‹glass, door, car›; (more violently) fracasser
(b) démanteler ‹drugs ring, gang›
(c) (Sport) to ∼ the ball faire un smash
⟦3⟧ vi se briser, se fracasser
smashing adj (GB) formidable (fam)
smattering n notions fpl (of de); to have a ∼ of Russian avoir quelques connaissances en russe
smear ⟦1⟧ n (a) (spot) tache f; (streak) traînée f
(b) (defamation) propos m diffamatoire
(c) (also ∼ **test**) (Med) frottis m
⟦2⟧ vtr (a) faire des taches sur ‹glass, window›; her face was ∼ed with jam elle avait le visage barbouillé de confiture
(b) (spread) étaler ‹butter, paint›; appliquer ‹lotion› (on sur)
⟦3⟧ vi ‹ink, paint› s'étaler; ‹lipstick, make-up› couler
smell ⟦1⟧ n (a) odeur f
(b) (sense) odorat m
⟦2⟧ vtr (prét, pp **smelled, smelt** (GB)) ‹person› sentir; ‹animal› renifler, sentir; I can ∼ burning ça sent le brûlé
⟦3⟧ vi (prét, pp **smelled, smelt** (GB)) sentir; that ∼s nice/horrible ça sent bon/très mauvais; to ∼ of sth sentir qch
smelling salts n pl sels mpl
smelly adj malodorant/-e, qui sent mauvais
ꝗ **smile** ⟦1⟧ n sourire m
⟦2⟧ vi sourire (at sb à qn)
■ **smile on**: ∼ on [sb/sth] ‹fortune, weather› sourire à; ‹person› être favorable à
smiley n (colloq) souriant m, smiley m (fam)

S

smirk ① *n* (self-satisfied) petit sourire *m* satisfait; (knowing) sourire *m* en coin
② *vi* (in a self-satisfied way) avoir un petit sourire satisfait; (knowingly) avoir un sourire en coin

smithereens *n pl* in ~ en mille morceaux; **to smash sth to** ~ faire voler qch en éclats

smock *n* blouse *f*, sarrau *m*

smog *n* smog *m*

smoke ① *n* fumée *f*
② *vtr* fumer
③ *vi* fumer

smoke alarm *n* détecteur *m* de fumée

smoked *adj* fumé/e

smoker *n* fumeur/-euse *m/f*

smoke screen *n* (Mil) écran *m* de fumée; (figurative) diversion *f*

smoking ① *n* ~ **and drinking** le tabac et l'alcool; **to give up** ~ arrêter de fumer; 'no ~' 'défense de fumer'
② *adj* ‹compartment, section› fumeurs) (*after n*)

smoking-related *adj* ‹disease› associé/-e au tabac

smoky *adj* ‹room› enfumé/-e; ‹cheese, bacon› fumé/-e

smooth ① *adj* (a) ‹stone, surface, skin, fabric› lisse; ‹curve, breathing› régulier/-ière; ‹sauce› homogène; ‹crossing, flight› sans heurts; ‹movement› aisé/-e
(b) ‹taste, wine, whisky› moelleux/-euse
(c) (suave) ‹person› mielleux/-euse; ‹manners, appearance› onctueux/-euse; **to be a** ~ **talker** être enjôleur/-euse
② *vtr* (a) (flatten out) lisser; (get creases out of) défroisser
(b) faciliter ‹transition, path›
■ **smooth over**: ~ over [sth] atténuer ‹differences›; aplanir ‹difficulties, problems›; **to** ~ **things over** arranger les choses

smooth-running *adj* ‹organization, event› qui marche bien

smother *vtr* étouffer

smoulder (GB), **smolder** (US) *vi*
(a) ‹cigarette, fire› se consumer
(b) ‹hatred, jealousy› couver; **to** ~ **with** être consumé/-e de

SMS *n* (*abbr* = **Short Message Service**) SMS *m*

smudge ① *n* trace *f*
② *vtr* étaler ‹make-up, print, ink, paint›; faire des traces sur ‹paper, paintwork›
③ *vi* ‹make-up, print, ink, paint› s'étaler

smug *adj* suffisant/-e

smuggle *vtr* faire du trafic de ‹arms, drugs›; faire passer [qch] en contrebande ‹watches, alcohol, cigarettes›; **to** ~ **sb/sth in** faire entrer qn/qch clandestinement

smuggler *n* contrebandier/-ière *m/f*; **drug/ arms** ~ passeur/-euse *m/f* de drogue/ d'armes

smuggling *n* contrebande *f*; **drug/arms** ~ trafic *m* de drogue/d'armes

smutty *adj* (a) (crude) grivois/-e
(b) (dirty) ‹face› noir/-e; ‹mark› noirâtre

snack ① *n* (a) (small meal) repas *m* léger; (instead of meal) casse-croûte *m inv*
(b) (crisps, peanuts) ~**s** amuse-gueule *m inv*
② *vi* grignoter, manger légèrement

snag *n* (a) (hitch) inconvénient *m* (in de)
(b) (tear) accroc *m* (in à)

snail *n* escargot *m*

snail mail *n* (colloq) courrier *m* postal

snake *n* serpent *m*

snap ① *n* (a) (of branch) craquement *m*; (of fingers, elastic) claquement *m*
(b) (colloq) (photograph) photo *f*
(c) (game) ≈ bataille *f*
② *adj* ‹decision, judgment, vote› rapide
③ *vtr* (*p prés etc* **-pp-**) (a) faire claquer ‹fingers, jaws, elastic›
(b) (break) (faire) casser net
(c) (say crossly) dire [qch] hargneusement
④ *vi* (*p prés etc* **-pp-**) (a) (break) se casser
(b) (speak sharply) parler hargneusement
■ **snap at** (a) (speak sharply) parler sèchement à
(b) ‹dog› essayer de mordre
■ **snap up** sauter sur ‹bargain›

snappy *adj* ‹rhythm, reply› rapide; ‹advertisement› accrocheur/-euse

snapshot *n* photo *f*

snare ① *n* piège *m*
② *vtr* prendre [qn/qch] au piège

snarl *vi* ‹animal› gronder férocement; ‹person› grogner

snarl-up *n* (in traffic) embouteillage *m*; (in distribution network) blocage *m*

snatch ① *n* (*pl* ~**es**) (a) (of conversation) bribe *f*; (of tune) quelques notes *fpl*
(b) (theft) vol *m*
② *vtr* (a) (grab) attraper ‹book, key›; **to** ~ **sth from sb** arracher qch à qn
(b) (colloq) (steal) voler ‹handbag› (from à)

sneak *vi* **to** ~ **in/out** entrer/sortir furtivement; **to** ~ **up on sb/sth** s'approcher sans bruit de qn/qch

sneaker *n* (US) basket *f*, (chaussure *f* de) tennis *f*

sneaking *adj* ‹suspicion› vague

sneaky *adj* sournois/-e

sneer ① *n* sourire *m* méprisant
② *vi* sourire avec mépris

sneeze ① *n* éternuement *m*
② *vi* éternuer

snide *adj* sournois/-e

sniff ① *n* reniflement *m*
② *vtr* ‹dog› flairer; ‹person› sentir ‹food›; inhaler ‹glue, cocaine›
③ *vi* renifler

snigger ① *n* ricanement *m*

···❯

2 *vi* ricaner

snip *vtr* (*p prés etc* **-pp-**) découper (à petits coups de ciseaux) ‹*fabric, paper*›; tailler ‹*hedge*›

■ **snip off** couper

sniper *n* tireur *m* embusqué

snippet *n* (of conversation, information) bribes *f*; (of text, fabric, music) fragment *m*

snivel *vi* (*p prés etc* **-ll-**) pleurnicher

snob *n* snob *mf*

snobbery *n* snobisme *m*

snobbish *adj* snob

snog **1** *n* bécotage *m* (fam)
2 *vtr, vi* (*p prés etc* **-gg-**) se bécoter (fam)

snooker **1** *n* (game) snooker *m*
2 *vtr* (a) (Sport, figurative) coincer ‹*player, person*›
(b) (US) (deceive) avoir (fam) ‹*person*›

snoop (colloq) **1** *n* fouineur/-euse *m/f*
2 *vi* fouiner, fureter

snooze (colloq) **1** *n* petit somme *m*
2 *vi* sommeiller

snore **1** *n* ronflement *m*
2 *vi* ronfler

snorkel *n* tuba *m*

snorkelling *n* plongée *f* avec tuba

snort **1** *vi* ‹*person, pig*› grogner; ‹*horse, bull*› s'ébrouer
2 *vtr* sniffer ‹*drugs*›

snout *n* museau *m*; (of pig) groin *m*

snow **1** *n* neige *f*
2 *v impers* neiger; **it's ~ing** il neige

snowball **1** *n* boule *f* de neige
2 *vi* faire boule de neige

snowboard **1** *n* surf *m* des neiges
2 *vi* faire du surf des neiges

snowdrift *n* congère *f*

snowdrop *n* perce-neige *m inv*

snowfall *n* chute *f* de neige

snowflake *n* flocon *m* de neige

snowman *n* bonhomme *m* de neige

snow mobile *n* motoneige *f*

snow plough (GB), **snow plow** (US) *n* chasse-neige *m inv*

snow shoe *n* raquette *f*

snub **1** *n* rebuffade *f*
2 *vtr* (*p prés etc* **-bb-**) rembarrer

snub-nosed *adj* au nez retroussé

snuff *n* tabac *m* à priser

snug *adj* ‹*bed, room*› douillet/-ette; ‹*coat*› chaud/-e

snuggle *vi* se blottir

ⓢ **so** **1** *adv* (a) (to such an extent) si, tellement; **~ happy/quickly** si *or* tellement heureux/-euse/vite; **~ much noise/many things** tant de bruit/de choses
(b) (in such a way) **~ arranged/worded that** organisé/rédigé d'une telle façon que; **and ~**

ⓢ *indicates a very frequent word*

on and ~ forth et ainsi de suite; **~ be it!** soit!
(c) (thus) ainsi; (therefore) donc; **~ that's the reason** voilà donc pourquoi; **~ you're going are you?** alors tu y vas?
(d) (true) **is that ~?** c'est vrai?; **if (that's) ~** si c'est vrai
(e) (also) aussi; **~ is she** elle aussi; **~ do I** moi aussi
(f) (colloq) (thereabouts) environ; **20 or ~** environ 20
(g) (other uses) **I think/don't think ~** je crois/ne crois pas; **I'm afraid ~** j'ai bien peur que oui *or* si; **~ it would appear** c'est ce qu'il semble; **~ to speak** si je puis dire; **I told you ~** je te l'avais bien dit; **~ I see** je le vois bien; **who says ~?** qui dit ça?; **only more ~** mais encore plus; **he dived and as he did ~…** il a plongé et en le faisant…; **'it's broken'—'~ it is'** 'c'est cassé'—'je le vois bien!'; **~ (what)?** et alors?

2 **so (that)** *phr* (in order that) pour que (+ subjunctive)

3 **so as** *phr* pour; **~ as to attract attention** pour attirer l'attention

4 **so much** *phr* tellement; **she worries ~ much** elle s'inquiète tellement; **she taught me ~ much** elle m'a tant appris; **thank you ~ much** merci beaucoup

IDIOMS **~ much the better** tant mieux; **~ ~** comme ci comme ça

soak **1** *vtr* (a) ‹*rain*› tremper ‹*person, clothes*›
(b) ‹*person*› faire tremper ‹*clothes, foods*›
2 *vi* (a) ‹*clothes, foods*› tremper
(b) ‹*liquid*› **to ~ into** être absorbé/-e par; **to ~ through** traverser

■ **soak up**: **1** ¶ **~ [sth] up, ~ up [sth]** absorber
2 ¶ **~ up [sth]** s'imprégner de ‹*atmosphere*›; **to ~ up the sun** faire le plein (fam) de soleil

soaked *adj* trempé/-e; **to be ~ through** *or* **~ to the skin** être trempé/-e jusqu'aux os

soaking *adj* trempé/-e

soap *n* savon *m*; **a bar of ~** un savon

soap opera *n* feuilleton *m*

soap powder *n* lessive *f* (en poudre)

soar *vi* (a) ‹*ball*› filer; ‹*bird, plane*› prendre son essor
(b) (glide) planer
(c) ‹*price, temperature, costs*› monter en flèche; ‹*hopes*› grandir considérablement
(d) ‹*tower, cliffs*› se dresser

soaring *adj* ‹*inflation, demand*› en forte progression; ‹*prices, temperatures*› en forte hausse

sob **1** *n* sanglot *m*
2 *vi* (*p prés etc* **-bb-**) sangloter

sober **1** *adj* (a) **I'm ~** (not drunk) je n'ai pas bu d'alcool; (in protest) je ne suis pas ivre
(b) (no longer drunk) dessoûlé/-e
(c) (serious) ‹*person*› sérieux/-ieuse; ‹*mood*› grave

(d) ‹colour, suit› sobre
2 vtr ‹news, reprimand› calmer
■ **sober up** dessoûler
sob story n (colloq) mélom (fam)
soccer n football m
sociable adj ‹person› sociable; ‹evening› agréable
⚡ **social** adj **(a)** (gen) social/-e
(b) ‹call, visit› amical/-e
social climber n (still rising) arriviste mf; (at his/her peak) parvenu/-e mf
social club n club m
social gathering n réunion f entre amis
socialism n socialisme m
socialist n, adj (also **Socialist**) socialiste mf
socialite n mondain/-e m/f
socialize vi rencontrer des gens; **to ∼ with sb** fréquenter qn
social life n (of person) vie f sociale; (of town) vie f culturelle
social mobility n mobilité f sociale
social networking site n (Comput) site m de réseau social
social science n science f sociale
social security n aide f sociale; **to be on ∼** recevoir l'aide sociale
Social Services n pl (GB) services mpl sociaux
social work n travail m social
social worker n travailleur/-euse m/f social/-e
⚡ **society** n **(a)** (gen) société f
(b) (club) société f; (for social contact) association f
(c) (also **high ∼**) haute société f
sociologist n sociologue mf
sociology n sociologie f
sock n (pl ∼s ou **sox** (US)) chaussette f
socket n **(a)** (for plug) prise f (de courant); (for bulb) douille f
(b) (of joint) cavité f articulaire; (of eye) orbite f
soda n **(a)** (chemical) soude f
(b) (also **washing ∼**) soude f ménagère
(c) (also **∼ water**) eau f de seltz; **whisky and ∼** whisky m soda
(d) (also **∼ pop**) (US) soda m
sodden adj ‹towel, clothing› trempé/-e; ‹ground› détrempé/-e
sofa n canapé m
sofa bed n canapé-lit m
⚡ **soft** adj **(a)** (gen) doux/douce; ‹ground› meuble; ‹bed, cushion› moelleux/-euse; ‹brush, hair› souple; ‹dough, butter› mou/ molle; ‹impact, touch› léger/-ère; ‹eyes, heart› tendre; ‹fold› souple
(b) (lenient) ‹parent, teacher› (trop) indulgent/-e
soft cheese n fromage m à pâte molle

soft drink n boisson f non alcoolisée
soft drug n drogue f douce
soften 1 vtr **(a)** adoucir ‹skin, water, light, outline›; ramollir ‹butter›
(b) atténuer ‹blow, shock, pain›
2 vi **(a)** ‹light, outline, music, colour› s'adoucir; ‹skin› devenir plus doux; ‹substance› se ramollir
(b) ‹person› s'assouplir (**towards sb** vis-à-vis de qn)
■ **soften up:** 1 ¶ ∼ **up** amollir
2 ¶ ∼ **[sb] up** affaiblir ‹enemy, opponent›; attendrir ‹customer›
softly adv ‹speak, touch, blow› doucement; ‹fall› en douceur
soft option n **to take the ∼** choisir la facilité
soft porn n (colloq) soft m (fam)
soft skills n pl compétences fpl douces
soft spot n (colloq) **to have a ∼ for sb** avoir un faible (fam) pour qn
soft-top n décapotable f
soft touch n (colloq) poire f (fam)
soft toy n peluche f
⚡ **software** n logiciel m
software house n fabricant m de logiciels
software package n progiciel m
software piracy n piratage m de logiciels
soggy adj ‹ground› détrempé/-e; ‹food› ramolli/-e
⚡ **soil** 1 n sol m, terre f
2 vtr salir
soiled adj **(a)** (dirty) sali/-e
(b) (also **shop-∼**) vendu/-e avec défaut
solace 1 n (feeling of comfort) consolation f; (source of comfort) réconfort m
2 vtr consoler (**for** de)
solar adj solaire
solar eclipse n éclipse f de soleil
solar power n énergie f solaire
solder vtr, vi souder (**onto, to** à)
⚡ **soldier** n soldat m
■ **soldier on** persévérer malgré tout
sole 1 n **(a)** (fish) sole f
(b) (of foot) plante f; (of shoe, sock) semelle f
2 adj **(a)** (single) seul/-e (before n), unique (before n)
(b) ‹agent, right› exclusif/-ive; ‹trader› indépendant
solely adv (wholly) entièrement; (exclusively) uniquement
solemn adj ‹occasion, person, voice› solennel/-elle; ‹duty, warning› formel/-elle
solicit 1 vtr solliciter ‹information, help, money, votes›; rechercher ‹business, investment, orders›
2 vi ‹prostitute› racoler
soliciting n racolage m

S

solicitor n (GB) (for documents, oaths) ≈ notaire m; (for court and police work) ≈ avocat/-e m/f

⚔ **solid** [1] n solide m

[2] adj (a) (gen) solide; **to go** or **become ~** se solidifier

(b) ‹gold, marble› massif/-ive; **the gate was made of ~ steel** le portail était tout en acier; **cut through ~ rock** taillé dans la roche

(c) ‹crowd› compact/-e; ‹line› continu/-e; **five ~ days, five days ~** cinq jours entiers

(d) ‹advice, worker› sérieux/-ieuse; ‹investment› sûr/-e

[3] adv ‹freeze› complètement; **to be packed ~** ‹hall› être bondé/-e; **the play is booked ~** la pièce affiche complet

solidarity n solidarité f

solidify [1] vtr solidifier

[2] vi ‹liquid› se solidifier; ‹honey, oil› se figer

solitary adj (a) (unaccompanied) ‹occupation, walker› solitaire

(b) (lonely) ‹person› très seul/-e; ‹farm, village› isolé/-e

(c) (single) seul/-e

solitary confinement n isolement m cellulaire

solo [1] n solo m

[2] adj, adv en solo

soloist n soliste mf

solstice n solstice m

soluble adj soluble

⚔ **solution** n solution f

⚔ **solve** vtr résoudre ‹equation, problem›; élucider ‹crime›; trouver la solution de ‹mystery›; trouver la solution à ‹clue, crossword›; trouver une solution à ‹crisis, poverty, unemployment›

solvent [1] n solvant m

[2] adj (in funds) solvable

sombre (GB), **somber** (US) adj sombre

⚔ **some**

■ **Note** When *some* is used to mean an unspecified amount of something, it is translated by *du*, *de l'* (before a vowel or mute 'h'), *de la* or *des* according to the gender and number of the noun that follows: *I'd like some bread* = je voudrais du pain; *have some water* = prenez de l'eau; *we've bought some beer* = nous avons acheté de la bière; *they've bought some peaches* = ils ont acheté des pêches.

— But note that when a plural noun is preceded by an adjective in French, *some* is translated by *de* alone: *some pretty dresses* = de jolies robes.

— When *some* is used as a pronoun, it is translated by *en* which is placed before the verb in French: *would you like some?* = est-ce que vous en voulez?; *I've got some* = j'en ai.

— For further examples, see the entry below.

[1] det (a) (an unspecified amount or number) du/de l'/de la/des; **~ old socks** de vieilles chaussettes; **~ red socks** des chaussettes rouges; **I need ~ help** j'ai besoin d'aide

(b) (certain) certain/-e (*before n*); **~ people say that** certaines personnes disent que; **to ~ extent** dans une certaine mesure

(c) (a considerable amount or number) **his suggestion was greeted with ~ hostility** sa suggestion a été accueillie avec hostilité; **it will take ~ doing** ça ne va pas être facile à faire; **we stayed there for ~ time** nous sommes restés là assez longtemps

(d) (a little, a slight) **the meeting did have ~ effect** la réunion a eu un certain effet; **you must have ~ idea where the house is** tu dois avoir une idée de l'endroit où se trouve la maison

(e) (an unknown) **he's doing ~ course** il suit des cours; **a car of ~ sort, ~ sort of car** une voiture quelconque

[2] pron, quantif (a) (an unspecified amount or number) en; **he took ~ of it/of them** il en a pris un peu/quelques-uns; **(do) have ~!** servez-vous!

(b) (certain ones) certain/-e; **~ (of them) are blue** certains sont bleus; **~ (of them) arrived early** certains d'entre eux sont arrivés tôt

[3] adv (a) (approximately) environ; **~ 20 people** environ 20 personnes

(b) (US) (colloq) un peu

⚔ **somebody** pron (*also* **someone**) quelqu'un; **~ famous** quelqu'un de célèbre

⚔ **somehow** adv (a) (*also* **~ or other**) (of future action) d'une manière ou d'une autre; (of past action) je ne sais comment; **we'll get there ~** on y arrivera d'une manière ou d'une autre; **we managed it ~** nous avons réussi je ne sais comment

(b) (for some reason) **~ it doesn't seem very important** en fait, ça ne semble pas très important

⚔ **someone** = SOMEBODY

somersault [1] n (of gymnast) roulade f; (of child) galipette f; (accidental) culbute f

[2] vi ‹gymnast› faire une roulade; ‹vehicle› faire un tonneau

⚔ **something** [1] pron quelque chose; **~ interesting** quelque chose d'intéressant; **~ to do** quelque chose à faire; **there's ~ wrong** il y a un problème; **~ or other** quelque chose; **in nineteen-sixty-~** en mille neuf cent soixante et quelques; **she's gone shopping or ~** elle est allée faire les courses ou quelque chose comme ça

[2] **something of** phr **she is ~ of an expert on...** elle est assez experte en...; **it was ~ of a surprise** c'était assez étonnant

sometime adv **we'll have to do it ~** il va falloir qu'on le fasse un jour ou l'autre; **I'll tell you about it ~** je te raconterai ça un de ces jours; **I'll phone you ~ next week** je te téléphonerai dans le courant de la semaine prochaine

⚔ **sometimes** adv parfois, quelquefois

somewhat *adv* (with adjective) plutôt; (with verb, adverb) un peu

somewhere *adv* (some place) quelque part; ~ hot un endroit chaud; ~ or other je ne sais où; ~ between 50 and 100 people entre 50 et 100 personnes

son *n* fils *m*

sonata *n* sonate *f*

song *n* chanson *f*; (of bird) chant *m*

songwriter *n* (of words) parolier/-ière *m/f*; (of words and music) auteur-compositeur *m* de chansons

sonic *adj* sonore

sonic boom *n* bang *m*

son-in-law *n* gendre *m*

sonnet *n* sonnet *m*

soon *adv* (a) (in a short time) bientôt; see you ~! à bientôt!
(b) (quickly) vite
(c) (early) tôt; the ~er the better le plus tôt sera le mieux; as ~ as possible dès que possible; as ~ as you can dès que tu pourras; as ~ as he has finished dès qu'il aura fini; ~er or later tôt ou tard
(d) (not long) ~ afterwards peu après; no ~er had I finished than… j'avais à peine fini que…

soot *n* suie *f*

soothe *vtr* calmer ⟨pain, nerves, person⟩; apaiser ⟨sunburn⟩

soothing *adj* ⟨music, voice⟩ apaisant/-e; ⟨cream, effect⟩ calmant/-e; ⟨words⟩ rassurant/-e

sophisticated *adj* (a) ⟨person⟩ (cultured) raffiné/-e; (affected) sophistiqué/-e; (elegant) chic; ⟨restaurant⟩ chic
(b) ⟨taste⟩ raffiné/-e; ⟨civilization⟩ évolué/-e
(c) ⟨equipment, technology⟩ sophistiqué/-e

soporific *adj* soporifique

soprano *n* (*pl* ~s) (person) soprano *mf*; (voice, instrument) soprano *m*

sorcerer *n* sorcier *m*

sordid *adj* sordide

sore ⓵ *n* plaie *f*
⓶ *adj* (a) ⟨eyes, gums⟩ irrité/-e; ⟨muscle, arm, foot⟩ endolori/-e; to have a ~ throat avoir mal à la gorge
(b) ⟨subject, point⟩ délicat/-e

sorrow *n* chagrin *m*

sorrowful *adj* ⟨look⟩ affligé/-e; ⟨voice⟩ triste

sorry ⓵ *adj* (a) désolé/-e; I'm terribly ~ je suis vraiment désolé, je suis navré; I'm ~ I'm late je suis désolé d'être en retard; to be ~ about sth s'excuser de qch; to say ~ s'excuser; to be ~ to do regretter de faire
(b) (pitying) to be *or* feel ~ for sb plaindre qn; to feel ~ for oneself s'apitoyer sur soi-même
(c) ⟨state, sight, business⟩ triste; ⟨person⟩ minable
⓶ *excl* (a) (apologizing) pardon!, désolé!
(b) (pardon) ~? pardon?

sort ⓵ *n* sorte *f*, genre *m*; books, records—that ~ of thing des livres, des disques, ce genre de choses; I'm not that ~ of person ce n'est pas mon genre; some ~ of computer une sorte d'ordinateur
⓶ *vtr* classer ⟨data, files, stamps⟩; trier ⟨letters, apples, potatoes⟩; to ~ books into piles ranger des livres en piles
⓷ of sorts, of a sort *phr* a duck of ~s *or* of a ~ une sorte de canard; progress of ~s un semblant de progrès
⓸ sort of *phr* (colloq) ~ of cute plutôt mignon/-onne; I ~ of understand je comprends plus ou moins; ~ of blue-green dans les bleu-vert; it just ~ of happened c'est arrivé comme ça
IDIOMS to be *or* feel out of ~s (ill) ne pas être dans son assiette; (grumpy) être de mauvais poil (fam); it takes all ~s (to make a world) il faut de tout pour faire un monde
■ **sort out** (a) régler ⟨problem, matter⟩
(b) s'occuper de ⟨details, arrangements⟩; I'll ~ it out je m'en occuperai
(c) ranger ⟨cupboard, desk⟩; classer ⟨files, documents⟩; mettre de l'ordre dans ⟨finances, affairs⟩; clarifier ⟨ideas⟩
(d) trier ⟨photos, clothes⟩

sort code *n* code *m* d'agence

SOS *n* SOS *m*

so-so (colloq) ⓵ *adj* moyen/-enne
⓶ *adv* comme ci comme ça (fam)

sought-after *adj* ⟨person, skill⟩ demandé/-e, recherché/-e; ⟨job, brand, area⟩ prisé/-e

soul *n* (a) (gen) âme *f*
(b) (*also* ~ **music**) soul *m*

soul-destroying *adj* abrutissant/-e

soul mate *n* âme *f* sœur

soul-searching *n* débat *m* intérieur

sound ⓵ *n* (a) (gen) son *m*; (noise) bruit *m* (of de); to turn the ~ up/down augmenter/baisser le volume; the ~ of voices un bruit de voix; a grating *or* rasping ~ un grincement; without a ~ sans bruit
(b) (figurative) by the ~ of it, we're in for a rough crossing d'après ce qu'on a dit, la traversée va être mauvaise
(c) (Med) sonde *f*
(d) (strait) détroit *m*
⓶ *adj* (a) ⟨heart, constitution⟩ solide; ⟨health⟩ bon/bonne (before *n*); to be of ~ mind être sain/-e d'esprit
(b) ⟨basis, argument⟩ solide; ⟨judgment⟩ sain/-e; ⟨advice, investment⟩ bon/bonne (before *n*), sûr/-e
⓷ *vtr* faire retentir ⟨siren, foghorn⟩; to ~ one's horn klaxonner; to ~ the alarm sonner l'alarme
⓸ *vi* (a) (seem) sembler; it ~s as if he's really in trouble il semble qu'il ait vraiment des ennuis; it ~s like it might be dangerous ça a l'air dangereux; to ~ boring paraître ennuyeux; it ~s like a flute on dirait une flûte ⋯⟫

S

(b) ‹alarm, buzzer, bugle› sonner
5 adv **to be** ∼ **asleep** dormir à poings fermés
■ **sound out** sonder, interroger ‹person›
sound barrier n mur m du son
sound bite n: bref extrait d'une interview enregistrée
sound card n (Comput) carte f son
sound effect n effet m sonore
soundly adv ‹sleep› à poings fermés; ‹defeat› à plates coutures
soundproof adj insonorisé/-e
sound system n (hi-fi) stéréo f (fam); (for disco etc) sono f (fam)
soundtrack n (of film) bande f sonore; (on record) bande f originale
soup n soupe f, potage m
soup kitchen n soupe f populaire
soup plate n assiette f creuse
soupspoon n cuillère f à soupe
sour **1** adj **(a)** aigre; **to go** ∼ ‹milk› tourner
(b) (bad-tempered) revêche
2 vtr gâter ‹relations, atmosphere›
◆ **source** n source f; **at** ∼ à la source; ∼ **of** source f de ‹anxiety, resentment, satisfaction›; cause f de ‹problem, error, infection, pollution›
sourdough n (US) levain m
◆ **south** **1** n **(a)** (compass direction) sud m
(b) (part of world, country) **the South** le Sud
2 adj (gen) sud inv; ‹wind› du sud; **in** ∼ **London** dans le sud de Londres
3 adv ‹move› vers le sud; ‹lie, live› au sud **(of** de)
South Africa pr n Afrique f du Sud
South America pr n Amérique f du Sud
southeast **1** n sud-est m
2 adj ‹coast, side› sud-est inv; ‹wind› de sud-est
3 adv ‹move› vers le sud-est; ‹lie, live› au sud-est **(of** de)
◆ **southern** adj ‹coast› sud inv; ‹town, accent› du sud; ‹hemisphere› Sud inv; ∼ **England** le sud de l'Angleterre
South Pole pr n pôle m Sud
southwest **1** n sud-ouest m
2 adj ‹coast› sud-ouest inv; ‹wind› de sud-ouest
3 adv ‹move› vers le sud-ouest; ‹lie, live› au sud-ouest **(of** de)
souvenir n souvenir m
sovereign **1** n **(a)** (monarch) souverain/-e m/f
(b) (coin) souverain m
2 adj souverain/-e **(after** n)
sovereignty n souveraineté f
Soviet Union pr n Union f soviétique
sow¹ n truie f

◆ indicates a very frequent word

sow² vtr (prét **sowed**, pp **sowed**, **sown**)
(a) semer ‹seeds, corn›
(b) ensemencer ‹field, garden› **(with** de)
(c) (figurative) semer
soya (GB), **soy** (US) n soja m
soya sauce, **soy sauce** n sauce f soja
spa n **(a)** (town) station f thermale
(b) (US) (health club) club m de remise en forme
◆ **space** **1** n **(a)** (also **outer** ∼) espace m
(b) (room) place f, espace m
(c) (gap) espace m **(between** entre); (on form) case f
(d) (interval of time) intervalle m; **in the** ∼ **of five minutes** en l'espace de cinq minutes
(e) (area of land) espace m; **open** ∼s espaces libres
2 adj ‹programme, rocket› spatial/-e
3 vtr espacer
■ **space out** espacer ‹words, objects›; échelonner ‹payments›
space-bar n barre f d'espacement
spaced out adj (colloq) **he's completely** ∼ il plane (fam) complètement
spaceship n vaisseau m spatial
space station n station f orbitale
spacesuit n combinaison f spatiale
spacing n espacement m; (of payments) échelonnement m; **in single/double** ∼ en simple/double interligne
spacious adj spacieux/-ieuse
spade n **(a)** (implement) bêche f, pelle f
(b) (in cards) pique m
spaghetti n spaghetti mpl inv
Spain pr n Espagne f
spamming n (Internet) envoi m de publicités à l'ensemble des connectés
span **1** n **(a)** (of time) durée f
(b) (of bridge) travée f; (wing) ∼ envergure f
2 vtr (p prés etc **-nn-**) **(a)** ‹bridge, arch› enjamber
(b) (figurative) s'étendre sur
Spaniard n Espagnol/-e m/f
spaniel n épagneul m
Spanish **1** n **(a)** (people) **the** ∼ les Espagnols mpl
(b) (language) espagnol m
2 adj (gen) espagnol/-e; ‹teacher, lesson› d'espagnol; ‹embassy› d'Espagne
spank vtr donner une fessée à
spanner n (GB) clé f (de serrage)
spar vi (p prés etc **-rr-**) ‹boxers› échanger des coups
spare **1** n (part) pièce f de rechange; (wheel) roue f de secours
2 adj **(a)** ‹cash› restant/-e; ‹seat› disponible; ‹copy› en plus; **I've got a** ∼ **ticket** j'ai un ticket en trop; **a** ∼ **moment** un moment de libre
(b) ‹part› de rechange; ‹wheel› de secours
(c) ‹person, build› élancé/-e

3 *vtr* **(a)** to have sth to ∼ avoir qch de disponible; **to catch the train with five minutes to** ∼ prendre le train avec cinq minutes d'avance; **can you** ∼ **a minute?** as-tu un moment?
(b) (treat leniently) épargner; **to** ∼ **sb sth** épargner qch à qn
(c) (manage without) se passer de ‹person›
IDIOM to ∼ **no effort** faire tout son possible

spare part *n* pièce *f* de rechange

spare room *n* chambre *f* d'amis

spare time *n* loisirs *mpl*

spare tyre (GB), **spare tire** (US) *n* pneu *m* de rechange

sparingly *adv* ‹use, add› en petite quantité

spark **1** *n* étincelle *f*
2 *vtr* (*also* ∼ **off** (GB)) provoquer ‹reaction, panic›; être à l'origine de ‹friendship, affair›

sparkle **1** *n* scintillement *m*; (in eye) éclair *m*
2 *vi* ‹flame, light› étinceler; ‹jewel, frost, metal, water› scintiller; ‹eyes› briller; ‹drink› pétiller

sparkler *n* cierge *m* magique

sparkling *adj* **(a)** ‹eyes› brillant/-e
(b) ‹wit› plein/-e de brio
(c) ‹drink› pétillant/-e

spark plug *n* bougie *f*

sparrow *n* moineau *m*

sparse *adj* clairsemé/-e

sparsely *adv* peu; ∼ **wooded** peu boisé/-e; ∼ **populated** à faible population

spasm *n* (of pain) spasme *m* (**of** de); (of panic, rage) accès *m* (**of** de)

spate *n* **(a)** **in full** ∼ (GB) ‹river› en pleine crue; ‹person› en plein discours
(b) **a** ∼ **of** une série de ‹incidents›

spatula *n* spatule *f*

ᵍ **speak** **1** *vtr* (*prét* **spoke**, *pp* **spoken**)
(a) parler ‹language›; **can you** ∼ **English?** parlez-vous (l')anglais?
(b) dire ‹truth›; prononcer ‹word, name›; **to** ∼ **one's mind** dire ce qu'on pense
2 *vi* (*prét* **spoke**, *pp* **spoken**) parler (**to, with** à; **about, of** de); **who's** ∼**ing?** (on phone) qui est à l'appareil?; **(this is) Eileen** ∼**ing** c'est Eileen; **generally** ∼**ing** en règle générale; **roughly** ∼**ing** en gros; **strictly** ∼**ing** à proprement parler
■ **speak out** se prononcer
■ **speak up (a)** (louder) parler plus fort
(b) (dare to speak) intervenir

speaker *n* **(a)** (person talking) personne *f* qui parle; (public speaker) orateur/-trice *m/f*
(b) **a French** ∼ un/-e francophone; **a Russian** ∼ un/-e russophone
(c) (on stereo system) haut-parleur *m*

-speaking *combining form* **English**-/ **French**-∼ anglophone/francophone; **Welsh**-∼ ‹person› qui parle le gallois

spear *n* lance *f*

spearhead *vtr* mener ‹campaign, revolt, reform›

spearmint *n* menthe *f* verte

ᵍ **special** *adj* (gen) spécial/-e; ‹case, reason, treatment› particulier/-ière; ‹friend› très cher/chère

special effect *n* effet *m* spécial

specialist *n* spécialiste *mf* (**in** de)

speciality (GB), **specialty** (US) *n* spécialité *f*

specialize *vi* se spécialiser

specially *adv* **(a)** (specifically) spécialement; **I made it** ∼ **for you** je l'ai fait exprès pour toi
(b) (particularly) particulièrement; ‹like, enjoy› surtout

special needs *n pl* (Sch) difficultés *fpl* d'apprentissage scolaire

special school *n* établissement *m* médico-éducatif pour enfants handicapés

ᵍ **species** *n* (*pl* ∼) espèce *f*

ᵍ **specific** *adj* précis/-e

ᵍ **specifically** *adv* **(a)** (specially) spécialement
(b) (explicitly) explicitement
(c) (in particular) en particulier

specify **1** *vtr* stipuler; ‹person› préciser
2 **specified** *pp adj* ‹amount, date, day› spécifié/-e

specimen *n* (of rock, urine, handwriting) échantillon *m*; (of blood, tissue) prélèvement; (of species, plant) spécimen *m*

speck *n* (of dust, soot) grain *m*; (of dirt, mud, blood) petite tache *f*; (of light) point *m*

spectacle **1** *n* spectacle *m*
2 **spectacles** *n pl* lunettes *fpl*

spectacular *adj* spectaculaire

spectator *n* spectateur/-trice *m/f*

spectre (GB), **specter** (US) *n* spectre *m*

spectrum *n* (*pl* **-tra, -trums**) **(a)** (of colours) spectre *m*
(b) (range) gamme *f*

speculate **1** *vtr* to ∼ **that** supposer que
2 *vi* spéculer (**on** sur; **about** à propos de)

speculation *n* **(a)** (conjecture) spéculations *fpl*
(b) (financial) spéculation *f* (**in** sur)

ᵍ **speech** *n* **(a)** discours *m* (**on** sur; **about** à propos de); **to give a** ∼ faire un discours
(b) (faculty) parole *f*
(c) (language) langage *m*

speech day *n* (GB Sch) (jour *m* de la) distribution *f* des prix

speech impediment *n* défaut *m* d'élocution

speechless *adj* muet/-ette (**with** de); **to be** ∼ **with** rester muet de; **I was** ∼ **at the news** la nouvelle m'a laissé sans voix

ᵍ **speed** **1** *n* **(a)** vitesse *f*; (of response, reaction) rapidité *f*; **at top** ∼ à toute vitesse
(b) (colloq) (drug) amphétamines *fpl*

S

····ᐳ

2 *vtr* (*prét*, *pp* **sped** *ou* **speeded**) hâter ‹*process, recovery*›

3 *vi* (*prét*, *pp* **sped**) (a) to ~ along ‹*driver, car*› rouler à toute allure; to ~ away s'éloigner à toute allure

(b) (drive too fast) conduire trop vite

▪ **speed up**: **1** ¶ ~ **up** ‹*walker*› aller plus vite; ‹*athlete, driver, car*› accélérer; ‹*worker*› travailler plus vite

2 ¶ ~ [sth] **up** accélérer

speedboat *n* hors-bord *m*

speed camera *n* ≈ cinémomètre *m*

speed dating *n* speed dating *m*, rencontres *fpl* rapides

speed dial *n* composition *f* abrégée

speed hump *n* ralentisseur *m*

speeding *n* excès *m* de vitesse

speed limit *n* limitation *f* de vitesse

speedometer *n* compteur *m* (de vitesse)

spell **1** *n* (a) (period) moment *m*, période *f*; **sunny** ~ éclaircie *f*

(b) (magic words) formule *f* magique; to be under a ~ être envoûté/-e; to cast *or* put a ~ on sb jeter un sort à qn; to be under sb's ~ être sous le charme de qn

2 *vtr* (*pp*, *prét* **spelled** *ou* **spelt**) (a) écrire ‹*word*›

(b) signifier ‹*danger, disaster*›

3 *vi* (*pp*, *prét* **spelled** *ou* **spelt**) he can't/ can ~ il a une mauvaise/bonne orthographe

▪ **spell out** (a) épeler ‹*word*›

(b) (explain) expliquer [qch] clairement

spellbound *adj* envoûté/-e (by par)

spellcheck *vtr* effectuer une correction orthographique sur ‹*document*›

spellchecker *n* correcteur *m* orthographique

spelling *n* orthographe *f*

ᵈ **spend** **1** *vtr* (*prét*, *pp* **spent**)

(a) dépenser ‹*money, salary*› (on en)

(b) passer ‹*time*› (doing à faire)

2 *vi* (*prét*, *pp* **spent**) dépenser

spending cut *n* réduction *f* des dépenses; (Pol) restriction *f* budgétaire

spending power *n* pouvoir *m* d'achat

spending spree *n* folie *f* (fam) (de dépense); to go on a ~ faire des folies (fam)

spendthrift *adj* ‹*person*› dépensier/-ière

sperm *n* sperme *m*

sperm donor *n* donneur *m* de sperme

spew *vtr* vomir

sphere *n* (a) (shape) sphère *f*

(b) (field) domaine *m* (of de); ~ of influence sphère *f* d'influence

spherical *adj* sphérique

spice *n* (Culin) épice *f*; (figurative) piment *m*

spick-and-span *adj* impeccable

spicy *adj* (a) ‹*food*› épicé/-e

(b) ‹*detail*› croustillant/-e

---

spider *n* araignée *f*

spiderweb *n* (US) toile *f* d'araignée

spike **1** *n* pointe *f*

2 *vtr* (colloq) corser ‹*drink*› (with de)

spiky *adj* ‹*hair*› en brosse *inv*; ‹*branch*› piquant/-e; ‹*object*› acéré/-e

spill **1** *vtr* (*prét*, *pp* **spilt** *ou* ~ed) renverser ‹*drink*› (on, over sur)

2 *vi* (*prét*, *pp* **spilt** *ou* ~ed) se répandre (onto sur; into dans)

▪ **spill over** déborder; to ~ over into dégénérer en ‹*looting, hostility*›

spin **1** *n* (a) (of wheel) tour *m*; (of dancer, skater) pirouette *f*

(b) to go into a ~ ‹*plane*› descendre en vrille

(c) to go for a ~ (in car) aller faire un tour

2 *vtr* (*p prés* -**nn**-, *prét*, *pp* **spun**)

(a) lancer ‹*top*›; faire tourner ‹*globe, wheel*›

(b) filer ‹*wool, thread*›

(c) ‹*spider*› tisser ‹*web*›

3 *vi* (*p prés* -**nn**-, *prét*, *pp* **spun**) tourner; ‹*weathercock, top*› tournoyer; ‹*dancer*› pirouetter; my head is ~ning j'ai la tête qui tourne

▪ **spin out** prolonger ‹*visit*›; faire traîner [qch] en longueur ‹*speech*›; faire durer ‹*work, money*›

▪ **spin round**: **1** ¶ ~ **round** ‹*person*› se retourner rapidement; ‹*dancer, skater*› pirouetter; ‹*car*› faire un tête-à-queue

2 ¶ ~ [sb/sth] **round** faire tourner ‹*wheel*›

spinach *n* (Culin) épinards *mpl*

spinal cord *n* moelle *f* épinière

spindly *adj* grêle

spin doctor *n* (Pol) consultant *m* en communication attaché à un parti politique

spin-drier, spin dryer *n* essoreuse *f*

spine *n* (a) (Anat) colonne *f* vertébrale

(b) (on hedgehog, cactus) piquant *m*

(c) (of book) dos *m*

spineless *adj* mou/molle

spin-off *n* (a) (incidental benefit) retombée *f* favorable

(b) (by-product) sous-produit *m*

spinster *n* célibataire *f*; (derogatory) vieille fille *f*

spiral **1** *n* spirale *f*

2 *adj* ‹*structure*› en spirale

3 *vi* (*p prés etc* -**ll**- (GB), -**l**- (US)) ‹*prices, costs*› monter en flèche

4 **spiralling** (GB), **spiraling** (US) *pres p adj* qui monte en flèche

spiral staircase *n* escalier *m* en colimaçon

spire *n* flèche *f*

ᵈ **spirit** **1** *n* (a) (gen) esprit *m*

(b) (courage, determination) courage *m*

2 **spirits** *n pl* (a) (alcohol) spiritueux *mpl*

(b) to be in good ~s être de bonne humeur; to be in high ~s être d'excellente humeur; to keep one's ~s up garder le moral

spirited adj ‹horse, debate, reply› fougueux/-euse; ‹attack, defence› vif/vive

spirit level n niveau m à bulle

spiritual ⸢1⸣ n spiritual m
⸢2⸣ adj spirituel/-elle

spit ⸢1⸣ n (a) (saliva) salive f
(b) (Culin) broche f
⸢2⸣ vtr (p prés **-tt-**, prét, pp **spat**) ‹person› cracher; ‹pan› projeter ‹oil›
⸢3⸣ vi (p prés **-tt-**, prét, pp **spat**) ‹cat, person› cracher (at, on sur); ‹oil, sausage› grésiller; ‹logs, fire› crépiter
⸢4⸣ v impers (p prés **-tt-**, prét, pp **spat**) it's ~**ting (with rain)** il bruine
IDIOM to be the ~**ting image of sb** être le portrait tout craché de qn

spite ⸢1⸣ n rancune f
⸢2⸣ vtr faire du mal à; (less strong) embêter
⸢3⸣ **in spite of** phr malgré; **in** ~ **of the fact that** bien que

spiteful adj ‹person› rancunier/-ière; ‹remark› méchant/-e

splash ⸢1⸣ n (a) (sound) plouf m
(b) (of mud) tache f; (of water, oil) éclaboussure f; (of colour) touche f; (of tonic, soda) goutte f
⸢2⸣ vtr éclabousser; to ~ **water on to one's face** s'asperger le visage d'eau
⸢3⸣ vi faire des éclaboussures
■ **splash out** (colloq) faire des folies (fam); to ~ **out on sth** se payer qch

splay vtr écarter ‹feet, fingers›

spleen n (Anat) rate f

splendid adj splendide; ‹idea, holiday, performance› merveilleux/-euse

splendour (GB), **splendor** (US) n splendeur f

splice vtr coller ‹tape, film›; épisser ‹ends of rope›

splint n (for injury) attelle f

splinter ⸢1⸣ n éclat m
⸢2⸣ vi ‹glass, windscreen› se briser; ‹wood› se fendre; ‹alliance› se scinder

splinter group n groupe m dissident

split ⸢1⸣ n (a) (in fabric) déchirure f; (in rock, wood) fissure f
(b) (in party, alliance) scission f (in de)
⸢2⸣ **splits** n pl **to do the** ~**s** faire le grand écart
⸢3⸣ adj ‹fabric› déchiré/-e; ‹seam› défait/-e; ‹log, lip› fendu/-e
⸢4⸣ vtr (p prés **-tt-**, prét, pp **split**) (a) fendre ‹log, rock› (in, into en); déchirer ‹garment›
(b) diviser ‹party›
(c) (share) partager (**between** entre)
⸢5⸣ vi (p prés **-tt-**, prét, pp **split**) (a) ‹wood, log, rock› se fendre (in, into en); ‹fabric, garment› se déchirer
(b) ‹party› se diviser
■ **split up**: ⸢1⸣ ¶ ~ **up** ‹couple, band› se séparer
⸢2⸣ ¶ ~ **[sth] up** diviser (**into** en)

split second n fraction f de seconde

splutter vi ‹person› bafouiller; ‹fire, fat› grésiller

spoil ⸢1⸣ vtr (pp ~**ed** ou ~**t** (GB)) (a) (mar) gâcher ‹event, view, game›; gâter ‹place, taste, effect›; **to** ~ **sth for sb** gâcher qch à qn
(b) (ruin) abîmer ‹garment, crops›
(c) (pamper) gâter ‹child, pet›
⸢2⸣ vi (pp ~**ed** ou ~**t** (GB)) ‹product, foodstuff› s'abîmer

spoiled, **spoilt** (GB) adj ‹child, dog› gâté/-e; **a** ~ **brat** un gamin pourri (fam)

spoiler n (Aut) becquet m

spoils n pl (of war) butin m (**of** de)

spoilsport n (colloq) **to be a** ~ être un rabat-joie

spoke n rayon m

⚥ **spokesman** n (pl ~**men**) porte-parole m inv

spokeswoman n (pl ~**women**) porte-parole m inv

sponge ⸢1⸣ n (a) éponge f
(b) (also ~ **cake**) génoise f
⸢2⸣ vtr éponger ‹material, stain, face›
⸢3⸣ vi (colloq) **to** ~ **off** or **on** vivre sur le dos de ‹family, state›

sponge bag n trousse f de toilette

sponsor ⸢1⸣ n (a) (advertiser, backer) sponsor m
(b) (patron) mécène m
⸢2⸣ vtr sponsoriser ‹event, team›; financer ‹student›; parrainer ‹child›

sponsorship n sponsorat m

spontaneous adj spontané/-e

spontaneously adv spontanément

spoof n (colloq) (parody) parodie f (**on** de)

spooky adj (colloq) ‹house, atmosphere› sinistre; ‹story› qui fait froid dans le dos

spool n bobine f

spoon n cuillère f; (teaspoon) petite cuillère f

spoonful n (pl **-fuls** ou **-sful**) cuillerée f, cuillère f

sporadic adj sporadique

⚥ **sport** n (a) sport m
(b) **he's a good** ~ (good loser) il est beau joueur

sporting adj (a) ‹fixture, event› sportif/-ive
(b) (fair, generous) généreux/-euse; **to have a** ~ **chance of doing** avoir de bonnes chances de faire

sports car n voiture f de sport

sports centre (GB), **-s center** (US) n centre m sportif

sports club n club m sportif

sports ground n (large) stade m; (in school, club) terrain m de sports

sports jacket n (GB) veste f en tweed

sportsman n (pl ~**men**) sportif m

sports star n vedette f sportive

sportswear n vêtements mpl de sport

sportswoman n (pl ~**women**) sportive f

sporty adj (colloq) sportif/-ive

S

ꝏ **spot** [1] *n* (a) (on animal) tache *f*; (on fabric) pois *m*; (on dice, domino) point *m*
(b) (stain) tache *f*
(c) (pimple) bouton *m*
(d) (place) endroit *m*; **on the ~** sur place; **to decide on the ~** décider sur-le-champ
(e) (colloq) (small amount) **a ~ of** un peu de
(f) (colloq) **to be in a (tight) ~** être dans une situation embêtante
[2] *vtr* (*p prés etc* -**tt**) (a) apercevoir ‹*person*›; repérer ‹*difference, mistake*›
(b) (stain) tacher

spot check *n* contrôle *m* surprise
spotless *adj* impeccable
spotlight *n* (a) (light) projecteur *m*; (in home) spot *m*
(b) (focus of attention) **to be in** *or* **under the ~** ‹*person*› être sur la sellette; **the ~ is on Aids** le sida fait la une; **to turn** *or* **put the ~ on sb/sth** attirer l'attention sur qn/qch
spotted *adj* ‹*fabric*› à pois; ‹*fur, dog*› tacheté/-e
spotty *adj* (pimply) ‹*skin*› boutonneux/-euse; **he's very ~** il est plein de boutons; (patterned) à pois (*after n*)
spouse *n* époux/épouse *m/f*
spout [1] *n* (of kettle, teapot) bec *m* verseur
[2] *vtr* (a) (spurt) faire jaillir ‹*water*›
(b) (recite) débiter ‹*poetry, statistics*›
[3] *vi* ‹*liquid*› jaillir (**from, out of** de)
sprain [1] *n* entorse *f*
[2] *vtr* **to ~ one's ankle** se faire une entorse à la cheville; (less severely) se fouler la cheville
sprawl [1] *n* (of suburbs, buildings) étendue *f*
[2] *vi* s'étaler
spray [1] *n* (a) (seawater) embruns *mpl*; (other) nuages *mpl* de (fines) gouttelettes
(b) (container) (for perfume) vaporisateur *m*; (can) bombe *f*; (for inhalant, throat, nose) pulvérisateur *m*
(c) (of flowers) (bunch) gerbe *f*; (single branch) rameau *m*
[2] *vtr* vaporiser ‹*liquid*›; asperger ‹*person*› (**with** de); **to ~ sth onto sth** (onto fire) projeter qch sur qch ‹*foam, water*›; (onto surface, flowers) vaporiser qch sur qch ‹*paint, water*›
spray can *n* bombe *f*, aérosol *m*
ꝏ **spread** [1] *n* (a) (of disease, drugs) propagation *f*; (of news, information) diffusion *f*
(b) (Culin) pâte *f* à tartiner
[2] *vtr* (*prét, pp* **spread**) (a) (unfold) étaler, étendre ‹*cloth, newspaper, map*› (**on, over** sur); ‹*bird*› déployer ‹*wings*›
(b) étaler ‹*butter, jam, glue*› (**on, over** sur)
(c) (distribute) disperser ‹*troops*›; répartir ‹*workload, responsibility*›
(d) (*also* **~ out**) étaler, échelonner ‹*payments, meetings*› (**over** sur)
(e) propager ‹*disease, fire*›; semer ‹*confusion,*

panic›; faire circuler ‹*rumour, story*›
[3] *vi* (*prét, pp* **spread**) (a) ‹*butter, jam, glue*› s'étaler
(b) ‹*forest, drought*› s'étendre (**over** sur); ‹*disease, fear, fire*› se propager; ‹*rumour, story*› circuler; ‹*stain, damp*› s'étaler
■ **spread out**: [1] ¶ **~ out** ‹*group*› se disperser (**over** sur); ‹*wings, tail*› se déployer
[2] ¶ **~ [sth] out** étaler, étendre ‹*cloth, map, rug*› (**on, over** sur)
spread-eagled *adj* bras et jambes écartés
spreadsheet *n* tableur *m*
spree *n* **to go on a ~** (drinking) faire la bringue (fam); **to go on a shopping ~** aller faire des folies dans les magasins
sprig *n* (of holly) petite branche *f*; (of parsley) brin *m*
sprightly *adj* alerte, gaillard
ꝏ **spring** [1] *n* (a) (season) printemps *m*; **in ~** au printemps
(b) (of wire) ressort *m*
(c) (leap) bond *m*
(d) (water source) source *f*
[2] *vtr* (*prét* **sprang**, *pp* **sprung**)
(a) déclencher ‹*trap, lock*›
(b) **to ~ a leak** ‹*tank, barrel*› commencer à fuir
(c) **to ~ sth on sb** annoncer qch de but en blanc à qn ‹*news, plan*›
[3] *vi* (*prét* **sprang**, *pp* **sprung**) (a) (jump) bondir (**onto** sur)
(b) (originate) **to ~ from** venir de
■ **spring up** ‹*new building*› apparaître
spring-clean *vtr* nettoyer [qch] de fond en comble ‹*house*›
spring onion *n* (GB) ciboule *f*
springtime *n* printemps *m*
springy *adj* ‹*mattress, seat*› élastique
sprinkle *vtr* **to ~ sth with** saupoudrer qch de ‹*salt, sugar*›; parsemer qch de ‹*herbs*›; **to ~ sth with water** humecter qch
sprinkler *n* (a) (for lawn) arroseur *m*
(b) (to extinguish fires) diffuseur *m*
sprint [1] *n* (race) sprint *m*, course *f* de vitesse
[2] *vi* (in athletics) sprinter; (to catch bus) courir (à toute vitesse)
sprout [1] *n* (*also* **Brussels ~**) chou *m* de Bruxelles
[2] *vi* ‹*seed, shoot*› germer; ‹*grass, weeds*› pousser
spruce [1] *n* (*also* **~ tree**) épicéa *m*
[2] *adj* ‹*person*› soigné/-e; ‹*house, garden*› bien tenu/-e
■ **spruce up** astiquer ‹*house*›; nettoyer ‹*garden*›; **to ~ oneself up** se faire beau/belle
spry *adj* alerte, leste
spun *adj* ‹*glass, gold, sugar*› filé/-e
spur [1] *n* (a) (for horse) éperon *m*; (figurative) aiguillon *m*
(b) (of rock) contrefort *m*

S

ꝏ indicates a very frequent word

② *vtr* (*p prés etc* **-rr-**) (*also* ~ **on**)
éperonner ‹horse›; aiguillonner ‹person›; **to
~ sb to do** inciter qn à faire
IDIOM **on the ~ of the moment** sur une
impulsion

spurn *vtr* refuser [qch] (avec mépris)

spurt ① *n* **(a)** (gush) (of water, oil, blood) giclée
f; (of flame) jaillissement *m*
(b) (of activity) regain *m*; (of energy) sursaut *m*;
(in growth) poussée *f*; **to put on a ~** ‹runner,
cyclist› pousser une pointe de vitesse
② *vi* (*also* ~ **out**) jaillir (**from, out of** de)

spy ① *n* espion/-ionne *m/f*
② *vtr* remarquer, discerner ‹figure, object›
③ *vi* **to ~ on sb/sth** espionner qn/qch

spying *n* espionnage *m*

squabble *vi* se disputer, se chamailler
(fam)

squad *n* (Mil) escouade *f*; (Sport) sélection *f*

squad car *n* voiture *f* de police

squadron *n* escadron *m*

squalid *adj* sordide

squall *n* (wind) bourrasque *f*, rafale *f*; (at sea)
grain *m*

squalor *n* (filth) saleté *f* repoussante;
(wretchedness) misère *f* (noire)

squandor *vtr* gaspiller

square ① *n* **(a)** (shape) carré *m*
(b) (in town) place *f*
(c) (in game, crossword) case *f*; (of glass, linoleum)
carreau *m*
(d) (colloq) (person) ringard/-e *m/f* (fam)
② *adj* **(a)** (in shape) carré/-e; **four ~ metres**
quatre mètres carrés
(b) (quits) **to be ~** ‹people› être quitte
③ *vtr* **(a) to ~ one's shoulders** redresser
les épaules
(b) (settle) régler ‹account, debt›
IDIOM **to go back to ~ one** retourner à la
case départ
■ **square up** (settle accounts) régler ses
comptes

square bracket *n* crochet *m*; **in ~s**
entre crochets

square root *n* racine *f* carrée

squash ① *n* **(a)** (Sport) squash *m*
(b) (drink) sirop *m*
(c) (vegetable) courge *f*
② *vtr* écraser
■ **squash up** (colloq) se serrer (**against**
contre)

squat ① *adj* ‹person, structure, object›
trapu/-e
② *vi* (*p prés etc* **-tt-**) **(a)** (crouch) s'accroupir
(b) to ~ in squatter ‹building›

squatter *n* squatter *m*

squawk *vi* ‹hen› pousser des gloussements;
‹duck, parrot› pousser des cris rauques

squeak ① *n* (of door, wheel, chalk)
grincement *m*; (of mouse, soft toy) couinement
m; (of furniture, shoes) craquement *m*

② *vi* ‹door, wheel, chalk› grincer; ‹mouse,
soft toy› couiner; ‹shoes, furniture› craquer
(on sur)

squeaky *adj* ‹voice› aigu/aiguë; ‹gate,
hinge, wheel› grinçant/-e

squeal *vi* ‹person, animal› pousser des cris
aigus

squeamish *adj* impressionnable, sensible

squeeze ① *n* **(a)** (on credit, finances)
resserrement *m* (**on** de)
(b) (colloq) (crush) **it will be a tight ~** ce sera
un peu juste
② *vtr* **(a)** presser ‹lemon, bottle, tube›;
serrer ‹arm, hand›; appuyer sur ‹trigger›;
percer ‹spot›; **to ~ water out of** essorer,
tordre ‹cloth›
(b) (figurative) réussir à obtenir ‹money› (**out
of** de); **to ~ the truth out of sb** arracher la
vérité à qn
(c) (fit) **to ~ sth into sth** entasser qch dans
qch
■ **squeeze in:** ① ¶ ~ **in** ‹person› se glisser
② ¶ ~ **sb in** ‹doctor etc› faire passer qn
entre deux rendez-vous
■ **squeeze past** ‹car, person› se passer

squelch *vi* ‹water, mud› glouglouter; **to ~
along** avancer en pataugeant

squid *n* calmar *m*, encornet *m*

squiggle *n* gribouillis *m*

squint ① *n* strabisme *m*; **to have a ~**
loucher
② *vi* **(a)** (look) plisser les yeux
(b) (have eye condition) loucher

squire *n* ≈ châtelain *m*

squirm *vi* (wriggle) se tortiller; ‹person› (in
pain) se tordre; (with embarrassment) être très
mal à l'aise

squirrel *n* écureuil *m*

squirt ① *vtr* faire gicler ‹liquid›
② *vi* ‹liquid› jaillir (**from, out of** de)

stab ① *n* **(a)** (act) coup *m* de couteau; **a ~
in the back** (figurative) un coup en traître
(b) (of pain) élancement *m* (**of** de)
② *vtr* (*p prés etc* **-bb-**) poignarder ‹person›

stabbing *n* agression *f* au couteau

stability *n* stabilité *f*

stabilize ① *vtr* stabiliser
② *vi* se stabiliser

stable ① *n* écurie *f*; **riding ~s** manège *m*
② *adj* **(a)** (steady) stable
(b) (psychologically) équilibré/-e

stack ① *n* (pile) pile *f*; (of hay, straw) meule *f*
② *vtr* **(a)** (*also* ~ **up**) ‹pile› empiler
(b) (fill) remplir ‹shelves›
(c) mettre [qch] en attente ‹planes, calls›

stadium *n* (*pl* **-iums** *ou* **-ia**) stade *m*

✓ **staff** *n* (*pl* ~) (of company) personnel *m*; (of a
school, college) personnel *m* enseignant

staff meeting *n* réunion *f* du personnel
enseignant

staff room *n* salle *f* des professeurs

stag n cerf m

⚹ **stage** ① n (a) (phase) (of illness, career, life) stade m (**of**, **in** de); (of project, process, plan) phase f (**of**, **in** de); (of journey, negotiations) étape f (**of**, **in** de)
(b) (raised platform) estrade f; (in theatre) scène f
② vtr (a) (organize) organiser ‹event, rebellion, strike›
(b) (fake) simuler ‹quarrel, scene›
(c) (in theatre) monter ‹play›

stagecoach n diligence f

stage fright n trac m

stage-manager n régisseur/-euse m/f

stagger ① vtr (a) (astonish) stupéfier, abasourdir
(b) échelonner ‹holidays, payments›
② vi (from weakness) chanceler; (drunkenly) tituber

staggering adj ‹amount, increase› prodigieux/-ieuse; ‹news› renversant/-e; ‹achievement, contrast› stupéfiant/-e; ‹success› étourdissant/-e

stagnant adj stagnant/-e

stagnate vi stagner

stag night, **stag party** n soirée f pour enterrer une vie de garçon

staid adj guindé/-e

stain ① n (a) (mark) tache f
(b) (dye) teinture f
② vtr (a) (soil) tacher ‹clothes, carpet, table›
(b) teindre ‹wood›

stained glass n verre m coloré

stained glass window n vitrail m

stainless steel n acier m inoxydable

stain remover n détachant m

stair ① n (step) marche f (d'escalier)
② **stairs** n pl the ~s l'escalier; **to fall down the** ~s tomber dans l'escalier

staircase, **stairway** n escalier m

stake ① n (a) (amount risked) enjeu m; **to be at** ~ être en jeu
(b) (investment) participation f (**in** dans)
(c) (post) pieu m
② vtr miser ‹money, property›; risquer ‹reputation›
■ **stake out**: ~ out [sth], ~ [sth] out surveiller ‹place›

stale adj ‹bread, cake› rassis/-e; ‹beer› éventé/-e; ‹smell› de renfermé; ‹ideas› éculé/-e

stalemate n (a) (in chess) pat m
(b) (deadlock) impasse f

stalk ① n (on plant, flower) tige f; (of leaf, apple) queue f; (of mushroom) pied m
② vtr ‹hunter, murderer› traquer ‹prey, victim›; ‹animal› chasser ‹prey›

stall ① n (a) (at market) éventaire m
(b) (in stable) stalle f
② **stalls** n pl (GB) orchestre m

⚹ indicates a very frequent word

③ vtr caler ‹engine, car›
④ vi (a) ‹car› caler
(b) (play for time) temporiser

stallholder n marchand/-e m/f

stallion n étalon m

stalwart adj loyal/-e

stamina n résistance f, endurance f

stammer ① n bégaiement m
② vi bégayer

stamp ① n (a) (for envelope) timbre m
(b) (on passport, document) cachet m
(c) (marker) (rubber) tampon m; (metal) cachet m
② vtr (a) apposer [qch] au tampon ‹date, name› (**on** sur); tamponner ‹ticket, book›; viser ‹document, passport›
(b) **to** ~ **one's foot** (in anger) taper du pied
③ vi ‹horse› piaffer; **to** ~ **on** écraser (du pied) ‹toy, foot›; piétiner ‹soil, ground›

stamp-collecting n philatélie f

stamped addressed envelope, **sae** n enveloppe f timbrée à votre/son etc adresse

stampede ① n débandade f
② vi s'enfuir (pris d'affolement)

stance n position f

⚹ **stand** ① n (a) (support, frame) support m; (for coats) portemanteau m
(b) (stall) (in market) éventaire m; (kiosk) kiosque m; (at exhibition, trade fair) stand m
(c) (in stadium) tribunes fpl
(d) (witness box) barre f
(e) (stance) **to take a** ~ **on sth** prendre position sur qch
(f) **(to make) a last** ~ (livrer) une dernière bataille
② vtr (prét, pp **stood**) (a) (place) mettre ‹person, object› (**against** contre; **in** dans; **on** sur)
(b) (bear) supporter ‹cold, weight›; tolérer ‹nonsense, bad behaviour›; **I can't** ~ **him** je ne peux pas le supporter or le sentir; **I can't** ~ **this town** je déteste cette ville; **I can't** ~ **doing** je déteste faire
(c) (colloq) **to** ~ **sb a drink** payer un verre à qn
(d) **to** ~ **trial** passer en jugement
③ vi (prét, pp **stood**) (a) (also ~ **up**) se lever
(b) (be upright) ‹person› se tenir debout; ‹object› tenir debout; **to remain** ~**ing** rester debout
(c) ‹building, village› se trouver, être
(d) (step) **to** ~ **on** marcher sur ‹insect, foot›
(e) (as things are) **as things** ~... étant donné l'état actuel des choses...; **the total** ~**s at 300** le total est de 300; **to** ~ **in sb's way** (figurative) faire obstacle à qn
(f) (remain valid) ‹offer, agreement› rester valable
(g) (be a candidate) se présenter (**as** comme); **to** ~ **for election** se présenter aux élections

■ **stand back** ‹person, crowd› reculer (**from** de); (figurative) prendre du recul (**from** par rapport à)

■ **stand by**: **1** ¶ ∼ **by** ‹doctor, army› être prêt/-e à intervenir

2 ¶ ∼ **by** [sb/sth] soutenir ‹person›; s'en tenir à ‹principles, decision›

■ **stand down** démissionner

■ **stand for** (a) (represent) représenter; ‹initials› vouloir dire

(b) (tolerate) tolérer

■ **stand in**: to ∼ **in for sb** remplacer qn

■ **stand out** ‹person› sortir de l'ordinaire; ‹work, ability› être remarquable

■ **stand up** **1** (a) (rise) se lever

(b) (stay upright) se tenir debout

(c) ‹theory, story› tenir debout

(d) to ∼ **up** tenir tête à ‹person›

(e) to ∼ **up for** défendre ‹person, rights›

2 ¶ ∼ [sth] **up** redresser ‹object›

3 ¶ ∼ [sb] **up** poser un lapin à (fam)

⚡ **standard** **1** n (a) (level) niveau m; **not to be up to** ∼ ne pas avoir le niveau requis

(b) (official specification) norme f (**for** de)

(c) (banner) étendard m

2 adj ‹size, rate, pay› standard inv; ‹procedure› habituel/-elle; ‹image› traditionnel/-elle; **it's** ∼ **practice** c'est l'usage

Standard Assessment Task n (GB Sch) test m d'aptitude scolaire (par tranches d'âge)

standardize vtr normaliser, standardiser

standard lamp n (GB) lampadaire m

standard of living n niveau m de vie

standby n (person) remplaçant/-e m/f; **to be on** ∼ ‹army, emergency services› être prêt/-e à intervenir; (for airline ticket) être en stand-by

stand-in n remplaçant/-e m/f

standing **1** n (a) (reputation) réputation f, rang m (**among** parmi; **with** chez)

(b) (length of time) **of long** ∼ de longue date

2 adj (a) ‹army, committee, force› actif/-ive

(b) ‹invitation› permanent/-e

standing charge n frais mpl d'abonnement

standing order n virement m automatique

stand-off n (US) impasse f

standpoint n point m de vue

standstill n **to be at a** ∼ ‹traffic› être à l'arrêt; ‹factory, port› être au point mort; ‹work› être arrêté/e; ‹talks› être arrivé/-e à une impasse; **to come to a** ∼ ‹person, car› s'arrêter

stand-up **1** n (also ∼ **comedy**) one man show m comique

2 adj ∼ **comedian** comique mf

Stanley knife® n cutter m

staple **1** n (a) (for paper) agrafe f

(b) (basic food) aliment m de base

2 adj ‹product, food, diet› de base

3 vtr agrafer (**to** à; **onto** sur)

stapler n agrafeuse f

⚡ **star** **1** n (a) (in sky) étoile f

(b) (celebrity) vedette f, star f

(c) (asterisk) astérisque m

(d) (ranking) **a three-**∼ **hotel** un hôtel (à) trois étoiles

2 n (p prés etc **-rr-**) ‹actor› jouer le rôle principal (**in** dans)

3 vtr (p prés etc **-rr-**) ‹film, play› avoir [qn] pour vedette ‹actor›

starch n (a) (carbohydrate) féculents mpl

(b) (for clothes) amidon m

stardom n célébrité f; **to rise to** ∼ devenir une vedette

⚡ **stare** **1** n regard m fixe

2 vi **to** ∼ **at sb/sth** regarder fixement qn/qch

starfish n étoile f de mer

stark adj ‹landscape› désolé/-e; ‹room, decor› nu/-e; **in** ∼ **contrast to** en opposition totale avec

IDIOM ∼ **naked** tout/-e nu/-e

starry adj ‹night, sky› étoilé/-e

starry-eyed adj ébloui/-e (**about** par)

star sign n signe m astrologique

star-studded adj ‹cast, line-up› avec de nombreuses vedettes

⚡ **start** **1** n (a) (beginning) début m

(b) (in sport) (advantage) avantage m; (in time, distance) avance f; (departure line) ligne f de départ

(c) (movement) **with a** ∼ en sursaut

2 vtr (a) (begin) commencer; entamer ‹bottle, packet›; **to** ∼ **doing** commencer à faire

(b) (cause, initiate) déclencher ‹quarrel, war›; lancer ‹fashion, rumour›

(c) faire démarrer ‹car›; mettre [qch] en marche ‹machine›

3 vi (a) (begin) commencer (**by doing** par faire); **to** ∼ **again** recommencer

(b) ‹car, engine, machine› démarrer

(c) (depart) partir

(d) (jump nervously) sursauter (**in** de)

4 **to start with** phr (a) (firstly) d'abord, premièrement

(b) (at first) au début

■ **start off**: **1** ¶ ∼ **off** (a) (set off) ‹train, bus› démarrer; ‹person› partir

(b) (begin) ‹person› commencer; ‹business, employee› débuter (**as** comme; **in** dans)

2 ¶ ∼ [sth] **off** (a) commencer ‹visit, talk› (**with** par)

(b) mettre [qch] en marche ‹machine›

■ **start out** (on journey) partir

■ **start over** recommencer (à zéro)

■ **start up**: **1** ¶ ∼ **up** ‹engine› démarrer

2 ¶ ∼ [sth] **up** faire démarrer ‹car›; ouvrir ‹shop›; créer ‹business›

starter n (a) (of race) starter m

(b) (on menu) hors-d'œuvre m inv

···❖

IDIOM for ∼s (colloq) pour commencer

startle *vtr* (a) (take aback) surprendre
(b) (alarm) effrayer

startling *adj* saisissant/-e

starvation *n* famine *f*; **to die of** ∼ mourir de faim

starve ⟦1⟧ *vtr* affamer; (figurative) priver (**of** de); **to** ∼ **oneself** se sous-alimenter
⟦2⟧ *vi* mourir de faim; **to be** ∼**d of** être en mal de ⟨*company, conversation*⟩

starving *adj* (hungry) **to be** ∼ mourir de faim; (hunger-stricken) affamé/-e

⚜ **state** ⟦1⟧ *n* (a) état *m*; **he's not in a fit** ∼ **to drive** il n'est pas en état de conduire
(b) (*also* **State**) (government, nation) État *m*
⟦2⟧ **States** *n pl* **the States** les États-Unis *mpl*
⟦3⟧ *adj* (a) ⟨*school, sector*⟩ public/-ique; ⟨*enterprise, pension*⟩ d'État; ⟨*subsidy*⟩ de l'État
(b) ⟨*occasion*⟩ d'apparat; ⟨*visit*⟩ officiel/-ielle
⟦4⟧ *vtr* (a) (declare) exposer ⟨*fact, opinion*⟩; indiquer ⟨*age, income*⟩; **to** ∼ **that** ⟨*person*⟩ déclarer que
(b) (specify) spécifier ⟨*amount, time, terms*⟩; exprimer ⟨*preference*⟩
IDIOM **to be in a** ∼ être dans tous ses états

State Department *n* (US) ministère *m* des Affaires étrangères

state-funded *adj* subventionné/-e par l'État

stateless *adj* apatride

stately *adj* imposant/-e

stately home *n* (GB) château *m*

⚜ **statement** *n* (a) déclaration *f*; (official) communiqué *m*
(b) (*also* **bank** ∼) relevé *m* de compte

state of the art *adj* ⟨*equipment*⟩ ultramoderne; ⟨*technology*⟩ de pointe

statesman *n* (*pl* **-men**) homme *m* d'État

static ⟦1⟧ *n* (a) (*also* ∼ **electricity**) électricité *f* statique
(b) (interference) parasites *mpl*
⟦2⟧ *adj* (a) (stationary) ⟨*image*⟩ fixe; ⟨*traffic*⟩ bloqué/-e
(b) (stable) ⟨*population, prices*⟩ stationnaire

⚜ **station** ⟦1⟧ *n* (a) (*also* **railway** ∼ (GB)) gare *f*
(b) (radio, TV) station *f*
(c) (*also* **police** ∼) commissariat *m*; (small) poste *m* de police
⟦2⟧ *vtr* poster ⟨*officer, guard*⟩; stationner ⟨*troops*⟩

stationary *adj* immobile, à l'arrêt

stationer *n* (*also* ∼'**s**) papeterie *f*

stationery *n* fournitures *fpl* de bureau; (writing paper) papier *m* à lettres

station wagon *n* (US) break *m*

⚜ indicates a very frequent word

statistic *n* statistique *f*; ∼**s show that...** d'après les statistiques...

statistical *adj* statistique

statue *n* statue *f*

stature *n* (a) (height) taille *f*
(b) (status) envergure *f*

⚜ **status** *n* (*pl* **-uses**) (a) (position) position *f*
(b) (prestige) prestige *m*
(c) (legal, professional) statut *m* (**as** de); **financial** ∼ situation *f* financière

status quo *n* statu quo *m*

status symbol *n* signe *m* de prestige

statute *n* texte *m* de loi; **by** ∼ par la loi

statutory *adj* légal/-e

staunch *adj* ⟨*supporter, defence*⟩ loyal/-e; ⟨*Catholic, communist*⟩ fervent/-e

stave *n* (Mus) portée *f*
■ **stave off** tromper ⟨*hunger, fatigue*⟩; écarter ⟨*threat*⟩

⚜ **stay** ⟦1⟧ *n* (a) (visit) séjour *m*
(b) ∼ **of execution** sursis *m*
⟦2⟧ *vi* (a) (remain) rester; **to** ∼ **for lunch** rester (à) déjeuner
(b) (have accommodation) loger; **to** ∼ **in a hotel/ with a friend** loger à l'hôtel/chez un ami; **to** ∼ **overnight** passer la nuit
(c) (visit) passer quelques jours (**with** chez)
■ **stay in** rester à la maison
■ **stay out**: **to** ∼ **out late/all night** rentrer tard/ne pas rentrer de la nuit; **to** ∼ **out of trouble** éviter les ennuis
■ **stay up** (a) (waiting for sb) veiller
(b) (as habit) se coucher tard
(c) (not fall down) tenir

staying-power *n* endurance *f*

steadfast *adj* tenace

steadily *adv* (a) (gradually) progressivement
(b) ⟨*work, rain*⟩ sans interruption

steady ⟦1⟧ *adj* (a) (continual) ⟨*stream, increase*⟩ constant/-e; ⟨*rain*⟩ incessant/-e; ⟨*breathing, progress*⟩ régulier/-ière
(b) (stable) stable; **to hold [sth]** ∼ bien tenir ⟨*ladder*⟩
(c) ⟨*voice, hand*⟩ ferme; ⟨*gaze*⟩ calme
(d) (reliable) ⟨*job*⟩ stable; ⟨*relationship*⟩ durable
⟦2⟧ *vtr* **to** ∼ **one's nerves** se calmer les nerfs

steak *n* (of beef) steak *m*; (of fish) darne *f*

⚜ **steal** ⟦1⟧ *vtr* (*prét* **stole**, *pp* **stolen**) voler (**from sb** à qn)
⟦2⟧ *vi* (*prét* **stole**, *pp* **stolen**) (a) (thieve) voler
(b) (creep) **to** ∼ **into/out of a room** entrer/ quitter une pièce subrepticement

stealing *n* vol *m*

stealthy *adj* ⟨*step, glance*⟩ furtif/-ive

steam ⟦1⟧ *n* vapeur *f*
⟦2⟧ *vtr* faire cuire [qch] à la vapeur ⟨*vegetables*⟩
⟦3⟧ *vi* fumer, dégager de la vapeur
IDIOMS **to run out of** ∼ s'essouffler; **to let off** ∼ décompresser

■ **steam up** ⟨*window, glasses*⟩ s'embuer

steam engine *n* locomotive *f* à vapeur

steamer *n* (boat) (bateau *m* à) vapeur *m*

steamroller *n* rouleau *m* compresseur

steamy *adj* (a) ⟨*window*⟩ embué/-e; ⟨*climate*⟩ chaud/-e et humide
(b) (colloq) (erotic) torride

steel ① *n* acier *m*
② *v refl* **to ~ oneself** s'armer de courage

steelworks, **steelyard** *n* installations *fpl* sidérurgiques

steep ① *adj* (a) ⟨*slope, stairs*⟩ raide; ⟨*street, path*⟩ escarpé/-e; ⟨*roof*⟩ en pente raide
(b) (sharp) ⟨*rise, fall*⟩ fort/-e (*before n*)
(c) (colloq) ⟨*price*⟩ exorbitant/-e
② *vtr* **to ~ sth in** faire tremper qch dans

steeple *n* (tower) clocher *m*; (spire) flèche *f*

steer ① *n* (animal) bouvillon *m*
② *vtr* (a) piloter ⟨*ship, car*⟩
(b) (guide) diriger ⟨*person*⟩
③ *vi* (in car) piloter; (in boat) gouverner
IDIOM **to ~ clear of sb/sth** se tenir à l'écart de qn/qch

steering lock *n* blocage *m* de direction

steering wheel *n* volant *m*

stem ① *n* (a) (of flower, leaf) tige *f*; (of fruit) queue *f*
(b) (of glass) pied *m*
② *vtr* (*p prés etc* **-mm-**) arrêter ⟨*flow*⟩; enrayer ⟨*advance, tide*⟩
③ *vi* (*p prés etc* **-mm-**) **to ~ from** provenir de

stem cell *n* cellule *f* mère, cellule *f* souche

stencil ① *n* pochoir *m*
② *vtr* décorer [qch] au pochoir ⟨*fabric, surface*⟩

stenography *n* (US) sténographie *f*

✍ **step** ① *n* (a) (pace) pas *m*
(b) (measure) mesure *f*; **to take ~s** prendre des mesures
(c) (stage) étape *f* (**in** dans)
(d) (stair) marche *f*; **~s** (small ladder) escabeau *m*
② *vi* (*p prés etc* **-pp-**) marcher (**in** dans; **on** sur); **to ~ into** entrer dans ⟨*lift*⟩; monter dans ⟨*dinghy*⟩; **to ~ off** descendre de ⟨*pavement*⟩; **to ~ over** enjamber ⟨*fence*⟩
IDIOM **one ~ at a time** chaque chose en son temps
■ **step back** (figurative) prendre du recul (**from** par rapport à)
■ **step down** se retirer; (as electoral candidate) se désister
■ **step in** intervenir (**and do** pour faire)
■ **step up** accroître ⟨*production*⟩; intensifier ⟨*campaign*⟩

step aerobics *n* step *m*

stepbrother *n* demi-frère *m*

step-by-step ① *adj* ⟨*guide*⟩ complet/-ète
② **step by step** *adv* ⟨*explain*⟩ étape par étape

stepchild *n* beau-fils/belle-fille *m/f*

stepdaughter *n* belle-fille *f*

stepfather *n* beau-père *m*

stepladder *n* escabeau *m*

stepmother *n* belle-mère *f*

stepping stone *n* pierre *f* de gué; (figurative) tremplin *m*

stepsister *n* demi-sœur *f*

stepson *n* beau-fils *m*

stereo *n* (a) (sound) stéréo *f*; **in ~** en stéréo
(b) (*also* **~ system**) chaîne *f* stéréo; **personal ~** baladeur *m*

stereotype *n* stéréotype *m*

sterile *adj* stérile

sterilize *vtr* stériliser

sterling *n* livre *f* sterling *inv*

stern ① *n* (of ship) poupe *f*
② *adj* sévère

steroid *n* stéroïde *m*

stew ① *n* ragoût *m*
② *vtr* cuire [qch] en ragoût ⟨*meat*⟩; faire cuire ⟨*fruit*⟩; **~ed apples** compote *f* de pommes

steward *n* (on plane, ship) steward *m*; (of club) intendant/-e *m/f*; (at races) organisateur *m*

stewardess *n* (on plane) hôtesse *f* (de l'air)

✍ **stick** ① *n* (a) (of wood, chalk, dynamite) bâton *m*
(b) (*also* **walking ~**) canne *f*
(c) (in hockey) crosse *f*
② *vtr* (*prét, pp* **stuck**) (a) **to ~ sth into sth** planter qch dans qch
(b) (colloq) (put) mettre
(c) (fix in place) coller ⟨*poster, stamp*⟩ (**on** sur; **to** à)
③ *vi* (*prét, pp* **stuck**) (a) **the thorn stuck in my finger** l'épine m'est restée dans le doigt
(b) ⟨*stamp, glue*⟩ coller; **to ~ to the pan** ⟨*sauce, rice*⟩ attacher (fam)
(c) ⟨*drawer, door, lift*⟩ se coincer
(d) (remain) rester; **to ~ in sb's mind** rester gravé dans la mémoire de qn
■ **stick at**: **~ at** [sth] persévérer dans ⟨*task*⟩
■ **stick out**: ① **~ out** ⟨*nail, sharp object*⟩ dépasser (**of** de); **his ears ~ out** il a les oreilles décollées
② **~ [sth] out**: **to ~ out one's hand/foot** tendre la main/le pied; **to ~ one's tongue out** tirer la langue
■ **stick to** (a) (keep to) s'en tenir à ⟨*facts, point*⟩; maintenir ⟨*story, version*⟩
(b) (follow) suivre ⟨*river, road*⟩
■ **stick together** (a) ⟨*pages*⟩ se coller
(b) (colloq) (be loyal) être solidaires
(c) (colloq) (not separate) rester ensemble
■ **stick up** (project) se dresser; **to ~ up for sb** défendre qn

sticker *n* autocollant *m*

sticking plaster *n* pansement *m* adhésif, sparadrap *m*

S

sticky adj (a) ⟨floor, fingers⟩ poisseux/-euse; ⟨label⟩ adhésif/-ive
(b) (sweaty) ⟨hand, palm⟩ moite
sticky tape n (colloq) Scotch® m, ruban m adhésif
stiff ⟨1⟩ adj (a) raide; (after sport, sleeping badly) courbaturé/-e; ~ **neck** torticolis m; **to have** ~ **legs** (after sport) avoir des courbatures dans les jambes
(b) ⟨lever, handle⟩ dur/-e à manier
(c) ⟨manner, style⟩ compassé/-e
(d) (tough) ⟨sentence⟩ sévère; ⟨exam, climb⟩ difficile; ⟨competition⟩ rude
(e) (high) ⟨charge, fine⟩ élevé/-e
(f) **a** ~ **drink** un remontant
⟨2⟩ adv (colloq) **to bore sb** ~ ennuyer qn à mourir; **to be scared** ~ avoir une peur bleue
stiffen ⟨1⟩ vtr renforcer ⟨card⟩; empeser ⟨fabric⟩
⟨2⟩ vi (a) ⟨person⟩ se raidir
(b) ⟨egg white⟩ devenir ferme; ⟨mixture⟩ prendre de la consistance
stifle vtr étouffer
stigma n (pl **-mas** ou **-mata**) stigmate m
stigmatize vtr stigmatiser
stile n échalier m
stiletto n (pl **-tos**) (also ~ **heel**) (shoe, heel) talon m aiguille
⚡ **still¹** adv (a) encore, toujours; **he's** ~ **as crazy as ever!** il est toujours aussi fou!; **they're** ~ **in town** ils sont encore en ville
(b) (referring to the future) encore; **I have four exams** ~ **to go** j'ai encore quatre examens à passer
(c) (nevertheless) quand même
(d) (with comparatives) encore; **better/worse** ~ encore mieux/pire
still² ⟨1⟩ n (a) (for making alcohol) alambic m
(b) (photograph) photo f de plateau
⟨2⟩ adj (a) (motionless) ⟨air, water⟩ calme; ⟨hand, person⟩ immobile
(b) (peaceful) ⟨countryside, streets⟩ tranquille
(c) ⟨drink⟩ non gazeux/-euse
⟨3⟩ adv ⟨lie, stay⟩ immobile; **to sit** ~ se tenir tranquille; **to stand** ~ ne pas bouger
still life n (pl **-lifes**) nature f morte
stilted adj guindé/-e
stimulant n stimulant m (**to** de)
stimulate vtr stimuler
stimulating adj stimulant/-e
stimulus n (pl **-li**) (a) (physical) stimulus m
(b) (boost) impulsion f
(c) (incentive) stimulant m
sting ⟨1⟩ n (a) (part of insect) aiguillon m
(b) (result of being stung) piqûre f
⟨2⟩ vtr (prét, pp **stung**) (a) ⟨insect⟩ piquer
(b) ⟨wind⟩ cingler
⟨3⟩ vi (prét, pp **stung**) (gen) piquer; ⟨cut⟩ cuire
stingy adj radin/-e (fam)
stink ⟨1⟩ n (mauvaise) odeur f

⚡ indicates a very frequent word

⟨2⟩ vi (prét **stank**, pp **stunk**) puer
stint ⟨1⟩ n **to do a three-year** ~ travailler trois ans
⟨2⟩ vi **to** ~ **on** lésiner sur ⟨drink, presents⟩
stipulate vtr stipuler (**that** que)
stir ⟨1⟩ n **to cause (quite) a** ~ faire sensation
⟨2⟩ vtr (p prés etc **-rr-**) (a) remuer ⟨liquid, sauce⟩; mélanger ⟨paint, powder⟩; **to** ~ **sth into sth** incorporer qch à qch
(b) ⟨breeze⟩ agiter ⟨leaves, papers⟩
⟨3⟩ vi (p prés etc **-rr-**) (a) ⟨leaves, papers⟩ trembler; ⟨curtains⟩ remuer
(b) (budge) bouger
■ **stir up** provoquer ⟨trouble⟩; attiser ⟨hatred, unrest⟩; exciter ⟨crowd⟩
stir-fry ⟨1⟩ n sauté m
⟨2⟩ vtr (prét, pp **-fried**) faire sauter ⟨beef, vegetables⟩
stirring adj ⟨story⟩ passionnant/-e; ⟨music, speech⟩ enthousiasmant/-e
stirrup n étrier m
stitch ⟨1⟩ n (a) (in sewing, embroidery) point m; (in knitting, crochet) maille f
(b) (in wound) point m de suture
(c) (pain) point m de côté
⟨2⟩ vtr coudre (**to, onto** à); recoudre ⟨wound⟩
stoat n hermine f
⚡ **stock** ⟨1⟩ n (a) (supply) stock m; **we're out of** ~ nous n'en avons plus
(b) (descent) souche f, origine f
(c) (Culin) bouillon m
(d) (livestock) bétail m
⟨2⟩ **stocks** n pl (a) (GB) (in finance) valeurs fpl, titres mpl; ~**s and shares** valeurs fpl mobilières
(b) (US) actions fpl
(c) **the** ~**s** le pilori
⟨3⟩ adj ⟨size⟩ courant/-e; ⟨answer⟩ classique; ⟨character⟩ stéréotypé/-e
⟨4⟩ vtr (a) (sell) avoir, vendre
(b) remplir ⟨fridge⟩; garnir ⟨shelves⟩; approvisionner ⟨shop⟩
IDIOM to take ~ faire le point (**of** sur)
■ **stock up** s'approvisionner (**with, on** en)
stockbroker n agent m de change
stock-cube n bouillon-cube® m
stock exchange n **the** ~ la Bourse
Stockholm pr n Stockholm
stocking n bas m
stock market n (a) (stock exchange) Bourse f (des valeurs)
(b) (prices, trading activity) marché m (des valeurs)
stockpile vtr stocker ⟨weapons⟩; faire des stocks de ⟨food, goods⟩
stock room n magasin m
stock-still adv **to stand** ~ rester cloué/-e sur place
stocktaking n inventaire m

stocky *adj* trapu/-e

stodgy *adj* ‹food› bourratif/-ive

stoical *adj* stoïque

stoke *vtr* (*also* ~ **up**) alimenter ‹fire, furnace›

stolid *adj* ‹person, character› flegmatique

stomach ⟦1⟧ *n* estomac *m*; (belly) ventre *m*
⟦2⟧ *vtr* supporter ‹person, attitude›

stomach ache *n* **to have (a)** ~ avoir mal au ventre

✔ **stone** ⟦1⟧ *n* (a) pierre *f*; (pebble) caillou *m*
(b) (in fruit) noyau *m*
(c) (GB) (weight) = *6.35 kg*
⟦2⟧ *vtr* dénoyauter ‹peach›

Stone Age *n* âge *m* de pierre

stone circle *n* enceinte *f* de monolithes, cromlech *m*

stone-cold *adj* glacé/-e

stone mason *n* tailleur *m* de pierre

stonewall *vi* faire de l'obstruction

stone-washed *adj* délavé/-e

stony *adj* (a) (rocky) pierreux/-euse
(b) ‹look, silence› glacial/-e

stool *n* tabouret *m*

stoop ⟦1⟧ *n* **to have a** ~ avoir le dos voûté
⟦2⟧ *vi* être voûté/-e; (bend down) se baisser; **to ~ so low as to do** s'abaisser jusqu'à faire

✔ **stop** ⟦1⟧ *n* (a) (gen) arrêt *m*; **to come to a** ~ ‹vehicle, work, progress› s'arrêter; **to put a** ~ **to** mettre fin à
(b) (in telegram) stop *m*
⟦2⟧ *vtr* (*p prés etc* **-pp-**) (a) (cease) arrêter; (temporarily) interrompre ‹activity›; **to ~ doing** arrêter de faire
(b) (prevent) empêcher; **to ~ sb (from) doing** empêcher qn de faire
(c) supprimer ‹allowance›; **to ~ a cheque** faire opposition à un chèque
(d) (plug) boucher ‹gap, hole, bottle›
⟦3⟧ *vi* (*p prés etc* **-pp-**) (a) s'arrêter
(b) (stay) rester; **to ~ for dinner** rester dîner; **I can't** ~ je n'ai vraiment pas le temps
⟦4⟧ *v refl* (*p près etc* **-pp-**) **to ~ oneself** se retenir
■ **stop off** (on journey) faire un arrêt
■ **stop up**: ~ **[sth] up**, ~ **up [sth]** boucher ‹hole›

stopgap *n* bouche-trou *m*

stop-off *n* (quick break) arrêt *m*; (longer) halte *f*

stopover *n* escale *f*

stoppage *n* (strike) arrêt *m* de travail

stopper *n* (for flask, jar) bouchon *m*

stop sign *n* (panneau *m* de) stop *m*

stopwatch *n* chronomètre *m*

storage ⟦1⟧ *n* (of food, fuel) stockage *m* (**of** de); **to be in** ~ ‹furniture› être au garde-meuble
⟦2⟧ *adj* ‹space› de rangement

storage heater *n* radiateur *m* électrique à accumulation

✔ **store** ⟦1⟧ *n* (a) (shop) magasin *m*; (smaller) boutique *f*
(b) (supply) provision *f*
(c) (place) (for food, fuel) réserve *f*; (for furniture) garde-meuble *m*
(d) **what does the future have in** ~ **for us?** qu'est-ce que l'avenir nous réserve?
⟦2⟧ *vtr* (a) conserver ‹food, information›; ranger ‹furniture›
(b) (Comput) mémoriser ‹data›

storekeeper *n* (US) commerçant/-e *m/f*

storeroom *n* (in house, school, office) réserve *f*; (in factory, shop) magasin *m*

storey (GB), **story** (US) *n* (*pl* **-reys** (GB), **-ries** (US)) étage *m*; **on the third** ~ au troisième étage (GB), au quatrième étage (US)

stork *n* cigogne *f*

storm ⟦1⟧ *n* tempête *f*; (thunderstorm) orage *m*
⟦2⟧ *vtr* prendre [qch] d'assaut ‹citadel, prison›
⟦3⟧ *vi* **he** ~**ed off in a temper** il est parti furibond

stormy *adj* orageux/-euse; ~ **scenes** éclats *mpl*

✔ **story** *n* (a) (gen) histoire *f* (**about, of** de); **a true** ~ une histoire vécue; **a ghost** ~ une histoire de fantômes
(b) (in newspaper) article *m* (**on, about** sur)
(c) (rumour) rumeur *f* (**about** sur); **the** ~ **goes that** on raconte que
(d) (US) (floor) étage *m*

storybook *n* livre *m* de contes

storyteller *n* conteur/-euse *m/f*

stout *adj* (a) (fat) corpulent/-e
(b) (strong) ‹wall› épais/-aisse

stove *n* (a) (cooker) cuisinière *f*
(b) (heater) poêle *m*

stovetop *n* (US) (on cooker) table *f* de cuisson

stow *vtr* ranger ‹baggage›

stowaway *n* passager/-ère *m/f* clandestin/-e

straddle *vtr* enfourcher ‹horse, bike›; s'asseoir à califourchon sur ‹chair›

straggle *vi* (a) ‹houses, villages› être disséminé/-e (**along** le long de)
(b) (dawdle) traîner

straggler *n* traînard/-e *m/f*

straggly *adj* ‹hair, beard› en désordre

✔ **straight** ⟦1⟧ *adj* (a) ‹line, nose, road› droit/-e; ‹hair› raide; **in a** ~ **line** en ligne droite
(b) (level, upright) bien droit/-e; **the picture isn't** ~ le tableau est de travers
(c) (tidy, in order) en ordre
(d) (clear) **to get sth** ~ comprendre qch; **to set the record** ~ mettre les choses au clair
(e) (honest, direct) ‹person› honnête, droit/-e; ····⟩

‹*answer, question*› clair/-e; **to be ~ with sb** jouer franc-jeu avec qn
(f) ‹*choice*› simple
(g) ‹*spirits, drink*› sec, sans eau
(h) ‹*actor, role*› sérieux/-ieuse
2 *adv* **(a)** droit; **stand up ~!** tenez-vous droit!; **to go/keep ~ ahead** aller/continuer tout droit; **to look ~ ahead** regarder droit devant soi
(b) (without delay) directement; **to go ~ back to Paris** rentrer directement à Paris
(c) (frankly) tout net; **I'll tell you ~** je vous le dirai tout net; **~ out** carrément
(d) (neat) ‹*drink*› sec, sans eau
IDIOM to keep a ~ face garder son sérieux

straightaway *adv* tout de suite

straighten *vtr* tendre ‹*arm, leg*›; redresser ‹*picture, teeth*›; ajuster ‹*tie, hat*›; défriser ‹*hair*›
■ **straighten out: to ~ things out** (resolve) arranger les choses
■ **straighten up:** **1** ¶ **~ up** ‹*person*› se redresser
2 ¶ **~ [sth] up** (tidy) ranger ‹*objects, room*›

straightforward *adj* ‹*answer, person*› franc/franche; ‹*account*› simple

straight-laced *adj* collet-monté *inv*

◆ **strain** **1** *n* **(a)** (force) effort *m* (**on** sur)
(b) (pressure) (on person) stress *m*; (in relations) tension *f*
(c) (of virus, bacteria) souche *f*
2 *vtr* **(a)** **to ~ one's eyes** (to see) plisser les yeux; **to ~ one's ears** tendre l'oreille
(b) (try) mettre [qch] à rude épreuve ‹*patience*›
(c) (injure) **to ~ a muscle** se froisser un muscle; **to ~ one's eyes** se fatiguer les yeux; **to ~ one's back** se faire un tour de reins
(d) (sieve) passer ‹*sauce*›; égoutter ‹*vegetables, pasta, rice*›
3 *vi* **to ~ at** tirer sur ‹*leash, rope*›

strained *adj* (tense) tendu/-e; (injured) ‹*muscle*› froissé/-e

strainer *n* passoire *f*

strait *n* détroit *m*
IDIOM to be in dire ~s être aux abois

straitjacket *n* camisole *f* de force

strand **1** *n* (gen) fil *m*; (of hair) mèche *f*
2 *vtr* **to be ~ed** être bloqué/-e; **to leave sb ~ed** laisser qn en rade (fam)

◆ **strange** *adj* **(a)** (unfamiliar) inconnu/-e; **a ~ man** un inconnu
(b) (odd) bizarre; **it is ~ (that)** il est bizarre que (+ *subjunctive*)

strangely *adv* ‹*behave, react*› d'une façon étrange; ‹*quiet, empty*› étrangement; **~ enough,...** chose étrange,...

stranger *n* (from elsewhere) étranger/-ère *m/f*; (unknown person) inconnu/-e *m/f*

strangle *vtr* étrangler

stranglehold *n* (control) mainmise *f*

strap **1** *n* (on shoe) bride *f*; (on case, harness) courroie *f*; (on watch) bracelet *m*; (on handbag) bandoulière *f*; (on dress, bra) bretelle *f*
2 *vtr* (*p prés etc* **-pp-**) attacher (**to** à)

strapless *adj* sans bretelles

strapped *adj* (colloq) **to be ~ for** être à court de ‹*cash, staff*›

strapping *adj* costaud/-e

stratagem *n* stratagème *m*

strategic *adj* stratégique

◆ **strategy** *n* stratégie *f*

straw *n* paille *f*
IDIOMS to clutch at ~s se raccrocher à n'importe quoi; **the last ~** la goutte qui fait déborder le vase

strawberry **1** *n* fraise *f*; **strawberries and cream** fraises à la crème
2 *adj* ‹*tart*› aux fraises; ‹*ice cream*› à la fraise; ‹*jam*› de fraises

straw poll *n* sondage *m* non-officiel

stray **1** *n* (dog) chien *m* errant; (cat) chat *m* vagabond
2 *adj* ‹*dog*› errant/-e; ‹*cat*› vagabond/-e; ‹*bullet*› perdu/-e; ‹*tourist*› isolé/-e
3 *vi* **(a)** (wander) s'égarer; **to ~ from the road** s'écarter de la route
(b) ‹*eyes, mind*› errer

streak **1** *n* **(a)** (in character) côté *m*
(b) (period) **a winning/losing ~** une bonne/mauvaise passe
(c) (of paint) traînée *f*; **~ of lightning** éclair *m*
(d) (in hair) mèche *f*
2 *vtr* **(a)** strier ‹*sea, sky*›
(b) **to get one's hair ~ed** se faire faire des mèches
3 *vi* **to ~ past** passer comme une flèche

streaky bacon *n* (GB) bacon *m* entrelardé

stream **1** *n* **(a)** (brook) ruisseau *m*
(b) **a ~ of** un flot de ‹*traffic, questions*›; **a ~ of abuse** un torrent d'insultes
2 *vi* **(a)** (flow) ruisseler; **sunlight was ~ing into the room** le soleil entrait à flots dans la pièce; **people ~ed out of the theatre** un flot de gens sortait du théâtre
(b) ‹*banners, hair*› **to ~ in the wind** flotter au vent
(c) ‹*eyes, nose*› couler

streamer *n* (of paper) banderole *f*

streamline *vtr* **(a)** (in design) caréner
(b) (make more efficient) rationaliser ‹*distribution, production*›
(c) (cut) dégraisser ‹*company*›

streamlined *adj* **(a)** ‹*cooker, furniture*› aux lignes modernes; ‹*hull, body*› caréné/-e
(b) ‹*production, system*› simplifié/-e

◆ **street** *n* rue *f*; **in** or **on the ~** dans la rue

street cred *n* (colloq) **to have ~** être dans le coup (fam)

◆ indicates a very frequent word

streetlamp n (old gas-lamp) réverbère m; (modern) lampadaire m

street market n marché m en plein air

street plan n indicateur m des rues

street value n valeur f à la revente

streetwise adj (colloq) dégourdi/-e (fam)

◆ **strength** n (of wind, person, government, bond, argument) force f; (of lens, magnet, voice, army) puissance f; (of structure, equipment) solidité f; (of material) résistance f; (of feeling) intensité f

strengthen vtr renforcer ‹building, argument, love, position›; consolider ‹bond, links›; affirmer ‹power, role›; fortifier ‹muscles›; raffermir ‹dollar›

strenuous adj ‹exercise› énergique; ‹activity, job› ardu/-e

◆ **stress** 1 n (a) (nervous) tension f, stress m; mental ~ tension nerveuse; to be under ~ être stressé/-e
(b) (emphasis) accent m (on sur); to lay ~ on insister sur ‹fact, problem›
(c) (in physics) effort m
(d) (in pronouncing) accent m
2 vtr mettre l'accent sur, insister sur; to ~ the importance of sth souligner l'importance f de qch; to ~ (that) souligner que
■ **stress out** (colloq): ~ [sb] out stresser [qn]

stressed adj (a) (also ~ out) stressé/-e
(b) ‹syllable› accentué/-e

stressful adj stressant/-e

◆ **stretch** 1 n (a) (of road, track) tronçon m; (of coastline, river) partie f
(b) (of water, countryside) étendue f
(c) (period) période f; to work for 12 hours at a ~ travailler 12 heures d'affilée
2 adj ‹cover, fabric, waist› extensible
3 vtr (a) (extend) tendre ‹rope, net›; étirer ‹arms, legs›; to ~ one's legs (figurative) se dégourdir les jambes
(b) étirer ‹elastic›; élargir ‹shoe›
(c) déformer ‹truth›
(d) utiliser [qch] au maximum ‹budget, resources›
4 vi (a) ‹person› s'étirer
(b) ‹road, track› s'étaler (for, over sur); ‹beach, moor› s'étendre (for sur)
(c) ‹elastic› s'étendre; ‹shoe› s'élargir
■ **stretch out**: 1 ¶ ~ out s'étendre
2 ¶ ~ [sth] out tendre ‹hand, foot› (towards vers); étirer ‹arm, leg›; étaler ‹nets, sheet›

stretcher n brancard m

strew vtr (prét **strewed**, pp **strewed** ou **strewn**) éparpiller ‹litter, paper› (on sur); ~n with jonché/-e de

stricken adj (a) ‹face› affligé/-e; ‹area› sinistré/-e; ~ by frappé/-e de ‹illness›; pris/-e de ‹fear›; accablé/-e de ‹guilt›
(b) ‹plane, ship› en détresse

strict adj ‹person› strict/-e (about sur); ‹view› rigide; ‹silence› absolu/-e; ‹Methodist, Catholic› de stricte observance; in ~

confidence à titre strictement confidentiel; in ~ secrecy dans le plus grand secret

strictly adv (a) ‹treat› avec sévérité
(b) ‹confidential, prohibited› strictement; ~ speaking à proprement parler

stride 1 n enjambée f
2 vi (prét **strode**, pp (rare) **stridden**) to ~ out/in sortir/entrer à grands pas; to ~ across sth enjamber qch
IDIOM to take sth in one's ~ prendre qch calmement

strife n conflits mpl

◆ **strike** 1 n (a) grève f; on ~ en grève
(b) (attack) attaque f
2 vtr (prét, pp **struck**) (a) (hit) frapper ‹person, vessel›; heurter ‹rock, tree, pedestrian›; he struck his head on the table il s'est cogné la tête contre la table; to be struck by lightning être frappé/-e par la foudre
(b) (afflict) frapper ‹area, people›
(c) ‹idea, thought› venir à l'esprit de ‹person›; ‹resemblance› frapper; to ~ sb as odd paraître étrange à qn
(d) (colloq) (find) tomber sur (fam) ‹oil, gold›
(e) (achieve) conclure ‹deal, bargain›; to ~ a balance trouver le juste milieu (between entre)
(f) frotter ‹match›
(g) ‹clock› sonner
3 vi (prét, pp **struck**) (a) (gen) frapper
(b) ‹workers› faire (la) grève
■ **strike down** terrasser ‹person›
■ **strike off**: 1 ¶ ~ [sth] off, ~ off [sth] (delete) rayer
2 ¶ ~ [sb] off radier ‹doctor›
3 ¶ ~ [sb/sth] off sth rayer [qn/qch] de ‹list›
■ **strike out**: 1 ¶ ~ out (hit out) frapper; to ~ out at attaquer ‹adversary›; s'en prendre à ‹critics›
2 ¶ ~ [sth] out rayer
■ **strike up**: 1 ¶ ~ up ‹orchestra› commencer à jouer
2 ¶ ~ up [sth]: to ~ up a conversation with engager la conversation avec; to ~ up a friendship with se lier d'amitié avec

strikebreaker n briseur/-euse m/f de grève

strikebreaking n retour m au travail

strike force n force f d'intervention

striker n (a) (person on strike) gréviste mf
(b) (in football) attaquant/-e m/f

striking adj ‹person› (good-looking) beau/ belle (before n); ‹design, contrast› frappant/-e

string 1 n (a) (twine) ficelle f; a piece of ~ un bout de ficelle
(b) (on bow, racket) corde f; (on puppet) fil m
(c) (series) a ~ of un défilé de ‹visitors›; une succession de ‹successes, awards›
(d) (set) ~ of pearls collier m de perles
2 **strings** n pl (Mus) the ~s les cordes fpl
3 vtr (prét, pp **strung**) enfiler ‹beads, pearls› (on sur)

⋯⟩

S

IDIOM **to pull ~s** faire jouer le piston (fam)
■ **string along**: 1 ¶ **~ along** suivre
2 ¶ **~ sb along** mener qn en bateau (fam)
■ **string together** aligner ‹words›
string bean n haricot m à écosser
stringed instrument n instrument m
à cordes
stringent adj rigoureux/-euse
strip 1 n bande f (**of** de)
2 vtr (p prés etc **-pp-**) (**a**) déshabiller
‹person›; vider ‹house, room›; défaire ‹bed›; **to
~ sb of** dépouiller qn de ‹belongings, rights›
(**b**) (remove paint from) décaper
(**c**) (dismantle) démonter
3 vi (p prés etc **-pp-**) se déshabiller
strip cartoon n bande f dessinée
stripe n (**a**) (on fabric, wallpaper) rayure f
(**b**) (on animal) (isolated) rayure f; (one of many)
zébrure f
striped adj rayé/-e
strip lighting n éclairage m au néon m
stripper n strip-teaseur/-euse m/f
strive vi (prét **strove**, pp **striven**)
s'efforcer (**to do** de faire)
stroke 1 n (**a**) (gen) coup m; **at a single
~** d'un seul coup; **a ~ of luck** un coup de
chance; **a ~ of genius** un trait de génie
(**b**) (in swimming) mouvement m des bras;
(particular style) nage f
(**c**) (of pen) trait m; (of brush) touche f
(**d**) (Med) congestion f cérébrale
2 vtr caresser
stroll 1 n promenade f, tour m
2 vi se promener; (aimlessly) flâner
stroller n (US) (pushchair) poussette f
✧ **strong** adj (**a**) (powerful) ‹arm, person,
current, wind› fort/-e; ‹army, swimmer,
country› puissant/-e
(**b**) ‹heart, fabric, table› solide; ‹candidate,
argument› de poids
(**c**) ‹tea, medicine, glue› fort/-e; ‹coffee›
serré/-e
(**d**) ‹smell, taste› fort/-e
(**e**) ‹desire, feeling› profond/-e
(**f**) ‹chance, possibility› fort/-e (before n)
IDIOMS **to be still going ~** ‹person› se porter
toujours très bien; ‹relationship› aller
toujours bien; **it's not my ~ point** ce n'est
pas mon fort
strongbox n coffre-fort m
stronghold n forteresse f; (figurative) fief m
✧ **strongly** adv (**a**) ‹oppose, advise› vivement;
‹protest, deny› énergiquement; ‹suspect›
fortement; ‹believe› fermement; **I feel ~
about this** c'est quelque chose qui me tient
à cœur
(**b**) (solidly) solidement
strongroom n chambre f forte
strong-willed adj obstiné/-e

✧ indicates a very frequent word

structural damage n dégâts mpl
matériels
✧ **structure** 1 n (**a**) (organization) structure f
(**b**) (building) construction f
2 vtr structurer ‹argument, essay, novel›;
organiser ‹day, life›
✧ **struggle** 1 n (gen) lutte f; (scuffle) rixe f
2 vi (**a**) (put up a fight) se débattre (**to do**
pour faire); (tussle, scuffle) se battre
(**b**) (try hard) lutter (**to do** pour faire; **for** pour)
struggling adj ‹writer, artist› qui essaie
de percer
strum vtr (p prés etc **-mm-**) (carelessly)
gratter ‹guitar, tune›; (gently) jouer
doucement de ‹guitar›
strung out adj **to be ~ on** être accro (fam)
à ‹drug›; **to be ~** (from drugs) être en état de
manque
strut 1 n montant m
2 vi (p prés etc **-tt-**) (also **~ about**, **~
around**) se pavaner
stub 1 n (of pencil) bout m; (of cheque, ticket)
talon m; (of cigarette) mégot m
2 vtr (p prés etc **-bb-**) **to ~ one's toe** se
cogner l'orteil
■ **stub out** écraser ‹cigarette›
stubble n (**a**) (straw) chaume m
(**b**) (beard) barbe f de plusieurs jours
stubborn adj ‹person, animal› entêté/-e;
‹behaviour› obstiné/-e; ‹refusal› opiniâtre;
‹stain› rebelle
stuck adj (**a**) (jammed, trapped) coincé/-e; **to
get ~ in** rester coincé/-e dans ‹lift›; s'enliser
dans ‹mud›
(**b**) **to be ~ for an answer** ne pas savoir quoi
répondre
stuck-up adj (colloq) bêcheur/-euse (fam)
stud n (**a**) (on jacket) clou m; (on door) clou m à
grosse tête; (on boot) crampon m
(**b**) (stallion) étalon m; (horse farm) haras m
(**c**) (earring) clou m d'oreille
✧ **student** n (university) étudiant/-e m/f; (US)
((high) school) élève mf
student grant n bourse f d'études
student ID card n carte f d'étudiant
student nurse n élève mf infirmier/-ière
student teacher n enseignant/-e m/f
stagiaire
student union n (building) maison f des
étudiants
studio n (pl **~s**) (gen) studio m; (of painter)
atelier m
studious adj studieux/-ieuse
✧ **study** 1 n (**a**) (work, research) étude f (**of,
on** de)
(**b**) (room) bureau m
2 n pl études fpl; **computer studies**
informatique f; **social studies** sciences fpl
humaines
3 adj ‹leave, group, visit› d'étude; **~ trip**

voyage *m* d'études

4 *vtr* étudier

5 *vi* faire ses études

study aid *n* outil *m* pédagogique (destiné à l'élève)

ꞏ **stuff** **1** *n* (things) choses *fpl*, trucs *mpl* (fam); (personal belongings) affaires *fpl*; (rubbish, junk) bazar *m* (fam); (substance) truc *m* (fam)

2 *vtr* **(a)** rembourrer ‹cushion› (**with** de); bourrer ‹suitcase, room› (**with** de)

(b) (shove) fourrer (fam) (**in, into** dans)

(c) (Culin) farcir ‹turkey, chicken›

(d) empailler ‹dead animal, bird›

stuffed *adj* ‹turkey, chicken› farci/-e; ‹toy animal› en peluche; ‹bird, fox› empaillé/-e

stuffing *n* **(a)** (Culin) farce *f*

(b) (of furniture, pillow) rembourrage *m*

stuffy *adj* **(a)** (airless) étouffant/-e

(b) (staid) guindé/-e

stumble *vi* **(a)** (trip) trébucher (**against** contre; **on, over** sur)

(b) (in speech) hésiter

■ **stumble across** tomber par hasard sur ‹rare find›

stumbling block *n* obstacle *m*

stump **1** *n* (of tree) souche *f*; (of candle, pencil, cigar) bout *m*; (of tooth) chicot *m*; (part of limb, tail) moignon *m*

2 *vtr* (colloq) **to be ~ed by sth** être en peine d'expliquer qch; **I'm ~ed!** (in quiz) je sèche! (fam); (nonplussed) aucune idée!

■ **stump up** (GB) (colloq) débourser (**for** pour)

stun *vtr* (*p prés etc* **-nn-**) **(a)** (daze) assommer

(b) (amaze) stupéfier

stunned *adj* **(a)** (dazed) assommé/-e

(b) (amazed) ‹person› stupéfait/-e; ‹silence› figé/-e

stunning *adj* (beautiful) sensationnel/-elle

stunt **1** *n* **(a)** (for attention) coup *m* organisé, truc *m* (fam)

(b) (in film) cascade *f*

2 *vtr* empêcher ‹development›; nuire à ‹plant growth›

stunted *adj* rabougri/-e

stuntman *n* cascadeur *m*

stupefying *adj* stupéfiant/-e

stupendous *adj* prodigieux/-ieuse

ꞏ **stupid** *adj* bête, stupide; **I've done something ~** j'ai fait une bêtise

stupidity *n* bêtise *f*

stupor *n* stupeur *f*; **in a drunken ~** hébété/-e par l'alcool

sturdy *adj* robuste, solide

stutter *vtr*, *vi* bégayer

St Valentine's Day *n* la Saint-Valentin

sty *n* **(a)** (for pigs) porcherie *f*

(b) (*also* **stye**) orgelet *m*

ꞏ **style** **1** *n* **(a)** (manner) style *m*

(b) (elegance) classe *f*; **to do things in ~** faire les choses en grand

(c) (design) (of car, clothing) modèle *m*; (of house) type *m*

(d) (fashion) mode *f*

2 *vtr* couper ‹hair›

styling **1** *n* **(a)** (design) conception *f*

(b) (in hairdressing) coupe *f*

2 *adj* ‹gel, mousse, product› coiffant/-e

stylish *adj* ‹car, coat, person› élégant/-e; ‹resort, restaurant› chic

stylist *n* **(a)** (hairdresser) coiffeur/-euse *m/f*

(b) (designer) concepteur/ trice *m/f*

stylistic *adj* stylistique

stylus *n* (*pl* **-li** *ou* **-luses**) pointe *f* de lecture

suave *adj* ‹person› mielleux/-euse

subconscious **1** *n* **the ~** le subconscient

2 *adj* inconscient/-e

subcontinent *n* sous-continent *m*

subcontract *vtr* sous-traiter (**out to** à)

subcontracting *n* sous-traitance *f*

subcontractor *n* sous-traitant *m*

subdivide *vtr* subdiviser

subdue *vtr* soumettre ‹people, nation›

subdued *adj* ‹person› silencieux/-ieuse; ‹excitement› contenu/-e; ‹lighting› tamisé/-e

subheading *n* sous-titre *m*

ꞏ **subject** **1** *n* **(a)** (topic) sujet *m*; **to change the ~** parler d'autre chose

(b) (at school, college) matière *f*; (for research, study) sujet *m*

(c) **to be the ~ of an inquiry** faire l'objet d'une enquête

(d) (citizen) sujet/-ette *m/f*

2 *adj* **(a)** (liable) **to be ~ to** être sujet/-ette à ‹flooding, fits›; être passible de ‹tax›

(b) (dependent) **to be ~ to** dépendre de ‹approval›; être soumis/-e à ‹law›

3 *vtr* **to ~ sb to sth** faire subir qch à qn

subject heading *n* sujet *m*

subjective *adj* subjectif/-ive

subjugate *vtr* subjuguer ‹country, people›

subjunctive *n* subjonctif *m*

sublet *vtr*, *vi* (*p prés* **-tt-**, *prét*, *pp* **-let**) sous-louer

sublime *adj* ‹beauty, genius› sublime; ‹indifference› suprême

subliminal *adj* subliminal/-e

submachine gun *n* mitraillette *f*

submarine *n* sous-marin *m*

submerge *vtr* ‹sea, flood› submerger; ‹person› immerger (**in** dans)

ꞏ **submission** *n* soumission *f* (**to** à)

submissive *adj* ‹person› soumis/-e; ‹behaviour› docile

ꞏ **submit** **1** *vtr* (*p prés etc* **-tt-**) soumettre ‹report, plan, script› (**to** à); présenter ‹bill, application›

2 *vi* (*p prés etc* **-tt-**) se soumettre; **to ~ to** subir ‹indignity, injustice›; céder à ‹will,   ·····>

S

demand›

subnormal *adj ‹person›* arriéré/-e

subordinate *n, adj* subalterne *mf*

subpoena *vtr (3ᵉ pers sg prés* ∼**s**, *prét, pp* ∼**ed**) assigner [qn] à comparaître

subprime mortgages *n pl* crédits *mpl* immobiliers à risque

subscribe *vi* (a) to ∼ to partager *‹view, values›*
(b) to ∼ to être abonné/-e à *‹magazine›*

subscriber *n* abonné/-e *m/f* (to de)

subscription *n* abonnement *m* (to à)

subsequent *adj* (in past) ultérieur/-e; (in future) à venir

subsequently *adv* par la suite

subservient *adj* servile (to envers)

subside *vi* (a) *‹storm, wind, noise›* s'apaiser; *‹emotion›* se calmer; *‹fever, excitement›* retomber
(b) *‹building, land›* s'affaisser

subsidiary ⓵ *n* (also ∼ **company**) filiale *f*
⓶ *adj* secondaire (to par rapport à)

subsidize *vtr* subventionner

subsidy *n* subvention *f* (to, for à)

subsist *vi* subsister

subsistence *n* subsistance *f*

subsistence level *n* niveau *m* minimum pour vivre

substance *n* (a) (gen) substance *f*
(b) (of argument, talks) essentiel *m*; (of claim, accusation) fondement *m*

substance abuse *n* abus *m* de substances toxiques

substandard *adj* de qualité inférieure

ᵈ **substantial** *adj* (a) (considerable) considérable; *‹sum, quantity›* important/-e; *‹meal›* substantiel/-ielle
(b) (solid) *‹proof, lock›* solide

substantiate *vtr* justifier *‹allegation›*; appuyer [qch] par des preuves *‹statement›*

substitute ⓵ *n* (a) (person) remplaçant/-e *m/f*
(b) (product, substance) succédané *m*
⓶ *vtr* substituer (for à)

subtitle *n* sous-titre *m*

subtitled *adj* sous-titré/-e

subtle *adj* (gen) subtil/-e; *‹change›* imperceptible; *‹hint›* voilé/-e; *‹lighting›* tamisé/-e

subtlety *n* subtilité *f*

subtotal *n* sous-total *m*

subtract *vtr* soustraire (from de)

subtraction *n* soustraction *f*

suburb ⓵ *n* banlieue *f*; **inner** ∼ faubourg *m*
⓶ **suburbs** *n pl* the ∼s la banlieue

suburban *adj ‹street, shop, train›* de banlieue; (US) *‹shopping mall›* à l'extérieur de la ville

suburbia *n* la banlieue *f*

subversive ⓵ *n* élément *m* subversif
⓶ *adj* subversif/-ive

subway *n* (a) (GB) (for pedestrians) passage *m* souterrain
(b) (US) (underground railway) métro *m*

sub-zero *adj* inférieur/-e à zéro

ᵈ **succeed** ⓵ *vtr* succéder à *‹person›*
⓶ *vi* réussir; to ∼ in doing réussir à faire

succeeding *adj* qui suit, suivant/-e

ᵈ **success** *n* succès *m*, réussite *f*; to be a ∼ *‹party›* être réussi/-e; *‹film, person›* avoir du succès

ᵈ **successful** *adj ‹attempt, operation›* réussi/-e; *‹plan, campaign›* couronné/-e de succès; *‹film, book, writer›* (profitable) à succès; (well regarded) apprécié/-e; *‹businessman›* prospère; *‹career›* brillant/-e; to be ∼ réussir (in doing à faire)

successfully *adv* avec succès

succession *n* (a) (sequence) série *f* (of de); in ∼ de suite; in close ∼ coup sur coup
(b) (inheriting) succession *f* (to à)

successive *adj* successif/-ive; *‹day, week›* consécutif/-ive

successor *n* successeur *m*

success rate *n* taux *m* de réussite

success story *n* réussite *f*

succinct *adj* succinct/-e

succulent *adj* succulent/-e

succumb *vi* succomber (to à)

ᵈ **such** ⓵ *det* tel/telle; (similar) pareil/-eille; ∼ **a situation** une telle situation; **in** ∼ **a situation** dans une situation pareille; **some** ∼ **remark** quelque chose comme ça; **there's no** ∼ **thing** ça n'existe pas; **you'll do no** ∼ **thing!** il n'en est pas question!; **in** ∼ **a way that** d'une telle façon que; ∼ **money as I have** le peu d'argent *or* tout l'argent que j'ai
⓶ *adv* (with adjectives) si, tellement; (with nouns) tel/telle; **in** ∼ **a persuasive way** d'une façon si convaincante; ∼ **a nice boy!** un garçon si gentil!; ∼ **good quality** une telle qualité; **I hadn't seen** ∼ **a good film for years** je n'avais pas vu un aussi bon film depuis des années; ∼ **a lot of problems** tant de problèmes; **there were (ever (colloq))** ∼ **a lot of people** il y avait beaucoup de monde
⓷ **such as** *phr* comme, tel/telle que; **a house** ∼ **as this** une maison comme celle-ci; **a person** ∼ **as her** une personne comme elle; **have you** ∼ **a thing as a screwdriver?** auriez-vous un tournevis par hasard?

such and such *det* tel/telle; **on** ∼ **a topic** sur tel ou tel sujet

suck ⓵ *vtr* sucer *‹thumb, fruit, lollipop, pencil›*; (drink in) aspirer *‹liquid, air›*
⓶ *vi* to ∼ at sucer; to ∼ on tirer sur *‹pipe›*

ᵈ indicates a very frequent word

■ **suck up**: ⬛1 ¶ ~ up faire de la lèche (fam); to ~ up to sb cirer les pompes à qn (fam) ⬛2 ¶ ~ [sth] up pomper ‹liquid›; aspirer ‹dirt›

sucker n (a) (colloq) (dupe) bonne poire f (fam) (b) (on plant) surgeon m (c) (pad) ventouse f

suction n succion f

suction pad n ventouse f

sudden adj (gen) soudain/-e; ‹movement› brusque; all of a ~ tout à coup

sudden death play-off n: penalties pour départager deux équipes

ᵔ **suddenly** adv ‹die, grow pale› subitement; ‹happen› tout à coup

sudoku n sudoku m

suds n pl (also **soap** ~) (foam) mousse f (de savon); (soapy water) eau f savonneuse

sue ⬛1 vtr intenter un procès à; to ~ sb for divorce demander le divorce à qn; to ~ sb for damages réclamer à qn des dommages-intérêts ⬛2 vi intenter un procès

suede ⬛1 n daim m ⬛2 adj ‹shoe, glove› en daim

ᵔ **suffer** ⬛1 vtr subir ‹loss, consequences, defeat›; to ~ a heart attack avoir une crise cardiaque ⬛2 vi (a) souffrir; to ~ from souffrir de ‹rheumatism, heat›; avoir ‹headache, high blood pressure, cold›; to ~ from depression être dépressif/-ive (b) (do badly) ‹company, profits› souffrir; ‹health, quality, work› s'en ressentir

sufferer n victime f; leukemia ~s les leucémiques mpl

suffering ⬛1 n souffrances fpl (of de) ⬛2 adj souffrant/-e

sufficient adj suffisamment de, assez de; to be ~ suffire

sufficiently adv suffisamment, assez

suffocate ⬛1 vtr ‹smoke, fumes› asphyxier; ‹person, anger› étouffer ⬛2 vi (a) (by smoke, fumes) être asphyxié/-e; (by pillow) être étouffé/-e (b) (figurative) suffoquer

suffocating adj ‹smoke› asphyxiant/-e; ‹atmosphere, heat› étouffant/-e

suffrage n (right) droit m de vote; (system) suffrage m

sugar n sucre m; brown ~ sucre m roux

sugar beet n betterave f à sucre

sugar cane n canne f à sucre

sugar-free adj sans sucre

sugar lump n morceau m de sucre

ᵔ **suggest** vtr suggérer; they ~ed that I (should) leave ils m'ont suggéré de partir

ᵔ **suggestion** n (a) (gen) suggestion f; at sb's ~ sur le conseil de qn (b) (hint) soupçon m (of de); (of smile) pointe f

suggestive adj suggestif/-ive

suicidal adj suicidaire

ᵔ **suicide** n (action) suicide m; (person) suicidé/-e m/f; to commit ~ se suicider

suicide attack n attentat m suicide

ᵔ **suit** ⬛1 n (a) (man's) costume m; (woman's) tailleur m; a ~ of armour une armure (complète) (b) (lawsuit) procès m (c) (in cards) couleur f ⬛2 vtr (a) ‹colour, outfit› aller à ‹person› (b) ‹date, climate, arrangement› convenir à ⬛3 vi convenir ⬛4 v refl to ~ oneself faire comme on veut

suitable adj ‹accommodation, clothing, employment› adéquat/-e; ‹candidate› apte; ‹gift, gesture› approprié/-e; ‹moment› opportun/-e; to be ~ for convenir à ‹person›; bien se prêter à ‹climate, activity, occasion›

suitably adv convenablement

suitcase n valise f

suite n (a) (gen) suite f (b) (furniture) mobilier m

suited adj to be ~ to ‹place, clothes› être commode pour; ‹game, style› convenir à; ‹person› être fait/-e pour

sulk vi bouder (about, over à cause de)

sulky adj boudeur/-euse; to look ~ faire la tête

sullen adj ‹person, expression› renfrogné/-e; ‹day, sky, mood› maussade

sulphur (GB), **sulfur** (US) n soufre m

sulphuric acid n acide m sulfurique

sultana n (Culin) raisin m de Smyrne

sultry adj (a) ‹day› étouffant/-e; ‹weather› lourd/-e (b) ‹look, smile› sensuel/-elle

sum n (a) (of money) somme f (b) (calculation) calcul m

■ **sum up**: ⬛1 ¶ ~ up récapituler ⬛2 ¶ ~ up [sth] résumer

summarize vtr résumer ‹book, problem›; récapituler ‹argument, speech›

summary n résumé m

ᵔ **summer** ⬛1 n été m; in ~ en été ⬛2 adj ‹evening, resort, clothes› d'été

summer camp n (US) colonie f de vacances

summer holiday (GB), **summer vacation** (US) n (gen) vacances fpl (d'été); (Sch, Univ) grandes vacances fpl

summerhouse n pavillon m (de jardin)

summer school n université f d'été

summertime n été m

summit n sommet m

summon vtr (a) (gen) faire venir (b) (Law) citer

■ **summon up** rassembler ‹energy, strength› (to do pour faire)

summons ⬛1 n (a) (Law) citation f   ⋯⟶

S

(b) (gen) injonction *f* (**from** de; **to** à)
② *vtr* citer (**to** à; **to do** à faire; **for** pour)
sumptuous *adj* somptueux/-euse
sum total *n* (of money) montant *m* total; (of achievements) ensemble *m*
ⱴ **sun** *n* soleil *m*; **in the** ∼ au soleil
sunbathe *vi* se faire bronzer
sunbed *n* (lounger) chaise *f* longue; (with sunlamp) lit *m* solaire
sun block *n* crème *f* écran total
sunburn *n* coup *m* de soleil
sunburned, sunburnt *adj* (burnt) brûlé/-e par le soleil; (tanned) (GB) bronzé/-e; **to get** ∼ attraper un coup de soleil
ⱴ **Sunday** *n* dimanche *m*
Sunday best *n* (dressed) **in one's** ∼ endimanché/-e
Sunday trading *n* commerce *m* dominical
sundial *n* cadran *m* solaire
sundress *n* robe *f* bain de soleil
sundries *n pl* articles *mpl* divers
sundry *adj* divers/-e; (**to**) **all and** ∼ (à) tout le monde
sunflower *n* tournesol *m*
sunglasses *n pl* lunettes *fpl* de soleil
sun hat *n* chapeau *m* de soleil
sunken *adj* **(a)** ⟨treasure, wreck⟩ immergé/-e
(b) ⟨cheek⟩ creux/creuse; ⟨eye⟩ cave
(c) ⟨bath⟩ encastré/-e; ⟨garden⟩ en contrebas
sunlamp *n* lampe *f* à bronzer
sunlight *n* lumière *f* du soleil
Sunni *n* **(a)** (religion) sunnisme
(b) (adherent) sunnite *mf*
sunny *adj* **(a)** ensoleillé/-e; **it's going to be** ∼ il va faire (du) soleil
(b) ⟨child, temperament⟩ enjoué/-e
sunrise *n* lever *m* du soleil
sunroof *n* toit *m* ouvrant
sunset *n* coucher *m* du soleil
sunshade *n* parasol *m*
sunshield *n* pare-soleil *m inv*
sunshine *n* soleil *m*
sunstroke *n* insolation *f*
suntan *n* bronzage *m*; **to get a** ∼ bronzer
suntan lotion *n* lotion *f* solaire
suntanned *adj* bronzé/-e
suntan oil *n* huile *f* solaire
super *adj, excl* (colloq) formidable
superb *adj* superbe
supercilious *adj* dédaigneux/-euse
superficial *adj* superficiel/-ielle
superfluous *adj* superflu/-e
superimpose *vtr* superposer (**on** à)
superintendent *n* **(a)** (supervisor) responsable *mf*
(b) (*also* **police** ∼) ≈ commissaire *m*

de police
(c) (US) (for apartments) concierge *mf*
(d) (*also* **school** ∼) (US) inspecteur/-trice *m/f*
superior ① *n* supérieur/-e *m/f*
② *adj* **(a)** supérieur/-e (**to** à; **in** en); ⟨product⟩ de qualité supérieure
(b) (condescending) condescendant/-e
superiority *n* supériorité *f*
superlative ① *n* superlatif *m*
② *adj* ⟨performance, service⟩ superbe
superman *n* (*pl* -**men**) surhomme *m*
supermarket *n* supermarché *m*
supermodel *n* top model *m*
supernatural ① *n* surnaturel *m*
② *adj* surnaturel/-elle
superpower *n* superpuissance *f*
supersede *vtr* remplacer
supersonic *adj* supersonique
superstar *n* superstar *f*
superstition *n* superstition *f*
superstitious *adj* superstitieux/-ieuse
superstore *n* (large supermarket) hypermarché *m*; (specialist shop) grande surface *f*
supervise *vtr* superviser ⟨activity, staff⟩; surveiller ⟨child, patient⟩
supervision *n* **(a)** (of staff, work) supervision *f*
(b) (of child, patient) surveillance *f*
supervisor *n* **(a)** (for staff) responsable *m*
(b) (GB for thesis) directeur/-trice *m/f* de thèse
(c) (US) (Sch) directeur/-trice *m/f* d'études
supper *n* (evening meal) dîner *m*; (late snack) collation *f* (du soir); (after a show) souper *m*; **the Last Supper** la Cène *f*
supple *adj* souple
supplement ① *n* **(a)** (fee) supplément *m*
(b) (to diet, income) complément *m* (**to** à)
(c) (in newspaper) supplément *m*
② *vtr* compléter ⟨diet, resources, training⟩ (**with** de); augmenter ⟨income, staff⟩ (**with** de)
supplementary *adj* supplémentaire
supplier *n* fournisseur *m* (**of, to** de)
ⱴ **supply** ① *n* **(a)** (stock) réserves *fpl*; **in short** ∼ difficile à obtenir; **to get in a** ∼ **of sth** s'approvisionner en qch
(b) (source) (of fuel, gas, oxygen) alimentation *f*; (of food) approvisionnement *m*; (of equipment) fourniture *f*
② **supplies** *n pl* **(a)** (equipment) réserves *fpl*; **food supplies** ravitaillement *m*
(b) (for office) fournitures *fpl*
③ *vtr* (provide) fournir approvisionner (**to, for** à); approvisionner ⟨factory, company⟩ (**with** en); (with fuel, food) ravitailler ⟨town, area⟩ (**with** en)
supply and demand *n* l'offre *f* et la demande
supply teacher *n* (GB) suppléant/-e *m/f*

ⱴ indicates a very frequent word

⚙ **support** **1** *n* **(a)** (moral, financial, political) soutien *m*, appui *m*; **to give sb/sth (one's)** ∼ apporter son soutien à qn/qch; **means of** ∼ (financial) moyens *mpl* de subsistance
(b) (physical, for weight) support *m*
(c) (person) soutien *m*; **to be a** ∼ **to sb** aider qn
2 *vtr* **(a)** (morally, financially) soutenir ‹*person, cause, organization, currency*›; donner à ‹*charity*›
(b) (physically) supporter ‹*weight*›; soutenir ‹*person*›
(c) confirmer ‹*argument, theory*›
(d) (maintain) ‹*breadwinner, farm*› subvenir aux besoins de

⚙ **supporter** *n* (gen) partisan *m*; (Sport) supporter *m*; (of political party) sympathisant/-e *m/f*

support group *n* groupe *m* de soutien

supporting *adj* ∼ **actor/actress** second rôle masculin/féminin; **the** ∼ **cast** les seconds rôles *mpl*

supportive *adj* ‹*person, organization*› d'un grand secours; ‹*role, network*› de soutien

⚙ **suppose** *vtr* **(a)** (assume) supposer (**that** que); **I** ∼ **so/not** je suppose que oui/non
(b) (think) **to** ∼ **(that)** penser *or* croire que

supposed *adj* **to be** ∼ **to do/be** être censé/-e faire/être; **it's** ∼ **to be a good hotel** il paraît que c'est un bon hôtel

supposing *conj* ∼ **(that) he says no?** et s'il dit non?; ∼ **your income is X** supposons que ton revenu soit de X

suppress *vtr* supprimer ‹*evidence, information*›; réprimer ‹*smile, urge, rebellion*›; étouffer ‹*scandal, yawn*›; dissimuler ‹*truth*›

supreme *adj* suprême

surcharge *n* supplément *m*

⚙ **sure** **1** *adj* (gen) sûr/-e (**about, of** de); **I'm not** ∼ **when he's coming** je ne sais pas trop quand il viendra; **we'll be there tomorrow for** ∼! on y sera demain sans faute!; **nobody knows for** ∼ personne ne (le) sait au juste; **to make** ∼ **that** (ascertain) s'assurer que; (ensure) faire en sorte que; **he's** ∼ **to fail** il va sûrement échouer; **to be** ∼ **of oneself** être sûr/-e de soi
2 *adv* '∼!' (of course) 'bien sûr!'; ∼ **enough** effectivement

sure-fire *adj* (colloq) garanti/-e

sure-footed *adj* agile

⚙ **surely** *adv* sûrement, certainement

surf **1** *n* (waves) vagues *fpl* (déferlantes); (foam) écume *f*
2 *vtr* **to** ∼ **the Internet** naviguer *or* surfer sur Internet
3 *vi* **(a)** (Sport) faire du surf
(b) (Comput) naviguer *or* surfer sur Internet

⚙ **surface** **1** *n* **(a)** surface *f*; **on the** ∼ (of liquid) à la surface; (of solid) sur la surface
(b) (of solid, cube) côté *m*

(c) (worktop) plan *m* de travail
2 *vi* **(a)** ‹*person, object*› remonter à la surface; ‹*submarine*› faire surface
(b) ‹*problem*› se manifester

surface area *n* superficie *f*

surfboard *n* planche *f* de surf

surfer *n* **(a)** (on water) surfeur/-euse *m/f*
(b) (Comput) internaute *mf*

surfing *n* surf *m*

surge **1** *n* **(a)** (of water, blood, energy) montée *f* (**of** de); (of anger, desire) accès *m* (**of** de)
(b) (in prices, unemployment) hausse *f* (**in** de); (in demand) accroissement *m* (**in** de)
2 *vi* **(a)** ‹*water, waves*› déferler; ‹*blood, energy, emotion*› monter; **to** ∼ **forward** ‹*crowd*› s'élancer en avant
(b) ‹*prices, demand*› monter en flèche

surgeon *n* chirurgien *m*

⚙ **surgery** *n* **(a)** (operation) chirurgie *f*; **to have** ∼ se faire opérer
(b) (GB Med) (premises) cabinet *m*

surgical *adj* ‹*instrument*› chirurgical/-e; ‹*boot, stocking*› orthopédique

surgical spirit *n* alcool *m* (à 90 degrés)

surly *adj* revêche

surname *n* nom *m* de famille

surpass **1** *vtr* surpasser (**in** en); dépasser ‹*expectations*›
2 *v refl* **to** ∼ **oneself** se surpasser

surplus **1** *n* (*pl* ∼**es**) surplus *m*; (in business) excédent *m*
2 *adj* (gen) en trop; (in business) excédentaire

⚙ **surprise** **1** *n* surprise *f*; **to take sb by** ∼ (gen) prendre qn au dépourvu; (Mil) surprendre qn
2 *vtr* **(a)** surprendre, étonner; **it** ∼**d them that no-one came** ils ont été surpris que personne ne vienne
(b) surprendre ‹*intruder*›; attaquer [qch] par surprise ‹*garrison*›

surprised *adj* étonné/-e; **I'm not** ∼ ça ne m'étonne pas

surprising *adj* étonnant/-e, surprenant/-e

surprisingly *adv* ‹*well, quickly*› étonnamment; ∼ **frank** d'une franchise étonnante

surreal *adj* surréaliste

surrealist *n, adj* surréaliste *mf*

surrender **1** *n* **(a)** (of army) capitulation *f* (**to** devant); (of soldier, town) reddition *f* (**to** à)
(b) (of territory, rights) abandon *m* (**to** à); (of weapons, document) remise *f* (**to** à)
2 *vtr* **(a)** livrer ‹*town*› (**to** à); céder ‹*weapons*› (**to** à)
(b) racheter ‹*insurance policy*›; rendre ‹*passport*› (**to** à)
3 *vi* ‹*army, soldier*› se rendre (**to** à); ‹*country*› capituler (**to** devant)

surrogate **1** *n* substitut *m* (**for** de)
2 *adj* de substitution

S

surrogate mother n mère f porteuse

ꞇ **surround** vtr (gen) entourer; ‹police› encercler ‹building›; cerner ‹person›

surrounding adj environnant/-e; **the ~ area** les environs mpl

surroundings n pl cadre m; (of town) environs mpl; **natural ~** milieu m naturel

surveillance n surveillance f

ꞇ **survey** 1 n (a) (of trends, prices) enquête f (**of** sur); (by questioning people) sondage m; (study) étude f (**of** de)
(b) (GB) (of house) expertise f (**on** de)
(c) (of land) étude f topographique; (map) levé m topographique
2 vtr (a) faire une étude de ‹market, trends›
(b) (GB) faire une expertise de ‹house›
(c) faire l'étude topographique de ‹area›
(d) contempler ‹scene, landscape›

surveyor n (a) (GB) (in housebuying) expert m (en immobilier)
(b) (for map-making) topographe mf

survival n (of person, animal) survie f (**of** de); (of custom, belief) survivance f (**of** de)

ꞇ **survive** 1 vtr (a) survivre à ‹winter, heart attack›; réchapper de ‹accident›; surmonter ‹crisis›
(b) survivre à ‹person›
2 vi survivre; **to ~ on sth** vivre de qch

surviving adj survivant/-e

survivor n (a) (of accident, attack) rescapé/-e m/f
(b) (Law) survivant/-e m/f

susceptible adj sensible (**to** à)

ꞇ **suspect** 1 n suspect/-e m/f
2 adj suspect/-e
3 vtr (a) (believe) soupçonner ‹murder, plot›; **to ~ that** penser que
(b) (doubt) douter de ‹truth, motives›
(c) (have under suspicion) soupçonner ‹person›

suspend vtr (a) (gen) suspendre
(b) exclure [qn] temporairement ‹pupil› (**from** de)

suspended sentence n condamnation f avec sursis

suspender belt n (GB) porte-jarretelles m inv

suspenders n pl (a) (GB) (for stockings) jarretelles fpl
(b) (US) (braces) bretelles fpl

suspense n (in film, novel) suspense m; **to leave sb in ~** laisser qn dans l'expectative

suspension n (a) (gen, Aut) suspension f
(b) (of pupil) exclusion f temporaire

suspicion n méfiance f (**of** de); **to arouse ~** éveiller des soupçons; **to have ~s about sb/sth** avoir des doutes mpl sur qn/qch

suspicious adj (a) (wary) méfiant/-e; **to be ~ of sth** se méfier de qch
(b) ‹person, object› suspect/-e; ‹behaviour,

activity› louche

sustain vtr (a) (maintain) maintenir ‹interest, success›
(b) (Mus) soutenir ‹note›
(c) (support) soutenir; (physically) donner des forces à; **to ~ life** rendre la vie possible
(d) recevoir ‹injury, burn›; éprouver ‹loss›

sustainable adj ‹development, forestry› durable; ‹resource› renouvelable; ‹growth› viable

sustenance n nourriture f

swab n (Med) tampon m

swagger vi (a) (walk) se pavaner
(b) (boast) fanfaronner

swallow 1 n (a) (bird) hirondelle f
(b) (gulp) gorgée f
2 vtr (a) (eat) avaler
(b) ravaler ‹pride›
(c) (colloq) (believe) avaler (fam)
3 vi avaler; (nervously) avaler sa salive

swamp 1 n marais m, marécage m
2 vtr inonder

swan n cygne m

swap (colloq) 1 n échange m
2 vtr (p prés etc **-pp-**) échanger; **to ~ sth for sth** échanger qch contre qch; **to ~ places** changer de place

swarm 1 n (of bees) essaim m; (of flies) nuée f
2 vi ‹bees› essaimer; **to be ~ing with** grouiller de ‹people, maggots›

swarthy adj basané/-e

swastika n croix f gammée, svastika m

swat vtr (p prés etc **-tt-**) écraser ‹fly, wasp› (**with** avec)

sway 1 n **to hold ~** avoir une grande influence; **to hold ~ over** dominer
2 vtr (a) (influence) influencer
(b) (rock) osciller
3 vi ‹tree, bridge› osciller; ‹person› chanceler; (to music) se balancer

swear 1 vtr (prét **swore**, pp **sworn**) jurer (**to do** de faire); **to ~ sb to secrecy** faire jurer le secret à qn
2 vi (prét **swore**, pp **sworn**) (a) (curse) jurer
(b) (attest) **to ~ to having done** jurer avoir fait
■ **swear by** (colloq): **~ by [sth/sb]** ne jurer que par ‹remedy, expert›
■ **swear in**: **~ in [sb]**, **~ [sb] in** faire prêter serment à

swearing n jurons mpl

swearword n juron m, gros mot m

sweat 1 n sueur f; **to break out into a ~** se mettre à suer; **to be in a cold ~ about sth** avoir des sueurs froides à l'idée de qch
2 **sweats** n pl (US) survêtement m
3 vi ‹person, horse› transpirer, suer; ‹hands, feet, cheese› transpirer

---

ꞇ indicates a very frequent word

sweatband *n* bandeau *m*

sweater *n* pull *m*

sweat pants *n pl* (US) pantalon *m* de survêtement

sweatshirt *n* sweatshirt *m*

sweatshop *n* atelier *m* où on exploite le personnel

sweaty *adj* ‹person› en sueur; ‹hand, palm› moite

swede *n* (GB) rutabaga *m*

Swede *n* Suédois/-e *m/f*

Sweden *pr n* Suède *f*

Swedish [1] *n* (language) suédois *m*
[2] *adj* suédois/-e

sweep [1] *n* (a) **to give sth a ~** donner un coup de balai à qch
(b) (movement) **with a ~ of his arm** d'un grand geste du bras
(c) (of land, woods) étendue *f*
(d) (*also* **chimney ~**) ramoneur *m*
[2] *vtr* (*prét, pp* **swept**) (a) balayer ‹floor, path›; ramoner ‹chimney›
(b) (push) **to ~ sth off the table** faire tomber qch de la table (d'un grand geste de la main); **to ~ sb off his/her feet** (figurative) faire perdre la tête à qn
(c) ‹beam, searchlight› balayer
[3] *vi* (*prét, pp* **swept**) (a) (clean) balayer
(b) **to ~ in/out** (majestically) entrer/sortir majestueusement
■ **sweep aside** écarter ‹person, objection›
■ **sweep up** balayer

sweeping *adj* (a) ‹change, review› radical/-e
(b) **~ generalization** généralisation *f* à l'emporte-pièce

✔ **sweet** [1] *n* (GB) (a) (candy) bonbon *m*
(b) (dessert) dessert *m*
[2] *adj* (a) (gen) doux/douce; ‹food, tea, taste› sucré/-e; **to have a ~ tooth** aimer les sucreries
(b) (kind) ‹person› gentil/-ille
(c) (cute) ‹baby, cottage› mignon/-onne
[3] *adv* **to taste ~** avoir un goût sucré; **to smell ~** sentir bon

sweet-and-sour *adj* aigre-doux/-douce

sweetcorn *n* maïs *m*

sweeten *vtr* (a) (Culin) sucrer (**with** avec)
(b) rendre [qch] plus tentant ‹offer›
■ **sweeten up** amadouer ‹person›

sweetener *n* (a) (in food) édulcorant *m*
(b) (colloq) (bribe) incitation *f*, (illegal) pot-de-vin *m*

sweetheart *n* (boyfriend) petit ami *m*; (girlfriend) petite amie *f*

sweetly *adv* ‹say, smile› gentiment

sweet potato *n* patate *f* douce

sweet-talk *vtr* (colloq) baratiner (fam)

swell [1] *n* (of waves, sea) houle *f*
[2] *vtr* (*prét* **swelled**, *pp* **swollen** *ou* **swelled**) gonfler ‹crowd, funds›; grossir ‹river›

[3] *vi* (*prét* **swelled** *pp* **swollen** *ou* **swelled**) ‹balloon, tyre, stomach› se gonfler; ‹wood› gonfler; ‹ankle, gland› enfler; ‹river› grossir; ‹crowd› s'accroître

swelling *n* (on limb, skin) enflure *f*; (on head) bosse *f*

sweltering *adj* (colloq) torride

swerve *vi* faire un écart; **to ~ off the road** sortir de la route

swift [1] *n* martinet *m*
[2] *adj* rapide, prompt/-e

swill *n* pâtée *f* (des porcs)

swim [1] *n* baignade *f*; **to go for a ~** (in sea, river) aller se baigner; (in pool) aller à la piscine
[2] *vtr* (*p prés* **-mm-**, *prét* **swam**, *pp* **swum**) nager ‹distance, stroke›
[3] *vi* (*p prés* **-mm-**, *prét* **swam**, *pp* **swum**) (a) nager; **to ~ across sth** traverser qch à la nage
(b) **to be ~ming in** baigner dans ‹sauce, oil›
(c) ‹scene, room› tourner

swimmer *n* nageur/-euse *m/f*

swimming *n* natation *f*

swimming costume *n* (GB) maillot *m* de bain

swimming pool *n* piscine *f*

swimming trunks *n pl* slip *m* de bain

swimsuit *n* maillot *m* de bain

swindle [1] *n* escroquerie *f*
[2] *vtr* escroquer; **to ~ sb out of sth** escroquer qch à qn

swindler *n* escroc *m*

swine flu *n* grippe *f* A

swing [1] *n* (a) (of pendulum, needle) oscillation *f*; (of hips, body) balancement *m*
(b) (in public opinion) revirement *m* (**in** de); (in prices, economy) fluctuation *f* (**in** de); (in mood) saute *f* (**in** de)
(c) (in playground) balançoire *f*
[2] *vtr* (*prét, pp* **swung**) (to and fro) balancer; **to ~ sb round and round** faire tournoyer qn
[3] *vi* (*prét, pp* **swung**) (a) (to and fro) se balancer; ‹pendulum› osciller
(b) **to ~ open** s'ouvrir; **the car swung into the drive** la voiture s'est engagée dans l'allée; **to ~ around** ‹person› se retourner (brusquement)
(c) (change) **to ~ from optimism to despair** passer de l'optimisme au désespoir; **the party swung towards the left** le parti a basculé vers la gauche
IDIOMS to get into the ~ of things se mettre dans le bain (fam); **to be in full ~** battre son plein (fam)

swing door (GB), **swinging door** (US) *n* porte *f* battante

swipe card *n* carte *f* à piste magnétique

swirl *vi* tourbillonner

Swiss [1] *n* Suisse *mf*

⋯⃗

2 *adj* suisse; ‹*embassy*› de Suisse
switch 1 *n* (a) (change) changement *m* (in de)
(b) (for light) interrupteur *m*; (on radio, appliance) bouton *m*
2 *vtr* (a) reporter ‹*attention*› (to sur); **to ~ flights** changer de vol
(b) intervertir ‹*objects, roles*›; **I've ~ed the furniture round** j'ai changé la disposition des meubles
3 *vi* changer
■ **switch off** éteindre ‹*appliance, light, engine*›; couper ‹*supply*›
■ **switch on** allumer ‹*appliance, light, engine*›
■ **switch over** (on TV) changer de chaîne
switchblade *n* (US) (couteau *m* à) cran *m* d'arrêt
switchboard *n* standard *m*
switchboard operator *n* standardiste *mf*
switchover *n* passage *m* (from de; to à)
Switzerland *pr n* Suisse *f*
swivel *vtr* (*p etc* **-ll-** (GB), **-l-** (US)) faire pivoter ‹*chair, camera*›; tourner ‹*head, body*›
■ **swivel round** pivoter
swivel chair, **swivel seat** *n* fauteuil *m* tournant, chaise *f* tournante
swollen *adj* ‹*ankle, gland*› enflé/-e; ‹*eyes*› gonflé/-e; ‹*river*› en crue
swoop *vi* (a) ‹*bird, bat, plane*› plonger; **to ~ down** descendre en piqué; **to ~ down on** fondre sur
(b) ‹*police, raider*› faire une descente
ơ **sword** *n* épée *f*
swordfish *n* espadon *m*
sworn *adj* (a) ‹*statement*› fait/-e sous serment
(b) ‹*enemy*› juré/-e; ‹*ally*› pour la vie
swot (GB) (colloq) 1 *n* bûcheur/-euse *m/f* (fam)
2 *vi* (*p prés etc* **-tt-**) bûcher (fam)
sycamore *n* (*also* **~ tree**) sycomore *m*
syllable *n* syllabe *f*
syllabus *n* (*pl* **-buses** *ou* **-bi**) programme *m*
symbol *n* symbole *m* (of, for de)
symbolic *adj* symbolique (of de)
symbolism *n* symbolisme *m*

symbolize *vtr* symboliser (by par)
symmetric(al) *adj* symétrique
sympathetic *adj* (compassionate) compatissant/-e (**to, towards** envers); (understanding) compréhensif/-ive; (kindly) gentil/-ille; (well disposed) bien disposé/-e (**to, towards** à l'égard de)
sympathize *vi* (a) témoigner de la sympathie (**with** à); **I ~ with you in your grief** je compatis à votre douleur
(b) (support) **to ~ with** souscrire à ‹*aims, views*›
sympathizer *n* sympathisant/-e *m/f* (of de)
sympathy *n* (a) (compassion) compassion *f*
(b) (solidarity) solidarité *f*
symphony *n* symphonie *f*
symphony orchestra *n* orchestre *m* symphonique
ơ **symptom** *n* symptôme *m*
synagogue *n* synagogue *f*
synchronize *vtr* synchroniser
syndicate *n* (gen) syndicat *m*; (of companies) consortium *m*
syndrome *n* syndrome *m*
synonymous *adj* synonyme (**with** de)
synopsis *n* (*pl* **-ses**) (of play) synopsis *m*; (of book) résumé *m*
syntax *n* syntaxe *f*
synthesis *n* (*pl* **-ses**) synthèse *f*
synthesizer *n* synthétiseur *m*
synthetic *adj* synthétique
syringe 1 *n* seringue *f*
2 *vtr* **to have one's ears ~d** se faire déboucher les oreilles (avec une seringue)
syrup *n* sirop *m*
ơ **system** *n* système *m* (**for doing, to do** pour faire); **road ~** réseau *m* routier; **reproductive ~** appareil *m* reproducteur; **to get sth out of one's ~** oublier qch
systematic *adj* (a) (efficient) méthodique
(b) (deliberate) systématique
systematically *adv* ‹*work, list*› méthodiquement; ‹*arrange, destroy*› systématiquement
systems analyst *n* analyste *mf* (de) systèmes
Szechuan *adj* sichuanais

S

___
ơ indicates a very frequent word

Tt

t, T *n* t, T *m*

tab *n* **(a)** (loop) attache *f*
(b) (on can) languette *f*
(c) (label) étiquette *f*
IDIOM **to keep ∼s on sb** (colloq) tenir qn à l'œil (fam)

tabby (cat) *n* chat/chatte *m/f* tigré/-e

♂ **table** **1** *n* **(a)** table *f*; **to set the ∼** mettre le couvert
(b) (list) table *f*, tableau *m*
2 *vtr* **(a)** (GB) (present) présenter
(b) (US) (postpone) ajourner

tablecloth *n* nappe *f*

table manners *n pl* **to have good/bad ∼** savoir/ne pas savoir se tenir à table

table mat *n* (under plate) set *m* de table; (under serving-dish) dessous-de-plat *m inv*

tablespoon *n* **(a)** (object) cuillère *f* de service
(b) (*also* **∼ful**) cuillerée *f* à soupe

tablet *n* comprimé *m* (**for** pour)

table tennis *n* tennis *m* de table, ping-pong® *m*

tabloid **1** *n* tabloïde *m*; **the ∼s** la presse populaire
2 *adj* ‹*journalism, press*› populaire

taboo *n*, *adj* tabou *m*

tacit *adj* tacite

tack **1** *n* **(a)** (nail) clou *m*
(b) (US) (drawing pin) punaise *f*
(c) (Naut) bordée *f*
(d) (tactic) tactique *f*
2 *vtr* **(a)** (nail) **to ∼ sth to** clouer qch à
(b) (in sewing) bâtir
3 *vi* ‹*sailor*› faire une bordée; ‹*yacht*› louvoyer
■ **tack on**: ∼ [sth] on, ∼ on [sth] ajouter [qch] après coup ‹*clause, ending, building*› (**to** à)

tackle **1** *n* **(a)** (in soccer, hockey) tacle *m*; (in rugby, American football) plaquage *m*
(b) (for fishing) articles *mpl* de pêche
(c) (on ship) gréement *m*; (for lifting) palan *m*
2 *vtr* **(a)** s'attaquer à ‹*task, problem*›
(b) (confront) **to ∼ sb about** parler à qn de
(c) (in soccer, hockey) tacler; (in rugby, American football) plaquer

tacky *adj* **(a)** (sticky) collant/-e
(b) (colloq) (cheap) tocard/-e (fam)

tact *n* tact *m*

tactful *adj* ‹*person, letter*› plein/-e de tact; ‹*enquiry*› discret/-ète

tactical *adj* tactique; ∼ **voting** vote *m* utile

tactics *n pl* tactique *f*

tactless *adj* ‹*person, question, suggestion*› indélicat/-e; **to be ∼** ‹*person, remark*› manquer de tact

tadpole *n* têtard *m*

tag *n* (label) étiquette *f*; (on cat, dog) plaque *f*; (on file) onglet *m*
■ **tag along** suivre

tail *n* queue *f*
■ **tail off** **(a)** ‹*figures, demand*› diminuer
(b) ‹*voice*› s'éteindre

tailback *n* bouchon *m*

tailgate *n* hayon *m*

tail-off *n* diminution *f*

tailor **1** *n* tailleur *m*
2 *vtr* **to ∼ sth to** adapter qch à ‹*needs, person*›

tailor-made *adj* ‹*garment*› fait/-e sur mesure; (figurative) conçu/-e spécialement

tails *n pl* **(a)** (tailcoat) habit *m*
(b) (of coin) pile *f*; **heads or ∼?** pile ou face?

tainted *adj* ‹*food*› avarié/-e; ‹*water, air*› pollué/-e (**with** par); ‹*reputation*› entaché/-e

♂ **take** **1** *n* **(a)** (in film-making) prise *f* (de vues); (Mus) enregistrement *m*
(b) (US) (takings) recette *f*
2 *vtr* (*prét* **took**, *pp* **taken**) **(a)** (gen) prendre; **he took the book off the shelf** il a pris le livre sur l'étagère; **she took a chocolate from the box** elle a pris un chocolat dans la boîte; **he took a pen out of his pocket** il a sorti un stylo de sa poche; **to ∼ an exam** passer un examen; **to ∼ a shower** prendre une douche; **to ∼ sb/sth seriously** prendre qn/qch au sérieux
(b) (carry with one) emporter, prendre ‹*object*›; (carry to a place) emporter, porter ‹*object*›; **to ∼ sb sth, to ∼ sth to sb** apporter qch à qn; **he took his umbrella with him** il a emporté son parapluie; **to ∼ a letter to the post office** porter une lettre à la poste; **to ∼ the car to the garage** emmener la voiture au garage; **to ∼ sth upstairs/downstairs** monter/descendre qch
(c) (accompany, lead) emmener ‹*person*›; **to ∼ sb to** ‹*bus*› emmener qn à ‹*place*›; ‹*road*› conduire *or* mener qn à ‹*place*›; **I'll ∼ you to your room** je vais vous conduire à votre chambre; **he took her home** il l'a raccompagnée; **to ∼ a dog/a child for a walk** promener un chien/emmener un enfant faire une promenade
(d) (accept) ‹*person*› accepter ‹*job, bribe*›; ‹*shop*› accepter ‹*credit card, cheque*›; ‹*person*› supporter ‹*pain, criticism*›; **she can't ∼ a joke** elle ne comprend pas la plaisanterie; **I can't ∼ any more!** je n'en peux plus!

⋯▸

(e) (require) demander, exiger ‹patience, skill, courage›; **it ~s patience to do** il faut de la patience pour faire; **it ~s three hours to get there** il faut trois heures pour y aller; **it won't ~ long** ça ne prendra pas longtemps; **it took her ten minutes to repair it** elle a mis dix minutes pour le réparer; **to have what it ~s** avoir tout ce qu'il faut **(to do** pour faire)
(f) (assume) **I ~ it that** je suppose que
(g) (hold) ‹hall, bus› pouvoir contenir ‹50 people›; ‹tank, container› avoir une capacité de ‹quantity›
(h) (wear) **what size do you ~?** (in clothes) quelle taille faites-vous?; (in shoes) quelle pointure faites-vous?; **I ~ a size 10** (in clothes) je m'habille en 36; **I ~ a size 5** (in shoes) je chausse du 38
(i) (subtract) soustraire ‹number, quantity› **(from** de)
3 vi (prét **took**, pp **taken**) ‹drug› faire effet; ‹dye, plant› prendre
IDIOMS **that's my last offer, ~ it or leave it!** c'est ma dernière proposition, c'est à prendre ou à laisser!; **to ~ a lot out of sb** fatiguer beaucoup qn
■ **take aback** interloquer; **to be ~n aback** rester interloqué/-e
■ **take after** tenir de ‹person›
■ **take apart** démonter ‹car, machine›
■ **take away (a)** (carry away) emporter
(b) (remove) enlever ‹object›; emmener ‹person›
(c) (subtract) soustraire ‹number›; **that doesn't ~ anything away from his achievement** ça n'enlève rien à ce qu'il a accompli
■ **take back (a)** (to shop) rapporter ‹goods›
(b) retirer ‹statement, words›
(c) (accompany) ramener ‹person›
(d) (accept again) reprendre
■ **take down (a)** enlever ‹picture, curtains›; démonter ‹tent, scaffolding›
(b) noter ‹name, details›
■ **take hold** ‹disease, epidemic› s'installer; ‹idea, ideology› se répandre; **to ~ hold of** prendre ‹object, hand›
■ **take in (a)** (deceive) tromper; **I wasn't taken in by him** je ne me suis pas laissé prendre à son jeu
(b) recueillir ‹refugee›; prendre ‹lodger›
(c) (understand) saisir, comprendre ‹situation›
(d) (observe) noter ‹detail›
(e) (encompass) inclure
(f) (absorb) absorber ‹nutrients, oxygen›
(g) ‹boat› prendre ‹water›
(h) (in sewing) reprendre ‹garment›
■ **take off**: **1** ¶ **~ off (a)** ‹plane› décoller
(b) ‹idea, fashion› prendre
2 ¶ **~ [sth] off (a) to ~ £10 off (the price)** réduire le prix de 10 livres sterling
(b) to ~ two days off prendre deux jours de congé
3 ¶ **~ off [sth]** enlever ‹clothing, shoes, lid›

ʂ indicates a very frequent word

4 ¶ **~ [sb] off** (imitate) imiter ‹person›
■ **take on (a)** (employ) embaucher ‹staff, worker›
(b) jouer contre ‹team, player›; (fight) se battre contre ‹person›
(c) (accept) prendre ‹responsibilities, work›
■ **take out: 1** ¶ **~ [sth] out (a)** sortir ‹object› **(from, of** de); extraire ‹tooth›; enlever ‹appendix›; retirer ‹money›
(b) (be successor) ‹person› prendre la suite; **to ~ over from** remplacer ‹predecessor›
2 ¶ **~ over [sth]** prendre le contrôle de ‹town, region›; reprendre ‹business›
■ **take part** prendre part; **to ~ part in** participer à
■ **take place** avoir lieu
■ **take to (a)** se prendre de sympathie pour ‹person›
(b) (begin) **to ~ to doing** se mettre à faire
(c) (go) se réfugier dans ‹forest, hills›; **to ~ to the streets** descendre dans la rue
■ **take up: 1 to ~ up with** s'attacher à ‹person, group›
2 ¶ **~ up [sth] (a)** (lift) enlever ‹carpet, pavement›
(b) (start) se mettre à ‹golf, guitar›; prendre ‹job›; **to ~ up one's duties** entrer dans ses fonctions
(c) (continue) reprendre ‹story, cry, refrain›
(d) (accept) accepter ‹offer, invitation›; relever ‹challenge›
(e) to ~ sth up with sb soulever [qch] avec qn ‹matter›
(f) (occupy) prendre ‹space, time, energy›
(g) prendre ‹position, stance›
(h) (shorten) raccourcir ‹skirt, curtains›
3 ¶ **~ sb up on (a)** reprendre qn sur ‹point, assertion›
(b) to ~ sb up on an offer accepter l'offre de qn
take-away n (GB) **(a)** (meal) repas m à emporter
(b) (restaurant) restaurant m qui fait des plats à emporter
take-home pay n salaire m net
taken adj **(a) to be ~** ‹seat, room› être occupé/-e
(b) (impressed) **to be ~ with** être emballé/-e (fam) par ‹idea, person›
take-off n **(a)** (by plane) décollage m
(b) (colloq) (imitation) imitation f **(of** de)
take-out adj (US) ‹food› à emporter
takeover n (of company) rachat m; (of political power) prise f de pouvoir
takeover bid n offre f publique d'achat, OPA f
taker n preneur/-euse m/f

■ take over: 1 ¶ **~ over (a)** ‹army, faction› prendre le pouvoir

takings *n pl* recette *f*

talc, talcum (powder) *n* talc *m*

tale *n* (story) histoire *f*; (fantasy story) conte *m*; (narrative, account) récit *m*

◆ **talent** *n* talent *m*

talent contest *n* concours *m* de jeunes talents *or* d'amateurs

talented *adj* doué/-e, talentueux/-euse

talisman *n* talisman *m*

◆ **talk** 1 *n* (a) (talking, gossip) propos *mpl*; **they are the ~ of the town** on ne parle que d'eux (b) (conversation) conversation *f*, discussion *f* (c) (speech) exposé *m* (**about, on** sur); (more informal) causerie *f*
2 **talks** *n pl* négociations *fpl*; (political) pourparlers *mpl*; **peace ~** pourparlers de paix
3 *vtr* parler; **to ~ business** parler affaires; **to ~ nonsense** raconter n'importe quoi; **to ~ sb into/out of doing** persuader/dissuader qn de faire; **he ~ed his way out of it** il s'en est tiré grâce à son bagout (fam)
4 *vi* parler; **to ~ to oneself** parler tout seul/toute seule

talkative *adj* bavard/-e

talking 1 *n* **I'll do the ~** c'est moi qui parlerai; **'no ~!'** 'silence!'
2 *adj* ‹bird, doll› qui parle

talking book *n* livre *m* enregistré (à l'usage des non-voyants)

talking-to *n* réprimande *f*

talk show *n* talk-show *m*

◆ **tall** *adj* ‹person› grand/-e; ‹building, tree, chimney› haut/-e; **he's six feet ~ ≈** il mesure un mètre quatre-vingts; **to grow ~er** grandir

tally 1 *n* compte *m*
2 *vi* concorder

tambourine *n* tambourin *m*

tame 1 *adj* (a) ‹animal› apprivoisé/-e (b) ‹story, party› sage; ‹reform› timide
2 *vtr* (a) apprivoiser ‹bird, wild animal›; dompter ‹lion, tiger› (b) soumettre ‹person›

tamper *vi* **to ~ with** tripoter ‹machinery, lock›; trafiquer ‹accounts, evidence›

tampon *n* tampon *m*

tan 1 *n* (a) (also **sun~**) bronzage *m* (b) (colour) fauve *m*
2 *adj* fauve
3 *vtr* (*p prés etc* **-nn-**) (a) bronzer ‹skin› (b) tanner ‹animal hide›
4 *vi* (*p prés etc* **-nn-**) ‹skin, person› bronzer

tandem *n* tandem *m*; **in ~** en tandem

tang *n* (taste) goût *m* acidulé; (smell) odeur *f* piquante

tangent *n* tangente *f*; **to go off on a ~** partir dans une digression

tangerine *n* tangerine *f*

tangible *adj* tangible

tangle 1 *n* (of hair, string, wires) enchevêtrement *m*; (of clothes, sheets) fouillis *m*
2 *vi* ‹hair, string, cable› s'emmêler
■ **tangle up** 1 **¶ ~ up** s'embrouiller
2 **to get ~d up** ‹hair, string, wires› s'emmêler

tangy *adj* acidulé/-e

tank *n* (a) (gen, Aut) réservoir *m*; (for oil) cuve *f*; (for water) citerne *f*; (for fish) aquarium *m* (b) (Mil) char *m* (de combat)

tankard *n* chope *f*

tanker *n* (a) (ship) navire-citerne *m*; **oil ~** pétrolier *m* (b) (lorry) camion-citerne *m*

tanned *adj* (*also* **sun~**) bronzé/-e

Tannoy® *n* (GB) **the ~** le système de haut-parleurs

tantalizing *adj* ‹suggestion› tentant/-e; ‹possibility› séduisant/-e; ‹glimpse› excitant/-e

tantamount *adj* **to be ~ to** équivaloir à, être équivalent/-e à

tantrum *n* crise *f* de colère; **to throw a ~** piquer une crise (fam)

tap 1 *n* (a) (GB) (for water, gas) robinet *m* (b) (blow) petit coup *m*
2 *vtr* (*p prés etc* **-pp-**) (a) (knock) taper (doucement); (repeatedly) tapoter (b) mettre [qch] sur écoute ‹telephone› (c) inciser ‹rubber tree›; exploiter ‹resources›
■ **tap in**: **~ [sth] in, ~ in [sth]** enfoncer ‹nail›; taper ‹information, number›

tap dance *n* (*also* **~ dancing**) claquettes *fpl*

tape 1 *n* (a) bande *f* (magnétique); (cassette) cassette *f*; (video) cassette *f* vidéo; (recording) enregistrement *m* (b) (*also* **adhesive ~**) scotch® *m*
2 *vtr* (a) (record) enregistrer (b) (stick) **to ~ sth to** coller qch à ‹surface, door›

tape deck *n* platine *f* cassette

tape measure *n* mètre *m* ruban

taper *vi* ‹sleeve, trouser leg› se resserrer; ‹column, spire› s'effiler

tape recorder *n* magnétophone *m*

tapestry *n* tapisserie *f*

tapeworm *n* ver *m* solitaire, ténia *m*

tap water *n* eau *f* du robinet

tar *n* goudron *m*; (on roads) bitume *m*

◆ **target** 1 *n* (a) (in archery, shooting) cible *f*; (Mil) objectif *f* (b) (butt) cible *f*; **to be the ~ of abuse** être insulté/-e (c) (goal) objectif *m*
2 *adj* ‹date, figure› prévu/-e; ‹audience, group› visé/-e, ciblé/-e
3 *vtr* (a) diriger ‹weapon, missile›; prendre [qch] pour cible ‹city, site›

⋯⋗

(b) (in marketing) viser ‹group, sector›

target language n langue f cible

tariff n (a) (price list) tarif m

(b) (customs duty) droit m de douane

tarmac n (a) (also **Tarmac**®) macadam m

(b) (GB) (of airfield) piste f

tarnish ① vtr ternir

② vi se ternir

tarpaulin n (material) toile f de bâche; (sheet) bâche f

tarragon n estragon m

tart n (small) tartelette f; (large) tarte f

■ **tart up**: (GB) (colloq) ① ¶ ~ [sth] up, ¶ ~ up [sth] retaper (fam) ‹house, room›

② ¶ ~ **oneself up** se pomponner (fam)

tartan adj écossais/-e

⚡ **task** n tâche f; a hard ~ une lourde tâche

task bar n barre f de tâches

task force n (Mil) corps m expéditionnaire; (committee) groupe m de travail

taskmaster n tyran m; to be a hard ~ être très exigeant/-e

tassel n gland m

⚡ **taste** ① n (a) (gen) goût m; that's a matter of ~ ça dépend des goûts; to be in bad ~ être de mauvais goût

(b) (brief experience) expérience f; (foretaste) avant-goût m

② vtr (a) (try) goûter ‹food, drink›

(b) I can ~ the brandy in this coffee je sens le (goût du) cognac dans ce café

(c) (experience) goûter à ‹freedom, success›

③ vi to ~ **sweet** avoir un goût sucré; to ~ **horrible** avoir mauvais goût; to ~ **like sth** avoir le goût de qch; to ~ **of** avoir un goût de

taste bud n papille f gustative

tasteful adj de bon goût

tasteless adj (a) ‹remark, joke› de mauvais goût

(b) ‹food, drink› insipide

tasty adj ‹food› succulent/-e

tatters n pl to be in ~ ‹clothing› être en lambeaux; ‹career, reputation› être en ruines

tattoo ① n tatouage m

② vtr tatouer (**on** sur)

tatty adj (colloq) ‹carpet, garment› miteux/-euse; ‹book, shoes› en mauvais état

taunt vtr railler ‹person›

Taurus n Taureau m

taut adj tendu/-e

tauten ① vtr tendre

② vi se tendre

⚡ **tax** ① n (on goods, services, property) taxe f; (on income, profits) impôt m

② vtr (a) imposer ‹earnings, person›; taxer ‹luxury goods›

(b) mettre [qch] à l'épreuve ‹patience›

taxation n (a) (imposition of taxes) imposition f

(b) (revenue from taxes) impôts mpl

tax bracket n tranche f d'imposition du revenu

tax collector n percepteur m

tax disc n vignette f (automobile)

tax evasion n fraude f fiscale

tax exile n: personne qui s'est expatriée pour raisons fiscales

tax-free adj exempt/-e d'impôt

tax haven n paradis m fiscal

taxi n taxi m; by ~ en taxi

taxing adj épuisant/-e

taxi rank (GB), **taxi stand** n station f de taxis

tax office n perception f

taxpayer n contribuable mf

tax return n (a) (form) feuille f d'impôts

(b) (declaration) déclaration f de revenus

TB n (abbr = **tuberculosis**) tuberculose f

tea n (a) (drink) thé m

(b) (GB) (afternoon meal) thé m; (for children) goûter m; (evening meal) dîner m

tea bag n sachet m de thé

tea break n (GB) pause-café f

⚡ **teach** ① vtr enseigner à ‹children, adults›; enseigner ‹subject›; to ~ sb enseigner [qch] à qn ‹academic subject›; apprendre [qch] à qn ‹practical skill›; to ~ **school** (US); être instituteur/-trice; to ~ sb a lesson ‹person› donner une bonne leçon à qn; ‹experience› servir de leçon à qn

② vi enseigner

⚡ **teacher** n (in general) enseignant/-e m/f; (secondary) professeur m; (primary) instituteur/-trice m/f; (special needs) éducateur/-trice m/f

teacher training n formation f pédagogique

⚡ **teaching** ① n enseignement m

② adj ‹post› d'enseignant; ‹method, qualification› pédagogique; ‹staff› enseignant/-e

teaching hospital n centre m hospitalo-universitaire, CHU m

teacup n tasse f à thé

teak n teck m

⚡ **team** n équipe f

team member n équipier/-ière m/f

team spirit n esprit m d'équipe

teamwork n collaboration f

teapot n théière f

tear¹ ① n (gen) accroc m; (Med) déchirure f

② vtr (prét **tore**, pp **torn**) déchirer ‹garment, paper›; to ~ sth out of arracher qch de ‹book, notepad›

③ vi (prét **tore**, pp **torn**) (a) (rip) se déchirer

(b) (rush) to ~ **out/off** sortir/partir en trombe

■ **tear apart** (a) mettre [qch] en pièces ‹prey›; déchirer ‹country›

⚡ indicates a very frequent word

(b) (separate) séparer
(c) (criticize) descendre [qn] en flammes
■ **tear off** (carefully) détacher; (violently) arracher
■ **tear open** ouvrir [qch] en le/la déchirant
■ **tear out** détacher ‹coupon, cheque›; arracher ‹page›
■ **tear up** déchirer ‹letter, document›
⚙ **tear²** n larme f; **to burst into ~s** fondre en larmes
tearful adj ‹person, face› en larmes; ‹voice› larmoyant/-e
tear gas n gaz m lacrymogène
tease vtr taquiner ‹person› (**about** à propos de); tourmenter ‹animal›
teasing n taquineries fpl
teaspoon n petite cuillère f, cuillère f à café
teaspoonful n cuillerée f à café
teat n **(a)** (of cow, goat, ewe) trayon m **(b)** (GB) (on baby's bottle) tétine f
teatime n l'heure f du thé
tea towel n (GB) torchon m (à vaisselle)
⚙ **technical** adj technique
technical college n institut m d'enseignement technique
technical drawing n dessin m industriel
technical hitch n incident m technique
technicality n **(a)** (technical detail) détail m technique (**of** de) **(b)** (minor detail) point m de détail **(c)** (technical nature) technicité f
technically adv **(a)** (strictly speaking) théoriquement **(b)** (technologically) techniquement
technician n technicien/-ienne m/f
⚙ **technique** n technique f
techno ① n techno f ② adj techno inv
technological adj technologique
⚙ **technology** n technologie f; **information ~** informatique f
teddy n (also **~ bear**) ours m en peluche
tedious adj ennuyeux/-euse
teem vi **to be ~ing with** grouiller de ‹people›
teenage adj ‹son, daughter› qui est adolescent/-e; ‹singer, player› jeune (before n); ‹fashion› des adolescents
teenager n jeune mf, adolescent/-e m/f
teens n pl adolescence f; **to be in one's ~** être adolescent/-e
tee-shirt n tee-shirt m, T-shirt m
teeter vi vaciller
teethe vi faire ses dents
teething troubles n pl difficultés fpl initiales
teetotal adj **I'm ~** je ne bois jamais d'alcool

teetotaller (GB), **teetotaler** (US) n personne f qui ne boit jamais d'alcool
TEFL n (abbr = **Teaching of English as a Foreign Language**) enseignement m de l'anglais langue étrangère
telecommunications n pl télécommunications fpl
telecommuting n télétravail m
teleconference n téléconférence f
telecottaging n télétravail m
telegram n télégramme m
telegraph ① n télégraphe m ② vtr télégraphier
telegraph pole n poteau m télégraphique
telemarketer n téléprospecteur/-trice m/f
telemarketing n télémarketing m
telepathy n télépathie f
telephone ① n téléphone m; **to be on the ~** (connected) avoir le téléphone; (talking) être au téléphone ② vtr téléphoner à ‹person›; téléphoner ‹instructions›; **to ~ France** appeler la France ③ vi appeler, téléphoner
telephone banking n transactions fpl bancaires télématiques
telephone booth, telephone box (GB) n cabine f téléphonique
telephone call n appel m téléphonique
telephone directory n annuaire m (du téléphone)
telephone number n numéro m de téléphone
telephone operator n standardiste mf
telephonist n (GB) standardiste mf
telephoto lens n téléobjectif m
telesales n télévente f
telescope n télescope m
teleshopping n téléachat m
teletext n télétexte m
televise vtr téléviser
⚙ **television** n **(a)** (medium) télévision f; **on ~** à la télévision **(b)** (set) téléviseur m
television licence n redevance f télévision
television programme n émission f de télévision
television set n téléviseur m, poste m de télévision
teleworking n télétravail m
telex ① n télex m ② vtr télexer
⚙ **tell** ① vtr (prét, pp **told**) **(a)** (gen) dire; raconter ‹joke, story›; prédire ‹future›; **to ~ sb about sth** parler de qch à qn; **to ~ sb to do** dire à qn de faire; **to ~ sb how to do/what to do** expliquer à qn comment faire/ce qu'il faut faire; **to ~ the time** ‹clock› indiquer ⋯⟶

or marquer l'heure; ⟨*person*⟩ lire l'heure; **can you ∼ me the time please?** peux-tu me dire l'heure (qu'il est), s'il te plaît?; **I was told that...** on m'a dit que...; **I told you so!** je te l'avais bien dit!
(b) (deduce) **you can ∼ (that) he's lying** on voit bien qu'il ment; **I can ∼ (that) he's disappointed** je sais qu'il est déçu
(c) (distinguish) distinguer; **can you ∼ the difference?** est-ce que vous voyez la différence?; **how can you ∼ them apart?** comment peut-on les distinguer l'un de l'autre?
2 *vi* (*prét, pp* **told**) **(a)** (reveal secret) **don't ∼!** ne le répète pas!
(b) (know) savoir; **as far as I can ∼** pour autant que je sache; **how can you ∼?** comment le sais-tu?
(c) (show effect) **her age is beginning to ∼** elle commence à faire son âge
■ **tell off** réprimander ⟨*person*⟩
■ **tell on (a)** dénoncer ⟨*person*⟩ **(to** à)
(b) the strain is beginning to ∼ on him on commence à voir sur lui les effets de la fatigue
telling *adj* ⟨*remark, omission*⟩ révélateur/-trice
tell-tale **1** *n* rapporteur/-euse *m/f*
2 *adj* ⟨*sign*⟩ révélateur/-trice
telly *n* (GB) (colloq) télé *f* (fam)
temp (GB) (colloq) **1** *n* intérimaire *mf*
2 *vi* travailler comme intérimaire
temper **1** *n* **(a)** (mood) humeur *f*; **to be in a good/bad ∼** être de bonne/mauvaise humeur
(b) to be in a ∼ être en colère; **to lose one's ∼** se mettre en colère **(with** contre)
(c) (nature) caractère *m*
2 *vtr* **(a)** (moderate) tempérer
(b) tremper ⟨*steel*⟩
temperament *n* **(a)** (nature) tempérament *m*
(b) (excitability) humeur *f*
temperamental *adj* (volatile) capricieux/-ieuse
temperate *adj* ⟨*climate, zone*⟩ tempéré/-e; ⟨*person, habit*⟩ modéré/-e
ᵍ **temperature** *n* température *f*; **to have a ∼** avoir de la température *or* de la fièvre
temper tantrum *n* caprice *m*
tempest *n* tempête *f*
tempestuous *adj* turbulent/-e
template *n* gabarit *m*; (Comput) modèle *m*
temple *n* **(a)** (building) temple *m*
(b) (Anat) tempe *f*
temporarily *adv* (for a limited time) temporairement; (provisionally) provisoirement
temporary *adj* ⟨*job, contract*⟩ temporaire; ⟨*manager, secretary*⟩ intérimaire; ⟨*arrangement, accommodation*⟩ provisoire

ᵍ indicates a very frequent word

tempt *vtr* tenter; **to be ∼ed to do** être tenté/-e de faire
temptation *n* tentation *f*
tempting *adj* ⟨*offer*⟩ alléchant/-e; ⟨*food, smell*⟩ appétissant/-e; ⟨*idea*⟩ tentant/-e
ᵍ **ten** *n, pron, det* dix *m inv*
tenacious *adj* tenace
tenancy *n* location *f*
tenant *n* locataire *mf*
ᵍ **tend** **1** *vtr* soigner ⟨*patient*⟩; entretenir ⟨*garden*⟩; s'occuper de ⟨*stall, store*⟩
2 *vi* **to ∼ to do** avoir tendance à faire
tendency *n* tendance *f* (**to do** à faire)
tender **1** *n* soumission *f*
2 *adj* **(a)** ⟨*meat*⟩ tendre
(b) ⟨*kiss, love, smile*⟩ tendre
(c) ⟨*bruise, skin*⟩ sensible
3 *vt* présenter ⟨*apology, fare*⟩; donner ⟨*resignation*⟩
tendon *n* tendon *m*
tendril *n* vrille *f*
tenement *n* immeuble *m* ancien
tenner *n* (GB) (colloq) (note) billet *m* de dix livres
tennis *n* tennis *m*
tennis court *n* court *m* de tennis, tennis *m inv*
tenor *n* (Mus) ténor *m*
tenpin bowling (GB), **tenpins** (US) *n* bowling *m* (à dix quilles)
tense **1** *n* temps *m*; **the present ∼** le présent; **in the past ∼** au passé
2 *adj* ⟨*person, atmosphere, conversation*⟩ tendu/-e; ⟨*moment*⟩ de tension; **to make sb ∼** rendre qn nerveux
3 *vtr* tendre ⟨*muscle*⟩; raidir ⟨*body*⟩
■ **tense up** ⟨*person*⟩ se crisper
tension *n* **(a)** (gen, Tech) tension *f*
(b) (suspense) suspense *m*
tent *n* tente *f*
tentacle *n* tentacule *m*
tentative *adj* ⟨*smile, suggestion*⟩ timide; ⟨*conclusion, offer*⟩ provisoire
tenterhooks *n pl*
IDIOMS to be on ∼ être sur des charbons ardents; **to keep sb on ∼** faire languir qn
tenth **1** *n* **(a)** (in order) dixième *mf*
(b) (of month) dix *m inv*
(c) (fraction) dixième *m*
2 *adj, adv* dixième
tenuous *adj* ⟨*link*⟩ ténu/-e; ⟨*distinction, theory*⟩ mince
tepid *adj* tiède
ᵍ **term** **1** *n* **(a)** (period of time) (gen) période *f*, terme *m*; (Sch, Univ) trimestre *m*; **autumn/spring/summer ∼** (Sch, Univ) premier/deuxième/troisième trimestre; **the president's first ∼ of office** le premier mandat du président
(b) (word, phrase) terme *m*

2 **terms** *n pl* **(a)** (conditions) termes *mpl*; (of financial arrangement) conditions *fpl* de paiement
(b) **to come to ~s with** assumer ‹*identity, past, disability*›; accepter ‹*death, defeat, failure*›; affronter ‹*issue*›
(c) (relations) termes *mpl*; **to be on good ~s with** être en bons termes avec
3 *vtr* appeler, nommer
4 **in terms of** *phr* du point de vue de, sur le plan de

terminal **1** *n* **(a)** (at station) terminus *m*; (in airport) aérogare *f*; **ferry ~** gare *f* maritime
(b) (Comput) terminal *m*
(c) (for electricity) borne *f*
2 *adj* ‹*stage*› terminal/-e; ‹*illness*› (incurable) incurable; (at final stage) en phase terminale

terminate **1** *vtr* mettre fin à ‹*meeting, phase, relationship*›; résilier ‹*contract*›; annuler ‹*agreement*›; interrompre ‹*pregnancy*›
2 *vi* se terminer

termination *n* **(a)** (of contract) résiliation *f*; (of service) interruption *f*
(b) (Med) interruption *f* de grossesse

terminology *n* terminologie *f*

terminus *n* (*pl* **-ni** *ou* **-nuses**) (GB) terminus *m*

terrace **1** *n* **(a)** (patio) terrasse *f*
(b) (row of houses) alignement *m* de maisons
2 **terraces** *n pl* (GB) (in stadium) gradins *mpl*

terrace(d) house *n* maison *f* (*située dans un alignement de maisons identiques et contiguës*)

terracotta *n* **(a)** (earthenware) terre *f* cuite
(b) (colour) ocre brun *m*

terrain *n* terrain *m*

terrible *adj* **(a)** ‹*pain, noise, sight*› épouvantable; ‹*accident, fight*› terrible; ‹*mistake*› grave
(b) (colloq) ‹*food, weather*› affreux/-euse

terribly *adv* **(a)** (very) ‹*pleased, obvious*› très; ‹*clever*› extrêmement; **I'm ~ sorry** je suis navré
(b) (badly) ‹*suffer*› horriblement; ‹*sing, drive*› affreusement mal

terrific *adj* **(a)** (huge) ‹*amount*› énorme; ‹*noise*› épouvantable; ‹*speed*› fou/folle; ‹*accident, shock*› terrible
(b) (colloq) (wonderful) formidable

terrifically *adv* extrêmement

terrified *adj* terrifié/-e; **to be ~ of** avoir une peur folle de

terrify *vtr* terrifier

terrifying *adj* (frightening) terrifiant/-e; (alarming) effroyable

territorial *adj* territorial/-e

✔ **territory** *n* territoire *m*; (figurative) domaine *m*

terror **1** *n* terreur *f*

2 *adj* ‹*tactic*› d'intimidation; **a ~ campaign** une vague terroriste

✔ **terrorism** *n* terrorisme *m*

✔ **terrorist** *n* terroriste *mf*

terrorize *vtr* terroriser

terry *n* (*also* **~ towelling** (GB), **~ cloth** (US)) tissu *m* éponge

terse *adj* ‹*style*› succinct/-e; ‹*person, statement*› laconique

tertiary *adj* ‹*sector*› tertiaire; ‹*education*› supérieur/-e

✔ **test** **1** *n* **(a)** (gen) test *m*; (Sch, Univ) (written) contrôle *m*; (oral) épreuve *f* orale; **to put sb/sth to the ~** mettre qn/qch à l'épreuve
(b) (of equipment, machine, new model) essai *m*
(c) (Med) (of blood, urine) analyse *f*; (of organ) examen *m*; (to detect virus, cancer) test *m* de dépistage; **to have a blood ~** se faire faire une analyse de sang
(d) (*also* **driving ~**) (Aut) examen *m* du permis de conduire
2 *vtr* **(a)** (gen) évaluer ‹*intelligence, efficiency*›; (Sch) (in classroom) interroger (**on** en); (at exam time) contrôler
(b) essayer ‹*new model, product*›; (Med) analyser ‹*blood, sample*›; expérimenter ‹*new drug*›; **to have one's eyes ~ed** se faire faire un examen des yeux
(c) mettre [qch] à l'épreuve ‹*strength, patience*›

testament *n* **(a)** (proof) témoignage *m*; **to be a ~ to sth** témoigner de qch
(b) **the Old/the New Testament** l'Ancien/le Nouveau Testament

test ban *n* interdiction *f* d'essais nucléaires

test case *n* procès *m* qui fait jurisprudence

test-drive *vtr* faire un essai de route à, essayer

testicle *n* testicule *m*

testify **1** *vtr* témoigner (**that** que)
2 *vi* témoigner; **to ~ to** témoigner de

testimony *n* témoignage *m*, déposition *f*

✔ **testing** *n* (of drug, cosmetic) expérimentation *f*; (of blood, water etc) analyse *f*; (Sch) contrôles *mpl*

test paper *n* (Sch) interrogation *f* écrite

test tube *n* éprouvette *f*

test-tube baby *n* bébé-éprouvette *m*

tetanus *n* tétanos *m*

tether **1** *n* longe *f* **2** *vtr* attacher (**to** à)
IDIOM **to be at the end of one's ~** être au bout du rouleau (fam)

✔ **text** **1** *n* **(a)** (document) texte *m*
(b) (SMS) texto *m*
2 *vtr* envoyer un texto à ‹*person*›

textbook **1** *n* manuel *m* (**about, on** sur)
2 *adj* ‹*case*› exemplaire; ‹*example*› parfait/-e

textile *n* textile *m*

textphone n textphone m

texture n texture f

Thames pr n the (river) ~ la Tamise

⚹ **than** [1] prep **(a)** (in comparisons) que; **he's taller ~ me** il est plus grand que moi; **he has more ~ me** il en a plus que moi
(b) (expressing quantity, degree, value) de; **more/less ~ 100** plus/moins de 100; **more ~ half** plus de la moitié; **temperatures lower ~ 30 degrees** des températures de moins de 30 degrés
[2] conj **(a)** (in comparisons) que; **he's older ~ I am** il est plus âgé que moi; **it took us longer ~ we expected** ça nous a pris plus de temps que prévu
(b) (expressing preferences) **I'd sooner** or **rather go to Rome ~ go to Venice** je préférerais aller à Rome que d'aller à Venise, j'aimerais mieux aller à Rome qu'à Venise
(c) (when) **hardly** or **no sooner had he left ~ the phone rang** à peine était-il parti que le téléphone a sonné
(d) (US) **to be different ~ sth** être différent/-e de qch

⚹ **thank** vtr remercier ⟨person⟩; **~ God!** Dieu merci!

thankful adj (grateful) reconnaissant/-e; (relieved) soulagé/-e

thankfully adv **(a)** (luckily) heureusement
(b) (with relief) avec soulagement; (with gratitude) avec gratitude

thankless adj ⟨task, person⟩ ingrat/-e

⚹ **thanks** [1] n pl remerciements mpl; **with ~** avec mes/nos remerciements
[2] adv (colloq) merci; **~ a lot** merci beaucoup; **no ~** non merci
[3] **thanks to** phr grâce à

Thanksgiving (Day) n (US) jour m d'Action de Grâces

thank you [1] n (also **thank-you, thankyou**) merci m; **to say ~ to sb** dire merci à qn
[2] adj ⟨letter, gift⟩ de remerciement
[3] adv merci; **~ for coming** merci d'être venu; **~ very much** merci beaucoup

⚹ **that**

■ **Note** As a determiner
— In French, determiners agree in gender and number with the noun that follows; that is translated by ce + masculine singular noun (ce monsieur), by cet + masculine singular noun beginning with a vowel or mute 'h' (cet arbre, cet homme) and by cette + feminine singular noun (cette femme). The plural form those is translated by ces.
— Note, however, that the above translations are also used for the English this (plural these). So when it is necessary to insist on that as opposed to others of the same sort -là is added to the noun: I prefer THAT version = je préfère cette version-là.

⚹ indicates a very frequent word

As a pronoun (meaning that one)
— In French, pronouns reflect the gender and number of the noun they are standing for. So that (meaning that one) is translated by celui-là for a masculine noun, celle-là for a feminine noun; those (meaning those ones) is translated by ceux-là for a masculine plural noun and celles-là for a feminine plural noun.

[1] det ce/cet/cette/ces; **~ chair** cette chaise; **those chairs** ces chaises; **at ~ moment** à ce moment-là; **at ~ time** à cette époque-là; **you can't do it ~ way** tu ne peux pas le faire comme ça; **he went ~ way** il est allé par là; **~ lazy son of yours** ton paresseux de fils
[2] dem pron (pl **those**) **(a)** (that one) celui-/celle-/ceux-/celles-là
(b) (that thing, that person) **what's ~?** qu'est-ce que c'est que ça?; **who's ~?** qui est-ce?; (on phone) qui est à l'appareil?; **is ~ Françoise?** c'est Françoise?; **who told you ~?** qui t'a dit ça?; **~'s how he did it** c'est comme ça qu'il l'a fait; **what did he mean by ~?** qu'est-ce qu'il entendait par là?; **~'s the kitchen** ça, c'est la cuisine
[3] rel pron **(a)** (as subject) qui; (as object) que; **the day ~ she arrived** le jour où elle est arrivée
(b) (with a preposition) lequel, laquelle, lesquels, lesquelles; **the chair ~ I was sitting on** la chaise sur laquelle j'étais assis
(c) (with prepositions translated by à) auquel, à laquelle, auxquels, auxquelles, **the girls ~ I was talking to** les filles auxquelles je parlais
(d) (with prepositions translated by de) dont; **the people ~ I've talked about** les personnes dont j'ai parlé
[4] conj que; **he said ~ he had finished** il a dit qu'il avait fini
[5] adv **it's about ~ thick** c'est à peu près épais comme ça; **I can't do ~ much work in one day** je ne peux pas faire autant de travail dans une journée; **he can't swim ~ far** il ne peut pas nager aussi loin
IDIOMS ~ is (to say)... c'est-à-dire...; **~'s it!** (that's right) c'est ça!; (that's enough) ça suffit!; **I don't want to see you again and ~'s ~!** je ne veux pas te revoir point final!

thatched cottage n chaumière f

thatched roof n toit m de chaume

thaw [1] n dégel m
[2] vtr faire fondre ⟨ice, snow⟩; décongeler ⟨frozen food⟩
[3] vi **(a)** ⟨snow⟩ fondre; ⟨ground, frozen food⟩ dégeler
(b) (figurative) se détendre

⚹ **the** det le/la/l'/les

■ **Note** In French, determiners agree in gender and number with the noun that follows. So the is translated by le or l' + masculine singular noun (le chien, l'ami), by la or l' + feminine singular noun (la chaise, l'amie) and by les + plural noun (les chaussures).

— When *the* is used with a preposition that translates by *de* in French *de* + *le* + masculine singular noun = *du* (*du fromage*) and *de* + *les* + plural noun = *des* (*des crayons*).
— When *the* is used with a preposition that translates by *à* in French *à* + *le* + masculine singular noun = *au* (*au cinéma*) and *à* + *les* + plural noun = *aux* (*aux enfants*).

two chapters of ∼ book deux chapitres du livre; I met them at ∼ supermarket je les ai rencontrés au supermarché; ∼ French les Français; ∼ wounded les blessés; she buys only ∼ best elle n'achète que ce qu'il y a de mieux; ∼ more I learn ∼ less I understand plus j'apprends moins je comprends; ∼ longer he waits ∼ harder it will be plus il attendra plus ce sera difficile; ∼ sooner ∼ better le plus tôt sera le mieux; ∼ fastest train le train le plus rapide; ∼ prettiest house in the village la plus jolie maison du village; THE book of the year le meilleur livre de l'année; do you mean THE Charlie Parker? tu veux dire le célèbre Charlie Parker?; Charles ∼ First Charles 1ᵉʳ *or* Premier; ∼ Smiths les Smith

⚜ **theatre** (GB), **theater** (US) *n* (a) théâtre *m*; to go to the ∼ aller au théâtre (b) (US) (cinema) cinéma *m*

theatregoer *n* amateur *mf* de théâtre

theatrical *adj* théâtral/-e; ‹group› de théâtre

theft *n* vol *m* (of de)

⚜ **their** *det* leur/leurs

■ Note In French, determiners agree in gender and number with the noun that follows. So *their* is translated by *leur* + masculine or feminine singular noun (*leur chien, leur maison*) and by *leurs* + plural noun (*leurs enfants*).
— When *their* is stressed, *à eux* is added after the noun: THEIR house = leur maison à eux.

theirs *pron*

■ Note In French, possessive pronouns reflect the gender and number of the noun they are standing for; *theirs* is translated by *le leur, la leur, les leurs*, according to what is being referred to.

my car is red but ∼ is blue ma voiture est rouge mais la leur est bleue; my children are older than ∼ mes enfants sont plus âgés que les leurs; which house is ∼? c'est laquelle leur maison?; the money wasn't ∼ to give away ils/elles n'avaient pas à donner cet argent

⚜ **them** *pron* (a) (direct object) les; I've seen ∼ je les ai vus; catch ∼! attrape-les!; don't eat ∼! ne les mange pas!
(b) (indirect object) leur; I gave it to ∼ je le leur ai donné; write to ∼! écris-leur!
(c) (with prepositions, with être) eux, elles; with ∼ avec eux/elles; it's ∼ c'est eux/elles; both of ∼ tous/toutes les deux; both of ∼ work in London ils/elles travaillent à Londres tous/toutes les deux; some of ∼ quelques-uns d'entre eux/quelques-unes d'entre elles

⚜ **theme** *n* thème *m*

theme park *n* parc *m* d'attractions (à thème)

theme song, theme tune *n* (of film) musique *f*; (of radio, TV programme) indicatif *m*

⚜ **themselves** *pron*

■ Note When used as a reflexive pronoun, direct and indirect, *themselves* is translated by *se* (or *s'* before a vowel or mute 'h').
— When used for emphasis, the translation is *eux-mêmes* in the masculine and *elles-mêmes* in the feminine: they did it themselves = ils l'ont fait eux-mêmes/elles l'ont fait elles-mêmes.
— After a preposition, the translation is *eux* or *elles* or *eux-mêmes* or *elles-mêmes*: they bought the painting for themselves = (*masculine or mixed gender*) ils ont acheté le tableau pour eux *or* pour eux-mêmes; (*feminine gender*) elles ont acheté le tableau pour elles *or* pour elles-mêmes.

(a) (reflexive) se, s'; they washed ∼ ils se sont lavés
(b) (emphatic) eux-mêmes/elles mêmes
(c) (after preposition) eux/elles, eux-mêmes/elles-mêmes; (all) by ∼ tout seuls/toutes seules

⚜ **then** *adv* (a) (at that time) alors, à ce moment-là; (implying more distant past) en ce temps-là; I was working in Oxford ∼ je travaillais alors à Oxford; since ∼ depuis
(b) (afterwards, next) puis, ensuite
(c) (in that case, so) alors
(d) (therefore) donc
(e) (in addition, besides) puis, aussi

thence *adv* de là

theology *n* théologie *f*

theorem *n* théorème *m*

theoretical *adj* théorique

theoretically *adv* théoriquement; ∼ speaking en théorie

⚜ **theory** *n* théorie *f*; in ∼ en théorie

therapeutic *adj* thérapeutique

therapist *n* thérapeute *mf*

⚜ **therapy** *n* thérapie *f*

⚜ **there**

■ Note *there* is generally translated by *là* after prepositions (*near there* = près de là) and when emphasizing the location of an object/a point etc visible to the speaker: put them there = mettez-les là.
— *voilà* is used to draw attention to a visible place/object/person: there's my watch = voilà ma montre, whereas *il y a* is used for generalizations: there's a village nearby = il y a un village tout près.
— *there*, when unstressed with verbs such as *aller* and *être*, is translated by *y*: we went there last year = nous y sommes allés l'année dernière, but not where emphasis is made: it was there that we went last year = c'est là que nous sommes allés l'année dernière.
— For examples of the above and further uses, ⋯⟡

see the entry below.

1 *pron* ~ **is/are** il y a; ~ **isn't any room** il n'y a pas de place; ~ **are many reasons** il y a beaucoup de raisons; ~ **are two** il y en a deux; ~ **is some left** il en reste; ~ **seems to be** il semble y avoir

2 *adv* **(a)** là; **up to** ~, **down to** ~ jusque là; **put it in** ~ mettez-le là-dedans; **stand** ~ mettez-vous là; **go over** ~ va là-bas; **will she be** ~ **now?** est-ce qu'elle y est maintenant? **(b)** (to draw attention) (to person, activity) voilà; ~ **you are** (seeing somebody arrive) vous voilà; (giving object) tenez, voilà; (that's done) et voilà; ~**'s a bus coming** voilà un bus; **that paragraph** ~ ce paragraphe

3 *excl* ~ ~! allez! allez!; ~, **I told you!** voilà, je te l'avais bien dit!; ~, **you've woken the baby!** c'est malin, tu as réveillé le bébé!

4 **there again** *phr* (on the other hand) d'un autre côté

thereabouts (GB), **thereabout** (US) *adv* **(a)** (in the vicinity) par là **(b)** (roughly) **100 dollars or** ~ 100 dollars environ

thereby *conj* ainsi

✓ **therefore** *adv* donc, par conséquent

thermal *adj* thermique; ⟨spring⟩ thermal/-e; ⟨garment⟩ en thermolactyl®

thermal imaging *n* thermographie *f*

thermometer *n* thermomètre *m*

Thermos® *n* (also ~ **flask**) bouteille *f* thermos®

thermostat *n* thermostat *m*

thesaurus *n* (*pl* **-ri** *ou* **-ruses**) dictionnaire *m* analogique

these ▸ THIS

thesis *n* (*pl* **theses**) **(a)** (Univ) (doctoral) thèse *f*; (master's) mémoire *m* **(b)** (theory) thèse *f*

✓ **they** *pron*

■ Note *they* is translated by ils (masculine) or elles (feminine). For a group of people or things of mixed gender, ils is always used. The emphatic form is eux (masculine) or elles (feminine).

~ **have already gone** (masculine or mixed) ils sont déjà partis; (feminine) elles sont déjà parties; **here** ~ **are!** les voici!; **there** ~ **are!** les voilà!

thick **1** *adj* **(a)** (gen) épais/épaisse; ⟨forest, vegetation, fog⟩ dense, épais/épaisse; **to be 6 cm** ~ faire 6 cm d'épaisseur **(b)** (colloq) (stupid) bête

2 *adv* **don't spread the butter on too** ~ ne mets pas trop de beurre; **the snow lay** ~ **on the ground** il y avait une épaisse couche de neige sur le sol

IDIOM **to be in the** ~ **of** être au beau milieu de

thicken **1** *vtr* épaissir **2** *vi* s'épaissir; ⟨voice⟩ s'enrouer

thicket *n* fourré *m*

✓ indicates a very frequent word

thickly *adv* ⟨spread⟩ en une couche épaisse; ⟨cut⟩ en morceaux épais

thickness *n* épaisseur *f*

thickset *adj* trapu/-e

thick-skinned *adj* insensible

thief *n* (*pl* **thieves**) voleur/-euse *m/f*

thieve *vtr, vi* voler

thigh *n* cuisse *f*

thimble *n* dé *m* à coudre

✓ **thin** **1** *adj* **(a)** ⟨nose, lips, wall⟩ mince; ⟨line, stripe, wire, paper⟩ fin/-e; ⟨slice, layer⟩ fin/-e, mince; ⟨fabric, mist⟩ léger/-ère **(b)** ⟨mixture⟩ liquide; ⟨soup, sauce⟩ clair/-e **(c)** ⟨person, body⟩ maigre; **to get** ~ maigrir **(d) to wear** ~ ⟨joke, excuse⟩ être usé/-e

2 *vtr* (*p prés etc* **-nn-**) diluer ⟨paint⟩; allonger ⟨sauce, soup⟩

3 *vi* (*p prés etc* **-nn-**) (also ~ **out**) ⟨hair⟩ se clairsemer

✓ **thing** **1** *n* **(a)** (object) chose *f*, truc *m* (fam); (action, task, event) chose *f*; **the best** ~ **(to do) would be to go and see her** le mieux serait d'aller la voir; **I couldn't hear a** ~ **(that)** he said je n'ai rien entendu de ce qu'il a dit; **the** ~ **is, (that)...** ce qu'il y a, c'est que...; **the only** ~ **is,...** la seule chose, c'est que... **(b)** (person, animal) **she's a pretty little** ~ c'est une jolie petite fille; **you lucky** ~! veinard/-e! (fam)

2 **things** *n pl* **(a)** (personal belongings, equipment) affaires *fpl* **(b)** (situation, circumstances, matters) les choses *fpl*; **how are** ~**s with you?** comment ça va?; **all** ~**s considered** tout compte fait

IDIOMS **for one** ~**... (and) for another** ~**...** premièrement... et deuxièmement...; **I must be seeing** ~**s!** je dois avoir des visions!

✓ **think** **1** *vtr* (*prét, pp* **thought**) **(a)** (believe) croire, penser; **I** ~ **so** je crois; **I don't** ~ **so** je ne crois pas; **what do you** ~ **it will cost?** combien ça va coûter à ton avis? **(b)** (imagine) imaginer, croire **(c)** (have opinion) **to** ~ **a lot/not much of** penser/ne pas penser beaucoup de bien de; **what do you** ~ **of him?** que penses-tu de lui?

2 *vi* (*prét, pp* **thought**) **(a)** penser; (carefully) réfléchir; **to** ~ **about** *or* **of sb/sth** penser à qn/qch; **I'll have to** ~ **about it** il faudra que j'y réfléchisse; **to** ~ **hard** bien réfléchir; **to be** ~**ing of doing** envisager de faire; **to** ~ **about doing** penser à faire **(b)** (consider) **to** ~ **of sb as** considérer qn comme **(c)** (remember) **to** ~ **of** se rappeler

■ **think again** (reflect more) se repencher sur la question; (change mind) changer d'avis

■ **think ahead** bien réfléchir (à l'avance)

■ **think back** se reporter en arrière (to à)

■ **think over**: ~ **over** [sth], ~ [sth] **over** réfléchir à

■ **think through** bien réfléchir à ⟨proposal, action⟩; faire le tour de ⟨problem, question⟩

thinking *n* (reflection) réflexion *f*; **current ~ is that…** la tendance actuelle de l'opinion est que…; **to my way of ~** à mon avis

think-tank *n* groupe *m* de réflexion

thinly *adv* ‹slice› en tranches fines; ‹spread› en couche mince; **~ disguised** à peine déguisé/-e

thinner *n* diluant *m*

✓ **third** **1** *n* **(a)** (in order) troisième *mf*
(b) (of month) trois *m inv*
(c) (fraction) tiers *m*
(d) (*also* **~-class honours degree**) (GB Univ) ≈ licence *f* avec mention passable
(e) (*also* **~ gear**) (Aut) troisième *f*
2 *adj* troisième
3 *adv* **(a)** ‹come, finish› troisième
(b) (*also* **thirdly**) troisièmement

third-class *adj* de troisième classe

third degree *n* (colloq) **to give sb the ~** ‹parent, teacher› soumettre qn à une interrogation

third party *n* tiers *m*

third sector *n* troisième secteur *m*

Third Way *n* (GB Pol) troisième voie *f*

Third World *n* tiers-monde *m*

thirst *n* soif *f* (**for** de)

thirsty *adj* assoiffé/-e; **to be ~** avoir soif; **to make sb ~** donner soif à qn

thirteen *n*, *pron*, *det* treize *m inv*

thirteenth **1** *n* **(a)** (in order) treizième *mf*
(b) (of month) treize *m inv*
(c) (fraction) treizième *m*
2 *adj*, *adv* treizième

thirties *n pl* **(a)** (era) **the ~** les années *fpl* trente
(b) (age) **to be in one's ~** avoir entre trente et quarante ans

thirtieth **1** *n* **(a)** (in order) trentième *mf*
(b) (of month) trente *m inv*
(c) (fraction) trentième *m*
2 *adj*, *adv* trentième

thirty *n*, *pron*, *det* trente *m inv*

thirty-first **1** *n* (of month) trente et un *m*
2 *adj* trente et unième

thirty something *n*: *jeune cadre de plus de trente ans qui s'installe, fonde une famille, etc*

✓ **this**

■ Note As a determiner
— In French, determiners agree in gender and number with the noun that follows; *this* is translated by *ce* + masculine singular noun (*ce monsieur*), BUT by *cet* + masculine singular noun beginning with a vowel or mute 'h' (*cet arbre, cet homme*) and by *cette* + feminine singular noun (*cette femme*). The plural form *these* is translated by *ces* (*ces livres, ces histoires*).
— Note, however, that the above translations are also used for the English *that* (plural *those*). So when it is necessary to insist on *this* as opposed to another or others of the same sort, the adverbial tag *-ci* (*this one here*) is added to the noun: *I prefer* THIS *version* = je préfère cette version-ci.

As a pronoun (*meaning this one*)
— In French, pronouns reflect the gender and number of the noun they are standing for. So *this* (meaning *this one*) is translated by *celui-ci* for a masculine noun, *celle-ci* for a feminine noun; *those* (meaning *those ones*) is translated by *ceux-ci* for a masculine plural noun, *celles-ci* for a feminine plural noun: *of all the dresses this is the prettiest one* = de toutes les robes celle-ci est la plus jolie.
— For other uses of *this*, see the entry below.

1 *det* **~ paper** ce papier; **~ lamp** cette lampe; **do it ~ way not that way** fais-le comme ça et pas comme ça
2 *pron* **what's ~?** qu'est-ce que c'est?; **who's ~?** qui est-ce?; (on telephone) qui est à l'appareil?; **whose is ~?** à qui appartient ceci?; **~ is the dining room** voici la salle à manger; **~ is my sister Moira** (introduction) voici ma sœur Moira; (on photo) c'est ma sœur, Moira; **~ is not the right one** ce n'est pas le bon; **who did ~?** qui a fait ça?; **~ is what happens when…** voilà ce qui se passe quand…
3 *adv* **it's ~ big** c'est grand comme ça
IDIOM **to talk about ~ and that** parler de tout et de rien

thistle *n* chardon *m*

thong *n* **(a)** (on whip) lanière *f*
(b) (on shoe, garment) lacet *m*
(c) (underwear) string *m* ficelle

thorn *n* épine *f*

thorough *adj* **(a)** (detailed) ‹analysis, knowledge› approfondi/-e; ‹search, work› minutieux/-ieuse
(b) (meticulous) minutieux/-ieuse

thoroughbred **1** *n* pur-sang *m*
2 *adj* de pure race

thoroughfare *n* rue *f*; '**no ~**' 'passage interdit'

thoroughly *adv* **(a)** (meticulously) ‹clean, examine, read› à fond; ‹check, search› minutieusement
(b) (completely) ‹clean, reliable, dangerous› tout à fait; ‹agree› parfaitement; ‹recommend› chaleureusement

those ▶ THAT

✓ **though** **1** *conj* bien que (+ *subjunctive*); **a foolish ~ courageous act** un acte stupide quoique courageux
2 *adv* quand même, pourtant; **it's very expensive, ~** c'est très cher, pourtant

✓ **thought** *n* **(a)** (idea) idée *f*, pensée *f*
(b) (reflection) pensée *f*; **deep in ~** plongé dans ses pensées
(c) (consideration) considération *f*; **to give ~ to sth** considérer qch

thoughtful *adj* **(a)** (reflective) pensif/-ive
(b) (considerate) ‹person, gesture› prévenant/-e; ‹letter› gentil/-ille

thoughtless *adj* irréfléchi/-e

thought-out *adj* well/badly ~ bien/mal conçu/-e

thought-provoking *adj* qui fait réfléchir

ℱ **thousand** *n, pron, det* mille *m inv*; a ~ and two mille deux; about a ~ un millier; four ~ pounds quatre mille livres sterling; ~s of des milliers de

thousandth *n, adj, adv* millième *mf*

thrash *vtr* (a) (whip) rouer [qn] de coups (b) (Mil, Sport) écraser

■ **thrash about, thrash around** se débattre

■ **thrash out** venir à bout de ‹problem›; réussir à élaborer ‹plan›

thrashing *n* raclée *f*

thread ① *n* (a) (for sewing) fil *m* (b) (of screw) filetage *m* (c) (of story, argument) fil *m* ② *vtr* enfiler ‹bead, needle›

threadbare *adj* usé/-e jusqu'à la corde

ℱ **threat** *n* menace *f* (to pour)

ℱ **threaten** ① *vtr* menacer; to ~ to do ‹person› menacer de faire; ‹event, thing› risquer de faire; to be ~ed with extinction risquer de disparaître ② *vi* menacer

ℱ **three** *n, pron, det* trois *m inv*

three-dimensional *adj* en trois dimensions

threefold ① *adj* triple ② *adv* triplement; to increase ~ tripler

three-piece suit *n* (costume *m*) trois-pièces *m inv*

three-piece suite *n* salon *m* trois pièces

three-quarters *n* trois-quarts *mpl*; ~ of an hour trois-quarts d'heure

thresh *vtr* battre

threshold *n* seuil *m*

thrift *n* économie *f*

thrifty *adj* ‹person› économe (in dans)

thrill ① *n* (a) (sensation) frisson *m* (b) (pleasure) plaisir *m* ② *vtr* transporter [qn] de joie ③ *vi* frissonner (at, to à)

thrilled *adj* ravi/-e; ~ed with enchanté/-e de

thriller *n* thriller *m*

thrilling *adj* ‹adventure, match, story› palpitant/-e; ‹concert, moment, sensation› exaltant/-e

thrive *vi* (*prét* **throve** *ou* **thrived**, *pp* **thriven** *ou* **thrived**) ‹person› se porter bien; ‹plant› pousser bien; ‹business, community› prospérer

thriving *adj* ‹business, community› florissant/-e; ‹plant, animal› en pleine santé

throat *n* gorge *f*; to have a sore ~ avoir mal à la gorge

ℱ indicates a very frequent word

throb *vi* (*p prés etc* **-bb-**) (a) ‹heart, pulse› battre; my head is ~bing ça me lance dans la tête (b) ‹motor› vibrer; ‹music, building› résonner

throbbing *adj* ‹pain, ache, music› lancinant/-e

throne *n* trône *m*

throng ① *n* foule *f* (of de) ② *vtr* envahir ‹street, town›

throttle *n* (accelerator) accélérateur *m*.

ℱ **through** ① *prep* (a) (from one side to the other) à travers; the nail went right ~ the wall le clou a traversé le mur (b) (via, by way of) to go ~ the town centre passer par le centre-ville; to look ~ regarder avec ‹telescope›; regarder par ‹hole, window›; it was ~ her that I got this job c'est par son intermédiaire que j'ai eu ce travail (c) (past) to go ~ brûler ‹red light›; to get or go ~ passer à travers ‹barricade›; passer ‹customs›; she's been ~ a lot elle en a vu des vertes et des pas mures (fam) (d) (because of) ~ carelessness par négligence; ~ illness pour cause de maladie (e) (until the end of) all or right ~ the day toute la journée (f) (up to and including) jusqu'à; from Friday ~ to Sunday de vendredi jusqu'à dimanche ② *adj* (a) ‹train, ticket, route› direct/-e; ‹freight› à forfait; 'no ~ road' 'voie sans issue' (b) (successful) to be ~ to the next round être sélectionné/-e pour le deuxième tour (c) (colloq) (finished) fini/-e; are you ~ with the paper? as-tu fini de lire le journal? ③ *adv* the water went ~ l'eau est passée à travers; to let sb ~ laisser passer qn; to read sth right ~ lire qch jusqu'au bout ④ **through and through** *phr* English ~ and ~ anglais jusqu'au bout des ongles

ℱ **throughout** ① *prep* (a) (all over) ~ France dans toute la France; ~ the world dans le monde entier (b) (for the duration of) tout au long de; ~ his life toute sa vie; ~ history à travers l'histoire ② *adv* (in every part) partout; (the whole time) tout le temps

throughway *n* (US) voie *f* rapide *or* express

ℱ **throw** ① *n* (in football) touche *f*; (of javelin) lancer *m*; (in judo, wrestling) jeté *m*; (of dice) coup *m* ② *vtr* (*prét* **threw**, *pp* **thrown**) (a) (with careful aim) lancer; (downwards) jeter; (with violence) projeter; to ~ sth at sb lancer qch à qn; to ~ a six (in dice) faire un six (b) ‹horse› désarçonner ‹rider› (c) lancer ‹punch›; jeter ‹glance›; projeter ‹light, shadow› (on sur) (d) (disconcert) désarçonner (e) to ~ a party faire une fête (fam) (f) (in pottery) tourner ③ *vi* (*prét* **threw**, *pp* **thrown**) lancer

■ **throw away** jeter ‹paper, old clothes›; gâcher ‹chance, life›

■ **throw back** rejeter ‹fish›; relancer ‹ball›

■ **throw in**: ∼ **in** [sth], ∼ [sth] **in** (give free) faire cadeau de; (add) ajouter

■ **throw out** (a) jeter ‹rubbish›; expulser ‹person› (of de)

(b) rejeter ‹application, decision›

■ **throw together**: 1 ¶ ∼ [sb] **together** réunir ‹people›

2 ¶ ∼ [sth] **together** improviser

■ **throw up**: 1 ¶ ∼ **up** vomir

2 ¶ ∼ [sth] **up** (a) lever ‹arms, hands›; lancer ‹ball›

(b) (abandon) laisser tomber ‹job›

throwaway adj (discardable) jetable; ‹society› de consommation; ‹remark› désinvolte

throwback n survivance f (**to** de)

thrush n (Zool) grive f

thrust 1 n (a) (gen, Mil, Tech) poussée f; **sword** ∼ coup m d'épée

(b) (of argument) portée f

2 vtr (prét, pp **thrust**) to ∼ **sth towards** or **at sb** mettre brusquement qch sous le nez de qn; to ∼ **sth into sth** enfoncer qch dans qch

thud 1 n bruit m sourd

2 vi (p prés etc **-dd-**) faire un bruit sourd

thug n voyou m

thumb 1 n pouce m

2 vtr (a) (also ∼ **through**) feuilleter ‹book, magazine›

(b) (colloq) to ∼ **a lift** faire du stop (fam)

IDIOM to be under sb's ∼ être sous la domination de qn

thumbs down n (colloq) to give sb/sth the ∼ rejeter qn/qch; to get the ∼ être rejeté/-e

thumbs up n (colloq) to give sb/sth the ∼ (approve) approuver qn/qch; **start the car when I give you the** ∼ démarre quand je te fais signe

thumbtack n punaise f

thump 1 n (a) (blow) (grand) coup m

(b) (sound) bruit m sourd

2 vtr taper sur; **he** ∼**ed me** il m'a tapé dessus

3 vi ‹heart› battre violemment; ‹music, rhythm› résonner

thunder 1 n (a) tonnerre m; **a peal of** ∼ un roulement de tonnerre

(b) (of hooves) fracas m; (of applause) tonnerre m

2 v impers tonner

thunderbolt n foudre f

thunderclap n coup m de tonnerre

thunderstorm n orage m

thunderstruck adj abasourdi/-e

✧ **Thursday** n jeudi m

✧ **thus** adv ainsi; ∼ **far** jusqu'à présent

thwart vtr contrarier ‹plan›; contrecarrer les desseins de ‹person›

thyme n thym m

thyroid n (also ∼ **gland**) thyroïde f

tiara n (woman's) diadème m; (Pope's) tiare f

Tibet pr n Tibet m

tick 1 n (a) (of clock) tic-tac m

(b) (mark) coche f

(c) (Zool) tique f

2 vtr cocher ‹box, name, answer›

3 vi ‹bomb, clock, watch› faire tic-tac

■ **tick off** cocher ‹name, item›

✧ **ticket** n (a) (for plane, train, cinema, exhibition) billet m (**for** pour); (for bus, underground, cloakroom, left-luggage) ticket m; (for library) carte f; (label) étiquette f

(b) (Aut) (colloq) (for fine) PV m (fam)

(c) (US) (of political party) liste f (électorale)

ticket office n (office) bureau m de vente (des billets); (booth) guichet m

tickle 1 n chatouillement m

2 vtr (a) ‹person, feather› chatouiller; ‹wool, garment› gratter

(b) (colloq) (gratify) chatouiller ‹palate, vanity›

(c) (amuse) amuser

3 vi chatouiller

tidal wave n raz-de-marée m inv

tide n marée f; (figurative) (of emotion) vague f; (of events) cours m

tidy 1 adj (a) ‹house, room, desk› bien rangé/-e; ‹garden, work, appearance› soigné/-e; ‹habits, person› ordonné/-e; ‹hair› bien coiffé/-e

(b) (colloq) ‹amount› beau/belle (before n)

2 vtr, vi = TIDY UP

■ **tidy up**: 1 ¶ ∼ **up** faire du rangement; to ∼ **up after** ranger derrière ‹person›

2 ¶ ∼ **up** [sth] ranger ‹house, room, objects›; arranger ‹appearance, hair›

✧ **tie** 1 n (a) (piece of clothing) cravate f

(b) (bond) lien m

(c) (constraint) contrainte f

(d) (draw) match m nul

2 vtr (p prés **tying**) (a) attacher ‹label, animal› (**to** à); ligoter ‹hands›; ficeler ‹parcel› (**with** avec); nouer ‹scarf, cravate›; attacher ‹laces›; to ∼ **a knot in sth** faire un nœud à qch

(b) (link) associer (**to** à)

(c) to be ∼**d to** être rivé/-e à ‹job›; être cloué/-e à (fam) ‹house›

3 vi (p prés **tying**) (a) (fasten) s'attacher

(b) (draw) (in match) faire match nul; (in race) être ex aequo; (in vote) obtenir le même nombre de voix

■ **tie back** nouer [qch] derrière ‹hair›

■ **tie down**: she feels ∼d down elle se sent coincée (fam); **he doesn't want to be** ∼d **down** il ne veut pas perdre sa liberté; to ∼ **sb down to sth** (limit) imposer qch à qn

■ **tie in with** concorder avec ‹fact, event›

■ **tie up** (a) ligoter ‹prisoner›; ficeler ‹parcel›; attacher ‹animal›

(b) (freeze) immobiliser ‹capital›

(c) to be ∼d **up** (busy) être pris/-e

(d) (finalize) conclure ‹deal›; to ∼ **up the loose ends** régler les derniers détails

tie break(er) n (in tennis) tie-break m; (in quiz) question f subsidiaire

tier n (of cake, sandwich) étage m; (of system) niveau m; (of seating) gradin m

tiff n (petite) querelle f

tiger n tigre m

✧ **tight** [1] adj (a) ⟨grip⟩ ferme; ⟨knot⟩ serré/-e; ⟨rope, voice⟩ tendu/-e
(b) ⟨space⟩ étroit/-e; ⟨clothing⟩ serré/-e; (closefitting) ⟨jacket, shirt⟩ ajusté/-e; **my shoes are too ~** mes chaussures me serrent
(c) (strict) ⟨security, deadline⟩ strict/-e; ⟨budget, credit, schedule⟩ serré/-e
[2] adv ⟨hold, grip⟩ fermement; **hold ~!** cramponne-toi!; **sit ~!** ne bouge pas!

tighten [1] vtr serrer ⟨lid, screw⟩; resserrer ⟨grip⟩; renforcer ⟨security, restrictions⟩
[2] vi ⟨lips⟩ se serrer; ⟨muscle⟩ se contracter

tight-fisted adj (colloq) radin/-e (fam)

tight-fitting adj ajusté/-e

tight-knit adj uni/-e

tightly adv ⟨grasp, hold⟩ fermement; ⟨embrace⟩ bien fort; ⟨fastened⟩ bien

tightrope n corde f raide

tightrope walker n funambule mf

tights n pl (GB) collant m

tile [1] n (for roof) tuile f; (for floor, wall) carreau m
[2] vtr poser des tuiles sur ⟨roof⟩; carreler ⟨floor, wall⟩

till¹ = UNTIL

till² n caisse f

tiller n barre f

till receipt n ticket m (de caisse)

tilt [1] vtr pencher ⟨table, sunshade⟩; incliner ⟨head⟩; rabattre ⟨hat, cap⟩
[2] vi (slant) pencher

timber n (for building) bois m (de construction); (trees) arbres mpl; (beam) poutre f

✧ **time** [1] n (a) temps m; **as ~ goes/went by** avec le temps; **you've got plenty of ~** tu as tout ton temps; **a long ~** longtemps; **a long ~ ago** il y a longtemps; **in five days' ~** dans cinq jours
(b) (hour of the day, night) heure f; **what ~ is it?, what's the ~?** quelle heure est-il?; **10 am French ~** 10 heures, heure française; **this ~ last week** il y a exactement huit jours; **on ~** à l'heure; **the train ~s** les horaires mpl des trains; **it's ~ for bed** c'est l'heure d'aller au lit; **it's ~ we started** il est temps de commencer; **about ~ too!** ce n'est pas trop tôt!; **in ~ for Christmas** à temps pour Noël
(c) (era, epoch) époque f; **at the ~** à l'époque; **in former ~s** autrefois; **it's just like old ~s** c'est comme au bon vieux temps
(d) (moment) moment m; **at ~s** par moments; **at the right ~** au bon moment; **this is no ~ for jokes** ce n'est pas le moment de plaisanter; **at all ~s** à tout moment; **any ~ now** d'un moment à l'autre; **by the ~**

I finished the letter the post had gone le temps de finir ma lettre et le courrier était parti; **some ~ next month** dans le courant du mois prochain; **for the ~ being** pour le moment
(e) (occasion) fois f; **nine ~s out of ten** neuf fois sur dix; **three ~s a month** trois fois par mois; **three at a ~** trois à la fois; **from ~ to ~** de temps en temps
(f) (experience) **to have a hard ~ doing** avoir du mal à faire; **he's having a hard ~** il traverse une période difficile; **we had a good ~** on s'est bien amusés
(g) (Mus) mesure f
(h) **ten ~s longer/stronger** dix fois plus long/plus fort; **eight ~s as much** huit fois autant
(i) (in mathematics) fois f
[2] vtr (a) (schedule) prévoir ⟨holiday, visit, attack⟩; fixer ⟨appointment, meeting⟩
(b) (judge) calculer ⟨blow, shot⟩
(c) chronométrer ⟨athlete, cyclist⟩
IDIOMS **all in good ~** chaque chose en son temps; **only ~ will tell** l'avenir nous le dira; **to have ~ on one's hands** (for brief period) avoir du temps devant soi; (longer) avoir beaucoup de temps libre

time bomb n bombe f à retardement

time-consuming adj qui prend du temps

time difference n décalage m horaire

time-frame n (period envisaged) calendrier m; (period allocated) délai m

timeless adj éternel/-elle

time-limit n (a) (deadline) date f limite
(b) (maximum duration) durée f maximum

timely adj opportun/-e

time management n gestion f du temps

time off n (leave) congé m; (free time) temps m libre

timer n (on light) minuterie f; (for cooking) minuteur m

timeshare n (house) maison f en multipropriété; (apartment) appartement m en multipropriété

time-sheet n feuille f de présence

timespan n durée f

timetable [1] n (Sch) emploi m du temps; (for plans, negotiations) calendrier m; (for buses, trains) horaire m
[2] vtr fixer l'heure de ⟨class⟩; fixer la date de ⟨meeting⟩

time zone n fuseau m horaire

timid adj timide; ⟨animal⟩ craintif/-ive

timing n (a) (gen) **the ~ of the announcement was unfortunate** le moment choisi pour la déclaration était inopportun
(b) (Aut) réglage m de l'allumage
(c) (Mus) sens m du rythme

tin n (a) (metal) étain m
(b) (GB) (can) boîte f (de conserve)
(c) (for biscuits, cake) boîte f; (for paint) pot m; (for

✧ indicates a very frequent word

baking) moule *m*; (for roasting) plat *m* (à rôtir)

tin can *n* boîte *f* en fer-blanc

tin foil *n* papier *m* (d')aluminium

tinge ⟦1⟧ *n* nuance *f*
⟦2⟧ *vtr* teinter (**with** de)

tingle ⟦1⟧ *n* (physical) picotement *m*;
(psychological) frisson *m*
⟦2⟧ *vi* (physically) picoter; (psychologically)
frissonner

tinker *vi* **to ~ with** bricoler ⟨*car*⟩; faire des
retouches à ⟨*document*⟩

tinkle ⟦1⟧ *n* tintement *m*
⟦2⟧ *vi* tinter

tinned *adj* (GB) ⟨*meat, fruit*⟩ en boîte, en
conserve

tinny *adj* ⟨*sound*⟩ grêle; (badly made) de
camelote (fam)

tin opener *n* (GB) ouvre-boîtes *m inv*

tinsel *n* guirlandes *fpl*

tint *n* (trace) nuance *f*; (pale colour) teinte *f*;
(hair colour) shampooing *m* colorant

tinted *adj* ⟨*glass, spectacles*⟩ fumé/-e, ⟨*hair*⟩
teint/-e

⚘ **tiny** *adj* tout/-e petit/-e

tip ⟦1⟧ *n* (a) (of stick, sword, pen, shoe, spire)
pointe *f*; (of branch, leaf, shoot, tail, feather)
extrémité *f*; (of finger, nose, tongue) bout *m*
(b) (gratuity) pourboire *m*
(c) (practical hint) truc *m* (fam), conseil *m*; (in
betting) tuyau *m* (fam)
⟦2⟧ *vtr* (*p prés etc* **-pp-**) (a) (tilt) incliner;
(pour) verser; (dump) déverser ⟨*waste, rubbish*⟩
(b) (predict) **to ~ sb/sth to win** prédire que
qn/qch va gagner
(c) donner un pourboire à ⟨*waiter, driver*⟩
⟦3⟧ *vi* (*p prés etc* **-pp-**) (tilt) s'incliner
■ **tip off**: **~ off** [sb], **~** [sb] **off** avertir
■ **tip over** faire basculer ⟨*chair*⟩; renverser
⟨*bucket, pile*⟩

tip-off *n* dénonciation *f*

tiptoe ⟦1⟧ *n* **on ~** sur la pointe des pieds
⟦2⟧ *vi* marcher sur la pointe des pieds

tire ⟦1⟧ *n* (US) pneu *m*
⟦2⟧ *vtr* fatiguer
⟦3⟧ *vi* (a) (get tired) se fatiguer
(b) (get bored) **to ~ of** se lasser de
■ **tire out** épuiser ⟨*person*⟩; **to be ~d out** être
éreinté/-e

⚘ **tired** *adj* (a) (weary) ⟨*person, face, legs*⟩
fatigué/-e; ⟨*voice*⟩ las/lasse
(b) (bored) **to be ~ of sth/of doing** en avoir
assez de qch/de faire; **to grow ~ of sth/of
doing** se lasser de qch/de faire

tiredness *n* fatigue *f*

tireless *adj* ⟨*person*⟩ inlassable, infatigable;
⟨*efforts*⟩ constant/-e

tiresome *adj* ⟨*person, habit*⟩ agaçant/-e;
⟨*problem, duty*⟩ fastidieux/-ieuse

tiring *adj* fatigant/-e (**to do** de faire)

⚘ **tissue** *n* (a) (handkerchief) mouchoir *m* en
papier

(b) (*also* **~ paper**) papier *m* de soie
(c) (Anat, Bot) tissu *m*

tit *n* (Zool) mésange *f*
IDIOM **~ for tat** un prêté pour un rendu

titbit *n* (GB) (of food) gâterie *f*; (of gossip)
cancan *m* (fam)

title ⟦1⟧ *n* titre *m*
⟦2⟧ **titles** *n pl* (in film) générique *m*
⟦3⟧ *vtr* intituler ⟨*book, play*⟩

title bar *n* (Comput) barre *f* de titre

titleholder *n* tenant/-e *m/f* du titre

title role *n* rôle *m* titre

titter ⟦1⟧ *n* ricanement *m*
⟦2⟧ *vi* ricaner

tizzy *n* (colloq) **to be in a ~** être dans tous
ses états

⚘ **to**

──────────

■ **Note** Remember that when *to* is translated by
à then à + *le* = *au* and à + *les* = *aux*.

⟦1⟧ *infinitive particle* (a) (expressing purpose)
pour; **to do sth ~ impress one's friends** faire
qch pour impressionner ses amis
(b) (linking consecutive acts) **he looked up ~
see…** en levant les yeux, il a vu…
(c) (after superlatives) à; **the youngest ~ do** le
or la plus jeune à faire
(d) (avoiding repetition of verb) **'did you go?'—'no
I promised not ~'** 'tu y es allé?'—'non j'avais
promis de ne pas le faire'; **'are you staying?'
—'I want ~ but…'** 'tu restes?'—'j'aimerais
bien mais…'
(e) (following impersonal verb) **it is difficult ~
do** il est difficile de faire; **it's difficult ~
understand** c'est difficile à comprendre; **it's
easy ~ read her writing** il est facile de lire
son écriture

⟦2⟧ *prep* (a) (in direction of) à ⟨*shops, school*⟩;
(with purpose of visiting) chez ⟨*doctor's*⟩; **she's
gone ~ Mary's** elle est partie chez Mary; **~
Paris** à Paris; **~ Spain** en Espagne; **~ town**
en ville; **the road ~ the village** la route qui
mène au village; **turned ~ the wall** tourné
vers le mur
(b) (up to) jusqu'à; **~ the end/this day** jusqu'à
la fin/ce jour
(c) (in telling time) **ten (minutes) ~ three** trois
heures moins dix; **it's five ~** il est moins cinq
(d) (introducing direct or indirect object) ⟨*give, offer*⟩
à; (to + personal pronoun) me/te/lui/nous/
vous/leur; **give the book ~ Sophie** donne le
livre à Sophie; **be nice ~ your brother** sois
gentil avec ton frère; **~ me it's just a minor
problem** pour moi ce n'est qu'un problème
mineur; **she gave it ~ them/him** elle le leur/
lui a donné
(e) (in toasts, dedications) à; **~ prosperity** à la
prospérité; **~ our dear son** (on tombstone) à
notre cher fils
(f) (in accordance with) **is it ~ your taste?** c'est
à ton goût?; **to dance ~ the music** danser
sur la musique
(g) (in relationships, comparisons) **to win by three** ⋯▸

goals ∼ **two** gagner par trois buts à deux;
next door ∼ **the school** à côté de l'école
(h) (showing accuracy) **three weeks** ∼ **the day**
trois semaines jour pour jour; ∼ **scale** à
l'échelle
(i) (showing reason) **to invite sb** ∼ **dinner**
inviter qn à dîner; ∼ **this end** à cette fin
(j) (belonging to) de; **the key** ∼ **the safe** la clé
du coffre; **a room** ∼ **myself** une chambre
pour moi tout seul; **personal assistant** ∼ **the**
director assistant du directeur
(k) ‹tied› à; ‹pinned› à ‹noticeboard›; sur
‹lapel, dress›
(l) (showing reaction) à; ∼ **his surprise/dismay**
à sa grande surprise/consternation

toad n crapaud m

toadstool n champignon m vénéneux

to and fro adv ‹swing› d'avant en arrière;
to go ∼ ‹person› aller et venir

toast ⟨1⟩ n **(a)** (bread) toast m; **a slice of** ∼
un toast
(b) (drink) toast m; **to drink a** ∼ lever son verre
⟨2⟩ vtr **(a)** faire griller ‹bread›
(b) porter un toast à ‹person, success›

toaster n grille-pain m inv

tobacco n (pl ∼s) tabac m

toboggan n luge f, toboggan m

⚘ **today** ⟨1⟩ n aujourd'hui m; ∼ **is Monday**
(aujourd'hui) nous sommes lundi
⟨2⟩ adv aujourd'hui; (nowadays) de nos jours;
∼ **week** dans une semaine aujourd'hui; **a**
week ago ∼ il y a une semaine aujourd'hui;
later ∼ plus tard dans la journée

toddler n très jeune enfant m

toe n **(a)** (Anat) orteil m; **big/little** ∼ gros/
petit orteil
(b) (of sock, shoe) bout m
IDIOMS **to** ∼ **the line** marcher droit; **from top**
to ∼ de la tête aux pieds

toehold n (in climbing) prise f; **to get** or
gain a ∼ **in** s'introduire dans ‹market,
organization›

toffee n caramel m (au beurre)

⚘ **together** ⟨1⟩ adv **(a)** ensemble; **to get**
back ∼ **again** se remettre ensemble; **to be**
close ∼ être rapprochés/-es; **she's cleverer**
than all the rest of them put ∼ elle est plus
intelligente que tous les autres réunis;
they belong ∼ (objects) ils vont ensemble;
(people) ils sont faits l'un pour l'autre; **the**
talks brought the two sides closer ∼ les
négociations ont rapproché les deux parties
(b) (at the same time) à la fois
⟨2⟩ **together with** phr (as well as) ainsi
que; (in the company of) avec
IDIOM **to get one's act** ∼ s'organiser

togetherness n (in team, friendship)
camaraderie f; (in family, couple) intimité f

toil ⟨1⟩ n labeur m
⟨2⟩ vi **(a)** (also **toil away**) ‹work› peiner

(b) (struggle) **to** ∼ **up the hill** monter
péniblement la côte

toilet n toilettes fpl; **public** ∼**(s)** toilettes
publiques

toilet bag n trousse f de toilette

toilet paper, toilet tissue n papier m
hygiénique

toiletries n pl articles mpl de toilette

toilet roll n (roll) rouleau m de papier
toilette; (tissue) papier m toilette

token ⟨1⟩ n **(a)** (for machine, phone) jeton m
(b) (voucher) bon m; **book/record** ∼ chèque-
cadeau m pour livre/pour disque
(c) témoignage m; **as a** ∼ **of** en signe de
⟨2⟩ adj symbolique; **to make a** ∼ **gesture**
faire un geste pour la forme

tolerable adj (bearable) tolérable; (adequate)
acceptable

tolerance n (gen, Med) tolérance f

tolerant adj tolérant/-e

tolerate vtr (permit) tolérer; (put up with)
supporter

toll ⟨1⟩ n **(a)** death ∼ nombre m de victimes
(from de)
(b) (levy) (on road, bridge) péage m
(c) (of bell) son m; (for funeral) glas m
⟨2⟩ vtr, vi sonner

toll call n (US) communication f
interurbaine

tomato ⟨1⟩ n (pl ∼es) tomate f
⟨2⟩ adj ‹puree› de tomate; ‹juice, salad› de
tomates; ‹soup› à la tomate

tomato sauce n sauce f tomate

tomb n tombeau m

tomboy n garçon m manqué

tombstone n pierre f tombale

tomcat n matou m

⚘ **tomorrow** ⟨1⟩ n demain m; **I'll do it by** ∼
je le ferai d'ici demain
⟨2⟩ adv demain; **see you** ∼! à demain!; ∼
week demain en huit; **a week ago** ∼ il y aura
une semaine demain

tomorrow afternoon n, adv demain
après-midi

tomorrow evening n, adv demain soir

tomorrow morning n, adv demain
matin

ton n **(a)** (in weight) (GB) (also **gross** ∼ or
long ∼) tonne f britannique (= 1.1016 kg);
(US) (also **net** ∼ or **short** ∼) tonne f
américaine (= 907 kg); **metric** ∼ tonne f
(b) (colloq) (a lot) ∼s of des tas de (fam) ‹food,
paper, bands›

⚘ **tone** ⟨1⟩ n **(a)** (gen) ton m; **his** ∼ **of voice**
son ton; **to set the** ∼ donner le ton (**for** à)
(b) (Mus) timbre m; (on phone) tonalité f
(c) (of muscle) tonus m
⟨2⟩ vtr (also ∼ **up**) tonifier ‹body, muscles›
⟨3⟩ vi (also ∼ **in**) (blend) ‹colours›
s'harmoniser

⚘ indicates a very frequent word

■ **tone down** atténuer ‹colours, criticism›; adoucir le ton de ‹letter, statement›

tone-deaf adj to be ~ ne pas avoir l'oreille musicale

tongs n pl (for coal) pincettes fpl; (in laboratory, for sugar) pince f

tongue n (a) (gen) langue f; to stick one's ~ out at sb tirer la langue à qn; to lose one's ~ (figurative) avaler sa langue
(b) (on shoe) languette f
IDIOMS I have his name on the tip of my ~ j'ai son nom sur le bout de la langue; a slip of the ~ un lapsus

tongue-in-cheek adj, adv au deuxième degré

tongue stud n piercing m de la langue

tongue-tied adj muet/-ette

tongue-twister n phrase f difficile à dire

tonic n (a) (also ~ **water**) eau f tonique; a gin and ~ un gin tonic
(b) (Med) remontant m

◦ **tonight** ⟦1⟧ n ce soir
⟦2⟧ adv (this evening) ce soir; (after bedtime) cette nuit

tonne n tonne f

tonsil n amygdale f; to have one's ~s out se faire opérer des amygdales

tonsillitis n amygdalite f

◦ **too** adv (a) (also) aussi; have you been to India ~? (like me) est-ce que toi aussi tu es allé en Inde?; (as well as other countries) est-ce que tu es allé en Inde aussi?
(b) (excessively) trop; ~ big trop grand/-e; ~ many/~ few people trop de/trop peu de gens; I ate ~ much j'ai trop mangé; you're ~ kind! vous êtes trop aimable!; I'm not ~ sure about that je n'en suis pas si sûr

◦ **tool** n outil m

tool bar n (Comput) barre f d'outils

toolbox n boîte f à outils

tool kit n trousse f à outils

◦ **tooth** n (pl **teeth**) dent f

toothache n mal m de dents; to have ~ (GB) or a ~ avoir mal aux dents

toothbrush n brosse f à dents

toothpaste n dentifrice m

toothpick n cure-dents m inv

◦ **top** ⟦1⟧ n (a) (of page, ladder, stairs, wall) haut m; (of list) tête f; (of mountain, hill) sommet m; (of garden, field) (autre) bout m; (of vegetable) fane f; (of box, cake) dessus m; (surface) surface f; at the ~ of en haut de ‹page, stairs, street, scale›; au sommet de ‹hill›; en tête de ‹list›; at the ~ of the building au dernier étage de l'immeuble; at the ~ of the table à la place d'honneur; to be at the ~ of the agenda être une priorité
(b) (highest position) to aim for the ~ viser haut; to get to or make it to the ~ réussir; to be ~ of the class être le premier/la première de la classe; to be ~ of the bill être

la tête d'affiche
(c) (cap, lid) (of pen) capuchon m; (of bottle) bouchon m; (with serrated edge) capsule f; (of paint-tin, saucepan) couvercle m
(d) (item of clothing) haut m
(e) (toy) toupie f

⟦2⟧ adj (a) (highest) ‹step, storey› dernier/-ière (before n); ‹bunk› de haut; ‹button, shelf› du haut; ‹layer, lip› supérieur/-e; ‹speed› maximum; ‹concern, priority› majeur/-e; in the ~ left-hand corner en haut à gauche; to get ~ marks (GB) (Sch) avoir dix sur dix or vingt sur vingt
(b) (furthest away) ‹field, house› du bout
(c) (leading) ‹adviser, politician› de haut niveau; ‹job› élevé/-e; ‹wine, restaurant› haut de gamme

⟦3⟧ vtr (p prés etc -**pp-**) (a) être en tête de ‹charts, polls›
(b) (exceed) dépasser ‹sum, figure›
(c) (finish off) compléter (**with** par); (Culin) recouvrir ‹cake›

⟦4⟧ **on top of** phr (a) (on) sur ‹cupboard, fridge, layer›
(b) (in addition to) en plus de ‹salary, workload›
IDIOMS on ~ of all this, to ~ it all par-dessus le marché (fam); from ~ to bottom de fond en comble; to be over the ~, to be OTT (colloq) ‹behaviour, reaction› être exagéré/-e; to feel on ~ of the world être aux anges; to shout at the ~ of one's voice crier à tue-tête

■ **top up** remplir (à nouveau) ‹tank, glass›; recharger ‹mobile phone›

topaz n topaze f

top hat n haut-de-forme m

top-heavy adj lourd/-e du haut

◦ **topic** n (of conversation, conference) sujet m; (of essay, research) thème m

topical adj d'actualité

topless adj ‹model› aux seins nus

top-level adj ‹talks, negotiations› au plus haut niveau

top management n (haute) direction f

top-of-the-range adj haut de gamme inv

topping n (of jam, cream) nappage m

topple ⟦1⟧ vtr renverser
⟦2⟧ vi (sway) ‹vase, pile of books› vaciller; (fall) (also ~ **over**) ‹vase, person› basculer; ‹pile of books› s'effondrer

top-ranking adj important/-e

top secret adj ultrasecret/-ète

topsy-turvy adj, adv (colloq) sens dessus dessous

top-up card n (for mobile phone) carte f de recharge

torch n (a) (GB) (flashlight) lampe f de poche
(b) (burning) flambeau m, torche f

torment ⟦1⟧ n supplice m
⟦2⟧ vtr tourmenter

tormentor n persécuteur/-trice m/f

torn adj déchiré/-e

tornado n (pl ~es ou ~s) tornade f
torpedo n torpille f
torrent n torrent m; (figurative) flot m
torrential adj torrentiel/-ielle
torrid adj torride
torso n (pl ~s) torse m
tortoise n tortue f
tortoiseshell n (shell) écaille f
tortuous adj tortueux/-euse
torture 1 n torture f; (figurative) supplice m
2 vtr torturer; (figurative) tourmenter
Tory n (GB) Tory mf, conservateur/-trice m/f
toss 1 n (pl ~es) (a) (throw) jet m; a ~ of
the head un mouvement brusque de la tête
(b) to decide sth on the ~ of a coin décider
qch à pile ou face
2 vtr (a) (throw) lancer ‹ball, stick, dice›;
faire sauter ‹pancake›; tourner ‹salad›; to ~
a coin jouer à pile ou face
(b) ‹animal› secouer ‹head, mane›; to ~
one's head ‹person› rejeter la tête en arrière
(c) ‹horse› désarçonner ‹rider›
(d) ‹wind› agiter ‹branches, leaves›
3 vi (a) ‹person› se retourner; I ~ed
and turned all night je me suis tourné et
retourné toute la nuit
(b) (flip a coin) tirer à pile ou face; to ~ for
first turn tirer le premier tour à pile ou face
■ **toss off** (colloq): ~ [sth] off, ~ off [sth]
expédier
■ **toss out**: 1 ¶ ~ [sth] out, ¶ ~ out [sth]
jeter ‹newspaper, empty bottles›
2 ¶ ~ [sb] out éjecter (from de)
tot n (a) (colloq) (toddler) tout/-e petit/-e enfant
m/f
(b) (GB) (of whisky, rum) petite dose f
✔ **total** 1 n total m; in ~ au total
2 adj (a) ‹cost, amount, profit› total/-e
(b) (complete) ‹effect› global/-e; ‹disaster,
eclipse› total/-e; ‹ignorance› complet/-ète
3 vtr (p prés etc -ll- (GB), -l- (US)) (a) (add
up) additionner ‹figures›
(b) ‹bill› se monter à ‹sum›
totalitarian n, adj totalitaire mf
✔ **totally** adv ‹blind, deaf› complètement;
‹unacceptable, convinced› totalement; ‹agree,
change, new, different› entièrement
totem n (pole) totem m; (symbol) symbole m
totter vi ‹person, regime, government›
chanceler; ‹drunk person› tituber; ‹baby›
trébucher; ‹pile of books, building› chanceler
✔ **touch** 1 n (a) contact m (physique); the ~
of her hand le contact de sa main
(b) (sense) toucher m
(c) (style, skill) (of artist, writer) touche f; (of
musician) toucher m; to lose one's ~ perdre
la main; that's a clever ~! ça, c'est génial!
(d) (little) a ~ un petit peu
(e) (communication) to get/stay in ~ with se
mettre/rester en contact avec; he's out of ~

with reality il est déconnecté de la réalité
(f) (Sport) touche f
2 vtr (a) toucher; (interfere with) toucher à; to
~ sb on the shoulder toucher l'épaule de qn;
I never ~ alcohol je ne prends jamais d'alcool
(b) (affect) toucher; (adversely) affecter; (as
matter of concern) concerner; we were most
~ed nous avons été très touchés
3 vi se toucher
IDIOMS to be a soft ~ être un pigeon (fam); it's
~ and go whether he'll make it through the
night il risque fort de ne pas passer la nuit
■ **touch down** (a) ‹plane› atterrir
(b) (Sport) (in rugby) marquer un essai
■ **touch (up)on** effleurer ‹topic›
touchdown n (a) (by plane) atterrissage m
(b) (Sport) essai m
touched adj (a) (emotionally) touché/-e
(b) (colloq) (mad) dérangé/-e (fam)
touching adj touchant/-e
touch line n ligne f de touche
touchpad n tablette f tactile
touch screen n écran m tactile
touch-tone adj ‹telephone› à touches
touch-type vi taper au toucher
touchy adj susceptible (about sur la
question de)
✔ **tough** 1 adj (a) ‹businessman› coriace;
‹criminal› endurci/-e; ‹policy, measure, law›
sévère; ‹opposition, competition› rude; a ~
guy un dur (fam)
(b) (difficult) difficile
(c) (robust) ‹person, animal› robuste; ‹plant,
material› résistant/-e
(d) ‹meat› coriace
(e) (rough) ‹area, school› dur/-e
2 excl (colloq) tant pis pour toi!
toughen vtr (a) renforcer ‹leather, plastic›;
tremper ‹glass, steel›; durcir ‹skin›
(b) (also ~ up) endurcir ‹person›; renforcer
‹law›
toupee n postiche m
✔ **tour** 1 n (a) (of country) circuit m; (of
city) tour m; (of building) visite f; (trip in bus)
excursion f
(b) (by team, band, theatre company) tournée f
2 vtr (a) visiter ‹building, country, gallery›
(b) ‹band, team› être en tournée in ‹country›;
‹theatre production› tourner en ‹country›
3 vi ‹orchestra, play, team› être en tournée
touring n (a) (by tourist) tourisme m
(b) (by team, theatre company, band) tournée f
tourism n tourisme m
✔ **tourist** n touriste mf
tourist class n (on flight) classe f touriste
tourist (information) office n
(in town) syndicat m d'initiative; (national
organization) office m du tourisme
tourist trap n piège m à touristes
touristy adj (colloq) envahi/-e par les
touristes

✔ indicates a very frequent word

tournament n tournoi m

tousle vtr ébouriffer ‹hair›

tousled adj ‹hair› ébouriffé/-e; ‹person, appearance› débraillé/-e

tout n (a) (selling tickets) revendeur m de billets au marché noir
(b) (soliciting custom) racoleur/-euse m/f
(c) (racing) vendeur m de tuyaux

tow ① n (Aut) **to be on ~** être en remorque ② vtr remorquer, tracter ‹trailer, caravan›
■ **tow away**: **~ away [sth]**, **~ [sth] away** ‹police› emmener [qch] à la fourrière; ‹recovery service› remorquer

✔ **towards** (GB), **toward** (US) prep

■ Note When towards is used to talk about direction or position, it is generally translated by vers: she ran toward(s) him = elle a couru vers lui.
— When toward(s) is used to mean in relation to, it is translated by envers: his attitude toward(s) his parents = son attitude envers ses parents. For further examples, see the entry below.

(a) vers; **~ the east** vers l'est; **he was standing with his back ~ me** il me tournait le dos; **~ evening** vers le soir; **~ the end of** vers la fin de ‹month, life›
(b) envers; **to be friendly/hostile ~ sb** se montrer cordial/hostile envers qn
(c) (as contribution) **the money will go ~ a new car** l'argent servira à payer une nouvelle voiture

towel n serviette f (de toilette)

towelling n (cloth) tissu m éponge

tower ① n (a) (structure) tour f
(b) (Comput) boîtier m vertical, tour f
② vi **to ~ above** or **over** dominer
IDIOM **to be a ~ of strength** être solide comme un roc

tower block n (GB) tour f (d'habitation)

towering adj imposant/-e

✔ **town** n ville f; **to go into ~** aller en ville
IDIOMS **to go to ~ on** ne pas lésiner sur ‹decor, catering›; exploiter [qch] à fond ‹story, scandal›; **he's the talk of the ~** on ne parle que de lui

town-and-country planning n aménagement m du territoire

town centre (GB), **town center** (US) n centre-ville m

town council n (GB) conseil m municipal

town hall n mairie f

town house n petite maison f en centre ville; (mansion) hôtel m particulier

town planning n (GB) urbanisme m

township n commune f; (in South Africa) township m

towpath n chemin m de halage

tow truck n dépanneuse f

toxic adj toxique

toxin n toxine f

toy ① n jouet m
② vi **to ~ with** jouer avec ‹object, feelings›; caresser ‹idea›; **to ~ with one's food** chipoter

toy boy n (GB) (colloq) gigolo m

toyshop n magasin m de jouets

trace ① n trace f
② vtr (a) (locate) retrouver ‹person, weapon, car›; dépister ‹fault›; déterminer ‹cause›; **the call was ~d to a London number** on a pu établir que le coup de téléphone venait d'un numéro à Londres
(b) (also **~ back**) faire remonter ‹origins, ancestry› (**to** à)
(c) (draw) tracer; (copy) décalquer ‹map, outline›

tracing paper n papier-calque m

✔ **track** ① n (a) (print) (of animal, person, vehicle) traces fpl
(b) (course, trajectory) (of person) trace f; (of missile, aircraft, storm) trajectoire f; **keep ~ of** ‹person› se tenir au courant de ‹developments, events›; suivre le fil de ‹conversation›; ‹police› suivre les mouvements de ‹criminal›; **to lose ~ of** perdre de vue ‹friend›; perdre la trace de ‹document, aircraft, suspect›; perdre le fil de ‹conversation›; **to lose ~ of (the) time** perdre la notion du temps
(c) (path, road) sentier m, chemin m; (Sport) piste f
(d) (railtrack) voie f ferrée; (US) (platform) quai m; **to leave the ~(s)** ‹train› dérailler
(e) (on record, tape, CD) morceau m
(f) (of tank, tractor) chenille f
(g) (US Sch) (stream) groupe m de niveau
② vtr suivre la trace de ‹person, animal›; suivre la trajectoire de ‹rocket, plane›
■ **track down** retrouver ‹person, object›

tracker ball n boule f de commande

tracker dog n chien m policier

track record n **to have a good ~** avoir de bons antécédents

track shoe n chaussure f de course à pointes

tracksuit n survêtement m

tract n (a) (of land) étendue f
(b) (pamphlet) pamphlet m

tractor n tracteur m

✔ **trade** ① n (a) (activity) commerce m; **to do a good ~** faire de bonnes affaires
(b) (sector of industry) industrie f
(c) (profession) (manual) métier m; (intellectual) profession f; **by ~** de métier
② vtr échanger (**for** contre)
③ vi faire du commerce
■ **trade in**: **he ~d in his old car for a new one** on lui a repris sa vieille voiture et il en a acheté une nouvelle

trade fair n salon m

trade-in n reprise f (d'un article usagé à l'achat d'un article neuf)

t

trademark n marque f déposée

trade name n nom m (de marque)

trade-off n compromis m

trader n (a) (shopkeeper, stallholder) commerçant/-e m/f
(b) (at stock exchange) opérateur/-trice m/f (en Bourse)

tradesman's entrance n entrée f de service

Trades Union Congress, TUC n (GB) Confédération f des syndicats (britanniques)

trade union n syndicat m

trade union member n syndiqué/-e m/f

trading n (a) (business) commerce m
(b) (at stock exchange) transactions fpl (boursières)

trading estate n (GB) zone f industrielle

⚜ **tradition** n tradition f

⚜ **traditional** adj traditionnel/-elle

traditionalist n, adj traditionaliste mf

⚜ **traffic** ① n (a) (on road) circulation f; (air, sea, rail) trafic m
(b) (in drugs, arms, slaves, goods) trafic m (**in** de)
② vi (p prés etc **-ck-**) **to ~ in** faire du trafic de ‹drugs, arms, stolen goods›

traffic calming n mesures fpl pour ralentir la circulation

traffic jam n embouteillage m

trafficker n trafiquant/-e m/f (**in** de)

traffic lights n pl feux mpl (de signalisation)

traffic warden n (GB) contractuel/-elle m/f

tragedy n tragédie f

tragic adj tragique

trail ① n (a) (path) chemin m, piste f
(b) (of blood, dust, slime) traînée f, trace f
(c) (trace) trace f, piste f
② vtr (a) (follow) ‹animal, person› suivre la piste de; ‹car› suivre
(b) (drag) traîner
③ vi (a) ‹skirt, scarf› traîner; ‹plant› pendre
(b) (shuffle) **to ~ in/out** entrer/sortir en traînant les pieds
(c) (lag) traîner; **our team were ~ing by 3 goals to 1** notre équipe avait un retard de 2 buts

trail bike n moto f tout terrain

trail blazer n pionnier/-ière m/f

trailer n (a) (vehicle, boat) remorque f
(b) (US) (caravan) caravane f
(c) (for film) bande-annonce f

trailer park n (US) terrain m de caravaning

⚜ **train** ① n (a) (means of transport) train m; (underground) rame f; **a ~ to Paris** un train pour Paris; **to go to Paris by ~** aller à Paris en train

⚜ indicates a very frequent word

(b) (succession) (of events) série f; **my ~ of thought** le fil de mes pensées
(c) (procession) (of animals, vehicles, people) file f; (of mourners) cortège m
(d) (of dress) traîne f
② vtr (a) former ‹staff, worker, musician›; entraîner ‹athlete, player›; dresser ‹circus animal, dog›
(b) (aim) braquer ‹gun, binoculars› (**on** sur)
③ vi (a) (for profession) être formé/-e, étudier; **he's ~ing to be/he ~ed as a doctor** il suit/il a reçu une formation de docteur
(b) (Sport) s'entraîner

trained adj ‹staff› qualifié/-e; ‹professional› diplômé/-e; ‹voice, eye, ear› exercé/-e; ‹singer, actor› professionnel/-elle; ‹animal› dressé/-e

trainee n stagiaire mf

trainer n (a) (of athlete, horse) entraîneur/-euse m/f; (of circus animal, dogs) dresseur/-euse m/f
(b) (GB) (shoe) (high) basket f; (low) tennis m

⚜ **training** n (a) (gen) formation f; (less specialized) apprentissage m
(b) (Mil, Sport) entraînement m

training college n (GB) école f professionnelle; (for teachers) centre m de formation pédagogique

training course n stage m de formation

train spotter n passionné/-e m/f de trains

trait n trait m

traitor n traître/traîtresse m/f (**to** à)

tram n (GB) tramway m

tramp n (rural) vagabond m; (urban) clochard/-e m/f

trample vtr piétiner

trampoline n trampoline m

trance n transe f; (figurative) état m second; **to go into a ~** entrer en transe

tranquil adj tranquille

tranquillizer (GB), **tranquilizer** (US) n tranquillisant m

transaction n transaction f

transatlantic adj ‹crossing, flight› transatlantique; ‹accent› d'outre-atlantique inv

transcend vtr (gen) transcender; (surpass) surpasser

transcribe vtr transcrire

transcript n (a) (copy) transcription f
(b) (US Sch) duplicata m de livret scolaire

⚜ **transfer** ① n (a) (gen) transfert m; (of property, debt) cession f; (of funds) virement m; (of employee) mutation f
(b) (GB) (on skin, china, paper) décalcomanie f; (on T-shirt) transfert m
② vtr (p prés etc **-rr-**) (a) transférer ‹data, baggage›; virer ‹money›; céder ‹property, power›; reporter ‹allegiance, support›; **I'm ~ring you to reception** je vous passe la réception
(b) (relocate) transférer ‹office, prisoner, player›; muter ‹employee›
③ vi (p prés etc **-rr-**) (a) ‹player, passenger›

être transféré/-e; ‹employee› être muté/-e
(b) ‹traveller› changer d'avion

transferable adj (gen) transmissible; (in finance) négociable

transfer passenger n passager/-ère m/f en transit

transferred charge call n appel m en PCV

transfixed adj (fascinated) fasciné/-e; (horrified) paralysé/-e d'horreur

⚡ **transform** vtr transformer

transformation n transformation f

transformer n transformateur m

transfusion n transfusion f

transgender adj transgenre inv

transgenic adj transgénique

transient adj ‹phase› transitoire; ‹emotion, beauty› éphémère; ‹population› de passage

transistor n transistor m

transit n transit m; in ∼ en transit

transition n transition f

transitional adj ‹arrangement, measure› transitoire; ‹period› de transition

transitive adj transitif/-ive

translate 1 vtr traduire
2 vi (a) ‹person› traduire
(b) ‹word, phrase, text› se traduire

translation n traduction f; (school exercise) version f

translator n traducteur/-trice m/f

transmission n transmission f

transmit 1 vtr (p prés etc **-tt-**) transmettre
2 vi (p prés etc **-tt-**) émettre

transmitter n (in radio, TV) émetteur m; (in telecommunications) capsule f microphonique

transparency n (slide) diapositive f; (for overhead projector) transparent m

transparent adj transparent/-e

transplant 1 n (operation) transplantation f; (organ, tissue transplanted) transplant m
2 vtr transplanter

⚡ **transport** 1 n (also **transportation** (US)) air/road ∼ transport m aérien/par route; to travel by public ∼ utiliser les transports en commun
2 vtr transporter

transportation n transport m

transpose vtr transposer

transsexual n, adj transsexuel/-elle m/f

transvestite n travesti/-e m/f

trap 1 n (a) (snare) piège m
(b) (vehicle) cabriolet m
2 vtr (p prés etc **-pp-**) (a) (snare) prendre [qn/qch] au piège
(b) (catch) coincer ‹person, finger›; retenir ‹heat›

trapdoor n trappe f

trash n (a) (US) (refuse) (in streets) déchets mpl; (from household) ordures fpl
(b) (colloq) (low-grade goods) camelote f (fam)
(c) (colloq) (nonsense) âneries fpl; the film is **(absolute)** ∼ le film est (complètement) nul (fam)

trashcan n (US) poubelle f

trashy adj (colloq) ‹novel, film› nul/nulle (fam); ‹goods› de pacotille

trauma n (pl **-as**, **-ata**) traumatisme m

traumatic adj (psychologically) traumatisant/-e; (Med) traumatique

traumatize vtr traumatiser

⚡ **travel** 1 n voyages mpl; foreign ∼ voyages à l'étranger
2 vtr (p prés etc **-ll-** (GB), **-l-** (US)) parcourir ‹country, road, distance›
3 vi (p prés etc **-ll-** (GB), **-l-** (US))
(a) (journey) voyager; he ∼s widely il voyage beaucoup; to ∼ abroad/to Brazil aller à l'étranger/au Brésil
(b) (move) ‹person, object, plane, boat› aller; ‹car, train› aller, rouler; ‹light, sound› se propager; to ∼ back in time remonter le temps
(c) to ∼ well ‹cheese, wine› supporter le transport

travel agency n agence f de voyages

travel agent n agent m de voyages

travel card n carte f de transport

travel insurance n assurance f voyage

traveller (GB), **traveler** (US) n
(a) (voyager) voyageur/-euse m/f
(b) (GB) (gypsy) nomade mf

traveller's cheque (GB), **traveler's check** (US) n chèque-voyage m

travelling (GB), **traveling** (US) 1 n (touring) voyages mpl; (on single occasion) voyage m; to go ∼ partir en voyage; the job involves ∼ le poste exige des déplacements
2 adj (a) ‹actor, company, circus› itinérant/-e
(b) ‹companion, rug› de voyage; ‹conditions› (on road) de route
(c) ‹allowance, expenses› de déplacement

travelling salesman n voyageur m de commerce

travel-sick adj to be or get ∼ souffrir du mal des transports

trawler n chalutier m

tray n plateau m

treacherous adj traître/traîtresse

treachery n traîtrise f

treacle n (GB) (black) mélasse f; (golden syrup) mélasse f raffinée

tread 1 n (of tyre) (pattern) sculptures fpl; (outer surface) chape f
2 vtr (prét **trod**, pp **trodden**) fouler ‹street, path, area›; to ∼ water nager sur place
3 vi (prét **trod**, pp **trodden**) marcher; to ···⟩

t

~ **on** (walk) marcher sur; (squash) piétiner; **to ~ carefully** (figurative) être prudent/-e

treason *n* trahison *f*; **high ~** haute trahison

treasure [1] *n* trésor *m*
[2] *vtr* (a) (cherish) chérir ‹person, gift›
(b) (prize) tenir beaucoup à ‹friendship›

treasurer *n* (a) (on committee) trésorier/-ière *m/f*
(b) (US) (in company) directeur *m* financier

Treasury *n* (also **~ Department**) ministère *m* des finances

⸕ **treat** [1] *n* (pleasure) (petit) plaisir *m*; (food) gâterie *f*; **I took them to the museum as a ~** je les ai emmenés au musée pour leur faire plaisir; **it's my ~** (colloq) c'est moi qui paie
[2] *vtr* (a) (gen, Med) traiter; **to ~ sb well/ badly** bien traiter/maltraiter qn; **to ~ sb/ sth with care** prendre soin de qn/qch; **they ~ the house like a hotel** ils prennent la maison pour un hôtel
(b) (pay for) **to ~ sb to sth** payer *or* offrir qch à qn; **to ~ oneself** to s'offrir ‹holiday, hairdo›

⸕ **treatment** *n* traitement *m*

treaty *n* traité *m*

treble [1] *adj* triple
[2] *vtr*, *vi* tripler

⸕ **tree** *n* arbre *m*; **an apple/a cherry ~** un pommier/un cerisier

tree stump *n* souche *f*

treetop *n* cime *f* (d'un arbre)

tree trunk *n* tronc *m* d'arbre

trek [1] *n* (long journey) randonnée *f*; (laborious) randonnée *f* pénible
[2] *vi* (*p prés etc* **-kk-**) **to ~ across** traverser péniblement ‹desert›

trekking *n* **to go ~** faire de la randonnée pédestre

tremble *vi* trembler

tremendous *adj* ‹effort, improvement, amount› énorme; ‹pleasure› immense; ‹storm, explosion› violent/-e; ‹success› fou/ folle (fam)

tremor *n* (a) (in voice) tremblement *m*
(b) (in earthquake) secousse *f*

trench *n* tranchée *f*

trench coat *n* imperméable *m*, trench-coat *m*

⸕ **trend** *n* (a) (tendency) tendance *f*
(b) (fashion) mode *f*; **to set a new ~** lancer une nouvelle mode

trendsetter *n* innovateur/-trice *m/f*; **to be a ~** lancer des modes

trendy *adj* (colloq) branché/-e (fam)

trespass *vi* s'introduire illégalement; **'no ~ing'** 'défense d'entrer'

trespasser *n* intrus/-e *m/f*

⸕ indicates a very frequent word

⸕ **trial** [1] *n* (a) (Law) procès *m*; **to go on ~, to stand ~** passer en jugement
(b) (test) (of machine, vehicle) essai *m*; (of drug, new product) test *m*; **on ~** à l'essai; **by ~ and error** ‹learn› par l'expérience; ‹proceed› par tâtonnements
(c) (Sport) épreuve *f*
(d) (trouble) épreuve *f*; (less strong) difficulté *f*
[2] *adj* ‹period, separation› d'essai; **on a ~ basis** à titre expérimental

trial run *n* essai *m*; **to take a car for a ~** essayer une voiture

triangle *n* triangle *m*

tribe *n* tribu *f*

tribunal *n* tribunal *m*

tributary *n* affluent *m*

tribute *n* hommage *m*; **to pay ~ to** rendre hommage à; **floral ~** (spray) gerbe *f*; (wreath) couronne *f*

trick [1] *n* (a) (to deceive) tour *m*, combine *f*; **to play a ~ on sb** jouer un tour à qn; **a ~ of the light** un effet de lumière
(b) (by magician, conjurer, dog) tour *m*; **to do a ~** faire un tour
(c) (knack, secret) astuce *f*
(d) (in cards) pli *m*; **to take** *or* **win a ~** faire un pli
[2] *adj* ‹photo, shot› truqué/-e
[3] *vtr* duper, rouler (fam); **to ~ sb into doing sth** amener qn à faire qch par la ruse
IDIOMS **the ~s of the trade** les ficelles du métier; **that'll do the ~** ça fera l'affaire

trickle [1] *n* (of liquid) filet *m*; (of powder, sand) écoulement *m*; (of investment, orders) petite quantité *f*; (of people) petit nombre *m*
[2] *vi* **to ~ down** dégouliner le long de ‹pane, wall›; **to ~ into** ‹liquid› s'écouler dans ‹container›; ‹people› entrer petit à petit ‹hall›
▪ **trickle away** ‹water› s'écouler lentement; ‹people› s'éloigner lentement

trick question *n* question *f* piège

tricky *adj* (a) ‹decision, task› difficile; ‹problem› épineux/-euse; ‹situation› délicat/-e
(b) (wily) malin/-igne

tricycle *n* (cycle) tricycle *m*

trifle [1] *n* (a) (GB Culin) ≈ diplomate *m*
(b) (triviality) bagatelle *f*
[2] *vi* **to ~ with** jouer avec ‹feelings, affections›; **to ~ with sb** traiter qn à la légère

trifling *adj* ‹sum, cost, detail› insignifiant/-e

trigger *n* (a) (on gun) gâchette *f*
(b) (on machine) manette *f*
▪ **trigger off** déclencher

trilogy *n* trilogie *f*

trim [1] *n* (a) (of hair) coupe *f* d'entretien
(b) (good condition) **to keep oneself in ~** se maintenir en bonne forme physique
[2] *adj* ‹garden› soigné/-e; ‹boat, house› bien tenu/-e; ‹figure› svelte; ‹waist› fin/-e
[3] *vtr* (*p prés etc* **-mm-**) (a) (cut) couper

⟨hair, grass, material⟩; tailler ⟨beard, hedge⟩
(b) (reduce) réduire (**by** de)
(c) (Culin) dégraisser ⟨meat⟩
(d) (decorate) décorer ⟨tree, furniture⟩; border ⟨dress, handkerchief⟩
trimming n (on clothing) garniture f; **~s** (Culin) (with dish) accompagnements mpl traditionnels
trinket n babiole f
trio n trio m (**of** de)
✤ **trip** ① n **(a)** (journey) (abroad) voyage m; (excursion) excursion f; **business ~** voyage d'affaires
(b) (colloq) trip m (fam)
② vtr (p prés etc **-pp-**) **(a)** (also **~ over, ~ up**) faire trébucher; (with foot) faire un croche-pied à
③ vi (p prés etc **-pp-**) **(a)** (also **~ over, ~ up**) (stumble) trébucher, faire un faux pas; **to ~ on** or **over** trébucher sur ⟨step, rock⟩; se prendre les pieds dans ⟨scarf, rope⟩
(b) (walk lightly) **to ~ along** ⟨child⟩ gambader; ⟨adult⟩ marcher d'un pas léger
triple adj triple
triplet n (child) triplé/-e m/f
triplicate: **in ~** phr en trois exemplaires
tripod n trépied m
triumph ① n triomphe m
② vi triompher (**over** de)
triumphant adj ⟨person, team⟩ triomphant/-e; ⟨return, success⟩ triomphal/-e
trivia n pl futilités fpl
trivial adj ⟨matter, scale, film⟩ insignifiant/-e; ⟨error, offence⟩ léger/-ère (before n); ⟨conversation, argument, person⟩ futile
trivialize vtr banaliser; minimiser ⟨role⟩
trolley n **(a)** (GB) (for food, drinks, luggage, shopping) chariot m
(b) (US) tramway m
trolley bus n trolleybus m
trolley car n tramway m, tram m
✤ **troop** n troupe f
trooper n **(a)** (Mil) homme m de troupe
(b) (US) (policeman) policier m
trophy n trophée m
tropic n tropique m; **in the ~s** sous les tropiques
tropical adj tropical/-e
trot ① n trot m; **at a ~** au trot
② vi (p prés etc **-tt-**) ⟨animal, rider⟩ trotter; ⟨person⟩ courir, trotter; ⟨child⟩ trottiner
IDIOM on the ~ (one after the other) coup sur coup; (continuously) d'affilée
■ **trot out** (colloq): **~ out [sth]** débiter ⟨excuse, explanation⟩
✤ **trouble** ① n **(a)** (problems) problèmes mpl; (personal) ennuis mpl; (difficulties) difficultés fpl; **to be in** or **get into ~** ⟨person⟩ avoir des ennuis; ⟨company⟩ avoir des difficultés; **to get sb into ~** créer des ennuis à qn; **back ~** mal m de dos; **what's the ~?** qu'est-ce qui

ne va pas?; **to have ~ doing** avoir du mal à faire; **to get sb out of ~** tirer qn d'affaire
(b) (effort, inconvenience) peine f; **it's not worth the ~** cela n'en vaut pas la peine; **to take the ~ to do, to go to the ~ of doing** se donner la peine de faire; **to save sb the ~ of doing** épargner à qn la peine de faire; **to go to a lot of ~** se donner beaucoup de mal
② **troubles** n pl soucis mpl; **money ~s** problèmes mpl d'argent
③ vtr **(a)** (disturb, inconvenience) déranger ⟨person⟩; **may** or **could I ~ you to...** puis-je vous demander de...
(b) (bother) **to be ~d by** être incommodé/-e par ⟨cough, pain⟩
(c) (worry) tracasser ⟨person⟩; **don't let that ~ you** ne te tracasse pas pour cela
troubled adj ⟨person, expression⟩ soucieux/-ieuse; ⟨mind⟩ inquiet/-iète; ⟨sleep, times, area⟩ agité/-e
troublefree adj sans problèmes
troublemaker n fauteur/-trice m/f de troubles
troubleshooter n consultant/-e m/f en gestion des entreprises
troublesome adj ⟨person⟩ ennuyeux/-euse; ⟨problem⟩ gênant/-e; ⟨cough, pain⟩ désagréable
trouble spot n point m chaud
trough n **(a)** (for drinking) abreuvoir m; (for animal feed) auge f
(b) (between waves, hills, on graph) creux m
(c) (in weather) zone f dépressionnaire
trousers n pl (GB) pantalon m; **short ~** culotte f courte
trout n (pl **~**) truite f
trowel n **(a)** (for cement) truelle f
(b) (for gardening) déplantoir m
truancy n absentéisme m
truant n **to play ~** faire l'école buissonnière
truce n trêve f
truck n **(a)** (lorry) camion m
(b) (rail wagon) wagon m de marchandises
truck driver, **trucker** (colloq) n routier m
trudge vi marcher d'un pas lourd; **to ~ through the snow** marcher péniblement dans la neige
✤ **true** ① adj **(a)** (based on fact, not a lie) ⟨news, fact, story⟩ vrai/-e; (from real life) ⟨story⟩ vécu/-e
(b) (real, genuine) vrai/-e (before n); ⟨identity, age⟩ véritable (before n); **to come ~** se réaliser
(c) (heartfelt, sincere) ⟨feeling, understanding⟩ sincère; **~ love** le véritable amour
(d) (accurate) ⟨copy⟩ conforme; ⟨assessment⟩ correct, juste
(e) (faithful, loyal) fidèle (**to** à)
(f) (Mus) ⟨note, instrument⟩ juste
② adv ⟨aim, fire⟩ juste
true-life adj ⟨adventure, story⟩ vécu/-e
truffle n truffe f

truly *adv* **(a)** (gen) vraiment; **well and ~** bel et bien
(b) (in letter) **yours ~** je vous prie d'agréer l'expression de mes sentiments distingués (formal)

trump *n* atout *m*
IDIOM **to come up ~s** sauver la situation

trumped-up *adj* ‹charge› forgé/-e de toutes pièces

trumpet *n* **(a)** (instrument, player) trompette *f*
(b) (elephant call) barrissement *m*
IDIOM **to blow one's own ~** vanter ses propres mérites

trumpeter *n* trompettiste *mf*

truncheon *n* matraque *f*

trunk *n* **(a)** (of tree, body) tronc *m*
(b) (of elephant) trompe *f*
(c) (for travel) malle *f*
(d) (US) (car boot) coffre *m*

trunks *n pl* slip *m* de bain

truss *n* (Med) bandage *m* herniaire
■ **truss up** brider, trousser ‹chicken›; ligoter ‹person›

trust ⓵ *n* **(a)** (faith) confiance *f*; **to put one's ~ in** se fier à
(b) (Law) (arrangement) fidéicommis *m*; (property involved) propriété *f* fiduciaire
⓶ *vtr* **(a)** (believe) se fier à ‹person, judgment›
(b) (rely on) faire confiance à
(c) (entrust) **to ~ sb with sth** confier qch à qn
⓷ *vi* **to ~ in** faire confiance à ‹person›; croire en ‹God, fortune›; **to ~ to luck** se fier au hasard
⓸ *v refl* **to ~ oneself to do** être sûr de pouvoir faire

trust company *n* société *f* fiduciaire

trusted *adj* ‹friend› fidèle

trusted third party, TTP *n* tierce partie *f* de confiance, TPC *f*

trustee *n* **(a)** (who administers property in trust) fiduciaire *m*
(b) (of company) administrateur/-trice *m/f* (of de)

trust fund *n* fonds *m* en fidéicommis

trusting *adj* ‹person› qui fait facilement confiance aux gens

trustworthy *adj* ‹staff, firm› sérieux/-ieuse; ‹friend, lover› digne de confiance

truth *n* (real facts) **the ~** la vérité; **there is some ~ in it** il y a du vrai dans cela

truthful *adj* ‹person› honnête; ‹account, version› vrai/-e

try ⓵ *n* (*pl* **tries**) **(a)** (attempt) essai *m*; **to have a ~** essayer (**at doing** de faire)
(b) (Sport) essai *m*
⓶ *vtr* (*prét, pp* **tried**) **(a)** (attempt) essayer de répondre à ‹exam question›; **to ~ doing** *or* **to do** essayer de faire; **to ~ hard to do** faire de gros efforts pour faire; **to ~ one's best to**

✍ indicates a very frequent word

do faire tout son possible pour faire
(b) (test out) essayer ‹tool, product, method, activity›; prendre [qn] à l'essai ‹person›; ‹thief› essayer d'ouvrir ‹door, window›; tourner ‹door knob›; **to ~ one's hand at sth** s'essayer à qch
(c) (taste) goûter ‹food›
(d) (consult) demander à ‹person›; consulter ‹book›; **~ the library** demandez à la bibliothèque
(e) (subject to stress) **to ~ sb's patience** pousser qn à bout
(f) (Law) juger ‹case, criminal›
⓷ *vi* (*prét, pp* **tried**) essayer; **to ~ again** (to perform task) recommencer; (to see somebody) repasser; (to phone) rappeler; **to ~ for** essayer d'obtenir ‹loan, university place›; essayer de battre ‹world record›; essayer d'avoir ‹baby›; **keep ~ing!** essaie encore!
■ **try on** (*pl* **tries**) essayer ‹hat, dress›
■ **try out**: (*pl* **tries**) **~ [sth] out, ~ out [sth]** essayer

trying *adj* ‹person› pénible; ‹experience› éprouvant/-e

T-shirt *n* T-shirt *m*

tub *n* **(a)** (for flowers, water) bac *m*; (of ice cream, pâté) pot *m*
(b) (US) (bath) baignoire *f*

tubby *adj* (colloq) grassouillet/-ette (fam)

tube *n* **(a)** (cylinder, container) tube *m*
(b) (GB) **the ~** le métro (londonien)
(c) (US) (colloq) (TV) télé *f* (fam)
(d) (in TV set) tube *m* cathodique
(e) (in tyre) chambre *f* à air

tuberculosis *n* tuberculose *f*

tuck ⓵ *n* (in sewing) pli *m*
⓶ *vtr* (put) glisser; **to ~ one's shirt into one's trousers** rentrer sa chemise dans son pantalon
■ **tuck away** (put away) ranger; **the house was ~ed away in the wood** la maison se cachait *or* était cachée dans le bois
■ **tuck in** rentrer ‹garment, shirt›; border ‹bedclothes, person›

Tuesday *n* mardi *m*

tuft *n* touffe *f*

tug ⓵ *n* **(a)** (pull) secousse *f*; **to give sth a ~** tirer sur qch
(b) (*also* **tug boat**) remorqueur *m*
⓶ *vtr* (*p prés etc* **-gg-**) (pull) tirer
⓷ *vi* (*p prés etc* **-gg-**) **to ~ at** *or* **on** tirer sur ‹rope, hair›

tug-of-love *n*: lutte entre les parents pour la garde de l'enfant

tug-of-war *n* (Sport) gagne-terrain *m*

tuition *n* cours *mpl*

tuition fees *n pl* frais *mpl* pédagogiques

tulip *n* tulipe *f*

tumble ⓵ *n* **(a)** (fall) chute *f*; **to take a ~** ‹person› faire une chute
(b) (of clown, acrobat) culbute *f*
⓶ *vi* **(a)** (fall) ‹person, object› tomber (**off,**

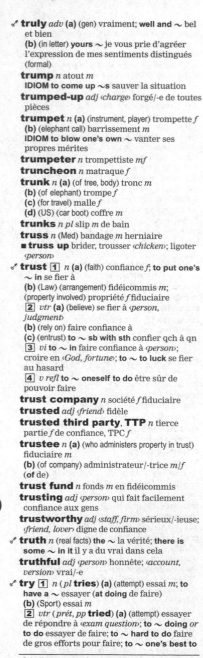

(b) ‹price, share, currency› chuter

(c) ‹clown, acrobat, child› faire des culbutes

■ **tumble down** ‹wall, building› s'écrouler

tumble-drier, tumble-dryer n sèche-linge m inv

tumble-dry vtr sécher (en machine)

tumbler n verre m droit

tummy n (colloq) ventre m

tumour (GB), **tumor** (US) n tumeur f

tumult n (a) (noise) tumulte m

(b) (disorder) agitation f

tuna n (also ~ **fish**) thon m

tune ① n air m; **to be in/out of ~** ‹instrument› être/ne pas être en accord; **to sing in/out of ~** chanter juste/faux

② vtr accorder ‹musical instrument›; régler ‹engine, radio, TV›

■ **tune in**: ① ~ **in** mettre la radio; **to ~ in to** se mettre à l'écoute de ‹programme›; régler sur ‹channel›

② ~ **[sth] in** régler (to sur)

tunic n (for gym) tunique f; (for nurse, schoolgirl) blouse f; (for soldier) vareuse f

tuning fork n diapason m

tunnel ① n tunnel m

② vtr, vi (p prés etc **-ll-** (GB), **-l-** (US)) creuser

tunnel vision n **to have ~** (figurative) avoir des œillères

turbine n turbine f

turbo n (engine) turbo m; (car) turbo f

turbocharged adj turbo inv

turbot n turbot m

turbulent adj (a) ‹water› agité/-e

(b) ‹times, situation› agité/-e; ‹career, history› mouvementé/-e; ‹passions, character, faction› turbulent/-e

tureen n soupière f

turf ① n (pl ~s, **turves**) (grass) gazon m; (peat) tourbe f

② vtr gazonner ‹lawn, pitch›

■ **turf out**: ~ **out [sb/sth]**, ~ **[sb/sth] out** virer (fam)

Turk n Turc/Turque m/f

turkey n (a) (bird) dinde f

(b) (US) (colloq) (flop) bide m (fam); (bad film) navet m (fam)

Turkey pr n Turquie f

Turkish ① n (language) turc m

② adj turc/turque

Turkish delight n loukoum m

turmoil n désarroi m

♂ **turn** ① n (a) (in games, sequence) tour m; **whose ~ is it?** c'est à qui le tour?; **to be sb's ~ to do** être le tour de qn de faire; **to take ~s at sleeping, to take it in ~s to sleep** dormir à tour de rôle; **by ~s** tour à tour; **to speak out of ~** commettre un impair

(b) (circular movement) tour m; **to give sth a ~**

tourner qch; **to do a ~** ‹dancer› faire un tour

(c) (in vehicle) virage m; **to make or do a left/right ~** tourner à gauche/à droite

(d) (bend, side road) tournant m, virage m; **take the next right ~, take the next ~ on the right** prenez la prochaine (rue) à droite

(e) (change, development) tournure f; **to take a ~ for the better** ‹things, events, situation› prendre une meilleure tournure; **to take a ~ for the worse** ‹situation› se dégrader; ‹health› s'aggraver

(f) (GB) (colloq) (attack) crise f; **a dizzy ~** un vertige; **it gave me quite a ~, it gave me a nasty ~** ça m'a fait un coup (fam)

(g) (act) numéro m

② vtr (a) (rotate) ‹person› tourner ‹wheel, handle›; serrer ‹screw›; ‹mechanism› faire tourner ‹cog, wheel›

(b) (turn over, reverse) retourner ‹mattress, soil, steak, collar›; tourner ‹page›; **it ~s my stomach** ça me soulève le cœur

(c) (change direction of) tourner ‹chair, head, face, car›

(d) (focus direction of) **to ~ [sth] on sb** braquer [qch] sur qn ‹gun, hose, torch›

(e) (transform) **to ~ sth white/black** blanchir/noircir qch; **to ~ sth opaque** rendre qch opaque; **to ~ sth into** transformer qch en ‹office, car park, desert›; **to ~ a book into a film** adapter un livre pour le cinéma; **to ~ sb into** ‹magician› changer qn en ‹frog›; ‹experience› faire de qn ‹extrovert, maniac›

(f) (colloq) (become) devenir ‹Conservative, Communist›; **businessman ~ed politician** ex-homme d'affaires devenu homme politique

(g) (deflect) détourner ‹person, conversation› (**towards** vers; **from** de)

(h) (colloq) (pass the age of) **he has ~ed 50** il a 50 ans passés; **she has just ~ed 30** elle vient d'avoir 30 ans

(i) (on lathe) tourner ‹wood, piece›

③ vi (a) (change direction) ‹person, car, plane, road› tourner; ‹ship› virer; **to ~ down** or **into** tourner dans ‹street, alley›; **to ~ towards** tourner en direction de ‹village, mountains›

(b) (reverse direction) ‹person, vehicle› faire demi-tour; ‹tide› changer; ‹luck› tourner

(c) (revolve) ‹key, wheel, planet› tourner; ‹person› se tourner

(d) (hinge) **to ~ on** ‹argument› tourner autour de ‹point, issue›; ‹outcome› dépendre de ‹factor›

(e) (spin round angrily) **to ~ on sb** ‹dog› attaquer qn; ‹person› se retourner contre qn

(f) (resort to) **to ~ to** se tourner vers ‹person, religion›; **to ~ to drink/drugs** se mettre à boire/se droguer; **I don't know where to ~** je ne sais plus où donner de la tête (fam)

(g) (change) **to ~ into** ‹person, tadpole› se transformer en ‹frog›; ‹sofa› se transformer en ‹bed›; ‹situation, evening› tourner à ‹farce, disaster›; **to ~ to** ‹substance› se changer ⋯⟩

en ‹ice, gold›; ‹fear, surprise› faire place à ‹horror, relief›

(h) (become by transformation) devenir ‹pale, cloudy, green›; **to ~ white/black/red** blanchir/noircir/rougir; **the weather is ~ing cold/warm** le temps se rafraîchit/se réchauffe

(i) (go sour) ‹milk› tourner

(j) ‹trees, leaves› jaunir

4 **in turn** phr ‹answer, speak› à tour de rôle; **she spoke to each of us in ~** elle nous a parlé chacun à notre tour

IDIOM to do sb a good ~ rendre un service à qn

■ **turn against**: 1 ¶ **~ against [sb/sth]** se retourner contre

2 ¶ **~ [sb] against** retourner [qn] contre

■ **turn around**: 1 ¶ **~ around (a)** (to face other way) ‹person› se retourner; ‹bus, vehicle› faire demi-tour

(b) (revolve, rotate) ‹object, windmill, dancer› tourner

2 ¶ **~ [sth] around** tourner [qch] dans l'autre sens ‹object›

■ **turn aside** se détourner (**from** de)

■ **turn away**: 1 ¶ **~ away** se détourner

2 ¶ **~ [sb] away** refuser ‹spectator, applicant›; ne pas laisser entrer ‹salesman, caller›

■ **turn back**: 1 ¶ **~ back (a)** (on foot) rebrousser chemin; **there's no ~ing back** il n'est pas question de revenir en arrière

(b) (in book) revenir

2 ¶ **~ [sth] back** reculer ‹dial, clock›

3 ¶ **~ [sb] back** refouler ‹people, vehicles›

■ **turn down (a)** (reduce) baisser ‹volume, radio, gas›

(b) (fold over) rabattre ‹sheet, collar›; retourner ‹corner of page›

(c) (refuse) refuser ‹person, request›; rejeter ‹offer, suggestion›

■ **turn off**: 1 ¶ **~ off (a)** ‹driver, walker› tourner

(b) ‹motor, fan› s'arrêter

2 ¶ **~ [sth] off** éteindre ‹light, oven, TV, radio›; fermer ‹tap›; couper ‹water, gas, engine›

3 ¶ **~ off [sth]** (leave) quitter ‹road›

4 ¶ **~ [sb] off** (colloq) rebuter

■ **turn on (a)** allumer ‹light, oven, TV, radio, gas›; ouvrir ‹tap›

(b) (colloq) exciter ‹person›

■ **turn out**: 1 ¶ **~ out (a)** (be eventually) **to ~ out well/badly** bien/mal se terminer; **it depends how things ~ out** cela dépend de la façon dont les choses vont tourner; **to ~ out to be wrong/easy** se révéler faux/facile; **it ~s out that they know each other already** il se trouve qu'ils se connaissent déjà

(b) (come out) ‹crowd, people› venir

2 ¶ **~ [sth] out (a)** (turn off) éteindre ‹light›

(b) (empty) vider ‹pocket, bag›; (Culin)

démouler ‹mousse›

(c) (produce) fabriquer ‹goods›; former ‹scientists, graduates›

3 ¶ **~ [sb] out** (evict) mettre [qn] à la porte

■ **turn over** 1 **~ over (a)** (roll over) ‹person, vehicle› se retourner

(b) (turn page) tourner la page

(c) ‹engine› se mettre en marche

2 **~ [sb/sth] over (a)** (turn) tourner ‹page, paper›; retourner ‹card, object, mattress, soil, patient›

(b) (hand over) remettre ‹object, money, find, papers›; livrer ‹person› (**to** à); remettre la succession de ‹company›

■ **turn round** (GB) = TURN AROUND

■ **turn up** 1 **~ up (a)** (arrive, show up) arriver, se pointer (fam); **don't worry—it will ~ up** ne t'inquiète pas—tu finiras par le retrouver

(b) (present itself) ‹opportunity, job› se présenter

(c) (point up) ‹corner, edge› être relevé/-e

2 **~ [sth] up (a)** (increase, intensify) augmenter ‹heating, volume, gas›; mettre [qch] plus fort ‹TV, radio, music›

(b) (point up) relever ‹collar›

turnaround n (in attitude) revirement m; (of fortune) revirement m (**in** de); (for the better) redressement m (**in** de)

turning n (GB) (in road) virage m

turning point n tournant m (**in, of** de)

turnip n navet m

turnoff n **(a)** (in road) embranchement m

(b) (colloq) (person) **to be a real ~** être vraiment repoussant/-e

turn of mind n tournure f d'esprit

turn of phrase n (expression) expression f

turnout n (to vote, strike, demonstrate) taux m de participation; **there was a magnificent ~ for the parade** beaucoup de gens sont venus voir le défilé

turnover n **(a)** (of company) chiffre m d'affaires

(b) (of stock) rotation f; (of staff) taux m de renouvellement

turnpike n (tollgate) barrière f de péage; (US) (toll expressway) autoroute f à péage

turnstile n (gate) tourniquet m; (to count number of visitors) compteur m pour entrées

turntable n (on record player) platine f

turnup n (GB) (of trousers) revers m

turpentine, turps (colloq) n térébenthine f

turret n tourelle f

turtle n (GB) tortue f marine; (US) tortue f

turtle dove n tourterelle f

turtleneck (sweater) n pull-over m à col cheminée

Tuscany pr n Toscane f

tusk n défense f

tussle n empoignade f (**for** pour)

ⱷ indicates a very frequent word

tutor n (a) (private teacher) professeur m particulier
(b) (GB Univ) chargé/-e m/f de travaux dirigés
(c) (US Univ) assistant/-e m/f
tutorial n (Univ) (group) classe f de travaux dirigés; (private) cours m privé
tuxedo n (US) smoking m
✯ **TV** n (colloq) (abbr = **television**) télé f (fam)
TV dinner n plateau m télé
TV screen n écran m télé
twang n (of string, wire) vibration f; (of tone) ton m nasillard
tweak vtr tordre ‹ear, nose›; tirer ‹hair, moustache›
tweezers n pl pincettes fpl; (for eyebrows) pince f à épiler
twelfth ⌐1⌐ n (a) (in order) douzième mf
(b) (of month) douze m inv
(c) (fraction) douzième m
⌐2⌐ adj, adv douzième
twelve n, pron, det douze m inv
twenties n pl (a) (era) the ~ les années fpl vingt
(b) (age) to be in one's ~ avoir entre vingt et trente ans
twentieth ⌐1⌐ n (a) (in order) vingtième mf
(b) (of month) vingt m
(c) (fraction) vingtième m
⌐2⌐ adj, adv vingtième
twenty n, pron, det vingt m inv
✯ **twice** adv deux fois; ~ a day or daily deux fois par jour; she's ~ his age elle a le double de son âge; ~ as much, ~ as many deux fois plus
twiddle vtr tripoter; to ~ one's thumbs se tourner les pouces
twig n brindille f
twilight n crépuscule m
twilight zone n zone f d'ombre
twin ⌐1⌐ n jumeau/-elle m/f
⌐2⌐ adj (a) ‹brother, sister› jumeau/-elle
(b) ‹masts, propellers, beds› jumeaux/-elles (after n); ‹speakers› jumelés
⌐3⌐ vtr (p prés etc -nn-) jumeler ‹town› (with avec)
twine n ficelle f
twinge n (of pain) élancement m; (of conscience, doubt) accès m; (of jealousy) pointe f
twinkle vi ‹light, star, jewel› scintiller; ‹eyes› pétiller
twin town n ville f jumelle
twirl ⌐1⌐ n tournoiement m
⌐2⌐ vtr faire tournoyer ‹baton, partner›; entortiller ‹ribbon, vine›
⌐3⌐ vi ‹dancer› tournoyer; to ~ round (turn round) se retourner brusquement
twist ⌐1⌐ n (a) (in rope, cord, wool) tortillon m; (in road) zigzag m; (in river) coude m
(b) (in play, story) coup m de théâtre; (in events) rebondissement m
(c) (small amount) (of yarn, thread, hair) torsade f;

a ~ of lemon une tranche de citron
⌐2⌐ vtr (a) (turn) tourner ‹knob, handle›; (open) dévisser ‹cap, lid›; (close) visser ‹cap, lid›; he ~ed around in his chair il s'est retourné dans son fauteuil
(b) (wind) enrouler; to ~ threads together torsader des fils
(c) (bend, distort) tordre ‹metal, rod, branch›; déformer ‹words, facts, meaning›; his face was ~ed with pain son visage était tordu de douleur
(d) (injure) to ~ one's ankle/wrist se tordre la cheville/le poignet; to ~ one's neck attraper un torticolis
⌐3⌐ vi (a) ‹person› to ~ round (turn round) se retourner
(b) ‹rope, flex, coil› s'entortiller; to ~ and turn ‹road, path› serpenter
twisted adj ‹wire, metal› tordu/-e; ‹cord› entortillé/-e; ‹ankle, wrist› tordu/-e; ‹sense of humour› malsain/-e
twit n (colloq) idiot/-e m/f
twitch ⌐1⌐ n (a) (tic) tic m
(b) (spasm) soubresaut m
⌐2⌐ vtr tirer sur [qch] d'un coup sec ‹fabric, curtain›
⌐3⌐ vi ‹person› avoir des tics; ‹mouth› trembler; ‹eye› cligner nerveusement; ‹limb, muscle› tressauter
twitchy adj agité/-e
twitter vi ‹bird› gazouiller
✯ **two** n, det, pron deux m inv; in ~s and threes par deux ou trois, deux ou trois à la fois; to break sth in ~ casser qch en deux
IDIOMS to be in ~ minds about doing hésiter à faire; to put ~ and ~ together faire le rapprochement
two-faced adj hypocrite, fourbe
twofold ⌐1⌐ adj double
⌐2⌐ adv doublement; to increase ~ doubler
two-piece n (also ~ suit) (woman's) tailleur m; (man's) costume m (deux-pièces)
two-seater n (car) voiture f à deux places; (plane) avion m à deux places
two-tier adj ‹society, health service› à deux vitesses
two-time vtr (colloq) être infidèle envers, tromper ‹partner›
two-way adj ‹street› à double sens; ‹traffic› dans les deux sens; ‹communication, exchange› bilatéral/-e
two-way mirror n glace f sans tain
two-way radio n émetteur-récepteur m
tycoon n magnat m
✯ **type** ⌐1⌐ n (a) (variety, kind) type m, genre m (of de)
(b) (in printing) caractères mpl
⌐2⌐ vtr taper (à la machine) ‹word, letter›; a ~d letter une lettre dactylographiée
⌐3⌐ vi taper (à la machine)
typecast vtr (prét, pp **-cast**) cataloguer ‹person›

t

typeface n police f (de caractères)
typewriter n machine f à écrire
typhoid n typhoïde f
typhoon n typhon m
✓ **typical** adj ⟨case, example, day, village⟩ typique; ⟨generosity, compassion⟩ caractéristique; **it's ~ of him to be late** cela ne m'étonne pas de lui qu'il soit en retard
typically adv ⟨react, behave⟩ (of person) comme à mon/ton etc habitude; **~ English** ⟨place, behaviour⟩ typiquement anglais; **she's ~ English** c'est l'Anglaise type

typify vtr ⟨feature, behaviour⟩ caractériser; ⟨person, institution⟩ être le type même de
typing n dactylo f
typist n dactylo mf
typographic(al) adj typographique
typography n typographie f
tyrannize vtr tyranniser
tyranny n tyrannie f (**over** sur)
tyrant n tyran m
tyre (GB), **tire** (US) n pneu m; **spare ~** (for car) pneu m de rechange; (fat) bourrelet m
tyre pressure n pression f des pneus

U u

u, U n u, U m
udder n pis m
UFO n (abbr = **unidentified flying object**) ovni m inv
ugly adj (a) ⟨person, building⟩ laid/-e
(b) ⟨situation⟩ dangereux/-euse
UK pr n (abbr = **United Kingdom**) Royaume-Uni m
Ukraine pr n the **~** l'Ukraine f
ulcer n ulcère m
ulterior adj **without any ~ motive** sans arrière-pensée
ultimate [1] n the **~ in** le nec plus ultra de ⟨comfort, luxury⟩
[2] adj ⟨result, destination⟩ final/-e; ⟨sacrifice⟩ ultime (before n)
✓ **ultimately** adv en fin de compte, au bout du compte
ultimatum n (pl **~s** ou **-mata**) ultimatum m
ultramarine n, adj outremer m inv
ultrasound n ultrasons mpl
ultrasound scan n échographie f
ultraviolet adj ultraviolet/-ette
umbilical cord n cordon m ombilical
umbrella n parapluie m
umpire n arbitre m
UN n (abbr = **United Nations**) the **~** l'ONU f
✓ **unable** adj **to be ~ to do** (lacking means or opportunity) ne pas pouvoir faire; (lacking knowledge or skill) ne pas savoir faire; (incapable, not qualified) être incapable de faire
unabridged adj intégral/-e
unacceptable adj ⟨proposal⟩ inacceptable; ⟨behaviour⟩ inadmissible

unaccompanied adj (a) ⟨child, baggage⟩ non accompagné/-e; ⟨man, woman⟩ seul/-e
(b) (Mus) sans accompagnement
unaccounted adj **to be ~ for** (gen) être introuvable; **two of the crew are still ~ for** deux membres de l'équipage sont toujours portés disparus
unaccustomed adj **to be ~ to sth/to doing** ne pas avoir l'habitude de qch/de faire
unaffected adj (a) **to be ~** ne pas être affecté/-e (**by** par)
(b) (natural) tout simple
unafraid adj ⟨person⟩ sans peur
unaided adv ⟨stand, sit, walk⟩ sans aide
unambiguous adj sans équivoque
unanimous adj unanime
unanimously adv ⟨agree, condemn⟩ unanimement; ⟨vote⟩ à l'unanimité
unannounced adv ⟨arrive, call⟩ sans prévenir
unanswered adj ⟨letter, question⟩ resté/-e sans réponse
unappetizing adj peu appétissant/-e
unappreciative adj ⟨person, audience⟩ ingrat/-e
unapproachable adj inaccessible
unarmed adj ⟨person⟩ non armé/-e; ⟨combat⟩ sans armes
unashamedly adv ouvertement
unasked adv ⟨come, attend⟩ sans être invité/-e; **to do sth ~** faire qch spontanément
unassuming adj modeste
unattached adj (a) ⟨part, element⟩ détaché/-e
(b) (single) ⟨person⟩ célibataire
unattainable adj inaccessible
unattractive adj ⟨person⟩ peu attirant/-e; ⟨proposition⟩ peu intéressant/-e (**to** pour)

✓ indicates a very frequent word

t
u

unauthorized *adj* fait/-e sans autorisation

unavailable *adj* to be ∼ ⟨person⟩ ne pas être disponible

unavoidable *adj* inévitable

unaware *adj* (a) (not informed) to be ∼ that ignorer que
(b) (not conscious) to be ∼ of sth ne pas être conscient/-e de qch

unawares *adv* to catch *or* take sb ∼ prendre qn au dépourvu

unbearable *adj* insupportable

unbeatable *adj* imbattable

unbeknown *adv* ∼ to sb à l'insu de qn

unbelievable *adj* incroyable

unbending *adj* inflexible

unbias(s)ed *adj* impartial/-e

unblock *vtr* déboucher ⟨pipe, sink⟩; désimlocker ⟨mobile phone⟩

unborn *adj* ⟨child⟩ à naître; her ∼ child l'enfant qu'elle porte/portait etc

unbreakable *adj* incassable

unbroken *adj* (a) ⟨sequence, silence, view⟩ ininterrompu/-e
(b) ⟨pottery⟩ intact/-e

unbuckle *vtr* déboucler ⟨belt⟩; défaire la boucle de ⟨shoe⟩

unbutton *vtr* déboutonner

uncalled-for *adj* ⟨remark⟩ déplacé/-e

uncanny *adj* ⟨resemblance⟩ étrange; ⟨accuracy⟩ étonnant/-e; ⟨silence⟩ troublant/-e

uncaring *adj* ⟨world⟩ indifférent/-e

uncertain ⟦1⟧ *adj* (a) (unsure) incertain/-e; to be ∼ about ne pas être certain/-e de
(b) (changeable) ⟨temper⟩ instable; ⟨weather⟩ variable
⟦2⟧ in no ∼ terms *phr* ⟨state⟩ en termes on ne peut plus clairs

uncertainty *n* incertitude *f*

unchallenged *adj* incontesté/-e; to go ∼ ⟨statement, decision⟩ ne pas être récusé/-e

unchanged *adj* inchangé/-e

uncharacteristic *adj* ⟨generosity⟩ peu habituel/-elle; it was ∼ of him to… ce n'est pas son genre de…

uncharitable *adj* peu charitable

unchecked *adv* de manière incontrôlée

uncivilized *adj* (a) (inhumane) ⟨treatment, conditions⟩ inhumain/-e
(b) (uncouth, rude) grossier/-ière
(c) (barbarous) ⟨people, nation⟩ non civilisé/-e

uncle *n* oncle *m*

unclear *adj* (a) ⟨motive, reason⟩ peu clair/-e; it is ∼ how/whether… on ne sait pas très bien comment/si…
(b) ⟨instructions, voice⟩ pas clair/-e; ⟨answer⟩ peu clair/-e; ⟨handwriting⟩ difficile à lire

uncomfortable *adj* (a) ⟨shoes, garment, seat⟩ inconfortable; ⟨journey, heat⟩ pénible; you look ∼ in that chair tu n'as pas l'air à l'aise dans ce fauteuil
(b) ⟨feeling, silence, situation⟩ pénible; to make sb (feel) ∼ mettre qn mal à l'aise

uncommon *adj* rare

uncommunicative *adj* peu communicatif/-ive

uncomplimentary *adj* peu flatteur/-euse

uncompromising *adj* intransigeant/-e

unconcerned *adj* (uninterested) indifférent/-e (with à); (not caring) insouciant/-e; (untroubled) imperturbable

unconditional *adj* ⟨obedience, support, love⟩ inconditionnel/-elle; ⟨offer, surrender⟩ sans condition

unconfirmed *adj* non confirmé/-e

unconnected *adj* ⟨incidents, facts⟩ sans lien entre eux/elles; to be ∼ with ⟨event, fact⟩ n'avoir aucun rapport avec; ⟨person⟩ n'avoir aucun lien avec

unconscious ⟦1⟧ *n* the ∼ l'inconscient *m*
⟦2⟧ *adj* (a) (insensible) sans connaissance; to knock sb ∼ assommer qn
(b) (unaware) to be ∼ of sth ne pas être conscient/-e de qch
(c) ⟨bias, hostility⟩ inconscient/-e

unconstitutional *adj* inconstitutionnel/-elle

uncontested *adj* ⟨leader, fact⟩ incontesté/-e; ⟨seat⟩ non disputé/-e

uncontrollable *adj* ⟨emotion⟩ incontrôlable; ⟨tears⟩ qu'on ne peut retenir

uncontrollably *adv* ⟨laugh, sob⟩ sans pouvoir se contrôler

unconventional *adj* peu conventionnel/-elle

unconvincing *adj* peu convaincant/-e

uncooked *adj* non cuit/-e

uncooperative *adj* peu coopératif/-ive

uncoordinated *adj* ⟨efforts, service⟩ désordonné/-e; to be ∼ ⟨person⟩ manquer de coordination

uncouth *adj* ⟨person⟩ grossier/-ière; ⟨accent⟩ peu raffiné/-e

uncover *vtr* dévoiler ⟨scandal⟩; découvrir ⟨evidence, body⟩

uncritical *adj* peu critique

unctuous *adj* onctueux/-euse, mielleux/-euse

uncut *adj* (a) ⟨film, version⟩ intégral/-e
(b) ⟨gem⟩ non taillé/-e

undamaged *adj* ⟨crops⟩ non endommagé/-e; ⟨building, reputation⟩ intact/-e

undecided *adj* ⟨person⟩ indécis/-e; ⟨outcome⟩ incertain/-e

undemanding *adj* ⟨task⟩ peu fatigant/-e; ⟨person⟩ peu exigeant/-e

undemocratic *adj* antidémocratique

undemonstrative *adj* peu démonstratif/-ive

undeniable *adj* indéniable

✔ **under** ① *prep* (a) sous; ~ **the bed** sous le lit; ~ **it** en dessous; **it's** ~ **there** c'est là-dessous; ~ **letter D** sous la lettre D
(b) (less than) ~ **£10** moins de 10 livres sterling; **children** ~ **five** les enfants de moins de cinq ans *or* au-dessous de cinq ans; **a number** ~ **ten** un nombre inférieur à dix; **temperatures** ~ **10°C** des températures inférieures à *or* au-dessous de 10°C
(c) (according to) ~ **the law** selon la loi
(d) (subordinate to) sous; **I have 50 people** ~ **me** j'ai 50 employés sous mes ordres
② *adv* (a) ‹crawl, sit, hide› en dessous; **to go** ~ ‹diver, swimmer› disparaître sous l'eau
(b) (less) moins; **£10 and** ~ 10 livres sterling et moins; **children of six and** ~ des enfants de six ans et au-dessous
(c) (anaesthetized) **to put sb** ~ endormir qn

underachieve *vi* (Sch) ne pas obtenir les résultats dont on est capable

underachiever *n* (Sch) sous-performant/-e *m/f*

underage *adj* ~ **drinking** la consommation d'alcool par les mineurs; **to be** ~ être mineur/-e

undercarriage *n* train *m* d'atterrissage

underclass *n* classe *f* sous-prolétariat

underclothes *n pl* sous-vêtements *mpl*

undercoat *n* couche *f* de fond

undercooked *adj* pas assez cuit/-e; **the meat is** ~ la viande n'est pas assez cuite

undercover *adj* ‹activity, group› clandestin/-e; ‹agent› secret/-ète

undercurrent *n* (in water) courant *m* profond; (in sea) courant *m* sous-marin; (figurative) courant *m* sous-jacent

undercut *vtr* (*p prés* **-tt-**, *prét, pp* **-cut**) concurrencer ‹prices›

underdeveloped *adj* ‹country› sous-développé/-e; ‹negative› pas assez développé/-e

underdog *n* (in society) opprimé/-e *m/f*; (in game, contest) perdant/-e *m/f*

underdone *adj* ‹food› pas assez cuit/-e; ‹steak› (GB) saignant/-e

underestimate *vtr* sous-estimer

underexpose *vtr* sous-exposer

underfed *adj* sous-alimenté/-e

underfoot *adv* sous les pieds; **the ground was wet** ~ le sol était humide

underfunded *adj* insuffisamment financé/-e

undergo *vtr* (*prét* **-went**, *pp* **-gone**) subir ‹change, test, operation›; suivre ‹treatment, training›; **to** ~ **surgery** subir une intervention chirurgicale

undergraduate *n* étudiant/-e *m/f*

✔ indicates a very frequent word

underground ① *n* (a) (GB) (subway) métro *m*; **on the** ~ dans le métro
(b) **the** ~ (political) la clandestinité; (artistic) l'underground *m*
② *adj* (a) (below ground) souterrain/-e
(b) (secret) clandestin/-e
(c) (artistic) underground *inv*
③ *adv* (a) (below ground) sous terre
(b) (secretly) **to go** ~ passer dans la clandestinité

underground train *n* rame *f* (de métro)

undergrowth *n* sous-bois *m*

underhand *adj* (*also* **underhanded**, (US)) ‹person, method› sournois/-e; ~ **dealings** magouilles *fpl* (fam)

underline *vtr* souligner

underling *n* subordonné/-e *m/f*

underlying *adj* ‹problem› sous-jacent/-e

undermine *vtr* saper ‹foundations, authority, efforts›; ébranler ‹confidence, position›

underneath ① *n* dessous *m*
② *adv* dessous, en dessous
③ *prep* sous, au-dessous de; **from** ~ **a pile of books** de dessous une pile de livres

undernourished *adj* sous-alimenté/-e

underpants *n pl* slip *m*; **a pair of** ~ un slip

underpass *n* (for traffic) voie *f* inférieure; (for pedestrians) passage *m* souterrain

underpay *vtr* (*prét, pp* **-paid**) sous-payer ‹employee›

underprivileged *adj* défavorisé/-e

underrate *vtr* sous-estimer

under-secretary *n* (*also* ~ **of state**) (GB); sous-secrétaire *mf* d'État

undersell ① *vtr* (*prét, pp* **-sold**) vendre moins cher que ‹competitor›
② *v refl* (*prét, pp* **-sold**) **to** ~ **oneself** se dévaloriser

undershirt *n* (US) maillot *m* de corps

understaffed *adj* **to be** ~ manquer de personnel

✔ **understand** ① *vtr* (*prét, pp* **-stood**)
(a) (gen) comprendre; **to make oneself understood** se faire comprendre
(b) (believe) **to** ~ **that** croire que
② *vi* (*prét, pp* **-stood**) comprendre (**about** à propos de)

understandable *adj* compréhensible; **it's** ~ ça se comprend

understandably *adv* naturellement

✔ **understanding** ① *n* (a) (grasp of subject, issue) compréhension *f*
(b) (arrangement) entente *f* (**about** sur; **between** entre)
(c) (sympathy) compréhension *f*
(d) (powers of reason) entendement *m*
② *adj* ‹tone› bienveillant/-e; ‹person› compréhensif/-ive

understatement *n* litote *f*

understudy n doublure f (to de)

undertake vtr (prét **-took**, pp **-taken**)
(a) entreprendre ‹search, study, trip›; se
charger de ‹mission, offensive›
(b) to ∼ to do s'engager à faire

undertaker n (GB) (person) entrepreneur
m de pompes funèbres; (company) entreprise f
de pompes funèbres

undertaking n (a) (venture) entreprise f
(b) (promise) garantie f

under-the-counter adj ‹goods, trade›
illicite; ‹payment› sous le manteau

undertone n (a) (low voice) voix f basse
(b) (hint) nuance f

undervalue vtr (a) (financially) sous-évaluer
(b) sous-estimer ‹person, quality›

underwater 1 adj ‹cable, exploration›
sous-marin/-e; ‹lighting› sous l'eau
2 adv sous l'eau

underway adj to get ∼ ‹vehicle› se mettre
en route; ‹season› commencer

underwear n sous-vêtements mpl

underweight adj trop maigre

underworld n milieu m, pègre f

undesirable adj ‹aspect, habit, result›
indésirable; ‹influence› néfaste; ‹friend› peu
recommandable

undetected adv ‹break in, listen› sans
être aperçu/-e; to go ∼ ‹person› rester
inaperçu/-e; ‹cancer› rester non décelé/-e;
‹crime› rester non découvert/-e

undeterred adj to be ∼ by sb/sth ne pas
se laisser démonter par qn/qch

undeveloped adj ‹person, organ, idea›
non développé/-e; ‹land› inexploité/-e;
‹country› sous-développé/-e

undignified adj indigne

undisciplined adj indiscipliné/-e

undiscovered adj ‹secret› non révélé/-e;
‹land› inexploré/-e; ‹crime, document› non
découvert/-e

undiscriminating adj sans
discernement

undisguised adj non déguisé/-e

undisputed adj incontesté/-e

undisturbed adj ‹sleep› paisible,
tranquille; to leave sb/sth ∼ ne pas
déranger qn/qch

undivided adj to give sb one's ∼ attention
accorder à qn toute son attention

undo vtr (3ᵉ pers sg prés **-does**, prét **-did**,
pp **-done**) (a) défaire ‹button, lock›; ouvrir
‹parcel›
(b) annuler ‹good, effort›

undocumented adj (a) (immigrant) sans
papiers
(b) (Comput) non documenté/-e

undone adj défait/-e; to come ∼ ‹parcel,
button› se défaire

undoubtedly adv indubitablement

undress 1 vtr déshabiller
2 vi se déshabiller

undrinkable adj (unpleasant) imbuvable;
(dangerous) non potable

undue adj excessif/-ive

unduly adv ‹optimistic, surprised›
excessivement; ‹neglect, worry› outre mesure

unearthly adj ‹light, landscape›
surnaturel/-elle; ‹cry, silence› étrange; at an
∼ hour à une heure indue

uneasily adv (a) (anxiously) avec inquiétude
(b) (uncomfortably) avec gêne

uneasiness n (worry) appréhension f
(about au sujet de); (dissatisfaction) malaise m

uneasy adj (a) ‹person› inquiet/-iète (about,
at au sujet de); ‹conscience› pas tranquille
(b) ‹compromise› difficile; ‹peace› boiteux/
-euse; ‹silence› gêné/-e
(c) ‹sleep› agité/-e

uneconomical adj ‹wasteful› pas
économique; (not profitable) pas rentable

uneducated adj (a) ‹person› sans
instruction
(b) ‹person, speech› inculte; ‹accent, tastes›
commun/-e

unemotional adj ‹person› impassible;
‹account, reunion› froid/-e

unemployed 1 n the ∼ les chômeurs
mpl
2 adj au chômage, sans emploi

unemployment n chômage m

unemployment benefit (GB),
unemployment compensation
(US) n allocations fpl de chômage

unemployment rate n taux m de
chômage

unenthusiastic adj peu enthousiaste

unenviable adj peu enviable

unequal adj ‹amounts, contest, pay›
inégal/-e

unequivocal adj ‹person, declaration›
explicite; ‹answer, support› sans équivoque

unethical adj (gen) contraire à la morale;
(Med) contraire à la déontologie

uneven adj ‹hem, teeth› irrégulier/-ière;
‹contest, surface› inégal/-e

uneventful adj ‹day, life, career› ordinaire;
‹journey, period› sans histoires

unexciting adj sans intérêt

unexpected adj ‹arrival, success›
imprévu/-e; ‹ally, outcome› inattendu/-e;
‹death› inopiné/-e

unexpectedly adv ‹happen›
à l'improviste; ‹large, small, fast›
étonnamment

unexplored adj inexploré/-e

unfailing adj ‹support› fidèle; ‹optimism› à
toute épreuve; ‹efforts› constant/-e

unfair adj injuste (to, on envers; to do
de faire); ‹play, tactics› irrégulier/-ière; ⋯⟩

⟨*trading*⟩ frauduleux/-euse
unfair dismissal n licenciement m abusif
unfairness n injustice f
unfaithful adj infidèle (**to** à)
unfamiliar adj (a) ⟨*face, name, place*⟩ inconnu/-e (**to** à); ⟨*concept, feeling, situation*⟩ inhabituel/-elle (**to** à)
(b) **to be** ~ **with** sth ne pas connaître qch
unfashionable adj qui n'est pas à la mode
unfasten vtr défaire ⟨*clothing, button*⟩; ouvrir ⟨*bag*⟩
unfavourable adj défavorable
unfinished adj ⟨*work*⟩ inachevé/-e; **to have** ~ **business** avoir des choses à régler
unfit adj (a) (out of condition) qui n'est pas en forme
(b) ⟨*housing*⟩ inadéquat/-e; ⟨*pitch, road*⟩ impraticable (**for** à); ~ **for human consumption** impropre à la consommation humaine
unflattering adj peu flatteur/-euse
unfold ⟨1⟩ vtr déplier ⟨*paper, map, deck chair*⟩; déployer ⟨*wings*⟩; décroiser ⟨*arms*⟩
⟨2⟩ vi (a) ⟨*leaf*⟩ s'ouvrir
(b) ⟨*scene*⟩ se dérouler; ⟨*mystery*⟩ se dévoiler
unforeseeable adj imprévisible
unforeseen adj imprévu/-e
unforgettable adj inoubliable
unforgivable adj impardonnable
unforgiving adj impitoyable
unfortunate adj (a) (pitiable) malheureux/-euse
(b) (regrettable) ⟨*incident, choice*⟩ malencontreux/-euse; ⟨*remark*⟩ fâcheux/-euse
(c) (unlucky) malchanceux/-euse
⚔ **unfortunately** adv malheureusement
unfounded adj sans fondement
unfriendly adj ⟨*person, attitude, reception*⟩ peu amical/-e; ⟨*place*⟩ inhospitalier/-ière
unfulfilled adj ⟨*ambition*⟩ non réalisé/-e; ⟨*desire, need*⟩ inassouvi/-e; **to feel** ~ se sentir insatisfait/-e
unfurnished adj non meublé/-e
ungracious adj désobligeant/-e (**of** de la part de)
ungrammatical adj incorrect/-e
ungrateful adj ingrat/-e (**of** de la part de; **towards** envers)
unhappily adv (a) (miserably) d'un air malheureux
(b) (unfortunately) malheureusement
(c) (inappropriately) malencontreusement
unhappiness n (a) (misery) tristesse f
(b) (dissatisfaction) mécontentement m

unhappy adj (a) ⟨*person, childhood, situation*⟩ malheureux/-euse; ⟨*face, occasion*⟩ triste
(b) (dissatisfied) mécontent/-e; **to be** ~ **with** sth ne pas être satisfait/-e de qch
(c) (concerned) inquiet/-iète
unharmed adj ⟨*person*⟩ indemne; ⟨*object*⟩ intact/-e
unhealthy adj (a) ⟨*person*⟩ maladif/-ive; ⟨*diet*⟩ malsain/-e; ⟨*conditions*⟩ insalubre
(b) (unwholesome) malsain/-e
unheard-of adj (a) (shocking) inouï/-e
(b) ⟨*price*⟩ record; ⟨*actor*⟩ inconnu/-e
unheeded adj **to go** ~ ⟨*warning, plea*⟩ rester vain/-e
unhelpful adj ⟨*employee*⟩ peu serviable; ⟨*attitude*⟩ peu obligeant/-e
unhindered adj ~ **by** sans être entravé/-e par ⟨*rules*⟩; sans être encombré/-e par ⟨*luggage*⟩
unhook vtr dégrafer ⟨*skirt*⟩; décrocher ⟨*picture*⟩ (**from** de)
unhurried adj ⟨*person*⟩ posé/-e; ⟨*pace, meal*⟩ tranquille
unhygienic adj ⟨*conditions*⟩ insalubre; ⟨*way, method*⟩ peu hygiénique
unidentified adj non identifié/-e
unification n unification f (**of** de)
uniform ⟨1⟩ n uniforme m
⟨2⟩ adj identique; ⟨*temperature*⟩ constant/-e
unify vtr unifier
unilateral adj unilatéral/-e
unimaginative adj ⟨*style*⟩ sans originalité; **to be** ~ manquer d'imagination
unimpeded adj ⟨*access, influx*⟩ libre
unimportant adj sans importance
unimpressed adj **to be** ~ être peu impressionné/-e par ⟨*person, performance*⟩; n'être guère convaincu/-e par ⟨*argument*⟩
uninhabitable adj inhabitable
uninhabited adj inhabité/-e
uninhibited adj ⟨*person*⟩ sans complexes (**about** en ce qui concerne)
uninitiated n **the** ~ les profanes
uninjured adj indemne
uninspired adj ⟨*approach*⟩ terne; ⟨*performance*⟩ honnête; **to be** ~ ⟨*person*⟩ manquer d'inspiration; ⟨*strategy*⟩ manquer d'imagination
unintelligible adj incompréhensible
unintended adj ⟨*slur, irony*⟩ involontaire; ⟨*consequence*⟩ non voulu/-e
unintentional adj involontaire
uninterested adj indifférent/-e (**in** à)
uninteresting adj sans intérêt
uninvited adj ⟨*attentions*⟩ non sollicité/-e; ⟨*remark*⟩ gratuit/-e; ~ **guest** intrus/-e m/f
uninviting adj ⟨*place*⟩ rébarbatif/-ive; ⟨*food*⟩ peu appétissant/-e

U

⚔ **union** n (a) (also **trade** ~) syndicat m

(b) (uniting) union *f*; (marriage) union *f*, mariage *m*

Unionist *n, adj* unioniste *mf*

Union Jack *n* drapeau *m* du Royaume-Uni

⟨ **unique** *adj* **(a)** (sole) unique; **to be ∼ to** être particulier/-ière à
(b) (remarkable) unique, exceptionnel/-elle

unisex *adj* unisexe

unison *n* **in ∼** à l'unisson

⟨ **unit** *n* **(a)** (gen) unité *f*
(b) (group) groupe *m*; (in army, police) unité *f*
(c) (department) (gen, Med) service *m*
(d) (piece of furniture) élément *m*

unite ☐1 *vtr* unir (**with** à)
☐2 *vi* s'unir (**with** à)

⟨ **united** *adj* ⟨group, front⟩ uni/-e (**in** dans); ⟨effort⟩ conjoint/-e

United Kingdom *pr n* Royaume-Uni *m*

United Nations (Organization) *n* (Organisation *f* des) Nations *fpl* unies

United States (of America) *pr n* États-Unis *mpl* (d'Amérique)

unit trust *n* ≈ société *f* d'investissement à capital variable, SICAV *f*

unity *n* unité *f*

universal *adj* ⟨acclaim, reaction⟩ général/-e; ⟨education⟩ pour tous; ⟨principle, truth⟩ universel/-elle

universally *adv* ⟨believed⟩ par tous, universellement; ⟨known, loved⟩ de tous

universe *n* univers *m*

⟨ **university** *n* université *f*

unjust *adj* injuste (**to** envers)

unjustified *adj* injustifié/-e

unkempt *adj* ⟨appearance⟩ négligé/-e; ⟨hair⟩ ébouriffé/-e; ⟨beard⟩ peu soigné/-e

unkind *adj* ⟨person, thought, act⟩ pas très gentil/-ille; ⟨remark⟩ désobligeant/-e; **to be ∼ to sb** (by deed) ne pas être gentil/-ille avec qn; (verbally) être méchant/-e avec qn

unknown ☐1 *n* **(a) the ∼** l'inconnu *m*
(b) (person) inconnu/-e *m/f*
☐2 *adj* inconnu/-e

unlace *vtr* délacer

unlawful *adj* ⟨activity⟩ illégal/-e; ⟨detention⟩ arbitraire; **∼ killing** meurtre *m*

unlawfully *adv* illégalement

unleaded petrol (GB), **unleaded gasoline** (US) *n* essence *f* sans plomb

unleavened *adj* sans levain

⟨ **unless** *conj* à moins que (+ *subjunctive*), à moins de (+ *infinitive*); **he won't come ∼ you invite him** il ne viendra pas à moins que tu (ne) l'invites; **she can't take the job ∼ she finds a nanny** elle ne peut pas accepter le poste à moins de trouver une nourrice

⟨ **unlike** *prep* **(a)** (in contrast to) contrairement à, à la différence de; **∼ me, he…** contrairement à moi, il…
(b) (different from) différent/-e de

(c) (uncharacteristic of) **it's ∼ her (to be so rude)** ça ne lui ressemble pas (d'être aussi impolie)

⟨ **unlikely** *adj* **(a)** (unexpected) improbable, peu probable; **it is ∼ that** il est peu probable que (+ *subjunctive*)
(b) ⟨partner, choice, situation⟩ inattendu/-e
(c) ⟨story⟩ invraisemblable

unlimited *adj* illimité/-e; ⟨access⟩ libre (*before n*)

unlined *adj* **(a)** ⟨garment, curtain⟩ sans doublure
(b) ⟨paper⟩ non réglé

unload ☐1 *vtr* **(a)** décharger ⟨goods, vessel, gun, camera⟩
(b) (get rid of) se décharger de ⟨feelings⟩ (**on(to)** sur); se débarrasser de ⟨goods⟩
☐2 *vi* ⟨truck, ship⟩ décharger

unlock *vtr* ouvrir ⟨door⟩; **to be ∼ed** ne pas être fermé/-e à clé

unluckily *adv* malheureusement (**for** pour)

unlucky *adj* **(a)** ⟨person⟩ malchanceux/-euse; ⟨event⟩ malencontreux/-euse; ⟨day⟩ de malchance
(b) ⟨number, colour⟩ néfaste, maléfique; **it's ∼ to do** ça porte malheur de faire

unmade *adj* ⟨bed⟩ défait/-e

unmanageable *adj* ⟨child, dog⟩ difficile; ⟨system⟩ ingérable; ⟨hair⟩ rebelle

unmarried *adj* célibataire

unmistakable *adj* **(a)** (recognizable) caractéristique (**of** de)
(b) (unambiguous) sans ambiguïté
(c) (marked) net/nette

unmotivated *adj* ⟨act⟩ gratuit/-e; ⟨person⟩ non motivé/-e

unmoved *adj* (unconcerned) indifférent/-e (**by** à); (emotionally) insensible (**by** à)

unnamed *adj* (name not divulged) ⟨company, source⟩ dont le nom n'a pas été divulgué; (without name) **as yet ∼** encore à la recherche d'un nom

unnatural *adj* **(a)** (odd) anormal/-e; **it is ∼ that** ce n'est pas normal que (+ *subjunctive*)
(b) ⟨style, laugh⟩ affecté/-e
(c) ⟨silence, colour⟩ insolite

unnecessarily *adv* inutilement

unnecessary *adj* **(a)** (not needed) inutile; **it is ∼ to do** il est inutile de faire; **it is ∼ for you to do** il est inutile que tu fasses
(b) (uncalled for) déplacé/-e

unnerve *vtr* décontenancer, rendre [qn] nerveux/-euse

unnoticed *adj* inaperçu/-e

unobstructed *adj* ⟨view, exit, road⟩ dégagé/-e

unobtainable *adj* ⟨supplies⟩ impossible à se procurer; ⟨number⟩ impossible à obtenir

unobtrusive *adj* ⟨person⟩ effacé/-e; ⟨site, object, noise⟩ discret/-ète

unoccupied *adj* ⟨house, shop⟩ inoccupé/-e; ⟨seat⟩ libre

u

unofficial adj ‹figure› officieux/-ieuse; ‹candidate› indépendant/-e; ‹strike› sauvage

unorthodox adj peu orthodoxe

unpack vtr défaire ‹suitcase›; déballer ‹belongings›

unpaid adj ‹bill, tax› impayé/-e; ‹debt› non acquitté/-e; ‹work› non rémunéré/-e; ~ leave congé m sans solde

unpalatable adj (a) ‹truth, statistic› inconfortable; ‹advice› dur/-e à avaler
(b) ‹food› qui n'a pas bon goût

unparalleled adj (a) ‹strength, luxury› sans égal; ‹success› hors pair
(b) (unprecedented) sans précédent

unpasteurized adj ‹milk› cru/-e; ‹cheese› au lait cru

unperturbed adj imperturbable

unplanned adj ‹stoppage, increase› imprévu/-e; ‹pregnancy, baby› non prévu/-e

unpleasant adj désagréable

unpleasantness n (a) (of odour, experience, remark) caractère m désagréable
(b) (bad feeling) dissensions fpl (between entre)

unplug vtr (p prés etc **-gg-**) débrancher ‹appliance›; déboucher ‹sink›

unpopular adj impopulaire

unprecedented adj sans précédent

unpredictable adj ‹event› imprévisible; ‹weather› incertain/-e; he's ~ on ne sait jamais à quoi s'attendre avec lui

unpremeditated adj non prémédité/-e

unprepared adj (a) ‹person› pas préparé/-e (for pour)
(b) ‹speech› improvisé/-e; ‹translation› non préparé/-e

unprepossessing adj peu avenant/-e

unpretentious adj sans prétention

unproductive adj improductif/-ive

unprofessional adj peu professionnel/-elle

unprofitable adj non rentable

unprotected adj ‹person, sex, area› sans protection (from contre)

unprovoked adj ‹attack, aggression› délibéré/-e

unqualified adj (a) ‹person› non qualifié/-e
(b) ‹support, respect› inconditionnel/-elle; ‹success› grand/-e (before n)

unquestionable adj incontestable

unravel ⟦1⟧ vtr (p prés etc **-ll-** (GB), **-l-** (US)) défaire ‹knitting›; démêler ‹thread, mystery›
⟦2⟧ vi (p prés etc **-ll-** (GB), **-l-** (US)) ‹knitting› se défaire; ‹mystery, thread› se démêler; ‹plot› se dénouer

unreal adj (a) (not real) irréel/-éelle
(b) (colloq) (unbelievable) incroyable

unrealistic adj irréaliste, peu réaliste

unreasonable adj (a) ‹behaviour, expectation› qui n'est pas raisonnable; he's being very ~ about it il n'est vraiment pas raisonnable
(b) ‹price, demand› excessif/-ive

unrecognizable adj méconnaissable

unrelated adj (a) (not connected) sans rapport (to avec)
(b) (as family) to be ~ ne pas avoir de lien de parenté

unrelenting adj ‹heat, stare, person› implacable; ‹pursuit, zeal› acharné/-e

unreliable adj ‹evidence› douteux/-euse; ‹method, employee› peu sûr/-e; ‹equipment› peu fiable; she's very ~ on ne peut pas compter sur elle

unrepentant adj impénitent/-e

unrequited adj ‹love› sans retour

unresolved adj irrésolu/-e

unrest n (a) (dissatisfaction) malaise m
(b) (agitation) troubles mpl

unrestricted adj ‹access› libre (before n); ‹power› illimité/-e

unrewarding adj (unfulfilling) peu gratifiant/-e; (thankless) ingrat/-e

unripe adj ‹fruit› pas mûr/-e

unrivalled adj sans égal

unroll vtr dérouler

unruffled adj (a) (calm) imperturbable
(b) ‹hair› lisse

unruly adj indiscipliné/-e

unsafe adj (a) ‹environment› malsain/-e; ‹drinking water› non potable; ‹goods, working conditions› dangereux/-euse
(b) (threatened) to feel ~ ne pas se sentir en sécurité

unsaid adj to leave sth ~ passer qch sous silence

unsatisfactory adj insatisfaisant/-e

unsatisfied adj ‹person› insatisfait/-e; ‹need› inassouvi/-e

unsatisfying adj peu satisfaisant/-e

unsavoury (GB), **unsavory** (US) adj ‹individual› louche, répugnant/-e

unscathed adj indemne

unscheduled adj ‹appearance, speech› surprise (after n); ‹flight› supplémentaire; ‹stop› qui n'a pas été prévu

unscrew vtr dévisser

unscrupulous adj ‹person› sans scrupules; ‹tactic› peu scrupuleux/-euse

unseat vtr désarçonner ‹rider›

unseen adv ‹escape, slip away› sans être vu/-e

unselfconscious adj (a) (natural) naturel/-elle
(b) (uninhibited) sans complexes

unselfish adj ‹person› qui pense aux autres; ‹act› désintéressé/-e

---

✧ indicates a very frequent word

unsentimental *adj* ‹*account, film*› qui ne donne pas dans la sensiblerie; ‹*person*› qui ne fait pas de sentiment

unsettled *adj* (a) ‹*weather, climate*› instable; ‹*person*› perturbé/-e
(b) ‹*account*› impayé/-e

unsettling *adj* ‹*question, experience*› troublant/-e; ‹*work of art*› dérangeant/-e

unshaken *adj* ‹*person*› imperturbable (**by** devant); ‹*belief*› inébranlable

unshaven *adj* pas rasé/-e

unskilled *adj* ‹*worker, labour*› non qualifié/-e; ‹*job, work*› qui n'exige pas de qualification professionnelle

unsociable *adj* peu sociable

unsocial *adj* to work ∼ hours travailler en dehors des heures normales

unsolicited *adj* non sollicité/-e

unsophisticated *adj* ‹*person*› sans façons; ‹*mind*› simple; ‹*analysis*› simpliste

unspeakable *adj* (a) (dreadful) ‹*pain, sorrow*› inexprimable; ‹*act*› innommable
(b) (inexpressible) (joy) indescriptible

unspoiled, **unspoilt** *adj* ‹*landscape, town*› préservé/-e intact

unspoken *adj* (a) (secret) inexprimé/-e
(b) (implicit) tacite

unstable *adj* instable

unsteady *adj* ‹*steps, legs, voice*› chancelant/-e; ‹*ladder*› instable; ‹*hand*› tremblant/-e; **to be** ∼ **on one's feet** marcher de façon mal assurée

unstoppable *adj* ‹*force, momentum*› irrésistible; ‹*athlete, leader*› imbattable

unstuck *adj* **to come** ∼ ‹*stamp*› se décoller; ‹*person*› connaître un échec

unsubscribe *vi* (Comput) se désabonner

unsubstantiated *adj* non corroboré/-e

unsuccessful *adj* (a) ‹*attempt, campaign*› infructueux/-euse; ‹*novel, film*› sans succès; ‹*effort, search*› vain/-e; **to be** ∼ ‹*attempt*› échouer
(b) ‹*candidate*› (for job) malchanceux/-euse; (in election) malheureux/-euse; ‹*businessperson*› malchanceux/-euse; ‹*artist*› inconnu/-e; **to be** ∼ **in doing** ne pas réussir à faire

unsuccessfully *adv* ‹*try*› en vain; ‹*challenge, bid*› sans succès

unsuitable *adj* ‹*location, clothing, accommodation, time*› inapproprié/-e; ‹*moment*› inopportun/-e; **to be** ∼ ne pas convenir (**for sb** à qn); **to be** ∼ **for a job** ne pas convenir pour un travail

unsupervised *adj* ‹*activity*› non encadré/-e; ‹*child*› laissé/-e sans surveillance

unsure *adj* peu sûr/-e (**of** de); **to be** ∼ **about how/why/where** ne pas savoir très bien comment/pourquoi/où; **to be** ∼ **of oneself** manquer de confiance en soi

unsuspecting *adj* ‹*person*› naïf/-ïve; ‹*public*› non averti/-e

unsweetened *adj* sans sucre, non sucré/-e

unsympathetic *adj* (a) (uncaring) ‹*person, attitude, tone*› peu compatissant/-e
(b) (unattractive) ‹*person, character*› antipathique

untaxed *adj* ‹*goods*› non taxé/-e; ‹*car*› sans vignette

untenable *adj* ‹*position*› intenable; ‹*claim, argument*› indéfendable

unthinkable *adj* impensable

untidily *adv* ‹*scattered, strewn*› en désordre; ∼ **dressed** habillé/-e de façon débraillée

untidy *adj* ‹*person*› (in habits) désordonné/-e; (in appearance) peu soigné/-e; ‹*habits, clothes*› négligé/-e; ‹*room*› en désordre

untie *vtr* (*p prés* **-tying**) défaire, dénouer ‹*knot, rope, laces*›; défaire ‹*parcel*›; délier ‹*hands, hostage*›

ᴓ **until**, *also* **till**

■ **Note** When used as a preposition in positive sentences, *until* is translated by *jusqu'à*: *they're staying until Monday* = ils restent jusqu'à lundi.
— Remember that *jusqu'à + le* becomes *jusqu'au* and *jusqu'à les* becomes *jusqu'aux*: *until the right moment* = jusqu'au bon moment; *until the exams* = jusqu'aux examens.
— In negative sentences, *not until* is translated by *ne…pas avant*: *I can't see you until Friday* = je ne peux pas vous voir avant vendredi.
— When used as a conjunction in positive sentences, *until* is translated by *jusqu'à ce que + subjunctive*: *we'll stay here until Maya comes back* = nous resterons ici jusqu'à ce que Maya revienne.
— In negative sentences where the two verbs have different subjects, *not until* is translated by *ne…pas avant que + subjunctive*: *we won't leave until Maya comes back* = nous ne partirons pas avant que Maya revienne.
— In negative sentences where the two verbs have the same subject, *not until* is translated by *pas avant de + infinitive*: *we won't leave until we've seen Claire* = nous ne partirons pas avant d'avoir vu Claire.
— For more examples and particular usages, see the entry below.

1 *prep* jusqu'à; (after negative verb) avant; ∼ **Tuesday** jusqu'à mardi; ∼ **the sixties** jusqu'aux années soixante; ∼ **now** jusqu'à présent; ∼ **then** jusqu'à ce moment-là, jusque-là; **(up)** ∼ **1901** jusqu'en *or* jusqu'à 1901; **valid (up)** ∼ **April 2006** valable jusqu'en avril 2006; **to work from Monday** ∼ **Saturday** travailler du lundi au samedi

2 *conj* jusqu'à ce que (+ *subjunctive*); (in negative constructions) avant que (+ *subjunctive*), avant de (+ *infinitive*); **we'll stay** ∼ **a solution is reached** nous resterons jusqu'à ce que nous trouvions une solution; **let's watch TV** ∼ **he's ready** regardons la télévision en attendant qu'il soit prêt; **I'll wait** ∼ **I get back** ⸽⸽⸽

u

j'attendrai d'être rentré (**before doing** pour faire); **she waited ~ they were alone** elle a attendu qu'ils soient seuls

untimely *adj* ‹*arrival, announcement*› inopportun/-e; ‹*death*› prématuré/-e

untold *adj* (not quantifiable) **~ millions** des millions et des millions; **~ damage** d'énormes dégâts; (endless) indicible

untrained *adj* ‹*worker*› sans formation; ‹*eye*› inexercé/-e; **to be ~** n'avoir aucune formation

untranslatable *adj* intraduisible (**into** en)

untroubled *adj* ‹*face, life*› paisible; **to be ~** (by news) ne pas être troublé/-e (**by** par)

untrue *adj* faux/fausse

untrustworthy *adj* ‹*information*› douteux/-euse; ‹*person*› indigne de confiance

unused¹ *adj* **to be ~ to sth/to doing** ne pas être habitué/-e à qch/à faire

unused² *adj* ‹*machine, building*› inutilisé/-e; ‹*stamp*› neuf/neuve

unusual *adj* ‹*colour, animal, flower*› peu commun/-e; ‹*feature, occurrence, skill*› peu commun/-e, inhabituel/-elle; ‹*dish, dress, person*› original/-e; **it is ~ to find/see** il est rare de trouver/voir; **there's nothing ~ about it** cela n'a rien d'extraordinaire

unusually *adv* exceptionnellement

unwanted *adj* ‹*goods, produce*› superflu/-e; ‹*pet*› abandonné/-e; ‹*visitor*› indésirable; ‹*child*› non souhaité/-e; **to feel ~** se sentir de trop

unwarranted *adj* injustifié/-e

unwary *n* **the ~** les imprudents *mpl*

unwelcome *adj* ‹*visitor, interruption*› importun/-e; ‹*news*› fâcheux/-euse

unwell *adj* souffrant/-e; **he is feeling ~** il ne se sent pas très bien

unwilling *adj* ‹*attention, departure*› forcé/-e; **he is ~ to do it** il n'est pas disposé à le faire; (stronger) il ne veut pas le faire

unwillingness *n* réticence *f* (**to do** à faire)

unwind **1** *vtr* (*prét, pp* **-wound**) dérouler ‹*cable, bandage, scarf*›
2 *vi* (*prét, pp* **-wound**) (a) ‹*tape, cable, scarf*› se dérouler
(b) (relax) se relaxer

unwise *adj* ‹*choice, loan, decision*› peu judicieux/-ieuse; ‹*person*› imprudent/-e

unwisely *adv* imprudemment

unwittingly *adv* (innocently) innocemment; (without wanting to) involontairement

unworthy *adj* indigne (**of** de)

unwrap *vtr* (*p prés etc* **-pp-**) déballer ‹*parcel*›

unwritten *adj* ‹*rule, agreement*› tacite

♪ indicates a very frequent word

unzip *vtr* (*p prés etc* **-pp-**) (a) (open) défaire la fermeture à glissière de ‹*garment, bag*›
(b) (Comput) dézipper, décompresser

♪ **up** **1** *adj* (a) (out of bed) **she's ~** elle est levée; **we were ~ very late last night** nous nous sommes couchés très tard hier soir; **they were ~ all night** ils ont veillé toute la nuit; **I was still ~ at 2 am** j'étais toujours debout à 2 heures du matin
(b) (higher in amount, level) **sales are ~ (by 10%)** les ventes ont augmenté (de 10%); **numbers of students are ~** le nombre d'étudiants est en hausse
(c) (colloq) (wrong) **what's ~?** qu'est-ce qui se passe?; **what's ~ with him?** qu'est-ce qu'il a?
(d) (erected, affixed) **the notice is ~ on the board** l'annonce est affichée sur le panneau; **is the tent ~?** est-ce que la tente est déjà montée?; **he had his hand ~ for five minutes** il a gardé la main levée pendant cinq minutes
(e) (open) **the blinds were ~** les stores étaient levés; **when the lever is ~ the machine is off** si le levier est vers le haut la machine est arrêtée
(f) (finished) **'time's ~!'** 'c'est l'heure!'; **when the four days were ~** à la fin des quatre jours
(g) (facing upwards) **'this side ~'** 'haut'; **she was floating face ~** elle flottait sur le dos
(h) (pinned up) **her hair was ~** elle avait les cheveux relevés
2 *adv* (a) **~ here/there** là-haut; **~ on the wardrobe** sur l'armoire; **~ in the tree/the clouds** dans l'arbre/les nuages; **~ in London** à Londres; **~ to/in Scotland** en Écosse; **~ North** au Nord; **four floors ~ from here** quatre étages au-dessus; **on the second shelf ~** sur la deuxième étagère en partant du bas
(b) (ahead) d'avance; **to be four points ~ (on sb)** avoir quatre points d'avance (sur qn)
(c) (upwards) **T-shirts from £2 ~** des T-shirts à partir de deux livres
3 *prep* **~ the tree** dans l'arbre; **the library is ~ the stairs** la bibliothèque se trouve en haut de l'escalier; **he ran ~ the stairs** il a monté l'escalier en courant; **he lives just ~ the road** il habite juste à côté; **to walk/drive ~ the road** remonter la rue; **he put it ~ his sleeve** il l'a mis dans sa manche
4 **up above** *phr* au-dessus; **~ above sth** au-dessus de qch
5 **up against** *phr* contre ‹*wall*›; **to come ~ against** rencontrer ‹*opposition*›
6 **up and about** *phr* debout; **to be ~ and about again** être de nouveau sur pied
7 **up and down** *phr* (a) (to and fro) **to walk ~ and down** aller et venir, faire les cent pas
(b) (throughout) **~ and down the country** dans tout le pays
8 **up to** *phr* (a) (to particular level) jusqu'à; **~ to here/there** jusqu'ici/jusque là

(b) (as many as) jusqu'à, près de;
∼ **to 20 people/50 dollars** jusqu'à
20 personnes/50 dollars
(c) (until) jusqu'à; ∼ **to 1964** jusqu'en 1964;
∼ **to 10.30 pm** jusqu'à 22 h 30; ∼ **to now**
jusqu'à maintenant
(d) I'm not ∼ **to it** (not capable) je n'en suis
pas capable; (not well enough) je n'en ai pas la
force; (can't face it) je n'en ai pas le courage
(e) it's ∼ **to him to do** c'est à lui de faire; **it's**
∼ **to you!** c'est à toi de décider!
(f) (doing) **what is he** ∼ **to?** qu'est-ce qu'il
fait?; **they're** ∼ **to something** ils mijotent
quelque chose (fam)
IDIOMS **to be one** ∼ **on sb** faire mieux que
qn; **to be (well)** ∼ **on** s'y connaître en ‹art,
history›; être au courant de ‹news›; **the** ∼**s
and downs** les hauts et les bas **(of de)**
up and coming adj prometteur/-euse
upbeat adj optimiste
upbringing n éducation f
update vtr **(a)** (revise) mettre or remettre
[qch] à jour ‹database, information›;
actualiser ‹price, value›
(b) (modernize) moderniser
(c) (inform) mettre [qn] au courant **(on** de)
upfront adj (colloq) **(a)** (frank) franc/franche
(b) ‹money› payé/-e d'avance
upgrade 1 n (new version) nouvelle
version f, mise f à jour; (in tourism)
surclassement m
2 vtr **(a)** (modernize) moderniser; (improve)
améliorer
(b) (Comput) améliorer ‹software, hardware›
(c) (raise) promouvoir ‹person›; revaloriser
‹job›
upheaval n **(a)** (disturbance) bouleversement
m
(b) (instability) (political, emotional)
bouleversements mpl; (physical) remue-
ménage m inv
uphill 1 adj **(a)** ‹road› qui monte; ∼ **slope**
côte f, montée f
(b) ‹task› difficile
2 adv **to go/walk** ∼ monter
uphold vtr (prét, pp **-held**) soutenir
‹right›; faire respecter ‹law›; confirmer
‹decision›
upholstery n **(a)** (covering) revêtement m
(b) (stuffing) rembourrage m
upkeep n **(a)** (of property) entretien m **(of** de)
(b) (cost) frais mpl d'entretien
uplifting adj tonique
upload vtr **to** ∼ **sth to a server** télécharger
qch vers un serveur
upmarket adj ‹car, hotel› haut de gamme;
‹area› riche
⚥ **upon** prep **(a)** (on) sur
(b) (linking two nouns) **thousands** ∼ **thousands
of people** des milliers et des milliers de
personnes
⚥ **upper** 1 n (of shoe) empeigne f

2 adj **(a)** ‹shelf, cupboard› du haut; ‹floor,
deck, lip› supérieur/-e; ‹teeth› du haut
(b) (in rank, scale) supérieur/-e
(c) the ∼ **limit** la limite maximale **(on** de)
IDIOM **to have/get the** ∼ **hand** avoir/prendre
le dessus
upper case adj ∼ **letters** (lettres fpl)
majuscules fpl
upper class n (pl ∼**es**) **the** ∼, **the** ∼**es**
l'aristocratie f et la haute bourgeoisie
uppermost adj **(a)** (highest) ‹branch› le
plus haut/la plus haute; (in rank) ‹echelon› le
plus élevé/la plus élevée
(b) to be ∼ **in sb's mind** être au premier
plan des préoccupations de qn
upper sixth n (GB Sch) ≈ (classe f)
terminale f
upright 1 adj **(a)** (physically) droit/-e; **to
stay** ∼ ‹person› rester debout
(b) (morally) droit/-e
2 adv **to stand** ∼ se tenir droit; **to sit** ∼
(action) se redresser
uprising n soulèvement m **(against** contre)
uproar n (noise) tumulte m; (protest)
protestations fpl
uproot vtr déraciner
upset 1 n **(a)** (surprise, setback) revers m
(b) (upheaval) bouleversement m
(c) (distress) peine f
(d) to have a stomach ∼ avoir l'estomac
détraqué
2 adj **to be** or **feel** ∼ (distressed) être très
affecté/-e; (annoyed) être contrarié/-e; **to get**
∼ (angry) se fâcher **(about** pour); (distressed)
se tracasser **(about** pour)
3 vtr (p prés **-tt-**, prét, pp **-set**) **(a)** (distress)
‹sight, news› bouleverser; ‹person› faire de
la peine à
(b) (annoy) contrarier
(c) bouleverser ‹plan›; déjouer ‹calculations›
(d) (destabilize) rompre ‹balance›
(e) (Med) rendre [qn] malade ‹person›;
perturber ‹digestion›
upsetting adj (distressing) navrant/-e;
(annoying) contrariant/-e
upside down 1 adj à l'envers
2 adv à l'envers; **to turn the house** ∼
mettre la maison sens dessus dessous
upstage vtr éclipser
upstairs 1 n haut m
2 adj ‹room› du haut; **an** ∼ **bedroom** une
chambre à l'étage
3 adv en haut; **to go** ∼ monter (l'escalier)
upstart n, adj arriviste mf
upstream adv ‹travel› vers l'amont; ∼
from here en amont d'ici
uptake n
IDIOM **to be quick/slow on the** ∼ (colloq)
comprendre/ne pas comprendre vite
uptight adj (colloq) **(a)** (tense) tendu/-e
(b) (inhibited) coincé/-e (fam)

u

up-to-date adj (a) ‹music, clothes› à la mode; ‹equipment› moderne
(b) ‹records, timetable› à jour; ‹information› récent/-e
(c) (informed) ‹person› au courant (with de)
up-to-the-minute adj ‹information› dernier/-ière
upward ⟦1⟧ adj ‹push, movement› vers le haut; ‹path, road› qui monte; ‹trend› à la hausse
⟦2⟧ adv (also **upwards**) to go or move ∼ monter; from £10 ∼ à partir de 10 livres sterling
upwardly mobile adj en pleine ascension sociale
upwards = UPWARD 2
uranium n uranium m
Uranus pr n Uranus f
⚜ **urban** adj urbain/-e
urban planning n urbanisme m
urban sprawl n mitage m
urchin n gamin m
Urdu n urdu m
⚜ **urge** ⟦1⟧ n forte envie f, désir m (to do de faire)
⟦2⟧ vtr conseiller vivement, préconiser ‹caution, restraint, resistance›; to ∼ sb to do conseiller vivement à qn de faire; (stronger) pousser qn à faire
urgency n (of situation, appeal, request) urgence f; (of voice, tone) insistance f; a matter of ∼ une affaire urgente
urgent adj (a) (pressing) ‹case, need› urgent/-e, pressant/-e; ‹message, demand› urgent/-e; ‹meeting, measures› d'urgence
(b) ‹request, tone› insistant/-e
urgently adv ‹request› d'urgence; ‹plead› instamment
urinal n (place) urinoir m; (fixture) urinal m
urinate vi uriner
urine n urine f
URL n (abbr = **Unified Resource Locator**) adresse f URL
urn n urne f
⚜ **us** pron nous; she knows ∼ elle nous connaît; both of ∼ tous/toutes les deux; every single one of ∼ chacun/-e d'entre nous; some of ∼ quelques-uns/-unes d'entre nous; she's one of ∼ elle est des nôtres
US pr n (abbr = **United States**) USA mpl
USA pr n (abbr = **United States of America**) USA mpl
USB key n clé f USB
⚜ **use** ⟦1⟧ n (a) (act of using) (of substance, object, machine) emploi m, utilisation f (of de); (of word, expression) emploi m, usage m (of de); for the ∼ of à l'usage de ‹customer, staff›; for my own ∼ pour mon usage personnel; to make ∼ of sth utiliser qch; to put sth to

⚜ indicates a very frequent word

good ∼ tirer parti de qch; while the machine is in ∼ lorsque la machine est en service or en fonctionnement; to have the ∼ of avoir l'usage de ‹house, car, kitchen›; avoir la jouissance de ‹garden›; to lose the ∼ of one's legs perdre l'usage de ses jambes
(b) (way of using) (of resource, object, material) utilisation f; (of term) emploi m; to have no further ∼ for sb/sth ne plus avoir besoin de qn/qch
(c) (usefulness) to be of ∼ être utile (to à); to be (of) no ∼ ‹object› ne servir à rien; ‹person› n'être bon/bonne à rien; what's the ∼ of crying? à quoi bon pleurer?; it's no ∼ (he won't listen) c'est inutile (il n'écoutera pas)
⟦2⟧ vtr (a) se servir de, utiliser ‹object, car, room, money›; employer ‹method, word›; profiter de, saisir ‹opportunity›; faire jouer ‹influence›; avoir recours à ‹blackmail›; utiliser ‹knowledge, talent›; to ∼ sb/sth as se servir de qn/qch comme; to ∼ sth to do se servir de qch pour faire
(b) (consume) consommer ‹fuel, food›; utiliser ‹water, leftovers›
(c) (exploit) se servir de ‹person›
⟦3⟧ **used** pp adj ‹car› d'occasion; ‹envelope› qui a déjà servi
■ **use up** finir ‹food›; dépenser ‹money›; épuiser ‹supplies›
used

■ Note To translate used to do, use the imperfect tense in French: he used to live in York = il habitait York.
— To emphasize a contrast between past and present, you can use avant: I used to love sport = avant, j'adorais le sport.

⟦1⟧ modal aux I ∼ to read a lot je lisais beaucoup; she ∼ to smoke, didn't she? elle fumait avant, non?; she doesn't smoke now, but she ∼ to elle ne fume plus maintenant, mais elle fumait avant; there ∼ to be a pub here il y avait un pub ici (dans le temps)
⟦2⟧ adj to be ∼ to sth avoir l'habitude de qch, être habitué/-e à qch; to get ∼ to s'habituer à; I'm not ∼ to it je n'ai pas l'habitude; you'll get ∼ to it tu t'y habitueras
⚜ **useful** adj utile
useless adj (a) (not helpful) inutile
(b) (not able to be used) inutilisable
(c) (colloq) (incompetent) incapable, nul/nulle (fam)
⚜ **user** n (of public service) usager m; (of product, machine) utilisateur/-trice m/f
user-friendly adj (Comput) convivial/-e; (gen) facile à utiliser
user group n groupe m d'utilisateurs
username n (Comput) nom m d'utilisateur
usher vtr conduire, escorter; to ∼ sb in/out faire entrer/sortir qn
usherette n ouvreuse f
USSR pr n (abbr = **Union of Soviet Socialist Republics**) URSS f

usual *adj* (gen) habituel/-elle; ‹word, term› usuel/-elle; **it is ∼ for sb to do** c'est normal pour qn de faire; **it is ∼ to do** il est d'usage de faire; **as ∼** comme d'habitude; **more/less than ∼** plus/moins que d'habitude

usually *adv* d'habitude, normalement

utensil *n* ustensile *m*

uterus *n* utérus *m*

utility **1** *n* **(a)** (usefulness) utilité *f*
(b) (*also* **public ∼**) (service) service *m* public
2 **utilities** *n pl* (US) factures *fpl*

utility bill *n* facture *f* de services publics

utility company *n* société *f* chargée d'assurer un service public

utmost **1** *n* **to do** *or* **try one's ∼ to do** faire tout son possible pour faire; **to the ∼ of**

one's abilities au maximum de ses capacités
2 *adj* ‹caution, ease, secrecy› le plus grand/ la plus grande (*before n*); ‹limit› extrême; **it is of the ∼ importance that** il est extrêmement important que (+ *subjunctive*)

Utopia *n* utopie *f*

utter **1** *adj* ‹disaster, boredom, despair› total/-e; ‹honesty, sincerity› absolu/-e; ‹fool, stranger› parfait/-e (*before n*)
2 *vtr* prononcer ‹word, curse›; pousser ‹cry›; émettre ‹sound›

utterly *adv* complètement; ‹condemn› avec vigueur

U-turn *n* demi-tour *m*; (figurative) volte-face *f inv*

UV *adj* (*abbr* = **ultraviolet**) ‹light, ray, radiation› ultraviolet/-ette

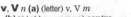

Vv

v, V *n* **(a)** (letter) v, V *m*
(b) v (*abbr* = **versus**) contre

vacancy *n* **(a)** (room) 'vacancies' 'chambres libres'; 'no vacancies' 'complet'
(b) (unfilled job) poste *m* à pourvoir, poste *m* vacant

vacant *adj* **(a)** ‹flat, room, seat› libre, disponible; ‹office, land› inoccupé/-e
(b) ‹job, post› vacant/-e, à pourvoir
(c) ‹look, stare› absent/-e; ‹expression› vide

vacant possession *n* jouissance *f* immédiate

vacate *vtr* quitter ‹house, premises, job›

vacation (US) *n* vacances *fpl*; **on ∼** en vacances

vacationer *n* (US) vacancier/-ière *m/f*

vaccinate *vtr* vacciner (**against** contre)

vaccination *n* vaccination *f* (**against** contre)

vaccine *n* vaccin *m* (**against** contre)

vacillate *vi* hésiter

vacuum **1** *n* **(a)** (gen) vide *m*
(b) (*also* **∼ cleaner**) aspirateur *m*
2 *vtr* passer [qch] à l'aspirateur ‹carpet›; passer l'aspirateur dans ‹room›

vacuum pack *vtr* emballer [qch] sous vide

vagrant *n, adj* vagabond/-e *m/f*

vague *adj* **(a)** (gen) vague; **to be ∼ about** rester vague sur *or* évasif/-ive au sujet de ‹plans, past›
(b) (distracted) ‹person, expression› distrait/-e

vaguely *adv* **(a)** (gen) vaguement
(b) (distractedly) ‹smile, gaze› d'un air distrait *or* vague

vain **1** *adj* **(a)** (conceited) vaniteux/-euse, vain/-e (*after n*)
(b) (futile) ‹attempt, promise, hope› vain/-e (*before n*)
2 **in vain** *phr* en vain

valentine card *n* carte *f* de la Saint-Valentin

Valentine('s) Day *n* la Saint-Valentin

valet *n* **(a)** (employee) valet *m* de chambre
(b) (US) (rack) valet *m* de nuit

valet parking *n* service *m* de voiturier

valiant *adj* ‹soldier› vaillant/-e; ‹attempt› courageux/-euse

valid *adj* **(a)** ‹passport, licence› valide; ‹ticket, offer› valable (**for** pour)
(b) ‹argument, excuse› valable; ‹complaint› fondé/-e; ‹point, comment› pertinent/-e

validate *vtr* **(a)** prouver le bien-fondé de ‹claim, theory›
(b) valider ‹document, passport›

valley *n* (*pl* ∼**s**) vallée *f*; (small) vallon *m*

valour (GB), **valor** (US) *n* bravoure *f*

valuable *adj* **(a)** ‹object, asset› de valeur; **to be ∼** avoir de la valeur; **a very ∼ ring** une bague de grande valeur
(b) ‹advice, information, lesson, member› précieux/-ieuse

valuables *n pl* objets *mpl* de valeur

valuation *n* (of house, land, company) évaluation *f*; (of antique, art) expertise *f*; **to have a ∼ done on sth** faire évaluer qch

value **1** *n* valeur *f*; **novelty ∼** caractère *m* nouveau; **to be good ∼** avoir un bon rapport qualité-prix; **to get ∼ for money** en avoir pour son argent

····›

2 vtr (a) évaluer ⟨house, asset, company⟩ (at à); expertiser ⟨antique, jewel, painting⟩
(b) (appreciate) apprécier ⟨person, friendship, opinion, help⟩; tenir à ⟨independence, life⟩
value pack n lot m économique
valve n (a) (in machine, engine) soupape f; (on tyre, football) valve f
(b) (Anat) valvule f
van n (a) (small, for deliveries) fourgonnette f, camionnette f; (larger, for removals) fourgon m
(b) (US) (camper) auto-caravane f, camping-car m
vandal n vandale mf
vandalism n vandalisme m
vandalize vtr vandaliser
van driver n chauffeur m de camionnette
vanguard n avant-garde f; in the ~ à l'avant-garde
vanilla n vanille f
vanish vi disparaître (from de); to ~ into thin air se volatiliser
vanity n vanité f
vantage point n point m de vue, position f élevée
vaporizer n vaporisateur m
vapour (GB), **vapor** (US) n vapeur f
vapour trail n traînée f de condensation, traînée f d'avion
variable n, adj variable f
variance n to be at ~ with ne pas concorder avec ⟨evidence, facts⟩
variant n variante f (of de; on par rapport à)
⚘ **variation** n (a) (change) variation f, différence f (in, in de)
(b) (new version) variante f (of de); (in music) variation f (on sur)
varied adj varié/-e
⚘ **variety** n (a) (diversity, range) variété f (in, of de); for a ~ of reasons pour diverses raisons; a ~ of sizes/colours un grand choix de tailles/de coloris
(b) (type) type m; (of plant) variété f
variety show n spectacle de variétés
⚘ **various** adj (a) (different) différents/-es (before n)
(b) (several) divers/-es
varnish **1** n vernis m
2 vtr vernir ⟨woodwork⟩; to ~ one's nails se vernir les ongles
⚘ **vary** **1** vtr varier ⟨menu, programme⟩; faire varier ⟨temperature⟩; changer de ⟨method, pace, route⟩
2 vi varier (with, according to selon); it varies from one town to another cela varie d'une ville à l'autre
varying adj variable
vase n vase m; flower ~ vase à fleurs

⚘ indicates a very frequent word

⚘ **vast** adj (a) ⟨amount, sum, improvement, difference⟩ énorme; the ~ majority la très grande majorité
(b) ⟨room, area, plain⟩ vaste (before n), immense
vat n cuve f; beer/wine ~ cuve à bière/vin
VAT n (GB) (abbr = **value-added tax**) TVA f, taxe f à la valeur ajoutée
Vatican pr n Vatican m; ~ **City** cité f du Vatican
vault **1** n (a) (roof) voûte f
(b) (also ~s) (of bank) chambre f forte; (for safe-deposit boxes) salle f des coffres; (of house, for wine) cave f
2 vtr sauter par-dessus ⟨fence, bar⟩
3 vi sauter (over par-dessus)
VCR n (abbr = **video cassette recorder**) magnétoscope m
VD n (abbr = **venereal disease**) MST f
VDU n (abbr = **visual display unit**) écran m de visualisation
veal n veau m
veer vi ⟨ship⟩ virer (also ~ off) ⟨person, road⟩ tourner; to ~ off course dévier de sa route
vegan n, adj végétalien/-ienne m/f
veganism n végétalisme m
vegeburger® ▶ VEGGIE BURGER
vegetable **1** n légume m
2 adj ⟨soup, patch⟩ de légumes; ⟨fat, oil⟩ végétal/-e; ~ **garden** potager m
vegetarian n, adj végétarien/-ienne m/f
vegetarianism n végétarisme m
vegetate vi végéter
vegetation n végétation f
veggie burger n croquette f pour végétariens
vehement adj véhément/-e
⚘ **vehicle** n véhicule m
veil **1** n (gen) (figurative) voile m; (on hat) voilette f
2 vtr ⟨mist, cloud⟩ voiler
veiled adj voilé/-e
vein n (blood vessel) veine f; (on insect wing, leaf) nervure f; (in cheese) veinure f; (of ore) veine f
velocity n vélocité f
velour(s) n velours m
velvet n velours m; **crushed** ~ velours frappé
velvety adj velouté/-e
vending machine n distributeur m automatique
vendor n (a) (in street, kiosk) marchand/-e m/f
(b) (as opposed to buyer) vendeur/-euse m/f
veneer n placage m; (figurative) vernis m
venereal disease n maladie f vénérienne
venetian blind n store m vénitien
Venezuela pr n Venezuela m

vengeance n vengeance f; **with a ~ de plus belle**

Venice pr n Venise

venison n (viande f de) chevreuil m

venom n venim m

venomous adj venimeux/-euse

vent ⓵ n (outlet for gas, pressure) bouche f, conduit m; **air ~** bouche d'aération; **to give ~ to** décharger ‹anger, feelings›
⓶ vtr décharger ‹anger, frustration› (**on** sur)

ventilate vtr aérer ‹room›

ventilation n (a) (gen) aération f, ventilation f
(b) (of patient) ventilation f artificielle

ventilator n (for patient) respirateur m artificiel

ventriloquist n ventriloque mf

venture ⓵ n (a) (undertaking) aventure f, entreprise f; **a commercial ~** une entreprise commerciale
(b) (experiment) essai m
⓶ vtr hasarder ‹opinion, suggestion›; **to ~ to do** se risquer à faire
⓷ vi **to ~ into** s'aventurer dans ‹place, street, city›; **to ~ out(doors)** s'aventurer dehors

venture capital n capital-risque m

venue n lieu m

Venus pr n Vénus f

verb n verbe m

verbal adj verbal/-e

verbatim ⓵ adj ‹report, account› textuel/ -elle
⓶ adv ‹describe, record› mot pour mot

verbose adj verbeux/-euse

verdict n (a) (Law) verdict m; **a ~ of guilty/ not guilty** un verdict positif/négatif
(b) (figurative) (opinion) verdict m; **well, what's the ~?** (colloq) eh bien, qu'est-ce que tu en penses?

verge n (a) (GB) (by road) accotement m, bas-côté m
(b) (brink) **on the ~ of** au bord de ‹tears›; au seuil de ‹adolescence, death›; **on the ~ of doing** sur le point de faire
■ **verge on** friser ‹panic, stupidity, contempt›

verification n vérification f

verify vtr vérifier

vermicelli n vermicelles mpl

vermilion n, adj vermillon m inv

vermin n (a) (rodents) animaux mpl nuisibles
(b) (lice, insects) vermine f

verruca n (pl **-cae** ou **-cas**) verrue f plantaire

versatile adj (a) ‹person› plein/-e de ressources, aux talents divers (after n); ‹mind› souple
(b) ‹vehicle› polyvalent/-e; ‹equipment› à

usages multiples

verse n (a) (poems) poésie f
(b) (form) vers mpl; **in ~** en vers
(c) (part of poem) strophe f, (of song) couplet m

⚡ **version** n version f (**of** de)

versus prep contre

vertebra n (pl **-brae**) vertèbre f

vertebrate n vertébré m

vertical adj vertical/-e; **a ~ drop** un à-pic

vertigo n (pl **-goes** ou **-gines**) vertige m; **to get ~** avoir le vertige

verve n brio m, verve f

⚡ **very** ⓵ adj (a) (actual) même (after n); **this ~ second** immédiatement
(b) (ideal) **the ~ person I need** exactement la personne qu'il me faut
(c) (ultimate) tout/-e; **from the ~ beginning** depuis le tout début; **at the ~ front** tout devant; **on the ~ edge** à l'extrême bord
(d) (mere) ‹mention, thought, word› seul/-e (before n); **the ~ idea!** quelle idée!
⓶ adv (a) (extremely) très; **I'm ~ sorry** je suis vraiment désolé; **~ well** très bien; **that's all ~ well but who's going to pay for it?** c'est bien beau, tout ça, mais qui va payer?; **~ much** beaucoup; **I didn't eat ~ much** je n'ai pas mangé grand-chose
(b) (absolutely) **the ~ best/worst thing** de loin la meilleure/pire chose; **at the ~ latest** au plus tard; **at the ~ least** tout au moins; **the ~ next day** le lendemain même; **a car of your ~ own** ta propre voiture

vessel n (a) (ship) vaisseau m
(b) (Anat) **blood ~** vaisseau m sanguin
(c) (container) vase m

vest n (a) (GB) (underwear) maillot m de corps
(b) (for sport, fashion) débardeur m
(c) (US) (waistcoat) gilet m

vested interest n **to have a ~** être personnellement intéressé/-e (**in** dans)

vestige n vestige m

vet ⓵ n (a) (abbr = **veterinary surgeon**) vétérinaire mf
(b) (US) (colloq, Mil) ancien combattant m, vétéran m
⓶ vtr (p prés etc **-tt-**) mener une enquête approfondie sur ‹person›; passer [qch] en revue ‹plan›; approuver ‹publication›

veteran ⓵ n vétéran m
⓶ adj ‹sportsman, politician› chevronné/-e

veterinarian n (US) vétérinaire mf

veterinary surgeon n vétérinaire mf

veterinary surgery n clinique f vétérinaire

veto ⓵ n (pl **-toes**) (a) (practice) veto m
(b) (right) droit m de veto (**over**, **on** sur)
⓶ vtr (prés **-toes**, prét, pp **-toed**) mettre or opposer son veto à

vetting n contrôle m

vex vtr (annoy) contrarier; (worry) tracasser

V

vexed adj (a) (annoyed) mécontent/-e (with de)
(b) ‹question, issue› épineux/-euse
VHF n (abbr = **very high frequency**) VHF
ơ **via** prep (a) (by way of) (on ticket, timetable) via; (other contexts) en passant par; **we came ~ Paris** nous sommes venus en passant par Paris
(b) (by means of) par
viability n (of company) viabilité f; (of project, idea) validité f
viable adj ‹company, government, farm› viable; ‹project, idea, plan› réalisable, valable
viaduct n viaduc m
vibrant adj ‹person, place, personality› plein/-e de vie; ‹colour› éclatant/-e
vibrate vi vibrer (with de)
vibration n vibration f
vicar n pasteur m
vicarage n presbytère m
vicarious adj ‹pleasure› indirect/-e
vice n (a) vice m; (amusing weakness) faiblesse f
(b) (also **vise** (US)) (tool) étau m
vice-captain n capitaine m en second
vice-chancellor n président/-e m/f d'Université
vice-president n vice-président/-e m/f
vice squad n brigade f des mœurs
vicinity n voisinage m; **in the (immediate) ~ of Oxford** à proximité (immédiate) d'Oxford
vicious adj ‹animal› malfaisant/-e; ‹speech, attack› brutal/-e; ‹rumour, person, lie› malveillant/-e
vicious circle n cercle m vicieux
ơ **victim** n victime f
victimization n persécution f
victimize vtr persécuter
victor n vainqueur m
Victorian adj victorien/-ienne
victorious adj victorieux/-ieuse (over sur)
ơ **victory** n victoire f
ơ **video** [1] n (pl ~**s**) (a) (also ~ **recorder**) magnétoscope m
(b) (also ~ **cassette**) cassette f vidéo; **on ~** en vidéo
(c) (also ~ **film**) vidéo f
[2] adj vidéo inv
[3] vtr (prés ~**s**, prét, pp ~**ed**) (a) (from TV) enregistrer [qch]
(b) (on camcorder) filmer [qch] en vidéo
video camera n caméra f vidéo
video card n (Comput) carte f vidéo
video clip n (from film) extrait m; (Mus) clip m
videoconference n vidéoconférence f

videoconferencing n vidéoconférence f
videodisc n vidéodisque m
video game n jeu m vidéo
video jock n (colloq) vidéo jockey mf
video nasty n vidéo f représentant des violences véritables
videophone n vidéophone m, visiophone m
video shop (GB), **video store** (US) n vidéoclub m
videotape n bande f vidéo
vie vi (p prés **vying**) rivaliser (with avec; for pour; to do pour faire)
Vienna pr n Vienne
ơ **view** [1] n (a) (gen) vue f; **in (full) ~ of sb** devant qn, sous les yeux de qn; **to disappear from ~** disparaître
(b) (personal opinion, attitude) avis m, opinion f; **point of ~** point m de vue; **in his ~** à son avis
[2] vtr (a) (consider) considérer; (envisage) envisager
(b) (look at) voir ‹scene, building, collection, exhibition›; visiter ‹house, castle›; regarder ‹programme›
(c) (Comput) visualiser
[3] **in view of** phr (considering) vu, étant donné
[4] **with a view to** phr with a ~ **to doing** en vue de faire, afin de faire
viewer n (a) (of TV) téléspectateur/-trice m/f
(b) (of property) visiteur/-euse m/f
(c) (on camera) visionneuse f
viewfinder n viseur m
viewing [1] n (of exhibition, house) visite f; (of film) projection f; (of new range) présentation f
[2] adj ‹habits, preferences› des téléspectateurs; ~ **figures** taux m d'écoute
viewpoint n (all contexts) point m de vue
vigil n (gen) veille f; (by sickbed) veillée f; (by demonstrators) manifestation f silencieuse
vigilant adj vigilant/-e
vigilante n membre m d'un groupe d'autodéfense
vigorous adj vigoureux/-euse
vigour (GB), **vigor** (US) n vigueur f
vile adj ‹smell› infect/-e; ‹weather› abominable; ‹place, colour› horrible; ‹mood› exécrable
villa n (in town) pavillon m; (in country, for holiday) villa f
ơ **village** n village m
village green n terrain m communal
village hall n salle f des fêtes
villager n villageois/-e m/f
villain n (in book, film) méchant m; (child) coquin/-e m/f; (criminal) bandit m
vindicate vtr justifier
vindictive adj vindicatif/-ive
vindictiveness n esprit m de vengeance

ơ indicates a very frequent word

v

vine *n* (a) (grapevine) vigne *f*
  (b) (climbing plant) plante *f* grimpante
vinegar *n* vinaigre *m*
vineyard *n* vignoble *m*
vintage ① *n* (wine) millésime *m*
  ② *adj* (a) ‹wine, champagne› millésimé/-e;
  ‹port› vieux/vieille
  (b) ‹comedy› classique
  (c) ‹clothes› vintage
vintage car *n* voiture *f* d'époque
vinyl ① *n* vinyle *m*
  ② *adj* en vinyle; ‹paint› vinylique
viola *n* (violon *m*) alto *m*
violate *vtr* (a) violer ‹law, agreement, rights›
  (b) profaner ‹sacred place›; troubler ‹peace›
violation *n* violation *f*; **traffic** ~ infraction
  f au code de la route
◆ **violence** *n* violence *f*
violent *adj* (a) ‹crime, behaviour, film,
  storm, emotion› violent/-e
  (b) ‹contrast› brutal/-e
  (c) ‹colour› criard/-e
violently *adv* ‹attack, react, shake›
  violemment; ‹brake, swerve› brusquement
violet ① *n* (a) (flower) violette *f*
  (b) (colour) violet *m*
  ② *adj* violet/-ette
violin *n* violon *m*
violinist *n* violoniste *mf*
VIP (*abbr* = **very important person**)
  ① *n* personnalité *f* (en vue)
  ② *adj* ‹area, lounge› réservé/-e aux
  personnalités; ~ **guest** hôte *mf* de marque;
  to give sb (the) ~ **treatment** recevoir qn en
  hôte de marque
viper *n* vipère *f*
virgin *n*, *adj* vierge *f*
Virgo *n* Vierge *f*
virile *adj* viril/-e
virtual *adj* (a) (gen) quasi-total/-e; **he was a**
  ~ **prisoner** il était pratiquement prisonnier
  (b) (Comput) virtuel/-elle
virtually *adv* pratiquement, presque; **it's** ~
  impossible c'est quasiment (fam) impossible
virtual reality *n* réalité *f* virtuelle
virtue ① *n* (a) (goodness) vertu *f*
  (b) (advantage) avantage *m*
  ② **by virtue of** *phr* en raison de
virtuoso *n* (*pl* **-sos** *ou* **-si**) virtuose *mf*
  (of de)
virtuous *adj* vertueux/-euse
virus *n* virus *m*
virus checker *n* (Comput) logiciel *m*
  antivirus
visa *n* visa *m*; **tourist** ~ visa de touriste
vis-à-vis *prep* (in relation to) par rapport à;
  (concerning) en ce qui concerne
visibility *n* visibilité *f*
visible *adj* (a) (able to be seen) visible; **clearly**
  ~ bien visible

  (b) (concrete) ‹improvement, sign› évident/-e
visibly *adv* ‹moved, shocked› manifestement
◆ **vision** *n* (a) (idea, mental picture, hallucination)
  vision *f*
  (b) (ability to see) vue *f*
  (c) (foresight) sagacité *f*
visionary *n*, *adj* visionnaire *mf*
◆ **visit** ① *n* (gen) visite *f*; (stay) séjour *m*; **a
  state** ~ une visite officielle; **to pay a** ~ **to
  sb, to pay sb a** ~ aller voir qn; (more formal)
  rendre visite à qn
  ② *vtr* (a) **to** ~ **Paris** (see) visiter Paris; (stay)
  faire un séjour à Paris, aller passer quelques
  jours à Paris; **to** ~ **sb** (call) aller voir qn;
  (more formal) rendre visite à qn; (stay with) aller
  (passer quelques jours) chez qn
  (b) (US) **to** ~ **with sb** aller voir qn
visiting card *n* (US) carte *f* de visite
visiting hours *n pl* heures *fpl* de visite
◆ **visitor** *n* (a) (caller) invité/-e *m/f*
  (b) (tourist) visiteur/-euse *m/f*
visitor centre *n* centre *m* d'accueil et
  d'information des visiteurs
visitors' book *n* (in exhibition) livre *m* d'or;
  (in hotel) registre *m*
visor *n* visière *f*
vista *n* panorama *m*; (figurative) perspective *f*
visual *adj* visuel/-elle
visual aid *n* support *m* visuel
visual arts *n pl* arts *mpl* plastiques
visualize *vtr* (a) (picture) s'imaginer
  (b) (envisage) envisager
visually impaired *n* **the** ~ les
  malvoyants *mpl*
◆ **vital** *adj* (a) (essential) (gen) primordial/-e;
  ‹match, point, support, factor› décisif/-ive;
  ‹service, help› indispensable; ‹treatment,
  organ, force› vital/-e; **of** ~ **importance** d'une
  importance capitale
  (b) ‹person› plein/-e de vie
vitality *n* vitalité *f*
vitally *adv* ‹important› extrêmement;
  ‹needed› absolument
vital statistics *n* (of woman)
  mensurations *fpl*
vitamin *n* vitamine *f*
viva ① *n* oral *m*
  ② *excl* vive!
vivacious *adj* plein/-e de vivacité
vivid *adj* (a) (bright) ‹colour, light› vif/vive
  (b) (graphic) ‹imagination› vif/vive; ‹memory,
  picture› net/nette; ‹dream, impression,
  description› frappant/-e
vividly *adv* ‹describe, illustrate› de façon
  très vivante; ‹remember, recall› très bien
vivisection *n* vivisection *f*
vixen *n* (a) (fox) renarde *f*
  (b) (woman) mégère *f*
viz *adv* (*abbr* = **videlicet**) à savoir
V-neck *n* (a) (neck) encolure *f* en V   ⋯⋯⟶

(b) (sweater) pull *m* en V

vocabulary *n* vocabulaire *m*

vocal *adj* (a) (concerning speech) vocal/-e
(b) (vociferous) ‹person› qui se fait entendre

vocalist *n* chanteur/-euse *m/f* (*dans un groupe pop*)

vocals *n pl* chant *m*; **to do the backing** ~ faire les chœurs

vocation *n* vocation *f*

vocational *adj* professionnel/-elle

vocational course *n* stage *m* de formation professionnelle

vociferous *adj* ‹person, protest› véhément/-e

vogue *n* vogue *f* (**for** de)

✧ **voice** ① *n* voix *f*; **in a loud** ~ à haute voix; **in a low** ~ à voix basse; **in a cross** ~ d'une voix irritée; **to have lost one's** ~ (when ill) être aphone; **at the top of one's** ~ à tue-tête
② *vtr* exprimer ‹concern, grievance›

voicemail *n* messagerie *f* vocale

voice-over *n* voix-off *f*

voice recognition *n* reconnaissance *f* vocale

void ① *n* vide *m*; **to fill the** ~ combler le vide
② *adj* (a) (Law) ‹contract, agreement› nul/nulle; ‹cheque› annulé/-e
(b) (empty) vide; ~ **of** dépourvu/-e de

volatile *adj* ‹situation› explosif/-ive; ‹person› lunatique; ‹market, exchange rate› instable

volcano *n* (*pl* **-noes** *ou* **-nos**) volcan *m*

volley ① *n* (a) (in tennis) volée *f*
(b) (of gunfire) salve *f* (**of** de)
(c) (series) **a** ~ **of** un feu roulant de ‹questions›; une bordée de ‹insults, oaths›
② *vtr* (in tennis) prendre [qch] de volée ‹ball›
③ *vi* (in tennis) jouer à la volée

volleyball *n* volley(-ball) *m*

volt *n* volt *m*

voltage *n* tension *f*

✧ **volume** *n* (a) (gen) volume *m* (**of** de); (of container) capacité *f*
(b) (book) volume *m*; (part of set) tome *m*

volume control *n* (bouton *m* de) réglage *m* du volume

voluntarily *adv* de plein gré, volontairement

voluntary *adj* (a) (gen) volontaire
(b) (unpaid) bénévole

voluntary redundancy *n* départ *m* volontaire

volunteer ① *n* (a) (offering to do sth) volontaire *mf*
(b) (unpaid worker) bénévole *mf*
② *vtr* (a) (offer) offrir; **to** ~ **to do** offrir de faire, se porter volontaire pour faire
(b) fournir [qch] spontanément ‹information›
③ *vi* (a) se porter volontaire (**for** pour)
(b) (as soldier) s'engager comme volontaire

voluptuous *adj* voluptueux/-euse

vomit ① *n* vomi *m*
② *vtr, vi* vomir

voodoo *n* vaudou *m*

voracious *adj* vorace

vortex *n* (*pl* ~**es** *ou* **-tices**) tourbillon *m*

✧ **vote** ① *n* (a) (gen) vote *m*
(b) (franchise) **the** ~ le droit de vote
② *vtr* (a) (gen) voter; **to** ~ **sb into/out of office** élire/ne pas réélire qn
(b) (colloq) (propose) proposer
③ *vi* voter (**on** sur; **for sb** pour qn; **against** contre); **let's** ~ **on it** mettons-le aux voix; **to** ~ **to strike** voter la grève

vote of confidence *n* vote *m* de confiance (**in** en)

vote of thanks *n* discours *m* de remerciement

✧ **voter** *n* électeur/-trice *m/f*

voting *n* scrutin *m*

voting age *n* majorité *f* électorale

vouch *v* ■ **vouch for** (a) (informally) répondre de ‹person›; témoigner de ‹fact›
(b) (officially) se porter garant de

voucher *n* bon *m*

vow ① *n* (religious) vœu *m*; (of honour) serment *m*; **marriage** *or* **wedding** ~**s** promesses *fpl* du mariage
② *vtr* faire vœu de ‹love, revenge, allegiance›; **to** ~ **to do** jurer de faire

vowel *n* voyelle *f*

voyage *n* voyage *m*

V-sign *n* (a) (victory sign) V *m* de la victoire
(b) (GB) (offensive gesture) geste *m* obscène

VSO *n* (*abbr* = **Voluntary Service Overseas**) (GB) coopération *f* civile

vulgar *adj* (a) (tasteless) ‹furniture, clothes› de mauvais goût; ‹taste› douteux/-euse; ‹person› vulgaire
(b) (rude) grossier/-ière

vulnerable *adj* vulnérable (**to** à)

vulture *n* vautour *m*

W w

w, W *n* w, W *m*

wad *n* (a) (of banknotes, paper) liasse *f* (of de) (b) (of cotton wool, padding) boule *f* (of de)

waddle *vi* ‹duck, person› se dandiner

wade *vi* (a) (in water) to ~ **into the water** entrer dans l'eau; to ~ **ashore** marcher dans l'eau jusqu'au rivage; to ~ **across** traverser à gué (b) he was wading through 'War and Peace' il lisait 'Guerre et Paix', mais ça avançait lentement

waders *n pl* cuissardes *fpl*

wafer *n* (Culin) gaufrette *f*

wafer-thin *adj* ‹slice› ultrafin/-e

waffle ① *n* (a) (Culin) gaufre *f* (b) (colloq) (empty words) verbiage *m* ② *vi (also ~ **on**)* (speaking) bavasser (fam); (writing) faire du remplissage

waft *vi* to ~ **towards** flotter vers; to ~ **up** monter

wag ① *vtr (p prés etc* **-gg-**) remuer ‹tail› ② *vi (p prés etc* **-gg-**) ‹tail› remuer, frétiller; **tongues will ~** ça va faire jaser

⚐ **wage** ① *n (also* ~**s** *pl*) salaire *m* ② *vtr* mener ‹campaign›; to ~ **(a) war against sb/sth** faire la guerre contre qn/qch

wage earner *n* (a) (person earning a wage) salarié/-e *m/f* (hebdomadaire) (b) (breadwinner) soutien *m* de famille

wage packet *n* (a) (envelope) enveloppe *f* de paie (b) (money) paie *f*

wager *n* pari *m*; to **make** *or* **lay a ~** parier, faire un pari

wage slip *n* feuille *f* de paie

waggon (GB), **wagon** *n* (a) (horse-drawn) chariot *m* (b) (GB) (on rail) wagon *m* (de marchandises) IDIOM to **be on the ~** (colloq) être au régime sec

wail ① *n* (of person) gémissement *m*; (of siren) hurlement *m*; (of musical instrument) son *m* plaintif ② *vi* ‹person, wind› gémir; ‹siren› hurler; ‹music› pleurer

waist *n* taille *f*

waistband *n* ceinture *f*

waistcoat *n* (GB) gilet *m*

waistline *n* taille *f*

waist measurement *n* tour *m* de taille

⚐ **wait** ① *n* attente *f*; **an hour's ~** une heure d'attente ② *vtr* (a) attendre ‹one's turn› (b) (US) to ~ **table** servir à table

③ *vi* attendre; to **keep sb ~ing** faire attendre qn; to ~ **for sb/sth** attendre qn/qch; to ~ **for sb/sth to do** attendre que qn/qch fasse; to ~ **to do** attendre de faire; I **can't ~ to do** j'ai hâte de faire; (stronger) je meurs d'impatience de faire; **you'll have to ~ and see** attends et tu verras IDIOM to **lie in ~ for sb** guetter qn

■ **wait around, wait about** (GB) attendre

■ **wait behind** attendre un peu; to ~ **behind for sb** attendre qn

■ **wait on** servir ‹person›; to ~ **on sb hand and foot** être aux petits soins pour qn

■ **wait up** (a) (stay awake) veiller; to ~ **up for sb** veiller jusqu'au retour de qn (b) (US) ~ **up!** attends!

waiter *n* serveur *m*; '~!' 'monsieur!'

waiting game *n* to **play a ~** attendre son heure; (in politics) faire de l'attentisme

waiting list *n* liste *f* d'attente

waiting room *n* salle *f* d'attente

waitress *n* serveuse *f*; '~!' 'madame!', 'mademoiselle!'

waive *vtr* déroger à ‹rule›; renoncer à ‹claim, right›; supprimer ‹fee›

⚐ **wake** ① *vtr (also* ~ **up**, *prét* **woke**, **waked**†, *pp* **woken**, **waked**†) réveiller; to ~ **sb from a dream** tirer qn d'un rêve ② *vi (also* ~ **up**, *prét* **woke**, **waked**†, *pp* **woken**, **waked**†) se réveiller

■ **wake up**: ① ¶ ~ **up** se réveiller; ~ **up!** réveille-toi!; (to reality) ouvre les yeux! ② ¶ ~ **[sb] up** réveiller

wake-up call *n* (a) réveil *m* téléphoné (b) (figurative) piqûre *f* de rappel

Wales *pr n* pays *m* de Galles

⚐ **walk** ① *n* (a) promenade *f*; (shorter) tour *m*; (hike) randonnée *f*; **it's about ten minutes' ~** c'est à environ dix minutes à pied; to **go for a ~** (aller) faire une promenade (b) (gait) démarche *f* (c) (pace) pas *m* (d) (path) allée *f* (e) (Sport) épreuve *f* de marche ② *vtr* (a) faire [qch] à pied ‹distance, path, road› (b) conduire ‹horse›; promener ‹dog›; to ~ **sb home** raccompagner qn chez lui/elle ③ *vi* (in general) marcher; (for pleasure) se promener; (not run) aller au pas; **it's not very far, let's ~** ce n'est pas très loin, allons-y à pied; **he ~ed up/down the road** il a remonté/descendu la rue (à pied)

■ **Note** *à pied* is often omitted with movement verbs if we already know that the person is on foot. If it is surprising or ambiguous, *à pied* should be included.

■ **walk around**: ⓵ ¶ ~ **around** se promener; (aimlessly) traîner
⓶ ¶ ~ **around [sth]** (to and fro) faire un tour dans; (make circuit of) faire le tour de
■ **walk away (a)** s'éloigner (**from** de)
(b) (refuse to face) **to ~ away from** se désintéresser de ⟨*problem*⟩
(c) (survive unscathed) sortir indemne (**from** de)
(d) (win easily) **to ~ away with** gagner [qch] haut la main ⟨*game, tournament*⟩; remporter [qch] haut la main ⟨*election*⟩; décrocher ⟨*prize, honour*⟩
■ **walk back** revenir sur ses pas (**to** jusqu'à); **we ~ed back (home)** nous sommes rentrés à pied
■ **walk in** entrer; **I'd just ~ed in when...** je venais à peine d'entrer quand...
■ **walk into (a)** ~ **into [sth]** (enter) entrer dans
(b) tomber dans ⟨*trap*⟩; se fourrer dans ⟨*tricky situation*⟩
(c) (bump into) rentrer dans ⟨*door, person*⟩
■ **walk off**: ⓵ **(a) to ~ off** partir brusquement
(b) to ~ off with sth (innocently) partir avec qch; (as theft) filer (fam) avec qch
⓶ **to ~ [sth] off** se promener pour faire passer ⟨*hangover, large meal*⟩
■ **walk out (a)** sortir (**of** de)
(b) (desert) partir; **to ~ out on** laisser tomber (fam) ⟨*lover*⟩; rompre ⟨*contract, undertaking*⟩
(c) (as protest) partir en signe de protestation; (on strike) se mettre en grève
■ **walk over**: ⓵ ¶ ~ **over** s'approcher (**to** de)
⓶ ¶ ~ **over [sb]** (colloq) **(a)** (defeat) battre [qn] à plates coutures
(b) (humiliate) marcher sur les pieds de
■ **walk round**: ⓵ ¶ ~ **round** faire le tour
⓶ ¶ ~ **round [sth]** (round edge of) faire le tour de; (visit) visiter ⟨*town*⟩
■ **walk through** traverser ⟨*house, forest*⟩; passer ⟨*door*⟩; parcourir ⟨*streets*⟩; marcher dans ⟨*snow, mud, grass*⟩
■ **walk up: to ~ up to** s'approcher de
walker *n* (for pleasure) promeneur/-euse *m/f*; (for exercise) marcheur/-euse *m/f*
walkie-talkie *n* talkie-walkie *m*
walking *n* (for pleasure) promenades *fpl* à pied; (for exercise) marche *f* à pied
walking boots *n pl* chaussures *fpl* de marche
walking distance *n* **to be within ~** être à quelques minutes de marche (**of** de)
walking pace *n* pas *m*; **at a ~** au pas
walking stick *n* canne *f*
walkman® *n* (*pl* **-mans**) walkman® *m*, baladeur *m*
walkout *n* (strike) grève *f* surprise
walkover *n* victoire *f* facile (**for** pour)

walkway *n* allée *f*
ᶠ **wall** *n* **(a)** (construction) mur *m*
(b) (of cave, tunnel) paroi *f*
(c) (Anat) paroi *f*
wall chart *n* affiche *f*
walled *adj* ⟨*city*⟩ fortifié/-e; ⟨*garden*⟩ clos/-e
wallet *n* (GB) (for notes) portefeuille *m*; (for documents) porte-documents *m inv*
wallflower *n* giroflée *f* jaune
IDIOM to be a ~ faire tapisserie
wall light *n* applique *f* murale
wall-mounted *adj* fixé/-e au mur
wallow *vi* **to ~ in** se vautrer dans ⟨*mud, luxury*⟩; se complaire dans ⟨*self-pity, nostalgia*⟩
wallpaper ⓵ *n* **(a)** (for walls) papier *m* peint
(b) (Comput) fond *m* d'écran
⓶ *vtr* tapisser ⟨*room*⟩
walnut *n* **(a)** (nut) noix *f*
(b) (tree, wood) noyer *m*
walrus *n* morse *m*
waltz ⓵ *n* valse *f*
⓶ *vi* danser la valse (**with** avec)
wand *n* baguette *f*
wander ⓵ *vtr* parcourir; **to ~ the streets** traîner dans la rue
⓶ *vi* **(a)** (walk, stroll) se promener; **to ~ around town** se balader en ville
(b) (stray) errer; **to ~ away** *or* **off** s'éloigner (**from** de)
(c) ⟨*eyes, hands*⟩ errer (**over** sur); ⟨*attention*⟩ se relâcher; **her mind is ~ing** elle divague
■ **wander about, wander around** (stroll) se balader; (when lost) errer
wane *vi* ⟨*moon*⟩ décroître; ⟨*enthusiasm, popularity*⟩ diminuer
wangle (colloq) ⓵ *n* combine *f* (fam)
⓶ *vtr* soutirer ⟨*money, promise*⟩; se débrouiller pour avoir ⟨*leave*⟩; **to ~ sth for sb** se débrouiller pour faire avoir qch à qn
wannabe(e) *n* (colloq): *personne qui rêve d'être célèbre*
ᶠ **want** ⓵ *n* **(a)** (need) besoin *m*
(b) (lack) défaut *m*; **for ~ of** à défaut *or* faute de; **it's not for ~ of trying** ce n'est pas faute d'avoir essayé
⓶ *vtr* **(a)** (desire) vouloir; **I ~** (as general statement) je veux; (would like) je voudrais; (am seeking) je souhaite; **I don't ~ to** je n'en ai pas envie; (flat refusal) je ne veux pas; **to ~ to do** vouloir faire; **to ~ sb to do** vouloir que qn fasse
(b) (colloq) (need) avoir besoin de
(c) (require presence of) demander; **if anyone ~s me** si quelqu'un me demande; **you're ~ed on the phone** on vous demande au téléphone; **to be ~ed by the police** être recherché/-e par la police
⓷ *vi* **to ~ for** manquer de
wanting *adj* **to be ~** faire défaut; **to be ~ in** manquer de; **to be found ~** s'avérer décevant/-e

wanton adj ‹cruelty, damage, waste› gratuit/-e; ‹disregard› délibéré/-e

⚓ **war** n guerre f; **in the** ∼ à la guerre; **to wage** ∼ **on** faire la guerre contre; (figurative) mener une lutte contre

ward n (a) (in hospital) (unit) service m; (room) unité f, (separate building) pavillon m; **maternity** ∼ service de maternité; **hospital** ∼ salle f d'hôpital

(b) (electoral) circonscription f électorale

(c) (also ∼ **of court**) (Law) pupille m

■ **ward off** chasser ‹evil, predator›; faire taire ‹accusations, criticism›; écarter ‹attack, threat›; éviter ‹disaster›

warden n (of institution, college) directeur/-trice m/f; (of park, estate) gardien/-ienne m/f

warder n (GB) gardien/-ienne m/f

wardrobe n (a) (furniture) armoire f

(b) (set of clothes) garde-robe f; (for theatre) costumes mpl

warehouse n entrepôt m

wares n pl marchandise f, marchandises fpl

warfare n guerre f

war game n jeu m de stratégie (militaire)

warhead n ogive f

warlike adj ‹people› guerrier/-ière; ‹mood, words› belliqueux/-euse

⚓ **warm** ① adj (a) ‹place, food, temperature, water, day, clothing› chaud/-e; **to be** ∼ ‹person› avoir chaud; **it's** ∼ il fait bon or chaud

(b) (affectionate) ‹person, atmosphere, welcome› chaleureux/-euse; ‹admiration, support› enthousiaste

(c) ‹colour› chaud/-e

② vtr chauffer ‹plate, food, water›; réchauffer ‹implement, bed›; **to** ∼ **oneself** se réchauffer; **to** ∼ **one's hands** se réchauffer les mains

③ vi ‹food, liquid, object› chauffer

■ **warm to**, **warm towards** se prendre de sympathie pour ‹person›; se faire à ‹idea›; prendre goût à ‹task›

■ **warm up** ① ∼ up (a) ‹person, room, house› se réchauffer; ‹food, liquid, engine› chauffer

(b) (become lively) s'animer

(c) ‹athlete› s'échauffer; ‹singer› s'échauffer la voix; ‹orchestra, musician› se préparer

② ¶ ∼ [sth] up réchauffer ‹room, bed, person›; faire réchauffer ‹food›

warm-hearted adj chaleureux/-euse

warmly adv ‹smile, thank, recommend› chaleureusement; ‹speak, praise› avec enthousiasme

warmth n chaleur f

warm-up n échauffement m

⚓ **warn** ① vtr avertir, prévenir; **to** ∼ **sb about** or **against sth** mettre qn en garde contre qch; **to** ∼ **sb to do** conseiller or dire à qn de faire; **to** ∼ **sb not to do** déconseiller

à qn de faire

② vi **to** ∼ **of sth** annoncer qch

⚓ **warning** n avertissement m; (by an authority) avis m; (by light, siren) alerte f; **to give sb** ∼ avertir qn (**of** de); **advance** ∼ préavis m; **health** ∼ mise f en garde; **flood** ∼ avis de crue

warning light n voyant m lumineux

warning shot n coup m de semonce

warning sign n (on road) panneau m d'avertissement; (of illness, stress) signe m annonciateur

warning triangle n (Aut) triangle m de présignalisation

warp ① vtr (a) déformer ‹metal, wood, record›

(b) pervertir ‹mind, personality›

② vi se déformer

warped adj (a) ‹metal, wood, record› déformé/-e

(b) ‹mind, humour› tordu/-e; ‹personality, sexuality› perverti/-e; ‹account, view› faussé/-e

warplane n avion m militaire

warrant ① n (Law) mandat m

② vtr justifier ‹action, measure›

warranty n garantie f

warren n (a) (rabbits') garenne f

(b) (building, maze of streets) labyrinthe m

warring adj en conflit

warrior n guerrier/-ière m/f

Warsaw pr n Varsovie

warship n navire m de guerre

wart n verrue f

wartime n **in** ∼ en temps de guerre

war-torn adj déchiré/-e par la guerre

war veteran n ancien combattant m

wary adj (a) (cautious) prudent/-e; **to be** ∼ montrer de la circonspection (**of** vis-à-vis de); **to be** ∼ **of doing** hésiter à faire

(b) (distrustful) méfiant/-e; **to be** ∼ se méfier (**of** de)

wash ① n (a) (clean) **to have a** ∼ se laver; **to give [sth] a** ∼ laver ‹window, floor›; nettoyer ‹object›; lessiver ‹paintwork, walls›; **to give [sb] a** ∼ débarbouiller ‹child›

(b) (laundry process) lavage m; **weekly** ∼ lessive f hebdomadaire; **in the** ∼ (about to be cleaned) au sale; (being cleaned) au lavage

(c) (from boat) remous m

② vtr laver ‹person, clothes, floor›; nettoyer ‹object, wound›; lessiver ‹paintwork, surface›; **to get** ∼**ed** se laver; **to** ∼ **one's hands/face** se laver les mains/le visage; **to** ∼ **the dishes** faire la vaisselle

③ vi (a) ‹person› se laver, faire sa toilette; ‹animal› faire sa toilette

(b) (do laundry) faire la lessive

■ **wash away** emporter ‹structure, debris, person›

■ **wash up** ① ∼ up (a) (GB) (do dishes) faire la vaisselle   ···∻

W

(b) (US) (clean oneself) faire un brin de toilette (fam)
2 ~ **[sth] up (a)** (clean) laver ‹plate›; nettoyer ‹pan›
(b) ‹tide› rejeter ‹debris›
washable adj lavable
washbasin n lavabo m
washbowl n (US) lavabo m
washcloth n (US) lavette f
washed-out adj **(a)** (faded) délavé/-e
(b) (tired) épuisé/-e, lessivé/-e (fam)
washed-up adj (colloq) fichu/-e (fam)
washer n (Tech) (as seal) joint m
washer-dryer n lave-linge/sèche-linge m inv
washing n (laundry) (to be cleaned) linge m sale; (when clean) linge m; **to do the** ~ faire la lessive
washing line n corde f à linge
washing machine n machine f à laver
washing powder n (GB) lessive f (en poudre)
washing-up n (GB) vaisselle f
washing-up liquid n (GB) liquide m (à) vaisselle
washout n **(a)** (colloq) (project, system) fiasco m
(b) (colloq) (person) nullité f (fam)
(c) (game, camp) fiasco m dû à la pluie
washroom n toilettes fpl
wash-stand n (US) lavabo m
wasp n guêpe f
waspish adj acerbe
wastage n **(a)** (of money, resources, talent) gaspillage m; (of heat, energy) déperdition f
(b) (also **natural** ~) élimination f naturelle
waste 1 n **(a)** (of food, money, energy) gaspillage m (**of** de); (of time) perte f (**of** de); **a** ~ **of effort** un effort inutile; **that car is such a** ~ **of money!** cette voiture, c'est vraiment de l'argent jeté par les fenêtres!; **to let sth go to** ~ gaspiller qch
(b) (detritus) (also **wastes** US) déchets mpl (**from** de)
2 **wastes** n pl **(a)** (wilderness) étendues fpl sauvages
(b) (US) = 1B
3 adj **(a)** ‹heat, energy› gaspillé/-e; ‹water› usé/-e; ~ **materials** déchets mpl
(b) ‹land› inculte
(c) to lay ~ **to** dévaster
4 vtr **(a)** (squander) gaspiller ‹food, resources, energy, money, talents›; perdre ‹time, opportunity›; user ‹strength›
(b) (make thinner) décharner; (make weaker) atrophier
wastebasket n corbeille f à papier
wastebin n (GB) (for paper) corbeille f à papier; (for rubbish) poubelle f

wasted adj **(a)** ‹effort, life, vote› inutile; ‹energy, years› gaspillé/-e
(b) (fleshless) ‹body, limb› décharné/-e; (weak) ‹body, limb› atrophié/-e
waste disposal n traitement m des déchets
waste disposal unit n (GB) broyeur m d'ordures
wasteful adj ‹product, machine› qui consomme beaucoup; ‹method, process› peu économique; ‹person› gaspilleur/-euse
wasteland n (urban) terrain m vague; (rural) terre f à l'abandon
wastepaper n papier m or papiers mpl à jeter
wastepaper basket, wastepaper bin (GB) n corbeille f à papier
waste pipe n tuyau m de vidange
wasting adj ‹disease› débilitant/-e
✔ **watch** 1 n **(a)** (timepiece) montre f
(b) (surveillance) surveillance f (**on** sur); **to keep** ~ monter la garde; **to keep (a)** ~ **on sb/sth** surveiller qn/qch
2 vtr **(a)** (look at) regarder; (observe) observer
(b) (monitor) suivre ‹career, development›; surveiller ‹situation›
(c) (keep under surveillance) surveiller ‹person, movements›
(d) (pay attention to) faire attention à ‹obstacle, dangerous object, money›; surveiller ‹language, manners, weight›; **to** ~ **one's step** (figurative) faire attention
(e) (look after) garder ‹person, property›
3 vi regarder (**from** de)
■ **watch for** guetter ‹person, chance›; surveiller l'apparition de ‹symptom›
■ **watch out** (be careful) faire attention (**for** à); (keep watch) guetter; ~ **out!** attention!
■ **watch over** veiller sur ‹person›; veiller à ‹interests, rights, welfare›
watchable adj qui se laisse regarder
watchband n (US) bracelet m de montre
watchdog n **(a)** (dog) chien m de garde
(b) (organization) organisme m de surveillance
watchmaker n horloger/-ère m/f
watchman n (guard) gardien m
watch strap n bracelet m de montre
watchword n slogan m
✔ **water** 1 n eau f
2 vtr arroser ‹lawn, plant›; irriguer ‹crop, field›; abreuver ‹livestock›
3 vi **the smell of cooking makes my mouth** ~ l'odeur de cuisine me fait venir l'eau à la bouche; **the smoke made her eyes** ~ la fumée l'a fait pleurer
■ **water down (a)** couper [qch] d'eau ‹beer, wine›; diluer ‹syrup›
(b) atténuer ‹effect, plans, policy›; édulcorer ‹description, story›
water bed n matelas m d'eau

water bird n oiseau m aquatique

water birth n accouchement m aquatique

water bottle n (for cyclist) bidon m

water cannon n canon m à eau

watercolour (GB), **watercolor** (US)
n (paint) peinture f pour aquarelle; (painting)
aquarelle f

watercress n cresson m (de fontaine)

waterfall n cascade f

water filter n filtre m à eau

waterfront n (on harbour) front m de mer;
(by lakeside, riverside) bord m de l'eau

water-heater n chauffe-eau m inv

watering can n arrosoir m

water jump n rivière f

water level n niveau m d'eau

water lily n nénuphar m

waterlogged adj ‹ground, pitch›
détrempé/-e

water main n canalisation f d'eau

watermark n (of sea) laisse f; (of river) ligne
f des hautes eaux; (on paper) filigrane m

watermelon n pastèque f

water power n énergie f hydraulique

waterproof adj ‹coat› imperméable;
‹make-up› résistant/-e à l'eau

waterproofs n pl vêtements mpl
imperméables

water-resistant adj qui résiste à l'eau

watershed n (a) (US) (area) bassin m
hydrographique
(b) (GB) (line) ligne f de partage des eaux;
(figurative) point m décisif

water-ski ① n ski m nautique
② vi faire du ski nautique

water-skiing n ski m nautique

water slide n toboggan m de piscine

water sport n sport m nautique

water supply n (in an area)
approvisionnement m en eau; (to a building)
alimentation f en eau

watertight adj (a) ‹container, seal› étanche
(b) ‹argument, case› incontestable; ‹alibi›
irréfutable

water tower n château m d'eau

water trough n abreuvoir m

waterway n voie f navigable

water wings n pl bracelets mpl de
natation

watery adj (a) ‹sauce, paint› trop liquide;
‹coffee› trop léger/-ère
(b) ‹colour, smile› pâle

watt n watt m

⚘ **wave** ① n (a) (of hand) signe m (de la main)
(b) (of water) vague f; **to make ~s** ‹wind› faire
des vagues; (cause a stir) faire du bruit; (cause
trouble) créer des histoires (fam)
(c) (outbreak, surge) vague f (**of** de)
(d) (of light, radio) onde f

(e) (in hair) cran m
② vtr (a) agiter ‹flag, ticket, banknote›;
brandir ‹umbrella, stick, gun›
(b) **to ~ goodbye to sb** faire au revoir de la
main à qn
③ vi (a) (with hand) **to ~ to** or **at sb** saluer
qn de la main
(b) ‹branches› être agité/-e par le vent; ‹corn›
ondoyer; ‹flag› flotter au vent

wave band n bande f de fréquence

wave farm n ferme f hydrolienne

wavelength n (on radio) longueur f d'onde
IDIOM **to be on the same ~ as sb** être sur la
même longueur d'onde que qn

waver vi (a) (weaken) ‹person› vaciller;
‹courage, love› faiblir; ‹voice› trembler
(b) (hesitate) hésiter (**between** entre; **over** sur)

wavy adj ‹hair, line› ondulé/-e

wax ① n (for candle, seal) cire f; (for skis) fart
m; (in ear) cérumen m
② vtr (a) cirer ‹floor›; lustrer ‹car›; farter
‹ski›
(b) (depilate) épiler [qch] à la cire ‹legs›
③ vi ‹moon› croître

waxed jacket n ciré m

wax paper n papier m paraffin

waxwork n personnage m en cire

waxworks n musée m de cire

waxy adj cireux/-euse

⚘ **way** ① n (a) (route, road) chemin m (**from**
de; **to** à); **the quickest ~ to town** le chemin
le plus court pour aller en ville; **to ask the
~ to the station** demander le chemin pour
aller à la gare; **there is no ~ around the
problem** il n'y a pas moyen de contourner
le problème; **on the ~ back** sur le chemin
du retour; **on the ~ back from the meeting**
en revenant de la réunion; **the ~ in** l'entrée
(**to** de); **the ~ out** la sortie (**of** de); **a ~ out of
our difficulties** un moyen de nous sortir de
nos difficultés; **the ~ up** la montée; **on the
~** en route; **to be out of sb's ~** ‹place› ne
pas être sur le chemin de qn; **don't go out of
your ~ to do** ne te donne pas de mal pour
faire; **out of the ~** (isolated) isolé/-e; (unusual)
extraordinaire; **by ~ of** (via) en passant par;
to make one's ~ towards se diriger vers; **to
make one's ~ along** avancer le long de;
to make one's own ~ there y aller par ses
propres moyens
(b) (direction) direction f, sens m; **which ~ did
he go?** dans quelle direction est-il parti?;
he went that ~ il est parti par là; **come this
~** suivez-moi, venez par ici; **'this ~ up'**
'haut'; **to look the other ~** (to see) regarder
de l'autre côté; (to avoid seeing unpleasant thing)
détourner les yeux; (to ignore wrongdoing)
fermer les yeux; **the other ~ up** dans l'autre
sens; **the right ~ up** dans le bon sens; **the
wrong ~ up** à l'envers; **to turn sth the other
~ around** retourner qch; **I didn't ask her, it
was the other ~ around** ce n'est pas moi qui ⋯⋗

W

le lui ai demandé, c'est l'inverse; **the wrong/right ~ around** dans le mauvais/bon sens
(c) (space in front, projected route) passage *m*; **to be in sb's ~** empêcher qn de passer; **to be in the ~** gêner le passage; **to get out of the ~** s'écarter (du chemin); **to get out of sb's ~** laisser passer qn; **to keep out of the ~** rester à l'écart; **to keep out of sb's ~** éviter qn; **to make ~** s'écarter; **to make ~ for sb/sth** faire place à qn/qch
(d) (distance) distance *f*; **it's a long ~** c'est loin (**to** jusqu'à); **to go all the ~ to China** aller jusqu'en Chine
(e) (manner) façon *f*, manière *f*; **do it this/that ~** fais-le comme ceci/cela; **to do another ~** faire autrement; **the French ~** à la française; **to write sth the right/wrong ~** écrire qch bien/mal; **try to see it my ~** mets-toi à ma place; **in his/her/its own ~** à sa façon; **to have a ~ with words** savoir manier les mots; **to have a ~ with children** savoir s'y prendre avec les enfants; **a ~ of doing** (method) une façon *or* manière de faire; (means) un moyen de faire; **I like the ~ he dresses** j'aime la façon dont il s'habille; **either ~, she's wrong** de toute façon, elle a tort; **one ~ or another** d'une façon ou d'une autre; **I don't care one ~ or the other** ça m'est égal; **you can't have it both ~s** on ne peut pas avoir le beurre et l'argent du beurre; **no ~!**(colloq) pas question! (fam); **~ of life** mode de vie
(f) (respect, aspect) sens *m*; **in a ~ it's sad** en un sens c'est triste; **in a ~ that's true** dans une certaine mesure c'est vrai; **in many ~s** à bien des égards; **in some ~s** à certains égards; **in no ~, not in any ~** aucunement
(g) (custom, manner) coutume *f*, manière *f*; **that's the modern ~** c'est ce qui se fait de nos jours; **I know all her little ~s** je connais toutes ses petites habitudes; **that's just his ~** il est comme ça; **it's the ~ of the world** c'est la vie
(h) (will, desire) **to get one's ~, to have one's own ~** faire à son idée; **she likes (to have) her own ~** elle aime n'en faire qu'à sa tête; **if I had my ~** si cela ne tenait qu'à moi; **have it your (own) ~** comme tu voudras
2 *adv* **we went ~ over budget** le budget a été largement dépassé; **to be ~ out** (in guess, estimate) être loin du compte; **that's ~ out of order** je trouve ça un peu fort
3 **by the way** *phr* en passant; **by the ~,...** à propos,...; **what time is it, by the ~?** quelle heure est-il, au fait?

waylay *vtr* (*prét, pp* **-laid**) ‹*attacker*› attaquer; ‹*beggar, friend*› arrêter, harponner (fam)

waymark *n* balise *f*

way-out *adj* (colloq) excentrique

wayside *n*
IDIOM **to fall by the ~** (stray morally) quitter le droit chemin; (fail, not stay the course)

abandonner en cours de route; (be cancelled, fall through) tomber à l'eau

wayward *adj* ‹*person, nature*› difficile; ‹*husband, wife*› volage

✔ **we** *pron* nous

> ■ **Note** In standard French, *we* is translated by nous but in informal French, *on* is frequently used: *we're going to the cinema* = nous allons au cinéma *or more informally* on va au cinéma.
> — *on* is also used in correct French to refer to a large, vaguely defined group: *we shouldn't lie to our children* = on ne devrait pas mentir à ses enfants.

~ saw her yesterday nous l'avons vue hier; **~ left at six** nous sommes partis à six heures; (informal) on est partis (fam) à six heures; **~ Scots like the sun** nous autres Écossais, nous aimons le soleil; **we didn't say that** nous, nous n'avons pas dit cela; (colloq) nous, on n'a pas dit ça (fam); **~ all make mistakes** tout le monde peut se tromper

✔ **weak** *adj* **(a)** ‹*person, animal, muscle, limb*› faible; ‹*health, ankle, heart, nerves*› fragile; ‹*stomach*› délicat/-e; ‹*intellect*› médiocre; ‹*chin*› fuyant/-e; **to be ~ with** *or* **from hunger** être affaibli/-e par la faim; **to grow** *or* **become ~(er)** ‹*person*› s'affaiblir; ‹*pulse, heartbeat*› faiblir
(b) ‹*beam, support*› peu solide; ‹*structure*› fragile
(c) (lacking authority, strength) ‹*government, team, pupil, president*› faible; ‹*parent, teacher*› (not firm) qui manque de fermeté; (poor) piètre ‹*before n*›; ‹*plot*› mince; ‹*actor, protest, excuse, argument*› peu convaincant/-e; **~ link** *or* **spot** point *m* faible
(d) (faint) ‹*light, current, concentration, sound*› faible; ‹*tea, coffee*› léger/-ère
(e) ‹*economy, dollar*› faible (**against** par rapport à)

weaken **1** *vtr* **(a)** (through illness, damage) affaiblir ‹*person, heart, structure*›; diminuer ‹*resistance*›; rendre [qch] moins solide ‹*joint, bank, wall*›
(b) (undermine) nuire à l'autorité de ‹*government, president*›; affaiblir ‹*team, company, authority, defence*›; amoindrir ‹*argument, power*›; nuire à ‹*morale*›
(c) (dilute) diluer
2 *vi* **(a)** (physically) s'affaiblir
(b) ‹*government, resolve*› fléchir; ‹*support, alliance*› se relâcher
(c) (Econ) ‹*economy, currency*› être en baisse

weakling *n* (physically) gringalet *m*; (morally) mauviette *f*

weakness *n* **(a)** (weak point) point *m* faible
(b) (liking) faible *m* (**for** pour)
(c) (physical, moral) faiblesse *f*
(d) (lack of authority) faiblesse *f*; (of evidence, position) fragilité *f*
(e) (of light, current, sound) faiblesse *f*; (of tea, solution) légèreté *f*

(f) (of economy, currency) faiblesse *f*
weak-willed *adj* to be ∼ manquer de fermeté
wealth *n* **(a)** (possessions) fortune *f*
(b) (state) richesse *f*
(c) (large amount) a ∼ of une mine de ‹information›; une profusion de ‹detail›; énormément de ‹experience, talent›
wealthy *adj* riche
wean *vtr* sevrer ‹baby›; to ∼ sb away from *or* off sth détourner qn de qch
✦ **weapon** *n* arme *f*; ∼s of mass destruction armes *fpl* de destruction massive
weaponry *n* matériel *m* de guerre
✦ **wear** **1** *n* **(a)** (clothing) children's/sports ∼ vêtements *mpl* pour enfants/de sport
(b) (use) for everyday ∼ de tous les jours; for summer ∼ pour l'été
(c) (damage) usure *f* (on de); ∼ and tear usure *f*; to be the worse for ∼ (drunk) être ivre; (tired) être épuisé/-e
2 *vtr* (*prét* **wore**, *pp* **worn**) **(a)** (be dressed in) porter; to ∼ blue s'habiller en bleu; to ∼ one's hair long/short avoir les cheveux longs/courts
(b) (put on, use) mettre; I haven't got a thing to ∼ je n'ai rien à me mettre; to ∼ make-up se maquiller
(c) (display) he wore a puzzled frown il fronçait les sourcils d'un air perplexe
(d) (damage by use) user; to ∼ a hole in trouer ‹garment, sheet›
3 *vi* (*prét* **wore**, *pp* **worn**) ‹carpet, shoes› s'user; my patience is ∼ing thin je commence à être à bout de patience
■ **wear away** ‹inscription› s'effacer; ‹tread, cliff, façade› s'user
■ **wear down**: **1** ¶ ∼ down s'user; to be worn down être usé/-e
2 ¶ ∼ [sth] down user ‹steps›; saper ‹resistance, resolve›
3 ¶ ∼ [sb] down épuiser
■ **wear off (a)** ‹drug, effect› se dissiper; ‹sensation› passer
(b) (come off) s'effacer
■ **wear out**: **1** ¶ ∼ out s'user
2 ¶ ∼ [sth] out user
3 ¶ ∼ [sb] out épuiser
■ **wear through** ‹elbow, trousers› se trouer; ‹sole, metal, fabric› se percer
weariness *n* lassitude *f*
wearing *adj* (exhausting) fatigant/-e; (irritating) pénible
weary **1** *adj* ‹person, smile, sigh, voice› las/lasse; ‹eyes, limbs, mind› fatigué/-e; to grow ∼ se lasser (of de; of doing de faire)
2 *vi* se lasser (of de; of doing de faire)
weasel *n* **(a)** (Zool) belette *f*
(b) (sly person) sournois/-e *m/f*
✦ **weather** **1** *n* temps *m*; what's the ∼ like? quel temps fait-il?; the ∼ here is hot il fait chaud ici; in hot/cold ∼ quand il fait chaud/

froid; ∼ permitting si le temps le permet; in all ∼s par tous les temps
2 *vtr* survivre à ‹crisis, upheaval›; to ∼ the storm (figurative) surmonter la crise
IDIOM to be under the ∼ ne pas se sentir bien
weatherbeaten *adj* ‹face› hâlé/-e; ‹rocks, landscape› battu/-e par les vents
weathercock *n* girouette *f*
weather forecast *n* bulletin *m* météorologique
weather forecaster *n* (on TV) présentateur/-trice *m/f* de la météo; (specialist) météorologue *mf*, météorologiste *mf*
weatherproof *adj* ‹garment, shoe› imperméable; ‹shelter, door› étanche
weave **1** *vtr* (*prét* **wove** *ou* **weaved**, *pp* **woven** *ou* **weaved**) **(a)** tisser ‹rug, fabric›
(b) tresser ‹cane, basket, wreath›
2 *vi* (*prét* **wove** *ou* **weaved**, *pp* **woven** *ou* **weaved**) to ∼ in and out se faufiler (of entre); to ∼ towards sth (drunk) s'approcher en titubant de qch
weaving *n* tissage *m*
✦ **web** *n* **(a)** (also **spider's** ∼ (GB), **spiderweb** (US)) toile *f* (d'araignée)
(b) (network) a ∼ of un réseau de ‹ropes, lines›; a ∼ of lies un tissu de mensonges
Web *n* the ∼ le Web *m*, la Toile *f*
webbing *n* (material) sangles *fpl*
Web cam *n* Webcam *f*
web foot *n* (*pl* **web feet**) patte *f* palmée
webinar *n* webinaire *m*
Webmaster *n* Webmestre *m*, Webmaster *m*
Web page *n* page *f* Web
Web server *n* serveur *m* Web
Website *n* site *m* Web
Web space *n* espace *m* Web
wed *n* the newly ∼s les jeunes mariés *mpl*
wedding *n* mariage *m*; a church ∼ un mariage religieux
wedding anniversary *n* anniversaire *m* de mariage
wedding day *n* jour *m* des noces
wedding dress, **wedding gown** *n* robe *f* de mariée
wedding reception *n* repas *m* de mariage
wedding ring *n* alliance *f*
wedge **1** *n* **(a)** (to insert in rock, wood) coin *m*; (to hold sth in position) cale *f*; (in rock climbing) piton *m*
(b) (of cake, pie, cheese) morceau *m*
2 *vtr* **(a)** to ∼ sth in place caler qch; to ∼ a door open caler une porte pour la tenir ouverte
(b) (jam) to ∼ sth into enfoncer qch dans; to be ∼d between être coincé/-e entre
IDIOM that's the thin end of the ∼ c'est le commencement de la fin

W

⚘ **Wednesday** n mercredi m

wee vi (GB) faire pipi (fam)

weed [1] n mauvaise herbe f; (in water) herbes fpl aquatiques
[2] vtr, vi désherber
■ **weed out**: [1] ¶ ∼ [sb] out, ∼ out [sb] (gen) éliminer; se débarrasser de ‹employee›
[2] ¶ ∼ [sth] out, ∼ out [sth] se débarrasser de ‹stock, items›

weedkiller n désherbant m, herbicide m

weedy adj (colloq) ‹person, build› malingre; ‹character, personality› faible

⚘ **week** n semaine f; last/next ∼ la semaine dernière/prochaine; this ∼ cette semaine; the ∼ before last il y a deux semaines; the ∼ after next dans deux semaines; every other ∼ tous les quinze jours; twice a ∼ deux fois par semaine; ∼ in ∼ out toutes les semaines; a ∼ today/on Monday (GB), today/ Monday ∼ aujourd'hui/lundi en huit; a ∼ yesterday (GB), a ∼ from yesterday (US) il y a eu huit jours or une semaine hier; in three ∼s' time dans trois semaines; the working or work (US) ∼ la semaine de travail

weekday n jour m de (la) semaine; on ∼s en semaine

⚘ **weekend** n week-end m; at the ∼ (GB), on the ∼ (US) pendant le week-end; at ∼s (GB), on ∼s (US) le week-end

weekend bag n petit sac m de voyage

weekend cottage n résidence f secondaire

weekly [1] n (newspaper) journal m hebdomadaire; (magazine) (revue f) hebdomadaire m
[2] adj hebdomadaire; on a ∼ basis à la semaine
[3] adv ‹pay› à la semaine; ‹meet, visit› une fois par semaine

weep vi (prét, pp **wept**) (a) (cry) pleurer (over sur)
(b) (ooze) suinter

weepy adj ‹mood, film› larmoyant/-e; to feel ∼ avoir envie de pleurer

weigh [1] vtr (a) (on scales) peser; to ∼ 10 kilos peser 10 kilos; how much or what do you ∼? combien pèses-tu?; to ∼ oneself se peser
(b) (assess) évaluer ‹arguments, advantages, options›; peser ‹consequences, risks, words›
[2] vi to ∼ on sb peser sur qn; to ∼ on sb's mind préoccuper qn
■ **weigh down**: [1] ¶ ∼ down on [sb/sth] peser sur
[2] ¶ ∼ [sb/sth] down surcharger ‹vehicle, boat›; faire plier ‹branches›; ‹responsibility, debt› accabler; to be ∼ed down with crouler sous le poids de ‹luggage›; être accablé/-e de ‹worry, guilt›
■ **weigh in** ‹boxer, wrestler› se faire peser;

⚘ indicates a very frequent word

‹jockey› aller au pesage
■ **weigh out** peser ‹ingredients, quantity›
■ **weigh up** évaluer ‹prospects, situation›; juger ‹person›; mettre [qch] en balance ‹options, benefits, risks›

weighing machine n (for people) balance f; (for luggage, freight) bascule f

⚘ **weight** [1] n poids m; to put on/lose ∼ prendre/perdre du poids
[2] vtr lester ‹net, arrow›
IDIOMS not to carry much ∼ ne pas peser lourd (with pour); to be a ∼ off one's mind être un grand soulagement; to pull one's ∼ faire sa part de travail; to throw one's ∼ about or around faire l'important/-e m/f

weightlessness n (in space) apesanteur f

weight-lifter n haltérophile m

weight-lifting n haltérophilie f

weight problem n problème m de poids

weight training n musculation f (en salle)

weighty adj (a) (serious) de grand poids
(b) (heavy) lourd/-e

weir n barrage m

weird adj (strange) bizarre; (eerie) mystérieux/-ieuse

⚘ **welcome** [1] n accueil m; to give sb a warm ∼ faire un accueil chaleureux à qn
[2] adj (a) bienvenu/-e; to be ∼ être le bienvenu/la bienvenue m/f; to make sb ∼ (on arrival) réserver un bon accueil à qn
(b) 'thanks'—'you're ∼' 'merci'—'de rien'
[3] excl (to respected guest) soyez le bienvenu/ la bienvenue m/f chez nous!; (greeting friend) entrez donc!; ∼ back!, ∼ home! je suis content que tu sois de retour!
[4] vtr accueillir ‹person›; se réjouir de ‹news, decision, change›; être heureux/-euse de recevoir ‹contribution›; accueillir favorablement ‹initiative, move›

welcoming adj ‹atmosphere, person› accueillant/-e; ‹ceremony, committee› d'accueil

weld vtr (also ∼ **together**) souder; to ∼ sth on or to souder qch à

welfare [1] n (a) (well-being) bien-être m inv; (interest) intérêt m
(b) (state assistance) assistance f sociale; (money) aide f sociale
[2] adj ‹system› de protection sociale; (US) ‹meal› gratuit/-e

welfare benefit n prestation f sociale

welfare services n pl services mpl sociaux

welfare spending n dépenses fpl sociales

welfare state n (as concept) État-providence m; (stressing state assistance) protection f sociale

⚘ **well**[1] [1] adj (comp **better**, superl **best**) bien; to feel ∼ se sentir bien; are you ∼? vous allez bien?/tu vas bien?; she's not ∼ enough to travel elle n'est pas en état de

voyager; **to get** ∼ se rétablir; **that's all very**
∼**, but…** tout ça c'est bien beau, mais…;
it would be just as ∼ **to check** il vaudrait
mieux vérifier; **it would be as** ∼ **for you not
to get involved** tu ferais mieux de ne pas t'en
mêler; **the flight was delayed, which was just
as** ∼ le vol a été retardé, ce qui n'était pas
plus mal
2 *adv* (*comp* **better,** *superl* **best**) bien;
to do ∼ **at school** être bon/bonne élève;
mother and baby are both doing ∼ la mère
et l'enfant se portent bien; **the operation
went** ∼ l'opération s'est bien passée; ∼
done! bravo!; **you may** ∼ **be right** il se
pourrait bien que tu aies raison; **we may as**
∼ **go home** on ferait aussi bien de rentrer; **it
was** ∼ **worth waiting for** ça valait vraiment
la peine d'attendre; **to wish sb** ∼ souhaiter
beaucoup de chance à qn
3 *excl* (expressing astonishment) eh bien!;
(expressing indignation, disgust) ça alors!;
(expressing disappointment) tant pis!; (qualifying
statement) enfin; ∼**, you may be right** après
tout, tu as peut-être raison; ∼**, that's too bad**
c'est vraiment dommage; ∼ **then, what's the
problem?** alors, quel est le problème?; **very**
∼ **then** très bien
4 **as well** *phr* aussi
5 **as well as** *phr* aussi bien que; **they
have a house in the country as** ∼ **as an
apartment in Paris** ils ont à la fois une
maison à la campagne et un appartement
à Paris
IDIOMS **to be** ∼ **in with sb** (colloq) être bien
avec qn (fam); **to be** ∼ **up in sth** s'y connaître
en qch; **to leave** ∼ **alone** (GB) *or* ∼ **enough
alone** (US) ne pas s'en mêler
well² *n* (sunk in ground) puits *m*; (pool) source *f*
well-balanced *adj* équilibré/-e
well-behaved *adj* ‹child› sage; ‹dog› bien
dressé/-e
well-being *n* bien-être *m inv*
well-defined *adj* ‹outline› net/nette; ‹role,
boundary› bien défini/-e
well-disposed *adj* **to be** ∼ **towards**
être bien disposé/-e envers ‹person›; être
favorable à ‹regime, idea, policy›
well done *adj* ‹steak› bien cuit/-e; ‹task›
bien fait/-e
well-educated *adj* (having a good education)
instruit/-e; (cultured) cultivé/-e
well-heeled *adj* (colloq) riche
well-informed *adj* bien informé/-e (**about**
sur); **he's very** ∼ il est très au courant de
l'actualité
wellington (boot) *n* (GB) botte *f* de
caoutchouc
well-kept *adj* ‹house, garden, village› bien
entretenu/-e
well-known *adj* ‹person, place› célèbre; **to
be** ∼ **to sb** être connu/-e de qn; **it is** ∼ **that, it
is a** ∼ **fact that** il est bien connu que
well-liked *adj* très apprécié/-e

well-made *adj* bien fait/-e
well-meaning *adj* ‹person› bien
intentionné/-e; ‹advice› qui part d'une bonne
intention
well-meant *adj* **his offer was** ∼ sa
proposition partait d'une bonne intention
well-off **1** *n* **the** ∼ les gens *mpl* aisés; **the
less** ∼ les plus défavorisés *mpl*
2 *adj* (wealthy) aisé/-e; **to be** ∼ **for** avoir
beaucoup de ‹space, provisions›
well-read *adj* cultivé/-e
well-respected *adj* très respecté/-e
well-rounded *adj* ‹education, programme›
complet/-ète; ‹individual› qui a reçu une
éducation complète
well-thought-out *adj* bien élaboré/-e
well-timed *adj* qui tombe/tombait à point;
that was well timed! (of entrance, phonecall etc)
c'est bien tombé!
well-to-do *adj* aisé/-e
well-wisher *n* personne *f* qui veut
témoigner sa sympathie
well-worn *adj* ‹carpet, garment› élimé/-e;
‹steps› usé/-e; ‹joke› rebattu/-e
Welsh **1** *n* (a) (people) **the** ∼ les Gallois *mpl*
(b) (language) gallois *m*
2 *adj* gallois/-e
welt *n* (on skin) marque *f* (de coup)
welterweight *n* poids *m* welter
west **1** *n* (a) (compass direction) ouest *m*
(b) **the West** l'Occident *m*, l'Ouest *m*; (part of
country) l'Ouest *m*; (political entity) l'Occident *m*
2 *adj* (gen) ouest *inv*; ‹wind› d'ouest
3 *adv* ‹move› vers l'ouest; ‹lie, live› à l'ouest
(**of** de)
West Bank *pr n* Cisjordanie *f*
western **1** *n* (film) western *m*
2 *adj* (a) ‹coast› ouest *inv*; ‹town, accent› de
l'ouest; ∼ **France** l'ouest de la France
(b) (Pol) occidental/-e
westerner *n* Occidental/-e *m/f*
westernize *vtr* occidentaliser; **to become**
∼**d** s'occidentaliser
west-facing *adj* exposé/-e à l'ouest
West Indian **1** *n* Antillais/-e *m/f*
2 *adj* antillais/-e
West Indies *pr n pl* Antilles *fpl*
wet **1** *adj* (a) (damp) ‹hair, clothes, grass,
surface› mouillé/-e; **to get** ∼ se faire
mouiller; **to get one's feet** ∼ se mouiller les
pieds; **to get the floor** ∼ tremper le sol; ∼
through trempé/-e
(b) (freshly applied) ‹cement, varnish› humide;
'∼ **paint**' 'peinture fraîche'
(c) (rainy) ‹weather, day, night› pluvieux/
-ieuse; ‹season› des pluies; **when it's** ∼ quand
il pleut
(d) (GB) ‹person› qui manque de caractère
2 *vtr* (*p prés* **-tt-,** *prét pp* ∼) (a) mouiller
‹floor, object, clothes›
(b) **to** ∼ **one's pants/the bed** ‹adult› mouiller
sa culotte/le lit; ‹child› faire pipi (fam) dans ···>

sa culotte/dans son lit

wet blanket n (colloq) rabat-joie mf inv

wet-look adj luisant/-e

wet suit n combinaison f de plongée

whack [1] n (blow) (grand) coup m

[2] excl paf!

[3] vtr (a) (hit) battre ‹person, animal›; frapper ‹ball›

(b) (GB) (defeat) piler (fam)

whacked adj (colloq) (tired) vanné/-e (fam)

whacky adj (colloq) ‹person› dingue (fam); ‹sense of humour› farfelu/-e (fam)

whale [1] n (a) (Zool) baleine f

(b) (colloq) to have a ~ of a time s'amuser comme un fou

[2] vtr (US) (colloq) (thrash) donner une raclée à (fam)

whaling n pêche f à la baleine

wharf n (pl **wharves**) quai m

♂ **what**

■ **Note** As a pronoun

— When used in questions as an object pronoun what is translated by qu'est-ce que (qu'est-ce qu' in front of a vowel or mute 'h'): what did you say? qu'est-ce que tu as dit? Alternatively you can use que (qu' before a vowel or mute 'h'), but note that subject and verb are reversed and a hyphen is inserted before a pronoun: what did you say? qu'as-tu dit?

— As a subject pronoun in questions what is translated by qu'est-ce qui: what is happening? qu'est-ce qui se passe? Alternatively que can be used and the subject and verb are reversed and the subject becomes il: what is happening? que se passe-t-il?

— When what is used to introduce a clause it is translated by ce que (ce qu') as the object of the verb: I don't know what you want je ne sais pas ce que tu veux. As the subject of the verb it is translated by ce qui: what matters is that… ce qui compte c'est que…

[1] pron with ~? avec quoi?; and ~ else? et quoi d'autre?; ~ for? (why) pourquoi?; (about what) à propos de quoi?; ~'s the matter? qu'est-ce qu'il y a?; ~'s her telephone number? quel est son numéro de téléphone?; ~'s that button for? à quoi sert ce bouton?; ~'s it like? comment c'est?; do ~ you want fais ce que tu veux; take ~ you need prends ce dont tu as besoin; ~ I need is... ce dont j'ai besoin c'est...; and ~'s more et en plus; and ~'s worse et en plus; he did ~? il a fait quoi?; **George** ~? George comment?

[2] det quel/quelle/quels/quelles; do you know ~ train he took? est-ce que tu sais quel train il a pris?; ~ a nice dress/car! quelle belle robe/voiture!; ~ a strange thing to do! quelle drôle d'idée!; ~ use is that? à quoi ça sert?; ~ money he earns he spends tout ce qu'il gagne, il le dépense; ~ few friends she **had** les quelques amis qu'elle avait

[3] **what about** phr (a) (to draw attention) ~ **about the children?** et les enfants (alors)?

(b) (to make suggestion) ~ **about a meal out?** et si on dînait au restaurant?; ~ **about Tuesday?** qu'est-ce que tu dirais de mardi?

[4] **what if** phr et si; ~ **if I bring the dessert?** et si j'apportais le dessert?

[5] excl quoi!, comment!

IDIOM ~ **with one thing and another** avec ceci et cela

what-d'yer-call-it n (colloq) machin m (fam)

♂ **whatever** [1] pron (a) (that which) (as subject) ce qui; (as object) ce que; **to do** ~ **one can** faire ce qu'on peut

(b) (anything that) (as subject) tout ce qui; (as object) tout ce que; **do** ~ **you like** fais tout ce que tu veux; ~ **you say** (as you like) tout ce qui vous plaira

(c) (no matter what) quoi que (+ subjunctive); ~ **happens** quoi qu'il arrive; ~ **she says, ignore it** quoi qu'elle dise n'en tiens pas compte; ~ **it costs it doesn't matter** quel que soit le prix, ça n'a pas d'importance

(d) (what on earth) (as subject) qu'est-ce qui; (as object) qu'est-ce que; ~**'s that?** qu'est-ce que c'est que ça?

[2] det (a) (any) **they eat** ~ **food they can get** ils mangent tout ce qu'ils trouvent à manger

(b) (no matter what) ~ **their arguments** quels que soient leurs arguments; ~ **the reason** quelle que soit la raison; **for** ~ **reason** pour je ne sais quelle raison

[3] adv (also **whatsoever**) **to have no idea** ~ ne pas avoir la moindre idée; '**any petrol?**'—'**none** ~' 'il y a de l'essence?'—'pas du tout'

what's-her-name n (colloq) Machin m (fam)

what's-his-name n (colloq) Machin m (fam)

wheat n blé m

wheat germ n germe m de blé

wheatmeal n farine f complète

wheedle vtr **to** ~ **sth out of sb** soutirer qch à qn par la cajolerie

wheel [1] n (a) (on vehicle) roue f; (on trolley, piece of furniture) roulette f

(b) (for steering) (in vehicle) volant m; (on boat) roue f (de gouvernail); **to be at** or **behind the** ~ être au volant

(c) (in watch, mechanism, machine) rouage m

(d) (for pottery) tour m

[2] vtr pousser ‹bicycle, barrow›; **they** ~**ed me into the operating theatre** ils m'ont emmené dans la salle d'opération sur un chariot

[3] vi (also ~ **round**) ‹person, regiment› faire demi-tour; ‹car, motorbike› braquer fortement; ‹ship› virer de bord

IDIOM **to** ~ **and deal** magouiller (fam)

wheelbarrow n brouette f

wheelchair n fauteuil m roulant

wheelclamp n (Aut) sabot m de Denver

wheeler dealer n (colloq) magouilleur/ -euse m/f (fam)

W

wheelie bin ···> which ····

wheelie bin n (GB) poubelle f à roulettes

wheeze vi avoir la respiration sifflante

wheezy adj ‹voice, cough› rauque; **to have a ~ chest** avoir la respiration sifflante

✧ **when**

■ Note When in questions is usually translated by quand.
— Note that there are three ways of asking questions using quand: when did she leave? = quand est-ce qu'elle est partie?, elle est partie quand?, quand est-elle partie?
— When talking about future time, quand will be used with the future tense of the verb: tell him when you see him = dis-lui quand tu le verras.

⬚1 adv (a) (in questions) quand; **~ are we leaving?** quand est-ce qu'on part?; **~ is the concert?** c'est quand le concert?; **I wonder ~ the film starts** je me demande à quelle heure commence le film; **say ~** dis-moi stop
(b) (whenever) quand; **he's only happy ~ he's moaning** il n'est content que quand il rouspète; **~ I eat ice cream, I feel ill** quand or chaque fois que je mange de la glace, j'ai mal au cœur
⬚2 rel pron où; **the week ~ it all happened** la semaine où tout cela s'est produit; **there are times ~ it's too stressful** il y a des moments où c'est trop stressant
⬚3 conj (a) (expressing time) quand; **~ he was at school** quand il était à l'école, lorsqu'il était à l'école; **~ I am 18** quand j'aurai 18 ans; **~ he arrives, I'll let you know** quand il arrivera or dès qu'il arrivera, je te le dirai
(b) (expressing contrast) alors que; **why buy their products ~ ours are cheaper?** pourquoi acheter leurs produits alors que les nôtres sont moins chers?
⬚4 pron quand; **until/since ~?** jusqu'à/depuis quand?; **1982, that's ~ I was born** 1982, c'est l'année où je suis né; **that's ~ I found out** c'est à ce moment-là que j'ai su

whenever adv (a) (no matter when) **~ you want** quand tu veux; **I'll come ~ it is convenient** je viendrai quand cela vous arrangera
(b) (every time that) chaque fois que; **~ I see a black cat, I make a wish** chaque fois que je vois un chat noir, je fais un vœu

✧ **where**

■ Note where in questions is usually translated by où: where are the plates? = où sont les assiettes?; I don't know where the plates are = je ne sais pas où sont les assiettes; do you know where he is? = est-ce que tu sais où il est?; do you know where Paul is? = est-ce que tu sais où est Paul?
— Note that où + est-ce que does not require a change in word order: where did you see her? = où est-ce que tu l'as vue?

⬚1 adv où; **~ is my coat?** où est mon manteau?; **~ do you work?** où est-ce que vous travaillez; **ask him ~ he went** demande-lui où il est allé; **do you know ~ she's going?** est-ce tu sais où elle va?; **sit ~ you like** asseyez-vous où vous voulez; **it's cold ~ we live** il fait froid là où nous habitons; **~ necessary** si nécessaire; **~ possible** dans la mesure du possible
⬚2 pron from **~?** d'où?; **that's ~ I fell** c'est là que je suis tombé; **that is ~ he is mistaken** c'est là qu'il se trompe

whereabouts n pl **do you know his ~?** savez-vous où il est?

✧ **whereas** conj **she likes dogs ~ I prefer cats** elle aime les chiens mais moi je préfère les chats; **he chose to stay quiet ~ I would have complained** il a choisi de ne rien dire alors que moi je me serais sûrement plaint

whereby conj **a system ~ all staff will carry identification** un système qui prévoit que tous les membres du personnel auront une carte

wherever adv (a) (in questions) **~ has he got to?** où est-ce qu'il a bien pu passer?
(b) (anywhere) **~ she goes I'll go** où qu'elle aille, j'irai; **~ you want** où tu veux; **we'll meet ~'s convenient for you** nous nous retrouverons là où ça t'arrange
(c) (whenever) **~ necessary** quand c'est nécessaire; **~ possible** dans la mesure du possible

whet vtr (p prés etc **-tt-**) **to ~ the appetite** stimuler l'appétit; **the books ~ted his appetite for travel** les livres lui donnèrent envie de voyager

✧ **whether** conj

■ Note When whether is used to mean if, it is translated by si. I wonder whether she got my letter = je me demande si elle a reçu ma lettre.
— In whether... or not sentences, whether is translated by que and the verb that follows is in the subjunctive.

(a) (when outcome is uncertain) si; **I wasn't sure ~ to answer or not** je ne savais pas s'il fallait répondre; **can you check ~ it's cooked?** est-ce que tu peux vérifier si c'est cuit?
(b) (no matter if) **you're coming ~ you like it or not!** tu viendras que cela te plaise ou non!; **~ you have children or not, this book should interest you** que vous ayez des enfants ou non, ce livre devrait vous intéresser

whew excl (in relief) ouf!; (in hot weather) pff!; (in surprise) hein!

✧ **which** ⬚1 pron (a) (in questions) lequel/laquelle/lesquels/lesquelles; **there are three peaches, ~ do you want?** il y a trois pêches, laquelle veux-tu?; **show her ~ you mean** montre-lui celui/celle etc dont tu parles; **I don't mind ~** ça m'est égal; **can you tell ~ is ~?** peux-tu les distinguer?
(b) (relative pronoun) (as subject) qui; (as object) que; (with a preposition) lequel/laquelle/lesquels/lesquelles; (with a preposition translated by de) dont; **the book ~ is on the table** le ···>

W

livre qui est sur la table; **the book ~ I am reading** le livre que je lis; **the contract ~ he's spoken about** le contrat dont il a parlé; **~ reminds me…** ce qui me fait penser que… **(c)** (with a superlative adjective) quel/quelle/quels/quelles; **~ is the biggest?** (of masculine objects) quel est le plus gros?

2 *det* quel/quelle/quels/quelles; **~ books?** quels livres?; **she asked me ~ coach was leaving first** elle m'a demandé lequel des cars allait partir le premier; **~ one of the children…?** lequel/laquelle des enfants…?; **you may wish to join, in ~ case…** vous voulez peut-être vous inscrire, auquel cas…

whichever 1 *pron* **(a)** (the one that) (as subject) celui *m* qui, celle *f* qui; (as object) celui *m* que, celle *f* que; **'which restaurant?'—'~ is nearest'** 'quel restaurant?'—'celui qui est le plus proche'; **come at 2 or 2.30, ~ suits you best** viens à 14 h ou 14 h 30, comme cela te convient le mieux
(b) (no matter which one) (as subject) quel *m* que soit celui qui, quelle *f* que soit celle qui; (as object) quel *m* que soit celui que, quelle *f* que soit celle que; **'do you want the big piece or the small piece?'—'~'** 'est-ce que tu veux le gros ou le petit morceau?'—'n'importe'
2 *det* **(a)** (the one that) **let's go to ~ station is nearest** allons à la gare la plus proche
(b) (no matter which) **I'll be happy ~ horse wins** quel que soit le cheval qui gagne je serai content

whiff *n* (of perfume, food) odeur *f*; (of smoke, garlic) bouffée *f*

♂ **while** 1 *conj* (*also* **whilst**) **(a)** (during the time that) pendant que; **he made a sandwich ~ I phoned** il s'est fait un sandwich pendant que je téléphonais; **~ in Spain, I visited Madrid** pendant que j'étais en Espagne, j'ai visité Madrid; **I fell asleep ~ watching TV** je me suis endormi en regardant la télé; **close the door ~ you're at it** ferme la porte pendant que tu y es
(b) (although) bien que (+ *subjunctive*), quoique (+ *subjunctive*)
(c) (whereas) alors que, tandis que; **she likes dogs ~ I prefer cats** elle aime les chiens mais moi je préfère les chats
2 *n* **a ~ ago** il y a quelque temps; **a ~ later** quelque temps plus tard; **for a good ~** pendant longtemps; **a short ~ ago** il y a peu de temps; **it will take a ~** cela va prendre un certain temps; **after a (short) ~** au bout d'un moment; **once in a ~** de temps en temps
■ **while away** tuer *‹time›* (doing, by doing en faisant)

whilst = WHILE 1

whim *n* caprice *m*; **on a ~** sur un coup de tête

whimper 1 *n* gémissement *m* (of de)
2 *vi* **(a)** *‹person, animal›* gémir

(b) (whinge) *‹person›* pleurnicher

whimsical *adj* *‹person›* fantasque; *‹play, tale, manner, idea›* saugrenu/-e

whine *vi* (complain) se plaindre (**about** de); (snivel) pleurnicher; *‹dog›* gémir

whinge *vi* (colloq) râler

whining 1 *n* (complaints) jérémiades *fpl*; (of dog) gémissements *mpl*
2 *adj* *‹voice›* geignard/-e; *‹child›* pleurnicheur/-euse

whinny *vi* *‹horse›* hennir doucement

whip 1 *n* **(a)** (for punishment) fouet *m*; (for horse) cravache *f*
(b) (Culin) mousse *f*
2 *vtr* (*p prés etc* **-pp-**) **(a)** (beat) fouetter
(b) (Culin) fouetter *‹cream›*; battre [qch] en neige *‹egg whites›*
(c) (colloq) **to ~ sth out** sortir qch brusquement; (remove quickly) **he ~ped the plates off the table** il a prestement retiré les assiettes de la table; **I ~ped the key out of his hand** je lui ai arraché la clé des mains; **to ~ the crowd up into a frenzy** mettre la foule en délire

whiplash injury *n* (Med) coup *m* du lapin

whip-round *n* (GB) (colloq) collecte *f*

whirl 1 *n* **(a)** (of activity, excitement) tourbillon *m* (**of** de)
(b) (spiral motif) spirale *f*
2 *vi* *‹dancer›* tournoyer; *‹blade, propeller›* tourner; *‹snowflakes, dust, thoughts›* tourbillonner
IDIOM to give sth a ~ (colloq) essayer qch
■ **whirl round** *‹person›* se retourner brusquement; *‹blade, clock hand›* tourner brusquement

whirlpool *n* tourbillon *m*

whirlpool bath *n* bain *m* bouillonnant

whirlwind *n* tourbillon *m*

whirr *vi* *‹motor›* vrombir; *‹camera, fan›* tourner; *‹insect›* bourdonner; *‹wings›* bruire

whisk 1 *n* (*also* **egg ~**) (manual) fouet *m*; (electric) batteur *m*
2 *vtr* **(a)** (Culin) battre
(b) (transport quickly) **he was ~ed off to meet the president** on l'a emmené sur le champ rencontrer le président; **she was ~ed off to hospital** elle a été emmenée d'urgence à l'hôpital

whisker 1 *n* (of animal) poil *m* de moustache
2 **whiskers** *n pl* (of animal) moustaches *fpl*; (of man) (beard) barbe *f*; (moustache) moustache *f*

♂ **whisper** 1 *n* chuchotement *m*; **to speak in a ~** *or* **in ~s** parler à voix basse
2 *vtr* chuchoter (**to** à); **to ~ sth to sb** chuchoter qch à qn; **'she's asleep', he ~ed** 'elle dort', dit-il en chuchotant
3 *vi* chuchoter; **to ~ to sb** parler à voix basse à qn

♂ indicates a very frequent word

whistle ① *n* **(a)** (object) sifflet *m*; **to blow the** *or* **one's ~** donner un coup de sifflet **(b)** (sound) (through mouth) sifflement *m*; (by referee) coup *m* de sifflet; (of bird, train) sifflement *m*
② *vtr* siffler; (casually) siffloter
③ *vi* siffler; **to ~ at sb/sth** siffler qn/qch; **to ~ for** siffler ‹dog›
IDIOM **to blow the ~ on sb** dénoncer qn

white ① *n* **(a)** (gen) blanc *m* **(b)** (*also* **White**) (Caucasian) Blanc/Blanche *m/f* **(c)** (in chess, draughts) blancs *mpl*
② *adj* **(a)** blanc/blanche; **bright ~ teeth** dents d'un blanc éclatant; **to go** *or* **turn ~** devenir blanc, blanchir; **to paint sth ~** peindre qch en blanc **(b)** ‹race, child, skin› blanc/blanche; ‹area› habité/-e par des Blancs; ‹culture, prejudice› des Blancs; **a ~ man/woman** un Blanc/une Blanche **(c)** (pale) pâle (with de); **to go** *or* **turn ~** pâlir (with de)

whitebait *n* (raw) blanchaille *f*; (fried) petite friture *f*

whiteboard *n* tableau *m* blanc

white coffee *n* (at home) café *m* au lait; (in café) (café *m*) crème *m*

white-collar *adj* ‹job, work› d'employé de bureau; ‹staff› de bureau, **~ worker** col *m* blanc, employé/-e *m/f* de bureau

white elephant *n* **(a)** (item, knickknack) bibelot *m* **(b)** (public project) réalisation *f* coûteuse et peu rentable

white goods *n pl* (appliances) gros électroménager *m*

white horses *n pl* (waves) moutons *mpl*

White House *n* **the ~** la Maison Blanche

white-knuckle ride *n* tour *m* de manège qui fait peur

white lie *n* pieux mensonge *m*

whitener *n* **(a)** (for clothes) agent *m* blanchissant **(b)** (for shoes) produit *m* pour blanchir **(c)** (for coffee, tea) succédané *m* de lait en poudre

whiteness *n* blancheur *f*

white spirit *n* white-spirit *m*

whitewash ① *n* **(a)** (for walls) lait *m* de chaux **(b)** (figurative) (cover-up) mise *f* en scène ② *vtr* **(a)** blanchir [qch] à la chaux ‹wall› **(b)** (*also* **~ over**) blanchir ‹facts›

white water *n* eau *f* vive

white water rafting *n* rafting *m* en eau vive

white wedding *n* mariage *m* en blanc

Whitsun *n* (*also* **Whitsuntide**) Pentecôte *f*

Whit Sunday *n* Pentecôte *f*

whittle *vtr* tailler [qch] au couteau; **to ~ sth away** *or* **down** réduire qch (**to** à)

whizz *vi* **to ~ by** *or* **past** ‹arrow, bullet› passer en sifflant; ‹car› passer à toute allure; ‹person› passer rapidement

whizz-kid *n* (colloq) jeune prodige *m*

who *pron*
■ **Note** Note that there are three ways of asking questions using *qui* as the object of the verb: *who did he call?* = qui est-ce qu'il a appelé?, qui a-t-il appelé?, il a appelé qui?

(a) (in questions) (as subject) qui (est-ce qui); (as object) qui (est-ce que); (after prepositions) qui; **~ knows the answer?** qui connaît la réponse?; **~'s going to be there?** qui sera là?; **~ did you invite?** qui est-ce que tu as invité?, qui as-tu invité?; **~ was she with?** avec qui était-elle?; **~ did you buy it for?** pour qui l'as-tu acheté?; **~ did you get it from?** qui te l'a donné?
(b) (relative) (as subject) qui; (as object) que; (after prepositions) qui; **his friend, ~ lives in Paris** son ami, qui habite Paris; **his friend ~ he sees once a week** l'ami qu'il voit une fois par semaine
(c) (whoever) **bring ~ you like** tu peux amener qui tu veux; **~ do you think you are?** tu te prends pour qui?

whodun(n)it *n* polar *m* (fam), roman *m* policier

whoever *pron* **(a)** (the one that) **~ wins the election** celui ou celle qui gagnera les élections **(b)** (anyone that) (as subject) quiconque; (as object) qui; **~ saw the accident should contact us** quiconque a assisté à l'accident devrait nous contacter; **invite ~ you like** invite qui tu veux **(c)** (no matter who) **~ you are** qui que vous soyez

whole ① *n* **(a)** (total unit) tout *m*; **as a ~** (not in separate parts) en entier; (overall) dans l'ensemble **(b)** (all) **the ~ of** tout/-e; **the ~ of the weekend/August** tout le week-end/mois d'août; **the ~ of London is talking about it** tout Londres en parle; **nearly the ~ of Berlin was destroyed** Berlin a été presque entièrement détruit
② *adj* **(a)** (entire) tout/-e, entier/-ière; (more emphatic) tout entier/-ière; **dans a ~ hour** une heure entière; **a ~ day** toute une journée; **for three ~ weeks** pendant trois semaines entières; **his ~ life** toute sa vie, sa vie entière; **the ~ truth** toute la vérité; **the most beautiful city in the ~ world** la plus belle ville du monde **(b)** (emphatic use) **a ~ new way of life** un mode de vie complètement différent; **that's the ~ point of the exercise** c'est tout l'intérêt de l'exercice **(c)** (intact) intact/-e
③ *adv* ‹swallow, cook› tout entier
④ **on the whole** *phr* dans l'ensemble

wholefood *n* (GB) produits *mpl* biologiques

W

wholehearted adj ‹approval, support›
sans réserve; **to be in ~ agreement with** être
en accord total avec

wholeheartedly adv sans réserve

wholemeal adj (GB) (also **wholewheat**)
complet/-ète

whole milk n lait m entier

wholesale ⓵ adj (a) ‹business› de gros
(b) (large-scale) ‹destruction› total/-e;
‹acceptance, rejection› en bloc; ‹attack› sur
tous les fronts
⓶ adv (a) ‹buy, sell› en gros
(b) ‹accept, reject› en bloc

wholesaler n grossiste mf, marchand/-e
m/f en gros

wholesome adj (a) (healthy) sain/-e
(b) (decent) ‹person, appearance› bien propre;
‹entertainment› innocent/-e

wholewheat = WHOLEMEAL

wholly adv entièrement, tout à fait

⚡ **whom** pron (a) (in questions) qui (est-ce
que); (after prepositions) qui; **~ did she meet?**
qui a-t-elle rencontré?, qui est-ce qu'elle a
rencontré?; **to ~ are you referring?** à qui
est-ce que vous faites allusion?
(b) (relative) que; (after prepositions) qui; **the
person to ~/of ~ I spoke** la personne à qui/
dont j'ai parlé

whooping cough n coqueluche f

whopper n (colloq) (large thing) monstre m

whopping adj (colloq) (also **~ great**)
monstre (fam)

whorl n (of cream, chocolate) spirale f; (on
fingerprint) volute f; (shell pattern) spire f; (of
petals) verticille m

⚡ **whose** ⓵ pron (a) (in questions) à qui; **~ is
this?** à qui est ceci?
(b) (relative) dont; **the boy ~ dog was killed**
le garçon dont le chien a été tué; **the man ~
daughter he was married to** l'homme dont il
avait épousé la fille
⓶ det **~ pen is that?** à qui est ce stylo?;
do you know ~ car was stolen? est-ce que
tu sais à qui appartenait la voiture volée?;
~ coat did you take? tu as pris le manteau
de qui?

⚡ **why**

■ **Note** Note that there are three ways of asking
questions using why:
— why did you go? = pourquoi est-ce que tu
y es allé?, pourquoi y es-tu allé?, tu y es allé
pourquoi?

⓵ adv (a) (in questions) pourquoi; **~
do you ask?** pourquoi est-ce que tu me
poses la question?, pourquoi me poses-
tu la question?; **~ bother?** pourquoi
se tracasser?; **~ the delay?** pourquoi
ce retard?; **~ not?** pourquoi pas?; **'tell
them'—'~ should I?'** 'dis-le-leur'—'et
pourquoi (est-ce que je devrais le faire)?'

⚡ indicates a very frequent word

(b) (making suggestions) pourquoi; **~ don't
we go away for the weekend?** pourquoi ne
pas partir quelque part pour le week-end?;
~ don't I invite them for dinner? et si je les
invitais à manger?
⓶ conj pour ça; **that is ~ they came** c'est
pour ça qu'ils sont venus; **I need to know the
reason ~** j'ai besoin de savoir pourquoi

wick n mèche f

wicked adj (a) (evil) ‹person› méchant/-e;
‹heart, deed› cruel/-elle; ‹plot› pernicieux/
-ieuse; ‹intention› mauvais/-e (before n)
(b) ‹grin, humour› malicieux/-ieuse;
‹thoughts› pervers/-e
(c) (vicious) ‹wind› méchant/-e; ‹weapon›
redoutable; **to have a ~ tongue** être
mauvaise langue

wicker ⓵ n (also **wickerwork**) osier m
⓶ adj ‹basket, furniture› en osier

⚡ **wide** ⓵ adj (a) (broad) ‹river, opening,
mouth› large; ‹margin› grand/-e; **how ~ is
your garden?** quelle est la largeur de votre
jardin?; **it's 30 cm ~** il fait 30 cm de large;
the river is 1 km across at its ~st le fleuve
fait or atteint 1 km à son point le plus large;
her eyes were ~ with fear ses yeux étaient
agrandis par la peur
(b) (immense) ‹ocean, desert, expanse› vaste
(before n)
(c) (extensive) ‹variety, choice› grand/-e (before
n); **a ~ range of opinions** une grande variété
d'opinions; **a ~ range of products** une vaste
gamme de produits
(d) (Sport) ‹ball, shot› perdu/-e
⓶ adv **to open one's eyes ~** ouvrir grand
les yeux; **to open the door/window ~** ouvrir
la porte/la fenêtre en grand; **his eyes are
(set) ~ apart** il a les yeux très écartés;
his legs were ~ apart il avait les jambes
écartées; **to be ~ of the mark** ‹ball, dart› être
à côté; ‹guess› être loin de la vérité

wide-angle lens n objectif m à grand
angle

wide awake adj complètement éveillé/-e

wide-eyed adj (a) (with surprise, fear)
he was ~ il ouvrait de grands yeux; **~
with fear/surprise** les yeux écarquillés de
peur/surprise; **she stared/listened ~** elle
regardait/écoutait les yeux écarquillés
(b) (naïve) ‹person, innocence› ingénu/-e

⚡ **widely** adv (a) (commonly) ‹accepted, used›
largement; **this product is now ~ available**
on trouve maintenant ce produit partout
(b) ‹spaced, planted› à de grands intervalles;
‹travel, differ, vary› beaucoup

widely-read adj ‹student› qui a beaucoup
lu; ‹author› très lu/-e

⚡ **widen** ⓵ vtr élargir ‹road, gap›; étendre
‹powers›; **this has ~ed their lead in the
opinion polls** ceci a renforcé leur position
dominante dans les sondages
⓶ vi s'élargir

widening adj ‹division› de plus en plus grand/-e; ‹gap› qui s'élargit de plus en plus

wide open adj (a) ‹door, window, eyes, mouth› grand/-e ouvert/-e
(b) **the race is** ~ l'issue de la course est indécise

wide-ranging adj ‹reforms› de grande envergure; ‹interests› très variés

wide screen n grand écran m

wide-screen TV n téléviseur m à grand écran

widespread adj ‹epidemic› généralisé/-e; ‹devastation› étendu/-e; ‹belief› très répandu/-e

widow ① n veuve f
② vtr **to be** ~ed devenir veuf/veuve m/f

widower n veuf m

width n (a) largeur f; **it is 30 metres in** ~ il fait or mesure 30 mètres de large
(b) (of fabric) lé m

wield vtr (a) brandir ‹weapon, tool›
(b) exercer ‹power› (over sur)

♂ **wife** n (pl **wives**) femme f; (more formally) épouse f; **the baker's/farmer's** ~ la boulangère/la fermière

Wi-Fi® n (abbr = **Wireless Fidelity**) Wi-Fi® m

wig n (whole head) perruque f; (partial) postiche m

wiggle (colloq) ① n a ~ **of the hips** un roulement des hanches
② vtr faire bouger ‹tooth, wedged object›; **to** ~ **one's hips** rouler les hanches; **to** ~ **one's fingers/toes** remuer les doigts/orteils
③ vi ‹snake, worm› se tortiller

♂ **wild** ① n **in the** ~ ‹conditions, life› en liberté; **to grow in the** ~ pousser à l'état sauvage; **the call of the** ~ l'appel de la nature
② adj (a) ‹animal, plant› sauvage; **the pony is still quite** ~ le poney est encore assez farouche
(b) ‹landscape› sauvage
(c) ‹wind› violent/-e; ‹sea› agité/-e; **it was a** ~ **night** c'était une nuit de tempête
(d) ‹party, laughter, person› fou/folle; ‹imagination› délirant/-e; ‹applause› déchaîné/-e; **to go** ~ se déchaîner
(e) (colloq) (furious) furieux/-ieuse; **he'll go** or **be** ~! ça va le mettre hors de lui!
(f) (colloq) (enthusiastic) **to be** ~ **about** être un/une fana (fam) de; **I'm not** ~ **about him/it** il/ça ne m'emballe (fam) pas
(g) (outlandish) ‹idea, plan› fou/folle; ‹claim, promise, accusation› extravagant/-e; ‹story› farfelu/-e (fam)
③ adv ‹grow› à l'état sauvage; **the garden had run** ~ le jardin était devenu une vraie jungle; **those children are allowed to run** ~! on permet à ces enfants de faire n'importe quoi!; **to let one's imagination run** ~ laisser libre cours à son imagination

wild boar n sanglier m

wilderness n étendue f sauvage et désolée

wild-eyed adj au regard égaré

wildfire n **to spread like** ~ se répandre comme une traînée de poudre

wild flower n fleur f des champs, fleur f sauvage

wild-goose chase n **it turned out to be a** ~ ça n'a abouti à rien; **to lead sb on a** ~ mettre qn sur une mauvaise piste

wildlife n (animals) faune f; (animals and plants) faune f et flore f

wildlife park, wildlife reserve, wildlife sanctuary n réserve f naturelle

wildly adv (a) ‹invest, spend, talk› de façon insensée; ‹fire, shoot› au hasard; **to hit out/run** ~ envoyer des coups/courir dans tous les sens
(b) ‹wave, gesture› de manière très agitée; ‹applaud› à tout rompre; **to beat** ~ subir des fluctuations violentes; **to beat** ~ ‹heart› battre à tout rompre
(c) ‹enthusiastic, optimistic› extrêmement

wilds n pl **to live in the** ~ **of Arizona** habiter au fin fond de l'Arizona

Wild West n Far West m

wilful (GB), **willful** (US) adj (a) ‹person, behaviour› volontaire
(b) ‹damage, disobedience› délibéré/-e

wilfully (GB), **willfully** (US) adv (a) (in headstrong way) obstinément
(b) (deliberately) délibérément

♂ **will¹** ① modal aux (a) (expressing the future) **I'll see you tomorrow** je te verrai demain; **it won't rain** il ne pleuvra pas; ~ **there be many people?** est-ce qu'il y aura beaucoup de monde?; **they'll come tomorrow** ils vont venir demain; **what** ~ **you do now?** qu'est-ce que tu vas faire maintenant?
(b) (expressing willingness or intention) ~ **you help me?** est-ce que tu m'aideras?; **we won't stay too long** nous ne resterons pas trop longtemps; **he won't cooperate** il ne veut pas coopérer
(c) (in requests, commands) ~ **you pass the salt please?** est-ce que tu peux me passer le sel s'il te plaît; ~ **you please be quiet!** est-ce que tu vas te taire?; **wait a minute,** ~ **you!** attends un peu!
(d) (in invitations) ~ **you have some tea?** est-ce que vous voulez du thé?; **won't you join us for dinner?** est-ce que tu veux dîner avec nous?; **what** ~ **you have to drink?** qu'est-ce que tu prends?
(e) (in assumptions) **he'll be about 30 now** il doit avoir 30 ans maintenant; **you'll be tired, I expect** tu dois être fatigué je suppose
(f) (indicating sth predictable or customary) **they** ~ **ask for a deposit** ils demandent une caution; **these things** ~ **happen** ce sont des choses qui arrivent; **you** ~ **keep contradicting her!** ⋯⋗

il faut toujours que tu la contredises! **(g)** (in short answers and tag questions) **you'll come again, won't you?** tu reviendras, n'est-ce pas?; **you won't forget, ~ you?** tu n'oublieras pas, n'est-ce pas?; **that'll be cheaper, won't it?** ça sera moins cher, non?; **'they won't be ready'—'yes, they ~'** 'ils ne seront pas prêts'—'(bien sûr que) si'; **'~ you call me?'—'yes, I ~'** 'est-ce que tu me téléphoneras?'—'bien sûr que oui'; **'she'll be furious'—'no, she won't!'** 'elle sera furieuse'—'bien sûr que non!'; **'I'll do it'—'no you won't!'** 'je le ferai'—'il n'en est pas question!'

2 *vtr* **(a)** (urge mentally) **to ~ sb to do** supplier mentalement qn de faire; **to ~ sb to live** prier pour que qn vive
(b) (wish, desire) vouloir
(c) (Law) léguer **(to** à)

will² **1** *n* **(a)** volonté *f* **(to do** de faire); **to have a ~ of one's own** n'en faire qu'à sa tête; **against my ~** contre mon gré; **to do with a ~** faire de bon cœur; **to lose the ~ to live** ne plus avoir envie de vivre
(b) (Law) testament *m*; **to leave sb sth in one's ~** léguer qch à qn
2 **at will** *phr* ‹select, take› à volonté; **they can wander about at ~** ils peuvent se promener comme ils veulent

◆ **willing** *adj* **(a)** (prepared) **to be ~ to do** être prêt/-e à faire
(b) (eager) ‹pupil, helper› de bonne volonté; ‹slave› consentant/-e; ‹recruit, victim› volontaire; **to show ~** faire preuve de bonne volonté

willingly *adv* ‹accept, help› volontiers; ‹work› avec bonne volonté

willingness *n* (readiness) volonté *f* **(to do** de faire)

willow *n* (also ~ **tree**) saule *m*

will power *n* volonté *f* **(to do** de faire)

willy-nilly *adv* **(a)** (regardless of choice) bon gré mal gré
(b) (haphazardly) au hasard

wilt *vi* **(a)** ‹plant, flower› se faner
(b) ‹person› (from heat, fatigue) se sentir faible; (at daunting prospect) perdre courage

wimp *n* (colloq) (ineffectual) lavette *f* (fam); (fearful) poule *f* mouillée (fam)

◆ **win** **1** *n* victoire *f* **(over** sur)
2 *vtr* (*p prés* **-nn-**, *prét, pp* **won**)
(a) gagner ‹match, bet, battle, money›; remporter ‹election›
(b) (acquire) obtenir ‹delay, reprieve›; gagner ‹friendship, heart›; s'attirer ‹sympathy›; s'acquérir ‹support› **(of** de); **to ~ sb's love/ respect** se faire aimer/respecter de qn
3 *vi* (*p prés* **-nn-**, *prét, pp* **won**) gagner; **to ~ against sb** l'emporter sur qn
■ **win back**: ¶ **~ [sth] back, ~ back [sth]** récupérer ‹support, votes› **(from sb** sur qn);

regagner ‹affection, respect›; reprendre ‹prize, territory› **(from** à)
■ **win over, win round** convaincre ‹person›

wince **1** *n* grimace *f*
2 *vi* grimacer, faire une grimace

winch **1** *n* treuil *m*
2 *vtr* **to ~ sth down/up** descendre/hisser qch au treuil

◆ **wind¹** **1** *n* **(a)** vent *m*; **the ~ is blowing** il y a du vent; **which way is the ~ blowing?** d'où vient le vent?
(b) (breath) **to knock the ~ out of sb** couper le souffle à qn; **to get one's ~** reprendre souffle
(c) (flatulence) vents *mpl*; **to break ~** lâcher un vent
2 *vtr* (*prét, pp* **winded**) **(a)** (make breathless) ‹blow, punch› couper la respiration à; ‹climb› essouffler
(b) faire faire son rot à ‹baby›

wind² **1** *vtr* (*prét, pp* **wound**) **(a)** (coil up) enrouler ‹hair, rope, wire› **(on, onto** sur; **round** autour de)
(b) (also ~ **up**) remonter ‹clock, toy›
(c) donner un tour de ‹handle›
(d) **to ~ its way** ‹procession, road, river› serpenter
2 *vi* (*prét, pp* **wound**) ‹road, river› serpenter (along le long de); ‹stairs› tourner
■ **wind down**: **1** ¶ **~ down**
(a) ‹organization› réduire ses activités; ‹activity, production› toucher à sa fin; ‹person› se détendre
(b) ‹clockwork› être sur le point de s'arrêter
2 ¶ **~ [sth] down (a)** baisser ‹car window›
(b) mettre fin à ‹activity, organization›
■ **wind up**: **1** ¶ **~ up (a)** (finish) ‹event› se terminer **(with** par); ‹speaker› conclure
(b) (colloq) (end up) finir, se retrouver
2 ¶ **~ [sth] up (a)** liquider ‹business›; mettre fin à ‹debate, meeting, project›
(b) remonter ‹clock, car window›
3 ¶ **~ [sb] up (a)** (tease) faire marcher ‹person›
(b) (make tense) énerver

wind chimes *n pl* carillon *m* éolien

wind energy *n* énergie *f* éolienne

windfall *n* fruit *m* tombé par terre; (figurative) aubaine *f*

windfall profit *n* profit *m* inattendu

wind farm *n* ferme *f* éolienne

winding *adj* ‹road, river› sinueux/-euse; ‹stairs› en spirale

wind instrument *n* instrument *m* à vent

windmill *n* moulin *m* à vent

◆ **window** *n* **(a)** (of house) fenêtre *f*; (of shop, public building) vitrine *f*; (of vehicle) (gen) vitre *f*; (of plane) hublot *m*; (stained glass) vitrail *m*; **to look out of** *or* **through the ~** regarder par la fenêtre
(b) (for service at bank or post office) guichet *m*

window blind *n* store *m*

window box *n* jardinière *f*

W

◆ indicates a very frequent word

window cleaner n laveur/-euse m/f de carreaux

window display n vitrine f

window ledge n appui m de fenêtre

windowpane n carreau m

window seat n (a) (in room) banquette f (b) (in plane, bus, train) place f côté vitre

window-shopping n to go ~ faire du lèche-vitrines m inv (fam)

windowsill n rebord m de fenêtre

windpipe n trachée-artère f

windpower n énergie f éolienne

windscreen (GB), **windshield** (US) n pare-brise m inv

windscreen wiper n (GB) essuie-glace m inv

windshield (US) = WINDSCREEN

windsurf vi faire de la planche à voile

windsurfer n (person) véliplanchiste mf; (board) planche f à voile

windswept adj venteux/-euse

windy adj ‹place› venteux/-euse; ‹day› de vent; **it was very** ~ il faisait beaucoup de vent

✓ **wine** n (a) (drink) vin m (b) (colour) lie-de-vin m

wine bar n bar m à vin

wine box n ≈ cubitainer® m

wine cellar n cave f

wine glass n verre m à vin

wine grower n viticulteur/-trice m/f

wine growing ① n viticulture f ② adj ‹region› vinicole

wine list n carte f des vins

wine rack n casier m à bouteilles

wine shop n marchand m de vin

wine tasting n dégustation f de vins

wine vinegar n vinaigre m de vin

wine waiter n sommelier/-ière m/f

✓ **wing** ① n aile f ② **wings** n pl (in theatre) **the** ~**s** les coulisses fpl; **to be waiting in the** ~**s** (figurative) attendre son heure

winger n (GB) ailier m

wing nut n écrou m à oreilles

wink ① n clin m d'œil; **we didn't get a** ~ **of sleep all night** nous n'avons pas fermé l'œil de la nuit ② vi cligner de l'œil; **to** ~ **at sb** faire un clin d'œil à qn

✓ **winner** n (a) (victor) gagnant/-e m/f (b) (success) **to be a** ~ ‹film, book, song› avoir un gros succès

winning adj (a) (victorious) gagnant/-e (b) ‹smile› engageant/-e; **to have** ~ **ways** avoir du charme

winning post n poteau m d'arrivée

winnings n pl gains mpl

winning streak n **to be on a** ~ être dans une bonne période

✓ **winter** ① n hiver m; **in** ~ en hiver ② adj ‹sports, clothes, weather› d'hiver ③ vi passer l'hiver

wintertime n hiver m

wipe ① n (a) **to give sth a** ~ (clean, dust) donner un coup de chiffon à qch; (dry) essuyer qch (b) (for face, baby) lingette f ② vtr essuyer ‹table, glass› (**on** sur; **with** avec); **to** ~ **one's hands/feet** s'essuyer les mains/les pieds; **to** ~ **one's nose** se moucher; **to** ~ **a baby's bottom** essuyer (les fesses d')un bébé; **to** ~ **the dishes** essuyer la vaisselle

■ **wipe away** essuyer ‹tears, sweat›; faire partir ‹dirt, mark›

■ **wipe out** (a) nettoyer ‹container, cupboard› (b) annuler ‹inflation›; anéantir ‹species, enemy, population›

■ **wipe up**: ① ¶ ~ up essuyer la vaisselle ② ¶ ~ [sth] up essuyer

wipe-clean adj facile à nettoyer

wire ① n (a) fil m; **electric/telephone** ~ fil électrique/téléphonique (b) (US) (telegram) télégramme m ② vtr (a) **to** ~ **a house** installer l'électricité dans une maison; **to** ~ **a plug/a lamp** connecter une prise/une lampe (b) (telegraph) télégraphier à ‹person›; télégraphier ‹money›

wireless ① n (GB) (Hist) radio f ② adj sans fil

wiring n (in house) installation f électrique; (in appliance) circuit m (électrique)

wiry adj (a) ‹person, body› mince et nerveux/-euse (b) ‹hair› rêche

wisdom n sagesse f

wisdom tooth n dent f de sagesse

wise ① adj ‹person, words, precaution, saying› sage; ‹choice, investment› judicieux/ -ieuse; ‹smile, nod› avisé/-e; **a** ~ **man** un sage; **a** ~ **move** une décision judicieuse; **to be none the** ~**r** (understand no better) ne pas être plus avancé/-e; (not realize) ne s'apercevoir de rien ② **-wise** combining form (a) (direction) dans le sens de; **length-**~ dans le sens de la longueur (b) (with regard to) pour ce qui est de; **work-**~ pour ce qui est du travail

wisecrack n vanne f (fam)

wise guy n (colloq) gros malin m (fam)

wisely adv judicieusement

✓ **wish** ① n (a) (request) souhait m (**for** de); **to make a** ~ faire un vœu; **her** ~ **came true** son souhait s'est réalisé (b) (desire) désir m (**for** de; **to do** de faire); **to go against sb's** ~**es** aller contre la volonté de qn

···⟩

Ⓦ

2 wishes n pl vœux mpl; **good** or **best ~es** meilleurs vœux; (ending letter) **bien amicalement**; **best ~es on your birthday** meilleurs vœux pour votre anniversaire; **please give him my best ~es** je vous prie de lui faire toutes mes amitiés

3 vtr **(a)** (expressing longing) **I ~ he were here/had been here** si seulement il était ici/avait été ici; **he ~ed he had written** il regrettait de ne pas avoir écrit

(b) (express congratulations, greetings) souhaiter; **I ~ you good luck/a happy birthday** je vous souhaite bonne chance/un bon anniversaire; **I ~ him well** je souhaite que tout aille bien pour lui

(c) (want) souhaiter, désirer

4 vi **(a)** (desire) vouloir; **just as you ~** comme vous voudrez

(b) (make a wish) faire un vœu

wishful thinking n **that's ~** c'est prendre ses désirs pour des réalités

wishy-washy adj (colloq) ‹colour› délavé/-e; ‹person› incolore et inodore (fam)

wisp n (of hair) mèche f; (of straw) brin m; (of smoke, cloud) volute f

wispy adj ‹hair, beard› fin/-e; ‹cloud, smoke› léger/-ère

wisteria n glycine f

wistful adj (sad) mélancolique; (nostalgic) nostalgique

wit **1** n **(a)** (sense of humour) esprit m
(b) (witty person) personne f spirituelle
2 to wit phr à savoir

witch n sorcière f

witchcraft n sorcellerie f

witch doctor n shaman m

witch-hunt n chasse f aux sorcières

❖ **with** prep **(a)** (gen) avec; **a meeting ~ sb** une réunion avec qn; **to hit sb ~ sth** frapper qn avec qch; **~ difficulty/pleasure** avec difficulté/plaisir; **to be patient ~ sb** être patient/-e avec qn; **delighted ~ sth** ravi/-e de qch; **to travel ~ sb** voyager avec qn; **to live ~ sb** (in one's own house) vivre avec qn; (in their house) vivre chez qn; **I'll be ~ you in a second** je suis à vous dans un instant; **take your umbrella ~ you** emporte ton parapluie; **bring the books back ~ you** rapporte les livres

(b) (in descriptions) à; **a girl ~ black hair** une fille aux cheveux noirs; **the boy ~ the broken leg** le garçon à la jambe cassée; **a boy ~ a broken leg** un garçon avec une jambe cassée; **a TV ~ remote control** une télévision avec télécommande; **furnished ~ antiques** meublé/-e avec des meubles anciens; **covered ~ mud** couvert/-e de boue; **to lie ~ one's eyes closed** être allongé/-e les yeux fermés; **to stand ~ one's arms folded** se tenir les bras croisés; **filled ~ sth**

rempli/-e de qch
(c) (according to) **to increase ~ time** augmenter avec le temps; **to vary ~ the temperature** varier selon la température
(d) (owning, bringing) **passengers ~ tickets** les passagers munis de billets; **people ~ qualifications** les gens qualifiés; **somebody ~ your experience** quelqu'un qui a ton expérience; **have you got the report ~ you?** est-ce que tu as (amené) le rapport?
(e) (as regards) **how are things ~ you?** comment ça va?; **what's up ~ you?** qu'est-ce que tu as?; **what do you want ~ another car?** qu'est-ce que tu veux faire d'une deuxième voiture?
(f) (because of) **sick ~ worry** malade d'inquiétude; **he can see better ~ his glasses on** il voit mieux avec ses lunettes; **I can't do it ~ you watching** je ne peux pas le faire si tu me regardes
(g) (suffering from) **people ~ Aids/leukemia** les personnes atteintes du sida/de leucémie; **to be ill ~ flu** avoir la grippe
(h) (employed by, customer of) **a reporter ~ the Gazette** un journaliste de la Gazette; **he's ~ the UN** il travaille pour l'ONU; **I'm ~ Chemco** je travaille chez Chemco; **we're ~ the National Bank** nous sommes à la National Bank
(i) (in the same direction as) **to sail ~ the wind** naviguer dans le sens du vent; **to drift ~ the tide** dériver avec le courant

withdraw **1** vtr (prét **-drew**, pp **-drawn**) retirer ‹hand, money, application, permission, troops›; renoncer à, retirer ‹claim›; rétracter ‹accusation, statement›
2 vi (prét **-drew**, pp **-drawn**) **(a)** (gen) se retirer (**from** de)
(b) (psychologically) se replier sur soi-même

withdrawal n **(a)** (of money, troops) retrait m (**of**, **from** de)
(b) (psychological reaction) repli m sur soi
(c) (of drug addict) état m de manque

withdrawal symptoms n pl symptômes mpl de manque; **to be suffering from ~** être en état de manque

withdrawn adj ‹person› renfermé/-e, replié/-e sur soi-même

wither **1** vtr flétrir
2 vi se flétrir

withering adj ‹look› plein/-e de mépris; ‹contempt, comment› cinglant/-e

withhold vtr (prét, pp **-held**) différer ‹payment›; retenir ‹tax, grant, rent›; refuser ‹consent, permission›; ne pas divulguer ‹information›

❖ **within** **1** prep **(a)** (inside) **~ the city walls** dans l'enceinte de la ville; **~ the party** au sein du parti; **it's a play ~ a play** c'est une pièce dans la pièce
(b) (in expressions of time) **I'll do it ~ the hour** je le ferai en moins d'une heure; **15 burglaries ~ a month** 15 cambriolages en (moins d')un

w

mois; **they died ~ a week of each other** ils sont morts à une semaine d'intervalle
(c) (not more than) **to be ~ several metres of sth** être à quelques mètres seulement de qch; **it's accurate to ~ a millimetre** c'est exact au millimètre près
(d) to live ~ one's income vivre selon ses moyens
2 *adv* à l'intérieur; **from ~** de l'intérieur

✓ **without** **1** *prep* sans; **~ a key** sans clé; **~ any money** sans argent; **she left ~ it** elle est partie sans; **they left ~ me** ils sont partis sans moi; **~ looking** sans regarder; **it goes ~ saying** cela va de soi
2 *adv* à l'extérieur; **from ~** de l'extérieur

withstand *vtr* (*prét, pp* **-stood**) résister à

✓ **witness** **1** *n* **(a)** (gen, Law) (person) témoin *m*; **she was a ~ to the accident** elle a été témoin de l'accident; **~ for the prosecution/ the defence** témoin à charge/à décharge
(b) (testimony) témoignage *m*; **to be** *or* **bear ~ to sth** témoigner de qch
2 *vtr* **(a)** (see) être témoin de, assister à ‹*incident, attack*›
(b) servir de témoin lors de la signature de ‹*will, treaty*›; être témoin à ‹*marriage*›

witness box (GB), **witness stand** (US) *n* barre *f* des témoins

wits *n pl* (intelligence) intelligence *f*; (presence of mind) présence *f* d'esprit; **to collect** *or* **gather one's ~** rassembler ses esprits; **to frighten sb out of their ~** faire une peur épouvantable à qn; **to live by one's ~** vivre d'expédients; **a battle of ~** une joute verbale
IDIOM **to be at one's ~ end** ne plus savoir quoi faire

witticism *n* bon mot *m*

witty *adj* spirituel/-elle

wizard *n* **(a)** (magician) magicien *m*
(b) (expert) **to be a ~ at chess/computing** être un as (fam) aux échecs/en informatique

wizened *adj* ratatiné/-e

wobble *vi* ‹*table, chair*› branler; ‹*pile of books, plates*› osciller; ‹*jelly*› trembloter; ‹*person*› (on bicycle) osciller; (on ladder, tightrope) chanceler

wobbly *adj* ‹*table, chair*› bancal/-e; ‹*tooth*› branlant/-e

woe *n* malheur *m*; **a tale of ~** une histoire pathétique

wolf *n* (*pl* **wolves**) loup *m*; **she-~** louve *f*
IDIOM **to cry ~** crier au loup

wolf-whistle **1** *n* sifflement *m*
2 *vi* siffler

✓ **woman** *n* (*pl* **women**) femme *f*; **a ~ Prime Minister** une femme premier ministre; **he's always criticizing women drivers** il est toujours en train de critiquer les femmes au volant

woman friend *n* amie *f*

womanizer *n* coureur *m* (de jupons)

womb *n* (Anat) uterus *m*

women's refuge *n* foyer *m* pour femmes battues

women's studies *n pl* études *fpl* féministes

✓ **wonder** **1** *n* **(a)** (miracle) merveille *f*; **to do** *or* **work ~s** faire des merveilles (**for** pour; **with** avec); **(it's) no ~ that he's late** (ce n'est) pas étonnant qu'il soit en retard
(b) (amazement) émerveillement *m*
2 *vtr* (ask oneself) se demander; **I ~ how/ why/whether** je me demande comment/ pourquoi/si; (as polite request) **I ~ if you could help me?** pourriez-vous m'aider?; **it makes you ~ why** c'est à se demander pourquoi
3 *vi* **(a)** (think) **to ~ about sth/about doing sth** penser à qch/à faire qch; **it makes you ~** cela donne à penser
(b) (be surprised) **to ~ at sth** s'étonner de qch; (admiringly) s'émerveiller de qch

✓ **wonderful** *adj* ‹*book, film, meal, experience, holiday*› merveilleux/-euse; ‹*musician, teacher*› excellent/-e

wonderfully *adv* ‹*funny, exciting, clever*› très; ‹*work, cope, drive*› admirablement

wonky *adj* (colloq) (crooked) de traviole (fam); (wobbly) ‹*furniture*› bancal/-e

wont *adj* **to be ~ to do** avoir coutume de faire; **as is his/their ~** comme à son/leur habitude

woo *vtr* courtiser

✓ **wood** **1** *n* bois *m*
2 **woods** *n pl* bois *mpl*
3 *adj* ‹*fire, smoke*› de bois; **~ floor** plancher *m*
IDIOMS **touch ~!** (GB) **knock on ~!** (US) touchons du bois!; **we are not out of the ~(s) yet** on n'est pas encore sorti de l'auberge

wooden *adj* **(a)** ‹*furniture, object, house*› en bois; ‹*leg, spoon*› de bois
(b) ‹*expression*› figé/-e

woodland *n* bois *m*

woodpecker *n* pic *m*

wood pigeon *n* pigeon *m* ramier

woodwind *n pl* bois *mpl*

woodwork *n* **(a)** (carpentry) menuiserie *f*
(b) (doors, windows) boiseries *fpl*

woodworm *n* ver *m* du bois

wool *n* laine *f*; **pure (new) ~** pure laine (vierge)
IDIOM **to pull the ~ over sb's eyes** duper qn

woollen (GB), **woolen** (US) **1** *n* (garment) lainage *m*
2 *adj* ‹*garment*› de laine

woolly (GB), **wooly** (US) **1** *n* lainage *m*
2 *adj* **(a)** ‹*garment*› de laine; ‹*animal coat, hair*› laineux/-euse; ‹*cloud*› cotonneux/-euse
(b) ‹*thinking*› flou/-e

✓ **word** **1** *n* **(a)** mot *m*; **to have the last ~** avoir le dernier mot; **I couldn't get a ~ in** je n'ai pas pu placer un mot; **in other ~s** en d'autres termes; **a ~ of warning** un ⋯⟶

W

avertissement; **a** ~ **of advice** un conseil; **too sad for** ~s trop triste; **I believed every** ~ he **said** je croyais tout ce qu'il me disait; **I mean every** ~ **of it** je pense ce que je dis; **a man of few** ~s un homme peu loquace; **not a** ~ **to anybody** pas un mot à qui que ce soit; **I don't believe a** ~ **of it** je n'en crois pas un mot
(b) (information) nouvelles *fpl* (**about** concernant); **there is no** ~ **of the missing climbers** on est sans nouvelles des alpinistes disparus; ~ **got out that…** la nouvelle a transpiré que…; **to bring/send** ~ **that** annoncer/faire savoir que
(c) (promise, affirmation) parole *f*; **he gave me his** ~ il m'a donné sa parole; **to keep/break one's** ~ tenir/ne pas tenir parole; **to take sb's** ~ **for it** croire qn sur parole; **take my** ~ **for it!** crois-moi!
(d) (rumour) ~ **has it that he's a millionaire** on dit qu'il est millionnaire; ~ **got around that…** le bruit a couru que…
(e) (command) ordre *m*; **to give the** ~ **to do** donner l'ordre de faire
2 words *n pl* (of play) texte *m*; (of song) paroles *fpl*
3 *vtr* formuler ‹*reply, letter, statement*›
IDIOMS **my** ~**!** (in surprise) ma parole!; **right from the** ~ **go** dès le départ; **to have a** ~ **with sb about sth** parler à qn à propos de qch; **to have** ~s **with sb** s'accrocher avec qn; **to put in a good** ~ **for sb** glisser un mot en faveur de qn

word for word *adv* ‹*copy, translate*› mot à mot; ‹*repeat*› mot pour mot

wording *n* formulation *f*

wordlist *n* liste *f* de mots

word-of-mouth **1** *adj* verbal/-e
2 by word of mouth *phr* verbalement

word processing, WP *n* traitement *m* de texte

word processor *n* machine *f* à traitement de texte

✧ **work** **1** *n* **(a)** (physical or mental activity) travail *m* (**on** sur); **it was hard** ~ **doing** ça a été dur de faire; **to be hard at** ~ travailler dur; **it's thirsty** ~ ça donne soif
(b) (occupation) travail *m*; **to be in** ~ avoir du travail *or* un emploi; **place of** ~ lieu *m* de travail; **to be off** ~ (on vacation) être en congé; **to be off** ~ **with flu** être en arrêt de travail parce qu'on a la grippe; **to be out of** ~ être au chômage
(c) (place of employment) **to go to** ~ aller au travail
(d) (building, construction) travaux *mpl* (**on** sur)
(e) (essay, report) travail *m*; (artwork, novel, sculpture) œuvre *f* (**by** de); (study) ouvrage *m* (**by** de; **on** sur); (research) recherches *fpl* (**on** sur); **a** ~ **of reference** un ouvrage de référence; **a** ~ **of fiction** une œuvre de fiction; **the** ~s **of Racine** l'œuvre *m* de

Racine; **this attack is the** ~ **of professionals** l'attaque est l'œuvre de professionnels
2 works *n pl* **(a)** (factory) usine *f*
(b) (building work) travaux *mpl*
(c) (colloq) (everything) **the (full** *or* **whole)** ~s toute la panoplie (fam)
3 *vtr* **(a)** (drive) **to** ~ **sb hard** surmener qn
(b) (labour) **to** ~ **days/nights** travailler de jour/de nuit; **to** ~ **a 40 hour week** faire la semaine de 40 heures; **he** ~**ed his way through college** il a travaillé pour payer ses études
(c) (operate) se servir de ‹*computer, machine*›
(d) (exploit commercially) exploiter ‹*mine, seam*›
(e) (bring about) **to** ~ **wonders** *or* **miracles** faire des merveilles
(f) (use to one's advantage) **to** ~ **the system** exploiter le système
(g) (fashion) travailler ‹*clay, metal*›
(h) (manoeuvre) **to** ~ **sth into** introduire qch dans ‹*slot, hole*›; **to** ~ **a lever up and down** actionner un levier
(i) (exercise) faire travailler ‹*muscles*›
(j) (move) **to** ~ **one's way through** se frayer un passage à travers ‹*crowd*›; **to** ~ **one's way along** avancer le long de ‹*ledge, windowsill*›; **to** ~ **one's hands free** se libérer les mains; **it** ~**ed its way loose, it** ~**ed itself loose** cela s'est desserré peu à peu
4 *vi* **(a)** (do a job) travailler (**doing** à faire); **to** ~ **for a living** gagner sa vie
(b) (strive) lutter (**against** contre; **for** pour; **to do** pour faire); **to** ~ **towards** aller vers ‹*solution*›; s'acheminer vers ‹*compromise*›; négocier ‹*agreement*›
(c) (function) fonctionner; **to** ~ **on electricity** marcher *or* fonctionner à l'électricité; **the washing machine isn't** ~**ing** la machine à laver est en panne
(d) (act, operate) **it doesn't** *or* **things don't** ~ **like that** ça ne marche pas comme ça; **to** ~ **in sb's favour** tourner à l'avantage de qn; **to** ~ **against sb** jouer en la défaveur de qn
(e) (be successful) ‹*treatment*› avoir de l'effet; ‹*detergent, drug*› agir (**against** contre; **on** sur); ‹*plan*› réussir; ‹*argument, theory*› tenir debout; **flattery won't** ~ **with me** la flatterie ne marche pas avec moi
(f) ‹*face, features*› se contracter
IDIOMS **to** ~ **one's way up** gravir tous les échelons; **to** ~ **one's way up the company** faire son chemin dans l'entreprise
∎ **work in:** ~ **in [sth],** ~ **[sth] in (a)** glisser ‹*joke*›; mentionner ‹*fact, name*›
(b) (Culin) incorporer
∎ **work off (a)** (remove) retirer ‹*lid*›
(b) (repay) travailler pour rembourser ‹*loan, debt*›
(c) (get rid of) se débarrasser de ‹*excess weight*›; dépenser ‹*excess energy*›; passer ‹*anger, frustration*›
∎ **work on:** **1** ~ **on** continuer à travailler
2 ~ **on [sb]** travailler (fam) ‹*person*›
3 ~ **on [sth]** travailler à ‹*book, report*›;

✧ indicates a very frequent word

W

travailler sur ‹project›; s'occuper de ‹case, problem›; chercher ‹cure, solution›; examiner ‹idea, theory›
■ **work out** 1 ~ out (a) (exercise) s'entraîner
(b) (go according to plan) marcher
(c) (add up) **to ~ out at** (GB) *or* **to** (US) s'élever à
2 ~ [sth] out (a) (calculate) calculer ‹amount›
(b) (solve) trouver ‹answer, reason, culprit›; résoudre ‹problem›; comprendre ‹clue›
(c) (devise) concevoir ‹plan, scheme›; trouver ‹route›
3 ¶ ~ [sb] out comprendre ‹person›
■ **work up**: 1 ¶ ~ up [sth] développer ‹interest›; accroître ‹support›; **to ~ up the courage to do** trouver le courage de faire; **to ~ up some enthusiasm for** s'enthousiasmer pour; **to ~ up an appetite** s'ouvrir l'appétit
2 ¶ ~ up to [sth] se préparer à ‹confrontation, announcement›
3 ¶ ~ [sb] up (a) (excite) exciter ‹child, crowd›
(b) (annoy) **to get ~ed up, to ~ oneself up** s'énerver

workable *adj* (a) ‹idea, plan, suggestion› réalisable; ‹system› pratique; ‹arrangement, compromise› possible
(b) ‹land, mine› exploitable; ‹cement› maniable

workaholic *n* (colloq) bourreau *m* de travail

workbook *n* (blank) cahier *m*; (with exercises) livre *m* d'exercices

ᵒ⸜ **worker** *n* (in manual job) ouvrier/-ière *m/f*; (in white-collar job) employé/-e *m/f*

work experience *n* stage *m*

workforce *n* (in industry) main-d'œuvre *f*; (in service sector) effectifs *mpl*

ᵒ⸜ **working** *adj* (a) ‹parent, woman› qui travaille; ‹conditions, environment, methods› de travail; ‹population, life› actif/-ive; ‹breakfast, lunch, day› de travail; **during ~ hours** (in office) pendant les heures de bureau; (in shop) pendant les heures d'ouverture
(b) (provisional) ‹document› de travail; ‹definition, title› provisoire
(c) (functional) ‹model› qui fonctionne; ‹farm, mine› en exploitation; **in full ~ order** en parfait état de marche

working class 1 *n* classe *f* ouvrière; **the ~es** les classes *fpl* laborieuses
2 **working-class** *adj* ‹area, background, family, life› ouvrier/-ière; ‹culture, London› prolétarien/-ienne; ‹person› de la classe ouvrière

workings *n pl* rouages *mpl*

workload *n* charge *f* de travail

workman *n* ouvrier *m*

workmanship *n* a carpenter famous for sound ~ un menuisier connu pour la qualité de son travail; **furniture of the finest ~** des meubles d'une belle facture; **a piece of poor** *or* **shoddy ~** du travail mal fait *or* bâclé

workmate *n* collègue *mf* de travail

work of art *n* œuvre *f* d'art

workout *n* séance *f* de mise en forme

workpack *n* fiches *fpl* de travail

work permit *n* permis *m* de travail

workplace *n* lieu *m* de travail

work-sharing *n* partage *m* du travail

worksheet *n* (Sch) feuille *f* de questions

workshop *n* atelier *m*

work station *n* poste *m* de travail

worktop *n* (GB) plan *m* de travail

work-to-rule *n* grève *f* du zèle

ᵒ⸜ **world** 1 *n* monde *m*; **throughout the ~** dans le monde entier; **to go round the ~** faire le tour du monde; **the biggest in the ~** le plus grand du monde; **more than anything in the ~** plus que tout au monde; **to go up in the ~** faire du chemin; **to go down in the ~** déchoir; **the Eastern/Western ~** les pays de l'Est/occidentaux; **the ancient ~** l'antiquité; **he lives in a ~ of his own** il vit dans un monde à part
2 *adj* ‹events, market, leader, politics, rights, scale› mondial/-e; ‹record, tour, championship› du monde; ‹cruise› autour du monde
IDIOMS **to be on top of the ~** être aux anges; **to get the best of both ~s** gagner sur les deux tableaux; **a man/woman of the ~** un homme/une femme d'expérience; **out of this ~** extraordinaire; **there's a ~ of difference** il y a une différence énorme; **it did him the** *or* **a ~ of good** ça lui a fait énormément de bien; **to think the ~ of sb** penser le plus grand bien de qn; **what/where/who in the ~?** que/où/qui etc diable?; **~s apart** diamétralement opposé

world-class *adj* de niveau mondial

World Cup *n* Coupe *f* du Monde

World Fair *n* Exposition *f* universelle

world-famous *adj* mondialement connu/-e

world leader *n* (a) (politician) chef *m* d'État
(b) (athlete) meilleur/-e *m/f* du monde; (company) leader *m* mondial

worldly *adj* (a) (not spiritual) matériel/-ielle
(b) (experienced) ‹person› avisé/-e, qui a de l'expérience

worldly-wise *adj* avisé/-e, qui a de l'expérience

world music *n* musiques *fpl* du monde

world power *n* puissance *f* mondiale

worldview *n* vision *f* du monde

world war *n* guerre *f* mondiale; **the First/ Second World War** la Première/Seconde ⋯⊱

Guerre mondiale

world-wide ① adj mondial/-e
② adv dans le monde entier

World Wide Web n the World Wide Web
la Toile f mondiale, le Web m

worm n ver m

worn adj ‹carpet, clothing, shoe, tyre› usé/-e;
‹stone› abîmé/-e; ‹tread› lisse

worn-out adj (a) ‹carpet, brake›
complètement usé/-e
(b) ‹person› épuisé/-e

✐ **worried** adj ‹person, face› inquiet/-iète;
to be ~ about sb/sth se faire du souci or
s'inquiéter pour qn/qch; I'm ~ (that) he
might get lost j'ai peur qu'il ne se perde

worrier n anxieux/-ieuse m/f

✐ **worry** ① n (a) (anxiety) soucis mpl (about,
over à propos de)
(b) (problem) souci m (about, over au sujet de)
② vtr (a) (concern) inquiéter; I ~ that he
won't come j'ai peur qu'il ne vienne pas; it
worried him that he couldn't find the keys ça
l'a inquiété de ne pas trouver les clés
(b) (bother) ennuyer; would it ~ you if I
opened the window? est-ce que ça vous
ennuierait que j'ouvre la fenêtre?
(c) ‹dog› harceler ‹sheep›
③ vi (be anxious) s'inquiéter; to ~ about or
over sb/sth s'inquiéter or se faire du souci
pour qn/qch; don't ~! ne t'inquiète pas!;
there's nothing to ~ about il n'y a pas lieu
de s'inquiéter
④ v refl to ~ oneself s'inquiéter, se faire du
souci (about sb au sujet de qn; about sth à
propos de qch); to ~ oneself sick over sth se
ronger les sangs (fam) au sujet de qch
▪ **worry at** ‹dog› mordiller, jouer avec ‹toy›;
‹person› retourner [qch] dans tous les sens
‹problem›

worry beads n pl chapelet m antistress

worrying adj inquiétant/-e

worse ① adj (comparative of **bad**)
pire (than que); to get ~ ‹pressure, noise›
augmenter; ‹conditions, weather› empirer;
‹illness, conflict› s'aggraver; he's getting ~
(in health) il va plus mal; the cough is getting
~ la toux empire; to feel ~ (more ill) se sentir
plus malade; (more unhappy) aller moins bien;
and what is ~... et le pire, c'est que...; and
to make matters ~, he lied et pour ne rien
arranger, il a menti
② n there is ~ to come ce n'est pas encore
le pire; to change for the ~ empirer
③ adv (comparative of **badly**) ‹play,
sing› moins bien (than que); to behave ~
se conduire plus mal; she could do ~ than
follow his example ce ne serait pas si mal si
elle suivait son exemple

worsen ① vtr aggraver ‹situation,
problem›
② vi ‹condition, health, weather, situation›

se détériorer; ‹problem, crisis, shortage,
flooding› s'aggraver

worsening ① n aggravation f (of de)
② adj ‹situation› en voie de détérioration;
‹problem, shortage› en voie d'aggravation

worse off adj (a) (less wealthy) to be ~
avoir moins d'argent (than que); I'm £10 a
week ~ j'ai dix livres de moins par semaine
(b) (in a worse situation) to be ~ être dans une
situation pire

worship ① n (a) (religious devotion) culte m;
sun/ancestor ~ culte du soleil/des ancêtres;
place of ~ lieu m de culte
(b) (veneration) vénération f
② Worship pr n (GB) Your Worship (to judge)
Monsieur le juge; (to mayor) Monsieur le
maire
③ vtr (p prés etc **-pp-**) (a) (venerate)
vénérer ‹God, Buddha›; (give praise to)
rendre hommage à
(b) adorer, avoir un culte pour ‹person›;
avoir le culte de ‹money, success›
④ vi (p prés etc **-pp-**) pratiquer sa religion

worshipper n fidèle m/f

worst ① n (a) (most difficult, unpleasant) the
~ le/la pire m/f; if the ~ came to the ~ (in
serious circumstances) dans le pire des cas;
(involving fatality) si le pire devait arriver
(b) (most negative trait) to bring out the ~ in sb
mettre à jour ce qu'il y a de plus mauvais
chez qn
(c) (of the lowest standard, quality) the ~ le plus
mauvais/la plus mauvaise m/f; he's one of
the ~ c'est un des plus mauvais; to be the ~
at French être le plus mauvais en français
② adj (superlative of **bad**) (a) (most
unsatisfactory, unpleasant) pire, plus mauvais/-e;
the ~ book I've ever read le plus mauvais
livre que j'aie jamais lu; the ~ thing about
the film is... ce qu'il y a de pire dans le film
c'est...
(b) (most serious) plus grave; one of the ~
recessions une des crises les plus graves
③ adv (most) the children suffer (the) ~ ce sont les
enfants qui souffrent le plus; they were (the)
~ hit by the strike ce sont eux qui ont été les
plus touchés par la grève; ~ of all,... le pire
de tout, c'est que...

✐ **worth** ① n (a) (quantity) five pounds' ~
of sth pour cinq livres de qch; thousands
of pounds' ~ of damage des milliers de
livres de dégâts; a week's ~ of supplies une
semaine de provisions; to get one's money's
~ en avoir pour son argent
(b) (value) valeur f; of great ~ de grande
valeur; of no ~ sans valeur
② adj (a) (of financial value) to be ~ sth
valoir qch; how much is it ~? combien cela
vaut-il?; the pound was ~ 10 francs then à
l'époque, la livre valait 10 francs
(b) (of abstract value) to be ~ sth valoir qch;
to be ~ it (en) valoir la peine; the book isn't
~ reading le livre ne vaut pas la peine d'être

✐ indicates a very frequent word

w

worthless ⇢ wreck

lu; **that's ~ knowing** cela est bon à savoir; **those little pleasures that make life ~ living** ces petits plaisirs qui rendent la vie agréable IDIOMS **for all one is ~** de toutes ses forces; **for what it's ~** pour ce que cela vaut; **to be ~ sb's while** valoir le coup

worthless *adj* sans valeur; **he's ~** c'est un bon à rien

worthwhile *adj* ‹discussion, undertaking, visit› qui en vaut la peine; ‹career, project› intéressant/-e; **to be ~ doing** valoir la peine de faire

worthy *adj* **(a)** (deserving) **to be ~ of sth** mériter qch, être digne de qch; **~ of note** digne d'intérêt; **to be ~ of doing** ‹person› être digne de faire
(b) (admirable) ‹cause› noble; ‹citizen, friend› digne

✱ **would** *modal aux* **(a)** (expressing the conditional) **it ~ be nice if everyone were there, wouldn't it?** ce serait bien si tout le monde était là, n'est-ce pas?; **if he had more money, he'd buy a car** s'il avait plus d'argent il achèterait une voiture; **we ~ have missed the train if we had left later** si nous étions partis plus tard, nous aurions raté le train; **we wouldn't have succeeded without him** nous n'aurions pas réussi sans lui
(b) (in indirect statements or questions) **we thought he'd forget** nous pensions qu'il oublierait; **did she say she ~ be coming?** est-ce qu'elle a dit qu'elle viendrait?; **I wish he ~ be quiet!** il ne pourrait pas se taire!
(c) (expressing willingness to act) **she wouldn't listen to me** elle ne voulait pas m'écouter; **he wouldn't do a thing to help us** il n'a rien voulu faire pour nous aider; **they asked me to leave but I wouldn't** ils m'ont demandé de partir mais j'ai refusé; **of course you ~ contradict him!** bien sûr il a fallu que tu le contredises!
(d) (in requests) **~ you give her the message?** est-ce que vous voulez bien lui transmettre le message?; **switch off the radio, ~ you?** éteins la radio, tu veux bien?; **~ you excuse me for a moment?** excusez-moi un instant
(e) (expressing one's wishes) **~ you like something to eat?** désirez-vous *or* voulez-vous manger quelque chose?; **I ~ like a beer** je voudrais une bière; **we ~ like to stay another night** nous aimerions rester une nuit de plus; **she'd have liked to stay here** elle aurait aimé rester ici; **I wouldn't mind another slice of cake** je prendrais bien un autre morceau de gâteau
(f) (offering advice) **if I were you, I wouldn't say anything** à ta place, je ne dirais rien; **it ~ be better to write** il vaudrait mieux écrire; **it ~ be a good idea to wait** ce serait une bonne idée d'attendre; **you ~ do well to check the timetable** tu ferais bien de vérifier l'horaire
(g) (in assumptions) **I ~ have been 12** je devais avoir 12 ans; **it ~ have been about midday** il devait être à peu près midi

(h) (used to) **she ~ talk for hours** elle parlait pendant des heures

would-be *adj* **(a)** (desirous of being) **~ emigrants/investors** personnes *fpl or* ceux qui désirent émigrer/investir
(b) (so-called) **~ intellectuals** les soi-disant intellectuels
(c) (having intended to be) **the ~ thieves were arrested** les voleurs ont été arrêtés avant qu'ils aient pu passer à l'acte

wound ① *n* **(a)** (injury) blessure *f*; (cut) plaie *f*; **bullet ~** blessure par balle; **knife ~** coup *m* de couteau; **a ~ to** *or* **in the head** une blessure à la tête
(b) (figurative) blessure *f*
② *vtr* blesser
IDIOMS **to lick one's ~s** panser ses blessures; **to rub salt into the ~** remuer le couteau dans la plaie

wounded ① *n* **the ~** les blessés/blessées *m/f*
② *adj* blessé/-e; **~ in the arm** blessé au bras

wrangle ① *n* querelle *f*
② *vi* se quereller (**over, about** sur, à propos de; **with** avec)

✱ **wrap** ① *n* (shawl) châle *m*; (stole) étole *f*
② *vtr* (*p prés etc* **-pp-**) (in paper) emballer (**in** dans); (in blanket, garment) envelopper (**in** dans); **to be ~ped in** être emmitouflé/-e dans ‹blanket›; être enveloppé/-e dans ‹newspaper›; être enveloppé/-e de ‹mystery›
IDIOM **to keep sth/to be under ~s** garder qch/être secret/-ète

■ **wrap up:** ① ¶**~ up** se couvrir; **~ up well** *or* **warm!** couvre-toi bien!
② **~ [sth] up (a)** faire ‹parcel›; envelopper ‹gift, purchase›; emballer ‹rubbish›
(b) to be ~ped up in ne s'occuper que de ‹person, child›; être absorbé/-e dans ‹activity, work›; **they are completely ~ped up in each other** ils ne vivent que l'un pour l'autre
(c) dissimuler ‹meaning, facts, ideas› (**in** derrière)

wraparound *adj* ‹window, windscreen› panoramique; ‹skirt› portefeuille

wraparound sunglasses *n pl* lunettes *fpl* de soleil enveloppantes

wrap-over *adj* ‹skirt› portefeuille; ‹dress› croisé/-e

wrapper *n* (of sweet) papier *m*

wrapping *n* emballage *m*

wrapping paper *n* (brown) papier *m* d'emballage; (decorative) papier *m* cadeau

wreak *vtr* assouvir ‹revenge› (**on** sur); **to ~ havoc** *or* **damage** infliger des dégâts; **to ~ havoc** *or* **damage on sth** dévaster qch

wreath *n* couronne *f*; **to lay a ~** déposer une gerbe

wreck ① *n* **(a)** (car, plane) (crashed) épave *f*; (burnt out) carcasse *f*
(b) (sunken ship) épave *f*
(c) (person) épave *f*
② *vtr* **(a)** ‹explosion, fire, vandals› dévaster ⇢

W

⟨building, machinery⟩; ⟨person, driver, impact⟩ détruire ⟨vehicle⟩
(b) ruiner ⟨career, chances, health, life, marriage⟩; gâcher ⟨holiday, weekend⟩

wreckage n **(a)** (of plane, car, ship) épave f; (of building) décombres mpl
(b) (of hopes, plans) naufrage m

wrecked adj **(a)** ⟨car, plane⟩ accidenté/-e; ⟨ship⟩ naufragé/-e; ⟨building⟩ démoli/-e
(b) ⟨life, career, marriage⟩ ruiné/-e

wren n roitelet m

wrench 1 n **(a)** (GB) (adjustable spanner) tourne-à-gauche m inv; (US) (spanner) clé f de serrage
(b) (emotional upheaval) déchirement m
2 vtr tirer violemment sur ⟨handle⟩; to ∼ one's ankle/knee se tordre la cheville/le genou; to ∼ sth from sb arracher qch à qn; to ∼ sth away from sb arracher qch de qch

wrestle 1 vtr to ∼ sb for sth lutter contre qn pour qch; to ∼ sb to the ground terrasser qn
2 vi **(a)** (Sport) faire du catch
(b) (struggle) to ∼ with se débattre avec ⟨person, problem, homework, conscience⟩; se battre avec ⟨controls, zip, suitcase⟩; lutter contre ⟨temptation⟩

wrestler n catcheur/-euse m/f

wrestling n catch m

wretched adj ⟨person⟩ infortuné/-e; ⟨existence, appearance, conditions⟩ misérable; ⟨weather⟩ affreux/-euse; ⟨accommodation⟩ minable; ⟨amount⟩ dérisoire

wriggle 1 vtr to ∼ one's toes/fingers remuer les orteils/doigts; to ∼ one's way out of sth se sortir de qch
2 vi ⟨person⟩ s'agiter, gigoter; ⟨snake, worm⟩ se tortiller; ⟨fish⟩ frétiller; to ∼ out of se défiler devant ⟨duty, task⟩

wring vtr (prét, pp **wrung**) **(a)** (also ∼ out) essorer ⟨clothes, cloth⟩
(b) (extract) arracher ⟨confession, money⟩ (from, out of à)
(c) (twist) to ∼ sb's/sth's neck tordre le cou à qn/qch; to ∼ one's hands se tordre les mains; (figurative) se lamenter

wrinkle 1 n (on skin) ride f; (in fabric) pli m
2 vtr **(a)** rider ⟨skin⟩; to ∼ one's nose faire la grimace (**at** devant)
(b) froisser ⟨fabric⟩
3 vi ⟨skin⟩ se rider; ⟨fabric⟩ se froisser; ⟨wallpaper⟩ gondoler

wrist n poignet m

wristband n (for tennis, on sleeve) poignet m

wristwatch n montre-bracelet f

writ n assignation f (for pour); to **issue** or **serve** a ∼ **against sb**, to serve sb with a ∼ assigner qn en justice

🔹 **write** 1 vtr (pp **written**) **(a)** écrire ⟨letter, poem, novel⟩ (to à); composer ⟨song,

symphony⟩; rédiger ⟨business letter, article, report, prescription⟩; faire ⟨cheque⟩; écrire ⟨software, program⟩; élaborer ⟨legislation⟩; **he wrote me a cheque for £100** il m'a fait un chèque de 100 livres sterling; **I wrote home** j'ai écrit à ma famille
(b) (US) écrire à ⟨person⟩
2 vi (pp **written**) écrire (**to sb** à qn)
■ **write back** répondre (to à)
■ **write down** noter ⟨details, name⟩; mettre [qch] par écrit ⟨ideas, suggestions⟩; consigner [qch] par écrit ⟨information, findings⟩
■ **write off**: 1 (pp **written**) to ∼ off écrire une lettre (to à); to ∼ off for écrire pour demander
2 (pp **written**) ∼ [sb/sth] off **(a)** (wreck) bousiller complètement (fam) ⟨car⟩
(b) (in bookkeeping) passer [qch] aux pertes et profits ⟨bad debt, loss⟩; amortir ⟨capital⟩
(c) (end) annuler ⟨debt, project, operation⟩
■ **write out (a)** (put down on paper) écrire
(b) (copy) copier

write-off n **(a)** (US) (in taxation) somme f déductible de la déclaration des revenus
(b) (wreck) épave f

write protect n (Comput) protection f en mode écriture

🔹 **writer** n (author) (professional) écrivain m; (nonprofessional) auteur m

writer's block n l'angoisse f de la page blanche

write-up n **(a)** (review) critique f
(b) (account) rapport m (of sur)

writhe vi (also ∼ **about**, ∼ **around**) se tortiller; to ∼ **in agony** se tordre de douleur

🔹 **writing** n **(a)** (activity) ∼ **is her life** écrire, c'est sa vie
(b) (handwriting) écriture f; **his ∼ is poor/good** il écrit mal/bien
(c) (words and letters) écriture f; to put sth in ∼ mettre qch par écrit
(d) (literature) littérature f

writing pad n bloc m de papier à lettres

writing paper n papier m à lettres

writing table n bureau m

written adj ⟨reply, guarantee, proof⟩ écrit/-e; **he failed the ∼ paper** il a échoué à l'écrit; ∼ **evidence** or **proof** (Law) preuves fpl écrites; **the ∼ word** l'écriture f

🔹 **wrong** 1 n **(a)** (evil) mal m
(b) (injustice) tort m; **to right a ∼** réparer un tort
2 adj **(a)** (incorrect) faux/fausse (before n); (ill-chosen) mauvais/-e (before n); **he took the ∼ key** il a pris la mauvaise clé; **it's the ∼ glue for the purpose** ce n'est pas la colle qu'il faut; **to go the ∼ way** se tromper de chemin; **I dialled the ∼ number** je me suis trompé de numéro, j'ai fait un faux or mauvais numéro; **you've got the ∼ number** vous faites erreur
(b) (reprehensible, unjust) **it is ∼ to cheat** c'est mal de tricher; **she hasn't done anything ∼**

🔹 indicates a very frequent word

w

elle n'a rien fait de mal; **it was ~ of me to do** je n'aurais pas dû faire; **it is ~ that** c'est injuste que; **there's nothing ~ with** or **in sth** il n'y a pas de mal à qch; **(so) what's ~ with that?** où est le mal?
(c) (mistaken) **to be ~** ‹person› avoir tort, se tromper; **to be ~ about** se tromper sur; **she was ~ about him** elle s'est trompée sur son compte; **to prove sb ~** donner tort à qn
(d) (not as it should be) **there is something (badly) ~** il y a quelque chose qui ne va pas (du tout); **there's something ~ with this computer** il y a un problème avec cet ordinateur; **the wording is all ~** la formulation ne va pas du tout; **what's ~ with your arm?** qu'est-ce que tu as au bras?; **what's ~ with you?** (to person suffering) qu'est-ce que tu as?; (to person behaving oddly) qu'est-ce qui t'arrive?; **your clock is ~** votre pendule n'est pas à l'heure
3 *adv* **to get [sth] ~** se tromper de ‹date, time, details›; se tromper dans ‹calculations›; **I think you've got it ~** je pense que tu te trompes; **to go ~** ‹person› se tromper;

‹machine› ne plus marcher
4 *vtr* faire du tort à ‹person, family›
IDIOMS to be in the ~ être dans mon/ton etc tort; **to get on the ~ side of sb** se faire mal voir de qn; **to go down the ~ way** ‹food, drink› passer de travers
wrongdoer *n* malfaiteur *m*
wrongfoot *vtr* (Sport) prendre [qn] à contre-pied; (figurative) prendre [qn] au dépourvu
wrongly *adv* mal; **he concluded, ~, that...** il a conclu, à tort, que...; **rightly or ~** à tort ou à raison
wrought *adj* ‹silver, gold› travaillé/-e
wrought iron *n* fer *m* forgé
wry *adj* ‹smile, look, humour› narquois/-e; **to have a ~ sense of humour** être pince-sans-rire
WTO (*abbr* = **World Trade Organization**) OMC *f*

---

x, X *n* **(a)** (letter) x, X *m*
(b) (standing for number, name) **for x people** pour x personnes; **Ms X** Mme X; **X marks the spot** l'endroit est marqué d'une croix
(c) (kisses ending letter) grosses bises
X-certificate *adj* ‹film› interdit/-e aux moins de 18 ans
xenophobia *n* xénophobie *f*
xerox® *vtr* photocopier

Xmas *n* Noël *m*
X-rated *adj* ‹film, video› interdit/-e aux moins de 18 ans
X-ray **1** *n* **(a)** (ray) rayon *m* X
(b) (photo) radiographie *f*, radio *f* (fam); **to have an ~** se faire radiographier; **to give sb an ~** faire une radiographie à qn
2 *vtr* radiographier
X-ray unit *n* service *m* de radiologie

---

y, Y *n* y, Y *m*
yacht *n* yacht *m*
yachting *n* yachting *m*; **to go ~** faire du yachting
yachtsman *n* yachtman *m*
yahoo **1** *n* abruti/-e *m* (fam)
2 *excl* hourra!
yak *n* yack *m*
Yale lock® *n* serrure *f* de sûreté
yam *n* igname *f*

yank **1** *n* coup *m* sec; **to give sth a ~** tirer qch d'un coup sec
2 *vtr* tirer ‹person, rope›
■ **yank out** arracher
Yank *n* (derogatory) yankee *mf*
Yankee *n* (derogatory) yankee *m*
yap **1** *n* jappement *m*
2 *vi* ‹dog› japper (**at** après)
yapping **1** *n* jappements *mpl*
2 *adj* ‹dog› jappeur/-euse
⚡ **yard** *n* **(a)** yard *m* (= 0.9144 m)   ⋯⟩

(b) (of house, farm, prison, hospital) cour *f*
(c) (US) (garden) jardin *m*
(d) (for storage) dépôt *m*; (for construction) chantier *m*; builder's ~ dépôt *m* de matériaux de construction

yardarm *n* bout *m* de vergue
yardstick *n* (figurative) critères *mpl*
yarn *n* **(a)** (fibre) fibre *f* textile; (wool) laine *f*
(b) (tale) histoire *f*; **to spin a ~** raconter des histoires

yashmak *n* voile *m* islamique
yawn ⓵ *n* bâillement *m*; **to give a ~** bâiller
  ⓶ *vi* **(a)** ‹person› bâiller
  (b) ‹abyss, chasm› béer

✔ **yeah** *particle* (colloq) ouais (fam), oui; **oh ~?** vraiment?

✔ **year** ⓵ *n* **(a)** (period of time) an *m*; (with emphasis on duration) année *f*; **in the ~ 1789/2000** en 1789/l'an 2000; **two ~s ago** il y a deux ans; **all (the) ~ round** toute l'année; **every ~** tous les ans *or* des années; **over the ~s** au cours des ans *or* des années; **the ~ before last** il y a deux ans; **every ~** tous les ans; **they have been living in Paris for ~s** ils habitent Paris depuis des années; **for the first time in ~s** pour la première fois depuis des années; **it's a ~ since I heard from him** je n'ai plus de ses nouvelles depuis un an; **they lived in Paris for ~s** ils ont habité Paris pendant des années; **to earn £30,000 a ~** gagner 30 000 livres sterling par an
  (b) (indicating age) **to be 19 ~s old** *or* **19 ~s of age** avoir 19 ans; **a two-~-old child** un enfant de deux ans
  (c) (pupil) **first/second-~** ≈ élève *mf* de sixième/cinquième
  ⓶ **years** *n pl* (colloq) (a long time) **that would take ~s!** ça prendrait une éternité!; **it's ~s since we last met!** ça fait un siècle qu'on ne s'est pas vus!
  IDIOM **this job has put ~s on me!** ce travail m'a vieilli de 10 ans!

yearbook *n* **(a)** (directory) annuaire *m*
  (b) (US) album *m* de promotion
yearlong *adj* ‹stay, course, absence› d'un an, d'une année
yearly ⓵ *adj* ‹visit, account, income› annuel/-elle
  ⓶ *adv* annuellement
yearn *vi* **(a)** **to ~ for** désirer (avoir) ‹child›; aspirer à ‹freedom, unity›; attendre ‹season, event›; **to ~ to do** avoir très envie de faire
  (b) (miss) **she ~s for her son** son fils lui manque terriblement
yearning ⓵ *n* désir *m* ardent (**for** de; **to do** de faire)
  ⓶ **yearnings** *n pl* aspirations *fpl*
  ⓷ *adj* ‹expression› plein/-e de désir
year out *n*: année d'interruption des études entre le lycée et l'université

year tutor *n*: professeur responsable de toutes les classes d'un même niveau
yeast *n* levure *f*
✔ **yell** ⓵ *n* (shout) cri *m*; (of rage, pain) hurlement *m*
  ⓶ *vtr* crier ‹warning›; (louder) hurler ‹insults›
  ⓷ *vi* crier; **to ~ at sb** crier après qn
yelling *n* cris *mpl*
✔ **yellow** ⓵ *n* jaune *m*
  ⓶ *adj* **(a)** (in colour) jaune; **to go** *or* **turn ~** jaunir
  (b) (colloq) (cowardly) trouillard/-e (fam)
  ⓷ *vi* jaunir
yellow-belly *n* (colloq) trouillard/-e *m/f* (fam)
yellow card *n* (Sport) carton *m* jaune
yellowish *adj* tirant sur le jaune; (unpleasantly) jaunâtre
Yellow Pages® *n pl* pages *fpl* jaunes
yelp ⓵ *n* glapissement *m*
  ⓶ *vi* glapir
Yemen *pr n* Yémen *m*
yen *n* **(a)** (currency) yen *m*
  (b) (colloq) (craving) **to have a ~ for sth/to do** avoir grande envie de qch/de faire
yeoman *n* (*pl* -**men**) (*also* ~ **farmer**) franc tenancier *m*
yeoman of the guard *n* (GB) membre *m* de la garde royale
yep, yup *particle* (colloq) (US) ouais (fam), oui
✔ **yes** *particle* oui; (in reply to negative question) si

────────────
■ Note *yes* is translated by *oui*, except when used in reply to a negative question in which case the translation is *si* or, more emphatically, *mais si*: 'did you see him?'—'yes (I did)' = 'est-ce que tu l'as vu?'—'oui (je l'ai vu)'; 'you're not hungry, are you?'—'yes I am' = 'tu n'as pas faim?'—'si (j'ai faim)'.
— Note that there are no direct equivalents in French for tag questions and short replies such as *yes I did, yes I am*.
— For some suggestions on how to translate these, see DO.
────────────

yes-man *n* (*pl* -**men**) (colloq) lèche-bottes *m inv*
✔ **yesterday** ⓵ *n* hier *m*; **~'s newspaper** le journal d'hier; **~ was a sad day for all of us** la journée d'hier a été triste pour nous tous; **~ was the fifth of April** hier nous étions le cinq avril; **the day before ~** avant-hier
  ⓶ *adv* hier; **only ~** pas plus tard qu'hier; **all day ~** toute la journée d'hier
yesterday afternoon *n*, *adv* hier après-midi
yesterday evening *n*, *adv* hier soir
yesterday morning *n*, *adv* hier matin
yesteryear *n* temps *m* jadis; **the fashions of ~** la mode d'antan *or* du temps jadis
yes-vote *n* oui *m*

────────────
✔ indicates a very frequent word

ᵍ **yet** ⸤1⸥ *conj* pourtant
⸤2⸥ *adv* **(a)** (up till now, so far) encore; (in
questions) déjà; (with superlatives) jusqu'ici; **it's
not ready ∼** ce n'est pas encore prêt; **has he
arrived ∼?** est-il (déjà) arrivé?; **not ∼** pas
encore, pas pour l'instant; **it's the best ∼**
jusqu'ici, c'est le meilleur
(b) (*also* **just ∼**) tout de suite, encore; **don't
start ∼** ne commence pas tout de suite
(c) (still) encore; **they may ∼ come** ils
pourraient encore arriver; **he'll finish it ∼** il
va le finir; **he won't come for hours ∼** il ne
viendra pas avant quelques heures
(d) (even, still) encore; **∼ more cars** encore
plus de voitures; **∼ another attack** encore
une autre attaque; **∼ again** encore une fois
yew *n* (*also* **∼ tree**) if *m*
Y-fronts *n pl* (GB) slip *m* ouvert
YHA *n* (GB) (*abbr* = **Youth Hostels
Association**) association *f* des auberges
de jeunesse
yield ⸤1⸥ *n* rendement *m*
⸤2⸥ *vtr* **(a)** (produce) produire
(b) (provide) donner, fournir ‹result, meaning›;
fournir ‹clue›
(c) (surrender) céder (**to** à); **to ∼ ground**
(figurative) céder du terrain
⸤3⸥ *vi* **(a)** (to person, temptation, pressure, threats)
céder (**to** à)
(b) (under weight, physical pressure) céder (**under**
sous)
(c) (be superseded) **to ∼ to** ‹technology,
phenomenon› céder le pas à
(d) (US) (driving) céder le passage
yob, yobbo *n* (GB) loubard *m* (fam), voyou *m*
yodel *vi* (*p prés etc* **-ll-**) jodler, iodler
yoga *n* yoga *m*
yoghurt *n* yaourt *m*, yoghourt *m*
yo-heave-ho *excl* oh! hisse!
yoke ⸤1⸥ *n* joug *m*
⸤2⸥ *vtr* (*also* **∼ up**) atteler
yokel *n* péquenaud/-e *m/f* (fam), plouc *mf* (fam)
yolk *n* jaune *m* (d'œuf)
yonks *n pl* (colloq) **I haven't seen him for ∼**
ça fait une éternité que je ne l'ai pas vu
ᵍ **you** *pron*

■ Note In French *you* has two forms: *tu* and
vous. The usual word to use to anyone you do
not know very well is *vous*, also called the polite
form: *can I help you?* = est-ce que je peux vous
aider? The more informal *tu* (plural *vous*) is used
between close friends and family members,
within groups of children and young people,
and by adults when talking to children: *there's
a biscuit for you* = il y a un biscuit pour toi. If in
doubt, use the *vous* form.

(a) (subject) tu, vous; (object) te, t', vous; (with
prepositions, for emphasis) toi, vous; **YOU would
never do that** (polite) vous, vous ne feriez
jamais cela; (informal) toi, tu ne ferais jamais
ça; **∼ English** vous autres Anglais; **∼ idiot!**
(colloq) espèce d'imbécile! (fam); **∼ two can**

stay vous deux, vous pouvez rester
(b) (as indefinite pronoun) (subject) on; (object,
indirect object) vous, te; **∼ never know!** on
ne sait jamais!; **it makes ∼ sleepy** ça fait
dormir
you-know-what *pron* (colloq) vous-savez-
quoi/tu-sais-quoi
you-know-who *pron* (colloq) qui-vous-
savez/qui-tu-sais
ᵍ **young** ⸤1⸥ *n* **(a)** (young people) **the ∼** les
jeunes *mpl*, la jeunesse *f*
(b) (animal's offspring) petits *mpl*
⸤2⸥ *adj* (not very old) jeune; **to be ∼ at heart**
avoir l'esprit jeune; **she is ten years ∼er
than him** elle a dix ans de moins que lui;
I feel ten years ∼er j'ai l'impression d'avoir
rajeuni de dix ans; **∼ lady** jeune femme *f*; **∼
people** jeunes gens *mpl*; **∼ person** jeune *m*;
the ∼er generation la jeune génération; **her
∼er brother** son frère cadet; **I'm not as ∼ as
I used to be** je n'ai plus 20 ans
young blood *n* sang *m* neuf
youngish *adj* assez jeune
young-looking *adj* **to be ∼** faire (très)
jeune
young offender *n* délinquant/-e *m/f*
young professional *n* jeune salarié/-e
m/f
youngster *n* **(a)** (young person) jeune *m*
(b) (child) enfant *mf*
ᵍ **your**

■ Note For a full note on the use of the *vous*
and *tu* forms in French, see the entry YOU.
— In French, determiners agree in gender and
number with the noun that follows: *your* + masculine singular noun = *ton, votre* (*your dog* ton/
votre chien); *your* + feminine singular noun = *ta,
votre* (*your house* ta/votre maison); *your* + plural
noun = *tes, vos* (*your parents* tes/vos parents).

det **(a)** votre/vos; (more informally) ton/ta/tes
(b) (used impersonally) son, sa, ses; **you buy
∼ tickets at the door** on prend ses billets
à l'entrée; **smoking is bad for ∼ health** le
tabac est mauvais pour la santé
(c) (for emphasis) à vous, à toi; **your house**
votre maison à vous/ta maison à toi
yours *pron*

■ Note For a full note on the use of the *vous*
and *tu* forms in French, see the boxed note for
the entry YOU.
— In French, possessive pronouns reflect
the gender and number of the noun they are
standing for. When *yours* is referring to only one
person, it is translated by *le vôtre, la vôtre, les
vôtres*, or more informally *le tien, la tienne, les
tiens, les tiennes*. When *yours* is referring to
more than one person, it is translated by *le vôtre,
la vôtre, les vôtres*.

my car is red but ∼ is blue ma voiture est
rouge mais la vôtre/la tienne est bleue; **her
children are older than ∼** ses enfants sont
plus âgés que les vôtres/les tiens; **which**   ⋯⟩

y

house is ∼? votre/ta maison c'est laquelle?;
he's a colleague of ∼ c'est un de vos/tes
collègues; it's not ∼ ce n'est pas à vous/à
toi; the money wasn't ∼ to give away vous
n'aviez pas à donner cet argent

✐ **yourself** *pron*

■ **Note** For a full note on the use of the *vous*
and *tu* forms in French, see the entry YOU.
— When used as a reflexive pronoun, direct
and indirect, *yourself* is translated by *vous* or
familiarly *te* (or *t'* before a vowel or mute 'h'):
you've hurt yourself = vous vous êtes fait mal/
tu t'es fait mal.
— In imperatives, the translation is *vous* or *toi*:
help yourself = servez-vous/sers-toi. (Note the
hyphens).
— When used for emphasis, the translation is
vous-même/toi-même: *you yourself don't know*
= vous ne savez pas vous-même/tu ne sais pas
toi-même.

(a) (reflexive) vous, te, t'; have you hurt ∼?
est-ce que tu t'es fait mal?
(b) (in imperatives) vous, toi
(c) (emphatic) vous-même, toi-même; you ∼
said that... vous avez dit vous-même que.../
tu as dit toi-même que...
(d) (after prepositions) vous, vous-même, toi,
toi-même
(e) (expressions) (all) by ∼ tout seul/toute
seule; you're not ∼ today tu n'as pas l'air
dans ton assiette aujourd'hui

yourselves *pron*

■ **Note** — When used as a reflexive pronoun,
direct and indirect, *yourselves* is translated by
vous: *help yourselves* ∼ = servez-vous.

— When used for emphasis, the translation is
vous-mêmes: *do it yourselves* = faites-le vous-
mêmes.

(a) (reflexive) vous; help ∼ servez-vous
(b) (emphatic) vous-mêmes
(c) (after prepositions) vous, vous-mêmes; all by
∼ tous seuls/toutes seules

✐ **youth** *n* (*pl* ∼s) **(a)** (young man) jeune
homme *m*; a gang of ∼s une bande de
jeunes gens
(b) (period, state of being young) jeunesse *f*;
because of his ∼ à cause de son jeune âge
(c) (young people) jeunes *mpl*

youth club *n* centre *m* de jeunes
youthful *adj* **(a)** (young) jeune
(b) (typical of youth) his ∼ looks son air jeune
youth hostel *n* auberge *f* de jeunesse
youth hostelling *n* logement *m* en
auberge de jeunesse
youth work *n* travail *m* social auprès des
jeunes
youth worker *n* éducateur/-trice *m/f*
yowl *vi* ‹person, dog› hurler; ‹cat› miauler;
‹baby› brailler
yoyo *n* yo-yo *m*
yuck *excl* (GB) berk (fam) !
yucky *adj* (GB) dégoûtant/-e
Yugoslavia *pr n* Yougoslavie *f*
Yule log *n* bûche *f* de Noël
yummy (colloq) **1** *adj* délicieux/-ieuse
2 *excl* miam-miam (fam)
yuppie **1** *n* jeune cadre *m* dynamique
2 *adj* ‹image, style, fashion› de jeune cadre
dynamique

Zz

z, Z *n* z, Z *m*
zany *adj* loufoque (fam)
zap (colloq) **1** *excl* paf !
2 *vtr* (*p prés etc* **-pp-**) **(a)** (destroy) détruire
‹town›; tuer ‹person, animal›
(b) (fire at) tirer sur ‹person›
(c) (delete from computer screen) supprimer
3 *vi* (*p prés etc* **-pp-**) to ∼ into town/a shop
faire un saut (fam) en ville/dans un magasin;
to ∼ from channel to channel zapper (fam)
zapper *n* (colloq) (TV remote control)
télécommande *f*
zeal *n* **(a)** (fanaticism) zèle *m*; (religious) ferveur
f
(b) (enthusiasm) ardeur *f*, zèle *m*
zealot *n* fanatique *mf*

zebra *n* zèbre *m*
zebra crossing *n* (GB) passage *m*
(protégé) pour piétons
zenith *n* (figurative) apogée *m*
zero **1** *n* zéro *m*
2 *adj* ‹altitude, growth, inflation, voltage›
zéro *inv*; ‹confidence, interest, involvement,
development› nul/nulle; sub-∼ temperatures
des températures en dessous de zéro
■ **zero in**: to ∼ in on [sth] (Mil) viser ‹target›;
(figurative) cerner ‹problem›; foncer droit sur
‹person›; repérer ‹place›
zero hour *n* heure *f* H
zest *n* (enthusiasm) entrain *m*; his ∼ for life
sa joie de vivre
zigzag **1** *n* zigzag *m*
2 *adj* ‹design, pattern› à zigzags; ‹route,
road› en zigzag

✐ indicates a very frequent word

y

z

3 vi (p prés etc **-gg-**) ⟨person, vehicle, road⟩ zigzaguer; ⟨river, path⟩ serpenter; **to ~ up/ down** monter/descendre en zigzag

zilch n (colloq) que dalle (pop)

zimmer® n déambulateur m

zing n (colloq) (energy) entrain m

zip 1 n **(a)** (also ~ **fastener**, **zipper** (US)) fermeture f à glissière, fermeture f éclair®; **to do up/undo a ~** tirer/défaire une fermeture à glissière
(b) (colloq) (energy) tonus m
(c) (also ~ **code**) (US) code m postal
2 vtr (p prés etc **-pp-**) **(a)** (close) **to ~ sth shut** fermer qch en tirant la fermeture à glissière
(b) (Comput) zipper, comprimer
3 vi (p prés etc **-pp-**) **to ~ along**, **to ~ past** filer à toute allure; **to ~ past sb/sth** dépasser qn/qch à toute allure
■ **zip through** (colloq): **to ~ through a book** lire un livre en diagonale (fam)
■ **zip up:** **1** ¶ ~ **up** ⟨garment, bag⟩ se fermer par une fermeture à glissière
2 ¶ ~ **[sth] up** remonter la fermeture à glissière de

zipper (US) = ZIP 1A

zip pocket n poche f à fermeture à glissière

zodiac n zodiaque m

zombie n zombi(e) m; (figurative) abruti/-e m/f (fam)

✓ **zone 1** n zone f
2 vtr (divide) diviser [qch] en zones

zonked (also **zonked out**) adj (colloq) (tired) crevé/-e (fam)

zoo n zoo m

zoo keeper n gardien/-ienne m/f de zoo

zoologist n zoologue mf, zoologiste mf

zoology n zoologie f

zoom 1 n (also ~ **lens**) zoom m
2 vi **(a)** (colloq) (move quickly) **to ~ past** passer en trombe; **to ~ around [sth]** passer à toute vitesse dans; **he's ~ed off to Paris** il a foncé (fam) à Paris
(b) (colloq) (rocket) ⟨prices, profits⟩ monter en flèche

zucchini n (pl ~ ou ~**s**) (US) courgette f

Z

Glossary of grammatical terms

Abbreviation A shortened form of a word or phrase made by leaving out some letters or by using only the initial letter of each word: etc., DNA

Active In the active form the subject of the verb performs the action: **she whistled** = **elle a sifflé**

Adjective A word describing a noun: a *red* pencil = un crayon *rouge*

Adverb A word that describes or changes the meaning of a verb, an adjective, or another adverb: **he drives** *fast* = **il conduit** *vite*; *fairly* often = *assez* souvent

Article The definite article, **the** = le, la, l', les, and indefinite article, **a/an** = un, une, are used in front of a noun

Attributive An adjective or noun is attributive when it is used directly before or directly after a noun: **the** *big* **dog** = **le** *grand* **chien**; *birthday* **card** = **carte d'anniversaire**

Auxiliary verb One of the verbs used to form the perfect, pluperfect, and future perfect tenses. In French the auxiliary verbs are avoir and être: **I have read the letter** = **j'***ai* **lu la lettre**; **he had already gone** = **il** *était* **déjà parti**

Cardinal number A whole number representing a quantity: **one, two, three** = **un/une, deux, trois**

Clause A self-contained section of a sentence that contains a subject and a verb

Collective noun A noun that is singular in form but refers to a group of persons or things, e.g. **royalty, grain**

Collocate A word that regularly occurs with another; for example **book** is a typical collocate of the verb **to read**

Comparative The form of an adjective or adverb for comparing two or more nouns or pronouns, often using **more, less** or **as** (plus, moins, aussi): **smaller = plus petit; more frequently = plus fréquement; as intelligent = aussi intelligent**

Compound adjective An adjective formed from two separate words : **tout-puissant = all-powerful; nord-américain = North American**

Compound noun A noun formed from two or more separate words: **porte-clés = keyring**

Conditional tense A tense of a verb that expresses what might happen if something else occurred: **I would invite them** = **je les inviterais**

Conjugation Variation of the form of a verb to show tense, person, etc.

Conjunction A word used to link clauses: **and = et, because = parce que**

Consonant All the letters other than a, e, i, o, u or y (y can be a vowel in French)

Definite article: the = le, la, l', les

Demonstrative adjective An adjective indicating the person or thing referred to: *this* car = *cette* voiture; *this* pen = *ce* stylo

Demonstrative pronoun A pronoun indicating the person or thing referred to: *this one* is cheaper = *celui-ci* est moins cher

Determiner A word used before a noun to make clear what is being referred to: **the** – **le, la, l', les; some** – **du/de l'/de la/des; my** = **mon/ma/mes**

Direct object the noun or pronoun directly affected by the verb: **she ate** *the apple* = **elle a mangé** *la pomme*

Direct speech A speaker's actual words or the use of these in writing

Elliptical Having a word or words omitted, especially where the sense can be guessed from the context

Ending Letters added to the stem of verbs, as well as to nouns and adjectives, according to tense, number, gender

Exclamation A sound, word, or remark expressing a strong feeling such as anger, fear, or joy: **ouch! = aïe!**

Feminine One of the two genders in French: **la femme = the woman; la carte = the card**

Future tense The tense of a verb that refers to something that will happen in the future: **I will go = j'irai**

Gender One of the two groups of nouns in French: masculine and feminine

Imperative A form of a verb that expresses a command: **hurry up! = dépêche-toi!**

Imperfect tense The tense of a verb that refers to an uncompleted or a habitual action in the past: **I went there every day = j'y allais tous les jours**

Impersonal verb A verb used in English only with 'it' and in French only with 'il': **it is raining = il pleut**

Indefinite article: a/an = **un, une**

Indefinite pronoun A pronoun that does not identify a specific person or object: **one = on; something = quelque chose**

Indicative form The form of a verb used when making a statement of fact or asking questions of fact in various tenses: **we like animals = nous aimons les animaux**

Indirect object The noun or pronoun indirectly affected by the verb, at which the direct object is aimed: **she gave *him* the key = elle *lui* a donné la clé**

Indirect speech A report of what someone has said which does not reproduce the exact words

Infinitive The basic form of a verb: **to play = jouer**

Inflect To change the ending or form of a word to show its tense or its grammatical relation to other words: **donne** and **donnez** are inflected forms of the verb **donner**

Interrogative pronoun A pronoun that asks a question: **who? = qui?**

Intransitive verb A verb that does not have a direct object: **he died yesterday = il est mort hier**

Invariable adjective An adjective that has the same form in the plural as the singular, as French **ivoire, transmanche**

Invariable noun A noun that has the same form in the plural as the singular, as English **sheep, species**, French **aide-mémoire, rabais**

Irregular verb A verb that does not follow one of the set patterns and has its own individual forms, e.g. English **to be**, French **être**

Masculine One of the two genders in French: **le garçon = the boy; le livre = the book**

Modal verb A verb that is used with another verb to express permission, obligation, possibility, such as **might, should**. The French modal verbs are **devoir, pouvoir, savoir, vouloir, falloir**

Negative Expressing refusal or denial: **there aren't any = il n'y en a pas; he won't go = il ne veut pas partir**

Noun A word that names a person, thing, or concept such as **Peter, a child, a book, peace**

Number The state of being either singular or plural

Object The word or group of words which is immediately affected by the action indicated by the verb, as **livre** in **il a lu le livre**, or **voiture** in **elle lave la voiture**

Ordinal number A number that shows the position of a person or thing in a series: **the *third* time = la *troisième* fois, the *fourth* door on the left = la *quatrième* porte à gauche**

Part of speech A grammatical term for the function of a word; noun, verb, adjective, etc., are parts of speech

Passive In the passive form the subject of the verb experiences the action rather than performs it: **he was punished = il a été puni**

Past participle The part of a verb used to form past tenses: **she had *gone* = elle était *partie***

Perfect tense The tense of a verb that refers to an action that has taken place in a period of time that includes the present: **I have already eaten = j'ai déjà mangé; my bike has been stolen = on m'a volé mon vélo**

Person Any of the three groups of personal pronouns and forms taken by verbs. In the singular the **first person** (e.g. **I/je**) refers to the person speaking; **the second person** (e.g. **you/tu**) refers to the person spoken to; the **third person** (e.g. **he, she, it/il, elle**) refers to the person spoken about. The corresponding plural forms are **we/nous, you/vous, they/ils, elles**

Personal pronoun A pronoun that refers to a person or thing

Phrasal verb A verb in English combined with a preposition or an adverb to have a particular meaning: **run away = se sauver**. There are no phrasal verbs in French

Phrase A self-contained section of a sentence that does not contain a full verb

Pluperfect tense The tense of a verb that refers to something that happened before a particular point in the past: **when I arrived, he *had* already *left* = quand je suis arrivé, il *était* déjà *parti***

Plural Of nouns, etc., referring to more than one: **the children = les enfants**

Possessive adjective An adjective that shows possession, belonging to someone or something: **my = mon/ma/mes**

Possessive pronoun a pronoun that shows possession, belonging to someone or something: **mine = le mien/la mienne/les miens/les miennes**

Postpositive Placed after the word to which it relates, as **in stock** in the phrase **items in stock**

Predicative An adjective is predicative when it comes after a verb such as **be** or **become** in English, or after **être** or **devenir** in French: **she is beautiful = elle est belle**

Prefix A group of letters added to the beginning of a word to change its meaning, e.g. **anti-, ultra-, non-**

Preposition A word that stands in front of a noun or pronoun, usually indicating movement, position or time: *on* **the chair =** *sur* **la chaise;** *towards* **the car =** *vers* **la voiture**

Present participle The part of a verb in English that ends in –ing; the corresponding ending in French is -ant

Present tense The tense of a verb that refers to something happening now: **I make = je fais**

Pronoun A word that stands instead of a noun: **he = il, she = elle, mine = le mien/ la mienne/les miens/les miennes**

Proper noun A name of a person, place, institution etc. written with a capital letter at the start; **France, the Alps, Madeleine, l'Europe** are all proper nouns

Reflexive pronoun A pronoun that goes with a reflexive verb: in French **me, te, se, nous, vous, se**

Reflexive verb A verb whose object is the same as its subject. In French it is used with a reflexive pronoun and conjugated with **être**: **he washed himself = il s'est lavé**

Regular verb A verb that follows a set pattern in its different forms

Relative pronoun A pronoun that introduces a subordinate clause, relating to a person or thing mentioned in the main clause: **the book** *which* **I chose = le livre** *que* **j'ai choisi**

Reported speech Another name for **Indirect speech**

Sentence A sequence of words, with a subject and a verb, that can stand on their own to make a statement, ask a question, or give a command

Singular Of nouns, etc., referring to just one: **the tree = l'arbre**

Stem The part of a verb to which endings are added; **donn-** is the stem of **donner**

Subject In a clause or sentence, the noun or pronoun that causes the action of the verb: *he* **caught the ball =** *il* **a attrapé le ballon**

Subjunctive A verb form that is used to express doubt or uncertainty in English. It is more widely used in French, particularly after certain conjunctions and with verbs of wishing, fearing, ordering, forbidding followed by **que: I want you to be good = je veux que tu sois sage; you may be right = il est possible que tu aies raison**

Subordinate clause A clause which adds information to the main clause of a sentence, but cannot function as a sentence by itself, e.g. **when it rang** in **she answered the phone when it rang**

Suffix A group of letters joined to the end of a word to form another word, as –**able** in **workable**, or in French as –**eur** in **grandeur** or –**able** in **véritable**

Superlative The form of an adjective or adverb that makes it the 'most' or 'least': the *biggest* **house =** *la plus grande* **maison; the** *cheapest* **CD = le CD** *le moins cher*

Tense The form of a verb that tells when the action takes place: present, future, imperfect, perfect, pluperfect are all tenses

Transitive verb A verb that is used with a direct object: **I wrote the letter = j'ai écrit la lettre**

Verb A word or group of words that describes an action: **the children are playing = les enfants jouent**

Vowel One of the following letters: **a, e, i, o, u** or **y** in French

Summary of French grammar

Grammar provides a description of the rules by which a language functions. Many of these rules are complex and there are many exceptions to them. The following pages offer a summary of some of the most important features of French grammar.

1 Nouns and Gender

All French nouns are either masculine or feminine. The gender of nouns is shown by the definite and indefinite articles. Most nouns relating to male people are masculine and most relating to female people are feminine. Inanimate objects can be either gender and other nouns may be a particular gender for no clear reason, *une personne* = a person. A few have different genders according to their sense: *le mode* = method; *la mode* = fashion.

1.1 The definite article (= *the*)

	Singular	Plural
Masculine	*le*	*les*
Feminine	*la*	*les*

- *le* and *la* are reduced to *l'* before:
  a singular noun starting with a vowel: *école* → *l'école*
  a singular noun starting with a silent *h*: *hôtel* → *l'hôtel*
- *les* is the plural in all cases: *les écoles, les hôtels*
- The preposition *à* + *le* become *au*: *au café* = at the café. Similarly *à* + *les* become *aux*

Note: Unlike in English, articles are rarely omitted, *les enfants aiment les bonbons* = children like sweets

1.2 The indefinite article (= *a* or *an*; plural = *some*)

	Singular	Plural
Masculine	*un*	*des*
Feminine	*une*	*des*

- *un* and *une* also indicate the number 1 in counting: *un couteau* = one knife; *une pomme* = one apple
- *des* is the plural form for both masculine and feminine nouns: *des couteaux, des pommes*

But when specifying someone's occupation or profession, the article is dropped:

il est boucher = he is a butcher   *ma sœur est avocat* = my sister is a lawyer

The article *le* is used to specify the day of the month:

aujourd'hui, c'est le six septembre = today is the 6th of September
c'est le mardi deux juillet = it's Tuesday 2 July

2 Nouns and Number

Nouns can be *singular* or *plural*, and this is referred to as *number*. This is an important consideration when choosing verb forms or adjectival agreements. Most nouns add an ending to form the plural.

2.1 Typical nouns:

Most nouns add -*s* in the plural:

chaise → *chaises* (= chairs)   *chien* → *chiens* (= dogs)
voiture → *voitures* (= cars)   *chat* → *chats* (= cats)

2.2 Nouns ending in -*au*, -*eu* or -*eau* usually add -*x* in the plural:

tuyau → *tuyaux* (= pipes)   *jeu* → *jeux* (= games)
neveu → *neveux* (= nephews)   *bureau* → *bureaux* (= desks)

2.3 Nouns ending in -*ail* usually add -*s*:

détail → *détails* (= details)

But there are exceptions:

travail → *travaux* (= works)

2.4 Nouns ending in -*al* usually change from -*al* to -*aux*:

rival → *rivaux* (= rivals)   *cheval* → *chevaux* (= horses)

But there are exceptions:

bal → *bals* (= dances)

2.5 Nouns ending in -*ou*:

These nouns usually add -*s* in the plural. But there are six common exceptions which add -*x*:

bijou → *bijoux* (= jewels)   *genou* → *genoux* (= knees)
caillou → *cailloux* (= pebbles)   *hibou* → *hiboux* (= owls)
chou → *choux* (= cabbages)   *joujou* → *joujoux* (= toys)

2.6 Some nouns have unusual plurals and these have to be learnt individually:

ciel → *cieux* (= skies)   *œil* → *yeux* (= eyes)

• •

Note the plurals in the group: *monsieur* → *messieurs*; *madame* → *mesdames*; *mademoiselle* → *mesdemoiselles*: mon-, ma- in these words meant 'my' originally (as in 'my lord', 'my lady').

Surnames are not used in the plural in phrases such as: *les Dupont* = the Duponts; names of dynasties do however take *-s* in the plural: *les Bourbons* = the Bourbons.

2.7 Hyphenated nouns

The plurals of this group of nouns vary and depend on how the word is formed, ADJECTIVE + NOUN, VERB + NOUN, etc. In cases where there is an ADJECTIVE + NOUN, it is normal for both words in the compound to change:

> *beau-père* → *beaux-pères* (= fathers-in-law)
> *chou-fleur* → *choux-fleurs* (= cauliflowers)

If an element of a compound is neither a noun nor an adjective, it does not change in the plural.

> *le tire-bouchon* = corkscrew → *les tire-bouchons* (*tire* is part of the verb *tirer*)
> *un passe-partout* = skeleton key → *des passe-partout* (no noun: *passe* is a verb, *partout* is an adverb)

If in doubt it can be helpful to translate the compound word for word and find which element would logically become plural in English:

> *arc-en-ciel* (= rainbow) → *arcs-en-ciel* (= rainbows)
> (literally 'arc in the sky' → 'arcs in the sky')

2.8 Nouns which do not change in the plural

Nouns already ending in *-s*: *bois* → *bois* (= woods)
Nouns already ending in *-x*: *voix* → *voix* (= voices)
Nouns ending in *-z*: *nez* → *nez* (= noses)

• •

3 *De* and expressions of quantity

De is used in many expressions of quantity. In many cases, it is translated in English by *some* or *any*.

Note how *de* is used with articles before nouns and how it may change:

> de + le → du   *le pain* → *du pain* = some bread
> de + la → de la   *la crème* → *de la crème* = some cream
> de + l' → de l'   *l'huile* → *de l'huile* = some oil
> de + les → des   *les oranges* → *des oranges* = some oranges

Note that after a negative the article is dropped and *de* alone is used:

> *j'ai du pain* = I have some bread
> *je n'ai pas de pain* = I don't have any bread
> *avez-vous de la crème* = do you have (some) cream?
> *nous n'avons pas de crème* = we do not have any cream

••

If *de* comes before a vowel or a silent *h*, it is written *d'*:

> *achetez des oranges/de l'huile* = buy some oranges/oil
> *n'achetez pas d'oranges/d'huile* = don't buy any oranges/oil

There is more on Negatives in section 11.

If *de* comes before an adjective which qualifies a noun, it often remains *de* or *d'* rather than *des*:

> *de jolies fleurs* = some pretty flowers
> *d'énormes problèmes* = enormous problems
> *d'autres amis* = other friends

Expressions of quantity. The following always use *de* or *d'* before a vowel or silent 'h'.

> *un verre de vin* = a glass of wine
> *un kilo de haricots verts* = a kilo of French beans
> *deux kilos de pommes* = two kilos of apples
> *beaucoup de farine* = a lot of flour
> *beaucoup de cerises* = a lot of cherries
> *peu de mots* = few words
> *peu d'habitants* = not many inhabitants

But note the following:

> *encore du pain, s'il vous plaît* = some more bread, please

•••

4 Pronouns

4.1 Subject pronouns

Pronouns such as *I*, *we*, *they*, etc replace nouns as the subjects of sentences, and can refer to people or things. Subject pronouns determine the choice of endings for verbs, *je chante* = I sing, *tu chantes* = you sing, *nous chantons* = we sing, *vous chantez* = you (plural) sing.

Singular	Plural
je = I	*nous* = we
tu = you	*vous* = you
il = he/it	*ils* = they [masculine or masculine + feminine]
elle = she/it	*elles* = they [feminine]
on = one*	

- *tu* is used to speak to a child or someone who is well known
- *vous* is used in polite speech or to more than one person
- *ils* means 'they' referring to a male group, or a mixed male and female group

*on is used as a less specific subject pronoun to mean 'one', 'you', 'we', 'people', 'they'. It always takes the endings of the third person singular, see the verb tables.

> *on mange ici?* = shall we eat here?   *on n'aime pas refuser* = one doesn't like to refuse

4.2 Object pronouns

4.2.a Direct object pronouns

Direct object pronouns in French, the equivalent of *it*, *her*, *him*, *us*, etc are used to replace noun objects. They can refer to people or things and can only be used with transitive verbs, marked *vtr* in this dictionary. Transitive verbs are those which affect or act on someone or something.

frapper *vtr* to hit: hit the ball; go on, hit it! = frappe la balle; allez, frappe-la!

French	English	French	English
me/m'	me	*nous*	us
te/t'	you [*singular*]	*vous*	you [*plural*]
le/l'	him /it	*les*	them
la/l'	her/it	*se/s'*	themselves
se/s'	himself/herself/itself		

- *m'/t'/l'/s'* are used if the word that follows begins with a vowel or a silent h:

  ils l'aiment = they love her
  elle l'héberge gratuitement = she puts him up for free

- Object pronouns can affect the endings of past participles in compound tenses if the object is feminine or plural:

  elle a poli la table → *elle l'a polie* (+e for feminine singular = she polished it)
  elle a poli les tables → *elle les a polies* (+es for feminine plural = she polished them)

4.2.b Indirect object pronouns

Indirect object pronouns in French, the equivalent of *to it*, *to her*, *to him*, *to us*, etc are used to replace indirect noun objects. They can refer to people or things and are indirectly affected by the action of the verb.

  donnez-lui la balle! = give the ball to him/to her
  il m'a montré la photo = he showed me the photo
  donne-le-leur! = give them that!/give that to them!

French	English	French	English
me/m'	(to) me	*nous*	(to) us
te/t'	(to) you [*singular*]	*vous*	(to) you [*plural*]
lui	(to) him or it	*leur*	(to) them
lui	(to) her or it		

4.2.c Indirect object pronouns *y* and *en*

y is used in sentences with verbs which govern a preposition, e.g. *s'intéresser à, s'opposer à, penser à*

  il ne s'y intéresse pas = he's not interested in it
  je m'y oppose = I'm against it
  j'y pense = I'm thinking about it

The indirect object pronoun referring to a quantity is: *en* = of it, of them, some

  j'en voudrais trois = I'd like three (of them)
  offrez-leur-en = offer them some

· ·

It is also used in sentences such as:

nous en parlerons ce soir = we'll talk about it this evening

4.3 Order of object pronouns in the sentence

Object pronouns come before most verb parts:

elle leur rend les livres = she is returning the books to them

Object pronouns come before an infinitive:

elle va leur rendre les livres = she is going to return the books to them

Object pronouns come before the first part of the compound tenses conjugated with *avoir* and *être*: see Verbs section 10.1.f

elle leur a rendu les livres = she returned the books to them
il y est allé = he went there

Object pronouns follow the imperative form of the verb and are linked to it by a hyphen:

rends-leur les livres! = give the books back to them!

Object pronouns return to normal order, object pronoun before verb, in imperative sentences if they are in the negative:

ne les rendez pas! = don't give them back!

Order of Object Pronouns (see 4.2 for meanings):

When more than one object pronouns occur in the same sentence, they keep a fixed sequence as follows:

me	*le*	*lui*	*y*	*en*
te	*la*	*leur*		
se	*les*			
nous				
vous				
se				

- any combination of object pronouns will follow the above order:

  nous le lui avons envoyé = we sent it to her/him
  ils le leur ont expliqué = they explained it to them
  elle leur en donne = she gives them some
  nous nous y opposons = we're against it

- *me*, *te*, *nous*, *vous* can be both direct and indirect objects. They are also used with reflexive verbs [see Verbs section 10.1]

- *se* means: (to) himself, (to) herself, (to) oneself, (to) themselves, and is used with reflexive verbs

4.4 Emphatic or disjunctive pronouns

moi	= me	*nous*	= us
toi	= you	*vous*	= you [plural or formal usage]
lui	= him	*eux*	= them
elle	= her	*elles*	= them [all female]

The emphatic pronouns are used in the following situations:

- after prepositions:

  avec moi = with me   *sans elle* = without her
  je pense à elle = I'm thinking of her

- after *que* or *qu'* in comparative sentences [see Comparison section 8.1]:

  plus petit que lui = smaller than him   *plus grand que toi* = bigger than you

- to emphasize the subject:

  lui, il n'aime pas le vin rouge mais elle, elle adore ça =
  he doesn't like red wine but she loves it

- with *c'est, ce sont*

  c'est moi! = it's me!   *ce sont eux* = it's them

- with *même* meaning 'self' (myself, yourself, etc.):

  toi-même = yourself   *vous-mêmes* = yourselves

Note: *-s* is added to *même* in the plural

Note: *moi* and *toi* are used in imperatives when pronouns follow the verb:

  donnez-le-moi! = give it to me!   *mets-toi là!* = sit yourself there!

5 Adjectives

Adjectives are listed alphabetically according to the masculine form in this dictionary. In those cases where the feminine form is the same as the masculine, no further information is given. When the feminine is formed by adding an ending to the masculine, this is shown by the symbol ∼ followed immediately by the ending: **lent, ∼e** *adj* slow. If the change involves a spelling change to the masculine form, this is clearly shown: **langoureux, -euse** *adj*. Many determiners *ce, mon, tout* etc (= *this, my, all* etc) are adjectival and therefore must also agree with the nouns they qualify

5.1 Common adjectival endings:

Adjectives which add *-e* to form the feminine:

  une jupe courte = a short skirt

Adjectives which add *-s* to form the masculine plural:

  des voyages intéressants = interesting journeys

All adjectives follow this pattern in the plural unless the ending is *-x*, *curieux* → masculine plural *curieux*, or there is already a final *-s*, *bas* → masculine plural *bas*

Adjectives which add *-s* to the feminine to form the feminine plural

  des histoires amusantes = funny stories

. . . .

5.2 Adjectives ending in -e

These are unchanged in the feminine: *aimable* → feminine *aimable*

-*s* is added in the normal way to form the plural for both masculine and feminine adjectives of this type: *aimable* → plural *aimables*

Note: If the adjective ends in -*é*, then the feminine form adds -*e*:

   aimé → feminine *aimée*   plural: *aimés* → feminine *aimées*

5.3 Table of adjective endings and their typical feminine variants:

The following double the last letter and add an -*e*

Typical ending	Adjective	Feminine	English
-as	*bas*	*basse*	low
-eil	*pareil*	*pareille*	similar
-el	*mortel*	*mortelle*	fatal
-en	*ancien*	*ancienne*	ancient
-et*	*muet*	*muette*	mute
-on	*bon*	*bonne*	good
-ul	*nul*	*nulle*	no good

*Note that some adjectives ending in -*et* follow a different pattern:
inquiet → *inquiète* = anxious

The following add a final -*e* and add an accent or change a consonant or consonant group

Typical ending	Adjective	Feminine	English
-er	*premier*	*première*	first
-ef	*bref*	*brève*	brief
-if	*actif*	*active*	active
-eux	*fameux*	*fameuse*	infamous
-eur	*menteur*	*menteuse*	untruthful
-nc	*blanc*	*blanche*	white
-ic	*public*	*publique*	public
-gu	*aigu*	*aiguë*	acute

The following are examples of irregular adjectives which show additional variations

doux → *douce* (= sweet)   *faux* → *fausse* (= false)
favori → *favorite* (= favourite)   *frais* → *fraîche* (= fresh)
gentil → *gentille* (= kind)   *jaloux* → *jalouse* (= jealous)
malin → *maligne* (= cunning)   *roux* → *rousse* (= red)
sot → *sotte* (= silly)

Summary of French grammar

5.4 Position of adjectives

In French most adjectives follow the noun:

un chocolat chaud (= a hot chocolate)
un homme grand (= a tall man)
un stylo noir (= a black pen)

Some adjectives go before the noun. These are usually common adjectives:
bon = good, *gros* = big, *joli* = pretty, *nouveau* = new, *grand* = big, *petit* = small

These may almost become part of the noun as a compound:

un jeune homme (= a young man)

They become part of a compound when they're joined to the noun by a hyphen:

les petits-enfants (= the grandchildren)

Some adjectives radically change their meaning depending on whether they precede or follow the noun, compare:

la pauvre fille (= the poor girl)   *la fille pauvre* (= the girl with little money)
la mauvaise clé (= the wrong key)   *un animal mauvais* (= a vicious animal)
un grand homme = a great man   *un homme grand* = a tall man

5.5 Adjectives which always precede the noun

The following classes of adjective always come before the nouns they qualify:

Numbers, cardinal and ordinal:

les trois filles = the three girls   *la troisième fois* = the third time

Possessive and demonstrative adjectives:

mon parapluie = my umbrella   *cette église* = this church

Indefinite adjectives such as:

chaque = each, *tel* = such, *autre* = other
chaque enfant = each child   *une telle personne* = such a person

beau, nouveau, vieux

These adjectives form a group because they have a variant spelling:

Masculine	Masculine with vowel*	Plural	Feminine	Plural	English
beau	bel	beaux	belle	belles	beautiful
nouveau	nouvel	nouveaux	nouvelle	nouvelles	new
vieux	vieil	vieux	vieille	vieilles	old

une belle femme (= a beautiful woman)
de nouveaux livres (= new books)
de vieilles histoires (= old stories)

*The variant spelling is used if the noun following is masculine and begins with a vowel or a silent *h*:

arbre → *un bel arbre* (= a lovely tree)

. . . .

6 Possession

6.1 Expressing possession

Possession is commonly expressed by *de*, meaning of.

le chien de Paul (= literally: the dog of Paul) = Paul's dog
les vêtements de Sophie (= literally: the clothes of Sophie) = Sophie's clothes

6.2 Possessive adjectives

The possessive adjectives are the equivalents of *my, your, his, her* etc.

POSSESSIVE ADJECTIVES

Masculine	Feminine	Plural	English
mon	ma	mes	my
ton	ta	tes	your
son	sa	ses	his/her/its/one's
notre	notre	nos	our
votre	votre	vos	your
leur	leur	leurs	their

- The possessive adjective matches the gender and number of what is possessed NOT the possessor:

  ma sœur = my sister (the speaker may be male)   *sa femme* = his wife

- the feminine forms *ma, ta,* and *sa* end in vowels and are not used before a vowel. Instead the masculine form is used:

  son élève = his or her student   *son obligation* = her or his obligation

6.3 Possessive Pronouns

These are the equivalents of English *mine, yours, ours* etc. In French they reflect the gender and number of what is possessed:

POSSESSIVE PRONOUNS

Masculine	Feminine	Masculine Plural	Feminine Plural	English
le mien	la mienne	les miens	les miennes	mine
le tien	la tienne	les tiens	les tiennes	yours
le sien	la sienne	les siens	les siennes	his/hers/its
le nôtre	la nôtre	les nôtres	les nôtres	ours
le vôtre	la vôtre	les vôtres	les vôtres	yours
le leur	la leur	les leurs	les leurs	theirs

ce n'est pas sa veste, c'est la mienne = it's not his jacket, it's mine (the speaker may be male)
ce ne sont pas ses chaussures, ce sont les miennes = these are not his shoes, they're mine

. . . .

7 Adverbs

Adverbs usually give additional information about a verb: i.e. they say 'how' (= in what way or manner), 'when', or 'where' something happens

• •

Most French adverbs are formed from the feminine adjective by adding
-ment

heureux → heureuse → heureusement (= happily, fortunately)
égal → égale → également (= equally)

Exceptions include:

7.1 masculine adjectives ending in a vowel

The adverb is formed from the masculine adjective rather than the
feminine:

hardi → hardiment (= robustly)   *résolu → résolument* (= resolutely)

7.2 adjectives ending in *-ant* or *-ent*

The *-nt* is dropped and the *-m-* is doubled:

constant → constamment (= constantly)   *intelligent → intelligemment* (= intelligently)

Note however *lent → lentement* (= slowly). Some adverbs are irregular in
their formation:

bon = good → *bien* = well   *bref* = brief → *brièvement* = briefly
gentil = kind → *gentiment* = kindly   *mauvais* = bad → *mal* = badly

• •

8 Comparison

8.1 Comparative of adjectives and adverbs

The comparative of adjectives and adverbs in English is usually expressed
by:

'more…'   *more interesting* – adjective; *more interestingly* – adverb
'as…'   *as easy* – adjective; *as easily* – adverb
'less…'   *less intelligent* – adjective; *less intelligently* – adverb

The comparative of adjectives and adverbs in French is expressed in most
cases by:

'plus…   *plus intéressant* – adjective; *plus facilement* – adverb
aussi…'   *aussi grand* – adjective (= as big); *aussi facilement* – adverb (= as easily)
'moins…'   *moins intelligent* – adjective (= *less intelligent*); *moins facilement* – adverb
             (= less easily)

Comparative adjectives and adverbs are followed by *que* (or *qu'* before a
vowel or silent *h*) to translate 'than' or 'as' in English.

plus intéressant que = more interesting than
aussi facilement que = as easily as
moins intelligent que = less intelligent than

The comparative adjective reflects the gender and number of the noun
described:

il est plus grand que toi = he is taller than you
cette rue est moins longue que celle-là = this road is shorter than that one

• •

SOME IRREGULAR:

ADJECTIVE COMPARATIVES			ADVERB COMPARATIVES		
Adjective	**Comparative**	**English**	**Adverb**	**Comparative**	**English**
bon = good	*meilleur*	better	*beaucoup* = much	plus	more
mauvais = bad	*pire*	worse	*bien* = well	*mieux*	better
			mal = badly	*pis*	worse
			peu = little	*moins*	less

8.2 Superlative of adjectives and adverbs

The superlative of adjectives and adverbs in English is expressed by 'most...'

most interesting – adjective, *most interestingly* – adverb

The superlative adjective in French is expressed in most cases by:

'le/la/les plus + *adjective*'   le plus intéressant

The article is repeated reflecting the gender and number of the noun described:

la ville la plus belle = the most beautiful city

Note how *de* (or *du*) following the superlative in French is translated by *in* or *of* in English in sentences like:

la ville la plus belle du monde = the most beautiful city IN the world
le meilleur épisode de la série = the best episode OF the series

The superlative of adverbs in French closely resembles the adjective, but the article is always *le* (never: *la* or *les*): *le plus facilement* = the most easily

• •

9 Time

Time phrases in French begin with *il est...* (= it is...) and the French equivalent of 'o'clock' is *heures*, except for 'one o'clock' *une heure*. The 24 hour clock is often used to distinguish between a.m. and p.m.

The number of hours is stated first and any minutes 'past' the hour are simply added to the end of the phrase:

il est sept heures dix = it's ten minutes past seven

'quarter past' is expressed by *et quart*:

il est sept heures et quart = it's quarter past seven or seven fifteen.

minutes 'to' the hour follow the word *moins* (= minus):

il est quatre heures moins cinq = it's five to four

'quarter to' is expressed by *moins le quart*:

il est quatre heures moins le quart = it's quarter to four

'half past' is expressed by *et demie*:

il est trois heures et demie = it's half past three

Note: *midi* (= midday) and *minuit* (= midnight) are masculine; therefore *et demie* changes to *et demi* with these two words:

> *il est midi/minuit et demi* = it's half past twelve (midday)/midnight

Examples:

> 1.00 = il est une heure
> 2.00 = il est deux heures
> 2.10 = il est deux heures dix
> 2.15 = il est deux heures et quart *or* il est deux heures quinze
> 2.30 = il est deux heures et demie *or* il est deux heures trente
> 2.35 = il est trois heures moins vingt-cinq *or* il est deux heures trente-cinq

10 Verbs

The infinitive is the basic form of the verb and the one you look up in the dictionary. Verbs are described as being *transitive* or *intransitive*. Transitive verbs, marked *vtr* in the dictionary, take an object. In *he kicks the ball*, 'kick' is the verb and 'the ball' is the object. Intransitive verbs, marked *vi*, function without objects; verbs like 'to die', 'to sleep', 'to live' are intransitive.

The tenses are the forms of the verb which convey the time at which something acts, happens, exists, etc. They are called the present tense, the future tense, the past tense etc. Verbs which follow the same pattern as others and make up a recognizable group are called regular verbs. Verbs which deviate from the general pattern or are unique in their verb forms are called irregular verbs. In the French-English section of the dictionary every French verb is cross-referenced to the verbs section by a number in square brackets, **déplacer** /deplase/ [12] ... This means that the relevant information will be found in table 12 of the section *French verbs*.

10.1 Verb patterns

In French there are three major groupings of regular verbs identified by their infinitive endings, *-er*, *-ir*, and *-re*. There are also many irregular verbs which don't follow the same patterns. Some verbs are reflexive which means that the object of the verb is the same as its subject.

> *je me lave* = I wash myself [see Pronouns section 4.3]

10.1.a Present tense

The present tense describes what is happening now (*it is raining*) or what regularly happens (*he plays football on Tuesdays*) or a current truth (*she loves chips*)

• •

parler 'to speak'	AN EXAMPLE OF AN -ER VERB
je parle = I speak	*nous parlons* = we speak
tu parles = you speak	*vous parlez* = you speak
il parle = he speaks	*ils parlent* = they speak (*masculine*)
elle parle = she speaks	*elles parlent* = they speak (*feminine*)

■ the translation *I speak*, etc., may also be *I am speaking* and *I do speak*

finir 'to finish'	AN EXAMPLE OF AN -IR VERB
je finis = I finish	*nous finissons* = we finish
tu finis = you finish	*vous finissez* = you finish
il finit = he finishes	*ils (masc) finissent* = they finish
elle finit = she finishes	*elles (fem) finissent* = they finish

■ note the lengthened stem *-iss-* in the plural

vendre 'to sell'	AN EXAMPLE OF AN -RE VERB
je vends = I sell	*nous vendons* = we sell
tu vends = you sell	*vous vendez* = you sell
il vend = he sells	*ils (masc) vendent* = they sell
elle vend = she sells	*elles (fem) vendent* = they sell

■ note the dropped verb ending with *il* and *elle*

10.1.b Imperative

The imperative is the form of the verb for giving orders. Three parts of the present tense are used: *tu, nous, vous*

The *-s* is dropped from the *tu* part of the verb:

parle! (= talk!); *parlons!* (= let's talk!); *parlez!* (= talk!)

But there are exceptions [see Verb Tables]:

aie! (= have!); *ayons!* (= let's have!); *ayez!* (= have!)
sois! (= be!); *soyons!* (= let's be!); *soyez!* (= be!)
sache! (= know!); *sachons!* (= let's know!); *sachez!* (= know!)

10.1.c Imperfect tense

The imperfect tense describes what was happening in the past (*it was raining*) or what used to be a fact or a regular occurrence (*he used to like chocolate; he used to go to classes*)

il jouait au football tous les jeudis = he played football/used to play football every Tuesday

Imperfect tense endings

-ais	*-ions*
-ais	*-iez*
-ait	*-aient*
-ait	*-aient*

These endings apply to all verbs and are added to the verb stem. The stem is taken from the *nous* form of the present tense, *nous finiss-ons* → *finiss-* → *je finissais*

The only irregular stem is *ét-* from *être: j'étais* (= I was), tu *étais* (= you were)... etc.

10.1.d Future tense

The future tense describes what will happen (*it will rain*) or what is expected to be a fact (*it will be easy*):

Future tense endings

-ai	*-ons*
-as	*-ez*
-a	*-ont*
-a	*-ont*

These endings apply to all verbs and are added to the infinitive, which acts as the 'stem' for most verbs in the future tense:

finir → *je finirai* (= I shall finish)

But *-re* verbs drop the final *-e* of the infinitive:

vendre → *je vendrai* (= I shall sell)

The future may also be expressed by: the verb *aller* + Infinitive

je vais finir… (= I am going to finish…)

Table of irregular future verb stems

Infinitive	Future Stem		Infinitive	Future Stem	
avoir	*j'aurai*	= I shall have	tenir	*je tiendrai*	= I shall hold
être	*je serai*	= I shall be	vouloir	*je voudrai*	= I shall want
faire	*je ferai*	= I shall make	pouvoir	*je pourrai*	= I shall be able
savoir	*je saurai*	= I shall know	recevoir	*je recevrai*	= I shall get
voir	*je verrai*	= I shall see	devoir	*je devrai*	= I shall have to
envoyer	*j'enverrai*	= I shall send	courir	*je courrai*	= I shall run
venir	*je viendrai*	= I shall come	mourir	*je mourrai*	= I shall die

Compounds of the above verbs take the same the same stem as the basic verb:

retenir (= to hold back) → *je retiendrai*   *défaire* (= to undo) → *je déferai*

10.1.e Conditional tense

The conditional tense describes what would happen (*it would make him angry*) or what would be a fact (*it would be easy*). Conditionals are often preceded or followed by a phrase introduced by *si* (= if).

Formation: The conditional is made up of the Future Stem + Imperfect Endings. This applies to all verbs.

il commencerait (= he would begin)
tu devrais (= you ought to)
il le ferait si tu le lui demandais = he'd do it if you asked him

10.1.f Perfect tense

The perfect tense describes what has happened (*it has snowed; they have written*). In French it is also used for what happened and remained the case until a specific point in time (*ils y sont restés jusqu'à mardi* = they stayed there until Tuesday) or to state an action as part of a series, each action

. . . .

being complete in itself (*je me suis approché de la maison, j'ai sonné à la porte...* = I went up to the house, rang the doorbell...)

Formation of the perfect tense:

Two common verbs are important in the formation of the perfect tense: *avoir* and *être*

avoir = to have		être = to be	
j'ai	*nous avons*	*je suis*	*nous sommes*
tu as	*vous avez*	*tu es*	*vous êtes*
il a	*ils ont*	*il est*	*ils sont*
elle a	*elles ont*	*elle est*	*elles sont*

There are three elements in the perfect tense:

SUBJECT + *avoir/être* + PAST PARTICIPLE

The past participle of regular verbs is formed by removing the last syllable of the infinitive (*regarder*, *choisir*, *rendre*) and by replacing it with *-é, -i, -u* respectively:

-ER verbs: *regarder → regardé → j'ai regardé* (= I have looked)
-IR verbs: *choisir → choisi → tu as choisi* (= you have chosen)
-RE verbs: *rendre → rendu → il a rendu* (= he has given back)

But some past participles are unique and have to be learnt by heart

Table of common irregular past participles following the auxiliary verb *avoir*:

Infinitive	Past Participle		Infinitive	Past Participle	
avoir	*j'ai eu*	= I have had	croire	*j'ai cru*	= I have believed
être	*j'ai été*	= I have been	savoir	*j'ai su*	= I have known
faire	*j'ai fait*	= I have made	voir	*j'ai vu*	= I have seen
boire	*j'ai bu*	= I have drunk	pleuvoir	*il a plu*	= it has rained
pouvoir	*j'ai pu*	= I have been able	dire	*j'ai dit*	= I have said
devoir	*j'ai dû*	= I have had to	écrire	*j'ai écrit*	= I have written
lire	*j'ai lu*	= I have read	mettre	*j'ai mis*	= I have put
vouloir	*j'ai voulu*	= I have wanted	prendre	*j'ai pris*	= I have taken

■ the past participle does not change its spelling after *avoir* unless there is a direct object preceding it: *j'ai vendu la table* (= I sold the table). No preceding direct object, no change to the past participle *vendu*. But in *tu l'as vendue* (= you've sold it), *l'* (referring to *la table*, feminine) makes *vendu* take the feminine ending *-e*.

Most verbs form their perfect tense with *avoir*. The exceptions are reflexive verbs and a small group of verbs of 'motion'. These take *être* and the past participle functions like an adjective qualifying the subject.

Summary of French grammar

• •

1 Reflexive verb: *se laver* = to get washed/to wash oneself

je me suis lavé(e) = I got washed   *nous nous sommes lavé(e)s* = we got washed
tu t'es lavé(e) = you got washed   *vous vous êtes lavé(e)(s)* = you got washed
il s'est lavé = he got washed   *ils se sont lavés* = they got washed
elle s'est lavée = she got washed   *elles se sont lavées* = they got washed

■ The alternatives in brackets depend on gender (masculine or feminine) and number (singular or plural) of the subject: *je, tu, elle, nous*, etc

2 Verbs of motion which take *être*

aller	*je suis allé(e)*	= I went	partir	*je suis parti(e)*	= I left
arriver	*je suis arrivé(e)*	= I arrived	rester	*je suis resté(e)*	= I stayed
descendre	*je suis descendu(e)*	= I went down	retourner	*je suis retourné(e)*	= I returned
entrer	*je suis entré(e)*	= I entered	revenir	*je suis revenu(e)*	= I came back
monter	*je suis monté(e)*	= I went up	sortir	*je suis sorti(e)*	= I went out
mourir	*je suis mort(e)*	= I died	tomber	*je suis tombé(e)*	= I fell
naître	*je suis né(e)*	= I was born	venir	*je suis venu(e)*	= I came

■ compounds of the above also take *être*: *devenir* (= to become) → *je suis devenu(e)*

10.1.g Pluperfect tense

The pluperfect tense describes what had happened (*it had snowed; they had written*) or what had been the case (*it had been easy*).

Formation: = Imperfect Tense of *avoir* or *être* + PAST PARTICIPLE

Examples:

j'avais fini = I had finished
nous avions vendu l'appartement = we had sold the flat
elle s'était réveillée = she had woken up
nous étions partis = we had left

■ As with the perfect tense, past participles after *être* function like adjectives. They qualify the subject of the verb and reflect its gender and number.

10.1.h Future perfect tense

The future perfect tense describes what will have happened (*he will have arrived*) or what will have been the case (*it will not have been easy*)

Formation: = Future Tense of *avoir* or *être* + PAST PARTICIPLE

Examples:

j'aurai fini = I shall have finished
nous aurons vendu la voiture = we shall have sold the car
nous serons descendus = we shall have gone down

■ As with the perfect tense, past participles after *être* function like adjectives. They qualify the subject of the verb and reflect its gender and number.

11 Negatives

Negative is the idea expressed by words such as *no*, *never*, *nobody*, *nothing*, etc in English and *non*, *jamais*, *personne*, *rien*, etc in French. The negative of French verbs is formed by using *ne* before the verb, and *pas*, *jamais*, *plus*, etc after the verb according to the sense required.

ne ... pas (= not)   ne ... jamais (= never)
ne ... personne (= nobody, no one)   ne ... plus (= no longer)
ne ... que (= only)   ne ... rien (= nothing)

In simple sentences *ne* is placed before the verb and *pas*, *jamais*, *plus* etc after it.

je ne lis pas = I am not reading

If there are pronouns before the verb, *ne* comes before them.

je ne le lui donne jamais = I never give it to him

If an auxiliary verb is used in a compound tense, it comes within *ne ... pas*, *jamais*, *plus* etc.

il n'a rien mangé = he didn't eat anything

If an infinitive is used in the sentence, it comes after *ne ... pas*, *jamais*, *plus* etc.

il ne veut pas manger = he doesn't want to eat

Neither ... nor is expressed by *ni ... ni*.

ni *Jean* ni *Luc ne voulaient venir* = neither Jean nor Luc wanted to come

If pronoun objects are used in the sentence they take the emphatic form.

ni lui ni sa femme n'étaient là = neither he nor his wife was there

If *personne* (= nobody) or *rien* (= nothing) is the subject it is followed only by *ne*:

personne ne vous dérangera = no one will disturb you
rien n'est impossible = nothing is impossible

Note also the following usage:

qui a frappé? – personne = who knocked? nobody
qu'est-ce qui se passe? – rien = what's going on? nothing

The use of the adjective *aucun/aucune* (= no) is very common; *aucun* is used with *ne* before the verb.

il n'a aucun talent = he has no talent
elle n'avait aucune nouvelle de lui = she hadn't heard from him

French verbs

Standard verb endings

	-er	-ir	-r, -re
Present			
Singular 1	-e	-is	-s *or* -e
2	-es	-is	-s *or* -es
3	-e	-it	-t *or* -e
Plural 1	-ons	-(iss)ons	-ons
2	-ez	-(iss)ez	-ez
3	-ent	-(iss)ent	-ent
Imperfect			
Singular 1	-ais	-(iss)ais	-ais
2	-ais	-(iss)ais	-ais
3	-ait	-(iss)ait	-ait
Plural 1	-ions	-(iss)ions	-ions
2	-iez	-(iss)iez	-iez
3	-aient	-(iss)aient	-aient
Past historic			
Singular 1	-ai	-is	-s
2	-as	-is	-s
3	-a	-it	-t
Plural 1	-âmes	-îmes	-mes
2	-âtes	-îtes	-tes
3	-èrent	-irent	-rent
Future			
Singular 1	-erai	-irai	-rai
2	-eras	-iras	-ras
3	-era	-ira	-ra
Plural 1	-erons	-irons	-rons
2	-erez	-irez	-rez
3	-eront	-iront	-ront
Present	-er	-ir	-r *or* -re

	-er	-ir	-r, -re
Present			
Singular 1	-e	-(iss)e	-e
2	-es	-(iss)es	-es
3	-e	-(iss)e	-e
Plural 1	-ions	-(iss)ions	-ions
2	-iez	-(iss)iez	-iez
3	-ent	-(iss)ent	-ent
Imperfect			
Singular 1	-asse	-isse	-sse
2	-asses	-isses	-sses
3	-ât	-ît	-ît *or* -ût
Plural 1	-assions	-issions	-ssions
2	-assiez	-issiez	-ssiez
3	-assent	-issent	-ssent
Present			
Singular 1			
2			
3	-e	-is	-s
Plural 1	-ons	-(iss)ons	-ons
2	-ez	-(iss)ez	-ez
Present			
Singular 1	-erais	-irais	-rais
2	-erais	-irais	-rais
3	-erait	-irait	-rait
Plural 1	-erions	-irions	-rions
2	-eriez	-iriez	-riez
3	-eraient	-iraient	-raient
Present	-ant	-(iss)ant	-ant
Past	-é	-i	-i *or* -u

1 aimer

Indicative

Present
j'	aime
tu	aimes
il	aime
nous	aimons
vous	aimez
ils	aiment

Imperfect
j'	aimais
tu	aimais
il	aimait
nous	aimions
vous	aimiez
ils	aimaient

Past historic
j'	aimai
tu	aimas
il	aima
nous	aimâmes
vous	aimâtes
ils	aimèrent

Future
j'	aimerai
tu	aimeras
il	aimera
nous	aimerons
vous	aimerez
ils	aimeront

Perfect
j'	ai	aimé
tu	as	aimé
il	a	aimé
nous	avons	aimé
vous	avez	aimé
ils	ont	aimé

Pluperfect
j'	avais	aimé
tu	avais	aimé
il	avait	aimé
nous	avions	aimé
vous	aviez	aimé
ils	avaient	aimé

Imperative

Present
	aime
	aimons
	aimez

Past
	aie	aimé
	ayons	aimé
	ayez	aimé

Subjunctive

Present
(que) j'	aime
(que) tu	aimes
(qu')il	aime
(que) nous	aimions
(que) vous	aimiez
(qu')ils	aiment

Perfect
(que) j'	aie	aimé
(que) tu	aies	aimé
(qu')il	ait	aimé
(que) nous	ayons	aimé
(que) vous	ayez	aimé
(qu')ils	aient	aimé

Pluperfect
(que) j'	eusse	aimé
(que) tu	eusses	aimé
(qu')il	eût	aimé
(que) nous	eussions aimé
(que) vous	eussiez	aimé
(qu')ils	eussent	aimé

Conditional

Present
j'	aimerais
tu	aimerais
il	aimerait
nous	aimerions
vous	aimeriez
ils	aimeraient

Past I
j'	aurais	aimé
tu	aurais	aimé
il	aurait	aimé
nous	aurions	aimé
vous	auriez	aimé
ils	auraient	aimé

Participle

Present	aimant
Past	aimé, -e
	ayant aimé

Infinitive

| Present | aimer |
| Past | avoir aimé |

2 plier

Indicative

Present
je	plie
tu	plies
il	plie
nous	plions
vous	pliez
ils	plient

Imperfect
je	pliais
tu	pliais
il	pliait
nous	pliions
vous	pliiez
ils	pliaient

Past historic
je	pliai
tu	plias
il	plia
nous	pliâmes
vous	pliâtes
ils	plièrent

Future
je	plierai
tu	plieras
il	pliera
nous	plierons
vous	plierez
ils	plieront

Perfect
j'	ai	plié
tu	as	plié
il	a	plié
nous	avons	plié
vous	avez	plié
ils	ont	plié

Pluperfect
j'	avais	plié
tu	avais	plié
il	avait	plié
nous	avions	plié
vous	aviez	plié
ils	avaient	plié

Imperative

Present
	plie
	plions
	pliez

Past
	aie	plié
	ayons	plié
	ayez	plié

Subjunctive

Present
(que) je	plie
(que) tu	plies
(qu')il	plie
(que) nous	pliions
(que) vous	pliiez
(qu')ils	plient

Perfect
(que) j'	aie	plié
(que) tu	aies	plié
(qu')il	ait	plié
(que) nous	ayons	plié
(que) vous	ayez	plié
(qu')ils	aient	plié

Pluperfect
(que) j'	eusse	plié
(que) tu	eusses	plié
(qu')il	eût	plié
(que) nous	eussions plié
(que) vous	eussiez plié
(qu')ils	eussent plié

Conditional

Present
je	plierais
tu	plierais
il	plierait
nous	plierions
vous	plieriez
ils	plieraient

Past I
j'	aurais	plié
tu	aurais	plié
il	aurait	plié
nous	aurions	plié
vous	auriez	plié
ils	auraient	plié

Participle

Present	pliant
Past	plié, -e
	ayant plié

Infinitive

| Present | plier |
| Past | avoir plié |

French verbs

3 finir

Indicative

Present

je	finis
tu	finis
il	finit
nous	finissons
vous	finissez
ils	finissent

Imperfect

je	finissais
tu	finissais
il	finissait
nous	finissions
vous	finissiez
ils	finissaient

Past historic

je	finis
tu	finis
il	finit
nous	finîmes
vous	finîtes
ils	finirent

Future

je	finirai
tu	finiras
il	finira
nous	finirons
vous	finirez
ils	finiront

Perfect

j'	ai	fini
tu	as	fini
il	a	fini
nous	avons	fini
vous	avez	fini
ils	ont	fini

Pluperfect

j'	avais	fini
tu	avais	fini
il	avait	fini
nous	avions	fini
vous	aviez	fini
ils	avaient	fini

Imperative

Present

	finis
	finissons
	finissez

Past

	aie fini
	ayons fini
	ayez fini

Subjunctive

Present

(que) je	finisse
(que) tu	finisses
(qu')il	finisse
(que) nous	finissions
(que) vous	finissiez
(qu')ils	finissent

Perfect

(que) j'	aie	fini
(que) tu	aies	fini
(qu')il	ait	fini
(que) nous	ayons	fini
(que) vous	ayez	fini
(qu')ils	aient	fini

Pluperfect

(que) j'	eusse	fini
(que) tu	eusses	fini
(qu')il	eût	fini
(que) nous	eussions	fini
(que) vous	eussiez	fini
(qu')ils	eussent	fini

Conditional

Present

je	finirais
tu	finirais
il	finirait
nous	finirions
vous	finiriez
ils	finiraient

Past I

j'	aurais	fini
tu	aurais	fini
il	aurait	fini
nous	aurions	fini
vous	auriez	fini
ils	auraient	fini

Participle

Present	finissant
Past	fini, -e
	ayant fini

Infinitive

Present	finir
Past	avoir fini

4 offrir

Indicative

Present

j'	offre
tu	offres
il	offre
nous	offrons
vous	offrez
ils	offrent

Imperfect

j'	offrais
tu	offrais
il	offrait
nous	offrions
vous	offriez
ils	offraient

Past historic

j'	offris
tu	offris
il	offrit
nous	offrîmes
vous	offrîtes
ils	offrirent

Future

j'	offrirai
tu	offriras
il	offrira
nous	offrirons
vous	offrirez
ils	offriront

Perfect

j'	ai	offert
tu	as	offert
il	a	offert
nous	avons	offert
vous	avez	offert
ils	ont	offert

Pluperfect

j'	avais	offert
tu	avais	offert
il	avait	offert
nous	avions	offert
vous	aviez	offert
ils	avaient	offert

Imperative

Present

	offre
	offrons
	offrez

Past

	aie offert
	ayons offert
	ayez offert

Subjunctive

Present

(que) j'	offre
(que) tu	offres
(qu')il	offre
(que) nous	offrions
(que) vous	offriez
(qu')ils	offrent

Perfect

(que) j'	aie	offert
(que) tu	aies	offert
(qu')il	ait	offert
(que) nous	ayons	offert
(que) vous	ayez	offert
(qu')ils	aient	offert

Pluperfect

(que) j'	eusse	offert
(que) tu	eusses	offert
(qu')il	eût	offert
(que) nous	eussions	offert
(que) vous	eussiez	offert
(qu')ils	eussent	offert

Conditional

Present

j'	offrirais
tu	offrirais
il	offrirait
nous	offririons
vous	offririez
ils	offriraient

Past I

j'	aurais	offert
tu	aurais	offert
il	aurait	offert
nous	aurions	offert
vous	auriez	offert
ils	auraient	offert

Participle

Present	offrant
Past	offert, -e
	ayant offert

Infinitive

Present	offrir
Past	avoir offert

5 recevoir

Indicative

Present

je	reçois
tu	reçois
il	reçoit
nous	recevons
vous	recevez
ils	reçoivent

Imperfect

je	recevais
tu	recevais
il	recevait
nous	recevions
vous	receviez
ils	recevaient

Past historic

je	reçus
tu	reçus
il	reçut
nous	reçûmes
vous	reçûtes
ils	reçurent

Future

je	recevrai
tu	recevras
il	recevra
nous	recevrons
vous	recevrez
ils	recevront

Perfect

j'	ai	reçu
tu	as	reçu
il	a	reçu
nous	avons	reçu
vous	avez	reçu
ils	ont	reçu

Pluperfect

j'	avais	reçu
tu	avais	reçu
il	avait	reçu
nous	avions	reçu
vous	aviez	reçu
ils	avaient	reçu

Imperative

Present

	reçois
	recevons
	recevez

Past

	aie reçu
	ayons reçu
	ayez reçu

Subjunctive

Present

(que) je	reçoive
(que) tu	reçoives
(qu')il	reçoive
(que) nous	recevions
(que) vous	receviez
(qu')ils	reçoivent

Perfect

(que) j'	aie	reçu
(que) tu	aies	reçu
(qu')il	ait	reçu
(que) nous	ayons	reçu
(que) vous	ayez	reçu
(qu')ils	aient	reçu

Pluperfect

(que) j'	eusse	reçu
(que) tu	eusses	reçu
(qu')il	eût	reçu
(que) nous	eussions	reçu
(que) vous	eussiez	reçu
(qu')ils	eussent	reçu

Conditional

Present

je	recevrais
tu	recevrais
il	recevrait
nous	recevrions
vous	recevriez
ils	recevraient

Past I

j'	aurais	reçu
tu	aurais	reçu
il	aurait	reçu
nous	aurions	reçu
vous	auriez	reçu
ils	auraient	reçu

Participle

Present recevant

Past reçu, -e
ayant reçu

Infinitive

Present recevoir

Past avoir reçu

6 rendre

Indicative

Present

je	rends
tu	rends
il	rend
nous	rendons
vous	rendez
ils	rendent

Imperfect

je	rendais
tu	rendais
il	rendait
nous	rendions
vous	rendiez
ils	rendaient

Past historic

je	rendis
tu	rendis
il	rendit
nous	rendîmes
vous	rendîtes
ils	rendirent

Future

je	rendrai
tu	rendras
il	rendra
nous	rendrons
vous	rendrez
ils	rendront

Perfect

j'	ai	rendu
tu	as	rendu
il	a	rendu
nous	avons	rendu
vous	avez	rendu
ils	ont	rendu

Pluperfect

j'	avais	rendu
tu	avais	rendu
il	avait	rendu
nous	avions	rendu
vous	aviez	rendu
ils	avaient	rendu

Imperative

Present

	rends
	rendons
	rendez

Past

	aie rendu
	ayons rendu
	ayez rendu

Subjunctive

Present

(que) je	rende
(que) tu	rendes
(qu')il	rende
(que) nous	rendions
(que) vous	rendiez
(qu')ils	rendent

Perfect

(que) j'	aie	rendu
(que) tu	aies	rendu
(qu')il	ait	rendu
(que) nous	ayons	rendu
(que) vous	ayez	rendu
(qu')ils	aient	rendu

Pluperfect

(que) j'	eusse	rendu
(que) tu	eusses	rendu
(qu')il	eût	rendu
(que) nous	eussions	rendu
(que) vous	eussiez	rendu
(qu')ils	eussent	rendu

Conditional

Present

je	rendrais
tu	rendrais
il	rendrait
nous	rendrions
vous	rendriez
ils	rendraient

Past I

j'	aurais	rendu
tu	aurais	rendu
il	aurait	rendu
nous	aurions	rendu
vous	auriez	rendu
ils	auraient	rendu

Participle

Present rendant

Past rendu, -e
ayant rendu

Infinitive

Present rendre

Past avoir rendu

7 être

Indicative

Present

je	suis
tu	es
il	est
nous	sommes
vous	êtes
ils	sont

Imperfect

j'	étais
tu	étais
il	était
nous	étions
vous	étiez
ils	étaient

Past historic

je	fus
tu	fus
il	fut
nous	fûmes
vous	fûtes
ils	furent

Future

je	serai
tu	seras
il	sera
nous	serons
vous	serez
ils	seront

Perfect

j'	ai	été
tu	as	été
il	a	été
nous	avons	été
vous	avez	été
ils	ont	été

Pluperfect

j'	avais	été
tu	avais	été
il	avait	été
nous	avions	été
vous	aviez	été
ils	avaient	été

Imperative

Present

	sois
	soyons
	soyez

Past

	aie	été
	ayons	été
	ayez	été

Subjunctive

Present

(que) je	sois
(que) tu	sois
(qu')il	soit
(que) nous	soyons
(que) vous	soyez
(qu')ils	soient

Perfect

(que) j'	aie	été
(que) tu	aies	été
(qu')il	ait	été
(que) nous	ayons	été
(que) vous	ayez	été
(qu')ils	aient	été

Pluperfect

(que) j'	eusse	été
(que) tu	eusses	été
(qu')il	eût	été
(que) nous	eussions	été
(que) vous	eussiez	été
(qu')ils	eussent	été

Conditional

Present

je	serais
tu	serais
il	serait
nous	serions
vous	seriez
ils	seraient

Past I

j'	aurais	été
tu	aurais	été
il	aurait	été
nous	aurions	été
vous	auriez	été
ils	auraient	été

Participle

Present	étant
Past	été (invariable)
	ayant été

Infinitive

Present	être
Past	avoir été

8 avoir

Indicative

Present

j'	ai
tu	as
il	a
nous	avons
vous	avez
ils	ont

Imperfect

j'	avais
tu	avais
il	avait
nous	avions
vous	aviez
ils	avaient

Past historic

j'	eus
tu	eus
il	eut
nous	eûmes
vous	eûtes
ils	eurent

Future

j'	aurai
tu	auras
il	aura
nous	aurons
vous	aurez
ils	auront

Perfect

j'	ai	eu
tu	as	eu
il	a	eu
nous	avons	eu
vous	avez	eu
ils	ont	eu

Pluperfect

j'	avais	eu
tu	avais	eu
il	avait	eu
nous	avions	eu
vous	aviez	eu
ils	avaient	eu

Imperative

Present

	aie
	ayons
	ayez

Past

	aie	eu
	ayons	eu
	ayez	eu

Subjunctive

Present

(que) j'	aie
(que) tu	aies
(qu')il	ait
(que) nous	ayons
(que) vous	ayez
(qu')ils	aient

Perfect

(que) j'	aie	eu
(que) tu	aies	eu
(qu')il	ait	eu
(que) nous	ayons	eu
(que) vous	ayez	eu
(qu')ils	aient	eu

Pluperfect

(que) j'	eusse	eu
(que) tu	eusses	eu
(qu')il	eût	eu
(que) nous	eussions	eu
(que) vous	eussiez	eu
(qu')ils	eussent	eu

Conditional

Present

j'	aurais
tu	aurais
il	aurait
nous	aurions
vous	auriez
ils	auraient

Past I

j'	aurais	eu
tu	aurais	eu
il	aurait	eu
nous	aurions	eu
vous	auriez	eu
ils	auraient	eu

Participle

Present	ayant
Past	eu, -e
	ayant eu

Infinitive

Present	avoir
Past	avoir eu

French verbs

9 aller

Indicative

Present

je	vais
tu	vas
il	va
nous	allons
vous	allez
ils	vont

Imperfect

j'	allais
tu	allais
il	allait
nous	allions
vous	alliez
ils	allaient

Past historic

j'	allai
tu	allas
il	alla
nous	allâmes
vous	allâtes
ils	allèrent

Future

j'	irai
tu	iras
il	ira
nous	irons
vous	irez
ils	iront

Perfect

je	suis	allé
tu	es	allé
il	est	allé
nous	sommes	allés
vous	êtes	allés
ils	sont	allés

Pluperfect

j'	étais	allé
tu	étais	allé
il	était	allé
nous	étions	allés
vous	étiez	allés
ils	étaient	allés

Imperative

Present

va	
allons	
allez	

Past	sois	allé
	soyons	allés
	soyez	allés

Subjunctive

Present

(que) j'	aille
(que) tu	ailles
(qu')il	aille
(que) nous	allions
(que) vous	alliez
(qu')ils	aillent

Perfect

(que) je	sois	allé
(que) tu	sois	allé
(qu')il	soit	allé
(que) nous	soyons	allés
(que) vous	soyez	allés
(qu')ils	soient	allés

Pluperfect

(que) je	fusse	allé
(que) tu	fusses	allé
(qu')il	fût	allé
(que) nous	fussions	allés
(que) vous	fussiez	allés
(qu')ils	fussent	allés

Conditional

Present

j'	irais
tu	irais
il	Irait
nous	irions
vous	iriez
ils	iraient

Past I

je	serais	allé
tu	serais	allé
il	serait	allé
nous	serions	allés
vous	seriez	allés
ils	seraient	allés

Participle

Present	allant

Past	allé, -e
	étant allé

Infinitive

Present	aller
Past	être allé

10 faire

Indicative

Present

je	fais
tu	fais
il	fait
nous	faisons
vous	faites
ils	font

Imperfect

je	faisais
tu	faisais
il	faisait
nous	faisions
vous	faisiez
ils	faisaient

Past historic

je	fis
tu	fis
il	fit
nous	fîmes
vous	fîtes
ils	firent

Future

je	ferai
tu	feras
il	fera
nous	ferons
vous	ferez
ils	feront

Perfect

j'	ai	fait
tu	as	fait
il	a	fait
nous	avons	fait
vous	avez	fait
ils	ont	fait

Pluperfect

j'	avais	fait
tu	avais	fait
il	avait	fait
nous	avions	fait
vous	aviez	fait
ils	avaient	fait

Imperative

Present

fais	
faisons	
faites	

Past	aie	fait
	ayons	fait
	ayez	fait

Subjunctive

Present

(que) je	fasse
(que) tu	fasses
(qu')il	fasse
(que) nous	fassions
(que) vous	fassiez
(qu')ils	fassent

Perfect

(que) j'	aie	fait
(que) tu	aies	fait
(qu')il	ait	fait
(que) nous	ayons	fait
(que) vous	ayez	fait
(qu')ils	aient	fait

Pluperfect

(que) j'	eusse	fait
(que) tu	eusses	fait
(qu')il	eût	fait
(que) nous	eussions	fait
(que) vous	eussiez	fait
(qu')ils	eussent	fait

Conditional

Present

je	ferais
tu	ferais
il	ferait
nous	ferions
vous	feriez
ils	feraient

Past I

j'	aurais	fait
tu	aurais	fait
il	aurait	fait
nous	aurions	fait
vous	auriez	fait
ils	auraient	fait

Participle

Present	faisant

Past	fait, -e
	ayant fait

Infinitive

Present	faire
Past	avoir fait

French verbs

Infinitive	Rules	Indicative Present	Imperfect	Past Historic	Future
11 créer	always é	je crée, -es, -e, -ent nous créons, -ez	je créais ...	je créai ...	je créerai ...
12 placer	c	je place, -es, -e, -ez, -ent	nous placions, -iez	ils placèrent	je placerai ...
	ç before a and o	nous plaçons	je plaçais, -ais, -ait, -aient	je plaçai, -as, -a, -âmes, -âtes	
13 manger	g	je mange, -es, -e, -ez, -ent	nous mangions, -iez	ils mangèrent	je mangerai ...
	ge before a and o	nous mangeons	je mangeais, -eais, -eait, -eaient	je mangeai, -as, -a, -âmes, -âtes	
14 céder	è before silent final syllable	je cède, -es, -e, -ent			
	é	nous cédons, -ez	je cédais ...	je cédai ...	je céderai ...
15 assiéger	è before silent final syllable	j'assiège, -es, -e, -ent			
	ge before a and o	nous assiégeons	j'assiégeais, -eais, -eait, -eaient	j'assiégeai	
	é before silent syllable				j'assiégerai ...
16 lever	è before silent syllable	je lève, -es, -e, -ent			je lèverai ...
	e	nous levons, -ez	je levais ...	je levai ...	
17 geler	è before silent syllable	je gèle, -es, -e, -ent			je gèlerai ...
	e	nous gelons, -ez	je gelais ...	je gelai ...	
18 acheter	è before silent syllable	j'achète, -es, -e, -ent			j'achèterai ...
	e	nous achetons, -ez	j'achetais ...	j'achetai ...	
19 appeler	ll before mute e	j'appelle, -es, -e, -ent			j'appellerai ...
	l	nous appelons, -ez	j'appelais ...	j'appelai ...	
20 jeter	tt before mute e	je jette, -es, -e, -ent			je jetterai ...
	t	nous jetons, -ez	je jetais ...	je jetai ...	
21 payer	i before mute e	je paie, -es, -e, -ent			je paierai ...
	or y	je paye, -es, -e, -ent nous payons, -ez	je payais ...	je payai ...	je payerai ...

Conditional	Subjunctive	Imperative	Participle		
Present	*Present*		*Present*	*Past*	
je créerais ...	que je crée ...	crée	créant	créé, -e	11
		créons, -ez			
je placerais ...	que je place ...	place, -ez		placé, -e	12
		plaçons	plaçant		
je mangerais ...	que je mange ...	mange, -ez		mangé, -e	13
		mangeons	mangeant		
	que je cède, -es, -e, -ent	cède			14
jc céderais ...	que nous cédions, -iez	cédons, -ez	cédant	cédé, -e	
	que j'assiège ...	assiège			15
j'assiégerais ...	que nous assiégions , -iez	assiégeons	assiégeant	assiégó, -e	
je lèverais ...	que je lève, -es, -e, -ent	lève			16
	que nous levions, -iez	levons, -ez	levant	levé, -e	
je gèlerais ...	que je gèle, -es, -e, -ent	gèle			17
	que nous gelions, -iez	gelons, -ez	gelant	gelé, -e	
j'achèterais ...	que j'achète, -es, -e, -ent	achète			18
	que nous achetions, -iez	achetons, -ez	achetant	acheté, -e	
j'appellerais ...	que j'appelle, -es, -e, -ent	appelle			19
	que nous appelions, -iez	appelons, -ez	appelant	appelé, -e	
je jetterais ...	que je jette, -es, -e, -ent	jette			20
	que nous jetions, -iez	jetons, -ez	jetant	jeté, -e	
je paierais ...	que je paie, -es, -e, -ent	paie			21
je payerais ...	que je paye, -es, -e, -ent	paye			
	que nous payions, -iez	payons, -ez	payant	payé, -e	

• •

Infinitive	Rules	Indicative			
		Present	Imperfect	Past Historic	Future
22 essuyer	i *before mute* e	j'essuie, -es, -e, -ent			j'essuierai ...
	y	nous essuyons, -ez	j'essuyais ...	j'essuyai ...	
23 employer	i *before mute* e	j'emploie, -es, -e, -ent			j'emploierai ...
	y	nous employons, -ez	j'employais ...	j'employai ...	
24 envoyer	i *before mute* e	j'envoie, -es, -e, -ent			
	y	nous envoyons, -ez	j'envoyais ...	j'envoyai ...	
	err				j'enverrai ...
25 haïr	i	je hais, -s, -t			
	ï	nous haïssons, -ez, -ent	je haïssais ...	je haïs ... (haïmes, haïtes)	je haïrai ...
26 courir		je cours ...	je courais ...	je courus ...	je courrai ...
27 cueillir		je cueille, -es, -e, nous cueillons ...	je cueillais ...	je cueillis ...	je cueillerai ...
28 assaillir		j'assaille, -es, -e, nous assaillons, -ez, -ent	j'assaillais ...	j'assaillis ...	j'assaillirai ...
29 fuir	i *before consonants and* e	je fuis, -s, -t, -ent		je fuis ...	je fuirai ...
	y *before* a, ez, i, o	nous fuyons, -ez	je fuyais ...		
30 partir	*without* t	je pars ...			
	with t	il part ...	je partais ...	je partis ...	je partirai ...
31 bouillir	ou	je bous, s, t			
	ouill	nous bouillons ...	je bouillais ...	je bouillis ...	je bouillirai ...
32 couvrir		je couvre, -es, -e, nous couvrons ...	je couvrais ...	je couvris ...	je couvrirai ...
33 vêtir		je vêts ...	je vêtais ...	je vêtis ...	je vêtirai ...
34 mourir	eur	je meurs, -s, -t, -ent			
	our	nous mourons, -ez	je mourais ...	je mourus ...	je mourrai ...
35 acquérir	quier	j'acquiers, -s, -t, -ièrent			
	quér	nous acquérons -ez	j'acquérais ...		j'acquerrai ...
	qu			j'acquis ...	

Conditional	Subjunctive	Imperative	Participle		
Present	Present		Present	Past	
j'essuierais ...	que j'essuie, -es, -e, -ent	essuie			22
	que nous essuyions, -iez	essuyons, -ez	essuyant	essuyé, e	
j'emploierais ...	que j'emploie, -es, -e, -ent	emploie			23
	que nous employions, -iez	employons, -ez	employant	employé, -e	
	que j'envoie, -es, -e, -ent	envoie			24
	que nous envoyions, -iez	envoyons, -ez	envoyant	envoyé, -e	
j'enverrais ...					
		hais			25
je haïrais ...	que je haïsse, qu'il haïsse	haïssons, haïssez	haïssant	haï, -e	
je courrais ...	que je coure ...	cours, courons, -ez	courant	couru, -e	26
je cueillerais ...	que je cueille ...	cueille cueillons, -ez	cueillant	cueilli, -e	27
		assaille			28
j'assaillirais ...	que j'assaille ...	assaillons, -ez	assaillant	assailli, -e	
je fuirais ...	que je fuie, -es, -e, -ent	fuis		fui, -e	29
	que nous fuyions, -iez	fuyons, -ez	fuyant		
		pars			30
je partirais ...	que je parte ...	partons, -ez	partant	parti, -e	
		bous			31
je bouillirais ...	que je bouille ...	bouillons, -ez	bouillant	bouilli, -e	
je couvrirais ...	que je couvre, -es, -e, que nous couvrions ...	couvre couvrons, -ez	couvrant	couvert, -e	32
je vêtirais ...	que je vête ...	vêts vêtons, vêtez	vêtant	vêtu, -e	33
	que je meure ...	meurs		mort, -e	34
je mourrais ...		mourons, -ez	mourant		
	que j'acquière, -es, -e, -ent	acquiers			35
j'acquerrais ...	que nous acquérions, -iez	acquérons, -ez	acquérant		
				acquis, -e	

Infinitive		Indicative			
	Rules	Present	Imperfect	Past Historic	Future
36 venir	i	je viens, -s, -t, -nent		je vins … ils vinrent	je viendrai …
	e	nous venons, -ez	je venais …		
37 gésir	Defective (only exists in certain tenses)	je gis, tu gis, il gît, nous gisons, -ez, -ent	je gisais …		
38 ouïr	Archaic	j'ois … nous oyons …	j'oyais …	j'ouïs …	j'ouïrai …
39 pleuvoir		il pleut ils pleuvent	il pleuvait ils pleuvaient	il plut ils plurent	il pleuvra ils pleuvront
40 pourvoir	i	je pourvois, -s, -t, -ent			je pourvoirai …
	y	nous pourvoyons, -ez	je pourvoyais …		
	u			je pourvus …	
41 asseoir	ie	j'assieds, -ds, -d			j'assiérai …
	ey	nous asseyons, -ez, -ent	j'asseyais …		
	i			j'assis …	
asseoir (oi/oy replace ie/ey)	oi	j'assois, -s, -t, -ent			j'assoirai …
	oy	nous assoyons, -ez	j'assoyais …		
42 prévoir	oi	je prévois, -s, -t, -ent			je prévoirai …
	oy	nous prévoyons, -ez	je prévoyais …		
	i/u			je prévis …	
43 mouvoir	eu	je meus, -s, -t, -vent			
	ou	nous mouvons, -ez	je mouvais …		je mouvrai …
	u			je mus, -s, -t, -(û)mes, -(û)tes, -rent	
44 devoir	û in the past participle masc. sing.	je dois, -s, -t -vent		je dus …	
		nous devons, -ez	je devais …		je devrai …
45 valoir	au, aille	je vaux, -x, -t			je vaudrai …
	al	nous valons, -ez, -ent	je valais …	je valus …	

prévaloir

Conditional	Subjunctive	Imperative	Participle		
Present	*Present*		*Present*	*Past*	
je viendrais ...	que je vienne, -es, -e, -ent	viens			36
	que nous venions, -iez	venons, -ez	venant	venu, -e	
					37
			gisant		
j'ouïrais ...	que j'oie ...	ois		ouï, -e	38
	que nous oyions ...	oyons, -ez	oyant		
il pleuvrait	qu'il pleuvo		pleuvant	plu	39
ils pleuvraient	qu'ils pleuvent				
je pourvoirais ...	que je pourvoie, -es, -e, -ent	pourvois			40
	que nous pourvoyions, -iez	pourvoyons, -ez	pourvoyant		
				pourvu, -e	
j'assiérais ...		assieds			41
	que j' asseye ...	asseyons, -ez	asséyant		
	que nous asseyions ...				
				assis, -e	
j'assoirais ...	que j'assoie, -es, -e, -ent	assois			
	que nous assoyions, -iez	assoyons, -ez	assoyant		
je prévoirais ...	que je prévoie, -es, -e, -ent	prévois			42
	que ns prévoyions, -iez	prévoyons, -ez	prévoyant		
				prévu, -e	
	que je meuve, -es, -e, -ent	meus			43
je mouvrais ...	que nous mouvions, -iez	mouvons, -ez	mouvant		
				mû, mue	
	que je doive, -es, -e, -ent	dois		dû, due	44
je devrais ...	que nous devions, -iez	devons, -ez	devant		
je vaudrais ...	que je vaille, -es, -e, -ent	vaux			45
	que nous valions, -iez	valons, -ez	valant	valu, -e	
	que je prévale, -es, -e				

Infinitive		Indicative			
	Rules	*Present*	*Imperfect*	*Past Historic*	*Future*
46 *voir*	oi	je vois, -s, -t, -ent			
	oy	nous voyons, -ez	je voyais ...		
	i/e/u			je vis ...	je verrai ...
47 *savoir*	5 forms	je sais, -s, -t,		je sus ...	je saurai ...
		nous savons, -ez, -ent	je savais ...		
48 *vouloir*	veu/veuil	je veux, -x, -t, veulent			
	voul/voudr	nous voulons, -ez	je voulais ...	je voulus ...	je voudrai ...
49 *pouvoir*	eu/u(i)	je peux, -x, -t, peuvent		je pus ...	
	ouv/our	nous pouvons, -ez	je pouvais ...		je pourrai ...
50 *falloir*	*Impersonal*	il faut	il fallait	il fallut	il faudra
51 *déchoir*	choir *and* échoir *are defective* (only exist in certain tenses)	je déchois, -s, -t, -ent			
		nous déchoyons, -ez	je déchoyais ...	je déchus ...	je décherrai ...
52 *prendre*	prend	je prends, -ds, -d			je prendrai ...
	pren	nous prenons, -ez ils prennent	je prenais ...		
	pri(s)			je pris ...	
53 *rompre*		je romps, -ps, -pt, nous rompons ...	je rompais ...	je rompis ...	je romprai ...
54 *craindre*	ain/aind	je crains, -s, -t			je craindrai ...
	aign	nous craignons, -ez, -ent	je craignais ...	je craignis ...	
55 *peindre*	ein	je peins, -s, -t			je peindrai ...
	eign	nous peignons, -ez, -ent	je peignais ...	je peignis ...	
56 *joindre*	oin/oind	je joins, -s, -t			je joindrai ...
	oign	nous joignons, -ez, -ent	je joignais ...	je joignis ...	
57 *vaincre*	ainc	je vaincs, -cs, -c			je vaincrai ...
	ainqu	nous vainquons, -ez, -ent	je vainquais ...	je vainquis ...	
58 *traire*	i	je trais, -s, -t, -ent		(obsolete)	je trairai ...
	y	nous trayons, -ez	je trayais ...		

Conditional	Subjunctive	Imperative	Participle		
Present	*Present*		*Present*	*Past*	
	que je voie, -es, -e, -ent	vois			46
	que nous voyions, -iez	voyons, -ez	voyant		
je verrais ...				vu, -e	
je saurais ...	que je sache ...	sache, -ons, -ez	sachant	su, -e	47
	que je veuille, -es, -e, -ent	veux (veuille)			48
je voudrais ...	que nous voulions, -iez	voulons, -ez (veuillez)	voulant	voulu, -e	
	que je puisse ...	(obsolete)		pu	49
je pourrais ...			pouvant		
il faudrait	qu'il faille	(no form)	(obsolete)	fallu	50
	que je déchoie, -es, -e, -ent	déchois	(no form but échéant)		51
je décherrais ...	que nous déchoyions, -iez	déchoyons, -ez		déchu, -e	
je prendrais ...		prends			52
	que je prenne ...	prenons, -ez	prenant		
				pris, -e	
je romprais ...	que je rompe ...	romps -pons, -pez	rompant	rompu, -e	53
je craindrais ...		crains		craint, -e	54
	que je craigne ...	craignons, -ez	craignant		
je peindrais ...		peins		peint, -e	55
	que je peigne ...	peignons, -ez	peignant		
je joindrais ...		joins		joint, -e	56
	que je joigne ...	joignons, -ez	joignant		
je vaincrais ...		vaincs		vaincu, -e	57
	que je vainque ...	vainquons, -ez	vainquant		
je trairais ...	que je traie, -es, -e, -ent	trais		trait, -e	58
	que nous trayions,	trayons, -ez	trayant		

Infinitive		Indicative			
	Rules	*Present*	*Imperfect*	*Past Historic*	*Future*
59 *plaire*	ai	je plais, tu plais, il plaît (but il tait) nous plaisons ...	je plaisais ...		je plairai ...
	u			je plus ...	
60 *mettre*	met	je mets, nous mettons	je mettais ...		je mettrai ...
	mis			je mis ...	
61 *battre*	t tt	je bats, -ts, -t nous battons ...	je battais ...	je battis ...	je battrai ...
62 *suivre*	ui uiv	je suis, -s, -t nous suivons ...	je suivais ...	je suivis ...	je suivrai ...
63 *vivre*	vi/viv	je vis, -s, -t, nous vivons ...	je vivais ...		je vivrai ...
	véc			je vécus ...	
64 *suffire*		je suffis, -s, -t, nous suffisons ...	je suffisais ...	je suffis ...	je suffirai ...
65 *médire*		je médis, -s, -t, nous médisons, vous médisez (but vous dites, redites)	je médisais ...	je médis ...	je médirai ...
66 *lire*	i is	je lis, -s, -t nous lisons, -ez, -ent	je lisais ...		je lirai ...
	u			je lus ...	
67 *écrire*	i iv	j'écris, -s, -t nous écrivons, -ez, -ent	j'écrivais ...	j'écrivis ...	j'écrirai ...
68 *rire*		je ris, -s, -t, nous rions ...	je riais ... nous riions, -iez	je ris ... nous rîmes ...	je rirai ...
69 *conduire*		je conduis ...	je conduisais ...	je conduisis...	je conduirai ...
70 *boire*	oi	je bois, -s, -t, -vent			je boirai ...
	u(v)	nous buvons, -ez	je buvais ...	je bus ...	
71 *croire*	oi	je crois, -s, -t, ils croient			je croirai ...
	oy u	nous croyons, -ez	je croyais ...	je crus ...	

• •

Conditional	Subjunctive	Imperative	Participle		
Present	*Present*		*Present*	*Past*	
je plairais ...	que je plaise ...	plais plaisons, -ez	plaisant		59
				plu	
je mettrais ...	que je mette ...	mets mettons, -ez	mettant		60
				mis, -e	
		bats			61
jo battrais ...	que je batte ...	battons, -ez	battant	battu, -e	
		suis			62
je suivrais ...	que je suive ...	suivons, -ez	suivant	suivi, -e	
je vivrais ...	que je vive ...	vis vivons, -ez	vivant		63
				vécu, -e	
je suffirais ...	que je suffise ...	suffis suffisons, -ez	suffisant	suffi (but confit, déconfit, frit, circoncis)	64
je médirais ...	que je médise ... que nous médisions, -iez	médis médisons médisez (but dites, redites)	médisant	médit	65
je lirais ...		lis			66
	que je lise ...	lisons, -ez	lisant		
				lu, -e	
j'écrirais ...		écris		écrit, -e	67
	que j'écrive ...	écrivons, -ez	écrivant		
je rirais ...	que je rie ...	ris, rions, riez	riant	ri	68
	que nous riions, -iez				
je conduirais ...	que je conduise ...	conduis conduisons, -ez	conduisant	conduit, -e (but lui, nui)	69
je boirais ...	que je boive, -es, -e, -ent	bois			70
	que nous buvions, -iez	buvons, -ez	buvant	bu, -e	
je croirais ...	que je croie ...	crois			71
		croyons, -ez	croyant		
				cru, -e	

Infinitive		Indicative			
	Rules	*Present*	*Imperfect*	*Past Historic*	*Future*
72 croître	oî	je croîs, -s, -t			je croîtrai ...
	oiss	nous croissons, -ez, -ent	je croissais ...		
	û			je crûs ...	
73 connaître		je connais, -s, -ssons, -ssez, -ssent	je connaissais ...	je connus ...	
	î before t	il connaît			je connaîtrai ...
74 naître		je nais, nais,			
	î before t	naît			je naîtrai ...
	naisse	nous naissons, -ez, -ent	je naissais ...		
	naqu			je naquis ...	
75 résoudre	ou	je résous, -s, -t		(absoudre	je résoudrai...
	ol/olv	nous résolvons, -ez, -ent	je résolvais ...	and dissoudre have no past historic)	
	olu			je résolus ...	
76 coudre	oud	je couds, -ds, -d			je coudrai ...
	ous	nous cousons, -ez, -ent	je cousais ...	je cousis ...	
77 moudre	moud	je mouds, -ds, -d			je moudrai ...
	moul	nous moulons, -ez, -ent	je moulais ...	je moulus ...	
78 conclure		je conclus, -s, -t, nous concluons, -ez, -ent	je concluais ...	je conclus ...	je conclurai ...
79 clore	Defective (only exists in certain tenses)	je clos, -os, -ôt ils closent	(obsolete)	(obsolete)	je clorai ...
80 maudire		je maudis, -s, -t nous maudissons, -ez, -ent	je maudissais ...	je maudis ...	je maudirai ...

· ·

Conditional	Subjunctive	Imperative	Participle		
Present	*Present*		*Present*	*Past*	
je croîtrais...		croîs			72
	que je croisse ...	croissons, -ez	croissant		
				crû, crue	
				(but accru, -e)	
	que je connaisse ...	connais,		connu, -e	73
		-ssons, -ssez	connaissant		
je connaîtrais ...					
		nais		né, -e	74
je naîtrais ...					
	que je naisse ...	naissons, -ez	naissant		
je résoudrais ...		résous		(absous, -oute;	75
	que je résolve ...	résolvons, -ez	résolvant	dissous, -oute)	
				résolu, -e	
je coudrais ...		couds			76
	que je couse ...	cousons, -ez	cousant	cousu, -e	
je moudrais ...		mouds			77
	que je moule ...	moulons, -ez	moulant	moulu, -e	
je conclurais ...	que je conclue ...	conclus	concluant	conclu, -e	78
		concluons, -ez		(but inclus, -e)	
je clorais ...	que je close ...	clos	closant	clos, -e	79
je maudirais ...	que je maudisse	maudis	maudissant	maudit, -e	80
	qu'il maudisse	-ssons, -ssez			

Numbers

Cardinal numbers

0 zéro*	16 seize	90 quatre-vingt-dix	1 200 mille** deux cents
1 un†	17 dix-sept	91 quatre-vingt-onze	2 000 deux mille††
2 deux	18 dix-huit	92 quatre-vingt-douze	10 000 dix mille
3 trois	19 dix-neuf	99 quatre-vingt-dix-neuf	100 000 cent mille
4 quatre	20 vingt	101 cent un†	102 000 cent deux mille
5 cinq	21 vingt et un	102 cent deux	1 000 000 un million‡‡
6 six	22 vingt-deux	110 cent dix	1 264 932 un million
7 sept	30 trente	187 cent quatre-vingt-	deux cent soixante-
8 huit	40 quarante	sept	quatre mille neuf cent
9 neuf	50 cinquante	200 deux cents	trente-deux
10 dix	60 soixante	250 deux cent◊	1 000 000 000 un
11 onze	70 soixante-dix	cinquante	milliard‡‡
12 douze	71 soixante et onze	1 000 mille∞	1 000 000 000 000 un
13 treize	80 quatre-vingts§	1 001 mille un†	billion‡‡
14 quatorze	81 quatre-vingt-un¶	1 002 mille deux	
15 quinze	82 quatre-vingt-deux	1 020 mille vingt	

* In English *0* may be called *nought, zero* or even *nothing*; French is always *zéro:* **a nought = un zéro.**

† **one** is **une** in French when it agrees with a feminine noun, so *un crayon* but *une table, une des tables, vingt et une tables,* etc.

§ Note that when *80* is used as a page number it has no *s:* **page eighty = page quatre-vingt.**

¶ **vingt** has no *s* when it is in the middle of a number. The only exception to this rule is when *quatre-vingts* is followed by *millions, milliards* or *billions,* eg **quatre-vingts millions, quatre-vingts billions** etc.

◊ **cent** does not take an *s* when it is in the middle of a number. The only exception to this rule is when it is followed by *millions, milliards* or *billions,* eg **trois cents millions, six cents billions** etc. It has a normal plural when it modifies other nouns: **200 inhabitants = deux cents habitants.**

∞ Where English would have a comma, French has simply a space. A full stop (period) can be used, e.g. **1.000.** As in English, there is no separation in dates between thousands and hundreds: **in 2004 = en 2004.**

** In dates, the spelling **mil** is preferred to **mille,** i.e. **en 1200 = en mil deux cents.** However, when the year is a round number of thousands, the spelling is always **mille,** so **en l'an mille, en l'an deux mille** etc.

†† **mille** is invariable; it never takes an *s.*

‡‡ The French words **million, milliard** and **billion** are nouns, and when written out in full they take **de** before another noun, eg **a million inhabitants = un million d'habitants.** However, when written in figures, **1,000,000 inhabitants = 1 000 000 habitants,** but is still spoken as *un million d'habitants.* When **million** etc. is part of a complex number, **de** is not used before the nouns, eg **6,000,210 people = six millions deux cent dix personnes.**

• •

Ordinal numbers§

1st	1er‡	premier (*fem.* première)
2nd	2e	second (*fem.* seconde) *or* deuxième
3rd	3e	troisième
4th	4e	quatrième
5th	5e	cinquième
6th	6e	sixième
7th	7e	septième
8th	8e	huitième
9th	9e	neuvième
10th	10e	dixième
11th	11e	onzième
12th	12e	douzième
13th	13e	treizième
14th	14e	quatorzième
15th	15e	quinzième
16th	16e	seizième
17th	17e	dix-septième
18th	18e	dix-huitième
19th	19e	dix-neuvième
20th	20e	vingtième
21st	21e	vingt et unième
22nd	22e	vingt-deuxième
23rd	23e	vingt-troisième
24th	24e	vingt-quatrième
25th	25e	vingt-cinquième

30th	30e	trentième
31st	31e	trente et unième
40th	40e	quarantième
50th	50e	cinquantième
60th	60e	soixantième
70th	70e	soixante-dixième
71st	71e	soixante et onzième
72nd	72e	soixante-douzième
73rd	73e	soixante-treizième
74th	74e	soixante-quartorzième
75th	75e	soixante-quinzième
79th	79e	soixante-dix-neuvième
80th	80e	quatre-vingtième
81st	81e	quatre-vingt-unième
90th	90e	quatre-vingt-dixième
91st	91e	quatre-vingt-onzième
99th	99e	quatre-vingt-dix-neuvième
100th	100e	centième
101st	101e	cent et unième
102nd	102e	cent-deuxième
200th	200e	deux centième
1,000th	1 000e	millième
2,000th	2 000e	deux millième
1,000,000th	1 000 000e	millionième

Like English, French makes nouns by adding the definite article:

the first . . . . = le premier (or la première, or les premiers *m pl* or les premières *f pl*)

the second . . . . = le second (or la seconde etc)

the first three . . . . = les trois premiers *or* les trois premières

Note the French word order in:

the third richest country in the world = le troisième pays le plus riche du monde

§ All the ordinal numbers in French behave like ordinary adjectives and take normal plural endings where appropriate.

‡ This is the masculine form; the feminine is **1re** and the plural **1ers** (m) or **1res** (f). All the other abbreviations of ordinal numbers are invariable.

Use of en

Note the use of *en* in the following examples:

there are six . . . . = il y en a six

I've got a hundred . . . . = j'en ai cent

en must be used when the thing you are talking about is not expressed (the French says literally *there of them are six, I of them have a hundred* etc.). However, *en* is not needed when the object is specified:

there are six apples . . . = il y a six pommes

Decimals in French

Note that French uses a comma where English has a decimal point.

written as	*spoken as*
0,25	zéro virgule vingt-cinq
0,05	zéro virgule zéro cinq
3,45	trois virgule quarante-cinq
8,195	huit virgule cent quatre-vingt-quinze

Numbers

Approximate numbers

When you want to say 'about ...' , remember the French ending *-aine*:

about ten . . . . = une dizaine
about ten books . . . . . . = une dizaine de livres
about fifteen . . . . = une quinzaine
about fifteen people . . . = une quinzaine de personnes

Similarly *une trentaine, une quarantaine, une cinquantaine, une soixantaine* and *une centaine* (and *une douzaine* means *a dozen*). For other numbers, use **environ** (*about*):

about thirty-five . . . . . . = environ trente-cinq
hundreds of books . . . . = des centaines de livres
thousands of books . . . = des milliers de livres
I've got thousands . . . . = j'en ai des milliers

Percentages in French

written as	*spoken as*
25%	vingt-cinq pour cent
50%	cinquante pour cent
100%	cent pour cent
200%	deux cents pour cent
365%	trois cent soixante-cinq pour cent
4,25%	quatre virgule vingt-cinq pour cent

Phrases

numbers up to ten . . . . = les nombres jusqu'à dix
to count up to ten . . . . = compter jusqu'à dix
almost ten . . . . = presque dix
less than ten . . . . = moins de dix
more than ten . . . . = plus de dix
all ten of them . . . . = tous les dix
all ten boys . . . . = les dix garçons
my last ten pounds . . . = mes dix dernières livres
the next twelve weeks . . = les douze prochaines semaines
the other two . . . . = les deux autres
the last four . . . . = les quatre derniers

Calculations in French

$10 + 3 = 13$ . . . . dix et trois font *or* égalent treize
$10 - 3 = 7$ . . . . trois ôté de dix il reste sept *or* dix moins trois égale sept
$10 \times 3 = 30$ . . . . . . dix fois trois égalent trente
$30 : 3 = 10$ . . . . . . trente divisé par trois
$(30 \div 3 = 10)$ . . . . . égale dix
5^2 . . . . cinq au carré
5^3 . . . . cinq puissance trois
$\sqrt{12}$ . . . . racine carrée de douze

Fractions in French

in figures	*in words*
$1/2$	un demi*
$1/3$	un tiers
$1/4$	un quart
$1/5$	un cinquième
$1/6$	un sixième
$1/7$	un septième
$1/8$	un huitième
$1/9$	un neuvième
$1/10$	un dixième
$1/11$	un onzième
$1/12$	un douzième (*etc*)

in figures	*in words*
$2/3$	deux tiers†
$2/5$	deux cinquièmes
$3/4$	trois quarts
$3/10$	trois dixièmes
$1\,1/2$	un et demi
$1\,1/3$	un (et) un tiers
$1\,1/4$	un et quart
$1\,1/5$	un (et) un cinquième
$5\,2/3$	cinq (et) deux tiers
$5\,3/4$	cinq (et) trois quarts

* Note that **half**, when not a fraction, is translated by the noun **moitié** or the adjective **demi**; see the dictionary entry.

† Note the use of **les** and **d'entre** when these fractions are used about a group of people or things: **two-thirds of them** = **les deux tiers d'entre eux**.